TRAVELING WITH YOUR PET
THE AAA PETBOOK®

The AAA guide to more than 14,000
pet-friendly, AAA Approved hotels
and campgrounds across the
United States and Canada.

14th Edition

AAA PUBLISHING

AAA wishes to acknowledge the following for their assistance:
Veterinary Emergency & Critical Care Society

Cover Photos

Front: Editors' Pick - Chase at Cannon Beach, Oregon
Submitted by owner Curtis H. Smith
Back: 1st place Photo Contest Winner: Lady at Crater Lake, Oregon
Submitted by owner Cassandra Basgall
Spine: 2nd place Photo Contest Winner: Maggie at Grand Teton National Park, Wyoming
Submitted by owner Wendy Gillroy

Published by AAA Publishing
1000 AAA Drive, Heathrow, Florida 32746

Fourteenth Edition Copyright © 2012 AAA Publishing. All rights reserved.
ISBN: 978-1-59508-503-0 Stock Number 552212
Printed in the USA by Rose Printing Company, Inc.

ABOUT THIS BOOK

Welcome to the 14th edition of *Traveling With Your Pet: The AAA PetBook®*. *Traveling With Your Pet* is a must for the traveler who's also an animal lover. This comprehensive book provides all the information you need to know about taking a four-legged friend on the road. Will Spot be a good car passenger? Is it safe to take Snowball on a plane? What are the important rules of pet etiquette? Is pet insurance a good idea? *Traveling With Your Pet* answers all of these questions and more. Here are just some of the features covered:

- Dog parks where you and your furry friends can play, exercise or just relax.
- An extensive listing of emergency animal clinics compiled by the Veterinary Emergency & Critical Care Society. Names, addresses and phone numbers provide valuable information for unexpected or emergency situations, both en route and at your destination.
- A roundup of pet-friendly attractions.
- National public lands in the United States and Canada that allow pets, along with recreation information.
- Border crossing procedures and tips for travelers — both entering Canada from the United States and vice versa.
- Policies pertaining to service animals.

Traveling With Your Pet lists more than 14,000 AAA Approved hotels and campgrounds. And the listings show AAA's trustworthy diamond ratings, the traveler's assurance of quality. Other handy features include:

- Informative highway directions.
- Specific information about lodgings' pet policies: deposits and fees (rounded to the nearest dollar), housekeeping service, designated rooms and other stipulations relating to travelers with pets.
- Additional details about the lodgings themselves, including icons for amenities, recreation, dining and accessibility.
- Icons designating AAA's member discount programs.
- Listings for AAA's highest rated campgrounds, including rate and pet policy information and service/amenity icons.

All of this valuable information is packaged in a contemporary, easy-to-read format, making *Traveling With Your Pet: The AAA PetBook®* as indispensable an on-the-road companion as Spot's water dish or Snowball's litter box. Don't leave home without it, and remember: It always pays to Travel With Someone You Trust®.

Have some great pictures from traveling with your pet? The AAA PetBook Photo Contest, sponsored by AAA and Best Western®, gives you a chance at winning some great prizes and seeing your pet's photo on a cover of *Traveling With Your Pet: The AAA PetBook®*. Check out more information about the contest winners on the next page and see some adorable photos of traveling pets in the middle section of this guide. For details on how to enter the annual Photo Contest and to obtain an entry form, please visit www.AAA.com/PetBook.

Picture Your Pet as the Next AAA PetBook® Cover Model!

For a chance to see your pet in an upcoming edition of **Traveling With Your Pet: The AAA PetBook®**, enter the AAA PetBook Photo Contest Sponsored by Best Western, open yearly from May 1 to Nov. 30. Visit **AAA.com/PetBook** for an entry form, prize listing, complete contest rules and photos of previous winners and runners up.

Editors' Pick — Chase

Every so often, we get a photo contest entry that's so compelling our editors simply insist on making it the cover photo. This year we awarded the honor to Chase, a frequent traveler and beach lover from Oregon.

As shown here vacationing at Cannon Beach, Oregon, Chase loves the beach. Owner Curtis Smith tells us that when Chase isn't on the beach trying to "herd" the waves, he is in town charming other tourists and trolling for head scratches. He also says Cannon Beach is a pet-friendly city with lots of open beach for dogs like Chase to run.

1st place winner — Lady

This delightful Tibetan Terrier from Torrance, California, caught our eye and stole our hearts. Shown here while vacationing in Crater Lake, Oregon, Lady steals first place and makes a stunning appearance on the book's back cover. Lady is an experienced traveler and often accompanies her human to dog shows. Lady's owner says she enjoys traveling with her dogs, especially to Oregon, where walks on beautiful, calm beaches are a treat.

2nd place winner — Maggie

Maggie is an American Eskimo/Pomeranian Mix who loves the outdoors. Proudly pictured on the book's spine as the second place winner, Maggie poses for a striking photo while exploring Grand Teton National Park in Wyoming. Maggie loves to go outdoors and her humans take her along whenever possible, saying their dogs are their kids. Maggie's first snow adventure took place while on a trip to Yellowstone. There she was unsure about the snow, but quickly dug a hole and stuck her face in it.

Turn to Page 361 to view a sampling of more highlights from the photo contest.

TABLE OF CONTENTS

AAA PetBook® Photo Contest

Traveling With Pets

Pet-Friendly Places

Pet-Friendly Lodgings

U.S. Lodgings

Canadian Lodgings

Pet-Friendly Campgrounds

Many people view their pets as full-fledged members of the family. Spot and Snowball often have their own beds, premium-quality foods, a basketful of toys and a special place in their humans' hearts.

Until it's time to go on vacation, that is. Then the family dog or cat is consigned to "watching the fort" at home while everyone else experiences the joy of traveling. Many animal lovers hesitate to take their pet with them because they don't think they'll be able to find accommodations that accept four-legged guests. Others aren't sure how — or if — their furry friends will adapt.

The truth is, including a pet in the family vacation is fairly easy, so long as you plan ahead. Most pets respond well to travel, a fact that isn't lost on the tourism industry. More than 14,000 AAA Approved hotels and campgrounds from coast to coast are pet-friendly, and airline bookings for pet passengers are on the rise. Great companions at home, pets are earning their stripes on the road, too.

So if you've been longing to hit the trail with a canine or feline companion, read the tips on the following pages. You may find that a getaway can be far more enjoyable with than without your pet.

Should Your Pet Travel?

Before you make reservations, determine if your pet is able to travel. Most animals can and do make the most of the experience, but a small percentage simply are not cut out for traveling. Illness, physical condition and temperament are important factors, as is your pet's ability to adjust to such stresses as changes to his environment and routine. When in doubt, check with your veterinarian. If you feel your pet isn't up to the trip, it's better for everyone if he stays home.

❀ **Rule 1: Pets who are very young, very old, pregnant, sick, injured, prone to biting or excessive vocalizing, or who cannot follow basic obedience commands should not travel.**

Even if Spot and Snowball are seasoned travelers, take into account the type of vacation and activities you have planned. No pet is going to be happy (or safe) cooped up in a car or hotel room. Likewise, the family dog may love camping and hiking, but the family cat may not. Putting a little thought toward your animal's needs and safety will pay off in a more enjoyable vacation for everyone.

❀ **Rule 2: If your pet can't actively participate in the trip, she should stay home.**

Most of the information in this book pertains to cats and dogs. If you own a bird, hamster, pig, ferret, lizard or other exotic creature, remember that unusual animals are not always accepted as readily as more conventional pets. Always specify the type of pet you have when making arrangements.

Also check states' animal policies. **Hawaii** imposes a 120-day quarantine for all imported dogs, cats and other carnivores to prevent the importation of rabies. In some cases, the quarantine period may be reduced to 5 days or less if a pet meets various pre- and post-arrival requirements. Guide dogs and service dogs are exempt from the quarantine provided they have: a standard health certificate issued within 30 days prior to arrival; a current rabies vaccination with documentation of the product name, lot number and lot expiration date; a successful result of an OIE-FAVN rabies blood test conducted after 1 year of age; and an electronic identification microchip implanted and operational. Upon arrival, guide dogs and service dogs still must be examined for external parasites. For additional details, obtain the Hawaii Rabies Quarantine Information Brochure from the Hawaii Department of Agriculture, Animal Quarantine Station, 99-951 Halawa Valley St., Aiea, HI 96701-5602; phone (808) 483-7151, e-mail rabiesfree@hawaii.gov. Further information also is available from the department's web site: www.hawaii.gov/hdoa/ai/aqs/info.

North Carolina has stringent restrictions regarding pets in lodgings. Make certain you understand an accommodation's specific policies before making reservations.

❀ **Rule 3: Be specific when making travel plans that include your pet. Nobody wants unpleasant surprises on vacation.**

If Spot and Snowball stay behind, leave them in good hands while you're gone. **Family, friends and neighbors** make good sitters (provided they're willing), especially if they know your pet and can care for him in your home. Provide detailed instructions for feeding, exercise and medication, as well as phone numbers for your destination, your veterinarian and your local animal emergency clinic.

Professional pet sitters offer a range of services, from feeding and walking your pet daily to full-time house sitting while you are gone. Interview several candidates, and always check credentials and references. For additional information, contact the National Association of Professional Pet Sitters or Pet Sitters International. *(See sidebars on p. 8 and p. 9.)*

Kennels board many animals simultaneously and generally are run by professionals who will provide food and exercise according to your instructions. Pets usually are kept in a run (dogs) or cage (cats and small dogs) and may not get the same level of human interaction as at home. Veterinary clinics also board pets and may be the best choice if yours is sick, injured or needs special medical care.

Veterinarians, fellow pet owners and professional associations are a good source of referrals for sitters and kennels.

❀ **Rule 4: Never leave your pet with someone you don't trust.**

Travelers Who Have Disabilities

Individuals with disabilities who own service animals to assist them with everyday activities undoubtedly face challenges, but traveling should not be one of them. Service animals (the accepted term for animals trained to help people with disabilities) are not pets and thus are not subject to many of the laws or policies pertaining to pets.

The Americans With Disabilities Act (ADA) defines a service animal as "any guide dog, signal dog or other animal individually trained to provide assistance to an individual with a disability." ADA regulations stipulate that public accommodations are required to modify policies, practices and procedures to permit the use of a service animal by an individual with a disability.

The purpose of these regulations is to provide equal access opportunities for people with disabilities and to ensure that they are not separated from their service animals. A tow truck operator, for example, must allow a service animal to ride in the truck with her owner rather than in the towed vehicle.

Public accommodations may charge a fee or deposit to an individual who has a disability — provided that fee or deposit is required of all customers — but no fees or deposits may be charged for the service animal, even those normally charged for pets.

The handler/owner is responsible for the animal's care and behavior; if the dog creates an altercation or poses a direct threat, the handler may be required to remove it from the premises and pay for any resulting damages.

CHOOSING A PET SITTER

Before hiring a pet sitter, ask:
- Is he or she insured (for commercial liability) and bonded?
- What is included in the fee?
- Does the sitter require that your pet have a current vaccination?
- What kind of animals does the sitter typically care for?
- How will a medical, weather or home emergency be handled?
- Does he or she fully understand your pet's medical or dietary needs?
- How much time will be spent with your pet?

The pet sitter should:
- Have a polished, professional attitude.
- Provide references.
- Have a standard contract outlining terms of service.
- Have experience in caring for animals.
- Insist on current vaccinations.
- Ask about your pet's health, temperament, schedule and needs.
- Visit and interact with your pet before you leave.
- Devote time and attention to your pet.
- Be affiliated with pet care organizations.

Be sure you:
- Explain your pet's personality — favorite toys, good and bad habits, hiding spots, general health, etc.
- Leave care instructions, keys, food and water dishes, extra supplies (food, medication, etc.), and phone numbers for your veterinarian and an emergency contact.
- Bring pets inside before leaving.

CHOOSING A KENNEL

Before reserving a kennel, ask:
- What is included in the fee?
- Are current vaccinations required?
- What kind of animals do they board?
- How will a medical or weather emergency be handled?
- Will your pet be kept in a cage or run?
- Will your pet receive daily exercise?
- Does the kennel fully understand your pet's medical or dietary needs?
- How and how often will staff interact with your pet?

The kennel should:
- Require proof of current vaccinations.
- Be clean, well-ventilated and offer adequate protection from the elements.
- Have separate areas for dogs, cats and other animals, with secure fencing and caging.
- Clean and disinfect facilities daily.
- Give your pet his regular food on his regular schedule.
- Provide soft bedding in runs/cages.
- Understand your pet's medical needs.
- Provide or obtain veterinary care if necessary.
- Offer sufficient supervision.
- Have a friendly, animal-loving staff.

Be sure you:
- Notify staff of behavior quirks (dislike of other animals, children, etc.).
- Provide food and medication.
- Leave a familiar object with your pet.
- Leave phone numbers for your veterinarian and an emergency contact.
- Spend time with your pet before boarding him.

The **Delta Society,** an organization devoted to companion and service animals, has information about laws that affect people and service animals in public accommodations. Phone (425) 679-5500 for a catalog, or visit www.deltasociety.org.

Preparing Your Pet for Travel

Happily, many vacations can be planned to include fun activities for pets. Trips to parks, nature trails, the ocean or lakes offer exposure to the world beyond the window or fence at home, as well as the chance to explore new sights and sounds. Even the streets of an unfamiliar city can provide a smorgasbord of discoveries for your animal friend to enjoy.

Once you decide Spot and Snowball are ready to hit the road, plan accordingly:

❧ **Get a clean bill of health from the veterinarian.** Update your pet's vaccinations, check his general physical condition and obtain a health certificate showing proof of up-to-date inoculations, particularly rabies, distemper and kennel cough. Such documentation will be necessary if you cross state or country lines, and also may come in handy in the unlikely event your pet gets lost and must be retrieved from the local shelter. Don't forget to ask the doctor about potential health risks at your destination (Lyme disease, heartworm infection) and the necessary preventive measures.

If your pet is taking prescribed medicine, pack a sufficient supply plus a few days' extra. Also take the prescription in case you need a refill. Be prepared for emergencies by getting the names and numbers of clinics or doctors at your destination from your veterinarian or the American Animal Hospital Association. **Hint:** Obtain these references before you leave and keep them handy throughout the trip.

Make sure your pet is in good physical shape overall, especially if you are planning an active vacation. If your animal is primarily sedentary or overweight, he may not be up to lengthy hikes through the woods.

Note: Some owners believe a sedated animal will travel more easily than one that is fully aware, but this is rarely the case. In fact, tranquilizing an animal can make travel much more stressful. Always consult a veterinarian about what is best for your pet, and administer sedatives only under the doctor's direction. In addition, never give an animal medication that is specifically prescribed for humans. The dosage may be too high for an animal's much smaller body mass, or may cause dangerous side effects.

❧ **Acclimate your pet to car travel.** Even if you're flying, your pet will have to ride in the car to get to the airport or terminal, and you don't want any unpleasant surprises before departure.

Some animals are used to riding in the car and even enjoy it. But most associate the inside of the carrier or the car with one thing only: the annual visit to the V-E-T. Considering that these visits usually end with a jab from a sharp needle, it's no wonder that some pets forget their training and act up in the car. If this is your situation, you

CONTACT INFORMATION

The following organizations offer information, tips, brochures and other travel materials designed to help you and your pet enjoy a happy and safe vacation.

American Animal Hospital Association
12575 W. Bayaud Ave., Lakewood, CO 80228
(303) 986-2800 — www.healthypet.com

American Society for the Prevention of Cruelty to Animals
424 E. 92nd St., New York, NY 10128-6804
(212) 876-7700 — www.aspca.org

American Veterinary Medical Association
1931 N. Meacham Rd., Suite 100
Schaumburg, IL 60173-4360
(800) 248-2862 — www.avma.org

The Humane Society of the United States
2100 L St. N.W., Washington, DC 20037
(202) 452-1100 — www.humanesociety.org

National Association of Professional Pet Sitters
15000 Commerce Pkwy., Suite C
Mt. Laurel, NJ 08054
(856) 439-0324 — www.petsitters.org

PetGroomer.com
P.O. Box 2489
Yelm, WA 98597
(360) 446-5348 — www.petgroomer.com

Pet Sitters International
201 E. King St., King, NC 27021
(336) 983-9222 — www.petsit.com

USDA-APHIS
USDA-APHIS-Animal Care
4700 River Rd., Unit 84
Riverdale, MD 20737-1234
(301) 734-7833 —
www.aphis.usda.gov/animal_welfare/index.shtml

will have to re-train your animal to view a drive as a reward, not a punishment.

Begin by allowing your pet to become used to the car without actually going anywhere. Then take short trips to places that are fun for animals, such as the park or the drive-through window at a fast-food restaurant. (Keep those indulgent snacks to a minimum!) Be sure to praise her for good behavior with words, petting and healthy treats. It shouldn't take long before you and your furry friend are enjoying leisurely drives without incident. *(See Traveling by Car, p. 12.)*

❧ **Brush up on behavior.** Will Snowball make a good travel companion? Or will he be an absolute terror on the road? Don't wait until the vacation is already under way to find out; review general behavioral guidelines with respect to your animal, keeping in mind that the unfamiliarity of travel situations may test the temperament of even the most well-behaved pet.

It's a good idea to socialize Spot by exposing her to other people and animals (especially if she normally stays inside). You're likely to encounter both on your trip, and it is important that she learns to behave properly in the company of strangers. Make her introduction to the outside world gradual, such as a walk in a new neighborhood or taking her along while you run errands. Exposure to new situations will help reduce fear of the unknown and result in more socially acceptable behavior.

Is your pet housebroken? How is he around children? Does he obey vocal commands? Be honest about your animal's ability to cope in unfamiliar surroundings. Depending on the length and nature of the trip and your pet's level of command response, an obedience refresher course might be a good idea.

❧ **Learn about your destination.** Check into quarantines or other restrictions well in advance, and make follow-up calls as your departure date approaches. Find out what types of documentation will be required — not just en route, but on the way home as well.

Be aware of potential safety or health risks where you're going, and plan accordingly. For example, the southeastern United States — particularly Florida — is home to alligators and heartworm-carrying mosquitoes, and many mountainous and wooded areas may harbor ticks that transmit Lyme disease.

Confirm all travel plans within a few days of your departure, especially with lodgings and airlines; their policies may have changed after you made the reservations. If you plan to visit state parks or attractions that accept pets on the premises, obtain their animal regulations in advance.

❧ **Determine the best mode of transportation.** Most people traveling with pets drive. Many airlines do accept animals in the passenger cabin or cargo hold, and as more people choose to fly with their pet airlines are becoming more pet-conscious. Restrictions vary as to the type and number of pets an airline will carry, however, so inquire about animal shipping and welfare policies before making reservations. If your pet must travel in the cargo

---

WHAT TO TAKE

- ❏ Carrier or crate. *(See Selecting a Carrier or Crate, p. 11, for specifications.)*
- ❏ Nylon or leather collar or harness, license tag, ID tag(s) and leash. All should be sturdy and should fit your pet properly.
- ❏ Food and water dishes.
- ❏ Can opener and spoon (for canned food).
- ❏ An ample supply of food, plus a few days' extra.
- ❏ Bottled water from home. (Many animals are finicky about their drinking water.)
- ❏ Cooler with ice.
- ❏ Healthy treats.
- ❏ Medications, if necessary.
- ❏ Health certificate and other required documents.
- ❏ A blanket or other bedding. (If your pet is used to sleeping on the furniture, bring an old blanket or sheet to place on top of the hotel's bedding.)
- ❏ Litter supplies (for cats or other small animals), a scooper and plastic bags (for dogs).
- ❏ Favorite toys.
- ❏ Carpet deodorizer.
- ❏ Chewing preventative.

- ❏ A recent photograph and a written description including name, breed, gender, height, weight, coloring and distinctive markings.
- ❏ Grooming supplies:
  comb/brush
  nail clippers
  shampoo
  cloth and paper towels
  cotton balls/tissues
- ❏ First-aid kit:
  gauze, bandages and adhesive tape
  hydrogen peroxide
  rubbing alcohol
  ointment
  muzzle
  scissors
  tweezers (for removing ticks, burrs, splinters, etc.)
  local emergency phone numbers
  first-aid guide (such as *Pet First Aid: Cats & Dogs*, published by The Humane Society of the United States and the American Red Cross)

hold, heed the cautionary advice in the Traveling by Air section. *(See p. 13.)*

Flying is really the only major alternative to car travel. Amtrak, as well as Greyhound and other interstate bus lines, do not accept pets. **Note:** Seeing-eye dogs and other service animals are exempt from the regulations prohibiting pets on Amtrak and interstate bus lines. Local rail and bus companies may allow pets in small carriers, but this is an exception rather than a rule.

The only cruise ship that currently permits pets is the Cunard Line's *Queen Mary 2* (on trans-Atlantic crossings only); kennels are provided, but animals are accepted on a very limited basis. Some small charter and sightseeing boat companies permit pets onboard, however.

A word of advice: Never try to sneak your pet onto any mode of public transportation where she is not permitted. You may face legal action or fines, and the animal may be confiscated if discovered.

❧ **Pack as carefully for your pet as you do for yourself.** *(See What To Take, p. 10.)* Make sure she has a collar with a license tag and ID tag(s) listing her name and yours, along with your address and phone number. As an added precaution, some owners outfit their dog with a second tag listing the name and number of a contact person at home. Popular backup identification methods are to have your animal tattooed with an ID number (usually a social security number) or to implant a microchip under her skin.

If your pet requires medication, make sure that is specified on his tag. This helps others understand your animal's needs and also may prevent people from keeping a found pet or from stealing one to sell.

Note: Choke chains, collars that tighten when they are pulled, may be useful during training sessions, but they do not make good full-time collars. If the chain catches on something, your pet could choke herself trying to pull free. For regular wear, use a harness or a conventional collar made of nylon or leather.

Selecting a Carrier or Crate

This is one of the most important steps in ensuring your pet's safety when traveling. A good-quality carrier not only contains your pet during transit, it also gives him a safe, reassuring place to stay when confinement is necessary at your destination. Acclimate the animal before the trip so he views the crate as a cozy den, not a place of exile.

If you plan to travel by car, a carrier will confine your pet en route, and also may come in handy if Spot or Snowball must stay in the room unsupervised. A secured crate will prevent your pet from escaping from the room when the cleaning staff arrives, or at night if camping in the open. *(See At Your Destination, p. 15.)*

Some airlines allow small pets to travel in the passenger cabin as carry-on luggage. There are no laws dictating the type of carrier to use, but remember that it must be small enough to fit under a standard airplane seat and should not exceed 45 linear inches (length + width + height), or roughly **22 by 14 by 9 inches.** Depending on the airline, carrier size limits may be even smaller. If your pet will be flying in the cargo hold, you must use a carrier that meets U.S. Department of Agriculture Animal and Plant Health Inspection Service (USDA-APHIS) specifications. *(See Traveling by Air, p. 13.)*

Crates are available at pet supply stores; some airlines also sell carriers. Soft-sided travel bags are handy for flyers with small pets. Before you make the investment, make sure your carrier is airline-approved.

Even if you never take to the skies, these common-sense guidelines provide a good rule of thumb in selecting a crate for other uses. USDA-APHIS rules stipulate the following:

❧ The crate must be enclosed, but with ventilation openings occupying at least 14 percent of total wall space, at least one-third of which must be located on the top half of the kennel. A three-quarter-inch lip or rim must surround the exterior to prevent air holes from being blocked.

❧ The crate must open easily, but must be sufficiently strong to hold up during normal cargo transit procedures (loading, unloading, etc.).

❧ The floor must be solid and leakproof, and must be covered with an absorbent lining or material (such as an old towel or litter).

❧ The crate must be just large enough to allow the animal to turn freely while standing, and to have a full range of normal movement while standing or lying down.

❧ The crate must offer exterior grips or handles so that handlers do not have to place their hands or fingers inside.

❧ Food and water dishes must be securely attached and accessible without opening the kennel.

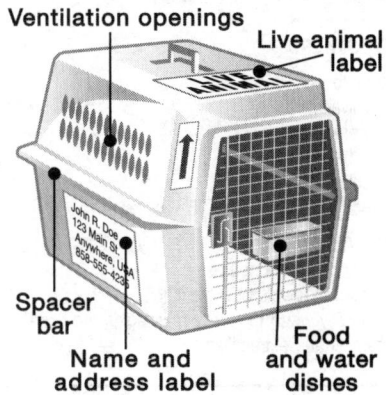

Ventilation openings · **Live animal label** · **Spacer bar** · **Name and address label** · **Food and water dishes**

HEATSTROKE AND HYPOTHERMIA

The best way to treat heatstroke or hypothermia is to prevent it. Do not leave pets unattended in a car, even if only for a few minutes. Also heed airlines' restrictions on pet travel, and carefully investigate animal welfare policies to make certain the airline has safeguards to protect your pet from both conditions.

Other preventive measures are to avoid strenuous exercise — including such activities as hiking and "fetch" — when the sun is strongest (10 a.m.-2 p.m.), and to provide your pet access to clean, fresh drinking water at all times.

Following are the warning signs and basic first aid for heatstroke and hypothermia. Always be alert to your pet's physical condition and watch for symptoms — immediate attention to the situation may mean the difference between life and death. If your pet is struck with either disorder, take him to an animal hospital or veterinarian as fast as safely possible.

HEATSTROKE

Symptoms
- rapid, shallow breathing
- excessive salivation
- heavy panting
- hot to the touch
- glazed eyes
- unsteadiness, dizziness
- deep red or purple tongue or gums
- vomiting
- body temperature of 104 F or higher

First Aid
- place pet in the shade
- quickly dampen with cool water, especially on the head and neck
- give small amounts of water

HYPOTHERMIA

Symptoms
- shivering
- weakness
- lethargy
- cold to the touch
- body temperature of 95 F or lower

First Aid
- place in a warm area
- wrap in towels or a blanket
- quickly warm by gently massaging the head, chest and extremities

❧ If the carrier has wheels, they must be removed or immobilized prior to loading.

❧ One-inch lettering stating "Live Animals" must be placed visibly on the exterior and must be accompanied by directional arrows showing the crate's proper orientation. It also is a good idea to label the crate with your name, home address and home phone number, as well as an address and phone number where you can be reached during the trip. **Hint:** Use an adhesive label or an indelible marker and write directly on the crate, as paper may be ripped off accidentally in transit.

❧ Attach a list of care instructions (feeding, watering, etc.) for a 24-hour period to the exterior of the carrier. This will help airport workers care for your pet if he is sent to the wrong destination.

❧ If you are traveling with multiple pets, note that crates may contain only one animal whose weight exceeds 20 pounds. Smaller animals may travel together under the following guidelines: one species to a crate, except compatible dogs and cats of similar size; two puppies or kittens under 6 months of age; 15 guinea pigs or rabbits; 50 hamsters. **Note:** These are federal limits; airlines may impose more stringent regulations.

Traveling by Car

The first step in ensuring your pet's well-being during a vacation is to train her to ride in the car. For safety reasons, pets should be confined to the back seat, either in a carrier or a harness attached to the car's seat belt. This keeps the animal from interfering with or distracting the driver, and also may save her life in the event of an accident. And a restrained animal will not be able to break free and run away the second the car door is opened.

To help prevent car sickness, feed your pet a light meal 4 to 6 hours before departing. Do not give an animal food or water in a moving vehicle.

Never allow your pet to ride in the bed of a pickup truck. It's illegal in some states; he also can jump out or be thrown, endangering himself and others on the road. Harnessing or leashing him to the truck bed is not advisable either: If he tries to jump out, he could be dragged along the road or the restraint could become a noose. Avoid placing animals in campers or trailers as well. **If your pet cannot ride in the car with you, leave him at home.**

Don't let your dog stick her head out the window, no matter how enjoyable it seems. Road debris and other flying objects can injure delicate eyes and ears, and the animal is at greater risk for severe injury if the vehicle should stop suddenly or be struck. If it is hot outside, run the air conditioner instead of opening the windows, and be sure that the air flow is reaching your pet.

AAA recommends that drivers stop every 2 hours to stretch their legs and take a quick break from driving. Your pet will appreciate the same break. Plan to visit a rest stop every 4 hours or so to let him have a drink and a chance to answer the call of nature. (Cat owners should bring along a litter box; dog owners should clean up afterward.)

Be sure your pet is leashed before opening the car door. This is not merely a courtesy to fellow travelers; it will prevent her from unexpectedly breaking free and running away. Keep in mind that even the most obedient pet may become disoriented during travel or in strange places and set off for home. **Hint:** If your pet is not used to traveling, use a harness instead of a collar; it is more difficult for an animal to wriggle out of a harness.

NEVER leave an animal in a parked car, even if the windows are partially open. Even on pleasant days the temperature inside a car can soar to well over 100 degrees in less than 10 minutes, placing your pet at risk for heatstroke and possibly death. On very cold days, hypothermia is a risk. Also, animals left unattended in parked cars frequently are stolen.

Traveling by Air

(Service animals are normally exempt from most of the regulations and fees specified in this section. Check policies with the airline when making reservations.)

Opinion is divided as to whether air travel is truly safe for pets. Statistically, it is less dangerous than being a passenger in a car, but some experts warn of potentially deadly conditions for animals. The truth lies somewhere in between: Most pets arrive at their destination in fine condition, but death or injury is always a possibility. Before you decide to fly, know the risk factors and the necessary precautions to keep your pet safe.

❖ **Determine whether your pet is fit to fly.** The Animal Welfare Act (AWA), administered by USDA-APHIS, specifies that dogs and cats must be at least 8 weeks old and weaned at least 5 days before air travel. Animals that are very young, very old, pregnant, ill or injured should not fly at all. Cats, snub-nosed dogs (pugs, boxers, etc.) and long-nosed dogs (shelties, collies, etc.) are prone to severe respiratory difficulties in an airplane's poorly ventilated cargo hold and should travel only in the passenger cabin (if size allows) with their owner. Some airlines will not accept snub-nosed breeds if the temperature exceeds 75 degrees anywhere in the routing. A few airlines may not allow snub-nosed breeds in the cargo hold at any time of year.

❖ **Decide where your pet will fly.** Most animals fly in the hold as checked baggage when traveling with their owners, or as cargo when they are unaccompanied. The AWA was enacted to ensure animals traveling in this manner are treated humanely and are not subjected to dangerous or life-threatening conditions. For specific requirements pertaining to your animal, check with the airline in advance, as policies vary. Some airlines will not ship dogs as checked baggage, and others will only accept dogs shipped as cargo from "known shippers"; i.e., commercial shippers or licensed pet breeders.

Items classified as "dangerous goods" (dry ice or toxic chemicals, for example) must be transported in a different part of the hold from where live animals are carried. Some planes are designed to have separate hold areas, but so-called "people mover" airlines that are primarily interested in getting human passengers from one point to another as quickly as possible may not give priority to this feature. Check your airline's specific baggage policies so you know exactly where in the hold your pet will be traveling.

Small pets may be taken into the passenger cabin with you as carry-on luggage on most airlines. This places the animal's welfare squarely in your hands but is feasible only if he is very well-behaved and fits comfortably in a container that meets standard carry-on regulations. *(See Selecting a Carrier or Crate, p. 11.)* Keep in mind that the carrier — with the animal inside — must be kept under the seat in front of you throughout the flight. Most airlines charge a fee (anywhere from $50-$125 each way) for

AIRLINE CONTACT INFORMATION

Following is a list of the major North American airlines and their toll-free reservation numbers.

Web site addresses include information about flying with animals. **Hint:** Look under links for baggage, cargo or special travel needs, or do a site search for "pets."

Air Canada . . . .(888) 247-2262
www.aircanada.com

Alaska Airlines . . . .(800) 252-7522
www.alaskaair.com

American Airlines . . . .(800) 433-7300
www.aa.com

Continental Airlines . . . .(800) 523-3273
www.continental.com

Delta Airlines . . . .(800) 221-1212
www.delta.com

JetBlue Airways . . . .(800) 538-2583
www.jetblue.com

Southwest Airlines . . . .(800) 435-9792
www.southwest.com

United Airlines . . . .(800) 864-8331
www.united.com

US Airways . . . .(800) 428-4322
www.usairways.com

carry-on pets. **Note:** AWA regulations do not apply to animals traveling in the cabin.

❦ **Do your homework.** Investigate the airline's animal transport and welfare policies, especially if you are flying with a small or commuter airline. All airlines are subject to basic AWA regulations, but specific standards of care vary greatly from one company to another. Do your research well in advance and confirm the information 24-48 hours before departing.

The more information an airline provides, the better care your pet is likely to receive. Beware of companies that have vague animal welfare guidelines, or none at all. All major airlines provide information about pet transport on their Web sites. Also talk to fellow travelers and pet owners about their experiences. Finally, keep in mind that airlines are not required to transport live animals and can refuse to carry them for any reason.

❦ **Protect your investment.** Most people think of their pets as part of the family, but the legal system assigns them the same value as a piece of luggage. Inquire about insurance — an airline that won't insure animals in its care may not be the right one for your pet. (Always read the fine print before purchasing any insurance

policy.) Also ask if the airline's workers are trained to handle animals. Few are, but it doesn't hurt to check. Remember, it's up to you to choose an airline that values pets and will treat yours with care.

❦ **Understand the potential hazards.** Because a plane's cargo hold is neither cooled nor heated until take-off, the most dangerous time for your pet is that spent on the ground in this unventilated compartment. In summer the space absorbs heat while the plane sits on the tarmac; the reverse is true in winter, when it is no warmer inside the hold than outside. Both instances expose pets to the possibility of serious injury or death from heatstroke or hypothermia. **Note:** The latter also may be a concern during flight if the hold's heater is disabled or turned off, allowing the temperature to drop to near-freezing levels.

To minimize these risks, USDA-APHIS rules prohibit animals from being kept in the hold or on the tarmac for more than 45 minutes when temperatures are above 85 F or below 45 F. Some airlines impose even tighter temperature restrictions and may not permit animals to fly on planes going to cities where the ground temperatures may exceed these limits. (Exceptions may be made for animals whose veterinarians certify they are acclimated to colder temperatures, but never warmer.)

❦ **Make stress-free travel arrangements.** Once you decide to fly, reserve space for Spot or Snowball when you arrange your own tickets, preferably well in advance of your travel date. Airlines accept only a limited number of animals per flight — usually two to four in the passenger cabin and one pet per passenger — on a first-come, first-served basis. More animals are generally allowed in the cargo hold.

Prepare to pay a fee each way; the cost is often greater for large animals traveling on a flight without their owner. Always reconfirm your reservations and flight information 24-48 hours before departure.

If your pet will be flying in the hold, travel on the same plane and reserve a nonstop flight. This not only reduces the danger of heatstroke or hypothermia during layovers, it also eliminates the possibility that she will be placed on the wrong connecting flight. In summer, fly during the early morning or late evening when temperatures are cooler. Because of large crowds and the chance of heavy air traffic causing delays, avoid holiday travel whenever possible.

Additional precautions may be necessary when traveling outside the United States and Canada. Other countries may impose lengthy quarantines, and airline workers outside North America may not be bound by animal welfare laws. *(See International Travel, p. 17.)*

❦ **Play an active role in your pet's well-being.** Flying safely with your pet requires careful planning and attention to his welfare. See the veterinarian within 10 days of departure for a health certificate (required by most airlines) and a pre-flight check-up.

PET INSURANCE

Just like their owners, pets can experience major medical problems at some point in their lifetime — even those that live indoors. And if illness strikes while you're on the road, it may be necessary to obtain care quickly. As a result, more and more people who travel with their devoted companion are considering pet health insurance.

Insurance plans run the gamut from basic coverage and routine care for illness and injury to comprehensive health maintenance, vaccinations and exams. Annual premiums range from less than $100 to more than $350, depending on the type of pet and plan. When choosing your plan, consider the following:

- What are the enrollment guidelines (age, breed, specific restrictions, etc.)?

- Which expenses are covered and which are excluded?

- What is the plan's policy concerning existing health problems?

- Does the plan allow you to use your own veterinarian?

- How are veterinary fees paid?

- Is a multiple pet discount offered?

Address any concerns you have about your pet traveling by air, especially if you are considering tranquilization. Sedation usually is not recommended for cats and dogs, regardless of whether they fly in the cabin or in the hold. Exposure to increased altitude pressure can create respiratory and cardiovascular problems; animals with short, wide heads are particularly susceptible to disorientation and possible injury. Sedation should never be administered without your veterinarian's approval.

Obtain an airline-approved carrier and acclimate your pet to its presence by leaving it open with a familiar object inside. A sturdy, well-ventilated crate adds an additional measure of protection.

Because animals are classified as luggage, they may be loaded on the plane via conveyor belt. If the crate falls off the belt, your pet could be injured or released. Ask that she be hand-carried on and off the plane, and that you be permitted to watch both procedures. Also ask about "counter-to-counter" shipping, in which the animal is loaded immediately before departure and unloaded immediately after arrival. There usually is an additional fee for this service.

Make sure you will have access to your pet if there is a lengthy layover or delay. Think twice about flying on an airline that won't allow you to check on your animal under such circumstances.

❧ **Prepare for the flight.** Keep in mind that traveling with an animal will require additional pre-flight time and preparation on your part. Exercise your pet before the flight, and arrive at least 2 but not more than 4 hours before departure. If he is traveling as carry-on luggage, check-in is normally at the passenger terminal; if he is traveling as checked baggage or as cargo in the cargo hold, proceed to the airline's cargo terminal, which is often in a different location. Find this out when making reservations and again when confirming flight information.

Make sure your animal's crate is properly labeled and secured, but do not lock it in case airline personnel have to provide emergency care. Include an ice pack for extra comfort on a hot day or a hot water bottle on a cold day. **Hint:** Wrap in a towel to prevent leaking.

Do not feed your pet less than 4 hours before departure, but provide water up until boarding. **Hint:** Freeze water in the bowl so that it melts throughout the trip, providing a constant drinking source.

Spot or Snowball should wear a sturdy collar (breakaway collars are recommended for cats) and two identification tags marked with your name, home address and phone number, and travel address and phone number. It's also a good idea to clip your pet's nails before departure so they won't accidentally get caught on any part of the carrier.

Note: You may be required to take your pet out of the carrier as you pass through security on your way to the gate. Make sure the animal is wearing a collar and leash or harness.

Attach food and water dishes inside the carrier so that airline workers can reach them without opening the door. If the trip will take longer than 12 hours, also attach a plastic bag with at least one meal's worth of dry food. Animals under 16 weeks of age must be fed every 12 hours, adult animals every 24 hours. Water must be provided at least every 12 hours, regardless of the animal's age.

Allow your pet to answer the call of nature before boarding, but do not take her out of the carrier while in the terminal. As a courtesy, wait until you are outside and away from fellow travelers. Keep her leash with you — do not leave it inside or attached to the kennel.

If your pet is traveling as carry-on luggage, let the passenger sitting next to you know. Someone with allergies may want to change seats.

Perhaps the most important precaution is to alert the flight crew and the captain that your pet is aboard. The pilot must activate the heater for the cargo hold; make sure this is done once you are in the air. If there are layovers or delays, ask the flight crew to be sure your pet has adequate shelter and/or ventilation; better yet, ask them to allow you to check in-person.

If you have arranged to watch your pet being unloaded, ask a flight attendant to call the baggage handlers and let them know you are on the way. Above all, do not hesitate to voice any concerns you have for your pet's welfare — it is your responsibility to do so.

❧ **Be prepared for emergencies.** In the unlikely event your pet gets lost en route, contact the airline, local humane shelters, animal control agencies or USDA-APHIS. Many airlines can trace a pet that was transferred to the wrong flight. If your pet is injured in transit, proceed to the nearest animal hospital; register any complaints with USDA-APHIS. **Hint:** Carry a list of emergency contact numbers and a current photograph of your pet in your wallet or purse, just in case.

At Your Destination

How well you and your companion behave on the road directly affects the way future furry travelers will be treated. Always clean up after your pet and keep him under your control. This is not only a courtesy to fellow human travelers; it's the surest way to enjoy a safe and happy vacation.

Inquire about pet policies before making lodging reservations. Properties may impose restrictions on the type or size of pet allowed, or they may designate only certain rooms, such as smoking rooms, for travelers with animals. If you have a dog, get a room on the first floor with direct access outside, preferably near a walking area; keep her leashed on any excursion.

Lodgings may have supervision policies requiring that pets be crated when unattended or that they may not be left alone at all. Allow your pet only in designated exercise or animal-approved areas; never take him into such off-limits places as the lobby, pool area, patio or restaurant. Prepare to receive limited housekeeping service, or none at all.

Expect to pay some type of additional charge, which may be per room or per pet and may include any of the following: refundable deposit, non-refundable deposit, daily fee, weekly fee.

If staying with friends or relatives, make certain your pet is a welcome guest. Know and respect their "house rules," especially if they have small children or pets of their own.

Once in the room, check for such hazards as chemically treated toilet water, hiding spaces and electrical cords before freeing your pet. Give her time to adjust to her new surroundings under your supervision.

Above all, practice good "petiquette":

❧ Try not to leave your pet alone, but if you must, crate or otherwise confine her.

❧ Crate at night as well.

❧ To keep your pet and the housekeeper from having an unexpected encounter, leave the "Do Not Disturb" sign on the door when you go out without him.

❧ Barking dogs make poor hotel neighbors — keep your pet quiet.

❧ Don't allow your pet on the furniture. If she insists on sleeping on the bed, bring a bedspread or sheet from home and place that on top of the hotel bedding.

❧ Clean up after your pet immediately — inside the room and out — and leave no trace of him behind when checking out.

❧ Dispose of litter and other "accidents" properly — check with housekeeping.

❧ Notify the management immediately if something is damaged, and be ready to pay for repairs.

❧ Add a little extra to the housekeeping tip.

❧ When you take your pet out of the room, keep her leashed, especially in wilderness areas and around small children. No matter how obedient she is at home, new stimuli and distractions may cause her to forget or ignore vocal commands. Know and obey animal policies at parks, beaches and other public areas. Check before arriving to make certain animals still are welcome, even if you've been there before — the rules may have changed.

❧ Look for outdoor cafes when selecting restaurants. For health reasons, pets are not permitted inside eating establishments, but many restaurants allow animals to sit quietly with their owners at outdoor tables. Drive-through restaurants are another alternative.

In Case of Emergency

Be prepared for any turn of events by knowing how to get to the nearest animal hospital. *(See Emergency Animal Clinics, p. 55.)* Also have the name and number of a local animal shelter and a local veterinarian handy — ask your veterinarian for a recommendation. Take first-aid supplies with you and know how to use them. An animal in pain may become aggressive, so exercise caution at all times.

Emergency evacuation shelters do not accept pets, and domesticated animals do not fare well if left to weather an emergency on their own, especially when far from home. Avert a potential tragedy by planning in advance where you will go with your pet in case of evacuation. Use the listings in this book to find other lodgings willing to take you and your pet. Above all, don't wait for disaster to strike. Leave as soon as the evacuation order is announced, and take your animal with you.

The Great Outdoors

Travelers planning an active or camping vacation should make some additional preparations. Check in advance to be sure your pet is permitted at campgrounds, parks, beaches, trails and anywhere else you will be visiting. If there are restrictions — and there usually are — follow them. Remember that pets other than service animals usually are not allowed in public buildings.

Note: It is not advisable to take animals other than dogs into wilderness areas. For example, bringing a pet is not recommended at some national parks in Alaska. Also keep in mind that rural areas often have few veterinarians and even fewer boarding kennels.

Use common sense. Clean up after your pet, do not allow excessive vocalizing and keep her under your control. If the property requires your pet to be leashed or crated at all times, do so. Few parks or natural areas will allow a pet to be unattended, even when chained — the risk of disagreeable encounters with other travelers or wildlife is too great. The National Park Service may confiscate pets that harm wildlife or other visitors.

If camping, crate your pet at night to protect him from the elements and predators. (Chaining confines the animal but won't keep him from becoming a midnight snack.)

When hiking, stick to the trail and keep your pet on a short leash. It is all too easy for an unleashed pet to wander off and get lost or fall prey to a larger animal. Keep an eye out for such wildlife as alligators, bears, big cats, porcupines and skunks, and avoid other dogs and small children. Be aware of indigenous poisonous plants, such as English ivy and oleander, or those causing physical injury, such as cactus, poison ivy or stinging nettle. Your veterinarian or local poison control center should be able to give you a full list of hazardous flora.

Before setting out on the trail, make sure both of you are in good physical shape. An animal that rarely exercises at home will not suddenly be ready for a 10-mile trek across uneven terrain. Plan a hike well within the limits of your pet's endurance, and don't push — remember, if Spot gets too tired to make it back on her own, you'll have to carry her.

Carry basic first-aid supplies, including a first-aid guide. *(See What To Take, p. 10.)* Also carry fresh drinking water for both of you — "found" water may contain harmful germs or toxins. Drink often, not just when thirst strikes, and have your pet do the same. Watch for signs of dehydration, leg or foot injuries, heat exhaustion or heatstroke. Stop immediately and return home or to camp if any of these occur.

Note: Dogs can carry their own backpacks (check your local pet store for specially designed packs), but should never carry more than one-third of their body weight. Train the dog to accept the pack beforehand, and only use it with a strong, healthy animal in excellent physical condition.

No matter where or how you spend your vacation, visit the veterinarian when you return home to check for injuries, parasites and general health.

Traveling Between the United States and Canada

Traveling across the international border with your pet — either from the United States into Canada or from Canada into the United States — should prove largely hassle-free, although some basic regulations need to be kept in mind. All U.S. and Canadian citizens traveling between the United States and Canada are required to show a passport or other accepted secure document. For additional information about secure documents visit www.travel.state.gov or phone (877) 487-2778.

U.S. Customs grants returning U.S. citizens who stay in Canada more than 48 hours an individual $800 duty-free exemption (if not used within the prior 30 days). Any amount over the $800 exemption is subject to duty.

The exemption is based on fair retail value and applies to goods acquired for personal or household use or as gifts but not intended for sale. All items for which the exemption is claimed must accompany you upon return.

A 5 percent goods and services tax (GST) is levied on most items sold and most services rendered in Canada. A 12 to 15 percent harmonized sales tax (HST), which includes the GST, is charged on goods and services in British Columbia, Ontario, New Brunswick, Nova Scotia and Newfoundland and Labrador.

U.S. citizens taking pet cats and dogs 3 months of age and older into Canada must carry a rabies vaccination certificate signed by a licensed veterinarian that describes the animal, provides proof of rabies vaccination and includes documentation of the product name, lot number and lot expiration date. Collar tags are not sufficient proof of immunization. The certificate also is needed to bring a pet dog back into the United States; make sure the vaccination doesn't expire while you're in Canada. **Note:** Pit bulls are not permitted to be taken into Ontario.

Service animals are exempt from import restrictions. Also exempt are puppies and kittens under 3 months old; obtain a certificate of health from your veterinarian indicating that the animal is too young to vaccinate. **Note:** For details on pet imports, contact the Canadian Embassy; 501 Pennsylvania Ave. N.W., Washington, DC 20001; phone (202) 682-1740. The Web site address is www.canadianembassy.org.

The Canadian Food Inspection Agency (CFIA) provides additional pet information; phone (800) 442-2342 or visit the Web site at www.inspection.gc.ca. If you need assistance while in Canada, contact the U.S. Embassy, P.O. Box 866/Station B, Ottawa, ON, Canada K1P 5T1; phone (613) 688-5335.

Canadian Customs allows Canadian citizens to bring back from the United States, duty and tax free, goods valued up to $400 any number of times per year, provided the visit is 48 hours or more. A $50 exemption, excluding alcoholic beverages and tobacco products, may be claimed if the visit is 24 hours or more and no other exemption is being used. If returning from a visit of 7 days or more (not counting the day of departure from Canada), the exemption goes up to $750.

Canadian travelers may take pet cats and dogs into the United States with no restrictions, but U.S. Customs requires that dogs have proof of rabies vaccination no less than 30 days before arrival. For additional information on U.S. regulations, contact the USDA-APHIS National Center for Import and Export, (301) 734-8364.

International Travel

If you plan to travel abroad with Spot or Snowball, prepare for a lengthy flight and at least a short quarantine period. Be aware that airline and animal workers in other countries may not be bound by the same animal welfare laws that exist in the United States and Canada. Contact the embassy or consulate at your destination for information about documentation and quarantine requirements, animal control laws and animal welfare regulations.

As with any trip, have your pet checked by your regular veterinarian within 10 days of departure to obtain a health certificate showing proof of rabies and other inoculations. If you are traveling with an animal other than a domesticated dog or cat, check with USDA-APHIS for restrictions or additional documentation required.

The booklet "Pets and Wildlife: Licensing and Health Requirements" has general information about traveling abroad with animals; write U.S. Customs & Border Protection, 1300 Pennsylvania Ave. N.W., Washington, DC 20229, or visit www.cbp.gov.

Note: Island nations such as Australia and the United Kingdom, which are rabies-free, have adopted the Pet Travel Scheme (PETS) to allow entry for dogs, cats and ferrets from the U.S. and Canada without the usual 6-month quarantine. Pets must be tested and vaccinated for rabies at least 21 days prior to travel, be implanted with microchip identification and receive a certificate of treatment from an official government veterinarian. For information, visit the U.K. Web site for the Department for Environment, Food and Rural Affairs (DEFRA) at www.defra.gov.uk. Hawaii, which has a standard 120-day quarantine for all imported animals except guide dogs, has adopted a similar expedited program of 5 days or less; a pet must have been vaccinated at least *twice* for rabies in its lifetime.

Loss Prevention Tips

Searching the woods or an unfamiliar town for a missing pet is easily prevented by following these helpful tips:

❧ Have your pet wear a sturdy nylon or leather collar with current ID and rabies tags firmly attached. Be sure the ID tag includes the phone number of an emergency contact. Consider having your pet implanted with microchip identification; it's a simple procedure similar to a vaccination.

❧ Keep your pet on a leash or harness. Even trained animals can become agitated or disoriented in unfamiliar surroundings and fail to obey vocal commands.

❧ Attach the leash or harness while your pet is still inside the closed car or crate.

❧ Do not leave your pet unattended at any time, anywhere. A stolen pet is extremely difficult to recover.

❧ Escape-proof your hotel room by crating your pet and asking hotel management to make certain no one enters your room while you are gone. (Inform the property that you're traveling with an animal when making reservations.)

❧ Take along a recent picture and a detailed written description of your pet.

If your pet gets lost these steps will improve your chances of recovery:

❧ If your pet is lost in transit, contact the airline immediately. Ask to trace the animal via the airline's automated baggage tracking system.

❧ Contact local police, animal control, animal shelters, humane organizations and veterinary clinics with a description and a recent photograph. Stay in contact until your pet is found, and provide your home and destination phone numbers.

❧ Post signs and place an ad in the local newspaper so that anyone who comes across your pet knows she is lost and how to reach you.

The Last Word

You are ultimately responsible for your pet's welfare and behavior while traveling. Since animals cannot speak for themselves, it is up to you to focus on your pet's well-being every step of the way. It also is important to make sure he conducts himself properly so that other pets will be welcome visitors in the future. Following the common-sense information in this book will help ensure that both you and your animal companion have a safe and happy trip.

Pet-Friendly
Places

in the United States and Canada

Dog Parks
Attractions
National Public Lands
Emergency Animal Clinics

DOG PARKS

A dog park is a place where people and their dogs can play together. These places offer dogs an area to play, exercise and socialize with other dogs while their owners enjoy the park-like setting. Dog park size and features vary greatly from location to location, from several hundred square feet in urban areas to several hundred acres in the suburbs and rural locations. Dog owners should remember to always keep their animal leashed until they reach the dog park entrance, to maintain voice control of their animal at all times, to bring their own supply of bags for picking up after their pet (and to be diligent in doing so), and to always have fresh water available for their dog. Please observe all dog park rules. The dog parks listed here welcome people who travel with their dogs; private parks or parks requiring local residency are not included. **Note:** Fence types and heights vary, and some areas have no fencing at all, requiring that the dog be under firm voice control.

United States

ARIZONA

Lewis Kingman Park - Kingman
parks.cityofkingman.gov
2201 E. Andy Devine Ave.
Daily 6 a.m.-10 p.m.
Fenced, 9 acres, double-gated entry, trees, shade, benches, shelter, picnic area and grills, multi-purpose field, separate areas for large and small dogs, water, disposal bags, parking, lights, restrooms, access for the disabled.

Countryside Park - Mesa
mesaaz.gov/parksrec
3130 E. Southern Ave., in Countryside Park.
Wed.-Mon. dawn to 10:00 p.m.
Fenced, 1.2 acres, park benches, separate areas for timid and active dogs, water fountains for both people and dogs, parking, disposal bags, trash cans.

Quail Run Park - Mesa
mesaaz.gov/parksrec
4155 E. Virginia, in Quail Run Park north of McDowell Road and off Greenfield
Daily dawn-10 p.m.; closed Thursdays for maintenance.
More than 3 acres, completely fenced, park benches, separate areas for active and timid dogs, water fountains for people and dogs, parking, disposal bags, trash cans.

Echo Mountain Off Leash Area - Phoenix
phoenix.gov, (602) 262-6696 (wet weather)
2302 E. Grovers Ave. (located in Grovers Basin on 20th Street at Cave Creek Road)
Daily 6:30 a.m.-10 p.m.
Fenced, 2.3 acres with grass surface, disposal bags, drinking fountains, trash cans, separate areas for large and small dogs.

PETsMART Dog Park at Washington Park - Phoenix
phoenix.gov, (602) 262-6971 (wet weather)
21st Avenue north of Maryland, between Bethany Home and Glendale roads
Daily 6:30 a.m.-10 p.m.
Fenced, 2.65 acres with grass surface, double-gated entries, benches, water fountain, two dog-watering stations, disposal bags, trash cans, separate areas for large and small dogs. Access for the disabled.

RJ Dog Park at Pecos Park - Phoenix
phoenix.gov, (602) 534-5252 (wet weather)
48th Street and Pecos Parkway (enter from 48th Street via Chandler Boulevard)
Daily 6 a.m.-11 p.m.
Fenced, 2 acres with grass surface, double-gated entry, benches, water fountain, separate areas for large and small dogs. Access for the disabled.

Rose Mofford Sports Complex - Phoenix
phoenix.gov, (602) 261-8011 (wet weather)
9833 N. 25th Ave. (north of Dunlap)
Daily 6:30 a.m.-10 p.m.
Fenced, 2.5 acres with grass surface, double-gated entries, benches, trees, water fountain, disposal bags, trash cans, separate areas for large and small dogs. Access for the disabled.

Steele Indian School Park - Phoenix
phoenix.gov, (602) 495-0739 (wet weather)
West side of 7th Street, just north of Indian School Road
Daily 6 a.m.-10 p.m.
Fenced, 1.83 acres with granite surface, double-gated entries, disposal bags, trash cans, separate areas for large and small dogs. Access for the disabled.

Chaparral Park - Scottsdale
scottsdaleaz.gov
5401 N. Hayden Rd. at McDonald Drive
Daily 5:30 a.m.-10 p.m., May-Oct.; 6 a.m.-10 p.m., rest of year. Closed for maintenance Tues. and Fri. 8-noon and in wet conditions. Phone (480) 312-2353 for status.
Fenced, 4 acres, benches, shade, restroom, water, lighted, separate areas for large and small dogs.

Horizon Park - Scottsdale
scottsdaleaz.gov
15444 N. 100th St. at Thompson Peak Parkway (east of SR 101 off Frank Lloyd Wright Boulevard)
Daily dawn-dusk. Closed Thursdays 9:30 a.m.-12:30 p.m. for maintenance.
Fenced, 2/3 acre, benches, shade structure, tables, disposal bags, trash cans, parking, phones, restrooms, people/dog drinking fountains.

Vista del Camino Park - Scottsdale
scottsdaleaz.gov
7800 E. Pierce St. (take Pierce Street heading west from Hayden Road)
Daily 5:30 a.m.-10 p.m.
Fenced, 1/2 acre, double-gated entry, lighted, grass turf, benches, restrooms nearby, water fountains for dogs and people, mutt mitt stations.

Creamery Park - Tempe
tempe.gov, (480) 350-5200
8th Street and Una Avenue (just south of University Drive near Rural Road)
Daily 6 a.m.-10 p.m.
Fenced, lighted, benches, disposal bags, trash cans, parking, water.

Jaycee Park - Tempe
tempe.gov, (480) 350-5200
5th Street and Hardy Drive
Daily 6 a.m.-10 p.m.
Fenced, lighted, trees, benches, disposal bags, trash cans, parking, water. Access for the disabled.

Mitchell Park - Tempe
tempe.gov, (480) 350-5200
Mitchell Drive and 9th Street
Daily 6 a.m.-10 p.m.; closed Mondays for maintenance.
Fenced, lighted, trees, benches, disposal bags, trash cans,
parking, water. Access for the disabled.

Papago Park - Tempe
tempe.gov, (480) 350-5200
Curry Road and College Avenue
Daily 6 a.m.-10 p.m.; closed Thursdays for maintenance.
Fenced, lighted, trees, disposal bags, trash cans, parking,
water.

Tempe Sports Complex - Tempe
tempe.gov, (480) 350-5200
Warner Road and Hardy Drive
Daily 6 a.m.-10 p.m.
Fenced, lighted, trees, disposal bags, trash cans, parking,
water.

Christopher Columbus Park - Tucson
tucsonaz.gov, (520) 791-4873
4600 N. Silverbell Rd.
Daily dawn-dusk.
Fenced, 1/3 acre, water fountain for dogs, scrambling area,
shaded area with ramada, scooper dispenser.

Reid Park - Miko's Corner Playground - Tucson
tucsonaz.gov, (520) 791-4873
Country Club Road and 22nd Street (use Picnic Place or
Concert Place entrances off Country Club Road)
Daily 7 a.m.-10 p.m.
Fenced, lighted, three double-entry gates, large turf areas,
divided 2-acre site for large and small dogs, dog-friendly
potable water fountains, scooper dispenser, ramada with tables.
Named after Miko, a Tucson police dog that lost its life in the
line of duty.

Jacobs Park - Tucson
tucsonaz.gov, (520) 791-4873
3300 N. Fairview Ave. on the west side of Jacobs Park
Daily dawn-dusk.
Fenced, turf area, walkway, picnic table, double-entry gate.

Palo Verde Park - Tucson
tucsonaz.gov, (520) 791-5930
300 S. Mann Ave. (south of Broadway Boulevard, west of Kolb
Road)
Daily 6 a.m.-10:30 p.m.
Fenced, separate areas for large and small dogs, both with
separate double-entry gates; entire facility lighted; DG/pea
gravel surface, no turf; picnic tables; trash cans; water
fountains for dogs on each side; scooper dispensers.

Sixth Avenue Dog Park - Tucson
tucsonaz.gov, (520) 791-4873
2075 N. Sixth Ave. (east side of Sixth Avenue across from
Northwest Center and Mansfield Park)
Daily dawn-dusk.
Fenced, ramada, tables, wash area, double-entry gate.

Udall Park - Tucson
tucsonaz.gov, (520) 791-4931
7290 E. Tanque Verde Rd.
Daily 6 a.m.-10 p.m.
Fenced, 1 acre, trash cans, seating, water for dogs.

CALIFORNIA

Calabasas Bark Park - Calabasas
cityofcalabasas.com
4232 Las Virgenes Rd. (approximately 2 miles west of US
101 on the south side)
Daily 5 a.m.-9 p.m.
Fenced, lighted, trees, benches, scoops, trash cans, paved
parking, water fountain for dogs, separate areas for large and
small dogs.

Canine Corral - Carmichael
carmichaelpark.com
5750 Grant Ave. at Fair Oaks Blvd.
Daily dawn-10 p.m.
Fenced, 1 acre, double-gated entry, trees, benches, shade,
small dog area, disposal bags, trash cans, water, parking,
lights. Access for the disabled.

Costa Mesa Bark Park - Costa Mesa
cmbarkpark.org, (949) 733-4101
890 Arlington Ave. at Newport Boulevard (across from the
Orange County Fairgrounds Equestrian Center)
Wed.-Mon. dawn-9 p.m.
Fenced, 2.1 acres, night lights dusk-9 p.m., grass turf, trees,
benches, tables, disposal bags, trash cans, parking, restrooms,
water fountains, water for dogs, separate small dog area.
Access for the disabled.

Ernie Smith Dog Park - El Verano
sonoma-county.org
18776 Gilman Dr.
Daily dawn-dusk.
Fenced, 1/2 acre, double-gated entry, water fountain for dogs,
picnic tables, disposal bags, trash can, free parking.

Elizabeth Anne Perrone Dog Park - Glen Ellen
sonoma-county.org
13630 Sonoma Hwy. in Sonoma Valley Regional Park (SR 12
between Arnold Drive and Madrone Road)
Daily dawn-dusk. Parking fee $5 or annual park pass.
Fenced, 1 acre, double-gated entry, covered gazebo, shade
trees, water fountain for dogs, disposal bags, trash can.

Badger Dog Park - Healdsburg
ci.healdsburg.ca.us
Heron Drive in Badger Park
Daily 6 a.m.-dusk.
Fenced, dog run best suited to small dogs, water, picnic table,
shade.

Villa Chanticleer Dog Park - Healdsburg
ci.healdsburg.ca.us
1248 N. Fitch Mountain Rd.
Daily dawn-dusk.
Fenced, 1.5 acres, water, picnic table, shade, information kiosk.

Huntington Dog Beach - Huntington Beach
dogbeach.org
Pacific Coast Highway between 21st and Seapoint streets
Daily 5 a.m.-10 p.m.; metered parking lots close at 10 p.m.
Unfenced, benches and tables on the bluffs above the beach,
disposal bags, trash cans, metered parking, restrooms. Dogs
may be off leash anywhere within dog beach boundaries while
under an owner's supervision. Access for the disabled to the
sand.

Laguna Niguel Pooch Park - Laguna Niguel
cityoflagunaniguel.org
31461 Golden Lantern near Fire Station #49
Tues.-Thurs. and Sat. 7 a.m.-dusk, Sun. 8 a.m.-dusk, Mon.
and Fri. noon-dusk.
Fenced, 1 acre, wood chip ground cover, picnic tables,
shelters, disposal bag dispenser, parking opposite the fire
station, restroom, water faucet with hose, separate fenced area
for small dogs. Access for the disabled.

Long Beach Recreation Dog Park - Long Beach
recreationdogpark.org
5201 E. 7th St. at Park Avenue
Daily 6 a.m.-10 p.m.; closed Mondays until noon for
maintenance
Fenced, 2 acres, lighted, trees, crushed-granite surface,
benches, tables, disposal bags, trash cans, parking, water,
separate fenced area for small dogs. Access for the disabled.

Mill Valley Dog Park - Mill Valley
millvalleydogpark.org
Camino Alto and Sycamore Ave.
Daily dawn-dusk.
Partially fenced, 3 acres, trees, shade, disposal bags, agility stations, trash cans, water. The park fronts Richardson Bay and is fenced on the land sides only. Parking is available about 350 feet from the park; dogs must be leashed from the parking areas to the park. Access for the disabled.

Morgan Hill Dog Park - Morgan Hill
morganhilldog.org
Edmundson Avenue and Monterey Road (entrance is shared with Centennial Recreation Center)
Daily dawn-dusk; closed Wednesday morning for maintenance
Fenced, between 2 and 3 acres, separate small dog area, natural grass, trees, tables, parking, water, double-gated entry, bulletin board, disposal bags, trash cans.

Palm Springs Dog Park - Palm Springs
palmspringsca.gov
3200 E. Tahquitz Canyon Way, behind City Hall
Daily 24 hours.
Fenced, 1.6 acres, lighted, double-gated entry, trees, benches, tables, shelter, disposal bags, trash cans, parking, phones, dual-level water fountains, separate areas for large and small dogs, antique fire hydrants, unusual iron fence created by sculptor Phill Evans. Access for the disabled.

Alice's Dog Park - Pasadena
pasadenapooch.org
3026 E. Orange Grove (located within Vina Vieja Park, east of Sierra Madre Boulevard)
Daily dawn-dusk.
Fenced, 2.5 acres for large dogs, 1 acre for small dogs, double-gated entry, trees, benches, water, shelter, disposal bags, trash cans, parking. Access for the disabled.

Rocky Memorial Park - Petaluma
cityofpetaluma.net
W. Casa Grande Road, southwest of Lakeville Hwy.
Daily 6 a.m. to 10 p.m.
Partially fenced, 9 acres, parking.

Redondo Beach Dog Park - Redondo Beach
rbdogpark.com
Southeast corner of 190th Street and Flagler Lane
Daily dawn-dusk; closed Wed. dawn-noon for maintenance.
Fenced, trees, benches, disposal bags, trash cans, parking, phones, water, separate fenced area for small dogs. Access for the disabled.

Bannon Creek Park - Sacramento
cityofsacramento.org
2780 Azevedo Dr., near West El Camino Avenue
Daily 5 a.m.-10 p.m.
Fenced, .6 acres, double-gated entry, benches, disposal bag dispensers, water fountain/faucet for dogs.

Glenbrook Dog Park - Sacramento
cityofsacramento.org
8500 La Riviera Dr. in Glenbrook Park, behind the little league fields
Daily 5 a.m.-10 p.m.
Fenced, 1 acre, double-gated entry, water fountain for dogs, shade, trees, seating, picnic tables.

Granite Dog Park - Sacramento
cityofsacramento.org
8200 Ramona Ave., off Power Inn Road in Granite Regional Park
Daily 5 a.m.-10 p.m.
Fenced, 2 acres, double-gated entry, lights, bench, disposal bags, trash cans, water spigot for dogs. Access for the disabled.

Jacinto Creek Park Dog Park - Sacramento
cityofsacramento.org
8600 W. Stockton Blvd., South Sacramento
Daily 5 a.m.-10 p.m.
Fenced, 2 acres, double-gated entry, drinking fountain for dogs, turf and decomposed granite areas, trees, obstacle course for dogs, benches.

North Natomas Regional Park Dog Park - Sacramento
cityofsacramento.org
2501 New Market Dr.
Daily dawn-dusk.
Fenced, 2.5 acres, separate small dog area, grass and crushed granite surface, benches, trash cans, water.

Partner Park - Sacramento
cityofsacramento.org
5699 South Land Park Dr. at Fruitridge Road, behind the Belle Cooledge Community Center. Parking available behind community center.
Daily 5 a.m.-10 p.m.
Fenced, 2 acres, lighted, double-gated entry, landscaped with turf and mature trees, bench, disposal bags, trash cans, water spigot for dogs. Access for the disabled.

Regency Community Park - Dog Park - Sacramento
cityofsacramento.org
5500 Honor Pkwy. in North Natomas
Daily 5 a.m.-10 p.m.
Fenced, 2 acres, double-gated entry, water fountain for dogs, turf and decomposed granite areas, trees, benches.

Sutters Landing Dog Park - Sacramento
cityofsacramento.org
20 28th St. (cross street is B Street)
Daily dawn-dusk.
Fenced, 2.5 acres, separate small dog area, trash cans, water.

Tanzanite Community Park - Sacramento
cityofsacramento.org
2220 Tanzanite Way in Tanzanite Community Park
Daily 5 a.m.-10 p.m.
Fenced, 2 acres, double-gated entry, landscaped with turf and native grass, trees, benches, disposal bags, trash cans, water fountain for dogs.

Balboa Park - San Diego
sandiego.gov
Daily 24 hours.
Unfenced, large field.
Two off-leash areas:
(1) Nate's Point at El Prado, on the south side of Cabrillo Bridge
(2) Morley Field, northwest of the tennis courts.

Cadman Community Park - San Diego
sandiego.gov
4280 Avati Dr.
Daily 7-9:30 a.m. and 5-7:30 p.m., in summer; 7:30-10 a.m. and 4:30-7 p.m., rest of year.
Unfenced; observe off-leash boundaries.

Capehart Park (Pacific Beach) - San Diego
sandiego.gov
Soledad Mountain Road and Feldspar Street
Daily 24 hours.
Fenced, 1 acre, picnic tables, benches, parking, separate grass-turf areas for large and small dogs, areas to provide water to dogs, water fountain.

Dog Beach - San Diego
sandiego.gov
Voltaire Street in Ocean Beach (enter the parking lot at the west end of Voltaire Street)
Daily 24 hours.
Unfenced, disposal bags, trash cans, water, restrooms nearby. Access for the disabled.

Doyle Community Park - San Diego
sandiego.gov
8175 Regents Rd. (behind the Doyle Recreation Center)
Daily 24 hours.
Fenced, no lights, separate grass-turf areas for large and small dogs.

Fiesta Island - San Diego
sandiego.gov
Part of Mission Bay Park
Daily 6 a.m.-10 p.m.
This island allows dogs anywhere outside the fenced areas.

Grape Street Park - San Diego
sandiego.gov
Grape Street and Granada Avenue
Mon.-Fri. 7:30 a.m.-9 p.m., Sat.-Sun. and holidays 9-9.
Unfenced, 5 acres, lighted, trees, benches, tables, trash cans, parking, restrooms, water.

Kearny Mesa Community Park - San Diego
sandiego.gov
3170 Armstrong St.
Daily 6:30 a.m.-10 p.m.
Unfenced, 1 acre, lights, water.

Rancho Penasquitos Park - San Diego
sandiego.gov
Salmon River Road at Fairgrove Lane
Daily dawn-dusk. Fenced, 1 acre, double-gated entry, benches, parking, separate large and small dog areas.

San Dimas Dog Park - San Dimas
sandimasdogpark.org
301 Horsethief Canyon Rd. (cross streets are Sycamore and San Dimas Canyon Road)
Daily dawn-dusk (closed alternating Wednesdays from noon-2 for maintenance and during wet weather).
Fenced, 1 acre, double-gated entry, trees, grass, benches, shelter, tables, separate small dog area, disposal bags, trash cans, water, parking. Access for the disabled.

San Francisco
San Francisco regularly reviews its off-leash ("dog play area") policies. Refer to www.sfrecpark.org/documents/DogBrochure.pdf for the most recent information on dog parks.

Alta Plaza Park - San Francisco
sfgov.org Clay Street between Scott and Steiner streets on the second terrace of the park
Daily 6 a.m.-10 p.m.
Unfenced, 1/2 acre; dogs must be under firm voice control.

Bernal Heights - San Francisco
sfgov.org
Bernal Heights Boulevard at the top of the hill
Daily 6 a.m.-10 p.m.
Unfenced; dogs must be under firm voice control.

Buena Vista Park - San Francisco
sfgov.org
Buena Vista West Avenue at Central Avenue
Daily 6 a.m.-10 p.m.
Unfenced; dogs must be under firm voice control.

Corona Heights - San Francisco
sfgov.org
Roosevelt Way and Museum Way in the field next to the Randall Museum
Daily 6 a.m.-10 p.m.
Fenced.

Dolores Park - San Francisco
sfgov.org
Between Church and Dolores streets, south of the tennis courts and soccer field
Daily 6 a.m.-10 p.m.
Unfenced; dogs must be under firm voice control.

Douglass Park - San Francisco
sfgov.org
27th and Douglass streets, upper field
Daily 6 a.m.-10 p.m.
Unfenced; dogs must be under firm voice control.

Eureka Valley Recreation Center - San Francisco
sfgov.org
Collingwood Street, adjacent to the tennis courts and east of the baseball diamond
Daily 6 a.m.-10 p.m.
Fenced.

Golden Gate Park - San Francisco
sfgov.org
Four off-leash areas:
(1) Southeast section bounded by Lincoln Way, King Drive and 5th and 7th avenues
(2) Northeast section at Stanyan and Grove streets
(3) South-central area bounded by King Drive, Middle Drive and 34th and 38th avenues
(4) Fenced dog-training area near 38th Avenue and Fulton Street.

Lafayette Park - San Francisco
sfgov.org
Near Sacramento Street between Octavia and Gough streets
Daily 6 a.m.-10 p.m.
Unfenced; dogs must be under firm voice control.

Lake Merced - San Francisco
sfgov.org
Lake Merced Boulevard and Middlefield Drive, northern lake area
Daily 6 a.m.-10 p.m.
Unfenced; dogs must be under firm voice control.

McKinley Square - San Francisco
sfgov.org
San Bruno Avenue and 20th Street, on the west slope
Daily 6 a.m.-10 p.m.
Unfenced; dogs must be under firm voice control.

McLaren Park - San Francisco
sfgov.org
Daily 6 a.m.-10 p.m.
Two off-leash areas:
(1) Top of hill at Shelly Drive and Mansell Street
(2) South entrance at 1600 block of Geneva Avenue, exclusive of habitat area (the open area fenced on roadway)

Mountain Lake Park - San Francisco
sfgov.org
North of Lake Street at 8th Avenue, east end of the park
Daily 6 a.m.-10 p.m.
Unfenced; dogs must be under firm voice control.

Potrero Hill Mini Park - San Francisco
sfgov.org
22nd Street between Arkansas and Connecticut streets
Daily 6 a.m.-10 p.m.
Unfenced; dogs must be under firm voice control.

St. Mary's Park - San Francisco
sfgov.org
Justin and Benton streets, lower terrace of the park
Daily 6 a.m.-10 p.m.
Fenced.

Stern Grove - San Francisco
sfgov.org
Wawona Street between 21st and 23rd avenues, north side
Daily 6 a.m.-10 p.m.
Unfenced; dogs must be under firm voice control.

Upper Noe Recreation Center - San Francisco
sfgov.org
30th Street between Church and Sanchez streets, adjacent to
ballfield (east of first base line, south of third base line)
Daily 6 a.m.-10 p.m.
Fenced.

Field of Dogs - San Rafael
fieldofdogs.org
3540 Civic Center Dr. (near the intersection of US 101 and
North San Pedro Road)
Daily dawn-dusk.
Fenced, double-gated entry, trees, benches, tables, shelter,
disposal bags, trash cans, parking, water. Access for the
disabled.

DeTurk Roundbarn Park - Santa Rosa
ci.santa-rosa.ca.us
819 Donahue St. (between West 8th and 9th streets)
Daily dawn-dusk (in winter, large dog area is closed; all dogs
use the small dog area).
Fenced, 1/4 acre, water.

Doyle Park Dog Park - Santa Rosa
ci.santa-rosa.ca.us
700 Hoen Ave. in Doyle Park (go west on Sonoma Avenue,
turn left on Hoen Avenue and then turn right into the parking
lot; the fenced dog park is behind the stadium)
Daily dawn-dusk (in winter, large dog area is closed; all dogs
use the small dog area).
Fenced, acre, bench, disposal bags, water, restrooms, separate
areas for large and small dogs.

Galvin Dog Park - Santa Rosa
ci.santa-rosa.ca.us
3330 Yulupa Ave. in Don Galvin Park (next to Bennet Valley
Golf Course)
Daily dawn-dusk (in winter, large dog area is closed; all dogs
use the small dog area).
Fenced, 1/2 acre, double-gated entry, trees, trash cans,
parking, water, picnic tables, restrooms. Access for the
disabled.

Northwest Community Dog Park - Santa Rosa
ci.santa-rosa.ca.us
2620 W. Steele Ln. in Northwest Community Park (go west on
Gurneville Road, turn right on Marlow Road and then turn right
at the first traffic light into the park's parking lot; walk east
along the path to the dog park on the left)
Daily dawn-dusk (in winter, large dog area is closed; all dogs
use the small dog area).
Fenced, 1/2 acre, benches, disposal bags, trash cans,
restrooms nearby, water, separate area for small dogs.

Rincon Valley Dog Park - Santa Rosa
ci.santa-rosa.ca.us
5108 Badger Rd. in Rincon Valley Community Park
Daily dawn-dusk (in winter, large dog area is closed; all dogs
use the small dog area).
Fenced, 1/2 acre, trees, benches, tables, disposal bags, trash
cans, parking, phones, restrooms, water, separate fenced
areas for large and small dogs (area for large dogs closed
during the winter), fenced pond area for dogs (open
year-round). Monitors are present during peak hours to enforce
rules. Access for the disabled.

Off-leash, unfenced, under voice control areas:

700 Doyle Park Drive - Santa Rosa
ci.santa-rosa.ca.us
700 Doyle Park Dr. (go west on Sonoma Avenue, turn left
on Hoen Avenue and then turn right into the parking lot; the
unfenced, off-leash area is to the right of the fenced dog
park)
Daily 6-8 a.m.

Franklin Park - Santa Rosa
ci.santa-rosa.ca.us
2095 Franklin Ave.
Daily 6-8 a.m.

Southwest Community - Santa Rosa
ci.santa-rosa.ca.us
1698 Hearn Ave.
Daily 6-8 a.m.

Youth Community - Santa Rosa
ci.santa-rosa.ca.us
1725 Fulton Rd.
Daily 6-8 a.m.

Remington Dog Park - Sausalito
sausalitodogpark.org
Ebbtide Avenue at Bridgeway Boulevard
Mon.-Fri. 7-7, Sat.-Sun. 8-7
Fenced, lighted, safety-gated entry, picnic tables, benches,
tents for shelter, scoops and scooper cleaning station, trash
cans, parking, water, tennis balls and racquets provided.

Animal Care Center Dog Park - Sebastopol
sonoma-county.org
500 Ragle Rd.
Daily dawn-dusk. Small dogs only Mon.-Fri. 11-noon, Sat.-Sun.
3-4. Parking fee $5 or annual park pass.
Fenced, 1/2 acre, double-gated entry, disposal bags, trash can,
parking, shade, water fountain for dogs.

Arbor Dog Park - Seal Beach
sealbeachca.gov
4665 Lampson Ave., between Valley View Street and Los
Alamitos Boulevard off Lampson Avenue
Daily dawn-dusk; closed Thursday 8 a.m.-noon for
maintenance. Non-resident user license available for a $12
annual fee; see Web site.
Fenced, 2.2 acres, double-gated entry, trees, benches, disposal
bags, trash cans, water, parking. Access for the disabled.

Sierra Madre Dog Park - Sierra Madre
cityofsierramadre.com
611 E. Sierra Madre Blvd. in Sierra Vista Park, south of the
tennis courts
Daily 6 a.m.-10 p.m. Permit required; daily permit $5. Daily and
annual permits are available at city hall.
Fenced, lighted, double-gated entry, trees, benches, disposal
bags, trash cans, parking, phones, restrooms, water, separate
fenced areas for large/active dogs and "special needs" dogs.
Access for the disabled.

Baldy View Dog Park - Upland
uplandpl.lib.ca.us
11th Street between Mountain Avenue and San Antonio
Avenue
Daily dawn-dusk. Annual family membership $25.
Fenced, 5 acres, double-gated entry and exit, grass turf, shade
trees, benches, free parking, separate areas for large and
small dogs, water stations for dogs.

Heather Farms Dog Park - Walnut Creek
walnut-creek.org
550 N. San Carlos Dr. in Heather Farms Park
Mon.-Fri. 7 a.m.-8 p.m., Sat.-Sun. and holidays 8-8. Park
closed during rainy weather; phone the Turf Hotline at (925)
256-3574 for status.
Fenced, double-gated entry, separate areas for large and small
dogs, grass, trees, benches, tables, disposal bags, water, trash
cans, parking. Access for the disabled.

COLORADO

Grandview Off-Leash Dog Park - Aurora
auroragov.org
17900 E. Quincy Ave. (just east of Pitkin Street, adjacent to Quincy Reservoir on the lake's west side)
Daily dawn-dusk.
Fenced, 5 acres, separate small dog area, shade, trash cans, parking, water.

East Boulder Community - Boulder City
bouldercolorado.gov
5660 Sioux Dr.
Daily dawn-dusk.
Fenced, 2.75 acres, separate areas for large and small dogs, disposal bags, trash cans, parking, water, fenced-off swimming area. Access for the disabled.

Foothills Community Park - Boulder City
bouldercolorado.gov
Locust Avenue and Lee Hill Road, west of Broadway Street
Daily dawn-dusk.
Fenced, 2 acres, separate areas for large and small dogs, disposal bags, trash cans, parking, water. Access for the disabled.

Howard H. Hueston Park - Boulder City
bouldercolorado.gov
34th Street near O'Neal Parkway
Daily dawn-dusk.
Unfenced, trees, benches, tables, trash cans, parking. Dogs must be under voice control and kept in sight at all times. Access for the disabled.

Valmont Dog Park - Boulder City
bouldercolorado.gov
5275 Valmont Rd. at Airport Road
Daily dawn-dusk.
Fenced, 3 acres, separate areas for large and small dogs, disposal bags, trash cans, parking, water (available seasonally). Access for the disabled.

Carter Park Dog Park - Breckenridge
townofbreckenridge.com
South end of High Street
Daily 24 hours.
Fenced, almost 1 acre, grass, trees, benches, tables, disposal bags, trash cans, water, parking. Please note there is no lighting. Access for the disabled.

Palmer Park - Colorado Springs
springsgov.com
Maizeland Road and Academy Boulevard
Daily 5 a.m.-11 p.m., May-Oct.; 5 a.m.-9 p.m., rest of year.
Fenced, benches, tables, disposal bags, trash cans, parking, restrooms, water. Access for the disabled.

Rampart Dog Park - Colorado Springs
springsgov.com
8270 Lexington Dr. (from the intersection of Lexington Drive and North Union Boulevard, go north on Lexington, then turn left into the park entrance)
Daily 5 a.m.-11 p.m., May-Oct.; 5 a.m.-9 p.m., rest of year.
Fenced, trees, benches, disposal bags, trash cans, parking, water. Access for the disabled.

Barnum Park - Denver
denvergov.org
Hooker Street and West 5th Avenue
Daily dawn-dusk.
Natural barriers (turf with split-rail fencing to delineate boundaries), 3 acres, trees, disposal bags, trash cans, parking, restroom, bulletin board.

Berkeley Park - Denver
denvergov.org
Sheridan Boulevard and West 46th Avenue, west of the lake
Daily dawn-dusk.
Fenced, 2 acres, turf, double-gate entry, trees, disposal bags, trash cans, parking, bulletin board.

Fuller Park - Denver
denvergov.org
Franklin Street and East 29th Avenue, northwest section (enter from 29th Avenue)
Daily dawn-dusk.
Fenced, 1 acre, turf, double-gate entry, disposal bags, trash cans, bulletin board, on-street neighborhood parking only.

Green Valley Ranch East Park - Denver
denvergov.org
Jebel Street and East 45th Avenue, southwest section (dog park accessible from parking lot)
Daily dawn-dusk.
Natural barriers (native vegetation and split-rail fencing to delineate boundaries), 2 acres, disposal bags, trash cans, parking.

Josephine Dog Park - Denver
denvergov.org
Josephine and 16th Avenue
Daily dawn-dusk.
Fenced, disposal bags, trash cans, benches.

Kennedy Park - Denver
denvergov.org
Hampden Avenue and South Dayton Street, southwest section
Daily dawn-dusk.
Natural barriers (native vegetation and split-rail fencing to delineate boundaries), 3 acres, disposal bags, trash cans, bulletin board, very limited parking (complex parking lot not open to dog park visitors).

Stapleton Dog Park - Denver
denvergov.org
E. 24th Avenue and Syracuse Street
Daily dawn-dusk.
Fenced, 3 acres, shade, water, street parking, disposal bags, trash cans.

Railyard Dog Park - Denver
denvergov.org
19th Avenue and Little Raven Street
Daily dawn-dusk.
Fenced, separate small dog area, water, shade, trees, disposal bags, trash cans.

City Bark at City Park - Pueblo
pueblo.us
800 Goodnight Ave.
Daily 6 a.m.-10 p.m.
Fenced, 2.3 acres, double-gated entry, trees, benches, shade, tables, disposal bags, trash cans, water, parking. Access for the disabled.

Westminster Dog Park - Westminster
ci.westminster.co.us
105th Avenue and Simms Street
Daily dawn-dusk.
Partially fenced, 420-acre open space, trees, benches, shelter, shade, disposal bags, trash cans, water, parking. Access for the disabled.

Little Dry Creek Dog Park - Westminster
ci.westminster.co.us
3655 W. 69th Pl.
Daily dawn-dusk.
Fenced, 1.75 acres, trees, benches, disposal bags, trash cans, water.

CONNECTICUT

Southbury Dog Park - Southbury
southbury-ct.org
Roxbury Road (Route 67), next to Red Sable Horse Farm
Daily dawn-dusk.
Fenced, double-gated entry, benches, tables, separate small dog area, disposal bags, trash cans, water, parking, onsite stream accessed by a staircase.

DELAWARE

Levels Road Park - Middletown
middletownde.org
Levels Road (Route 15), located within Levels Road Park
Daily 7 a.m.-dusk.
Fenced, 5-acre large dog area, 3-acre small dog area, double-gated entry, trees, benches, shade, grass, disposal bags, trash cans, water available spring-fall, parking.

Rockford Park Off-Leash Area - Wilmington
destateparks.com
Park Drive and Red Oak Road
Daily 8 a.m.-dusk.
Unfenced, more than 5 acres, trees, benches, shade, disposal bags, trash cans, water.

FLORIDA

Canine Cove at South County Regional Park - Boca Raton
pbcgov.com
12551 Glades Rd., west of Boca Raton in South County Regional Park
Daily dawn-dusk; closed Wednesday noon-3 for maintenance.
Fenced, 4 acres, paved pathways, shaded sitting areas, disposal bag dispensers and receptacles, trash cans, restrooms and parking nearby, gazebos, separate areas for large and small dogs, canine drinking stations, dog wash area.

Happy Tails Canine Park - Bradenton
mymanatee.org
51st Street West at G.T. Bray Park, about halfway between Manatee Avenue and Cortez Road
Daily dawn-dusk. Closed Thurs. 7-10 and last Fri. of the month 2-dusk for maintenance.
Eight-foot fence, 3 acres, separate area for small dogs, trees, benches, tables, disposal bags, trash cans, parking, restrooms nearby, water.

Dr. Paul's Memorial Dog Park - Coral Springs
toppetcare.com/petutopiawelcome.html
2915 Sportsplex Dr. in the Sportsplex Regional Park Complex (park off Sportsplex Drive at the west pedestrian entrance)
Daily dawn - 9:30 p.m.
Enclosed, lighted, trees, shaded area, paved running path, picnic table, gazebo, disposal bag dispensers, trash cans, indoor restroom, separate areas for large and small dogs, water fountains for dogs and people, dog shower, dog statues, weatherproof dog agility equipment.

The Dog Park in Lake Ida Park - Delray Beach
pbcgov.com
1455 Lake Ida Rd. (take the Atlantic Avenue West exit off I-95, proceed west to Congress Avenue, go north on Congress for 1 mile, turn right onto Lake Ida Road and proceed east under I-95; park entrance is on the left)
Daily dawn-dusk; closed Thurs. noon-3 for maintenance.
Fenced, 2.5 acres, partial paved pathway, eight shaded sitting areas, disposal bag dispensers and receptacles, restrooms and parking nearby, separate fenced areas for large and small dogs, two canine drinking stations, dog washing area, information kiosk.

Pooch Pines Dog Park at Okeeheelee Park - Delray Beach
pbcgov.com
7715 Forest Hill Blvd. (off I-95 exit Forest Hill Boulevard, west to the main Okeeheelee Park entrance on the north side of the road; follow the park road to the Pooch Pines sign, turn right and continue to the top of the hill)
Daily dawn-dusk; closed Wed. noon-3 for maintenance.
Fenced, 5 acres, paved pathways, shaded sitting areas, disposal bag dispensers and receptacles, trash cans, restrooms and parking nearby, separate areas for large and small dogs, canine drinking stations, dog washing area.

Bark Park at Snyder Park - Fort Lauderdale
fortlauderdale.gov
3299 S.W. 4th Ave.
Daily 7 a.m.-7 p.m.; closed Thurs. 8-11 for maintenance.
Closed Jan. 1 and Dec. 25.
Entry fee varies; canine beach $7.
Fenced, two open-air pavilions, benches, disposal bags, trash cans, parking, restrooms, water, separate area for small dogs, two hose stations, water fountains, agility equipment, small nature area with more than 20 labeled native trees, canine swimming in East Lake, canine beach (hours vary). Access for the disabled. Note: Dogs must remain in the car until arrival at Bark Park and are not permitted in the remainder of Snyder Park.

Millennium Dog Park - Ocala
millenniumdogpark.com
2513 S.E. 32nd Ave.
Mon.-Wed. and Sat.-Sun. 8 a.m.-7 p.m., in summer; 8-6, in winter.
Fenced, 4.5 acres, double-gated entry, grass, trees, benches, shelter, shade, small dog area, disposal bags, trash cans, water, parking. Access for the disabled.

Dog Leg Park at Buffalo Creek - Palmetto
mymanatee.org
7550 69th St. E.
Daily dawn-dusk. Closed Thurs. 7 a.m.-10 a.m. and last Fri. of the month 2-dusk for maintenance.
Fenced, 3 acres, trees, separate small dog area, disposal bags, doggie drinking fountains, shelter.

Paw Park of Historic Sanford - Sanford
pawparksanford.org
427 French Ave. (US 17/92) in Sanford's Historic District, 20 minutes north of downtown Orlando. From I-4, take the SR 46 exit (exit 101C, Sanford/Mount Dora), proceed east on SR 46 approximately 4 miles to French Ave., turn right (southbound) and get into the left thru-lane; the Paw Park is on the left just past the Burger King.
Daily 7:30 a.m.-8 p.m.
Fenced, double-gated entry, shaded with mature oak trees, historic lighting, paved walkway, benches, tables, disposal bag dispensers, parking, self-watering bowls, water misting station, dog showers, separate area for small dogs, community bulletin board. Access for the disabled.

17th Street Paw Park - Sarasota
scgov.net
4570-4730 17th St.
Daily dawn-dusk.
Fenced, separate areas for large and small dogs, tables, benches, shade, drinking fountain for dogs, disposal bags, trash cans.

Lakeview Paw Park - Sarasota
scgov.net
7150 Lago St.
Daily dawn-dusk.
Fenced, separate areas for large and small dogs, water, disposal bags, trash cans.

Davis Islands Dog Park - Tampa
tampagov.net
1002 Severn St.
Daily dawn-dusk.
Fenced, with two areas at the south end of the island: a 1-acre dry area and a 1.5-acre beach with more than 200 feet of waterfront. Both areas have double-gated entries, disposal bags, trash cans and water. Designated off-leash area on the beach.

Gadsden Park - Tampa
tampagov.net
6901 S. MacDill Ave., southwest corner of the grounds.
Daily dawn-dusk.
Fenced, 1 acre, double-gated entry, water, disposal bags, trash cans, benches, tables, shade trees.

Giddens Park - Tampa
tampagov.net
5202 N. 12th St.
Daily dawn-dusk.
Fenced, 1 acre, double-gated entry, drinking fountains for dogs and people, disposal bags, trash cans, benches, tables, shade trees.

James Urbanski Dog Park at Al Lopez Park - Tampa
tampagov.net
4810 N. Himes Ave.
Daily dawn-dusk.
Fenced, 1.5 acres, separate area for small dogs, double-gated entry, disposal bags, trash cans, benches, tables, shade trees.

Palma Ceia Park - Tampa
tampagov.net
2200 Marti St.
Mon.-Fri. 8 a.m.-dusk or 7:15 p.m. (whichever is earlier), Sat.-Sun. 9 a.m.-dusk or 7:15 p.m. (whichever is earlier).
Fenced, 3/4 acre, double-gated entry, disposal bags, trash cans, benches, tables, shade trees.

Picnic Island Park - Tampa
tampagov.net
7409 Picnic Island Blvd.
Daily dawn-dusk.
Fenced, double-gated entry, disposal bags, trash cans, benches, tables, shade trees. Designated off-leash area on beach.

Rowlett Park - Tampa
tampagov.net
2401 E. Yukon St.
Daily dawn-dusk.
Fenced, 1.75 acre, double-gated entry, disposal bags, trash cans, benches, tables, shade trees, separate areas for large and small dogs, agility equipment.

Lake Idamere Park - Tavares
lakecountyfl.gov
12335 County Rd. 448
Daily dawn-dusk.
Fenced, separate small-dog area, trees, benches, shade, disposal bags, water, trash cans.

North Lake Community Park Dog Park - Umatilla
lakecountyfl.gov
40730 Roger Giles Rd., within North Lake Community Park
Daily 6:30 a.m.-10 p.m.
Fenced, double-gated entry, trees, benches, shelter, shade, disposal bags, grass, trash cans, water, parking, lights. Access for the disabled.

Brohard Beach & Paw Park - Venice
venicegov.com
1600 Harbor Dr. S.
Daily 7 a.m.-dusk.
Six-foot fence, trees, benches, tables, shelter, disposal bags, trash cans, parking, water, dog shower, separate area for small dogs, community bulletin board. Dog Beach is accessed by a boardwalk from Paw Park. Dogs are permitted in a restricted area along Brohard Beach as indicated by beach signs. Access for the disabled.

Woodmere Park & Woodmere Paw Park - Venice
scgov.net
3951 Woodmere Park Blvd. (2 blocks north of US 41 on Jacaranda Boulevard)
Daily dawn-dusk.
Fenced, 2.5 acres, double-gated entry, trees, benches, tables, disposal bags, trash cans, parking, restrooms, water, double-gated section for small dogs near the front gate, dog shower, community bulletin board.

IDAHO

Moscow Dog Park - Moscow
dogparkfriends.org
2019 White Ave. (next to the Humane Society of the Palouse)
Daily dawn-dusk.
Fenced, 1 acre, grass, two double-gated entries, trees, shade, tables, benches, disposal bags, trash cans, water, parking, large tire structures for dogs to climb on or run through. Access for the disabled.

Nampa Dog Park - Nampa
nampaparks.org
East Amity Avenue and 2nd Street South, near the Kings Road overpass
Daily half an hour before dawn to half an hour after dusk.
Fenced, 6 acres, grass, double-gated entry, trees, benches, walking trails, shelter, shade, tables, separate small dog area, disposal bags, trash cans, water, parking. Access for the disabled.

ILLINOIS

Rover's Run Dog Park - Homewood
hfparks.com, (708) 957-0300
Near 191st Street and Center Avenue in Apollo Park
Daily dawn-dusk.
Annual membership fee $25 (non-residents); $15 (residents). A list of current vaccinations is required.
Fenced, 3 acres, double-gated entry, separate training area and entrance, benches, covered picnic tables, free parking, walking path, water fountain for dogs and people.

Bradley Dog Park - Peoria
peoriaparks.org
1314 N. Park Rd. (cross street is Farmington Road)
Daily dawn-dusk.
Fenced, 5 acres, double-gated entry, trees, benches, shade, tables, separate small dog area, disposal bags, trash cans, water, parking, grass and wood mulch. Access for the disabled.

East Side Sports Complex Dog Park - St. Charles
stcparks.org
3565 Legacy Blvd. (east of Kirk Road and about 1 mile south of Rt. 64)
Daily 9 a.m.-dusk (weather permitting).
Fenced, just under 1 acre, separate small dog area, interactive play equipment, water.

James O. Breen Community Park Dog Park - St. Charles
stcparks.org
Corner of Campton Hills and Peck Road
Daily 9 a.m.-dusk (weather permitting).
Fenced, 2.5 acres, double-gated entry, trees, benches, activity stations, disposal bags, trash cans, parking, dog water fountain.

IOWA

Rita's Ranch Off Leash Dog Park - Iowa City
jcdogpac.org
Scott Boulevard between E. Court and Muscatine Avenue
Daily dawn-dusk.
Day pass $5, yearly tag $25 ($5 discount for spayed/neutered dogs)
Fenced, approximately 3 acres, double-gated entry, disposal bags, trash cans, parking.

Thornberry Off Leash Dog Park - Iowa City
jcdogpak.org
End of Foster Road; closest cross street is Canton Street
Daily dawn-dusk.
Day pass $5, yearly tag $25 ($5 discount for spayed/neutered dogs)
Fenced, 10 acres, four separately fenced areas (all dogs, small dogs, training area and a pond for dog swimming and wading), grass, trees, disposal bags, trash cans, asphalt walking path, parking. Water is trucked in except during winter; bring your own container. Access for the disabled.

Lewis and Clark Dog Park at Bacon Creek Park - Sioux City
sioux-city.org
5100 Correctionville Rd.
Daily 7 a.m.-dusk.
Fenced, 4 acres for larger dogs, 1 acre for small dogs, double-gated entry, trees, grass, benches, trash cans, water, parking, disposal bags. Access for the disabled.

KANSAS

El Dorado Dog Park - El Dorado
eldoks.com
400 E. Locust Ave.
Daily dawn-dusk.
Fenced, 1/2 acre, double-gated entry, trees, grass, benches, water, disposal bags, trash cans, parking. Access for the disabled.

KENTUCKY

Kenton County Kentucky Paw Park - Covington
kentonpawpark.com
3950 Madison Pike (Rt. 17) at Pioneer Park
Daily dawn-dusk.
Fenced, 2 acres, double-gated entry, trees, grass, benches, tables, separate areas for large and small dogs, disposal bags. Beautiful creekside setting with additional area for agility (not always available).

Judy Rains Memorial Dog Park - Richmond
parks.richmond.ky.us
299 Lake Reba Dr. (in Lake Reba Park)
Daily 8 a.m.-dusk.
Fenced, 1/2 acre, double-gated entry, trees, grass, benches, tables, separate small dog area, disposal bags, trash cans, water, parking, lights.

MARYLAND

Rebel's Dog Park - Fallston
HarfordShelter.org
2208 Connolly Rd. (at the junction with Rt. 152)
Mon.-Fri. 10-6, Sat. 10-5, Sun. noon-4.
Fenced, double-gated entry, benches, shade, separate small dog area, disposal bags, trash cans, water, parking.

MASSACHUSETTS

The South Boston Bark Park - Boston
sbbarkpark.org
Columbia Road and Day Boulevard
Daily 6 a.m.-8 p.m.
Fenced, 3,000 square feet, double-gated entry, trees, benches, separate small dog area, trash cans, water, pea stone with cement walkways, street parking. Access for the disabled.

Pilgrim Bark Park - Provincetown
provincetowndogpark.org
Shank Painter Road at Rt. 6. Do not park on Shank Painter Road; park on the east side of Rt. 6.
Daily dawn-dusk.
Fenced, nearly 1 acre, separate small dog area, disposal bags, trash cans. Many features, like the custom benches and welcome sign, have been made by local artists.

MICHIGAN

Pet Supplies "Plus" Dog Park at Hillcrest Park - Grand Rapids
grand-rapids.mi.us
1415 Lyon St. N.E. and Benjamin Street N.E. at Hillcrest Park
Daily dawn-dusk.
Fenced, 1 acre, double-gated entry, separate small dog area, shade, water, disposal bags. Street parking is available, or park at Fuller Park and walk to Hillcrest.

Meadow Run Dog Park - Kalamazoo
meadowrunpark.com
900 S. 8th St.
Open daily to members 7 a.m.-8 p.m. Sept.-May, 6 a.m.-9 p.m. June-Aug.; visitors during office hours 10-6 or park close.
Visitor day pass $15 first dog, $5 each additional dog. See site for membership fees.
Fenced, 25 acres, double-gated entry, separate small dog area, agility equipment, swimming area with beach, dock diving area, benches, water, disposal bags, restrooms. Paths plowed in winter. Parking.

Orion Oaks Bark Park - Lake Orion
oakgov.com
South of Clarkston Road on Joslyn Road (park at the north Joslyn Road entrance and follow the signs)
Daily 8 a.m. to half-hour after dusk, or as posted.
A park pass is required; a daily pass is available at the Lake Orion Township office (open Mon.-Fri.) on Joslyn Road south of the park; or at the Independence Oaks County Park (open daily) on Sashabaw Road, 2.5 miles north of I-75.
Day pass per private vehicle $10 (non-resident); $5 (resident); $4 (ages 63+). Annual pass per private vehicle $46 (non-resident); $30 (ages 63+ and resident).
Fenced, 7 acres, trees, benches, tables, disposal bags, trash cans, parking, portable toilet, water. A portion of Lake Sixteen is reserved for canine swimming. Access for the disabled.

Soldan Dog Park at Hawk Island County Park - Lansing
lansingdogparks.com
1601 E. Cavanaugh Rd., just north of Hawk Island County Park; the dog park main entrance is through the park. The dog park also can be accessed from the west off the River Trail in Scott Woods; drive to the very north end of the Hawk Island parking area, then walk a short distance (with your dog or dogs on-leash) past the Hawk Island Maintenance Building to the main dog park entrance.
Daily 6 a.m. to half an hour after dusk, May 15-Aug. 15; daily 7 a.m. to half an hour after dusk, Aug. 16-Sept. 14; daily 8 a.m. to half an hour after dusk, rest of year.
Parking fee Tues.-Sun. $2 for residents, $4 for non-residents
Fenced, 17 acres, double-gated entry, diverse natural area with trails, a large pond and an open field, disposal bags, parking, dog and human drinking fountains. Access for the disabled.

Lyon Oaks Bark Park - Lyon Township
oakgov.com
Pontiac Trail between Wixom and Old Plank roads
Daily 8 a.m. to half-hour after dusk, or as posted.
A park pass is required and is available at park banquet center
(Mon.-Fri. 9-5)
Day pass per private vehicle $10 (non-resident); $5 (resident);
$4 (ages 63+). Annual pass per private vehicle $46
(non-resident); $30 (ages 63+ and resident).
Fenced, 13 acres of open fields, benches, tables, disposal
bags, trash cans, parking, restrooms, water pump.

Red Oaks Dog Park - Madison Heights
oakgov.com
Dequindre Road, adjacent to Red Oaks Waterpark
Daily 8 a.m. to 9 p.m., or as posted. Day permit available
Wed., Sat.-Sun. 10-5.
Fenced, 5.2 acres, 4 separate large and small dog areas,
shelter, water, tables, benches, disposal bags, trash cans,
paved parking.

MINNESOTA

Note: In the greater Minneapolis area there are multiple
off-leash sites within a 15-minute drive of downtown
Minneapolis/St. Paul. There are additional sites in rural/
suburban areas of the seven-county metropolitan area. Some
parks require a permit for use. Please read descriptions
carefully.

Alimagnet Dog Park - Burnsville (south metro suburb)
alimagnetdogpark.org
1200 Alimagnet Pkwy. (from central St. Paul, go south on
I-35E to the CR 42 exit, east to CR 11, then north on CR 11
to Alimagnet Parkway and turn right; the dog park is on the
right)
Daily 5 a.m.-10 p.m. Permit required; for more information visit
the Web site or phone the Recreation Department at (952)
895-4500.
Fenced, 7 acres, double-gated entry, wooded areas, open
fields, mowed prairie-grass trail, benches, tables, disposal bags,
trash cans, lights, parking, phones, restrooms, water, pond.

Dakota Woods Dog Park (south metro rural)
co.dakota.mn.us
16470 Blaine Ave. south of CR 46 (160th Street East) in the
center of Dakota County near Coates Daily 5 a.m.-10 p.m.
Permit required.
Fenced, 16 acres of wooded and open spaces with a walking
trail loop, tables, disposal bag dispensers, trash cans, parking,
portable toilets, no surface water; bring your own water.

Elm Creek Park Reserve - Dayton (northwest metro rural)
threeriversparkdistrict.org
13080 Territorial Rd.
Daily 5 a.m.-10 p.m. Permit required; day permits are available
at the site. Annual special-use permits may be obtained online.
Fenced, 30 acres with a mowed trail, trees, tables, trash cans,
parking, restrooms.

**Battle Creek Off-Leash Site - Maplewood (east central
metro)**
co.ramsey.mn.us
Lower Afton and McKnight roads
Daily dawn-dusk except during deer hunts (see Web site for
dates). No permit required.
Partially fenced, 35 acres, tables, trash cans, parking.

Franklin Terrace - Minneapolis
minneapolisparks.org
925 Franklin Terr. and 30th Avenue South
Daily 6 a.m.-10 p.m. Permit required.
Fully fenced, 1.4 acres, double-gated entry at the east and
west ends of the site, bench, disposal bag dispensers,
on-street parking.

Lake of the Isles Park - Minneapolis
minneapolisparks.org
2845 Lake of the Isles Pkwy. W. at West 28th Street
Daily 6 a.m.-10 p.m. Permit required.
Fully fenced, 1.8 acres, double-gated entry at the northern end
of the site, separate small dog area, lighted at the southern
end, benches, disposal bag dispensers.

Loring Park - Minneapolis
minneapolisparks.org
132 Willow St. at Maple Street and Harmon Place
Daily 6 a.m.-10 p.m. Permit required.
Fenced, 1/4 acre, disposal bag dispensers, limestone boulders
for climbing and sitting, crushed limestone surface.

Minnehaha Park - Minneapolis
minneapolisparks.org
5399 S. Minnehaha Park Dr. and East 54th Street
Daily 6 a.m.-10 p.m. Permit required.
Partially fenced, 7.5 acres along the Mississippi River (where
dogs can swim), disposal bag dispensers, lighted parking area
(parking permit required), portable toilet in parking area.

St. Anthony Parkway - Minneapolis
minneapolisparks.org
700 St. Anthony Pkwy., off Central Avenue
Daily 6 a.m.-10 p.m. Permit required.
Fully fenced, 2 acres, double-gated entry at the east and west
ends of the park, bench, disposal bag dispensers, parking.

Egan Park's Off-Leash Area - Plymouth
ci.plymouth.mn.us
CR 47 in northwest Plymouth, about 2 blocks west of Dunkirk
Lane on the south side of CR 47
Daily dawn-dusk. No permit required.
Unfenced, 10 acres, separate area for small dogs, trash cans;
bring your own water and disposal bags.

Cleary Lake Regional Park - Prior Lake (south metro rural)
threeriversparkdistrict.org
18106 Texas Ave.
Daily 5 a.m.-10 p.m. Permit required; day permits are available
at the site. Annual special-use permits may be obtained online.
Fenced, 35 acres, tables, trash cans, parking, restrooms, pond.
Trails are mowed in summer, packed in winter.

**Crow-Hassan Park Reserve - Rogers (northwest metro
rural)**
threeriversparkdistrict.org
Sylvan Lake Road west of Rogers (from I-94, take the Rogers
exit and go south through town to the T intersection, turn right
on CR 116 and proceed to CR 203, turn left and follow CR
203 to the park entrance)
Daily 5 a.m.-10 p.m. Permit required; day permits are available
at the site. Annual special-use permits may be obtained online.
Fenced, 30 acres with a mowed trail, trees, tables, trash cans,
parking, restrooms.

Woodview Dog Park - Roseville (central)
co.ramsey.mn.us
Larpenteur Avenue, just east of Dale Street (access gate to
main off-leash area is about 100 yards down the bike trail)
Daily dawn-dusk; small dog play times posted online. No
permit required.
Partially fenced (along bike trail only), 4 acres, trees, tables,
disposal bags, trash cans, parking, water, separate fenced area
for small dogs. Access for the disabled during all open hours
regardless of dog size.

Arlington-Arkwright (ArlArk) Dog Park - St. Paul
stpaul.gov
Arkwright Street at Arlington Avenue (from I-35E, take the Maryland Avenue exit east to Arkwright Street, then go north; the park is on the right)
Daily dawn-dusk. No permit required.
Fenced, 4.5 acres with trails and woods, tables, disposal bags, trash cans, parking. Park users sometimes leave gates open; keep your dog under voice control to prevent escapes, bring your own water.

Rice Creek Off-Leash Site - Shoreview (northeast metro)
co.ramsey.mn.us
Lexington Avenue, just south of CR J
Daily dawn-dusk. No permit required.
Unfenced, 13 acres of flat prairie vegetation, tables, trash cans, parking, small pond.

Otter Lake Dog Park - White Bear Township (northeast suburban)
co.ramsey.mn.us
Otter Lake Road (take I-35E to the CR J exit, then CR J east to Otter Lake Road, following it south to the dog park; the entrance is next to the boat launch)
Daily dawn-dusk except during deer hunts (see Web site for dates). No permit required.
Partially fenced, 10 acres of rolling hills with wooded and open prairie vegetation, separate 1-acre fenced area for small dogs. The park is fenced adjacent to Otter Lake Road and along most of the south boundary, bounded on the east by a large wetland and on the north by Otter Lake.

NEBRASKA

Omaha Dog Park/Hefflinger Dog Park - Omaha
omahadogpark.org
11111 W. Maple Rd. (Old Maple Road and N. 112th Avenue)
Daily dawn-dusk.
Fenced, 7.5 acres, double-gated entry, separate small dog area, trees, benches, shade, tables, disposal bags, trash cans, parking. Water is available Memorial Day through Labor Day. The off-leash area is inside the dog park gates; a leash is required in all other areas.

Scottsbluff Dog Park - Scottsbluff
scottsbluff.org
1600 S. Beltline Hwy. West (within Riverside Park and behind the zoo)
Daily dawn-dusk.
Fenced, double-gated entry, separate small dog area, disposal bags, swimming areas, parking; bring your own water. Access for the disabled. The surface is kennel rock, mulch and natural turf (near the river).

NEVADA

Note: All Clark County/Las Vegas dog park areas include water, seating and waste receptacles.

Desert Breeze Park Dog Park - Clark County/Las Vegas (NW)
clarkcountynv.gov
8425 W. Spring Mountain Rd. at Durango Drive
Daily 6 a.m. - 11 p.m.
Three runs, trees.

Desert Inn Dog Park - Clark County/Las Vegas (SE)
clarkcountynv.gov
3570 Vista del Monte Dr. (near Lamb Boulevard and Boulder Highway)
Daily 6 a.m.-11 p.m.

Dog Fancier's Park - Clark County/Las Vegas (SE)
clarkcountynv.gov, (702) 455-8200
5800 E. Flamingo Rd. at Jimmy Durante Boulevard
Daily 6 a.m.-11 p.m. Since this 12-acre park also is used for dog shows and training, phone ahead to confirm schedule.

Molasky Park Dog Park - Clark County/Las Vegas (SE)
clarkcountynv.gov
1065 E. Twain Ave. (west of Maryland Parkway; dog run is south of Twain Avenue)
Daily 6 a.m.-11 p.m.
10 acres.

Shadow Rock Dog Park - Clark County/Las Vegas (NE)
clarkcountynv.gov
2650 Los Feliz St. at Lake Mead Boulevard (east of Hollywood Boulevard; dog run is east of the park area)
Daily 6 a.m.-11 p.m.
Tree, two shade shelters.

Silverado Ranch Park Dog Park - Clark County/Las Vegas (SE)
clarkcountynv.gov
9855 S. Gillespie St.
Daily 6 a.m.-11 p.m.
Two runs, one for dogs under 30 pounds and another for dogs over 29 pounds; lights.

Spring Valley Dog Park - Clark County/Las Vegas (SW)
clarkcountynv.gov
7600 W. Flamingo Rd.
Daily 6 a.m.-11 p.m.
Three runs, lights.

Sunset Park - Clark County/Las Vegas (SE)
clarkcountynv.gov
2601 E. Sunset Rd. (closest parking is off Eastern Avenue between Sunset and Warm Springs roads)
Daily 6 a.m.-11 p.m.
Two runs for large and small dogs.

NEW HAMPSHIRE

Derry Dog Park - Derry
derry.nh.us
45 Fordway St.
Daily dawn-dusk.
Fenced, 1/2 acre, double-gated entry, gazebo, picnic tables, separate area for small dogs, bone-shaped dog pool (open in summer only). Tunnel, seesaw, tire jump and other agility items are provided. Children under 9 are not permitted. Rules are posted on fence inside and out. Parking is free but somewhat limited after 25 vehicles.

Dog Park at South Mill Pond - Portsmouth
portcitydogs.org
South Mill Pond at Junkins Avenue and South Street
Daily dawn-dusk.
Fenced, double-gated entry, separate large and small dog areas, stone and grass surface, benches, shelter, tables, disposal bags, trash cans, water, parking.

NEW MEXICO

Coronado Dog Park - Albuquerque
cabq.gov
301 McKnight Ave. N.W.
Daily 6 a.m.-10 p.m.
Fenced, double-gated entry, no water.

Los Altos Dog Park - Albuquerque
cabq.gov
821 Eubank Blvd. N.E.
Daily 6 a.m.-10 p.m.
Fenced, double-gated entry, no water, lights.

Montessa Dog Park - Albuquerque
cabq.gov
3615 Los Picaros Rd. S.E.
Daily 6 a.m.-10 p.m.
Fenced, double-gated entry, no water.

North Domingo Baca Dog Park - Albuquerque
cabq.gov
7520 Corona Ave. N.E.
Daily 6 a.m.-10 p.m.
Fenced, double-gated entry, no water, lights.

Ouray Dog Park - Albuquerque
cabq.gov
7500 Ouray Rd. N.W.
Daily 6 a.m.-10 p.m.
Fenced, 2 acres, water, parking. Access for the disabled.

Rio Grande Triangle Dog Park - Albuquerque
cabq.gov
1451 Kit Carson Ave. S.E.
Daily 6 a.m.-10 p.m.
Fenced, double-gated entry, no water, lights.

Roosevelt Dog Park - Albuquerque
cabq.gov
500 Spruce St. S.E.
Mon.-Fri 6 a.m.-10 a.m. Apr.-Sept.; Mon.-Fri. 6 a.m.-11 a.m., rest of year. Closed holidays.
Fenced, double-gated entry, no water.

Santa Fe Village Dog Park - Albuquerque
cabq.gov
5700 Bogart St. N.W.
Daily 6 a.m.-10 p.m.
Fenced, double-gated entry, trees, benches, shade, disposal bags, trash cans, water. Access for the disabled.

Tom Bolak Urban Forest Dog Park - Albuquerque
cabq.gov
2000 Dakota St. N.E.
Daily 6 a.m.-10 p.m.
Fenced, double-gated entry, water.

Tower Pond Dog Park - Albuquerque
cabq.gov
Tower Road S.W. and 86th Street S.W.
Daily 6 a.m.-10 p.m.
Fenced, double-gated entry, no water.

USS Bullhead Dog Park - Albuquerque
cabq.gov
1606 San Pedro Dr. S.E.
Daily 6 a.m.-10 p.m.
Fenced, double-gated entry, no water, lights.

Westgate Community Dog Park - Albuquerque
cabq.gov
Cartagena Avenue and Valley View Drive
Daily 6 a.m.-10 p.m.
Fenced, double-gated entry, no water, lights.

NEW YORK

Barkyard-LaSalle Off-Leash Dog Park - Buffalo
thebarkyard.org
101-397 Dar Dr.
Daily dawn-dusk. Small dog hours: Tues. 4-6, Sun. 1-3.
Fenced, 1.6 acres, double-gated entry, benches, trash cans. Access for the disabled.

Wegmans Good Dog Park - Liverpool
onondagacountyparks.com
2500 Cold Springs Tr., Onondaga Lake Park
Daily dawn-dusk.
Fenced, 1 acre, double-gated entry, playground quality pea gravel and grass, trees, separate small dog area, agility equipment, benches, water (May-Oct.), disposal bags, trash cans, parking.

New York City (Manhattan and boroughs)
urbanhound.com
nycgovparks.org

Canine Court, Van Cortlandt Park - Bronx
West 252nd Street and Broadway (enter on the path on 252nd and follow it about 100 feet to the left)
Daily dawn-dusk.
Fenced with two large runs: a basic dog run and a canine agility playground with teeter-totter, hurdles, ladder, three chutes and a hanging tire.

Ewen Park ("John's Run") - Bronx (Riverdale)
Riverdale to Johnson avenues, south of West 232nd Street and down the steps in the clearing on the right
Daily dawn-dusk.
Unfenced, plastic lawn furniture, scenic views.

Seton Park - Bronx (Riverdale)
West 235th Street and Independence Avenue (west of Independence on 235th Street, near the Spuyten Duyvil Library)
Daily dawn-dusk.

Prospect Park - Brooklyn
fidobrooklyn.org
Grand Army Plaza and Flatbush; off-leash areas may be accessed from all park entrances
Daily 9 p.m.-1 a.m. and 5-9 a.m. At all other times dogs must be on a leash; minimum fine for non-compliance $100.
Off-leash areas are the Long Meadow, Nethermead and Peninsula open meadows. Ball fields are off-limits to dogs at all times. **Note:** Use of the park is at the owner's risk. Dogs may be off-leash with appropriate supervision in the three large meadows at the hours specified above; please observe all off-leash rules. Rules are posted online and at park entrances. Dogs must be on a leash at all other places and times.

Owl's Head Park - Brooklyn (Bay Ridge)
68th Street and Shore Road
Tree, grass surface, disposal bags.

Hillside Park - Brooklyn Heights
Columbia Heights and Middagh Street
Daily 24 hours.
Fenced.

Palmetto Playground - Brooklyn Heights
Columbia Place and State Street (in the corner by the Brooklyn-Queens Expressway)
Daily 24 hours.
Benches, one park light, water.

Tompkins Square Park - Manhattan (East Village)
East 9th Street at Avenue B
Daily 6 a.m.-midnight.
Benches, picnic tables, water, a canine memorial. Access for the disabled.

Madison Square Park - Manhattan (Gramercy/Flatiron/ Union Square)
East 24th Street at Fifth Avenue
Daily 6 a.m.-midnight. Trees, benches, disposal bags, water.

Thomas Jefferson Park - Manhattan (Harlem)
East 112th Street at First Avenue
Daily 24 hours.
Benches, wood chip surface.

J. Hood Wright Park - Manhattan (Inwood/Ft. George/ Washington Heights)
West 173rd Street between Fort Washington Avenue and Haven Avenue

Fishbridge Park - Manhattan (Lower East Side)
Dover Street at Pearl Street, just south of the Brooklyn Bridge
Daily dawn-dusk.
Benches, water hose, wading pool (open in summer only), lockbox for toys, lockbox with newspapers for picking up after your dog.

Peter Detmold Park - Manhattan (Midtown East)
East 49th Street at FDR Drive (behind Beekman Place)
Daily dawn-9 p.m., June-Sept.; dawn-8 p.m., Mar.-May and
Oct.-Nov.; dawn-7 p.m., rest of year.
Trees, benches, historical lamps, disposal bags.

Carl Schurz Park - Manhattan (Upper East Side)
East 86th Street at East End Avenue
Daily dawn-1 a.m.
Benches, scoops, pea gravel surface. A second run for small
dogs (past the main run, toward the East River) has a scenic
view of the river and the 59th Street Bridge.

**Riverside Park at 72nd Street - Manhattan (Upper West
Side/Morningside Heights)**
West 72nd Street
Daily 6 a.m.-1 a.m.
Bench, hanging flowerpots, disposal bags, scoopers.

**Riverside Park at 87th Street - Manhattan (Upper West
Side/Morningside Heights)**
West 87th Street
Daily dawn-dusk.
Separate areas for large and small dogs, water fountain and
hose.

**Riverside Park at 105th Street - Manhattan (Upper West
Side/Morningside Heights)**
riversidedog.org
West 105th Street, Riverside Park Central Promenade
Daily dawn-dusk.
Trees, crushed granite surface, benches, disposal bag
dispensers, water fountain, water faucet for dogs, separate
area for small dogs.

**Theodore Roosevelt Park - Manhattan (Upper West
Side/Morningside Heights)**
West 81st Street at Columbus Avenue
Daily 8 a.m.-10 p.m.
Shade trees, benches, dog water faucet, separate run for small
dogs.

Washington Square Park - Manhattan (West Village)
West 4th Street at Thompson Street
Daily 6 a.m.-midnight.
Trees, pea gravel surface, benches, scoopers, water hose,
water bowls.

Freeway Dog Park - Queens (Rockaway Beach)
arfarfrockaway.org
Rockaway Freeway between Beach 83rd and Beach 81st
streets
Daily 8 a.m.-9 p.m.
Fenced, double-gated entry, trees, separate small dog area,
benches, disposal bags. Access for the disabled.

Doughboy Plaza - Queens (Woodside)
Woodside Avenue from 54th to 56th streets (also south of
Woodside at 56th Street) at Windmuller Park
Daily dawn-dusk.
Fenced, trash can.

NORTH CAROLINA

Poston Dog Park - Gastonia Co.
gastongov.com
1101 Lowell Spencer Mountain Rd.
Daily 7 a.m.-dusk.
Fenced, 5 acres, double-gated entry, separate small dog area,
trees, benches, grass, disposal bags, trash cans, water,
parking.

Down East Dog Park - New Bern
newbern-nc.org
303 Glenburnie Dr. in Glenburnie Park
Daily dawn-dusk.
Annual fee $35 for the first dog, $20 for each additional dog.
Weekend pass $15. Proof of current rabies vaccination is
required. Phone (252) 639-2901 for more information.
Fenced. The main 1-acre area is for large dogs over 25
pounds, but dogs of any size may use it; a separate area is
set aside for puppies and small dogs.

OHIO

Park 4 Paws - Avon Lake
avonlake.org
33401 Weber Rd. at Weiss Field
Daily 7 a.m.-9 p.m.
Fenced, double-gated entry, trees, benches, shade, separate
small dog area, disposal bags, trash cans, water, parking.
Access for the disabled.

Armleder Park Dog Park - Cincinnati
greatparks.org
5057 Wooster Pl.
Daily dawn-dusk. (check Web site for dog park opening status)
Fenced, trees, shelter, parking, separate large and small dog
areas, canine showers and drinking fountains, paved walking
trail.

Mt. Airy Dog Park - Cincinnati
cincyparks.com
Westwood Northern Boulevard in Mt. Airy Forest's Highpoint
Picnic Area, between Montana Avenue and North Bend Road
Daily dawn-dusk.
Fenced, 2 acres, trees, benches, tables, shelter, trash cans,
parking, restrooms, water. Access for the disabled.

Big Walnut Dog Park - Columbus
parks.columbus.gov
5000 E. Livingston Ave. in Big Walnut Park (across from
Walnut Ridge High School)
Daily 7 a.m.-11 p.m.
Fenced, 3 acres, two double-gated entries, swimming pond,
shade trees, picnic tables, paved parking.

Three Creeks Dog Park - Columbus parks
columbus.gov
2748 Spangler Rd.
Daily 8 a.m.-dusk.
Fenced, 5 acres, separate small dog area, walking paths,
water.

Wheeler Dog Park - Columbus parks
columbus.gov
725 Thurber Dr. W.
Daily 7 a.m.-11 p.m.
Fenced, 1.5 acres, benches, lights, walking paths, water, street
parking.

Pooch Playground - Gahanna
gahanna.gov
940 Pizzurro Pkwy. From I-270 South, take exit 37 to Hamilton
Road. Turn right (south) onto Hamilton and immediately get in
the left lane to turn left into Pizzurro Park.
Daily dawn-dusk.
Fenced, 4 acres, double-gated entry, trees, benches, separate
small dog area, agility area, disposal bags, trash cans, water
(spring through fall), parking. Access for the disabled. There
are trees along the perimeter and in the small dog area. Dogs
may swim in the creek outside the fenced enclosure.

Mentor Dog Park - Mentor
cityofmentor.com
6647 Hopkins Rd.
Daily dawn-dusk.
Fenced, 3/4 acre, double-gated entry, benches, shelter, agility equipment, shade, tables, separate small dog area, disposal bags, trash cans, dog water fountain, parking. Access for the disabled.

OKLAHOMA

Joe Station Bark Park - Tulsa
cityoftulsa.org
2279 Charles Page Blvd.
Daily 5 a.m.-11 p.m., in summer; 5 a.m.-9 p.m., in winter. Closed Wed. until noon for maintenance.
Fenced, separate small dog area, water, shade, parking, lights. Located at a former baseball field and named for one of the trolley stops along the historic Interurban Line that once connected Tulsa and Sand Springs.

OREGON

Awbrey Reservoir - Bend
DogPAC.org
N.W. 10th and Trenton
Daily dawn-dusk.
Unfenced 5-acre area with access to trails, parking.

Big Sky - Bend
DogPAC.org
21690 Neff Rd.
Daily dawn-dusk.
5 fenced acres, 6 unfenced acres.

Deschutes River Trail - Bend
DogPAC.org
Meadow Camp downstream to Sunrise Village
Daily dawn-dusk.
Year-round off-leash section starts a quarter of a mile downstream from the parking area. From Meadow Camp upstream to Benham Falls, a leash is required May 15-Sept. 15.

Gooddog! Offleash Area - Bend
DogPAC.org
Century Drive, west of Entrada Lodge
Daily dawn-dusk.
Unfenced, several miles of trails with river access.

Hollinshead Dog Park - Bend
DogPAC.org
1235 N.E. Jones Rd.
Daily dawn-dusk.
Unfenced, 3 acres.

Overturf Butte Reservoir - Bend
DogPAC.org
Skyliner Summit Loop
Daily dawn-dusk.
4 partially fenced acres.

Pine Nursery - Bend
DogPAC.org
Deschutes Market Road and Yeoman Road (entrance on Yeoman Road)
Daily dawn-dusk.
18 fenced acres with an open area.

Ponderosa Dog Park - Bend
DogPAC.org
225 S.E. 15th St., south of Bear Creek Road
Daily dawn-dusk.
4 fenced acres.

Riverbend Beach - Bend
DogPAC.org
799 N.W. Columbia St.
Daily dawn-dusk.
Fenced, double-gated entry, benches, disposal bags, trash cans, water, swimming access.

Alton Baker Park - Eugene
eugene-or.gov
South of Leo Harris Parkway (park in the lot south of Autzen Stadium and cross the pedestrian bridge to the dog park)
Daily 6 a.m.-11 p.m.
Fenced, benches, tables, simple shelters for protection from sun and rain, disposal bag receptacles, water.

Amazon Park - Eugene
eugene-or.gov
East of 29th Street and Amazon Parkway
Daily 6 a.m.-11 p.m.
Fenced, benches, tables, simple shelters for protection from sun and rain, disposal bag receptacles, water, parking nearby.

Candlelight Park - Eugene
eugene-or.gov
Royal Avenue and Throne Drive
Daily 6 a.m.-11 p.m.
Fenced, benches, tables, disposal bag receptacles.

Wayne Morse Family Farm - Eugene
eugene-or.gov
Crest Drive and Lincoln Street (park in the main parking area at 595 Crest Dr. and take the trail east)
Daily 6 a.m.-11 p.m.
Fenced, benches, tables, simple shelters for protection from sun and rain, disposal bag receptacles, water.

Brentwood Park - Portland
portlandonline.com
Southeast 60th Avenue and Duke Street
Daily 5 a.m.-midnight.
Fenced.

Chimney Park - Portland
portlandonline.com
9360 N. Columbia Blvd.
Daily 5 a.m.-midnight.
Fenced, 6 acres of off-leash meadow and trails. Dogs should be under excellent voice command.

Delta Park - Portland
portlandonline.com
North Denver Avenue and Martin Luther King Jr. Boulevard (off I-5 exit 307 across from the East Delta Sports Complex)
Daily 6 a.m.-midnight, May-Oct. (open during dry season only).
Fenced, 5 acres of off-leash field, trees, benches; bring your own water. Dogs are not allowed on the sports fields.

Gabriel Park - Portland
portlandonline.com
Southwest 45th Avenue and Vermont Street
Daily 5 a.m.-midnight, May-Oct. (open during dry season only).
Fenced, off-leash area, trees, picnic tables, water. Dogs must remain leashed when not in the off-leash area.

Normandale Park - Portland
portlandonline.com
Northeast 57th Avenue and Halsey Street
Daily 5 a.m.-midnight.
Fenced.

Sacajawea Dog Park - Portland
portlandonline.com
Northeast 75th Ave. and Roselawn Street
Daily 5 a.m.-midnight.
Fenced.

Wallace Park - Portland
portlandonline.com
Northwest 25th Avenue and Raleigh Street
Daily 5 a.m.-midnight.
Fenced.

PENNSYLVANIA

Conneaut Lake Bark Park - Conneaut Lake
conneautlakebarkpark.com
12810 Foust Rd.
Membership required, ranges from $4 (Mon.-Fri.), $8 (Sat.-Sun.) through annual plan. Proof of current vaccinations required. Contact (814) 382-2478 for more information.
Daily 7:30 a.m.-dusk (weather permitting).
Four fenced areas within 45 acres, water stations, swimming pond and regulation dock diving platform, walking trail, parking, picnic tables, portable restroom, disposal bags, trash cans.

Canine Meadows Off-Leash Dog Area - York
yorkcountyparks.org
400 Mundis Race Rd.
Daily 8 a.m.-dusk. Area is closed during wet conditions; phone (717) 840-7440 for information.
Fenced, 13.5 acres, double-gated entry, three separate dog areas, information kiosk, disposal bags, water, trash cans, parking.

TEXAS

White Rock Lake Dog Park - Dallas
whiterockdogpark.org
8000 Mockingbird Point within White Rock Lake Park
Daily 5 a.m.-11 p.m. (weather permitting); closed for maintenance second and fourth Mon. of the month.
Fenced, 2.5 acres, trees, benches, disposal bags, trash cans, parking, restrooms, water fountains, separate fenced areas for large and small dogs, fenced swimming area for dogs in White Rock Lake.

Independence Dog Park - Pearland
pearlandparks.com
3919 Liberty Dr.
Daily 6 a.m.-10 p.m.
Fenced, separate small dog area, agility equipment, covered picnic area, disposal bags, water.

Southdown Dog Park - Pearland
pearlandparks.com
2150 Countryplace Pkwy., within Southdown Park near the Westside Event Center
Daily 6 a.m.-10 p.m.
Fenced, separate small dog area, agility equipment, shade, disposal bags, water.

Jack Carter Park - Plano
plano.gov
Pleasant Valley Drive and Spring Creek Parkway (half block north of the intersection on Pleasant Valley Drive)
Daily dawn-dusk (weather permitting); closed for maintenance first and third Tues. of the month.
Fenced, 2 acres, double-gated entry, benches, disposal bags, trash cans, parking, water fountains for dogs and people.

Round Rock Dog Depot - Round Rock
roundrocktexas.gov
800 Deerfoot Dr.
Daily 6 a.m.-8 p.m., Apr. 1-Oct. 1; daily 6-6, rest of year.
Fenced, approximately 2 acres, grass, agility equipment, double-gated entry, disposal bags, separate areas for large and small dogs, has a train depot theme with a windmill and a water tower that acts as a mister for hot dogs in summer.

VIRGINIA

Note: Disposal bag receptacles are provided at Alexandria parks; patrons must provide their own bags.

Ben Brenman Park - Alexandria
alexandriava.gov
Cameron Station along Backlick Creek
Daily 6 a.m.-10 p.m.
Fenced, disposal bag receptacles, trash cans, parking.

Dog Park - Alexandria
alexandriava.gov
5000 block of Duke Street east of the Charles E. Beatley Jr. Library
Daily 6 a.m.-10 p.m.
Fenced, disposal bag receptacles, trash cans, parking.

Dog Run at Carlyle - Alexandria
alexandriava.gov
450 Andrews Ln.
Daily 6 a.m.-10 p.m.
Fenced, disposal bag receptacles, trash cans, parking.

Montgomery Park - Alexandria
alexandriava.gov
Fairfax and 1st streets
Daily 6 a.m.-10 p.m.
Fenced, disposal bag receptacles, trash cans, parking.

Simpson Stadium Park - Alexandria
alexandriava.gov
Monroe Avenue
Daily 6 a.m.-10 p.m.
Fenced, disposal bag receptacles, trash cans, parking, water fountains for dogs.

Off-leash, unfenced, under voice control areas:

Braddock Road - Alexandria
alexandriava.gov
Southeast corner of Braddock Road and Commonwealth Avenue
Daily 6 a.m.-10 p.m.
Unfenced.

Chambliss Street - Alexandria
alexandriava.gov
Chambliss Street at Grigsby Avenue, south of the tennis courts
Daily 6 a.m.-10 p.m.
Unfenced; area is marked by traffic barriers.

Chinquapin Park - Alexandria
alexandriava.gov
King Street at the east end of the loop road
Daily 6 a.m.-10 p.m.
Unfenced; area is marked by traffic barriers.

Edison Street - Alexandria
alexandriava.gov
Edison Street, west of the cul-de-sac between the bike trail and Berkey Photo Processing
Daily 6 a.m.-10 p.m.
Unfenced; area is marked by traffic barriers.

Ft. Williams - Alexandria
alexandriava.gov
Ft. Williams and New Ft. Williams Parkway
Daily 6 a.m.-10 p.m.
Unfenced; area is marked by traffic barriers.

Founders Park - Alexandria
alexandriava.gov
Oronoco Street and Union Street, northeast corner
Daily 6 a.m.-10 p.m.
Unfenced; 100-by-100-foot area is marked by traffic barriers.

Hooff's Run - Alexandria
alexandriava.gov
East of Commonwealth Avenue between Oak and
Chapman streets
Daily 6 a.m.-10 p.m.
Unfenced; area is marked by traffic barriers.

Monticello Park - Alexandria
alexandriava.gov
Beverly Drive, east of the entrance
Daily 6 a.m.-10 p.m.
Unfenced; 50-by-200-foot area is marked by traffic barriers.

North Fort Ward Park - Alexandria
alexandriava.gov
Braddock Road, east side of entrance
Daily 6 a.m.-10 p.m.
Unfenced; 100-by-100-foot area is marked by traffic barriers.

Tarleton Park - Alexandria
alexandriava.gov
Mill Run west of Gordon Street
Daily 6 a.m.-10 p.m.
Unfenced.

Timberbranch Parkway - Alexandria
alexandriava.gov
Median to Timberbranch Parkway between Braddock Road
and Oakley Place
Daily 6 a.m.-10 p.m.
Unfenced; area is marked by traffic barriers.

Windmill Hill Park - Alexandria
alexandriava.gov
Gibbon and Union streets
Daily 6 a.m.-10 p.m.
Unfenced.

W&OD Railroad - Alexandria
alexandriava.gov
Raymond Avenue (200 feet of the W&OD Railroad
right-of-way south of Raymond)
Daily 6 a.m.-10 p.m.
Unfenced; area is marked by traffic barriers.

Benjamin Banneker Park - Arlington County
arlingtondogs.wordpress.com
1701 N. Sycamore St. (take I-66 west to Sycamore Street/exit
69, turn left on Sycamore and proceed past the East Falls
Church Metro Station, turn right onto North 16th Street and
take the first right, which dead-ends at the dog exercise area)
Daily dawn to half-hour after dusk.
Fully fenced, 11 acres, picnic table, benches, lights, water.

Fort Barnard Park - Arlington County
arlingtondogs.wordpress.com
South Pollard Street and South Walter Reed Drive (from Rt.
50, take Glebe Road south, turn right on South Walter Reed
Drive and proceed to Pollard Street; the park is on the right)
Daily dawn to half-hour after dusk.
Fully fenced, picnic table, benches, lights, water.

Glencarlyn Park - Arlington County
arlingtondogs.wordpress.com
301 S. Harrison St. (from Rt. 50, head west to Carlin Springs
Road, exit right and then turn left at the stop sign, pass under
Rt. 50 and follow Carlin Springs to 4th Street, turn left on 4th
Street and proceed 5 blocks until the road ends at the
Glencarlyn Park sign, following the park road until it ends; park
and walk over a small bridge and stream to the exercise area)
Daily dawn to half-hour after dusk.
Unfenced area near a creek and woods, picnic table, benches.

Shirlington Park - Arlington County
arlingtondogs.wordpress.com
2601 S. Arlington Mill Dr., bordering South Four Mile Run
between Shirlington Road and South Walter Reed Drive along
the bicycle path between a storage facility and the water, near
but not in Jennie Dean Park (from South Four Mile Run, turn
south onto Nelson and park behind the storage facility; there
are no signs indicating the dog park)
Daily dawn to half-hour after dusk.
Partially fenced, picnic table, benches, water.

Towers Park - Arlington County
arlingtondogs.wordpress.com
801 S. Scott St., behind the tennis courts
Daily dawn to half-hour after dusk.
Fully fenced, 3.5 acres, separate small dog area, lights,
parking.

The Hanover Dog Park - Ashland
co.hanover.va.us
13017 Taylor Complex Ln.
Daily dawn-dusk.
Fenced, grass, dog agility equipment, water, disposal bags,
benches, parking.

Red Wing Park - Virginia Beach
vbgov.com
1398 General Booth Blvd.
Daily 7:30 a.m.-dusk.
Annual fee for first-time visitors $10; owners must register at
the park office, show proof of pet's rabies shot and vaccines,
and obtain a city dog license.
Fenced, benches, disposal bags, parking, restrooms, water.
Access for the disabled.

Woodstock Community Park - Virginia Beach
vbgov.com
5709 Providence Rd.
Daily 7:30 a.m.-dusk.
Annual fee for first-time visitors $10; owners must register at
the park office, show proof of pet's rabies shot and vaccines,
and obtain a city dog license.
Fenced, benches, disposal bags, restrooms, parking. Access
for the disabled.

WASHINGTON

Cedar River Dog Park - Renton
rentonoffleash.org
1156 S. 3rd St., next to Cedar River Trail
Daily dawn-dusk.
Fenced, 3.5 acres with 8,000 square feet reserved for
small/shy dogs, short grass, mulch, gravel, water, benches,
trees, shelter, tables, parking.

I-5 Colonnade Park - Seattle
coladog.org
Lakeview Boulevard and Franklin Avenue East in the Eastlake
neighborhood beneath I-5, south of East Howe Street
Daily 6 a.m.-11 p.m.
Fenced, 1.2 acres, double-gated entry, water fountain for dogs;
the I-5 freeway deck provides shelter from the elements.

I-90 "Blue Dog Pond" - Seattle
coladog.org
Martin Luther King Jr. Way and South Massachusetts Street,
on the northwest corner
Daily 6 a.m.-11 p.m.
Fenced, 1 acre, parking, water fountain for dogs, Blue Dog
sculpture. No off-leash areas in I-90 Lid Park, just east of Blue
Dog Pond.

Dr. Jose Rizal Park - Seattle
coladog.org
1008 12th Ave. S. on North Beacon Hill; off-leash area is in the lower portion of the park
Daily 6 a.m.-11 p.m.
Fenced, 4 acres, double-gated entry, parking, water fountain for dogs, scenic view of downtown.

Genesee Park - Seattle
coladog.org
46th Avenue South and South Genesee Street
Daily 6 a.m.-11 p.m.
Fenced, 3 acres, double-gated entry, parking, water fountain for dogs.

Golden Gardens Park - Seattle
coladog.org
8498 Seaview Pl. N.W. in Ballard
Daily 6 a.m.-11 p.m.
Fenced, 1 acre, lighted, parking, water fountain for dogs. The off-leash area is in the upper (eastern) portion of the park; dogs are not allowed on the lower beach area.

Magnuson Park - Seattle
coladog.org
6500 Sandpoint Way N.E. (enter the park at 74th Street and drive to the end of the road)
Daily 6 a.m.-11 p.m.
Fenced, 9 acres, double-gated entry, shelter, parking, separate area for small/shy dogs, water fountain for dogs, beach access.

Northacres Park - Seattle
coladog.org
North 130th Street, west of I-5; off-leash area is in the northeast corner of the park at 12530 Third Ave. N.E., north of the ball field. Parking is available on the west side of the park along 1st Street Northeast and on the south side along North 125th Street
Daily 6 a.m.-11 p.m.
Fenced, double-gated entry, parking, water fountain for dogs.

Plymouth Pillars Park - Seattle
coladog.org
Boren Avenue and Pike Street on Capitol Hill above I-5
Daily 6 a.m.-11 p.m.
Fenced, 9,800 square feet, double-gated entry, water fountain for dogs, scenic view of downtown Seattle.

Regrade Park - Seattle
coladog.org
3rd Avenue and Bell Street, downtown
Fenced, 13,000 square feet, double-gated entry, water fountain for dogs.

Westcrest Park - Seattle
coladog.org
8806 8th Ave. S.W. in West Seattle
Daily 6 a.m.-11 p.m.
Fenced, 5 acres, shelters, lights, separate area for small dogs, parking, water fountain for dogs. The off-leash area is along the east side of the reservoir.

Woodland Park - Seattle
coladog.org
West Green Lake Way North, west of the tennis courts
Daily 6 a.m.-11 p.m.
Fenced, 1 acre, double-gated entry, parking, water fountain for dogs.

Patricia Simonet Laughing Dog Park - Spokane
spokanecounty.org
26715 E. Spokane Bridge Rd. in Gateway Park
Daily dawn-dusk.
Fenced, 3.5 acres, grass and wooded walking area, double-gated entry, parking, water fountain for dogs (not available in winter), restrooms, disposal bags, trash cans. Access for the disabled.

Canada

ALBERTA

91 Street Right of Way - Edmonton
edmonton.ca, (780) 496-1475
Berm east of 91 Street from 10 Avenue north to Whitemud Freeway and east to 76 Street
Unfenced.

Buena Vista Great Meadow - Edmonton
edmonton.ca, (780) 496-1475
North of Laurier Park and Buena Vista Drive and south of Melton Ravine in the vicinity of 88 Avenue
Unfenced; area does not include the pedestrian bridge access trail, Yorath property or the trail north to McKenzie Ravine. This is a hot-air balloon site, so please leash your dog during balloon launches.

Hermitage Park North - Edmonton
edmonton.ca, (780) 496-1475
129 Avenue to 137 Avenue; also 22 Street along the riverbank where signs designate an off-leash area.
Unfenced. This is a multiuse area in the valley north of the park's fishing pond and picnic area.

Jackie Parker Park - Edmonton
edmonton.ca, (780) 496-1475
Whitemud Freeway and 50th Street
Unfenced. Includes the area south of the 44 Avenue entrance; dogs are not allowed on the golf course or north of the service road playground.

Keehewin Blackmud - Edmonton
edmonton.ca, (780) 496-1475
Pipeline corridor, 104 Street and 20 Avenue to the south end of 109 Street (excludes Bearspaw Drive West and Blackmud Creek and Ravine)
Unfenced.

Kennedale - Edmonton
edmonton.ca, (780) 496-1475
Ravine west of the 40 Street loop, west to 47 Street and the top of the bank
Unfenced.

Lauderdale - Edmonton
edmonton.ca, (780) 496-1475
South end of Grand Trunk Park, from 127 to 129 Avenue and 113A to 109 Street
Unfenced.

Mill Creek Ravine - Edmonton
edmonton.ca, (780) 496-1475
68 Avenue and 93 Street, accessible from the west or north sides of Argyll Park
Unfenced. A granular trail along the bottom of the ravine leads to the Whyte (82) Avenue overpass.

Terwillegar Park - Edmonton
edmonton.ca, (780) 496-1475
Rabbit Hill Road
Unfenced. This is a multiuse area.

MANITOBA

Bourkevale Park - Winnipeg
winnipeg.ca
100 Ferry Rd., south of the dike along the riverbank
Daily 6 a.m.-10 p.m.
Unfenced, trash cans, parking; bring your own disposal bags.

Juba Park & Pioneer Avenue - Winnipeg
winnipeg.ca
Pioneer Avenue, all vacant land west of the walkway to Juba Park
Daily 6 a.m.-10 p.m.
Unfenced, trash cans, parking; bring your own disposal bags.

Kil-Cona Park - Winnipeg
winnipeg.ca
Lagimodiere Boulevard in the area north of the west parking lot. Parking available near McIvor entrance.
Daily 6 a.m.-10 p.m.
Unfenced, trash cans, parking; bring your own disposal bags.

King's Park - Winnipeg
winnipeg.ca
Kilkenny Drive and King's Drive, northeast of the retention pond.
Daily 6 a.m.-10 p.m.
Unfenced, trash cans, parking; bring your own disposal bags.

Little Mountain Park - Winnipeg
winnipeg.ca
Northwest corner of the park adjacent to Klimpike Road and Farmer Avenue
Daily 6 a.m.-10 p.m.
Unfenced, trash cans, parking; bring your own disposal bags.

Maple Grove Park - Winnipeg
winnipeg.ca
Frobisher Road, north area of the park
Daily 6 a.m.-10 p.m.
Unfenced, separate fenced area for puppies, trash cans, parking; bring your own disposal bags.

Mazenod Park - Winnipeg
winnipeg.ca
Area surrounding retention pond, bordered by Mazenod Road, Camiel Sys Street and Beghin Street
Daily 6 a.m.-10 p.m.
Unfenced, trash cans, parking; bring your own disposal bags.

Westview Park - Winnipeg
winnipeg.ca
Midland Street and Saskatchewan Avenue; entire park is an off-leash area
Daily 6 a.m.-10 p.m.
Unfenced, trash cans, parking; bring your own disposal bags.

Woodsworth Park - Winnipeg
winnipeg.ca
West of Hekla off Keewatin Street, northeast of King Edward Avenue and Park Lane
Daily 6 a.m.-10 p.m.
Unfenced, trash cans, parking; bring your own disposal bags.

ATTRACTIONS
United States

CALIFORNIA

 Disneyland® Resort

(714) 781-4400, 1313 Harbor Blvd., is off I-5 Disneyland Dr. and Disney Way exits at 1313 Harbor Blvd., Anaheim
Disneyland® Resort consists of two family-oriented theme parks—Disneyland® and Disney California Adventure™ Park—and the shops, restaurants and entertainment of Downtown Disney® District. Indoor kennel facilities. Both theme parks are open daily with extended hours during the summer, on some holidays and on weekends. Cost: One-day one-park ticket $80; $74 (ages 3-9). One-day Park Hopper Ticket $105; $99 (ages 3-9). Two-day Park Hopper Ticket $173; $161 (ages 3-9). Three-day Park Hopper Ticket $224; $208 (ages 3-9). Validity periods for Park Hopper tickets vary according to ticket type. Select theme park tickets are available at participating AAA/CAA Travel offices. Pets can be left at the resort's kennel for a fee. Parking: $15 (autos or motorcycles); $20 (RVs). Disneyland.com

LEGOLAND California

(760) 918-5346, One LEGOLAND Dr., off I-5 exit Cannon Road E. at LEGOLAND Dr., Carlsbad
The more than 60 rides—including three roller coasters—shows and attractions in this 128-acre family theme park are geared for kids ages 2 to 12. Free kennels are available on a first-come, first-served basis. Open daily mid-May to Labor Day and holidays. Open Thurs.-Mon. rest of year. Days closed and closing times may be extended in the off-season. Cost: One-day admission $69; $59 (ages 3-12 and 60+). Resort Hopper (1-day admission includes LEGOLAND, LEGOLAND Water Park and SEA LIFE Carlsbad) $89; $79 (ages 3-12 and 60+); $3 (ages 1-2). Water Park Hopper (1-day admission includes LEGOLAND and LEGOLAND Water Park) $81; $71 (ages 3-12 and 60+); $3 (ages 1-2). Two-day admission tickets also are available. Parking: $12; $15 (RVs); $5 (motorcycles). california.legoland.com

SeaWorld San Diego

(800) 257-4268, 500 SeaWorld Dr., on SeaWorld Dr., off I-5 on Mission Bay's south shore, San Diego
SeaWorld San Diego offers animal shows, rides and exhibits featuring marine creatures from around the world, including killer whales, sharks, penguins and sea lions. Talented dolphins, pilot whales, birds and humans perform in the Blue Horizons show. Pet facility provided for a nominal charge on a first-come, first-served basis. Opens daily at 9 or 10; closing times vary. Hours vary and may be extended during summer and holiday periods. Cost: $69.99; $61.99 (ages 3-9). An additional fee is charged for some rides. Kennel $10. Parking: $12; $8 (motorcycles); $17 (RVs and preferred). seaworldparks.com/en/seaworld-sandiego

Six Flags Magic Mountain

(661) 255-4111, 26101 Magic Mountain Pkwy., off I-5 Magic Mountain Pkwy. exit, Valencia
Thrill rides, Looney Tunes and Justice League characters, action shows—there is something here to amuse almost everyone. Free kennel facilities are available in the main parking lot. Opens daily at 10:30, late Mar.-Labor Day; Fri.-Sun. at 10:30, day after Labor Day-Oct. 31; Sat.-Sun. and holidays at 10:30, rest of year. Closing times vary. Cost: $61.99; $36.99 (under 48 inches tall); free (ages 0-2). Prices may vary; phone ahead. Parking: $15; $20 (RVs and buses). www.sixflags.com

Universal Studios Hollywood

(800) 864-8377, 100 Universal Dr., off Hollywood Frwy. (US 101) at Lankershim Blvd. For guests arriving by Metro, a free shuttle across the street from the station provides transportation to the gate entrance, Universal City
In addition to thrill rides and attractions, Universal Studios gives visitors a behind-the-scenes look at the workings of a major film and TV studio. Complimentary kennel service. Daily 9-9, in summer; 10-6, rest of year. The Studio Tour is offered continuously; last tour departs 2 hours, 45 minutes before closing during summer. Cost: $72; $62 (under 48 inches tall). Front of Line passes are available; details are available at the front gate. Rates and availability of attractions may vary; phone ahead. Members save 10 percent on select dining and souvenirs at Universal Studios Hollywood and Universal CityWalk Hollywood. Parking: $15 (per private vehicle); $10 (per private vehicle after 3 p.m.); $17 (RVs); $20 (preferred). www.universalstudios.com

DISTRICT OF COLUMBIA

Washington Monument

(202) 426-6841, 15th St. & Constitution Ave. N.W., near the center of the National Mall; the grounds extend from 14th to 17th sts. and from Constitution to Independence aves. N.W., Washington, D.C.
This instantly recognizable 555-foot marble obelisk commemorates our nation's first president and is surrounded by expansive grounds. Pets on leash. Daily 9-5 (also 5-10, Memorial Day-Labor Day). Last tour begins about 15 minutes before closing. Cost: Advance ticket reservations $2 per ticket. www.nps.gov/wamo

FLORIDA

Busch Gardens Tampa Bay

(888) 800-5447, 3000 E. Busch Blvd. (SR 580), 2 mi. e. of jct. I-275 exit 50 or 2 mi. w. of I-75 exit 265, Tampa
This family entertainment park combines world-class thrill rides, live entertainment and one of North America's largest zoos, providing an adventure for the entire family. Indoor kennel facilities. Generally opens daily between 9 and 10; closing times vary. Cost: $77.99; $69.99 (ages 3-9). Admission includes a second visit within 7 days of first visit. There is an additional fee for the Serengeti Safari Tour. The Length of Stay ticket, a 14-day combination ticket with Adventure Island, is $92.99; $84.99 (ages 3-9). Parking: $13; $15 (RVs); $18 (preferred). www.buschgardens.com

SeaWorld Orlando

(800) 327-2420, 7007 SeaWorld Dr., at jct. I-4 and SR 528 (Beachline Expwy.), Orlando
This marine life adventure park presents crowd-pleasing animal shows starring a family of performing killer whales. SeaWorld also features numerous attractions and rides, including Manta, a flying coaster, as well as a penguin encounter area and simulated helicopter rides. Air-conditioned kennels. Opens daily at 9; closing times vary. Last admission 1 hour before closing. Cost: $81.99; $73.99 (ages 3-9). Admission includes a second visit within 7 days of first visit. Fourteen-day combination ticket with Aquatica $119.99; $111.99 (ages 3-9). There is an additional fee for VIP tours. AAA members save on the Makahiki Luau and Dine with Shamu. Reservations are required for these dining experiences; visit Guest Relations for details. Parking: $14; $15 (RVs); $20 (preferred).
www.seaworld.com/orlando

Universal Orlando Resort

(407) 363-8000, 1000 Universal Studios Plaza, off I-4 exit 75A (eastbound) or 74B (westbound), Orlando
At Universal Orlando you can "ride the movies" at the Universal Studios® theme park, cavort with superheroes and cartoon characters at Universal's Islands of Adventure® theme park, or visit the specialty shops, themed restaurants and entertainment venues at Universal CityWalk®. Air-conditioned kennels. The theme parks generally open daily at 9; closing times vary by season. Universal CityWalk open daily 8 a.m.-2 a.m. Theme park and CityWalk hours may vary; phone ahead. Cost: A 1-day Base ticket to either Universal Studios Florida or Universal's Islands of Adventure is $85; $79 (ages 3-9). A 1-day Park-to-Park ticket, which allows same-day access to both Universal Studios Florida and Universal's Islands of Adventure, is $120; $114 (ages 3-9). A 2-day Base ticket, which allows access to one park per day, is $135.99; $125.99 (ages 3-9). A 2-day Park-to-Park ticket, which allows same-day access to both parks, is $155.99; $145.99 (ages 3-9). Tickets are also available for 3-, 4- and 7-day access to parks. Multiday tickets include admission to select live entertainment venues at Universal CityWalk. Special advance purchase discount tickets are available at participating AAA offices. Members can show their AAA/CAA card and save 10 percent at select merchandise and restaurant locations within the resort (excluding food or merchandise carts, tobacco, candy, film, collectibles, and clearance and sundry items). Parking: $15; $3 (6-10 p.m.); free (after 10 p.m.). Valet parking $25.

Walt Disney World® Resort

(407) 824-4321, 3111 World Dr., accessible from Florida's Tpke., US 192, Osceola Pkwy. and several exits off I-4 s. of Orlando, depending on the park destination, Lake Buena Vista
The sprawling complex includes Magic Kingdom® Park, Epcot®, Disney's Hollywood Studios™, Disney's Animal Kingdom® Theme Park, family water parks and numerous entertainment, shopping and dining facilities.
With the exception of service dogs for guests with disabilities, pets are not permitted in the Theme Parks or Disney Resort hotels, or on Disney buses. Best Friends Pet Care boarding facility offers air-conditioned accommodations for pets across from Disney's Port Orleans Resort at 2510 Bonnet Creek Pkwy. Reservations at Best Friends Pet Care are not required but are suggested. Disney Resort hotel reservations do not guarantee space for pets. Phone (877) 4 WDW-PETS for information and reservations. WDW.BestFriendsPetCare.com
Theme parks open daily generally at 9; closing times vary. Cost: One-day, one-park admission $85; $79 (ages 3-9). Ticket options for additional fees include admission to other entertainment areas and "hopping" between theme parks. Select theme park tickets are available at participating AAA/CAA Travel offices. Parking: $14; $15 (camper or trailer); free (Disney resort guests with valid resort ID). The fee allows parking at any of the theme parks for that entire day. Disneyworld.com

GEORGIA

Six Flags Over Georgia

(770) 948-9290, 275 Riverside Pkwy., 7.4 mi. s.e. on I-20, Austell
Six Flags offers rides, attractions and live shows. Kennel facilities are available. Opens daily at 10:30, late May-early Aug.; Sat.-Sun. at 10:30, early Mar.-late May and early Aug.-late Sept. Closing times vary. The park also is open for Fright Fest late Sept.-early Nov. Cost: All-inclusive 1-day $49.99; $34.99 (children under 48 inches tall); free (ages 0-2). AAA members save on select services and merchandise. See Guest Relations for details. Parking: $15.
www.sixflags.com/parks/overgeorgia/index.asp

ILLINOIS

Six Flags Great America

(847) 249-4636, 542 SR 21N, 1 mi. e. of I-94 on Grand Ave. (SR 132), Gurnee
Six Flags Great America offers 14 coasters, a water park, shows, parades, rides and attractions for the whole family. Kennel facilities are available. Theme park open daily at 10, mid-May to late Aug.; Sat.-Sun. at 10, first three weeks in Sept.; Fri. at 5, Sat.-Sun. at 10, in Oct. Closing times vary. Water park days and hours vary. Cost: (Includes Six Flags Hurricane Harbor) $59.99; $39.99 (children under 48 inches tall); free (ages 0-2). Prices may vary; phone ahead. AAA members save on select services and merchandise. See guest relations for details. Parking: $20.
www.sixflags.com/parks/greatamerica/ParkInfo/index.asp

IOWA

 Pella Historical Village

(641) 628-4311, jct. E. First and Franklin sts., Pella
A country store, log cabin, grist mill, windmill, smithy and other buildings (including Wyatt Earp's boyhood home) are reminders of this town's Dutch Heritage. Leashed pets are permitted but are not allowed in the windmill. Mon.-Sat. 9-4, mid-Mar. through Dec. 31. Cost: $8; $2 (ages 5-18). www.pellatuliptime.com

MASSACHUSETTS

 Bunker Hill Monument

(617) 242-5641, in Monument Square on Breed's Hill in Charlestown (T: Community College), Boston
Part of Boston National Historical Park, this 221-foot-tall granite obelisk commemorates the site of the Battle of Bunker Hill, which occurred on June 17, 1775. Leashed pets are permitted on the grounds but not inside the monument. Daily 9-5 (also 5-6, July-Aug.). Cost: Free.
www.nps.gov/bost/historyculture/bhm.htm

MISSOURI

 The Gateway Arch

(314) 655-1700, Memorial Dr. and Market St. within Jefferson National Expansion Memorial park, St. Louis
This curved, stainless steel monument soars 630 feet high and symbolizes the gateway to the West. A tram ride takes visitors to an observation deck. Pets on leashes are permitted on the grounds. Ticket center open daily 8 a.m.-10 p.m., Memorial Day-Labor Day; 9-6, rest of year. Last tram departs 50 minutes before closing. Cost: Tram ride $10; $5 (ages 3-15). Individual movie admission $7; $2.50 (ages 3-15). Combination tickets $14; $7.50 (ages 3-15). www.nps.gov/archive/jeff/arch.html

 Six Flags St. Louis

(636) 938-5300, I-44 & Allenton Rd., off I-44 at 4900 Six Flags Rd., Eureka
Themed areas showcase a variety of shows, rides and attractions; kids will have a ball exploring Bugs Bunny National Park. Air-conditioned kennel facilities are at the parking lot entrance. Pets cannot be kept overnight, and must have current vaccinations and registration tags. Park open mid-Apr. through Oct. 31; days and hours vary. Hurricane Harbor open Memorial Day weekend-Labor Day; days and hours vary. Cost: (Includes Hurricane Harbor) $49.99; $36.99 (children under 48 inches tall); free (ages 0-2). Prices may vary; phone ahead. AAA members save on select services and merchandise. See guest relations for details. Parking: $15.
www.sixflags.com/parks/stlouis/parkinfo/index.asp

NORTH CAROLINA

 Carowinds

(704) 588-2600, 14523 Carowinds Blvd., 10 mi. s. on I-77 to exit 90, Charlotte
Depicting the past and present of the Carolinas, the themed areas at this park offer roller coasters, water rides, children's play areas and other family entertainment. Air-conditioned kennels are available. Park opens daily at 10, early June to mid-Aug.; Sat.-Sun. at 10, mid-Mar. to early June and mid-Aug. to early Oct. Closing times vary. Cost: Park (all-inclusive) $51.99; $24.99 (ages 62+, under 48 inches tall and to all after 4 p.m.); free (ages 0-2). Two-day pass $56.99. Parking: $10.
www.carowinds.com

OHIO

 Kings Island

(513) 754-5700, 6300 Kings Island Dr., off I-71 exits 24 and 25 on Kings Island Dr., Kings Mills
Kings Island is a family entertainment park featuring 14 hair-raising roller coasters; Soak City Waterpark, the park's 33-acre water playground; costumed Peanuts cartoon characters; and a variety of live shows. A day-use pet kennel is available for a fee. Park opens daily at 10 a.m., late May-late Aug.; Sat.-Sun. at 10 a.m., late Apr. to late May and first weekend in Sept.; Fri.-Sun. at 11, in Oct. Closing times vary. Soak City Waterpark daily 11-7, late May-late Aug. Cost: (includes Soak City Waterpark) $52.99; $32.99 (ages 3-6, ages 62+ and children under 48 inches tall). Prices vary throughout the season; phone ahead to confirm. Parking: $12.
www.visitkingsisland.com

PENNSYLVANIA

 Hersheypark

(800) 437-7439, 100 W. Hersheypark Dr., just off SR 743 and US 422, Hershey
Hersheypark has more than 65 rides and attractions—including 12 roller coasters—plus live entertainment. Visitors can enjoy a marine mammal show, song and dance reviews and concerts highlighting big-name performers. ZooAmerica North American Wildlife Park covers 11 acres. Open daily at 10, Memorial Day-Labor Day; Sat.-Sun. at 10, in May; Sat.-Sun. at 10, select weekends in Sept. after Labor Day. Closing times vary; phone ahead. Phone for Springtime and Halloween schedules. Cost: (includes ZooAmerica North American Wildlife Park) $56.95; $35.95 (ages 3-8 and 55-69); $22.95 (ages 70+). Sunset admission (after 3 when park closes at 6, after 4 when park closes at 8, after 5 when park closes at 10 and 11) $28.95; $24.95 (ages 3-8 and 55-69); $17.95 (ages 70+). Other admission packages, including multiday options, are available.
www.hersheypark.com

TEXAS

 SeaWorld San Antonio

(800) 700-7786, 10500 SeaWorld Dr., 16 mi. n.w. off SR 151 between loops 410 and 1604 at jct. Westover Hills Blvd. and Ellison Dr., San Antonio

A 250-acre marine life adventure park, SeaWorld San Antonio entertains and educates with shark exhibits, a penguin habitat, the "Believe" show starring world-famous killer whale Shamu, and a high-energy whale and dolphin show. Such thrill rides as Journey to Atlantis, the Steel Eel and Great White coasters, and the Rio Loco and Texas splashdown water rides add to the excitement. Outdoor kennel facilities (owner must provide food). Park open late Feb.-Dec. 31; days and hours vary. Cost: $59.99; $49.99 (ages 3-9). Admission and parking prices may vary; phone ahead. Parking: $15; $20 (preferred). seaworldparks.com/en/seaworld-sanantonio

 Six Flags Fiesta Texas

(210) 697-5050, 17000 I-10W, 15 mi. n.w. off I-10W exit 555, just n. of Loop 1604, San Antonio

Housed in a former rock quarry, the park celebrates Texas and the Southwest with thrill and family-style rides, live entertainment and themed areas. Kennel facilities are located to the right of the main entrance. Pets cannot be kept overnight and must have current vaccinations and registration tags. Park open daily Memorial Day weekend-Labor Day (also in mid-Mar. for spring break); Sat.-Sun., early Mar.-day before Memorial Day weekend and day after Labor Day to mid-Sept.; schedule varies mid-Sept. to early Jan. Water park open daily mid-June through Labor Day weekend; Sat.-Sun., May 1 to mid-June. Hours vary. Cost: $53.99; $38.99 (under 48 inches tall); free (ages 0-2). Rates may vary; phone ahead. AAA members save on select services and merchandise. See guest relations for details. Parking: $15. www.sixflags.com

 Six Flags Over Texas

(817) 530-6000, 2201 Road to Six Flags, s.w. at jct. I-30 and SR 360 (Angus Wynne Jr. Frwy.) exit 30, following signs, Arlington

Themed areas, each featuring thrill rides, food and entertainment, depict Texas under six different flags: Spain, France, Mexico, the Republic of Texas, the Confederate States of America and the United States. Air-conditioned kennels (fee). Daily late May-early Aug.; Sat.-Sun., Mar. 1-late May, mid-Aug. through Oct. 31 and day after Thanksgiving-Dec. 31. Hours vary. Cost: $56.99; $36.99 (under 48 inches tall); free (ages 0-2). AAA members save on select services and merchandise. See guest relations for details. Parking: $15; $20 (preferred). www.sixflags.com

VIRGINIA

 Busch Gardens Williamsburg

(800) 343-7946, 1 Busch Gardens Blvd., 3 mi. e. on US 60 or off I-64 exit 243A, Williamsburg

This European-themed adventure park offers something for the entire family, from thrill rides to entertaining shows to villages representing England, Germany, France and other nations. Kennel facilities (England parking lot); fee $10 per pet per day. Open Mar.-Dec.; days and hours vary. Cost: $63.99; $53.99 (ages 3-9). Multiday and combination tickets with Water Country USA are available. Parking: $13. www.buschgardens.com/bgw/default.aspx

 Kings Dominion

(804) 876-5000, 16000 Theme Park Dr., .5 mi. e. off I-95 exit 98 on SR 30, Doswell

The 400-acre park features a water park, thrill rides, children's play areas, costumed characters, live shows and specialty shopping. Kennels are available. Park open daily, Memorial Day-Labor Day; Sat.-Sun., late Mar.-Apr. 30; Fri.-Sun., May 1-day before Memorial Day and late Sept.-late Oct. WaterWorks open daily, Memorial Day-Labor Day. Hours of operation vary depending on the season; phone ahead. Cost: (includes WaterWorks in season) $58.99; $36.99 (ages 62+ and under 48 inches tall); free (ages 0-2). Parking: $12. www.kingsdominion.com

WASHINGTON

Hovander Homestead Park

(360) 384-3444, 1 mi. s. via Hovander Rd. to 5299 Nielsen Ave., Ferndale

This restored house, dating from 1903 and furnished with antiques, is within a large park encompassing gardens, picnic sites and a children's farm area. Dogs are allowed in on-leash areas of the park. Grounds open daily 8 a.m.-dusk. House open Thurs.-Sun. 12:30-4:30, Memorial Day-Labor Day. The house is not always open during scheduled times; phone ahead to confirm. The boardwalk may be closed during designated hunting season. Cost: House $1; 50c (ages 0-12). www.co.whatcom.wa.us/parks/hovander/hovander.jsp

Canada

ONTARIO

 Canada's Wonderland

(905) 832-7000, off Hwy. 400, Rutherford Rd. exit northbound
or Major MacKenzie Dr. E. exit southbound at 9580 Jane St.,
Vaughan

Thrill rides at this theme park include the hair-raising Behemoth
rollercoaster and the Backlot Stunt Coaster, while Nickelodeon
Central and Hanna-Barbera Land will entertain little ones.
Air-conditioned kennels are available for a fee. Daily late
May-Labour Day; open some weekends early May-late May and
day after Labour Day-late Oct. Gates open at 10; closing time
varies. Phone to verify schedule and admission. Cost: Passport
for grounds and most rides $39.99; $32.99 (ages 3-6 and 60+).
Concerts are available at an extra charge. Height restrictions
apply to some rides. Parking: $10.
www.canadaswonderland.com

Upper Canada Village

(613) 543-4328, 13740 CR 2, 11 km (7 mi.) e. on CR 2 off
Hwy. 401, Morrisburg

Upper Canada Village re-creates life during the 1860s through a
working community of artisans and costumed interpreters who
perform chores typical of the era. Seeing eye and hearing aid
dogs are welcome. All other pets must be kept on a leash and
may not enter historic buildings. Daily 9:30-5, Victoria Day
weekend-Labour Day; Wed.-Sun. 9:30-5, day after Labour
Day-Thanksgiving. Cost: Village $19.95; $18.95 (ages 65+);
$11.95 (ages 5-18); $3.95 (ages 2-4). Visitor center $4; free
(ages 0-12). Rates may vary; phone ahead.
www.uppercanadavillage.com

NATIONAL PUBLIC LANDS

The National Public Lands listed below permit pets on a leash. Keep in mind that animals may be prohibited from entering public buildings and even some areas outdoors, particularly those that are ecologically sensitive. Where swimming is permitted, there are usually no lifeguards on duty; people and pets swim at their own risk. Specific pet policies vary from park to park and are subject to change. Always check in advance regarding any applicable regulations and to confirm that pets are still permitted where you are going.

Be aware of dangers to your pet in natural areas, including snakes, ticks and fast-moving currents in rivers and streams. An unleashed dog may chase after a wild animal and become separated from its owner, increasing the risk of loss or injury. Never leave your pet unattended. Keep him leashed or crated at all times. Follow park guidelines faithfully, and monitor your pet's behavior; the National Park Service may confiscate pets that harm wildlife or other visitors. *For additional information on outdoor vacations, see The Great Outdoors, p. 16.*

United States

ALABAMA

Conecuh National Forest
On the Alabama-Florida border.
(334) 222-2555
🚴 🏕 🥾 ⛱ 🏊

Horseshoe Bend National Military Park
12 mi. n. of Dadeville on SR 49.
(256) 234-7111
🥾 ⛱ 🏊 👥

Talladega National Forest
In central Alabama.
(256) 362-2909
🏕 🥾 ⛱ 🏊

Tuskegee National Forest
Northeast of Tuskegee.
(334) 727-2652
🚴 🏕 🥾 ⛱

William B. Bankhead National Forest
In northwestern Alabama.
(205) 489-5111
🚴 🏕 🥾 ⛱ 🏊

ALASKA

Chugach National Forest
Along the Gulf of Alaska from Cape Suckling to Seward.
(907) 743-9500
🚴 🏕 🥾 ⛱ 👥

Denali National Park and Preserve
In south-central Alaska.
(907) 683-2294
🏕 🥾 ⛱ 👥 🍽

Glacier Bay National Park and Preserve
North of Cross Sound to the Canadian border.
(907) 697-2230
🏕 🥾 👥 🍽

Kenai Fjords National Park
Southeastern side of the Kenai Peninsula.
(907) 224-7500 or (907) 224-2132
🏕 🥾 ⛱ 👥

Lake Clark National Park and Preserve
In southern Alaska.
(907) 644-3626
🏕 👥

Tongass National Forest
In southeastern Alaska.
(907) 228-6220
🏕 🥾 ⛱ 👥

Wrangell-St. Elias National Park and Preserve
In southeastern Alaska, northwest of Tongass National Forest.
(907) 822-7250
🏕 🥾 ⛱ 👥

ARIZONA

Apache-Sitgreaves National Forests
In east-central Arizona.
(928) 333-4301
🚴 🏕 🥾 ⛱ 👥 🍽

Coconino National Forest
In north-central Arizona.
(928) 527-3600
🏕 🥾 ⛱ 🏊 🍽

Coronado National Forest
In southeastern Arizona and southwestern New Mexico.
(520) 388-8300
🚴 🏕 🥾 ⛱ 👥

Glen Canyon National Recreation Area
In northern Arizona and Southern Utah.
(928) 608-6200
🏕 🥾 ⛱ 🏊 👥 🍽

Grand Canyon National Park
In northwestern Arizona.
(928) 638-2901
🏕 🥾 ⛱ 👥 🍽

Kaibab National Forest
In north-central Arizona.
(928) 643-7298
🚴 🏕 🥾 ⛱ 👥 🍽

🚴 Bicycling Trails   🏕 Camping   🥾 Hiking Trails   ⛱ Picnic Facilities
🏊 Swimming   👥 Visitor Center   🍽 Food Service

Petrified Forest National Park
In east-central Arizona, east of Holbrook.
(928) 524-6228
🐎 ⛱ 🏚 🍴

Prescott National Forest
In central Arizona.
(928) 443-8000
⛰ 🐎 ⛱ 🍴

Saguaro National Park
Two districts, 15 mi. east and west of Tucson.
(520) 733-5153
🚲 ⛰ 🐎 ⛱ 🏚

Tonto National Forest
In central Arizona.
(602) 225-5200
🚲 ⛰ 🐎 ⛱ 🏊 🍴

ARKANSAS

Buffalo National River
In northwestern Arkansas.
(870) 439-2502
⛰ 🐎 ⛱ 🏊 🏚 🍴

Hot Springs National Park
In western Arkansas.
(501) 620-6701
⛰ 🐎 ⛱ 🏚

Ouachita National Forest
In west-central Arkansas and southeastern Oklahoma.
(501) 321-5202
🚲 ⛰ 🐎 ⛱ 🏊 🏚

Ozark National Forest
In northwestern Arkansas.
(479) 964-7200
🚲 ⛰ 🐎 ⛱ 🏊 🏚

St. Francis National Forest
In east-central Arkansas.
(479) 964-7200
🚲 ⛰ 🐎 ⛱ 🏊

CALIFORNIA

Angeles National Forest
In southern California.
(626) 574-5200
🚲 ⛰ 🐎 ⛱ 🏊 🏚 🍴

Cleveland National Forest
In southwestern California.
(858) 673-6180
🚲 ⛰ 🐎 ⛱ 🏚 🍴

Death Valley National Park
Along the Nevada border in east-central California.
(760) 786-3200
⛰ 🐎 ⛱ 🏊 🏚

Eldorado National Forest
In central California.
(530) 644-6048
🚲 ⛰ 🐎 ⛱ 🏊 🏚 🍴

Golden Gate National Recreation Area
North of the Golden Gate Bridge and in northern and western San Francisco.
(415) 561-4700
🚲 ⛰ 🐎 ⛱ 🏊 🏚 🍴

Inyo National Forest
In east-central California.
(760) 873-2400
🚲 ⛰ 🐎 ⛱ 🏊 🏚 🍴

Joshua Tree National Park
East of Desert Hot Springs.
(760) 367-5500
⛰ 🐎 ⛱ 🏚

King Range National Conservation Area
In northwestern California.
(707) 825-2300
🚲 ⛰ 🐎 ⛱ 🏊 🏚 🍴

Klamath National Forest
In northern California.
(530) 842-6131
🚲 ⛰ 🐎 ⛱ 🏊 🏚

Lassen National Forest
In northeastern California.
(530) 257-2151
🚲 ⛰ 🐎 ⛱ 🏊 🏚 🍴

Lassen Volcanic National Park
In northeastern California.
(530) 595-4444
⛰ 🐎 ⛱ 🏊 🏚 🍴

Los Padres National Forest
In southern California.
(805) 968-6640
🚲 ⛰ 🐎 ⛱ 🏊 🏚

Mendocino National Forest
In northwestern California.
(530) 934-2350
🚲 ⛰ 🐎 ⛱ 🏊 🏚 🍴

Modoc National Forest
In northeastern California.
(530) 233-5811
🚲 ⛰ 🐎 ⛱ 🏊 🏚

Mojave National Preserve
Between I-15 and I-40 in southeastern California.
(760) 252-6108
⛰ 🐎 ⛱ 🏚 🍴

Plumas National Forest
In northern California.
(530) 283-2050
🚲 ⛰ 🐎 ⛱ 🏊 🏚 🍴

🚲 Bicycling Trails   ⛰ Camping   🐎 Hiking Trails   ⛱ Picnic Facilities
🏊 Swimming   🏚 Visitor Center   🍴 Food Service

Point Reyes National Seashore
Along the California coast just north of San Francisco.
(415) 464-5100
♿ ⛺ 🚴 ⛲ 🚶 🍴

Redwood National and State Parks
On the northern California coast.
(707) 465-7765
♿ ⛺ 🚴 ⛲ 🚣 🚶 🍴

San Bernardino National Forest
In southern California.
(909) 382-2600
♿ ⛺ 🚴 ⛲ 🚣 🚶 🍴

Santa Monica Mountains National Recreation Area
West from Griffith Park in Los Angeles past the Ventura
County line.
(805) 370-2301
♿ ⛺ 🚴 ⛲ 🚣 🚶 🍴

Sequoia and Kings Canyon National Parks
In east-central California.
(559) 565-3341
⛺ 🚴 ⛲ 🚶

Sequoia National Forest
In south-central California.
(559) 784-1500
♿ ⛺ 🚴 ⛲ 🚣 🚶 🍴

Shasta-Trinity National Forests
In northern California.
(530) 226-2500
♿ ⛺ 🚴 ⛲ 🚣 🚶 🍴

Sierra National Forest
In central California.
(559) 297-0706
♿ ⛺ 🚴 ⛲ 🚣 🚶 🍴

Six Rivers National Forest
In northwestern California.
(707) 442-1721
♿ ⛺ 🚴 ⛲ 🚣 🚶 🍴

Smith River National Recreation Area
Within Six Rivers National Forest in northwestern
California.
(707) 457-3131
♿ ⛺ 🚴 ⛲ 🚣

Stanislaus National Forest
Within Six Rivers National Forest in northwestern
California.
(707) 457-3131
♿ ⛺ 🚴 ⛲ 🚣 🍴

Tahoe National Forest
In north-central California.
(530) 265-4531
⛺ 🚴 ⛲ 🚣 🚶 🍴

Whiskeytown-Shasta-Trinity National Recreation Area
North and west of Redding.
(530) 242-3400
♿ ⛺ 🚴 ⛲ 🚣 🚶 🍴

Yosemite National Park
In central California.
(209) 372-0200
♿ ⛺ 🚴 ⛲ 🚣 🚶 🍴

COLORADO

Arapaho and Roosevelt National Forests and Pawnee National Grassland
In north-central Colorado.
(970) 295-6700
♿ ⛺ 🚴 ⛲ 🚣 🚶

Arapaho National Recreation Area
In north-central Colorado.
(970) 887-4100
♿ ⛺ 🚴 ⛲ 🚣 🚶

Black Canyon of The Gunnison National Park
In western Colorado.
(970) 249-1914
⛺ 🚴 ⛲ 🚶

Curecanti National Recreation Area
In south-central Colorado between Gunnison and
Montrose, paralleling US 50.
(970) 641-2337
⛺ 🚴 ⛲ 🚣 🚶 🍴

Grand Mesa—Uncompahgre—Gunnison National Forests
In west-central Colorado.
(970) 874-6600
♿ ⛺ 🚴 ⛲ 🚶 🍴

Great Sand Dunes National Park and Preserve
Northeast of Alamosa.
(719) 378-6399
⛺ 🚴 ⛲ 🚶

Mesa Verde National Park
In southwestern Colorado.
(970) 529-4465
⛺ 🚴 ⛲ 🚶

Pikes Peak and Pike National Forest
In south-central Colorado.
(719) 553-1400
♿ ⛺ 🚴 ⛲ 🚶 🍴

Rio Grande National Forest
In south-central Colorado.
(719) 852-5941
♿ ⛺ 🚴 ⛲ 🚣 🚶

Rocky Mountain National Park
In north-central Colorado.
(970) 586-1206
⛺ 🚴 ⛲ 🚶

Routt National Forest
In northwestern Colorado.
(970) 638-4516
♿ ⛺ 🚴 ⛲ 🚣 🚶

San Juan National Forest
In southwestern Colorado.
(970) 247-4874
♿ ⛺ 🚴 ⛲ 🚣 🚶 🍴

White River National Forest
In west-central Colorado.
(970) 945-2521
🚲 ⛺ 🥾 ⛱ 🏊 👤 🍴

FLORIDA
Apalachicola National Forest
In northwestern Florida.
(850) 926-3561
🚲 ⛺ 🥾 ⛱ 🏊

Biscayne National Park
In southeast Florida.
(305) 230-7275
⛺ 🥾 ⛱ 🏊 👤 🍴

Ocala National Forest
In north-central Florida.
(352) 236-0288
🚲 ⛺ 🥾 ⛱ 🏊 👤 🍴

Osceola National Forest
Near the Georgia border.
(386) 752-2577
🚲 ⛺ 🥾 ⛱ 🏊

GEORGIA
Chattahoochee River National Recreation Area
North of Atlanta.
(678) 538-1200
🚲 🥾 ⛱ 🏊 👤

Chattahoochee and Oconee National Forests
In central and northern Georgia.
(770) 297-3000
🚲 ⛺ 🥾 ⛱ 🏊 👤

IDAHO
Boise National Forest
In southwestern Idaho.
(208) 373-4007
🚲 ⛺ 🥾 ⛱ 🏊 👤

Caribou-Targhee National Forest
In southeastern Idaho.
(208) 524-7500
⛺ 🥾 ⛱ 🏊 👤

Clearwater National Forest
In northeastern Idaho.
(208) 476-4541
⛺ 🥾 ⛱ 🏊 👤

Idaho Panhandle National Forests
In northern and northwestern Idaho.
(208) 765-7223
🚲 ⛺ 🥾 ⛱ 🏊

Nez Perce National Forest
In northwestern Idaho.
(208) 983-1950
🚲 ⛺ 🥾 ⛱ 🏊 👤

Payette National Forest
In west-central Idaho.
(208) 634-0700
🚲 ⛺ 🥾 ⛱ 🏊 👤

Salmon-Challis National Forest
In east-central Idaho.
(208) 756-5100
⛺ 🥾 ⛱ 🏊 🍴

Sawtooth National Forest
In south-central Idaho.
(208) 737-3200
🚲 ⛺ 🥾 ⛱ 🏊 👤 🍴

Sawtooth National Recreation Area
In south-central Idaho.
(208) 727-5013
🚲 ⛺ 🥾 ⛱ 🏊 👤 🍴

ILLINOIS
Shawnee National Forest
In southern Illinois.
(618) 253-7114
⛺ 🥾 ⛱ 🏊 👤

INDIANA
Hoosier National Forest
In southern Indiana.
(812) 275-5987
🚲 ⛺ 🥾 ⛱ 🏊

Indiana Dunes National Lakeshore
On the southern shore of Lake Michigan.
(219) 926-7561
⛺ 🥾 ⛱ 🏊 👤

KENTUCKY
Daniel Boone National Forest
Five districts in eastern and southeastern Kentucky.
(859) 745-3100
🚲 ⛺ 🥾 ⛱ 👤 🍴

Daniel Boone National Forest (Laurel River Lake)
Off I-75 west of Corbin.
(606) 864-4163
🚲 ⛺ 🥾 ⛱ 🏊

Daniel Boone National Forest (Red River Gorge Geological Area)
Off SR 15.
(606) 663-8100
⛺ 🥾 ⛱ 👤

Daniel Boone National Forest (Rockcastle)
22 mi. southwest of London via SR 192/3497.
(606) 864-4163
⛺ 🥾 ⛱ 🏊

🚲 Bicycling Trails   ⛺ Camping   🥾 Hiking Trails   ⛱ Picnic Facilities
🏊 Swimming   👤 Visitor Center   🍴 Food Service

Daniel Boone National Forest (Sawyer)
5 mi. west of Cumberland Falls on SR 90, then 7 mi.
north on SR 896 following signs.
(606) 376-5323

Daniel Boone National Forest (S-Tree)
.5 mi. west of McKee on US 421, 3 mi. south on SR 89,
1 mi. west on FR 43, then south on FR 20 following
signs.
(606) 864-4163

Daniel Boone National Forest (Turkey Foot)
3 mi. north of McKee on SR 89, then east on FR 4
following signs for 3 mi.
(606) 864-4163

Land Between The Lakes National Recreation Area
In western Kentucky and Tennessee.
(270) 924-2000

Mammoth Cave National Park
In south-central Kentucky 10 mi. west of Cave City.
(270) 758-2180

LOUISIANA
Bayou Sauvage National Wildlife Refuge
Within the New Orleans city limits.
(985) 882-2000

Kisatchie National Forest
In central and northern Louisiana.
(318) 473-7160

Sabine National Wildlife Refuge
In southwestern Louisiana.
(337) 762-3816

MAINE
Acadia National Park
Along the Atlantic coast southeast of Bangor.
(207) 288-3338

MICHIGAN
Hiawatha National Forest
In Michigan's Upper Peninsula.
(906) 786-4062

Huron-Manistee National Forests
In the northern part of the Lower Peninsula.
(231) 775-2421

Ottawa National Forest
In Michigan's Upper Peninsula.
(906) 932-1330

Pictured Rocks National Lakeshore
Along Lake Superior in Michigan's Upper Peninsula.
906-387-3700

Sleeping Bear Dunes National Lakeshore
Along Lake Michigan in the northwestern part of the Lower
Peninsula.
(231) 326-5134

MINNESOTA
Chippewa National Forest
In north-central Minnesota.
(218) 335-8600

Superior National Forest
In northeastern Minnesota.
(218) 626-4300

MISSISSIPPI
Bienville National Forest
In central Mississippi.
(601) 469-3811

Gulf Islands National Seashore
Along the Gulf of Mexico in southern Mississippi.
(228) 875-9057

MISSOURI
Mark Twain National Forest
Southern Missouri.
(573) 364-4621

Mark Twain National Forest (Big Bay)
1 mi. southeast of Shell Knob on SR 39, then 3 mi.
southeast on CR YY.
(573) 364-4621

Mark Twain National Forest (Crane Lake)
12 mi. south of Ironton off SR 49 and CR E.
(573) 364-4621

Mark Twain National Forest (Fourche Lake)
18 mi. west of Doniphan on US 160.
(573) 364-4621

Mark Twain National Forest (Noblett Lake)
8 mi. west of Willow Springs on SR 76, then 1.4 mi. south
on SR 181, 3 mi. southeast on CR AP and 1 mi.
southwest on CR 857.
(573) 364-4621

Mark Twain National Forest (Pinewoods Lake)
2 mi. west of Ellsinore on SR 60.
(573) 364-4621

Mark Twain National Forest (Red Bluff)
1 mi. east of Davisville on CR V, then 1 mi. north on FR 2011.
(573) 364-4621
🔺 🥾 🌲 🏊

Ozarks and Ozark National Scenic Riverways
In southeastern Missouri.
(573) 323-4236
🔺 🥾 🌲 🏊 🏢 🍴

MONTANA
Beaverhead-Deerlodge National Forest
In southwestern Montana.
(406) 683-3900
🚲 🔺 🥾 🌲 🏊

Bighorn Canyon National Recreation Area
In southern Montana and northern Wyoming.
(406) 666-2412
🔺 🥾 🌲 🏊 🏢 🍴

Bitterroot National Forest
In western Montana.
(406) 363-7100
🚲 🔺 🥾 🌲 🏊 🏢

Custer National Forest
In southeastern Montana.
(406) 657-6200
🚲 🔺 🥾 🌲 🏊 🍴

Flathead National Forest
In northwestern Montana.
(406) 758-5204
🚲 🔺 🥾 🌲 🏊 🏢

Gallatin National Forest
In south-central Montana.
(406) 522-2520
🚲 🔺 🥾 🌲 🏊 🏢 🍴

Glacier National Park
In northwestern Montana.
(406) 888-7800
🔺 🥾 🌲 🏊 🏢 🍴

Helena National Forest
In west-central Montana.
(406) 449-5201
🔺 🥾 🌲 🏊

Kootenai National Forest
In northwestern Montana.
(406) 293-6211
🚲 🔺 🥾 🌲 🏊 🏢 🍴

Lewis and Clark National Forest
In central Montana.
(406) 791-7700
🔺 🥾 🌲 🏊

NEVADA
Great Basin National Park
In central Nevada, 5 mi. west of Baker near the Nevada-Utah border.
(775) 234-7331
🔺 🥾 🌲 🏢 🍴

Humboldt-Toiyabe National Forest
In central, western, northern and southern Nevada and eastern California.
(775) 331-6444
🚲 🔺 🥾 🌲

Lake Mead National Recreation Area
In northwestern Arizona and southeastern Nevada.
(702) 293-8990
🚲 🔺 🥾 🌲 🏊 🏢 🍴

NEW HAMPSHIRE
White Mountains and White Mountain National Forest
In northern New Hampshire.
(603) 528-8721
🚲 🔺 🥾 🌲 🏊 🏢

NEW JERSEY
Gateway National Recreation Area (Sandy Hook Unit)
In northeastern New Jersey.
(732) 872-5970
🚲 🥾 🌲 🏊 🏢 🍴

NEW MEXICO
Carson National Forest
In north-central New Mexico.
(575) 758-6200
🚲 🔺 🥾 🌲 🏢

Chaco Culture National Historical Park
In northwestern New Mexico.
(505) 786-7014
🚲 🔺 🥾 🌲 🏢

Cibola National Forest
In central New Mexico.
(505) 856-7325
🚲 🔺 🥾 🌲 🏊 🏢

El Malpais National Monument and National Conservation Area
23 mi. south of I-40 via SRs 53 and 117.
(505) 783-4774
🚲 🔺 🥾 🌲 🏢

Gila National Forest
In southwestern New Mexico.
(575) 388-8201
🚲 🔺 🥾 🌲 🏊 🏢

Lincoln National Forest
In south-central New Mexico.
(575) 434-7200
🚲 🔺 🥾 🌲 🍴

🚲 Bicycling Trails   🔺 Camping   🥾 Hiking Trails   🌲 Picnic Facilities
🏊 Swimming   🏢 Visitor Center   🍴 Food Service

Santa Fe National Forest
In north-central New Mexico between the Jemez
Mountains and the Sangre de Cristo Mountains.
(505) 438-5300
⬤ ⬤ ⬤ ⬤ ⬤

NEW YORK
Finger Lakes National Forest
In south-central New York on a ridge between Seneca
and Cayuga lakes, via I-90, I-81 and SR 17.
(607) 546-4470
⬤ ⬤ ⬤ ⬤ ⬤

Gateway National Recreation Area (Jamaica Bay Unit)
In Brooklyn and Queens boroughs in New York City.
(718) 338-3799
⬤ ⬤ ⬤ ⬤ ⬤ ⬤ ⬤

Gateway National Recreation Area (Staten Island Unit)
On Staten Island borough in New York City.
(718) 354-4500
⬤ ⬤ ⬤ ⬤ ⬤ ⬤

NORTH CAROLINA
Cape Hatteras National Seashore
In eastern North Carolina along the Outer Banks.
(252) 473-2111
⬤ ⬤ ⬤ ⬤ ⬤

Croatan National Forest
In southeastern North Carolina.
(252) 638-5628
⬤ ⬤ ⬤ ⬤ ⬤

Croatan National Forest (Cedar Point)
1.25 mi. north jct. SRs 24 and 58, 3 mi. southeast of
Swansboro.
(252) 638-5628
⬤ ⬤ ⬤

Nantahala National Forest
At North Carolina's southwestern tip.
(828) 257-4200
⬤ ⬤ ⬤ ⬤ ⬤

Nantahala National Forest (Hanging Dog)
21 acres 5 mi. northwest of Murphy on SR 1326.
(828) 837-5152
⬤ ⬤ ⬤

Nantahala National Forest (Jackrabbit Mountain)
10 mi. northeast of Hayesville via US 64, SR 175 and SR
1155.
(828) 524-6441
⬤ ⬤ ⬤ ⬤

Nantahala National Forest (Standing Indian Mountain)
9 mi. west of Franklin on US 64, 2 mi. east on old US 64,
then 2 mi. south on FR 67.
(828) 524-6441
⬤ ⬤ ⬤

Pisgah National Forest
In western North Carolina.
(828) 257-4200
⬤ ⬤ ⬤ ⬤ ⬤ ⬤

Pisgah National Forest (Lake Powhatan)
7 mi. southwest of Asheville on SR 191 and FR 3484.
(828) 670-5627
⬤ ⬤ ⬤ ⬤ ⬤

Pisgah National Forest (Rocky Bluff)
3 mi. south of Hot Springs on SR 209.
(828) 682-6146
⬤ ⬤ ⬤

Uwharrie National Forest
In central North Carolina.
(910) 576-6391
⬤ ⬤ ⬤ ⬤ ⬤

Uwharrie National Forest (Badin Lake)
10 mi. north of Troy on SR 109.
(910) 576-6391
⬤ ⬤ ⬤ ⬤

NORTH DAKOTA
Theodore Roosevelt National Park (North Unit)
In western North Dakota.
(701) 842-2333
⬤ ⬤ ⬤ ⬤

Theodore Roosevelt National Park (South Unit)
In western North Dakota.
(701) 623-4466
⬤ ⬤ ⬤ ⬤

OHIO
Cuyahoga Valley National Park
In northeastern Ohio.
(800) 257-9477
⬤ ⬤ ⬤ ⬤ ⬤ ⬤

OKLAHOMA
Black Kettle National Grasslands
Off SR 283 in Cheyenne.
(580) 497-2143
⬤ ⬤ ⬤ ⬤ ⬤

Chickasaw National Recreation Area
In south-central Oklahoma.
(580) 622-3161
⬤ ⬤ ⬤ ⬤ ⬤ ⬤

OREGON
Crater Lake National Park
On the crest of the Cascade Range off SR 62.
(541) 594-3100
⬤ ⬤ ⬤ ⬤ ⬤ ⬤

Deschutes National Forest
In central Oregon 6 mi. south of Bend via US 97.
(541) 383-5300
⬤ ⬤ ⬤ ⬤ ⬤ ⬤ ⬤

Fremont-Winema National Forests
In south-central Oregon.
(541) 947-2151
⬤ ⬤ ⬤ ⬤ ⬤ ⬤ ⬤

Hells Canyon National Recreation Area
In northeastern Oregon and western Idaho.
(509) 758-0616
🅰 🏃 ⛱ 🏠

Malheur National Forest
In eastern Oregon.
(541) 575-3000
🚲 🅰 🏃 ⛱ 🏊

Mt. Hood and Mt. Hood National Forest
In northwestern Oregon.
(888) 622-4822
🚲 🅰 🏃 ⛱ 🏊 🏠 🍴

Ochoco National Forest
In central Oregon off US 26.
(541) 416-6500
🚲 🅰 🏃 ⛱ 🏊

Oregon Dunes National Recreation Area
Between North Bend and Florence.
(541) 750-7000
🅰 🏃 ⛱ 🏊 🏠

Rogue River–Siskiyou National Forest
In southwestern Oregon off I-5 from Medford.
(541) 858-2200
🚲 🅰 🏃 ⛱ 🏊 🏠

Siuslaw National Forest
In western Oregon.
(541) 750-7000
🚲 🅰 🏃 ⛱ 🏊 🏠

Umatilla National Forest
In northeastern Oregon.
(541) 278-3716
🚲 🅰 🏃 ⛱ 🏊 🏠

Umpqua National Forest
In southwestern Oregon 33 mi. east of Roseburg on SR 138.
(541) 672-6601
🚲 🅰 🏃 ⛱ 🏊 🏠 🍴

Wallowa-Whitman National Forest
In northeastern Oregon.
(541) 523-6391
🅰 🏃 ⛱ 🏊

Willamette National Forest
In western Oregon.
(541) 225-6300
🚲 🅰 🏃 ⛱ 🏊 🍴

PENNSYLVANIA
Allegheny National Forest
In northwestern Pennsylvania.
(814) 723-5150
🚲 🅰 🏃 ⛱ 🏊 🏠 🍴

Delaware Water Gap National Recreation Area
In eastern Pennsylvania and northwestern New Jersey.
(570) 426-2457
🅰 🏃 ⛱ 🏊 🏠

SOUTH CAROLINA
Congaree National Park
Southeast of Hopkins.
(803) 776-4396
🅰 🏃 ⛱ 🏠

Francis Marion National Forest
On the Coastal Plain north of Charleston.
(803) 561-4000
🚲 🅰 🏃 ⛱ 🏠

Sumter National Forest
In western South Carolina.
(803) 561-4000
🚲 🅰 🏃 ⛱ 🏊

SOUTH DAKOTA
Badlands National Park
In southwestern South Dakota.
(605) 433-5361
🅰 🏃 ⛱ 🏠 🍴

Black Hills National Forest
In southwestern South Dakota.
(605) 673-9200
🚲 🅰 🏃 ⛱ 🏊 🏠 🍴

Wind Cave National Park
In southwestern South Dakota.
(605) 745-4600
🚲 🅰 🏃 ⛱ 🏠 🍴

TENNESSEE
Big South Fork National River and Recreation Area
In northeastern Tennessee and southeastern Kentucky.
(423) 286-7275
🚲 🅰 🏃 ⛱ 🏊 🏠 🍴

Cherokee National Forest
In eastern Tennessee.
(423) 476-9700
🚲 🅰 🏃 ⛱ 🏊 🏠

TEXAS
Amistad National Recreation Area
Northwest of Del Rio via US 90.
(830) 775-7491
🅰 🏃 ⛱ 🏊

Angelina National Forest
In east Texas.
(936) 897-1068
🅰 🏃 ⛱ 🏊

🚲 Bicycling Trails   🅰 Camping   🏃 Hiking Trails   ⛱ Picnic Facilities
🏊 Swimming   🏠 Visitor Center   🍴 Food Service

Big Bend National Park
In southwest Texas.
(432) 477-2251
[icons]

Davy Crockett National Forest
In east Texas.
(936) 655-2299
[icons]

Guadalupe Mountains National Park
110 mi. east of El Paso on US 62/180.
(915) 828-3251
[icons]

Lake Meredith National Recreation Area
45 mi. northeast of Amarillo and 9 mi. west of Borger via SR 136.
(806) 857-3151
[icons]

Padre Island National Seashore
On Padre Island near Corpus Christi.
(361) 949-8068
[icons]

Sabine National Forest
In east Texas.
(409) 625-1940
[icons]

Sam Houston National Forest
40 mi. north of Houston in east Texas.
(936) 344-6205
[icons]

UTAH
Ashley National Forest
In northeastern Utah.
(435) 789-1181
[icons]

Canyonlands National Park
In southeastern Utah.
(435) 719-2313
[icons]

Capitol Reef National Park
10 mi. east of Torrey on SR 24.
(435) 425-3791
[icons]

Dixie National Forest
In southwestern Utah.
(435) 865-3700
[icons]

Fishlake National Forest
In south-central Utah.
(435) 896-9233
[icons]

Flaming Gorge National Recreation Area
In northeastern Utah on the Wyoming-Utah border.
(435) 784-3445
[icons]

Manti-La Sal National Forest
In southeastern Utah.
(435) 637-2817
[icons]

Uinta National Forest
In north-central, central and northeastern Utah.
(801) 342-5100
[icons]

Zion National Park
In southwestern Utah.
(435) 772-3256
[icons]

VERMONT
Green Mountains and Green Mountain National Forest
In south-central Vermont.
(802) 747-6700
[icons]

VIRGINIA
George Washington and Jefferson National Forests
In western Virginia and the eastern edge of West Virginia.
(540) 265-5100
[icons]

Mount Rogers National Recreation Area
In southwestern Virginia.
(276) 783-5196
[icons]

Shenandoah National Park
In northwestern Virginia.
(540) 999-3500
[icons]

WASHINGTON
Colville National Forest
In northeastern Washington.
(509) 684-7000
[icons]

Gifford Pinchot National Forest
In southwestern Washington.
(360) 891-5000
[icons]

Gifford Pinchot National Forest (Goose Lake)
13 mi. west of Trout Lake via SR 141, FR 24 and FR 60.
(509) 395-3400
[icons]

Gifford Pinchot National Forest (Takhlakh Lake)
32 mi. southeast of Randle via SR 131, FR 23 and FR 2329.
(360) 497-1100
[icons]

Lake Chelan National Recreation Area
In north-central Washington.
(509) 682-1900
[icons]

Lake Roosevelt National Recreation Area
In northeastern Washington.
(509) 633-9441
🖾 🛦 🏊 👬 🍽

Mount Baker-Snoqualmie National Forest
2 mi. east of Glacier on SR 542.
(425) 783-6000
🚲 🛦 🥾 🏕 🏊 👬 🍽

Mount Baker-Snoqualmie National Forest (Douglas Fir)
2 mi. east of Glacier on SR 542.
(425) 783-6000
🛦 🥾 🏕

Mount Baker-Snoqualmie National Forest (Horseshoe Cove)
14 mi. north of Concrete on Baker Lake.
(360) 599-2714
🛦 🥾 🏊

Mount Baker-Snoqualmie National Forest (Shannon Creek)
24 mi. north of Concrete on Baker Lake.
(360) 599-2714
🛦 🥾 🏕 🏊

Okanogan-Wenatchee National Forest
In north-central Washington.
(509) 826-3275
🚲 🛦 🥾 🏕 🏊 👬 🍽

Okanogan-Wenatchee National Forest (Bonaparte Lake)
7 mi. northwest of Wauconda via SR 20 and CR 4953.
(509) 664-9200
🛦 🏕 🏊

Okanogan-Wenatchee National Forest (Bumping Lake)
3 mi. south of Goose Prairie.
(509) 664-9200
🛦 🏕 🏊

Okanogan-Wenatchee National Forest (Kachess)
15 mi. north of Easton via I-90 and FR 49.
(509) 852-1100
🚲 🛦 🥾 🏕 🏊

Okanogan-Wenatchee National Forest (Lost Lake)
17 mi. northwest of Wauconda via SR 20, CR 4953, FR 32 and FR 33.
(509) 852-1100
🛦 🏕 🏊

Okanogan-Wenatchee National Forest (Rimrock Lake Area)
At Rimrock off US 12.
(509) 653-1401
🛦 🏕 🏊

Olympic National Forest
In northwestern Washington.
(360) 956-2402
🚲 🛦 🥾 🏕 🏊 👬 🍽

Olympic National Forest (Falls Creek)
3 mi. east of US 101 on Quinault Lake.
(360) 956-2402
🛦 🥾 🏕 🏊

Olympic National Forest (Willaby)
2 mi. east of US 101 on Quinault Lake.
(360) 956-2402
🛦 🥾 🏕 🏊

Olympic National Forest (Wynoochee Lake-Coho)
1 mi. west of Montesano on US 12, then 37 mi. north on FR 22 (Old Wynoochee Valley Rd.).
(360) 956-2402
🚲 🛦 🥾 🏕 🏊

Ross Lake National Recreation Area
Between the north and south sections of North Cascades National Park.
(360) 854-7200
🛦 🥾 🏕 👬 🍽

WEST VIRGINIA

Monongahela National Forest
In eastern West Virginia.
(304) 636-1800
🚲 🛦 🥾 🏕 🏊 👬 🍽

Monongahela National Forest (Lake Sherwood)
11 mi. northeast of Neola on SR 14.
(304) 636-1800
🚲 🛦 🥾 🏕 🏊

New River Gorge National River
Between Fayetteville and Hinton.
(304) 465-0508
🚲 🥾 🏕 🏊 👬

Spruce Knob-Seneca Rocks National Recreation Area
In east-central West Virginia.
(304) 257-4488
🛦 🥾 🏕 🏊 👬

WISCONSIN

Apostle Islands National Lakeshore
Off northern Wisconsin's Bayfield Peninsula in Lake Superior.
(715) 779-3397
🛦 🥾 🏕 🏊 👬

Chequamegon-Nicolet National Forest
In north-central and northeastern Wisconsin.
(715) 362-1300
🚲 🛦 🥾 🏕 🏊 🍽

St. Croix National Scenic Riverway
Running 252 mi. from Cable to Prescott.
(715) 483-2274
🛦 🥾 🏕 🏊 👬

🚲 Bicycling Trails   🛦 Camping   🥾 Hiking Trails   🏕 Picnic Facilities
🏊 Swimming   👬 Visitor Center   🍽 Food Service

WYOMING
Bighorn National Forest
In north-central Wyoming.
(307) 674-2600

Devils Tower National Monument
Between Sundance and Hulett.
(307) 467-5283

Grand Teton National Park
In northwestern Wyoming.
(307) 739-3300

Medicine Bow National Forest
In southeastern Wyoming.
(307) 745-2300

Shoshone National Forest
In northwestern Wyoming.
(307) 527-6241

Yellowstone National Park
In northwestern Wyoming.
(307) 344-7381

Canada

ALBERTA
Banff National Park of Canada
In southwestern Alberta, west of Calgary.
(403) 762-1550

Elk Island National Park of Canada
In central Alberta, east of Edmonton.
(780) 992-2950

Jasper National Park of Canada
In west-central Alberta along the British Columbia border.
(780) 852-3858

Waterton Lakes National Park of Canada
In Alberta's southwestern corner.
(403) 859-2224

BRITISH COLUMBIA
Glacier National Park of Canada
In southeastern British Columbia.
(250) 837-7500

Gulf Islands National Park Reserve of Canada
Off the southeast coast of Vancouver Island.
(250) 654-4000

Kootenay National Park of Canada
In southeastern British Columbia.
(250) 343-6783

Mount Revelstoke National Park of Canada
In southeastern British Columbia.
(250) 837-7500

Pacific Rim National Park Reserve of Canada
On the southwestern coast of Vancouver Island.
(250) 726-7721

Yoho National Park of Canada
On the British Columbia-Alberta border.
(250) 343-6783

MANITOBA
Riding Mountain National Park of Canada
In southwestern Manitoba.
(204) 848-7275

NEW BRUNSWICK
Fundy National Park of Canada
On Hwy. 114, 130 km. southwest of Moncton.
(506) 887-6000

Kouchibouguac National Park of Canada
On Hwy. 134, north of Moncton.
(506) 876-2443

NEWFOUNDLAND AND LABRADOR
Gros Morne National Park of Canada
On Newfoundland's western coast.
(709) 458-2417

Terra Nova National Park of Canada
In eastern Newfoundland.
(709) 533-2801

NORTHWEST TERRITORIES
Wood Buffalo National Park of Canada
On the Northwest Territories-Alberta border.
(867) 872-7900

NOVA SCOTIA
Cape Breton Highlands National Park of Canada
5 km. northeast of Che'ticamp on Cabot Tr.
(902) 224-2306

Kejimkujik National Park and National Historic Site of Canada
In southwestern Nova Scotia off Hwy. 8 at Maitland Bridge.
(902) 682-2772
🚴 🔺 🚶 🏕 🏊 👥 🍽

ONTARIO
Bruce Peninsula National Park of Canada
In southwestern Ontario.
(519) 596-2233
🔺 🚶 🏕 🏊

Georgian Bay Islands National Park of Canada
Along the southeastern portion of Georgian Bay.
(705) 526-9804
🚴 🔺 🚶 🏕 🏊 👥

Point Pelee National Park of Canada
South of Leamington.
(519) 322-2365
🚴 🚶 🏕 🏊 👥 🍽

Pukaskwa National Park of Canada
On the north shore of Lake Superior.
(807) 229-0801
🔺 🚶 🏕 🏊 👥

St. Lawrence Islands National Park of Canada
In the St. Lawrence River between Kingston and Brockville.
(613) 923-5261
🔺 🚶 🏕 🏊 👥

PRINCE EDWARD ISLAND
Prince Edward Island National Park of Canada
Along the island's northern shore.
(902) 672-6350
🚴 🔺 🚶 🏕 🏊 👥 🍽

QUEBEC
Forillon National Park of Canada
20 km. northeast of Gaspe´ via Hwy. 132.
(418) 368-5505
🚴 🔺 🚶 🏕 🏊 👥 🍽

La Mauricie National Park of Canada
North of Trois-Rivie´res via Hwy. 55.
(819) 538-3232
🚴 🔺 🚶 🏕 🏊 👥 🍽

SASKATCHEWAN
Grasslands National Park of Canada
Between Val Marie and Killdeer in southern Saskatchewan.
(306) 298-2257
🔺 🚶 🏕 👥

Prince Albert National Park of Canada
In central Saskatchewan.
(306) 663-4522
🚴 🔺 🚶 🏕 🏊 👥 🍽

🚴 Bicycling Trails   🔺 Camping   🚶 Hiking Trails   🏕 Picnic Facilities
🏊 Swimming   👥 Visitor Center   🍽 Food Service

EMERGENCY ANIMAL CLINICS

This list of emergency animal clinics in the United States and Canada is provided by the Veterinary Emergency & Critical Care Society (VECCS) as a service to the community for information purposes only. This is not to be construed as a certification or an endorsement of any clinic listed. For further information, contact the society at (210) 698-5575 or online at www.veccs.org. Note: Hours frequently change, and not all clinics are open 24 hours or in the evening. In addition, not all facilities listed here are emergency clinics. In non-emergency situations, it's best to call first.

If you are traveling to an area not covered in this list, be prepared for an emergency by asking your regular veterinarian to recommend a clinic or veterinarian at your destination. The American Animal Hospital Association also can recommend veterinary clinics that meet the association's high standards for veterinary care. For additional information contact the association at (303) 986-2800.

United States

ALABAMA
Animal Medical Center
2864 Acton Rd., Birmingham
(205) 967-7389

Emergency Pet Care
4524 Southlake Pkwy., Suite 28, Birmingham
(205) 988-5988

Southern Regional Veterinary Emergency Services
301 Westgate Pkwy., Dothan
(334) 699-7787

Animal Emergency Clinic of North Alabama
2112 Memorial Pkwy. S.W., Huntsville
(256) 533-7600

Animal Emergency & Referral Center of Mobile
2573 Government Blvd., Mobile
(251) 706-0890

ALASKA
Pet Emergency Treatment, Inc.
2320 E. Dowling Rd., Anchorage
(907) 274-5636

After Hours Veterinary Emergency Clinic
8 Bonnie Ave., Fairbanks
(907) 479-2700

ARIZONA
First Regional Animal Hospital
1233 W. Warner Rd., Chandler
(480) 732-0335

Emergency Animal Clinic, PLC
86 W. Juniper, Gilbert
(480) 497-0222

1st Emergency Pet Care
1423 S. Highley Rd., #102, Mesa
(408) 924-1123

Emergency Animal Clinic
1235 S. Gilbert Rd., Suite 24, Mesa
(480) 497-0222

Mesa Veterinary Hospital
858 N. Country Club Dr., Mesa
(480) 833-7330

Emergency Animal Clinic
9875 W. Peoria Ave., Peoria
(623) 974-1520

Emergency Animal Clinic, PLC
2260 W. Glendale Ave., Phoenix
(602) 995-3757

North Valley Animal Emergency Center
3134 W. Carefree Hwy., Suite A-2, Phoenix
(623) 516-8571

Sonora Veterinary Specialists
4015 E. Cactus Rd., Phoenix
(602) 765-3700

Emergency Animal Clinic
14202 N. Scottsdale Rd., Suite 163, Scottsdale
(480) 949-8001

Paradise Valley Emergency Animal Clinic
6969 E. Shea Blvd., Suite 225, Scottsdale
(480) 991-1848

Arizona Veterinary Surgery
4131 E. Speedway Blvd., Tucson
(520) 795-9955

Ina Road Animal Hospital
7320 N. La Cholla Blvd., Suite 114, Tucson
(520) 544-7700

Pima Pet Clinic / Animal Emergency Service
4832 E. Speedway Blvd., Tucson
(520) 327-5624

Southern Arizona Veterinary Specialty and Emergency Center
141 E. Fort Lowell Rd., Tucson
(520) 888-3177

Southern Arizona Veterinary Specialty and Emergency Center
7474 E. Broadway Blvd., Tucson
(520) 888-3177

Valley Animal Hospital, P.C.
4984 E. 22nd St., Tucson
(520) 748-0331

Veterinary Specialty Center of Tucson
4909 N. La Canada Dr., Tucson
(520) 795-9955

ARKANSAS
Ft. Smith Animal Emergency Clinic
4301 Regions Park Dr., Suite 3, Fort Smith
(479) 649-3100

Pulaski County Veterinary Emergency Clinic
801 John Barrow #6, Little Rock
(501) 224-3784

After Hour Animal Hospital
290 Smokey Ln., North Little Rock
(501) 955-0911

Animal Emergency & Specialty Clinic
8735 Sheltie Dr., Suite G, North Little Rock
(501) 224-3784

Animal Emergency Clinic of Northwest Arkansas
1110 Mathias Dr., Suite E, Springdale
(501) 927-0007

CALIFORNIA
East Bay Veterinary Emergency
1312 Sunset Dr., Antioch
(925) 754-5001

Central Coast Pet Emergency Clinic
1558 W. Branch St., Arroyo Grande
(805) 489-6573

Atascadero Pet Hospital and Emergency Center
9575 El Camino Real, Atascadero
(805) 466-3880

Animal Emergency & Urgent Care
4300 Easton Dr., Suite 1, Bakersfield
(661) 322-6019

Pet Emergency Treatment and Specialty (PETS) Referral Center
1048 University Ave., Berkeley
(510) 548-6684

United Emergency Animal Clinic
1657 S. Bascom Ave., Campbell
(408) 371-6282

Pacific Veterinary Specialists and Emergency Critical Care Center
1980 41st Ave., Capitola
(831) 476-2584

North Valley Emergency Veterinary Clinic
2500 Zanella Way, Chico
(530) 899-1720

Contra Costa Veterinary Emergency Center
1410 Monument Blvd., Suite 108, Concord
(925) 798-2900

VCA Aacacia Animal Hospital
939 W. 6th St., Corona
(951) 371-1002

Advanced Critical Care and Internal Medicine Los Angeles
9599 Jefferson Blvd., Culver City
(310) 558-6100

UC Davis Veterinary Medical Teaching Hospital - Small Animal Clinic
1 Garrod Dr., Davis
(530) 752-1393

Tri-Valley Animal Emergency Center
7111 Amador Plaza Rd., Dublin
(925) 771-5630

Vetcare Emergency & Specialty Care Center
7660 Amador Valley Blvd., Dublin
(925) 556-1234

Emergency Pet Clinic of San Gabriel Valley
3254 Santa Anita Ave., El Monte
(626) 579-4550

North Coast Veterinary and Emergency
414 Encinitas Blvd., Encinitas
(760) 632-1072

Animal Urgent Care
2430 S. Escondido Blvd., Escondido
(760) 738-9600

Animal Emergency Center
3954 A Jacobs Ave., Eureka
(707) 443-2776

Solano-Napa Pet Emergency Clinic
4437 Central Pl., Fairfield
(707) 864-1444

VCA All-Care Animal Referral Center
18440 Amistad St., Suite E, Fountain Valley
(714) 963-0909

Ohlone Veterinary Emergency Clinic
1618 Washington Blvd., Fremont
(510) 657-6620

Central California Veterinary Specialty Center
6606 N. Blackstone Ave., Fresno
(559) 451-0800

Fresno Pet Emergency & Referral Center, Inc.
7375 N. Palm Bluffs Ave., Fresno
(559) 437-3766

Veterinary Emergency Service, Inc.
1639 N. Fresno St., Fresno
(559) 486-0520

Orange County Emergency Pet Clinic
12750 Garden Grove Blvd., Garden Grove
(714) 537-3032

eMash, Inc.
10825 Watsonville Rd., Gilroy
(408) 847-1122

Animal Emergency Clinic
12022 La Crosse Ave., Grand Terrace
(909) 825-9350

Irvine Regional Animal Emergency Hospital
1371 Reynolds Ave., Irvine
(949) 833-9020

North Orange County Emergency Pet Clinic
1474 S. Harbor Blvd., La Habra
(714) 441-2925

Pet Emergency & Specialty Center
5232 Jackson Dr., Suite 105, La Mesa
(619) 462-4800

Animal Emergency Clinic
1055 W. Avenue M, Suite 101, Lancaster
(661) 723-3959

Animal Specialty Group
4641 Colorado Blvd., Los Angeles
(818) 244-7977

Animal Surgical & Emergency Center
1535 S. Sepulveda Blvd., Los Angeles
(310) 473-1561

Animal Surgical and Emergency Center (ASEC)
1535 S. Sepulveda Blvd., Los Angeles
(310) 473-5906

Eagle Rock Emergency Pet Clinic
4254 Eagle Rock Blvd., Los Angeles
(323) 254-7382

VCA West Los Angeles Animal Hospital
1818 S. Sepulveda Blvd., Los Angeles
(310) 473-2951

Animal Urgent Care
2805 Hillcrest, Mission Viejo
(949) 364-6228

Portola Plaza Veterinary Hospital
27752 Santa Margarita Pkwy., Mission Viejo
(949) 859-2101

Modesto Veterinary Emergency Clinic
1800 Prescott Rd., Suite E, Modesto
(209) 527-8844

Monterey Peninsula Veterinary Emergency & Specialty Center
20 Lower Ragsdale Dr., Suite 150, Monterey
(831) 373-7374

All Creatures Emergency Center
22722 Lyons Ave., #5, Newhall
(661) 291-1121

Central Orange County Emergency Animal Clinic
3720 Campus Drive, Suite D, Newport Beach
(949) 261-7979

Crossroads Animal Emergency and Referral Clinic
11057 E. Rosecrans Ave., Norwalk
(562) 863-2522

Orange Veterinary Hospital
1100 W. Chapman Ave., Orange
(714) 997-8200

Extraordinary Veterinary Services
5714 Los Coyotes Dr., Palm Springs
(760) 202-8710

South Peninsula Veterinary Emergency Clinic
3045 Middlefield Rd., Palo Alto
(650) 494-1461

Animal Emergency Clinic of Pasadena
2121 E. Foothill Blvd., Pasadena
(626) 564-0704

Animal Emergency Clinic of San Diego
12775 Poway Rd., Poway
(858) 748-7387

Animal Care Center
6470 Redwood Dr., Rohnert Park
(707) 584-4343

Atlantic St. Veterinary Hospital and Pet Emergency Center, Inc.
1100 Atlantic St., Roseville
(916) 783-4655

El Camino Veterinary Hospital
4000 El Camino Ave., Sacramento
(916) 488-6878

Mueller Animal Hospital
6420 Freeport Blvd., Sacramento
(916) 428-9202

Northern California Veterinary Specialists
7425 Greenhaven Dr., Sacramento
(916) 231-0696

VCA Sacramento Veterinary Referral Center
9801 Old Winery Pl., Sacramento
(916) 362-3111

Animal ER of San Diego
5610 Kearny Mesa Rd., Suite A, San Diego
(858) 569-0600

VCA Emergency Animal Hospital and Referral Center
2317 Hotel Cir. S., San Diego
(619) 299-2400

Veterinary Specialty Hospital
10435 Sorrento Valley Rd., San Diego
(858) 875-7500

All Animals Emergency Hospital
1333 Ninth Ave., San Francisco
(415) 566-0531

Pets Unlimited
2343 Fillmore St., San Francisco
(415) 563-6700

San Francisco Veterinary Specialists
600 Alabama St., San Francisco
(415) 401-9200

Emergency Animal Clinic of South San Jose
5440 Thornwood Dr., Suite E, San Jose
(408) 578-5622

Bay Area Veterinary Emergency Clinic
14790 Washington Ave., San Leandro
(510) 352-6080

California Veterinary Specialists
100 N. Rancho Santa Fe Rd., San Marcos
(760) 734-4433

North Peninsula Veterinary Emergency Clinic, Inc.
227 N. Amphlett Blvd., San Mateo
(650) 348-2575

The Pet Emergency and Specialty Center of Marin
901 E. Francisco Blvd., Suite C, San Rafael
(415) 456-7372

California Animal Referral & Emergency Hospital
301 E. Haley St., Santa Barbara
(805) 899-2273

Santa Cruz Veterinary Hospital
2585 Soquel Dr., Santa Cruz
(831) 475-5400

North Bay Animal Emergency Hospital
1304 Wilshire Blvd., Santa Monica
(310) 451-8962

Emergency Animal Hospital of Santa Rosa
1946 Santa Rosa Ave., Santa Rosa
(707) 544-1647

PetCare Veterinary Hospital
1370 Fulton Rd., Santa Rosa
(707) 579-5900

Beverly Oaks Animal Hospital and Emergency Animal Clinic
14302 Ventura Blvd., Sherman Oaks
(818) 788-7860

TLC Pet Medical Centers - South Pasadena
1412 Huntington Dr., South Pasadena
(626) 441-8555

Associated Veterinary Emergency Services
3008 E. Hammer Ln., #115, Stockton
(209) 952-8387

Animal Emergency Centre
11730 Ventura Blvd., Studio City
(818) 760-3882

Emergency Pet Clinic of Temecula
27443 Jefferson Ave., Temecula
(951) 695-5044

Pet Emergency Clinic
2967 N. Moorepark Rd., Thousand Oaks
(805) 492-2436

Animal Emergency Referral Center
3511 Pacific Coast Hwy., Suite A, Torrance
(310) 325-3000

Emergency Pet Clinic of South Bay
2325 Torrance Blvd., Torrance
(310) 320-8300

Monte Vista Small Animal Hospital
901 E. Monte Vista Ave., Turlock
(209) 634-0023

Advanced Critical Care & Internal Medicine
2965 Edinger Ave., Tustin
(949) 654-8950

Inland Valley Emergency Pet Clinic
10 W. 7th St., Upland
(909) 931-7871

Pet Emergency Clinic
2301 S. Victoria Ave., Ventura
(805) 642-8562

Veterinary Medical and Surgical Group
2199 Sperry Ave., Ventura
(805) 339-2290

Animal Emergency Clinic
15532 Bear Valley Rd., Victorville
(760) 962-1122

Pinnacle Veterinary Service, Inc.
2300 S. Divisadero St., Visalia
(559) 732-8000

Tulare-Kings Veterinary Emergency Service
4240 W. Mineral King, Visalia
(559) 739-7054

TLC Pet Medical Centers - West Hollywood
8725 Santa Monica Blvd., West Hollywood
(310) 859-4852

COLORADO
Animal Urgent Care
7851 Indiana St., Arvada
(303) 420-7387

Aurora Veterinary Emergency Center
18511 E. Hampden Ave., Aurora
(303) 699-1665

Valley Emergency Pet Care
180 Fiou Ln., Suite 101, Basalt
(970) 927-5066

Alpenglow Veterinary Specialty & Emergency Center
3640 Walnut St., Boulder
(303) 443-4569

Animal Emergency & Referral Center
1480 W. Midway Blvd., Boulder
(303) 464-7744

Boulder Emergency Pet Clinic
1658 30th St., Boulder
(303) 440 7722

VCA Douglas County Animal Hospital
531 Jerry St., Castle Rock
(303) 688-2480

Animal Emergency Care Centers -North
5520 N. Nevada Ave., Colorado Springs
(719) 260-7141

Animal Emergency Care Centers- South
3775 Airport Rd., Colorado Springs
(719) 578-9300

Animal Emergency Care, Inc.
5752 N. Academy Blvd., Colorado Springs
(719) 260-7141

VCA Alameda East Veterinary Hospital
9770 E. Alameda Ave., Denver
(303) 366-2639

Central Veterinary Emergency Services
3550 S. Jason St., Englewood
(303) 874-7387

Pets of Northern Colorado
3629 23rd Ave., Evans
(970) 339-8700

Fort Collins Veterinary Emergency Hospital
816 S. Lemay Ave., Fort Collins
(970) 484-8080

James L. Voss Veterinary Teaching Hospital Colorado State University
300 W. Drake Rd., Fort Collins
(970) 221-4535

Grand Valley Veterinary Emergency Center
1660 North Ave., Grand Junction
(970) 255 1911

Animal Hospital Specialty Center
5640 County Line Pl., Suite 1, Highlands Ranch
(303) 740-9595

Animal Critical Care & Emergency Services, Inc.
1597 Wadsworth Blvd., Lakewood
(303) 239-1200

Animal E.R.
221 W. County Line Rd., Littleton
(720) 283-9348

Columbine Animal Hospital & Emergency Clinic
5546 W. Canyon Tr., Littleton
(303) 929-4040

Animal Emergency & Critical Care
230 S. Main St., Longmont
(303) 678-8844

Animal Emergency Services of Northern Colorado
201 W. 67th Ct., Loveland
(970) 663-5760

Animal Emergency & Urgent Care
17701 Cottonwood Dr., Parker
(720) 842-5050

Emergency Animal Hospital of Pueblo
472 S. Joe Martinez Blvd., Pueblo
(719) 229-7030

Pueblo Area Pet Emergency Hospital
712 Fortino Blvd., Pueblo
(719) 544-7788

Northside Emergency Pet Clinic, P.C.
945 W. 124th Ave., Westminster
(303) 252-7722

Wheat Ridge Animal Hospital / Wheat Ridge Veterinary Specialists
3695 Kipling St., Wheat Ridge
(303) 424-3325

CONNECTICUT
Farmington Valley Veterinary Emergency Hospital
9 Avonwood Rd., Avon
(860) 674-1886

VCA Cheshire Veterinary Hospital
1572 S. Main St., Cheshire
(203) 271-1577

Veterinary Emergency Treatment Services (VETS)
8 Enterprise Ln., Montville
(860) 444-8870

New Haven Hospital for Veterinary Medicine, Inc.
843 State St., New Haven
(203) 865-0878

VCA Veterinary Referral & Emergency Center
123 W. Cedar St., Norwalk
(203) 854-9960

V-E-T-S (Veterinary Emergency Treatment Services)
8 Enterprise Ln., Oakdale
(860) 444 8870

Animal Emergency Hospital Of Central Connecticut
588 Cromwell Ave., Rocky Hill
(860) 563-4447

Shoreline Animal Emergency Clinic
7365 Main St., Stratford
(203) 375-6500

Connecticut Veterinary Center
470 Oakwood Ave., West Hartford
(860) 233-8564

DELAWARE
VCA Newark Animal Hospital
1360 Marrows Rd., Newark
(302) 737-8100

Veterinary Emergency Center of Delaware
1212 E. Newport Pike, Wilmington
(302) 691-3647

Windcrest Animal Emergency Hospital
3705 Lancaster Pike, Wilmington
(302) 998-2995

DISTRICT OF COLUMBIA
Friendship Hospital for Animals
4105 Brandywine St., Washington
(202) 363-7300

FLORIDA
Calusa Veterinary Center
6900 Congress Ave., Boca Raton
(561) 999-3000

Southwest Florida Veterinary Specialists & 24 Hour Emergency Hospital
28400 Old 41 Rd., Suite 1, Bonita Springs
(239) 992-8387

PetPB Animal Emergency & Referral Center
2246 N. Congress Ave., Boynton Beach
(561) 752-3232

Animal Emergency Clinic of Brandon
693 W. Lumsden Rd., Brandon
(813) 684-3013

Animal ER of SW Florida
1327 N.E. Pine Island Rd., Suite 110, Cape Coral
(239) 673-7426

Veterinary Emergency Clinic of Central Florida - Casselberry
195 Concord Dr., Casselberry
(407) 644-4449

Animal Emergency and Critical Care Services of S. Florida
9410 Stirling Rd., Cooper City
(954) 432-5611

Coral Springs Animal Hospital
2160 N. University Dr., Coral Springs
(954) 753-1800

Florida Veterinary Referral Center & 24 Hour Emergency & Critical Care
9220 Estero Park Commons Blvd., Suite 7, Estero
(239) 992-8878

Animal Emergency Trauma Center
2200 W. Oakland Park Blvd., Fort Lauderdale
(954) 731-4228

Pet Emergency Center
921 E. Cypress Creek Rd., Fort Lauderdale
(954) 772-0420

Emergency Veterinary Clinic, Inc.
2045 Collier Ave., Fort Myers
(239) 939-5542

Animal Emergency and Referral Center
3984 S. US 1, Fort Pierce
(772) 466-3441

Affiliated Pet Emergency Services
7314 W. University Ave., Gainesville
(352) 373-4444

Miami Veterinary Specialists
8601 Sunset Dr., Glenvar Heights
(305) 665-2820

Hollywood Animal Hospital
2864 Hollywood Blvd., Hollywood
(954) 920-3556

Animal ER
3444 Southside Blvd., Suite 101, Jacksonville
(904) 642-4357

Emergency Pet Care, LLC
14185 Beach Blvd., Suite 7, Jacksonville
(904) 223-8000

First Coast Animal ER
3444 Southside Blvd., Suite 101, Jacksonville
(904) 642-4357

Emergency Pet Care of Jupiter
300 Central Blvd., Jupiter
(561) 746-0555

Tampa Bay Veterinary Emergency Service
1501-A Belcher Rd., Suite 1A, Largo
(727) 531-5752

Veterinary Emergency Clinic of Central Florida - Leesburg
33040 Professional Dr., Leesburg
(352) 728-4440

Animal Emergency and Critical Care Center of Brevard
2281 W. Eau Gallie Blvd., Melbourne
(321) 725-5365

AEC-Animal Emergency Clinic South
8429 S.W. 132nd St., Miami
(305) 251-2096

Doral Centre Animal Clinic
9589 N.W. 41st St., Miami
(305) 598-1234

Knowles Animal Clinic - Snapper Creek Emergency Clinic
9933 Sunset Dr., Miami
(305) 279-2323

Miami Pet Emergency
11774 N. Kendall Dr., Miami
(305) 273-8100

The Pet Emergency Room
6394 S. Dixie Hwy., Miami
(305) 666-4142

Animal Specialty Hospital of Florida (ASH)
10130 Market St., Suite 1, Naples
(239) 263-0480

Emergency Pet Hospital of Collier Co.
6530 Dudley Dr., Naples
(941) 263-8010

Ocala Animal Emergency Hospital
1815 N.E. Jacksonville Rd., Ocala
(352) 840-0044

Clay-Duval Pet Emergency Clinic
275 Corporate Way, Suite 200, Orange Park
(904) 264-8281

Veterinary Emergency Clinic of Central Florida - South Orlando
2080 Principal Row, Orlando
(407) 438-4449

Pet Emergency and Critical Care Clinic
3816 Northlake Blvd., Palm Beach Gardens
(561) 691-9999

A.A.Animal ER Center, LLC
36401 US 19N, Palm Harbor
(727) 787-5402

Animal Emergency of Countryside, Inc.
30610 US 19N, Palm Harbor
(727) 786-5755

St. Francis Emergency Animal Hospital
6602 Pines Blvd., Pembroke Pines
(954) 962-0300

Veterinary Emergency Referral Center
4800 N. Davis Hwy., Pensacola
(850) 477-3914

The Veterinary Emergency Clinic
17829 Murdock Cir., Port Charlotte
(941) 255-5222

Animal Specialty and Emergency Hospital
5775 Schenck Ave., Rockledge
(321) 752-7600

Critical Care & Veterinary Specialists of Sarasota
4937 S Tamiami Tr., Sarasota
(941) 929-1818

Sarasota Veterinary Emergency Hospital
7515-7517 S. Tamiami Tr., Sarasota
(941) 923-7260

Animal Emergency Clinic of St. Petersburg
3165 22nd Ave. N., St. Petersburg
(727) 323-1311

Noahs Animal Hospital and 24 Hour Emergency
2050 62nd Ave. N., St. Petersburg
(727) 522-6640

Pet Emergency & Critical Care Clinic, Inc.
2239 S. Kanner Hwy., Stuart
(772) 781-3302

FVS (Florida Veterinary Specialists)
3000 Busch Lake Blvd., Tampa
(813) 933-8944

Tampa Bay Veterinary Emergency Service
238 E. Bearss Ave., Tampa
(813) 265-4043

Animal E.R.
8237 Cooper Creek Blvd., University Park
(941) 355-2884

Animal Emergency Clinic
3425 Forest Hill Blvd., West Palm Beach
(561) 433-2244

Palm Beach Veterinary Specialists
3884 Forest Hill Blvd., West Palm Beach
(561) 434-5700

VCA Cabrera Animal Hospital
6390 S.W. 8th St., West Miami
(305) 261-2374

GEORGIA

All Pets Emergency and Referral Center, P.C.
6460 Highway 9N, Alpharetta
(678) 366-2125

University of Georgia - Vet Teaching Hospital
College of Veterinary Medicine, Athens
(706) 542-3221

Georgia Veterinary Specialists & Emergency Care
455 Abernathy Rd. N.E., Atlanta
(404) 459-0963

East Metro Animal Emergency Clinic, LLC
6225 Hwy. 278 N.W., Covington
(678) 212-0300

PetFirst 24 Hour Animal Hospital
4075 Pleasant Hill Rd., Duluth
(678) 745-1262

Southern Crescent Animal Emergency Clinic
1270 Hwy. 54 E., Fayetteville
(770) 460-8166

An-Emerge Animal Emergency Clinic
275 Pearl Nix Pkwy., Suite 3, Gainesville
(770) 534-2911

Eastside Animal Medical Center
1835 Grayson Hwy., Grayson
(678) 958-5530

Animal Emergency Center of Gwinnett
1956 Lawrenceville-Suwanee Rd., Lawrenceville
(770) 277-3220

Cobb Emergency Veterinary Clinic
630 Cobb Pkwy. N., Suite C, Marietta
(770) 424-9157

Animal Emergency Center of North Fulton
900 Mansell Rd., Suite 19, Roswell
(770) 594-2266

Animal Emergency Center of Sandy Springs
228 Sandy Springs Pl. N.E., Sandy Springs
(404) 252-7881

Savannah Veterinary Emergency Clinic
317 Eisenhower Dr., Savannah
(912) 355-6113

DeKalb-Gwinnett Animal Emergency Clinic
6430 Lawrenceville Hwy., Tucker
(770) 491-0661

Cherokee Emergency Veterinary Clinic
7800 Hwy. 92, Woodstock
(678) 238-0700

IDAHO

Mountain View Animal Hospital / Pet ER
3435 N. Cole Rd., Boise
(208) 375-0251

WestVet Animal Emergency & Specialty Center
5019 N. Sawyer Ave., Garden City
(208) 375-1600

Idaho Falls Veterinary Emergency Clinic
3151 McNeil Dr., Idaho Falls
(208) 552-0662

All Valley Animal Care Center
2326 E. Cinema Dr., Meridian
(208) 888-0818

WestVet Animal Emergency
3085 E. Magic View Dr., Suite. 110, Meridian
(208) 288-0400

North Idaho Pet Emergency
2700 E. Seltice Way, Suite 12, Post Falls
(208) 777-2707

ILLINOIS

Animal E.R. of Arlington Heights
1195 E. Palatine Rd., Arlington Heights
(847) 394-6049

VCA Aurora Animal Hospital
2600 W. Galena Blvd., Aurora
(630) 896-8541

Animal Emergency Clinic of McLean County
2505 E. Oakland Ave., Bloomington
(309) 665-5020

Veterinary Specialty Center
1515 Busch Pkwy., Buffalo Grove
(847) 459-7535

Animal Emergency Clinic of Champaign County
1713 S. State St., Unit 4, Champaign
(217) 359-1977

Chicago Veterinary Emergency & Specialty Center
3123 N. Clybourne Ave., Chicago
(773) 281-7110

Animal Emergency Center
2005 Mall St., Collinsville
(618) 346-1898

Emergency Veterinary Care South
13715 S. Cicero Ave., Crestwood
(708) 388-3771

Animal Emergency of McHenry County
1095 Pingree Rd., Suite 120, Crystal Lake
(815) 479-9119

Arboretum View Animal Hospital
2551 Warrenville Rd., Downers Grove
(630) 963-0424

Dundee Animal Hospital
199 Penny Ave., Dundee
(847) 428-6114

Midwest Animal Emergency Hospital
7510 W. North Ave., Elmwood Park
(708) 453-4755

VCA Franklin Park Animal Hospital
9846 W. Grand Ave., Franklin Park
(847) 455-4922

Hawthorne Animal Hospital
5 Cougar Dr., Glen Carbon
(618) 288-3971

Animal Emergency & Treatment Center
1810 E. Belvidere Rd., Grayslake
(847) 548-5300

Emergency Veterinary Services
820 Ogden Ave., Lisle
(630) 960-2900

Animal Emergency of Mokena
19110 S. 88th Ave., Mokena
(708) 326-4800

Animal Emergency & Critical Care Center
1810 Frontage Rd., Northbrook
(847) 564-5775

Tri-County Animal Emergency Clinic
1800 N. Sterling Ave., Peoria
(309) 672-1565

Animal Emergency Clinic of Rockford
4236 Maray Dr., Rockford
(815) 229-7791

Animal 911
3735 W. Dempster St., Skokie
(847) 673-9110

Animal Emergency Clinic of Springfield
1333 W. Wabash Ave., Springfield
(617) 698-0870

Emergency Veterinary Services of St. Charles
530 Dunham Rd., St. Charles
(630) 584-7447

ASPCA Animal Poison Control Center
1717 S. Philo Rd., Suite 36, Urbana
(217) 337-5030

University of Illinois College of Veterinary Medicine
1008 W. Hazelwood Dr., Urbana
(217) 333-5300

INDIANA

VCA Northwood Animal Hospital
3255 N. SR 9, Anderson
(765) 649-5218

St. Francis Family Pet Health Care
822 W. Plymouth St., Bremen
(574) 546-9005

Circle City Veterinary Specialty & Emergency Hospital
9650 Mayflower Park Dr., Carmel
(317) 872-8387

Northeast Indiana Veterinary Emergency & Specialty Hospital
5818 Maplecrest Rd., Fort Wayne
(260) 426-1062

Airport Animal Emergi-Center, P.C.
5235 W. Washington St., Indianapolis
(317) 248-0832

Indianapolis Veterinary Emergency Center
5425 Victory Dr., Indianapolis
(317) 782-4484

Noah's Animal Hospital & 24 Hour Emergency Center
5510 Millersville Rd., Indianapolis
(317) 253-1327

VCA Indiana Veterinary Specialists & Emergency Center
8250 Bash St., Indianapolis
(317) 849-4925

Animal Emergency Clinic of Tippecanoe County
1343 Sagamore Pkwy. N., Lafayette
(765) 449-2001

Animal Emergency Clinic
2324 Grape Rd., Mishawaka
(574) 259-8387

Calumet Emergency Veterinary Clinic
216 W. Lincoln Hwy., Schererville
(219) 865-0970

North Central Veterinary Emergency Center
1645 S. US 421, Westville
(219) 785-7300

IOWA

Iowa State University Veterinary Clinical Sciences Teaching Hospital
1600 S. 16th St., Ames
(515) 294-4900

Animal Emergency Center of the Quad Cities
1510 State St., Bettendorf
(563) 344-9599

Eastern Iowa Veterinary Specialty Center
755 Capital Dr. S.W., Cedar Rapids
(319) 841-5161

Animal Emergency & Referral Center of Central Iowa
6110 Creston Ave., Des Moines
(515) 280-3051

KANSAS
Kansas State University Vet. Med. Teaching Hospital
1800 Denison Ave., Manhattan
(785) 532-4100

Mission MedVet
5914 Johnson Dr., Mission
(913) 722-5566

BluePearl Veterinary Partners
11950 W. 110th St., Overland Park
(913) 642-9563

Central Kansas Veterinary Center
515 W. Blanchard Ave., South Hutchinson
(620) 663 8387

Emergency Animal Clinic of Topeka
839 S.W. Fairlawn Rd., Topeka
(785) 272-2926

Veterinary Emergency & Specialty Hospital of Wichita
727 S. Washington St., Wichita
(316) 262-5321

KENTUCKY
AA Small Animal Emergency Service
150 Dennis Dr., Lexington
(859) 276-2505

Hagyard & Davidson- McGee, PLCC
4250 Iron Works Pike, Lexington
(859) 253-0002

Jefferson Animal Hospital & Regional Emergency Center
4504 Outer Loop, Louisville
(502) 966-4104

Louisville Veterinary Specialty & Emergency Services
13160 Magisterial Dr., Louisville
(502) 244-3036

Greater Cincinnati Veterinary Specialists & Emergency Services
11 Beacon Dr., Wilder
(859) 572-0560

LOUISIANA
Animal Emergency Clinic of Baton Rouge
7353 Jefferson Hwy., Baton Rouge
(225) 927-8800

Baton Rouge Pet Emergency Hospital
1514 Cottondale Dr., Baton Rouge
(225) 925-5566

Veterinary Emergency and Critical Care, LLC
2611 Florida St., Mandeville
(985) 626-4862

Southeast Veterinary Emergency & Critical Care
3409 Division St., Metairie
(504) 219-0444

MAINE
Eastern Maine Emergency Veterinary Clinic
15 Dirigo Dr., Brewer
(207) 989-6267

Animal Emergency Clinic of Mid-Maine
37 Strawberry Ave., Lewiston
(207) 777-1110

Animal Emergency Clinic
739 Warren Ave., Portland
(207) 878-3121

Maine Veterinary Referral Center
1500 Technology Way, Enterprise Business Park
Scarborough
(207) 885-1290

MARYLAND
AAVEC, Inc.
808 Bestgate Rd., Annapolis
(410) 224-0331

Anne Arundel Veterinary Emergency Clinic
808 Bestgate Rd., Annapolis
(410) 224-0331

Emergency Veterinary Clinic
32 Mellor Ave., Baltimore
(410) 788-7040

Falls Road Animal Hospital
6314 Falls Rd., Baltimore
(410) 825-9100

Animal Emergency Hospital
807B Belair Rd., Bel Air
(410) 420-7297

Harford Emergency Veterinary Services
526 Underwood Ln., Bel Air
(410) 420-8000

Emergency Veterinary Clinic, Inc.
32 Mellor Ave., Catonsville
(410) 788-7042

Emergency Animal Hospital of Ellicott City
10270 Baltimore National Pike (US 40W), Ellicott City
(410) 750-1177

Crossroads Animal Referral and Emergency CARE
1080 W. Patrick St., Frederick
(301) 662-2273

Frederick Emergency Animal Hospital
434 Prospect Blvd., Frederick
(301) 662-6622

VCA Veterinary Referral Associates
500 Perry Pkwy., Gaithersburg
(301) 926-3300, ext. 140

Mountain View Animal Emergency
17747 Virginia Ave., Hagerstown
(301) 733-7339

Metropolitan Emergency Animal Clinic
12106 Nebel St., Rockville
(301) 770-5226

Pets ER Gateway Crossing
329 Tilghman Rd., Suite 100, Salisbury
(410) 543-8400

PET ER
1209 Cromwell Bridge Rd., Towson
(410) 252-8387

Southern Maryland Veterinary Referral Center
3485 Rockefeller Ct., Waldorf
(301) 638-0988

Central Carroll Animal Emergency
1030 Baltimore Blvd., Suite 180, Westminster
(410) 871-9001

Westminster Veterinary Hospital & Emergency / Trauma Center
269 W. Main St., Westminster
(410) 848-3363

MASSACHUSETTS

Animal Emergency Care
164 Great Rd., Acton
(978) 263-1742

Angell Memorial Animal Hospital
350 S. Huntington Ave., Boston
(617) 522-7282

Cape Cod Veterinary Specialists Emergency Service
230 Main St., Buzzards Bay
(508) 759-5125

Wignall Animal Hospital
1837 Bridge St., Dracut
(978) 454 8272

Fall River Animal Hospital, Inc.
33 18th St., Fall River
(508) 675-6374

Essex County Veterinary Emergency Hospital
247 Chickering Rd., North Andover
(978) 725-5544

Tufts University School of Veterinary Medicine
200 Westboro Rd., North Grafton
(508) 839-7826

Animal ER
1634 W. Housatonic St., Pittsfield
(413) 997-3425

Veterinary Emergency & Specialty Hospital
141 Greenfield Rd., South Deerfield
(413) 665-4911

Cape Animal Referral & Emergency Center
79 Theophilus Smith Rd., South Dennis
(508) 398-7575

VCA South Shore Animal Hospital
595 Columbian St., South Weymouth
(781) 337-6622

Boston Road Animal Hospital
1235 Boston Rd., Springfield
(413) 783-1203

Mass-RI Veterinary ER
477 Milford Rd., Swansea
(508) 730-1112

Tufts Veterinary Emergency Treatment and Specialties (Tufts VETS)
525 South St., Walpole
(508) 668-5454

Vetcision
293 Second Ave., Waltham
(781) 810-1010

Veterinary Emergency & Specialty Center of New England
180 Bear Hill Rd., Waltham
(781) 684-8387

New England Animal Medical Center
595 W. Center St., West Bridgewater
(508) 580-2515

Massachusetts Veterinary Referral Hospital
20 Cabot Rd., Woburn
(781) 932-5802

Woburn Animal Hospital
373 Russell St., Woburn
(718) 933-0170

MICHIGAN

Affiliated Veterinary Emergency Service, P.C.
15220 Southfield Rd., Allen Park
(313) 389-1700

Animal Emergency Clinic
4126 Packard Rd., Ann Arbor
(734) 971-8774

Ann Arbor Animal Hospital
2150 W. Liberty St., Ann Arbor
(734) 662-4474

Michigan Veterinary Specialists
3412 E. Walton Blvd., Auburn Hills
(248) 371-3713

Oakland Veterinary Emergency & Critical Care
1400 Telegraph Rd., Bloomfield Hills
(248) 334-6877

Oakland Veterinary Emergency Group
1948 Telegraph Rd., Bloomfield Hills
(248) 334-1555

Animal Emergency Hospital of Macomb
43731 N. Gratiot Ave., Clinton Township
(586) 307-3730

Animal ER Center
1120 Welch Rd., Commerce
(248) 960-7200

Michigan State University Veterinary Teaching Hospital
Michigan State University, Wilson Rd., East Lansing
(517) 353-5420

Animal Emergency Hospital
1007 S. Ballenger Hwy., Flint
(810) 238-7557

Animal Emergency Hospital
3260 Plainfield Ave. N.E., Grand Rapids
(616) 361-9911

Michigan Veterinary Specialists
1425 Michigan St. N.E., Suite F, Grand Rapids
(616) 284-5300

Southwest Michigan Animal Emergency Hospital
3301 S. Burdick St., Kalamazoo
(616) 381-5228

Lansing Veterinary Urgent Care
3276 E. Jolly Rd., Lansing
(517) 393-9200

Veterinary Emergency Service - East
28223 John R Rd., Madison Heights
(248) 547-4677

Veterinary Care Specialists
205 Rowe Rd., Milford
(248) 684-0468

Animal Emergency Center
24360 Novi Rd., Novi
(248) 348-1788

Veterinary Emergency Service - West
40850 Ann Arbor Rd., Plymouth
(734) 207-8500

Great Lakes Pet Emergencies
1221 Tittabawassee Rd., Saginaw
(989) 752-1960

Michigan Veterinary Specialists
29080 Inkster Rd., Southfield
(248) 354-6660

MINNESOTA
South Metro Animal Emergency Care
14690 Pennock Ave., Apple Valley
(952) 953-3737

Affiliated Emergency Veterinary Service
11850 Aberdeen St. N.E., Blaine
(763) 754-5000

Affiliated Emergency Veterinary Service
1615 Coon Rapids Blvd., Coon Rapids
(763) 754-9434

Affiliated Emergency Veterinary Service
2314 W. Michigan St., Duluth
(218) 302-8000

Affiliated Emergency Veterinary Service
7717 Flying Cloud Dr., Eden Prairie
(952) 942-8272

Affiliated Emergency Veterinary Service
4708 Hwy. 55, Golden Valley
(763) 529-6560

Animal Emergency Clinic
1163 Helmo Ave. N., Oakdale
(651) 501-3766

Affiliated Emergency Veterinary Service
121 23rd Ave. S.W., Rochester
(507) 424-3976

Affiliated Emergency Veterinary Service
4180 Thielman Ln., St. Cloud
(320) 258-3481

Animal Emergency Clinic
301 University Ave., St. Paul
(651) 293-1800

University of Minnesota, College of Veterinary Medicine - Veterinary Medical Center
1365 Gortner Ave., St. Paul
(612) 626-8387

MISSISSIPPI
Gulf Coast Veterinary Emergency Hospital
13095 Hwy. 67, Biloxi
(228) 392-7474

MISSOURI
Animal Emergency Clinic
7095 Metropolitan Blvd., Suite G, Barnhart
(636) 464-2846

Animal Emergency Clinic
12501 Natural Bridge Rd., Bridgeton
(314) 739-1500

University of Missouri - Veterinary Med. Teaching Hospital
900 E. Campus Dr., Columbia
(573) 882-7821

Animal Emergency Center
8141 N. Oak Trfy., Kansas City
(816) 455-5430

Animal Emergency & Referral Hospital
3495 N.E. Ralph Powell Rd., Lee's Summit
(816) 554-4990

VSS Emergency Center
1021 Howard George Dr., Manchester
(636) 227-6100

Animal Emergency Clinic
334 Fort Zumwalt Sq., O'Fallon
(636) 240-5496

Emergency Veterinary Clinic of Southwest Missouri
400 S. Glenstone Ave., Springfield
(417) 890-1600

Animal Emergency Clinic
9937 Big Bend Blvd., St. Louis
(314) 822-7600

Animal Emergency & Referral Center
16457 Village Plaza View Dr., Wildwood
(636) 458-1777

MONTANA
Emergency Animal Clinic of Western Montana
1914 S. Reserve St., Missoula
(406) 829-9300

NEBRASKA
United Vet Emergency Treatment Services
3700 S. 9th St., Lincoln
(402) 489-6800

Animal Emergency Clinic, P.C.
9664 Mockingbird Dr., Omaha
(402) 339-6232

NEVADA
Animal Emergency Center of Las Vegas
3340 E. Patrick Ln., Las Vegas
(702) 457-8050

Las Vegas Animal Emergency Hospital
5231 W. Charleston Blvd., Las Vegas
(702) 822-1045

Warm Springs Veterinary Emergency Clinic
2500 W. Warm Springs Rd., Las Vegas
(702) 614-5454

Animal Emergency Center of Reno
6425 S. Virginia St., Reno
(775) 851-3600

NEW HAMPSHIRE
Capital Area Veterinary Emergency Service
1 Intervale Rd., Concord
(603) 227-1199

Small Animal Veterinary Emergency Service
63 Evans Dr., Lebanon
(603) 306-0007

Veterinary Emergency Center of Manchester
336 Abby Rd., Manchester
(603) 666-6677

Winnipesaukee Veterinary Emergency Center
8 Maple Street, Suite 2, Meredith
(603) 279-1117

The Animal Hospital of Nashua
168 Main Dunstable Rd., Nashua
(603) 880-3034

Animal Medical Center of New England
168 Main Dunstable Rd., Nashua
(603) 821-7222

The Veterinary Emergency, Critical Care & Cancer Center of New Hampshire
15 Piscataqua Dr., Portsmouth
(603) 431-3600

Port City Veterinary Referral Hospital
215 Commerce Way, Suite 100, Portsmouth
(603) 433-0056

Rockingham Emergency Veterinary Hospital
3 Cobbetts Pond Rd., Windham
(603) 870-9770

NEW JERSEY
Animal Emergency & Referral Associates
1237 Bloomfield Ave., Fairfield
(973) 226-3282

Central Jersey Veterinary Emergency Service
643 Rt. 27, Iselin
(732) 283-3535

Jersey Shore Veterinary Emergency Service
1000 Rt. 70, Lakewood
(732) 363-3200

Crown Veterinary Specialists
23 Blossom Hill Rd., Lebanon
(908) 236-4120

Red Bank Veterinary Hospital Linwood
535 Maple Ave., Linwood
(609) 926-5300

North Jersey Veterinary Emergency Services
724 Ridge Rd., Lyndhurst
(201) 438-7122

Animal Emergency Service of South Jersey
220 Moorestown-Mount Laurel Rd., Mount Laurel
(856) 727-1332

Newton Veterinary Hospital
116 Hampton House Rd., Newton
(973) 383-4321

Oradell Animal Hospital
580 Winters Ave., Paramus
(201) 262-0010

Alliance Emergency Veterinary Clinic
540 Rt. 10 W., Randolph
(973) 328-2844

Animerge
21 Rt. 206 N., Raritan
(908) 707-9077

NorthStar VETS
315 Robbinsville-Allentown Rd., Robbinsville
(609) 259-8300

Garden State Veterinary Specialists
1 Pine St., Tinton Falls
(732) 922-0011

Red Bank Veterinary Hospital
197 Hance Ave., Tinton Falls
(732) 747-3636

Regional Veterinary Emergency & Specialty Center
4250 Rt. 42, Turnersville
(856) 728-1400

NEW MEXICO
Staley's Veterinary Medical Clinic
1407 Indian Wells Rd., Alamogordo
(505) 437-3063

Veterinary Emergency & Specialty Center of New Mexico
4000 Montgomery Blvd. N.E., Albuquerque
(505) 884-3433

ABQ PetCare
9032 Montgomery Blvd. N.E., Albuquerque
(505) 299-8387

Veterinary Emergency & Specialty Center of Santa Fe
2001 Vivigen Way, Santa Fe
(505) 984-0625

NEW YORK

Greater Buffalo Veterinary Emergency Clinic
4949 Main St., Amherst
(716) 839-4044

Veterinary Emergency & Critical Care Center
2115 Downer Street Rd., Baldwinsville
(315) 638-3500

Katonah Bedford Veterinary Center
546 N. Bedford Rd., Bedford Hills
(914) 241-7700

Atlantic Coast Veterinary Specialists
3250 Veterans Memorial Hwy., Bohemia
(631) 285-7780

Veterinary Emergency & Referral Group
318 Warren St., Brooklyn
(718) 522-9400

Animal Emergency Service
6230-C Jericho Tpke., Commack
(631) 462-6044

Veterinary Medical Center of Central New York
5841 Bridge St., Suite 200, East Syracuse
(315) 446-7933

New York Veterinary Specialty & Emergency Center
2233 Broadhollow Rd., Farmingdale
(631) 694-3400

Natural Vet For Pets, P.C.
585 Warburton Ave., Hastings-on-Hudson
(914) 478-4100

Animal Emergency Clinic of the Hudson Valley
1112 Morton Blvd., Kingston
(845) 336-0713

Capital District Animal Emergency Clinic
222 Troy Schenectady Rd., Latham
(518) 785-1094

Orange County Animal Emergency Service
517 Rt 211 E., Middletown
(845) 692-0260

Ultracare Veterinary Hospital & Specialty Center
220 E. Jericho Tpke., Mineola
(516) 294-6680

BluePearl - Manhattan
410 W. 55th St., New York
(212) 767-0099

Fifth Avenue Veterinary Specialists
1 W. 15th St., New York
(212) 924-3311

Manhattan Veterinary Group
240 E. 80th St., New York
(212) 988-1000

Orchard Park Veterinary Medical Center
3930 N. Buffalo Rd., Orchard Park
(716) 662-6660

Long Island Veterinary Specialists / Animal Emergency & Critical Care Center
163 S. Service Rd., Plainview
(516) 501-1700

Animal Emergency Clinic of the Hudson Valley
84 Patrick Ln., Poughkeepsie
(845) 471-8242

East End Veterinary Emergency Center
67 Commerce Dr., Riverhead
(631) 369-4513

Animal Hospital of Pittsford
2816 Monroe Ave., Rochester
(716) 271-7700

Veterinary Specialists & Emergency Service of Rochester
825 White Spruce Blvd., Rochester
(585) 424-1277

Animal Emergency Service
280-L Middle Country Rd., Selden
(631) 698-2225

Valley Cottage Animal Hospital
202 Rt. 303, Valley Cottage
(845) 268-9263

Central Veterinary Associates
73 W. Merrick Rd., Valley Stream
(516) 825-3066

BrightHeart Veterinary Referral & Emergency Center
609-5 Cantiague Rock Rd., Westbury
(516) 420-0000

Nassau Animal Emergency Hospital
740 Old Country Rd., Westbury
(516) 333-6262

The Veterinary Emergency Group
193 Tarrytown Rd., White Plains
(914) 949-8779

Animal Specialty Center
9 Odell Plaza, Yonkers
(914) 457-4000

NORTH CAROLINA

Small Animal Emergency Services
1335 N. Sandhills Blvd., Aberdeen
(910) 944-0405

Regional Emergency Animal Care Hospital (REACH)
677 Brevard Rd., Asheville
(828) 665-4399

Animal Emergency Clinic of the High Country
1126 Blowing Rock Rd., Suite A, Boone
(828) 268-2833

Animal Emergency Clinic of Cary
220 High House Rd., Cary
(919) 462-8989

Veterinary Specialty Hospital of the Carolinas
6405 Tryon Rd., Cary
(919) 233-4911

Animal Medical Hospital
3832 Monroe Rd., Charlotte
(704) 334-4684

Carolina Veterinary Specialists - Animal Emergency & Trauma Center
2225 Township Rd., Charlotte
(704) 504-9608

Triangle Veterinary Referral Hospital
608 Morreene Rd., Durham
(919) 489-0615

After Hours Veterinary Emergency Clinic
5505 W. Friendly Ave., Greensboro
(336) 851-1990

Carolina Veterinary Specialists - Animal Emergency & Trauma Center
501 Nicholas Rd., Greensboro
(336) 632-0605

Happy Tails Veterinary Emergency Clinic
2936 Battleground Ave., Greensboro
(336) 288-2688

Pet Emergency Clinic of Pitt County
2207-A Evans St., Greenville
(252) 321-1521

Carolina Veterinary Specialists - Animal Emergency & Trauma Center
12117 Statesville Rd., Huntersville
(704) 949-1100

Cabarrus Emergency Veterinary Clinic
1317 S. Cannon Blvd., Kannapolis
(704) 932-1182

Charlotte Veterinary Emergency & Trauma Services
2440 Plantation Center Dr., Matthews
(704) 844-6440

After Hours Animal Emergency Clinic
409 Vick Ave., Raleigh
(919) 781-5145

North Carolina State University Small Animal Emergency Service
4700 Hillsborough St., Raleigh
(919) 513-6130

Quail Corners Animal Hospital & 24 Hour Emergency Care
1613 E. Millbrook Rd., Raleigh
(919) 876-0739

Thomasville Veterinary Hospital, P.A.
303 National Hwy., Thomasville
(336) 475-9119

Eastern Carolina Veterinary Emergency Treatment Services
4909-D Expressway Dr., Wilson
(252) 265-9920

Animal Emergency Services of Forsyth County
7781 North Point Blvd., Winston-Salem
(336) 377-2866

Carolina Veterinary Specialists - Animal Emergency & Trauma Center
1600 Hanes Mall Blvd., Winston-Salem
336-896-0902

NORTH DAKOTA
Red River Animal Emergency Clinic
1401 Oak Manor Ave. S., Suite 2, Fargo
701-478-9299

OHIO
Akron Veterinary Referral & Emergency Center
1321 Centerview Cir., Akron
(330) 665-4996

Metropolitan Veterinary Hospital
1053 S. Cleveland-Massillon Rd., Akron
(330) 666-2976

Great Lakes Veterinary Specialists
5035 Richmond Rd., Bedford Heights
(216) 831-6789

Animal Emergency Clinic West
5320 W. 140th St., Brook Park
(216) 362-6000

Stark County Veterinary Emergency Clinic, LLC
2705 Fulton Dr. N.W., Canton
(330) 452-5117

Cincinnati Animal Referral and Emergency Care Center
6995 E. Kemper Rd., Cincinnati
(513) 530-0911

Capital Veterinary Referral & Emergency Center
5230 Renner Rd., Columbus
(614) 870-0480

Ohio State University Veterinary Medical Center
601 Vernon L. Tharp St., Columbus
·(614) 292-3551

Dayton Care Center
6405 Clyo Rd., Dayton
(937) 428-0911

Dayton Emergency Veterinary Clinic
2714 Springboro W., Dayton
(937) 293-2714

After Hours Animal Emergency Clinic, Inc.
2680 W. Liberty St., Girard
(330) 530-8387

Animal Emergency & Specialty Center
5152 Grove Ave., Lorain
(440) 240-1400

Aaron Animal Clinic and Emergency Hospital
7640 Broadview Rd., Parma
(216) 901-9980

Animal Emergency & Critical Care Center of Toledo, Inc.
2785 W. Central Ave., Toledo
(419) 473-0328

VCA Green Animal Medical Center
1620 Corporate Woods Cir., Uniontown
(330) 896-4040

Cleveland Road Animal Hospital
2752 Cleveland Rd., Wooster
(330) 345-6063

MedVet Associates, Ltd.
300 E. Wilson Bridge Rd., Worthington
(614) 846-5800

OKLAHOMA

Animal Emergency Center
931 S.W. 74th St., Oklahoma City
(405) 631-7828

Neel Veterinary Hospital
2700 N. MacArthur Blvd., Oklahoma City
(405) 947-8387

Veterinary Emergency and Critical Care Hospital
1800 W. Memorial Rd., Oklahoma City
(405) 749-6989

Animal Emergency Center, Inc.
4055 S. 102nd Ave., Tulsa
(918) 665-0508

OREGON

Animal Emergency Center of Central Oregon
1245 S.E. 3rd St., Suite C3, Bend
(541) 385-9110

Northwest Veterinary Specialists Emergency Service
16756 S.E. 82nd Dr., Clackamas
(503) 656-3999

Animal Emergency & Critical Care Center
1562 S.W. 3rd St., Corvallis
(541) 753-5750

Southern Oregon Veterinary Specialty Center
3265 Biddle Rd., Medford
(541) 282-7711

Dove Lewis Emergency Animal Hospital
1945 N.W. Pettygrove St., Portland
(503) 228-7281

VCA Southeast Portland Animal Hospital
13830 S.E. Stark St., Portland
(503) 255-8139

Salem Veterinary Emergency Clinic
3215 Market St. N.E., Salem
(503) 588-8082

Emergency Veterinary Hospital
103 W. Q St., Springfield
(541) 746-0112

Emergency Veterinary Clinic of Tualatin
19314 S.W. Mohave Ct., Tualatin
(503) 691-7922

PENNSYLVANIA

Veterinary Referral and Emergency Center
318 Northern Blvd., Clarks Summit
(570) 587-7777

Northwest Pennsylvania Pet Emergency Center
429 W. 38th St., Erie
(814) 866-5920

Keystone Veterinary Emergency and Referral
1200 W. Chester Pike, Havertown
(484) 454-5412

Center for Animal Referral and Emergency Services (CARES)
2010 Cabot Blvd. W., Suite D, Langhorne
(215) 750-2774

Gwynedd Veterinary Hospital
1615 W. Point Pike, Lansdale
(215) 699-9294

Veterinary Specialty & Emergency Center
301 Veterans Hwy., Levittown
(215) 750-7884

Allegheny Veterinary Emergency Trauma & Specialty (AVETS)
4224 Northern Pike, Monroeville
(412) 373-4200

Metropolitan Veterinary Associates
2626 Van Buren Ave., Norristown
(610) 666-1050

Matthew J. Ryan Hospital for Small Animals at the University of Pennsylvania
3850 Spruce St., Philadelphia
(215) 898-4685

Pittsburgh Veterinary Specialty & Emergency Center
807 Camp Horn Rd., Pittsburgh
(412) 366-3400

VCA Castle Shannon Animal Hospital Service
3610 Library Rd., Pittsburgh
(412) 885-2500

Animal Emergency & Referral Hospital
755 S. Township Blvd., Pittston
(570) 655-3600

Hickory Veterinary Hospital
2303 Hickory Rd., Plymouth Meeting
(610) 828-3054

Creature Comforts Veterinary Service
Old Route 115, Saylorsburg
(570) 992-0400

Central Pennsylvania Veterinary Emergency Treatment Services
1522 Martin St., State College
(814) 237-4670

Bucks County Veterinary Emergency Trauma Service
978 Easton Rd., Warrington
(215) 918-2200

Animal Emergency Center
395 Susquehanna Tr., Watsontown
(570) 742-7400

Valley Central Emergency Veterinary Hospital
210 Fullerton Ave., Whitehall
(610) 435-5588

Animal Emergency & Referral Center of York
1640 S. Queen St., York
(717) 767-5355

RHODE ISLAND
Ocean State Veterinary Specialists
1480 S. County Tr., East Greenwich
(401) 886-6787

SOUTH CAROLINA
Charleston Veterinary Referral Center
3484 Shelby Ray Ct., Charleston
(843) 614-8387

Palmetto Regional Emergency Hospital for Animals
10298 Two Notch Rd., Columbia
(803) 865-1418

South Carolina Veterinary Emergency Care
3924 Fernandina Rd., Columbia
(803) 798-3837

Animal Emergency Clinic
393 Woods Lake Rd., Greenville
(864) 232-1878

Veterinary Emergency Care - Mt. Pleasant
930-B Pine Hollow Rd., Mt. Pleasant
(843) 216-7554

Animal Emergency Hospital of the Strand
303 Hwy. 15, Suite 1, Myrtle Beach
(843) 445-9797

Veterinary Emergency Care - North Charleston
3163 W. Montague Ave., North Charleston
(843) 744-3372

Care Animal Regional Emergency Clinic of Spartanburg
1291 Asheville Hwy., Spartanburg
(864) 591-1923

SOUTH DAKOTA
Veterinary Emergency Hospital
3508 S. Minnesota Ave., Suite 104, Sioux Falls
(605) 977-6200

TENNESSEE
Midland Pet Emergency Center, Inc.
235 Calderwood St., Alcoa
(865) 982-1007

Airport Pet Emergency Clinic
2436 Hwy. 75, Blountville
(423) 279-0574

Affiliated Veterinary Specialists
1668 Mallory Ln., Brentwood
(615) 333-1212

Regional Institute for Veterinary Emergencies & Referrals
2132 Amnicola Hwy., Chattanooga
(423) 698-4612

Animal Emergency Clinic of Maury County, LLC
1900B Shady Brook St., Columbia
(931) 380-1929

PetMed Emergency Center, LLC
830 N. Germantown Pkwy., Suite 105, Cordova
(901) 624-9002

Jackson Pet Emergency Clinic, LLC
2815-D N. Highland, Jackson
(731) 660-4343

Knoxville Pet Emergency Clinic
1819 Ailor Ave., Knoxville
(865) 637-0114

University of Tennessee Veterinary Teaching Hospital
2407 River Dr., Knoxville
(865) 974-8387

Animal Medical Center
234 River Rock Blvd., Murfreesboro
(615) 867-7575

Nashville Pet Emergency Clinic
2000 12th Ave. S., Nashville
(615) 383-2600

Nashville Veterinary Specialists & Animal Emergency
2971 Sidco Dr., Nashville
(615) 386-0107

TEXAS
I-20 Animal Medical Center
5820 W. I-20, Arlington
(817) 478-9238

AM/PM Animal Hospital
2239 S. Lamar Blvd., Austin
(512) 448-2676

Austin Vet Care - Central
4106 N. Lamar Blvd., Austin
(512) 459-4336

Emergency Animal Hospital of Northwest Austin - North Branch
12034 Research Blvd., Suite 8, Austin
(512) 331-6121

Emergency Animal Hospital of Northwest Austin - South Branch
4434 Frontier Tr., Austin
(512) 899-0955

White Angel Animal Hospital
1901 RR 620 N., Austin
(512) 266-7838

Southeast Texas Animal Emergency Clinic
3420 W. Cardinal Dr., Beaumont
(409) 842-3239

Burleson Animal Emergency Hospital
805 N.E. Alsbury Blvd., Burleson
(817) 447-9194

North Texas Emergency Pet Clinic
1712 W. Frankford Rd., Suite 108, Carrolton
(972) 323-1310

Texas A&M University Veterinary Teaching Hospital
4475 TAMU, College Station
(979) 845-3541

Heritage Veterinary Hospital
3930 Glade Rd., Suite 120, Colleyville
(817) 358-0404

Emergency Animal Clinic
12101 Greenville Ave., Suite 118, Dallas
(972) 994-9110

The E-Clinic, Inc.
3337 Fitzhugh Ave., Dallas
(214) 520-8388

Grayson County Animal Emergency Clinic
3301 Woodlawn Blvd., Denison
(903) 337-0898

Denton County Animal Emergency Room
4145 S. I-35E, Suite 101, Denton
(940) 271-1200

El Paso Animal Emergency Center
1220 Airway Blvd., El Paso
(915) 203-0818

Airport Freeway Animal Emergency Clinic
411 N. Main St., Euless
(817) 571-2088

DFW North Emergency Veterinary Clinic
2311 Cross Timbers, Suite 319, Flower Mound
(469) 464-2964

Metro West Emergency Veterinary Center
3201 Hulen St., Fort Worth
(817) 731-3734

Animal Emergency Hospital of North Texas
2700 W. Hwy. 114, Grapevine
(817) 410-2273

Animal Emergency Center of West Houston
4823 Hwy. 6N, Houston
(832) 593-8387

Animal Emergency Clinic SH 249
18707 SH 249, Houston
(281) 890-8875

Animal Emergency Clinic Southeast
10331 Gulf Frwy., Houston
(713) 941-8460

Houston Veterinary Services, Inc.
111 West Loop S., #200, Houston
(713) 693-1100

Veterinary Emergency Referral Group, Inc.
8921 Katy Frwy., Houston
(713) 932-9589

Animal Emergency Clinic North East
10205 Birchridge Dr., Humble
(281) 446-4900

Metroplex Animal Hospital & Pet Lodge
700 W. Airport Frwy., Irving
(972) 438-7113

After Hours Veterinary Services
2501 S. W.S. Young, Suite 413, Killeen
(254) 628-5017

Animal Emergency Hospital Southeast - Calder Rd
1108 Gulf Frwy. S., Suite 280, League City
(281) 332-1678

Lake Ray Hubbard Emergency Pet Care Center
4651 N. Belt Line Rd., Mesquite
(214) 763-4243

Lake Ray Hubbard Emergency Pet Care Center
4651 N. Beltline Rd., Mesquite
(972) 226-3377

Angel of Mercy Animal Critical Care, Inc.
8734 Grissom Rd., San Antonio
(210) 684-2105

Animal Emergency Room
4315 Fredericksburg Rd., Suite 2, San Antonio
(210) 737-7380

Emergency Pet Clinic
8503 Broadway #105, San Antonio
(210) 822-2873

Emergency Pet Clinic
503 E. Sonterra Blvd., San Antonio
(210) 404-2873

I-10 Pet Emergency
10822 Fredericksburg Rd., San Antonio
(210) 691-0900

Northeast Emergency Animal Clinic
8365 Perrin Beitel, San Antonio
(210) 650-3141

Animal Emergency Clinic - Sugar Land
9920 Hwy. 90A, Suite 100C, Sugar Land
(281) 340-8387

Southwest Freeway Animal Hospital & Emergency Center
15575 Southwest Frwy., Sugar Land
(281) 491-8387

Sugar Land Veterinary Specialists & Emergency Center
1515 Lake Pointe Pkwy., Sugar Land
(281) 491-7800

Texas Animal Medical Center
4900 Steinbeck Bend, Waco
(254) 753-0901

Animal Emergency & Urgent Care Center of the Woodlands
27870 I-45 N., The Woodlands
(281) 367-5444

UTAH
Central Emergency Animal Hospital
55 E. Miller Ave., Salt Lake City
(801) 487-1325

Pet E.R. - The Pet Emergency Room
6360 S. Highland Dr., Salt Lake City
(801) 278-3367

Animal Emergency Center
2465 N. Main St., Suite 5, Sunset
(801) 776-8118

VERMONT
Burlington Emergency & Veterinary Specialists
200 Commerce St., Williston
(802) 863-2387

VIRGINIA
Alexandria Veterinary Emergency Service
2660 Duke St., Alexandria
(703) 823-3601

Veterinary Emergency Treatment Services, Inc.
370 Greenbrier Dr., Suite A-2, Charlottesville
(434) 973-3519

Greenbrier Veterinary Emergency Center
1100 Eden Way N., Suite 101B, Chesapeake
(757) 366-9000

SouthPaws Veterinary Referral Center
8500 Arlington Blvd., Fairfax
(703) 752-9100

Fredericksburg Regional Veterinary Emergency Center, LLC
2301 1/2 Jefferson Davis Hwy., Fredericksburg
(540) 372-3470

Animal Emergency Critical Care Associates
165 Fort Evans Rd. N.E., Leesburg
(703) 777-5755

Animal Emergency & Critical Care of Lynchburg
3432 Odd Fellows Rd., Lynchburg
(434) 846-1504

Veterinary Referral & Critical Care (VRCC)
1596 Hockett Rd., Manakin Sabot
(804) 784-8722

Prince William Emergency Veterinary Clinic
8610 Centreville Rd., Manassas
(703) 361-8287

Veterinary Emergency & Specialty Center - Midlothian
2460 Colony Crossing Pl., Midlothian
(804) 744-9800

Blue Ridge Veterinary Associates
120 E. Cornwell Ln., Purcellville
(540) 338-7387

Veterinary Emergency Center, Inc.
3312 W. Cary St., Richmond
(804) 353-9000

Emergency Veterinary Services of Roanoke
4902 Frontage Rd. N.W., Roanoke
(540) 563-8575

Regional Veterinary Referral Center
6651 Backlick Rd., Springfield
(703) 451-8900

The Hope Center for Advanced Veterinary Medicine
140 Park St. S.E., Vienna
(703) 242-4732

Beach Veterinary Emergency Clinic
1124 Lynnhaven Pkwy., Virginia Beach
(757) 468-4900

Tidewater Veterinary Emergency & Critical Care Center
364 S. Independence Blvd., Virginia Beach
(757) 499-5463

Valley Emergency Veterinary Clinic, LLC
164-4 Garber Ln., Winchester
(540) 662-7811

Woodbridge Animal Hospital
2703 Caton Hill Rd., Woodbridge
(703) 897-5665

Animal Emergency Center
5007 Victory Blvd., Yorktown
(757) 234-0461

Peninsula Emergency Veterinary Clinic
1120 Hwy. 17, Yorktown
(757) 874-8115

WASHINGTON
After Hours Animal Emergency Clinic
718 Auburn Way N., Auburn
(253) 939-6272

Animal Emergency Care
317 Telegraph Rd., Bellingham
(360) 758-2200

Animal Emergency Clinic of Everett
3625 Rucker Ave., Everett
(425) 258-4466

VCA Alpine Animal Hospital
888 N.W. Sammamish Rd., Issaquah
(425) 392-8888

Animal Emergency Service, East
636 7th Ave., Kirkland
(425) 827-8727

Seattle Veterinary Specialists
11814 115th Ave. N.E., Suite 102, Kirkland
(425) 823-9111

Agape Pet Emergency Center
16418 7th Pl. W., Lynnwood
(425) 741-2688

VCA Veterinary Specialty Center of Seattle
20115 44th Ave. W., Lynnwood
(425) 697-6106

Pet Emergency Center
14434 Avon Allen Rd., Mount Vernon
(360) 848-5911

Mid-Columbia Pet Emergency Services
8913 Sandifur Pkwy., Pasco
(509) 547-3577

Animal Emergency & Trauma Center
320 Lindvig Way, Poulsbo
(360) 697-7771

VCA Central Kitsap Animal Hospital
10310 Central Valley Rd. N.E., Poulsbo
(360) 692-6162

Washington State University
Veterinary Teaching Hospital, 100 Grimes Way, Pullman
(509) 335-0711

Animal Critical Care & Emergency Services (ACCES)
11536 Lake City Way, N.E., Seattle
(206) 364-1660

Emerald City Emergency Clinic
4102 Stone Way N., Seattle
(206) 634-9000

Five Corners Veterinary Hospital
15707 1st Ave. S., Seattle
(206) 243-2982

Animal Medical Center Of Seattle
14810 15th Ave N.E., Shoreline
(206) 204-3366

PSCVM Small Animal Emergency and Critical Care Center
11308 92nd St. S.E., Snohomish
(360) 563-5300

Pet Emergency Clinic
21 E. Mission Ave., Spokane
(509) 326-6670

Puget Sound Veterinary Referral Center - The Animal Emergency Clinic
5608 S. Durango St., Tacoma
(253) 474-0791

Summit Veterinary Referral Center
2505 S. 80th St., Tacoma
(253) 983-1114

Columbia River Veterinary Specialists
6818 N.E. Fourth Plain Blvd., Suite C, Vancouver
(360) 694-3007

St. Francis 24 Hr. Animal Hospital
12010 N.E. 65th St., Vancouver
(360) 253-5446

Yakima Pet Emergency Service
510 W. Chestnut Ave., Yakima
(509) 452-4138

WEST VIRGINIA
Kanawha Valley Animal Emergency Clinic
5304 MacCorkle Ave. S.W., Charleston
(304) 768-2911

Animal Urgent Care, Inc.
4201 Wood St., Wheeling
(304) 233-0002

WISCONSIN
Fox Valley Animal Referral Center
4706 New Horizons Blvd., Appleton
(920) 993-9193

Animal Emergency Center
2100 W. Silver Spring Dr., Glendale
(414) 540-6710

Green Bay Animal Emergency Center
933 Anderson Dr., Suite F, Green Bay
(920) 494-9400

Crawford Animal Hospital
4607 S. 108th St., Greenfield
(414) 543-3499

Emergency Clinic for Animals
229 W. Beltline Hwy., Madison
(608) 274-7772

University of Wisconsin Veterinary Teaching Hospital
2015 Linden Dr., Madison
(608) 263-7600

Veterinary Emergency Service
4902 E. Broadway, Madison
(608) 222-2455

Veterinary Emergency Service
1612 N. High Point Rd., Suite 100, Middleton
(608) 831-1101

Central Wisconsin Animal Emergency Center
1420 Kronenwetter Dr., Mosinee
(715) 693-6934

Lakeshore Veterinary Specialists & Emergency Hospital
207 W. Seven Hills Rd., Port Washington
(262) 268-7800

Animal ER / Critical Care of Southeast Wisconsin
4333 S. Green Bay Rd., Racine
(262) 553-9223

Wisconsin Veterinary Referral Center
360 Bluemound Rd., Waukesha
(262) 542-3241

Canada

ALBERTA
Calgary Animal Referral and Emergency Centre
7140 12th St. S.E., Calgary
(403) 520-8387

Calgary North Veterinary Hospital and Emergency Service
4204 4th St. N.W., Calgary
(403) 277-0135

McKnight 24 Hour Veterinary Hospital
34-5010 4th St. N.E., Calgary
(403) 457-0911

Western Veterinary Specialist & Emergency Centre
1802 10th Ave. S.W., Calgary
(403) 770-1340

Animal Emergency Hospital South, Ltd.
3823 99 St., Edmonton
(780) 436-5880

Edmonton Veterinarians Emergency Clinic
11104 102nd Ave., Edmonton
(780) 433-9505

BRITISH COLUMBIA
Animal Critical Care Group
1410 Boundary Rd., Burnaby
(604) 473-4882

Central Animal Emergency Clinic
812 Roderick Ave., Coquitlam
(604) 931-1911

Animal Emergency Clinic of the Fraser Valley
306-6325 204th St., Langley
(604) 514-1711

Mainland Animal Emergency Clinic
15338 Fraser Hwy., Surrey
(604) 588-4000

Vancouver Animal Emergency Clinic, Ltd.
1590 W. 4th St., Vancouver
(604) 734-5104

Central Victoria Veterinary Hospital
760 Roderick St., Victoria
(250) 475-2495

MANITOBA
Winnipeg Animal Emergency Clinic
400 Pembina Hwy., Winnipeg
(204) 452-9427

NOVA SCOTIA
Metro Animal Emergency Clinic
201 Brownlow Ave., Unit 32, Dartmouth
(902) 468-0674

ONTARIO
Veterinary Emergency Clinic of York Region
14879 Yonge St., Aurora
(905) 713-2323

Huronia Veterinary Emergency Clinic
115 Bell Farm Rd., Barrie
(705) 722-0377

Emergency Veterinary Clinic
#1 Wexford Rd., Brampton
(905) 495-9907

North Town Veterinary Hospital
496 Main St. N., Brampton
(905) 451-2000

Burgess Veterinary Emergency Clinic
775 Woodview Rd., Burlington
(905) 637-8111

Alta Vista Animal Hospital
2616 Bank St., Gloucester
(613) 731-9911

Halton-Wentworth Emergency Vet Clinic
505 King St. W., Hamilton
(905) 529-1004

London Veterinary Emergency Clinic
41 Adelaide St. N., Unit 43, London
(519) 432-7341

Mississauga-Oakville Veterinary Emergency Hospital
2285 Bristol Cir., Oakville
(905) 829-9444

Alta Vista Animal Hospital
2616 Bank St., Ottawa
(613) 731-9911

Vaughan-Richmond Hill Veterinary Emergency Clinic
10303 Yonge St., Richmond Hill
(905) 884-1832

Niagara Veterinary Emergency Clinic
2F Tremont Dr., Unit 1, St. Catharines
(905) 641-3185

Toronto Veterinary Emergency Hospital
21 Rolark Dr., Scarborough
(416) 247-8387

Veterinary Emergency Clinic
920 Yonge St., #117, Toronto
(416) 920-2002

Animal Emergency Clinic
1910 Dundas St. E., Unit 122, Whitby
(905) 576-3031

QUEBEC
DMV Veterinary Centre
2300 54e Ave., Lachine
(514) 633-8888

University of Montreal / Companion Animal Clinic
3200 Sicotte St., St.-Hyacinthe
(450) 778-8111

Pet-Friendly Lodgings

HOW TO USE THE LISTINGS

Some 14,000 AAA Approved hotels and campgrounds across North America accept traveling pets. This guide provides listings for those lodgings in the United States and Canada that roll out the welcome mat for pets as well as the people who love them.

For the purpose of this book, "pets" are domestic cats or dogs. If you are planning to travel with any other kind of animal — particularly such exotic pets as birds or reptiles — check with the property before making definite plans. Expect to keep nontraditional pets crated at all times.

Note: Always inform the management that you are traveling with an animal; you may be fined if you do not declare your pet. Many properties require guests with pets to sign a waiver or release form and to pay for the room with a credit card. Of course, whether you pay in cash or by credit card, you will be held liable for any damages caused by your pet, even if the property does not charge a deposit or pet fee. It is not a good idea to leave your pet unattended in the room, but if you must, crate him and notify management. When in public areas, keep your pet leashed and do not allow him to disturb other guests.

About the Listings

Geographic listings are used for accuracy and consistency; lodgings are listed under the city or town in which they physically are located — or in some cases under the nearest recognized city or town. For a complete list of all cities within a state or province, see the comprehensive City Index at the beginning of the corresponding section.

U.S. properties are shown first, followed by Canadian properties. Most listings are alphabetically organized by state or province, city and establishment name. Reflecting contemporary travel patterns, properties in some cities or towns may instead be listed within destination cities or areas. Such "vicinity cities" and their listings will be shown alphabetically in the destination city or area, and the vicinity city also will appear in alphabetical order in the City Index, along with the page number on which the listings begin.

Each listing provides the following information (see sample listing, next page):

❶ Symbol denoting Official Appointment (OA) properties. The OA program permits properties to display and advertise the 🅐🅐🅐 or 🅐🅐 logo. OAs have a special interest in serving AAA/CAA members. Ask if they offer special member amenities such as free breakfast, early check-in/late check-out, free room upgrade, free local phone calls, etc.

❷ Diamond Rating

❸ Property name

❹ Lodging classification
(see next page for descriptions)

❺ Special amenities offered. These properties provide an additional benefit to pets, such as treats, toys or gifts, pet sitting and/or walking, a pet menu, food/water dishes, pet sheets or pillows, pet beds or other extras.

❻ Telephone number

❼ Two-person (2P) rate year-round, and cancellation notice validity period (if more than 48 hours). Rates listed are daily. **Note:** Most properties accept any or all of the major credit cards, including American Express, MasterCard and VISA. If a property accepts only cash, the phrase "(no credit cards)" follows the rates. "Call for rates" indicates rates were not available at time of printing. Please contact property for current rate information.

❽ Physical address and/or highway location, if available

❾ Exterior or interior corridors

❿ Pet policies. If the phrase "pets accepted" appears, the property does accept pets but specific information was unavailable at press time. Otherwise, pet-specific policies are denoted as follows:
Size. "Very small" denotes pets weighing up to 10 pounds; "small," up to 25 pounds; "medium," up to 50 pounds; and "large," up to 100 pounds. If no size is specified, the property accepts pets of all sizes.
Species. "Other" indicates the property accepts animals other than dogs and cats. Always call ahead and specify the type of pet you plan to bring.
Deposits and fees. Includes the dollar amount, the type of charge (refundable deposit or nonrefundable fee), the frequency of the charge and whether the charge is per pet or per room.
Designated rooms. Guests with pets are placed in certain rooms, often smoking rooms or those on the ground floor.
Housekeeping service. The phrase "service with restrictions" denotes properties that require the pet to be crated, removed or attended by the owner during housekeeping service.
Supervision. The pet is required to be supervised at all times.
Crate. The pet must be crated when the owner is not present.

⓫ Member values, services and facilities:
🌱 Indicates lodgings that have been certified by well-established government and/or private eco-certification organizations. For more information about these organizations and their programs, visit AAA.com/eco.

💾 Discounted standard room rate or lowest public rate available at time of booking for dates of stay

📶 Wireless Internet service on premises

⊠ Smoke-free premises

♿ Accessible features
(call property for available services and amenities)

🔌 Refrigerator

☕ Coffee maker

(II) Restaurant on premises

(≥) Pool

(⊠) Recreational activities

(✗) No air conditioning

(✗) No TV

(✗) No telephones

Please note: Some in-room amenities represented by the icons in the listings may be available only in selected rooms, and may incur an extra fee. Please inquire when making your reservations.

It is important to remember that animal policies do change; always confirm policies, restrictions and fees with the lodging when making reservations and again 1-2 days before departure.

Listing information is subject to change. All listing information was accurate at press time. However, lodging rates and policies change and the publisher cannot be held liable for changes occurring after publication. AAA cannot guarantee the safety of guests or their pets at any facility.

AAA Diamond Ratings

Before a property is listed by AAA, it must satisfy a set of minimum standards regarding basic lodging needs as identified by AAA members. If a property meets those requirements (determined during an unannounced evaluation by a AAA inspector), it is assigned a Diamond Rating.

Once an establishment becomes AAA Approved, it is then assigned a rating of one to five Diamonds, indicating the extensiveness of its facilities, amenities and services, from basic to moderate to luxury. The Diamond Ratings guide members in selecting establishments appropriately matched to their needs and expectations.

❖ Budget-oriented, offering basic comfort and hospitality.

❖❖ Affordable, with modestly enhanced facilities, décor and amenities.

❖❖❖ Distinguished, multi-faceted with enhanced physical attributes, amenities and guest comforts.

❖❖❖❖ Refined, stylish with upscale physical attributes, extensive amenities and a high degree of hospitality, service and attention to detail.

❖❖❖❖❖ Ultimate luxury, sophistication and comfort with extraordinary physical attributes, meticulous personalized service, extensive amenities and impeccable standard of excellence.

Lodging Classifications

BB Bed & Breakfast: Typically smaller scale properties emphasizing a high degree of personal touches that provide guests an "at home" feeling. Guest units tend to be individually decorated. Rooms may not include some modern amenities such as televisions and telephones, and may have a shared bathroom. Usually owner-operated with a common room or parlor separate from the innkeeper's living quarters, where guests and operators can interact during evening and breakfast hours. Evening office closures are normal. A continental or full, hot breakfast is served and is included in the room rate.

CA Cabin/Cottage: Vacation-oriented, small-scale, free-standing houses or cabins. Units vary in design and décor and often contain one or more bedrooms, living room, kitchen, dining area and bathroom. Studio-type models combine the sleeping and living areas into one room. Typically, basic cleaning supplies, kitchen utensils, and complete bed and bath linens are supplied. The guest registration area may be located off-site.

CO Condominium: Vacation-oriented — commonly for extended-stay purposes — apartment-style accommodations of varying design or décor. Routinely available for rent through a management company, units often contain one or more bedrooms, a living room, full kitchen, and an

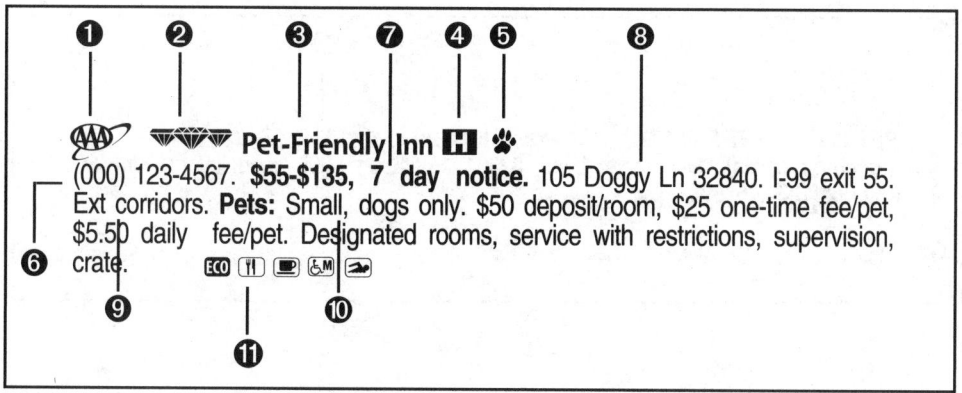

eating area. Studio-type models combine the sleeping and living areas into one room. As a rule, basic cleaning supplies, kitchen utensils, and complete bed and bath linens are supplied. The guest registration area may be located off site.

CI Country Inn: Although similar in definition to a bed and breakfast, country inns are usually larger in scale with spacious public areas and offer a dining facility that serves at least breakfast and dinner.

H Hotel: Commonly, a multistory establishment with interior room entrances offering a variety of guest unit styles. The magnitude of the public areas is determined by the overall theme, location and service level, but may include a variety of facilities such as a restaurant, shops, fitness center, spa, business center, and/or meeting rooms.

M Motel: Commonly, a one- or two-story establishment with exterior room entrances and drive up parking. Typically, guest units have one bedroom with a bathroom of similar décor and design. Public areas and facilities are often limited in size and/or availability.

RA Ranch: Typically a working ranch with an obvious rustic, Western theme featuring equestrian-related activities and a variety of guest unit styles.

VH Vacation Rental House: Vacation-oriented — commonly for extended-stay purposes — typically larger scale, freestanding, and of varying design or décor. Routinely available for rent through a management company, houses often contain two or more bedrooms, a living room, full kitchen, dining room, and multiple bathrooms. As a rule, basic cleaning supplies, kitchen utensils, and complete bed and bath linens are supplied. The guest registration area may be located off site.

Campground Listings

Camping information provided by Woodall's®

Geographic listings are used for accuracy and consistency. Campgrounds are listed under the city or town in which they physically are located — or in some cases under the nearest recognized city or town. Not all listings include physical addresses. U.S. campgrounds are listed first, followed by Canadian campgrounds. Listings are alphabetically organized by state or province, city and campground name.

Note: Call first before taking your pet on a camping trip, as campground policies regarding pets may change, including any possible fees that may be assessed.

Each listing provides the following information (see sample listing):

❶ Location

❷ Campground name

❸ Symbol denoting Official Appointment (OA) campgrounds. The OA program permits privately operated Campgrounds to display and advertise the AAA or CAA logo. OAs have a special interest in serving AAA/CAA members.

❹ Telephone number

❺ Rates are provided as a comparative overview of camping fees within a general area. The fee will typically be shown as a range of rates for either a specific number of persons, a family (2 adults, 2 children) or per vehicle. The range represents the low to high ranges and may or may not include hookups.

❻ Most campgrounds accept any or all of the major credit cards, including American Express, MasterCard and Visa. If a campground accepts only cash, the phrase "(no credit cards)" appears.

❼ Physical address and/or highway location and mailing address (if available).

❽ Member values, services and facilities:

    ⑤ᴅ Senior discount

    🚫 No Tents

    ⊅ Pool

    ☒ Recreational activities

    &ᴍ Accessible features
    (call property for available services and amenities)

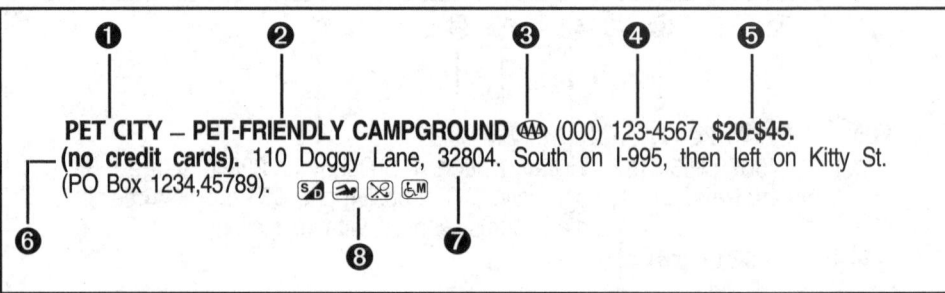

United States Lodgings

ALABAMA

ABBEVILLE

Best Western-Abbeville Inn M

(334) 585-5060. $59-$89. 1237 US Hwy 431 S 36310. Jct SR 27. Ext corridors. Pets: Large, other species. $8 daily fee/pet. Service with restrictions, supervision.

ALBERTVILLE

Jameson Inn H

(256) 891-2600. $74-$94. 315 Martling Rd 35950. On US 431, just e of SR 75. Ext corridors. Pets: Medium. $15 daily fee/room. Service with restrictions, supervision.

Microtel Inn & Suites H

(256) 894-4000. $59-$62. 220 Hwy 75 N 35951. Jct US 431 and SR 75, just ne. Int corridors. Pets: Accepted.

ALEXANDER CITY

Jameson Inn H

(256) 234-7099. $79-$99. 4335 US Hwy 280 35010. US 280, just s of jct SR 22; just w of jct SR 63. Ext corridors. Pets: Medium. $15 daily fee/room. Service with restrictions, supervision.

ANDALUSIA

Days Inn & Suites M

(334) 427-0050. $63-$82. 1604 Dr MLK Jr Expwy 36420. On US 84 Bypass. Ext corridors. Pets: Accepted.

Econo Lodge M

(334) 222-7511. Call for rates. 1421 Dr MLK Jr Expwy 36420. On US 84 Bypass. Ext corridors. Pets: Medium. $10 daily fee/pet. Service with restrictions, supervision.

ANNISTON

Super 8 M

(256) 820-1000. $46-$90. 6220 McClellan Blvd 36206. I-20 exit 185, 9 mi n on SR 21. Ext corridors. Pets: Accepted.

The Victoria, A Country Inn CI

(256) 236-0503. Call for rates. 1600 Quintard Ave 36201. I-20 exit 185, 4 mi n on SR 21/US 431. Ext/int corridors. Pets: Accepted.

ARAB

Jameson Inn H

(256) 586-5777. $79-$99. 706 N Brindlee Mountain Pkwy 35016. On US 231, 0.5 mi n of jct SR 69. Ext corridors. Pets: Medium. $15 daily fee/room. Service with restrictions, supervision.

ATHENS

Best Western Athens Inn H

(256) 233-4030. $68-$90. 1329 Hwy 72 35611. I-65 exit 351, just w. Ext corridors. Pets: Small, dogs only. $20 one-time fee/pet. Designated rooms, service with restrictions, supervision.

Sleep Inn Athens H

(256) 232-4700. $72-$90. 1115 Audubon Ln 35611. I-65 exit 351, just nw. Int corridors. Pets: Accepted.

ATMORE

Holiday Inn Express H

(251) 368-1585. Call for rates. 111 Lakeview Cir 36504. I-65 exit 57, just s. Int corridors. Pets: Accepted.

Muskogee Inn H

(251) 368-8182. $89-$128, 3 day notice. 6141 Hwy 21 36502. I-65 exit 57, just e. Int corridors. Pets: Medium. $30 deposit/room. Service with restrictions, supervision.

ATTALLA

Days Inn Attalla H

(256) 538-7861. $50-$120. 801 Cleveland Ave 35954. I-59 exit 183 northbound, just e; exit southbound, thru first set of lights, then just e. Ext corridors. Pets: Accepted.

AUBURN

The Crenshaw Guest House BB

(334) 821-1131. Call for rates. 371 N College St 36830. Just w of downtown. Ext/int corridors. Pets: Accepted.

The Hotel at Auburn University & Dixon Conference Center H

(334) 821-8200. $99-$229. 241 S College St 36830. Just e of downtown. Int corridors. Pets: Accepted.

Jameson Inn M

(334) 502-5020. $74-$94. 1212 Mall Pkwy 36831. Adjacent to Colonial Mall. Ext corridors. Pets: Medium. $15 daily fee/room. Service with restrictions, supervision.

Lexington Hotel University Convention Center H

(334) 821-7001. $100-$260. 1577 S College St 36832. I-85 exit 51, 1.4 mi w on US 29/SR 147. Ext corridors. Pets: Accepted.

Quality Inn H

(334) 821-6699. $65-$200. 2283 S College St 36832. I-85 exit 51, just ne. Int corridors. Pets: Medium. $10 daily fee/pet. Service with restrictions, supervision.

BIRMINGHAM METROPOLITAN AREA

BESSEMER

Best Western Plus Bessemer Hotel & Suites 🅷 ❀

(205) 481-1950. **$90-$100.** 5041 Academy Ln 35022. I-20/59 exit 108, just sw. Int corridors. **Pets:** Large. $20 daily fee/pet. Designated rooms, service with restrictions, supervision. [SAVE] 🛜 ⊠ 🛏 💻 ➰

Jameson Inn 🅷

(205) 428-3194. **$79-$99.** 5021 Academy Ln 35022. I-20/59 exit 108, just sw. Ext corridors. **Pets:** Medium. $15 daily fee/room. Service with restrictions, supervision. 🛜 🛏 💻 ➰

Sleep Inn 🅷

(205) 424-0000. **$69-$190.** 1259 Greenmor Dr 35022. I-459 exit 6, just s, then just w. Int corridors. **Pets:** Accepted. 🛜 🛏 💻 ➰

BIRMINGHAM

Comfort Inn Birmingham Airport 🅷

(205) 957-0084. **$80-$150.** 4965 Montevallo Rd 35210. I-20 exit 132B, just s. Int corridors. **Pets:** Accepted. 🛜 🛗 🛏 💻 ➰

Days Inn 🅷

(205) 324-4510. **$54-$126.** 905 11th Ct W 35204. I-20/59 exit 123, just sw. Ext/int corridors. **Pets:** $10 daily fee/pet. Service with restrictions, supervision. 🛜 🛏 💻 ➰

Days Inn Highway 280 Ⓜ

(205) 991-9977. **$70-$100.** 4627 Hwy 280 E 35242. I-459 exit 19 (US 280), 1.4 mi e. Ext corridors. **Pets:** Accepted. 🛜 🛏 💻 ➰ ⊠

Drury Inn & Suites-Birmingham Southeast 🅷

(205) 967-2450. **$85-$164.** 3510 Grandview Pkwy 35243. I-459 exit 19 (US 280), just e; in Grandview. Int corridors. **Pets:** Accepted. 🛜 🛏 💻 ➰

Embassy Suites Birmingham 🅷

(205) 879-7400. **$139-$179.** 2300 Woodcrest Pl 35209. Just n of jct US 31 and 280 exit 21st Ave southbound, 0.3 mi s. Int corridors. **Pets:** Accepted. 🛜 🛗 🛏 💻 🍽 ➰ ⊠

Homestead Studio Suites-Birmingham Perimeter Park South 🅷 ❀

(205) 967-3800. **$60-$110.** 12 Perimeter Park S 35243. I-459 exit 19 (US 280), 0.5 mi e, then just s. Ext corridors. **Pets:** Other species. $25 daily fee/pet. Service with restrictions. 🛜 🛏 💻

The Hotel Highland at Five Points South, an Ascend Collection hotel 🅷

(205) 933-9555. **$109-$299.** 1023 20th St S 35205. 1.5 mi s; in Five Points South. Int corridors. **Pets:** Accepted. 🛜 ⊠ 🛏 💻

La Quinta Inn Birmingham / Cahaba Park South 🅷

(205) 995-9990. **$54-$111.** 513 Cahaba Park Cir 35242. I-459 exit 19 (US 280), 1.2 mi e. Int corridors. **Pets:** Medium, other species. Service with restrictions, supervision. 🛜 🛏 💻

Residence Inn Birmingham 🅷

(205) 991-8686. **$80-$180.** 3 Greenhill Pkwy 35242. I-459 exit 19 (US 280), 2 mi e. Ext corridors. **Pets:** Accepted. [SAVE] 🛜 ⊠ 🛏 💻 ➰ ⊠

Residence Inn Birmingham Downtown @ UAB 🅷

(205) 731-9595. **$103-$169.** 821 20th St S 35205. Jct University Blvd, just s; corner 8th Ct S. Int corridors. **Pets:** Accepted. [SAVE] 🛜 ⊠ 🛗 🛏 💻 ➰

Sheraton Birmingham Hotel 🅷

(205) 324-5000. **$89-$299.** 2101 Richard Arrington Jr Blvd N 35203. I-20/59 exit 22nd St. Int corridors. **Pets:** Accepted. [SAVE] 🛜 ⊠ 🛏 💻 🍽 ➰ ⊠

CALERA

Quality Inn 🅷

(205) 668-3641. **$75-$96.** 357 Hwy 304 35040. I-65 exit 231, just se. Ext corridors. **Pets:** Other species. $20 daily fee/room. Service with restrictions, supervision. 🛜 🛏 💻 ➰

FULTONDALE

Holiday Inn Express Fultondale 🅷

(205) 439-6300. **$89-$149.** 1733 Fulton Rd 35068. I-65 exit 267, just e. Int corridors. **Pets:** Accepted. 🛏 💻 ➰

GARDENDALE

Microtel Inn & Suites-Birmingham North-Gardendale 🅷

(205) 631-6320. **$62-$100.** 850 Odum Rd 35071. I-65 exit 271, just e, then just s. Int corridors. **Pets:** Small. $25 one-time fee/room. Designated rooms, no service. 🛜 🛏 💻 ➰

HOMEWOOD

Aloft Birmingham Soho Square 🅷

(205) 874-8055. **$109-$229.** 1903 29th Ave S 35209. I-59 exit 126A, 3.5 mi s on US 31, then just w. Int corridors. **Pets:** Accepted. [SAVE] 🛜 ⊠ 🛗 🛏 💻 🍽 ➰

Best Western Plus Carlton Suites 🅷

(205) 940-9990. **$85-$160.** 140 State Farm Pkwy 35209. I-65 exit 255, just w to Wildwood Pkwy, then just n. Int corridors. **Pets:** Small, dogs only. $20 one-time fee/pet. Designated rooms, no service, supervision. [SAVE] 🛜 🛗 🛏 💻 ➰

Drury Inn & Suites-Birmingham Southwest 🅷

(205) 940-9500. **$100-$189.** 160 State Farm Pkwy 35209. I-65 exit 255, 0.5 mi on northwest frontage road. Int corridors. **Pets:** Accepted. 🛜 🛏 💻 ➰

La Quinta Inn & Suites Birmingham (Homewood) 🅷

(205) 290-0150. **$74-$133.** 60 State Farm Pkwy 35209. I-65 exit 255, 0.9 mi on northwest frontage road. Int corridors. **Pets:** Medium, other species. Service with restrictions, supervision. 🛜 🛏 💻 ➰

Quality Inn 🅷

(205) 945-9600. **$63-$140.** 155 Vulcan Rd 35209. I-65 exit 256 northbound; exit 256A southbound, just nw. Ext/int corridors. **Pets:** Other species. $20 daily fee/pet. Service with restrictions, supervision. 🛜 🛗 🛏 💻 ➰

Residence Inn Birmingham Homewood 🅷

(205) 943-0044. **$89-$177.** 50 State Farm Pkwy 35209. I-65 exit 255, 1 mi on northwest frontage road. Int corridors. **Pets:** Accepted. [SAVE] 🛜 ⊠ 🛗 🛏 💻 ➰ ⊠

Super 8 🅷

(205) 945-9888. **$45-$60, 7 day notice.** 140 Vulcan Rd 35209. I-65 exit 256 northbound; exit 256A southbound, just nw. Int corridors. **Pets:** Large. $5 daily fee/pet. Service with restrictions, supervision. 🛜 🛏 💻

TownePlace Suites Birmingham Homewood 🅷

(205) 943-0114. **$76-$169.** 500 Wildwood Cir 35209. I-65 exit 255, 0.6 mi w, then just n. Int corridors. **Pets:** Accepted. [ECO] [SAVE] ⊠ 🛗 🛏 💻 ➰

HOOVER

▼▼ Days Inn at the Galleria 🄷
(205) 985-7500. **$62-$122.** 1800 Riverchase Dr 35244. I-459 exit 13, 0.5 mi s on US 31, then 0.4 mi w on SR 150. Ext corridors. **Pets:** Small. $25 daily fee/pet. Service with restrictions, supervision. 🛜 🛅 🖵 ⌷

▼▼▼ Homewood Suites Birmingham-SW/Riverchase Galleria 🄷
(205) 637-2900. **$99-$269.** 121 Riverchase Pkwy E 35244. I-65 exit 247, just sw on Valleydale Rd, then just n. Int corridors. **Pets:** Accepted. 🛜 🖄 🛅 🖵 ⌷ ⌧

▼▼▼ Homewood Suites by Hilton 🄷
(205) 995-9823. **$99-$149.** 215 Inverness Center Dr 35242. I-459 exit 19 (US 280), 1.8 mi e, then just s. Int corridors. **Pets:** Accepted. 🛜 🛅 🖵 ⌷ ⌧

▼▼ La Quinta Inn & Suites Birmingham Hoover 🄷
(205) 403-0096. **$62-$126.** 120 Riverchase Pkwy E 35244. I-65 exit 247, just sw on Valleydale Rd, then just n. Int corridors. **Pets:** Medium, other species. Service with restrictions, supervision. 🛜 🖄 🛅 🖵 ⌷

▼▼▼ Residence Inn by Marriott Birmingham/Hoover 🄷
(205) 733-1655. **$93-$139.** 2725 John Hawkins Pkwy 35244. I-459 exit 13A, 0.5 mi se to SR 150, then 1.5 mi s. Int corridors. **Pets:** Small, other species. $100 one-time fee/room. Service with restrictions. 🛜 ⌧ 🖄 🛅 🖵 ⌷

▼▼▼ The Wynfrey Hotel 🄷 ❀
(205) 987-1600. **$109-$1200.** 1000 Riverchase Galleria 35244. I-459 exit 13 (US 31). Int corridors. **Pets:** Small. $50 one-time fee/room. Service with restrictions. 🛜 ⌧ 🖵 🍴 ⌷ ⌧

IRONDALE

▼▼▼ Holiday Inn Express Hotel & Suites Birmingham East 🄷
(205) 957-0555. **$89-$179.** 811 Old Grants Mill Rd 35210. I-20 exit 133, just sw on Crescent Blvd, then just s. Int corridors. **Pets:** Accepted. 🛜 🛅 🖵 ⌷

▼▼ Quality Inn Birmingham East 🄷
(205) 956-4100. **$70-$85.** 3910 Kilgore Memorial Dr 35210. I-20 exit 133, just e. Ext corridors. **Pets:** Accepted. 🛜 🛅 🖵 ⌷

LEEDS

◈◈◈ ▼▼ Days Inn of Leeds Ⓜ
(205) 699-9833. **$68-$221.** 1838 Ashville Rd 35094. I-20 exit 144A eastbound; exit 144B westbound, just s. Ext corridors. **Pets:** Other species. $10 daily fee/pet. Service with restrictions, crate. [SAVE] 🛜 🛅 🖵 ⌷

ONEONTA

◈◈◈ ▼▼▼ Colonial Inn Oneonta 🄷
(205) 274-2200. **Call for rates.** 293 Valley Rd 35121. On SR 75, 0.5 mi n of jct US 231. Ext corridors. **Pets:** Accepted. [SAVE] 🛜 🛅 🖵 ⌷

PELHAM

◈◈◈ ▼▼▼ Best Western Plus Oak Mountain Inn 🄷
(205) 982-1113. **$90-$175.** 100 Bishop Cir 35124. I-65 exit 246, just sw, then just s on State Park Rd. Int corridors. **Pets:** Accepted. [SAVE] 🛜 🛅 🖵 ⌷

◈◈◈ ▼▼ Quality Inn 🄷
(205) 444-9200. **Call for rates.** 110 Cahaba Valley Pkwy 35124. I-65 exit 246, just nw. Ext corridors. **Pets:** Accepted. [SAVE] 🛜 🛅 🖵 ⌷

TRUSSVILLE

▼▼ Jameson Inn 🄷
(205) 661-9323. **$79-$99.** 4730 Norrell Dr 35173. I-59 exit 141, just e on Chalkville Rd, then just n. Ext corridors. **Pets:** Medium. $15 daily fee/room. Service with restrictions, supervision. 🛜 🛅 🖵 ⌷

END METROPOLITAN AREA

CHILDERSBURG

▼▼ Key West Inn Childersburg Ⓜ
(256) 378-0337. **Call for rates.** 32210 US Hwy 280 35044. Just s of jct CR 235. Ext corridors. **Pets:** Dogs only. $25 one-time fee/room. Service with restrictions, supervision. 🛜 🛅 🖵 ⌷

CLANTON

◈◈◈ ▼▼▼ Best Western Inn 🄷
(205) 280-1006. **$65-$100.** 801 Bradberry Ln 35046. I-65 exit 205, 0.5 mi e. Ext corridors. **Pets:** Small, dogs only. $10 daily fee/pet. Service with restrictions, supervision. [SAVE] 🛜 🛅 🖵 ⌷

▼▼ GuestHouse International Inn Ⓜ ❀
(205) 280-0306. **$59-$73.** 946 Lake Mitchell Rd 35045. I-65 exit 208, just w. Ext corridors. **Pets:** Other species. $6 daily fee/pet. Service with restrictions, supervision. 🛜 🛅 🖵 ⌷

CULLMAN

◈◈◈ ▼▼ Best Western Fairwinds Inn 🄷
(256) 737-5009. **$59-$159.** 1917 Commerce Ave NW 35055. I-65 exit 310, just e. Ext corridors. **Pets:** Very small, dogs only. $10 daily fee/pet. No service. [SAVE] 🛜 🛅 🖵 ⌷

▼▼ Days Inn 🄷
(256) 739-3800. **$52-$54.** 1841 4th St SW 35055. I-65 exit 308 (US 278), just e. Ext corridors. **Pets:** Medium, dogs only. $10 daily fee/pet. Service with restrictions, supervision. 🛜 🛅 🖵 ⌷

▼▼ Sleep Inn & Suites 🄷
(256) 734-6166. **$65-$110.** 2050 Old Hwy 157 35057. I-65 exit 310, just ne. Int corridors. **Pets:** Accepted. 🛜 🛅 🖵 ⌷

DAPHNE

▼▼▼ Homewood Suites by Hilton Mobile East Bay/Daphne 🄷
(251) 621-0100. **$149-$249.** 29474 N Main St 36526. I-10 exit 35A eastbound; exit 35 westbound, just s. Int corridors. **Pets:** Accepted. 🛜 🖄 🛅 🖵 ⌷

DECATUR

◈◈◈ ▼▼▼ Best Western River City Hotel 🄷
(256) 301-1388. **$77.** 1305 Front Ave 35603. I-65 exit 334, 8 mi n. Int corridors. **Pets:** Medium. $20 daily fee/room. Service with restrictions, supervision. [SAVE] 🛜 🖄 🛅 🖵 ⌷

▼▼▼ Holiday Inn Hotel & Suites 🄷
(256) 355-3150. **$79-$139.** 1101 6th Ave NE 35601. Just w of jct US 31, 72A and SR 20. Ext/int corridors. **Pets:** Small. $15 one-time fee/room. Designated rooms, service with restrictions, supervision. 🛜 ⌧ 🛅 🖵 🍴 ⌷

▼▼ Jameson Inn 🄷
(256) 355-2229. **$64-$84.** 2120 Jameson Pl SW 35603. SR 67, 1.6 mi s of jct US 72A; 3.9 mi n of jct US 31. Ext corridors. **Pets:** Medium. $15 daily fee/room. Service with restrictions, supervision. 🛜 🛅 🖵 ⌷

▼▼ **La Quinta Inn Decatur** Ⓜ
(256) 355-9977. **$62-$120.** 918 Beltline Rd SW 35601. Jct US 31 and SR 67, 1.6 mi w. Int corridors. **Pets:** Medium, other species. Service with restrictions, supervision. 📶 🛗 🍴 💻 🏊

▼▼ **Microtel Inn & Suites** Ⓗ
(256) 301-9995. **$53-$62, 14 day notice.** 2226 Beltline Rd SW 35601. On SR 67, 4 mi w of jct US 31. Int corridors. **Pets:** Large. $50 one-time fee/pet. Service with restrictions, crate. 📶 🛗 🍴 💻 🏊

DEMOPOLIS

🔷⃞ ▼▼▼ **Best Western Plus Two Rivers Hotel & Suites** Ⓗ
(334) 289-2611. **$110.** 662 US Hwy 80 W 36732. Jct US 43, 0.8 mi w. Int corridors. **Pets:** Accepted. [SAVE] 📶 ✕ 🍴 💻 🏊

DOTHAN

🔷⃞ ▼ **Americas Best Value Inn & Suites** Ⓜ
(334) 793-5200. **$45-$99.** 2901 Ross Clark Cir 36301. 0.8 mi s of jct US 84; west end of town. Ext corridors. **Pets:** Accepted.
[SAVE] 📶 🍴 💻 🏊

🔷⃞ ▼▼ **Days Inn** Ⓜ
(334) 671-3700. **$58.** 3071 Ross Clark Cir 36301. Just s of jct US 84; west end of town. Ext corridors. **Pets:** Accepted.
[SAVE] 📶 🛗 🍴 💻

▼▼ **Howard Johnson Inn** Ⓜ
(334) 792-3339. **$53-$116.** 2244 Ross Clark Cir 36301. 1.4 mi s of jct SR 52; west end of town. Ext corridors. **Pets:** Accepted.
📶 🍴 💻 🏊

▼🔷▼ **La Quinta Inn & Suites-Dothan** Ⓗ
(334) 793-9090. **$89-$150.** 3593 Ross Clark Cir 36303. Just w of jct US 231; northwest part of town. Int corridors. **Pets:** Medium, other species. Service with restrictions, supervision. 📶 🛗 🍴 💻 🏊

ENTERPRISE

▼▼ **Comfort Inn** Ⓜ
(334) 393-2304. **$65-$99.** 615 Boll Weevil Cir 36330. On US 84 Bypass. Ext corridors. **Pets:** Accepted. 📶 🍴 💻 🏊

EUFAULA

🔷🔷🔷 **Eufaula Comfort Suites** Ⓗ
(334) 616-0114. **Call for rates.** 12 Paul Lee Pkwy 36027. 1.7 mi s on US 431 from jct US 82 E, then just e. Int corridors. **Pets:** $25 one-time fee/pet. Service with restrictions, crate.
📶 ✕ 🛗 🍴 💻 🏊 ✕

▼▼ **Jameson Inn** Ⓜ
(334) 687-7747. **$74-$94.** 136 Towne Center Blvd 36027. On US 431, 1 mi s of US 82 E. Ext corridors. **Pets:** Medium. $15 daily fee/room. Service with restrictions, supervision. 📶 🍴 💻 🏊

EVERGREEN

🔷⃞ ▼▼▼ **Comfort Inn** Ⓜ
(251) 578-4701. **$64.** 1571 Ted Bates Rd 36401. I-65 exit 96, just w. Ext corridors. **Pets:** Other species. $10 daily fee/pet. Service with restrictions, crate. [SAVE] 📶 🍴 💻 🏊

▼▼ **Days Inn of Evergreen** Ⓜ
(251) 578-2100. **$65.** 215 Hwy 83 36401. I-65 exit 96, just w. Ext corridors. **Pets:** Accepted. 📶 🍴 💻

FAIRHOPE

▼🔷▼ **Holiday Inn Express** Ⓗ
(251) 928-9191. **Call for rates.** 19751 Greeno Rd 36532. On US 98, 2.2 mi s of jct SR 104. Int corridors. **Pets:** Accepted.
📶 ✕ 🍴 💻 🏊

▼▼ **Key West Inn** Ⓜ
(251) 990-7373. **$59-$109.** 231 S Greeno Rd 36532. On US 98, 1.9 mi s of jct SR 104. Ext corridors. **Pets:** Small. $15 daily fee/pet. Designated rooms, service with restrictions, supervision. 📶 🍴 💻 🏊

FLORENCE

▼▼ **Jameson Inn** Ⓗ
(256) 764-5326. **$69-$84.** 115 Ana Dr 35630. On US 43/72, just nw of jct SR 133 (Cox Creek Pkwy). Ext corridors. **Pets:** Medium. $15 daily fee/room. Service with restrictions, supervision. 📶 🍴 💻 🏊

🔷⃞ ▼▼▼ **Marriott Shoals Hotel and Spa** Ⓗ
(256) 246-3600. **$138-$193.** 800 Cox Creek Pkwy S 35630. US 43/72 and SR 133 (Cox Creek Pkwy), 1.5 mi s; at Wilson Dam. Int corridors. **Pets:** Accepted. [SAVE] 📶 ✕ 🛗 🍴 💻 🍴 🏊 ✕

🔷⃞ ▼▼ **Quality Inn** Ⓗ
(256) 740-0444. **$75-$89.** 150 Etta Gray Dr 35630. US 43/72, just se of jct SR 133 (Cox Creek Pkwy). Int corridors. **Pets:** Medium. $10 daily fee/pet. Designated rooms, service with restrictions, supervision.
[SAVE] 📶 ✕ 🍴 💻 🏊

FOLEY

🔷⃞ ▼▼ **Econo Lodge & Suites** Ⓗ
(251) 943-9100. **$60-$199.** 2682 S McKenzie St 36535. On SR 59, 1.9 mi s of jct US 98. Ext corridors. **Pets:** Small, other species. $20 one-time fee/room. Service with restrictions, crate. [SAVE] 📶 🛗 🍴 💻 🏊

GENEVA

▼ **Briarwood Inn of Geneva** Ⓜ
(334) 684-7715. **$69-$100.** 1503 W Magnolia Ave 36340. On SR 52, 0.3 mi w of jct SR 196. Ext corridors. **Pets:** Very small, dogs only. $10 daily fee/pet. Designated rooms, no service, supervision. 📶 🍴 🏊

GREENVILLE

🔷⃞ ▼▼ **Best Western Inn** Ⓜ
(334) 382-9200. **$59-$89.** 56 Cahaba Rd 36037. I-65 exit 130, just n on SR 185. Ext corridors. **Pets:** Accepted. [SAVE] 📶 🍴 💻 🏊

🔷⃞ ▼▼ **Comfort Inn** Ⓗ
(334) 383-9595. **$62-$94.** 1029 Fort Dale Rd 36037. I-65 exit 130, just n on SR 185. Int corridors. **Pets:** Small. $20 daily fee/pet. Service with restrictions, supervision. [SAVE] 📶 🛗 🍴 💻 🏊

🔷⃞ ▼▼ **Days Inn** Ⓜ
(334) 382-3118. **$60-$69.** 946 Fort Dale Rd 36037. I-65 exit 130, just s on SR 185. Ext corridors. **Pets:** Accepted. [SAVE] 📶 🍴 💻 🏊

▼▼ **Jameson Inn** Ⓜ
(334) 382-6300. **$64-$84.** 71 Jameson Ln 36037. I-65 exit 130, just n on SR 185, then just w on Cahaba Rd. Ext corridors. **Pets:** Medium. $15 daily fee/room. Service with restrictions, supervision. 📶 🍴 💻 🏊

GULF SHORES

▼▼▼ **Staybridge Suites** Ⓗ ❀
(251) 975-1030. **$99-$179.** 3947 Hwy 59 36542. On Gulf Shores Pkwy (SR 59), 3.1 mi n of jct SR 180. Int corridors. **Pets:** Other species. $75 one-time fee/room. Service with restrictions. 📶 🛗 🍴 💻 🏊

GUNTERSVILLE

🔷⃞ ▼▼▼ **Best Western Plus Lake Guntersville Hotel** Ⓗ
(256) 582-2220. **$90-$117.** 2140 Gunter Ave 35976. Jct US 431 (Gunter Ave) and SR 79. Ext corridors. **Pets:** Accepted.
[SAVE] 📶 🛗 🍴 💻 🍴 🏊 ✕

▼ **Super 8-Guntersville** Ⓜ
(256) 582-8444. **$40-$96.** 14341 Hwy 431 S 35976. Jct SR 69, 2 mi s. Ext corridors. **Pets:** Accepted. 📶 🍴 💻

HAMILTON

▼▼ Days Inn H

(205) 921-1790. **$57-$109.** 1849 Military St S 35570. US 78 exit 14, 1 mi n, then 1 mi w on US 43. Ext corridors. **Pets:** Medium. $10 daily fee/pet. Service with restrictions, supervision. 🛜 📶 💻 🏊

HUNTSVILLE

▼▼ Extended StayAmerica Huntsville-U.S. Space and Rocket Center H 🐾

(256) 830-9110. **$65-$100.** 4751 Governors House Dr 35805. I-565 exit 17A, just s, then 0.5 mi w. Ext corridors. **Pets:** Other species. $25 daily fee/pet. Service with restrictions. 🛜 ♿ 📶 💻

▼▼▼ Holiday Inn Express Hotel & Suites H

(256) 721-1000. **$86-$135.** 3808 University Dr 35816. I-565 exit 17A, just e. Int corridors. **Pets:** Small. $50 one-time fee/room. Designated rooms, service with restrictions, supervision. 🛜 📶 💻 🏊

▲▲▲ ▼▼▼ Holiday Inn Huntsville Downtown H

(256) 533-1400. **$89-$159.** 401 Williams Ave SW 35801. Just w of Church St; downtown. Int corridors. **Pets:** Small, dogs only. $30 one-time fee/room. Service with restrictions, supervision.

[SAVE] 🛜 📶 💻 🍴 🏊

▼▼ La Quinta Inn & Suites Huntsville Madison Square H

(256) 830-8999. **$74-$133.** 4890 University Dr NW 35816. I-565 exit 14B, 2.6 mi n on SR 255 (Research Park Blvd), then 0.9 mi e on US 72. Int corridors. **Pets:** Medium, other species. Service with restrictions, supervision. 🛜 📶 💻 🏊

▼▼ La Quinta Inn Huntsville (Research Park) H

(256) 830-2070. **$64-$122.** 4870 University Dr NW 35816. I-565 exit 14B, 2.6 mi n on SR 255 (Research Park Blvd), then 1.1 mi e on US 72. Ext corridors. **Pets:** Medium, other species. Service with restrictions, supervision. 🛜 📶 💻 🏊

▼▼ La Quinta Inn Huntsville (Space Center) H

(256) 533-0756. **$58-$115.** 3141 University Dr NW 35816. I-565 exit 17A, 1.1 mi n on SR 53 (Jordan Ln), then 0.6 mi e on US 72. Ext corridors. **Pets:** Medium, other species. Service with restrictions, supervision.

🛜 📶 💻 🏊

▼▼ Microtel Inn & Suites H

(256) 859-6655. **$47-$63.** 1820 Chase Creek Row 35811. Jct US 72 and Shields Rd, just n, then just w. Int corridors. **Pets:** Other species. $15 one-time fee/room. Service with restrictions. 🛜 ♿ 📶 💻 🏊

▼▼▼ TownePlace Suites Huntsville H

(256) 971-5277. **$94-$164.** 1125 McMurtrie Dr 35806. I-565 exit 14B, 2.6 mi n on SR 255 (Research Park Blvd), 0.8 mi w on US 72, then just s. Int corridors. **Pets:** $100 one-time fee/room. Designated rooms, service with restrictions, crate. 🛜 ✂ ♿ 📶 💻 🏊

▲▲▲ ▼▼▼▼ The Westin Huntsville H 🐾

(256) 428-2000. **$119-$299.** 6800 Governors West NW 35806. I-565 exit 14A, 0.5 mi w on SR 255 (Research Park Blvd), just w on Old Madison Pike, then 0.5 mi n. Int corridors. **Pets:** Medium, dogs only. $50 one-time fee/room, $15 daily fee/pet. Designated rooms, service with restrictions, supervision. [SAVE] 🛜 ✂ ♿ 📶 💻 🍴 🏊 ✂

JASPER

▼▼ Jameson Inn H

(205) 387-7710. **$74-$94.** 1100 Hwy 78/118 E 35501. SR 118, 1.8 mi w of jct SR 69. Ext corridors. **Pets:** Medium. $15 daily fee/room. Service with restrictions, supervision. 🛜 ♿ 📶 💻 🏊

LINCOLN

▲▲▲ ▼▼▼ Comfort Inn H

(205) 763-9777. **$70-$90.** 850/A Speedway Industrial Dr 35096. I-20 exit 168, just se. Int corridors. **Pets:** Medium. $10 daily fee/pet. Service with restrictions, supervision. [SAVE] 🛜 ♿ 📶 💻 🏊

MADISON

▼▼▼ Country Inn & Suites By Carlson H

(256) 325-0007. **$75-$200.** 101 Westchester Dr 35758. I-565 exit 8, just n, then just w. Int corridors. **Pets:** Medium, dogs only. $15 daily fee/pet. Designated rooms, service with restrictions, supervision.

🛜 ♿ 📶 💻 🏊

MILLBROOK

▼▼ Key West Inn M

(334) 309-2004. **$69-$120.** 2275 Cobbs Ford Rd 36054. I-65 exit 179, just w. Ext corridors. **Pets:** Medium. $10 daily fee/pet. Designated rooms, service with restrictions, supervision. 🛜 📶 💻 🏊

MOBILE

▲▲▲ ▼▼▼ Best Western Battleship Inn M

(251) 432-2703. **$89-$109.** 2701 Battleship Pkwy 36602. I-10 exit 27, just e. Ext corridors. **Pets:** Other species. $25 one-time fee/room. Service with restrictions, supervision. [SAVE] 🛜 📶 💻 🍴 🏊

▼▼▼ Drury Inn-Mobile H

(251) 344-7700. **$90-$139.** 824 W I-65 Service Rd S 36609. I-65 exit 3 (Airport Blvd), just w, then just s on service road. Int corridors. **Pets:** Accepted. 🛜 📶 💻 🏊

▼▼ Extended StayAmerica Mobile-Spring Hill H 🐾

(251) 344-2514. **$50-$120.** 508 Spring Hill Plaza Ct 36608. I-65 exit 5A, just w, then just n. Ext corridors. **Pets:** Other species. $25 daily fee/pet. Service with restrictions. 🛜 📶 💻

▼▼ La Quinta Inn Mobile M

(251) 343-4051. **$68-$126.** 816 W I-65 Service Rd S 36609. I-65 exit 3 (Airport Blvd), just w, then just s. Ext/int corridors. **Pets:** Medium, other species. Service with restrictions, supervision. 🛜 📶 💻 🏊

▲▲▲ ▼▼▼ ▼▼▼ Renaissance-The Battle House Mobile Hotel & Spa H

(251) 338-2000. **$154-$239.** 26 N Royal St 36602. I-10 exit 26B (Water St) eastbound, w on Government St, then just n. Int corridors. **Pets:** Accepted. [SAVE] 🛜 ✂ ♿ 📶 💻 🍴 🏊 ✂

▼▼▼ Residence Inn by Marriott Mobile H

(251) 304-0570. **$107-$179.** 950 W I-65 Service Rd S 36609. I-65 exit 3 (Airport Blvd), just w, then 0.4 mi s. Int corridors. **Pets:** Accepted. 🛜 ✂ 📶 💻 🏊 ✂

▼▼▼ TownePlace Suites Mobile H

(251) 345-9588. **$80-$159.** 1075 Montlimar Dr 36609. I-65 exit 3 (Airport Blvd), 0.5 mi w, then 0.5 mi s. Int corridors. **Pets:** Large, other species. $75 one-time fee/room. Service with restrictions, crate. 🛜 ✂ 📶 💻 🏊

MONROEVILLE

▼▼ Americas Best Value Inn M

(251) 743-3154. **Call for rates.** 50 Hwy 21 S 36460. On SR 21, just s of jct US 84. Ext corridors. **Pets:** Accepted. 🛜 📶

▲▲▲ ▼▼▼ Best Western of Monroeville M

(251) 575-9999. **$77-$90.** 4419 S Alabama Ave 36460. On SR 21, 0.5 mi n of jct US 84. Ext corridors. **Pets:** Accepted.

[SAVE] 🛜 📶 💻 🏊

▼▼ Days Inn of Monroeville M

(251) 743-3297. **$59-$108.** 4389 S Alabama Ave 36460. On SR 21, 0.5 mi n of jct US 84. Ext corridors. **Pets:** Accepted. 🛜 📶 💻 🏊

▲▲▲ ▼▼▼ Holiday Inn Express H

(251) 743-3333. **Call for rates.** 120 Hwy 21 S 36460. On SR 21, just s of jct US 84. Int corridors. **Pets:** Accepted.

[SAVE] 🛜 ♿ 📶 💻 🏊

MONTGOMERY

♦♦ Baymont Inn & Suites M
(334) 277-4442. **$54-$67.** 5837 Monticello Dr 36117. I-85 exit 6, just n, then just e. Ext corridors. **Pets:** Accepted. 🛜 🍴 🛗 💻 🏊

♦♦♦ Candlewood Suites at Eastchase H
(334) 277-0677. **$70-$119.** 9151 Boyd Cooper Pkwy 36117. I-85 exit 11, just sw. Int corridors. **Pets:** Accepted. 🛜 ✖ 🕹 🛗 💻

AAA ♦♦♦ Days Inn Midtown M
(334) 269-9611. **$40-$49.** 2625 Zelda Rd 36107. I-85 exit 3, just s on Ann St. Ext corridors. **Pets:** $10 daily fee/pet. Service with restrictions, supervision. SAVE 🛜 🛗 💻 🏊

♦♦♦ Drury Inn & Suites-Montgomery H
(334) 273-1101. **$90-$164.** 1124 Eastern Blvd 36117. I-85 exit 6, just n. Int corridors. **Pets:** Accepted. 🛜 🕹 🛗 💻 🏊

♦ Embassy Suites Montgomery Conference Center H 🐾
(334) 269-5055. **Call for rates.** 300 Tallapoosa St 36104. Between Molton and Commerce sts; in historic downtown. Int corridors. **Pets:** Medium. $50 one-time fee/room. 🛜 🕹 🛗 💻 🍴 🏊

♦♦♦ Holiday Inn Express Hotel & Suites H
(334) 288-8844. **$89-$99.** 4273 Troy Hwy 36116. 1 mi s of jct US 80 and 231 (Troy Hwy). Int corridors. **Pets:** Accepted. 🛜 🛗 💻 🏊

♦♦♦ Homewood Suites by Hilton H
(334) 272-3010. **$104-$179.** 1800 Interstate Park Dr 36109. I-85 exit 4, just n on Perry Hill, then just e. Int corridors. **Pets:** Accepted.
🛜 🕹 🛗 💻 🏊

♦♦ La Quinta Inn & Suites Montgomery Carmichael Road H
(334) 277-6000. **$58-$122.** 5225 Carmichael Rd 36106. I-85 exit 6, just s on Eastern Blvd, then just w. Int corridors. **Pets:** Medium, other species. Service with restrictions, supervision. 🛜 🛗 💻 🏊

♦♦ La Quinta Inn Montgomery Eastern Bypass M
(334) 271-1620. **$48-$104.** 1280 East Blvd 36117. I-85 exit 6, just s. Ext corridors. **Pets:** Medium, other species. Service with restrictions, supervision. 🛜 🛗 💻 🏊

♦ Motel 6 #4263 M
(334) 280-1866. **$46-$60.** 7760 Slade Plaza Blvd 36105. I-65 exit 164, just s. Int corridors. **Pets:** Other species. Service with restrictions, supervision. 🛜 🛗 🏊

♦♦ Red Roof Inn Montgomery H
(334) 270-0007. **$59-$79.** 5601 Carmichael Rd 36117. I-85 exit 6, just s on Eastern Blvd, then just e. Ext/int corridors. **Pets:** Large, other species. No service, supervision. 🛜 🛗 🏊

♦♦♦ Residence Inn Montgomery H
(334) 270-3300. **$84-$142.** 1200 Hilmar Ct 36117. I-85 exit 6, just s on Eastern Blvd, then just e. Ext/int corridors. **Pets:** Accepted.
🛜 ✖ 🛗 💻 🏊 ✖

♦ Sleep Inn & Suites H
(334) 387-1004. **$70-$90.** 5005 Carmichael Rd 36106. I-85 exit 6, just s. Int corridors. **Pets:** Accepted. 🛜 🛗 💻 🏊

♦♦♦ Staybridge Suites-EastChase H
(334) 277-9383. **$99-$119.** 7800 EastChase Pkwy 36117. I-85 exit 9 (Taylor Rd), just s, then 1 mi e; in The Shoppes of EastChase. Int corridors. **Pets:** Accepted. 🛜 🕹 🛗 💻 🏊

♦ StudioPLUS Montgomery-Carmichael Rd H 🐾
(334) 273-0075. **$50-$90.** 5115 Carmichael Rd 36106. I-85 exit 6, just s, then just w. Int corridors. **Pets:** Other species. $25 daily fee/pet. Service with restrictions. 🛜 🛗 💻 🏊

♦♦ TownePlace Suites Montgomery H
(334) 396-5505. **$84-$129.** 5047 TownePlace Dr 36106. I-85 exit 6, just s on Eastern Blvd, then just w on Carmichael Rd. Int corridors.
Pets: Accepted. 🛜 ✖ 🕹 🛗 💻 🏊

OXFORD

♦♦ Baymont Inn Anniston/Oxford M
(256) 835-1492. **$50-$270.** 1600 Hwy 21 S 36203. I-20 exit 185, just s. Ext corridors. **Pets:** Accepted. 🛜 🛗 💻 🏊

♦♦ Comfort Inn M
(256) 831-0860. **Call for rates.** 138 Elm St 36203. I-20 exit 185, just s. Ext corridors. **Pets:** Accepted. 🛜 🛗 💻 🏊

AAA ♦♦ Hampton Inn & Suites H
(256) 831-8958. **$84-$117.** 210 Colonial Dr 36203. I-20 exit 188, just n, then w. Int corridors. **Pets:** Accepted.
SAVE 🛜 ✖ 🕹 🛗 💻 🏊 ✖

AAA ♦♦♦ Holiday Inn Express & Suites Anniston/Oxford H
(256) 835-8768. **$89-$144.** 160 Colonial Dr 36203. I-20 exit 188, just n, then w. Int corridors. **Pets:** Other species. $25 daily fee/room. Service with restrictions, supervision. SAVE 🛜 🕹 🛗 💻 🏊 ✖

♦♦ Jameson Inn Oxford M
(256) 835-2170. **$59-$79.** 161 Colonial Dr 36203. I-20 exit 188, just n, then w. Ext corridors. **Pets:** Medium. $15 daily fee/room. Service with restrictions, supervision. 🛜 🛗 💻 🏊

OZARK

AAA ♦♦ All American Ozark Inn M
(334) 774-5166. **$40-$45.** 2064 Hwy 231 S 36360. 1 mi s of jct SR 249. Ext corridors. **Pets:** Other species. $50 deposit/pet. Service with restrictions, supervision. SAVE 🛜 🛗 💻 🏊

♦♦ Jameson Inn M
(334) 774-0233. **$74-$94.** 1360 S US Hwy 231 36360. 0.3 mi s of jct SR 249. Ext corridors. **Pets:** Medium. $15 daily fee/room. Service with restrictions, supervision. 🛜 🕹 🛗 💻 🏊

PHENIX CITY

♦♦♦ Quality Inn H
(334) 298-9321. **$65-$129.** 1700 E US 280 Bypass 36867. On US 280/431 Bypass. Ext corridors. **Pets:** Accepted. 🛜 🛗 💻 🍴 🏊

PRATTVILLE

♦♦ Jameson Inn H
(334) 361-6463. **$69-$89.** 104 Jameson Ct 36067. I-65 exit 179, 1 mi w. Ext corridors. **Pets:** Medium. $15 daily fee/room. Service with restrictions, supervision. 🛜 🛗 💻 🏊

♦♦♦ La Quinta Inn & Suites H
(334) 358-5454. **$69-$119.** 261 Interstate Commercial Park Loop 36066. I-65 exit 181, just w. Int corridors. **Pets:** Medium, other species. Service with restrictions, supervision. 🛜 ✖ 🛗 💻 🏊

♦♦ Quality Inn H
(334) 365-6003. **$75-$90.** 797 Business Park Dr 36066. I-65 exit 181, just sw, then just n. Int corridors. **Pets:** Medium. $10 daily fee/pet. Service with restrictions, supervision. 🛜 🕹 🛗 💻 🏊

PRICEVILLE

♦♦ Comfort Inn H
(256) 355-1037. **Call for rates.** 3239 Point Mallard Pkwy 35601. I-65 exit 334, just w. Int corridors. **Pets:** Accepted. 🛜 🛗 💻 🏊

♦♦ Super 8 Decatur/Priceville M
(256) 355-2525. **$41-$60.** 70 Marco Dr 35603. I-65 exit 334, just e. Ext corridors. **Pets:** Small, dogs only. $10 one-time fee/pet. Service with restrictions. 🛜 🛗 💻 🏊

SCOTTSBORO

▼▼ ▼ Jameson Inn [H]
(256) 574-6666. **$74-$94.** 208 Micah Way 35768. On US 72, just s of jct SR 35. Ext corridors. **Pets:** Medium. $15 daily fee/room. Service with restrictions, supervision. 🛜 🖨 💻 🏊

SELMA

▼▼ Jameson Inn [M]
(334) 874-8600. **$69-$89.** 2420 Broad St 36701. On SR 22, just n of jct US 80. Ext corridors. **Pets:** Medium. $15 daily fee/room. Service with restrictions, supervision. 🛜 🖨 💻 🏊

▼▼ Ramada Inn Selma [H]
(334) 872-0461. **$52-$55, 3 day notice.** 1710 W Highland Ave 36701. On US 80. Ext corridors. **Pets:** Accepted. 🛜 🖨 💻 🍽 🏊

SHEFFIELD

▼▼▼ Emerald River Hotel [H]
(256) 381-4710. **$69-$79.** 4900 Hatch Blvd 35660. 4 mi n on US 43 from jct US 72. Ext/int corridors. **Pets:** Accepted. 🛜 🖨 💻 🍽 🏊

STEVENSON

▼ Budget Host Inn [M]
(256) 437-2215. **$55-$75, 3 day notice.** 42973 US Hwy 72 35772. On US 72, just s of CR 85. Ext corridors. **Pets:** Accepted. 🛜 🖨 💻

SYLACAUGA

▼▼ Jameson Inn [H]
(256) 245-4141. **$69-$89.** 89 Gene Stewart Blvd 35151. Off US 280, just s. Ext corridors. **Pets:** Medium. $15 daily fee/room. Service with restrictions, supervision. 🛜 🖨 💻 🏊

TROY

AAA ▼▼ ▼ Econo Lodge of Troy [M]
(334) 566-7799. **$50-$80.** 811 Hwy 231 S 36081. On US 231, 1.5 mi s of jct US 29. Ext corridors. **Pets:** Accepted. SAVE 🛜 🖨 💻 🏊

▼▼ Motel 6 [H]
(334) 670-0012. **Call for rates.** 204B US Hwy 231 36081. On US 231, just n of jct US 29. Ext corridors. **Pets:** Other species. Service with restrictions, supervision. 🛜 🖨

▼▼▼ Quality Inn of Troy [H]
(334) 566-1150. **$64-$110.** 204 US Hwy 231 N 36081. On US 231, just n of jct US 29. Ext corridors. **Pets:** Small, other species. $20 one-time fee/pet. Service with restrictions. 🛜 🖨 💻 🏊

AAA ▼▼ ▼ Super 8 [M]
(334) 566-4960. **$49-$58.** 1013 Hwy 231 S 36081. On US 231, 2 mi s of jct US 29. Ext corridors. **Pets:** Accepted. SAVE 🛜 🖨 💻 🏊

TUSCALOOSA

AAA ▼▼ ▼ Comfort Inn [H]
(205) 556-3232. **$76-$250.** 4700 Doris Pate Dr 35405. I-59/20 exit 76, just n. Int corridors. **Pets:** Small, other species. $10 one-time fee/room. Service with restrictions, crate. SAVE 🛜 🖨 💻 🏊

▼▼ ▼ Jameson Inn [H]
(205) 345-5018. **$74-$94.** 5021 Oscar Baxter Dr 35403. I-59/20 exit 71A, just s. Ext corridors. **Pets:** Medium. $15 daily fee/room. Service with restrictions, supervision. 🛜 🖨 💻 🏊

▼▼ ▼ La Quinta Inn Tuscaloosa [M]
(205) 349-3270. **$62-$122.** 4122 McFarland Blvd E 35405. I-59/20 exit 73, just sw on US 82. Ext corridors. **Pets:** Medium, other species. Service with restrictions, supervision. 🛜 🖨 💻 🏊

▼ Masters Inn [M]
(205) 556-2010. **$45-$150, 3 day notice.** 3600 McFarland Blvd 35405. I-59/20 exit 73, just nw on US 82. Ext corridors. **Pets:** Accepted. 🛜 🖨 🏊

▼▼▼ Wingate by Wyndham Tuscaloosa [H]
(205) 553-5400. **Call for rates.** 4918 Skyland Blvd E 35405. I-59/20 exit 76, just n. Int corridors. **Pets:** Accepted. 🛜 🗙 🛄 🖨 💻 🏊

TUSCUMBIA

▼▼ Microtel Inn & Suites [H]
(256) 248-0055. **Call for rates.** 1852 Hwy 72 E 35674. Just w of jct US 72 and 43. Int corridors. **Pets:** Small. $15 daily fee/pet. Designated rooms, service with restrictions, supervision.
🛜 🗙 🛄 🖨 💻 🏊

ALASKA

CITY INDEX

ANCHORAGE

AAA ▼▼▼ Clarion Suites Downtown [H]
(907) 222-5005. **$99-$249, 3 day notice.** 1110 W 8th Ave 99501. Corner of L St and W 8th Ave. Int corridors. **Pets:** Large, dogs only. $150 one-time fee/room. Designated rooms, service with restrictions, supervision. SAVE 🛜 🗙 🛄 🖨 💻 🏊

▼▼ ▼ Hilton Anchorage [H]
(907) 272-7411. **$180-$285.** 500 W 3rd Ave 99501. At E St; downtown. Int corridors. **Pets:** Accepted. 🛜 🛄 💻 🍽 🏊 🗙

▼▼ Microtel Inn & Suites [M]
(907) 245-5002. **$58-$135.** 5205 Northwood Dr 99517. Jct International Airport Rd, just n. Int corridors. **Pets:** Accepted. 🛜 🛄 🖨 💻

▼▼ Millennium Alaskan Hotel Anchorage [H] 🐾
(907) 243-2300. **Call for rates.** 4800 Spenard Rd 99517. Jct International Airport Rd, just n. Int corridors. **Pets:** Large. $25 one-time fee/room. Crate. 🛜 🗙 🛄 🖨 💻 🍽 🗙

▼ Motel 6 - 4216 [M]
(907) 677-8000. **Call for rates.** 5000 A St 99503. Jct C St, just n on A St, then just n. Int corridors. **Pets:** Other species. Service with restrictions, supervision. 🛄 🖨

▼▼ ▼ Residence Inn by Marriott [H]
(907) 563-9844. **$169-$299.** 1025 E 35th Ave 99508. Corner of SR 1 (Seward Hwy) and 36th Ave. Int corridors. **Pets:** Accepted.
🛜 🗙 🛄 🖨 💻 🏊 🗙

AAA ◆◆◆ Sheraton Anchorage Hotel & SPA 🅷
(907) 276-8700. **$219-$369.** 401 E 6th Ave 99501. 6th Ave and Denali St. Int corridors. **Pets:** Accepted. (SAVE) 📶 ✕ ♿ 🛏 💻 🍴

CANTWELL

AAA ◆ Backwoods Lodge 🅼
(907) 768-2232. **$90-$170, 10 day notice.** Denali Hwy MM 133.8 99729. Parks Hwy (Milepost 210), just e. Ext corridors. **Pets:** Large. Supervision. (SAVE) ✕ 🛏 💻 🅐🅒

DENALI NATIONAL PARK AND PRESERVE

◆◆◆ Denali Bluffs Hotel 🅷
(907) 683-7000. **$99-$239, 3 day notice.** Milepost 238.4 Parks Hwy 99755. 1 mi n of park entrance. Ext corridors. **Pets:** Accepted.
📶 ✕ ♿ 💻 🍴 🅐🅒

◆◆◆ Grande Denali Lodge 🅷
(907) 683-5100. **$149-$299, 3 day notice.** Milepost 238.2 Parks Hwy 99755. SR 3 (Parks Hwy), at Milepost 238.2, on east side of road, 0.7 mi ne on Grande Dr. Ext/int corridors. **Pets:** Accepted. ✕ ♿ 💻 🍴

◆◆◆ McKinley Chalet Resort 🅷
(907) 683-8200. **Call for rates.** Milepost 238.5 Parks Hwy 99755. Milepost 238.5 on SR 3 (Parks Hwy). Ext/int corridors. **Pets:** Accepted.
📶 ✕ ♿ 💻 🍴 🅐🅒

FAIRBANKS

AAA ◆◆◆ Pike's Waterfront Lodge 🅷 🐾
(907) 456-4500. **$89-$450, 3 day notice.** 1850 Hoselton Rd 99709. Jct Airport Way and Hoselton Rd. Ext/int corridors. **Pets:** Other species. $25 daily fee/pet. Designated rooms, service with restrictions, crate.
(SAVE) 📶 ✕ ♿ 🛏 💻 🍴 ✕

AAA ◆◆◆ Westmark Fairbanks Hotel & Conference Center 🅷
(907) 456-7722. **$94-$239.** 813 Noble St 99701. Just n of Airport Way at 10th Ave; just w of SR 2; downtown. Int corridors. **Pets:** Accepted.
(SAVE) 📶 ✕ ♿ 🛏 💻 🍴

HAINES

AAA ◆ Captain's Choice Motel 🅼
(907) 766-3111. **$137-$184.** 108 2nd Ave N 99827. Jct 2nd Ave and Dalton St. Ext corridors. **Pets:** Other species. $25 one-time fee/room. Service with restrictions, supervision. (SAVE) 📶 🛏 💻 🅐🅒

HOMER

AAA ◆◆◆ Best Western Plus Bidarka Inn 🅷 🐾
(907) 235-8148. **$169-$209.** 575 Sterling Hwy 99603. Just n of Pioneer Ave on Sterling Hwy (SR 1). Ext/int corridors. **Pets:** Large, other species. $15 daily fee/pet. Designated rooms, service with restrictions, supervision.
(SAVE) 📶 ♿ 🛏 💻 🍴

JUNEAU

AAA ◆◆◆ Westmark Baranof Hotel 🅷
(907) 586-2660. **$149-$279.** 127 N Franklin St 99801. At 2nd and Franklin sts; downtown. Int corridors. **Pets:** Accepted.
(SAVE) 📶 ✕ 🛏 💻 🍴 🅐🅒

KETCHIKAN

AAA ◆◆◆ Best Western Plus Landing Hotel 🅷 🐾
(907) 225-5166. **$143-$246.** 3434 Tongass Ave 99901. Across from Alaska Marine Hwy ferry terminal. Ext/int corridors. **Pets:** Medium, other species. $50 deposit/room, $10 daily fee/pet. Designated rooms, service with restrictions, supervision. (SAVE) 📶 ♿ 🛏 💻 🍴

◆◆◆ Cape Fox Lodge 🅷
(907) 225-8001. **$115-$225.** 800 Venetia Way 99901. Above Creek St (tramway from Creek St). Ext/int corridors. **Pets:** Accepted.
(SAVE) 📶 ♿ 🛏 💻 🍴 🅐🅒

KODIAK

AAA ◆◆◆ Best Western Kodiak Inn & Convention Center 🅷
(907) 486-5712. **$100-$205.** 236 W Rezanof Dr 99615. 0.3 mi w of ferry terminal; center. Ext/int corridors. **Pets:** Medium. $50 deposit/room, $25 one-time fee/pet. Designated rooms, service with restrictions, supervision.
(SAVE) 📶 ♿ 🛏 💻 🍴 🅐🅒

◆◆◆ Comfort Inn Kodiak 🅷
(907) 487-2700. **Call for rates.** 1395 Airport Way 99615. Adjacent to Kodiak Airport. Int corridors. **Pets:** Accepted.
📶 ♿ 🛏 💻 🍴 🅐🅒

SEWARD

AAA ◆◆◆ Hotel Seward 🅷
(907) 224-8001. **$59-$379, 3 day notice.** 221 Fifth Ave 99664. Just n of Alaska SeaLife Center; downtown. Int corridors. **Pets:** Medium, dogs only. $25 daily fee/pet. Designated rooms, service with restrictions, supervision.
(SAVE) 📶 ✕ ♿ 🛏 💻 🍴 🅐🅒

SITKA

AAA ◆◆◆ Shee Atika Totem Square Inn 🅷 🐾
(907) 747-3693. **$149-$289.** 201 Katlian St 99835. In Totem Square Complex near Municipal Office. Int corridors. **Pets:** Small, other species. $50 deposit/room, $10 daily fee/pet. Service with restrictions, supervision.
(SAVE) 📶 ✕ ♿ 🛏 💻 🍴 🅐🅒

◆◆ Super 8-Sitka 🅷
(907) 747-8804. **$71-$125.** 404 Sawmill Creek Rd 99835. Just e from corner of Lake St and Halibut Point/Sawmill Creek Rd; center. Int corridors. **Pets:** Other species. $15 daily fee/pet. Designated rooms, service with restrictions, supervision. 📶 ♿ 🛏 💻

◆◆◆ Westmark Sitka 🅷
(907) 747-6241. **$139-$179.** 330 Seward St 99835. Center. Int corridors. **Pets:** Accepted. 📶 ✕ ♿ 💻 🍴 🅐🅒

SKAGWAY

AAA ◆ Westmark Inn Skagway 🅼
(907) 983-6000. **$115-$145, 14 day notice.** 3rd Ave & Spring St 99840. Downtown. Ext/int corridors. **Pets:** Accepted.
(SAVE) 📶 ✕ ♿ 🛏 💻 🍴 🅐🅒

TOK

AAA ◆◆◆ Cleft of the Rock Bed & Breakfast 🅒🅐
(907) 883-4219. **$110-$165, 3 day notice.** 0.5 Sundog Tr 99780. Jct SR 1 and 2 (Alaskan Hwy), 2.5 mi w on SR 2 (Alaskan Hwy) to Sundog Tr, then 0.5 mi n. Ext/int corridors. **Pets:** Accepted.
(SAVE) 📶 ✕ 🛏 💻 🍴 🅐🅒

AAA ◆◆◆ Westmark Inn Tok 🅼
(907) 883-5174. **$139-$250.** Jct Alaska & Glenn Hwys 99780. On SR 1; jct SR 2 (Alaskan Hwy). Ext corridors. **Pets:** Accepted.
(SAVE) 📶 ✕ ♿ 💻 🍴

TRAPPER CREEK

◆◆◆ Gate Creek Cabins 🅒🅐
(907) 733-1393. **$120-$520, 10 day notice.** Mile 10.5 Petersville Rd 99683. MM 114 (Parks Hwy), 10.5 mi w at Petersville Rd. Ext corridors. **Pets:** Accepted. 📶 ✕ 🛏 💻 ✕ 🅐🅒 ✍

◆◆◆ Trapper Creek Inn & RV Park 🅼
(907) 733-2302. **$99-$139, 10 day notice.** Mile 114.6 Parks Hwy 99683. George Parks Hwy (SR 3), Milepost 114. Ext corridors. **Pets:** $50 deposit/pet. Service with restrictions, supervision.
📶 ✕ 🛏 💻 🍴 🅐🅒 ✍

VALDEZ

Best Western Valdez Harbor Inn 🄷
(907) 835-3434. **$100-$211.** 100 N Harbor Dr 99686. Just s at Meals Ave. Int corridors. **Pets:** Medium, dogs only. $100 deposit/room, $10 daily fee/pet. Designated rooms, service with restrictions, supervision.
SAVE 🛜 🄼 🛄 🖵 🍴 🐾

WASILLA

Best Western Lake Lucille Inn 🄷
(907) 373-1776. **$100-$190.** 1300 W Lake Lucille Dr 99654. SR 3 (George Parks Hwy), just w on Hallea Ln; center. Int corridors. **Pets:** Medium. $20 daily fee/pet. Supervision.
SAVE 🛜 ❌ 🄼 🛄 🖵 🐾

WHITTIER

The Inn at Whittier 🄷
(907) 472-3200. **$109-$299.** 5A Harbor Loop 99693. At harbor. Int corridors. **Pets:** Accepted. SAVE 🛜 ❌ 🛄 🖵 🍴 🐾

ARIZONA

CITY INDEX

AJO

La Siesta Motel 🄼
(520) 387-6569. **Call for rates.** 2561 N Ajo-Gila Bend Hwy 85321. On SR 85, 1.8 mi n of town plaza. Ext corridors. **Pets:** Accepted.
🛜 ❌ 🛄 🖵 🏊 🐾

AMADO

Amado Territory Inn 🄱🄱
(520) 398-8684. **Call for rates.** 3001 E Frontage Rd 85645. I-19 exit 48, just e, then just s. Int corridors. **Pets:** Accepted.
🛜 ❌ 🛄 🖵 🍴

BENSON

Best Western Plus Quail Hollow Inn 🄷 🌸
(520) 586-3646. **$100-$130.** 699 N Ocotillo Rd 85602. I-10 exit 304 (Ocotillo Rd), just s. Ext corridors. **Pets:** Other species. $20 daily fee/pet. Designated rooms, service with restrictions, supervision.
SAVE 🛜 🛄 🖵 🏊

Super 8 🄼
(520) 586-1530. **$44-$80.** 855 N Ocotillo Rd 85602. I-10 exit 304 (Ocotillo Rd), just s. Ext corridors. **Pets:** Other species. $10 one-time fee/room. Designated rooms, service with restrictions, supervision.
🛜 🛄 🖵 🏊

BISBEE

Americas Best Value Inn & Suites 🄼
(520) 432-2293. **$70-$360.** 1372 Hwy 92 85603. 0.8 mi w of jct Naco Hwy; sw of downtown. Ext corridors. **Pets:** Medium, dogs only. $10 daily fee/pet. Designated rooms, service with restrictions, supervision.
SAVE 🛜 ❌ 🛄 🖵

Audrey's Inn 🄲🄾
(520) 227-6120. **$105-$125.** 20 Brewery Ave 85603. Just ne of Main St; in historic district. Int corridors. **Pets:** Accepted. 🛜 ❌ 🛄 🖵

San Jose Lodge 🄼
(520) 432-5761. **$60-$180.** 2102 Naco Hwy 85603. SR 92 W, 1.5 mi s. Ext corridors. **Pets:** Dogs only. $10 daily fee/pet. Designated rooms, service with restrictions, supervision. SAVE 🛜 🛄 🖵 🍴 🏊

BULLHEAD CITY

Best Western Bullhead City Inn 🄷
(928) 754-3000. **Call for rates.** 1126 Hwy 95 86429. 1.8 mi s of Laughlin Bridge. Ext corridors. **Pets:** Accepted. SAVE 🛜 🛄 🖵 🏊

Lake Mohave Resort Motel 🄼
(928) 754-3245. **Call for rates.** 2690 E Katherine Spur Rd 86429. Jct SR 95, 1.5 mi e on SR 68, 1 mi n, then 5.4 mi e; at Katherine Landing; in Lake Mead National Recreation area. Ext corridors. **Pets:** Other species. $10 daily fee/pet. Service with restrictions, crate. 🛄 🖵 🗙

Lodge on The River 🄼
(928) 758-8080. **$45-$125, 7 day notice.** 1717 Hwy 95 86442. 3.8 mi s of Laughlin Bridge. Ext corridors. **Pets:** $10 daily fee/pet. Service with restrictions, supervision. SAVE 🛜 🛄 🖵 🏊

CAMERON

Cameron Trading Post Motel, Restaurant & Gift Shop 🄼
(928) 679-2231. **$59-$109.** 466 N Hwy 89 86020. 1 mi from east gate turn off. Ext corridors. **Pets:** Accepted. SAVE 🛜 ❌ 🛄 🖵 🍴

CAMP VERDE

Cliff Castle Casino Hotel 🄷
(928) 567-6611. **Call for rates.** 333 Middle Verde Rd 86322. I-17 exit 289, 0.4 mi se. Ext corridors. **Pets:** Accepted.
SAVE 🛜 ❌ 🛄 🖵 🍴

ⱯⱯⱯ ▽▽ Comfort Inn-Camp Verde 🅗 ❀
(928) 567-9000. **$59-$209.** 340 N Goswick Way 86322. I-17 exit 287, just e, then just s. Int corridors. **Pets:** Large, other species. $15 one-time fee/pet. Designated rooms, service with restrictions, supervision.
SAVE 📶 🛄 💻 �

▽ Super 8-Camp Verde 🅜
(928) 567-2622. **$56-$94.** 1550 W Hwy 260 86322. I-17 exit 287, just e. Int corridors. **Pets:** Accepted. 📶 🛄 💻 🌫

CASA GRANDE

ⱯⱯⱯ ▽▽▽ Holiday Inn Express & Suites Casa Grande 🅗
(520) 509-6333. **$85-$145.** 805 N Cacheries Ct 85122. I-10 exit 194 (SR 287), 0.6 mi w. Int corridors. **Pets:** $20 daily fee/room. Service with restrictions, supervision. SAVE 📶 ✕ 🅼 🛄 💻 🌫

ⱯⱯⱯ ▽▽▽ Holiday Inn Hotel Casa Grande 🅗
(520) 426-3500. **$79-$199, 3 day notice.** 777 N Pinal Ave 85122. I-10 exit 194 (SR 287), 3.9 mi w. Int corridors. **Pets:** Small. $20 one-time fee/pet. Designated rooms, service with restrictions, supervision.
SAVE 📶 🛄 💻 🍽 🌫

ⱯⱯⱯ ▽▽ Super 8 🅗
(520) 836-8800. **$50-$81.** 2066 E Florence Blvd 85222. I-10 exit 194 (SR 287), 0.6 mi w. Int corridors. **Pets:** Other species. $10 daily fee/pet. Service with restrictions, supervision. SAVE 📶 🛄 💻 🌫

COTTONWOOD

ⱯⱯⱯ ▽▽▽ Best Western Cottonwood Inn 🅗
(928) 634-5575. **$90-$120.** 993 S Main St 86326. On SR 89A, at SR 260. Ext corridors. **Pets:** Small, dogs only. $15 daily fee/pet. Designated rooms, service with restrictions, supervision.
SAVE 📶 ✕ 🛄 💻 🌫

▽ Little Daisy Motel 🅜
(928) 634-7865. **Call for rates.** 34 S Main St 86326. On SR 89A, just n. Ext corridors. **Pets:** Accepted. 📶 🛄

▽▽ Motel 6 🅜
(928) 634-3678. **$55-$149.** 1089 S SR 260 86326. On SR 260, just e of jct SR 89A. Ext corridors. **Pets:** Other species. Service with restrictions, supervision. 📶 ✕ 🛄

▽▽ Pines Motel 🅜
(928) 634-9975. **$59-$99.** 920 S Camino Real 86326. Jct SR 260, just nw on SR 89A, then just s. Ext corridors. **Pets:** $20 one-time fee/room, $5 daily fee/room. Designated rooms, service with restrictions, supervision.
ECO 📶 ✕ 🛄 💻 🌫

ⱯⱯⱯ ▽ The View Motel 🅜
(928) 634-7581. **$59-$129.** 818 S Main St 86326. On SR 89A, 0.4 mi nw of jct SR 260. Ext corridors. **Pets:** Accepted. SAVE 📶 🛄 🌫

DOUGLAS

▽ Motel 6 #305 🅜
(520) 364-2457. **$45-$61.** 111 16th St (SR 80) 85607. 1.2 mi e of jct SR 191. Ext corridors. **Pets:** Other species. Service with restrictions, supervision. 📶 🛄 🌫

EAGAR

ⱯⱯⱯ ▽▽ Best Western Sunrise Inn 🅜
(928) 333-2540. **$90-$123.** 128 N Main St 85925. Jct SR 260, just n; jct US 60, 1.5 mi s. Ext corridors. **Pets:** Accepted. SAVE 📶 🛄 💻

EHRENBERG

ⱯⱯⱯ ▽▽▽ Best Western Desert Oasis 🅗 ❀
(928) 923-9711. **Call for rates.** S Frontage Rd 85334. I-10 exit 1, just s; 0.5 mi e of Colorado River. Int corridors. **Pets:** Other species. No service, crate. SAVE 📶 🛄 💻 🌫

ELOY

▽ Motel 6 - 1263 🅜
(520) 836-3323. **$45-$61.** 4965 S Sunland Gin Rd 85231. I-10 exit 200, just w. Ext corridors. **Pets:** Other species. Service with restrictions, supervision. 📶 🛄 🌫

FLAGSTAFF

ⱯⱯⱯ ▽▽ Best Western Pony Soldier Inn & Suites 🅗 ❀
(928) 526-2388. **$65-$150.** 3030 E Route 66 86004. I-40 exit 201, just n, then 1 mi w. Int corridors. **Pets:** Large, other species. $20 one-time fee/room. Designated rooms, service with restrictions, supervision.
SAVE 📶 ✕ 🛄 💻 🌫

▽▽▽ Comfort Inn I-17/I-40 🅗
(928) 774-2225. **$80-$200.** 2355 S Beulah Blvd 86001. I-40 exit 195, just n to Forest Meadows St, then 1 blk w. Int corridors. **Pets:** Accepted.
📶 🛄 💻 🌫

ⱯⱯⱯ ▽▽ Days Inn & Suites 🅗
(928) 527-1477. **$56-$138.** 3601 E Lockett Rd 86004. I-40 exit 201, 0.5 mi w on I-40 business loop, then just n on Fanning Dr. Int corridors. **Pets:** Medium. $25 one-time fee/room. Service with restrictions, supervision. SAVE 📶 ✕ 🛄 💻 🌫

▽▽▽ Drury Inn & Suites-Flagstaff 🅗
(928) 773-4900. **$105-$234.** 300 S Milton Rd 86001. I-40 exit 195, 1.8 mi n on SR 89A (Milton Rd). Int corridors. **Pets:** Accepted.
ECO 📶 ✕ 🅼 🛄 💻 🌫

ⱯⱯⱯ ▽▽▽ Econo Lodge-University 🅜 ❀
(928) 774-7326. **$60-$130.** 914 S Milton Rd 86001. I-40 exit 195, 1.2 mi n on SR 89A (Milton Rd). Ext corridors. **Pets:** Other species. $10 daily fee/pet. Service with restrictions, supervision. SAVE 📶 🛄 💻 🌫

▽▽▽ La Quinta Inn & Suites Flagstaff 🅗
(928) 556-8666. **$84-$192.** 2015 S Beulah Blvd 86001. I-40 exit 195, just n to Forest Meadows St, then just w. Int corridors. **Pets:** Medium, other species. Service with restrictions, supervision. 📶 🛄 💻 🌫

▽▽ Motel 6-Flagstaff West #1000 🅜
(928) 779-3757. **$45-$65.** 2745 S Woodlands Village Blvd 86001. I-40 exit 195, just n to Forest Meadows St, w to Beulah Blvd, just s, then just w. Ext corridors. **Pets:** Other species. Service with restrictions, supervision. 📶 🅼 🛄 🌫

ⱯⱯⱯ ▽▽ Quality Inn I-40/I-17 🅗
(928) 774-8771. **$50-$140.** 2000 S Milton Rd 86001. I-40 exit 195, just n to Forest Meadows St, then right. Int corridors. **Pets:** Other species. $10 daily fee/room. Service with restrictions, supervision.
SAVE 📶 ✕ 💻 🌫

▽▽ Ramada Inn-Lucky Lane 🅗
(928) 779-3614. **$49-$199.** 2350 E Lucky Ln 86004. I-40 exit 198 (Butler Ave), just n, then just e. Ext corridors. **Pets:** Accepted.
📶 🛄 💻 🌫

ⱯⱯⱯ ▽▽▽ Residence Inn by Marriott Flagstaff 🅗
(928) 526-5555. **$98-$134.** 3440 N Country Club Dr 86004. I-40 exit 201, 0.5 mi s. Ext/int corridors. **Pets:** Accepted.
SAVE 📶 ✕ 🛄 💻 🌫 ✕

ⱯⱯⱯ ▽▽ Super 8 - Flagstaff Mall 🅜
(928) 526-0818. **$45-$95.** 3725 N Kasper Ave 86004. I-40 exit 201, just n, 0.5 mi w on I-40 business loop, then just n. Int corridors.
Pets: Accepted. SAVE 📶 🛄 💻

ⱯⱯⱯ ▽▽ Travel Inn 🅜
(928) 774-3381. **$39-$119, 3 day notice.** 801 W Route 66 86001. I-40 exit 195, 1.2 mi n on SR 89A (Milton Rd), then just w. Ext corridors. **Pets:** Small. $10 daily fee/pet. Service with restrictions, supervision.
SAVE 📶 🛄

FLORENCE

▼▼▼▼ Rancho Sonora Inn [CI]

(520) 868-8000. **$79-$225, 3 day notice.** 9198 N Hwy 79 85232. On SR 79, 5 mi s of SR 287. Ext corridors. **Pets:** $10 daily fee/pet. Designated rooms, service with restrictions, crate. 🛜 ⊠ 🛎 💻 🏊

FOREST LAKES

🔷 ▼ Forest Lakes Lodge [M]

(928) 535-4727. **$54-$85.** 2823 SR 260 85931. On SR 260; between MM 288 and 289. Ext corridors. **Pets:** Small. $15 one-time fee/room. Service with restrictions, supervision. [SAVE] 🛜 🛎 🐾

GILA BEND

▼ America's Choice Inn & Suites [M]

(928) 683-6311. **$65.** 2888 Butterfield Tr 85337. I-8 exit 119, just nw. Int corridors. **Pets:** Accepted. 🛜 ⊠ 🛎 🐾

▼▼▼ Best Western Space Age Lodge [M]

(928) 683-2273. **$109-$189.** 401 E Pima St 85337. Business Loop I-8; center. Ext corridors. **Pets:** Medium, other species. $20 one-time fee/pet. Service with restrictions, crate. [SAVE] 🛜 ⊠ 🛎 💻 🍽 🐾

GLOBE

▼▼ Quality Inn [M]

(928) 425-7575. **Call for rates.** 1515 South St 85501. On US 60, 1 mi e of town. Ext corridors. **Pets:** Small, other species. $15 one-time fee/pet. Service with restrictions, supervision. 🛜 ⊠ 🛎 💻 🐾

GRAND CANYON NATIONAL PARK AREA

GRAND CANYON NATIONAL PARK - SOUTH RIM

🔷 ▼▼ Canyon Plaza Resort Grand Canyon [H] ✿

(928) 638-2673. **$83-$268.** 406 Canyon Plaza Ln 86023. On SR 64; 2 mi s of South Rim entrance. Ext/int corridors. **Pets:** Medium, other species. $50 one-time fee/room. Designated rooms, service with restrictions, supervision. [SAVE] 🛜 🛎 💻 🍽 🐾

🔷 ▼▼▼ The Grand Hotel [H]

(928) 638-3333. **$119-$259, 3 day notice.** Hwy 64 86023. On SR 64; 2 mi s of South Rim entrance. Int corridors. **Pets:** Accepted.

[SAVE] 🛜 ⊠ 🛎 💻 🍽 🐾 ⊠

▼▼ Red Feather Lodge [H]

(928) 638-2414. **$75-$250.** 300 SR 64 86023. On SR 64; 2 mi s of South Rim entrance. Ext/int corridors. **Pets:** Accepted.

[SAVE] 🛜 🛎 💻 🐾

END AREA

HEBER

🔷 ▼▼ Best Western Sawmill Inn [M] ✿

(928) 535-5053. **$60-$92.** 1877 Hwy 260 85928. 0.5 mi e of center. Ext corridors. **Pets:** Large, dogs only. $10 daily fee/pet. Designated rooms, service with restrictions, crate. [ECO] [SAVE] 🛜 🛎 💻

HOLBROOK

🔷 ▼▼ Best Western Adobe Inn [M]

(928) 524-3948. **$80-$130.** 615 W Hopi Dr 86025. I-40 exit 285, 1 mi e on US 180 (Hopi Dr). Ext corridors. **Pets:** Accepted.

[SAVE] 🛜 🛎 💻 🐾

🔷 ▼▼ Best Western Arizonian Inn [H]

(928) 524-2611. **Call for rates.** 2508 Navajo Blvd 86025. I-40 exit 289, 0.5 mi w. Ext corridors. **Pets:** Accepted. [SAVE] 🛜 ⊠ 🛎 💻 🐾

🔷 ▼▼ Comfort Inn [H]

(928) 524-6131. **$70-$99.** 2602 E Navajo Blvd 86025. I-40 exit 289, just w. Ext corridors. **Pets:** Accepted. [SAVE] 🛜 🛎 💻 🐾

🔷 ▼▼ Ramada Limited [H]

(928) 524-2566. **$54-$79.** 2608 E Navajo Blvd 86025. I-40 exit 289, just w. Ext corridors. **Pets:** Dogs only. $11 daily fee/pet. Designated rooms, service with restrictions, supervision. [SAVE] 🛜 🛎 💻

JEROME

🔷 ▼▼▼ Connor Hotel of Jerome [H] ✿

(928) 634-5006. **$95-$175, 3 day notice.** 160 S Main St 86331. Center. Int corridors. **Pets:** Other species. Supervision. [SAVE] 🛜 🛎 💻

KAYENTA

▼▼▼ Hampton Inn of Kayenta [H]

(928) 697-3170. **Call for rates.** Hwy 160 86033. Just w of US 163. Int corridors. **Pets:** Accepted. 🛜 ⊠ 🛎 💻 🍽 🐾

KINGMAN

🔷 ▼▼▼ Best Western Plus A Wayfarer's Inn & Suites [H]

(928) 753-6271. **$96-$128.** 2815 E Andy Devine Ave 86401. I-40 exit 53, 0.5 mi w on Route 66. Ext corridors. **Pets:** Medium. $10 one-time fee/pet. Service with restrictions, supervision. [SAVE] 🛜 🛎 💻 🐾

🔷 ▼▼▼ Best Western Plus King's Inn & Suites [H]

(928) 753-6101. **$94-$128.** 2930 E Andy Devine Ave 86401. I-40 exit 53, just w on Route 66. Ext corridors. **Pets:** Accepted.

[SAVE] 🛜 🛎 💻 🐾

▼▼ Comfort Inn [M]

(928) 718-1717. **$95-$170.** 3129 E Andy Devine Ave 86401. I-40 exit 53, just w on Route 66. Int corridors. **Pets:** Medium, dogs only. $20 one-time fee/room. Designated rooms, service with restrictions, supervision.

🛜 🛎 💻 🐾

🔷 ▼▼ Days Inn West [M] ✿

(928) 753-7500. **$44-$72.** 3023 E Andy Devine Ave 86401. I-40 exit 53, just w on Route 66. Ext corridors. **Pets:** Other species. $10 daily fee/pet. Service with restrictions, supervision. [SAVE] 🛜 🛎 💻 🐾

🔷 ▼▼▼ Holiday Inn Express Hotel & Suites [H]

(928) 718-4343. **$109-$219.** 3031 E Andy Devine Ave 86401. I-40 exit 53, just w on Route 66. Int corridors. **Pets:** Accepted.

[SAVE] 🛜 🛎 💻 🐾

Motel 6 - 1114 **M**
(928) 753-9222. **$39-$52.** 424 W Beale St 86401. I-40 exit 48, just se on Business Loop I-40/US 93. Ext corridors. **Pets:** Other species. Service with restrictions, supervision.

SpringHill Suites by Marriott **H**
(928) 753-8766. **$98-$123.** 3101 E Andy Devine Ave 86401. I-40 exit 53, just w on Route 66. Int corridors. **Pets:** Accepted.

Travelodge **M**
(928) 757-1188. **$50-$59.** 3275 E Andy Devine Ave 86401. I-40 exit 53, just e on Route 66. Ext corridors. **Pets:** Medium. $10 one-time fee/room. Designated rooms, service with restrictions, supervision.

KOHLS RANCH
Kohl's Ranch Lodge **CO**
(928) 478-4211. **Call for rates.** 202 S Kohl's Ranch Lodge Rd 85541. SR 87, 16.6 mi e on US 260, MM 238-239. Ext/int corridors. **Pets:** $20 daily fee/pet. Designated rooms, supervision.

LAKE HAVASU CITY
Days Inn Lake Havasu **M**
(928) 855-7841. **$40-$118.** 1700 McCulloch Blvd N 86403. Just ne of Lake Havasu Ave; center. Ext corridors. **Pets:** Other species. $5 daily fee/pet. Service with restrictions.

Hampton Inn Lake Havasu **H** ❧
(928) 855-4071. **$119-$149.** 245 London Bridge Rd 86403. 0.5 mi n of London Bridge. Ext/int corridors. **Pets:** Large, other species. Designated rooms, service with restrictions, supervision.

Havasu Travelodge **M**
(928) 680-9202. **$57-$144, 3 day notice.** 480 London Bridge Rd 86403. 1 mi n of London Bridge. Int corridors. **Pets:** Accepted.

Island Inn Hotel **H**
(928) 680-0606. **Call for rates.** 1300 W McCulloch Blvd 86403. 0.7 mi w of London Bridge/SR 95. Int corridors. **Pets:** Accepted.

Island Suites **H**
(928) 855-7333. **Call for rates.** 236 S Lake Havasu Ave 86403. Just s of jct McCulloch Blvd. Int corridors. **Pets:** Accepted.

Lake Havasu City Super 8 **M**
(928) 855-8844. **$50-$89.** 305 London Bridge Rd 86403. Just w of SR 95 exit Palo Verde Blvd; 0.5 mi n of London Bridge. Int corridors. **Pets:** Accepted.

Motel 6 Lakeside - #4067 **M**
(928) 855-3200. **Call for rates.** 111 London Bridge Rd 86403. 0.3 mi n of London Bridge. Int corridors. **Pets:** Other species. Service with restrictions, supervision.

The Nautical Beachfront Resort **H**
(928) 855-2141. **$69-$550, 3 day notice.** 1000 McCulloch Blvd N 86403. 1.4 mi w of London Bridge/SR 95, follow signs. Ext corridors. **Pets:** Accepted.

Quality Inn & Suites **M**
(928) 855-1111. **$65-$129.** 271 S Lake Havasu Ave 86403. SR 95, just e on Swanson Ave, then just s. Ext corridors. **Pets:** Other species. $50 deposit/room, $20 one-time fee/room. Service with restrictions.

MUNDS PARK
Motel In The Pines **M**
(928) 286-9699. **$39-$89.** 80 W Pinewood Rd 86017. I-17 exit 322, just e. Ext corridors. **Pets:** Large, other species. $15 daily fee/pet. Service with restrictions, supervision.

NOGALES
Candlewood Suites **H**
(520) 281-1111. **$99-$149.** 875 N Frank Reed Rd 85621. I-19 exit 4, just w to Frank Reed Rd, then just nw. Int corridors. **Pets:** Accepted.

Holiday Inn Express Hotel Nogales **H**
(520) 281-0123. **$99-$159.** 850 W Shell Rd 85621. I-19 exit 4, just w to Frank Reed Rd, then just nw. Int corridors. **Pets:** Accepted.

Motel 6 Nogales #71 **M**
(520) 281-2951. **$45-$61.** 141 W Mariposa Rd 85621. I-19 exit 4, 0.9 mi e. Ext corridors. **Pets:** Other species. Service with restrictions, supervision.

Siesta Motel **M**
(520) 287-4671. **$50-$60.** 673 N Grand Ave 85621. On Business Loop I-19, 1 mi n of International border. Ext corridors. **Pets:** Small, dogs only. $10 daily fee/pet. Designated rooms, service with restrictions, supervision.

PAGE
Lake Powell Days Inn & Suites **H**
(928) 645-2800. **$50-$163.** 961 N Hwy 89 86040. On US 89, just s. Int corridors. **Pets:** Other species. $15 daily fee/pet. Designated rooms, service with restrictions, supervision.

Lake Powell Resort and Marina **H** ❧
(928) 645-2433. **Call for rates.** 100 Lakeshore Dr 86040. 4 mi n of Glen Canyon Dam via US 89. Int corridors. **Pets:** $20 one-time fee/room. Designated rooms, service with restrictions, supervision.

PARKER
Best Western Parker Inn **M**
(928) 669-6060. **$69-$85.** 1012 Geronimo Ave 85344. SR 95, just e. Int corridors. **Pets:** Accepted.

Blue Water Resort & Casino **H**
(928) 669-7000. **Call for rates.** 11300 Resort Dr 85344. Jct SR 62, 1.3 mi nw on SR 95. Ext corridors. **Pets:** Accepted.

PAYSON
Americas Best Value Inn **M**
(928) 474-2283. **$50-$121.** 811 S Beeline Hwy 85541. SR 87, 0.7 mi s of SR 260. Ext/int corridors. **Pets:** Small, dogs only. $15 daily fee/pet. Designated rooms, service with restrictions, supervision.

Best Western Payson Inn **H** ❧
(928) 474-3241. **$60-$160.** 801 N Beeline Hwy 85541. SR 87, 0.6 mi n of SR 260. Ext corridors. **Pets:** Other species. $20 daily fee/room. Designated rooms, service with restrictions, supervision.

Paysonglo Lodge **M**
(928) 474-2382. **$49-$119.** 1005 S Beeline Hwy 85541. SR 87, 0.9 mi s of SR 260. Ext corridors. **Pets:** Medium. $15 daily fee/pet. Designated rooms, service with restrictions, supervision.

▼▼ **Wooden Nickel Cabins** 🄲🄰
(928) 478-4519. **Call for rates.** 165 Hunter Creek Dr 85541. SR 87, 22 mi e on SR 260, then 0.7 mi n; just w of MM 275, follow signs. Ext corridors. **Pets:** Accepted. ⊠ 🛆 💻 🗙 🏊

PEACH SPRINGS

🄰🄰🄰 ▼▼▼▼ **Hualapai Lodge** 🄷
(928) 769-2230. **$100-$120, 3 day notice.** 900 Historic Route 66 86434. Center. Int corridors. **Pets:** Medium. $25 daily fee/room. Designated rooms, service with restrictions, crate.

🆂🅰🆅🅴 📶 🛆🄼 🛆 💻 🍽 🏊

PHOENIX METROPOLITAN AREA

APACHE JUNCTION

🄰🄰🄰 ▼ **Apache Junction Motel** 🄼
(480) 982-7702. **$49-$89, 3 day notice.** 1680 W Apache Tr 85120. US 60 exit 195, 2 mi n, then just w. Ext corridors. **Pets:** Accepted.
🆂🅰🆅🅴 📶 🛆 💻

BUCKEYE

🄰🄰🄰 ▼▼▼ **Days Inn-Buckeye** 🄷
(623) 386-5400. **$56-$158.** 25205 W Yuma Rd 85326. I-10 exit 114 (Miller Rd), just sw. Ext corridors. **Pets:** Other species. $15 daily fee/pet. Service with restrictions, supervision. 🆂🅰🆅🅴 📶 🛆 💻 🏊

CAREFREE

🄰🄰🄰 ▼▼▼▼ **The Boulders, A Waldorf Astoria**
Resort 🄷
(480) 488-9009. **$149-$449.** 34631 N Tom Darlington Dr 85377. Scottsdale Rd, 11 mi n of Bell Rd. Ext corridors. **Pets:** Other species. $100 one-time fee/room. Supervision. 🆂🅰🆅🅴 📶 🗙 💻 🍽 🏊 🗙

🄰🄰🄰 ▼▼▼▼ **Carefree Resort & Conference Center** 🄷
(480) 488-5300. **$59-$870, 3 day notice.** 37220 Mule Train Rd 85377. SR 101 exit 36 (Pima Rd), 12.2 mi n to Cave Creek Rd, 1 mi w, then 0.4 mi n. Ext/int corridors. **Pets:** Medium, dogs only. $75 one-time fee/pet. Service with restrictions, supervision.
🆂🅰🆅🅴 📶 🗙 🛆 💻 🍽 🏊 🗙

CHANDLER

▼▼ **Chandler Super 8** 🄷 🐾
(480) 961-3888. **Call for rates.** 7171 W Chandler Blvd 85226. I-10 exit 160 (Chandler Blvd), just e. Int corridors. **Pets:** Large, other species. $100 deposit/room, $5 daily fee/pet. Designated rooms, service with restrictions, supervision. 📶 🛆 💻 🏊

🄰🄰🄰 ▼▼▼▼ **Crowne Plaza San Marcos Golf Resort** 🄷
(480) 812-0900. **$79-$229.** 1 San Marcos Pl 85225. Jct Chandler Blvd, just s on Arizona Ave, then just w on Buffalo St; in historic downtown. Ext corridors. **Pets:** Small. $50 one-time fee/room. Designated rooms, service with restrictions, supervision. 🆂🅰🆅🅴 📶 🛆 💻 🍽 🗙

🄰🄰🄰 ▼▼▼ **Hawthorn Suites by**
Wyndham-Chandler 🄷
(480) 705-8881. **$79-$199.** 5858 W Chandler Blvd 85226. I-10 exit 160 (Chandler Blvd), 1.5 mi e. Int corridors. **Pets:** Accepted.
🆂🅰🆅🅴 📶 🛆 💻 🏊

▼▼▼▼ **Hilton Phoenix Chandler** 🄷 🐾
(480) 899-7400. **$109-$229.** 2929 W Frye Rd 85224. SR 202 exit 50B (Price Rd), 0.4 mi n, then just w. Int corridors. **Pets:** Medium. $75 one-time fee/room. Service with restrictions. 📶 🛆 💻 🍽 🏊

▼▼▼▼ **Homewood Suites by Hilton Phoenix-Chandler** 🄷
(480) 753-6200. **$99-$189.** 7373 W Detroit St 85226. I-10 exit 160 (Chandler Blvd), 0.4 mi e, n on 54th St, then just w. Int corridors. **Pets:** Medium. $75 one-time fee/room. 📶 🛆🄼 🛆 💻 🏊 🗙

▼▼▼▼ **Homewood Suites by Hilton-Phoenix Chandler/**
Fashion Center 🄷
(480) 963-5700. **$109-$219.** 1221 S Spectrum Blvd 85286. SR 202 exit 50B (Price Rd), just s. Int corridors. **Pets:** Accepted.
📶 🛆🄼 🛆 💻 🏊 🗙

🄰🄰🄰 ▼▼▼ **Quality Inn** 🄷
(480) 705-0922. **$59-$139.** 255 N Kyrene Rd 85226. I-10 exit 160 (Chandler Blvd), 1.5 mi e, then just n. Int corridors. **Pets:** Other species. $20 one-time fee/room. 🆂🅰🆅🅴 📶 🗙 🛆🄼 🛆 💻 🏊

🄰🄰🄰 ▼▼▼ **Red Roof Inn-Chandler** 🄷
(480) 857-4969. **$75-$135.** 7400 W Boston St 85226. I-10 exit 160 (Chandler Blvd), just e, then s on Southgate Dr. Int corridors. **Pets:** Large, other species. No service, supervision.
🆂🅰🆅🅴 📶 🛆🄼 🛆 🏊

▼▼▼▼ **Residence Inn-Chandler Fashion Center** 🄷
(480) 782-1551. **$100-$190.** 200 N Federal St 85226. I-10 exit 160 (Chandler Blvd), 4.2 mi e, just n on N Metro Blvd, then just e. Int corridors. **Pets:** Accepted. 📶 🗙 🛆🄼 🛆 💻 🏊

🄰🄰🄰 ▼▼▼ **Sheraton Wild Horse Pass Resort &**
Spa 🄷 ❄
(602) 225-0100. **$319-$969, 7 day notice.** 5594 W Wild Horse Pass Blvd 85226. I-10 exit 162, 2.4 mi w. Int corridors. **Pets:** Medium, dogs only. Designated rooms, service with restrictions, supervision.
🆂🅰🆅🅴 📶 🗙 🛆 💻 🍽 🏊 🗙

🄰🄰🄰 ▼▼▼ **Windmill Suites of Chandler** 🄷
(480) 812-9600. **$80-$155.** 3535 W Chandler Blvd 85226. I-10 exit 160 (Chandler Blvd), 4 mi e. Int corridors. **Pets:** Accepted.
🆂🅰🆅🅴 📶 🗙 🛆 💻 🏊 🗙

FOUNTAIN HILLS

🄰🄰🄰 ▼▼▼ **Comfort Inn** 🄷
(480) 837-5343. **$100-$120.** 17105 E Shea Blvd 85268. 0.5 mi w of SR 87 (Beeline Hwy). Int corridors. **Pets:** Small. $30 deposit/pet, $15 one-time fee/pet. Designated rooms, service with restrictions, supervision.
🆂🅰🆅🅴 📶 🛆 💻 🏊

▼▼▼▼ **Holiday Inn Hotel & Suites-Fountain Hills/Mayo**
Clinic 🄷
(480) 837-6565. **$49-$159, 3 day notice.** 12800 N Saguaro Blvd 85268. Jct Shea Blvd, 2.2 mi n; center. Int corridors. **Pets:** Accepted.
📶 🗙 🛆🄼 🛆 💻 🏊 🗙

▼▼▼▼ **Inn at Eagle Mountain** 🄲🄸
(480) 816-3000. **$89-$279, 3 day notice.** 9800 N Summer Hill Blvd 85268. Loop 101 exit 41, 7.3 mi e on Shea Blvd, 0.3 mi e on Eagle Mountain Pkwy, then just w. Ext corridors. **Pets:** Accepted.
📶 🗙 🛆 💻 🍽 🏊 🗙

GLENDALE

🄰🄰🄰 ▼▼▼▼ **Comfort Suites Glendale** 🄷
(623) 271-9005. **$89-$299.** 9824 W Camelback Rd 85305. Loop 101 exit 5 (Camelback Rd), just w to 99th St, then just n. Int corridors.
Pets: Accepted. 🆂🅰🆅🅴 📶 🗙 🛆🄼 🛆 💻 🏊

▼▼▼▼ **Residence Inn Phoenix Glendale Sports &**
Entertainment District 🄷
(623) 772-8900. **$97-$219.** 7350 W Zanjero Blvd 85305. Loop 101 exit 7 (Glendale Ave), then e. Int corridors. **Pets:** Accepted.
📶 🗙 🛆🄼 🛆 💻 🏊 🗙

WWWW Staybridge Suites **H** ❖
(623) 842-0000. **$79-$340.** 9340 W Cabela Dr 85305. Loop 101 exit 7
(Glendale Ave), e on Zanjero Blvd, then left. Int corridors. **Pets:** Medium,
other species. $50 one-time fee/room. Service with restrictions.
📶 ✕ ⓜ 🛗 🖵 🏊

GOODYEAR

AAA WWWW Best Western Plus Phoenix Goodyear
Inn **H** ❖
(623) 932-3210. **$80-$170.** 55 N Litchfield Rd 85338. I-10 exit 128, 0.8
mi s. Ext/int corridors. **Pets:** $15 daily fee/room. Service with restrictions.
SAVE 📶 🛗 🖵 🍴 🏊

AAA WWWW Comfort Suites Goodyear **H** ❖
(623) 266-2884. **Call for rates.** 15575 W Roosevelt St 85338. I-10 exit
126, just s on Estrella Pkwy, then just w. Int corridors. **Pets:** Medium. $25
one-time fee/pet. Designated rooms, service with restrictions, supervision.
SAVE 📶 ✕ ⓜ 🛗 🖵 🏊

WWWW Hampton Inn & Suites **H**
(623) 536-1313. **Call for rates.** 2000 N Litchfield Rd 85395. I-10 exit
128, 0.5 mi n. Int corridors. **Pets:** Accepted.
📶 ⓜ 🛗 🖵 🏊 ✕

WWWW Holiday Inn Hotel & Suites **H** ❖
(623) 547-1313. **$159-$195.** 1188 N Dysart Rd 85395. I-10 exit 129
(Dysart Rd), just n. Int corridors. **Pets:** $35 one-time fee/room. Service
with restrictions, crate. 📶 🛗 🖵 🏊

WWWW Holiday Inn Express West Phoenix/Goodyear **H**
(623) 535-1313. **$109-$199.** 1313 N Litchfield Rd 85395. I-10 exit 128,
just n. Int corridors. **Pets:** Other species. $35 one-time fee/room. Service
with restrictions. 📶 ⓜ 🛗 🖵 🏊 ✕

WWWW Quality Inn & Suites Goodyear **H** ❖
(623) 932-9191. **$65-$180.** 950 N Dysart Rd 85338. I-10 exit 129 (Dysart
Rd), just s. Ext corridors. **Pets:** Medium, other species. $50 deposit/pet,
$15 daily fee/pet. Service with restrictions, supervision.
📶 🛗 🖵 🏊

WWWW Residence Inn by Marriott **H**
(623) 866-1313. **$82-$239.** 2020 N Litchfield Rd 85395. I-10 exit 128, 0.6
mi n. Int corridors. **Pets:** Accepted. 📶 ✕ 🛗 🖵 🏊 ✕

WWWW TownePlace Suites by Marriott
Phoenix/Goodyear **H** ❖
(623) 535-5009. **$74-$219.** 13971 W Fillmore St 85338. I-10 exit 128,
just s, then just w. Int corridors. **Pets:** Large, other species. $100 one-
time fee/room. Service with restrictions, crate.
📶 ✕ ⓜ 🛗 🖵 🏊

LITCHFIELD PARK

AAA WWWW WWWW The Wigwam **H**
(623) 935-3811. **$99-$1800, 3 day notice.** 300 Wigwam Blvd 85340.
I-10 exit 128 (Litchfield Rd), 2.4 mi n, then 0.4 mi e. Ext corridors.
Pets: Other species. $15 daily fee/room. Service with restrictions, crate.
SAVE 📶 ✕ 🛗 🖵 🍴 🏊 ✕

MESA

AAA WWWW Arizona Golf Resort & Conference
Center **H**
(480) 832-3202. **$89-$209.** 425 S Power Rd 85206. 1.3 mi n of US 60
(Superstition Frwy) exit 188 (Power Rd); southeast corner of Broadway
and Power rds; entrance on Broadway Rd. Ext corridors. **Pets:** Accepted.
SAVE 📶 ✕ 🛗 🖵 🍴 🏊 ✕

AAA WWWW Best Western Mezona Inn **H** ❖
(480) 834-9233. **$76-$175.** 250 W Main St 85201. Just e of Country
Club Dr; downtown. Ext corridors. **Pets:** $20 one-time fee/room. Desig-
nated rooms, service with restrictions, supervision.
SAVE 📶 🛗 🖵 🏊

AAA WWWW Best Western Superstition Springs **H** ❖
(480) 641-1164. **$75-$176.** 1342 S Power Rd 85206. Just n of US 60
(Superstition Frwy) exit 188 (Power Rd); northwest corner of Power Rd
and Hampton Ave. Ext corridors. **Pets:** Medium. $10 daily fee/pet. Desig-
nated rooms, service with restrictions, supervision.
SAVE 📶 🛗 🖵 🏊

WWWW Days Hotel **H**
(480) 844-8900. **$50-$126.** 333 W Juanita Ave 85210. US 60 (Superstition Frwy) exit 179 (Country Club Dr), just s, then just e. Int corridors.
Pets: Other species. $5 daily fee/pet. Service with restrictions, supervi-
sion. 📶 ✕ 🛗 🖵 🏊

AAA WWW Days Inn & Suites Mesa **H**
(480) 969-3600. **$40-$86.** 1750 E Main St 85203. US 60 (Superstition
Frwy) exit 182 (Gilbert Rd), 2.1 mi n, then 0.3 mi w. Ext corridors.
Pets: Accepted. SAVE 📶 🛗 🖵 🏊

AAA WWW Days Inn-East Mesa **H**
(480) 981-8111. **$45-$99.** 5531 E Main St 85205. 0.4 mi e of Higley Rd.
Ext corridors. **Pets:** Small, dogs only. $10 daily fee/pet. Designated
rooms, service with restrictions, crate. 📶 🛗 🖵 🏊

AAA WWWW Dobson Ranch Inn & Resort **H**
(480) 831-7000. **$72-$165.** 1666 S Dobson Rd 85202. Just s of US 60
(Superstition Frwy) exit 177 (Dobson Rd). Ext/int corridors. **Pets:** Medium,
dogs only. $50 deposit/room. Designated rooms, service with restrictions,
crate. SAVE 📶 ✕ 🛗 🖵 🍴 🏊

WWW Extended StayAmerica-Phoenix/Mesa **H** ❖
(480) 632-0201. **$60-$85.** 455 W Baseline Rd 85210. US 60 (Superstition
Frwy) exit 179 (Country Club Dr), 0.4 mi s on SR 87, then just w. Int
corridors. **Pets:** Other species. $25 daily fee/room. Service with restrictions.
📶 🛗 🖵

AAA WWWW Hilton Phoenix East/Mesa **H** ❖
(480) 833-5555. **$79-$189.** 1011 W Holmes Ave 85210. US 60 (Superstition Frwy) exit 178 (Alma School Rd), just n, then just e. Int corridors.
Pets: Medium. $75 one-time fee/room. Designated rooms, service with
restrictions, supervision. SAVE 📶 🛗 🖵 🍴 🏊 ✕

WWWW Holiday Inn Hotel & Suites **H**
(480) 964-7000. **$79-$209.** 1600 S Country Club Dr 85210. US 60
(Superstition Frwy) exit 179 (Country Club Dr), just s. Ext/int corridors.
Pets: Small. $50 one-time fee/room. Designated rooms, service with
restrictions, supervision. 📶 ✕ 🛗 🖵 🍴 🏊

WWW Homestead Studio Suites Hotel
Phoenix-Mesa **H** ❖
(480) 752-2266. **$60-$80.** 1920 W Isabella Ave 85202. Just s of US 60
(Superstition Frwy) exit 177 (Dobson Rd). Ext corridors. **Pets:** Other species. $25 daily fee/pet. Service with restrictions. 📶 🛗 🖵

WWWW Howard Johnson Inn Mesa **H** ❖
(480) 964-8000. **$50-$120.** 1625 E Main St 85203. 2 mi n of US 60
(Superstition Frwy) exit Stapley Dr, 0.5 mi e. Ext corridors. **Pets:** Medium,
other species. $10 daily fee/pet. Designated rooms, service with restric-
tions, supervision. 📶 🛗 🖵 🏊

WWWW La Quinta Inn & Suites Phoenix Mesa East **H**
(480) 654-1970. **$78-$192.** 6530 E Superstition Springs Blvd 85206. US
60 (Superstition Frwy) exit 187 (Superstition Springs Blvd) eastbound, just
se; exit 188 (Power Rd) westbound, just sw. Int corridors. **Pets:** Medium,
other species. Service with restrictions, supervision.
📶 ⓜ 🛗 🖵 🏊

WWWW La Quinta Inn & Suites Phoenix Mesa West **H**
(480) 844-8747. **$68-$170.** 902 W Grove Ave 85210. US 60 (Superstition
Frwy) exit 178 (Alma School Rd), just n, then just e. Int corridors. **Pets:**
Medium, other species. Service with restrictions, supervision.
📶 🛗 🖵 🏊

WWW Motel 6-Mesa South #1030 **M**
(480) 834-0066. **$45-$65.** 1511 S Country Club Dr 85210. US 60 (Superstition Frwy) exit 179 (Country Club Dr), northeast corner. Ext corridors.
Pets: Other species. Service with restrictions, supervision.
📶 ⓜ 🛗 🏊

▼▼ Quality Inn & Suites Mesa/Phoenix 🄷
(480) 964-2897. **$49-$109.** 1410 S Country Club Dr 85210. US 60 (Superstition Frwy) exit 179 (Country Club Dr), just n. Ext corridors. **Pets:** $10 daily fee/pet. Service with restrictions, supervision.
🛜 🔌 💻 🏊

▼▼▼ Residence Inn by Marriott Phoenix Mesa 🄷
(480) 610-0100. **$79-$229.** 941 W Grove Ave 85210. US 60 (Superstition Frwy) exit 178 (Alma School Rd), just n, then just e. Int corridors. **Pets:** Accepted. 🛜 ❌ 🅫 🔌 💻 🏊 🅧

▼▼ Sleep Inn of Mesa 🄷
(480) 807-7760. **$50-$160.** 6347 E Southern Ave 85206. US 60 (Superstition Frwy) exit 188 (Power Rd), 0.8 mi n, then 0.4 mi w to mall entrance. Int corridors. **Pets:** Accepted. 🛜 🔌 💻 🏊

▼ Travelodge Suites Mesa 🄷 🌢
(480) 832-5961. **$50-$200.** 4244 E Main St 85205. US 60 (Superstition Frwy) exit 185 (Greenfield Rd), 2 mi n, then just w. Ext corridors. **Pets:** Other species. $10 daily fee/pet. Designated rooms, service with restrictions, supervision. 🛜 🔌 💻 🏊

PARADISE VALLEY

▼▼▼ Hermosa Inn 🄷 🌢
(602) 955-8614. **$199-$549, 7 day notice.** 5532 N Palo Cristi Rd 85253. 1 mi s of Lincoln Dr; corner of Stanford Dr. Ext corridors. **Pets:** Dogs only. Designated rooms, service with restrictions, supervision.
🛜 ❌ 🔌 💻 🍽 🅧

⟨AAA⟩ ▼▼▼▼ Montelucia Resort & Spa 🄷 🌢
(480) 627-3200. **Call for rates.** 4949 E Lincoln Dr 85253. Southeast corner of Lincoln Dr and Tatum Blvd, enter from Lincoln Dr. Ext/int corridors. **Pets:** Small. $100 one-time fee/room. Service with restrictions, supervision. 🆂🅰🆅🅴 🛜 🔌 💻 🍽 🏊 🅧

⟨AAA⟩ ▼▼▼▼ Sanctuary on Camelback Mountain 🄷 🌢
(480) 948-2100. **$199-$849, 7 day notice.** 5700 E McDonald Dr 85253. SR 101 exit McDonald Dr, 3.9 mi w; 1.8 mi w of jct Scottsdale Rd. Ext corridors. **Pets:** Medium. $100 one-time fee/room. Service with restrictions, supervision. 🆂🅰🆅🅴 🛜 ❌ 💻 🍽 🏊 🅧

PEORIA

▼▼ Comfort Suites by Choice Hotels/Peoria Sports Complex 🄷
(623) 334-3993. **$59-$199.** 8473 W Paradise Ln 85382. Loop 101 exit 14 (Bell Rd), just e to 83rd Ave, just s, then just w. Int corridors. **Pets:** Accepted. 🛜 ❌ 🔌 💻 🏊

▼▼ Extended StayAmerica Phoenix-Peoria 🄷 🌢
(623) 487-0020. **$60-$80.** 7345 W Bell Rd 85382. Loop 101 exit 14 (Bell Rd), 1.2 mi e. Int corridors. **Pets:** Other species. $25 daily fee/pet. Service with restrictions. 🛜 🔌 💻

▼▼▼ Hampton Inn 🄷
(623) 486-9918. **$69-$199.** 8408 W Paradise Ln 85382. Loop 101 exit 14 (Bell Rd), just e to 83rd Ave, just s, then just w. Int corridors. **Pets:** Accepted. 🛜 🔌 💻 🏊

▼▼▼ Holiday Inn Express Hotel & Suites Peoria North/Glendale 🄷
(623) 853-1313. **$79-$229.** 16771 N 84th Ave 85382. Loop 101 exit 14 (Bell Rd), just w, then just s. Int corridors. **Pets:** Accepted.
🛜 🅫 🔌 💻 🏊

▼▼▼ La Quinta Inn & Suites Phoenix West Peoria 🄷
(623) 487-1900. **$78-$280.** 16321 N 83rd Ave 85382. Loop 101 exit 14 (Bell Rd), just e, then just s. Int corridors. **Pets:** Medium, other species. Service with restrictions, supervision. 🛜 ❌ 🔌 💻 🏊

▼▼ Ramada Peoria Convention Center 🄷 🌢
(623) 979-7200. **Call for rates.** 8955 W Grand Ave 85345. Loop 101 N exit 11 (Grand Ave), 0.5 mi e. Int corridors. **Pets:** Medium, other species. $10 daily fee/pet. Designated rooms, supervision.
🛜 ❌ 🔌 🍽 🏊

▼▼▼ Residence Inn by Marriott 🄷 🌢
(623) 979-2074. **$95-$285.** 8435 W Paradise Ln 85382. Loop 101 exit 14 (Bell Rd), just e, just s on 83rd Ave, then just w. Int corridors. **Pets:** Medium, other species. $100 one-time fee/room. Service with restrictions, supervision. 🛜 ❌ 🔌 💻 🏊 🅧

PHOENIX

⟨AAA⟩ ▼▼▼ Aloft Phoenix Airport Hotel 🄷 🌢
(602) 275-6300. **$79-$229.** 4450 E Washington St 85034. SR 143 exit Washington St, just w. Int corridors. **Pets:** Medium, dogs only. Service with restrictions, supervision. 🆂🅰🆅🅴 🛜 ❌ 🅫 🔌 💻 🏊

⟨AAA⟩ ▼▼▼▼ Arizona Biltmore, A Waldorf Astoria Hotel 🄷
(602) 955-6600. **$109-$299.** 2400 E Missouri Ave 85016. Jct Camelback Rd, 0.5 mi n on 24th St, then 0.4 mi e. Ext/int corridors. **Pets:** Accepted.
🄴🄲🄾 🆂🅰🆅🅴 🛜 🔌 💻 🍽 🏊

⟨AAA⟩ ▼▼▼ Best Western Phoenix I-17 MetroCenter Inn 🄷 🌢
(602) 864-6233. **Call for rates.** 8101 N Black Canyon Hwy 85021. I-17 exit 206 (Northern Ave), just e, then just n; on east side of freeway. Ext corridors. **Pets:** Other species. $100 deposit/room, $20 daily fee/pet. Designated rooms, service with restrictions, supervision.
🆂🅰🆅🅴 🛜 🔌 💻 🏊

⟨AAA⟩ ▼▼▼ Best Western Plus InnSuites Phoenix Hotel & Suites 🄷 🌢
(602) 997-6285. **$75-$159.** 1615 E Northern Ave 85020. SR 51 exit 7, 0.6 mi w. Ext corridors. **Pets:** Large. $25 one-time fee/room. Designated rooms, service with restrictions, crate. 🆂🅰🆅🅴 🛜 🔌 💻 🏊

▼▼ Candlewood Suites Phoenix 🄷
(602) 861-6940. **$79-$139.** 11411 N Black Canyon Hwy 85029. I-17 exit 208 (Peoria Ave), just e, then 0.4 mi n. Int corridors. **Pets:** Accepted.
🔌 💻 🏊

⟨AAA⟩ ▼▼▼ Clarion Hotel @ Phoenix Tech Center 🄷
(480) 893-3900. **$59-$189.** 5121 E La Puenta Ave 85044. I-10 exit 157 (Elliot Rd), just w, just n on 51st St, then just e. Ext corridors. **Pets:** Other species. $25 one-time fee/room. Service with restrictions, supervision. 🆂🅰🆅🅴 🛜 🔌 💻 🏊

⟨AAA⟩ ▼▼ Comfort Inn I-10 West/Central 🄷
(602) 415-1623. **Call for rates.** 1344 N 27th Ave 85009. I-10 exit 27th Ave eastbound, just n; exit 141 (35th Ave) westbound, just n, 1 mi e on McDowell Rd, then s. Int corridors. **Pets:** Accepted.
🆂🅰🆅🅴 🛜 🔌 💻 🏊

⟨AAA⟩ ▼▼▼▼ Comfort Inn-Phoenix North 🄷
(602) 978-2222. **$59-$129.** 2641 W Union Hills Dr 85027. I-17 exit 214A (Union Hills Dr), just w. Int corridors. **Pets:** Medium, other species. $10 daily fee/room. Service with restrictions, supervision.
🆂🅰🆅🅴 🛜 🔌 💻 🍽 🏊

▼▼▼ Comfort Suites by Choice Hotels 🄷 🌢
(602) 861-3900. **$59-$150.** 10210 N 26th Dr 85021. I-17 exit 208 (Peoria Ave), just e, just s on 25th Ave, then 0.3 mi w on W Beryl Ave. Int corridors. **Pets:** Large. $25 one-time fee/pet. Service with restrictions.
🛜 ❌ 🅫 🔌 💻 🏊

▼▼▼ Crowne Plaza Phoenix 🄷
(602) 943-2341. **$99-$179.** 2532 W Peoria Ave 85029. I-17 exit 208 (Peoria Ave), just e, then just n on 25th Ave. Int corridors. **Pets:** Accepted. 🛜 ❌ 🅫 🔌 🍽 🏊

⟨AAA⟩ ▼▼▼ Crowne Plaza Phoenix Airport 🄷
(602) 273-7778. **$79-$169.** 4300 E Washington St 85034. SR 202 exit 2 (44th St), 0.7 mi s. Int corridors. **Pets:** Accepted.
🆂🅰🆅🅴 🛜 🔌 💻 🍽 🏊

▼▼▼▼ **Drury Inn & Suites Phoenix Pinnacle Peak** �H
(623) 879-8800. **$85-$204.** 2335 W Pinnacle Peak Rd 85027. I-17 exit 217 (Pinnacle Peak Rd), just e. Int corridors. **Pets:** Accepted.
📶 🔊 🛏 💻 🏊

🅐🅐🅐 ▼▼▼ **Econo Lodge Airport** Ⓜ
(602) 273-1601. **$55-$65.** 3037 E Van Buren St 85008. SR 202 exit 1C (32nd St), 0.6 mi s, then just w. Ext corridors. **Pets:** Accepted.
SAVE 📶 🏊

🅐🅐🅐 ▼▼▼ **Embassy Suites Phoenix Airport at 24th St** �H
(602) 957-1910. **$79-$209.** 2333 E Thomas Rd 85016. SR 51 exit 2 (44th St), just e. Ext corridors. **Pets:** Accepted.
SAVE 📶 🛏 💻 🍴 🏊

▼▼▼▼ **Embassy Suites Phoenix-Biltmore** �H
(602) 955-3992. **$99-$299.** 2630 E Camelback Rd 85016. Just n of Camelback Rd, on 26th St. Int corridors. **Pets:** Medium. $50 one-time fee/room. Service with restrictions, supervision. 📶 🛏 💻 🍴 🏊

🅐🅐🅐 ▼▼▼ **Embassy Suites Phoenix North** �H
(602) 375-1777. **$59-$159.** 2577 W Greenway Rd 85023. I-17 exit 211, just e. Ext corridors. **Pets:** $50 one-time fee/room. Service with restrictions, supervision. SAVE 📶 🛏 💻 🍴 🏊 ❌

▼▼ ▼▼ **Extended StayAmerica-Phoenix-Chandler** �H ✿
(480) 785-0464. **$65-$90.** 14245 S 50th St 85044. I-10 exit 159, just w on Ray Rd, just s, then just e. Int corridors. **Pets:** Other species. $25 daily fee/pet. Service with restrictions. 📶 🔊 🛏 💻

▼▼ ▼▼ **Extended StayAmerica Phoenix-Chandler-E Chandler Blvd** �H ✿
(480) 753-6700. **$65-$90.** 5035 E Chandler Blvd 85048. I-10 exit 160 (Chandler Blvd), just w. Ext corridors. **Pets:** Other species. $25 daily fee/pet. Service with restrictions. 📶 🛏 💻 🏊

▼▼ ▼▼ **Extended StayAmerica Phoenix-Deer Valley** �H ✿
(623) 879-6609. **$50-$75.** 20827 N 27th Ave 85027. I-10 exit 215 (Rose Garden Ln) northbound, just w; exit 215B southbound, just w, then 0.4 mi s. Int corridors. **Pets:** Other species. $25 daily fee/pet. Service with restrictions. 📶 🛏 💻

▼▼ ▼▼ **Extended Stay Deluxe Phoenix-Biltmore** �H ✿
(602) 265-6800. **$75-$105.** 5235 N 16th St 85016. Jct SR 51, just w on Camelback Rd, then just n. Int corridors. **Pets:** Other species. $25 daily fee/pet. Service with restrictions. 📶 🛏 💻 🏊

▼▼ ▼▼ **Extended Stay Deluxe (Phoenix/Midtown)** �H ✿
(602) 279-9000. **$75-$95.** 217 W Osborn Rd 85013. Just w of Central Ave; between Indian School and Thomas rds. Int corridors. **Pets:** Other species. $25 daily fee/pet. Service with restrictions.
📶 🔊 🛏 💻 🏊

🅐🅐🅐 ▼▼▼▼ **Hilton Phoenix Airport** �H ✿
(480) 894-1600. **$109-$229.** 2435 S 47th St 85034. I-10 exit 151 (University Dr), 2 mi n, then just w. Int corridors. **Pets:** Large, dogs only. $25 one-time fee/pet. Service with restrictions, supervision.
SAVE 📶 🛏 💻 🍴 🏊

▼▼▼▼ **Hilton Suites-Phoenix** �H
(602) 222-1111. **$79-$269.** 10 E Thomas Rd 85012. Just e of Central Ave; in Phoenix Plaza. Int corridors. **Pets:** Accepted.
📶 🔊 🛏 💻 🍴 🏊 ❌

▼▼▼▼ **Holiday Inn Phoenix West** �H
(602) 484-9009. **$89-$149.** 1500 N 51st Ave 85043. I-10 exit 139 (51st Ave), just n. Int corridors. **Pets:** Accepted.
📶 🔊 🛏 💻 🍴 🏊

▼▼▼▼ **Homewood Suites by Hilton Phoenix-Biltmore** �H ✿
(602) 508-0937. **$89-$159.** 2001 E Highland Ave 85016. Just e of 20th St. Int corridors. **Pets:** Large. $75 one-time fee/room. Crate.
📶 🛏 💻 ❌

▼▼▼▼ **Homewood Suites by Hilton Phoenix Metrocenter** �H
(602) 674-8900. **$72-$189.** 2536 W Beryl Ave 85021. I-17 exit 208 (Peoria Ave), just e, just s on 25th Ave, then just w. Int corridors. **Pets:** Medium, other species. $50 one-time fee/room. Service with restrictions. 📶 🔊 🛏 💻

▼▼▼▼ **Homewood Suites Phoenix North/Happy Valley** �H
(623) 580-1800. **$99-$199.** 2470 W Charlotte Dr 85085. I-17 exit 217 (Pinnacle Peak Rd), 0.6 mi n on Frontage Rd. Int corridors.
Pets: Accepted. 📶 🔊 🛏 💻 🏊 ❌

▼▼▼▼ **Hotel Highland at Biltmore** �H
(602) 956-5221. **$69-$189.** 2310 E Highland Ave 85016. Just sw of Camelback Rd and 24th St. Int corridors. **Pets:** Accepted.
📶 ❌ 🔊 🛏 💻

🅐🅐🅐 ▼▼▼ **Howard Johnson Inn Airport Downtown** Ⓜ
(602) 275-5746. **$49-$100.** 4120 E Van Buren St 85008. SR 202 exit 2 (44th St), 0.5 mi s, then just w. Ext corridors. **Pets:** Very small, dogs only. $10 daily fee/pet. Designated rooms, service with restrictions, supervision. SAVE 📶 🛏 💻 🏊

▼▼▼▼ **La Quinta Inn & Suites Phoenix Chandler** �H
(480) 961-7700. **$58-$177.** 15241 S 50th St 85044. I-10 exit 160 (Chandler Blvd), just w, then just n. Int corridors. **Pets:** Medium, other species. Service with restrictions, supervision. 📶 🔊 🛏 💻 🏊

▼▼▼▼ **La Quinta Inn & Suites Phoenix I-10 West** �H
(602) 595-7601. **$81-$179.** 4929 W McDowell Rd 85035. I-10 exit 139 (51st Ave), just n, then just e. Int corridors. **Pets:** Medium, other species. Service with restrictions, supervision. 📶 ❌ 🛏 💻 🏊

▼▼ ▼▼ **La Quinta Inn Phoenix-Arcadia** �H
(602) 956-6500. **$71-$134.** 4727 E Thomas Rd 85018. Just w of 48th St. Ext/int corridors. **Pets:** Medium, other species. Service with restrictions, supervision. 📶 ❌ 🛏 💻 🏊

▼▼ ▼▼ **La Quinta Inn Phoenix North** �H
(602) 993-0800. **$48-$166.** 2510 W Greenway Rd 85023. I-17 exit 211, just e. Ext corridors. **Pets:** Medium, other species. Service with restrictions, supervision. 📶 🛏 💻 🏊 ❌

▼▼ ▼▼ **La Quinta Inn Phoenix Thomas Road** Ⓜ
(602) 258-6271. **$52-$144.** 2725 N Black Canyon Hwy 85009. I-17 exit 201 (Thomas Rd), just e, then just s; on east side of freeway. Ext corridors. **Pets:** Medium, other species. Service with restrictions, supervision.
📶 ❌ 🔊 🛏 💻 🏊

▼▼ **Motel 6 Phoenix East #18** Ⓜ
(602) 267-8555. **$45-$55.** 5315 E Van Buren St 85008. SR 202 E exit 4 (52nd St/Van Buren St), just s, then just e. Ext corridors. **Pets:** Other species. Service with restrictions, supervision. 📶 🛏 🏊

▼▼ **Motel 6 Phoenix-North #344** Ⓜ
(602) 993-2353. **$49-$59.** 2330 W Bell Rd 85023. I-17 exit 212, just e. Ext corridors. **Pets:** Other species. Service with restrictions, supervision.
📶 🏊

▼▼ **Motel 6 Phoenix West #696** Ⓜ
(602) 272-0220. **$49-$59.** 1530 N 52nd Dr 85043. I-10 exit 139 (51st Ave), just n to McDowell Rd, just w, then just s. Ext corridors.
Pets: Other species. Service with restrictions, supervision. 🛏 🏊

🅐🅐🅐 ▼▼▼▼ **Pointe Hilton Squaw Peak Resort** �H ✿
(602) 997-2626. **$89-$219.** 7677 N 16th St 85020. SR 51 exit Glendale Ave, 0.4 mi w, then 0.6 mi n. Ext corridors. **Pets:** Other species. $75 one-time fee/room. Service with restrictions.
SAVE ❌ 🛏 💻 🍴 🏊 ❌

⚑ ▼▼▼ ▼▼▼ Pointe Hilton Tapatio Cliffs Resort H
(602) 866-7500. **$89-$219.** 11111 N 7th St 85020. I-17 exit 207 (Dunlap Ave), 3 mi e, then 2 mi n. Ext corridors. **Pets:** Accepted.
[ECO] [SAVE] 🛰 ✕ 🔥M 🛏 💻 🛎 🏊 ✕

⚑ ▼▼ Quality Inn & Suites H
(602) 242-8011. **$55-$80.** 5050 N Black Canyon Hwy 85017. I-17 exit 203 (Camelback Rd), just w, then just n; on west side of freeway. Ext corridors. **Pets:** Small, dogs only. $15 one-time fee/pet. Designated rooms, service with restrictions, supervision. [SAVE] 🛰 🛏 💻 🏊

⚑ ▼▼ Red Roof Inn Phoenix West H
(602) 233-8004. **$50-$126.** 5215 W Willetta 85043. I-10 exit 139 (51st Ave), just n, just e on McDowell Rd, then just s. Int corridors. **Pets:** Large, other species. No service, supervision.
[SAVE] 🛰 🔥M 🛏 💻 🏊

▼▼▼ Residence Inn by Marriott Phoenix H
(602) 864-1900. **Call for rates.** 8242 N Black Canyon Hwy 85051. I-17 exit 207 (Dunlap Ave), just w, then 0.8 mi s; on frontage road. Ext/int corridors. **Pets:** Accepted. 🛰 ✕ 🔥M 🛏 💻 🏊 ✕

▼▼▼ Residence Inn by Marriott Phoenix Airport H
(602) 273-9220. **$119-$239.** 801 N 44th St 85008. SR 202 exit 2 (44th St), just s. Int corridors. **Pets:** Accepted.
[ECO] 🛰 ✕ 🔥M 🛏 💻 🏊 ✕

▼▼▼ Residence Inn by Marriott Phoenix North/Happy Valley H
(623) 580-8833. **$79-$154.** 2035 W Whispering Wind Dr 85085. I-17 exit 128 (Happy Valley Rd), 0.4 mi e to 23rd Ave, just s, then just e. Int corridors. **Pets:** Accepted. 🛰 ✕ 🛏 💻 🏊 ✕

▼▼▼ The Ritz-Carlton, Phoenix H
(602) 468-0700. **Call for rates.** 2401 E Camelback Rd 85016. Southeast corner of Camelback Rd and 24th St. Int corridors. **Pets:** Accepted.
🛰 ✕ 🛏 💻 🍴 🏊 ✕

⚑ ▼▼ ▼▼ Royal Palms Resort and Spa H
(602) 840-3610. **$179-$599, 7 day notice.** 5200 E Camelback Rd 85018. Just e of 52nd St. Ext/int corridors. **Pets:** Accepted.
[ECO] [SAVE] 🛰 ✕ 🛏 💻 🍴 🏊 ✕

⚑ ▼▼▼ Sheraton Crescent Hotel H ❀
(602) 943-8200. **$125-$635.** 2620 W Dunlap Ave 85021. I-17 exit 207 (Dunlap Ave), just e. Int corridors. **Pets:** Medium. Service with restrictions, crate. [SAVE] 🛰 ✕ 🔥M 🛏 💻 🍴 🏊 ✕

⚑ ▼▼ ▼▼ Sheraton Phoenix Downtown Hotel H
(602) 262-2500. **$299-$729.** 340 N 3rd St 85004. I-10 exit 145A (7th St), 0.5 mi s to Fillmore St, just w, then just s. Int corridors. **Pets:** Accepted.
[ECO] [SAVE] 🛰 🔥M 🛏 💻 🍴 🏊 ✕

⚑ ▼▼ Sleep Inn Phoenix Airport H
(480) 967-7100. **$60-$150.** 2621 S 47th Pl 85034. I-10 exit 151 (University Dr), 2 mi n, then just w. Int corridors. **Pets:** Accepted.
[SAVE] 🛰 🛏 💻 🏊

⚑ ▼▼ Sleep Inn Phoenix North H
(602) 504-1200. **$60-$130.** 18235 N 27th Ave 85053. I-17 exit 214A (Union Hills Dr), just w, then just s. Int corridors. **Pets:** Small. $50 deposit/pet, $15 daily fee/pet. Designated rooms, service with restrictions, crate. [SAVE] 🛰 🔥M 🛏 💻 🏊

⚑ ▼▼ ▼▼ Super 8-Downtown Phoenix M
(602) 252-6823. **$45-$63.** 965 E Van Buren St 85006. I-10 exit 145 (7th St), just s, then just e. Ext corridors. **Pets:** Medium, other species. $25 one-time fee/room. Designated rooms, service with restrictions, supervision. [SAVE] 🛰 ✕ 🛏 💻 🏊

⚑ ▼▼ ▼▼ Super 8 Phoenix Metro North M
(602) 995-8451. **$33-$71.** 8130 N Black Canyon Hwy 85051. I-17 exit 206 (Northern Ave), just w, then just n on west side of freeway. Ext corridors. **Pets:** Medium, other species. $10 daily fee/pet. Service with restrictions, supervision. [SAVE] 🛰 🛏 💻 🏊

▼▼ ▼▼ Super 8-Phoenix West H
(602) 415-0888. **$45-$81.** 1242 N 53rd Ave 85043. I-10 exit 139 (51st Ave), just s to Latham Rd, then just w. Int corridors. **Pets:** Small. $20 daily fee/pet. Service with restrictions, crate. 🛰 🛏 💻 🏊

▼▼ ▼▼ TownePlace Suites Phoenix North H
(602) 943-9510. **$59-$149.** 9425 N Black Canyon Frwy 85021. I-17 exit 207 (Dunlap Ave), just e, then 0.3 mi n. Int corridors. **Pets:** Accepted.
🛰 ✕ 🛏 💻 🏊

⚑ ▼▼ ▼▼ The Westin Phoenix Downtown H
(602) 429-3500. **$369-$589, 3 day notice.** 333 N Central Ave 85004. Northeast corner of Central Ave and Van Buren St. Int corridors.
Pets: Accepted. [SAVE] 🛰 ✕ 🔥M 🛏 💻 🍴 🏊

SCOTTSDALE

⚑ ▼▼▼ Best Western Plus Sundial H
(480) 994-4170. **$100-$250.** 7320 E Camelback Rd 85251. Just e of Scottsdale Rd. Ext corridors. **Pets:** Accepted.
[SAVE] 🛰 ✕ 🔥M 🛏 💻 🏊

⚑ ▼▼▼ The Canyon Suites at The Phoenician H ❀
(480) 423-2880. **$299-$2500, 7 day notice.** 6000 E Camelback Rd 85251. 0.5 mi w of 64th St; in The Phoenician. Int corridors.
Pets: Medium. Designated rooms, service with restrictions, supervision.
[SAVE] 🛰 🔥M 🍴 🏊 ✕

⚑ ▼▼▼ Chaparral Suites Scottsdale H 🐾
(480) 949-1414. **$99-$279.** 5001 N Scottsdale Rd 85250. At Chaparral Rd. Ext corridors. **Pets:** Dogs only. $25 one-time fee/pet. Service with restrictions, supervision. [SAVE] 🛰 🔥M 🛏 💻 🍴 🏊 ✕

⚑ ▼▼▼ Clarion Hotel Scottsdale H
(480) 945-4392. **$79-$119.** 5101 N Scottsdale Rd 85250. Just n of Chaparral Rd. Ext corridors. **Pets:** Accepted.
[SAVE] 🛰 ✕ 🔥M 🛏 💻 🍴 🏊

▼▼ ▼▼ Comfort Suites by Choice Hotels-Old Town H 🐾
(480) 946-1111. **$70-$170.** 3275 N Drinkwater Blvd 85251. N of Thomas Rd; just e of Scottsdale Rd. Int corridors. **Pets:** Medium. $25 one-time fee/pet. Designated rooms, service with restrictions, supervision.
🛰 ✕ 🔥M 🛏 💻 🏊

▼▼ ▼▼ Country Inn & Suites By Carlson H 🐾
(480) 314-1200. **$59-$209, 3 day notice.** 10801 N 89th Pl 85260. SR 101 exit 41, just e on Shea Blvd, then just n. Int corridors. **Pets:** Small. $15 daily fee/room. Designated rooms, service with restrictions, supervision. 🛰 ✕ 🛏 💻 🏊

⚑ ▼▼ ▼▼ Courtyard Scottsdale at Mayo Clinic H ❀
(480) 860-4000. **$75-$195.** 13444 E Shea Blvd 85259. SR 101 exit 41, 5.8 mi e. Int corridors. **Pets:** Small. $50 one-time fee/pet. Service with restrictions, crate. [ECO] [SAVE] 🛰 ✕ 🔥M 🛏 💻 🍴 🏊

⚑ ▼▼ ▼▼ Days Inn Scottsdale Fashion Square M ❀
(480) 947-5411. **$44-$144.** 4710 N Scottsdale Rd 85251. Just n of Camelback Rd. Ext corridors. **Pets:** Medium, other species. $25 one-time fee/room. Service with restrictions, crate. [SAVE] 🛰 🛏 💻 🏊

⚑ ▼▼▼ ▼▼ DoubleTree Resort by Hilton Paradise Valley - Scottsdale H
(480) 947-5400. **$89-$239.** 5401 N Scottsdale Rd 85250. Just n of Chaparral Rd; on east side of Scottsdale Rd. Ext corridors. **Pets:** Accepted.
[SAVE] 🛰 🛏 💻 🍴 🏊 ✕

▼▼ ▼▼ Extended StayAmerica-Phoenix-Scottsdale H ❀
(480) 607-3767. **$70-$95.** 15501 N Scottsdale Rd 85254. SR 101 exit Frank Lloyd Wright Blvd, 2 mi w, 0.5 mi s on Scottsdale Rd, then just e on Tierra Buena Ln. Ext corridors. **Pets:** Other species. $25 daily fee/pet. Service with restrictions. 🛰 🛏 💻

Extended Stay Deluxe Phoenix-Scottsdale 🏨 🐾
(480) 483-1333. **$75-$110.** 10660 N 69th St 85254. Jct Scottsdale Rd, just w on Shea Blvd, then just n. Int corridors. **Pets:** Other species. $25 daily fee/pet. Service with restrictions. 🛰️🍴💻🏊

Fairmont Scottsdale Princess 🏨 🐾
(480) 585-4848. **$134-$2699, 7 day notice.** 7575 E Princess Dr 85255. SR 101 exit 34 (Scottsdale Rd), 0.8 mi s, then just e; 0.6 mi n of Bell Rd. Ext/int corridors. **Pets:** Small. $25 daily fee/pet. Designated rooms, service with restrictions, supervision.
🌿 💾 🛰️ 🖥️ 🍴 💻 🍴 🏊 ⚔️

FireSky Resort & Spa, A Kimpton Hotel 🏨
(480) 945-7666. **$115-$469, 3 day notice.** 4925 N Scottsdale Rd 85251. Southeast corner of Scottsdale and Chaparral rds. Int corridors.
Pets: Accepted. 🌿 💾 🛰️ ⚔️ 🖥️ 🍴 💻 🏊 ⚔️

Four Seasons Resort Scottsdale at Troon North 🏨
(480) 515-5700. **$129-$719, 7 day notice.** 10600 E Crescent Moon Dr 85262. SR 101 exit 36 (Pima Rd), 4.7 mi n, 2 mi e on Happy Valley Rd, then 1.5 mi n on Alma School Rd. Ext corridors. **Pets:** Accepted.
💾 🛰️ ⚔️ 🖥️ 🍴 💻 🍴 🏊 ⚔️

Gainey Suites Hotel 🏨
(480) 922-6969. **$99-$259.** 7300 E Gainey Suites Dr 85258. Just e of Scottsdale Rd. Int corridors. **Pets:** Small, dogs only. $100 deposit/room. Service with restrictions, crate. 💾 🛰️ ⚔️ 🍴 💻 🏊 ⚔️

Hampton Inn Scottsdale 🏨
(480) 443-3233. **$59-$199.** 10101 N Scottsdale Rd 85253. Just s of Shea Blvd. Int corridors. **Pets:** Accepted. 🛰️ ⚔️ 🖥️ 🍴 💻 🏊

Hilton Scottsdale Resort & Villas 🏨
(480) 948-7750. **$99-$249.** 6333 N Scottsdale Rd 85250. SR 101 exit 45, 2.1 mi w on McDonald Dr, then 0.3 mi n. Int corridors.
Pets: Accepted. 💾 🛰️ ⚔️ 🖥️ 🍴 💻 🍴 🏊 ⚔️

Holiday Inn Express Hotel & Suites-Scottsdale 🏨
(480) 675-7665. **$69-$229, 3 day notice.** 3131 N Scottsdale Rd 85251. Northeast corner of Scottsdale Rd and Earll Dr. Int corridors.
Pets: Accepted. 💾 🛰️ 🖥️ 🍴 💻 🏊

Holiday Inn Express Scottsdale North 🏨
(480) 596-6559. **$119-$249, 3 day notice.** 7350 E Gold Dust Ave 85258. Just e of Scottsdale Rd; just s of Shea Blvd; on north side of Gold Dust Ave. Int corridors. **Pets:** Accepted.
🛰️ ⚔️ 🖥️ 🍴 💻 🏊

Homestead Studio Suites Hotel-Phoenix-Scottsdale Ⓜ 🐾
(480) 994-0297. **$65-$85.** 3560 N Marshall Way 85251. Just w of Scottsdale Rd on Goldwater, just s. Ext corridors. **Pets:** Other species. $25 daily fee/pet. Service with restrictions. 🛰️ 🖥️ 🍴 💻 🏊

Homewood Suites by Hilton Scottsdale 🏨
(480) 368-8705. **$59-$269.** 9880 N Scottsdale Rd 85253. 0.5 mi s of Shea Blvd. Int corridors. **Pets:** Accepted. 🛰️ 🍴 💻 ⚔️

Hotel Indigo Scottsdale 🏨 🐾
(480) 941-9400. **$99-$259.** 4415 N Civic Center Plaza 85251. Scottsdale Rd, just e on Camelback Rd, just s on 75th St. Ext/int corridors. **Pets:** Medium, dogs only. Service with restrictions, supervision.
💾 🛰️ ⚔️ 🖥️ 🍴 💻 🍴 🏊

Hotel Valley Ho 🏨
(480) 248-2000. **$89-$359.** 6850 E Main St 85251. 0.4 mi w of Scottsdale Rd, just s of Indian School Rd; on north side of Main St. Ext/int corridors. **Pets:** Accepted.
🌿 💾 🛰️ ⚔️ 🍴 💻 🍴 🏊 ⚔️

Hyatt Summerfield Suites Scottsdale/Old Town 🏨
(480) 946-7700. **$79-$499.** 4245 N Drinkwater Blvd 85251. 0.3 mi e of Scottsdale Rd. Ext corridors. **Pets:** Accepted.
💾 🛰️ ⚔️ 🍴 🍴 💻 🏊

Hyatt Regency Scottsdale Resort & Spa at Gainey Ranch 🏨 🐾
(480) 444-1234. **$129-$605, 3 day notice.** 7500 E Doubletree Ranch Rd 85258. SR 101 exit 43, 2.6 mi w on Via de Ventura. Ext/int corridors. **Pets:** Medium, other species. $50 daily fee/pet. Designated rooms, service with restrictions. 🌿 💾 🛰️ 🍴 🍴 💻 🍴 🏊 ⚔️

JW Marriott Camelback Inn Resort & Spa 🏨
(480) 948-1700. **$134-$549, 3 day notice.** 5402 E Lincoln Dr 85253. 0.5 mi e of Tatum Blvd; on north side of Lincoln Dr. Ext corridors. **Pets:** Large. $75 one-time fee/room. Service with restrictions, crate.
💾 🛰️ ⚔️ 🍴 🍴 💻 🍴 🏊 ⚔️

La Quinta Inn & Suites Phoenix Scottsdale 🏨
(480) 614-5300. **$64-$192.** 8888 E Shea Blvd 85260. SR 101 exit Shea Blvd; northeast corner. Int corridors. **Pets:** Medium, other species. Service with restrictions, supervision. 🛰️ ⚔️ 🍴 🍴 💻

Marriott Scottsdale McDowell Mountain 🏨
(480) 502-3836. **$139-$379.** 16770 N Perimeter Dr 85260. SR 101 exit 36 (Princess Dr), just w to N Perimeter Dr, then 0.6 mi s. Int corridors.
Pets: Accepted. 💾 🛰️ ⚔️ 🍴 🍴 💻 🍴 🏊 ⚔️

Millennium Resort Scottsdale McCormick Ranch 🏨
(480) 948-5050. **$59-$339, 3 day notice.** 7401 N Scottsdale Rd 85253. 0.8 mi n of Indian Bend Rd. Int corridors. **Pets:** Accepted.
💾 🛰️ ⚔️ 🍴 🍴 💻 🍴 🏊 ⚔️

Motel 6 Scottsdale #29 Ⓜ
(480) 946-2280. **$51-$85.** 6848 E Camelback Rd 85251. Just w of Scottsdale Rd. Ext corridors. **Pets:** Other species. Service with restrictions, supervision. 🛰️ 🍴 🍴 🏊

The Phoenician 🏨 🐾
(480) 941-8200. **$199-$2500, 7 day notice.** 6000 E Camelback Rd 85251. 0.5 mi w of 64th St. Ext/int corridors. **Pets:** Medium. Designated rooms, service with restrictions, supervision.
🌿 💾 🛰️ ⚔️ 🍴 🍴 💻 🍴 🏊 ⚔️

The Pima Inn & Suites Ⓒ
(480) 948-3800. **$79-$219.** 7330 N Pima Rd 85258. 0.4 mi n of Indian Bend Rd; on west side of Pima Rd. Ext/int corridors. **Pets:** Accepted.
🛰️ ⚔️ 🍴 🍴 💻 🏊 ⚔️

Radisson Fort McDowell Resort & Casino 🏨
(480) 789-5300. **$79-$499.** 10438 N Ft. McDowell Rd 85264. Jct Shea Blvd, 1.6 mi ne on SR 87. Int corridors. **Pets:** Accepted.
💾 🛰️ ⚔️ ⚔️ 🍴 🍴 💻 🍴 🏊 ⚔️

Residence Inn by Marriott, Scottsdale/ Paradise Valley 🏨
(480) 948-8666. **$179-$269.** 6040 N Scottsdale Rd 85253. Just n of McDonald Dr. Ext/int corridors. **Pets:** Other species. $100 one-time fee/room. Service with restrictions.
💾 🛰️ ⚔️ ⚔️ 🍴 🍴 💻 🏊 ⚔️

Residence Inn Scottsdale North 🏨
(480) 563-4120. **$79-$257.** 17011 N Scottsdale Rd 85255. SR 101 exit 34 (Scottsdale Rd), 1.1 mi s; northeast corner of Frank Lloyd Wright Blvd and Scottsdale Rd. Int corridors. **Pets:** Accepted.
🛰️ ⚔️ 🍴 💻 🏊 ⚔️

◬ ◈◈◈◈ Scottsdale Cottonwoods Resort 🄷

(480) 991-1414. **Call for rates.** 6160 N Scottsdale Rd 85253. Just n of McDonald Dr. Ext corridors. **Pets:** Medium. $75 one-time fee/room. Service with restrictions, supervision.

SAVE 📶 ✕ 🔥M 🔋 💻 ⊇ ✕

◬ ◈◈◈ Scottsdale Resort & Athletic Club 🄷

(480) 344-0600. **$89-$609.** 8235 E Indian Bend Rd 85250. 1.5 mi e of Scottsdale Rd. Ext corridors. **Pets:** Medium. $100 deposit/room. Designated rooms, service with restrictions.

SAVE 📶 ✕ 🔥M 🔋 💻 🍴 ⊇ ✕

◬ ◈◈◈ Scottsdale Resort & Conference Center 🄷

(480) 991-9000. **$79-$359, 3 day notice.** 7700 E McCormick Pkwy 85258. Just w of Hayden Rd; 0.7 mi e of Scottsdale Rd. Ext/int corridors. **Pets:** $150 deposit/room. Service with restrictions, crate.

ECO SAVE 📶 ✕ 🔋 💻 🍴 ⊇ ✕

◈◈◈ Scottsdale Thunderbird Suites 🄷 🐾

(480) 951-4000. **$59-$189.** 7515 E Butherus Dr 85260. 0.8 mi n of Thunderbird Rd; 0.5 mi e of Scottsdale Rd. Ext/int corridors. **Pets:** Medium. $15 daily fee/pet. Service with restrictions.

📶 ✕ 🔋 💻 🍴 ⊇

◈◈◈ SpringHill Suites by Marriott-Scottsdale North 🄷

(480) 922-8700. **$59-$199.** 17020 N Scottsdale Rd 85255. Just n of Frank Lloyd Wright Blvd. Int corridors. **Pets:** Accepted.

📶 ✕ 🔥M 🔋 💻 ⊇ ✕

◈◈◈ TownePlace Suites Scottsdale by Marriott 🄷

(480) 551-1100. **$59-$209.** 10740 N 90th St 85260. SR 101 exit Shea Blvd, just e to 90th St, then just n. Int corridors. **Pets:** Accepted.

ECO 📶 ✕ 🔥M 🔋 💻 ⊇

◬ ◈◈◈◈ The Westin Kierland Resort & Spa 🄷

(480) 624-1000. **$139-$709, 7 day notice.** 6902 E Greenway Pkwy 85254. 0.5 mi w of Scottsdale Rd. Int corridors. **Pets:** Accepted.

ECO SAVE 📶 ✕ 🔋 💻 🍴 ⊇ ✕

◬ ◈◈◈◈ W Scottsdale 🄷

(480) 970-2100. **$129-$699.** 7277 E Camelback Rd 85251. Just e of Scottsdale Rd. Int corridors. **Pets:** Accepted.

SAVE 📶 🔥M 🔋 💻 🍴 ⊇

◈◈◈ Xona Resort Suites, an Ascend Collection hotel 🄷

(480) 585-1234. **$79-$399.** 7677 E Princess Blvd 85255. SR 101 exit 34 (Scottsdale Rd), 0.8 mi s, then just e. Ext corridors. **Pets:** Accepted.

📶 ✕ 🔋 💻 🍴 ⊇ ✕

SURPRISE

◬ ◈◈◈ Comfort Inn & Suites of Surprise 🄷 🐾

(623) 544-6874. **$79-$139.** 13337 W Grand Ave 85374. Jct Bell Rd, 0.4 mi se. Int corridors. **Pets:** Medium, dogs only. $20 one-time fee/pet. Service with restrictions, supervision. SAVE 📶 ✕ 🔥M 🔋 💻 ⊇

◬ ◈◈◈ Hampton Inn & Suites Surprise 🄷 🐾

(623) 537-9122. **$80-$179.** 14783 W Grand Ave 85374. Jct Bell Rd, 2 mi nw. Int corridors. **Pets:** Medium, other species. Designated rooms, service with restrictions. SAVE 📶 ✕ 🔥M 🔋 💻 ⊇

◈◈◈ Quality Inn & Suites 🄷

(623) 583-3500. **$59-$169.** 16741 N Greasewood St 85374. US 60 (Grand Ave), 1.1 mi e on Bell Rd, then just s. Int corridors. **Pets:** Accepted. 📶 ✕ 🔋 💻 ⊇

◬ ◈◈◈◈ Residence Inn by Marriott Phoenix NW Surprise 🄷

(623) 249-6333. **$100-$120.** 16418 N Bullard Ave 85374. Jct US 60 (Grand Ave), 1.4 mi w on Bell Rd, then just s. Int corridors. **Pets:** Accepted. SAVE 📶 ✕ 🔥M 🔋 💻 ⊇ ✕

◬ ◈◈◈ Windmill Suites in Surprise 🄷

(623) 583-0133. **Call for rates.** 12545 W Bell Rd 85374. US 60 (Grand Ave), 1 mi e. Int corridors. **Pets:** Accepted.

SAVE 📶 ✕ 🔋 💻 ⊇ ✕

TEMPE

◬ ◈◈◈ Aloft Tempe 🄷 🐾

(480) 621-3300. **$99-$279.** 951 E Playa Del Norte Dr 85281. SR 202 Loop (Red Mountain Frwy) exit 7 (Rural Rd), just s on Scottsdale Rd, then just e. Int corridors. **Pets:** Medium, dogs only. Designated rooms, service with restrictions, supervision.

ECO SAVE 📶 ✕ 🔥M 🔋 💻 ⊇

◬ ◈◈◈ Best Western Inn of Tempe 🄷 🐾

(480) 784-2233. **$70-$140.** 670 N Scottsdale Rd 85281. SR 202 Loop (Red Mountain Frwy) exit 7 (Rural Rd S), just s. Int corridors. **Pets:** Medium, dogs only. $10 daily fee/pet. Service with restrictions, supervision. SAVE 📶 ✕ 🔋 💻

◬ ◈◈◈ Best Western Plus Tempe by the Mall 🄷 🐾

(480) 820-7500. **$70-$140.** 5300 S Priest Dr 85283. I-10 exit 155 (Baseline Rd), 0.4 mi e, then just s. Int corridors. **Pets:** Medium. $10 daily fee/pet. Designated rooms, service with restrictions, supervision.

SAVE 📶 ✕ 🔋 💻 ⊇

◬ ◈◈◈ Country Inn & Suites By Carlson, Phoenix Airport at Tempe 🄷

(480) 858-9898. **$79-$209.** 808 N Scottsdale Rd 85281. SR 202 Loop (Red Mountain Frwy) exit 7 (Rural Rd S), just n. Int corridors. **Pets:** Accepted. SAVE 📶 ✕ 🔥M 🔋 💻 ⊇

◬ ◈◈◈ Days Inn & Suites 🄷

(480) 345-8585. **Call for rates.** 1660 W Elliot Rd 85284. I-10 exit 157, just e. Ext corridors. **Pets:** Accepted. SAVE 📶 🔋 💻 ⊇

◬ ◈◈◈ Fiesta Resort Conference Center 🄷

(480) 967-1441. **$79-$159.** 2100 S Priest Dr 85282. I-10 exit 153 (Broadway Rd), 0.5 mi e. Ext corridors. **Pets:** Accepted.

SAVE 📶 ✕ 🔋 💻 🍴 ⊇ ✕

◬ ◈◈◈ Four Points by Sheraton Tempe 🄷

(480) 968-3451. **$75-$225.** 1333 S Rural Rd 85281. US 60 (Superstition Frwy) exit 174 (Rural Rd), 2 mi n. Int corridors. **Pets:** Accepted.

SAVE 📶 ✕ 🔥M 🔋 💻 🍴 ⊇

◈◈◈ Hampton Inn & Suites 🄷

(480) 675-9799. **$69-$149.** 1429 N Scottsdale Rd 85281. SR 202 Loop (Red Mountain Frwy) exit 7 (Rural Rd S), 0.5 mi n. Ext corridors. **Pets:** Medium, other species. Service with restrictions, supervision.

📶 ✕ 🔋 💻 ⊇ ✕

◈◈◈ Homestead Studio Suites Hotel-Phoenix/Airport/Tempe 🄷 🐾

(480) 557-8880. **$55-$75.** 2165 W 15th St 85281. I-10 exit 153 (Broadway Rd), 0.3 mi ne, just nw on S 52nd St, then just w. Int corridors. **Pets:** Other species. $25 daily fee/pet. Service with restrictions.

📶 🔋 💻 ⊇

◈◈◈ Hotel Tempe InnSuites Airport @ the Mall 🄷

(480) 897-7900. **$69-$199.** 1651 W Baseline Rd 85283. I-10 exit 155 (Baseline Rd), just e. Ext corridors. **Pets:** Accepted.

📶 🔋 💻 ⊇ ✕

◈◈◈ La Quinta Inn Phoenix Sky Harbor Airport South 🄷

(480) 967-4465. **$54-$148.** 911 S 48th St 85281. I-10 exit 153 (Broadway Rd) eastbound; exit 153A (University Dr) westbound, 0.8 mi n; on south side of University Dr; east side of SR 143 (Hohokam Expwy). Ext/int corridors. **Pets:** Medium, other species. Service with restrictions, supervision. 📶 🔋 💻 ⊇

Quality Suites near Old Town Scottsdale H

(480) 947-3711. **$44-$79.** 1635 N Scottsdale Rd 85281. SR 202 Loop (Red Mountain Frwy) exit 7, 0.6 mi n. Ext corridors. **Pets:** Medium, other species. $10 daily fee/room. Supervision.

Ramada Inn - Arizona Mills Mall H

(480) 413-1188. **$59-$119.** 1701 W Baseline Rd 85283. I-10 exit 155 (Baseline Rd), just e. Ext corridors. **Pets:** Accepted.

Ramada Limited Tempe-University M ✿

(480) 736-1700. **$49-$119.** 1915 E Apache Blvd 85281. US 60 (Superstition Frwy) exit 175, 1.9 mi n on McClintock Dr, then 0.3 mi e. Ext corridors. **Pets:** Medium, dogs only. $50 deposit/room, $15 one-time fee/pet. Service with restrictions, supervision.

Red Roof Inn Phoenix Airport H

(480) 449-3205. **$49-$118.** 2135 W 15th St 85281. I-10 exit 153 (Broadway Rd), just nw on S 52nd St, then just w. Ext corridors. **Pets:** Large, other species. No service, supervision.

Residence Inn by Marriott H

(480) 756-2122. **$104-$170.** 5075 S Priest Dr 85282. I-10 exit 155 (Baseline Rd), 0.4 mi e, then just n. Ext/int corridors. **Pets:** Medium, other species. $100 one-time fee/room. Service with restrictions, supervision.

Sheraton Phoenix Airport Hotel-Tempe H

(480) 967-6600. **$79-$359, 3 day notice.** 1600 S 52nd St 85281. I-10 exit 153B (Broadway Rd) westbound; exit 153A (48th St) eastbound, 0.3 mi ne. Int corridors. **Pets:** Accepted.

Studio 6 Extended Stay #6031 M

(602) 414-4470. **$53-$63.** 4909 S Wendler Dr 85282. I-10 exit 155 (Baseline Rd), just w, then 0.4 mi n. Ext corridors. **Pets:** Other species. $10 daily fee/room. Service with restrictions, supervision.

Super 8 Tempe/ASU M

(480) 967-8891. **$53-$98.** 1020 E Apache Blvd 85281. Just e of Rural Rd; just e of ASU main campus. Ext corridors. **Pets:** Small, dogs only. $10 daily fee/pet. Designated rooms, service with restrictions, supervision.

Tempe Mission Palms Hotel H

(480) 894-1400. **$99-$319.** 60 E 5th St 85281. Jct University Dr, just n on Mill Ave, then just e; downtown. Int corridors. **Pets:** Accepted.

TOLLESON

Premier Inns H

(623) 533-4660. **Call for rates.** 8399 W Lynwood St 85353. I-10 exit 135 (83rd Ave), just n, then just w. Ext corridors. **Pets:** Accepted.

YOUNGTOWN

Best Western Inn & Suites of Sun City H

(623) 933-8211. **$60-$130.** 11201 Grand Ave 85363. On US 60, just se of 113th Ave. Ext/int corridors. **Pets:** Accepted.

END METROPOLITAN AREA

PINETOP-LAKESIDE

Best Western Inn of Pinetop M

(928) 367-6667. **$75-$139.** 404 E White Mountain Blvd 85935. On SR 260. Ext corridors. **Pets:** Large, other species. $10 daily fee/pet. Service with restrictions, crate.

Executive Inn & Suites M

(928) 367-4146. **$49-$89.** 1023 E White Mountain Blvd 85935. On SR 260; east end of town. Ext corridors. **Pets:** Small, dogs only. $10 daily fee/pet. Designated rooms, service with restrictions, supervision.

Hon-Dah Resort Casino & Conference Center H ✿

(928) 369-0299. **$109-$200.** 777 Hwy 260 85935. Jct SR 260 and 73; east end of town. Int corridors. **Pets:** Other species. $50 one-time fee/room. Service with restrictions, supervision.

Northwoods Resort CA

(928) 367-2966. **Call for rates.** 165 E White Mountain Blvd 85935. On SR 260, MM 352. Ext corridors. **Pets:** Accepted.

Super 8 H

(928) 367-3161. **$58-$99.** 1202 E White Mountain Blvd 85935. On SR 260; east end of town. Int corridors. **Pets:** Accepted.

TimberLodge Inn M

(928) 367-4463. **$45-$99.** 1078 E White Mountain Blvd 85935. On SR 260; east end of town. Ext corridors. **Pets:** Other species. $10 daily fee/pet. Designated rooms, service with restrictions, crate.

Woodland Inn & Suites M ✿

(928) 367-3636. **$74-$169, 3 day notice.** 458 E White Mountain Blvd 85935. On SR 260; east end of town. Ext corridors. **Pets:** Medium, other species. $10 daily fee/pet. Supervision.

PRESCOTT

Americas Best Value Inn M

(928) 776-1282. **$60-$120.** 1105 E Sheldon St 86301. 0.4 mi e of jct SR 89. Int corridors. **Pets:** Accepted.

Best Western Prescottonian M

(928) 445-3096. **$80-$130.** 1317 E Gurley St 86301. On SR 89, just s of jct SR 69. Ext corridors. **Pets:** Other species. $10 daily fee/pet. Service with restrictions, supervision.

Comfort Inn of Prescott M

(928) 778-5770. **Call for rates.** 1290 White Spar Rd 86303. On SR 89, 1.5 mi s of town center. Ext corridors. **Pets:** Accepted.

Forest Villas Hotel H

(928) 717-1200. **$87-$109.** 3645 Lee Cir 86301. Jct SR 69, just n on Lee Blvd, then just e. Int corridors. **Pets:** Very small. $35 one-time fee/pet. Designated rooms, service with restrictions, supervision.

Hassayampa Inn H

(928) 778-9434. **$89-$219.** 122 E Gurley St 86301. Jct Marina St; downtown. Int corridors. **Pets:** Accepted.

Motel 6 #0166 M

(928) 776-0160. **$45-$65.** 1111 E Sheldon St 86301. 0.4 mi e of jct SR 89; center. Ext corridors. **Pets:** Other species. Service with restrictions, supervision.

◈◈◈ Prescott Cabin Rentals- Lynx Creek Farm 🅲🅰
(928) 778-9573. **$99-$219, 31 day notice.** 5555 Onyx Dr 86303. Jct SR 89, 5 mi e on SR 69, 0.4 mi s on dirt/gravel road. Ext corridors. **Pets:** Other species. $10 daily fee/pet. No service, crate.
📶 ❌ 🛏 💻 ⌖ 🔌

◈◈◈ Residence Inn by Marriott 🅷
(928) 775-2232. **$99-$189.** 3599 Lee Cir 86301. Jct SR 69, just n on Lee Blvd, then just e. Int corridors. **Pets:** Other species. $50 one-time fee/room. Service with restrictions, crate.
📶 ❌ ♿ 🛏 💻 ⌖ 🔌

◈◈◈ SpringHill Suites by Marriott 🅷
(928) 776-0998. **$99-$189.** 200 E Sheldon St 86301. On SR 89; at Marina St. Int corridors. **Pets:** Accepted. 📶 ❌ ♿ 🛏 💻 ⌖

◈◈ ◈◈◈ Wyndham Garden Hotel Prescott 🅷
(928) 777-0770. **Call for rates.** 4499 E SR 69 86301. On SR 69, 3.6 mi e of jct SR 89. Int corridors. **Pets:** Accepted.
SAVE 📶 ❌ 🛏 💻 🍴 ⌖ 🔌

PRESCOTT VALLEY

◈◈ ◈◈◈ Americas Best Value Inn 🅷
(928) 772-2200. **$59-$155.** 8383 E SR 69 86314. On SR 69, just w of N Navajo Dr. Int corridors. **Pets:** Accepted. SAVE 📶 🛏 💻 ⌖

◈◈ ◈◈◈◈ Comfort Suites Prescott Valley 🅷 🐾
(928) 771-2100. **$89-$150.** 2601 N Crownpointe Dr 86314. Just w on SR 69, then n on Market St. Int corridors. **Pets:** Medium. $40 one-time fee/room. Designated rooms, service with restrictions, supervision.
SAVE 📶 ❌ ♿ 🛏 💻 ⌖

◈◈◈ Days Inn/Prescott Valley 🅷
(928) 772-8600. **$45-$88.** 7875 E Hwy 69 86314. On SR 69; corner of Windsong Rd. Ext corridors. **Pets:** Other species. $50 deposit/room. Service with restrictions. 📶 🛏 💻 ⌖

QUARTZSITE

◈◈◈ Super 8-Quartzsite 🅼 🐾
(928) 927-8080. **$72-$117, 14 day notice.** 2050 Dome Rock Rd 85359. I-10 exit 17, just s to Frontage Rd, then 0.6 mi w. Int corridors. **Pets:** Other species. $10 daily fee/pet. Service with restrictions, supervision. 📶 🛏 💻

RIO RICO

◈◈ ◈◈◈◈ Esplendor Resort at Rio Rico 🅷
(520) 281-1901. **$99-$249.** 1069 Camino Caralampi 85648. I-19 exit 17 (Rio Rico Dr), just w to Camino Caralampi, then just s. Ext corridors. **Pets:** Large. $25 one-time fee/room. Supervision.
SAVE 📶 ♿ 🛏 💻 🍴 ⌖ 🔌

SAFFORD

◈◈ ◈◈ Best Western Desert Inn 🅼
(928) 428-0521. **$75-$85.** 1391 W Thatcher Blvd 85546. US 191, 1 mi w on US 70. Ext corridors. **Pets:** Accepted. SAVE 📶 🛏 💻 ⌖

◈◈ ◈◈ Days Inn 🅼
(928) 428-5000. **$57-$109.** 520 E Hwy 70 85546. US 191, 0.5 mi e. Ext corridors. **Pets:** Small. $20 daily fee/pet. Service with restrictions, crate.
📶 ♿ 🛏 💻 ⌖

ST. JOHNS

◈◈◈ Days Inn 🅼
(928) 337-4422. **$64-$99.** 125 E Commercial St 85936. On US 191/SR 61; center. Ext corridors. **Pets:** Dogs only. $10 daily fee/pet. Designated rooms, service with restrictions. 📶 🛏 💻

SEDONA

◈◈ ◈◈◈ ◈◈◈ Amara Hotel, Restaurant & Spa 🅷
(928) 282-4828. **$155-$295, 3 day notice.** 100 Amara Ln 86336. Jct SR 179, 0.4 mi ne; center. Int corridors. **Pets:** Accepted.
SAVE 📶 ❌ 🛏 💻 🍴 ⌖ 🔌

◈◈ ◈◈◈ ◈◈◈ Best Western Plus Inn of Sedona 🅷 🐾
(928) 282-3072. **$109-$249.** 1200 W SR 89A 86336. Jct SR 179, 1.2 mi w. Ext corridors. **Pets:** Medium, other species. $20 daily fee/room. Designated rooms, service with restrictions, supervision.
ECO SAVE 📶 ❌ 🛏 💻 ⌖

◈◈ ◈◈◈ ◈◈◈ Casa Sedona Bed and Breakfast Inn 🅱🅱 🐾
(928) 282-2938. **$139-$279, 7 day notice.** 55 Hozoni Dr 86336. Jct SR 179, 3 mi w on SR 89A, then 3 blks nw via Tortilla, Southwest and Hozoni drs. Ext/int corridors. **Pets:** Small, dogs only. $25 daily fee/pet. Designated rooms, service with restrictions, supervision.
SAVE 📶 ❌ 🛏 💻 🔌

◈◈ ◈◈◈ Desert Quail Inn 🅷
(928) 284-1433. **$69-$189.** 6626 Hwy 179 86351. Jct Bell Rock Blvd, 0.9 mi s. Ext corridors. **Pets:** Medium, dogs only. $20 daily fee/pet. Designated rooms, service with restrictions, supervision.
SAVE 📶 ❌ 🛏 💻 ⌖

◈◈ ◈◈◈ ◈◈◈ El Portal Sedona Luxury Inn 🅷 🐾
(928) 203-9405. **$179-$399, 15 day notice.** 95 Portal Ln 86336. Jct SR 89A, just s on SR 179, then just w. Ext/int corridors. **Pets:** Other species. Designated rooms, service with restrictions, crate. SAVE 📶 ❌ 🛏

◈◈ ◈◈◈ Hilton Sedona Resort & Spa 🅷
(928) 284-4040. **$135-$269.** 90 Ridge Trail Dr 86351. Jct SR 89A, 7.3 mi s on SR 179. Int corridors. **Pets:** Accepted.
SAVE 📶 ❌ 🛏 💻 🍴 ⌖ 🔌

◈◈ ◈◈ King's Ransom Sedona Hotel 🅷
(928) 282-7151. **$99-$225.** 771 SR 179 86336. 0.7 mi s of jct SR 89A. Ext/int corridors. **Pets:** Accepted. 📶 ❌ 🛏 💻 🍴 ⌖

◈◈ ◈◈◈ ◈◈◈ La Quinta Inn Sedona / Village of Oak Creek 🅷
(928) 284-0711. **$89-$179.** 6176 SR 179 86351. Jct Bell Rock Blvd, just s. Int corridors. **Pets:** Medium, other species. Service with restrictions, supervision. SAVE 📶 ♿ 🛏 💻 ⌖

◈◈ ◈◈◈ ◈◈◈ L'Auberge de Sedona Inn and Spa 🅷 🐾
(928) 282-1661. **$229-$725, 7 day notice.** 301 L'Auberge Ln 86336. Jct SR 179, just n on SR 89A, then ne; down the hill. Ext/int corridors. **Pets:** Medium, dogs only. $35 daily fee/pet. Designated rooms, service with restrictions. SAVE 📶 ❌ 🛏 💻 🍴 🔌

◈◈◈ The Lodge at Sedona 🅱🅱 🐾
(928) 204-1942. **$189-$349, 14 day notice.** 125 Kallof Pl 86336. Jct SR 179, 1.8 mi w on SR 89A, then just s. Ext/int corridors. **Pets:** Medium, dogs only. $35 daily fee/pet. Designated rooms, service with restrictions, supervision. 📶 ❌ 🛏 🔌

◈◈ ◈◈◈ Matterhorn Inn 🅼 🐾
(928) 282-7176. **$99-$179.** 230 Apple Ave 86336. Jct SR 179, just ne on SR 89A; uptown. Ext corridors. **Pets:** Large. $10 daily fee/pet. Designated rooms, service with restrictions, crate. SAVE 📶 ❌ 🛏 💻 ⌖

◈◈ ◈◈◈ Orchards Inn of Sedona 🅷
(928) 282-2405. **Call for rates.** 254 N SR 89A 86336. Jct SR 179, just ne on SR 89A. Ext corridors. **Pets:** Accepted.
SAVE 📶 ❌ 🛏 💻 🍴 ⌖

◈◈ ◈◈◈ Sedona Real Inn & Suites 🅷 🐾
(928) 282-1414. **$95-$340.** 95 Arroyo Piñon Dr 86336. Jct SR 179, 3.4 mi w on SR 89A, just sw. Ext corridors. **Pets:** Large, other species. $30 one-time fee/pet. Designated rooms, service with restrictions, crate.
SAVE 📶 ❌ 🛏 💻 ⌖ 🔌

Sedona Rouge Hotel & Spa [H]
(928) 203-4111. **$209-$279, 3 day notice.** 2250 W Hwy 89A 86336. Jct SR 179, 2 mi w. Ext/int corridors. **Pets:** Medium, dogs only. $100 deposit/pet, $50 one-time fee/pet. Designated rooms, service with restrictions, supervision. [ECO] [SAVE] 🛰 ⊠ ⬛ 💻 🍴 ⇌ ⊠

Sedona Super 8 [H]
(928) 282-1533. **$77-$126.** 2545 W Hwy 89A 86336. Jct SR 179, 2.4 mi w. Int corridors. **Pets:** Medium. $25 one-time fee/pet. Designated rooms, service with restrictions, supervision. 🛰 ⊠ ⬛ 💻 ⇌

Sky Ranch Lodge [M]
(928) 282-6400. **$80-$250.** 1105 Airport Rd 86336. Jct SR 179, 1 mi w on SR 89A, then 1 mi s. Ext corridors. **Pets:** Large, other species. $10 daily fee/pet. Service with restrictions, supervision. 🛰 ⬛ 💻 ⇌

Southwest Inn at Sedona [H]
(928) 282-3344. **Call for rates.** 3250 W Hwy 89A 86336. Jct SR 179, 3.5 mi w. Ext corridors. **Pets:** Accepted. 🛰 ⊠ ⬛ 💻 ⇌

Village Lodge [M]
(928) 284-3626. **$49-$89, 3 day notice.** 105 Bell Rock Plaza 86351. Jct SR 179, just w. Ext/int corridors. **Pets:** Small, dogs only. Designated rooms, service with restrictions, supervision. 🛰 ⊠ ⬛ 💻

SELIGMAN

Canyon Lodge [M]
(928) 422-3255. **Call for rates.** 22340 Old Hwy 66 86337. I-40 exit 121, 1 mi n, then 0.7 mi e. Ext corridors. **Pets:** Large, other species. $10 daily fee/pet. Service with restrictions, supervision.
[SAVE] 🛰 ⊠ ⬛ 💻

Deluxe Inn Motel [M]
(928) 422-3244. **$48-$57.** 22295 Old Hwy 66 86337. I-40 exit 121 eastbound, 1 mi n, then 0.7 mi e; exit 123 westbound, just ne on I-40 business loop, then 2.4 mi w. Ext corridors. **Pets:** Medium, other species. $10 one-time fee/pet. Designated rooms, service with restrictions, supervision.
[SAVE] 🛰 ⬛

SHOW LOW

Best Western Paint Pony Lodge [M]
(928) 537-5773. **$80-$120.** 581 W Deuce of Clubs Ave 85901. On US 60 and SR 260. Ext corridors. **Pets:** Large, other species. $10 daily fee/pet. Designated rooms, service with restrictions, supervision.
[SAVE] 🛰 ⬛ 💻

Days Inn [M]
(928) 537-4356. **$44-$140, 3 day notice.** 480 W Deuce of Clubs Ave 85901. On US 60 and SR 260. Ext/int corridors. **Pets:** Accepted.
🛰 ⬛ 💻 🍴 ⇌

Kiva Motel [M]
(928) 537-4542. **$58-$68, 3 day notice.** 261 E Deuce of Clubs Ave 85901. On US 60 and SR 260; center. Ext corridors. **Pets:** Small, dogs only. $5 daily fee/pet. Service with restrictions, supervision.
[SAVE] 🛰 ⬛ 💻

Sleep Inn [H]
(928) 532-7323. **Call for rates.** 1751 W Deuce of Clubs Ave 85901. 2 mi w of jct US 60 and SR 260, south side. Int corridors. **Pets:** Other species. $15 daily fee/pet. Service with restrictions, supervision.
🛰 ⬛M ⬛ 💻 ⇌

SIERRA VISTA

Americas Best Value Inn [M]
(520) 459-5380. **Call for rates.** 100 Fab Ave 85635. Jct Business SR 90 and Fry Blvd, then just e of main gate to Fort Huachuca. Ext corridors. **Pets:** Small, dogs only. $15 daily fee/pet. Service with restrictions, supervision. [SAVE] 🛰 ⬛ 💻 ⇌

Best Western Mission Inn [H]
(520) 458-8500. **$79-$129.** 3460 E Fry Blvd 85635. Just w of jct SR 90 and 92. Ext corridors. **Pets:** Large, other species. $10 daily fee/pet. Service with restrictions, supervision. [SAVE] 🛰 ⊠ ⬛M ⬛ 💻 ⇌

Candlewood Suites [H]
(520) 439-8200. **$119-$152.** 1904 S Hwy 92 85635. Jct SR 90 and 92, 1.4 mi s. Int corridors. **Pets:** Accepted. 🛰 ⊠ ⬛ 💻 ⇌

Holiday Inn Express [H] 🐾
(520) 439-8800. **$99-$119.** 1902 S Hwy 92 85635. Jct SR 90 and 92, 1.4 mi s. Int corridors. **Pets:** Large, other species. $15 one-time fee/pet. Service with restrictions, crate. 🛰 ⬛ 💻 ⇌

Quality Inn [H]
(520) 458-7900. **$61-$67.** 1631 S Hwy 92 85635. On SR 92, 1 mi s of jct SR 90. Int corridors. **Pets:** Large. $10 daily fee/pet. Designated rooms, service with restrictions, crate. [SAVE] 🛰 ⬛ 💻 ⇌

Sun Canyon Inn [H]
(520) 459-0610. **$93-$104, 3 day notice.** 260 N Garden Ave 85635. Just n of Fry Blvd; just e of main gate to Fort Huachuca. Int corridors. **Pets:** $20 daily fee/pet. Service with restrictions, supervision.
[SAVE] 🛰 ⬛ 💻 ⇌

TownePlace Suites by Marriott [H]
(520) 515-9900. **$107-$170.** 3399 Rodeo Dr 85635. Jct SR 90, 1.5 mi s on SR 92, just w on Avenida Cochise, just s on Oakmont Dr, then just e. Int corridors. **Pets:** Accepted. 🛰 ⊠ ⬛ 💻 ⇌

SNOWFLAKE

Comfort Inn [H]
(928) 536-3888. **$60-$130.** 2055 S Main St 85937. SR 77, just s of town. Int corridors. **Pets:** Other species. $15 daily fee/pet. Service with restrictions, supervision. 🛰 ⬛ 💻 ⇌

TAYLOR

Rodeway Inn - Silver Creek Inn [M]
(928) 536-2600. **Call for rates.** 825 N Main St 85939. On SR 77. Ext corridors. **Pets:** Accepted. [SAVE] 🛰 ⬛ 💻

TOMBSTONE

Best Western Lookout Lodge [H]
(520) 457-2223. **$108-$130.** 781 N Hwy 80 85638. On SR 80, 1 mi n. Ext corridors. **Pets:** Accepted. [SAVE] 🛰 ⊠ ⬛ 💻 🍴 ⇌

TUBAC

Tubac Golf Resort & Spa [H] 🐾
(520) 398-2211. **$129-$289, 3 day notice.** 1 Otero Rd 85646. I-19 exit 40 (Chavez Siding Rd), on east side, then 2 mi s. Ext corridors. **Pets:** $25 daily fee/pet. Designated rooms, service with restrictions, crate.
[ECO] [SAVE] 🛰 ⊠ ⬛ 💻 🍴 ⇌ ⊠

TUBA CITY

Quality Inn Navajo Nation [H]
(928) 283-4545. **$89-$119.** 10 N Main St 86045. 1 mi n of US 160. Int corridors. **Pets:** Other species. $10 daily fee/pet. Service with restrictions, supervision. [SAVE] 🛰 ⬛ 💻 🍴

TUCSON METROPOLITAN AREA

CATALINA

Best Western Catalina Inn
(520) 818-9500. **$69-$120.** 15691 N Oracle Rd 85739. 4.6 mi n of Tangerine Rd. Ext/int corridors. **Pets:** Medium, dogs only. $100 one-time fee/pet, $20 daily fee/pet. Service with restrictions, supervision.

GREEN VALLEY

Comfort Inn
(520) 399-3736. **$110-$120.** 90 W Esperanza Blvd 85614. I-19 exit 65, just w. Int corridors. **Pets:** Medium. $20 daily fee/pet. Service with restrictions, supervision.

Holiday Inn Express
(520) 625-0900. **Call for rates.** 19200 S I-19 Frontage Rd 85614. I-19 exit 69 (Duval Mine Rd), west side of interstate, then just s. Int corridors. **Pets:** Accepted.

MARANA

La Quinta Inn & Suites NW Tucson Marana
(520) 572-4235. **$139-$215.** 6020 W Hospitality Rd 85743. I-10 exit 246 (Cortaro Rd), just w, then just n. Int corridors. **Pets:** Medium, other species. Service with restrictions, supervision.

Red Roof Inn Tucson North
(520) 744-8199. **$41-$125.** 4940 W Ina Rd 85743. I-10 exit 248 (Ina Rd), just w. Int corridors. **Pets:** Large, other species. No service, supervision.

The Ritz-Carlton, Dove Mountain
(520) 572-3000. **$179-$559.** 15000 N Secret Springs Dr 85658. I-10 exit 240 (Tangerine Rd), 5 mi e to Dove Mountain Dr, then 4.5 mi n, follow signs. Int corridors. **Pets:** Small, dogs only. $125 one-time fee/room. Designated rooms, service with restrictions, supervision.

ORO VALLEY

Hilton Tucson El Conquistador Golf & Tennis Resort
(520) 544-5000. **Call for rates.** 10000 N Oracle Rd 85704. I-10 exit 248 (Ina Rd); jct Ina Rd, 4.4 mi n. Ext/int corridors. **Pets:** Medium, other species. $50 one-time fee/room. Designated rooms, service with restrictions.

TUCSON

Americas Best Value Inn-Tucson
(520) 884-5800. **$44-$160.** 810 E Benson Hwy 85713. I-10 exit 262, just s. Ext corridors. **Pets:** Other species. $25 deposit/room. Service with restrictions, supervision.

Arizona Riverpark Inn
(520) 239-2300. **$69-$299, 3 day notice.** 350 S Freeway 85745. I-10 exit 258 (Broadway Blvd/Congress St), just w, then 0.4 mi s. Ext/int corridors. **Pets:** Accepted.

Best Western Plus InnSuites Tucson Foothills Hotel & Suites
(520) 297-8111. **$79-$169.** 6201 N Oracle Rd 85704. I-10 exit 250 (Orange Grove Rd), 4 mi e, then just s. Ext corridors. **Pets:** Medium, other species. $20 one-time fee/room. Designated rooms, service with restrictions, crate.

Best Western Plus Royal Sun Inn & Suites
(520) 622-8871. **$70-$170.** 1015 N Stone Ave 85705. I-10 exit 257 (Speedway Blvd), 0.8 mi e, then just s. Ext corridors. **Pets:** Medium. $25 daily fee/pet. Service with restrictions, supervision.

Catalina Park Inn Bed and Breakfast
(520) 792-4541. **$139-$189, 14 day notice.** 309 E 1st St 85705. I-10 exit 257 (Speedway Blvd), 1 mi e to 5th Ave, just s, then just e. Ext/int corridors. **Pets:** Medium, dogs only. Designated rooms, service with restrictions, supervision.

Comfort Suites at Sabino Canyon
(520) 298-2300. **$89-$139.** 7007 E Tanque Verde Rd 85715. Jct Grand Rd, 0.4 mi ne. Ext corridors. **Pets:** Medium. $25 daily fee/pet. Designated rooms, service with restrictions, supervision.

Comfort Suites at Tucson Mall
(520) 888-6676. **$100-$220.** 515 W Auto Mall Dr 85705. I-10 exit 254 (Prince Rd), 1.9 mi e, then 1.2 mi n. Int corridors. **Pets:** Accepted.

Comfort Suites Tucson Airport
(520) 295-4400. **$79-$169.** 6935 S Tucson Blvd 85756. Just n of Tucson International Airport. Int corridors. **Pets:** Accepted.

Country Inn & Suites By Carlson, Tucson-Airport
(520) 741-9000. **$79-$169.** 6681 S Tucson Blvd 85756. 0.4 mi n of Tucson International Airport entrance. Int corridors. **Pets:** Other species. $25 one-time fee/room. Service with restrictions.

Country Inn & Suites Tucson City Center
(520) 867-6200. **$69-$199.** 705 N Freeway 85745. I-10 exit 257 (St. Mary's Rd/Speedway Blvd), just w, then just s. Int corridors.
Pets: Accepted.

Crossland Economy Studios-Tucson-Butterfield Dr
(520) 745-3612. **$55-$70.** 4800 S Butterfield Dr 85714. I-10 exit 264B eastbound, just n to Irvington Rd, just e to Hotel Dr, then just n; exit 264 westbound, just n. Ext corridors. **Pets:** Other species. $25 daily fee/pet. Service with restrictions.

DoubleTree by Hilton Tucson - Reid Park
(520) 881-4200. **$109-$299.** 445 S Alvernon Way 85711. I-10 exit 259 (22nd St), 4 mi e, then just n. Ext/int corridors. **Pets:** Medium, other species. $50 one-time fee/room. Designated rooms, service with restrictions, crate.

Econo Lodge
(520) 622-6714. **Call for rates.** 1136 N Stone Ave 85705. I-10 exit 257 (Speedway Blvd) eastbound, just e, then just n. Ext corridors.
Pets: Medium, dogs only. $15 deposit/pet, $15 one-time fee/pet. Designated rooms, service with restrictions.

Extended StayAmerica-Tucson-Grant Rd
(520) 795-9510. **$60-$80.** 5050 E Grant Rd 85712. 0.5 mi e of Swan Rd. Ext corridors. **Pets:** Other species. $25 daily fee/pet. Service with restrictions.

Four Points by Sheraton Tucson University Plaza
(520) 327-7341. **$60-$260.** 1900 E Speedway Blvd 85719. Southeast corner of Speedway Blvd and Campbell Ave. Int corridors.
Pets: Accepted.

Hampton Inn Tucson North
(520) 206-0602. **$89-$159.** 1375 W Grant Rd 85745. I-10 exit 256 (Grant Rd), just w. Int corridors. **Pets:** Other species. Designated rooms, service with restrictions, supervision.

Hilton Tucson East H
(520) 721-5600. **$79-$159.** 7600 E Broadway Blvd 85710. 0.5 mi e of Kolb Rd. Int corridors. **Pets:** Medium. $50 one-time fee/room. Designated rooms, service with restrictions, crate.

Holiday Inn Express Tucson Airport H
(520) 889-6600. **$109-$189.** 2548 E Medina Rd 85756. 0.5 mi n of Tucson International Airport entrance. Int corridors. **Pets:** Accepted.

Holiday Inn Hotel & Suites-Tucson Airport North H
(520) 746-1161. **$59-$189.** 4550 S Palo Verde Blvd 85714. I-10 exit 264 westbound; exit 264B eastbound, 0.5 mi n. Ext/int corridors. **Pets:** Accepted.

La Posada Lodge & Casitas H
(520) 887-4800. **$105-$172.** 5900 N Oracle Rd 85704. 0.5 mi s of Orange Grove Rd. Ext corridors. **Pets:** Accepted.

La Quinta Inn & Suites Tucson Airport H
(520) 573-3333. **$68-$159.** 7001 S Tucson Blvd 85706. Just n of Tucson International Airport. Int corridors. **Pets:** Medium, other species. Service with restrictions, supervision.

La Quinta Inn Tucson East H
(520) 747-1414. **$58-$144.** 6404 E Broadway Blvd 85710. Just e of Wilmot Rd. Ext corridors. **Pets:** Medium, other species. Service with restrictions, supervision.

Lodge on the Desert H
(520) 320-2000. **$109-$429, 3 day notice.** 306 N Alvernon Way 85711. I-10 exit 258 (Broadway Blvd/Congress St), 4 mi e, then just n. Ext corridors. **Pets:** Dogs only. $25 daily fee/pet. Designated rooms, supervision.

The Lodge @ Ventana Canyon H
(520) 577-1400. **$99-$799, 21 day notice.** 6200 N Clubhouse Ln 85750. I-10 exit 256 (Grant Rd), 8.6 mi e, 0.6 mi e on Tanque Verde Rd, 2 mi n on Sabino Canyon Rd, then 3.2 mi n on Kolb Rd. Ext/int corridors. **Pets:** Dogs only. $100 one-time fee/room. Designated rooms, service with restrictions, supervision.

Loews Ventana Canyon H
(520) 299-2020. **$149-$449, 3 day notice.** 7000 N Resort Dr 85750. I-10 exit 256 (Grant Rd), 8.6 mi e, 0.6 mi ne on Tanque Verde Rd, 2 mi n on Sabino Canyon Rd, then 3.5 mi n on Kolb Rd. Ext/int corridors. **Pets:** Large, other species. $25 one-time fee/room. Designated rooms, no service.

Motel 6 Tucson North #1127 H
(520) 744-9300. **$45-$61.** 4630 W Ina Rd 85741. I-10 exit 248 (Ina Rd), just e to Camino de Oeste, then just n. Int corridors. **Pets:** Other species. Service with restrictions, supervision.

Omni Tucson National Resort H
(520) 297-2271. **$109-$459, 3 day notice.** 2727 W Club Dr 85742. I-10 exit 246 (Cortaro Rd), 3.5 mi e, then n on Shannon Rd. Ext corridors. **Pets:** Large. $75 one-time fee/room. Designated rooms, service with restrictions.

Oracle Foothills Quality Inn & Suites H
(520) 575-9255. **Call for rates.** 7411 N Oracle Rd 85704. SR 77 (Oracle Rd), just n of Ina Rd. Ext corridors. **Pets:** Accepted.

Quality Inn at Tucson Airport H
(520) 294-2500. **$59-$139.** 2803 E Valencia Rd 85706. 1 mi ne of Tucson International Airport; just e of Tucson Blvd. Ext/int corridors. **Pets:** Medium. $10 one-time fee/pet. Service with restrictions, supervision.

Radisson Suites Tucson H
(520) 721-7100. **$76-$269.** 6555 E Speedway Blvd 85710. Just e of Wilmot Rd. Ext corridors. **Pets:** Large. $25 one-time fee/room. Designated rooms, service with restrictions, supervision.

Ramada Foothills Inn & Suites H
(520) 886-9595. **$64-$169.** 6944 E Tanque Verde Rd 85715. Jct Campbell Ave, 5.5 mi e on Grant Rd, then just ne. Ext corridors. **Pets:** Very small. $25 daily fee/pet. Service with restrictions, supervision.

Red Roof Inn-Tucson South H
(520) 571-1400. **$39-$120.** 3704 E Irvington Rd 85714. I-10 exit 264 westbound; exit 264B eastbound. Ext corridors. **Pets:** Large, other species. No service, supervision.

Residence Inn by Marriott-Tucson H
(520) 721-0991. **$99-$209.** 6477 E Speedway Blvd 85710. Just e of Wilmot Rd. Ext corridors. **Pets:** Other species. $100 one-time fee/room. Designated rooms.

Residence Inn by Marriott Williams Centre H
(520) 790-6100. **$98-$359.** 5400 E Williams Cir 85711. Jct Campbell Ave, 3.8 mi e on Broadway Blvd, then just s and just e on Williams Blvd. Int corridors. **Pets:** Accepted.

Residence Inn Tucson Airport H
(520) 294-5522. **$89-$249.** 2660 E Medina Rd 85756. 0.5 mi n of airport entrance on Tucson Blvd, just e. Int corridors. **Pets:** $100 one-time fee/room. Supervision.

Rodeway Inn-University of AZ M
(520) 622-6446. **Call for rates.** 1248 N Stone Ave 85705. I-10 exit 257 (Speedway Blvd) eastbound, just e, then just n. Ext corridors. **Pets:** Small. $10 daily fee/pet. Service with restrictions, supervision.

Staybridge Suites Tucson Airport H
(520) 807-1004. **$109-$249.** 2705 E Executive Dr 85756. 0.7 mi n of Tucson International Airport. Int corridors. **Pets:** Accepted.

Studio 6 Extended Stay #6002 M
(520) 746-0030. **$49-$63.** 4950 S Outlet Center Dr 85706. I-10 exit 264A eastbound; exit 264B westbound, just s, then just nw on Julian Dr. Ext corridors. **Pets:** Other species. $10 daily fee/room. Service with restrictions, supervision.

Super 8 Central East M
(520) 790-6021. **$36-$80, 3 day notice.** 1990 S Craycroft Rd 85711. I-10 exit 265 (Alvernon Way), 4.4 mi ne on Alvernon Way Golflinks Rd, then 0.4 mi n. Ext corridors. **Pets:** Small, dogs only. $10 daily fee/pet. Service with restrictions, supervision.

TownePlace Suites by Marriott H
(520) 292-9697. **$99-$199.** 405 W Rudasill Rd 85704. Jct Orange Grove Rd, 0.5 mi s on Oracle Rd, then just e. Int corridors. **Pets:** Other species. $75 one-time fee/room. Service with restrictions, crate.

Radisson Suites Hotel Tucson Airport H
(520) 225-0800. **$89-$189.** 7051 S Tucson Blvd 85756. At entrance to Tucson International Airport. Ext corridors. **Pets:** Large. $25 one-time fee/pet. Service with restrictions, crate.

The Westin La Paloma Resort & Spa H
(520) 742-6000. **$99-$539, 7 day notice.** 3800 E Sunrise Dr 85718. SR 77 (Oracle Rd), 4.6 mi e on Ina Rd via Skyline and Sunrise drs, then just s on Via Palomita. Ext corridors. **Pets:** Medium, dogs only. Designated rooms.

Westward Look Resort H
(520) 297-1151. **$149-$449, 7 day notice.** 245 E Ina Rd 85704. I-10 exit 248 (Ina Rd), 6 mi e, then just n on Westward Look Dr. Ext corridors. **Pets:** Other species. $75 one-time fee/room. Designated rooms, service with restrictions. ECO SAVE 🛜 🛗 🖥 🍽 ⊷ ⊗

Windmill Suites at St. Philip's Plaza H ❀
(520) 577-0007. **Call for rates.** 4250 N Campbell Ave 85718. I-10 exit 254 (Prince Rd), 4 mi e, then 1 mi n. Int corridors. **Pets:** Other species. Designated rooms, service with restrictions, supervision. SAVE 🛜 ⊗ 🛗 🖥 ⊷ ⊗

END METROPOLITAN AREA

WELLTON

Microtel Inn & Suites at Coyote Wash H
(928) 785-3777. **$53-$69.** 28784 Commerce Way 85356. I-8 exit 30, just s. Int corridors. **Pets:** Accepted. 🛜 ⊗ 🛗 🖥 ⊷

WICKENBURG

Best Western Rancho Grande H
(928) 684-5445. **Call for rates.** 293 E Wickenburg Way 85390. On US 60; center. Ext corridors. **Pets:** Accepted. SAVE 🛜 🛗 🖥 ⊷ ⊗

Super 8 Wickenburg M ❀
(928) 684-0808. **$58-$126.** 1021 N Tegner St 85390. 1 mi n of US 60 and 93. Ext/int corridors. **Pets:** Small. $10 daily fee/pet. Service with restrictions, supervision. SAVE 🛜 🛗 🖥

Wickenburg Inn H
(928) 684-5461. **$69-$95, 5 day notice.** 850 E Wickenburg Way 85390. 1.3 mi se on US 60. Int corridors. **Pets:** Medium. $10 daily fee/pet. Designated rooms, service with restrictions, supervision.
🛜 ⊗ 🛗 🖥 ⊷

WILLCOX

Days Inn M
(520) 384-4222. **$43-$75.** 724 N Bisbee Ave 85643. I-10 exit 340, just s. Ext corridors. **Pets:** Large. $5 daily fee/pet. Service with restrictions, supervision. SAVE 🛜 🛗 🖥 ⊷

Holiday Inn Express & Suites Willcox H
(520) 384-3333. **$84-$129.** 1251 N Virginia Ave 85643. I-10 exit 340, just n. Int corridors. **Pets:** Medium. $20 daily fee/pet. Designated rooms, service with restrictions, supervision. 🛜 🛗 🖥 ⊷

Quality Inn H
(520) 384-3556. **Call for rates.** 1100 W Rex Allen Dr 85643. I-10 exit 340, just s. Ext corridors. **Pets:** Accepted. 🛜 🛗 🖥 🍽 ⊷

Super 8 H
(520) 384-0888. **$43-$58.** 1500 W Ft. Grant Rd 85643. I-10 exit 340, just n. Int corridors. **Pets:** Small. $6 daily fee/pet. Designated rooms, service with restrictions, supervision. 🛜 🛗 🖥 ⊷

WILLIAMS

Best Western Plus Inn of Williams H
(928) 635-4400. **$79-$199.** 2600 W Route 66 86046. I-40 exit 161, just e. Int corridors. **Pets:** Accepted. SAVE 🛜 ⊗ 🛗 🖥 🍽 ⊷

Days Inn of Williams M
(928) 635-4051. **$50-$118.** 2488 W Route 66 86046. I-40 exit 161, just e. Int corridors. **Pets:** $20 daily fee/room. Service with restrictions, supervision. 🛜 ⊗ 🛗 🖥 ⊷

Holiday Inn Williams H
(928) 635-4114. **$109-$159.** 950 N Grand Canyon Blvd 86046. I-40 exit 163, just s. Int corridors. **Pets:** Other species. No service, crate.
🛜 🛗 🖥 🍽 ⊷

Quality Inn Mountain Ranch Resort H
(928) 635-2693. **$79-$169.** 6701 E Mountain Ranch Rd 86046. I-40 exit 171 (Deer Farm Rd), just s. Ext corridors. **Pets:** Medium. $45 one-time fee/room. Designated rooms, service with restrictions, supervision.
SAVE 🛜 ⊗ 🛗 🖥 🍽 ⊷ ⊗

Travelodge Williams M
(928) 635-2651. **$36-$144.** 430 E Route 66 86046. I-40 exit 163, 0.5 mi s, then just e. Ext corridors. **Pets:** Dogs only. $10 daily fee/pet. Designated rooms, service with restrictions. SAVE 🛜 🛗 🖥 ⊷

WINDOW ROCK

Quality Inn Navajo Nation Capital H
(928) 871-4108. **$81-$101.** 48 W Hwy 264 86515. Center. Ext corridors. **Pets:** Other species. $50 deposit/pet. Service with restrictions, supervision. SAVE 🛜 🛗 🖥 🍽

WINSLOW

Best Western Plus Winslow Inn H
(928) 289-2960. **$70-$140.** 816 Transcon Ln 86047. I-40 exit 255, just n. Int corridors. **Pets:** Dogs only. $20 one-time fee/room. Service with restrictions, supervision. SAVE 🛜 ⊗ 🛗 🖥 ⊷

Econo Lodge at I-40 M
(928) 289-4687. **$54-$63.** 1706 N Park Dr 86047. I-40 exit 253, just s. Ext corridors. **Pets:** Large, other species. Service with restrictions, crate. SAVE 🛜 🛗 🖥 ⊷

La Posada Hotel H
(928) 289-4366. **$109-$169, 7 day notice.** 303 E 2nd St 86047. I-40 exit 253, 1 mi s to Route 66 (2nd St), then just e; in historic downtown. Int corridors. **Pets:** Accepted. 🛜 ⊗ 🛗 🍽 ⊗

YUMA

Candlewood Suites H
(928) 726-2800. **$90-$189.** 2036 S Ave 3 E 85365. I-8 exit 3, just n, then just w on Frontage Rd. Int corridors. **Pets:** Accepted.
🛜 ⊗ 🛗 🖥

Clarion Suites H
(928) 726-4830. **$79-$152.** 2600 S 4th Ave 85364. I-8 exit 2 (16th St/US 95) eastbound, 1 mi w, then 1.3 mi s; exit 3 (SR 280) westbound, 0.5 mi s, then 2 mi w. Ext corridors. **Pets:** Small, dogs only. $100 deposit/room, $20 one-time fee/pet. Designated rooms, service with restrictions, supervision. 🛜 ⊗ 🛗 🖥 ⊷ ⊗

Comfort Inn H
(928) 782-1200. **$69-$99.** 1691 S Riley Ave 85365. I-8 exit 2 (16th St/US 95), just w. Int corridors. **Pets:** Medium. $10 daily fee/room. Designated rooms, service with restrictions, crate. 🛜 🛗 🖥 ⊷

Holiday Inn H ❀
(928) 782-9300. **$99-$169.** 1901 E 18th St 85365. I-8 exit 2 (16th St/US 95), 0.4 mi e on 16th St, just s on Pacific Ave, then just w. Int corridors. **Pets:** Medium, dogs only. $15 daily fee/pet. No service, supervision.
🛜 ⊗ 🛗 🖥 🍽 ⊷

Holiday Inn Express H
(928) 317-1400. **$89-$169.** 2044 S Ave 3 E 85365. I-8 exit 3, just n, then just w on Frontage Rd. Int corridors. **Pets:** Small. $15 daily fee/pet. Designated rooms, service with restrictions, supervision.
🛜 ⊗ 🛗 🖥 ⊷

WWWW **Homewood Suites by Hilton** H
(928) 782-4100. **$109-$309.** 1955 E 16th St 85365. I-8 exit 2 (16th St/US 95), 0.4 mi e. Int corridors. **Pets:** Accepted.
🛜 🛒 📵 📖 🌊 ✖️

WW **Howard Johnson Inn** H
(928) 344-1420. **$56-$122.** 3181 S 4th Ave 85364. I-8 exit 3E (SR 280 S), 1 mi s to 32nd St, then 2 mi w. Ext corridors. **Pets:** Large, other species. $10 daily fee/room. Service with restrictions, supervision.
🛜 ✖️ 📵 📖 🌊

AAA WWW **La Fuente Inn & Suites** H
(928) 329-1814. **$80-$179.** 1513 E 16th St 85365. I-8 exit 2 (16th St/US 95), just e. Ext corridors. **Pets:** Accepted.
SAVE 🛜 📵 📖 🌊 ✖️

WW **Microtel Inn & Suites** H
(928) 345-1777. **$69-$74.** 11274 S Fortuna Rd 85367. I-8 exit 12 (Fortuna Rd), just s, then w on frontage road. Int corridors. **Pets:** Accepted.
🛜 ✖️ 📵 📖 🌊

AAA WWW **Oak Tree Inn** H 🐾
(928) 539-9000. **$69-$99, 3 day notice.** 1731 Sunridge Dr 85365. I-8 exit 2 (16th St/US 95), just e, then just s. Int corridors. **Pets:** Service with restrictions, crate. SAVE 🛜 ✖️ 📵 📖 🌊

WWWW **Radisson Hotel Yuma** H
(928) 783-8000. **$99-$180.** 1501 S Redondo Center Dr 85365. I-8 exit 2 (16th St/US 95), just w, then just n. Int corridors. **Pets:** $15 daily fee/pet. Designated rooms, service with restrictions, supervision.
ECO 🛜 📵 📖 🍴 🌊

AAA WWW **Shilo Inn Hotel & Suites-Yuma** H
(928) 782-9511. **$70-$170.** 1550 S Castle Dome Ave 85365. I-8 exit 2 (16th St/US 95), just e to Yuma Palms Pkwy, just n, then just w. Int corridors. **Pets:** Dogs only. $25 one-time fee/room. Designated rooms, service with restrictions, crate. SAVE 🛜 ✖️ 🛒 📵 📖 🌊 ✖️

WWW **TownePlace Suites by Marriott** H
(928) 783-6900. **$107-$134.** 1726 S Sunridge Dr 85365. I-8 exit 2 (16th St/US 95), just e to Sunridge Dr, then just s. Int corridors.
Pets: Accepted. 🛜 ✖️ 🛒 📵 📖 🌊

AAA WWW **Yuma Cabana Motel** M
(928) 783-8311. **$46-$130, 3 day notice.** 2151 S 4th Ave 85364. I-8 exit 2 (16th St/US 95), 1 mi w, then 0.5 mi s. Int corridors. **Pets:** Small, dogs only. $6 daily fee/pet. Service with restrictions, supervision.
SAVE 🛜 ✖️ 📵 📖 🌊

ARKANSAS

CITY INDEX

ALMA
WW WW **Comfort Inn & Suites** H
(479) 632-4141. **Call for rates.** 439 Hwy 71 N 72921. I-40 exit 13, just n. Ext/int corridors. **Pets:** Accepted. 🛜 📵 📖

ARKADELPHIA
AAA WW WW **Best Western Continental Inn** H 🐾
(870) 246-5592. **$65-$79.** 136 Valley St 71923. I-30 exit 78, just e. Ext corridors. **Pets:** Large. $10 daily fee/pet. Designated rooms, service with restrictions. SAVE 🛜 📵 📖 🌊

BATESVILLE
WW WW **Ramada** H
(870) 698-1800. **$68-$155.** 1325 N St. Louis St 72501. 1 mi n on US 167. Ext corridors. **Pets:** Small. $20 daily fee/pet. Designated rooms, service with restrictions, crate. 🛜 📵 📖 🍴 🌊

WW **Super 8-Batesville** M
(870) 793-5888. **$35-$59.** 1287 N St. Louis St 72501. 1 mi n on US 167. Int corridors. **Pets:** Medium. $25 one-time fee/pet. Service with restrictions, supervision. 🛜 📵 📖

BENTON
AAA WW WW **Best Western Inn** H
(501) 778-9695. **$75-$80.** 17036 I-30 72019. I-30 exit 117 southbound; exit 118 northbound, just w. Ext corridors. **Pets:** Large, other species. $11 daily fee/pet. Service with restrictions, crate. SAVE 🛜 📵 📖 🌊

BENTONVILLE
AAA WWW **Comfort Suites Bentonville/Rogers** H
(479) 439-8373. **$65-$119.** 2011 SE Walton Blvd 72712. I-540 exit 85, just w. Int corridors. **Pets:** $50 one-time fee/room.
SAVE 🛜 ✖️ 📵 📖 🌊 ✖️

WWWW **La Quinta Inn & Suites Bentonville** H
(479) 271-7555. **$71-$159.** 1001 SE Walton Blvd 72712. I-540 exit 85, 0.7 mi w. Int corridors. **Pets:** Medium, other species. Service with restrictions, supervision. 🛜 🛒 📵 📖 🌊 ✖️

WW WW **Suburban Extended Stay Hotel** H
(479) 268-4400. **$50-$60.** 200 SW Suburban Ln 72712. I-540 exit 85, 1.6 mi w. Int corridors. **Pets:** Accepted. 🛜 📵 📖

WW WW **TownePlace Suites by Marriott Bentonville/Rogers** H
(479) 621-0202. **$71-$180.** 3100 SE 14th St 72712. I-540 exit 86, just e. Int corridors. **Pets:** Other species. $50 one-time fee/room. Service with restrictions, crate. 🛜 ✖️ 🛒 📵 📖 🌊

WW WW **Wingate by Wyndham** H
(479) 418-5400. **$63-$123.** 7400 SW Old Farm Blvd 72712. 7.4 mi w of jct Walton and SW Regional Airport blvds. Int corridors. **Pets:** Other species. $75 one-time fee/room. Designated rooms, service with restrictions.
🛜 ✖️ 🛒 📵 📖 🌊 ✖️

BLYTHEVILLE
AAA WW WW **Best Western Blytheville Inn** H
(870) 762-5200. **$70-$80.** 1101 Kari Ln 72315. I-55 exit 63, just nw. Ext corridors. **Pets:** Accepted. SAVE 🛜 📵 📖 🌊

♦♦♦ **Holiday Inn** 🅷
(870) 763-5800. **$95-$159.** 1121 E Main St 72315. I-55 exit 67, just w. Ext/int corridors. **Pets:** Accepted. 📶 ◘ ▣ 🍴 🏊

♦♦ **Quality Inn** 🅷
(870) 763-7081. **Call for rates.** 1520 E Main St 72315. I-55 exit 67, just w. Ext corridors. **Pets:** Accepted. 📶 ◘ ▣ 🍴 🏊

BRYANT

♦♦ **Americas Best Value Inn** 🅼
(501) 653-7800. **$55-$90.** 407 W Commerce St 72022. I-30 exit 123, just sw. Ext corridors. **Pets:** Accepted. 📶 ◘ ▣

♦♦♦ **Comfort Inn & Suites** 🅷
(501) 653-4000. **$75-$125.** 209 W Commerce St 72022. I-30 exit 123, just w. Int corridors. **Pets:** Accepted. 📶 ◘ ▣ 🏊 ✂

AAA ♦♦♦ **Holiday Inn Express** 🅷
(501) 847-0900. **$89-$119.** 2915 Main St 72022. I-30 exit 123, just n on west service road. Int corridors. **Pets:** Medium, dogs only. $25 one-time fee/pet. Designated rooms, service with restrictions, supervision.
SAVE 📶 ♿ ◘ ▣ 🏊

AAA ♦♦ **Hometown Hotel.com** 🅷 🐾
(501) 653-0123. **$59-$84.** 2921 Main St 72022. I-30 exit 123, just nw. Ext/int corridors. **Pets:** Medium, dogs only. $15 one-time fee/pet. Service with restrictions, supervision. SAVE 📶 ⊠ ♿ ◘ ▣

♦♦♦ **La Quinta Inn & Suites Bryant** 🅷
(501) 847-9494. **$94-$155.** 408 W Commerce St 72022. I-30 exit 123, just sw. Int corridors. **Pets:** Medium, other species. Service with restrictions, supervision. 📶 ⊠ ◘ ▣ 🏊

♦♦ **Super 8** 🅼
(501) 847-7888. **$45-$54.** 201 Dell Dr 72022. I-30 exit 123, just e. Ext corridors. **Pets:** Medium, dogs only. $20 deposit/room, $10 one-time fee/pet. Designated rooms, service with restrictions, supervision.
📶 ◘ ▣

♦♦ **Vista Inn & Suites** 🅷
(501) 847-7120. **$65-$96, 7 day notice.** 210 Office Park Dr 72022. I-30 exit 123, just w. Ext corridors. **Pets:** Accepted. 📶 ◘ ▣ 🏊

CABOT

♦♦ **Days Inn & Suites - Cabot** 🅷
(501) 605-1810. **Call for rates.** 1302 W Locust St 72023. US 67/167 exit 19, just ne. Int corridors. **Pets:** Medium. $10 one-time fee/pet. Service with restrictions, supervision. 📶 ⊠ ◘ ▣ 🏊

CLARKSVILLE

AAA ♦♦ **Best Western Sherwood Inn** 🅷 🐾
(479) 754-7900. **$64-$79.** 1207 S Rogers Ave 72830. I-40 exit 58, just n. Ext corridors. **Pets:** $10 one-time fee/room. Service with restrictions, supervision. SAVE 📶 ◘ ▣ 🏊

CLINTON

AAA ♦♦ **Best Western Hillside Inn** 🅷
(501) 745-4700. **$72-$82.** 1025 Hwy 65 B 72031. Just w of jct US 62. Ext corridors. **Pets:** Medium. $8 daily fee/pet. Service with restrictions, supervision. SAVE 📶 ⊠ ◘ ▣ 🏊

CONWAY

AAA ♦♦ **Best Western Conway** 🅷
(501) 329-9855. **$70.** 816 E Oak St 72032. I-40 exit 127, just n. Ext corridors. **Pets:** Accepted. SAVE 📶 ◘ ▣

AAA ♦♦ **Candlewood Suites** 🅷
(501) 329-8551. **$82-$109.** 2360 Sanders St 72033. I-40 exit 125, just se. Int corridors. **Pets:** Medium, other species. $75 one-time fee/room. Service with restrictions, crate. SAVE 📶 ◘ ▣

♦♦♦ **La Quinta Inn & Suites** 🅷
(501) 328-5100. **Call for rates.** 2350 Sanders Rd 72032. I-40 exit 125, just se. Int corridors. **Pets:** Medium, other species. Service with restrictions, supervision. 📶 ⊠ ♿ ◘ ▣ 🏊

♦♦ **Microtel Inn & Suites Conway** 🅷
(501) 327-0898. **$70-$130.** 2475 Sanders St 72032. I-40 exit 125, just se. Int corridors. **Pets:** Small, dogs only. $25 one-time fee/room. Service with restrictions, supervision. 📶 ◘ ▣

EL DORADO

♦♦♦ **La Quinta Inn El Dorado** 🅷
(870) 863-6677. **$67-$125.** 2303 Junction City Rd 71730. Just e of jct US 167 and 82 business route. Int corridors. **Pets:** Medium, other species. Service with restrictions, supervision. 📶 ◘ ▣ 🏊

EUREKA SPRINGS

AAA ♦♦♦ **1886 Crescent Hotel & Spa** 🅷
(479) 253-9766. **$169-$219, 3 day notice.** 75 Prospect Ave 72632. 1.3 mi n of jct SR 23 on US 62B Historic Loop. Int corridors. **Pets:** Other species. $25 daily fee/pet. Service with restrictions, crate.
SAVE 📶 ⊠ ◘ ▣ 🍴 🏊

♦♦♦ **Arsenic & Old Lace B&B** 🅱🅱 🐾
(479) 253-5454. **$149-$299, 15 day notice.** 60 Hillside Ave 72632. 1.2 mi n on SR 23, just sw; downtown. Ext/int corridors. **Pets:** Dogs only. $30 one-time fee/room. Designated rooms, service with restrictions, crate.
📶 ⊠ ◘

AAA ♦♦ **Basin Park Hotel - A Magnuson Grand Hotel** 🅷
(479) 253-7837. **$84-$159, 3 day notice.** 12 Spring St 72632. 0.7 mi n of jct US 62 via SR 23 N; downtown. Int corridors. **Pets:** Medium. $25 one-time fee/room. Service with restrictions, crate.
SAVE 📶 ⊠ ◘ ▣ 🍴

AAA ♦♦ **Best Western Eureka Inn** 🅷
(479) 253-9551. **$60-$129.** 101 E Van Buren 72632. Just w of jct US 62 and SR 23 N. Ext/int corridors. **Pets:** Accepted.
SAVE 📶 ⊠ ◘ ▣ 🏊 ✂

AAA ♦♦ **Best Western Inn of the Ozarks** 🅷 🐾
(479) 253-9768. **$70-$130.** 207 W Van Buren 72632. 0.5 mi w of jct US 62 and SR 23. Ext corridors. **Pets:** Medium, dogs only. $10 daily fee/pet. Service with restrictions, supervision.
SAVE 📶 ◘ ▣ 🍴 🏊 ✂

♦♦ **Days Inn** 🅼 🐾
(479) 253-8863. **$63-$160, 3 day notice.** 120 W Van Buren 72632. Just w of jct US 62 and SR 23. Ext corridors. **Pets:** Dogs only. $15 daily fee/room. Service with restrictions, supervision. 📶 ◘ ▣ 🏊

AAA ♦♦ **Quality Inn & Suites** 🅷
(479) 253-5040. **$80-$109.** 3010 E Van Buren 72632. 0.8 mi e of jct US 62 and SR 23. Ext/int corridors. **Pets:** Accepted.
SAVE 📶 ⊠ ◘ ▣ 🏊

FAYETTEVILLE

AAA ♦♦ **Best Western Windsor Suites** 🅷 🐾
(479) 587-1400. **$80-$95.** 1122 S Futrall Dr 72701. I-540 exit 62, just se. Ext corridors. **Pets:** $20 one-time fee/room. Designated rooms, service with restrictions. SAVE 📶 ◘ ▣ 🏊

♦♦♦ **Comfort Inn & Suites** 🅷
(479) 571-5177. **$80-$125.** 1234 Steamboat Dr 72704. I-540 exit 64, just nw. Int corridors. **Pets:** Small. $25 daily fee/pet. Service with restrictions, crate. 📶 ◘ ▣ 🏊

♦♦ **Sleep Inn by Choice Hotels** 🅷
(479) 587-8700. **$64-$190.** 728 E Millsap Rd 72703. I-540 exit 67, 1.6 mi e, then just s on US 71B. Int corridors. **Pets:** Large, other species. $25 daily fee/pet. Service with restrictions, crate. 📶 ◘ ▣

▼▼▼ **Staybridge Suites** 🚫
(479) 695-2400. **$89-$219.** 1577 W 15th St 72701. Just w of jct Razorback Rd. Int corridors. **Pets:** Accepted.

FORDYCE

▼▼ **Days Inn** 🚫
(870) 352-2400. **$69-$97.** 2500 W 4th St 71742. US 79/167, 1 mi w. Ext/int corridors. **Pets:** Medium. $10 one-time fee/pet. Service with restrictions, supervision.

FORREST CITY

🆔 ▼▼ **Best Western Colony Inn** 🚫 🐾
(870) 633-0870. **$85-$100.** 2333 N Washington St 72335. I-40 exit 241A, just s. Ext corridors. **Pets:** Large, other species. $20 daily fee/pet. Service with restrictions, supervision.

▼▼▼ **Days Inn Forrest City** 🚫
(870) 633-6300. **$70-$120.** 200 Holiday Dr 72335. I-40 exit 241B, just n. Ext corridors. **Pets:** Accepted.

FORT SMITH

▼▼ **AmericInn of Fort Smith** 🚫
(479) 484-0227. **Call for rates.** 2120 Burnham Rd 72903. I-540 exit 8A (Rogers Ave), just w. Int corridors. **Pets:** Accepted.

▼▼ **Aspen Hotel & Suites** 🚫
(479) 452-9000. **$89-$119.** 2900 S 68th St 72903. I-540 exit 8B (Rogers Ave), just e. Int corridors. **Pets:** Accepted.

▼▼ **Baymont Inn & Suites Fort Smith** 🚫
(479) 484-5770. **$50-$75.** 2123 Burnham Rd 72903. I-540 exit 8A (Rogers Ave), just w. Int corridors. **Pets:** Other species. Service with restrictions.

▼▼▼ **Beland Manor Bed & Breakfast** 🅱🅱
(479) 782-3300. **Call for rates.** 1320 S Albert Pike 72903. I-540 exit 8A (Rogers Ave), 1.3 mi w. Int corridors. **Pets:** Accepted.

▼▼▼ **Courtyard by Marriott Downtown Fort Smith** 🚫
(479) 783-2100. **$99-$149.** 900 Rogers Ave 72901. Just s of US 64 (Garrison Ave); downtown. Int corridors. **Pets:** Accepted.

▼▼ **GuestHouse Inn** 🚫
(479) 646-5100. **$65-$80.** 3600 Grinnell Ave 72908. I-540 exit 12, 0.5 mi se. Int corridors. **Pets:** Accepted.

▼▼ **Holiday Inn City Center Fort Smith** 🚫
(479) 783-1000. **$99-$139.** 700 Rogers Ave 72901. Just s of US 64 (Garrison Ave); downtown. Int corridors. **Pets:** Accepted.

▼▼ **Holiday Inn Express** 🚫
(479) 452-7500. **Call for rates.** 6813 Phoenix Ave 72903. I-540 exit 8B (Rogers Ave), 0.6 mi e, then 0.5 mi s. Int corridors. **Pets:** Large. $25 daily fee/pet. Designated rooms, supervision.

🆔 ▼▼ **Residence Inn by Marriott** 🚫
(479) 478-8300. **$94-$123.** 3005 S 74th St 72903. I-540 exit 8A (Rogers Ave), 0.8 mi e. Int corridors. **Pets:** $75 one-time fee/room. Service with restrictions, crate.

HARDY

🆔 ▼▼ **Best Western Village Inn** Ⓜ
(870) 856-2176. **$72-$80.** 3587 Hwy 62/412 72542. 2 mi sw on US 62/412. Ext corridors. **Pets:** Small, dogs only. $25 daily fee/pet. Designated rooms, service with restrictions, supervision.

HARRISON

▼▼▼ **Holiday Inn Express Hotel & Suites** 🚫
(870) 741-3636. **Call for rates.** 117 Hwy 43 E 72601. Just e of jct US 62/65/412 and SR 43. Int corridors. **Pets:** Small. $25 one-time fee/pet. Service with restrictions, supervision.

▼▼ **Quality Inn** 🚫
(870) 741-7676. **$70-$80.** 1210 Hwy 62/65 N 72601. 1 mi e on US 62/65/412. Ext/int corridors. **Pets:** Small, other species. $25 one-time fee/pet. Service with restrictions, supervision.

HELENA-WEST HELENA

🆔 ▼▼▼ **Best Western Inn** 🚫
(870) 572-2592. **$80-$90.** 1053 Hwy 49 W 72390. US 49, 3 mi w. Ext corridors. **Pets:** Accepted.

HOPE

🆔 ▼▼▼ **Best Western of Hope** 🚫 🐾
(870) 777-9222. **$75-$95.** 1800 Holiday Dr 71801. I-30 exit 30, just nw. Ext corridors. **Pets:** Other species. $10 daily fee/room. Service with restrictions, supervision.

HOT SPRINGS

🆔 ▼▼▼ **Best Western Winner's Circle Inn** 🚫 🐾
(501) 624-2531. **$90-$190, 7 day notice.** 2520 Central Ave 71901. 1.3 mi n of jct US 270 and SR 7. Ext corridors. **Pets:** Medium, dogs only. $25 one-time fee/room. Designated rooms, service with restrictions, crate.

🆔 ▼▼▼ **Clarion Resort** 🚫
(501) 525-1391. **$90-$150.** 4813 Central Ave 71913. 5.5 mi s of jct US 270 and SR 7. Int corridors. **Pets:** Small. $25 one-time fee/room, $10 daily fee/room. Designated rooms, service with restrictions, supervision.

🆔 ▼▼▼ **Staybridge Suites** 🚫
(501) 525-6500. **$89-$199.** 103 Lookout Cir 71913. 3.5 mi s of jct US 270 and SR 7. Int corridors. **Pets:** Large, other species. $75 one-time fee/room. Supervision.

JACKSONVILLE

▼▼ **Super 8** 🚫
(501) 982-9219. **$62-$90.** 1850 John Harden Dr 72076. US 67/167 exit 10B southbound; exit 11 northbound. Ext corridors. **Pets:** Other species. $10 daily fee/pet. Designated rooms, service with restrictions, supervision.

JOHNSON

▼▼▼ **TownePlace Suites by Marriott Fayetteville North/Springdale** 🚫 🐾
(479) 439-1905. **$89-$194.** 5437 S 48th St 72741. I-540 exit 69, just se. Int corridors. **Pets:** Small, other species. $75 one-time fee/room. Service with restrictions, crate.

JONESBORO

▼▼ **Comfort Inn & Suites** 🚫
(870) 972-9000. **Call for rates.** 2911 Gilmore Dr 72401. Just ne of jct US 63 and Caraway Rd. Int corridors. **Pets:** Accepted.

▼▼▼ **Fairfield Inn & Suites Jonesboro** 🚫 🐾
(870) 277-1870. **$80-$123.** 3408 Access Rd 72401. 0.7 mi e of jct Stadium Blvd and Phillips Dr. Int corridors. **Pets:** $75 one-time fee/room. Service with restrictions, supervision.

▼▼▼ **Holiday Inn of Jonesboro** 🚫
(870) 935-2030. **Call for rates.** 3006 S Caraway Rd 72401. Just n of jct US 63. Ext/int corridors. **Pets:** Medium. $15 one-time fee/room. Service with restrictions.

LITTLE ROCK

Comfort Inn & Suites, Downtown Little Rock @ The Clinton Library H

(501) 687-7700. **$89-$110.** 707 I-30 72202. I-30 exit 140A, just e. Int corridors. **Pets:** Medium. $50 one-time fee/room. Service with restrictions, supervision.

Comfort Inn & Suites Little Rock Airport H

(501) 376-2466. **$76-$96.** 4301 E Roosevelt Rd 72206. I-440 exit 3, just n. Int corridors. **Pets:** Other species. $25 one-time fee/room. Designated rooms, service with restrictions, supervision.

Embassy Suites Hotel Little Rock H

(501) 312-9000. **$120-$169.** 11301 Financial Centre Pkwy 72211. Jct I-430 and 630, just w. Int corridors. **Pets:** Medium. $50 one-time fee/room. Designated rooms, service with restrictions, crate.

Hilton Little Rock H

(501) 664-5020. **$109-$129.** 925 S University Ave 72204. I-630 exit 5 (University Ave), just s. Int corridors. **Pets:** Medium. $50 one-time fee/room. No service.

Holiday Inn Airport Conference Center H

(501) 490-1000. **$89-$129.** 3201 Bankhead Dr 72206. I-440 exit 3, just s. Int corridors. **Pets:** Accepted.

Holiday Inn Express Airport H

(501) 490-4000. **$85-$105.** 3121 Bankhead Dr 72206. I-440 exit 3, just s. Ext/int corridors. **Pets:** $25 one-time fee/pet. Service with restrictions, supervision.

Residence Inn by Marriott H

(501) 312-0200. **$125-$139.** 1401 S Shackleford Rd 72211. I-430 exit 5, just n. Int corridors. **Pets:** Accepted.

TownePlace Suites by Marriott - Little Rock H

(501) 708-1917. **$85-$123.** 12 Crossings Ct 72205. I-430 exit 5, 0.6 mi e. Int corridors. **Pets:** Other species. $75 one-time fee/room. Service with restrictions.

LONOKE

Days Inn H

(501) 676-5138. **$55-$64.** 105 Dee Dee Ln 72086. I-40 exit 175, just n. Ext corridors. **Pets:** Medium. $10 daily fee/pet. Service with restrictions, supervision.

Holiday Inn Express Hotel & Suites H

(501) 676-7800. **$104-$151.** 104 Dee Dee Ln 72086. I-40 exit 175, just n. Int corridors. **Pets:** Medium. $25 daily fee/pet. Service with restrictions, supervision.

Super 8 H

(501) 676-8880. **$63-$76.** 102 Dee Dee Ln 72086. I-40 exit 175, just n. Int corridors. **Pets:** Small, dogs only. $10 daily fee/pet. Designated rooms, service with restrictions, supervision.

MARION

Best Western-Regency Motor Inn H

(870) 739-3278. **$50-$64.** 3635 I-55 72364. I-55 exit 10, just nw. Ext corridors. **Pets:** Small. Designated rooms, service with restrictions, crate.

MCGEHEE

Best Western McGehee M

(870) 222-3564. **$77-$81.** 1202 Hwy 65 N 71654. Center. Ext corridors. **Pets:** Accepted.

MOUNTAIN HOME

Comfort Inn H

(870) 424-9000. **$80-$165.** 1031 Highland Cir 72653. 1.5 mi e on US 62B. Ext/int corridors. **Pets:** Accepted.

Days Inn H

(870) 425-1010. **$65-$77.** 1746 E Hwy 62B 72653. 2.3 mi e on US 62B. Int corridors. **Pets:** Accepted.

Holiday Inn Express H

(870) 425-6200. **$115-$135.** 1005 Coley Dr 72653. 1.4 mi e on US 62B. Int corridors. **Pets:** Accepted.

Super 8-Mountain Home M

(870) 424-5600. **$54-$60.** 865 Hwy 62 E 72653. 1.3 mi e on US 62B. Int corridors. **Pets:** $10 daily fee/pet. No service, supervision.

Teal Point Resort CA

(870) 492-5145. **$80-$410.** 715 Teal Point Rd 72653. 3.5 mi e of jct US 62 and 62 business route, 0.6 mi n on CR 406, follow signs. Ext corridors. **Pets:** $7 daily fee/pet. Designated rooms, crate.

MOUNTAIN VIEW

Best Western Fiddlers Inn M

(870) 269-2828. **$70-$90, 7 day notice.** 601 Sylamore Ave 72560. 1 mi n on SR 5, 9 and 14. Ext corridors. **Pets:** Medium, dogs only. $15 daily fee/pet. Service with restrictions, crate.

NORTH LITTLE ROCK

Holiday Inn-North H

(501) 758-1851. **$89-$99.** 120 W Pershing Blvd 72114. I-40 exit 152 westbound; exit 153A eastbound. Int corridors. **Pets:** Accepted.

La Quinta Inn & Suites Little Rock N - McCain Mall H

(501) 945-0808. **$68-$137.** 4311 Warden Rd 72116. US 67/167 exit 1B northbound; exit 1 southbound. Int corridors. **Pets:** Medium, other species. Service with restrictions, supervision.

La Quinta Inn Little Rock North Landers Road H

(501) 758-8888. **$58-$115.** 4100 E McCain Blvd 72117. Jct US 67/167 exit 1A northbound; exit 1 southbound. Ext corridors. **Pets:** Medium, other species. Service with restrictions, supervision.

Quality Inn H

(501) 771-2090. **$69-$79.** 500 W 29th St 72114. I-40 exit 152, just s. Int corridors. **Pets:** Accepted.

Red Roof Inn H

(501) 945-0080. **$49-$64.** 5711 Pritchard Dr 72117. I-40 exit 157, just sw. Int corridors. **Pets:** Large, other species. No service, supervision.

Residence Inn by Marriott-North H

(501) 945-7777. **$108-$130.** 4110 Healthcare Dr 72117. I-40 exit 156, just nw. Int corridors. **Pets:** Accepted.

PINE BLUFF

Best Western Plus Presidential Hotel & Suites H

(870) 535-6300. **$69-$139.** 3104 Market St 71601. I-530 exit 46, just n. Int corridors. **Pets:** Accepted.

Comfort Inn H

(870) 535-5300. **$55-$109.** 2809 Pines Mall Dr 71601. I-530 exit 46, just n. Int corridors. **Pets:** Service with restrictions, crate.

▼▼ Days Inn & Suites 🅷
(870) 534-1800. **$53-$99.** 406 N Blake St 71601. Just n of jct US 65B and 79B. Ext corridors. **Pets:** Accepted. 📶 🛗 💻 ➳

▼▼ Holiday Inn Express Hotel & Suites 🅷
(870) 879-3800. **Call for rates.** 3620 Camden Rd 71603. I-530 exit 39, just sw. Int corridors. **Pets:** Accepted. 📶 ♿ 🛗 💻 ➳

POCAHONTAS
▼▼ Days Inn & Suites 🅷
(870) 892-9500. **$75.** 2805 Hwy 67 S 72455. 1.7 mi s. Int corridors. **Pets:** Other species. $25 deposit/pet, $10 daily fee/pet. Designated rooms, service with restrictions, supervision. 📶 🛗 💻 ➳

ROGERS
AAA ▼▼▼▼ Aloft Rogers-Bentonville 🅷 🐾
(479) 268-6799. **$90-$170.** 1103 S 52nd St 72758. I-540 exit 83, just nw. Int corridors. **Pets:** Medium. No service, supervision.

▼▼ Candlewood Suites 🅷
(479) 636-2783. **$99-$122.** 4601 W Rozell St 72757. I-540 exit 85, 0.5 mi n on 46th St. Int corridors. **Pets:** Accepted. 📶 🛗 💻 ➳

▼▼▼▼ Country Inn & Suites By Carlson 🅷
(479) 633-0055. **Call for rates.** 4304 W Walnut St 72756. I-540 exit 85, just e. Int corridors. **Pets:** Accepted. 📶 ✕ 🛗 💻 ➳

▼▼▼▼ Embassy Suites Northwest Arkansas 🅷 🐾
(479) 254-8400. **$114-$189.** 3303 Pinnacle Hills Pkwy 72758. I-540 exit 83, just w, then 0.6 mi s. Int corridors. **Pets:** Medium, other species. $50 one-time fee/room. Designated rooms, service with restrictions, crate.
📶 ♿ 🛗 💻 🍽 ➳ ✕

▼▼ Microtel Inn & Suites 🅷
(479) 636-5551. **$45-$54.** 909 S 8th St 72756. 0.5 mi s of jct Walnut Blvd. Int corridors. **Pets:** Accepted. 📶 ✕ 🛗 💻

AAA ▼▼▼▼ Residence Inn by Marriott 🅷
(479) 636-5900. **$69-$199.** 4611 W Locust St 72756. I-540 exit 85, 0.4 mi n on 46th St. Int corridors. **Pets:** Accepted.
SAVE 📶 ✕ ♿ 🛗 💻 ➳ ✕

▼▼▼▼ Staybridge Suites Rogers-Bentonville 🅷
(479) 845-5701. **Call for rates.** 1801 S 52nd St 72758. I-540 exit 83, just nw. Int corridors. **Pets:** Medium. $15 daily fee/room. Service with restrictions, crate. 📶 ✕ ♿ 🛗 💻

RUSSELLVILLE
▼▼▼▼ La Quinta Inn & Suites 🅷
(479) 967-2299. **Call for rates.** 111 E Harrell Dr 72802. I-40 exit 81, just se. Int corridors. **Pets:** Medium, other species. Service with restrictions, supervision. 📶 ✕ 🛗 💻 ➳ ✕

▼▼ Quality Inn 🅷
(479) 967-7500. **$65-$70.** 3019 E Parkway Dr 72802. I-40 exit 84, just s. Ext corridors. **Pets:** Medium. $10 daily fee/pet. Service with restrictions, supervision. 📶 🛗 💻 ➳

SPRINGDALE
▼▼▼ Hampton Inn & Suites 🅷
(479) 756-3500. **$89-$179.** 1700 S 48th St 72762. I-540 exit 72, just e. Int corridors. **Pets:** Accepted. 📶 ♿ 🛗 💻 ➳

▼▼▼ Holiday Inn Northwest AR Hotel & Convention Center 🅷
(479) 751-8300. **$89-$159.** 1500 S 48th St 72762. I-540 exit 72, just e. Int corridors. **Pets:** Small. $39 daily fee/room. No service, supervision.
📶 ✕ 🛗 💻 🍽 ➳ ✕

▼▼▼ La Quinta Inn & Suites Springdale 🅷
(479) 751-2626. **$67-$135.** 1300 S 48th St 72764. I-540 exit 72, just e. Int corridors. **Pets:** Medium, other species. Service with restrictions, supervision. 📶 ♿ 🛗 💻 ➳ ✕

AAA ▼▼▼▼ Residence Inn by Marriott 🅷
(479) 872-9100. **$71-$156.** 1740 S 48th St 72762. I-540 exit 72, just e to 48th St, then just s. Int corridors. **Pets:** Accepted.
SAVE 📶 ✕ 🛗 💻 ➳ ✕

STAR CITY
▼▼ Star City Inn & Suites 🅷
(870) 628-6883. **$57-$95.** 1308 N Lincoln Ave 71667. Just n on US 425. Int corridors. **Pets:** Small, dogs only. $5 daily fee/pet. Service with restrictions, supervision. 🛗 💻 ➳

STUTTGART
▼▼ Days Inn & Suites 🅷
(870) 673-3616. **$65-$113.** 708 W Michigan St 72160. Just w on US 63/79. Ext corridors. **Pets:** Accepted. 📶 🛗 💻 ➳

TEXARKANA
▼▼ La Quinta Inn & Suites Texarkana 🅷
(870) 773-1000. **$82-$149.** 5102 N State Line Ave 71854. I-30 exit 223B, just n. Int corridors. **Pets:** Medium, other species. Service with restrictions, supervision. 📶 🛗 💻 ➳

VAN BUREN
AAA ▼▼ Best Western Van Buren Inn 🅷
(479) 474-8100. **$85.** 1903 N 6th St 72956. I-40 exit 5, just n. Ext corridors. **Pets:** Accepted. SAVE 📶 💻 ➳

▼▼▼▼ Sleep Inn & Suites 🅷
(479) 262-6776. **$75-$90.** 1633 N 12th Ct 72956. 0.6 mi e of jct SR 59. Int corridors. **Pets:** Medium, other species. $15 deposit/pet.
📶 ✕ ♿ 🛗 💻 ➳

CALIFORNIA

CITY INDEX

ALPINE

▼▼▼▼ Ayres Inn Alpine  ❀

(619) 445-5800. **$99-$139.** 1251 Tavern Rd 91901. I-8 exit 30 (Tavern Rd), just s. Ext corridors. **Pets:** Small, dogs only. $45 one-time fee/pet. Designated rooms, service with restrictions, supervision.

🛜 🛗 📺

ALTURAS

▲▲▲ ▼▼ Best Western Trailside Inn M

(530) 233-4111. **$82-$91.** 343 N Main St 96101. Just s of jct US 395/SR 299 and Main St; jct W 4th St; center. Ext corridors. **Pets:** Medium, dogs only. $15 daily fee/pet. Designated rooms, service with restrictions, supervision. SAVE 🛜 🛗 📺 🏊

▲▲▲ ▼▼ Rim Rock Motel M

(530) 233-5455. **$58-$75.** 22760 US 395 96101. Jct SR 299 and US 395, 0.7 mi ne. Ext corridors. **Pets:** Small, dogs only. $10 one-time fee/pet. Designated rooms, service with restrictions, supervision.

SAVE 🛜 🛗 📺

▲▲▲ ▼▼ Super 8 M

(530) 233-3545. **$59-$67.** 511 N Main St 96101. Jct SR 299 and US 395, 0.4 mi s on US 395; at W 5th St. Ext corridors. **Pets:** Accepted.

SAVE 🛜 🛗 📺

ANAHEIM

▲▲▲ ▼▼ Anaheim Plaza Hotel & Suites H

(714) 772-5900. **$89-$218.** 1700 S Harbor Blvd 92802. I-5 exit 110 (Harbor Blvd/Ball Rd) northbound; exit 110A (Harbor Blvd) southbound, 0.6 mi s. Ext corridors. **Pets:** Medium. $15 daily fee/pet. Service with restrictions, supervision. SAVE 🛜 ♿ 🛗 📺 🍽 🏊

▲▲▲ ▼▼ Clarion Hotel Anaheim Resort H

(714) 750-3131. **$69-$199.** 616 Convention Way 92802. I-5 exit 109 (Katella Ave/Disney Way) northbound; exit 109A (Katella Ave/Orangewood Ave) southbound, 0.8 mi w to Harbor Blvd, just s, then just w. Int corridors. **Pets:** Small. $25 one-time fee/pet, $10 daily fee/pet. Designated rooms, service with restrictions, crate.

SAVE 🛜 ♿ 🛗 📺 🍽 🏊

▼▼▼ Embassy Suites Hotel Anaheim-North H

(714) 632-1221. **$99-$199.** 3100 E Frontera St 92806. SR 91 exit 31 (Kramer Blvd/Glasset St) eastbound; exit 32 westbound just s, then just e. Int corridors. **Pets:** Accepted. ECO 🛜 🛗 📺 🍽 🏊

▼▼ Extended StayAmerica-Orange County-Anaheim Convention Center H ❀

(714) 502-9988. **$59-$89.** 1742 S Clementine St 92802. I-5 exit 109 (Katella Ave/Disney Way) northbound; exit 109A (Katella Ave/Orangewood Ave) southbound, just w, then just n. Int corridors. **Pets:** Other species. $25 daily fee/pet. Service with restrictions. 🛜 🛗 📺 🏊

▼▼▼ Hilton Anaheim H

(714) 750-4321. **$109-$299.** 777 Convention Way 92802. I-5 exit 109 (Katella Ave/Disney Way) northbound; exit 109A (Katella Ave/Orangewood Ave) southbound, 0.8 mi w on Katella Ave, just s on Harbor Blvd, then just w. Int corridors. **Pets:** Accepted.

ECO 🛜 ✖ ♿ 🛗 📺 🍽 🏊 ✖

▼▼ Hotel Menage H

(714) 758-0900. **$129-$299.** 1221 S Harbor Blvd 92805. I-5 exit 110 (Harbor Blvd/Ball Rd) northbound; exit 110A (Harbor Blvd) southbound, just n. Ext corridors. **Pets:** Accepted. 🛜 ✖ 🛗 📺 🍽 🏊

▼▼ La Quinta Inn & Suites Anaheim Disneyland H

(714) 635-5000. **$89-$169.** 1752 S Clementine St 92802. I-5 exit 109 (Katella Ave/Disney Way) northbound; exit 109A (Katella Ave/Orangewood Ave) southbound, just w, then just n. Int corridors. **Pets:** Medium, other species. Service with restrictions, supervision.

🛜 ✖ 🛗 📺 🏊 ✖

▼▼ Motel 6 Anaheim-Maingate #1066 M

(714) 520-9696. **$55-$85.** 100 W Disney Way 92802. I-5 exit 109 (Katella Ave/Disney Way) northbound; exit 109B (Disney Way/Anaheim Blvd) southbound, just w, just n on Anaheim Blvd, then just w. Ext corridors. **Pets:** Other species. Service with restrictions, supervision. 🛜 🛗 🏊

▲▲▲ ▼▼▼ Red Lion Hotel Anaheim H

(714) 750-2801. **$99-$250, 3 day notice.** 1850 S Harbor Blvd 92802. I-5 exit 109 (Katella Ave/Disney Way) northbound; exit 109A (Katella Ave/Orangewood Ave) southbound, 0.8 mi w, then just s. Int corridors. **Pets:** Accepted. SAVE 🛜 ✖ 🛗 📺 🍽 🏊

▼▼▼ Residence Inn by Marriott Anaheim Maingate H ❀

(714) 533-3555. **$113-$219.** 1700 S Clementine St 92802. I-5 exit 109 (Katella Ave/Disney Way) northbound; exit 109A (Katella Ave/Orangewood Ave) southbound, just w, then just n. Ext corridors. **Pets:** Medium. $100 one-time fee/room. Designated rooms, service with restrictions, supervision. 🛜 ✖ ♿ 🛗 📺 🏊 ✖

▲▲▲ ▼▼▼ Sheraton Anaheim Hotel H ❀

(714) 778-1700. **$139-$189.** 900 S Disneyland Dr 92802. I-5 exit 110 (Harbor Blvd/Ball Rd) northbound; exit 110A (Harbor Blvd) southbound, just n, just w on Ball Rd, then just n. Int corridors. **Pets:** Other species. $25 one-time fee/room. Service with restrictions.

SAVE 🛜 ✖ ♿ 🛗 📺 🍽 🏊 ✖

▲▲▲ ▼▼▼ Sheraton Park Hotel at the Anaheim Resort H ❀

(714) 750-1811. **$129-$295, 3 day notice.** 1855 S Harbor Blvd 92802. I-5 exit 109 (Katella Ave/Disney Way) northbound; exit 109A (Katella Ave/Orangewood Ave) southbound, 0.8 mi w, then just s. Int corridors. **Pets:** Medium, other species. $50 one-time fee/room. Designated rooms, service with restrictions, supervision.

SAVE 🛜 ✖ 🛗 📺 🏊

▼▼▼ Staybridge Suites -Anaheim Resort H

(714) 748-7700. **$89-$139, 3 day notice.** 1855 S Manchester Ave 92802. I-5 exit 109 (Katella Ave/Disney Way) northbound; exit 109A (Katella Ave/Orangewood Ave) southbound, just w, then 0.3 mi s; adjacent to west side of freeway. Int corridors. **Pets:** Medium, dogs only. $15 one-time fee/room. Service with restrictions, crate.

🛜 ♿ 🛗 📺 🏊

▲▲▲ ▼▼▼ TownePlace Suites Anaheim Maingate Near Angel Stadium M

(714) 939-9700. **$89-$139.** 1730 S State College Blvd 92806. I-5 exit 109 (Katella Ave/Disney Way) northbound; exit 109A (Katella Ave/Orangewood Ave) southbound, 0.7 mi e, then just n. Int corridors. **Pets:** Accepted. SAVE 🛜 ✖ 🛗 📺 🏊 ✖

ANAHEIM HILLS

▲▲▲ ▼▼▼ Best Western Anaheim Hills H

(714) 779-0252. **$72-$120.** 5710 E La Palma Ave 92807. SR 91 exit 36 (SR 90/Imperial Hwy), just n. Ext corridors. **Pets:** Medium. $15 daily fee/pet. Designated rooms, service with restrictions, supervision.

SAVE 🛜 🛗 📺 🏊 ✖

ANDERSON

▲▲▲ ▼▼▼ Best Western Anderson Inn H

(530) 365-2753. **$90-$150.** 2688 Gateway Dr 96007. I-5 exit 668 (Central Anderson) northbound, just e; exit southbound, just e, just s on McMurry Dr, then just e. Ext corridors. **Pets:** Medium. $15 daily fee/pet. Designated rooms, service with restrictions, supervision.

SAVE 🛜 ♿ 🛗 📺 🏊

▼▼▼ Gaia Hotel Shasta, Woodside Grill Restaurant & Lotus Spa H

(530) 365-7077. **Call for rates.** 4125 Riverside Pl 96007. I-5 exit 670 (Riverside Ave), just e. Ext corridors. **Pets:** Accepted.

ECO 🛜 ✖ 🛗 📺 🍽 🏊 ✖

ANGELS CAMP

AAA ♦♦♦ Angels Inn Motel **H**
(209) 736-4242. **$69-$189.** 600 N Main St 95221. On SR 49; north end of town. Ext corridors. **Pets:** Dogs only. $10 daily fee/pet. Service with restrictions, supervision. SAVE 🛜 ⌖M 🛢 🖵 🏊

AAA ♦♦♦ Best Western Plus Cedar Inn & Suites **H**
(209) 736-4000. **$79-$199.** 444 S Main St 95222. On SR 49; center. Ext/int corridors. **Pets:** Accepted. SAVE 🛜 ✕ ⌖M 🛢 🖵 🏊

AAA ♦♦ Jumping Frog Motel **M**
(209) 736-2191. **$60-$150, 3 day notice.** 330 Murphys Grade Rd 95222. Just e of jct SR 49; center. Ext corridors. **Pets:** Small, dogs only. $10 one-time fee/pet, $10 daily fee/pet. Service with restrictions, supervision. SAVE 🛢 🖵

ANTIOCH

♦♦♦♦ Comfort Suites Antioch-Oakley **H**
(925) 755-1222. **$89-$139.** 5549 Bridgehead Rd 94561. In Oakley; just e of SR 160 and 4; just n of Main St. Int corridors. **Pets:** Medium, dogs only. $25 daily fee/pet. Designated rooms, service with restrictions, supervision. 🛜 ✕ ⌖M 🛢 🖵 🏊

APTOS

♦♦♦ Bayview Hotel **CI**
(831) 688-8654. **Call for rates.** 8041 Soquel Dr 95003. SR 1 exit State Park Dr E, 0.8 mi s. Int corridors. **Pets:** Accepted. 🛜 ✕ 🍴

ARCATA

♦♦♦ Arcata Redwood Inn **M**
(707) 826-2827. **Call for rates.** 4701 Valley West Blvd 95521. US 101 exit Giuntoli Ln/Janes Rd, just e, then just s. Ext corridors. **Pets:** Medium, dogs only. $20 daily fee/room. Designated rooms, service with restrictions, supervision. 🛜 ⌖M 🛢 🖵 🏊

♦♦ Arcata Super 8 **H**
(707) 822-8888. **$49-$134.** 4887 Valley West Blvd 95521. US 101 exit Giuntoli Ln/Janes Rd, just e, then just s. Int corridors. **Pets:** Accepted. 🛜 🛢 🖵

AAA ♦♦♦ Best Western Arcata Inn **M** ❀
(707) 826-0313. **$90-$186.** 4827 Valley West Blvd 95521. US 101 exit Giuntoli Ln/Janes Rd, just e, then just s. Ext corridors. **Pets:** Dogs only. $20 one-time fee/room. Service with restrictions, crate. SAVE 🛜 🛢 🖵 🏊

♦♦ Hotel Arcata **H**
(707) 826-0217. **$85-$156.** 708 9th St 95521. Corner of G St; downtown; in Plaza. Int corridors. **Pets:** Accepted. 🛜 🖵 🍴 🐾

AAA ♦♦♦ Quality Inn Arcata **H**
(707) 822-0409. **$79-$125.** 3535 Janes Rd 95521. US 101 exit Giuntoli Ln/Janes Rd, just w. Int corridors. **Pets:** Other species. $10 one-time fee/pet. Service with restrictions, supervision. SAVE 🛜 🛢 🖵 🏊

ARNOLD

AAA ♦♦♦ Arnold Meadowmont Lodge **M**
(209) 795-1394. **$65-$155.** 2011 Hwy 4 95223. On SR 4; west end of town. Ext corridors. **Pets:** Dogs only. $20 daily fee/room. Service with restrictions, supervision. SAVE 🛜 ⌖M 🛢 🖵 🐾

ARROYO GRANDE

AAA ♦♦♦ Best Western Casa Grande Inn **M**
(805) 481-7398. **$59-$165.** 850 Oak Park Rd 93420. US 101 exit 188 (Oak Park Rd), just e. Ext/int corridors. **Pets:** Accepted. SAVE 🛜 🛢 🖵 🏊 ✕

AUBURN

AAA ♦♦♦♦ Best Western Golden Key **H** ❀
(530) 885-8611. **$99-$170.** 13450 Lincoln Way 95603. I-80 exit 121 (Foresthill Rd-Auburn Ravine Rd), just e, then n. Ext corridors. **Pets:** Other species. $15 one-time fee/pet. Designated rooms, service with restrictions, supervision. SAVE 🛜 ⌖M 🛢 🖵 🏊

AAA ♦♦♦ Comfort Inn **H**
(530) 885-1800. **$86-$90.** 1875 Auburn Ravine Rd 95603. I-80 exit 121 (Foresthill Rd-Auburn Ravine Rd), just w, then just s. Int corridors. **Pets:** Small, other species. $15 one-time fee/pet, $15 daily fee/pet. Designated rooms, service with restrictions, supervision.
SAVE 🛜 🛢 🖵 🏊

♦♦♦ Foothills Motel **M**
(530) 885-8444. **Call for rates.** 13431 Bowman Rd 95603. I-80 exit 121 (Foresthill Rd-Auburn Ravine Rd), just w, then just n. Ext corridors. **Pets:** Accepted. 🛜 ⌖M 🛢 🏊

♦♦♦ Holiday Inn-Auburn **H** ❀
(530) 887-8787. **$109-$209.** 120 Grass Valley Hwy 95603. I-80 exit SR 49, just nw. Int corridors. **Pets:** Medium, dogs only. $30 one-time fee/room. Service with restrictions, crate.
ECO 🛜 ⌖M 🛢 🖵 🍴 🏊

♦♦ Motel 6 #4152 **M**
(530) 888-7829. **$72-$78.** 1819 Auburn Ravine Rd 95603. I-80 exit 121 (Foresthill-Auburn Ravine rds), just w, then just s. Int corridors. **Pets:** Other species. Service with restrictions, supervision.
🛜 ⌖M 🛢 🏊

AAA ♦♦♦ Quality Inn Gold Country **M**
(530) 885-7025. **$70-$120.** 13490 Lincoln Way 95603. I-80 exit 121 (Foresthill-Auburn Ravine rds), just e, then just n. Ext/int corridors. **Pets:** Accepted. SAVE 🛜 ⌖M 🛢 🖵 🏊

AVILA BEACH

♦♦♦ Avila Village Inn **H**
(805) 627-1810. **$139-$399.** 6655 Bay Laurel Dr 93424. US 101 exit 195 (Avila Beach Dr), 1.2 mi w to San Luis Bay Dr, then just w. Int corridors. **Pets:** $25 daily fee/room. Designated rooms, service with restrictions, supervision. 🛜 ✕ ⌖M 🛢

BAKERSFIELD

AAA ♦♦ Americas Best Value Inn **M**
(661) 366-1630. **$50-$85.** 8230 E Brundage Ln 93307. SR 99 exit 24 (SR 58 E), 7 mi e, exit 117 (SR 184/Weedpatch Hwy), just n, then just e. Ext/int corridors. **Pets:** Medium, other species. $5 daily fee/pet. Service with restrictions, supervision. SAVE 🛜 🛢 🖵 🏊

AAA ♦♦♦ Best Western Crystal Palace Inn & Suites **H**
(661) 327-9651. **$76-$90, 3 day notice.** 2620 Buck Owens Blvd 93308. SR 99 exit 26B (Buck Owens Blvd) northbound, just s; exit 26 (SR 58 W/SR 178 E) southbound, just e, then just n. Int corridors. **Pets:** Large, other species. $10 one-time fee/pet. Designated rooms, service with restrictions, supervision. SAVE 🛜 ⌖M 🛢 🖵 🍴 🏊

AAA ♦♦♦ Best Western Heritage Inn **M**
(661) 764-6268. **$90-$106.** 253 Trask St 93314. I-5 exit 253 (Stockdale Hwy), just e. Ext corridors. **Pets:** Small. $10 daily fee/pet. Designated rooms, service with restrictions, supervision.
SAVE 🛜 ⌖M 🛢 🖵 🏊

AAA ♦♦♦ Best Western Plus Hill House **H** ❀
(661) 327-4064. **$72-$139.** 700 Truxtun Ave 93301. SR 99 exit 25 (California Ave), 1.2 mi e, 0.4 mi n on Chester Ave, then 0.4 mi e. Int corridors. **Pets:** Medium. $15 daily fee/pet. Designated rooms, service with restrictions, supervision. SAVE 🛜 ⌖M 🛢 🖵 🍴 🏊

♦♦ California Best Inn **M**
(661) 834-3377. **Call for rates.** 1030 Wible Rd 93304. SR 99 exit 23 (Ming Ave), just e, then 0.7 mi n. Ext corridors. **Pets:** Accepted.
🛜 🛢 🖵 🏊

▼▼▼▼ DoubleTree by Hilton Hotel Bakersfield H
(661) 323-7111. **$89-$116.** 3100 Camino Del Rio Ct 93308. SR 99 exit 26 (SR 58 W/Rosedale Hwy), just w, then just s. Int corridors.
Pets: Accepted. ⬛ 🛜 ⊠ ⚿M 🔋 💻 ⑪ ➿

▼▼ Extended StayAmerica-Bakersfield-California Avenue H 🐾
(661) 322-6888. **$69-$84.** 3318 California Ave 93304. SR 99 exit 25 (California Ave), on east side of freeway, then just n. Ext corridors.
Pets: Other species. $25 daily fee/pet. Service with restrictions.
🛜 🔋 💻

▼▼ Extended Stay Deluxe Bakersfield-Chester Lane H 🐾
(661) 328-8181. **$95-$110.** 3600 Chester Ln 93309. SR 99 exit 25 (California Ave), just w to Real Rd, just s, then just w. Int corridors.
Pets: Other species. $25 daily fee/pet. Service with restrictions.
🛜 🔋 💻

◈◈◇ ▼▼ Garden Suites Inn H
(661) 833-6066. **$55-$89.** 2310 Wible Rd 93304. SR 99 exit 23 (Ming Ave), just e. Int corridors. **Pets:** Medium. $5 daily fee/pet. Service with restrictions, supervision. ⬛ 🛜 🔋 💻 ➿

▼▼▼▼ Hampton Inn & Suites Bakersfield East H
(661) 321-9424. **$99-$119.** 7941 E Brundage Ln 93307. SR 99 exit 24 (SR 58), 7 mi e; exit 117 (SR 184/Weedpatch Hwy), just n, then just w. Int corridors. **Pets:** Designated rooms, service with restrictions, supervision. 🛜 ⊠ 🔋 💻 ➿

▼▼▼▼ Hampton Inn & Suites Bakersfield North/Airport H
(661) 391-0600. **$89-$129.** 8818 Spectrum Park Way 93308. SR 99 exit 30 (SR 65) northbound, just e to Merle Haggard Dr, just n to Spectrum Park Way, then just s; exit 31 (7th Standard Rd) southbound, 0.5 mi e, then just s. Int corridors. **Pets:** Large. Service with restrictions, crate.
🛜 🔋 💻 ➿

▼▼▼▼ Holiday Inn Hotel & Suites H
(661) 377-8000. **$89-$119.** 3927 Marriott Dr 93308. SR 99 exit 26A (SR 58 W/Rosedale Hwy), just w, just s on Camino Del Rio Ct, then just w. Int corridors. **Pets:** Accepted. 🛜 ⚿M 🔋 💻 ⑪ ➿

▼▼▼▼ Homewood Suites H
(661) 664-0400. **$124-$179.** 1505 Mill Rock Way 93311. SR 99 exit 23 (Ming Ave), 4 mi w, then just n. Int corridors. **Pets:** Accepted.
🛜 🔋 💻 ➿

▼▼▼▼ Howard Johnson Inn H
(661) 396-1425. **$46-$54.** 2700 White Ln 93304. SR 99 exit 21 (White Ln), just e. Ext corridors. **Pets:** Accepted. 🛜 🔋 💻 ➿

▼▼▼▼ La Quinta Inn & Suites Bakersfield North H
(661) 393-7775. **$71-$139.** 8858 Spectrum Park Way 93308. SR 99 exit 30 (SR 65) northbound, just e to Merle Haggard Dr, just n to Spectrum Park Way, then just s; exit 31 (7th Standard Rd) southbound, just e, then just s. Int corridors. **Pets:** Medium, other species. Service with restrictions, supervision. 🛜 ⚿M 🔋 💻 ➿

◈◈◈◇ ▼▼ La Quinta Inn Bakersfield South M
(661) 325-7400. **$67-$132.** 3232 Riverside Dr 93308. SR 99 exit 26A (SR 58 W/Rosedale Hwy) southbound, just e, then just n; exit 26B (Buck Owens Blvd) northbound, just s. Ext corridors. **Pets:** Medium, other species. Service with restrictions, supervision. 🛜 ⚿M 🔋 💻 ➿

◈◈◇ ▼▼ Ramada Limited-Central M
(661) 831-1922. **$49-$119.** 830 Wible Rd 93304. SR 99 exit 23 (Ming Ave), just e, then 0.8 mi n. Ext corridors. **Pets:** Accepted.
⬛ 🛜 🔋 💻 ➿

▼▼▼▼ Residence Inn by Marriott H
(661) 321-9800. **$89-$229.** 4241 Chester Ln 93309. SR 99 exit 25 (California Ave), 0.5 mi w, then just n. Ext corridors. **Pets:** Other species. $100 one-time fee/room. Service with restrictions.
⬛ 🛜 ⊠ 🔋 💻 ➿ ⊠

◈◈◇ ▼▼ Sleep Inn H
(661) 399-2100. **$49-$149.** 6257 Knudson Dr 93308. SR 99 exit 28 (Olive Dr), just w, then just n. Int corridors. **Pets:** Large. $10 daily fee/pet. Service with restrictions. ⬛ 🛜 ⊠ ⚿M 🔋 💻

◈◈◇ ▼▼▼ Super 8 M
(661) 833-1000. **$45-$69.** 3620 Wible Rd 93309. SR 99 exit 21 (White Ln), just w, then 0.3 mi n. Ext corridors. **Pets:** Medium, other species. $5 daily fee/pet. Service with restrictions, supervision.
⬛ 🛜 🔋 💻 ➿

◈◈◇ ▼▼▼ Super 8 Bakersfield M
(661) 322-1012. **$50-$63.** 901 Real Rd 93309. SR 99 exit 25 (California Ave), just w, then just s. Ext corridors. **Pets:** Small. $10 daily fee/pet. Designated rooms, service with restrictions, supervision.
⬛ 🛜 🔋 💻 ➿

▼▼ Travelodge of Bakersfield M
(661) 325-0772. **$49-$58.** 1011 Oak St 93304. SR 99 exit 25 (California Ave), just e, then just s. Ext/int corridors. **Pets:** Accepted.
🛜 🔋 💻 ➿

▼▼ Vagabond Inn Bakersfield / I5 M
(661) 764-5221. **Call for rates.** 200 Trask St 93314. I-5 exit 253 (Stockdale Hwy), just e. Ext corridors. **Pets:** Medium. $10 daily fee/pet. Service with restrictions, supervision. 🛜 🔋 💻 ➿

▼▼ Vagabond Inn South M
(661) 831-9200. **Call for rates.** 6501 Colony St 93307. SR 99 exit 20 (Panama Ln), just e, then just s. Ext corridors. **Pets:** Accepted.
🛜 🔋 💻 ➿

BANNING

◈◈◇ ▼▼ Banning Travelodge M
(951) 849-1000. **$54-$126.** 1700 W Ramsey St 92220. I-10 exit 99 (22nd St), just n, then 0.4 mi e. Ext corridors. **Pets:** Medium, dogs only. $10 daily fee/pet. Service with restrictions, supervision.
⬛ 🛜 🔋 💻 ➿

▼▼ Country Inn M
(951) 849-6733. **Call for rates.** 932 E Ramsey St 92220. I-10 exit 101 (Hargrave St), just n, then just e. Ext corridors. **Pets:** Small. $15 daily fee/pet. Designated rooms, service with restrictions, supervision.
🛜 🔋

◈◈◇ ▼▼ Days Inn M
(951) 849-0092. **$51-$116.** 2320 W Ramsey St 92220. I-10 exit 99 (22nd St), just n, then just w. Ext corridors. **Pets:** Dogs only. $10 daily fee/pet. No service, supervision. ⬛ 🛜 🔋 💻 ➿

▼▼▼▼ Hampton Inn & Suites H
(951) 922-1000. **$89-$229.** 6071 Joshua Palmer Way 92220. I-10 exit 96 (Highland Springs Ave), just n, then just e. Int corridors. **Pets:** Medium. $25 daily fee/pet. Service with restrictions, supervision.
🛜 🔋 💻 ➿

◈◈◇ ▼▼ Super 8 M
(951) 849-8888. **$54-$108.** 1690 W Ramsey St 92220. I-10 exit 99 (22nd St), just n, then 0.4 mi e. Int corridors. **Pets:** Medium, dogs only. $10 daily fee/pet. Service with restrictions, supervision.
⬛ 🛜 🔋 💻 ➿

BARSTOW

▼▼ Barstow-Super 8 M
(760) 256-8443. **$59-$64.** 170 Coolwater Ln 92311. I-15 exit 184B (E Main St) northbound; exit 184 (E Main St/I-40 E/Needles) southbound, 0.3 mi w, then just s. Ext corridors. **Pets:** Other species. $10 daily fee/pet. Service with restrictions, supervision. 🛜 🔋 💻 ➿

◈◈◇ ▼▼▼▼ Best Western Plus Desert Villa Inn M
(760) 256-1781. **$79-$119.** 1984 E Main St 92311. I-15 exit 184B (E Main St) northbound; exit 184 (E Main St/I-40/Needles) southbound, 0.5 mi e. Ext corridors. **Pets:** Accepted. ⬛ 🛜 ⚿M 🔋 💻 ➿

▼▼▼ Comfort Suites 🄷

(760) 253-3600. **$99-$149.** 2571 Fisher Blvd 92311. I-15 exit 178 (Lenwood Rd), just ne; n of Barstow Outlets. Int corridors. **Pets:** Medium, other species. $25 one-time fee/room. Designated rooms, service with restrictions, crate. 🛜 ⊠ 🕭 🛏 💻 🏊

▼▼▼ Country Inn & Suites By Carlson 🄷 🐾

(760) 307-3121. **$99-$199.** 2812 Lenwood Rd 92311. I-15 exit 178 (Lenwood Rd), just se, then just s. Int corridors. **Pets:** Medium, other species. $50 deposit/pet, $20 daily fee/pet. Designated rooms, service with restrictions, supervision. 🛜 ⊠ 🛏 💻 🏊

⬢⬢ ▼▼ Days Inn South at Lenwood 🄼

(760) 253-2121. **$61-$82.** 2551 Commerce Pkwy 92311. I-15 exit 178 (Lenwood Rd), just w, then just n; 8 mi s of town. Ext corridors. **Pets:** Accepted. (SAVE) 🛜 🛏 💻 🏊

▼▼▼ Econo Lodge 🄼

(760) 256-2133. **$54-$58.** 1230 E Main St 92311. I-15 exit 184B (E Main St) northbound; exit 184 (E Main St/I-40 E/Needles) southbound; 0.9 mi w. Ext corridors. **Pets:** Accepted. 🛜 🛏 💻 🏊

▼▼▼ Hampton Inn & Suites 🄷

(760) 253-2600. **$109-$209.** 2710 Lenwood Rd 92311. I-15 exit 178 (Lenwood Rd), just se, then 0.5 mi s. Int corridors. **Pets:** Other species. Service with restrictions, crate. 🛜 🕭 🛏 💻 🏊

▼▼▼ Holiday Inn Express, Barstow-Historic Route 66 🄷

(760) 256-1300. **$104-$135.** 1861 W Main St 92311. I-15 exit 181 (L St), 0.5 mi n, then just e. Int corridors. **Pets:** $25 one-time fee/room. No service, supervision. 🛜 🛏 💻 🏊

▼▼▼ Holiday Inn Express Hotel & Suites 🄷 🐾

(760) 253-9200. **$116-$202.** 2700 Lenwood Rd 92311. I-15 exit 178 (Lenwood Rd), just se, then 0.5 mi s. Int corridors. **Pets:** Other species. $25 deposit/room. Service with restrictions, supervision.
🛜 🕭 🛏 💻 🏊 ⊠

▼▼ Quality Inn 🄼 🐾

(760) 256-6891. **$85-$169.** 1520 E Main St 92311. I-15 exit 184B (E Main St) northbound; exit 184 (E Main St/I-40 E/Needles) southbound, 0.3 mi w. Ext corridors. **Pets:** Small, dogs only. $100 deposit/room. Designated rooms, service with restrictions. 🛜 🛏 💻 🍴 🏊

⬢⬢ ▼▼ Rodeway Inn 🄼

(760) 256-7581. **Call for rates.** 1261 E Main St 92311. I-15 exit 184B (E Main St) northbound; exit 184 (E Main St/I-40 E/Needles) southbound, 0.8 mi w. Ext corridors. **Pets:** Medium. $10 daily fee/room. Designated rooms, service with restrictions, supervision.
(SAVE) 🛜 ⊠ 🛏 💻 🏊

⬢⬢ ▼ Stardust Inn 🄼

(760) 256-7116. **$40-$60.** 901 E Main St 92311. I-15 exit 183 (Barstow Rd), 0.8 mi n, then 0.4 mi e. Ext corridors. **Pets:** Accepted.
(SAVE) 🛜 🛏 💻 🏊

BASS LAKE

▼▼▼ The Pines Resort Chalets 🄲🄰

(559) 642-3121. **Call for rates.** 54449 Rd 432 93604. 6 mi e of SR 41 exit CR 222, e on CR 274, then s on CR 434. Ext corridors.
Pets: Accepted. ⊠ 🛏 💻 🍴 🏊 ⊠

BEAUMONT

⬢⬢ ▼▼ Best Western El Rancho Motor Inn 🄼

(951) 845-2176. **$73-$99.** 480 E 5th St 92223. I-10 exit 94 (SR 79/Beaumont Ave), just n, then just e. Ext corridors. **Pets:** Accepted.
(SAVE) 🛜 🛏 💻 🏊

⬢⬢ ▼ Rodeway Inn 🄼

(951) 845-1436. **$50-$300.** 1265 E 6th St 92223. I-10 exit 94 (SR 79/Beaumont Ave), just n, then 0.7 mi e. Ext corridors. **Pets:** Medium, dogs only. $10 daily fee/pet. Service with restrictions, supervision.
(SAVE) 🛜 🛏 💻 🏊

BENICIA

⬢⬢ ▼▼▼ Best Western Plus Heritage Inn 🄷 🐾

(707) 746-0401. **$119-$150.** 1955 E 2nd St 94510. I-780 exit Central Benicia/E 2nd St, just e. Ext/int corridors. **Pets:** Medium. $20 daily fee/pet. Service with restrictions, supervision. (SAVE) 🛜 🛏 💻 🏊

BERKELEY

⬢⬢ ▼ Best Value Golden Bear Inn 🄼 🐾

(510) 525-6770. **$80-$160.** 1620 San Pablo Ave 94702. I-80 exit 12 (Gilman St), 0.5 mi e, then just s. Ext corridors. **Pets:** Other species. $10 daily fee/pet. Service with restrictions, supervision.
(SAVE) 🛜 🛏 💻 🎾

⬢⬢ ▼▼▼ Claremont Hotel Club & Spa 🄷

(510) 843-3000. **$169-$389.** 41 Tunnel Rd 94705. SR 13 and 24 exit SR 24 (Claremont Ave) eastbound, 1 mi n; I-80 exit 11 (University Ave E), just e, then 1.5 mi s on San Pablo Ave, 2.6 mi w on Ashby Ave, then just e. Int corridors. **Pets:** Accepted. (SAVE) 🛜 🕭 💻 🍴 🏊 ⊠

⬢⬢ ▼▼▼ DoubleTree by Hilton Hotel Berkeley Marina 🄷

(510) 548-7920. **$89-$229.** 200 Marina Blvd 94710. I-80 exit 11 (University Ave), 0.5 mi w; on Berkeley Marina. Int corridors. **Pets:** Accepted.
(ECO) (SAVE) 🛜 ⊠ 🕭 🛏 💻 🍴 🏊 ⊠

▼▼▼ Hotel Durant, a Joie de Vivre hotel 🄷

(510) 845-8981. **$99-$445.** 2600 Durant Ave 94704. I-80 exit 11 (University Ave E), 2 mi e to Oxford St, 0.3 mi s, then 0.5 mi e; jct Bowditch St. Int corridors. **Pets:** Large, other species. Service with restrictions, supervision. (ECO) 🛜 ⊠ 💻 🍴

BIG BEAR LAKE

▼▼▼ Bay Meadows Resort 🄲🄰

(909) 866-4666. **$79-$369, 3 day notice.** 39756 Big Bear Blvd 92315. SR 18, 1 mi w of Village. Ext corridors. **Pets:** Accepted.
🛜 ⊠ 🛏 💻 🏊 🎾

▼▼ Bear Manor Cabins 🄲🄰

(909) 866-6800. **$69-$499, 30 day notice.** 40393 Big Bear Blvd 92315. SR 18, 0.8 mi w of village. Ext corridors. **Pets:** Accepted.
🛜 ⊠ 🛏 💻 🎾

⬢⬢ ▼▼▼ Best Western Plus Big Bear Chateau 🄷 🐾

(909) 866-6666. **$100-$310.** 42200 Moonridge Rd 92315. SR 18, 1.5 mi e of Pine Knot Ave, 0.5 mi s. Int corridors. **Pets:** $30 one-time fee/room. Designated rooms, service with restrictions, supervision.
(SAVE) 🛜 ⊠ 🛏 💻 🏊 ⊠ 🎾

▼▼ Eagle's Nest Bed & Breakfast 🄱🄱 🐾

(909) 866-6465. **$115-$185, 5 day notice.** 41675 Big Bear Blvd 92315. SR 18, 1 mi e of Pine Knot Ave. Ext/int corridors. **Pets:** Other species. $10 daily fee/pet. Designated rooms, service with restrictions, supervision.
🛜 ⊠ 🛏 💻

⬢⬢ ▼▼ Golden Bear Cottages 🄲🄰 🐾

(909) 866-2010. **$99-$799, 90 day notice.** 39367 Big Bear Blvd 92315. SR 18, 2 mi w of village. Ext corridors. **Pets:** Other species. $10 one-time fee/pet. Designated rooms, service with restrictions, crate.
(SAVE) 🛜 ⊠ 🛏 💻 🏊 ⊠ 🎾

⬢⬢ ▼▼▼ Grey Squirrel Resort 🄲🄰

(909) 866-4335. **$79-$450, 30 day notice.** 39372 Big Bear Blvd 92315. SR 18, 2 mi w of village. Ext corridors. **Pets:** $10 daily fee/pet. Service with restrictions, crate. (SAVE) 🛜 ⊠ 🛏 💻 🏊 ⊠ 🎾

▼▼ Pine Knot Guest Ranch 🄲🄰 🐾

(909) 866-6500. **$99-$199, 7 day notice.** 908 Pine Knot Ave 92315. Just s of SR 18 and downtown area. Ext corridors. **Pets:** Other species. $10 daily fee/pet. Service with restrictions. 🛜 ⊠ 🛏 💻

WW WW Sleepy Forest Cottages CA
(909) 866-7444. **$79-$299, 15 day notice.** 426 Eureka Dr 92315. SR 18, 0.7 mi e of Pine Knot Ave, then just n. Ext corridors. **Pets:** Dogs only. $25 daily fee/pet. Service with restrictions, supervision.
🛜 ✕ 🛏 💻 🐾

WW WW Timber Haven Lodge CA
(909) 866-7207. **$113-$340, 7 day notice.** 877 Tulip Ln 92315. SR 18, 1.8 mi w of Pine Knot Ave, 0.4 mi s. Ext corridors. **Pets:** Accepted.
🛜 ✕ 🛏 💻 ✕ 🐾

BIG PINE
WW WW Big Pine Motel M
(760) 938-2282. **Call for rates.** 370 S Main St 93513. On US 395. Ext corridors. **Pets:** Accepted. 🛜 ✕ 🛏 💻

AAA WW WW Bristlecone Motel M 🐾
(760) 938-2067. **$55-$80.** 101 N Main St 93513. On US 395. Ext corridors. **Pets:** Other species. Service with restrictions, crate.
SAVE 🛜 ✕ 🛏 💻

BISHOP
AAA WW WW Americas Best Value Inn M
(760) 873-4912. **$65-$195.** 192 Short St 93514. US 395 to Short St, just e. Ext corridors. **Pets:** Medium. $10 daily fee/pet. Designated rooms, service with restrictions, supervision. SAVE 🛜 🛏 💻

AAA WWWW Best Western Plus Bishop Holiday Spa Lodge M 🐾
(760) 873-3543. **$100-$200.** 1025 N Main St 93514. On US 395. Ext corridors. **Pets:** Small, dogs only. $20 daily fee/pet. Designated rooms, service with restrictions, supervision. SAVE 🛜 🛜 🛏 💻 🏊

WWWW Chalfant House Bed & Breakfast BB
(760) 872-1790. **$85-$115.** 213 Academy St 93514. On US 395, just w. Ext/int corridors. **Pets:** $20 daily fee/pet. Designated rooms, service with restrictions, supervision. 🛜 ✕ ☎

WWWW Comfort Inn M
(760) 873-4284. **$79-$129.** 805 N Main St 93514. On US 395. Ext corridors. **Pets:** Accepted. 🛜 🛜 🛏 💻

AAA WWWW Holiday Inn Express Hotel & Suites H
(760) 872-2423. **$119-$279.** 636 N Main St 93514. On US 395. Int corridors. **Pets:** Accepted. SAVE 🛜 ✕ 🛜 🛏 💻 🏊 ✕

WWWW Joseph House Inn BB
(760) 872-3389. **$148-$178, 14 day notice.** 376 W Yaney St 93514. 0.3 mi w of US 395. Int corridors. **Pets:** Accepted. 🛜 ✕ ☎

WW WW La Quinta Inn Bishop - Mammoth Lakes H
(760) 873-6380. **$85-$166.** 651 N Main St 93514. On US 395. Int corridors. **Pets:** Medium, other species. Service with restrictions, supervision.
🛜 🛜 🛏 💻

WW WW Motel 6 - #4094 M
(760) 873-8426. **$65-$220.** 1005 N Main St 93514. On US 395. Ext corridors. **Pets:** Other species. Service with restrictions, supervision.
🛜 🛜 🛏 🏊

AAA WW WW Ramada Limited M 🐾
(760) 872-1771. **$69-$159.** 155 E Elm St 93514. On US 395, just e. Ext corridors. **Pets:** Other species. $15 daily fee/pet. Service with restrictions, supervision. SAVE 🛜 🛜 🛏 💻 🏊

WW WW Super 8 M
(760) 872-1386. **$54-$198.** 535 S Main St 93514. On US 395. Ext corridors. **Pets:** Other species. 🛜 🛏 💻 🏊

AAA WWWW Vagabond Inn M 🐾
(760) 873-6351. **$80-$195.** 1030 N Main St 93514. On US 395. Ext corridors. **Pets:** $15 daily fee/pet. Designated rooms, service with restrictions, supervision. SAVE 🛜 🛜 🛏 💻 🏊

BLYTHE
AAA WWWW Best Western Sahara Motel M 🐾
(760) 922-7105. **$99-$159.** 825 W Hobsonway 92225. I-10 exit 239 (Lovekin Blvd), just n, then just w. Ext corridors. **Pets:** Medium. $15 one-time fee/pet. Service with restrictions, supervision.
SAVE 🛜 🛏 💻 🏊

WWWW Regency Inn & Suites M
(760) 922-4146. **$65-$169.** 903 W Hobsonway 92225. I-10 exit 239 (Lovekin Blvd), just n, then just w. Ext corridors. **Pets:** Accepted.
🛜 🛏 💻 🏊

BORREGO SPRINGS
WWWW Palm Canyon Resort & RV Park M
(760) 767-5341. **Call for rates.** 221 Palm Canyon Dr 92004. 1.5 mi w on CR S-22. Ext corridors. **Pets:** Accepted. ✕ 🛏 💻 🍴 🏊

BRAWLEY
AAA WWWW Best Western Plus Main Street Inn M
(760) 351-9800. **$104-$115.** 1562 E Main St 92227. On SR 78 and 111. Ext/int corridors. **Pets:** $20 daily fee/pet. Service with restrictions, supervision. SAVE 🛜 🛏 💻 🏊

BREA
WWWW Chase Suite Hotels M
(714) 579-3200. **$109-$299.** 3100 E Imperial Hwy 92821. SR 57 exit 9 (SR 90), 1.5 mi e on Imperial Hwy. Ext corridors. **Pets:** Medium. $150 deposit/room, $10 daily fee/pet. Designated rooms, service with restrictions, supervision. 🛜 ✕ 🛏 💻 🏊

WWWW Embassy Suites Hotel H
(714) 990-6000. **$109-$179.** 900 E Birch St 92821. SR 57 exit 9 (SR 90), 0.5 mi w on Imperial Hwy, 0.3 mi n on Randolph, then just e. Int corridors. **Pets:** Accepted. 🛜 🛏 💻 🍴 🏊

BRIDGEPORT
AAA WW WW Redwood Motel M 🐾
(760) 932-7060. **$59-$250.** 425 Main St 93517. On US 395; on north side of town. Ext corridors. **Pets:** Large. $10 daily fee/room. Designated rooms, service with restrictions, supervision. SAVE 🛜 🛏 💻

AAA WW WW Ruby Inn M 🐾
(760) 932-7241. **$125-$200.** 333 Main St 93517. On US 395; center. Ext corridors. **Pets:** Small. Supervision. SAVE 🛜 ✕ 🛏 💻

AAA WW WW Silver Maple Inn M 🐾
(760) 932-7383. **$80-$140.** 310 Main St 93517. On US 395; center. Ext corridors. **Pets:** Other species. Service with restrictions, supervision.
SAVE 🛜 ✕ 🛏 💻 🐾

AAA WW WW Walker River Lodge M
(760) 932-7021. **$85-$220.** 100 Main St 93517. On US 395; at south end of town. Ext corridors. **Pets:** Other species. Service with restrictions, supervision. SAVE 🛜 🛏 💻 🏊

BUELLTON
AAA WW WW Quality Inn Santa Ynez Valley M
(805) 688-0022. **$72-$126.** 630 Ave of the Flags 93427. US 101 exit 140B (Ave of the Flags) southbound, just s; exit 140A (SR 246) northbound, just w, then just n. Ext/int corridors. **Pets:** Accepted.
SAVE 🛜 🛏 💻

◊◊◊ ▼▼▼▼ **Santa Ynez Valley Marriott** 🅷 🐾
(805) 688-1000. **$142-$227.** 555 McMurray Rd 93427. US 101 exit 140A (SR 246), just e, then just n. Int corridors. **Pets:** Other species. $80 one-time fee/room. Service with restrictions.
SAVE 📶 ⊠ 🛢 🖵 🍴 🏊 ⊠

BUENA PARK

◊◊◊ ▼▼▼▼ **InnSuites Hotel & Suites Buena Park/Anaheim** 🅼
(714) 522-7360. **$69-$119.** 7555 Beach Blvd 90620. SR 91 exit 23B (Beach Blvd/SR 39), just s. Ext corridors. **Pets:** Accepted.
📶 🛢 🖵 🏊 ⊠

◊◊◊ ▼▼▼ **Red Roof Inn** 🅼
(714) 670-9000. **$50-$129.** 7121 Beach Blvd 90620. SR 91 exit 23B (Beach Blvd/SR 39), just n. Int corridors. **Pets:** Large, other species. No service, supervision. SAVE 📶 🛢 🏊

BURNEY

◊◊◊ ▼ **Charm Motel** 🅼 🐾
(530) 335-3300. **$69-$99.** 37363 Main St 96013. 0.5 mi ne on SR 299; jct Roff Way. Ext corridors. **Pets:** Other species. $10 daily fee/pet. Service with restrictions, supervision. SAVE 📶 🛢 🖵

◊◊◊ ▼▼ **Green Gables Motel** 🅼 🐾
(530) 335-3300. **$69-$99.** 37385 Main St 96013. 0.5 mi ne on SR 299; jct Roff Way and SR 299. Ext corridors. **Pets:** Other species. $10 daily fee/pet. Service with restrictions, supervision.
SAVE 📶 ⊠ 🛢 🖵 🏊

CALEXICO

◊◊◊ ▼▼ **Best Western John Jay Inn** 🅼
(760) 768-0442. **Call for rates.** 2421 Scaroni Ave 92231. I-8 exit 118A (SR 111 S), 5.5 mi s, just w on W Cole Rd, then just n. Int corridors. **Pets:** Dogs only. $100 deposit/room, $20 daily fee/pet. Service with restrictions, supervision. SAVE 📶 ♿ 🛢 🖵 🏊

▼▼ **Quality Inn** 🅷
(760) 357-3271. **$75-$90.** 801 Imperial Ave 92231. SR 111, 0.5 mi n of Mexico Border. Int corridors. **Pets:** Large. $40 deposit/pet, $10 daily fee/pet. Designated rooms, service with restrictions, supervision.
📶 ⊠ 🛢 🖵 🍴 🏊

CALIMESA

◊◊◊ ▼▼ **Calimesa Inn Motel** 🅼
(909) 795-2536. **$60-$110.** 1205 Calimesa Blvd 92320. I-10 exit 88 (Calimesa Blvd), just ne. Ext corridors. **Pets:** Small, dogs only. $10 daily fee/pet. Designated rooms, service with restrictions, supervision.
SAVE 📶 🛢 🏊

CAMARILLO

◊◊◊ ▼▼▼ **Best Western Camarillo Inn** 🅼 🐾
(805) 987-4991. **$87-$127.** 295 E Daily Dr 93010. US 101 exit 55 (Las Posas Rd), just n, then just e. Ext corridors. **Pets:** $20 daily fee/room. Designated rooms, service with restrictions, supervision.
SAVE 📶 🛢 🖵 🏊

▼▼▼▼ **Camarillo Residence Inn by Marriott** 🅷
(805) 388-7997. **$123-$169.** 2912 Petit St 93012. US 101 exit 53A (Flynn Rd) northbound, 0.8 mi n, then just w; exit Dawson Dr southbound, just w. Int corridors. **Pets:** Other species. $100 one-time fee/room. Service with restrictions, supervision. 📶 ⊠ 🛢 🖵 🏊 ⊠

CAMBRIA

◊◊◊ ▼▼▼▼ **Best Western Plus Fireside Inn On Moonstone Beach** 🅼
(805) 927-8661. **$129-$279, 7 day notice.** 6700 Moonstone Beach Dr 93428. SR 1 exit Moonstone Beach Dr, just w, then 0.5 mi s. Ext/int corridors. **Pets:** Accepted. SAVE 📶 ⊠ ♿ 🛢 🖵 🏊 🐾

▼▼▼▼ **Blue Dolphin Inn** 🅷 🐾
(805) 927-3300. **$129-$349.** 6470 Moonstone Beach Dr 93428. SR 1 exit Moonstone Beach Dr, 0.7 mi n. Int corridors. **Pets:** Medium, other species. $25 daily fee/pet. Designated rooms, service with restrictions, supervision. 📶 ⊠ 🛢 🖵 🐾

◊◊◊ ▼▼▼▼ **Blue Whale Inn Bed & Breakfast** 🅱🅱
(805) 927-4647. **$347-$470, 10 day notice.** 6736 Moonstone Beach Dr 93428. SR 1 exit Moonstone Beach Dr, just w, then 0.5 mi s. Ext corridors. **Pets:** $25 one-time fee/room. Service with restrictions, supervision.
SAVE 📶 ⊠ 🛢 🖵 🐾

▼▼▼ **Cambria Shores Inn** 🅼 🐾
(805) 927-8644. **$169-$350, 7 day notice.** 6276 Moonstone Beach Dr 93428. SR 1 exit Moonstone Beach Dr, just w, then 0.8 mi s. Ext corridors. **Pets:** Dogs only. $15 daily fee/pet. Service with restrictions, supervision. 📶 ⊠ 🛢 🖵

▼▼▼▼ **Fog Catcher Inn** 🅼 🐾
(805) 927-1400. **$139-$500.** 6400 Moonstone Beach Dr 93428. SR 1 exit Moonstone Beach Dr, just w, then 0.7 mi s. Ext corridors. **Pets:** $25 daily fee/room. Designated rooms, service with restrictions, supervision.
📶 ⊠ 🛢 🖵 🏊 🐾

▼▼▼▼ **Pelican Cove Inn** 🅷
(805) 927-1500. **Call for rates.** 6316 Moonstone Beach Dr 93428. SR 1 exit Moonstone Beach Dr, just w, then 0.8 mi s. Ext/int corridors.
Pets: Accepted. 📶 ⊠ ♿ 🛢 🖵 🏊

▼▼▼▼ **Sand Pebbles Inn** 🅷 🐾
(805) 927-5600. **$109-$299.** 6252 Moonstone Beach Dr 93428. SR 1 exit Moonstone Beach Dr, just w, then 0.9 mi s. Int corridors. **Pets:** Medium, other species. $25 daily fee/pet. Designated rooms, service with restrictions, supervision. 📶 ⊠ 🛢 🖵 🐾

▼▼▼ **Sea Otter Inn** 🅼
(805) 927-5888. **$99-$329, 3 day notice.** 6656 Moonstone Beach Dr 93428. SR 1 exit Moonstone Beach Dr, just w, then 0.5 mi s. Ext corridors. **Pets:** Accepted. 📶 ⊠ 🛢 🖵 🏊 🐾

▼▼ **White Water Inn** 🅼
(805) 927-1066. **$129-$289, 7 day notice.** 6790 Moonstone Beach Dr 93428. SR 1 exit Moonstone Beach Dr, just w, then 0.4 mi s. Ext corridors. **Pets:** Accepted. 📶 ⊠ 🛢 🐾

CAMPBELL

◊◊◊ ▼▼▼ **Campbell Inn** 🅷
(408) 374-4300. **$99-$249.** 675 E Campbell Ave 95008. SR 17 exit Hamilton Ave E, 0.3 mi to Bascom Ave, 0.3 mi s, then 0.3 mi w. Ext corridors. **Pets:** Medium. $30 one-time fee/pet. Designated rooms, service with restrictions, crate. SAVE 📶 🛢 🖵 🏊 ⊠

▼▼▼ **Residence Inn by Marriott-San Jose** 🅷
(408) 559-1551. **Call for rates.** 2761 S Bascom Ave 95008. SR 17 exit Camden Ave E, just n. Ext corridors. **Pets:** Accepted.
📶 ⊠ ♿ 🛢 🖵

▼▼▼▼ **TownePlace Suites by Marriott-San Jose/Campbell** 🅷 🐾
(408) 370-4510. **$129-$209.** 700 E Campbell Ave 95008. SR 17 exit Hamilton Ave E, 0.3 mi to Bascom Ave, 0.3 mi s, then 0.3 mi w. Int corridors. **Pets:** Large, other species. $75 one-time fee/room. Designated rooms, service with restrictions, crate. 📶 ⊠ ♿ 🛢 🖵

CAPITOLA

◊◊◊ ▼▼▼ **Capitola Inn** 🅼 🐾
(831) 462-3004. **$69-$300.** 720 Hill St 95010. SR 1 exit Bay Ave, just w. Ext/int corridors. **Pets:** Large, other species. $10 daily fee/pet. Designated rooms, service with restrictions. SAVE 📶 ⊠ ♿ 🛢 🖵 🏊

CARLSBAD

▼▼▼▼ Carlsbad by the Sea Resort 🅷
(760) 438-7880. **$109-$279.** 850 Palomar Airport Rd 92011. I-5 exit 47 (Palomar Airport Rd), just e. Ext corridors. **Pets:** Accepted.
📶 👤M 🛏 💻 🍴 🏊

▼▼▼▼ Homewood Suites by Hilton Carlsbad-North San Diego County 🅷
(760) 431-2266. **$159-$229.** 2223 Palomar Airport Rd 92011. I-5 exit 47 (Palomar Airport Rd), 3.1 mi e. Int corridors. **Pets:** Medium. $100 one-time fee/room. Designated rooms, service with restrictions.
📶 ✖ 👤M 🛏 💻 🏊 ✖

🏵 ▼▼▼▼ Hyatt Summerfield Suites San Diego/Carlsbad 🅷
(760) 929-8200. **$169-$359.** 5010 Avenida Encinas 92008. I-5 exit 48 (Cannon Rd), just w, then just s. Int corridors. **Pets:** Medium. $200 one-time fee/room. Designated rooms, service with restrictions, supervision.
SAVE 📶 ✖ 👤M 🛏 💻 🏊

▼▼▼▼ La Quinta Inn San Diego Carlsbad Ⓜ
(760) 438-2828. **$116-$179.** 760 Macadamia Dr 92011. I-5 exit 45 (Poinsettia Ln/Aviara Pkwy), just w to Ave Encinas, just n, then just e. Ext corridors. **Pets:** Medium, other species. Service with restrictions, supervision. 📶 ✖ 🛏 💻 🏊

🏵 ▼▼▼▼ Park Hyatt Aviara Resort, Golf Club & Spa 🅷 🐾
(760) 603-6800. **$250-$575, 7 day notice.** 7100 Aviara Resort Dr 92011. I-5 exit 45 (Poinsettia Ln/Aviara Pkwy); 1 mi e on Poinsettia Ln, 1 mi s on Aviara Pkwy, then just sw. Int corridors. **Pets:** Small. $75 one-time fee/room. Designated rooms, service with restrictions.
SAVE 📶 ✖ 🛏 💻 🍴 🏊 ✖

▼▼▼▼ Quality Inn & Suites North Legoland Area Ⓜ
(760) 931-1185. **$75-$199.** 751 Raintree Dr 92011. I-5 exit 45 (Poinsettia Ln/Aviara Pkwy, just w to Ave Encinas, then just n. Ext corridors. **Pets:** Accepted. 📶 🛏 💻 🏊

▼▼▼ Ramada Inn & Suites Ⓜ
(760) 438-2285. **$89-$206.** 751 Macadamia Dr 92011. I-5 exit 45 (Poinsettia Ln), just w to Ave Encinas, then 0.3 mi n. Ext corridors. **Pets:** Medium, other species. Designated rooms, service with restrictions, supervision. 📶 ✖ 🛏 💻 🏊

▼▼▼ West Inn & Suites 🅷 🐾
(760) 448-4500. **$159-$399, 3 day notice.** 4970 Avenida Encinas 92008. I-5 exit 48 (Cannon Rd), just w, then just n. Int corridors. **Pets:** $75 one-time fee/room. Designated rooms, service with restrictions, supervision. 📶 ✖ 👤M 🛏 💻 🏊

CARPINTERIA

▼▼▼ Holiday Inn Express & Suites 🅷
(805) 566-9499. **$109-$249.** 5606 Carpinteria Ave 93013. US 101 exit 86A (Casitas Pass Rd), just s, then just e. Int corridors. **Pets:** Large. $15 daily fee/room. Designated rooms, service with restrictions, supervision.
📶 ✖ 👤M 🛏 💻 🏊

CASTAIC

🏵 ▼▼▼ Rodeway Inn Ⓜ
(661) 295-1100. **Call for rates.** 31558 Castaic Rd 91384. I-5 exit 175A (Parker Rd) northbound, just e on Ridge Route Rd, then just n; exit 176 (Lake Hughes Rd/Castaic) southbound, just s on The Old Rd, just e on Sloan Canyon Rd, then 0.4 mi s. Ext corridors. **Pets:** Medium. $10 one-time fee/pet. Designated rooms, service with restrictions, supervision.
SAVE 📶 🛏 💻 🏊

CASTRO VALLEY

▼▼▼ Quality Inn 🅷
(510) 538-9501. **$69-$189.** 2532 Castro Valley Blvd 94546. I-580 exit Castro Valley Blvd, 0.3 mi n. Int corridors. **Pets:** Small. $10 daily fee/pet. Service with restrictions, supervision. 📶 👤M 🛏 💻 🏊

CATALINA ISLAND

▼▼ Hotel Catalina Courtyard Garden Wing Ⓜ
(310) 510-0027. **Call for rates.** 108 Marilla Ave 90704. In Avalon; just off Crescent Ave. Ext corridors. **Pets:** Accepted. 🛏 💻

CATHEDRAL CITY

▼▼▼▼ Doral Desert Princess Resort, Palm Springs 🅷
(760) 322-7000. **$139-$379, 3 day notice.** 67-967 Vista Chino 92234. I-10 exit 126 (Date Palm Dr), 0.5 mi s, then 1 mi w. Int corridors. **Pets:** Medium. $75 one-time fee/room. Designated rooms, service with restrictions, supervision. 📶 ✖ 🛏 💻 🍴 🏊 ✖

▼▼ Quality Inn & Suites Date Palm Ⓜ
(760) 324-5939. **$69-$319.** 69-151 E Palm Canyon Dr 92234. I-10 exit 126 (Date Palm Dr), 5 mi s, then just e. Ext corridors. **Pets:** Accepted.
📶 ✖ 🛏 💻 🏊

CAYUCOS

▼▼ Beachwalker Inn Ⓜ
(805) 995-2133. **Call for rates.** 501 S Ocean Ave 93430. On SR 1 business route. Ext corridors. **Pets:** Accepted. 📶 ✖ 🛏 💻 🐾

▼▼▼ Cayucos Beach Inn Ⓜ 🐾
(805) 995-2828. **$85-$195, 3 day notice.** 333 S Ocean Ave 93430. On SR 1 business route. Ext corridors. **Pets:** Medium, dogs only. $15 daily fee/room. Designated rooms, no service, supervision.
📶 ✖ 👤M 🛏 💻

🏵 ▼▼▼ Cypress Tree Motel Ⓜ
(805) 995-3917. **$50-$117.** 125 S Ocean Ave 93430. On SR 1 business route. Ext corridors. **Pets:** Accepted. SAVE 📶 ✖ 🛏 💻 🐾

▼ Estero Bay Motel Ⓜ
(805) 995-3614. **$60-$160, 3 day notice.** 25 S Ocean Ave 93430. On SR 1 business route. Ext corridors. **Pets:** Medium, dogs only. $10 daily fee/pet. Designated rooms, no service, supervision.
📶 ✖ 🛏 💻 🐾

🏵 ▼▼▼ Shoreline Inn On The Beach Ⓜ 🐾
(805) 995-3681. **$105-$225, 3 day notice.** 1 N Ocean Ave 93430. On SR 1 business route. Ext corridors. **Pets:** Other species. $20 one-time fee/pet. Service with restrictions, supervision. SAVE 📶 🛏 💻 🐾

CEDARVILLE

🏵 ▼▼▼ Sunrise Motel Ⓜ
(530) 279-2161. **$69-$79, 7 day notice.** 62271 Hwy 299 W 96104. Jct SR 299 and CR 1, 0.6 mi w on CR 1. Ext corridors. **Pets:** Medium. $10 daily fee/pet. Designated rooms, service with restrictions, supervision.
SAVE 📶 🛏 💻 🐾

CHESTER

🏵 ▼▼▼▼ Best Western Rose Quartz Inn 🅷
(530) 258-2002. **$110-$170.** 306 Main St 96020. 0.3 mi w of center on SR 36. Int corridors. **Pets:** Medium, other species. $30 daily fee/pet. Designated rooms, service with restrictions, supervision.
SAVE 📶 👤M 🛏 💻

CHICO

🏵 ▼▼▼▼ Best Western Plus Heritage Inn - Chico 🅷 🐾
(530) 894-8600. **$95-$120.** 25 Heritage Ln 95926. Just e of SR 99, via Cohasset Rd. Int corridors. **Pets:** $30 one-time fee/room. Designated rooms, service with restrictions, supervision.
SAVE 📶 👤M 🛏 💻 🏊

🏵 ▼▼▼ Heritage Inn Express Ⓜ
(530) 343-4527. **$89-$120.** 725 Broadway 95928. SR 99 exit 385 (SR 32), 1.1 mi w; jct W 8th St; downtown. Ext corridors. **Pets:** Accepted.
SAVE 📶 🛏 💻 🏊

⚛ ▼▼▼ Holiday Inn Chico & Conference Center H ☙

(530) 345-2491. **$89-$115.** 685 Manzanita Ct 95926. SR 99 exit 387A (Mangrove Ave/Cohasset Rd), follow Mangrove Ave, just sw. Int corridors. **Pets:** $30 one-time fee/room. Designated rooms, no service, supervision.
SAVE 📶 🅼 🛏 🖵 🍴 🌊

▼▼▼ Oxford Suites H ☙

(530) 899-9090. **$99-$179.** 2035 Business Ln 95928. SR 99 exit 384 (E 20th St), just e, then just s. Int corridors. **Pets:** Medium. $35 one-time fee/room. Designated rooms, service with restrictions, supervision.
📶 🅼 🛏 🖵 🌊 🗙

⚛ ▼▼▼ Residence Inn by Marriott Chico H

(530) 894-5500. **$94-$127.** 2485 Carmichael Dr 95928. SR 99 exit 383 (Skyway/Park Ave), just w, then just n. Int corridors. **Pets:** Accepted.
SAVE 📶 🗙 🛏 🖵 🌊 🗙

⚛ ▼▼ Super 8 H

(530) 345-2533. **$51-$180.** 655 Manzanita Ct 95926. SR 99 exit 387A (Mangrove Ave/Cohasset Rd), follow Mangrove Ave, then just se. Int corridors. **Pets:** Small. $10 one-time fee/pet. Service with restrictions, supervision. SAVE 📶 🛏 🖵 🌊

CHOWCHILLA

▼▼▼ Days Inn M

(559) 665-4821. **$53-$62.** 220 E Robertson Blvd 93610. SR 99 exit Robertson Blvd W. Ext corridors. **Pets:** Accepted. 📶 🛏 🖵 🌊

▼▼▼ Holiday Inn Express & Suites Gateway to Yosemite H

(559) 665-3300. **$79-$169.** 309 Prosperity Blvd 93610. SR 99 exit Robertson Blvd, just w. Int corridors. **Pets:** Large, other species. $25 daily fee/pet. Designated rooms, service with restrictions, supervision.
📶 🗙 🅼 🛏 🖵 🌊

CLOVIS

⚛ ▼▼▼ Comfort Suites H ☙

(559) 299-9992. **$79-$159.** 143 Clovis Ave 93612. SR 168 exit Herndon Ave E, just s. Int corridors. **Pets:** Other species. $35 one-time fee/room. Service with restrictions, crate. SAVE 📶 🗙 🅼 🛏 🖵 🌊

COALINGA

⚛ ▼▼▼ Best Western Big Country Inn M

(559) 935-0866. **$109-$139.** 25020 W Dorris Ave 93210. I-5 exit SR 198/Hanford-Lemoore, just w. Ext corridors. **Pets:** Accepted.
SAVE 📶 🅼 🛏 🖵 🌊

⚛ ▼▼▼ The Inn at Harris Ranch H

(559) 935-0717. **$155-$350.** 24505 W Dorris Ave 93210. I-5 exit SR 198/Hanford-Lemoore, just e. Ext/int corridors. **Pets:** Accepted.
SAVE 📶 🅼 🛏 🖵 🍴 🌊

COLTON

▼▼▼ Holiday Inn Express H

(951) 788-9900. **$98-$128.** 2830 S Iowa Ave 92324. I-215 exit 37 (La Cadena Dr) northbound; exit 37 (Iowa Ave) southbound, just se. Int corridors. **Pets:** $25 deposit/room, $50 one-time fee/room. Service with restrictions, supervision. 📶 🛏 🖵 🌊

COLUMBIA

▼ Columbia Gem Motel M

(209) 532-4508. **$99-$159.** 22131 Parrotts Ferry Rd 95370. 3 mi n of Sonora; 1 mi from Columbia State Historic Park. Ext corridors.
Pets: Dogs only. Service with restrictions, supervision. 🛏 🖵 🍽

CONCORD

⚛ ▼▼▼ Best Western Plus Heritage Inn H

(925) 686-4466. **$80-$105.** 4600 Clayton Rd 94521. I-680 exit Treat Blvd/Geary Rd, 4.8 mi ne, then 0.4 mi e. Ext corridors. **Pets:** Accepted.
SAVE 📶 🅼 🛏 🖵 🌊

⚛ ▼▼▼ Crowne Plaza Hotel Concord/Walnut Creek H ☙

(925) 825-7700. **$109-$189.** 45 John Glenn Dr 94520. I-680 exit Concord Ave, just e. Int corridors. **Pets:** Small, other species. $35 one-time fee/pet. Service with restrictions, crate.
SAVE 📶 🅼 🛏 🖵 🍴 🌊 🗙

⚛ ▼▼ Days Inn Concord H

(925) 674-9400. **Call for rates.** 5370 Clayton Rd 94521. 6.5 mi e of jct I-680 and SR 24; I-680 exit SR 242 to Clayton Rd, 5.5 mi e. Ext corridors. **Pets:** Medium. $100 deposit/pet. Designated rooms, crate.
SAVE 📶 🅼 🛏 🖵 🌊

⚛ ▼▼▼ Hilton Concord H ☙

(925) 827-2000. **$119-$199.** 1970 Diamond Blvd 94520. I-680 exit Willow Pass Rd, just e. Int corridors. **Pets:** Medium. $250 deposit/room, $50 one-time fee/room. Designated rooms, service with restrictions, crate.
ECO SAVE 📶 🅼 🛏 🖵 🍴 🌊

▼▼ Premier Inns H

(925) 674-8000. **$52-$72.** 1581 Concord Ave 94520. SR 242 exit Clayton Rd northbound; exit Concord Ave southbound, just e. Ext corridors.
Pets: Accepted. 📶 🅼 🛏 🌊

CORNING

⚛ ▼▼▼ Best Western Corning Inn and Suites H

(530) 824-5200. **$90-$160.** 910 Hwy 99 W 96021. I-5 exit 631 (Central Corning), just e. Int corridors. **Pets:** $15 one-time fee/pet. Designated rooms, service with restrictions, supervision. SAVE 📶 🛏 🖵 🌊

⚛ ▼▼▼ Days Inn H

(530) 824-2000. **$63-$135.** 3475 Hwy 99 W 96021. I-5 exit 630 (South Ave), just e, then just s. Int corridors. **Pets:** Small. $10 daily fee/pet. Service with restrictions, supervision. SAVE 📶 🅼 🛏 🖵 🌊

⚛ ▼▼▼ Holiday Inn Express Hotel & Suites H ☙

(530) 824-6400. **$95-$125.** 3350 Sunrise Way 96021. I-5 exit 630 (South Ave), just e, then just s. Int corridors. **Pets:** $10 daily fee/pet. Designated rooms, service with restrictions, supervision.
SAVE 📶 🛏 🖵 🌊 🗙

⚛ ▼▼◆ Super 8 Corning M

(530) 824-2468. **$80-$90.** 2165 Solano St 96021. I-5 exit 631 (Central Corning), just e. Ext corridors. **Pets:** $15 one-time fee/pet. Designated rooms, service with restrictions, supervision.
SAVE 📶 🅼 🛏 🖵 🌊

CORONA

▼▼▼ Ayres Suites Corona West H

(951) 738-9113. **$89-$169.** 1900 Frontage Rd 92882. SR 91 exit 48 (Maple/W 6th Sts) eastbound; exit Maple St westbound, just sw. Ext/int corridors. **Pets:** Accepted. 📶 🛏 🖵 🌊

⚛ ▼▼▼ Best Western Kings Inn M ☙

(951) 734-4241. **$84-$119.** 1084 Pomona Rd 92882. SR 91 exit 49 (Lincoln Ave), just ne. Ext corridors. **Pets:** Small, dogs only. $100 deposit/room, $10 daily fee/pet. Designated rooms, service with restrictions, supervision. SAVE 📶 🛏 🖵 🌊

▼▼▼ Hotel Paseo M

(951) 371-7185. **Call for rates.** 1805 W 6th St 92882. SR 91 exit 48 (Maple/W 6th Sts) eastbound; exit Maple St westbound, just se. Ext corridors. **Pets:** Small. $25 one-time fee/room.
📶 🗙 🛏 🖵 🌊 🗙

▼▼▼ Residence Inn by Marriott Corona H ☙

(951) 371-0107. **$104-$123.** 1015 Montecito Dr 92879. I-15 exit 95 (Magnolia Ave), just e, just n on El Camino, just w on Carly Way, then just n. Int corridors. **Pets:** Medium. $125 one-time fee/room. Service with restrictions, crate. 📶 🗙 🅼 🛏 🖵 🌊 🗙

COSTA MESA

▼▼◆▼ Hilton Orange County/Costa Mesa **H**
(714) 540-7000. **$123-$180.** 3050 Bristol St 92626. I-405 exit 9B (Bristol St), just s. Int corridors. **Pets:** Accepted.
ECO 🛜 ✕ 🅼 🔒 💻 🍽 ⊇

🔷 ▼▼◆▼ The Hotel Hanford **H**
(714) 557-3000. **$109-$269.** 3131 S Bristol St 92626. I-405 exit 9B (Bristol St), just s. Int corridors. **Pets:** Medium, other species. $50 one-time fee/room. Service with restrictions, supervision.
SAVE 🛜 ✕ 🔒 💻 🍽 ⊇

🔷 ▼▼◆▼ Ramada Inn & Suites **H**
(949) 645-2221. **$49-$179.** 1680 Superior Ave 92627. SR 55 terminus; just w of Newport Blvd at 17th St. Ext corridors. **Pets:** Other species. $150 deposit/room, $5 daily fee/pet. Designated rooms, service with restrictions, supervision. SAVE 🛜 ✕ 🅼 🔒 💻 🍽 ⊇

▼▼◆▼ Residence Inn by Marriott **H**
(714) 241-8800. **$119-$249.** 881 W Baker St 92626. SR 73 exit 17B (Bear St); SR 55 exit 5B (Baker St). Ext corridors. **Pets:** Other species. $100 one-time fee/room. ECO 🛜 ✕ 🔒 💻 ⊇ ✕

🔷 ▼▼◆▼ Travelodge-Orange County Airport **M**
(714) 557-8700. **$68-$125.** 1400 Bristol St 92626. I-405 exit 9B (Bristol St), 2 mi se. Ext corridors. **Pets:** Small. $50 one-time fee/pet. Designated rooms, no service, crate. SAVE 🛜 🔒 💻 ⊇

🔷 ▼▼ Vagabond Inn **M** ❀
(714) 557-8360. **$59-$119.** 3205 Harbor Blvd 92626. I-405 exit 11 (Harbor Blvd), just s; entrance from Gisler Ave, just w of harbor. Ext corridors. **Pets:** Small, other species. $10 daily fee/pet. Designated rooms, service with restrictions, supervision. SAVE 🛜 🔒 💻 ⊇

🔷 ▼▼◆▼ The Westin South Coast Plaza Hotel **H**
(714) 540-2500. **$129-$375.** 686 Anton Blvd 92626. I-405 exit 9B (Bristol St), just n, then just e. Int corridors. **Pets:** Accepted.
ECO SAVE 🛜 ✕ 🅼 💻 🍽 ⊇ ✕

CRESCENT CITY

🔷 ▼ Americas Best Value Inn **M** ❀
(707) 464-4141. **$50-$125.** 440 Hwy 101 N 95531. Between Cooper and 9th sts; across from Del Norte County Fairground. Ext corridors. **Pets:** Medium, dogs only. $10 daily fee/pet. Designated rooms, service with restrictions, supervision. SAVE 🛜 🔒 💻 📵

🔷 ▼▼ Econo Lodge Crescent City **M**
(707) 464-6106. **Call for rates.** 725 Hwy 101 N 95531. On US 101, jct Northcrest St. Ext corridors. **Pets:** Accepted. SAVE 🛜 🔒 💻 📵

🔷 ▼ Hiouchi Motel **M**
(707) 458-3041. **Call for rates.** 2097 Hwy 199 95531. On US 199, 5.5 mi e of jct US 101. Ext corridors. **Pets:** Accepted.
SAVE 🛜 ✕ 🔒 💻 📵 🗲

🔷 ▼▼ Quality Inn & Suites **H** ❀
(707) 464-3885. **$84-$149.** 100 Walton St 95531. Just w of US 101. Ext corridors. **Pets:** Medium. $15 daily fee/pet. Designated rooms, service with restrictions, supervision. SAVE 🛜 ✕ 🔒 💻

🔷 ▼▼ Super 8 **M** ❀
(707) 464-4111. **$50-$117.** 685 Hwy 101 S/Redwood Hwy 95531. On US 101. Ext corridors. **Pets:** Small, dogs only. $15 daily fee/pet. Designated rooms, service with restrictions, supervision. SAVE 🛜 🔒 💻 📵

CUPERTINO

🔷 ▼▼◆▼ Cypress Hotel **H** ❀
(408) 253-8900. **$84-$299.** 10050 S De Anza Blvd 95014. I-280 exit De Anza Blvd, 0.7 mi s. Int corridors. **Pets:** Other species. Service with restrictions, supervision. ECO SAVE 🛜 ✕ 🅼 🍽 ⊇

CYPRESS

🔷 ▼▼ Hyatt Summerfield Suites Cypress/Anaheim **H**
(714) 828-4000. **$89-$299.** 5905 Corporate Ave 90630. I-605 exit 1D (Katella Ave) southbound; exit 1B (Katella Ave/Willow St) northbound, 3 mi e, 0.4 mi n on Valley View Ave, then just w. Int corridors.
Pets: Accepted. SAVE 🛜 ✕ 🔒 💻 ⊇

DANA POINT

▼▼◆▼ Blue Lantern Inn **BB** ❀
(949) 661-1304. **$200-$600, 7 day notice.** 34343 Street of Blue Lantern 92629. I-5 exit 79 (Pacific Coast Highway) southbound; exit 79 (Beach Cities Dr) northbound, 1.5 mi n on Pacific Coast Hwy, then just w. Int corridors. **Pets:** Medium, dogs only. $65 one-time fee/room. Designated rooms, service with restrictions, supervision. 🛜 ✕ 🔒 💻 ✕

▼▼◆▼ DoubleTree Suites by Hilton Hotel Dana Point - Doheny Beach **H**
(949) 661-1100. **$109-$289.** 34402 Pacific Coast Hwy 92629. I-5 exit 79 (Beach Cities Dr) northbound; exit 79 (Pacific Coast Hwy) southbound, 0.6 mi w, U-turn at Doheny Park Plaza Dr, then 0.8 mi s. Int corridors.
Pets: Accepted. ECO 🛜 🔒 💻 🍽 ⊇ ✕

🔷 ▼▼◆▼ Holiday Inn Express Hotel & Suites **H**
(949) 248-1000. **$99-$399.** 34280 Pacific Coast Hwy 92629. I-5 exit 79 (Pacific Coast Hwy) southbound; exit 79 (Beach Cities Dr) northbound, 0.6 mi w, then 0.5 mi n. Ext/int corridors. **Pets:** Accepted.
SAVE 🛜 ✕ 🅼 🔒 💻 ⊇

🔷 ▼▼◆▼ The Ritz-Carlton, Laguna Niguel **H**
(949) 240-2000. **$425-$595, 3 day notice.** One Ritz-Carlton Dr 92629. I-5 exit 79 (Pacific Coast Hwy) northbound, 3 mi n, then just w; exit 86 (Crown Valley Pkwy) southbound, 3 mi w, 1 mi s on Pacific Coast Hwy, then just w. Int corridors. **Pets:** Accepted.
SAVE 🛜 ✕ 🅼 🔒 💻 🍽 ⊇ ✕

🔷 ▼▼◆▼ St. Regis Resort, Monarch Beach **H** ❀
(949) 234-3200. **$625-$6000, 7 day notice.** One Monarch Beach Resort 92629. I-5 exit 79 (Pacific Coast Hwy) northbound, 3 mi n, then 0.5 mi e on Niguel Rd; exit 86 (Crown Valley Pkwy) southbound, 3 mi w, 1 mi s on Pacific Coast Hwy, then 0.5 mi e on Niguel Rd. Int corridors. **Pets:** Small, other species. $150 one-time fee/room. Designated rooms, service with restrictions, supervision.
SAVE 🛜 ✕ 🅼 🔒 🍽 ⊇ ✕

DANVILLE

🔷 ▼▼◆▼ Best Western Plus Danville Sycamore Inn **H** ❀
(925) 855-8888. **$85-$135.** 803 Camino Ramon 94526. I-680 exit Sycamore Valley Rd, just e, then just s. Ext/int corridors. **Pets:** Medium. $15 daily fee/pet. Designated rooms, service with restrictions, supervision.
SAVE 🛜 🅼 🔒 💻 ⊇

DAVIS

🔷 ▼▼ Best Western University Lodge **M**
(530) 756-7890. **$90-$230.** 123 B St 95616. I-80 exit 72B (Richards Blvd) westbound, just nw to 1st St, just w to B St, then just n; exit 72 (Richards Blvd) eastbound, just nw to 1st St, just w to B St, then just n; at 2nd and B sts. Ext corridors. **Pets:** Medium. $10 daily fee/pet. Supervision. SAVE 🛜 🔒 💻 ✕

🔷 ▼▼◆▼ La Quinta Inn & Suites Davis **H**
(530) 758-2600. **$112-$175.** 1771 Research Park Dr 95616. I-80 exit 72A (Richards Blvd) westbound, just se, then just n; exit 72 (Richards Blvd) eastbound. Int corridors. **Pets:** Medium, other species. Service with restrictions, supervision. SAVE 🛜 ✕ 🔒 💻 ⊇

🔷 ▼▼◆▼ University Park Inn & Suites **H**
(530) 756-0910. **$80-$189.** 1111 Richards Blvd 95616. I-80 exit 72A (Richards Blvd) westbound; exit 72 (Richards Blvd) eastbound, just nw. Ext corridors. **Pets:** Medium. $10 daily fee/pet. Designated rooms, service with restrictions, supervision. SAVE 🛜 🅼 🔒 💻 ⊇

DEATH VALLEY NATIONAL PARK

▼▼ Stovepipe Wells Village **M**

(760) 786-2387. **Call for rates.** SR 190 92328. On SR 190; 24 mi nw of visitor center. Ext corridors. **Pets:** Accepted.

(icons)

DELANO

ⱯⱯⱯ ▼▼▼ Best Western Liberty Inn **M**

(661) 725-0976. **$76-$199.** 14394 County Line Rd 93215. SR 99 exit 58 (County Line Rd), just e, then just n on Girard St. Int corridors. **Pets:** $20 daily fee/room. Service with restrictions, supervision.

(icons)

ⱯⱯⱯ ▼▼▼ Rodeway Inn **M**

(661) 725-1022. **$70-$129.** 2211 Girard St 93215. SR 99 exit 58 (County Line Rd), just e, then just s. Ext corridors. **Pets:** Medium. $10 daily fee/pet. Service with restrictions, supervision. (icons)

DINUBA

▼▼▼ Holiday Inn Express Hotel & Suites Dinuba **M**

(559) 595-1500. **$91-$200, 3 day notice.** 375 S Alta Ave 93618. Center. Int corridors. **Pets:** $50 one-time fee/pet. Designated rooms, service with restrictions, supervision. (icons)

▼▼▼ Reedley Country Inn Bed & Breakfast **BB** ❀

(559) 638-2585. **$85-$95, 3 day notice.** 43137 Rd 52 93618. SR 99 exit 121 (Manning Ave), 10 mi e, then 1 mi s. Ext/int corridors. **Pets:** Medium. $20 one-time fee/pet. Designated rooms, no service. (icons)

DIXON

ⱯⱯⱯ ▼▼▼ Best Western Plus Inn Dixon **H** ❀

(707) 678-1400. **$89-$179.** 1345 Commercial Way 95620. I-80 exit 64 (Pitt School Rd), just s, then just e. Ext/int corridors. **Pets:** Medium. $15 daily fee/room. Designated rooms, service with restrictions, supervision.

(icons)

▼▼▼ Comfort Suites - West of UC Davis **H**

(707) 676-5000. **$80-$300.** 155 Dorset Dr 95620. I-80 exit 66A (Currey Rd) westbound, follow SR 113 S; exit 66 (Currey Rd) eastbound, just s on SR 113. Int corridors. **Pets:** Large. $25 one-time fee/pet. Designated rooms, service with restrictions, crate. (icons)

▼▼ Super 8 **H**

(707) 678-3399. **$50-$77.** 2500 Plaza Ct 95620. I-80 exit West A St, follow signs for West A St, just n on Gateway Dr. Int corridors. **Pets:** Accepted. (icons)

DORRIS

ⱯⱯⱯ ▼ Golden Eagle Motel **M**

(530) 397-3114. **$39-$99.** 100 W 1st St 96023. US 97; center. Ext corridors. **Pets:** Medium. $5 daily fee/pet. Designated rooms, service with restrictions, supervision. (icons)

DOWNIEVILLE

ⱯⱯⱯ ▼▼▼ Riverside Inn **M** ❀

(530) 289-1000. **$88-$180, 3 day notice.** 206 Commercial St (SR 49) 95936. On SR 49; center. Ext corridors. **Pets:** Medium, other species. $15 one-time fee/pet. Service with restrictions, supervision.

(icons)

DUBLIN

▼▼▼ La Quinta Inn & Suites Dublin - Pleasanton **H**

(925) 828-9393. **$98-$179.** 6275 Dublin Blvd 94568. I-580 exit Hopyard/Dougherty Rd, just n. Int corridors. **Pets:** Medium, other species. Service with restrictions, supervision. (icons)

DUNSMUIR

▼▼ Oak Tree Inn **H**

(530) 235-4100. **$90-$141.** 4000 Siskiyou Ave 96025. I-5 exit 732 (Siskiyou Ave), just e. Int corridors. **Pets:** Accepted.

(icons)

EAST PALO ALTO

▼▼ ▼▼ Four Seasons Hotel Silicon Valley at East Palo Alto **H** ❀

(650) 566-1200. **Call for rates.** 2050 University Ave 94303. US 101 exit University Ave. Int corridors. **Pets:** Medium. Service with restrictions.

(icons)

EL CENTRO

▼▼ Comfort Inn & Suites **M**

(760) 335-3502. **$80-$100.** 2354 S 4th St 92243. I-8 exit 115 (4th St/SR 86), just s. Int corridors. **Pets:** Small, other species. $25 one-time fee/room. Designated rooms, service with restrictions, supervision.

(icons)

▼▼ Rodeway Inn & Suites **M**

(760) 352-6620. **Call for rates.** 455 W Wake Ave 92243. I-8 exit 115 (4th St/SR 86), just s, then just w. Ext corridors. **Pets:** Accepted.

(icons)

▼▼▼ TownePlace Suites by Marriott **H**

(760) 370-3800. **$102-$117.** 3003 S Dogwood Rd 92243. I-8 exit 116 (Dogwood Rd), 0.5 mi s. Int corridors. **Pets:** Accepted.

(icons)

ELK GROVE

▼▼ Extended StayAmerica-Sacramento-Elk Grove **H** ❀

(916) 683-3753. **$79-$94.** 2201 Longport Ct 95758. I-5 exit 508 (Laguna Blvd), 0.5 mi e, just s on Harbour Point Dr, then just w. Int corridors. **Pets:** Other species. $25 daily fee/pet. Service with restrictions.

(icons)

ⱯⱯⱯ ▼▼▼ Fairfield Inn & Suites by Marriott Sacramento Elk Grove **H**

(916) 681-5400. **$99-$169.** 8058 Orchard Loop Ln 95624. SR 99 exit 289 (Cosumnes River Blvd/Calvine Rd), just e to Calvine Rd, then just s. Int corridors. **Pets:** Medium. $35 daily fee/room. Service with restrictions, supervision.

(icons)

ⱯⱯⱯ ▼▼▼ Holiday Inn Express Hotel & Suites **H** ❀

(916) 478-9000. **$116-$152.** 9175 W Stockton Blvd 95758. SR 99 exit 287 (Laguna Blvd), just w; in Laguna Gateway Shopping Center. Int corridors. **Pets:** Medium. $35 one-time fee/pet. Designated rooms, service with restrictions, supervision. (icons)

EL PORTAL

ⱯⱯⱯ ▼▼▼ Yosemite View Lodge **H**

(209) 379-2681. **$95-$729, 7 day notice.** 11136 Hwy 140 95318. Just w of Yosemite National Park West Gate. Ext corridors. **Pets:** $10 one-time fee/pet. Service with restrictions, supervision.

(icons)

EMERYVILLE

ⱯⱯⱯ ▼▼▼ Hyatt Summerfield Suites Emeryville/San Francisco Bay Area **H**

(510) 601-5880. **$139-$239.** 5800 Shellmound St 94608. I-80 exit Powell St, just e. Int corridors. **Pets:** Accepted.

(icons)

ENCINITAS

ⱯⱯⱯ ▼▼▼ Best Western Encinitas Inn & Suites at Moonlight Beach **M** ❀

(760) 942-7455. **$110-$170.** 85 Encinitas Blvd 92024. I-5 exit 41B (Encinitas Blvd), just w. Ext corridors. **Pets:** Medium, other species. $20 daily fee/pet. Designated rooms, service with restrictions, supervision.

(icons)

▼▼▼ Econo Lodge Moonlight Beach Encinitas Ⓜ
(760) 436-4999. **$79-$179.** 410 N Coast Hwy 101 92024. I-5 exit 41B (Encinitas Blvd), 0.6 mi w, then 0.6 mi n. Ext/int corridors. **Pets:** Small, other species. $20 daily fee/pet. Designated rooms, service with restrictions, supervision. 〔SAVE〕 ⊛ ⊠ ▤ 🖵 ⇋

▼▼ Howard Johnson-Encinitas Ⓜ
(760) 944-3800. **$53-$104.** 607 Leucadia Blvd 92024. I-5 exit 43 (Leucadia Blvd), just e. Ext corridors. **Pets:** Accepted. ⊛ ▤ 🖵 ⇋

ESCONDIDO

▲▲▲ ▼▼▼ Best Western Escondido Hotel Ⓗ
(760) 740-1700. **$110-$130.** 1700 Seven Oaks Rd 92026. I-15 exit 33 (El Norte Pkwy), just e, then just n. Int corridors. **Pets:** Medium, other species. $25 one-time fee/pet. Designated rooms, service with restrictions, supervision. 〔SAVE〕 ⊛ ▤ 🖵 ⇋

▼▼ Comfort Inn San Diego/Escondido Ⓗ
(760) 489-1010. **$100.** 1290 W Valley Pkwy 92029. I-15 exit 31 (Valley Pkwy), just w. Int corridors. **Pets:** Accepted. ⊛ ▤ 🖵 ⇋

▲▲▲ ▼▼ Econo Lodge Ⓜ
(760) 743-9733. **$50-$199.** 2650 S Escondido Blvd 92025. I-15 exit 29 (Felicita Rd/Citracado Pkwy), 0.8 mi e on Citracado Pkwy, then just s. Ext corridors. **Pets:** Accepted. 〔SAVE〕 ⊛ ▤ 🖵 ⇋

▲▲▲ ▼▼▼ Rodeway Inn Ⓜ 🐾
(760) 746-0441. **$58-$159.** 250 W El Norte Pkwy 92026. I-15 exit 33 (El Norte Pkwy), 1 mi e. Ext corridors. **Pets:** Medium. $25 daily fee/pet. Designated rooms, service with restrictions, supervision. 〔SAVE〕 ⊛ ▤ 🖵

EUREKA

▲▲▲ ▼▼▼ Best Western Plus Bayshore Inn Ⓗ 🐾
(707) 268-8005. **$90-$230.** 3500 Broadway 95503. US 101; south end of town. Ext corridors. **Pets:** Large, dogs only. $20 one-time fee/pet. Designated rooms, service with restrictions, supervision.
〔SAVE〕 ⊛ ▤ 🖵 ⊺¹ ⇋ ⊠

▼▼▼ Carter House Inns Ⓒ 🐾
(707) 444-8062. **$159-$612, 3 day notice.** 301 L St 95501. Just w of US 101 S. Int corridors. **Pets:** Medium, dogs only. $50 one-time fee/room. Designated rooms, no service, supervision.
⊛ ⊠ ▤ ⊺¹ 🎬

▲▲▲ ▼▼ Eureka Town House Motel Ⓜ
(707) 443-4536. **$55-$150.** 933 4th St 95501. On US 101 southbound; corner of K St. Ext corridors. **Pets:** Medium, dogs only. $10 daily fee/pet. Designated rooms, service with restrictions, supervision.
〔SAVE〕 ⊛ 🖵 🎬

▲▲▲ ▼▼ Quality Inn Eureka Ⓜ
(707) 443-1601. **Call for rates.** 1209 4th St 95501. On US 101 southbound; between M and N sts. Ext corridors. **Pets:** Accepted.
〔SAVE〕 ⊛ ▤ 🖵 ⇋ 🎬

▲▲▲ ▼▼▼ Red Lion Hotel Eureka Ⓗ
(707) 445-0844. **$99-$149.** 1929 4th St 95501. On US 101 southbound; between T and V sts. Int corridors. **Pets:** Accepted.
〔SAVE〕 ⊛ ⊠ ▤ 🖵 ⊺¹ ⇋

FAIRFIELD

▼▼▼ Extended StayAmerica-Fairfield-Napa Valley Ⓗ 🐾
(707) 438-0932. **$94-$109.** 1019 Oliver Rd 94534. I-80 exit Texas St, just w. Int corridors. **Pets:** Other species. $25 daily fee/pet. Service with restrictions. ⊛ ⊾ᴹ ▤ 🖵

▼▼▼▼ Homewood Suites Fairfield-Napa Valley Area Ⓗ
(707) 863-0300. **$119-$179.** 4755 Business Center Dr 94534. I-80 exit Green Valley Rd/Suisun Valley Rd, n on Green Valley Rd, then just e. Int corridors. **Pets:** Medium. $75 one-time fee/room. Designated rooms, no service, supervision. ⊛ ⊾ᴹ ▤ 🖵 ⇋ ⊠

▼▼▼▼ Staybridge Suites Fairfield-Napa Valley Area Ⓗ
(707) 863-0900. **$99-$179, 3 day notice.** 4775 Business Center Dr 94534. I-80 exit Green Valley Rd/Suisun Valley Rd, n on Green Valley Rd, then just e. Int corridors. **Pets:** Accepted.
⊛ ⊠ ⊾ᴹ ▤ 🖵 ⇋

FALLBROOK

▼▼▼▼ Pala Mesa Resort Ⓗ
(760) 728-5881. **$109-$275.** 2001 Old Hwy 395 92028. I-15 exit 46 (SR 76/Pala Rd/Oceanside), just w, then 2 mi n. Ext corridors.
Pets: Accepted. ⊛ ▤ 🖵 ⊺¹ ⇋ ⊠

FALL RIVER MILLS

▲▲▲ ▼▼▼ Hi-Mont Motel Ⓜ
(530) 336-5541. **$69-$99.** 43000 Bridge St 96028. 0.4 mi sw on SR 299; jct SR 299 E and Bridge St. Ext corridors. **Pets:** Accepted.
〔SAVE〕 ⊛ ▤ 🖵

FERNDALE

▲▲▲ ▼▼▼▼ Shaw House Inn ⒷⒷ 🐾
(707) 786-9958. **$125-$275, 15 day notice.** 703 Main St 95536. Center. Ext/int corridors. **Pets:** Medium, other species. $35 one-time fee/pet. Designated rooms, service with restrictions, crate. 〔SAVE〕 ⊛ ⊠ 🎬 🎬

FIREBAUGH

▲▲▲ ▼▼▼ Best Western Apricot Inn Ⓜ
(559) 659-1444. **$89-$110.** 46290 W Panoche Rd 93622. I-5 exit W Panoche Rd, just w. Ext corridors. **Pets:** Medium, other species. $25 one-time fee/room. Service with restrictions, supervision.
〔SAVE〕 ⊛ ⊾ᴹ ▤ 🖵 ⇋

FISH CAMP

▲▲▲ ▼▼▼▼ The Cottages at Tenaya Lodge Ⓗ
(559) 683-6555. **$129-$425, 7 day notice.** 1122 Hwy 41 93623. 2 mi from Yosemite National Park South Gate. Ext corridors. **Pets:** Accepted.
〔SAVE〕 ⊛ ⊠ ⊾ᴹ ▤ 🖵 ⇋ ⊠

▼▼▼ The Narrow Gauge Inn Ⓗ 🐾
(559) 683-7720. **$79-$250, 4 day notice.** 48571 Hwy 41 93623. 4 mi from Yosemite National Park South Gate. Ext corridors. **Pets:** Other species. $25 one-time fee/pet. Designated rooms, service with restrictions, supervision. ⊛ 🖵 ⊺¹ ⇋

▲▲▲ ▼▼▼ Tenaya Lodge at Yosemite Ⓗ
(559) 683-6555. **$129-$425, 7 day notice.** 1122 Hwy 41 93623. 2 mi from Yosemite National Park South Gate. Int corridors. **Pets:** Accepted.
〔SAVE〕 ⊛ ⊠ ⊾ᴹ ▤ 🖵 ⊺¹ ⇋ ⊠

FOLSOM

▲▲▲ ▼▼▼▼ Lake Natoma Inn Ⓗ
(916) 351-1500. **$89-$169.** 702 Gold Lake Dr 95630. US 50 exit Folsom Blvd, 3 mi n, 0.5 mi e on Riley St; behind The Lakes Specialty Shopping Center. Int corridors. **Pets:** Other species. $45 one-time fee/room, $15 daily fee/pet. Service with restrictions, crate.
〔SAVE〕 ⊛ ⊾ᴹ ▤ 🖵 ⊺¹ ⇋ ⊠

▼▼▼ Residence Inn by Marriott Ⓗ
(916) 983-7289. **$110-$150.** 2555 Iron Point Rd 95630. US 50 exit Bidwell St, just n, then just w. Int corridors. **Pets:** Accepted.
⊛ ⊠ ⊾ᴹ ▤ 🖵 ⇋ ⊠

FORTUNA

▲▲▲ ▼▼▼ Best Western Country Inn Ⓜ 🐾
(707) 725-6822. **$80-$150.** 2025 Riverwalk Dr 95540. US 101 exit 687 (Kenmar Rd), just w. Ext corridors. **Pets:** Dogs only. $20 one-time fee/room. Service with restrictions, supervision.
〔SAVE〕 ⊛ ⊾ᴹ ▤ 🖵 ⇋

Fortuna Super 8 M
(707) 725-2888. **$72-$175.** 1805 Alamar Way 95540. US 101 exit 687 (Kenmar Rd), 0.3 mi w on Riverwalk Dr. Ext corridors. **Pets:** Dogs only. $15 daily fee/pet. Designated rooms, service with restrictions, supervision.

Holiday Inn Express H
(707) 725-5500. **$99-$179.** 1859 Alamar Way 95540. US 101 exit 687 (Kenmar Rd), 0.3 mi w on Riverwalk Dr. Ext corridors. **Pets:** Accepted.

FOUNTAIN VALLEY

Residence Inn by Marriott H
(714) 965-8000. **$169-$209.** 9930 Slater Ave 92708. I-405 exit 14 (Brookhurst St), just n, then just w. Ext corridors. **Pets:** Accepted.

FREMONT

Best Western Plus Garden Court Inn H
(510) 792-4300. **$90-$120.** 5400 Mowry Ave 94538. I-880 exit Mowry Ave, just e. Int corridors. **Pets:** Accepted.

Comfort Inn by Choice Hotels H
(510) 490-2900. **$60-$104.** 47031 Kato Rd 94538. I-880 exit Warren Ave/Mission Blvd E, just e. Int corridors. **Pets:** Accepted.

Extended StayAmerica-Fremont-Newark H ❖
(510) 794-8040. **$84-$99.** 5355 Farwell Pl 94536. I-880 exit Mowry Ave, just e. Int corridors. **Pets:** Other species. $25 daily fee/pet. Service with restrictions.

La Quinta Inn & Suites Fremont H
(510) 445-0808. **$71-$155.** 46200 Landing Pkwy 94538. I-880 exit Fremont Blvd/Cushing Pkwy, just w. Int corridors. **Pets:** Medium, other species. Service with restrictions, supervision.

Residence Inn by Marriott H ❖
(510) 794-5900. **Call for rates.** 5400 Farwell Pl 94536. I-880 exit Mowry Ave, just e. Ext corridors. **Pets:** Other species. $100 one-time fee/room. Service with restrictions, crate.

FRESNO

Ambassador Inn & Suites M
(559) 442-1082. **$55-$80.** 1804 W Olive Ave 93728. SR 99 exit Olive Ave, just w. Ext corridors. **Pets:** Medium. $20 deposit/pet. Service with restrictions, supervision.

Americas Best Value Inn - Water Tree Inn H
(559) 222-4445. **$69-$99.** 4141 N Blackstone Ave 93726. SR 41 exit Ashlan Ave, 0.3 mi w. Int corridors. **Pets:** Very small. $50 deposit/pet, $25 one-time fee/pet. Designated rooms, service with restrictions, supervision.

Best Western Plus Village Inn H
(559) 226-2110. **$70-$100.** 3110 N Blackstone Ave 93703. SR 41 exit Shields Ave, 0.3 mi w. Int corridors. **Pets:** Accepted.

Days Inn-Parkway M
(559) 268-6211. **$47-$64.** 1101 N Parkway Dr 93728. SR 99 exit Olive Ave, just w. Ext corridors. **Pets:** Accepted.

Extended StayAmerica Fresno-North H ❖
(559) 438-7105. **$79-$94.** 7135 N Fresno St 93720. SR 41 exit Herndon Ave E, just n. Ext corridors. **Pets:** Other species. $25 daily fee/pet. Service with restrictions.

La Quinta Inn & Suites Fresno
Riverpark H
(559) 449-0928. **$116-$179.** 330 E Fir Ave 93720. SR 41 exit Herndon Ave, just e. Int corridors. **Pets:** Medium, other species. Service with restrictions, supervision.

La Quinta Inn Fresno Yosemite H
(559) 442-1110. **$67-$134.** 2926 Tulare St 93721. SR 99 exit Fresno St, 1 mi e to R St, then s, then just e. Ext/int corridors. **Pets:** Medium, other species. Service with restrictions, supervision.

Motel 6 Fresno #4390 M
(559) 276-1910. **$50-$80, 14 day notice.** 5021 N Barcus Ave 93722. SR 99 exit Shaw Ave, just e. Ext corridors. **Pets:** Other species. Service with restrictions, supervision.

Quality Inn-Fresno M
(559) 275-2727. **$70-$110.** 4278 W Ashlan Ave 93722. SR 99 exit Ashlan Ave, just w. Ext corridors. **Pets:** Accepted.

Residence Inn by Marriott H
(559) 222-8900. **$98-$189.** 5322 N Diana St 93710. SR 41 exit Shaw Ave, 0.3 mi w, n on Blackstone Ave, then e on Barstow Ave. Int corridors. **Pets:** Accepted.

Rodeway Inn H
(559) 431-3557. **Call for rates.** 6730 N Blackstone Ave 93710. SR 41 exit Herndon Ave, then w. Ext corridors. **Pets:** Accepted.

Super 8-Parkway M
(559) 268-0741. **$41-$86.** 1087 N Parkway Dr 93728. SR 99 exit Olive Ave, just w. Ext corridors. **Pets:** $10 daily fee/pet. Service with restrictions, supervision.

TownePlace Suites by Marriott H
(559) 435-4600. **$69-$119.** 7127 N Fresno St 93720. SR 41 exit Herndon Ave E. Int corridors. **Pets:** Accepted.

FULLERTON

Fullerton Marriott Hotel at California State
University H
(714) 738-7800. **$79-$189.** 2701 E Nutwood Ave 92831. SR 57 exit 7 (Nutwood Ave) northbound; exit 7 (Nutwood Ave/Chapman Ave) southbound, just w. Int corridors. **Pets:** Accepted.

GARBERVILLE

Benbow Inn H
(707) 923-2124. **$99-$695, 5 day notice.** 445 Lake Benbow Dr 95542. US 101 exit Benbow Lake Rd, just w; 2 mi s of downtown. Int corridors. **Pets:** Accepted.

Best Western Plus Humboldt House
Inn M ❖
(707) 923-2771. **$123-$157.** 701 Redwood Dr 95542. US 101 exit Garberville, just e. Ext corridors. **Pets:** Medium, dogs only. $15 one-time fee/pet. Designated rooms, service with restrictions, supervision.

GARDEN GROVE

Anaheim Marriott Suites H
(714) 750-1000. **$99-$279.** 12015 Harbor Blvd 92840. I-5 exit 107B (Chapman Ave) northbound, 1.5 mi w on Chapman Ave, then just s; exit 107C (State College/The City Dr) southbound, just s on State College Blvd, 1.5 mi w on Chapman Ave, then just s. Int corridors. **Pets:** Accepted.

Candlewood Suites Anaheim-South H
(714) 539-4200. **$69-$140.** 12901 Garden Grove Blvd 92843. SR 22 exit 13 (Haster St) westbound; exit 13 (Fairview St) eastbound, just n, then just w. Int corridors. **Pets:** Accepted.

▼▼▼ **Residence Inn Anaheim Resort Area** 🄷
(714) 591-4000. **$119-$289.** 11931 Harbor Blvd 92840. I-5 exit 107B (Chapman Ave) northbound, 1.5 mi w, then just n; exit 107C (State College Blvd/The City Dr) southbound, just s on State College Blvd, 1.5 mi w on Chapman Ave, then just n. Int corridors. **Pets:** Accepted.
🛜 ⊠ 🅖M 📁 🖥 🌊 📷

🄰🄰🄰 ▼▼▼▼ **Sheraton Garden Grove Anaheim South** 🄷
(714) 703-8400. **$159-$189.** 12221 Harbor Blvd 92840. I-5 exit 110 (Harbor Blvd/Ball Rd), 2.2 mi s. Int corridors. **Pets:** Accepted.
SAVE 🛜 ⊠ 📁 🖥 🍽 🌊

GILROY

🄰🄰🄰 ▼▼▼▼ **Best Western Plus Forest Park Inn** 🄷 🐾
(408) 848-5144. **$100-$239.** 375 Leavesley Rd 95020. US 101 exit Leavesley Rd, just w. Int corridors. **Pets:** Medium, dogs only. $20 daily fee/pet. Designated rooms, service with restrictions, supervision.
SAVE 🛜 ⊠ 🅖M 📁 🖥 🌊 📷

▼▼▼▼ **Hilton Garden Inn Gilroy** 🄷
(408) 840-7000. **$109-$199.** 6070 Monterey Rd 95020. US 101 exit Monterey Rd, just w. Int corridors. **Pets:** Accepted.
🛜 🅖M 📁 🖥 🍽 🌊

🄰🄰🄰 ▼▼▼ **Quality Inn & Suites** 🄷 🐾
(408) 847-5500. **$79-$249.** 8430 Murray Ave 95020. US 101 exit Leavesley Rd, just w. Ext corridors. **Pets:** Other species. $10 daily fee/pet. Service with restrictions, supervision. SAVE 🛜 📁 🖥 🌊

GLENNVILLE

▼▼▼ **The Bunkhouse Motel** 🄼 🐾
(661) 536-9100. **$65-$75, 3 day notice.** 12044 Hwy 155 93226. On SR 155 at Granite Rd. Ext corridors. **Pets:** $15 one-time fee/room. Service with restrictions.
📁 🖥 🍽

GRAEAGLE

▼▼▼ **Chalet View Lodge** 🄷
(530) 832-5528. **$89-$315, 7 day notice.** 72056 Hwy 70 96103. Jct SR 70 and 89, 5.7 mi e on SR 70. Ext corridors. **Pets:** Other species. $25 one-time fee/room. Service with restrictions, supervision.
🛜 ⊠ 📁 🖥 🍽 🌊 📷

GRASS VALLEY

🄰🄰🄰 ▼▼▼▼ **Best Western Gold Country Inn** 🄼
(530) 273-1393. **$90-$120.** 972 Sutton Way 95945. SR 20 and 49 exit 183 (Brunswick Rd), just e; midway between Grass Valley and Nevada City. Ext corridors. **Pets:** Accepted. SAVE 🛜 📁 🖥 🌊

🄰🄰🄰 ▼▼ **Golden Chain Resort Motel** 🄼
(530) 273-7279. **$55-$99.** 13413 State Hwy 49 95949. On SR 49, 2.5 mi s. Ext corridors. **Pets:** Accepted. SAVE 🛜 🅖M 📁 🖥 🌊

🄰🄰🄰 ▼▼▼ **Grass Valley Courtyard Suites** 🄷
(530) 272-7696. **$150-$360, 3 day notice.** 210 N Auburn St 95945. SR 49 exit 182A (SR 174/Colfax Ave) southbound, just w to S Auburn St, then just n; exit northbound, just n on S Auburn St; jct Richardson St. Ext corridors. **Pets:** Accepted. SAVE 🛜 🅖M 🖥 🌊 📷

▼▼▼ **Holiday Inn Express Hotel & Suites** 🄷 🐾
(530) 477-1700. **$129-$194.** 121 Bank St 95945. SR 49 exit 182A (SR 174/Colfax Ave) northbound, just n on Auburn St, then just e; exit 182B (SR 174/Colfax Ave) southbound, just n on Auburn St, then just e. Int corridors. **Pets:** $50 one-time fee/room. Service with restrictions, supervision.
🛜 ⊠ 🅖M 📁 🖥

GROVELAND

🄰🄰🄰 ▼▼▼ **Groveland Hotel at Yosemite National Park** 🄲🄸
(209) 962-4000. **$145-$345.** 18767 Main St 95321. Center. Int corridors. **Pets:** Accepted. SAVE 🛜 🖥 🍽

HANFORD

🄰🄰🄰 ▼▼▼ **Sequoia Inn** 🄷
(559) 582-0338. **$72-$89.** 1655 Mall Dr 93230. SR 198 exit 12th Ave N, just e. Int corridors. **Pets:** Other species. $100 deposit/room, $25 one-time fee/room. Service with restrictions, supervision.
SAVE 🛜 📁 🖥 🌊

HAWAIIAN GARDENS

▼▼▼ **La Quinta Inn & Suites Hawaiian Gardens** 🄷
(562) 860-2500. **$94-$181.** 12441 Carson St 90716. I-605 exit 3 (Carson St), 1 mi e. Int corridors. **Pets:** Medium, other species. Service with restrictions, supervision. 🛜 ⊠ 🅖M 📁 🖥

HAYWARD

🄰🄰🄰 ▼▼▼▼ **La Quinta Inn & Suites Hayward Oakland Airport** 🄷
(510) 732-6300. **$84-$181.** 20777 Hesperian Blvd 94541. I-880 exit A St, 0.5 mi w. Int corridors. **Pets:** Medium, other species. Service with restrictions, supervision. SAVE 🛜 🅖M 📁 🖥 🌊

HEMET

🄰🄰🄰 ▼▼▼ **Best Western Inn of Hemet** 🄼
(951) 925-6605. **$80-$110.** 2625 W Florida Ave 92545. 2.4 mi w of SR 79 N (San Jacinto St) on SR 74/79. Ext corridors. **Pets:** Accepted.
SAVE 🛜 📁 🖥 🌊

🄰🄰🄰 ▼▼▼ **Quality Inn** 🄼
(951) 766-1902. **$90-$110.** 1201 W Florida Ave 92543. 1.5 mi w of SR 79 N (San Jacinto St) on SR 74/79. Ext corridors. **Pets:** Small. $20 daily fee/pet. Designated rooms, service with restrictions, supervision.
ECO SAVE 🛜 🅖M 📁 🖥 🌊

HESPERIA

▼▼▼ **Econo Lodge** 🄼 🐾
(760) 949-1515. **$55-$100.** 11976 Mariposa Rd 92345. I-15 exit 147 (Bear Valley Rd), just e, then just s. Ext corridors. **Pets:** Medium, dogs only. $10 daily fee/pet. Service with restrictions, supervision.
🛜 📁 🖥

▼▼▼ **Holiday Inn Express Hotel & Suites** 🄷 🐾
(760) 244-7674. **$65-$99.** 9750 Key Pointe Dr 92345. I-15 exit 143 (Hesperia/Main St), just w on Main St, then just n. Int corridors. **Pets:** Medium. $25 daily fee/pet. Designated rooms, service with restrictions, supervision. 🛜 ⊠ 🅖M 📁 🖥

▼▼▼ **La Quinta Inn & Suites Victorville/Hesperia** 🄷
(760) 949-9900. **$94-$155.** 12000 Mariposa Rd 92345. I-15 exit 147 (Bear Valley Rd), just e, then just s. Int corridors. **Pets:** Medium, other species. Service with restrictions, supervision. 🛜 🅖M 📁 🖥 🌊

HUNTINGTON BEACH

🄰🄰🄰 ▼▼▼ **Best Western Harbour Inn & Suites** 🄷
(562) 592-4770. **$129-$199.** 16912 Pacific Coast Hwy 90742. I-405 exit 15 (Magnolia St/Warner Ave W), 6 mi s, then 0.5 mi n. Int corridors. **Pets:** Accepted. SAVE 🛜 ⊠ 📁 🖥

🄰🄰🄰 ▼▼▼▼ **Hyatt Regency Huntington Beach Resort & Spa** 🄷 🐾
(714) 698-1234. **$179-$499, 7 day notice.** 21500 Pacific Coast Hwy 92648. I-405 exit 16 (Beach Blvd), 6.5 mi s. Int corridors. **Pets:** Medium, dogs only. $50 daily fee/room. Designated rooms, service with restrictions, supervision. ECO SAVE 🛜 🅖M 📁 🖥 🍽 🌊 📷

🄰🄰🄰 ▼▼▼▼ **The Waterfront Beach Resort A Hilton Hotel** 🄷 🐾
(714) 845-8000. **$209-$539.** 21100 Pacific Coast Hwy 92648. I-405 exit 16 (Beach Blvd), 6 mi s, then just w. Int corridors. **Pets:** Medium. $50 one-time fee/room. Designated rooms, service with restrictions, supervision.
ECO SAVE 🛜 ⊠ 🅖M 📁 🖥 🍽 🌊 📷

IDYLLWILD

▼▼ Quiet Creek Inn CA ❀
(951) 659-6110. **$89-$165, 14 day notice.** 26345 Delano Dr 92549. SR 243, 0.8 mi sw of town center, 0.4 mi w on Toll Gate Rd, then just n. Ext corridors. **Pets:** Other species. $35 one-time fee/room. Supervision.
🛜 ⊗ 🛏 💻 🗙 ☎

▼ **Strawberry Creek Bunkhouse** M
(951) 659-2201. **Call for rates.** 25525 Hwy 243 92549. SR 243, 0.5 mi n of town center. Ext corridors. **Pets:** Accepted.
🛜 ⊗ 🛏 💻 ☎

▼▼ Woodland Park Manor CA
(951) 659-2657. **$99-$205, 10 day notice.** 55350 S Circle Dr 92549. From SR 243 and town center, 1.5 mi ne. Ext corridors. **Pets:** Other species. $15 one-time fee/room. Designated rooms, supervision.
🛜 ⊗ 🛏 💻 ➰ 🗙 ☎

INDIAN WELLS

AAA **▼▼▼▼ Hyatt Grand Champions Resort** H
(760) 341-1000. **$89-$429, 7 day notice.** 44-600 Indian Wells Ln 92210. I-10 exit 134 (Cook St), 4.4 mi s, 1.5 mi e on SR 111, then just n. Ext/int corridors. **Pets:** Accepted.
ECO SAVE 🛜 ♿ 🛏 💻 🍴 ➰ 🗙

AAA **▼▼▼▼ Miramonte Resort and Spa** H ❀
(760) 341-2200. **$99-$499, 3 day notice.** 45-000 Indian Wells Ln 92210. I-10 exit 134 (Cook St), 4.4 mi s, 1.5 mi e on SR 111, then just s. Ext/int corridors. **Pets:** Medium, dogs only. $50 deposit/room, $50 one-time fee/room. Designated rooms, service with restrictions, supervision.
ECO SAVE 🛜 ⊗ 🛏 💻 🍴 ➰ 🗙

INDIO

AAA **▼▼ Best Western Date Tree Hotel** M ❀
(760) 347-3421. **$59-$350.** 81-909 Indio Blvd 92201. I-10 exit 139 (Jefferson St/Indio Blvd), 2.5 mi se. Int corridors. **Pets:** Other species. $15 daily fee/room. Service with restrictions, crate. SAVE 🛜 ⊗ 🛏 💻 ➰

▼▼ Indian Palms Country Club & Resort H ❀
(760) 775-4444. **$84-$209.** 48-630 Monroe St 92201. I-10 exit 142 (Monroe St), 3 mi s. Ext corridors. **Pets:** Medium, dogs only. $15 daily fee/room. Service with restrictions, supervision.
🛜 ⊗ 🛏 💻 🍴 ➰ 🗙

IRVINE

▼▼▼▼ Embassy Suites Hotel-Orange County Airport H
(949) 553-8332. **$99-$209.** 2120 Main St 92614. I-405 exit 8 (MacArthur Blvd/John Wayne Airport), just n, then just 0.5 mi e. Int corridors.
Pets: Accepted. ECO 🛜 ♿ 🛏 💻 🍴 ➰

AAA **▼▼▼▼ Hilton Irvine/Orange County Airport** H
(949) 833-9999. **Call for rates.** 18800 MacArthur Blvd 92612. I-405 exit 8 (MacArthur Blvd/John Wayne Airport), 0.5 mi s. Int corridors.
Pets: Medium. $75 one-time fee/room. Designated rooms, service with restrictions, supervision. ECO SAVE 🛜 ♿ 🛏 💻 🍴 ➰ 🗙

AAA **▼▼▼▼ Hyatt Regency Irvine** H
(949) 975-1234. **$89-$329.** 17900 Jamboree Rd 92614. I-405 exit 7 (Jamboree Blvd), just ne. Int corridors. **Pets:** Accepted.
ECO SAVE 🛜 ♿ 🛏 💻 🍴 ➰ 🗙

▼▼▼▼ Residence Inn by Marriott Irvine John Wayne Airport H
(949) 261-2020. **$119-$279.** 2855 Main St 92614. I-405 exit 7 (Jamboree Blvd), just n, then just e. Int corridors. **Pets:** Large, other species. $100 one-time fee/room. Service with restrictions.
🛜 ⊗ ♿ 🛏 💻 ➰ 🗙

▼▼▼▼ Residence Inn by Marriott-Irvine Spectrum H
(949) 380-3000. **$109-$229.** 10 Morgan 92618. I-5 exit 94 (Alton Pkwy) southbound; exit 94B (Alton Pkwy) northbound, 2 mi e. Ext corridors. **Pets:** Large, other species. $110 one-time fee/room. Service with restrictions, crate. ECO 🛜 ⊗ ♿ 🛏 💻 ➰ 🗙

JACKSON

AAA **▼▼ Best Western Amador Inn** H
(209) 223-0211. **$89-$99.** 200 S Hwy 49 95642. Just se of jct SR 49 and 88. Int corridors. **Pets:** Large. $15 daily fee/pet. Service with restrictions, supervision. SAVE 🛜 🛏 💻 ➰

AAA **▼▼ The Jackson Lodge** M
(209) 223-0486. **$65-$145.** 850 N Hwy 49 95642. On SR 49 and 88, 0.5 mi w. Ext corridors. **Pets:** $15 daily fee/pet. Designated rooms, service with restrictions, supervision. SAVE 🛜 🛏 💻 ➰

JAMESTOWN

AAA **▼▼▼▼ 1859 Historic National Hotel, A Country Inn** CI ❀
(209) 984-3446. **$140-$160, 3 day notice.** 18183 Main St 95327. In historic downtown. Int corridors. **Pets:** Medium, dogs only. $25 daily fee/pet. Service with restrictions, supervision. SAVE 🛜 ⊗ 🍴 🗙 ☎

AAA **▼▼ Country Inn Sonora** M
(209) 984-0315. **$59-$289.** 18730 Hwy 108 95327. SR 108 and 49, 1 mi e of town. Ext corridors. **Pets:** Medium. $10 daily fee/pet. Service with restrictions, supervision. SAVE 🛜 🛏 💻 ➰

AAA **▼ Jamestown Railtown Motel** M
(209) 984-3332. **$40-$80, 3 day notice.** 10301 Willow St 95327. Center. Ext corridors. **Pets:** Accepted. SAVE 🛜 🛏 ➰

▼▼▼▼ Victorian Gold Bed & Breakfast BB
(209) 984-3429. **$115-$185, 5 day notice.** 10382 Willow St 95327. Center; in historic downtown. Int corridors. **Pets:** Accepted.
🛜 ⊗ 🛏 ☎

JUNE LAKE

AAA **▼▼▼▼ Double Eagle Resort/Spa** CA
(760) 648-7004. **$169-$400, 30 day notice.** 5587 Hwy 158 93529. On SR 158; 3 mi w of village. Ext corridors. **Pets:** $50 one-time fee/room. Service with restrictions, crate.
SAVE 🛜 ⊗ ♿ 🛏 💻 🍴 ➰ 🗙 ♿

▼▼ Gull Lake Lodge M
(760) 648-7516. **$79-$204, 7 day notice.** 132 Leonard Ave 93529. Just n of SR 158, via Knoll and Bruce sts; in village. Ext corridors.
Pets: Other species. Designated rooms, service with restrictions, supervision. 🛜 ⊗ 🛏 💻 ♿ ☎

KERNVILLE

▼▼ Barewood Inn & Suites M
(760) 376-1910. **$75-$195.** 7013 Wofford Blvd 93285. In Wofford Heights. Ext corridors. **Pets:** Accepted. 🛜 🗙 🛏 💻

▼▼ River View Lodge M
(760) 376-6019. **$79-$129, 3 day notice.** 2 Sirretta St 93238. On Kernville Rd; at the bridge. Ext corridors. **Pets:** Accepted. 🛜 🗙 🛏

KETTLEMAN CITY

AAA **▼▼▼▼ Best Western Kettleman Inn & Suites** M
(559) 386-0804. **$111-$126.** 33410 Powers Dr 93239. E of and adjacent to I-5 exit SR 41 N, 0.3 mi to Bernard Dr, then 0.3 mi n. Ext corridors. **Pets:** Accepted. SAVE 🛜 ♿ 🛏 💻 ➰

AAA **▼▼ Super 8** M
(559) 386-9530. **$62-$68.** 33415 Powers Dr 93239. E of and adjacent to I-5 exit SR 41 N, 0.3 mi to Bernard, then 0.3 mi n. Ext corridors.
Pets: Accepted. SAVE 🛜 🛏 💻 ➰

KING CITY

AAA **▼▼▼ Courtesy Inn** M
(831) 385-4646. **$59-$199.** 4 Broadway Cir 93930. US 101 exit Broadway St, just w. Ext corridors. **Pets:** $10 daily fee/pet. Service with restrictions, supervision. SAVE 🛜 ♿ 🛏 💻 ➰

KLAMATH

⬥⬥ ▼ Motel Trees M
(707) 482-3152. **$70-$145.** 15495 Hwy 101 N 95548. On US 101, 4.5 mi n of Klamath. Ext corridors. **Pets:** Accepted.
[SAVE] 🛰 🛢 🖵 📶 🔏

LAGUNA BEACH

▼ ▼ Art Hotel-Laguna Beach M
(949) 494-6464. **$99-$199, 3 day notice.** 1404 N Coast Hwy 92651. SR 133 to Coast Hwy, then 1.1 mi n on SR 1. Ext corridors. **Pets:** Other species. Designated rooms. 🛰 ✕ 🛢 🖵 ⮌

▼▼▼ The Carriage House-Bed & Breakfast BB
(949) 494-8945. **$160-$225, 3 day notice.** 1322 Catalina St 92651. SR 133 to Coast Hwy, 1 mi s on SR 1 to Cress St, then just e. Ext corridors. **Pets:** Other species. $20 daily fee/pet. Supervision.
🛰 ✕ 🛢 🖵 🔏 🐾

▼▼▼ Casa Laguna Inn & Spa BB 🐾
(949) 494-2996. **$150-$650, 5 day notice.** 2510 S Coast Hwy 92651. SR 133 to Coast Hwy, then 1.3 mi s on SR 1. Ext corridors. **Pets:** Medium, dogs only. $25 daily fee/pet. Service with restrictions, supervision. 🛰 ✕ 🛢 🖵 ⮌

▼▼▼ Holiday Inn Laguna Beach H
(949) 494-1001. **$109-$449.** 696 S Coast Hwy 92651. SR 133 to Coast Hwy, then 0.5 mi s on SR 1. Ext corridors. **Pets:** Accepted.
🛰 ✕ 🛢 🖵 📶 ⮌

▼▼▼ Laguna Cliffs Inn M
(949) 497-6645. **Call for rates.** 475 N Coast Hwy 92651. SR 133 to Coast Hwy, then 0.5 mi n on SR 1. Ext corridors. **Pets:** Accepted.
🛰 ✕ 🛢 🖵 ⮌

▼▼▼▼ Montage Laguna Beach H
(949) 715-6000. **Call for rates.** 30801 S Coast Hwy 92651. SR 133 to Coast Hwy, then 3 mi s on SR 1. Ext/int corridors. **Pets:** Accepted.
[ECO] 🛰 ✕ 🛢 🖵 📶 ⮌ ✕

▼▼▼▼ Surf & Sand Resort H 🐾
(949) 497-4477. **$435-$705, 3 day notice.** 1555 S Coast Hwy 92651. SR 133, 1 mi s. Ext corridors. **Pets:** Small, other species. $100 one-time fee/room. Designated rooms, service with restrictions, supervision.
🛰 ✕ 🖢 🛢 🖵 📶 ⮌ ✕

▼▼ The Tides Laguna Beach M 🐾
(949) 494-2494. **$99-$305, 3 day notice.** 460 N Coast Hwy 92651. SR 133 to Coast Hwy, then 0.5 mi n on SR 1. Ext corridors. **Pets:** $25 daily fee/pet. Designated rooms, service with restrictions, supervision.
🛰 ✕ 🛢 🖵 ⮌

LAGUNA HILLS

▼▼▼ The Hills Hotel, an Ascend Collection hotel H
(949) 586-5000. **$89-$189.** 25205 La Paz Rd 92653. I-5 exit 89 (La Paz Rd), just w. Int corridors. **Pets:** Medium, other species. $30 daily fee/pet. Designated rooms, service with restrictions.
🛰 ✕ 🖢 🛢 🖵 📶 ⮌

LAKE ARROWHEAD

▼▼▼ Arrowhead Saddleback Inn CI
(909) 336-3571. **$137-$648, 7 day notice.** 300 S SR 173 92352. On SR 173, jct SR 189. Ext/int corridors. **Pets:** Other species. $8 daily fee/pet. Designated rooms, service with restrictions, supervision.
🛰 🛢 🖵 📶

▼▼ Arrowhead Tree Top Lodge M
(909) 337-2311. **$79-$217, 7 day notice.** 27992 Rainbow Dr 92352. 0.3 mi s of Lake Arrowhead Village on SR 173. Ext corridors.
Pets: Accepted. 🛰 ✕ 🛢 🖵 ⮌ 🔏 🐾

⬥⬥ ▼▼▼▼ Lake Arrowhead Resort and Spa H 🐾
(909) 336-1511. **$169-$449, 3 day notice.** 27984 Hwy 189 92352. Just w of SR 173; in Lake Arrowhead Village. Int corridors. **Pets:** Other species. $25 daily fee/pet. Designated rooms, service with restrictions, supervision. [SAVE] 🛰 ✕ 🖢 🛢 🖵 📶 ⮌ ✕

LAKE ELSINORE

▼▼▼ Holiday Inn Express Hotel & Suites H 🐾
(951) 674-4333. **$89-$109.** 31573 Canyon Estates Dr 92532. I-15 exit 73 (Diamond Dr/Railroad Canyon Rd), just e, just ne on Summerhill Dr, then just n. Int corridors. **Pets:** $300 deposit/room, $75 one-time fee/room. Designated rooms, service with restrictions, supervision.
🛰 ✕ 🖢 🛢 🖵 ⮌

▼▼ Quality Inn Lake Elsinore M
(951) 674-9694. **$59-$130.** 31808 Casino Dr 92530. I-15 exit 73 (Diamond Dr/Railroad Canyon Rd), just w, then 0.5 mi s. Ext corridors. **Pets:** Small. $75 deposit/room, $20 daily fee/pet. Designated rooms, service with restrictions, supervision. 🛰 🛢 🖵 ⮌

LAKE FOREST

⬥⬥ ▼▼▼ The Prominence Hotel and Suites H
(949) 900-1288. **$89-$199.** 20768 Lake Forest Dr 92630. I-5 exit 92A (Lake Forest Dr) northbound; exit 92 (Bake Pkwy/Lake Forest Dr) southbound, 4 mi e. Int corridors. **Pets:** Accepted.
[SAVE] 🛰 ✕ 🖢 🛢 🖵 ⮌

▼▼ Quality Inn & Suites H
(949) 458-1900. **$90-$120.** 23702 Rockfield Blvd 92630. I-5 exit 92A (Lake Forest Dr) northbound; exit 92 (Bake Pkwy/Lake Forest Dr) southbound, 0.5 mi e on Lake Forest Dr, then just s. Int corridors.
Pets: Accepted. 🛰 🛢 🖵 📶 ⮌

▼▼▼ Staybridge Suites Irvine East/Lake Forest H
(949) 462-9500. **$119-$209.** 2 Orchard Rd 92630. I-5 exit 92B (Bake Pkwy) northbound; exit 92 (Bake Pkwy/Lake Forest Dr) southbound, 4.7 mi e on Bake Pkwy, just n on Rancho Pkwy southbound, then just w. Int corridors. **Pets:** Accepted. 🛰 🖢 🛢 🖵 ⮌ ✕

LAKE TAHOE AREA

SOUTH LAKE TAHOE

▼▼ Alpenrose Inn M
(530) 544-2985. **$49-$199, 7 day notice.** 4074 Pine Blvd 96150. Just s of casino area to Stateline Ave, 0.3 mi w to Pine Blvd, then just s. Ext corridors. **Pets:** Medium, dogs only. $50 deposit/room, $15 daily fee/pet. Designated rooms, service with restrictions, crate. 🛰 ✕ 🛢 🖵

▼ Ambassador Motor Lodge M
(530) 544-6461. **Call for rates.** 4130 Manzanita Ave 96150. Just s of casino area, just w on Stateline Ave to Manzanita Ave, then just s. Ext corridors. **Pets:** Accepted. 🛰 🛢 🖵 ⮌ 🔏

⬥⬥ ▼▼▼ Best Western Plus Timber Cove Lodge H 🐾
(530) 541-6722. **$110-$400, 7 day notice.** 3411 Lake Tahoe Blvd 96150. 1.8 mi s of casino area on US 50. Ext corridors. **Pets:** Medium, dogs only. $10 daily fee/pet. Designated rooms, supervision.
[SAVE] 🛰 🖢 🛢 🖵 📶 ⮌ ✕

▼ Big Pines Mountain House of Tahoe M
(530) 541-5155. **Call for rates.** 4083 Cedar Ave 96150. Just s of casino area to Stateline Ave, just w, then just s. Ext corridors. **Pets:** Accepted.
🛰 🖢 🛢 🖵 ⮌

Capri Motel M
(530) 544-3665. **$40-$300, 3 day notice.** 932 Stateline Ave 96150. Just s of casino area to Stateline Ave, then just w. Ext corridors.
Pets: Accepted. SAVE 📶 🚻 🖥 🏊 ❄

Fireside Lodge - An All Inclusive Premier Bed & Breakfast BB ❖
(530) 544-5515. **$119-$225, 7 day notice.** 515 Emerald Bay Rd 96150. 1.3 mi n of jct US 50 and SR 89. Ext corridors. **Pets:** Other species. $25 daily fee/pet. SAVE 📶 ❌ 🚻 🖥 ❄

Highland Inn M ❖
(530) 544-3862. **$69-$299, 3 day notice.** 3979 Lake Tahoe Blvd 96150. 0.4 mi sw of casino area; near Heavenly Village. Ext corridors.
Pets: Dogs only. $20 daily fee/pet. Service with restrictions. 📶 🚻

Howard Johnson Inn M
(530) 541-4000. **$63-$269.** 3489 Lake Tahoe Blvd 96150. 1.5 mi s of casino area. Ext corridors. **Pets:** $100 deposit/pet, $10 daily fee/pet. Designated rooms, service with restrictions, supervision. 📶 🚻 🖥 🏊

Inn By The Lake H ❖
(530) 542-0330. **$108-$508, 3 day notice.** 3300 Lake Tahoe Blvd 96150. 2.2 mi sw of casino area on US 50. Int corridors. **Pets:** Medium, dogs only. $20 daily fee/pet. Designated rooms, service with restrictions, supervision. SAVE 📶 ❌ 🚻 🖥 🍽 🏊 ❄

Park Tahoe Inn M
(530) 544-6000. **$39-$349, 3 day notice.** 4011 Lake Tahoe Blvd 96150. 0.4 mi sw of casino area; at Park Ave and Lake Tahoe Blvd (US 50); across from Heavenly Village. Ext corridors. **Pets:** $25 daily fee/pet. Designated rooms, service with restrictions, supervision.
📶 ❌ 🚻 🖥

Rodeway Inn Casino Center M ❖
(530) 541-7150. **$45-$165, 3 day notice.** 4127 Pine Blvd 96150. 0.3 mi w on Stateline Ave, just s on Pine Blvd. Ext/int corridors. **Pets:** Other species. $15 one-time fee/pet. Designated rooms, service with restrictions.
SAVE 📶 ❌ 🚻 🖥 🏊

Tahoe Chalet Inn-The Theme Inn M
(530) 544-3311. **$45-$195, 3 day notice.** 3860 Lake Tahoe Blvd 96150. 0.7 mi s of casino area on US 50. Ext corridors. **Pets:** Accepted.
📶 ❌ ❄ 🚻 🖥

Tahoe Keys Resort CO ❖
(530) 544-5397. **$112-$1700.** 599 Tahoe Keys Blvd 96150. 0.5 mi e of jct US 50 and SR 89, 1 mi n. Ext corridors. **Pets:** Dogs only. $25 one-time fee/pet. Service with restrictions, supervision.
SAVE 📶 🚻 🖥 🏊 ❄

Tahoe Valley Lodge M
(530) 541-0353. **$125-$495, 7 day notice.** 2241 Lake Tahoe Blvd 96150. 0.5 mi e of jct US 50 and SR 89. Ext corridors. **Pets:** Very small, dogs only. $20 daily fee/pet. Designated rooms, service with restrictions, supervision. SAVE 📶 ❌ 🚻 🖥 🏊

TAHOE CITY

Granlibakken Lodge & Conference Center CO
(530) 583-4242. **$143-$215, 30 day notice.** 725 Granlibakken Rd 96145. 0.8 mi s of jct SR 89 and 28, 0.6 mi w. Ext/int corridors.
Pets: Accepted. SAVE 📶 ❄ 🚻 🖥 🍽 🏊 ❄

Mother Nature's Inn M ❖
(530) 581-4278. **$59-$159, 5 day notice.** 551 N Lake Blvd 96145. SR 28, 0.5 mi e of jct SR 89; behind Mother Nature's Store. Int corridors.
Pets: Other species. $15 daily fee/pet. Designated rooms, service with restrictions, supervision. 📶 ❌ 🚻 🖥

River Ranch Lodge M
(530) 583-4264. **Call for rates.** SR 89 & Alpine Meadows Rd 96145. I-80 exit SR 89, 11 mi s; 3.5 mi n from city center. Ext/int corridors.
Pets: Accepted. 📶 ❄ 🍽 ❄

TAHOE VISTA

Cedar Glen Lodge M ❖
(530) 546-4281. **$53-$216.** 6589 N Lake Blvd 96148. SR 28, 1.5 mi w of SR 267. Ext corridors. **Pets:** Medium. $30 one-time fee/room. Designated rooms, service with restrictions, supervision.
📶 ❄ 🚻 🖥 🏊 ❄

Holiday House M ❖
(530) 546-2369. **$125-$225.** 7276 N Lake Blvd 96148. SR 28, 1 mi w of SR 267. Ext corridors. **Pets:** Other species. $30 one-time fee/pet. Supervision. 📶 ❄ 🚻 🖥 ❄

TRUCKEE

The Cedar House Sport Hotel H ❖
(530) 582-5655. **$170-$320, 3 day notice.** 10918 Brockway Rd 96161. I-80 exit 188 (SR 267) westbound; exit 188B (SR 267) eastbound, 1.5 mi s, then 0.8 mi nw. Int corridors. **Pets:** Large, dogs only. $50 one-time fee/pet. Designated rooms, service with restrictions, supervision.
📶 ❌ 🚻 🖥

The Inn at Truckee H ❖
(530) 587-8888. **$80-$155.** 11506 Deerfield Dr 96161. I-80 exit 185 (SR 89), just s, then just w. Int corridors. **Pets:** Medium, other species. $15 daily fee/pet. Service with restrictions, supervision. 📶 ❌ 🚻

The Ritz-Carlton, Lake Tahoe H ❖
(530) 562-3000. **$249-$699, 7 day notice.** 13031 Ritz-Carlton Highlands Ct 96161. I-80 exit 188 (SR 267) westbound; exit 188B (SR 267) eastbound, 6.5 mi se, then 2.8 mi w. Int corridors. **Pets:** Medium. $125 one-time fee/room. Service with restrictions, crate.
ECO SAVE 📶 ❌ ❄ 🖥 🍽 🏊 ❄

END AREA

LANCASTER

Comfort Inn & Suites H
(661) 723-2001. **$101-$104.** 1825 W Ave J-12 93534. SR 14 exit 43 (Ave J) northbound; exit 43 (20th St) southbound, just s, then just e. Int corridors. **Pets:** Small. $200 deposit/room, $30 daily fee/pet. Service with restrictions, supervision. 📶 ❄ 🚻 🖥 🏊 ❄

Holiday Inn Express H
(661) 951-8848. **$109-$199.** 43719 17th St W 93534. SR 14 exit 42 (Ave K), just e, then just n. Int corridors. **Pets:** Dogs only. $100 deposit/room, $10 daily fee/pet. Designated rooms, service with restrictions, supervision. SAVE 📶 ❄ 🚻 🖥 🏊

Homewood Suites Lancaster H
(661) 723-8040. **$149-$189.** 2320 W Double Play Way 93536. SR 14 exit 44 (Ave I) just w, s on Valley Central Way, then just e. Int corridors.
Pets: Accepted. 📶 ❄ 🚻 🖥 🏊 ❄

Inn of Lancaster M ❖
(661) 945-8771. **$69-$89.** 44131 Sierra Hwy 93534. SR 14 exit 42 (Ave K), 2 mi n. Ext corridors. **Pets:** Medium. $100 deposit/room. Service with restrictions, supervision. SAVE 📶 🚻 🖥 🏊 ❄

Oxford Inn & Suites M ❖
(661) 949-3423. **$79-$139.** 1651 W Ave K 93534. SR 14 exit 42 (Ave K), just w. Int corridors. **Pets:** $25 daily fee/pet. Designated rooms, service with restrictions, supervision. 📶 ❄ 🚻 🖥 🏊

LA PALMA

◆◆◆ **La Quinta Inn & Suites Buena Park** 🄷
(714) 670-1400. **$85-$149.** 3 Centerpointe Dr 90623. SR 91 exit 21 (Orangethorpe Ave/Valley View St) eastbound; exit 22 (Orangethorpe Ave/Valley View St) westbound, just n. Int corridors. **Pets:** Medium, other species. Service with restrictions, supervision. 🛜 🔌 💻 🏊

LA QUINTA

◆◆◆ **Embassy Suites La Quinta-Hotel & Spa** 🄷
(760) 777-1711. **$89-$299.** 50-777 Santa Rosa Plaza 92253. I-10 exit 137 (Washington St), 6 mi s, then 0.4 mi on Calle Tampico. Ext/int corridors. **Pets:** Accepted. 🛜 ♿ 🔌 💻 🍴 🏊 ✖

◆◆◆◆ **La Quinta Resort & Club, A Waldorf Astoria Resort** 🄷
(760) 564-4111. **$129-$399.** 49-499 Eisenhower Dr 92253. I-10 exit 137 (Washington St), 4.7 mi s, then 1 mi w. Ext corridors. **Pets:** Accepted.
🛜 ✖ 🔌 💻 🍴 🏊 ✖

LATHROP

◆◆ **Days Inn** 🄷
(209) 982-1959. **$63-$67.** 14750 S Harlan Rd 95330. I-5 exit Lathrop Rd, just e. Int corridors. **Pets:** Accepted. 🛜 ♿ 🔌 💻 🏊

LEBEC

◆◆◆ **Holiday Inn Express Frazier Park/Lebec** 🄷
(661) 248-1600. **$99-$159.** 612 Wainright Ct 93243. I-5 exit 205 (Frazier Mountain Rd), just n. Int corridors. **Pets:** Accepted.
🛜 ✖ 🔌 💻 🏊

◆◆◆ **Ramada Limited Grapevine** 🄼
(661) 248-1530. **$59-$89.** 9000 Country Side Ct 93243. I-5 exit 215 (Grapevine Rd), just w. Ext corridors. **Pets:** Medium. $20 daily fee/pet. Designated rooms, service with restrictions, supervision.
[SAVE] 🛜 🔌 💻 🏊

LEE VINING

◆◆◆ **Murphey's Motel** 🄼
(760) 647-6316. **$58-$123.** 51493 Hwy 395 93541. US 395; in town. Ext corridors. **Pets:** Medium. $5 daily fee/room. Designated rooms, service with restrictions, supervision. [SAVE] 🛜 ✖ 🔌 💻

LINDSAY

◆◆ **Super 8** 🄼 🐾
(559) 562-5188. **$68-$162.** 390 N Hwy 65 93247. On SR 65. Ext corridors. **Pets:** Small, dogs only. $15 daily fee/room. Service with restrictions, supervision. 🛜 🔌 💻 🏊

LIVERMORE

◆◆◆ **Holiday Inn Express Hotel & Suites-Livermore** 🄷
(925) 961-9600. **$89-$129.** 3000 Constitution Dr 94551. I-580 exit Airway Blvd/Collier Canyon Rd, just n. Int corridors. **Pets:** Medium. $30 daily fee/pet. Designated rooms, service with restrictions, supervision.
🛜 ♿ 🔌 💻 🏊

◆◆ **La Quinta Inn Livermore** 🄷
(925) 373-9600. **$93-$154.** 7700 Southfront Rd 94551. I-580 exit Greenville Rd, just s. Int corridors. **Pets:** Medium, other species. Service with restrictions, supervision. 🛜 ♿ 🔌 💻 🏊 ✖

◆◆◆ **Residence Inn by Marriott** 🄷
(925) 373-1800. **$149-$179.** 1000 Airway Blvd 94551. I-580 exit Airway Blvd/Collier Canyon Rd, just n. Ext corridors. **Pets:** Accepted.
🛜 ✖ ♿ 🔌 💻 🏊 ✖

LODI

◆◆◆ **Best Western Royal Host Inn** 🄷
(209) 369-8484. **$69-$119.** 710 S Cherokee Ln 95240. 0.8 mi s on SR 99 business route. Ext corridors. **Pets:** Accepted.
[SAVE] 🛜 ♿ 🔌 💻 🏊

◆◆ **Holiday Inn Express** 🄷
(209) 210-0150. **$109-$199.** 1337 E Kettleman Ln 95240. SR 99 exit Kettleman Ln, 0.4 mi e. Int corridors. **Pets:** Accepted.
🛜 ✖ ♿ 🔌 💻 🏊

◆◆◆ **Microtel Inn & Suites** 🄷 🐾
(209) 367-9700. **$62-$81.** 6428 W Banner St 95242. I-5 exit SR 12, just e. Int corridors. **Pets:** $10 daily fee/pet. Service with restrictions, supervision. [SAVE] 🛜 🔌 💻 🏊

◆◆◆ **Motel 6 Lodi** 🄷
(209) 334-6422. **Call for rates.** 1140 S Cherokee Ln 95240. SR 99 exit Kettleman Ln W, just n. Ext corridors. **Pets:** Other species. Service with restrictions, supervision. 🛜 ♿ 🔌 💻

◆◆◆ **Wine & Roses Hotel and Restaurant** 🄲
(209) 334-6988. **$169-$495.** 2505 W Turner Rd 95242. I-5 exit Turner Rd, 5 mi e; SR 99 exit Turner Rd, 2 mi w. Ext corridors. **Pets:** Medium. $45 daily fee/room. Designated rooms, service with restrictions, crate.
🛜 ♿ 🔌 💻 🍴 🏊 ✖

LOMA LINDA

◆◆ **Loma Linda Inn** 🄼
(909) 583-2500. **$75-$85, 10 day notice.** 24532 University Ave 92354. I-10 exit 74 (Tippecanoe Ave), 1 mi s, just w on Stewart St, just s on Campus, then just w. Ext corridors. **Pets:** Accepted.
🛜 ✖ ♿ 🔌 💻

LOMPOC

◆◆◆ **Comfort Inn & Suites** 🄷 🐾
(805) 735-8555. **$89-$149.** 1621 N H St 93436. SR 1, 1.8 mi n of Ocean Ave. Int corridors. **Pets:** Medium, other species. $25 one-time fee/pet. Service with restrictions, supervision. [SAVE] 🛜 🔌 💻 🏊

◆◆◆ **Days Inn** 🄼
(805) 735-7744. **$81-$126.** 1122 N H St 93436. SR 1, 1.2 mi n of Ocean Ave. Ext/int corridors. **Pets:** $25 one-time fee/room. Service with restrictions, supervision. 🛜 🔌 💻 🏊

◆◆◆ **Embassy Suites Hotel** 🄷
(805) 735-8311. **$108-$171.** 1117 N H St 93436. SR 1, 1.3 mi n of Ocean Ave. Ext corridors. **Pets:** Small, dogs only. $25 daily fee/pet. Designated rooms, service with restrictions, crate. 🛜 ♿ 🔌 💻 🏊

◆◆ **O'Cairns Inn** 🄼
(805) 735-6444. **Call for rates.** 1020 E Ocean Ave 93436. SR 1, 1.5 mi w of H St. Ext corridors. **Pets:** Accepted. 🛜 🔌 💻

◆◆ **Rodeway Inn** 🄼
(805) 735-3737. **$55-$165.** 1200 N H St 93436. SR 1, 1.3 mi n of Ocean Ave. Ext/int corridors. **Pets:** Accepted. 🛜 ♿ 🔌 💻 🄰🄲

LONE PINE

◆◆◆ **Best Western Plus Frontier Motel** 🄷
(760) 876-5571. **$91-$144.** 1008 S Main St 93545. US 395; south end of town. Ext corridors. **Pets:** Other species. Designated rooms, service with restrictions, supervision. [SAVE] 🛜 ♿ 🔌 💻 🏊

◆◆◆ **Comfort Inn** 🄷 🐾
(760) 876-8700. **$89-$199.** 1920 S Main St 93545. US 395, 1.5 mi s of town. Int corridors. **Pets:** Medium. $20 daily fee/pet. Designated rooms, service with restrictions, supervision. [SAVE] 🛜 ✖ 🔌 💻 🏊

◆◆◆ **Dow Villa Motel** 🄼
(760) 876-5521. **$74-$155.** 310 S Main St 93545. US 395; center of town. Ext corridors. **Pets:** Medium, other species. $50 deposit/room. Designated rooms, service with restrictions, supervision.
[SAVE] 🛜 ✖ ♿ 🔌 💻 🏊

◆◆ **Timberline Motel** 🄼
(760) 876-4555. **$45-$99, 3 day notice.** 215 E Post St 93545. US 395, just e. Ext corridors. **Pets:** Accepted. [SAVE] 🛜 🔌 💻 ✖

LOS ALAMITOS

▼▼▼ Residence Inn by Marriott-Cypress/Los
Alamitos ℍ ✿

(714) 484-5700. **$139-$159.** 4931 Katella Ave 90720. I-605 exit 1D (Katella Ave) southbound; exit 1B (Katella Ave/Willow St) northbound, 1.9 mi e. Int corridors. **Pets:** Small, other species. $100 one-time fee/room. Supervision. 🐾 🛜 ✕ 🛏 💻 🛋 🗙

LOS ALTOS

▼▼▼ Residence Inn-Palo Alto/Los Altos ℍ

(650) 559-7890. **$134-$251.** 4460 El Camino Real 94022. US 101 exit San Antonio Rd, 2 mi w to SR 82, then just n. Int corridors.
Pets: Accepted. 🛜 ✕ 🛋 🛏 💻 🛋 🗙

LOS ANGELES METROPOLITAN AREA

ALHAMBRA

𝔸𝔸𝔸 ▼▼▼ Super 8 Los Angeles/Alhambra Ⓜ

(323) 225-2310. **$58-$117.** 5350 S Huntington Dr 90032. I-10 exit 22 (Fremont Ave), 2.5 mi n, then 0.5 mi w. Ext corridors. **Pets:** Accepted.

🗠 🛋 🛏 💻

ARCADIA

▼▼▼ Extended StayAmerica-Los Angeles-Arcadia ℍ ✿

(626) 446-6422. **$95-$110.** 401 E Santa Clara St 91006. I-210 exit 33 (Huntington Dr), just w to 5th Ave, just n, then just w. Int corridors. **Pets:** Other species. $25 daily fee/pet. Service with restrictions.

🛜 🛋 🛏 💻

▼▼▼ Residence Inn by Marriott ℍ

(626) 446-6500. **$107-$152.** 321 E Huntington Dr 91006. I-210 exit 33 (Huntington Dr), 0.5 mi w, then just n on Gateway Dr. Ext corridors.
Pets: Accepted. 🐾 🛜 ✕ 🛋 🛏 💻 🛋 🗙

BEVERLY HILLS

▼▼▼ Avalon Hotel ℍ

(310) 277-5221. **Call for rates.** 9400 W Olympic Blvd 90212. I-10 exit 6 (Robertson Blvd), 1.7 mi n, then 0.8 mi w. Ext/int corridors.
Pets: Accepted. 🐾 🛜 💻 🍴 🛋

𝔸𝔸𝔸 ▼▼▼▼ The Beverly Hills Hotel and
Bungalows ℍ ✿

(310) 276-2251. **$560-$810, 3 day notice.** 9641 Sunset Blvd 90210. I-405 exit 57 (Sunset Blvd), 3.7 mi e. Ext/int corridors. **Pets:** Small, dogs only. $200 one-time fee/room. Designated rooms, service with restrictions, crate. 🅂🄰🅅🄴 🛜 ✕ 🛋 🛏 💻 🍴 🛋 🗙

▼▼▼ The Beverly Hilton ℍ

(310) 274-7777. **$169-$459.** 9876 Wilshire Blvd 90210. I-405 exit 55 (Wilshire Blvd), 2.2 mi e. Int corridors. **Pets:** Small, dogs only. $25 daily fee/room. Service with restrictions, crate.

🐾 🛜 ✕ 🛋 🍴 🛋 🗙

𝔸𝔸𝔸 ▼▼▼▼ Beverly Wilshire A Four Seasons
Hotel ℍ

(310) 275-5200. **$500-$1575.** 9500 Wilshire Blvd 90212. I-405 exit 55 (Wilshire Blvd), 4.5 mi e. Int corridors. **Pets:** Accepted.

🅂🄰🅅🄴 🛜 ✕ 🛋 🍴 🛋 🗙

𝔸𝔸𝔸 ▼▼▼▼ L'Ermitage Beverly Hills ℍ

(310) 278-3344. **$355-$1530.** 9291 Burton Way 90210. I-10 exit 6 (Robertson Blvd), 3.1 mi n, then just w. Int corridors. **Pets:** Accepted.

🅂🄰🅅🄴 🛜 ✕ 🛋 🍴 🛋 🗙

𝔸𝔸𝔸 ▼▼▼▼ Montage Beverly Hills ℍ

(310) 860-7800. **Call for rates.** 225 N Canon Dr 90210. I-405 exit 55A (Santa Monica Blvd), 3.4 mi e, then 0.4 mi s. Int corridors.
Pets: Accepted. 🐾 🅂🄰🅅🄴 🛜 ✕ 🛋 🍴 🛋 🗙

𝔸𝔸𝔸 ▼▼▼▼ The Peninsula Beverly Hills ℍ ✿

(310) 551-2888. **$475-$7250.** 9882 S Santa Monica Blvd 90212. I-405 exit 55A (Santa Monica Blvd), 2.2 mi e at Wilshire Blvd. Int corridors.
Pets: Other species. $35 daily fee/pet.

🅂🄰🅅🄴 🛜 ✕ 🛋 🛏 💻 🍴 🛋 🗙

𝔸𝔸𝔸 ▼▼▼▼ SLS Hotel at Beverly Hills ℍ

(310) 247-0400. **$599-$7000.** 465 S La Cienega Blvd 90048. I-10 exit 7A (La Cienega Blvd), 2.5 mi n. Ext corridors. **Pets:** Accepted.

🅂🄰🅅🄴 🛜 🛋 🍴 🛋 🗙

BURBANK

▼▼▼ Holiday Inn-Burbank ℍ

(818) 841-4770. **$171-$181.** 150 E Angeleno Ave 91502. I-5 exit 146A (Olive Ave) northbound; exit 146A (Verdugo Ave) southbound, just e. Int corridors. **Pets:** Accepted. 🛜 🛋 🛏 💻 🍴 🛋 🗙

𝔸𝔸𝔸 ▼▼▼ ▼▼▼ Hotel Amarano Burbank ℍ

(818) 842-8887. **$159-$585.** 322 N Pass Ave 91505. SR 134 exit 2 (Hollywood Way) westbound, just w on Alameda Ave, then 0.5 mi n; exit 2 (Pass Ave) eastbound, 0.5 mi n. Ext corridors. **Pets:** Accepted.

🅂🄰🅅🄴 🛜 ✕ 🛋 🛏 💻 🍴 🗙

▼▼▼▼ Los Angeles Marriott Burbank Airport Hotel ℍ

(818) 843-6000. **$89-$229.** 2500 Hollywood Way 91505. I-5 exit 149 (Hollywood Way), 1 mi s. Int corridors. **Pets:** Small, dogs only. $75 one-time fee/room. Service with restrictions, supervision.

🐾 🛜 ✕ 🛋 🛏 💻 🍴 🛋

▼▼▼▼ Residence Inn by Marriott Burbank Downtown ℍ

(818) 260-8787. **$151-$299.** 321 S First St 91502. I-5 exit 146A (Olive Ave) northbound, just e on Angeleno Ave, then just s; exit 146A (Verdugo Ave) southbound, just s on Front St, just e on Verdugo Ave, then just n. Int corridors. **Pets:** Accepted. 🛜 ✕ 🛋 🛏 💻 🛋

CALABASAS

𝔸𝔸𝔸 ▼▼▼▼ Country Inn & Suites By Carlson ℍ

(818) 222-5300. **$119-$159.** 23627 Calabasas Rd 91302. US 101 exit 29 (Valley Cir/Mulholland Dr), just w, then 0.6 mi n. Int corridors.
Pets: Accepted. 🅂🄰🅅🄴 🛜 ✕ 🛋 🛏 💻 🛋

CARSON

▼▼▼ Extended StayAmerica-Los Angeles/Carson ℍ ✿

(310) 323-2080. **$64-$94.** 401 E Albertoni St 90746. SR 91 exit 7B (Avalon Blvd) just s, then just w. Int corridors. **Pets:** Other species. $25 daily fee/pet. Service with restrictions. 🛜 🛋 🛏 💻

CERRITOS

𝔸𝔸𝔸 ▼▼▼ Sheraton Cerritos Hotel at Towne
Center ℍ ✿

(562) 809-1500. **$99-$219, 7 day notice.** 12725 Center Court Dr 90703. SR 91 exit 19B (Artesia/Bloomfield Dr), just s to Towne Center Dr, just e, then just s. Int corridors. **Pets:** Medium, dogs only. Service with restrictions, supervision. 🅂🄰🅅🄴 🛜 ✕ 💻 🍴 🛋

CHATSWORTH

𝔸𝔸𝔸 ▼▼▼ Ramada ℍ

(818) 998-5289. **$49-$139.** 21340 Devonshire St 91311. SR 118 exit 35 (De Soto Ave), 1.5 mi s, then 0.5 mi w. Int corridors. **Pets:** Small. $10 daily fee/pet. Designated rooms, service with restrictions, supervision.

🅂🄰🅅🄴 🛜 🛋 🛏 💻 🍴 🛋

▼▼▼ Staybridge Suites ℍ

(818) 773-0707. **$104-$159.** 21902 Lassen St 91311. SR 118 exit 34 (Topanga Canyon Blvd), 2 mi s, then just e. Ext corridors.
Pets: Accepted. 🛜 🛋 🛏 💻 🛋

CHINO

WW WW Extended StayAmerica Los Angeles-Chino Valley 🏨 ❀

(909) 597-8675. **$59-$79.** 4325 Corporate Center Ave 91710. SR 71 exit 8 (Chino Hills Pkwy), just e to Ramona Ave, just n, then just w. Int corridors. **Pets:** Other species. $25 daily fee/pet. Service with restrictions.

🛜 📶 🛏 💻

CLAREMONT

WWW Hotel Casa 425 🏨 ❀

(909) 624-2272. **$195-$400, 3 day notice.** 425 W First St 91711. I-10 exit 47 (Indian Hill Blvd N), 1.2 mi n, then just w. Ext corridors. **Pets:** Medium, dogs only. $65 one-time fee/room. Designated rooms, service with restrictions, supervision. 🛜 ✖ 📶 🛏 💻

WW WW Hotel Claremont & Tennis Club Ⓜ ❀

(909) 621-4831. **$59-$69.** 840 S Indian Hill Blvd 91711. I-10 exit 47 (Indian Hill Blvd), just s; enter on Auto Center Dr. Ext corridors. **Pets:** Other species. Service with restrictions.

🛜 📶 🛏 💻 🏊 ✖

COMMERCE

AAA WWWW DoubleTree by Hilton Hotel Los Angeles - Commerce 🏨

(323) 887-8100. **$89-$219.** 5757 Telegraph Rd 90040. I-5 exit 128B (Washington Blvd), just e, then just s. Int corridors. **Pets:** Accepted.

SAVE 🛜 📶 🛏 💻 🍴 🏊 ✖

COVINA

WWWW Radisson Suites Hotel 🏨

(626) 915-3441. **$99-$149.** 1211 E Garvey St 91724. I-10 exit 38B (Holt Ave), just n, then just w. Ext corridors. **Pets:** Accepted.

ECO 🛜 📶 🛏 💻 🍴 🏊

CULVER CITY

AAA WWWW Four Points by Sheraton LA Westside 🏨

(310) 641-7740. **$99-$199.** 5990 Green Valley Cir 90230. I-405 exit 49 (Howard Hughes Pkwy), just n, then just e. Int corridors. **Pets:** Medium. $25 daily fee/room. Designated rooms, service with restrictions, supervision. SAVE 🛜 ✖ 🛏 💻 🍴 🏊

DIAMOND BAR

WWW Ayres Suites Diamond Bar 🏨

(909) 860-6290. **$99-$159.** 21951 Golden Springs Dr 91765. SR 57/60 exit 24B (Grand Ave), just s, then 0.5 mi w. Int corridors. **Pets:** Accepted.

🛜 🛏 💻 🏊 ✖

DOWNEY

WWWW Embassy Suites Hotel 🏨

(562) 861-1900. **$135-$209.** 8425 Firestone Blvd 90241. I-605 exit 10 (Firestone Blvd), 2 mi w. Int corridors. **Pets:** Accepted.

🛜 📶 🛏 💻 🍴 🏊 ✖

EL MONTE

AAA WWW Americas Best Value Inn & Suites Ⓜ

(626) 442-8354. **$77-$98.** 12040 Garvey Ave 91732. I-10 exit 30 (Garvey Ave) westbound, just w; exit 29A (Peck Rd) eastbound, just s to Garvey Ave, then 0.6 mi e. Ext corridors. **Pets:** Accepted.

SAVE 🛜 🛏 💻 🏊

EL SEGUNDO

WWWW Embassy Suites-LAX South 🏨

(310) 640-3600. **$109-$229.** 1440 E Imperial Ave 90245. I-405 exit 45B (Imperial Hwy), 1.6 mi w. Int corridors. **Pets:** Small, other species. $35 daily fee/pet. Service with restrictions.

🛜 📶 🛏 💻 🍴 🏊

WW WW Homestead Studio Suites Hotel-Los Angeles-LAX Airport-El Segundo Ⓜ ❀

(310) 607-4000. **$84-$119.** 1910 E Mariposa Ave 90245. I-105 exit 1B (Sepulveda Blvd), 1 mi s. Ext corridors. **Pets:** Other species. $25 daily fee/pet. Service with restrictions. 🛜 📶 🛏 💻

AAA WWWW Hyatt Summerfield Suites Los Angeles LAX/El Segundo 🏨

(310) 725-0100. **$139-$189.** 810 S Douglas St 90245. I-405 exit 43 (Rosecrans Ave), 0.5 mi e, then just n. Ext corridors. **Pets:** Accepted.

SAVE 🛜 ✖ 📶 🛏 💻 🏊 ✖

WWWW Residence Inn by Marriott-LAX/El Segundo 🏨

(310) 333-0888. **$119-$199.** 2135 E El Segundo Blvd 90245. I-405 exit 44 (El Segundo Blvd), 1.4 mi w. Int corridors. **Pets:** Accepted.

🛜 ✖ 📶 🛏 💻 🏊 ✖

GLENDALE

AAA WWWWW Hilton Los Angeles North/Glendale & Executive Meeting Center 🏨

(818) 956-5466. **$109-$249.** 100 W Glenoaks Blvd 91202. SR 134 exit 7B (Brand Blvd), just n, then just w. Int corridors. **Pets:** Accepted.

ECO SAVE 🛜 📶 🛏 💻 🍴 🏊 ✖

WW WW Homestead Studio Suites Hotel-Los Angeles-Glendale 🏨 ❀

(818) 956-6665. **$110-$125.** 1377 W Glenoaks Blvd 91201. I-5 exit 145A (Western Ave), 0.4 mi e, then 0.6 mi s. Int corridors. **Pets:** Other species. $25 daily fee/pet. Service with restrictions. 🛜 📶 🛏 💻

WW WW Los Angeles Days Inn-Glendale 🏨

(818) 956-0202. **$85-$143.** 450 W Pioneer Dr 91203. SR 134 exit 7A (Pacific Ave), just s, then just e. Int corridors. **Pets:** Medium. $50 deposit/room. Designated rooms, service with restrictions, supervision.

🛜 🛏 💻 🍴 🏊

WW WW Vagabond Inn Glendale Ⓜ

(818) 240-1700. **$94-$104.** 120 W Colorado St 91204. SR 134 exit 7B (Brand Blvd), 1 mi s, then just w. Ext corridors. **Pets:** Accepted.

🛜 ✖ 🛏 💻 🏊

HAWTHORNE

WW WW Candlewood Suites LAX Hawthorne 🏨 ❀

(310) 973-3331. **$99-$129.** 11410 Hawthorne Blvd 90250. I-105 exit 3 (Hawthorne Blvd/Prairie Ave), 0.6 mi s. Int corridors. **Pets:** Medium, other species. $75 deposit/pet, $75 one-time fee/pet. Service with restrictions, supervision. 🛜 ✖ 🛏 💻 🏊

WW WW TownePlace Suites by Marriott Ⓜ

(310) 725-9696. **$99-$209.** 14400 Aviation Blvd 90250. I-405 exit 43 (Rosecrans Ave), 0.4 mi w. Int corridors. **Pets:** Accepted.

ECO 🛜 ✖ 🛏 💻 🏊

HERMOSA BEACH

WWWW Quality Inn & Suites 🏨

(310) 374-2666. **$99-$119.** 901 Aviation Blvd 90254. SR 1 (Pacific Coast Hwy), just e. Ext/int corridors. **Pets:** Other species. $20 daily fee/room. Designated rooms, service with restrictions, supervision. 🛜 🛏 💻

HOLLYWOOD

AAA WWWW Hilton Garden Inn Los Angeles/Hollywood 🏨

(323) 876-8600. **Call for rates.** 2005 N Highland Ave 90068. US 101 exit Highland Ave, just s. Int corridors. **Pets:** Accepted.

SAVE 🛜 ✖ 📶 🛏 💻 🍴 🏊

WWWW Hollywood Hotel 🏨

(323) 315-1800. **$99-$249, 7 day notice.** 1160 N Vermont Ave 90029. US 101 exit 6A (Vermont Ave), 0.5 mi n. Int corridors. **Pets:** Medium. $35 daily fee/pet. Service with restrictions, supervision.

SAVE 🛜 ✖ 📶 🛏 💻

AAA WW WW Motel 6 Los Angeles - Hollywood #4044 Ⓜ

(323) 464-6006. **$75-$150.** 1738 N Whitley Ave 90028. US 101 exit 9C southbound, just s, just w, then just s. Int corridors. **Pets:** Other species. Service with restrictions, supervision. SAVE 🛜 ✖ 🛏

△△△ ▼▼▼ ▼▼▼ W Hollywood ⊞ ❀

(323) 798-1300. **$639-$10000, 3 day notice.** 6250 Hollywood Blvd 90028. US 101 exit 8B (Hollywood Blvd), 0.5 mi w. Int corridors. **Pets:** Medium. $100 one-time fee/room, $25 daily fee/room. Service with restrictions. ⌨ 🅂 📶 ✕ 🄼 🛗 📲 🍴 🏊 ✕

HUNTINGTON PARK

▼▼ ▼▼ Rodeway Inn Near LA Live Ⓜ

(323) 589-5971. **Call for rates.** 6340 Santa Fe Ave 90255. I-710 exit 17B (Atlantic Blvd) southbound, 1.1 mi w on Bandini Blvd, 2.6 mi w on Slauson Ave, 0.4 mi s on Alameda St, then just e; exit 17A northbound, 1.1 mi se on Bandini Blvd, 4 mi w on Slauson Ave, 0.4 mi s on Alameda St, then just e. Ext/int corridors. **Pets:** Medium. $10 daily fee/pet. Service with restrictions, supervision. 📶 ✕ 🛗

INDUSTRY

▼▼▼ Pacific Palms Resort ⊞

(626) 810-4455. **$159-$210.** One Industry Hills Pkwy 91744. SR 60 exit 18 (Azusa Ave), 1.3 mi n, 0.5 mi w. Int corridors. **Pets:** Accepted.

📶 🄼 🖥 🍴 🏊 ✕

LA MIRADA

▼▼▼ Residence Inn by Marriott ⊞

(714) 523-2800. **$125-$179.** 14419 Firestone Blvd 90638. I-5 exit 118 (Valley View Ave), just n, then 0.5 mi e. Ext corridors. **Pets:** Accepted.

📶 ✕ 🄼 🛗 📲 🏊 ✕

LONG BEACH

▼▼ ▼▼ Extended StayAmerica-Los Angeles-Long Beach ⊞ ❀

(562) 989-4601. **$69-$99.** 4105 E Willow St 90815. I-405 exit 27 (Lakewood Blvd), 0.3 mi sw. Int corridors. **Pets:** Other species. $25 daily fee/pet. Service with restrictions. 📶 🄼 🖥 🛗 📲

▼▼▼ ▼▼▼ Hilton Long Beach ⊞

(562) 983-3400. **$109-$299.** 701 W Ocean Blvd 90831. I-710 exit Downtown/Broadway, just e to Daisy Ave, just s to Ocean Blvd, then just w. Int corridors. **Pets:** Accepted. ⌨ 📶 🄼 🛗 📲 🍴 🏊

▼▼▼ ▼▼▼ Hotel Current Ⓜ ❀

(562) 597-1341. **$129-$189.** 5325 E Pacific Coast Hwy 90804. I-405 exit 23 (SR 22/Long Beach) northbound, 2 mi nw; exit 27 (Lakewood Blvd) southbound, 2 mi se on SR 1. Ext corridors. **Pets:** $200 deposit/pet, $50 one-time fee/pet. Service with restrictions, crate.

⌨ 📶 ✕ 🛗 📲 🏊

▼▼▼ ▼▼▼ Hotel Maya - a DoubleTree by Hilton Hotel ⊞

(562) 435-7676. **$129-$299.** 700 Queensway Dr 90802. I-710 exit 14 (Harbor Scenic Dr/Queen Mary), 1 mi s. Ext corridors. **Pets:** Accepted.

📶 ✕ 📲 🍴 🏊 ✕

△△△ ▼▼▼ ▼▼ Renaissance Long Beach Hotel ⊞

(562) 437-5900. **$118-$229.** 111 E Ocean Blvd 90802. I-710 exit Downtown/Broadway, 0.8 mi e to Long Beach Blvd, just s, then just w. Int corridors. **Pets:** Accepted.

⌨ 🅂 📶 ✕ 🄼 🛗 📲 🍴 🏊 ✕

▼▼▼ ▼▼ Residence Inn by Marriott Long Beach ⊞

(562) 595-0909. **$149-$189.** 4111 E Willow St 90815. I-405 exit 27 (Lakewood Blvd), just s, then just w. Ext corridors. **Pets:** Other species. $100 one-time fee/room. Service with restrictions.

⌨ 📶 ✕ 🄼 🛗 📲 ✕

△△△ ▼▼▼ ▼▼ Residence Inn Long Beach Downtown South Waterfront ⊞

(562) 495-0700. **$149-$159.** 600 Queensway Dr 90802. I-710 exit 14 (Harbor Scenic Dr/Queen Mary), 1.3 mi s. Int corridors. **Pets:** Large, other species. $100 one-time fee/room. Service with restrictions.

🅂 📶 ✕ 🛗 📲 🏊

LOS ANGELES

△△△ ▼▼▼ ▼▼▼ Best Western Plus Dragon Gate Inn ⊞ ❀

(213) 617-3077. **$100-$180.** 818 N Hill St 90012. US 101 exit 2C (Broadway), 0.6 mi n to Alpine St, just e, then just n. Ext corridors. **Pets:** Medium, other species. $20 daily fee/pet. Designated rooms, service with restrictions, supervision. 🅂 📶 ✕ 🛗

△△△ ▼▼▼ Beverly Laurel Motor Hotel Ⓜ

(323) 651-2441. **$114-$155.** 8018 Beverly Blvd 90048. I-10 exit 7B (Fairfax Ave), 2.8 mi n, then just w. Ext corridors. **Pets:** Medium. $25 daily fee/pet. Service with restrictions, supervision. 🅂 📶 🛗 🍴 🏊

▼▼▼ ▼▼▼ Extended StayAmerica-Los Angeles/LAX Airport ⊞ ❀

(310) 568-9337. **$99-$129.** 6531 S Sepulveda Blvd 90045. I-405 exit 49 (Howard Hughes Pkwy), 0.9 mi w, then just n. Int corridors. **Pets:** Other species. $25 daily fee/pet. Service with restrictions. 📶 🄼 🖥

△△△ ▼▼▼ ▼▼▼ Four Points by Sheraton LAX ⊞

(310) 645-4600. **$85-$230.** 9750 Airport Blvd 90045. I-405 exit 46 (Century Blvd), 1.5 mi w, then just n. Int corridors. **Pets:** Accepted.

🅂 📶 ✕ 🛗 🖥 🍴 🏊

▼▼▼ ▼▼▼ Four Seasons Hotel Los Angeles at Beverly Hills ⊞ ❀

(310) 273-2222. **$505-$10500.** 300 S Doheny Dr 90048. I-10 exit 6 (Robertson Blvd), 3 mi n to Burton Way, then just w. Int corridors. **Pets:** Small. Service with restrictions, supervision.

📶 ✕ 🄼 🖥 🍴 🏊 ✕

△△△ ▼▼▼ ▼▼▼ Hilton Checkers Los Angeles ⊞

(213) 624-0000. **$139-$299.** 535 S Grand Ave 90071. SR 110 exit 6th St, just w to Olive St, just n to 5th St, then just s. Int corridors. **Pets:** Accepted. 🅂 📶 🛗 🖥 🍴 🏊 ✕

△△△ ▼▼▼ ▼▼▼ Hilton Los Angeles Airport ⊞

(310) 410-4000. **$89-$209.** 5711 W Century Blvd 90045. I-405 exit 46 (Century Blvd), 0.8 mi w. Int corridors. **Pets:** Medium. $50 one-time fee/pet. Service with restrictions. ⌨ 📶 🛗 🖥 🍴 🏊

△△△ ▼▼▼ ▼▼▼ Hotel Palomar LA Westwood ⊞

(310) 475-8711. **$199-$389.** 10740 Wilshire Blvd 90024. I-405 exit 55B (Wilshire Blvd), 1 mi w; in Westwood. Int corridors. **Pets:** Accepted.

⌨ 🅂 📶 ✕ 🍴 🏊

△△△ ▼▼▼ ▼▼▼ Hyatt Regency Century Plaza & Spa ⊞ ❀

(310) 228-1234. **$179-$499.** 2025 Avenue of the Stars 90067. I-10 exit 6 (Robertson Blvd), 2.7 mi n to Olympic Blvd, 1.9 mi w, then just n. Int corridors. **Pets:** Small, dogs only. $35 daily fee/room. Designated rooms, service with restrictions, supervision.

🅂 📶 🄼 🖥 🍴 🏊 ✕

▼▼▼ ▼▼▼ InterContinental Los Angeles Century City ⊞

(310) 284-6500. **$249-$399.** 2151 Avenue of the Stars 90067. I-10 exit 6 (Robertson Blvd), 2.7 mi n to Olympic Blvd, 1.9 mi w, then just n. Int corridors. **Pets:** Accepted. 📶 ✕ 🖥 🍴 🏊 ✕

▼▼▼ ▼▼▼ La Quinta Inn & Suites LAX ⊞

(310) 645-2200. **$98-$182.** 5249 W Century Blvd 90045. I-405 exit 46 (Century Blvd), just w. Int corridors. **Pets:** Medium, other species. Service with restrictions, supervision. 📶 🛗 🖥 🍴 🏊

▼▼▼ ▼▼▼ Luxe City Center Hotel ⊞

(213) 748-1291. **$159-$349.** 1020 S Figueroa St 90015. SR 110 exit Olympic southbound, just e; exit 9th St northbound, just e to Flower St, just s to 11th St, just w, then just n. Int corridors. **Pets:** Accepted.

📶 🄼 🛗 🖥 🍴

 Luxe Hotel Sunset Boulevard 🏨 🐾
(310) 476-6571. **$209-$490.** 11461 Sunset Blvd 90049. I-405 exit 57 (Sunset Blvd), just w. Int corridors. **Pets:** Medium. $250 one-time fee/room. Service with restrictions, supervision.

Omni Los Angeles Hotel at California Plaza 🏨 🐾
(213) 617-3300. **$169-$700.** 251 S Olive St 90012. SR 110 exit 4th St southbound; exit 6th St northbound, just e, then just n. Int corridors. **Pets:** Medium, dogs only. $50 one-time fee/room. Designated rooms, service with restrictions, supervision.

The Orlando Hotel 🏨
(323) 658-6600. **$229-$1500.** 8384 W 3rd St 90048. I-10 exit 7A (La Cienega Blvd), 2.3 mi n, then just e. Int corridors. **Pets:** Accepted.

Radisson Hotel at Los Angeles Airport 🏨
(310) 670-9000. **$89-$269.** 6225 W Century Blvd at Sepulveda Blvd 90045. I-405 exit 46 (Century Blvd), 1.6 mi w. Int corridors. **Pets:** Accepted.

Radisson Hotel Midtown Los Angeles at USC 🏨
(213) 748-4141. **Call for rates.** 3540 S Figueroa St 90007. SR 110 exit Exposition Blvd, just w, then just n. Int corridors. **Pets:** Accepted.

Residence Inn by Marriott-Beverly Hills 🏨 🐾
(310) 228-4100. **$169-$309.** 1177 S Beverly Dr 90035. I-10 exit 6 (Robertson Blvd), 1.6 mi n to Pico Blvd, then 0.6 mi w. Int corridors. **Pets:** $100 one-time fee/room, $10 daily fee/pet. Designated rooms, service with restrictions.

Sheraton Gateway, Los Angeles 🏨 🐾
(310) 642-1111. **$329-$349.** 6101 W Century Blvd 90045. I-405 exit 46 (Century Blvd), 1.3 mi w. Int corridors. **Pets:** Medium, dogs only. $25 daily fee/room. Service with restrictions, supervision.

Sheraton Los Angeles Downtown Hotel 🏨 🐾
(213) 488-3500. **$119-$322.** 711 S Hope St 90017. SR 110 exit 6th St southbound, just e, then just s. Int corridors. **Pets:** Medium, other species. $35 one-time fee/pet. Designated rooms, service with restrictions, supervision.

Sofitel Los Angeles 🏨
(310) 278-5444. **$235-$2000, 3 day notice.** 8555 Beverly Blvd 90048. I-10 exit 7A (La Cienega Blvd), 2.5 mi n. Int corridors. **Pets:** Accepted.

Travelodge Hotel at Lax 🏨 🐾
(310) 649-4000. **$49-$85.** 5547 W Century Blvd 90045. I-405 exit 46 (Century Blvd), 0.5 mi w. Ext/int corridors. **Pets:** Other species. $20 daily fee/pet. Designated rooms, service with restrictions, supervision.

The Westin Bonaventure Hotel & Suites 🏨
(213) 624-1000. **$119-$2500, 3 day notice.** 404 S Figueroa St 90071. SR 110 exit 6th St, just n, e on 4th St, then s on Flower St. Int corridors. **Pets:** Accepted.

The Westin Hotel-Los Angeles Airport 🏨
(310) 216-5858. **$124-$324.** 5400 W Century Blvd 90045. I-405 exit 46 (Century Blvd), just w. Int corridors. **Pets:** Accepted.

MANHATTAN BEACH
Manhattan Beach Marriott 🏨
(310) 546-7511. **$89-$289.** 1400 Parkview Ave 90266. I-405 exit 43 (Rosecrans Ave), 1 mi w, then just s. Int corridors. **Pets:** Accepted.

Residence Inn by Marriott 🏨 🐾
(310) 421-3100. **$190-$219.** 1700 N Sepulveda Blvd 90266. I-405 exit 43B (Rosecrans Ave), 1.5 mi w, then 1 mi s on SR 1. Ext corridors. **Pets:** Medium, other species. $100 one-time fee/room. Service with restrictions, crate.

MARINA DEL REY
The Ritz-Carlton, Marina del Rey 🏨
(310) 823-1700. **$299-$599.** 4375 Admiralty Way 90292. SR 90 (Marina Frwy), just s on Lincoln Blvd (SR 1), just w on Bali Way. Int corridors. **Pets:** Accepted.

MONROVIA
DoubleTree by Hilton Hotel Monrovia - Pasadena Area 🏨
(626) 357-1900. **$119-$179.** 924 W Huntington Dr 91016. I-210 exit 33 (Huntington Dr), just s. Int corridors. **Pets:** Accepted.

Homestead Studio Suites Hotel-Los Angeles-Monrovia 🏨 🐾
(626) 256-6999. **$95-$110.** 930 S Fifth Ave 91016. I-210 exit 33 (Huntington Dr), just w, then just n. Int corridors. **Pets:** Other species. $25 daily fee/pet. Service with restrictions.

NORTH HOLLYWOOD
Colony Inn Ⓜ
(818) 763-2787. **$80-$150.** 4917 Vineland Ave 91601. US 101 exit 12C (Vineland Ave), 1 mi n. Ext corridors. **Pets:** Small. $25 one-time fee/pet. Service with restrictions, crate.

NORTHRIDGE
Extended StayAmerica-Los Angeles/Northridge 🏨 🐾
(818) 734-1787. **$100-$115.** 19325 Londelius St 91324. SR 118 exit 37 (Tampa Ave), 3 mi s. Int corridors. **Pets:** Other species. $25 daily fee/pet. Service with restrictions.

PASADENA
Hilton Pasadena 🏨
(626) 577-1000. **$109-$189.** 168 S Los Robles Ave 91101. I-210 exit 26B (Lake Ave), 0.3 mi s to Colorado Blvd, then 0.4 mi w. Int corridors. **Pets:** Accepted.

Howard Johnson Pasadena Ⓜ
(626) 304-9678. **$89-$600.** 1599 E Colorado Blvd 91106. I-210 exit 27B (Allen Ave) westbound; exit 27 (Hill Ave) eastbound, 0.8 mi s. Ext corridors. **Pets:** Medium. $25 daily fee/pet. Designated rooms.

Quality Inn Pasadena Ⓜ
(626) 796-9291. **$83-$139.** 3321 E Colorado Blvd 91107. I-210 exit 29B (Madre St), just s, then 0.3 mi e. Ext corridors. **Pets:** $20 daily fee/pet. Service with restrictions, supervision.

Sheraton Pasadena Hotel 🏨 🐾
(626) 449-4000. **$139-$379.** 303 E Cordova St 91101. I-210 exit 26B (Lake Ave), 0.7 mi s, then just w. Int corridors. **Pets:** Dogs only. Designated rooms, service with restrictions, supervision.

Super 8 Ⓜ
(626) 449-3020. **$59-$153.** 2863 E Colorado Blvd 91107. I-210 exit 29A (San Gabriel Blvd), 0.3 mi s, then just e. Ext corridors. **Pets:** Small. $20 daily fee/pet. Designated rooms, service with restrictions, supervision.

Vagabond Inn Executive Ⓜ
(626) 449-3170. **$90-$500.** 1203 E Colorado Blvd 91106. I-210 exit 27A (Hill Ave), just s, then just w. Ext/int corridors. **Pets:** Accepted.

The Westin-Pasadena H ❖
(626) 792-2727. **$149-$399.** 191 N Los Robles Ave 91101. I-210 exit Los Robles Ave, just s; in Plaza Las Fuentes. Int corridors. **Pets:** Dogs only. Designated rooms, supervision.

POMONA

Sheraton Fairplex H ❖
(909) 622-2220. **$109-$249.** 601 W McKinley Ave 91768. I-10 exit 45A (White Ave) eastbound, 0.5 mi n, then just w; exit 43 (Fairplex Dr) westbound, 1 mi n, then 0.7 mi e. Int corridors. **Pets:** Medium, other species. $200 deposit/room. Designated rooms, service with restrictions, crate.

Shilo Inn Suites Hotel - Pomona Hilltop H
(909) 598-7666. **$109-$199.** 3101 Temple Ave 91768. SR 57 exit 20 (Temple Ave), just w. Int corridors. **Pets:** Dogs only. $25 one-time fee/ room. Designated rooms, service with restrictions, crate.

RANCHO PALOS VERDES

Terranea Resort H
(310) 265-2800. **Call for rates.** 100 Terranea Way 90275. I-110 exit Gaffey St, 1.5 mi s, 6.5 mi w on 25th St (which becomes Palos Verdes Dr S), then just w into resort. Ext/int corridors. **Pets:** Accepted.

REDONDO BEACH

Best Western Plus Sunrise Hotel at Redondo Beach Marina H
(310) 376-0746. **$139-$219.** 400 N Harbor Dr 90277. I-405 exit 40A (Artesia Blvd) northbound; exit 40B (Redondo Beach Blvd) southbound, 0.5 mi w to Artesia Blvd, 1.5 mi w to Aviation Blvd, 1.2 mi sw to Pacific Coast Hwy, 1 mi s to Beryl St, then 0.4 mi w. Int corridors. **Pets:** Medium. $100 deposit/room, $20 daily fee/room. Designated rooms, service with restrictions, supervision.

SAN GABRIEL

Hilton Los Angeles/San Gabriel H
(626) 270-2700. **$139-$209.** 225 W Valley Blvd 91776. I-10 exit 24 (New Ave), 0.6 mi n, then 0.3 mi e. Int corridors. **Pets:** Accepted.

SAN PEDRO

DoubleTree by Hilton Hotel San Pedro H
(310) 514-3344. **$139-$159.** 2800 Via Cabrillo Marina 90731. I-110 exit Gaffey St, 1.5 mi s, 0.5 mi e on 22nd St. Int corridors. **Pets:** Small. $75 one-time fee/pet. Designated rooms, service with restrictions, supervision.

Vagabond Inn San Pedro M
(310) 831-8911. **$74-$109.** 215 S Gaffey St 90731. I-110 exit Gaffey St, just s. Int corridors. **Pets:** Medium. $25 one-time fee/room. Designated rooms.

SANTA CLARITA

Best Western Valencia Inn M
(661) 255-0555. **$90-$170.** 27413 Wayne Mills Pl 91355. I-5 exit 170 (Magic Mountain Pkwy), just e. Ext corridors. **Pets:** Accepted.

Embassy Suites Valencia H
(661) 257-3111. **$119-$149.** 28508 Westinghouse Pl 91355. I-5 exit 172 (SR 126/Newhall Ranch Rd), just se, just e on Vanderbuilt Way, then just n. Int corridors. **Pets:** Accepted.

Extended StayAmerica Los Angeles-Valencia H ❖
(661) 255-1044. **$100-$115.** 24940 W Pico Canyon Rd 91381. I-5 exit 167 (Lyons Ave), just w. Int corridors. **Pets:** Other species. $25 daily fee/pet. Service with restrictions.

Fairfield Inn by Marriott M
(661) 290-2828. **$99-$129.** 25340 The Old Rd 91381. I-5 exit 167 (Lyons Ave), just w. Ext/int corridors. **Pets:** Accepted.

Hilton Garden Inn Valencia Six Flags H
(661) 254-8800. **$109-$159.** 27710 The Old Rd 91355. I-5 exit 170 (Magic Mountain Pkwy), 0.3 mi nw. Int corridors. **Pets:** Accepted.

La Quinta Inn & Suites Santa Clarita - Valencia H
(661) 286-1111. **$84-$164.** 25201 The Old Rd 91381. I-5 exit 167 (Lyons Ave), just w to Chiquella Ln, just s, then just sw. Int corridors. **Pets:** Medium, other species. Service with restrictions, supervision.

Residence Inn by Marriott H
(661) 290-2800. **$129-$329.** 25320 The Old Rd 91381. I-5 exit 167 (Lyons Ave), just w. Int corridors. **Pets:** Accepted.

Super 8-Santa Clarita M
(661) 252-1722. **$63-$102.** 17901 Sierra Hwy 91351. SR 14 exit 6A (Sierra Hwy/Via Princessa), 1.5 mi n. Int corridors. **Pets:** Large. $20 one-time fee/room. Designated rooms, service with restrictions, supervision.

SANTA MONICA

The Ambrose H
(310) 315-1555. **$225-$289.** 1255 20th St 90404. I-10 exit 1C (Cloverfield Blvd), 0.5 mi n, just w on Santa Monica Blvd, then just n. Int corridors. **Pets:** Small, dogs only. $30 daily fee/room. Designated rooms, service with restrictions, supervision.

The Fairmont Miramar Hotel & Bungalows H ❖
(310) 576-7777. **Call for rates.** 101 Wilshire Blvd 90401. I-10 exit 1B (Lincoln Blvd), 0.6 mi n, then 0.6 mi w. Ext/int corridors. **Pets:** Other species. Supervision.

The Georgian Hotel H ❖
(310) 395-9945. **$252-$528.** 1415 Ocean Ave 90401. I-10 exit 1B (Lincoln Blvd), just n, then 0.5 mi w on Broadway. Int corridors. **Pets:** Medium. $150 one-time fee/pet. Service with restrictions, supervision.

JW Marriott Santa Monica Le Merigot H
(310) 395-9700. **$380-$460.** 1740 Ocean Ave 90401. I-10 exit 1B (Lincoln Blvd), 0.3 mi s, 0.6 mi w on Pico Blvd, then just n. Int corridors. **Pets:** Accepted.

Loews Santa Monica Beach Hotel H ❖
(310) 458-6700. **$299-$3600.** 1700 Ocean Ave 90401. I-10 exit 1B (Lincoln Blvd), 0.3 mi s, 0.6 mi w on Pico Blvd, then just n. **Pets:** Other species. $25 one-time fee/room. Service with restrictions.

Sheraton Delfina Santa Monica H
(310) 399-9344. **$249-$599.** 530 Pico Blvd 90405. I-10 exit 1B (Lincoln Blvd), just s. Int corridors. **Pets:** Accepted.

Travelodge-Santa Monica/Pico Blvd M
(310) 450-5766. **$89-$134.** 3102 Pico Blvd 90405. I-10 exit 2 (Centinela Ave), just s, then just w. Ext corridors. **Pets:** Small. Designated rooms, service with restrictions, supervision.

Viceroy Santa Monica H
(310) 260-7500. **Call for rates.** 1819 Ocean Ave 90404. I-10 exit 1B (Lincoln Blvd), 0.3 mi s, 0.6 mi w on Pico Blvd, then just n. Int corridors. **Pets:** Accepted.

SEAL BEACH

AAA **WWWW** **The Pacific Inn** **H**
(562) 493-7501. **$109-$189.** 600 Marina Dr 90740. I-405 exit 22 (Seal Beach Blvd/Los Alamitos Blvd)), 2.6 mi s, 0.5 mi w, then just s. Ext/int corridors. **Pets:** Other species. $50 one-time fee/room. Service with restrictions, supervision. [SAVE] [icons]

SHERMAN OAKS

AAA **WWWW** **Best Western Plus Carriage Inn** **M**
(818) 787-2300. **$109-$189.** 5525 Sepulveda Blvd 91411. I-405 exit 64 (Burbank Blvd), just e, then just s. Ext/int corridors. **Pets:** Accepted. [SAVE] [icons]

SOUTH PASADENA

WWWW **Arroyo Vista Inn** **BB**
(323) 478-7300. **Call for rates.** 335 Monterey Rd 91030. SR 110 exit 64 (Marmion Way) northbound, 0.8 mi e, then just n; exit 31A (Orange Grove Ave) southbound, 0.3 mi e, 0.6 mi s, then just n. Int corridors. **Pets:** Accepted. [icons]

STUDIO CITY

WWWW **Sportsmen's Lodge Hotel** **H**
(818) 769-4700. **Call for rates.** 12825 Ventura Blvd 91604. US 101 exit 15 (Coldwater Canyon Ave), 0.8 mi s, then just e. Int corridors. **Pets:** Small, dogs only. $75 one-time fee/pet. Designated rooms, service with restrictions, supervision. [icons]

TARZANA

AAA **WWW** **St. George Inn & Suites** **M** ❀
(818) 345-6911. **$68-$105.** 19454 Ventura Blvd 91356. US 101 exit 24 (Tampa Ave), just s, then just w. Ext corridors. **Pets:** Medium. $125 deposit/pet, $25 one-time fee/pet. Designated rooms, service with restrictions, supervision. [SAVE] [icons]

TORRANCE

AAA **WWW** **Ramada Inn** **M** ❀
(310) 325-0660. **$55-$149.** 2880 Pacific Coast Hwy 90505. I-405 exit 39 (Crenshaw Blvd), 5.2 mi s, then just w. Ext corridors. **Pets:** Small. $20 daily fee/pet. Designated rooms, service with restrictions, supervision. [SAVE] [icons]

WWWW **Residence Inn by Marriott** **H**
(310) 543-4566. **$139-$189.** 3701 Torrance Blvd 90503. I-405 exit 42A (Hawthorne Blvd), 3.2 mi s, then just e. Ext corridors. **Pets:** Other species. $100 one-time fee/room. Service with restrictions. [icons]

WWWW **Staybridge Suites** **M**
(310) 371-8525. **$99-$199.** 19901 Prairie Ave 90503. I-405 exit 39 (Crenshaw Blvd), 0.4 mi s to 190th St, 0.9 mi w, then 0.4 mi s. Ext/int corridors. **Pets:** Medium, other species. $15 one-time fee/pet, $10 daily fee/pet. Service with restrictions, supervision. [icons]

UNIVERSAL CITY

AAA **WWWW** **Hilton Los Angeles/Universal City** **H** ❀
(818) 506-2500. **$155-$185.** 555 Universal Hollywood Dr 91608. US 101 exit 12A (Lankershim Blvd), just n, then just e. Int corridors. **Pets:** Large. $50 one-time fee/room. Designated rooms, service with restrictions, supervision. [ECO] [SAVE] [icons]

AAA **WWWW** **Sheraton Universal Hotel, at Universal Studios** **H** ❀
(818) 980-1212. **$159-$409.** 333 Universal Hollywood Dr 91608. US 101 exit 12A (Lankershim Blvd), just n, then just e. Int corridors. **Pets:** Small, other species. Service with restrictions, supervision. [SAVE] [icons]

WALNUT

WWW **Quality Inn & Suites** **H**
(909) 594-9999. **$69-$129.** 1170 Fairway Dr 91789. SR 60 exit 21 (Fairway Dr), 0.3 mi s. Int corridors. **Pets:** Accepted. [icons]

WEST HOLLYWOOD

AAA **WWWW** **Andaz West Hollywood** **H**
(323) 656-1234. **$245-$545, 3 day notice.** 8401 Sunset Blvd 90069. I-10 exit 7A (La Cienega Blvd), 4.4 mi n, then just e. Int corridors. **Pets:** Accepted. [ECO] [SAVE] [icons]

WWW **Chamberlain West Hollywood** **H** ❀
(310) 657-7400. **$259-$330.** 1000 Westmount Dr 90069. I-10 exit 7A (La Cienega Blvd), 4 mi n to Santa Monica Blvd, just w, then just n. Int corridors. **Pets:** Small, dogs only. $125 one-time fee/room. Service with restrictions, supervision. [icons]

AAA **WWWW** **The Grafton on Sunset** **H**
(323) 654-4600. **$189-$369.** 8462 Sunset Blvd 90069. I-10 exit 7A (La Cienega Blvd), 4.4 mi n, then just e. Int corridors. **Pets:** Accepted. [SAVE] [icons]

WWWW **Le Montrose Suite Hotel** **H**
(310) 855-1115. **$189-$569.** 900 Hammond St at Cynthia St 90069. I-10 exit 7A (La Cienega Blvd), 2.6 mi n to San Vicente Blvd, 1.3 mi nw, then just w on Cynthia St. Int corridors. **Pets:** Accepted. [icons]

WWWW **Le Parc Suite Hotel** **H** ❀
(310) 855-8888. **$259-$499.** 733 N West Knoll Dr 90069. I-10 exit 7A (La Cienega Blvd), 3.5 mi n, just w on Melrose Ave, then just n. Int corridors. **Pets:** Medium. $75 one-time fee/room. Service with restrictions, crate. [icons]

WWWW **The London West Hollywood** **H**
(310) 854-1111. **$249-$499.** 1020 N San Vicente Blvd 90069. I-10 exit 7A (La Cienega Blvd), 2.6 mi n, then 1.5 mi nw. Int corridors. **Pets:** Accepted. [icons]

WWWW **Sunset Marquis Hotel & Villas** **H**
(310) 657-1333. **$250-$850.** 1200 N Alta Loma Rd 90069. I-10 exit 7A (La Cienega Blvd), 4.5 mi n to Holloway Dr, just w, then just n. Int corridors. **Pets:** Accepted. [icons]

WHITTIER

AAA **WWW** **Vagabond Inn** **M**
(562) 698-9701. **$70-$120.** 14125 E Whittier Blvd 90605. I-605 exit 15 (Whittier Blvd), 3.5 mi e. Ext corridors. **Pets:** Large, other species. $15 daily fee/pet. Designated rooms, service with restrictions, supervision. [SAVE] [icons]

WOODLAND HILLS

WWW **Extended StayAmerica-Los Angeles-Woodland Hills** **H** ❀
(818) 710-1170. **$85-$100.** 20205 Ventura Blvd 91364. US 101 exit 25 (Winnetka Ave), just s, then just w. Int corridors. **Pets:** Other species. $25 daily fee/pet. Service with restrictions. [icons]

WWW **Hilton Woodland Hills/Los Angeles** **H** ❀
(818) 595-1000. **$99-$199.** 6360 Canoga Ave 91367. US 101 exit 26B (Canoga Ave), 1 mi n. Int corridors. **Pets:** Medium. $50 one-time fee/room. Designated rooms, service with restrictions, supervision. [icons]

WWW **Holiday Inn Express & Suites** **H**
(818) 222-2299. **$99-$129.** 22617 Ventura Blvd 91364. US 101 exit 28 (Fallbrook) southbound, n to Ventura Blvd, just e; exit 27C northbound, just w. Ext/int corridors. **Pets:** Small, dogs only. $25 daily fee/pet. Designated rooms, service with restrictions, supervision. [icons]

Holiday Inn-Woodland Hills H
(818) 883-6110. **$99-$199.** 21101 Ventura Blvd 91364. US 101 exit 26A (De Soto Ave), just s, then just w. Int corridors. **Pets:** Accepted.

Warner Center Marriott Hotel H
(818) 887-4800. **$129-$224.** 21850 Oxnard St 91367. US 101 exit 27A (Topanga Canyon Blvd N), 0.6 mi n, then just e. Int corridors.
Pets: Accepted.

END METROPOLITAN AREA

LOS BAÑOS

Americas Best Value Inn M
(209) 826-5002. **$62-$82.** 330 W Pacheco Blvd 93635. On SR 152; center. Ext corridors. **Pets:** Small. $10 daily fee/pet. Service with restrictions, supervision.

Best Western Executive Inn H ❀
(209) 827-0954. **$78-$85.** 301 W Pacheco Blvd 93635. On SR 152; center. Int corridors. **Pets:** Medium. $20 daily fee/room. Designated rooms, service with restrictions, supervision.

Vagabond Inn Executive H ❀
(209) 827-4677. **Call for rates.** 20 W Pacheco Blvd 93635. On SR 152; center. Int corridors. **Pets:** Medium, dogs only. $10 daily fee/pet. Designated rooms, service with restrictions, supervision.

LOS GATOS

Los Gatos Lodge H
(408) 354-3300. **$109-$229.** 50 Los Gatos Saratoga Rd 95032. SR 17 exit E Los Gatos, just e. Ext/int corridors. **Pets:** Accepted.

MADERA

Madera Valley Inn H
(559) 664-0100. **$59-$169.** 317 North G St 93637. SR 99 exit Central Madera, just e. Int corridors. **Pets:** $15 one-time fee/room. Service with restrictions, supervision.

Super 8 M
(559) 661-1131. **$54-$63.** 1855 W Cleveland Ave 93637. SR 99 exit Cleveland Ave, just w. Ext corridors. **Pets:** Accepted.

MAMMOTH LAKES

Mammoth Mountain Inn H
(760) 934-2581. **$129-$239, 14 day notice.** 1 Minaret Rd 93546. 5 mi w of town on SR 203. Int corridors. **Pets:** Accepted.

Shilo Inn Suites-Mammoth Lakes H
(760) 934-4500. **$110-$230.** 2963 Main St 93546. On SR 203, just e of Old Mammoth Rd. Int corridors. **Pets:** Dogs only. $25 one-time fee/room. Designated rooms, service with restrictions, crate.

Sierra Lodge H
(760) 934-8881. **$69-$199.** 3540 Main St 93546. On SR 203, 0.6 mi w of Old Mammoth Rd. Int corridors. **Pets:** $10 daily fee/pet. Designated rooms, service with restrictions.

Sierra Nevada Lodge H ❀
(760) 934-2515. **$129-$999, 14 day notice.** 164 Old Mammoth Rd 93546. Just s of SR 203. Ext/int corridors. **Pets:** Dogs only. $20 daily fee/pet. Designated rooms, service with restrictions, supervision.

The Westin Monache Resort H ❀
(760) 934-0400. **$169-$1399.** 50 Hillside Dr 93546. SR 203, 1 mi w to Minaret Rd, 0.3 mi n to Forest Tr, just w, then just nw. Int corridors. **Pets:** Large, dogs only. Service with restrictions, supervision.

MANTECA

Americas Best Value Inn H
(209) 239-6115. **$70-$100.** 1920 E Yosemite Ave 95336. SR 99 exit SR 120, 0.5 mi e. Ext corridors. **Pets:** Accepted.

Best Western Plus Executive Inn & Suites H
(209) 825-1415. **$72-$85.** 1415 E Yosemite Ave 95336. Jct SR 99 and 120 exit E Yosemite Ave, just w. Ext corridors. **Pets:** Accepted.

MARIPOSA

Best Western Yosemite Way Station Motel H ❀
(209) 966-7545. **$59-$229.** 4999 Hwy 140 95338. SR 140 at SR 49 S. Ext corridors. **Pets:** Small, other species. $20 daily fee/pet. Designated rooms, service with restrictions, supervision.

Comfort Inn Yosemite Valley Gateway H
(209) 966-4344. **Call for rates.** 4994 Bullion St 95338. Jct SR 140 and 49 S, just e. Ext corridors. **Pets:** Small. $15 daily fee/pet. Service with restrictions, supervision.

The Mariposa Lodge H
(209) 966-3607. **$59-$139.** 5052 Hwy 140 95338. Center. Ext corridors. **Pets:** Medium. $10 daily fee/pet. Designated rooms, service with restrictions, supervision.

Miners Inn Motel M
(209) 742-7777. **$69-$249.** 5181 Hwy 49 N 95338. On SR 49, n at SR 140. Ext/int corridors. **Pets:** $15 daily fee/pet. Designated rooms, service with restrictions, supervision.

MARTINEZ

Best Western Plus John Muir Inn H
(925) 229-1010. **$111-$129.** 445 Muir Station Rd 94553. Jct I-680 and SR 4, 2.3 mi w on SR 4 to Pine St/Center Ave exit, then just s. Int corridors. **Pets:** Accepted.

MARYSVILLE

Baymont Inn & Suites H ❀
(530) 742-2700. **$62-$107.** 1111 N Beale Rd 95901. SR 70 exit 20A (Feather River Blvd/Yuba College) northbound; exit 20B (N Beale Rd) southbound, just w. Int corridors. **Pets:** Other species. $50 deposit/room, $10 daily fee/pet. Service with restrictions, crate.

Comfort Suites H
(530) 742-9200. **$79-$144.** 1034 N Beale Rd 95901. SR 70 exit 20A (Feather River Blvd/Yuba College) northbound; exit 20B (N Beale Rd) southbound, just e. Int corridors. **Pets:** Medium. $10 daily fee/pet. Designated rooms, service with restrictions, supervision.

MCCLOUD

McCloud Dance Country RV Resort CA
(530) 964-2252. **$100-$190, 7 day notice.** 480 Hwy 89 96057. Jct SR 89 and Squaw Valley Rd, just s; behind big red barn. Ext corridors. **Pets:** Accepted.

▼▼▼ McCloud Mercantile Hotel �H ❀
(530) 964-2330. **$129-$250, 10 day notice.** 241 Main St 96057. Jct SR 89 and W Minnesota Ave, 0.3 mi se on W Minnesota Ave to Main St, then just n. Int corridors. **Pets:** Large. Designated rooms, service with restrictions, supervision.

MENLO PARK

△△△ ▼▼▼ Red Cottage Inn & Suites Ⓜ
(650) 326-9010. **$129-$219.** 1704 El Camino Real 94025. US 101 exit 406 (Marsh Rd), 0.4 mi s on Middlefield Rd, 0.6 mi w on Encinal Rd, then just n. Ext corridors. **Pets:** Accepted.

MERCED

△△△ ▼▼▼ Best Western Plus Inn �H
(209) 723-2163. **$84-$95.** 1033 Motel Dr 95341. SR 99 exit E Childs Ave or SR 140, just e. Ext corridors. **Pets:** Accepted.

▼▼ Comfort Inn Merced �H
(209) 383-0333. **$69-$99.** 730 Motel Dr 95341. SR 99 exit SR 140, just e. Ext corridors. **Pets:** Accepted.

▼▼ Merced-Yosemite Travelodge Ⓜ
(209) 722-6224. **$54-$72.** 1260 Yosemite Pkwy 95340. SR 99 exit SR 140, just e. Ext corridors. **Pets:** Accepted.

▼▼ Ramada Inn �H
(209) 723-3121. **$49-$139.** 2010 E Childs Ave 95340. SR 99 exit E Childs Ave, just e. Ext/int corridors. **Pets:** Accepted.

MILPITAS

△△△ ▼▼▼ Best Western Plus Brookside Inn �H
(408) 263-5566. **$79-$139.** 400 Valley Way 95035. I-880 exit Calaveras Blvd (SR 237), just e. Ext/int corridors. **Pets:** Accepted.

△△△ ▼▼▼ Beverly Heritage Hotel �H
(408) 943-9080. **$69-$239.** 1820 Barber Ln 95035. Northwest quadrant of I-880 and Montague Expwy. Int corridors. **Pets:** Medium, other species. $35 one-time fee/room. Service with restrictions, crate.

▼▼▼ Residence Inn by Marriott �H
(408) 941-9222. **$85-$179.** 1501 California Cir 95035. I-880 exit Dixon Landing Rd E, just s. Int corridors. **Pets:** Medium, other species. $100 one-time fee/pet. Service with restrictions, supervision.

△△△ ▼▼▼ Sheraton San Jose Hotel �H
(408) 943-0600. **$99-$269.** 1801 Barber Ln 95035. 4 mi n of San Jose International Airport; 0.3 mi nw of I-880 and Montague Expwy. Ext/int corridors. **Pets:** Accepted.

▼▼▼ TownePlace Suites by Marriott �H
(408) 719-1959. **$80-$179.** 1428 Falcon Dr 95035. I-680 exit Montague Expwy, just w, then just n. Int corridors. **Pets:** Accepted.

MIRANDA

△△△ ▼▼▼ Miranda Gardens Resort ⒸⒶ
(707) 943-3011. **$105-$265, 7 day notice.** 6766 Ave of the Giants 95553. US 101 exit 650, 0.3 mi s on Maple Hills Rd, then 1.5 mi e. Ext corridors. **Pets:** Accepted.

MI-WUK VILLAGE

△△△ ▼▼▼ Christmas Tree Inn �H
(209) 586-1005. **$89-$129, 3 day notice.** 24685 Hwy 108 95346. On SR 108, 15 mi e of Sonora. Ext corridors. **Pets:** Medium, dogs only. $20 daily fee/room. Designated rooms, service with restrictions, supervision.

MODESTO

△△△ ▼▼▼ Best Western Town House Lodge �H ❀
(209) 524-7261. **$71-$85.** 909 16th St 95354. SR 99 exit Central Modesto, 1 mi e; at I St. Ext corridors. **Pets:** Small. $25 one-time fee/room. Service with restrictions, crate.

△△△ ▼▼▼ Courtyard by Marriott �H
(209) 577-3825. **$94-$116.** 1720 Sisk Rd 95350. SR 99 exit Briggsmore Ave, 0.3 mi n. Int corridors. **Pets:** Accepted.

▼▼ Days Inn �H
(209) 527-1010. **$57-$80.** 1312 McHenry Ave 95350. SR 99 exit Briggsmore Ave, 2.3 mi e, then 0.5 mi s. Ext/int corridors. **Pets:** Accepted.

△△△ ▼▼▼▼ DoubleTree by Hilton Hotel Modesto �H
(209) 526-6000. **Call for rates.** 1150 9th St 95354. SR 99 exit Central Modesto northbound; exit Maze Blvd southbound, just e. Int corridors. **Pets:** Accepted.

△△△ ▼▼▼ Howard Johnson Express Inn Ⓜ
(209) 537-4821. **$58-$66.** 1672 Herndon Rd 95307. SR 99 exit Hatch Rd E, then s. Ext corridors. **Pets:** Other species. $50 deposit/room. Service with restrictions, crate.

△△△ ▼▼▼ Microtel Inn & Suites �H
(209) 538-6466. **$59-$80.** 1760 Herndon Rd 95307. SR 99 exit Hatch Rd E, just s. Int corridors. **Pets:** Other species. $100 deposit/room. Service with restrictions, crate.

△△△ ▼▼ Quality Inn �H
(209) 578-5400. **$60-$100.** 500 Kansas Ave 95351. SR 99 exit Kansas Ave, just e. Int corridors. **Pets:** Accepted.

▼▼▼ Super 8 �H
(209) 543-9000. **$62-$66.** 4100 Salida Blvd 95358. SR 99 exit Pelandale Ave, just w. Ext corridors. **Pets:** Medium, other species. $25 one-time fee/pet. Designated rooms, service with restrictions, crate.

MOJAVE

△△△ ▼▼▼ Best Western Plus Desert Winds Ⓜ
(661) 824-3601. **$92-$102.** 16200 Sierra Hwy 93501. On SR 14 and 58; center. Ext corridors. **Pets:** Medium. $20 one-time fee/room. Designated rooms, service with restrictions, supervision.

▼▼▼ Days Inn-Mojave Ⓜ
(661) 824-2421. **$72-$122.** 16100 Sierra Hwy 93501. On SR 14; center. Ext corridors. **Pets:** Medium. $10 daily fee/pet. Service with restrictions, supervision.

△△△ ▼▼▼ Desert Inn Ⓜ
(661) 824-2518. **$45-$65.** 1954 Hwy 58 93501. Just e of SR 14. Ext corridors. **Pets:** Medium. Service with restrictions, crate.

△△△ ▼▼▼ Mariah Country Inn & Suites �H
(661) 824-4980. **$89-$139.** 1385 Hwy 58 93501. SR 14 exit 172 Business Rt 58, 1.5 mi e. Int corridors. **Pets:** Medium. $20 one-time fee/room. Service with restrictions, supervision.

MONTEREY PENINSULA AREA

CARMEL-BY-THE-SEA

Briarwood Inn BB ❀
(831) 626-9056. **$99-$249, 3 day notice.** San Carlos St 93921. 3 blks n of Ocean Ave; at 4th Ave. Ext corridors. **Pets:** Small, dogs only. $25 daily fee/pet. Designated rooms, service with restrictions, supervision.
SAVE 🛜 ✕ 🛏 🖵 AC

Carmel Country Inn BB ❀
(831) 625-3263. **$275-$425, 7 day notice.** Dolores St & 3rd Ave 93921. 4 blks n of Ocean Ave. Ext corridors. **Pets:** Other species. $20 daily fee/pet. Service with restrictions, supervision. 🛜 ✕ 🛏 🖵 AC

Carmel Fireplace Inn Bed & Breakfast BB ❀
(831) 624-4862. **$99-$249, 3 day notice.** San Carlos St & 4th Ave 93921. 3 blks n of Ocean Ave. Ext corridors. **Pets:** Small, dogs only. $25 daily fee/pet. Designated rooms, service with restrictions, supervision.
SAVE 🛜 ✕ 🛏 🖵 AC

Carmel Garden Court BB
(831) 624-6926. **$150-$400, 7 day notice.** 4th Ave & Torres St 93923. 3 blks n of Ocean Ave. Ext corridors. **Pets:** $50 one-time fee/pet. Service with restrictions, supervision. 🛏 🖵 AC

Carmel Lodge H ❀
(831) 624-1255. **$119-$309, 5 day notice.** San Carlos St & 5th Ave 93921. 2 blks n of Ocean Ave. Ext/int corridors. **Pets:** Dogs only. $35 daily fee/pet. Designated rooms, service with restrictions.
SAVE 🛜 🛏 🖵 ❤ ⛝ AC

Carmel Mission Inn H
(831) 624-1841. **$99-$529.** 3665 Rio Rd 93923. 1 mi s on SR 1. Ext/int corridors. **Pets:** Large. $35 one-time fee/room. Designated rooms, service with restrictions, supervision. 🛜 ✕ ⛝ 🛏 🖵 ❤ ❤

Carmel Resort Inn M
(831) 624-3113. **Call for rates.** Carpenter St & 1st Ave 93923. SR 1 exit Carpenter St, 0.5 mi w. Ext corridors. **Pets:** Accepted.
🛜 🛏 🖵 AC

Carmel River Inn M
(831) 624-1575. **$99-$369, 3 day notice.** 26600 Oliver Rd 93922. 1 mi s on SR 1; n of Carmel River Bridge. Ext corridors. **Pets:** Accepted.
🛜 🛏 🖵 ❤ AC

Coachman's Inn H
(831) 624-6421. **$145-$435, 3 day notice.** San Carlos St at 7th Ave 93921. Just s of Ocean Ave on San Carlos St; between 7th and 8th aves. Ext corridors. **Pets:** Dogs only. $25 daily fee/pet. Designated rooms, service with restrictions, supervision.
SAVE 🛜 ⛝ 🛏 🖵 AC

Cypress Inn H
(831) 624-3871. **Call for rates.** Lincoln & 7th Ave 93922. Just s off Ocean Ave. Ext/int corridors. **Pets:** Accepted. 🛜 ✕ 🛏 ❤ AC

Hofsas House H ❀
(831) 624-2745. **$90-$400, 3 day notice.** San Carlos St 93921. 3 blks n off Ocean Ave; between 3rd and 4th aves. Ext corridors. **Pets:** Dogs only. $25 daily fee/pet. Designated rooms, service with restrictions, supervision. SAVE 🛜 🛏 🖵 ❤ AC

Horizon Inn & Ocean View Lodge H ❀
(831) 624-5327. **$106-$390, 3 day notice.** 3rd Ave & Junipero Ave 93921. 4 blks n off Ocean Ave. Ext corridors. **Pets:** Dogs only. $20 daily fee/pet. Designated rooms, service with restrictions, supervision.
SAVE 🛜 ✕ ⛝ 🛏 🖵 AC

Svendsgaard's H ❀
(831) 624-1511. **$119-$259, 3 day notice.** 4th Ave & San Carlos St 93921. 3 blks n off Ocean Ave. Ext corridors. **Pets:** $25 daily fee/pet. Designated rooms, service with restrictions, supervision.
SAVE 🛜 🛏 🖵 ❤ AC

Tradewinds Carmel H ❀
(831) 624-2776. **$225-$550, 7 day notice.** Mission St & 3rd Ave 93921. 4 blks n off Ocean Ave. Ext corridors. **Pets:** Other species. $25 daily fee/pet. Designated rooms, service with restrictions, supervision.
🛜 ✕ 🛏 🖵 AC

CARMEL VALLEY

Carmel Valley Ranch H
(831) 625-9500. **$300-$1200, 7 day notice.** One Old Ranch Rd 93923. 6.3 mi e of SR 1 via Carmel Valley Rd to Robinson Canyon Rd exit, follow signs. Ext corridors. **Pets:** Accepted.
SAVE 🛜 ⛛M 🛏 🖵 🍴 ❤ ⛝

Los Laureles Lodge H
(831) 659-2233. **$125-$650, 3 day notice.** 313 W Carmel Valley Rd 93924. 10.5 mi e of SR 1. Ext corridors. **Pets:** Accepted.
🛜 🛏 🖵 🍴 ❤ AC

MARINA

The Sanctuary Beach Resort H ❀
(831) 883-9478. **$169-$550, 3 day notice.** 3295 Dunes Dr 93933. SR 1 exit Reservation Rd, just w. Ext corridors. **Pets:** Medium. $40 daily fee/pet. Designated rooms, service with restrictions, supervision.
🛜 ⛛M 🛏 🖵 🍴 ❤ AC

MONTEREY

Bay Park Hotel H ❀
(831) 649-1020. **$99-$350.** 1425 Munras Ave 93940. SR 1 exit Soledad Dr/Munras Ave, just w. Int corridors. **Pets:** Medium, other species. $20 daily fee/pet. Designated rooms, service with restrictions, supervision.
SAVE 🛜 ✕ ⛛M 🛏 🖵 🍴 ❤

Best Western Plus Beach Resort Monterey H ❀
(831) 394-3321. **Call for rates.** 2600 Sand Dunes Dr 93940. SR 1 exit Del Rey Oaks, just w. Ext corridors. **Pets:** Other species. $20 daily fee/room. Designated rooms, service with restrictions, supervision.
SAVE 🛜 ⛛M 🛏 🖵 🍴 ❤

Best Western Plus Victorian Inn H ❀
(831) 373-8000. **$79-$379, 3 day notice.** 487 Foam St 93940. SR 1 exit Monterey, 3.4 mi w. Ext/int corridors. **Pets:** $30 daily fee/room. Designated rooms, supervision. SAVE 🛜 ⛛M 🛏 🖵 AC

Comfort Inn-Monterey Bay H
(831) 373-3081. **$69-$300.** 2050 N Fremont St 93940. SR 1 exit Fremont St or Casa Verde Way, 0.3 mi e. Ext corridors. **Pets:** Small. $250 deposit/room, $25 daily fee/pet. Designated rooms, service with restrictions, supervision. SAVE 🛜 ⛛M 🛏 🖵

Comfort Inn-Monterey by the Sea H
(831) 372-2908. **$69-$300.** 1252 Munras Ave 93940. SR 1 exit Soledad Dr/Munras Ave, just s. Ext corridors. **Pets:** Medium. $250 deposit/room, $25 daily fee/pet. Designated rooms, service with restrictions, supervision.
ECO SAVE 🛜 ✕ ⛛M 🛏 🖵 ❤

El Adobe Inn M
(831) 372-5409. **$49-$299, 3 day notice.** 936 Munras Ave 93940. SR 1 exit Soledad Dr/Munras Ave, 0.6 mi w. Ext corridors. **Pets:** Medium, dogs only. $15 daily fee/pet. Designated rooms, service with restrictions, supervision. SAVE 🛜 ✕ 🛏 🖵 AC

Hotel Abrego H

(831) 372-7551. **$99-$700, 3 day notice.** 755 Abrego St 93940. SR 1 exit Fremont St, 0.8 mi w. Ext/int corridors. **Pets:** Large. $30 daily fee/room. Designated rooms, supervision.

SAVE 🛰 ✕ 🅻ᴹ 🔌 💻 📺

Hotel Pacific H

(831) 373-5700. **$149-$700, 3 day notice.** 300 Pacific St 93940. SR 1 exit Del Monte Ave, 2.2 mi w. Ext/int corridors. **Pets:** Accepted.

🛰 ✕ 🅻ᴹ 🔌 💻 📺

Hyatt Regency Monterey Hotel & Spa H

(831) 372-1234. **$99-$439, 3 day notice.** 1 Old Golf Course Rd 93940. SR 1 exit Aguajito Rd northbound; exit Monterey southbound, just e. Int corridors. **Pets:** Accepted.

ECO SAVE 🛰 🅻ᴹ 🔌 💻 🍴 🏊 ✕ 📺

InterContinental The Clement Monterey H

(831) 375-4500. **$179-$399.** 750 Cannery Row 93940. Between Prescott and David aves. Int corridors. **Pets:** Accepted.

SAVE 🛰 ✕ 🅻ᴹ 🔌 💻 🍴 🏊 ✕

Mariposa Inn & Suites H 🐾

(831) 649-1414. **$149-$419, 3 day notice.** 1386 Munras Ave 93940. SR 1 exit Soledad Dr/Munras Ave, just w. Ext/int corridors. **Pets:** Medium, dogs only. $40 daily fee/pet. Service with restrictions, supervision.

🛰 🅻ᴹ 🔌 💻 🏊

Monterey Bay Lodge H

(831) 372-8057. **$79-$349.** 55 Camino Aguajito 93940. SR 1 exit Aguajito Rd, just w. Ext corridors. **Pets:** Medium, dogs only. $15 daily fee/pet. Designated rooms, service with restrictions, supervision.

SAVE 🛰 🅻ᴹ 🔌 💻 🍴 🏊

Monterey Bay Travelodge H

(831) 373-3381. **$62-$169, 14 day notice.** 2030 N Fremont St 93940. Jct SR 1 and Fremont St, at SR 68. Ext/int corridors. **Pets:** Medium. $20 daily fee/pet. Designated rooms, service with restrictions, supervision.

SAVE 🛰 🅻ᴹ 🔌 💻 🍴 🏊 📺

Monterey Fireside Lodge M

(831) 373-4172. **$69-$599, 3 day notice.** 1131 10th St 93940. SR 1 exit Aguajito Rd or Monterey, just w. Ext corridors. **Pets:** Large, other species. $20 daily fee/pet. Designated rooms, no service, supervision.

SAVE 🛰 🔌 📺

Old Monterey Inn BB 🐾

(831) 375-8284. **$219-$449, 14 day notice.** 500 Martin St 93940. SR 1 exit Soledad Dr/Munras Ave, 1 mi w; from Fisherman's Wharf, 1 mi s on Pacific St to Martin St, 2 blks w. Ext/int corridors. **Pets:** Small, dogs only. $25 daily fee/room. Designated rooms. SAVE 🛰 ✕

Portola Hotel & Spa H

(831) 649-4511. **$179-$525, 3 day notice.** 2 Portola Plaza 93940. 2 mi w of SR 1 exit Del Monte or Munras aves; near Fisherman's Wharf; downtown. Int corridors. **Pets:** Accepted.

ECO SAVE 🛰 🅻ᴹ 🔌 💻 🍴 🏊 ✕

PACIFIC GROVE

Bide-A-Wee Inn & Cottages M 🐾

(831) 372-2330. **$69-$409, 3 day notice.** 221 Asilomar Ave 93950. 1 mi n of SR 68. Ext corridors. **Pets:** Medium, dogs only. $25 daily fee/pet. Designated rooms, service with restrictions, supervision.

SAVE 🛰 🔌 💻 📺

Deer Haven Inn & Suites H

(831) 373-7784. **Call for rates.** 740 Crocker Ave 93950. Just e of SR 68 via Sinex Ave. Ext corridors. **Pets:** Accepted.

🛰 ✕ 🔌 💻 📺

The Inn at 213 Seventeen Mile Drive BB

(831) 642-9514. **Call for rates.** 213 Seventeen Mile Dr 93950. At Lighthouse Ave. Ext/int corridors. **Pets:** Accepted. SAVE 🛰 ✕ 📺

Lighthouse Lodge & Suites M 🐾

(831) 655-2111. **$75-$800, 3 day notice.** 1150 Lighthouse Ave 93950. 0.5 mi w of Seventeen Mile Dr. Ext corridors. **Pets:** Other species. $25 daily fee/pet. Designated rooms, service with restrictions, supervision.

🛰 🅻ᴹ 🔌 💻 🏊 📺

Pacific Gardens Inn H

(831) 646-9414. **$90-$203, 7 day notice.** 701 Asilomar Blvd 93950. Just n of SR 68. Ext corridors. **Pets:** Other species. Designated rooms, service with restrictions. SAVE 🛰 ✕ 🔌 💻 📺

Sea Breeze Inn and Cottages H 🐾

(831) 372-7771. **$79-$499.** 1100 Lighthouse Ave 93950. Just w of Seventeen Mile Dr; jct Lighthouse and Grove Acre aves. Ext/int corridors. **Pets:** $25 one-time fee/pet. Designated rooms, service with restrictions, supervision. 🛰 🔌 💻 🍴 📺

Sea Breeze Lodge M 🐾

(831) 372-3431. **$79-$499.** 1101 Lighthouse Ave 93950. Just w of Seventeen Mile Dr. Ext corridors. **Pets:** $25 one-time fee/pet. Designated rooms, service with restrictions, supervision. 🛰 🔌 💻 🏊 📺

PEBBLE BEACH

The Lodge at Pebble Beach H

(831) 624-3811. **Call for rates.** 1700 Seventeen Mile Dr 93953. Off SR 1. Ext/int corridors. **Pets:** Accepted. 🛰 🅻ᴹ 💻 🍴 🏊 ✕ 📺

SEASIDE

Econo Lodge Bay Breeze M

(831) 899-7111. **$50-$240.** 2049 Fremont Blvd 93955. SR 1 exit Sand City/Seaside, just e. Ext/int corridors. **Pets:** Small. $20 daily fee/pet. Designated rooms, service with restrictions, supervision.

SAVE 🛰 🔌 💻 📺

Thunderbird Motel M

(831) 394-6797. **$39-$249, 3 day notice.** 1933 Fremont Blvd 93955. SR 1 business route, 0.3 mi n. Ext corridors. **Pets:** Small. $50 deposit/pet. Service with restrictions, supervision. SAVE 🛰 🔌 📺

END AREA

MORENO VALLEY

Best Western Moreno Hotel & Suites M 🐾

(951) 924-4546. **$85-$95.** 24840 Elder Ave 92557. SR 60 exit 62 (Perris Blvd) westbound, just n, then just w; eastbound, just e on Sunnymead Blvd, just n on Perris Blvd, then just w. Ext corridors. **Pets:** Medium, dogs only. $25 daily fee/pet. Designated rooms, supervision.

SAVE 🛰 🔌 💻 🏊

Comfort Inn M

(951) 242-0699. **$70-$109.** 23330 Sunnymead Blvd 92553. SR 60 exit 60 (Frederick St/Pigeon Pass Rd), just s, then 0.4 mi e. Ext/int corridors. **Pets:** Medium. $50 deposit/pet, $10 daily fee/pet. Service with restrictions, crate. 🛰 🔌 💻 🏊

La Quinta Inn & Suites H

(951) 486-9000. **$71-$239.** 23090 Sunnymead Blvd 92553. SR 60 exit 60 (Frederick St/Pigeon Pass Rd), just s, then just e. Int corridors. **Pets:** Medium, other species. Service with restrictions, supervision.

SAVE 🛰 ✕ 🅻ᴹ 🔌 💻 🏊

MORGAN HILL

 Extended StayAmerica-San Jose-Morgan Hill ☑ ☙

(408) 779-9660. **$79-$94.** 605 Jarvis Dr 95037. US 101 exit Cochrane W, s on Sutter Blvd, then just e. Int corridors. **Pets:** Other species. $25 daily fee/pet. Service with restrictions. 🛜 🛢M 📞 💻

Ⓐ Ramada Morgan Hill ☑

(408) 779-7666. **$59-$179.** 16115 Condit Rd 95037. US 101 exit Tennant Ave, just e. Int corridors. **Pets:** Medium, other species. $30 one-time fee/room. Service with restrictions. SAVE 🛜 🛢M 📞 💻 🏊

Residence Inn by Marriott ☑ ☙

(408) 782-8311. **$110-$180.** 18620 Madrone Pkwy 95037. US 101 exit Cochrane W, just n. Int corridors. **Pets:** Medium, other species. $100 one-time fee/room. Service with restrictions, supervision.
🛜 ✕ 🛢M 📞 💻 🏊

MORRO BAY

Beach Bungalow Inn & Suites 🄲 ☙

(805) 772-9700. **$109-$269, 3 day notice.** 1050 Morro Ave 93442. SR 1 exit Morro Bay Blvd, 0.8 mi w, then just n. Ext corridors. **Pets:** Small, dogs only. $20 daily fee/pet. Designated rooms, service with restrictions, supervision. 🛜 ✕ 📞 💻 🅰🄲

Ⓐ Best Western El Rancho Ⓜ ☙

(805) 772-2212. **$65-$205, 3 day notice.** 2460 Main St 93442. SR 1 exit Morro Bay Blvd, 0.5 mi n. Ext corridors. **Pets:** Large. $12 daily fee/pet. Designated rooms, service with restrictions.
SAVE 🛜 🛢M 📞 💻 🏊 🅰🄲

Days Inn Ⓜ

(805) 772-2711. **$69-$210.** 1095 Main St 93442. SR 1 exit Morro Bay Blvd, 0.7 mi w, then just n. Ext corridors. **Pets:** $22 daily fee/pet. Service with restrictions, supervision. 🛜 ✕ 📞 💻 🅰🄲

Econo Lodge Ⓜ

(805) 772-5609. **Call for rates.** 1100 Main St 93442. SR 1 exit Morro Bay Blvd, 0.7 mi w, then just n. Ext corridors. **Pets:** Accepted.
🛜 ✕ 📞 💻

Ⓐ The Inn at Morro Bay ☑

(805) 772-5651. **$99-$425.** 60 State Park Rd 93442. SR 1 exit Morro Bay Blvd, 0.7 mi w, then 1 mi s on Main St. Ext corridors.
Pets: Accepted. SAVE 🛜 ✕ 🛢M 📞 💻 🍴 🏊 ✕ 🅰🄲

Rodeway Inn - Morro Bay Ⓜ

(805) 772-7503. **Call for rates.** 540 Main St 93442. SR 1 exit Morro Bay Blvd, 0.7 mi w, then 0.4 mi s. Ext corridors. **Pets:** Accepted.
🛜 ✕ 📞 💻 🅰🄲

Sea Pines Golf Resort ☑

(805) 528-5252. **$99-$219.** 1945 Solano St 93402. SR 1 exit Los Osos/Baywood Park, 4 mi s on S Bay Blvd, 1.6 mi w on Los Osos Valley Rd, 0.3 mi. n on Pecho Rd, then just w on Skyline Dr; in Los Osos. Ext corridors. **Pets:** Dogs only. $25 daily fee/room. Designated rooms, service with restrictions, crate. 🛜 ✕ 📞 💻 🍴 ✕

MOUNTAIN VIEW

Homestead Studio Suites Hotel-San Jose, Mountain View ☑ ☙

(650) 962-1500. **$119-$134.** 190 E El Camino Real 94040. SR 82, just w of SR 85. Ext corridors. **Pets:** Other species. $25 daily fee/pet. Service with restrictions. 🛜 🛢M 📞 💻

Hotel Avante, a Joie de Vivre hotel ☑ ☙

(650) 940-1000. **$89-$239.** 860 E El Camino Real 94040. US 101 exit 398B (SR 85/Cupertino); exit SR 82 S (Sunnyvale), 0.5 mi e. Int corridors. **Pets:** Dogs only. Designated rooms, service with restrictions, supervision. 🄴🄲🄾 ✕ 🛢M 💻 🏊

Residence Inn by Marriott - Palo Alto/Mountain View ☑

(650) 940-1300. **Call for rates.** 1854 W El Camino Real 94040. US 101 exit 399 (Shoreline Blvd/Mountain View), 2 mi to SR 82, then 0.5 mi n. Ext corridors. **Pets:** Accepted. 🛜 ✕ 🛢M 📞 💻 🏊 ✕

MOUNT SHASTA

Ⓐ Best Western Plus Tree House ☑ ☙

(530) 926-3101. **$129-$184.** 111 Morgan Way 96067. I-5 exit 738 (Central Mount Shasta), just e. Ext/int corridors. **Pets:** Medium, other species. $15 one-time fee/pet. Service with restrictions, crate.
SAVE 🛜 ✕ 📞 💻 🍴 🏊

Ⓐ Cold Creek Inn Ⓜ ☙

(530) 926-9851. **$69-$129.** 724 N Mount Shasta Blvd 96067. I-5 exit 738 (Central Mount Shasta), 0.5 mi ne on W Lake St, then 0.4 mi nw. Ext corridors. **Pets:** Other species. $10 daily fee/pet. Service with restrictions, supervision. SAVE 🛜 ✕ 📞 💻

Mt Shasta Ranch Bed & Breakfast 🄱🄱

(530) 926-3870. **$80-$150, 3 day notice.** 1008 W A Barr Rd 96067. I-5 exit 738 (Central Mount Shasta), 0.4 mi w, then 0.8 mi s; jct W Ream Ave. Ext/int corridors. **Pets:** Accepted. 🛜 ✕ 📞 💻 ✉

Ⓐ Swiss Holiday Lodge Ⓜ

(530) 926-3446. **$65-$180.** 2400 S Mount Shasta Blvd 96067. I-5 exit 736 (McCloud/SR 89), just ne on SR 89, then just nw. Ext corridors. **Pets:** Small. $10 daily fee/pet. Service with restrictions, supervision.
SAVE 🛜 ✕ 📞 🏊

MYERS FLAT

Ⓐ Myers Inn 🄱🄱

(707) 943-3259. **$185-$250, 14 day notice.** 12913 Ave of the Giants 95554. US 101 exit Myers Flat, just w. Int corridors. **Pets:** Accepted.
SAVE 🛜 ✕ 🅰🄲 ✉

NEEDLES

Americas Best Value Inn Ⓜ ☙

(760) 326-4501. **$49-$199, 3 day notice.** 1102 E Broadway 92363. I-40 exit 144 (US 95/E Broadway), just sw. Ext corridors. **Pets:** Other species. $10 daily fee/pet. Designated rooms. 🛜 📞 💻 🏊

Ⓐ Best Western Colorado River Inn Ⓜ ☙

(760) 326-4552. **$79-$129.** 2371 W Broadway 92363. I-40 exit 141 (W Broadway/River Rd), 0.3 mi se; on Business Loop I-40. Ext corridors. **Pets:** Other species. $15 daily fee/pet. Designated rooms, service with restrictions, supervision. SAVE 🛜 ✕ 📞 💻

Ⓐ Rio del Sol Inn Ⓜ ☙

(760) 326-5660. **Call for rates.** 1111 Pashard St 92363. I-40 exit 141 (W Broadway/River Rd), just sw. Ext corridors. **Pets:** Other species. $15 daily fee/room. Service with restrictions, supervision.
SAVE 🛜 📞 💻 🏊

NEWARK

Chase Suite Hotel ☑

(510) 795-1200. **Call for rates.** 39150 Cedar Blvd 94560. I-880 exit Mowry Ave, just w, then 0.3 mi s. Ext corridors. **Pets:** Accepted.
🛜 ✕ 📞 💻 🏊

Hilton Newark/Fremont ☑ ☙

(510) 490-8390. **$89-$189.** 39900 Balentine Dr 94560. I-880 exit Stevenson Blvd, just w. Int corridors. **Pets:** $50 one-time fee/room. Designated rooms, service with restrictions, supervision.
🛜 🛢M 📞 💻 🍴 🏊

Homewood Suites by Hilton ☑

(510) 791-7700. **$71-$139.** 39270 Cedar Blvd 94560. I-880 exit Mowry Ave, w to Cedar Blvd, then 0.3 mi s. Int corridors. **Pets:** Accepted.
🛜 🛢M 📞 💻 🏊 ✕

ΔΔΔ ▼▼▼▼ Residence Inn by Marriott Newark/Silicon Valley **H** ❀

(510) 739-6000. **$76-$142.** 35466 Dumbarton Ct 94560. SR 84 exit Newark Blvd, just s. Int corridors. **Pets:** $100 one-time fee/room. Service with restrictions, supervision. (ECO) (SAVE) 🛜 ✕ (ᴦᴹ) 🛢 🖵 🍽 🏊 ⊠

NEWPORT BEACH

ΔΔΔ ▼▼▼▼ ▼▼▼▼ The Balboa Bay Club & Resort **H**

(949) 645-5000. **$195-$525.** 1221 W Coast Hwy 92663. SR 73 exit 15 (Jamboree Rd), 3.5 mi s, then just w. Int corridors. **Pets:** Medium, dogs only. $100 one-time fee/pet. Service with restrictions, supervision. (SAVE) 🛜 (ᴦᴹ) 🛢 🖵 🍴 🏊 ⊠

ΔΔΔ ▼▼▼ Best Western Plus Newport Beach Inn **M**

(949) 642-8252. **$109-$299.** 6208 W Coast Hwy 92663. SR 55, 1 mi nw on SR 1. Int corridors. **Pets:** Accepted. (SAVE) 🛜 ✕ 🛢 🖵 🏊

▼▼▼ Extended StayAmerica-Orange County/John Wayne Airport **H** ❀

(949) 851-2711. **$69-$104.** 4881 Birch St 92660. I-405 exit 8 (MacArthur Blvd), 0.8 mi s, then just e. Int corridors. **Pets:** Other species. $25 daily fee/pet. Service with restrictions. 🛜 (ᴦᴹ) 🛢 🖵

ΔΔΔ ▼▼▼ ▼▼▼ Fairmont Newport Beach **H** ❀

(949) 476-2001. **$139-$299, 3 day notice.** 4500 MacArthur Blvd 92660. I-405 exit 8 (MacArthur Blvd), 1 mi s. Int corridors. **Pets:** Small. $25 daily fee/pet. Designated rooms, service with restrictions, supervision. (ECO) (SAVE) 🛜 (ᴦᴹ) 🛢 🖵 🍴 🏊 ⊠

ΔΔΔ ▼▼▼ ▼▼▼ Hyatt Regency Newport Beach **H** ❀

(949) 729-1234. **$99-$289.** 1107 Jamboree Rd 92660. SR 73 exit 15 (Jamboree Rd), 3 mi s. Ext/int corridors. **Pets:** Medium, dogs only. $50 daily fee/room. Designated rooms, service with restrictions, supervision. (ECO) (SAVE) 🛜 (ᴦᴹ) 🛢 🖵 🏊 ⊠

ΔΔΔ ▼▼▼▼ ▼▼▼▼ Island Hotel Newport Beach **H** ❀

(949) 759-0808. **$219-$5000.** 690 Newport Center Dr 92660. SR 73 exit 14 (MacArthur Blvd) northbound, 3 mi s to San Joaquin Hills Rd, then 0.5 mi w; exit 15 (Jamboree Rd) southbound, 2.5 mi s to San Joaquin Hills Rd, then 0.5 mi e. Int corridors. **Pets:** Medium. $100 one-time fee/room. Service with restrictions, supervision. (SAVE) 🛜 ✕ (ᴦᴹ) 🛢 🍴 🏊 ⊠

NIPOMO

▼▼ ▼▼ Kaleidoscope Inn & Gardens B&B **BB**

(805) 929-5444. **$125-$160, 7 day notice.** 130 E Dana St 93444. US 101 exit 179 (Tefft St), 0.7 mi e, just s on Thompson Rd, then just e. Ext/int corridors. **Pets:** Other species. Designated rooms, service with restrictions, crate. 🛜 ✕ ☎

NOVATO

ΔΔΔ ▼▼▼ ▼▼▼ Inn Marin **M** ❀

(415) 883-5952. **$119-$329.** 250 Entrada Dr 94949. US 101 exit Ignacio Blvd, just w, just n on Enfrente Rd, then just e. Ext corridors. **Pets:** Other species. $20 one-time fee/pet. Service with restrictions, supervision. (ECO) (SAVE) 🛜 (ᴦᴹ) 🛢 🖵 🍴 🏊

OAKHURST

ΔΔΔ ▼▼▼ ▼▼▼ Best Western Plus Yosemite Gateway Inn **H**

(559) 683-2378. **$71-$192.** 40530 Hwy 41 93644. SR 49, 0.8 mi n. Ext corridors. **Pets:** Accepted. (SAVE) 🛜 ✕ (ᴦᴹ) 🛢 🖵 🍴 🏊 ⊠

ΔΔΔ ▼▼▼ ▼▼▼ Château du Sureau **CI**

(559) 683-6860. **$385-$585, 14 day notice.** 48688 Victoria Ln 93644. Just w of jct SR 41 and 49. Ext/int corridors. **Pets:** Accepted. (SAVE) 🛜 ✕ 🍴 🏊 ᴡ

ΔΔΔ ▼▼▼ Comfort Inn Yosemite Area **H**

(559) 683-8282. **$60-$200.** 40489 Hwy 41 93644. SR 49, 0.5 mi n. Ext corridors. **Pets:** Other species. $20 daily fee/room. Designated rooms, service with restrictions, supervision. (SAVE) 🛜 ✕ 🛢 🖵 🏊

ΔΔΔ ▼▼▼▼ Shilo Inn Suites-Oakhurst **H**

(559) 683-3555. **$130-$230.** 40644 Hwy 41 93644. SR 49, 0.8 mi n. Int corridors. **Pets:** Dogs only. $25 one-time fee/room. Designated rooms, service with restrictions, crate. (SAVE) 🛜 ✕ (ᴦᴹ) 🛢 🖵 🏊 ⊠

OAKLAND

▼▼▼▼ Hilton Oakland Airport **H**

(510) 635-5000. **$99-$199.** 1 Hegenberger Rd 94621. I-880 exit Hegenberger Rd, 1 mi w; 1.3 mi e of Metropolitan Oakland International Airport. Int corridors. **Pets:** Accepted. (ECO) 🛜 (ᴦᴹ) 🛢 🖵 🍴 🏊

ΔΔΔ ▼▼▼ ▼▼▼ Homewood Suites **H**

(510) 663-2700. **$169-$350.** 1103 Embarcadero 94606. I-880 exit 16th Ave/Embarcadero southbound; exit 5th Ave/Embarcadero northbound, just w. Int corridors. **Pets:** Medium. $75 one-time fee/room. Service with restrictions, crate. (ECO) (SAVE) 🛜 (ᴦᴹ) 🛢 🖵 🏊

ΔΔΔ ▼▼▼ ▼▼▼ La Quinta Inn Oakland Airport Coliseum **H**

(510) 632-8900. **$89-$150.** 8465 Enterprise Way 94621. I-880 exit Hegenberger Rd, just e. Int corridors. **Pets:** Medium, other species. Service with restrictions, supervision. (SAVE) 🛜 (ᴦᴹ) 🛢 🖵 🏊

ΔΔΔ ▼▼▼ Quality Inn **H**

(510) 562-4888. **$59-$169.** 8471 Enterprise Way 94621. I-880 exit Hegenberger Rd, just e. Ext corridors. **Pets:** Small, dogs only. $100 deposit/room, $10 daily fee/pet. Service with restrictions, supervision. (SAVE) 🛜 (ᴦᴹ) 🛢 🖵 🏊

ΔΔΔ ▼▼▼ Red Lion Hotel Oakland International Airport **H**

(510) 635-5300. **$89-$179.** 150 Hegenberger Rd 94621. I-880 exit Hegenberger Rd, 0.8 mi w. Int corridors. **Pets:** Accepted. (SAVE) 🛜 (ᴦᴹ) 🛢 🖵 🍴 🏊

ΔΔΔ ▼▼▼ Waterfront Hotel, a Joie de Vivre hotel **H** ❀

(510) 836-3800. **$105-$359.** Ten Washington St 94607. I-880 exit Broadway, 0.5 mi w. Int corridors. **Pets:** Other species. Supervision. (ECO) (SAVE) 🛜 (ᴦᴹ) 🖵 🍴 🏊

OCEANO

▼▼ ▼▼ Oceano Inn **M**

(805) 473-0032. **$69-$219, 3 day notice.** 1252 Pacific Blvd 93445. On SR 1. Ext corridors. **Pets:** Medium, dogs only. $20 daily fee/pet. Service with restrictions, supervision. 🛜 ✕ (ᴦᴹ) 🛢 🖵

OCEANSIDE

▼▼▼ La Quinta Inn San Diego Oceanside **H**

(760) 450-0730. **$80-$159.** 937 N Coast Hwy 92054. I-5 exit 54B (Coast Hwy/Oceanside) southbound; exit 54B (Camp Pendleton) northbound, just w. Int corridors. **Pets:** Medium, other species. Service with restrictions, supervision. 🛜 ✕ 🛢 🖵

ΔΔΔ ▼▼▼ Motel 6 #4208 **M**

(760) 721-1543. **$55-$129.** 909 N Coast Hwy 92054. I-5 exit 54B (Coast Hwy/Oceanside) southbound; exit 54B (Camp Pendleton) northbound, just w. Int corridors. **Pets:** Other species. Service with restrictions, supervision. (ECO) (SAVE) 🛜 (ᴦᴹ) 🛢 🖵 🏊

▼▼▼ Residence Inn by Marriott San Diego/Oceanside **H** ❀

(760) 722-9600. **$159-$229.** 3603 Ocean Ranch Blvd 92056. I-5 exit 52 (Oceanside Blvd), 3.3 mi e, 0.5 mi n on Rancho del Oro Rd, then just e. Int corridors. **Pets:** Large, other species. $100 one-time fee/room. Service with restrictions, supervision. 🛜 ✕ 🛢 🖵 🏊 ⊠

Super 8 Oceanside M
(760) 757-7700. **Call for rates.** 3240 Mission Ave 92058. I-5 exit 53 (Mission Ave), 2 mi e. Ext/int corridors. **Pets:** Small, dogs only. $10 daily fee/pet. Service with restrictions, supervision.

OJAI

Blue Iguana Inn M
(805) 646-5277. **$119-$299, 7 day notice.** 11794 N Ventura Ave 93023. 2.5 mi w of town on SR 33. Ext corridors. **Pets:** Medium, dogs only. $100 deposit/room, $20 daily fee/pet. Service with restrictions, supervision.

Casa Ojai Inn M
(805) 646-8175. **$90-$170.** 1302 E Ojai Ave 93023. 0.8 mi e on SR 150. Ext corridors. **Pets:** Medium. $25 daily fee/pet. Designated rooms, service with restrictions, crate.

Oakridge Inn M
(805) 649-4018. **$65-$140, 3 day notice.** 780 N Ventura Ave 93022. 4 mi s on SR 33; 2 mi e of Lake Casitas; in Oak View. Ext corridors. **Pets:** Medium. $10 daily fee/pet. Designated rooms, service with restrictions, supervision.

Ojai Valley Inn & Spa H
(805) 646-1111. **$325-$650, 3 day notice.** 905 Country Club Rd 93023. 1 mi w on SR 150, 0.3 mi s. Ext/int corridors. **Pets:** $125 one-time fee/pet. Designated rooms, service with restrictions, supervision.

ONTARIO

Ayres Boutique Suites Ontario Airport H
(909) 937-9700. **$89-$169.** 204 N Vineyard Ave 91764. I-10 exit 54 (Vineyard Ave), 0.3 mi s. Int corridors. **Pets:** Medium. $45 one-time fee/room. Designated rooms, service with restrictions, supervision.

Best Western Plus InnSuites Airpark Ontario Hotel & Suites H
(909) 466-9600. **$89-$149.** 3400 Shelby St 91764. I-10 exit 56 (Haven Ave), just n to Inland Empire Blvd, just w, then just se. Ext corridors. **Pets:** Medium. $20 one-time fee/room. Service with restrictions.

DoubleTree by Hilton Hotel Ontario Airport H
(909) 937-0900. **$89-$134.** 222 N Vineyard Ave 91764. I-10 exit 54 (Vineyard Ave), 0.4 mi s. Int corridors. **Pets:** Small, other species. $50 one-time fee/room. Crate.

Extended StayAmerica-Los Angeles-Ontario Airport H
(909) 944-8900. **$69-$89.** 3990 E Inland Empire Blvd 91764. I-10 exit 56 (Haven Ave), just n, then 0.5 mi e. Int corridors. **Pets:** Other species. $25 daily fee/pet. Service with restrictions.

Hilton Ontario Airport H
(909) 980-0400. **$99-$179.** 700 N Haven Ave 91764. I-10 exit 56 (Haven Ave), just n. Int corridors. **Pets:** Accepted.

La Quinta Inn & Suites Ontario Airport H
(909) 476-1112. **$89-$149.** 3555 Inland Empire Blvd 91764. I-10 exit 56 (Haven Ave), just n, then just e. Int corridors. **Pets:** Medium, other species. Service with restrictions, supervision.

Quality Inn Ontario Airport M
(909) 937-2999. **$72-$109.** 514 N Vineyard Ave 91764. I-10 exit 54 (Vineyard Ave), just s. Ext corridors. **Pets:** Small. $20 daily fee/pet. Service with restrictions, supervision.

Residence Inn Ontario - Airport H
(909) 937-6788. **$99-$169.** 2025 Convention Center Way 91764. I-10 exit 54 (Vineyard Ave), just s, then 1 blk e. Ext corridors. **Pets:** Accepted.

Sheraton Ontario Airport Hotel H
(909) 937-8000. **$89-$259.** 429 N Vineyard Ave 91764. I-10 exit 54 (Vineyard Ave), just s. Int corridors. **Pets:** Accepted.

ORANGE

Ayres Inn Orange H
(714) 978-9168. **$99-$139.** 3737 W Chapman Ave 92868. I-5 exit 107B (Chapman Ave) northbound, just w; exit 107C (State College/The City Dr) southbound, just s on State College Blvd, then just w. Int corridors. **Pets:** Large. $45 one-time fee/room. Designated rooms, supervision.

DoubleTree by Hilton Hotel Anaheim - Orange County H
(714) 634-4500. **$99-$199.** 100 The City Dr 92868. I-5 exit 107B (Chapman Ave) northbound, just w; exit 107C (State College Blvd/The City Dr) southbound, just s on State College Blvd, then just w. Int corridors. **Pets:** Accepted.

ORICK

Elk Meadow Cabins CA
(707) 488-2222. **$200-$300, 14 day notice.** 7 Valley Green Camp Rd 95555. US 101, milepost 124. Ext corridors. **Pets:** Medium. $15 daily fee/pet. Designated rooms, no service, supervision.

ORLAND

Orland Inn M
(530) 865-7632. **$69-$79.** 1052 South St 95963. I-5 exit 618 (CR 16/South St), just ne; in Stony Creek Shopping Center. Ext corridors. **Pets:** Medium, other species. $5 daily fee/pet. Service with restrictions, crate.

OROVILLE

Americas Best Value Inn & Suites M
(530) 533-7070. **$65-$95.** 580 Oro Dam Blvd 95965. SR 70 exit SR 162 (Oro Dam Blvd), 0.3 mi e. Ext corridors. **Pets:** Accepted.

Days Inn-Oroville M
(530) 533-3297. **$59-$68.** 1745 Feather River Blvd 95965. SR 70 exit 47 (E Montgomery St), just e to Feather River Blvd, then 0.5 mi s. Ext corridors. **Pets:** Accepted.

Comfort Inn H
(530) 533-9673. **$89-$149.** 1470 Feather River Blvd 95965. SR 70 exit 47 (Montgomery St), just ne, then s. Int corridors. **Pets:** Accepted.

OXNARD

Best Western Plus Oxnard Inn M
(805) 483-9581. **$100-$110.** 1156 S Oxnard Blvd 93030. US 101 exit 61 (Rose Ave) northbound, 3 mi s, then 1 mi se; exit 62B (Oxnard Blvd) southbound, 3.5 mi s. Ext corridors. **Pets:** Small, dogs only. $40 one-time fee/pet. Designated rooms, service with restrictions, supervision.

Comfort Inn-Oxnard/Camarillo M
(805) 201-6000. **$99-$149.** 1001 E Channel Islands Blvd 93033. US 101 exit 61 (Rose Ave), 3.5 mi s, then 1.5 mi w. Ext corridors. **Pets:** Small. $35 one-time fee/pet. Service with restrictions, supervision.

Embassy Suites Mandalay Beach Resort H
(805) 984-2500. **$149-$369.** 2101 Mandalay Beach Rd 93035. US 101 exit 64 (Victoria Ave), 5.5 mi s to Channel Islands Blvd, 0.5 mi w to Harbor Blvd, 0.3 mi n to Costa De Oro, then just w. Ext/int corridors. **Pets:** Accepted.

GrandStay Residential Suites Hotel 🅷 🐾
(805) 983-6808. **$110-$150.** 2211 E Gonzales Rd 93036. US 101 exit Santa Clara Ave to Rice Ave, 0.4 mi w, then just n. Int corridors. **Pets:** Medium. $200 deposit/pet, $20 daily fee/room. Service with restrictions. 〔SAVE〕 🛜 🖩 🍴 💻 🏊

Residence Inn by Marriott at River Ridge 🅷
(805) 278-2200. **$107-$217.** 2101 W Vineyard Ave 93036. US 101 exit 62A (Vineyard Ave), 1.8 mi w. Ext corridors. **Pets:** Accepted.
〔SAVE〕 🛜 🗙 🖩 🍴 💻 🏊 🗙

PALMDALE

Holiday Inn Palmdale-Lancaster 🅷
(661) 947-8055. **$99-$159.** 38630 5th St W 93551. SR 14 exit 35 (Palmdale Blvd), 0.5 mi w. Int corridors. **Pets:** Large, other species. $150 one-time fee/pet. Service with restrictions, supervision.
🛜 🗙 🖩 🍴 💻 🍽 🏊 🗙

Residence Inn by Marriott 🅷
(661) 947-4204. **$115-$160.** 514 W Ave P 93551. SR 14 exit 37 (Rancho Vista Blvd/Ave P), just e. Int corridors. **Pets:** Accepted.
🛜 🗙 🖩 🍴 💻 🏊 🗙

Staybridge Suites 🅷 🐾
(661) 947-9300. **$159-$179, 3 day notice.** 420 W Park Dr 93551. SR 14 exit 35 (Palmdale Blvd), 0.5 mi w. Int corridors. **Pets:** Other species. $75 deposit/room. 🛜 🗙 🖩 🍴 💻 🏊 🗙

PALM DESERT

Best Western Plus Palm Desert Resort Ⓜ
(760) 340-4441. **$80-$300.** 74-695 Hwy 111 92260. I-10 exit 134 (Cook St), 4.4 mi s, then 0.3 mi w. Ext corridors. **Pets:** Other species. $10 daily fee/room. Service with restrictions, supervision.
〔SAVE〕 🛜 🗙 🖩 🍴 💻 🏊 🗙

Comfort Suites Ⓜ
(760) 360-3337. **$89-$119.** 39585 Washington St 92211. I-10 exit 137 (Washington St), just n. Int corridors. **Pets:** Other species. $20 daily fee/room. Service with restrictions, supervision.
〔ECO〕 🛜 🗙 🖩 🍴 💻 🏊 🗙

Embassy Suites Hotel 🅷
(760) 340-6600. **$89-$299.** 74-700 Hwy 111 92260. I-10 exit 134 (Cook St), 4.4 mi s, then 0.3 mi w. Ext corridors. **Pets:** Accepted.
〔ECO〕 🛜 🖩 💻 🍽 🏊 🗙

Holiday Inn Express 🅷
(760) 340-4303. **$59-$159.** 74-675 Hwy 111 92260. I-10 exit 134 (Cook St), 4.4 mi s, then 0.3 mi w. Int corridors. **Pets:** Accepted.
🛜 🗙 🖩 🍴 💻 🏊 🗙

Homewood Suites by Hilton-Palm Desert 🅷 🐾
(760) 568-1600. **$80-$198.** 36-999 Cook St 92211. I-10 exit 134 (Cook St), 0.5 mi s; in The Village at University Park. Int corridors. **Pets:** Medium. $75 one-time fee/room. Service with restrictions, supervision. 🛜 🖩 💻 🏊 🗙

Residence Inn by Marriott 🅷
(760) 776-0050. **$84-$288.** 38-305 Cook St 92211. I-10 exit 134 (Cook St), 0.8 mi s. Ext corridors. **Pets:** Accepted.
〔SAVE〕 🛜 🗙 🖩 💻 🏊 🗙

PALM SPRINGS

A Place In The Sun Ⓜ 🐾
(760) 325-0254. **$99-$379, 7 day notice.** 754 E San Lorenzo Rd 92264. Just e of Palm Canyon Dr on Mesquite Ave, just n on Random Rd, then just e. Ext corridors. **Pets:** Other species. $15 one-time fee/pet.
🛜 🗙 🖩 💻 🏊

Best Western Inn At Palm Springs Ⓜ
(760) 325-9177. **$70-$230.** 1633 S Palm Canyon Dr 92264. 1.3 mi s of Tahquitz Canyon Way. Ext corridors. **Pets:** Medium. $23 daily fee/pet. Designated rooms, service with restrictions, supervision.
〔SAVE〕 🛜 🗙 🖩 🍴 💻 🏊

Casa Cody Country Inn Ⓜ
(760) 320-9346. **$89-$639, 3 day notice.** 175 S Cahuilla Rd 92262. Just s of Tahquitz Canyon Way, just w of Palm Canyon Dr. Ext corridors. **Pets:** Other species. $15 deposit/pet. Supervision.
🛜 🗙 🖩 💻 🏊

Hilton Palm Springs 🅷
(760) 320-6868. **$100-$355.** 400 E Tahquitz Canyon Way 92262. Just e of Indian Canyon Dr. Int corridors. **Pets:** Medium, dogs only. $75 one-time fee/room. Designated rooms, service with restrictions, supervision.
🛜 🖩 💻 🍽 🏊 🗙

Holiday Inn Resort Palm Springs 🅷
(760) 323-1711. **$89-$209, 3 day notice.** 1800 E Palm Canyon Dr 92264. 2.5 mi se of Tahquitz Canyon Way. Ext/int corridors.
Pets: Accepted. 🛜 🗙 🖩 🍴 💻 🍽 🏊 🗙

Hotel Zoso 🅷
(760) 325-9676. **$99-$349, 3 day notice.** 150 S Indian Canyon Dr 92262. Just s of Tahquitz Canyon Way. Int corridors. **Pets:** Accepted.
🛜 🗙 🖩 💻 🍽 🏊

Hyatt Regency Suites Palm Springs 🅷 🐾
(760) 322-9000. **$75-$429, 3 day notice.** 285 N Palm Canyon Dr 92262. Downtown. Ext/int corridors. **Pets:** Large. $25 daily fee/pet. Service with restrictions, supervision.
〔SAVE〕 🛜 🖩 🍴 💻 🍽 🏊 🗙

Palm Springs Travelodge 🅷
(760) 327-1211. **Call for rates.** 333 E Palm Canyon Dr 92264. 1.5 mi se of Tahquitz Canyon Way. Ext corridors. **Pets:** Accepted.
🛜 🗙 🖩 💻 🏊

Quality Inn Palm Springs Ⓜ
(760) 323-2775. **$59-$350.** 1269 E Palm Canyon Dr 92264. 2.4 mi se of Tahquitz Canyon Way. Ext corridors. **Pets:** Designated rooms, service with restrictions, supervision. 🛜 🖩 💻 🏊

Ramada Palm Springs Ⓜ
(760) 320-0555. **$49-$149, 3 day notice.** 2000 N Palm Canyon Dr 92262. 1.5 mi n of Tahquitz Canyon Way. Ext corridors. **Pets:** Accepted.
🛜 🗙 🖩 💻 🍽 🏊

Renaissance Palm Springs Hotel 🅷
(760) 322-6000. **$74-$194, 3 day notice.** 888 Tahquitz Canyon Way 92262. 0.4 mi e of Indian Canyon Dr. Int corridors. **Pets:** Accepted.
🛜 🗙 🖩 🍴 💻 🍽 🏊 🗙

Shilo Inn Suites - Palm Springs Ⓜ
(760) 320-7676. **$75-$225.** 1875 N Palm Canyon Dr 92262. 1.4 mi n of Tahquitz Canyon Way. Ext corridors. **Pets:** Dogs only. $25 one-time fee/room. Designated rooms, service with restrictions, crate.
〔SAVE〕 🛜 🗙 🖩 💻 🏊 🗙

Villa Royale Inn ⒸⒾ 🐾
(760) 327-2314. **$89-$500, 3 day notice.** 1620 S Indian Tr 92264. 2 mi se of Tahquitz Canyon Way on Palm Canyon Dr, then just n. Ext corridors. **Pets:** Small, dogs only. $75 one-time fee/pet. Service with restrictions, supervision. 🛜 🗙 🖩 🍴 💻 🍽 🏊 🗙

PALO ALTO

Comfort Inn Palo Alto/Stanford Area Ⓜ
(650) 493-3141. **$95-$250.** 3945 El Camino Real 94306. US 101 exit Oregon Expwy/Page Mill Rd, 1 mi s. Ext corridors. **Pets:** Large, other species. $20 daily fee/pet. Designated rooms, service with restrictions, supervision. 〔SAVE〕 🛜 🗙 🖩 🍴 💻

Crowne Plaza Cabana Hotel H
(650) 857-0787. **$109-$529.** 4290 El Camino Real 94306. US 101 exit San Antonio Rd, 0.4 mi n. Ext/int corridors. **Pets:** Small. $50 one-time fee/pet. Designated rooms, service with restrictions, supervision.

Days Inn Stanford University M
(650) 493-4222. **$71-$171.** 4238 El Camino Real 94306. US 101 exit San Antonio Rd, 2 mi w to SR 82, then 1 mi n. Ext corridors. **Pets:** Medium, other species. $15 daily fee/pet. Service with restrictions.

Dinah's Garden Hotel H
(650) 493-2844. **$99-$750.** 4261 El Camino Real 94306. US 101 exit San Antonio Rd S, 0.4 mi n on SR 82. Ext/int corridors. **Pets:** Accepted.

Quality Inn Palo Alto/Stanford Area M
(650) 493-2760. **$85-$250.** 3901 El Camino Real 94306. US 101 exit Oregon Expwy/Page Mill Rd, 2 mi w to SR 82, then se to Ventura Ave. Ext corridors. **Pets:** Large, other species. $20 daily fee/pet. Designated rooms, service with restrictions, supervision.

Sheraton Palo Alto Hotel H ☙
(650) 328-2800. **$99-$459, 3 day notice.** 625 El Camino Real 94301. US 101 exit 402 (Embarcadero Rd), 1.8 mi w, then just n on SR 82. Int corridors. **Pets:** Medium, other species. Service with restrictions, supervision.

Stanford Terrace Inn H
(650) 857-0333. **$199-$469, 3 day notice.** 531 Stanford Ave 94306. US 101 exit Oregon Expwy, 0.4 mi n on SR 82, then just w. Ext corridors. **Pets:** Accepted.

The Westin Palo Alto H ☙
(650) 321-4422. **$129-$529, 3 day notice.** 675 El Camino Real 94301. US 101 exit 402 (Embarcadero Rd), 1.8 mi w, then just n on SR 82. Int corridors. **Pets:** Medium, other species. Service with restrictions, supervision.

PARADISE

Comfort Inn H ☙
(530) 876-0191. **$79-$199.** 5475 Clark Rd 95969. SR 191 (Skyway Rd), 1.1 mi e on Pearson Rd, 0.3 mi s. Int corridors. **Pets:** Dogs only. $100 deposit/room, $10 daily fee/pet. Designated rooms, service with restrictions, supervision.

Lantern Inn M
(530) 877-5553. **$55-$82.** 5799 Wildwood Ln 95969. Just n of jct Pearson and Skyway rds, then 1 blk w off Skyway Rd. Ext corridors. **Pets:** $10 daily fee/pet. No service, supervision.

Ponderosa Gardens Motel M
(530) 872-9094. **Call for rates.** 7010 Skyway Rd 95969. 2 blks e; center. Ext corridors. **Pets:** Accepted.

PASO ROBLES

Holiday Inn Express Hotel & Suites H
(805) 238-6500. **$119-$299.** 2455 Riverside Ave 93446. US 101 exit 231B (SR 46 E), just w, then just n. Int corridors. **Pets:** Accepted.

La Quinta Inn & Suites Paso Robles H
(805) 239-3004. **$125-$229.** 2615 Buena Vista Dr 93446. US 101 exit 234 northbound; exit 231B (SR 46 E) southbound, 0.3 mi e, then just n. Int corridors. **Pets:** Medium, other species. Service with restrictions, supervision.

PATTERSON

Best Western Plus Villa Del Lago Inn H
(209) 892-5300. **$80-$159.** 2959 Speno Dr 95363. I-5 exit Sperry Rd, just e. Int corridors. **Pets:** Accepted.

PHELAN

Best Western Cajon Pass M
(760) 249-6777. **$60-$90.** 8317 Hwy 138 92371. I-15 exit 131 (SR 138/Palmdale), just w. Ext corridors. **Pets:** Accepted.

PISMO BEACH

Cliffs Resort H
(805) 773-5000. **$149-$429, 3 day notice.** 2757 Shell Beach Rd 93449. US 101 exit 193 (Spyglass Dr) northbound; exit 193 (Shell Beach Rd) southbound, just w, then just n. Int corridors. **Pets:** Accepted.

Cottage Inn by the Sea M ☙
(805) 773-4617. **$109-$399.** 2351 Price St 93449. US 101 exit 191B (Shell Beach Rd) northbound, just w, then 0.5 mi s; exit 191B (Price St) southbound, just w, then just s. Ext corridors. **Pets:** Medium, other species. $20 daily fee/room. Designated rooms, service with restrictions, supervision.

Dolphin Bay Resort & Spa CO
(805) 773-4300. **$335-$1160.** 2727 Shell Beach Rd 93449. US 101 exit 193 (Spyglass Dr) northbound; exit 193 (Shell Beach Rd) southbound, just w, then just n; in Shell Beach area. Ext corridors. **Pets:** Accepted.

Edgewater Inn & Suites M
(805) 773-4811. **$89-$269.** 280 Wadsworth Ave 93449. US 101 exit 191A (Wadsworth Ave) northbound, just w; exit 191B (Price St) southbound, just w, then 0.4 mi s on Dolliver St. Ext corridors. **Pets:** Small, dogs only. $50 deposit/room. Service with restrictions, supervision.

Oxford Suites H ☙
(805) 773-3773. **$95-$229.** 651 Five Cities Dr 93449. US 101 exit 189 (4th St), just w, then just s. Ext corridors. **Pets:** Medium. $25 one-time fee/room. Designated rooms, service with restrictions, supervision.

Sandcastle Inn M ☙
(805) 773-2422. **$135-$499.** 100 Stimson Ave 93449. US 101 exit 190 (Price St) northbound, 0.3 mi s, then just w; exit 190B (Hinds Ave) southbound, just w, then just s. Ext/int corridors. **Pets:** $20 one-time fee/room. Designated rooms, service with restrictions, supervision.

SeaCrest OceanFront Hotel M ☙
(805) 773-4608. **$139-$399.** 2241 Price St 93449. US 101 exit 191B (Shell Beach Rd) northbound, just w, then 0.5 mi s; exit 191B (Price St) southbound, just w, then just s. Ext/int corridors. **Pets:** Designated rooms, service with restrictions, crate.

Sea Gypsy Motel M
(805) 773-1801. **$60-$265.** 1020 Cypress St 93449. US 101 exit 191A (Wadsworth Ave) northbound, 0.3 mi w to Cypress St, then just s; exit 191A (SR 1) southbound, just w on Wadsworth Ave, then just s. Ext/int corridors. **Pets:** Other species. $15 daily fee/room. Service with restrictions, supervision.

Shell Beach Inn M
(805) 773-4373. **$65-$225.** 653 Shell Beach Rd 93449. US 101 exit 191B (Shell Beach Rd) northbound, just w, then 1.2 mi s; exit 191B (Price St) southbound, just w, then 1 mi n; in Shell Beach area. Ext corridors. **Pets:** Large, dogs only. $20 one-time fee/pet. Service with restrictions, supervision.

▼▼▼▼ Spyglass Inn 🅗
(805) 773-4855. **$99-$349.** 2705 Spyglass Dr 93449. US 101 exit 193 (Spyglass Dr) northbound; exit 193 (Shell Beach Rd) southbound, just w, then just n. Ext corridors. **Pets:** Accepted.
🛜 ✕ 🔥M 🔋 🖥 🏊 🎾

PLACENTIA

▼▼▼▼ Residence Inn by Marriott 🅗
(714) 996-0555. **$89-$139.** 700 W Kimberly Ave 92870. SR 57 exit 6 (Orangethorpe Ave) southbound; exit 6A (Orangethorpe Ave) northbound, just w, just n on Placentia Ave, then just e. Ext corridors. **Pets:** $100 one-time fee/room. Service with restrictions, crate.
🛜 ✕ 🔋 🖥 🏊 ✕

PLACERVILLE

ⒶⒶⒶ ▼▼▼▼ Best Western Plus Placerville Inn 🅗
(530) 622-9100. **$80-$300.** 6850 Green Leaf Dr 95667. US 50 exit 44A (Missouri Flat Rd S), just e. Int corridors. **Pets:** Large. $20 daily fee/room. Designated rooms, service with restrictions, supervision.
SAVE 🛜 🔥M 🖥 🏊

PLEASANT HILL

▼▼▼ Extended StayAmerica-Pleasant Hill-Buskirk Ave 🅗 🐾
(925) 945-6788. **$99-$114.** 3220 Buskirk Ave 94523. I-680 exit Treat Blvd/Geary Rd E, just n. Int corridors. **Pets:** Other species. $25 daily fee/pet. Service with restrictions. 🛜 🔥M 🔋 🖥

ⒶⒶⒶ ▼▼▼▼ Hyatt Summerfield Suites Pleasant Hill 🅗 🐾
(925) 934-3343. **$89-$209.** 2611 Contra Costa Blvd 94523. I-680 exit Contra Costa Blvd, then w. Int corridors. **Pets:** Medium. $100 one-time fee/room. Service with restrictions, crate.
SAVE 🛜 ✕ 🔥M 🔋 🖥 🏊 ✕

▼▼▼▼ Residence Inn by Marriott-Pleasant Hill 🅗
(925) 689-1010. **$113-$199.** 700 Ellinwood Way 94523. I-680 exit Willow Pass Rd W to S Contra Costa Blvd, e on Ellinwood Dr, then n. Ext/int corridors. **Pets:** Large, other species. $100 one-time fee/room. Service with restrictions, crate. ECO 🛜 ✕ 🔥M 🖥 🏊 ✕

PLEASANTON

ⒶⒶⒶ ▼▼▼▼ Best Western Plus Pleasanton Inn 🅗 🐾
(925) 463-1300. **$79-$109.** 5375 Owens Ct 94588. I-580 exit Hopyard Rd, just s. Ext corridors. **Pets:** Medium, dogs only. $50 deposit/room, $35 daily fee/pet. Designated rooms, service with restrictions, supervision.
SAVE 🛜 🔥M 🖥 🏊

▼▼▼▼ Hilton Pleasanton at the Club 🅗
(925) 463-8000. **$79-$229.** 7050 Johnson Dr 94588. In southeast quadrant of jct I-580 and 680. Int corridors. **Pets:** $50 one-time fee/room. Service with restrictions, crate. 🛜 🔥M 🔋 🖥 🍴 🏊 ✕

ⒶⒶⒶ ▼▼▼▼ Pleasanton Marriott 🅗
(925) 847-6000. **$75-$170.** 11950 Dublin Canyon Rd 94588. I-580 exit Foothill Rd, 0.3 mi s. Int corridors. **Pets:** Dogs only. $75 one-time fee/room. Service with restrictions, supervision.
SAVE 🛜 ✕ 🔥M 🔋 🖥 🍴 🏊

▼▼▼▼ Residence Inn by Marriott 🅗
(925) 227-0500. **$179-$209.** 11920 Dublin Canyon Rd 94588. I-580 exit Foothill Rd S, then w. Int corridors. **Pets:** Accepted.
🛜 ✕ 🔋 🖥 ✕

ⒶⒶⒶ ▼▼▼▼ Sheraton Pleasanton Hotel 🅗
(925) 463-3330. **$89-$219.** 5990 Stoneridge Mall Rd 94588. Jct I-580 and 680, 0.5 mi sw; I-580 exit Foothill Rd, 0.3 mi s, then 0.3 mi e on Canyon Way. Int corridors. **Pets:** Accepted.
SAVE 🛜 🔥M 🔋 🖥 🍴 🏊

PLYMOUTH

ⒶⒶ ▼▼▼▼ Shenandoah Inn 🅗
(209) 245-4491. **$69-$149, 3 day notice.** 17674 Village Dr 95669. On SR 49, south end of town. Ext corridors. **Pets:** Small. $10 daily fee/pet. Designated rooms, supervision. SAVE 🛜 🔋 🖥 🏊 🎾

POLLOCK PINES

ⒶⒶⒶ ▼▼▼▼ Best Western Stagecoach Inn Ⓜ
(530) 644-2029. **$119-$149.** 5940 Pony Express Tr 95726. US 50 exit 57 (Pollock Pines) eastbound, just n, then 1 mi e; exit Sly Park Rd westbound, just n, then 1 mi w. Ext corridors. **Pets:** Accepted.
SAVE 🛜 🔥M 🔋 🖥 🏊

PORTERVILLE

ⒶⒶⒶ ▼▼▼▼ Best Western Plus Porterville Inn 🅗
(559) 781-7411. **$79-$189.** 350 W Montgomery Ave 93257. SR 65, 0.8 mi e on SR 190, just s on Jaye St, then just e. Int corridors. **Pets:** Dogs only. $35 one-time fee/pet. Designated rooms, service with restrictions, supervision. SAVE 🛜 ✕ 🔥M 🔋 🖥 🏊

PORT HUENEME

▼▼▼ Country Inn & Suites By Carlson 🅗
(805) 986-5353. **$117-$229.** 350 E Port Hueneme Rd 93041. US 101 exit 62A (Vineyard Rd), just s to Oxnard Blvd, 2 mi s to Wooley Rd, 1 mi w to Ventura Rd, then 3 mi s. Int corridors. **Pets:** Small, dogs only. $25 daily fee/pet. Designated rooms, service with restrictions, supervision.
🛜 🔋 🖥 🏊

PORTOLA

▼ Sleepy Pines Motel Ⓜ
(530) 832-4291. **$67-$140, 3 day notice.** 74631 Hwy 70 96122. 1 mi w of center on SR 70. Ext corridors. **Pets:** Accepted. 🛜 🔋 🖥

RAMONA

ⒶⒶⒶ ▼▼ Ramona Valley Inn Ⓜ
(760) 789-6433. **$68-$125.** 416 Main St 92065. SR 78, 0.5 mi e of jct SR 67. Ext corridors. **Pets:** $15 daily fee/room. Service with restrictions, supervision. SAVE 🛜 🔋 🏊 🎾

RANCHO CORDOVA

▼▼ Extended StayAmerica-Sacramento-White Rock Rd 🅗 🐾
(916) 635-2363. **$69-$84.** 10721 White Rock Rd 95670. US 50 exit Zinfandel Dr, just s. Ext corridors. **Pets:** Other species. $25 daily fee/pet. Service with restrictions. 🛜 🔋 🖥

ⒶⒶⒶ ▼▼▼▼ Fairfield Inn & Suites by Marriott 🅗
(916) 858-8680. **$69-$119.** 10745 Gold Center Dr 95670. US 50 exit Zinfandel Dr, just s to White Rock Rd, just e, then just n; jct Gold Center Dr. Int corridors. **Pets:** Accepted. SAVE 🛜 ✕ 🔥M 🔋 🖥 🏊

ⒶⒶⒶ ▼▼▼▼ Holiday Inn Rancho Cordova 🅗
(916) 635-4040. **$99-$149.** 11269 Point East Dr 95742. US 50 exit Sunrise Blvd S, e on Folsom Blvd, then just n. Int corridors. **Pets:** Accepted.
ECO SAVE 🛜 ✕ 🔥M 🔋 🖥 🍴 🏊 ✕

ⒶⒶⒶ ▼▼▼▼ Hyatt Place Sacramento/Rancho Cordova 🅗
(916) 635-4799. **$79-$209.** 10744 Gold Center Dr 95670. US 50 exit Zinfandel Dr, just s to White Rock Rd, just e, then just n; jct Gold Center Dr. Int corridors. **Pets:** Accepted.
SAVE 🛜 ✕ 🔥M 🔋 🖥 🍴 🏊

▼▼▼ La Quinta Inn & Suites Rancho Cordova Sacramento 🅗
(916) 638-1111. **$88-$148.** 11131 Folsom Blvd 95670. US 50 exit Sunrise Blvd, just s, then just w. Int corridors. **Pets:** Medium, other species. Service with restrictions, supervision. 🛜 🔥M 🔋 🖥 🏊

▼▼ **Red Lion Inn** 🅷

(916) 631-7500. **$69-$99.** 10713 White Rock Rd 95670. US 50 exit Zinfandel Dr, just s, then just w. Ext/int corridors. **Pets:** Accepted.

🛜 ⬛ 🛏 💻 🏊

▼▼ **Residence Inn by Marriott** 🅷

(916) 851-1550. **$114-$143.** 2779 Prospect Park Dr 95670. US 50 exit Zinfandel Dr, just s to White Rock Rd, just e, then just n; jct Gold Center Dr. Int corridors. **Pets:** Accepted. 🛜 ⬛ ⬛ 🛏 💻 🏊 ⬛

RANCHO CUCAMONGA

AAA ▼▼▼ **Aloft Ontario-Rancho Cucamonga** 🅷

(909) 484-2018. **$69-$299, 7 day notice.** 10480 4th St 91730. I-10 exit 59 (Haven Ave), 0.3 m n, then just w. Int corridors. **Pets:** Accepted.

SAVE 🛜 ⬛ ⬛ 🛏 💻 🏊

AAA ▼▼▼ **Four Points by Sheraton** 🅷

(909) 204-6100. **$85-$255.** 11960 Foothill Blvd 91739. I-15 exit 112 (Foothill Blvd), 0.8 mi w. Int corridors. **Pets:** Small. $75 one-time fee/room. Designated rooms, service with restrictions, supervision.

SAVE 🛜 ⬛ 🛏 💻 🍴 🏊

▼▼▼ **Homewood Suites** 🅷

(909) 481-6480. **$104-$151.** 11433 Mission Vista Dr 91730. I-15 exit 110 (4th St), just w to Richmond Pl, just n, then just w. Int corridors. **Pets:** Accepted. 🛜 ⬛ 🛏 💻 🏊 ⬛

AAA ▼▼▼ **TownePlace Suites by Marriott** 🅷

(909) 466-1100. **$89-$139.** 9625 Milliken Ave 91730. I-10 exit 57 (Milliken Ave), 0.6 mi n. Int corridors. **Pets:** Other species. $100 one-time fee/room. Service with restrictions, supervision.

SAVE 🛜 ⬛ 🛏 💻 🏊

RANCHO MIRAGE

AAA ▼▼▼▼ **The Westin Mission Hills Resort & Spa** 🅷 ❀

(760) 328-5955. **$89-$1499, 3 day notice.** 71-333 Dinah Shore Dr 92270. I-10 exit 130 (Ramon Rd/Bob Hope Dr), 1 mi s on Bob Hope Dr, then 0.6 mi w. Ext corridors. **Pets:** Medium, dogs only. Designated rooms, service with restrictions, supervision.

SAVE 🛜 ⬛ 🛏 💻 🍴 🏊 ⬛

RED BLUFF

AAA ▼▼▼ **Best Western Plus Antelope Inn** 🅷

(530) 527-8882. **$84-$149.** 203 Antelope Blvd 96080. I-5 exit 649 (SR 36), just e. Int corridors. **Pets:** Large, other species. $14 daily fee/pet. Service with restrictions, supervision. SAVE 🛜 🛏 💻 🏊

AAA ▼▼▼ **Comfort Inn** 🅷

(530) 529-7060. **$90-$175.** 90 Sale Ln 96080. I-5 exit 649 (SR 36), 0.3 mi e. Int corridors. **Pets:** Accepted. SAVE 🛜 ⬛ 🛏 💻 🏊

AAA ▼▼ **Sportsman Lodge** Ⓜ

(530) 527-2888. **$55-$150, 3 day notice.** 768 Antelope Blvd 96080. I-5 exit 649 (SR 36), 1.5 mi e. Ext corridors. **Pets:** $7 daily fee/pet. Service with restrictions, supervision. SAVE 🛜 🛏 💻 🏊

AAA ▼▼▼ **Super 8 Red Bluff** Ⓜ

(530) 529-2028. **$54-$63.** 30 Gilmore Rd 96080. I-5 exit 649 (SR 36), just w, then just s. Ext corridors. **Pets:** Accepted.

SAVE 🛜 ⬛ 🛏 💻 🏊

REDCREST

AAA ▼ **Redcrest Resort** ⒸⒶ ❀

(707) 722-4208. **$65-$230, 14 day notice.** 26459 Ave of the Giants 95569. US 101 exit Redcrest southbound; exit Redcrest/Holmes northbound, just e, then just n. Ext corridors. **Pets:** Large. $10 daily fee/pet. Designated rooms, service with restrictions, supervision.

SAVE 🛜 🛏 💻 ⬛ Ⓧ 📞

REDDING

AAA ▼▼▼ **Baymont Inn & Suites Redding** 🅷

(530) 722-9100. **$71-$135.** 2600 Larkspur Ln 96002. I-5 exit 677 (Cypress Ave), just e, then just s. Int corridors. **Pets:** Medium, dogs only. $30 daily fee/pet. Designated rooms, service with restrictions, supervision.

SAVE 🛜 ⬛ ⬛ 🛏 💻 🏊

AAA ▼▼▼ **Best Western Plus Twin View Inn & Suites** 🅷

(530) 241-5500. **$89-$124.** 1080 Twin View Blvd 96003. I-5 exit 681 (Twin View Blvd), just w. Int corridors. **Pets:** Medium, dogs only. $30 daily fee/pet. Designated rooms, service with restrictions, supervision.

SAVE 🛜 ⬛ ⬛ 🛏 💻 🏊

AAA ▼▼▼ **Bridge Bay Resort** Ⓜ ❀

(530) 275-3021. **$85-$190, 3 day notice.** 10300 Bridge Bay Rd 96003. I-5 exit 690, just w. Ext corridors. **Pets:** Medium. $50 deposit/pet, $50 one-time fee/pet, $10 daily fee/pet. Designated rooms, service with restrictions, supervision. SAVE 🛏 💻 🍴 🏊 ⬛

AAA ▼▼▼ **Comfort Inn** 🅷

(530) 221-4472. **$78-$132.** 850 Mistletoe Ln 96002. I-5 exit 677 (Cypress Ave), 0.8 mi n on Hilltop Dr, then just e. Int corridors. **Pets:** Medium, other species. $10 daily fee/pet. Designated rooms, service with restrictions, supervision. SAVE 🛜 ⬛ 🛏 💻

▼▼▼ **Fairfield Inn & Suites** 🅷

(530) 243-3200. **$99-$132.** 5164 Caterpillar Rd 96003. I-5 exit 681 (Twin View Blvd) northbound; exit 681B southbound, just w, then just n. Int corridors. **Pets:** Accepted. 🛜 ⬛ ⬛ 🛏 💻 🏊

▼▼ **Fawndale Lodge & RV Resort** Ⓜ

(530) 275-8000. **$63-$123, 5 day notice.** 15215 Fawndale Rd 96003. I-5 exit 689 (Fawndale Rd), just e, then 0.3 mi s; 10 mi n of town; 1 mi s of Shasta Lake. Ext corridors. **Pets:** Accepted.

🛜 ⬛ 🛏 💻 🏊 ⬛

AAA ▼▼▼ **Holiday Inn** 🅷

(530) 221-7500. **$125-$185.** 1900 Hilltop Dr 96002. I-5 exit 677 (Cypress Ave), just e, then 0.8 mi n. Int corridors. **Pets:** Dogs only. $10 daily fee/pet. Designated rooms, service with restrictions, supervision.

SAVE 🛜 🛏 💻 🍴 🏊

AAA ▼▼▼ **Oxford Suites** 🅷 ❀

(530) 221-0100. **$109-$159.** 1967 Hilltop Dr 96002. I-5 exit 677 (Cypress Ave), just e, then just n. Ext/int corridors. **Pets:** Small, other species. $25 one-time fee/pet. Designated rooms, service with restrictions, supervision.

🛜 ⬛ 🛏 💻

AAA ▼▼ **Quality Inn** Ⓜ

(530) 221-6530. **Call for rates.** 2059 Hilltop Dr 96002. I-5 exit 677 (Cypress Ave), just e, then 0.4 mi n. Ext corridors. **Pets:** Small. $15 one-time fee/room. Service with restrictions, crate. SAVE 🛜 🛏 💻 🏊

AAA ▼▼ **Redding Travelodge** 🅷

(530) 243-5291. **$68-$106.** 540 N Market St 96003. I-5 exit 680 (Lake Blvd) northbound, 0.5 mi w to Market St, then 0.5 mi s; exit Market St southbound, 2 mi s. Ext corridors. **Pets:** Other species. $8 daily fee/pet. Designated rooms, service with restrictions, supervision.

SAVE 🛜 ⬛ 🛏 💻 🏊

▼▼▼ **Red Lion Hotel Redding** 🅷

(530) 221-8700. **$109-$189.** 1830 Hilltop Dr 96002. I-5 exit SR 44 (Hilltop Dr) southbound, just e, then just s; exit 677 (Cypress Ave) northbound, just e, then 0.6 mi n. Int corridors. **Pets:** Accepted.

🛜 ⬛ 🛏 💻 🍴 🏊

REDLANDS

▼▼▼ **Ayres Hotel Redlands** 🅷 ❀

(909) 335-9024. **$99-$169.** 1015 W Colton Ave 92374. I-10 exit 77B (Tennessee St) westbound; exit 77C (Tennessee St) eastbound, just s, then just e. Ext corridors. **Pets:** $45 one-time fee/room. Designated rooms, service with restrictions, crate.

ECO 🛜 ⬛ 🛏 💻 🏊 ⬛

▼▼▼▼ Dynasty Suites-Redlands M
(909) 793-6648. **$79-$149, 3 day notice.** 1235 W Colton Ave 92374. I-10 exit 77C (Tennessee St) eastbound; exit 77B (Tennessee St) westbound, just s, then just w. Ext corridors. **Pets:** Small, dogs only. $15 daily fee/pet. Designated rooms, service with restrictions, supervision.
ECO 📶 🛏 🖥 🏊 ⌧

REDWOOD CITY

▲▲▲ ▼▼▼ ▼▼▼ Sofitel San Francisco Bay H 🐾
(650) 598-9000. **$96-$275, 7 day notice.** 223 Twin Dolphin Dr 94065. US 101 exit Marine Pkwy E, 0.5 mi s. Int corridors. **Pets:** $300 deposit/room. Designated rooms, no service, supervision.
ECO SAVE 📶 ⌧ 🔥M 🛏 🖥 🍴 🏊

▼▼▼▼ TownePlace Suites by Marriott H
(650) 593-4100. **$129-$209.** 1000 Twin Dolphin Dr 94065. US 101 exit Redwood Shores Pkwy, 0.3 mi e, then just s. Int corridors. **Pets:** $75 one-time/room. Service with restrictions. 📶 ⌧ 🔥M 🛏 🖥

REEDLEY

▲▲▲ ▼▼ ▼▼ Edgewater Inn M
(559) 637-7777. **$75-$79.** 1977 W Manning Ave 93654. 12 mi e of SR 99 via Manning Ave. Ext corridors. **Pets:** $10 daily fee/room. Service with restrictions, supervision. SAVE 📶 🛏 🖥 🏊

RIALTO

▼▼ ▼▼ Days Inn Fontana / Rialto M
(909) 877-0690. **Call for rates.** 475 W Valley Blvd 92376. I-10 exit 68 (Riverside Ave), just n, then 0.5 mi w. Ext corridors. **Pets:** Medium. $40 deposit/pet, $15 daily fee/pet. Service with restrictions, supervision.
📶 🛏 🖥 🍴 🏊

RIDGECREST

▲▲▲ ▼▼▼▼ Best Western Plus China Lake Inn M
(760) 371-2300. **$85-$130.** 400 S China Lake Blvd 93555. On US 395 business route. Ext corridors. **Pets:** Large. $25 daily fee/pet. Service with restrictions, crate. SAVE 📶 🔥M 🛏 🏊

▲▲▲ ▼▼ ▼▼ Carriage Inn M
(760) 446-7910. **$109-$169.** 901 N China Lake Blvd 93555. On SR 178 and US 395 business route; center. Ext corridors. **Pets:** Small. $75 one-time fee/pet. Designated rooms, service with restrictions, supervision.
SAVE 📶 🔥M 🛏 🖥 🍴 🏊 ⌧

▲▲▲ ▼▼▼▼ Comfort Inn M 🐾
(760) 375-9731. **$84-$124.** 507 S China Lake Blvd 93555. On US 395 business route; south end of town. Ext corridors. **Pets:** Medium. $25 daily fee/pet. Designated rooms, service with restrictions, supervision.
SAVE 📶 ⌧ 🛏 🖥 🏊

▲▲▲ ▼▼▼▼ Econo Lodge Inn & Suites M
(760) 446-2551. **$63-$83.** 201 Inyokern Rd 93555. SR 178 and US 395 business route, just w of China Lake Blvd. Ext corridors. **Pets:** Small, dogs only. $10 one-time fee/pet. Service with restrictions, supervision.
SAVE 📶 🛏 🖥 🏊

▲▲▲ ▼▼▼▼ Heritage Inn & Suites H
(760) 446-6543. **$83-$96.** 1050 N Norma St 93555. On US 395 business route, just w. Int corridors. **Pets:** Other species. $100 deposit/room. Service with restrictions, crate. SAVE 📶 🔥M 🛏 🖥 🍴 🏊

▼▼ ▼▼ Vagabond Inn M
(760) 375-2220. **Call for rates.** 426 China Lake Blvd 93555. On US 395 business route; south end of town. Ext corridors. **Pets:** Accepted.
📶 🔥M 🛏 🖥

RIO DELL

▲▲▲ ▼▼ Humboldt Gables Motel M
(707) 764-5609. **$60-$135.** 40 W Davis St 95562. US 101 exit Wildwood Ave, 0.5 mi w. Ext corridors. **Pets:** Small, dogs only. $20 daily fee/room. Supervision. SAVE 📶 ⌧ 🔥M 🛏 🖥 🐾

RIPON

▲▲▲ ▼▼▼▼ La Quinta Inn & Suites Manteca - Ripon H
(209) 599-8999. **$70-$176.** 1524 Colony Rd 95366. SR 99 exit Jack Tone Rd, just e. Int corridors. **Pets:** Medium, other species. Service with restrictions, supervision. SAVE 📶 🔥M 🛏 🖥 🏊

RIVERSIDE

▼▼▼ Comfort Inn University M
(951) 683-6000. **$80-$120.** 1590 University Ave 92507. I-215 and SR 60 exit 32 (University Ave), 0.5 mi w. Ext corridors. **Pets:** Small. $15 daily fee/pet. Service with restrictions, crate. 📶 🛏 🖥 🏊

▼▼ ▼▼ Econo Lodge M
(951) 351-2424. **$59-$64.** 10705 Magnolia Ave 92505. SR 91 exit 55B (La Sierra), just n, then 0.5 mi e. Ext/int corridors. **Pets:** Dogs only. $7 daily fee/pet. Designated rooms, service with restrictions, supervision.
SAVE 📶 🛏 🏊

▼▼▼▼ Hampton Inn & Suites Riverside/Corona East H
(951) 352-5020. **$84-$139.** 4250 Riverwalk Pkwy 92505. SR 91 exit 54 (Pierce St/Riverwalk Pkwy) eastbound, 0.4 mi n; exit 55A (Magnolia Ave) westbound, just w, then 0.5 mi n. Int corridors. **Pets:** Medium. $40 one-time fee/room. Service with restrictions, supervision.
📶 🔥M 🛏 🖥 🏊

▼▼ ▼▼ Quality Inn & Suites M
(951) 688-5000. **$69-$149.** 11043 Magnolia Ave 92505. SR 91 exit 55B (La Sierra), just n, then just e. Ext corridors. **Pets:** Accepted.
📶 🛏 🏊

▲▲▲ ▼▼ ▼▼ Rodeway Inn Riverside M
(951) 359-0770. **Call for rates.** 10518 Magnolia Ave 92505. SR 91 exit 56 (Tyler St), 0.5 mi n, then 0.3 mi w. Ext corridors. **Pets:** Other species. $100 deposit/pet, $20 daily fee/pet. Designated rooms, service with restrictions, crate. SAVE 📶 🛏 🖥 🏊

ROCKLIN

▲▲▲ ▼▼ ▼▼ Heritage Inn Express, Rocklin H
(916) 632-3366. **$65-$75.** 4480 Rocklin Rd 95677. I-80 exit Rocklin Rd, just w, then just s. Int corridors. **Pets:** Accepted.
SAVE 📶 🛏 🖥 🏊

▲▲▲ ▼▼ ▼▼ Howard Johnson Hotel H
(916) 624-4500. **$54-$63.** 4420 Rocklin Rd 95677. I-80 exit Rocklin Rd, just w, then just s. Int corridors. **Pets:** Accepted.
SAVE 📶 🔥M 🛏 🖥 🏊

▼▼▼▼ Staybridge Suites H 🐾
(916) 781-7500. **$99-$169.** 6664 Lonetree Blvd 95765. SR 65 exit Blue Oaks Blvd, just e, just n to Redwood Dr, then just w; behind Blue Oaks Town Center. Int corridors. **Pets:** Medium. $35 one-time fee/pet. Service with restrictions, crate. 📶 🔥M 🛏 🖥 🏊

ROSEVILLE

▲▲▲ ▼▼▼▼ Best Western Plus Roseville Inn H
(916) 782-4434. **$77-$82.** 220 Harding Blvd 95678. I-80 exit 103 westbound; exit 103B eastbound, just w, then just n. Ext corridors.
Pets: Accepted. SAVE 📶 🔥M 🛏 🖥 🏊

▼▼ ▼▼ Extended StayAmerica-Sacramento-Roseville H 🐾
(916) 781-9001. **$84-$99.** 1000 Lead Hill Blvd 95678. I-80 exit 103A westbound; exit 103B eastbound, just w, then 0.6 mi n on Harding Blvd. Int corridors. **Pets:** Other species. $25 daily fee/pet. Service with restrictions. 📶 🛏 🖥

▼▼▼▼ Homewood Suites by Hilton H
(916) 783-7455. **$119-$179.** 401 Creekside Ridge Ct 95678. I-80 exit SR 65, 1 mi w to Galleria Blvd, 0.5 mi s to Antelope Creek Rd, then just e. Int corridors. **Pets:** Accepted. 📶 🔥M 🛏 🖥 🏊

Orchid Suites Roseville H ❀
(916) 784-2222. **$80-$199.** 130 N Sunrise Ave 95661. I-80 exit Douglas Blvd, just e, then 0.3 mi n. Ext/int corridors. **Pets:** Medium. $20 daily fee/pet. Designated rooms, service with restrictions, supervision.
SAVE 🛜 ⓜ 🔒 🖥 ☒

Residence Inn by Marriott H
(916) 772-5500. **$100-$140.** 1930 Taylor Rd 95661. I-80 exit 105A (Atlantic St/Eureka Rd), just n. Int corridors. **Pets:** Accepted.
🛜 ☒ ⓜ 🔒 🖥 ⌘ ☒

TownePlace Suites by Marriott Roseville H
(916) 782-2232. **$104-$149.** 10569 Fairway Dr 95678. SR 65 exit Blue Oaks Blvd, just e. Int corridors. **Pets:** Accepted.
🛜 ☒ ⓜ 🔒 🖥 ⌘ ☒

SACRAMENTO

Best Western Expo Inn & Suites H
(916) 922-9833. **$90-$110.** 1413 Howe Ave 95825. US 50 exit Howe Ave, 2.5 mi n; I-80 business route exit Howe Ave, 2 mi s; just n of jct Hurley and Howe aves. Int corridors. **Pets:** Accepted.
SAVE 🛜 ⓜ 🔒 🖥 ⌘

Best Western John Jay Inn H
(916) 689-4425. **$72-$130, 3 day notice.** 15 Massie Ct 95823. SR 99 exit Stockton Blvd/Mack Rd northbound, 0.8 mi n; exit Mack Rd E southbound, just e, just n on Stockton Blvd, then just w. Int corridors. **Pets:** Small, dogs only. $20 one-time fee/pet. Service with restrictions, supervision. SAVE 🛜 ⓜ 🔒 🖥 ⌘ ☒

Best Western Sandman Motel H ❀
(916) 443-6515. **$82-$97.** 236 Jibboom St 95814. I-5 exit Richards Blvd, just w. Ext corridors. **Pets:** Large, other species. $15 daily fee/room. Designated rooms, service with restrictions, supervision.
SAVE 🛜 ⓜ 🔒 🖥 🍴 ⌘

The Citizen, a Joie de Vivre hotel H
(916) 447-2700. **$119-$299.** 926 J St 95814. I-5 exit J St (Old Sacramento), 0.6 mi e; jct 10th St; downtown. Int corridors. **Pets:** Other species. Service with restrictions. ECO 🛜 ⓜ 🔒 🖥 🍴

Days Inn-Sacramento Downtown H
(916) 443-4811. **$45-$99.** 228 Jibboom St 95814. I-5 exit Richards Blvd, just w. Int corridors. **Pets:** Medium, dogs only. $10 daily fee/pet. Service with restrictions, supervision. SAVE 🛜 ⓜ 🔒 🖥 ⌘

DoubleTree by Hilton Hotel Sacramento H
(916) 929-8855. **$79-$199.** 2001 Point West Way 95815. Business Rt I-80 exit Arden Way, just e. Int corridors. **Pets:** Medium. $50 one-time fee/room. Service with restrictions, supervision.
ECO SAVE 🛜 ⓜ 🔒 🖥 🍴 ⌘

Econo Lodge M
(916) 443-6631. **$55-$125.** 711 16th St 95814. Business Rt I-80 exit SR 160, 3.5 mi sw to N 12th St, 0.5 mi s, just e on H St, then just n; I-5 exit J St (Old Sacramento), 1 mi e, then just n. Ext corridors. **Pets:** Small, dogs only. $6 daily fee/pet. Designated rooms, service with restrictions.
SAVE 🛜 ⓜ 🔒

Extended StayAmerica-Sacramento-Arden Way H ❀
(916) 921-9942. **$76-$91.** 2100 Harvard St 95815. I-80 business route exit Arden Way, just w. Ext corridors. **Pets:** Other species. $25 daily fee/pet. Service with restrictions. 🛜 ⓜ 🔒 🖥

Hilton Sacramento Arden West H
(916) 922-4700. **$79-$208.** 2200 Harvard St 95815. Business Rt I-80 exit Arden Way, just w, then just n. Int corridors. **Pets:** Accepted.
SAVE 🛜 ⓜ 🖥 🍴 ⌘

Holiday Inn Express Sacramento Convention Center H
(916) 444-4436. **$99-$209.** 728 16th St 95814. Jct H and 16th sts; downtown. Int corridors. **Pets:** Medium, other species. $75 one-time fee/room. Designated rooms, service with restrictions, supervision.
ECO SAVE 🛜 ☒ ⓜ 🔒 🖥

La Quinta Inn Sacramento Downtown H
(916) 448-8100. **$64-$139.** 200 Jibboom St 95814. I-5 exit Richards Blvd, just w. Ext corridors. **Pets:** Medium, other species. Service with restrictions, supervision. 🛜 ⓜ 🖥 ⌘

La Quinta Inn Sacramento North H
(916) 348-0900. **$71-$132.** 4604 Madison Ave 95841. I-80 exit Madison Ave, 0.3 mi e. Ext corridors. **Pets:** Medium, other species. Service with restrictions, supervision. 🛜 ⓜ 🖥 ⌘

Lions Gate Hotel & Conference Center H ❀
(916) 643-6222. **Call for rates.** 3410 Westover St 95652. I-80 exit Watt Ave, 1.3 mi n to Palm St, just w, then just s on Arnold Ave. Ext/int corridors. **Pets:** Other species. $25 one-time fee/pet. Service with restrictions, crate. SAVE 🛜 ⓜ 🔒 🖥 🍴 ⌘

Quality Inn Natomas H
(916) 927-7117. **$59-$109.** 3796 Northgate Blvd 95834. I-80 exit Northgate Blvd, just s. Ext corridors. **Pets:** Medium, other species. $25 one-time fee/pet. Designated rooms, service with restrictions, supervision.
SAVE 🛜 ⓜ 🔒 🖥 ⌘

Ramada Limited-Discovery Park H
(916) 442-6971. **$59-$99.** 350 Bercut Dr 95814. I-5 exit Richards Blvd, just e, then just n. Ext corridors. **Pets:** Accepted.
🛜 ⓜ 🔒 🖥 ⌘

Residence Inn by Marriott-Sacramento Airport Natomas H
(916) 649-1300. **$89-$179.** 2410 W El Camino Ave 95833. I-5 exit 521B (W El Camino Ave) northbound only, just w, then just s on Gateway Oaks Dr; I-80 exit W El Camino Ave, 1.5 mi e, then just s on Gateway Oaks Dr. Ext corridors. **Pets:** Accepted.
SAVE 🛜 ☒ ⓜ 🔒 🖥 ⌘ ☒

Residence Inn by Marriott- Sacramento at Capitol Park H
(916) 443-0500. **$107-$183.** 1121 15th St 95814. Jct 15th and L sts; just e of state capitol; downtown. Int corridors. **Pets:** Accepted.
🛜 ☒ ⓜ 🔒 🖥 🍴 ⌘ ☒

Sheraton Grand Sacramento Hotel H
(916) 447-1700. **$119-$359.** 1230 J St 95814. I-5 exit J St (Old Sacramento), 1 mi e; jct 12th St; downtown. Int corridors. **Pets:** Accepted.
ECO SAVE 🛜 ⓜ 🖥 🍴 ⌘

Staybridge Suites Sacramento Airport/Natomas H
(916) 575-7907. **$99-$159.** 140 Promenade Cir 95834. I-80 exit Truxel Rd, just nw, n on Gateway Park Blvd, e on N Freeway Blvd, then just s. Int corridors. **Pets:** Accepted. ECO 🛜 ⓜ 🔒 🖥 ⌘ ☒

TownePlace Suites by Marriott Sacramento Cal Expo H
(916) 920-5400. **$89-$149.** 1784 Tribute Rd 95815. Business Rt I-80 exit Cal Expo westbound; exit Exposition Blvd eastbound, just w, then just s. Int corridors. **Pets:** Accepted. SAVE 🛜 ☒ 🔒 🖥 ⌘ ☒

Vagabond Executive Inn Old Town H
(916) 446-1481. **$79-$150.** 909 3rd St 95814. I-5 exit J St (Old Sacramento); 8 blks w of state capitol; jct J and 3rd sts; downtown. Ext corridors. **Pets:** Medium. $10 daily fee/pet. Designated rooms, service with restrictions, supervision. 🛜 ⓜ 🔒 🖥 ⌘

Radisson Hotel
(916) 922-2020. **$89-$209.** 500 Leisure Ln 95815. Business Rt I-80 exit Cal Expo/Exposition Blvd, 0.4 mi w on Exposition Blvd; SR 160 exit 47B (Exposition Blvd) eastbound, just sw; SR 160 exit 47A (Leisure Ln/Canterbury Rd) westbound, just e. Ext corridors. **Pets:** Small, dogs only. $50 one-time fee/pet. Service with restrictions, supervision.

SALIDA

La Quinta Inn & Suites Modesto Salida
(209) 579-8723. **$81-$144.** 4909 Sisk Rd 95368. SR 99 exit SR 219, just e. Int corridors. **Pets:** Medium, other species. Service with restrictions, supervision.

SALINAS

Residence Inn by Marriott-Salinas
(831) 775-0410. **$130-$190.** 17215 El Rancho Way 93907. US 101 exit Laurel Dr, just w. Int corridors. **Pets:** Medium. $100 one-time fee/room. Designated rooms, service with restrictions, supervision.

Super 8 Motel
(831) 758-4693. **$62-$229.** 131 Kern St 93905. US 101 exit Market St, just e. Ext corridors. **Pets:** Accepted.

SAN ANDREAS

The Robins Nest
(209) 754-1076. **$100-$175, 7 day notice.** 247 W St. Charles St 95249. SR 49; north end of town. Int corridors. **Pets:** Other species. Designated rooms, service with restrictions, crate.

SAN BERNARDINO

Best Western Hospitality Lane
(909) 381-1681. **$100-$150.** 294 E Hospitality Ln 92408. I-10 exit 73 (Waterman Ave) westbound; exit 73B (Waterman Ave) eastbound, just nw. Ext corridors. **Pets:** Medium. $10 daily fee/pet. Service with restrictions, supervision.

Hilton-San Bernardino
(909) 889-0133. **$89-$169.** 285 E Hospitality Ln 92408. I-10 exit 73 (Waterman Ave) westbound; exit 73B (Waterman Ave) eastbound, just n, then just w. Int corridors. **Pets:** Accepted.

La Quinta Inn San Bernardino
(909) 888-7571. **$67-$125.** 205 E Hospitality Ln 92408. I-10 exit 73 (Waterman Ave) westbound; 73B (Waterman Ave N) eastbound, just n, then 0.3 mi w. Ext/int corridors. **Pets:** Medium, other species. Service with restrictions, supervision.

Quality Inn
(909) 888-4827. **$75-$149.** 1750 S Waterman Ave 92408. I-10 exit 73 (Waterman Ave), 0.5 mi n. Ext corridors. **Pets:** Accepted.

Residence Inn San Bernardino
(909) 382-4564. **$114-$171.** 1040 E Harriman Pl 92408. I-10 exit 74 (Tippecanoe Ave) eastbound; exit 74 (Anderson St/Tippecanoe Ave) westbound, just n, then just w. Int corridors. **Pets:** Accepted.

SAN CLEMENTE

Best Western Plus Casablanca Inn
(949) 361-1644. **$90-$200.** 1601 N El Camino Real 92672. I-5 exit 76 (Avenida Pico), 0.8 mi sw, then just s. Ext/int corridors. **Pets:** Other species. $20 daily fee/room. Designated rooms, service with restrictions, supervision.

Holiday Inn-San Clemente Resort
(949) 361-3000. **$119-$250.** 111 S Avenida de Estrella 92672. I-5 exit 75 (Avenida Palizada) southbound, just w, then just s; exit Avenida Presidio northbound, just w, then just n. Int corridors. **Pets:** Accepted.

SAN DIEGO METROPOLITAN AREA

CHULA VISTA

Comfort Inn & Suites
(619) 426-2500. **$80-$200.** 632 East St 91910. I-5 exit 8B (E St), just e. Int corridors. **Pets:** Small, dogs only. $25 one-time fee/pet. Designated rooms, service with restrictions, supervision.

La Quinta Inn San Diego Chula Vista
(619) 691-1211. **$76-$159.** 150 Bonita Rd 91910. I-805 exit 7C (E St/Bonita Rd), just w. Ext/int corridors. **Pets:** Medium, other species. Service with restrictions, supervision.

CORONADO

Crown City Inn
(619) 435-3116. **$100-$300.** 520 Orange Ave 92118. I-5 exit 14A (Coronado Bridge), 2.4 mi nw, then just sw. Ext corridors. **Pets:** Other species. $25 daily fee/pet. Designated rooms, supervision.

Loews Coronado Bay
(619) 424-4000. **Call for rates.** 4000 Loews Coronado Bay Rd 92118. I-5 exit 14A (Coronado Bridge), 2.4 mi nw to Orange Ave, 1 mi sw to Silver Strand Blvd, 4.5 mi s to Coronado Cays, then just e. Ext/int corridors. **Pets:** Other species. $25 one-time fee/pet. Designated rooms, supervision.

DEL MAR

Hilton San Diego Del Mar
(858) 792-5200. **$119-$289.** 15575 Jimmy Durante Blvd 92014. I-5 exit 36 (Via de la Valle), just w, then just s. Int corridors. **Pets:** Accepted.

Hotel Indigo Del Mar
(858) 755-1501. **$129-$309, 3 day notice.** 710 Camino Del Mar 92014. I-5 exit 34 (Del Mar Heights Rd), 1 mi w, then just n. Ext corridors. **Pets:** Accepted.

L'Auberge Del Mar
(858) 259-1515. **$275-$700, 3 day notice.** 1540 Camino Del Mar 92014. I-5 exit 34 (Del Mar Heights Rd), 1 mi w, then 1 mi n. Int corridors. **Pets:** Very small, dogs only. $75 one-time fee/room. Service with restrictions, supervision.

EL CAJON

Best Western Courtesy Inn
(619) 440-7378. **$59-$89.** 1355 E Main St 92021. I-8 exit 19 (2nd St), 0.5 mi s, then just e. Ext corridors. **Pets:** Other species. $20 daily fee/pet. Designated rooms, service with restrictions, crate.

Quality Inn & Suites San Diego East County
(619) 588-8808. **$60-$100.** 1250 El Cajon Blvd 92020. I-8 exit 14C (Severin Dr) westbound, 1 mi e on Murray Dr; exit 15 (El Cajon Blvd) eastbound, 0.5 mi w. Ext corridors. **Pets:** Small. $20 daily fee/pet. Designated rooms, service with restrictions, supervision.

LA JOLLA

Hilton La Jolla Torrey Pines
(858) 558-1500. **$159-$299.** 10950 N Torrey Pines Rd 92037. I-5 exit 29 (Genesee Ave), 0.7 mi w, then just n. Int corridors. **Pets:** Medium. $75 one-time fee/room. Service with restrictions.

▼▼▼▼ Hotel La Jolla At The Shores 🄷

(858) 459-0261. **Call for rates.** 7955 La Jolla Shores Dr 92037. I-5 exit 28 (La Jolla Village Dr) southbound, 0.7 mi w to Torrey Pines Rd, 1.7 mi sw, then just n; exit 26A (La Jolla Pkwy) northbound, 1.5 mi n to Torrey Pines Rd, just w, then just n. Ext corridors. **Pets:** Accepted.

🛜 ✕ 🖥 🔲 🍽 🏊 ✕

AAA ▼▼▼ ▼▼▼ Hyatt Regency La Jolla 🄷

(858) 552-1234. **$85-$399, 3 day notice.** 3777 La Jolla Village Dr 92122. I-5 exit 28 (La Jolla Village Dr), just e. Int corridors.
Pets: Accepted. 🄴🄲🄾 🅂🄰🅅🄴 🛜 📶 🖥 🔲 🍽 🏊 ✕

AAA ▼▼▼ ▼▼▼ La Valencia Hotel 🄷

(858) 454-0771. **$279-$795, 3 day notice.** 1132 Prospect St 92037. I-5 exit 26A (La Jolla Pkwy) northbound, 1.5 mi n to Torrey Pines Rd, 1 mi sw to Prospect St, then 0.6 mi sw; exit 28 (La Jolla Village Dr) southbound, 0.7 mi w to Torrey Pines Rd, 2.5 mi sw to Prospect St, then 0.6 mi sw. Ext/int corridors. **Pets:** Accepted.

🅂🄰🅅🄴 🛜 ✕ 🖥 🔲 🍽 🏊 ✕

▼▼▼▼ Residence Inn San Diego La Jolla 🄷 🐾

(858) 587-1770. **$129-$259.** 8901 Gilman Dr 92037. I-5 exit 27 (Gilman Dr), 1.3 mi nw. Ext corridors. **Pets:** Other species. $100 one-time fee/room. Service with restrictions, supervision.

🄴🄲🄾 🛜 ✕ 🅂🄼 🖥 🔲 🏊 ✕

▼▼▼▼ San Diego Marriott La Jolla 🄷 🐾

(858) 587-1414. **$129-$259.** 4240 La Jolla Village Dr 92037. I-5 exit 28 (La Jolla Village Dr), 0.8 mi e. Int corridors. **Pets:** $75 one-time fee/room. Service with restrictions, supervision.

🛜 ✕ 🅂🄼 🖥 🔲 🍽 🏊 ✕

▼▼▼ Scripps Inn 🄼

(858) 454-3391. **$185-$475, 7 day notice.** 555 Coast Blvd S 92037. I-5 exit 28 (La Jolla Village Dr) southbound, 0.7 mi w to Torrey Pines Rd, 2.5 mi sw to Prospect St, 1 mi sw to Cuvier St, just w, then just s; exit 26A (La Jolla Pkwy) northbound, 1.5 mi n to Torrey Pines Rd, 1 mi sw to Prospect St, 1 mi sw to Cuvier St, just w, then just s. Ext corridors.
Pets: Accepted. 🛜 ✕ 🖥 🔲 ✕

AAA ▼▼▼ ▼▼▼ Sheraton La Jolla Hotel 🄷

(858) 453-5500. **$149-$295.** 3299 Holiday Ct 92037. I-5 exit 28 (La Jolla Village Dr), just w to Villa La Jolla Dr, just s, then just e. Ext/int corridors. **Pets:** Medium, dogs only. $40 one-time fee/room. Service with restrictions, supervision. 🄴🄲🄾 🅂🄰🅅🄴 🛜 ✕ 🅂🄼 🖥 🔲 🍽 🏊 ✕

NATIONAL CITY

AAA ▼▼▼ Best Western Plus Marina Gateway Hotel 🄷

(619) 259-2800. **$110-$150.** 800 Bay Marina Dr 91950. I-5 exit 10 (Bay Marina Dr), just w. Int corridors. **Pets:** Small. $150 deposit/room, $25 daily fee/pet. Designated rooms, service with restrictions, supervision.

🅂🄰🅅🄴 🛜 ✕ 🅂🄼 🖥 🔲 🏊

▼▼ ▼▼ Comfort Inn San Diego South Bay 🄼

(619) 474-2400. **$79-$249.** 1645 E Plaza Blvd 91950. I-805 exit 10 (Plaza Blvd), just w. Int corridors. **Pets:** Accepted.

🄴🄲🄾 🛜 ✕ 🅂🄼 🖥 🔲 🏊

POWAY

AAA ▼▼▼ Best Western Plus Poway/San Diego Hotel 🄼

(858) 748-6320. **$79-$189.** 13845 Poway Rd 92064. I-15 exit 18 (Poway Rd), 4.5 mi e. Ext corridors. **Pets:** Medium, dogs only. $10 daily fee/pet. Designated rooms, service with restrictions, supervision.

🄴🄲🄾 🅂🄰🅅🄴 🛜 🖥 🔲 🏊

▼▼ ▼▼ Ramada Hotel 🄷

(858) 748-7311. **$49-$179.** 12448 Poway Rd 92064. I-15 exit 18 (Poway Rd), 3 mi e. Ext corridors. **Pets:** Accepted. 🛜 ✕ 🖥 🔲 🏊

RANCHO BERNARDO

AAA ▼▼▼▼ DoubleTree by Hilton Golf Resort San Diego 🄷

(858) 672-9100. **$99-$229.** 14455 Penasquitos Dr 92129. I-15 exit 21 (Carmel Mountain Rd), just w. Ext corridors. **Pets:** Accepted.

🄴🄲🄾 🅂🄰🅅🄴 🛜 ✕ 🖥 🔲 🍽 🏊 ✕

▼▼▼▼ La Quinta Inn San Diego Scripps Poway 🄷

(858) 484-8800. **$73-$149.** 10185 Paseo Montril 92129. I-15 exit 18 (Rancho Penasquitos Blvd), just w. Ext/int corridors. **Pets:** Medium, other species. Service with restrictions, supervision. 🛜 🖥 🔲 🏊

▼▼▼▼ Radisson Hotel San Diego-Rancho Bernardo 🄷

(858) 451-6600. **$149-$199.** 11520 W Bernardo Ct 92127. I-15 exit 24 (Rancho Bernardo Rd), just w, then 0.5 mi s on W Bernardo Dr, then just w. Ext corridors. **Pets:** Medium, dogs only. $25 one-time fee/pet. Designated rooms, service with restrictions, crate.

🛜 ✕ 🖥 🔲 🍽 🏊

▼▼▼▼ Rancho Bernardo Inn 🄷

(858) 675-8500. **$199-$359, 3 day notice.** 17550 Bernardo Oaks Dr 92128. I-15 exit 24 (Rancho Bernardo Rd), 1 mi e, then 1 mi n. Ext/int corridors. **Pets:** Small, other species. $100 one-time fee/room. Designated rooms, service with restrictions, crate.

🛜 ✕ 🅂🄼 🖥 🔲 🍽 🏊 ✕

RANCHO SANTA FE

▼▼▼▼ The Inn at Rancho Santa Fe 🄷

(858) 756-1131. **$229-$1500, 3 day notice.** 5951 Linea del Cielo 92067. I-5 exit 37 (Lomas Santa Fe Dr), 4 mi e on CR S-8. Ext/int corridors. **Pets:** Medium. $125 one-time fee/room. Designated rooms, service with restrictions, supervision. 🛜 ✕ 🖥 🔲 🍽 🏊 ✕

▼▼▼▼ Morgan Run Resort & Club 🄷

(858) 756-2471. **$129-$299.** 5690 Cancha de Golf 92091. I-5 exit 36 (Via de la Valle), 3 mi e. Int corridors. **Pets:** Medium, other species. $25 daily fee/room. Service with restrictions, supervision.

🛜 ✕ 🖥 🔲 🏊 ✕

AAA ▼▼▼ ▼▼▼ Rancho Valencia an Auberge Resort 🄷 🐾

(858) 756-1123. **$490-$928, 7 day notice.** 5921 Valencia Cir 92067. I-5 exit 36 (Via de la Valle), 1.3 mi e, 0.5 mi s on El Camino Real, 2.5 mi e on San Dieguito Rd, just e on Rancho Diegueno Rd, 1 mi ne on Rancho Valencia, then just e at main gate. Ext corridors. **Pets:** Medium, dogs only. $75 one-time fee/pet. Service with restrictions, supervision.

🅂🄰🅅🄴 🛜 ✕ 🖥 🔲 🍽 🏊 ✕

SAN DIEGO

AAA ▼▼▼ Andaz San Diego 🄷 🐾

(619) 849-1234. **$199-$499, 3 day notice.** 600 F St 92101. I-5 exit 16B (6th Ave) northbound, 1 mi s, then just e; exit 17 (Front St) southbound, 0.9 mi s to Broadway, 0.5 mi e to 8th Ave, just s, then just w. Int corridors. **Pets:** Medium. $40 daily fee/pet. Service with restrictions.

🅂🄰🅅🄴 🛜 ✕ 🔲 🍽 🏊

AAA ▼◆▼ Best Western Lamplighter Inn & Suites at SDSU 🄼 🐾

(619) 582-3088. **$90-$190.** 6474 El Cajon Blvd 92115. I-8 exit 11 (70th St/Lake Murray Blvd), 0.4 mi s on 70th St, then 0.8 mi w. Ext corridors. **Pets:** Medium, dogs only. $15 daily fee/pet. Service with restrictions, crate. 🅂🄰🅅🄴 🛜 🖥 🔲 🏊

AAA ▼◆▼ Best Western Mission Bay 🄼

(619) 275-5700. **$79-$179.** 2575 Clairemont Dr 92117. I-5 exit 22 (Clairemont Dr/Mission Bay Dr), just e. Ext corridors. **Pets:** Accepted.

🅂🄰🅅🄴 🛜 🖥 🔲 🏊

AAA ▼▼▼▼ Best Western Plus Hacienda Hotel Old Town 🄷 🐾

(619) 298-4707. **$169-$249, 3 day notice.** 4041 Harney St 92110. I-5 exit 19 (Old Town Ave), just e, 0.3 mi n on San Diego Ave, then just e. Ext corridors. **Pets:** Medium. $50 one-time fee/pet, $20 daily fee/pet. Designated rooms, service with restrictions, crate.

🅂🄰🅅🄴 🛜 ✕ 🅂🄼 🖥 🔲 🍽 🏊

Best Western Plus San Diego/Miramar Hotel M

(858) 578-6600. **$79-$189.** 9310 Kearny Mesa Rd 92121. I-15 exit 14 (Miramar Rd/Pomerado Rd), just w, then just s. Ext corridors. **Pets:** Small, other species. $25 daily fee/pet. Designated rooms, service with restrictions, supervision. ECO SAVE 🛜 🖬 📺 ➿

The Bristol H

(619) 232-6141. **$139-$329.** 1055 First Ave 92101. I-5 exit 17 (Front St) southbound, 0.5 mi s, just e on C St, then just s; exit 15B (B St) northbound, 1 mi w to 1st Ave, then just s. Int corridors. **Pets:** Accepted.
ECO SAVE 🛜 ✕ 📺 🍴

Catamaran Resort Hotel & Spa H

(858) 488-1081. **$139-$595.** 3999 Mission Blvd 92109. I-5 exit 23A (Garnet Ave), via Mission Bay to Garnet Ave, 2.2 mi w, then 0.5 mi s. Ext/int corridors. **Pets:** Medium, dogs only. $75 one-time fee/pet. Service with restrictions, supervision. ECO SAVE 🛜 ✕ 🖬 📺 🍴 ➿ ✕

Country Inn & Suites By Carlson San Diego North H ❀

(858) 558-1818. **$99-$199.** 5975 Lusk Blvd 92121. I-805 exit 27 (Mira Mesa Blvd), 1 mi e, then just n. Int corridors. **Pets:** Dogs only. $75 one-time fee/room. Designated rooms, service with restrictions, supervision.
ECO 🛜 ✕ 🖬 📺 🍴 ➿

Crowne Plaza San Diego H ❀

(619) 297-1101. **$139-$209.** 2270 Hotel Cir N 92108. I-8 exit 3 (Taylor St), just n, then just e. Ext corridors. **Pets:** Medium, other species. $75 one-time fee/room. Designated rooms, service with restrictions, supervision. ECO 🛜 ✕ 🖬 📺 🍴 ➿ ✕

DoubleTree by Hilton Hotel San Diego - Del Mar H

(858) 481-5900. **$99-$249.** 11915 El Camino Real 92130. I-5 exit 33 (Carmel Valley Rd), 0.3 mi e, then just n. Int corridors. **Pets:** Accepted.
ECO SAVE 🛜 ✕ 🖬 📺 🍴 ➿

Embassy Suites Hotel San Diego Bay-Downtown H ❀

(619) 239-2400. **Call for rates.** 601 Pacific Hwy 92101. I-5 exit 17 (Front St) southbound, 1.2 mi s to Market St, then just w; exit 16B (6th Ave) northbound, just s to Market St, then 1.4 mi w. Int corridors. **Pets:** $50 one-time fee/room. Service with restrictions, crate.
🛜 🖬 🖬 📺 🍴 ➿

Extended StayAmerica-San Diego/Hotel Circle H ❀

(619) 296-5570. **$74-$109.** 2087 Hotel Cir S 92108. I-8 exit 4A (Hotel Cir), south side. Int corridors. **Pets:** Other species. $25 daily fee/pet. Service with restrictions. 🛜 🖬 🖬 📺

The Grand Del Mar H

(858) 314-2000. **$395-$495, 7 day notice.** 5300 Grand Del Mar Ct 92130. I-5 exit 33 (Carmel Valley Rd), 1.5 mi e on SR 56, 0.5 mi s on Carmel Country Rd, 0.5 mi e on Grand Del Mar Way, then just se. Int corridors. **Pets:** Accepted.
ECO SAVE 🛜 ✕ 🖬 📺 🍴 ➿ ✕

Hampton Inn-Del Mar H

(858) 792-5557. **Call for rates.** 11920 El Camino Real 92130. I-5 exit 33 (Carmel Valley Rd), just ne. Int corridors. **Pets:** Large. $50 one-time fee/room. Service with restrictions, supervision. 🛜 ✕ 🖬 📺

Handlery Hotel & Resort H

(619) 298-0511. **$109-$249.** 950 Hotel Cir N 92108. I-8 exit 4A (Hotel Cir), north side. Ext/int corridors. **Pets:** Accepted.
ECO 🛜 ✕ 🖬 📺 🍴 ➿

Heritage Inn San Diego - SeaWorld M

(619) 223-9500. **Call for rates.** 3333 Channel Way 92110. I-8 exit 1 (W Mission Bay/Sports Arena Blvd), just s, then just e. Ext corridors. **Pets:** Accepted. SAVE 🛜 🖬 🖬 📺 ➿

Hilton San Diego Airport/Harbor Island H

(619) 291-6700. **$129-$229.** 1960 Harbor Island Dr 92101. I-5 exit 184 (Laurel St) southbound, 1.5 mi w; exit 17 (Hawthorn St) northbound, 0.5 mi w to Harbor Dr, 1.5 mi nw. Int corridors. **Pets:** Accepted.
ECO SAVE 🛜 🖬 🖬 📺 ➿

Hilton San Diego Bayfront H ❀

(619) 564-3333. **$179-$599.** One Park Blvd 92101. I-5 exit 17 (Front St) southbound, 1.5 mi s, just w to Harbor Dr, then just s; exit 16B (6th Ave) northbound, 1.3 mi s, just w on Market, just s on Front St, just w to Harbor Dr, then just s. Int corridors. **Pets:** Medium. $50 one-time fee/room. Designated rooms, service with restrictions.
ECO SAVE 🛜 ✕ 🖬 📺 🍴 ➿ ✕

Hilton San Diego Gaslamp Quarter H

(619) 231-4040. **$199-$359.** 401 K St 92101. I-5 exit 7B (J St) northbound, 0.8 mi w to 4th Ave, then just s; exit 17 (Front St) southbound, 0.5 mi e to 4th Ave, then 1 mi s; in Historic Gaslamp Quarter. Int corridors. **Pets:** Accepted. 🛜 ✕ 🖬 🖬 📺 🍴 ➿

Hilton San Diego Mission Valley H ❀

(619) 543-9000. **Call for rates.** 901 Camino del Rio S 92108. I-8 exit 5 (Mission Center Rd), just s, then just w. Int corridors. **Pets:** Small. $75 one-time fee/pet. Designated rooms, service with restrictions, supervision.
ECO 🛜 ✕ 🖬 🖬 📺 🍴 ➿

Holiday Inn on the Bay H

(619) 232-3861. **$49-$225, 3 day notice.** 1355 N Harbor Dr 92101. I-5 exit 17 (Hawthorn St) northbound, 0.4 mi w, then 0.4 mi s; exit 17 (Front St) southbound, 0.5 mi s to Ash St, then just w. Int corridors.
Pets: Accepted. ECO 🛜 ✕ 🖬 📺 🍴 ➿

Hotel Indigo San Diego Gaslamp Quarter H ❀

(619) 727-4000. **$129-$399.** 509 9th Ave 92101. I-5 exit 17 (Front St) southbound, 0.3 mi s, 0.5 mi e on A St, 0.5 mi s on 6th Ave, then just e on island; exit 16B (6th Ave) northbound, 0.5 mi s, then just e on island. Int corridors. **Pets:** Other species. Service with restrictions, supervision. ECO 🛜 ✕ 🖬 🖬 📺 🍴

Howard Johnson Near SeaWorld M

(619) 224-8266. **$59-$178.** 3330 Rosecrans St 92110. I-5 exit 20 (Rosecrans St) southbound, 0.4 mi nw, just nw; exit 18A (Pacific Hwy) northbound, 1.5 mi n, just nw on Barnett Ave, 0.5 mi n on Midway Dr, then just w. Ext corridors. **Pets:** Small. $50 one-time fee/pet. Designated rooms, service with restrictions, supervision. ECO 🛜 ✕ 🖬 📺 ➿

Hyatt Summerfield Suites San Diego/Sorrento Mesa H ❀

(858) 597-0500. **$109-$399.** 10044 Pacific Mesa Blvd 92121. I-805 exit 27 (Mira Mesa Blvd), 1.5 mi e, just n on Pacific Heights, then just w. Int corridors. **Pets:** Medium. $150 one-time fee/room. Service with restrictions, crate. SAVE 🛜 ✕ 🖬 🖬 📺 🍴 ➿

Hyatt Regency Mission Bay Spa and Marina H ❀

(619) 224-1234. **$129-$459.** 1441 Quivira Rd 92109. I-8 exit 1 (Ingraham/Mission Bay Dr), 0.7 mi n, just w on Mission Bay Dr, then just sw. Ext/int corridors. **Pets:** Medium, dogs only. $50 daily fee/room. Designated rooms, service with restrictions, supervision.
ECO SAVE 🛜 🖬 🖬 📺 🍴 ➿ ✕

Kona Kai Resort Spa & Marina H

(619) 221-8000. **$139-$229.** 1551 Shelter Island Dr 92106. I-5 exit 20 (Rosecrans St) southbound, 3 mi sw, then 1.5 mi sw; exit 17 (Hawthorn St) northbound, 3 mi nw on Harbor Dr to Scott Rd, then 1.5 mi sw. Ext/int corridors. **Pets:** Medium. $75 one-time fee/room. Service with restrictions, supervision. SAVE 🛜 🖬 🖬 📺 🍴 ➿ ✕

La Quinta Inn & Suites San Diego Mission Valley M

(619) 295-6886. **$116-$189.** 641 Camino Del Rio S 92108. I-8 exit 5 (Mission Center Rd), just s, then just w. Ext corridors. **Pets:** Medium, other species. Service with restrictions, supervision.
🛜 ✕ 🖬 🖬 📺 ➿

▼▼▼▼ La Quinta Inn San Diego Old Town/Airport Ⓜ
(619) 291-9100. **$143-$210.** 2380 Moore St 92110. I-5 exit 19 (Old Town Ave), just n via Frontage Rd; on east side of freeway. Ext/int corridors. **Pets:** Medium, other species. Service with restrictions, supervision.

🔽 🛜 ✖ 🛗 📶 🅿 🏊

Ⓐ ▼▼▼ Manchester Grand Hyatt San Diego Ⓗ
(619) 232-1234. **$109-$459, 7 day notice.** One Market Pl 92101. I-5 exit 17 (Front St), 1.3 mi s, then just w. Int corridors. **Pets:** Accepted.

SAVE 🛜 🛗 📶 🅿 🍴 🏊 ✖

Ⓐ ▼▼▼ Marina Inn & Suites Ⓜ
(619) 232-7551. **$49-$289.** 1943 Pacific Hwy 92101. I-5 exit 17 (Front St) southbound, just s to Cedar St, 0.3 mi w, then just n; exit 17 (Hawthorn St) northbound, 0.4 mi w, then just s. Ext corridors. **Pets:** Large, other species. $20 daily fee/pet. Designated rooms, service with restrictions, crate. SAVE 🛜 📶 🅿

▼▼ Old Town Inn Ⓜ
(619) 260-8024. **$75-$200.** 4444 Pacific Hwy 92110. I-5 exit 21 (Sea-World Dr/Tecolote St), just sw, then 1 mi se. Ext corridors. **Pets:** Medium. $15 daily fee/pet. Service with restrictions, supervision.

🛜 📶 🅿 🏊

▼▼▼ ▼▼▼ Omni San Diego Hotel Ⓗ 🐾
(619) 231-6664. **Call for rates.** 675 L St 92101. I-5 exit 17 (Front St) southbound, 0.3 mi s, 0.3 mi e on A St, 0.6 mi s on 6th Ave, then just e; exit 16B (6th Ave) northbound, just s on 6th Ave, then just e; connected via skybridge to Petco Park. Int corridors. **Pets:** Small. $50 one-time fee/ pet. Designated rooms, service with restrictions, supervision.

🛜 📶 🅿 🏊 ✖

Ⓐ ▼▼▼ Pacific Inn Hotel & Suites Ⓜ
(619) 232-6391. **$49-$289.** 1655 Pacific Hwy 92101. I-5 exit 17 (Front St) southbound, just s to Cedar St, 0.5 mi w, then just n; exit 17 (Hawthorn St) northbound, 0.6 mi w, then just s. Ext corridors. **Pets:** Large, other species. $20 daily fee/pet. Designated rooms, service with restrictions, crate. SAVE 🛜 📶 🅿 🏊

Ⓐ ▼▼▼ Pacific Shores Inn Ⓜ
(858) 483-6300. **$109-$269, 3 day notice.** 4802 Mission Blvd 92109. I-5 exit 23A (Garnet Ave), via Mission Bay Dr to Garnet Ave, 2.2 mi w, then 0.3 mi n. Ext corridors. **Pets:** Medium. $35 one-time fee/room. Service with restrictions, crate. SAVE 🛜 ✖ 🏊

Ⓐ ▼▼▼ Paradise Point Ⓗ
(858) 274-4630. **$150-$450, 7 day notice.** 1404 Vacation Rd 92109. I-5 exit 21 (SeaWorld Dr/Tecolote Rd), 2.4 mi sw via Ingraham St, then just w. Ext corridors. **Pets:** Small. $150 deposit/pet, $100 one-time fee/pet. Service with restrictions, crate. SAVE 🛜 ✖ 📶 🅿 🍴 🏊 ✖

Ⓐ ▼▼▼ Point Loma Inn & Suites Ⓜ
(619) 222-4704. **$39-$129.** 2933 Fenelon St 92106. I-8 exit Nimitz Blvd, 2 mi s, then 0.4 mi sw. Ext corridors. **Pets:** Large, other species. $20 daily fee/pet. Designated rooms, service with restrictions, crate.

SAVE 🛜 📶 🅿

▼▼▼ Porto Vista Hotel Ⓗ 🐾
(619) 544-0164. **Call for rates.** 1835 Columbia St 92101. I-5 exit 17 (Front St) southbound, just w on Cedar St, then just n on State St; exit 17 (Hawthorn St) northbound, just e, then just s. Ext/int corridors. **Pets:** Medium. $75 one-time fee/room. Service with restrictions, crate.

🛜 ✖ 📶 🅿 🍴

▼▼▼ Residence Inn by Marriott-San Diego Central Ⓗ
(858) 278-2100. **$99-$389.** 5400 Kearny Mesa Rd 92111. SR 163 exit 8 (Clairemont Mesa Blvd) just w, then just n. Ext corridors. **Pets:** Accepted.
🛜 ✖ 📶 📶 🅿 🏊 ✖

▼▼▼ Residence Inn by Marriott San Diego Downtown Ⓗ
(619) 338-8200. **$179-$239.** 1747 Pacific Hwy 92101. I-5 exit 17 (Front St) southbound, just s to Cedar St, 0.3 mi w, then just n; exit 17 (Hawthorn St) northbound, 0.4 mi w, then just s. Int corridors. **Pets:** Medium. $100 one-time fee/room. Service with restrictions.

🛜 ✖ 📶 📶 🅿 🏊

▼▼▼ Residence Inn San Diego Downtown Gaslamp Quarter Ⓗ
(619) 487-1200. **$135-$289.** 356 6th Ave 92101. I-5 exit 17 (Front St/Civic Center) southbound, 0.3 mi s, 0.3 mi e on A St, then 0.6 mi s; exit 16B (6th Ave) northbound, 1 mi s. Int corridors. **Pets:** Other species. $100 one-time fee/room. Service with restrictions, crate.

🛜 ✖ 📶 📶 🅿 🏊

▼▼▼ Residence Inn San Diego/Mission Valley/SeaWorld Area Ⓗ
(619) 881-3600. **$169-$289.** 1865 Hotel Cir S 92108. I-8 exit 4A (Hotel Cir), south side. Int corridors. **Pets:** Other species. $100 one-time fee/ room. Designated rooms, service with restrictions, crate.

🛜 ✖ 📶 📶 🅿 🏊 ✖

▼▼▼ Residence Inn San Diego Rancho Bernardo/Scripps Poway Ⓗ
(858) 635-5724. **$171-$238.** 12011 Scripps Highland Dr 92131. I-805 exit 17 (Mercy Rd/Scripps Poway Pkwy), just e, then just n. Int corridors. **Pets:** Accepted. 🛜 ✖ 📶 📶 🅿 🏊 ✖

▼▼▼ Residence Inn San Diego-Sorrento Mesa Ⓗ
(858) 552-9100. **$129-$209.** 5995 Pacific Mesa Ct 92121. I-805 exit 27 (Mira Mesa Blvd), 1.5 mi e, just n on Pacific Heights, then just se. Int corridors. **Pets:** Accepted. 🔽 🛜 📶 📶 🅿 🏊 ✖

▼▼▼ San Diego Marriott Del Mar Ⓗ
(858) 523-1700. **$129-$259.** 11966 El Camino Real 92130. I-5 exit 33 (Carmel Valley Rd), just ne. Int corridors. **Pets:** Medium. $75 one-time fee/room. Service with restrictions, supervision.

🔽 🛜 ✖ 📶 📶 🅿 🍴 🏊

▼▼▼ ▼▼▼ San Diego Marriott Marquis & Marina Ⓗ
(619) 234-1500. **$220-$290.** 333 W Harbor Dr 92101. I-5 exit 17 (Front St) southbound, 1.5 mi s, then just w; exit 16B (6th Ave) northbound, 1.3 mi s, just w on Market St, just s on Front St, then just w. Int corridors. **Pets:** Accepted. 🛜 ✖ 📶 📶 🅿 🍴 🏊 ✖

▼▼▼ San Diego Marriott Mission Valley Ⓗ
(619) 692-3800. **$129-$259.** 8757 Rio San Diego Dr 92108. I-8 exit 6A (Qualcomm Way), just n. Int corridors. **Pets:** Accepted.
🔽 🛜 ✖ 📶 📶 🅿 🍴 🏊 ✖

Ⓐ ▼▼▼ Sheraton Mission Valley, San Diego Hotel Ⓗ
(619) 260-0111. **$99-$299.** 1433 Camino del Rio S 92108. I-8 exit 5 (Mission Center Rd), south side. Int corridors. **Pets:** Medium, dogs only. Service with restrictions, supervision.

SAVE 🛜 ✖ 📶 📶 🅿 🍴 🏊

Ⓐ ▼▼▼ Sheraton San Diego Hotel & Marina Ⓗ
(619) 291-2900. **$119-$469, 3 day notice.** 1380 Harbor Island Dr 92101. I-5 exit 17 (Hawthorn St) northbound, just e to Harbor Dr, 1.5 mi w, then just s; exit 18A (Kettner/Hancock) southbound, just s to Laurel St, just w to Harbor Dr, 1.5 mi w, then just s. Ext/int corridors.
Pets: Accepted. 🔽 SAVE 🛜 ✖ 📶 📶 🅿 🍴 🏊 ✖

Ⓐ ▼▼▼ Sheraton Suites San Diego at Symphony Hall Ⓗ 🐾
(619) 696-9800. **$139-$299.** 701 A St 92101. I-5 exit 16 (10th Ave) southbound, just s to B St, just w, then just n on 7th St; exit 16B (6th Ave) northbound, just s, then just e. Int corridors. **Pets:** Medium, other species. Designated rooms, service with restrictions, supervision.

SAVE 🛜 ✖ 📶 🅿 🍴 🏊

Ⓐ ▼▼▼ The Sofia Hotel Ⓗ 🐾
(619) 234-9200. **$149-$229, 3 day notice.** 150 W Broadway 92101. I-5 exit 17 (Front St) southbound, 0.5 mi s, just w on Broadway; exit 15B (B St) northbound, 1 mi w to 3rd Ave, just s to Broadway, then just w. Int corridors. **Pets:** Other species. $25 daily fee/pet. Designated rooms, supervision. SAVE 🛜 ✖ 📶 📶 🅿 🍴

▼▼▼ Sommerset Suites Hotel Ⓗ
(619) 692-5200. **$119-$329.** 606 Washington St 92103. SR 163 exit 2B (Washington St), just w. Ext/int corridors. **Pets:** Accepted.

🛜 ✖ 📶 🅿 🏊

▼▼▼▼ **Staybridge Suites San Diego-Rancho Bernardo** H
(858) 487-0900. **$119-$169.** 11855 Ave of Industry 92128. I-15 exit 21 (Carmel Mountain Rd), 1 mi ne to second Rancho Carmel Dr, just w to Innovation Dr, just n, then just e. Int corridors. **Pets:** Accepted.
🛜 🕭ᴹ 📶 📲 ⇌ ⊠

▼▼▼▼ **Staybridge Suites-Sorrento Mesa** H
(858) 453-5343. **$169-$199.** 6639 Mira Mesa Blvd 92121. I-805 exit 27 (Mira Mesa Blvd), 2.3 mi e. Int corridors. **Pets:** Other species. $15 daily fee/room. Service with restrictions. 🛜 🕭ᴹ 📶 📲 ⇌

🅐🅐🅐 ▼▼▼▼ ▼▼▼▼ **The US Grant, A Luxury Collection**
Hotel H
(619) 232-3121. **$229-$619, 3 day notice.** 326 Broadway 92101. I-5 exit 17 (Front St) southbound, 0.9 mi s to Broadway, then just e; exit 16B (6th Ave) northbound, 0.6 mi s, then just w. Int corridors. **Pets:** Accepted.
🄴🄲🄾 🆂🅰🆅🅴 🛜 ⊠ 🕭ᴹ 📶 📲 🍴

▼▼ ▼▼ **Vagabond Inn-Point Loma** M
(619) 224-3371. **Call for rates.** 1325 Scott St 92106. I-8 exit Nimitz Blvd, 2 mi s to Rosecrans St, just w to Jarvis St, then just s. Ext corridors. **Pets:** Accepted. 🛜 📶 📲 ⇌

🅐🅐🅐 ▼▼ ▼▼ **Vagabond Inn SeaWorld** M
(619) 297-1691. **$49-$289.** 625 Hotel Cir S 92108. I-8 exit 4A (Hotel Cir), south side. Ext corridors. **Pets:** Large, other species. $20 daily fee/pet. Designated rooms, service with restrictions, crate.
🆂🅰🆅🅴 🛜 📶 📲 ⇌

🅐🅐🅐 ▼▼▼▼ **The Westin Gaslamp Quarter** H 🐾
(619) 239-2200. **$169-$449, 3 day notice.** 910 Broadway Cir 92101. I-5 exit 17 (Front St) southbound, 0.9 mi s to Broadway, just e, then just s; exit 16B (6th Ave) northbound, 0.6 mi s, just w, then just s. Int corridors. **Pets:** Medium, dogs only. Designated rooms, service with restrictions, supervision. 🆂🅰🆅🅴 🛜 ⊠ 🕭ᴹ 📶 📲 🍴 ⇌ ⊠

🅐🅐🅐 ▼▼▼▼ ▼▼▼▼ **The Westin San Diego** H
(619) 239-4500. **$129-$459.** 400 W Broadway 92101. I-5 exit 17 (Front St) southbound, 0.9 mi s, then just w; exit 16B (6th Ave) northbound, 0.6 mi s, just w. Int corridors. **Pets:** Accepted.
🆂🅰🆅🅴 🛜 ⊠ 🕭ᴹ 📶 📲 🍴 ⇌ ⊠

🅐🅐🅐 ▼▼▼▼ **W San Diego** H
(619) 398-3100. **$179-$469, 3 day notice.** 421 W B St 92101. I-5 exit 17 (Front St) southbound, 0.6 mi s, then just w; exit 16B (6th St) northbound, just s, then just w. Int corridors. **Pets:** Accepted.
🆂🅰🆅🅴 🛜 ⊠ 📲 🍴 ⇌

SANTEE

🅐🅐🅐 ▼▼ ▼▼ **Best Western Santee Lodge** M
(619) 449-2626. **$75-$159.** 10726 Woodside Ave 92071. SR 52 exit 14 (Mission Gorge Rd), 2 mi e. Ext corridors. **Pets:** Small. $10 daily fee/room. Service with restrictions, supervision.
🆂🅰🆅🅴 🛜 🕭ᴹ 📶 📲 ⇌

END METROPOLITAN AREA

SAN FRANCISCO METROPOLITAN AREA

BELMONT

🅐🅐🅐 ▼▼▼▼ **Hyatt Summerfield Suites-Belmont/Redwood**
Shores H
(650) 591-8600. **$109-$209.** 400 Concourse Dr 94002. US 101 exit 412 (Ralston Ave/Belmont), just e, then 0.3 mi n on Island Pkwy. Ext corridors. **Pets:** Accepted. 🆂🅰🆅🅴 🛜 ⊠ 🕭ᴹ 📶 📲 ⇌ ⊠

BURLINGAME

▼▼▼▼ **Crowne Plaza** H
(650) 342-9200. **$99-$169, 3 day notice.** 1177 Airport Blvd 94010. US 101 exit Broadway-Burlingame or Old Bayshore Hwy, just e. Int corridors. **Pets:** Accepted. 🛜 🕭ᴹ 📶 📲 🍴 ⇌

🅐🅐🅐 ▼▼▼▼ **DoubleTree by Hilton Hotel San Francisco**
Airport H
(650) 344-5500. **$89-$189.** 835 Airport Blvd 94010. US 101 exit Broadway-Burlingame or Anza Blvd, just e. Int corridors. **Pets:** Accepted.
🄴🄲🄾 🆂🅰🆅🅴 🛜 🕭ᴹ 📶 📲 🍴

▼▼▼▼ **Embassy Suites-San Francisco**
Airport-Burlingame H
(650) 342-4600. **$89-$189.** 150 Anza Blvd 94010. US 101 exit Broadway-Burlingame, just e. Int corridors. **Pets:** Other species. $50 one-time fee/pet. Service with restrictions, supervision.
🄴🄲🄾 🛜 🕭ᴹ 📶 📲 🍴 ⇌ ⊠

🅐🅐🅐 ▼▼▼▼ **Hilton San Francisco Airport** H 🐾
(650) 340-8500. **$99-$309.** 600 Airport Blvd 94010. US 101 exit Broadway-Burlingame or Anza Blvd, 0.3 mi e. Int corridors. **Pets:** Medium. $50 one-time fee/room. Service with restrictions, supervision. 🆂🅰🆅🅴 🛜 🕭ᴹ 📶 📲 🍴 ⇌

🅐🅐🅐 ▼▼ ▼▼ **Red Roof Inn** M
(650) 342-7772. **$60-$140.** 777 Airport Blvd 94010. US 101 exit Broadway-Burlingame or E Anza Blvd; just s of airport. Ext corridors. **Pets:** Large, other species. No service, supervision.
🆂🅰🆅🅴 🛜 🕭ᴹ 📶 🍴 ⇌

▼▼▼▼ **San Francisco Airport Marriott Waterfront** H
(650) 692-9100. **$139-$349.** 1800 Old Bayshore Hwy 94010. US 101 exit Millbrae Ave, just e. Int corridors. **Pets:** Medium, other species. $75 one-time fee/room. 🄴🄲🄾 🛜 ⊠ 🕭ᴹ 📶 📲 🍴 ⇌ ⊠

CORTE MADERA

🅐🅐🅐 ▼▼▼▼ **Marin Suites Hotel** H 🐾
(415) 924-3608. **$109-$209.** 45 Tamal Vista Blvd 94925. US 101 exit Lucky Dr southbound, just w on Fifer Ave, 0.4 mi s; exit Tamalpais Rd/Paradise Dr northbound, 0.5 mi n on Madera Blvd (which becomes Tamal Vista Blvd). Ext corridors. **Pets:** $20 daily fee/pet. Designated rooms, service with restrictions, supervision.
🆂🅰🆅🅴 🛜 ⊠ 🕭ᴹ 📶 📲 ⇌ ⊠ 🐾

HALF MOON BAY

🅐🅐🅐 ▼▼▼▼ **Best Western Plus Half Moon Bay**
Lodge H 🐾
(650) 726-9000. **$129-$249.** 2400 Cabrillo Hwy S 94019. 2.5 mi s of jct SR 92 and 1, just w. Ext corridors. **Pets:** Small, dogs only. $20 daily fee/pet. Designated rooms, service with restrictions, supervision.
🆂🅰🆅🅴 🛜 ⊠ 🕭ᴹ 📶 📲 ⇌ ⊠ 🐾

🅐🅐🅐 ▼▼▼▼ **Coastside Inn Half Moon Bay** H
(650) 726-3400. **$98-$239.** 230 S Cabrillo Hwy 94019. On SR 1, just s of SR 92. Ext corridors. **Pets:** Other species. $15 daily fee/pet. Designated rooms, service with restrictions, supervision.
🄴🄲🄾 🆂🅰🆅🅴 🛜 ⊠ 🕭ᴹ 📶 📲

🅐🅐🅐 ▼▼▼▼ **Comfort Inn Half Moon Bay** H 🐾
(650) 712-1999. **$105-$300.** 2930 Cabrillo Hwy N 94019. On SR 1, 2 mi n of jct SR 92 and 1. Ext corridors. **Pets:** Medium. $10 daily fee/pet. Designated rooms, service with restrictions, supervision.
🆂🅰🆅🅴 🛜 ⊠ 🕭ᴹ 📶 📲

🅐🅐🅐 ▼▼ ▼▼ **Harbor View Inn** M
(650) 726-2329. **$69-$249.** 51 Ave Alhambra 94018. SR 1 exit Capistrano Ave, just e; 4 mi n of jct SR 92. Ext corridors. **Pets:** Accepted.
🆂🅰🆅🅴 🛜 ⊠ 🕭ᴹ 📶 📲 🐾

Landis Shores Oceanfront Inn BB
(650) 726-6642. **$225-$345, 7 day notice.** 211 Mirada Rd 94019. 3 mi n of jct SR 92 and 1 exit SR 1 W at Medio Ave, just n. Int corridors. **Pets:** Medium, dogs only. $30 daily fee/pet. Designated rooms, service with restrictions, supervision.

The Ritz-Carlton, Half Moon Bay H
(650) 712-7000. **$320-$3200.** 1 Miramontes Point Rd 94019. 3 mi s of jct SR 92 and 1; w of SR 1 at Miramontes Point Rd. Ext/int corridors. **Pets:** Accepted.

Seal Cove Inn BB ❀
(650) 728-4114. **$245-$375, 7 day notice.** 221 Cypress Ave 94038. 6 mi n of jct SR 92 and 1; w of SR 1. Int corridors. **Pets:** Medium, dogs only. $65 one-time fee/room. Designated rooms, service with restrictions, supervision.

MILLBRAE

The Westin San Francisco Airport H ❀
(650) 692-3500. **$99-$409.** 1 Old Bayshore Hwy 94030. Just e of US 101 exit Millbrae Ave. Int corridors. **Pets:** Medium, dogs only. Service with restrictions, supervision.

MILL VALLEY

Acqua Hotel, a Joie de Vivre hotel H ❀
(415) 380-0400. **$129-$279.** 555 Redwood Hwy 94941. US 101 exit Seminary Dr. Ext/int corridors. **Pets:** Designated rooms, no service, supervision.

SAN BRUNO

Staybridge Suites H
(650) 588-0770. **$119-$309.** 1350 Huntington Ave 94066. I-380 exit El Camino Real N, e on Sneath Ln, then just n. Ext corridors. **Pets:** Large, other species. $15 daily fee/room.

SAN FRANCISCO

Argonaut Hotel H
(415) 563-0800. **$199-$719.** 495 Jefferson St 94109. Fisherman's Wharf; adjacent to The Cannery. Int corridors. **Pets:** Accepted.

Beresford Arms Hotel & Suites H ❀
(415) 673-2600. **$89-$209.** 701 Post St 94109. 3 blks w of Union Square; at Jones St. Int corridors. **Pets:** Medium, other species. $25 one-time fee/pet. Designated rooms, service with restrictions, supervision.

Beresford Hotel H ❀
(415) 673-9900. **$79-$139.** 635 Sutter St 94102. 1 blk nw of Union Square at Mason St. Int corridors. **Pets:** Medium, other species. $25 one-time fee/pet. Designated rooms, service with restrictions, supervision.

Best Western Plus Americania H
(415) 626-0200. **$109-$199.** 121 7th St 94103. Just s of Market St; between Minna and Natoma sts. Ext corridors. **Pets:** Accepted.

Best Western Plus Tuscan Inn at Fisherman's Wharf H
(415) 561-1100. **$199-$349.** 425 Northpoint St 94133. Just s of Fisherman's Wharf at Mason St. Int corridors. **Pets:** Accepted.

Best Western The Hotel California H
(415) 441-2700. **Call for rates.** 580 Geary St 94102. 0.3 mi w of Union Square at Jones St. Int corridors. **Pets:** Accepted.

Executive Hotel Vintage Court H
(415) 392-4666. **$219-$349.** 650 Bush St 94108. Between Powell and Stockton sts; 2 blks n of Union Square. Int corridors. **Pets:** Accepted.

The Fairmont San Francisco H
(415) 772-5000. **$199-$999.** 950 Mason St (atop Nob Hill) 94108. Atop Nob Hill at California St. Int corridors. **Pets:** Accepted.

Four Seasons Hotel San Francisco H ❀
(415) 633-3000. **$445-$595, 3 day notice.** 757 Market St 94103. Between 3rd and 4th sts. Int corridors. **Pets:** Small, other species. Service with restrictions, crate.

Galleria Park Hotel, a Joie de Vivre hotel H
(415) 781-3060. **Call for rates.** 191 Sutter St 94104. 2 blks ne of Union Square; between Kearny and Trinity sts. Int corridors. **Pets:** Accepted.

Good Hotel, a Haiyi Hotel H
(415) 621-7001. **$99-$199.** 112 7th St 94103. Just s of Market St; at Mission St. Int corridors. **Pets:** Accepted.

Grand Hyatt San Francisco H
(415) 398-1234. **$139-$439.** 345 Stockton St 94108. On Union Square at Sutter St. Int corridors. **Pets:** Accepted.

The Handlery Union Square Hotel H
(415) 781-7800. **$169-$329.** 351 Geary St 94102. Between Powell and Mason sts; just sw of Union Square. Int corridors. **Pets:** Small, dogs only. $20 daily fee/room. Service with restrictions, supervision.

Harbor Court Hotel H ❀
(415) 882-1300. **$209-$359.** 165 Steuart St 94105. On Embarcadero; between Howard and Mission sts. Int corridors. **Pets:** Other species. Designated rooms, service with restrictions, supervision.

Hilton San Francisco Financial District H
(415) 433-6600. **$109-$455.** 750 Kearny St 94108. Between Clay and Washington sts. Int corridors. **Pets:** Accepted.

Hilton San Francisco Union Square H
(415) 771-1400. **Call for rates.** 333 O'Farrell St 94102. Just w of Union Square at Mason St. Int corridors. **Pets:** Accepted.

Holiday Inn Civic Center H
(415) 626-6103. **$109-$339.** 50 8th St 94103. Between Market and Mission sts. Int corridors. **Pets:** Small. $75 one-time fee/room. Designated rooms, service with restrictions, supervision.

Holiday Inn Fisherman's Wharf H
(415) 771-9000. **$119-$325.** 1300 Columbus Ave 94133. Jct North Point St. Int corridors. **Pets:** Medium. $85 one-time fee/room. Designated rooms, no service, supervision.

Holiday Inn Golden Gateway H
(415) 441-4000. **$119-$259.** 1500 Van Ness Ave 94109. US 101 (Van Ness Ave) at Pine St. Int corridors. **Pets:** Accepted.

Hotel Carlton, a Joie de Vivre hotel H
(415) 673-0242. **Call for rates.** 1075 Sutter St 94109. 0.5 mi w of Union Square; between Hyde and Larkin sts. Int corridors. **Pets:** Accepted.

Hotel Del Sol, a Joie de Vivre hotel
(415) 921-5520. **$109-$269.** 3100 Webster St 94123. Just s of Lombard St at Greenwich St. Ext corridors. **Pets:** Dogs only. Service with restrictions, supervision.

Hotel Diva
(415) 885-0200. **$129-$369.** 440 Geary St 94102. Between Taylor and Mason sts; on Theater Row. Int corridors. **Pets:** Medium, dogs only. $25 one-time fee/pet. Service with restrictions, crate.

Hotel Frank
(415) 986-2000. **$109-$399.** 386 Geary St 94102. Just w of Union Square at Mason St. Int corridors. **Pets:** Medium, dogs only. $25 one-time fee/pet. Supervision.

Hotel Kabuki, a Joie de Vivre hotel
(415) 922-3200. **Call for rates.** 1625 Post St 94115. Jct Laguna St; in Japan Center. Int corridors. **Pets:** Accepted.

Hotel Monaco
(415) 292-0100. **$189-$459.** 501 Geary St 94102. Just w of Union Square at Taylor St. Int corridors. **Pets:** Accepted.

Hotel Nikko San Francisco
(415) 394-1111. **Call for rates.** 222 Mason St 94102. At O'Farrell St. Int corridors. **Pets:** Accepted.

Hotel Palomar
(415) 348-1111. **Call for rates.** 12 4th St 94103. At Market St. Int corridors. **Pets:** Accepted.

Hotel Triton
(415) 394-0500. **Call for rates.** 342 Grant Ave 94108. Near Union Square at Bush St. Int corridors. **Pets:** Accepted.

Hotel Union Square
(415) 397-3000. **$129-$369.** 114 Powell St 94102. At Ellis St; just n of cable car turnaround. Int corridors. **Pets:** Small, dogs only. $25 one-time fee/pet. Service with restrictions, crate.

Hotel Vertigo
(415) 885-6800. **$119-$309.** 940 Sutter St 94109. Between Leavenworth and Hyde sts. Int corridors. **Pets:** Medium, other species. $25 one-time fee/pet. Service with restrictions, supervision.

Hotel Vitale, a Joie de Vivre hotel
(415) 278-3700. **$399-$2000.** 8 Mission St 94105. At Embarcadero. Int corridors. **Pets:** Medium, dogs only. Designated rooms, service with restrictions, crate.

InterContinental Mark Hopkins San Francisco
(415) 392-3434. **$179-$359.** One Nob Hill 94108. Corner of California and Mason sts. Int corridors. **Pets:** Small. $50 daily fee/pet. Service with restrictions, supervision.

InterContinental San Francisco
(415) 616-6500. **$159-$489.** 888 Howard St 94103. Between 4th and 5th sts; in SoMa District. Int corridors. **Pets:** Medium, other species. $50 daily fee/room. Designated rooms, service with restrictions, supervision.

JW Marriott San Francisco
(415) 771-8600. **$249-$399.** 500 Post St 94102. Just w of Union Square at Mason St. Int corridors. **Pets:** Accepted.

Kensington Park Hotel
(415) 788-6400. **Call for rates.** 450 Post St 94102. Just w of Union Square. Int corridors. **Pets:** Medium, dogs only. $25 one-time fee/pet. Service with restrictions, supervision.

Laurel Inn, a Joie de Vivre hotel
(415) 567-8467. **$159-$329.** 444 Presidio Ave 94115. 1 mi w of US 101 (Van Ness Ave); 1 mi e of Park Presidio Blvd (SR 1); at California St. Int corridors. **Pets:** Large, other species. Service with restrictions, supervision.

Le Meridien San Francisco
(415) 296-2900. **$179-$549.** 333 Battery St 94111. At Clay St; in Financial District. Int corridors. **Pets:** Medium. Service with restrictions, supervision.

Mandarin Oriental, San Francisco
(415) 276-9888. **$445-$4200.** 222 Sansome St 94104. Between Pine and California sts; in Financial District. Int corridors. **Pets:** Small, dogs only. $25 daily fee/pet. Service with restrictions, supervision.

Marina Motel
(415) 921-9406. **Call for rates.** 2576 Lombard St 94123. Between Broderick and Divisadero sts. Int corridors. **Pets:** Dogs only. $10 daily fee/pet. Designated rooms, service with restrictions, crate.

Motel Capri
(415) 346-4667. **$80-$170.** 2015 Greenwich St 94123. Just s of US 101 (Lombard St) at Buchanan St. Ext corridors. **Pets:** Accepted.

Omni San Francisco Hotel
(415) 677-9494. **$189-$699.** 500 California St 94104. At Montgomery St; in Financial District. Int corridors. **Pets:** Medium. $50 one-time fee/room. Designated rooms, service with restrictions, supervision.

Palace Hotel
(415) 512-1111. **$179-$619.** 2 New Montgomery St 94105. Just e of Union Square; at Market St. Int corridors. **Pets:** Medium, other species. $100 one-time fee/room. Service with restrictions, supervision.

Parc 55 Wyndham San Francisco Union Square
(415) 392-8000. **$159-$379, 3 day notice.** 55 Cyril Magnin St 94102. Corner of Cyril Magnin and Eddy sts; just sw of Union Square. Int corridors. **Pets:** Medium. $50 one-time fee/pet. No service, supervision.

The Powell Hotel
(415) 398-3200. **$250-$300.** 28 Cyril Magnin St 94102. At Powell St cable car turnaround. Int corridors. **Pets:** Accepted.

The Prescott Hotel
(415) 563-0303. **Call for rates.** 545 Post St 94102. Just w of Union Square. Int corridors. **Pets:** Accepted.

Radisson Hotel Fisherman's Wharf
(415) 392-6700. **$119-$409.** 250 Beach St 94133. At Powell St. Int corridors. **Pets:** Medium. $75 one-time fee/pet. Service with restrictions, supervision.

The Ritz-Carlton, San Francisco
(415) 296-7465. **Call for rates.** 600 Stockton St 94108. Just n of Union Square at California St. Int corridors. **Pets:** Accepted.

AAA ▼▼▼▼ St. Regis Hotel San Francisco H
(415) 284-4000. **$329-$649.** 125 3rd St 94103. At Mission St. Int corridors. **Pets:** Accepted. SAVE 🛜 ✕ ♿M ▯ ➖ ✕

AAA ▼▼▼ San Francisco Marriott Fisherman's Wharf H
(415) 775-7555. **$143-$369.** 1250 Columbus Ave 94133. Just s of Fisherman's Wharf at Bay St. Int corridors. **Pets:** Accepted.
SAVE 🛜 ✕ ♿M ▯ ▯ ▯

AAA ▼▼▼ Serrano Hotel H ❖
(415) 885-2500. **Call for rates.** 405 Taylor St 94102. Just w of Union Square at O'Farrell St. Int corridors. **Pets:** Other species. Service with restrictions, supervision. ECO SAVE 🛜 ✕ ♿M ✕

AAA ▼▼▼ Sheraton Fisherman's Wharf H
(415) 362-5500. **$109-$419.** 2500 Mason St 94133. Just se of Fisherman's Wharf at Beach St. Int corridors. **Pets:** Medium, dogs only. Service with restrictions, supervision.
ECO SAVE 🛜 ✕ ♿M ▯ ▯ ▯ ➖

AAA ▼▼▼ Sir Francis Drake Hotel H
(415) 392-7755. **$129-$449.** 450 Powell St 94102. Just n of Union Square at Sutter St. Int corridors. **Pets:** Accepted.
ECO SAVE 🛜 ♿M ▯

AAA ▼▼▼ The Stanford Court, A Renaissance Hotel H
(415) 989-3500. **$180-$218.** 905 California St 94108. Atop Nob Hill; corner of California and Powell sts. Int corridors. **Pets:** Accepted.
ECO SAVE 🛜 ✕ ♿M ▯ ▯ ▯

▼▼▼▼ Taj Campton Place San Francisco H ❖
(415) 781-5555. **Call for rates.** 340 Stockton St 94108. Just n of Union Square; jct Sutter St. Int corridors. **Pets:** Dogs only. $100 one-time fee/room. Crate. ECO 🛜 ♿M ▯

▼▼ Travelodge at the Presidio M ❖
(415) 931-8581. **$89-$143.** 2755 Lombard St 94123. Between Lyon and Baker sts. Ext corridors. **Pets:** Medium. $20 daily fee/pet. Service with restrictions, supervision. 🛜 ✕ ▯ ▯

▼▼ Travelodge By The Bay M ❖
(415) 673-0691. **$67-$157.** 1450 Lombard St 94123. On US 101 (Lombard St); between Van Ness Ave and Franklin St. Ext/int corridors. **Pets:** Medium, dogs only. $20 daily fee/pet. Designated rooms, service with restrictions, crate. SAVE 🛜 ✕ ♿M ▯ ▯

AAA ▼▼▼ The Westin St. Francis San Francisco on Union Square H
(415) 397-7000. **$199-$599, 3 day notice.** 335 Powell St 94102. On Union Square. Int corridors. **Pets:** Accepted.
SAVE 🛜 ✕ ♿M ▯ ▯ ▯ ✕

AAA ▼▼▼▼ Westin San Francisco Market Street H ❖
(415) 974-6400. **$159-$589.** 50 3rd St 94103. Just n of Moscone Convention Center; between Jessie and Stevenson sts. Int corridors. **Pets:** Medium, dogs only. Service with restrictions, supervision.
SAVE 🛜 ✕ ♿M ▯ ▯

AAA ▼▼▼ The Wharf Inn M
(415) 673-7411. **$119-$225.** 2601 Mason St 94133. At Beach St; adjacent to Fisherman's Wharf and San Francisco Bay. Ext corridors.
Pets: Accepted. SAVE 🛜 ✕ ♿M ▯

AAA ▼▼▼ W San Francisco H ❖
(415) 777-5300. **$249-$669.** 181 3rd St 94103. At Howard St. Int corridors. **Pets:** Medium. $100 one-time fee/room. Designated rooms, service with restrictions, crate. ECO SAVE 🛜 ✕ ♿M ▯ ▯ ➖ ✕

SAN MATEO

▼▼ Comfort Inn H
(650) 344-6376. **$100-$170.** 350 N Bayshore Blvd 94401. US 101 exit Dore Ave northbound; exit 3rd Ave E southbound, re-enter US 101 exit Dore Ave. Ext/int corridors. **Pets:** Medium. $35 one-time fee/pet. Service with restrictions, supervision. 🛜 ♿M ▯ ▯

▼▼▼ Residence Inn by Marriott H
(650) 574-4700. **$113-$218.** 2000 Winward Way 94404. US 101 exit 414B (SR 92/E Hayward/Fashion Island) to Mariners Island exit, then just e. Ext corridors. **Pets:** Accepted. 🛜 ✕ ♿M ▯ ▯ ➖ ✕

SAN RAFAEL

▼▼ Gerstle Park Inn BB
(415) 721-7611. **$189-$275, 3 day notice.** 34 Grove St 94901. US 101 exit Central San Rafael, 0.5 mi w on 4th St, 0.5 mi s on D St, then just w on San Rafael Ave. Ext/int corridors. **Pets:** Accepted. 🛜 ✕ ♿M

SOUTH SAN FRANCISCO

▼▼▼ Embassy Suites San Francisco Airport-South San Francisco H ❖
(650) 589-3400. **$134-$229.** 250 Gateway Blvd 94080. US 101 exit 425A (Grand Ave), just e. Int corridors. **Pets:** Medium. $50 one-time fee/room. Designated rooms, service with restrictions.
ECO 🛜 ♿M ▯ ▯ ▯ ➖

▼▼▼ Residence Inn by Marriott at Oyster Point H ❖
(650) 837-9000. **$140-$349.** 1350 Veterans Blvd 94080. US 101 exit 425B (Oyster Point Blvd), just ne. Int corridors. **Pets:** Other species. $110 one-time fee/room. Service with restrictions.
ECO 🛜 ✕ ♿M ▯ ▯ ▯ ➖ ✕

END METROPOLITAN AREA

SANGER

▼▼▼ Blossom Trail Bed & Breakfast BB
(559) 875-6036. **Call for rates.** 3700 S Newmark Ave 93657. SR 180, 3.5 mi s on Reed Ave, 5 mi w on Goodfellow Ave to Newmark Ave, then just n. Ext/int corridors. **Pets:** Accepted. 🛜 ✕ ▯ ▯

▼▼ Wonder Valley Ranch Resort H
(559) 787-2551. **$149-$278.** 6450 Elwood Rd 93657. SR 180, 5 mi n on Piedra Rd, 3 mi e. Ext corridors. **Pets:** Small, dogs only. $25 daily fee/pet. Designated rooms, supervision. 🛜 ♿M ▯ ▯ ➖ ✕

SAN JOSE

▼▼▼ Crowne Plaza San Jose - Downtown H
(408) 998-0400. **Call for rates.** 282 Almaden Blvd 95113. I-280 exit Almaden-Vine, 6 blks n. Int corridors. **Pets:** Accepted.
🛜 ✕ ♿M ▯ ▯ ▯

AAA ▼▼▼▼ DoubleTree by Hilton Hotel San Jose H ❖
(408) 453-4000. **$99-$299.** 2050 Gateway Pl 95110. 0.3 mi e of Norman Y. Mineta San Jose International Airport via Airport Blvd; w of US 101 exit N 1st St; US 101 exit Brokaw Rd northbound. Int corridors. **Pets:** Other species. $50 one-time fee/room. Service with restrictions.
ECO SAVE 🛜 ✕ ♿M ▯ ▯ ▯ ➖

▼▼▼▼ Extended Stay Deluxe-San Jose-Downtown H ❀

(408) 453-3000. **$134-$149.** 55 E Brokaw Rd 95112. US 101 exit 1st St/Brokaw Rd, just e. Int corridors. **Pets:** Other species. $25 daily fee/pet. Service with restrictions. 🛜 ⓜ 🗄 💻 ≋

▼▼▼▼ Fairfield Inn & Suites H

(408) 453-3133. **$122-$139.** 1755 N 1st St 95112. US 101 exit N 1st St, just w. Int corridors. **Pets:** Accepted.
SAVE 🛜 ✕ ⓜ 🗄 💻 ≋

▼▼▼▼ The Fairmont San Jose H

(408) 998-1900. **$129-$429.** 170 S Market St 95113. At Fairmont Plaza. Int corridors. **Pets:** Accepted.
ECO SAVE 🛜 ✕ ⓜ 💻 🍴 ≋ ✕

▼▼▼▼ Hilton San Jose H

(408) 287-2100. **$99-$329.** 300 Almaden Blvd 95110. SR 87 exit Santa Clara St E, 0.4 mi s; at W San Carlos St. Int corridors. **Pets:** Accepted.
SAVE 🛜 ✕ ⓜ 🗄 💻 🍴 ≋

▼▼ Homestead Studio Suites Hotel-San Jose-Downtown H 🐾

(408) 573-0648. **$89-$104.** 1560 N 1st St 95112. 1 mi e of Norman Y. Mineta San Jose International Airport; US 101 exit N 1st St, then s. Int corridors. **Pets:** Other species. $25 daily fee/pet. Service with restrictions.
🛜 ⓜ 🗄 💻

▼▼▼▼ Homewood Suites by Hilton H

(408) 428-9900. **$115-$249.** 10 W Trimble Rd 95131. US 101 exit Trimble Rd, 1.3 mi e; 2 mi ne of Norman Y. Mineta San Jose International Airport. Ext/int corridors. **Pets:** Accepted.
🛜 ⓜ 🗄 💻 ≋ ✕

▼▼▼▼ Hotel De Anza H 🐾

(408) 286-1000. **$129-$399.** 233 W Santa Clara St 95113. SR 87 exit Santa Clara St, just e. Int corridors. **Pets:** Small. $50 one-time fee/room. Designated rooms, service with restrictions, crate.
SAVE 🛜 ✕ ⓜ 💻 🍴

▼▼▼ Hotel Elan M

(408) 280-5300. **$84-$225.** 1215 S 1st St 95110. Jct I-280 and SR 82, 0.8 mi s. Ext corridors. **Pets:** Medium, other species. $50 deposit/room, $10 one-time fee/pet, $10 daily fee/pet. Service with restrictions.
SAVE 🛜 ⓜ 🗄 💻

▼▼▼▼ La Quinta Inn San Jose Airport H

(408) 435-8800. **$72-$148, 7 day notice.** 2585 Seaboard Ave 95131. US 101 exit Trimble Rd E; 1 mi ne of Norman Y. Mineta San Jose International Airport. Int corridors. **Pets:** Medium, other species. Service with restrictions, supervision. SAVE 🛜 ⓜ 🗄 🗄 💻 ≋

▼▼▼ Residence Inn by Marriott H

(408) 226-7676. **Call for rates.** 6111 San Ignacio Ave 95119. US 101 exit Bernal Rd W, just n. Int corridors. **Pets:** Accepted.
🛜 ✕ ⓜ 🗄 💻 ≋ ✕

▼▼▼▼ San Jose Airport Garden Hotel H

(408) 793-3300. **$89-$209.** 1740 N 1st St 95112. W of US 101 exit N 1st St; 0.5 mi e of Norman Y. Mineta San Jose International Airport via Airport Pkwy. Int corridors. **Pets:** Small, dogs only. $50 one-time fee/room. Service with restrictions, supervision.
SAVE 🛜 ✕ ⓜ 🗄 💻 🍴 ≋ ✕

▼▼▼▼ San Jose Marriott H 🐾

(408) 280-1300. **$116-$227.** 301 S Market St 95113. SR 87 exit Santa Clara St E, s on Almaden Blvd, then just e on San Carlos St. Int corridors. **Pets:** Medium. $75 one-time fee/room. Designated rooms, service with restrictions, supervision.
ECO SAVE 🛜 ✕ ⓜ 🗄 💻 🍴 ≋

▼▼▼ Staybridge Suites San Jose H 🐾

(408) 436-1600. **$129-$225.** 1602 Crane Ct 95112. US 101 exit 1st St/Brokaw Rd, 0.4 mi e to Bering Dr, then 0.5 mi s. Ext corridors. **Pets:** Medium. $20 daily fee/room. Service with restrictions, supervision.
🛜 ⓜ 🗄 💻 ≋

▼▼▼▼ Holiday Inn Silicon Valley South H

(408) 972-7800. **$89-$144.** 399 Silicon Valley Blvd 95138. US 101 exit Bernal Rd, just e. Int corridors. **Pets:** Accepted.
🛜 ⓜ 🗄 💻 🍴 ≋

▼▼▼▼ TownePlace Suites by Marriott San Jose/Cupertino H

(408) 984-5903. **$85-$199.** 440 Saratoga Ave 95129. I-280 exit Saratoga Ave, just n. Int corridors. **Pets:** Accepted. 🛜 ✕ ⓜ 🗄 💻 ≋

SAN JUAN BAUTISTA

▼▼▼ San Juan Inn M

(831) 623-4380. **$69-$99.** 410 The Alameda 95045. Jct SR 156. Ext corridors. **Pets:** Medium. $10 daily fee/pet. Designated rooms, service with restrictions. SAVE 🛜 ⓜ 🗄 💻 ≋

SAN JUAN CAPISTRANO

▼▼▼▼ Best Western Capistrano Inn M

(949) 493-5661. **$90-$150.** 27174 Ortega Hwy 92675. I-5 exit 82 (SR 74/Ortega Hwy), just e. Ext corridors. **Pets:** Other species. $20 daily fee/room. Service with restrictions. SAVE 🛜 🗄 💻 ≋

SAN LUIS OBISPO

▼▼▼ Best Western Plus Royal Oak Hotel M

(805) 544-4410. **$99-$259.** 214 Madonna Rd 93405. US 101 exit 201 (Madonna Rd), just s. Ext/int corridors. **Pets:** Accepted.
SAVE 🛜 ⓜ 🗄 💻 ≋

▼▼▼ Donnington-Days Inn San Luis Obispo H 🐾

(805) 549-9911. **$67-$359.** 2050 Garfield St 93401. US 101 exit 204 (Monterey St), just sw. Ext corridors. **Pets:** Dogs only. $15 daily fee/pet. Designated rooms, service with restrictions, crate.
SAVE 🛜 ✕ ⓜ 🗄 💻 ≋

▼▼▼ Embassy Suites Hotel H

(805) 549-0800. **$119-$319.** 333 Madonna Rd 93405. US 101 exit 201 (Madonna Rd), 0.5 mi sw. Int corridors. **Pets:** Small, dogs only. $10 daily fee/pet. Designated rooms, no service, supervision.
🛜 ⓜ 🗄 💻 🍴 ≋ ✕

▼▼▼ Heritage Inn Bed & Breakfast BB 🐾

(805) 544-7440. **$65-$165, 7 day notice.** 978 Olive St 93405. US 101 exit 203B (SR 1/Morro Bay) northbound, just w on Santa Rosa St, then just s; exit 203A (Santa Rosa St) southbound, just ne. Int corridors. **Pets:** Medium, other species. $100 deposit/room, $35 one-time fee/room. Designated rooms, service with restrictions, supervision.
🛜 ✕ Ⓚ Ⓦ ☎

▼▼▼▼ Holiday Inn Express H

(805) 544-8600. **$119-$259.** 1800 Monterey St 93401. US 101 exit 204 (Monterey St), just w. Int corridors. **Pets:** Accepted.
🛜 ✕ ⓜ 🗄 💻 ≋

▼▼▼▼ Petit Soleil Bed & Breakfast BB

(805) 549-0321. **$159-$309, 3 day notice.** 1473 Monterey St 93401. US 101 exit 204 (Monterey St), 0.3 mi sw. Ext corridors. **Pets:** Accepted.
🛜 ✕ 🗄 Ⓚ

▼▼▼ Ramada Inn Olive Tree M

(805) 544-2800. **$49-$219.** 1000 Olive St 93405. US 101 exit 203B (Morro Bay) northbound, just w on Santa Rosa St, then just s; exit 203A (Santa Rosa St) southbound, just ne. Ext corridors. **Pets:** Accepted.
SAVE 🛜 ✕ ⓜ 🗄 💻 ≋

▼▼▼ Sands Inn & Suites M

(805) 544-0500. **$79-$249.** 1930 Monterey St 93401. US 101 exit 204 (Monterey St), just sw. Ext corridors. **Pets:** Other species. $25 one-time fee/room. Service with restrictions, supervision.
SAVE 🛜 ✕ ⓜ 🗄 💻 ≋

 Super 8 M

(805) 544-6888. **$53-$161.** 1951 Monterey St 93401. US 101 exit 204 (Monterey St), just e. Ext corridors. **Pets:** Accepted.

SAN MARCOS

Residence Inn by Marriott San Diego North/San Marcos ⛨ ✿

(760) 591-9828. **$125-$209.** 1245 Los Vallecitos Blvd 92069. SR 78 exit Las Posas Rd, just ne. Int corridors. **Pets:** Small. $100 one-time fee/room. Service with restrictions, supervision.

SAN RAMON

Homestead Studio Suites Hotel-San Ramon-Bishop Ranch ⛨ ✿

(925) 277-0833. **$94-$109.** 18000 San Ramon Valley Blvd 94583. I-680 exit Bollinger Canyon Rd E, just n. Ext corridors. **Pets:** Other species. $25 daily fee/pet. Service with restrictions.

Residence Inn by Marriott ⛨

(925) 277-9292. **$104-$229.** 1071 Market Pl 94583. I-680 exit Bollinger Canyon Rd E, 0.5 mi e. Ext corridors. **Pets:** Large. $100 one-time fee/room. Service with restrictions, crate.

San Ramon Marriott at Bishop Ranch ⛨

(925) 867-9200. **$94-$239.** 2600 Bishop Dr 94583. I-680 exit Bollinger Canyon Rd E, n on Sunset, then just w. Int corridors. **Pets:** Accepted.

SAN SIMEON

Best Western Plus Cavalier Oceanfront Resort ⛨

(805) 927-4688. **$99-$319, 3 day notice.** 9415 Hearst Dr 93452. Just w of SR 1. Ext corridors. **Pets:** Accepted.

Courtesy Inn M

(805) 927-4691. **$69-$109, 7 day notice.** 9450 Castillo Dr 93452. Just e of SR 1. Ext corridors. **Pets:** Dogs only. $25 daily fee/pet. Designated rooms, service with restrictions, supervision.

The Morgan San Simeon ⛨

(805) 927-3878. **$99-$309.** 9135 Hearst Dr 93452. Just w of SR 1. Int corridors. **Pets:** Accepted.

Sands by the Sea M

(805) 927-3243. **$69-$119, 3 day notice.** 9355 Hearst Dr 93452. Just w of SR 1. Ext corridors. **Pets:** Accepted.

San Simeon Lodge ⛨ ✿

(805) 927-4601. **$50-$240, 3 day notice.** 9520 Castillo Dr 93452. On SR 1. Ext corridors. **Pets:** Small, dogs only. $10 daily fee/pet. Designated rooms, service with restrictions, supervision.

Silver Surf Motel M

(805) 927-4661. **$59-$189.** 9390 Castillo Dr 93452. Just e of SR 1. Ext corridors. **Pets:** Medium. $15 daily fee/pet. Designated rooms, service with restrictions, supervision.

SANTA ANA

Embassy Suites/Santa Ana Orange County ⛨

(714) 241-3800. **$119-$209.** 1325 E Dyer Rd 92705. SR 55 exit 8 (Dyer Rd) northbound; exit 8B (Dyer Rd W) southbound, just w. Int corridors. **Pets:** Accepted.

La Quinta Inn & Suites Orange County - Santa Ana M

(714) 540-1111. **$94-$155.** 2721 Hotel Terrace Dr 92705. SR 55 exit 8 (Dyer Rd) northbound; exit 8B (Dyer Rd W) southbound, just w, then just s. Ext corridors. **Pets:** Medium, other species. Service with restrictions, supervision.

Red Roof Inn M

(714) 542-0311. **$59-$100.** 2600 N Main St 92701. I-5 exit 105B (Main St), 0.3 mi n. Ext/int corridors. **Pets:** Large, other species. No service, supervision.

SANTA BARBARA

Best Western Beachside Inn M

(805) 965-6556. **$109-$399.** 336 W Cabrillo Blvd 93101. US 101 exit 96 (Garden St) northbound, just w; exit 97 (Castillo St/Harbor) southbound, 0.3 mi w to Cabrillo Blvd, then 0.5 mi n; corner of Cabrillo Blvd and Castillo St. Ext corridors. **Pets:** Medium, dogs only. $20 daily fee/pet. Designated rooms, service with restrictions, supervision.

Blue Sands Motel M

(805) 965-1624. **$95-$275, 3 day notice.** 421 S Milpas St 93103. US 101 exit 96A (Milpas St), 0.3 mi s. Ext corridors. **Pets:** Dogs only. $15 daily fee/pet. Service with restrictions.

Extended StayAmerica Santa Barbara-Calle Real ⛨ ✿

(805) 692-1882. **$125-$140.** 4870 Calle Real 93111. US 101 exit Turnpike Rd, just e, then just n. Int corridors. **Pets:** Other species. $25 daily fee/pet. Service with restrictions.

Fess Parker's DoubleTree Resort by Hilton ⛨ ✿

(805) 564-4333. **$215-$495.** 633 E Cabrillo Blvd 93103. US 101 exit 96A (Milpas St), just s, then just w. Ext/int corridors. **Pets:** Other species. $25 daily fee/room. Designated rooms, service with restrictions, supervision.

Four Seasons Biltmore Santa Barbara ⛨

(805) 969-2261. **Call for rates.** 1260 Channel Dr 93108. US 101 exit 94A (Olive Mill Rd), 0.3 mi s; in Montecito. Ext corridors. **Pets:** Accepted.

Hyatt Santa Barbara ⛨

(805) 963-0744. **Call for rates.** 1111 E Cabrillo Blvd 93103. US 101 exit 96A (Milpas St), 0.3 mi s, then just e. Int corridors. **Pets:** Medium. $75 one-time fee/room. Designated rooms, service with restrictions, supervision.

Marina Beach Motel M

(805) 963-9311. **$115-$285.** 21 Bath St 93101. US 101 exit 96B (Garden St), 0.3 mi w to Cabrillo Blvd, 0.4 mi n to Bath St, then just e. Ext corridors. **Pets:** Medium. $15 daily fee/pet. Designated rooms, service with restrictions, supervision.

Pacifica Suites ⛨

(805) 683-6722. **$179-$419.** 5490 Hollister Ave 93111. US 101 exit 104A (Patterson Ave), 0.5 mi w, then 0.5 mi n. Ext/int corridors. **Pets:** Medium, dogs only. $20 daily fee/pet. Service with restrictions, supervision.

The Parkside Inn M

(805) 963-0744. **$79-$249, 3 day notice.** 424 Por La Mar 93103. I-101 exit 96A (Milpas St), 0.3 mi s, just e on Cabrillo Blvd, just n, then just n. Int corridors. **Pets:** Accepted.

The Secret Garden & Cottages BB

(805) 687-2300. **Call for rates.** 1908 Bath St 93101. US 101 exit 98B (Arrellaga St) northbound, just e, then just n; exit 99 (Mission St) southbound, just e, then just s. Ext/int corridors. **Pets:** Other species. $20 daily fee/room. Designated rooms, service with restrictions, supervision.

SANTA CLARA

◆◇ ▼▼▼ Avatar Hotel Great America 🅷
(408) 235-8900. **Call for rates.** 4200 Great America Pkwy 95054. 0.5 mi e off US 101 exit Great America Pkwy; 0.8 mi s of Great America Theme Park. Ext corridors. **Pets:** Dogs only. Service with restrictions.
🅴🅲🅾 💲ᴬⱽᴱ 🛜 🔥ᴹ 🖥 💻 🏊

◆◇ ▼▼▼ Biltmore Hotel & Suites/Silicon Valley 🅷 🐾
(408) 988-8411. **$79-$199.** 2151 Laurelwood Rd 95054. US 101 exit Montague Expwy, just e; 1 mi s of Great America Pkwy. Ext/int corridors. **Pets:** Small. $50 one-time fee/room. Designated rooms, service with restrictions, supervision. 💲ᴬⱽᴱ 🛜 🔥ᴹ 🖥 💻 🍽 🏊

◆◇ ▼▼▼ ▼▼▼ Hilton Santa Clara Hotel 🅷
(408) 330-0001. **$99-$329.** 4949 Great America Pkwy 95054. US 101 exit Great America Pkwy, 0.5 mi n. Int corridors. **Pets:** Large. $75 daily fee/room. Service with restrictions, supervision.
🅴🅲🅾 💲ᴬⱽᴱ 🛜 🔥ᴹ 🖥 💻 🍽 🏊

◆◇ ▼▼▼ ▼▼▼ Hyatt Regency Santa Clara 🅷
(408) 200-1234. **$79-$309.** 5101 Great America Pkwy 95054. US 101 exit Great America Pkwy, 0.8 mi e. Int corridors. **Pets:** Accepted.
💲ᴬⱽᴱ 🛜 ✖ 🔥ᴹ 🖥 💻 🍽 🏊 🏊

◆◇ ▼▼ ▼▼ Quality Inn & Suites Silicon Valley Ⓜ
(408) 241-3010. **$80-$140.** 2930 El Camino Real 95051. SR 82, 0.5 mi w of San Tomas Expwy; US 101 exit S Bowers Ave. Ext corridors. **Pets:** Small. $20 daily fee/pet. Designated rooms, service with restrictions, supervision. 💲ᴬⱽᴱ 🛜 🔥ᴹ 🖥 💻

▼▼▼ Santa Clara Marriott Hotel 🅷 🐾
(408) 988-1500. **$89-$259.** 2700 Mission College Blvd 95054. 0.5 mi e off US 101 exit Great America Pkwy; 0.8 mi s of Great America Theme Park. Int corridors. **Pets:** Small. $75 one-time fee/room. Designated rooms, service with restrictions, supervision.
🅴🅲🅾 🛜 ✖ 🔥ᴹ 🖥 💻 🍽 🏊

◆◇ ▼▼ ▼▼ The Vagabond Inn Ⓜ
(408) 241-0771. **$59-$199.** 3580 El Camino Real 95051. On SR 82, southeast corner of Lawrence Expwy cloverleaf. Ext corridors. **Pets:** Accepted. 💲ᴬⱽᴱ 🛜 🖥 💻 🏊

SANTA CRUZ

◆◇ ▼▼▼ ▼▼▼ Chaminade Resort & Spa 🅷
(831) 475-5600. **$199-$439, 3 day notice.** 1 Chaminade Ln 95065. 1.5 mi e of SR 1 and 17; SR 1 exit Soquel Ave, just w to Paul Sweet Rd, then 0.5 mi n. Int corridors. **Pets:** Medium, dogs only. $75 one-time fee/room. Designated rooms, service with restrictions, supervision.
💲ᴬⱽᴱ 🛜 🔥ᴹ 🖥 💻 🍽 🏊

◆◇ ▼▼▼ Hilton Santa Cruz/Scotts Valley 🅷 🐾
(831) 440-1000. **$129-$299.** 6001 La Madrona Dr 95060. SR 17 exit Mt. Hermon Rd. Int corridors. **Pets:** Dogs only. $50 one-time fee/pet. Service with restrictions, supervision. 💲ᴬⱽᴱ 🛜 ✖ 🔥ᴹ 🖥 💻 🍽 🏊

◆◇ ▼▼▼ The Inn at Pasatiempo 🅷
(831) 423-5000. **$75-$305.** 555 Hwy 17 95060. 0.8 mi n of jct SR 1 and 17; SR 17 exit Pasatiempo Dr. Ext corridors. **Pets:** Small, dogs only. $25 daily fee/pet. Designated rooms, service with restrictions, crate.
💲ᴬⱽᴱ 🛜 🔥ᴹ 🖥 💻 🍽 🏊 🅺

◆◇ ▼▼ ▼▼ Ocean Pacific Lodge 🅷 🐾
(831) 457-1234. **$69-$299.** 301 Pacific Ave 95060. SR 1 and 17 exit w via Ocean St, 1 mi w to Broadway, turn right, left on Front St to Pacific Ave, then just right. Ext corridors. **Pets:** Medium. $30 daily fee/pet. Designated rooms, service with restrictions, supervision.
💲ᴬⱽᴱ 🛜 🔥ᴹ 🖥 💻 🏊

◆◇ ▼▼ ▼▼ Pacific Inn Santa Cruz 🅷 🐾
(831) 425-3722. **$70-$249, 3 day notice.** 330 Ocean St 95060. Jct SR 1 and 17 exit Ocean Ave, 1 mi w. Int corridors. **Pets:** Dogs only. $15 daily fee/pet. Service with restrictions, supervision.
💲ᴬⱽᴱ 🛜 🖥 💻 🏊

SANTA MARIA

◆◇ ▼▼▼ Best Western Plus Big America Ⓜ
(805) 922-5200. **$108-$128.** 1725 N Broadway 93454. US 101 exit 173 (SR 135/S Broadway), 0.5 mi s. Ext corridors. **Pets:** Other species. Service with restrictions, supervision. 💲ᴬⱽᴱ 🛜 ✖ 🖥 💻 🏊

▼▼ Candlewood Suites 🅷
(805) 928-4155. **$89-$159, 3 day notice.** 2079 N Roemer Ct 93454. US 101 exit 173 (SR 135/S Broadway), 0.8 mi sw, then just s. Int corridors. **Pets:** Accepted. 🛜 ✖ 🖥 💻

▼▼▼ Historic Santa Maria Inn 🅷 🐾
(805) 928-7777. **$121-$157.** 801 S Broadway 93454. US 101 exit 171 (Main St), 1 mi w, then 0.5 mi s. Int corridors. **Pets:** Other species. $50 one-time fee/room. Service with restrictions, supervision.
🛜 🖥 💻 🍽 🏊 ✖

▼▼▼ Holiday Inn & Suites 🅷
(805) 928-6000. **$122-$194.** 2100 N Broadway 93454. US 101 exit 173 (SR 135/S Broadway), just s. Int corridors. **Pets:** Accepted.
🛜 🔥ᴹ 🖥 💻 🍽 🏊

◆◇ ▼▼▼ Quality Inn & Suites Ⓜ
(805) 922-5891. **$95-$105.** 210 S Nicholson Ave 93454. US 101 exit 171 (Main St), just e, then just s. Int corridors. **Pets:** Medium, dogs only. $25 one-time fee/pet. Service with restrictions, supervision.
💲ᴬⱽᴱ 🛜 🖥 💻

◆◇ ▼▼▼ Radisson Hotel Santa Maria 🅷
(805) 928-8000. **$107-$159.** 3455 Skyway Dr 93455. US 101 exit 169 (Betteravia Rd), 2.3 mi w, then 1.8 mi s. Ext/int corridors. **Pets:** Medium. $50 one-time fee/room. Designated rooms, service with restrictions, supervision. 💲ᴬⱽᴱ 🛜 🖥 💻 🍽 🏊 ✖

SANTA NELLA

◆◇ ▼▼ Best Western Andersen's Inn 🅷
(209) 826-5534. **$94-$124.** 12367 Hwy 33 S 95322. I-5 exit 407 (SR 33), just e. Ext corridors. **Pets:** Dogs only. $20 one-time fee/room. No service, supervision. 💲ᴬⱽᴱ 🛜 🔥ᴹ 🖥 💻

◆◇ ▼▼ Holiday Inn Express 🅷
(209) 826-8282. **$79-$99.** 28976 Plaza Dr 95322. I-5 exit 407 (SR 33), just e. Ext corridors. **Pets:** Medium, dogs only. $12 one-time fee/pet. Designated rooms, service with restrictions, supervision.
💲ᴬⱽᴱ 🛜 🔥ᴹ 🖥 💻

◆◇ ▼▼ Motel 6 of Santa Nella 🅷
(209) 827-8700. **$45-$99.** 28821 W Gonzaga Rd 95322. 2.5 mi w of I-5; SR 152 exit Gonzaga Rd, just s. Ext corridors. **Pets:** Other species. Service with restrictions, supervision. 💲ᴬⱽᴱ 🛜 🔥ᴹ 🖥 💻 🏊

SANTA PAULA

▼▼▼ Glen Tavern Inn 🅷 🐾
(805) 933-5550. **$79-$99.** 134 N Mill St 93060. SR 126 exit 12 (10th St) northbound, 0.5 mi w, just s on Santa Barbara St, then just e. Int corridors. **Pets:** Small. $10 daily fee/pet. Designated rooms, service with restrictions, supervision. 🛜 ✖ 🖥 💻 🏊

SCOTTS VALLEY

◆◇ ▼▼▼ Best Western Plus Inn Scotts Valley 🅷
(831) 438-6666. **$79-$169.** 6020 Scotts Valley Dr 95066. SR 17 exit Granite Creek, just w. Ext corridors. **Pets:** Accepted.
💲ᴬⱽᴱ 🛜 🔥ᴹ 🖥 💻 🏊

SELMA

▼▼▼ Holiday Inn-Swan Court 🅷
(559) 891-8000. **$94-$104, 3 day notice.** 2950 Pea Soup Anderson Blvd 93662. SR 99 exit Floral Ave, just w. Int corridors. **Pets:** Accepted.
🛜 ✖ 🔥ᴹ 🖥 💻 🍽 🏊

AAA ▼▼▼ Super 8 Selma/Fresno Area H
(559) 896-2800. **$43-$113.** 3142 S Highland Ave 93662. SR 99 exit Floral Ave, just e. Int corridors. **Pets:** Small. $10 daily fee/pet. Designated rooms, service with restrictions, supervision. [SAVE] 🛜 🍴 💻 🏊

SIERRA CITY

AAA ▼▼▼ Herrington's Sierra Pines M
(530) 862-1151. **$79-$140, 10 day notice.** 104 Main St 96125. 0.5 mi w of center on SR 49; 12 mi n of Downieville. Ext corridors.
Pets: Accepted. [SAVE] 🛜 ✕ 💻 🍴 🐾 🔑 🏊

SIMI VALLEY

▼▼ Extended StayAmerica-Los Angeles-Simi Valley H 🐾
(805) 584-8880. **$94-$109.** 2498 Stearns St 93063. SR 118 exit 28 (Stearns St), just s. Int corridors. **Pets:** Other species. $25 daily fee/pet. Service with restrictions. 🛜 🍴 💻

SOLVANG

AAA ▼▼▼ Hadsten House Inn M
(805) 688-3210. **$164-$254, 7 day notice.** 1450 Mission Dr 93463. On SR 246. Ext corridors. **Pets:** Medium, other species. $25 one-time fee/room. Designated rooms, service with restrictions, supervision.
[SAVE] 🛜 ✕ 💪 🍴 💻 🍴 🏊

▼▼ Meadowlark Inn M 🐾
(805) 688-4631. **$135-$285, 7 day notice.** 2644 Mission Dr 93463. SR 246, 1.6 mi e. Ext corridors. **Pets:** Medium, dogs only. $100 deposit/pet, $25 daily fee/pet. Designated rooms, service with restrictions, supervision.
🛜 🍴 💻 🏊

AAA ▼▼▼ Royal Copenhagen Inn M
(805) 688-5561. **$85-$275, 3 day notice.** 1579 Mission Dr 93463. On SR 246. Ext corridors. **Pets:** Large, other species. $15 daily fee/pet. Designated rooms, service with restrictions, supervision.
[SAVE] 🛜 🍴 💻 🏊

AAA ▼▼ Viking Motel M
(805) 688-1337. **$59-$180, 3 day notice.** 1506 Mission Dr 93463. On SR 246. Ext corridors. **Pets:** Small. $15 daily fee/pet. Designated rooms, service with restrictions, supervision. [SAVE] 🛜 🍴

AAA ▼▼▼ Wine Valley Inn & Cottages H 🐾
(805) 688-2111. **$119-$399.** 1564 Copenhagen Dr 93463. SR 246, just s on 5th St. Ext/int corridors. **Pets:** Other species. $50 one-time fee/pet. Service with restrictions, supervision. [SAVE] 🛜 ✕ 🍴 💻

SONORA

AAA ▼▼▼ Aladdin Motor Inn H
(209) 533-4971. **$81-$119.** 14260 Mono Way (Hwy 108) 95370. On SR 108, 3.5 mi e. Ext/int corridors. **Pets:** Other species. $15 one-time fee/room. Designated rooms, supervision. [SAVE] 🛜 🍴 💻 🏊

▼▼▼ Barretta Gardens Inn BB
(209) 532-6039. **$140-$250, 14 day notice.** 700 S Barretta St 95370. Downtown. Int corridors. **Pets:** Dogs only. Designated rooms, service with restrictions, supervision. 🛜 🎲

AAA ▼▼ Best Western Plus Sonora Oaks Hotel & Conference Center H 🐾
(209) 533-4400. **$99-$149.** 19551 Hess Ave 95370. 3.5 mi e on SR 108. Ext/int corridors. **Pets:** Medium, dogs only. $20 daily fee/room. Designated rooms, service with restrictions, supervision.
[SAVE] 🛜 🍴 💻 🏊

AAA ▼▼ Inns of California-Sonora H
(209) 532-3633. **$70-$180.** 350 S Washington St 95370. 3 blks e of jct SR 49 and 108; downtown. Ext corridors. **Pets:** $100 deposit/room, $25 one-time fee/room. Designated rooms, service with restrictions, supervision. [SAVE] 🛜 🍴 💻 🏊

AAA ▼▼ Miner's Motel M
(209) 532-7850. **$40-$80.** 18740 SR 108 95327. On SR 108, 1 mi e of Jamestown. Ext corridors. **Pets:** Small, dogs only. $10 daily fee/pet. Service with restrictions. [SAVE] 🛜 🍴 💻 🏊

▼▼▼ Union Hill Inn BB
(209) 533-1494. **$150-$195, 3 day notice.** 21645 Parrotts Ferry Rd 95370. Jct SR 49 and Parrotts Ferry Rd; 3 mi n of downtown. Ext corridors. **Pets:** Accepted. 🛜 ✕ 🍴 💻 🏊 🎲

STOCKTON

AAA ▼▼▼▼ Best Western Plus Heritage Inn H
(209) 474-3301. **$60-$100.** 111 E March Ln 95207. I-5 exit March Ln, 2.5 mi e; corner of El Dorado St. Int corridors. **Pets:** Accepted.
[SAVE] 🛜 💪 🍴 💻 🍴 🏊

▼▼▼▼ Clarion Inn & Suites H 🐾
(209) 931-3131. **$79-$109.** 4219 E Waterloo Rd 95215. E of SR 99; jct SR 88. Int corridors. **Pets:** Small, dogs only. $25 daily fee/pet. Designated rooms, service with restrictions, supervision.
🛜 💪 🍴 💻 🍴 🏊

▼▼▼ La Quinta Inn Stockton H
(209) 952-7800. **$64-$132.** 2710 W March Ln 95219. I-5 exit March Ln, just w. Ext corridors. **Pets:** Medium, other species. Service with restrictions, supervision. 🛜 💪 🍴 💻 🏊

▼▼▼ Residence Inn by Marriott H
(209) 472-9800. **$123-$143.** 3240 W March Ln 95219. I-5 exit March Ln, 0.5 mi w. Int corridors. **Pets:** Medium. $100 one-time fee/room. Service with restrictions, supervision. 🛜 ✕ 💪 🍴 💻 🏊 ✕

AAA ▼▼▼▼ University Plaza Waterfront Hotel H
(209) 944-1140. **$89-$149.** 110 W Fremont St 95202. SR 4 exit downtown Stockton, 0.5 mi n on El Dorado St, then just w. Int corridors. **Pets:** Medium, other species. $20 one-time fee/room. Service with restrictions, supervision. [ECO] [SAVE] 🛜 ✕ 💪 🍴 💻 🍴

SUISUN CITY

▼▼▼ Hampton Inn & Suites Suisun City Waterfront H 🐾
(707) 429-0900. **$99-$134.** 2 Harbor Center Dr 94585. I-80 exit SR 12, 2.6 mi e to Suisun City exit, then just s. Int corridors. **Pets:** Medium. Designated rooms, service with restrictions, crate.
[ECO] 🛜 ✕ 💪 🍴 💻 🏊

SUN CITY

▼▼ Motel 6 Menifee #4599 M
(951) 679-1133. **$57-$90.** 27955 Encanto Dr 92586. I-215 exit 12 (McCall Blvd), just e, then just s. Ext corridors. **Pets:** Other species. Service with restrictions, supervision. 🛜 💪 🍴 💻 🏊

SUNNYVALE

AAA ▼▼▼ Maple Tree Inn H 🐾
(408) 720-9700. **$109-$169.** 711 E El Camino Real 94087. US 101 exit 394 (Lawrence Expwy), 2.9 mi w to El Camino Real exit, then 1.8 mi n. Int corridors. **Pets:** Medium. $10 daily fee/pet. Service with restrictions, supervision. [SAVE] 🛜 ✕ 💪 🍴 💻 🏊

▼▼▼ Quality Inn Santa Clara Convention Center H
(408) 744-1100. **$79-$179.** 1280 Persian Dr 94089. US 101 exit Lawrence Expwy N, 1 mi n to Persian Dr, then 0.3 mi w. Int corridors. **Pets:** Accepted. 🛜 💪 🍴 💻 🏊

AAA ▼▼▼ Ramada Inn-Silicon Valley H
(408) 245-5330. **$69-$119.** 1217 Wildwood Ave 94089. US 101 exit Lawrence Expwy N, just n. Ext corridors. **Pets:** Accepted.
[SAVE] 🛜 💪 🍴 💻 🍴 🏊

▼▼▼ Residence Inn by Marriott Silicon Valley I H
(408) 720-1000. **Call for rates.** 750 Lakeway Dr 94085. US 101 exit Lawrence Expwy S, e on Oakmead Pkwy. Ext corridors. **Pets:** Accepted.
🛜 ✕ 💪 🍴 💻 🏊 ✕

▽▽▽ Residence Inn by Marriott Sunnyvale Silicon Valley II 🅷

(408) 720-8893. **Call for rates.** 1080 Stewart Dr 94086. US 101 exit Lawrence Expwy S, w on Duane Ave. Ext corridors. **Pets:** Accepted.

🛜 ⊠ 🛏 🍴 ▭ ⇌ 🚫

📣 ▽▽▽ Sheraton Sunnyvale 🅷

(408) 745-6000. **$89-$429.** 1100 N Mathilda Ave 94089. US 101 exit Mathilda Ave. Int corridors. **Pets:** Medium, other species. Service with restrictions, supervision. 🆂🅰🆅🅴 🛜 ⊠ 🛏 ▭ 🍴 ⇌

📣 ▽▽▽ Staybridge Suites 🅷

(408) 745-1515. **$119-$189.** 900 Hamlin Ct 94089. SR 237 exit Mathilda Ave S, w on Ross Dr. Ext corridors. **Pets:** Accepted.

🆂🅰🆅🅴 🛜 🛏 ▭ ⇌ 🚫

▽▽▽ TownePlace Suites by Marriott Sunnyvale/Mountain View 🅷

(408) 733-4200. **$85-$209.** 606 S Bernardo Ave 94087. SR 85 exit SR 82, 0.5 mi s. Int corridors. **Pets:** Accepted. 🛜 ⊠ 🛏 ▭

▽▽ Vagabond Inn 🅼

(408) 734-4607. **Call for rates.** 816 Ahwanee Ave 94085. US 101 exit Mathilda Ave S, then s. Ext corridors. **Pets:** Accepted.

🛜 🛏 ▭ ⇌

▽▽▽ Wild Palms Hotel 🅷

(408) 738-0500. **Call for rates.** 910 E Fremont Ave 94087. US 101 exit Lawrence Expwy S, 1.5 mi s, 0.9 mi n on E El Camino Real, just w on S Wolfe Rd, then just s. Ext/int corridors. **Pets:** Accepted.

🅴🅲🅾 🛜 ⊠ 🛏 ▭ ⇌

SUSANVILLE

📣 ▽▽▽▽ Best Western Plus Trailside Inn 🅼

(530) 257-4123. **$80-$86.** 2785 Main St 96130. 0.7 mi se of jct SR 36 (Main St) and 139. Ext corridors. **Pets:** Accepted.

🆂🅰🆅🅴 🛜 ⊠ 🛏 ▭ 🍴 ⇌

📣 ▽▽▽ River Inn Motel 🅼

(530) 257-6051. **$60-$75.** 1710 Main St 96130. Jct SR 36 and 139, just e on SR 36. Ext corridors. **Pets:** Accepted. 🆂🅰🆅🅴 🛜 🛏 🍴 ⇌

▽▽▽ The Roseberry House Bed & Breakfast 🅱🅱

(530) 257-5675. **$110-$135, 5 day notice.** 609 North St 96130. Jct SR 36 and 139, 0.7 mi nw to N Lassen St, then just ne. Int corridors. **Pets:** Other species. $10 daily fee/pet. No service, supervision.

🛜 ⊠ 🇿

📣 ▽▽ Super 8 🅼

(530) 257-2782. **$60-$69.** 2975 Johnstonville Rd 96130. Jct SR 36 and 139, 1 mi se on SR 139. Ext corridors. **Pets:** Accepted.

🆂🅰🆅🅴 🛜 🛏 ▭ ⇌

TEHACHAPI

📣 ▽▽ Best Western Mountain Inn 🅼 ❁

(661) 822-5591. **Call for rates.** 418 W Tehachapi Blvd 93561. SR 58 exit 148 (SR 202), 1 mi s, then e. Ext corridors. **Pets:** Other species. Designated rooms, service with restrictions, supervision.

🆂🅰🆅🅴 🛜 🛏 ▭ ⇌

▽▽▽ Holiday Inn Express & Suites 🅷

(661) 822-9837. **$99-$126.** 901 Capital Hills Pkwy 93561. SR 58 exit 149 (Mill St), just n. Int corridors. **Pets:** Medium. $40 one-time fee/pet. Designated rooms, service with restrictions, supervision.

🛜 🆅🅼 🛏 ▭ ⇌

▽▽ La Quinta Inn Tehachapi 🅼

(661) 823-8000. **$93-$154.** 500 E Steuber Rd 93561. SR 58 exit 151 (Monolith St/Tehachapi Blvd), just s. Int corridors. **Pets:** Medium, other species. Service with restrictions, supervision. 🛜 ⊠ 🛏 ▭ ⇌

TEMECULA

▽▽▽ Embassy Suites 🅷

(951) 676-5656. **$129-$219.** 29345 Rancho California Rd 92591. I-15 exit 59 (Rancho California Rd), just e. Int corridors. **Pets:** Accepted.

🛜 🛏 ▭ 🍴 ⇌

▽▽▽ La Quinta Inn & Suites Temecula 🅷

(951) 296-1003. **$102-$199.** 27330 Jefferson Ave 92590. I-15 exit 61 (SR 79 N/Winchester Rd), just w, then just n; east side of Rancho Temecula Plaza. Int corridors. **Pets:** Medium, other species. Service with restrictions, supervision. 🛜 ⊠ 🛏 ▭ ⇌

▽▽ Quality Inn Temecula Wine Country 🅼

(951) 296-3788. **$67-$139.** 27338 Jefferson Ave 92590. I-15 exit 61 (SR 79 N/ Winchester Rd), just w, then just n; east side of Rancho Temecula Plaza. Ext corridors. **Pets:** Medium, dogs only. $20 daily fee/room. Designated rooms, service with restrictions, supervision.

🛜 ⊠ 🛏 ▭ ⇌

▽▽▽ Temecula Creek Inn 🅷

(951) 694-1000. **$119-$249, 3 day notice.** 44501 Rainbow Canyon Rd 92592. I-15 exit 58 (SR 79 S), 1 mi e to Pechanga Pkwy, then 0.5 mi s. Ext corridors. **Pets:** Accepted. 🛜 ⊠ 🛏 ▭ 🍴 ⇌ 🚫

THOUSAND OAKS

▽▽▽ La Quinta Inn & Suites Thousand Oaks Newbury Park 🅼

(805) 499-5910. **$88-$148.** 1320 Newbury Rd 91320. US 101 exit 46 (Ventu Park Rd), just se. Ext corridors. **Pets:** Medium, other species. Service with restrictions, supervision. 🛜 🆅🅼 🛏 ▭ ⇌

▽ Motel 6 #1360 Thousand Oaks 🅼

(805) 499-0711. **$55-$65.** 1516 Newbury Rd 91320. US 101 exit 46 (Ventu Park Rd), just w, then just n. Ext corridors. **Pets:** Other species. Service with restrictions, supervision. 🛜 ⇌

📣 ▽▽▽ Palm Garden Hotel 🅷

(805) 716-4200. **$89-$295.** 495 N Ventu Park Rd 91320. US 101 exit 46 (Ventu Park Rd), just n. Ext corridors. **Pets:** Small. $30 one-time fee/ room. Designated rooms, service with restrictions.

🆂🅰🆅🅴 🛜 🆅🅼 🛏 ▭ 🍴 ⇌ 🚫

▽▽ Premier Inn 🅼

(805) 499-0755. **Call for rates.** 2434 W Hillcrest Dr 91320. US 101 exit 47B (Borchard Rd), just e, then just n. Ext corridors. **Pets:** Accepted.

🛜 🛏 ⇌

▽▽▽ TownePlace Suites by Marriott 🅷 ❁

(805) 499-3111. **$94-$142.** 1712 Newbury Rd 91320. US 101 exit 46 (Ventu Park Rd), just w, then just n. Int corridors. **Pets:** Other species. $100 one-time fee/room. Service with restrictions.

🛜 ⊠ 🛏 ▭ ⇌

THREE RIVERS

📣 ▽▽ Americas Best Value Inn - Lazy J Ranch 🅼

(559) 561-4449. **$100-$125, 3 day notice.** 39625 Sierra Dr 93271. SR 198, 3 mi sw of town center. Ext corridors. **Pets:** Accepted.

🆂🅰🆅🅴 🛜 ⊠ 🛏 ▭ ⇌ 🚫

📣 ▽▽ Buckeye Tree Lodge 🅼

(559) 561-5900. **$73-$156, 7 day notice.** 46000 Sierra Dr 93271. SR 198, north end of town, 0.5 mi from national forest gate. Ext corridors. **Pets:** Other species. $10 daily fee/pet. Service with restrictions, supervision. 🆂🅰🆅🅴 🛜 ⊠ 🛏 ▭ ⇌

📣 ▽▽▽ Comfort Inn & Suites 🅼

(559) 561-9000. **$80-$189.** 40820 Sierra Dr 93271. SR 198, 1.5 mi sw of town center. Ext/int corridors. **Pets:** Small, other species. $35 one-time fee/pet. Designated rooms, service with restrictions, crate.

🆂🅰🆅🅴 🛜 ⊠ 🆅🅼 🛏 ▭ ⇌ 🚫

▼▼ Gateway Lodge M
(559) 561-4133. **$79-$179, 3 day notice.** 45978 Sierra Dr 93271. SR 198, 6 mi ne of town center; 0.5 mi sw of entrance to Sequoia National Park. Ext corridors. **Pets:** $10 daily fee/pet. Service with restrictions.

▼▼ Sequoia River Dance Bed & Breakfast BB ❖
(559) 561-4411. **$105-$145, 10 day notice.** 40534 Cherokee Oaks Dr 93271. SR 198, 2 mi sw of town center, then 0.3 mi e. Int corridors. **Pets:** $10 daily fee/pet. Service with restrictions, supervision.

AAA ▼▼ Sequoia Village Inn M
(559) 561-3652. **$73-$305, 7 day notice.** 45971 Sierra Dr 93271. SR 198, 6 mi ne of town center; 0.5 mi sw of entrance to Sequoia National Park. Ext corridors. **Pets:** Other species. $10 daily fee/pet. Service with restrictions, supervision.

TRACY

AAA ▼▼ Best Western Luxury Inn H
(209) 832-0271. **$65-$70.** 811 W Clover Rd 95376. I-205 exit Central Tracy, just s, then just w. Int corridors. **Pets:** Medium. $10 daily fee/pet. Service with restrictions, crate.

AAA ▼▼ Quality Inn-Tracy H
(209) 835-1335. **$59-$189.** 3511 N Tracy Blvd 95376. I-205 exit Central Tracy/Tracy Blvd, just s. Ext/int corridors. **Pets:** Accepted.

TRINIDAD

AAA ▼▼ Emerald Forest of Trinidad CA
(707) 677-3554. **$120-$185, 5 day notice.** 753 Patrick's Point Dr 95570. US 101 exit Trinidad, just w on Main St, then 0.7 mi n. Ext corridors. **Pets:** Accepted.

▼▼▼ Lost Whale Bed & Breakfast Inn BB
(707) 677-3425. **$199-$315, 7 day notice.** 3452 Patrick's Point Dr 95570. US 101 exit Patrick's Point Dr, 1.1 mi w. Int corridors. **Pets:** Accepted.

AAA ▼▼ Trinidad Inn M ❖
(707) 677-3349. **$110-$180.** 1170 Patrick's Point Dr 95570. US 101 exit Trinidad, just w on Main St, then 1.3 mi n. Ext corridors. **Pets:** Dogs only. $10 daily fee/pet. Designated rooms, supervision.

TULARE

AAA ▼▼▼ Charter Inn & Suites H ❖
(559) 685-9500. **$89-$199.** 1016 E Prosperity Ave 93274. SR 99 exit 88 (Prosperity Ave/Blackstone St), just e. Int corridors. **Pets:** Small. $100 deposit/room, $10 daily fee/pet. Service with restrictions, crate.

▼▼▼ La Quinta Inn & Suites Tulare H
(559) 685-8900. **$84-$174.** 1500 Cherry Ct 93274. SR 99 exit 88 (Prosperity Ave/Blackstone St), just w. Int corridors. **Pets:** Medium, other species. Service with restrictions, supervision.

AAA ▼▼▼ Quality Inn M
(559) 686-3432. **$70-$135.** 1010 E Prosperity Ave 93274. SR 99 exit 88 (Prosperity Ave/Blackstone St), just e. Int corridors. **Pets:** Small, dogs only. $15 daily fee/pet. Service with restrictions, supervision.

TURLOCK

AAA ▼▼▼ Best Western Plus Orchard Inn H
(209) 667-2827. **$59-$79.** 5025 N Golden State Blvd 95382. SR 99 exit Taylor Rd, just e. Ext corridors. **Pets:** Accepted.

▼▼▼ Candlewood Suites H
(209) 250-1501. **$59-$149.** 1000 Powers Ct 95380. SR 99 exit Monte Vista Ave, just w. Int corridors. **Pets:** Accepted.

AAA ▼▼ Comfort Suites H
(209) 667-7777. **$79-$104.** 191 N Tully Rd 95380. SR 99 exit West Main St E, just n. Int corridors. **Pets:** Medium, other species. $20 one-time fee/pet. Designated rooms, service with restrictions, supervision.

TWAIN HARTE

AAA ▼▼ ▼▼ McCaffrey House Bed & Breakfast Inn BB ❖
(209) 586-0757. **$139-$199, 8 day notice.** 23251 Hwy 108 95383. On SR 108, 0.5 mi e; just beyond 4000' elevation marker. Int corridors. **Pets:** $25 daily fee/pet. Designated rooms, service with restrictions, supervision.

TWENTYNINE PALMS

▼▼▼ Roughley Manor BB
(760) 367-3238. **Call for rates.** 74744 Joe Davis Rd 92277. SR 62, 0.7 mi n on Utah Tr, 0.4 mi e on Joe Davis Rd, then just n. Ext/int corridors. **Pets:** Dogs only. Designated rooms, service with restrictions, supervision.

▼▼ Sunnyvale Garden Suites Hotel H
(760) 361-3939. **$99-$120.** 73843 Sunnyvale Dr 92277. SR 62, 0.7 mi n on Adobe Rd, just e on S Slope Dr, just n on Ocotillo, then just e. Ext corridors. **Pets:** Accepted.

UPLAND

▼▼▼ GuestHouse Inn & Suites H
(909) 949-4800. **$79-$99.** 1191 E Foothill Blvd 91786. I-10 exit 51 (Euclid Ave), 1.3 mi n, then 0.8 mi e. Ext/int corridors. **Pets:** Accepted.

VACAVILLE

AAA ▼▼ Best Western Heritage Inn M
(707) 448-8453. **$60-$100.** 1420 E Monte Vista Ave 95688. I-80 exit Monte Vista Ave, just nw. Ext corridors. **Pets:** Accepted.

▼▼ Extended StayAmerica-Sacramento-Vacaville H ❖
(707) 469-1371. **$74-$89.** 799 Orange Dr 95687. I-80 exit Leisure Town Rd, just s; just e of I-505 interchange. Int corridors. **Pets:** Other species. $25 daily fee/pet. Service with restrictions.

AAA ▼▼▼ Hampton Inn & Suites Vacaville/Napa Valley H ❖
(707) 469-6200. **$99-$129.** 800 Mason St 95688. I-80 exit Davis St eastbound, just n, then ne on Porter Way; exit Mason St westbound, just w; jct Porter Way. Int corridors. **Pets:** Other species. Supervision.

▼▼ Quality Inn & Suites Vacaville M
(707) 446-8888. **$69-$269.** 1050 Orange Dr 95687. I-80 exit Leisure Town Rd, just s, then just e. Ext corridors. **Pets:** Other species. $99 daily fee/room. Designated rooms, service with restrictions, supervision.

▼▼▼ Residence Inn by Marriott H
(707) 469-0300. **$139-$189.** 360 Orange Dr 95687. I-80 exit Orange Dr eastbound, 0.5 mi ne; exit Monte Vista Ave westbound to freeway overpass to E Nut Tree Pkwy, then just ne. Int corridors. **Pets:** $100 one-time fee/room. Service with restrictions, supervision.

AAA ▼▼▼ Vacaville Courtyard by Marriott H
(707) 451-9000. **$99-$149.** 120 Nut Tree Pkwy 95687. I-80 exit Orange Dr eastbound, just w; exit Monte Vista Ave westbound, just ne to freeway overpass to E Nut Tree Pkwy, then just w. Int corridors. **Pets:** Dogs only. $75 one-time fee/room. Service with restrictions, supervision.

VALLEJO

Best Western Plus Inn & Suites at Discovery Kingdom H

(707) 554-9655. **$60-$170.** 1596 Fairgrounds Dr 94589. I-80 exit SR 37 N (Marine World Pkwy), 0.3 mi w. Int corridors. **Pets:** Large, other species. $70 one-time fee/pet. Designated rooms, service with restrictions, crate.

Courtyard by Marriott H

(707) 644-1200. **$98-$134.** 1000 Fairgrounds Dr 94589. I-80 exit SR 37 (Marine World Pkwy), 0.3 mi n. Int corridors. **Pets:** Small, dogs only. $75 one-time fee/room. Service with restrictions, supervision.

VENTURA

Crowne Plaza Ventura Beach Resort H

(805) 648-2100. **$84-$199.** 450 E Harbor Blvd 93001. US 101 exit 70A (California St) northbound, just s; exit 71 (Main St) southbound, 0.5 mi e to California St, then just s. Int corridors. **Pets:** Accepted.

Four Points by Sheraton Ventura Harbor Resort H

(805) 658-1212. **$115-$350.** 1050 Schooner Dr 93001. US 101 exit 68 (Seaward Ave), just w, then 1.5 mi s on Harbor Blvd; at Ventura Harbor. Ext/int corridors. **Pets:** $75 one-time fee/room. Designated rooms, service with restrictions, supervision.

Holiday Inn Express Ventura Harbor H

(805) 856-9533. **$119-$225.** 1080 Navigator Dr 93001. US 101 exit 68 (Seaward Ave), just w, then 1.5 mi s; at Ventura Harbor. Ext/int corridors. **Pets:** $75 one-time fee/room. Designated rooms, service with restrictions, supervision.

La Quinta Inn Ventura M

(805) 658-6200. **$73-$155.** 5818 Valentine Rd 93003. US 101 exit 64 (Victoria Ave), just s, then just n. Ext/int corridors. **Pets:** Medium, other species. Service with restrictions, supervision.

Marriott Ventura Beach Hotel H

(805) 643-6000. **$139-$161.** 2055 E Harbor Blvd 93001. US 101 exit 68 (Seaward Ave), just w, then 0.5 mi n. Int corridors. **Pets:** Accepted.

Pierpont Inn H

(805) 643-6144. **Call for rates.** 550 Sanjon Rd 93001. US 101 exit 69 (Sanjon Rd) northbound; exit 68 (Seaward Ave) southbound, just w, then 1 mi on Harbor Blvd. Ext/int corridors. **Pets:** Accepted.

Vagabond Inn Ventura M

(805) 648-5371. **$69-$249.** 756 E Thompson Blvd 93001. US 101 exit 70A (California St) northbound, just n, then just e; exit 70A (Ventura Ave) southbound, 0.6 mi e. Ext corridors. **Pets:** Other species. $10 daily fee/room. Service with restrictions, supervision.

VICTORVILLE

Comfort Suites H

(760) 245-6777. **$89-$299.** 12281 Mariposa Rd 92395. I-15 exit 147 (Bear Valley Rd), just e, then just n. Int corridors. **Pets:** Accepted.

Hawthorn Suites H

(760) 949-4700. **Call for rates.** 11750 Dunia Rd 92392. I-15 exit 147 (Bear Valley Rd), just w, 0.3 mi s on Amargosa Rd, then just w. Int corridors. **Pets:** Other species. $100 deposit/room, $5 daily fee/pet. Service with restrictions, supervision.

VISALIA

Ben Maddox House BB

(559) 739-0721. **Call for rates.** 601 N Encina St 93291. SR 198 exit 107A (Central Visalia/SR 63 N), 0.4 mi n to Murray St, just w, then just n. Ext/int corridors. **Pets:** Accepted.

Comfort Inn & Suites H

(559) 651-3700. **$79-$129.** 9300 W Airport Dr 93277. SR 198 exit 102 (Plaza Dr), just s, then just w. Int corridors. **Pets:** Medium. $25 one-time fee/room. Designated rooms, service with restrictions.

Holiday Inn Hotel & Conference Center H 🐾

(559) 651-5000. **$90-$139.** 9000 W Airport Dr 93277. SR 198 exit 102 (Plaza Dr), just s. Int corridors. **Pets:** Medium. $25 daily fee/pet. Designated rooms, no service, supervision.

Lamp Liter Inn M

(559) 732-4511. **$79-$149.** 3300 W Mineral King Ave 93291. SR 198 exit 105B (SR 63 S/Mooney Blvd) westbound, 0.5 mi w; exit eastbound, just n, then 0.5 mi w. Ext corridors. **Pets:** Small. $25 daily fee/room. Service with restrictions, supervision.

La Quinta Inn & Suites Visalia/Sequoia Gateway H

(559) 739-9800. **$102-$164.** 5438 W Cypress Ave 93277. SR 198 exit 104 (Akers St), just s, then just w. Int corridors. **Pets:** Medium, other species. Service with restrictions, supervision.

Marriott Visalia at the Convention Center H

(559) 636-1111. **$109-$179.** 300 S Court St 93291. SR 198 exit 107A (Central Visalia/SR 63 N), just ne. Int corridors. **Pets:** Accepted.

VISTA

Americas Best Value Inn & Suites M

(760) 726-2900. **$59-$189.** 330 Mar Vista Dr 92083. SR 78 exit Mar Vista Dr, just ne. Ext corridors. **Pets:** Very small, dogs only. $100 deposit/pet, $10 daily fee/pet. Designated rooms, service with restrictions.

La Quinta Inn San Diego Vista M

(760) 727-8180. **$64-$139.** 630 Sycamore Ave 92083. SR 78 exit Sycamore Ave, just sw. Ext/int corridors. **Pets:** Medium, other species. Service with restrictions, supervision.

WALNUT CREEK

Holiday Inn Express Walnut Creek H

(925) 932-3332. **$89-$209.** 2730 N Main St 94597. I-680 exit N Main St, just n. Int corridors. **Pets:** Small, dogs only. $20 daily fee/pet. Designated rooms, service with restrictions, supervision.

Walnut Creek Marriott H 🐾

(925) 934-2000. **$109-$229.** 2355 N Main St 94596. I-680 exit N Main St, 0.3 mi e, then s at Parkside Dr. Int corridors. **Pets:** Medium, other species. $35 daily fee/room. Service with restrictions, supervision.

WATSONVILLE

Best Western Plus Rose Garden Inn H

(831) 724-3367. **$100-$250.** 740 Freedom Blvd 95076. On SR 152. Ext corridors. **Pets:** Large. $20 daily fee/room. Designated rooms, service with restrictions, crate.

WEAVERVILLE

49er Gold Country Inn M

(530) 623-4937. **$50-$120, 3 day notice.** 880 Main St (Hwy 299) 96093. Jct SR 3 and 299, just se on SR 299. Ext corridors. **Pets:** Accepted.

Motel Trinity M 🐾

(530) 623-2129. **$50-$75, 3 day notice.** 1270 Main St 96093. Jct SR 3 and 299, 0.7 mi se on SR 299. Ext corridors. **Pets:** Dogs only. $5 daily fee/room. Service with restrictions, supervision.

◈ Red Hill Motel CA

(530) 623-4331. **$37-$95, 7 day notice.** Red Hill Rd 96093. Jct SR 3 and 299, just nw on SR 299, then just n. Ext corridors. **Pets:** Other species. $5 one-time fee/pet. Service with restrictions, supervision.

⊠ 🖥 🖵

◈◈ Weaverville Victorian Inn M

(530) 623-4432. **$79-$169.** 2051 Main St 96093. Jct SR 3 and 299, 1.5 mi se on SR 299. Ext corridors. **Pets:** Accepted. 📶 🖥 🖵 ⪼

WEED

◭ ◈◈ Comfort Inn H

(530) 938-1982. **$90-$100.** 1844 Shastina Dr 96094. I-5 exit 745 (S Weed Blvd), just e, then just n. Int corridors. **Pets:** Large, dogs only. $10 daily fee/pet. Designated rooms, service with restrictions, supervision.

SAVE 📶 🖥 🖵 ⪼

◭ ◈ Sis-Q-Inn Motel M ❀

(530) 938-4194. **$65-$150.** 1825 Shastina Dr 96094. I-5 exit 745 (S Weed Blvd), just e, then just n. Int corridors. **Pets:** Small. $10 daily fee/pet. Service with restrictions, supervision. SAVE 📶 🖥

WESTLAKE VILLAGE

◭ ◈◈◈◈ Four Seasons Hotel Westlake Village H ❀

(818) 575-3000. **$235-$525.** Two Dole Dr 91362. US 101 exit 39 (Lindero Canyon Rd), just e, then just n on Via Colinas. Int corridors. **Pets:** Very small, other species. $50 one-time fee/room.

ECO SAVE 📶 ⊠ 🖥 🖵 🍴 ⪼ ⊠

◭ ◈◈◈ Hyatt Westlake Plaza Hotel H ❀

(805) 557-1234. **$99-$309.** 880 S Westlake Blvd 91361. US 101 exit 40 (Westlake Blvd), just s. Int corridors. **Pets:** Medium. $50 daily fee/room. Designated rooms, service with restrictions, supervision.

ECO SAVE 📶 ⊠ 🖥 🖵 ⪼ ⊠

◈◈◈ Residence Inn by Marriott H

(818) 707-4411. **$108-$163.** 30950 Russell Ranch Rd 91362. US 101 exit 39 (Lindero Canyon Rd), just e, then just s. Int corridors. **Pets:** Small. $100 one-time fee/room. Service with restrictions.

📶 ⊠ 🖥 🖵 ⪼ ⊠

WESTLEY

◭ ◈◈ Econo Lodge M

(209) 894-3900. **$59-$149.** 7100 McCracken Rd 95387. I-5 exit Westley, just e. Ext corridors. **Pets:** Medium. $10 daily fee/pet. No service, supervision. SAVE 📶 🖥 🖵 ⪼

◈◈◈ Holiday Inn Express H ❀

(209) 894-8940. **$74-$129.** 4525 Howard Rd 95387. I-5 exit Westley, just e. Int corridors. **Pets:** Other species. $20 one-time fee/room. Designated rooms, service with restrictions, crate. 📶 🖥 🖵 ⪼

WESTMORLAND

◈◈ Americas Best Value Inn M

(760) 351-7100. **$90-$140.** 351 W Main St 92281. On SR 86/78. Int corridors. **Pets:** Medium. $20 daily fee/pet. Service with restrictions, supervision. 📶 🖥 🖵 ⪼

WEST SACRAMENTO

◈◈ Extended StayAmerica-Sacramento-West Sacramento H ❀

(916) 371-1270. **$84-$99.** 795 Stillwater Rd 95605. I-80 exit Reed Ave, just n, just w, then just s. Int corridors. **Pets:** Other species. $25 daily fee/pet. Service with restrictions. 📶 🖥 🖵

◭ ◈◈◈ Ramada Inn & Plaza Harbor Conference Center H

(916) 371-2100. **$55-$200.** 1250 Halyard Dr 95691. Business Rt I-80 (Capital City Frwy) exit 1 (Harbour Blvd S), just s to Beacon Blvd, just w, then just n. Ext/int corridors. **Pets:** Large, other species. $25 daily fee/room. Designated rooms, service with restrictions, crate.

SAVE 📶 ♿ 🖥 🖵 🍴 ⪼ ⊠

◭ ◈ Rodeway Inn Capitol M

(916) 371-6983. **Call for rates.** 817 W Capitol Ave 95691. Business Rt I-80 (Capital City Frwy) exit Jefferson Blvd westbound, 0.3 mi n, then just e; exit Jefferson Blvd eastbound, just s (make U-turn), 0.3 mi n on Jefferson Blvd, then just e. Ext corridors. **Pets:** Medium, dogs only. Service with restrictions, supervision. SAVE 📶 🖥 🖵

WILLIAMS

◭ ◈◈ Quality Inn M

(530) 473-2381. **$70-$130.** 400 C St 95987. I-5 exit 577 (Williams), just w on E St (SR 20 business route), just n on 4th St; at 76 gas station, then just e. Ext corridors. **Pets:** Accepted.

SAVE 📶 ♿ 🖥 🖵 ⪼

◭ ◈◈ Ramada H

(530) 473-5120. **$49-$99.** 374 Ruggeri Way 95987. I-5 exit 577 (Williams), just e. Int corridors. **Pets:** Accepted.

SAVE 📶 ⊠ ♿ 🖥 🖵

◭ ◈ Stage Stop Inn M

(530) 473-2281. **$45-$55.** 330 7th St 95987. I-5 exit 577 (Williams), just w on E St (SR 20 business route), then just n. Ext corridors. **Pets:** Accepted. SAVE 📶 🖥 🖵 ⪼

◭ ◈ Traveler's Inn M

(530) 473-5387. **$38-$60.** 215 N 7th St 95987. I-5 exit 577 (Williams), just w on E St (SR 20 business route), then 0.3 mi n. Ext corridors. **Pets:** $10 daily fee/pet. Service with restrictions, supervision. SAVE 📶 ⊠ ♿ 🖥 ⪼

WILLOW CREEK

◈ Bigfoot Motel M

(530) 629-2142. **Call for rates.** 39039 Hwy 299 95573. On SR 299; just e of SR 96; center. Ext corridors. **Pets:** Accepted. 📶 🖥 ⪼

WILLOWS

◭ ◈◈◈ Baymont Inn & Suites Willows H

(530) 934-9700. **$63-$117.** 199 N Humboldt Ave 95988. I-5 exit 603 (SR 162 Willows/Oroville), just e, then s. Int corridors. **Pets:** Medium. $10 one-time fee/pet. Designated rooms, service with restrictions, supervision.

SAVE 📶 🖥 🖵 ⪼

◭ ◈◈ Days Inn M

(530) 934-4444. **$72-$167.** 475 N Humboldt Ave 95988. I-5 exit 603 (SR 162 Willows/Oroville), just e, then just n. Ext corridors. **Pets:** $15 daily fee/pet. Designated rooms, service with restrictions, supervision.

SAVE 📶 ♿ 🖥 🖵 ⪼

◭ ◈ Economy Inn M

(530) 934-4224. **$60-$85, 3 day notice.** 435 N Tehama St 95988. I-5 exit 603 (SR 162 Willows/Oroville), 1 mi e, then just n. Ext corridors. **Pets:** Small. $5 one-time fee/pet. Designated rooms, service with restrictions, supervision. SAVE 📶 🖥 🖵

◭ ◈◈◈ Holiday Inn Express Willows H

(530) 934-8900. **$99-$139.** 545 N Humboldt Ave 95988. I-5 exit 603 (SR 162 Willows/Oroville), just e, then just n. Int corridors. **Pets:** Accepted.

SAVE 📶 ♿ 🖥 🖵 ⪼

◭ ◈ Motel 6 #4273 M

(530) 934-7026. **$49-$99.** 452 N Humboldt Ave 95988. I-5 exit 603 (SR 162 Willows/Oroville), just e, then just n. Ext corridors. **Pets:** Other species. Service with restrictions, supervision. SAVE 📶 🖥 ⪼

WINE COUNTRY AREA

ALBION

▼▼ Fensalden Inn BB

(707) 937-4042. **$139-$253, 7 day notice.** 33810 Navarro Ridge Rd 95410. 1.5 mi s on SR 1, 0.5 mi e. Ext/int corridors. **Pets:** Other species. $25 one-time fee/room. Designated rooms, service with restrictions, supervision. 📶 ⊠ 🛁 💷 🐾 🐾 ⓩ

CALISTOGA

AAA ▼▼ Brannan Cottage Inn BB 🐾

(707) 942-4200. **$160-$280, 7 day notice.** 109 Wapoo Ave 94515. At Lincoln Ave. Ext corridors. **Pets:** Other species. $100 deposit/room, $25 daily fee/pet. Designated rooms, service with restrictions, crate. SAVE 📶 ⊠ 🛁 ⓩ

CLEARLAKE

AAA ▼▼ Clear Lake Cottages and Marina CA 🐾

(707) 995-5253. **$119-$209, 8 day notice.** 13885 Lakeshore Dr 95422. SR 53 exit Lakeshore Dr, 2.1 mi w. Ext corridors. **Pets:** Other species. $20 daily fee/pet. Designated rooms, service with restrictions. SAVE 📶 ⊠ 🛁 💷 🐊 ⓩ

CLOVERDALE

▼▼▼ Auberge on the Vineyard BB

(707) 894-5956. **$125-$315, 7 day notice.** 29955 River Rd 95425. US 101 exit Citrus Fair Dr, just e, 0.5 mi n on Asti Rd, then 0.8 mi e on Crocker Rd. Int corridors. **Pets:** Accepted. 📶 ⊠ 🛁 💷 ⓩ

AAA ▼▼▼ Old Crocker Inn BB

(707) 894-4000. **$165-$255, 8 day notice.** 1126 Old Crocker Inn Rd 95425. US 101 exit Citrus Fair Dr, just e, 0.5 mi n on Asti Rd, 0.8 mi e on Crocker Rd, 3.8 mi n on River Rd, 1.1 mi e on Asti Ridge Rd, then just n. Ext corridors. **Pets:** Dogs only. Designated rooms, service with restrictions, supervision. SAVE 📶 ⊠ 🛁 🐊 ⓩ

FORT BRAGG

AAA ▼▼▼▼ Beachcomber Motel M 🐾

(707) 964-2402. **$119-$269, 3 day notice.** 1111 N Main St 95437. 1 mi n on SR 1. Ext corridors. **Pets:** Medium, other species. $20 daily fee/pet. Service with restrictions, supervision. SAVE 📶 ⊠ 🛁 💷 🐾

AAA ▼▼ Beach House Inn M

(707) 961-1700. **$69-$250.** 100 Pudding Creek Rd 95437. 0.7 mi n on SR 1. Int corridors. **Pets:** Other species. $20 daily fee/pet. Service with restrictions, supervision. SAVE 📶 ⊠ 🛁 💷 🐾

▼▼ Coast Inn and Spa M 🐾

(707) 964-2852. **$80-$390, 3 day notice.** 18661 N Hwy 1 95437. 0.3 mi s of SR 20. Ext corridors. **Pets:** Large, dogs only. $20 daily fee/pet. Designated rooms, service with restrictions, supervision. 📶 ⊠ 🛁 💷 🍴 🐾

AAA ▼▼▼▼ Emerald Dolphin Inn & Mini Golf H 🐾

(707) 964-6699. **$65-$175, 7 day notice.** 1211 S Main St 95437. On SR 1; at Harbor View Dr. Ext corridors. **Pets:** Dogs only. $10 daily fee/room. Designated rooms, service with restrictions, supervision. SAVE 📶 🛁 🛁 💷 ⊠ 🐾

AAA ▼▼▼▼ Holiday Inn Express H

(707) 964-1100. **$119-$199.** 250 Hwy 20 95437. On SR 20, just e of jct SR 1. Ext/int corridors. **Pets:** Accepted. SAVE 📶 🛁 🛁 💷 🐊

AAA ▼▼ Seabird Lodge M 🐾

(707) 964-4731. **$75-$150, 3 day notice.** 191 South St 95437. 0.8 mi n of Noyo River Bridge; 1 blk e off SR 1. Ext corridors. **Pets:** Other species. $10 daily fee/room. Service with restrictions, supervision. SAVE 📶 🛁 💷 🐊 🐾

▼▼ Shoreline Cottages CA

(707) 964-2977. **$95-$160, 3 day notice.** 18725 N Hwy 1 95437. On SR 1, 0.3 mi s of SR 20. Ext corridors. **Pets:** Accepted. 📶 ⊠ 🛁 💷 🐾 ⓩ

▼▼ Super 8 M 🐾

(707) 964-4003. **$56-$116.** 888 S Main St 95437. 0.5 mi s on SR 1; north end of Noyo River Bridge. Ext corridors. **Pets:** Medium. $10 one-time fee/pet. Designated rooms, service with restrictions, supervision. 📶 🛁 💷

AAA ▼▼ Surf Motel & Gardens M 🐾

(707) 964-5361. **$49-$275, 3 day notice.** 1220 S Main St 95437. At Oceanview Dr. Ext corridors. **Pets:** Dogs only. $10 daily fee/pet. Designated rooms, service with restrictions, supervision. SAVE 📶 🛁 💷 🐾

▼▼▼▼ The Weller House Inn BB

(707) 964-4415. **Call for rates.** 524 Stewart St 95437. Just w of SR 1 via Pine St, just n. Int corridors. **Pets:** Accepted. 📶 ⊠ 🛁 🐾 ⓩ

GUALALA

▼▼ Gualala Country Inn M

(707) 884-4343. **$77-$190, 3 day notice.** 47975 Center St 95445. South end of town; just n of Old State Hwy. Ext/int corridors. **Pets:** Accepted. 📶 🛁 💷 🐾

AAA ▼▼▼▼ North Coast Country Inn BB

(707) 884-4537. **$164-$245, 3 day notice.** 34591 S Hwy 1 95445. On SR 1, 4.5 mi n. Ext corridors. **Pets:** Dogs only. $35 daily fee/pet. Designated rooms, service with restrictions, supervision. SAVE 📶 ⊠ 🛁 💷 🐾 🐾 ⓩ

AAA ▼▼ Surf Motel M 🐾

(707) 884-3571. **$89-$209, 3 day notice.** 39170 S SR 1 95445. Center. Ext/int corridors. **Pets:** Other species. $15 daily fee/pet. Service with restrictions, supervision. SAVE 📶 ⊠ 🛁 💷 🐾

GUERNEVILLE

AAA ▼▼ Ferngrove Cottages CA 🐾

(707) 869-8105. **$89-$269, 3 day notice.** 16650 Hwy 116 95446. Just w of downtown. Ext corridors. **Pets:** Large, other species. $25 daily fee/pet. Designated rooms, service with restrictions, supervision. SAVE 📶 ⊠ 🛁 💷 🐊 🐾 ⓩ

HEALDSBURG

AAA ▼▼ Americas Best Value Inn & Suites M

(707) 433-5548. **$79-$219.** 74 Healdsburg Ave 95448. US 101 exit Central Healdsburg, just se. Ext corridors. **Pets:** Small. $15 daily fee/pet. Service with restrictions, supervision. SAVE 📶 ⊠ 🛁 🛁 💷 🐊

▼▼▼▼ Bella Villa Messina BB

(707) 433-6655. **$220-$390, 7 day notice.** 316 Burgundy Rd 95448. US 101 exit Dry Creek Rd, just e to Grove St, 0.5 mi n to Chiquita Rd, then 0.5 mi w. Int corridors. **Pets:** Accepted. 📶 ⊠ 🛁

AAA ▼▼▼▼ Best Western Plus Dry Creek Inn H

(707) 433-0300. **$79-$299.** 198 Dry Creek Rd 95448. US 101 exit Dry Creek Rd, just se. Ext corridors. **Pets:** $30 daily fee/room. Designated rooms, service with restrictions, supervision. SAVE 📶 🛁 🛁 💷 🐊 ⊠

JENNER

▼▼ Jenner Inn & Cottages CI

(707) 865-2377. **$118-$348, 10 day notice.** 10400 Hwy 1 95450. On SR 1, 1 mi n of SR 116. Ext corridors. **Pets:** Accepted. 📶 ⊠ 🛁 🛁 💷 🍴 ⊠ 🐾

KENWOOD

AAA **WW** Birmingham Bed & Breakfast **BB** ❀
(707) 833-6996. **$160-$295, 14 day notice.** 8790 Hwy 12 95452. SR 12, just n of town. Int corridors. **Pets:** Dogs only. $10 daily fee/pet. Designated rooms, service with restrictions, crate. 〔SAVE〕 ⊚ ⊠ ☎

LAKEPORT

W Rainbow Lodge **M**
(707) 263-4309. **Call for rates.** 2569 Lakeshore Blvd 95453. SR 29 exit 103 (11th St), 0.8 mi e, just n on Main St, just w on Clearlake Ave, 0.4 mi n on N High St, then 0.6 mi n. Ext corridors. **Pets:** Accepted.
⊚ ⊠ 🖥 ⊡ ⊡

LEGGETT

AAA **W** Redwoods River Resort **CA**
(707) 925-6249. **$75-$175, 7 day notice.** 75000 Hwy 101 95585. 6.5 mi n of jct SR 1. Ext corridors. **Pets:** Accepted.
〔SAVE〕 ⊚ ⊠ 🖥 ⊡ ⊡ ⊱ ⊠ 🐾 ☎

LITTLE RIVER

WWW The Inn at Schoolhouse Creek **CI**
(707) 937-5525. **$175-$399, 14 day notice.** 7051 N SR 1 95456. SR 1, 0.8 mi s of Van Damme State Park entrance. Ext corridors.
Pets: Accepted. ⊚ ⊠ 🖥 ⊡ ⊡ ⊪ ⊠ 🐾

WWW Little River Inn **CI** ❀
(707) 937-5942. **$130-$365, 5 day notice.** 7901 N SR 1 95456. On SR 1, just s of Van Damme State Park entrance. Ext/int corridors.
Pets: Other species. $25 one-time fee/pet. Designated rooms, service with restrictions, supervision. ⊚ ⊠ 🖥 ⊡ ⊡ ⊪ ⊠ 🐾

AAA **WWWW** Stevenswood Spa Resort **CI** ❀
(707) 937-2810. **$159-$399, 99 day notice.** 8211 N Hwy 1 95456. On SR 1, 0.4 mi n of Van Damme State Park entrance. Int corridors.
Pets: $25 one-time fee/pet. 〔SAVE〕 ⊚ ⊠ ⊡ ⊪ ⊠ 🐾

MENDOCINO

WWWW Agate Cove Inn **CA** ❀
(707) 937-0551. **$179-$329, 14 day notice.** 11201 N Lansing St 95460. Just w on Little Lake Rd from jct SR 1, then 0.6 mi n. Ext corridors. **Pets:** $20 daily fee/room. Designated rooms, service with restrictions, supervision. ⊚ ⊠ 🖥 ⊡ 🐾 ☎

AAA **WW** Blackberry Inn **M**
(707) 937-5281. **$100-$255, 7 day notice.** 44951 Larkin Rd 95460. 0.5 mi n on SR 1, then just e. Ext corridors. **Pets:** Accepted.
〔SAVE〕 ⊚ ⊠ 🖥 ⊡ 🐾

AAA **WWWW** Hill House Inn **H**
(707) 937-0554. **Call for rates.** 10701 Pallette Dr 95460. Just w on Little Lake St from jct SR 1, then just n on Lansing St. Ext corridors.
Pets: Accepted. 〔SAVE〕 ⊚ ⊠ 🖥 ⊡ ⊡ 🐾

WW Mendocino Hotel & Garden Suites **H**
(707) 937-0511. **Call for rates.** 45080 Main St 95460. 0.4 mi w on Main St from jct SR 1. Ext/int corridors. **Pets:** Accepted.
⊚ ⊠ ⊡ ⊪ 🐾

AAA **WWW** Mendocino Seaside Cottage **BB** ❀
(707) 485-0239. **$187-$299, 7 day notice.** 10940 Lansing St 95460. Just w on Little Lake Rd from jct SR 1, 0.3 mi n. Ext/int corridors.
Pets: $25 one-time fee/pet. Service with restrictions, supervision.
〔SAVE〕 ⊚ ⊠ 🖥 ⊡ 🐾

WW Nicholson House Inn **BB** ❀
(707) 937-0934. **$99-$229, 3 day notice.** 951 Ukiah St 95460. Just e of Lansing St; center. Ext/int corridors. **Pets:** Other species. $35 one-time fee/room. Service with restrictions, supervision.
⊚ ⊠ 🖥 ⊡ 🐾 ☎

AAA **WWW WWW** Stanford Inn by the Sea
Eco-Lodge **CI** ❀
(707) 937-5615. **$189-$490, 7 day notice.** 44850 Comptche-Ukiah Rd 95460. SR 1 exit Comptche-Ukiah Rd, just e. Ext corridors. **Pets:** Other species. $45 one-time fee/pet. Supervision.
〔SAVE〕 ⊚ ⊠ 🖥 ⊡ ⊡ ⊪ ⊱ ⊠ 🐾

MIDDLETOWN

WWW Backyard Garden Oasis Bed and Breakfast
Inn **BB** ❀
(707) 987-0505. **$139-$159, 5 day notice.** 24019 Hilderbrand Dr 95461. 3.9 mi s on SR 29, just e. Ext/int corridors. **Pets:** Dogs only. $20 one-time fee/pet. Designated rooms, service with restrictions, supervision.
⊚ ⊠ 🖥 ⊡

MONTE RIO

WW Rio Villa Beach Resort **M**
(707) 865-1143. **$100-$300, 7 day notice.** 20292 Hwy 116 95462. Center. Ext corridors. **Pets:** Small. $25 daily fee/room. Designated rooms, service with restrictions, crate. ⊚ ⊠ 🖥 ⊡

NAPA

AAA **WWWW** Bel Abri **BB**
(707) 253-2100. **$149-$310, 7 day notice.** 837 California Blvd 94559. SR 29 exit 1st St, just e. Int corridors. **Pets:** Accepted.
〔SAVE〕 ⊚ ⊠ 🅼 🖥 ⊡

WWW Blackbird Inn **BB** ❀
(707) 226-2450. **$185-$325, 7 day notice.** 1755 1st St 94559. SR 29 exit 1st St, 0.5 mi e to Jefferson St, then just n. Int corridors.
Pets: Medium, dogs only. $65 one-time fee/room. Designated rooms, service with restrictions, supervision. ⊚ ⊠ 🅼

WW The Chablis Inn **M** ❀
(707) 257-1944. **$79-$179, 3 day notice.** 3360 Solano Ave 94558. Just w off SR 29 via Redwood Rd, then just s. Ext corridors. **Pets:** Small, dogs only. $25 one-time fee/room. Service with restrictions, crate.
⊚ ⊠ 🅼 🖥 ⊡

WWW Embassy Suites Napa Valley **H**
(707) 253-9540. **$159-$399.** 1075 California Blvd 94559. SR 29 exit 1st St E. Ext/int corridors. **Pets:** Medium, other species. $75 one-time fee/room. Service with restrictions, crate.
〔ECO〕 ⊚ ⊠ 🅼 🖥 ⊡ ⊡ ⊪ ⊱ ⊠

AAA **WWW** The Inn on First **BB**
(707) 253-1331. **$199-$375, 30 day notice.** 1938 1st St 94559. SR 29 exit 1st St, just e via Clay St. Ext/int corridors. **Pets:** Accepted.
〔ECO〕 〔SAVE〕 ⊚ ⊠ 🅼 🖥 ⊡

AAA **WWW** John Muir Inn **H**
(707) 257-7220. **$120-$275.** 1998 Trower Ave 94558. SR 29 exit E Trower Ave. Int corridors. **Pets:** $30 one-time fee/room. Designated rooms, service with restrictions, crate.
〔SAVE〕 ⊚ ⊠ 🅼 🖥 ⊡ ⊱

AAA **WWW WWW** The Meritage Resort and Spa **H**
(707) 251-1900. **$159-$469.** 875 Bordeaux Way 94558. 0.5 mi n of jct SR 29 and 121; SR 121 N, follow Downtown Napa/Lake Berryessa, w on Napa Valley Corporate Way, then just s. Int corridors. **Pets:** Accepted.
〔SAVE〕 ⊚ ⊠ 🅼 🖥 ⊡ ⊪ ⊱ ⊠

AAA **W** Napa Valley Redwood Inn **M**
(707) 257-6111. **$67-$150, 3 day notice.** 3380 Solano Ave 94558. Just w off SR 29 via Redwood Rd, just s. Ext corridors. **Pets:** Other species. $10 daily fee/pet. Service with restrictions, supervision.
〔SAVE〕 ⊚ ⊠ 🅼 🖥 ⊱

The Napa Inn BB
(707) 257-1444. **$149-$295, 10 day notice.** 1137 Warren St 94559. SR 29 exit 1st St, 0.5 mi e, then 0.3 mi n. Int corridors. **Pets:** Accepted.

Napa River Inn H
(707) 251-8500. **$179-$599.** 500 Main St 94559. Downtown. Int corridors. **Pets:** Medium. $25 daily fee/room. Designated rooms, service with restrictions, supervision.

The Westin Verasa, Napa H
(707) 257-1800. **$129-$599, 3 day notice.** 1314 McKinstry St 94559. Jct Soscol Ave. Int corridors. **Pets:** Medium, dogs only. Service with restrictions, supervision.

NICE

Featherbed Railroad Co. BB
(707) 274-8378. **$99-$220, 3 day notice.** 2870 Lakeshore Blvd 95464. 0.5 mi s of SR 20. Ext corridors. **Pets:** Small. $30 one-time fee/pet. Designated rooms, service with restrictions, crate.

Gingerbread Cottages B & B CA
(707) 274-0200. **$125-$195, 7 day notice.** 4057 E Hwy 20 95464. On SR 20, south of town. Ext corridors. **Pets:** Accepted.

OCCIDENTAL

Inn at Occidental BB
(707) 874-1047. **$209-$359, 10 day notice.** 3657 Church St 95465. Town center. Ext/int corridors. **Pets:** Medium, dogs only. $40 daily fee/pet. Designated rooms, service with restrictions, supervision.

Occidental Lodge M
(707) 874-3623. **$95-$180.** 3610 Bohemian Hwy 95465. In the village. Ext corridors. **Pets:** Medium, dogs only. $15 daily fee/pet. Service with restrictions, supervision.

PETALUMA

Best Western Petaluma Inn H
(707) 763-0994. **$80-$130.** 200 S McDowell Blvd 94954. US 101 exit Washington St, just e. Ext corridors. **Pets:** Accepted.

Quality Inn-Petaluma H
(707) 664-1155. **$89-$219.** 5100 Montero Way 94954. US 101 exit Old Redwood Hwy-Penngrove northbound; exit Petaluma Blvd N-Penngrove southbound (east side), just n on N McDowell Blvd, then just e. Ext/int corridors. **Pets:** Large. $15 daily fee/room. Service with restrictions, supervision.

Sheraton Sonoma County-Petaluma H
(707) 283-2888. **$109-$339.** 745 Baywood Dr 94954. US 101 exit SR 116 (Lakeville Hwy), just se. Int corridors. **Pets:** Accepted.

POINT ARENA

Wharf Master's Inn H
(707) 882-3171. **$105-$395, 3 day notice.** 785 Port Rd 95468. 1 mi w on Iversen Ave from jct SR 1; at wharf. Ext corridors. **Pets:** Accepted.

ROHNERT PARK

Best Western Inn M
(707) 584-7435. **$95-$135.** 6500 Redwood Dr 94928. US 101 exit Rohnert Park Expwy, just w. Ext corridors. **Pets:** Medium, other species. $20 one-time fee/room. Designated rooms, service with restrictions, supervision.

DoubleTree by Hilton Hotel Sonoma - Wine Country H
(707) 584-5466. **$99-$179.** One Doubletree Dr 94928. US 101 exit Golf Course Dr; 3 mi s of Santa Rosa. Int corridors. **Pets:** Medium, dogs only. $50 one-time fee/pet. Designated rooms, service with restrictions, crate.

Rodeway Inn H
(707) 584-1600. **Call for rates.** 6288 Redwood Dr 94928. US 101 exit W Rohnert Park Expwy, just n. Ext corridors. **Pets:** Accepted.

RUTHERFORD

Rancho Caymus H
(707) 963-1777. **$149-$449, 3 day notice.** 1140 Rutherford Rd 94573. Just e of SR 29 and 128; 4 mi s of St. Helena. Ext corridors. **Pets:** Accepted.

ST. HELENA

El Bonita Motel H
(707) 963-3216. **$80-$280, 3 day notice.** 195 Main St 94574. 0.8 mi s on SR 29. Ext corridors. **Pets:** Medium, other species. $15 daily fee/pet. Service with restrictions.

Harvest Inn H
(707) 963-9463. **$229-$899, 14 day notice.** One Main St 94574. 1.5 mi s on SR 29. Ext corridors. **Pets:** Accepted.

SANTA ROSA

Americas Best Value Inn M
(707) 523-3480. **$70-$179.** 1800 Santa Rosa Ave 95407. US 101 exit Baker Ave northbound; exit Corby Ave southbound. Ext corridors. **Pets:** Accepted.

Best Western Plus Garden Inn H
(707) 546-4031. **$99-$154.** 1500 Santa Rosa Ave 95404. US 101 exit Baker Ave northbound, just n; exit Corby Ave southbound. Ext corridors. **Pets:** Medium, dogs only. $15 daily fee/pet. Designated rooms, service with restrictions, supervision.

Best Western Plus Wine Country Inn & Suites H
(707) 545-9000. **$99-$179.** 870 Hopper Ave 95403. US 101 exit Mendocino Ave/Old Redwood Hwy northbound, just w; exit Hopper Ave southbound. Ext corridors. **Pets:** Medium, dogs only. $20 one-time fee/room. Designated rooms, service with restrictions, supervision.

Courtyard by Marriott H
(707) 573-9000. **$119-$309.** 175 Railroad St 95401. US 101 exit downtown Santa Rosa, just w; jct 3rd and Railroad sts. Int corridors. **Pets:** Small. $25 daily fee/pet. Service with restrictions, supervision.

Extended StayAmerica-Santa Rosa-North H
(707) 541-0959. **$89-$104.** 100 Fountain Grove Pkwy 95403. US 101 exit Mendocino Ave/Old Redwood Hwy northbound, 0.3 mi e; exit Hopper Ave southbound, 0.6 mi e. Int corridors. **Pets:** Other species. $25 daily fee/pet. Service with restrictions.

Extended StayAmerica-Santa Rosa-South H
(707) 546-4808. **$79-$94.** 2600 Corby Ave 95407. US 101 exit Hearn Ave/Yolanda Ave northbound; exit Hearn Ave southbound. Ext corridors. **Pets:** Other species. $25 daily fee/pet. Service with restrictions.

Flamingo Conference Resort and Spa H ❀

(707) 545-8530. **$99-$299.** 2777 4th St 95405. Off SR 12; at Farmers Ln. Int corridors. **Pets:** Medium, other species. $50 one-time fee/room. Designated rooms, service with restrictions, supervision.

Fountaingrove Inn, Hotel & Conference Center H

(707) 578-6101. **$99-$299.** 101 Fountaingrove Pkwy 95403. 2.5 mi n on US 101 exit Mendocino Ave/Old Redwood Hwy, just e. Int corridors. **Pets:** Small, dogs only. $25 daily fee/room. Service with restrictions, crate.

Hillside Inn Motel M

(707) 546-9353. **$84-$99, 3 day notice.** 2901 4th St 95409. US 101, 2.5 mi e on SR 12; at Farmers Ln and 4th St. Ext corridors. **Pets:** Very small, other species. Service with restrictions, supervision.

Hilton Sonoma Wine Country H ❀

(707) 523-7555. **$129-$309.** 3555 Round Barn Blvd 95403. US 101 exit Mendocino Ave/Old Redwood Hwy; just ne at top of hill. Int corridors. **Pets:** Medium, dogs only. $50 one-time fee/pet. Service with restrictions, crate.

Quality Inn & Suites Santa Rosa H

(707) 521-2100. **$79-$249.** 3000 Santa Rosa Ave 95407. US 101 exit Todd Rd, 1.2 mi n. Int corridors. **Pets:** $15 daily fee/pet. Service with restrictions, supervision.

Sandman Inn H ❀

(707) 544-8570. **$89-$125.** 3421 Cleveland Ave 95403. US 101 exit W Mendocino Ave/Old Redwood Hwy. Ext corridors. **Pets:** $25 one-time fee/pet. Service with restrictions, supervision.

Santa Rosa Downtown Travelodge M

(707) 544-4141. **$72-$108.** 635 Healdsburg Ave 95401. US 101 exit College Ave, 0.3 mi e, then just s; at Mendocino Ave. Ext corridors. **Pets:** Accepted.

Travelodge M

(707) 542-3472. **$72-$161.** 1815 Santa Rosa Ave 95407. US 101 exit Baker Ave northbound; exit Corby Ave southbound. Ext corridors. **Pets:** Accepted.

Santa Rosa Inn M

(707) 542-5544. **Call for rates.** 2632 Cleveland Ave 95403. US 101 exit Steele Ln, 1 mi n. Int corridors. **Pets:** $15 daily fee/pet. Service with restrictions.

SONOMA

Best Western Plus Sonoma Valley Inn & Krug Event Center H

(707) 938-9200. **$99-$389.** 550 2nd St W 95476. 1 blk w of town plaza. Ext corridors. **Pets:** $20 daily fee/pet. Designated rooms, service with restrictions, supervision.

The Fairmont Sonoma Mission Inn & Spa H

(707) 938-9000. **$199-$549, 5 day notice.** 100 Boyes Blvd 95476. 2.5 mi n on SR 12. Ext/int corridors. **Pets:** Accepted.

Inn at Sonoma BB ❀

(707) 939-1340. **$225-$325, 7 day notice.** 630 Broadway 95476. On SR 12, just s of Sonoma Plaza. Int corridors. **Pets:** Medium, dogs only. $65 one-time fee/room. Designated rooms, service with restrictions, supervision.

The Lodge at Sonoma, A Renaissance Resort & Spa H

(707) 935-6600. **$199-$429, 3 day notice.** 1325 Broadway 95476. On SR 12, 1 mi s of Sonoma Plaza. Ext/int corridors. **Pets:** Accepted.

Sonoma Creek Inn M ❀

(707) 939-9463. **$89-$199, 7 day notice.** 239 Boyes Blvd 95476. SR 12, 0.5 mi w. Ext corridors. **Pets:** Medium, dogs only. $35 one-time fee/room. Designated rooms, service with restrictions, supervision.

UKIAH

Best Western Plus Orchard Inn H

(707) 462-1514. **$90-$120.** 555 S Orchard Ave 95482. US 101 exit Gobbi St, 0.5 mi w. Int corridors. **Pets:** Accepted.

Comfort Inn & Suites H ❀

(707) 462-3442. **$89-$159.** 1220 Airport Park Blvd 95482. US 101 exit Talmage Rd, just w, then just s. Int corridors. **Pets:** Medium. $20 daily fee/pet. Designated rooms, service with restrictions.

Days Inn M

(707) 462-7584. **$47-$80.** 950 N State St 95482. US 101 exit N State St, 0.5 mi s. Ext corridors. **Pets:** Medium. $10 daily fee/pet. Designated rooms, service with restrictions, supervision.

Discovery Inn H ❀

(707) 462-8873. **$79-$129.** 1340 N State St 95482. US 101 exit N State St, just sw. Ext corridors. **Pets:** Medium, other species. $25 one-time fee/pet. Designated rooms, service with restrictions, supervision.

Quality Inn M

(707) 462-2906. **$80-$140.** 1050 S State St 95482. US 101 exit Talmage Rd, 0.4 mi w, then just n. Ext corridors. **Pets:** Accepted.

Super 8 Ukiah M ❀

(707) 468-8181. **$49-$76.** 693 S Orchard Ave 95482. US 101 exit Gobbi St W, just nw. Ext corridors. **Pets:** $10 daily fee/pet. Supervision.

Travelodge Ukiah H ❀

(707) 462-5745. **$69-$199.** 1720 N State St 95482. US 101 exit N State St. Ext corridors. **Pets:** Other species. $20 daily fee/pet. Designated rooms, service with restrictions, supervision.

UPPER LAKE

Super 8 M

(707) 275-0888. **$59-$125, 3 day notice.** 450 E Hwy 20 95485. Jct SR 29, 0.5 mi e. Ext corridors. **Pets:** Dogs only. $10 daily fee. Service with restrictions, supervision.

Tallman Hotel CI

(707) 275-2244. **$149-$249, 30 day notice.** 9550 Main St 95485. Just n of SR 20; downtown. Ext/int corridors. **Pets:** Accepted.

WILLITS

Baechtel Creek Inn & Spa, an Ascend Collection hotel H ❀

(707) 459-9063. **$100-$180.** 101 Gregory Ln 95490. US 101, just w. Ext corridors. **Pets:** Medium, dogs only. $20 daily fee/pet. Designated rooms, service with restrictions, supervision.

◈ ▼▼▼ Old West Inn M
(707) 459-4201. **$55-$95.** 1221 S Main St 95490. US 101, 0.5 mi s of jct SR 20. Ext corridors. **Pets:** Small. $10 daily fee/pet. Service with restrictions, supervision. (SAVE) 🛰 🖥 💻

YOUNTVILLE
◈ ▼▼▼ ▼▼▼ Vintage Inn H ❀
(707) 944-1112. **$225-$700, 7 day notice.** 6541 Washington St 94599. SR 29 exit Yountville; center. Ext corridors. **Pets:** Other species. $40 one-time fee/room. Designated rooms, service with restrictions, supervision. (SAVE) 🛰 ♿ 🖥 💻 ➰ ✖

END AREA

WOODLAND
◈ ▼▼ Days Inn H
(530) 666-3800. **$55-$74.** 1524 E Main St 95776. I-5 exit 537 (Main St) northbound; exit SR 113 (Davis) southbound, just w; behind McDonalds. Int corridors. **Pets:** Medium. $10 daily fee/pet. Service with restrictions, supervision. (SAVE) 🛰 🖥 💻 ➰

◈ ▼▼▼▼ Holiday Inn Express Hotel & Suites H
(530) 662-7750. **$109-$179.** 2070 Freeway Dr 95776. I-5 exit 536 (CR 102), just n, then just e. Int corridors. **Pets:** Small. $20 daily fee/pet. Designated rooms, service with restrictions, supervision.
(SAVE) 🛰 ✖ ♿ 🖥 💻 ⟋

YERMO
◈ ▼▼ Oak Tree Inn H
(760) 254-1148. **Call for rates.** 35450 Yermo Rd 92398. I-15 exit 191 (Ghost Town Rd), just se. Int corridors. **Pets:** Accepted.
(SAVE) 🛰 ✖ 🖥 💻 🍴 ➰

YOSEMITE NATIONAL PARK
▼▼ The Redwoods In Yosemite VH
(209) 375-6666. **$190-$1300, 30 day notice.** 8038 Chilnualna Falls Rd 95389. 6 mi inside southern entrance via SR 41 and Chilnualna Falls Rd. Ext corridors. **Pets:** Accepted. 🖥 💻

YREKA
◈ ▼▼▼ Baymont Inn & Suites H ❀
(530) 841-1300. **$68-$95.** 148 Moonlit Oaks Ave 96097. I-5 exit 773, just w. Int corridors. **Pets:** Medium. $10 one-time fee/pet. Service with restrictions, supervision. (SAVE) 🛰 🖥 💻 ➰ ✖

◈ ▼▼▼ Best Western Miner's Inn M ❀
(530) 842-4355. **$103-$144.** 122 E Miner St 96097. I-5 exit 776 southbound, just w to N Main St, then just s; exit 775 northbound, just w to N Main St, then just n. Ext corridors. **Pets:** Medium. $10 daily fee/pet. Designated rooms, service with restrictions, supervision.
(SAVE) 🛰 🖥 💻 ➰ ✖

◈ ▼▼ Comfort Inn H
(530) 842-1612. **$70-$130.** 1804-B Fort Jones Rd 96097. I-5 exit 773, just w. Int corridors. **Pets:** Accepted. (SAVE) 🛰 🖥 💻 ➰

◈ ▼ Econo Lodge Inn & Suites M
(530) 842-4404. **$45-$95.** 526 S Main St 96097. I-5 exit 775, just w to Main St, then just s. Ext corridors. **Pets:** Medium. $20 deposit/pet, $10 daily fee/pet. Service with restrictions, supervision.
(SAVE) 🛰 🖥 💻 ➰

◈ ▼ Klamath Motor Lodge M
(530) 842-2751. **$50-$65.** 1111 S Main St 96097. I-5 exit 775 southbound, just w to Main St, then 0.9 mi s; exit 773 northbound, just w to Main St, then 1.1 mi n. Ext corridors. **Pets:** Medium. $5 daily fee/pet. Designated rooms, service with restrictions, supervision.
(SAVE) 🛰 🖥 💻 ➰

◈ ▼ Mountain View Inn/Motel M
(530) 842-1940. **$48-$68.** 801 N Main St 96097. I-5 exit 776, just w. Ext corridors. **Pets:** Accepted. (SAVE) 🛰 ✖ 🖥 💻

◈ ▼ Rodeway Inn M ❀
(530) 842-4412. **$48-$54.** 1235 S Main St 96097. I-5 exit 775 southbound, just w to Main St, then 0.9 mi s; exit 773 northbound, just w to Main St, then 1.1 mi n. Ext corridors. **Pets:** Medium. $25 deposit/room, $7 daily fee/pet. Designated rooms, service with restrictions, supervision.
(SAVE) 🛰 🖥 💻 ➰

◈ ▼▼ Super 8-Yreka M
(530) 842-5781. **$50-$69.** 136 Montague Rd 96097. I-5 exit 776, just w. Ext corridors. **Pets:** $10 daily fee/pet. Designated rooms, service with restrictions, supervision. (SAVE) 🛰 🖥 💻 ⟋

YUBA CITY
◈ ▼▼▼ Best Western Yuba City Inn M
(530) 674-1650. **$90-$160.** 894 W Onstott Rd 95991. Just s of jct SR 99 and 20. Ext corridors. **Pets:** Accepted. (SAVE) ♿ 🖥 💻 ➰ ✖

◈ ▼▼◈ Econo Lodge Inn & Suites H
(530) 674-1592. **$50-$100.** 730 Palora Ave 95991. 0.5 mi s of jct SR 99 and 20, just e on Bridge St, then just n. Int corridors. **Pets:** Accepted.
(SAVE) 🛰 ♿ 🖥 💻 ➰

COLORADO

ALAMOSA

Best Western Alamosa Inn

(719) 589-2567. **$93-$140.** 2005 W Main St 81101. On US 160, 1 mi w. Ext corridors. **Pets:** Medium, dogs only. $10 one-time fee/pet. Designated rooms, service with restrictions, supervision.

Comfort Inn of Alamosa

(719) 587-9000. **$71-$159.** 6301 Rd 107 S 81101. On US 160, 2.3 mi w. Int corridors. **Pets:** Medium, dogs only. $20 daily fee/pet. Designated rooms, service with restrictions, supervision.

Holiday Inn Express

(719) 589-4026. **$108-$148, 3 day notice.** 3418 Mariposa St 81101. On US 160, 1.8 mi w. Int corridors. **Pets:** Accepted.

ASPEN

Aspen Meadows Resort, A Dolce Resort

(970) 925-4240. **$125-$800, 30 day notice.** 845 Meadows Rd 81611. 0.3 mi n of SR 82 via 7th Ave, just w. Ext/int corridors. **Pets:** $25 daily fee/room.

Aspen Mountain Lodge

(970) 925-7650. **$116-$435, 7 day notice.** 311 W Main St 81611. 0.3 mi w on SR 82; between 2nd and 3rd sts. Int corridors. **Pets:** Dogs only. $20 daily fee/pet. No service, crate.

Hotel Jerome

(970) 920-1000. **$180-$1850, 30 day notice.** 330 E Main St 81611. Jct Main and Mill sts. Int corridors. **Pets:** Accepted.

Hotel Lenado

(970) 925-6246. **$145-$645, 30 day notice.** 200 S Aspen St 81611. 0.3 mi w on SR 82, just s via Aspen St to Hopkins St. Ext/int corridors. **Pets:** Other species.

Limelight Lodge

(970) 925-3025. **$115-$2520, 14 day notice.** 355 S Monarch St 81611. Just s of SR 82; at Monarch and Cooper sts. Int corridors. **Pets:** $25 daily fee/pet. Designated rooms, service with restrictions, supervision.

The Little Nell

(970) 920-4600. **$255-$3300, 30 day notice.** 675 E Durant Ave 81611. 0.3 mi e on SR 82, 0.3 mi s on Spring St; jct Durant Ave and Spring St; beside gondola at base of Aspen Mountain. Int corridors. **Pets:** Dogs only. $125 one-time fee/room, $25 daily fee/pet.

Mountain House Lodge

(970) 920-2550. **$79-$299, 30 day notice.** 905 E Hopkins St 81611. 0.3 mi e on SR 82, just e. Int corridors. **Pets:** Accepted.

The Residence Hotel

(970) 920-6532. **$199-$1195.** 305 S Galena St 81611. Jct S Galena St and E Hyman Ave; downtown. Int corridors. **Pets:** Accepted.

St. Regis Aspen Resort

(970) 920-3300. **$199-$2099, 60 day notice.** 315 E Dean St 81611. Just w on SR 82; jct Monarch and Dean sts. Int corridors. **Pets:** Accepted.

Sky Hotel

(970) 925-6760. **$200-$869, 30 day notice.** 709 E Durant Ave 81611. At base of Aspen Mountain. Ext/int corridors. **Pets:** Other species. Service with restrictions, supervision.

AVON

Comfort Inn Vail/Beaver Creek

(970) 949-5511. **$100-$225.** 161 W Beaver Creek Blvd 81620. I-70 exit 167, just s on Avon Rd, then just w. Int corridors. **Pets:** Large. $25 one-time fee/room. Service with restrictions, supervision.

Westin Riverfront Resort & Spa, Avon

(970) 790-6000. **$179-$889, 30 day notice.** 126 Riverfront Ln 81620. I-70 exit 167, 0.6 mi s on Avon Rd, then just w. Int corridors. **Pets:** Dogs only. Service with restrictions, supervision.

BAYFIELD

Wilderness Trails Ranch

(970) 247-0722. **$199-$2495, 120 day notice.** 23486 CR 501 81122. 35 mi e of Durango to CR 501 via US 160, continue 8 mi nw and 11 mi ne on CR 501, then 4.5 mi se on dirt road via CR 501. Ext corridors. **Pets:** Accepted.

BEAVER CREEK

Park Hyatt Beaver Creek Resort & Spa

(970) 949-1234. **$119-$949, 3 day notice.** 136 E Thomas Pl 81620. I-70 exit 167, 3 mi s on Avon and Village rds to Offerson Rd, then 0.4 mi e. Int corridors. **Pets:** Medium, dogs only. $50 one-time fee/room. Designated rooms, service with restrictions.

AAA ◈◈◈◈ **The Ritz-Carlton, Bachelor Gulch** H
(970) 748-6200. **Call for rates.** 130 Daybreak Ridge 81620. I-70 exit 167, just s past the Beaver Creek Village gatehouse to Prater Rd, then just w; follow signs to Bachelor Gulch Village. Int corridors.
Pets: Accepted. [SAVE] 🛜 ✕ &M 🛏 💻 🍴 ⇶ ✕

BOULDER

AAA ◈◈◈ **Best Western Plus Boulder Inn** H
(303) 449-3800. **$110-$190.** 770 28th St 80303. US 36 (28th St) at Baseline Rd. Int corridors. **Pets:** $50 deposit/room. Designated rooms, supervision. [SAVE] 🛜 🛏 💻 ⇶ ✕

AAA ◈◈◈ **Boulder Outlook Hotel & Suites** H ☙
(303) 443-3322. **$79-$159.** 800 28th St 80303. US 36 (28th St) exit Baseline Rd via Frontage Rd. Ext/int corridors. **Pets:** $10 daily fee/room. Designated rooms, service with restrictions, supervision.
[SAVE] 🛜 🛏 💻 🍴 ⇶ ✕

AAA ◈◈ **Boulder University Inn** M ☙
(303) 417-1700. **$79-$179.** 1632 Broadway 80302. US 36 (28th St) exit Baseline Rd, 0.3 mi s, then 3 mi nw. Ext corridors. **Pets:** Medium, other species. $100 deposit/room, $15 daily fee/room. Designated rooms, service with restrictions, supervision. [ECO] [SAVE] 🛜 🛏 💻 ⇶

AAA ◈ **Foot of The Mountain Motel** M
(303) 442-5688. **$80-$90.** 200 Arapahoe Ave 80302. 1.8 mi w of US 36 (28th St). Ext corridors. **Pets:** Large. $50 deposit/room, $5 daily fee/pet. Service with restrictions, supervision. [SAVE] 🛜 🛏 💻 [AC]

AAA ◈◈ **Holiday Inn Express** H
(303) 442-6600. **$99-$199.** 4777 N Broadway 80304. 3 mi n of Pearl Street Pedestrian Mall; jct US 36 (28th St), 0.3 mi s. Int corridors. **Pets:** Other species. $25 one-time fee/room. Service with restrictions, supervision. [SAVE] 🛜 ✕ 🛏 💻 ⇶

◈◈◈ **Homewood Suites by Hilton** H ☙
(303) 499-9922. **$159-$229.** 4950 Baseline Rd 80303. 1.2 mi e of US 36 (28th St); jct SR 157 (Foothills Pkwy), just w; entry off Baseline Rd. Ext/int corridors. **Pets:** Other species. $50 one-time fee/room. Designated rooms, service with restrictions. 🛜 🛏 💻 ⇶ ✕

AAA ◈◈◈ **Quality Inn & Suites Boulder Creek** H ☙
(303) 449-7550. **$120-$170.** 2020 Arapahoe Ave 80302. US 36 (28th St), 0.5 mi w. Ext/int corridors. **Pets:** $100 deposit/room, $15 daily fee/pet. Designated rooms, service with restrictions, supervision.
[SAVE] 🛜 🛏 💻 ⇶ ✕

◈◈◈ **Residence Inn by Marriott** H
(303) 449-5545. **$119-$309.** 3030 Center Green Dr 80301. 0.5 mi e of US 36 (28th St), e on Valmont Rd; from Foothills Pkwy, just w on Valmont Rd. Ext corridors. **Pets:** Accepted.
[ECO] 🛜 ✕ 🛏 💻 ⇶ ✕

BRECKENRIDGE

AAA ◈◈◈ **Beaver Run Resort & Conference Center** H ☙
(970) 453-6000. **$105-$585, 3 day notice.** 620 Village Rd 80424. 0.3 mi w of SR 9, on S Park Ave and Village Rd; at base of peak 9. Int corridors. **Pets:** Medium, dogs only. $40 daily fee/pet. Designated rooms, supervision. [SAVE] 🛜 🛏 💻 🍴 ⇶ ✕ [AC]

◈◈◈ **DoubleTree by Hilton Breckenridge** H
(970) 547-5550. **$129-$299.** 550 Village Rd 80424. Jct Main St, just w on S Park Ave, then just sw. Int corridors. **Pets:** Accepted.
[ECO] 🛜 ✕ 🛏 💻 🍴 ⇶ ✕ [AC]

AAA ◈◈◈ **The Lodge & Spa at Breckenridge** H
(970) 453-9300. **$79-$340.** 112 Overlook Dr 80424. Jct Main St and Park Ave, just s to Boreas Pass Rd, 2.1 mi w. Ext/int corridors.
Pets: Accepted. [SAVE] 🛜 ✕ 🛏 💻 [AC]

BROOMFIELD

AAA ◈◈◈ **Aloft Broomfield Denver** H ☙
(303) 635-2000. **$89-$169.** 8300 Arista Pl 80021. US 36 (Boulder Tpke) exit US 287/CR 121, 0.6 mi s, then 0.4 mi w on Uptown Ave. Int corridors. **Pets:** Medium, dogs only. Designated rooms, service with restrictions, crate. [SAVE] 🛜 ✕ 🛏 💻 ⇶ ✕

AAA ◈◈◈ **Hyatt Summerfield Suites Boulder/Broomfield** H
(720) 890-4811. **$89-$239.** 13351 W Midway Blvd 80020. US 36 (Boulder Tpke) exit Storagetek Dr/Interlocken Loop, 0.3 mi n, then just e on Via Varra Rd. Int corridors. **Pets:** Medium. $200 one-time fee/pet, $10 daily fee/pet. Service with restrictions, supervision.
[SAVE] 🛜 ✕ 🛏 💻 ⇶

AAA ◈◈◈◈ **Omni Interlocken Resort** H
(303) 438-6600. **$119-$389.** 500 Interlocken Blvd 80021. US 36 (Boulder Tpke) exit Interlocken Loop, 0.4 mi s, then 0.4 mi e. Int corridors.
Pets: Accepted. [SAVE] 🛜 ✕ &M 🛏 💻 🍴 ⇶ ✕

AAA ◈◈◈ **TownePlace Suites by Marriott Boulder/Broomfield** H
(303) 466-2200. **$179-$196.** 480 Flatiron Blvd 80021. US 36 (Boulder Tpke) exit Interlocken Loop, 0.4 mi s, just w on Interlocken Blvd, then just s. Int corridors. **Pets:** Accepted. [SAVE] 🛜 ✕ &M 🛏 💻 ⇶

BURLINGTON

AAA ◈◈ **Chaparral Motor Inn** M
(719) 346-5361. **$49-$65.** 405 S Lincoln St 80807. I-70 exit 437, just n on US 385. Ext corridors. **Pets:** $7 one-time fee/pet. Designated rooms, service with restrictions, supervision. [SAVE] 🛜 🛏 💻 ⇶

◈◈◈ **Comfort Inn Burlington** H
(719) 346-7676. **$70-$149.** 282 S Lincoln St 80807. I-70 exit 437, just n on US 385. Int corridors. **Pets:** Large. $15 daily fee/room. Designated rooms, service with restrictions, supervision. 🛜 ✕ 🛏 💻 ⇶

CAÑON CITY

◈◈ **Barrymore Hotel** H
(719) 275-2400. **$80-$149.** 110 Latigo Ln 81212. From 9th St, 3 mi e on US 50, then just n. Int corridors. **Pets:** Other species. $15 daily fee/pet. Designated rooms, crate. 🛜 ✕ 🛏 💻 ⇶

◈◈◈ **Hampton Inn** H
(719) 269-1112. **$105-$155.** 102 McCormick Pkwy 81212. From 9th St, 2.7 mi e on US 50, then just n. **Pets:** Accepted.
🛜 💻 ⇶

CARBONDALE

◈◈ **Comfort Inn & Suites** H
(970) 963-8880. **$79-$169.** 920 Cowen Dr 81623. Jct SR 82 and 133, just s. Int corridors. **Pets:** Accepted. 🛜 ✕ 🛏 💻 ⇶ ✕

CASTLE ROCK

AAA ◈◈◈ **Best Western Inn & Suites of Castle Rock** H ☙
(303) 814-8800. **$85-$130.** 595 Genoa Way 80109. I-25 exit 184 (Meadows Pkwy), just w to Castleton Way, just s, then e. Int corridors.
Pets: $20 daily fee/room. Service with restrictions, supervision.
[SAVE] 🛜 ✕ 🛏 💻 ⇶

◈◈◈ **Hampton Inn** H ☙
(303) 660-9800. **$89-$149.** 4830 Castleton Way 80104. I-25 exit 184 (Meadows Pkwy), sw to N Castleton Rd, just s, then e. Int corridors.
Pets: Medium. Service with restrictions, crate. 🛜 &M 🛏 💻 ⇶

CEDAREDGE

◈◈ **Howard Johnson Express Inn** M
(970) 856-7824. **$59-$90.** 530 S Grand Mesa Dr 81413. 0.3 mi s of Main St on SR 65. Int corridors. **Pets:** Accepted. 🛜 🛏 💻 ⇶

CIMARRON

▼▼ The Inn at Arrowhead ◆

(970) 862-8206. **$135-$175, 14 day notice.** 21401 Alpine Plateau Rd 81220. 11 mi e of Montrose on US 50, 5.1 mi s, follow signs. Int corridors. **Pets:** Accepted. 🖼 🍴 ⊠ ℳ 🎦 🐾

CLIFTON

◆◆◆◇ ▼▼◆▼ Best Western Grande River Inn & Suites ◆ ❀

(970) 434-3400. **$80-$150.** 3228 I-70 Business Loop 81520. I-70 exit 37, 0.8 mi s. Ext corridors. **Pets:** Medium. $20 daily fee/pet. Service with restrictions, supervision. 🅂🅰🆅🅴 🖼 🛡 💻 🐾

COLORADO SPRINGS METROPOLITAN AREA

CHIPITA PARK

▼▼▼ Chipita Lodge B & B 🅱🅱 ❀

(719) 684-8454. **$125-$190, 7 day notice.** 9090 Chipita Park Rd 80809. Jct US 24, just s on Fountain Blvd (Pine Peak Hwy), then 1.5 mi w; right at fork. Ext/int corridors. **Pets:** Dogs only. $25 one-time fee/pet. Designated rooms, no service, supervision. 🖼 ⊠ ℳ 🎦 🐾

COLORADO SPRINGS

◆◆◆ ▼▼ ▼ The Academy Hotel Colorado Springs ◆

(719) 598-5770. **Call for rates.** 8110 N Academy Blvd 80920. I-25 exit 150, just s. Int corridors. **Pets:** Medium. $10 daily fee/room. Designated rooms, service with restrictions, crate.
🅂🅰🆅🅴 🖼 ⊠ 🅰ℳ 🛡 💻 🍴 🐾 ⊠

◆◆◆ ▼▼▼ ▼▼ Antlers Hilton Colorado Springs ◆

(719) 473-5600. **Call for rates.** 4 S Cascade Ave 80903. I-25 exit 142 (Bijou St), just e, then just s; downtown. Int corridors. **Pets:** Accepted.
🅂🅰🆅🅴 🖼 🅰ℳ 🛡 💻 🍴 🐾 ⊠

◆◆◆ ▼▼ ▼ Best Western Executive Inn & Suites ◆ ❀

(719) 576-2371. **$80-$140.** 1440 Harrison Rd 80905. I-25 exit 138, just w; on northwest corner of interchange; entrance through restaurant. Int corridors. **Pets:** $10 daily fee/room. Designated rooms, service with restrictions, crate. 🅂🅰🆅🅴 🖼 🅰ℳ 🛡 💻 🐾

◆◆◆ ▼▼◆▼◆▼ The Broadmoor ◆ ❀

(719) 634-7711. **$300-$7500, 7 day notice.** 1 Lake Ave 80906. I-25 exit 138, 3 mi w on Circle Dr (which becomes Lake Ave). Ext/int corridors. **Pets:** $50 daily fee/pet. Service with restrictions.
🅂🅰🆅🅴 🖼 ⊠ 🅰ℳ 🛡 💻 🍴 🐾 ⊠

◆◆◆ ▼▼◆▼ ▼▼ Cheyenne Mountain Resort ◆ ❀

(719) 538-4000. **$99-$349.** 3225 Broadmoor Valley Rd 80906. I-25 exit 138, 1.4 mi w to SR 115, 0.5 mi s, just w on Cheyenne Mountain Blvd, then just s. Ext/int corridors. **Pets:** Small, dogs only. $125 one-time fee/pet. Designated rooms, service with restrictions, crate.
🅂🅰🆅🅴 🖼 ⊠ 🅰ℳ 🛡 💻 🍴 🐾 ⊠

◆◆◆ ▼▼ ▼ Comfort Inn ◆

(719) 380-9000. **$90-$160.** 2115 Aerotech Dr 80916. I-25 exit 139, 4.2 mi e on US 24 Bypass, 0.4 mi s on Powers Blvd, just w on Astrozon Blvd, then just n. Int corridors. **Pets:** Accepted. 🅂🅰🆅🅴 🖼 🛡 💻 🐾

◆◆◆ ▼▼ ▼ Comfort Inn South ◆

(719) 579-6900. **$79-$139.** 1410 Harrison Rd 80905. I-25 exit 138, just w to Rand Rd, then ne. Int corridors. **Pets:** Accepted.
🅂🅰🆅🅴 🖼 🛡 💻 🐾

◆◆◆ ▼▼◆▼ Crowne Plaza Colorado Springs ◆ ❀

(719) 576-5900. **$75-$169.** 2886 S Circle Dr 80906. I-25 exit 138, just e. Int corridors. **Pets:** Medium, dogs only. $50 one-time fee/pet. Service with restrictions, supervision. 🅂🅰🆅🅴 🖼 ⊠ 🛡 💻 🍴 🐾 ⊠

▼▼ ▼ Drury Inn-Pikes Peak ◆

(719) 598-2500. **$70-$154.** 8155 N Academy Blvd 80920. I-25 exit 150, just s, then e. Int corridors. **Pets:** Accepted. 🖼 🛡 💻 🐾

▼▼◆▼ ▼ Embassy Suites Hotel Colorado Springs ◆

(719) 599-9100. **$139-$159.** 7290 Commerce Center Dr 80919. I-25 exit 149 (Woodmen Rd), just w, then n. Int corridors. **Pets:** Medium, dogs only. $50 deposit/pet. Service with restrictions, supervision.
🖼 🛡 💻 🍴 🐾 ⊠

◆◆◆ ▼▼◆▼ ▼▼ Fairfield Inn & Suites Colorado Springs Air Force Academy ◆

(719) 488-4644. **$98-$120.** 15275 W Struthers Rd 80921. I-25 exit 158, just e on Baptist Rd, then just s. Int corridors. **Pets:** Accepted.
🅂🅰🆅🅴 🖼 ⊠ 🅰ℳ 🛡 💻 🐾 ⊠

▼▼◆▼ ▼ Fairfield Inn & Suites Colorado Springs/South ◆

(719) 576-1717. **$79-$189.** 2725 Geyser Dr 80906. I-25 exit 138, just w to E Cheyenne Mountain Blvd, then just s. Int corridors. **Pets:** Accepted.
🖼 ⊠ 🅰ℳ 🛡 💻 🐾 ⊠

◆◆◆ ▼▼ ▼ Garden of the Gods Motel ⓜ

(719) 636-5271. **$48-$125.** 2922 W Colorado Ave 80904. I-25 exit 141, 2.5 mi nw on US 24, just n on 31st St, then e. Ext/int corridors. **Pets:** Other species. $15 one-time fee/pet. Crate. 🅂🅰🆅🅴 🖼 🛡 🐾

◆◆◆ ▼▼◆▼ ▼▼ Hampton Inn & Suites Colorado Springs Air Force Academy/I-25 North @ Interquest ◆

(719) 598-6911. **$79-$189.** 1307 Republic Dr 80921. I-25 exit 153, 0.5 mi e, then just s. Int corridors. **Pets:** $50 one-time fee/room. Designated rooms, crate. 🅂🅰🆅🅴 🖼 ⊠ 🛡 💻 🐾

◆◆◆ ▼▼◆▼ Holiday Inn Express Air Force Academy ◆

(719) 592-9800. **$79-$209.** 7110 Commerce Center Dr 80919. I-25 exit 149 (Woodmen Rd), just w, then just n. Int corridors. **Pets:** Large, dogs only. $25 daily fee/pet. Designated rooms, service with restrictions, crate.
🅂🅰🆅🅴 🖼 🅰ℳ 🛡 💻 🐾 ⊠

▼▼◆▼◆▼ Homewood Suites by Hilton Colorado Springs-North ◆

(719) 265-6600. **$114-$134.** 9130 Explorer Dr 80920. I-25 exit 151 (Briargate Pkwy), 0.8 mi e; across from Focus on the Family. Int corridors. **Pets:** Accepted. 🖼 🅰ℳ 🛡 💻 🐾

▼▼ ▼ La Quinta Inn Colorado Springs Garden of the Gods ◆

(719) 528-5060. **$58-$165.** 4385 Sinton Rd 80907. I-25 exit 146 (Garden of the Gods Rd), just e. Ext/int corridors. **Pets:** Medium, other species. Service with restrictions, supervision. 🖼 💻 🐾

◆◆◆ ▼▼ ▼ Microtel Inn & Suites ◆ ❀

(719) 598-7500. **$53-$71.** 7265 Commerce Center Dr 80919. I-25 exit 149 (Woodmen Rd), just w, then n. Int corridors. **Pets:** Other species. $20 one-time fee/room. Designated rooms, service with restrictions.
🅂🅰🆅🅴 🖼 🅰ℳ 🛡 💻 🐾

◆◆◆ ▼▼◆▼ ▼ Radisson Hotel Colorado Springs Airport ◆ ❀

(719) 597-7000. **$119-$185.** 1645 N Newport Rd 80916. I-25 exit 139, 4.5 mi e on US 24 Bypass. Int corridors. **Pets:** Medium, dogs only. $100 deposit/room, $25 one-time fee/pet. Designated rooms, service with restrictions, crate. 🅂🅰🆅🅴 🖼 ⊠ 🅰ℳ 🛡 💻 🍴 🐾 ⊠

◆◆◆ ▼▼◆▼ ▼▼ Residence Inn by Marriott Colorado Springs Central ◆

(719) 574-0370. **$149-$229.** 3880 N Academy Blvd 80917. I-25 exit 146 (Garden of the Gods Rd), 4.5 mi e, then 0.3 mi s. Ext corridors. **Pets:** Accepted. 🅂🅰🆅🅴 🖼 ⊠ 🛡 💻 🐾 ⊠

▼▼▼▼ Residence Inn by Marriott Colorado Springs North at Interquest Pkwy 🅗

(719) 388-9300. **$89-$349.** 9805 Federal Dr 80921. I-25 exit 153, just e, then s. Int corridors. **Pets:** Medium. $75 one-time fee/pet. Service with restrictions, supervision. 🛰 ⊠ ⓛᴹ 🛌 💻 ⊱ ⊠

▼▼▼▼ Residence Inn by Marriott-Colorado Springs South 🅗

(719) 576-0101. **$109-$259.** 2765 Geyser Dr 80906. I-25 exit 138, just w to E Cheyenne Mountain Blvd, then just s. Int corridors. **Pets:** Accepted. 🛰 ⊠ ⓛᴹ 🛌 💻 ⊱ ⊠

🔗 ▼▼▼ Sleep Inn 🅗

(719) 260-6969. **$45-$129.** 1075 Kelly Johnson Blvd 80920. I-25 exit 150, just s on Academy Blvd to Kelly Johnson Blvd, then w. Int corridors. **Pets:** Small. $10 daily fee/pet. Service with restrictions, supervision. SAVE 🛰 ⓛᴹ 💻

🔗 ▼▼▼▼ Staybridge Suites-Air Force Academy 🅗

(719) 590-7829. **$89-$159, 3 day notice.** 7130 Commerce Center Dr 80919. I-25 exit 149 (Woodmen Rd), just w, then n. Int corridors. **Pets:** Accepted. SAVE 🛰 ⓛᴹ 🛌 💻 ⊱ ⊠

▼▼ ▼▼ TownePlace Suites by Marriott-Colorado Springs 🅗 ❄

(719) 594-4447. **$129-$159.** 4760 Centennial Blvd 80919. I-25 exit 146 (Garden of the Gods Rd), 1 mi w, then just n. Int corridors. **Pets:** Other species. $100 one-time fee/room. Service with restrictions. 🛰 ⊠ ⓛᴹ 🛌 💻 ⊱

▼▼▼▼ TownePlace Suites Colorado Springs South 🅗

(719) 638-0800. **$119-$139.** 1530 N Newport Rd 80916. I-25 exit 139, 5 mi e on US 24 Bypass, then just n. Int corridors. **Pets:** Accepted. 🛰 ⊠ 🛌 💻 ⊱

🔗 ▼▼ Travelodge 🅗

(719) 632-4600. **$45-$94.** 2625 Ore Mill Rd 80904. I-25 exit 141, 2.3 mi nw on US 24; entry via 26th St. Int corridors. **Pets:** Accepted. SAVE 🛰 ⊠ 🛌 💻 ⊱

MANITOU SPRINGS

🔗 ▼▼▼ El Colorado Lodge 🅒🅐

(719) 685-5485. **$56-$175, 14 day notice.** 23 Manitou Ave 80829. I-25 exit 141, 4 mi w on US 24, then just ne on US 24 business route. Ext corridors. **Pets:** Large. $75 deposit/room. Designated rooms, service with restrictions, crate. SAVE 🛰 ⊠ 🛌 💻 ⊱ ⊠

🔗 ▼▼▼ Park Row Lodge 🅜

(719) 685-5216. **$49-$89.** 54 Manitou Ave 80829. I-25 exit 141, 4 mi w on US 24, then just ne on US 24 business route. Ext corridors. **Pets:** Accepted. SAVE 🛰 🛌

▼ Red Wing Motel 🅜

(719) 685-9547. **Call for rates.** 56 El Paso Blvd 80829. I-25 exit 141, 4 mi w on US 24, just ne on US 24 business route/Manitou Ave, then just w on Beckers Ln. Ext corridors. **Pets:** Accepted. 🛰 🛌 💻 ⊱

🔗 ▼▼ Silver Saddle Motel 🅜 ❄

(719) 685-5611. **$59-$129.** 215 Manitou Ave 80829. I-25 exit 141, 4 mi w on US 24, then just sw on US 24 business route. Ext corridors. **Pets:** Medium. Designated rooms, service with restrictions, supervision. SAVE 🛰 ⊠ 🛌 💻 ⊱

END METROPOLITAN AREA

CORTEZ

▼▼ Baymont Inn & Suites 🅗

(970) 565-3400. **$94-$117.** 2321 E Main St 81321. 1.3 mi e on US 160. Ext/int corridors. **Pets:** Other species. $10 one-time fee/room. Designated rooms, service with restrictions. 🛰 ⊠ 🛌 💻 ⊱

🔗 ▼▼▼ Best Western Turquoise Inn & Suites 🅜 ❄

(970) 565-3778. **$110-$130, 14 day notice.** 535 E Main St 81321. 0.6 mi e of center on US 160. Ext corridors. **Pets:** Small, dogs only. $25 one-time fee/pet. Designated rooms, service with restrictions, supervision. SAVE 🛰 🛌 💻 ⊱

🔗 ▼ Budget Host Inn 🅜

(970) 565-3738. **$49-$108.** 2040 E Main St 81321. 1.3 mi e of center on US 160 (Main St). Ext corridors. **Pets:** Other species. $10 daily fee/pet. Designated rooms, service with restrictions, supervision. SAVE 🛰 🛌 💻 ⊱

▼▼ Econo Lodge 🅜 ❄

(970) 565-3474. **$60-$150.** 2020 E Main St 81321. 1.3 mi e on US 160. Ext corridors. **Pets:** Other species. $10 daily fee/pet. Designated rooms, service with restrictions, crate. 🛰 🛌 💻 ⊱

🔗 ▼▼▼ Holiday Inn Express 🅗

(970) 565-6000. **$119-$189.** 2121 E Main St 81321. 1.3 mi e on US 160. Int corridors. **Pets:** Accepted. SAVE 🛰 🛌 💻 🍴 ⊱ ⊠

🔗 ▼▼ Tomahawk Lodge 🅜

(970) 565-8521. **$49-$99.** 728 S Broadway 81321. 1 mi w of center on US 160. Ext corridors. **Pets:** Dogs only. $25 deposit/pet. Designated rooms, service with restrictions, supervision. SAVE 🛰 ⊱

CRAIG

🔗 ▼▼▼▼ Best Western Plus Deer Park Inn & Suites 🅗

(970) 824-9282. **$90-$300.** 262 Commerce St 81625. 0.3 mi s of jct US 40 and SR 13. Int corridors. **Pets:** Accepted. SAVE 🛰 ⊠ 🛌 💻 ⊱

▼▼▼▼ Candlewood Suites - Craig 🅗 ❄

(970) 824-8400. **$89-$169.** 92 Commerce St 81625. 0.4 mi s of jct US 40 and SR 13, just e. Int corridors. **Pets:** Medium, other species. $150 one-time fee/room. Service with restrictions, crate. 🛰 ⊠ 🛌 💻

CRESTED BUTTE

▼▼▼▼ Elevation Hotel & Spa 🅗 ❄

(970) 251-3000. **$167-$375, 3 day notice.** 500 Gothic Rd 81225. 5.9 mi n; in Mt Crested Butte. Int corridors. **Pets:** Dogs only. $35 daily fee/pet. Service with restrictions, crate. 🛰 ⊠ 🛌 💻 🍴 ⊱ ⊠ 🎾

▼▼▼▼ Elk Mountain Lodge 🅑🅑

(970) 349-7533. **$119-$189, 14 day notice.** 129 Gothic Ave 81224. 0.3 mi w on Elk Ave, then just n on 2nd St. Int corridors. **Pets:** Medium, dogs only. $25 one-time fee/room. Designated rooms, supervision. 🛰 ⊠ ⊠ 🎾

▼▼▼▼ Grand Lodge Hotel & Suites 🅗

(970) 349-8000. **$95-$269, 3 day notice.** 6 Emmons Loop 81225. 2.3 mi n; in Mt. Crested Butte. Int corridors. **Pets:** Accepted. 🛰 🛌 💻 🍴 ⊱ ⊠ 🎾

▼▼ Old Town Inn 🅜 ❄

(970) 349-6184. **$89-$149, 14 day notice.** 708 6th St 81224. On SR 135, just s of Elk Ave. Int corridors. **Pets:** $10 daily fee/room. Designated rooms, service with restrictions. 🛰

▼▼▼ WestWall Lodge 🆔

(970) 349-1280. **$250-$2300, 30 day notice.** 14 Hunter Hill Rd 81225. 2.2 mi n, then just e; in Mt. Crested Butte. Int corridors. **Pets:** Accepted.

🛰 ⊠ 🛏 🖵 🏊 ⊠ 🐾

CRIPPLE CREEK

🔷🔷🔷 ▼▼▼ Gold King Mountain Inn at Wildwood Casino 🆔

(719) 689-2600. **$79-$209.** 601 E Galena Ave 80813. 0.3 mi e off SR 67. Int corridors. **Pets:** Accepted. 🆂🆅🅴 🛰 🛏 🖵 🏊 ⊠

DELTA

🔷🔷🔷 ▼ ▼ Best Western Sundance Ⓜ

(970) 874-9781. **$89-$111.** 903 Main St 81416. 0.5 mi s on US 50. Ext corridors. **Pets:** $10 daily fee/room. Designated rooms, service with restrictions, supervision. 🆂🆅🅴 🛰 🛏 🖵 🍴 🏊

▼▼ Comfort Inn 🆔

(970) 874-1000. **Call for rates.** 180 Gunnison River Dr 81416. Just n of jct US 50 and SR 92. Int corridors. **Pets:** Accepted. 🛰 🛏 🖵

DENVER METROPOLITAN AREA

AURORA

🔷🔷🔷 ▼▼▼▼ Aloft Denver International Airport 🆔

(303) 371-9500. **$79-$199.** 16470 E 40th Cir 80011. I-70 exit 283 (Chambers Rd), just n, 0.7 mi e, then just s. Int corridors. **Pets:** Accepted. 🆂🆅🅴 🛰 ⊠ 🛏 🖵 🍴 🏊

🔷🔷🔷 ▼▼▼▼ Best Western Plus Gateway Inn & Suites 🆔

(720) 748-4800. **$79-$150.** 800 S Abilene St 80012. I-225 exit 7 (Mississippi Ave), just e, then 0.3 mi n. Int corridors. **Pets:** Medium. $15 daily fee/room. Service with restrictions, supervision.

🆂🆅🅴 🛰 ♿ᴹ 🛏 🖵 🏊 ⊠

▼▼▼▼ Holiday Inn Express & Suites Denver-Aurora 🆔 🐾

(303) 369-8400. **Call for rates.** 1500 S Abilene St 80012. I-225 exit 7 (Mississippi Ave), just e, then 0.5 mi s. Int corridors. **Pets:** $50 one-time fee/room. Designated rooms, service with restrictions, crate.

🛰 ⊠ ♿ᴹ 🛏 🖵 🏊

▼▼▼▼ Residence Inn by Marriott 🆔

(303) 459-8000. **$98-$152.** 16490 E 40th Cir 80011. I-70 exit 283 (Chambers Rd), just n, 0.5 mi e, then just s. Int corridors. **Pets:** Medium, other species. $75 one-time fee/room. Service with restrictions.

🛰 ⊠ ♿ᴹ 🛏 🖵 🏊

🔷🔷🔷 ▼▼ ▼ Sleep Inn Denver International Airport 🆔

(303) 373-1616. **$69-$130.** 15900 E 40th Ave 80011. I-70 exit 283 (Chambers Rd); from airport, Pena Blvd S to 40th Ave W. Int corridors. **Pets:** Medium, other species. $15 one-time fee/room. Designated rooms, service with restrictions. 🆂🆅🅴 🛰 ⊠ ♿ᴹ 🛏 🖵 🏊

BRIGHTON

🔷🔷🔷 ▼▼ ▼ Best Western Brighton Inn 🆔

(303) 637-7710. **$99-$119.** 15151 Brighton Rd 80601. US 85, 1 mi s of jct SR 7, just w. Int corridors. **Pets:** Accepted.

🆂🆅🅴 🛰 ♿ᴹ 🛏 🖵 🏊

CENTENNIAL

🔷🔷🔷 ▼▼ ▼ Candlewood Suites 🆔

(303) 792-5393. **$49-$99.** 6780 S Galena St 80112. I-25 exit 197 (Arapahoe Rd), 0.7 mi e, then just s. Int corridors. **Pets:** Accepted.

🆂🆅🅴 🛰 🛏 🖵

▼▼▼ Drury Inn & Suites-Denver Near the Tech Center 🆔

(303) 694-3400. **$85-$139.** 9445 E Dry Creek Rd 80112. I-25 exit 196 (Dry Creek Rd), just w; on northwest corner. Int corridors. **Pets:** Accepted. 🛰 🛏 🖵 🏊

🔷🔷🔷 ▼▼▼▼ Embassy Suites Denver Tech Center 🆔 🐾

(303) 792-0433. **$129-$199.** 10250 E Costilla Ave 80112. I-25 exit 197 (Arapahoe Rd), 1 mi e, 0.3 mi s on Havana St, then w. Int corridors. **Pets:** Large. $75 one-time fee/pet. Designated rooms, service with restrictions, supervision. 🆂🆅🅴 🛰 ♿ᴹ 🛏 🖵 🍴 🏊

▼▼ ▼ Extended Stay Deluxe-Denver Tech Center South 🆔 🐾

(303) 858-0292. **$80-$90.** 9604 E Easter Ave 80112. I-25 exit 197 (Arapahoe Rd), just e to Clinton St, 0.5 mi s, then just e. Int corridors. **Pets:** Other species. $25 daily fee/pet. Service with restrictions.

🛰 🛏 🖵 🏊

▼▼▼▼ Staybridge Suites Denver Tech Center 🆔

(303) 858-9990. **$85-$105.** 7150 S Clinton St 80112. I-25 exit 197 (Arapahoe Rd), just e to Clinton St, 0.5 mi s, then just e. Int corridors. **Pets:** Medium, other species. $20 daily fee/room. Designated rooms, service with restrictions. 🛰 ⊠ ♿ᴹ 🛏 🖵 🏊

🔷🔷🔷 ▼▼ ▼ TownePlace Suites Denver Tech Center 🆔

(720) 875-1113. **$69-$149.** 7877 S Chester St 80112. I-25 exit 196 (Dry Creek Rd), just w to Chester St, then 0.3 mi s. Int corridors. **Pets:** Accepted. 🆂🆅🅴 🛰 ⊠ ♿ᴹ 🛏 🖵 🏊

DENVER

🔷🔷🔷 ▼▼▼▼ Best Western Plus Denver Hotel 🆔

(303) 388-6161. **Call for rates.** 3737 Quebec St 80207. I-70 exit 278, just s. Int corridors. **Pets:** Accepted. 🆂🆅🅴 🛰 ⊠ 🛏 🖵 🏊

🔷🔷🔷 ▼▼▼▼ Brown Palace Hotel and Spa 🆔

(303) 297-3111. **Call for rates.** 321 17th St 80202. From Broadway and Tremont Pl, just sw. Int corridors. **Pets:** Accepted.

🆂🆅🅴 🛰 ⊠ 🛏 🖵 🍴 ⊠

🔷🔷🔷 ▼▼ ▼ Comfort Inn Central 🆔

(303) 297-1717. **$84-$109.** 401 E 58th Ave 80216. I-25 exit 215, just e, then n on Logan St; connected to Denver Merchandise Mart. Int corridors. **Pets:** Large, other species. $10 daily fee/pet. Designated rooms, service with restrictions, crate. 🆂🆅🅴 🛰 ♿ᴹ 🛏 🖵 🏊

🔷🔷🔷 ▼▼▼▼ Comfort Inn Downtown Denver 🆔 🐾

(303) 296-0400. **$99-$299.** 401 17th St 80202. From Broadway and Tremont Pl, just sw. Int corridors. **Pets:** Dogs only. $50 deposit/room. Supervision. 🆂🆅🅴 🛰 ⊠ 🛏 🖵

▼▼▼▼ Courtyard by Marriott Denver Stapleton 🆔

(303) 333-3303. **$59-$119.** 7415 E 41st Ave 80216. I-70 exit 278, s on Quebec St to Smith Rd exit, then e to Frontage Rd; I-270 exit 4. Int corridors. **Pets:** Accepted. 🅴🅲🅾 🛰 ⊠ 🛏 🖵 🍴 🏊

🔷🔷🔷 ▼▼▼▼ Crowne Plaza Denver International Airport 🆔

(303) 371-9494. **$89-$199.** 15500 E 40th Ave 80239. I-70 exit 283 (Chambers Rd), just n, then just e. Int corridors. **Pets:** Accepted.

🆂🆅🅴 🛰 ⊠ ♿ᴹ 🛏 🖵 🍴 🏊

▼▼▼▼ the Curtis Denver - a DoubleTree by Hilton Hotel 🆔 🐾

(303) 571-0300. **$119-$309.** 1405 Curtis St 80202. I-25 exit 212 (Speer Blvd S), s to Lawrence St, just ne, just se on 14th St, then just n. Int corridors. **Pets:** Large, other species. $25 daily fee/room. Service with restrictions, supervision. 🆂🆅🅴 🛰 ⊠ ♿ᴹ 🛏 🖵 🍴

DoubleTree by Hilton Hotel Denver H
(303) 321-3333. **$79-$224.** 3203 Quebec St 80207. I-70 exit 278, 0.5 mi s; I-270 exit 4. Int corridors. **Pets:** Accepted.

Drury Inn-Denver East H
(303) 373-1983. **$85-$139.** 4380 Peoria St 80239. I-70 exit 281 eastbound; exit 282 westbound, just n. Int corridors. **Pets:** Accepted.

Embassy Suites Denver-Aurora H
(303) 375-0400. **$109-$249.** 4444 N Havana St 80239. I-70 exit 280, just n. Int corridors. **Pets:** Accepted.

Embassy Suites Denver Southeast H
(303) 696-6644. **$119-$139.** 7525 E Hampden Ave 80231. I-25 exit 201, 1 mi e. Int corridors. **Pets:** Accepted.

Four Seasons Hotel Denver H ❀
(303) 389-3000. **$245-$4000.** 1111 14th St 80202. Between Lawrence and Arapahoe sts. Int corridors. **Pets:** Small, other species. Service with restrictions, supervision.

Grand Hyatt Denver H ❀
(303) 295-1234. **$99-$399.** 1750 Welton St 80202. Between 17th and 18th sts. Int corridors. **Pets:** Medium, dogs only. $40 daily fee/room. Designated rooms, service with restrictions, crate.

Hampton Inn & Suites Denver Tech Center H
(303) 804-9900. **$69-$159.** 5001 S Ulster St 80237. I-25 exit 199, e to Ulster St, then just n. Int corridors. **Pets:** Large. $25 one-time fee/room. Designated rooms, service with restrictions, crate.

Hampton Inn DIA H
(303) 371-0200. **$115-$135.** 6290 Tower Rd 80249. I-70 exit 286 (Tower Rd), 3.5 mi n. Int corridors. **Pets:** Accepted.

Holiday Chalet A Victorian Bed & Breakfast BB ❀
(303) 437-8245. **$94-$160.** 1820 E Colfax Ave 80218. Between Williams and High sts. Int corridors. **Pets:** Other species. $5 daily fee/pet. Service with restrictions, supervision.

Holiday Inn Denver East - Stapleton H
(303) 321-3500. **Call for rates.** 3333 Quebec St 80207. I-70 exit 278, 0.3 mi s; I-270 exit 4. Int corridors. **Pets:** Accepted.

Hotel Monaco Denver H
(303) 296-1717. **$159-$399.** 1717 Champa St 80202. Between 17th and 18th sts. Int corridors. **Pets:** Accepted.

Hotel Teatro H
(303) 228-1100. **$159-$1500.** 1100 14th St 80202. Between Lawrence and Arapahoe sts. Int corridors. **Pets:** Accepted.

Hyatt Summerfield Suites Denver Airport H
(303) 628-7777. **$89-$149.** 18741 E 71st Ave 80249. I-70 exit 286 (Tower Rd), 4.6 mi n, then just e; Pena Blvd exit 5 (Tower Rd/SR 32), just s. Int corridors. **Pets:** Large. $100 one-time fee/room. Designated rooms, service with restrictions, crate.

Hyatt Regency Denver Tech Center H ❀
(303) 779-1234. **$69-$319.** 7800 E Tufts Ave 80237. I-225 exit 2 (Tamarac St), just s to Tufts Ave; I-25 exit 199 (Belleview Ave), e to S Ulster St, then 0.5 mi n. Int corridors. **Pets:** Medium, dogs only. $25 one-time fee/room. Designated rooms, service with restrictions.

The Inn at Cherry Creek H
(303) 350-4440. **$199-$425.** 233 Clayton St 80206. Between 2nd and 3rd aves; in Cherry Creek Village. Int corridors. **Pets:** Accepted.

JW Marriott Denver At Cherry Creek H
(303) 316-2700. **$199-$399.** 150 Clayton Ln 80206. I-25 exit 205 (University Blvd), 2.4 mi n to 1st Ave, just e, then just n. Int corridors. **Pets:** Accepted.

La Quinta Inn & Suites Denver Airport DIA H
(303) 371-0888. **$88-$170.** 6801 Tower Rd 80249. I-70 exit 286 (Tower Rd), 4.2 mi n; 0.8 mi s of Pena Blvd. Int corridors. **Pets:** Medium, other species. Service with restrictions, supervision.

La Quinta Inn & Suites Denver Gateway Park H
(303) 373-2525. **Call for rates.** 4460 Peoria St 80239. I-70 exit 281, just n. Int corridors. **Pets:** Medium, other species. Service with restrictions, supervision.

La Quinta Inn Denver Cherry Creek H
(303) 758-8886. **$78-$170.** 1975 S Colorado Blvd 80222. I-25 exit 204, just s. Ext corridors. **Pets:** Medium, other species. Service with restrictions, supervision.

The Oxford Hotel H
(303) 628-5400. **$180-$380.** 1600 17th St 80202. Corner of 17th and Wazee sts. Int corridors. **Pets:** Accepted.

Quality Inn & Suites-DIA H
(303) 371-5300. **$79-$159.** 6890 Tower Rd 80249. I-70 exit 286 (Tower Rd), 4.2 mi n; 0.8 mi s of Pena Blvd. Int corridors. **Pets:** Accepted.

Quality Inn Denver East H ❀
(303) 371-5640. **$62-$119.** 3975 Peoria Way 80239. I-70 exit 281 eastbound; exit 282 westbound, just s. Ext corridors. **Pets:** Small. $10 daily fee/room. Designated rooms, service with restrictions, supervision.

Red Lion Denver Central H
(303) 321-6666. **Call for rates.** 4040 Quebec St 80216. I-70 exit 278, s on Quebec St to Smith Rd exit, then e to Frontage Rd. Int corridors. **Pets:** Accepted.

Renaissance Denver Hotel H
(303) 399-7500. **$170-$208.** 3801 Quebec St 80207. I-70 exit 278, just s via Smith Rd exit. Int corridors. **Pets:** Dogs only. $75 one-time fee/room. Designated rooms, service with restrictions, supervision.

Residence Inn by Marriott Denver City Center H ❀
(303) 296-3444. **$107-$319.** 1725 Champa St 80202. Between 17th and 18th sts. Int corridors. **Pets:** Other species. $75 one-time fee/room.

Residence Inn by Marriott Denver Downtown H
(303) 458-5318. **$159-$179.** 2777 Zuni St 80211. I-25 exit 212B (Speer Blvd) southbound; exit 212A (Speer Blvd S) northbound, just w, then just n. Ext corridors. **Pets:** Accepted.

The Ritz-Carlton, Denver H
(303) 312-3800. **Call for rates.** 1881 Curtis St 80202. Between 18th and 19th sts. Int corridors. **Pets:** Accepted.
[SAVE] [icons]

Sheraton Denver Downtown Hotel H ❄
(303) 893-3333. **$119-$369.** 1550 Court Pl 80202. Int corridors. **Pets:** Medium, dogs only. Service with restrictions, supervision.
[SAVE] [icons]

Staybridge Suites H ❄
(303) 574-0888. **$79-$179.** 6951 Tower Rd 80249. Just s of jct Pena Blvd. Int corridors. **Pets:** Medium. $75 one-time fee/room. Service with restrictions, crate. [icons]

Timbers Hotel H
(303) 373-1444. **Call for rates.** 4411 Peoria St 80239. I-70 exit 281, just n. Int corridors. **Pets:** Accepted. [SAVE] [icons]

TownePlace Suites by Marriott-Denver Southeast H
(303) 759-9393. **$69-$149.** 3699 S Monaco Pkwy 80237. I-25 exit 201, just e to Monaco Pkwy, then s. Int corridors. **Pets:** Other species. $100 one-time fee/room. Service with restrictions.
[SAVE] [icons]

TownePlace Suites by Marriott Downtown Denver H ❄
(303) 722-2322. **$99-$299.** 685 Speer Blvd 80204. I-25 exit 209A (6th Ave), 1.4 mi w, then just n on Acoma St. Int corridors. **Pets:** Other species. $100 one-time fee/room. Service with restrictions.
[icons]

Warwick Denver Hotel H ❄
(303) 861-2000. **$109-$499.** 1776 Grant St 80203. Between 17th and 18th aves. Int corridors. **Pets:** Medium, dogs only. $50 one-time fee/room. Designated rooms, service with restrictions, supervision.
[SAVE] [icons]

The Westin Denver Downtown H ❄
(303) 572-9100. **$169-$369.** 1672 Lawrence St 80202. Between 16th and 17th sts. Int corridors. **Pets:** Medium, dogs only. Service with restrictions, supervision. [SAVE] [icons]

ENGLEWOOD

Homewood Suites by Hilton - DTC/Inverness H
(303) 706-0102. **$89-$209.** 199 Inverness Dr W 80112. I-25 exit 195 (County Line Rd), 0.3 mi ne to traffic light, then just n. Int corridors. **Pets:** Medium. $100 one-time fee/pet. Designated rooms, service with restrictions, supervision. [icons]

Residence Inn Park Meadows H
(720) 895-0200. **$149-$169.** 8322 S Valley Hwy 80112. I-25 exit 195 (County Line Rd), just e to S Valley Hwy, then just s. Int corridors. **Pets:** Accepted. [icons]

GLENDALE

Loews Denver Hotel H ❄
(303) 782-9300. **$89-$279.** 4150 E Mississippi Ave 80246. I-25 exit 204, 0.8 mi n on Colorado Blvd, then just e. Int corridors. **Pets:** Large, other species. $25 one-time fee/pet. Supervision.
[SAVE] [icons]

GOLDEN

Candlewood Suites Lakewood/Golden H
(303) 232-7171. **Call for rates.** 895 Tabor St 80401. US 6 exit Simms St/Union Blvd, just n to 8th St, then just w. Int corridors. **Pets:** Accepted.
[SAVE] [icons]

The Golden Hotel, an Ascend Collection hotel H ❄
(303) 279-0100. **$139-$189.** 800 11th St 80401. At 11th St and Washington Ave; downtown. Int corridors. **Pets:** Large. $100 deposit/room, $15 daily fee/room. Designated rooms, service with restrictions, supervision.
[icons]

Residence Inn by Marriott Denver West/Golden H
(303) 271-0909. **$79-$249.** 14600 W 6th Ave, Frontage Rd 80401. US 6 exit Indiana Ave, just s to frontage road, then just e. Int corridors. **Pets:** Other species. $25 daily fee/pet. Service with restrictions.
[icons]

Table Mountain Inn H ❄
(303) 277-9898. **$135-$249.** 1310 Washington Ave 80401. US 6 exit 19th St, 0.5 mi n to Washington Ave, 0.5 mi w; downtown, just s of arch. Int corridors. **Pets:** $10 daily fee/pet. Designated rooms, service with restrictions, crate. [SAVE] [icons]

GREENWOOD VILLAGE

Hampton Inn Denver Southeast H
(303) 792-9999. **Call for rates.** 9231 E Arapahoe Rd 80112. I-25 exit 197 (Arapahoe Rd), just e. Int corridors. **Pets:** Accepted.
[icons]

Hyatt Summerfield Suites Denver Tech Center H
(303) 706-1945. **$79-$219.** 9280 E Costilla Ave 80112. I-25 exit 197 (Arapahoe Rd), e to Clinton St, then just s. Int corridors. **Pets:** Medium. $200 one-time fee/room. Service with restrictions, supervision.
[SAVE] [icons]

La Quinta Inn & Suites Denver Tech Center H
(303) 649-9969. **$64-$165.** 7077 S Clinton St 80112. I-25 exit 197 (Arapahoe Rd), e to Clinton St, then 0.5 mi s. Int corridors. **Pets:** Medium, other species. Service with restrictions, supervision.
[icons]

Residence Inn by Marriott-Denver Tech Center H
(303) 740-7177. **$189-$209.** 6565 S Yosemite St 80111. I-25 exit 197 (Arapahoe Rd), just w, then n. Ext corridors. **Pets:** Medium, other species. $75 one-time fee/room. Service with restrictions.
[icons]

Sheraton Denver Tech Center Hotel H
(303) 799-6200. **$149-$179.** 7007 S Clinton St 80112. I-25 exit 197 (Arapahoe Rd), just e, then s. Int corridors. **Pets:** Accepted.
[SAVE] [icons]

HIGHLANDS RANCH

Comfort Suites-Denver South H ❄
(303) 770-5400. **$69-$199.** 7060 E County Line Rd 80126. SR 470 exit Quebec St, just n to County Line Rd, just w, then just s; at Quebec Highlands Center. Int corridors. **Pets:** Medium. $50 deposit/room, $15 one-time fee/pet. Designated rooms, service with restrictions, supervision.
[SAVE] [icons]

Residence Inn by Marriott Denver Highlands Ranch H
(303) 683-5500. **$159-$179.** 93 Centennial Blvd 80126. SR 470 exit Broadway, just s, then w. Int corridors. **Pets:** Accepted.
[icons]

LAKEWOOD

AmericInn Hotel & Suites/Denver West- Federal Center H
(303) 231-9929. **Call for rates.** 11909 W 6th Ave 80401. US 6 exit Simms St/Union Blvd, westbound turn right at traffic light, but do not use right turn lane, follow signs to frontage road. Int corridors. **Pets:** Accepted.
[icons]

Best Western Denver Southwest H
(303) 989-5500. **$85-$119.** 3440 S Vance St 80227. Just ne of jct US 285 (Hampden Ave) and S Wadsworth Blvd, e on Girton Dr, then just s. Int corridors. **Pets:** Designated rooms, service with restrictions, supervision. SAVE 🛰 ☒ 🛏 💻 🏊

Holiday Inn Denver Lakewood H
(303) 980-9200. **$89-$129.** 7390 W Hampden Ave 80227. US 285 (W Hampden Ave) exit S Wadsworth Blvd, just e on Jefferson Ave, then n on Vance St. Int corridors. **Pets:** Medium. $50 one-time fee/room. Designated rooms, service with restrictions.
SAVE 🛰 🛏 💻 🍴 🏊 ☒

Lakewood Comfort Suites H
(303) 988-8600. **$100.** 7260 W Jefferson Ave 80235. Just se of US 285 (W Hampden Ave) and S Wadsworth Blvd, then e. Int corridors. **Pets:** $15 daily fee/pet. Designated rooms, service with restrictions, supervision. 🛰 ☒ 🛏 💻 🏊

Residence Inn by Marriott Denver SW/Lakewood H
(303) 985-7676. **$79-$219.** 7050 W Hampden Ave 80227. Just se of jct US 285 (W Hampden Ave) and Wadsworth Blvd, e on Jefferson Ave, then n on frontage road. Int corridors. **Pets:** Other species. $100 one-time fee/room. Service with restrictions, supervision.
🛰 ☒ 🛗 🛏 💻 🏊 ☒

Sheraton-Denver West Hotel H
(303) 987-2000. **$89-$279.** 360 Union Blvd 80228. US 6 exit Simms St/Union Blvd, just s on Union Blvd; 3 mi e of jct I-70 exit 261. Int corridors. **Pets:** Accepted. SAVE 🛰 ☒ 🛏 💻 🍴 🏊 ☒

TownePlace Suites by Marriott-Denver West/Federal Center H
(303) 232-7790. **$79-$169.** 800 Tabor St 80401. US 6 exit Simms St/Union Blvd, just n to 8th St, then w. Int corridors. **Pets:** $100 one-time fee/room. Designated rooms, service with restrictions, crate.
SAVE 🛰 ☒ 🛗 🛏 💻 🏊

LITTLETON

Hampton Inn & Suites Denver Littleton H
(303) 973-2400. **$79-$129.** 7611 Shaffer Pkwy 80127. SR 470 exit Ken Caryl Ave, just e, then just s. Int corridors. **Pets:** Accepted.
🛰 🛗 🛏 💻 🏊

Holiday Inn Express Hotel & Suites H
(720) 981-1000. **$89-$119.** 12683 W Indore Pl 80127. I-70 to SR 470 and Ken Caryl Ave; I-25 to SR 470 and Ken Caryl Ave, to Shaffer Ave, just n, then w. Int corridors. **Pets:** Accepted.
SAVE 🛰 🛗 🛏 💻 🏊

Homewood Suites by Hilton-Denver Littleton H 🐾
(720) 981-4763. **$99-$299.** 7630 Shaffer Pkwy 80127. SR 470 exit Ken Caryl Ave, just e, then just s. Int corridors. **Pets:** Other species. $50 one-time fee/room. Service with restrictions, supervision.
SAVE 🛰 🛗 🛏 💻 🏊 ☒

TownePlace Suites by Marriott-Littleton Denver Southwest H
(303) 972-0555. **$149-$164.** 10902 W Toller Dr 80127. SR 470 exit Kipling Pkwy, just s then 0.4 mi w on Ute St. Int corridors. **Pets:** Accepted.
SAVE 🛰 ☒ 🛏 💻 🏊

LONE TREE

Element Denver Park Meadows H
(303) 790-2100. **$89-$199.** 9985 Park Meadows Dr 80124. SR 470 exit Yosemite St, just s, then 0.4 mi e. Int corridors. **Pets:** Accepted.
ECO SAVE 🛰 ☒ 🛏 💻 🏊

Staybridge Suites Denver South-Lone Tree H
(303) 649-1010. **$79-$189.** 7820 Park Meadows Dr 80124. I-25 exit 195 (County Line Rd), w to Acres Green Dr, s to E Park Meadows Dr, then just w; SR 470 exit Quebec St, just s, then just e. Int corridors. **Pets:** Accepted. 🛰 🛗 🛏 💻 🏊

THORNTON

Sleep Inn North Denver H
(303) 280-9818. **$70-$75.** 12101 Grant St 80241. I-25 exit 223, e to Grant St, then n. Int corridors. **Pets:** Accepted.
SAVE 🛰 🛗 🛏 💻 🏊

WESTMINSTER

Comfort Inn Northwest H 🐾
(303) 428-3333. **$59-$135.** 8500 Turnpike Dr 80031. US 36 (Boulder Tpke) exit Sheridan Ave, just s, left on Turnpike Dr at 87th Ave, then 0.4 mi. Int corridors. **Pets:** Medium. $10 daily fee/pet. Designated rooms, service with restrictions, crate. SAVE 🛰 ☒ 🛗 🛏 💻 🏊

Comfort Suites Denver North H
(303) 429-5500. **$69-$124.** 12085 Delaware St 80234. I-25 exit 223, just w. Int corridors. **Pets:** $25 one-time fee/pet. Designated rooms, service with restrictions, supervision. SAVE 🛰 ☒ 🛏 💻 🏊

DoubleTree by Hilton Hotel Denver - Westminster H 🐾
(303) 427-4000. **$89-$189.** 8773 Yates Dr 80031. US 36 (Boulder Tpke) exit Sheridan Ave, n to 92nd Ave, e to Yates Dr, then 0.5 mi s. Int corridors. **Pets:** Other species. $25 one-time fee/room. Service with restrictions, crate. SAVE 🛰 🛏 💻 🍴 🏊

Residence Inn by Marriott H
(303) 427-9500. **$153-$187.** 5010 W 88th Pl 80031. US 36 (Boulder Tpke) exit Sheridan Ave, n to 92nd Ave, e to Yates Dr, then s. Int corridors. **Pets:** Accepted. 🛰 ☒ 🛗 🛏 💻 🏊 ☒

The Westin Westminster H 🐾
(303) 410-5000. **$109-$329, 3 day notice.** 10600 Westminster Blvd 80020. US 36 (Boulder Tpke) exit 104th Ave, just n. Int corridors. **Pets:** Large, dogs only. Designated rooms, service with restrictions, supervision. SAVE 🛰 ☒ 🛗 🛏 💻 🍴 🏊 ☒

END METROPOLITAN AREA

DILLON

Best Western Ptarmigan Lodge H
(970) 468-2341. **$76-$186.** 652 Lake Dillon Dr 80435. I-70 exit 205, 1.3 mi se on US 6 to Lake Dillon Dr, then 0.3 mi s. Ext/int corridors. **Pets:** $50 deposit/room, $10 daily fee/pet. Designated rooms, service with restrictions, supervision. SAVE 🛰 ☒ 🛏 💻 ☒ 🎿

Super 8 Dillon M
(970) 468-8888. **$49-$136.** 808 Little Beaver Tr 80435. I-70 exit 205, 0.3 mi s, then just e. Int corridors. **Pets:** Accepted. 🛰 🛏 💻

DURANGO

Apple Orchard Inn BB 🐾
(970) 247-0751. **$90-$250, 21 day notice.** 7758 CR 203 81301. 8.5 mi n on US 550, just w at Trimble Ln, then 1.3 mi n. Ext/int corridors. **Pets:** Dogs only. $20 daily fee/pet. Designated rooms, service with restrictions, supervision. SAVE 🛰 ☒ 🛏 💻 🎿

Best Western Durango Inn & Suites M
(970) 247-3251. **$79-$189.** 21382 US Hwy 160 W 81303. On US 160, 1 mi w. Ext corridors. **Pets:** Accepted. SAVE 🛰 🛏 💻 🍴 🏊

▼▼ **Caboose Motel** Ⓜ
(970) 247-1191. **$58-$190.** 3363 Main Ave 81301. 2.5 mi n on US 550. Ext corridors. **Pets:** Medium, dogs only. $10 daily fee/pet. Designated rooms, service with restrictions, supervision. 🛰❌📶📺🖥

▼▼▼ **DoubleTree by Hilton Hotel Durango** Ⓗ
(970) 259-6580. **$109-$269.** 501 Camino Del Rio 81301. Jct US 160 and 550. Int corridors. **Pets:** Accepted. ECO🛰📶📺🍴🏊❌

AAA ▼▼▼ **Durango Downtown Inn** Ⓜ ❖
(970) 247-5393. **$109-$189.** 800 Camino Del Rio 81301. On US 550, just n of jct US 160. Ext corridors. **Pets:** $10 daily fee/pet. Designated rooms, service with restrictions, supervision.
SAVE🛰📺🍴🏊❌

▼▼▼ **Leland House Bed & Breakfast Suites** BB ❖
(970) 385-1920. **$129-$399, 14 day notice.** 721 E 2nd Ave 81301. Just e of Main Ave via 7th St, then just n. Ext/int corridors. **Pets:** Other species. $20 daily fee/pet. Designated rooms, supervision.
🛰❌📶📺

▼▼ **Lightner Creek Inn** BB
(970) 259-1226. **$99-$199, 14 day notice.** 999 Lightner Creek Rd, CR 207 81301. 3 mi w on US 160, 1 mi n. Ext/int corridors. **Pets:** Accepted.
🛰❌📶📺❌🐾

▼▼ **Quality Inn** Ⓜ ❖
(970) 259-5373. **$79-$159.** 2930 N Main Ave 81301. 2 mi n on US 550. Ext corridors. **Pets:** Large, other species. $15 daily fee/pet. Designated rooms, service with restrictions, supervision. 🛰📺🏊

▼▼▼ **Residence Inn by Marriott** Ⓗ
(970) 259-6200. **$116-$242.** 21691 Hwy 160 W 81301. On US 160, just w. Int corridors. **Pets:** Accepted. 🛰❌📶📺🏊❌

▼▼ **The Rochester Hotel** BB ❖
(970) 385-1920. **$129-$399, 14 day notice.** 726 E 2nd Ave 81301. Just e of Main Ave via 7th St, then just n. Int corridors. **Pets:** Other species. $20 daily fee/pet. Designated rooms, supervision. 🛰❌📶

▼ **Siesta Motel** Ⓜ
(970) 247-0741. **$58-$145.** 3475 N Main Ave 81301. 2.6 mi n on US 550. Ext corridors. **Pets:** Accepted. 🛰📶📺

AAA ▼▼▼ **Strater Hotel** Ⓗ ❖
(970) 247-4431. **$119-$289.** 699 Main Ave 81301. Corner of 7th St and Main Ave; historic downtown. Int corridors. **Pets:** Small, dogs only. $125 deposit/pet. Designated rooms, service with restrictions, supervision.
ECO SAVE 🛰❌🍴

ESTES PARK

AAA ▼▼▼ **Castle Mountain Lodge** CA ❖
(970) 586-3664. **$75-$575, 30 day notice.** 1520 Fall River Rd 80517. 1 mi w on US 34. Ext corridors. **Pets:** Dogs only. $15 daily fee/pet. Designated rooms, service with restrictions, supervision.
SAVE 🛰❌📶📺❌🐾🖥

▼▼ **Mountain Shadows Resort** CA ❖
(970) 577-0397. **Call for rates.** 871 Riverside Dr 80517. Just s of jct Elkhorn and Moraine aves to Riverside Dr, then 1.2 mi sw. Ext corridors. **Pets:** Dogs only. $10 daily fee/pet. Designated rooms, service with restrictions, crate. 🛰❌📶📺🐾🖥

AAA ▼▼▼ **Rocky Mountain Park Inn** Ⓗ ❖
(970) 586-2332. **$100-$200.** 101 S Saint Vrain Ave 80517. 0.4 mi se on US 36 to US 7, then just s. Int corridors. **Pets:** Other species. $15 daily fee/room. Designated rooms, service with restrictions, supervision.
SAVE 🛰❌📶📺🍴🏊

▼▼▼ **Silver Moon Inn** Ⓜ
(970) 586-6006. **$80-$300.** 175 Spruce Dr 80517. Just w of jct Elkhorn and Moraine aves; west end of downtown. Ext/int corridors. **Pets:** Other species. Designated rooms, supervision. 🛰❌📶📺🏊❌

▼▼ ▼▼ **Tyrol Mountain Inn** Ⓜ
(970) 586-3382. **$69-$179, 3 day notice.** 1240 Big Thompson Ave 80517. 0.8 mi e of jct US 34 and 36. Ext corridors. **Pets:** Accepted.
🛰❌📶📺🏊❌

EVERGREEN

▼▼▼ **Comfort Suites at Evergreen Parkway** Ⓗ ❖
(303) 526-2000. **$114-$149.** 29300 US Hwy 40 80439. I-70 exit 252 (Evergreen Pkwy) westbound; exit 251 eastbound; on west side of El Rancho Restaurant. Int corridors. **Pets:** Large. $10 daily fee/pet. Designated rooms, service with restrictions, supervision.
🛰❌📶📶📺🏊❌

FIRESTONE

AAA ▼▼ **Best Western Firestone Inn & Suites** Ⓗ
(720) 494-1925. **$90-$130.** 11228 Business Park Cir 80504. I-25 exit 240, just e. Int corridors. **Pets:** Small, dogs only. $20 daily fee/pet. Designated rooms, service with restrictions.
SAVE 🛰❌📶📶📺🏊

AAA ▼▼ **Comfort Suites** Ⓗ
(720) 864-2970. **Call for rates.** 11292 Business Park Cir 80504. I-25 exit 240, just e on Firestone Blvd, just n on Frontage Rd, then just e. Int corridors. **Pets:** Accepted. SAVE 🛰❌📶📺🏊

FORT COLLINS

AAA ▼▼▼ **Best Western Kiva Inn** Ⓗ ❖
(970) 484-2444. **$70-$130.** 1638 E Mulberry St 80524. I-25 exit 269B, 1.5 mi w on SR 14. Ext/int corridors. **Pets:** Medium, dogs only. $10 daily fee/pet. Designated rooms, service with restrictions, supervision.
SAVE 🛰📶📺🏊❌

AAA ▼▼▼ **Best Western University Inn** Ⓜ
(970) 484-1984. **$79-$159.** 914 S College Ave 80524. I-25 exit 268, 4 mi w to College Ave, then just n on US 287. Ext/int corridors.
Pets: Accepted. SAVE 🛰❌📶📺🖥

▼▼ **Comfort Suites Fort Collins** Ⓗ
(970) 206-4597. **$59-$169.** 1415 Oakridge Dr 80525. I-25 exit 265 (Harmony Rd), 3.3 mi w to McMurry Ave, just s, then w. Int corridors. **Pets:** Medium, other species. $15 one-time fee/room. Service with restrictions, crate. 🛰❌📶📺🏊

▼▼▼ **Courtyard by Marriott** Ⓗ
(970) 282-1700. **$89-$119.** 1200 Oakridge Dr 80525. I-25 exit 265 (Harmony Rd), 3.3 mi w; entry via Lemay Ave. Int corridors. **Pets:** Accepted.
ECO 🛰❌📶📺🍴🏊

▼▼▼ **Fort Collins Marriott** Ⓗ
(970) 226-5200. **$80-$149.** 350 E Horsetooth Rd 80525. I-25 exit 265 (Harmony Rd), 4 mi w to John F Kennedy Pkwy, then n; just beyond Horsetooth Rd. Int corridors. **Pets:** Accepted.
ECO 🛰❌📶📶📺🍴🏊

▼▼▼ **Hampton Inn** Ⓗ
(970) 229-5927. **$109-$139.** 1620 Oakridge Dr 80525. I-25 exit 265 (Harmony Rd), 3.3 mi w, just s on McMurry Ave, then just e. Int corridors.
Pets: Accepted. 🛰📶📶📺🏊

▼▼▼ **Hilton Ft Collins** Ⓗ
(970) 482-2626. **$109-$189.** 425 W Prospect Rd 80526. I-25 exit 268, 4.3 mi w. Int corridors. **Pets:** Accepted. 🛰📶📺🍴🏊❌

▼▼▼ **Holiday Inn Express & Suites** Ⓗ ❖
(970) 225-2200. **Call for rates.** 1426 Oakridge Dr 80525. I-25 exit 265 (Harmony Rd), 3 mi w, just s on McMurry Ave, then just w. Int corridors. **Pets:** Medium, dogs only. $30 one-time fee/pet. Service with restrictions, supervision. 🛰❌📶📺🏊

AAA ▼▼▼ Homewood Suites by Hilton Fort Collins H
(970) 225-2400. **$119-$159.** 1521 Oakridge Dr 80525. I-25 exit 265 (Harmony Rd), 3 mi w, just s on McMurry Ave, then just w. Int corridors. **Pets:** Small. $75 one-time fee/room. Designated rooms, service with restrictions, supervision. 〔SAVE〕 📶 🍴 💻 🎇 ⊠

AAA ▼▼▼ La Quinta Inn Fort Collins H
(970) 493-7800. **$76-$149.** 3709 E Mulberry St 80524. I-25 exit 269B, just w, then just sw on frontage road. Int corridors. **Pets:** Medium, other species. Service with restrictions, supervision.
〔SAVE〕 📶 🍴 💻 🎇 ⊠

▼▼ Quality Inn & Suites H
(970) 282-9047. **$89-$199.** 4001 S Mason St 80525. I-25 exit 265 (Harmony Rd), 4.6 mi w to Mason St, then 0.5 mi n. Int corridors.
Pets: Accepted. 📶 ⊠ 〔ᴸᴹ〕 🍴 💻 🎇

▼▼▼ Residence Inn Fort Collins H
(970) 223-5700. **$89-$209.** 1127 Oakridge Dr 80525. I-25 exit 265 (Harmony Rd), 3.3 mi w to Lemay Ave, then s to Oakridge Dr. Int corridors.
Pets: Accepted. 〔ECO〕 📶 ⊠ 🍴 💻 🎇 ⊠

▼▼ Super 8 H
(970) 493-7701. **$55-$98.** 409 Centro Way 80524. I-25 exit 269B, just w. Int corridors. **Pets:** Other species. $10 daily fee/pet. Service with restrictions, crate. 📶 🍴 💻 ⊠

FORT MORGAN

AAA ▼▼▼ Central Motel M
(970) 867-2401. **$52-$69.** 201 W Platte Ave 80701. I-76 exit 80, 0.6 mi s, then w on US 34. Ext corridors. **Pets:** Accepted. 〔SAVE〕 🍴 💻

▼▼▼ Clarion Inn Fort Morgan H
(970) 867-8200. **Call for rates.** 14378 Hwy 34 80701. I-76 exit 75, 0.3 mi s. Int corridors. **Pets:** Accepted. 📶 ⊠ 🍴 💻 🍴 🎇

▼▼ Fort Morgan Super 8 H
(970) 867-9443. **$58-$70.** 1220 N Main St 80701. I-76 exit 80, just s, then just e. Int corridors. **Pets:** Accepted. 📶 🍴 💻

▼▼ Rodeway Inn M 🐾
(970) 867-9481. **$60-$120.** 1409 Barlow Rd 80701. I-76 exit 82 (Barlow Rd), just n. Ext/int corridors. **Pets:** Medium, other species. $15 one-time fee/pet. Service with restrictions, supervision. 📶 🍴 💻 🍴

FRISCO

AAA ▼▼▼ Best Western Lake Dillon Lodge H
(970) 668-5094. **$70-$295.** 1202 N Summit Blvd 80443. I-70 exit 203, just s. Int corridors. **Pets:** $15 daily fee/room. Designated rooms, service with restrictions, supervision. 〔SAVE〕 📶 ⊠ 🍴 💻 🎇 ⊠

▼▼ Hotel Frisco H 🐾
(970) 668-5009. **$79-$319, 14 day notice.** 308 Main St 80443. I-70 exit 201, 0.7 mi e. Int corridors. **Pets:** Other species. $10 daily fee/pet. No service, supervision. 📶 ⊠ 🍴 💻 〔AC〕

AAA ▼▼▼ New Summit Inn H
(970) 668-3220. **$49-$159, 15 day notice.** 1205 N Summit Blvd 80443. I-70 exit 203, just s, then just e. Int corridors. **Pets:** Dogs only. $10 daily fee/pet. Designated rooms, service with restrictions, supervision. 〔SAVE〕 📶 ⊠ 🍴 💻

AAA ▼▼▼ Ramada Limited Frisco H 🐾
(970) 668-8783. **$58-$176.** 990 Lakepoint Dr 80443. I-70 exit 203, just s, then just e. Int corridors. **Pets:** Other species. $10 daily fee/room. Designated rooms, no service, supervision. 〔SAVE〕 📶 🍴 💻

FRUITA

▼▼ Balanced Rock Motel M
(970) 858-7333. **$55-$65.** 126 S Coulson St 81521. I-70 exit 19, just n to Aspen Ave, then just w. Ext corridors. **Pets:** Accepted. 📶 🍴

▼▼ Comfort Inn H
(970) 858-1333. **$69-$139.** 400 Jurassic Ave 81521. I-70 exit 19, 0.3 mi s; just e of Dinosaur Journey Museum. Int corridors. **Pets:** Accepted.
📶 🍴 💻 🎇

AAA ▼▼▼ La Quinta Inn & Suites Fruita H
(970) 858-8850. **$116-$189.** 570 Raptor Rd 81521. I-70 exit 19, 0.3 mi s. Int corridors. **Pets:** Medium, other species. Service with restrictions, supervision. 〔SAVE〕 📶 🍴 💻 🎇

AAA ▼▼▼ Super 8 M
(970) 858-0808. **$66-$98.** 399 Jurassic Ave 81521. I-70 exit 19, 0.3 mi s; just e of Dinosaur Journey Museum. Int corridors. **Pets:** Large. $5 daily fee/pet. Designated rooms, service with restrictions, supervision.
〔SAVE〕 📶 🍴 💻 🎇

GLENWOOD SPRINGS

AAA ▼▼▼ Best Western Antlers M
(970) 945-8535. **$96-$176.** 171 W 6th St 81601. I-70 exit 116, just n, then just w. Ext corridors. **Pets:** Accepted.
〔SAVE〕 📶 ⊠ 🍴 💻 🎇 ⊠

AAA ▼▼▼ Hotel Colorado H 🐾
(970) 945-6511. **Call for rates.** 526 Pine St 81601. I-70 exit 116, just ne. Int corridors. **Pets:** Large, dogs only. $25 daily fee/pet. Designated rooms, service with restrictions, supervision.
〔SAVE〕 📶 ⊠ 🍴 💻 🍴 〔AC〕

▼▼▼ The Hotel Denver H
(970) 945-6565. **$124-$339.** 402 7th St 81601. I-70 exit 116; across from historic train station; in town center. Int corridors. **Pets:** Dogs only. Designated rooms, service with restrictions. 📶 ⊠ 🍴 💻 🍴

▼▼▼ The Hotel Glenwood Springs H
(970) 928-8188. **$99-$235.** 52000 Two Rivers Plaza Rd 81601. I-70 exit 116, 0.3 mi w on US 6 and 24. Int corridors. **Pets:** Dogs only. $15 daily fee/room. Designated rooms, service with restrictions.
📶 ⊠ 🍴 💻 🎇 ⊠

▼▼▼ Quality Inn & Suites H
(970) 945-5995. **$79-$149.** 2650 Gilstrap Ct 81601. I-70 exit 114, just s, then just w. Int corridors. **Pets:** Accepted. 📶 🍴 💻 🎇

▼▼▼ Residence Inn by Marriott H
(970) 928-0900. **$152-$186.** 125 Wulfsohn Rd 81601. I-70 exit 114, 2nd exit at roundabout, 1.5 mi e on Midland Ave, then just s. Int corridors.
Pets: Accepted. 📶 ⊠ 🍴 💻 🎇 ⊠

GRAND JUNCTION

AAA ▼▼ Americas Best Value Inn M 🐾
(970) 245-1410. **$62-$120.** 754 Horizon Dr 81506. I-70 exit 31, just n. Ext corridors. **Pets:** Other species. $10 daily fee/pet. Designated rooms, service with restrictions, supervision. 〔SAVE〕 📶 🍴 💻 🎇

AAA ▼▼▼ Best Western Sandman Motel M
(970) 243-4150. **$70-$125.** 708 Horizon Dr 81506. I-70 exit 31, 0.3 mi s. Ext corridors. **Pets:** Accepted. 〔SAVE〕 📶 🍴 💻 🎇

▼▼▼ Candlewood Suites Grand Junction H
(970) 255-8093. **Call for rates.** 654 Market St 81506. I-70 exit 28 (24 Rd), 1.3 mi s to F Rd, just e, then just n. Int corridors. **Pets:** Accepted.
📶 ⊠ 🍴 💻

AAA ▼▼▼ Clarion Inn H
(970) 243-6790. **$84-$109.** 755 Horizon Dr 81506. I-70 exit 31, just n. Ext/int corridors. **Pets:** Other species. Designated rooms, service with restrictions, supervision. 〔SAVE〕 📶 🍴 💻 🍴 🎇

▼▼▼ Fairfield Inn & Suites Grand Junction H
(970) 242-2525. **$99-$199.** 225 Main St 81501. At 2nd and Main sts; downtown. Int corridors. **Pets:** Accepted. 📶 🍴 💻 🎇

La Quinta Inn & Suites Grand Junction 🅗
(970) 241-2929. **$88-$192.** 2761 Crossroads Blvd 81506. I-70 exit 31, 0.3 mi n, then 0.3 mi w. Int corridors. **Pets:** Medium, other species. Service with restrictions, supervision. 📶 🔳 🛁 💻 🏊

Quality Inn of Grand Junction 🅗
(970) 245-7200. **$70-$129.** 733 Horizon Dr 81506. I-70 exit 31, just s. Int corridors. **Pets:** $10 daily fee/room. Designated rooms, service with restrictions, supervision. SAVE 📶 🛁 💻 🍴 🏊

Residence Inn by Marriott 🅗 🐾
(970) 263-4004. **$99-$149.** 767 Horizon Dr 81506. I-70 exit 31, 0.3 mi n. Int corridors. **Pets:** Large, other species. $100 one-time fee/room. Service with restrictions. 📶 🔳 🛁 💻 🏊 🔳

SpringHill Suites Grand Junction Downtown/Historic Main Street 🅗 🐾
(970) 424-5777. **$99-$199.** 236 Main St 81501. At 3rd and Main sts; west end of Main St. Int corridors. **Pets:** Dogs only. $25 daily fee/pet. Service with restrictions, crate. 📶 🔳 🛁 💻 🏊

Super 8 🅼 🐾
(970) 248-8080. **$58-$80.** 728 Horizon Dr 81506. I-70 exit 31, just s. Int corridors. **Pets:** Large. $10 daily fee/pet. Designated rooms, service with restrictions, supervision. SAVE 📶 💻 🏊

GRAND LAKE
Spirit Lake Lodge 🅼
(970) 627-3344. **$55-$200, 7 day notice.** 829 Grand Ave 80447. 0.3 mi e to Grand Ave, then 0.4 mi e. Ext corridors. **Pets:** Other species. $10 daily fee/pet. Service with restrictions, supervision.
SAVE 📶 🔳 🛁 💻 🐾

GREELEY
Comfort Inn-Greeley 🅗 🐾
(970) 330-6380. **$90-$120.** 2467 W 29th St 80631. US 34 Bypass exit 23rd Ave, just sw. Int corridors. **Pets:** Other species. $15 daily fee/pet. Service with restrictions, crate. SAVE 📶 🔳 🛁 💻 🏊

Country Inn & Suites By Carlson 🅗 🐾
(970) 330-3404. **$95-$180, 3 day notice.** 2501 W 29th St 80631. US 34 Bypass exit 23rd Ave, just s, then w. Int corridors. **Pets:** Other species. $15 daily fee/room. Service with restrictions, crate.
📶 🔳 💻 🏊

GUNNISON
Alpine Inn 🅼
(970) 641-2804. **$56-$180.** 1011 W Rio Grande 81230. 1.1 mi w of center, then just s. Int corridors. **Pets:** Small. $10 one-time fee/pet. Designated rooms, supervision. 📶 🛁 💻 🏊

Rodeway Inn 🅼
(970) 641-0500. **Call for rates.** 37760 W Hwy 50 81230. 2.3 mi w of center. Ext corridors. **Pets:** Accepted. 📶 🛁 💻

The Seasons Inn 🅼
(970) 641-0700. **Call for rates.** 412 E Tomichi Ave 81230. 0.3 mi e of center. Ext corridors. **Pets:** $10 daily fee/room. Supervision.
SAVE 📶 🛁

Super 8 🅼
(970) 641-3068. **$40-$149.** 411 E Tomichi Ave 81230. 0.3 mi e of center. Int corridors. **Pets:** Accepted. 📶 🛁 💻

Water Wheel Inn 🅗 🐾
(970) 641-1650. **$69-$109.** 37478 W Hwy 50 81230. On US 50, 2.5 mi w. Ext/int corridors. **Pets:** Other species. $5 daily fee/pet. Designated rooms, service with restrictions, supervision. SAVE 📶 🛁 💻 🔳

HOT SULPHUR SPRINGS
Canyon Motel 🅼 🐾
(970) 725-3395. **$59-$139.** 221 Byers Ave 80451. Just e on US 40. Ext corridors. **Pets:** Other species. $10 one-time fee/room. Service with restrictions, supervision. SAVE 📶 🔳 🛁 💻 🔳

IGNACIO
Sky Ute Casino Resort 🅗
(970) 563-3000. **$100-$300.** 14324 Hwy 172 N 81137. Jct US 172 and CR 517. Int corridors. **Pets:** Medium. $50 one-time fee/room. Designated rooms, service with restrictions, crate.
SAVE 📶 🛁 💻 🍴 🏊 🔳

KEYSTONE
The Inn at Keystone 🅗 🐾
(970) 496-4825. **$119-$249, 21 day notice.** 23044 Hwy 6 80435. I-70 exit 205, 6.5 mi e (on south side of US 6). Int corridors. **Pets:** Dogs only. $25 daily fee/room. Designated rooms, service with restrictions.
📶 🔳 🛁 💻 🍴 🔳 🔳

KREMMLING
Allington Inn & Suites 🅗
(970) 724-9800. **$97-$117.** 215 W Central Ave 80459. Just n on 2nd St. Int corridors. **Pets:** Accepted. SAVE 📶 🔳 🛁 💻 🏊

LA JUNTA
Holiday Inn Express 🅗
(719) 384-2900. **$99-$119.** 27994 US Hwy 50 Frontage Rd 81050. On US 50, 0.8 mi w. Int corridors. **Pets:** $20 daily fee/room. Service with restrictions, supervision. 📶 🛁 💻 🏊

Stagecoach Motel 🅼
(719) 384-5476. **$50-$70.** 905 W 3rd St 81050. US 50 and 350. Ext corridors. **Pets:** Medium. $10 daily fee/pet. Designated rooms, service with restrictions, supervision. SAVE 📶 🛁 💻 🏊

LAKE GEORGE
Mule Creek Outfitters/M Lazy C Ranch 🆁🅰
(719) 748-3398. **$75-$110, 30 day notice.** 801 CR 453 80827. 5 mi w on US 24, then 1 mi n on dirt road. Ext corridors. **Pets:** Dogs only. $5 daily fee/pet. Designated rooms, no service, supervision.
SAVE 📶 🔳 🛁 💻 🔳 🔳 🔳 🔳

LAMAR
Blue Spruce Motel 🅼
(719) 336-7454. **$55-$85.** 1801 S Main St 81052. 1.3 mi s on US 287 and 385. Ext corridors. **Pets:** Medium, other species. $7 daily fee/pet. Designated rooms, service with restrictions, supervision.
SAVE 📶 🛁 💻 🏊

Chek Inn 🅼
(719) 336-4331. **$50-$75.** 1210 S Main St 81052. 1 mi s on US 287 and 385. Ext corridors. **Pets:** Medium, other species. $7 daily fee/pet. Designated rooms, service with restrictions, supervision.
SAVE 📶 🛁 💻 🏊

Days Inn 🅗
(719) 336-5340. **Call for rates.** 1302 N Main St 81052. 0.8 mi n on US 50 and 287. Int corridors. **Pets:** Medium, dogs only. $15 daily fee/pet. Designated rooms, service with restrictions, supervision.
📶 🛁 💻 🏊

Holiday Inn Express & Suites 🅗
(719) 931-4010. **Call for rates.** 1304 N Main St 81052. 0.8 mi n on US 50 and 287. Int corridors. **Pets:** Accepted.
📶 🔳 🔳 🛁 💻 🏊

LAS ANIMAS

◆◆ Bent's Fort Inn  M

(719) 456-0011. **Call for rates.** 10950 E US 50 81054. On US 50, 1.5 mi e on frontage road. Int corridors. **Pets:** Accepted.

LEADVILLE

AAA ◆◆ Alps Motel M

(719) 486-1223. **$60-$85, 5 day notice.** 207 Elm St 80461. Just s of center on US 24. Ext corridors. **Pets:** Other species. $18 daily fee/pet. Service with restrictions, supervision.

LIMON

AAA ◆ Safari Inn M

(719) 775-2363. **$45-$130.** 637 Main St 80828. I-70 exit 361, 0.8 mi w. Ext corridors. **Pets:** Other species. $10 daily fee/pet. Designated rooms, service with restrictions, supervision.

LONGMONT

◆◆◆ Holiday Inn Express & Suites H

(303) 684-0404. **$133-$169.** 1355 Dry Creek Dr 80503. Jct Main St and Ken Pratt Blvd (SR 119), 2.2 mi w, just n, then just ne. Int corridors. **Pets:** Other species. $30 one-time fee/room. Service with restrictions, supervision.

AAA ◆◆◆ Plaza Hotel Longmont H

(303) 776-2000. **$100-$170.** 1450 Ken Pratt Blvd 80501. Jct US 287, 1.3 mi sw on Ken Pratt Blvd (SR 119). Int corridors. **Pets:** Other species. $50 one-time fee/room. Designated rooms, service with restrictions, supervision.

◆◆◆ Residence Inn by Marriott Boulder/Longmont H

(303) 702-9933. **$105-$210.** 1450 Dry Creek Dr 80503. Jct Main St and Ken Pratt Blvd (SR 119), 2.2 mi w, just n, then just ne; jct Hoover Rd and SR 119. Int corridors. **Pets:** Accepted.

AAA ◆◆ Super 8 Twin Peaks, Longmont H ❧

(303) 772-8106. **$57-$89.** 2446 N Main St 80501. I-25 exit 240, 6.9 mi w to US 287, then 3.5 mi n; jct SR 66. Int corridors. **Pets:** Small. $10 daily fee/pet. Designated rooms, service with restrictions, supervision.

LOUISVILLE

◆◆ Quality Inn in Boulder County H ❧

(303) 604-0181. **$59-$159.** 1196 Dillon Rd 80027. US 36 (Boulder Tpke) exit Superior (SR 170), just n on McCaslin Blvd, then just w. Int corridors. **Pets:** Medium, dogs only. $15 daily fee/pet. Designated rooms, service with restrictions, supervision.

◆◆◆ Residence Inn by Marriott-Boulder/Louisville H

(303) 665-2661. **$100-$200.** 845 Coal Creek Cir 80027. US 36 (Boulder Tpke) exit Superior (SR 170), n on McCaslin Blvd to Dillon Rd, then 0.6 mi e. Int corridors. **Pets:** Accepted.

LOVELAND

AAA ◆◆◆ Best Western Plus Crossroads Inn & Conference Center H ❧

(970) 667-7810. **$80-$200.** 5542 E US Hwy 34 80537. I-25 exit 257B, just w. Ext/int corridors. **Pets:** Other species. $18 daily fee/pet. Service with restrictions.

◆◆◆ Embassy Suites Loveland H

(970) 593-6200. **$129-$159.** 4705 Clydesdale Pkwy 80538. I-25 exit 259, just e, then just n. Int corridors. **Pets:** Accepted.

◆◆◆ La Quinta Inn & Suites Loveland H

(970) 622-8600. **$79-$179.** 1450 Cascade Ave 80538. I-25 exit 257B, 7.3 mi w. Int corridors. **Pets:** Medium, other species. Service with restrictions, supervision.

◆◆◆ Residence Inn By Marriott Loveland H

(970) 622-7000. **$149-$164.** 5450 McWhinney Blvd 80538. I-25 exit 257B, 0.5 mi w to outlet mall entry, just n, then just e. Int corridors. **Pets:** Accepted.

MANCOS

AAA ◆ Mesa Verde Motel M ❧

(970) 533-7741. **$55-$108, 3 day notice.** 191 W Railroad Ave 81328. On US 160 at SR 184; 7 mi e of Mesa Verde National Park entrance. Ext corridors. **Pets:** Other species. $15 one-time fee/room. Designated rooms.

MESA VERDE NATIONAL PARK

AAA ◆◆ Far View Lodge M

(970) 529-4421. **$110-$153, 3 day notice.** 1 Navajo Hill, MM 15 81330. 14 mi from park gate. Ext corridors. **Pets:** Accepted.

MONTE VISTA

AAA ◆◆ Best Western Movie Manor H

(719) 852-5921. **$85-$150.** 2830 W Hwy 160 81144. On US 160, 2 mi w. Ext corridors. **Pets:** Accepted.

MONTROSE

AAA ◆◆◆ Best Western Red Arrow H ❧

(970) 249-9641. **$69-$129.** 1702 E Main St 81401. 1 mi e on US 50. Ext/int corridors. **Pets:** $10 one-time fee/pet. Designated rooms, service with restrictions, supervision.

◆◆ Days Inn H

(970) 249-4507. **$68-$125.** 1417 E Main St 81401. 0.8 mi e on US 50. Ext corridors. **Pets:** Large. $10 daily fee/pet. Service with restrictions, supervision.

◆◆◆ Hampton Inn H

(970) 252-3300. **$109-$159.** 1980 N Townsend Ave 81401. 1.5 mi n on US 550. Int corridors. **Pets:** Accepted.

◆◆ Quality Inn & Suites H ❧

(970) 249-1011. **$80-$159.** 2751 Commercial Way 81401. 2 mi s on US 550, just w on O'Delle Rd. Int corridors. **Pets:** Medium. $10 daily fee/pet. Service with restrictions, supervision.

◆◆ Uncompahgre Bed & Breakfast BB

(970) 240-4000. **$90-$150.** 21049 Uncompahgre Rd 81401. 8 mi s on US 550 (east side). Int corridors. **Pets:** Dogs only. Designated rooms, service with restrictions, supervision.

◆ Western Motel M

(970) 249-3481. **Call for rates.** 1200 E Main St 81401. 0.8 mi e on US 50. Ext corridors. **Pets:** Accepted.

NEDERLAND

AAA ◆◆◆ Best Western Lodge at Nederland H

(303) 258-9463. **Call for rates.** 55 Lakeview Dr 80466. SR 119; across from Visitor's Center. Int corridors. **Pets:** Accepted.

NEW CASTLE

AAA ◆◆ Rodeway Inn M ❧

(970) 984-2363. **Call for rates.** 781 Burning Mountain Ave 81647. I-70 exit 105, just n, then w. Int corridors. **Pets:** Other species. $10 daily fee/pet. Supervision.

OURAY

Best Western Plus Twin Peaks Lodge & Hot Springs H ✿

(970) 325-4427. **$100-$399.** 125 3rd Ave 81427. Just s on US 550 (Main St), then just w on 3rd Ave. Ext corridors. **Pets:** Dogs only. $20 daily fee/pet. Designated rooms, service with restrictions, supervision.

SAVE 🛰 ✕ 🛏 🖵 🍽 ⊠

Comfort Inn M

(970) 325-7203. **$64-$149.** 191 5th Ave 81427. Just w of US 550 (Main St) via 5th Ave. Ext corridors. **Pets:** Accepted. 🛰 🔥M 🛏 🖵

Ouray Riverside Inn & Cabins M

(970) 325-4061. **$62-$212, 3 day notice.** 1804 N Main St 81427. 1 mi n of center on US 550 (Main St). Ext corridors. **Pets:** Other species. $5 daily fee/pet. Designated rooms, service with restrictions, supervision.

SAVE 🛰 ✕ 🛏 🖵 ⊠

Ouray Victorian Inn M 🐾

(970) 325-7222. **$72-$199.** 50 3rd Ave 81427. Just w of US 550 (Main St) via 3rd Ave. Ext corridors. **Pets:** Dogs only. $10 daily fee/pet. Designated rooms, service with restrictions, crate. SAVE 🛰 ✕ 🛏 🖵

River's Edge Motel M

(970) 325-4621. **$51-$150.** 110 7th Ave 81427. Just w of US 550 (Main St) via 7th Ave. Ext corridors. **Pets:** Accepted. SAVE 🛰 ✕ 🛏 🖵

PAGOSA SPRINGS

Alpine Inn of Pagosa Springs M

(970) 731-4005. **Call for rates.** 8 Solomon Dr 81147. 2.5 mi w on US 160, just w on Piedra Rd. Ext/int corridors. **Pets:** Accepted.

SAVE 🛰 🛏 🖵

Fireside Inn Cabins CA ✿

(970) 264-9204. **$105-$194, 30 day notice.** 1600 E Hwy 160 81147. 1.3 mi e on US 160. Ext corridors. **Pets:** Dogs only. $10 daily fee/pet. Designated rooms, no service, crate. 🛰 🛏 🖵 ⊠ 🐾

High Country Lodge & Cabins M ✿

(970) 264-4181. **$79-$210.** 3821 E Hwy 160 81147. On US 160, 3 mi e. Ext corridors. **Pets:** $10 daily fee/pet. Supervision. 🛰 🛏 🖵 ⊠

Pagosa Lodge H

(970) 731-4141. **Call for rates.** 3505 W Hwy 160 81147. On US 160, 3.5 mi w. Int corridors. **Pets:** Accepted. 🛰 ✕ 🛏 🖵 🏊 ⊠

Pagosa Springs Inn & Suites M

(970) 731-3400. **$65-$189.** 519 Village Dr 81147. 3.8 mi w on US 160. Int corridors. **Pets:** Medium. $10 daily fee/pet. Designated rooms, service with restrictions, supervision. 🛰 🛏 🖵 🏊

PALISADE

Wine Country Inn H

(970) 464-5777. **$105-$275.** 777 Grande River Dr 81526. I-70 exit 42, 0.3 mi w. Int corridors. **Pets:** Medium, dogs only. $50 deposit/room, $35 one-time fee/room. Designated rooms, service with restrictions, supervision. SAVE 🛰 🔥M 🛏 🖵 🍽 🏊

PARKER

Holiday Inn H

(303) 248-2147. **$127-$147.** 19308 Cottonwood Dr 80138. E470 toll road exit 5 (Parker Rd/SR 83) eastbound, straight at light, follow signs to Cottonwood Dr; exit westbound, just s to Crown Crest Blvd, follow signs to Cottonwood Dr. Int corridors. **Pets:** Medium. $75 one-time fee/room. Service with restrictions, supervision. 🛰 ✕ 🛏 🖵 🍽 🏊

Super 8-Parker H ✿

(720) 851-2644. **$71-$98.** 6230 E Pine Ln 80138. E470 toll road exit 5 (Parker Rd/SR 83), 0.4 mi se, then just e. Int corridors. **Pets:** $25 one-time fee/pet. Designated rooms, service with restrictions, crate.

🛰 🛏 🖵

PUEBLO

Best Western Eagleridge Inn & Suites H ✿

(719) 543-4644. **$89-$100.** 4727 N Elizabeth St 81008. I-25 exit 102, just w, then just n. Int corridors. **Pets:** Large. $20 one-time fee/room. Designated rooms, service with restrictions, crate.

SAVE 🛰 ✕ 🛏 🖵 ⊠

Holiday Inn & Suites H

(719) 542-8888. **$79-$159.** 4530 Dillon Dr 81008. I-25 exit 102, just e, then just s. Int corridors. **Pets:** Accepted.

🛰 ✕ 🔥M 🛏 🖵 🍽 🏊

La Quinta Inn & Suites Pueblo H

(719) 542-3500. **$88-$174.** 4801 N Elizabeth St 81008. I-25 exit 102, just nw. Int corridors. **Pets:** Medium, other species. Service with restrictions, supervision. 🛰 🛏 🖵 🏊

Microtel Inn & Suites H

(719) 242-2020. **$44-$71.** 3343 Gateway Dr 81004. I-25 exit 94, just w, then just s. Int corridors. **Pets:** Accepted. 🛰 🛏 🖵

Pueblo Marriott at the Convention Center ◆

(719) 542-3200. **$161-$197.** 110 W 1st St 81003. I-25 exit 98B, just w. Int corridors. **Pets:** Accepted. SAVE 🛰 ✕ 🔥M 🛏 🖵 🍽 🏊

RIDGWAY

Ridgway Lodge & Suites H

(970) 626-5444. **$79-$99.** 373 Palomino Tr 81432. Jct US 550 and SR 62, just e, just s. Int corridors. **Pets:** $15 daily fee/pet. Designated rooms, service with restrictions, supervision. 🛰 ✕ 🛏 🖵 🏊 ⊠

RIFLE

Comfort Inn & Suites Rifle H ✿

(970) 625-9912. **$71-$166.** 301 S 7th St 81650. I-70 exit 90, just s, then just w. Int corridors. **Pets:** Other species. $10 daily fee/pet. Designated rooms, service with restrictions, supervision.

🛰 ✕ 🛏 🖵 ⊠

Hampton Inn & Suites Rifle H ✿

(970) 625-1500. **$89-$119.** 499 Airport Rd 81650. I-70 exit 90, just s, then just e. Int corridors. **Pets:** Medium, other species. No service.

SAVE 🛰 ✕ 🛏 🖵 🏊

La Quinta Inn & Suites Rifle H

(970) 625-2676. **$82-$148.** 600 Wapiti Ct 81650. I-70 exit 90, just s, then just e. Int corridors. **Pets:** Medium, other species. Service with restrictions, supervision. 🛰 ✕ 🛏 🖵 🏊

Rusty Cannon Motel M

(970) 625-4004. **$76-$129.** 701 Taughenbaugh Blvd 81650. I-70 exit 90, just s of roundabout. Ext corridors. **Pets:** Accepted.

SAVE 🛰 🛏 🖵 🏊

SALIDA

Aspen Leaf Lodge M ✿

(719) 539-6733. **$45-$99.** 7350 W Hwy 50 81201. 0.3 mi w of Hot Springs Pool. Ext corridors. **Pets:** Medium, other species. $5 daily fee/pet. Service with restrictions, supervision. 🛰 🛏

Chalets at Tudor Rose VH ✿

(719) 539-2002. **$200-$300, 30 day notice.** 6720 CR 104 81201. Just e on US 50, just s on CR 104, then 0.5 mi up the hill, follow signs. Ext corridors. **Pets:** Dogs only. $10 daily fee/pet. No service, crate.

🛰 ✕ 🔥M 🛏 🖵 🐾

Silver Ridge Lodge M ✿

(719) 539-2553. **$50-$100.** 545 W Rainbow Blvd 81201. On US 50. Ext corridors. **Pets:** Small, dogs only. $20 daily fee/pet. Designated rooms, service with restrictions, supervision. SAVE 🛰 🛏 🖵 🏊

▼▼ Super 8 **M**
(719) 539-6689. **$85-$126.** 525 W Rainbow Blvd 81201. On US 50. Ext corridors. **Pets:** Accepted. 🛰 🔒 🖥 🏊

△△△ ▼ ▼ ▼ Woodland Motel **M** 🐾
(719) 539-4980. **$55-$165.** 903 W 1st St 81201. 0.5 mi w on 1st St (SR 291); just w of historic district. Ext corridors. **Pets:** Other species.
🆂🅰🆅🅴 🛰 🔒 🖥

SILVERTHORNE
▼▼ Quality Inn & Suites **H**
(970) 513-1222. **$129-$189.** 530 Silverthorne Ln 80498. I-70 exit 205, just n on SR 9, just e on Rainbow Dr, then just e on Tanglewood Ln. Int corridors. **Pets:** Accepted. 🛰 🔒 🖥 🏊

SILVERTON
△△△ ▼▼▼ Silverton's Inn of the Rockies at the Historic Alma House **BB**
(970) 387-5336. **$99-$149, 7 day notice.** 220 E 10th St 81433. Just se of 10th and Main sts. Int corridors. **Pets:** Dogs only. $20 daily fee/pet. Service with restrictions, supervision. 🆂🅰🆅🅴 🛰 ✕ 🐾 🄯

▼▼ Villa Dallavalle Inn **BB**
(970) 387-5555. **$109-$125.** 1257 Blair St 81433. Corner of 13th and Blair sts. Int corridors. **Pets:** Dogs only. $15 one-time fee/room.
🛰 ✕ 🔒 🖥 🐾

▼▼▼ The Wyman Hotel & Inn **BB**
(970) 387-5372. **Call for rates.** 1371 Greene St 81433. Corner of 14th and Main sts. Int corridors. **Pets:** Accepted.
🛰 ✕ 🔒 🖥 ✕ 🐾

SOUTH FORK
▼▼ Ute Bluff Lodge & Cabins **M**
(719) 873-5595. **$49-$208, 14 day notice.** 27680 W Hwy 160 81154. Jct US 160 and SR 149, 2.7 mi e. Ext corridors. **Pets:** Accepted.
🛰 🔒 🖥 🐾

STEAMBOAT SPRINGS
△△△ ▼▼ Fairfield Inn & Suites by Marriott **H**
(970) 870-9000. **$143-$175.** 3200 S Lincoln Ave 80477. 3 mi s on US 40. Int corridors. **Pets:** $20 daily fee/pet. Designated rooms, service with restrictions, supervision. 🆂🅰🆅🅴 🛰 ✕ 🔒 🖥 🏊

▼▼▼ Hampton Inn & Suites
(970) 871-8900. **$116-$152.** 725 S Lincoln Ave 80487. 1.1 mi e on US 40. Int corridors. **Pets:** Accepted. 🛰 🅼 🔒 🖥 🏊

▼▼▼ Holiday Inn Steamboat Springs **H** 🐾
(970) 879-2250. **$99-$199, 3 day notice.** 3190 S Lincoln Ave 80487. 3 mi e on US 40. Int corridors. **Pets:** Other species. $20 daily fee/room. Designated rooms, service with restrictions, supervision.
🛰 ✕ 🅼 🔒 🖥 🍴 🏊 ✕

▼▼ La Quinta Inn Steamboat Springs **H**
(970) 871-1219. **$89-$189.** 3155 Ingles Ln 80487. 3 mi s on US 40, then just e. Int corridors. **Pets:** Medium, other species. Service with restrictions, supervision. 🛰 ✕ 🔒 🖥 🏊

▼▼ Nordic Lodge **M**
(970) 879-0531. **Call for rates.** 1036 Lincoln Ave 80477. Between 10th and 11th sts; downtown. Ext corridors. **Pets:** Accepted.
🛰 ✕ 🔒 🏊 ✕

△△△ ▼▼ Quality Inn & Suites **H** 🐾
(970) 879-6669. **$80-$200.** 1055 Walton Creek Rd 80487. 2.8 mi e on US 40. Int corridors. **Pets:** Other species. $50 deposit/pet, $20 daily fee/pet. Designated rooms, supervision. 🆂🅰🆅🅴 🛰 ✕ 🅼 🔒 🖥 🏊

▼▼ Rabbit Ears Motel **M**
(970) 879-1150. **$89-$189, 3 day notice.** 201 Lincoln Ave 80477. Just e on US 40. Ext corridors. **Pets:** Accepted. 🛰 🔒 🖥

△△△ ▼▼▼ Sheraton Steamboat Resort **H** 🐾
(970) 879-2220. **$149-$519, 30 day notice.** 2200 Village Inn Ct 80487. 2.3 mi s from center on US 40 to Mt. Werner Rd exit, 0.8 mi e, 0.3 mi ne on Mt. Werner Cir, just ne at Ski Time Sq, then just s. Int corridors. **Pets:** Medium, dogs only. Designated rooms, service with restrictions, supervision. 🆂🅰🆅🅴 🛰 ✕ 🔒 🖥 🍴 🏊 ✕

STERLING
△△△ ▼▼▼ Best Western Sundowner **M** 🐾
(970) 522-2265. **$90-$140.** 125 Overland Trail St 80751. I-76 exit 125, just w. Ext/int corridors. **Pets:** Large, other species. $20 daily fee/room. Designated rooms, service with restrictions, supervision.
🆂🅰🆅🅴 🛰 ✕ 🔒 🖥 🏊

▼▼ Ramada Inn **H**
(970) 522-2625. **$71-$109.** 22140 E Hwy 6 80751. I-76 exit 125, 0.5 mi e on US 6. Ext/int corridors. **Pets:** $25 deposit/room. Designated rooms, service with restrictions, supervision. 🛰 🔒 🖥 🍴 🏊 ✕

STRATTON
△△△ ▼▼ Best Western Golden Prairie Inn **H**
(719) 348-5311. **$96-$120.** 700 Colorado Ave 80836. I-70 exit 419, just n. Ext corridors. **Pets:** Accepted. 🆂🅰🆅🅴 🛰 🔒 🖥 🏊

TELLURIDE
▼▼▼ Fairmont Heritage Place Franz Klammer Lodge **CO**
(970) 728-3318. **$250-$2200, 45 day notice.** 567 Mountain Village Blvd 81435. 2.3 mi e; in Mountain Village. Int corridors. **Pets:** Accepted.
🄴🄲🄾 🛰 ✕ 🔒 🖥 🏊 ✕ 🐾

△△△ ▼▼▼ Hotel Columbia **H** 🐾
(970) 728-0660. **$175-$1625, 30 day notice.** 301 W San Juan Ave 81435. At Aspen St and San Juan Ave; opposite gondola. Int corridors. **Pets:** Dogs only. $25 daily fee/pet. Service with restrictions, supervision.
🆂🅰🆅🅴 🛰 ✕ 🖥 🍴

▼▼▼ Hotel Madeline Telluride **H**
(970) 369-0880. **$150-$1675, 30 day notice.** 568 Mountain Village Blvd 81435. 2.2 mi e; in Mountain Village. Int corridors. **Pets:** Accepted.
🛰 ✕ 🔒 🖥 🍴 🏊 ✕

▼▼▼ The Hotel Telluride **H**
(970) 369-1188. **Call for rates.** 199 N Cornet St 81435. Just s of round-about, then just e. Int corridors. **Pets:** Accepted.
🛰 ✕ 🅼 🔒 🖥 🍴 ✕

▼▼▼ Ice House Lodge & Condominiums **H**
(970) 728-6300. **$185-$595, 30 day notice.** 310 S Fir St 81435. Just s of SR 145 (Colorado Ave); end of Fir St. Int corridors. **Pets:** Other species. $20 daily fee/pet. Designated rooms, service with restrictions, supervision. 🛰 ✕ 🔒 🖥 🏊 ✕ 🐾

▼▼▼ The Peaks, A Grand Heritage Resort & Spa **H**
(970) 728-6800. **Call for rates.** 136 Country Club Dr 81435. 2.5 mi e; in Mountain Village. Int corridors. **Pets:** Accepted.
🛰 ✕ 🔒 🖥 🍴 🏊 ✕ 🐾

TRINIDAD
△△△ ▼▼ Best Western Trinidad Inn **M**
(719) 846-2215. **$59-$119.** 900 W Adams St 81082. I-25 exit 13A north-bound; exit Cross Bridge southbound, just ne. Ext corridors. **Pets:** Medium. $10 daily fee/pet. Designated rooms, service with restrictions, supervision. 🆂🅰🆅🅴 🛰 🔒 🖥 🏊

▼▼▼ Holiday Inn Hotel & Suites **H**
(719) 845-8400. **$79-$159.** 3130 Santa Fe Trail Dr 81082. I-25 exit 11, just e, then 1.2 mi n. Int corridors. **Pets:** Accepted.
🛰 ✕ 🅼 🔒 🖥 🍴 ✕

▼▼▼ **La Quinta Inn & Suites Trinidad** H
(719) 845-0102. **$79-$179.** 2833 Toupal Dr 81082. I-25 exit 11, just w, then n. Int corridors. **Pets:** Medium, other species. Service with restrictions, supervision. 🛜 ⊠ 📧 💻 ⊇ ⊠

▼ **Super 8** M
(719) 846-8280. **$63-$85.** 1924 Freedom Rd 81082. I-25 exit 15, just ne. Int corridors. **Pets:** Accepted. 🛜 📧 💻

VAIL

▲▲▲ ▼▼▼ ▼▼▼ **The Arrabelle at Vail Square, A RockResort** H ❀
(970) 754-7777. **Call for rates.** 675 Lionshead Pl 81657. I-70 exit 176, 1 mi w on S Frontage Rd, then just e. Int corridors. **Pets:** Dogs only. $50 daily fee/room. Designated rooms.
SAVE 🛜 ⊠ 📧 💻 🍴 ⊇ ⊠

▼▼▼ **Evergreen Lodge at Vail** H
(970) 476-7810. **$120-$570, 30 day notice.** 250 S Frontage Rd W 81657. I-70 exit 176, just w on Frontage Rd. Int corridors. **Pets:** Other species. $25 daily fee/room. Designated rooms, service with restrictions, crate. 🛜 ⊠ 📧 💻 ⊇ ⊠ 🐾

▼▼▼ **Four Seasons Resort Vail** H
(970) 477-8600. **Call for rates.** One Vail Rd 81657. I-70 exit 176, just w of roundabout. Int corridors. **Pets:** Accepted.
🛜 ⊠ 📧 💻 🍴 ⊇ ⊠

▼▼▼ **Holiday Inn Apex Vail** H
(970) 476-2739. **$99-$249.** 2211 N Frontage Rd 81657. I-70 exit 173, just nw, then 0.3 mi ne. Int corridors. **Pets:** Medium, dogs only. $25 daily fee/pet. Designated rooms, service with restrictions, supervision.
🛜 ⊠ 📧 💻 🍴 ⊇ ⊠

▼▼▼ **The Lodge at Vail, A RockResort & Spa** H
(970) 476-5011. **Call for rates.** 174 E Gore Creek Dr 81657. I-70 exit 176, 0.3 mi s on Vail Rd to Gore Creek Dr. Ext/int corridors.
Pets: Accepted. 🛜 ⊠ 📧 💻 🍴 ⊇ ⊠

▲▲▲ ▼▼▼ ▼▼▼ **The Sebastian Vail** H 🐾
(970) 477-8000. **$199-$1800, 31 day notice.** 16 Vail Rd 81657. I-70 exit 176, 2nd exit at roundabout (Vail Rd); just s of S Frontage and Vail rds. Int corridors. **Pets:** Medium, dogs only. $150 one-time fee/pet. Designated rooms, service with restrictions, supervision.
SAVE 🛜 ⊠ 📶 📧 💻 🍴 ⊇ ⊠

▲▲▲ ▼▼▼ **Sonnenalp Resort of Vail** H
(970) 476-5656. **$160-$3500, 30 day notice.** 20 Vail Rd 81657. I-70 exit 176, 2nd exit at the roundabout, then just s. Int corridors.
Pets: Accepted. ECO SAVE 🛜 🍴 ⊇ ⊠

▲▲▲ ▼▼▼ ▼▼▼ **Vail Cascade Resort & Spa** H
(970) 476-7111. **$99-$659, 3 day notice.** 1300 Westhaven Dr 81657. I-70 exit 176, 1.3 mi w via S Frontage Rd; 1 mi e of exit 173. Int corridors. **Pets:** Medium, dogs only. $25 daily fee/pet. Designated rooms, service with restrictions, supervision.
SAVE 🛜 ⊠ 📶 📧 💻 🍴 ⊇ ⊠

WALSENBURG

▲▲▲ ▼▼▼ **Best Western Rambler** H
(719) 738-1121. **$94-$112, 3 day notice.** 457 US Hwy 85-87 81089. I-25 exit 52, just w. Ext/int corridors. **Pets:** Accepted.
SAVE 🛜 📧 💻 ⊇

WINDSOR

▼▼ **Super 8 Motel** H
(970) 686-5996. **$63-$72.** 1265 Main St 80550. I-25 exit 262, 3.8 mi e; in shopping and restaurant complex. Int corridors. **Pets:** Accepted.
🛜 ⊠ 📶 📧 💻

WINTER PARK

▲▲▲ ▼▼▼ **Best Western Alpenglo Lodge** H ❀
(970) 726-8088. **$79-$167.** 78665 US Hwy 40 80482. 0.3 mi n of center. Int corridors. **Pets:** Other species. $10 daily fee/pet. Designated rooms, service with restrictions, supervision. SAVE 🛜 ⊠ 📶 📧 💻

WOODLAND PARK

▼▼▼ **Bristlecone Lodge** CA
(719) 687-9518. **$89-$140, 14 day notice.** 510 N Hwy 67 80863. 0.5 mi n. Ext corridors. **Pets:** Dogs only. $10 daily fee/pet. Designated rooms, service with restrictions, supervision. 🛜 ⊠ 📧 💻 🐾 🔋

YAMPA

▼▼ **Oak Tree Inn** M
(970) 638-1000. **$76-$125.** 98 Moffat Ave 80483. 0.3 mi w of SR 131. Int corridors. **Pets:** $10 daily fee/room. Service with restrictions, supervision. 🛜 ⊠ 📧 💻 🍴

CONNECTICUT

CITY INDEX

BETHEL

▼▼ **Microtel Inn & Suites** H
(203) 748-8318. **$63-$71.** 80 Benedict Rd 06801. I-84 exit 8, 1 mi e on US 6. Int corridors. **Pets:** Accepted. 🛜 📧 💻

BRANFORD

▼▼ **Baymont Inn & Suites** H
(203) 488-4991. **$80-$143.** 3 Business Park Dr 06405. I-95 exit 56, just n. Int corridors. **Pets:** Medium. $50 deposit/room, $20 daily fee/room. Service with restrictions, supervision. 🛜 📧 💻 ⊇ ⊠

BRIDGEPORT

▼▼▼ **Bridgeport Holiday Inn & Convention Center** H
(203) 334-1234. **$119-$159.** 1070 Main St 06604. SR 8 exit 2 northbound, 0.7 mi se; exit southbound, just s, then just e. Int corridors.
Pets: Accepted. 🛜 📶 📧 💻 🍴 ⊇

BROOKFIELD

▼▼ **The Newbury Inn** M
(203) 775-0220. **$79-$119, 3 day notice.** 1030 Federal Rd 06804. Jct SR 25, 0.9 mi nw. Ext/int corridors. **Pets:** Accepted. 🛜 📧 💻

DANBURY

▼▼▼ **Crowne Plaza Danbury** H ❀
(203) 794-0600. **$109-$229.** 18 Old Ridgebury Rd 06810. I-84 exit 2 eastbound; exit 2A westbound. Int corridors. **Pets:** Medium, dogs only. $75 deposit/room. Designated rooms, service with restrictions.
🛰 🛜 📶 🖵 🍴

▼▼▼ **Ethan Allen Hotel** H
(203) 744-1776. **$99-$159.** 21 Lake Ave Ext 06811. I-84 exit 4, 0.3 mi w on US 6 and 202. Int corridors. **Pets:** Accepted.
🛰 ⊠ 📶 🖵 🍴 ⤷

▲▲▲ ▼▼▼ **Holiday Inn** H
(203) 792-4000. **$89-$159.** 80 Newtown Rd 06810. I-84 exit 8 (Newtown Rd), 0.5 mi s on US 6 W. Int corridors. **Pets:** Accepted.
SAVE 🛰 🖵 🍴 ⤷

▲▲▲ ▼▼▼ **La Quinta Inn & Suites** H
(203) 798-1200. **$95-$180.** 116 Newtown Rd 06810. I-84 exit 8 (Newtown Rd), just sw. Int corridors. **Pets:** Medium, other species. Service with restrictions, supervision. SAVE 🛰 📶 🖵 🍴

▼▼▼ **Maron Hotel & Suites** H
(203) 791-2200. **$99-$199.** 42 Lake Ave Ext 06811. I-84 exit 4, 0.5 mi w on US 6 and 202. Int corridors. **Pets:** Accepted.
🛰 🛜 📶 🖵 🍴

▼▼▼ **Residence Inn Danbury** H
(203) 797-1256. **$113-$199.** 22 Segar St 06810. I-84 exit 4 eastbound, just n; exit westbound, just e on Lake Ave Ext, then just s. Int corridors.
Pets: Accepted. ECO 🛰 ⊠ 📶 🖵 ⤷

DAYVILLE

▼▼▼ **Comfort Inn & Suites** H
(860) 779-3200. **$125-$143.** 16 Tracy Rd 06241. I-395 exit 94, just w. Int corridors. **Pets:** Medium. $15 daily fee/pet. Service with restrictions, supervision. 🛰 🛜 📶 🖵 ⤷

FAIRFIELD

▲▲▲ ▼▼▼ **Best Western Plus Black Rock Inn** H
(203) 659-2200. **$109-$149, 3 day notice.** 100 Kings Hwy Cutoff 06824. I-95 exit 24, just sw. Int corridors. **Pets:** Medium, dogs only. $25 deposit/pet. Designated rooms, service with restrictions, supervision.
SAVE 🛰 ⊠ 🛜 📶 🖵

GREENWICH

▼▼▼ **The Stanton House Inn** BB
(203) 869-2110. **$159-$239, 7 day notice.** 76 Maple Ave 06830. Just n of US 1; center. Ext/int corridors. **Pets:** Small, dogs only. $25 daily fee/pet. Designated rooms, service with restrictions, supervision.
🛰 ⊠ 📶 ⤷

HAMDEN

▼▼▼ **Clarion Hotel & Suites Hamden-New Haven** M ❀
(203) 288-3831. **$119-$229.** 2260 Whitney Ave 06518. Just n off SR 15 exit 61. Int corridors. **Pets:** Medium. $50 deposit/room. Service with restrictions, supervision. 🛰 ⊠ 🛜 📶 🖵 ⤷

HARTFORD METROPOLITAN AREA

AVON

▼▼▼ **Avon Old Farms Hotel** H
(860) 677-1651. **$109-$259.** 279 Avon Mountain Rd 06001. Jct US 44 and SR 10. Ext/int corridors. **Pets:** Accepted. 🛰 📶 🖵 🍴 ⤷

▼▼▼ **Residence Inn by Marriott Hartford-Avon** H
(860) 678-1666. **$135-$170.** 55 Simsbury Rd (SR 202 & SR 10) 06001. Jct US 44, just n. Int corridors. **Pets:** Accepted.
🛰 ⊠ 🛜 📶 🖵 ⤷ ⊠

EAST HARTFORD

▼▼▼ **The Hartford Plaza Hotel** H
(860) 528-9703. **Call for rates.** 100 E River Dr 06108. I-84 exit 53 eastbound, just s; exit 54 westbound to exit 3 (Darlin St), just n. Int corridors.
Pets: Accepted. 🛰 ⊠ 🛜 📶 🖵 🍴 ⤷

▲▲▲ ▼▼▼ **Ramada East Hartford** H
(860) 528-9611. **Call for rates.** 363 Roberts St 06108. I-84 exit 58, just w. Int corridors. **Pets:** Medium, other species. $35 one-time fee/room. Designated rooms, service with restrictions, supervision.
SAVE 🛰 🛜 📶 🖵 🍴 ⤷

EAST WINDSOR

▲▲▲ ▼▼▼ **Baymont Inn & Suites East Windsor** H
(860) 627-6585. **$99-$129.** 260 Main St (US 5) 06088. I-91 exit 44, just s. Int corridors. **Pets:** Medium, other species. $35 one-time fee/room. Service with restrictions, crate. SAVE 🛰 🛜 📶 🖵 ⤷

ENFIELD

▼▼▼ **Holiday Inn Hotel Enfield-Springfield** H ❀
(860) 741-2211. **$99-$189.** 1 Bright Meadow Blvd 06082. I-91 exit 49, just e on service road. Int corridors. **Pets:** Medium, dogs only. $50 one-time fee/room. Designated rooms, service with restrictions, supervision.
🛰 🛜 📶 🖵 🍴 ⤷ ⊠

▲▲▲ ▼ **Red Roof Inn # 7105** M
(860) 741-2571. **$65-$112.** 5 Hazard Ave 06082. I-91 exit 47E. Ext corridors. **Pets:** Large, other species. No service, supervision.
SAVE 🛰 🛜

FARMINGTON

▲▲▲ ▼▼▼ **Centennial Inn Hotel & Apartments** H
(860) 677-4647. **$121-$181.** 5 Spring Ln 06032. US 6, 0.3 mi e of jct SR 177. Ext/int corridors. **Pets:** $20 daily fee/pet. Designated rooms, service with restrictions, crate. SAVE 🛰 🛜 📶 🖵 ⤷

▼▼▼ **Extended Stay Deluxe Hartford-Farmington** H ❀
(860) 676-2790. **$105-$139.** 1 Batterson Park Rd 06032. I-84 exit 37, just ne. Int corridors. **Pets:** Other species. $25 daily fee/pet. Service with restrictions. 🛰 🛜 📶 🖵

▼▼▼ **The Farmington Inn** H
(860) 269-3401. **$109-$179.** 827 Farmington Ave 06032. I-84 exit 39, 1.8 mi w on SR 4. Int corridors. **Pets:** Accepted. 🛰 ⊠ 📶 🖵

▼▼▼ **Homewood Suites by Hilton Hartford-Farmington** H
(860) 321-0000. **$135-$159.** 2 Farm Glen Blvd 06032. I-84 exit 39, 0.6 mi e on SR 4. Int corridors. **Pets:** Accepted. 🛰 🛜 📶 🖵 ⤷

GLASTONBURY

▲▲▲ ▼▼▼ **Homewood Suites by Hilton Hartford South-Glastonbury** H
(860) 652-8111. **$99-$209.** 65 Glastonbury Blvd 06033. SR 3 exit Main St, just se. Int corridors. **Pets:** Accepted. SAVE 🛰 🛜 📶 🖵 ⤷

HARTFORD

▼▼▼ **The Hilton Hartford Hotel** H
(860) 728-5151. **$139-$319.** 315 Trumbull St 06103. Downtown. Int corridors. **Pets:** Accepted. ECO 🛰 🛜 📶 🖵 🍴 ⤷ ⊠

▼▼▼ Holiday Inn Express Downtown Hartford 🅗
(860) 246-9900. **Call for rates.** 440 Asylum St 06103. I-84 exit 48, just
se via Spring St. Int corridors. **Pets:** Accepted. 🛜 🍴 💻

▼▼▼ Holiday Inn Express Hotel & Suites Hartford 🅗
(860) 525-1000. **$99-$155.** 185 Brainard Rd 06114. I-91 exit 27, just e,
then just s. Int corridors. **Pets:** Accepted. 🛜 🍴 💻 🌊

▼▼▼ Homewood Suites by Hilton Hartford
Downtown 🅗
(860) 524-0223. **Call for rates.** 338 Asylum St 06103. Between Ann and
High sts; downtown. Int corridors. **Pets:** Accepted. 🛜 🅰M 🍴 💻

▼▼▼ Ramada Plaza Hartford Downtown 🅗
(860) 549-2400. **$149-$179.** 50 Morgan St 06120. I-91 exit 32B; I-84 exit
50 eastbound; exit 52 westbound. Int corridors. **Pets:** Accepted.
🛜 🅰M 🍴 💻 🌊

▼▼▼ Residence Inn by Marriott Downtown Hartford 🅗
(860) 524-5550. **$234-$315.** 942 Main St 06103. I-91 exit 29A northbound; exit 31 southbound. Int corridors. **Pets:** Other species. $100 one-
time fee/pet. 🅴🅲🅾 🛜 ⊠ 🍴 💻

MANCHESTER

▼▼ Extended StayAmerica Hartford-Manchester 🅗 🐾
(860) 643-5140. **$85-$119.** 340 Tolland Tpke 06040. I-84 exit 63, 0.3 mi
se on SR 30, then just sw. Int corridors. **Pets:** Other species. $25 daily
fee/pet. Service with restrictions. 🛜 🅰M 🍴 💻

▼▼▼ Residence Inn Hartford/Manchester 🅗 🐾
(860) 432-4242. **$166-$222.** 201 Hale Rd 06042. I-84 exit 63, 0.5 mi nw,
then 0.6 mi sw. Int corridors. **Pets:** Other species. $75 one-time fee/room.
Service with restrictions, supervision.
🛜 ⊠ 🅰M 🍴 💻 🌊 ⊠

NEW BRITAIN

▼▼▼ La Quinta Inn & Suites New Britain/Hartford
South 🅗
(860) 348-1463. **$55-$121.** 65 Columbus Blvd 06051. SR 9 exit 26 northbound; exit 27 southbound, then just nw. Int corridors. **Pets:** Medium,
other species. Service with restrictions, supervision. 🛜 ♿ 🍴 💻

ROCKY HILL

▼▼▼ Residence Inn by Marriott Hartford-Rocky
Hill 🅗 🐾
(860) 257-7500. **$100-$260.** 680 Cromwell Ave 06067. I-91 exit 23, 0.4
mi w on West St, then just n. Int corridors. **Pets:** Other species. $100
one-time fee/room. Service with restrictions.
🛜 ⊠ 🅰M 🍴 💻 🌊 ⊠

SIMSBURY

▼▼▼ Simsbury Inn 🅗
(860) 651-5700. **Call for rates.** 397 Hopmeadow St 06070. On US
202/SR 10, 0.4 mi n of jct SR 185. Int corridors. **Pets:** Accepted.
🛜 ⊠ 🅰M 🍴 💻 🍴 🌊 ⊠

SOUTHINGTON

▼▼▼ Residence Inn Southington 🅗 🐾
(860) 621-4440. **$143-$170.** 778 West St 06489. I-84 exit 31, just s. Int
corridors. **Pets:** $100 one-time fee/pet. Service with restrictions, crate.
🅴🅲🅾 🛜 ⊠ 🅰M 🍴 💻 🌊 ⊠

WINDSOR

◈◈◈ ▼▼▼ Hyatt house Hartford
North/Windsor 🅗 🐾
(860) 298-8000. **$89-$189.** 200 Corporate Dr 06095. I-91 exit 38 northbound; exit 38B southbound. Int corridors. **Pets:** Medium. $200 one-time
fee/room. Designated rooms, service with restrictions, supervision.
🆂🅰🆅🅴 🛜 ⊠ 🅰M 🍴 💻 🌊 ⊠

▼▼▼ Residence Inn by Marriott Hartford-Windsor 🅗
(860) 688-7474. **$126-$153.** 100 Dunfey Ln 06095. I-91 exit 37, just w
on SR 305 to Dunfey Ln, then 0.3 mi n. Ext corridors. **Pets:** Accepted.
🛜 ⊠ 🅰M 🍴 💻 🌊 ⊠

WINDSOR LOCKS

▼▼▼ Candlewood Suites 🅗
(860) 623-2000. **$99-$149.** 149 Ella T Grasso Tpke 06096. I-91 exit 40,
2.5 mi w on SR 20, then 0.6 mi n on SR 75. Int corridors.
Pets: Accepted. 🛜 🅰M 🍴 💻 🌊

▼▼▼ La Quinta Inn Hartford Bradley Airport 🅗
(860) 623-3336. **$62-$135.** 64 Ella T Grasso Tpke 06096. I-91 exit 40,
2.5 mi w on SR 20, then just n on SR 75. Int corridors. **Pets:** Medium,
other species. Service with restrictions, supervision. 🛜 🅰M 🍴 💻

▼▼▼ Ramada Inn Bradley International Airport 🅗
(860) 623-9494. **$71-$134.** 5 Ella T Grasso Tpke 06096. I-91 exit 40, 2.5
mi w on SR 20, then just n on SR 75. Int corridors. **Pets:** Accepted.
🛜 🍴 💻 🍴 🌊

◈◈◈ ▼▼▼ Sheraton Hartford Hotel At Bradley
Airport 🅗 🐾
(860) 627-5311. **$109-$299, 3 day notice.** 1 Bradley International Airport 06096. Jct SR 75, 0.6 mi w on Schoephoester Rd, 0.5 mi nw on
Terminal Rd. Int corridors. **Pets:** Medium. Service with restrictions, supervision. 🅴🅲🅾 🆂🅰🆅🅴 🛜 ⊠ 🅰M 🍴 💻 🍴 🌊

END METROPOLITAN AREA

IVORYTON

◈◈◈ ▼▼▼▼ The Copper Beech Inn 🅒🅘
(860) 767-0330. **$209-$400, 14 day notice.** 46 Main St 06442. SR 9
exit 3, 1.7 mi w. Int corridors. **Pets:** Accepted. 🆂🅰🆅🅴 🛜 ⊠ 🍴

LAKEVILLE

◈◈◈ ▼▼▼▼ Interlaken Inn Resort and Conference
Center 🅗 🐾
(860) 435-9878. **$179-$289, 7 day notice.** 74 Interlaken Rd 06039. On
SR 112, 0.5 mi w of jct SR 41. Ext/int corridors. **Pets:** $15 daily fee/
room. Designated rooms, service with restrictions, supervision.
🅴🅲🅾 🆂🅰🆅🅴 🛜 ⊠ 🍴 💻 🍴 🌊 ⊠

LEDYARD

▼▼▼ Almost In Mystic/Mares Inn 🅱🅱
(860) 572-7556. **$125-$225, 14 day notice.** 333 Colonel Ledyard Hwy
06339. I-95 exit 89, 1 mi ne to Gold Star Hwy, 0.6 mi w, then 0.7 mi n.
Int corridors. **Pets:** Accepted. 🛜 ⊠ 🍴 💻 ⊘

LITCHFIELD

▼▼▼ Litchfield Inn 🅒🅘
(860) 567-4503. **$159-$279.** 432 Bantam Rd 06759. 1.5 mi w on US
202. Int corridors. **Pets:** Accepted. 🛜 ⊠ 🍴 💻 🍴

MASHANTUCKET

◈◈◈ ▼▼▼ Two Trees Inn at Foxwoods Resort
Casino 🅗
(860) 312-3000. **$79-$499.** 240 Indiantown Rd 06339. Jct SR 214 and 2.
Int corridors. **Pets:** Accepted. 🆂🅰🆅🅴 🛜 🅰M 🍴 💻 🍴 🌊 ⊠

MERIDEN

◆◆ Extended StayAmerica Hartford-Meriden 🅷 ❖
(203) 630-1927. **$85-$119.** 366 Bee St 06450. I-91 exit 17 northbound, just e on E Main St, then 0.7 mi n; exit 19 southbound, 0.5 mi w on Baldwin Ave, then 0.6 mi s. Int corridors. **Pets:** Other species. $25 daily fee/pet. Service with restrictions. 🛜 🛏 🖵

◆◆◆ ◆◆ Four Points by Sheraton Meriden 🅷
(203) 238-2380. **$80-$180.** 275 Research Pkwy 06450. I-91 exit 17 southbound; exit 16 northbound, 0.5 mi e, then 0.5 mi s. Int corridors. **Pets:** Accepted. SAVE 🛜 ✕ 🅼 🛏 🖵 🍴 🏊

◆◆ Hawthorn Suites by Wyndham - Meriden 🅷 ❖
(203) 634-7770. **Call for rates.** 390 Bee St 06450. I-91 exit 16 northbound, just e on E Main St, then 0.7 mi n; exit 19 southbound, 0.5 mi w on Baldwin Ave, then 0.5 mi s. Ext/int corridors. **Pets:** Other species. $75 one-time fee/pet. Service with restrictions, supervision.
🛜 ✕ 🅼 🛏 🖵 🏊

MILFORD

◆◆◆ ◆◆ The Red Roof Inn 🅼
(203) 877-6060. **$60-$120.** 10 Rowe Ave 06460. I-95 exit 35, just nw. Ext corridors. **Pets:** Large, other species. No service, supervision.
SAVE 🛜 🛏

◆◆◆ Residence Inn Milford 🅷
(203) 283-2100. **$89-$209.** 62 Rowe Ave 06460. I-95 exit 35, just nw. Int corridors. **Pets:** Accepted. 🛜 ✕ 🛏 🖵 🏊

MORRIS

◆◆◆ ◆◆◆ Winvian 🅷 🐾
(860) 567-9600. **$650-$2300, 60 day notice.** 155 Alain White Rd 06763. Jct SR 109, 1 mi n. Ext/int corridors. **Pets:** Dogs only. Service with restrictions, supervision. SAVE 🛜 ✕ 🛏 🖵 🍴 ✕

MYSTIC

◆◆◆ ◆◆ Comfort Inn of Mystic 🅷
(860) 572-8531. **$76-$269.** 48 Whitehall Ave 06355. I-95 exit 90, just n on SR 27. Int corridors. **Pets:** Small, other species. $75 one-time fee/pet. Designated rooms, service with restrictions, crate.
ECO SAVE 🛜 🅼 🛏 🖵 🏊

◆◆◆◆ Hampton Inn & Suites/Mystic 🅷 ❖
(860) 536-2536. **$79-$259.** 6 Hendel Dr 06355. I-95 exit 90. Int corridors. **Pets:** Other species. Designated rooms, service with restrictions, crate.
🛜 ✕ 🅼 🛏 🖵 🏊

◆◆◆ ◆◆◆ Hilton Mystic 🅷
(860) 572-0731. **Call for rates.** 20 Coogan Blvd 06355. I-95 exit 90, 0.5 mi s, then e. Int corridors. **Pets:** Accepted.
SAVE 🛜 ✕ 🛏 🖵 🍴 🏊

◆◆◆ ◆◆◆ Inn at Mystic 🅼
(860) 536-9604. **$115-$275.** 3 Williams Ave 06355. On US 1 at SR 27. Ext/int corridors. **Pets:** Other species. $15 deposit/pet, $15 daily fee/pet. Designated rooms, service with restrictions, supervision.
SAVE 🛜 ✕ 🛏 🖵 🍴 🏊 ✕

◆◆◆◆ Residence Inn by Marriott 🅷
(860) 536-5150. **$116-$368.** 40 Whitehall Ave 06355. I-95 exit 90, just n on SR 27. Int corridors. **Pets:** Other species. $100 one-time fee/room. Designated rooms, service with restrictions, supervision.
ECO 🛜 ✕ 🛏 🖵 🏊 ✕

NAUGATUCK

◆◆◆ ◆ Comfort Inn Naugatuck 🅷
(203) 723-9356. **Call for rates.** 716 New Haven Rd 06770. Jct SR 63 and 8, 0.8 mi s. Int corridors. **Pets:** Small. $25 daily fee/pet. Designated rooms, service with restrictions, supervision. 🛜 🅼 🛏 🖵

NEW HAVEN

◆◆◆◆ La Quinta Inn & Suites New Haven 🅷
(203) 562-1111. **$62-$156.** 400 Sargent Dr 06511. I-95 exit 46. Int corridors. **Pets:** Medium, other species. Service with restrictions, supervision.
🛜 🛏 🖵 🍴 🏊

◆◆◆◆ Omni New Haven Hotel at Yale 🅷 🐾
(203) 772-6664. **Call for rates.** 155 Temple St 06510. Between Chapel and Crown sts; downtown. Int corridors. **Pets:** Small, other species. $50 one-time fee/room. Service with restrictions, crate.
ECO 🛜 🅼 🛏 🖵 🍴 ✕

◆◆◆ ◆◆◆ Premiere Hotel & Suites 🅷
(203) 777-5337. **$149-$239.** 3 Long Wharf Dr 06511. I-95 exit 46, 0.6 mi nw. Ext corridors. **Pets:** Medium, other species. $75 one-time fee/room. Service with restrictions. ECO SAVE 🛜 ✕ 🅼 🛏 🖵

NEW LONDON

◆◆◆◆ Clarion Inn 🅷
(860) 442-0631. **Call for rates.** 269 N Frontage Rd 06320. I-95 exit 82A northbound, 0.8 mi n, just w on Colman St, then 0.6 mi s; exit 83 southbound, 0.6 mi s. Int corridors. **Pets:** Small. $10 daily fee/pet. Designated rooms, service with restrictions, supervision.
🛜 🅼 🛏 🖵 🍴 🏊

◆◆◆ ◆ Red Roof Inn #7145 🅼
(860) 444-0001. **$49-$110.** 707 Colman St 06320. I-95 exit 82A northbound, 0.4 mi e, then just n; exit 83 southbound, 0.6 mi s. Ext corridors. **Pets:** Large, other species. No service, supervision. SAVE 🛜 🛏

NEW MILFORD

◆◆◆◆ The Homestead Inn 🅱🅱
(860) 354-4080. **$105-$250.** 5 Elm St 06776. Jct US 202, just w. Ext/int corridors. **Pets:** Other species. $10 one-time fee/room. Designated rooms, service with restrictions, crate. 🛜 ✕ 🛏

NIANTIC

◆ Motel 6 - 1063 🅼
(860) 739-6991. **$45-$65.** 269 Flanders Rd 06357. I-95 exit 74, just s. Ext corridors. **Pets:** Other species. Service with restrictions, supervision.
🛜 🛏 🏊

NORTH STONINGTON

◆◆◆◆ The Inn at Lower Farm B & B 🅱🅱
(860) 535-9075. **$105-$185, 7 day notice.** 119 Mystic Rd 06359. I-95 exit 90, 1.5 mi n on SR 27, 1.4 mi e on SR 184, then 3.4 mi n on SR 201. Int corridors. **Pets:** Medium. $10 daily fee/pet. Designated rooms, service with restrictions, supervision. ECO 🛜 ✕ 🅿 🆉

NORWALK

◆◆◆ ◆◆◆ Four Points by Sheraton Norwalk 🅷 ❖
(203) 849-9828. **$89-$209.** 426 Main Ave 06851. I-95 exit 15, 3.5 mi n on US 7, just e, then 0.7 mi s. Int corridors. **Pets:** Medium, other species. $50 one-time fee/room. Service with restrictions.
ECO SAVE 🛜 ✕ 🅼 🛏 🖵 🍴

◆◆◆◆ Homestead Studio Suites-Norwalk-Stamford 🅷 ❖
(203) 847-6888. **$120-$199.** 400 Main Ave 06851. I-95 exit 15, 3.5 mi n on US 7, just e, then 1 mi s. Int corridors. **Pets:** Other species. $25 daily fee/pet. Service with restrictions. 🛜 🛏 🖵

OLD SAYBROOK

◆◆◆ Days Inn 🅼
(860) 388-3453. **$62-$189.** 1430 Boston Post Rd 06475. I-95 exit 66, 0.3 mi s on SR 166, then 0.5 mi e on US 1 N. Ext corridors. **Pets:** Accepted.
🛜 🛏 🖵

◆◆ Liberty Inn 🅼
(860) 388-1777. **$58-$130.** 55 Spring Brook Rd 06475. I-95 exit 68 southbound; exit 67 northbound, 0.9 mi n on US 1, then w. Ext corridors. **Pets:** Dogs only. $15 daily fee/pet. Service with restrictions, supervision.
🛜 🛏 🖵

Saybrook Point Inn & Spa H
(860) 395-2000. **$229-$899, 3 day notice.** 2 Bridge St 06475. On SR 154, 2.2 mi s of jct US 1; at Saybrook Point. Int corridors.
Pets: Accepted.

PAWCATUCK

La Quinta Inn & Suites H
(860) 599-2400. **$97-$185.** 349 Liberty St 06379. I-95 exit 92, 1 mi s on SR 2. Int corridors. Pets: Medium, other species. Service with restrictions, supervision.

PLAINFIELD

Quality Inn H
(860) 564-4021. **Call for rates.** 55 Lathrop Rd 06374. I-395 exit 87, just se. Int corridors. Pets: Accepted.

RIVERTON

Old Riverton Inn CI
(860) 379-8678. **$99-$225, 10 day notice.** 436 E River Rd (SR 20) 06065. Center. Int corridors. Pets: Accepted.

SHELTON

Homestead Studio Suites-Shelton-Fairfield County H
(203) 926-6868. **$105-$199.** 945 Bridgeport Ave 06484. SR 8 exit 11, 0.5 mi w. Int corridors. Pets: Other species. $25 daily fee/pet. Service with restrictions.

Residence Inn Shelton Fairfield County H
(203) 926-9000. **$89-$249.** 1001 Bridgeport Ave 06484. SR 8 exit 11, 0.3 mi w. Ext corridors. Pets: Accepted.

SOUTHBURY

Cornucopia at Oldfield Bed and Breakfast BB
(203) 267-6772. **$160-$275, 14 day notice.** 782 Main St N 06488. I-84 exit 15, 1.5 mi n. Int corridors. Pets: Small, dogs only. $25 daily fee/pet. Designated rooms, service with restrictions, supervision.

Crowne Plaza Southbury H
(203) 598-7600. **$108-$159.** 1284 Strongtown Rd 06488. I-84 exit 16, just n on SR 188. Int corridors. Pets: $25 one-time fee/pet. Designated rooms, service with restrictions.

Heritage Hotel H
(203) 264-8200. **$99-$179.** 522 Heritage Rd 06488. I-84 exit 15, 0.4 mi n on SR 67, then 1 mi w. Int corridors. Pets: $25 one-time fee/pet. Designated rooms, service with restrictions, supervision.

SOUTHPORT

Delamar Southport H
(203) 259-2800. **$355.** 275 Old Post Rd 06890. I-95 exit 19, just e. Int corridors. Pets: Medium, dogs only. $50 daily fee/pet. Crate.

STAMFORD

Amsterdam Hotel - Greenwich/Stamford H
(203) 327-4300. **$90-$120.** 19 Clarks Hill Ave 06902. I-95 exit 8 northbound, just n on Atlantic St, 0.6 mi ne on Tresser Blvd, then just s; exit southbound, just nw on Elm St, ne on Main St, then just s. Int corridors. Pets: $30 daily fee/pet. Designated rooms, service with restrictions, supervision.

Hilton Stamford Hotel & Executive Meeting Center H
(203) 967-2222. **$109-$229.** 1 First Stamford Pl 06902. I-95 exit 7 northbound, just s on Greenwich Ave, then just w; exit 6 southbound, just s on West Ave, 0.3 mi w on Baxter Ave, just n on Fairfield Ave, then just e. Int corridors. Pets: Accepted.

La Quinta Inn & Suites Stamford / New York City H
(203) 357-7100. **$72-$167.** 135 Harvard Ave 06902. I-95 exit 6 northbound, just s; exit southbound, just w on Grenhart Rd, then just s. Int corridors. Pets: Medium, other species. Service with restrictions, supervision.

Sheraton Stamford Hotel H ✿
(203) 358-8400. **$109-$329.** 700 E Main St 06901. I-95 exit 8 southbound, just n on Elm St; exit northbound, n on Atlantic St, 0.3 mi e on Tresser Blvd, then just n on Elm St; downtown. Int corridors. Pets: Other species. Designated rooms, service with restrictions, supervision.

Stamford Marriott Hotel & Spa H ✿
(203) 357-9555. **$107-$240.** 243 Tresser Blvd 06901. I-95 exit 8, just n under viaduct, then n. Int corridors. Pets: $49 one-time fee/room. Designated rooms, service with restrictions.

STONINGTON

Another Second Penny Inn BB
(860) 535-1710. **$109-$199, 7 day notice.** 870 Pequot Tr 06378. I-95 exit 91, 0.8 mi s on SR 234. Int corridors. Pets: Accepted.

STRATFORD

Homewood Suites by Hilton H
(203) 377-3322. **$179-$209.** 6905 Main St 06614. SR 15 exit 53, just n. Int corridors. Pets: Accepted.

WALLINGFORD

Homewood Suites by Hilton New Haven/Wallingford H
(203) 284-2600. **Call for rates.** 90 Miles Dr 06492. I-91 exit 15, nw on SR 68, then just s. Int corridors. Pets: Accepted.

WATERFORD

Oakdell Motel M
(860) 442-9446. **$60-$150.** 983 Hartford Tpke 06385. I-95 exit 82, 2 mi n on SR 85. Ext/int corridors. Pets: Medium, dogs only.

Rodeway Inn at Crossroad M
(860) 442-7227. **Call for rates.** 211 Parkway N 06385. I-95 exit 81 northbound, just nw; exit southbound, 0.6 mi w. Ext corridors. Pets: $25 daily fee/pet. Designated rooms.

WESTPORT

The Westport Inn, an Ascend Collection hotel H
(203) 259-5236. **$129-$309.** 1595 Post Rd E 06880. I-95 exit 18 northbound, n to US 1, then 1.5 mi e; exit 19 southbound, 1 mi w. Ext/int corridors. Pets: Accepted.

WOODSTOCK

Inn at Woodstock Hill CI
(860) 928-0528. **$135-$250, 3 day notice.** 94 Plaine Hill Rd 06281. 0.8 mi n on SR 169. Int corridors. Pets: Other species. $25 deposit/room. Designated rooms.

DELAWARE

BEAR

▼▼▼▼ Best Western PLUS of Newark/Christiana Inn 🅗

(302) 326-2500. **Call for rates.** 875 Pulaski Hwy 19701. I-95 exit 4, 3.3 mi se on SR 1 exit 160, then just e on US 40. Int corridors.
Pets: Accepted. 📶 ✕ ৬M 🛏 💻 🏊

DEWEY BEACH

▼▼ ▼▼ Bellbuoy Motel Ⓜ 🐾

(302) 227-6000. **$49-$375, 3 day notice.** 21 Van Dyke St 19971. SR 1; on ocean side. Ext corridors. **Pets:** Dogs only. $10 daily fee/pet. Designated rooms, service with restrictions. 📶 ✕ 🛏 ☎

🄰🄰🄰 ▼▼ ▼▼ Sea-Esta Motel III Ⓜ

(302) 227-4343. **$55-$279, 3 day notice.** 1409 Coastal Hwy 19971. Jct SR 1 and Rodney St. Ext corridors. **Pets:** Medium, other species. $10 daily fee/pet. Service with restrictions, supervision. SAVE 📶 🛏 💻

DOVER

▼▼ ▼▼ Days Inn Dover Ⓜ

(302) 674-8002. **$62-$585.** 272 N DuPont Hwy 19901. SR 1 exit 104, 2.8 mi s on US 13. Ext corridors. **Pets:** Accepted. 📶 🛏 💻

▼▼▼▼ Hampton Inn-Dover 🅗

(302) 736-3500. **$89-$188.** 1568 N DuPont Hwy 19901. SR 1 exit 104, 1 mi s. Int corridors. **Pets:** Accepted. 📶 ৬M 🛏 💻 🏊

▼▼▼▼ Holiday Inn Express Hotel & Suites Dover 🅗

(302) 678-0600. **Call for rates.** 1780 N DuPont Hwy 19901. SR 1 exit 104, just s on US 13. Int corridors. **Pets:** Large, other species. $20 daily fee/room. Service with restrictions, crate. 📶 ৬M 🛏 💻 🏊

▼▼▼▼ MainStay Suites Dover 🅗

(302) 678-8383. **Call for rates.** 201 Stover Blvd 19901. SR 1 exit 95 on S Bay Rd, then just n. Int corridors. **Pets:** Accepted.
ECO 📶 ৬M 🛏 💻 🏊

▼▼▼▼ Residence Inn by Marriott-Dover 🅗

(302) 677-0777. **$101-$159.** 600 Jefferic Blvd 19901. SR 1 exit 104, 2.7 mi s on US 13. Int corridors. **Pets:** Other species. $100 one-time fee/room. Service with restrictions, crate.
📶 ✕ ৬M 🛏 💻 🏊 ✕

🄰🄰🄰 ▼▼▼▼ Sheraton Dover Hotel 🅗 🐾

(302) 678-8500. **$109-$219.** 1570 N DuPont Hwy 19901. SR 1 exit 104, 1 mi s on US 13. Int corridors. **Pets:** Medium, dogs only. Designated rooms, service with supervision.
SAVE 📶 ✕ 🛏 💻 🍴 🏊

▼▼ ▼▼ Sleep Inn & Suites Dover 🅗

(302) 735-7770. **Call for rates.** 1784 N DuPont Hwy 19901. SR 1 exit 104 just s on US 13. Int corridors. **Pets:** Large, other species. $10 daily fee/room. Service with restrictions, crate. 📶 ✕ ৬M 🛏 💻 🏊

GEORGETOWN

▼▼▼▼ Comfort Inn & Suites-Georgetown 🅗

(302) 854-9400. **Call for rates.** 20530 DuPont Blvd 19947. On US 113, 0.5 mi n of jct SR 404. Int corridors. **Pets:** Accepted.
📶 🛏 💻 🏊

HARRINGTON

▼▼▼ AmericInn Lodge & Suites of Harrington 🅗

(302) 398-3900. **$89-$169.** 1259 Corn Crib Rd 19952. On US 13, 0.6 mi s of jct SR 14. Int corridors. **Pets:** Small, dogs only. $25 daily fee/pet. Designated rooms, service with restrictions, supervision.
📶 ✕ ৬M 🛏 💻 🏊

LEWES

🄰🄰🄰 ▼▼▼▼ The Inn at Canal Square 🅗

(302) 644-3377. **$105-$310, 7 day notice.** 122 Market St 19958. On the canal. Int corridors. **Pets:** Medium. Designated rooms, service with restrictions, supervision. SAVE 📶 ✕ 🛏 💻 ✕

▼▼ ▼▼ Sleep Inn & Suites 🅗

(302) 645-6464. **Call for rates.** 18451 Coastal Hwy 19958. On SR 1, 1.5 mi s. Int corridors. **Pets:** Medium. $25 daily fee/pet. Designated rooms, service with restrictions, supervision. 📶 🛏 💻 🏊

LONG NECK

🄰🄰🄰 ▼▼ ▼▼ Sea-Esta II Ⓜ

(302) 945-5900. **$39-$249.** 100 Rudder Rd 19966. On SR 23, 1.1 mi s of jct SR 24, 5 and 23. Ext corridors. **Pets:** Medium, other species. $10 daily fee/pet. Service with restrictions, supervision.
SAVE 📶 ✕ 🛏 💻 🏊

MILLSBORO

▼▼ ▼▼ Atlantic Inn-Millsboro Ⓜ

(302) 934-6711. **$89-$159.** 28534 DuPont Blvd 19966. US 113, just s of SR 24. Ext corridors. **Pets:** Dogs only. $25 daily fee/pet. No service.
📶 🛏 🏊

NEWARK

🄰🄰🄰 ▼▼▼▼ Courtyard by Marriott-Newark at the
University of Delaware 🅗

(302) 737-0900. **$139-$219.** 400 David Hollowell Dr 19716. I-95 exit 1B, 0.6 mi n on SR 896. Int corridors. **Pets:** Accepted.
ECO SAVE 📶 ✕ ৬M 🛏 💻 🍴 🏊

▼▼ ▼▼ Days Inn Wilmington/Newark Ⓜ

(302) 368-2400. **$67-$162.** 900 Churchmans Rd 19713. I-95 exit 4B, 0.3 mi n on SR 7 exit 166, then 0.3 mi w on SR 58 (Churchmans Rd). Ext corridors. **Pets:** Accepted. 📶 🛏 💻 🏊

▼▼▼▼ Hilton Wilmington/Christiana 🅗 🐾

(302) 454-1500. **$98-$237.** 100 Continental Dr 19713. I-95 exit 4B, 0.3 mi n on SR 7 exit 166, then 0.4 mi w on SR 58 (Churchmans Rd). Int corridors. **Pets:** Medium. $49 one-time fee/room. Designated rooms, service with restrictions, supervision. ECO 📶 🛏 💻 🍴 🏊 ✕

▼▼ ▼▼ Homestead Studio Suites
Hotel-Newark/Christiana 🅗 🐾

(302) 283-0800. **$94-$174.** 333 Continental Dr 19713. I-95 exit 4B, 0.3 mi n on SR 7 exit 166, then 0.4 mi w on SR 58 (Churchmans Rd). Int corridors. **Pets:** Other species. $25 daily fee/pet. Service with restrictions.
📶 ৬M 🛏 💻

▼▼▼▼ Homewood Suites by Hilton Newark/Wilmington
South 🅗

(302) 453-9700. **$109-$199.** 640 S College Ave 19713. I-95 exit 1B southbound; exit 1 northbound, 0.8 mi n on SR 896. Int corridors.
Pets: Accepted. 📶 ৬M 🛏 💻 🏊

Red Roof Inn-Wilmington M
(302) 292-2870. **$75-$130.** 415 Stanton Christiana Rd 19713. I-95 exit 4B, 0.5 mi n on SR 7. Ext corridors. **Pets:** Large, other species. No service, supervision. (SAVE) 🛜 (&M) 🛏

Residence Inn by Marriott Wilmington/Newark H
(302) 453-9200. **$179-$241.** 240 Chapman Rd 19702. I-95 exit 3 southbound; exit 3A northbound, 0.3 mi e on SR 273 E, then 0.5 mi s. Ext corridors. **Pets:** Accepted. 🛜 (X) 🛏 🖵 🛋 (X)

Staybridge Suites-Newark/Wilmington H
(302) 366-8097. **$129-$299.** 270 Chapman Rd 19702. I-95 exit 3 southbound; exit 3A northbound, 0.3 mi e on SR 273 E, then just n. Int corridors. **Pets:** Accepted. 🛜 (X) (&M) 🛏 🖵 🛋

TownePlace Suites by Marriott-Wilmington/Christiana/Newark H
(302) 369-6212. **$116-$159.** 410 Eagle Run Rd 19702. I-95 exit 3 southbound; exit 3A northbound, just e. Int corridors. **Pets:** Accepted.
(SAVE) 🛜 (X) (&M) 🛏 🖵

NEW CASTLE
Clarion Hotel - The Belle H
(302) 428-1000. **$83-$170.** 1612 N DuPont Hwy 19720. Jct I-295, just n on SR 13. Int corridors. **Pets:** Accepted.
(ECO) 🛜 (&M) 🛏 🖵 (¶) 🛋

REHOBOTH BEACH
AmericInn Lodge & Suites of Rehoboth Beach H
(302) 226-0700. **$99-$299, 3 day notice.** 36012 Airport Rd 19971. Just w of SR 1; just w on Miller Rd, then just s. Int corridors. **Pets:** Accepted.
🛜 (X) (&M) 🛏 🖵 🛋

The Breakers Hotel & Suites M
(302) 227-6688. **$49-$299, 3 day notice.** 105 2nd St 19971. Just n of Rehoboth Ave. Ext corridors. **Pets:** Dogs only. $50 daily fee/pet. Designated rooms, service with restrictions. 🛜 (X) 🛏 🖵 🛋

Sea-Esta IV M
(302) 227-5882. **$38-$209, 3 day notice.** 20902 Coastal Hwy 19971. 1 mi s of jct SR 24. Ext corridors. **Pets:** Medium, other species. $10 daily fee/pet. Service with restrictions, supervision.
(SAVE) 🛜 (X) 🛏 🖵 🛋

SEAFORD
Comfort Suites H
(302) 628-5400. **Call for rates.** 23420 Sussex Hwy 19973. On US 13, just n jct SR 20. Int corridors. **Pets:** Accepted.
🛜 (X) (&M) 🛏 🖵 🛋

Holiday Inn Express-Seaford H
(302) 629-2000. **$99-$299.** 24058 N Sussex Hwy 19973. On US 13, just s of SR 20 W. Int corridors. **Pets:** Accepted. 🛜 (&M) 🛏 🖵 🛋

WILMINGTON
Best Western Plus Brandywine Valley Inn H
(302) 656-9436. **$139-$169.** 1807 Concord Pike 19803. I-95 exit 8, 1 mi n on US 202. Ext corridors. **Pets:** Other species. $25 one-time fee/room. Designated rooms, service with restrictions, crate.
(SAVE) 🛜 🛏 🖵 🛋

Hotel du Pont H
(302) 594-3100. **$139-$899.** 1007 Market St 19801. I-95 exit 7, 0.5 mi se; downtown at 11th St. Int corridors. **Pets:** Small, dogs only. $100 one-time fee/pet. Service with restrictions, crate.
(SAVE) 🛜 (X) 🛏 🖵 (¶) (X)

Quality Inn & Suites Wilmington H
(302) 478-2222. **Call for rates.** 4000 Concord Pike 19803. I-95 exit 8, 3 mi n on US 202. Ext corridors. **Pets:** Medium, other species. Designated rooms, service with restrictions, crate. 🛜 🛏 🖵 🛋

Sheraton Suites Wilmington H
(302) 654-8300. **$129-$349.** 422 Delaware Ave 19801. I-95 exit 7 northbound; exit 7A southbound, 0.3 mi e; downtown. Int corridors.
Pets: Accepted. (SAVE) 🛜 (X) (&M) 🛏 🖵 (¶) 🛋

DISTRICT OF COLUMBIA

WASHINGTON, D.C. METROPOLITAN AREA

WASHINGTON, D.C.
Capitol Hill Suites H
(202) 543-6000. **$129-$799.** 200 C St SE 20003. 2 blks from Capitol grounds; at 2nd and C sts SE. Int corridors. **Pets:** Accepted.
(SAVE) 🛜 (X) 🛏 🖵

DoubleTree Suites by Hilton Hotel Washington DC H
(202) 785-2000. **$269-$319.** 801 New Hampshire Ave NW 20037. Just sw at Washington Circle. Int corridors. **Pets:** Accepted.
🛜 (&M) 🛏 🖵 🛋

The Dupont Circle Hotel H
(202) 483-6000. **$159-$549.** 1500 New Hampshire Ave NW 20036. At Dupont Circle, Connecticut and Massachusetts aves NW. Int corridors.
Pets: Accepted. (SAVE) 🛜 (X) (¶)

The Fairmont Washington, D.C. H ✿
(202) 429-2400. **$189-$950.** 2401 M St NW 20037. 24th and M sts NW. Int corridors. **Pets:** Other species. Service with restrictions, supervision.
(ECO) (SAVE) 🛜 (&M) 🛏 🖵 (¶) 🛋 (X)

Four Seasons Hotel Washington, D.C. H
(202) 342-0444. **$595-$1975, 30 day notice.** 2800 Pennsylvania Ave NW 20007. In Georgetown. Int corridors. **Pets:** Accepted.
(SAVE) 🛜 (&M) 🛏 🖵 (¶) 🛋 (X)

Hamilton Crowne Plaza Hotel Washington DC H
(202) 682-0111. **Call for rates.** 1001 14th St NW 20005. 14th and K sts NW. Int corridors. **Pets:** Accepted. (SAVE) 🛜 (X) (&M) 🛏 🖵 (¶)

The Hay-Adams H
(202) 638-6600. **$1000-$1300.** 800 16th St NW 20006. 16th and H sts NW; just n of the White House. Int corridors. **Pets:** Accepted.
(ECO) (SAVE) 🛜 🛏 (¶)

Hotel George-A Kimpton Hotel H
(202) 347-4200. **Call for rates.** 15 E St NW 20001. On Capitol Hill, just n of Capitol grounds. Int corridors. **Pets:** Accepted.
(ECO) (SAVE) 🛜 (X) (&M) 🛏 🖵 (¶)

Hotel Helix-A Kimpton Hotel H ✿
(202) 462-9001. **Call for rates.** 1430 Rhode Island Ave NW 20005. Just e of Scott Circle. Int corridors. **Pets:** Other species. Service with restrictions, crate. (ECO) (SAVE) 🛜 (X) 🛏 (¶)

Hotel Madera-A Kimpton Hotel H
(202) 296-7600. **Call for rates.** 1310 New Hampshire Ave NW 20036. Between 20th and N sts NW. Int corridors. **Pets:** Accepted.
ECO SAVE 🛜 ✖ 🔒 🍽

Hotel Monaco Washington DC-A Kimpton Hotel H
(202) 628-7177. **Call for rates.** 700 F St NW 20004. Between 7th and 8th sts NW. Int corridors. **Pets:** Accepted.
ECO SAVE 🛜 ✖ 🍽 ✖

Palomar Washington, DC-A Kimpton Hotel H ✿
(202) 448-1800. **$159-$459.** 2121 P St NW 20037. Between 21st and 22nd sts NW; just w of Dupont Circle. Int corridors. **Pets:** Other species. Service with restrictions, supervision.
ECO SAVE 🛜 ✖ 🔒 🍽 ➰

Hotel Rouge-A Kimpton Hotel H
(202) 232-8000. **Call for rates.** 1315 16th St NW 20036. Just n of Scott Circle. Int corridors. **Pets:** Accepted.
ECO SAVE 🛜 ✖ 🔒 🖥 🍽

The Jefferson, Washington D.C. H
(202) 448-2300. **Call for rates.** 1200 16th St NW 20036. 16th and M sts NW; just s of Scott Circle. Int corridors. **Pets:** Accepted.
🛜 ✖ 🔒 🖥 🍽 ✖

The Latham Hotel H
(202) 726-5000. **$99-$349.** 3000 M St NW 20007. Between 30th and 31st sts NW; in Georgetown. Int corridors. **Pets:** Accepted.
SAVE 🛜 🔒 🖥 ➰

L'Enfant Plaza Hotel H
(202) 484-1000. **$99-$579.** 480 L'Enfant Plaza SW 20024. I-395 exit L'Enfant Plaza/12th St. Int corridors. **Pets:** Accepted.
🛜 ✖ 🔒 🖥 🍽 ➰ ✖

The Liaison Capitol Hill, An Affinia Hotel H
(202) 638-1616. **Call for rates.** 415 New Jersey Ave NW 20001. On Capitol Hill. Int corridors. **Pets:** Accepted.
SAVE 🛜 ✖ 🔒 🖥 🍽 ✖

The Madison H
(202) 862-1600. **Call for rates.** 1177 15th St NW 20005. 15th and M sts NW. Int corridors. **Pets:** Accepted. SAVE 🛜 ✖ 🖥 🍽 ✖

Mandarin Oriental, Washington D.C. H ✿
(202) 554-8588. **Call for rates.** 1330 Maryland Ave SW 20024. Jct Independence Ave SW, just s on 12th St SW. Int corridors. **Pets:** Very small. $50 one-time fee/room, $50 daily fee/pet. Service with restrictions, supervision. 🛜 🔒 🍽 ➰ ✖

The Mayflower-A Renaissance Hotel H ✿
(202) 347-3000. **$389-$729.** 1127 Connecticut Ave NW 20036. Just n of K St NW; in business district. Int corridors. **Pets:** Medium, dogs only. $100 one-time fee/pet. Service with restrictions.
SAVE 🛜 ✖ 🔒 🖥 🍽 ✖

The Melrose Hotel, Washington DC H
(202) 955-6400. **$129-$589.** 2430 Pennsylvania Ave NW 20037. Between 24th and 25th sts NW. Int corridors. **Pets:** Accepted.
🛜 🔒 🖥 🍽

The Normandy Hotel H ✿
(202) 483-1350. **Call for rates.** 2118 Wyoming Ave NW 20008. Just w of Connecticut Ave. Int corridors. **Pets:** Medium, dogs only. Designated rooms, service with restrictions, supervision. SAVE 🛜 ✖ 🔒 🖥

Omni Shoreham Hotel H
(202) 234-0700. **$149-$499.** 2500 Calvert St NW 20008. Just w of Connecticut Ave. Int corridors. **Pets:** Accepted.
SAVE 🛜 ✖ 🔒 🖥 🍽 ➰ ✖

Park Hyatt Washington D. C. H 🐾
(202) 789-1234. **$249-$595, 3 day notice.** 1201 24th St NW 20037. 24th and M sts NW. Int corridors. **Pets:** Dogs only. $150 one-time fee/ room. Supervision. ECO SAVE 🛜 ♿M 🔒 🖥 🍽 ➰ ✖

The Quincy H
(202) 223-4320. **$99-$539.** 1823 L St NW 20036. Between 18th and 19th sts NW. Int corridors. **Pets:** Medium. $150 one-time fee/pet. Service with restrictions, crate. 🛜 ✖ 🔒 🖥 🍽

Residence Inn by Marriott Capitol H
(202) 484-8280. **$161-$529.** 333 E St SW 20024. Between 3rd and 4th sts SW. Int corridors. **Pets:** Accepted. 🛜 ✖ ♿M 🔒 🖥 ➰

Residence Inn by Marriott-Dupont Circle H
(202) 466-6800. **$142-$370.** 2120 P St NW 20037. Between 21st and 22nd sts NW; just w of Dupont Circle. Int corridors. **Pets:** Accepted.
🛜 ✖ ♿M 🔒 🖥

Residence Inn by Marriott-Washington DC-Vermont Ave H ✿
(202) 898-1100. **$142-$449.** 1199 Vermont Ave NW 20005. Jct 14th St and Vermont Ave NW, at Thomas Circle. Int corridors. **Pets:** Medium. $175 one-time fee/room. Designated rooms, service with restrictions, supervision. ECO 🛜 ✖ ♿M 🔒 🖥

The Ritz-Carlton Georgetown, Washington DC H
(202) 912-4100. **Call for rates.** 3100 S South St NW 20007. Just s of jct M St and Wisconsin Ave; in Georgetown. Int corridors.
Pets: Accepted. 🛜 ✖ ♿M 🔒 🍽 ✖

The Ritz-Carlton, Washington, D.C. H
(202) 835-0500. **Call for rates.** 1150 22nd St NW 20037. At 22nd and M sts NW. Int corridors. **Pets:** Accepted.
SAVE 🛜 ✖ ♿M 🔒 🖥 🍽 ➰ ✖

The River Inn H
(202) 337-7600. **Call for rates.** 924 25th St NW 20037. Between K and I sts NW. Int corridors. **Pets:** Accepted. 🛜 ✖ 🔒 🖥 🍽

The St. Regis Washington, D.C. H
(202) 638-2626. **$301-$1200.** 923 16th St NW 20006. 16th and K sts; just n of the White House. Int corridors. **Pets:** Accepted. SAVE 🛜 🍽

Sofitel Washington DC Lafayette Square H
(202) 730-8800. **Call for rates.** 806 15th St NW 20005. Jct 15th and H sts NW. Int corridors. **Pets:** Accepted. ECO 🛜 ✖ ♿M 🔒 🖥

Topaz Hotel-A Kimpton Hotel H
(202) 393-3000. **Call for rates.** 1733 N St NW 20036. Just e of Connecticut Ave. Int corridors. **Pets:** Accepted.
ECO SAVE 🛜 ✖ 🔒 🖥 🍽

Washington Hilton H
(202) 483-3000. **$119-$399.** 1919 Connecticut Ave NW 20009. Just n of Dupont Circle at T St NW. Int corridors. **Pets:** Accepted.
🛜 🔒 🖥 🍽 ➰

Washington Marriott Wardman Park H
(202) 328-2000. **$94-$341.** 2660 Woodley Rd NW 20008. Just w of Connecticut Ave; at Woodley Park/Zoo Metro Station. Int corridors.
Pets: Accepted. SAVE 🛜 ✖ ♿M 🔒 🖥 🍽 ➰ ✖

Washington Suites Georgetown H
(202) 333-8060. **Call for rates.** 2500 Pennsylvania Ave NW 20037. Jct 25th St NW and Pennsylvania Ave; 2 blks from Foggy Bottom Metro Station. Int corridors. **Pets:** Accepted. 🛜 ✖ ♿M 🔒 🖥

(AAA) ▼▼▼▼ The Westin Georgetown, Washington, D.C. H ❀

(202) 429-0100. **$149-$649, 3 day notice.** 2350 M St NW 20037. 24th and M sts NW. Int corridors. **Pets:** Small, dogs only. Designated rooms, service with restrictions, supervision.

[SAVE] 📶 ✕ 🛏 💷 🍽 ⌁

(AAA) ▼▼▼▼ The Westin Washington DC City Center Hotel H

(202) 429-1700. **$120-$500.** 1400 M St NW 20005. Just w of Thomas Circle. Int corridors. **Pets:** Accepted. [SAVE] 📶 ✕ 🛏 💷 🍽

(AAA) ▼▼▼▼ The Willard InterContinental H

(202) 628-9100. **$229-$629.** 1401 Pennsylvania Ave NW 20004. Just e of the White House; jct 14th St NW. Int corridors. **Pets:** Accepted.

[SAVE] 📶 ✕ 🛏M 💷 🍽 ⌁

(AAA) ▼▼▼▼ W Washington, D.C. H

(202) 661-2400. **$359-$1450.** 515 15th St NW 20004. 15th St and Pennsylvania Ave NW. Int corridors. **Pets:** Accepted.

[SAVE] 📶 ✕ 🛏M 🍽 ⌁

END METROPOLITAN AREA

FLORIDA

CITY INDEX

APALACHICOLA

(AAA) ▼▼▼▼ Coombs House Inn BB ❀

(850) 653-9199. **$119-$269, 7 day notice.** 80 Sixth St 32320. US 98 (Market St) and Ave E. Int corridors. **Pets:** Medium, other species. $25 daily fee/pet. Designated rooms, service with restrictions, supervision.

[SAVE] 📶 ✕ 🛏 💷

(AAA) ▼▼▼▼ Gibson Inn H ❀

(850) 653-2191. **$115-$260, 14 day notice.** 51 Ave C 32329. US 98 at west end of bridge; downtown. Int corridors. **Pets:** Other species. $25 daily fee/pet. Designated rooms, service with restrictions, supervision.

[SAVE] 📶 ✕

(AAA) ▼▼▼▼ Water Street Hotel & Marina CO ❀

(850) 653-3700. **Call for rates.** 329 Water St 32320. Jct Ave I. Ext corridors. **Pets:** Other species. $25 daily fee/pet. Service with restrictions, supervision. [SAVE] 📶 ✕ 🛏M 🛏 💷 ⌁ ⊠

ARCADIA

(AAA) ▼▼▼ Knights Inn-Arcadia M

(863) 494-4884. **$45-$54.** 504 S Brevard Ave 34266. 0.6 mi s of SR 70; on US 17. Ext corridors. **Pets:** Accepted. [SAVE] 📶 🛏 💷 ⌁

BOCA RATON

▼▼▼▼ Boca Raton Bridge Hotel H

(561) 368-9500. **$89-$409.** 999 E Camino Real 33432. I-95 exit 44 (Palmetto Park Rd), 2.1 mi e to US 1 (Federal Hwy), 0.7 mi s to E Camino Real, then 0.8 mi e. Int corridors. **Pets:** Medium, dogs only. $100 onetime fee/room. Service with restrictions, crate.

📶 ✕ 🛏 💷 🍽 ⌁ ⊠

(AAA) ▼▼▼ ▼▼▼ Boca Raton Resort & Club, A Waldorf Astoria Resort H ❀

(561) 447-3000. **$169-$349.** 501 E Camino Real 33432. I-95 exit 44 (Palmetto Park Rd), 1.9 mi e to Federal Hwy, just s to Camino Real, then 0.5 mi e. Ext/int corridors. **Pets:** Small, dogs only. $125 one-time fee/pet. Designated rooms, service with restrictions, crate.

[ECO] [SAVE] 📶 🛏M 🛏 💷 🍽 ⌁ ⊠

▼▼▼▼ **Fairfield Inn & Suites Boca Raton - Airport** H
(561) 417-8585. **$89-$189.** 3400 Airport Rd 33431. I-95 exit 45 (SR 808/Glades Rd), just e to Airport Rd, then 1.1 mi n. Int corridors.
Pets: Accepted. 🌱 🤙 ✕ 🔥 ❚ 🖵 🏊

AAA ▼▼▼▼ **Hilton Suites Boca Raton** H ✿
(561) 483-3600. **$89-$259.** 7920 Glades Rd 33434. I-95 exit 45 (SR 808/Glades Rd), 3.4 mi w; Florida Tpke exit 75 (SR 808/Glades Rd), just e; in Arvida Parkway Center. Int corridors. **Pets:** Small. $50 one-time fee/room. Service with restrictions, supervision.
🌱 SAVE 🤙 ✕ ❚ 🖵 🏊 ✕

AAA ▼▼▼ **Quality Inn - Boca Raton** M
(561) 395-7172. **$74-$199.** 2899 N Federal Hwy 33431. I-95 exit 48 (Yamato Rd), 1.2 mi e to US 1 (Federal Hwy), then 1.3 mi s. Ext corridors. **Pets:** Other species. $25 one-time fee/room. Service with restrictions. SAVE 🤙 ❚ 🖵 🏊

AAA ▼▼▼▼ **Residence Inn by Marriott-Boca Raton** H
(561) 994-3222. **$94-$229.** 525 NW 77th St 33487. I-95 exit 50 (Congress Ave), merge onto NW 82nd St, left on Congress Ave, left on NW 6th Ave, then left; in Boca Commerce Center. Ext corridors. **Pets:** Other species. $85 one-time fee/room. Service with restrictions, crate.
SAVE 🤙 ✕ ❚ 🖵 🏊

AAA ▼▼▼▼ **TownePlace Suites Boca Raton** H
(561) 994-7232. **$86-$225.** 5110 NW 8th Ave 33487. I-95 exit 48B (Yamato Rd), just w; in Arvida Park of Commerce. Int corridors.
Pets: Accepted. 🌱 SAVE 🤙 ✕ 🔥 ❚ 🖵 🏊

AAA ▼▼▼▼ **Wyndham Garden Hotel - Boca Raton** H ✿
(561) 368-5200. **$129-$309.** 1950 Glades Rd 33431. I-95 exit 45 (SR 808/Glades Rd), just w. Ext/int corridors. **Pets:** Small, dogs only. $100 one-time fee/room. Designated rooms, service with restrictions, supervision. 🌱 SAVE 🤙 ✕ 🔥 ❚ 🖵 🏊

BONITA SPRINGS

▼▼▼ **Bonita Springs Lodge & Suites** H
(239) 495-9255. **$56-$109.** 28600 Trails Edge Blvd 34134. I-75 exit 116, 3.5 mi w on Bonita Beach Rd (CR 865), 0.7 mi s on US 41 (Tamiami Tr), just w; in Woods Edge. Int corridors. **Pets:** Accepted.
🤙 🔥 ❚ 🖵 🏊

AAA ▼▼▼▼ **Holiday Inn Express Hotel & Suites Bonita Springs** H ✿
(239) 948-0699. **$69-$149.** 27891 Crown Lake Blvd 34135. I-75 exit 116, 3.4 mi w on Bonita Beach Rd SE (CR 865), then just n. Int corridors.
Pets: Medium. $25 one-time fee/room. Designated rooms, service with restrictions, crate. 🌱 SAVE 🤙 🔥 ❚ 🖵 🏊

AAA ▼▼▼ ▼▼▼ **Hyatt Regency Coconut Point Resort & Spa** H
(239) 444-1234. **$139-$399, 3 day notice.** 5001 Coconut Rd 34134. I-75 exit 123, 1.9 mi w on Corkscrew Rd, 2.3 mi s on US 41 (Tamiami Tr), then 1.5 mi w. Int corridors. **Pets:** Accepted.
🌱 SAVE 🤙 ❚ 🖵 🍴 🏊 ✕

BRADENTON

▼▼▼▼ **Country Inn & Suites By Carlson-Bradenton** H
(941) 363-4000. **$79-$169.** 5610 Manor Hill Ln 34203. I-75 exit 217, just w on SR 70, then just s. Int corridors. **Pets:** Accepted.
🤙 ✕ 🔥 ❚ 🖵 🏊

AAA ▼▼▼ **Quality Inn North** M
(941) 758-7199. **$59-$179.** 6727 14th St W 34207. On US 41, 2 mi s of jct SR 70. Ext corridors. **Pets:** Small, dogs only. $10 daily fee/pet. Designated rooms, service with restrictions, supervision.
SAVE 🤙 ❚ 🖵 🏊

AAA ▼▼▼ **Super 8-Bradenton** M
(941) 756-6656. **$49-$71.** 6516 14 St W 34207. On US 41, 1.5 mi s of jct SR 70. Ext corridors. **Pets:** Small, dogs only. $10 daily fee/pet. Service with restrictions, supervision. SAVE ❚ 🏊

BRADENTON BEACH

AAA ▼▼▼▼ **Tortuga Inn Beach Resort** CO ✿
(941) 778-6611. **$120-$445, 14 day notice.** 1325 Gulf Dr N 34217. On Sarasota Bay and Anna Maria Island; on SR 789, 0.3 mi n of jct SR 684 (Cortez Rd). Ext corridors. **Pets:** Large. $50 one-time fee/pet. Designated rooms, service with restrictions, supervision. SAVE 🤙 ❚ 🖵 🏊

AAA ▼▼▼▼ **Tradewinds Resort** CA
(941) 779-0010. **$140-$360, 14 day notice.** 1603 Gulf Dr N 34217. On Sarasota Bay and Anna Maria Island; on SR 789, 0.5 mi n of jct SR 684 (Cortez Rd). Ext corridors. **Pets:** Accepted. SAVE 🤙 ❚ 🖵 🏊

BROOKSVILLE

▼▼▼ **Microtel Inn & Suites** H
(352) 796-9025. **$54-$99.** 6298 Nature Coast Blvd 34602. I-75 exit 301, just w on US 98/SR 50, then just s. Int corridors. **Pets:** Accepted.
🤙 🔥 ❚ 🖵 🏊

AAA ▼▼▼ **Quality Inn & Suites** M
(352) 796-9481. **$85-$129.** 30307 Cortez Blvd 34602. I-75 exit 301, just w on US 98/SR 50. Ext corridors. **Pets:** Accepted.
SAVE 🤙 🔥 ❚ 🖵 🍴 🏊

CAPE CANAVERAL

▼▼▼▼ **Residence Inn by Marriott Cape Canaveral/Cocoa Beach** H ✿
(321) 323-1100. **$169-$209.** 8959 Astronaut Blvd 32920. On SR A1A, 0.3 mi s of jct SR 528. Int corridors. **Pets:** Other species. $100 one-time fee/room. Service with restrictions, crate.
🌱 🤙 ✕ ❚ 🖵 🏊 ✕

CAPE CORAL

▼▼▼ **Holiday Inn Express Cape Coral** H
(239) 542-2121. **$89-$189.** 1538 Cape Coral Pkwy E 33904. Jct Del Prado Blvd. Int corridors. **Pets:** Accepted. 🤙 🔥 ❚ 🖵 🏊

CARRABELLE

▼▼▼ **The Moorings At Carrabelle** M ✿
(850) 697-2800. **$70-$150.** 1000 US 98 32322. On US 98/319, jct 10th St, just e of bridge. Ext corridors. **Pets:** Other species. $50 deposit/room, $10 daily fee/pet. 🤙 ❚ 🖵 🍴 🏊 ✕

CEDAR KEY

AAA ▼▼▼ **Cedar Key Bed and Breakfast** BB
(352) 543-9000. **$105-$245, 7 day notice.** 810 3rd St 32625. 0.3 mi sw of SR 24. Ext/int corridors. **Pets:** Accepted. SAVE 🤙 ❚ 🖵 🏊

AAA ▼▼▼ **Park Place Motel & Condominiums** M
(352) 543-5737. **$65-$115.** 211 2nd St 32625. Just ne of jct SR 24; at A St. Ext corridors. **Pets:** Small, other species. $7 daily fee/pet. Designated rooms, service with restrictions, supervision. 🌱 SAVE 🤙 ❚ 🖵

▼▼▼ **Seahorse Landing Condominiums** CO
(352) 543-5860. **$100-$175, 3 day notice.** 4050 G St 32625. Just sw of jct SR 24, on 6th St. Ext corridors. **Pets:** Large, dogs only. $15 daily fee/room. Designated rooms, no service, crate.
🌱 🤙 ❚ 🖵 🏊 ✕

CHARLOTTE HARBOR

▼▼▼ **Banana Bay On Charlotte Harbor** M
(941) 743-4441. **$59-$119.** 23285 Bayshore Rd 33980. Jct US 41/SR 45. Ext corridors. **Pets:** Medium, other species. $4 daily fee/pet. Supervision.
✕ ❚ 🖵 🏊 ✕

CHIEFLAND

AAA ▼▼▼ **Best Western Suwannee Valley Inn** H
(352) 493-0663. **$83-$100.** 1125 N Young Blvd 32626. On Alternate Rt US 27/19/98, just n of jct US 129. Ext corridors. **Pets:** Medium. $20 daily fee/pet. Service with restrictions, supervision. SAVE 🤙 ❚ 🖵 🏊

♥♥ Days Inn Chiefland H

(352) 493-9400. **$70-$81.** 809 NW 21st Ave 32626. Just e of US 19/98; 1 mi n of jct US 129. Ext corridors. **Pets:** Accepted.

CHIPLEY

♥♥ Super 8 M

(850) 638-8530. **$45-$58.** 1150 Motel Dr 32428. I-10 exit 120, just n. Ext corridors. **Pets:** Other species. $10 daily fee/pet. Service with restrictions, supervision.

COCOA

♥♥ Econo Lodge Space Center M

(321) 632-4561. **$45-$79.** 3220 N Cocoa Blvd 32926. US 1, just n of jct SR 528. Ext corridors. **Pets:** Medium. $25 one-time fee/pet. Designated rooms, service with restrictions, crate.

COCOA BEACH

♥♥ Best Western Ocean Beach Hotel & Suites H

(321) 783-7621. **$79-$199.** 5600 N Atlantic Ave 32931. SR A1A, 0.8 mi n of jct SR 520. Ext/int corridors. **Pets:** Accepted.

♥♥ Cocoa Beach Suites H

(321) 783-6868. **$70-$150.** 3655 N Atlantic Ave 32931. SR A1A, 0.3 mi s of jct SR 520. Int corridors. **Pets:** Small, dogs only. $100 deposit/room. Service with restrictions, supervision.

♥♥♥ Four Points by Sheraton Cocoa Beach H

(321) 783-8717. **$95-$145.** 4001 N Atlantic Ave 32931. SR A1A, just s of jct SR 520. Int corridors. **Pets:** Accepted.

♥♥ International Palms Resort - Cocoa Beach H

(321) 783-2271. **$79-$259.** 1300 N Atlantic Ave 32931. SR A1A, 1.8 mi s of jct SR 520. Ext corridors. **Pets:** Large. $25 daily fee/room. Designated rooms, service with restrictions, supervision.

♥♥ La Quinta Inn Cocoa Beach H

(321) 783-2252. **$103-$185.** 1275 N Atlantic Ave 32931. SR A1A, 1.7 mi s of SR 520. Ext corridors. **Pets:** Medium, other species. Service with restrictions, supervision.

♥ Surf Studio Beach Resort M

(321) 783-7100. **$110-$265, 7 day notice.** 1801 S Atlantic Ave 32931. SR A1A northbound, 5 mi s of jct SR 520 at Francis St; 1.3 mi n of Patrick AFB. Ext corridors. **Pets:** Medium. $25 daily fee/pet. Service with restrictions.

CRESCENT BEACH

♥♥ Beacher's Lodge Oceanfront Suites H

(904) 471-8849. **$79-$225.** 6970 A1A S 32080. Just s of jct SR 206. Ext corridors. **Pets:** Other species. $50 one-time fee/pet. Designated rooms, service with restrictions.

CRESTVIEW

♥♥ Comfort Inn & Suites H

(850) 682-1481. **$85-$126.** 900 Southcrest Dr 32536. I-10 exit 56, just se. Int corridors. **Pets:** Accepted.

♥♥ Jameson Inn H

(850) 683-1778. **$79-$99.** 151 Cracker Barrel Dr 32536. I-10 exit 56, just s. Int corridors. **Pets:** Medium. $15 daily fee/room. Service with restrictions, supervision.

♥♥ Super 8 M

(850) 682-9649. **$39-$43.** 3925 S Ferdon Blvd 32539. I-10 exit 56, 0.3 mi s. Ext corridors. **Pets:** Accepted.

CRYSTAL RIVER

♥♥ Best Western Crystal River Resort H ♣

(352) 795-3171. **$114-$150.** 614 NW Hwy 19 34428. On US 19/98, 0.8 mi n of jct SR 44. Ext corridors. **Pets:** Medium, other species. $5 daily fee/pet. Service with restrictions, supervision.

♥♥ Days Inn M

(352) 795-2111. **$63-$96.** 2380 NW Hwy 19 34428. On US 19, 2.2 mi n of jct SR 44. Ext corridors. **Pets:** $15 daily fee/pet. Designated rooms, service with restrictions, supervision.

DAYTONA BEACH

♥♥♥ Comfort Inn & Suites Oceanfront H

(386) 255-5491. **$90-$320.** 730 N Atlantic Ave 32118. On SR A1A, 1.1 mi n of jct US 92. Ext/int corridors. **Pets:** Accepted.

♥♥ Extended Stay Deluxe Daytona Beach-International Speedway H ♣

(386) 257-4311. **$70-$500.** 255 Bill France Blvd 32114. I-95 exit 261 (International Speedway Blvd/US 92), 2.1 mi e to Bill France Blvd, then just n. Int corridors. **Pets:** Other species. $25 daily fee/pet. Service with restrictions.

♥♥♥ Hilton Daytona Beach Oceanfront Resort H

(386) 254-8200. **$99-$299.** 100 N Atlantic Ave 32118. I-95 exit 261 (International Speedway Blvd/US 92), 6.1 mi e to Atlantic Ave (SR A1A), then 0.5 mi n. Int corridors. **Pets:** Medium. $50 one-time fee/pet. Designated rooms, service with restrictions.

♥♥♥ Holiday Inn Daytona Beach LPGA H

(386) 236-0200. **$79-$99.** 137 AutoMall Cir 32124. I-95 exit 265, just sw. Int corridors. **Pets:** Accepted.

♥♥♥ Homewood Suites by Hilton Daytona Speedway-Airport H

(386) 258-2828. **$99-$299.** 165 Bill France Blvd 32114. I-95 exit 261 (International Speedway Blvd/US 92), 2.1 mi e to Bill France Blvd, then just n. Int corridors. **Pets:** Other species. $50 one-time fee/room. Designated rooms, service with restrictions.

♥♥ La Quinta Inn - Daytona Beach International Speedway H

(386) 255-7412. **$58-$115.** 2725 W International Speedway Blvd 32114. I-95 exit 261 (International Speedway Blvd/US 92), just e. Int corridors. **Pets:** Medium, other species. Service with restrictions, supervision.

♥♥ Ramada Inn Speedway H

(386) 255-2422. **$59-$399, 30 day notice.** 1798 W International Speedway Blvd 32114. I-95 exit 261 (International Speedway Blvd/US 92), 2.2 mi e. Ext corridors. **Pets:** Accepted.

♥♥♥ Residence Inn Daytona Beach H ♣

(386) 252-3949. **$104-$459.** 1725 Richard Petty Blvd 32114. I-95 exit 261 (International Speedway Blvd/US 92), 2.4 mi e to Midway Ave, just s to Richard Petty Blvd, then just e. Int corridors. **Pets:** Other species. $80 one-time fee/room. Service with restrictions, supervision.

♥ Scottish Inns M

(386) 258-5742. **$40-$250, 5 day notice.** 1515 S Ridgewood Ave 32114. I-95 exit 260A (SR 400/Beville Rd), 4.7 mi e to US 1/Ridgewood Ave, then just n. Ext corridors. **Pets:** Accepted.

DAYTONA BEACH SHORES

♥♥ Atlantic Ocean Palm Inn M ♣

(386) 761-8450. **$49-$199, 30 day notice.** 3247 S Atlantic Ave 32118. On SR A1A, 5 mi s of jct US 92. Ext corridors. **Pets:** Small, dogs only. $15 daily fee/pet. Designated rooms, service with restrictions, supervision.

AAA ◆◆◆ The Shores Resort & Spa H ❀

(386) 767-7350. **$119-$569, 3 day notice.** 2637 S Atlantic Ave 32118. On SR A1A, 3.2 mi s of jct US 92. Int corridors. **Pets:** Medium, other species. $200 deposit/room, $50 daily fee/room. Service with restrictions, crate. ECO SAVE 📶 ✕ ♿M ⬛ 🖵 ▥ ⛱ ✕

DE FUNIAK SPRINGS

AAA ◆◆ Best Western Crossroads Inn H

(850) 892-5111. **$59-$100, 30 day notice.** 2343 US Hwy 331 S 32435. I-10 exit 85, just s. Ext/int corridors. **Pets:** Medium, other species. $10 one-time fee/room. Designated rooms, service with restrictions, supervision. SAVE 📶 ⬛ 🖵 ▥ ⛱

◆◆◆ Comfort Inn & Suites H

(850) 951-2225. **$69-$79.** 326 Coy Burgess Loop 32435. I-10 exit 85, just s, then just w. Int corridors. **Pets:** Accepted.
📶 ✕ ⬛ 🖵 ⛱

DELAND

AAA ◆◆ University Inn M

(386) 734-5711. **$79-$199.** 644 N Woodland Blvd 32720. US 17, 0.9 mi n of jct SR 44; next to Stetson University. Ext corridors. **Pets:** Small. $10 daily fee/pet. Designated rooms, service with restrictions, crate.
SAVE 📶 ⬛ 🖵 ⛱

DELRAY BEACH

AAA ◆◆◆ Colony Hotel & Cabana Club H ❀

(561) 276-4123. **$99-$329, 3 day notice.** 525 E Atlantic Ave 33483. On SR 806 (Atlantic Ave) at US 1 northbound; downtown. Int corridors. **Pets:** Other species. $25 daily fee/pet. ECO SAVE 📶 ✕ ⛱

◆◆◆ Residence Inn Delray Beach H ❀

(561) 276-7441. **$125-$339.** 1111 E Atlantic Ave 33483. I-95 exit 52 (SR 806/Atlantic Ave), 1.7 mi e. Int corridors. **Pets:** Other species. $100 one-time fee/room. Service with restrictions, crate.
ECO 📶 ✕ ♿M ⬛ 🖵 ⛱

◆◆◆ Sundy House H

(561) 272-5678. **Call for rates.** 106 S Swinton Ave 33444. I-95 exit 52 (SR 806/Atlantic Ave), 1.1 mi e to Swinton Ave, then just s. Ext corridors. **Pets:** Accepted. 📶 ✕ ⬛ 🖵 ▥ ⛱

DELTONA

AAA ◆◆ Best Western Deltona Inn H ❀

(386) 860-3000. **$75-$180.** 481 Deltona Blvd 32725. I-4 exit 108, just ne. Ext corridors. **Pets:** Medium, dogs only. $10 daily fee/pet. Service with restrictions, supervision. SAVE 📶 ⬛ 🖵 ▥ ⛱

DESTIN

AAA ◆◆◆ Residence Inn Sandestin at Grand Boulevard H

(850) 650-7811. **$107-$207.** 300 Grand Blvd 32550. On US 98, jct Baytowne Ln. Int corridors. **Pets:** Medium, other species. $100 one-time fee/room. Service with restrictions, supervision.
ECO SAVE 📶 ✕ ♿M ⬛ 🖵 ⛱

AAA ◆◆◆ Sandestin Golf and Beach Resort CO

(850) 267-8000. **$89-$1349, 7 day notice.** 9300 Emerald Coast Pkwy W 32550. On US 98; jct Sandestin Dr. Ext/int corridors. **Pets:** Accepted. SAVE 📶 ⬛ 🖵 ▥ ⛱ ✕

◆◆◆ SummerPlace Inn H ❀

(850) 650-8003. **$80-$200.** 14047 Emerald Coast Pkwy 32541. Jct SR 293 and US 98, 2.5 mi w. Int corridors. **Pets:** Other species. $25 one-time fee/pet. Designated rooms, service with restrictions, crate.
📶 ✕ ⬛ 🖵 ⛱

ELKTON

AAA ◆◆◆ Quality Inn St. Augustine M ❀

(904) 829-3435. **$60-$190.** 2625 SR 207 32033. I-95 exit 311, just w. Ext corridors. **Pets:** Other species. $15 daily fee/pet. Service with restrictions, supervision. SAVE 📶 ⬛ 🖵 ⛱

FLAGLER BEACH

AAA ◆◆ Topaz Motel M ❀

(386) 439-3301. **$75-$195, 14 day notice.** 1224 S Oceanshore Blvd 32136. I-95 exit 284 (SR 100), 3.5 mi e to Oceanshore Blvd (SR A1A), then 0.6 mi s. Ext/int corridors. **Pets:** Dogs only. $15 one-time fee/pet. Service with restrictions. SAVE 📶 ⬛ 🖵 ▥ ⛱

FLORAL CITY

◆◆ Moonrise Resort CA ❀

(352) 726-2553. **$85-$1800 (no credit cards), 14 day notice.** 8801 E Moonrise Ln, Lot 18 34436. Just e on CR 48, then 1.5 mi n on Old Floral City Rd. Ext corridors. **Pets:** Dogs only. $20 daily fee/pet. No service.
⬛ ✕ ☏

THE FLORIDA KEYS AREA

DUCK KEY

AAA ◆◆◆ Hawks Cay Resort H

(305) 743-7000. **$149-$369, 3 day notice.** MM 61 33050. 0.5 mi s of US 1 (Overseas Hwy). Int corridors. **Pets:** Accepted.
SAVE 📶 ⬛ 🖵 ▥ ⛱ ✕

ISLAMORADA

◆◆◆ Islander Resort M ❀

(305) 664-2031. **Call for rates.** 82100 Overseas Hwy 33036. US 1 at MM 82.1. Ext corridors. **Pets:** Other species. $75 one-time fee/pet. Designated rooms, service with restrictions, supervision.
📶 ✕ ⬛ 🖵 ▥ ⛱ ✕

AAA ◆◆◆ Sands of Islamorada M

(305) 664-2791. **$120-$350, 3 day notice.** 80051 Overseas Hwy 33036. US 1 at MM 80. Ext corridors. **Pets:** Accepted.
SAVE 📶 ✕ ⬛ 🖵 ⛱ ✕

KEY LARGO

AAA ◆◆◆ Hilton Key Largo Resort H

(305) 852-5553. **$149-$399.** 97000 S Overseas Hwy 33037. US 1 at MM 97; bayside. Ext corridors. **Pets:** Accepted.
SAVE 📶 ⬛ 🖵 ▥ ⛱ ✕

◆◆◆ Tarpon Flats Inn & Marina BB

(305) 453-1313. **$150-$200, 30 day notice.** 29 Shoreland Dr 33037. US 1 at MM 103.5, 0.3 mi e on Transylvania Ave, then s on Oceanview to Shoreland Dr. Ext corridors. **Pets:** Accepted.
📶 ✕ ⬛ 🖵 ⛱ ✕

KEY WEST

AAA ◆◆◆ Best Western Key Ambassador Resort Inn M

(305) 296-3500. **$130-$300.** 3755 S Roosevelt Blvd 33040. On SR A1A, 1 mi s of jct US 1. Ext corridors. **Pets:** Accepted.
SAVE 📶 ⬛ 🖵 ⛱

Casa Marina, A Waldorf Astoria Resort H

(305) 296-3535. **$170-$436.** 1500 Reynolds St 33040. 4 mi s on Flagler Ave (CR 5A) from jct SR A1A. Ext/int corridors. **Pets:** Accepted.

Chelsea House Pool & Gardens BB

(305) 296-2211. **$119-$389, 7 day notice.** 709 Truman Ave 33040. Corner of Elizabeth St and Truman Ave. Ext/int corridors. **Pets:** Other species. $20 daily fee/pet. Designated rooms, service with restrictions, supervision.

Courtney's Place Historic Cottages & Inn CA

(305) 294-3480. **$109-$349, 21 day notice.** 720 Whitmarsh Ln 33040. Just e of jct Petronia and Simonton sts; in Old Town. Ext corridors. **Pets:** Other species. $25 one-time fee/pet. Service with restrictions.

Curry Mansion Inn BB

(305) 294-5349. **$195-$365, 14 day notice.** 511 Caroline St 33040. Just n of jct Duval St; in Old Town. Ext/int corridors. **Pets:** Very small. Service with restrictions, supervision.

Cypress House Bed & Breakfast BB

(305) 294-6969. **$159-$550, 30 day notice.** 601 Caroline St 33040. Jct Simonton St; in Old Town. Ext/int corridors. **Pets:** Medium. Supervision.

DoubleTree Resort by Hilton Hotel Grand Key - Key West H

(305) 293-1818. **$120-$595.** 3990 S Roosevelt Blvd 33040. From US 1, 0.5 mi s on SR A1A. Int corridors. **Pets:** Medium. $75 one-time fee/room. Designated rooms, service with restrictions.

Frances Street Bottle Inn BB

(305) 294-8530. **Call for rates.** 535 Frances St 33040. US 1/Roosevelt Blvd, w on White St, then just s on Southard St; corner of Frances and Southard sts; in Old Town. Ext/int corridors. **Pets:** Accepted.

Hyatt Key West Resort & Spa H

(305) 809-1234. **$219-$595, 7 day notice.** 601 Front St 33040. Simonton and Front sts; just n of Mallory Square; in Old Town. Ext corridors. **Pets:** Medium, dogs only. $35 daily fee/room. Service with restrictions, supervision.

The Palms Hotel BB

(305) 294-3146. **$90-$280, 7 day notice.** 820 White St 33040. Just w of Truman Ave. Ext corridors. **Pets:** Medium. $40 daily fee/room. Designated rooms, service with restrictions, crate.

The Reach, A Waldorf Astoria Resort H

(305) 296-5000. **$170-$379.** 1435 Simonton St 33040. Just s of jct Truman Ave and Simonton St. Ext corridors. **Pets:** Accepted.

Sheraton Suites-Key West H

(305) 292-9800. **$149-$469, 3 day notice.** 2001 S Roosevelt Blvd 33040. Jct US 1 and SR A1A, 3 mi s. Ext/int corridors. **Pets:** Medium. Service with restrictions, supervision.

The Westin Key West Resort & Marina H

(305) 294-4000. **$229-$599, 3 day notice.** 245 Front St 33040. Adjacent to Mallory Square; in Old Town. Ext/int corridors. **Pets:** Medium, dogs only. Service with restrictions, supervision.

MARATHON

Royal Hawaiian Motel/Botel M

(305) 743-7500. **$95-$175, 30 day notice.** 12020 Overseas Hwy 33050. US 1 at MM 53; gulfside. Ext corridors. **Pets:** Small. $25 one-time fee/pet. Service with restrictions.

END AREA

FORT LAUDERDALE METROPOLITAN AREA

CORAL SPRINGS

La Quinta Inn & Suites Coral Springs University Dr H

(954) 753-9000. **$73-$169.** 3701 N University Dr 33065. SR 869 (Sawgrass Expwy) exit 15 (University Dr/SR 817), 1.9 mi s. Int corridors. **Pets:** Medium, other species. Service with restrictions, supervision.

La Quinta Inn & Suites - Ft. Lauderdale University Dr H

(954) 344-2200. **$71-$169.** 3100 N University Dr 33065. SR 869 (Sawgrass Expwy) exit 15 (University Dr/SR 817), 2.4 mi s. Int corridors. **Pets:** Medium, other species. Service with restrictions, supervision.

DANIA BEACH

Hilton Fort Lauderdale Airport Hotel H

(954) 920-3300. **$79-$199.** 1870 Griffin Rd 33004. I-95 exit 23 (Griffin Rd), just e. Ext/int corridors. **Pets:** Accepted.

Hyatt Summerfield Suites Fort Lauderdale Airport - South H

(954) 922-0271. **$99-$219.** 90 SW 18th Ave 33004. I-95 exit 22 (Stirling Rd), just e to SW 18th Ave, then just n. Int corridors. **Pets:** Accepted.

Sheraton Fort Lauderdale Airport & Cruise Port Hotel H

(954) 920-3500. **$89-$329.** 1825 Griffin Rd 33004. I-95 exit 23 (Griffin Rd), just e. Int corridors. **Pets:** Medium, dogs only. Service with restrictions, supervision.

DEERFIELD BEACH

Comfort Inn Oceanside H

(954) 428-0650. **$62-$250.** 50 S Ocean Dr (SR A1A) 33441. I-95 exit 42 (Hillsboro Blvd), 2.6 mi e; jct Hillsboro Blvd and SR A1A. Int corridors. **Pets:** Accepted.

Comfort Suites Deerfield Beach H

(954) 570-8887. **$50-$130.** 1040 E Newport Center Dr 33442. I-95 exit 41 (SW 10th St), just w; in Newport Center Complex. Ext corridors. **Pets:** Accepted.

WW Extended StayAmerica - Fort Lauderdale - Deerfield Beach H ☙

(954) 428-5997. **$60-$140.** 1200 FAU Research Park Blvd 33441. I-95 exit 41 (SW 10th St), just e to FAU Research Park Rd, then just s. Int corridors. **Pets:** Other species. $25 daily fee/pet. Service with restrictions.

AAA WWWW Hilton Deerfield Beach/Boca Raton H ☙

(954) 427-7700. **$99-$219.** 100 Fairway Dr 33441. I-95 exit 42A (Hillsboro Blvd E), just e to Fairway Dr. Int corridors. **Pets:** Medium. $50 one-time fee/room. Designated rooms, service with restrictions, crate.

WW WW La Quinta Inn & Suites Deerfield Beach I-95 H

(954) 428-0661. **$64-$169.** 100 SW 12th Ave 33442. I-95 exit 42B (Hillsboro Blvd), just w, then just s. Int corridors. **Pets:** Medium, other species. Service with restrictions, supervision.

WW WW La Quinta Inn Deerfield Beach I-95 At Hillsboro East H

(954) 421-1004. **$71-$159.** 351 W Hillsboro Blvd 33441. I-95 exit 42A (Hillsboro Blvd), 0.3 mi e. Ext/int corridors. **Pets:** Medium, other species. Service with restrictions, supervision.

WWWW Wyndham Deerfield Beach Resort H

(954) 428-2850. **$152-$242.** 2096 NE 2nd St 33441. I-95 exit 42 (Hillsboro Blvd), 2.6 mi e to SR A1A (Ocean Blvd), then just ne. Int corridors. **Pets:** Accepted.

FORT LAUDERDALE

AAA WWWW Bahia Mar Beach Resort & Yachting Center H

(954) 764-2233. **Call for rates.** 801 Seabreeze Blvd 33316. SR A1A, 0.5 mi s of Las Olas Blvd. Int corridors. **Pets:** Accepted.

AAA WWWW Candlewood Suites Fort Lauderdale Airport/ Cruise Port H

(954) 522-8822. **$79-$269.** 1120 W State Road 84 33315. I-95 exit 25 (SR 84 E), 0.8 mi e. Int corridors. **Pets:** Medium, other species. $75 one-time fee/room. Service with restrictions, crate.

WWWW Embassy Suites Fort Lauderdale - 17th Street H

(954) 527-2700. **$129-$299.** 1100 SE 17th St 33316. I-95 exit 25 (SR 84), 2 mi e to US 1 (SE 6th Ave), 0.5 mi n to SE 17th St, then 0.3 mi e. Int corridors. **Pets:** Accepted.

WW WW Extended StayAmerica - Fort Lauderdale - Airport - Cruiseport H ☙

(954) 761-9055. **$60-$140.** 1450 SE 17th St Cswy 33316. 0.5 mi e of US 1 (Federal Hwy) on SE 17th St. Int corridors. **Pets:** Other species. $25 daily fee/pet. Service with restrictions.

WW WW Extended StayAmerica-Fort Lauderdale-Cypress Creek-Andrews Ave M ☙

(954) 776-9447. **$60-$140.** 5851 N Andrews Ave Ext 33309. I-95 exit 33 (Cypress Creek), just w to N Andrews Ave, then 0.3 mi s. Ext corridors. **Pets:** Other species. $25 daily fee/pet. Service with restrictions.

WW WW Extended Stay Deluxe - Fort Lauderdale - Cypress Creek - NW 6th Way H ☙

(954) 772-3155. **$60-$140.** 6001 NW 6th Way 33309. I-95 exit 33 (Cypress Creek), 0.4 mi w, then just s. Int corridors. **Pets:** Other species. $25 daily fee/pet. Service with restrictions.

WWWW Hampton Inn Fort Lauderdale Airport North H

(954) 524-9900. **$99-$229.** 2301 SW 12th Ave 33315. I-95 exit 25 (SR 84 E), 0.7 mi e to SW 12th Ave, then just n. Int corridors.
Pets: Accepted.

WWWW Hampton Inn Ft. Lauderdale-Cypress Creek H

(954) 776-7677. **$99-$159.** 720 E Cypress Creek Rd 33334. I-95 exit 33 (Cypress Creek Rd), just e. Int corridors. **Pets:** Accepted.

AAA WWWW Hilton Fort Lauderdale Marina H

(954) 463-4000. **$129-$359.** 1881 SE 17th St Cswy 33316. I-95 exit 25 (SR 84), 2 mi e to US 1/SE 6th Ave, 0.5 mi n SE 17th St/SR A1A, then 1 mi e. Ext/int corridors. **Pets:** Accepted.

WWWW Holiday Inn Express & Suites - Ft Lauderdale Executive Airport H

(954) 772-3032. **$99-$199.** 1500 W Commercial Blvd 33309. I-95 exit 32 (Commercial Blvd), 0.7 mi w. Int corridors. **Pets:** Small, dogs only. $25 daily fee/room. Service with restrictions, supervision.

AAA WWWW Il Lugano Suite Hotel H

(954) 564-4400. **$119-$999, 3 day notice.** 3333 NE 32nd Ave 33308. 1.4 mi s of Commercial Blvd on N Ocean Dr (SR A1A), w on NE 34th St; on Intracoastal Waterway. Int corridors. **Pets:** Accepted.

WWWW La Quinta Inn & Suites Fort Lauderdale Cypress Creek H

(954) 491-7666. **$62-$165.** 999 W Cypress Creek Rd 33309. I-95 exit 33 (Cypress Creek Rd), 0.7 mi w. Int corridors. **Pets:** Medium, other species. Service with restrictions, supervision.

WWWW La Quinta Inn-Fort Lauderdale NE H

(954) 491-2500. **$71-$159.** 5727 N Federal Hwy 33308. US 1 (Federal Hwy), 0.5 mi n of SR 870 (Commercial Blvd). Ext/int corridors. **Pets:** Medium, other species. Service with restrictions, supervision.

AAA WWWW Renaissance Fort Lauderdale Cruise Port Hotel H

(954) 626-1700. **$113-$289.** 1617 SE 17th St Cswy 33316. I-95 exit 25 (SR 84), 2 mi e to US 1 (SE 6th Ave), 0.5 mi n to SE 17th St, then 0.7 mi e. Int corridors. **Pets:** Accepted.

AAA WWWW The Ritz-Carlton, Fort Lauderdale H ☙

(954) 465-2300. **$199-$2499, 7 day notice.** 1 N Fort Lauderdale Beach Blvd 33304. I-95 exit 29 (Sunrise Blvd), 4.2 mi e to Fort Lauderdale Beach Blvd (SR A1A), then 1 mi s. Int corridors. **Pets:** Small. $250 one-time fee/room. Supervision.

AAA WWWW Sheraton Fort Lauderdale Beach Hotel H

(954) 524-5551. **$109-$850, 3 day notice.** 1140 Seabreeze Blvd 33316. SR A1A, just s of Bahia Mar Marina. Ext/int corridors. **Pets:** Accepted.

AAA WWWW Sheraton Suites Cypress Creek Ft Lauderdale H ☙

(954) 772-5400. **$99-$269.** 555 NW 62nd St 33309. I-95 exit 33 (Cypress Creek Rd), just w. Int corridors. **Pets:** Medium, dogs only. $25 daily fee/room. Service with restrictions, supervision.

AAA WWWW TownePlace Suites by Marriott Fort Lauderdale West H

(954) 484-2214. **$170-$259.** 3100 Prospect Rd 33309. I-95 exit 33 (Cypress Creek Rd), 2.7 mi w to NW 31st St, then 0.5 mi s. Int corridors. **Pets:** Accepted.

AAA WWWW The Westin Beach Resort & Spa, Fort Lauderdale H

(954) 467-1111. **$169-$1100, 3 day notice.** 321 N Fort Lauderdale Beach Blvd (SR A1A) 33304. I-95 exit 29 (Sunrise Blvd), 4.2 mi e to SR A1A (Ft Lauderdale Beach Blvd), then 0.8 mi s. Int corridors.
Pets: Accepted.

▲▲▲ ▼▼▼ The Westin Fort Lauderdale 🅷
(954) 772-1331. **$79-$499.** 400 Corporate Dr 33334-3642. I-95 exit 33 (Cypress Creek Rd), just e; in Radice Corporate Park. Int corridors. **Pets:** Accepted. 🆂🅰🆅🅴 📶 ☒ 🖥 🍴 🏊 ☒

▲▲▲ ▼▼▼ ▼▼▼ W Fort Lauderdale 🅷 🐾
(954) 414-8200. **$199-$499, 3 day notice.** 401 N Fort Lauderdale Beach Blvd 33304. I-95 exit 29 (Sunrise Blvd), 4.2 mi e to SR A1A (Fort Lauderdale Beach Blvd), then 0.7 mi s. Int corridors. **Pets:** Medium. $100 one-time fee/room, $25 daily fee/room. Service with restrictions, crate.
🆂🅰🆅🅴 📶 ☒ 🅼 🖥 🍴 🏊 ☒

HOLLYWOOD

▲▲▲ ▼▼▼ Comfort Inn - Ft. Lauderdale Airport/Cruise Port South 🅷
(954) 922-1600. **$89-$189.** 2520 Stirling Rd 33020. I-95 exit 22 (Stirling Rd), 0.4 mi e. Ext corridors. **Pets:** Accepted.
🆂🅰🆅🅴 📶 🅼 🖥 🏊

▼▼▼ Days Inn - Fort Lauderdale/Hollywood Airport South 🅷
(954) 923-7300. **$60-$299.** 2601 N 29th Ave 33020. I-95 exit 21 (Sheridan St), just w, then just n. Int corridors. **Pets:** Small, other species. $10 daily fee/pet. Designated rooms, service with restrictions, crate.
🅴🅲🅾 📶 🖥 🏊

▼▼▼ La Quinta Inn & Suites Ft. Lauderdale (Airport) 🅷
(954) 922-2295. **$94-$225.** 2620 N 26th Ave 33020. I-95 exit 21 (Sheridan St), just e to Oakwood Blvd (N 26th Ave), then just n. Int corridors. **Pets:** Medium, other species. Service with restrictions, supervision.
📶 🅼 🖥 🏊

▲▲▲ ▼▼▼ Quality Inn & Suites - Hollywood Blvd 🅼
(954) 981-1800. **Call for rates.** 4900 Hollywood Blvd 33021. I-95 exit 20 (Hollywood Blvd), 1.6 mi w; Florida Tpke exit 49, 1.3 mi e. Ext corridors. **Pets:** Accepted. 🆂🅰🆅🅴 📶 🖥 🏊

▲▲▲ ▼▼▼ ▼▼▼ Seminole Hard Rock Hotel & Casino Hollywood 🅷
(954) 327-7625. **Call for rates.** 1 Seminole Way 33314. I-95 exit 22 (Stirling Rd), 2.9 mi w, then just n on SR 7/US 441; Florida Tpke exit 53, 0.5 mi e, then 0.8 mi s. Int corridors. **Pets:** Accepted.
🅴🅲🅾 🆂🅰🆅🅴 📶 🅼 🖥 🍴 🏊 ☒

▼ Swan 🅼
(954) 893-8020. **Call for rates.** 345 Cleveland St 33019. I-95 exit 21 (Sheridan St), 3.1 mi e to SR A1A (N Ocean Dr), then 0.7 mi s to Cleveland St. Ext corridors. **Pets:** Accepted. 📶 ☒ 🖥 🏊

MIRAMAR

▼▼▼ Residence Inn by Marriott Fort Lauderdale SW/Miramar 🅷
(954) 450-2717. **$119-$285.** 14700 Hotel Rd 33027. I-75 exit 7A (Miramar Pkwy), just e to SW 145th Ave, then n. Int corridors. **Pets:** Other species. $100 one-time fee/room. Service with restrictions, crate.
🅴🅲🅾 📶 ☒ 🅼 🖥 🏊

PLANTATION

▼▼▼ Extended StayAmerica - Fort Lauderdale/Plantation 🅷 🐾
(954) 382-8888. **$60-$140.** 7755 SW 6th St 33324. I-595 exit 5 (SR 817/University Dr), 1.2 mi w to University Dr, 1 mi n to SW 6th St, then just w. Int corridors. **Pets:** Other species. $25 daily fee/pet. Service with restrictions. 📶 🖥 🏊

▲▲▲ ▼▼▼ Holiday Inn Express Hotel & Suites Plantation 🅷
(954) 472-5600. **$99-$189.** 1701 N University Dr 33322. SR 817 (University Dr), just s of jct SR 838 (Sunrise Blvd). Int corridors. **Pets:** Accepted.
🆂🅰🆅🅴 📶 🖥 🏊

▼▼▼ La Quinta Inn 🅷
(954) 473-8257. **$80-$165.** 7901 SW 6th St 33324. I-595 exit 5 (SR 817/University Dr), 1.2 mi w to University Dr, 1 mi n to SW 6th St, then 0.3 mi w; in Wellesley Corporate Plaza. Int corridors. **Pets:** Medium, other species. Service with restrictions, supervision. 📶 🖥 🏊

▼▼▼ La Quinta Inn & Suites - Ft. Lauderdale Plantation 🅷
(954) 476-6047. **$85-$165.** 8101 Peters Rd 33324. I-595 exit 5 (SR 817 N/University Dr), just n, then just w; in Crossroad Office Park. Int corridors. **Pets:** Medium, other species. Service with restrictions, supervision. 📶 🅼 🖥 🏊

▲▲▲ ▼▼▼ Quality Inn Sawgrass Conference Center 🅷
(954) 556-8200. **$69-$200.** 1711 N University Dr 33322. On SR 817 (University Dr), just s of Sunrise Blvd (SR 838). Ext corridors. **Pets:** Accepted. 🆂🅰🆅🅴 📶 🖥 🍴 🏊

▼▼▼ Residence Inn by Marriott - Fort Lauderdale Plantation 🅷
(954) 723-0300. **$85-$239.** 130 N University Dr 33324. I-95 exit 27 (Broward Blvd), 5.2 mi w, then just n. Int corridors. **Pets:** Other species. $100 one-time fee/room. Designated rooms, service with restrictions, supervision. 🅴🅲🅾 📶 ☒ 🅼 🖥 🏊 ☒

▲▲▲ ▼▼▼ ▼▼▼ Sheraton Suites - Plantation 🅷 🐾
(954) 424-3300. **$109-$189.** 311 N University Dr 33324. I-595 exit 5 (SR 817/University Dr), 1.2 mi w to University Dr, then 1.8 mi n; at Fashion Mall. Int corridors. **Pets:** Medium. No service, supervision.
🅴🅲🅾 🆂🅰🆅🅴 📶 ☒ 🅼 🖥 🍴 🏊 ☒

▼▼▼ Staybridge Suites Ft. Lauderdale - Plantation 🅷
(954) 577-9696. **$109-$229.** 410 N Pine Island Rd 33324. I-595 exit 4 (Pine Island Rd), 1.7 mi n. Int corridors. **Pets:** Accepted.
📶 🅼 🖥 🏊

POMPANO BEACH

▼▼▼ Ebb Tide Resort 🅼
(954) 941-7200. **$89-$179, 7 day notice.** 300 Briny Ave 33062. I-95 exit 36A (Atlantic Blvd/SR 814), 3.3 mi e to Briny Ave, then just s. Ext corridors. **Pets:** Accepted. 📶 ☒ 🖥 🏊

▼▼▼ Extended Stay Deluxe - Cypress Creek Park North 🅷 🐾
(954) 783-1050. **$60-$140.** 1401 W McNab Rd 33069. I-95 exit 33B (Cypress Creek Rd), just w to Andrews Ave, 0.7 mi n to McNab Rd, then just w. Int corridors. **Pets:** Other species. $25 daily fee/pet. Service with restrictions. 📶 🖥 🏊

▼▼▼ Residence Inn by Marriott - Ft. Lauderdale Pompano Beach/Oceanfront 🅷
(954) 590-1000. **$279-$469.** 1350 N Ocean Blvd 33062. I-95 exit 36 (Atlantic Blvd/SR 814), 2.7 mi e to SR A1A/Ocean Blvd, then 1.3 mi n. Ext/int corridors. **Pets:** Accepted.
📶 ☒ 🅼 🖥 🍴 🏊 ☒

SUNRISE

▼▼▼ La Quinta Inn & Suites Sunrise 🅷
(954) 845-9929. **$80-$169.** 13600 NW 2nd St 33325. I-595 exit 1A (SR 84), 0.5 mi w to NW 136th Ave, 0.4 mi n to NW 2nd St, then just w. Int corridors. **Pets:** Medium, other species. Service with restrictions, supervision. 📶 🖥 🏊

▼▼▼ La Quinta Inn & Suites Sunrise Sawgrass Mills 🅷
(954) 846-1200. **$80-$169.** 13651 NW 2nd St 33325. I-595 exit 1A (SR 84), 0.5 mi w to NW 136th Ave, 0.4 mi n to NW 2nd St, then just w. Int corridors. **Pets:** Medium, other species. Service with restrictions, supervision. 📶 🖥 🏊

TAMARAC

▼▼ **La Quinta Inn & Suites Fort Lauderdale Tamarac** 🅷
(954) 484-6909. **$67-$159.** 5070 N SR 7 33319. I-95 exit 32 (Commercial Blvd), 3.2 mi w to SR 7 (US 441), then just n; Florida Tpke exit 62, 0.5 mi e to SR 7 (US 441), then just n. Int corridors. **Pets:** Medium, other species. Service with restrictions, supervision. 🛜 🗄 💻 ≋

▼▼ **La Quinta Inn-Fort Lauderdale Tamarac East** 🅷
(954) 485-7900. **$62-$159.** 3800 W Commercial Blvd 33309. On SR 870 (Commercial Blvd), 0.8 mi e of Florida Tpke exit 62. Int corridors. **Pets:** Medium, other species. Service with restrictions, supervision.
🛜 🗄 💻 ≋

WESTON

Ⓐⓐⓐ ▼▼▼▼ **Hawthorn Suites by Wyndham** 🅷
(954) 659-1555. **$100-$300.** 2201 N Commerce Pkwy 33326. I-75 exit 15 (Royal Palm Blvd), just w to Weston Rd, n to N Commerce Pkwy, then just e. Int corridors. **Pets:** Small, other species. $10 daily fee/pet. Service with restrictions, crate. 🆂🅰🆅🅴 🛜 ♿ 🗄 💻 ≋

Ⓐⓐⓐ ▼▼▼▼ **Hyatt Regency Bonaventure Conference Center & Spa** 🅷 🐾
(954) 616-1234. **$99-$499.** 250 Racquet Club Rd 33326. I-75 exit 21, 0.5 mi w to Indian Trace, just s to SR 84, 1.3 mi e to W Mall Rd, just s to Racquet Club Rd, then just e. Ext corridors. **Pets:** Medium. $50 one-time fee/pet. Designated rooms, service with restrictions, crate.
🄴🄲🄾 🆂🅰🆅🅴 🛜 ✕ 🗄 💻 🍴 ≋ ✕

▼▼▼ **Residence Inn by Marriott Weston** 🅷
(954) 659-8585. **$94-$294.** 2605 Weston Rd 33331. I-75 exit 15 (Royal Palm Blvd), 0.3 mi w to Weston Rd, then just s. Int corridors. **Pets:** Other species. $100 one-time fee/room. Service with restrictions, crate.
🛜 ✕ ♿ 🗄 💻 ≋ ✕

▼▼▼ **TownePlace Suites Fort Lauderdale-Weston** 🅷
(954) 659-2234. **$123-$256.** 1545 Three Village Rd 33326. I-75 exit 15 (Royal Palm Blvd), 1.1 mi e to Bonaventure Blvd, 0.4 mi n to Three Village Rd, then just w. Int corridors. **Pets:** Medium, other species. $100 one-time fee/pet. Designated rooms, service with restrictions, crate.
🛜 ✕ ♿ 🗄 💻 ≋

END METROPOLITAN AREA

FORT MYERS

Ⓐⓐⓐ ▼▼ **Best Western Airport Inn** 🅷
(239) 561-7000. **$70-$130.** 8955 Daniels Pkwy 33912. I-75 exit 131, 0.6 mi w on CR 879 (Daniels Pkwy). Int corridors. **Pets:** Large. $20 daily fee/pet. Designated rooms, service with restrictions, supervision.
🆂🅰🆅🅴 🛜 🗄 💻 ≋ ✕

▼▼▼ **Candlewood Suites** 🅷
(239) 344-4400. **$69-$149.** 3626 Colonial Ct 33913. I-75 exit 136, just e on SR 884 (Colonial Blvd), then just s; in Colonial Plaza. Int corridors. **Pets:** Accepted. 🛜 ♿ 🗄 💻

▼▼▼ **Candlewood Suites Fort Myers Sanibel Gateway** 🅷
(239) 210-7777. **$79-$109.** 9740 Commerce Center Ct 33908. Just e of Summerlin Rd on Bass Rd, just sw in Summerlin Park. Int corridors. **Pets:** Accepted. 🛜 ✕ ♿ 🗄 💻 ≋

▼▼▼ **Country Inn & Suites By Carlson, Sanibel-Gateway** 🅷
(239) 454-9292. **Call for rates.** 13901 Shell Point Plaza 33908. Just w of jct McGregor Blvd. Int corridors. **Pets:** Accepted.
🄴🄲🄾 🛜 ♿ 🗄 💻 ≋

▼▼▼ **Days Inn Springs Resort** 🅼
(239) 267-7900. **$64-$109.** 18051 S Tamiami Tr 33908. On US 41; jct Constitution Blvd. Ext corridors. **Pets:** Accepted. 🛜 🗄 💻 ≋

Ⓐⓐⓐ ▼▼▼ **GrandStay Hotel & Suites** 🅷
(239) 791-5000. **$69-$259.** 10150 Daniels Pkwy 33913. I-75 exit 131, just e on CR 879 (Daniels Pkwy). Int corridors. **Pets:** Accepted.
🆂🅰🆅🅴 🛜 ✕ ♿ 🗄 💻 ≋

▼▼▼ **Hilton Garden Inn Fort Myers Airport/FGCU** 🅷
(239) 210-7200. **$89-$149.** 16410 Corporate Commerce Way 33913. I-75 exit 128, 0.6 mi e on CR 840 (Alico Rd), just n on Ben Hill Griffin Pkwy, then just w; in Gulfcoast Landings. Int corridors. **Pets:** Accepted.
🛜 ♿ 🗄 💻 🍴 ≋ ✕

▼▼▼ **Holiday Inn Downtown Historic District** 🅷
(239) 332-3232. **Call for rates.** 2431 Cleveland Ave 33901. On US 41, just s of jct Edison Ave. Int corridors. **Pets:** Accepted.
🄴🄲🄾 🛜 ♿ 🗄 💻 🍴 ≋

▼▼▼ **Homewood Suites by Hilton Fort Myers Airport/FGCU** 🅷 🐾
(239) 210-7300. **$89-$159.** 16450 Corporate Commerce Way 33913. I-75 exit 128, 0.6 mi e on CR 840 (Alico Rd), just n on Ben Hill Griffin Pkwy, then just w; in Gulfcoast Landings. Int corridors. **Pets:** Medium, other species. $75 one-time fee/pet. Service with restrictions, crate.
🛜 ♿ 🗄 💻 ≋

▼▼▼ **Homewood Suites by Hilton-Ft. Myers** 🅷
(239) 275-6000. **$119-$299.** 5255 Big Pine Way 33907. Just e of jct US 41; just n of jct Daniels Pkwy; in Bell Tower Shops. Int corridors. **Pets:** Medium. $75 one-time fee/room. Designated rooms, service with restrictions, supervision. 🄴🄲🄾 ♿ 🗄 💻 ≋ ✕

▼▼▼ **Hotel Indigo-Ft. Myers-River District Downtown** 🅷
(239) 337-3446. **$99-$189.** 1520 Broadway Ave 33901. Between First and Main sts; downtown. Int corridors. **Pets:** Accepted.
🄴🄲🄾 🛜 ♿ 🗄 💻 🍴 ≋

Ⓐⓐⓐ ▼▼▼ **La Quinta Inn & Suites-Airport** 🅷
(239) 466-0012. **$107-$169.** 9521 Marketplace Rd 33912. I-75 exit 131, 0.4 mi w on CR 879 (Daniels Pkwy), then just n on Danport Blvd. Int corridors. **Pets:** Medium, other species. Service with restrictions, supervision. 🄴🄲🄾 🆂🅰🆅🅴 🛜 ✕ ♿ 🗄 💻 ≋

▼▼ **La Quinta Inn & Suites Fort Myers Central** 🅼
(239) 275-3300. **$64-$169.** 4850 S Cleveland Ave 33907. On US 41, just s of jct N Airport Rd. Ext corridors. **Pets:** Medium, other species. Service with restrictions, supervision. 🛜 ♿ 🗄 💻 ≋

▼▼▼ **La Quinta Inn & Suites Ft. Myers - Sanibel Gateway** 🅷
(239) 466-1200. **$67-$189.** 20091 Summerlin Rd SW 33908. Jct John Morris Rd. Ext corridors. **Pets:** Medium, other species. Service with restrictions, supervision. 🛜 ♿ 🗄 💻 ≋

▼▼▼ **Mainstay Suites Fort Myers** 🅷
(239) 454-6363. **$99-$159.** 9200 College Pkwy 33919. 1.3 mi w of US 41 at McGregor Blvd; in Southpointe Commons. Int corridors. **Pets:** Accepted. 🛜 🗄 💻 ≋ ✕

▼▼▼ **Residence Inn Fort Myers** 🅷 🐾
(239) 936-0110. **$101-$199.** 2960 Colonial Blvd 33912. I-75 exit 136, 3.5 mi w on SR 884 (Colonial Blvd). Int corridors. **Pets:** Other species. $100 one-time fee/room. 🄴🄲🄾 🛜 ✕ ♿ 🗄 💻 ≋ ✕

AAA **WWWW** Residence Inn Ft. Myers - Sanibel **H** ❀
(239) 415-4150. **$116-$249.** 20371 Summerlin Rd 33908. On CR 869, just ne of jct McGregor Blvd. Int corridors. **Pets:** Large, other species. $100 one-time fee/room. Designated rooms, service with restrictions, supervision. SAVE 📶 ✕ &M 🖥 🖵 ➰ ✕

WWWW Suburban Extended Stay Hotel **H**
(239) 938-0100. **$62-$124.** 10150 Metro Pkwy 33912. I-75 exit 136, 3.4 mi w on SR 884 (Colonial Blvd); just s on SR 739. Int corridors. **Pets:** Accepted. ECO &M 🖥 🖵 ➰

FORT MYERS BEACH

AAA **WWWW** Best Western Plus Beach Resort **H** ❀
(239) 463-6000. **$179-$349, 7 day notice.** 684 Estero Blvd 33931. 0.4 mi n of Matanzas Pass Bridge (SR 865). Ext corridors. **Pets:** Small. $20 daily fee/pet. Service with restrictions, supervision.
SAVE 📶 ✕ &M 🖥 🖵 ➰

AAA **WWWW** Hampton Inn & Suites Ft. Myers Beach-Sanibel Gateway **H**
(239) 437-8888. **$89-$199.** 11281 Summerlin Square Rd 33931. Just e of jct San Carlos Blvd (SR 865). Int corridors. **Pets:** Service with restrictions, supervision. ECO SAVE 📶 &M 🖥 🖵 ➰

AAA **WW WW** Lighthouse Resort Inn & Suites **H**
(239) 463-9392. **$72-$325, 3 day notice.** 1051 5th St 33931. Jct Matanzas Pass Bridge (SR 865). Ext corridors. **Pets:** Small. $25 daily fee/pet. Service with restrictions, supervision. SAVE 📶 🖥 🖵 🍴 ➰

AAA **WW WW** Matanzas Inn **M**
(239) 463-9258. **$79-$199, 30 day notice.** 414 Crescent St 33931. Just e of Matanzas Pass Bridge (SR 865), then just n. Ext corridors. **Pets:** Small, dogs only. $30 one-time fee/room. Designated rooms, service with restrictions, supervision. SAVE 📶 🖥 🖵 ➰ ✕

WW WW R&L Ambassador Suites **H**
(239) 463-6662. **$85-$275, 14 day notice.** 6950 Estero Blvd 33931. 4.8 mi se of Matanzas Pass Bridge (SR 865); jct Lenell Rd. Ext corridors. **Pets:** Accepted. ✕ &M 🖥 🖵 ➰

FORT PIERCE

WW WW Econo Lodge - Ft. Pierce **M**
(772) 461-2323. **Call for rates.** 3236 S US 1 34982. Jct SR 70, 1.3 mi s. Ext corridors. **Pets:** Accepted. 📶 🖥 ➰

WW Fountain Resort **M**
(772) 466-7041. **Call for rates.** 4889 N US 1 34946. I-95 exit 138 (Indrio Rd), 5.5 mi e, then just n. Ext corridors. **Pets:** Small. $30 one-time fee/pet. Service with restrictions, supervision. 📶 ✕ 🖥 🖵 ➰

WWWW Holiday Inn Express & Suites - Fort Pierce West **H**
(772) 464-5000. **Call for rates.** 7151 Okeechobee Rd 34945. I-95 exit 129 (Okeechobee Rd), 0.7 mi w; Florida Tpke exit 152, just e. Int corridors. **Pets:** Accepted. 📶 &M 🖥 🖵 ➰

AAA **WW WW** Royal Inn Beach - Hutchinson Island **M**
(772) 672-8888. **$69-$179.** 222 Hernando St 34949. 2.5 mi e on SR A1A southbound to Hernando St, then just s. Ext corridors. **Pets:** Small. $25 daily fee/pet. Service with restrictions. SAVE 📶 ✕ 🖥

AAA **WW WW** The Sandhurst Hotel & Suites **H**
(772) 595-0711. **$79-$169.** 1230 Seaway Dr 34949. Jct US 1 and SR A1A southbound, 2 mi e. Int corridors. **Pets:** Accepted.
SAVE 📶 ✕ 🖥 🖵 ➰ ✕

FORT WALTON BEACH

AAA **WW WW** La Quinta Inn & Suites Fort Walton Beach **H**
(850) 244-1500. **$80-$154.** 3 SW Miracle Strip Pkwy 32548. Jct SR 189 and US 98. Int corridors. **Pets:** Medium, other species. Service with restrictions, supervision. SAVE 📶 ✕ 🖥 🖵 ➰

GAINESVILLE

AAA **WWWW** Best Western Plus Gateway Grand **H** ❀
(352) 331-3336. **$99-$249.** 4200 NW 97th Blvd 32606. I-75 exit 390, just n of SR 222, then just w. Int corridors. **Pets:** Other species. $20 daily fee/room. Designated rooms, service with restrictions, supervision.
ECO SAVE 📶 ✕ &M 🖥 🖵 🍴 ➰ ✕

WWWW Comfort Inn West **H**
(352) 264-1771. **$90-$220.** 3440 SW 40th Blvd 32608. I-75 exit 384, just e, then just n. Int corridors. **Pets:** Accepted. 📶 &M 🖥 🖵 ➰

WWWW Extended StayAmerica Gainesville-I-75 **H** ❀
(352) 375-0073. **$60-$130.** 3600 SW 42nd St 32608. I-75 exit 384, just e. Ext corridors. **Pets:** Other species. $25 daily fee/pet. Service with restrictions. 📶 🖥 🖵

AAA **WW WW** Fairfield Inn Gainesville **H**
(352) 332-8292. **$63-$114.** 6901 NW 4th Blvd 32607. I-75 exit 387, just w on SR 26 to 75th St, just s to NW 4th Blvd, then e. Ext/int corridors. **Pets:** Accepted. SAVE 📶 ✕ 🖥 🖵 ➰

AAA **WW WW** Hilton University of Florida Conference Center Gainesville **H** ❀
(352) 371-3600. **$120-$189.** 1714 SW 34th St 32607. I-75 exit 384, 0.9 mi e on SR 24, then 0.7 mi n on SR 121; in University of Florida. Int corridors. **Pets:** Medium, dogs only. $75 one-time fee/room. Designated rooms, service with restrictions, supervision.
ECO SAVE 📶 &M 🖥 🖵 🍴 ➰ ✕

AAA **WW WW** Holiday Inn Express **H**
(352) 376-0004. **$112-$205.** 3905 SW 43rd St 32608. I-75 exit 384, just w. Int corridors. **Pets:** Medium, other species. $10 daily fee/room. Designated rooms, service with restrictions, supervision.
SAVE 📶 &M 🖥 🖵 ➰

WW WW Homewood Suites **H**
(352) 335-3133. **$139-$299.** 3333 SW 42nd St 32608. I-75 exit 384, just e. Int corridors. **Pets:** Accepted. ECO 📶 &M 🖥 🖵 ➰ ✕

WW WW La Quinta Inn Gainesville FL **H**
(352) 332-6466. **$64-$134.** 920 NW 69th Terr 32605. I-75 exit 387, just e, then just n. Ext corridors. **Pets:** Medium, other species. Service with restrictions, supervision. 📶 🖥 🖵 ➰

WW WW Quality Inn **H**
(352) 378-2405. **$70-$180.** 3455 SW Williston Rd 32608. I-75 exit 382, just w. Int corridors. **Pets:** Accepted. 📶 🖥 🖵 ➰

AAA **WW WW** Quality Inn - University **H**
(352) 373-6500. **$75-$160.** 2435 SW 13th St 32608. I-75 exit 382, 2 mi ne on SR 331, then 1 mi n on US 441. Ext corridors. **Pets:** Medium. $10 daily fee/pet. Service with restrictions, crate. SAVE 📶 🖥 🖵 ➰

WW WW Red Roof Inn-Gainesville **H**
(352) 336-3311. **$52-$199.** 3500 SW 42nd St 32608. I-75 exit 384, just e. Int corridors. **Pets:** Large, other species. No service, supervision.
📶 &M 🖥 ➰

AAA **WWWW** Residence Inn Gainesville I-75 **H**
(352) 264-0000. **$99-$359.** 3275 SW 40th Blvd 32608. I-75 exit 384, just e to SW 40th Blvd, then n. Int corridors. **Pets:** Other species. $75 one-time fee/room. Service with restrictions, crate.
ECO SAVE 📶 ✕ 🖥 🖵 ➰

AAA **WWWW** SpringHill Suites Gainesville **H**
(352) 376-8873. **$87-$103.** 4155 SW 40th Blvd 32608. I-75 exit 384, just e, then just s. Int corridors. **Pets:** Accepted.
ECO SAVE 📶 ✕ 🖥 🖵 ➰

AAA **WWWW** Sweetwater Branch Inn Bed & Breakfast **BB**
(352) 373-6760. **Call for rates.** 625 E University Ave 32601. 1.3 mi e of the University on SR 26; 7.3 mi e of I-75 exit 387. Int corridors. **Pets:** Accepted. SAVE 📶 🖥 🖵

HERNANDO

♨♨ Citrus Hills Lodge M
(352) 527-0015. **Call for rates.** 350 E Norvell Bryant Hwy 34442. On CR 486 at Citrus Hills Blvd, 3.6 mi w of US 41. Int corridors.
Pets: Accepted. 🛜 &M 🛏 💻 🌊

INDIALANTIC

♨ ♨♨ **DoubleTree Suites by Hilton Hotel Melbourne Beach Oceanfront H**
(321) 723-4222. **$119-$159.** 1665 N SR A1A 32903. On SR A1A, 1.5 mi n of jct US 192. Ext corridors. **Pets:** Accepted.
ECO SAVE 🛜 ✖ 🛏 💻 ⊺⊺ 🌊 ✖

♨♨♨ Oceanfront Cottages CA
(321) 725-8474. **$150-$225, 60 day notice.** 612 Wavecrest Ave 32903. Just s of east end of US 192. Ext corridors. **Pets:** Dogs only. $100 one-time fee/pet. No service, supervision. 🛜 ✖ 🛏 💻 🌊

INGLIS

♨♨♨ Pine Lodge Bed & Breakfast BB
(352) 447-7463. **Call for rates.** 649 CR 40 W 34449. 1.5 mi w of US 19, on Follow That Dream Pkwy. Ext/int corridors. **Pets:** Accepted.
ECO 🛜 ✖ 🛏 💻 🌊 ✄

JACKSONVILLE METROPOLITAN AREA

ATLANTIC BEACH

♨ ♨♨♨ **One Ocean Resort Hotel & Spa H**
(904) 241-4321. **$199-$449.** 1 Ocean Blvd 32233. Jct SR A1A, just e on Atlantic Blvd. Int corridors. **Pets:** Accepted.
ECO SAVE 🛜 ✖ &M 🛏 ⊺⊺ 🌊 ✖

BALDWIN

♨ ♨♨ **Best Western Baldwin Inn M**
(904) 266-9759. **$63-$70.** 1088 US 301 S 32234. I-10 exit 343, just s. Ext corridors. **Pets:** Other species. $10 daily fee/pet. Service with restrictions, supervision. SAVE 🛜 🛏 💻 🌊

FERNANDINA BEACH

♨♨ Amelia Island Hampton Inn H ✿
(904) 321-1111. **Call for rates.** 2549 Sadler Rd 32034. In Fernandina Beach; just w of jct SR A1A and Sadler Rd. Int corridors. **Pets:** Medium, other species. $25 one-time fee/pet. Designated rooms, service with restrictions. 🛜 &M 🛏 💻 🌊

♨♨♨ Comfort Suites Amelia Island H
(904) 261-0193. **$85-$240.** 2801 Atlantic Ave 32034. In Fernandina Beach; SR A1A, 1.5 mi e of downtown. Int corridors. **Pets:** Small. $25 daily fee/pet. Designated rooms, service with restrictions, supervision. 🛜 ✖ &M 🛏 💻 🌊

♨♨ Days Inn & Suites H
(904) 277-2300. **$63-$125.** 2707 Sadler Rd 32034. In Fernandina Beach; 12.3 mi e on SR 200/A1A, 1.2 mi e. Ext corridors. **Pets:** Other species. $25 one-time fee/room. Designated rooms, service with restrictions, supervision. 🛜 🛏 💻 🌊 ✖

♨ ♨♨♨ **Omni Amelia Island Plantation Resort H**
(904) 261-6161. **$219-$499, 7 day notice.** 6800 First Coast Hwy 32034. In Fernandina Beach, 6.5 mi s of the bridge. Ext corridors. **Pets:** Medium. $50 one-time fee/pet. Designated rooms, service with restrictions. ECO SAVE 🛜 ✖ 🛏 💻 ⊺⊺ 🌊 ✖

♨ ♨♨♨ **Residence Inn - Amelia Island H ✿**
(904) 277-2440. **$116-$238.** 2301 Sadler Rd 32034. In Fernandina Beach; on east side of island, just w of jct SR A1A and Sadler Rd. Int corridors. **Pets:** Medium. $50 one-time fee/room. Designated rooms, service with restrictions, supervision. ECO SAVE 🛜 ✖ &M 🛏 💻 🌊 ✖

JACKSONVILLE

♨ ♨♨ **Best Western Hotel - JTB/Southpoint H ✿**
(904) 281-0900. **$70-$160.** 4660 Salisbury Rd 32256. I-95 exit 344 (SR 202), just ne, then just s. Int corridors. **Pets:** Medium. $10 daily fee/pet. Designated rooms, service with restrictions.
SAVE 🛜 🛏 💻 🌊 ✖

♨ ♨♨ **Best Western Jacksonville Airport H**
(904) 741-4980. **$70-$150.** 1170 Airport Entrance Rd 32218. I-95 exit 363B, just w, then just s on Duval Rd. Ext corridors. **Pets:** Accepted.
SAVE 🛜 &M 🛏 💻 🌊

♨♨ Candlewood Suites H ✿
(904) 296-7785. **$52-$73.** 4990 Belfort Rd 32256. I-95 exit 344 (SR 202), ne to Belfort Rd, then just s. Int corridors. **Pets:** Medium. $15 daily fee/room. Designated rooms, service with restrictions, crate. &M 🛏 💻

♨♨ Comfort Suites H
(904) 737-4477. **$60-$130.** 8277 Western Way Cir 32256. I-95 exit 341 (Baymeadows Rd/SR 152), just e. Int corridors. **Pets:** Accepted.
🛜 ✖ &M 🛏 💻 🌊

♨♨♨ Courtyard Jacksonville Airport Northeast H
(904) 741-1122. **$80-$145.** 14668 Duval Rd 32218. I-95 exit 363B, just w on Airport Rd, then just s. Int corridors. **Pets:** Small. $75 one-time fee/room. Service with restrictions, crate.
🛜 ✖ &M 🛏 💻 ⊺⊺ 🌊

♨ ♨♨♨ **Crowne Plaza Jacksonville Airport H**
(904) 741-4404. **$89-$179.** 14670 Duval Rd 32218. I-95 exit 363, just w. Int corridors. **Pets:** Accepted. SAVE 🛜 &M 💻 ⊺⊺ 🌊

♨♨♨ Embassy Suites Jacksonville - Baymeadows H
(904) 731-3555. **$89-$189.** 9300 Baymeadows Rd 32256. I-95 exit 341 (Baymeadows Rd/SR 152), 0.5 mi e. Int corridors. **Pets:** Medium, other species. $50 one-time fee/room. Designated rooms, service with restrictions. ECO 🛜 &M 🛏 💻 ⊺⊺ 🌊

♨♨ Extended StayAmerica-Jacksonville-Butler Blvd H ✿
(904) 296-0181. **$50-$70.** 6961 Lenoir Ave 32216. I-95 exit 344 (SR 202), just sw, then 0.3 mi n. Int corridors. **Pets:** Other species. $25 daily fee/pet. Service with restrictions. 🛜 🛏 💻

♨♨ Extended Stay Deluxe-Jacksonville-Butler Blvd H ✿
(904) 332-6512. **$55-$80.** 4699 Lenoir Ave S 32216. I-95 exit 344 (SR 202), just sw, then just n. Int corridors. **Pets:** Other species. $25 daily fee/pet. Service with restrictions. 🛜 🛏 💻 🌊

♨♨ Extended Stay Deluxe (Jacksonville/Deerwood Park) H ✿
(904) 620-9008. **$60-$90.** 8801 Perimeter Park Blvd 32216. I-95 exit 344 (SR 202), 2.5 mi e on J Turner Butler Blvd to Southside Blvd, then just n on west side of road. Int corridors. **Pets:** Other species. $25 daily fee/pet. Service with restrictions. 🛜 &M 🛏 💻 🌊

♨♨♨ Hampton Inn & Suites Deerwood Park H
(904) 997-9100. **$80-$125.** 4415 Southside Blvd 32216. I-95 exit 344 (SR 202), 2.5 mi e on J Turner Butler Blvd, then 0.9 mi n on SR 115. Int corridors. **Pets:** Service with restrictions, supervision.
🛜 ✖ 🛏 💻 🌊

▼▼▼▼ Holiday Inn Express & Suites Jacksonville H ❀

(904) 696-3333. **$82-$109.** 10148 New Berlin Rd 32226. I-95 exit 362A southbound, 4.9 mi s on SR 9A to Heckscher Dr, then just w; exit 358A northbound, 5.8 mi ne on Heckscher Dr; 0.6 mi from Jaxport Cruise Terminal. Int corridors. **Pets:** Other species. $15 daily fee/room. Service with restrictions, crate. 🛜 🖥 💻 🏊

▼▼▼▼ Holiday Inn Express Hotel & Suites H

(904) 652-2782. **$89-$109.** 537 Chaffee Point Blvd 32221. I-10 exit 351 (Chaffee Rd), just se. Int corridors. **Pets:** Accepted.
🛜 ✕ ♿ 🖥 💻 🏊

▼▼▼▼ Holiday Inn Express Hotel & Suites Jacksonville Mayport/Beach H

(904) 435-0700. **$99-$149.** 2040 Mayport Rd 32233. On SR AIA, 1.2 mi n of Atlantic Blvd (SR 10). Int corridors. **Pets:** Accepted.
🛜 ✕ ♿ 🖥 💻 🏊

▼▼▼▼ Homewood Suites by Hilton - Jacksonville H

(904) 733-9299. **$70-$140.** 8737 Baymeadows Rd 32256. I-95 exit 341 (Baymeadows Rd/SR 152), 0.3 mi w. Ext/int corridors. **Pets:** Medium. $75 one-time fee/room. Designated rooms, service with restrictions, crate.
🛜 🖥 💻 🏊 ✕

▼▼▼▼ Homewood Suites by Hilton Jacksonville South/Town Center H

(904) 641-7988. **$109-$249.** 10434 Midtown Pkwy 32246. I-95 exit 344 (SR 202), 3.5 mi e on J Turner Butler Blvd to Gate Pkwy, 0.3 mi n to Town Center Pkwy, 0.5 mi e to Midtown Pkwy, then 0.3 mi s. Int corridors. **Pets:** Accepted. 🛜 🖥 💻 🏊 ✕

▼▼▼ Hotel Indigo Jacksonville-Deerwood Park H

(904) 996-7199. **$75-$175.** 9840 Tapestry Park Cir 32246. I-95 exit 340, 4.5 mi to Southside Blvd, then e. Int corridors. **Pets:** Accepted.
🛜 ✕ 🖥 💻 🍴 🏊

∆∆∆▷ ▼▼▼▼ Hyatt Regency Jacksonville Riverfront H

(904) 588-1234. **$89-$399.** 225 Coast Line Dr E 32202. Downtown; just e of The Landing. Int corridors. **Pets:** Accepted.
ECO SAVE 🛜 🖥 💻 🍴 🏊 ✕

▼▼ Jameson Inn H

(904) 296-0968. **$64-$84.** 7030 Bonneval Rd 32216. I-95 exit 344 (SR 202), just w. Int corridors. **Pets:** Medium. $15 daily fee/room. Service with restrictions, supervision. 🛜 🖥 💻 🏊

▼▼▼▼ La Quinta Inn & Suites Jacksonville (Butler Blvd) H

(904) 296-0703. **$67-$125.** 4686 Lenoir Ave S 32216. I-95 exit 344 (SR 202), just sw, then just nw. Int corridors. **Pets:** Medium, other species. Service with restrictions, supervision. 🛜 ♿ 🖥 💻 🏊

▼▼ La Quinta Inn & Suites - Jacksonville Mandarin/San Jose H

(904) 268-9999. **$62-$119.** 3199 Hartley Rd 32257. I-295 exit 5A northbound; exit 5 (SR 13) southbound, just n and e. Int corridors.
Pets: Medium, other species. Service with restrictions, supervision.
🛜 🖥 💻 🏊

▼▼▼ La Quinta Inn Jacksonville (Orange Park) H

(904) 778-9539. **$55-$112.** 8555 Blanding Blvd 32244. I-295 exit 12, just s on SR 21. Ext corridors. **Pets:** Medium, other species. Service with restrictions, supervision. 🛜 ♿ 🖥 💻 🏊

∆∆∆▷ ▼▼▼▼ Omni Jacksonville Hotel H ❀

(904) 355-6664. **$139-$349, 5 day notice.** 245 Water St 32202. Corner of Pearl and Water sts; on north side of St. Johns River; downtown; adjacent to The Landing. Int corridors. **Pets:** Medium. $50 one-time fee/pet. Service with restrictions, supervision.
ECO SAVE 🛜 🖥 💻 🍴 🏊

▼▼ Quality Inn H

(904) 781-6000. **$49-$199.** 6802 Commonwealth Ave 32254. I-295 exit 22, just e. Ext/int corridors. **Pets:** Accepted.
🛜 🖥 💻 🍴 🏊 ✕

▼▼ Ramada Conference Center - Mandarin H

(904) 268-8080. **$69-$225.** 3130 Hartley Rd 32257. I-295 exit 5A northbound; exit 5 southbound, then just n on SR 13. Ext corridors.
Pets: Large. Designated rooms, service with restrictions, crate.
🛜 ✕ 🖥 💻 🍴 🏊

▼▼▼▼ Residence Inn by Marriott Butler Blvd H

(904) 996-8900. **$89-$249.** 10551 Deerwood Park Blvd 32256. I-95 exit 344 (SR 202/Butler Blvd), 3.3 mi e to Gate Parkway exit, just s to Deerwood Park Blvd, then just w. Int corridors. **Pets:** Accepted.
🛜 ✕ ♿ 🖥 💻 🏊 ✕

∆∆∆▷ ▼▼▼▼ Residence Inn by Marriott Jacksonville Baymeadows H

(904) 733-8088. **$80-$129.** 8365 Dix Ellis Tr 32256. I-95 exit 341 (Baymeadows Rd/SR 152), just w to Freedom Commerce Pkwy, then just s. Ext corridors. **Pets:** Accepted. SAVE 🛜 ✕ 🖥 💻 🏊 ✕

▼▼▼ St. Johns Suites H

(904) 997-9190. **$63-$72, 3 day notice.** 53 Jefferson Rd 32225. Jct SR 9A and Atlantic Blvd, just ne. Int corridors. **Pets:** Accepted.
🛜 ✕ 🖥 💻 🏊

∆∆∆▷ ▼▼▼▼ Sheraton Jacksonville Hotel H ❀

(904) 564-4772. **$99-$399.** 10605 Deerwood Park Blvd 32256. I-95 exit 344 (SR 202/Butler Blvd), 3.3 mi e to Gate Parkway exit, just s to Deerwood Park Blvd, then just w. Int corridors. **Pets:** Medium, other species. Designated rooms, service with restrictions, supervision.
SAVE 🛜 ✕ ♿ 🖥 🍴 🏊

▼▼▼ TownePlace Suites Jacksonville Butler Blvd H

(904) 296-1661. **$80-$149.** 4801 Lenoir Ave 32216. I-95 exit 344 (SR 202), just w, then just n. Int corridors. **Pets:** Medium. $75 one-time fee/room. Service with restrictions, supervision.
🛜 ✕ ♿ 🖥 💻 🏊

∆∆∆▷ ▼▼▼ Travelodge Inn & Suites H

(904) 741-4600. **$45-$61.** 1153 Airport Rd 32218. I-95 exit 363B, just w. Ext corridors. **Pets:** Accepted. SAVE 🛜 🖥 💻 🏊

JACKSONVILLE BEACH

∆∆∆▷ ▼▼▼▼ Holiday Inn Express-Jacksonville Beach H

(904) 435-3000. **$119-$169.** 1101 Beach Blvd 32250. 0.7 mi w of 3rd St/SR A1A. Int corridors. **Pets:** Medium. $25 daily fee/pet. Service with restrictions, supervision. ECO SAVE 🛜 ✕ ♿ 🖥 💻 🏊 ✕

∆∆∆▷ ▼▼▼▼ Quality Suites Oceanfront H ❀

(904) 435-3535. **$179-$359.** 11 1st St N 32250. Just n of Beach Blvd (US 90). Int corridors. **Pets:** Medium. $35 daily fee/pet. Service with restrictions, supervision. ECO SAVE 🛜 ✕ ♿ 🖥 💻 🏊 ✕

NEPTUNE BEACH

∆∆∆▷ ▼▼▼ Days Inn Neptune Beach-Mayo Clinic NE H

(904) 249-2777. **Call for rates.** 1401 Atlantic Blvd 32266. SR 9A exit SR 10, 6.9 mi e. Int corridors. **Pets:** $15 daily fee/pet. Designated rooms, service with restrictions. SAVE 🛜 🖥 💻 🏊

ORANGE PARK

▼▼ Comfort Inn H ❀

(904) 644-4444. **$59-$99.** 341 Park Ave 32073. I-295 exit 10 (US 17), just s. Ext corridors. **Pets:** Medium, other species. $30 one-time fee/pet. Service with restrictions, supervision. 🛜 🖥 💻 🏊

YULEE

◆◆ Comfort Inn 🅗
(904) 225-2600. **$65-$150.** 76043 Sidney Pl 32097. I-95 exit 373, just e on SR 200/A1A. Int corridors. **Pets:** Accepted. 🛜 🔌 💻 🏊

◍ ◆◆◆ Country Inn & Suites By Carlson 🅗 🐾
(904) 225-0182. **$79-$129.** 462577 SR 200 32097. I-95 exit 373, just e on SR 200/A1A. Int corridors. **Pets:** Medium. $25 deposit/room, $15 daily fee/room. Service with restrictions, supervision.
SAVE 🛜 ✖ 🅼 🔌 💻 🏊

END METROPOLITAN AREA

JUNO BEACH

 Holiday Inn Express - Juno Beach 🅗
(561) 622-4366. **$99-$239.** 13950 US Hwy 1 33408. I-95 exit 83 (Donald Ross Rd), 4.5 mi e; jct US 1 and Donald Ross Rd. Int corridors. **Pets:** $25 daily fee/pet. Service with restrictions, supervision.
🛜 ✖ 🔌 💻 🏊

JUPITER

◆◆◆ Fairfield Inn & Suites West Palm Beach Jupiter 🅗
(561) 748-5252. **$87-$279.** 6748 W Indiantown Rd 33458. I-95 exit 87A (Indiantown Rd), 0.8 mi e. Int corridors. **Pets:** Accepted.
ECO 🛜 ✖ 🔌 💻 🏊

LAKE CITY

◍ ◆◆◆ Best Western Lake City Inn 🅗
(386) 752-3801. **$78-$89.** 3598 W Hwy 90 32055. I-75 exit 427, just w. Ext corridors. **Pets:** Medium, other species. $15 daily fee/room. Designated rooms, no service, supervision. SAVE 🛜 🔌 💻 🏊 ✖

◍ ◆◆ Days Inn I-10 🅗
(386) 758-4224. **$41-$79.** 3430 N Hwy 441 32055. I-10 exit 303, just s. Ext corridors. **Pets:** Other species. $10 daily fee/pet. Service with restrictions, crate. SAVE 🛜 🔌 💻 🏊

◍ ◆◆ Driftwood Inn 🅜
(386) 755-3545. **$42-$70.** 2764 W Hwy 90 32055. I-75 exit 427, 0.7 mi e. Ext corridors. **Pets:** Small, dogs only. $10 daily fee/pet. Designated rooms, service with restrictions, supervision. SAVE 🛜 🔌

◆◆◆ Holiday Inn Hotel & Suites 🅗
(386) 754-1411. **$89-$149.** 213 SW Commerce Dr 32025. I-75 exit 427, just e. Int corridors. **Pets:** Accepted.
ECO 🛜 ✖ 🔌 💻 🍴 🏊 ✖

◆◆ Red Roof Inn 🅗
(386) 752-6693. **$59-$89.** 414 SW Florida Gateway Dr 32024. I-75 exit 427, just w, then 0.4 mi s. Ext corridors. **Pets:** Large, other species. No service, supervision. 🛜 🔌 🏊

◍ ◆◆ Rodeway Inn 🅜
(386) 755-5203. **Call for rates.** 205 SW Commerce Dr 32025. I-75 exit 427, just e. Ext corridors. **Pets:** Accepted. SAVE 🛜 🔌 💻

LAKELAND

◆◆◆ Crestwood Suites Lakeland 🅗
(863) 904-2050. **$89-$109.** 4360 Lakeland Park Dr 33809. I-4 exit 33, 0.6 mi se on SR 33; 0.4 mi n on Socrum Loop, just s. Int corridors. **Pets:** Small. $15 daily fee/room. Designated rooms, service with restrictions, supervision. 🛜 🅼 🔌 💻 🏊

◆◆ Jameson Inn 🅗
(863) 858-9070. **$64-$84.** 4375 Lakeland Park Dr 33809. I-4 exit 33, 0.6 mi s on SR 33, just nw on N Socrum Loop Rd, just w. Int corridors. **Pets:** Medium. $15 daily fee/room. Service with restrictions, supervision.
🛜 🅼 🔌 💻 🏊

◆◆ La Quinta Inn & Suites Lakeland East 🅗
(863) 815-0606. **$67-$135.** 4315 Lakeland Park Dr 33809. I-4 exit 33, 0.6 mi sw on SR 33, just s on N Socrum Loop Rd, then just w. Int corridors. **Pets:** Medium, other species. Service with restrictions, supervision.
🛜 🅼 🔌 💻 🏊

◆◆ La Quinta Inn & Suites Lakeland West 🅗
(863) 859-2866. **$67-$159.** 1024 Crevasse St 33809. I-4 exit 32, just n on US 98. Int corridors. **Pets:** Medium, other species. Service with restrictions, supervision. 🛜 🅼 🔌 💻 🏊

◆◆◆ Ramada Inn Lakeland 🅗
(863) 577-0977. **$62-$161, 7 day notice.** 4620 N Socrum Loop Rd 33809. I-4 exit 33, 0.6 mi sw on SR 33, then 0.4 mi n. Int corridors. **Pets:** Accepted. 🛜 🔌 💻 🏊

◆◆◆ Residence Inn Lakeland 🅗
(863) 680-2323. **$132-$379.** 3701 Harden Blvd 33803. SR 570 (Polk Pkwy) exit 5, just n. Int corridors. **Pets:** Accepted.
🛜 ✖ 🔌 💻 🏊 ✖

LAKE WORTH

◍ ◆◆◆ ◆◆◆ Sabal Palm House B & B Inn 🅱🅱
(561) 582-1090. **$99-$249, 14 day notice.** 109 N Golfview Rd 33460. Just n of SR 802; west side of Intracoastal Bridge. Ext/int corridors. **Pets:** Medium, dogs only. $15 daily fee/room. Designated rooms.
SAVE 🛜 ✖ 🔌 💻

LANTANA

◍ ◆◆◆ Super 8 Lantana 🅜
(561) 585-3970. **$59-$71.** 1255 Hypoluxo Rd 33462. I-95 exit 60 (Hypoluxo Rd), just e; on north side. Ext corridors. **Pets:** Accepted.
SAVE 🛜 🔌 💻

LECANTO

◆◆◆ Holiday Inn Express Hotel & Suites 🅗
(352) 341-3515. **$80-$160.** 903 E Gulf to Lake Hwy 34461. On SR 44, 4.2 mi e. Int corridors. **Pets:** Other species. $50 daily fee/pet. Designated rooms, service with restrictions, supervision.
ECO 🛜 ✖ 🅼 🔌 💻 🏊

LIVE OAK

◍ ◆◆◆ Best Western Suwannee River Inn 🅗
(386) 362-6000. **$76-$251, 7 day notice.** 6819 US 129 N 32060. I-10 exit 283, 0.3 mi s. Ext corridors. **Pets:** Medium. $20 daily fee/pet. Service with restrictions, supervision. SAVE 🛜 🔌 💻 🏊

◍ ◆◆◆ Econo Lodge 🅗
(386) 362-7459. **Call for rates.** 6811 N US 129 & I-10 32060. I-10 exit 283, just s. Ext corridors. **Pets:** Accepted. SAVE 🛜 🔌 💻 🏊

LYNN HAVEN

◆◆◆ Wingate by Wyndham Lynn Haven 🅗
(850) 248-8080. **$77-$147.** 2610 Lynn Haven Pkwy 32444. On SR 77, 1.8 mi n of jct SR 368. Int corridors. **Pets:** Medium, dogs only. $60 one-time fee/pet. Designated rooms, service with restrictions, crate.
🛜 ✖ 🅼 🔌 💻 🏊 ✖

MACCLENNY

◍ ◆◆◆ Econo Lodge 🅜
(904) 259-3000. **$50-$55.** 151 Woodlawn Rd 32063. I-10 exit 335, just s of jct SR 121. Ext corridors. **Pets:** Accepted. SAVE 🛜 🔌 💻 🏊

MANALAPAN

◇◇◇ ▼▼▼▼▼ The Ritz-Carlton, Palm Beach 🅷
(561) 533-6000. **$199-$749.** 100 S Ocean Blvd 33462. I-95 exit 61 (Lantana Rd), 1.1 mi e to US 1 (Federal Hwy), just s to Ocean Ave, then 0.8 mi e. Int corridors. **Pets:** Accepted.
🔲 🔲 🔲 🔲 🔲 🔲 🔲

MARIANNA

▼▼ ▼▼ Americas Best Value Inn 🅷 ❖
(850) 526-5666. **Call for rates.** 2086 Hwy 71 S 32448. I-10 exit 142, 0.3 mi s. Ext corridors. **Pets:** Medium. $12 daily fee/pet. Service with restrictions, supervision. 🔲 🔲 🔲 🔲

▼▼ ▼▼ Days Inn Marianna 🅷
(850) 526-1006. **Call for rates.** 2185 Hwy 71 S 32448. I-10 exit 142, just nw. Ext corridors. **Pets:** Accepted. 🔲 🔲 🔲 🔲

▼▼ ▼▼ Microtel Inn & Suites 🅷
(850) 526-5005. **$49-$76.** 4959 White Tail Dr 32448. I-10 exit 142, just n. Int corridors. **Pets:** Small, dogs only. $25 one-time fee/room. Service with restrictions, crate. 🔲 🔲 🔲 🔲 🔲

◇◇◇ ▼▼ ▼▼ Quality Inn 🅷 ❖
(850) 526-5600. **Call for rates.** 2175 Hwy 71 S 32448. I-10 exit 142, just n. Ext corridors. **Pets:** Medium. $12 daily fee/pet. Service with restrictions, supervision. 🔲 🔲 🔲 🔲 🔲

MELBOURNE

▼▼▼▼▼ Candlewood Suites Hotel 🅷 ❖
(321) 821-9009. **$89-$119.** 2930 Pineda Plaza Way 32940. I-95 exit 191 (CR 509/Wickham Rd), 4.5 mi e, then just n. Int corridors. **Pets:** Medium. $25 daily fee/room. Service with restrictions, supervision. 🔲 🔲 🔲

▼▼▼▼ Crane Creek Inn Waterfront Bed & Breakfast 🅱🅱 ❖
(321) 768-6416. **Call for rates.** 907 E Melbourne Ave 32901. Jct US 192, just s on Babcock St, 0.9 mi e. Ext/int corridors. **Pets:** Medium, dogs only. $20 daily fee/pet. Designated rooms, service with restrictions, crate. 🔲 🔲 🔲 🔲 🔲

▼▼▼ Extended Stay Deluxe Melbourne-Airport 🅷 ❖
(321) 733-6050. **$70-$120.** 1701 Evans Rd 32904. I-95 exit 180 (US 192/New Haven Ave), 3.2 mi e to Evans Rd, then 0.4 mi n. Int corridors. **Pets:** Other species. $25 daily fee/pet. Service with restrictions.
🔲 🔲 🔲 🔲

◇◇◇ ▼▼▼▼ Hilton Melbourne Beach Oceanfront 🅷
(321) 777-5000. **$119-$159.** 3003 N SR A1A 32903. 3 mi n of jct US 192. Int corridors. **Pets:** Medium, other species. $50 one-time fee/room. Service with restrictions, supervision.
🔲 🔲 🔲 🔲 🔲 🔲 🔲

▼▼▼▼ Hilton Melbourne Rialto Place 🅷
(321) 768-0200. **$89-$229.** 200 Rialto Pl 32901. I-95 exit 180 (US 192/New Haven Ave), 4.8 mi e to Airport Blvd, then 0.8 mi n to Rialto Pl. Int corridors. **Pets:** Medium. $50 one-time fee/room. Service with restrictions.
🔲 🔲 🔲 🔲 🔲 🔲

▼▼ ▼▼ La Quinta Inn & Suites - Melbourne 🅷
(321) 242-9400. **$73-$159.** 7200 George T Edwards Dr 32940. I-95 exit 191 (CR 509/Wickham Rd), just w. Int corridors. **Pets:** Medium, other species. Service with restrictions, supervision. 🔲 🔲 🔲 🔲

◇◇◇ ▼▼▼▼ Residence Inn by Marriott Melbourne 🅷
(321) 723-5740. **$94-$180.** 1430 S Babcock St 32901. I-95 exit 180 (US 192/New Haven Ave), 5.1 mi e to Babcock St, then 0.5 mi n. Int corridors. **Pets:** Large, other species. $100 one-time fee/room. Service with restrictions, supervision. 🔲 🔲 🔲 🔲 🔲 🔲 🔲 🔲

MIAMI-MIAMI BEACH METROPOLITAN AREA

AVENTURA

◇◇◇ ▼▼▼▼ Residence Inn by Marriott-Aventura Mall 🅷 ❖
(786) 528-1001. **$161-$419, 3 day notice.** 19900 W Country Club Dr 33180. I-95 exit 16 (Ives Dairy Rd), 1.1 mi e to US 1/Biscayne Blvd, 0.5 mi s to 199th St, 0.5 mi e to W Country Club Dr, then just s. Int corridors. **Pets:** Medium. $100 one-time fee/room. Designated rooms, service with restrictions, supervision.
🔲 🔲 🔲 🔲 🔲 🔲 🔲 🔲

◇◇◇ ▼▼▼▼ ▼▼ Turnberry Isle Miami 🅷 ❖
(305) 932-6200. **$119-$3900, 3 day notice.** 19999 W Country Club Dr 33180. I-95 exit 16 (Ives Dairy Rd), 1.1 mi e to US 1 (Biscayne Blvd), just s to 199th St (Aventura Blvd), 0.5 mi e to Country Club Dr, then just s. Ext/int corridors. **Pets:** Small. $25 daily fee/room. Service with restrictions, supervision. 🔲 🔲 🔲 🔲 🔲 🔲 🔲 🔲 🔲

BAL HARBOUR

◇◇◇ ▼▼▼▼ ▼▼▼▼ ONE Bal Harbour Resort & Spa 🅷
(305) 455-5400. **Call for rates.** 10295 Collins Ave 33154. On Collins Ave (SR A1A); at Haulover Cswy. Int corridors. **Pets:** Accepted.
🔲 🔲 🔲 🔲 🔲 🔲 🔲 🔲

COCONUT GROVE

◇◇◇ ▼▼▼▼ ▼▼▼▼ Mayfair Hotel & Spa 🅷 ❖
(305) 441-0000. **$139-$339.** 3000 Florida Ave 33133. At Florida Ave and Virginia St; center. Ext/int corridors. **Pets:** Other species. $25 one-time fee/pet. Service with restrictions, supervision.
🔲 🔲 🔲 🔲 🔲 🔲

◇◇◇ ▼▼▼▼ Residence Inn by Marriott Miami Coconut Grove 🅷
(305) 285-9303. **$125-$242.** 2835 Tigertail Ave 33133. S Bayshore Dr, w on SW 27th Ave/Cornelia Dr, then s. Ext corridors. **Pets:** Other species. $100 one-time fee/room. Supervision. 🔲 🔲 🔲 🔲 🔲 🔲

CORAL GABLES

▼▼▼▼ ▼▼▼▼ The Biltmore Hotel Coral Gables 🅷
(305) 445-1926. **$195-$440.** 1200 Anastasia Ave 33134. From US 1, 1.4 mi w on Bird Rd (SW 40th St) to Granada Blvd, 0.5 mi n to Anastasia Ave, then just w. Int corridors. **Pets:** Accepted.
🔲 🔲 🔲 🔲 🔲 🔲

▼▼▼▼ Extended StayAmerica-Miami-Coral Gables 🅷 ❖
(305) 443-7444. **$60-$140.** 3640 Coral Way/SW 22nd St 33145. Just e of Douglas Rd. Int corridors. **Pets:** Other species. $25 daily fee/pet. Service with restrictions. 🔲 🔲 🔲 🔲

◇◇◇ ▼▼▼▼ ▼▼▼▼ The Westin Colonnade Coral Gables 🅷
(305) 441-2600. **$109-$559.** 180 Aragon Ave 33134. At Aragon Ave and Ponce de Leon Blvd; downtown. Int corridors. **Pets:** Accepted.
🔲 🔲 🔲 🔲 🔲 🔲 🔲

FLORIDA CITY

◇◇◇ ▼▼ ▼▼ Travelodge 🅼
(305) 248-9777. **$66-$188.** 409 SE 1st Ave 33034. On US 1, just s of Florida Tpke terminus. Ext corridors. **Pets:** Other species. $10 daily fee/pet. Service with restrictions, supervision. 🔲 🔲 🔲 🔲 🔲

KEY BISCAYNE

◇◇◇ ▼▼▼▼ ▼▼▼▼ The Ritz-Carlton, Key Biscayne 🅷 ❖
(305) 365-4500. **Call for rates.** 455 Grand Bay Dr 33149. Jct Crandon Blvd, just e. Int corridors. **Pets:** Medium. $150 one-time fee/room, $85 daily fee/room. Designated rooms, service with restrictions, supervision.
🔲 🔲 🔲 🔲 🔲 🔲 🔲 🔲 🔲

MIAMI

▼▼ Candlewood Suites Miami Airport West ☐
(305) 591-9099. **$99-$159.** 8855 NW 27th St 33172. SR 826 (Palmetto Expwy) 0.8 mi w on nw 36th St, 0.4 mi s. Int corridors. **Pets:** Accepted.
🛰 🛗ᴹ 🛄 💻 🐾

▲ ▼▼◆ DoubleTree by Hilton Hotel Miami Airport & Convention Center ☐
(305) 261-3800. **$119-$159.** 711 NW 72nd Ave 33126. SR 836 exit NW 57th Ave/Red Rd, 0.6 mi s to NW 7th St, 1.5 mi w to NW 72nd Ave/ Milam Dairy Rd, then just n. Int corridors. **Pets:** Accepted.
[SAVE] 🛰 💻 🍽 🐾 ✕

▲ ▼▼◆ ▼▼◆ Epic Hotel ☐
(305) 424-5226. **$269-$839.** 270 Biscayne Boulevard Way 33131. Just e of US 1 (SE 2nd Ave). Int corridors. **Pets:** Accepted.
[ECO] [SAVE] 🛰 ✕ 🛗ᴹ 🍽 🐾 ✕

▼▼ Extended Stay Deluxe-Miami Airport-Doral ☐ 🐾
(305) 716-9005. **$55-$130.** 7750 NW 25th St 33122. SR 836 (Dolphin Expwy) exit NW 25th St, then w; turn into The Shoppes at MICC Center. Int corridors. **Pets:** Other species. $25 daily fee/pet. Service with restrictions. 🛰 🛗ᴹ 🛄 💻 🐾

▲ ▼▼◆ Four Seasons Hotel Miami ☐ 🐾
(305) 358-3535. **$395-$3750, 3 day notice.** 1435 Brickell Ave 33131. Jct 14th Terr on US 1. Int corridors. **Pets:** Very small. Designated rooms, service with restrictions, supervision.
[ECO] [SAVE] 🛰 🛗ᴹ 🛄 💻 🍽 🐾 ✕

▲ ▼▼◆ Hilton Miami Downtown ☐
(305) 374-0000. **$99-$379.** 1601 Biscayne Blvd 33132. On US 1 (Biscayne Blvd), just n of NE 15th St. Int corridors. **Pets:** Accepted.
[ECO] [SAVE] 🛰 ✕ 🛗ᴹ 🛄 💻 🐾

▼▼ Homestead Studio Suites Hotel - Miami Airport - Blue Lagoon ☐ 🐾
(305) 260-0085. **$60-$140.** 6605 NW 7th St 33126. SR 836 (Dolphin Expwy) exit Milam Dairy Rd S, 0.3 mi e. Ext corridors. **Pets:** Other species. $25 daily fee/pet. Service with restrictions. 🛰 🛗ᴹ 🛄 💻

▲ ▼▼◆ Hotel Indigo Miami-Dadeland ☐ 🐾
(305) 595-6000. **$109-$199.** 7600 N Kendall Dr 33156. SR 826 (Palmetto Expwy) exit SW 88th St (N Kendall Dr), just w. Int corridors. **Pets:** Medium. $20 daily fee/pet. Designated rooms, service with restrictions, supervision. [SAVE] 🛰 ✕ 🛗ᴹ 🛄 💻 🍽 🐾

▲ ▼▼◆ Hyatt Summerfield Suites Miami Airport ☐
(305) 269-1922. **$84-$389.** 5710 Blue Lagoon Dr 33126. SR 836 (Dolphin Expwy) exit NW 57th Ave/Red Rd, just s. Int corridors.
Pets: Accepted. [SAVE] 🛰 ✕ 🛗ᴹ 🛄 💻 🐾

▼▼◆ La Quinta Inn & Suites - Miami Airport West ☐
(305) 436-0830. **$85-$202.** 8730 NW 27th St 33172. SR 836 (Dolphin Expwy) just n on 87th NW Ave. Int corridors. **Pets:** Medium, other species. Service with restrictions, supervision. 🛰 🛗ᴹ 🛄 💻 🐾

▼▼◆ Mandarin Oriental, Miami ☐ 🐾
(305) 913-8288. **$249-$775.** 500 Brickell Key Dr 33131. US 1 (Brickell Ave), just e on SE 8th St (Brickell Key Dr). Int corridors. **Pets:** Small. $100 deposit/room, $100 one-time fee/room. Supervision.
[ECO] 🛰 🛗ᴹ 🛄 💻 🐾

▲ ▼▼◆ Quality Inn-South at The Falls Ⓜ
(305) 251-2000. **$83-$200.** 14501 S Dixie Hwy (US 1) 33176. US 1 at SW 145th St. Ext corridors. **Pets:** Medium, other species. $10 daily fee/ room. Service with restrictions. [SAVE] 🛰 🛄 💻 🍽 🐾

▲ ▼▼◆ Residence Inn by Marriott Miami Airport South ☐
(305) 642-8570. **$139-$199.** 1201 NW LeJeune Rd 33126. SR 836 (Dolphin Expwy) exit LeJeune Rd (NW 42nd Ave), just s. Int corridors.
Pets: Accepted. [SAVE] 🛰 ✕ 🛗ᴹ 🛄 💻

▼▼◆ Residence Inn - Miami Airport West/Doral Area ☐
(305) 591-2211. **$116-$179.** 1212 NW 82nd Ave 33126. SR 826 (Palmetto Expwy) exit NW 25th St/PBA Memorial Blvd, 0.5 mi w to NW 82nd Ave, then 1 mi s. Ext corridors. **Pets:** Accepted.
🛰 ✕ 🛄 💻 🐾

▼▼◆ Sofitel Miami ☐
(305) 264-4888. **Call for rates.** 5800 Blue Lagoon Dr 33126. SR 836 (Dolphin Expwy) exit Red Rd/SR 959, just s to Blue Lagoon Dr, then just w. Int corridors. **Pets:** Accepted. [ECO] 🛰 💻 🍽 🐾 ✕

▼▼◆ Staybridge Suites Miami - Doral Area ☐
(305) 500-9100. **$129-$149, 3 day notice.** 3265 NW 87th Ave 33172. 0.4 mi s of jct NW 36th St. Int corridors. **Pets:** Accepted.
🛰 🛄 💻 🐾

▲ ▼▼◆ TownePlace Suites Miami Airport West/Doral Area ☐
(305) 718-4144. **$89-$156.** 10505 NW 36th St 33178. Florida Tpke exit 29, 1.2 mi e to 107th Ave, then just s. **Pets:** Other species.
$100 one-time fee/room. [SAVE] 🛰 ✕ 🛄 💻 🐾

MIAMI BEACH

▲ ▼▼◆ ▼▼◆ Eden Roc Renaissance Miami Beach ☐
(305) 531-0000. **$189-$332, 3 day notice.** 4525 Collins Ave 33140. SR A1A (Collins Ave), just n of 41st St. Int corridors. **Pets:** Accepted.
[SAVE] 🛰 ✕ 🛄 💻 🐾 ✕

▲ ▼▼◆ ▼▼◆ Fontainebleau Miami Beach ☐ 🐾
(305) 538-2000. **$269-$1349, 3 day notice.** 4441 Collins Ave 33140. SR A1A (Collins Ave); just n of Arthur Godfrey Rd. Int corridors.
Pets: Other species. $100 one-time fee/pet. Service with restrictions, crate. [ECO] [SAVE] 🛰 🛄 💻 🍽 🐾 ✕

▲ ▼▼◆ ▼▼◆ Hilton Bentley Miami/South Beach ☐
(305) 938-4600. **$229-$799.** 101 Ocean Dr 33139. Just e of SR A1A (Collins Ave); corner of Ocean Dr and 1st St. Int corridors.
Pets: Accepted. [SAVE] 🛰 ✕ 🛗ᴹ 🛄 💻 🍽 🐾 ✕

▼▼◆ The Kent Hotel ☐
(305) 604-5068. **Call for rates.** 1131 Collins Ave 33139. On SR A1A, jct Collins Ave and 11th St. Int corridors. **Pets:** Accepted. 🛰 🛄 🍽

▲ ▼▼◆ ▼▼◆ Loews Miami Beach Hotel ☐
(305) 604-1601. **Call for rates.** 1601 Collins Ave 33139. SR A1A, jct Collins and 16th aves. Int corridors. **Pets:** Accepted.
[SAVE] 🛰 ✕ 🛗ᴹ 💻 🍽 🐾 ✕

▲ ▼▼◆ ▼▼◆ Marriott South Beach ☐
(305) 536-7700. **$215-$521, 3 day notice.** 161 Ocean Dr 33139. Just e of SR A1A (Collins Ave); just s of 2nd St. Int corridors. **Pets:** Accepted.
[SAVE] 🛰 ✕ 🛄 💻 🐾 ✕

▲ ▼▼◆ ▼▼◆ The National Hotel ☐
(305) 532-2311. **Call for rates.** 1677 Collins Ave 33139. On SR A1A (Collins Ave) and 16th St. Int corridors. **Pets:** Accepted.
[SAVE] 🛰 🍽 🐾 ✕

▼▼◆ ▼▼◆ The Ritz-Carlton, South Beach ☐
(786) 276-4000. **Call for rates.** 1 Lincoln Rd 33139. Jct SR A1A (Collins Ave). Int corridors. **Pets:** Accepted.
[ECO] 🛰 ✕ 🛗ᴹ 🛄 💻 🍽 🐾 ✕

▲ ▼▼◆ ▼▼◆ The Setai, South Beach ☐
(305) 520-6000. **$550-$1400, 14 day notice.** 2001 Collins Ave 33139. On SR A1A (Collins Ave); at 20th St. Int corridors. **Pets:** Accepted.
[ECO] [SAVE] 🛰 ✕ 🛗ᴹ 🛄 💻 🍽 🐾 ✕

▲ ▼▼◆ ▼▼◆ W South Beach ☐
(305) 938-3000. **$369-$1099, 3 day notice.** 2201 Collins Ave 33139. Jct Collins Ave and 22nd St. Int corridors. **Pets:** Accepted.
[SAVE] 🛰 ✕ 🛗ᴹ 🛄 💻 🍽 🐾 ✕

MIAMI LAKES

La Quinta Inn & Suites Miami Lakes ⬨
(305) 821-8274. **$94-$189.** 7925 NW 154th St 33016. Jct SR 826 (Palmetto Expwy) just w. Int corridors. **Pets:** Medium, other species. Service with restrictions, supervision. 🛜 🍴 💻 🏊

TownePlace Suites Miami Lakes ⬨
(305) 512-9191. **$89-$156.** 8079 NW 154th St 33016. SR 826 (Palmetto Expwy) exit 154th St, 0.4 mi w. Int corridors. **Pets:** Accepted.
🆂🅰🆅🅴 🛜 ✖ 👪 🍴 💻 🏊

MIAMI SPRINGS

Homestead Studio Suites Hotel-Miami/Airport/Miami Springs ⬨ 🐾
(305) 870-0448. **$55-$130.** 101 Fairway Dr 33166. I-95 to SR 112 W exit NW 36th St, 1.2 mi w to Palmetto Dr, then just n to Fairway Dr; property on right. Int corridors. **Pets:** Other species. $25 daily fee/pet. Service with restrictions. 🛜 🍴 💻 🏊 ✖

La Quinta Inn & Suites - Miami Airport East ⬨
(305) 871-1777. **$85-$179.** 3501 NW LeJeune Rd 33142. LeJeune Rd (NW 42nd Ave), just s of SR 112. Int corridors. **Pets:** Medium, other species. Service with restrictions, supervision. 🛜 🍴 💻 🏊

Red Roof Inn - Miami Airport ⬨
(305) 871-4221. **$79-$269.** 3401 NW LeJeune Rd (NW 42nd Ave) 33142. On LeJeune Rd (NW 42nd Ave), just s of SR 112. Int corridors. **Pets:** Large, other species. No service, supervision. 🛜 🍴 🏊

SUNNY ISLES BEACH

Acqualina Resort & Spa on the Beach ⬨ 🐾
(305) 918-8000. **$575-$3250, 30 day notice.** 17875 Collins Ave 33160. I-95 exit 16 (Ives Dairy Rd), 1.2 mi e to US 1 (Biscayne Blvd), 0.6 mi s to William Lehman Cswy, 1.6 mi e to SR A1A (Collins Ave), then 0.8 mi s. Int corridors. **Pets:** Small, dogs only. $150 one-time fee/pet. Service with restrictions, crate. 🆂🅰🆅🅴 🛜 ✖ 👪 🍴 💻 🍽 🏊 ✖

END METROPOLITAN AREA

MIDWAY

Best Western Plus Panhandle Capital Inn & Suites ⬨
(850) 514-2222. **$69-$169.** 85 River Park Dr 32343. I-10 exit 192, just s. Int corridors. **Pets:** Accepted. 🆂🅰🆅🅴 🛜 🍴 💻 🏊

MILTON

Comfort Inn ⬨
(850) 623-1511. **$59-$149.** 8936 Hwy 87 S 32583. I-10 exit 31, just s. Int corridors. **Pets:** Small. $20 daily fee/room. Designated rooms, service with restrictions, supervision. 🆂🅰🆅🅴 🛜 👪 🍴 💻 🏊

Red Roof Inn & Suites ⬨
(850) 995-6100. **$70-$104.** 2672 Avalon Blvd 32583. I-10 exit 22, just s. Int corridors. **Pets:** Large, other species. No service, supervision.
🆂🅰🆅🅴 🛜 👪 🍴 💻 🏊

NAPLES

Hawthorn Suites by Wyndham, Naples ⬨ 🐾
(239) 593-1300. **$159-$279.** 3557 Pine Ridge Rd 34109. I-75 exit 107 (Pine Ridge Rd), 0.5 mi w on CR 896. Int corridors. **Pets:** Medium, dogs only. $125 one-time fee/room. Designated rooms, service with restrictions, supervision. 🅴🅲🅾 🆂🅰🆅🅴 🛜 ✖ 👪 🍴 💻 🏊 ✖

Hilton Naples ⬨ 🐾
(239) 430-4900. **$99-$299.** 5111 Tamiami Tr N 34103. Just s of jct CR 896 (Pine Ridge Rd). Int corridors. **Pets:** Dogs only. $75 one-time fee/room. Service with restrictions, supervision.
🅴🅲🅾 🆂🅰🆅🅴 🛜 ✖ 👪 🍴 💻 🍽 🏊 ✖

La Quinta Inn & Suites - Naples Downtown ⬨
(239) 793-4646. **$75-$189.** 1555 5th Ave S 34102. Just w of jct SR 84 (Davis Blvd) and US 41 (Tamiami Tr). Int corridors. **Pets:** Medium, other species. Service with restrictions, supervision. 🛜 🍴 💻 🏊

La Quinta Inn & Suites Naples East (I-75) ⬨
(239) 352-8400. **$58-$155.** 185 Bedzel Cir 34104. I-75 exit 101, just w on SR 84 (Davis Blvd). Int corridors. **Pets:** Medium, other species. Service with restrictions, supervision. 🛜 👪 🍴 💻 🏊

Ramada Inn of Naples Ⓜ
(239) 263-3434. **$69-$189.** 1100 Tamiami Tr N 34102. US 41 (Tamiami Tr), jct 13th Ave n. Ext corridors. **Pets:** Large, other species. $25 daily fee/room. Designated rooms, service with restrictions.
🅴🅲🅾 🆂🅰🆅🅴 🛜 🍴 💻 🍽 🏊

Residence Inn by Marriott, Naples ⬨ 🐾
(239) 659-1300. **$93-$247.** 4075 Tamiami Tr N 34103. I-75 exit 107 (Pine Ridge Rd), 3.8 mi w, then 1 mi s on US 41 (Tamiami Tr). Int corridors. **Pets:** Medium, other species. $75 one-time fee/room. Service with restrictions, crate. 🛜 ✖ 👪 🍴 💻 🏊 ✖

The Ritz-Carlton Golf Resort, Naples ⬨
(239) 593-2000. **$129-$579, 3 day notice.** 2600 Tiburon Dr 34109. I-75 exit 111 (Immokalee Rd), 1.6 mi w, then 1.3 mi s on CR 31 (Airport-Pulling Rd), just e. Int corridors. **Pets:** Accepted.
🅴🅲🅾 🆂🅰🆅🅴 🛜 ✖ 👪 🍴 💻 🍽 🏊 ✖

Staybridge Suites by Holiday Inn ⬨
(239) 643-8002. **$59-$199.** 4805 Tamiami Tr N 34103. I-75 exit 107 (Pine Ridge Rd), 3.8 mi w, then 0.9 mi s on US 41 (Tamiami Tr). Int corridors. **Pets:** Accepted. 🛜 👪 🍴 💻 🏊

NAVARRE

Days Inn & Suites Navarre Conference Center Ⓜ
(850) 939-1761. **$72-$144.** 8700 Navarre Pkwy 32566. US 98, 0.3 mi e of Navarre Beach Bridge. Ext corridors. **Pets:** Accepted.
🛜 🍴 💻 🏊

NEW SMYRNA BEACH

Buena Vista Inn Ⓜ
(386) 428-5565. **$75-$130, 14 day notice.** 500 N Causeway 32169. Jct SR 44, 2 mi e on SR 44 business route; at west end of North Causeway Bridge. Ext corridors. **Pets:** Accepted. 🛜 ✖ 🍴 💻

Longboard Inn Ⓑ Ⓑ
(386) 428-3499. **$115-$160, 14 day notice.** 312 Washington St 32168. Just e of US 1 (Dixie Frwy); 0.3 mi w of jct N Riverside Dr. Ext corridors. **Pets:** Accepted. 🆂🅰🆅🅴 🛜 ✖ 🍴

Night Swan Intracoastal Bed & Breakfast Ⓑ Ⓑ
(386) 423-4940. **$110-$200, 3 day notice.** 512 S Riverside Dr 32168. I-95 exit 249 (SR 44), 4 mi e to Live Oak St, just s to Andrews St, just e to S Riverside Dr, then just s; on west side of Intracoastal Waterway. Ext/int corridors. **Pets:** Medium. Designated rooms, service with restrictions. 🅴🅲🅾 🛜 ✖ 🍴 💻

NORTH FORT MYERS

Best Western Ft. Myers Waterfront ⬨
(239) 997-5511. **$90-$150.** 13021 N Cleveland Ave 33903. On US 41, 0.6 mi s of SR 78A (Pondella Rd), jct N Bay Dr and Caloosahatchee Bridge. Ext corridors. **Pets:** Accepted.
🆂🅰🆅🅴 🛜 ✖ 👪 🍴 💻 🍽 🏊 ✖

OCALA

◇◇◇ ▼▼▼ Hilton Ocala H
(352) 854-1400. **$69-$599.** 3600 SW 36th Ave 34474. I-75 exit 350, 0.3 mi e on SR 200. Int corridors. **Pets:** Accepted.
[ECO] [SAVE] 🛜 🖦M 🛏 🖵 🍴 🏊 ✕

◇◇◇ ▼▼▼ Holiday Inn Express Midtown Medical H
(352) 629-7300. **$78-$119.** 1212 S Pine Ave 34474. 0.8 mi s on US 27, 301 and 441; just s of SR 200. Int corridors. **Pets:** Small. $25 one-time fee/pet. Designated rooms, service with restrictions, supervision.
[SAVE] 🛜 ✕ 🖦M 🛏 🖵 🏊

▼▼▼ La Quinta Inn & Suites Ocala H
(352) 861-1137. **$67-$169.** 3530 SW 36th Ave 34474. I-75 exit 350, just e on SR 200. Int corridors. **Pets:** Medium, other species. Service with restrictions, supervision. 🛜 🖦M 🛏 🖵 🏊

▼▼▼ Red Roof Inn & Suites H
(352) 732-4590. **$60-$150.** 120 NW 40th Ave 34482. I-75 exit 352, just w on SR 40. Int corridors. **Pets:** Large, other species. No service, supervision. [SAVE] 🛜 🛏 🖵 🏊

◇◇◇ ▼▼▼ Residence Inn by Marriott Ocala H 🐾
(352) 547-1600. **$109-$249.** 3610 SW 38th Ave 34474. I-75 exit 350, just w on SR 200, then n. Int corridors. **Pets:** Large, other species. $75 one-time fee/room. Service with restrictions, crate.
[ECO] [SAVE] 🛜 ✕ 🛏 🖵 🏊 ✕

OKEECHOBEE

▼ Economy Inn M
(863) 763-1148. **Call for rates.** 507 N Parrott Ave 34972. On US 441, 0.3 mi n of jct SR 70/710. Ext corridors. **Pets:** Small. $10 daily fee/pet. Designated rooms, service with restrictions, supervision. 🛜 🛏

ORANGE CITY

▼▼▼ Alling House Bed and Breakfast BB
(386) 775-7648. **$105-$155, 7 day notice.** 215 E French Ave 32763. I-4 exit 114, 3 mi nw on SR 472, 2.3 mi s on US 17-92, then just e. Ext/int corridors. **Pets:** Accepted. 🛜 ✕ 🛏 🖵 🎬

▼▼ Days Inn M
(386) 775-4522. **$49-$207.** 2501 N Volusia Ave 32763. I-4 exit 114, 2.8 mi w on SR 472, then 0.3 mi s on US 17-92. Ext corridors. **Pets:** Accepted. 🛜 🛏 🖵 🏊

▼▼ Quality Inn M
(386) 775-7444. **$70-$225.** 445 S Volusia Ave 32763. I-4 exit 114, 2.8 mi w on SR 472, then 2 mi s on US 17-92. Ext corridors. **Pets:** Accepted.
🛜 ✕ 🛏 🖵 🏊

ORLANDO METROPOLITAN AREA

ALTAMONTE SPRINGS

▼▼ Candlewood Suites H
(407) 767-5757. **Call for rates.** 644 Raymond Ave 32701. I-4 exit 92, just w to Douglas Ave, 0.8 mi n to Central Pkwy, then just e. Int corridors. **Pets:** Accepted. 🖦M 🛏 🖵 🏊

◇◇◇ ▼▼ Days Inn & Suites H
(407) 788-1411. **$55-$90.** 150 S Westmonte Dr 32714. I-4 exit 92, 0.3 mi w on SR 436, then just s. Ext corridors. **Pets:** Large. $10 daily fee/pet. Service with restrictions, supervision. [SAVE] 🛜 🛏 🖵 🏊

◇◇◇ ▼▼ Embassy Suites Orlando North H 🐾
(407) 834-2400. **$109-$219.** 225 Shorecrest Dr 32701. I-4 exit 92, 0.3 mi e on SR 436, then just n on N Lake Blvd. Int corridors. **Pets:** Medium. $50 one-time fee/pet. Designated rooms, service with restrictions, crate.
[ECO] [SAVE] 🛜 🖦M 🛏 🖵 🍴 🏊 ✕

▼▼ Hilton Orlando/Altamonte Springs H
(407) 830-1985. **$79-$139.** 350 S North Lake Blvd 32701. I-4 exit 92, just e on SR 436, then 0.5 mi s. Int corridors. **Pets:** Accepted.
[ECO] 🛜 🖦M 🛏 🖵 🍴 🏊 ✕

▼▼▼ Homestead Studio Suites Hotel-Orlando/Altamonte Springs H 🐾
(407) 332-9300. **$54-$134.** 302 North Lake Blvd 32701. I-4 exit 92, e, then 0.3 mi s. Int corridors. **Pets:** Other species. $25 daily fee/pet. Service with restrictions. 🛜 🖦M 🛏 🖵

▼▼▼ Howard Johnson Plaza Altamonte H 🐾
(407) 862-4455. **Call for rates.** 230 W SR 436 32714. I-4 exit 92, just sw. Ext/int corridors. **Pets:** Other species. $10 daily fee/pet. Designated rooms, service with restrictions, supervision.
🛜 ✕ 🖦M 🛏 🖵 🍴 🏊

▼▼▼ Residence Inn Orlando Altamonte Springs/Maitland H
(407) 788-7991. **$89-$149.** 270 Douglas Ave 32714. I-4 exit 92, just w on SR 436, then just n. Ext corridors. **Pets:** Accepted.
🛜 ✕ 🖦M 🛏 🖵 🏊 ✕

CELEBRATION

◇◇◇ ▼▼▼▼ Bohemian Hotel Celebration, Autograph Collection H 🐾
(407) 566-6000. **$152-$279, 3 day notice.** 700 Bloom St 34747. SR 417 exit 2 (Celebration Ave), 0.9 mi sw to Campus St, then just s; downtown. Int corridors. **Pets:** Small, dogs only. $150 one-time fee/pet. Designated rooms, service with restrictions, crate.
[SAVE] 🛜 ✕ 🖦M 🛏 🖵 🏊 ✕

CHAMPIONSGATE

◇◇◇ ▼▼▼ Omni Orlando Resort at ChampionsGate H
(407) 390-6664. **Call for rates.** 1500 Masters Blvd 33896. I-4 exit 58 (CR 532), 0.5 mi w on ChampionsGate Blvd (CR 532) to Masters Blvd, then just n. Int corridors. **Pets:** Accepted.
[ECO] [SAVE] 🛜 🖦M 🖵 🍴 🏊 ✕

CLERMONT

◇◇◇ ▼▼▼ Fairfield Inn & Suites Clermont H 🐾
(352) 394-6585. **$94-$104.** 1750 Hunt Trace Blvd 34711. Jct SR 50 and US 27, 0.5 mi e on SR 50, just n. Int corridors. **Pets:** Other species. $75 one-time fee/room. Designated rooms, service with restrictions, crate.
[ECO] [SAVE] 🛜 ✕ 🛏 🖵 🏊

◇◇◇ ▼▼▼ Holiday Inn Express Clermont H
(352) 243-7878. **$99-$159.** 1810 S US Hwy 27 34711. Just s of SR 50. Int corridors. **Pets:** Medium, other species. $50 one-time fee/room. Designated rooms, service with restrictions, crate.
[SAVE] 🛜 🖦M 🛏 🖵 🏊

DAVENPORT

▼▼ Days Inn & Suites M
(863) 424-2596. **$37-$81.** 2425 Frontage Rd 33837. I-4 exit 55, just s. Ext corridors. **Pets:** Medium. $15 daily fee/pet. Designated rooms, service with restrictions, supervision. 🛜 🛏 🖵 🏊

FERN PARK

▼▼ Days Inn North Orlando H
(407) 339-3333. **$45-$90.** 8245 S Hwy 17-92 32730. Jct SR 436 and US 17-92, 1.3 mi s on US 17-92. Ext corridors. **Pets:** Accepted.
🛜 🛏 🖵 🏊

KISSIMMEE

Baymont Inn & Suites Kissimmee H
(407) 994-1900. **$45-$84, 3 day notice.** 4156 W Vine St 34741. I-4 exit 64 (US 192), 7.8 mi se. Ext corridors. **Pets:** Medium. $10 daily fee/pet. Designated rooms, service with restrictions, supervision.

Celebration Suites H
(407) 396-7900. **Call for rates.** 5820 W Irlo Bronson Memorial Hwy 34746. I-4 exit 64 (US 192), 2.2 mi e. Ext corridors. **Pets:** Accepted.

Champions World Resort H
(407) 396-4500. **$29-$69.** 8660 W Irlo Bronson Memorial Hwy 34747. I-4 exit 64 (US 192), 6.7 mi w. Ext corridors. **Pets:** Accepted.

Clarion Resort & Water Park H ✿
(407) 846-2221. **$59-$109.** 2261 E Irlo Bronson Memorial Hwy 34744. Florida Tpke exit 244, just w. Ext corridors. **Pets:** Medium. $30 daily fee/room. Designated rooms, service with restrictions, crate.

Palms Hotel and Villas CO ✿
(407) 396-2229. **$59-$199.** 3100 Parkway Blvd 34747. I-4 exit 64 (US 192), 1.2 mi e to Parkway Blvd, then 0.4 mi n. Ext/int corridors. **Pets:** Medium, dogs only. $100 one-time fee/room. Service with restrictions, crate.

Ramada Gateway Hotel H ✿
(407) 396-4400. **Call for rates.** 7470 W Irlo Bronson Memorial Hwy 34747. I-4 exit 64 (US 192), 3.4 mi w. Ext/int corridors. **Pets:** Medium, other species. $50 one-time fee/room. Designated rooms, service with restrictions, supervision.

Seralago Hotel & Suites Main Gate East H
(407) 396-4488. **$45-$89.** 5678 W Irlo Bronson Memorial Hwy 34746. I-4 exit 64 (US 192), 2.5 mi e. Ext corridors. **Pets:** Medium, dogs only. $40 one-time fee/room. Designated rooms, service with restrictions.

Venetian Bay - Ventura Resort Rentals CO ✿
(407) 273-8770. **$79-$500, 15 day notice.** 4008 San Gallo Dr 34747. SR 417 exit 11, 3 mi s on Orange Blossom Tr, then 2 mi w on West Carroll. Ext corridors. **Pets:** Small, other species. $100 deposit/pet, $100 one-time fee/pet. Designated rooms, service with restrictions, crate.

Westgate Vacation Villas CO
(407) 239-0510. **$79-$209, 3 day notice.** 2770 Old Lake Wilson Rd 34747. I-4 exit 64 (US 192), 3.5 mi w to Old Lake Wilson Rd, then 0.5 mi s. Ext corridors. **Pets:** Accepted.

LADY LAKE

Comfort Suites in the Villages H
(352) 259-6578. **$89-$175.** 1202 Avenida Central N 32159. Just n on US 441. Int corridors. **Pets:** Medium. $35 one-time fee/pet. Service with restrictions, crate.

Holiday Inn Express Hotel & Suites H
(352) 750-3888. **$89-$129.** 1205 Avenida Central N 32159. Just n on US 441. Int corridors. **Pets:** Medium, other species. $35 one-time fee/pet. Designated rooms, service with restrictions, supervision.

Microtel Inn & Suites H
(352) 259-0184. **$68-$77.** 850 US 27/441 32159. 1 mi s of downtown. Int corridors. **Pets:** Accepted.

TownePlace Suites The Villages H
(352) 753-8686. **$84-$199.** 1141 Alonzo Ave 32159. US 441/27 to Main St. Int corridors. **Pets:** Accepted.

LAKE BUENA VISTA

Clarion Inn Lake Buena Vista H
(407) 996-7300. **$59-$99.** 8442 Palm Pkwy 32836. I-4 exit 68, 0.6 mi n on SR 535, then 0.5 mi e. Ext corridors. **Pets:** Accepted.

Holiday Inn Express Lake Buena Vista H
(407) 239-8400. **Call for rates.** 8686 Palm Pkwy 32836. I-4 exit 68, 0.5 mi n on SR 535, then 0.3 mi e. Int corridors. **Pets:** Medium, other species. $50 one-time fee/room. Designated rooms, service with restrictions, crate. ECO

Hyatt Regency Grand Cypress H ✿
(407) 239-1234. **$99-$299, 3 day notice.** 1 Grand Cypress Blvd 32836. I-4 exit 68, just w on SR 535; near entrance to Walt Disney World Village. Int corridors. **Pets:** Medium, dogs only. $100 one-time fee/room, $50 daily fee/room. Designated rooms, service with restrictions, supervision.

Orlando Vista Hotel, an Ascend Collection hotel H
(407) 239-4646. **$60-$99.** 12490 Apopka-Vineland Rd 32836. I-4 exit 68, 0.4 mi n on SR 535. Int corridors. **Pets:** Accepted.

Residence Inn Orlando Lake Buena Vista H ✿
(407) 465-0075. **$89-$299, 3 day notice.** 11450 Marbella Palms Ct 32836. I-4 exit 68, 0.4 mi n on SR 535, then 0.5 mi e on Palm Pkwy. Int corridors. **Pets:** Medium. $100 one-time fee/room. No service.

Sheraton Safari Hotel & Suites H
(407) 239-0444. **$89-$219.** 12205 Apopka-Vineland Rd 32836. I-4 exit 68, 0.5 mi n on SR 535. Ext/int corridors. **Pets:** Medium, dogs only. Designated rooms, no service, supervision. ECO

LAKE MARY

Candlewood Suites Lake Mary-Heathrow H
(407) 585-3000. **Call for rates.** 1130 Greenwood Blvd 32746. I-4 exit 98, just e to Lake Emma Rd, then 0.5 mi s. Int corridors. **Pets:** Accepted.

Extended StayAmerica/Lake Mary/Sanford H ✿
(407) 833-0011. **$49-$115.** 1036 Greenwood Blvd 32746. I-4 exit 98, just e to Lake Emma Rd, then 0.5 mi. Int corridors. **Pets:** Other species. $25 daily fee/pet. Service with restrictions.

Hilton Garden Inn Lake Mary H ✿
(407) 531-9900. **$69-$179.** 705 Currency Cir 32746. I-4 exit 98, just ne via Lake Mary and Primera blvds. Int corridors. **Pets:** Large. $100 one-time fee/room. Designated rooms, service with restrictions.

Homestead Studio Suites - Lake Mary/Sanford H ✿
(407) 829-2332. **$54-$134.** 1040 Greenwood Blvd 32746. I-4 exit 98, 0.5 mi s on Lake Emma Rd; in Commerce Park. Int corridors. **Pets:** Other species. $25 daily fee/pet. Service with restrictions.

La Quinta Inn & Suites Orlando (Lake Mary) H
(407) 805-9901. **$62-$139.** 1060 Greenwood Blvd 32746. I-4 exit 98, just e to Lake Emma Rd, then 0.5 mi s. Int corridors. **Pets:** Medium, other species. Service with restrictions, supervision.

Residence Inn by Marriott Lake Mary H ✿
(407) 995-3400. **$99-$190.** 825 Heathrow Park Lane Pkwy 32746. I-4 exit 101A, just w, then just s on International Pkwy. Int corridors. **Pets:** Medium, other species. $112 one-time fee/room. Designated rooms, service with restrictions.

AAA ◇◇◇ **The Westin Lake Mary Orlando North** H ❖

(407) 531-3555. **$119-$279.** 2974 International Pkwy 32746. I-4 exit 101C, just w. Int corridors. **Pets:** Medium, dogs only. Designated rooms, service with restrictions. [SAVE] 📶 ✕ 💻 ❙❙ 🏊 ✕

LEESBURG

AAA ◇◇◇ **Best Western Plus Chain of Lakes Inn & Suites** H

(352) 460-0118. **$80-$140, 7 day notice.** 1321 N 14th St 34748. Florida Tpke exit 285 (US 27), 15.9 mi n; jct US 27 and 441. Int corridors. **Pets:** Small, dogs only. $20 daily fee/pet. Designated rooms, service with restrictions, supervision. [SAVE] 📶 ✕ ♿ ❙ 💻 🏊

MAITLAND

◇◇ **Extended Stay Deluxe-Orlando-Maitland-Pembrook Dr** H ❖

(407) 475-1675. **$55-$120.** 1776 Pembrook Dr 32810. I-4 exit 90B, 0.5 mi w. Int corridors. **Pets:** Other species. $25 daily fee/pet. Service with restrictions. 📶 ❙ 💻 🏊

AAA ◇◇◇ **Homewood Suites by Hilton Orlando North** H ❖

(407) 875-8777. **$114-$174.** 290 Southhall Ln 32751. I-4 exit 90, just w, then just s on Lake Destiny. Int corridors. **Pets:** Large. $75 one-time fee/pet. Service with restrictions, crate. [SAVE] 📶 ♿ ❙ 💻 🏊

AAA ◇◇◇ **Sheraton Orlando North** H

(407) 660-9000. **$99-$189.** 600 N Lake Destiny Dr 32751. I-4 exit 90B, just w. Int corridors. **Pets:** Accepted.
[ECO] [SAVE] 📶 ✕ ♿ ❙ 💻 ❙❙ 🏊 ✕

MOUNT DORA

◇◇ ◇◇ **Heron Cay Lakeview Bed & Breakfast** BB ❖

(352) 383-4050. **$120-$295.** 495 Old US Hwy 441 32757. On CR 441 (Old US 441), 0.3 mi w. Int corridors. **Pets:** Large, other species. $25 daily fee/room. Designated rooms, service with restrictions.
📶 ✕ ❙ 🏊 🅩

OCOEE

◇◇◇ **Red Roof Inn Orlando West** H

(407) 347-0140. **$55-$83.** 11241 W Colonial Dr 34761. I-4 exit 84, 10 mi w on SR 50; Florida Tpke exit 267, 0.6 mi e. Int corridors. **Pets:** Large, other species. No service, supervision. 📶 ❙ 🏊

ORLANDO

AAA ◇◇◇ **Baymont Inn & Suites Florida Mall** H ❖

(407) 851-8200. **$44-$52.** 8820 S Orange Blossom Tr 32809. Florida Tpke exit 254, just n. Int corridors. **Pets:** Medium. $10 daily fee/room. Designated rooms, service with restrictions, supervision.
[SAVE] 📶 ❙ 💻 🏊

AAA ◇◇◇ **Best Western Inn & Suites-East Orlando** H ❖

(407) 282-3900. **$89-$119, 3 day notice.** 8750 E Colonial Dr 32817. SR 417 exit 34. Ext corridors. **Pets:** Small. $20 daily fee/pet. Designated rooms, service with restrictions, crate. [SAVE] 📶 ❙ 💻 🏊

AAA ◇◇◇ **Best Western Orlando West** H

(407) 841-8600. **$69-$200.** 2014 W Colonial Dr 32804. I-4 exit 84, 1.5 mi w on SR 50 (Colonial Dr); 0.4 mi e of SR 423. Int corridors. **Pets:** Accepted. [SAVE] 📶 ❙ 💻 ❙❙

AAA ◇◇◇ **Best Western Plus Orlando Gateway Hotel** H ❖

(407) 351-5009. **$90-$160.** 7299 Universal Blvd 32819. I-4 exit 75A, just e of International Dr. Int corridors. **Pets:** Large. $20 daily fee/room. Service with restrictions. [SAVE] 📶 ✕ ♿ ❙ 💻 ❙❙ 🏊 ✕

AAA ◇◇◇ **Comfort Suites Downtown** H

(407) 228-4007. **$111-$160.** 2416 N Orange Ave 32804. I-4 exit 85, just e on Princeton, then just n. Int corridors. **Pets:** Small. $15 daily fee/pet. Service with restrictions, crate. [ECO] [SAVE] 📶 ✕ ❙ 💻 🏊

◇◇◇ **Country Inn & Suites By Carlson-Orlando International Airport** H

(407) 856-8896. **$79-$129.** 5440 Forbes Pl 32812. SR 528 (Beachline Expwy) exit 11, 0.6 mi n on SR 436, then just w. Int corridors. **Pets:** Accepted. 📶 ❙ 💻 🏊

AAA ◇◇◇ **Days Inn Florida Mall/Airport** M

(407) 855-0308. **$55-$117.** 9301 S Orange Blossom Tr 32837. SR 528 (Beachline Expwy) exit 4, just s on US 17-92/441. Ext corridors. **Pets:** Accepted. [SAVE] 📶 ❙ 💻 🏊

AAA ◇◇◇◇ **DoubleTree by Hilton Orlando at SeaWorld** H ❖

(407) 352-1100. **$109-$229.** 10100 International Dr 32821. I-4 exit 72, 0.5 mi e on SR 528 (Beachline Expwy) exit 1 (International Dr), just e. Ext/int corridors. **Pets:** Small. $75 one-time fee/room. Designated rooms, service with restrictions, crate.
[ECO] [SAVE] 📶 ♿ ❙ 💻 ❙❙ 🏊 ✕

◇◇ **Extended StayAmerica/Orlando Convention Center/ Westwood Blvd** H ❖

(407) 352-3454. **$55-$175.** 6451 Westwood Blvd 32821. I-4 exit 72, just e on SR 528 (Beachline Expwy) to exit 1 (International Dr), just s, then just w. Int corridors. **Pets:** Other species. $25 daily fee/pet. Service with restrictions. 📶 ❙ 💻

◇◇ **Extended StayAmerica-Orlando Universal Studios** H ❖

(407) 351-1788. **$55-$175.** 5620 Major Blvd 32819. I-4 exit 75B, just n, then just e. Int corridors. **Pets:** Other species. $25 daily fee/pet. Service with restrictions. 📶 ❙ 💻

◇◇ **ExtendedStay Deluxe Orlando Convention Center/ Pointe Orlando** H ❖

(407) 903-1500. **$60-$180.** 8750 Universal Blvd 32819. I-4 exit 74A, 0.5 mi e on SR 482 (Sand Lake Rd), then 0.7 mi s. Int corridors. **Pets:** Other species. $25 daily fee/pet. Service with restrictions. 📶 ♿ ❙ 💻 🏊

◇◇ **Extended Stay Deluxe/Orlando Convention Center/ Westwood Blvd** H ❖

(407) 351-1982. **$60-$180.** 6443 Westwood Blvd 32821. I-4 exit 72, just e on SR 528 (Beachline Expwy) to exit 1 (International Dr), just s, then just w. Int corridors. **Pets:** Other species. $25 daily fee/pet. Service with restrictions. 📶 ❙ 💻 🏊

◇◇ **Extended Stay Deluxe Orlando-Universal Studios** H ❖

(407) 370-4428. **$60-$180.** 5610 Vineland Rd 32819. I-4 exit 75B, just n, then e. Int corridors. **Pets:** Other species. $25 daily fee/pet. Service with restrictions. 📶 ♿ ❙ 💻 🏊

AAA ◇◇◇ **The Florida Hotel and Conference Center** H ❖

(407) 859-1500. **$89-$239, 3 day notice.** 1500 Sand Lake Rd 32809. Just s of jct Sand Lake Rd and S Orange Blossom Tr; south end of Florida Mall. Int corridors. **Pets:** Small, other species. $50 one-time fee/room. Designated rooms, service with restrictions, crate.
[ECO] [SAVE] 📶 ✕ ♿ ❙ 💻 ❙❙ 🏊 ✕

AAA ◇◇◇ **Floridays Resort Orlando** CO ❖

(407) 238-7700. **$150-$450, 3 day notice.** 12562 International Dr 32821. I-4 exit 72, 0.5 mi e on SR 528 (Beachline Expwy) exit 1, then 3 mi s. Ext corridors. **Pets:** Medium, other species. $200 one-time fee/pet. Service with restrictions.
[ECO] [SAVE] 📶 ✕ ♿ ❙ 💻 ❙❙ 🏊 ✕

The Grand Bohemian Hotel Autograph Collection 🅗

(407) 313-9000. **$152-$333.** 325 S Orange Ave 32801. I-4 exit 82B, just e on South St, jct Jackson St. Int corridors. **Pets:** Accepted.

ECO SAVE 🛜 ✕ ♿M 💻 🍴 🏊 ✕

Hard Rock Hotel® at Universal Orlando 🅗 ❖

(407) 503-2000. **$249-$544, 5 day notice.** 5800 Universal Blvd 32819. I-4 exit 74B; exit 75A eastbound, 1 mi n. Int corridors. **Pets:** Other species. $25 one-time fee/room. Designated rooms, service with restrictions.

ECO SAVE 🛜 ♿M 🛏 💻 🍴 🏊 ✕

Holiday Inn Resort Orlando-The Castle 🅗

(407) 345-1511. **$119-$219.** 8629 International Dr 32819. I-4 exit 74A, 1 mi se, just e of International Dr; 0.5 mi s of SR 482 (Sand Lake Rd). Int corridors. **Pets:** Medium. $75 daily fee/pet. Designated rooms, service with restrictions, crate. 🛜 ♿M 🛏 💻 🍴 🏊

International Palms Resort - Orlando 🅗

(407) 351-3500. **$59-$109.** 6515 International Dr 32819. I-4 exit 74A, just e on SR 482 (Sand Lake Rd), then 0.5 mi n. Ext/int corridors.

Pets: Accepted. SAVE 🛜 ♿M 🛏 💻 🍴 🏊 ✕

La Quinta Inn & Suites Orlando (Convention Center) 🅗

(407) 345-1365. **$73-$155.** 8504 Universal Blvd 32819. I-4 exit 74A, 0.5 mi e on SR 482 (Sand Lake Rd), then 0.5 mi s at jct Via Mercado W. Int corridors. **Pets:** Medium, other species. Service with restrictions, supervision. 🛜 ♿M 🛏 💻

La Quinta Inn & Suites Orlando South 🅗

(407) 240-0500. **$62-$145.** 2051 Consulate Dr 32837. SR 528 (Beachline Expwy) exit 4, just se; Florida Tpke exit 254, s on US 441, then right. Int corridors. **Pets:** Medium, other species. Service with restrictions, supervision. 🛜 🛏 💻 🏊

La Quinta Inn & Suites Orlando (U.C.F.) 🅗

(407) 737-6075. **$80-$159.** 11805 Research Pkwy 32826. Just se of jct SR 434 (Alafaya Tr). Int corridors. **Pets:** Medium, other species. Service with restrictions, supervision. 🛜 ♿M 🛏 💻

La Quinta Inn Orlando International Drive North 🅗

(407) 351-4100. **$90-$160.** 5825 International Dr 32819. I-4 exit 75A, just w. Int corridors. **Pets:** Medium, other species. Service with restrictions, supervision. 🛜 🛏 💻 🏊

Loews Portofino Bay Hotel at Universal Orlando® 🅗

(407) 503-1000. **$274-$574, 5 day notice.** 5601 Universal Blvd 32819. I-4 exit 74B westbound; exit 75A eastbound, 1 mi n. Int corridors. **Pets:** Accepted. ECO SAVE 🛜 ✕ ♿M 🛏 💻 🍴 🏊 ✕

Loews Royal Pacific Resort at Universal Orlando® 🅗 ❖

(407) 503-3000. **$219-$489, 5 day notice.** 6300 Hollywood Way 32819. I-4 exit 74B westbound; exit 75A eastbound, just n on Universal Blvd, just w. Int corridors. **Pets:** Other species. $25 one-time fee/room. Designated rooms, service with restrictions, supervision.

ECO SAVE 🛜 ✕ 🛏 💻 🍴 🏊 ✕

Motel 6 Orlando-International Drive #1079 🅗

(407) 351-6500. **$49-$59.** 5909 American Way 32819. I-4 exit 75A, just w of SR 435 (Kirkman Rd), then just n. Int corridors. **Pets:** Other species. Service with restrictions, supervision. 🛜 🛏 🏊

Quality Inn & Suites 🅗

(407) 996-4600. **$44-$139.** 8700 S Orange Blossom Tr 32809. On US 17-92 and 441, 0.5 mi n of SR 528 (Beachline Expwy) and Florida Tpke exit 254. Ext corridors. **Pets:** Accepted. SAVE 🛜 🛏 🏊

Quality Inn International 🅗 ❖

(407) 996-1600. **$60-$110.** 7600 International Dr 32819. I-4 exit 74A, just e on SR 482 (Sand Lake Rd), then just n. Ext corridors. **Pets:** Medium, other species. $10 daily fee/pet. Service with restrictions, crate.

SAVE 🛜 ♿M 🛏 💻 🍴 🏊

Red Roof Inn Convention Center 🅗

(407) 352-1507. **$50-$126.** 9922 Hawaiian Ct 32819. I-4 exit 72, 0.9 mi e on SR 528 (Beachline Expwy) to exit 1 (International Dr), then just n. Ext corridors. **Pets:** Large, other species. No service, supervision.

♿M 🛏 🏊

Residence Inn by Marriott Orlando Convention Center 🅗

(407) 226-0288. **$89-$199.** 8800 Universal Blvd 32819. I-4 exit 74A, 0.5 mi e on SR 482 (Sand Lake Rd), then 0.8 mi s. Int corridors. **Pets:** Medium. $75 one-time fee/room. Service with restrictions.

SAVE 🛜 ✕ ♿M 🛏 💻 🏊 ✕

Residence Inn by Marriott/Orlando East UCF 🅗 ❖

(407) 513-9000. **$116-$162.** 11651 University Blvd 32817. 2.2 mi e of SR 417 on University Blvd; just w of SR 434 (Alafaya Tr). Int corridors. **Pets:** Small. $100 one-time fee/room. Service with restrictions.

🛜 ✕ 🛏 💻 🏊 ✕

Residence Inn by Marriott Orlando International Airport 🅗

(407) 856-2444. **$119-$169.** 7024 Augusta National Dr 32822. SR 528 (Beach Line Expwy) exit 11, 1 mi n; 1 mi e of Orlando International Airport. Int corridors. **Pets:** Accepted.

SAVE 🛜 ✕ ♿M 🛏 💻 🏊 ✕

Residence Inn by Marriott-Orlando International Dr 🅗

(407) 345-0117. **$97-$199.** 7975 Canada Ave 32819. I-4 exit 74A, just e on SR 482 (Sand Lake Rd). Ext corridors. **Pets:** Other species. $75 one-time fee/room. Service with restrictions, crate.

SAVE 🛜 ✕ 🛏 💻 🏊 ✕

Residence Inn SeaWorld International Center 🅗

(407) 313-3600. **$89-$247.** 11000 Westwood Blvd 32821. I-4 exit 72. Int corridors. **Pets:** Accepted.

SAVE 🛜 ✕ ♿M 🛏 💻 🍴 🏊 ✕

Rosen Inn 🅗

(407) 996-4444. **Call for rates.** 6327 International Dr 32819. I-4 exit 74A, just e on SR 482 (Sand Lake Rd), then 0.7 mi n. Ext/int corridors.

Pets: Accepted. SAVE 🛜 ✕ ♿M 🛏 💻 🍴 🏊

Rosen Inn at Pointe Orlando 🅗 ❖

(407) 996-8585. **$59-$129.** 9000 International Dr 32819. I-4 exit 74A, just e on SR 482 (Sand Lake Rd), then 1 mi s, jct Samoan Ct. Ext corridors. **Pets:** Medium. $10 daily fee/pet. Designated rooms, service with restrictions. SAVE 🛜 ✕ ♿M 🛏 💻 🍴 🏊 ✕

Sheraton Orlando Downtown Hotel 🅗 ❖

(407) 843-6664. **$108-$207.** 400 W Livingston St 32801. I-4 exit 84 (SR 50/Colonial Dr) westbound; exit 83A (Robinson St) eastbound, just w; jct Livingston and Hughey sts. Int corridors. **Pets:** Medium, dogs only. Designated rooms, service with restrictions, supervision.

ECO SAVE 🛜 ✕ ♿M 🛏 💻 🍴 🏊

Sheraton Suites Orlando Airport 🅗

(407) 240-5555. **$89-$279.** 7550 Augusta National Dr 32822. 2 mi n of airport terminal via SR 436 and TG Lee Blvd. Int corridors.

Pets: Accepted. ECO SAVE 🛜 ✕ ♿M 🛏 💻 🍴 🏊

Hawthorn Suites Orlando Airport 🅗

(407) 438-2121. **$95-$250.** 7450 Augusta National Dr 32822. SR 528 (Beachline Expwy) exit 11, 0.5 mi n on SR 436, just e, then just s. Int corridors. **Pets:** Accepted. ECO 🛜 ✕ ♿M 🛏 💻 🏊 ✕

▼▼▼▼ TownePlace Suites by Marriott Orlando East/UCF 🅷 ❀

(407) 243-6100. **$139-$179.** 11801 High Tech Ave 32817. 2.2 mi e of SR 417 on University Blvd; 1.2 mi w of jct SR 434 (Alafaya Tr), just n on Quadrangle Blvd. Int corridors. **Pets:** Small, dogs only. $100 one-time fee/room. Service with restrictions, crate. 🛜 ✖ 🍴 🖥 ➥

▼▼▼▼ Ventura Cove-Ventura Country Club-Ventura Resort Rentals 🆅🅷 ❀

(407) 273-8770. **$79-$500, 15 day notice.** 3763 Ventura Club 32822. 0.6 mi e of SR 436 (Semoran Blvd). Ext corridors. **Pets:** Small, other species. $100 deposit/pet, $100 one-time fee/pet. Designated rooms, service with restrictions, crate. 🍴 🖥 ➥ ✖

🅰🅰🅰 ▼▼▼ ▼▼▼ Villas Of Grand Cypress Golf Resort 🅷

(407) 239-4700. **$175-$2000, 3 day notice.** 1 N Jacaranda 32836. I-4 exit 68, 2.3 mi nw on SR 535. Ext corridors. **Pets:** Small, dogs only. $150 one-time fee/room. Service with restrictions, crate. 🎗 🆂🅰🆅🅴 🛜 ✖ 🍴 🖥 🍴 ➥ ✖

🅰🅰🅰 ▼▼▼ ▼▼▼ Westgate Palace 🆎

(407) 996-6000. **$125-$206, 3 day notice.** 6145 Carrier Dr 32819. I-4 exit 74A, just e on SR 482 (Sand Lake Rd), 0.6 mi n on International Dr, then just e. Int corridors. **Pets:** Accepted.
🆂🅰🆅🅴 🛜 🆂🅼 🍴 🖥 🍴 ➥ ✖

🅰🅰🅰 ▼▼▼▼ Wyndham Orlando Resort 🅷 ❀

(407) 351-2420. **$113-$194, 3 day notice.** 8001 International Dr 32819. I-4 exit 74A, just e on SR 482 (Sand Lake Rd). Ext/int corridors. **Pets:** Large, other species. $50 one-time fee/room. Service with restrictions, supervision. 🆂🅰🆅🅴 🛜 🆂🅼 🍴 🖥 🍴 ➥ ✖

ST. CLOUD

🅰🅰🅰 ▼▼▼▼ Budget Inn of St Cloud 🅼

(407) 892-2858. **$35-$90, 3 day notice.** 602 13th St 34769. On US 192, 0.5 mi e of The Water Tower, 2 mi w of jct CR 15. Ext corridors. **Pets:** Very small, dogs only. $10 daily fee/pet. Service with restrictions, crate. 🆂🅰🆅🅴 🛜 🍴 🖥

SANFORD

▼▼▼▼ Holiday Inn Express-Sanford/Lake Mary 🅷

(407) 320-0845. **$70-$109.** 3401 S Orlando Dr 32773. I-4 exit 98, e on Lake Mary Blvd, then 0.5 mi n on US 17-92. Int corridors. **Pets:** Accepted. 🛜 ✖ 🆂🅼 🍴 🖥 ➥

WINTER PARK

🅰🅰🅰 ▼▼▼▼ Best Western Mt. Vernon Inn 🅷 ❀

(407) 647-1166. **$129-$159.** 110 S Orlando Ave 32789. I-4 exit 87 (Fairbanks Ave), 1 mi e, then 0.3 mi n on US 17-92. Ext/int corridors. **Pets:** Dogs only. $15 daily fee/pet. Designated rooms, service with restrictions, supervision. 🆂🅰🆅🅴 🛜 🍴 🖥 🍴 ➥

END METROPOLITAN AREA

ORMOND BEACH

▼▼▼ Mainsail Inn & Suites 🅷

(386) 677-2131. **$60-$200, 3 day notice.** 281 S Atlantic Ave 32176. I-95 exit 268 (SR 40/Granada Blvd), 5.4 mi e to SR A1A (Atlantic Ave), then 0.6 mi s. Ext/int corridors. **Pets:** Accepted. 🛜 🍴 🖥 ➥

🅰🅰🅰 ▼▼▼▼ Destination Daytona Hotel & Suites 🅷

(386) 944-1500. **$84-$500, 7 day notice.** 1635 N US Hwy 1 32174. I-95 exit 273 (US 1), just nw. Int corridors. **Pets:** Accepted.
🆂🅰🆅🅴 🍴 🖥 ➥

▼▼▼▼ Hampton Inn Daytona/Ormond Beach 🅷

(386) 677-9999. **$110-$350.** 155 Interchange Blvd 32174. I-95 exit 268 (SR 40/Granada Blvd), just w to Interchange Blvd, then just s. Int corridors. **Pets:** Accepted. 🛜 🆂🅼 🍴 🖥 ➥

▼▼▼▼ Jameson Inn 🅷

(386) 672-3675. **$74-$94.** 175 Interchange Blvd 32174. I-95 exit 268 (SR 40/Granada Blvd), just w to Interchange Blvd, then just s. Int corridors. **Pets:** Medium. $15 daily fee/room. Service with restrictions, supervision. 🛜 🍴 🖥 ➥

PALATKA

▼▼ Quality Inn & Suites Riverfront 🅷

(386) 328-3481. **Call for rates.** 201 N First St 32177. On US 17; at foot of St. Johns River Bridge. Ext corridors. **Pets:** Accepted. 🛜 🍴 🖥 🍴 ➥

▼▼ Sleep Inn & Suites 🅷

(386) 325-8889. **Call for rates.** 3805 Reid St 32177. 2 mi n on SR 100, jct SR 19. Int corridors. **Pets:** Accepted. 🛜 🍴 🖥 ➥

PALM BAY

▼▼▼▼ Holiday Inn Express Hotel & Suites-Palm Bay 🅷

(321) 220-2003. **Call for rates.** 1206 SE Malabar Rd 32907. I-95 exit 173 (SR 514/Malabar Rd), just e. Int corridors. **Pets:** Accepted. 🛜 🍴 🖥 ➥

▼▼ Jameson Inn 🅷

(321) 725-2952. **$74-$94.** 890 Palm Bay Rd NE 32905. I-95 exit 176 (Palm Bay Rd NE), 0.5 mi e. Int corridors. **Pets:** Medium. $15 daily fee/room. Service with restrictions, supervision. 🛜 🆂🅼 🍴 🖥 ➥

PALM BEACH

🅰🅰🅰 ▼▼▼ ▼▼▼ The Brazilian Court Hotel & Beach Club 🅷 ❀

(561) 655-7740. **$249-$2999, 14 day notice.** 301 Australian Ave 33480. From Royal Palm Way, just s on Cocoanut Row to Australian Ave, then just e; corner of Hibiscus and Australian aves. Int corridors. **Pets:** Small. $100 one-time fee/pet. Service with restrictions, supervision.
🆂🅰🆅🅴 🛜 ✖ 🍴 🍴 ➥ ✖

🅰🅰🅰 ▼▼▼ ▼▼▼ The Chesterfield Hotel Palm Beach 🅷

(561) 659-5800. **$179-$929, 3 day notice.** 363 Cocoanut Row 33480. Jct Australian Ave and Cocoanut Row; 2 blks n of Worth Ave. Int corridors. **Pets:** Accepted. 🆂🅰🆅🅴 🛜 🍴 🍴 ➥ ✖

▼▼▼▼ The Colony 🅷

(561) 655-5430. **$190-$2500, 3 day notice.** 155 Hammon Ave 33480. 1 blk s of Worth Ave; between S County Rd and SR A1A (S Ocean Blvd). Int corridors. **Pets:** Accepted. 🛜 ✖ 🍴 ➥ ✖

🅰🅰🅰 ▼▼▼ ▼▼▼ Four Seasons Resort Palm Beach 🅷

(561) 582-2800. **$245-$4500, 14 day notice.** 2800 S Ocean Blvd 33480. On SR A1A, 0.4 mi n of SR 802 (Lake Ave). Int corridors. **Pets:** Accepted. 🎗 🆂🅰🆅🅴 🛜 ✖ 🆂🅼 🍴 ➥ ✖

▼▼▼ ▼▼▼ The Omphoy Ocean Resort 🅷

(561) 540-6440. **$149-$1099, 14 day notice.** 2842 S Ocean Blvd 33480. On SR A1A (S Ocean Blvd), 0.4 mi n of SR 802 (Lake Ave). Int corridors. **Pets:** Accepted. 🛜 ✖ 🍴 ➥ ✖

PALM BEACH GARDENS

🅰🅰🅰 ▼▼▼ ▼▼▼ DoubleTree by Hilton Hotel and Executive Meeting Center Palm Beach Gardens 🅷

(561) 622-2260. **$79-$189.** 4431 PGA Blvd 33410. I-95 exit 79B (PGA Blvd W), just w. Int corridors. **Pets:** Accepted.
🎗 🆂🅰🆅🅴 🛜 🆂🅼 🍴 🖥 🍴 ➥ ✖

Homewood Suites by Hilton - Palm Beach Gardens H ❖

(561) 622-7799. **$139-$249.** 4700 Donald Ross Rd 33418. I-95 exit 83 (Donald Ross Rd), 1.1 mi e; in Donald Ross Village. Int corridors. **Pets:** Medium. $75 one-time fee/room. Designated rooms, service with restrictions, crate.

PGA National Resort & Spa H

(561) 627-2000. **$149-$969, 3 day notice.** 400 Ave of the Champions 33418. I-95 exit 79B (PGA Blvd), 2 mi w; Florida Tpke exit 109, just w. Int corridors. **Pets:** Medium. $150 one-time fee/pet. Designated rooms.

Windsor Gardens Hotel & Conference Center H

(561) 844-8448. **Call for rates.** 11360 US Hwy 1 33408. I-95 exit 79A (PGA Blvd), 2.9 mi e, then just s. Int corridors. **Pets:** Large, other species. $35 one-time fee/pet. Designated rooms, service with restrictions, crate.

PALM BEACH SHORES

Hilton Singer Island Oceanfront Resort H

(561) 848-3888. **$129-$329.** 3700 N Ocean Dr 33404. On Singer Island; 1.8 mi n, e on SR A1A from jct US 1. Int corridors. **Pets:** Accepted.

SeaSpray Inn Beach Resort H

(561) 844-0233. **Call for rates.** 123 S Ocean Ave 33404. On Singer Island; 0.5 mi s of SR A1A. Int corridors. **Pets:** Accepted.

PALM COAST

Best Western Palm Coast M

(386) 446-4457. **$70-$100.** 5 Kingswood Dr 32137. I-95 exit 289 (Palm Coast Pkwy), just e to Kingswood Dr, then just s; in Kingswood Center. Ext corridors. **Pets:** Medium, other species. $20 daily fee/room. Service with restrictions, supervision.

Days Inn Palm Coast H

(386) 627-7734. **Call for rates.** 120 Garden St N 32137. I-95 exit 289 (Palm Coast Pkwy), just w Boulder Rock Dr, just n to Garden St, then just e. Int corridors. **Pets:** Other species. $15 one-time fee/pet. Service with restrictions.

Fairfield Inn & Suites Palm Coast I-95 H

(386) 445-3450. **$64-$260.** 400 Old Kings Rd N 32137. I-95 exit 289 (Palm Coast Pkwy), just e Kingswood Dr, then 0.3 mi s. Int corridors. **Pets:** Accepted.

Holiday Inn Express Hotel & Suites H

(386) 439-3939. **$89-$189.** 200 Flagler Plaza Dr 32137. I-95 exit 284 (SR 100), just e. Int corridors. **Pets:** Other species. $50 deposit/room, $15 daily fee/pet. Service with restrictions.

Microtel Inn & Suites H

(386) 445-8976. **$45-$117.** 16 Kingswood Dr 32137. I-95 exit 289 (Palm Coast Pkwy), just e to Kingswood Dr, then just sw. Int corridors. **Pets:** Accepted.

Palm Coast Villas M

(386) 445-3525. **Call for rates.** 5454 N Oceanshore Blvd 32137. I-95 exit 289 (Palm Coast Pkwy), 3 mi ne to Camino Del Mar, just nw to Oceanshore Blvd, then 1.8 mi n. Ext corridors. **Pets:** Accepted.

PANAMA CITY

Comfort Inn & Conference Center M

(850) 769-6969. **$59-$149.** 1013 E 23rd St 32405. On SR 368, just w of jct US 231. Ext corridors. **Pets:** Large, other species. $50 deposit/room, $10 daily fee/pet. Designated rooms, service with restrictions, supervision.

La Quinta Inn & Suites H

(850) 914-0022. **$88-$159.** 1030 E 23rd St 32405. On SR 368, jct US 231. Int corridors. **Pets:** Medium, other species. Service with restrictions, supervision.

Red Roof Inn-Panama City H

(850) 215-2727. **$59-$129.** 217 N Hwy 231 32401. On US 231, just ne of jct US 98. Int corridors. **Pets:** Large, other species. No service, supervision.

Super 8-Panama City M

(850) 784-1988. **$51-$99.** 207 Hwy 231 N 32405. On US 231, just ne of jct US 98. Ext/int corridors. **Pets:** Dogs only. $15 daily fee/pet. Service with restrictions, crate.

TownePlace Suites by Marriott Panama City H

(850) 747-0609. **$89-$169.** 903 E 23rd Pl 32405. Just e of jct SR 77 (Martin Luther King Jr Blvd) on 23rd St (SR 368), n on Palo Alto Ave. Int corridors. **Pets:** Other species. $100 one-time fee/room. Service with restrictions, supervision.

PENSACOLA

La Quinta Inn Pensacola H

(850) 474-0411. **$68-$165.** 7750 N Davis Hwy 32514. I-10 exit 13, just n. Ext corridors. **Pets:** Medium, other species. Service with restrictions, supervision.

MainStay Suites H

(850) 479-1000. **$84-$129.** 7230 Plantation Rd 32504. I-10 exit 13, just s, then 0.3 mi w. Ext corridors. **Pets:** Medium, other species. $25 daily fee/room. Designated rooms, service with restrictions, crate.

Red Roof Inn M

(850) 476-7960. **$55-$89.** 7340 Plantation Rd 32504. I-10 exit 13, just s. Ext corridors. **Pets:** Large, other species. No service, supervision.

Red Roof Inn Pensacola West H

(850) 941-0908. **$55-$90.** 2591 Wilde Lake Blvd 32526. I-10 exit 7, just s. Int corridors. **Pets:** Large, other species. No service, supervision.

TownePlace Suites Pensacola H

(850) 484-7022. **$89-$149.** 481 Creighton Rd 32504. I-10 exit 13, 0.3 mi s, then just w. Int corridors. **Pets:** Accepted.

PERRY

Econo Lodge M ❖

(850) 584-6231. **Call for rates.** 2220 US 19 S 32348. On US Alt 27/19/ 98, 0.4 mi s of jct US 221. Ext corridors. **Pets:** Medium. $10 one-time fee/pet, $10 daily fee/pet. Designated rooms, service with restrictions, crate.

PORT CHARLOTTE

Country Inn & Suites By Carlson H

(941) 235-1035. **$69-$179.** 24244 Corporate Ct 33954. I-75 exit 170, just w on CR 769 (Kings Hwy). Int corridors. **Pets:** $10 daily fee/room. Service with restrictions, crate.

Days Inn of Port Charlotte H ❖

(941) 627-8900. **$71-$125.** 1941 Tamiami Tr 33948. US 41, 2.3 mi s of jct Toledo Blade Blvd (CR 779). Ext corridors. **Pets:** Small, other species. $10 daily fee/pet. Designated rooms, service with restrictions, supervision.

La Quinta Inn & Suites Port Charlotte H

(941) 979-4200. **$84-$144.** 812 Kings Hwy 33980. I-75 exit 170, just w on CR 769 (Kings Hwy), then just s on Veterans Blvd. Int corridors. **Pets:** Medium, other species. Service with restrictions, supervision.

PORT ORANGE

▼▼▼▼ **La Quinta Inn & Suites - Port Orange** H
(386) 756-3440. **$76-$155.** 1791 Dunlawton Ave 32129. I-95 exit 256, just e. Int corridors. **Pets:** Medium, other species. Service with restrictions, supervision. 🛜 ⊠ 🔏 🚪 🖵 🏊

PORT ST. JOE

⚫⚫⚫ ▼▼▼▼ **MainStay Suites By Choice Hotels** H
(850) 229-6246. **$89-$199.** 3951 E Hwy 98 32456. On US 98, 3 mi e of jct SR 71. Int corridors. **Pets:** Small. $25 daily fee/room. Designated rooms, service with restrictions, supervision.
🌿 💰 🛜 ⊠ 🔏 🚪 🖵 🏊

PORT ST. LUCIE

▼▼▼ **Holiday Inn-Port St Lucie** H
(772) 337-2200. **$80-$159.** 10120 S Federal Hwy 34952. On US 1, 0.6 mi n of jct SR 716 (Port St Lucie Blvd). Int corridors. **Pets:** $50 one-time fee/room. Designated rooms, service with restrictions, crate.
🌿 🛜 🔏 🚪 🖵 🍴 🏊 ⊠

▼▼▼ **Homewood Suites by Hilton Port St. Lucie-Tradition** H
(772) 345-5300. **$84-$144.** 10301 SW Innovation Way 34987. I-95 exit 118 (Gatlin Rd), 0.5 mi w to Village Pkwy, then just s. Int corridors. **Pets:** Accepted. 🛜 🔏 🚪 🖵 🏊

▼▼▼ **MainStay Suites at PGA Village** H
(772) 460-8882. **$65-$169.** 8501 Champions Way 34986. I-95 exit 121 (St. Lucie West Blvd), just w. Int corridors. **Pets:** Accepted.
🛜 🔏 🚪 🖵 🏊

▼▼▼ **Residence Inn by Marriott Port St. Lucie** H 🐾
(772) 344-7814. **$84-$149.** 1920 SW Fountainview Blvd 34986. I-95 exit 121 (St Lucie West Blvd), just e to Paramount Dr, just s to SW Fountainview Blvd, then just sw. Int corridors. **Pets:** Large. $100 one-time fee/room. Service with restrictions, crate. 🛜 ⊠ 🔏 🚪 🖵 🏊

PUNTA GORDA

⚫⚫⚫ ▼▼▼ **Best Western Waterfront** H
(941) 639-1165. **$80-$140.** 300 Retta Esplanade 33950. Jct US 41 southbound, just s of jct US 41 northbound. Int corridors. **Pets:** Accepted.
💰 🛜 🔏 🚪 🖵 🍴 🏊 ⊠

⚫⚫⚫ ▼▼▼ **Four Points by Sheraton Punta Gorda Harborside** H
(941) 637-6770. **$89-$209.** 33 Tamiami Tr 33950. On US 41; at Peace River Bridge. Int corridors. **Pets:** Accepted.
💰 🛜 ⊠ 🔏 🚪 🖵 🍴 🏊 ⊠

⚫⚫⚫ ▼▼▼▼ **Wyvern Hotel** H
(941) 639-7700. **Call for rates.** 101 E Retta Esplanade 33950. Jct US 41 northbound; just e of jct US 41 southbound. Int corridors.
Pets: Accepted. 💰 🛜 🔏 🚪 🖵 🍴 🏊

QUINCY

▼▼▼ **Allison House Inn** BB 🐾
(850) 875-2511. **$85-$175, 21 day notice.** 215 N Madison St 32351. Just e of town center; in historic district. **Pets:** Small, dogs only. Designated rooms, service with restrictions, crate. 🛜 ⊠

RIVER RANCH

⚫⚫⚫ ▼▼▼ **Westgate River Ranch Resort** M
(863) 692-1321. **$79-$179, 7 day notice.** 3200 River Ranch Rd 33867. Florida Tpke exit 193 (SR 60), 22 mi w to River Ranch Blvd, then 2.7 mi s. Ext corridors. **Pets:** Accepted.
💰 🛜 ⊠ 🔏 🚪 🖵 🍴 🏊 ⊠

⚫⚫⚫ ▼▼▼▼ **Westgate River Ranch Resort Cabins** CA
(863) 692-1321. **$129-$319, 3 day notice.** 3200 River Ranch Blvd 33867. Florida Tpke exit 193 (SR 60), 22 mi w to River Ranch Blvd, then 2.7 mi s. Ext corridors. **Pets:** Medium. $25 daily fee/room. Service with restrictions, supervision. 💰 🛜 ⊠ 🔏 🚪 🖵 🍴 🏊 ⊠

ST. AUGUSTINE

⚫⚫⚫⚫ ▼▼▼ ▼▼▼ **Autograph Collection Casa Monica** H
(904) 827-1888. **$179-$399, 3 day notice.** 95 Cordova St 32084. Downtown; across from Lightner Museum and Flagler College. Int corridors. **Pets:** Medium, dogs only. $150 one-time fee/room. Designated rooms, service with restrictions, supervision.
🌿 💰 🛜 ⊠ 🔏 🚪 🖵 🍴 🏊 ⊠

▼▼▼ **Bayfront Marin House Bed & Breakfast Inn** BB 🐾
(904) 824-4301. **$119-$299, 7 day notice.** 142 Avenida Menendez 32084. 1 blk s of Bridge of Lions. Ext corridors. **Pets:** $30 daily fee/pet. Designated rooms, service with restrictions. 🛜 ⊠

⚫⚫⚫ ▼▼▼ **Best Western I-95 St. Augustine** M
(904) 829-1999. **$80-$150.** 2445 SR 16 32092. I-95 exit 318, just w. Ext corridors. **Pets:** Accepted. 💰 🛜 🖵 🏊

⚫⚫⚫ ▼▼▼ **Casablanca Inn on the Bay** BB
(904) 829-0928. **$99-$379, 7 day notice.** 24 Avenida Menendez 32084. I-95 exit 318 (SR 16), 5.5 mi e to San Marco Ave, then 1.8 mi s; in historic district. Ext/int corridors. **Pets:** $15 daily fee/room. Designated rooms, service with restrictions. 💰 🛜 ⊠ 🔏 🏊

▼▼▼ **Casa De Solana Bed & Breakfast Inn** BB
(904) 824-3555. **Call for rates.** 21 Aviles St 32084. Aviles St at Cadiz St; in historic district. Int corridors. **Pets:** Accepted. 🛜 ⊠ 🔏 🕿

⚫⚫⚫ ▼▼▼ **The Cozy Inn** M
(904) 824-2449. **$59-$209, 30 day notice.** 202 San Marco Ave 32084. I-95 exit 318 (SR 16), 5.5 mi e to San Marco Ave, the 0.4 mi s. Ext corridors. **Pets:** Accepted. 💰 🛜 🔏 🖵

▼▼▼ **The Inn At Camachee Harbor** CO 🐾
(904) 825-0003. **$99-$169, 7 day notice.** 201 Yacht Club Dr 32084. On Intracoastal Waterway at west side of Usina Bridge; 1 mi e of jct N SR A1A and San Marco Blvd. Ext/int corridors. **Pets:** Medium, other species. $15 daily fee/pet. Designated rooms, service with restrictions, crate.
🛜 ⊠ 🔏 🖵

▼▼▼ **La Quinta Inn & Suites St. Augustine** H
(904) 209-2580. **$125-$208.** 250 Prime Outlet Blvd 32084. I-95 exit 318 (SR 16), just e to Prime Outlet Blvd, then n. Int corridors. **Pets:** Medium, other species. Service with restrictions, supervision.
🛜 ⊠ 🔏 🖵 🏊

⚫⚫⚫ ▼▼▼ **Monterey Inn** M
(904) 824-4482. **$89-$129.** 16 Avenida Menendez 32084. I-95 exit 318 (SR 16), 5.5 mi e to San Marco Ave, then 1.7 mi s; in historic district. Ext corridors. **Pets:** Small, other species. $20 daily fee/pet. Service with restrictions, supervision. 💰 🛜 🔏 🖵 🏊

▼▼▼ **Peace and Plenty Inn** BB
(904) 829-8209. **$89-$189, 7 day notice.** 87 Cedar St 32084. From King St, just s on Granada St, then just w. Int corridors. **Pets:** Medium, dogs only. $35 one-time fee/pet. Designated rooms, service with restrictions, supervision. 🛜 ⊠ 🔏 🕿

⚫⚫⚫ ▼▼▼ **Quality Inn** M
(904) 823-8636. **$60-$170.** 2310 SR 16 32084. I-95 exit 318 (SR 16), just e. Ext corridors. **Pets:** Dogs only. $15 daily fee/room. Designated rooms, service with restrictions, supervision. 💰 🛜 🔏 🖵 🏊

⚫⚫⚫ ▼▼▼ **Ramada Limited St. Augustine** M
(904) 829-5643. **$60-$130.** 2535 SR 16 32092. I-95 exit 318 (SR 16), just w. Ext corridors. **Pets:** Other species. $10 daily fee/room. Service with restrictions. 💰 🛜 🔏 🖵 🏊

▼▼▼ **St. Francis Inn** BB 🐾
(904) 824-6068. **Call for rates.** 279 St. George St 32084. 0.3 mi s of jct King and St. George sts; in historic district. Ext/int corridors. **Pets:** Medium, other species. $15 daily fee/pet. Service with restrictions. 🌿 🛜 ⊠ 🔏 🖵 🏊

ST. AUGUSTINE BEACH

AAA **WWW** **Comfort Inn at St. Augustine Beach** M
(904) 471-1474. **$79-$159.** 901 A1A Beach Blvd 32080. On Business Rt SR A1A, 1.6 mi s of jct SR 312 and A1A. Ext corridors. **Pets:** $20 daily fee/pet. Designated rooms, service with restrictions.
SAVE 🛜 ✕ 🛏 💷 ➸

AAA **WWW** **Holiday Isle Oceanfront Resort** H ❀
(904) 471-2555. **$99-$189.** 860 A1A Beach Blvd 32080. On Business Rt SR A1A, 1.8 mi s of jct SR 312 and A1A. Int corridors. **Pets:** Other species. $20 daily fee/pet. Designated rooms, service with restrictions, supervision. ECO SAVE 🛜 ✕ ᏭM 🛏 💷 ¶ ➸

AAA **WWW** **House of Sea and Sun** BB ❀
(904) 461-1716. **$169-$229, 7 day notice.** 2 B St 32080. Jct SR 312 and A1A, 1.9 mi s to B St, then just e. Ext/int corridors. **Pets:** Large, other species. Service with restrictions. SAVE 🛜 ✕

WW **St. Augustine Island Inn** H
(904) 471-1440. **$59-$249, 3 day notice.** 894 A1A Beach Blvd 32080. On Business Rt SR A1A, 2 mi s of jct SR 312 and A1A. Int corridors. **Pets:** Medium. $20 daily fee/pet. Service with restrictions, supervision. 🛜 🛏 💷 ➸

ST. PETERSBURG-CLEARWATER AND BEACHES AREA

CLEARWATER

AAA **WWW** **Candlewood Suites Clearwater-St. Petersburg** H
(727) 573-3344. **$69-$149, 3 day notice.** 13231 49th St N 33762. I-275 exit 31 southbound, 3 mi w on SR 688 (Ulmerton Rd), then just s; exit 30 northbound, 1.4 mi w on SR 686, 1.6 mi w on SR 688 (Ulmerton Rd), then just s. Int corridors. **Pets:** Medium. $15 daily fee/room. Service with restrictions, supervision. ᏭM 🛏 💷 ➸

AAA **WWW** **Days Inn Clearwater/St. Petersburg Airport** H
(727) 573-3334. **$47-$79.** 3910 Ulmerton Rd 33762. I-275 exit 31 southbound, 2 mi w on SR 688 (Ulmerton Rd); exit 30 northbound, 1.4 mi w on SR 686, 0.7 mi w. Int corridors. **Pets:** Accepted.
SAVE 🛜 ᏭM 🛏 💷 ➸

WWW **Extended StayAmerica-St. Petersburg-Clearwater** H ❀
(727) 561-9032. **$50-$120.** 3089 Executive Dr 33762. I-275 exit 31 southbound, 1.7 mi w on SR 688 (Ulmerton Rd); exit 30 northbound, 1.4 mi w on SR 686, just n on 34th St N, then 0.3 mi ne. Int corridors. **Pets:** Other species. $25 daily fee/pet. Service with restrictions.
🛜 ᏭM 🛏 💷

WWW **Homestead Studio Suites Hotel-St Petersburg-Clearwater** M ❀
(727) 572-4800. **$55-$130.** 2311 Ulmerton Rd 33762. I-275 exit 31 southbound, 1.3 mi w on SR 688 (Ulmerton Rd); exit 30 northbound, 1.4 mi w on SR 686, then 0.6 mi e on SR 688 (Ulmerton Rd). Ext corridors. **Pets:** Other species. $25 daily fee/pet. Service with restrictions.
🛜 ᏭM 🛏 💷 ➸

WWWW **Homewood Suites by Hilton Clearwater** H
(727) 573-1500. **$129-$289.** 2233 Ulmerton Rd 33762. I-275 exit 31 southbound, 1.3 mi w on SR 688 (Ulmerton Rd); exit 30 northbound, 1.4 mi w on SR 686, then 0.6 mi e on SR 688 (Ulmerton Rd). Int corridors. **Pets:** Accepted. 🛜 ᏭM 🛏 💷 ➸

WWW **Howard Johnson Inn & Suites** M
(727) 796-0135. **$58-$99.** 27988 US Hwy 19 N 33761. On US 19, 0.6 mi n of jct SR 580. Ext corridors. **Pets:** Medium, other species. $50 deposit/room, $10 daily fee/pet. Designated rooms, service with restrictions, crate.
🛜 🛏 💷 ➸

WW **La Quinta Inn Tampa Bay (Clearwater Airport)** H
(727) 572-7222. **$58-$149.** 3301 Ulmerton Rd 33762. I-275 exit 31 southbound, 1.7 mi w on SR 688 (Ulmerton Rd); exit 30 northbound, 1.4 mi w on SR 686, then just w on SR 688 (Ulmerton Rd); in The Centres Office Park. Int corridors. **Pets:** Medium, other species. Service with restrictions, supervision. 🛜 🛏 💷 ➸ ✕

AAA **WWWW** **Residence Inn by Marriott Clearwater Downtown** H ❀
(727) 562-5400. **$116-$269.** 940 Court St 33756. On SR 60 at jct S Prospect Ave. Int corridors. **Pets:** $100 one-time fee/room. Designated rooms, service with restrictions. SAVE 🛜 ✕ ᏭM 🛏 💷 ➸

AAA **WWWW** **Residence Inn by Marriott St. Petersburg/Clearwater** H
(727) 573-4444. **$79-$259.** 5050 Ulmerton Rd 33760. I-275 exit 31 southbound, 3.1 mi w on SR 688 (Ulmerton Rd); exit 30 northbound, 1.4 mi w on SR 686, then 1.7 mi w on SR 688 (Ulmerton Rd). Ext corridors. **Pets:** Other species. $100 one-time fee/room.
SAVE ✕ 🛏 💷 ➸ ✕

AAA **WWWW** **Super 8 Clearwater/St. Petersburg Airport/Tampa Bay** H
(727) 572-8881. **$35-$109.** 13260 34th St N 33762. I-275 exit 31 southbound, 1.8 mi w on SR 688 (Ulmerton Rd), then just s; exit 30 northbound, 1.4 mi w on SR 686. Int corridors. **Pets:** Small, other species. $10 daily fee/pet. Designated rooms, service with restrictions, supervision. SAVE 🛜 🛏 💷 ➸

WWWW **TownePlace Suites by Marriott St. Petersburg/Clearwater** H
(727) 299-9229. **$99-$184.** 13200 49th St N 33762. I-275 exit 31 southbound; exit 30 northbound, 1.4 mi w on SR 686, 3 mi w on SR 688 (Ulmerton Rd), then just s; in Turtle Creek. Int corridors. **Pets:** Small. $100 one-time fee/pet. Service with restrictions.
🛜 ✕ ᏭM 🛏 💷 ➸

INDIAN ROCKS BEACH
WW **Sea Star Motel & Apartments** M
(727) 596-2525. **$75-$135, 30 day notice.** 1805 Gulf Blvd 33785. On SR 699, 1.2 mi n of jct SR 688 (Walsingham Rd). Ext corridors. **Pets:** $10 daily fee/pet. Designated rooms, no service.
🛜 🛏 💷 ✕ 🐾

INDIAN SHORES
AAA **WWW** **Sea Club Resort Condominiums** CO
(727) 596-2046. **$80-$165 (no credit cards), 45 day notice.** 19725 Gulf Blvd 33785. On SR 699, 1.1 mi n of jct CR 694. Ext corridors. **Pets:** Small. $50 one-time fee/room. Service with restrictions, crate.
SAVE 🛜 🛏 ➸ ✕

LARGO
AAA **WWW** **Hampton Inn & Suites** H
(727) 585-3333. **$99-$189.** 100 E Bay Dr 33770. On SR 686 (W Bay/E Bay drs), 3.4 mi w of jct US 19; jct Alternate Rt US 19 (Seminole Blvd). Int corridors. **Pets:** Medium. Service with restrictions, supervision.
ECO SAVE ᏭM 🛏 💷 ➸

AAA **WWW** **Holiday Inn Express & Suites** H
(727) 581-3900. **$99-$159.** 210 Seminole Blvd 33770. On Alternate Rt US 19, just s of jct SR 686 (W Bay/E Bay drs). Int corridors. **Pets:** Medium. $35 deposit/room. Service with restrictions, crate.
SAVE 🛜 ✕ ᏭM 🛏 💷 ➸

MADEIRA BEACH
AAA **WWW** **Snug Harbor Inn Waterfront Bed & Breakfast** M ❀
(727) 395-9256. **$75-$140, 21 day notice.** 13655 Gulf Blvd 33708. On SR 699, 0.9 mi s of jct SR 666 (Tom Stuart Cswy). Ext corridors. **Pets:** Other species. Service with restrictions.
SAVE 🛜 🛏 💷 ➸ ✕

NEW PORT RICHEY

△△△△ ▼▼▼ River Side Inn M

(727) 845-4990. **$50-$100.** 7631 US 19 34652. On US 19, 0.8 mi n of jct Main St. Ext corridors. **Pets:** Small. $6 daily fee/room. Designated rooms, no service, supervision. ⟨SAVE⟩ 🛜 📵 📺 🏊

OLDSMAR

△△△△ ▼▼▼▼ Residence Inn Tampa/Oldsmar H

(813) 818-9400. **$104-$198.** 4012 Tampa Rd 34677. On SR 580; jct St. Pete Dr. Int corridors. **Pets:** Other species. $100 one-time fee/room.

⟨ECO⟩ ⟨SAVE⟩ 🛜 ✕ ♿ 📵 📺 🏊 ✕

PALM HARBOR

▼▼ Knights Inn-Clearwater/Palm Harbor M

(727) 789-2002. **$40-$50.** 34106 US 19 N 34684. On US 19, 1.8 mi n of CR 752 (Tampa Rd). Ext corridors. **Pets:** Other species. $10 daily fee/room. Designated rooms, service with restrictions.

🛜 ♿ 📵 📺 🏊

PINELLAS PARK

▼▼ La Quinta Inn Tampa Bay Pinellas Park Clearwater H

(727) 545-5611. **$58-$129.** 7500 US Hwy 19 N 33781. I-275 exit 28, 1.4 mi s on Gandy Blvd (SR 694), then just n. Ext/int corridors. **Pets:** Medium, other species. Service with restrictions, supervision.

🛜 ♿ 📵 📺 🏊

PORT RICHEY

▼▼▼ Homewood Suites by Hilton Tampa/Port Richey H

(727) 819-1000. **$99-$149.** 11115 US 19 N 34668. On US 19, 0.5 mi s mi of jct SR 52; jct Hammock/Ranch Rd. Int corridors. **Pets:** Large. $75 one-time fee/room. Designated rooms, service with restrictions, supervision. 🛜 ♿ 📵 📺 🏊 ✕

ST. PETE BEACH

△△△△ ▼▼▼ Alden Beach Resort H ❀

(727) 360-7081. **$129-$349.** 5900 Gulf Blvd 33706. On SR 699, 1.7 mi n of Pinellas Bayway. Ext corridors. **Pets:** Medium, dogs only. $25 one-time fee/room. Designated rooms, service with restrictions, crate.

⟨SAVE⟩ 🛜 📵 📺 🏊 ✕

△△△ ▼▼▼ Bay Palms Waterfront Resort M

(727) 360-7642. **$59-$229, 14 day notice.** 4237 Gulf Blvd 33706. On SR 699, 0.6 mi n of Pinellas Bayway. Ext corridors. **Pets:** Accepted.

⟨ECO⟩ ⟨SAVE⟩ 🛜 📵 ✕

△△△△ ▼▼▼ Bayview Plaza Waterfront Resort M

(727) 367-2791. **$59-$229, 14 day notice.** 4321 Gulf Blvd 33706. On SR 699, 0.6 mi n of Pinellas Bayway. Ext/int corridors. **Pets:** Accepted.

⟨ECO⟩ ⟨SAVE⟩ 📵 ✕

△△△ ▼▼▼ Beach House Suites By The Don Cesar H

(727) 363-0001. **$159-$539, 3 day notice.** 3860 Gulf Blvd 33706. On SR 699, 0.4 mi n of jct Pinellas Bayway. Ext corridors. **Pets:** Accepted.

⟨SAVE⟩ 🛜 📵 📺 🏊 ✕

△△△ ▼▼▼ ▼▼ Don CeSar Beach Resort, A Loews Hotel H ❀

(727) 360-1881. **$169-$699, 3 day notice.** 3400 Gulf Blvd 33706. On SR 699, jct Pinellas Bayway. Int corridors. **Pets:** Other species. $25 one-time fee/room. Designated rooms, service with restrictions, crate.

⟨ECO⟩ ⟨SAVE⟩ 🛜 ♿ 📵 📺 🏊 ✕

△△△ ▼▼▼ Postcard Inn on the Beach M

(727) 367-2711. **$89-$299, 3 day notice.** 6300 Gulf Blvd 33706. On SR 699, 2 mi n of Pinellas Bayway. Ext corridors. **Pets:** Accepted.

⟨SAVE⟩ 🛜 ♿ 📵 🍴 🏊 ✕

△△△ ▼▼▼ TradeWinds Island Grand Beach Resort H ❀

(727) 363-2200. **$176-$517.** 5500 Gulf Blvd 33706. On SR 699, 1 mi n of Pinellas Bayway. Ext/int corridors. **Pets:** Large, other species. $100 deposit/room, $30 daily fee/room. Designated rooms, service with restrictions. ⟨ECO⟩ ⟨SAVE⟩ 🛜 📵 📺 🍴 🏊 ✕

ST. PETERSBURG

△△△△ ▼▼▼ Hotel Indigo-Downtown St Petersburg H

(727) 822-4814. **$99-$229.** 234 3rd Ave N 33701. Jct 2nd St N. Int corridors. **Pets:** Accepted. ⟨SAVE⟩ 🛜 ✕ ♿ 📵 📺 🍴 🏊 ✕

▼▼▼ La Quinta Inn & Suites St. Petersburg Northeast H

(727) 525-1800. **$92-$153.** 6638 4th St N 33702. I-275 exit 26, 1.7 mi e on 54th Ave N (CR 202), then 0.8 mi n. Int corridors. **Pets:** Medium, other species. Service with restrictions, supervision.

🛜 ♿ 📵 📺 🏊

▼▼▼ La Quinta Inn Tampa Bay St. Petersburg M

(727) 527-8421. **$58-$134.** 4999 34th St N 33714. I-275 exit 26 southbound; exit 26B northbound, just w on 54th Ave N, then just s on US 19. Ext corridors. **Pets:** Medium, other species. Service with restrictions, supervision. 🛜 ♿ 📵 📺 🏊

△△△ ▼▼▼ Magnuson Hotel Marina Cove M ❀

(727) 867-1151. **$80-$180.** 6800 Sunshine Skyway Ln S 33711. I-275 exit 16, just e on Pinellas Point Dr S, then just s. Ext/int corridors. **Pets:** Medium. $20 daily fee/pet. Designated rooms, service with restrictions, crate. ⟨SAVE⟩ 🛜 ♿ 📵 📺 🍴 🏊

▼▼▼ Mansion House B & B BB

(727) 821-9391. **Call for rates.** 105 5th Ave NE 33701. 0.5 mi n at 1st St N. Ext/int corridors. **Pets:** Accepted. 🛜 📵 📺

TREASURE ISLAND

△△△ ▼▼▼ Residence Inn St. Petersburg/Treasure Island H ❀

(727) 367-2761. **$159-$399, 3 day notice.** 11908 Gulf Blvd 33706. On SR 699, 0.7 mi n of jct Treasure Island Cswy. Ext/int corridors. **Pets:** Medium. $100 one-time fee/room. Designated rooms, service with restrictions, supervision. ⟨SAVE⟩ 🛜 ✕ ♿ 📵 📺 🏊

△△△ ▼ Tahitian Resort M

(727) 360-6264. **$65-$169, 7 day notice.** 11320 Gulf Blvd 33706. On SR 699, 0.4 mi n of jct 107th Ave (Central Ave). Ext corridors. **Pets:** Other species. Designated rooms, service with restrictions.

⟨SAVE⟩ 📵 📺 🏊

END AREA

SARASOTA

▼▼ ▼▼ Comfort Inn, Sarasota I-75 H ❀

(941) 921-7750. **$70-$130.** 5778 Clark Rd 34233. I-75 exit 205, just w on SR 72 (Clark Rd). Int corridors. **Pets:** Medium. $10 daily fee/room. Designated rooms, service with restrictions, supervision.

⟨ECO⟩ 🛜 ♿ 📵 📺 🏊

▼▼▼ Hampton Inn & Suites Sarasota Bradenton Airport H

(941) 355-8140. **$109-$159.** 975 University Pkwy 34243. Just e of jct US 41 (N Tamiami Tr). Int corridors. **Pets:** Accepted.

🛜 ♿ 📵 📺 🏊

Country Inn & Suites By Carlson, Sarasota I-75 H

(941) 925-0631. **$89-$269.** 5730 Gantt Rd 34233. I-75 exit 205, 0.3 mi w on SR 72 (Clark Rd), then just n on Hospitality Way. Int corridors. **Pets:** Accepted.

Holiday Inn Sarasota Bradenton Airport H ✿

(941) 355-9000. **$99-$199.** 8009 Fifteenth St E 34243. 1.2 mi nw on W University Pkwy from jct University Pkwy. Int corridors. **Pets:** Medium. $150 one-time fee/pet. Designated rooms, service with restrictions, supervision.

Homewood Suites by Hilton H

(941) 365-7300. **$99-$179.** 3470 Fruitville Rd 34237. I-75 exit 210, 3.2 mi w on SR 780 (Fruitville Rd). Int corridors. **Pets:** Accepted.

Hotel Indigo H

(941) 487-3800. **$134-$254.** 1223 Boulevard of the Arts 34236. Jct US 41 (N Tamiami Tr). Int corridors. **Pets:** Accepted.

Hyatt Regency Sarasota H ✿

(941) 953-1234. **$99-$369, 3 day notice.** 1000 Boulevard of the Arts 34236. Just w of jct US 41 (Tamiami Tr). Int corridors. **Pets:** Medium. $40 one-time fee/pet. Designated rooms, service with restrictions, crate.

La Quinta Inn & Suites Sarasota H

(941) 366-5128. **$89-$189.** 1803 N Tamiami Tr 34234. On US 41, 1 mi n of jct SR 780 (Fruitville Rd). Int corridors. **Pets:** Medium, other species. Service with restrictions, supervision.

Residence Inn by Marriott Sarasota-Bradenton H ✿

(941) 358-1468. **$98-$189.** 1040 University Pkwy 34234. Just e of jct US 41 (Tamiami Tr). Int corridors. **Pets:** Other species. $75 one-time fee/room. Service with restrictions.

The Ritz-Carlton, Sarasota H

(941) 309-2000. **Call for rates.** 1111 Ritz-Carlton Dr 34236. On US 41, jct John Ringling Blvd. Int corridors. **Pets:** Accepted.

SEBRING

Inn On The Lakes H ✿

(863) 471-9400. **$69-$219.** 3101 Golfview Rd 33875. On US 27, 4.9 mi n of jct SR 98. Ext/int corridors. **Pets:** Large, other species. $40 one-time fee/room. Designated rooms, service with restrictions.

La Quinta Inn & Suites-Sebring H

(863) 386-1000. **$71-$175.** 4115 US Hwy 27 S 33870. On US 27, just n of Sebring Pkwy. Int corridors. **Pets:** Medium, other species. Service with restrictions, supervision.

Residence Inn Sebring H ✿

(863) 314-9100. **$97-$127.** 3221 Tubbs Rd 33875. On US 27, 4.5 mi n of jct SR 98; south side of Lake Jackson. Int corridors. **Pets:** Medium. $10 daily fee/pet. Designated rooms, service with restrictions, crate.

SIESTA KEY

Tropical Breeze Resort CO ✿

(941) 349-1125. **$99-$329.** 140 Columbus Ave 34242. Jct Ocean Blvd; in Siesta Village. Ext corridors. **Pets:** Other species. $10 daily fee/pet. Service with restrictions.

SILVER SPRINGS

Holiday Inn Express Hotel & Suites H

(352) 304-6111. **$70-$160.** 5360 E Silver Springs Blvd 34488. On SR 40, just e of jct NE 25th St. Int corridors. **Pets:** Medium. $15 daily fee/pet. Supervision.

SPRING HILL

Quality Inn Weeki Wachee M

(352) 596-2007. **$65-$149.** 6172 Commercial Way 34606. On US 19, jct SR 50 (Cortez Blvd). Ext corridors. **Pets:** Other species. $15 daily fee/pet. Service with restrictions, supervision.

STARKE

Best Western Starke H

(904) 964-6744. **$68-$125.** 1290 N Temple Ave 32091. 1 mi n on US 301 from jct SR 100 (Reid St). Ext corridors. **Pets:** Medium. $10 daily fee/pet. Service with restrictions, supervision.

Econo Lodge H

(904) 964-7357. **Call for rates.** 880 N Temple Ave 32091. 0.7 mi n on US 301 from jct SR 100. Ext corridors. **Pets:** Accepted.

STUART

Best Western Plus Downtown Stuart M ✿

(772) 287-6200. **$80-$130.** 1209 S Federal Hwy 34994. US 1, 0.5 mi s of jct SR 76. Ext corridors. **Pets:** Medium. $15 daily fee/room. Designated rooms, service with restrictions, supervision.

Courtyard by Marriott Stuart H

(772) 781-3344. **$111-$269.** 7615 SW Lost River Rd 34997. I-95 exit 101 (SR 76), 0.7 mi e to SW Lost River Rd, then just nw. Int corridors. **Pets:** Medium, other species. $50 one-time fee/pet. Service with restrictions, supervision.

Hampton Inn & Suites Stuart-North H

(772) 692-6922. **$119-$169.** 1150 NW Federal Hwy 34994. On US 1 (Federal Hwy), 2.1 mi nw of SR 76 (SW Kanner Hwy). Int corridors. **Pets:** Small, dogs only. Designated rooms, service with restrictions, supervision.

Monterey Inn & Marina M ✿

(772) 283-3500. **$65-$129.** 300 SW Monterey Rd 34994. Jct SR 76 (S Kanner Hwy) and CR 714 (SW Monterey Rd), just w; base of east side of Palm City Bridge. Ext corridors. **Pets:** Other species. $20 one-time fee/pet. Designated rooms, no service.

Pirate's Cove Resort & Marina H

(772) 287-2500. **Call for rates.** 4307 SE Bayview St 34997. From US 1, 0.4 mi ne on SE Indian St to SE Dixie Hwy, 2 mi se to SE Bayview St, then 0.3 mi e. Ext corridors. **Pets:** Other species. $20 daily fee/pet. Designated rooms, service with restrictions, supervision.

TALLAHASSEE

Aloft Tallahassee Downtown H ✿

(850) 513-0313. **$109-$249.** 200 N Monroe St 32301. 0.4 mi n of Capitol. Int corridors. **Pets:** Medium.

Best Western Pride Inn & Suites H

(850) 656-6312. **$65-$219, 7 day notice.** 2016 Apalachee Pkwy 32301. 1 mi se of US 27. Ext corridors. **Pets:** Other species. $10 daily fee/pet. No service, supervision.

Best Western Seminole Inn M

(850) 656-2938. **$60-$70.** 6737 Mahan Dr 32308. I-10 exit 209A, just w on US 90. Ext corridors. **Pets:** Medium. $10 daily fee/pet. Service with restrictions, supervision.

Cabot Lodge-Thomasville Rd 🏨 ❀

(850) 386-7500. **$89-$299, 7 day notice.** 1653 Raymond Diehl Rd 32308. I-10 exit 203, 0.4 mi se. Int corridors. **Pets:** Medium, other species. $75 one-time fee/room. Designated rooms, service with restrictions.

Econo Lodge 🅼

(850) 385-6155. **$41-$129.** 2681 N Monroe St 32303. I-10 exit 199, 0.5 mi s. Ext corridors. **Pets:** Large, other species. $15 one-time fee/room. Service with restrictions, supervision.

Four Points by Sheraton Tallahassee North 🏨

(850) 671-2020. **$85-$225, 3 day notice.** 1978 Village Green Way 32308. I-10 exit 203, southeast corner. Int corridors. **Pets:** Accepted.

Holiday Inn Capital Center 🏨

(850) 877-3171. **$89-$269.** 1355 Apalachee Pkwy 32301. 1.3 mi se on US 27. Int corridors. **Pets:** Accepted.

Homewood Suites by Hilton 🏨

(850) 402-9400. **$119-$249.** 2987 Apalachee Pkwy 32301. US 27, 3.5 mi s. Int corridors. **Pets:** Accepted.

La Quinta Inn Tallahassee (North) 🏨

(850) 385-7172. **$54-$119.** 2905 N Monroe St 32303. I-10 exit 199, just s on US 27. Ext corridors. **Pets:** Medium, other species. Service with restrictions, supervision.

La Quinta Inn Tallahassee (South) 🏨

(850) 878-5099. **$62-$122.** 2850 Apalachee Pkwy 32301. 3 mi se on US 27. Ext corridors. **Pets:** Medium, other species. Service with restrictions, supervision.

Motel 6 #420 🅼

(850) 668-2600. **$33-$45.** 1481 Timberlane Rd 32308. I-10 exit 203, just n, then w. Ext corridors. **Pets:** Other species. Service with restrictions, supervision.

Quality Inn & Suites 🏨 ❀

(850) 877-4437. **$60-$175.** 2020 Apalachee Pkwy 32301. 2.2 mi s on US 27. Int corridors. **Pets:** Medium, other species. $50 one-time fee/room. Designated rooms, service with restrictions, supervision.

Residence Inn by Marriott Tallahassee Universities at the Capitol 🏨

(850) 329-9080. **$149-$219.** 600 W Gaines St 32304. 0.5 mi w of S Monroe St; downtown. Int corridors. **Pets:** Medium, other species. $100 one-time fee/room.

Residence Inn Tallahassee North I-10 Capital Circle 🏨

(850) 422-0093. **$98-$323.** 1880 Raymond Diehl Rd 32308. I-10 exit 203, just s. Int corridors. **Pets:** Accepted.

Staybridge Suites Tallahassee 🏨

(850) 219-7000. **Call for rates.** 1600 Summit Lake Dr 32317. I-10 exit 209B, just n. Int corridors. **Pets:** Accepted.

StudioPLUS-Tallahassee-Killearn 🏨 ❀

(850) 383-1700. **$60-$190.** 1950 Raymond Diehl Rd 32308. I-10 exit 203, 2.4 mi s, then just n. Int corridors. **Pets:** Other species. $25 daily fee/pet. Service with restrictions.

Super 8 🏨

(850) 386-8286. **$40-$150.** 2801 N Monroe St 32303. I-10 exit 199, just s. Ext corridors. **Pets:** Accepted.

TownePlace Suites Tallahassee North/Capital Circle 🏨

(850) 219-0122. **$80-$288.** 1876 Capital Cir NE 32308. 3.3 mi e on US 90, 1 mi n on US 319. Int corridors. **Pets:** Accepted.

TAMPA METROPOLITAN AREA

BRANDON

Homestead Studio Suites Hotel-Tampa/Brandon 🅼 ❀

(813) 643-5900. **$60-$130.** 330 Grand Regency Blvd 33510. I-75 exit 257, just e on SR 60, then 0.4 mi n; in Regency Corporate Park. Ext corridors. **Pets:** Other species. $25 daily fee/pet. Service with restrictions.

La Quinta Inn & Suites Tampa Brandon Regency Park 🏨

(813) 643-0574. **$82-$154.** 310 Grand Regency Blvd 33510. I-75 exit 257, just e on SR 60, then 0.5 mi n; in Regency Corporate Office Park. Int corridors. **Pets:** Medium, other species. Service with restrictions, supervision.

LUTZ

Residence Inn Tampa Suncoast Parkway at NorthPointe Village 🏨 ❀

(813) 792-8400. **$122-$170.** 2101 NorthPointe Pkwy 33558. Suncoast Pkwy exit 19, just w on SR 54, then just ne; in NorthPointe at Suncoast Crossings. Int corridors. **Pets:** $100 one-time fee/room. Service with restrictions, crate.

PLANT CITY

Comfort Inn of Plant City 🏨

(813) 707-6000. **$69-$159.** 2003 S Frontage Rd 33566. I-4 exit 22, just s on Park Rd. Int corridors. **Pets:** Accepted.

Red Rose Inn & Suites 🅼

(813) 752-3141. **Call for rates.** 2011 N Wheeler St 33563. I-4 exit 21, 0.4 mi se on SR 39. Ext corridors. **Pets:** Medium, other species. Designated rooms, service with restrictions, crate.

RUSKIN

Southern Comfort Bed & Breakfast 🅱🅱 ❀

(813) 645-6361. **Call for rates.** 2409 Ravine Dr W 33570. Jct US 41, 1.1 mi sw on 1st St, just w on 24th Ave SW, then just s. Ext/int corridors. **Pets:** Medium. $10 daily fee/room. Designated rooms, service with restrictions.

SEFFNER

Country Inn & Suites By Carlson, Tampa East 🏨

(813) 675-8600. **$79-$199.** 11551 Discovery Ln 33584. I-4 exit 10, just n on CR 579. Int corridors. **Pets:** Medium, other species. $25 daily fee/pet. Designated rooms, service with restrictions, crate.

TAMPA

Baymont Inn & Suites Tampa Conference Center 🅼

(813) 622-8557. **$64-$99.** 10007 Princess Palm Ave 33619. I-75 exit 260 southbound; exit 260B northbound, 0.5 mi w on SR 574 (Dr. Martin Luther King Jr Blvd), just s on Falkenburg Rd, then just w; in Sabal Corporate Park. Int corridors. **Pets:** Other species. $20 daily fee/pet. No service.

Best Western Brandon Hotel & Conference Center M

(813) 621-5555. **$59-$99.** 9331 Adamo Dr 33619. I-75 exit 257, 1.2 mi w on SR 60 (Adamo Dr). Ext corridors. **Pets:** $35 one-time fee/room. Service with restrictions, crate.

Extended Stay Deluxe Tampa - Airport H

(813) 886-5253. **$70-$300.** 4811 Memorial Hwy 33634. Veteran's Expwy exit 3, just sw on CR 576. Int corridors. **Pets:** Other species. $25 daily fee/pet. Service with restrictions.

Extended Stay Deluxe-Tampa-Airport-N West Shore Blvd H

(813) 637-8990. **$70-$300.** 1805 N Westshore Blvd 33607. I-275 exit 40A southbound, 0.5 mi nw; exit 39A northbound, 1 mi e on Kennedy Blvd, then 1.3 mi nw. Int corridors. **Pets:** Other species. $25 daily fee/pet. Service with restrictions.

Grand Hyatt Tampa Bay H

(813) 874-1234. **$99-$399.** 2900 Bayport Dr 33607. On SR 60 (Kennedy Blvd), east end of Courtney Campbell Cswy. Ext/int corridors.
Pets: Accepted.

Hampton Inn-Tampa Veterans Expressway H

(813) 901-5900. **$79-$149.** 5628 W Waters Ave 33634. SR 589 (Veteran's Expwy) exit 6A, just e on CR 584. Int corridors. **Pets:** Accepted.

Holiday Inn Express Hotel & Suites H

(813) 910-7171. **$89-$139, 3 day notice.** 8310 Galbraith Rd 33647. I-75 exit 270, 0.3 mi n on CR 581 (Bruce B Downs Blvd), just w on Highwoods Preserve Pkwy, then just n; in Highwoods Preserve. Int corridors. **Pets:** Medium, other species. $50 one-time fee/room. Designated rooms, service with restrictions, supervision.

Homewood Suites by Hilton Tampa Airport/Westshore H

(813) 282-1950. **$109-$209.** 5325 Avion Park Dr 33607. I-275 exit 40A southbound, 0.7 mi n on Westshore Blvd; exit 39A northbound, 1 mi e on Kennedy Blvd (SR 60), 1.2 mi n on Westshore Blvd, just w on Spruce St, then just s on O'Brien St; in Avion Park Westshore. Int corridors. **Pets:** Medium. $100 one-time fee/pet. Service with restrictions, supervision.

Homewood Suites by Hilton Tampa/Brandon H

(813) 685-7099. **$99-$159.** 10240 Palm River Rd 33619. I-75 exit 257, 0.4 mi w on SR 60 (Adamo Dr), just s on S Falkenburg Rd, then 0.3 mi e. Int corridors. **Pets:** Medium. $100 one-time fee/room.

La Quinta Inn & Suites Tampa East Fairgrounds H

(813) 626-0885. **$64-$125.** 4811 US 301 N 33610. I-4 exit 7 westbound; exit 7A eastbound, just se. Int corridors. **Pets:** Medium, other species. Service with restrictions, supervision.

La Quinta Inn & Suites Tampa Brandon West H

(813) 684-4007. **$62-$135.** 602 S Falkenburg Rd 33619. I-75 exit 257, just w on SR 60 (Adamo Dr), then just n. Int corridors. **Pets:** Medium, other species. Service with restrictions, supervision.

La Quinta Inn & Suites Tampa Central H

(813) 490-9090. **$107-$169.** 3826 W Waters Ave 33614. Just w of jct US 92 (Dale Mabry Hwy). Int corridors. **Pets:** Medium, other species. Service with restrictions, supervision.

La Quinta Inn & Suites USF (near Busch Gardens) H

(813) 910-7500. **$93-$164.** 3701 E Fowler Ave 33612. I-275 exit 51, 2.2 mi e on SR 582 (Fowler Ave). Int corridors. **Pets:** Medium, other species. Service with restrictions, supervision.

La Quinta Inn Tampa South H

(813) 835-6262. **$80-$150.** 4620 W Gandy Blvd 33611. Just ne of jct S Westshore Blvd. Int corridors. **Pets:** Medium, other species. Service with restrictions, supervision.

Mainsail Suites Hotel & Conference Center H

(813) 243-2600. **Call for rates.** 5108 Eisenhower Blvd 33634. SR 589 (Veteran's Expwy) exit 4, just w on SR 580; main entrance on Hillsborough Ave. Ext corridors. **Pets:** Accepted.

Quality Inn & Suites- Tampa M

(813) 623-6000. **$50-$229.** 4955 E 18th Ave 33605. I-4 exit 3, just n on US 41 (50th St), just w on W Melbourne Blvd, then just s on N 49th St. Int corridors. **Pets:** Accepted.

Red Roof Inn-Brandon H

(813) 681-8484. **$40-$100.** 10121 Horace Ave 33619. I-75 exit 257, just w on SR 60 (Adamo Dr), just n on Falkenburg Rd, then just e. Ext corridors. **Pets:** Large, other species. No service, supervision.

Red Roof Inn-Fairgrounds M

(813) 623-5245. **$40-$129.** 5001 N US 301 33610. I-4 exit 7 westbound; exit 7A eastbound, just se. Ext corridors. **Pets:** Large, other species. No service, supervision.

Residence Inn by Marriott Tampa Downtown H

(813) 221-4224. **$109-$119.** 101 E Tyler St 33602. I-275 exit 44, 0.5 mi se on W Ashley Dr/Tampa St; exit 45A southbound, 1.5 mi se on W Ashley Dr. Int corridors. **Pets:** Accepted.

Residence Inn by Marriott Tampa Westshore/Airport H

(813) 877-7988. **$93-$199.** 4312 W Boy Scout Blvd 33607. I-275 exit 40B, 0.8 mi n on Lois Ave. Int corridors. **Pets:** Accepted.

Residence Inn Tampa Sabal Park/Brandon H

(813) 627-8855. **$85-$171.** 9719 Princess Palm Ave 33619. I-75 exit 260 southbound; exit 260B northbound, just w on SR 574 (Dr. Martin Luther King Jr Blvd), just s on Falkenburg Rd, then 0.4 mi w; in Sabal Corporate Center. Int corridors. **Pets:** Accepted.

Seminole Hard Rock Hotel & Casino Tampa H

(813) 627-7625. **$189-$449.** 5223 N Orient Rd 33610. I-4 exit 6, just w. Int corridors. **Pets:** Accepted.

Sheraton Suites Tampa Airport Westshore H

(813) 873-8675. **$99-$405.** 4400 W Cypress St 33607. I-275 exit 40A southbound, just nw on CR 587; exit 39A northbound, just nw on Westshore Blvd (CR 587), then just e. Int corridors. **Pets:** Medium, dogs only. Service with restrictions, supervision.

Sheraton Tampa Riverwalk H

(813) 223-2222. **$99-$339.** 200 N Ashley Dr 33602. I-275 exit 44, 0.8 mi s. Int corridors. **Pets:** Accepted.

Staybridge Suites Tampa-Sabal Park H

(813) 227-4000. **$99-$269.** 3624 N Falkenburg Rd 33619. I-75 exit 260 southbound; exit 260B northbound, just w on SR 574 (Dr. Martin Luther King Jr Blvd), then just s. Int corridors. **Pets:** Accepted.

▼▼▼▼ TownePlace Suites by Marriott Tampa
Westshore/Airport H

(813) 282-1081. **$85-$169.** 5302 Avion Park Dr 33607. I-275 exit 40A southbound, 0.7 mi n on Westshore Blvd; exit 39A northbound, 1 mi e on Kennedy Blvd (SR 60), 1.2 mi n on Westshore Blvd, just w on Spruce St, then just s on O'Brien St; in Avion Park Westshore. Int corridors. **Pets:** Medium, other species. $100 one-time fee/room. Service with restrictions. ECO 📶 ✕ ⚙M 🛏 💻 ⚓

₳₳₳ ▼▼▼▼ The Westin Tampa Bay H

(813) 281-0000. **$109-$469.** 7627 Courtney Campbell Cswy 33607. On SR 60, at east end of Courtney Campbell Cswy. Int corridors.
Pets: Accepted. SAVE 📶 ✕ ⚙M 🛏 💻 🍽 ⚓ ✕

₳₳₳ ▼▼▼▼ The Westin Tampa Harbour Island H

(813) 229-5000. **$109-$439, 3 day notice.** 725 S Harbour Island Blvd 33602. I-275 exit 44, 2.4 mi e on W Ashley Dr/Tampa St, on Harbour Island; exit 45A southbound, 3.9 mi e. Int corridors. **Pets:** Accepted.
ECO SAVE 📶 ✕ ⚙M 🛏 💻 🍽 ⚓ ✕

₳₳₳ ▼▼▼▼ Wyndham Tampa Westshore H ☙

(813) 289-8200. **$99-$239.** 700 N Westshore Blvd 33609. I-275 exit 40A southbound, just nw on CR 587; exit 39A northbound, 1 mi n on Kennedy Blvd, then 0.9 mi nw on CR 587, jct W Cypress St. Int corridors. **Pets:** Medium. $25 one-time fee/room. Designated rooms, service with restrictions. SAVE 📶 ⚙M 🛏 💻 🍽 ⚓ ✕

TEMPLE TERRACE

▼▼ ▼▼ Extended Stay America-Tampa North-USF
Attractions H ☙

(813) 989-2264. **$60-$130.** 12242 Morris Bridge Rd 33637. I-75 exit 266, just w on Fletcher Ave (CR 582A). Int corridors. **Pets:** Other species. $25 daily fee/pet. Service with restrictions. 📶 ⚙M 🛏 💻

▼▼▼▼ Holiday Inn Express Tampa North/Telecom
Park H ☙

(813) 972-9800. **$75-$125.** 13294 Telecom Dr 33637. I-75 exit 266, 1.4 mi w on Fletcher Ave (CR 582A), just s; in Rivers Edge at Telecom Park. Int corridors. **Pets:** Medium. $15 daily fee/room. Designated rooms, service with restrictions, supervision. ECO 📶 ✕ ⚙M 🛏 💻 ⚓

▼▼▼▼ Residence Inn Tampa North I-75 Fletcher H

(813) 972-4400. **$80-$180.** 13420 N Telecom Pkwy 33637. I-75 exit 266, 1.1 mi w on Fletcher Ave (CR 582A), just s; in Telecom Tampa Park. Int corridors. **Pets:** Accepted. 📶 ✕ ⚙M 🛏 💻 ⚓ ✕

▼▼▼▼ TownePlace Suites Tampa North/I-75 Fletcher H

(813) 975-9777. **$62-$149.** 6800 Woodstork Rd 33637. I-75 exit 266, 1.1 mi w on Fletcher Ave (CR 582A), then just s on N Telecom Dr; in Telecom Tampa Park. Int corridors. **Pets:** Accepted.
📶 ✕ 🛏 💻 ⚓

WESLEY CHAPEL

₳₳₳ ▼▼▼ Holiday Inn Express H

(813) 907-1379. **$65-$85.** 27615 SR 54 W 33543. I-75 exit 279, just w. Int corridors. **Pets:** Medium. $25 one-time fee/room. Designated rooms, service with restrictions, supervision. SAVE ⚙M 🛏 💻 ⚓

ZEPHYRHILLS

▼▼ ▼▼ Microtel Inn & Suites H

(813) 783-2211. **$54-$63.** 7839 Gall Blvd 33541. On US 301; 0.9 mi n of jct Daugherty Rd. Int corridors. **Pets:** Small, dogs only. $25 one-time fee/room. Service with restrictions, crate. 📶 ⚙M 🛏 💻 ⚓

END METROPOLITAN AREA

TITUSVILLE

₳₳₳ ▼▼ ▼▼ Best Western Space Shuttle Inn Kennedy
Space Center H

(321) 269-9100. **$60-$310.** 3455 Cheney Hwy 32780. I-95 exit 215 (SR 50), just e. Ext corridors. **Pets:** Other species. $10 daily fee/room. Designated rooms, service with restrictions, crate.
SAVE 📶 🛏 💻 🍽 ⚓

₳₳₳ ▼▼ ▼▼ Days Inn Titusville Kennedy Space
Center M

(321) 269-4480. **$53-$170.** 3755 Cheney Hwy 32780. I-95 exit 215 (SR 50), just w. Ext corridors. **Pets:** Accepted.
SAVE 📶 🛏 💻 🍽 ⚓

₳₳₳ ▼▼ ▼▼ Fairfield Inn & Suites Titusville Kennedy
Space Center H ☙

(321) 385-1818. **$89-$171.** 4735 Helen Hauser Blvd 32780. I-95 exit 215 (SR 50), just w. Int corridors. **Pets:** Small, dogs only. $50 one-time fee/ room. Designated rooms, service with restrictions, supervision.
SAVE 📶 ✕ ⚙M 🛏 💻 ⚓

▼▼ ▼▼ Holiday Inn, Titusville, Kennedy Space Center H

(321) 383-0200. **$119-$139.** 4715 Helen Hauser Blvd 32780. I-95 exit 215 (SR 50), just w to Helen Hauser Blvd, then just n. Int corridors.
Pets: Large. $25 daily fee/room. Service with restrictions, supervision.
📶 ⚙M 🛏 💻 🍽 ⚓

VENICE

▼▼▼▼ Holiday Inn Express Hotel & Suites H ☙

(941) 584-6800. **$99-$159.** 380 Commercial Ct 34292. I-75 exit 193, just w on Jacaranda Blvd (CR 765), then just n. Int corridors. **Pets:** $30 one-time fee/room. Service with restrictions, crate. 📶 ⚙M 🛏 💻 ⚓

▼▼▼▼ Horse and Chaise Inn A Bed & Breakfast BB

(941) 488-2702. **$115-$189, 14 day notice.** 317 Ponce de Leon 34285. Just s of jct Venice Ave on Nassau St, just sw; downtown. Ext/int corridors. **Pets:** Medium. Designated rooms. 📶 🛏 ✕

VERO BEACH

₳₳₳ ▼▼▼▼ The Caribbean Court Boutique
Hotel H ☙

(772) 231-7211. **$99-$299.** 1601 S Ocean Dr 32963. US 1, 4.3 mi n on Indian River Blvd (CR 603), 1.3 mi w on 17th St (SR 656) to Ocean Dr, then just s; jct Ocean Dr and Jasmine Ln. Ext corridors. **Pets:** Other species. Designated rooms, service with restrictions.
SAVE 📶 🛏 💻 🍽 ⚓

▼▼▼▼ Country Inn & Suites By Carlson, Vero Beach
I-95 H

(772) 257-0252. **$69-$199.** 9330 19th Ln 32966. I-95 exit 147 (20th St/SR 60), just w. Int corridors. **Pets:** Small, other species. $25 one-time fee/room. Service with restrictions, crate. 📶 🛏 💻 ⚓

▼▼ ▼▼ Holiday Inn Hotel & Suites - Oceanside H

(772) 231-2300. **$139-$299.** 3384 Ocean Dr 32963. E of SR A1A; at end of SR 60. Ext corridors. **Pets:** Accepted.
ECO 📶 ✕ 🛏 💻 🍽 ⚓

₳₳₳ ▼▼▼▼ Vero Beach Hotel & Spa H ☙

(772) 231-5666. **Call for rates.** 3500 Ocean Dr 32963. On Ocean Dr, just n of SR 60. Ext/int corridors. **Pets:** Other species. Service with restrictions. ECO SAVE 📶 ✕ ⚙M 🛏 🍽 ⚓ ✕

WEEKI WACHEE

₳₳₳ ▼▼▼▼ Best Western Nature Coast M

(352) 596-9000. **$60-$90.** 9373 Cortez Blvd 34613. On SR 50, just e of jct US 19. Ext corridors. **Pets:** Accepted. SAVE 📶 🛏 💻 ⚓

WEST MELBOURNE

Fairfield Inn & Suites by Marriott - Melbourne H

(321) 722-2220. **$75-$227.** 4355 W New Haven Ave 32904. I-95 exit 180 (US 192/New Haven Ave), just e. Int corridors. **Pets:** Accepted.

WEST PALM BEACH

Best Western Palm Beach Lakes Inn H

(561) 683-8810. **$79-$129.** 1800 Palm Beach Lakes Blvd 33401. I-95 exit 71 (Palm Beach Lakes Blvd), just e. Ext/int corridors. **Pets:** Medium. $100 deposit/pet, $15 daily fee/pet. Designated rooms, service with restrictions, supervision.

Comfort Inn & Conference Center H

(561) 689-6100. **$89-$119.** 1901 Palm Beach Lakes Blvd 33409. I-95 exit 71 (Palm Beach Lakes Blvd), just w. Int corridors. **Pets:** Medium. $10 daily fee/room. Designated rooms, service with restrictions, crate.

Extended Stay Deluxe - West Palm Beach - Northpoint Corporate Park H

(561) 683-5332. **$60-$140.** 700 Northpoint Pkwy 33407. I-95 exit 74 (45th St), just w to Northpoint Pkwy, then n. Int corridors. **Pets:** Other species. $25 daily fee/pet. Service with restrictions.

La Quinta Inn & Suites - West Palm Beach CityPlace M

(561) 697-3388. **$73-$159.** 5981 Okeechobee Blvd 33417. I-95 exit 70B (Okeechobee Blvd), 3.6 mi w; Florida Tpke exit 99 (Okeechobee Blvd), just e. Ext corridors. **Pets:** Medium, other species. Service with restrictions, supervision.

Red Roof Inn - West Palm Beach H

(561) 697-7710. **$45-$129.** 2421 Metrocentre Blvd E 33407. I-95 exit 74 (45th St), just w to Metrocentre Blvd; in Metrocentre Corporate Park. Ext/int corridors. **Pets:** Large, other species. No service, supervision.

Residence Inn by Marriott - West Palm Beach H

(561) 687-4747. **$89-$189.** 2461 Metrocentre Blvd E 33407. I-95 exit 74 (45th St), just w to Metrocentre Blvd; in Metrocentre Corporate Park. Int corridors. **Pets:** Accepted.

Stay Inn West Palm Beach Airport Hotel M

(561) 471-8700. **$80-$180.** 1505 Belvedere Rd 33406. I-95 exit 69 (Belvedere Rd), just w. Ext corridors. **Pets:** Medium. $20 daily fee/pet. Service with restrictions, crate.

WILDWOOD

Sleep Inn & Suites H

(352) 748-0507. **$69-$199.** 1224 S Main St 34785. Florida Tpke exit 304, just e. Int corridors. **Pets:** Accepted.

GEORGIA

CITY INDEX

ADAIRSVILLE

Quality Inn M

(770) 773-2886. **$65-$100.** 107 Princeton Blvd 30103. I-75 exit 306, just w. Ext corridors. **Pets:** Medium. $15 daily fee/pet. Service with restrictions, supervision.

Ramada Limited M

(770) 769-9726. **$53-$100.** 500 Georgia North Cir 30103. I-75 exit 306, 0.3 mi w. Ext corridors. **Pets:** Accepted.

ADEL

Days Inn H

(229) 896-4574. **$25-$74.** 1204 W 4th St 31620. I-75 exit 39, just w. Ext corridors. **Pets:** Medium, other species. $10 daily fee/pet. Service with restrictions, supervision.

Hampton Inn H

(229) 896-3099. **Call for rates.** 1500 W 4th St 31620. I-75 exit 39, just w. Int corridors. **Pets:** Other species. Designated rooms, service with restrictions, supervision.

ALBANY

Best Western Albany Mall Inn & Suites H

(229) 446-2001. **$90-$120.** 2729 Pointe North Blvd 31721. Just se of jct Dawson Rd and US 82 W. Int corridors. **Pets:** Accepted.

Jameson Inn H

(229) 435-3737. **$75-$95.** 2720 Dawson Rd 31707. 0.5 mi se of jct US 82 and SR 520. Ext corridors. **Pets:** Medium. $15 daily fee/room. Service with restrictions, supervision.

▼▼ ▼▼ **Merry Acres Inn** Ⓜ

(229) 435-7721. **Call for rates.** 1500 Dawson Rd 31707. 3.3 mi w. Ext corridors. **Pets:** Accepted. 🛜 📶 💻 🏊

▼▼▼▼ **Wingate by Wyndham** Ⓗ

(229) 883-9800. **$86-$116.** 2735 Dawson Rd 31707. Jct US 82 and SR 520, 0.4 mi se. Int corridors. **Pets:** Accepted. 🛜 ☾M 📶 💻 🏊

ALMA

▼▼ ▼▼ **Days Inn** Ⓜ

(912) 632-7000. **$49-$64.** 930 S Pierce St 31510. Jct SR 32/US 1, 0.4 mi s on US 1. Ext corridors. **Pets:** Accepted. 🛜 📶 💻 🏊

AMERICUS

▼▼ ▼▼ **1906 Pathway Inn Bed & Breakfast** ⒷⒷ

(229) 928-2078. **$99-$145, 3 day notice.** 501 S Lee St 31709. 0.5 mi s of US 280 on SR 377. Int corridors. **Pets:** Accepted. 🛜 ☒

▼▼ ▼▼ **Quality Inn** Ⓗ

(229) 924-4431. **$68-$90.** 1205 Martin Luther King Jr Blvd 31709. On US 19 S, 1 mi w of downtown. Ext corridors. **Pets:** Small. $10 daily fee/pet. Designated rooms, service with restrictions, crate.
🛜 📶 💻 🍽 🏊

ASHBURN

ⒶⒶⒶ ▼▼ ▼▼ **Best Western Ashburn Inn** Ⓗ

(229) 567-0080. **$59-$68.** 820 Shoney's Dr 31714. I-75 exit 82, just w. Ext corridors. **Pets:** Medium, dogs only. $10 daily fee/pet. Designated rooms, service with restrictions, supervision. 🅂🄰🅅🄴 🛜 📶 💻 🏊

ⒶⒶⒶ ▼▼ ▼▼ **Days Inn** Ⓗ

(229) 567-3346. **$35-$54.** 823 E Washington Ave 31714. I-75 exit 82, just w on SR 112. Ext corridors. **Pets:** Medium. $10 daily fee/pet. Designated rooms, service with restrictions, supervision.
🅂🄰🅅🄴 🛜 📶 💻 🏊

▼▼ ▼▼ **Super 8** Ⓗ

(229) 567-4688. **$40-$42.** 749 E Washington Ave 31714. I-75 exit 82, just w. Ext corridors. **Pets:** Medium, other species. $5 daily fee/pet. Service with restrictions, crate. 🛜 📶 💻

ATHENS

ⒶⒶⒶ ▼▼ ▼▼ **Best Western Athens** Ⓜ

(706) 546-7311. **$65-$300, 14 day notice.** 170 N Milledge Ave 30601. Jct US 78 business route (Broad St), 0.5 mi w on SR 15. Ext corridors. **Pets:** Small. $10 daily fee/pet. Designated rooms, service with restrictions, crate. 🅂🄰🅅🄴 🛜 📶 💻 🏊

▼▼▼▼ **Candlewood Suites** Ⓗ 🐾

(706) 548-9663. **$69-$199.** 156 Classic Rd 30622. Jct SR 8/10 Loop and US 29/78, 1.1 mi w on US 29/78 to Classic Rd, then just s. Int corridors. **Pets:** Medium, other species. $75 one-time fee/pet. Service with restrictions, supervision. 🛜 ☾M 📶 💻 🏊

ⒶⒶⒶ ▼▼▼▼ **Comfort Suites Downtown Athens** Ⓗ

(706) 995-4000. **$77-$129.** 255 North Ave 30601. SR 10 Loop exit 11B (Dougherty St/North Ave); 1 mi n of downtown. Int corridors. **Pets:** Small. $25 daily fee/pet. Service with restrictions, supervision.
🅂🄰🅅🄴 🛜 ☒ 📶 💻 🏊

▼▼▼▼ **Foundry Park Inn & Spa** Ⓗ 🐾

(706) 549-7020. **$107-$145, 10 day notice.** 295 E Dougherty St 30601. Jct Thomas and Dougherty sts; downtown. Ext corridors. **Pets:** Small, dogs only. $25 one-time fee/pet. Designated rooms, service with restrictions. 🛜 📶 💻 🍽 🏊

▼▼▼▼ **Holiday Inn** Ⓗ

(706) 549-4433. **$99-$109.** 197 E Broad St 30603. On US 78 business route (Broad St); jct N Hull St; center. Int corridors. **Pets:** Accepted.
🛜 📶 💻 🍽 🏊

ⒶⒶⒶ ▼▼▼▼ **Hotel Indigo** Ⓗ 🐾

(706) 546-0430. **$99-$199.** 500 College Ave 30601. Just n of center. Int corridors. **Pets:** Medium. $75 one-time fee/room. Service with restrictions, crate. 🄴🄲🄾 🅂🄰🅅🄴 🛜 ☾M 📶 💻 🍽

ⒶⒶⒶ ▼▼ ▼▼ **Microtel Inn** Ⓗ

(706) 548-5676. **$45-$158.** 1050 Ultimate Dr 30605. Jct US 78 business route (Broad St) and SR 10 Loop, 1.4 mi e. Int corridors. **Pets:** Medium, dogs only. $25 one-time fee/pet. Designated rooms, service with restrictions, crate. 🅂🄰🅅🄴 🛜 ☾M 📶 💻

▼▼ ▼▼ **Sleep Inn & Suites** Ⓗ

(706) 850-1261. **$69-$230.** 109 Florence Dr 30622. Jct SR 8/10 Loop and US 29/78, 1.2 mi w on US 29/78 to Florence Rd, then just s. Int corridors. **Pets:** Accepted. 🛜 ☾M 📶 💻 🏊

ATLANTA METROPOLITAN AREA

ACWORTH

ⒶⒶⒶ ▼▼ ▼▼ **America's Best Inn** Ⓜ

(770) 974-5400. **$45-$50.** 5320 Cherokee St 30101. I-75 exit 278, just w. Ext corridors. **Pets:** $5 daily fee/pet. Designated rooms, service with restrictions, supervision. 🅂🄰🅅🄴 🛜 📶 🏊

ⒶⒶⒶ ▼▼ ▼▼ **Best Western Acworth Inn** Ⓜ

(770) 974-0116. **$70-$95.** 5155 Cowan Rd 30101. I-75 exit 277, just w. Ext corridors. **Pets:** Other species. $10 daily fee/pet. Service with restrictions, supervision. 🅂🄰🅅🄴 🛜 📶 💻 🏊

▼▼▼▼ **Econo Lodge** Ⓜ

(770) 974-1922. **$55-$75.** 4980 Cowan Rd 30101. I-75 exit 277, just w. Ext corridors. **Pets:** Accepted. 🛜 🏊

▼▼▼▼ **La Quinta Inn Acworth** Ⓗ

(770) 975-9920. **$80-$140.** 184 N Point Way 30102. I-75 exit 277, just e. Ext/int corridors. **Pets:** Medium, other species. Service with restrictions, supervision. 🛜 ☾M 📶 💻 🏊

▼▼▼▼ **Super 8** Ⓜ

(770) 966-9700. **$43-$70.** 4970 Cowan Rd 30101. I-75 exit 277, just w. Ext corridors. **Pets:** Medium. $10 daily fee/pet. Service with restrictions, supervision. 🛜 📶 💻 🏊

ALPHARETTA

▼▼▼▼ **Embassy Suites Hotel Alpharetta** Ⓗ

(678) 566-8800. **$99-$199.** 5955 North Point Pkwy 30022. SR 400, just e to North Point Pkwy, then just n. Int corridors. **Pets:** Small, dogs only. $25 daily fee/pet. Designated rooms, service with restrictions, supervision.
🛜 ☾M 📶 💻 🍽 🏊

▼▼▼▼ **Holiday Inn Express Alpharetta** Ⓗ

(770) 552-0006. **$59-$199.** 2950 Mansell Rd 30022. SR 400 exit 8, 0.7 mi e. Int corridors. **Pets:** Accepted. 🛜 ☾M 📶 💻 🏊

▼▼▼▼ **Homewood Suites** Ⓗ

(770) 998-1622. **$65-$139.** 10775 Davis Dr 30009. SR 400 exit 8, northwest corner. Int corridors. **Pets:** Accepted. 🛜 ☾M 📶 💻 🏊

▼▼▼▼ **La Quinta Inn & Suites Atlanta (Alpharetta)** Ⓗ

(770) 754-7800. **$48-$148.** 1350 North Point Dr 30022. SR 400 exit 9, 0.5 mi e. Int corridors. **Pets:** Medium, other species. Service with restrictions, supervision. 🛜 ☾M 📶 💻 🏊

▼▼▼▼ **Residence Inn Atlanta Alpharetta North Point Mall** Ⓗ

(770) 587-1151. **$65-$151.** 1325 North Point Dr 30022. SR 400 exit 9, just e to North Point Dr, then just s. Int corridors. **Pets:** Accepted.
🛜 ☒ ☾M 📶 💻 🏊 ☒

▼▼▼▼ Residence Inn Atlanta Alpharetta/Windward 🅷
(770) 664-0664. **$61-$156.** 5465 Windward Pkwy W 30004. SR 400 exit 11, 0.4 mi w. Ext/int corridors. **Pets:** Accepted.
📶 ✕ 🔥 🍴 💻 🏊

▼▼▼▼ Staybridge Suites 🅷
(770) 569-7200. **$74-$162.** 3980 North Point Pkwy 30005. SR 400 exit 10, 0.5 mi e. Int corridors. **Pets:** Accepted.
📶 🔥 🍴 💻 🏊 ✕

▼▼▼▼ StudioPLUS-Atlanta-Alpharetta-Northpoint 🅷 🐾
(770) 475-7871. **$53-$88.** 3331 Old Milton Pkwy 30005. SR 400 exit 10, just e. Int corridors. **Pets:** Other species. $25 daily fee/pet. Service with restrictions. 📶 🔥 🍴 💻 🏊

▼▼▼▼ TownePlace Suites Alpharetta 🅷
(770) 664-1300. **$56-$133.** 7925 Westside Pkwy 30009. SR 400 exit 9, 0.3 mi w. Int corridors. **Pets:** Accepted. 📶 ✕ 🔥 🍴 💻 🏊

▼▼▼▼ Wingate by Wyndham Alpharetta 🅷
(770) 649-0955. **$39-$62.** 1005 Kingswood Pl 30004. SR 400 exit 8, 0.7 mi w. Int corridors. **Pets:** Accepted. 📶 🔥 🍴 🍴 💻

ATLANTA

▼▼▼▼ Artmore Hotel 🅷
(404) 876-6100. **Call for rates.** 1302 W Peachtree St 30309. I-75/85 exit 250 (14th St), just e, then just n on W Peachtree St to 16th St. Int corridors. **Pets:** Accepted. 📶 ✕ 🔥 💻 🍴

AAA ▼▼▼▼ Atlanta Marriott Perimeter Center 🅷
(770) 394-6500. **$89-$199.** 246 Perimeter Center Pkwy 30346. I-285 exit 29 (Ashford-Dunwoody Rd), just n, 0.3 mi w on Hammond Dr, then just s. Int corridors. **Pets:** Accepted.
ECO SAVE 📶 ✕ 🔥 🍴 💻 🍴 🏊 ✕

AAA ◆◆◆◆ Atlanta Perimeter Hotel & Suites 🅷
(770) 396-6800. **$99-$469.** 111 Perimeter Center W 30346. I-285 E exit 29 (Ashford-Dunwoody Rd), 0.5 mi n. Int corridors. **Pets:** Accepted.
SAVE 📶 ✕ 🔥 🍴 🍴 🏊 ✕

AAA ◆◆◆◆ Best Western Plus Inn at the Peachtrees 🅷
(404) 577-6970. **$99-$209.** 330 W Peachtree St 30308. I-75/85 exit 248C northbound, 0.4 mi w to Peachtree St, then 0.3 mi n; exit 249C southbound, just s to Peachtree Pl, then just e. Ext/int corridors. **Pets:** Medium. $20 one-time fee/pet. Service with restrictions, supervision.
SAVE 📶 ✕ 🔥 🍴 💻

▼▼▼ Beverly Hills Inn 🅱🅱
(404) 233-8520. **$129-$249, 3 day notice.** 65 Sheridan Dr NE 30305. Jct Piedmont and Peachtree rds, 1.1 mi s on Peachtree Rd to Sheridan Dr, then just e. Int corridors. **Pets:** Other species. $50 one-time fee/room. Service with restrictions, supervision. 📶 🔥 💻

▼▼▼ Budgetel Inn Atlanta Northeast 🅼
(678) 808-8100. **Call for rates.** 3585 Chamblee Tucker Rd 30341. I-285 exit 34, just e. Ext corridors. **Pets:** Accepted. 📶 🔥 🏊

◆◆◆◆ Courtyard by Marriott-Atlanta Vinings 🅷
(770) 432-5555. **$76-$171.** 2857 Paces Ferry Rd 30339. I-285 exit 18, 0.6 mi e. Int corridors. **Pets:** Accepted.
📶 ✕ 🔥 🍴 💻 🍴 🏊

▼▼▼ Crowne Plaza Atlanta Perimeter Galleria 🅷
(770) 955-1700. **$69-$189.** 6345 Powers Ferry Rd NW 30339. I-285 exit 22, just s. Int corridors. **Pets:** Accepted.
📶 ✕ 🔥 🍴 🍴 💻 🍴 🏊

▼▼ Extended StayAmerica Atlanta-Clairmont 🅷 🐾
(404) 679-4333. **$65-$100.** 3115 Clairmont Rd 30329. I-85 exit 91, 0.6 mi w. Int corridors. **Pets:** Other species. $25 daily fee/pet. Service with restrictions. 📶 🔥 🍴 💻

▼▼▼ Extended StayAmerica Atlanta-Perimeter 🅷 🐾
(770) 396-5600. **$65-$100.** 905 S Crestline Pkwy 30328. I-285 exit 28 westbound, 0.7 mi n; exit 26 eastbound, 0.5 mi n to Hammond Dr, 0.5 mi e, then 0.3 mi n. Int corridors. **Pets:** Other species. $25 daily fee/pet. Service with restrictions. 📶 🔥 🍴 💻

◆◆◆ Extended Stay Deluxe Atlanta-Lenox 🅷 🐾
(404) 237-9100. **$83-$110.** 3967 Peachtree Rd 30319. I-85 exit 89, 2.8 mi w. Int corridors. **Pets:** Other species. $25 daily fee/pet. Service with restrictions. 📶 🔥 🍴 💻 🏊

◆◆◆ Extended Stay Deluxe (Atlanta/Marietta/Powers Ferry Rd) 🅷 🐾
(770) 933-8010. **$63-$98.** 2010 Powers Ferry Rd 30339. I-75 exit 260 (Windy Hill Rd), 0.5 mi e, then just s. Int corridors. **Pets:** Other species. $25 daily fee/pet. Service with restrictions. 📶 🔥 🍴 💻 🏊

▼▼▼ Extended Stay Deluxe (Atlanta/Marietta/Windy Hill/Int N Pkwy) 🅷 🐾
(770) 226-0242. **$65-$90.** 2225 Interstate North Pkwy 30339. I-75 exit 260 (Windy Hill Rd), just e to Interstate North Pkwy, then just s. Int corridors. **Pets:** Other species. $25 daily fee/pet. Service with restrictions.
📶 🔥 🍴 💻 🏊

▼▼▼ Extended Stay Deluxe Atlanta-Perimeter 🅷 🐾
(770) 379-0111. **$75-$110.** 6330 Peachtree-Dunwoody Rd NE 30328. I-285 exit 28 westbound, 0.7 mi n; exit 26 eastbound, 0.5 mi n to Hammond Dr, 0.5 mi e, then 0.3 mi n. Int corridors. **Pets:** Other species. $25 daily fee/pet. Service with restrictions. 📶 🔥 🍴 💻 🏊

▼▼▼ Extended Stay Deluxe Atlanta-Vinings 🅷 🐾
(770) 436-1511. **$65-$100.** 2474 Cumberland Pkwy SE 30339. I-285 exit 18, just e. Int corridors. **Pets:** Other species. $25 daily fee/pet. Service with restrictions. 📶 🔥 🍴 💻 🏊

▼▼▼ Fairview Inn at Six Flags Atlanta 🅷
(404) 505-8880. **$50-$70.** 4330 Fulton Industrial Blvd 30336. I-20 exit 49, just s. Int corridors. **Pets:** Accepted. 📶 🔥 💻 🏊

AAA ◆◆◆◆ Four Seasons Hotel Atlanta 🅷
(404) 881-9898. **$400-$4000.** 75 14th St 30309. I-75/85 exit 250 (14th St), 0.3 mi e. Int corridors. **Pets:** Accepted.
SAVE 📶 🔥 🍴 🏊 ✕

AAA ◆◆◆◆ The Georgian Terrace Hotel 🅷
(404) 897-1991. **Call for rates.** 659 Peachtree St 30308. I-75/85 exit 249D, 0.5 mi e to Peachtree St, then just n. Int corridors. **Pets:** Accepted.
SAVE 📶 ✕ 🔥 💻 🍴 🏊

AAA ◆◆◆◆ Glenn Hotel, Autograph Collection 🅷
(404) 521-2250. **$107-$218.** 110 Marietta St NW 30303. I-75/85 exit 248C northbound, 0.8 mi w, then just s; exit 249A southbound, just s to Baker St, just w, then just s. Int corridors. **Pets:** Accepted.
SAVE 📶 ✕ 🔥 🔥 💻 🍴

AAA ◆◆◆ ◆◆◆ Grand Hyatt Atlanta 🅷
(404) 237-1234. **$139-$409.** 3300 Peachtree Rd NE 30305. Corner of Peachtree and Piedmont rds. Int corridors. **Pets:** Accepted.
ECO SAVE 📶 🔥 🔥 🍴 💻 🍴 🏊 ✕

AAA ◆◆◆◆ Hawthorn Suites by Wyndham Atlanta Northwest 🅷
(770) 952-9595. **$129-$149.** 1500 Parkwood Cir 30339. I-75 exit 260 (Windy Hill Rd), 0.5 mi e, then 0.3 mi s on Powers Ferry Rd. Ext corridors. **Pets:** Accepted. SAVE 📶 🔥 💻 🏊 ✕

◆◆◆ Hilton Atlanta 🅷
(404) 659-2000. **$99-$209.** 255 Courtland St NE 30303. I-75/85 exit 249A southbound; exit 248C northbound, just w to Piedmont Ave, just n to Baker St, then just w. Int corridors. **Pets:** Accepted.
ECO 📶 🔥 💻 🍴 🏊 ✕

◥◤◥◤ Hilton Suites Atlanta Perimeter H

(770) 668-0808. **$99-$179.** 6120 Peachtree-Dunwoody Rd 30328. I-285 exit 28 westbound, 0.4 mi n; exit 26 eastbound, 0.5 mi n to Hammond Dr, 0.5 mi e to Peachtree-Dunwoody Rd, then just n. Int corridors. **Pets:** Accepted. 📶 ᠔M 🛗 💻 🍴 ⊷

◢◣ ◥◤◥◤ Holiday Inn Atlanta Perimeter H

(770) 457-6363. **$79-$129.** 4386 Chamblee-Dunwoody Rd 30341. I-285 exit 30 eastbound, just s; exit westbound, follow access road 1.3 mi to Chamblee-Dunwoody Rd, then just s. Int corridors. **Pets:** Other species. $35 one-time fee/room. Designated rooms.

SAVE 📶 ᠔M 🛗 💻 🍴 ⊷

◥◤◥◤ Wingate by Wyndham Atlanta Clairmont Rd H

(404) 248-1550. **$85-$129.** 2920 Clairmont Rd 30329. I-85 exit 91, just w. Int corridors. **Pets:** Accepted. 📶 ᠔M 🛗 💻

**◥◤◥◤ Homestead Studio Suites
Hotel-Atlanta/Perimeter** H 🐾

(770) 522-0025. **$65-$100.** 1050 Hammond Dr 30328. I-285 exit 26 eastbound, 0.5 mi n to Hammond Dr, then 0.5 mi e; exit 28 westbound, just n to Hammond Dr, then just w. Ext corridors. **Pets:** Other species. $25 daily fee/pet. Service with restrictions. 📶 ᠔M 🛗 💻

◥◤◥◤ Homewood Suites-Atlanta Buckhead H

(404) 365-0001. **$109-$179.** 3566 Piedmont Rd 30305. SR 400 exit 2, just s to Piedmont Rd, then 1 mi w. Int corridors. **Pets:** Accepted. 📶 ᠔M 🛗 💻 ⊷

◥◤◥◤ Homewood Suites-Cumberland H

(770) 988-9449. **$99-$169.** 3200 Cobb Pkwy SW 30339. I-285 exit 19 eastbound; exit 20 westbound, 0.7 mi se on US 41 (Cobb Pkwy). Ext/int corridors. **Pets:** Medium, other species. $25 daily fee/room. Service with restrictions, crate. 📶 ᠔M 🛗 💻 ⊷ ⊠

◥◤◥◤ Hotel Indigo Atlanta Midtown H 🐾

(404) 874-9200. **$99-$259.** 683 Peachtree St NE 30308. I-75/85 exit 249D, 0.5 mi e to Peachtree St, then just n. Int corridors. **Pets:** Designated rooms, service with restrictions. 📶 ᠔M 🛗 💻 🍴

**◢◣ ◥◤◥◤ InterContinental Buckhead
Atlanta** H 🐾

(404) 946-9000. **$159-$349.** 3315 Peachtree Rd NE 30326. Jct Piedmont and Peachtree rds NE, just e. Int corridors. **Pets:** Small. $100 one-time fee/pet. Service with restrictions, supervision.

SAVE 📶 ᠔M 💻 🍴 ⊷ ⊠

**◥◤◥◤ La Quinta Inn & Suites Atlanta (Paces
Ferry/Vinings)** H

(770) 801-9002. **$64-$154.** 2415 Paces Ferry Rd SE 30339. I-285 exit 18, just w. Int corridors. **Pets:** Medium, other species. Service with restrictions, supervision. 📶 ᠔M 🛗 💻 ⊷

**◥◤◥◤ La Quinta Inn & Suites Atlanta (Perimeter/Medical
Center)** H

(770) 350-6177. **$58-$143.** 6260 Peachtree-Dunwoody 30328. I-285 exit 28 westbound, 0.7 mi n; exit 26 eastbound, 0.5 mi n to Hammond Dr, 0.7 mi e, then 0.5 mi n. Int corridors. **Pets:** Medium, other species. Service with restrictions, supervision. 📶 ᠔M 🛗 💻 ⊷

◥◤ ◥◤ La Quinta Inn Atlanta Lenox Buckhead H

(404) 321-0999. **$62-$137.** 2535 Chantilly Dr NE 30324. I-85 exit 88 southbound; exit 86 northbound, 2 mi on Buford Hwy to Lenox Rd, then just e under highway. Int corridors. **Pets:** Medium, other species. Service with restrictions, supervision. 📶 🛗 💻

◥◤◥◤ Loews Hotel Atlanta H

(404) 745-5000. **$189-$349.** 1075 Peachtree St NE 30309. I-75/85 exit 251 (10th St), 0.5 mi e to Peachtree St NE, then just n. Int corridors. **Pets:** Accepted. 📶 ⊠ ᠔M 🛗 💻 🍴 ⊠

◥◤ ◥◤ Microtel Inn & Suites H

(404) 325-4446. **$62-$71.** 1840 Corporate Blvd 30329. I-85 exit 89, just w to Buford Hwy, 0.3 mi n to Corporate Blvd, then just e. Int corridors. **Pets:** Medium. $25 one-time fee/room. Service with restrictions, crate. 📶 ᠔M 🛗 💻

◢◣ ◥◤◥◤◥◤ Omni Hotel at CNN Center H

(404) 659-0000. **Call for rates.** 100 CNN Center 30303. I-75/85 exit 248C northbound, 0.8 mi w; exit 249C southbound to International Blvd, then 0.5 mi w. Int corridors. **Pets:** Accepted.

SAVE 📶 💻 🍴 ⊷ ⊠

◥◤◥◤ Red Roof Inn-Druid Hills M

(404) 321-1653. **$49-$84.** 1960 N Druid Hills Rd 30329. I-85 exit 89, just w. Ext corridors. **Pets:** Large, other species. No service, supervision. 📶 🛗

◢◣ ◥◤◥◤◥◤ Renaissance Atlanta Midtown H

(678) 412-2400. **$123-$279.** 866 W Peachtree St NW 30308. I-75/85 exit 249D, just e to W Peachtree St NW, then 0.6 mi n. Int corridors. **Pets:** Accepted. ECO SAVE 📶 ⊠ 💻 🍴

**◢◣ ◥◤◥◤ Residence Inn Atlanta Buckhead/Lenox
Park** H

(404) 467-1660. **$85-$162.** 2220 Lake Blvd 30319. I-85 exit 89, 1.6 mi w on N Druid Hills (which becomes E Roxboro Rd), then just n on Lenox Park Blvd. Int corridors. **Pets:** Medium, other species. $100 one-time fee/room. Service with restrictions, crate.

SAVE 📶 ⊠ ᠔M 🛗 💻 ⊷ ⊠

◥◤◥◤ Residence Inn Atlanta - Downtown H

(404) 522-0950. **$89-$299.** 134 Peachtree St NW 30303. I-75/85 exit 248C northbound, 0.4 mi w, then just s; exit 249A southbound to International Blvd, just w, then just s. Int corridors. **Pets:** Medium. $100 one-time fee/room. Service with restrictions, crate. 📶 ⊠ 🛗 💻

◥◤◥◤ Residence Inn Atlanta Midtown at 17th Street H

(404) 745-1000. **$98-$195.** 1365 Peachtree St 30309. I-75/85 exit 250 (14th St), 0.5 mi e to Peachtree St, then 0.3 mi n. Int corridors. **Pets:** Accepted. 📶 ⊠ ᠔M 🛗 💻

◥◤◥◤ Residence Inn Atlanta - Midtown/Historic H

(404) 872-8885. **$98-$171.** 1041 W Peachtree St 30309. I-75/85 exit 250 (10th St), just e to W Peachtree St, then just n; corner of 11th St. Int corridors. **Pets:** Accepted. 📶 ⊠ ᠔M 🛗 💻

**◢◣ ◥◤◥◤ Residence Inn Atlanta - Perimeter
Center** H

(404) 252-5066. **$75-$149.** 6096 Barfield Rd 30328. I-285 exit 26 eastbound, 0.5 mi n on Glenridge to Hammond Dr, then 0.3 mi e to Barfield Rd; exit 28 westbound (Peachtree-Dunwoody Rd), 0.5 mi n to Hammond Dr, then just w. Ext corridors. **Pets:** Accepted.

SAVE 📶 ⊠ 🛗 💻 ⊷ ⊠

**◢◣ ◥◤◥◤ Residence Inn Atlanta
Perimeter/Dunwoody** H

(770) 455-4446. **$75-$139.** 1901 Savoy Dr 30341. I-285 exit 30, just e. Ext corridors. **Pets:** Accepted. SAVE 📶 ⊠ 🛗 💻 ⊷ ⊠

**◢◣ ◥◤◥◤ Residence Inn by
Marriott-Atlanta/Buckhead** H 🐾

(404) 239-0677. **$87-$171.** 2960 Piedmont Rd NE 30305. Jct Piedmont and Pharr rds, just s. Ext corridors. **Pets:** Other species. $100 one-time fee/room. Service with restrictions. SAVE 📶 ⊠ 🛗 💻 ⊷ ⊠

◢◣ ◥◤◥◤◥◤ The Ritz-Carlton, Buckhead H

(404) 237-2700. **$209-$499.** 3434 Peachtree Rd NE 30326. I-85 exit 86, 1.8 mi n on Lenox Rd. Int corridors. **Pets:** Accepted.

SAVE 📶 ⊠ ᠔M 🛗 💻 🍴 ⊷ ⊠

**◢◣ ◥◤◥◤◥◤ St. Regis Atlanta Hotel &
Residences** H 🐾

(404) 563-7900. **$610-$630.** 88 W Paces Ferry Rd 30305. Jct Peachtree and W Paces Ferry rds, just w. Int corridors. **Pets:** Small, other species. $100 one-time fee/pet, $25 daily fee/pet. Service with restrictions.

SAVE 📶 ᠔M 🍴 ⊷ ⊠

Sheraton Atlanta Hotel H
(404) 659-6500. **$120-$400, 3 day notice.** 165 Courtland St NE 30303. I-75/85 exit 249A southbound; exit 248C northbound, just w. Int corridors. **Pets:** Accepted. [SAVE] [icons]

Sheraton Suites Galleria H ❧
(770) 955-3900. **$99-$279.** 2844 Cobb Pkwy SE 30339. I-285 exit 20 westbound; exit 19 eastbound, just s on US 41 (Cobb Pkwy). Int corridors. **Pets:** Medium. $25 one-time fee/room. Service with restrictions.
[SAVE] [icons]

Staybridge Suites H ❧
(404) 842-0800. **$99-$220.** 540 Pharr Rd 30305. Jct Pharr and Piedmont rds, just w. Int corridors. **Pets:** Medium. $75 daily fee/room. Service with restrictions. [icons]

Staybridge Suites-Atlanta-Mt. Vernon H
(404) 250-0110. **$106-$136.** 760 Mt Vernon Hwy NE 30328. I-285 exit 25, 0.8 mi n on Roswell Rd, then 1 mi e. Ext/int corridors. **Pets:** Accepted. [icons]

Staybridge Suites Atlanta Perimeter H
(678) 320-0111. **$134-$164.** 4601 Ridgeview Rd 30338. I-285 exit 29 (Ashford-Dunwoody Rd), 0.5 mi n, 0.5 mi w on Perimeter Center W to Crowne Pointe Dr, then just n. Int corridors. **Pets:** Accepted.
[icons]

Stonehurst Place Bed & Breakfast BB
(404) 881-0722. **$159-$649, 3 day notice.** 923 Piedmont Ave 30309. I-75 exit 251 (10th St), 0.6 mi e to Juniper St, just s to 8th St, just e to Piedmont Ave, then just n. Int corridors. **Pets:** Accepted. [icons]

Super 8 M
(404) 873-5731. **$63-$108.** 1641 Peachtree St NE 30309. I-75/85 exit 250 (14th St), 0.3 mi e to Peachtree St, then 1 mi n. Ext/int corridors. **Pets:** Dogs only. $10 daily fee/pet. Service with restrictions, supervision.
[icons]

TownePlace Suites Atlanta Buckhead H
(404) 949-4820. **$69-$199.** 820 Sidney Marcus Blvd 30324. I-85 exit 86 northbound, 1.9 mi n to Sidney Marcus Blvd, then just w; exit 88 southbound, just w to Sidney Marcus Blvd, then just w. Int corridors. **Pets:** Accepted. [icons]

University Inn at Emory M ❧
(404) 634-7327. **$80-$175.** 1767 N Decatur Rd 30307. Adjacent to Emory University. Ext corridors. **Pets:** Large, other species. $25 daily fee/room. Designated rooms, service with restrictions.
[SAVE] [icons]

W Atlanta Buckhead H
(678) 500-3100. **$99-$559.** 3377 Peachtree Rd NE 30326. Jct Piedmont and Peachtree rds, 0.3 mi e. Int corridors. **Pets:** Accepted.
[SAVE] [icons]

W Atlanta Downtown H ❧
(404) 582-5800. **$199-$539.** 45 Ivan Allen Jr Blvd 30308. I-75/85 exit 249C, just s. Int corridors. **Pets:** Medium, other species. $100 one-time fee/pet, $25 daily fee/pet. No service. [SAVE] [icons]

W Atlanta Midtown H
(404) 892-6000. **$139-$379.** 188 14th St NE 30361. I-75/85 exit 250 (14th St), 0.5 mi. Int corridors. **Pets:** Accepted.
[SAVE] [icons]

The Westin Atlanta North H
(770) 395-3900. **$109-$359.** 7 Concourse Pkwy 30328. I-285 exit 28 westbound; exit 26 eastbound, 0.5 mi n to Hammond Dr, then 0.4 mi e. Int corridors. **Pets:** Accepted.
[SAVE] [icons]

The Westin Buckhead Atlanta H
(404) 365-0065. **$129-$479.** 3391 Peachtree Rd NE 30326. Adjacent to Lenox Square Mall. Int corridors. **Pets:** Accepted.
[SAVE] [icons]

The Westin Peachtree Plaza H
(404) 659-1400. **$120-$400.** 210 Peachtree St 30303. I-75/85 exit 248C northbound, 0.4 mi w; exit 249C southbound, 0.5 mi s. Int corridors. **Pets:** Accepted. [ECO] [SAVE] [icons]

AUSTELL

Quality Inn & Suites of Six Flags M
(770) 941-1499. **$60-$75.** 1100 N Blairs Bridge Rd 30168. I-20 exit 44, just n, then just e. Ext corridors. **Pets:** Other species. $15 daily fee/pet. No service. [icons]

Super 8 Austell/Six Flags M
(770) 944-2110. **Call for rates.** 7377 Six Flags Dr 30168. I-20 exit 46 eastbound; exit 46B westbound, just n. Ext/int corridors. **Pets:** Accepted.
[icons]

COLLEGE PARK

Best Western Plus Hotel & Suites Airport South H
(770) 996-5800. **$69-$129.** 1556 Phoenix Blvd 30349. I-285 exit 60 (Riverdale Rd N), just s to Phoenix Blvd, then just w. Int corridors. **Pets:** Accepted. [SAVE] [icons]

Econo Lodge M
(404) 768-1241. **Call for rates.** 4874 Old National Hwy 30337. I-285 exit 62, just n. Ext corridors. **Pets:** Very small, dogs only. $10 daily fee/pet. Service with restrictions, crate. [icons]

Embassy Suites Hotel at Atlanta Airport H
(404) 767-1988. **$89-$199.** 4700 Southport Rd 30337. I-85 exit 71, 0.3 mi w on Riverdale Rd. Int corridors. **Pets:** Accepted.
[icons]

Holiday Inn Express-Atlanta Airport H
(404) 761-6500. **$79-$139.** 4601 Best Rd 30337. I-85 exit 71; northwest corner. Int corridors. **Pets:** Accepted. [icons]

La Quinta Inn & Suites Atlanta Airport H
(770) 996-0000. **$94-$160.** 4820 Massachusetts Blvd 30337. I-85 exit 71, just e to Airport Rd, then just s. Int corridors. **Pets:** Medium, other species. Service with restrictions, supervision. [icons]

Microtel Inn-Atlanta Airport H
(770) 994-3003. **$45-$90.** 4839 Massachusetts Blvd 30337. I-85 exit 71, just e to Airport Rd, then just s; I-285 exit 60 (Riverdale Rd N), 1 mi to Sullivan Rd, then just s. Int corridors. **Pets:** Accepted. [icons]

Quality Hotel & Conference Center-Atlanta Airport H
(770) 996-4321. **$69-$89.** 1551 Phoenix Blvd 30349. I-285 exit 60 (Riverdale Rd N), just sw. Ext/int corridors. **Pets:** Accepted.
[icons]

Sheraton Gateway Hotel, Atlanta Airport H
(770) 997-1100. **$79-$279.** 1900 Sullivan Rd 30337. I-85 exit 71, just e to Airport Rd, then just s. Int corridors. **Pets:** Accepted.
[SAVE] [icons]

The Westin Hotel-Atlanta Airport H ❧
(404) 762-7676. **$99-$359.** 4736 Best Rd 30337. I-85 exit 71, just w, se on access road to Best Rd, then just s. Int corridors. **Pets:** Medium. $100 one-time fee/room. Service with restrictions, crate.
[SAVE] [icons]

DECATUR

America's Best Inn & Suites M
(404) 286-2500. **$60.** 4095 Covington Hwy 30032. I-285 exit 43, just w. Ext corridors. **Pets:** $10 daily fee/pet. Service with restrictions, supervision. [icons]

◆◆◆ Decatur Hotel & Conference Center 🏨
(404) 371-0204. **Call for rates.** 130 Clairmont Ave 30030. Downtown. Int corridors. **Pets:** Accepted. 🛰 🔌 📶 ❄ 🍴 ➿

◆◆◆ Super 8 Ⓜ
(404) 378-3765. **$65-$150.** 917 Church St 30030. Downtown. Ext corridors. **Pets:** Accepted. (SAVE) 🛰 📶 🔌 📟

DORAVILLE

◆◆◆◆ Metro Hotel 🏨
(770) 455-3700. **$69-$99.** 2001 Clearview Ave 30340. I-285 exit 32, southeast corner. Int corridors. **Pets:** Medium. $25 one-time fee/pet. Designated rooms, service with restrictions, supervision.
🛰 📶 🔌 📟 🍴 ➿

◆◆◆ Super 8 Atlanta NE Ⓜ
(770) 458-2671. **$36-$54.** 2822 Chamblee Tucker Rd 30341. I-85 exit 94, just w. Ext corridors. **Pets:** Accepted. (SAVE) 🛰 🔌 📟

DOUGLASVILLE

◆◆ Days Inn Ⓜ
(770) 949-1499. **$50-$67.** 5489 Westmoreland Plaza 30134. I-20 exit 37, just n. Ext corridors. **Pets:** Accepted. 🛰 🔌 📟 ➿

◆◆◆ Best Western Garden Inn & Suites 🏨 🐾
(770) 489-4863. **$60-$80.** 8304 Cherokee Blvd 30134. I-20 exit 37, just n to Cherokee Blvd, then just e. Int corridors. **Pets:** Small. $15 daily fee/pet. Service with restrictions, supervision. (SAVE) 🛰 📶 🔌 📟 ➿

◆◆◆ La Quinta Inn & Suites Atlanta Douglasville 🏨
(770) 577-3838. **$80-$139.** 1000 Linnenkohl Dr 30134. I-20 exit 34, just n. Int corridors. **Pets:** Medium, other species. Service with restrictions, supervision. 🛰 📶 🔌 📟 ➿

DULUTH

◆◆◆ Candlewood Suites-Atlanta 🏨
(678) 380-0414. **$60-$75.** 3665 Shackleford Rd 30096. I-85 exit 104, just e, then just s. Int corridors. **Pets:** Accepted. 🛰 📶 🔌 📟

◆◆◆ Extended Stay Deluxe Atlanta-Gwinnett Place 🏨 🐾
(770) 623-6800. **$65-$200.** 3390 Venture Pkwy NW 30096. I-85 exit 104, just w to Venture Pkwy, then just n. Int corridors. **Pets:** Other species. $25 daily fee/pet. Service with restrictions. 🛰 📶 🔌 📟 ➿

◆◆◆ Holiday Inn Express 🏨
(770) 935-7171. **$74-$94.** 3670 Shackleford Rd 30096. I-85 exit 104, just e to Shackleford Rd, then just s. Int corridors. **Pets:** Accepted.
🛰 📶 🔌 📟 ➿

◆◆◆ Holiday Inn-Gwinnett Center 🏨
(770) 476-2022. **$69-$169.** 6310 Sugarloaf Pkwy 30097. I-85 exit 108, just w. Int corridors. **Pets:** Accepted. 🛰 📶 🔌 📟 🍴 ➿

◆◆◆ La Quinta Inn Atlanta Duluth 🏨
(678) 957-0500. **$62-$149.** 2370 Stephen Center Dr 30096. I-85 exit 107 southbound, just w; exit 105 northbound, to Boggs Rd, 0.5 mi w to Satellite Blvd, then 0.5 mi n. Int corridors. **Pets:** Medium, other species. Service with restrictions, supervision. (SAVE) 🛰 ✖ 📶 🔌 📟 ➿

◆◆ Quality Inn - Gwinnett Mall Ⓜ
(770) 623-9300. **$50-$100.** 3500 Venture Pkwy 30096. I-85 exit 104, just w to Venture Pkwy, then just n. Ext/int corridors. **Pets:** Medium, other species. $10 daily fee/pet. Service with restrictions, supervision.
🛰 📶 🔌 📟 ➿

◆◆◆ Residence Inn Atlanta Gwinnett Place 🏨
(770) 921-2202. **$95-$162.** 1760 Pineland Rd 30096. I-85 exit 104, just e to Shackleford Rd, just s to Pineland Rd, then just e. Int corridors.
Pets: Accepted. 🛰 ✖ 📶 🔌 📟 ➿

◆◆ Studio 6 #6023 Ⓜ
(770) 931-3113. **$43-$53.** 3525 Breckinridge Blvd 30096. I-85 exit 104, just e to Breckinridge Blvd, then just n. Ext corridors. **Pets:** Other species. $10 daily fee/room. Service with restrictions, supervision.
🛰 📶 🔌 📟

EAST POINT

◆◆ Comfort Inn & Suites Atlanta Airport Camp Creek 🏨
(404) 762-5566. **$59-$79.** 3601 N Desert Dr 30344. I-285 exit 2, just e. Int corridors. **Pets:** Small. $50 one-time fee/pet. Service with restrictions, supervision. 🛰 📶 🔌 📟 ➿

◆◆◆ Crowne Plaza Atlanta Airport 🏨
(404) 768-6660. **$89-$189.** 1325 Virginia Ave 30344. I-85 exit 73 southbound; exit 73B northbound, just w. Int corridors. **Pets:** Accepted.
🛰 ✖ 📶 🔌 📟 🍴 ➿

◆◆◆ Drury Inn & Suites-Atlanta Airport 🏨
(404) 761-4900. **$90-$169.** 1270 Virginia Ave 30344. I-85 exit 73 southbound; exit 73A northbound, just e. Int corridors. **Pets:** Accepted.
🛰 📶 🔌 📟 ➿

◆◆ Motel 6 Atlanta Airport North #4589 🏨
(404) 209-1800. **$50-$70.** 1200 Virginia Ave 30344. I-85 exit 73 southbound; exit 73A northbound, just e. Int corridors. **Pets:** Other species. Service with restrictions, supervision. 🛰 📶 🔌 ➿

FAIRBURN

◆◆◆ Country Inn & Suites By Carlson 🏨
(678) 782-4900. **$89-$109.** 7815 Senoia Rd 30213. I-85 exit 61, just e. Int corridors. **Pets:** Accepted. 🛰 📶 🔌 📟 ➿

◆◆◆ Sleep Inn & Suites 🏨
(678) 782-4700. **Call for rates.** 1005 Oakley Industrial Blvd 30213. I-85 exit 61, just e. Int corridors. **Pets:** Accepted. 🛰 📶 🔌 📟 ➿

FOREST PARK

◆◆ Days Inn-Airport East Ⓜ
(404) 768-6400. **$35-$56, 14 day notice.** 5116 Hwy 85 30297. I-75 exit 237A southbound; exit 237 northbound, 0.5 mi w. Ext corridors.
Pets: Small, other species. $25 one-time fee/pet. Service with restrictions, crate. 🛰 🔌 📟 ➿

◆◆ Econo Lodge Ⓜ 🐾
(404) 363-6429. **$45.** 5060 Frontage Rd 30297. I-75 exit 237, just e to Frontage Rd, then just s. Ext corridors. **Pets:** Other species. $15 daily fee/pet. Service with restrictions, supervision. 🛰 🔌

◆◆ Super 8 Ⓜ
(404) 363-8811. **$41-$90.** 410 Old Dixie Way 30297. I-75 exit 235, just e. Ext corridors. **Pets:** Accepted. 🛰 🔌 📟 ➿

HAPEVILLE

◆◆◆ Hilton Atlanta Airport 🏨 🐾
(404) 767-9000. **$99-$229.** 1031 Virginia Ave 30354. I-85 exit 73 southbound; exit 73A northbound, just e. Int corridors. **Pets:** Large, other species. $50 one-time fee/pet. Service with restrictions, crate.
(SAVE) 🛰 📶 🔌 📟 🍴 ➿ ✖

◆◆◆ Residence Inn Atlanta Airport North/Virginia Avenue 🏨
(404) 761-0511. **$104-$169.** 3401 International Blvd 30354. I-85 exit 73 southbound; exit 73A northbound, 0.5 mi e to International Blvd, then just n. Ext/int corridors. **Pets:** Accepted.
(SAVE) 🛰 ✖ 📶 🔌 📟 ➿ ✖

JONESBORO

◆◆◆ Clarion Hotel Atlanta Airport South 🏨
(770) 968-4300. **$59-$79.** 6288 Old Dixie Hwy 30236. I-75 exit 235, just w. Int corridors. **Pets:** Accepted. 🛰 📶 🔌 📟 🍴 ➿

KENNESAW

Best Western Kennesaw Inn M ❀
(770) 424-7666. **$68-$75.** 3375 Busbee Dr 30144. I-75 exit 271, just e. Ext corridors. **Pets:** Large. $10 daily fee/pet. Service with restrictions, supervision. [SAVE] [📶] [🔌] [💻] [🏊]

Days Inn M
(770) 419-1576. **$45-$72.** 760 Cobb Place Blvd 30144. I-75 exit 269, just w. Ext corridors. **Pets:** Medium. $15 daily fee/pet. Designated rooms, service with restrictions, supervision. [📶] [🔌] [💻]

Embassy Suites Atlanta-Kennesaw Town Center H
(770) 420-2505. **$99-$159.** 620 Chastain Rd 30144. I-75 exit 271, 0.4 mi w. Int corridors. **Pets:** Accepted. [📶] [🔌] [🔌] [💻] [🍽] [🏊]

Extended StayAmerica Atlanta Kennesaw H ❀
(770) 422-1403. **$52-$87.** 3000 George Busbee Pkwy 30144. I-75 exit 269, just e to George Busbee Pkwy, then 0.8 mi n. Int corridors. **Pets:** Other species. $25 daily fee/pet. Service with restrictions. [📶] [🔌] [🔌] [💻]

Green Roof Inn & Suites M
(770) 529-3370. **Call for rates.** 3027 Cobb Pkwy NW 30152. I-75 exit 271, 2.5 mi w, then 2.2 mi n on US 41. Ext corridors. **Pets:** Accepted. [📶] [🔌] [🔌] [💻]

La Quinta Inn Kennesaw H
(770) 426-0045. **$85-$145.** 2625 George Busbee Pkwy 30144. I-75 exit 269, just e to George Busbee Pkwy, then just n. Int corridors. **Pets:** Medium, other species. Service with restrictions, supervision. [📶] [🔌] [🔌] [💻] [🏊]

Quality Inn M
(770) 419-1530. **$60-$85.** 750 Cobb Place Blvd 30144. I-75 exit 269, just w. Ext corridors. **Pets:** Medium. $15 daily fee/pet. Designated rooms, service with restrictions, supervision. [📶] [🔌] [🔌] [💻]

Red Roof Inn-Town Center Mall M
(770) 429-0323. **$44-$69.** 520 Roberts Ct NW 30144. I-75 exit 269, just e. Ext corridors. **Pets:** Large, other species. No service, supervision. [📶] [🔌] [🔌]

Residence Inn Atlanta Kennesaw/Town Center H
(770) 218-1018. **$149-$249.** 3443 Busbee Dr 30144. I-75 exit 271, just e. Int corridors. **Pets:** Accepted. [SAVE] [📶] [✕] [🔌] [🔌] [💻] [🏊] [✕]

StudioPLUS Atlanta-Kennesaw H ❀
(770) 425-6101. **$52-$87.** 3316 Busbee Dr 30144. I-75 exit 271, just e to Busbee Dr, then just s. Int corridors. **Pets:** Other species. $25 daily fee/pet. Service with restrictions. [📶] [🔌] [🔌] [💻] [🏊]

Travelodge M
(770) 590-0519. **$41-$74.** 1460 George Busbee Pkwy 30144. I-75 exit 273, just e. Ext corridors. **Pets:** Accepted. [📶] [🔌] [💻] [🏊]

LAWRENCEVILLE

Days Inn M
(770) 995-7782. **$48-$65.** 731 Duluth Hwy 30045. Jct SR 316, just e on SR 120. Ext corridors. **Pets:** $25 one-time fee/pet. Service with restrictions, supervision. [SAVE] [📶] [🔌] [💻]

Extended StayAmerica Atlanta-Lawrenceville H ❀
(770) 962-5660. **$50-$200.** 474 W Pike St 30045. SR 316 exit SR 120, 0.8 mi s. Ext corridors. **Pets:** Other species. $25 daily fee/pet. Service with restrictions. [📶] [🔌] [🔌] [💻]

Magnuson Hotel Lawrenceville H
(770) 513-0028. **$50-$80.** 571 Buford Dr 30045. Jct SR 316 and 20/124, 0.5 mi s. Int corridors. **Pets:** Accepted. [📶] [🔌] [🔌] [💻] [🏊]

LITHONIA

Red Roof Inn H
(770) 322-1400. **$69-$90.** 5400 Fairington Rd 30038. I-20 exit 71, just s to Fairington Rd, then just ne. Int corridors. **Pets:** Large, other species. No service, supervision. [SAVE] [📶] [🔌] [🔌] [💻]

MARIETTA

Americas Best Value Inn H
(770) 952-0052. **$50-$100.** 1940 Leland Dr 30067. I-75 exit 260, just e, then 0.3 mi n. Ext/int corridors. **Pets:** Small. $10 daily fee/pet. No service, supervision. [📶] [🔌] [💻]

Clarion Hotel H
(770) 428-4400. **Call for rates.** 1775 Parkway Pl NW 30067. I-75 exit 263, just w. Int corridors. **Pets:** Accepted. [📶] [🔌] [🔌] [💻] [🍽] [🏊] .

Comfort Inn-Marietta M
(770) 952-3000. **$55-$80.** 2100 Northwest Pkwy 30067. I-75 exit 261, 0.3 mi w to Franklin Rd, then just s. Ext corridors. **Pets:** Medium. $25 one-time fee/pet. Service with restrictions, supervision. [📶] [🔌] [💻] [🏊]

Days Inn M
(770) 952-9863. **$45-$72.** 2191 Northwest Pkwy 30067. I-75 exit 261, just w on Delk Rd to Franklin Rd, just s to Northwest Pkwy, then just e. Ext/int corridors. **Pets:** Accepted. [📶] [🔌] [🔌] [💻] [🏊]

Drury Inn & Suites-Atlanta Northwest H
(770) 612-0900. **$80-$149.** 1170 Powers Ferry Pl 30067. I-75 exit 261, just e. Int corridors. **Pets:** Accepted. [📶] [🔌] [🔌] [💻] [🏊]

Extended StayAmerica Atlanta-Marietta Windy Hill H ❀
(770) 690-9477. **$45-$70.** 1967 Leland Dr 30067. I-75 exit 260, just e to Leland Dr, then just n. Int corridors. **Pets:** Other species. $25 daily fee/pet. Service with restrictions. [📶] [🔌] [🔌] [💻]

Hilton Atlanta/Marietta Hotel & Conference Center H
(770) 427-2500. **Call for rates.** 500 Powder Springs St 30064. I-75 exit 263, 3.5 mi w to Powder Springs St, then just w. Int corridors. **Pets:** Accepted. [SAVE] [📶] [🔌] [🔌] [💻] [🍽] [🏊] [✕]

Homestead Studio Suites Hotel-Atlanta-Marietta-Powers Ferry Rd H ❀
(770) 303-0043. **$51-$86.** 2239 Powers Ferry Rd 30067. I-285 exit 22, just n. Int corridors. **Pets:** Other species. $25 daily fee/pet. Service with restrictions. [📶] [🔌] [🔌] [💻]

Hometown Inn Atlanta-Marietta-Canton Rd M
(770) 499-9550. **Call for rates.** 1051 Canton Rd 30066. I-75 exit 267A northbound, 1.8 mi w. Ext corridors. **Pets:** Accepted. [📶] [🔌] [💻]

Hyatt Regency Suites Atlanta NW H
(770) 956-1234. **$79-$269, 3 day notice.** 2999 Windy Hill Rd 30067. I-75 exit 260, 0.5 mi e at Powers Ferry Rd. Int corridors. **Pets:** Accepted. [SAVE] [📶] [🔌] [🔌] [💻] [🍽] [🏊]

La Quinta Inn M
(770) 951-0026. **$52-$108.** 2170 Delk Rd 30067-8761. I-75 exit 261, 0.3 mi w. Ext/int corridors. **Pets:** Medium, other species. Service with restrictions, supervision. [📶] [🔌] [💻] [🏊]

Masters Inn Marietta M
(770) 951-2005. **$45-$75.** 2682 Windy Hill Rd 30067. I-75 exit 260, just w to Circle 75 Pkwy, then just s. Ext corridors. **Pets:** Accepted. [📶] [🔌]

Ramada H
(770) 952-9005. **$49-$71.** 1175 Powers Ferry Pl 30067. I-75 exit 261, just e. Int corridors. **Pets:** Accepted. [📶] [🔌] [🔌] [💻] [🏊]

MORROW

🐾 ▼▼ Best Western Southlake Inn Ⓜ
(770) 961-6300. **Call for rates.** 6437 Jonesboro Rd 30260. I-75 exit 233, just e. Ext corridors. **Pets:** Accepted. 🆂🆅🅴 🔌 💻 🏊

▼▼ Drury Inn & Suites-Atlanta South Ⓗ
(770) 960-0500. **$85-$154.** 6520 S Lee St 30260. I-75 exit 233, just e. Int corridors. **Pets:** Accepted. 🛜 🆓 🔌 💻 🏊

▼▼ Extended StayAmerica-Atlanta-Morrow Ⓗ ❄
(770) 472-0727. **$55-$90.** 2265 Mt. Zion Pkwy 30260. I-75 exit 231, just w, then just s. Int corridors. **Pets:** Other species. $25 daily fee/pet. Service with restrictions. 🛜 🔌 💻

▼▼ Red Roof Inn-South Ⓜ
(770) 968-1483. **$45-$69.** 1348 Southlake Plaza Dr 30260. I-75 exit 233, just e to Southlake Plaza Dr, then just n. Ext corridors. **Pets:** Large, other species. No service, supervision. 🛜 🆓 🔌

🐾 ▼▼ Sleep Inn Ⓗ
(770) 472-9800. **$40-$110.** 2185 Mt. Zion Pkwy 30260. I-75 exit 231, just w to Mt. Zion Pkwy, then just s. Int corridors. **Pets:** Medium. $50 deposit/room, $10 daily fee/pet. Designated rooms, service with restrictions, supervision. 🆂🆅🅴 🛜 🆓 🔌 💻 🏊

NORCROSS

▼▼▼ Comfort Inn & Suites Ⓗ
(770) 263-8883. **$70-$90.** 5200 Peachtree Industrial Blvd 30071. I-285 exit 31B, 5.5 mi n; I-85 exit 99, 4 mi w to Peachtree Industrial Blvd, then 1.5 mi n. Int corridors. **Pets:** Accepted. 🛜 🆓 🔌 💻 🏊

▼▼ Days Inn & Suites Ⓗ
(770) 416-9021. **$45-$80.** 5385 Peachtree Industrial Blvd 30092. I-285 exit 31B, 5.5 mi n; I-85 exit 99, 4 mi w to Peachtree Industrial Blvd, then 1.5 mi n. Int corridors. **Pets:** Accepted. 🛜 🆓 🔌 💻 🏊

🐾 ▼▼ Days Inn Atlanta NE Ⓜ
(770) 368-0218. **$45-$70.** 5990 Western Hills Dr 30071. I-85 exit 99, 0.8 mi w to Norcross Tucker Rd to Western Hills Dr, then just n. Ext corridors. **Pets:** Accepted. 🆂🆅🅴 🛜 🔌 💻 🏊

▼▼ Drury Inn & Suites-Atlanta Northeast Ⓗ
(770) 729-0060. **$75-$154.** 5655 Jimmy Carter Blvd 30071. I-85 exit 99, just w. Int corridors. **Pets:** Accepted. 🛜 🆓 🔌 💻 🏊

▼▼ Extended StayAmerica Atlanta-Jimmy Carter Blvd Ⓜ ❄
(770) 446-9245. **$55-$200.** 6295 Jimmy Carter Blvd 30071. I-85 exit 99, 1.5 mi w. Ext corridors. **Pets:** Other species. $25 daily fee/pet. Service with restrictions. 🛜 🆓 🔌

▼▼ Extended StayAmerica Atlanta-Norcross Ⓜ ❄
(770) 729-8100. **$50-$200.** 200 Lawrenceville St 30071. Downtown; behind post office. Ext corridors. **Pets:** Other species. $25 daily fee/pet. Service with restrictions. 🛜 🆓 🔌 💻

▼▼▼ Hilton Atlanta Northeast Ⓗ
(770) 447-4747. **$79-$149.** 5993 Peachtree Industrial Blvd 30092. I-285 exit 31B, 4.5 mi ne. Int corridors. **Pets:** Accepted.
🛜 🆓 🔌 💻 🍴 🏊

▼▼ Homestead Studio Suites Hotel-Atlanta/Peachtree Corners Ⓜ ❄
(770) 449-9966. **$55-$200.** 7049 Jimmy Carter Blvd 30092. I-85 exit 99, 4 mi n; I-285 exit 31B, 4 mi n. Ext corridors. **Pets:** Other species. $25 daily fee/pet. Service with restrictions. 🛜 🆓 🔌 💻

▼▼ Homewood Suites by Hilton Ⓗ
(770) 448-4663. **$99-$179.** 450 Technology Pkwy 30092. I-85 exit 99, 4 mi w to Peachtree Industrial Blvd, 0.4 mi n, w on Holcomb Bridge Rd, then 2 blks n on Peachtree Pkwy; I-285 exit 31B, 5 mi n on SR 141. Ext/int corridors. **Pets:** Accepted. 🛜 🆓 🔌 💻 🏊 ✖

▼▼ Horizon Inn & Suites Ⓜ
(770) 448-8686. **Call for rates.** 6187 Dawson Blvd 30093. I-85 exit 99, just e to McDonough Dr, then just s. Ext corridors. **Pets:** Accepted.
🛜 🔌 🏊

▼▼ Howard Johnson Ⓗ
(678) 736-6610. **$36-$40.** 5375 Peachtree Industrial Blvd 30092. I-285 exit 31B, 5.5 mi n; I-85 exit 99, 4 mi w to Peachtree Industrial Blvd, then 1.5 mi n. Ext/int corridors. **Pets:** Medium, other species. $50 deposit/room, $10 daily fee/pet. Designated rooms, service with restrictions, supervision. 🛜 🔌 💻

▼▼▼ La Quinta Inn Norcross Ⓗ
(770) 368-9400. **$80-$144.** 5945 Oakbrook Pkwy 30093. I-85 exit 99, 0.5 mi e to Live Oak Pkwy, then 0.8 mi w. Int corridors. **Pets:** Medium, other species. Service with restrictions, supervision. 🛜 🔌 💻 🏊

▼▼ Red Roof Inn-Indian Trail Ⓜ
(770) 448-8944. **$36-$55.** 5171 Brook Hollow Pkwy 30071. I-85 exit 101, just w to Brook Hollow Pkwy, then just s. Ext corridors. **Pets:** Large, other species. No service, supervision. 🛜

▼▼ StudioPLUS-Atlanta Peachtree Corners Ⓗ ❄
(770) 582-9984. **$55-$200.** 7065 Jimmy Carter Blvd 30092. I-85 exit 99, 4 mi n; I-285 exit 31B, 4 mi n. Int corridors. **Pets:** Other species. $25 daily fee/pet. Service with restrictions. 🛜 🆓 🔌 💻 🏊

▼▼ TownePlace Suites Atlanta Norcross/Peachtree Corners Ⓗ
(770) 447-8446. **$56-$123.** 6640 Bay Cir 30071. I-285 exit 31B, 3 mi n on Peachtree Industrial Blvd to Jones Mill Rd. Int corridors.
Pets: Accepted. 🄴🄲🄾 🛜 ✖ 🆓 🔌 💻 🏊

ROSWELL

▼▼ La Quinta Inn & Suites Atlanta Roswell Ⓗ
(770) 552-0200. **$54-$111.** 575 Old Holcomb Bridge Rd 30076. SR 400 exit 7B, 0.3 mi w. Int corridors. **Pets:** Medium, other species. Service with restrictions, supervision. 🛜 🆓 🔌 💻 🏊

▼▼ Studio 6 #6025 Ⓜ
(770) 992-9449. **$47-$57.** 9955 Old Dogwood Rd 30076. SR 400 exit 7B, just w. Ext corridors. **Pets:** Other species. $10 daily fee/room. Service with restrictions, supervision. 🛜 🆓 🔌 💻

SMYRNA

▼▼ Baymont Inn & Suites Ⓗ
(404) 794-1600. **$59-$80.** 5130 S Cobb Dr 30082. I-285 exit 15, 0.3 mi w. Int corridors. **Pets:** Medium. $20 daily fee/pet. Service with restrictions, supervision. 🛜 🆓 🔌 💻 🏊

🐾 ▼▼ Cobb Galleria Inn Ⓗ
(770) 435-4990. **$69-$169.** 2855 Spring Hill Pkwy 30080. I-285 exit 20 westbound; exit 19 eastbound, just n on US 41 (Cobb Pkwy), then just w on Spring Rd. Int corridors. **Pets:** Other species. Service with restrictions, crate. 🆂🆅🅴 🛜 🆓 🔌 💻 🏊

▼▼ Homestead Studio Suites Hotel-Atlanta/Cumberland Mall Ⓜ ❄
(770) 432-4000. **$50-$85.** 3103 Sports Ave 30080. I-285 exit 20 westbound; exit 19 eastbound, just n to Spring Rd, then 0.3 mi w. Ext corridors. **Pets:** Other species. $25 daily fee/pet. Service with restrictions.
🛜 🆓 🔌 💻

▼▼ Red Roof Inn-North Ⓜ
(770) 952-6966. **$39-$69.** 2200 Corporate Plaza 30080. I-75 exit 260, just w to Corporate Plaza, then just s. Ext corridors. **Pets:** Large, other species. No service, supervision. 🛜 🆓 🔌

🐾 ▼▼▼ Residence Inn-Atlanta Cumberland Ⓗ ❄
(770) 433-8877. **$85-$154.** 2771 Cumberland Blvd 30080. I-285 exit 20 westbound; exit 19 eastbound, just n to Spring Rd, 0.3 mi w to Cumberland Blvd, then just n. Ext corridors. **Pets:** Medium, other species. $100 one-time fee/room. 🆂🆅🅴 🛜 ✖ 🆓 🔌 💻 🏊 ✖

SNELLVILLE

▼▼▼ Crestwood Suites 🏠

(770) 982-5250. **$55-$72.** 1784 Presidential Cir 30078. Jct Ronald Reagan Pkwy and SR 124, just w. Int corridors. **Pets:** Small. $15 daily fee/pet. Designated rooms, service with restrictions, supervision.

🛜 🛗 💻

◯◯◯ ▼▼▼▼ La Quinta Inn & Suites Snellville - Stone Mountain 🏠

(770) 736-4723. **$85-$190.** 2971 Main St W 30078. Jct US 78 and SR 124, 0.9 mi w. Int corridors. **Pets:** Medium, other species. Service with restrictions, supervision. SAVE 🛜 🛗 🛗 💻 🌊

STONE MOUNTAIN

◯◯◯ ▼▼▼ Best Western Stone Mountain M

(770) 465-1022. **$80-$116.** 1595 E Park Place Blvd 30087. US 78 exit 9, just n. Ext corridors. **Pets:** Medium. $25 daily fee/pet. Designated rooms, service with restrictions, supervision. SAVE 🛜 🛗 💻 🌊

SUWANEE

◯◯◯ ▼▼▼ Comfort Inn M ✿

(770) 945-1608. **Call for rates.** 2945 Lawrenceville Suwanee Rd 30024. I-85 exit 111, just e. Ext corridors. **Pets:** $25 one-time fee/pet. Service with restrictions. SAVE 🛜 🛗 💻 🌊

▼▼▼ Motel 6 Gwinnett Center 🏠

(770) 271-5559. **Call for rates.** 77 Gwinco Blvd 30024. I-85 exit 111, just e to Gwinco Blvd, then just s. Int corridors. **Pets:** Other species. Service with restrictions, supervision. 🛜 🛗 🛗 🌊

TUCKER

◯◯◯ ▼▼▼▼ DoubleTree by Hilton Hotel Atlanta - Northlake 🏠

(770) 938-1026. **$79-$119.** 4156 Lavista Rd 30084. I-285 exit 37, just w. Int corridors. **Pets:** Accepted. SAVE 🛜 🛗 💻 🍽 🌊

◯◯◯ ▼▼▼ Econo Lodge M

(770) 939-8440. **$50-$65.** 1820 Mountain Industrial Blvd 30084. US 78 exit 4, just n. Int corridors. **Pets:** Medium, dogs only. $10 daily fee/pet. Service with restrictions, supervision. SAVE 🛜 🛗 💻

◯◯◯ ◇ Masters Inn Tucker M

(770) 938-3552. **$42-$75.** 1435 Montreal Rd 30084. I-285 exit 38, just w. Ext corridors. **Pets:** Other species. $10 one-time fee/pet. Service with restrictions, supervision. SAVE 🛜 🛗 🌊

◯◯◯ ▼▼▼ Quality Inn Atlanta/Northlake M

(770) 491-7444. **$67-$99.** 2155 Ranchwood Dr 30345. I-285 exit 37, 0.4 mi w, then just n. Ext/int corridors. **Pets:** Small. $15 daily fee/pet. Designated rooms, service with restrictions, supervision. SAVE 🛜 🛗 🛗 💻 🌊

▼▼▼ TownePlace Suites Atlanta Northlake 🏠

(770) 938-0408. **$67-$125.** 3300 Northlake Pkwy 30345. I-285 exit 36 southbound, just w; exit 37 northbound, just w to Parklake Dr, 0.5 mi n, then just w. Int corridors. **Pets:** Accepted. ECO 🛜 ✖ 🛗 🛗 💻 🌊

UNION CITY

▼▼▼ Days Inn M

(770) 306-6067. **$50-$63.** 6840 Shannon Pkwy S 30291. I-85 exit 64, 0.3 mi w to Shannon Pkwy, then just s. Ext corridors. **Pets:** Medium, dogs only. $12 daily fee/pet. Service with restrictions, supervision. 🛜 🛗 💻 🌊

▼▼▼ Garden Inn Suites M

(770) 892-3128. **Call for rates.** 6701 Shannon Pkwy 30291. I-85 exit 64, 0.3 mi w to Shannon Pkwy, then just n. Ext corridors. **Pets:** Accepted. 🛜 🛗 💻 🌊

◯◯◯ ▼▼▼ Microtel Inn & Suites 🏠

(770) 306-3800. **$41-$117.** 6690 Shannon Pkwy 30291. I-85 exit 64, 0.3 mi w to Shannon Pkwy, then just n. Int corridors. **Pets:** Accepted. SAVE 🛜 🛗 🛗 💻

END METROPOLITAN AREA

AUGUSTA

◯◯◯ ▼▼▼▼ Augusta Marriott At The Convention Center 🏠

(706) 722-8900. **$125-$149.** 2 10th St 30901. I-20 exit 200 (River Watch Pkwy), 5.4 mi se, then just n; downtown. Int corridors. **Pets:** Medium, other species. $25 one-time fee/room. Service with restrictions, crate. SAVE 🛜 ✖ 🛗 🛗 💻 🍽 🌊 ✖

▼▼▼▼ Candlewood Suites Augusta 🏠

(706) 733-3300. **$70-$86.** 1080 Claussen Rd 30907. I-20 exit 200 (River Watch Pkwy), just nw, then just sw. Int corridors. **Pets:** Accepted. 🛜 🛗 🛗 💻

◯◯◯ ▼▼▼ Clarion Suites M

(706) 868-1800. **$79-$129.** 3038 Washington Rd 30907. I-20 exit 199 (Washington Rd), just w. Ext corridors. **Pets:** Small. $25 one-time fee/pet. Service with restrictions, crate. SAVE 🛜 🛗 💻 🍽 🌊

▼▼▼▼ DoubleTree by Hilton Hotel Augusta 🏠

(706) 855-8100. **Call for rates.** 2651 Perimeter Pkwy 30909. I-520 exit 1C (Wheeler Rd), just w to Perimeter Pkwy, then just n. Int corridors. **Pets:** Accepted. 🛜 🛗 🛗 💻 🍽 🌊 ✖

◯◯◯ ▼▼▼ Holiday Inn Gordon Highway at Bobby Jones M

(706) 737-2300. **$75-$89.** 2155 Gordon Hwy 30909. I-520 exit 3A (US 78), just w. Ext corridors. **Pets:** Accepted. SAVE 🛜 ✖ 🛗 💻 🍽 🌊

▼▼▼ Jameson Suites 🏠

(706) 733-4656. **$80-$105.** 1062 Clausen Rd 30907. I-20 exit 200 (River Watch Pkwy), just nw, then just sw. Int corridors. **Pets:** Medium. $15 daily fee/room. Service with restrictions, supervision. 🛜 🛗 🛗 💻 🌊

▼▼▼ La Quinta Inn Augusta M

(706) 733-2660. **$64-$122.** 3020 Washington Rd 30907. I-20 exit 199 (Washington Rd), just w. Ext/int corridors. **Pets:** Medium, other species. Service with restrictions, supervision. 🛜 🛗 🛗 💻 🌊

▼▼▼ The Partridge Inn 🏠

(706) 737-8888. **Call for rates.** 2110 Walton Way 30904. 1.3 mi w off 15th St. Int corridors. **Pets:** Accepted. 🛜 🛗 💻 🍽 🌊

◯◯◯ ▼▼▼▼ Sheraton Augusta Hotel 🏠

(706) 396-1000. **$99-$179.** 1069 Stevens Creek Rd 30907. I-20 exit 199 (Washington Rd), just w, then just ne. Int corridors. **Pets:** Accepted. SAVE 🛜 ✖ 🛗 💻 🍽 🌊

▼▼▼▼ Staybridge Suites 🏠

(706) 733-0000. **$106-$159.** 2540 Center West Pkwy 30909. I-20 exit 199 (Washington Rd), just e, then just n. Int corridors. **Pets:** Accepted. 🛜 ✖ 🛗 🛗 💻 ✖

BAINBRIDGE

▼▼▼ Jameson Inn 🏠

(229) 243-7000. **$75-$95.** 1403 Tallahassee Hwy 39819. Just s of US 84 Bypass on US 27. Ext corridors. **Pets:** Medium. $15 daily fee/room. Service with restrictions, supervision. 🛜 🛗 💻 🌊

BLUE RIDGE

AAA ▼▼▼ **The Blue Ridge Lodge by Comfort Inn & Suites** **H**
(706) 946-3333. **$63-$90.** 83 Blue Ridge Overlook 30513. Just off SR 515 and US 76; behind Arby's. Int corridors. **Pets:** Accepted.
SAVE 🛜 ✕ ⚙ 🛏 💻 🏊

▼▼ **Days Inn** **M**
(706) 632-2100. **$45-$95.** 4970 Appalachian Hwy 30513. On SR 515 and US 76. Ext corridors. **Pets:** Accepted. 🛜 🛏 💻 🏊

▼▼ **Douglas Inn & Suites** **M**
(706) 258-3600. **Call for rates.** 1192 Windy Ridge Rd 30513. Just off SR 515 and US 76; behind Wendy's. Ext corridors. **Pets:** Accepted.
🛜 ⚙ 🛏 💻 🏊

BRASELTON

AAA ▼▼▼ **Best Western Braselton Inn** **H** ❀
(706) 654-3081. **$90-$170.** 303 Zion Church Rd 30517. I-85 exit 129, just e, then 0.3 mi n. Ext corridors. **Pets:** Medium. $15 daily fee/pet. Designated rooms, service with restrictions, supervision.
SAVE 🛜 🛏 💻 🏊

BREMEN

▼▼ **Days Inn** **M**
(770) 537-4646. **$48-$69, 14 day notice.** 35 Price Creek Rd 30110. I-20 exit 11, just n. Ext corridors. **Pets:** Dogs only. $10 one-time fee/pet. Service with restrictions, supervision. 🛜 ⚙ 🛏 💻 🏊

AAA ▼▼▼ **Holiday Inn Express Hotel & Suites** **H**
(770) 537-3770. **$79-$129.** 125 US Hwy 27 Bypass 30110. I-20 exit 11, just n. Int corridors. **Pets:** Accepted. SAVE 🛜 ⚙ 🛏 💻 🏊

AAA ▼▼▼ **Quality Inn & Suites** **H**
(770) 824-5105. **$52-$79.** 1077 Alabama Ave 30110. I-20 exit 11, just n. Ext corridors. **Pets:** Small. $10 daily fee/pet. Service with restrictions, supervision. SAVE 🛜 🛏 💻 🏊

BRUNSWICK

AAA ▼▼▼ **Hampton Inn Brunswick** **H**
(912) 261-0002. **Call for rates.** 230 Warren Mason Blvd 31520. I-95 exit 36A (New Jesup Hwy/US 25), just se, then just sw on Tourist Dr. Ext/int corridors. **Pets:** Medium. Service with restrictions, supervision.
SAVE 🛜 ✕ 🛏 💻 🏊

▼▼ **La Quinta Inn & Suites Brunswick** **H**
(912) 265-7725. **$62-$119.** 165 Warren Mason Blvd 31520. I-95 exit 36A (New Jesup Hwy/US 25), just se, then sw on Tourist Dr. Int corridors. **Pets:** Medium, other species. Service with restrictions, supervision.
🛜 🛏 💻 🏊

AAA ▼ **Super 8** **H**
(912) 264-8800. **$45-$59.** 5280 New Jesup Hwy 31523. I-95 exit 36B (New Jesup Hwy/US 25), just nw. Int corridors. **Pets:** $10 daily fee/pet. Service with restrictions. SAVE 🛜 🛏 💻

BYRON

AAA ▼▼▼ **Best Western Inn & Suites** **H** ❀
(478) 956-3056. **$70-$78.** 101 Dunbar Rd 31008. I-75 exit 149 (SR 49), just ne. Ext corridors. **Pets:** Other species. $10 daily fee/pet. Service with restrictions, supervision. SAVE 🛜 🛏 💻 🏊

AAA ▼▼▼ **Econo Lodge** **H** ❀
(478) 956-2800. **$50-$60.** 12003 Watson Blvd 31008. I-75 exit 146, just nw. Ext corridors. **Pets:** Large, other species. $10 daily fee/pet. Designated rooms, service with restrictions. SAVE 🛜 🛏 💻

CAIRO

AAA ▼▼▼ **Best Western Executive Inn** **H**
(229) 377-8000. **$70-$90.** 2800 Hwy 84 E 39828. 2 mi e. Ext corridors. **Pets:** Accepted. SAVE 🛜 🛏 💻 🍴 🏊

CALHOUN

▼▼ **Country Inn & Suites By Carlson** **H**
(706) 625-6500. **$80-$179, 3 day notice.** 1033 Fairmount Hwy 30701. I-75 exit 312, just e. Int corridors. **Pets:** Medium. Service with restrictions, supervision. 🛜 ⚙ 🛏 💻 🏊

▼▼ **Days Inn** **M**
(706) 629-9501. **$48-$60.** 915 Hwy 53 E SE 30701. I-75 exit 312, just e. Ext corridors. **Pets:** Accepted. 🛜 ⚙ 🛏 💻 🍴 🏊

▼▼ **Jameson Inn** **M**
(706) 629-8133. **$70-$90.** 189 Jameson St 30701. I-75 exit 312, just w. Ext corridors. **Pets:** Medium. $15 daily fee/room. Service with restrictions, supervision. 🛜 ⚙ 🛏 💻 🏊

▼▼ **La Quinta Inn** **H**
(706) 629-2559. **$84-$144.** 150 Cracker Barrel Dr 30701. I-75 exit 312, just e. Int corridors. **Pets:** Medium, other species. Service with restrictions, supervision. 🛜 ⚙ 🛏 💻 🏊

▼▼ **Motel 6** **M**
(706) 629-8271. **$44-$69.** 742 Hwy 53 SE 30701. I-75 exit 312, just w. Ext corridors. **Pets:** Other species. Service with restrictions, supervision. 🛜 🛏 🍴 🏊

▼▼ **Ramada Calhoun** **M**
(706) 629-9207. **$60-$95.** 1204 Red Bud Rd NE 30701. I-75 exit 315, just w. Ext corridors. **Pets:** Small. $10 daily fee/pet. Designated rooms, service with restrictions, supervision. 🛜 🛏 💻 🏊

CANTON

▼▼ **Comfort Inn** **H**
(770) 345-1994. **$69-$79.** 138 Keith Dr 30114. I-575 exit 20, just e. Int corridors. **Pets:** Small. $25 daily fee/pet. Service with restrictions, supervision. 🛜 ⚙ 🛏 💻 🏊

▼▼ **Microtel Inn & Suites** **H**
(770) 345-8700. **$67-$76.** 114 River Pointe Pkwy 30114. I-575 exit 20, just e. Int corridors. **Pets:** Accepted. 🛜 ✕ ⚙ 🛏 💻

CARROLLTON

▼▼ **Jameson Inn** **M**
(770) 834-2600. **$70-$90.** 700 S Park St 30117. On US 27, just s of downtown. Ext corridors. **Pets:** Medium. $15 daily fee/room. Service with restrictions, supervision. 🛜 ⚙ 🛏 💻 🏊

CARTERSVILLE

▼▼ **America's Best Inn & Suites** **M**
(770) 387-9577. **$40-$45.** 35 Carson Loop 30184. I-75 exit 296, just w. Ext corridors. **Pets:** Accepted. 🛜 🛏 🍴 🏊

AAA ▼▼▼ **Best Western Garden Inn & Suites** **M**
(770) 386-1569. **$67-$104.** 5663 Hwy 20 NE 30121. I-75 exit 290, 0.3 mi e. Ext corridors. **Pets:** Accepted. SAVE 🛜 ⚙ 🛏 💻 🏊

▼▼▼ **Country Inn & Suites By Carlson** **H**
(770) 386-5888. **$80-$169, 3 day notice.** 43 SR 20 Spur 30121. I-75 exit 290, 0.3 mi se. Int corridors. **Pets:** Accepted.
🛜 ⚙ 🛏 💻 🏊

▼▼ **Days Inn** **M**
(770) 382-1824. **$50-$95.** 5618 Hwy 20 SE 30120. I-75 exit 290, just w. Ext corridors. **Pets:** Accepted. 🛜 🛏 💻 🏊

▼▼ **Delux Inn** **M**
(770) 386-0510. **Call for rates.** 235 Dixie Ave 30120. I-75 exit 288, 2.5 mi w. Ext corridors. **Pets:** Accepted. 🛜 🛏 💻 🍴 🏊

▼▼ **Holiday Inn** **H**
(770) 386-0830. **$87-$88, 3 day notice.** 2336 Hwy 411 30120. I-75 exit 293; southwest corner. Int corridors. **Pets:** Accepted.
🛜 ⚙ 🛏 💻 🍴 🏊

▼▼ Howard Johnson Express M
(770) 386-0700. **$45.** 25 Carson Loop NW 30121. I-75 exit 296, just w. Ext corridors. **Pets:** Accepted. 🛰️ 🍴 💻 🏊

AAA ▼▼ Knights Inn M
(770) 386-7263. **$32-$54.** 420 E Church St 30121. I-75 exit 288, 1.5 mi w. Ext corridors. **Pets:** Accepted. [SAVE] 🛰️ 🍴 🏊

▼▼ Motel 6 - 4046 M
(770) 386-1449. **$43-$47.** 5657 Hwy 20 NE 30121. I-75 exit 290, 0.3 mi e. Ext corridors. **Pets:** Other species. Service with restrictions, supervision. 🛰️ 🍴 🏊

▼▼ Red Roof Inn M
(770) 387-1800. **$49-$79.** 28 SR 20 Spur 30121. I-75 exit 290, 0.3 mi se. Ext corridors. **Pets:** Large, other species. No service, supervision. 🛰️ 🍴 💻 🏊

▼▼▼ Sleep Inn H
(770) 386-9259. **$74.** 11 Kent Dr 30121. I-75 exit 296, just e. Int corridors. **Pets:** Accepted. 🛰️ 🔥M 🍴 💻 🏊

▼▼ Super 8 H
(770) 382-8881. **$50-$90.** 41 SR 20 Spur SE 30121. I-75 exit 290, 0.3 mi e. Int corridors. **Pets:** Accepted. 🛰️ 🍴 💻 🏊

CEDARTOWN

▼▼ Country Hearth Inn H
(770) 749-9951. **Call for rates.** 925 N Main St 30125. 1.5 mi n on US 27. Int corridors. **Pets:** Accepted. 🛰️ 🔥M 🍴 💻

CHATSWORTH

AAA ▼▼ Best Western Fairwinds Inn & Suites M
(706) 695-1411. **Call for rates.** 613 S 3rd Ave 30705. On US 76/441, 0.3 mi s. Ext corridors. **Pets:** Accepted. [SAVE] 🛰️ 🔥M 🍴 💻 🏊

▼▼ Key West Inn M
(706) 517-1155. **Call for rates.** 501 GI Maddox Pkwy 30705. Jct US 76/411. Ext corridors. **Pets:** Accepted. 🛰️ 🍴

CLAYTON

▼▼ Americas Best Value Inn H
(706) 782-4702. **$45-$95.** 698 Hwy 441 S 30525. 0.8 mi s. Int corridors. **Pets:** Accepted. 🛰️ 🍴 💻

▼▼ Days Inn M
(706) 782-4258. **$50-$88.** 54 Hwy 441 30525. Center. Ext corridors. **Pets:** Accepted. 🛰️ 🍴 💻 🏊

▼▼ Historic Old Clayton Inn H
(706) 782-7722. **$69-$119, 7 day notice.** 60 S Main St 30525. 1 blk s of US 76; 2 blks w of US 441; downtown. Int corridors. **Pets:** Medium. $100 deposit/pet. Service with restrictions. 🛰️ 🍴

AAA ▼ Regal Inn M
(706) 782-4269. **$40-$95.** 707 Hwy 441 S 30525. 0.8 mi s. Ext corridors. **Pets:** Small, dogs only. $10 one-time fee/pet. Designated rooms, service with restrictions, supervision. [SAVE] 🛰️ 🍴 💻

COLQUITT

▼▼▼ Tarrer Inn CI ✿
(229) 758-2888. **$99-$149, 7 day notice.** 155 S Cuthbert St 39837. Corner of SR 91 and 27; center of town square. Int corridors. **Pets:** Small. $25 one-time fee/room. Supervision. 🛰️ ✖️ 🔥M 💻 🍴

COLUMBUS

AAA ▼▼ Best Western Columbus M
(706) 568-3300. **$80-$110.** 3443B Macon Rd 31907. I-185 exit 6, just e. Ext corridors. **Pets:** Accepted. [SAVE] 🛰️ 🍴 💻 🏊

▼▼ Extended StayAmerica-Columbus-Airport M 🐾
(706) 653-0131. **$55-$75.** 5020 Armour Rd 31904. I-185 exit 8, 1.5 mi e, then 0.5 mi n. Ext corridors. **Pets:** Other species. $25 daily fee/pet. Service with restrictions. 🛰️ 🍴 💻

▼▼ Extended StayAmerica-Columbus-Bradley Park H 🐾
(706) 653-9938. **$65-$85.** 1721 Rollins Way 31904. I-185 exit 10 (US 80 and SR 22), 1.5 mi w on US 80 exit 3A, just s to Whittlesey Rd, 0.3 mi e to Rollins Way, then just n. Int corridors. **Pets:** Other species. $25 daily fee/pet. Service with restrictions. 🛰️ 🍴 💻

▼▼▼ Holiday Inn Express & Suites H
(706) 507-7080. **$129-$149, 3 day notice.** 3901 Victory Dr 31903. I-185 exit 1B, 1 mi w. Int corridors. **Pets:** Accepted. 🛰️ 🔥M 🍴 💻 🏊

AAA ▼▼▼ Holiday Inn North H
(706) 324-0231. **$59-$149.** 2800 Manchester Expy 31904. I-185 exit 7 (Manchester Expwy), just w. Int corridors. **Pets:** Accepted. [SAVE] 🛰️ ✖️ 🍴 💻 🍴 🏊

▼▼ La Quinta Inn Columbus Midtown M
(706) 568-1740. **$62-$126.** 3201 Macon Rd, Suite 200 31906. I-185 exit 6, just w. Ext/int corridors. **Pets:** Medium, other species. Service with restrictions, supervision. 🛰️ 💻 🏊

▼▼ La Quinta Inn Columbus State University H
(706) 323-4344. **$68-$137.** 2919 Warm Springs Rd 31909. I-185 exit 7 southbound; exit 7A northbound, just e. Int corridors. **Pets:** Medium, other species. Service with restrictions, supervision. 🛰️ 🔥M 🍴 💻 🏊

▼▼ Microtel Inn & Suites of North Columbus H
(706) 653-7004. **$59-$68.** 1728 Fountain Ct 31904. I-185 exit 12, just w. Int corridors. **Pets:** Accepted. 🛰️ 🔥M 🍴 💻

▼ Motel 6 #58 M
(706) 687-7214. **$45-$55.** 3050 Victory Dr 31903. I-185 exit 1B, 3 mi w. Ext corridors. **Pets:** Other species. Service with restrictions, supervision. 🛰️ 🍴 🏊

▼▼▼ Rothschild-Pound House Inn BB
(706) 322-4075. **Call for rates.** 201 7th St 31901. Jct US 27 (Veterans Pkwy/7th St), just w; downtown. Ext/int corridors. **Pets:** Accepted. 🛰️ ✖️ 🍴 💻 ✉️

AAA ▼▼▼ Staybridge Suites H
(706) 507-7700. **$98-$126.** 1694 Whittlesey Rd 31904. I-185 exit 8, just w on Whitesville Rd, then just s. Int corridors. **Pets:** Accepted. [SAVE] 🛰️ 🍴 💻 🏊

COMMERCE

AAA ▼▼ Best Western Commerce Inn H
(706) 335-3640. **$60-$169.** 157 Eisenhower Dr 30529. I-85 exit 149, just ne. Int corridors. **Pets:** Medium. $10 daily fee/pet. Designated rooms, service with restrictions, supervision. [SAVE] 🛰️ 🔥M 🍴 💻 🏊

AAA ▼▼▼ Comfort Suites Commerce H 🐾
(706) 336-0000. **$79-$129.** 30490 Hwy 441 S 30529. I-85 exit 149, just w. Int corridors. **Pets:** Medium. $25 one-time fee/room. Crate. [SAVE] 🛰️ ✖️ 🔥M 🍴 💻 🏊

▼▼▼ Howard Johnson Inn Commerce GA M
(706) 335-5581. **$44-$140.** 148 Eisenhower Dr 30529. I-85 exit 149, just w. Ext corridors. **Pets:** Large. $10 one-time fee/pet. Service with restrictions, supervision. 🛰️ 🍴 💻 🏊

▼▼ Quality Inn M
(706) 335-9001. **$40-$90.** 165 Eisenhower Dr 30529. I-85 exit 149, just w. Ext corridors. **Pets:** Accepted. 🛰️ 🍴 💻 🏊

▼▼ Super 8 M
(706) 336-8008. **$39-$119.** 152 Eisenhower Dr 30529. I-85 exit 149, just w. Ext corridors. **Pets:** Large. $10 one-time fee/pet. Service with restrictions, supervision.

CONYERS

▲▲▲ ▼▼▼ Comfort Inn H
(770) 760-0300. **$70-$80.** 1363 Klondike Rd 30094. I-20 exit 80, just s. Int corridors. **Pets:** Small. $25 one-time fee/pet. Designated rooms, no service, supervision.

▼▼▼ Country Inn & Suites By Carlson H
(770) 785-2400. **$87-$120, 3 day notice.** 1312 Old Covington Hwy SE 30013. I-20 exit 82, just n. Int corridors. **Pets:** Medium. $45 one-time fee/pet. Designated rooms, service with restrictions, supervision.

▼▼▼ Hampton Inn H 🐾
(770) 483-8838. **$79-$159.** 1340 Dogwood Dr 30013. I-20 exit 82, just n, then just e. Int corridors. **Pets:** Other species. Designated rooms, service with restrictions.

▼▼ Jameson Inn M
(770) 760-1230. **$60-$80.** 1164 Dogwood Dr 30012. I-20 exit 82, just n, then just w. Ext corridors. **Pets:** Medium. $15 daily fee/room. Service with restrictions, supervision.

▼▼▼ La Quinta Inn & Suites Atlanta (Conyers) H
(770) 918-0092. **$78-$137.** 1184 Dogwood Dr 30012. I-20 exit 82, just n, then just w. Int corridors. **Pets:** Medium, other species. Service with restrictions, supervision.

▲▲▲ ▼▼▼ Ramada Inn & Conference Center M
(770) 483-3220. **$66-$94.** 1351 Dogwood Dr SW 30012. I-20 exit 80, just n, then 0.4 mi w. Ext corridors. **Pets:** Accepted.

CORDELE

▲▲▲ ▼▼▼ Best Western Colonial Inn H 🐾
(229) 273-5420. **$59-$65.** 1706 E 16th Ave (US 280) 31015. I-75 exit 101 (US 280), just w. Ext/int corridors. **Pets:** Medium, other species. $10 daily fee/pet. Designated rooms, service with restrictions, supervision.

▼▼ Comfort Inn & Suites H
(229) 273-9477. **Call for rates.** 416 S Greer St 31015. I-75 exit 101 (US 280), just w, then just n. Int corridors. **Pets:** Accepted.

▼▼ Hampton Inn H
(229) 273-0737. **$87-$99.** 1603 16th Ave E (US 280) 31015. I-75 exit 101 (US 280), just w. Ext corridors. **Pets:** Medium. Designated rooms, service with restrictions.

▲▲▲ ▼▼▼ Lake Blackshear Resort & Golf Club H 🐾
(229) 276-1004. **$99-$199, 7 day notice.** 2459-H US 280 W 31015. I-75 exit 101 (US 280), 10 mi w. Ext/int corridors. **Pets:** Other species. Designated rooms, service with restrictions.

▲▲▲ ▼▼▼ Quality Inn Cordele H
(229) 273-2371. **$59-$125.** 1601 E 16th Ave (US 280) 31015. I-75 exit 101 (US 280), just w. Ext corridors. **Pets:** Accepted.

▲▲▲ ▼▼▼ Ramada Cordele H 🐾
(229) 273-5000. **$54.** 2016 E 16th Ave (US 280) 31015. I-75 exit 101 (US 280), just e. Ext corridors. **Pets:** Medium. $10 daily fee/pet. Service with restrictions, supervision.

CORNELIA

▼▼ America's Best Inn & Suites H
(706) 778-9573. **$60-$175.** 2965 J Warren Rd 30531. Jct SR 365 and US 441 business route, just w. Int corridors. **Pets:** Medium, dogs only. $25 daily fee/pet. Designated rooms, service with restrictions, crate.

COVINGTON

▲▲▲ ▼▼▼ Baymont Inn & Suites M
(770) 787-4900. **$50-$103.** 10111 Alcovy Rd 30014. I-20 exit 92, just n. Ext corridors. **Pets:** Small. $15 daily fee/pet. Service with restrictions, supervision.

▼▼ Quality Inn M
(770) 784-1849. **$42-$119.** 10225 Hwy 142 N 30014. I-20 exit 93, just s. Ext corridors. **Pets:** Small, other species. $50 deposit/room, $15 daily fee/pet. Designated rooms, service with restrictions, supervision.

DAHLONEGA

▲▲▲ ▼▼▼ Quality Inn Dahlonega M
(706) 864-6191. **$70-$120.** 619 N Grove St 30533. 0.5 mi n on US 19 business route. Ext corridors. **Pets:** Small, dogs only. $10 daily fee/pet. Designated rooms, service with restrictions, supervision.

▼▼▼ Super 8 M
(706) 864-4343. **$45-$82, 7 day notice.** 20 Mountain Dr 30533. 0.5 mi s on US 19 and SR 60. Ext corridors. **Pets:** Accepted.

DALLAS

▼▼ Days Inn M
(770) 505-4567. **$49-$62.** 1007 Old Harris Rd 30132. Jct Business Rt SR 6 (Atlanta Hwy). Ext corridors. **Pets:** Accepted.

DALTON

▼▼ Baymont Dalton M
(706) 226-5022. **Call for rates.** 2106 Chattanooga Rd 30720. I-75 exit 336, just w. Ext corridors. **Pets:** Accepted.

▼▼▼ Comfort Inn & Suites H
(706) 259-2583. **$85-$120.** 905 Westbridge Rd 30720. I-75 exit 333, just w to Westbridge Rd, then just s. Int corridors. **Pets:** Accepted.

▼▼ Dalton Inn M
(706) 278-4300. **Call for rates.** 2007 Tampico Way 30720. I-75 exit 336, just e. Int corridors. **Pets:** Accepted.

▼▼▼ Holiday Inn & Suites Dalton H
(706) 529-6000. **$114-$180.** 879 College Dr 30720. I-75 exit 333, just w. Int corridors. **Pets:** Medium. $40 daily fee/pet. Service with restrictions, supervision.

▼▼ Jameson Inn M
(706) 281-1880. **$70-$90.** 790 College Dr 30720. I-75 exit 333, just w, then 0.3 mi n. Ext corridors. **Pets:** Medium. $15 daily fee/room. Service with restrictions, supervision.

▼▼▼ La Quinta Inn & Suites Dalton H
(706) 272-9099. **$78-$154.** 715 College Dr 30720. I-75 exit 333, just w to Holiday Dr, then 0.5 mi n. Int corridors. **Pets:** Medium, other species. Service with restrictions, supervision.

▼▼ Quality Inn M
(706) 278-0500. **$65-$99.** 875 College Dr 30720. I-75 exit 333, just w. Ext corridors. **Pets:** Accepted.

DARIEN

AAA ▼▼▼ Comfort Inn H
(912) 437-4200. **$55.** 12924 GA Hwy 251 Rd 31305. I-95 exit 49 (SR 251), just nw. Int corridors. **Pets:** Large. $15 daily fee/pet. Designated rooms, service with restrictions, supervision. [SAVE] 🛜 📶 💻 🏊

DAWSONVILLE

AAA ▼▼▼ Best Western Dawson Village Inn H
(706) 216-4410. **$70-$73.** 76 N Georgia Ave 30534. Jct SR 400/53, 0.5 mi s. Int corridors. **Pets:** Dogs only. $20 daily fee/pet. Service with restrictions, supervision. [SAVE] 🛜 ✕ &M 📶 💻 🏊

▼▼▼ Comfort Inn H
(706) 216-1900. **$64-$94.** 127 Beartooth Pkwy 30534. Jct SR 400/53, 0.5 mi s. Int corridors. **Pets:** Accepted. 🛜 ✕ &M 📶 💻 🏊

▼▼ Super 8 H
(706) 216-6801. **$45-$63, 6 day notice.** 205 N 400 Center Ln 30534. Jct SR 400/53, just n. Int corridors. **Pets:** Medium, other species. $10 daily fee/pet. Service with restrictions, supervision.
🛜 &M 📶 💻 🏊

DILLARD

AAA ▼▼▼ Dillard House M
(706) 746-5348. **$69-$179, 3 day notice.** 768 Franklin St 30537. US 441, just e via Old Dillard Rd. Ext corridors. **Pets:** Accepted.
[SAVE] 🛜 📶 💻 ¶ 🏊 ✕

AAA ▼▼▼ Mountain Valley Inn M
(706) 746-5373. **$35-$110.** 13 Royalty Ln 30537. Just n of town center. Ext corridors. **Pets:** Small. $10 daily fee/pet. Service with restrictions, supervision. [SAVE] 🛜 📶 💻 🏊

DOUGLAS

▼▼ Jameson Inn H
(912) 384-9432. **$63-$83.** 1628 S Peterson Ave 31535. Jct US 221/441/SR 31 and SR 206/353, just s. Ext corridors. **Pets:** Medium. $15 daily fee/room. Service with restrictions, supervision. 🛜 📶 💻 🏊

DUBLIN

▼▼ Jameson Inn H
(478) 275-3008. **$75-$95.** 100 PM Watson Dr 31021. I-16 exit 51 (US 441), just n. Ext corridors. **Pets:** Medium. $15 daily fee/room. Service with restrictions, supervision. 🛜 📶 💻 🏊

▼▼▼ La Quinta Inn & Suites Dublin H
(478) 272-3110. **$84-$149.** 101 Travel Center Blvd 31021. I-16 exit 51 (US 441), just s. Int corridors. **Pets:** Medium, other species. Service with restrictions, supervision. 🛜 ✕ 📶 💻 🏊

AAA ▼▼▼ Quality Inn & Suites H
(478) 274-8000. **Call for rates.** 2110 Hwy 441 S 31021. I-16 exit 51 (US 441), 0.6 mi n. Ext corridors. **Pets:** Accepted.
[SAVE] 🛜 &M 📶 💻 🏊

EAST ELLIJAY

AAA ▼▼▼ Best Western Mountain View Inn H
(706) 515-1500. **$74-$120.** 43 Coosawattee Dr 30539. 0.8 mi s on SR 515. Int corridors. **Pets:** Small. $10 daily fee/pet. Service with restrictions, supervision. [SAVE] 🛜 &M 📶 💻 🏊

AAA ▼▼▼ Stratford Motor Inn M
(706) 276-1080. **$60-$100.** 79 Maddox Cir 30540. Jct Maddox Cir and SR 515; behind Waffle King. Ext corridors. **Pets:** Medium, other species. $10 one-time fee/pet. Designated rooms, service with restrictions, supervision. [SAVE] 🛜 📶 💻 🏊

EATONTON

▼▼▼▼ The Lodge on Lake Oconee H
(706) 485-7785. **Call for rates.** 930 Lake Oconee Pkwy 31024. I-20 exit 130 (SR 44), 12.3 mi s. Int corridors. **Pets:** Accepted.
🛜 ✕ 📶 💻 🏊 ✕

FITZGERALD

▼▼ Western Motel H
(229) 424-9500. **Call for rates.** 111 Bull Run Rd 31750. Just n of US 319/107, on US 129. Ext corridors. **Pets:** Accepted. 🛜 📶 💻 🏊

FORSYTH

AAA ▼▼▼ Comfort Inn H
(478) 994-3400. **$69-$99.** 333 Harold G Clark Pkwy 31029. I-75 exit 185 (SR 18), just w. Ext corridors. **Pets:** Accepted. [SAVE] 🛜 📶 💻 🏊

AAA ▼▼▼ Econo Lodge M 🐾
(478) 994-5603. **Call for rates.** 320 Cabiness Rd 31029. I-75 exit 187, just e. Int corridors. **Pets:** Medium, other species. $6 daily fee/pet. Service with restrictions, supervision. [SAVE] 🛜 📶

AAA ▼▼▼ Hilltop Garden Inn M
(478) 994-9260. **$60-$80.** 951 Hwy 42 N 31029. I-75 exit 188, just e, via Frontage Rd. Ext corridors. **Pets:** Accepted. [SAVE] 🛜 📶 💻 🏊

▼▼ Holiday Inn Express H
(478) 994-9697. **$88-$124.** 520 Holiday Cir 31029. I-75 exit 186 (Juliette Rd), just w, then just s on Aaron St. Int corridors. **Pets:** Accepted.
🛜 &M 📶 💻 🏊

▼▼ Ramada Conference Center Forsyth H
(478) 994-5691. **Call for rates.** 480 Holiday Cir 31029. I-75 exit 186 (Juliette Rd), just w, then just s on Aaron St. Ext corridors.
Pets: Accepted. 🛜 📶 💻 🏊

▼▼ Super 8 H
(478) 994-5101. **$50-$65.** 436 Tift College Dr 31029. I-75 exit 186 (Juliette Rd), just w. Ext/int corridors. **Pets:** Medium. $15 daily fee/pet. Service with restrictions, supervision. 🛜 📶 💻 🏊

FORT OGLETHORPE

AAA ▼▼▼ Best Western Battlefield Inn M
(706) 866-0222. **$60-$150.** 2120 Lafayette Rd 30742. Jct US 27 and SR 2, just n. Ext corridors. **Pets:** Small. $15 daily fee/pet. Service with restrictions, supervision. [SAVE] 🛜 📶 💻 🏊

GAINESVILLE

▼▼▼ Country Hearth Inn & Suites M
(770) 287-3205. **$55-$60.** 766 Jesse Jewell Pkwy SW 30501. I-985 exit 20, 1.9 mi w to Jesse Jewell Pkwy, then just s. Ext corridors.
Pets: Accepted. 🛜 📶 💻

▼▼▼ GuestHouse Inn & Suites M
(770) 535-8100. **$54-$99.** 520 Queen City Pkwy SW 30501. I-985 exit 20, 1.8 mi nw on SR 60/Queen City Pkwy. Ext corridors. **Pets:** Other species. $15 daily fee/pet. Designated rooms, service with restrictions, crate. 🛜 📶 💻 🏊

GARDEN CITY

▼▼ Baymont Inn & Suites H
(912) 964-8669. **$81-$124.** 357 Main St 31408. I-95 exit 109 (SR 21), 6.5 mi se to Spur SR 21 (Brampton Rd), 0.3 mi n to Coastal Hwy/Main St, then just se. Int corridors. **Pets:** Accepted. 🛜 📶 💻 🏊

GOLDEN ISLES AREA

JEKYLL ISLAND

Hampton Inn & Suites Jekyll Island 🅷
(912) 635-3733. **$99-$229.** 200 S Beachview Dr 31527. Jct Ben Fortson Pkwy (SR 520/Beachview Dr), 2 mi s. Int corridors. **Pets:** Accepted.
[SAVE] 🛜 ✕ 🕭ᴹ 🔌 💻 🍴 ≈ ⊠

Villas by the Sea 🆑 🐾
(912) 635-2521. **$128-$369, 7 day notice.** 1175 N Beachview Dr 31527. Jct Ben Fortson Pkwy (SR 520/Beachview Dr), 4 mi n. Ext corridors. **Pets:** Other species. $100 one-time fee/room.
[SAVE] 🛜 🕭ᴹ 🔌 💻 🍴 ≈ ⊠

ST. SIMONS ISLAND

The Lodge at Sea Island 🅷 🐾
(912) 634-3992. **$349-$595, 7 day notice.** 100 Retreat Ave 31522. FJ Torras Cswy, 1.6 mi se on Kings Way, just s. Int corridors. **Pets:** Small. $175 one-time fee/room. Service with restrictions.
[SAVE] 🛜 ✕ 🍴 ⊠

Sea Palms Inn 🅷
(912) 634-0660. **$109-$149.** 411 Longview Plaza 31522. Jct Frederica and Demere rds, 0.4 mi n on Frederica Rd. Ext corridors.
Pets: Accepted. 🛜 🔌 💻 ≈ ⊠

END AREA

GREENSBORO

The Ritz-Carlton Lodge, Reynolds Plantation 🅷
(706) 467-0600. **Call for rates.** One Lake Oconee Tr 30642. I-20 exit 130, 7.2 mi sw on SR 44 (Old Eatonton Rd), 1.5 mi e on Linger Longer Rd, then 2 mi ne. Ext/int corridors. **Pets:** Accepted.
🛜 ✕ 🕭ᴹ 🔌 💻 🍴 ≈ ⊠

GRIFFIN

Comfort Inn & Suites 🅷
(770) 233-4747. **$76-$215.** 1906 N Expressway 30224. 2 mi n on US 41 and 19. Int corridors. **Pets:** Medium, other species. $10 daily fee/pet. Designated rooms, service with restrictions, crate.
[SAVE] 🛜 🕭ᴹ 🔌 💻

GROVETOWN

Hawthorn Suites by Wyndham Augusta 🅷
(706) 228-1990. **Call for rates.** 4049 Jimmie Dyess Pkwy 30909. I-20 exit 194 (SR 383), 0.5 mi s. Int corridors. **Pets:** Accepted.
🛜 🕭ᴹ 🔌 💻 ≈

Super 8-Augusta 🅷
(706) 396-1600. **$54-$243.** 456 Park West Dr 30813. I-20 exit 194 (SR 383), just s, then w. Int corridors. **Pets:** Accepted. 🛜 🔌 💻 ≈

HAMPTON

Western Inn 🅷
(770) 707-1477. **Call for rates.** 1078 Bear Creek Blvd 30228. 1 mi w of center of town; at US 41 and 19. Int corridors. **Pets:** Accepted.
🛜 🕭ᴹ 🔌 💻

HARTWELL

Best Western Lake Hartwell Inn & Suites 🅷
(706) 376-4700. **$64-$99.** 1357 E Franklin St 30643. I-85 exit 177, 2 mi on US 29 E. Int corridors. **Pets:** Other species. $25 one-time fee/room. Service with restrictions, supervision. [SAVE] 🛜 ✕ 🔌 💻 ≈

HAWKINSVILLE

Budget Inn Ⓜ
(478) 783-2002. **Call for rates.** 509 Broad St 31036. Downtown. Ext corridors. **Pets:** Small. $20 one-time fee/pet. No service, crate.
🛜 🔌 💻 ≈

HELEN

The Helendorf River Inn & Conference Center Ⓜ
(706) 878-2271. **$44-$169, 10 day notice.** 33 Munich Strasse 30545. SR 17 and 75; center. Ext corridors. **Pets:** Other species. $20 daily fee/pet. Designated rooms, service with restrictions, supervision.
🛜 🔌 💻 ≈

Kountry Peddler Tanglewood Resort Cabins 🅲🅰
(706) 878-3286. **Call for rates.** 3387 Hwy 356 30571. 1 mi n on SR 75, then 3 mi ne. Ext corridors. **Pets:** Accepted. 🛜 🔌 💻

Quality Inn Ⓜ
(706) 878-2268. **$55-$299.** 15 Yonah St 30545. Just w of Mack St. Ext corridors. **Pets:** Accepted. [SAVE] 🛜 🔌 💻 ≈

Riverbend Motel & Cabins Ⓜ
(706) 878-2155. **$49-$289, 3 day notice.** 134 River St 30545. Just w off Main St. Ext corridors. **Pets:** Accepted. [SAVE] 🛜 🔌 💻

HIAWASSEE

Enota B & B, Cabins & Conference Lodge 🅲🅰
(706) 896-9966. **Call for rates.** 1000 Hwy 180 30546. E on US 76 to SR 75/17, 6 mi s to SR 180, then 2.5 mi w. Ext corridors. **Pets:** Other species. $15 daily fee/pet. No service, supervision.
🛜 ✕ 🔌 💻 ⊠ ✍

Ramada Lake Chatuge Lodge of Hiawassee 🅷
(706) 896-5253. **$62-$167.** 653 US Hwy 76 30546. 1 mi w. Int corridors. **Pets:** Small. $25 deposit/room. Designated rooms, service with restrictions, supervision. 🛜 🕭ᴹ 🔌 💻

HIRAM

Country Inn & Suites By Carlson 🅷
(770) 222-0456. **$75-$120.** 70 Enterprise Path 30134. Jct SR 92/6 and US 278, 0.3 mi w. Int corridors. **Pets:** Small. $15 daily fee/pet. Service with restrictions, supervision. 🛜 🔌 💻 ≈

HOGANSVILLE

Woodstream Inn Ⓜ
(706) 637-9395. **$50-$120.** 1888 E Main St 30230. I-85 exit 28, just w. Ext corridors. **Pets:** Accepted. 🛜 🔌 💻 ≈

JASPER

Microtel Inn & Suites 🅷
(706) 299-5500. **$58-$71.** 171 H Mullins Ct 30143. Jct SR 515/53, 0.9 mi n. Int corridors. **Pets:** Small, other species. $25 one-time fee/pet. Service with restrictions, supervision. 🛜 🕭ᴹ 🔌 💻

Super 8 Ⓜ
(706) 253-3297. **$51-$84.** 100 Whitfield Dr 30143. Jct SR 515/53; in Lawsons Crossing. Ext corridors. **Pets:** Accepted.
🛜 🕭ᴹ 🔌 💻 ≈

JESUP

Jameson Inn of Jesup 🅷
(912) 427-6800. **$65-$85.** 205 N Hwy 301 31545. Jct US 341, just n. Ext corridors. **Pets:** Medium. $15 daily fee/room. Service with restrictions, supervision. 🛜 🔌 💻 ≈

KINGSLAND

▼▼▼▼ Country Inn & Suites By Carlson 🅗
(912) 576-1616. **Call for rates.** 135 The Lakes Blvd 31548. I-95 exit 3
(SR 40), just se. Int corridors. **Pets:** Accepted. 🛜 🛗Ⓜ 🛏 🖵 🏊

▼▼ Jameson Inn 🅗
(912) 729-9600. **$65-$85.** 105 May Creek Blvd 31548. I-95 exit 3 (SR
40), just w, then s at Boone Ave. Ext corridors. **Pets:** Medium. $15 daily
fee/room. Service with restrictions, supervision. 🛜 🛗Ⓜ 🛏 🖵 🏊

ⒶⒶⒶ ▼▼▼▼ La Quinta Inn & Suites Kingsland 🅗
(912) 882-8010. **$76-$135.** 104 May Creek Dr 31548. I-95 exit 3 (SR
40), just sw. Int corridors. **Pets:** Medium, other species. Service with
restrictions, supervision. 🆂🅰🆅🅴 🛜 ⓧ 🛗Ⓜ 🛏 🖵 🏊

ⒶⒶⒶ ▼▼▼ Microtel Inn & Suites 🅗
(912) 729-1555. **$45-$68.** 1325 E King Ave 31548. I-95 exit 3 (SR 40),
just ne. Int corridors. **Pets:** Large, other species. $10 daily fee/pet. Desig-
nated rooms, service with restrictions, supervision.
🆂🅰🆅🅴 🛜 🛏 🖵 🏊

▼▼ Sleep Inn & Suites 🅗
(912) 673-7116. **$49-$89.** 1321 Hospitality Ave 31548. I-95 exit 3 (SR
40), just e. Int corridors. **Pets:** Accepted. 🛜 🛗Ⓜ 🛏 🖵 🏊

LA FAYETTE

▼▼ Days Inn Ⓜ
(706) 639-9362. **$40-$85.** 2209 N Main St 30728. 2.5 mi n on US 27.
Ext corridors. **Pets:** $10 daily fee/pet. Designated rooms, service with
restrictions, supervision. 🛜 🛏 🖵 🏊

▼▼ Key West Inn Ⓜ
(706) 638-8200. **$49-$89.** 2221 N Main St 30728. 2.5 mi n on US 27.
Ext corridors. **Pets:** Accepted. 🛜 🛗Ⓜ 🛏 🏊

LAGRANGE

▼▼ Baymont Inn & Suites 🅗
(706) 885-9002. **$63-$79.** 107 Hoffman Dr 30240. I-85 exit 18 (Lafayette
Pkwy), just w. Int corridors. **Pets:** Medium. $10 daily fee/pet. Service with
restrictions, crate. 🛜 🛏 🖵 🏊 ⓧ

ⒶⒶⒶ ▼▼▼▼ Best Western Plus Lafayette Garden Inn &
Conference Center Ⓜ
(706) 884-6175. **$65-$80.** 1513 Lafayette Pkwy 30241. I-85 exit 18
(Lafayette Pkwy), just w. Ext corridors. **Pets:** Accepted.
🆂🅰🆅🅴 🛜 🛏 🖵 🍽 🏊

ⒶⒶⒶ ▼▼▼ Days Inn-LaGrange/Callaway Gardens Ⓜ
(706) 882-8881. **$45-$64.** 2606 Whitesville Rd 30240. I-85 exit 13, just e.
Ext corridors. **Pets:** Other species. $15 daily fee/pet. Service with restric-
tions, supervision. 🆂🅰🆅🅴 🛜 🛏 🖵 🏊

▼▼ Jameson Inn Ⓜ
(706) 882-8700. **$70-$90.** 110 Jameson Dr 30240. I-85 exit 18 (Lafayette
Pkwy), 0.3 mi w. Ext corridors. **Pets:** Medium. $15 daily fee/room. Service
with restrictions, supervision. 🛜 🛗Ⓜ 🛏 🖵 🏊

▼▼ Red Roof Inn LaGrange Ⓜ
(706) 882-9540. **$59-$99.** 1601 Lafayette Pkwy 30241. I-85 exit 18
(Lafayette Pkwy), just e. Ext corridors. **Pets:** Large, other species. No
service, supervision. 🛜 🛏 🖵 🏊

LAKE PARK

ⒶⒶⒶ ▼▼▼ Days Inn 🅗
(229) 559-0229. **$50-$70.** 4913 Timber Dr 31636. I-75 exit 5, just nw. Ext
corridors. **Pets:** Medium. $10 one-time fee/pet. Service with restrictions,
supervision. 🆂🅰🆅🅴 🛜 ⓧ 🛏 🖵 🏊

LAVONIA

▼▼▼ Holiday Inn Express & Suites 🅗
(706) 356-2100. **Call for rates.** 110 Owens Dr 30553. I-85 exit 173, just
w. Int corridors. **Pets:** Small. $30 one-time fee/room. Designated rooms,
service with restrictions, supervision. 🛜 🛗Ⓜ 🛏 🖵 🏊

▼▼ Regency Inn & Suites Ⓜ 🐾
(706) 356-4000. **Call for rates.** 13705 Jones St 30553. I-85 exit 173,
just e. Ext corridors. **Pets:** Other species. $15 one-time fee/room.
🛜 🛏 🖵 🏊

▼▼ Super 8-Lavonia Ⓜ
(706) 356-8848. **$46-$66.** 14227 Jones St 30553. I-85 exit 173, just w.
Ext corridors. **Pets:** Accepted. 🛜 🛗Ⓜ 🛏 🖵 🏊

LOCUST GROVE

ⒶⒶⒶ ▼▼▼▼ La Quinta Inn & Suites Locust Grove 🅗
(678) 583-8088. **$84-$144.** 4832 Bill Gardner Pkwy 30248. I-75 exit 212,
just e. Int corridors. **Pets:** Medium, other species. Service with restrictions,
supervision. 🆂🅰🆅🅴 🛜 🛗Ⓜ 🛏 🖵 🏊

ⒶⒶⒶ ▼▼▼▼ Red Roof Inn 🅗
(678) 583-0004. **$59-$89.** 4840 Bill Gardner Pkwy 30248. I-75 exit 212,
just e. Int corridors. **Pets:** Large, other species. No service, supervision.
🆂🅰🆅🅴 🛜 🛗Ⓜ 🛏 🏊

ⒶⒶⒶ ▼▼▼ Super 8 Ⓜ
(770) 957-2936. **$49-$87, 3 day notice.** 4605 Bill Gardner Pkwy 30248.
I-75 exit 212, just w. Ext corridors. **Pets:** Small, dogs only. $15 daily fee/
pet. Designated rooms, service with restrictions. 🆂🅰🆅🅴 🛜 🛏 🖵

MACON

ⒶⒶⒶ ▼▼▼ Best Western Inn & Suites of
Macon Ⓜ 🐾
(478) 781-5300. **$70-$80.** 4681 Chambers Rd 31206. I-475 exit 3 (Eisenhower Pkwy/US 80), just ne, then just se. Ext corridors. **Pets:** Medium.
$10 daily fee/room. Service with restrictions. 🆂🅰🆅🅴 🛜 🛏 🖵 🏊

▼▼ Candlewood Suites 🅗
(478) 254-3530. **$81-$89.** 3957 River Place Dr 31210. I-75 exit 169 (Arkwright Rd), just e, then just s. Int corridors. **Pets:** Accepted.
🛜 🛗Ⓜ 🛏 🖵 🏊

ⒶⒶⒶ ▼▼▼ Comfort Inn & Suites 🅗
(478) 757-8688. **$63-$74.** 3935 Arkwright Rd 31210. I-75 exit 169 (Arkwright Rd), just n. Int corridors. **Pets:** Accepted.
🆂🅰🆅🅴 🛜 🛏 🖵 🏊

▼▼ Extended Stay Deluxe Macon-North 🅗 🐾
(478) 474-2805. **$65-$100.** 3980 Riverside Dr 31210. I-75 exit 169 (Arkwright Rd), just sw, then 0.4 mi nw. Int corridors. **Pets:** Other species.
$25 daily fee/pet. Service with restrictions. 🛜 🛏 🖵 🏊

▼▼▼ La Quinta Inn & Suites Macon 🅗
(478) 475-0206. **$64-$137.** 3944 River Place Dr 31210. I-75 exit 169
(Arkwright Rd), just n, then e. Int corridors. **Pets:** Medium, other species.
Service with restrictions, supervision. 🛜 🛗Ⓜ 🛏 🖵 🏊

▼▼▼ La Quinta Inn & Suites Macon West 🅗
(478) 788-6226. **$75-$150.** 4615 Chambers Rd 31206. I-475 exit 3
(Eisenhower Pkwy/US 80), just e, then 0.5 mi s. Int corridors.
Pets: Medium, other species. Service with restrictions, supervision.
🛜 ⓧ 🛏 🖵 🏊

▼▼ Ramada Inn Macon West 🅗
(478) 788-0120. **$45-$63.** 4755 Chambers Rd 31206. I-475 exit 3 (Eisenhower Pkwy/US 80), just e. Ext corridors. **Pets:** Other species. $15 one-
time fee/pet. Designated rooms, service with restrictions, supervision.
🛜 🛏 🖵 🏊

Rodeway Inn M ❀
(478) 781-4343. **$49-$59.** 4999 Eisenhower Pkwy 31206. I-475 exit 3 (Eisenhower Pkwy/US 80), just ne. Ext corridors. **Pets:** Medium. $10 daily fee/pet. Service with restrictions, crate. SAVE 📶 🛏 💻 🏊

SpringHill Suites Macon H
(478) 803-9100. **$115-$144.** 4630 Sheraton Dr 31210. I-75 exit 169 (Arkwright Rd), just n, then 1.5 mi nw. Int corridors. **Pets:** Accepted.
SAVE 📶 ✕ 🛗 🛏 💻 🏊

MCDONOUGH

Comfort Inn/McDonough M
(770) 954-9110. **Call for rates.** 80 Hwy 81 W 30253. I-75 exit 218, just nw. Ext corridors. **Pets:** Small. $10 daily fee/pet. Service with restrictions, crate. SAVE 📶 🛏 💻 🏊

Country Inn & Suites By Carlson H
(770) 957-0082. **$89-$190.** 115 E Greenwood Rd 30253. I-75 exit 216, just w. Int corridors. **Pets:** Small. $20 one-time fee/room. Designated rooms, service with restrictions, crate. 📶 🛗 🛏 💻 🏊

Days Inn M
(770) 957-5261. **$40-$60.** 744 Hwy 155 S 30253. I-75 exit 216, just e. Ext corridors. **Pets:** Accepted. 📶 🛏 💻 🏊

Econo Lodge M ❀
(770) 957-2651. **$40-$100.** 1279 Hwy 20 W 30253. I-75 exit 218, just w. Ext corridors. **Pets:** Small. $10 daily fee/pet. Designated rooms, supervision. SAVE 📶 🛏 💻

Quality Inn & Suites Conference Center M ❀
(770) 957-5291. **$75-$80.** 930 Hwy 155 S 30253. I-75 exit 216, just w. Ext corridors. **Pets:** Large. $10 daily fee/room. Service with restrictions, crate. SAVE 📶 🛗 🛏 💻 🍴 🏊

Sleep Inn H
(770) 898-0804. **Call for rates.** 945 Hwy 155 S 30253. I-75 exit 216, just w. Int corridors. **Pets:** Accepted. SAVE 📶 🛗 🛏 🏊

MILLEDGEVILLE

Antebellum Inn BB
(478) 453-3993. **$119-$199, 3 day notice.** 200 N Columbia St 31061. Just s of Business Rt US 441 (Columbia St); between SR 22 and 49; downtown. Int corridors. **Pets:** Small, dogs only. $25 daily fee/pet. Designated rooms, service with restrictions, supervision. 📶 ✕ 🏊 🚭

Holiday Inn Express Hotel & Suites H
(478) 454-9000. **$79-$199.** 1839 N Columbia St 31061. US 441, 2 mi n of downtown. Int corridors. **Pets:** Accepted. 📶 🛗 🛏 💻 🏊

Super 8 Milledgeville H
(478) 453-9491. **$49-$60.** 2474 N Columbia St 31061. US 441, 2.6 mi n of downtown. Ext corridors. **Pets:** Medium. $10 daily fee/pet. Service with restrictions, supervision. 📶 🛏 💻

MOULTRIE

Econo Lodge H
(229) 890-8652. **Call for rates.** 1300 Veterans Pkwy 31788. Northern jct US 319 and 319 business route, just e. Int corridors. **Pets:** Accepted.
📶 🛏 💻 🏊

NEWNAN

Best Western Shenandoah Inn M
(770) 304-9700. **$55-$109.** 620 Hwy 34 E 30265. I-85 exit 47, just w. Ext corridors. **Pets:** Medium. $10 daily fee/pet. Service with restrictions, supervision. SAVE 📶 🛗 🛏 💻 🏊

Howard Johnson Inn M
(770) 683-1499. **$43-$53.** 1310 Hwy 29 S 30263. I-85 exit 41, just w. Ext corridors. **Pets:** Medium. $10 daily fee/pet. Service with restrictions, supervision. 📶 🛏 💻 🏊

La Quinta Inn & Suites Atlanta South - Newnan H
(770) 502-8430. **$67-$125.** 600 Bullsboro Dr 30265. I-85 exit 47, 0.3 mi w. Int corridors. **Pets:** Medium, other species. Service with restrictions, supervision. 📶 🛗 🛏 💻

OAKWOOD

Country Inn & Suites By Carlson H
(770) 535-8080. **Call for rates.** 4535 Oakwood Rd 30566. I-985 exit 16, just sw. Int corridors. **Pets:** Accepted. 📶 🛏 💻 🏊

Jameson Inn M
(770) 533-9400. **$70-$90.** 3780 Merchants Way 30566. I-985 exit 16, 0.4 mi w. Ext corridors. **Pets:** Medium. $15 daily fee/room. Service with restrictions, supervision. 📶 🛗 🛏 💻 🏊

PEACHTREE CITY

Best Western Inn & Suites M
(770) 632-9700. **$63-$80.** 976 Crosstown Dr 30269. Jct SR 74 and 54, 2.1 mi s on SR 74. Ext corridors. **Pets:** Accepted.
SAVE 📶 🛗 🛏 💻 🏊

Wyndham Peachtree Hotel & Conference Center H
(770) 487-2000. **$89-$199.** 2443 Hwy 54 W 30269. Jct SR 74 and 54, 1 mi e. Int corridors. **Pets:** Accepted. 📶 ✕ 🛗 💻 🍴 🏊 ✕

PERRY

Econo Lodge M
(478) 987-2142. **$50-$100.** 102 Valley Dr 31069. I-75 exit 136, just w, then just s. Int corridors. **Pets:** Medium, dogs only. $10 daily fee/pet. Service with restrictions, supervision. 📶 🛏 🏊

Jameson Inn-Perry M
(478) 987-5060. **$55-$75.** 200 Market Place Dr 31069. I-75 exit 136 (Sam Nunn Blvd), just e, then s. Ext corridors. **Pets:** Medium. $15 daily fee/room. Service with restrictions, supervision. 📶 🛏 💻 🏊

Microtel Inn & Suites H
(478) 987-4004. **$53-$71.** 110 Fairview Dr 31069. I-75 exit 134, just nw. Int corridors. **Pets:** Accepted. 📶 ✕ 🛗 🛏 💻 🏊

Ramada Inn H ❀
(478) 987-3313. **$63-$81.** 200 Valley Dr 31069. I-75 exit 136 (Sam Nunn Blvd), just w, then s. Ext corridors. **Pets:** Medium. $35 daily fee/room. Designated rooms, service with restrictions, crate.
📶 🛏 💻 🍴 🏊 ✕

PINE MOUNTAIN

Mountain Creek Inn at Callaway Gardens M
(706) 663-2281. **$119-$199, 7 day notice.** 17800 Hwy 27 31822. Jct SR 354, 1.5 mi s on US 27/SR 1; in Callaway Gardens. Ext corridors.
Pets: Accepted. SAVE 📶 🛗 🛏 💻 🍴 🏊 ✕

White Columns Motel M ❀
(706) 663-2312. **$59-$80, 3 day notice.** 524 S Main Ave 31822. Jct SR 354, just n on US 27/SR 1. Ext corridors. **Pets:** Large. $20 daily fee/pet. Designated rooms, service with restrictions, supervision. 📶 🛏

POOLER

Best Western Bradbury Suites H
(912) 330-0330. **$85-$109.** 155 Bourne Ave 31322. I-95 exit 102 (US 80), just e. Int corridors. **Pets:** Accepted.
SAVE 📶 🛗 🛏 💻 🏊 ✕

Jameson Inn H

(912) 748-0017. **$70-$90.** 125 Bourne Ave 31322. I-95 exit 102 (US 80), just w. Int corridors. **Pets:** Medium. $15 daily fee/room. Service with restrictions, supervision.

La Quinta Inn & Suites Savannah Airport - Pooler H

(912) 748-3771. **$84-$144.** 414 Gray St 31322. I-95 exit 102 (US 80), just w. Int corridors. **Pets:** Medium, other species. Service with restrictions, supervision.

Travelodge Suites H

(912) 748-6363. **$47-$76.** 130 Continental Blvd 31322. I-95 exit 102 (US 80), just e. Int corridors. **Pets:** Accepted.

PORT WENTWORTH

Comfort Suites Savannah North H

(912) 965-1445. **$79-$200.** 115 Travelers Way 31407. I-95 exit 109 (SR 21), just nw. Int corridors. **Pets:** Accepted.

Hampton Inn Savannah North H

(912) 966-2000. **$69-$116.** 7050 Hwy 21 31407. I-95 exit 109 (SR 21), just e. Int corridors. **Pets:** Large. Designated rooms, service with restrictions, crate.

Wingate by Wyndham H

(912) 964-0840. **$76-$94.** 115 O' Leary Rd 31407. I-95 exit 109 (SR 21), just e, then just n. Int corridors. **Pets:** Accepted.

RICHMOND HILL

Best Western Plus Richmond Hill Inn H

(912) 756-7070. **$59-$119.** 4564 Hwy 17 31324. I-95 exit 87 (Ocean Hwy/US 17), just w. Int corridors. **Pets:** Accepted.

Comfort Suites H

(912) 756-6668. **$79-$139.** 4601 Hwy 17 31324. I-95 exit 87 (Ocean Hwy/US 17), 0.4 mi sw. Int corridors. **Pets:** $10 daily fee/pet. Supervision.

RINGGOLD

Hometown Inn H

(706) 937-7070. **$60-$99.** 22 Gateway Business Park Dr 30736. I-75 exit 350, just e. Int corridors. **Pets:** Other species. $10 daily fee/pet. Designated rooms, service with restrictions, supervision.

ROCKMART

Days Inn M

(770) 684-9955. **$49-$90.** 105 GTM Pkwy 30165. Jct US 278 and SR 101, just n. Ext corridors. **Pets:** Accepted.

ROME

Jameson Inn H

(706) 291-7797. **$80-$100.** 40 Grace Dr 30161. On US 411, 2.2 mi e. Int corridors. **Pets:** Medium. $15 daily fee/room. Service with restrictions, supervision.

La Quinta Inn & Suites H

(706) 291-1034. **$84-$144.** 15 Chateau Dr SE 30161. 2 mi e on US 411. Int corridors. **Pets:** Medium, other species. Service with restrictions, supervision.

ST. MARYS

Cumberland Inn & Suites Kings Bay H

(912) 882-6250. **$79-$129.** 2710 Osborne Rd 31558. I-95 exit 3 (SR 40), 5.5 mi e. Ext corridors. **Pets:** Medium. $25 one-time fee/room. Service with restrictions, supervision.

SANDERSVILLE

Days Inn Sandersville M

(478) 553-0393. **$59-$99.** 128 Commerce St 31082. On SR 15, jct SR 24/88, just s. Ext corridors. **Pets:** Accepted.

SAVANNAH

Baymont Inn & Suites H ❀

(912) 925-9494. **$71-$89.** 393 Canebrake Rd 31419. I-95 exit 94 (SR 204/Abercorn St), just se. Int corridors. **Pets:** Medium. $20 daily fee/pet. Designated rooms, service with restrictions, supervision.

Best Western Plus Savannah Historic District H ❀

(912) 233-1011. **Call for rates.** 412 W Bay St 31401. I-16 exit 167 (Montgomery St), just ne. Ext corridors. **Pets:** Large, dogs only. $50 deposit/room, $20 daily fee/room. Service with restrictions, supervision.

Bohemian Hotel Savannah Riverfront, Autograph Collection H ❀

(912) 721-3800. **$189-$449, 3 day notice.** 102 W Bay St 31401. Between Bull and Whitaker sts. Int corridors. **Pets:** Medium, dogs only. $100 one-time fee/room. Service with restrictions, supervision.

Candlewood Suites H ❀

(912) 966-9644. **$59-$119.** 50 Stephen S Green Dr 31408. I-95 exit 104, just e, then s. Int corridors. **Pets:** $25 one-time fee/pet. Service with restrictions, supervision.

Catherine Ward House Inn BB

(912) 234-8564. **$149-$249, 3 day notice.** 118 E Waldburg St 31401. Between Drayton and Abercorn sts. Ext/int corridors. **Pets:** Dogs only. $35 one-time fee/room. Designated rooms, service with restrictions.

Clarion Inn & Suites H

(912) 920-3200. **$75-$135.** 16 Gateway Blvd E 31419. I-95 exit 94 (SR 204/Abercorn St), just e. Int corridors. **Pets:** Accepted.

Comfort Suites Historic District H ❀

(912) 629-2001. **$99-$299.** 630 W Bay St 31401. I-16 exit 167 (Montgomery St), 0.9 mi n to Bay St, then just w. Int corridors. **Pets:** Small, other species. $50 one-time fee/room. Designated rooms, service with restrictions, supervision.

East Bay Inn CI

(912) 238-1225. **$189-$325, 7 day notice.** 225 E Bay St 31401. I-16 exit 167 (Montgomery St), 0.8 mi n, then 0.4 mi se; in historic district. Int corridors. **Pets:** Accepted.

Extended StayAmerica Savannah-Midtown H ❀

(912) 692-0076. **$60-$110.** 5511 Abercorn St 31405. Jct SR 21 and 204 (Abercorn St), just s. Int corridors. **Pets:** Other species. $25 daily fee/pet. Service with restrictions.

Foley House Inn BB

(912) 232-6622. **$199-$399, 3 day notice.** 14 W Hull St 31401. Between Bull and Whitaker sts; in historic district on Chippewa Square. Ext/int corridors. **Pets:** Accepted.

The Forsyth Park Inn BB

(912) 233-6800. **Call for rates.** 102 W Hall St 31401. Between Whitaker and Howard sts; across from Forsyth Park. Int corridors. **Pets:** Accepted.

Hamilton-Turner Inn BB

(912) 233-1833. **$189-$369, 10 day notice.** 330 Abercorn St 31401. Between E Charlton and E Harris sts; overlooking Lafayette Square; in historic district. Ext/int corridors. **Pets:** Small, other species. $50 one-time fee/room. Designated rooms, service with restrictions, crate.

Hilton Savannah DeSoto
(912) 232-9000. **$109-$279.** 15 E Liberty St 31401. Between Bull and Drayton sts; in historic district. Int corridors. **Pets:** Accepted.

Homewood Suites by Hilton
(912) 353-8500. **$109-$199.** 5820 White Bluff Rd 31405. Jct SR 21 and 204 (Abercorn St), 0.5 mi s. Ext/int corridors. **Pets:** Medium, other species. $75 one-time fee/room. Service with restrictions.

Joan's on Jones B & B
(912) 234-3863. **$160-$185 (no credit cards), 7 day notice.** 17 W Jones St 31401. Between Whitaker and Bull sts. Ext corridors. **Pets:** Dogs only. $50 one-time fee/room.

La Quinta Inn & Suites
(912) 927-7660. **$72-$155.** 8484 Abercorn St 31406. 2.4 mi s of jct SR 21 and 204 (Abercorn St). Int corridors. **Pets:** Medium, other species. Service with restrictions, supervision.

La Quinta Inn Savannah (I-95)
(912) 925-9505. **$58-$126.** 6 Gateway Blvd S 31419. I-95 exit 94 (SR 204/Abercorn St), just e, then just s. Ext corridors. **Pets:** Medium, other species. Service with restrictions, supervision.

Mansion on Forsyth Park Hotel and Spa, Autograph Collection
(912) 238-5158. **$159-$379, 3 day notice.** 700 Drayton St 31401. Between E Hall and E Gwinnett sts; on Forsyth Park. Int corridors. **Pets:** Accepted.

The Mulberry-A Holiday Inn Hotel
(912) 238-1200. **$129-$249.** 601 E Bay St 31401. Between Broad and Houston sts; east side of historic district. Ext/int corridors. **Pets:** Accepted.

Olde Harbour Inn
(912) 234-4100. **$159-$300, 7 day notice.** 508 E Factors Walk 31401. Lincoln St ramp off E Bay St; in historic riverfront district. Ext corridors. **Pets:** Accepted.

Quality Inn Heart of Savannah
(912) 236-6321. **$99-$159.** 300 W Bay St 31401. Between N Montgomery and N Jefferson sts; in historic district. Ext corridors. **Pets:** Accepted.

Quality Inn Midtown
(912) 352-7100. **$55-$85.** 7100 Abercorn St 31406. Jct SR 21, 1.2 mi s on SR 204 (Abercorn St). Ext corridors. **Pets:** Accepted.

Red Roof Inn Midtown
(912) 355-4100. **$45-$99.** 201 Stephenson Ave 31405. 1.1 mi s of jct SR 21 and 204 (Abercorn St), just e. Ext corridors. **Pets:** Large, other species. No service, supervision.

Residence Inn Savannah Midtown
(912) 356-3266. **$104-$142.** 5710 White Bluff Rd 31405. Jct SR 21, 0.5 mi s. Int corridors. **Pets:** Accepted.

Staybridge Suites Savannah Historic District
(912) 721-9000. **$99-$199.** 301 E Bay St 31401. Corner of Lincoln St; in historic district. Int corridors. **Pets:** Medium. $75 one-time fee/room. Designated rooms, service with restrictions, supervision.

Super 8 Gateway
(912) 925-6996. **$54-$90.** 387 Canebrake Rd 31419. I-95 exit 94 (SR 204/Abercorn St), just e, then s. Int corridors. **Pets:** Small. Designated rooms, service with restrictions, supervision.

TownePlace Suites Savannah Airport
(912) 629-7775. **$89-$153.** 4 Jay R Turner Dr 31408. I-95 exit 104, just e. Int corridors. **Pets:** Other species. $25 daily fee/room. Service with restrictions.

TownePlace Suites Savannah Midtown
(912) 920-9080. **$94-$152.** 11309 Abercorn St 31419. Jct SR 21 and 204 (Abercorn St), 4.6 mi s. Int corridors. **Pets:** Other species. $100 one-time fee/room. Service with restrictions.

The Westin Savannah Harbor Golf Resort and Spa
(912) 201-2000. **$139-$449, 3 day notice.** 1 Resort Dr 31421. On Hutchinson Island; 1 mi se of first exit after Eugene Talmadge Memorial Bridge and US 17. Int corridors. **Pets:** Accepted.

Wingate by Wyndham Savannah Airport
(912) 544-1180. **$89-$167.** 15 Sylvester C Formey Dr 31408. I-95 exit 104, 0.4 mi e. Int corridors. **Pets:** Accepted.

STATESBORO

Best Western University Inn
(912) 681-7900. **$55-$85.** 1 Jameson Ave 30458. Jct US 25/301 and SR 67, 0.9 mi s on US 25/301. Ext corridors. **Pets:** Accepted.

La Quinta Inn Statesboro
(912) 871-2525. **$58-$122.** 225 Lanier Dr 30458. Jct US 301 Bypass and SR 67, 1.2 mi w on US 301, just n of Georgia Southern University. Int corridors. **Pets:** Medium, other species. Service with restrictions, supervision.

STOCKBRIDGE

La Quinta Inn & Suites Atlanta Stockbridge
(770) 506-9991. **$80-$154.** 3581 Cameron Pkwy 30281. I-75 exit 228, just e on SR 138, then just n; I-675 exit 1, just w on SR 138, then just n. Int corridors. **Pets:** Medium, other species. Service with restrictions, supervision.

Microtel Inn & Suites
(678) 782-6100. **$48-$104, 21 day notice.** 195 Country Club Dr 30281. I-75 exit 224, just e, then just s. Int corridors. **Pets:** Small. $15 daily fee/pet. Designated rooms, no service, supervision.

Quality Inn & Suites
(770) 507-7911. **$54-$69.** 7325 Davidson Pkwy N 30281. I-675 exit 1, just e, then just n; I-75 exit 228, 1 mi e, then just n. Ext corridors. **Pets:** Small. $10 daily fee/pet. Designated rooms, service with restrictions, supervision.

Sleep Inn & Suites
(770) 474-3870. **$60-$70.** 7423 Davidson Cir W 30281. I-675 exit 1, just e, then just s; I-75 exit 228, 1 mi e, then just s. Int corridors. **Pets:** Accepted.

Super 8 Stockbridge
(770) 474-5758. **$50-$86.** 1451 Hudson Bridge Rd 30281. I-75 exit 224, just w. Ext corridors. **Pets:** Accepted.

SWAINSBORO

Best Western Bradford Inn
(478) 237-2400. **$58-$65.** 688 S Main St 30401. I-16 exit 90 (US 1), 12.4 mi n. Ext corridors. **Pets:** Medium. $10 daily fee/pet. Supervision.

THOMASTON

▼▼ Jameson Inn **M**

(706) 648-2232. **$65-$85.** 1010 Hwy 19 N 30286. Jct SR 74, 2.3 mi n. Ext corridors. **Pets:** Medium. $15 daily fee/room. Service with restrictions, supervision. 🛜 📶 🛑 💻 🌊

THOMASVILLE

▼▼ Jameson Inn **M**

(229) 227-9500. **$70-$90.** 1470 Remington Ave 31792. Jct US 19 and SR 122, just w. Ext corridors. **Pets:** Medium. $15 daily fee/room. Service with restrictions, supervision. 🛜 📶 🛑 💻 🌊

AAA ▼▼ Quality Inn & Suites Conference Center **M** 🐾

(229) 225-2134. **$59-$75.** 15138 US Hwy 19 S 31757. 0.3 mi s of US 319. Ext corridors. **Pets:** Medium. $10 daily fee/room. Designated rooms, service with restrictions, supervision.

SAVE 🛜 📶 🛑 💻 🍴 🌊

THOMSON

AAA ▼▼ Best Western White Columns Inn **M** 🐾

(706) 595-8000. **$87-$97.** 1890 Washington Rd 30824. I-20 exit 172 (US 78), just s. Ext corridors. **Pets:** $50 deposit/room, $10 daily fee/pet. Designated rooms, no service, crate. SAVE 🛜 🛑 💻 🍴 🌊

TIFTON

▼▼▼ Country Inn & Suites By Carlson **M**

(229) 382-8100. **Call for rates.** 310 S Virginia Ave W 31794. I-75 exit 62, just e on US 82 and 319. Int corridors. **Pets:** Accepted.

🛜 🛑 💻 🌊

▼▼ Days Inn & Suites **H**

(229) 382-8505. **$44-$120.** 1199 Hwy 82 W 31793. I-75 exit 62, just w. Int corridors. **Pets:** Other species. $10 daily fee/pet. Service with restrictions, supervision. 🛜 🛑 💻

▼▼ Hampton Inn **H**

(229) 382-8800. **$79-$99.** 720 Hwy 319 S 31794. I-75 exit 62, just e. Ext corridors. **Pets:** Accepted. 🛜 🛑 💻 🌊

▼▼ Ramada Limited and Conference Center **H**

(229) 382-8500. **$42-$55.** 1211 Hwy 82 W 31793. I-75 exit 62, just w. Ext corridors. **Pets:** Other species. $10 one-time fee/pet. Service with restrictions, supervision. 🛜 🛑 💻 🌊

VALDOSTA

AAA ▼▼▼ Best Western Plus Valdosta Hotel & Suites **H** 🐾

(229) 241-9221. **$109-$199.** 4025 Northlake Dr 31602. I-75 exit 22, just e on N Valdosta Rd, then just n. Int corridors. **Pets:** Other species. $20 daily fee/pet. Designated rooms, service with restrictions.

SAVE 🛜 ⊠ 📶 🛑 💻 🌊

AAA ▼▼▼ Clarion Inn Conference Center **H**

(229) 242-1212. **$74-$146.** 2101 W Hill Ave 31602. I-75 exit 16, just w. Ext/int corridors. **Pets:** Small. $25 one-time fee/room. Service with restrictions, crate. SAVE 🛜 🛑 💻 🌊 ⊠

▼▼ Days Inn I-75 North **H**

(229) 244-4460. **$42-$51.** 4598 N Valdosta Rd 31602. I-75 exit 22, just w. Ext corridors. **Pets:** Medium. $10 daily fee/pet. Service with restrictions, supervision. 🛜 🛑 💻 🌊

AAA ▼▼▼ Econo Lodge **H**

(229) 671-1511. **$50-$90.** 3022 James Cir 31602. I-75 exit 18, just w. Int corridors. **Pets:** Accepted. SAVE 🛜 📶 🛑 💻 🌊

AAA ▼▼▼ La Quinta Inn & Suites Valdosta / Moody AFB **H**

(229) 247-7755. **$111-$179.** 1800 Clubhouse Dr 31601. I-75 exit 18, 0.3 mi e, then just s off SR 94. Int corridors. **Pets:** Medium, other species. Service with restrictions, supervision. SAVE 🛜 🛑 💻 🌊 ⊠

▼▼ Quality Inn South **H**

(229) 244-4520. **$56-$76.** 1902 W Hill Ave 31601. I-75 exit 16, just e on US 84. Ext corridors. **Pets:** Medium, other species. $8 daily fee/pet. Service with restrictions, crate. 🛜 🛑 💻 🌊

AAA ▼▼▼ Travelodge **H**

(229) 244-7600. **$64-$69, 7 day notice.** 1403 N St Augustine Rd 31602. I-75 exit 18, just w off SR 94. Ext corridors. **Pets:** Accepted. SAVE 🛜 🛑 💻 🌊

AAA ▼▼▼▼ Wingate by Wyndham Valdosta/Moody AFB **H**

(229) 242-1225. **$94-$180, 3 day notice.** 2010 W Hill Ave 31601. I-75 exit 16, just e. Int corridors. **Pets:** Accepted. ECO SAVE 🛜 ⊠ 📶 🛑 💻 🌊 ⊠

VILLA RICA

▼▼ Days Inn **H**

(770) 459-8888. **$50-$94.** 195 Hwy 61 Connector 30180. I-20 exit 24, just n. Int corridors. **Pets:** $10 daily fee/pet. Designated rooms, service with restrictions, supervision. 🛜 📶 🛑 💻 🌊

▼▼ Super 8 **M**

(770) 459-8000. **$41-$77, 7 day notice.** 128 Hwy 61 Connector 30180. I-20 exit 24, just n. Ext corridors. **Pets:** Accepted. 🛜 🛑 💻 🌊

WARM SPRINGS

AAA ▼▼▼ Best Western White House Inn **H** 🐾

(706) 655-2750. **Call for rates.** 2526 White House Pkwy 31830. Jct US 27 and 41, 0.5 mi s. Ext/int corridors. **Pets:** Medium, dogs only. $25 daily fee/pet. Designated rooms, service with restrictions, supervision.

SAVE 🛜 🛑 💻 🌊

WARNER ROBINS

AAA ▼▼▼ Best Western Peach Inn **H**

(478) 953-3800. **$49-$63.** 2739 Watson Blvd 31093. I-75 exit 146 (SR 247C), 4.1 mi e. Ext corridors. **Pets:** Large. $8 daily fee/pet. Designated rooms, service with restrictions, crate. SAVE 🛜 🛑 💻 🌊

▼▼ Comfort Inn & Suites **H**

(478) 922-7555. **$77-$81.** 95 S Hwy 247 31088. Jct SR 247C and US 129/SR 247, 1.6 mi s on US 129/SR 247. Ext/int corridors. **Pets:** Accepted. 🛜 🛑 💻 🌊

▼▼ Days Inn & Suites-Warner Robins **M**

(478) 953-6866. **$45-$99.** 215 Margie Dr 31088. I-75 exit 146 (SR 247C), 3.2 mi e, then just s. Ext corridors. **Pets:** Accepted. 🛜 🛑 💻 🌊

▼▼ Jameson Inn-Warner Robins **H**

(478) 953-5522. **$70-$90.** 2731 Watson Blvd 31093. I-75 exit 146 (SR 247C), 4.1 mi e. Ext corridors. **Pets:** Medium. $15 daily fee/room. Service with restrictions, supervision. 🛜 🛑 💻 🌊

▼▼▼ La Quinta Inn & Suites Warner Robins **H**

(478) 333-3444. **$89-$149.** 109 Willie Lee Pkwy 31088. I-75 exit 146 (SR 247C), 2.8 mi e. Int corridors. **Pets:** Medium, other species. Service with restrictions, supervision. 🛜 ⊠ 📶 🛑 💻 🌊

WAYCROSS

▼▼▼ Comfort Suites **H**

(912) 548-0555. **$75-$85.** 1922 Memorial Dr 31501. Between US 1 and 82. Int corridors. **Pets:** Medium, dogs only. $20 one-time fee/pet. Designated rooms, service with restrictions, supervision.

🛜 ⊠ 🛑 💻 🌊

▼▼ Econo Lodge M
(912) 283-3300. **Call for rates.** 1903 Memorial Dr 31501. Between US 1 and 82, at S City Blvd. Ext corridors. **Pets:** Accepted.

▼▼▼ Holiday Inn Express & Suites H
(912) 548-0720. **$77-$99.** 1761 Memorial Dr 31501. Between US 1 and 82. Int corridors. **Pets:** Accepted.

▼▼ Jameson Inn M
(912) 283-3800. **$65-$85.** 950 City Blvd 31501. Between US 1 and 82; east of city. Ext corridors. **Pets:** Medium. $15 daily fee/room. Service with restrictions, supervision.

WAYNESBORO
▼▼ Jameson Inn M
(706) 437-0500. **$75-$95.** 1436 N Liberty St 30830. 0.9 mi n of downtown center on US 25. Ext corridors. **Pets:** Medium. $15 daily fee/room. Service with restrictions, supervision.

WINDER
(AAA) ▼▼ Best Western Winder Hotel H
(770) 868-5303. **$80-$140.** 177 W Athens St 30680. Jct Broad St, 0.8 mi n; downtown. Int corridors. **Pets:** Accepted.

▼▼ Jameson Inn M
(770) 867-1880. **$60-$80.** 9 Stafford St 30680. Jct SR 81, 11, 53 and 8; center. Ext corridors. **Pets:** Medium. $15 daily fee/room. Service with restrictions, supervision.

YOUNG HARRIS
▼▼▼ Brasstown Valley Resort H
(706) 379-9900. **$129-$239, 7 day notice.** 6321 US Hwy 76 30582. US 76 and US 76/SR 515. Int corridors. **Pets:** Accepted.

HAWAII

HONOLULU METROPOLITAN AREA

HONOLULU
▼▼ Aqua Waikiki Wave Hotel H
(808) 922-1262. **Call for rates.** 2299 Kuhio Ave 96815. Just s of Seaside Ave. Int corridors. **Pets:** Accepted.

(AAA) ▼▼▼ Best Western The Plaza Hotel H ❖
(808) 836-3636. **$107-$139, 3 day notice.** 3253 N Nimitz Hwy 96819. Just e of jct Paiea St. Ext/int corridors. **Pets:** Medium. $25 daily fee/pet. Service with restrictions, supervision.

(AAA) ▼▼▼▼ DoubleTree by Hilton Alana Waikiki Hotel H
(808) 941-7275. **$95-$218.** 1956 Ala Moana Blvd 96815. Between Ena Rd and Kalakaua Ave. Int corridors. **Pets:** Medium, other species. $100 one-time fee/room. Service with restrictions, crate.

▼▼▼ Hotel Renew H
(808) 687-7700. **$159-$369, 3 day notice.** 129 Paoakalani Ave 96815. Between Kalakaua Ave and Lemon Rd. Int corridors. **Pets:** Accepted.

(AAA) ▼▼▼ ▼▼ The Kahala Hotel & Resort H ❖
(808) 739-8888. **$525-$10000, 3 day notice.** 5000 Kahala Ave 96816. E of Diamond Head at end of Kahala Ave. Int corridors. **Pets:** Medium, dogs only. $150 one-time fee/room. Service with restrictions, supervision.

▼▼▼ ▼▼▼ The Waikiki EDITION H
(808) 943-5800. **$350-$995, 3 day notice.** 1775 Ala Moana Blvd 96815. Jct Hobron Ln. Int corridors. **Pets:** Accepted.

(AAA) ▼▼▼ OHANA Honolulu Airport Hotel H ❖
(808) 836-0661. **$107-$139, 3 day notice.** 3401 N Nimitz Hwy 96819. Jct Rodgers Blvd. Int corridors. **Pets:** Small, other species. $25 daily fee/pet. Designated rooms, service with restrictions, crate.

▼▼▼ ▼▼▼ Trump International Hotel Waikiki Beach Walk H ❖
(808) 683-7777. **Call for rates.** 223 Saratoga Rd 96815. Jct Kalia Rd. Int corridors. **Pets:** Small, dogs only. $250 one-time fee/room. Service with restrictions, supervision.

KAHUKU
▼▼▼ Turtle Bay Resort H ❖
(808) 293-6000. **$249-$1399, 7 day notice.** 57-091 Kamehameha Hwy 96731. 3 mi nw off SR 83. Ext/int corridors. **Pets:** Small, dogs only. $250 one-time fee/room. Designated rooms, service with restrictions, supervision.

END METROPOLITAN AREA

KAUPULEHU
(AAA) ▼▼▼▼▼ Four Seasons Resort Hualalai at Historic Ka'upulehu H
(808) 325-8000. **$635-$1295, 21 day notice.** 72-100 Ka'upulehu Dr 96740. Off SR 19, 6 mi n of Kona International Airport, 1.3 mi sw. Ext corridors. **Pets:** Accepted.

KOHALA COAST
(AAA) ▼▼▼ ▼▼ The Fairmont Orchid, Hawaii H
(808) 885-2000. **$329-$3900, 14 day notice.** 1 N Kaniku Dr 96743. On SR 19, 19 mi n of Kona International Airport, 2 mi w; in Mauna Lani resort area. Int corridors. **Pets:** Accepted.

LĀNA'I CITY

AAA ▼▼▼▼ Four Seasons Resort Lana'i at Manele Bay H

(808) 565-2000. **$425-$7500, 21 day notice.** 1 Manele Bay Rd 96763. From airport, 4 mi e on Kaumalapau Hwy to Lana'i City, 7 mi s on SR 440. Ext corridors. **Pets:** Accepted.

SAVE 🛜 ✕ ᴋM 🗎 🖵 ꭱꭲ ➦ ✕

AAA ▼▼▼▼ Four Seasons Resort Lana'i, The Lodge at Koele H

(808) 565-4000. **$295-$1750, 21 day notice.** One Keomoku Hwy 96763. From airport, 4 mi e on Kaumalapau Hwy to Lana'i City, 2 mi n on SR 440, follow signs. Int corridors. **Pets:** Accepted.

SAVE 🛜 ✕ ᴋM 🗎 🖵 ꭱꭲ ➦ ✕

WAILEA

AAA ▼▼▼▼ Four Seasons Resort Maui at Wailea H

(808) 874-8000. **$465-$1595, 21 day notice.** 3900 Wailea Alanui Dr 96753. From end of SR 31, 0.5 mi s. Int corridors. **Pets:** Accepted.

SAVE 🛜 ✕ ᴋM 🗎 🖵 ꭱꭲ ➦ ✕

IDAHO

CITY INDEX

AHSAHKA

AAA ▼▼▼▼ The High Country Inn - Orofino BB ☘

(208) 476-7570. **$89-$135, 7 day notice.** 70 High Country Ln 83520. 0.5 mi w to Dworshak Visitors Center Rd, 2 mi n, just w, follow signs. Ext/int corridors. **Pets:** Large, other species. $25 one-time fee/room. Designated rooms. SAVE 🛜 ✕ 🖵 ꮃ ✍

BLACKFOOT

AAA ▼▼ Best Western Blackfoot Inn H ☘

(208) 785-4144. **$69-$149.** 750 Jensen Grove Dr 83221. I-15 exit 93, 0.3 mi e to Parkway Dr, then 0.4 mi n. Int corridors. **Pets:** Dogs only. Service with restrictions, supervision. SAVE 🛜 🗎 🖵 ➦

▼▼ Super 8 M

(208) 785-9333. **$56-$94.** 1279 Parkway Dr 83221. I-15 exit 93, just se, then just w. Int corridors. **Pets:** Other species. $10 one-time fee/room. Service with restrictions, crate. 🛜 🗎 🖵

BOISE

AAA ▼▼ Best Western Airport Inn H

(208) 384-5000. **$70-$100.** 2660 Airport Way 83705. I-84 exit 53 (Vista Ave), just s, then just e. Ext corridors. **Pets:** Medium, dogs only. $10 daily fee/pet. Service with restrictions, supervision.

SAVE 🛜 🗎 🖵 ➦

AAA ▼▼ Best Western Plus Northwest Lodge H ☘

(208) 287-2300. **$79-$99.** 6989 Federal Way 83716. I-84 exit 57, just e, then just s. Int corridors. **Pets:** Medium, dogs only. $20 daily fee/room. Designated rooms, supervision. SAVE 🛜 🗎 🖵 ➦ ✕

AAA ▼▼▼ Best Western Plus Vista Inn at the Airport H

(208) 336-8100. **$79-$99.** 2645 Airport Way 83705. I-84 exit 53 (Vista Ave), just s. Ext/int corridors. **Pets:** Medium, dogs only. $20 daily fee/room. Designated rooms, service with restrictions, crate.

SAVE 🛜 🗎 🖵 ➦

▼▼ The Boise Hotel & Conference Center H ☘

(208) 343-4900. **$59-$119, 3 day notice.** 3300 S Vista Ave 83705. I-84 exit 53 (Vista Ave), just n. Int corridors. **Pets:** Dogs only. Designated rooms, service with restrictions. 🛜 ᴋM 🗎 🖵 ꭱꭲ ➦ ✕

▼▼▼ Candlewood Suites Boise Towne Square H

(208) 322-4300. **$59-$99.** 700 N Cole Rd 83704. I-184 exit 1B westbound, just n; exit 1A eastbound, just e, then 0.5 mi n. Int corridors. **Pets:** Accepted. 🛜 ᴋM 🗎 🖵

▼▼▼ DoubleTree Club by Hilton Hotel Boise H

(208) 345-2002. **$75-$159.** 475 W Parkcenter Blvd 83706. I-84 exit 54 (Broadway Ave), 2 mi n, then 0.3 mi e on Beacon St and Parkcenter Blvd. Int corridors. **Pets:** Accepted. 🛜 🖵 ꭱꭲ ➦

AAA ▼▼▼ Fairfield Inn by Marriott H

(208) 331-5656. **$71-$111.** 3300 S Shoshone St 83705. I-84 exit 53 (Vista Ave), just n to Elder St, then just w. Int corridors. **Pets:** Other species. $20 daily fee/pet. Designated rooms, service with restrictions, supervision. SAVE 🛜 ✕ ᴋM 🗎 🖵 ➦ ✕

▼▼▼ Hampton Inn H

(208) 331-5600. **$85-$139.** 3270 S Shoshone St 83705. I-84 exit 53 (Vista Ave), just n to Elder St, then just w. Int corridors. **Pets:** Small. Designated rooms, service with restrictions, supervision.

🛜 ᴋM 🗎 🖵 ➦

▼▼ Holiday Inn Express H

(208) 388-0800. **Call for rates.** 2613 S Vista Ave 83705. I-84 exit 53 (Vista Ave), 0.5 mi n. Int corridors. **Pets:** Medium, other species. $20 daily fee/pet. Designated rooms, service with restrictions.

🛜 ᴋM 🗎 🖵 ➦

AAA ▼▼▼ Inn America H

(208) 389-9800. **$46-$66.** 2275 Airport Way 83705. I-84 exit 53 (Vista Ave), 0.3 mi se. Int corridors. **Pets:** Medium, dogs only. $20 daily fee/room. Designated rooms, supervision. SAVE 🛜 ᴋM 🗎 🖵 ➦

▼▼▼ Modern Hotel & Bar H

(208) 424-8244. **$96-$119.** 1314 W Grove St 83702. Corner of 14th and W Grove sts; downtown. Ext/int corridors. **Pets:** Accepted. 🛜 🗎 🖵 ꭱꭲ

▼▼▼ Oxford Suites Boise H

(208) 322-8000. **$89-$169.** 1426 S Entertainment Ave 83709. I-84 exit 50A, just s to Spectrum Way, just w, then just n. Int corridors. **Pets:** Other species. $25 one-time fee/pet. Designated rooms, service with restrictions, supervision. 🛜 ✕ ᴋM 🗎 🖵 ➦ ✕

▼▼▼▼ Red Lion Hotel Boise Downtowner 🅷
(208) 344-7691. **$69-$249.** 1800 Fairview Ave 83702. I-184 exit 3 (Fairview Ave), 1 mi n. Int corridors. **Pets:** Accepted.
🛜 ❌ 📶 🍽 🏨 🛥

🆑 ▼▼▼ Residence Inn by Marriott Boise West 🅷
(208) 385-9000. **$69-$129.** 7303 W Denton St 83704. I-84 exit 50A westbound; exit 50B eastbound, 2 mi n on Cole Rd, then just w. Int corridors. **Pets:** Medium. $100 one-time fee/room. Designated rooms, service with restrictions, crate. [SAVE] 🛜 ❌ 📶 🏨 🍽 🛥 ❌

🆑 ▼▼▼ Residence Inn by Marriott Downtown 🅷
(208) 344-1200. **$79-$199.** 1401 S Lusk Ave 83706. I-84 exit 53 (Vista Ave), 2.4 mi n, just w on Ann Morrison, then just s on Lois Ave. Ext corridors. **Pets:** Accepted. [SAVE] 🛜 ❌ 📶 🍽 🛥 ❌

▼▼▼ Safari Inn Downtown 🅷
(208) 344-6556. **$69-$99.** 1070 Grove St 83702. Corner of 11th and Grove sts. Int corridors. **Pets:** $10 one-time fee/room. Designated rooms, service with restrictions, supervision. 🛜 ❌ 📶 🍽 🛥 ❌

🆑 ▼▼▼ Shilo Inn Suites - Boise Airport 🅷
(208) 343-7662. **$59-$120.** 4111 Broadway Ave 83705. I-84 exit 54 (Broadway Ave), just sw. Int corridors. **Pets:** Dogs only. $25 one-time fee/room. Designated rooms, service with restrictions, crate.
[SAVE] 🛜 ❌ 📶 🍽 🛥 ❌

🆑 ▼▼▼ SpringHill Suites by Marriott Boise 🅷
(208) 939-8266. **$88-$98.** 6325 N Cloverdale Rd 83713. I-84 exit 46 (Eagle Rd), 4.3 mi n to Chinden, 0.9 mi e, then just s. Int corridors. **Pets:** Accepted. [SAVE] 🛜 ❌ 📶 🏨 🍽 🛥 ❌

▼▼▼▼ SpringHill Suites by Marriott Boise ParkCenter 🅷
(208) 342-1044. **$79-$149.** 424 E Parkcenter Blvd 83706. I-84 exit 54 (Broadway Ave), 2.3 mi n, then 0.3 mi e on Beacon St and Parkcenter Blvd. Int corridors. **Pets:** Accepted. 🛜 ❌ 📶 🏨 🍽 🛥 ❌

🆑 ▼▼▼ TownePlace Suites by Marriott Downtown 🅷
(208) 429-8881. **$76-$149.** 1455 S Capitol Blvd 83706. I-84 exit 53 (Vista Ave), 2.4 mi n. Int corridors. **Pets:** Large, other species. $25 daily fee/room. Service with restrictions, supervision.
[SAVE] 🛜 ❌ 📶 🏨 🍽 🛥

BONNERS FERRY

🆑 ▼▼▼▼ Best Western Plus Kootenai River Inn Casino & Spa 🅷
(208) 267-8511. **$140-$150.** 7169 Plaza St 83805. On US 95; city center. Int corridors. **Pets:** Medium. $20 daily fee/room. Service with restrictions, supervision. [SAVE] 🛜 ❌ 📶 🍽 🍽 🛥 ❌

▼▼▼▼ Northside School Bed & Breakfast 🅱🅱
(208) 267-1826. **$70-$140.** 6497 Comanche St 83805. US 95, w on Chinook St, just n on Bingham St, then just e. Int corridors. **Pets:** Small, dogs only. $10 one-time fee/room. Service with restrictions, supervision.
🛜 ❌ 📶 🍽 🛥 🐾 ✉

BURLEY

🆑 ▼▼▼ Best Western Plus Burley Inn & Convention Center 🅷
(208) 678-3501. **$75-$100.** 800 N Overland Ave 83318. I-84 exit 208, just s. Ext/int corridors. **Pets:** Accepted.
[SAVE] 🛜 📶 🍽 🍽 🛥 ❌

🆑 ▼▼▼ Super 8 Burley 🅷
(208) 678-7000. **$63-$85.** 336 S 600 W 83318. I-84 exit 208, just n. Int corridors. **Pets:** Accepted. [SAVE] 🛜 📶 🍽 🛥

CALDWELL

🆑 ▼▼▼▼ Best Western Plus Caldwell Inn & Suites 🅷 🐾
(208) 454-7225. **$72-$92.** 908 Specht Ave 83605. I-84 exit 29, just s. Int corridors. **Pets:** Other species. $5 daily fee/pet. Supervision.
[SAVE] 🛜 📶 🍽 🛥

▼▼▼ La Quinta Inn Caldwell 🅷
(208) 454-2222. **$80-$174.** 901 Specht Ave 83605. I-84 exit 29, just s. Int corridors. **Pets:** Medium, other species. Service with restrictions, supervision. 🛜 📶 🍽 🛥

COEUR D'ALENE

🆑 ▼▼▼▼ Best Western Plus Coeur d'Alene Inn 🅷
(208) 765-3200. **$99-$159.** W 506 Appleway Ave 83814. I-90 exit 12, just nw. Int corridors. **Pets:** Accepted.
[SAVE] 🛜 ❌ 📶 🏨 🍽 🍽 🛥

▼▼▼ ▼▼▼ The Coeur d'Alene Resort 🅷
(208) 765-4000. **$119-$539, 3 day notice.** 115 S 2nd St 83814. I-90 exit 11 (Northwest Blvd), 2 mi s. Ext/int corridors. **Pets:** $75 one-time fee/pet. Service with restrictions, crate. 🛜 ❌ 📶 🍽 🍽 🛥 ❌

▼▼▼ Comfort Inn Coeur d'Alene 🅷
(208) 664-1649. **Call for rates.** 2303 N 4th St 83814. I-90 exit 13, just n. Int corridors. **Pets:** Accepted. 🛜 ❌ 📶 🍽 🛥

▼▼▼ Days Inn-Coeur d'Alene 🅷
(208) 667-8668. **$51-$176.** 2200 Northwest Blvd 83814. I-90 exit 11 (Northwest Blvd), just se. Int corridors. **Pets:** Accepted.
🛜 ❌ 📶 🏨 🍽 ❌

▼▼▼ Guest House Inn & Suites 🅷
(208) 765-3011. **$45-$159.** 330 W Appleway Ave 83814. I-90 exit 12, just n, then just e. Int corridors. **Pets:** $10 one-time fee/room, $10 daily fee/room. Designated rooms, supervision. 🛜 📶 🍽

▼▼▼ ▼ Holiday Inn Express Hotel & Suites Coeur d'Alene 🅷 🐾
(208) 667-3100. **$99-$159.** 2300 W Seltice Way 83814. I-90 exit 11 (Northwest Blvd), just s. Int corridors. **Pets:** Large, dogs only. $15 one-time fee/room. Service with restrictions, supervision.
🛜 ❌ 📶 🍽 🛥

▼▼▼ Japan House Suites 🅷 🐾
(208) 667-0600. **Call for rates.** 2113 E Sherman Ave 83814. I-90 exit 15 (Sherman Ave), just s. Int corridors. **Pets:** Small, dogs only. $15 daily fee/pet. Designated rooms, service with restrictions, supervision.
🛜 ❌ 📶 🍽

▼▼▼ La Quinta Inn & Suites Coeur d'Alene East 🅷
(208) 667-6777. **$125-$189.** 2209 E Sherman Ave 83814. I-90 exit 15 (Sherman Ave), just s. Int corridors. **Pets:** Medium, other species. Service with restrictions, supervision. 🛜 📶 🍽 🛥

▼▼▼ La Quinta Inn Coeur d'Alene Appleway 🅷
(208) 765-5500. **$71-$179.** 280 W Appleway Ave 83814. I-90 exit 12, just ne. Int corridors. **Pets:** Medium, other species. Service with restrictions, supervision. 🛜 ❌ 📶 🍽 🛥 ❌

🆑 ▼▼▼ Resort City Inn 🅼
(208) 676-1225. **$59-$129, 3 day notice.** 621 Sherman Ave 83814. I-90 exit 11 (Northwest Blvd), 2.5 mi e via Northwest Blvd and Sherman Ave; downtown. Ext corridors. **Pets:** Other species. $25 one-time fee/room. Designated rooms, service with restrictions, supervision.
[SAVE] 🛜 ❌ 📶 🍽

▼▼▼▼ The Roosevelt Inn and Spa 🅱🅱
(208) 765-5200. **$89-$319, 14 day notice.** 105 E Wallace Ave 83814. I-90 exit 13, 2 mi s, then just w; downtown. Int corridors. **Pets:** Accepted.
🛜 ❌ ❌ 🅆 ✉

AAA ▼▼▼ Shilo Inn Suites - Coeur d'Alene H
(208) 664-2300. **$60-$130.** 702 W Appleway Ave 83814. I-90 exit 12,
just n, then just w. Int corridors. **Pets:** Dogs only. $25 one-time fee/room.
Designated rooms, service with restrictions, crate.
[SAVE] 🛜 ✕ ⟨M 🛏 💻 🐾 ✕

GRANGEVILLE

AAA ▼▼▼ Gateway Inn - Grangeville M
(208) 983-2500. **$55-$99.** 700 W Main St 83530. Jct US 95 and SR 13.
Ext corridors. **Pets:** $10 daily fee/room. Designated rooms, service with
restrictions, supervision. [SAVE] 🛜 ✕ 🛏 💻 🐾

HAGERMAN

AAA ▼▼▼ Hagerman Valley Inn M
(208) 837-6196. **$63-$108.** 661 Frog's Landing 83332. South end of town
on US 30. Ext/int corridors. **Pets:** $7 daily fee/pet. Designated rooms,
service with restrictions, supervision. [SAVE] 🛜 ✕ 🛏 💻

HAILEY

▼▼ Airport Inn M 🐾
(208) 788-2477. **$80-$150, 3 day notice.** 820 4th Ave S 83333. 0.8 mi
se of center; across from airport. Ext corridors. **Pets:** Large. $10 daily
fee/pet. Service with restrictions, supervision. 🛜 🛏 💻

▼▼▼ AmericInn Lodge & Suites of Hailey H
(208) 788-7950. **$89-$200, 3 day notice.** 51 Cobblestone Ln 83333. 0.5
mi n of center. Int corridors. **Pets:** Dogs only. $25 one-time fee/room.
Designated rooms, supervision. 🛜 ✕ 🛏 💻 🐾 ✕

▼▼ Wood River Inn H
(208) 578-0600. **$89-$159.** 603 N Main St 83333. 0.3 mi n of center. Int
corridors. **Pets:** Accepted. 🛜 🛏 💻 🐾 ✕

HAYDEN

▼▼▼ Holiday Inn Express Hotel & Suites H 🐾
(208) 772-7900. **$90-$399.** 151 W Orchard Ave 83835. I-90 exit 12, 3.5
mi n. Int corridors. **Pets:** $10 daily fee/pet. Service with restrictions, super-
vision. 🛜 ✕ ⟨M 🛏 💻 ✕

IDAHO FALLS

AAA ▼▼▼ Best Western Plus CottonTree Inn H
(208) 523-6000. **$90-$190.** 900 Lindsay Blvd 83402. I-15 exit 119, just e.
Int corridors. **Pets:** Small. $15 daily fee/pet. Designated rooms, service
with restrictions, supervision. [ECO] [SAVE] 🛜 🛏 💻 🐾

AAA ▼▼▼ Best Western Plus Driftwood Inn M 🐾
(208) 523-2242. **$79-$149.** 575 River Pkwy 83402. I-15 exit 118 (Broadway), 0.5 mi e, then 0.3 mi n. Ext corridors. **Pets:** Other species. $10
daily fee/room. Supervision. [SAVE] 🛜 ✕ 🛏 💻 🐾

▼▼ Candlewood Suites H 🐾
(208) 525-9800. **$79-$159.** 665 Pancheri Dr 83402. I-15 exit 118 (Broadway), 1 mi e (cross bridge), 0.5 mi s on S Capital Ave. Int corridors.
Pets: Large, other species. $15 one-time fee/room. Crate.
🛜 ⟨M 🛏 💻

AAA ▼▼▼ Le Ritz Hotel & Suites H 🐾
(208) 528-0880. **$78-$128.** 720 Lindsay Blvd 83402. I-15 exit 118
(Broadway), 0.5 mi e, then just n. Int corridors. **Pets:** $15 daily fee/room.
Designated rooms, service with restrictions.
[SAVE] 🛜 ⟨M 🛏 💻 🐾

▼▼ Red Lion Hotel on the Falls H
(208) 523-8000. **$79-$300.** 475 River Pkwy 83402. I-15 exit 118 (Broadway), 0.5 mi e, then just n. Ext/int corridors. **Pets:** Accepted.
🛜 🛏 💻 🍴 🐾 ✕

AAA ▼▼ Shilo Inn Suites Hotel Idaho Falls H
(208) 523-0088. **$79-$170.** 780 Lindsay Blvd 83402. I-15 exit 119, just
se. Int corridors. **Pets:** Dogs only. $25 one-time fee/room. Designated
rooms, service with restrictions, crate.
[SAVE] 🛜 ✕ 🛏 💻 🍴 🐾 ✕

JACKSON HOLE AREA (NEARBY WYOMING)

DRIGGS

▼ Teton Valley Cabins M
(208) 354-8153. **$69-$99, 7 day notice.** 388 Ski Hill Rd 83422. 0.8 mi e
on Little Ave from SR 33 E. Ext corridors. **Pets:** Accepted.
🛜 ✕ 🛏 💻 ✕ 🎿

END AREA

JEROME

**AAA ▼▼▼ Best Western Plus Sawtooth Inn &
Suites H 🐾**
(208) 324-9200. **Call for rates.** 2653 S Lincoln Ave 83338. I-84 exit 168,
just n. Int corridors. **Pets:** Other species. $100 deposit/room. Designated
rooms, service with restrictions, crate. [SAVE] 🛜 ✕ 🛏 💻 🐾

KAMIAH

▼▼ Clearwater 12 Motel M
(208) 935-2671. **Call for rates.** 108 E 3rd St (Hwy 12) 83536. On SR
12, just e of center. Ext corridors. **Pets:** Accepted. 🛜 🛏 💻

KELLOGG

▼▼ GuestHouse Inn & Suites H
(208) 783-1234. **$69-$209.** 601 Bunker Ave 83837. I-90 exit 49, 0.5 mi
se. Int corridors. **Pets:** Other species. $15 daily fee/pet. Service with
restrictions, supervision. 🛜 ⟨M 🛏 💻 🐾 ✕

▼▼▼ Morning Star Lodge CO
(208) 783-0202. **$101-$400.** 602 Bunker Ave 83837. I-90 exit 49, 0.5 mi
se. Int corridors. **Pets:** Accepted. ✕ 🛏 💻 🍴 ✕

▼ Silverhorn Motor Inn H 🐾
(208) 783-1151. **$69-$120.** 699 W Cameron Ave 83837. I-90 exit 49, just
ne. Int corridors. **Pets:** Other species. Supervision. 🛜 🛏 🍴

KETCHUM

AAA ▼▼▼ Best Western Tyrolean Lodge **H**
(208) 726-5336. **$89-$159, 3 day notice.** 260 Cottonwood St 83340. Just s of center to Rivers St, w to 2nd Ave, s to Cottonwood St, then just w. Int corridors. **Pets:** Accepted. (SAVE) 🛰 🖪 🖭 ⚟ 🖾

▼▼ Tamarack Lodge **M** 🐾
(208) 726-3344. **Call for rates.** 291 Walnut Ave N 83340. 0.3 mi e on Sun Valley Rd. Ext/int corridors. **Pets:** Large, other species. $25 one-time fee/room. Designated rooms, service with restrictions, supervision.
🛰 🖪 🖭 ⚟

KOOSKIA

▼▼▼ River Dance Lodge Resort **CA**
(208) 926-4300. **$129-$329, 45 day notice.** 7743 Hwy 12 83539. On SR 12, 16 mi e of Kooskia at MM 89. Ext corridors. **Pets:** $15 one-time fee/pet. Designated rooms, supervision.
🛰 🖪 🖭 🍽 🖾 🎾 ⚟

LEWISTON

AAA ▼▼▼ Holiday Inn Express **H** 🐾
(208) 750-1600. **$109-$189.** 2425 Nez Perce Dr 83501. 1.2 mi s on US 12 from jct US 95, 1.2 mi s on 21st St, then just e. Int corridors. **Pets:** $10 daily fee/room. Service with restrictions, crate.
(SAVE) 🛰 🖾 🖭 🖪 🖭 🖾

▼▼ Inn America **M**
(208) 746-4600. **Call for rates.** 702 21st St 83501. 1.2 mi s on US 12 from jct US 95, just s. Int corridors. **Pets:** Accepted.
🛰 🖭 🖪 🖭 ⚟

MCCALL

AAA ▼▼▼ Best Western Plus McCall Lodge & Suites **H** 🐾
(208) 634-2230. **$120-$150.** 211 S 3rd St 83638. 1 mi s of center on SR 55. Int corridors. **Pets:** Medium, dogs only. $20 daily fee/pet. Designated rooms, service with restrictions, supervision.
(SAVE) 🛰 🖾 🖪 🖭 ⚟ 🖾

▼▼ Super 8 - McCall **M**
(208) 634-4637. **$67-$98.** 303 S 3rd St 83638. 1.1 mi s of center on SR 55. Int corridors. **Pets:** Accepted. 🛰 🖭 🖪 🖭

▼▼ Western Mountain Lodge **H**
(208) 634-6300. **Call for rates.** 415 N 3rd St 83638. 0.4 mi s of center on SR 55. Int corridors. **Pets:** Accepted. 🛰 🖭 🖪 🖭 ⚟

MERIDIAN

▼▼▼ Candlewood Suites Boise-Meridian **H** 🐾
(208) 888-5121. **$85-$104.** 1855 S Silverstone Way 83642. I-84 exit 46 (Eagle Rd), 0.6 mi s, just e on Overland Rd, then just s. Int corridors. **Pets:** Small. $12 daily fee/room. Service with restrictions, supervision.
🛰 🖭 🖪 🖭 🖾

AAA ▼▼▼ Comfort Suites Meridian/West Boise **H**
(208) 288-2060. **$68-$77.** 2610 E Freeway Dr 83642. I-84 exit 46 (Eagle Rd), just n to St Lukes Rd, then just w to Allen St, follow signs. Int corridors. **Pets:** Accepted. (SAVE) 🛰 🖾 🖾 🖪 🖭 ⚟

AAA ▼▼▼ Country Inn & Suites By Carlson, Boise West **H**
(208) 639-3300. **$89-$129.** 3355 E Pine Ave 83642. I-84 exit 46 (Eagle Rd), 0.7 mi n, then just e. Int corridors. **Pets:** Accepted.
(SAVE) 🛰 🖾 🖾 🖪 🖭 ⚟

AAA ▼▼▼ TownePlace Suites Boise West/Meridian **H**
(208) 884-8550. **$72-$94.** 1415 S Eagle Rd 83642. I-84 exit 46 (Eagle Rd), just s. Int corridors. **Pets:** Accepted. (SAVE) 🛰 🖾 🖪 🖭 ⚟

MONTPELIER

AAA ▼▼▼ Clover Creek Inn & Suites **H** 🐾
(208) 847-1782. **$68-$110.** 243 N 4th St 83254. Just n on US 30 from jct US 89 S. Ext corridors. **Pets:** Dogs only. $10 one-time fee/room. Service with restrictions, supervision. (SAVE) 🛰 🖪 🖭

MOSCOW

AAA ▼▼▼▼ Best Western Plus University Inn **H** 🐾
(208) 882-0550. **$100-$200.** 1516 Pullman Rd 83843. Jct US 95, 1 mi w on SR 8. Int corridors. **Pets:** Small. $20 daily fee/room. Designated rooms, service with restrictions, crate.
(SAVE) 🛰 🖾 🖾 🖪 🖭 🍽 ⚟ 🖾

▼▼▼▼ La Quinta Inn & Suites Moscow Pullman **H**
(208) 882-5365. **$89-$165.** 185 Warbonnet Dr 83843. 1.6 mi w on SR 8 from jct US 93, just n. Int corridors. **Pets:** Medium, other species. Service with restrictions, supervision. 🛰 🖾 🖪 🖭 ⚟

▼▼ Super 8 **H**
(208) 883-1503. **$58-$158.** 175 Peterson Dr 83843. Jct US 95, 0.8 mi w on SR 8, just n. Int corridors. **Pets:** Accepted. 🛰 🖪 🖭

MOUNTAIN HOME

AAA ▼▼▼▼ Best Western Foothills Inn **M** 🐾
(208) 587-8477. **$94-$134.** 1080 Hwy 20 83647. I-84 exit 95, just n. Ext corridors. **Pets:** Large, dogs only. $15 daily fee/room. Designated rooms, service with restrictions, supervision. (SAVE) 🛰 🖪 🖭 ⚟

▼▼ Sleep Inn **M**
(208) 587-9743. **$82-$99.** 1180 Hwy 20 83647. I-84 exit 95, just n. Int corridors. **Pets:** Medium. $10 daily fee/room. Designated rooms, service with restrictions, supervision. 🛰 🖪 🖭

NAMPA

AAA ▼▼▼ Shilo Inn Suites Hotel Nampa **H**
(208) 465-3250. **$59-$120.** 1401 Shilo Dr 83687. I-84 exit 36 (Franklin Blvd), just nw. Int corridors. **Pets:** Dogs only. $25 one-time fee/room. Designated rooms, service with restrictions, crate.
(SAVE) 🛰 🖾 🖪 🖭 🍽 ⚟ 🖾

▼▼ Sleep Inn Nampa **H**
(208) 463-6300. **Call for rates.** 1315 Industrial Rd 83687. I-84 exit 36 (Franklin Blvd), just s. Int corridors. **Pets:** $25 one-time fee/room. Designated rooms, service with restrictions, supervision. 🛰 🖪 🖭 ⚟

OROFINO

AAA ▼▼▼ Best Western Plus Lodge at River's Edge **H** 🐾
(208) 476-9999. **$92-$112.** 615 Main St 83544. From US 12, 0.3 mi e to Main St, then 0.3 mi s. Int corridors. **Pets:** Small, dogs only. $20 daily fee/pet. Designated rooms, service with restrictions, supervision.
(SAVE) 🛰 🖾 🖪 🖭 🍽 ⚟ 🖾

▼▼ Helgeson Hotel **H** 🐾
(208) 476-5729. **$56-$77.** 125 Johnson Ave 83544. US 12, 0.3 mi e. Int corridors. **Pets:** Medium, dogs only. $20 daily fee/pet. Designated rooms, service with restrictions, supervision. 🛰 🖾 🖪 🖭

AAA ▼▼ Konkolville Motel **M**
(208) 476-5584. **$60-$90.** 2600 Michigan Ave 83544. US 12, 3 mi e. Ext corridors. **Pets:** Other species. $10 daily fee/pet. Service with restrictions, supervision. (SAVE) 🛰 🖾 🖪 🖭 ⚟

POCATELLO

AAA ▼▼▼ Best Western Plus CottonTree Inn **H**
(208) 237-7650. **$90-$95.** 1415 Bench Rd 83201. I-15 exit 71, just e. Int corridors. **Pets:** Accepted. (SAVE) 🛰 🖾 🖪 🖭 ⚟

▼▼▼▼ Clarion Inn 🄷

(208) 237-1400. **Call for rates.** 1399 Bench Rd 83201. I-15 exit 71, just e. Ext/int corridors. **Pets:** Large, other species. $10 one-time fee/room. Designated rooms, service with restrictions, supervision.

🛜 🛏 🖨 🍴 🛆 ⊠

🔴 ▼▼▼ Red Lion Hotel Pocatello 🄷

(208) 233-2200. **$75-$130.** 1555 Pocatello Creek Rd 83201. I-15 exit 71, just e. Int corridors. **Pets:** Accepted.

SAVE 🛜 ⊠ 🛏 🖨 🍴 🛆

🔴 ▼▼▼ Super 8 Pocatello 🄷 ❀

(208) 234-0888. **$63-$81.** 1330 Bench Rd 83201. I-15 exit 71, just e. Int corridors. **Pets:** $15 one-time fee/room. Designated rooms, no service, supervision. SAVE 🛜 🛏 🖨

▼▼ Thunderbird Motel 🄼

(208) 232-6330. **$44-$69.** 1415 S 5th Ave 83201. I-15 exit 67 (5th Ave), 1.3 mi n; just s of Idaho State University. Ext corridors. **Pets:** Other species. $5 daily fee/pet. Service with restrictions, supervision.

🛜 🛏 🛆

🔴 ▼▼▼▼ TownePlace Suites by Marriott 🄷

(208) 478-7000. **$99-$129.** 2376 Via Caporatti Dr 83201. I-15 exit 69 (Clark St), just e. Int corridors. **Pets:** Medium. $100 one-time fee/room. Service with restrictions, supervision.

SAVE 🛜 ⊠ 🛐 🛏 🖨 🛆

PONDERAY

▼▼ GuestHouse Lodge-Sandpoint 🄷

(208) 263-2210. **$45-$153.** 476841 Hwy 95 N 83852. 0.7 mi n on US 95 from jct SR 200. Int corridors. **Pets:** Accepted. 🛜 🛐 🛏 🖨

▼▼▼ Holiday Inn Express & Suites 🄷

(208) 255-4500. **$119-$249.** 477326 Hwy 95 N 83852. 0.7 mi n on US 95 from jct SR 200. Int corridors. **Pets:** Small. $10 daily fee/room. Designated rooms, service with restrictions, supervision.

🛜 ⊠ 🛐 🛏 🖨 🛆

▼▼ Howard Johnson Sandpoint/Ponderay 🄷

(208) 263-5383. **$45-$99.** 477255 Hwy 95 N 83852. 1.2 mi n on US 95 from jct SR 200. Int corridors. **Pets:** Accepted. 🛜 🛐 🛏 🖨

POST FALLS

🔴 ▼▼▼ Red Lion Templin's Hotel on the River - Post Falls 🄷

(208) 773-1611. **$99-$199.** 414 E First Ave 83854. I-90 exit 5 eastbound, just s to First Ave; exit 6 westbound, 0.7 mi w on Seltice Way to Spokane St, 0.5 mi s, then just e. Int corridors. **Pets:** Accepted.

SAVE 🛜 ⊠ 🛐 🛏 🖨 🍴 🛆 ⊠

▼▼ Sleep Inn 🄷 ❀

(208) 777-9394. **$59-$149.** 157 S Pleasant View Rd 83854. I-90 exit 2, just s. Int corridors. **Pets:** Dogs only. $15 one-time fee/room. Service with restrictions, supervision. 🛜 🛐 🛏 🖨 🛆

PRIEST RIVER

▼▼ Eagle's Nest Motel 🄼

(208) 448-2000. **$59-$105, 3 day notice.** 5722 Hwy 2 83856. US 2, 0.5 mi w. Ext corridors. **Pets:** Other species. $10 daily fee/pet. Designated rooms, service with restrictions, supervision. 🛜 🛐 🛏 🖨

REXBURG

🔴 ▼▼ AmericInn Lodge & Suites of Rexburg 🄷

(208) 356-5333. **$80-$210.** 1098 Golden Beauty Dr 83440. US 20 exit 332 (S Rexburg). Int corridors. **Pets:** Other species. $20 one-time fee/room. Designated rooms, service with restrictions, crate.

SAVE 🛜 ⊠ 🛏 🖨 🛆 ⊠

🔴 ▼▼ Quality Inn 🄷 ❀

(208) 359-1311. **$90-$130.** 885 W Main St 83440. US 20 exit 333 (Salmon), just e. Int corridors. **Pets:** Large. Designated rooms, service with restrictions, supervision. SAVE 🛜 🛏 🖨 🛆

RIGBY

▼▼▼ Blue Heron Inn 🄱🄱 ❀

(208) 745-9922. **$109-$199, 7 day notice.** 706 N Yellowstone Hwy 83442. US 20 exit 325, just e. Ext/int corridors. **Pets:** Designated rooms, service with restrictions, supervision. 🛜 ⊠ 🛐 ⊠ 🕿

RIGGINS

🔴 ▼▼▼ Best Western Plus Salmon Rapids Lodge 🄷 ❀

(208) 628-2743. **$90-$108.** 1010 S Main St 83549. 0.3 mi s of center. Int corridors. **Pets:** Other species. $15 daily fee/pet. Designated rooms, service with restrictions, supervision. SAVE 🛜 ⊠ 🛏 🖨 🛆

▼▼ Pinehurst Resort Cabins 🄲🄰

(208) 628-3323. **$65-$95.** 5604 Hwy 95 83654. MM 182 on US 95; 13 mi s of center. Ext corridors. **Pets:** Accepted.

🛜 ⊠ 🛏 🖨 🎦 🕿

SAGLE

▼▼ Bottle Bay Resort & Marina 🄲🄰

(208) 265-0951. **$142-$172.** 115 Resort Rd 83860. 8.3 mi e on Bottle Bay Rd from US 95. Ext corridors. **Pets:** Accepted.

⊠ 🛏 🖨 🍴 ⊠ 🎦 🕿

🔴 ▼▼▼▼ The Lodge at Sandpoint 🄷

(208) 263-2211. **$99-$459, 14 day notice.** 41 Lakeshore Dr 83860. 1 mi s of Sandpoint on US 95; just s of Longbridge. Int corridors. **Pets:** Small. $20 daily fee/room. Designated rooms.

SAVE 🛜 ⊠ 🛏 🖨 🍴 ⊠

ST. ANTHONY

▼▼ GuestHouse International Henry's Fork Inn 🄷 ❀

(208) 624-3711. **$60-$98.** 115 S Bridge St 83445. US 20 exit 346, just e. Ext corridors. **Pets:** $10 daily fee/pet. Designated rooms, service with restrictions, supervision. 🛜 🛏 🖨

SALMON

▼▼ Stagecoach Inn 🄼

(208) 756-2919. **Call for rates.** 201 Riverfront Dr (US 93 N) 83467. Just n on US 93 from jct SR 28. Int corridors. **Pets:** Accepted.

🛜 🛏 🖨 🛆

SANDPOINT

🔴 ▼▼▼ Best Western Plus Edgewater Resort 🄷

(208) 263-3194. **$99-$229.** 56 Bridge St 83864. Just e of US 95 N; downtown. Int corridors. **Pets:** Accepted.

SAVE 🛜 ⊠ 🛏 🖨 🍴 🛆 ⊠

▼▼▼ La Quinta Inn Sandpoint 🄷

(208) 263-9581. **$84-$189.** 415 Cedar St 83864. Jct US 2 and 95; downtown. Ext/int corridors. **Pets:** Medium, other species. Service with restrictions, supervision. 🛜 ⊠ 🛐 🛏 🖨 🍴 🛆

▼▼ Quality Inn Sandpoint 🄷

(208) 263-2111. **$79-$159.** 807 N 5th Ave 83864. US 2 and 95, just s of jct SR 200. Int corridors. **Pets:** Accepted. 🛜 🛏 🖨 🛆

STANLEY

🔴 ▼ Jerrys Country Store, Cabins & Motel 🄼

(208) 774-3566. **$70-$135, 7 day notice.** 55 Lower Stanley (US Hwy 75) 83278. 1 mi n of jct US 75 and SR 21. Ext corridors. **Pets:** $10 daily fee/pet. Service with restrictions, supervision. SAVE 🛏 🖨 🎦

TWIN FALLS

▼▼▼ AmericInn Hotel & Suites of Twin Falls 🄷

(208) 734-7494. **$89-$149.** 1910 Fillmore St N 83301. I-84 exit 173, 3 mi s to Fillmore St, then 0.5 mi w. Int corridors. **Pets:** Medium, other species. $20 daily fee/pet. Service with restrictions, supervision.

🛜 🛏 🖨 🛆

 **Best Western Plus Twin Falls Hotel** 🏨 ❀

(208) 736-8000. **$90-$120.** 1377 Blue Lakes Blvd N 83301. I-84 exit 173, 4 mi s on US 93. Int corridors. **Pets:** Large, other species. $20 daily fee/ room. Designated rooms, service with restrictions, crate.

Days Inn Jerome/Twin Falls 🏨

(208) 324-6400. **$49-$77.** 1200 Centennial Spur 83338. I-84 exit 173, just n on US 93. Int corridors. **Pets:** Accepted.

 **La Quinta Inn & Suites Twin Falls** 🏨

(208) 736-9600. **Call for rates.** 539 Pole Line Rd 83301. I-84 exit 173, 3 mi s to Pole Line Rd, then just w. Int corridors. **Pets:** Medium, other species. Service with restrictions, supervision.

 **Red Lion Hotel Canyon Springs** 🏨

(208) 734-5000. **$80-$169.** 1357 Blue Lakes Blvd N 83301. I-84 exit 173, 4 mi s on US 93. Int corridors. **Pets:** Accepted.

Shilo Inn Suites Hotel - Twin Falls 🏨

(208) 733-7545. **$77-$160.** 1586 Blue Lakes Blvd N 83301. I-84 exit 173, 3.7 mi s on US 93. Int corridors. **Pets:** Dogs only. $25 one-time fee/room. Designated rooms, service with restrictions, crate.

Super 8 Twin Falls Ⓜ

(208) 734-5801. **$55-$90.** 1260 Blue Lakes Blvd N 83301. I-84 exit 173, 4.1 mi s on US 93. Int corridors. **Pets:** Other species. $10 daily fee/pet. Service with restrictions, supervision.

WALLACE

The Wallace Inn 🏨

(208) 752-1252. **$72-$175.** 100 Front St 83873. I-90 exit 61 (Business Rt 90), just se. Int corridors. **Pets:** Other species. $20 daily fee/room. Service with restrictions, supervision.

WHITE BIRD

Hells Canyon Jet Boat Trips & Lodging Ⓜ ❀

(208) 839-2255. **$70-$80, 7 day notice.** 3252 Waterfront Dr 83554. Take the White Bird exit off US 95, then 1 mi s of center. Ext corridors. **Pets:** Large. $15 daily fee/pet. Service with restrictions, supervision.

WORLEY

Coeur d'Alene Casino Resort Hotel 🏨

(208) 769-2600. **Call for rates.** 27068 S Hwy 95 83876. On US 95, 3 mi n. Int corridors. **Pets:** Accepted.

ILLINOIS

CITY INDEX

ALTON

 **Best Western Plus Parkway Hotel** 🏨 ❀

(618) 433-9900. **$90-$120.** 1900 Homer Adams Pkwy 62002. On SR 111, 1.8 mi e of jct US 67. Int corridors. **Pets:** Other species. $10 daily fee/pet. Service with restrictions, supervision.

Comfort Inn 🏨

(618) 465-9999. **Call for rates.** 11 Crossroads Ct 62002. Off SR 3, jct SR 140. Int corridors. **Pets:** Other species. Service with restrictions, supervision.

ANNAWAN

Best Western Annawan Inn 🏨

(309) 935-6565. **Call for rates.** 315 N Canal St 61234. I-80 exit 33, just s. Int corridors. **Pets:** $25 daily fee/pet. Service with restrictions, supervision.

ARCOLA

Comfort Inn 🏨

(217) 268-4000. **Call for rates.** 610 E Springfield Rd 61910. I-57 exit 203 (SR 133), just w. Int corridors. **Pets:** Small. $10 daily fee/pet. Service with restrictions, supervision.

BLOOMINGTON

▼▼▼▼ The Chateau Hotel and Conference Center H
(309) 662-2020. **$79-$119.** 1601 Jumer Dr 61704. I-55 exit 167, follow I-55 business route (Veterans Pkwy), just e; 1.3 mi n of jct SR 9; 1 mi s of jct I-55. Int corridors. **Pets:** Small. $25 one-time fee/room. Designated rooms, service with restrictions, crate.

▼▼ Country Inn & Suites By Carlson Bloomington/Normal West H
(309) 828-7177. **Call for rates.** 923 Maple Hill Rd 61704. I-55/74 exit 160 (SR 9), 0.3 mi w to Wylie Dr, just n, then just e. Int corridors. **Pets:** Accepted.

▼▼▼▼ Doubletree Hotel & Conference Center-Bloomington H
(309) 664-6446. **$90-$97.** 10 Brickyard Dr 61701. I-55 business route (Veterans Pkwy), just n of US 150. Int corridors. **Pets:** Accepted.

▼▼▼ Eastland Suites Hotel & Conference Center H
(309) 662-0000. **Call for rates.** 1801 Eastland Dr 61704. Jct I-55 business route (Veterans Pkwy) and SR 9, just s to Eastland Dr, then just e. Ext/int corridors. **Pets:** Small, other species. $50 one-time fee/pet. Designated rooms, service with restrictions, crate.

▼▼▼ Holiday Inn Hotel & Suites H ❀
(309) 662-4700. **Call for rates.** 3202 E Empire St 61704. Jct I-55 business route (Veterans Pkwy) and SR 9, 2.3 mi e on SR 9. Int corridors. **Pets:** Dogs only. $20 one-time fee/room. Designated rooms, service with restrictions, supervision.

▼▼ La Quinta Inn Bloomington - Normal H
(309) 828-6000. **$80-$145.** 505 Brock Dr 61701. I-55/74 exit 160 (SR 9), just e. Int corridors. **Pets:** Medium, other species. Service with restrictions, supervision.

▼▼ Ramada Limited and Suites Bloomington H
(309) 828-0900. **$55-$109.** 919 Maple Hill Rd 61705. I-55/74 exit 160 (SR 9), 0.3 mi w to Wylie Dr, just n, then just e. Int corridors. **Pets:** $25 daily fee/room. Service with restrictions, crate.

CARBONDALE

▼▼▼ Hampton Inn H
(618) 549-6900. **$99-$109.** 2175 Reed Station Pkwy 62901. I-57 exit 54B, 11.7 mi w on SR 13. Int corridors. **Pets:** Accepted.

▼▼▼ Holiday Inn Hotel and Conference Center H
(618) 549-2600. **$119-$139.** 2300 Reed Station Pkwy 62901. I-57 exit 54B, 12 mi w on SR 13. Int corridors. **Pets:** Accepted.

▼ Super 8 H
(618) 457-8822. **$54-$76.** 1180 E Main St 62901. I-57 exit 54B, 13.9 mi w on SR 13. Int corridors. **Pets:** Accepted.

CHAMPAIGN

▼▼ Baymont Inn & Suites H
(217) 356-8900. **$67-$179.** 302 W Anthony Dr 61822. I-74 exit 182 (Neil St), just nw. Int corridors. **Pets:** Medium, other species. $10 daily fee/pet. Designated rooms, service with restrictions, crate.

▼▼▼ Drury Inn & Suites-Champaign H
(217) 398-0030. **$100-$219.** 905 W Anthony Dr 61821. I-74 exit 181 (Prospect Ave), just n. Int corridors. **Pets:** Accepted.

▼▼ Extended StayAmerica-Champaign-Urbana H ❀
(217) 351-8899. **$59-$84.** 610 W Marketview Dr 61822. I-74 exit 181 (Prospect Ave), just n, then just e. Int corridors. **Pets:** Other species. $25 daily fee/pet. Service with restrictions.

⊕⊕⊕ ▼▼▼ Hawthorn Suites by Wyndham H
(217) 398-3400. **$90-$230.** 101 Trade Centre Dr 61820. I-74 exit 182 (Neil St), 2.7 mi s. Int corridors. **Pets:** $25 daily fee/pet. Service with restrictions, crate. SAVE

▼▼ La Quinta Inn Champaign H
(217) 356-4000. **$64-$137.** 1900 Center Dr 61820. I-74 exit 182 (Neil St), just n. Int corridors. **Pets:** Medium, other species. Service with restrictions, supervision.

CHESTER

⊕⊕⊕ ▼▼▼ Best Western Reid's Inn H
(618) 826-3034. **$80.** 2150 State St 62233. SR 150, 1 mi e of SR 3. Int corridors. **Pets:** Small, dogs only. $25 deposit/pet, $5 daily fee/pet. Designated rooms, service with restrictions, supervision.
SAVE

CHICAGO METROPOLITAN AREA

ALSIP

▼▼ Baymont Inn & Suites Chicago/Alsip H
(708) 597-3900. **$71-$144.** 12801 S Cicero Ave 60803. I-294 exit SR 50 (Cicero Ave S). Int corridors. **Pets:** Medium. $50 deposit/room, $10 one-time fee/pet. Designated rooms, service with restrictions, crate.

ANTIOCH

▼▼ Comfort Inn & Suites by Choice Hotels H
(847) 395-3606. **Call for rates.** 350 Rt 173 60002. SR 173, 0.5 mi w of jct SR 83. Int corridors. **Pets:** Accepted.

ARLINGTON HEIGHTS

▼▼▼▼ DoubleTree by Hilton Hotel Chicago - Arlington Heights H
(847) 364-7600. **$109-$139.** 75 W Algonquin Rd 60005. I-90 exit Arlington Heights Rd, just n to Algonquin Rd, then just w. Int corridors. **Pets:** Accepted.

▼▼▼ Holiday Inn Express H
(847) 593-9400. **Call for rates.** 2120 S Arlington Heights Rd 60005. I-90 exit Arlington Heights Rd, 0.6 mi n. Int corridors. **Pets:** Small. $15 daily fee/pet. Designated rooms, service with restrictions, supervision.

▼▼ Jameson Suites Chicago-Arlington Heights H
(847) 956-1400. **$75-$95.** 2111 S Arlington Heights Rd 60005. I-90 exit Arlington Heights Rd, 0.6 mi n. Int corridors. **Pets:** Medium. $15 daily fee/room. Service with restrictions, supervision.

▼▼ La Quinta Inn Chicago Arlington Heights H
(847) 253-8777. **$58-$133.** 1415 W Dundee Rd 60004. SR 53 exit Dundee Rd, just e. Int corridors. **Pets:** Medium, other species. Service with restrictions, supervision.

⊕⊕⊕ Red Roof Inn #102 M
(847) 228-6650. **$45-$90.** 22 W Algonquin Rd 60005. I-90 exit Arlington Heights Rd, 0.5 mi n, then just w. Ext corridors. **Pets:** Large, other species. No service, supervision. SAVE

AURORA

▼▼▼▼ Staybridge Suites Aurora/Naperville H
(630) 978-2222. **$89-$159.** 4320 Meridian Pkwy 60504. I-88 exit SR 59, 2 mi s to Meridian Pkwy, then just w. Int corridors. **Pets:** Accepted.

BANNOCKBURN

▼▼▼▼ **La Quinta Inn & Suites Chicago North Shore** H
(847) 317-7300. **$78-$159.** 2000 S Lakeside Dr 60015. I-94 exit Half Day
Rd (SR 22), just e to Lakeside Dr, then just s. Int corridors.
Pets: Medium, other species. Service with restrictions, supervision.
🛜 ⟨M⟩ 🛏 💻 🕰 ⊠

BEDFORD PARK

▼▼ **Extended StayAmerica Chicago-Midway** H ✿
(708) 496-8211. **$70-$120.** 7524 State Rd 60638. Jct SR 50, just w. Int
corridors. **Pets:** Other species. $25 daily fee/pet. Service with restrictions.
🛜 ⟨M⟩ 🛏 💻

▼▼▼ **Residence Inn Chicago Midway Airport** H
(708) 458-7790. **$139-$209.** 6638 S Cicero Ave 60638. Jct 65th St. Int
corridors. **Pets:** Accepted. 🛜 ⊠ ⟨M⟩ 🛏 💻 🕰 ⊠

BLOOMINGDALE

▼▼▼ **Courtyard by Marriott** H
(630) 529-9200. **$129-$179.** 275 Knollwood Dr 60108. I-355 exit Army
Trail Rd, 4 mi w, then just n. Int corridors. **Pets:** Accepted.
🛜 ⊠ ⟨M⟩ 🛏 💻 🍴 🕰

▲▲▲ ▼▼▼▼ **Hilton Chicago Indian Lakes Resort** H
(630) 529-0200. **$99-$179.** 250 W Schick Rd 60108. I-355 exit Lake St
(US 20), 2.5 mi w, just s on Bloomingdale Rd, then 0.6 mi w. Int corridors. **Pets:** Accepted. SAVE 🛜 💻 🍴 🕰 ⊠

▼▼▼ **Residence Inn by Marriott** H
(630) 893-9200. **$139-$159.** 295 Knollwood Dr 60108. I-355 exit Army
Trail Rd, 4 mi w, then just n. Int corridors. **Pets:** Accepted.
🛜 ⊠ ⟨M⟩ 🛏 💻 🕰 ⊠

BOLINGBROOK

▲▲▲ ▼▼▼▼ **Aloft Bolingbrook** H
(630) 410-6367. **$89-$199.** 500 Janes Ave 60440. I-355 exit Boughton
Rd, just sw. Int corridors. **Pets:** Accepted.
SAVE 🛜 ⊠ ⟨M⟩ 🛏 💻 🕰

▲▲▲ ▼▼▼ **AmericInn Lodge & Suites of**
Bolingbrook H ✿
(630) 378-5300. **$89-$119, 7 day notice.** 175 W Remington Blvd
60440. I-55 exit 267, just n on SR 53. Int corridors. **Pets:** Medium, dogs
only. $25 one-time fee/pet. Service with restrictions, supervision.
SAVE 🛜 ⟨M⟩ 🛏 💻 🕰

▼▼ **La Quinta Inn & Suites Bolingbrook** H
(630) 226-0000. **$75-$189.** 225 W South Frontage Rd 60440. I-55 exit
267, 0.5 mi sw. Int corridors. **Pets:** Medium, other species. Service with
restrictions, supervision. 🛜 🛏 💻 🕰

BRIDGEVIEW

▼ **Days Inn Bridgeview** H
(708) 430-1818. **$67-$152.** 9625 S 76th Ave 60455. I-294 exit 95th St,
just sw. Int corridors. **Pets:** Other species. $25 daily fee/room. Service
with restrictions, supervision. 🛜 🛏 💻

BUFFALO GROVE

▼▼ **Extended StayAmerica-Chicago-Buffalo**
Grove-Deerfield H ✿
(847) 215-0641. **$55-$105.** 1525 Busch Pkwy 60089. I-94 exit W Lake
Cook Rd, 2 mi w to Milwaukee Ave (US 45/SR 21), then 1.3 mi n. Int
corridors. **Pets:** Other species. $25 daily fee/pet. Service with restrictions.
🛜 🛏 💻

BURR RIDGE

▼▼ **Extended StayAmerica Chicago-Burr Ridge** H ✿
(630) 323-6630. **$55-$100.** 15 W 122nd S Frontage Rd 60527. I-55 exit
276A (County Line Rd), just sw. Int corridors. **Pets:** Other species. $25
daily fee/pet. Service with restrictions. 🛜 🛏 💻

▼▼▼ **Quality Inn & Conference Center** H
(630) 325-2900. **$70-$180.** 300 S Frontage Rd 60527. I-55 exit 276A
(County Line Rd), just sw. Int corridors. **Pets:** Accepted.
🛜 🛏 💻 🕰

CHICAGO

▲▲▲ ▼▼▼▼ **Affinia Chicago Hotel** H
(312) 787-6000. **$169-$499, 3 day notice.** 166 E Superior St 60611.
Just e of Michigan Ave. Int corridors. **Pets:** Accepted.
SAVE 🛜 ⊠ 🛏 💻 🍴

▲▲▲ ▼▼▼▼ **Allegro Chicago, A Kimpton Hotel** H
(312) 236-0123. **Call for rates.** 171 W Randolph St 60601. Jct La Salle
St; in theater district. Int corridors. **Pets:** Accepted.
ECO SAVE 🛜 ⊠ 💻 🍴

▼▼▼ **Amalfi Hotel Chicago** H
(312) 395-9000. **$139-$649.** 20 W Kinzie St 60654. Between State and
Dearborn sts. Int corridors. **Pets:** Accepted.
🛜 ⊠ ⟨M⟩ 🛏 💻 ⊠

▼▼▼ **Avenue Crowne Plaza Chicago Downtown**
Magnificent Mile H
(312) 787-2900. **$109-$379.** 160 E Huron St 60611. Just e of N Michigan Ave. Int corridors. **Pets:** Accepted. 🛜 ⊠ 🛏 💻 🍴 🕰

▲▲▲ ▼▼▼▼ **The Blackstone, A Renaissance**
Hotel H
(312) 447-0955. **$159-$309.** 636 S Michigan Ave 60605. Jct Congress
Pkwy, just s. Int corridors. **Pets:** Accepted.
SAVE 🛜 ⊠ 🛏 💻 🍴

▲▲▲ ▼▼▼ **Carlton Inn Midway** M ✿
(773) 582-0900. **$89-$189.** 4944 S Archer Ave 60632. I-55 exit 287
(Pulaski Rd), 1.8 mi s to Archer Ave, then just e. Ext corridors.
Pets: Medium. $50 deposit/room, $10 daily fee/room. Designated rooms,
service with restrictions, supervision. SAVE 🛜 🛏 💻

▲▲▲ ▼▼▼▼ **Conrad Chicago** H ✿
(312) 645-1500. **$175-$355.** 521 N Rush St 60611. Jct Grand Ave. Int
corridors. **Pets:** Small. Designated rooms, service with restrictions, supervision. SAVE 🛜 ⊠ ⟨M⟩ 🛏 💻 🍴 ⊠

▲▲▲ ▼▼▼▼ **Crowne Plaza Chicago Metro** H
(312) 829-5000. **$116-$229.** 733 W Madison St 60661. I-90/94 exit 51D
(Madison St); jct Halsted St. Int corridors. **Pets:** Accepted.
SAVE 🛜 💻 🍴

▲▲▲ ▼▼▼ ▼▼▼ **The Drake Hotel, Chicago** H ✿
(312) 787-2200. **$119-$389.** 140 E Walton Pl 60611. Jct N Michigan Ave
and Lake Shore Dr. Int corridors. **Pets:** Medium. $75 one-time fee/pet.
Service with restrictions. SAVE 🛜 ⊠ 🛏 💻 🍴 ⊠

▲▲▲ ▼▼▼▼ ▼▼▼ **Fairmont Chicago, Millennium**
Park H ✿
(312) 565-8000. **Call for rates.** 200 N Columbus Dr 60601. Jct Michigan
Ave and Wacker Dr, just e. Int corridors. **Pets:** Small. $25 daily fee/room.
Service with restrictions, supervision. ECO SAVE 🛜 ⟨M⟩ 🍴

▲▲▲ ▼▼▼▼ ▼▼▼ **Four Seasons Hotel Chicago** H ✿
(312) 280-8800. **Call for rates.** 120 E Delaware Pl 60611. Jct Michigan
Ave; just nw of John Hancock Building. Int corridors. **Pets:** Very small.
Designated rooms, service with restrictions, supervision.
ECO SAVE 🛜 ⟨M⟩ 🛏 💻 🍴 🕰 ⊠

▲▲▲ ▼▼▼▼ ▼▼▼ **Hard Rock Hotel Chicago** H
(312) 345-1000. **$109-$529.** 230 N Michigan Ave 60601. Between Lake
St and Wacker Dr. Int corridors. **Pets:** Medium. $25 daily fee/room. Serv-
ice with restrictions, supervision. SAVE 🛜 ⊠ ⟨M⟩ 💻 🍴 ⊠

AAA ▼▼▼ ▼▼▼ **Hilton Chicago** H ❀
(312) 922-4400. **$119-$559.** 720 S Michigan Ave 60605. I-290 (Congress Pkwy) exit Michigan Ave, just s. Int corridors. **Pets:** Large, other species. $50 one-time fee/room. Service with restrictions, crate.
ECO SAVE 🛰 💻 🍴 ➰ ✕

AAA ▼▼▼ ▼▼▼ **Hilton Chicago O'Hare Airport** H ❀
(773) 686-8000. **$109-$399.** O'Hare Int'l Airport 60666. Opposite and connected to terminal buildings at Chicago O'Hare International Airport, accessed via I-190. Int corridors. **Pets:** Medium. $50 one-time fee/room. Designated rooms, service with restrictions, supervision.
SAVE 🛰 💻 🍴 ➰ ✕

AAA ▼▼▼ ▼▼▼ **Hilton Suites Chicago/Magnificent Mile** H
(312) 664-1100. **$129-$389.** 198 E Delaware Pl 60611. Just e of Michigan Ave. Int corridors. **Pets:** Accepted.
SAVE 🛰 ♿ 🖥 💻 🍴 ➰ ✕

AAA ▼▼▼ **Holiday Inn & Suites Downtown Chicago** H ❀
(312) 957-9100. **$129-$349.** 506 W Harrison St 60607. I-290 exit Canal St, just s. Int corridors. **Pets:** Small, dogs only. $100 one-time fee/pet, $25 daily fee/pet. Designated rooms, service with restrictions, supervision.
SAVE 🛰 🖥 💻 🍴 ➰

AAA ▼▼▼ **Holiday Inn Chicago O'Hare** H
(773) 693-5800. **Call for rates.** 5615 N Cumberland Ave 60631. I-90 exit 79B (N Cumberland Ave), just s. Int corridors. **Pets:** Accepted.
SAVE 🛰 ♿ 🖥 💻 🍴 ➰

AAA ▼▼▼ **Hotel Burnham Chicago** H
(312) 782-1111. **Call for rates.** One W Washington St 60602. Jct State St. Int corridors. **Pets:** Accepted. ECO SAVE 🛰 ✕ 💻 🍴

▼▼▼ **Hotel Indigo Chicago Downtown Gold Coast** H
(312) 787-4980. **$139-$399.** 1244 N Dearborn St 60610. Just n of Division St. Int corridors. **Pets:** Accepted. 🛰 💻 🍴

AAA ▼▼▼ ▼▼▼ **Hotel Monaco Chicago** H ❀
(312) 960-8500. **Call for rates.** 225 N Wabash Ave 60601. Jct Wacker Dr. Int corridors. **Pets:** Other species. Service with restrictions, crate.
ECO SAVE 🛰 ✕ 💻 🍴 ✕

AAA ▼▼▼ ▼▼▼ **Hotel Palomar Chicago** H ❀
(312) 755-9703. **$129-$799.** 505 N State St 60654. Between Grand and Illinois sts. Int corridors. **Pets:** Other species. Service with restrictions.
🛰 ✕ ♿ 🍴 ➰

▼▼▼ ▼▼▼ **InterContinental Chicago Magnificent Mile** H
(312) 944-4100. **$129-$549.** 505 N Michigan Ave 60611. Just n of Chicago River; between E Grand Ave and E Illinois St. Int corridors.
Pets: Medium. $50 deposit/pet, $50 one-time fee/pet. Service with restrictions, crate. ECO 🛰 ✕ 💻 🍴 ➰ ✕

▼▼▼ ▼▼▼ **The James Chicago** H
(312) 337-1000. **$179-$599, 3 day notice.** 55 E Ontario St 60611. Just w of N Michigan Ave. Int corridors. **Pets:** Accepted.
🛰 ♿ 💻 🍴 ✕

▼▼▼ ▼▼▼ **La Quinta Inn & Suites Chicago Downtown** H
(312) 558-1020. **$137-$302.** 1 S Franklin St 60606. Jct Madison Ave. Int corridors. **Pets:** Medium, other species. Service with restrictions, supervision. 🛰 ♿ 🖥 💻 🍴 ➰ ✕

AAA ▼▼▼ ▼▼▼ **Omni Chicago Hotel** H ❀
(312) 944-6664. **Call for rates.** 676 N Michigan Ave 60611. Jct Huron St. Int corridors. **Pets:** Small. $50 one-time fee/room. Service with restrictions. SAVE 🛰 ✕ ♿ 🖥 💻 🍴 ➰ ✕

AAA ▼▼▼ ▼▼▼ **Palmer House - A Hilton Hotel** H ❀
(312) 726-7500. **$119-$459.** 17 E Monroe St 60603. Between State St and Wabash Ave. Int corridors. **Pets:** Other species. $50 one-time fee/room. Service with restrictions, supervision.
ECO SAVE 🛰 🖥 💻 🍴 ➰ ✕

AAA ▼▼▼ ▼▼▼ **Park Hyatt Chicago** H
(312) 335-1234. **$295-$495, 3 day notice.** 800 N Michigan Ave 60611. Jct Chicago Ave at Water Tower Square. Int corridors. **Pets:** Accepted.
ECO SAVE 🛰 🍴 ➰ ✕

AAA ▼▼▼ ▼▼▼ **The Peninsula Chicago** H
(312) 337-2888. **$440-$1395.** 108 E Superior St 60611. Jct Michigan Ave. Int corridors. **Pets:** Accepted. SAVE 🛰 ♿ 🖥 🍴 ➰ ✕

AAA ▼▼▼ ▼▼▼ **Renaissance Chicago Downtown** H
(312) 372-7200. **$209-$489.** 1 W Wacker Dr 60601. Jct State St. Int corridors. **Pets:** Accepted.
SAVE 🛰 ✕ ♿ 🖥 💻 🍴 ➰ ✕

AAA ▼▼▼ **Residence Inn by Marriott Chicago Downtown/ Magnificent Mile** H ❀
(312) 943-9800. **$129-$469.** 201 E Walton Pl 60611. Just e of Michigan Ave at Mies van der Rohe Way. Int corridors. **Pets:** Other species. $100 one-time fee/room. SAVE 🛰 ✕ ♿ 🖥 💻

▼▼▼ ▼▼▼ **Residence Inn by Marriott Chicago Downtown River North** H
(312) 494-9301. **$209-$319.** 410 N Dearborn St 60654. Between W Kinzie and W Hubbard sts. Int corridors. **Pets:** Accepted.
🛰 ✕ ♿ 🖥 💻

AAA ▼▼▼ ▼▼▼ **The Ritz-Carlton Chicago (A Four Seasons Hotel)** H
(312) 266-1000. **Call for rates.** 160 E Pearson St 60611. Jct N Michigan Ave. Int corridors. **Pets:** Accepted.
ECO SAVE 🛰 ✕ ♿ 🖥 💻 🍴 ➰ ✕

AAA ▼▼▼ ▼▼▼ **Sheraton Chicago Hotel & Towers** H ❀
(312) 464-1000. **$109-$659.** 301 E North Water St 60611. Columbus Dr at Chicago River; just e of Michigan Ave. Int corridors. **Pets:** Large, dogs only. Service with restrictions, supervision.
ECO SAVE 🛰 ✕ 🖥 💻 🍴 ➰ ✕

AAA ▼▼▼ ▼▼▼ **Sofitel Chicago Water Tower** H
(312) 324-4000. **$175-$496.** 20 E Chestnut St 60611. Jct Wabash Ave and Chestnut St, 1/2 blk w of Rush St. Int corridors. **Pets:** Accepted.
ECO SAVE 🛰 ♿ 💻 🍴 ✕

AAA ▼▼▼ **The Sutton Place Hotel** H
(312) 266-2100. **Call for rates.** 21 E Bellevue Pl 60611. Jct Rush St. Int corridors. **Pets:** Accepted. SAVE 🛰 🍴

AAA ▼▼▼ ▼▼▼ **Swissotel Chicago** H
(312) 565-0565. **$99-$599.** 323 E Wacker Dr 60601. Just e of Michigan Ave. Int corridors. **Pets:** Accepted.
SAVE 🛰 ✕ ♿ 💻 🍴 ➰ ✕

AAA ▼▼▼ ▼▼▼ **Trump International Hotel & Tower** H
(312) 588-8000. **$395-$2000.** 401 N Wabash Ave 60611. Between Hubbard and Kinzie sts; just s of Kinzie St. Int corridors. **Pets:** Accepted.
SAVE 🛰 ✕ ♿ 🖥 💻 🍴 ➰ ✕

AAA ▼▼▼ ▼▼▼ **Waldorf Astoria Chicago formerly "Elysian"** H
(312) 646-1300. **$555-$6000, 3 day notice.** 11 E Walton St 60611. Between State and Rush sts. Int corridors. **Pets:** Accepted.
SAVE 🛰 ✕ ♿ 🖥 🍴 ➰ ✕

AAA ▼▼▼ ▼▼▼ **W Chicago-City Center** H
(312) 332-1200. **$169-$529.** 172 W Adams St 60603. Between La Salle and Wells sts. Int corridors. **Pets:** Accepted. SAVE 🛰 ✕ 🖥 🍴

AAA ▼▼▼ ▼▼▼ **W Chicago Lakeshore** H ❀
(312) 943-9200. **$159-$739.** 644 N Lake Shore Dr 60611. Jct Ontario St. Int corridors. **Pets:** Medium. $100 one-time fee/room, $25 daily fee/pet. Designated rooms, service with restrictions, crate. SAVE 🛰 🍴 ➰

◬◬◬ ▼▼▼ ▼▼▼ **The Westin Chicago River North** 🅗
(312) 744-1900. **$129-$659.** 320 N Dearborn St 60654. Just n of Chicago River; between Dearborn and Clark sts. Int corridors.
Pets: Accepted. 🆂🅰🆅🅴 🛜 ⊠ 🛗 📞 💻 🍴 🚫

◬◬◬ ▼▼▼ ▼▼▼ **The Westin Michigan Avenue Chicago** 🅗 ❄
(312) 943-7200. **$679.** 909 N Michigan Ave 60611. Across from John Hancock Center. Int corridors. **Pets:** Medium, dogs only. Designated rooms, service with restrictions, supervision.
🅴🅲🅾 🆂🅰🆅🅴 🛜 ⊠ 🛗 💻 🍴 🚫

CRYSTAL LAKE
▼▼ ▼▼ **Comfort Inn by Choice Hotels** 🅗
(815) 444-0040. **$89-$119.** 595 Tracy Tr 60014. Jct US 14 and SR 31, 0.4 mi w, just n on Pingree Rd, then just n. Int corridors. **Pets:** Accepted.
🛜 🛗 💻 🛟

▼▼▼ ▼▼▼ **Holiday Inn Chicago-Crystal Lake** 🅗
(815) 477-7000. **Call for rates.** 800 S SR 31 60014. At Three Oaks Rd, 0.3 mi s of jct US 14. Int corridors. **Pets:** Small, dogs only. $20 daily fee/pet. Designated rooms, service with restrictions, supervision.
🛜 🛗 💻 🍴 🛟

▼▼ ▼▼ **Super 8** 🅗
(815) 788-8888. **$52-$84.** 577 Crystal Point Dr 60014. On US 14, 1 mi w of jct SR 31. Int corridors. **Pets:** Accepted. 🛜 🛗 💻

DARIEN
▼▼ ▼▼ **Extended StayAmerica Chicago-Darien** 🅗 ❄
(630) 985-4708. **$55-$100.** 2345 Sokol Ct 60561. I-55 exit 271A, 0.5 mi s to Westgate Rd, then 0.5 mi ne via frontage road. Int corridors.
Pets: Other species. $25 daily fee/pet. Service with restrictions.
🛜 🛗 💻

DEERFIELD
◬◬◬ ▼▼▼ ▼▼▼ **Chicago Marriott Suites Deerfield** 🅗
(847) 405-9666. **$74-$229.** 2 Parkway North 60015. I-94 exit Deerfield Rd northbound, just w; exit Lake Cook Rd southbound, 0.3 mi e to Saunders Rd, then 0.5 mi n. Int corridors. **Pets:** Small. $75 one-time fee/room, $10 daily fee/room. Designated rooms, service with restrictions, supervision. 🆂🅰🆅🅴 🛜 ⊠ 🛗 💻 🛟 🚫

◬◬◬ ▼ **Red Roof Inn #188** Ⓜ
(847) 205-1755. **$54-$78.** 340 S Waukegan Rd 60015. I-94 exit SR 43 (Waukegan Rd). Ext corridors. **Pets:** Large, other species. No service, supervision. 🆂🅰🆅🅴 🛜 🛗 💻

▼▼▼ ▼▼▼ **Residence Inn by Marriott Chicago/Deerfield** 🅗
(847) 940-4644. **$199-$219.** 530 Lake Cook Rd 60015. I-94 exit Lake Cook Rd, 1.8 mi e, then 3 blks n on Corporate 500 Dr access road. Ext corridors. **Pets:** Accepted. 🛜 ⊠ 🛗 💻 🛟 🚫

DES PLAINES
◬◬◬ ▼▼ ▼▼ **Comfort Inn O'Hare** 🅗
(847) 635-1300. **$90-$190.** 2175 E Touhy Ave 60018. I-294 exit Touhy Ave westbound, just w; exit Golf Rd (SR 58) eastbound, 0.3 mi w to River Rd, then 5.5 mi s. Int corridors. **Pets:** Accepted.
🆂🅰🆅🅴 🛜 ⊠ 🛗 💻

▼▼ ▼▼ **Extended StayAmerica-Chicago O'Hare** 🅗 ❄
(847) 294-9693. **$55-$110.** 1201 E Touhy Ave 60018. SR 72 (Higgins Rd), 0.6 mi, w of US 12/45 (Mannheim Rd). Int corridors. **Pets:** Other species. $25 daily fee/pet. Service with restrictions. 🛜 🅼 🛗 💻

▼▼ ▼▼ **Extended Stay Deluxe Chicago O'Hare** 🅗 ❄
(847) 768-0395. **$60-$120.** 1207 E Touhy Ave 60018. SR 72 (Higgins Rd), 0.6 mi w of US 12/45 (Mannheim Rd). Int corridors. **Pets:** Other species. $25 daily fee/pet. Service with restrictions. 🛜 🅼 🛗 💻

▼▼▼ ▼▼▼ **Hilton Garden Inn Chicago-O'Hare Airport** 🅗
(847) 296-8900. **$95-$219.** 2930 S River Rd 60018. I-294 exit Touhy Ave westbound, just w to River Rd, then 0.3 mi s; exit Golf Rd (SR 58) eastbound, 0.3 mi w to River Rd, then 6 mi s. Int corridors. **Pets:** Medium. $50 one-time fee/pet. Service with restrictions, supervision.
🛜 ⊠ 🅼 🛗 💻 🍴 🛟 🚫

DOWNERS GROVE
▼▼ ▼▼ **Holiday Inn Express** 🅗
(630) 810-9500. **$79-$209.** 3031 Finley Rd 60515. I-355 exit Butterfield Rd (SR 56), just e. Int corridors. **Pets:** Accepted. 🛜 🛗 💻

◬◬◬ ▼ **Red Roof Inn Downers Grove/Lombard** Ⓜ
(630) 963-4205. **$59-$94.** 1113 Butterfield Rd 60515. I-355 exit Butterfield Rd (SR 56), on frontage road; I-88 exit Highland Ave N, just w. Ext corridors. **Pets:** Large, other species. No service, supervision. 🆂🅰🆅🅴 🛜 🛗

ELGIN
▼▼ ▼▼ **Quality Inn-Elgin** 🅗
(847) 608-7300. **$72-$89.** 500 Tollgate Rd 60123. I-90 exit SR 31 N, just n. Int corridors. **Pets:** Accepted. 🛜 🅼 🛗 💻

ELK GROVE VILLAGE
▼ **Baymont Inn & Suites** 🅗
(847) 803-9400. **$53-$107.** 2881 Touhy Ave 60007. Jct SR 72 (Higgins Rd) and 83 (Busse Rd), 1.5 mi e on SR 72 (Higgins Rd). Int corridors.
Pets: Accepted. 🛜 🛗 💻

▼ **Days Inn Schaumburg/Elk Grove** 🅗
(847) 895-2085. **$49-$80.** 1000 W Devon Ave 60007. I-290 exit Thorndale Ave, 0.5 mi w to Rohlwing Rd, 0.3 mi n to Devon Ave, then 0.3 mi e. Int corridors. **Pets:** Accepted. 🛜 🛗 💻

▼▼ ▼▼ **La Quinta Inn Chicago O'Hare Airport** 🅗
(847) 439-6767. **$67-$180.** 1900 E Oakton St 60007. Jct SR 72 (Higgins Rd) and 83 (Busse Rd). Int corridors. **Pets:** Medium, other species. Service with restrictions, supervision. 🛜 🛗 💻 🛟

◬◬◬ ▼▼▼ ▼▼▼ **Sheraton Suites Chicago Elk Grove** 🅗
(847) 290-1600. **$99-$159.** 121 Northwest Point Blvd 60007. I-90 exit Arlington Heights Rd, just s; in Northwest Point Corporate Park. Int corridors. **Pets:** Accepted. 🆂🅰🆅🅴 🛜 ⊠ 🅼 🛗 💻 🍴 🛟 🚫

◬◬◬ ▼▼ ▼▼ **Super 8 O'Hare** 🅗
(847) 827-3133. **$47-$92.** 2951 Touhy Ave 60007. Jct SR 72 (Higgins Rd) and 83 (Busse Rd); 1.5 mi e on SR 72 (Higgins Rd). Int corridors. **Pets:** Medium. $20 daily fee/pet. Designated rooms, service with restrictions, supervision. 🆂🅰🆅🅴 🛜 🅼 🛗 💻 🛟

ELMHURST
◬◬◬ ▼▼▼ ▼▼▼ **Clarion Inn Waterford Convention Center** 🅗
(630) 279-0700. **Call for rates.** 933 S Riverside Dr 60126. 2.4 mi s of SR 64 (North Ave), just off SR 83. Int corridors. **Pets:** Small, other species. $25 one-time fee/pet. Designated rooms, service with restrictions, crate. 🆂🅰🆅🅴 🛜 🛗 💻 🛟

▼▼ ▼▼ **Extended StayAmerica Chicago-Elmhurst-O'Hare** 🅗 ❄
(630) 530-4353. **$50-$100.** 550 W Grand Ave 60126. Jct US 20 (Lake St), 0.4 mi ne; adjacent to I-290 overpass. Int corridors. **Pets:** Other species. $25 daily fee/pet. Service with restrictions. 🛜 🅼 🛗 💻

EVANSTON
◬◬◬ ▼▼▼ ▼▼▼ **Hilton Orrington/Evanston** 🅗 ❄
(847) 866-8700. **$129-$209.** 1710 Orrington Ave 60201. Jct Church St. Int corridors. **Pets:** Medium. $50 one-time fee/room. Designated rooms, service with restrictions. 🆂🅰🆅🅴 🛜 🅼 🛗 💻 🍴 🚫

GLEN ELLYN

▼▼▼▼ Crowne Plaza Glen Ellyn-Lombard 🏨
(630) 629-6000. **$110-$210.** 1250 Roosevelt Rd 60137. I-355 exit Roosevelt Rd, 0.8 mi e on SR 38. Int corridors. **Pets:** Designated rooms, service with restrictions, crate. 📶 ⊗ 🕭 🛢 💻 🍽 🏊

GLENVIEW

▼▼▼▼ Staybridge Suites 🏨
(847) 657-0002. **$89-$169.** 2600 Lehigh Ave 60026. I-294 exit Willow Rd, 2.4 mi e. Int corridors. **Pets:** Accepted. 📶 ⊗ 🕭 🛢 💻 🏊

▼▼▼▼ Wyndham Glenview Suites 🏨
(847) 803-9800. **$98-$233.** 1400 N Milwaukee Ave 60025. I-294 exit Willow Rd, 0.3 mi w to Sanders Rd, 1.3 mi s to Milwaukee Ave (SR 21), then 1 mi s. Int corridors. **Pets:** Accepted.

📶 ⊗ 🛢 💻 🍽 🏊 ⊗

GRAYSLAKE

▼▼▼▼ Comfort Suites by Choice Hotels 🏨
(847) 223-5050. **$72-$147.** 1775 E Belvidere Rd 60030. Just w of jct US 45. Int corridors. **Pets:** Medium. $35 one-time fee/pet. Designated rooms, service with restrictions, supervision. 📶 ⊗ 🛢 💻 🏊 ⊗

GURNEE

🆔 ▼▼▼ Best Western Gurnee Hotel & Suites 🏨
(847) 782-0890. **$79-$159.** 5430 Grand Ave 60031. I-94 exit Grand Ave (SR 132 E), 0.5 mi e. Int corridors. **Pets:** Accepted.
SAVE 📶 ⊗ 🕭 🛢 💻 🏊

▼▼▼ Comfort Inn by Choice Hotels 🏨
(847) 855-8866. **$59-$140.** 6080 Gurnee Mills Cir E 60031. I-94 exit Grand Ave (SR 132 W), just nw. Int corridors. **Pets:** Accepted.
📶 🛢 💻 🏊

▼▼▼ Country Inn & Suites By Carlson 🏨
(847) 625-9700. **Call for rates.** 5420 Grand Ave 60031. I-94 exit Grand Ave (SR 132 E), 0.5 mi e. Int corridors. **Pets:** Accepted.
📶 ⊗ 🕭 🛢 💻 🏊

▼▼ Fairfield Inn by Marriott 🏨
(847) 855-8868. **$109-$149.** 6090 Gurnee Mills Cir E 60031. I-94 exit Grand Ave (SR 132 W), just nw. Int corridors. **Pets:** Medium, dogs only. $50 one-time fee/room. Designated rooms, service with restrictions, supervision. 📶 ⊗ 🛢 💻 🏊

▼▼ La Quinta Inn & Suites Chicago Gurnee 🏨
(847) 662-7600. **$62-$155.** 5688 Northridge Dr 60031. I-94 exit Grand Ave (SR 132 E), just e via service road. Int corridors. **Pets:** Medium, other species. Service with restrictions, supervision.
📶 🕭 🛢 💻 🏊

HANOVER PARK

▼▼▼ Extended StayAmerica-Chicago-Hanover Park 🏨 🐾
(630) 893-4823. **$55-$100.** 1075 Lake St 60133. On US 20; between Gary Ave and Elgin-O'Hare Expwy. Int corridors. **Pets:** Other species. $25 daily fee/pet. Service with restrictions. 📶 🛢 💻

HILLSIDE

🆔 ▼▼▼▼ Best Western Plus Chicago Hillside 🏨
(708) 544-9300. **$89-$139.** 4400 Frontage Rd 60162. I-290 exit 14B eastbound to US 12/45 (Mannheim Rd), just nw via frontage road; exit 17 westbound to US 12/45 (Mannheim Rd), just nw via frontage road. Int corridors. **Pets:** Medium. $50 one-time fee/room. Designated rooms, service with restrictions, crate. SAVE 📶 🛢 💻 🍽 🏊

HOFFMAN ESTATES

▼▼▼ La Quinta Inn Chicago Hoffman Estates 🏨
(847) 882-3312. **$54-$144.** 2280 Barrington Rd 60169. I-90 exit Barrington Rd westbound, 0.3 mi s; exit SR 59 eastbound, 0.5 mi n to SR 72 (Higgins Rd), 2 mi e to Barrington Rd, then just n. Int corridors. **Pets:** Medium, other species. Service with restrictions, supervision.
📶 🛢 💻 🏊

▼▼▼ Red Roof Inn #199 Ⓜ
(847) 885-7877. **$50-$90.** 2500 Hassell Rd 60169. I-90 exit Barrington Rd westbound, 0.3 mi s; exit SR 59 eastbound, 0.5 mi n to SR 72 (Higgins Rd), 2 mi e to Barrington Rd, then just n. Ext corridors. **Pets:** Large, other species. No service, supervision. SAVE 📶 🛢

ITASCA

▼▼▼ Extended StayAmerica-Chicago-Itasca 🏨 🐾
(630) 250-1111. **$50-$100.** 1181 Rohlwing Rd 60143. I-290 exit Thorndale Ave, 0.5 mi w. Int corridors. **Pets:** Other species. $25 daily fee/pet. Service with restrictions. 📶 🕭 🛢 💻

🆔 ▼▼▼ ▼▼▼ The Westin Chicago Northwest 🏨 🐾
(630) 773-4000. **$99-$349, 3 day notice.** 400 Park Blvd 60143. I-290 exit Thorndale Ave, just e. Int corridors. **Pets:** Medium. Crate.
SAVE 📶 ⊗ 🛢 💻 🍽 🏊 ⊗

JOLIET

▼▼ ▼▼ Comfort Inn by Choice Hotels Joliet North 🏨
(815) 436-5141. **$75-$190.** 3235 Norman Ave 60435. I-55 exit 257, just e. Int corridors. **Pets:** Accepted. 📶 🛢 💻 🏊

▼▼ ▼▼ Comfort Inn by Choice Hotels-South 🏨
(815) 744-1770. **$80-$190.** 135 S Larkin Ave 60436. I-80 exit 130B, 0.5 mi n. Int corridors. **Pets:** Accepted. 📶 🛢 💻 🏊

▼▼ ▼▼ Fairfield Inn by Marriott Joliet South 🏨
(815) 741-3499. **$120-$260.** 1501 Riverboat Center Dr 60436. I-80 exit 127, just n. Int corridors. **Pets:** Accepted. 📶 ⊗ 🕭 🛢 💻 🏊

🆔 ▼▼ Red Roof Inn #10071 Ⓜ
(815) 741-2304. **$50-$131.** 1750 McDonough St 60436. I-80 exit 130B, just off Larkin Ave. Ext corridors. **Pets:** Large, other species. No service, supervision. SAVE 📶 🏊

🆔 ▼▼▼ ▼▼▼ TownePlace Suites by Marriott Joliet 🏨 🐾
(815) 741-2400. **$129-$199.** 1515 Riverboat Center Dr 60431. I-80 exit 127, just n. Int corridors. **Pets:** Large, other species. $50 one-time fee/room. Service with restrictions, supervision.
SAVE 📶 ⊗ 🕭 🛢 💻 🏊 ⊗

LAKE ZURICH

▼▼▼▼ Holiday Inn Express & Suites Lake Zurich-Barrington 🏨
(847) 726-7500. **$89-$129.** 197 S Rand Rd 60047. On US 12, 0.3 mi nw of SR 22. Int corridors. **Pets:** Medium, other species. $30 one-time fee/pet. Designated rooms, service with restrictions, supervision.
📶 ⊗ 🕭 🛢 💻 🏊 ⊗

LANSING

▼▼ ▼▼ Extended StayAmerica-Chicago-Lansing 🏨 🐾
(708) 895-6402. **$55-$110.** 2520 173rd St 60438. I-80/94 exit 161 (Torrence Ave), just n to 173rd St, then just e. Int corridors. **Pets:** Other species. $25 daily fee/pet. Service with restrictions. 📶 🕭 🛢 💻

LIBERTYVILLE

▼▼ ▼▼ Candlewood Suites Chicago-Libertyville 🏨
(847) 247-9900. **$109-$139.** 1100 N US 45 60048. I-94 exit SR 137 (Buckley Rd), 5.6 mi w to US 45, then 1.4 mi s. Int corridors. **Pets:** Accepted. 📶 🕭 🛢 💻

▼▼ ▼▼ Holiday Inn Express Hotel & Suites 🏨
(847) 549-7878. **$79-$139.** 77 Buckley Rd 60048. I-94 exit SR 137 (Buckley Rd), 2.3 mi w. Int corridors. **Pets:** $50 one-time fee/pet. Service with restrictions, supervision. 📶 🛢 💻 🏊

LINCOLNSHIRE

▼▼▼▼▼ Homewood Suites by Hilton Chicago-Lincolnshire 🏨
(847) 945-9300. **$99-$179.** 10 Westminster Way 60069. I-94 exit Half Day Rd, just w. Int corridors. **Pets:** Accepted. 📶 🛢 💻 🏊

▼▼▼ **Staybridge Suites Lincolnshire** H
(847) 821-0002. **Call for rates.** 100 Barclay Blvd 60069. I-94 exit Half Day Rd, 2.2 mi w to Barclay Blvd, then just s; just w of jct US 45 and SR 21; in Lincolnshire Corporate Center. Int corridors. **Pets:** Medium, other species. $150 one-time fee/room, $10 daily fee/room. Designated rooms, service with restrictions, supervision.

LISLE

▼▼ **Extended StayAmerica-Chicago-Lisle** H ✿
(630) 434-7710. **$45-$95.** 445 Warrenville Rd 60532. I-355 exit Ogden Ave, just nw. Int corridors. **Pets:** Other species. $25 daily fee/pet. Service with restrictions.

ΔΔΔ ▼▼▼ **Hyatt Lisle** H
(630) 852-1234. **$49-$239.** 1400 Corporetum Dr 60532. I-88 exit SR 53 westbound, 0.3 mi s; exit Naperville Rd eastbound to Warrenville Rd, 2 mi e to jct SR 53. Int corridors. **Pets:** Accepted.

▼▼▼▼ **Marriott Hickory Ridge Conference Hotel** H
(630) 971-5000. **$129-$144.** 1195 Summerhill Dr 60532. I-88 exit SR 53, 2.5 mi s, then just w. Int corridors. **Pets:** Accepted.

LOMBARD

ΔΔ ▼▼▼▼ **Embassy Suites Hotel Chicago-Lombard/Oak Brook** H
(630) 969-7500. **$109-$199.** 707 E Butterfield Rd 60148. I-88 exit Highland Ave, just n to Butterfield Rd (SR 56), then 0.5 mi e. Int corridors. **Pets:** Medium, other species. $50 one-time fee/pet. Service with restrictions, crate.

▼▼ **Extended Stay Deluxe-Chicago-Lombard-Oak Brook** H ✿
(630) 424-1000. **$65-$105.** 260 E 22nd St 60148. I-88 exit Highland Ave, 0.8 mi n to 22nd St, then just e. Int corridors. **Pets:** Other species. $25 daily fee/pet. Service with restrictions.

▼▼ **Homestead Studio Suites Hotel-Chicago/Lombard-Oak Brook** H ✿
(630) 928-0202. **$45-$100.** 2701 Technology Dr 60148. I-88 exit Highland Ave, just n, 0.6 mi e on Butterfield Rd (SR 56), then just s. Int corridors. **Pets:** Other species. $25 daily fee/pet. Service with restrictions.

ΔΔΔ ▼▼▼ **Residence Inn by Marriott Chicago-Lombard** H ✿
(630) 629-7800. **$99-$199.** 2001 S Highland Ave 60148. I-88 exit Highland Ave, 0.8 mi n. Ext corridors. **Pets:** Large, other species. $75 one-time fee/room. Service with restrictions.

ΔΔΔ ▼▼◆ **TownePlace Suites by Marriott Chicago Lombard** H
(630) 932-4400. **$89-$189.** 455 E 22nd St 60148. I-88 exit Highland Ave, 0.8 mi n, then 0.3 mi e. Int corridors. **Pets:** Accepted.

ΔΔΔ ▼▼▼▼ **The Westin Lombard Yorktown Center** H ✿
(630) 719-8000. **$199-$309.** 70 Yorktown Center 60148. I-88 exit Highland Ave, just n to Butterfield Rd (SR 56), then just e; in The Shops on Butterfield. Int corridors. **Pets:** Small, dogs only. Service with restrictions, supervision.

MATTESON

▼▼ **La Quinta Inn Chicago Matteson** H
(708) 503-0999. **$67-$165.** 5210 Southwick Dr 60443. I-57 exit 340A, 0.3 mi e on US 30, then 0.3 mi s on Cicero Ave (SR 50). Int corridors. **Pets:** Medium, other species. Service with restrictions, supervision.

METTAWA

▼▼▼ **Residence Inn by Marriott Chicago Lake Forest-Mettawa** H
(847) 615-2701. **$79-$209.** 26325 N Riverwoods Blvd 60045. I-94 exit SR 60 (Townline Rd), just nw. Int corridors. **Pets:** Accepted.

MORTON GROVE

ΔΔΔ ▼▼▼ **Best Western Morton Grove Inn** M
(847) 965-6400. **$69-$159.** 9424 Waukegan Rd 60053. SR 43, just s of Golf Rd (SR 58). Ext corridors. **Pets:** Accepted.

MUNDELEIN

▼▼▼ **DoubleTree by Hilton Hotel Libertyville - Mundelein** H
(847) 949-5100. **$89-$199.** 510 E Illinois (Rt 83) 60060. Jct US 45. Int corridors. **Pets:** Accepted.

NAPERVILLE

▼ **Baymont Inn & Suites Naperville** H
(630) 357-0022. **$53-$62.** 1585 Naperville/Wheaton Rd 60563. I-88 exit Naperville Rd, 0.5 mi s. Int corridors. **Pets:** Accepted.

ΔΔΔ ▼▼▼ **Best Western Naperville Inn** H ✿
(630) 505-0200. **$73-$110.** 1617 N Naperville Wheaton Rd 60563. I-88 exit Naperville Rd, just e on Diehl Rd to Naperville Rd, then just s. Ext/int corridors. **Pets:** Medium, dogs only. $10 daily fee/pet. Designated rooms, service with restrictions, supervision.

ΔΔΔ ▼▼◆ **Country Inn & Suites By Carlson** H ✿
(630) 505-3353. **$79-$179.** 1837 Centre Point Cir 60563. I-88 exit Naperville Rd, 0.3 mi s to Diehl Rd, 0.7 mi w, then just n. Int corridors. **Pets:** Other species. $100 one-time fee/room. Designated rooms, service with restrictions, crate.

▼▼ **Homestead Studio Suites Hotel-Chicago-Naperville** H ✿
(630) 577-0200. **$50-$100.** 1827 Centre Point Cir 60563. I-88 exit Naperville Rd, just s to Diehl Rd, 0.8 mi w, then just n. Int corridors. **Pets:** Other species. $25 daily fee/pet. Service with restrictions.

ΔΔΔ ▼▼◆◆ **Hotel Arista at CityGate Centre** H ✿
(630) 579-4100. **Call for rates.** 2139 CityGate Ln 60563. I-88 exit SR 59, just n. Int corridors. **Pets:** Small. $250 one-time fee/room. Designated rooms, service with restrictions, supervision.

ΔΔΔ ▼ **Red Roof Inn #195** M
(630) 369-2500. **$55-$90.** 1698 W Diehl Rd 60563. I-88 exit SR 59, just s. Ext corridors. **Pets:** Large, other species. No service, supervision.

ΔΔΔ ▼▼ **Sleep Inn by Choice Hotels** H
(630) 778-5900. **$75-$85.** 1831 W Diehl Rd 60563. I-88 exit SR 59, just sw. Int corridors. **Pets:** Small, other species. $30 one-time fee/room. Designated rooms, service with restrictions, supervision.

▼▼▼ **TownePlace Suites by Marriott Naperville** H
(630) 548-0881. **$110-$190.** 1843 W Diehl Rd 60563. I-88 exit SR 59, just s to Diehl Rd, then just w. Int corridors. **Pets:** Accepted.

NORTHBROOK

ΔΔΔ ▼▼▼ **Hilton Chicago/Northbrook** H ✿
(847) 480-7500. **$99-$209.** 2855 N Milwaukee Ave 60062. On SR 21, s of jct US 45 and Willow Rd. Int corridors. **Pets:** Medium. $50 one-time fee/room. Service with restrictions.

△△△ ▼▼▼ ▼▼▼ **Renaissance Chicago North Shore** H
(847) 498-6500. **$98-$349.** 933 Skokie Blvd 60062. I-94 exit Dundee Rd
W northbound; exit SR 43 (Waukegan Rd) southbound, 0.5 mi s to SR
68, then 1.5 mi e. Int corridors. **Pets:** Other species. $75 one-time fee/
room. Designated rooms. SAVE 🛜 ✕ 🗄 💷 ▮▮ ⊇ ⊠

△△△ ▼▼▼▼ **Sheraton Chicago Northbrook Hotel** H
(847) 480-1900. **$99-$339, 3 day notice.** 1110 Willow Rd 60062. 2 mi
w of jct I-94; 3.2 mi e of jct I-294. Int corridors. **Pets:** Accepted.
SAVE 🛜 ✕ 🗄ᴹ 🗄 💷 ▮▮ ⊇

OAK BROOK

▼▼▼▼ **Residence Inn by Marriott Chicago/Oak Brook** H
(630) 571-1200. **$162-$198.** 790 Jorie Blvd 60523. I-88 exit Midwest Rd
eastbound, just n to 22nd St (Cermak Rd), 1.7 mi e to Jorie Blvd, then
just sw; exit 22nd St (Cermak Rd) westbound, 0.4 mi e to Jorie Blvd. Int
corridors. **Pets:** Accepted. 🛜 ✕ 🗄ᴹ 🗄 💷 ⊇ ⊠

OAKBROOK TERRACE

△△△ ▼▼▼▼ **Holiday Inn Chicago-Oak Brook** H
(630) 833-3600. **$79-$209.** 17 W 350 22nd St 60181. I-88 exit Midwest
Rd eastbound, 0.4 mi n to 22nd St (Cermak Rd), then just e; exit 22nd
St (Cermak Rd) westbound, then 0.9 mi w. Int corridors. **Pets:** Accepted.
SAVE 🛜 🗄 💷 ▮▮ ⊇

△△△ ▼▼ ▼▼ **La Quinta Inn Chicago Oakbrook Terrace** H
(630) 495-4600. **$64-$152.** 1 S 666 Midwest Rd 60181. I-88 exit Midwest
Rd eastbound, 0.4 mi n, then just n of 22nd St (Cermak Rd); exit 22nd
St (Cermak Rd) westbound, 1.1 mi w to Midwest Rd, then just n. Int cor-
ridors. **Pets:** Medium, other species. Service with restrictions, supervision.
SAVE 🛜 🗄 💷

△△△ ▼▼▼▼ **Staybridge Suites Chicago-Oakbrook**
Terrace H
(630) 953-9393. **$70-$150.** 200 Royce Blvd 60181. I-88 exit Midwest Rd
eastbound to 22nd St (Cermak Rd), 0.4 mi w to Butterfield Rd (SR 56),
just n, then just n on Renaissance Blvd; exit 22nd St (Cermak Rd) westbound, 2.5 mi w on 22nd St to SR 56, just n, then just n on Renaissance
Blvd. Int corridors. **Pets:** Medium, other species. $15 daily fee/pet. Serv-
ice with restrictions. SAVE 🛜 🗄ᴹ 🗄 💷

PALATINE

▼▼▼▼ **Holiday Inn Express Palatine/Arlington Heights** H
(847) 934-4900. **$72-$108.** 1550 E Dundee Rd 60074. SR 53 exit
Dundee Rd (SR 68), just w. Int corridors. **Pets:** Dogs only. $50 one-time
fee/room. Designated rooms, service with restrictions.
🛜 🗄ᴹ 🗄 💷 ⊠

PROSPECT HEIGHTS

▼▼ **Super 8-Prospect Heights** H
(847) 459-0545. **$45-$99.** 540 N Milwaukee Ave 60070. Jct SR 21 and
US 45. Int corridors. **Pets:** Medium. $25 one-time fee/room. Service with
restrictions, crate. 🛜 🗄 💷

RICHMOND

▼▼ ▼▼ **Super 8 Richmond/Geneva Lakes** H
(815) 678-4711. **$58-$152.** 11200 N Rt 12 60071. 0.5 mi n of jct SR
173. Int corridors. **Pets:** Small, dogs only. $100 deposit/room, $20 daily
fee/pet. Designated rooms, service with restrictions, supervision.
🛜 🗄 💷

ROMEOVILLE

▼▼▼▼ **Country Inn & Suites By Carlson, Romeoville**
(Chicago) H
(630) 378-1052. **Call for rates.** 1265 Lakeview Dr 60446. I-55 exit 263,
just n. Int corridors. **Pets:** Accepted. 🛜 🗄 💷 ⊇

▼▼ ▼▼ **Extended StayAmerica Chicago-Romeoville** H 🐾
(630) 226-8966. **$60-$105.** 1225 Lakeview Dr 60446. I-55 exit 263, just
n. Int corridors. **Pets:** Other species. $25 daily fee/pet. Service with
restrictions. 🛜 🗄 💷

ROSEMONT

△△△ ▼▼▼▼ **Aloft Chicago O'Hare** H
(847) 671-4444. **$89-$309.** 9700 Balmoral Ave 60018. I-190 exit 1B, just
s. Int corridors. **Pets:** Accepted. SAVE 🛜 ✕ 🗄ᴹ 🗄 💷 ⊇

△△△ ▼▼▼▼ **Crowne Plaza Chicago O'Hare Hotel &**
Conference Center H
(847) 671-6350. **$69-$159.** 5440 N River Rd 60018. I-190 exit 1B (River
Rd), just s. Int corridors. **Pets:** Accepted.
SAVE 🛜 🗄ᴹ 🗄 💷 ▮▮ ⊇

△△△ ▼▼▼▼ **DoubleTree by Hilton Hotel Chicago**
O'Hare Airport - Rosemont H
(847) 292-9100. **$99-$299.** 5460 N River Rd 60018. I-190 exit 1B (River
Rd), just s. Int corridors. **Pets:** Medium. $25 one-time fee/room. Service
with restrictions, crate. SAVE 🛜 🗄ᴹ 🗄 💷 ▮▮ ⊠

△△△ ▼▼▼▼ **Embassy Suites Hotel O'Hare**
Rosemont H
(847) 678-4000. **$119-$309.** 5500 N River Rd 60018. I-190 exit 1B
(River Rd), just s. Int corridors. **Pets:** Medium. $25 one-time fee/room.
Service with restrictions, crate. SAVE 🛜 🗄 💷 ▮▮ ⊇

△△△ ▼▼▼▼ **Hilton Rosemont Chicago**
O'Hare H 🐾
(847) 678-4488. **$109-$359.** 5550 N River Rd 60018. I-190 exit 1B
(River Rd), just s. Int corridors. **Pets:** Medium, dogs only. $75 one-time
fee/room. Service with restrictions, supervision.
SAVE 🛜 🗄ᴹ 💷 ▮▮ ⊇

△△△ ▼▼▼▼ **InterContinental Chicago O'Hare** H
(847) 544-5300. **Call for rates.** 5300 N River Rd 60018. I-190 exit 1B
(River Rd), 0.4 mi s. Int corridors. **Pets:** Accepted.
SAVE 🛜 ✕ 🗄ᴹ 💷 ▮▮

▼▼▼▼ **Residence Inn by Marriott Chicago-O'Hare** H
(847) 375-9000. **$179-$219.** 7101 Chestnut St 60018. Jct US 12, 45 and
Touhy Ave. Int corridors. **Pets:** Accepted. 🛜 ✕ 🗄 💷 ⊇ ⊠

△△△ ▼▼▼▼ **Sheraton Chicago O'Hare** H 🐾
(847) 699-6300. **$99-$399, 3 day notice.** 6501 N Mannheim Rd 60018.
On US 12 and 45, at SR 72 (Higgins Rd). Int corridors. **Pets:** Medium,
dogs only. $50 deposit/room. Service with restrictions, supervision.
SAVE 🛜 ✕ 🗄 💷 ▮▮ ⊇

△△△ ▼▼▼▼ **The Westin O'Hare** H
(847) 698-6000. **$99-$259.** 6100 N River Rd 60018. I-190 exit 1B (River
Rd), just n. Int corridors. **Pets:** Accepted.
SAVE 🛜 ✕ 🗄ᴹ 🗄 💷 ▮▮ ⊇ ⊠

ST. CHARLES

△△△ ▼▼▼▼ **Best Western Inn of St. Charles** H 🐾
(630) 584-4550. **$80-$140.** 1635 E Main St 60174. On SR 64, 0.5 mi e
of SR 25. Ext/int corridors. **Pets:** Dogs only. $10 daily fee/pet. Designated
rooms, service with restrictions, supervision. SAVE 🛜 🗄 💷 ⊇

▼▼▼▼ **Country Inn & Suites By Carlson** H
(630) 587-6564. **Call for rates.** 155 38th Ave 60174. On SR 64, 3.1 mi
w of SR 59. Int corridors. **Pets:** Accepted.
🛜 🗄ᴹ 🗄 💷 ⊇ ⊠

▼▼▼▼ **Courtyard by Marriott Chicago-St Charles** H
(630) 377-6370. **$79-$169.** 700 Courtyard Dr 60174. Jct SR 59 and 64,
3.4 mi w on SR 64, just n on Kirk Rd, then just w on Foxfield. Int corridors. **Pets:** Medium. $75 one-time fee/room. Service with restrictions,
crate. ECO 🛜 ✕ 🗄ᴹ 🗄 💷 ▮▮ ⊇ ⊠

△△△ ▼▼▼▼ **Holiday Inn Express** H
(630) 584-5300. **Call for rates.** 1600 E Main St 60174. On SR 64, 0.5
mi e of SR 25. Int corridors. **Pets:** Accepted. SAVE 🛜 🗄 💷 ⊇

SCHAUMBURG

▼▼/▼▼ Candlewood Suites Schaumburg 🅗
(847) 517-7644. **$80-$119.** 1200 E Bank Dr 60173. I-290 exit SR 72 (Higgins Rd), 0.8 mi w to National Pkwy, then just n. Int corridors. **Pets:** Accepted. 🛜 🔒 💻

▼▼ Extended StayAmerica Chicago-Schaumburg Convention Center 🅗 🐾
(847) 882-7011. **$48-$95.** 2000 N Roselle Rd 60195. I-90 exit Roselle Rd, just sw. Int corridors. **Pets:** Other species. $25 daily fee/pet. Service with restrictions. 🛜 🔒 💻

▼▼ Extended StayAmerica-Chicago-Woodfield 🅗 🐾
(847) 517-7255. **$55-$105.** 1200 American Ln 60173. I-290 exit SR 72 (Higgins Rd), 0.5 mi w to Meacham Rd, 0.5 mi n to American Ln, then just w. Int corridors. **Pets:** Other species. $25 daily fee/pet. Service with restrictions. 🛜 🔒 💻

▼▼ Homestead Studio Suites Chicago-Schaumburg 🅗 🐾
(847) 882-6900. **$50-$100.** 51 E State Pkwy 60173. I-90 exit Roselle Rd, 0.8 mi s, then just e. Int corridors. **Pets:** Other species. $25 daily fee/pet. Service with restrictions. 🛜 🔒 💻

▼▼/▼▼ Homewood Suites by Hilton-Schaumburg 🅗
(847) 605-0400. **$89-$159.** 815 E American Ln 60173. I-290 exit SR 72 (Higgins Rd), 1.5 mi w, then 0.4 mi n on Plum Grove Rd. Ext/int corridors. **Pets:** Accepted. 🛜 🔒 💻 ⤳ ✕

Ⓐ ▼▼/▼▼ Hyatt Summerfield Suites Chicago/Schaumburg 🅗
(847) 706-9007. **$79-$139.** 1251 E American Ln 60173. I-290 exit SR 72 (Higgins Rd), 0.5 mi w to Meacham Rd, 0.5 mi n to American Ln, then just w. Int corridors. **Pets:** Accepted.
SAVE 🛜 ✕ 🔒 💻 ⤳ ✕

▼▼ La Quinta Inn (Schaumburg) 🅗
(847) 517-8484. **$54-$155.** 1730 E Higgins Rd 60173. I-290 exit SR 72 (Higgins Rd), just w. Int corridors. **Pets:** Medium, other species. Service with restrictions, supervision. 🛜 🔒 💻 ⤳

▼▼/▼▼ Residence Inn by Marriott-Chicago/Schaumburg 🅗
(847) 517-9200. **$170-$190.** 1610 McConnor Pkwy 60173. I-290 exit 1A (Woodfield Rd/Golf Rd) northbound, follow signs just n to Golf Rd, just w to McConnor Pkwy, then 0.8 mi n; exit 1B (Woodfield Rd/Golf Rd) southbound. Int corridors. **Pets:** Accepted.
🛜 ✕ 🔒 💻 ⤳ ✕

▼▼ Staybridge Suites Chicago/Schaumburg 🅗
(847) 619-6677. **$99-$189.** 901 E Woodfield Office Ct 60173. I-290 exit SR 72 (Higgins Rd), 1.5 mi w, then 0.3 mi n on Plum Grove Rd. Ext/int corridors. **Pets:** Accepted. 🛜 🔒 💻 ⤳ ✕

SCHILLER PARK

▼▼/▼▼ Comfort Suites O'Hare Airport 🅗
(847) 233-9000. **$69-$159.** 4200 N River Rd 60176. Jct SR 19 (Irving Park Rd) and Des Plaines St/River Rd, just n. Int corridors. **Pets:** Other species. $50 one-time fee/pet. Service with restrictions, crate.
🛜 ✕ 🔒 💻 🍽

Ⓐ ▼▼/▼▼ Four Points by Sheraton Chicago O'Hare Airport 🅗
(847) 671-6000. **$79-$250.** 10249 W Irving Park Rd 60176. Jct US 12, 45 and SR 19 (Irving Park Rd). Int corridors. **Pets:** Accepted.
SAVE 🛜 ✕ 🔒 🔒 💻 🍽 ⤳ ✕

▼▼/▼▼ Hampton Inn Chicago O'Hare Airport 🅗 🐾
(847) 671-1700. **$89-$139.** 3939 N Mannheim Rd 60176. Jct US 12 and 45, 0.5 mi s of SR 19 (Irving Park Rd). Int corridors. **Pets:** Small. $50 one-time fee/pet. Designated rooms, service with restrictions, supervision.
🛜 🔒 💻 ⤳ ✕

SKOKIE

Ⓐ ▼▼/▼▼ Comfort Inn Northshore-Skokie 🅗 🐾
(847) 679-4200. **$90-$209.** 9333 Skokie Blvd 60077. I-94 exit 35 (Old Orchard Rd), 0.4 mi e to Skokie Blvd (US 41), then 0.3 mi s. Int corridors. **Pets:** Other species. $15 daily fee/room. Designated rooms, service with restrictions, crate. SAVE 🛜 🔒 💻 ⤳

▼▼/▼▼ Extended StayAmerica-Chicago-Skokie 🅗 🐾
(847) 663-9031. **$60-$115.** 5211 Old Orchard Rd 60077. I-94 exit 35 (Old Orchard Rd). Int corridors. **Pets:** Other species. $25 daily fee/pet. Service with restrictions. 🛜 🔒 💻

Ⓐ ▼▼/▼▼ Holiday Inn Chicago North Shore 🅗
(847) 679-8900. **Call for rates.** 5300 W Touhy Ave 60077. I-94 exit 39A, 0.5 mi w. Int corridors. **Pets:** Accepted. SAVE 🛜 🔒 💻 🍽 ⤳

TINLEY PARK

▼▼/▼▼ La Quinta Inn & Suites Chicago-Tinley Park 🅗
(708) 633-1200. **$80-$175.** 7255 W 183rd St 60477. I-80 exit 148B, 0.5 mi n to 183rd St, then just w to North Creek Business Center. Int corridors. **Pets:** Medium, other species. Service with restrictions, supervision.
🛜 ⓜ 🔒 💻 ⤳

VERNON HILLS

▼▼/▼▼ Extended StayAmerica-Chicago-Vernon Hills-Lake Forest 🅗 🐾
(847) 821-7101. **$55-$105.** 215 N Milwaukee Ave 60061. I-94 exit SR 60 (Townline Rd), 2.1 mi w to SR 21 (Milwaukee Ave), then 0.3 mi s; in The Marketplace At Vernon Hills. Int corridors. **Pets:** Other species. $25 daily fee/pet. Service with restrictions. 🛜 ⓜ 🔒 💻

▼▼/▼▼ Holiday Inn Express/Vernon Hills 🅗
(847) 367-8031. **Call for rates.** 975 Lakeview Pkwy 60061. Jct SR 21 (Milwaukee Ave), 0.7 mi w on SR 60 (Townline Rd) to Lakeview Pkwy, then just n. Int corridors. **Pets:** Accepted. 🛜 ✕ ⓜ 🔒 💻 ⤳

▼▼/▼▼ Homestead Studio Suites Hotel-Chicago/Vernon Hills-Lincolnshire 🅗 🐾
(847) 955-1111. **$55-$110.** 675 Woodlands Pkwy 60061. I-94 exit SR 60 (Townline Rd), 2.1 mi w to SR 21 (Milwaukee Ave), 1.9 mi s to Woodlands Pkwy, then just w. Int corridors. **Pets:** Other species. $25 daily fee/pet. Service with restrictions. 🛜 🔒 💻

▼▼/▼▼ Hotel Indigo Chicago/Vernon Hills 🅗
(847) 918-1400. **$89-$189.** 450 N Milwaukee Ave 60061. I-94 exit SR 60 (Townline Rd), 2.1 mi w to SR 21 (Milwaukee Ave), then 0.3 mi s. Int corridors. **Pets:** Accepted. 🛜 ✕ 🔒 💻 🍽 ⤳

WARRENVILLE

Ⓐ ▼▼/▼▼ Hyatt Summerfield Suites Chicago/Naperville/Warrenville 🅗
(630) 836-2960. **$79-$259.** 27554 Maecliff Dr 60555. I-88 exit Winfield Rd, just n to Ferry Rd, then just e. Int corridors. **Pets:** Large. $200 one-time fee/room. Service with restrictions.
SAVE 🛜 ✕ ⓜ 🔒 💻 ⤳

▼▼/▼▼ Residence Inn by Marriott Chicago Naperville/Warrenville 🅗
(630) 393-3444. **$79-$169.** 28500 Bella Vista Pkwy 60555. I-88 exit Winfield Rd, just n to Ferry Rd, then just e. Int corridors. **Pets:** Accepted.
🛜 ✕ ⓜ 🔒 💻 ⤳ ✕

WAUKEGAN

▼▼/▼▼ Candlewood Suites Chicago/Waukegan 🅗
(847) 578-5250. **$119-$149.** 1151 S Waukegan Rd 60085. I-94 exit SR 137 (Buckley Rd), 0.5 mi e to SR 43 (Waukegan Rd), then 1.9 mi n. Int corridors. **Pets:** Large. $15 one-time fee/room, $10 daily fee/room. Service with restrictions, crate. 🛜 🔒 💻

▼▼ Crossland Studios-Chicago-Waukegan 🅜 🐾
(847) 688-0402. **$45-$85.** 1177 S Northpoint Blvd 60085. Between US 41 and SR 43. Ext corridors. **Pets:** Other species. $25 daily fee/pet. Service with restrictions. 🛜 🔒 💻

 **Residence Inn by Marriott
Chicago-Waukegan/Gurnee** H

(847) 689-9240. **$114-$194.** 1440 S White Oak Dr 60085. I-94 exit SR 137 (Buckley Rd), 0.5 mi e to SR 43 (Waukegan Rd), 1.5 mi n to Lakeside Dr, then just e. Int corridors. **Pets:** Accepted.

[ECO] 📶 ✕ 👤 🖥 🏊 ✕

WEST DUNDEE

 **TownePlace Suites by Marriott Chicago West
Dundee/Elgin** H

(847) 608-6320. **$89-$149.** 2185 Marriott Dr 60118. I-90 exit SR 31, 0.4 mi n to Marriott Dr, then just e. Int corridors. **Pets:** Accepted.

[ECO] 📶 ✕ 👤 🖥 🏊

WESTMONT

ClubHouse Inn & Suites H

(630) 920-2200. **$79-$139.** 630 Pasquinelli Dr 60559. Just off US 34 (Ogden Ave), 0.3 mi nw of jct SR 83. Int corridors. **Pets:** Small. $10 daily fee/pet. Designated rooms, service with restrictions, supervision.

[SAVE] 📶 ✕ 👤 🖥 🏊

Homestead Studio Suites - Chicago - Westmont - Oak Brook H 🐾

(630) 323-9292. **$50-$100.** 855 Pasquinelli Dr 60559. SR 83 exit US 34 (Ogden Ave), just w to Pasquinelli Dr, then 0.5 mi n. Int corridors. **Pets:** Other species. $25 daily fee/pet. Service with restrictions.

📶 🖥 👤 🖥

WHEELING

The Westin Chicago North Shore H

(847) 777-6500. **$99-$349.** 601 N Milwaukee Ave 60090. Jct Lake Cook Rd, just s. Int corridors. **Pets:** Accepted.

[SAVE] 📶 ✕ 🖥 👤 🖥 🍴 🏊 ✕

WILLOWBROOK

La Quinta Inn Chicago-Willowbrook H

(630) 654-0077. **$68-$137.** 855 79th St 60527. I-55 exit 274, just n. Int corridors. **Pets:** Medium, other species. Service with restrictions, supervision. 📶 👤 🖥

Red Roof Inn #0167 M

(630) 323-8811. **$54-$77.** 7535 Kingery Hwy Route 83 60527. I-55 exit 274, 0.5 mi n on SR 83. Ext corridors. **Pets:** Large, other species. No service, supervision. [SAVE] 📶 👤

WOODSTOCK

Super 8 H

(815) 337-8808. **$46-$75.** 1220 Davis Rd 60098. On SR 47, s of jct US 14. Int corridors. **Pets:** Accepted. 📶 👤 🖥

END METROPOLITAN AREA

COLLINSVILLE

DoubleTree by Hilton Hotel Collinsville - St. Louis H

(618) 345-2800. **$99-$139.** 1000 Eastport Plaza Dr 62234. I-55/70 exit 11 (SR 157), just nw. Int corridors. **Pets:** Medium. $50 one-time fee/room. Service with restrictions, crate. [SAVE] 📶 ✕ 🖥 🍴 🏊

Drury Inn-St. Louis/Collinsville H

(618) 345-7700. **$90-$164.** 602 N Bluff Rd 62234. I-55/70 exit 11 (SR 157), just n. Int corridors. **Pets:** Accepted. 📶 🖥 👤 🖥 🏊

Super 8-Collinsville H

(618) 345-8008. **$47-$75.** 2 Gateway Dr 62234. I-55/70 exit 11 (SR 157), just n. Int corridors. **Pets:** Other species. $35 deposit/room, $15 one-time fee/room. Service with restrictions, supervision. 📶 👤 🖥

COLUMBIA

Hampton Inn H

(618) 281-9000. **$85-$104.** 165 Admiral Trost Dr 62236. I-255 exit 6 (SR 3), 2 mi s, then just e. Int corridors. **Pets:** Accepted.

📶 ✕ 🖥 👤 🖥 🏊

DANVILLE

Best Western Regency Inn H

(217) 446-2111. **$65-$199.** 360 Eastgate Dr 61834. I-74 exit 220 (Lynch Dr), just n. Ext/int corridors. **Pets:** Accepted. [SAVE] 📶 👤 🖥 🏊

Sleep Inn & Suites H 🐾

(217) 442-6600. **$74-$99.** 361 Lynch Dr 61834. I-74 exit 220 (Lynch Dr), just n. Int corridors. **Pets:** Medium. $15 daily fee/pet. Service with restrictions, crate. 📶 👤 🖥 🏊

Super 8 H

(217) 443-4499. **$54-$82.** 377 Lynch Dr 61834. I-74 exit 220 (Lynch Dr), just n. Int corridors. **Pets:** Accepted. 📶 👤 🖥

DECATUR

Decatur Conference Center & Hotel H

(217) 422-8800. **$99, 3 day notice.** 4191 W Hwy 36 62522. I-72 exit 133A (US 36), 1 mi e. Int corridors. **Pets:** Other species. $35 one-time fee/room. Designated rooms, service with restrictions, crate.

📶 🖥 👤 🖥 🍴 🏊 ✕

Sleep Inn H

(217) 872-7700. **$65-$100.** 3920 E Hospitality Ln 62521. I-72 exit 144 (SR 48), just s to Brush College Rd, then just e. Int corridors. **Pets:** Accepted. 📶 👤 🖥 🏊

DEKALB

Best Western DeKalb Inn & Suites H

(815) 758-8661. **$79-$139.** 1212 W Lincoln Hwy 60115. I-88 exit Annie Glidden Rd, 2 mi n to W Lincoln Hwy (SR 38), then just w. Ext/int corridors. **Pets:** Accepted. [SAVE] 📶 👤 🖥 🏊

DIXON

Comfort Inn by Choice Hotels H

(815) 284-0500. **$80-$105.** 136 Plaza Dr 61021. I-88 exit SR 26, just n, then just e. Int corridors. **Pets:** Medium. $15 daily fee/pet. Service with restrictions, crate. [SAVE] 📶 👤 🖥 🏊 ✕

EAST MOLINE

Comfort Inn & Suites H

(309) 792-4660. **$80-$150.** 2209 John Deere Expwy 61244. I-74 exit 4B (John Deere Rd), 5 mi e; I-80 exit 4A, 6 mi w on SR 5. Int corridors. **Pets:** Accepted. 📶 ✕ 🖥 👤 🖥 🏊

Super 8-East Moline H

(309) 796-1999. **$40-$86.** 2201 John Deere Rd 61244. I-74 exit 4B (John Deere Rd), 5.5 mi e on SR 5. Int corridors. **Pets:** Accepted.

📶 👤 🖥

EAST PEORIA

Stoney Creek Inn & Conference Center H

(309) 694-1300. **Call for rates.** 101 Mariners Way 61611. I-74 exit 95 (Main St) westbound; exit 95A eastbound, just n. Int corridors. **Pets:** Accepted. 📶 ✕ 🖥 👤 🖥 🏊 ✕

▼▼ Super 8 H
(309) 698-8889. **$44-$75.** 725 Taylor St 61611. I-74 exit 96, just e. Int corridors. **Pets:** Accepted. 📶 🛄 💻

EFFINGHAM

🔺 ▼▼ Best Western Raintree Inn H
(217) 342-4121. **$62-$72.** 1811 W Fayette Ave 62401. I-57/70 exit 159, just n. Ext/int corridors. **Pets:** Other species. Crate.
SAVE 📶 💻 🍴 🛄

▼▼▼ Comfort Suites H
(217) 342-3151. **$90-$135.** 1310 W Fayette Ave 62401. I-57/70 exit 159, 0.4 mi e. Int corridors. **Pets:** Other species. $10 one-time fee/room. Service with restrictions, supervision. 📶 ✖ ♿ 🛄 💻 🛄

🔺 ▼▼ Days Inn H
(217) 347-7131. **$45-$79.** 1205 N Keller Dr 62401. I-57/70 exit 160 (SR 32/33), just n. Int corridors. **Pets:** Other species. $10 daily fee/pet. Service with restrictions, supervision. SAVE 📶 🛄 💻

▼▼▼ Fairfield Inn & Suites H
(217) 540-5454. **$84-$129.** 1111 N Henrietta St 62401. I-57/70 exit 160 (SR 32/33), just se. Int corridors. **Pets:** Accepted.
📶 ✖ ♿ 🛄 💻 🛄

▼▼ Holiday Inn Express H
(217) 540-1111. **Call for rates.** 1103 Ave of Mid-America 62401. I-57/70 exit 160 (SR 32/33), just n. Int corridors. **Pets:** Accepted.
📶 ♿ 🛄 💻 🛄

▼▼ Quality Inn H 🐾
(217) 347-5050. **$69-$78.** 1304 W Evergreen Dr 62401. I-57/70 exit 160 (SR 32/33), just e, then just n. Int corridors. **Pets:** Large, other species. $10 daily fee/pet. Service with restrictions, supervision.
📶 🛄 💻 🛄

▼ Super 8-Effingham M
(217) 342-6888. **$48-$100.** 1400 Thelma Keller Ave 62401. I-57/70 exit 160 (SR 32/33), 0.5 mi n. Int corridors. **Pets:** Other species. Service with restrictions, supervision. 📶 🛄 💻

FAIRFIELD

▼▼▼ Briarwood Inn Fairfield H 🐾
(618) 842-3667. **$79-$104.** 116 N Market Ave 62837. West end of town. Int corridors. **Pets:** Small. $10 daily fee/pet. Designated rooms, service with restrictions, supervision. 📶 ♿ 🛄 💻 🛄

FAIRVIEW HEIGHTS

🔺 ▼▼ Best Western Camelot Inn of Fairview Heights H 🐾
(618) 624-3636. **$60-$90.** 305 Salem Pl 62208. I-64 exit 12 (SR 159), just n. Int corridors. **Pets:** Large. $20 daily fee/pet. Designated rooms, service with restrictions, supervision. SAVE 📶 🛄 💻 🛄

▼▼▼ Comfort Suites H
(618) 394-0202. **Call for rates.** 137 Ludwig Dr 62208. I-64 exit 12 (SR 159), just n to Ludwig Dr, then 0.4 mi w. Int corridors. **Pets:** Medium. $50 deposit/room, $10 daily fee/pet. Service with restrictions, supervision.
📶 ✖ ♿ 🛄 💻 🛄

▼▼▼ Drury Inn & Suites-Fairview Heights H
(618) 398-8530. **$90-$169.** 12 Ludwig Dr 62208. I-64 exit 12 (SR 159), just n. Int corridors. **Pets:** Accepted. 📶 🛄 💻 🛄 ✖

▼▼ Fairfield Inn by Marriott H 🐾
(618) 398-7124. **$90-$108.** 140 Ludwig Dr 62208. I-64 exit 12 (SR 159), 1 mi nw. Int corridors. **Pets:** Other species. $25 daily fee/room. Designated rooms, service with restrictions, crate.
📶 ✖ ♿ 🛄 💻 🛄

▼▼▼ Hampton Inn by Hilton H
(618) 397-9705. **$89-$119.** 150 Ludwig Dr 62208. I-64 exit 12 (SR 159), 1 mi nw. Int corridors. **Pets:** Accepted. 📶 ♿ 🛄 💻 🛄

▼▼ Ramada Fairview Heights H
(618) 632-4747. **$59-$99.** 6900 N Illinois St 62208. I-64 exit 12 (SR 159), just n. Int corridors. **Pets:** Accepted. 📶 🛄 💻 🍴 🛄 ✖

FLORA

🔺 ▼▼ Best Western Lorson Inn H
(618) 662-3054. **$75-$95.** 201 Hagen Dr 62839. Jct US 45 and 50. Int corridors. **Pets:** Accepted. SAVE 📶 ♿ 🛄 💻

FORSYTH

▼▼▼ Hampton Inn Decatur-Forsyth H
(217) 877-5577. **$89-$109.** 1429 Hickory Point Dr 62535. I-72 exit 141B (US 51), 0.5 mi n. Int corridors. **Pets:** Accepted.
📶 ♿ 🛄 💻 🛄 ✖

FREEPORT

▼▼ Baymont Inn & Suites-Freeport H 🐾
(815) 599-8510. **$71-$89.** 1060 Rt 26 61032. Jct US 20 Bypass and SR 26, just s. Int corridors. **Pets:** Large, other species. $35 one-time fee/room. Service with restrictions, crate. 📶 🛄 💻 🛄

🔺 ▼▼ Hampton Inn H
(815) 232-7100. **$89-$134.** 109 S Galena Ave 61032. Jct Main St; downtown. Int corridors. **Pets:** Other species. Service with restrictions, supervision. SAVE 📶 ♿ 🛄 💻 🍴 🛄

▼▼ Super 8 H
(815) 232-4455. **$54-$86.** 1551 S Sleezer Home Rd 61032. Jct SR 26 and South St, 1.1 mi e on South St. Int corridors. **Pets:** Small. $50 deposit/pet, $15 one-time fee/pet, $15 daily fee/pet. Designated rooms, no service, supervision. 📶 ♿ 🛄 💻 🛄

GALENA

🔺 ▼▼ Best Western Designer Inn & Suites H 🐾
(815) 777-2577. **$90-$170.** 9923 US Rt 20 W 61036. On US 20, 1 mi e. Ext/int corridors. **Pets:** Small, dogs only. $15 one-time fee/pet. Designated rooms, service with restrictions. SAVE 📶 🛄 💻 🛄

🔺 ▼▼ Eagle Ridge Resort & Spa H
(815) 777-5000. **$139-$319, 7 day notice.** 444 Eagle Ridge Dr 61036. US 20, 6 mi e to E Glen Hollow Rd, 4.5 mi n. Ext/int corridors. **Pets:** Medium, dogs only. $75 one-time fee/pet. Designated rooms, service with restrictions, crate. SAVE 📶 🛄 💻 🍴 🛄 ✖

▼▼ Stoney Creek Inn H 🐾
(815) 777-2223. **Call for rates.** 940 Galena Square Dr 61036. On US 20, 1.8 mi w. Int corridors. **Pets:** Medium, other species. $25 daily fee/pet. Designated rooms, supervision. 📶 ✖ 🛄 💻 🛄 ✖

GALESBURG

🔺 ▼▼▼ Best Western Plus Prairie Inn H
(309) 343-7151. **$69-$125.** 300 S Soangetaha Rd 61401. I-74 exit 48 (Main St), just e, then just s. Int corridors. **Pets:** Large, other species. $20 daily fee/room. Service with restrictions, supervision.
SAVE 📶 🛄 💻 🍴 🛄

▼▼ Comfort Inn by Choice Hotels H
(309) 344-5445. **$69-$140.** 907 W Carl Sandburg Dr 61401. US 34 exit US 150 E. Int corridors. **Pets:** Accepted. 📶 ♿ 🛄 💻

▼▼▼ Holiday Inn Express H
(309) 343-7100. **$89-$159.** 2285 Washington St 61401. I-74 exit 48A (US 150), just w to Michigan Ave, just s to Washington St, then just e. Int corridors. **Pets:** Other species. $25 one-time fee/room. Service with restrictions, supervision. 📶 ♿ 🛄 💻 🛄 ✖

GILMAN

Super 8
(815) 265-7000. **$50-$65.** 1301 S Crescent St 60938. I-57 exit 283, 0.3 mi e. Int corridors. **Pets:** Small. $25 deposit/pet, $10 daily fee/pet. Service with restrictions, supervision.

GRAYVILLE

Super 8
(618) 375-7288. **$43-$90.** 2060 CR 2450 N 62844. I-64 exit 130 (SR 1), just n. Int corridors. **Pets:** Other species. $15 one-time fee/room. Service with restrictions, supervision.

GREENVILLE

Super 8-Greenville
(618) 664-0800. **$46-$80.** 1700 SR 127 S 62246. I-70 exit 45, just n. Int corridors. **Pets:** Accepted.

JACKSONVILLE

Starlite Motel
(217) 245-7184. **$40-$65.** 1910 W Morton Ave 62650. I-72 exit 64, 2.3 mi n on SR 267 (Main St) to SR 104 (Morton Ave), then 1.8 mi w. Ext corridors. **Pets:** Very small. $5 daily fee/pet. Service with restrictions.

Super 8
(217) 479-0303. **$50-$90.** 1003 W Morton Ave 62650. I-72 exit 64, 2.3 mi n on SR 267 (Main St) to SR 104 (Morton Ave), then 0.8 mi w. Int corridors. **Pets:** Small, other species. $10 daily fee/pet. Service with restrictions.

KEWANEE

AmericInn Lodge & Suites of Kewanee
(309) 856-7200. **$100-$160.** 925 S Tenney St 61443. On SR 78, 1.9 mi s of jct US 34. Int corridors. **Pets:** Accepted.

LEROY

Holiday Inn Express
(309) 962-4439. **$85-$109.** 705 S Persimmons Ct 61752. I-74 exit 149, just ne. Int corridors. **Pets:** Accepted.

Red Roof Inn Le Roy
(309) 962-4700. **$71-$111.** 1 Demma Dr 61752. I-74 exit 149, just sw. Ext/int corridors. **Pets:** Large, other species. No service, supervision.

LINCOLN

Best Western Plus Lincoln Inn
(217) 732-9641. **$80-$90.** 1750 5th St 62656. I-55 exit 126 (US 121), 1.6 mi e to Lincoln Pkwy, then 0.5 mi s. Int corridors. **Pets:** Medium. $15 daily fee/room. Service with restrictions, supervision.

Hampton Inn - Lincoln
(217) 732-6729. **$70-$95.** 1019 N Heitman Dr 62656. I-55 exit 126 (US 121), just e. Int corridors. **Pets:** Accepted.

Holiday Inn Express
(217) 735-5800. **$74-$89.** 130 Olson Dr 62656. I-55 exit 126 (US 121), just e. Int corridors. **Pets:** Medium, dogs only. Service with restrictions, supervision.

LITCHFIELD

Hampton Inn
(217) 324-4441. **$71-$139.** 11 Thunderbird Cir 62056. I-55 exit 52 (SR 16), on Corvette Dr, then just e. Int corridors. **Pets:** Large. $50 deposit/room. Service with restrictions, crate.

Holiday Inn Express
(217) 324-4556. **$99-$139.** 1405 W Hudson Dr 62056. I-55 exit 52 (SR 16), just e to Ohren Ln, just s to W Hudson Dr, then just w. Int corridors. **Pets:** Other species. Designated rooms, service with restrictions, supervision.

Quality Inn & Suites Litchfield
(217) 324-9260. **$70-$74.** 1010 E Columbian Blvd N 62056. I-55 exit 52 (SR 16), just e to Ohren Ln, just s to W Hudson Dr, then just w. Int corridors. **Pets:** Small. $10 daily fee/pet. Service with restrictions, crate.

LOVES PARK

Holiday Inn Express Hotel & Suites Rockford North
(815) 654-4100. **$100-$130.** 7552 Park Pl 61111. I-39/90 exit E Riverside Blvd, just nw. Int corridors. **Pets:** Accepted.

Quality Inn & Suites Rockford/Loves Park
(815) 282-9300. **Call for rates.** 4313 Bell School Rd 61111. I-39/90 exit E Riverside Blvd, just nw. Int corridors. **Pets:** Small. $10 daily fee/pet. No service, supervision.

MACOMB

Super 8
(309) 836-8888. **$49-$108.** 313 University Dr 61455. 1.1 mi n on US 67 to University Dr, 0.5 mi w. Int corridors. **Pets:** Accepted.

MANTENO

Country Inn & Suites By Carlson
(815) 468-2600. **$79-$199.** 380 S Cypress St 60950. I-57 exit 322, just se via frontage road. Int corridors. **Pets:** Accepted.

MARION

Drury Inn-Marion
(618) 997-9600. **$100-$169.** 2706 W DeYoung St 62959. I-57 exit 54B (SR 13), 0.5 mi w. Int corridors. **Pets:** Accepted.

Super 8
(618) 993-5577. **$53-$69.** 2601 W Vernell Rd 62959. I-57 exit 54B (SR 13), just w. Int corridors. **Pets:** Accepted.

MASCOUTAH

La Quinta Inn & Suites O'Fallon / Mascoutah
(618) 808-0280. **$80-$169.** 9730 Hayden Dr 62258. I-64 exit 23, just n. Int corridors. **Pets:** Medium, other species. Service with restrictions, supervision.

MATTOON

Baymont Inn & Suites
(217) 234-2420. **$62-$169.** 206 McFall Rd 61938. I-57 exit 190B, just w. Int corridors. **Pets:** Accepted.

Holiday Inn Express Hotel & Suites
(217) 235-2060. **$94-$159.** 121 Swords Dr 61938. I-57 exit 190B, just w. Int corridors. **Pets:** $10 daily fee/pet. Designated rooms, service with restrictions, supervision.

Super 8
(217) 235-8888. **$50-$72.** 205 McFall Rd 61938. I-57 exit 190B, just w. Int corridors. **Pets:** Medium, other species. $10 one-time fee/pet. Designated rooms, service with restrictions, supervision.

MONMOUTH

 **Americlnn Lodge & Suites of Monmouth** 🏨 ✿
(309) 734-9958. **$90-$170.** 1 Americlnn Way 61462. Jct US 34 and N
Main St, just s; 18 mi w of jct I-74 and US 34. Int corridors. **Pets:** Small,
dogs only. $75 one-time fee/room. Designated rooms, service with restric-
tions, supervision. 📶 ✕ ⓜ 🛏 💻 🏊

MONTICELLO

🔷 **Best Western Monticello Gateway Inn** 🏨
(217) 762-9436. **$75-$110, 3 day notice.** 805 Iron Horse Pl 61856. I-72
exit 166, just s. Ext/int corridors. **Pets:** Accepted.
⟨SAVE⟩ 📶 ✕ 🛏 💻 🏊

MORRIS

🔷 **Comfort Inn by Choice Hotels** 🏨
(815) 942-1433. **Call for rates.** 70 Gore Rd W 60450. I-80 exit 112 (SR
47), 0.3 mi nw. Int corridors. **Pets:** Accepted. 📶 🛏 💻 🏊

🔷 **Holiday Inn Express & Suites** 🏨
(815) 941-8700. **$114-$249.** 222 Gore Rd 60450. I-80 exit 112 (SR 47),
just nw. Int corridors. **Pets:** Accepted. 📶 ⓜ 🛏 💻 🏊

MORTON

🔷 **Baymont Inn & Suites** 🏨
(309) 266-8888. **$67-$103.** 210 E Ashland St 61550. I-74 exit 102, 0.4
mi ne. Int corridors. **Pets:** Accepted. ⟨SAVE⟩ 📶 🛏 💻 🏊

🔷 **Best Western Ashland House & Conference
Center** 🏨
(309) 263-5116. **$85-$100.** 201 E Ashland St 61550. I-74 exit 102, 0.3
mi ne. Int corridors. **Pets:** Medium, dogs only. $15 one-time fee/pet. Des-
ignated rooms, service with restrictions, supervision.
⟨SAVE⟩ 📶 🛏 💻 🍽 🏊

🔷 **Quality Inn by Choice Hotels** 🏨
(309) 266-8310. **$72-$85.** 115 E Ashland Ave 61550. I-74 exit 102B, just
w. Ext/int corridors. **Pets:** Accepted. 📶 🛏 💻

MOUNT VERNON

🔷 **Comfort Suites** 🏨
(618) 244-2700. **$80-$126.** 404 S 44th St 62864. I-57/64 exit 95 (SR 15),
just e. Int corridors. **Pets:** Accepted. 📶 ✕ ⓜ 🛏 💻 🏊

🔷 **Drury Inn-Mount Vernon** 🏨
(618) 244-4550. **$95-$134.** 145 N 44th St 62864. I-57/64 exit 95 (SR
15), just e, then just n; entry through restaurant parking lot. Int corridors.
Pets: Accepted. 📶 🛏 💻 🏊

🔷 **Holiday Inn** 🏨
(618) 244-7100. **$77-$110.** 222 Potomac Blvd 62864. I-57/64 exit 95 (SR
15), just w to Potomac Blvd, then just n. Int corridors. **Pets:** Medium,
other species. $20 one-time fee/pet. Designated rooms, service with
restrictions, crate. 📶 ⓜ 🛏 💻 🍽 🏊 ✕

🔷 **Thrifty Inn-Mt. Vernon** 🏨
(618) 244-7750. **$45-$94.** 100 N 44th St 62864. I-57/64 exit 95 (SR 15),
just e. Ext corridors. **Pets:** Accepted. 📶 🛏 💻

NASHVILLE

🔷 **Best Western U.S. Inn** 🏨
(618) 478-5341. **$65-$85.** 11640 SR 127 62263. I-64 exit 50 (SR 127),
0.3 mi s. Int corridors. **Pets:** Medium. $10 daily fee/pet. Designated
rooms, service with restrictions, supervision.
⟨SAVE⟩ 📶 ⓜ 🏊

NORMAL

🔷 **Americas Best Value - University Inn** 🏨
(309) 454-4070. **Call for rates.** 6 Traders Cir 61761. I-55 exit 165A (US
51), just s, then return on frontage road. Int corridors. **Pets:** Accepted.
⟨SAVE⟩ 📶 🛏 💻 🏊

🔷 **Comfort Suites by Choice Hotels
Bloomington/Normal** 🏨
(309) 452-8588. **$74-$149.** 310 B Greenbriar Dr 61761. I-55 exit 167,
follow I-55 business route (Veterans Pkwy), 1.3 mi s; jct Fort Jesse Rd.
Int corridors. **Pets:** Other species. $20 daily fee/room. Service with restric-
tions, supervision. 📶 ✕ ⓜ 🛏 💻 🏊

O'FALLON

🔷 **Candlewood Suites** 🏨
(618) 622-9555. **$84-$139.** 1332 Park Plaza Dr 62269. I-64 exit 14 (US
50), just s on Lincoln Hwy, 0.5 mi w on Hartman Ln, then just n on 2nd
entrance to Park Plaza Dr. Int corridors. **Pets:** Accepted.
📶 ⓜ 🛏 💻

🔷 **Drury Inn & Suites-O'Fallon** 🏨
(618) 624-2211. **$100-$194.** 1118 Central Park Dr 62269. I-64 exit 16,
just s. Int corridors. **Pets:** Accepted. 📶 ⓜ 🛏 💻 🏊

🔷 **Extended StayAmerica-St. Louis-O'Fallon** 🏨 ✿
(618) 624-1757. **$59-$84.** 154 Regency Park Dr 62269. I-64 exit 14 (US
50), just w to Regency Park Dr, then 0.4 mi s. Int corridors. **Pets:** Other
species. $25 daily fee/pet. Service with restrictions. 📶 ⓜ 🛏 💻

🔷 **Settle Inn & Suites** 🏨
(618) 624-6060. **$69-$149.** 1100 Eastgate Dr 62269. I-64 exit 19B (SR
158), 0.5 mi n, then just sw. Int corridors. **Pets:** Other species. $50
deposit/pet. Service with restrictions. ⟨SAVE⟩ 📶 🛏 💻 🏊

🔷 **Suburban Extended Stay Hotel** 🏨
(618) 589-3696. **$65-$85.** 148 Regency Park Dr 62269. I-64 exit 14 (US
50), 0.5 mi e. Int corridors. **Pets:** Accepted. 📶 🛏 💻 🏊

OGLESBY

🔷 **Best Western Oglesby Inn** 🏨 ✿
(815) 883-3535. **$80-$120.** 900 Holiday St 61348. I-39 exit 54, just e. Int
corridors. **Pets:** Medium. $35 one-time fee/room. Service with restrictions,
crate. ⟨SAVE⟩ 📶 🛏 💻

🔷 **Days Inn Oglesby/Starved Rock** 🏨
(815) 883-9600. **Call for rates.** 120 N Lewis Ave 61348. I-39 exit 54,
just e. Int corridors. **Pets:** Medium. $15 one-time fee/pet. Designated
rooms, service with restrictions, supervision.
⟨SAVE⟩ 📶 ✕ ⓜ 🛏 💻 🏊

OSWEGO

🔷 **Americlnn Lodge & Suites of Oswego** 🏨 ✿
(630) 554-9090. **$95-$162.** 1050 Douglas Rd 60543. Between US 30
and 34. Int corridors. **Pets:** Medium, dogs only. $15 daily fee/pet. Desig-
nated rooms, service with restrictions, supervision.
📶 ⓜ 🛏 💻 🏊 ✕

OTTAWA

🔷 **Fairfield Inn & Suites Ottawa/Starved Rock
Area** 🏨
(815) 431-8955. **$121-$147.** 3000 Fairfield Ln 61350. I-80 exit 90 (SR
23), just s to Etna Rd, then just e. Int corridors. **Pets:** Accepted.
📶 ✕ ⓜ 🛏 💻 🏊

🔷 **Hampton Inn-Starved Rock Area** 🏨
(815) 434-6040. **Call for rates.** 4115 Holiday Ln 61350. I-80 exit 90 (SR
23), just n. Int corridors. **Pets:** Accepted. 📶 ⓜ 🛏 💻 🏊

PEORIA

🔷 **Americlnn Lodge & Suites of Peoria** 🏨
(309) 692-9200. **Call for rates.** 9106 N Lindbergh Dr 61615. SR 6 exit
6, 0.5 mi s. Int corridors. **Pets:** Accepted. 📶 🛏 💻 🏊 ✕

🔷 **Candlewood Suites Peoria at Grand Prairie** 🏨
(309) 691-1690. **$109-$139.** 5300 W Landens Way 61615. SR 6 exit 2
(US 150/War Memorial Dr), follow US 150 NW to Summershade Cir, then
just w. Int corridors. **Pets:** Medium. $75 one-time fee/pet. Service with
restrictions, supervision. 📶 ⓜ 🛏 💻

▼▼▼ Comfort Suites by Choice Hotels 🅗

(309) 688-3800. **$100-$130.** 1812 W War Memorial Dr 61614. I-74 exit 89 (US 150/War Memorial Dr), just e, then just s. Int corridors. **Pets:** Accepted. 🛜 ⊠ 🛏 💻 🌊

▼▼▼ Country Inn & Suites By Carlson Peoria-North 🅗 🐾

(309) 589-0044. **Call for rates.** 5309 W Landens Way 61615. SR 6 exit 2 (US 150/War Memorial Dr), just n. Int corridors. **Pets:** $75 one-time fee/room. Service with restrictions, supervision.

🛜 ⊠ 🅜 🛏 💻 🌊 ⊠

▼▼▼ Jameson Inn & Suites 🅗

(309) 685-2556. **$95-$115.** 4112 N Brandywine Dr 61614. I-74 exit 89 (US 150/War Memorial Dr), just e. Int corridors. **Pets:** Medium. $15 daily fee/room. Service with restrictions, supervision. 🛜 🛏 💻 🌊

⍟ ▼ Red Roof Inn #057 🅜

(309) 685-3911. **$47-$70.** 1822 W War Memorial Dr 61614. I-74 exit 89 (US 150/War Memorial Dr), just e. Ext corridors. **Pets:** Large, other species. No service, supervision. [SAVE] 🛜 🛏

▼▼▼ Residence Inn by Marriott 🅗

(309) 681-9000. **$152-$186.** 2000 W War Memorial Dr 61614. I-74 exit 89 (US 150/War Memorial Dr), just w; entrance through Northwoods Mall. Int corridors. **Pets:** Accepted. 🛜 ⊠ 🛏 💻 🌊 ⊠

▼▼ Super 8 🅗

(309) 688-8074. **$42-$74.** 1816 W War Memorial Dr 61614. I-74 exit 89 (US 150/War Memorial Dr), just e. Int corridors. **Pets:** Accepted.
🛜 🛏 💻

▼▼▼ Wingate by Wyndham Peoria 🅗

(309) 589-0033. **$107-$125.** 7708 N Rt 91 61615. SR 6 exit 2 (US 150/War Memorial Dr), just w, then 0.3 mi n. Int corridors. **Pets:** Accepted.
🛜 ⊠ 🅜 🛏 💻 🌊 ⊠

PERU

▼▼▼ La Quinta Inn & Suites Peru 🅗

(815) 224-9000. **$89-$170.** 4389 Venture Dr 61354. I-80 exit 75 (SR 251), 0.4 mi s to 38th St, just w to Venture Dr, then 0.4 mi nw. Int corridors. **Pets:** Medium, other species. Service with restrictions, supervision.
🛜 🛏 💻 🌊

QUAD CITIES AREA

MOLINE

▼▼ Comfort Inn by Choice Hotels 🅗

(309) 762-7000. **$79-$99.** 2600 52nd Ave 61265. I-280/74 exit 18A eastbound; exit 5B westbound, just s on US 6 and 150, then 0.5 mi nw on 27th St. Int corridors. **Pets:** Large. $10 daily fee/pet. Designated rooms, service with restrictions, supervision. 🛜 🛏 💻 🌊

▼▼ Days Inn & Suites 🅗

(309) 762-8300. **$45-$162.** 6910 27th St 61265. I-280/74 exit 18A eastbound; exit 5B westbound, just s on US 6 and 150, then just nw. Int corridors. **Pets:** Accepted. 🛜 🛏 💻

▼▼ Fairfield Inn by Marriott 🅗

(309) 762-9083. **$109-$129.** 2705 48th Ave 61265. I-280/74 exit 5B westbound; exit 18A eastbound, just s on US 6 to traffic light, then 1 mi nw on 27th St. Int corridors. **Pets:** Accepted.
🛜 ⊠ 🅜 🛏 💻 🌊

▼▼ La Quinta Inn Moline Airport 🅗

(309) 762-9008. **$64-$122.** 5450 27th St 61265. I-280/74 exit 18A eastbound; exit 5B westbound, just s on US 6 and 150 to traffic light, then just nw. Int corridors. **Pets:** Medium, other species. Service with restrictions, supervision. 🛜 🛏 💻 🌊

▼▼ Ramada Airport Conference Center 🅗

(309) 762-8811. **$51-$81.** 6902 27th St 61265. I-280/74 exit 18A eastbound; exit 5B westbound, just s on US 6 and 150, then just nw. Int corridors. **Pets:** Accepted. 🛜 🛏 💻 🌊 ⊠

▼▼ Super 8 🅗

(309) 797-5580. **$45-$81.** 2501 52nd Ave 61265. I-280/74 exit 18A eastbound; exit 5B westbound, just s on US 6 and 150, then 1 mi nw on 27th St. Int corridors. **Pets:** Accepted. 🛜 🛏 💻

END AREA

QUINCY

▼▼ Comfort Inn by Choice Hotels 🅗 🐾

(217) 228-2700. **$65-$120.** 4122 Broadway 62305. I-172 exit 14 (SR 104), 1.3 mi w. Int corridors. **Pets:** $10 daily fee/pet. Designated rooms, service with restrictions, supervision. 🛜 🛏 💻 🌊

▼▼ Microtel Inn & Suites Quincy 🅗

(217) 222-5620. **$62-$109.** 200 S 3rd St 62301. Jct US 24 and SR 57, just sw. Int corridors. **Pets:** Accepted. 🛜 🛏 💻 🌊

▼▼ Stoney Creek Inn 🅗

(217) 223-2255. **Call for rates.** 3809 Broadway 62305. I-172 exit 14 (SR 104), 1 mi w. Int corridors. **Pets:** Accepted.
🛜 ⊠ 🛏 💻 🌊 ⊠

▼▼ Super 8 🅗

(217) 228-8808. **$51-$71.** 224 N 36th St 62301. I-172 exit 14 (SR 104), 1.8 mi w, then just s. Int corridors. **Pets:** Accepted. 🛜 🅜 🛏 💻

RANTOUL

⍟ ▼▼▼ Magnuson Hotel Heritage Inn 🅜

(217) 892-9292. **Call for rates.** 420 S Murray Rd 61866. I-57 exit 250 (US 136), 0.5 mi e, then just s. Ext corridors. **Pets:** Medium. $8 daily fee/pet. Service with restrictions, supervision. [SAVE] 🛜 🛏 💻 🌊

▼▼ Super 8 🅗

(217) 893-8888. **$44-$129.** 207 S Murray Rd 61866. I-57 exit 250 (US 136), just e. Int corridors. **Pets:** Small, dogs only. $10 daily fee/pet. Designated rooms, service with restrictions, supervision. 🛜 🛏 💻

RAYMOND

⍟ ▼▼▼ Magnuson Grand Hotel & Conference Center 🅗

(217) 324-2100. **$80-$120.** 19067 W Frontage Rd 62560. I-55 exit 60 (SR 108), just w. Int corridors. **Pets:** Medium, other species. $15 daily fee/pet. Designated rooms, service with restrictions, supervision.
[SAVE] 🛜 ⊠ 🛏 💻 🍴 🌊

ROBINSON

⍟ ▼▼▼ Best Western Robinson Inn 🅗 🐾

(618) 544-8448. **$85-$112.** 1500 W Main St 62454. 1.2 mi w on SR 33. Int corridors. **Pets:** Other species. $5 daily fee/room. Service with restrictions, supervision. [SAVE] 🛜 🛏 💻

ROCHELLE

⍟ ▼▼▼▼ Comfort Inn & Suites by Choice Hotels 🅗

(815) 562-5551. **$69-$110.** 1133 N 7th St 61068. I-39 exit 99 (SR 38), 2.5 mi w; jct SR 38 and 251; downtown. Int corridors. **Pets:** Accepted.
[SAVE] 🛜 🛏 💻 🍴 🌊 ⊠

Holiday Inn Express
(815) 562-9994. **$89-$119.** 1240 Dement Rd 61068. I-39 exit 99 (SR 38), just nw. Int corridors. **Pets:** Medium. $25 one-time fee/pet. Designated rooms, no service, supervision.

ROCKFORD

Baymont Inn & Suites Rockford
(815) 229-8200. **$63-$126.** 662 N Lyford Rd 61107. I-90 exit US 20 business route, just e, then just n. Int corridors. **Pets:** Other species. $10 daily fee/pet. Designated rooms, service with restrictions, supervision.

Candlewood Suites
(815) 229-9300. **$99-$129.** 7555 Walton St 61108. I-90 exit US 20 business route, 0.3 mi e to Bell School Rd, just s to Walton St, then just e. Int corridors. **Pets:** Large, other species. $75 one-time fee/pet. Designated rooms, service with restrictions, crate.

Comfort Inn by Choice Hotels
(815) 398-7061. **$79-$159.** 7392 Argus Dr 61107. I-90 exit US 20 business route, just w to Bell School Rd, then just n. Int corridors.
Pets: Accepted.

Days Inn Rockford
(815) 332-4915. **$54-$72.** 220 S Lyford Rd 61108. I-90 exit US 20 business route, just e, then just s. Int corridors. **Pets:** Accepted.

Extended StayAmerica-Rockford East
(815) 226-8969. **$45-$85.** 653 Clark Dr 61107. I-90 exit US 20 business route, just w. Int corridors. **Pets:** Other species. $25 daily fee/pet. Service with restrictions.

Holiday Inn
(815) 398-2200. **$79-$150.** 7550 E State St 61108. I-90 exit US 20 business route, 0.3 mi w to Bell School Rd. Int corridors. **Pets:** Other species. $25 daily fee/room. Designated rooms, service with restrictions, crate.

Red Roof Inn #7035
(815) 398-9750. **$54-$90.** 7434 E State St 61108. I-90 exit US 20 business route, just w. Ext corridors. **Pets:** Large, other species. No service, supervision.

Residence Inn by Marriott
(815) 227-0013. **$150-$165.** 7542 Colosseum Dr 61107. I-90 exit US 20 business route, 0.3 mi w to Bell School Rd, then just n. Int corridors.
Pets: Large. $100 one-time fee/room. Designated rooms, service with restrictions, crate.

Sleep Inn-Rockford
(815) 398-8900. **Call for rates.** 725 Clark Dr 61107. I-90 exit US 20 business route, just w to Bell School Rd, just n to Clark Dr, then 0.4 mi ne. Int corridors. **Pets:** Medium. $20 daily fee/pet. Service with restrictions, supervision.

Staybridge Suites
(815) 397-0200. **$99-$249, 3 day notice.** 633 N Bell School Rd 61107. I-90 exit US 20 business route, 0.3 mi w to Bell School Rd, then just n. Int corridors. **Pets:** Accepted.

StudioPLUS Deluxe Studios Rockfort-East
(815) 397-8316. **$58-$90.** 747 N Bell School Rd 61107. I-90 exit US 20 business route, just w to Bell School Rd, then 0.3 mi n. Int corridors. **Pets:** Other species. $25 daily fee/pet. Service with restrictions.

SALEM

Super 8
(618) 548-5882. **$58-$87.** 118 Woods Ln 62881. I-57 exit 116 (US 50), just w. Ext/int corridors. **Pets:** Medium. Service with restrictions, supervision.

SAVOY

Best Western Paradise Inn
(217) 356-1824. **$75-$101.** 709 N Dunlap Ave 61874. I-57 exit 229, 2.5 mi e to US 45, then 2.5 mi n. Ext corridors. **Pets:** Accepted.

SOUTH BELOIT

Best Western Legacy Inn & Suites Beloit/ South Beloit
(815) 389-4211. **$79-$149.** 5910 Technology Dr 61080. I-90/39 exit 1, just sw. Int corridors. **Pets:** Accepted.

SOUTH JACKSONVILLE

Comfort Inn by Choice Hotels-South Jacksonville
(217) 245-8372. **Call for rates.** 200 Comfort Dr 62650. I-72 exit 64, just n. Int corridors. **Pets:** Accepted.

Holiday Inn Express & Suites Jacksonville
(217) 245-6500. **$109-$159.** 2501 Holliday Ln 62650. I-72 exit 64, just n. Int corridors. **Pets:** Accepted.

SPRINGFIELD

Baymont Inn & Suites Springfield
(217) 529-6655. **$57-$123.** 5871 S 6th St 62703. I-55 exit 90 (Toronto Rd), just e to 6th St, then just n. Int corridors. **Pets:** Accepted.

Best Western Clearlake Plaza
(217) 525-7420. **$100-$135.** 3440 E Clearlake Ave 62702. I-55 exit 98B, just w. Int corridors. **Pets:** Large. $20 daily fee/room. Service with restrictions, supervision.

Candlewood Suites
(217) 522-5100. **$75-$119.** 2501 Sunrise Dr 62703. I-55 exit 94 (Stevenson Dr), just w to Dirksen Pkwy, then 0.4 mi n. Int corridors. **Pets:** Other species. $75 one-time fee/room. Service with restrictions.

Comfort Inn by Choice Hotels
(217) 787-2250. **$80-$120.** 3442 Freedom Dr 62704. I-72 exit 93 (Veterans Pkwy), 0.7 mi n to Lindbergh Blvd, just w to Freedom Dr, then just s. Int corridors. **Pets:** Accepted.

Drury Inn & Suites-Springfield
(217) 529-3900. **$100-$169.** 3180 S Dirksen Pkwy 62703. I-55 exit 94 (Stevenson Dr), just w to Dirksen Pkwy, then just n. Int corridors.
Pets: Accepted.

Fairfield Inn by Marriott
(217) 793-9277. **$99-$159.** 3446 Freedom Dr 62704. I-72 exit 93 (Veterans Pkwy), 0.7 mi n to Lindbergh Blvd, just w to Freedom Dr, then just s. Int corridors. **Pets:** Accepted.

Holiday Inn Express Hotel & Suites
(217) 529-7771. **$79-$119.** 3050 S Dirksen Pkwy 62703. I-55 exit 94 (Stevenson Dr), just w to S Dirksen Pkwy, then 0.4 mi n. Int corridors.
Pets: Medium, other species. $25 one-time fee/room. Service with restrictions, supervision.

Mansion View Inn & Suites
(217) 544-7411. **$89.** 529 S 4th St 62701. I-55 exit 92 (6th St), 3.9 mi n to Edwards St, then just w, follow signs. Ext/int corridors. **Pets:** Accepted.

Microtel Inn & Suites
(217) 753-2636. **$67-$85.** 2636 Sunrise Dr 62703. I-55 exit 94 (Stevenson Dr), just w to Dirksen Pkwy, then 0.4 mi n. Int corridors. **Pets:** Small, dogs only. $5 daily fee/pet. Service with restrictions, crate.

▼▼▼ Sleep Inn by Choice Hotels 🅷

(217) 787-6200. **$50-$150.** 3470 Freedom Dr 62704. I-72 exit 93 (Veterans Pkwy), 0.7 mi n to Lindbergh Blvd, just w to Freedom Dr, then just s. Int corridors. **Pets:** Accepted. 📶 🔲 💻

▼▼▼▼ Staybridge Suites Springfield South 🅷 🐾

(217) 793-6700. **$124-$184, 3 day notice.** 4231 Schooner Dr 62711. I-72 exit 93 (Veterans Pkwy), 0.4 mi se. Int corridors. **Pets:** Large, other species. $75 one-time fee/room. Service with restrictions, crate. 📶 ⓜ 🔲 💻 🏊 ☒

STAUNTON

▼▼▼ Staunton Super 8 🅷

(618) 635-5353. **$45-$70.** 1527 Herman Rd 62088. I-55 exit 41, 0.5 mi w. Int corridors. **Pets:** Medium. $10 one-time fee/room. Service with restrictions, supervision. 📶 🔲 💻

STOCKTON

▼▼▼ Country Inn & Suites By Carlson 🅷 🐾

(815) 947-6060. **$89-$142.** 200 Dillon Ave 61085. On US 20, just e of SR 78. Int corridors. **Pets:** Medium. $20 daily fee/pet. Designated rooms, service with restrictions, supervision. 📶 ⓜ 🔲 💻 🏊

STREATOR

Ⓐ ▼▼ Budget Inn & Suites Ⓜ

(815) 672-0080. **$71-$99.** 1705 N Bloomington St 61364. Jct SR 18 and 23, 1.5 mi n. Int corridors. **Pets:** Other species. $15 daily fee/pet. Designated rooms, no service, supervision. SAVE 📶 ⓜ 🔲 💻 🏊

SYCAMORE

▼▼ Motel 6 Sycamore #4628 🅷

(815) 899-6500. **Call for rates.** 1860 Dekalb Ave 60178. On SR 23, 0.9 mi s of Peace Rd. Int corridors. **Pets:** Other species. Service with restrictions, supervision. 📶 ⓜ 🔲 💻

TROY

Ⓐ ▼▼ Super 8 🅷

(618) 667-8888. **$46-$74, 3 day notice.** 910 Edwardsville Rd 62294. I-55/70 exit 18, just w. Int corridors. **Pets:** Accepted. SAVE 📶 🔲 💻 🏊

TUSCOLA

▼▼ Baymont Inn & Suites 🅷

(217) 253-3500. **$71-$98.** 1006 Southline Rd 61953. I-57 exit 212 (US 36), 0.3 mi w. Int corridors. **Pets:** Small. $10 daily fee/pet. Service with restrictions, supervision. 📶 ⓜ 🔲 💻 🏊

▼▼▼ Holiday Inn Express 🅷

(217) 253-6363. **$99-$125.** 1201 Tuscola Blvd 61953. I-57 exit 212 (US 36), 0.3 mi w to Progress Blvd, just s to Tuscola Blvd, then 0.4 mi se. Int corridors. **Pets:** Medium. Service with restrictions, supervision. 📶 🔲 💻 🏊

▼▼ Super 8-Tuscola 🅷

(217) 253-5488. **$39-$65.** 1007 E Southline Rd 61953. I-57 exit 212 (US 36), 0.4 mi w. Int corridors. **Pets:** Other species. $10 daily fee/pet. No service, supervision. 📶 🔲 💻

URBANA

▼▼▼▼ Comfort Suites by Choice Hotels Urbana/Champaign 🅷

(217) 328-3500. **$99-$115.** 2001 N Lincoln Ave 61801. I-74 exit 183 (Lincoln Ave), 0.5 mi s. Int corridors. **Pets:** $20 one-time fee/room. Service with restrictions, crate. 📶 ☒ ⓜ 🔲 💻 🏊

Ⓐ ▼▼▼ Ramada-Urbana/Champaign 🅷

(217) 328-4400. **$69-$102.** 902 W Killarney St 61801. I-74 exit 183 (Lincoln Ave), just s to Killarney St, then just w. Int corridors. **Pets:** Small. $25 deposit/pet. Service with restrictions, supervision. SAVE 📶 🔲 💻 🏊

Ⓐ ▼▼▼ Sleep Inn by Choice Hotels 🅷

(217) 367-6000. **Call for rates.** 1908 N Lincoln Ave 61801. I-74 exit 183 (Lincoln Ave), 0.5 mi s. Int corridors. **Pets:** Other species. $10 daily fee/pet. Service with restrictions, supervision. SAVE 📶 🔲 💻 🏊

VANDALIA

▼▼ Days Inn-Vandalia 🅷

(618) 283-4400. **Call for rates.** 1920 Kennedy Blvd 62471. I-70 exit 63 (US 51), 0.6 mi n. Ext corridors. **Pets:** Accepted. 📶 🔲 💻 🍴 🏊

▼▼▼▼ Holiday Inn Express Hotel & Suites 🅷

(618) 283-0010. **Call for rates.** 21 Mattes Ave 62471. I-70 exit 61, just s. Int corridors. **Pets:** Accepted. 📶 ☒ ⓜ 🔲 💻 🏊

Ⓐ ▼▼▼ Jay's Inn Ⓜ

(618) 283-1200. **$56-$65.** 720 Gochenour St 62471. I-70 exit 63 (US 51), just s. Ext corridors. **Pets:** Other species. Service with restrictions. SAVE 📶 🔲 💻

▼▼ Ramada Vandalia 🅷

(618) 283-1400. **$55-$89.** 2707 Veterans Ave 62471. I-70 exit 61, just s. Int corridors. **Pets:** Accepted. 📶 🔲 💻

WASHINGTON

▼▼ Super 8 🅷

(309) 444-8881. **$45-$68.** 1884 Washington Rd 61571. On Business Rt US 24, 1.5 mi w. Int corridors. **Pets:** Accepted. 📶 🔲 💻

WATSEKA

Ⓐ ▼▼ Super 8 🅷

(815) 432-6000. **$52-$78.** 710 W Walnut St 60970. On US 24; center of downtown. Int corridors. **Pets:** Small. $25 deposit/pet, $10 daily fee/pet. Service with restrictions, supervision. SAVE 📶 🔲 💻

WENONA

▼▼ Super 8 🅷

(815) 853-4371. **$40-$63.** 5 Cavalry Dr 61377. I-39 exit 35. Int corridors. **Pets:** Medium. $5 daily fee/pet. Designated rooms, service with restrictions, supervision. 📶 🔲 💻

INDIANA

ANGOLA

 **Ramada Angola Hotel** H
(260) 665-9471. **$68-$153.** 3855 N SR 127 & I-69 exit 154 46703. I-69 exit 154, just e, then 0.4 mi s. Int corridors. **Pets:** Other species. $25 daily fee/room. Service with restrictions, crate.

AUBURN

Quality Inn H
(260) 925-6363. **Call for rates.** 225 Touring Dr 46706. I-69 exit 129 (SR 8), just e, then just s. Int corridors. **Pets:** Accepted.

Super 8-Auburn H
(260) 927-8800. **$57-$152.** 503 Ley Dr 46706. I-69 exit 129 (SR 8), just e, then just s. Int corridors. **Pets:** Accepted.

BEDFORD

Bedford Comfort Inn H
(812) 279-8111. **$70-$200.** 911 Constitution Ave 47421. Jct SR 37 and 58, just s on SR 37. Int corridors. **Pets:** Accepted.

Bedford Super 8 H
(812) 275-8881. **$59-$131.** 501 Bell Back Rd 47421. Jct SR 37 and 58, just e on SR 58. Int corridors. **Pets:** $10 daily fee/pet. Service with restrictions, crate.

Holiday Inn Express & Suites H
(812) 279-1206. **$120-$160.** 2800 Express Ln 47421. On US 50/SR 37, 1.4 mi s of jct SR 450. Int corridors. **Pets:** Accepted.

BERNE

Black Bear Inn & Suites H
(260) 589-8955. **$68-$73.** 1335 US 27 N 46711. On US 27, 1 mi n. Int corridors. **Pets:** Medium. $10 one-time fee/room. Designated rooms, service with restrictions.

BLOOMINGTON

Comfort Inn Bloomington H 🐾
(812) 650-0010. **$99-$299.** 1700 N Kinser Pike 47404. On SR 45 and 45 Bypass, 1 mi e of jct SR 37. Int corridors. **Pets:** Medium, other species. $25 one-time fee/room. Designated rooms, service with restrictions.

Fairfield Inn by Marriott H
(812) 331-1122. **$109-$499.** 120 Fairfield Dr 47404. Just e from SR 37 at 3rd St. Int corridors. **Pets:** Accepted.

Hampton Inn H
(812) 334-2100. **$99-$129.** 2100 N Walnut St 47404. 1 mi e of jct SR 37 on SR 45 and 46 Bypass, then just s on College Ave/Walnut St. Int corridors. **Pets:** Accepted.

Holiday Inn Bloomington H
(812) 334-3252. **$89-$229.** 1710 N Kinser Pike 47404. On SR 45 and 46 Bypass, 1 mi e of jct SR 37. Int corridors. **Pets:** Accepted.

TownePlace Suites By Marriott H 🐾
(812) 334-1234. **$109-$399.** 105 S Franklin Rd 47404. Just e from SR 37 at 3rd St, then 0.3 mi n. Int corridors. **Pets:** Other species. $75 one-time fee/room. Service with restrictions, crate.

BLUFFTON

Bluffton Inn & Suites H
(260) 824-5553. **$64-$89.** 100 Charles Deam Ct 46714. Jct SR 1 and 124 (E Division Rd), just n. Int corridors. **Pets:** Accepted.

BREMEN

Scottish Bed and Breakfast BB
(574) 220-6672. **$109-$149, 14 day notice.** 2180 Miami Tr 46506. Jct SR 331, 2 mi w on SR 106, just s. Int corridors. **Pets:** Dogs only. $25 one-time fee/pet. Designated rooms, service with restrictions, crate.

CENTERVILLE

Historic Lantz House Inn BB 🐾
(765) 855-2936. **$103-$139, 5 day notice.** 214 W Main St 47330. I-70 exit 145, 3 mi s to US 40 (W Main St), then just w. Int corridors. **Pets:** Medium. $20 one-time fee/room. Designated rooms, crate.

CHESTERTON

Gray Goose Inn BB 🐾
(219) 926-5781. **$110-$195, 10 day notice.** 350 Indian Boundary Rd 46304. I-94 exit 26A, 0.6 mi s, then just w. Int corridors. **Pets:** $25 one-time fee/pet. Service with restrictions, crate.

CINCINNATI METROPOLITAN AREA (NEARBY OHIO)

BATESVILLE

Hampton Inn Batesville H
(812) 934-6262. **$90-$125.** 1030 SR 229 N 47006. I-74 exit 149, just n. Int corridors. **Pets:** Medium. Designated rooms, service with restrictions, supervision. SAVE

LAWRENCEBURG

Comfort Inn & Suites H
(812) 539-3600. **$80-$170.** 1610 Flossie Dr 47025. I-275 exit 16, 0.3 mi e. Int corridors. **Pets:** Accepted.

Quality Inn & Suites H
(812) 539-4770. **Call for rates.** 1000 E Eads Pkwy 47025. I-275 exit 16, 0.5 mi w on US 50. Int corridors. **Pets:** $20 daily fee/pet. Service with restrictions, supervision.

END METROPOLITAN AREA

CLARKSVILLE

Best Western Green Tree Inn M
(812) 288-9281. **$85-$120.** 1425 Broadway St 47129. I-65 exit 4, just w. Ext corridors. **Pets:** Dogs only. Service with restrictions, crate.

Candlewood Suites Louisville North H
(812) 284-6113. **$89-$116.** 1419 Bales Ln 47129. I-65 exit 4, just w. Int corridors. **Pets:** Large, other species. $75 one-time fee/room. Service with restrictions, crate. SAVE

CLOVERDALE

Super 8 Cloverdale/Greencastle H
(765) 795-7373. **$51-$159.** 1020 N Main St 46120. I-70 exit 41, just s on US 231. Int corridors. **Pets:** Medium, dogs only. Service with restrictions, crate.

COLUMBIA CITY

Quality Inn H
(260) 248-4551. **$74-$79.** 701 W Connexion Way 46725. 1 mi w of SR 9, just off US 30. Int corridors. **Pets:** Accepted.

COLUMBUS

Clarion Hotel and Conference Center H
(812) 372-1541. **$89-$199.** 2480 Jonathan Moore Pike 47201. I-65 exit 68, just w on SR 46. Ext/int corridors. **Pets:** Accepted.

Hotel Indigo H
(812) 375-9100. **$99-$189.** 400 Brown St 47201. Jct 4th St. Int corridors. **Pets:** Medium, dogs only. $35 one-time fee/room. Service with restrictions, crate.

La Quinta Inn & Suites H
(812) 379-4657. **Call for rates.** 101 Carrie Ln 47201. I-65 exit 68, just w on SR 46. Int corridors. **Pets:** Medium, other species. Service with restrictions, supervision.

Residence Inn by Marriott H
(812) 342-2400. **$116-$142.** 4525 W SR 46 47201. I-65 exit 68, 0.8 mi w on SR 46. Int corridors. **Pets:** Accepted.

CORYDON

Holiday Inn Express H
(812) 738-1623. **$94-$119.** 249 Federal Dr 47112. I-64 exit 105, 0.6 mi s, then just w. Int corridors. **Pets:** Accepted.

CRAWFORDSVILLE

Comfort Inn H
(765) 361-0665. **Call for rates.** 2991 N Gandhi Dr 47933. I-74 exit 34, just s on US 231. Int corridors. **Pets:** $15 daily fee/pet. Service with restrictions, supervision. SAVE

Hampton Inn & Suites H
(765) 362-8884. **$90-$159.** 2895 Gandhi Dr 47933. I-74 exit 34, just s on US 231. Int corridors. **Pets:** Accepted.

Holiday Inn Express Hotel & Suites H
(765) 323-4575. **$99-$109.** 2506 N Lafayette Rd 47933. I-74 exit 34, 0.3 mi s on US 231. Int corridors. **Pets:** Accepted.

Quality Inn Crawfordsville H
(765) 362-8700. **Call for rates.** 2500 N Lafayette Rd 47933. I-74 exit 34, 0.3 mi s on US 231. Ext corridors. **Pets:** Accepted.

DALE

Best Western Plus Lincoln Land Inn H
(812) 937-7000. **$80-$200, 3 day notice.** 1339 N Washington St 47523. I-64 exit 57A, just s. Int corridors. **Pets:** Accepted. SAVE

DECATUR

Baymont Inn & Suites H
(260) 728-4600. **$67-$80.** 1201 S 13th St 46733. On US 27 and 33, 1 mi s of jct US 224. Int corridors. **Pets:** Accepted.

ELKHART

Candlewood Suites H
(574) 262-8600. **$80-$225.** 300 Northpointe Blvd 46514. I-80/90 exit 92, just n on SR 19, then just w. Int corridors. **Pets:** Large, other species. $20 daily fee/pet. Service with restrictions, supervision.

Jameson Inn Elkhart H
(574) 264-7222. **$80-$100.** 3010 Brittany Ct 46514. I-80/90 exit 92, 0.3 mi s on SR 19. Int corridors. **Pets:** Medium. $15 daily fee/room. Service with restrictions, supervision.

Staybridge Suites Elkhart North H
(574) 970-8488. **$99-$139.** 3252 Cassopolis St 46514. I-80/90 exit 92, just n on SR 19. Int corridors. **Pets:** Medium, other species. $25 daily fee/room. Designated rooms, service with restrictions, supervision. SAVE

EVANSVILLE

▼▼▼▼ **Baymont Inn & Suites Evansville East** 🅷
(812) 477-2677. **$67-$126.** 8005 E Division St 47715. I-164 exit 7B (SR 66/Lloyd Expwy), 0.5 mi w to Cross Pointe Blvd, just n to Division St, then 0.5 mi e. Int corridors. **Pets:** Medium, other species. $10 daily fee/room. Service with restrictions, supervision. 🛜 &M 🔌 💻 🏊

🅰🅰🅰 ▼▼▼ **Best Western Plus Gateway Inn & Suites** 🅷
(812) 868-8000. **$80-$160.** 324 Rusher Creek Rd 47725. I-64 exit 25A (US 41), 0.5 mi s, then just w. Int corridors. **Pets:** Accepted.
SAVE 🛜 &M 🔌 💻 🏊

🅰🅰🅰 ▼▼▼▼ **Casino Aztar Hotel** 🅷
(812) 433-4000. **Call for rates.** 421 NW Riverside Dr 47708. SR 62 (Lloyd Expwy), just s on Fulton. Int corridors. **Pets:** Medium. $100 deposit/pet. Designated rooms, service with restrictions.
SAVE 🛜 &M 🔌 💻 🍴

▼▼ **Comfort Inn East** 🅷
(812) 476-3600. **Call for rates.** 8331 E Walnut St 47715. I-164 exit 7B (SR 66/Lloyd Expwy), 0.5 mi w to Eagle Crest Blvd, 0.3 mi se to Fuquay St, just s to Walnut St, then 0.4 mi e. Int corridors. **Pets:** Accepted.
🛜 &M 🔌 💻 🏊

▼▼ **Comfort Inn North** 🅷
(812) 867-1600. **Call for rates.** 19622 Elpers Rd 47725. I-64 exit 25A (US 41), 0.5 mi s, then just w. Int corridors. **Pets:** Accepted.
🛜 🔌 💻 🏊

▼▼▼▼ **Drury Inn & Suites-Evansville East** 🅷
(812) 471-3400. **$95-$174.** 100 Cross Pointe Blvd 47715. I-164 exit 7B (SR 66/Lloyd Expwy), 0.5 mi w. Int corridors. **Pets:** Accepted.
🛜 &M 🔌 💻 🏊 ✖

▼▼▼▼ **Drury Inn & Suites-Evansville North** 🅷
(812) 423-5818. **$95-$159.** 3901 US 41 N 47711. US 41, 2.5 mi n of jct SR 62 and 66 (Lloyd Expwy), 3.3 mi sw of Evansville Regional Airport entrance. Int corridors. **Pets:** Accepted. 🛜 &M 🔌 💻 🏊

▼▼▼ **Holiday Inn Express - Evansville West** 🅷 🐾
(812) 421-9773. **Call for rates.** 5737 Pearl Dr 47712. Jct US 41 and SR 62, 5.7 mi w on SR 62, then just s on Boehne Camp Rd. Int corridors. **Pets:** Medium. $15 one-time fee/room. Service with restrictions, supervision. 🛜 &M 🔌 💻 🏊

▼▼ **HomeLife Studios & Suites** Ⓜ
(812) 475-1900. **$59-$119.** 100 S Green River Rd 47715. I-164 exit 7B (SR 66/Lloyd Expwy), 2 mi w to Green River Rd, then just s. Ext corridors. **Pets:** Small. $50 one-time fee/room. Service with restrictions, crate.
🛜 🔌 💻 🏊

▼▼▼▼ **Jameson Inn Evansville** 🅷
(812) 476-9626. **$80-$100.** 1101 N Green River Rd 47715. I-164 exit 9 (SR 62 E/Morgan Ave), 1.5 mi w on SR 62, then just s. Int corridors. **Pets:** Medium. $15 daily fee/room. Service with restrictions, supervision.
🛜 &M 🔌 💻 🏊

▼▼▼▼ **La Quinta Inn & Suites Evansville** 🅷
(812) 471-3414. **$170-$240.** 8015 E Division St 47715. I-164 exit 7B (SR 66/ Lloyd Expwy), 0.5 mi w to Cross Pointe Blvd, just n, then 0.5 mi e. Int corridors. **Pets:** Medium, other species. Service with restrictions, supervision. 🛜 🔌 💻 🏊

▼▼ **Residence Inn by Marriott Evansville East** 🅷
(812) 471-7191. **$89-$159.** 8283 E Walnut St 47715. I-164 exit 7B (SR 66/Lloyd Expwy), 0.5 mi w to Eagle Crest Blvd, 0.3 mi se to Fuquay St, then 0.3 mi e. Int corridors. **Pets:** Accepted.
🛜 ✖ &M 🔌 💻 🏊 ✖

▼▼ **StudioPLUS Evansville East** 🅷 🐾
(812) 479-0103. **$50-$85.** 301 Eagle Crest Dr 47715. I-164 exit 7B (SR 66/Lloyd Expwy), 0.5 mi w to Eagle Crest Blvd, 0.5 mi s, then just e. Int corridors. **Pets:** Other species. $25 daily fee/pet. Service with restrictions.
🛜 🔌 🏊

FERDINAND

▼▼ **Comfort Inn** 🅷
(812) 367-1122. **$69-$299.** 440 S Main St 47532. I-64 exit 63. Int corridors. **Pets:** Medium, other species. $10 one-time fee/pet. Designated rooms, service with restrictions, supervision. 🛜 &M 🔌 💻 🏊

FORT WAYNE

▼▼ **Baymont Inn Fort Wayne** 🅷
(260) 489-2220. **$58-$67.** 1005 W Washington Center Rd 46825. I-69 exit 111B, just n on SR 3, then 0.4 mi e. Int corridors. **Pets:** Accepted.
🛜 🔌 💻

🅰🅰🅰 ▼▼◆ **Best Western Luxbury Inn Fort Wayne** 🅷
(260) 436-0242. **$70-$100.** 5501 Coventry Ln 46804. I-69 exit 102, just w. Int corridors. **Pets:** Medium. $20 one-time fee/room. Designated rooms, service with restrictions, supervision. SAVE 🛜 🔌 💻 🏊

▼▼▼ **Candlewood Suites** 🅷
(260) 484-1400. **$89-$149.** 5250 Distribution Dr 46825. I-69 exit 111A, just e. Int corridors. **Pets:** Accepted. 🛜 &M 🔌 💻 🏊

▼▼ **Don Hall's Guesthouse** 🅷
(260) 489-2524. **$89-$99, 3 day notice.** 1313 W Washington Center Rd 46825. I-69 exit 111B, just n on SR 3, then 0.3 mi e. Ext/int corridors. **Pets:** Large, dogs only. $10 daily fee/pet. Service with restrictions, crate.
🛜 🔌 💻 🍴 🏊 ✖

▼▼ **Extended StayAmerica-Fort Wayne-South** 🅷 🐾
(260) 432-1916. **$50-$90.** 8309 W Jefferson Blvd 46804. I-69 exit 102, 0.4 mi e on US 24, then 0.6 mi s. Int corridors. **Pets:** Other species. $25 daily fee/room. Service with restrictions. 🛜 🔌 💻

🅰🅰🅰 ▼▼▼▼ **Hilton Fort Wayne at Grand Wayne Convention Center** 🅷 🐾
(260) 420-1100. **$99-$189.** 1020 S Calhoun St 46802. Jct Jefferson Blvd; center. Int corridors. **Pets:** $50 one-time fee/room. Service with restrictions, crate. SAVE 🛜 &M 🔌 💻 🍴 🏊

🅰🅰🅰 ▼▼▼▼ **Holiday Inn at IPFW & The Coliseum** 🅷
(260) 482-3800. **$110-$150.** 4111 Paul Shaffer Dr 46825. I-69 exit 111A, 1.2 mi s on Lima Rd, then 1.5 mi e. Int corridors. **Pets:** Accepted.
SAVE 🛜 ✖ &M 🔌 💻 🍴 🏊 ✖

🅰🅰🅰 ▼▼▼ **Quality Inn** 🅷
(260) 489-5554. **$75-$100.** 1734 W Washington Center Rd 46818. I-69 exit 111B, just n on SR 3. Int corridors. **Pets:** Medium. $15 daily fee/pet. Service with restrictions, crate. SAVE 🛜 🔌 💻 🏊

▼▼▼▼ **Residence Inn Southwest** 🅷
(260) 432-8000. **$121-$147.** 7811 W Jefferson Blvd 46804. I-69 exit 102, 0.5 mi e. Int corridors. **Pets:** Accepted. 🛜 ✖ 🔌 💻 🏊 ✖

▼▼▼ **Staybridge Suites** 🅷
(260) 432-2427. **Call for rates.** 5925 Ellison Rd 46804. I-69 exit 102, just w. Int corridors. **Pets:** Accepted. 🛜 &M 🔌 💻 🏊 ✖

▼▼▼ **Stay Inn Suites** 🅷
(260) 484-4700. **$161-$206.** 4919 Lima Rd 46808. I-69 exit 111A, 0.4 mi s on US 27. Ext corridors. **Pets:** Accepted.
🛜 ✖ 🔌 💻 🏊 ✖

FRENCH LICK

▼▼▼ **Comfort Suites** 🅷
(812) 936-5300. **$105-$135.** 9530 W SR 56 47432. Jct SR 145, 1.2 mi sw. Int corridors. **Pets:** $25 one-time fee/pet. Designated rooms, service with restrictions, supervision. 🛜 ✖ &M 🔌 💻 🏊

🅰🅰🅰 ▼▼▼◆ **French Lick Resort** 🅷
(812) 936-9300. **$139-$299.** 8670 W SR 56 47432. Jct SR 145. Int corridors. **Pets:** Accepted. SAVE 🛜 ✖ &M 🔌 💻 🍴 🏊 ✖

GAS CITY

△△△ ▼▼▼▼ Best Western Plus Gas City H
(765) 998-2331. **$90-$145.** 4936 Kaybee Dr 46933. I-69 exit 59, just e. Int corridors. **Pets:** Medium. $20 one-time fee/pet. Designated rooms, service with restrictions, crate. [SAVE] 📶 ♿ 🍴 💻 🏊

GOSHEN

△△△ ▼▼▼ Best Western Inn M
(574) 533-0408. **$79-$99.** 900 Lincolnway E 46526. 1 mi se on US 33. Ext corridors. **Pets:** Service with restrictions, crate. [SAVE] 📶 ♿ 💻

GREENSBURG

▼▼▼▼ Hampton Inn & Suites H ❀
(812) 663-5000. **$79-$109.** 2075 N Michigan Ave 47240. I-74 exit 132, just se. Int corridors. **Pets:** Medium. Service with restrictions.
📶 ♿ 🍴 💻 🏊

▼▼▼ Holiday Inn Express H ❀
(812) 663-5500. **$89-$119.** 915 Ann Blvd 47240. I-74 exit 134A, 1.4 mi s on SR 3. Int corridors. **Pets:** Other species. $15 daily fee/pet. Designated rooms, service with restrictions, supervision. 📶 ♿ 🍴 💻 🏊

HAMMOND

△△△ ▼▼ Best Western Northwest Indiana Inn H
(219) 844-2140. **$102-$130.** 3830 179th St 46323. I-80/94 exit 5, 0.6 mi s on Cline Ave (SR 912), then 0.6 mi n on frontage road (179th St). Int corridors. **Pets:** Medium. $55 deposit/pet, $10 daily fee/pet. Designated rooms, service with restrictions, supervision.
[SAVE] 📶 🍴 💻 🍴 🏊

▼▼▼ Residence Inn by Marriott Chicago Southeast H ❀
(219) 844-8440. **$119-$199.** 7740 Corinne Dr 46323. I-80/94 exit 3 (Kennedy Ave S), just s. Int corridors. **Pets:** Medium, other species. $100 one-time fee/room. Service with restrictions, supervision.
📶 ❌ ♿ 🍴 💻 🏊 ❌

HOWE

▼▼▼▼ Holiday Inn Express-Howe/Sturgis H
(260) 562-3660. **$99-$159.** 45 W 750 N 46746. I-80/90 exit 121 (US 66). Int corridors. **Pets:** $35 one-time fee/room. Service with restrictions, supervision. 📶 ❌ ♿ 🍴 💻 🏊

HUNTINGTON

▼▼▼ Super 8 H
(260) 358-8888. **$58-$63.** 2801 Guilford St 46750. US 24, just n. Int corridors. **Pets:** Accepted. 📶 🍴 💻 🏊

INDIANAPOLIS METROPOLITAN AREA

BROWNSBURG

▼▼▼▼ Holiday Inn Express Brownsburg H
(317) 852-5353. **Call for rates.** 31 Maplehurst Dr 46112. I-74 exit 66, just n on SR 267. Int corridors. **Pets:** Accepted. 📶 🍴 💻 🏊

CARMEL

▼▼▼▼ Jameson Inn Carmel H
(317) 816-1616. **Call for rates.** 10201 N Meridian St 46290. I-465 exit 31, 0.3 mi n on US 31. Int corridors. **Pets:** Medium. $15 daily fee/room. Service with restrictions, supervision. 📶 ♿ 🍴 💻 🏊 ❌

▼▼▼ Residence Inn by Marriott Indianapolis/Carmel H ❀
(317) 846-2000. **$109-$189.** 11895 N Meridian St 46032. I-465 exit 31, 2 mi n on US 31, just e on 116th St, then just n on Pennsylvania Rd. Int corridors. **Pets:** Other species. $100 one-time fee/room. Service with restrictions, supervision. 📶 ❌ ♿ 🍴 💻 🏊 ❌

▼▼▼▼ Staybridge Suites Indianapolis-Carmel H
(317) 582-1500. **$89-$199.** 10675 N Pennsylvania St 46280. I-465 exit 31, 0.7 mi n to 106th St, just e, then just n. Int corridors. **Pets:** Accepted.
📶 ❌ ♿ 🍴 💻 🏊

EDINBURGH

△△△ ▼▼▼ Best Western Horizon Inn H
(812) 526-9883. **$95-$113.** 11780 N US 31 46124. I-65 exit 76B, just n. Int corridors. **Pets:** Accepted. [SAVE] 📶 🍴 💻 🏊

FISHERS

△△△ ▼▼▼▼ Comfort Suites H
(317) 578-1200. **$82-$250.** 9760 Crosspoint Blvd 46256. I-69 exit 3, just w on 96th St, then just n. Int corridors. **Pets:** $10 daily fee/pet. Service with restrictions. [SAVE] 📶 ❌ 🍴 💻 🏊

▼▼▼ Holiday Inn Express-Fishers H
(317) 578-2000. **$79-$159.** 9790 North by Northeast Blvd 46038. I-69 exit 3, just ne. Int corridors. **Pets:** Accepted. 📶 ♿ 🍴 💻 🏊

▼▼▼ Hotel Indigo H
(317) 558-4100. **Call for rates.** 9791 North by Northeast Blvd 46037. I-69 exit 3, just ne. Int corridors. **Pets:** Accepted.
📶 ❌ ♿ 🍴 💻 🍴 🏊

▼▼▼ Residence Inn by Marriott Indianapolis/Fishers H
(317) 842-1111. **$99-$149.** 9765 Crosspoint Blvd 46256. I-69 exit 3, just nw. Int corridors. **Pets:** Accepted. 📶 ❌ ♿ 🍴 💻 🏊 ❌

▼▼▼ Staybridge Suites Indianapolis-Fishers H
(317) 577-9500. **$89-$149.** 9780 Crosspoint Blvd 46256. I-69 exit 3, just nw. Int corridors. **Pets:** Accepted. 📶 ♿ 🍴 💻 🏊 ❌

GREENFIELD

△△△ ▼▼▼ Comfort Inn-Greenfield/Indianapolis H
(317) 467-9999. **$90-$499.** 178 E Martindale Dr 46140. I-70 exit 104, 0.4 mi s on State St. Int corridors. **Pets:** Accepted.
[SAVE] 📶 🍴 💻 🏊

△△△ ▼▼▼ Quality Inn Greenfield H
(317) 462-7112. **$59-$89.** 2270 N State St 46140. I-70 exit 104, just s. Int corridors. **Pets:** Accepted. [SAVE] 📶 🍴 💻 🏊

GREENWOOD

▼▼▼▼ Candlewood Suites Indy-South H
(317) 882-4300. **$89-$99.** 1190 N Graham Rd 46143. I-65 exit 101, just e. Int corridors. **Pets:** Large, other species. $75 one-time fee/room. Service with restrictions, crate. 📶 ♿ 🍴 💻

△△△ ▼▼▼ Red Roof Inn M
(317) 887-1515. **$59-$199.** 110 Sheek Rd 46143. I-65 exit 99, just w. Ext corridors. **Pets:** Large, other species. No service, supervision.
[SAVE] 📶 🍴 🏊

INDIANAPOLIS

▼▼▼ Baymont Inn & Suites H
(317) 322-2000. **$98-$143, 3 day notice.** 1540 Brookville Crossing Way 46239. I-465 exit 47, 0.3 mi e. Int corridors. **Pets:** Accepted.
📶 ♿ 🍴 💻 🏊

△△△ ▼▼▼▼ Best Western Airport Suites H
(317) 246-1505. **$80-$180.** 55 S High School Rd 46241. I-465 exit 13B, just w. Int corridors. **Pets:** Accepted. [SAVE] 📶 🍴 💻

▼▼ **Candlewood Suites Indianapolis NE** �H 🐾
(317) 595-9292. **$89-$129.** 8111 Bash St 46250. I-69 exit 1, just w. Int corridors. **Pets:** Large, other species. $25 one-time fee/room.
🛜 🛏 💻 ⊇ ⊠

▼▼▼ **Candlewood Suites Indianapolis NW** �H 🐾
(317) 298-8000. **$89-$109.** 7455 Woodland Dr 46278. I-465 exit 21 (73rd St), just n. Int corridors. **Pets:** Other species. $25 one-time fee/room. Service with restrictions. 🛜 🛗 🛏 💻 ⊇

▼▼▼ **Caribbean Cove Hotel & Water Park** �H
(317) 872-9790. **$94-$119.** 3850 Depauw Blvd 46268. I-465 exit 27, just s. Int corridors. **Pets:** Accepted. 🛜 🛏 💻 🍴 ⊇ ⊠

ⒶⒶⒶ ▼▼ **Comfort Inn & Suites North** �H
(317) 875-7676. **Call for rates.** 9090 Wesleyan Rd 46268. I-465 exit 27, just s to Depauw Blvd, just e, then just s. Int corridors. **Pets:** Accepted.
SAVE 🛜 🛏 💻 ⊇

▼▼ **Comfort Inn-East** �H
(317) 359-9999. **$69-$89.** 2295 N Shadeland Ave 46219. I-70 exit 89, 0.5 mi w of jct I-465. Int corridors. **Pets:** Other species. $25 one-time fee/room. Service with restrictions. 🛜 🛗 🛏 💻 ⊇

▼▼▼ **Conrad Indianapolis** �H
(317) 713-5000. **$189-$399.** 50 W Washington St 46204. Jct Illinois St. Int corridors. **Pets:** Accepted. 🛜 🛗 🛏 💻 🍴 ⊇ ⊠

▼▼▼ **Drury Inn & Suites Indianapolis Northeast** �H
(317) 849-8900. **$105-$219.** 8180 N Shadeland Ave 46250. I-69 exit 1, just e. Int corridors. **Pets:** Accepted. 🛜 🛗 🛏 💻 ⊇

▼▼▼ **Drury Inn-Indianapolis** �H
(317) 876-9777. **$70-$164.** 9320 N Michigan Rd 46268. I-465 exit 27, just s. Int corridors. **Pets:** Accepted. 🛜 🛏 💻 ⊇

▼▼ **Extended StayAmerica Indianapolis Castleton** �H 🐾
(317) 596-1288. **$42-$90.** 7940 N Shadeland Ave 46250. I-69 exit 1, 0.5 mi s. Int corridors. **Pets:** Other species. $25 daily fee/pet. Service with restrictions. 🛜 🛏 💻

▼▼ **Extended StayAmerica Indianapolis - North - Carmel** �H 🐾
(317) 843-1181. **$47-$100.** 9750 Lakeshore Dr 46280. I-465 exit 33, 0.4 mi n on Keystone Dr, 0.6 mi e on 96th St, then just n on Bauer Dr. Int corridors. **Pets:** Other species. $25 daily fee/pet. Service with restrictions.
🛜 🛏 💻

▼▼ **Extended StayAmerica-Indianapolis-Northwest-College Park** �H 🐾
(317) 872-3090. **$40-$100.** 9030 Wesleyan Rd 46268. I-465 exit 27, just s to Depauw Blvd, just e, then just s. Int corridors. **Pets:** Other species. $25 daily fee/pet. Service with restrictions. 🛜 🛏 💻

ⒶⒶⒶ ▼▼▼ **Hilton Indianapolis Hotel & Suites** �H 🐾
(317) 972-0600. **$99-$259.** 120 W Market St 46204. Jct Illinois St. Int corridors. **Pets:** Medium, other species. $50 one-time fee/room. Service with restrictions, supervision. SAVE 🛜 🛗 🛏 💻 🍴 ⊇ ⊠

ⒶⒶⒶ ▼▼ ▼▼ **The Historic Canterbury Hotel** �H
(317) 634-3000. **$129-$399.** 123 S Illinois St 46225. Between Georgia and Maryland sts. Int corridors. **Pets:** Accepted.
SAVE 🛜 ⊠ 🛏 💻 🍴

▼▼▼ **Holiday Inn Express South** �H
(317) 783-5151. **$92-$119.** 5151 S East St 46227. I-465 exit 2B, 0.3 mi s. Int corridors. **Pets:** Large, other species. $50 one-time fee/room. Designated rooms, service with restrictions. 🛜 🛏 💻 ⊇ ⊠

▼▼ **Homestead Studio Suites Hotel-Indianapolis/Northwest** �H 🐾
(317) 334-7829. **$50-$100.** 8520 Northwest Blvd 46278. I-465 exit 23, just e. Int corridors. **Pets:** Other species. $25 daily fee/pet. Service with restrictions. 🛜 🛗 🛏 💻 ⊇

ⒶⒶⒶ ▼▼▼ **Indianapolis Marriott East** �H
(317) 352-1231. **$108-$144.** 7202 E 21st St 46219. I-70 exit 89, 0.3 mi se; 0.5 mi w of jct I-465. Int corridors. **Pets:** Accepted.
SAVE 🛜 ⊠ 🛗 🛏 💻 🍴 ⊇

▼▼▼ **Jameson Inn Indianapolis Castleton** �H
(317) 849-8555. **$80-$100.** 8380 Kelly Ln 46250. I-465 exit 35 (Allisonville Rd), just s. Int corridors. **Pets:** Medium. $15 daily fee/room. Service with restrictions, supervision. 🛜 🛗 🛏 💻

▼▼▼ **Jameson Inn Indianapolis South** �H
(317) 784-7006. **$85-$105.** 4402 E Creekview Dr 46237. I-65 exit 103, just w. Int corridors. **Pets:** Medium. $15 daily fee/room. Service with restrictions, supervision. 🛜 🛏 💻

▼▼▼ **Jameson Inn Indy West** �H
(317) 299-6165. **$85-$105.** 3850 Eagle View Dr 46254. I-465 exit 17, just w on 38th St, then just n. Int corridors. **Pets:** Medium. $15 daily fee/room. Service with restrictions, supervision. 🛜 🛗 🛏 💻 ⊇

▼▼ **La Quinta Inn Indianapolis Airport Executive Drive** �H
(317) 244-8100. **$71-$129.** 2650 Executive Dr 46241. I-465 exit 11 southbound; exit 11B northbound, 0.3 mi e. Int corridors. **Pets:** Medium, other species. Service with restrictions, supervision. 🛜 🛗 🛏 💻

▼▼ **La Quinta Inn Indianapolis Airport Lynhurst** �H
(317) 247-4281. **$62-$125.** 5316 W Southern Ave 46241. I-465 exit 11A, 0.5 mi e on Sam Jones Expwy to Lynhurst Dr. Int corridors. **Pets:** Medium, other species. Service with restrictions, supervision.
🛜 🛏 💻 ⊇

▼▼ **La Quinta Inn Indianapolis East** �H
(317) 359-1021. **$84-$149.** 7304 E 21st St 46219. I-70 exit 89, just s, then just e; 0.5 mi w of jct I-465. Int corridors. **Pets:** Medium, other species. Service with restrictions, supervision. 🛜 🛏 💻 ⊇

ⒶⒶⒶ ▼▼▼ **Magnuson Hotel Castleton Inn** �H
(317) 842-9190. **$59-$150.** 8300 Craig St 46250. I-69 exit 1, 0.5 mi w. Int corridors. **Pets:** Accepted. SAVE 🛜 🛏 💻 ⊇

ⒶⒶⒶ ▼▼▼ ▼▼▼ **Omni Severin Hotel** �H
(317) 634-6664. **$129-$289.** 40 W Jackson Pl 46225. Corner of Illinois and Georgia sts. Int corridors. **Pets:** Accepted.
SAVE 🛜 ⊠ 🛏 💻 🍴 ⊇

▼▼ **Quality Inn & Suites Airport** �H
(317) 381-1000. **$65-$160.** 2631 S Lynhurst Dr 46241. I-465 exit 11A, 0.5 mi e on Sam Jones Expwy to Lynhurst Dr. Int corridors.
Pets: Accepted. 🛜 🛏 💻 ⊇

▼▼ **Ramada Limited** Ⓜ
(317) 297-1848. **$70-$76, 30 day notice.** 3851 Shore Dr 46254. I-465 exit 17, just w on 38th St, then just n. Ext corridors. **Pets:** Other species. $15 daily fee/pet. Service with restrictions, crate. 🛜 🛏 💻 ⊇

▼▼▼ **Residence Inn by Marriott Indianapolis Airport** �H
(317) 244-1500. **$89-$209.** 5224 W Southern Ave 46241. I-465 exit 11A, 0.5 mi e on Sam Jones Expwy exit Lynhurst Dr. Int corridors.
Pets: Accepted. 🛜 ⊠ 🛗 🛏 💻 ⊇ ⊠

▼▼▼ **Residence Inn by Marriott Indianapolis Downtown on the Canal** �H
(317) 822-0840. **$119-$249.** 350 W New York St 46202. Jct Senate Ave. Int corridors. **Pets:** Accepted. 🛜 ⊠ 🛗 🛏 💻 ⊇

Residence Inn by Marriott Northwest-Indianapolis H
(317) 275-6000. **$119-$229.** 6220 Digital Way 46278. I-465 exit 21, just w. Int corridors. **Pets:** Accepted.

Sheraton Hotel City Centre H
(317) 635-2000. **$99-$209.** 31 W Ohio St 46204. Jct Meridian St; just n of Monument Cir. Int corridors. **Pets:** Accepted.

Sheraton Indianapolis at Keystone Crossing H
(317) 846-2700. **$119-$750.** 8787 Keystone Crossing 46240. I-465 exit 33, 0.5 mi s on SR 431, just e on 86th St, then just n. Int corridors.
Pets: Accepted.

Staybridge Suites City Centre H
(317) 536-7500. **Call for rates.** 535 S West St 46225. Just s of South St. Int corridors. **Pets:** Accepted.

Suburban Extended Stay Hotel H
(317) 598-1914. **$54-$69.** 8055 Bash St 46250. I-69 exit 1, just w. Int corridors. **Pets:** Accepted.

TownePlace Suites by Marriott Keystone H
(317) 255-3700. **$89-$149.** 8468 Union Chapel Rd 46240. I-465 exit 33, 0.5 mi s on SR 431, just e on 86th St, then just s. Int corridors.
Pets: Medium, other species. $50 one-time fee/room. Service with restrictions, supervision.

TownePlace Suites by Marriott Park 100 H
(317) 290-8900. **$79-$89.** 5802 W 71st St 46278. I-465 exit 21, 0.3 mi e. Int corridors. **Pets:** $50 one-time fee/room. Designated rooms, service with restrictions, crate.

The Westin Indianapolis H ❀
(317) 262-8100. **$159-$420.** 50 S Capitol Ave 46204. Jct Washington and Maryland sts. Int corridors. **Pets:** Medium. Service with restrictions, supervision.

Wingate Inn-Airport H
(317) 243-8310. **$45-$180.** 5797 Rockville Rd 46224. I-465 exit 13A, just e. Int corridors. **Pets:** Accepted.

Wyndham Indianapolis West H
(317) 248-2481. **$89-$299.** 2544 Executive Dr 46241. I-465 exit 11A southbound; exit 11B northbound, just e on Sam Jones Expwy to Executive Dr. Int corridors. **Pets:** Dogs only. $50 one-time fee/pet. Designated rooms, no service, crate.

LEBANON

Holiday Inn Express H
(765) 483-4100. **$99-$139.** 335 N Mt Zion Rd 46052. I-65 exit 140, just w. Int corridors. **Pets:** Medium. $15 daily fee/pet. Designated rooms, no service, supervision.

Super 8 H
(765) 482-9999. **$54-$148.** 405 N Mt Zion Rd 46052. I-65 exit 140, just w. Int corridors. **Pets:** Accepted.

MARTINSVILLE

Best Western Martinsville Inn H
(765) 342-1842. **Call for rates.** 50 Bill's Blvd 46151. SR 37 to Ohio St, just w. Int corridors. **Pets:** Accepted.

NOBLESVILLE

Quality Inn & Suites H
(317) 770-6772. **Call for rates.** 16025 Prosperity Dr 46060. I-69 exit 5, 4 mi n on SR 37. Int corridors. **Pets:** Accepted.

Super 8 Noblesville H
(317) 776-7088. **$53-$125.** 17070 Dragonfly Dr 46060. Jct SR 37 and 38, 0.5 mi s on SR 37. Int corridors. **Pets:** Accepted.

PLAINFIELD

La Quinta Inn & Suites Indianapolis Airport-Plainfield H
(317) 279-2650. **Call for rates.** 2251 Manchester Dr 46168. I-70 exit 66, 0.4 mi n on SR 267, just e on Perry Rd. Int corridors. **Pets:** Medium, other species. Service with restrictions, supervision.

Staybridge Suites Indianapolis Airport H
(317) 839-2700. **$114-$199.** 6295 Cambridge Way 46168. I-70 exit 66, 0.4 mi n on SR 267, just e on Hadley Rd, then just s. Int corridors.
Pets: Accepted.

END METROPOLITAN AREA

JASPER
Days Inn Jasper H
(812) 482-6000. **$69-$96.** 272 Brucke Strasse 47546. Jct SR 164, just w. Ext/int corridors. **Pets:** Medium. $20 daily fee/pet. Designated rooms, service with restrictions, crate.

JEFFERSONVILLE
Comfort Suites Louisville North H
(812) 282-2100. **$79-$350.** 360 Eastern Blvd 47130. I-65 exit 2 (Eastern Blvd), just e. Int corridors. **Pets:** Accepted.

Sheraton Louisville Riverside Hotel H ❀
(812) 284-6711. **$89-$349.** 700 W Riverside Dr 47130. I-65 exit 0, just w. Int corridors. **Pets:** Other species. Designated rooms, service with restrictions.

TownePlace Suites by Marriott H 🐾
(812) 280-8200. **$109-$425.** 703 N Shore Dr 47130. I-65 exit 0, just w. Int corridors. **Pets:** Medium. $100 one-time fee/room. Service with restrictions, crate.

KENDALLVILLE
Holiday Inn Express Kendallville H
(260) 343-0000. **$65-$155.** 1917 Dowling St 46755. I-69 exit 134, 9.3 mi e on US 6. Int corridors. **Pets:** Medium, other species. $15 daily fee/pet. Designated rooms, service with restrictions, supervision.

KOKOMO
Comfort Inn by Choice Hotels H
(765) 452-5050. **$59-$100.** 522 Essex Dr 46901. Jct US 35, 0.3 mi n on US 31. Int corridors. **Pets:** Accepted.

Fairfield Inn by Marriott H
(765) 453-8822. **$79-$159.** 1717 E Lincoln Rd 46902. US 31, 2 mi s of jct US 35. Int corridors. **Pets:** Accepted.

Hampton Inn & Suites H
(765) 455-2900. **$99-$119.** 2920 S Reed Rd (US Hwy 31) 46902. US 31, 2 mi s of jct US 35. Int corridors. **Pets:** Accepted.

LAFAYETTE

 **Baymont Inn & Suites** H

(765) 449-4808. **$74-$99.** 201 Frontage Rd 47905. I-65 exit 172, just e on SR 26, then just n. Int corridors. **Pets:** Medium, dogs only. $10 daily fee/pet. Service with restrictions, supervision. (SAVE) 🤏 📱

Best Western Lafayette Executive Plaza & Conference Center H

(765) 447-0575. **$110-$160.** 4343 SR 26 E 47905. I-65 exit 172, just w. Int corridors. **Pets:** Accepted.
(SAVE) 🤏 ✖ 🔥 📱 🍽 🏊 ✖

Candlewood Suites H

(765) 807-5735. **Call for rates.** 240 Meijer Dr 47905. I-65 exit 172, just e on SR 26. Int corridors. **Pets:** $75 one-time fee/pet. Service with restrictions, crate. 🤏 ✖ 🔥 📱 🏊

Comfort Inn H

(765) 447-3434. **$79-$179.** 4701 Meijer Ct 47905. I-65 exit 172, just e on SR 26. Int corridors. **Pets:** Medium, other species. $15 one-time fee/pet. Designated rooms, service with restrictions, supervision.
🤏 📱

Days Inn & Suites H

(765) 446-8558. **$62-$135.** 151 Frontage Rd 47905. I-65 exit 172, just e. Int corridors. **Pets:** Accepted. 🤏 📱

Homewood Suites by Hilton H ✿

(765) 448-9700. **$139-$149.** 3939 SR 26 E 47905. I-65 exit 172, 0.8 mi w. Ext/int corridors. **Pets:** Other species. $250 deposit/room, $10 daily fee/pet. 🤏 📱 🏊 ✖

Motel 6 #4291 M

(765) 447-7566. **$50-$119.** 139 Frontage Rd 47905. I-65 exit 172. Ext corridors. **Pets:** Other species. Service with restrictions, supervision.
🤏 📱

Quality Inn & Suites H

(765) 447-9460. **Call for rates.** 4221 SR 26 E 47905. I-65 exit 172, 0.3 mi w. Int corridors. **Pets:** Accepted. 🤏 📱 🏊 ✖

Red Roof Inn-Lafayette #7062 M

(765) 448-4671. **$52-$119.** 4201 SR 26 E 47905. I-65 exit 172, 0.3 mi w. Ext corridors. **Pets:** Large, other species. No service, supervision.
🤏 📱

TownePlace Suites by Marriott H

(765) 446-8668. **$109-$159.** 163 Frontage Rd 47905. I-65 exit 172, just e. Int corridors. **Pets:** $75 one-time fee/room. Service with restrictions, crate. (SAVE) 🤏 ✖ 📱 🏊

LA PORTE

Best Western Plus LaPorte Hotel & Conference Center H

(219) 362-4585. **$109.** 444 Pine Lake Ave 46350. 1.5 mi n on US 35. Int corridors. **Pets:** Accepted. (SAVE) 🤏 📱 🍽 🏊 ✖

LOGANSPORT

Ramada H

(574) 753-6351. **$54-$135.** 3550 E Market St 46947-0813. 2.5 mi e on Business Rt US 24. Int corridors. **Pets:** Small. $15 one-time fee/room. Service with restrictions, crate. 🤏 📱 🍽 🏊

MERRILLVILLE

Candlewood Suites H ✿

(219) 791-9100. **$99-$109.** 8339 Ohio St 46410. I-65 exit 253, 0.3 mi e, just s on Mississippi St, 0.4 mi w on 83rd Ave, then just s. Int corridors. **Pets:** Medium. $75 one-time fee/room. Service with restrictions, crate.
🤏 📱

Extended StayAmerica-Merrillville-US Rte 30 H ✿

(219) 769-4740. **$60-$100.** 1355 E 83rd Ave 46410. I-65 exit 253, 0.3 mi e on US 30, just s on Mississippi St, then 0.4 mi w. Int corridors. **Pets:** Other species. $25 daily fee/pet. Service with restrictions.
🤏 📱

Residence Inn by Marriott Merrillville H

(219) 791-9000. **$120-$215.** 8018 Delaware Pl 46410. I-65 exit 253, 0.3 mi nw. Int corridors. **Pets:** Accepted.
🤏 ✖ 🔥 📱 🏊 ✖

MISHAWAKA

Country Inn & Suites By Carlson H

(574) 271-1700. **Call for rates.** 120 W University Dr 46545. I-80/90 exit 83, just n on SR 331 to SR 23, 0.6 mi sw on SR 23, then just s on Main St. Int corridors. **Pets:** Accepted. 🤏 🔥 📱 🏊

Holiday Inn Express Mishawaka H

(574) 277-2520. **$99-$299.** 420 W University Dr 46545. I-80/90 exit 83, just n on SR 331 to SR 23, 1.6 mi sw to Main St, just s to University Dr, then just w. Int corridors. **Pets:** Accepted. 🤏 🔥 📱 🏊

Residence Inn by Marriott South Bend/Mishawaka H

(574) 271-9283. **$89-$349.** 231 Park Pl 46545. I-80/90 exit 83, just n on SR 331 to SR 23, 1.6 mi sw, then 1.3 mi s on Main St. Int corridors. **Pets:** Accepted. 🤏 ✖ 🔥 📱 🏊 ✖

MONTGOMERY

Gasthof Amish Village Inn H

(812) 486-2600. **Call for rates.** 6747 E Gasthof Village Rd 47558. US 50, 0.8 mi n on First St. Int corridors. **Pets:** Accepted.
🤏 📱 🍽 🏊

MOUNT VERNON

Four Seasons Motel M

(812) 838-4821. **$58-$100.** 70 Hwy 62 W 47620. 1.8 mi w. Ext corridors. **Pets:** Small, other species. $25 one-time fee/pet. Service with restrictions, supervision. 🤏 📱 🏊

MUNCIE

Super 8 H

(765) 286-4333. **$43-$106, 3 day notice.** 3601 W Fox Ridge Ln 47304. I-69 exit 41, 6.3 mi e on SR 332. Int corridors. **Pets:** Small, dogs only. $10 daily fee/pet. Service with restrictions, supervision. 🤏 📱

NORTH VERNON

Comfort Inn H

(812) 352-9999. **$90-$110.** 150 FDR Dr 47265. Jct US 50, 0.6 mi n on SR 7. Int corridors. **Pets:** Accepted. 🤏 📱 🏊

PERU

Best Western Circus City Inn H ✿

(765) 473-8800. **$90-$100.** 2642 Business Rt US 31 S 46970. Just e of jct US 31. Int corridors. **Pets:** Large, other species. $10 daily fee/pet. Supervision. (SAVE) 🤏 📱 🏊

PLYMOUTH

Super 8 H

(574) 936-8856. **$56-$111.** 2160 N Oak Rd 46563. Jct US 30, just s. Int corridors. **Pets:** Accepted. 🤏 📱 🏊

PORTAGE

Comfort Inn H

(219) 763-7177. **$69-$179.** 2300 Willowcreek Rd 46368. I-80/90 exit 23; I-94 exit 19, 1.5 mi s on CR 249. Int corridors. **Pets:** Medium, dogs only. $20 one-time fee/pet. Service with restrictions, supervision.
🤏 📱

▼▼ Super 8 Portage H

(219) 762-8857. **$50-$66.** 6118 Melton Rd 46368. I-94 exit 19, just s on CR 249, then just w on US 20; I-80 exit 23, 1.2 mi n on CR 249, then just w on US 20. Int corridors. **Pets:** Accepted. 🛰️ 🛢️ 💻

PRINCETON

▼▼ Fairfield Inn by Marriott H

(812) 385-4300. **$89-$115.** 2828 Dixon St 47670. Jct US 41 and SR 64, 0.3 mi w. Int corridors. **Pets:** Small. $25 one-time fee/room. Service with restrictions, supervision. 🛰️ ✖️ ♿ 🛢️ 💻 🏊

RICHMOND

▲▲ ▼▼ Best Western Classic Inn H ❀

(765) 939-9500. **$84-$119.** 533 W Eaton Pike 47374. I-70 exit 156A, just s. Int corridors. **Pets:** Medium. $10 daily fee/pet. Designated rooms, supervision. SAVE 🛰️ 🛢️ 💻 🏊

▼▼ Days Inn M

(765) 966-4900. **$46-$76.** 5775 National Rd E 47374. I-70 exit 156A, just s. Ext corridors. **Pets:** Other species. $10 daily fee/pet. Designated rooms, service with restrictions. 🛰️ 🛢️ 💻

▲▲ ▼▼ Knights Inn M

(765) 966-1505. **$45-$58.** 3020 E Main St 47374. I-70 exit 156A, 2 mi w. Ext corridors. **Pets:** Small. $10 daily fee/pet. Service with restrictions, supervision. SAVE 🛰️ 🛢️ 💻

▼▼▼ Quality Inn Richmond Conference Center H ❀

(765) 966-7511. **$89-$225, 3 day notice.** 5501 National Rd E 47374. I-70 exit 156A, 0.3 mi w. Int corridors. **Pets:** $20 one-time fee/room. Designated rooms, service with restrictions, crate.

🛰️ ♿ 🛢️ 💻 🏊 ✖️

RUSHVILLE

▼▼▼ Comfort Inn H

(765) 932-2999. **Call for rates.** 320 Conrad Harcourt Way 46173. Just e of SR 3. Int corridors. **Pets:** Small, dogs only. $20 daily fee/room. Service with restrictions, supervision. 🛰️ 🛢️ 💻

SCOTTSBURG

▼▼▼ Hampton Inn & Suites H

(812) 752-1999. **$80-$129.** 1535 W McClain Ave 47170. I-65 exit 29, just w. Int corridors. **Pets:** Accepted. 🛰️ 🛢️ 💻 🏊

SELLERSBURG

▼▼ Home Lodge H

(812) 246-6332. **Call for rates.** 363 Triangle Dr 47172. I-65 exit 9, just e. Int corridors. **Pets:** Accepted. 🛰️ 🛢️ 💻

▼▼ Ramada H

(812) 246-3131. **$59-$359.** 360 Triangle Dr 47172. I-65 exit 9, just e. Int corridors. **Pets:** Accepted. 🛰️ ✖️ 🛢️ 💻 🏊

SOUTH BEND

▼▼▼ Comfort Suites University Area H ❀

(574) 272-1500. **$79-$354.** 52939 SR 933 N 46637. I-80/90 exit 77, just e to Business Rt US 31/SR 933, then 1 mi n. Int corridors. **Pets:** Large, other species. $20 one-time fee/room. Designated rooms, service with restrictions, crate. 🛰️ ✖️ 🛢️ 💻 🏊 ✖️

▲▲ ▼▼▼ Cushing Manor Inn BB

(574) 288-1990. **$115-$155, 14 day notice.** 508 W Washington St 46601. 0.4 mi w of jct SR 933 and Business Rt US 31. Int corridors. **Pets:** Accepted. SAVE 🛰️ ✖️

▼▼▼▼ Oliver Inn Bed & Breakfast BB

(574) 232-4545. **$135-$339, 14 day notice.** 630 W Washington St 46601. 0.3 mi w of SR 933 and Business Rt US 31. Int corridors. **Pets:** $25 daily fee/room. Designated rooms, service with restrictions, supervision. 🛰️ ✖️ 🛢️ 💻

▲▲ ▼▼▼▼ Sleep Inn H ❀

(574) 232-3200. **$70-$250.** 4134 Lincolnway W 46628. I-80/90 exit 72, 1.5 mi s on US 31 to South Bend Regional Airport exit, then 2 mi e. Int corridors. **Pets:** Medium. $10 daily fee/pet. Designated rooms, service with restrictions, crate. SAVE 🛰️ 🛢️ 💻

▼▼▼ Staybridge Suites South Bend-University Area H

(574) 968-7440. **Call for rates.** 52860 SR 933 N 46637. I-80/90 exit 77, 1 mi n. Int corridors. **Pets:** Medium. $75 one-time fee/room. Designated rooms, service with restrictions. 🛰️ ♿ 🛢️ 💻 🏊

▼▼ Suburban Extended Stay Hotel H

(574) 968-4737. **$54-$129.** 52825 SR 933 N 46637. I-80/90 exit 77, 1 mi n. Int corridors. **Pets:** Accepted. 🛰️ ♿ 🛢️ 💻 🏊

▲▲ ▼▼▼ Super 8 - South Bend H

(574) 243-0200. **$54-$198, 30 day notice.** 4124 Ameritech Dr 46628. I-80/90 exit 72, 0.7 mi n on US 31, just e on Cleveland Rd, then just s. Int corridors. **Pets:** Medium. $10 daily fee/pet. Designated rooms, service with restrictions, supervision. SAVE 🛰️ 🛢️ 💻 🏊

▼▼▼ Waterford Estates Lodge H

(574) 272-5220. **$109-$119.** 52890 SR 933 N 46637. I-80/90 exit 77, 1 mi n. Int corridors. **Pets:** Other species. $30 one-time fee/room. Service with restrictions, supervision. 🛰️ ✖️ ♿ 🛢️ 💻 🍴 🏊

TAYLORSVILLE

▼▼ Red Roof Inn M

(812) 526-9747. **$65-$95.** 10330 US 31 47280. I-65 exit 76A, just s. Ext corridors. **Pets:** Large, other species. No service, supervision.

🛰️ 🛢️ 💻 🏊

TELL CITY

▼▼▼ Holiday Inn Express H

(812) 547-0800. **$97-$140.** 310 Orchard Hill Dr 47586. Just off SR 66, 1.7 mi se of jct SR 37. Int corridors. **Pets:** Accepted.

🛰️ ♿ 🛢️ 💻 🏊

▼▼ Ramada Limited H

(812) 547-3234. **$57-$107.** 235 Orchard Hill Dr 47586. Just off SR 66, 1.7 mi se of jct SR 37. Int corridors. **Pets:** Small, dogs only. $10 daily fee/pet. Designated rooms, service with restrictions, supervision.

🛰️ 🛢️ 💻 🏊

TERRE HAUTE

▼▼▼ Candlewood Suites H

(812) 234-3400. **Call for rates.** 721 Wabash Ave 47807. I-70 exit 7 (US 41/150), 2.2 mi n, 0.4 mi e, then just s. Int corridors. **Pets:** Accepted.

🛰️ ♿ 🛢️ 💻

▲▲ ▼▼▼ Days Inn & Suites M

(812) 232-8006. **$45-$125.** 101 E Margaret Ave 47802. I-70 exit 7 (US 41/150), just nw. Ext corridors. **Pets:** Medium, other species. $5 daily fee/pet. Service with restrictions, supervision. SAVE 🛰️ 🛢️ 💻 ✖️

▼▼▼ Drury Inn-Terre Haute H

(812) 238-1206. **$100-$174.** 3040 Hwy 41 S 47802. I-70 exit 7 (US 41/150), just n. Int corridors. **Pets:** Accepted.

🛰️ ♿ 🛢️ 💻 🏊 ✖️

▼▼▼ Holiday Inn H ❀

(812) 232-6081. **$89-$109.** 3300 US 41 S 47802. I-70 exit 7 (US 41/150), just s. Int corridors. **Pets:** Small. $25 one-time fee/room. Service with restrictions, crate. 🛰️ 🛢️ 💻 🍴 🏊 ✖️

▼▼ Pear Tree Inn by Drury-Terre Haute H

(812) 234-4268. **$65-$129.** 3050 US 41 S 47802. I-70 exit 7 (US 41/150), just n. Int corridors. **Pets:** Accepted. 🛰️ 🛢️ 💻

▼▼ Super 8-Terre Haute H

(812) 232-4890. **$48-$68.** 3089 S 1st St 47802. I-70 exit 7 (US 41/150), just nw. Int corridors. **Pets:** Accepted. 🛰️ 🛢️

VALPARAISO

▼▼▼▼ Courtyard by Marriott Valparaiso [H]

(219) 465-1700. **$85-$120.** 2301 E Morthland Dr 46383. US 30, just w of jct SR 49. Int corridors. **Pets:** Dogs only. $75 one-time fee/room. No service. 🛜 ✕ 📦 📖 🏊

(AAA) ▼▼▼▼ The Inn at Aberdeen [BB]

(219) 465-3753. **$106-$201.** 3158 S SR 2 46385. Jct US 30, 2.7 mi w, just n. Int corridors. **Pets:** $25 daily fee/room. Designated rooms, service with restrictions, supervision. [SAVE] 🛜 ✕ 📦 📖

WARREN

▼▼▼ Comfort Inn Warren [H]

(260) 375-4800. **Call for rates.** 7275 S 75 E 46792. I-69 exit 78, just n on SR 5. Int corridors. **Pets:** Accepted. 🛜 ♿ 📦 📖 🏊 ✕

WARSAW

▼▼▼▼ Holiday Inn Express Hotel & Suites-Warsaw [H]

(574) 268-1600. **$109-$149.** 3825 Lake City Hwy 46580. Jct US 30 and SR 15, 4 mi e on US 30. Int corridors. **Pets:** Small. $15 daily fee/pet. Designated rooms, service with restrictions. 🛜 ✕ 📦 📖 🏊

▼▼▼ Ramada Plaza of Warsaw [H]

(574) 269-2323. **$65-$159.** 2519 E Center St 46580. 2.8 mi e of SR 15 on US 30, just s. Int corridors. **Pets:** Accepted.
🛜 ✕ 📦 📖 🍴 🏊 ✕

WASHINGTON

▼▼▼ Baymont Inn & Suites Washington [H]

(812) 254-7000. **$77-$104.** 7 Cumberland Dr 47501. Just ne of jct US 50 and SR 257. Int corridors. **Pets:** Accepted.
🛜 ✕ 📦 📖 🏊 ✕

▼▼▼ Holiday Inn Express [H]

(812) 254-6666. **Call for rates.** 1808 E National Hwy 47501. On US 50 business route, 0.4 mi e of SR 257. Int corridors. **Pets:** Accepted.
🛜 📦 📖 🏊

WEST BADEN SPRINGS

(AAA) ▼▼▼▼▼ West Baden Springs Hotel [H]

(812) 936-1902. **$180-$325.** 8538 W Baden Ave 47469. On SR 56. Int corridors. **Pets:** Accepted.
[SAVE] 🛜 ✕ ♿ 📦 📖 🍴 🏊 ✕

IOWA

CITY INDEX

ADAIR

(AAA) ▼ Adair Budget Inn [M]

(641) 742-5553. **$40-$54.** 100 S 5th St 50002. I-80 exit 76, just n. Ext corridors. **Pets:** $20 deposit/room. Designated rooms, service with restrictions, supervision. [SAVE] 🛜 📦

ALBIA

▼▼ ▼▼ Indian Hills Inn [H] 🐾

(641) 932-7181. **$68-$149.** 100 Hwy 34 E 52531. Just e of jct US 34 and SR 5. Ext/int corridors. **Pets:** Medium. $10 daily fee/pet. Designated rooms, service with restrictions, supervision. 🛜 📦 📖 🍴 🏊

ALGONA

▼▼ ▼▼ AmericInn Lodge & Suites of Algona [H]

(515) 295-3333. **$91-$156.** 600 Hwy 18 W 50511. Just w of jct US 169/18. Int corridors. **Pets:** Accepted. 🛜 ✕ ♿ 📦 📖 🏊

ALTOONA

▼▼ ▼▼ Settle Inn & Suites-Altoona [H]

(515) 967-7888. **Call for rates.** 2101 Adventureland Dr 50009. I-80 exit 142A, just se. Int corridors. **Pets:** Accepted. 🛜 📦 📖 🏊

AMES

(AAA) ▼▼▼▼ Best Western Plus University Park Inn & Suites [H]

(515) 296-2500. **$90-$150.** 2500 University Blvd 50010. I-35 exit 111B, 3.5 mi w on US 30 exit 146 (University Blvd), then just s. Int corridors. **Pets:** Medium. $10 one-time fee/room. Service with restrictions, supervision. [SAVE] 🛜 📦 📖 🏊

(AAA) ▼▼▼ Comfort Inn-Ames [H]

(515) 232-0689. **$80-$125.** 1605 S Dayton Pl 50010. I-35 exit 111B, just w on US 30 exit 150. Int corridors. **Pets:** Accepted.
[SAVE] 🛜 📦 📖 🏊

▼▼▼ Gateway Hotel & Conference Center [H]

(515) 292-8600. **$69-$199.** 2100 Green Hills Dr 50014. I-35 exit 111B, 3.5 mi w on US 30 exit 146 (University Blvd). Int corridors.
Pets: Accepted. 🛜 ✕ ♿ 📦 📖 🍴 🏊 ✕

(AAA) ▼▼▼ GrandStay Residential Suites Hotel [H]

(515) 232-8363. **Call for rates.** 1606 S Kellogg Ave 50010. I-35 exit 111B, 1 mi w, then just nw on Duff Ave to Kellogg Ave. Int corridors.
Pets: Accepted. [SAVE] 🛜 ✕ ♿ 📦 📖 🏊 ✕

▼▼▼ Holiday Inn Ames Conference Center-ISU [H]

(515) 268-8808. **$79-$299.** 2609 University Blvd 50010. I-35 exit 111B, 3.5 mi w on US 30 exit 146 (University Blvd), then just s. Int corridors.
Pets: Accepted. 🛜 ♿ 📦 📖 🍴 🏊

▼▼ Microtel Inn & Suites 🅷 ❀
(515) 233-4444. **$49-$94.** 2216 SE 16th St 50010. I-35 exit 111B, just w on US 30 exit 150. Int corridors. **Pets:** Other species. $10 daily fee/pet. Designated rooms, service with restrictions, crate. 🛜 📶 🔋 🔲

▼▼▼ Quality Inn & Suites Starlite Village Conference Center 🅷
(515) 232-9260. **Call for rates.** 2601 E 13th St 50010. I-35 exit 113 (13th St), 0.5 mi w. Int corridors. **Pets:** Accepted.
🛜 📶 🔋 🔲 🍴 🏊

ANAMOSA
▼▼▼ AmericInn Lodge & Suites 🅷
(319) 462-4119. **$90-$165.** 101 Harley Ave 52205. US 151 exit 54, 1 mi n. Int corridors. **Pets:** Accepted. 🛜 ✖ 📶 🔋 🔲 🏊

▼▼ Super 8-Anamosa 🅷
(319) 462-3888. **$45-$72.** 100 Grant Wood Dr 52205. US 151 exit 54, just e on SR 64. Int corridors. **Pets:** Accepted. 🛜 🔋 🔲

ANKENY
🅰🅰🅰 ▼▼▼ Comfort Inn 🅷
(515) 963-1100. **$89-$169.** 2602 SE Creekview Dr 50021. I-35 exit 90, just ne. Int corridors. **Pets:** Accepted. 🅢🅐🅥🅔 🛜 🔋 🔲 🏊

🅰🅰🅰 ▼▼ Days Inn 🄼
(515) 965-1995. **$59-$89.** 105 NE Delaware Ave 50021. I-35 exit 92, just w. Int corridors. **Pets:** Dogs only. No service, supervision.
🅢🅐🅥🅔 🛜 🔋 🔲

ARNOLDS PARK
🅰🅰🅰 ▼▼▼▼ Bridges Bay Resort 🄲🄾
(712) 332-2202. **$79-$750.** 630 Linden Dr 51331. Just e of US 71. Int corridors. **Pets:** Medium. Service with restrictions, supervision.
🅢🅐🅥🅔 🛜 ✖ 🔋 🔲 🍴 🏊 ✖

▼▼ Fillenwarth Beach 🄼
(712) 332-5646. **$114-$1680 (no credit cards), 60 day notice.** 87 Lake Shore Dr 51331. Just w of US 71; on West Lake Okoboji. Ext corridors. **Pets:** Other species. Service with restrictions.
🛜 ✖ 🔋 🔲 🏊 ✖

ATLANTIC
▼▼ Americas Best Value Inn 🅷
(712) 243-4067. **$60-$90.** 64968 Boston Rd 50022. I-80 exit 60 (US 71), 0.3 mi s. Int corridors. **Pets:** Large, other species. Designated rooms, service with restrictions, supervision. 🛜 🔋 🔲 🏊

▼▼ Super 8 🅷
(712) 243-4723. **$63-$89.** 1902 E 7th St 50022. I-80 exit 60 (US 71), 6 mi s, then 2 mi w; east side of town. Int corridors. **Pets:** Other species. $20 deposit/room, $10 one-time fee/room. Designated rooms, service with restrictions, crate. 🛜 ✖ 📶 🔋 🔲 🏊

BURLINGTON
🅰🅰🅰 ▼▼▼ Comfort Suites Hotel & Conference Center 🅷
(319) 753-1300. **$90-$116.** 1780 Stonegate Center Dr 52601. On US 61, 2 mi s of US 34. Int corridors. **Pets:** Large. $15 daily fee/pet. Designated rooms, service with restrictions, crate.
🅢🅐🅥🅔 🛜 ✖ 📶 🔋 🔲 🍴 🏊 ✖

🅰🅰🅰 ▼▼▼ Quality Inn 🅷
(319) 753-0000. **Call for rates.** 3051 Kirkwood St 52601. Jct US 61 and 34, just n. Int corridors. **Pets:** Medium. $10 daily fee/pet. Service with restrictions, supervision. 🅢🅐🅥🅔 🛜 🔋 🔲 🏊

▼▼ Super 8 🅷
(319) 752-9806. **$49-$55.** 3001 Kirkwood St 52601. Jct US 61 and 34, just n. Int corridors. **Pets:** Accepted. 🛜 🔋 🔲

CARTER LAKE
🅰🅰🅰 ▼▼▼▼ Holiday Inn Express & Suites-Omaha Airport 🅷
(402) 505-4900. **Call for rates.** 2510 Abbott Plaza 51510. I-480 W exit 4 to 10th St, 2 mi n, follow Eppley Airfield signs. Int corridors.
Pets: Accepted. 🅢🅐🅥🅔 🛜 ✖ 📶 🔋 🔲 🏊

🅰🅰🅰 ▼▼▼▼ La Quinta Inn & Suites Omaha Airport - Carter Lake 🅷
(712) 347-6595. **$84-$189.** 1201 Ave H 51510. I-480 W exit 4 to 10th St, 2 mi n, follow Eppley Airfield signs. Int corridors. **Pets:** Medium, other species. Service with restrictions, supervision.
🅢🅐🅥🅔 🛜 📶 🔋 🔲 🏊

▼▼ Super 8 🅷
(712) 347-5588. **$67-$99.** 3000 Airport Dr 51510. I-480 W exit 4 to 10th St, 2.3 mi n, follow Eppley Airfield signs. Int corridors. **Pets:** Accepted.
🛜 ✖ 🔋 🔲 🏊

CEDAR FALLS
▼▼▼ Comfort Suites 🅷
(319) 273-9999. **$90-$140.** 7402 Nordic Dr 50613. US 20 exit 225, just nw. Int corridors. **Pets:** Accepted. 🛜 ✖ 📶 🔋 🔲 🏊

🅰🅰🅰 ▼▼ University Inn 🅷
(319) 277-1412. **$50-$112.** 4711 University Ave 50613. 1.6 mi e of jct SR 58. Ext/int corridors. **Pets:** Large, dogs only. $50 deposit/pet. Designated rooms, service with restrictions, supervision. 🅢🅐🅥🅔 🛜 🔋 🔲

CEDAR RAPIDS
▼▼ AmericInn Lodge & Suites of Cedar Rapids 🅷
(319) 632-1800. **$90-$196.** 8910 6th St SW 52404. I-380 exit 13, just nw. Int corridors. **Pets:** Medium. $25 daily fee/pet. Designated rooms, service with restrictions, supervision. 🛜 📶 🔋 🔲 🏊 ✖

🅰🅰🅰 ▼▼▼ Baymont Inn & Suites 🅷
(319) 378-8000. **$58-$95.** 1220 Park Pl NE 52402. I-380 exit 24A (SR 100/Collins Rd), 0.9 mi e, then just n. Int corridors. **Pets:** $15 one-time fee/pet. Designated rooms, service with restrictions.
🅢🅐🅥🅔 🛜 ✖ 📶 🔋 🔲 🏊

🅰🅰🅰 ▼▼▼ Best Western Cooper's Mill Hotel 🅷
(319) 366-5323. **$115-$140.** 100 F Ave NW 52405. I-380 exit 19C northbound, s at end of exit, make immediate U-turn and go under I-380; exit 20A southbound, cross river, just n on 1st St NW. Int corridors.
Pets: Large. $10 daily fee/pet. Service with restrictions, supervision.
🅢🅐🅥🅔 🛜 🔋 🔲 🍴 🏊 ✖

🅰🅰🅰 ▼▼▼▼ Best Western Plus Longbranch Hotel & Convention Center 🅷 ❀
(319) 377-6386. **$120-$140.** 90 Twixt Town Rd NE 52402. I-380 exit 24A (SR 100/Collins Rd), 2.5 mi e, then just n. Int corridors. **Pets:** Medium, other species. $10 daily fee/pet. Designated rooms, service with restrictions. 🅢🅐🅥🅔 🛜 🔋 🔲 🍴 🏊 ✖

▼▼ Clarion Hotel & Convention Center 🅷
(319) 366-8671. **$85-$175.** 525 33rd Ave SW 52404. I-380 exit 17 (33rd Ave SW), just w. Int corridors. **Pets:** Accepted.
🛜 🔋 🔲 🍴 🏊 ✖

▼▼ Collins Inn & Suites 🅷
(319) 378-8888. **$76-$126.** 2025 Werner Ave NE 52402. I-380 exit 24A (SR 100/Collins Rd), just se. Int corridors. **Pets:** Small. $10 daily fee/pet. Service with restrictions, crate. 🛜 🔋 🔲

▼▼ Comfort Inn by Choice Hotels North 🅷
(319) 393-8247. **$75-$110.** 5055 Rockwell Dr NE 52402. I-380 exit 24A (SR 100/Collins Rd), 1 mi e. Int corridors. **Pets:** Accepted.
🛜 🔋 🔲

▼▼ Comfort Inn by Choice Hotels South 🅷
(319) 363-7934. **$69-$169.** 390 33rd Ave SW 52404. I-380 exit 17 (33rd Ave SW), just w. Int corridors. **Pets:** Accepted. 🛜 🔋 🔲

△△△ ▼▼ **Country Inn & Suites By Carlson, Cedar Rapids Airport** 🅷
(319) 363-3789. **$89-$179.** 9100 Atlantic Dr SW 52405. I-380 exit 13, just w. Int corridors. **Pets:** Small. $25 one-time fee/room, $10 daily fee/pet. Designated rooms, service with restrictions, supervision.
SAVE 🛜 🅼 🛏 💻 🏊

▼▼▼ **Homewood Suites** 🅷
(319) 378-1140. **$109-$199.** 1140 Park Pl NE 52402. I-380 exit 24A (SR 100/Collins Rd) to Collins Rd, n on Council St, then just e. Int corridors. **Pets:** Accepted. 🛜 🅼 🛏 💻 🏊

▼▼▼ **Howard Johnson** 🅼
(319) 366-2475. **$50-$67.** 616 33rd Ave SW 52404. I-380 exit 17 (33rd Ave SW), 0.3 mi w. Int corridors. **Pets:** Accepted. 🛜 🛏 💻

▼▼▼ **MainStay Suites** 🅷
(319) 363-7829. **$69-$250.** 5145 Rockwell Dr NE 52402. I-380 exit 24A (SR 100/Collins Rd), 1 mi e, then just n. Int corridors. **Pets:** Small. $25 daily fee/pet. Designated rooms, service with restrictions, crate.
🛜 🅼 🛏 💻 🏊

▼▼▼ **Red Roof Inn Cedar Rapids** 🅷
(319) 364-2000. **$54-$89.** 3243 South Ridge Dr SW 52404. I-380 exit 17 (33rd Ave SW), just nw. Ext/int corridors. **Pets:** Large, other species. No service, supervision. 🛜 🅼 🏊

▼▼▼ **Residence Inn by Marriott** 🅷
(319) 395-0111. **$105-$158.** 1900 Dodge Rd NE 52402. I-380 exit 24A (SR 100/Collins Rd), just e. Int corridors. **Pets:** Accepted.
🛜 ❌ 🅼 🛏 💻 🏊 ❌

▼▼▼ **Super 8** 🅷
(319) 362-6002. **$45-$90, 3 day notice.** 720 33rd Ave SW 52404. I-380 exit 17 (33rd Ave SW), 0.4 mi w. Int corridors. **Pets:** Accepted.
🛜 🛏 💻

CHARLES CITY
▼▼▼ **Sleep Inn & Suites** 🅷
(641) 257-6700. **Call for rates.** 1416 S Grand Ave 50616. US 218/18 exit 218, 0.7 mi n on US 218 business route; south side of town. Int corridors. **Pets:** Accepted. 🛜 🅼 🛏 💻 🏊

▼▼▼ **Super 8 - Charles City** 🅷
(641) 228-2888. **$47-$90.** 1411 S Grand Ave 50616. US 218/18 exit 218, 0.8 mi n on US 218 business route; south side of town. Int corridors. **Pets:** Medium. $10 daily fee/pet. Designated rooms, service with restrictions, supervision. 🛜 🅼 🛏 💻

CHEROKEE
△△△ ▼▼ **Best Western La Grande Hacienda** 🅷
(712) 225-5701. **$85-$90, 3 day notice.** 1401 N 2nd St 51012. Just s of jct SR 3 and US 59 (N 2nd St). Int corridors. **Pets:** Medium, other species. $50 deposit/room. Service with restrictions, supervision.
SAVE 🛜 ❌ 🅼 💻 🍴 🏊

CLARINDA
▼▼ **Clarinda Super 8** 🅷
(712) 542-6333. **$53-$57.** 1203 S 12th St 51632. Jct US 71 and SR 2, just e. Int corridors. **Pets:** Accepted. 🛜 🅼 🛏 💻 🏊

CLEAR LAKE
▼▼ **AmericInn Lodge & Suites of Clear Lake** 🅷
(641) 357-8954. **$91-$111.** 1406 N 25th St 50428. I-35 exit 194 (US 18), just nw. Int corridors. **Pets:** Accepted. 🛜 🛏 💻 🏊

△△△ ▼▼ **Best Western Holiday Lodge** 🅷 🐾
(641) 357-5253. **$89-$119.** 2023 7th Ave N 50428. I-35 exit 194 (US 18), 0.3 mi w. Ext/int corridors. **Pets:** $25 one-time fee/room, $10 daily fee/room. Service with restrictions, supervision.
SAVE 🛜 🅼 🛏 💻 🍴 🏊

▼▼ **Budget Inn** 🅼
(641) 357-8700. **Call for rates.** 1306 N 25th St 50428. I-35 exit 194 (US 18), just nw. Int corridors. **Pets:** Accepted. 🛜 🛏 🏊

▼▼ **Lake Country Inn** 🅼
(641) 357-2184. **$55-$75.** 518 US 18 50428. I-35 exit 194 (US 18), 1.9 mi w. Ext corridors. **Pets:** Accepted. 🛜 🛏

▼▼ **Microtel Inn** 🅷
(641) 357-0966. **$56-$100.** 1305 N 25th St 50428. I-35 exit 194 (US 18), just nw. Int corridors. **Pets:** Accepted. 🛜 🅼 🛏 💻

CLINTON
△△△ ▼▼ **Country Inn & Suites By Carlson** 🅷
(563) 244-9922. **$89-$149.** 2224 Lincoln Way 52732. On US 30, just e of jct US 30 and 67. Int corridors. **Pets:** $10 daily fee/pet. Service with restrictions, supervision. SAVE 🛜 🅼 🛏 💻 🏊

▼▼ **Oak Tree Inn** 🅷
(563) 243-1000. **$72-$79.** 2300 Valley West Ct 52732. Just n of jct US 30 and 67; west side of town. Int corridors. **Pets:** Accepted.
🛜 ❌ 🅼 🛏 💻

CLIVE
△△△ ▼▼▼ **Best Western Plus Des Moines West Inn & Suites** 🅷 ✿
(515) 221-2345. **$85-$110.** 1450 NW 118th St 50325. I-80/35 exit 124 (University Ave), just nw. Int corridors. **Pets:** Dogs only. $15 daily fee/pet. Service with restrictions, supervision. SAVE 🛜 🅼 🛏 💻 🏊

▼▼▼ **Chase Suites Hotel by Woodfin** 🅷
(515) 223-7700. **$109-$159.** 11428 Forest Ave 50325. I-80/35 exit 124 (University Ave), just ne. Ext corridors. **Pets:** Accepted.
🛜 ❌ 🅼 🛏 💻 🏊

▼▼ **La Quinta Inn & Suites Des Moines West Clive** 🅷
(515) 221-9200. **$74-$133.** 1390 NW 118th St 50325. I-80/35 exit 124 (University Ave). Int corridors. **Pets:** Medium, other species. Service with restrictions, supervision. 🛜 🅼 🛏 💻 🏊

▼▼ **Super 8** 🅷
(515) 226-0414. **Call for rates.** 11414 Forest Ave 50325. I-80/35 exit 124 (University Ave), just e. Int corridors. **Pets:** Accepted. 🛜 🛏 💻

COLFAX
▼▼ **Colfax Inn & Suites** 🅷 ✿
(515) 674-4455. **$75-$169.** 1402 N Walnut St 50054. I-80 exit 155 (SR 117), just ne. Int corridors. **Pets:** Medium. $15 daily fee/room. Service with restrictions, supervision. 🛜 🅼 🛏 💻 🏊

△△△ ▼▼ **Microtel Inn & Suites** 🅷
(515) 674-0600. **$53-$116.** 11000 Federal Ave 50054. I-80 exit 155 (SR 117). Int corridors. **Pets:** Other species. $10 daily fee/room. Service with restrictions, crate. SAVE 🛜 🅼 🛏 🏊

CORALVILLE
△△△ ▼▼ **Baymont Inn & Suites** 🅷
(319) 337-9797. **$72-$190.** 200 6th St 52241. I-80 exit 242, just s on 1st Ave, then just w. Int corridors. **Pets:** Accepted. SAVE 🛜 🛏 💻 🏊

△△△ ▼▼ **Best Western Cantebury Inn & Suites** 🅷
(319) 351-0400. **$85-$140.** 704 1st Ave 52241. I-80 exit 242, just s. Int corridors. **Pets:** Medium. $20 daily fee/pet. Designated rooms, service with restrictions. SAVE 🛜 🛏 💻 🍴 🏊 ❌

▼▼ **Comfort Inn by Choice Hotels** 🅷
(319) 351-8144. **$75-$129.** 209 W 9th St 52241. I-80 exit 242, just s. Int corridors. **Pets:** Accepted. 🛜 🅼 🛏 💻 🏊

Fairfield Inn by Marriott H
(319) 337-8382. **$130-$300.** 214 W 9th St 52241. I-80 exit 242, just s.
Int corridors. **Pets:** $25 one-time fee/room. Service with restrictions,
supervision.

Holiday Inn H
(319) 351-5049. **$89-$269.** 1220 1st Ave 52241. I-80 exit 242, just n. Int
corridors. **Pets:** $20 one-time fee/room. Designated rooms, service with
restrictions, supervision.

Super 8 H
(319) 337-8388. **$59-$117.** 611 1st Ave 52241. I-80 exit 242, 0.4 mi s.
Int corridors. **Pets:** Other species. $10 one-time fee/room. Service with
restrictions.

COUNCIL BLUFFS

AmericInn H
(712) 322-8400. **$80-$150.** 1000 Woodbury Ave 51503. I-80 exit 5 (Madison Ave). Int corridors. **Pets:** Large, dogs only. $5 daily fee/pet. Designated rooms, service with restrictions, supervision.

Best Western Crossroads of the Bluffs H
(712) 322-3150. **Call for rates.** 2216 27th Ave 51501. I-29/80 exit 1B
(24th St), just ne. Int corridors. **Pets:** Accepted.

Comfort Suites H
(712) 323-9760. **$90-$210.** 1801 S 35th St 51503. I-29 exit 52, just e. Int
corridors. **Pets:** Accepted.

Days Inn H
(712) 366-9699. **$50-$119.** 3208 S 7th St 51501. I-29/80 exit 3 (US 92),
just sw. Int corridors. **Pets:** Accepted.

Days Inn H
(712) 323-2200. **$45-$162.** 3619 9th Ave 51501. I-29 exit 53A (9th Ave).
Int corridors. **Pets:** Accepted.

Harrah's Casino & Hotel H
(712) 329-6000. **Call for rates.** 1 Harrahs Blvd 51501. I-29 exit 53A (9th
Ave), just w. Int corridors. **Pets:** Accepted.

Microtel Inn & Suites - Council Bluffs H
(712) 256-2900. **$77-$189.** 2141 S 35th St 51501. I-29/80 exit 1B (24th
St), 0.4 mi n, then 0.8 mi w on 23rd Ave. Int corridors. **Pets:** Other species. $25 one-time fee/room. Service with restrictions, crate.

Super 8 H
(712) 322-2888. **$56-$78.** 2712 S 24th St 51501. I-29/80 exit 1B (24th
St), just nw. Int corridors. **Pets:** Service with restrictions, supervision.

Western Inn H
(712) 322-4499. **$59-$145.** 1842 Madison Ave 51503. I-80 exit 5 (Madison Ave), just s. Int corridors. **Pets:** Small, other species. $10 daily fee/
pet.

CRESCO

Cresco Motel M
(563) 547-2240. **$53-$81.** 620 2nd Ave SE (SR 9) 52136. East side of
town. Ext corridors. **Pets:** Dogs only. Service with restrictions, supervision.

CRESTON

Super 8-Creston H
(641) 782-6541. **$49-$63.** 804 W Taylor St 50801. Jct US 34 and SR 25,
on US 34. Int corridors. **Pets:** Accepted.

DECORAH

Quality Inn & Suites H
(563) 382-2269. **$84-$169.** 705 Commerce Dr 52101. Jct US 52, 1.5 mi
e on SR 9. Int corridors. **Pets:** Small, dogs only. $25 daily fee/pet. Designated rooms, service with restrictions, supervision.

DENISON

Denison Super 8 H
(712) 263-5081. **$57-$65.** 502 Boyer Valley Rd 51442. Jct US 30/59 and
SR 141, 0.3 mi sw. Int corridors. **Pets:** Accepted.

DES MOINES

Comfort Inn H
(515) 266-6800. **Call for rates.** 4950 NE 14th St 50313. I-80 exit 136
(US 69). Int corridors. **Pets:** Small, dogs only. $10 daily fee/room. Service
with restrictions, supervision.

Comfort Inn by Choice Hotels H
(515) 287-3434. **$69-$129.** 5231 Fleur Dr 50321. Opposite the airport. Int
corridors. **Pets:** Large. $10 daily fee/pet. Service with restrictions, crate.

Des Moines Marriott Downtown H
(515) 245-5500. **$116-$299.** 700 Grand Ave 50309. Downtown. Int corridors. **Pets:** Other species. $75 one-time fee/room. Service with restrictions.

Econo Lodge H
(515) 278-8858. **Call for rates.** 4755 Merle Hay Rd 50322. I-80/35 exit
131 (Merle Hay Rd), just s. Int corridors. **Pets:** $10 daily fee/room. Service with restrictions, supervision.

Holiday Inn Airport & Conference Center H
(515) 287-2400. **$125-$185.** 6111 Fleur Dr 50321. SR 5 exit 97, 1 mi n;
opposite the airport. Int corridors. **Pets:** Dogs only. $25 one-time fee/
room. Designated rooms, service with restrictions, supervision.

**Best Western Plus Marquis Des Moines
Airport Hotel** H
(515) 287-6464. **$99-$130.** 1810 Army Post Rd 50315. SR 5 exit 97, 1
mi n, then just e; just e of airport. Int corridors. **Pets:** Accepted.

Quality Inn & Suites Event Center H
(515) 282-5251. **Call for rates.** 929 3rd St 50309. I-235 exit 3rd St;
downtown. Int corridors. **Pets:** Accepted.

DE WITT

De Witt Super 8 H
(563) 659-8888. **$46-$81.** 918 Westwood Dr 52742. Just e of jct US 30
and 61, on US 30. Int corridors. **Pets:** Accepted.

DUBUQUE

**Best Western Plus Dubuque Hotel &
Conference Center** H
(563) 557-8000. **$90-$190.** 3100 Dodge St 52003. US 20, 2.3 mi w of jct
US 52/61/151 and Mississippi Bridge. Int corridors. **Pets:** Large, other
species. $15 daily fee/pet. Designated rooms, service with restrictions,
supervision.

Comfort Inn by Choice Hotels H
(563) 556-3006. **$65-$130.** 4055 McDonald Dr 52002. US 20, 3.8 mi w
of jct US 52/61/151 and Mississippi Bridge. Int corridors. **Pets:** Accepted.

△△△ **▽▽▽** **Days Inn** **H**
(563) 583-3297. **$54-$81.** 1111 Dodge St 52003. US 20, 0.8 mi w of jct US 52/61/151 and Mississippi Bridge exit Hill/Bryant. Ext corridors. **Pets:** Medium. $10 one-time fee/pet. Service with restrictions, crate.
[SAVE] 🛰 🖥 🖾

△△△ **▽▽▽▽** **Holiday Inn Dubuque/Galena** **H**
(563) 556-2000. **$79-$117.** 450 Main St 52001. At Main and 4th sts; downtown. Int corridors. **Pets:** Accepted.
[SAVE] 🛰 ᴋᴹ 🖥 🖾 🍴 🏊 ⊠

▽▽▽▽ **MainStay Suites** **H**
(563) 557-7829. **$79-$170.** 1275 Associates Dr 52002. Just n of jct US 20 and NW Arterial Rd; west side of town. Int corridors. **Pets:** Accepted.
🛰 ᴋᴹ 🖥 🖾

DYERSVILLE
▽▽▽ **Comfort Inn** **H**
(563) 875-7700. **$81-$110.** 527 16th Ave SE 52040. US 20 exit 294 (SR 136), just nw. Int corridors. **Pets:** Small. $20 daily fee/room. Designated rooms, service with restrictions, supervision. 🛰 🖥 🖾 🔁

▽▽▽ **Super 8** **H**
(563) 875-8885. **$45-$72.** 925 15th Ave SE 52040. US 20 exit 294 (SR 136), just n. Int corridors. **Pets:** Small. $15 daily fee/pet. Designated rooms, service with restrictions, supervision. 🛰 🖥 🖾

EMMETSBURG
▽▽▽ **Super 8** **H**
(712) 852-2667. **$54-$81.** 3501 Main St 50536. Jct US 18 and SR 4, 0.8 mi w. Int corridors. **Pets:** $10 daily fee/pet. Designated rooms, crate.
🛰 ⊠ 🖥 🖾

ESTHERVILLE
△△△ **▽▽▽▽** **Sleep Inn & Suites** **H** 🐾
(712) 362-5522. **$100-$125.** 2008 Central Ave 51334. Jct SR 4 and 9, 1 mi e. Int corridors. **Pets:** Medium, other species. $20 one-time fee/room. Designated rooms, service with restrictions, supervision.
[SAVE] 🛰 🖥 🖾 🔁

▽▽▽ **Super 8** **H**
(712) 362-2400. **$52-$71.** 1919 Central Ave 51334. Jct SR 4 and 9, 1 mi e. Int corridors. **Pets:** Small, dogs only. $6 daily fee/pet. Service with restrictions, supervision. 🛰 🖥 🖾

EVANSDALE
▽▽▽ **Days Inn** **H**
(319) 235-1111. **$71-$80.** 450 Evansdale Dr 50707. I-380/US 20 exit 68, just n. Int corridors. **Pets:** Accepted. 🛰 ᴋᴹ 🖥 🖾 🔁

FAIRFIELD
△△△ **▽▽▽** **Best Western Fairfield Inn** **H**
(641) 472-2200. **$85-$95.** 2200 W Burlington Ave 52556. On US 34, 1 mi w of jct SR 1. Int corridors. **Pets:** Accepted.
[SAVE] 🛰 🖥 🖾 🍴 🔁

△△△ **▽▽▽** **Super 8** **H**
(641) 469-2000. **$52-$78.** 3001 W Burlington Ave 52556. On US 34, 1.5 mi w of jct SR 1. Int corridors. **Pets:** $50 deposit/room, $5 daily fee/pet. No service, supervision. [SAVE] 🛰 🖥 🖾 🔁

FORT DODGE
▽▽▽ **AmericInn Lodge & Suites of Fort Dodge** **H**
(515) 576-2100. **$120-$225.** 100 W Kenyon Rd 50501. 3 mi n of jct US 20 and 169. Int corridors. **Pets:** Accepted. 🛰 ᴋᴹ 🖥 🖾 🔁

▽▽▽ **Comfort Inn** **H**
(515) 573-5000. **$99-$149.** 2938 5th Ave S 50501. US 20 exit 124 (Coalville), 3.5 mi n on CR P59, then 1.3 mi w on 5th Ave and Business Rt US 20. Int corridors. **Pets:** Accepted. 🛰 ᴋᴹ 🖥 🖾 🔁

▽▽▽ **Fort Dodge Inn** **H**
(515) 576-8000. **$71-$86, 7 day notice.** 3040 5th Ave S 50501. US 20 exit 124 (Coalville), 3.5 mi n on CR P59, then 1.2 mi w on Business Rt US 20. Int corridors. **Pets:** Accepted. 🛰 🖥 🖾

FORT MADISON
▽▽▽▽ **Comfort Inn & Suites** **H**
(319) 372-6800. **Call for rates.** 6169 Reve Ct 52627. Just e of jct US 61 and SR 2, on US 61. Int corridors. **Pets:** Accepted.
🛰 🖥 🖾 🔁 ⊠

▽▽▽ **Knights Inn** **M**
(319) 372-7740. **$45-$52, 7 day notice.** 3440 Ave L 52627. 2.1 mi e of jct US 61 and SR 2. Ext corridors. **Pets:** Small. $10 daily fee/pet. Designated rooms, service with restrictions, supervision. 🛰 🖥 🖾

▽▽▽ **Super 8-Ft Madison** **H**
(319) 372-8500. **$50-$62.** 5107 Ave O 52627. 1 mi e of jct US 61 and SR 2. Int corridors. **Pets:** Accepted. 🛰 🖥 🖾

GRINNELL
△△△ **▽▽▽▽** **Best Western Plus Pioneer Inn & Suites** **H**
(641) 236-6116. **$100-$110.** 2210 West St S 50112. I-80 exit 182, just n. Int corridors. **Pets:** Medium. $20 daily fee/pet. Designated rooms, service with restrictions, supervision. [SAVE] 🛰 ᴋᴹ 🖥 🖾 🔁

▽▽▽ **Comfort Inn & Suites** **H**
(641) 236-5236. **$65-$199.** 1630 West St S 50112. I-80 exit 182, 0.7 mi n. Int corridors. **Pets:** Accepted. 🛰 ⊠ ᴋᴹ 🖥 🖾 🔁

GRUNDY CENTER
▽▽▽ **AmericInn Motel & Suites of Grundy Center** **H**
(319) 824-5272. **$79-$114.** 2101 Commerce Dr 50638. SR 175, 1.2 mi w of jct SR 14 and 175; west side of town. Int corridors. **Pets:** Medium. $25 one-time fee/room. Designated rooms, service with restrictions.
🛰 ᴋᴹ 🖥 🖾 🔁 ⊠

HAMPTON
△△△ **▽▽▽** **AmericInn Lodge & Suites of Hampton** **H**
(641) 456-5559. **$81-$146.** 702 Central Ave W 50441. On SR 3 (Central Ave W), 0.7 mi w of jct US 65 and SR 3. Int corridors. **Pets:** Other species. $15 daily fee/pet. Designated rooms, service with restrictions, supervision. [SAVE] 🛰 🖥 🖾 🔁 ⊠

IDA GROVE
▽▽▽ **Super 8** **H**
(712) 364-3988. **$54-$63.** 90 E Hwy 175 51445. Just n of SR 175. Int corridors. **Pets:** Accepted. 🛰 ᴋᴹ 🖥 🖾

INDEPENDENCE
▽▽▽ **Super 8** **H**
(319) 334-7041. **$53-$100.** 2000 1st St W 50644. US 20 exit 252, 1.4 mi n. Int corridors. **Pets:** Very small. $15 daily fee/pet. Service with restrictions. 🛰 ᴋᴹ 🖥 🖾

IOWA CITY
△△△ **▽▽▽◇** **Alexis Park Inn & Suites** **H**
(319) 337-8665. **$75-$350, 3 day notice.** 1165 S Riverside Dr 52246. I-80 exit 239 (US 218), 2 mi e on US 6, then just s. Ext corridors. **Pets:** Medium. $100 deposit/room, $15 one-time fee/pet. Designated rooms, service with restrictions, supervision. [SAVE] 🛰 🖥 🖾 🔁

△△△ **▽▽▽▽** **hotelVetro conference center** **H** 🌸
(319) 337-4961. **$139-$399.** 201 S Linn St 52240. I-80 exit 244, s on Dubuque St, e on Washington St, then just s. Int corridors. **Pets:** Dogs only. $50 one-time fee/room. Service with restrictions, supervision.
[SAVE] 🛰 ⊠ ᴋᴹ 🖥 🖾 🔁

WWWW Sheraton Iowa City Hotel **H** ☆
(319) 337-4058. **$119-$369.** 210 S Dubuque St 52240. Jct Dubuque and Burlington sts (SR 1); downtown. Int corridors. **Pets:** Dogs only. Service with restrictions, supervision. [SAVE] 🛜 ✕ ᴹ 💻 🍴 ➿

IOWA FALLS

WW Iowa Falls Super 8 **H**
(641) 648-4618. **$55-$90.** 839 S Oak St 50126. Jct US 65 and Washington Ave, 1 mi s; US 20 exit 168, 3.8 mi n. Int corridors. **Pets:** Accepted.
🛜 🛏 💻 ➿

JOHNSTON

WWWW Stoney Creek Inn **H** ☆
(515) 334-9000. **Call for rates.** 5291 Stoney Creek Ct 50131. I-80/35 exit 129 (86th St), just ne. Int corridors. **Pets:** Small, dogs only. $25 one-time fee/pet. Supervision. 🛜 ✕ 🛏 💻 ➿ ✕

KEOKUK

WWWW Holiday Inn Express **H**
(319) 524-8000. **$81-$96.** 325 Main St 52632. 4th and Main sts; downtown. Int corridors. **Pets:** Accepted. 🛜 ᴹ 🛏 💻 ➿ ✕

WWWW Super 8-Keokuk **H**
(319) 524-3888. **$53-$59.** 3511 Main St 52632. On Business Rt US 61/218, 2 mi n of jct US 136. Int corridors. **Pets:** Accepted.
🛜 ᴹ 🛏 💻

LE CLAIRE

WW Comfort Inn & Suites-Riverview **H** ☆
(563) 289-4747. **$85-$145.** 902 Mississippi View Ct 52753. I-80 exit 306 (US 67), 0.5 mi n to Eagle Ridge Rd, then just sw. Int corridors. **Pets:** Medium. $10 daily fee/pet. Service with restrictions, crate.
🛜 ᴹ 🛏 💻 ➿

WWWW Holiday Inn Express **H**
(563) 289-9978. **Call for rates.** 1201 Canal Shore Dr 52753. I-80 exit 306 (US 67), just n. Int corridors. **Pets:** Large. $25 one-time fee/room. Service with restrictions, supervision. 🛜 🛏 💻 ➿

WW Super 8 of Le Claire **H** ☆
(563) 289-5888. **$66-$96.** 1552 Welcome Center Dr 52753. I-80 exit 306 (US 67), 0.5 mi n to Eagle Ridge Rd, then just sw to Mississippi View Ct. Int corridors. **Pets:** Medium. $10 daily fee/pet. Service with restrictions, crate. 🛜 ᴹ 🛏 💻

LE MARS

WWW Baymont Inn & Suites **H**
(712) 548-4910. **$71-$113.** 1314 12th St SW 51031. US 75 exit 116, 1.7 mi ne. Int corridors. **Pets:** Other species. $10 one-time fee/room. Service with restrictions. [SAVE] 🛜 ᴹ 🛏 💻 ➿ ✕

WW Econo Lodge **H**
(712) 546-8800. **Call for rates.** 1201 Hawkeye Ave SW 51031. US 75 exit 116, 1.6 mi ne. Int corridors. **Pets:** Accepted.
🛜 ᴹ 🛏 💻 ➿

MANCHESTER

WWW Super 8 **H**
(563) 927-2533. **$48-$85.** 1020 W Main St 52057. Jct US 20 and SR 13 exit 275, 1.3 mi n, then 0.3 mi e. Int corridors. **Pets:** Accepted.
🛜 ᴹ 🛏 💻

MARQUETTE

W The Frontier Motel **M**
(563) 873-3497. **$55-$110.** 101 S 1st St 52158. Just s of jct US 18 and SR 76; between Mississippi River Bridge and casino. Ext corridors.
Pets: Accepted. 🛜 🛏 💻 ➿

MARSHALLTOWN

WWW Best Western Regency Inn **H**
(641) 752-6321. **$70-$175.** 3303 S Center St 50158. Jct US 30 and SR 14. Int corridors. **Pets:** Medium. $50 deposit/room, $10 daily fee/room. Designated rooms, service with restrictions, supervision.
[SAVE] 🛜 ᴹ 🛏 💻 🍴 ➿

WW Comfort Inn **H**
(641) 752-6000. **$70-$90.** 2613 S Center St 50158. 0.5 mi n of jct US 30 and SR 14. Int corridors. **Pets:** Accepted. 🛜 🛏 💻 ➿

WW Super 8 **H**
(641) 753-3333. **$45-$80.** 3315 S Center St 50158. Just n of jct US 30 and SR 14. Int corridors. **Pets:** Medium. $50 deposit/room, $10 daily fee/room. Designated rooms, service with restrictions, supervision.
🛜 🛏 💻

MASON CITY

WWWW Clarion Inn **H** ☆
(641) 423-1640. **Call for rates.** 2101 4th St SW (Hwy 122) 50401. I-35 exit 194 (SR 122), 6 mi e. Ext/int corridors. **Pets:** $100 deposit/room, $25 one-time fee/room. [SAVE] 🛜 ᴹ 🛏 💻 🍴 ➿ ✕

W Days Inn Mason City **H**
(641) 424-0210. **$53-$131.** 2301 4th St SW 50401. I-35 exit 194 (SR 122), 6 mi e. Int corridors. **Pets:** Accepted. 🛜 🛏 💻

WW Mason City Super 8 **H**
(641) 423-8855. **Call for rates.** 3010 4th St SW 50401. I-35 exit 194 (SR 122), 5.3 mi e. Int corridors. **Pets:** Other species. $10 daily fee/pet. Service with restrictions, supervision. 🛜 ᴹ 🛏 💻 ➿

MISSOURI VALLEY

WWW Oak Tree Inn **H**
(712) 642-3000. **Call for rates.** 128 S Willow Rd 51555. I-29 exit 75, 0.4 mi ne. Int corridors. **Pets:** Other species. $5 daily fee/pet. Designated rooms, service with restrictions, supervision.
[SAVE] 🛜 ✕ ᴹ 🛏 💻

MORAVIA

WWWW Honey Creek Resort State Park on Rathbun Lake **H**
(641) 724-9100. **$99-$189, 14 day notice.** 12633 Resort Dr 52571. Jct SR 5 and CR J18, 5.4 mi on CR J18, then 1.3 mi s. Int corridors. **Pets:** Other species. $20 one-time fee/room. Designated rooms, no service, supervision. [ECO] [SAVE] 🛜 ✕ ᴹ 💻 🍴 ➿ ✕

MOUNT PLEASANT

WWWW Best Western Mt. Pleasant Inn **H**
(319) 385-2102. **$67-$200.** 810 N Grand Ave 52641. US 218 exit 45, 0.6 mi s. Int corridors. **Pets:** Accepted. [SAVE] 🛜 ✕ 🛏 💻 ➿ ✕

WWWW Comfort Inn & Suites **H**
(319) 385-0571. **Call for rates.** 1200 E Baker St 52641. US 218 exit 45, 0.6 mi s. Int corridors. **Pets:** Accepted. 🛜 ✕ ᴹ 🛏 💻 ➿

WW Super 8 **H** ☆
(319) 385-8888. **$51-$88.** 1000 N Grand Ave 52641. US 218/SR 27 exit 45, 0.6 mi s. Int corridors. **Pets:** $10 daily fee/pet. Service with restrictions, supervision. 🛜 🛏 💻

MOUNT VERNON

WWWW Sleep Inn & Suites **H**
(319) 895-0055. **Call for rates.** 310 Virgil Ave 52314. Jct US 30 and SR 1, just se. Int corridors. **Pets:** Large, dogs only. $13 daily fee/room. Service with restrictions, supervision. 🛜 ᴹ 🛏 💻 ➿

MUSCATINE

AmericInn Lodge & Suites of Muscatine H
(563) 263-0880. **Call for rates.** 3115 Hwy 61 N 52761. Jct US 61 and SR 38, just n. Int corridors. **Pets:** Accepted.
[SAVE] 🛜 &M 🛠 🖵 🌊

Muscatine Super 8 H
(563) 263-9100. **$53-$62.** 2900 N Hwy 61 52761. Jct US 61 and SR 38. Int corridors. **Pets:** Accepted. 🛜 🛠 🖵

NEW HAMPTON

Super 8-New Hampton H
(641) 394-3838. **$57-$118.** 825 S Linn Ave 50659. US 63 exit 201, 1.5 mi ne on US 63 business route. Int corridors. **Pets:** Accepted.
🛜 🗙 &M 🛠 🖵 🌊 🗙

NEWTON

AmericInn of Newton H
(641) 791-1160. **$105-$180.** 4401 S 22nd Ave E 50208. I-80 exit 168, just sw. Int corridors. **Pets:** Small. $10 daily fee/pet. Designated rooms, service with restrictions, supervision. 🛜 &M 🛠 🖵 🌊

Holiday Inn Express H
(641) 792-3333. **Call for rates.** 208 W 4th St N 50208. Downtown. Int corridors. **Pets:** Accepted. 🛜 &M 🛠 🖵 🌊

NORTH LIBERTY

Sleep Inn & Suites H
(319) 665-2700. **$81-$91.** 485 Madison Ave N 52317. I-380 exit 4. Int corridors. **Pets:** Small, dogs only. $13 daily fee/pet. Designated rooms, no service, supervision. 🛜 &M 🛠 🖵 🌊

NORTHWOOD

Country Inn & Suites By Carlson H
(641) 323-7000. **$120-$130, 14 day notice.** 711 Diamond Jo Ln 50459. I-35 exit 214, just nw. Int corridors. **Pets:** Medium. $25 one-time fee/room. Service with restrictions, supervision. 🛜 &M 🛠 🖵 🌊

Holiday Inn Express & Suites H 🐾
(641) 323-7500. **Call for rates.** 4712 Wheelenwood Rd 50459. I-35 exit 214, just nw. Int corridors. **Pets:** Dogs only. Designated rooms, service with restrictions, crate. [SAVE] 🛜 🗙 &M 🛠 🖵 🌊

OELWEIN

Super 8-Oelwein M
(319) 283-2888. **$55-$109.** 210 10th St SE 50662. Jct SR 3 and 150, 1 mi s on SR 150; south end of downtown. Int corridors. **Pets:** Accepted.
🛜 🛠 🖵

OKOBOJI

AmericInn Lodge & Suites of Okoboji H
(712) 332-9000. **$89-$289, 7 day notice.** 1005 Brooks Park Dr 51355. Jct US 71 and SR 9, 2.5 mi s on US 71. Int corridors. **Pets:** Medium, dogs only. $25 one-time fee/pet. Service with restrictions, supervision.
🛜 🗙 &M 🛠 🖵 🌊

Arrowwood Resort & Conference Center by ClubHouse H
(712) 332-2161. **$79-$219.** 1405 US 71 S 51355. Jct US 71 and SR 9, 3 mi s. Ext/int corridors. **Pets:** Accepted.
[SAVE] 🛜 &M 🛠 🖵 🍴 🌊 🗙

OSCEOLA

Americas Best Value Inn M
(641) 342-2123. **$75-$77.** 1520 Jeffreys Dr 50213. I-35 exit 33 (Osceola/US 34), just e. Int corridors. **Pets:** Service with restrictions, crate. [SAVE] 🛜 🖵

AmericInn Lodge & Suites of Osceola H
(641) 342-9400. **$90-$160.** 111 Ariel Cir 50213. I-35 exit 33 (Osceola/US 34), just w. Int corridors. **Pets:** Accepted. 🛜 &M 🛠 🖵 🌊

Days Inn H
(641) 342-6666. **$58-$108.** 710 Warren Ave 50213. I-35 exit 33 (Osceola/US 34), just e. Int corridors. **Pets:** Accepted.
🛜 🛠 🖵 🌊

OSKALOOSA

Comfort Inn H
(641) 676-6000. **$99-$149.** 2401 A Ave W 52577. SR 163 exit 57 (SR 92), just e. Int corridors. **Pets:** Accepted. 🛜 🛠 🖵 🌊

Super 8-Oskaloosa H
(641) 673-8481. **$45-$72.** 306 S 17th St 52577. Just s of SR 92 and 23. Int corridors. **Pets:** Small, dogs only. $10 daily fee/pet. Designated rooms, service with restrictions, supervision. 🛜 &M 🛠 🖵

OTTUMWA

AmericInn of Ottumwa H 🐾
(641) 684-8222. **$72-$122.** 222 W 2nd St 52501. Just se of US 63 and W 4th; downtown. Int corridors. **Pets:** Dogs only. $50 deposit/room, $20 one-time fee/room. Designated rooms, service with restrictions, supervision. 🛜 &M 🛠 🖵 🌊

Quality Inn & Suites H
(641) 682-8526. **$69-$129.** 125 W Joseph Ave 52501. Jct US 34, 2 mi n on US 63. Int corridors. **Pets:** Medium. $15 daily fee/pet. Designated rooms, service with restrictions, supervision.
[SAVE] 🛜 🗙 🛠 🖵 🌊

PELLA

Super 8 H 🐾
(641) 628-8181. **$49-$90.** 105 E Oskaloosa St 50219. SR 163 exit 42, 1 mi n, then 0.5 mi e. Int corridors. **Pets:** Large. $10 daily fee/pet. Designated rooms, service with restrictions, crate. [SAVE] 🛜 &M 🛠 🖵

PLEASANT HILL

Sleep Inn & Suites H
(515) 299-9922. **$90-$160.** 5850 Morning Star Ct 50327. US 65 exit 79 (SR 163/E University Ave), just e. Int corridors. **Pets:** Other species. $15 daily fee/pet. Designated rooms, service with restrictions, supervision.
🛜 &M 🛠 🖵 🌊

QUAD CITIES AREA

BETTENDORF

Econo Lodge Inn & Suites H
(563) 355-6336. **$73-$180.** 815 Golden Valley Dr 52722. I-74 exit 2, just e, just n on Utica Ridge Rd, then just w. Int corridors. **Pets:** Medium, dogs only. $10 daily fee/pet. Service with restrictions, supervision.
[SAVE] 🛜 🛠 🖵 🌊

The Lodge Hotel & Conference Center H
(563) 359-7141. **Call for rates.** 900 Spruce Hills Dr 52722. I-74 exit 2, just e. Int corridors. **Pets:** Accepted. 🛜 🛠 🖵 🍴 🌊 🗙

Ramada Bettendorf/Davenport H
(563) 355-7575. **$52-$158.** 3020 Utica Ridge Rd 52722. I-74 exit 2, just e. Int corridors. **Pets:** Accepted. [SAVE] 🛜 &M 🛠 🖵 🌊

DAVENPORT

Best Western Plus Steeplegate Inn H 🐾
(563) 386-6900. **$100-$140.** 100 W 76th St 52806. I-80 exit 295A (US 61), 0.5 mi s to 65th St and west frontage road entrance, then just nw. Int corridors. **Pets:** Medium. $10 daily fee/pet. Designated rooms, no service, supervision. [SAVE] 🛜 &M 🛠 🖵 🍴 🌊

WWWW Clarion Hotel & Conference Center H
(563) 391-1230. **$75-$159.** 5202 Brady St 52806. I-80 exit 295A (US 61), 1.6 mi s. Int corridors. **Pets:** Other species. $10 one-time fee/pet. Designated rooms, service with restrictions, supervision.
SAVE 🛰 🖥 🗐 🖳 🍴 🏊 ⊗

WWWW Comfort Inn & Suites-Davenport H
(563) 324-8300. **$100-$115.** 8300 Northwest Blvd 52806. I-80 exit 292 (Northwest Blvd), just n. Int corridors. **Pets:** Accepted.
SAVE 🛰 ⊠ 🖥 🗐 🖳 🏊

WW Country Inn & Suites By Carlson H
(563) 388-6444. **Call for rates.** 140 E 55th St 52806. I-80 exit 295A (US 61), 1.4 mi s. Int corridors. **Pets:** Accepted. 🛰 🖥 🗐 🖳 🏊

WW Days Inn Davenport H
(563) 391-8222. **Call for rates.** 7222 Northwest Blvd 52806. I-80 exit 292 (Northwest Blvd), 0.3 mi s. Ext corridors. **Pets:** Accepted.
🛰 🖥 🗐 🖳

WW Fairfield Inn by Marriott H
(563) 355-2264. **$110-$130.** 3206 E Kimberly Rd 52807. I-74 exit 2, just w. Int corridors. **Pets:** $35 one-time fee/room. Service with restrictions, supervision. 🛰 ⊠ 🖥 🗐 🖳 🏊

WWWW Residence Inn by Marriott H
(563) 391-8877. **$130-$200.** 120 E 55th St 52806. I-80 exit 295A (US 61), 1.4 mi s. Int corridors. **Pets:** Accepted.
🛰 ⊠ 🖥 🗐 🖳 🏊 ⊗

WWWW Staybridge Suites H
(563) 359-7829. **$99-$159.** 4729 Progress Dr 52807. I-74 exit 1 (53rd St), 0.5 mi e, then 0.4 mi s on CR 216 (Utica Ridge Rd). Int corridors. **Pets:** Medium, other species. $10 daily fee/pet. Service with restrictions, crate. 🛰 ⊠ 🖥 🗐 🖳

WW Super 8 H
(563) 388-9810. **$50-$76.** 410 E 65th St 52807. I-80 exit 295A (US 61), 0.5 mi s, then just e. Int corridors. **Pets:** Accepted. 🛰 🖥 🖳

END AREA

RIVERSIDE
WWWW Riverside Casino & Golf Resort H
(319) 648-1234. **$70-$250.** 3184 Hwy 22 52327. I-218 exit 80, 1.5 mi ne. Int corridors. **Pets:** Accepted. 🖥 🗐 🖳 🍴 🏊 ⊗

ROCK RAPIDS
WW Four Seasons Motel M
(712) 472-2565. **$52-$82.** 810 First Ave 51246. Jct US 75, just w on SR 9. Ext/int corridors. **Pets:** Medium, dogs only. Service with restrictions, crate. SAVE 🛰 🖥 🖳

SHELDON
WW Super 8 H
(712) 324-8400. **$74-$90.** 210 N 2nd Ave 51201. SR 60 exit 34, 2 mi w on US 18, then just n on Business Rt SR 60. Int corridors.
Pets: Accepted. 🛰 🖥 🗐 🖳 🏊

SIBLEY
WW Super 8 H
(712) 754-3603. **$58-$69.** 1108 2nd Ave 51249. SR 60 exit 48, 1 mi w. Int corridors. **Pets:** Accepted. 🛰 🖥 🗐 🖳

SIGOURNEY
WW Belva Deer Inn H
(641) 622-3200. **$74-$99.** 21638 Hwy 92 52591. Jct SR 149 and 92, 1.1 mi e. Int corridors. **Pets:** Accepted. 🛰 ⊠ 🖥 🗐 🖳

SIOUX CENTER
WW Econo Lodge H
(712) 722-4000. **Call for rates.** 86 9th St Cir NE 51250. On US 75, 1 mi n of jct SR 840; north side of town. Ext/int corridors. **Pets:** $10 daily fee/pet. Designated rooms, service with restrictions, supervision.
🛰 🖥 🗐 🖳

SIOUX CITY
WW AmericInn Lodge & Suites of Sioux City H
(712) 255-1800. **$77-$160.** 4230 S Lewis Blvd 51106. I-29 exit 143, just e. Int corridors. **Pets:** Other species. $10 daily fee/room. Designated rooms, service with restrictions, crate. 🛰 🖥 🗐 🖳 🏊 ⊗

WW Comfort Inn by Choice Hotels H
(712) 274-1300. **Call for rates.** 4202 S Lakeport St 51106. I-29 exit 144A, 1 mi e on US 20, then just s. Int corridors. **Pets:** Large, other species. $15 one-time fee/room. Service with restrictions, supervision.
🛰 🖥 🗐 🖳 🏊

WW Fairfield Inn by Marriott H
(712) 276-5600. **$99-$109.** 4716 Southern Hills Dr 51106. I-29 exit 144A, 1 mi e on US 20, then just s. Int corridors. **Pets:** $15 daily fee/room. Designated rooms, service with restrictions, supervision.
🛰 ⊠ 🖥 🗐 🖳

WWW Hilton Garden Inn - Sioux City Riverfront H
(712) 255-4200. **$104-$129.** 1132 Larsen Park Rd 51103. I-29 exit 149, just sw. Int corridors. **Pets:** Accepted. 🛰 ⊠ 🖥 🗐 🖳 🏊

WW Holiday Inn Express H
(712) 274-1400. **Call for rates.** 4230 S Lakeport St 51106. I-29 exit 144A, 1 mi e on US 20, then just s. Int corridors. **Pets:** Accepted.
🛰 🖥 🖳

WWW Ramada City Centre H
(712) 277-1550. **$60-$129.** 130 Nebraska St 51101. I-29 exit 147B (Tyson Event Center), just w on US 20 (Gordon Dr), then just n. Int corridors. **Pets:** Medium. $10 one-time fee/pet. Designated rooms, service with restrictions, supervision. SAVE 🛰 🖥 🖳 🏊

WWWW Stoney Creek Inn H
(712) 234-1100. **Call for rates.** 300 3rd St 51101. I-29 exit 147B (Tyson Event Center), 0.3 mi w on US 20 (Gordon Dr), then just n. Int corridors. **Pets:** Accepted. 🛰 ⊠ 🖥 🗐 🖳 🏊 ⊗

WW Super 8 H
(712) 274-1520. **$50-$78.** 4307 Stone Ave 51106. I-29 exit 144A northbound, US 75 exit 4B, 1.5 mi w on Gordon Dr; exit 147B southbound to Gordon Dr, 3 mi e. Int corridors. **Pets:** $10 daily fee/pet. Service with restrictions, crate. 🛰 🖥 🖳

SLOAN
WW WinnaVegas Inn H
(712) 428-4280. **$79-$189.** 1862 Hwy 141 51055. I-29 exit 127, just e. Int corridors. **Pets:** Accepted. 🛰 ⊠ 🖥 🗐 🖳

SPIRIT LAKE
WW Spirit Lake Super 8 H 🐾
(712) 336-4901. **$99-$167.** 2203 Circle Dr W 51360. Jct US 71 and SR 9. Int corridors. **Pets:** Other species. $10 one-time fee/room. Service with restrictions, supervision. 🛰 🖥 🖳

STORM LAKE
WWWW King's Pointe Waterpark Resort H
(712) 213-4500. **$99-$399, 3 day notice.** 1520 E Lakeshore Dr 50588. Just n of jct US 71 business route and SR 7. Int corridors. **Pets:** Medium. $75 one-time fee/room. Designated rooms, service with restrictions, supervision. SAVE 🛰 ⊠ 🖥 🗐 🖳 🍴 🏊 ⊗

STORY CITY

◆◆◆◆ Comfort Inn ⊞
(515) 733-6363. **Call for rates.** 425 Timberland Dr 50248. I-35 exit 124, just sw. Int corridors. **Pets:** Other species. $13 one-time fee/room. Service with restrictions, supervision. 🛜 ♿ 🍴 💻 🏊

◆◆◆ Super 8 ⊞
(515) 733-5281. **$48-$76.** 515 Factory Outlet Dr 50248. I-35 exit 124, just sw. Int corridors. **Pets:** Accepted. 🛜 🍴 💻

STUART

◆◆◆ AmericInn Lodge & Suites of Stuart ⊞
(515) 523-9000. **Call for rates.** 420 SW 8th St 50250. I-80 exit 93, just w. Int corridors. **Pets:** $15 daily fee/room. Designated rooms, service with restrictions, supervision. 🛜 ❌ ♿ 🍴 💻 🏊

◆◆ Super 8 ⊞
(515) 523-2888. **$45-$81.** 203 SE 7th St 50250. I-80 exit 93, just ne. Int corridors. **Pets:** Accepted. 🛜 ♿ 🍴 💻 🏊

TOLEDO

◆◆◆ Designer Inn & Suites ⊞
(641) 484-5678. **$45-$199.** 403 US 30 W 52342. On US 30, just w of jct US 63 and 30. Int corridors. **Pets:** Accepted. 🛜 🍴 💻 🏊

◆◆ Super 8-Toledo ⊞
(641) 484-5888. **$50-$99.** 207 Hwy 30 W 52342. On US 30, just w of jct US 63 and 30. Ext/int corridors. **Pets:** Accepted. 🛜 🍴 💻

URBANA

◆◆◆ Urbana Inn & Suites ⊞
(319) 443-8888. **$59-$71.** 5369 Hutton Dr 52345. I-380 exit 43, just s on east access road. Int corridors. **Pets:** Small. $15 one-time fee/room. Designated rooms, service with restrictions, supervision.
🛜 ❌ ♿ 🍴 💻 🏊 ❌

URBANDALE

◆◆◆ Extended StayAmerica Des Moines-Urbandale ⊞ ❀
(515) 276-1929. **$59-$74.** 3940 114th St 50322. I-35/80 exit 126 (Douglas Ave), just e to 114th St, then 0.4 mi nw. Int corridors. **Pets:** Other species. $25 daily fee/pet. Service with restrictions. 🛜 ♿ 🍴 💻

AAA ◆◆◆ Holiday Inn Hotel & Suites Northwest ⊞
(515) 278-4755. **$89-$129.** 4800 Merle Hay Rd 50322. I-35/80 exit 131 (Merle Hay Rd), just s. Int corridors. **Pets:** Accepted.
SAVE 🛜 ❌ ♿ 🍴 💻 🍴 🏊 ❌

◆◆◆ Microtel Inn & Suites ⊞
(515) 727-5424. **$49-$62.** 8711 Plum Dr 50322. I-35/80 exit 129 (86th St). Int corridors. **Pets:** Accepted. 🛜 ♿ 🍴 💻

◆◆◆ Ramada Tropics Resort/Conference Center Des Moines ⊞
(515) 278-0271. **$79-$180.** 5000 Merle Hay Rd 50322. I-35/80 exit 131 (Merle Hay Rd), just s. Ext/int corridors. **Pets:** Accepted.
🛜 ❌ 🍴 💻 🍴 🏊 ❌

◆◆◆ Sleep Inn ⊞
(515) 270-2424. **$79-$149.** 11211 Hickman Rd 50322. I-35/80 exit 125 (Hickman Rd), just ne. Int corridors. **Pets:** Accepted.
🛜 ♿ 🍴 💻 🏊

◆◆◆◆ TownePlace Suites by Marriott Des Moines/Urbandale ⊞
(515) 727-4066. **$69-$144.** 8800 Northpark Dr 50131. I-35/80 exit 129 (86th St), just nw. Int corridors. **Pets:** Other species. $100 one-time fee/room. Service with restrictions. 🛜 ❌ 🍴 💻 🏊

WALCOTT

AAA ◆◆◆ Davenport/Walcott Comfort Inn ⊞ ❀
(563) 284-9000. **$79-$190.** 501 W Walker St 52773. I-80 exit 284, just nw. Int corridors. **Pets:** Small, other species. $50 deposit/pet, $15 daily fee/pet. Designated rooms, service with restrictions, supervision.
SAVE 🛜 ♿ 💻 🏊

WALNUT

◆◆◆ Super 8 ⊞
(712) 784-2221. **$58-$100.** 2109 Antique City Dr 51577. I-80 exit 46, just n. Int corridors. **Pets:** Other species. Designated rooms, service with restrictions, supervision. 🛜 ♿ 🍴 💻 🏊

WATERLOO

◆◆◆ Baymont Inn & Suites ⊞
(319) 233-9191. **$71-$76.** 2141 La Porte Rd 50702. I-380 exit 72 (E San Marnan Dr). Int corridors. **Pets:** Accepted. 🛜 ♿ 🍴 💻 🏊

◆◆◆ Candlewood Suites ⊞
(319) 235-7000. **$89-$139.** 2056 La Porte Rd 50702. I-380 exit 72 (E San Marnan Dr), just sw. Int corridors. **Pets:** Accepted.
🛜 ♿ 🍴 💻 🏊

◆◆◆ Comfort Inn by Choice Hotels ⊞
(319) 234-7411. **$79-$129.** 1945 La Porte Rd 50702. I-380 exit 72 (E San Marnan Dr). Int corridors. **Pets:** Other species. Designated rooms, service with restrictions, supervision. 🛜 🍴 💻 🏊

◆◆◆ Days Inn & Suites ⊞
(319) 235-4461. **$71-$100.** 1809 La Porte Rd 50702. I-380 exit 72 (E San Marnan Dr), just nw. Int corridors. **Pets:** Accepted.
🛜 🍴 💻 🏊

◆◆◆ Fairfield Inn by Marriott ⊞
(319) 234-5452. **$90-$99.** 2011 La Porte Rd 50702. I-380 exit 72 (E San Marnan Dr), just w. Int corridors. **Pets:** Medium, other species. $25 one-time fee/room. Service with restrictions, supervision.
🛜 ❌ ♿ 🍴 💻 🏊

◆◆◆ Howard Johnson ⊞
(319) 232-7467. **$63-$95.** 3052 Marnie Ave 50701. 1 mi n of jct US 20 and 63 exit 227. Int corridors. **Pets:** $10 daily fee/pet. Designated rooms, service with restrictions, supervision. 🛜 🍴 💻 🏊

◆◆◆ Ramada Hotel & Convention Center ⊞
(319) 233-7560. **$50-$150.** 205 W 4th St 50701. At 4th and Commercial sts; downtown. Int corridors. **Pets:** Accepted.
🛜 ♿ 🍴 💻 🍴 🏊 ❌

◆◆◆ Super 8 ⊞
(319) 233-1800. **$47-$62.** 1825 La Porte Rd 50702. I-380 exit 72 (E San Marnan Dr), just nw. Int corridors. **Pets:** Accepted. 🛜 🍴 💻

WAUKON

◆◆◆ Stoney Creek Inn ⊞
(563) 568-2220. **$69-$142.** 407 Rossville Rd 52172. Jct SR 9 and 76, 1.7 mi n. Int corridors. **Pets:** Accepted. 🛜 ♿ 🍴 💻

WAVERLY

◆◆◆ Comfort Inn ⊞
(319) 352-0399. **Call for rates.** 404 29th Ave SW 50677. US 218 exit 198, 0.7 mi n. Int corridors. **Pets:** Medium, dogs only. $10 daily fee/pet. Designated rooms, service with restrictions, supervision.
🛜 ♿ 🍴 💻 🏊 ❌

◆◆◆ Super 8 Waverly ⊞
(319) 352-0888. **$56-$107.** 301 13th Ave SW 50677. US 218 exit 198, 1.4 mi n. Int corridors. **Pets:** Accepted. 🛜 ♿ 🍴 💻

WEBSTER CITY

Americinn Motel & Suites of Webster City 🅷

(515) 832-3999. **$75-$125.** 411 Closz Dr 50595. Just s of jct US 20 and SR 17. Int corridors. **Pets:** Other species. $25 one-time fee/room. Service with restrictions, crate.

WEST BEND

Park View Inn & Suites 🅷

(515) 887-3611. **Call for rates.** 13 4th St NE 50597. Jct CR B63, 1 mi n on SR 15, then just w. Int corridors. **Pets:** Accepted.

WEST BURLINGTON

Americinn Lodge & Suites of Burlington 🅷

(319) 758-9000. **$70-$150.** 628 S Gear Ave 52655. US 34 exit 260 (Gear Ave), just ne. Int corridors. **Pets:** $20 daily fee/pet. Designated rooms, service with restrictions, supervision.

WEST DES MOINES

Candlewood Suites-West Des Moines 🅷

(515) 221-0001. **Call for rates.** 7625 Office Plaza Dr N 50266. I-80 exit 121 (Jordan Creek Pkwy), just sw. Int corridors. **Pets:** Accepted.

Drury Inn & Suites 🅷

(515) 457-9500. **$110-$199.** 5505 Mills Civic Pkwy 50266. I-35 exit 70 (Mills Civic Pkwy), just w. Int corridors. **Pets:** Accepted.

Residence Inn-Des Moines West 🅷

(515) 267-0338. **$110-$250.** 160 S Jordan Creek Pkwy 50266. I-35 exit 70 (Mills Civic Pkwy), 1.2 mi w o 68th St, then just nw. Int corridors. **Pets:** Accepted.

Sheraton West Des Moines 🅷 ❀

(515) 223-1800. **$59-$200, 3 day notice.** 1800 50th St 50266. I-35/80 exit 124 (University Ave), just e. Int corridors. **Pets:** Medium. $50 deposit/room. Designated rooms, service with restrictions, crate.

Staybridge Suites 🅷

(515) 223-0000. **Call for rates.** 6905 Lake Dr 50266. I-80 exit 121 (Jordan Creek Pkwy), just ne. Int corridors. **Pets:** Accepted.

West Des Moines Marriott 🅷

(515) 267-1500. **$119-$209.** 1250 Jordan Creek Pkwy 50266. I-80 exit 121 (Jordan Creek Pkwy), just sw. Int corridors. **Pets:** $75 one-time fee/room. Service with restrictions, crate.

WILLIAMS

Best Western Norseman Inn Ⓜ

(515) 854-2281. **$69-$80.** 3086 220th St 50271. I-35 exit 144, just e. Int corridors. **Pets:** Medium, dogs only. $10 one-time fee/pet. Designated rooms, service with restrictions, supervision.

WILLIAMSBURG

Best Western Cozy House & Suites 🅷 🐾

(319) 668-9777. **$100-$150.** 1708 N Highland St 52361. I-80 exit 220, 0.8 mi n. Int corridors. **Pets:** Medium. $20 daily fee/pet. Designated rooms, service with restrictions, supervision.

Crest Motel Ⓜ

(319) 668-1522. **$70-$90.** 340 W Evans St 52361. I-80 exit 220, just nw. Ext corridors. **Pets:** Accepted.

Heritage Inn Hotel & Suites Amana Colonies 🅷

(319) 668-2700. **$77-$160.** 2185 U Ave 52361. I-80 exit 225 (US 151), just n. Int corridors. **Pets:** Accepted.

Super 8 🅷

(319) 668-9718. **$54-$83.** 1708 N Highland St 52361. I-80 exit 220, 0.8 mi n. Ext/int corridors. **Pets:** Medium. $17 daily fee/pet. Designated rooms, service with restrictions, supervision.

KANSAS

CITY INDEX

ABILENE

Diamond Motel Ⓜ

(785) 263-2360. **$40-$75.** 1407 NW 3rd St 67410. I-70 exit 275, 1.3 mi s, then 1 mi w. Ext corridors. **Pets:** Dogs only. $7 daily fee/pet. Designated rooms, service with restrictions, supervision.

Holiday Inn Express Hotel & Suites 🅷

(785) 263-4049. **$106-$121.** 110 E Lafayette Ave 67410. I-70 exit 275, just n. Int corridors. **Pets:** Accepted.

ANDOVER

Andover Express Inn Ⓜ

(316) 733-8881. **$55-$63.** 222 W US Hwy 54 67002. 2.2 mi e of jct SR 96. Ext corridors. **Pets:** Medium, dogs only. $10 daily fee/pet. Service with restrictions, supervision.

Holiday Inn Express & Suites 🅷

(316) 733-8833. **$90-$119.** 600 S Allen St 67002. 2.2 mi e of jct SR 96 and US 54, then just s. Int corridors. **Pets:** Small. $10 one-time fee/pet. Designated rooms, service with restrictions, supervision.

BELOIT

▼▼ ▼▼ **Super 8** 🄷
(785) 738-4300. **$49-$69, 3 day notice.** 3018 W Hwy 24 67420. Just e of jct SR 14. Ext/int corridors. **Pets:** Medium, dogs only. $10 daily fee/pet. Designated rooms, service with restrictions, supervision.
🛜 ✕ ♿ 🍴 📺

BURLINGTON

▼▼ ▼▼ **Country Haven Inn** 🄷
(620) 364-8260. **$67-$75.** 207 Cross St 66839. Just e of US 75; 1 mi n of center. Int corridors. **Pets:** Accepted. 🛜 ♿ 🍴 📺

CHANUTE

▼ **Knight's Inn** 🄼
(620) 431-9460. **Call for rates.** 3428 S Santa Fe Ave 66720. US 169 exit 35th St, 1.5 mi e. Ext corridors. **Pets:** Accepted. 🛜 🍴 ≋

CLAY CENTER

▼▼ ▼▼ **Cedar Court Motel** 🄼
(785) 632-2148. **$55-$80.** 905 Crawford St 67432. On US 24, just e of jct SR 15. Ext corridors. **Pets:** Accepted. 🛜 ♿ 🍴 📺 ≋

COFFEYVILLE

Ⓐ ▼▼ ▼▼ **Best Western Bricktown Lodge** 🄷
(620) 251-3700. **$88-$93.** 605 Northeast St 67337. 1 mi e of center. Int corridors. **Pets:** Large. $20 daily fee/pet. Designated rooms, service with restrictions, supervision. 💰 🛜 ✕ ♿ 🍴 📺 ≋

COLBY

▼▼ ▼▼ **Comfort Inn** 🄷 🐾
(785) 462-3833. **$79-$139.** 2225 S Range Ave 67701. I-70 exit 53 (SR 25), just s. Int corridors. **Pets:** Other species. $10 daily fee/pet. Designated rooms, service with restrictions, supervision.
🛜 ♿ 🍴 📺 🍴 ≋

Ⓐ ▼▼ ▼▼ **Crown Inn** 🄼
(785) 462-3943. **$47-$65.** 2320 S Range Ave 67701. I-70 exit 53 (SR 25), just s. Ext corridors. **Pets:** Accepted. 💰 🛜 🍴 📺 ≋

Ⓐ ▼▼ ▼▼ **Days Inn** 🄷
(785) 462-8691. **$67-$72.** 1925 S Range Ave 67701. I-70 exit 53 (SR 25), 0.3 mi n. Int corridors. **Pets:** Medium, dogs only. $10 daily fee/pet. Designated rooms, service with restrictions, supervision.
💰 🛜 🍴 📺 ≋

▼▼ ▼▼ ▼▼ **Hampton Inn** 🄷
(785) 460-2333. **Call for rates.** 1000 E Willow Dr 67701. I-70 exit 54, just n, then just e. Int corridors. **Pets:** Small, dogs only. Designated rooms, service with restrictions, supervision. 🛜 ✕ 📺 ≋

Ⓐ ▼▼ ▼▼ ▼▼ **Holiday Inn Express Hotel & Suites** 🄷
(785) 462-8787. **$115-$125.** 645 W Willow St 67701. I-70 exit 53 (SR 25), just ne. Int corridors. **Pets:** Medium, other species. $25 one-time fee/room. Designated rooms, service with restrictions, supervision.
💰 🛜 ✕ ♿ 🍴 📺 ≋

Ⓐ ▼ **Motel 6 #4245** 🄷
(785) 462-8201. **$40-$72.** 1985 S Range Ave 67701. I-70 exit 53 (SR 25), just n. Ext/int corridors. **Pets:** Other species. Service with restrictions, supervision. 💰 🛜 🍴

Ⓐ ▼▼ ▼▼ **Super 8** 🄷
(785) 462-8248. **$54-$63.** 1040 Zelfer Ave 67701. I-70 exit 53 (SR 25), 0.3 mi n, then just w. Int corridors. **Pets:** $10 daily fee/pet. Designated rooms, service with restrictions, supervision. 💰 🛜 🍴 📺

COTTONWOOD FALLS

Ⓐ ▼▼ ▼▼ ▼▼ **Grand Central Hotel** 🄲
(620) 273-6763. **$160-$190.** 215 Broadway 66845. US 177, just w on Main St, then just s; center of downtown. Int corridors. **Pets:** Service with restrictions, supervision. 💰 🛜 ✕ 📺 🍴

DERBY

▼▼ ▼▼ ▼▼ **Hampton Inn Derby** 🄷
(316) 425-7900. **$119-$179.** 1701 Cambridge St 67037. Just sw of jct Rock Rd. Int corridors. **Pets:** Accepted. 🛜 ✕ ♿ 🍴 📺 ≋

DODGE CITY

Ⓐ ▼▼ ▼▼ ▼▼ **Best Western Plus Country Inn & Suites** 🄷
(620) 225-7378. **$120.** 506 N 14th Ave 67801. Just n of jct US 50 business route. Ext/int corridors. **Pets:** Dogs only. $20 daily fee/room. Designated rooms, service with restrictions, supervision.
💰 🛜 ✕ ♿ 🍴 📺 ≋

▼▼ ▼▼ **Comfort Inn** 🄷
(620) 338-8700. **Call for rates.** 2000 W Wyatt Earp Blvd 67801. 1.3 mi w on US 50 business route. Int corridors. **Pets:** Accepted.
🛜 🍴 📺 ≋

▼▼ ▼▼ ▼▼ **Holiday Inn Express** 🄷
(620) 227-5000. **$99-$119.** 2320 W Wyatt Earp Blvd 67801. 1.4 mi w on US 50 business route. Int corridors. **Pets:** $25 one-time fee/room. Service with restrictions, crate. 🛜 🍴 📺 ≋

▼▼ ▼▼ ▼▼ **La Quinta Inn & Suites Dodge City** 🄷
(620) 225-7373. **$85-$179.** 2400 W Wyatt Earp Blvd 67801. 1.4 mi w on US 50 business route. Int corridors. **Pets:** Medium, other species. Service with restrictions, supervision. 🛜 ♿ 🍴 📺 ≋

▼▼ ▼▼ **Super 8** 🄷
(620) 225-3924. **$60-$72.** 1708 W Wyatt Earp Blvd 67801. 1.2 mi w on US 50 business route. Int corridors. **Pets:** Accepted. 🛜 🍴 📺 ≋

EL DORADO

Ⓐ ▼▼ ▼▼ **Best Western Red Coach Inn** 🄷
(316) 321-6900. **$73.** 2525 W Central Ave 67042. I-35 exit 71, 0.5 mi e. Ext corridors. **Pets:** Very small, dogs only. $15 daily fee/pet. Designated rooms, service with restrictions, supervision. 💰 🛜 🍴 📺 ≋

▼ **Super 8-El Dorado** 🄼
(316) 321-4888. **$50-$63.** 2530 W Central Ave 67042. I-35 exit 71, 0.5 mi e. Int corridors. **Pets:** Accepted. 🛜 🍴 📺

ELLIS

▼▼ ▼▼ ▼▼ **Days Inn** 🄷
(785) 726-2511. **$75-$90.** 205 N Washington St 67637. I-70 exit 145, just s. Int corridors. **Pets:** Accepted. 🛜 ✕ ♿ 🍴 📺 ≋

ELLSWORTH

Ⓐ ▼▼ ▼▼ **Americas Best Value Inn** 🄷
(785) 472-3116. **Call for rates.** 1414 Foster Rd 67439. Jct SR 140 and 156. Ext corridors. **Pets:** Accepted. 💰 🛜 ♿ 🍴 📺 ≋

EMPORIA

Ⓐ ▼▼ ▼▼ **Best Western Hospitality House** 🄷
(620) 342-7587. **$80-$100.** 3021 W Hwy 50 66801. I-35 exit 127A, just s to US 50, follow roundabout directions, then 0.5 mi e. Ext/int corridors. **Pets:** Other species. $10 daily fee/room. Designated rooms, service with restrictions, crate. 💰 🛜 ✕ 🍴 📺 🍴 ≋

▼▼ ▼▼ **Candlewood Suites** 🄷
(620) 343-7756. **Call for rates.** 2602 Candlewood Dr 66801. I-35 exit 128 (Industrial St), just n, then just e. Int corridors. **Pets:** Medium. $13 daily fee/room. Service with restrictions, crate. 🛜 ✕ 🍴 📺

Ⓐ ▼▼ ▼▼ **Comfort Inn** 🄷
(620) 342-9700. **$81-$90.** 2836 W 18th Ave 66801. I-35 exit 128 (Industrial St), just nw. Int corridors. **Pets:** Small, other species. $15 daily fee/room. Service with restrictions, supervision.
💰 🛜 ✕ 🍴 📺 ≋

Super 8 M

(620) 342-7567. **$54-$90.** 2913 W Hwy 50 66801. I-35 exit 127A, just s to US 50, follow roundabout directions, then 0.7 mi e. Int corridors. **Pets:** Small, other species. $10 daily fee/pet. Designated rooms, service with restrictions, supervision. SAVE 🛜 ⊠ 🛏 🖵

FORT SCOTT

Lyons' Twin Mansions B & B Hotel and Spa BB

(620) 223-3644. **Call for rates.** 742 S National Ave 66701. Jct US 69 and 54 E, 0.3 mi w on Wall St, then 0.6 mi s. Int corridors. **Pets:** Dogs only. Designated rooms, service with restrictions, supervision.
🛜 ⊠ 🛏 🖵 🍴 ⊠

GARDEN CITY

AmericInn Lodge & Suites of Garden City H 🐾

(620) 272-9860. **$89-$165.** 3020 E Kansas Ave 67846. Jct US 50, 83 and SR 156. Int corridors. **Pets:** Medium. $100 deposit/pet, $10 one-time fee/room. Designated rooms, service with restrictions, supervision.
🛜 ⊠ 🛏 🖵 🏊 ⊠

Best Western Red Baron Hotel H

(620) 275-4164. **$99-$109.** 2205 E Fulton St 67846. 2.3 mi e on US 50 business route, at US 83 Bypass. Ext corridors. **Pets:** Accepted.
SAVE 🛜 🛏 🖵 🏊

Clarion Inn & Conference Center H

(620) 275-7471. **$110-$135.** 1911 E Kansas Ave 67846. 0.5 mi w of US 50 and 83 Bypass, on SR 156. Int corridors. **Pets:** Accepted.
🛜 ⊠ 🛏 🖵 🍴 🏊

Comfort Inn H

(620) 275-5800. **Call for rates.** 2608 E Kansas Ave 67846. Jct US 50, 83 and SR 156. Int corridors. **Pets:** Accepted.
🛜 ⊠ 🛏 🖵 🏊 ⊠

Hampton Inn H

(620) 272-0454. **$94-$114.** 2505 E Crestway Dr 67846. US 50/83/400 exit SR 156, just sw. Int corridors. **Pets:** Accepted.
🛜 ⊠ �Ɱ 🛏 🖵 🏊

Holiday Inn Express Hotel & Suites H

(620) 275-5900. **$109-$114.** 2502 E Kansas Ave 67846. Jct US 50, 83 and SR 156. Int corridors. **Pets:** Accepted. 🛜 ⊠ 🛏 🖵 🏊

GOODLAND

Comfort Inn H

(785) 899-7181. **Call for rates.** 2519 Enterprise Rd 67735. I-70 exit 17 (SR 27), just n. Int corridors. **Pets:** $15 daily fee/pet. Designated rooms, service with restrictions, supervision. SAVE 🛜 🛛Ɱ 🛏 🖵 🏊

Holiday Inn Express Hotel & Suites H

(785) 890-9060. **$109-$129.** 2631 Enterprise Rd 67735. I-70 exit 17 (SR 27), just s. Int corridors. **Pets:** Other species. $25 one-time fee/room. Designated rooms, service with restrictions, supervision.
SAVE 🛜 ⊠ 🛛Ɱ 🛏 🖵 🏊

Super 8 H

(785) 890-7566. **$47-$61.** 2520 Commerce Rd 67735. I-70 exit 17 (SR 27), just n. Ext corridors. **Pets:** Accepted. 🛜 🛏 🖵

GREAT BEND

Best Western Angus Inn H

(620) 792-3541. **$74-$82.** 2920 10th St 67530. 0.8 mi w on US 56 and SR 96/156. Ext/int corridors. **Pets:** Large, other species. $10 daily fee/pet. Designated rooms, service with restrictions, crate.
SAVE 🛜 🛏 🖵 🍴 🏊 ⊠

GREENSBURG

Best Western Plus Night Watchman Inn & Suites H ❄

(620) 723-2244. **$100-$150.** 515 W Kansas Ave 67054. US 54, just e of US 183 and 54. Int corridors. **Pets:** Large. $25 deposit/pet. Service with restrictions. SAVE 🛜 ⊠ 🛏 🖵 🏊

HAYS

Americas Best Value Inn Vagabond M

(785) 625-2511. **$60-$163.** 2524 Vine St 67601. I-70 exit 159 (US 183), 1 mi s. Ext corridors. **Pets:** $5 daily fee/room. Designated rooms, service with restrictions, supervision. 🛜 🛏 🖵 🏊

Fairfield Inn Hays H

(785) 625-3344. **$95-$113.** 377 Mopar Dr 67601. I-70 exit 159 (US 183), just n to 43rd St, then just w. Int corridors. **Pets:** Accepted.
🛜 ⊠ 🛛Ɱ 🛏 🖵 🏊

Hampton Inn H

(785) 621-4444. **Call for rates.** 4002 General Hays Rd 67601. I-70 exit 159 (US 183), just n, then e. Int corridors. **Pets:** Accepted.
🛜 🛛Ɱ 🛏 🖵 🏊

HERINGTON

Herington Inn & Suites H

(785) 258-3300. **$70-$92.** 565 Hwy 77 67449. US 77, just w. Int corridors. **Pets:** Accepted. 🛛Ɱ 🛏 🖵

HESSTON

AmericInn Lodge & Suites of Hesston H

(620) 327-2053. **$70-$160.** 2 Leonard Ct 67062. I-135 exit 40, just e. Int corridors. **Pets:** Small. $30 one-time fee/room. Service with restrictions, crate. 🛜 🛏 🖵 🏊

HILLSBORO

Country Haven Inn H

(620) 947-2929. **$72-$85.** 804 Western Heights Cir 67063. On US 56; center. Int corridors. **Pets:** Accepted. 🛜 ⊠ 🛏

HUTCHINSON

Comfort Inn H

(620) 663-7822. **$59-$169.** 1621 Super Plaza 67501. Just w of jct SR 61 and N 17th Ave. Int corridors. **Pets:** Small, other species. $10 one-time fee/pet. Designated rooms, service with restrictions, supervision.
🛜 🛏 🖵 🏊

Holiday Inn Express Hotel & Suites H

(620) 669-5200. **$105-$165.** 1601 Super Plaza 67501. Just w of jct SR 61 and N 17th Ave. Int corridors. **Pets:** Accepted.
🛜 🛛Ɱ 🛏 🖵 🏊

INDEPENDENCE

Appletree Inn H

(620) 331-5500. **$99-$145.** 201 N 8th St 67301. At 8th and Laurel sts. Ext/int corridors. **Pets:** Accepted. 🛜 🛏 🖵 🏊

IOLA

Best Western Inn M

(620) 365-5161. **$66-$79.** 1315 N State St 66749. Jct US 54 and 169, 1.5 mi w on US 54, then 0.8 mi n. Ext corridors. **Pets:** Accepted.
SAVE 🛜 🛛Ɱ 🛏 🖵 🍴 🏊

JUNCTION CITY

Best Western J.C. Inn H

(785) 210-1212. **$80-$100.** 604 E Chestnut St 66441. I-70 exit 298, just w. Int corridors. **Pets:** Accepted. SAVE 🛜 🛛Ɱ 🛏 🖵 🏊

▼▼▼ Candlewood Suites 🏠
(785) 238-1454. **$86-$115, 3 day notice.** 100 S Hammons Dr 66441. I-70 exit 298, just w. Int corridors. **Pets:** Accepted.
📶 ♿ 🍴 🖥 ❌

▼▼▼ Courtyard by Marriott Junction City 🏠
(785) 210-1500. **$94-$159.** 310 Hammons Dr 66441. I-70 exit 298, just w. Int corridors. **Pets:** Accepted. 📶 ❌ ♿ 🍴 🖥 🏊

▼▼▼ Holiday Inn Express 🏠
(785) 762-4200. **$105-$150.** 120 N East St 66441. I-70 exit 298, just nw. Int corridors. **Pets:** Medium. $5 daily fee/pet. Service with restrictions, supervision. 📶 ♿ 🍴 🖥 🏊

KANSAS CITY METROPOLITAN AREA

BONNER SPRINGS

▼▼▼ Holiday Inn Express 🏠 ❀
(913) 721-5300. **Call for rates.** 13031 Ridge Ave 66012. I-70 exit 224. Int corridors. **Pets:** Other species. $20 one-time fee/room. Service with restrictions, supervision. 📶 ♿ 🍴 🖥 🏊

GARDNER

▼▼ Super 8 🏠
(913) 856-8887. **$58-$144.** 2001 E Santa Fe 66030. I-35 exit 210. Int corridors. **Pets:** Other species. $10 daily fee/pet. Service with restrictions, supervision. 📶 ♿ 🍴 🖥 🏊

KANSAS CITY

△△△ ▼▼▼ Best Western Kansas City Inn 🏠
(913) 677-3060. **$90-$100.** 501 Southwest Blvd 66103. I-35 exit 234 (7th St), 0.4 mi s to Southwest Blvd, then just w. Int corridors. **Pets:** Other species. $25 one-time fee/room. Service with restrictions, supervision.
SAVE 📶 🍴 🖥 🏊

▼▼▼ Candlewood Suites 🏠
(913) 788-9929. **Call for rates.** 10920 Parallel Pkwy 66109. I-435 exit 14B, just w. Int corridors. **Pets:** Accepted. 📶 ♿ 🍴 🖥

LEAWOOD

△△△ ▼▼▼ Aloft Leawood-Overland Park 🏠 ❀
(913) 345-9430. **$99-$229.** 11620 Ash St 66211. I-435 exit 77B (Nall Ave), 1.1 mi s, then just e; in Town Center shopping area. Int corridors. **Pets:** Medium, dogs only. Service with restrictions, crate.
SAVE 📶 ❌ ♿ 🍴 🖥 🏊

LENEXA

▼▼ Extended StayAmerica-Kansas City-Lenexa-87th St 🏠 ❀
(913) 894-5550. **$65-$99.** 8015 Lenexa Dr 66215. I-35 exit 227 (75th St), 1 mi s on east frontage road. Ext corridors. **Pets:** Other species. $25 daily fee/pet. Service with restrictions.
📶 ❌ ♿ 🍴 🖥 🏊 ❌

▼▼ La Quinta Inn Kansas City Lenexa 🏠
(913) 492-5500. **$58-$115.** 9461 Lenexa Dr 66215. I-35 exit 224 (95th St), just ne; entrance left on Monrovia Rd off 95th St. Int corridors. **Pets:** Medium, other species. Service with restrictions, supervision.
📶 ❌ 🍴 🖥 🏊

△△△ ▼▼ Super 8-Lenexa 🏠
(913) 888-8899. **$50-$108.** 9401 Westgate Dr 66215. I-35 exit 224 (95th St), just se. Int corridors. **Pets:** Medium, dogs only. $10 daily fee/pet. Designated rooms, service with restrictions, supervision.
SAVE 📶 ❌ ♿ 🍴 🖥

MERRIAM

▼▼ Drury Inn-Merriam/Shawnee Mission Parkway 🏠
(913) 236-9200. **$75-$154.** 9009 W Shawnee Mission Pkwy 66202. I-35 exit 228B (Shawnee Mission Pkwy), just se. Int corridors. **Pets:** Accepted.
📶 ♿ 🍴 🖥 🏊

▼▼ Homestead Studio Suites Hotel-Kansas City-Shawnee Mission 🏠 ❀
(913) 236-6006. **$59-$104.** 6451 E Frontage Rd 66202. I-35 exit 228B (Shawnee Mission Pkwy), just se. Ext corridors. **Pets:** Other species. $25 daily fee/pet. Service with restrictions. 📶 ♿ 🍴 🖥

OLATHE

△△△ ▼▼▼ Best Western Plus Olathe Hotel & Suites 🏠 ❀
(913) 440-9762. **$90-$190.** 1580 S Hamilton Cir 66061. I-35 exit 215 (151st St), just nw. Int corridors. **Pets:** Medium. $10 daily fee/pet. Designated rooms, service with restrictions, crate.
SAVE 📶 ❌ 🍴 🖥 🏊

▼▼ Candlewood Suites Olathe 🏠
(913) 768-8888. **$85-$99.** 15490 S Rogers Rd 66062. I-35 exit 215 (151st St), just sw. Int corridors. **Pets:** $75 deposit/room. Service with restrictions, crate. 📶 ♿ 🍴 🖥

▼▼ Days Inn Olathe Medical Center 🏠
(913) 390-9500. **Call for rates.** 20662 W 151st St 66061. I-35 exit 215 (151st St), 0.4 mi sw, follow signs. Int corridors. **Pets:** Accepted.
📶 ♿ 🍴 🖥 🏊

▼▼▼ Holiday Inn at Olathe Medical Center 🏠 ❀
(913) 829-4000. **$84-$154.** 101 W 151st St 66061. I-35 exit 215 (151st St). Int corridors. **Pets:** Small. $30 one-time fee/room. Service with restrictions, supervision. 📶 ❌ 🍴 🖥 🍴 🏊

△△△ ▼▼▼ La Quinta Inn & Suites Olathe 🏠
(913) 254-0111. **$71-$190.** 20570 W 151st St 66061. I-35 exit 215 (151st St), just w. Int corridors. **Pets:** Medium, other species. Service with restrictions, supervision. SAVE 📶 ❌ ♿ 🍴 🖥 🏊

△△△ ▼▼▼ Residence Inn by Marriott 🏠
(913) 829-6700. **$108-$219.** 12215 S Strang Line Rd 66062. I-35 exit 220 (119th St), just e to Strang Line Rd, then 0.8 mi s. Int corridors. **Pets:** Accepted. SAVE 📶 ❌ ♿ 🍴 🖥 🏊 ❌

OVERLAND PARK

▼▼▼ Candlewood Suites 🏠
(913) 469-5557. **Call for rates.** 11001 Oakmont St 66210. I-435 exit 82 (Quivira Rd), 0.5 mi s, 0.3 mi w on College Ave, then just n. Int corridors. **Pets:** Accepted. ❌ ♿ 🍴 🖥

▼▼▼ Chase Suite Hotels - Overland Park 🏠
(913) 491-3333. **$79-$139.** 6300 W 110th St 66211. I-435 exit 79 (Metcalf Ave/US 169), 0.3 mi s on US 169, 0.5 mi e on College Blvd to Lamar Ave, then just n. Ext corridors. **Pets:** Accepted.
📶 ❌ 🍴 🖥 🏊

▼▼▼ Clarion Hotel 🏠
(913) 383-2550. **Call for rates.** 7000 W 108th St 66211. I-435 exit 79 (Metcalf Ave/US 169), just ne. Int corridors. **Pets:** Accepted.
📶 ❌ ♿ 🍴 🖥 🍴 🏊

△△△ ▼▼▼ Comfort Inn & Suites 🏠
(913) 648-7858. **$89-$149.** 7200 W 107th St 66212. I-435 exit 79 (Metcalf Ave/US 169), just nw. Int corridors. **Pets:** Accepted.
SAVE 📶 ❌ ♿ 🍴 🖥 🏊

▼▼ Days Inn Overland Park 🏠
(913) 341-0100. **Call for rates.** 6800 W 108th St 66211. I-435 exit 79 (Metcalf Ave/US 169), just ne. Ext corridors. **Pets:** Accepted.
📶 ❌ ♿

▼▼▼▼ Drury Inn & Suites-Overland Park H
(913) 345-1500. **$80-$209.** 10963 Metcalf Ave 66210. I-435 exit 79 (Metcalf Ave/US 169), just se. Int corridors. **Pets:** Accepted.
🛜 ⊠ &M 🚻 💻 ⇴ 🐾

▼▼ Econo Lodge Inn & Suites H
(913) 262-9600. **Call for rates.** 7508 Shawnee Mission Pkwy 66202. I-35 exit 228B, 0.5 mi e. Ext corridors. **Pets:** Accepted.
🛜 ⊠ 🚻 💻 ⇴

▼▼ Extended StayAmerica-Kansas City-Overland Park H ❀
(913) 661-9299. **$64-$99.** 10750 Quivira Rd 66210. I-435 exit 82 (Quivira Rd), just sw. Int corridors. **Pets:** Other species. $25 daily fee/pet. Service with restrictions. 🛜 ⊠ &M 🚻 💻

▼▼▼▼ La Quinta Inn & Suites Overland Park H
(913) 648-5555. **$71-$129.** 10610 Marty St 66212. I-435 exit 79 (Metcalf Ave/US 169), just nw. Int corridors. **Pets:** Medium, other species. Service with restrictions, supervision. 🛜 ⊠ 🚻 💻 ⇴

▼▼▼▼ Pear Tree Inn by Drury-Overland Park H
(913) 451-0200. **$65-$129.** 10951 Metcalf Ave 66210. I-435 exit 79 (Metcalf Ave/US 169), just se. Int corridors. **Pets:** Accepted.
🛜 ⊠ &M 🚻 💻 ⇴

▼▼▼▼ Residence Inn by Marriott H
(913) 491-4444. **$94-$180.** 12010 Blue Valley Pkwy 66213. I-435 exit 79 (Metcalf Ave/US 169), 1.3 mi s. Int corridors. **Pets:** Medium. $75 one-time fee/room. Service with restrictions, supervision.
🛜 ⊠ &M 🚻 💻 ⇴ 🐾

AAA ▼▼▼▼ Sheraton Overland Park Hotel at the Convention Center H ❀
(913) 234-2100. **$89-$259.** 6100 College Blvd 66211. I-435 exit 79 (Metcalf Ave/US 169), just s to College Blvd, then 0.6 mi e. Int corridors. **Pets:** Medium, dogs only. $50 deposit/room. Designated rooms, service with restrictions, supervision. ECO SAVE 🛜 ⊠ &M 💻 🍴 ⇴

END METROPOLITAN AREA

LANSING
▼▼ Econo Lodge H
(913) 727-2777. **$68-$78.** 504 N Main 66043. I-70 exit 224 (Leavenworth), 10 mi n on US 73 and SR 7. Int corridors. **Pets:** Accepted.
🛜 🚻 💻

LARNED
▼▼ Townsman Inn H
(620) 285-3114. **Call for rates.** 123 E 14th St 67550. Jct US 56 and SR 156. Ext corridors. **Pets:** Other species. Service with restrictions, supervision. 🛜 🚻 💻 ⇴

LAWRENCE
AAA ▼▼▼▼ Baymont Inn & Suites H
(785) 838-4242. **$63-$135.** 740 Iowa St 66044. I-70 exit 202, 1 mi s on US 59. Int corridors. **Pets:** Medium. $15 daily fee/pet. Designated rooms, service with restrictions, supervision. SAVE 🛜 &M 🚻 💻 ⇴

AAA ▼▼▼▼ Best Western Lawrence H ❀
(785) 843-9100. **$76-$110.** 2309 Iowa St 66046. On US 59; jct SR 10. Ext/int corridors. **Pets:** Dogs only. $8 daily fee/pet. Designated rooms, service with restrictions, supervision.
SAVE 🛜 &M 🚻 💻 ⇴ 🐾

AAA ▼▼▼▼ Holiday Inn Express Hotel & Suites H ❀
(785) 749-7555. **$99-$149.** 3411 SW Iowa St 66046. I-70 exit 197 (SR 10), 8.4 mi e to US 59, then just n. Int corridors. **Pets:** Small, other species. $20 daily fee/pet. Designated rooms, service with restrictions, supervision. SAVE 🛜 ⊠ &M 🚻 💻 ⇴ 🐾

▼▼▼▼ Holiday Inn Hotel & Convention Center H
(785) 841-7077. **$99-$199.** 200 McDonald Dr 66044. I-70 exit 202, 0.5 mi s on US 59. Int corridors. **Pets:** $25 one-time fee/room. Service with restrictions, supervision. 🛜 ⊠ 🚻 💻 🍴 ⇴ 🐾

▼▼ Quality Inn M
(785) 842-5100. **Call for rates.** 801 Iowa St 66049. I-70 exit 202, 1 mi s on US 59. Ext/int corridors. **Pets:** Medium, dogs only. $10 daily fee/pet. Designated rooms, service with restrictions, supervision.
🛜 🚻 💻 ⇴

AAA ▼▼▼ Super 8 H
(785) 842-5721. **$43-$99.** 515 McDonald Dr 66049. I-70 exit 202, 0.8 mi s, then just w. Int corridors. **Pets:** Medium, dogs only. $10 daily fee/room. Service with restrictions, supervision. SAVE 🛜 🚻 💻

LIBERAL
AAA ▼▼ Americas Best Value Inn M
(620) 624-6203. **$54-$64.** 564 E Pancake Blvd 67901. 0.8 w of jct US 54 and 83. Ext corridors. **Pets:** Medium. $10 daily fee/pet. Designated rooms, service with restrictions, supervision. SAVE 🛜 🚻 💻

LYONS
▼▼ Celebration Centre Inn & Suites M
(620) 680-6022. **$65-$100.** 1108 E Hwy 56 67554. 2 mi e of jct SR 14 and US 56. Int corridors. **Pets:** $20 one-time fee/room. Designated rooms, service with restrictions, supervision. 🛜 🚻 💻

MANHATTAN
AAA ▼▼▼▼ Best Western Manhattan Inn H ❀
(785) 537-8300. **$79-$99.** 601 E Poyntz Ave 66502. SR 177, 0.5 mi e on US 24 (Frontage Rd). Int corridors. **Pets:** Large, other species. $10 daily fee/pet. Service with restrictions, supervision.
SAVE 🛜 ⊠ &M 🚻 💻 ⇴

▼▼▼▼ Clarion Hotel H
(785) 539-5311. **$69-$169.** 530 Richards Dr 66502. On SR 18 (Ft. Riley Blvd), 0.3 mi e of jct SR 113. Ext/int corridors. **Pets:** Accepted.
🛜 ⊠ 🚻 💻 🍴 ⇴ 🐾

▼▼▼▼ Holiday Inn at the Campus H
(785) 539-7531. **$99-$219.** 1641 Anderson Ave 66502. 1 mi n of SR 18 (Ft. Riley Blvd). Int corridors. **Pets:** Accepted.
🛜 ⊠ 🚻 💻 🍴 ⇴

AAA ▼▼▼▼ Parkwood Inn & Suites H ❀
(785) 320-5440. **Call for rates.** 505 S 17th St 66502. 1.5 mi w of jct SR 177 and 18 (Ft. Riley Blvd), just n. Int corridors. **Pets:** $10 daily fee/pet. Service with restrictions, crate. SAVE 🛜 ⊠ 🚻 💻

MARYSVILLE
▼▼ Heritage Inn Express H
(785) 562-5588. **$54-$95.** 1155 Pony Express Hwy 66508. 2 mi e on US 36 (Pony Express Hwy). Int corridors. **Pets:** Other species. $10 one-time fee/room. Designated rooms, service with restrictions, supervision.
🛜 🚻 💻

▼▼ Marysville Surf Motel M
(785) 562-2354. **Call for rates.** 2105 Center St 66508. 1 mi e on US 36 (Pony Express Hwy). Ext/int corridors. **Pets:** Accepted. 🛜 🚻 💻

AAA ▼▼▼ Oak Tree Inn H
(785) 562-1234. **$79.** 1127 Pony Express Hwy 66508. 1.6 mi e on US 36 (Pony Express Hwy). Int corridors. **Pets:** Other species. Service with restrictions, crate. SAVE 📶 ✕ 🛗 💻

MCPHERSON

AAA ▼▼▼ Best Western Holiday Manor H 🐾
(620) 241-5343. **$80-$115.** 2211 E Kansas Ave 67460. I-135 exit 60, just w. Ext/int corridors. **Pets:** Other species. $10 daily fee/pet. Service with restrictions, supervision. SAVE 📶 🛗 💻 🍴 ⊿

MEADE

▼ Dalton's Bedpost Motel M
(620) 873-2131. **$54-$65.** 519 E Carthage St 67864. On US 54. Ext corridors. **Pets:** Large. Service with restrictions, crate. 📶 🛗 💻

NEWTON

AAA ▼▼▼ Best Western Red Coach Inn H
(316) 283-9120. **$80-$100.** 1301 E 1st St 67114. I-135 exit 31, just w; exit southbound, just w at 2nd roundabout. Ext/int corridors. **Pets:** Accepted. SAVE 📶 ✕ 🛗 💻 ⊿ ✕

AAA ▼▼▼ Comfort Inn & Suites H
(316) 804-4866. **Call for rates.** 1205 E 1st St 67114. I-135 exit 31 northbound, just w; southbound, w at second roundabout. Int corridors. **Pets:** Accepted. SAVE 📶 ✕ 🛗 💻 ⊿

OAKLEY

AAA ▼▼▼ Sleep Inn & Suites of Oakley H
(785) 671-1111. **$79-$129.** 3596 E Hwy 40 67748. I-70 exit 76, just w. Int corridors. **Pets:** Medium. $10 daily fee/pet. Designated rooms, service with restrictions, supervision. SAVE 📶 ✕ 🛗 💻 ⊿

OTTAWA

AAA ▼▼▼ Best Western Ottawa Inn H
(785) 242-2224. **$90-$100.** 212 E 23rd St 66067. I-35 exit 183 (US 59). Ext/int corridors. **Pets:** Medium. $20 daily fee/pet. Service with restrictions, crate. SAVE 📶 🛗 🛗 💻 ⊿

PAOLA

▼▼ Paola Inn & Suites H
(913) 294-3700. **$95-$98.** 1600 E Hedge Lane Ct 66071. US 169 exit 127 (Baptiste Dr), just w. Int corridors. **Pets:** Large, other species. $10 daily fee/room. Designated rooms, service with restrictions, crate. 📶 ✕ 🛗 🛗 💻 ⊿

PARK CITY

AAA ▼▼▼ Best Western Wichita North Hotel & Suites H
(316) 832-9387. **$84.** 915 E 53rd St N 67219. I-135 exit 13, just w. Ext/int corridors. **Pets:** Accepted. SAVE 📶 🛗 💻 🍴 ⊿ ✕

AAA ▼▼▼ Park City Express Inn & Suites H
(316) 927-3900. **$63-$80.** 792 Beaumont St 67219. I-135 exit 14, just sw. Int corridors. **Pets:** Medium, dogs only. $10 daily fee/pet. Service with restrictions, supervision. SAVE 📶 🛗 💻 ⊿

▼ Super 8-Wichita North/Park City M
(316) 744-2071. **$39-$63.** 6075 Air Cap Dr 67219. I-135 exit 14, just sw. Int corridors. **Pets:** Accepted. 📶 🛗 💻 ⊿

PARSONS

AAA ▼▼▼ Best Western Parsons Inn H
(620) 423-0303. **$85-$95.** 101 E Main St 67357. 1.5 mi e. Int corridors. **Pets:** Small. $20 daily fee/pet. Service with restrictions, supervision. SAVE 📶 🛗 💻 ⊿

AAA ▼▼▼ Sleep Inn & Suites H
(620) 421-6126. **$90-$100.** 1807 Harding Dr 67357. Just sw of jct US 59 and 400. Int corridors. **Pets:** Very small. $25 one-time fee/room. Service with restrictions, supervision. SAVE 📶 ✕ 🛗 🛗 💻 ⊿

PHILLIPSBURG

▼ Cottonwood Inn M
(785) 543-2125. **$69-$199, 7 day notice.** 1200 State St 67661. 1 mi e on US 36/183. Ext corridors. **Pets:** Accepted. 📶 🛗 ⊿

PITTSBURG

AAA ▼▼▼▼ Lamplighter Inn & Suites H
(620) 231-8700. **$79-$129.** 4020 Parkview Dr 66762. 2.3 mi n on US 69 from jct SR 126. Ext/int corridors. **Pets:** Small, dogs only. $10 daily fee/pet. Designated rooms, service with restrictions, supervision. SAVE 📶 🛗 🛗 💻 ⊿

▼▼ Super 8 H
(620) 232-1881. **$60-$69.** 3108 N Broadway Ave 66762. 2.1 mi n on US 69 from jct SR 126. Int corridors. **Pets:** Accepted. 📶 🛗 💻

PRATT

AAA ▼▼▼ Comfort Suites H
(620) 672-9999. **$100-$120.** 704 Allison Ln 67124. Jct US 54 and SR 61, just n. Int corridors. **Pets:** Medium. $25 daily fee/room. Service with restrictions, crate. SAVE 📶 ✕ 🛗 💻 ⊿

▼ Evergreen Inn & RV Park M
(620) 672-6431. **$59-$100.** 20001 W US Hwy 54 67124. 3 mi w. Ext corridors. **Pets:** Medium, dogs only. $5 one-time fee/pet. Service with restrictions, supervision. 📶 🛗 ⊿

SALINA

▼▼▼ AmericInn Hotel & Suites Salina H
(785) 826-1711. **$89-$140.** 1820 W Crawford St 67401. I-135 exit 92, just e. Int corridors. **Pets:** Small. $25 daily fee/pet. Service with restrictions, supervision. 📶 ✕ 🛗 🛗 💻 ⊿

▼▼ Candlewood Suites H
(785) 823-6939. **$69-$109.** 2650 Planet Ave 67401. I-135 exit 89 (Schilling Rd), just e to S 9th St, 0.5 mi n to Belmont, then just w. Int corridors. **Pets:** Medium. $20 one-time fee/pet. Service with restrictions, supervision. 📶 ✕ 🛗 🛗 💻

▼▼ Days Inn H
(785) 823-9791. **$67-$72.** 407 W Diamond Dr 67401. I-70 exit 252, just n. Int corridors. **Pets:** Medium, dogs only. $15 daily fee/room. Designated rooms, service with restrictions, supervision. 📶 ✕ 🛗 💻 ⊿

▼▼ Days Inn Salina South H
(785) 827-9315. **Call for rates.** 632 Westport Blvd 67401. I-135 exit 92, just e. Ext/int corridors. **Pets:** Accepted. 📶 ✕ 💻 ⊿

▼▼▼▼ La Quinta Inn & Suites H
(785) 827-9000. **Call for rates.** 201 E Diamond Dr 67401. I-70 exit 252, just ne. Int corridors. **Pets:** Medium, other species. Service with restrictions, supervision. 📶 ✕ 🛗 🛗 💻 ⊿

▼▼ Rodeway Inn Salina M
(785) 827-0356. **Call for rates.** 1846 N 9th St 67401. I-70 exit 252, just s. Ext corridors. **Pets:** Accepted. 📶 ✕ 🛗 💻 ⊿

▼▼▼ Sleep Inn & Suites H 🐾
(785) 404-6777. **$69-$89.** 3932 S 9th St 67401. I-135 exit 88, just e, then just s. Int corridors. **Pets:** Other species. Service with restrictions, supervision. 📶 ✕ 🛗 💻 ⊿

▼▼ Super 8 I-70 H
(785) 823-8808. **$68-$76.** 120 E Diamond Dr 67401. I-70 exit 252, just ne. Int corridors. **Pets:** Accepted. 📶 ✕ 🛗 🛗 💻 ⊿

SHARON SPRINGS

▼▼▼ Oak Tree Inn 🅗
(785) 852-4664. **Call for rates.** 801 N Hwy 27 67758. Jct US 40 and
SR 27. Ext/int corridors. **Pets:** Accepted. 🛜 ⊠ 🚭M 🖬 🖵 🍴

TOPEKA

🅐🅐🅐 **▼▼▼** Best Western Topeka Inn & Suites 🅗
(785) 228-2223. **$70-$110.** 700 SW Fairlawn Rd 66606. I-70 exit 357A,
just ne. Int corridors. **Pets:** Large. $25 one-time fee/pet. Service with
restrictions, supervision. [SAVE] 🛜 🖬 🖵 ⊸

▼▼▼▼ Capitol Plaza Hotel 🅗 ❀
(785) 431-7200. **$79-$149.** 1717 SW Topeka Blvd 66612. I-70 exit 362B
(SE 8th Ave), 1.6 mi s; I-470 exit 177 (Topeka Blvd), 2.9 mi n. Int corridors. **Pets:** Dogs only. $50 one-time fee/room. Service with restrictions,
crate. 🛜 ⊠ 🚭M 🖬 🖵 🍴 ⊸ ⊠

🅐🅐🅐 **▼▼▼▼** ClubHouse Inn & Suites 🅗 ❀
(785) 273-8888. **$82-$122.** 924 SW Henderson 66615. I-70 exit 356
(Wanamaker Rd), just sw. Int corridors. **Pets:** $10 daily fee/room. Super-
vision. [SAVE] 🛜 🖬 🖵 ⊸

▼▼▼▼ Courtyard by Marriott 🅗
(785) 271-6165. **$90-$149.** 2033 SW Wanamaker Rd 66604. I-70 exit
356 (Wanamaker Rd), 1.5 mi s. Int corridors. **Pets:** Accepted.
🛜 ⊠ 🚭M 🖬 🖵 ⊸

▼▼▼▼ Ramada Convention Center Downtown Topeka 🅗
(785) 234-5400. **$76-$94.** 420 SE 6th Ave 66607. I-70 exit 362B, just e.
Int corridors. **Pets:** Accepted. 🛜 ⊠ 🚭M 🖬 🖵 🍴 ⊠

▼▼▼▼ Residence Inn by Marriott 🅗
(785) 271-8903. **$94-$299.** 1620 SW Westport Dr 66604. I-470 exit 1
(Wanamaker Rd), just se. Int corridors. **Pets:** Accepted.
🛜 ⊠ 🚭M 🖬 🖵 ⊸ ⊠

▼▼▼ Sleep Inn & Suites 🅗
(785) 228-2500. **$65-$99.** 1024 SW Wanamaker Rd 66604. I-70 exit 356
(Wanamaker Rd), just s. Int corridors. **Pets:** Medium, other species. $10
daily fee/pet. Service with restrictions, supervision.
🛜 🚭M 🖬 🖵 ⊸

🅐🅐🅐 **▼▼▼** Super 8 at Forbes Landing 🅗 ❀
(785) 862-2222. **$63-$121.** 5922 SW Topeka Blvd 66619. I-470 exit 6,
2.2 mi s. Int corridors. **Pets:** $20 one-time fee/room. Service with restric-
tions, crate. [SAVE] 🛜 🚭M 🖬 🖵 ⊸

ULYSSES

▼▼▼ Single Tree Inn 🅗
(620) 356-1500. **Call for rates.** 2033 W Oklahoma Ave 67880. 1.5 mi w
on US 160. Int corridors. **Pets:** Very small, dogs only. $10 daily fee/pet.
Service with restrictions, supervision. 🛜 ⊠ 🖬 🖵

UNIONTOWN

▼ Wyatt Earp Inn & Hotel 🅗
(620) 756-4990. **$64.** 100 5th St 66779. On SR 3; west side of town. Int
corridors. **Pets:** Accepted. 🛜 🖬 🖵

WAKEENEY

🅐🅐🅐 **▼▼▼▼** Best Western Plus Wakeeney Inn &
Suites 🅗 ❀
(785) 743-2700. **$100.** 525 S 1st St 67672. I-70 exit 127, just n. Int corri-
dors. **Pets:** Other species. $10 daily fee/pet. Designated rooms, service
with restrictions, supervision. [SAVE] 🛜 ⊠ 🚭M 🖬 🖵 ⊸

🅐🅐🅐 **▼▼▼** Super 8 🅗 ❀
(785) 743-6442. **$53-$59.** 709 S 13th St 67672. I-70 exit 128, just n. Int
corridors. **Pets:** Other species. $10 daily fee/pet. Designated rooms, serv-
ice with restrictions, supervision. [SAVE] 🛜 🖬 🖵

WICHITA

🅐🅐🅐 **▼▼▼** Best Western Airport Inn & Conference
Center 🅗 ❀
(316) 942-5600. **$120-$140.** 6815 W Kellogg St 67209. I-235 exit 7, 0.6
mi w on US 54 (S Frontage Rd). Int corridors. **Pets:** Small, dogs only.
Service with restrictions, crate. [SAVE] 🛜 ⊠ 🖬 🖵 🍴 ⊸ ⊠

🅐🅐🅐 **▼▼▼** Best Western Governors Inn & Suites 🅗
(316) 522-0775. **$77-$90.** 4742 S Emporia St 67216. I-135 exit 1A/B
(47th St S), just sw. Int corridors. **Pets:** Small, dogs only. $10 daily fee/
pet. Service with restrictions, supervision. [SAVE] 🛜 🖬 🖵

▼▼ Candlewood Suites 🅗 ❀
(316) 942-0400. **$69-$119.** 570 S Julia St 67209. I-235 exit 7, 0.3 mi w
to Dugan St, just n to Taft St, just e, then just s. Int corridors.
Pets: Other species. $15 one-time fee/room, $10 daily fee/room. Service
with restrictions, crate. 🖬 🖵

▼▼ Candlewood Suites-Wichita Northeast 🅗 ❀
(316) 634-6070. **$69-$119.** 3141 N Webb Rd 67226. SR 96 exit Webb
Rd, just nw. Int corridors. **Pets:** Medium, dogs only. $15 daily fee/pet.
Service with restrictions, crate. 🚭M 🖬 🖵

🅐🅐🅐 **▼▼** Comfort Inn 🅗 ❀
(316) 522-1800. **$70-$150.** 4849 S Laura St 67216. I-135 exit 1A/B (47th
St S), just e. Int corridors. **Pets:** Large, other species. $10 daily fee/pet.
Service with restrictions, supervision. [SAVE] 🛜 🖬 🖵 ⊸

▼▼ Comfort Inn by Choice Hotels 🅗
(316) 686-2844. **$72-$81.** 9525 E Corporate Hills Dr 67207. I-35 exit 50,
just ne. Int corridors. **Pets:** Accepted. 🛜 🖬 🖵 ⊸

▼▼ Cresthill Suites Hotel 🅗
(316) 689-8000. **$108.** 12111 E Central Ave 67206. 1.7 mi e of jct Webb
Rd. Int corridors. **Pets:** Accepted. 🖬 🖵 ⊸

▼▼▼ Hampton Inn by Hilton 🅗
(316) 686-3576. **Call for rates.** 9449 E Corporate Hills Dr 67207. I-35
exit 50, just ne. Int corridors. **Pets:** Accepted. 🛜 🚭M 🖬 🖵 ⊸

▼▼▼ Homewood Suites by Hilton at The Waterfront 🅗
(316) 260-8844. **$129-$299.** 1550 N Waterfront Pkwy 67206. Just e of jct
13th and Webb rds. Int corridors. **Pets:** Accepted.
🛜 🚭M 🖬 🖵 ⊸ ⊠

▼▼▼▼ La Quinta Inn & Suites Wichita Airport 🅗
(316) 943-2181. **$116-$189.** 5500 W Kellogg Dr 67209. I-235 exit 7, just
nw. Int corridors. **Pets:** Medium, other species. Service with restrictions,
supervision. 🛜 ⊠ 🖬 🖵 🍴 ⊸

▼▼▼▼ Residence Inn by Marriott at Plazzio 🅗
(316) 682-7300. **$89-$199.** 1212 N Greenwich Rd 67206. SR 96 exit
13th St, 0.5 mi sw. Int corridors. **Pets:** Accepted.
🛜 ⊠ 🚭M 🖬 🖵 ⊸ ⊠

▼▼▼ Staybridge Suites 🅗
(316) 927-3888. **$99-$189.** 2250 N Greenwich Rd 67226. Just e of jct
21st St and Greenwich Rd. Int corridors. **Pets:** Accepted.
🛜 🚭M 🖬 🖵 ⊸

🅐🅐🅐 **▼▼▼** Super 8-Wichita/East 🅗
(316) 686-3888. **$41-$62.** 527 S Webb Rd 67207. I-35 exit 50, just e. Int
corridors. **Pets:** Large, other species. $10 one-time fee/pet. Service with
restrictions, supervision. [SAVE] 🛜 🖬 🖵

▼▼ TownePlace Suites by Marriott 🅗
(316) 631-3773. **$71-$104.** 9444 E 29th St N 67226. SR 96 exit Webb
Rd, just sw. Int corridors. **Pets:** Large, other species. $75 one-time fee/
room. Service with restrictions, supervision. 🛜 ⊠ 🚭M 🖬 🖵

▼▼ Wesley Inn H

(316) 858-3343. **$91.** 3343 E Central Ave 67208. Just e of jct Hillside St. Int corridors. **Pets:** Small. $25 one-time fee/room. Crate.

▼▼ Wichita Inn-North H

(316) 636-2022. **$59-$79.** 3741 N Rock Rd 67226. SR 96 exit Rock Rd, just n. Int corridors. **Pets:** Small, other species. $10 one-time fee/pet. Designated rooms, service with restrictions, supervision.

WINFIELD

▼▼▼ Comfort Inn H

(620) 221-7529. **Call for rates.** 3800 S Pike Rd 67156. On US 77, 1 mi s. Ext/int corridors. **Pets:** Accepted.

KENTUCKY

CITY INDEX

ASHLAND

AAA ▼▼▼▼ Best Western River Cities H

(606) 326-0357. **$100-$128, 3 day notice.** 31 Russell Plaza Dr 41101. I-64 exit 185, 6 mi nw on US 60, then 3 mi n on US 23. Int corridors. **Pets:** Medium, dogs only. $10 daily fee/pet. Designated rooms, service with restrictions, supervision.

▼▼ Quality Inn H

(606) 325-8989. **$62-$69.** 4708 Winchester Ave 41101. I-64 exit 191, 4.8 mi n on US 23. Ext corridors. **Pets:** Other species. $15 daily fee/pet. Service with restrictions, supervision.

BARDSTOWN

AAA ▼ Bardstown-Parkview Motel M

(502) 348-5983. **$45-$100.** 418 E Stephen Foster Ave 40004. 0.5 mi e on US 150; e of jct US 62. Ext corridors. **Pets:** Accepted.

AAA ▼▼ Best Western General Nelson H 🐾

(502) 348-3977. **$65-$130.** 411 W Stephen Foster Ave 40004. 0.5 mi w on US 62. Ext corridors. **Pets:** Large, dogs only. $15 one-time fee/room. Service with restrictions, crate.

▼▼▼ Hampton Inn H

(502) 349-0100. **$99-$119.** 985 Chambers Blvd 40004. Just s of US 245. Int corridors. **Pets:** Accepted.

BENTON

▼▼▼ Comfort Inn & Suites H

(270) 527-5300. **$110.** 173 Carroll Rd 42025. Just ne of jct US 68/641. Int corridors. **Pets:** $10 one-time fee/pet. Crate.

BEREA

AAA ▼▼▼ Boone Tavern Hotel & Restaurant of Berea College H

(859) 985-3700. **$99-$165.** 100 Main St 40404. I-75 exit 76, 1.5 mi ne on SR 21. Int corridors. **Pets:** Accepted.

▼▼▼ Comfort Inn & Suites H

(859) 985-5500. **$89-$99.** 219 Paint Lick Rd 40403. I-75 exit 76, just w. Int corridors. **Pets:** Medium, other species. $10 daily fee/pet. Service with restrictions, supervision.

BOWLING GREEN

AAA ▼▼▼▼ Best Western Plus Motor Inn H 🐾

(270) 782-3800. **$70-$100.** 166 Cumberland Trace Rd 42103. I-65 exit 22 (Scottsville Rd), just e. Int corridors. **Pets:** Medium. $10 daily fee/pet. Service with restrictions, supervision.

AAA ▼▼▼ Candlewood Suites H

(270) 843-5505. **$99-$159.** 540 Wall St 42103. I-65 exit 22 (Scottsville Rd), just n. Int corridors. **Pets:** Accepted.

AAA ▼▼▼ Country Hearth Inn H

(270) 783-4443. **$45-$90.** 395 Corvette Dr 42101. I-65 exit 28, just w. Int corridors. **Pets:** Small. $5 daily fee/pet. Service with restrictions, supervision.

▼▼▼ Country Inn & Suites By Carlson H

(270) 781-7200. **$89-$249.** 535 Wall St 42104. I-65 exit 22 (Scottsville Rd), just w. Int corridors. **Pets:** Accepted.

▼▼▼ Drury Inn-Bowling Green H

(270) 842-7100. **$100-$174.** 3250 Scottsville Rd 42104. I-65 exit 22 (Scottsville Rd), just w. Int corridors. **Pets:** Accepted.

▼▼▼ Hampton Inn H

(270) 842-4100. **$84-$99.** 233 Three Springs Rd 42104. I-65 exit 22 (Scottsville Rd), 0.3 mi w. Int corridors. **Pets:** Accepted.

▼▼▼ Holiday Inn University Plaza H

(270) 745-0088. **$99-$179.** 1021 Wilkinson Trace 42103. I-65 exit 22 (Scottsville Rd), 2.5 mi w, then just n. Int corridors. **Pets:** Accepted.

▼▼▼▼ **La Quinta Inn & Suites** 🅷
(270) 783-0083. **Call for rates.** 1953 Mel Browning St 42104. I-65 exit 22 (Scottsville Rd), just e. Int corridors. **Pets:** Medium, other species. Service with restrictions, supervision. 🛜 ⊠ 🛌 💻 🖭 ➰

AAA ▼▼ ▼ **News Inn of Bowling Green** Ⓜ
(270) 781-3460. **$49-$89.** 3160 Scottsville Rd 42104. I-65 exit 22 (Scottsville Rd), just w. Ext corridors. **Pets:** $5 daily fee/pet. Designated rooms, service with restrictions, supervision. [SAVE] 🛜 🛌 💻 ➰

AAA ▼▼ ▼ **Red Roof Inn** 🅷
(270) 781-6550. **$50-$109.** 3140 Scottsville Rd 42104. I-65 exit 22 (Scottsville Rd), 0.3 mi w. Ext corridors. **Pets:** Large, other species. No service, supervision. [SAVE] 🛜 🛌

BUCKHORN LAKE STATE RESORT PARK

▼▼ ▼ **Buckhorn Lake State Resort Park** 🅷
(606) 398-7510. **$50-$120.** 4441 Hwy 1833 41721. 5 mi off SR 28 via SR 1833. Ext corridors. **Pets:** Accepted. 🛜 🛌 💻 🖭 ➰ ⊠

BURKESVILLE

▼▼ ▼ **Dale Hollow Lake State Resort Park** 🅷
(270) 433-7431. **$60-$140.** 5970 State Park Rd 42717. Jct SR 449 and 1206. Ext corridors. **Pets:** Accepted.
🛜 ⊠ 🛌 💻 🖭 ➰ ⊠

CADIZ

▼▼ ▼▼ **Lake Barkley State Resort Park** 🅷
(270) 924-1131. **$60-$140.** 3500 State Park Rd 42211. I-24 exit 65, 9.1 mi sw on US 68 and SR 80 to SR 1489, 3.3 mi nw to State Park Rd, then n, follow signs. Ext corridors. **Pets:** Accepted.
🛜 ⊠ 🛌 💻 🖭 ➰ ⊠

CALVERT CITY

▼▼ ▼ **Super 8 Calvert City/KY Lake Area** 🅷
(270) 395-5566. **$45-$80.** 86 Campbell Dr 42029. I-24 exit 27 (US 62), just e. Int corridors. **Pets:** Small, dogs only. $10 one-time fee/pet. Designated rooms, service with restrictions. 🛜 🛌 🛌 💻 ➰

CARROLLTON

AAA ▼▼ ▼ **Best Western Executive Inn** 🅷
(502) 732-8444. **$50-$80.** 10 Slumber Ln 41008. I-71 exit 44, just nw. Int corridors. **Pets:** Accepted. [SAVE] 🛜 🛌 🛌 💻 ➰

▼▼ ▼ **General Butler State Resort Park** 🅷
(502) 732-4384. **$60-$130.** 1608 Hwy 227 41008. I-71 exit 44, 2 mi n. Ext/int corridors. **Pets:** Accepted. 🛜 🛌 🛌 💻 🖭 ➰ ⊠

▼▼ ▼ **Super 8 Carrollton** 🅷
(502) 732-0252. **$54-$90.** 130 Slumber Ln 41008. I-71 exit 44, just nw. Int corridors. **Pets:** Accepted. 🛜 🛌 💻

CATLETTSBURG

▼▼ ▼ **Ramada Limited Hotel** 🅷
(606) 739-5700. **$85-$105.** 6000 Crider Dr 41129. I-64 exit 191, 0.5 mi n on US 23. Int corridors. **Pets:** Accepted. 🛜 🛌 💻 ➰

CAVE CITY

AAA ▼▼ ▼ **Super 8** Ⓜ
(270) 773-2500. **$35-$100.** 799 Mammoth Cave St 42127. I-65 exit 53, just ne. Ext corridors. **Pets:** Medium. $10 daily fee/pet. Designated rooms, service with restrictions, crate. [SAVE] 🛜 🛌 🛌 💻 ➰

CORBIN

AAA ▼▼ ▼ **Best Western Corbin Inn** Ⓜ
(606) 528-2100. **$80-$100.** 2630 Cumberland Falls Hwy 40701. I-75 exit 25, just w. Ext corridors. **Pets:** Other species. $15 daily fee/pet. Service with restrictions, supervision. [SAVE] 🛜 🛌 💻 ➰

COVINGTON

AAA ▼▼ ▼ **Embassy Suites Cincinnati Rivercenter** 🅷 ❀
(859) 261-8400. **$139-$209.** 10 E Rivercenter Blvd 41011. I-71/75 exit 192, 0.8 mi e on 5th St, then 0.3 mi n on Madison Ave. Int corridors. **Pets:** Small. $50 one-time fee/pet. Designated rooms, service with restrictions, crate. [SAVE] 🛜 🛌 🛌 💻 🖭 🍴 ➰ ⊠

CUMBERLAND FALLS STATE RESORT PARK

▼▼ ▼▼ **Cumberland Falls State Resort Park** 🅷
(606) 528-4121. **$60-$140.** 7351 Hwy 90 40701. Jct SR 25 W and 90, 8 mi w. Ext/int corridors. **Pets:** Accepted.
🛜 🛌 🛌 💻 🖭 🍴 ➰ ⊠

DANVILLE

AAA ▼▼ ▼ **Best Western Danville Inn** 🅷
(859) 236-5525. **Call for rates.** 210 Brenda Ave 40422. Just e on US 127 Bypass and 150 (Perryville Rd). Int corridors. **Pets:** Accepted. [SAVE] 🛜 🛌 🛌 💻 ➰

AAA ▼▼ ▼ **Comfort Suites** 🅷
(859) 936-9300. **Call for rates.** 864 Ben Ali Dr 40422. On US 127 Bypass and 150 (Perryville Rd). Int corridors. **Pets:** Accepted. [SAVE] 🛜 ⊠ 🛌 🛌 💻 ➰

▼▼ ▼▼ **Quality Inn** 🅷
(859) 236-8600. **$65-$130.** 96 Daniel Dr 40422. Just e of US 127 on US 150 Bypass. Int corridors. **Pets:** Accepted. 🛜 🛌 🛌 💻 ➰

DAWSON SPRINGS

▼▼ ▼ **Pennyrile Forest State Resort Park** 🅷
(270) 797-3421. **$50-$120.** 20781 Pennyrile Lodge Rd 42408. Western Kentucky Pkwy exit 24, 9.5 mi se on SR 109, then 1.8 mi w on SR 398. Ext corridors. **Pets:** Accepted. 🛜 ⊠ 🛌 🛌 💻 🍴 ➰ ⊠

DRY RIDGE

▼▼ ▼ **Comfort Inn** 🅷
(859) 824-7121. **$70-$99.** 1050 Fashion Ridge Rd 41035. I-75 exit 159, just nw. Int corridors. **Pets:** Accepted. 🛜 🛌 💻

▼▼ ▼ **Hampton Inn** 🅷
(859) 823-7111. **$85-$98.** 1200 Cull Rd 41035. I-75 exit 159, just nw. Int corridors. **Pets:** Accepted. 🛜 🛌 💻 ➰

EDDYVILLE

▼▼ ▼ **Eddy Creek Marina Resort** Ⓜ
(270) 388-2271. **$82-$195, 45 day notice.** 7612 SR 93 S 42038. I-24 exit 45, 4 mi s. Ext corridors. **Pets:** $15 daily fee/pet. Service with restrictions, crate. 🛜 ⊠ 🛌 💻 🍴 ➰ ⊠ ✍

▼▼ ▼ **Holiday Hills Resort Townhouses** Ⓒⓞ
(270) 388-7236. **Call for rates.** 5631 Kentucky 93 S 42038. I-24 exit 45, 2 mi s. Ext corridors. **Pets:** Accepted. 🛜 🛌 💻 ➰ ⊠ ✍

ELIZABETHTOWN

▼▼ ▼ **Baymont Inn & Suites** 🅷
(270) 769-9616. **$61-$97.** 209 Commerce Dr 42701. I-65 exit 94, just nw. Int corridors. **Pets:** Accepted. 🛜 🛌 🛌 💻 ➰

AAA ▼▼ ▼ **Best Western Atrium Gardens** 🅷 ❀
(270) 769-3030. **$79-$80.** 1043 Executive Dr 42702. I-65 exit 94, just nw. Int corridors. **Pets:** Other species. $20 one-time fee/room. Service with restrictions. [SAVE] 🛜 🛌 💻 ➰

▼▼ ▼ **Comfort Inn** 🅷
(270) 765-4166. **$77-$99.** 2009 N Mulberry St 42701. I-65 exit 94, just sw. Int corridors. **Pets:** Medium, other species. $10 daily fee/pet. Designated rooms, no service, supervision. 🛜 🛌 🛌 💻 ➰

▽▽ Holiday Inn Express **H**

(270) 769-1334. **Call for rates.** 107 Buffalo Creek Dr 42701. I-65 exit 94, just w. Int corridors. **Pets:** Small. $50 daily fee/pet. Service with restrictions, crate. 🛰️ 🔊 **H** 💻 ➿

▽▽ Howard Johnson Inn **H**

(270) 769-2344. **$80-$84.** 1058 N Mulberry St 42701. I-65 exit 94, just nw. Ext corridors. **Pets:** Service with restrictions.

🛰️ **H** 💻 🍴 ➿

ⒶⒶⒶ ▽▽▽ La Quinta Inn & Suites Elizabethtown **H**

(270) 765-4747. **$85-$190.** 210 Commerce Dr 42701. I-65 exit 94, just nw. Int corridors. **Pets:** Medium, other species. Service with restrictions, supervision. (SAVE) 🛰️ ⊠ 🔊 **H** 💻 ➿

ERLANGER

▽▽▽ Residence Inn by Marriott, Cincinnati
   Airport **H** 🐾

(859) 282-7400. **$109-$190.** 2811 Circleport Dr 41018. I-275 exit 2, just s. Int corridors. **Pets:** Other species. $100 one-time fee/room. Service with restrictions. 🛰️ ⊠ 🔊 **H** 💻 ➿ ⊠

FALLS OF ROUGH

▽▽ Rough River Dam State Resort Park **H**

(270) 257-2311. **$60-$130.** 450 Lodge Rd 40119. On SR 79, at Rough River Dam. Ext corridors. **Pets:** Accepted.

🛰️ **H** 💻 🍴 ➿ ⊠

FLORENCE

▽▽▽ Ashley Quarters Hotel **H**

(859) 525-9997. **Call for rates.** 4880 Houston Rd 41042. I-71/75 exit 182, 0.6 mi w on Turfway and Houston rds. Int corridors. **Pets:** Accepted.

🛰️ **H** 💻 ➿

ⒶⒶⒶ ▽▽▽ Best Western Inn Florence **H**

(859) 525-0090. **$60-$250.** 7821 Commerce Dr 41042. I-71/75 exit 181, just ne. Int corridors. **Pets:** Medium, dogs only. $15 one-time fee/pet. Service with restrictions, supervision. (SAVE) 🛰️ 🔊 **H** 💻 ➿

ⒶⒶⒶ ▽▽ Comfort Inn Greater Cincinnati Airport on
   Turfway Rd **M**

(859) 647-2700. **Call for rates.** 7454 Turfway Rd 41042. I-71/75 exit 182, 0.8 mi sw. Int corridors. **Pets:** Medium. $10 daily fee/pet. Service with restrictions, supervision. (SAVE) 🛰️ **H** 💻

▽▽ Extended StayAmerica-Cincinnati-Florence **H** 🐾

(859) 282-7829. **$60-$77.** 7350 Turfway Rd 41042. I-71/75 exit 182, just w. Int corridors. **Pets:** Other species. $25 daily fee/pet. Service with restrictions. 🛰️ 🔊 **H** 💻

ⒶⒶⒶ ▽▽ Florence Super 8 **H** 🐾

(859) 283-1221. **$45-$90.** 7928 Dream St 41042. I-71/75 exit 180, just e on US 42, then just n. Int corridors. **Pets:** Other species. $5 daily fee/pet. Service with restrictions, supervision. (SAVE) 🛰️ **H** 💻 ➿

ⒶⒶⒶ ▽▽▽ Hilton Cincinnati Airport **H**

(859) 371-4400. **$90-$159.** 7373 Turfway Rd 41042. I-71/75 exit 182, 0.4 mi sw. Int corridors. **Pets:** Large, dogs only. $50 one-time fee/room. Service with restrictions, supervision. (SAVE) 🛰️ 🔊 **H** 💻 🍴 ➿

▽▽▽ Homewood Suites **H**

(859) 283-2111. **$109-$159.** 1090 Vandercar Way 41042. I-75 exit 182, just w. Int corridors. **Pets:** Accepted. 🛰️ **H** 💻 ➿ ⊠

▽▽▽ La Quinta Inn & Suites Cincinnati Airport
   Florence **H**

(859) 282-8212. **$93-$154.** 350 Meijer Dr 41042. I-71/75 exit 182, 0.4 mi sw. Int corridors. **Pets:** Medium, other species. Service with restrictions, supervision. 🛰️ ⊠ 🔊 **H** 💻 ➿

▽▽ Microtel Inn & Suites **H**

(859) 746-8100. **$54-$90.** 7490 Woodspoint Dr 41042. I-71/75 exit 181, just w. Int corridors. **Pets:** Accepted. 🛰️ 🔊 **H** 💻

FRANKFORT

ⒶⒶⒶ ▽▽▽ Best Western Parkside Inn **H** 🐾

(502) 695-6111. **$80-$99.** 80 Chenault Rd 40601. I-64 exit 58, just e. Ext/int corridors. **Pets:** Large. $20 daily fee/pet. Designated rooms, service with restrictions, crate. (SAVE) 🛰️ **H** 💻 ➿

▽▽▽▽ Capital Plaza Hotel **H**

(502) 227-5100. **Call for rates.** 405 Wilkinson Blvd 40601. Adjacent to Frankfort Convention Center. Int corridors. **Pets:** Accepted.

🛰️ 🔊 **H** 💻 🍴 ➿

FRANKLIN

ⒶⒶⒶ ▽▽▽ Franklin Comfort Inn & Suites **H**

(270) 586-3832. **Call for rates.** 105 Trotters Ln 42134. I-65 exit 6, just w. Int corridors. **Pets:** Accepted. (SAVE) 🛰️ 🔊 **H** 💻 ➿

▽▽▽ Holiday Inn Express & Suites-Franklin **H**

(270) 586-7626. **$98-$169.** 85 Neha Dr 42134. I-65 exit 2, just n. Int corridors. **Pets:** Accepted. 🛰️ ⊠ 🔊 **H** 💻

GILBERTSVILLE

▽▽▽ Kentucky Dam Village State Resort Park **H**

(270) 362-4271. **$60-$140.** 166 Upper Village Dr 42044. I-24 exit 27, 2 mi w on US 62, follow signs. Ext/int corridors. **Pets:** Accepted.

🛰️ **H** 💻 🍴 ➿ ⊠

GLASGOW

▽▽ Comfort Inn **M**

(270) 651-9099. **$75-$200.** 210 Calvary Dr 42141. Cumberland Pkwy exit 11, just n. Ext corridors. **Pets:** Accepted. 🛰️ **H** 💻 ➿

GRAND RIVERS

▽▽ Americas Best Value Inn **M**

(270) 928-2700. **Call for rates.** 720 Complex Dr 42045. I-24 exit 31 (SR 453), just s. Ext/int corridors. **Pets:** Accepted. 🛰️ **H** 💻 ➿

GRAYSON

▽▽ Quality Inn-Grayson, KY **M**

(606) 474-7854. **Call for rates.** 205 SR 1947 41143. I-64 exit 172, just n. Ext corridors. **Pets:** Accepted. 🛰️ 🔊 **H** 💻 ➿

▽▽ Super 8 **H**

(606) 474-8811. **$53-$100.** 125 Super 8 Ln 41143. I-64 exit 172, just s. Int corridors. **Pets:** Small. $10 daily fee/pet. Designated rooms, service with restrictions, supervision. 🛰️ 🔊 **H** 💻

GREENUP

▽▽ Greenbo Lake State Resort Park **H**

(606) 473-7324. **$50-$120.** 965 Lodge Rd 41144. I-64 exit 172, 15 mi ne on SR 1. Ext corridors. **Pets:** Accepted. 🛰️ **H** 💻 🍴 ➿ ⊠

HARDIN

▽▽ Kenlake State Resort Park **H**

(270) 474-2211. **$50-$120.** 542 Kenlake Rd 42048. Just se of jct US 68 and SR 80. Int corridors. **Pets:** Accepted.

🛰️ 🔊 **H** 💻 🍴 ➿ ⊠

HARLAN

▽▽ Holiday Inn Express Harlan **H**

(606) 573-3385. **Call for rates.** 2608 S Hwy 421 40831. On US 421, 2.8 mi s. Int corridors. **Pets:** Small. $10 daily fee/pet. Service with restrictions, crate. 🛰️ **H** 💻 ➿

HARRODSBURG

▼▼ ▼▼ Country Hearth Inn **H**

(859) 734-2400. **$65-$130.** 105 Commercial Dr 40330. 0.6 mi n on College St. Int corridors. **Pets:** Small. $20 one-time fee/pet. Service with restrictions, supervision. 🛜 🔊 ⬛ 💻

▼▼ ▼▼ Shaker Village of Pleasant Hill **CI**

(859) 734-5411. **$95-$250.** 3501 Lexington Rd 40330. On US 68, 7 mi ne. Ext/int corridors. **Pets:** Other species. $20 daily fee/pet. Designated rooms, service with restrictions, supervision. 🛜 ✕ ⬛ 💻 🍽

HEBRON

AAA▷ ▼▼▼▼ DoubleTree by Hilton Hotel Cincinnati Airport **H**

(859) 371-6166. **$90-$160.** 2826 Terminal Dr 41048. I-71/75 exit 185 (I-275), 4 mi w, exit 4B (SR 212), then 1.3 mi w. Int corridors. **Pets:** Dogs only. Designated rooms, service with restrictions, supervision. SAVE 🛜 ✕ 🔊 ⬛ 💻 🍽 🏊

HENDERSON

▼▼ ▼▼ Ramada Inn **H**

(270) 826-6600. **$49-$104.** 2044 US 41 N 42420. On US 41, 1 mi n. Int corridors. **Pets:** Accepted. 🛜 ⬛ 💻 🏊

HOPKINSVILLE

AAA▷ ▼▼▼▼ Holiday Inn **H**

(270) 886-4413. **$89-$109.** 2910 Ft Campbell Blvd 42240. Pennyrile Pkwy exit 7A, 0.6 mi n on US 41A. Int corridors. **Pets:** Accepted. SAVE 🛜 ⬛ 💻 🍽 🏊 ✕

JAMESTOWN

▼▼ ▼▼ Lake Cumberland State Resort Park **H**

(270) 343-3111. **$60-$140.** 5465 State Park Rd 42629. Jct SR 55 and US 127, 2 mi n. Ext/int corridors. **Pets:** Accepted. 🛜 🔊 ⬛ 💻 🍽 🏊 ✕

KUTTAWA

▼▼ ▼▼ Days Inn **M**

(270) 388-4060. **$54-$72.** 139 Days Inn Dr 42055. I-24 exit 40 (US 62), just s. Ext corridors. **Pets:** Accepted. 🛜 🔊 ⬛ 💻 🏊

AAA▷ ▼▼ ▼▼ Relax Inn **M**

(270) 388-2285. **$45-$80.** 224 New Circle Dr 42055. I-24 exit 40 (US 62), just e. Ext corridors. **Pets:** Accepted. SAVE 🛜 ⬛

LEBANON

▼▼▼▼ Hampton Inn Lebanon **H**

(270) 699-4000. **$94-$130.** 1125 Loretto Rd 40033. Jct SR 49 and 84. Int corridors. **Pets:** Medium, other species. $45 one-time fee/room. Service with restrictions, crate. 🛜 🔊 ⬛ 💻 🏊

LEITCHFIELD

▼▼ ▼▼ Hatfield Inn **H**

(270) 259-0464. **$83-$135.** 769 White St 42754. Western Kentucky Pkwy exit 107, just nw. Int corridors. **Pets:** Medium. $20 daily fee/pet. Service with restrictions, supervision. 🛜 ⬛ 💻

LEWISPORT

AAA▷ ▼▼ ▼▼ Best Western Hancock Inn **M**

(270) 295-3234. **$70-$100.** 9040 US Hwy 60 W 42351. On US 60. Int corridors. **Pets:** Accepted. SAVE 🛜 ⬛ 💻 🏊

LEXINGTON

AAA▷ ▼▼ ▼▼ Best Western Lexington Conference Center Hotel **H**

(859) 263-5241. **$85-$110.** 5532 Athens-Boonesboro Rd 40509. I-75 exit 104, just e. Int corridors. **Pets:** Medium, other species. $20 daily fee/room. Service with restrictions, crate. SAVE 🛜 ⬛ 💻 🏊 ✕

▼▼▼▼ Candlewood Suites **H** ❀

(859) 967-1940. **$60-$150.** 603 Adcolor Dr 40511. Jct SR 4 (New Circle Rd) and Newtown Pike, just s. Int corridors. **Pets:** $25 one-time fee/pet. Service with restrictions, supervision. 🛜 🔊 ⬛ 💻 🏊

AAA▷ ▼▼▼▼ Clarion Hotel **H** ❀

(859) 233-0512. **Call for rates.** 1950 Newtown Pike 40511. I-75/64 exit 115, just s. Ext/int corridors. **Pets:** Small, other species. $35 one-time fee/room. Service with restrictions, supervision. SAVE 🛜 🔊 ⬛ 💻 🍽 🏊 ✕

▼▼▼▼ Comfort Suites by Choice Hotels **H**

(859) 296-4446. **$89-$119.** 3060 Fieldstone Way 40513. Jct New Circle and Harrodsburg rds, just sw. Int corridors. **Pets:** Accepted. 🛜 ✕ 🔊 ⬛ 💻 🏊 ✕

▼▼ ▼▼ Crowne Plaza Lexington -The Campbell House **H**

(859) 255-4281. **$79-$229.** 1375 S Broadway 40504. I-75/64 exit 113, 4.8 mi sw. Int corridors. **Pets:** Accepted. 🛜 🔊 ⬛ 💻 🍽 🏊

▼▼ ▼▼ Days Inn-South **M**

(859) 263-3100. **$45-$65.** 5575 Athens-Boonesboro Rd 40509. I-75 exit 104, just e. Ext corridors. **Pets:** Accepted. 🛜 ⬛ 💻

▼▼▼▼ DoubleTree Suites by Hilton Hotel Lexington **H**

(859) 268-0060. **$99-$159.** 2601 Richmond Rd 40509. I-75 exit 104, 5.5 mi w. Int corridors. **Pets:** Accepted. 🛜 🔊 ⬛ 💻 🍽 🏊

▼▼▼▼ Fairfield Inn & Suites by Marriott - Lexington North **H**

(859) 977-5870. **$99-$159.** 2100 Hackney Pl 40511. I-64/75 exit 9B, just n, then 0.3 mi e on Stanton Way. Int corridors. **Pets:** Large, other species. $75 one-time fee/room. Service with restrictions, supervision. 🛜 ✕ 🔊 ⬛ 💻 🏊

AAA▷ ▼▼▼▼ Four Points by Sheraton Hotel **H**

(859) 259-1311. **$69-$169, 3 day notice.** 1938 Stanton Way 40511. I-75/64 exit 115, just se on SR 922. Int corridors. **Pets:** Large, dogs only. $25 daily fee/room. Service with restrictions, crate. SAVE 🛜 ✕ 🔊 ⬛ 💻 🍽 🏊

▼▼▼▼ Hampton Inn I-75 **H**

(859) 299-2613. **Call for rates.** 2251 Elkhorn Rd 40505. I-75 exit 110, 0.4 mi nw. Int corridors. **Pets:** Large. Service with restrictions, supervision. 🛜 🔊 ⬛ 💻 🏊

▼▼▼▼ Hilton Lexington/Downtown **H** ❀

(859) 231-9000. **$109-$269.** 369 W Vine St 40507. Corner of Vine St and Broadway. Int corridors. **Pets:** $200 one-time fee/room. Service with restrictions, supervision. 🛜 🔊 ⬛ 💻 🍽 🏊 ✕

▼▼▼▼ Hilton Suites of Lexington Green **H**

(859) 271-4000. **$139-$349.** 245 Lexington Green Cir 40503. SR 4 (New Circle Rd) exit 19, just s. Int corridors. **Pets:** Accepted. 🛜 🔊 ⬛ 💻 🍽 🏊

▼▼▼▼ Holiday Inn Express Hotel & Suites-Lexington **H**

(859) 389-6800. **$99-$299.** 1000 Export St 40504. I-75 exit 113, 4.5 mi s, then just e. Int corridors. **Pets:** $25 one-time fee/room. Service with restrictions, crate. 🛜 🔊 ⬛ 💻 🏊

▼▼▼▼ La Quinta Inn & Suites Lexington South/Hamburg **H**

(859) 543-1877. **Call for rates.** 100 Canebrake Dr 40509. I-75 exit 104, just e. Int corridors. **Pets:** Medium, other species. Service with restrictions, supervision. 🛜 🔊 ⬛ 💻 🏊

▼▼▼▼ Lyndon House Bed & Breakfast **BB**

(859) 420-2683. **$159-$249.** 507 N Broadway 40508. I-75/64 exit 113, 2.5 mi w on US 27, then just n. Int corridors. **Pets:** Accepted. 🛜 ✕ 📱

▼▼▼▼ Marriott Griffin Gate Resort & Spa 🅗
(859) 231-5100. **$179-$199.** 1800 Newtown Pike 40511. I-75/64 exit 115, 0.5 mi sw. Int corridors. **Pets:** Large. $100 one-time fee/room. Designated rooms, service with restrictions, supervision.
🛜 ✕ 🅼 🔲 🍴 🏊 ✕

🆎 ▼▼ Red Roof Inn-North 🅗
(859) 293-2626. **$45-$99.** 1980 Haggard Ct 40505. I-75/64 exit 113, 0.3 mi nw. Ext corridors. **Pets:** Large, other species. No service, supervision.
SAVE 🛜 🔲

🆎 ▼▼ Red Roof Inn South 🅗
(859) 277-9400. **$50-$80.** 2651 Wilhite Dr 40503. Jct US 27 and SR 4 (New Circle Rd). Ext corridors. **Pets:** Large, other species. No service, supervision. SAVE 🛜 🅼 🔲

▼▼▼ Residence Inn by Marriott 🅗
(859) 296-0460. **$139-$153.** 3110 Wall St 40513. Jct New Circle and Harrodsburg rds. Int corridors. **Pets:** Accepted.
🛜 ✕ 🅼 🔲 🏊 ✕

▼▼▼▼ Residence Inn Lexington North 🅗 🐾
(859) 231-6191. **$143-$175.** 1080 Newtown Pike 40511. I-75/64 exit 115, 1 mi s on SR 922. Ext corridors. **Pets:** $75 one-time fee/room. Service with restrictions, crate. 🛜 ✕ 🔲 🏊

▼▼▼ Residence Inn Lexington South/Hamburg Place 🅗 🐾
(859) 263-9979. **$109-$189.** 2688 Pink Pigeon Pkwy 40509. I-75 exit 108, just se. Int corridors. **Pets:** Other species. $75 one-time fee/room. Service with restrictions, crate. 🛜 ✕ 🅼 🔲 🍴 🏊 ✕

▼▼ Sleep Inn Lexington 🅗
(859) 543-8400. **$72-$117.** 1920 Plaudit Pl 40509. I-75 exit 108, just sw. Int corridors. **Pets:** Accepted. 🛜 🔲 🏊

LONDON

▼▼ Budget Host Westgate Inn 🅜 🐾
(606) 878-7330. **$47-$59.** 254 Russell Dyche Memorial Hwy & Bravo Ln 40741. I-75 exit 41, just w on SR 80. Ext/int corridors. **Pets:** Small. Designated rooms, service with restrictions, supervision. 🛜 🔲 🏊

▼▼ Red Roof Inn 🅗
(606) 862-8844. **$59-$114.** 110 Melcon Ln 40741. I-75 exit 41, southwest corner. Int corridors. **Pets:** Large, other species. No service, supervision.
🛜 🅼 🔲 🏊

LOUISA

▼▼ Super 8-Louisa 🅗
(606) 638-7888. **$53-$104.** 191 Falls Creek Dr 41230. Jct US 23 and SR 3. Int corridors. **Pets:** Accepted. 🛜 🅼 🔲

LOUISVILLE METROPOLITAN AREA

BROOKS

▼▼◆ Baymont Inn 🅗
(502) 957-6900. **$62-$260.** 149 Willabrook Dr 40109. I-65 exit 121, just nw. Int corridors. **Pets:** Accepted. 🛜 🔲 🏊

HURSTBOURNE

▼▼▼ Drury Inn & Suites-Louisville 🅗
(502) 326-4170. **$95-$179.** 9501 Blairwood Rd 40222. I-64 exit 15, just n. Int corridors. **Pets:** Accepted. 🛜 🅼 🔲 🏊 ✕

🆎 ▼▼ Red Roof Inn Louisville - East #034 🅗
(502) 426-7621. **$49-$199.** 9330 Blairwood Rd 40222. I-64 exit 15, 0.3 mi nw of Hurstbourne Pkwy. Ext corridors. **Pets:** Large, other species. No service, supervision. SAVE 🛜 🅼 🔲

JEFFERSONTOWN

▼▼▼ Holiday Inn-Hurstbourne 🅗
(502) 426-2600. **$79-$450.** 1325 S Hurstbourne Pkwy 40222. I-64 exit 15, just n. Ext/int corridors. **Pets:** Other species. $39 one-time fee/pet. Service with restrictions, crate. 🛜 🅼 🔲 🍴 🏊 ✕

▼▼ Jameson Inn Louisville East 🅗
(502) 267-8100. **$80-$100.** 1301 Kentucky Mills Dr 40299. I-64 exit 17, just s. Ext/int corridors. **Pets:** Medium. $15 daily fee/room. Service with restrictions, supervision. 🛜 🅼 🔲 🏊

🆎 ▼▼◆ La Quinta Inn & Suites Louisville Expo East 🅗
(502) 267-8889. **Call for rates.** 1501 Alliant Ave 40299. I-64 exit 17, just e. Int corridors. **Pets:** Medium, other species. Service with restrictions, supervision. SAVE 🛜 ✕ 🅼 🔲 🏊

▼▼ Microtel Inn Louisville East 🅗
(502) 266-6590. **$45-$250.** 1221 Kentucky Mills Dr 40299. I-64 exit 17, just s. Int corridors. **Pets:** Medium. $20 one-time fee/pet. Designated rooms, service with restrictions, supervision. 🛜 🅼

LA GRANGE

🆎 ▼▼▼◆ Holiday Inn Express 🅗
(502) 222-5678. **Call for rates.** 1001 Paige Pl 40031. I-71 exit 22, just se. Int corridors. **Pets:** $25 daily fee/pet. Designated rooms, service with restrictions, supervision. SAVE 🛜 🅼 🔲 🏊

LOUISVILLE

▼▼▼▼ 21c Museum Hotel 🅗
(502) 217-6300. **Call for rates.** 700 W Main St 40202. Jct 7th and Main sts. Int corridors. **Pets:** Accepted. 🛜 ✕ 🅼 🔲 🍴 ✕

▼▼▼ Aleksander House Bed and Breakfast 🅑🅑
(502) 637-4985. **$124-$195, 14 day notice.** 1213 S 1st St 40203. I-65 exit 135 (St Catherine St), just s. Int corridors. **Pets:** Accepted.
🛜 ✕ 🔲

🆎 ▼▼▼ Best Western Plus Airport East/Expo Center 🅗
(502) 456-4411. **$62-$159.** 1921 Bishop Ln 40218. I-264 exit 15B westbound, 0.3 mi s; exit 15 eastbound. Int corridors. **Pets:** Other species. $25 one-time fee/room. Service with restrictions, crate.
SAVE 🛜 🅼 🔲 🍴 🏊

▼▼ Candlewood Suites Louisville Airport 🅗
(502) 357-3577. **Call for rates.** 1367 Gardiner Ln 40213. I-264 exit 14, just s, then just e. Int corridors. **Pets:** Medium. $75 one-time fee/room. Service with restrictions, supervision. 🛜 🔲 ✕

▼▼▼ Crowne Plaza Louisville 🅗
(502) 367-2251. **$99-$299, 3 day notice.** 830 Phillips Ln 40209. I-264 exit 11 (Fairgrounds/Expo Center Main Gate). Int corridors. **Pets:** Other species. $250 one-time fee/room. Service with restrictions, crate.
🛜 ✕ 🅼 🔲 🍴 🏊

▼▼ Homewood Suites 🅗
(502) 429-9070. **$144-$249.** 9401 Hurstbourne Trace 40222. I-64 exit 15, 2.5 mi n. Int corridors. **Pets:** Large. $100 one-time fee/room. Service with restrictions, crate. 🛜 🅼 🔲 🏊 ✕

▼▼ Jameson Inn Airport South 🅗
(502) 968-4100. **$85-$105.** 6515 Signature Dr 40213. I-65 exit 128 (Fern Valley Rd); on southeast corner. Int corridors. **Pets:** Medium. $15 daily fee/room. Service with restrictions, supervision. 🛜 🔲 🏊

🆎 ▼▼▼◆ La Quinta Inn & Suites Louisville Airport Expo 🅗
(502) 368-0007. **$85-$155.** 4125 Preston Hwy 40213. I-65 exit 130, 1 mi n. Int corridors. **Pets:** Medium, other species. Service with restrictions, supervision. SAVE 🛜 ✕ 🅼 🔲 🏊

▼▼ Ramada Limited Airport & Fair/Expo Center 🏨
(502) 637-6336. **Call for rates.** 2912 Crittenden Dr 40209. I-264 exit 11 (Fairgrounds/Expo Center Main Gate), 0.6 mi n. Int corridors. **Pets:** $25 one-time fee/pet. Service with restrictions, supervision.
🛜 ❌ 🛏 💻 🕽

🌀 ▼▼ Red Roof Inn-Airport-Fairgrounds 🏨
(502) 968-0151. **$46-$111.** 4704 Preston Hwy 40213. I-65 exit 130, northeast corner. Ext corridors. **Pets:** Large, other species. No service, supervision. 🆂🅰🆅🅴 🛜 🛏

🌀 ▼▼ Red Roof Inn-Southeast-Fairgrounds 🏨
(502) 456-2993. **$55-$250.** 3322 Red Roof Inn Pl 40218. I-264 exit 15B westbound, 0.3 mi s; exit 15 eastbound. Ext corridors. **Pets:** Large, other species. No service, supervision. 🆂🅰🆅🅴 🛜 🛏 💻

▼▼▼ Residence Inn by Marriott-Louisville Airport 🏨
(502) 363-8800. **$134-$164.** 700 Phillips Ln 40209. I-264 exit 11 (Fairgrounds/Expo Center Main Gate), 0.4 mi w. Int corridors.
Pets: Accepted. 🛜 ❌ 🛡 🛏 💻 🕽 ❌

▼▼▼ Residence Inn by Marriott Louisville Downtown 🏨
(502) 589-8998. **$103-$159.** 333 E Market St 40202. Corner of Preston and E Market sts. Int corridors. **Pets:** Accepted.
🛜 ❌ 🛡 🛏 💻 🕽 ❌

▼▼▼ Residence Inn by Marriott-Louisville NE 🏨
(502) 412-1311. **$95-$133.** 3500 Springhurst Commons Dr 40241. I-265 exit 32, 0.5 mi w on Westport Rd, then just n. Int corridors.
Pets: Accepted. 🛜 ❌ 🛡 🛏 💻 🕽 ❌

▼▼▼ Residence Inn Louisville East 🏨
(502) 425-1821. **$109-$149.** 120 N Hurstbourne Pkwy 40222. I-64 exit 15, 1.8 mi n. Ext corridors. **Pets:** Accepted.
🛜 ❌ 🛏 💻 🕽 ❌

🌀 ▼▼▼ ▼▼▼ The Seelbach Hilton Louisville 🏨
(502) 585-3200. **$149-$229.** 500 4th St 40202. I-65 exit 136C (Muhammad Ali Blvd), 0.3 mi w, then just s. Int corridors. **Pets:** Accepted.
🆂🅰🆅🅴 🛜 ❌ 🛡 🛏 💻 🍴 ❌

▼▼ Sleep Inn Fairgrounds 🏨
(502) 368-9597. **$89-$109.** 3330 Preston Hwy 40213. I-264 exit 11 (Fairgrounds/Expo Center Main Gate), 0.5 mi e on Phillips Ln, then just n. Int corridors. **Pets:** Other species. $25 one-time fee/room. Supervision.
🛜 ❌ 🛡 🛏 💻 🕽

▼▼▼ Staybridge Suites Louisville East 🏨
(502) 244-9511. **$75-$189.** 11711 Gateworth Way 40299. I-64 exit 17, just n. Int corridors. **Pets:** Accepted. 🛜 🛡 🛏 💻 🕽

▼▼ Super 8 🏨
(502) 635-0799. **$50-$100.** 101 Central Ave 40209. I-65 exit 132, just s. Int corridors. **Pets:** Accepted. 🛜 🛡 🛏 💻

SHEPHERDSVILLE

🌀 ▼▼▼ Best Western Plus South 🏨
(502) 543-7097. **$79-$99.** 211 S Lakeview Dr 40165. I-65 exit 117 (SR 44 W), just se. Int corridors. **Pets:** Medium. Service with restrictions, supervision. 🆂🅰🆅🅴 🛜 🛏 💻 🕽

▼▼▼ Fairfield Inn Louisville South 🏨
(502) 955-5533. **$103-$125.** 362 Brenton Way 40165. I-65 exit 121, just ne. Int corridors. **Pets:** Accepted. 🛜 ❌ 🛡 🛏 💻 🕽 ❌

▼▼▼ Sleep Inn & Suites - Louisville South 🏨
(502) 921-1001. **Call for rates.** 130 Spring Pointe Dr 40165. I-65 exit 117 (SR 44 W), just e. Int corridors. **Pets:** Accepted.
🛜 🛡 🛏 💻 🕽

▼▼ Super 8 🏨
(502) 543-8870. **$50-$99.** 275 Keystone Crossroads 40165. I-65 exit 117 (SR 44 W), just w. Int corridors. **Pets:** Accepted. 🛜 🛏 💻 🕽

SHIVELY

▼▼▼ Holiday Inn Southwest Fair Expo 🏨
(502) 448-2020. **$109-$169.** 4110 Dixie Hwy 40216. I-264 exit 8B, just n on US 31 W and 60. Int corridors. **Pets:** Accepted.
🛜 🛡 🛏 💻 🍴 🕽

END METROPOLITAN AREA

LUCAS

▼▼ Barren River Lake State Resort Park 🏨
(270) 646-2151. **$60-$140.** 1149 State Park Rd 42156. Cumberland Pkwy exit 11, 10 mi s on US 31 E. Ext corridors. **Pets:** Small. $25 one-time fee/room. Designated rooms, service with restrictions, crate.
🛜 🛏 💻 🍴 🕽 ❌

MADISONVILLE

🌀 ▼▼▼ Best Western Plus Madisonville Inn 🏨 🐾
(270) 821-2121. **$90-$100.** 1891 Lantaff Blvd 42431. Pennyrile Pkwy exit 44. Int corridors. **Pets:** Medium. $10 daily fee/pet. Service with restrictions, supervision. 🆂🅰🆅🅴 🛜 🛡 🛏 💻

MANCHESTER

🌀 ▼▼ Best Western of Manchester 🏨
(606) 598-1800. **$75.** 363 Hwy 80 40962. Hal Roders Pkwy exit 20. Ext corridors. **Pets:** Accepted. 🆂🅰🆅🅴 🛜 🛡 🛏 💻 🕽

MAYSVILLE

▼▼ Super 8 🏨
(606) 759-8888. **$43-$80.** 550 Tucker Dr 41056. Just e of US 68. Int corridors. **Pets:** Accepted. 🛜 🛡 🛏 💻

MOREHEAD

🌀 ▼▼▼ Comfort Inn & Suites 🏨
(606) 780-7378. **$69-$129.** 2650 Kentucky 801 N 40351. I-64 exit 133, just s. Int corridors. **Pets:** Accepted. 🆂🅰🆅🅴 🛜 🛡 🛏 💻 🕽

▼▼▼ Holiday Inn Express of Morehead 🏨
(606) 784-5796. **$99-$129.** 110 Toms Dr 40351. I-64 exit 137 (SR 32), just sw. Int corridors. **Pets:** Medium, other species. $15 daily fee/pet. Service with restrictions, supervision. 🛜 🛡 🛏 💻 🕽

MORTONS GAP

🌀 ▼▼ Executive Pennyrile Inn 🏨
(270) 258-5201. **Call for rates.** White City Rd 42440. Pennyrile Pkwy exit 37 (US 41). Ext corridors. **Pets:** Accepted. 🆂🅰🆅🅴 🛜 🛏 💻 🕽

MOUNT OLIVET

▼▼ Blue Licks Battlefield State Resort Park 🏨
(859) 289-5507. **$50-$120.** 10299 Maysville Rd 41064. I-75/64 exit 113, 45 mi n on US 68. Ext corridors. **Pets:** Accepted.
🛜 ❌ 🛡 🛏 💻 🍴 🕽 ❌

MOUNT VERNON

▼▼ Days Inn-Renfro Valley 🏨
(606) 256-3300. **$49-$95.** 1630 Richmond St 40456. I-75 exit 62, just n. Ext corridors. **Pets:** Small. $15 one-time fee/pet. Service with restrictions, supervision. 🛜 🛡 💻

MURRAY

Best Western University Inn [H]
(270) 753-5353. **$55-$85.** 1503 N 12th St 42071. 1.9 mi n on US 641.
Ext corridors. **Pets:** Accepted. [SAVE] 🛜 🔲 🖵 🏊

OAK GROVE

Holiday Inn Express [H]
(270) 439-0022. **$95-$99.** 12759 Ft Campbell Blvd 42262. I-24 exit 86,
just s. Int corridors. **Pets:** Small. $10 daily fee/pet. Designated rooms,
service with restrictions, crate. 🛜 🖑M 🔲 🖵

Quality Inn @ Ft. Campbell [H]
(270) 439-3311. **$75-$90.** 201 Auburn St 42262. I-24 exit 86, just se. Ext
corridors. **Pets:** Medium. $20 daily fee/pet. Designated rooms, no service,
supervision. [SAVE] 🛜 🖑M 🔲 🖵

OLIVE HILL

Carter Caves State Resort Park [H]
(606) 286-4411. **$60-$130.** 344 Caveland Dr 41164. I-64 exit 161, just n.
Ext corridors. **Pets:** Accepted. 🛜 🔲 🖵 🍴 🏊 ⊠

OWENSBORO

Super 8-Owensboro [H]
(270) 685-3388. **$63-$90.** 1027 Goetz Dr 42301. US 60 Bypass exit 4 at
US 431. Int corridors. **Pets:** Other species. $20 one-time fee/pet. Service
with restrictions, crate. 🛜 🔲 🖵

PADUCAH

Americas Best Value Inn [H]
(270) 575-9605. **$50-$60.** 5125 Old Cairo Rd 42001. I-24 exit 3 (SR
305), just e. Ext corridors. **Pets:** Accepted. [SAVE] 🛜 🔲

Candlewood Suites [H] 🐾
(270) 442-3969. **$65-$119.** 3940 Coleman Crossing Cir 42001. I-24 exit
4 (US 60), just ne. Int corridors. **Pets:** Large, other species. $25 one-time
fee/room. Service with restrictions, crate. 🛜 🖑M 🔲 🖵

Days Inn [H]
(270) 442-7500. **$53-$59.** 3901 Hinkleville Rd 42001. I-24 exit 4 (US 60),
just e. Ext corridors. **Pets:** Accepted. 🛜 🔲 🖵 🏊

Drury Inn [H]
(270) 443-3313. **$105-$149.** 3975 Hinkleville Rd 42001. I-24 exit 4 (US
60), just e. Int corridors. **Pets:** Accepted. 🛜 🔲 🖵 🏊 ⊠

Drury Suites [H]
(270) 441-0024. **$100-$144.** 2930 James Sanders Blvd 42001. I-24 exit
4 (US 60), just w. Int corridors. **Pets:** Accepted.
🛜 🖑M 🔲 🖵 🏊 ⊠

Holiday Inn Express [H]
(270) 442-8874. **$99-$169.** 3994 Hinkleville Rd 42001. I-24 exit 4 (US
60), just se. Int corridors. **Pets:** Accepted. 🛜 🔲 🖵 🏊

Pear Tree Inn by Drury [H]
(270) 444-7200. **$75-$124.** 5006 Hinkleville Rd 42001. I-24 exit 4 (US
60), just w. Int corridors. **Pets:** Accepted. 🛜 🔲 🖵 🏊

Residence Inn by Marriott [H] 🐾
(270) 444-3966. **$109-$149.** 3900 Coleman Crossing Cir 42001. I-24 exit
4 (US 60), just ne. Int corridors. **Pets:** Medium, other species. $50 one-
time fee/room. Designated rooms, crate.
🛜 ⊠ 🖑M 🔲 🖵 🏊 ⊠

PINEVILLE

Pine Mountain State Resort Park [H]
(606) 337-3066. **$60-$130.** 1050 State Park Rd 40977. Jct US 25 E and
SR 190, 5.5 mi w. Ext corridors. **Pets:** Accepted.
🛜 🔲 🖵 🍴 🏊 ⊠

PRESTONSBURG

Heritage House Hotel [H]
(606) 886-0001. **$62-$72, 10 day notice.** 1887 N US 23 41653. On US
23, 2 mi s. Ext corridors. **Pets:** Accepted.
🛜 🖑M 🔲 🖵 🏊 ⊠

Jenny Wiley State Resort Park [H]
(606) 889-1790. **$60-$130.** 75 Theatre Ct 41653-9799. 3.5 mi s on US
23 and 460, 3 mi e on SR 3; SR 80, 4 mi n on SR 302. Ext corridors.
Pets: Accepted. 🛜 🖑M 🔲 🖵 🍴 🏊 ⊠

RICHMOND

Comfort Suites [H]
(859) 624-0770. **Call for rates.** 2007 Colby Taylor Dr 40475. I-75 exit
87, just e. Int corridors. **Pets:** Accepted. 🛜 ⊠ 🖑M 🔲 🖵 🏊

Holiday Inn Express Hotel & Suites [H]
(859) 624-4055. **$109-$119.** 1990 Colby Taylor Dr 40745. I-75 exit 87,
just w. Int corridors. **Pets:** $25 daily fee/pet. Service with restrictions,
crate. 🛜 🖑M 🔲 🖵 🏊

Jameson Inn [H]
(859) 623-0063. **$85-$105.** 1007 Colby Taylor Dr 40475. I-75 exit 87, just
w. Int corridors. **Pets:** Medium. $15 daily fee/room. Service with restric-
tions, supervision. 🛜 🖑M 🔲 🖵 🏊

Super 8 [H] 🐾
(859) 624-1550. **$36-$75.** 107 N Keeneland Dr 40475. I-75 exit 90. Int
corridors. **Pets:** Small, dogs only. $25 daily fee/pet. Designated rooms,
service with restrictions, supervision. [SAVE] 🛜 🔲 🖵

RUSSELLVILLE

Econo Lodge [H]
(270) 726-2488. **Call for rates.** 1450 Bowling Green Rd 42276. 1.4 mi e
on SR 80 and US 68. Ext corridors. **Pets:** Accepted.
🛜 🔲 🖵 🏊

SHELBYVILLE

Best Western Shelbyville Lodge [H]
(502) 633-4400. **$80-$191.** 115 Isaac Shelby Dr 40065. I-64 exit 32, 0.5
mi n on SR 55. Int corridors. **Pets:** Accepted. [SAVE] 🛜 🔲 🖵 🏊

Country Hearth Inn [H]
(502) 633-5771. **$55-$145.** 100 Howard Dr 40065. I-64 exit 32, 0.5 mi n
on SR 55. Int corridors. **Pets:** Accepted. [SAVE] 🛜 🔲 🖵

Ramada [H]
(502) 633-9933. **$59-$299, 3 day notice.** 251 Breighton Cir 40065. I-64
exit 32, just s. Int corridors. **Pets:** Accepted.
🛜 ⊠ 🖑M 🔲 🖵 🏊

SLADE

Natural Bridge State Resort Park [H]
(606) 663-2214. **$60-$140.** 2135 Natural Bridge Rd 40376. Mountain
Pkwy exit 33, 2 mi s on SR 11. Ext/int corridors. **Pets:** Accepted.
🛜 🖑M 🔲 🖵 🍴 🏊 ⊠

SMITHS GROVE

Bryce Inn [M]
(270) 563-5141. **$53-$75.** 592 S Main St 42171. I-65 exit 38, 0.3 mi w.
Ext corridors. **Pets:** Small, dogs only. $10 one-time fee/room. Service with
restrictions, supervision. 🛜 🔲 🖵 🏊

SPARTA

Ramada at the Kentucky Speedway [H]
(859) 567-7223. **$59-$270, 3 day notice.** 525 Dale Dr 41086. I-71 exit
57, just w. Int corridors. **Pets:** Medium. $25 one-time fee/room. Service
with restrictions, crate. 🛜 🖑M 🔲 🖵 🏊

VERSAILLES
▼▼▼▼ 1823 Historic Rose Hill Inn BB

(859) 873-5957. **Call for rates.** 233 Rose Hill Ave 40383. Just s on SR 33 (S Main St), then just w. Ext/int corridors. **Pets:** Accepted.
🛜 🖼 💻

WEST LIBERTY
▼▼ ▼▼ Days Inn H

(606) 743-4206. **$63-$81.** 1613 W Main St 41472. Jct SR 519 and 460, just w. Int corridors. **Pets:** Accepted. 🛜 🖼 🔲 💻

WILLIAMSBURG
📞 ▼▼▼▼ Cumberland Inn H

(606) 539-4100. **$80-$85.** 649 S 10th St 40769. I-75 exit 11, just e. Int corridors. **Pets:** Small. $15 daily fee/pet. Designated rooms, service with restrictions, supervision. 💾 🛜 🖼 🔲 💻 🍽 ≈

LOUISIANA

CITY INDEX

ALEXANDRIA
▼▼▼▼ La Quinta Inn & Suites Alexandria H

(318) 442-3700. **$98-$175.** 6116 W Calhoun Dr 71303. I-49 exit 90 (Air Base Rd), just w. Int corridors. **Pets:** Medium, other species. Service with restrictions, supervision. 🛜 🖼 🔲 💻 ≈

📞 ▼▼ Ramada H

(318) 448-1611. **$59-$99.** 742 MacArthur Dr 71303. 0.4 mi s of jct SR 28 and US 71/165 (MacArthur Dr). Ext corridors. **Pets:** Accepted.
💾 🛜 🔲 💻 ≈

BATON ROUGE
📞 ▼▼ ▼▼ Best Western Chateau Louisianne Suite Hotel H

(225) 927-6700. **$79-$129.** 710 N Lobdell Blvd 70806. 4.6 mi e on Florida Blvd, then 0.3 mi n. Int corridors. **Pets:** Accepted.
💾 🛜 🔲 💻 ≈ 🖾

📞 ▼▼▼▼ Best Western Plus Richmond Inn & Suites - Baton Rouge H 🐾

(225) 924-6500. **$100-$160.** 5668 Hilton Ave 70808. I-10 exit 158 (College Dr), just ne. Int corridors. **Pets:** Other species. $20 daily fee/room. Service with restrictions, supervision.
💾 🛜 🖾 🔲 💻 ≈ 🖾

▼▼▼▼ Chase Suites by Woodfin H

(225) 927-5630. **Call for rates.** 5522 Corporate Blvd 70808. I-10 exit 158 (College Dr), just n, then just e. Ext corridors. **Pets:** Accepted.
🛜 🖾 🔲 💻 🖾

📞 ▼▼▼▼ Courtyard Baton Rouge Acadian Center H

(225) 924-6400. **$89-$219.** 2421 S Acadian Thruway 70808. I-10 exit 157B, just s. Int corridors. **Pets:** Accepted.
🔳ECO 💾 🛜 🖾 🖼 🔲 💻 🍽 ≈

📞 ▼▼▼▼ Crowne Plaza Executive Center H

(225) 925-2244. **$109-$189.** 4728 Constitution Ave 70808. I-10 exit 158 (College Dr), just s, then just e. Int corridors. **Pets:** Accepted.
💾 🛜 🖼 🔲 💻 🍽 ≈

▼▼▼▼ Drury Inn & Suites Baton Rouge H

(225) 766-2022. **$90-$224.** 7939 Essen Park Ave 70809. I-10 exit 160 (Essen Ln), just s. Int corridors. **Pets:** Accepted.
🛜 🖼 🔲 💻 ≈

📞 ▼▼▼▼ Hilton Baton Rouge Capitol Center H

(225) 344-5866. **$139-$249.** 201 Lafayette St 70801. I-110 exit 1C (Florida Blvd), 0.5 mi w to Lafayette St, then just s. Int corridors. **Pets:** Accepted. 💾 🛜 🖾 🔲 💻 🍽 ≈

📞 ▼▼▼▼ Holiday Inn-College @ I-10 H

(225) 448-2030. **$99-$119.** 4848 Constitution Ave 70808. I-10 exit 158 (College Dr), just s, then just e. Int corridors. **Pets:** Accepted.
💾 🛜 🔲 💻 🍽 ≈

▼▼▼▼ Holiday Inn-South H

(225) 924-7021. **$99-$119.** 9940 Airline Hwy 70816. I-12 exit 2B, just n on US 61. Ext/int corridors. **Pets:** Accepted. 🛜 🔲 💻 🍽 ≈

📞 ▼▼▼▼ Hotel Indigo Baton Rouge Downtown Riverfront H

(225) 343-1515. **$189-$249.** 200 Convention St 70801. Corner of Lafayette St; downtown. Int corridors. **Pets:** Medium. $50 one-time fee/room. Designated rooms, service with restrictions, supervision.
💾 🛜 🖾 🖼 🔲 💻 🍽 🖾

▼▼▼▼ La Quinta Inn Baton Rouge-Siegen Lane H

(225) 291-6600. **$71-$132.** 10555 Reiger Rd 70809. I-10 exit 163 (Siegen Ln), just n, then just e. Int corridors. **Pets:** Medium, other species. Service with restrictions, supervision. 🛜 🔲 💻 ≈

▼▼▼▼ La Quinta Inn Baton Rouge University Area M

(225) 924-9600. **$80-$142.** 2333 S Acadian Thruway 70808. I-10 exit 157B, just n. Ext corridors. **Pets:** Medium, other species. Service with restrictions, supervision. 🛜 🔲 💻 ≈

📞 ▼▼▼▼ Microtel Inn & Suites Baton Rouge Airport H

(225) 356-9191. **$80-$107.** 3444 Harding Blvd 70807. I-110 exit 6, just e. Int corridors. **Pets:** Accepted. 💾 🛜 🖾 🖼 🔲 💻 ≈

▼▼▼▼ Radisson Hotel Baton Rouge H

(225) 236-4000. **$129-$409, 3 day notice.** 2445 S Acadian Thruway 70808. I-10 exit 157B, just n. Int corridors. **Pets:** Accepted.
🛜 🖾 🔲 💻 🍽 ≈ 🖾

▼▼▼▼ Residence Inn by Marriott-Baton Rouge-Siegen Lane H

(225) 293-8700. **$93-$169.** 10333 N Mall Dr 70809. I-10 exit 163 westbound, just s on Siegen Ln, then just e; exit eastbound, 0.5 mi to S Mall Dr, just e to Andrea (at Lowe's), then just n. Int corridors. **Pets:** Accepted.
🛜 🖾 🖼 🔲 💻 ≈ 🖾

◇◇◇ ▼▼▼ Residence Inn by Marriott Baton
Rouge-Towne Center at Cedar Lodge 🏠
(225) 925-9100. **$132-$199.** 7061 Commerce Cir 70809. I-10 exit 158
(College Dr), just n to Corporate Blvd, then 1.8 mi e. Int corridors.
Pets: Medium, other species. $75 one-time fee/room. Service with restrictions, crate. (SAVE) 🛰 ⊠ 🐾 🛗 📺 ➰ 🐾

▼▼ TownePlace Suites Baton Rouge South 🏠 ❀
(225) 819-2112. **$59-$89.** 8735 Summa Ave 70809. I-10 exit 162 (Bluebonnet Blvd), just s to Picardy, just w to Summa Ave, then 0.5 mi nw. Int corridors. **Pets:** Other species. $50 one-time fee/room. Service with restrictions. 🛰 ⊠ 🐾 🛗 📺 ➰

BOSSIER CITY
▼▼▼ Hampton Inn 🏠
(318) 752-1112. **$99-$139.** 1005 Gould Dr 71111. I-20 exit 21, just n,
then 0.5 mi e. Int corridors. **Pets:** Accepted. 🛰 🐾 🛗 📺 ➰

◇◇◇ ▼▼▼ MainStay Suites 🏠 ❀
(318) 747-6220. **$130-$150.** 1001 Gould Dr 71111. I-20 exit 21, just ne.
Ext corridors. **Pets:** Medium, other species. $100 one-time fee/pet. Service with restrictions, supervision. (SAVE) 🛰 ⊠ 🐾 🛗 📺 ➰ 🐾

▼▼ Microtel Inn & Suites 🏠
(318) 742-7882. **$63-$99.** 2713 Village Ln 71112. I-20 exit 22 (Airline Dr),
just s, then just w. Int corridors. **Pets:** Accepted. 🛰 🐾 🛗 📺

▼▼ Quality Inn & Suites 🏠
(318) 742-7890. **Call for rates.** 2717 Village Ln 71112. I-20 exit 22 (Airline Dr), just s, then just w. Int corridors. **Pets:** Accepted.
🛰 🐾 🛗 📺 ➰

BREAUX BRIDGE
▼▼ Holiday Inn Express of Breaux Bridge 🏠
(337) 667-8913. **$85-$120.** 2942 H Grand Point Hwy 70517. I-10 exit
115, just n. Int corridors. **Pets:** Other species. $25 deposit/room, $25
one-time fee/room. Designated rooms, service with restrictions, supervision. 🛰 🐾 🛗 📺 ➰

BROUSSARD
▼▼▼ La Quinta Inn & Suites Broussard - Lafayette
Area 🏠
(337) 330-8081. **$93-$159.** 104 Sweetland Dr 70518. On US 90. Int corridors. **Pets:** Medium, other species. Service with restrictions, supervision. 🛰 ⊠ 🐾 🛗 📺 ➰

DELHI
◇◇◇ ▼▼▼ Best Western Delhi Inn 🅼
(318) 878-5126. **$85-$95.** 135 Snider Rd 71232. I-20 exit 153, just s. Ext
corridors. **Pets:** Accepted. (SAVE) 🛗 📺 ➰

FRANKLIN
▼▼ Comfort Inn & Suites 🏠
(337) 828-1134. **$80-$100.** 1819 Main St 70538. SR 182, 0.4 mi e of jct
SR 182 and 3211. Int corridors. **Pets:** Accepted.
🛰 🐾 🛗 📺 ➰

HAMMOND
◇◇◇ ▼▼▼ Best Western University Inn 🏠
(985) 345-0003. **$90-$129.** 46053 N Puma Dr 70401. I-55 exit 32
(Wardline/University), just e. Ext corridors. **Pets:** Accepted.
(SAVE) 🛰 🛗 📺 ➰

▼▼▼ La Quinta Inn & Suites Hammond 🏠
(985) 345-4742. **$98-$159.** 42126 Veterans Ave 70403. I-12 exit 40 (US
51), just s. Int corridors. **Pets:** Medium, other species. Service with restrictions, supervision. 🛰 ⊠ 🐾 🛗 📺 ➰

◇◇◇ ▼▼▼ Michabelle Inn 🅲🅸
(985) 419-0550. **$75-$125, 10 day notice.** 1106 S Holly St 70403. I-12
exit 40 (US 51), 0.8 mi n, just e on Old Covington Hwy, then n, follow
signs. Ext/int corridors. **Pets:** Accepted.
(SAVE) 🛰 ⊠ 🛗 📺 ⑪ ☎

HOUMA
▼▼▼ La Quinta Inn & Suites Houma 🏠
(985) 879-1646. **$84-$144.** 189 Synergy Center Blvd 70364. US 90 exit
202, 3.4 mi s on Main St to Martin Luther King Jr Blvd, then just w. Int
corridors. **Pets:** Medium, other species. Service with restrictions, supervision. 🛰 ⊠ 🐾 🛗 📺 ➰

IOWA
▼▼▼ Howard Johnson Express Inn 🏠
(337) 582-2440. **$81.** 107 E Frontage Rd 70647. I-10 exit 43, just n, then
just e. Int corridors. **Pets:** Other species. $20 one-time fee/pet. Service
with restrictions, crate. 🛰 🛗 📺 ➰

▼▼▼ La Quinta & Suites Iowa 🏠
(337) 582-2261. **$93-$154.** 204 W Frontage Rd 70647. I-10 exit 43, just
n. Int corridors. **Pets:** Medium, other species. Service with restrictions,
supervision. 🛰 ⊠ 🛗 📺 ➰

KINDER
◇◇◇ ▼▼▼ Best Western Inn At Coushatta 🏠 ❀
(337) 738-4800. **$79-$109.** 12102 US Hwy 165 N 70648. 5 mi n of jct
US 190/165. Int corridors. **Pets:** Other species. $25 deposit/pet. Service
with restrictions. (SAVE) 🛰 🐾 🛗 📺 ➰

LAFAYETTE
▼▼ Best Western Lafayette Inn 🏠 ❀
(337) 769-2900. **$67-$99.** 2207 NW Evangeline Thruway 70501. I-10 exit
103A, just s. Int corridors. **Pets:** Medium. $15 one-time fee/pet. Service
with restrictions, crate. 🛰 🛗 📺 ➰

▼▼▼ Candlewood Suites 🏠
(337) 984-6900. **$99-$125.** 2105 Kaliste Saloom Rd 70508. I-10 exit
103A, 3.9 mi s, then 3.6 mi w. Int corridors. **Pets:** Accepted.
🛰 ⊠ 🐾 🛗 📺

◇◇◇ ▼▼ ▼▼ Carriage House Hotel 🏠
(337) 769-8400. **$199-$299.** 603 Silverstone Rd 70508. I-10 exit 103A,
3.5 mi s to Pinhook Rd, 1.6 mi sw to Kaliste Saloom Rd, 2 mi w to
Camellia Blvd, 0.4 mi n to Silverstone Rd, then just w. Int corridors.
Pets: Accepted. (SAVE) 🛰 ⊠ 🛗 📺 ⑪ ➰ 🐾

▼▼▼ Drury Inn & Suites-Lafayette 🏠
(337) 262-0202. **$95-$154.** 120 Alcide Dominique 70502. I-10 exit 101
(SR 182), just s on University Ave, then just w. Int corridors.
Pets: Accepted. 🛰 🐾 🛗 📺 ➰

▼▼▼ Fairfield Inn & Suites by Marriott I-10 🏠
(337) 235-9898. **$81-$149.** 2225 NW Evangeline Thruway 70501. I-10
exit 103A, just sw. Int corridors. **Pets:** $35 one-time fee/room. Designated
rooms, service with restrictions, supervision.
🛰 ⊠ 🐾 🛗 📺 ➰

◇◇◇ ▼▼▼ Hilton Lafayette 🏠
(337) 235-6111. **$89-$189.** 1521 W Pinhook Rd 70503. I-10 exit 103A,
3.5 mi s, then 1.3 mi w. Int corridors. **Pets:** Medium. $50 one-time fee/
room. Designated rooms, service with restrictions, crate.
(SAVE) 🛰 🛗 📺 ⑪ ➰

◇◇◇ ▼▼▼ Holiday Inn Lafayette Conference
Center 🏠
(337) 233-6815. **$89-$189.** 2032 NE Evangeline Thruway 70501. I-10
exit 103A, just s. Ext/int corridors. **Pets:** Accepted.
(SAVE) 🛰 🛗 📺 ⑪ ➰ 🐾

◆◆ ◆◆ Jameson Inn of Lafayette 🅷
(337) 291-2916. **$69-$89.** 2200 NE Evangeline Thruway 70501. I-10 exit
103A, just s. Int corridors. **Pets:** Medium. $15 daily fee/room. Service with
restrictions, supervision. 📶 🛗 💻 🏊

◆◆◆◆ La Quinta Inn & Suites Lafayette Oil Center 🅷
(337) 291-1088. **$94-$155.** 1015 W Pinhook Rd 70503. I-10 exit 101
(University Ave), 3.5 mi to SR 182 (Pinhook Rd), then 0.5 mi w. Int corridors. **Pets:** Medium, other species. Service with restrictions, supervision.
📶 🛗 💻 🏊

◆◆ ◆◆ La Quinta Inn Lafayette North Ⓜ
(337) 233-5610. **$58-$119.** 2100 NE Evangeline Thruway 70501. I-10
exit 103A, 0.3 mi s on US 167. Ext corridors. **Pets:** Medium, other species. Service with restrictions, supervision. 📶 🛗 💻 🏊

◆◆ ◆◆ Pear Tree Inn By Drury 🅷
(337) 289-9907. **$80-$129.** 126 Alcide Dominique 70502. I-10 exit 101,
just s on University Ave, then just w. Int corridors. **Pets:** Accepted.
📶 🛗ᴹ 💻 🏊

◆◆ ◆◆ Ramada 🅷
(337) 235-0858. **$49-$89.** 120 E Kaliste Saloom Rd 70508. I-10 exit
103A, 3.9 mi s on US 90 to Kaliste Saloom Rd, then 1 mi w. Ext corridors. **Pets:** Accepted. 📶 🛗 💻 🏊

◆◆◆◆ Residence Inn by Marriott, Lafayette Airport 🅷
(337) 232-3341. **$107-$189.** 128 James Comeaux Rd 70508. I-10 exit
103A, 3.9 mi s to Kaliste Saloom Rd, then 1 mi w. Int corridors.
Pets: Large, other species. $100 one-time fee/room. Service with restric-
tions, crate. 📶 ❌ 🛗ᴹ 🛗 💻 🏊 ❌

◆◆◆◆ Staybridge Suites Lafayette Airport 🅷
(337) 267-4666. **$89-$219.** 129 E Kaliste Saloom Rd 70508. I-10 exit
103A, 3.9 mi s on US 90 to Kaliste Saloom Rd, then 0.7 mi w. Int corridors. **Pets:** Medium, other species. $15 one-time fee/pet, $10 daily fee/
pet. Designated rooms, supervision. 📶 ❌ 🛗ᴹ 🛗 💻 🏊 ❌

LAKE CHARLES

◆◆◆ ◆◆◆◆ La Quinta Inn & Suites-Prien 🅷
(337) 478-9889. **$120-$184.** 1201 W Prien Lake Rd 70601. I-210 exit 4
(Nelson Rd), just n, then just e. Int corridors. **Pets:** Medium, other species. Service with restrictions, supervision.
[SAVE] 📶 ❌ 🛗 💻 🏊

◆◆ ◆◆ Super 8-Lake Charles 🅷 ❀
(337) 477-1606. **$50-$150, 7 day notice.** 1350 E Prien Lake Rd 70601.
I-210 exit 6B (Enterprise Blvd), just n, then just e. Int corridors.
Pets: Small. $20 one-time fee/pet, $20 daily fee/pet. Service with restrictions, supervision. 📶 🛗 💻 🏊

MANY

**◆◆◆ ◆◆◆◆ Cypress Bend Resort Golf, Spa & Conference
Center** 🅷
(318) 590-1500. **$129-$189, 3 day notice.** 2000 Cypress Bend Pkwy
71449. 13 mi w on SR 6, 3 mi s on SR 191, 3 mi w on Cypress Bend
Dr, then 1.5 mi w. Int corridors. **Pets:** $50 one-time fee/room. Service
with restrictions, crate. [SAVE] 📶 ❌ 🛗ᴹ 🛗 💻 🍴 🏊 ❌

MINDEN

◆◆◆ ◆◆ ◆◆ Best Western Minden Inn 🅷
(318) 377-1001. **$85-$95.** 1411 Sibley Rd 71055. I-20 exit 47, just n. Ext
corridors. **Pets:** Medium. $15 daily fee/pet. Service with restrictions,
supervision. [SAVE] 📶 🛗 💻 🏊

MONROE

◆◆ ◆◆ Clarion Inn & Suites and Conference Center 🅷
(318) 387-5100. **$69-$89.** 1051 Hwy 165 Bypass 71203. I-20 exit 118B,
just ne on US 165 service road. Ext/int corridors. **Pets:** Accepted.
📶 🛗 💻 🍴 🏊 ❌

◆◆◆ ◆◆◆◆ Residence Inn by Marriott 🅷
(318) 387-0210. **$89-$159.** 4960 Millhaven Rd 71203. I-20 exit 120, just
n of Pecanland Mall. Int corridors. **Pets:** Accepted.
[SAVE] 📶 ❌ 🛗ᴹ 🛗 💻 🏊 ❌

MORGAN CITY

◆◆ ◆◆ Holiday Inn-Morgan City 🅷
(985) 385-2200. **$99-$229.** 520 Roderick St 70380. 1.5 mi s of jct US 90
and SR 70. Ext corridors. **Pets:** Accepted.
📶 🛗ᴹ 🛗 💻 🍴 🏊

◆◆ ◆◆ ◆◆ La Quinta Inn & Suites Morgan City 🅷
(985) 300-0200. **$93-$154.** 2018 Allison St 70380. US 90 exit Dr Martin
Luther King Jr Blvd, just s. Int corridors. **Pets:** Medium, other species.
Service with restrictions, supervision. 📶 ❌ 🛗ᴹ 🛗 💻 🏊

NATCHITOCHES

◆◆◆ ◆◆ ◆◆ Best Western Natchitoches Inn 🅷
(318) 352-6655. **$113-$130.** 5131 University Pkwy 71457. I-49 exit 138,
just e. Int corridors. **Pets:** Large, other species. $20 daily fee/room. Serv-
ice with restrictions, crate. [SAVE] 📶 🛗 💻 🏊

NEW IBERIA

◆◆◆ ◆◆◆◆ La Quinta Inn & Suites 🅷
(337) 321-6000. **$89-$149.** 611A Queen City Dr 70560. US 90 exit SR
14, just e. Int corridors. **Pets:** Medium, other species. Service with restrictions, supervision. [SAVE] 📶 ❌ 🛗 💻 🏊

◆◆ ◆◆ Super 8 of New Iberia 🅷
(337) 364-3030. **Call for rates.** 2714 Hwy 14 70560. 0.3 mi e of jct US
90. Ext/int corridors. **Pets:** Other species. $25 one-time fee/room. Supervi-
sion. 📶 🛗 💻 🍴 🏊

NEW ORLEANS METROPOLITAN AREA

COVINGTON

◆◆◆ ◆◆ ◆◆ Best Western Northpark Inn 🅷 ❀
(985) 892-2681. **$75-$299.** 625 N Hwy 190 70433. I-12 exit 63B, just n.
Ext/int corridors. **Pets:** Large, other species. $20 daily fee/room. Desig-
nated rooms, service with restrictions, crate. [SAVE] 📶 🛗 💻 🏊

**◆◆◆ ◆◆◆◆ Residence Inn New Orleans Covington/North
Shore** 🅷 ❀
(985) 246-7222. **$116-$243.** 101 Park Place Blvd 70433. I-12 exit 63B,
0.5 mi n, then just w. Int corridors. **Pets:** Other species. $75 one-time
fee/room. Service with restrictions, supervision.
[SAVE] 📶 ❌ 🛗 💻 🏊 ❌

◆◆◆◆ Staybridge Suites Covington-Northpark 🅷
(985) 892-0003. **$119-$129.** 140 Holiday Blvd 70433. I-12 exit 63B, just
n, then just w. Int corridors. **Pets:** Medium, other species. $75 one-time
fee/room. Service with restrictions, supervision. 📶 🛗 💻 🏊 ❌

◆◆◆ ◆◆ Super 8 Covington Ⓜ
(985) 892-4470. **$70-$90.** 120 Holiday Blvd 70433. I-12 exit 63B, just nw.
Ext corridors. **Pets:** Small, dogs only. $20 one-time fee/pet. Service with
restrictions, supervision. [SAVE] 📶 🛗 💻 🏊

GRETNA

▼▼ **La Quinta Inn New Orleans West Bank / Gretna** H
(504) 368-5600. **$80-$142.** 50 Terry Pkwy 70056. S US 90 business route exit 9A (Terry Pkwy); N US 90 (Westbank Expwy) exit 9 (Terry Pkwy/General DeGaulle). Ext corridors. **Pets:** Medium, other species. Service with restrictions, supervision. 🛜 🗄 💻 ➰

KENNER

▼▼▼ **Days Inn New Orleans Airport** H
(504) 464-1644. **$62-$107.** 1021 Airline Dr 70062. US 61, 0.6 mi w from jct SR 49. Ext corridors. **Pets:** Other species. $50 deposit/room, $15 one-time fee/room. Service with restrictions, crate. 🛜 🗄 💻 🍴 ➰

▼▼▼ **DoubleTree by Hilton Hotel New Orleans Airport** H
(504) 467-3111. **$99-$169.** 2150 Veterans Blvd 70062. I-10 exit 223A (Williams Blvd), just s, then just e. Int corridors. **Pets:** Accepted.
🛜 ✖ 🗄 💻 🍴 ➰

🔷 ▼▼▼▼ **Hilton New Orleans Airport** H ❀
(504) 469-5000. **$99-$179.** 901 Airline Dr 70062. I-10 exit 223A (Williams Blvd), 2 mi s, then 0.8 mi w. Int corridors. **Pets:** Medium. $50 one-time fee/room. Designated rooms, service with restrictions, supervision.
🆂🅰🆅🅴 🛜 🗄 💻 🍴 ➰

▼▼▼▼ **La Quinta Inn New Orleans (Airport)** H
(504) 466-1401. **$68-$139.** 2610 Williams Blvd 70062. I-10 exit 223A (Williams Blvd), 0.3 mi s. Int corridors. **Pets:** Medium, other species. Service with restrictions, supervision. 🛜 🅼 🗄 💻 🍴 ➰

LA PLACE

🔷 ▼▼ **Best Western La Place Inn** H
(985) 651-4000. **$70-$140.** 4289 Main St 70068. I-10 exit 209, just s. Ext corridors. **Pets:** Small, dogs only. $25 daily fee/pet. Designated rooms, service with restrictions, supervision. 🆂🅰🆅🅴 🛜 🗄 💻 ➰

METAIRIE

▼▼ **La Quinta Inn New Orleans Causeway** H
(504) 835-8511. **$71-$134.** 3100 S I-10 Service Rd 70001. I-10 exit 228 (Causeway Blvd), just s. Ext corridors. **Pets:** Medium, other species. Service with restrictions, supervision. 🛜 🅼 🗄 💻 ➰

NEW ORLEANS

🔷 ▼▼▼ **Best Western Plus St. Charles Inn** H
(504) 899-8888. **$119-$229.** 3636 St. Charles Ave 70115. US 90 business route exit St. Charles Ave, 1.8 mi s. Int corridors. **Pets:** Accepted.
🆂🅰🆅🅴 🛜 ✖ 🗄 💻 ➰

🔷 ▼▼▼ **Best Western Plus St. Christopher Hotel** H
(504) 648-0444. **$89-$299, 3 day notice.** 114 Magazine St 70130. Between Canal and Common sts. Int corridors. **Pets:** Medium, other species. $50 deposit/room, $20 one-time fee/room. Designated rooms, service with restrictions, crate. 🆂🅰🆅🅴 🛜 💻

🔷 ▼▼▼ **The Bienville House Hotel** H ❀
(504) 529-2345. **$79-$289, 3 day notice.** 320 Decatur St 70130. Between Conti and Bienville sts. Ext/int corridors. **Pets:** $100 one-time fee/pet, $25 daily fee/pet. Service with restrictions, supervision.
🆂🅰🆅🅴 🛜 ✖ 🗄 💻 🍴 ➰

▼▼▼ **Clarion Inn & Suites** H
(504) 299-9900. **Call for rates.** 1300 Canal St 70112. Jct Saratoga St. Int corridors. **Pets:** Medium. $75 one-time fee/room. Designated rooms, service with restrictions, crate. 🛜 ✖ 🗄 💻

▼▼▼ **Drury Inn & Suites-New Orleans** H
(504) 529-7800. **$110-$274.** 820 Poydras St 70112. Between Baronne and Carondelet sts. Int corridors. **Pets:** Accepted.
🛜 🅼 🗄 💻 ➰

🔷 ▼▼▼▼ **Elysian Fields Inn** BB
(504) 948-9420. **$109-$269, 15 day notice.** 930 Elysian Fields Ave 70117. I-610 exit 3 (Elysian Fields Ave), 1.2 mi s. Int corridors. **Pets:** Large. $30 daily fee/pet. No service, crate. 🆂🅰🆅🅴 🛜 ✖

🔷 ▼▼▼▼ **Hilton New Orleans St. Charles Avenue** H
(504) 524-8890. **Call for rates.** 333 St. Charles Ave 70130. Jct Perdido St. Int corridors. **Pets:** Accepted. 🆂🅰🆅🅴 🛜 🅼 🗄 💻 🍴 ➰

🔷 ▼▼▼▼ **Hotel Monteleone** H ❀
(504) 523-3341. **$169-$399, 3 day notice.** 214 Royal St 70130. Between Iberville and Bienville sts. Int corridors. **Pets:** Other species. $100 one-time fee/room, $25 daily fee/room. Service with restrictions, supervision. 🅴🅲🅾 🆂🅰🆅🅴 🛜 ✖ 🗄 💻 🍴 ➰

🔷 ▼▼▼▼ **InterContinental New Orleans** H
(504) 525-5566. **$79-$459.** 444 St Charles Ave 70130. Between Perdido and Poydras sts. Int corridors. **Pets:** Accepted.
🆂🅰🆅🅴 🛜 🗄 💻 🍴 ➰

▼▼▼ **La Quinta Inn & Suites New Orleans Downtown** H
(504) 598-9977. **$98-$192.** 301 Camp St 70130. Corner of Gravier and Camp sts. Int corridors. **Pets:** Medium, other species. Service with restrictions, supervision. 🛜 🅼 🗄 💻 ➰

🔷 ▼▼▼▼ **Loews New Orleans Hotel** H ❀
(504) 595-3300. **$149-$750.** 300 Poydras St 70130. Corner of S Peters St. Int corridors. **Pets:** $25 one-time fee/room. Designated rooms, service with restrictions, supervision. 🆂🅰🆅🅴 🛜 💻 🍴 ➰ ✖

🔷 ▼▼▼▼ **Maison Dupuy Hotel** H
(504) 586-8000. **$89-$249, 3 day notice.** 1001 Toulouse St 70112. Between Burgundy and Rampart sts. Int corridors. **Pets:** Small, dogs only. $50 one-time fee/pet. No service, supervision.
🆂🅰🆅🅴 🛜 🗄 🍴 ➰ ✖

🔷 ▼▼▼▼ **Omni Royal Crescent Hotel** H
(504) 527-0006. **$99-$289, 3 day notice.** 535 Gravier St 70130. 0.3 mi w of Canal St. Int corridors. **Pets:** Accepted.
🆂🅰🆅🅴 🛜 ✖ 🗄 💻 🍴 ✖

🔷 ▼▼▼▼ **Omni Royal Orleans Hotel** H ❀
(504) 529-5333. **$119-$359, 3 day notice.** 621 St. Louis St 70140. At Royal and St. Louis sts. Int corridors. **Pets:** Medium. $50 one-time fee/room. Designated rooms, service with restrictions, supervision.
🆂🅰🆅🅴 🛜 🗄 💻 🍴 ➰

🔷 ▼▼▼ **Quality Inn & Suites Maison St. Charles** H
(504) 522-0187. **Call for rates.** 1319 St. Charles Ave 70130. Just s of US 90 business route (Pontchartrain Expwy). Ext corridors. **Pets:** Medium. $50 one-time fee/pet. Service with restrictions.
🆂🅰🆅🅴 🛜 ✖ 🗄 💻 ➰

🔷 ▼▼▼▼ **The Ritz-Carlton, New Orleans** H
(504) 524-1331. **Call for rates.** 921 Canal St 70112. Between Dauphine and Burgundy sts. Int corridors. **Pets:** Accepted.
🆂🅰🆅🅴 🛜 ✖ 🅼 🍴 ✖

🔷 ▼▼▼▼ **The Roosevelt New Orleans, A Waldorf Astoria Hotel** H
(504) 648-1200. **$159-$499.** 123 Baronne St 70112. Just s of Canal St. Int corridors. **Pets:** Small, other species. $175 one-time fee/room. Service with restrictions, crate. 🆂🅰🆅🅴 🛜 ✖ 🅼 🗄 🍴 ➰ ✖

🔷 ▼▼▼▼ **Royal Sonesta Hotel New Orleans** H
(504) 586-0300. **Call for rates.** 300 Bourbon St 70130. Garage entrance on Conti or Bienville sts. Int corridors. **Pets:** Small. $50 one-time fee/room. Service with restrictions, supervision.
🆂🅰🆅🅴 🛜 🅼 🗄 🍴 ➰

▼▼▼ **St. James Hotel** H
(504) 304-4000. **Call for rates.** 330 Magazine St 70130. Jct Magazine and Natchez sts. Int corridors. **Pets:** Accepted. 📶 ⊠ 🖥 💻 🍴

▲▲▲ ▼▼▼ **Sheraton New Orleans Hotel** H 🐾
(504) 525-2500. **$89-$389, 3 day notice.** 500 Canal St 70130. Between Camp and Magazine sts. Int corridors. **Pets:** Medium, dogs only. Service with restrictions, supervision. SAVE 📶 ⊠ 🖥 💻 🍴 🏊 ⊠

▼▼▼ **Staybridge Suites Hotel** H
(504) 571-1818. **Call for rates.** 501 Tchoupitoulas St 70130. Corner of Poydras St. Int corridors. **Pets:** $15 daily fee/room. Designated rooms, service with restrictions, supervision. 📶 🖥 🖥 💻 🏊

▲▲▲ ▼▼▼ ▼▼▼ **Westin New Orleans Canal Place** H
(504) 566-7006. **$99-$329, 3 day notice.** 100 Iberville St 70130. At Canal Place, near Mississippi River. Int corridors. **Pets:** Accepted.
SAVE 📶 ⊠ 🖥 💻 🍴 🏊

▲▲▲ ▼▼▼ **W French Quarter** H
(504) 581-1200. **$119-$529, 3 day notice.** 316 Chartres St 70130. Between Conti and Bienville sts. Int corridors. **Pets:** Accepted.
SAVE 📶 🏊

▲▲▲ ▼▼▼ ▼▼▼ **Windsor Court Hotel** H
(504) 523-6000. **$190-$685, 3 day notice.** 300 Gravier St 70130. Between Magazine and Tchoupitoulas sts. Int corridors. **Pets:** Accepted.
SAVE 📶 🖥 🍴 🏊 ⊠

▲▲▲ ▼▼▼ ▼▼▼ **W New Orleans** H
(504) 525-9444. **$109-$509, 3 day notice.** 333 Poydras St 70130. Jct Poydras and S Peters sts; close to Riverfront area/convention center. Int corridors. **Pets:** Accepted. SAVE 📶 🖥 🍴 🏊

PEARL RIVER
▲▲▲ ▼▼▼ **Microtel Inn & Suites** H
(985) 863-7310. **Call for rates.** 63537 Hwy 1090 70452. I-59 exit 3, just w. Int corridors. **Pets:** Accepted. SAVE 📶 ⊠ 🖥 💻

SLIDELL
▼▼▼ **La Quinta Inn New Orleans/Slidell** H
(985) 643-9770. **$71-$132.** 794 E I-10 Service Rd 70461. I-10 exit 266 (Gause Blvd), just se. Ext corridors. **Pets:** Medium, other species. Service with restrictions, supervision. 📶 🖥 💻 🏊

END METROPOLITAN AREA

PONCHATOULA
▼▼ ▼▼ **Microtel Inn & Suites** H
(985) 370-7378. **$71-$89.** 727 W Pine St 70454. I-55 exit 26, just e on SR 22. Int corridors. **Pets:** Accepted. 📶 🖥 🖥 💻 🏊

RUSTON
▼▼ ▼▼ **Days Inn** H
(318) 251-2360. **$63-$135.** 1801 N Service Rd E 71270. I-20 exit 86, just ne. Ext corridors. **Pets:** Medium. $50 deposit/room. Service with restrictions, supervision. 📶 🖥 💻 🏊

ST. FRANCISVILLE
▼▼ ▼▼ **Lake Rosemound Inn Bed & Breakfast** BB
(225) 635-3176. **$80-$135, 4 day notice.** 10473 Lindsey Ln 70775. 13 mi n on SR 61, then 3 mi w using Rosemound Loop, Sligo Rd, Lake Rosemound Rd and Lindsey Ln, follow signs. Ext/int corridors.
Pets: Dogs only. No service, supervision. 📶 ⊠

SCOTT
▼▼ ▼▼ **Howard Johnson Inn Lafayette West** H
(337) 593-0849. **$54-$58.** 103 Harold Gauthe Dr 70583. I-10 exit 97, just s. Int corridors. **Pets:** Accepted. 📶 🖥 💻 🏊

SHREVEPORT
▼▼▼ **Candlewood Suites** H
(318) 635-8062. **$79-$119.** 5020 Hollywood Ave 71109. I-20 exit 13, 0.4 mi s, then just e. Int corridors. **Pets:** Accepted.
📶 ⊠ 🖥 🖥 💻 🏊

▲▲▲ ▼▼▼ **Holiday Inn Shreveport West** H
(318) 688-3000. **$92-$139.** 5555 Financial Plaza 71129. I-20 exit 10 (Pines Rd), 1 mi e on frontage road. Int corridors. **Pets:** Other species. $25 daily fee/pet. Service with restrictions.
SAVE 📶 ⊠ 🖥 💻 🍴 🏊 ⊠

▼▼▼ ▼▼▼ **Homewood Suites - Shreveport** H
(318) 549-2000. **$109-$121.** 5485 Financial Plaza 71129. I-20 exit 10 (Pines Rd), just s, then 1.2 mi e. Int corridors. **Pets:** Accepted.
📶 🖥 💻 🏊 ⊠

▼▼▼ ▼▼▼ **La Quinta Inn & Suites Shreveport Airport** H
(318) 671-1100. **$91-$169.** 6700 Financial Cir 71129. I-20 exit 10 (Pines Rd), 0.5 mi e on frontage road. Int corridors. **Pets:** Medium, other species. Service with restrictions, supervision. 📶 🖥 🖥 💻 🏊

▲▲▲ ▼▼▼ **Residence Inn by Marriott Shreveport - Airport** H
(318) 635-8000. **$113-$199.** 4910 W Monkhouse Dr 71109. I-20 exit 13, just nw. Int corridors. **Pets:** Other species. $100 one-time fee/room. Designated rooms, service with restrictions, crate.
SAVE 📶 ⊠ 🖥 🖥 💻 🏊 ⊠

SULPHUR
▼▼▼ **Quality Inn & Suites** H
(337) 626-7000. **$72-$250.** 320 S Cities Service Hwy 70663. I-10 exit 23, just n. Int corridors. **Pets:** Small, other species. $25 one-time fee/pet. Service with restrictions, crate. 📶 🖥 💻 🏊

▼▼▼ ▼▼▼ **Wingate by Wyndham** H
(337) 527-5151. **$87-$99.** 300 Arena Rd 70665. I-10 exit 20, just s, then just w. Int corridors. **Pets:** Medium. $35 one-time fee/room. Designated rooms, service with restrictions, crate. 📶 🖥 💻 🏊

VILLE PLATTE
▲▲▲ ▼▼▼ **Best Western Ville Platte** H
(337) 360-9961. **$91.** 1919 E Main St (Hwy 167) 70586. Jct SR 1168. Int corridors. **Pets:** Accepted. SAVE 📶 🖥 💻 🏊

WALKER
▼▼▼ ▼▼▼ **La Quinta Inn & Suites Walker** H
(225) 667-1966. **$89-$149.** 13450 Vera McGowan 70785. I-12 exit 15, just n. Int corridors. **Pets:** Medium, other species. Service with restrictions, supervision. 📶 ⊠ 🖥 💻 🏊

WEST MONROE
▼▼ ▼▼ **Jameson Inn** H
(318) 361-0750. **$74-$94.** 213 Constitution Dr 71292. I-20 exit 114 (Thomas Rd), just s to Constitution Dr, then just w. Int corridors. **Pets:** Medium. $15 daily fee/room. Service with restrictions, supervision.
📶 🖥 💻 🏊

▼▼ ▼▼ **Quality Inn & Suites-West Monroe** H
(318) 387-2711. **$81-$99.** 503 Constitution Dr 71292. I-20 exit 114 (Thomas Rd), just s to Constitution Dr, then 0.6 mi w. Int corridors. **Pets:** Large, other species. $25 one-time fee/room. Service with restrictions, crate. 📶 🖥 🖥 💻 🏊

WINNFIELD

Best Western of Winnfield M

(318) 628-3993. **$66-$85.** 700 W Court St 71483. Jct US 84 and 167, just e. Ext corridors. **Pets:** Other species. $10 daily fee/pet. Service with restrictions, crate.

ZACHARY

Best Western Zachary Inn H

(225) 658-2550. **$88.** 4030 Hwy 19 70791. Just s of jct SR 64. Int corridors. **Pets:** Other species. $20 daily fee/room. Service with restrictions, supervision.

MAINE

CITY INDEX

AUBURN

A Fireside Inn & Suites H

(207) 777-1777. **$90-$250.** 1777 Washington St 04210. I-95 exit 75, 0.5 mi s on US 202, SR 4 and 100. Ext/int corridors. **Pets:** $20 daily fee/pet. Designated rooms, service with restrictions, crate.

Residence Inn by Marriott Auburn H

(207) 777-3400. **$119-$189.** 670 Turner St 04210. I-95 exit 80 southbound; exit 75 northbound; from SR 100, just w. Int corridors. **Pets:** Accepted.

Sleepy Time Motel M

(207) 783-1435. **$89-$99.** 46 Danville Corner Rd 04210. I-95 exit 75, 0.5 mi ne on US 202, then just e. Ext corridors. **Pets:** Medium, other species. $10 daily fee/pet. Service with restrictions, supervision. .

AUGUSTA

Best Western Plus Augusta Civic Center H

(207) 622-4751. **$89-$179.** 110 Community Dr 04330. I-95 exit 112A northbound; exit 112 southbound, just s on SR 8, 11 and 27. Int corridors. **Pets:** Other species. $10 daily fee/room. Service with restrictions, supervision.

Comfort Inn H

(207) 623-1000. **Call for rates.** 281 Civic Center Dr 04330. I-95 exit 112B northbound; exit 112 southbound. Int corridors. **Pets:** Other species. $10 daily fee/room. Designated rooms, service with restrictions, supervision.

Senator Inn & Spa H

(207) 622-5804. **$80-$229.** 284 Western Ave 04330. I-95 exit 109 northbound; exit 109A southbound, on US 202, SR 11 and 100. Ext/int corridors. **Pets:** Other species. $12 daily fee/room. Designated rooms, service with restrictions.

BANGOR

Best Western White House H

(207) 862-3737. **$110-$155.** 155 Littlefield Ave 04401. I-95 exit 180 (Coldbrook Rd), 5.5 mi s of downtown. Ext/int corridors. **Pets:** Large, other species. $10 daily fee/pet. Designated rooms, service with restrictions, supervision.

Econo Lodge Inn & Suites M

(207) 945-0111. **$69-$200.** 327 Odlin Rd 04401. I-95 exit 182B, just e on US 2 and SR 100. Int corridors. **Pets:** $10 one-time fee/room. Service with restrictions, supervision.

Fairfield Inn Bangor H

(207) 990-0001. **$129-$179.** 300 Odlin Rd 04401. I-95 exit 182B, just e on US 2 and SR 100. Int corridors. **Pets:** Accepted.

Fireside Inn & Suites H

(207) 942-1234. **$89-$179, 7 day notice.** 570 Main St 04401. I-395 exit 3B. Int corridors. **Pets:** $10 daily fee/pet. Service with restrictions, supervision.

Four Points by Sheraton Bangor H

(207) 947-6721. **$159-$199.** 308 Godfrey Blvd 04401. At Bangor International Airport. Int corridors. **Pets:** Accepted.

Holiday Inn-Bangor H

(207) 947-0101. **Call for rates.** 404 Odlin Rd 04401. I-95 exit 182B; jct Odlin Rd and I-395. Int corridors. **Pets:** Designated rooms, service with restrictions, supervision.

Howard Johnson Inn H

(207) 942-5251. **$43-$72.** 336 Odlin Rd 04401. I-95 exit 182B; jct Odlin Rd and I-395. Int corridors. **Pets:** Accepted.

Quality Inn Bangor H

(207) 942-7899. **Call for rates.** 750 Hogan Rd 04401. I-95 exit 187 (Hogan Rd), 0.5 mi nw. Int corridors. **Pets:** Service with restrictions, supervision.

Ramada H

(207) 947-6961. **$80-$107.** 357 Odlin Rd 04401. I-95 exit 182B; jct Odlin Rd and I-395. Int corridors. **Pets:** Accepted.

Riverside Inn H

(207) 973-4100. **Call for rates.** 495 State St 04401. Adjacent to Eastern Maine Medical Center. Int corridors. **Pets:** Accepted.

BAR HARBOR

Atlantic Eyrie Lodge H

(207) 288-9786. **$83-$244, 7 day notice.** 6 Norman Rd 04609. 1 mi w on SR 3 to Highbrook Rd. Ext corridors. **Pets:** Medium. $35 one-time fee/room. Designated rooms, service with restrictions, supervision.

Atlantic Oceanside Hotel & Conference Center H

(207) 288-5801. **$119-$399, 7 day notice.** 119 Eden St 04609. 1.8 mi w on SR 3. Ext/int corridors. **Pets:** Dogs only. $35 daily fee/room. Designated rooms, service with restrictions, supervision.

ECO SAVE 🛜 🗙 🛡 💻 ⟿

A Wonder View Inn & Suites H ❀

(207) 288-3358. **$89-$269, 3 day notice.** 50 Eden St 04609. 0.5 mi w on SR 3. Ext corridors. **Pets:** $20 one-time fee/pet. Service with restrictions, supervision. SAVE 🛜 🗙 🛡 💻 🍴 ⟿

Balance Rock Inn 1903 BB

(207) 288-2610. **$155-$635, 14 day notice.** 21 Albert Meadow 04609. Just s of Main St; center. Ext/int corridors. **Pets:** Other species. $40 daily fee/pet. Designated rooms, service with restrictions, supervision.

SAVE 🛜 🗙 🛡 💻 ⟿

Hutchins Mountain View Cottages CA ❀

(207) 288-4833. **$70-$98, 14 day notice.** 286 State Rt 3 04609. On SR 3, 4 mi w. Ext corridors. **Pets:** Other species. Service with restrictions, crate. ECO 🛜 🗙 🛡 💻 ⟿ 🎾 🖊

Quimby House Inn H ❀

(207) 288-5811. **$79-$199, 10 day notice.** 109 Cottage St 04609. Center. Ext/int corridors. **Pets:** $15 daily fee/pet. Designated rooms, service with restrictions, supervision. 🛜 🗙 ♿ 🛡 💻

BATH

Holiday Inn Bath/Brunswick H

(207) 443-9741. **$79-$199.** 139 Richardson St 04530. 0.3 mi s on US 1. Int corridors. **Pets:** Other species. Designated rooms, service with restrictions, crate. ECO SAVE 🛜 ♿ 🛡 💻 🍴 ⟿

BELFAST

Belfast Harbor Inn H ❀

(207) 338-2740. **$64-$169.** 91 Searsport Ave (Rt 1) 04915. On US 1, 1.2 mi n from jct SR 3. Ext/int corridors. **Pets:** Dogs only. $10 daily fee/pet. Designated rooms, service with restrictions, supervision.

SAVE 🛜 🛡 ⟿

Comfort Inn Ocean's Edge H

(207) 338-2090. **$79-$259.** 159 Searsport Ave 04915. On US 1, 2 mi n from jct SR 3. Int corridors. **Pets:** Accepted.

ECO 🛜 ♿ 🛡 💻 🍴 ⟿ 🖊

Gull Motel M ❀

(207) 338-4030. **$59-$119, 3 day notice.** 196 Searsport Ave 04915. On US 1, 3 mi n from jct SR 3. Ext corridors. **Pets:** Small, dogs only. $10 daily fee/pet. Service with restrictions, supervision. 🛜 🛡

BETHEL

The Inn At the Rostay M

(207) 824-3111. **$68-$140, 14 day notice.** 186 Mayville Rd (US 2) 04217. On US 2, 2 mi e. Ext corridors. **Pets:** Other species. $20 daily fee/pet. Designated rooms, service with restrictions, supervision.

🛜 🗙 🛡 ⟿

BOOTHBAY

The Boothbay Resort M ❀

(207) 633-3411. **$89-$239, 14 day notice.** 301 Adams Pond Rd 04537. US 1, 9 mi s on SR 27, then just w. Ext/int corridors. **Pets:** Medium, dogs only. Designated rooms, service with restrictions.

ECO 🛜 🗙 🛡 💻 ⟿ 🖊

White Anchor Inn M

(207) 633-3788. **$59-$95, 7 day notice.** 609 Wiscasset Rd 04537. US 1 to SR 27, 7.5 mi s. Ext/int corridors. **Pets:** Other species. $15 one-time fee/room. Designated rooms, service with restrictions, supervision.

SAVE 🛜 🗙 🛡

BOOTHBAY HARBOR

Beach Cove Hotel and Resort M

(207) 633-0353. **Call for rates.** 48 Lakeview Rd 04538. Off SR 27. Ext corridors. **Pets:** Accepted. 🛜 🗙 🛡 💻 ⟿

Cap'n Fish's Waterfront Inn H

(207) 633-6605. **$75-$175, 7 day notice.** 65 Atlantic Ave 04538. 0.3 mi se of SR 27, on east side of Boothbay Harbor. Ext corridors.
Pets: Accepted. 🛜 🛡 💻

Flagship Inn M ❀

(207) 633-5094. **$74-$144, 3 day notice.** 200 Townsend Ave 04538. On SR 27, just n of jct SR 96. Ext corridors. **Pets:** Other species. $10 daily fee/pet. Designated rooms, service with restrictions, supervision.

ECO SAVE 🛜 🛡 ⟿

Tugboat Inn H ❀

(207) 633-4434. **$85-$260, 3 day notice.** 80 Commercial St 04538. Center. Ext corridors. **Pets:** $100 deposit/room, $20 daily fee/pet. Designated rooms, service with restrictions, supervision.

SAVE 🛜 🗙 🛡 💻 🍴

BRUNSWICK

Days Inn Brunswick H

(207) 725-8883. **$68-$153.** 224 Bath Rd 04011. US 1 exit Cooks Corner, left on Bath Rd, then 0.3 mi w. Int corridors. **Pets:** Accepted.

SAVE 🛜 ♿ 🛡 💻

BRYANT POND

Mollyockett Motel & Swim Spa M

(207) 674-2345. **$70-$99.** 1132 S Main St 04219. 1.3 mi n on SR 26 from jct SR 219. Ext/int corridors. **Pets:** Dogs only. Service with restrictions, supervision. 🛜 🗙 🛡 💻 🍴 ⟿ 🖊

BUCKSPORT

Bucksport Motor Inn M

(207) 469-3111. **$69-$109.** 70 US Route 1 04416. Center. Ext corridors. **Pets:** Large, dogs only. $10 one-time fee/room. Designated rooms, service with restrictions, supervision. 🛜 🛡 💻

CAMDEN

The Camden Riverhouse Hotel & Inns H ❀

(207) 236-0500. **$109-$250, 14 day notice.** 11 Tannery Ln 04843. Center; just e of Washington St. Int corridors. **Pets:** Dogs only. $15 daily fee/pet. Designated rooms, service with restrictions, supervision.

ECO 🛜 🗙 🛡 💻 🖊

Hartstone Inn and Hideaway CI

(207) 236-4259. **$105-$295, 14 day notice.** 41 Elm St 04843. US 1, just s of Washington St; center. Ext/int corridors. **Pets:** Medium, dogs only. $25 one-time fee/room. SAVE 🛜 🗙 💻 🍴

Inns at Blackberry Common BB

(207) 236-6060. **$125-$285, 14 day notice.** 82 Elm St 04843. Center; on US 1. Ext/int corridors. **Pets:** Accepted.

ECO 🛜 🗙 🛡 💻 🖊

Lord Camden Inn H ❀

(207) 236-4325. **$99-$339.** 24 Main St 04843. Center; just n of Washington St. Int corridors. **Pets:** $25 daily fee/pet. Designated rooms, service with restrictions, supervision. ECO SAVE 🛜 🗙 🛡 💻

CAPE ELIZABETH

Inn by the Sea H ❀

(207) 799-3134. **$199-$1099, 14 day notice.** 40 Bowery Beach Rd (SR 77) 04107. On SR 77, 7 mi s. Ext/int corridors. **Pets:** Designated rooms, service with restrictions, supervision.

ECO SAVE 🛜 🗙 ♿ 🛡 💻 🍴 ⟿ 🖊

CARIBOU

Caribou Inn & Convention Center H ❀
(207) 498-3733. **$98-$146.** 19 Main St 04736. 3 mi s on US 1. Int corridors. **Pets:** Other species. $35 one-time fee/pet. Service with restrictions.

Crown Park Inn H
(207) 493-3311. **$74-$104.** 30 Access Hwy 04736. On SR 89, 0.4 mi e of jct US 1. Int corridors. **Pets:** Dogs only. Service with restrictions, supervision.

CASCO

Alyssas Motel on Thomas Pond M
(207) 655-2223. **$75-$169, 30 day notice.** 11 Roosevelt Tr 04015. On US 302 at the Casco/Raymond line. Ext corridors. **Pets:** Accepted.

CASTINE

Pentagoet Inn CI
(207) 326-8616. **Call for rates.** 26 Main St 04421. Center. Int corridors. **Pets:** Accepted.

EAGLE LAKE

Overlook Motel & Lakeside Cabins M
(207) 444-4535. **$76.** 3232 Aroostook Rd 04739. On SR 11; center. Ext/int corridors. **Pets:** Other species. $10 daily fee/pet. Service with restrictions, supervision.

EDGECOMB

Sheepscot Harbour Village & Resort H
(207) 882-6343. **$119-$369, 7 day notice.** 306 Eddy Rd 04556. 1 mi w on US 1; on east side of Davies Bridge; 1 mi e of Wiscasset. Ext/int corridors. **Pets:** Accepted.

ELLSWORTH

Acadia Birches Knights Inn M
(207) 667-3621. **Call for rates.** 19 Thorsen Rd 04605. US 1, 1.5 mi n of SR 3. Ext corridors. **Pets:** Dogs only. $25 one-time fee/pet. Designated rooms, service with restrictions, supervision.

Comfort Inn H ❀
(207) 667-1345. **$109-$159.** 130 High St 04605. Center. Int corridors. **Pets:** $25 daily fee/pet. Designated rooms.

Ellsworth Ramada H
(207) 667-9341. **$82-$157.** 215 High St 04605. Jct US 1, 1A and SR 3. Int corridors. **Pets:** Dogs only. $20 daily fee/pet. Designated rooms, service with restrictions, supervision.

Sunset Motel CA
(207) 667-8390. **$65-$78, 3 day notice.** 210 Twin Hill Rd 04605. 6 mi s on US 1 and SR 3. Ext corridors. **Pets:** Accepted.

Twilite Motel M ❀
(207) 667-8165. **$54-$126.** 147 Bucksport Rd 04605. Jct US 1A, 1.5 mi w on US 1 and SR 3. Ext corridors. **Pets:** Small, dogs only. $10 daily fee/room. Designated rooms, supervision.

FALMOUTH

Falmouth Inn M
(207) 781-2120. **$65-$136.** 209 US 1 04105. I-295 exit 10, just e on Buckman Rd, then just s. Ext corridors. **Pets:** Dogs only. $10 one-time fee/room. Designated rooms, service with restrictions, supervision.

FREEPORT

Best Western Plus Freeport Inn H ❀
(207) 865-3106. **$80-$200.** 31 US 1 04032. I-295 exit 17, 1 mi n. Ext/int corridors. **Pets:** Other species. $10 daily fee/room. Designated rooms, service with restrictions.

Captain Briggs House B & B BB
(207) 865-1868. **$105-$235, 5 day notice.** 8 Maple Ave 04032. Just n of downtown, then just w. Int corridors. **Pets:** Dogs only.

Econo Lodge M
(207) 865-3777. **$58-$130.** 537 US Rt 1 04032. I-295 exit 20, 0.3 mi s. Ext corridors. **Pets:** Medium, other species. $10 daily fee/room. Designated rooms, service with restrictions, supervision.

Harraseeket Inn CI ❀
(207) 865-9377. **$135-$305, 3 day notice.** 162 Main St 04032. I-295 exit 22, 0.5 mi e. Int corridors. **Pets:** Other species. $25 daily fee/pet. Designated rooms, service with restrictions.

White Cedar Inn BB ❀
(207) 865-9099. **$140-$250, 7 day notice.** 178 Main St 04032. I-295 exit 22, 0.5 mi e, then just w on US 1. Ext/int corridors. **Pets:** Dogs only. $25 one-time fee/room. Designated rooms, service with restrictions, supervision.

GREENVILLE

Chalet Moosehead Lakefront Motel M
(207) 695-2950. **$79-$165, 7 day notice.** 12 N Birch St 04442. 1.5 mi w on SR 15. Ext corridors. **Pets:** Accepted.

Kineo View Motor Lodge M
(207) 695-4470. **$69-$199.** 50 Overlook Dr 04441. 2.5 mi s on SR 15; gravel access road from highway. Ext corridors. **Pets:** $10 daily fee/room. Designated rooms, service with restrictions, supervision.

The Lodge at Moosehead Lake CI
(207) 695-4400. **$219-$680, 21 day notice.** 368 Lily Bay Rd 04441. 2.5 mi n. Int corridors. **Pets:** Accepted.

HANCOCK

Le Domaine Inn CI
(207) 422-3395. **Call for rates.** 1513 US Rt 1 04640. On US 1, 9 mi e of Ellsworth; center. Ext corridors. **Pets:** Accepted.

HOULTON

Shiretown Inn & Suites H
(207) 532-9421. **Call for rates.** 282 North St 04730. I-95 exit 302, 0.3 mi n on US 1. Ext/int corridors. **Pets:** Accepted.

JACKMAN

Bishop's Country Inn Motel M
(207) 668-3231. **$65-$100.** 461 Main St 04945. On US 201; center. Ext corridors. **Pets:** $10 daily fee/pet. Service with restrictions, crate..

KENNEBUNK

Econo Lodge M
(207) 985-6100. **Call for rates.** 55 York St (US 1) 04043. Jct SR 35 (US 1), 0.7 mi s. Ext corridors. **Pets:** Accepted.

Kennebunk Gallery Motel & Cottages CA
(207) 985-4543. **$55-$144, 28 day notice.** 65 York St (US 1) 04043. 0.5 mi s of center on US 1. Ext corridors. **Pets:** Accepted.

◇▽◇ ▽▽ ▽▽ Turnpike Motel M
(207) 985-4404. **$59-$125.** 77 Old Alewive Rd 04043. I-95 exit 25, just e on SR 35, then just n. Ext/int corridors. **Pets:** Other species. $10 daily fee/pet. Supervision. [SAVE] 🛜 📶

KENNEBUNKPORT

▽▽ ▽▽ The Captain Jefferds Inn BB
(207) 967-2311. **Call for rates.** 5 Pearl St 04046. From Dock Square, 0.3 mi s on Ocean Ave, just ne; corner of Pearl and Pleasant sts. Ext/int corridors. **Pets:** Accepted. 🛜 ✖ 📶

◇▽◇ ▽▽▽▽ The Colony Hotel H ❖
(207) 967-3331. **$119-$699, 7 day notice.** 140 Ocean Ave 04046. From Dock Square, 1 mi s. Int corridors. **Pets:** Other species. $30 daily fee/pet. Service with restrictions. [ECO] [SAVE] 🛜 📶 🍴 ≈ ✖

▽▽ ▽▽ Lodge At Turbat's Creek M ❖
(207) 967-8700. **$69-$179, 14 day notice.** 7 Turbats Creek Rd 04046. From Dock Square, 0.5 mi se on Maine St, 0.6 mi ne on Wildes District Rd, then just se. Ext corridors. **Pets:** Other species. $15 daily fee/pet. Designated rooms, service with restrictions, crate.
🛜 ✖ ⓜ 📶 ≈

◇▽◇ ▽▽▽▽ The Yachtsman Lodge & Marina M
(207) 967-2511. **$129-$399, 30 day notice.** 57 Ocean Ave 04046. From Dock Square, just s. Ext corridors. **Pets:** Accepted.
[SAVE] 🛜 ✖ 📶 💻 ✖

KITTERY

◇▽◇ ▽▽ ▽▽ The Coachman Inn H
(207) 439-4434. **$69-$189.** 380 US Rt 1 03904. I-95 exit 2, 1 mi n. Ext/int corridors. **Pets:** $10 daily fee/pet. Designated rooms, service with restrictions, supervision. [SAVE] 🛜 ✖ ⓜ 📶 ≈

LINCOLNVILLE

▽▽ Abbingtons Seaview Motel & Cottages CA ❖
(207) 236-3471. **$74-$149, 5 day notice.** 4 Seaview Dr 04849. US 1, 1.2 mi s of jct SR 173. Ext corridors. **Pets:** Other species. $15 daily fee/pet. Designated rooms, service with restrictions, supervision.
🛜 ✖ 📶 💻 ≈

▽▽ ▽▽ Victorian By The Sea BB
(207) 236-3785. **$139-$259, 10 day notice.** 33 Seaview Dr 04849. On US 1, 1.2 mi s of jct SR 173. Int corridors. **Pets:** Small. $15 daily fee/room. Designated rooms, service with restrictions.
🛜 ✖ 🎦 📺 📠

LUBEC

▽▽ The Eastland Motel M ❖
(207) 733-5501. **$70-$85.** 385 County Rd 04652. Jct US 1 and SR 189, 8.4 mi e on SR 189. Ext/int corridors. **Pets:** Dogs only. $10 one-time fee/pet. Designated rooms, service with restrictions, crate.
🛜 ✖ 📶 💻

MACHIAS

◇▽◇ ▽▽ The Bluebird Motel M
(207) 255-3332. **$75-$85, 7 day notice.** 231 Dublin St 04654. On US 1, 1 mi s. Ext corridors. **Pets:** Accepted. [SAVE] 🛜 ⓜ 📶

◇▽◇ ▽▽▽▽ Machias Motor Inn M
(207) 255-4861. **$84-$124.** 103 Main St 04654. 0.5 mi e on US 1. Ext corridors. **Pets:** Dogs only. $10 daily fee/pet. Designated rooms, service with restrictions, supervision. [SAVE] 🛜 📶 💻

MILFORD

◇▽◇ ▽▽▽▽ Milford Motel On The River M
(207) 827-3200. **$69-$125, 3 day notice.** 174 Main Rd 04461. 0.5 mi n on US 2. Ext/int corridors. **Pets:** Small, dogs only. Designated rooms, service with restrictions, supervision. [SAVE] 🛜 📶 💻

MILLINOCKET

▽▽ ▽▽ Baxter Park Inn H
(207) 723-9777. **$79-$129.** 935 Central St 04462. 0.8 mi e on SR 11 and 157. Int corridors. **Pets:** $15 daily fee/pet. Service with restrictions, supervision. 🛜 📶 💻 ≈

NAPLES

▽▽▽▽ Augustus Bove House BB
(207) 693-6365. **Call for rates.** 11 Sebago Rd 04055. Corner of US 302 and SR 114. Int corridors. **Pets:** Accepted. 🛜 ✖ 📶 💻

NEWCASTLE

▽▽▽▽ Newcastle Inn BB
(207) 563-5685. **$155-$275, 21 day notice.** 60 River Rd 04553. Jct US 1 and River Rd, 0.5 mi nw. Ext/int corridors. **Pets:** Accepted.
🛜 ✖ 📠

NORTHPORT

◇▽◇ ▽▽▽▽ Point Lookout Resort & Conference Center CA
(207) 789-2000. **$129-$349, 14 day notice.** 67 Atlantic Hwy 04849. 4 mi s on US 1; at Lincolnville town line. Ext corridors. **Pets:** Accepted.
[ECO] [SAVE] 🛜 ✖ 📶 💻 🍴 ✖

OGUNQUIT

▽▽ ▽▽ Studio East Motor Inn M
(207) 646-7297. **$59-$199, 7 day notice.** 267 Main St 03907. On US 1; center. Ext corridors. **Pets:** Accepted. 🛜 ✖ 📶

OLD ORCHARD BEACH

◇▽◇ ▽▽ Sea View Inn H
(207) 934-4180. **$60-$300, 7 day notice.** 65 W Grand Ave (SR 9) 04064. 0.5 mi w on SR 9 (W Grand Ave). Ext corridors. **Pets:** Medium, dogs only. $10 daily fee/pet. Service with restrictions, supervision.
[SAVE] 🛜 ✖ 📶 💻 ≈

ORONO

▽▽ ▽▽ Black Bear Inn Conference Center & Suites H
(207) 866-7120. **$99-$179.** 4 Godfrey Dr 04473. I-95 exit 193 (Stillwater Ave). Int corridors. **Pets:** $10 daily fee/pet. Designated rooms, service with restrictions, supervision. 🛜 ✖ ⓜ 📶 💻

▽▽ ▽▽ University Inn Academic Suites H
(207) 866-4921. **$86-$135.** 5 College Ave 04473. I-95 exit 191, 1.6 mi n on US 2; 8 mi n of Bangor. Int corridors. **Pets:** Accepted.
🛜 ✖ 📶 💻 ≈

POLAND SPRING

▽▽▽▽ Wolf Cove Inn BB ❖
(207) 998-4976. **$129-$169, 14 day notice.** 5 Jordan Shore Dr 04274. Just w of SR 11. Int corridors. **Pets:** $25 one-time fee/room. Designated rooms, supervision. 🛜 ✖ 📠

PORTLAND

▽▽▽▽ Clarion Portland H
(207) 774-5611. **$79-$219.** 1230 Congress St 04102. I-295 exit 5, w on SR 22. Int corridors. **Pets:** Accepted.
🛜 ✖ ⓜ 📶 💻 🍴 ≈

▽▽▽▽ Eastland Park Hotel H
(207) 775-5411. **$79-$359, 3 day notice.** 157 High St 04101. At Congress Square; center. Int corridors. **Pets:** Accepted.
🛜 📶 💻 🍴 ✖

◇▽◇ ▽▽▽▽ Embassy Suites Hotel H
(207) 775-2200. **$129-$289.** 1050 Westbrook St 04102. At Portland International Jetport. Int corridors. **Pets:** Large. $50 one-time fee/room. Designated rooms, service with restrictions, supervision.
[SAVE] 🛜 ⓜ 📶 💻 🍴 ≈ ✖

AAA ▼▼▼ Fireside Inn & Suites H

(207) 774-5601. **$110-$240.** 81 Riverside St 04103. I-95 exit 48. Int corridors. **Pets:** Small. $35 one-time fee/room. Service with restrictions, supervision. SAVE 🛜 ⛾M 🛏 🖵 🍽 🛳 ✕

▼▼▼ Hampton Inn Portland Downtown - Waterfront H

(207) 775-1454. **$139-$349.** 209 Fore St 04101. In the Old Port; between Franklin and India sts. Int corridors. **Pets:** Accepted. 🛜 ⛾M 🛏 🖵 🛳

AAA ▼▼▼ Hilton Garden Inn Portland Airport H

(207) 828-1117. **$99-$299.** 145 Jetport Blvd 04102. At Portland International Jetport. Int corridors. **Pets:** Medium, dogs only. $50 one-time fee/pet. Designated rooms, service with restrictions, crate. SAVE 🛜 ⛾M 🛏 🖵 🍽 🛳

▼▼▼ Hilton Garden Inn Portland Downtown Waterfront H

(207) 780-0780. **$129-$309.** 65 Commercial St 04101. In the Old Port; across from Casco Bay ferry terminal. Int corridors. **Pets:** Accepted. 🛜 ✕ ⛾M 🛏 🖵 🍽 🛳

▼▼ Howard Johnson Plaza Hotel H

(207) 774-5861. **$72-$166.** 155 Riverside St 04103. I-95 exit 48, jct SR 25. Int corridors. **Pets:** $50 deposit/room. Service with restrictions. 🛜 🛏 🖵 🍽 🛳

▼▼ La Quinta Inn & Suites Portland H

(207) 871-0611. **$72-$188.** 340 Park Ave 04102. I-295 exit 5A southbound; exit 5 northbound, e on SR 22. Int corridors. **Pets:** Medium, other species. Service with restrictions, supervision. 🛜 ⛾M 🛏 🖵 🛳

AAA ▼▼▼▼ Portland Harbor Hotel H ❀

(207) 775-9090. **$179-$379.** 468 Fore St 04101. In the Old Port. Int corridors. **Pets:** Other species. $35 one-time fee/room. Designated rooms, service with restrictions, supervision. SAVE 🛜 ✕ ⛾M 🛏 🍽

▼▼▼ Residence Inn by Marriott Portland Downtown/Waterfront H

(207) 761-1660. **$125-$290.** 145 Fore St 04101. In the Old Port; across from Casco Bay ferry terminal. Int corridors. **Pets:** Large. $100 one-time fee/room. Designated rooms, service with restrictions, supervision. 🛜 ✕ ⛾M 🛏 🖵 🛳

PRESQUE ISLE

▼ Budget Traveler Inn & Suites M

(207) 769-0111. **Call for rates.** 71 Main St 04769. 1.3 mi s on US 1. Int corridors. **Pets:** Accepted. 🛜 🛏

AAA ▼▼ Presque Isle Inn & Convention Center H ❀

(207) 764-3321. **$88-$150.** 116 Main St 04769. 1 mi s on US 1. Int corridors. **Pets:** Other species. $25 one-time fee/room. Service with restrictions. SAVE 🛜 🛏 🖵 🍽 🛳 ✕

RANGELEY

AAA ▼▼ Rangeley Saddleback Inn H ❀

(207) 864-3434. **$85-$250, 3 day notice.** 2303 Main St 04970. On SR 4, just s of village. Ext corridors. **Pets:** Other species. $10 daily fee/room. Designated rooms, service with restrictions. SAVE 🛜 ✕ ⛾M 🛏 🖵 🍽 🛳

ROCKLAND

▼▼ Navigator Motor Inn H

(207) 594-2131. **$79-$169.** 520 Main St 04841. On US 1 N between Talbot and Summer sts. Int corridors. **Pets:** Accepted. 🛜 ✕ 🛏 🍽

AAA ▼▼ Trade Winds Motor Inn H

(207) 596-6661. **$64-$224.** 2 Park Dr 04841. On US 1; center. Ext/int corridors. **Pets:** Accepted. SAVE 🛜 ✕ 🛏 🖵 🍽 🛳 ✕

ROCKPORT

AAA ▼▼▼ The Country Inn At Camden/Rockport H

(207) 236-2725. **$109-$239.** 8 Country Inn Way 04858. Jct SR 90, 0.9 mi n on US 1. Ext/int corridors. **Pets:** Accepted. SAVE 🛜 ✕ 🛏 🖵 🛳 ✕

AAA ▼▼▼ Glen Cove Inn & Suites M

(207) 594-4062. **$59-$199.** 866 Commercial St 04856. Jct SR 90, 3 mi s on US 1. Ext corridors. **Pets:** Medium, dogs only. Designated rooms, service with restrictions, crate. SAVE 🛜 ✕ 🛏 🛳

AAA ▼▼▼▼ Samoset Resort H

(207) 594-2511. **$159-$1599, 3 day notice.** 220 Warrenton Ave 04856. 3.5 mi s on US 1, then 0.5 mi e on Waldo Rd. Int corridors. **Pets:** Accepted. ECO SAVE 🛜 ✕ ⛾M 🛏 🖵 🍽 🛳 ✕

SACO

AAA ▼▼▼ Hampton Inn H

(207) 282-7222. **$99-$259.** 48 Industrial Park Rd 04072. I-95 exit 36 (I-195) exit 1 (Industrial Park Rd), just ne. Int corridors. **Pets:** Other species. Designated rooms, service with restrictions, supervision. SAVE 🛜 ⛾M 🛏 🖵 🛳

AAA ▼▼▼ Ramada Saco Old Orchard Beach Area H

(207) 286-9600. **$60-$190.** 352 North St (SR 112) 04072. I-95 exit 36 (I-195), exit 1 (Industrial Park Rd), 0.6 mi sw to SR 112, then 0.4 mi nw. Int corridors. **Pets:** Accepted. SAVE 🛜 ✕ ⛾M 🛏 🖵 🍽 🛳

AAA ▼ Saco Motel M

(207) 284-6952. **$50-$90, 3 day notice.** 473 Main St 04072. I-95 exit 36 (I-195), exit 2A (US 1 S), just sw. Ext corridors. **Pets:** Medium, dogs only. $10 daily fee/pet. Designated rooms, service with restrictions, supervision. SAVE 🛜 ✕ 🛏 🛳

▼▼ Wagon Wheel Motel M

(207) 283-3258. **Call for rates.** 726 Portland Rd (US 1) 04072. I-95 exit 36 (I-195), 1.5 mi se to US 1, then 0.7 mi ne. Ext corridors. **Pets:** Accepted. 🛜 ✕ 🛏 🖵 🛳 ☎

SANFORD

▼▼ Super 8 H ❀

(207) 324-8823. **$47-$99.** 1892 Main St (Rt 109) 04073. I-95 exit 19, 7 mi nw. Int corridors. **Pets:** Large. $15 daily fee/pet. Service with restrictions, supervision. 🛜 🛏 🖵

SCARBOROUGH

AAA ▼▼▼ Comfort Inn & Suites Scarborough H

(207) 883-2700. **$90-$190.** 329 US 1 04074. I-95 exit 42, 0.6 mi n. Int corridors. **Pets:** Accepted. SAVE 🛜 ✕ 🛏 🖵 🛳

▼▼ Extended StayAmerica Portland-Scarborough H ❀

(207) 883-0554. **$90-$169.** 2 Ashley Dr 04074. I-95 exit 42, just n. Int corridors. **Pets:** Other species. $25 daily fee/pet. Service with restrictions. 🛜 🛏 🖵

AAA ▼▼▼ Homewood Suites Portland H ❀

(207) 775-2700. **$139-$299.** 200 Southborough Dr 04074. I-95 exit 45, just s. Int corridors. **Pets:** $75 one-time fee/room. Designated rooms, service with restrictions, supervision. SAVE 🛜 ⛾M 🛏 🖵 🛳 ✕

▼ Pride Motel & Cottages CA

(207) 883-4816. **$65-$225, 7 day notice.** 677 US Rt 1 04074. I-95 exit 36, 0.5 mi e to US 1, then 4.5 mi n. Ext corridors. **Pets:** Medium, dogs only. $15 daily fee/pet. Service with restrictions, supervision. ECO 🛜 ✕ 🛏 🛳 ✕ ☎

▼▼▼ Residence Inn by Marriott H

(207) 883-0400. **$89-$289.** 800 Roundwood Dr 04074. I-95 exit 42, 1.5 mi n on Payne Rd. Int corridors. **Pets:** Accepted. 🛜 ✕ ⛾M 🛏 🖵 🛳 ✕

▼▼▼ TownePlace Suites by Marriott [H]
(207) 883-6800. **$99-$180.** 700 Roundwood Dr 04074. I-95 exit 42, 1.5 mi n on Payne Rd. Int corridors. **Pets:** Accepted.
🛜 ⊠ 🔗M 🗄 💻 🏊

SKOWHEGAN

◁AAA▷ ▼▼ Belmont Motel [M]
(207) 474-8315. **$85-$125.** 273 Madison Ave 04976. 1 mi n on US 201. Ext corridors. **Pets:** Accepted. [SAVE] 🛜 🔗M 🗄 💻 🏊

SOUTHPORT

◁AAA▷ ▼▼▼ Ocean Gate Resort [H]
(207) 633-3321. **$104-$384, 7 day notice.** 70 Ocean Gate Rd 04576. SR 27, 2.5 mi s of Boothbay Harbor, 0.5 mi s of bridge to Southport Island. Ext corridors. **Pets:** Accepted.
[SAVE] 🛜 ⊠ 🗄 💻 🏊 ⊠

SOUTH PORTLAND

▼ Anchor Motel [M]
(207) 775-9011. **$55-$85.** 715 Main St 04106. I-95 exit 48, 1.5 mi e to US 1. Ext corridors. **Pets:** Service with restrictions, supervision. 🗄

◁AAA▷ ▼▼▼ Best Western Merry Manor Inn [H] 🐾
(207) 774-6151. **$110-$198, 30 day notice.** 700 Main St 04106. I-95 exit 45, 1.3 mi e to US 1. Ext/int corridors. **Pets:** $10 daily fee/pet. Designated rooms, service with restrictions, supervision.
[SAVE] 🛜 ⊠ 🔗M 🗄 💻 🍽 🏊 ⊠

◁AAA▷ ▼▼ Comfort Inn [H] 🐾
(207) 775-0409. **$79-$179.** 90 Maine Mall Rd 04106. I-95 exit 45, 1 mi n. Int corridors. **Pets:** Medium. $10 daily fee/pet. Service with restrictions, supervision. [ECO] [SAVE] 🛜 ⊠ 🔗M 🗄 💻

◁AAA▷ ▼▼▼ Days Inn Portland-South Portland [H]
(207) 772-3450. **$54-$135.** 461 Maine Mall Rd 04106. I-95 exit 45. Int corridors. **Pets:** Accepted. [SAVE] 🛜 🗄 💻 🏊

◁AAA▷ ▼▼▼ DoubleTree by Hilton [H] 🐾
(207) 775-6161. **$99-$339.** 363 Maine Mall Rd 04106. I-95 exit 45. Int corridors. **Pets:** Medium, other species. Designated rooms, service with restrictions, supervision. [SAVE] 🛜 🔗M 🗄 💻 🍽 🏊

▼▼▼ Hampton Inn Portland Airport [H]
(207) 773-4400. **$89-$269.** 171 Philbrook Ave 04106. I-95 exit 45, just ne. Int corridors. **Pets:** Accepted. 🛜 ⊠ 🔗M 🗄 💻 🏊 ⊠

◁AAA▷ ▼▼▼ Holiday Inn Express & Suites [H]
(207) 775-3900. **$89-$219.** 303 Sable Oaks Dr 04106. I-95 exit 45, just n on Maine Mall Rd, then just w on Running Hill Rd. Int corridors. **Pets:** Accepted. [ECO] [SAVE] 🛜 ⊠ 🗄 💻 🏊

▼▼ Howard Johnson Hotel [H]
(207) 775-5343. **$67-$139.** 675 Main St 04106. I-95 exit 45, 1.3 mi e to US 1. Int corridors. **Pets:** Accepted. 🛜 🗄 💻 🏊

◁AAA▷ ▼▼▼ Portland Marriott at Sable Oaks [H]
(207) 871-8000. **$119-$379.** 200 Sable Oaks Dr 04106. I-95 exit 45, just n on Maine Mall Rd, then just w on Running Hill Rd. Int corridors. **Pets:** Medium, dogs only. $50 one-time fee/room. Designated rooms, service with restrictions, supervision.
[ECO] [SAVE] 🛜 ⊠ 🔗M 🗄 💻 🍽 🏊 ⊠

SPRUCE HEAD

▼▼ The Craignair Inn & Restaurant [CI]
(207) 594-7644. **$100-$200, 14 day notice.** 5 Third St 04859. 2.5 mi w on SR 73, 1.5 mi s on Clark Island Rd; 10 mi s of Rockland. Ext/int corridors. **Pets:** $10 daily fee/pet. Designated rooms, service with restrictions, supervision. [ECO] 🛜 ⊠ 🍽

STANDISH

▼▼ Sebago Lake Lodge and Cottages [BB]
(207) 892-2698. **$62-$275, 30 day notice.** 661 White's Bridge Rd 04084. 1 mi w on US 302. Ext/int corridors. **Pets:** Accepted.
🛜 ⊠ 🗄 💻 ⊠ 🐾 🖾

WATERVILLE

◁AAA▷ ▼▼◆ Best Western Plus Waterville Grand Hotel [H]
(207) 873-0111. **$110-$259, 14 day notice.** 375 Main St 04901. I-95 exit 130 (Main St), on SR 104. Int corridors. **Pets:** Accepted.
[ECO] [SAVE] 🛜 🗄 💻 🍽 🏊 ⊠

▼▼ Comfort Inn & Suites [H]
(207) 873-2777. **Call for rates.** 332 Main St 04901. I-95 exit 130 (Main St), 0.4 mi e on SR 104. Int corridors. **Pets:** Accepted.
🛜 🗄 💻 🏊

▼▼ Fireside Inn & Suites [H] 🐾
(207) 873-3335. **$89-$209.** 356 Main St 04901. I-95 exit 130 (Main St). Int corridors. **Pets:** Large, other species. $20 one-time fee/room. Designated rooms, service with restrictions, supervision.
[ECO] 🛜 🗄 💻 🍽 🏊 ⊠

WELLS

▼▼ Wells-Moody Motel [M]
(207) 646-5601. **$49-$149, 10 day notice.** 119 Post Rd (US 1) 04054. I-95 exit 19; jct SR 109/US 1, 3.4 mi s. Ext corridors. **Pets:** Accepted.
🛜 ⊠ 🗄 🏊

WESTBROOK

◁AAA▷ ▼▼◆ Super 8 [H]
(207) 854-1881. **$60-$125.** 208 Larrabee Rd 04092. I-95 exit 48. Int corridors. **Pets:** $25 one-time fee/room. Designated rooms, service with restrictions, supervision. [SAVE] 🛜 🗄 💻 🏊

WEST FORKS

◁AAA▷ ▼▼ Inn by the River [CI] 🐾
(207) 663-2181. **$89-$129, 30 day notice.** 2777 US Rt 201 04985. Center. Int corridors. **Pets:** $25 daily fee/pet. Designated rooms, service with restrictions, supervision. [SAVE] 🛜 ⊠ 💻 🍽 ⊠ 🐾 🖾

WESTPORT

▼▼▼ The Squire Tarbox Inn [CI]
(207) 882-7693. **$115-$199, 14 day notice.** 1181 Main Rd 04578. Jct US 1 and SR 144; in Wiscasset; 8.5 mi s on SR 144, follow signs. Ext/int corridors. **Pets:** Accepted. 🛜 ⊠ 🍽 ⊠ 🐾 🖾

WILTON

▼▼▼ Farmington/Wilton Comfort Inn & Suites [H] 🐾
(207) 645-5155. **$110-$130.** 1026 US Rt 2 04294. On US 2, just w of jct SR 133. Int corridors. **Pets:** $35 one-time fee/room. Designated rooms, service with restrictions, crate. 🛜 🔗M 🗄 💻 🏊

YARMOUTH

◁AAA▷ ▼▼ Down-East Village Motel [M]
(207) 846-5161. **Call for rates.** 705 US Rt 1 04096. I-295 exit 15 northbound; exit 17 southbound. Ext corridors. **Pets:** Accepted.
[SAVE] 🛜 ⊠ 🗄 💻 🏊

YORK HARBOR

▼▼▼ Inn at Harmon Park [BB]
(207) 363-2031. **$79-$139 (no credit cards), 7 day notice.** 415 York St 03911. I-95 exit 7, 0.3 mi s on US 1, then 1.5 mi n; to York Village. Int corridors. **Pets:** Service with restrictions, supervision. 🛜 ⊠ 🖾

▼▼▼ York Harbor Inn [CI]
(207) 363-5119. **$109-$349, 14 day notice.** 480 York St 03911. On US 1A; center. Ext/int corridors. **Pets:** Accepted. [ECO] 🛜 ⊠ 🍽

MARYLAND

BALTIMORE METROPOLITAN AREA

ABERDEEN

▼▼ Clarion Aberdeen 🅷 ❀
(410) 273-6300. **$79-$129.** 980 Hospitality Way 21001. I-95 exit 85, just e on SR 22. Int corridors. **Pets:** Other species. Service with restrictions, crate. 📶 🛏 🖥 🍴 🏊

▼▼ La Quinta Inn Aberdeen 🅷
(410) 272-6000. **$75-$169.** 793 W Bel Air Ave 21001. I-95 exit 85, just e. Int corridors. **Pets:** Medium, other species. Service with restrictions, supervision. 📶 🛏 🖥 🍴 🏊

🔷 ▼▼ Red Roof Inn Aberdeen 🅼
(410) 273-7800. **$50-$75.** 988 Hospitality Way 21001. I-95 exit 85, just e on SR 22. Ext corridors. **Pets:** Large, other species. No service, supervision. 🅂🅰🆅🅴 📶 🛏

◇◇◇ Residence Inn by Marriott Aberdeen at Ripken Stadium 🅷
(410) 272-0440. **$125-$179.** 830 Long Dr 21001. I-95 exit 85, 0.5 mi w on SR 22, then 0.5 mi n. Int corridors. **Pets:** Accepted.
📶 ✖ 🏋 🛏 🖥 🏊

🔷 ▼ Super 8 Aberdeen 🅼
(410) 272-5420. **$54-$63.** 1008 Beards Hill Rd 21001. I-95 exit 85, just e on SR 22. Int corridors. **Pets:** $10 daily fee/pet. Service with restrictions, supervision. 🅂🅰🆅🅴 📶 🛏 🖥

ANNAPOLIS

🔷 ▼▼▼ DoubleTree by Hilton Hotel Annapolis 🅷
(410) 224-3150. **$79-$209.** 210 Holiday Ct 21401. 2.3 mi sw on US 50 and 301 exit 22 to Riva Rd, 0.3 mi n. Int corridors. **Pets:** Accepted.
🅂🅰🆅🅴 📶 🛏 🖥 🍴 🏊

▼▼ Extended StayAmerica-Annapolis/Naval Academy 🅼 ❀
(410) 571-9988. **$99-$299.** 1 Womack Dr 21401. 2.3 mi sw on US 50 and 301 exit 22, just s on Admiral Cochrane Dr, then just n on Spruill Rd. Int corridors. **Pets:** Other species. $25 daily fee/pet. Service with restrictions. 📶 🛏 🖥

▼▼▼ Hampton Inn & Suites-Annapolis 🅷 ❀
(410) 571-0200. **$99-$284.** 124 Womack Dr 21401. 2.3 mi sw on US 50 and 301 exit 22, just s, then just e on Admiral Cochrane Dr, just n on Spruill Rd, then just w. Int corridors. **Pets:** Service with restrictions, crate. 📶 🏋 🛏 🖥 🏊 ✖

▼▼ Homestead Studio Suites Hotel-Annapolis-Naval Academy 🅷 ❀
(410) 571-6600. **$109-$309.** 120 Admiral Cochrane Dr 21401. 2.3 mi sw on US 50 and 301 exit 22, just s, then just e. Int corridors. **Pets:** Other species. $25 daily fee/pet. Service with restrictions. 📶 🏋 🛏 🖥

🔷 ▼▼▼ Loews Annapolis Hotel 🅷
(410) 263-7777. **Call for rates.** 126 West St 21401. US 50 and 301 exit 24 eastbound; exit 24A westbound, 1.4 mi s on SR 70, just sw on Calvert St, then just w. Int corridors. **Pets:** Accepted.
🄴🄲🄾 🅂🅰🆅🅴 📶 ✖ 🛏 🖥 🍴

▼▼ Quality Inn 🅼
(410) 974-4440. **$90-$139.** 1542 Whitehall Rd 21409. 1 mi w of Chesapeake Bay Bridge, off US 50 and 301 exit 30 eastbound; exit 32 westbound. Int corridors. **Pets:** Accepted. 📶 🛏 🖥

🔷 ▼▼▼ Sheraton Annapolis Hotel 🅷
(410) 266-3131. **$109-$249.** 173 Jennifer Rd 21401. North side of US 50 and 301 exit 23B westbound; exit 23 eastbound. Int corridors. **Pets:** Medium, dogs only. $50 one-time fee/room. Designated rooms, service with restrictions, crate. 🅂🅰🆅🅴 📶 ✖ 🏋 🛏 🖥 🍴 🏊 ✖

🔷 ▼▼▼ The Westin Annapolis 🅷 ❀
(410) 972-4300. **$159-$1599.** 100 Westgate Cir 21401. US 50 and 301 exit 24 eastbound; exit 24A westbound, 0.7 mi s on SR 70, then 0.8 mi e on SR 435; 0.5 mi n of Church Cir. Int corridors. **Pets:** Medium, dogs only. Designated rooms, service with restrictions, supervision.
🅂🅰🆅🅴 📶 ✖ 🏋 🛏 🖥 🍴 🏊 ✖

BALTIMORE

▼▼▼ Admiral Fell Inn 🅷
(410) 522-7377. **Call for rates.** 888 S Broadway St 21231. Corner of Broadway and Thames sts; facing the waterfront. Int corridors. **Pets:** Accepted. 📶 ✖ 🛏 🖥 🍴

▼▼ Brookshire Suites 🅷
(410) 625-1300. **Call for rates.** 120 E Lombard St 21202. Corner of Calvert and Lombard sts. Int corridors. **Pets:** Accepted.
📶 ✖ 🛏 🖥

▼▼▼ Celie's Waterfront Inn 🅱🅱
(410) 522-2323. **$149-$349, 15 day notice.** 1714 Thames St 21231. In historic Fells Point area. Int corridors. **Pets:** Accepted.
📶 ✖ 🛏 🖥 🎿

🔷 ▼▼▼ Days Inn Inner Harbor Baltimore 🅷
(410) 576-1000. **$143-$206.** 100 Hopkins Pl 21201. Opposite First Mariner Arena; 1 blk from Baltimore Convention Center. Int corridors. **Pets:** Accepted. 🅂🅰🆅🅴 📶 ✖ 🛏 🖥 🍴 🏊

▼▼▼ Hilton Baltimore 🅷
(443) 573-8700. **$159-$359.** 401 W Pratt St 21201. I-95 exit 53, just w of Camden Yards. Int corridors. **Pets:** Accepted.
📶 ✖ 🏋 🛏 🖥 🍴 🏊 ✖

▼▼▼ Holiday Inn Express Baltimore/Downtown 🅷
(410) 400-8045. **$99-$169.** 221 N Gay St 21202. Jct N Gay St and Fallsway. Int corridors. **Pets:** Small. $50 one-time fee/pet. Service with restrictions, crate. 📶 ✖ 🏋 🛏 🖥

AAA ▼▼▼ Holiday Inn-Inner Harbor H
(410) 685-3500. **$139-$279.** 301 W Lombard St 21201. Just w of Camden Yards. Int corridors. **Pets:** Medium, other species. $25 one-time fee/room. [SAVE] 🛜 ✖ 🛏 💻 🍴 ≈ 🐾

▼▼▼ Home2 Suites by Hilton-Downtown Baltimore H
(410) 576-1200. **$149-$199.** & E Pleasant St 21202. Just s of US 40 E, off Charles St. Int corridors. **Pets:** Accepted. 🛜 🛏 💻

▼▼ Homewood Suites by Hilton Baltimore Inner Harbor H
(410) 234-0999. **$149-$349.** 625 S President St 21202. In Harbor East section of Inner Harbor. Int corridors. **Pets:** Accepted.
🛜 ♿ 🛏 💻 ≈ 🐾

▼▼ Hotel Brexton H
(443) 478-2100. **$129-$199.** 868 Park Ave 21201. Between Tyson and Brexton sts; 1 blk e of Martin Luther King Jr Blvd. Int corridors. **Pets:** Small. $50 daily fee/pet. Designated rooms. 🛜 ✖ 🛏 💻

▼▼ ▼▼ Hotel Monaco Baltimore H
(443) 692-6170. **$139-$329.** 2 N Charles St 21201. Jct Baltimore and N Charles sts. Int corridors. **Pets:** Accepted.
🔲 🛜 ✖ 🛏 💻 🍴

▼▼▼ Inn at The Colonnade Baltimore - A DoubleTree by Hilton Hotel H
(410) 235-5400. **$143-$226.** 4 W University Pkwy 21218. I-83 exit 9A, 0.5 mi e on Cold Springs Ln to Roland Ave/University Pkwy, then 1 mi s. Int corridors. **Pets:** Accepted. [ECO] 🛜 ✖ 🛏 💻 🍴 ≈ 🐾

AAA ▼▼▼▼ InterContinental Harbor Court H
(410) 234-0550. **$169-$479.** 550 Light St 21202. Facing Inner Harbor. Int corridors. **Pets:** Medium. $150 one-time fee/room. Designated rooms, service with restrictions, supervision.
[SAVE] 🛜 ✖ ♿ 🛏 💻 🍴 ≈ 🐾

▼▼▼ Pier 5 Hotel H
(410) 539-2000. **Call for rates.** 711 Eastern Ave 21202. On the Inner Harbor, at Pier 5. Int corridors. **Pets:** Accepted.
🛜 ✖ 🛏 💻 🍴

▼▼▼ Radisson Hotel at Cross Keys H
(410) 532-6900. **$109-$179.** 100 Village Sq 21210. I-83 exit 10A (Northern Pkwy), just e, then 0.4 mi s on Falls Rd; in Village of Cross Keys. Int corridors. **Pets:** Accepted. 🛜 ✖ ♿ 🛏 💻 🍴 ≈ 🐾

AAA ▼▼▼▼ Radisson Plaza Lord Baltimore H
(410) 539-8400. **Call for rates.** 20 W Baltimore St 21201. At Baltimore and Hanover sts. Int corridors. **Pets:** Medium, dogs only. $50 one-time fee/pet. [ECO] [SAVE] 🛜 ✖ ♿ 🛏 💻

▼▼▼ Residence Inn by Marriott-Baltimore Downtown/Inner Harbor H
(410) 962-1220. **$161-$218.** 17 Light St 21202. Jct Redwood and Light sts. Int corridors. **Pets:** Accepted. 🛜 ✖ ♿ 🛏 💻 🍴

AAA ▼▼▼ Sheraton Baltimore City Center Hotel H 🐾
(410) 752-1100. **$100-$380.** 101 W Fayette St 21201. Between Charles and Liberty sts. Int corridors. **Pets:** Small, dogs only. $250 deposit/pet. Designated rooms, service with restrictions, supervision.
[SAVE] 🛜 ✖ 🛏 💻 🍴 ≈

AAA ▼▼▼ Sheraton Inner Harbor Hotel H
(410) 962-8300. **$159-$454, 3 day notice.** 300 S Charles St 21201. At Conway St; 1 blk from the Inner Harbor. Int corridors. **Pets:** Accepted.
[SAVE] 🛜 ✖ 🛏 💻 🍴 ≈ 🐾

AAA ▼▼ Sleep Inn & Suites Downtown/Inner Harbor H 🐾
(410) 779-6166. **Call for rates.** 301 Fallsway 21202. Between E Lexington and Gay sts. Int corridors. **Pets:** Large, other species. $35 daily fee/room. [SAVE] 🛜 ✖ ♿ 🛏 💻

▼▼▼ Tremont Plaza Hotel H
(410) 727-2222. **$99-$389.** 222 St. Paul Pl 21202. At St. Paul Pl and Saratoga St. Int corridors. **Pets:** Accepted.
🛜 ✖ 🛏 💻 🍴 ≈ 🐾

AAA ▼▼▼ Wyndham Baltimore Peabody Court H
(410) 727-7101. **Call for rates.** 612 Cathedral St 21201. Cathedral St and Mt. Vernon Square. Int corridors. **Pets:** Small, other species. $50 one-time fee/room. Service with restrictions, crate.
[SAVE] 🛜 ✖ 🛏 💻 🍴

BELCAMP

▼▼ Candlewood Suites Aberdeen H 🐾
(410) 914-3060. **$99-$129.** 4216 Philadelphia Rd 21015. I-95 exit 80 (SR 543), just s to SR 7 (Philadelphia Rd N), then just w. Int corridors. **Pets:** Large, other species. $25 one-time fee/pet. Designated rooms, service with restrictions, supervision. 🛜 ♿ 🛏 💻

▼▼ Extended StayAmerica-Baltimore-Bel Air H 🐾
(410) 273-0194. **$99-$289.** 1361 James Way 21015. I-95 exit 80 (SR 543), just ne. Int corridors. **Pets:** Other species. $25 daily fee/pet. Service with restrictions. 🛜 ♿ 🛏 💻

COLUMBIA

▼▼ Extended Stay Deluxe Columbia Corporate Park H 🐾
(410) 872-2994. **$109-$309.** 8890 Stanford Blvd 21045. I-95 exit 41B, 1.3 mi w on SR 175, 0.5 mi s on Snowden River Pkwy, just w on McGaw Rd, then 0.3 mi nw. Int corridors. **Pets:** Other species. $25 daily fee/pet. Service with restrictions. 🛜 🛏 💻

▼▼▼ Homewood Suites by Hilton Columbia H
(410) 872-9200. **Call for rates.** 8320 Benson Dr 21045. I-95 exit 41B, 0.5 mi w on SR 175, just nw on SR 108, then just w on Lark Brown Rd. Int corridors. **Pets:** Other species. $15 daily fee/room. Service with restrictions, crate. 🛜 ♿ 🛏 💻 ≈ 🐾

AAA ▼▼▼▼ Sheraton Columbia Town Center Hotel H
(410) 730-3900. **$119-$299.** 10207 Wincopin Cir 21044. 1.2 mi w on SR 175 (Little Patuxent Pkwy) from jct US 29, then just s; center. Int corridors. **Pets:** Accepted. [ECO] [SAVE] 🛜 ✖ 🛏 💻 🍴 ≈ 🐾

▼▼▼ Staybridge Suites Baltimore-Columbia H
(410) 964-9494. **$89-$159.** 8844 Columbia 100 Pkwy 21045. I-95 exit 43B, 4 mi w on SR 100 exit 1B, then just e. Int corridors. **Pets:** Accepted. 🛜 ♿ 🛏 💻 ≈ 🐾

▼▼ StudioPLUS Columbia Gateway Drive H 🐾
(410) 312-1557. **$89-$279.** 6620 Eli Whitney Dr 21046. I-95 exit 41, 1 mi w on SR 175, then just se on Columbia Gateway Dr. Int corridors. **Pets:** Other species. $25 daily fee/pet. Service with restrictions.
🛜 🛏 💻

EDGEWOOD

AAA ▼▼ Best Western Invitation Inn M
(410) 679-9700. **$74-$99.** 1709 Edgewood Rd 21040. I-95 exit 77A, just e on SR 24. Ext corridors. **Pets:** Accepted. [SAVE] 🛜 🛏 💻 ≈

AAA ▼▼ La Quinta Inn & Suites H
(410) 676-6969. **Call for rates.** 2112B Emmorton Park Rd 21040. I-95 exit 77A, just e on SR 24. Int corridors. **Pets:** Medium, other species. Service with restrictions, supervision. [SAVE] 🛜 ✖ ♿ 🛏 💻

ELLICOTT CITY

▼▼▼ Residence Inn by Marriott Columbia H
(410) 997-7200. **$95-$192.** 4950 Beaver Run Ct 21043. I-95 exit 43B, 4 mi w on SR 100 exit 1B (Executive Park Dr). Int corridors.
Pets: Accepted. [ECO] 🛜 ✖ ♿ 🛏 💻 ≈ 🐾

AAA ▼▼▼ Turf Valley H
(410) 465-1500. **$104-$269, 3 day notice.** 2700 Turf Valley Rd 21042. I-70 exit 82 eastbound, 1.5 mi e on US 40 exit 83 westbound, 0.6 mi s on Marriottsville Rd, then 0.8 mi e on US 40. Int corridors.
Pets: Accepted. [ECO] [SAVE] 🛜 ✖ 🛏 💻 🍴 ≈ 🐾

ESSEX

▼▼ **Super 8 Baltimore/Essex** ⊞

(410) 780-0030. **$79-$105.** 98 Stemmers Run Rd 21221. I-695 exit 36 (SR 702 S) to SR 150 E Chase exit. Int corridors. **Pets:** Small. $11 daily fee/pet. Service with restrictions, supervision. 🐾 🛏 💻

GLEN BURNIE

 ▼▼▼ **Days Inn-Baltimore South/Glen Burnie** Ⓜ

(410) 761-8300. **$58-$107.** 6600 Ritchie Hwy 21061. I-695 exit 3B eastbound; exit 2 westbound, 0.5 mi s on SR 2. Ext corridors. **Pets:** Medium. $20 daily fee/pet. Designated rooms, service with restrictions, supervision. 🅂🅰🆅🅴 🐾 🛏 💻 ≈

▼▼ **Extended StayAmerica Baltimore-Glen Burnie** ⊞ 🐾

(410) 761-2708. **$99-$289.** 104 Chesapeake Centre Ct 21061. I-695 exit 3B, 0.9 mi s on SR 2, just e on E Ordnance Rd, then just s. Int corridors. **Pets:** Other species. $25 daily fee/pet. Service with restrictions. 🐾 🅢🅜 🛏 💻

 ▼▼▼ **La Quinta Inn & Suites Baltimore South Glen Burnie** ⊞

(410) 636-4300. **$83-$159.** 6323 Ritchie Hwy 21061. I-695 exit 3A eastbound; exit 2 westbound, jct SR 2. Int corridors. **Pets:** Medium, other species. Service with restrictions, supervision. 🅂🅰🆅🅴 🐾 🅢🅜 🛏 💻 ≈ 🗙

HANOVER

 ▼▼▼ **Aloft Arundel Mills** ⊞

(443) 577-0077. **$99-$250.** 7520 Teague Rd 21076. I-95 exit 43A, 3.6 mi e on SR 100 exit 10A (Arundel Mills Blvd), then 0.4 mi s to SR 713. Int corridors. **Pets:** Accepted. 🅂🅰🆅🅴 🐾 🗙 🅢🅜 🛏 💻 ≈

 ▼▼▼ **Element by Westin at Arundel Mills** ⊞

(443) 577-0050. **$99-$250.** 7522 Teague Rd 21076. I-95 exit 43A, 3.6 mi e on SR 100 exit 10A (Arundel Mills Blvd), then 0.4 mi s to SR 713. Int corridors. **Pets:** Accepted. 🅂🅰🆅🅴 🐾 🗙 🅢🅜 🛏 💻 ≈

▼▼▼▼ **Homewood Suites by Hilton Baltimore/Arundel Mills** ⊞

(410) 878-7201. **$129-$269.** 7491-B New Ridge Rd 21076. SR 100 exit 10B, 0.3 mi n on SR 713. Int corridors. **Pets:** Accepted. 🐾 🅢🅜 🛏 💻 ≈ 🗙

 ▼▼▼ **Red Roof Inn-BWI Parkway** Ⓜ

(410) 712-4070. **$60-$130.** 7306 Parkway Dr S 21076. I-95 exit 43A, 2 mi e on SR 100 exit 8 (Coca Cola Dr), then 0.5 mi se. Ext corridors. **Pets:** Large, other species. No service, supervision. 🅂🅰🆅🅴 🐾 🅢🅜 🛏

▼▼▼▼ **Residence Inn by Marriott-Arundel Mills/BWI** ⊞ 🐾

(410) 799-7332. **$142-$189.** 7035 Arundel Mills Cir 21076. I-95 exit 43A, 3.6 mi e on SR 100 exit 10A (Arundel Mills Blvd). Int corridors. **Pets:** Medium, other species. $100 one-time fee/room. Designated rooms, service with restrictions, crate. 🐾 🗙 🅢🅜 🛏 💻 ≈ 🗙

▼▼▼▼ **TownePlace Suites by Marriott Arundel Mills/BWI** ⊞

(410) 379-9000. **$113-$170.** 7021 Arundel Mills Cir 21076. I-95 exit 43A, 3.6 mi e on SR 100 exit 10A (Arundel Mills Blvd). Int corridors. **Pets:** Accepted. 🐾 🗙 🅢🅜 🛏 💻 ≈ 🗙

HAVRE DE GRACE

▼▼ **Super 8 Havre de Grace** Ⓜ

(410) 939-1880. **$53-$78.** 929 Pulaski Hwy 21078. I-95 exit 89, 2.5 mi e on SR 155, then 0.3 mi w on US 40. Int corridors. **Pets:** Medium, other species. $10 daily fee/pet. Service with restrictions, supervision. 🐾 🛏 💻

HUNT VALLEY

▼▼▼▼ **Residence Inn by Marriott Baltimore Hunt Valley** ⊞

(410) 527-2333. **$132-$161.** 45 Schilling Rd 21031. I-83 exit 20A (Shawan Rd), just e on Shawan Rd, just s on McCormick Rd, then just e. Int corridors. **Pets:** Accepted. 🐾 🗙 🅢🅜 🛏 💻 ≈ 🗙

JESSUP

▼▼ **Extended StayAmerica-Columbia-Laurel** ⊞ 🐾

(301) 725-3877. **$99-$289.** 8550 Washington Blvd 20794. I-95 exit 38A, 1.4 mi e on SR 32, then 0.5 mi n on US 1. Int corridors. **Pets:** Other species. $25 daily fee/pet. Service with restrictions. 🐾 🛏 💻

▼▼▼ **La Quinta Inn & Suites Columbia Jessup** ⊞

(410) 799-1500. **$89-$175.** 7300 Crestmount Rd 20794. I-95 exit 41A, just s of jct US 1 and SR 175. Int corridors. **Pets:** Medium, other species. Service with restrictions, supervision. 🐾 🅢🅜 🛏 💻

 ▼▼▼ **Red Roof Inn-Columbia/Fort Meade** Ⓜ

(410) 796-0380. **$60-$130.** 8000 Washington Blvd 20794. I-95 exit 41A, 0.3 mi s of jct US 1 and SR 175. Ext corridors. **Pets:** Large, other species. No service, supervision. 🅂🅰🆅🅴 🐾 🅢🅜 🛏

LINTHICUM HEIGHTS

 ▼▼▼ **Aloft Baltimore Washington Intl Airport** ⊞ 🐾

(410) 691-6969. **$149-$299.** 1741 W Nursery Rd 21090. I-695 exit 7A, 1 mi s on SR 295, then 1.2 mi e. Int corridors. **Pets:** Medium, dogs only. Service with restrictions. 🅂🅰🆅🅴 🐾 🗙 🅢🅜 🛏 💻 ≈

▼▼▼ **Candlewood Suites-BWI** ⊞

(410) 850-9214. **$99-$149.** 1247 Winterson Rd 21090. I-695 exit 7A, 1 mi s on SR 295, 1.3 mi e on W Nursery Rd, then 0.3 mi w. Int corridors. **Pets:** Large. $150 one-time fee/pet, $15 daily fee/pet. Service with restrictions, crate. 🐾 🛏 💻

▼▼▼▼ **Comfort Suites-BWI Airport** ⊞ 🐾

(410) 691-1000. **$67-$162.** 815 Elkridge Landing Rd 21090. I-695 exit 7A, 1 mi s on SR 295, then 1.3 mi e on W Nursery Rd. Int corridors. **Pets:** Other species. $30 one-time fee/room. Service with restrictions, crate. 🐾 🗙 🅢🅜 🛏 💻

▼▼▼▼ **Holiday Inn-BWI Airport Conference Center** ⊞

(410) 859-8400. **$99-$239.** 890 Elkridge Landing Rd 21090. I-695 exit 7A, 1 mi s on SR 295, 1.3 mi e on W Nursery Rd, then 0.5 mi w. Int corridors. **Pets:** Accepted. 🐾 🅢🅜 🛏 💻 🍴 ≈

 ▼▼▼ **Four Points by Sheraton BWI Airport** ⊞

(410) 859-3300. **$90-$190, 7 day notice.** 7032 Elm Rd 21240. I-195 exit 1A, 0.5 mi n on SR 170, then just e. Int corridors. **Pets:** $25 daily fee/pet. Service with restrictions. 🅂🅰🆅🅴 🐾 🗙 🅢🅜 🛏 💻 🍴 ≈

▼▼▼ **Hampton Inn BWI Airport** ⊞

(410) 850-0600. **$79-$199.** 829 Elkridge Landing Rd 21090. I-695 exit 7A, 1 mi s on SR 295, 1.3 mi e on W Nursery Rd, then just w. Int corridors. **Pets:** Accepted. 🐾 🗙 🅢🅜 🛏 💻

▼▼▼ **Homestead Studio Suites Hotel-Baltimore-BWI Airport** Ⓜ 🐾

(410) 691-2500. **$99-$289.** 939 International Dr 21090. I-695 exit 7A, 1 mi s on SR 295, then 0.6 mi e on W Nursery Rd. Ext corridors. **Pets:** Other species. $25 daily fee/pet. Service with restrictions. 🐾 🅢🅜 🛏 💻

▼▼▼ **La Quinta Inn & Suites BWI Airport** ⊞

(410) 859-2333. **$94-$189.** 1734 W Nursery Rd 21090. I-695 exit 7A, 1 mi s on SR 295, then 1.3 mi e on W Nursery Rd. Int corridors. **Pets:** Medium, other species. Service with restrictions, supervision. 🐾 🛏 💻 ≈

Red Roof Inn-BWI Airport M
(410) 850-7600. **$60-$110.** 827 Elkridge Landing Rd 21090. I-695 exit 7A, 1 mi s on SR 295, 1.3 mi e on W Nursery Rd, then just w. Ext corridors. **Pets:** Large, other species. No service, supervision.
SAVE 🛰 🍴 🖼 🖵

Residence Inn by Marriott-BWI Airport H
(410) 691-0255. **$114-$229.** 1160 Winterson Rd 21090. I-695 exit 7A, 1 mi s on SR 295, 0.7 mi e on W Nursery Rd, then just n. Int corridors. **Pets:** Medium. $75 one-time fee/room. Service with restrictions, supervision. ECO SAVE 🛰 ✕ 🔊M 🍴 🖵 ➰ ✕

Sheraton Baltimore Washington Airport Hotel H
(443) 577-2100. **$99-$300.** 1100 Old Elkridge Landing Rd 21090. I-695 exit 7A, 1 mi s on SR 295, 1.3 mi e on W Nursery Rd, then 0.4 mi w on Winterson Rd. Int corridors. **Pets:** Accepted.
SAVE 🛰 ✕ 🔊M 🍴 🖵 🍴 ➰ ✕

Sleep Inn & Suites BWI Airport H
(410) 789-7223. **$79-$129.** 6055 Belle Grove Rd 21225. I-695 exit 6A eastbound; exit 5 westbound, 0.3 mi n to jct SR 170/648. Int corridors. **Pets:** Accepted. 🛰 🔊M 🍴 🖵

Staybridge Suites BWI H
(410) 850-5666. **$109-$359.** 1301 Winterson Rd 21090. I-695 exit 7A, 1 mi s on SR 295, 1.3 mi e on Nursery Rd, then 0.4 mi w. Int corridors. **Pets:** Medium. $150 one-time fee/pet. Service with restrictions, crate.
🛰 🔊M 🍴 🖵 ➰

TownePlace Suites by Marriott Baltimore/BWI Airport H ✿
(410) 694-0060. **$119-$139.** 1171 Winterson Rd 21090. I-695 exit 7A, 1 mi s on SR 295, 0.7 mi e on W Nursery Rd, then just n. **Pets:** Medium, other species. $100 one-time fee/room. Service with restrictions, supervision. ECO SAVE 🛰 ✕ 🔊M 🍴 🖵 ➰

The Westin-Baltimore Washington Airport H ✿
(443) 577-2300. **$119-$350.** 1110 Old Elkridge Landing Rd 21090. I-695 exit 7A, 1 mi s on SR 295, 1.3 mi e on W Nursery Rd, then 0.4 mi w on Winterson Rd. Int corridors. **Pets:** Small, dogs only. $25 one-time fee/room. Designated rooms, service with restrictions.
SAVE 🛰 ✕ 🔊M 🖵 🍴 ➰ ✕

ROSEDALE

La Quinta Inn & Suites Baltimore North H
(410) 574-8100. **$94-$165.** 4 Philadelphia Ct 21237. I-695 exit 34, just n. Int corridors. **Pets:** Medium, other species. Service with restrictions, supervision. 🛰 🍴 🖵 ➰

SYKESVILLE

Inn at Norwood BB
(410) 549-7868. **$135-$225, 7 day notice.** 7514 Norwood Ave 21784. I-70 exit 80 (SR 32), 3.6 mi n, 0.6 mi w on West Friendship Rd (which becomes Main St), then just s on Church St. Int corridors. **Pets:** Dogs only. $20 one-time fee/pet, $20 daily fee/pet. Designated rooms, service with restrictions, crate. 🛰 ✕ 🍴 🖵 🐾

TIMONIUM

Red Roof Inn-Timonium M
(410) 666-0380. **$60-$110.** 111 W Timonium Rd 21093. I-83 exit 16A northbound; exit 16 southbound, just e. Ext corridors. **Pets:** Large, other species. No service, supervision. SAVE 🛰 🔊M 🍴

TOWSON

Sheraton Baltimore North Hotel H
(410) 321-7400. **$99-$259.** 903 Dulaney Valley Rd 21204. I-695 exit 27A (Dulaney Valley Rd), 0.3 mi s. Int corridors. **Pets:** Accepted.
SAVE 🛰 ✕ 🍴 🖵 🍴 ➰ ✕

WESTMINSTER

Best Western Westminster Catering & Conference Ctr. H ✿
(410) 857-1900. **$83-$160.** 451 WMC Dr 21158. 1.7 mi w on SR 140 from jct SR 27. Int corridors. **Pets:** Medium, dogs only. $20 daily fee/room. Service with restrictions, supervision.
SAVE 🛰 ✕ 🍴 🖵 ➰

The Boston Inn M
(410) 848-9095. **$47-$75.** 533 Baltimore Blvd 21157. 0.9 mi se on SR 97/140 from jct SR 27. Ext corridors. **Pets:** Dogs only. Service with restrictions, crate. 🛰 🍴 🖵 ➰

WHITE MARSH

Residence Inn by Marriott Baltimore/White Marsh H
(410) 933-9554. **$149-$194.** 4980 Mercantile Rd 21236. I-95 exit 67B, 0.5 mi w on SR 43 (White Marsh Blvd), just s to Mercantile Rd, then just e. Int corridors. **Pets:** Other species. $75 one-time fee/room. Service with restrictions, supervision. 🛰 ✕ 🔊M 🍴 🖵 ➰ ✕

END METROPOLITAN AREA

CALIFORNIA

La Quinta Inn & Suites Lexington Park - Patuxent H
(301) 862-4100. **$116-$210.** 22769 Three Notch Rd 20619. 3.2 mi n on SR 235. Int corridors. **Pets:** Medium, other species. Service with restrictions, supervision. 🛰 ✕ 🍴 🖵 ➰

CAMBRIDGE

Comfort Inn & Suites Cambridge H
(410) 901-0926. **Call for rates.** 2936 Ocean Gateway 21613. On US 50, 0.8 mi e of jct SR 16. Int corridors. **Pets:** Accepted.
🛰 ✕ 🔊M 🍴 🖵 ➰

Hyatt Regency Chesapeake Bay Golf Resort, Spa and Marina H ✿
(410) 901-1234. **$139-$459, 3 day notice.** 100 Heron Blvd 21613. US 50 E, 1.2 mi e of Frederick C Malkus Jr Bridge. Int corridors. **Pets:** Large, dogs only. $50 daily fee/pet. Designated rooms, service with restrictions. ECO SAVE 🛰 🔊M 🍴 🖵 🍴 ➰ ✕

CUMBERLAND

Holiday Inn H
(301) 724-8800. **$99-$169.** 100 S George St 21502. I-68 exit 43C, just n; downtown. Int corridors. **Pets:** Accepted. 🛰 🍴 🖵 🍴 ➰

EASTON

Inn at 202 Dover CI
(410) 819-8007. **$279-$475, 7 day notice.** 202 E Dover St 21601. 0.7 mi w on SR 331 from jct US 50. Int corridors. **Pets:** Accepted.
SAVE 🛰 ✕ 🍴

ELKTON

▼▼▼▼ Elk Forge Inn & Spa 🄱🄱
(410) 392-9007. **$109-$289, 10 day notice.** 807 Elk Mills Rd 21921.
I-95 exit 109B, 1 mi w on SR 279 to Fletchwood Rd (SR 277), then 2 mi
s. Ext/int corridors. **Pets:** Accepted. 🖥 ✕ 🔲 🐾

EMMITSBURG

▼▼▼ Sleep Inn & Suites in Emmitsburg 🄷
(301) 447-0044. **Call for rates.** 501 Silo Hill Pkwy 21727. US 15 exit SR
140, just w, then just n. Int corridors. **Pets:** Medium. $25 one-time fee/
room. Designated rooms, service with restrictions, crate.
🖥 ✕ 🔲 🔲 🐾

FREDERICK

ⓐⓐ ▼▼▼▼ Comfort Inn Frederick 🄷
(301) 668-7272. **$90-$109.** 7300 Executive Way 21704. I-270 exit 31B,
0.9 mi sw on SR 85. Int corridors. **Pets:** Medium. $10 daily fee/pet. Des-
ignated rooms, service with restrictions, supervision.
🅂🄰🅅🄴 🖥 🔲 🔲

▼▼▼ Days Inn 🄼
(301) 694-6600. **$67-$74, 3 day notice.** 5646 Buckeystown Pike 21704.
I-270 exit 31A, 0.5 mi e on SR 85; I-70 exit 54, 0.5 mi w. Ext corridors.
Pets: Accepted. 🖥 🔲 🔲 🏊

▼▼ Extended StayAmerica-Frederick-Westview Dr 🄼 🐾
(301) 668-0808. **$89-$279.** 5240 Westview Dr 21703. I-270 exit 31B, 0.5
mi sw on SR 85, then 0.4 mi n. Int corridors. **Pets:** Other species. $25
daily fee/pet. Service with restrictions. 🖥 🔲 🔲

ⓐⓐ ▼▼▼▼ Hampton Inn Frederick 🄷
(301) 698-2500. **$99-$159.** 5311 Buckeystown Pike (SR 85) 21704. I-270
exit 31B, 0.6 mi w. Int corridors. **Pets:** Accepted.
🅂🄰🅅🄴 🖥 🔲 🔲 🍴 🏊

▼▼▼ Holiday Inn & Conference Center 🄷
(301) 694-7500. **$109-$189.** 5400 Holiday Dr 21703. I-270 exit 31A, just
se of SR 85. Int corridors. **Pets:** Accepted.
🖥 🔲 🔲 🍴 🏊 🚫

▼▼▼ Holiday Inn Express-FSK Mall 🄼
(301) 695-2881. **$99-$179.** 5579 Spectrum Dr 21703. I-270 exit 31A, just
e on SR 85. Int corridors. **Pets:** Accepted. 🖥 🔲 🔲

ⓐⓐ ▼▼▼▼ MainStay Suites Frederick 🄷
(301) 668-4600. **$90-$110.** 7310 Executive Way 21704. I-270 exit 31B,
0.7 mi sw on SR 85. Int corridors. **Pets:** Medium. $10 daily fee/pet. Des-
ignated rooms, service with restrictions, supervision.
🅂🄰🅅🄴 🖥 🔲 🔲 🏊

▼▼▼▼ Residence Inn by Marriott Frederick 🄷 🐾
(301) 360-0010. **$139-$229.** 5230 Westview Dr 21703. I-270 exit 31B,
0.5 mi sw on SR 85, then 0.3 mi n on Crestwood Blvd. Int corridors.
Pets: Medium, other species. $100 one-time fee/room. Service with
restrictions, crate. 🖥 ✕ 🔲 🔲 🏊 🚫

ⓐⓐ ▼▼▼ Travelodge Frederick 🄷
(301) 663-0500. **$52-$79.** 20 E Monocacy Blvd 21704. I-70 exit 54, just
n. Int corridors. **Pets:** Medium. $25 deposit/room. Designated rooms,
service with restrictions, supervision. 🅂🄰🅅🄴 🖥 🔲 🔲

FROSTBURG

ⓐⓐ ▼▼▼ Days Inn & Suites 🄼
(301) 689-2050. **$76-$114.** 11100 New Georges Creek Rd 21532. I-68
exit 34, 1 mi n on SR 36. Int corridors. **Pets:** Accepted.
🅂🄰🅅🄴 🖥 🔲 🔲 🚫

GRASONVILLE

ⓐⓐ ▼▼▼ Best Western Kent Narrows Inn 🄼 🐾
(410) 827-6767. **$85-$219.** 3101 Main St 21638. US 50 and 301 exit 42;
at Kent Narrows Bridge. Ext corridors. **Pets:** Small, other species. $10
daily fee/pet. Designated rooms, service with restrictions.
🅂🄰🅅🄴 🖥 🔲 🔲 🏊 🚫

HAGERSTOWN

▼▼▼ Econo Lodge Inn & Suites 🄼
(301) 733-2700. **$50-$170.** 1101 Dual Hwy 21740. I-70 exit 32B, 2.2 mi
w on US 40. Int corridors. **Pets:** $11 daily fee/pet. Designated rooms,
service with restrictions, supervision. 🖥 🔲 🔲

▼▼▼ Halfway Hagerstown Super 8 🄼
(301) 582-1992. **$57-$80.** 16805 Blake Rd 21740. I-81 exit 5B, just w. Int
corridors. **Pets:** Medium. $10 daily fee/pet. Designated rooms, service
with restrictions, supervision. 🖥 🔲 🔲

ⓐⓐ ▼▼▼▼ Holiday Inn Express Hotel & Suites 🄷
(301) 745-5644. **$109-$134.** 241 Railway Ln 21740. I-81 exit 5A, just e.
Int corridors. **Pets:** Accepted. 🅂🄰🅅🄴 🖥 🅶🄼 🔲 🔲 🏊 🚫

ⓐⓐ ▼▼▼▼ Homewood Suites by Hilton 🄷
(301) 665-3816. **$129-$159.** 1650 Pullman Ln 21740. I-81 exit 5, 6.3 mi
e; 0.5 mi n of jct I-70 and 81. Int corridors. **Pets:** Accepted.
🅂🄰🅅🄴 🖥 🔲 🔲 🏊 🚫

ⓐⓐ ▼▼▼ Sleep Inn & Suites 🄷
(301) 766-9449. **$72-$108.** 18216 Col Henry K Douglas Dr 21740. I-70
exit 29, just s. Int corridors. **Pets:** $10 daily fee/pet. Designated rooms,
service with restrictions, supervision. 🅂🄰🅅🄴 🖥 🔲 🔲 🏊

INDIAN HEAD

ⓐⓐ ▼▼▼ Super 8 Indian Head 🄼
(301) 753-8100. **$53-$67.** 4694 Indian Head Hwy 20640. SR 210, 0.6 mi
s of jct SR 225. Int corridors. **Pets:** Medium, dogs only. $10 daily fee/pet.
Service with restrictions, supervision. 🅂🄰🅅🄴 🖥 🅶🄼 🔲 🔲

LA VALE

ⓐⓐ ▼▼▼▼ Best Western Plus Braddock Motor Inn 🄷
(301) 729-3300. **$70-$120.** 1268 National Hwy 21502. On US 40, jct SR
53, adjacent to I-68 exit 39W/40E. Int corridors. **Pets:** Accepted.
🅂🄰🅅🄴 🖥 🔲 🔲 🍴 🏊 🚫

LEXINGTON PARK

**▼▼▼ TownePlace Suites by Marriott Patuxent River Naval
Air Station** 🄷
(301) 863-1111. **$199-$249.** 22520 Three Notch Rd 20653. From Gate 1
at Patuxent River Naval Air Station, 1 mi n on SR 235. Int corridors.
Pets: Accepted. 🖥 ✕ 🅶🄼 🔲 🔲 🏊

MCHENRY

▼▼▼ Wisp Resort Hotel & Conference Center 🄷
(301) 387-5581. **$59-$369, 7 day notice.** 290 Marsh Hill Rd 21541. 1
mi s on US 219 from jct SR 42, just w on Sang Run Rd, then 0.3 mi s.
Int corridors. **Pets:** Medium, dogs only. $50 one-time fee/room. Desig-
nated rooms, service with restrictions, supervision.
🖥 ✕ 🔲 🔲 🍴 🏊 🚫

NORTH EAST

ⓐⓐ ▼▼▼ Best Western North East Inn 🄷
(410) 287-5450. **$90-$140.** 39 Elwoods Rd 21901. I-95 exit 100 southbound; exit 100B northbound, 0.5 mi n on SR 272, then just w on Joseph
Biggs Hwy to Old Bayview Rd. Int corridors. **Pets:** Large, other species.
$10 daily fee/pet. Designated rooms, service with restrictions.
🅂🄰🅅🄴 🖥 🔲 🔲 🏊

▼▼▼ Comfort Inn & Suites North East 🄷
(410) 287-7100. **$100-$110.** 1 Center Dr 21901. I-95 exit 100 southbound; exit 100A northbound, just s on SR 272. Int corridors.
Pets: Small, dogs only. $15 daily fee/pet. Designated rooms, service with
restrictions, supervision. 🖥 🔲 🔲 🏊

OCEAN CITY

ⓐⓐ ▼▼▼ Clarion Resort Fontainebleau Hotel 🄷
(410) 524-3535. **$89-$399.** 10100 Coastal Hwy 21842. At 101st St. Int
corridors. **Pets:** Accepted. 🅂🄰🅅🄴 🖥 ✕ 🔲 🔲 🍴 🏊 🚫

▼▼▼ Comfort Suites Ocean City ⊞
(410) 213-7171. **Call for rates.** 12718 Ocean Gateway 21842. US 50;
0.7 mi w of Ocean City Bridge. Int corridors. **Pets:** Accepted.

PERRYVILLE

▼▼ Ramada Perryville Ⓜ
(410) 642-2866. **$58-$95.** 61 Heather Ln 21903. I-95 exit 93, just e. Ext
corridors. **Pets:** Accepted.

ROCK HALL

▼▼▼ Inn at Huntingfield Creek ⒝⒝ ❀
(410) 639-7779. **$179-$285, 14 day notice.** 4928 Eastern Neck Rd
21661. 1.8 mi s on SR 445 from jct SR 20. Ext/int corridors. **Pets:** Dogs
only. $30 daily fee/pet. Designated rooms, no service.

▼ Mariners Motel Ⓜ
(410) 639-2291. **$70-$95.** 5681 S Hawthorne Ave 21661. 0.3 mi e of SR
20. Ext corridors. **Pets:** Other species. $10 one-time fee/room. Service
with restrictions, supervision.

ST. MICHAELS

ⒶⒶⒶ ▼▼▼ St. Michaels Harbour Inn, Marina & Spa ⊞
(410) 745-9001. **$129-$525, 3 day notice.** 101 N Harbor Rd 21663. 0.3
mi e on SR 33, just n on Seymour Ave, then just w on Meadow St. Int
corridors. **Pets:** Accepted.

SALISBURY

ⒶⒶⒶ ▼▼ Best Western Salisbury Plaza Ⓜ
(410) 546-1300. **$59-$129.** 1735 N Salisbury Blvd 21801. US 13 business route, 0.5 mi s of US 50 Bypass. Ext corridors. **Pets:** Large. Service
with restrictions, supervision.

▼▼▼ Holiday Inn Salisbury Downtown ⊞
(410) 546-4400. **$99-$250.** 300 S Salisbury Blvd 21801. US 13 business
route, 0.4 mi s of jct US 50 business route; downtown. Int corridors.
Pets: Accepted.

▼▼▼ Residence Inn by Marriott Salisbury ⊞
(410) 543-0033. **$109-$179.** 140 Centre Rd 21801. Just off US 13 business route at US 50. Int corridors. **Pets:** Accepted.

SNOW HILL

ⒶⒶⒶ ▼▼▼ River House Inn ⒝⒝
(410) 632-2722. **$99-$300, 7 day notice.** 201 E Market St 21863. 1 mi
w on SR 394 from jct SR 113. Ext/int corridors. **Pets:** Accepted.

THURMONT

ⒶⒶⒶ ▼▼▼ Cozy Country Inn Ⓜ
(301) 271-4301. **$67-$150.** 103 Frederick Rd 21788. US 15, just e to SR
806, 0.4 mi n. Ext corridors. **Pets:** Accepted.

▼▼ Super 8-Thurmont Ⓜ
(301) 271-7888. **$69-$85.** 300 Tippin Dr 21788. US 15, just w on SR
806. Int corridors. **Pets:** Medium, other species. $10 daily fee/pet. Service
with restrictions, supervision.

WALDORF

▼▼ La Quinta Inn Waldorf ⊞
(301) 645-0022. **$71-$190.** 11770 Business Park Dr 20601. 1 mi n on
US 301 from jct SR 228. Int corridors. **Pets:** Medium, other species.
Service with restrictions, supervision.

▼▼▼ Residence Inn by Marriott Waldorf ⊞
(301) 632-2111. **$113-$132.** 3020 Technology Pl 20601. SR 228, just w
of jct US 301. Int corridors. **Pets:** Accepted.

WASHINGTON, D.C. METROPOLITAN AREA

BELTSVILLE

▼▼▼ Comfort Inn Capital Beltway/I-95 North ⊞
(301) 572-7100. **$89-$249.** 4050 Powder Mill Rd 20705. I-95 exit 29B,
just w on SR 212. Int corridors. **Pets:** Accepted.

ⒶⒶⒶ ▼▼▼ Sheraton Washington North Hotel ⊞
(301) 937-4422. **$89-$199.** 4095 Powder Mill Rd 20705. I-95 exit 29B,
just w on SR 212; 2 mi n of I-495. Int corridors. **Pets:** Accepted.

BETHESDA

▼▼▼ Residence Inn by Marriott-Bethesda Downtown ⊞
(301) 718-0200. **$149-$349.** 7335 Wisconsin Ave 20814. I-495 exit 34,
2.5 mi s on SR 355; entrance on Waverly St. Int corridors.
Pets: Accepted.

BOWIE

ⒶⒶⒶ ▼▼▼ Comfort Inn Hotel & Conference
Center-Bowie ⊞
(301) 464-0089. **$89-$135.** 4500 NW Crain Hwy 20716. US 50 exit 13A,
jct US 50/301 and SR 3. Int corridors. **Pets:** Large, other species. $15
daily fee/pet. Designated rooms, service with restrictions, crate.

▼▼▼ Hampton Inn-Bowie ⊞
(301) 809-1800. **$119-$149.** 15202 Major Lansdale Blvd 20716. US 50
exit 11, 0.4 mi s on SR 197. Int corridors. **Pets:** Accepted.

CAMP SPRINGS

▼▼▼ Country Inn & Suites By Carlson Andrews Air Force
Base/DC Area ⊞
(240) 492-1070. **Call for rates.** 4950 Mercedes Blvd 20746. I-95/495 exit
7B, just e to Auth Rd, then just n. Int corridors. **Pets:** Accepted.

▼▼ Quality Inn Camp Springs/Andrews Air Force
Base ⊞
(301) 420-2800. **$69-$139.** 4783 Allentown Rd 20746. I-95/495 exit 9.
Ext/int corridors. **Pets:** Medium. $25 one-time fee/pet. Designated rooms,
service with restrictions, crate.

CHEVERLY

▼▼ Howard Johnson Inn Cheverly ⊞
(301) 779-7700. **$104-$170.** 5811 Annapolis Rd 20784. Jct Baltimore-
Washington Pkwy and SR 450. Int corridors. **Pets:** Accepted.

CLINTON

ⒶⒶⒶ ▼▼▼ Comfort Inn at Joint Base Andrews ⊞
(301) 856-5200. **$99-$189.** 7979 Malcolm Rd 20735. I-95/495 exit 7A,
3.2 mi s on SR 5. Int corridors. **Pets:** Accepted.

 TownePlace Suites by Marriott Clinton/Andrews AFB 🏨 ✿

(301) 856-2266. **$132-$227.** 7800 Ferry Ave 20735. I-95/495 exit 7A, 2.9 mi s on SR 5 exit Coventry Way E, follow signs to Andrews AFB, then 0.5 mi ne on Old Alexandria Ferry Rd. Int corridors. **Pets:** Small. $100 one-time fee/room. Designated rooms, service with restrictions, supervision.

COLLEGE PARK

Comfort Inn & Suites College Park 🏨

(301) 441-8110. **$79-$219.** 9020 Baltimore Ave 20740. I-95/495 exit 25 northbound; exit 25B southbound, 1.3 mi s on US 1. Int corridors. **Pets:** Medium. $25 daily fee/pet. Designated rooms, service with restrictions, supervision.

Super 8-College Park 🅜

(301) 474-0894. **$79-$105.** 9150 Baltimore Ave 20740. I-95/495 exit 25 northbound; exit 25B southbound, 0.9 mi s on US 1. Int corridors. **Pets:** Small. $10 daily fee/pet. Designated rooms, service with restrictions, supervision.

GAITHERSBURG

Comfort Inn Shady Grove 🏨 ✿

(301) 330-0023. **$79-$159.** 16216 Frederick Rd 20877. I-270 exit 8, 1 mi e on Shady Grove Rd at SR 355. Int corridors. **Pets:** Large, other species. $15 daily fee/pet. Service with restrictions.

Extended Stay Deluxe-Washington, DC-Gaithersburg 🏨 ✿

(301) 963-3539. **$119-$329.** 201 Professional Dr 20879. I-270 exit 11, 0.4 mi e, then 0.9 mi n on SR 355. Int corridors. **Pets:** Other species. $25 daily fee/pet. Service with restrictions.

Hilton Washington DC North/Gaithersburg 🏨

(301) 977-8900. **$89-$219.** 620 Perry Pkwy 20877. I-270 exit 11, then e. Int corridors. **Pets:** Accepted.

Holiday Inn-Gaithersburg 🏨

(301) 948-8900. **Call for rates.** 2 Montgomery Village Ave 20879. I-270 exit 11, 0.3 mi e. Int corridors. **Pets:** Medium. Designated rooms, service with restrictions, supervision.

Homestead Studio Suites Hotel-Washington DC-Gaithersburg-Rockville 🏨 ✿

(301) 987-9100. **$109-$299.** 2621 Research Blvd 20850. I-270 exit 8, just w, then just n. Int corridors. **Pets:** Other species. $25 daily fee/pet. Service with restrictions.

Hyatt Summerfield Suites Gaithersburg 🏨 ✿

(301) 527-6000. **$79-$219.** 200 Skidmore Blvd 20877. I-370 exit SR 355, just n to Westland Rd. Ext corridors. **Pets:** Medium, other species. $150 one-time fee/room. Designated rooms, service with restrictions, crate.

Residence Inn by Marriott-Gaithersburg 🏨

(301) 590-3003. **$80-$189.** 9721 Washingtonian Blvd 20878. I-270 exit 9B (I-370/Sam Eig Hwy), just w to Fields Rd, 0.8 mi se, then just ne. Int corridors. **Pets:** Accepted.

TownePlace Suites by Marriott-Gaithersburg 🏨

(301) 590-2300. **$139-$209.** 212 Perry Pkwy 20877. I-270 exit 10 northbound, just e; exit 11 southbound, just e on SR 124 to SR 355, 0.3 mi s, then 0.5 mi sw. Int corridors. **Pets:** Accepted.

GREENBELT

Residence Inn by Marriott-Greenbelt 🏨

(301) 982-1600. **$79-$229.** 6320 Golden Triangle Dr 20770. I-95/495 exit 23, 0.5 mi sw of jct SR 201; off SR 193 (Greenbelt Rd), just n on Walker Dr. Int corridors. **Pets:** Accepted.

LAUREL

Comfort Suites Laurel Lakes 🏨

(301) 206-2600. **$79-$170.** 14402 Laurel Pl 20707. On US 1, 0.9 mi s of jct SR 198. Int corridors. **Pets:** Accepted.

Holiday Inn Laurel-West 🏨 ✿

(301) 776-5300. **$79-$169.** 15101 Sweitzer Ln 20707. I-95 exit 33B, just w on SR 198. Ext/int corridors. **Pets:** Large. $50 one-time fee/room. Service with restrictions, supervision.

NATIONAL HARBOR

Aloft Washington National Harbor 🏨

(301) 749-9000. **$119-$299.** 156 Waterfront St 20745. I-95/495 exit 2A, 0.5 mi e. Int corridors. **Pets:** Accepted.

Residence Inn by Marriott National Harbor 🏨

(301) 749-4755. **$151-$284.** 192 Waterfront St 20745. I-95/495 exit 2A, 0.5 mi e. Int corridors. **Pets:** $200 one-time fee/room. Service with restrictions, supervision.

The Westin Washington National Harbor 🏨 ✿

(301) 567-3999. **$309.** 171 Waterfront St 20745. I-95/495 exit 2A, just e. Int corridors. **Pets:** Small, dogs only. Designated rooms, service with restrictions, crate.

ROCKVILLE

Best Western Plus Rockville Hotel & Suites 🏨

(301) 424-4940. **$99-$149.** 1251 W Montgomery Ave 20850. I-270 exit 6B, just w on SR 28. Int corridors. **Pets:** Accepted.

Hilton Rockville Hotel & Executive Meeting Center 🏨

(301) 468-1100. **$89-$249.** 1750 Rockville Pike 20852. SR 355, 2 mi s of jct SR 28. Int corridors. **Pets:** Accepted.

Red Roof Inn-Rockville 🅜

(301) 987-0965. **$70-$145.** 16001 Shady Grove Rd 20850. I-270 exit 8 (Shady Grove Rd), 0.5 mi e. Ext corridors. **Pets:** Large, other species. No service, supervision.

Sheraton Rockville 🏨

(240) 912-8200. **$89-$400.** 920 King Farm Blvd 20850. I-270 exit 8 (Shady Grove Rd) northbound to Redland Blvd, just n on Piccard Dr; exit 8 southbound, 0.3 mi e to Choke Cherry Rd, just s to Piccard Dr, then just sw; 1 mi w of SR 355 via Redland Blvd. Int corridors. **Pets:** Accepted.

Sleep Inn-Rockville 🏨

(301) 948-8000. **$79-$159.** 2 Research Ct 20850. I-270 exit 8 (Shady Grove Rd), just sw. Int corridors. **Pets:** Accepted.

SILVER SPRING

 Crowne Plaza Washington, D.C.-Silver Spring 🏨

(301) 589-0800. **$99-$229.** 8777 Georgia Ave 20910. I-495 exit 31B, 1 mi s. Int corridors. **Pets:** Accepted.

▼▼▼▼ Residence Inn by Marriott Silver Spring 🄷
(301) 572-2322. **$109-$349.** 12000 Plum Orchard Dr 20904. I-95 exit 29B, 1.2 mi w on SR 212, then 1 mi n on Cherry Hill Rd. Int corridors.
Pets: Accepted. 🅴🄲🄾 📶 ⌧ 🖫 🄷 💻 🏊 ⌧

UPPER MARLBORO

🄰🄰🄰 ▼▼▼ **Executive Inn & Suites** 🄼
(301) 627-3969. **$70-$120.** 2901 Crain Hwy 20774. On US 301, 2.5 mi n of jct SR 4; 7 mi s of jct US 50. Ext corridors. **Pets:** $5 daily fee/pet. Service with restrictions, supervision. 🆂🅰🆅🅴 📶 🖫 🄷 💻

END METROPOLITAN AREA

WILLIAMSPORT

🄰🄰🄰 ▼▼▼ **Red Roof Inn** 🄼
(301) 582-3500. **$50-$80.** 310 E Potomac St 21795. I-81 exit 2, 0.3 mi sw on US 11. Ext corridors. **Pets:** Large, other species. No service, supervision. 🆂🅰🆅🅴 📶 🄷

MASSACHUSETTS

CITY INDEX

AMHERST

▼▼▼ **University Lodge** 🄼
(413) 256-8111. **$59-$159.** 345 N Pleasant St 01002. 0.6 mi n. Ext corridors. **Pets:** Large. $20 daily fee/room. Designated rooms, service with restrictions. 🄷 💻

AUBURN

▼▼▼▼ **Comfort Inn** 🄷
(508) 832-8300. **Call for rates.** 426 Southbridge St 01501. I-90 exit 10, 1 mi n on SR 12; I-290 exit 9 to SR 12. Int corridors. **Pets:** Accepted.
📶 🖫 🄷 💻

▼▼▼ **La Quinta Inn Auburn Worcester** 🄷
(508) 832-7000. **$62-$125.** 446 Southbridge St 01501. I-90 exit 10, 1.2 mi n on SR 12. Int corridors. **Pets:** Medium, other species. Service with restrictions, supervision. 📶 🄷 💻

BARRE

▼▼▼▼ **Jenkins Inn** 🄲🄸 🐾
(978) 355-6444. **$185-$260, 7 day notice.** 7 West St 01005. On SR 122 and 32. Int corridors. **Pets:** Dogs only. $10 daily fee/pet. Service with restrictions, supervision. 📶 ⌧ 🄷 💻 🍴

BOSTON METROPOLITAN AREA

ANDOVER

🄰🄰🄰 ▼▼▼▼ **Homewood Suites by Hilton Boston/Andover** 🄷
(978) 475-6000. **$129-$259.** 4 Riverside Dr 01810. I-93 exit 45, 0.5 mi e. Int corridors. **Pets:** Accepted. 🆂🅰🆅🅴 📶 🖫 🄷 💻 🏊 ⌧

▼▼▼▼ **La Quinta Inn & Suites Andover** 🄷
(978) 685-6200. **$62-$135.** 131 River Rd 01810. I-93 exit 45, just w; I-495 exit 40B, 2 mi n. Int corridors. **Pets:** Medium, other species. Service with restrictions, supervision. 📶 🖫 🄷 💻

▼▼▼▼ **Residence Inn by Marriott Boston-Andover** 🄷
(978) 683-0382. **$99-$179.** 500 Minuteman Rd 01810. I-93 exit 45, 0.3 mi w, then 0.5 mi n. Int corridors. **Pets:** Accepted.
📶 ⌧ 🖫 🄷 💻 🏊 ⌧

▼▼▼▼ **Staybridge Suites Boston/Andover** 🄷
(978) 686-2000. **$129-$149.** 4 Tech Dr 01810. I-93 exit 45, just sw via Shattuck Rd. Int corridors. **Pets:** Accepted. 📶 🖫 🄷 💻 🏊

🄰🄰🄰 ▼▼▼▼ **Wyndham Boston/Andover Hotel** 🄷 🐾
(978) 975-3600. **$109-$199.** 123 Old River Rd 01810. I-93 exit 45, just e on River Rd. Int corridors. **Pets:** Medium, other species. $50 one-time fee/room. Service with restrictions, crate.
🆂🅰🆅🅴 📶 ⌧ 🄷 💻 🍴 🏊

ARLINGTON

🄰🄰🄰 ▼▼▼▼ **Homewood Suites by Hilton-Cambridge/Arlington** 🄷
(781) 643-7258. **$159-$339.** 1 Massachusetts Ave 02474. On SR 2A, just n of SR 16. Int corridors. **Pets:** Accepted. 🆂🅰🆅🅴 📶 🖫 🄷 💻

BEDFORD

DoubleTree by Hilton Hotel Boston - Bedford Glen H
(781) 275-5500. **$89-$199.** 44 Middlesex Tpke 01730. I-95 exit 32B, 2.5 mi n. Int corridors. **Pets:** Accepted.
SAVE 🛜 ⌖M 🛄 💻 🍴 🏊 ⊗

BILLERICA

Homewood Suites by Hilton H 🐾
(978) 670-7111. **$129-$189.** 35 Middlesex Tpke 01821. I-95 exit 32B, 2.5 mi n. Int corridors. **Pets:** Large, other species. $50 one-time fee/room. Designated rooms, service with restrictions, crate.
🛜 ⌖M 🛄 💻 🏊

BOSTON

Ames, A Morgans Original H
(617) 979-8100. **$200-$700.** 1 Court St 02108. Across from Old State House. Int corridors. **Pets:** Small. $100 one-time fee/room. Service with restrictions, supervision. SAVE 🛜 ⊗ ⌖M 🍴

Best Western Plus Roundhouse Suites H
(617) 989-1000. **$169.** 891 Massachusetts Ave 02118. I-93 exit 18, just sw; just n of Newmarket Square. Int corridors. **Pets:** Medium. $25 daily fee/pet. Designated rooms, service with restrictions, crate.
SAVE 🛜 ⊗ ⌖M 🛄 💻

Boston Harbor Hotel H
(617) 439-7000. **$285-$950.** 70 Rowes Wharf 02110. At Rowes Wharf. Int corridors. **Pets:** Accepted. SAVE 🛜 ⊗ 🍴 🏊 ⊗

The Boston Park Plaza Hotel & Towers H
(617) 426-2000. **Call for rates.** 50 Park Plaza at Arlington St 02116. Just s of Boston Common and Public Gardens. Int corridors. **Pets:** Medium, dogs only. $50 one-time fee/room. Service with restrictions, supervision. SAVE 🛜 ⊗ 🍴

Bulfinch Hotel H 🐾
(617) 624-0202. **Call for rates.** 107 Merrimac St 02114. At Lancaster St. Int corridors. **Pets:** Other species. Service with restrictions, supervision.
🛜 ⊗ 💻 🍴

The Colonnade Hotel Boston H
(617) 424-7000. **Call for rates.** 120 Huntington Ave 02116. Just s of Copley Square. Int corridors. **Pets:** Accepted.
SAVE 🛜 ⊗ 💻 🍴 🏊

Comfort Inn Boston H
(617) 287-9200. **$99-$189.** 900 William T Morrissey Blvd 02122. I-93 exit 13 northbound, 0.5 mi sw; exit 12 southbound, follow signs. Int corridors. **Pets:** Service with restrictions, supervision. SAVE 🛜 ⊗ 🛄 💻

Copley Square Hotel H 🐾
(617) 536-9000. **$159-$599.** 47 Huntington Ave 02116. I-90 exit 22, just n. Int corridors. **Pets:** Medium. $60 one-time fee/pet. Service with restrictions, supervision. SAVE 🛜 ⊗ 🍴

DoubleTree Suites by Hilton Hotel Boston H
(617) 783-0090. **$129-$399.** 400 Soldiers Field Rd 02134. I-90 exit 20 westbound; exit 18 eastbound. Int corridors. **Pets:** Designated rooms, service with restrictions, supervision.
SAVE 🛜 ⊗ 🛄 💻 🍴 🏊

The Eliot Hotel H 🐾
(617) 267-1607. **$285-$545.** 370 Commonwealth Ave 02215. Corner of Commonwealth and Massachusetts aves. Int corridors. **Pets:** Other species. Service with restrictions, crate. SAVE 🛜 ⊗ 🍴

Fairmont Battery Wharf H 🐾
(617) 994-9000. **$209-$2200.** Three Battery Wharf 02109. At Battery Wharf, e of north end. Int corridors. **Pets:** Small. $25 daily fee/pet. Service with restrictions, supervision.
ECO SAVE 🛜 ⊗ ⌖M 💻 🍴 ⊗

The Fairmont Copley Plaza Boston H 🐾
(617) 267-5300. **$219-$579.** 138 St. James Ave 02116. At Copley Square. Int corridors. **Pets:** $25 daily fee/pet. No service, supervision.
ECO SAVE 🛜 ⊗ ⌖M

Fifteen Beacon H 🐾
(617) 670-1500. **$325-$1600.** 15 Beacon St 02108. Center. Int corridors. **Pets:** Dogs only. Service with restrictions, supervision.
SAVE 🛜 ⊗ 🍴

Four Seasons Hotel Boston H
(617) 338-4400. **$395-$995.** 200 Boylston St 02116. Between Arlington and Charles sts. Int corridors. **Pets:** Accepted.
SAVE 🛜 ⊗ ⌖M 🍴 🏊 ⊗

Hilton Boston Back Bay H
(617) 867-6000. **$169-$549.** 40 Dalton St 02115. At Dalton and Belvidere sts. Int corridors. **Pets:** Accepted. 🛜 ⊗ 🛄 💻 🍴 🏊

Hilton Boston Financial District H 🐾
(617) 556-0006. **$119-$539.** 89 Broad St 02110. Corner of Broad and Franklin sts. Int corridors. **Pets:** Medium, other species. Service with restrictions, crate. 🛜 ⊗ ⌖M 🍴

Hilton Boston Logan Airport H
(617) 568-6700. **$159-$399.** 1 Hotel Dr 02128. At Boston Logan International Airport. Int corridors. **Pets:** Large, dogs only. Service with restrictions, supervision. SAVE 🛜 ⊗ ⌖M 🛄 💻 🍴 🏊 ⊗

Hotel Commonwealth H 🐾
(617) 933-5000. **$179-$498.** 500 Commonwealth Ave 02215. On SR 2 at Beacon St and Brookline Ave. Int corridors. **Pets:** Dogs only. $125 one-time fee/room. Supervision. SAVE 🛜 ⊗ ⌖M 🛄 🍴

Howard Johnson Hotel Fenway M
(617) 267-8300. **$125-$179.** 1271 Boylston St 02215. I-90 exit Brookline Ave S, backing onto Fenway Park. Int corridors. **Pets:** Accepted.
🛜 ⊗ 🛄 💻 🍴 🏊

Hyatt Regency Boston H
(617) 912-1234. **$129-$499.** 1 Ave De Lafayette 02111. Just e of Boston Common at Lafayette Pl. Int corridors. **Pets:** Accepted.
ECO SAVE 🛜 ⊗ ⌖M 💻 🍴 🏊 ⊗

InterContinental Boston H
(617) 747-1000. **$299-$599.** 510 Atlantic Ave 02210. I-93 exit 23 southbound; exit 20 northbound; at Pearl St. Int corridors. **Pets:** Accepted.
SAVE 🛜 ⊗ ⌖M 💻

The Langham, Boston H 🐾
(617) 451-1900. **$205-$575.** 250 Franklin St 02110. On Post Office Square; center. Int corridors. **Pets:** Medium, dogs only. $100 one-time fee/room. Service with restrictions, crate.
ECO SAVE 🛜 ⊗ 💻 🍴 🏊 ⊗

The Lenox Hotel H
(617) 536-5300. **$195-$465.** 61 Exeter St 02116. I-90 exit 22, just n at Boylston. Int corridors. **Pets:** Accepted. ECO SAVE 🛜 ⊗ 🛄 🍴

The Liberty Hotel H
(617) 224-4000. **$275-$650.** 215 Charles St 02114. I-93 exit 26 (Storrow Dr). Int corridors. **Pets:** Accepted. SAVE 🛜 ⊗ ⌖M 🍴

Mandarin Oriental, Boston H
(617) 535-8888. **$345-$995.** 776 Boylston St 02199. At Prudential Center. Int corridors. **Pets:** Accepted. SAVE 🛜 ⊗ ⌖M 🛄 🍴

The Midtown Hotel H 🐾
(617) 262-1000. **$99-$309.** 220 Huntington Ave 02115. 3 blks sw of Copley Pl; just n of Symphony Hall and Massachusetts Ave. Int corridors. **Pets:** $50 one-time fee/pet. Designated rooms, service with restrictions, supervision. SAVE 🛜 ⊗ 🛄 💻 🍴 🏊

◉ ▼▼▼ ▼▼▼ Nine Zero Hotel H
(617) 772-5800. **$209-$539.** 90 Tremont St 02108. Just ne of Boston Common; motor entrance on Bosworth. Int corridors. **Pets:** Accepted.
[ECO] [SAVE] [📶] [✕] [&M] [¶]

◉ ▼▼▼ ▼▼▼ Omni Parker House H
(617) 227-8600. **$99-$449.** 60 School St 02108. Corner of Tremont and School sts; northeast corner of Boston Common. Int corridors.
Pets: Small. $50 one-time fee/room. Service with restrictions, supervision.
[SAVE] [📶] [✕] [💻] [¶]

◉ ▼▼▼ ▼▼▼ Onyx Hotel H
(617) 557-9955. **Call for rates.** 155 Portland St 02114. Just n, corner of Merrimac and Traverse sts, 3 blks s of TD Bank North Garden. Int corridors. **Pets:** Accepted. [ECO] [SAVE] [📶] [✕] [¶]

▼▼ ▼▼ Ramada Boston H
(617) 287-9100. **$74-$143.** 800 William T Morrissey Blvd 02122. I-93 exit 13 northbound, 0.5 mi sw; exit 12 southbound, follow signs. Int corridors. **Pets:** Service with restrictions, supervision. [📶] [✕] [🅱] [💻] [➷]

◉ ▼▼▼ ▼▼▼ Residence Inn by Marriott Boston Harbor on Tudor Wharf H
(617) 242-9000. **$299-$549.** 34-44 Charles River Ave 02129. Just se of SR 99 at Charlestown Bridge. Int corridors. **Pets:** Accepted.
[SAVE] [📶] [✕] [&M] [🅱] [💻] [¶] [➷]

◉ ▼▼▼ ▼▼▼ The Ritz-Carlton, Boston Common H ❖
(617) 574-7100. **Call for rates.** 10 Avery St 02111. At Washington and Avery sts; 1 blk e of Boston Common. Int corridors. **Pets:** Medium, other species. $125 one-time fee/room. Service with restrictions.
[SAVE] [📶] [✕] [&M] [¶] [✕]

◉ ▼▼▼ ▼▼▼ Seaport Hotel & Seaport World Trade Center H
(617) 385-4000. **$149-$499.** 1 Seaport Ln 02210. At Seaport World Trade Center. Int corridors. **Pets:** Accepted.
[ECO] [SAVE] [📶] [✕] [&M] [🅱] [💻] [¶] [➷] [✕]

◉ ▼▼▼ ▼▼▼ Sheraton Boston H
(617) 236-2000. **$229-$559, 3 day notice.** 39 Dalton St 02199. I-90 exit 22. Int corridors. **Pets:** Accepted.
[ECO] [SAVE] [📶] [✕] [💻] [🅱] [💻] [¶] [➷]

◉ ▼▼▼ ▼▼▼ Taj Boston H ❖
(617) 536-5700. **$249-$5000.** 15 Arlington St 02117. At Arlington and Newbury sts; overlooks the Public Gardens. Int corridors. **Pets:** Large. $125 one-time fee/room. Service with restrictions, supervision.
[ECO] [SAVE] [📶] [✕] [¶] [✕]

◉ ▼▼▼ ▼▼▼ W Boston Hotel & Residences H ❖
(617) 261-8700. **$219-$619.** 100 Stuart St 02116. At Tremont St. Int corridors. **Pets:** Medium. $45 one-time fee/room. Designated rooms, service with restrictions, supervision. [SAVE] [📶] [✕] [¶]

◉ ▼▼▼ ▼▼▼ Westin Boston Waterfront H ❖
(617) 532-4600. **$499-$579.** 425 Summer St 02210. I-93 exit 23, 1 mi se via Purchase St to Summer St. Int corridors. **Pets:** Medium, other species. Service with restrictions, supervision.
[SAVE] [📶] [✕] [🅱] [💻] [¶] [➷]

◉ ▼▼▼ ▼▼▼ The Westin Copley Place Boston H ❖
(617) 262-9600. **$279-$639.** 10 Huntington Ave 02116. I-90 exit 22, at Copley Square. Int corridors. **Pets:** Small, dogs only. Service with restrictions, supervision. [ECO] [SAVE] [📶] [✕] [💻] [¶] [➷] [✕]

BOXBOROUGH

▼▼▼ ▼▼▼ Holiday Inn Boxborough Woods H
(978) 263-8701. **$99-$169.** 242 Adams Pl 01719. I-495 exit 28, just e on SR 111. Int corridors. **Pets:** Accepted. [📶] [✕] [🅱] [💻] [¶] [➷]

BRAINTREE

▼▼ ▼▼ Candlewood Suites Boston - Braintree H
(781) 849-7450. **Call for rates.** 235 Wood Rd 02184. I-93 exit 6, just n on SR 37, then 0.5 mi w. Int corridors. **Pets:** Accepted. [📶] [🅱] [💻]

▼▼ ▼▼ Extended StayAmerica Boston-Braintree H ❖
(781) 356-8333. **$125-$169.** 20 Rockdale St 02184. I-93 exit 6, just se. Int corridors. **Pets:** Other species. $25 daily fee/pet. Service with restrictions. [📶] [&M] [🅱] [💻]

◉ ▼▼▼ ▼▼▼ Hampton Inn Braintree H
(781) 380-3300. **$119-$249.** 215 Wood Rd 02184. I-93 exit 6, just n on SR 37, then 0.5 mi w. Int corridors. **Pets:** Designated rooms, service with restrictions, supervision. [SAVE] [📶] [&M] [🅱] [💻] [➷]

BROOKLINE

▼▼▼ ▼▼▼ Holiday Inn Boston-Brookline H
(617) 277-1200. **$189-$299.** 1200 Beacon St 02446. 1 mi sw of Kenmore Square; at Beacon and St. Paul sts. Int corridors. **Pets:** Medium. $25 one-time fee/room. Service with restrictions, supervision.
[📶] [✕] [&M] [🅱] [💻] [¶] [➷]

BURLINGTON

▼▼ ▼▼ Candlewood Suites Boston-Burlington H
(781) 229-4300. **$69-$149.** 130 Middlesex Tpke 01803. I-95 exit 32B, just n. Int corridors. **Pets:** Accepted. [📶] [&M] [🅱] [💻]

◉ ▼▼▼ ▼▼▼ Hyatt house Boston/Burlington H
(781) 270-0800. **$89-$229.** 2 Van de Graaff Dr 01803. I-95 exit 33A, just s on US 3, then 0.5 mi w on Wayside Rd. Int corridors. **Pets:** Accepted.
[SAVE] [📶] [✕] [&M] [🅱] [💻] [➷] [✕]

CAMBRIDGE

◉ ▼▼▼ ▼▼▼ Best Western Plus Hotel Tria H ❖
(617) 491-8000. **$149-$359.** 220 Alewife Brook Pkwy 02138. Jct SR 2, 16 and US 3; I-90 (Massachusetts Tpke) exit Cambridge/Allston to SR 2 W (Fresh Pond Pkwy). Int corridors. **Pets:** Medium. $20 daily fee/room. Designated rooms, service with restrictions.
[SAVE] [📶] [&M] [🅱] [💻] [¶]

◉ ▼▼▼ ▼▼▼ The Charles Hotel, Harvard Square H
(617) 864-1200. **Call for rates.** One Bennett St 02138. Just s of Harvard Square, at Eliot St. Int corridors. **Pets:** Accepted.
[SAVE] [📶] [✕] [&M] [🅱] [¶] [➷] [✕]

◉ ▼▼▼ ▼▼▼ Hotel Marlowe H
(617) 868-8000. **$159-$569.** 25 Edwin H Land Blvd 02141. Just sw of jct SR 28. Int corridors. **Pets:** Accepted.
[ECO] [SAVE] [📶] [✕] [&M] [✕]

◉ ▼▼▼ ▼▼▼ Hyatt Regency Cambridge H
(617) 492-1234. **$99-$459.** 575 Memorial Dr 02139. On US 3 and SR 2. Int corridors. **Pets:** Accepted. [SAVE] [📶] [&M] [🅱] [💻] [¶] [➷] [✕]

◉ ▼▼▼ ▼▼▼ Le Meridien Cambridge H
(617) 577-0200. **$139-$499, 3 day notice.** 20 Sidney St 02139. On SR 2A, 1 mi n of river. Int corridors. **Pets:** Large. $150 deposit/pet. Service with restrictions, supervision. [SAVE] [📶] [✕] [&M] [💻] [¶]

▼▼▼ ▼▼▼ Residence Inn Boston Cambridge Center H
(617) 349-0700. **$129-$499.** 6 Cambridge Center 02142. Corner of Ames St and Broadway. Int corridors. **Pets:** Accepted.
[📶] [✕] [&M] [🅱] [💻] [➷]

◉ ▼▼▼ ▼▼▼ Sheraton Commander Hotel H ❖
(617) 547-4800. **$119-$800.** 16 Garden St 02138. Just n of Harvard Square. Int corridors. **Pets:** Medium, dogs only. Service with restrictions, supervision. [SAVE] [📶] [✕] [💻] [¶]

CONCORD

Best Western Plus at Historic Concord H
(978) 369-6100. **$129-$179.** 740 Elm St 01742. 1.8 mi w, just off SR 2 and 2A. Int corridors. **Pets:** $15 daily fee/pet. Designated rooms, service with restrictions, supervision. [SAVE] 🛜 ⊠ 🖪 💻 🌊

The Hawthorne Inn BB
(978) 369-5610. **$149-$359, 14 day notice.** 462 Lexington Rd 01742. 0.8 mi e of town square. Int corridors. **Pets:** Medium, other species. $35 daily fee/pet. Designated rooms, service with restrictions, supervision. 🛜 ⊠ 🕅

DANVERS

Comfort Inn North Shore H
(978) 777-1700. **$80-$180.** 50 Dayton St 01923. Just w of US 1; 0.8 mi n of jct SR 114 exit Center St northbound, w under US 1; exit Dayton St southbound. Int corridors. **Pets:** Accepted. [SAVE] 🛜 🕹M 🖪 💻 🌊

DoubleTree by Hilton Boston North Shore H
(978) 777-2500. **$114-$254.** 50 Ferncroft Rd 01923. I-95 exit 50, follow signs for US 1 S to Ferncroft Village. Int corridors. **Pets:** Accepted. [SAVE] 🛜 ⊠ 🕹M 🖪 💻 🍴 🌊 🕱

Residence Inn Boston-North Shore/Danvers H
(978) 777-7171. **$139-$186.** 51 Newbury St 01923. US 1 N, just s of jct SR 114. Ext corridors. **Pets:** Accepted. 🛜 ⊠ 🖪 💻 🌊 🕱

TownePlace Suites Boston-North Shore/Danvers H
(978) 777-6222. **$99-$199.** 238 Andover St 01923. Southwest corner of jct US 1 and SR 114; SR 114 eastbound, enter just w of US 1 (no westbound entrance); US 1 southbound, enter through shopping center. Int corridors. **Pets:** Accepted. [ECO] 🛜 ⊠ 🕹M 🖪 💻 🌊

DEDHAM

Hilton Boston/Dedham H
(781) 329-7900. **$99-$229.** 25 Allied Dr 02026. I-95 exit 14, just e. Int corridors. **Pets:** Medium, dogs only. $75 daily fee/room. Designated rooms, service with restrictions, supervision. [SAVE] 🛜 🖪 💻 🍴 🌊 🕱

Residence Inn by Marriott H
(781) 407-0999. **$149-$209.** 259 Elm St 02026. I-95 exit 15A, just n, then 0.4 mi e. Int corridors. **Pets:** Accepted. 🛜 ⊠ 🖪 💻 🌊 🕱

FOXBORO

Foxborough Residence Inn by Marriott H
(508) 698-2800. **$113-$259.** 250 Foxborough Blvd 02035. I-95 exit 7A, 0.6 mi s on SR 140, 0.7 mi e, then just n. Int corridors. **Pets:** Accepted. 🛜 ⊠ 🕹M 🖪 💻 🌊 🕱

FRAMINGHAM

Best Western Framingham H
(508) 872-8811. **$115.** 130 Worcester Rd 01702. I-90 exit 13, 0.5 mi s to SR 9; 1 mi w of Speen St; just w of Shopper's World Mall. Int corridors. **Pets:** Medium, other species. Designated rooms, service with restrictions, supervision. [SAVE] 🛜 🖪 💻 🍴 🌊

Red Roof Inn #068 M
(508) 872-4499. **$65-$119.** 650 Cochituate Rd 01701. I-90 exit 13, follow SR 30 E. Ext corridors. **Pets:** Large, other species. No service, supervision. [SAVE] 🛜 🖪

Residence Inn Boston/Framingham H
(508) 370-0001. **$206-$277.** 400 Staples Dr 01702. SR 9 W to Crossing Blvd, then s. Int corridors. **Pets:** Accepted. [SAVE] 🛜 ⊠ 🕹M 🖪 💻 🌊

Sheraton Framingham Hotel & Conference Center H
(508) 879-7200. **$95-$285.** 1657 Worcester Rd 01701. I-90 exit 12, follow signs to SR 9 W. Int corridors. **Pets:** Accepted. [SAVE] 🛜 ⊠ 🖪 💻 🍴 🌊

FRANKLIN

Hawthorn Suites by Wyndham H
(508) 553-3500. **$109-$139.** 835 Upper Union St 02038. I-495 exit 16, just s, then 0.3 mi e. Int corridors. **Pets:** Accepted. [SAVE] 🛜 ⊠ 🕹M 🖪 💻 🌊 🕱

Residence Inn by Marriott-Franklin H
(508) 541-8188. **$90-$219.** 4 Forge Pkwy 02038. I-495 exit 17, 0.7 mi nw off SR 140 N. Int corridors. **Pets:** Accepted. 🛜 ⊠ 🕹M 🖪 💻 🌊 🕱

GLOUCESTER

Cape Ann Motor Inn M 🐾
(978) 281-2900. **$85-$185, 7 day notice.** 33 Rockport Rd 01930. 2 mi n of terminus of SR 128 via SR 127A. Ext corridors. **Pets:** Large. Service with restrictions, supervision. [SAVE] 🛜 ⊠ 🖪 🎵

HAVERHILL

Best Western Plus Merrimack Valley H
(978) 373-1511. **$109-$209.** 401 Lowell Ave 01832. I-495 exit 49 (SR 110). Int corridors. **Pets:** Accepted. [SAVE] 🛜 ⊠ 🖪 💻 🌊

LAWRENCE

Holiday Inn Express H
(978) 975-4050. **$79-$129.** 224 Winthrop Ave 01843. I-495 exit 42A, just s on SR 114. Int corridors. **Pets:** Accepted. [SAVE] 🛜 ⊠ 🕹M 💻

LEXINGTON

Aloft Lexington H
(781) 761-1700. **$99-$349.** 727 Marrett Rd - A 02421. I-95 exit 30B, just w. Int corridors. **Pets:** Accepted. [SAVE] 🛜 ⊠ 🖪 💻 🌊

Element Lexington H
(781) 761-1750. **$109-$369.** 727 Marrett Rd - B 02421. I-95 exit 30B. Int corridors. **Pets:** Accepted. [ECO] [SAVE] 🛜 ⊠ 🕹M 🖪 💻 🌊

Quality Inn & Suites H
(781) 861-0850. **$62-$89.** 440 Bedford St 02420. I-95 exit 31B, just n on SR 4 and 225, continue n and use jughandle to reverse direction. Ext corridors. **Pets:** Medium. $25 daily fee/pet. Designated rooms, service with restrictions, crate. [SAVE] 🛜 🕹M 🖪 💻 🌊

LOWELL

UMass Lowell Inn & Conference Center H
(978) 934-6920. **$89-$189.** 50 Warren St 01852. I-495 exit 35C via Gorham and Church sts, follow signs; 0.5 mi from end of Lowell connector; center. Int corridors. **Pets:** Accepted. 🛜 ⊠ 🕹M 💻 🍴

MARLBOROUGH

Best Western Royal Plaza Hotel & Trade Center H
(508) 460-0700. **$120-$160.** 181 Boston Post Rd W 01752. I-495 exit 24B, 1 mi w on US 20. Int corridors. **Pets:** Medium, dogs only. $25 daily fee/room. Service with restrictions, supervision. [SAVE] 🛜 🖪 💻 🍴 🌊

Courtyard Boston Marlborough H
(508) 480-0015. **$89-$199.** 75 Felton St 01752. I-495 exit 24B, just w; just off US 20. Int corridors. **Pets:** Accepted. 🛜 ⊠ 🕹M 🖪 💻 🍴 🌊

Embassy Suites Hotel-Boston Marlborough H
(508) 485-5900. **$123-$209.** 123 Boston Post Rd W 01752. I-495 exit 24B, 0.5 mi w; just off US 20. Int corridors. **Pets:** Accepted. 🛜 🕹M 🖪 💻 🍴 🌊 🕱

WWWW Residence Inn By Marriott Boston Marlborough H

(508) 481-1500. **$134-$180.** 112 Donald Lynch Blvd 01752. I-290 exit 25B, 3 mi ne. Int corridors. **Pets:** Accepted.

NATICK

AAA WWWW Crowne Plaza Boston-Natick H

(508) 653-8800. **$139-$279.** 1360 Worcester St 01760. I-90 exit 12, 5 mi e; SR 9, 4 mi e of Framingham Center. Int corridors. **Pets:** Other species. $150 one-time fee/room. Designated rooms, service with restrictions.

NEEDHAM

AAA WWWW Sheraton Needham Hotel H ❀

(781) 444-1110. **$99-$349.** 100 Cabot St 02494. I-95 exit 19A, just e. Int corridors. **Pets:** Medium, dogs only. Designated rooms, service with restrictions, supervision.

NEWBURYPORT

WWWW Garrison Inn H ❀

(978) 499-8500. **$190-$350, 7 day notice.** 11 Brown Square 01950. I-95 exit 57, 2.6 mi e on SR 1A, just n on Green St, just w on Pleasant St, then just s. Int corridors. **Pets:** Other species. $30 daily fee/pet. Service with restrictions, supervision.

NEWTON

WWWW Crowne Plaza Boston/Newton H

(617) 969-3010. **$99-$359.** 320 Washington St 02458. I-90 exit 17. Int corridors. **Pets:** Accepted.

AAA WWWW Hotel Indigo Boston-Newton Riverside H ❀

(617) 969-5300. **$119-$259.** 399 Grove St 02462. I-95 exit 22, just e. Int corridors. **Pets:** Large, other species. $75 one-time fee/pet. Service with restrictions, supervision.

NORTH CHELMSFORD

AAA WWWW Hawthorn Suites by Wyndham H

(978) 256-5151. **$90-$99.** 25 Research Pl 01863. US 3 exit 32, 0.3 mi ne on SR 4. Int corridors. **Pets:** Medium, other species. $25 one-time fee/pet. Service with restrictions, supervision.

NORWOOD

WWWW Hampton Inn Boston - Norwood H

(781) 769-7000. **$91-$135.** 434 Providence Hwy 02062. I-95 exit 9 northbound, 5.9 mi ne on US 1; exit 11B southbound, 1.3 mi nw on Neponset St, then 0.4 mi n on US 1. Int corridors. **Pets:** Accepted.

AAA WWWW Residence Inn Boston-Norwood H

(781) 278-9595. **$188-$253.** 275 Norwood S 02062. I-95 exit 9 northbound, 3.7 mi n on US 1; exit 11B southbound, 0.5 mi nw on Neponset St, 0.6 mi w on Dean St, then 0.8 mi s on US 1. Int corridors. **Pets:** Other species. $100 one-time fee/room. Service with restrictions, supervision.

PEABODY

WW Homestead Studio Suites Hotel-Boston/Peabody H ❀

(978) 531-6632. **$100-$169.** 200 Jubilee Dr 01960. SR 128 exit 28, just s to Centennial Dr, w to the end, n to Jubilee Dr, then 1.1 mi e. Int corridors. **Pets:** Other species. $25 daily fee/pet. Service with restrictions.

WWWW Homewood Suites by Hilton H

(978) 536-5050. **$109-$229.** 57 Newbury St 01960. On US 1 northbound. Int corridors. **Pets:** Accepted.

REVERE

WWW Comfort Inn & Suites Boston Airport H

(781) 485-3600. **$69-$249.** 85 American Legion Hwy 02151. Jct SR 1A and 60, 3 mi n of Boston Logan International Airport. Int corridors. **Pets:** Accepted. ECO

WWWW Hampton Inn Boston Logan Airport H

(781) 286-5665. **$119-$299.** 230 Lee Burbank Hwy 02151. On SR 1A, 0.6 mi s of terminus SR 60, 1.9 mi n of Boston Logan International Airport. Int corridors. **Pets:** Accepted.

ROCKPORT

AAA WWWW Rockport Inn & Suites H ❀

(978) 546-3300. **$109-$259, 3 day notice.** 183 Main St 01966. On SR 127. Ext corridors. **Pets:** $30 daily fee/pet. Service with restrictions.

ROWLEY

AAA WWWW Country Garden Inn & Spa M

(978) 948-7773. **$99-$329, 10 day notice.** 101 Main St 01969. On SR 1A. Ext corridors. **Pets:** Accepted.

SALEM

AAA WWWW Hawthorne Hotel H

(978) 744-4080. **$114-$224, 3 day notice.** 18 Washington Square W 01970. On SR 1A. Int corridors. **Pets:** Accepted.

WWWW The Salem Inn BB

(978) 741-0680. **$119-$350, 7 day notice.** 7 Summer St 01970. On SR 114 at Essex St; SR 128 exit 25A, 3 mi e. Int corridors. **Pets:** Other species. $15 daily fee/pet. Designated rooms, service with restrictions.

SAUGUS

AAA WWW Red Roof Inn #1305 H

(781) 941-1400. **$89-$189.** 920 Broadway 01906. I-95 exit 44 northbound, 3.2 mi s on US 1 exit Main St/Saugus southbound to U-turn. Int corridors. **Pets:** Large, other species. No service, supervision.

SOMERVILLE

WWWWW La Quinta Inn & Suites Boston Somerville H

(617) 625-5300. **$93-$198.** 23 Cummings St 02143. I-93 exit 29 northbound, just ne on SR 28, then just s on Middlesex Ave; exit 31 southbound 1 mi e on SR 16, then 0.5 mi s on SR 28 to Middlesex Ave. Int corridors. **Pets:** Medium, other species. Service with restrictions, supervision.

TEWKSBURY

WW WW Extended StayAmerica Boston-Tewksbury H ❀

(978) 863-9888. **$90-$139.** 1910 Andover St 01876. I-93 exit 43B, just w; I-495 exit 39, just e. Int corridors. **Pets:** Other species. $25 daily fee/pet. Service with restrictions.

AAA WWWW Holiday Inn Tewksbury-Andover H

(978) 640-9000. **Call for rates.** 4 Highwood Dr 01876. I-495 exit 39, just w on SR 133. Int corridors. **Pets:** Accepted.

WWWW Residence Inn by Marriott Boston-Tewksbury-Andover H ❀

(978) 640-1003. **$80-$179.** 1775 Andover St 01876. I-495 exit 39, 0.3 mi w on SR 133. Ext corridors. **Pets:** Other species. $100 one-time fee/room. Designated rooms, service with restrictions.

WWWW TownePlace Suites Boston Tewksbury H

(978) 863-9800. **$89-$159.** 20 International Pl 01876. I-495 exit 39, 0.3 mi nw. Int corridors. **Pets:** Accepted. ECO

WAKEFIELD

◇◇◇ Sheraton Colonial Hotel Boston North & Conference Center 🅷

(781) 245-9300. **$105-$255.** 1 Audubon Rd 01880. I-95 exit 42, just n. Int corridors. **Pets:** Accepted. 🆂🅰🆅🅴 📶 ⊗ 🅖🅼 🛏 💻 🍴 ⊃ ⊗

WALTHAM

◇◇◇ Courtyard by Marriott Boston-Waltham 🅷

(781) 419-0900. **$99-$239.** 387 Winter St 02451. I-95 exit 27B northbound; exit 27A southbound, on northeast corner. Int corridors.
Pets: Accepted. 📶 ⊗ 🅖🅼 🛏 💻 🍴 ⊃

◇◇ Extended Stay Deluxe Boston-Waltham 🅷 ✿

(781) 622-1900. **$110-$249.** 32 4th Ave 02451. I-95 exit 27A, just se. Int corridors. **Pets:** Other species. $25 daily fee/pet. Service with restrictions.
📶 🅖🅼 🛏 💻 ⊃

◇◇◇ Hilton Garden Inn Boston/Waltham 🅷

(781) 890-0100. **$79-$255.** 420 Totten Pond Rd 02451. I-95 exit 27A, just e. Int corridors. **Pets:** Accepted.
📶 ⊗ 🅖🅼 🛏 💻 🍴 ⊃

◇◇◇ Holiday Inn Express Boston/Waltham 🅷

(781) 890-2800. **$99-$189.** 385 Winter St 02451. I-95 exit 27B northbound; exit 27A southbound, just ne. Int corridors. **Pets:** Large, other species. $50 one-time fee/room. Service with restrictions.
📶 ⊗ 🅖🅼 🛏 💻 ⊃

◇◇◇◇ The Westin Waltham-Boston 🅷 ✿

(781) 290-5600. **$109-$349.** 70 3rd Ave 02451. I-95 exit 27A, just se. Int corridors. **Pets:** Medium, dogs only. Service with restrictions, supervision.
🄴🄲🄾 🆂🅰🆅🅴 📶 ⊗ 🅖🅼 💻 🍴 ⊃ ⊗

WESTFORD

◇◇◇ Residence Inn Boston Westford 🅷

(978) 392-1407. **$170-$229.** 7 Lan Dr 01886. I-495 exit 32, just s, then 0.5 w on SR 110. Int corridors. **Pets:** Accepted.
📶 ⊗ 🅖🅼 🛏 💻 ⊃ ⊗

WOBURN

◇◇◇ Best Western Plus New Englander 🅷

(781) 935-8160. **Call for rates.** 1 Rainin Rd 01801. I-93 exit 36, just e. Int corridors. **Pets:** Accepted. 🆂🅰🆅🅴 📶 🅖🅼 🛏 💻 🍴 ⊃

◇◇ Extended Stay Deluxe Boston-Woburn 🅷 ✿

(781) 938-3737. **$110-$199.** 831 Main St 01801. I-95 exit 35, just n on SR 38. Int corridors. **Pets:** Other species. $25 daily fee/pet. Service with restrictions. 📶 🅖🅼 🛏 💻 ⊃

◇◇◇ Hilton Boston/Woburn 🅷

(781) 932-0999. **Call for rates.** 2 Forbes Rd 01801. I-95 exit 36, 0.5 mi s via Washington St, then just e at Lukoil; jct Cedar St. Int corridors.
Pets: Accepted. 📶 🛏 💻 ⊃

◇◇◇ Holiday Inn Select 🅷

(781) 935-8760. **$109-$199.** 15 Middlesex Canal Park Rd 01801. I-95 exit 35, s via SR 38. Int corridors. **Pets:** Accepted.
📶 🅖🅼 🛏 💻 🍴 ⊃

◇◇ Red Roof Inn Woburn #238 🅷

(781) 935-7110. **$79-$180.** 19 Commerce Way 01801. I-95 exit 36, just n, then just w on Mishawum Rd. Int corridors. **Pets:** Large, other species. No service, supervision. 🆂🅰🆅🅴 📶 🅖🅼 🛏 💻 ⊃

◇◇◇ Residence Inn by Marriott-Boston/Woburn 🅷

(781) 376-4000. **$109-$289.** 300 Presidential Way 01801. I-93 exit 37C, just nw. Int corridors. **Pets:** Accepted.
🆂🅰🆅🅴 📶 ⊗ 🅖🅼 🛏 💻 ⊃ ⊗

END METROPOLITAN AREA

BROCKTON

◇◇◇ Residence Inn Boston Brockton 🅷

(508) 583-3600. **$161-$217.** 124 Liberty St 02301. SR 24 exit 17B, just w, just s on Pearl St, then 0.3 mi se via Mill St connector. Int corridors.
Pets: Accepted. 📶 ⊗ 🅖🅼 🛏 💻 ⊃ ⊗

CAPE COD AREA

BUZZARDS BAY

◇ Bay Motor Inn 🅼

(508) 759-3989. **$72-$149, 7 day notice.** 223 Main St 02532. SR 25, 0.5 mi w of Bourne rotary, exit 3. **Pets:** $15 daily fee/room. Service with restrictions, supervision. 🆂🅰🆅🅴 📶 ⊗ 🛏 💻

EAST FALMOUTH

◇◇ Capewind Waterfront Motel 🅼

(508) 548-3400. **$109-$289, 30 day notice.** 34 Maravista Ext 02536. 2.2 mi e via SR 28, just s, follow signs. Ext corridors. **Pets:** Accepted.
📶 ⊗ 🛏 💻 ⊃ ⊗

EASTHAM

◇ Ocean Park Inn 🅼

(508) 255-1132. **$69-$179, 7 day notice.** 3900 State Hwy 02642. On US 6; 1 mi n of National Seashore Visitor's Center. Ext corridors.
Pets: $25 daily fee/pet. Designated rooms, no service, supervision.
📶 ⊗ 🛏 ⊃

FALMOUTH

◇◇ Mariner Motel 🅼

(508) 548-1331. **$69-$189, 14 day notice.** 555 Main St 02540. 0.5 mi e on SR 28. Ext corridors. **Pets:** Accepted. 🆂🅰🆅🅴 📶 ⊗ 🛏 ⊃

◇◇ Seaside Inn 🅼 ✿

(508) 540-4120. **$59-$345, 14 day notice.** 263 Grand Ave 02540. Jct SR 28, 1.3 mi s via Falmouth Heights Rd. Ext/int corridors.
Pets: Medium. $15 daily fee/pet. Designated rooms, service with restrictions, crate. 🆂🅰🆅🅴 📶 ⊗ 🛏 💻

HYANNIS

◇ Cape Cod Harbor House Inn 🅼

(508) 771-1880. **Call for rates.** 119 Ocean St 02601. Opposite ferry docks. Ext corridors. **Pets:** Accepted. 📶 ⊗ 🛏 💻

◇◇ Comfort Inn Cape Cod 🅷

(508) 771-4804. **Call for rates.** 1470 Iyannough Rd 02601. US 6 exit 6, 1.3 mi se on SR 132. Ext/int corridors. **Pets:** Large. $25 daily fee/pet. Designated rooms, service with restrictions, supervision.
📶 ⊗ 🛏 💻 ⊃ ⊗

ORLEANS

▼▼ Governor Prence Inn **M**

(508) 255-1216. **$99-$169, 10 day notice.** 66 SR 6A 02653. 0.5 mi w of rotary. Ext corridors. **Pets:** Accepted. 🛰 ⊠ 🛏 ⊇

▼▼ Orleans Inn **CI**

(508) 255-2222. **$250-$450.** 21 SR 6A 02653. On SR 28 and 6A exit rotary, just w. Int corridors. **Pets:** Dogs only. 🛰 ⊠ 🛏 🍴

◆◆ ▼▼ Skaket Beach Motel **M** ❀

(508) 255-1020. **$65-$175, 10 day notice.** 203 Cranberry Hwy (Rt 6A) 02653. US 6 exit 12, just e. Ext corridors. **Pets:** Dogs only. $12 daily fee/pet. Service with restrictions, supervision. [SAVE] 🛰 🛏 ⊇ ⊇

PROVINCETOWN

▼▼ Bayshore & Chandler **CO** ❀

(508) 487-9133. **$105-$325, 30 day notice.** 493 Commercial St 02657. 0.8 mi e of Town Hall. Ext corridors. **Pets:** $20 daily fee/pet. Service with restrictions. 🛰 ⊠ 🛏 ⊇

◆◆ ▼▼▼▼ Crowne Pointe Historic Inn & Spa **CI**

(508) 487-6767. **$99-$499, 21 day notice.** 82 Bradford St 02657. On SR 6A, just w of Town Hall. Ext/int corridors. **Pets:** Accepted.
[SAVE] 🛰 ⊠ 🛏 ⊇ 🍴 ⊇ ⊠

▼▼▼ White Wind Inn **BB**

(508) 487-1526. **$85-$300, 14 day notice.** 174 Commercial St 02657. Just w of Town Hall. Int corridors. **Pets:** Accepted. 🛰 ⊠ 🛏 ⊇

SANDWICH

▼ Shady Nook Inn & Motel **M**

(508) 888-0409. **$59-$199, 21 day notice.** 14 Old Kings Hwy (SR 6A) 02563. On SR 6A, 1.5 mi w. Ext corridors. **Pets:** Other species. $10 daily fee/pet. Service with restrictions. 🛰 ⊠ 🛏 ⊇ ⊇

SOUTH YARMOUTH

◆◆◆ ▼▼▼ Ambassador Inn & Suites **H**

(508) 394-4000. **$60-$199.** 1314 Main St 02664. On SR 28, just w of Bass River Bridge. Int corridors. **Pets:** Large, other species. $20 daily fee/pet. Designated rooms, service with restrictions, supervision.
[SAVE] 🛰 🛏 ⊇ ⊇ ⊠

◆◆◆ ▼▼▼ Blue Rock Golf Resort **M**

(508) 398-6962. **$89-$219, 10 day notice.** 39 Todd Rd 02664. SR 28, 1 mi ne via N Main St and High Bank Rd, then 0.5 mi nw on Country Club Dr, follow signs. Ext corridors. **Pets:** Accepted.
[SAVE] 🛰 ⊠ 🛏 ⊇ 🍴 ⊇ ⊠

◆◆◆ ▼▼▼ Blue Water on The Ocean **H** ❀

(508) 398-2288. **$100-$395, 30 day notice.** 291 S Shore Dr 02664. 1 mi s off SR 28. Ext/int corridors. **Pets:** Other species. $35 daily fee/pet. Designated rooms, service with restrictions, supervision.
[SAVE] 🛰 ⊠ 🛏 ⊇ 🍴 ⊇ ⊠

◆◆◆ ▼▼▼ Red Jacket Riviera Beach Resort **H** ❀

(508) 398-2273. **$135-$550, 10 day notice.** 327 S Shore Dr 02664. 1 mi s off SR 28. Ext/int corridors. **Pets:** Other species. $35 daily fee/pet. Designated rooms, service with restrictions, crate.
[SAVE] 🛰 ⊠ 🛏 🍴 ⊇ ⊠

WEST DENNIS

▼▼ Inn at Swan River **M**

(508) 394-5415. **$119-$319, 14 day notice.** 829 Main St 02670. On SR 28, just w of SR 134. Ext corridors. **Pets:** Other species. $35 daily fee/room. Designated rooms, service with restrictions, crate.
🛰 ⊠ 🛏 ⊇

WEST YARMOUTH

▼▼ The Yarmouth Resort **M**

(508) 775-5155. **Call for rates.** 343 Main St 02673. On SR 28, 2 mi e of jct SR 132. Ext/int corridors. **Pets:** Accepted.
🛰 🛏 ⊇ ⊇ ⊠

END AREA

EAST WAREHAM

◆◆◆ ▼ Atlantic Motel **M**

(508) 295-0210. **$80-$200, 10 day notice.** 7 Depot St 02538. Between eastbound and westbound lanes of US 6/SR 28; jct SR 25 exit 1. Ext corridors. **Pets:** Medium, dogs only. $25 daily fee/pet. Designated rooms, service with restrictions, supervision. [SAVE] 🛰 🛏 ⊇ ⊇

FAIRHAVEN

◆◆ ▼▼▼ Seaport Inn Conference Center & Marina **H**

(508) 997-1281. **$109-$159.** 110 Middle St 02719. I-195 exit 15, 1 mi s, then just off US 6. Int corridors. **Pets:** $25 one-time fee/room. Designated rooms, service with restrictions. [SAVE] 🛰 🛏 ⊇ 🍴

FALL RIVER

▼▼▼ Comfort Inn & Suites **H**

(508) 672-0011. **$89-$169.** 360 Airport Rd 02720. SR 79 and 24 exit 8; at Fall River Airport. Int corridors. **Pets:** Accepted.
🛰 ⊠ 🛏 ⊇ ⊇

FITCHBURG

▼▼▼ Courtyard by Marriott Fitchburg **H**

(978) 342-7100. **$107-$144.** 150 Royal Plaza Dr 01420. SR 2 exit 28, just s on SR 31. Int corridors. **Pets:** Accepted.
🛰 ⊠ &M 🛏 🍴 ⊇

GARDNER

▼▼▼ Colonial Hotel **H**

(978) 630-2500. **$99-$149.** 625 Betty Spring Rd 01440. SR 2 exit 24 eastbound; exit 24B westbound, 0.9 mi n on SR 140, then 0.5 mi w. Int corridors. **Pets:** Accepted. 🛰 🛏 ⊇ 🍴 ⊇ ⊠

▼ Super 8 **M**

(978) 630-2888. **$62-$84.** 22 Pearson Blvd 01440. SR 2 exit 23, just n. Int corridors. **Pets:** Medium. $15 daily fee/pet. Service with restrictions, supervision. 🛰 🛏 ⊇

GREENFIELD

◆◆◆ ▼▼▼ The Brandt House B&B **BB**

(413) 774-3329. **$105-$359, 30 day notice.** 29 Highland Ave 01301. I-91 exit 26, 1.8 mi e on SR 2A, then se via Crescent St. Int corridors. **Pets:** Medium, dogs only. $25 one-time fee/pet. Service with restrictions, supervision. [SAVE] 🛰 ⊠

HADLEY

◆◆◆ ▼▼▼ Comfort Inn **H**

(413) 584-9816. **$89-$159.** 237 Russell St 01035. I-91 exit 19 northbound; exit 20 southbound, 3 mi e on SR 9. Int corridors. **Pets:** Medium, dogs only. $25 daily fee/room. Designated rooms, service with restrictions, supervision. [SAVE] 🛰 🛏 ⊇ ⊇

◆◆◆ ▼▼▼ Howard Johnson Express Inn-Hadley **H**

(413) 586-0114. **$63-$189.** 401 Russell St 01035. I-91 exit 19 northbound, 4.3 mi e on SR 9; exit 24 southbound, 10 mi s on SR 116, then just w on SR 9. Int corridors. **Pets:** Accepted.
[SAVE] 🛰 &M 🛏 ⊇ ⊇

HOLLAND

▼▼▼ The Inn at Restful Paws BB ❖

(413) 245-7792. **$174, 14 day notice.** 70 Allen Hill Rd 01521. SR 20, 2.1 mi s on E Brimfield Rd, 0.4 mi on Alexander Rd, then 0.7 mi n. Int corridors. **Pets:** No service, supervision. 🛜 ✕ 🖵 🕅 🖉

HOLYOKE

▼▼▼ Homewood Suites by Hilton Holyoke-Springfield North ▣

(413) 532-3100. **$119-$229.** 375 Whitney Ave 01040. I-91 exit 15, just w on Lower Westfield Rd, then 0.4 mi s. Int corridors. **Pets:** Accepted.
🛜 🛁 🛠 🖵 ⫘ ✕

LENOX

◭ ▼▼ ▼▼ Blantyre ◐

(413) 637-3556. **$675-$2000, 30 day notice.** 16 Blantyre Rd 01240. US 20, 1 mi s from jct SR 183. Int corridors. **Pets:** Accepted.
[SAVE] 🛜 ✕ 🛠 🖵 ⫘ ✕

The Kemble Inn BB

(413) 637-4113. **$175-$475, 15 day notice.** 2 Kemble St 01240. Jct SR 183 and 7A. Int corridors. **Pets:** Accepted. 🛜 ✕

MANSFIELD

▼▼▼ Holiday Inn Mansfield ▣

(508) 339-2200. **$99-$169.** 31 Hampshire St 02048. I-95 exit 7A, 0.5 mi s on SR 140, then 1 mi w on Forbes Rd; I-495 exit 12, 2 mi n on SR 140, then w on Forbes Rd. Int corridors. **Pets:** Small. $15 daily fee/room. Service with restrictions, supervision. 🛜 🛠 🖵 ⫙ ⫘ ✕

◭ ▼▼▼ Red Roof Inn - Mansfield/Foxboro ▣

(508) 339-2323. **$46-$150.** 60 Forbes Blvd 02048. I-95 exit 7A, 1.3 mi n; I-495 exit 12, just off SR 140. Int corridors. **Pets:** Large, other species. No service, supervision. [SAVE] 🛜 🛠 ⫘

MARTHA'S VINEYARD AREA

EDGARTOWN

▼▼▼ Vineyard Square Hotel & Suites ◐

(508) 627-4711. **$95-$945, 14 day notice.** 38 N Water St 02539. Just n from Main St. Int corridors. **Pets:** Accepted. 🛜 ✕ 🛠 🖵 ⫙

OAK BLUFFS

▼▼▼ The Dockside Inn BB

(508) 693-2966. **Call for rates.** 9 Circuit Ave Ext 02557. Center. Ext corridors. **Pets:** Accepted. 🛜 ✕ 🛠 🖵

VINEYARD HAVEN

▼▼▼ The Doctor's House Bed & Breakfast BB

(508) 696-0859. **Call for rates.** 60 Mt. Aldworth Rd 02568. 0.4 mi sw to road to Edgartown, 1 blk e. Int corridors. **Pets:** Accepted. 🛜 ✕ 🖉

END AREA

MILFORD

▼▼▼ Holiday Inn Express ▣

(508) 478-7010. **$79-$139.** 50 Fortune Blvd 01757. I-495 exit 20, just sw on SR 85, then just se. Int corridors. **Pets:** Accepted.
🛜 ⫛ 🛠 🖵 ⫘

NORTHAMPTON

▼▼ Clarion Hotel & Conference Center ▣

(413) 586-1211. **Call for rates.** 1 Atwood Dr 01060. I-91 exit 18, just s on US 5. Int corridors. **Pets:** Large, other species. $20 daily fee/room. Designated rooms, service with restrictions, crate.
🛜 ⫛ 🛠 🖵 ⫙ ⫘ ✕

NORTH DARTMOUTH

◭ ▼▼▼ Residence Inn New Bedford/Dartmouth ▣

(508) 984-5858. **$89-$249.** 181 Faunce Corner Rd 02747. I-195 exit 12A westbound; exit 12 eastbound, just s. Int corridors. **Pets:** Other species. $100 one-time fee/room. Service with restrictions.
[SAVE] 🛜 ✕ ⫛ 🛠 🖵 ⫘ ✕

NORTON

▼▼ ▼▼ Extended StayAmerica-Foxboro-Norton ▣ ❖

(508) 285-7800. **$100-$149.** 280 S Washington St 02766. I-495 exit 9, 0.3 mi se on Bay St, then 0.5 mi nw via Industrial Park Rd. Int corridors. **Pets:** Other species. $25 daily fee/pet. Service with restrictions.
🛜 ⫛ 🛠 🖵

PITTSFIELD

▼▼▼ Crowne Plaza Hotel Pittsfield Berkshires ▣ ❖

(413) 499-2000. **$99-$349, 3 day notice.** 1 West St 01201. Center. Int corridors. **Pets:** Medium, other species. $50 one-time fee/pet. Designated rooms, service with restrictions, supervision.
🛜 ⫛ 🛠 🖵 ⫙ ⫘ ✕

PLYMOUTH

▼▼▼ Hampton Inn & Suites - Plymouth Kingston ▣

(508) 747-5000. **$109-$199.** 10 Plaza Way 02360. SR 3 exit 7. Int corridors. **Pets:** Accepted. 🛜 ⫛ 🛠 🖵 ⫘

RAYNHAM

◭ ▼▼ Quality Inn of Raynham-Taunton ▥

(508) 824-8647. **$79-$129.** 164 New State Hwy 02767. SR 24 exit 13B, 0.8 mi w on US 44. Ext/int corridors. **Pets:** Medium. $10 daily fee/pet. Designated rooms, service with restrictions, supervision.
[SAVE] 🛜 🛠 🖵

REHOBOTH

▼▼▼ Five Bridge Inn Bed & Breakfast BB ❖

(508) 252-3190. **$110-$145, 3 day notice.** 154 Pine St 02769. 1.6 mi n of US 44; 3.3 mi w of jct SR 118; US 44, n on Blanding Rd, e on Broad St, n on Salisbury St, then w. Int corridors. **Pets:** Medium. $20 one-time fee/room. Designated rooms, service with restrictions, supervision.
🛜 ✕ 🛠 🖵 ⫘ ✕ 🖉

RICHMOND

▼▼▼ The Inn at Richmond BB

(413) 698-2566. **Call for rates.** 802 State Rd (SR 41) 01254. 2.5 mi s of jct US 20. Ext/int corridors. **Pets:** Accepted. 🛜 ✕ 🛠 🖵 ✕

ROCKLAND

◭ ▼▼ Best Western Rockland ▣

(781) 871-5660. **$100-$180.** 909 Hingham St 02370. SR 3 exit 14, 0.3 mi sw on SR 228. Int corridors. **Pets:** Accepted. [SAVE] 🛜 🛠 🖵

SEEKONK

▼ Motel 6 - 1289 M
(508) 336-7800. **$55-$65.** 821 Fall River Ave 02771. I-195 exit 1, just n on SR 114A. Int corridors. **Pets:** Other species. Service with restrictions, supervision. 🛰 &M

▼▼ Ramada Providence Conference Center H
(508) 336-7300. **$74-$152.** 940 Fall River Ave 02771. I-195 exit 1, just s. Int corridors. **Pets:** Accepted. 🛰 🛄 🖵 🍽 🐾 ⊠

SOMERSET

▲▲▲ ▼▼▼ Quality Inn-Fall River/Somerset H ❖
(508) 678-4545. **$85-$209.** 1878 Wilbur Ave 02725. Jct SR 103 and I-195 exit 4 eastbound; exit 4A westbound. Int corridors. **Pets:** $50 deposit/pet. Designated rooms, service with restrictions, supervision.
SAVE 🛰 🛄 🖵 🐾 ⊠

SOUTHBOROUGH

▲▲▲ ▼▼▼ Red Roof Inn # 7075 M
(508) 481-3904. **$49-$89.** 367 Turnpike Rd 01772. I-495 exit 23A, just e on SR 9. Ext corridors. **Pets:** Large, other species. No service, supervision. SAVE 🛰 🛄

SOUTH DEERFIELD

▲▲▲ ▼▼▼ Red Roof Inn M
(413) 665-7161. **$55-$125.** 9 Greenfield Rd 01373. I-91 exit 24 northbound; exit 25 southbound, on SR 5 and 10. Int corridors. **Pets:** Large, other species. No service, supervision. SAVE 🛰 🛄 🐾

SPRINGFIELD

▲▲▲ ▼▼▼▼ Sheraton Springfield Monarch Place H
(413) 781-1010. **$119-$239.** 1 Boland Way 01144. I-91 exit 6 northbound; exit 7 southbound, just n; downtown. Int corridors. **Pets:** Accepted.
SAVE 🛰 ⊠ &M 🛄 🖵 🍽 🐾 ⊠

STURBRIDGE

▲▲▲ ▼▼▼▼ Comfort Inn & Suites Colonial H 🐾
(508) 347-3306. **Call for rates.** 215 Charlton Rd 01566. I-90 exit 9, 0.5 mi e; I-84 exit 3A. Ext/int corridors. **Pets:** Medium. Designated rooms, service with restrictions. SAVE 🛰 ⊠ &M 🛄 🖵

▼▼▼ Days Inn M
(508) 347-3391. **$63-$134.** 66-68 Haynes St (SR 15) 01566. I-84 exit 2, 0.5 mi n, follow signs to SR 131, on I-84 service road. Ext/int corridors. **Pets:** Accepted. 🛰 🛄 🖵 🐾

▼▼▼ Publick House Historic Inn & Country Lodge H
(508) 347-3313. **Call for rates.** 277 Main St 01566. I-90 exit 9; I-84 exit 3B, 0.5 mi s of jct US 20. Ext/int corridors. **Pets:** Accepted.
🛰 🛄 🖵 🍽 🐾

▲▲▲ ▼▼▼▼ Sturbridge Host Hotel & Conference Center on Cedar Lake H
(508) 347-7393. **$115-$199.** 366 Main St 01566. I-90 exit 9, just w on US 20; I-84 exit 3B. Int corridors. **Pets:** Other species. $25 daily fee/pet. Designated rooms, service with restrictions, supervision.
SAVE 🛰 🛄 🖵 🍽 🐾 ⊠

▲▲▲ ▼▼▼ Super 8 Sturbridge M
(508) 347-9000. **$62-$225.** 358 Main St 01566. I-90 exit 9; I-84 exit 3B on US 20. Ext corridors. **Pets:** Accepted. SAVE 🛰 🛄 🖵 🐾

WESTBOROUGH

▼▼▼ Extended Stay Deluxe-Boston-Westborough H 🐾
(508) 616-9213. **$90-$129.** 180 E Main St 01581. I-495 exit 23B, 1.4 mi w, then just sw on SR 30. Int corridors. **Pets:** Other species. $25 daily fee/pet. Service with restrictions. 🛰 &M 🛄 🖵

▼▼▼ Residence Inn by Marriott Boston/Westborough H
(508) 366-7700. **$159-$197.** 25 Connector Rd 01581. I-495 exit 23B, just w on SR 9 exit Computer and Research drs, then 0.3 mi s. Ext/int corridors. **Pets:** Accepted. ECO 🛰 ⊠ &M 🛄 🖵 🐾 ⊠

WESTMINSTER

▲▲▲ ▼▼▼ Wachusett Village Inn & Conference Center H
(978) 874-2000. **$99-$189.** 9 Village Inn Rd 01473. SR 2 exit 27 westbound, 0.3 mi e; exit 26 eastbound. Ext/int corridors. **Pets:** Accepted.
SAVE 🛰 🛄 🖵 🍽 🐾 ⊠

WESTPORT

▼▼▼▼ Hampton Inn-Fall River-Westport H 🐾
(508) 675-8500. **$99-$199.** 53 Old Bedford Rd 02790. I-195 exit 9 eastbound; exit 10 westbound, just s to US 6, then 1.3 mi w. Int corridors. **Pets:** Medium. $35 daily fee/room. Designated rooms, service with restrictions, supervision. 🛰 🛄 🖵 🐾 ⊠

WEST SPRINGFIELD

▼▼▼▼ Candlewood Suites H
(413) 739-1122. **Call for rates.** 572 Riverdale St 01089. I-91 exit 13B, 1.3 mi s. Int corridors. **Pets:** Accepted. 🛰 &M 🛄 🖵 🐾

▼▼▼▼ Hampton Inn H
(413) 732-1300. **$129-$199.** 1011 Riverdale St (US 5) 01089. I-91 exit 13B, 0.3 mi s. Int corridors. **Pets:** Accepted.
🛰 ⊠ &M 🛄 🖵 🐾

▼▼▼▼ Residence Inn West Springfield H
(413) 732-9543. **$129-$339.** 64 Border Way 01089. I-91 exit 13A on US 5. Int corridors. **Pets:** Medium. $75 one-time fee/room. Service with restrictions, crate. 🛰 ⊠ &M 🛄 🖵 🐾 ⊠

WILLIAMSTOWN

▼▼▼ Berkshire Hills Motel M
(413) 458-3950. **Call for rates.** 1146 Cold Spring Rd 01267. 2.3 mi s on US 7 and SR 2. Ext corridors. **Pets:** Accepted. 🛰 ⊠ 🐾

▲▲▲ ▼▼ Cozy Corner Motel M
(413) 458-8006. **$50-$135, 7 day notice.** 284 Sand Springs Rd (Rt 7) 01267. On US 7, 1.5 mi n of jct SR 2. Ext corridors. **Pets:** Medium. $50 deposit/pet, $15 one-time fee/pet, $25 daily fee/pet. Designated rooms, no service, crate. SAVE 🛰 ⊠ 🛄

▼▼▼ Maple Terrace Motel M 🐾
(413) 458-9677. **$68-$185, 10 day notice.** 555 Main St 01267. On SR 2, 1 mi e of jct US 7. Ext corridors. **Pets:** Dogs only. $17 one-time fee/pet. Designated rooms, service with restrictions, supervision.
🛰 ⊠ 🛄 🖵 🐾

▲▲▲ ▼▼ The Villager Motel M
(413) 458-4046. **Call for rates.** 953 Simonds Rd 01267. On US 7, 1.7 mi n of jct SR 2. Ext corridors. **Pets:** Accepted.
SAVE 🛰 ⊠ 🛄 🖵

WORCESTER

▲▲▲ ▼▼▼▼▼ Beechwood Hotel H
(508) 754-5789. **$159-$390.** 363 Plantation St 01605. I-290 exit 22 westbound, 0.5 mi w on Lincoln St, then 1.5 mi s; exit 21 eastbound, 1.3 mi s. Int corridors. **Pets:** Small. $50 daily fee/pet. Service with restrictions, supervision. SAVE 🛰 ⊠ &M 🛄 🖵 🍽 ⊠

▼▼▼▼ Residence Inn by Marriott Worcester H
(508) 753-6300. **$89-$229.** 503 Plantation St 01605. I-290 exit 21, 0.5 mi sw. Int corridors. **Pets:** Accepted. 🛰 ⊠ &M 🛄 🖵 🐾

MICHIGAN

ACME

▼▼ ▼▼ **Sleep Inn & Suites** 🅷

(231) 938-7000. **$60-$190.** 5520 US 31 N 49610. Jct US 31 and SR 72, 0.5 mi sw. Int corridors. **Pets:** Accepted. 🅰️ ✖️ 🅜 🅸 💻 🏊

ADRIAN

▼▼▼▼ **Carlton Lodge** 🅷

(517) 263-7000. **Call for rates.** 1629 W Maumee St 49221. Jct US 223 and SR 52, 3 mi w on US 223. Int corridors. **Pets:** Accepted.

🅰️ ✖️ 🅸 💻 🍴 🏊

▼▼▼▼ **Holiday Inn Express** 🅷

(517) 265-5700. **Call for rates.** 1077 W US 223 49221. Jct US 223 and SR 52, just w. Int corridors. **Pets:** Medium. $50 one-time fee/room. Service with restrictions. 🅰️ ✖️ 🅸 💻 🏊

▼▼ ▼▼ **Super 8** 🅷

(517) 265-8888. **$76-$248.** 1091 W US 223 49221. Jct US 223 and SR 52, just w. Int corridors. **Pets:** Other species. $25 one-time fee/room. Service with restrictions, supervision. 🅰️ ✖️ 🅸 💻

ALGONAC

▼▼ ▼▼ **Linda's Lighthouse Inn** 🅱🅱

(810) 794-2992. **$95-$135, 14 day notice.** 5965 Pointe Tremble Rd (SR 29) 48001. I-94 exit 243 (23 Mile Rd), 14.3 mi e. Int corridors. **Pets:** Accepted. 🅰️ ✖️ 🆇 🆆 🆉

ALMA

🆀 ▼▼ ▼▼ **Triangle Motel** 🅼

(989) 463-2296. **$50-$65.** 131 W Lincoln Rd 48801. US 127 exit 123 (Lincoln Rd) northbound; exit 124 (State Rd) southbound, just w on US 127 business route. Ext corridors. **Pets:** Small, dogs only. Designated rooms, service with restrictions, supervision. 🆂🅰️🆅🅴 🅰️ ✖️ 🅸

ALPENA

🆀 ▼▼ ▼▼ **Best Western of Alpena** 🅷

(989) 356-9087. **$79-$92.** 1286 Hwy M-32 W 49707. 2.3 mi w of jct US 23. Ext/int corridors. **Pets:** Dogs only. $5 daily fee/pet. Service with restrictions, supervision. 🆂🅰️🆅🅴 🅰️ ✖️ 🅸 💻 🏊 🆇

▼▼ ▼▼ **Days Inn** 🅷

(989) 356-6118. **$67-$108.** 1496 Hwy M-32 49707. 2.5 mi w of jct US 23. Int corridors. **Pets:** Dogs only. $100 deposit/room, $10 daily fee/room. Service with restrictions, supervision. 🅰️ ✖️ 🅸 💻 🏊 🆇

▼▼ ▼▼ **Holiday Inn** 🅷

(989) 356-2151. **$99-$159.** 1000 Hwy 23 N 49707. On US 23, 1 mi n. Int corridors. **Pets:** Accepted. 🅰️ ✖️ 🅸 💻 🍴 🏊 🆇

ANN ARBOR

▼▼ ▼▼ **Candlewood Suites** 🅷

(734) 663-2818. **$79-$140.** 701 Waymarket Way 48103. I-94 exit 175 (Ann Arbor/Saline Rd), just e on Eisenhower Rd. Int corridors. **Pets:** Accepted. 🅰️ ✖️ 🅜 🅸 💻

▼▼ ▼▼ **Extended Stay Deluxe Detroit-Ann Arbor** 🅷 🐾

(734) 997-7623. **$77-$112.** 3265 Boardwalk St 48108. I-94 exit 177 (State St), just n, then just e on Victors Way. Int corridors. **Pets:** Other species. $25 daily fee/pet. Service with restrictions. 🅰️ ✖️ 🅸 💻

▼▼ ▼▼ **Hampton Inn-North** 🅷

(734) 996-4444. **$99-$299.** 2300 Green Rd 48105. US 23 exit 41 (Plymouth Rd), just nw. Int corridors. **Pets:** Accepted. 🅰️ ✖️ 🅜 🅸 💻 🍴 🏊

▼▼ ▼▼ **Hawthorn Suites** 🅷

(734) 327-0011. **Call for rates.** 3535 Green Ct 48105. US 23 exit 41 (Plymouth Rd), just sw. Int corridors. **Pets:** Accepted. 🅰️ ✖️ 🅜 🅸 💻 🏊 🆇

🆀 ▼▼▼▼ **Holiday Inn Near the University of Michigan** 🅷

(734) 769-9800. **$149-$209.** 3600 Plymouth Rd 48105. US 23 exit 41 (Plymouth Rd), just sw. Int corridors. **Pets:** $20 daily fee/room. Service with restrictions, crate. 🆂🅰️🆅🅴 🅰️ ✖️ 🅸 💻 🍴 🏊 🆇

🆀 ▼▼ ▼▼ **Red Roof Inn #7045** 🅼

(734) 996-5800. **$60-$190.** 3621 Plymouth Rd 48105. US 23 exit 41 (Plymouth Rd), just nw. Ext corridors. **Pets:** Large, other species. No service, supervision. 🆂🅰️🆅🅴 🅰️ ✖️ 🅜 🅸 💻

▼▼ ▼▼ **Residence Inn by Marriott** 🅷

(734) 996-5666. **$99-$149.** 800 Victors Way 48108. I-94 exit 177 (State St), just ne. Ext/int corridors. **Pets:** Accepted. 🅰️ ✖️ 🅜 🅸 💻 🏊 🆇

AU GRES

▼▼ ▼▼ **Econo Lodge Inn** 🅷

(989) 876-4060. **Call for rates.** 510 W US 23 48703. On US 23, just w. Int corridors. **Pets:** Accepted. 🅰️ ✖️ 🅸 💻 🏊

BAD AXE

▼▼ **Econo Lodge Inn & Suites** 🅷 ❀
(989) 269-3200. **Call for rates.** 898 N Van Dyke Rd 48413. 1.3 mi n of jct SR 142 and 53 (Van Dyke Rd). Int corridors. **Pets:** Medium. $25 daily fee/pet. Designated rooms, service with restrictions, supervision.
🛜 ⊠ 🛢 💻 ❙❙ ⇌ ⊠

BATTLE CREEK

▼▼ **Baymont Inn & Suites-Battle Creek** 🅷 ❀
(269) 979-5400. **$79-$143.** 4725 Beckley Rd 49015. I-94 exit 97 (Capital Ave), just sw. Int corridors. **Pets:** Other species. $10 one-time fee/pet. Service with restrictions, crate. 🛜 ⊠ 🛢 💻 ⇌

BAY CITY

▼▼ **Bay Valley Resort & Conference Center** 🅷
(989) 686-3500. **Call for rates.** 2470 Old Bridge Rd 48706. 0.3 mi nw of jct I-75 and SR 84 exit 160. Int corridors. **Pets:** Accepted.
🛜 ⊠ 🛢 💻 ❙❙ ⇌ ⊠

▼▼ **Fairfield Inn by Marriott** 🅷
(989) 667-7050. **$100-$130.** 4015 E Wilder Rd 48706. 1 mi e of SR 13. Int corridors. **Pets:** Accepted. 🛜 ⊠ 🛢 💻 ⇌

▼▼▼ **Holiday Inn Express & Suites** 🅷
(989) 667-3800. **$99-$169.** 3959 Traxler Ct 48706. I-75 exit 164 (SR 13/Wilder Rd), 0.3 mi e. Int corridors. **Pets:** Accepted.
🛜 ⊠ 🅜 🛢 💻 ⇌

BEAR LAKE

🇦🇦🇦 ▼ **Bella Vista Inn** 🅼
(231) 864-3000. **$55-$106, 7 day notice.** 12273 West St 49614. On US 31; center. Ext corridors. **Pets:** Large, dogs only. $15 daily fee/pet. Service with restrictions, supervision. SAVE 🛜 ⊠ 🛢 ⇌

BEULAH

🇦🇦🇦 ▼▼▼ **Best Western Scenic Hill Resort** 🅷
(231) 882-7754. **$80-$176.** 1400 US Hwy 31 49617. On US 31, 0.8 mi e. Int corridors. **Pets:** Large. $50 deposit/room, $20 daily fee/pet. Service with restrictions, supervision. SAVE 🛜 ⊠ 🛢 💻 ⇌ ⊠

BIG RAPIDS

▼▼ **Holiday Inn Hotel & Conference Center** 🅷
(231) 796-4400. **$119-$174.** 1005 Perry St 49307. US 131 exit 139, 1.3 mi e on SR 20. Int corridors. **Pets:** Accepted.
🛜 ⊠ 🅜 🛢 💻 ❙❙ ⇌ ⊠

▼▼ **Quality Inn & Suites** 🅼
(231) 592-5150. **$55-$89.** 1705 S State St 49307. US 131 exit 139, 1.5 mi e on SR 20, then 0.8 mi s. Ext/int corridors. **Pets:** Medium. $10 daily fee/pet. Designated rooms, service with restrictions, supervision.
🛜 ⊠ 🛢 💻 ⇌

BIRCH RUN

◆◆◆ **Americas Best Value Inn & Suites** 🅷
(989) 624-4440. **$50-$140.** 9235 E Birch Run Rd 48415. I-75 exit 136 (Birch Run Rd), just e. Int corridors. **Pets:** Accepted. 🛜 ⊠ 🛢 💻

🇦🇦🇦 ◆◆◆ **Best Western of Birch Run/Frankenmuth** 🅷
(989) 624-9395. **$70-$130.** 9087 Birch Run Rd 48415. I-75 exit 136 (Birch Run Rd), just e. Ext/int corridors. **Pets:** $20 one-time fee/room. Designated rooms, service with restrictions, supervision.
SAVE ◆ ⊠ 🅜 🛢 💻 ❙❙ ⇌ ⊠

◆◆◆ **Holiday Inn Express** 🅷
(989) 624-9300. **Call for rates.** 12150 Dixie Hwy 48415. I-75 exit 136 (Birch Run Rd), just e. Int corridors. **Pets:** Accepted.
🛜 ⊠ 🛢 💻 ⇌ ⊠

BRIDGEPORT

▼▼◆ **Baymont Inn & Suites-Frankenmuth/Bridgeport** 🅷
(989) 777-3000. **$62-$159.** 6460 Dixie Hwy 48722. I-75 exit 144A. Int corridors. **Pets:** Accepted. 🛜 ⊠ 🅜 🛢 💻 ⇌

BRIGHTON

🇦🇦🇦 ▼◆◆ **Courtyard by Marriott** 🅷
(810) 225-9200. **$107-$131.** 7799 Conference Center Dr 48114. I-96 exit 145 (Grand River Ave S), just ne. Int corridors. **Pets:** Accepted.
SAVE 🛜 ⊠ 🅜 🛢 💻 ⇌

BROOKLYN

▼▼ **Super 8 - Brooklyn** 🅷
(517) 592-0888. **$54-$135.** 155 Wamplers Lake Rd 49230. Jct SR 50 (Main St) and 124; downtown. Int corridors. **Pets:** $5 daily fee/pet. Service with restrictions, supervision. 🛜 ⊠ 🅜 💻

BYRON CENTER

▼▼▼ **Comfort Suites-Grand Rapids South** 🅷
(616) 301-2255. **$75-$135.** 7644 Caterpillar Ct SW 49548. US 131 exit 75. Int corridors. **Pets:** Accepted. 🛜 ⊠ 🅜 🛢 💻 ⇌ ⊠

CADILLAC

🇦🇦🇦 ▼◆◆ **McGuire's Resort** 🅷 🐾
(231) 775-9947. **$79-$119, 7 day notice.** 7880 Mackinaw Tr 49601. US 131 exit 177, 0.7 mi n, then 0.5 mi w. Int corridors. **Pets:** Other species. $20 daily fee/room. Designated rooms, service with restrictions.
SAVE 🛜 ⊠ 🛢 💻 ❙❙ ⇌ ⊠

CALUMET

▼▼ **AmericInn Lodge & Suites of Calumet** 🅷 ❀
(906) 337-6463. **$95-$146.** 56925 S 6th St 49913. On US 41; just w of Visitors Center. Int corridors. **Pets:** Medium, dogs only. $20 one-time fee/room. Designated rooms, service with restrictions, supervision.
🛜 ⊠ 🛢 💻 ⇌ ⊠

CASCADE

▼▼ **Baymont Inn-Grand Rapids Airport** 🅷
(616) 956-3300. **$58-$146.** 2873 Kraft Ave SE 49512. I-96 exit 43B, just e. Int corridors. **Pets:** $10 daily fee/pet. Designated rooms, service with restrictions, supervision. 🛜 ⊠ 🛢 💻

🇦🇦🇦 ▼◆◆ **Best Western Hospitality Hotel &**
Suites 🅷 🐾
(616) 949-8400. **$69-$109.** 5500 28th St SE 49512. I-96 exit 43B, just e on SR 11. Int corridors. **Pets:** Medium, other species. $10 daily fee/pet. Designated rooms, service with restrictions, supervision.
SAVE 🛜 ⊠ 🛢 💻 ⇌ ⊠

▼▼ **Clarion Inn & Suites Grand Rapids Airport** 🅷
(616) 956-9304. **$84-$139.** 4981 28th St SE 49512. I-96 exit 43A, 0.5 mi w on SR 11. Int corridors. **Pets:** Accepted. 🛜 ⊠ 🛢 💻 ⇌

🇦🇦🇦 ▼◆◆ **Country Inn & Suites By Carlson** 🅷 ❀
(616) 977-0909. **$79-$114.** 5399 28th St SE 49512. I-96 exit 43B, just e on SR 11. Int corridors. **Pets:** Other species. $10 one-time fee/pet. Designated rooms, supervision. SAVE 🛜 ⊠ 🛢 💻 ⇌

▼▼▼ **Crowne Plaza Grand Rapids** 🅷
(616) 957-1770. **$82-$189.** 5700 28th St SE 49546. I-96 exit 43B, 0.3 mi e on SR 11. Int corridors. **Pets:** Accepted.
🛜 ⊠ 🅜 🛢 💻 ❙❙ ⇌ ⊠

▼▼ **Holiday Inn Express Suites Airport** 🅷
(616) 940-8100. **Call for rates.** 5401 28th St Ct SE 49546. I-96 exit 43B, just e on SR 11. Int corridors. **Pets:** Other species. $10 one-time fee/room. Designated rooms, crate. 🛜 ⊠ 🅜 🛢 💻 ⇌ ⊠

AAA **W** Red Roof Inn #7011 **M**

(616) 942-0800. **$52-$70.** 5131 28th St SE 49512. I-96 exit 43A, 0.3 mi w on SR 11. Ext corridors. **Pets:** Large, other species. No service, supervision. SAVE 🛰 ✕ 🔒 💻

WW Super 8-Grand Rapids Airport **H**

(616) 957-3000. **$47-$81.** 4855 28th St SE 49512. I-96 exit 43A, 0.5 mi w on SR 11. Int corridors. **Pets:** Accepted. 🛰 ✕ 🔒 💻

CHARLEVOIX

WW AmericInn Lodge & Suites of Charlevoix **H**

(231) 237-0988. **$59-$200.** 11800 US 31 N 49720. On US 31, 2.4 mi n. Int corridors. **Pets:** Accepted. 🛰 ✕ 🖐M 🔒 💻 🛏

CHARLOTTE

WW Super 8 **H**

(517) 543-8288. **$62-$122.** 828 E Shepherd St 48813. I-69 exit 60 (SR 50), just w. Int corridors. **Pets:** Accepted. 🛰 ✕ 🔒 💻

CHEBOYGAN

AAA **WW** Best Western River Terrace **M**

(231) 627-5688. **$89-$179.** 847 S Main St 49721. 1 mi s on SR 27. Ext/int corridors. **Pets:** Accepted. SAVE 🛰 ✕ 🔒 💻 🛏 🐾

W Birch Haus Motel **M**

(231) 627-5862. **$40-$85.** 1301 Mackinaw Ave 49721. On US 23, 0.8 mi nw. Ext corridors. **Pets:** Small, dogs only. $5 daily fee/pet. Service with restrictions, supervision. 🛰 ✕ 🔒

WW Continental Inn **M**

(231) 627-7164. **$39-$99.** 613 N Main St 49721. Jct US 23 and SR 27. Ext corridors. **Pets:** Medium, dogs only. $10 daily fee/room. Designated rooms, service with restrictions, crate. 🛰 ✕ 🔒 💻 🛏

CHELSEA

WWW Chelsea Comfort Inn & Village Conference Center **H**

(734) 433-8000. **$82-$113.** 1645 Commerce Park Dr 48118. I-94 exit 159 (SR 52/Main St), just n. Int corridors. **Pets:** Other species. $20 daily fee/room. Service with restrictions, supervision.
🛰 ✕ 🖐M 🔒 💻 🛏 🐾

WWW Holiday Inn Express **H** 🐾

(734) 433-1600. **$94-$266.** 1540 Commerce Park Dr 48118. I-94 exit 159 (SR 52/Main St), 0.3 mi n. Int corridors. **Pets:** $100 deposit/pet, $75 one-time fee/room. Designated rooms, service with restrictions, supervision.
🛰 ✕ 🖐M 🔒 💻 🛏

CHESANING

AAA **W** Colonial Motel **M**

(989) 845-3292. **$60-$130, 3 day notice.** 9475 E M-57 48616. On SR 57, 0.5 mi e. Ext corridors. **Pets:** Accepted. SAVE 🛰 ✕ 🔒 💻

CLARE

WW Days Inn of Clare **H**

(989) 386-1111. **$70-$120.** 10318 S Clare Ave 48617. On Business Rt US 10 and 127; just w of jct US 127 and Old US 27. Int corridors. **Pets:** Dogs only. $10 daily fee/pet. Designated rooms, service with restrictions, supervision. 🛰 ✕ 🔒 💻 🛏

COMSTOCK PARK

WWW Comfort Suites Grand Rapids North **H**

(616) 785-7899. **$89-$149.** 350 Dodge St 49321. US 131 exit 91. Int corridors. **Pets:** Accepted. 🛰 ✕ 🖐M 🔒 💻 🛏

COPPER HARBOR

W Lake Fanny Hooe Resort **M**

(906) 289-4451. **$95-$130, 7 day notice.** 505 2nd St 49918. Just s on Manganese Rd. Ext corridors. **Pets:** Other species. $10 daily fee/pet. Service with restrictions, supervision.
🛰 ✕ 🔒 💻 ✕ 🎿 ✉

DETROIT METROPOLITAN AREA

ALLEN PARK

AAA **WWWW** Best Western Greenfield Inn **H** 🐾

(313) 271-1600. **$92-$115.** 3000 Enterprise Dr 48101. I-94 exit 206 (Oakwood Blvd), just s, then just w. Int corridors. **Pets:** Dogs only. Service with restrictions, supervision. SAVE 🛰 ✕ 🔒 💻 🍴 🛏 ✕

AUBURN HILLS

WW Candlewood Suites **H**

(248) 373-3342. **$65-$104.** 1650 N Opdyke Rd 48326. I-75 exit 79 (University Dr), just w, then 0.4 mi n. Int corridors. **Pets:** Accepted.
🛰 ✕ 🔒 💻

WW Extended Stay Deluxe-Detroit Auburn Hills-Featherstone **H** 🐾

(248) 335-5200. **$75-$100.** 2100 Featherstone Rd 48326. I-75 exit 79 (University Dr), just w to Opdyke Rd, s to Featherstone Rd, then just e. Int corridors. **Pets:** Other species. $25 daily fee/pet. Service with restrictions. 🛰 ✕ 🖐M 🔒 💻

WWWW Hilton Suites Auburn Hills **H**

(248) 334-2222. **$89-$149.** 2300 Featherstone Rd 48326. I-75 exit 79 (University Dr), just w, 0.5 mi s on Opdyke Rd, then just e. Int corridors. **Pets:** Accepted. 🛰 ✕ 🔒 💻 🍴 🛏 ✕

WWWW Homestead Studio Suites Hotel-Detroit/Auburn Hills **H** 🐾

(248) 340-8888. **$72-$95.** 3315 University Dr 48326. I-75 exit 79 (University Dr), 0.9 mi e. Int corridors. **Pets:** Other species. $25 daily fee/pet. Service with restrictions. 🛰 ✕ 🔒 💻

WWW Staybridge Suites **H**

(248) 322-4600. **$79-$149.** 2050 Featherstone Rd 48326. I-75 exit 79 (University Dr), just w, 0.5 mi s on Opdyke Rd, then just e. Int corridors. **Pets:** Large. $25 daily fee/room. Service with restrictions, crate.
🛰 ✕ 🔒 💻 🛏

BELLEVILLE

WWWW Holiday Inn Express Hotel & Suites **H** 🐾

(734) 857-6200. **$119-$139.** 46194 N I-94 Service Dr 48111. I-94 exit 190 (Belleville Rd), just n, then just w. Int corridors. **Pets:** Medium, other species. $50 one-time fee/pet. Designated rooms, service with restrictions.
🛰 ✕ 🖐M 🔒 💻 🛏 ✕

AAA **WWW** Red Roof Inn Metro Airport #7183 **M**

(734) 697-2244. **$49-$79.** 45501 N I-94 Service Dr 48111. I-94 exit 190 (Belleville Rd), just n. Ext corridors. **Pets:** Large, other species. No service, supervision. SAVE 🛰 ✕ 🔒

BIRMINGHAM

AAA **WWWW** The Townsend Hotel **H** 🐾

(248) 642-7900. **$320-$440.** 100 Townsend St 48009. Center. Int corridors. **Pets:** Large, dogs only. $150 one-time fee/room, $5 daily fee/room. Service with restrictions, supervision.
ECO SAVE 🛰 ✕ 🖐M 💻 🍴 ✕

CANTON

WWW La Quinta Inn Detroit Canton **H**

(734) 981-1808. **$67-$129.** 41211 Ford Rd 48187. I-275 exit 25 (Ford Rd), just w to jct Haggerty Rd. Int corridors. **Pets:** Medium, other species. Service with restrictions, supervision. 🛰 ✕ 🔒 💻

▼▼ **Super 8-Canton** H
(734) 722-8880. **Call for rates.** 3933 Lotz Rd 48188. I-275 exit 22 (Michigan Ave), just e on US 12, then just s. Int corridors. **Pets:** Small. $10 daily fee/pet. Service with restrictions, supervision.
📶 ⊠ 🛗 💻

DEARBORN

▼▼ **Extended StayAmerica Detroit Dearborn** H ☆
(313) 336-0021. **$85-$112.** 260 Towne Center Dr 48126. SR 39 (Southfield Frwy); between Ford Rd and Michigan Ave exits; just w of jct Service and Hubbard drs. Int corridors. **Pets:** Other species. $25 daily fee/pet. Service with restrictions. 📶 ♿ 🛗 💻

🌀 ▼▼▼▼ **The Henry, Autograph Collection** H
(313) 441-2000. **$125-$279.** 300 Town Center Dr 48126. SR 39 (Southfield Frwy); between Ford Rd and Michigan Ave exits, on Service Dr. Int corridors. **Pets:** Accepted.
SAVE 📶 ⊠ 🛗 ♿ 💻 🍽 ⊅ ⊠

🌀 ▼▼▼▼ **Hyatt Regency Dearborn** H 🐾
(313) 593-1234. **$99-$399.** 600 Town Center Dr 48126. Jct SR 39 (Southfield Frwy), 0.3 mi w on Michigan Ave, 0.3 mi n on Evergreen Rd, then e on Fairlane Rd. Int corridors. **Pets:** Medium, other species. $50 one-time fee/pet. Service with restrictions, supervision.
ECO SAVE 📶 ⊠ ♿ 🛗 💻 🍽 ⊅ ⊠

🌀 ▼▼ ▼▼ **Red Roof Inn-Dearborn #7182** M
(313) 278-9732. **$61-$96.** 24130 Michigan Ave 48124. Jct US 24 (Telegraph Rd) and 12 (Michigan Ave). Ext corridors. **Pets:** Large, other species. No service, supervision. SAVE 📶 ⊠ ♿ 🛗

▼▼ **TownePlace Suites** H
(313) 271-0200. **$132-$170.** 6141 Mercury Dr 48126. SR 39 (Southfield Frwy) exit 7 (Ford Rd), just e, then 0.8 mi n. Int corridors. **Pets:** Small. $100 one-time fee/room. Service with restrictions.
📶 ⊠ ♿ 🛗 💻 ⊅

DETROIT

▼▼▼▼ **DoubleTree Suites by Hilton Hotel Detroit Downtown - Fort Shelby** H
(313) 963-5600. **$119-$229.** 525 W Lafayette Blvd 48226. Jct First Ave. Int corridors. **Pets:** Accepted. 📶 ⊠ 🛗 💻 🍽

▼▼▼▼ **Hawthorn Suites by Wyndham** H
(313) 441-1700. **$79-$159.** 5777 Southfield Service Dr 48228. SR 39 (Southfield Frwy) exit Ford Rd, just w. Ext corridors. **Pets:** Accepted.
📶 ⊠ 🛗 💻 ⊅ ⊠

▼▼▼▼ **Holiday Inn Express** H
(313) 887-7000. **Call for rates.** 1020 Washington Blvd 48226. Corner of Washington Blvd and Michigan Ave. Int corridors. **Pets:** Accepted.
📶 ⊠ ♿ 🛗 💻 🍽 ⊅

🌀 ▼▼▼▼ **MotorCity Casino Hotel** H
(313) 237-7711. **$179-$599.** 2901 Grand River Ave 48201. I-75 exit 50 (Grand River Ave), just n. Int corridors. **Pets:** Accepted.
SAVE 📶 ⊠ ♿ 🛗 💻 🍽 ⊠

🌀 ▼▼▼▼ **The Westin Book Cadillac Detroit** H 🐾
(313) 442-1600. **$179-$424.** 1114 Washington Blvd 48226. Corner of Washington Blvd and Michigan Ave. Int corridors. **Pets:** Medium, dogs only. Service with restrictions, supervision.
SAVE 📶 ⊠ ♿ 🛗 💻 🍽 ⊅ ⊠

FARMINGTON HILLS

▼▼ **Candlewood Suites** H
(248) 324-0540. **$77-$124.** 37555 Hills Tech Dr 48331. I-696 exit I-96 E/I-275 S/SR 5, just s to SR 5 N, 2 mi n to 12 Mile Rd, 1.3 mi n, then 0.3 mi s on Halsted Rd. Int corridors. **Pets:** Accepted.
⊠ ♿ 🛗 💻

▼▼◆ **Extended StayAmerica Detroit-Farmington Hills** H ☆
(248) 473-4000. **$60-$82.** 27775 Stansbury Blvd 48334. I-696 exit 5 (Orchard Lake Rd), just n, just e on 12 Mile Rd, then just s. Int corridors. **Pets:** Other species. $25 daily fee/pet. Service with restrictions.
📶 ⊠ ♿ 🛗 💻

🌀 ▼▼▼ **Holiday Inn & Suites** H
(248) 477-7800. **$99-$160.** 37529 Grand River Ave 48335. I-275 exit 165 (SR 5/Grand River Ave), 1 mi e. Int corridors. **Pets:** Accepted.
SAVE 📶 ⊠ ♿ 🛗 💻 🍽 ⊅ ⊠

🌀 ▼▼▼ **Red Roof Inn-Farmington Hills #7038** M
(248) 478-8640. **$42-$73.** 24300 Sinacola Ct 48335. I-96/275 and SR 5 exit 165 (Grand River Ave), just w. Ext corridors. **Pets:** Large, other species. No service, supervision. SAVE 📶 ⊠ ♿ 🛗

LAKE ORION

▼▼ **Palace Inn** H
(248) 391-2755. **Call for rates.** 2755 N Lapeer Rd 48360. I-75 exit 81 (Lapeer Rd), 3.3 mi n. Ext/int corridors. **Pets:** Accepted.
📶 ⊠ ♿ 🛗 💻 ⊅

LIVONIA

▼▼▼▼ **Embassy Suites Hotel** H
(734) 462-6000. **$99-$149.** 19525 Victor Pkwy 48152. I-275 exit 169 (7 Mile Rd), just e, then 0.5 mi n. Int corridors. **Pets:** Accepted.
📶 ⊠ 🛗 💻 ⊅

▼▼▼▼ **Livonia Marriott** H
(734) 462-3100. **$89-$129.** 17100 Laurel Park Dr N 48152. I-275 exit 170 (6 Mile Rd), just w. Int corridors. **Pets:** Accepted.
ECO 📶 ⊠ 🛗 💻 🍽 ⊅

▼▼▼▼ **Residence Inn Detroit-Livonia** H
(734) 462-4201. **$149-$239.** 17250 Fox Dr 48152. I-275 exit 170 (6 Mile Rd), just w. Int corridors. **Pets:** Accepted.
📶 ⊠ ♿ 🛗 💻 ⊅ ⊠

▼▼ **TownePlace Suites by Marriott** H ☆
(734) 542-7400. **$69-$134.** 17450 Fox Dr 48152. I-275 exit 170 (6 Mile Rd), just nw. Int corridors. **Pets:** Other species. $100 one-time fee/room. Designated rooms. 📶 ⊠ ♿ 🛗 💻 ⊅

MADISON HEIGHTS

▼ **Motel 6 Madison Heights #1109** M
(248) 583-0500. **$43-$53.** 32700 Barrington Rd 48071. I-75 exit 65A (14 Mile Rd), just e. Ext corridors. **Pets:** Other species. Service with restrictions, supervision. 📶 ♿ 🛗

🌀 ▼▼▼ **Red Roof Inn #7084** M
(248) 583-4700. **$49-$85.** 32511 Concord Dr 48071. I-75 exit 65A (14 Mile Rd), just e, then just s. Ext corridors. **Pets:** Large, other species. No service, supervision. SAVE 📶 ⊠ 🛗

▼▼▼ **Residence Inn by Marriott-Detroit Troy/Madison Heights** H
(248) 583-4322. **$170-$208.** 32650 Stephenson Hwy 48071. I-75 exit 65B (14 Mile Rd), just w, then just s. Ext corridors. **Pets:** Other species. $75 one-time fee/room. Service with restrictions.
📶 ⊠ 🛗 💻 ⊅ ⊠

MOUNT CLEMENS

▼▼▼ **Concorde Inn of Clinton Township** H
(586) 493-7300. **$79-$190.** 44315 Gratiot Ave 48036. I-94 exit 240B (SR 59), 0.3 mi w, then 0.3 mi s. Int corridors. **Pets:** Accepted.
📶 ⊠ ♿ 🛗 💻 ⊅ ⊠

NOVI

▼▼ **Extended StayAmerica-Detroit-Novi** H ☆
(248) 305-9955. **$80-$105.** 21555 Haggerty Rd 48375. I-275 exit 167 (8 Mile Rd), just w, then 0.5 mi n. Int corridors. **Pets:** Other species. $25 daily fee/pet. Service with restrictions. 📶 ⊠ ♿ 🛗 💻

▼▼▼ Residence Inn by Marriott-Detroit/Novi H

(248) 735-7400. **$90-$250.** 27477 Cabaret Dr 48377. I-96 exit 162 (Novi Rd), just n to 12 Mile Rd, then just w. Int corridors. **Pets:** Accepted.

AAA ▼▼▼▼ Sheraton-Detroit-Novi H

(248) 349-4000. **$87-$229.** 21111 Haggerty Rd 48375. I-275 exit 167 (8 Mile Rd), just w to Haggerty Rd, then just n. Int corridors. **Pets:** Accepted.

▼▼▼▼ Staybridge Suites H

(248) 349-4600. **$125-$199, 3 day notice.** 27000 Providence 48374. I-96 exit 160 (Beck Rd), just s to Grand River Ave, then 0.6 mi w. Int corridors. **Pets:** Medium, dogs only. $75 one-time fee/pet. Designated rooms, service with restrictions, crate.

▼▼▼ TownePlace Suites H

(248) 305-5533. **$69-$104.** 42600 11 Mile Rd 48375. I-96 exit 162 (Novi Rd), just s, 0.5 mi e on Crescent Dr, then just s on Town Center Dr. Int corridors. **Pets:** Accepted.

PLYMOUTH

AAA ▼▼▼ Comfort Inn Plymouth Clocktower H

(734) 455-8100. **$72-$99.** 40455 Ann Arbor Rd 48170. I-275 exit 28 (Ann Arbor Rd), just w; entry on Massey Dr. Int corridors. **Pets:** Medium. $25 one-time fee/room, $10 daily fee/pet. Service with restrictions, supervision.

AAA ▼▼▼ Red Roof Inn-Plymouth #7016 M

(734) 459-3300. **$45-$110.** 39700 Ann Arbor Rd 48170. I-275 exit 28 (Ann Arbor Rd), just e. Ext corridors. **Pets:** Large, other species. No service, supervision.

PONTIAC

▼▼▼ Residence Inn by Marriott Detroit Pontiac/Auburn Hills H

(248) 858-8664. **$145-$165.** 3333 Centerpoint Pkwy 48341. I-75 exit 75 (Square Lake Rd), w via Opdyke Rd. Int corridors. **Pets:** Accepted.

ROCHESTER HILLS

AAA ▼▼▼ Red Roof Inn #7191 M

(248) 853-6400. **$45-$99.** 2580 Crooks Rd 48309. Jct Hall Rd (SR 59). Ext corridors. **Pets:** Large, other species. No service, supervision.

ROMULUS

▼▼▼ Baymont Inn & Suites Detroit-Airport H

(734) 722-6000. **$44-$71.** 9000 Wickham Rd 48174. I-94 exit 198 (Merriman Rd), just n, then just w. Int corridors. **Pets:** Accepted.

AAA ▼▼▼ Best Western Gateway International Hotel H

(734) 728-2800. **$75-$200.** 9191 Wickham Rd 48174. I-94 exit 198 (Merriman Rd), just n, then just w. Int corridors. **Pets:** Accepted.

▼▼▼ Days Inn and Suites H

(734) 946-4300. **$54-$63.** 9501 Middlebelt Rd 48174. I-94 exit 199 (Middlebelt Rd), 0.4 mi s. Int corridors. **Pets:** Small. $20 daily fee/pet. Designated rooms, service with restrictions, crate.

▼▼▼▼ Detroit Metro Airport Marriott H

(734) 729-7555. **$72-$149.** 30559 Flynn Dr 48174. I-94 exit 198 (Merriman Rd), just n, then 0.3 mi e. Int corridors. **Pets:** Accepted.

▼▼ Extended StayAmerica Detroit-Metro Airport H ❀

(734) 722-7780. **$65-$88.** 30325 Flynn Dr 48174. I-94 exit 198 (Merriman Rd), just n, then 0.4 mi e. Int corridors. **Pets:** Other species. $25 daily fee/pet. Service with restrictions.

▼▼▼ La Quinta Inn Detroit Airport Romulus H

(734) 641-9006. **$80-$170.** 7680 Merriman Rd 48174. I-94 exit 198 (Merriman Rd), 0.4 mi n. Int corridors. **Pets:** Medium, other species. Service with restrictions, supervision.

▼▼ Red Roof Inn H

(734) 595-7400. **$39-$60.** 9095 Wickham Rd 48174. I-94 exit 198 (Merriman Rd), just n, then just w. Int corridors. **Pets:** Large, other species. No service, supervision.

▼▼▼ Romulus Quality Inn & Suites H

(734) 946-1400. **$54-$79.** 9555 Middlebelt Rd 48174. I-94 exit 199 (Middlebelt Rd), 0.4 mi s. Int corridors. **Pets:** Accepted.

AAA ▼▼▼ Sheraton Detroit Metro Airport H

(734) 729-2600. **$89-$189.** 8000 Merriman Rd 48174. I-94 exit 198 (Merriman Rd), 0.4 mi n. Int corridors. **Pets:** Accepted.

AAA ▼▼▼ ▼▼▼ The Westin Detroit Metropolitan Airport H

(734) 942-6500. **$99-$329.** 2501 Worldgateway Pl 48242. I-94 exit 198 (Merriman Rd); at McNamara Terminal. Int corridors. **Pets:** Accepted.

ROSEVILLE

AAA ▼▼▼ Best Western Plus Georgian Inn M

(586) 294-0400. **$74-$94.** 31327 Gratiot Ave 48066. I-94 exit 232 (Little Mack Ave), just s, 0.5 mi n on 13 Mile Rd, then just n. Ext corridors. **Pets:** Dogs only. $8 daily fee/pet. Service with restrictions, supervision.

AAA ▼▼▼ Red Roof Inn #10012 M

(586) 296-0310. **$45-$89.** 31800 Little Mack Ave 48066. I-94 exit 232 (Little Mack Ave), just n. Ext corridors. **Pets:** Large, other species. No service, supervision.

SOUTHFIELD

▼▼▼ Candlewood Suites H

(248) 945-0010. **$69-$129.** 1 Corporate Dr 48076. SR 10 (Northwestern Hwy) exit Lahser Rd, just e. Int corridors. **Pets:** Medium, other species. $10 daily fee/room. Service with restrictions.

▼▼▼ Hampton Inn-Southfield H

(248) 356-5500. **$99-$159.** 27500 Northwestern Service Dr 48034. I-696 exit 9 (Telegraph Rd N), just n to 11 Mile Rd, then 0.5 mi e. Int corridors. **Pets:** Accepted.

AAA ▼▼▼ Red Roof Inn-Southfield #7133 M

(248) 353-7200. **$49-$111.** 27660 Northwestern Hwy 48034. I-696 exit 9 (Telegraph Rd), just nw. Ext corridors. **Pets:** Large, other species. No service, supervision.

AAA ▼▼▼ ▼▼▼ The Westin Southfield Detroit H

(248) 827-4000. **$99-$309.** 1500 Town Center 48075. SR 10 (Northwestern Hwy) exit 10 (10 Mile Rd/Evergreen Rd), 0.3 mi n. Int corridors. **Pets:** Accepted.

SOUTHGATE

▼▼▼ La Quinta Inn Detroit Southgate H

(734) 374-3000. **$71-$129.** 12888 Reeck Rd 48195. I-75 exit 37 (Northline Rd), just w. Int corridors. **Pets:** Medium, other species. Service with restrictions, supervision.

STERLING HEIGHTS

▼▼▼ TownePlace Suites H

(586) 566-0900. **$120-$132.** 14800 Lakeside Cir 48313. 1 mi e of jct SR 53 (Van Dyke Ave) and 59 (Hall Rd). Int corridors. **Pets:** Accepted.

TAYLOR

◆◆◆ ▼▼▼ Red Roof Inn-Taylor #7189 M
(734) 374-1150. **$38-$75.** 21230 Eureka Rd 48180. I-75 exit 36 (Eureka Rd), just w. Ext corridors. **Pets:** Large, other species. No service, supervision. [SAVE] 📶 ⊠ 🖥

TROY

▼▼▼ Drury Inn & Suites-Troy H
(248) 528-3330. **$85-$234.** 575 W Big Beaver Rd 48084. I-75 exit 69 (Big Beaver Rd), just e. Int corridors. **Pets:** Accepted.
📶 ⊠ 🖥 💻 🍴 🏊

▼▼ The Gatehouse Suites Troy Hotel H
(248) 689-6856. **Call for rates.** 2600 Livernois Rd 48083. I-75 exit 69 (Big Beaver Rd), 0.5 mi e to Livernois Rd, then 0.5 mi s. Ext corridors. **Pets:** Accepted. 📶 ⊠ 🖥 💻 🏊 ⊠

▼▼ Holiday Inn-Troy H
(248) 689-7500. **Call for rates.** 2537 Rochester Ct 48083. I-75 exit 67 (Rochester Rd), 0.3 mi sw, then just w. Int corridors. **Pets:** Accepted.
[ECO] 📶 ⊠ 🖥 💻 🍴 🏊

▼▼ The MET Hotel Troy Detroit H
(248) 879-2100. **$69-$199, 3 day notice.** 5500 Crooks Rd 48098. I-75 exit 72 (Crooks Rd), just n. Int corridors. **Pets:** Accepted.
📶 ⊠ 🕪 🖥 💻 🏊

◆◆◆ ▼▼▼ Red Roof Inn-Troy #7021 M
(248) 689-4391. **$56-$66.** 2350 Rochester Ct 48083. I-75 exit 67 (Rochester Rd), 0.3 mi sw. Ext corridors. **Pets:** Large, other species. No service, supervision. [SAVE] 📶 ⊠ 🕪 🖥

UTICA

◆◆◆ ▼▼▼ Comfort Inn H ❀
(586) 739-7111. **$80-$190.** 11401 Hall Rd 48317. Jct Van Dyke Ave (SR 53). Int corridors. **Pets:** Medium, dogs only. $50 deposit/room. Service with restrictions, supervision. [SAVE] 📶 ⊠ 🖥 💻

▼▼▼ La Quinta Inn & Suites Detroit Utica H
(586) 731-4700. **$89-$149.** 45311 Park Ave 48315. Jct Van Dyke Ave (SR 53) and Hall Rd (SR 59), just n. Int corridors. **Pets:** Medium, other species. Service with restrictions, supervision. 📶 ⊠ 🖥 💻 🏊

▼▼▼ Staybridge Suites-Utica H ❀
(586) 323-0101. **$129-$189.** 46155 Utica Park Blvd 48315. Jct Van Dyke Ave (SR 53) and Hall Rd (SR 59), just n. Int corridors. **Pets:** Medium. $75 one-time fee/room. Service with restrictions, crate.
📶 ⊠ 🕪 🖥 🏊

WARREN

▼▼▼ Candlewood Suites-Detroit Warren H
(586) 978-1261. **Call for rates.** 7010 Convention Blvd 48092. I-696 exit 23 (Van Dyke Ave), 2.8 mi n. Int corridors. **Pets:** Accepted.
📶 ⊠ 🕪 🖥 💻

▼▼ Extended Stay Deluxe Detroit-Warren H ❀
(586) 558-5554. **$68-$78.** 30125 N Civic Center Blvd 48093. I-696 exit 23 (Van Dyke Ave), 1.5 mi n, then just e. Int corridors. **Pets:** Other species. $25 daily fee/pet. Service with restrictions.
📶 ⊠ 🕪 🖥 💻

▼▼ Hawthorn Suites H
(586) 558-7870. **$99-$119, 3 day notice.** 30180 N Civic Center Blvd 48093. I-696 exit 23 (Van Dyke Ave), 1.8 mi n. Int corridors. **Pets:** Small. $100 one-time fee/pet. Designated rooms, service with restrictions, supervision. 📶 ⊠ 🕪 🖥 💻 🏊

▼▼ La Quinta Inn Detroit Warren Tech Center H
(586) 574-0550. **$58-$115.** 30900 Van Dyke Ave 48093. I-696 exit 23 (Van Dyke Ave), 1.8 mi n on SR 53. Int corridors. **Pets:** Medium, other species. Service with restrictions, supervision. 📶 ⊠ 🕪 🖥 💻

◆◆◆ ▼▼▼ Red Roof Inn-Warren #070 M
(586) 573-4300. **$54-$74.** 26300 Dequindre Rd 48091. I-696 exit 20 (Dequindre Rd), just ne. Ext corridors. **Pets:** Large, other species. No service, supervision. [SAVE] 📶 ⊠ 🖥 💻

◆◆◆ ▼▼▼▼ TownePlace Suites by Marriott-Warren H
(586) 264-8800. **$99-$129.** 7601 Chicago Rd 48092. I-696 exit 23 (Van Dyke Ave), 2 mi n. Int corridors. **Pets:** Accepted.
[SAVE] 📶 ⊠ 🕪 🖥 💻 🏊

WATERFORD

▼▼▼ Comfort Inn H
(248) 666-8555. **Call for rates.** 7076 Highland Rd 48327. Jct SR 59 (Highland Rd) and Airport Rd, 1 mi w. Int corridors. **Pets:** Accepted.
📶 ⊠ 🖥 💻 🏊 ⊠

END METROPOLITAN AREA

DEWITT

▼▼ Magnuson Hotels H
(517) 374-0000. **$67-$116.** 1055 Aaron Dr 48820. I-69 exit 87 (Old US 27), just s. Int corridors. **Pets:** Accepted. 📶 ⊠ 🕪 🖥 💻 🏊

◆◆◆ ▼▼ Sleep Inn H
(517) 669-8823. **$69-$129.** 1101 Commerce Park Dr 48820. I-69 exit 87 (Old US 27), 0.8 mi n. Int corridors. **Pets:** Small, dogs only. $10 daily fee/pet. Service with restrictions, supervision.
[SAVE] 📶 ⊠ 🖥 💻 🏊

DOUGLAS

▼▼ AmericInn Lodge & Suites of Douglas H
(269) 857-8581. **$89-$249.** 2905 Blue Star Hwy 49406. I-196 exit 36, 0.3 mi n. Int corridors. **Pets:** Accepted. 📶 ⊠ 🕪 🖥 💻 🏊

◆◆◆ ▼▼▼ The Kirby House BB
(269) 857-2904. **$100-$225, 14 day notice.** 294 W Center St 49406. Center. Int corridors. **Pets:** Small, dogs only. $25 daily fee/pet. Service with restrictions, crate. [SAVE] 📶 ⊠ 🏊 📷

EAST LANSING

▼▼▼ Gatehouse Suites East Lansing H
(517) 332-7711. **$89-$399.** 1600 E Grand River Ave 48823. US 127 exit Grand River Ave, 2.6 mi se on SR 43. Ext corridors. **Pets:** Other species. $75 one-time fee/room. Service with restrictions.
📶 ⊠ 🖥 💻 🏊 ⊠

▼▼▼ Hampton Inn East Lansing H
(517) 324-2072. **$129-$179.** 2500 Coolidge Rd 48823. US 127 exit 79 (Lake Lansing Rd), just e. Int corridors. **Pets:** Accepted.
📶 ⊠ 🖥 💻

◆◆◆ ▼▼▼ Howard Johnson Inn M
(517) 351-5500. **$67-$143.** 1100 Trowbridge Rd 48823. US 127 exit 75 (Trowbridge Rd), just e. Ext/int corridors. **Pets:** Accepted.
[SAVE] 📶 ⊠ 🖥 💻 🏊

EAST TAWAS

◆◆◆ ▼▼▼ Tawas Bay Beach Resort H
(989) 362-8600. **$70-$189, 3 day notice.** 300 E Bay St 48730. On US 23 W. Int corridors. **Pets:** Accepted.
[SAVE] 📶 ⊠ 🖥 💻 🍴 🏊 📷

ESCANABA

▼▼ Bay View Motel **M**
(906) 786-2843. **$45-$65, 4 day notice.** 7110 US Hwy 2 & 41 & M35 49837. 4.5 mi n on US 2/41 and SR 35. Ext/int corridors.
Pets: Accepted. 📶 ✕ 🛢 💻 ✕

▼▼ Econo Lodge **H**
(906) 789-1066. **$70-$99.** 921 N Lincoln Rd 49829. 0.5 mi n on US 2/41 and SR 35. Int corridors. **Pets:** Small. $10 daily fee/pet. Service with restrictions, supervision. SAVE 📶 ✕ 🛢 💻

FENTON

▼▼▼ Holiday Inn Express & Suites **H**
(810) 714-7171. **$89-$129.** 17800 Silver Pkwy 48430. US 23 exit 78 (Owen Rd), just w, then 0.4 mi n. Int corridors. **Pets:** Accepted.
📶 ✕ 🛢M 🛢 💻 ✕

FLINT

▲▲ ▼▼ AmericInn Flint Airport **H**
(810) 233-9000. **$79-$109.** 6075 Hill 23 Dr 48507. US 23 exit 90 (Hill Rd), just w. Int corridors. **Pets:** $25 one-time fee/pet. Service with restrictions, supervision. SAVE 📶 ✕ 🛢M 🛢 💻 ✕ ✕

▼▼ Baymont Inn & Suites-Flint/Flushing **H**
(810) 732-2300. **Call for rates.** 4160 Pier North Blvd 48504. I-75 exit 122 (Pierson Rd), just w. Int corridors. **Pets:** Accepted.
📶 ✕ 🛢 💻 ✕

▼▼▼ Courtyard by Marriott **H**
(810) 232-3500. **$116-$142.** 5205 Gateway Center 48507. US 23 exit 90 (Hill Rd), just e to Gateway Center, then just n. Int corridors.
Pets: Accepted. 📶 ✕ 🛢M 🛢 💻 ✕

▼▼▼ Holiday Inn Express Flint Campus Area **H**
(810) 238-7744. **Call for rates.** 1150 Robert T Longway Blvd 48503. I-475 exit 8A (Robert T Longway Blvd), just w. Int corridors.
Pets: Accepted. 📶 ✕ 🛢M 🛢 💻

▼▼▼ Residence Inn by Marriott **H**
(810) 424-7000. **$99-$169.** 2202 W Hill Rd 48507. US 23 exit 90 (Hill Rd), just e. Int corridors. **Pets:** Accepted.
📶 ✕ 🛢M 🛢 💻 ✕ ✕

FRANKENMUTH

▼▼ Drury Inn & Suites **H**
(989) 652-2800. **$115-$204.** 260 S Main St 48734. On SR 83; downtown. Int corridors. **Pets:** Accepted. 📶 ✕ 🛢M 🛢 💻 ✕

▼ Frankenmuth Motel **M**
(989) 652-6171. **$50-$99.** 1218 Weiss St 48734. Just e of SR 83. Ext corridors. **Pets:** Accepted. 📶 ✕ 🛢

GAYLORD

▼▼ Alpine Lodge **H**
(989) 732-2431. **$69-$119, 14 day notice.** 833 W Main St 49735. I-75 exit 282, 0.3 mi e on SR 32. Ext/int corridors. **Pets:** Small, dogs only. Service with restrictions, supervision.
📶 ✕ 🛢 💻 ✕ ✕ ✕

▲▲ ▼ Downtown Motel **M**
(989) 732-5010. **$40-$66.** 208 S Otsego Ave 49735. I-75 exit 282, 0.5 mi e, then 0.3 mi s on I-75 business loop. Ext corridors. **Pets:** Dogs only. $5 daily fee/pet. Service with restrictions, supervision. SAVE 📶 ✕ 🛢

▼▼ Econo Lodge **H**
(989) 732-6451. **Call for rates.** 803 S Otsego Ave 49735. I-75 exit 279, 2.3 mi ne on I-75 business loop. Int corridors. **Pets:** Accepted.
📶 ✕ 🛢 💻 ✕ ✕

GRAND BLANC

▼▼ ▼ Comfort Inn **H**
(810) 694-0000. **Call for rates.** 9040 Holly Rd 48439. I-75 exit 108 (Holly Rd), just e. Int corridors. **Pets:** Accepted.
📶 ✕ 🛢M 🛢 💻 ✕

GRAND HAVEN

▼▼ Days Inn **H**
(616) 842-1999. **$73-$145.** 1500 S Beacon Blvd 49417. 1.5 mi s on US 31. Int corridors. **Pets:** $150 deposit/room, $10 daily fee/pet. Designated rooms, service with restrictions. 📶 ✕ 🛢 💻 ✕

GRAND RAPIDS

▲▲ ▼▼▼ Holiday Inn Grand Rapids Downtown **H**
(616) 235-7611. **$133-$159.** 310 Pearl St NW 49504. US 131 exit 85B (Pearl St), just e. Int corridors. **Pets:** Other species. $25 daily fee/room. Designated rooms, service with restrictions, crate.
ECO SAVE 📶 ✕ 🛢 💻 🍴 ✕ ✕

▼▼▼ Homewood Suites by Hilton **H** 🐾
(616) 285-7100. **$99-$179.** 3920 Stahl Dr SE 49546. I-96 exit 43A (28th St SW), 1.5 mi w to E Paris Ave, then just n. Int corridors. **Pets:** Large. Service with restrictions, supervision. 📶 ✕ 🛢M 🛢 💻 ✕

▲▲ ▼▼▼ Radisson Hotel Grand Rapids Riverfront **H**
(616) 363-9001. **$99-$179.** 270 Ann St NW 49504. US 131 exit 88, just e. Int corridors. **Pets:** Accepted. SAVE 📶 ✕ 🛢 💻 🍴 ✕

GRANDVILLE

▼▼ Days Inn & Suites **H**
(616) 531-5263. **$60-$63.** 3825 28th St SW 49418. I-196 exit 70/70A, 0.3 mi e. Int corridors. **Pets:** Accepted. 📶 ✕ 🛢 💻

▼▼▼ Residence Inn by Marriott Grand Rapids West **H** 🐾
(616) 538-1100. **$109-$159.** 3451 Rivertown Point Ct SW 49418. I-196 exit 67, 1.7 mi e. Int corridors. **Pets:** Large, other species. $75 one-time fee/room. Service with restrictions.
ECO 📶 ✕ 🛢M 🛢 💻 ✕ ✕

GRAYLING

▼▼ Ramada Hotel & Conference Center **H**
(989) 348-7611. **Call for rates.** 2650 S Business Loop 49738. I-75 business loop, 0.8 mi s. Ext/int corridors. **Pets:** Accepted.
📶 ✕ 🛢M 🛢 💻 🍴 ✕ ✕

▼▼ Super 8 **H** 🐾
(989) 348-8888. **$48-$101.** 5828 Nelson A Miles Pkwy 49738. I-75 exit 251, just w. Int corridors. **Pets:** Other species. $8 daily fee/pet. Designated rooms, service with restrictions, crate.
📶 ✕ 🛢 💻 ✕ ✕

GREENVILLE

▼▼ AmericInn Lodge & Suites of Greenville **H**
(616) 754-4500. **$90-$105.** 2525 W Washington St 48838. US 131 exit 101 (SR 57), 13 mi e. Int corridors. **Pets:** Accepted.
📶 ✕ 🛢M 🛢 💻 ✕ ✕

HANCOCK

▲▲ ▼▼▼ Magnuson Hotel Copper Crown **H**
(906) 482-6111. **$71.** 235 Hancock St 49930. On US 41 S; downtown. Ext/int corridors. **Pets:** Accepted. SAVE 📶 ✕ 🛢 💻 ✕

HARRISON

▲▲ ▼ Lakeside Motel & Cottages **M** 🐾
(989) 539-3796. **$62-$99.** 515 E Park St, Business US 127 48625. US 127 exit US 127 business route/SR 61, 2.2 mi w. Ext corridors.
Pets: Other species. Service with restrictions, supervision.
SAVE 📶 ✕ 🛢 💻 ✕

HILLMAN

▼▼ **Thunder Bay Golf Resort** Ⓜ

(989) 742-4502. **Call for rates.** 27800 Hwy M-32 E 49746. On SR 32, just e. Ext corridors. **Pets:** Accepted. 🛰 ✕ 🖪 💻 🍴 ✕

HOLLAND

▼▼ **Country Inn & Suites By Carlson** Ⓗ

(616) 396-6677. **Call for rates.** 12260 James St 49424. Jct US 31 N and James St, just e. Int corridors. **Pets:** Accepted.
🛰 ✕ 🖪 💻 ⇌

▼▼▼ **Residence Inn by Marriott** Ⓗ ❀

(616) 393-6900. **$169-$199.** 631 Southpoint Ridge Rd 49423. I-196 exit 49, 0.7 mi n on SR 40. Int corridors. **Pets:** Other species. $75 one-time fee/room. Service with restrictions, crate.
🛰 ✕ 🖪 🖪 💻 ⇌ ✕

HOUGHTON

▼▼▼ **Country Inn & Suites By Carlson** Ⓗ

(906) 487-6700. **$89-$179.** 919 Razorback Dr 49931. 1.3 mi w on SR 26. Int corridors. **Pets:** Medium, dogs only. $25 daily fee/room. Designated rooms, service with restrictions, supervision.
🛰 ✕ 🖪 🖪 💻 ⇌ ✕

▼▼ **Magnuson Hotel - Franklin Square Inn** Ⓗ

(906) 487-1700. **Call for rates.** 820 Shelden Ave 49931. On US 41; downtown. Int corridors. **Pets:** Accepted.
🛰 ✕ 🖪 💻 🍴 ⇌ ✕

HOUGHTON LAKE

▼▼ **Super 8** Ⓗ

(989) 422-3119. **$54-$99.** 9580 W Lake City Rd 48629. Jct US 127 and SR 55. Int corridors. **Pets:** Other species. $10 daily fee/pet. Service with restrictions, supervision. 🛰 ✕ 🖪 💻 ⇌ ✕

HOWELL

▼▼ **Baymont Inn & Suites-Howell** Ⓗ

(517) 546-0712. **$67-$95.** 4120 Lambert Dr 48855. I-96 exit 133 (US 59/Grand River Ave), just n, then 0.5 mi e. Int corridors. **Pets:** Accepted.
🛰 ✕ 🖪 🖪 💻 ⇌

(AAA) ▼▼ **Best Western Howell** Ⓜ

(517) 548-2900. **$89-$155.** 1500 Pinckney Rd 48843. I-96 exit 137 (Pinckney Rd), just s on CR D19. Ext corridors. **Pets:** Small, dogs only. $20 daily fee/pet. Designated rooms, service with restrictions, supervision.
SAVE 🛰 ✕ 🖪 💻 ⇌

▼▼ **Holiday Inn Express & Suites** Ⓗ

(517) 548-0100. **$86-$129.** 1397 N Burkhart Rd 48855. I-96 exit 133 (US 59/Grand River Ave), just n, then 0.5 mi e. Int corridors. **Pets:** $25 one-time fee/pet. Service with restrictions, supervision.
🛰 ✕ 🖪 🖪 💻 ⇌

IMLAY CITY

▼▼ **Super 8-Imlay City** Ⓗ

(810) 724-8700. **$48-$68.** 6951 Newark Rd 48444. I-69 exit 168 (SR 53/Van Dyke Rd), just n, then just e. Int corridors. **Pets:** Accepted.
🛰 ✕ 🖪 💻 ✕

IRON MOUNTAIN

(AAA) ▼ **Budget Host Inn** Ⓜ ❀

(906) 774-6797. **$52-$60.** 1585 N Stephenson Ave 49801. On US 2 and 141, 1.5 mi nw. Ext corridors. **Pets:** Medium. $5 one-time fee/room. Designated rooms, service with restrictions, supervision. SAVE 🛰 ✕ 🖪

(AAA) ▼▼ **Comfort Inn** Ⓗ ❀

(906) 774-5505. **$89-$119.** 1565 N Stephenson Ave 49801. On US 2, 1.3 mi nw. Int corridors. **Pets:** Medium, dogs only. $15 daily fee/pet. Designated rooms, service with restrictions, supervision.
SAVE 🛰 ✕ 🖪 💻

▼▼ **Country Inn & Suites By Carlson** Ⓗ ❀

(906) 774-1900. **$86-$160.** 2005 S Stephenson Ave 49801. Jct SR 141, 0.8 mi w on US 2. Int corridors. **Pets:** Dogs only. $20 daily fee/room. Designated rooms, service with restrictions, supervision.
🛰 ✕ 🖪 🖪 💻 ⇌

IRON RIVER

▼▼ **AmericInn Lodge & Suites of Iron River** Ⓗ ❀

(906) 265-9100. **$99-$136.** 40 E Adams St 49935. On US 2; downtown. Int corridors. **Pets:** Dogs only. $10 daily fee/room. Designated rooms, service with restrictions, supervision. 🛰 ✕ 🖪 🖪 💻 ⇌ ✕

IRONWOOD

▼ **Americas Best Value Inn** Ⓗ

(906) 932-3395. **$60-$120.** 160 E Cloverland Dr 49938. Jct US 2 and 2 business route. Int corridors. **Pets:** Accepted. 🛰 ✕ 🖪 💻 ✕

▼▼ **AmericInn of Ironwood** Ⓗ

(906) 932-7200. **$69-$185.** 1117 E Cloverland Dr 49938. 0.8 mi e on US 2. Int corridors. **Pets:** Accepted. 🛰 ✕ 🖪 🖪 💻 ⇌

ISHPEMING

(AAA) ▼▼ **Best Western Country Inn** Ⓗ

(906) 485-6345. **$91-$108.** 850 US 41 W 49849. US 41, just n of town. Int corridors. **Pets:** Designated rooms, service with restrictions, supervision. SAVE 🛰 ✕ 💻 🍴 ⇌

JACKSON

▼▼ **Baymont Inn-Jackson** Ⓗ

(517) 789-6000. **$71-$180.** 2035 Holiday Inn Dr 49202. I-94 exit 138 (US 127), just nw. Int corridors. **Pets:** Accepted. 🛰 ✕ 🖪 💻

▼▼▼ **Hampton Inn by Hilton** Ⓗ

(517) 789-5151. **$99-$159.** 2225 Shirley Dr 49202. I-94 exit 138 (US 127), just n to Springport Rd, then just e. Int corridors. **Pets:** Small, other species. Designated rooms, service with restrictions, supervision.
🛰 ✕ 🖪 🖪 💻 ⇌

KALAMAZOO

▼▼ **Baymont Inn & Suites** Ⓗ

(269) 372-7999. **$58-$170.** 2203 S 11th St 49009. US 131 exit 36B (Stadium Dr), just w. Int corridors. **Pets:** Accepted. 🛰 ✕ 🖪 💻

(AAA) ▼▼ **Best Western Hospitality Inn** Ⓗ

(269) 381-1900. **$100-$130.** 3640 E Cork St 49001. I-94 exit 80 (Sprinkle Rd), just nw. Int corridors. **Pets:** Accepted.
SAVE 🛰 ✕ 🖪 💻 ⇌ ✕

(AAA) ▼▼▼ **Best Western Plus Kalamazoo Suites** Ⓗ

(269) 350-5522. **$100-$170.** 2575 S 11th St 49009. US 131 exit 36B (Stadium Dr), just w. Int corridors. **Pets:** $25 one-time fee/room. Service with restrictions, supervision. SAVE 🛰 ✕ 🖪 🖪 💻 ⇌

▼▼ **Candlewood Suites** Ⓗ

(269) 270-3203. **$109-$139.** 3443 Retail Place Dr 49048. I-94 exit 80 (Sprinkle Rd), just s. Int corridors. **Pets:** Accepted.
🛰 ✕ 🖪 🖪 💻

(AAA) ▼▼▼ **Four Points by Sheraton** Ⓗ

(269) 385-3922. **$95-$125.** 3600 E Cork St 49001. I-94 exit 80 (Sprinkle Rd), just n, then just w. Int corridors. **Pets:** Medium, dogs only. $25 one-time fee/pet. Service with restrictions, crate.
SAVE 🛰 ✕ 🖪 🖪 💻 🍴 ⇌

(AAA) ▼▼▼ **Holiday Inn-West** Ⓗ

(269) 375-6000. **$129-$134.** 2747 S 11th St 49009. US 131 exit 36B (Stadium Dr), just w. Int corridors. **Pets:** Accepted.
ECO SAVE 🛰 ✕ 🖪 🖪 💻 🍴 ⇌ ✕

AAA ◆◆◆ **Quality Inn** H

(269) 381-7000. **Call for rates.** 3820 S Sprinkle Rd 49001. I-94 exit 80 (Sprinkle Rd), 0.3 mi s. Int corridors. **Pets:** Accepted.

SAVE 📶 ✕ 🖥 🖵 🛏️

AAA ◆◆◆ **Red Roof Inn-West #7025** H

(269) 375-7400. **$49-$110.** 5425 W Michigan Ave 49009. US 131 exit 36B (Stadium Dr), just nw. Ext corridors. **Pets:** Large, other species. No service, supervision. SAVE 📶 ✕ 🖥 🖵

◆◆◆◆ **Residence Inn by Marriott** H

(269) 349-0855. **$125-$170.** 1500 E Kilgore Rd 49001. I-94 exit 78 (Portage Rd), just n, then just w. Int corridors. **Pets:** Accepted.

ECO 📶 ✕ 🖥 🖵 🛏️ ✕

◆◆◆◆ **Staybridge Suites-Kalamazoo** H ❖

(269) 372-8000. **$79-$199.** 2001 Seneca Ln 49008. US 131 exit 36A (Stadium Dr), 0.3 mi e. Int corridors. **Pets:** Medium, other species. $25 one-time fee/pet. Service with restrictions, supervision.

📶 ✕ 🖥 🖵 🛏️

◆◆◆◆ **TownePlace Suites by Marriott Kalamazoo** H

(269) 353-1500. **$129-$159.** 5683 S 9th St 49009. I-94 exit 72 (9th St), just s. Int corridors. **Pets:** Accepted. 📶 ✕ 🖥 🖵 🛏️

KENTWOOD

◆◆ **Comfort Inn** H

(616) 957-2080. **$70-$140.** 4155 28th St SE 49512. I-96 exit 43A, 1.5 mi w on SR 11. Int corridors. **Pets:** Accepted. 📶 ✕ 🖥 🖵

◆ **Extended StayAmerica Grand Rapids-Kentwood** H ❖

(616) 977-6750. **$45-$80.** 3747 29th St SE 49512. I-96 exit 43A, 2 mi w on SR 11, then just s. Int corridors. **Pets:** Other species. $25 daily fee/pet. Service with restrictions. 📶 ✕ 🖥 🖵

◆◆◆ **The Gatehouse Suites** H ❖

(616) 957-8111. **Call for rates.** 2701 E Beltline Ave 49546. Jct SR 11 and E Beltline Ave (SR 37). Ext corridors. **Pets:** Large, other species. $50 one-time fee/room. Service with restrictions, crate.

📶 ✕ 🖥 🖵 🛏️ ✕

◆◆◆ **Sleep Inn & Suites** H

(616) 975-9000. **$55-$120.** 4284 29th St SE 49512. I-96 exit 43A, 1 mi w on SR 11, then just s on Acquest Ave. Int corridors. **Pets:** $10 daily fee/room. Service with restrictions, supervision.

📶 ✕ 🖥 🖵 🛏️ ✕

◆◆◆ **Staybridge Suites** H

(616) 464-3200. **$129-$149.** 3000 Lake Eastbrook Blvd SE 49512. I-96 exit 43A, 2 mi w on SR 11, then just s. Int corridors. **Pets:** Small. $15 daily fee/room. Service with restrictions, crate.

📶 ✕ 🖥 🖵 🛏️

LANSING

AAA ◆◆◆ **Candlewood Suites** H ❖

(517) 351-8181. **$59-$189.** 3545 Forest Rd 48910. I-496 exit 11 (Jolly Rd), 0.3 mi e to Collins Rd, 0.7 mi n, then just e. Int corridors. **Pets:** Medium. $75 one-time fee/room. Service with restrictions, crate.

SAVE 📶 ✕ 🖥 🖵 🍴 🛏️

AAA ◆◆◆ **Courtyard by Marriott** H

(517) 482-0500. **$134-$164.** 2710 Lake Lansing Rd 48912. US 127 exit 79 (Lake Lansing Rd), just w. Int corridors. **Pets:** Accepted.

SAVE 📶 ✕ 🖥 🖵 🍴 🛏️

◆◆◆ **Hampton Inn of Lansing** H

(517) 627-8381. **$85-$99.** 525 N Canal Rd 48917. I-96 exit 93B (SR 43/Saginaw Hwy), just e. Int corridors. **Pets:** Medium. $50 deposit/pet. Designated rooms, service with restrictions, supervision.

📶 ✕ 🖥 🖵 🛏️ ✕

◆◆◆ **Lexington Lansing Hotel** H ❖

(517) 323-7100. **$150-$300.** 925 S Creyts Rd 48917. I-496 exit 1 (Creyts Rd), just n. Int corridors. **Pets:** Medium, dogs only. $30 one-time fee/room. Service with restrictions.

SAVE 📶 ✕ 🖥 🖵 🍴 🛏️ ✕

AAA ◆◆◆ **Quality Suites Hotel** H ❖

(517) 886-0600. **$79-$109.** 901 Delta Commerce Dr 48917. I-96 exit 93B (SR 43/Saginaw Hwy), 0.3 mi e to Bennigan's, then just n. Int corridors. **Pets:** Other species. $25 one-time fee/room. Service with restrictions.

ECO SAVE 📶 ✕ 🖥 🖵 ✕

AAA ◆◆◆ **Red Roof Inn-West #7020** H

(517) 321-7246. **$47-$68.** 7412 W Saginaw Hwy 48917. I-96 exit 93B (SR 43/Saginaw Hwy), just e. Ext corridors. **Pets:** Large, other species. No service, supervision. SAVE 📶 ✕ 🖥 🖵

◆◆◆ **Residence Inn by Marriott West** H

(517) 886-5030. **$100-$110.** 922 Delta Commerce Dr 48917. I-96 exit 93B (SR 43/Saginaw Hwy), 0.4 mi e; behind Bennigan's. Int corridors. **Pets:** Accepted. 📶 ✕ 🖥 🖵 🛏️ ✕

LUDINGTON

AAA ◆◆◆ **Best Western Splash Park Inn** H

(231) 843-2140. **$59-$249.** 5005 W US 10 49431. US 31 exit 170B, 1 mi w. Int corridors. **Pets:** Accepted. SAVE 📶 ✕ 🖥 🖵 🛏️ ✕

◆◆◆ **Holiday Inn Express** H ❖

(231) 845-7004. **$89-$249, 3 day notice.** 5323 W US 10 49431. US 31 exit 170B, 1.3 mi w. Int corridors. **Pets:** Dogs only. $10 daily fee/pet. Designated rooms, service with restrictions, supervision.

ECO 📶 ✕ 🖥 🖵 🛏️ ✕

MACKINAW CITY

◆◆ **Americas Best Value Inn Mackinaw City** M ❖

(231) 436-5544. **$49-$209.** 112 Old US 31 49701. I-75 exit 337 northbound, 0.5 mi n; exit 338 southbound, 0.5 mi s. Ext corridors. **Pets:** $25 one-time fee/room. Service with restrictions, supervision.

📶 ✕ 🖥 🖵 🛏️

◆◆◆ **Baymont Inn & Suites-Mackinaw City** H

(231) 436-7737. **$89-$220.** 109 S Nicolet St 49701. I-75 exit 338 southbound, just n. Int corridors. **Pets:** Accepted. 📶 ✕ 🖥 🖵 🛏️

◆◆ **The Beach House** CA

(231) 436-5353. **$49-$197, 14 day notice.** 11490 W US 23 49701. 1.3 mi s. Ext corridors. **Pets:** Accepted. 📶 ✕ 🖥 🛏️ ✕ 🐾

◆◆◆ **Days Inn & Suites "Bridgeview Lodge"** M

(231) 436-8961. **$39-$199.** 206 N Nicolet St 49701. I-75 exit 339; at bridge. Ext/int corridors. **Pets:** Medium, dogs only. $50 deposit/pet. Designated rooms, service with restrictions, supervision.

📶 ✕ 🖥 🖵 🛏️

AAA ◆◆ **Days Inn Lakeview** M

(231) 436-5557. **$39-$199, 3 day notice.** 825 S Huron Ave 49701. I-75 exit 337 northbound, 0.5 mi n to US 23, then 0.3 mi e; exit 338 southbound, 0.8 mi se on US 23. Ext corridors. **Pets:** Small, dogs only. $25 daily fee/pet. Service with restrictions, crate.

SAVE 📶 ✕ 🖥 🖵 🛏️ ✕

◆ **Econo Lodge at the Bridge** M

(231) 436-5026. **Call for rates.** 412 N Nicolet St 49701. I-75 exit 339. Ext corridors. **Pets:** Medium, dogs only. $10 daily fee/pet. Supervision.

📶 ✕ 🖥 🖵

AAA ◆◆◆ **Econo Lodge Bayview** M

(231) 436-5777. **$39-$199, 3 day notice.** 712 S Huron Ave 49701. I-75 exit 337 northbound, 0.5 mi n to US 23, 0.3 mi e, then just n; exit 338 southbound, 0.8 mi se on US 23, then just n. Ext corridors. **Pets:** Medium. $25 daily fee/room. Crate.

SAVE 📶 ✕ 🖥 🖵 🛏️ ✕

◉ ▼▼▼ Fairview Beachfront Inn Ⓜ
(231) 436-8831. **$38-$198, 3 day notice.** 907 S Huron St 49701. 0.8 mi se on US 23. Ext corridors. **Pets:** Dogs only. $25 one-time fee/pet. Service with restrictions, crate. ⟨SAVE⟩ 🛜 ✕ 🛏 🖵 ⇌

▼▼ Holiday Inn Express at the Bridge Ⓗ
(231) 436-7100. **$49-$199.** 364 Louvigny 49701. I-75 exit 339. Int corridors. **Pets:** Small, dogs only. Designated rooms, service with restrictions, supervision. 🛜 ✕ ♿ᴹ 🛏 🖵 ⇌ ⊗

▼ Lamplighter Motel Ⓜ
(231) 436-5350. **$32-$97.** 303 Jamet St 49701. I-75 exit 339, just n of town. Ext corridors. **Pets:** Medium. $10 daily fee/pet. No service, supervision. 🛜 ✕ 🛏 🖵

◉ ▼▼▼ Super 8-Beachfront Ⓜ
(231) 436-7111. **$39-$199, 3 day notice.** 519 S Huron Ave 49701. I-75 exit 337 northbound, 0.5 mi n to US 23, 0.3 mi e, then just n; exit 338 southbound, 0.8 mi se on US 23, then just n. Ext corridors. **Pets:** Dogs only. $25 one-time fee/pet. Service with restrictions, crate.
⟨SAVE⟩ 🛜 ✕ 🛏 🖵 ⇌

◉ ▼▼▼ Super 8 Bridgeview Ⓗ
(231) 436-5252. **$39-$199, 3 day notice.** 601 N Huron Ave 49701. I-75 exit 339 northbound, just n, then just e. Ext/int corridors. **Pets:** Small, dogs only. $100 deposit/room. Crate.
⟨SAVE⟩ 🛜 ✕ 🛏 🖵 ⇌ ⊗

◉ ▼▼▼ Thunderbird Inn Mackinaw City Ⓜ
(231) 436-5433. **$49-$99.** 146 Old US 31 49701. I-75 exit 337 northbound, just ne; exit 338 southbound, 0.7 mi se. Ext corridors.
Pets: Accepted. ⟨SAVE⟩ 🛜 ✕ 🛏 🖵 ⇌

MANISTIQUE

▼▼ Comfort Inn by Choice Hotels Ⓗ
(906) 341-6981. **$80-$159.** 617 E Lakeshore Dr 49854. 0.5 mi e on US 2. Int corridors. **Pets:** Other species. $10 daily fee/pet. Service with restrictions, supervision. 🛜 ✕ 🛏 🖵

▼▼ Econo Lodge Lakeshore Ⓜ
(906) 341-6014. **Call for rates.** 1101 E Lakeshore Dr 49854. 1.5 mi e on US 2. Ext/int corridors. **Pets:** Accepted. 🛜 ✕ 🛏 🖵

▼▼ Peninsula Pointe Hotel Ⓗ
(906) 341-3777. **$79-$129.** 955 E Lakeshore Dr 49854. 1.4 mi e on US 2. Int corridors. **Pets:** Other species. $10 daily fee/pet. Supervision.
🛜 ✕ 🛏 🖵

MARQUETTE

◉ ▼ Birchmont Motel Ⓜ
(906) 228-7538. **$49-$80.** 2090 US 41 S 49855. On US 41, 1.8 mi n of jct SR 28; 4.3 mi s of downtown. Ext corridors. **Pets:** Accepted.
⟨SAVE⟩ 🛜 ✕ 🛏 ⇌

▼▼ Days Inn Ⓗ
(906) 225-1393. **$71-$91, 3 day notice.** 2403 US 41 W 49855. On US 41 and SR 28, 2.3 mi w. Int corridors. **Pets:** Accepted.
🛜 ✕ 🛏 🖵 ⇌ ⊗

▼▼ Holiday Inn Ⓗ
(906) 225-1351. **$139-$199.** 1951 US 41 W 49855. On US 41 and SR 28, 1.8 mi w. Int corridors. **Pets:** Dogs only. $25 daily fee/room. Service with restrictions, supervision. 🛜 ✕ ♿ᴹ 🛏 🖵 🍽 ⇌ ⊗

▼▼ Ramada Marquette Ⓗ
(906) 228-6000. **$89-$169.** 412 W Washington St 49855. 0.5 mi w on US 42 business route. Int corridors. **Pets:** $25 one-time fee/pet. Service with restrictions, crate. 🛜 ✕ 🛏 🖵 🍽 ⇌ ⊗

▼▼ Super 8 Ⓗ 🐾
(906) 228-8100. **$58-$81.** 1275 US 41 W 49855. On US 41 and SR 28, 1 mi w. Int corridors. **Pets:** Dogs only. $20 one-time fee/room. Designated rooms, service with restrictions, supervision. 🛜 ✕ 🛏 🖵 ⇌

MARSHALL

◉ ▼ Arbor Inn of Historic Marshall Ⓜ
(269) 781-7772. **$45-$69.** 15435 W Michigan Ave 49068. I-69 exit 36 (Michigan Ave), just w. Ext corridors. **Pets:** Accepted.
⟨SAVE⟩ 🛜 ✕ 🛏 ⇌

▼▼ Comfort Inn Ⓗ
(269) 789-7890. **$99-$189.** 204 Winston Dr 49068. I-69 exit 36 (Michigan Ave), just se. Int corridors. **Pets:** Accepted.
🛜 ✕ ♿ᴹ 🛏 🖵 ⇌ ⊗

▼▼▼ Hampton Inn-Marshall Ⓗ
(269) 789-0131. **$116-$125.** 325 Sam Hill Dr 49068. I-94 exit 110 (SR 227), just s. Int corridors. **Pets:** Other species. $25 daily fee/room. Service with restrictions, crate. 🛜 ✕ ♿ᴹ 🛏 🖵 ⇌

▼▼▼ Holiday Inn Express-Marshall Ⓗ
(269) 789-9301. **$109-$149.** 329 Sam Hill Dr 49068. I-94 exit 110 (SR 227), just s. Int corridors. **Pets:** $35 daily fee/room. Service with restrictions, crate. 🛜 ✕ ♿ᴹ 🛏 🖵 ⇌

MENOMINEE

▼▼▼ Econo Lodge On The Bay Ⓗ 🐾
(906) 863-4431. **$50-$80.** 2516 10th St 49858. 1 mi n on US 41. Int corridors. **Pets:** $10 daily fee/pet. Designated rooms, service with restrictions, supervision. 🛜 ✕ 🛏 🖵 ⊗

MIDLAND

◉ ▼▼▼ Best Western Valley Plaza Inn Ⓗ
(989) 496-2700. **Call for rates.** 5221 Bay City Rd 48642. US 10 exit Midland/Bay City Rd. Int corridors. **Pets:** Accepted.
⟨SAVE⟩ 🛜 ✕ 🛏 🖵 🍴 ⇌ ⊗

▼▼ Fairview Inn & Suites Ⓗ
(989) 631-0070. **$89-$125.** 2200 W Wackerly St 48640. Jct US 10 and Eastman Ave. Int corridors. **Pets:** Accepted. 🛜 ✕ 🛏 🖵 ⇌

▼▼ Sleep Inn of Midland Ⓗ
(989) 837-1010. **$85-$130.** 2100 W Wackerly St 48640. Jct US 10 and Eastman Ave. Int corridors. **Pets:** Other species. $10 daily fee/room. Service with restrictions, supervision. 🛜 ✕ 🛏 🖵 ⇌

MILAN

◉ ▼▼▼ Sleep Inn & Suites Ⓗ
(734) 439-1400. **$60-$200.** 1230 Dexter St 48160. US 23 exit 27 (Carpenter Rd), just w. Int corridors. **Pets:** Accepted.
⟨SAVE⟩ 🛜 ✕ ♿ᴹ 🛏 🖵 ⇌

MOUNT PLEASANT

◉ ▼▼▼ Comfort Inn & Suites Hotel and Conference Center Ⓗ
(989) 772-4000. **Call for rates.** 2424 S Mission St 48858. 2 mi s on US 127 business route. Int corridors. **Pets:** Accepted.
⟨SAVE⟩ 🛜 ✕ 🛏 🖵 ⇌

▼▼▼ Fairfield Inn & Suites Ⓗ
(989) 775-5000. **$103-$125.** 2525 S University Park Dr 48858. 2.5 mi s on US 127 business route. Int corridors. **Pets:** Other species. $20 daily fee/room. Service with restrictions, supervision.
🛜 ✕ 🛏 🖵 ⇌ ⊗

▼▼ Super 8 Ⓗ
(989) 773-8888. **$63-$148.** 2323 S Mission St 48858. 1.8 mi s on US 127 business route. Int corridors. **Pets:** Accepted.
🛜 ✕ ♿ᴹ 🛏 🖵

MUNISING

▼ Alger Falls Motel Ⓜ
(906) 387-3536. **$45-$175.** E9427 Hwy M-28 49862. 2 mi e on SR 28 and 94. Ext corridors. **Pets:** Accepted. 🛜 ✕ 🛏

◆◆ **AmericInn Lodge & Suites of Munising** [H]
(906) 387-2000. **$70-$170.** E9926 Hwy M-28 49854. On SR 28, 2.7 mi e. Int corridors. **Pets:** Accepted. 📶 🚭 ♿ ▣ 🖥 🏊 🏋

◆◆◆ **Holiday Inn Express Lakeview** [H]
(906) 387-4800. **Call for rates.** E8890 M-28 49862. On SR 28, 2 mi w of town. Int corridors. **Pets:** Accepted.
📶 🚭 ♿ ▣ 🖥 🏊 🏋

AAA ◆ **Terrace Motel** [M]
(906) 387-2735. **$50-$65.** 420 Prospect St 49862. 0.5 mi e, just off SR 28. Ext corridors. **Pets:** Accepted. [SAVE] 📶 🚭 🏋 ❄ ☎

NEW BUFFALO

◆◆◆ **Fairfield Inn & Suites** [H]
(269) 586-2222. **$126-$154.** 11400 Holiday Dr 49117. I-94 exit 1 (La Porte Rd). Int corridors. **Pets:** Accepted. 📶 🚭 ♿ ▣ 🖥 🏊

◆◆◆ **Holiday Inn Express Hotel & Suites** [H]
(269) 469-1400. **Call for rates.** 11500 Holiday Dr 49117. I-94 exit 1 (La Porte Rd), just w. Int corridors. **Pets:** Accepted.
📶 🚭 ♿ ▣ 🖥 🏊

NILES

◆◆ **Comfort Inn & Suites** [H]
(269) 684-3900. **Call for rates.** 1265 S 11th St (M-51) 49120. I-80/90 exit 77, n on SR 933 (which becomes SR 51), then 3.5 mi n. Int corridors. **Pets:** Accepted. 📶 🚭 ▣ 🖥 🏊

NORWAY

◆◆ **AmericInn Lodge & Suites of Norway** [H]
(906) 563-7500. **$81-$88.** W6002 US Hwy 2 49870. 0.7 mi w. Int corridors. **Pets:** Accepted. 📶 🚭 ▣ 🖥 🏊 🏋

OKEMOS

◆◆◆ **Comfort Inn-E Lansing/Okemos** [H]
(517) 347-6690. **$76-$171.** 2187 University Park Dr 48864. I-96 exit 110 (Okemos Rd), just n, then just e. Int corridors. **Pets:** Accepted.
📶 🚭 ♿ ▣ 🖥

◆◆◆ **Holiday Inn Express & Suites** [H]
(517) 349-8700. **$104-$114.** 2209 University Park Dr 48864. I-96 exit 110 (Okemos Rd), just n, then just e. Int corridors. **Pets:** Large, dogs only. $25 one-time fee/pet. Designated rooms, service with restrictions, crate.
📶 🚭 ♿ ▣ 🖥 🏊 🏋

◆◆◆ **Staybridge Suites - Lansing/Okemos** [H] 🐾
(517) 347-3044. **$89-$199.** 3553 Meridian Crossing Dr 48864. I-96 exit 110 (Okemos Rd), just n. Int corridors. **Pets:** Large. $75 one-time fee/room. Service with restrictions, crate. 📶 🚭 ♿ ▣ 🖥 🏊

PAW PAW

◆◆ **Comfort Inn & Suites** [H]
(269) 655-0303. **$72-$149.** 153 Ampey Rd 49079. I-94 exit 60 (SR 40), just nw. Int corridors. **Pets:** Large, other species. Service with restrictions, supervision. 📶 🚭 ♿ ▣ 🖥 🏊

PETOSKEY

AAA ◆◆ **Days Inn Petoskey** [M]
(231) 348-3900. **$53-$116.** 1420 Spring St 49770. 1.3 mi s on US 131. Ext corridors. **Pets:** Large, other species. $9 daily fee/pet. Service with restrictions, supervision. [SAVE] 📶 🚭 ▣ 🖥 🍴

◆◆◆ **Holiday Inn Express Hotel & Suites** [H]
(231) 487-0991. **$79-$299.** 1751 US 131 S 49770. I-75 exit 282, w on SR 32 to US 131 N. Int corridors. **Pets:** Medium, dogs only. $50 deposit/pet. Designated rooms, supervision. 📶 🚭 ▣ 🖥 🏊 🏋

PLAINWELL

AAA ◆◆◆ **Comfort Inn** [H]
(269) 685-9891. **$89-$125.** 622 Allegan St 49080. US 131 exit 49A, just e. Int corridors. **Pets:** Small. $15 daily fee/pet. Designated rooms, service with restrictions, supervision. [SAVE] 📶 🚭 ▣ 🖥 🏊

PORT HURON

AAA ◆◆ **Baymont Inn & Suites** [H]
(810) 364-8000. **$62-$107.** 1611 Range Rd 48074. I-94 exit 269 (Range Rd), just w. Int corridors. **Pets:** Medium. $15 daily fee/pet. Designated rooms, service with restrictions, supervision.
[SAVE] 📶 🚭 ▣ 🖥 🏊

◆◆ **Comfort Inn** [H]
(810) 982-5500. **$85-$170.** 1700 Yeager St 48060. I-94 exit 274 (Water St), just s, then just w. Int corridors. **Pets:** Dogs only. $50 deposit/room, $15 daily fee/pet. Designated rooms, service with restrictions, supervision.
📶 🚭 ▣ 🖥 🏊

PORTLAND

AAA ◆◆ **American Heritage Inn** [H]
(517) 647-2200. **$69-$149.** 1681 Grand River Ave 48875. I-96 exit 77, just n. Int corridors. **Pets:** Small, dogs only. $10 one-time fee/pet. Service with restrictions, supervision. [SAVE] 📶 🚭 ♿ ▣ 🖥 🏊

SAGINAW

◆◆ **Americas Best Value Inn Saginaw** [H]
(989) 755-0461. **Call for rates.** 1408 S Outer Dr 48601. I-75 exit 149B (SR 46), just w. Int corridors. **Pets:** Accepted.
📶 🚭 ▣ 🖥 🏊 🏋

◆◆ **Comfort Suites by Choice Hotels** [H]
(989) 797-8000. **$90-$179.** 5180 Fashion Square Blvd 48603. I-675 exit 6, 0.6 mi w on Tittabawassee Rd. Int corridors. **Pets:** Medium, other species. $50 one-time fee/room. Service with restrictions, supervision.
📶 🚭 ♿ ▣ 🖥 🏊

◆◆ **Country Inn & Suites Saginaw** [H]
(989) 792-7666. **Call for rates.** 2222 Tittabawassee Rd 48604. I-675 exit 6, just w. Int corridors. **Pets:** Accepted. 📶 🚭 ▣ 🖥 🏊

◆◆◆ **Residence Inn by Marriott** [H]
(989) 799-9000. **$149-$204.** 5230 Fashion Square Blvd 48604. I-675 exit 6, 0.8 mi w, then just n. Int corridors. **Pets:** Accepted.
📶 🚭 ▣ 🖥 🏊 🏋

ST. IGNACE

AAA ◆◆ **Budget Host Inn & Suites** [H]
(906) 643-9666. **$68-$154.** 700 N State St 49781. 1.8 mi n of bridge tollgate on I-75 business route. Ext/int corridors. **Pets:** Other species. $40 deposit/room. Service with restrictions, supervision.
[SAVE] 📶 🚭 ▣ 🖥 🏊 🏋

ST. JOSEPH

◆◆ **Silver Beach Hotel** [H]
(269) 983-7341. **Call for rates.** 100 Main St 49085. I-94 exit 23, 6 mi nw on Business Rt I-94. Int corridors. **Pets:** Accepted.
📶 🚭 ▣ 🖥 🏊 🏋

SANDUSKY

◆◆ **DeMott's West Park Inn** [H]
(810) 648-4300. **Call for rates.** 440 W Sanilac Rd 48471. On SR 46; center. Ext/int corridors. **Pets:** Small. Supervision.
📶 🚭 ▣ 🖥 🍴

SAULT STE. MARIE

◆◆ **Americas Best Value Inn** [H]
(906) 632-8882. **$53-$72.** 3826 I-75 Business Loop 49783. I-75 exit 392, 0.5 mi ne. Int corridors. **Pets:** Accepted. 📶 🚭 ▣ 🖥

Budget Host Crestview Inn M

(906) 635-5213. $59-$99. 1200 Ashmun St 49783. I-75 exit 392, 2.8 mi ne on I-75 business loop. Ext corridors. **Pets:** Other species. $15 daily fee/room. Designated rooms, service with restrictions, supervision.

Days Inn H

(906) 635-5200. $56-$90. 3651 I-75 Business Spur 49783. I-75 exit 392, 0.8 mi ne on I-75 business loop. Int corridors. **Pets:** Other species. $5 daily fee/room. Service with restrictions, crate.

Park Inn by Radisson Sault Sainte Marie, MI H

(906) 632-6000. $55-$90. 3525 I-75 Business Spur 49783. I-75 exit 392, 0.7 mi ne. Int corridors. **Pets:** Dogs only. $10 daily fee/room. Designated rooms, service with restrictions, supervision.

Ramada Plaza Ojibway Hotel H

(906) 632-4100. $79-$189. 240 Portage St W 49783. Just w of jct Ashmun St; downtown. Int corridors. **Pets:** Small, other species. $25 one-time fee/room. Designated rooms.

SOUTH HAVEN

Comfort Suites H

(269) 639-2014. $79-$209. 1755 Phoenix St 49090. I-196 exit 20, 0.5 mi e. Int corridors. **Pets:** Small, other species. $25 daily fee/pet. Service with restrictions, crate.

SPRING LAKE

Grand Haven Waterfront Holiday Inn H

(616) 846-1000. $99-$499. 940 W Savidge St 49456. On SR 104, just e of US 31. Int corridors. **Pets:** Accepted.

STEVENSVILLE

Candlewood Suites H

(269) 428-4400. **Call for rates.** 2567 W Marquette Woods Rd 49127. I-94 exit 23 (Red Arrow Hwy), just w. Int corridors. **Pets:** Accepted.

Hampton Inn of St. Joseph I-94 H

(269) 429-2700. $104-$189. 5050 Red Arrow Hwy 49127. I-94 exit 23 (Red Arrow Hwy), just se. Int corridors. **Pets:** Accepted.

SUTTONS BAY

Red Lion Motor Lodge M

(231) 271-6694. $59-$195. 4290 S West Bay Shore Rd 49682. 5 mi s on SR 22. Ext corridors. **Pets:** Accepted.

TAWAS CITY

Bay Inn Tawas H

(989) 362-0088. $63-$135, 3 day notice. 1020 W Lake St 48763. 1.5 mi s on US 23. Int corridors. **Pets:** $200 deposit/room. Service with restrictions, supervision.

THOMPSONVILLE

Crystal Mountain Resort & Spa H

(231) 378-2000. $149-$309, 14 day notice. 12500 Crystal Mountain Dr 49683. On SR 115, 2 mi w. Ext/int corridors. **Pets:** $35 one-time fee/room. Designated rooms, no service, supervision.

THREE RIVERS

Super 8 H

(269) 279-8888. $62-$115. 689 Super 8 Way 49093. Jct US 131 and SR 60 (W Broadway St), 0.3 mi s on US 131. Int corridors. **Pets:** Very small, dogs only. $50 deposit/pet, $11 daily fee/pet. Designated rooms, service with restrictions, supervision.

TRAVERSE CITY

Baymont Inn & Suites-Traverse City H

(231) 933-4454. $76-$144. 2326 N US 31 S 49684. 3.5 mi s on SR 37. Int corridors. **Pets:** Accepted.

Best Western Four Seasons H

(231) 946-8424. $49-$279. 305 Munson Ave 49686. 2 mi e on US 31. Int corridors. **Pets:** Other species. $15 daily fee/room. Service with restrictions, supervision.

Days Inn & Suites H

(231) 941-0208. $51-$153. 420 Munson Ave 49686. 2 mi e on US 31. Int corridors. **Pets:** Accepted.

Holiday Inn, West Bay H 🐾

(231) 947-3700. $79-$219. 615 E Front St 49686. 0.5 mi e on US 31. Int corridors. **Pets:** Large, other species. $15 daily fee/pet. Designated rooms, service with restrictions, supervision.

Park Place Hotel H

(231) 946-5000. $90-$290, 3 day notice. 300 E State St 49684. Corner of E State and Park sts; downtown. Int corridors. **Pets:** Accepted.

Quality Inn H 🐾

(231) 929-4423. $50-$200. 1492 US 31 N 49686. On US 31, 3.3 mi n. Ext/int corridors. **Pets:** Other species. $10 daily fee/room. Service with restrictions, supervision.

Traverse Victorian Inn H

(231) 947-5525. **Call for rates.** 461 Munson Ave 49686. 2.4 mi e on US 31. Int corridors. **Pets:** Small, dogs only. $25 one-time fee/pet. Service with restrictions, supervision.

WALKER

Baymont Inn & Suites-Grand Rapids North H

(616) 735-9595. $76-$134. 2151 Holton Ct NW 49544. I-96 exit 28 (Walker Ave), just s. Int corridors. **Pets:** Accepted.

Hampton Inn- Grand Rapids North H

(616) 647-1000. $99-$159. 500 Center Dr NW 49544. I-96 exit 30, just n on Alpine Rd, then 0.3 mi e. Int corridors. **Pets:** Service with restrictions, crate.

Quality Inn Grand Rapids North H

(616) 791-8500. $70-$129. 2171 Holton Ct 49544. I-96 exit 28 (Walker Ave), just s. Int corridors. **Pets:** Accepted.

SpringHill Suites by Marriott H

(616) 785-1600. $89-$149. 450 Center Dr 49544. I-96 exit 30, just n on Alpine Rd, then 0.3 mi e. Int corridors. **Pets:** Accepted.

WATERSMEET

Dancing Eagles Resort Lac Vieux Desert Casino H

(906) 358-4949. $45-$90. N5384 US Hwy 45 49969. 1.8 mi n of US 2. Int corridors. **Pets:** Accepted.

WHITEHALL

Comfort Inn H

(231) 893-4833. **Call for rates.** 2822 N Durham Rd 49461. US 31 exit 128, just e. Int corridors. **Pets:** Accepted.

WHITMORE LAKE

Best Western of Whitmore Lake M

(734) 449-2058. $90-$130. 9897 Main St 48189. US 23 exit 53, just e. Ext corridors. **Pets:** $20 daily fee/pet. Designated rooms, service with restrictions, crate.

MINNESOTA

AITKIN

▼ **Ripple River Motel & RV Park** M

(218) 927-3734. **$55-$90.** 701 Minnesota Ave S 56431. US 169, 0.8 mi s of jct SR 210. Ext corridors. **Pets:** Dogs only. $10 daily fee/pet. Designated rooms, service with restrictions, supervision. 🛜 🍴

ALBERT LEA

▼▼▼ **AmericInn Lodge & Suites of Albert Lea** H

(507) 373-4324. **Call for rates.** 811 E Plaza St 56007. I-90 exit 157 (CR 22), just se. Int corridors. **Pets:** Accepted. 🛜 🍴 🖥 🏊 ⊗

⦿ ▼▼▼▼ **Best Western Plus Albert Lea I-90 Hotel** H

(507) 373-4000. **$90-$130.** 821 Plaza St 56007. I-90 exit 157 (CR 22), just se. Int corridors. **Pets:** Accepted.
SAVE 🛜 ⊗ ⌖ 🍴 🖥 🏊

▼▼▼▼ **Comfort Inn** H

(507) 377-1100. **$89-$99.** 810 Happy Trails Ln 56007. I-35 exit 11, just se. Int corridors. **Pets:** Medium. $25 one-time fee/pet. Supervision.
🛜 ⌖ 🍴 🖥 🏊 ⊗

▼▼▼▼ **Country Inn & Suites By Carlson** H

(507) 373-5513. **$95-$180.** 2214 E Main St 56007. I-35 exit 12 southbound; exit 11 northbound, 1 mi w. Int corridors. **Pets:** $20 one-time fee/room. Designated rooms, service with restrictions, supervision.
🛜 ⌖ 🍴 🖥 🏊

ALEXANDRIA

⦿ ▼▼ **Best Western Alexandria Inn** H

(320) 762-5161. **$79-$120.** 508 Twin Blvd 56308. I-94 exit 103, just n, then just e on 50th St. Int corridors. **Pets:** Large. $10 daily fee/pet. Service with restrictions, supervision. SAVE 🛜 🍴 🖥 🏊 ⊗

⦿ ▼▼ **Country Inn & Suites By Carlson** H

(320) 763-9900. **$79-$139.** 5304 Hwy 29 S 56308. I-94 exit 103, just sw. Int corridors. **Pets:** Small, dogs only. $10 one-time fee/room. Designated rooms, service with restrictions, supervision.
SAVE 🛜 ⌖ 🍴 🖥 🏊 ⊗

▼▼▼▼ **Holiday Inn Alexandria** H

(320) 763-6577. **$120-$180.** 5637 State Hwy 29 S 56308. I-94 exit 103, just s. Int corridors. **Pets:** Accepted. 🛜 🍴 🖥 ⌖ 🏊 ⊗

▼▼ **Super 8** H

(320) 763-6552. **$57-$85, 7 day notice.** 4620 Hwy 29 S 56308. I-94 exit 103, 0.3 mi nw. Int corridors. **Pets:** Small, dogs only. $10 one-time fee/pet. Designated rooms, service with restrictions, supervision.
🛜 🍴

AUSTIN

▼▼▼ **Days Inn** H

(507) 433-8600. **$66.** 700 16th Ave NW 55912. I-90 exit 178A (4th St NW), just nw. Int corridors. **Pets:** Accepted. 🛜 🍴 🖥

▼▼▼ **Holiday Inn & Austin Conference Center** H

(507) 433-1000. **Call for rates.** 1701 4th St NW 55912. I-90 exit 178A (4th St NW), just nw. Int corridors. **Pets:** Accepted.
🛜 ⌖ 🍴 🖥 🍴 🏊 ⊗

BABBITT

▼▼▼ **Timber Bay Lodge & Houseboats** CA 🐾

(218) 827-3682. **$165-$798, 60 day notice.** 8347 Timber Bay Rd 55706. 2.8 mi e of jct CR 21 via CR 70 and 623. Ext corridors.
Pets: $15 daily fee/pet. No service, crate. 🛜 🍴 🖥 ⊗ 🏊

BAUDETTE

▼▼ **AmericInn Lodge & Suites of Baudette** H

(218) 634-3200. **Call for rates.** 1179 Main St W 56623. 0.5 mi w on SR 11. Int corridors. **Pets:** Accepted. 🛜 ⌖ 🍴 🖥 🏊 ⊗

BAXTER

▼▼▼ **Country Inn & Suites By Carlson** H

(218) 828-2161. **$89-$139.** 15058 Dellwood Dr N 56425. Jct SR 371 and 210, 1 mi n on SR 371. Int corridors. **Pets:** Medium. $30 one-time fee/room. Designated rooms, service with restrictions, supervision.
🛜 ⌖ 🍴 🖥 🏊

▼▼▼ **Holiday Inn Express, Three Bear Waterpark** H

(218) 824-3232. **Call for rates.** 15739 Audubon Way 56425. Just se of jct SR 371 and CR 77. Int corridors. **Pets:** Accepted.
⊗ ⌖ 🍴 🖥

⦿ ▼▼ **Super 8** M

(218) 828-4288. **$63-$149.** 14341 Edgewood Dr 56425. 0.5 mi n of jct SR 371 on SR 210. Int corridors. **Pets:** Service with restrictions, supervision. SAVE 🛜 🍴 🖥

BEMIDJI

AmericInn Lodge & Suites of Bemidji H
(218) 751-3000. **$80-$160.** 1200 Paul Bunyan Dr NW 56601. 0.5 mi e of northwest jct US 2, 71 and SR 197. Int corridors. **Pets:** Medium, dogs only. $30 one-time fee/pet. Designated rooms, service with restrictions, supervision. SAVE

Best Western Bemidji Inn H
(218) 751-0390. **$94-$104.** 2420 Paul Bunyan Dr 56601. Jct US 71 N and SR 197. Int corridors. **Pets:** Large, other species. $15 daily fee/room.
SAVE

Ruttger's Birchmont Lodge CA
(218) 444-3463. **$52-$390, 30 day notice.** 7598 Bemidji Rd NE 56601. Jct SR 197, 3.6 mi n on CR 21 (Bemidji Ave N). Ext/int corridors.
Pets: Accepted. SAVE

BRECKENRIDGE

Select Inn of Breckenridge/Wahpeton H
(218) 643-9201. **$62.** 821 Hwy 75 N 56520. Just sw of jct US 75 N and 210. Int corridors. **Pets:** Large. $10 daily fee/pet. Designated rooms, service with restrictions, supervision.

CALEDONIA

Caledonia Inn Lodge & Suites H
(507) 725-8000. **$90-$150.** 508 N Kruckow Ave 55921. Jct SR 44 and 76, just sw. Int corridors. **Pets:** Supervision.

CANBY

Canby Inn & Suites H ❀
(507) 223-6868. **$90-$175.** 127 1st St W 56220. Just w of US 75; center. Int corridors. **Pets:** $20 one-time fee/room. Designated rooms, service with restrictions, crate.

CANNON FALLS

Best Western Saratoga Inn H
(507) 263-7272. **$70-$140.** 31591 64th Ave 55009. Jct SR 19, 1 mi sw on US 52. Int corridors. **Pets:** Accepted. SAVE

CLOQUET

AmericInn Lodge & Suites of Cloquet H
(218) 879-1231. **Call for rates.** 111 Big Lake Rd 55720. I-35 exit 237 (SR 33), 2 mi nw. Int corridors. **Pets:** Dogs only. $50 deposit/room, $12 one-time fee/room. Designated rooms, supervision.

Super 8 H
(218) 879-1250. **$63-$125.** 121 Big Lake Rd 55720. I-35 exit 237 (SR 33), 2 mi nw. Int corridors. **Pets:** Accepted.

COOK

Ludlow's Island Resort CA ❀
(218) 666-5407. **$200-$600, 90 day notice.** 8166 Ludlow Dr 55723. US 53, 3.5 mi ne on CR 24, 5.1 mi e on CR 78 and 540. Ext corridors.
Pets: $30 daily fee/pet. Designated rooms, no service, supervision.

CROSSLAKE

Pine Peaks Lodge and Suites H
(218) 692-7829. **$80-$170, 3 day notice.** 14047 Swann Dr 56442. Jct CR 66 and Swann Dr. Int corridors. **Pets:** Accepted.

DEER RIVER

White Oak Inn & Suites H
(218) 246-9400. **$57-$160.** 201 4th Ave NW 56636. On US 2. Int corridors. **Pets:** $15 one-time fee/pet. Designated rooms, service with restrictions, supervision. SAVE

DEERWOOD

Country Inn of Deerwood H ❀
(218) 534-3101. **$79-$139.** 23885 Front St 56444. On SR 6 and 210, e of jct CR 12. Int corridors. **Pets:** Large. $10 daily fee/pet. Service with restrictions, supervision. SAVE

DETROIT LAKES

AmericInn Lodge & Suites of Detroit Lakes H
(218) 847-8795. **$80-$190.** 777 Hwy 10 E 56501. 1.4 mi se. Int corridors. **Pets:** Other species. $10 one-time fee/room, $5 daily fee/room. Service with restrictions, crate. SAVE

Best Western Plus Holland House H ❀
(218) 847-4483. **$89-$329, 3 day notice.** 615 Hwy 10 E 56501. 1.3 mi se. Ext/int corridors. **Pets:** Medium. $15 daily fee/pet. Designated rooms, service with restrictions, supervision. SAVE

Country Inn & Suites By Carlson H
(218) 847-2000. **Call for rates.** 1330 Hwy 10 E 56501. Just e of jct US 10 and CR 54 E. Int corridors. **Pets:** Accepted.
SAVE

Holiday Inn on the Lake H
(218) 847-2121. **Call for rates.** 1155 US 10 E 56501. 2 mi se. Int corridors. **Pets:** Accepted.

DULUTH

AmericInn Hotel & Suites of Duluth South H
(218) 624-1026. **$84-$210.** 185 US 2 55810. Jct I-35 and US 2, 0.8 mi n. Int corridors. **Pets:** $25 one-time fee/room. Service with restrictions, supervision. SAVE

Best Western Downtown Motel M
(218) 727-6851. **$60-$200.** 131 W 2nd St 55802. 2nd St at 2nd Ave W; center. Ext/int corridors. **Pets:** Accepted. SAVE

Country Inn & Suites By Carlson North H
(218) 740-4500. **$119-$229.** 4257 Haines Rd 55811. Just n of US 53. Int corridors. **Pets:** Accepted.

Country Inn & Suites By Carlson South H ❀
(218) 628-0668. **$65-$350.** 9330 W Skyline Pkwy 55810. I-35 exit 249 (Boundary Ave), just se. Int corridors. **Pets:** Dogs only. $20 one-time fee/pet. Designated rooms, service with restrictions, supervision.
SAVE

Days Inn-Duluth H
(218) 727-3110. **$52-$181.** 909 Cottonwood Ave 55811. SR 194, just n of jct US 53. Int corridors. **Pets:** Other species. $5 daily fee/room. Service with restrictions, supervision.

Econo Lodge Airport H ❀
(218) 722-5522. **$79-$139.** 4197 Haines Rd 55811. Just s of US 53. Int corridors. **Pets:** Other species. $10 one-time fee/room. Service with restrictions, supervision. SAVE

Edgewater Resort & Waterpark H ❀
(218) 728-3601. **$79-$329.** 2400 London Rd 55812. I-35 exit 258 (21st Ave E), just nw. Ext/int corridors. **Pets:** Other species. $20 daily fee/pet. Service with restrictions, supervision.

Fitger's Inn H
(218) 722-8826. **$129-$349.** 600 E Superior St 55802. I-35 exit 256B (Lake Ave), just ne. Int corridors. **Pets:** Large, other species. Designated rooms, service with restrictions, supervision.
SAVE

The Inn on Lake Superior H
(218) 726-1111. **$99-$329.** 350 Canal Park Dr 55802. In Canal Park area. Int corridors. **Pets:** Accepted.

Radisson Hotel Duluth-Harborview H
(218) 727-8981. **$89-$229.** 505 W Superior St 55802. At 5th Ave W; center. Int corridors. **Pets:** Accepted.

Residence Inn by Marriott H
(218) 279-2885. **$129-$159.** 517 W Central Entrance 55811. Just e on SR 194 from jct US 53. Int corridors. **Pets:** Large. $75 one-time fee/room. Service with restrictions, supervision.

Sheraton Duluth Hotel H
(218) 733-5660. **$99-$299.** 301 E Superior St 55802. I-35 exit 256B (Lake Ave), just nw. Int corridors. **Pets:** Large, dogs only. Designated rooms, service with restrictions, supervision.

The Suites Hotel at Waterfront Plaza H
(218) 727-4663. **$89-$549.** 325 Lake Ave S 55802. In Canal Park area. Int corridors. **Pets:** Medium. $15 daily fee/pet. Service with restrictions, supervision.

Voyageur Lakewalk Inn M
(218) 722-3911. **$40-$94.** 333 E Superior St 55802. I-35 exit 256 (Superior St), just n at jct 4th Ave E and Superior St. Ext corridors. **Pets:** $15 one-time fee/room. Designated rooms, service with restrictions, supervision.

ELY

Grand Ely Lodge Resort and Conference Center H
(218) 365-6565. **$109-$290, 14 day notice.** 400 N Pioneer Rd 55731. SR 169 to Central Ave, just n to Pioneer Rd, then 1 mi n. Ext/int corridors. **Pets:** $15 daily fee/pet. Designated rooms, service with restrictions, supervision.

Motel Ely-Budget Host M
(218) 365-3237. **$50-$130, 3 day notice.** 1047 E Sheridan St 55731. SR 1 and 169. Ext corridors. **Pets:** Dogs only. $10 one-time fee/room. Designated rooms, service with restrictions, supervision.

EVELETH

Super 8 H
(218) 744-1661. **$67-$134.** 1080 Industrial Park Dr 55734. On US 53, 0.5 mi n of jct SR 37. Int corridors. **Pets:** Dogs only. $15 daily fee/pet. Designated rooms, service with restrictions, supervision.

FAIRMONT

Comfort Inn H
(507) 238-5444. **Call for rates.** 2225 N State St 56031. I-90 exit 102 (SR 15), just s. Int corridors. **Pets:** Accepted.

Hampton Inn Fairmont H
(507) 235-2626. **$129-$159.** 100 Hampton Dr 56031. I-90 exit 102 (SR 15), just sw. Int corridors. **Pets:** Accepted.

Holiday Inn H
(507) 238-4771. **$109-$149.** 1201 Torgerson Dr 56031. I-90 exit 102 (SR 15), just s. Int corridors. **Pets:** Other species. $25 daily fee/room. Service with restrictions, supervision.

Super 8 H
(507) 238-9444. **$72.** 1200 Torgerson Dr 56031. I-90 exit 102 (SR 15), just s. Int corridors. **Pets:** Other species. $25 one-time fee/room. Service with restrictions, supervision.

FARIBAULT

AmericInn Motel & Suites of Faribault H
(507) 334-9464. **Call for rates.** 1801 Lavender Dr 55021. I-35 exit 59 (SR 21), 0.3 mi e. Int corridors. **Pets:** Accepted.

Days Inn & Suites H
(507) 334-6835. **$60-$102.** 1920 Cardinal Ln 55021. I-35 exit 59 (SR 21), just ne. Int corridors. **Pets:** Accepted.

FERGUS FALLS

AmericInn Lodge & Suites of Fergus Falls H 🐾
(218) 739-3900. **$84-$155.** 526 Western Ave N 56537. I-94 exit 54 (SR 210), just se. Int corridors. **Pets:** Other species. $10 one-time fee/room. Designated rooms, service with restrictions, supervision.

FINLAYSON

Americas Best Value Inn H
(320) 245-5284. **Call for rates.** 60671 State Hwy 23 55735. I-35 exit 195 (SR 23), just ne. Int corridors. **Pets:** Accepted.

FOSSTON

Super 8 H
(218) 435-1088. **$52-$83.** 108 S Amber Ave 56542. US 2, 0.5 mi e. Int corridors. **Pets:** Accepted.

GARRISON

Garrison Inn & Suites H
(320) 692-4050. **$75-$149.** 9243 Hwy 169 56540. SR 169, just s of jct SR 18. Int corridors. **Pets:** Small. $25 daily fee/pet. Designated rooms, service with restrictions, supervision.

GAYLORD

America's Best Inn & Suites M
(507) 237-5860. **Call for rates.** 330 Main Ave E 55334. 1.5 mi e. Int corridors. **Pets:** Accepted.

GRAND MARAIS

Best Western Plus Superior Inn & Suites H 🐾
(218) 387-2240. **$99-$359, 3 day notice.** 104 1st Ave E 55604. SR 61, just ne of center. Int corridors. **Pets:** Large. $15 daily fee/pet. Designated rooms, service with restrictions, supervision.

Gunflint Lodge VH 🐾
(218) 388-2294. **$99-$399, 31 day notice.** 143 S Gunflint Lake 55604. 43 mi nw on CR 12 (Gunflint Tr) from jct SR 61; 0.8 mi e on CR 50. Ext corridors. **Pets:** Other species. $20 daily fee/pet. Service with restrictions, crate.

Nor'Wester Lodge and Outfitter CA
(218) 388-2252. **$99-$259, 60 day notice.** 7778 Gunflint Tr 55604. 30 mi nw on CR 12 (Gunflint Tr) from jct SR 61. Ext corridors. **Pets:** Large, other species. $15 daily fee/pet. Service with restrictions, supervision.

Outpost Motel M
(218) 387-1833. **$49-$89.** 2935 SR 61 E 55604. SR 61, 9 mi ne. Ext corridors. **Pets:** Other species. $10 daily fee/pet. Supervision.

Wedgewood Motel M
(218) 387-2944. **$55-$85, 3 day notice.** 1663 E Hwy 61 55604. SR 61, 2.5 mi ne. Ext corridors. **Pets:** Dogs only. $5 daily fee/pet. Supervision.

GRAND RAPIDS

AAA ◆◆◆◆ **Country Inn & Suites By Carlson** **H** ✿

(218) 327-4960. **Call for rates.** 2601 S Hwy 169 55744. US 2, 2 mi s. Int corridors. **Pets:** Medium, dogs only. Supervision.

[SAVE] 📶 ᴋM 🛏 🖵 ➤

AAA ◆◆◆◆ **Sawmill Inn** **H**

(218) 326-8501. **$69-$109.** 2301 S Hwy 169 55744. US 2, 2 mi s on US 169. Ext/int corridors. **Pets:** Large, other species. Service with restrictions, supervision. [SAVE] 📶 🛏 🖵 ❜❜ ➤ ✕

GRANITE FALLS

◆◆ **Granite Falls Super Motel** **H**

(320) 564-4075. **$59-$129.** 845 W SR 212 56241. Jct SR 23, 0.5 mi w. Int corridors. **Pets:** Small. $25 one-time fee/pet. Designated rooms, service with restrictions, crate. 📶 ᴋM 🛏 ➤

HUTCHINSON

◆◆ **AmericInn of Hutchinson** **H** ✿

(320) 587-5515. **$76-$136.** 1115 Hwy 7 E 55350. 1 mi e of jct SR 15. Int corridors. **Pets:** Dogs only. $15 daily fee/room. Designated rooms, service with restrictions, supervision. 📶 ᴋM 🛏 🖵 ➤ ✕

AAA ◆◆ **Best Western Victorian Inn** **H**

(320) 587-6030. **$73-$90.** 1000 Hwy 7 W 55350. SR 15, 1 mi w. Int corridors. **Pets:** $10 one-time fee/room. Service with restrictions, supervision. [SAVE] 📶 🛏 🖵 ❜❜ ➤

INTERNATIONAL FALLS

◆◆ **AmericInn of International Falls** **H**

(218) 283-8000. **Call for rates.** 1500 US 71 W 56649. 1.5 mi w on US 71 and SR 11 W. Int corridors. **Pets:** $10 one-time fee/pet. Designated rooms, supervision. 📶 🛏 🖵 ❜❜ ➤ ✕

AAA ◆◆ **Hilltop Motel** **M**

(218) 283-2505. **$56-$89.** 2002 2nd Ave W 56649. US 53, 1 mi s of jct US 53 and SR 11. Ext corridors. **Pets:** Accepted. [SAVE] 📶 ✕

JACKSON

AAA ◆◆◆◆ **AmericInn Lodge & Suites of Jackson** **H**

(507) 847-2444. **$85-$180.** 110 Belmont Ln 56143. I-90 exit 73 (US 71), just sw. Int corridors. **Pets:** Small, dogs only. $10 daily fee/pet. Designated rooms, service with restrictions, supervision.

[SAVE] 📶 ᴋM 🛏 🖵 ➤

◆◆ **Econo Lodge** **H**

(507) 847-3110. **Call for rates.** 2007 US 71 N 56143. I-90 exit 73 (US 71), just nw. Ext/int corridors. **Pets:** $15 daily fee/pet. Designated rooms, service with restrictions, supervision. 📶 🛏 🖵 ❜❜ ➤

KASSON

◆◆ **AmericInn Motel & Suites of Kasson** **H**

(507) 634-3444. **$79-$159.** 301 8th St SE 55944. Just se of jct US 14 and SR 57. Int corridors. **Pets:** Accepted. 📶 ᴋM 🛏 🖵 ➤

LAMBERTON

◆ **Lamberton Motel** **M**

(507) 752-7242. **Call for rates.** 601 1st Ave W 56152. Just s of jct US 14 and Ilex St. Ext corridors. **Pets:** Accepted. 📶 🛏 🖵

LE CENTER

◆◆ **Guardian Inn Motel** **M**

(507) 357-2239. **Call for rates.** 550 Commerce Dr 56057. 1 mi e on SR 99. Ext/int corridors. **Pets:** Accepted. 📶 ✕ 🛏 🖵

LITCHFIELD

AAA ◆◆ **Knights Inn** **M**

(320) 693-2496. **Call for rates.** 1017 E Frontage Rd 55355. On US 12. Int corridors. **Pets:** Accepted. [SAVE] 📶 🛏 ➤

LONG PRAIRIE

AAA ◆◆◆ **Budget Host Inn** **M**

(320) 732-6118. **$66-$89, 3 day notice.** 417 Lake St 56347. On US 71 and SR 27, just s of jct SR 287. Ext corridors. **Pets:** $15 daily fee/pet. Designated rooms, service with restrictions, supervision.

[SAVE] 📶 🛏 🖵

LUTSEN

◆◆ **Solbakken Resort** **M**

(218) 663-7566. **$59-$89, 14 day notice.** 4874 W SR 61 55612. SR 61, 1.3 mi n of jct CR 4 (Caribou Tr). Ext corridors. **Pets:** Other species. $10 daily fee/pet. Designated rooms, no service, supervision.

✕ 🛏 🖵 ✕ ᴋ

MADELIA

AAA ◆◆◆ **Madelia Lodge & Suites** **H**

(507) 642-2004. **Call for rates.** 620 Haynes Ave NE 56062. Just nw of jct SR 60 and CR 3. Int corridors. **Pets:** Accepted.

[SAVE] 📶 ᴋM 🛏 🖵 ➤ ✕

MAHNOMEN

◆◆ **Shooting Star Casino Hotel & Events Center** **H**

(218) 935-2701. **Call for rates.** 777 Casino Rd 56557. 1 mi s on SR 59. Int corridors. **Pets:** Accepted. 📶 ᴋM 🛏 ❜❜ ➤ ✕

MANKATO

AAA ◆◆◆◆ **Best Western Plus Hotel & Restaurant** **H** ✿

(507) 625-9333. **$80-$115.** 1111 Range St 56003. 0.6 mi s of jct US 169 and 14. Int corridors. **Pets:** $10 daily fee/room. Designated rooms, service with restrictions, supervision. [SAVE] 📶 🛏 🖵 ❜❜ ➤ ✕

◆◆◆ **Comfort Inn by Choice Hotels** **H**

(507) 388-5107. **$65-$150.** 131 Apache Pl 56001. Just s of jct US 14 and SR 22 S. Int corridors. **Pets:** $10 daily fee/room. Designated rooms, service with restrictions, supervision. 📶 🛏 🖵 ➤

◆◆◆ **Days Inn** **H** ✿

(507) 387-3332. **$49-$76.** 1285 Range St 56001. 0.3 mi s of jct US 169 and 14. Int corridors. **Pets:** $10 daily fee/pet. Designated rooms, service with restrictions, supervision. 📶 🛏 🖵 ➤

AAA ◆◆◆◆ **GrandStay Residential Suites Hotel** **H**

(507) 388-8688. **$80-$150.** 1000 Raintree Rd 56001. 0.4 mi se of jct US 14 and CR 3. Int corridors. **Pets:** Small. $10 daily fee/pet. Service with restrictions, supervision. [SAVE] 📶 🛏 🖵 ➤ ✕

AAA ◆◆◆◆ **Mankato City Center Hotel** **H**

(507) 345-1234. **$80-$120.** 101 E Main St 56001. Main St at Riverfront Dr; downtown. Int corridors. **Pets:** Other species. $35 one-time fee/room. Service with restrictions, crate.

[SAVE] 📶 ✕ ᴋM 🛏 🖵 ❜❜ ➤ ✕

◆◆ **Microtel Inn & Suites** **H**

(507) 388-2818. **$56-$74.** 200 St. Andrews Dr 56001. US 14 exit CR 3, 0.4 mi n. Int corridors. **Pets:** Accepted. 📶 🛏 🖵

◆◆ **Super 8** **H**

(507) 387-0600. **$49-$81, 3 day notice.** 51578 US Hwy 169 N 56001. Jct US 169 and 14, just n. Int corridors. **Pets:** Accepted. 📶 🛏 🖵

MARSHALL

◆◆ **Comfort Inn** **H** ✿

(507) 532-3070. **$72-$108.** 1511 E College Dr 56258. SR 19, w of jct SR 23. Int corridors. **Pets:** $10 daily fee/pet. Service with restrictions, crate. 📶 ✕ ᴋM 🛏 🖵 ➤

◆◆ **Ramada Marshall** **H**

(507) 532-3221. **$92-$169.** 1500 E College Dr 56258. SR 19, just w of jct SR 23. Int corridors. **Pets:** Accepted.

📶 ✕ 🛏 🖵 ❜❜ ➤ ✕

▼▼ Super 8 H
(507) 537-1461. **$57-$70.** 1106 E Main St 56258. 0.3 mi se on US 59 from jct SR 23. Int corridors. **Pets:** Accepted. 🛜 🍴 💻

MCGREGOR
▼▼ Country Meadows Inn H
(218) 768-7378. **$65-$125.** 403 Meadows Dr 55760. Jct SR 65 and 210. Int corridors. **Pets:** Accepted. 🛜 🍴 💻 🏊

MINNEAPOLIS-ST. PAUL METROPOLITAN AREA

ANNANDALE
▼▼ AmericInn Lodge & Suites of Annandale H
(320) 274-3006. **$70-$139.** 620 Elm St E 55302. On SR 55. Int corridors. **Pets:** Accepted. 🛜 ⓜ 🍴 💻 🏊

BECKER
🔷 ▼▼▼ Crossings by GrandStay Inn & Suites of
Becker H
(763) 262-7700. **$69-$100.** 14435 Bank St 55308. Just e on US 10. Int corridors. **Pets:** $10 daily fee/pet. Service with restrictions, supervision.
SAVE 🛜 🍴 💻 🏊 ✖

BLAINE
🔷 ▼▼▼ Comfort Suites H
(763) 792-0750. **Call for rates.** 10580 Baltimore St NE 55449. 1.5 mi n of jct SR 65 and US 10 to 107th Ave NE, just e to Baltimore St NE, then just s. Int corridors. **Pets:** Accepted.
SAVE 🛜 ✖ ⓜ 🍴 💻 🏊 ✖

▼▼ Super 8 H
(763) 786-8888. **$72-$179.** 9410 Baltimore St NE 55449. Just n of jct US 10 and SR 65 to 93rd Ln, just e to Baltimore St NE, then just n. Int corridors. **Pets:** Small. $10 daily fee/pet. Designated rooms, service with restrictions, supervision. 🛜 ⓜ 🍴 💻 🏊

BLOOMINGTON
🔷 ▼▼▼ Best Western Plus Bloomington
Hotel H ❖
(952) 854-8200. **$130-$160.** 1901 Killebrew Dr 55425. Corner of SR 77 and Killebrew Dr. Int corridors. **Pets:** Medium. $20 daily fee/pet. Designated rooms, service with restrictions, supervision.
SAVE 🛜 ✖ 🍴 💻 🏊

🔷 ▼▼▼ DoubleTree by Hilton Bloomington -
Minneapolis South H
(952) 835-7800. **$79-$186.** 7800 Normandale Blvd 55439. Just nw of jct I-494 and SR 100, access via SR 100 and Industrial Blvd. Int corridors. **Pets:** Accepted. SAVE 🛜 ✖ 🍴 💻 🍴 🏊 ✖

▼▼ Extended StayAmerica
Minneapolis-Bloomington H ❖
(952) 884-1400. **$69-$84.** 7956 Lyndale Ave 55420. I-494 exit 4B (Lyndale Ave), just sw. Int corridors. **Pets:** Other species. $25 daily fee/pet. Service with restrictions. 🛜 🍴 💻

🔷 ▼▼▼ Hilton Minneapolis/Bloomington H
(952) 893-9500. **$89-$239.** 3900 American Blvd W 55437. I-494 exit 6B (France Ave), just sw. Int corridors. **Pets:** Accepted.
SAVE 🛜 🍴 💻 🍴 🏊

🔷 ▼▼▼ Hilton Minneapolis/St. Paul Airport Mall of
America H
(952) 854-2100. **$89-$209.** 3800 American Blvd E 55425. I-494 exit 1B (34th Ave), just se. Int corridors. **Pets:** Accepted.
SAVE 🛜 ⓜ 🍴 💻 🍴 🏊

🔷 ▼▼▼ Homewood Suites by Hilton H
(952) 854-0900. **$129-$199.** 2261 Killebrew Dr 55425. I-494 exit 2A (24th Ave), 1 mi s, then just w. Int corridors. **Pets:** Accepted.
SAVE 🛜 🍴 💻 🏊

▼▼ La Quinta Inn & Suites Minneapolis Bloomington
NW H
(952) 830-1300. **$64-$155.** 5151 American Blvd W 55437. I-494 exit 6B (France Ave), just se of SR 100, 1 mi w on frontage road. Int corridors. **Pets:** Medium, other species. Service with restrictions, supervision.
🛜 ⓜ 🍴 💻 🍴 🏊 ✖

▼▼ La Quinta Inn Minneapolis Airport Bloomington H
(952) 881-7311. **$64-$126.** 7815 Nicollet Ave S 55420. I-494 exit 4A (Nicollet Ave), just s. Int corridors. **Pets:** Medium, other species. Service with restrictions, supervision. 🍴 💻

🔷 ▼▼▼ Le Bourget Aero Suites, an Ascend Collection
hotel H ❖
(952) 893-9999. **$89-$149.** 7770 Johnson Ave 55435. I-494 exit 6B (France Ave), 0.5 mi nw on frontage road (78th St). Int corridors. **Pets:** Other species. $10 daily fee/pet. Service with restrictions, supervision. SAVE 🛜 ⓜ 🍴 💻 🍴 🏊

▼▼ Park Plaza Hotel Bloomington H
(952) 831-3131. **Call for rates.** 4460 W 78th Street Cir 55435. I-494 exit 6B (France Ave), 0.5 mi nw. Int corridors. **Pets:** Accepted.
ECO 🛜 🍴 💻 🍴 🏊 ✖

🔷 ▼▼▼ Ramada Mall of America - Airport H
(952) 854-3411. **$79-$189.** 2300 E American Blvd 55425. I-494 exit 2A (24th Ave), just s. Int corridors. **Pets:** Accepted.
SAVE 🛜 ⓜ 🍴 💻 🍴 🏊 ✖

▼▼▼ Residence Inn by Marriott H ❖
(952) 876-0900. **$199-$219.** 7850 Bloomington Ave S 55425. I-494 exit 3 (Portland/12th Ave), on south frontage road; behind Courtyard by Marriott Minneapolis/Bloomington. Int corridors. **Pets:** Large, other species. $75 one-time fee/room. 🛜 ✖ 🍴 💻 🏊 ✖

🔷 ▼▼▼▼ Sofitel Minneapolis H
(952) 835-1900. **$109-$299.** 5601 W 78th St 55439. Just nw of jct I-494 and SR 100, access via SR 100 and Industrial Blvd. Int corridors. **Pets:** Accepted. ECO SAVE 🛜 ✖ ⓜ 🍴 🍴

▼▼▼ Staybridge Suites H
(952) 831-7900. **$89-$269.** 5150 American Blvd 55437. I-494 exit 6B (France Ave), just se of SR 100, then 1 mi w on frontage road. Int corridors. **Pets:** Accepted. 🛜 ⓜ 🍴 💻 🏊

🔷 ▼▼▼ Super 8 H
(952) 888-8800. **$58-$71.** 7800 S 2nd Ave 55420. I-494 exit 4A (Nicollet Ave), just se. Int corridors. **Pets:** Medium. $10 daily fee/pet. Service with restrictions, supervision. SAVE 🛜 🍴 💻 ✖

BROOKLYN CENTER
▼▼ Comfort Inn by Choice Hotels H ❖
(763) 560-7464. **$70-$109.** 1600 James Cir N 55430. I-94/694 exit 34 (Shingle Creek Pkwy), just ne. Int corridors. **Pets:** Other species. $20 one-time fee/pet. 🛜 ⓜ 🍴 💻

🔷 ▼▼▼ Country Inn & Suites By Carlson H
(763) 561-0900. **$81-$159.** 2550 Freeway Blvd 55430. I-94/694 exit 34 (Shingle Creek Pkwy), just nw. Int corridors. **Pets:** Accepted.
ECO SAVE 🛜 🍴 💻 🏊

▼▼ **Extended StayAmerica-Minneapolis-Brooklyn Center** 🏠 ☼

(763) 549-5571. **$59-$79.** 2701 Freeway Blvd 55430. I-94/694 exit 34 (Shingle Creek Pkwy), 0.5 mi nw. Int corridors. **Pets:** Other species. $25 daily fee/pet. Service with restrictions. 🛰 🔋 💻

BROOKLYN PARK

▼▼ **La Quinta Inn & Suites Brooklyn Park** 🏠

(763) 971-8000. **$54-$114.** 7011 Northland Cir 55428. I-94/694 exit 30 (Boone Ave), just ne. Int corridors. **Pets:** Medium, other species. Service with restrictions, supervision. 🛰 🔋 🔋 💻 🌊

BURNSVILLE

 ▼▼▼ **Best Western Premier Nicollet Inn** 🏠 ☼

(952) 435-2100. **$110-$140.** 14201 Nicollet Ave S 55337. Just n of jct I-35W and CR 42. Int corridors. **Pets:** Large. $20 one-time fee/pet. Designated rooms, service with restrictions, crate.

[SAVE] 🛰 ✖ 🔋 🔋 💻 🍴 🌊

CHANHASSEN

 ▼▼▼ **AmericInn of Chanhassen** 🏠 ☼

(952) 934-3888. **$109-$195.** 570 Pond Promenade 55317. Just se of jct SR 5 and 101 S. Int corridors. **Pets:** Medium. $100 deposit/room, $30 one-time fee/room. Designated rooms, service with restrictions.

[SAVE] 🛰 ✖ 🔋 🔋 💻 🌊 ✖

COON RAPIDS

▼▼ **Country Inn & Suites By Carlson, Coon Rapids** 🏠

(763) 780-3797. **Call for rates.** 155 Coon Rapids Blvd 55433. US 10 exit Foley Blvd, 0.8 mi s to Coon Rapids Blvd, 0.5 mi e to Springbrook Dr, then just n. Int corridors. **Pets:** Accepted. 🛰 🔋 💻 🌊

▲▲▲ ▼ **Quality Inn Northtown** 🏠

(763) 785-4746. **Call for rates.** 9052 University Ave NW 55448. US 10 exit Foley Blvd, 0.6 mi. Int corridors. **Pets:** Accepted.

[SAVE] 🛰 🔋 💻 🌊

EAGAN

▲▲▲ ▼▼▼ **Best Western Plus Dakota Ridge** 🏠

(651) 452-0100. **$90-$140.** 3450 Washington Dr 55122. I-35E exit 97B (Yankee Doodle Rd), just sw. Int corridors. **Pets:** Medium, dogs only. $50 deposit/room, $20 daily fee/room. Designated rooms, service with restrictions, supervision. [SAVE] 🛰 ✖ 🔋 💻

▼▼ **Days Inn** 🏠

(651) 681-1770. **$68-$90.** 4510 Erin Dr 55122. Just ne of jct SR 77 and Cliff Rd. Int corridors. **Pets:** Accepted. 🛰 🔋 🔋 💻 🌊 ✖

▼▼ **Extended StayAmerica Minneapolis-Airport-Eagan** 🏠 ☼

(651) 681-9991. **$69-$79.** 3384 Norwest Ct 55121. I-35E exit 97, just nw. Int corridors. **Pets:** Other species. $25 daily fee/pet. Service with restrictions. 🛰 🔋 💻

▼▼ **Homestead Studio Suites Hotel-Minneapolis-Airport-Eagan** 🏠 ☼

(651) 905-1778. **$69-$79.** 3015 Denmark Ave 55121. I-35E exit 98 (Lone Oak Rd), just se. Int corridors. **Pets:** Other species. $25 daily fee/pet. Service with restrictions. 🛰 🔋 💻

▼▼ **Microtel Inn & Suites** 🏠

(651) 405-0988. **$45-$81, 7 day notice.** 3000 Denmark Ave 55121. I-35E exit 98 (Lone Oak Rd), just se. Int corridors. **Pets:** Medium, other species. $15 daily fee/room. Service with restrictions, supervision.
🛰 🔋 💻

▲▲▲ ▼▼ **Residence Inn Minneapolis-St. Paul Airport/Eagan** 🏠 ☼

(651) 688-0363. **$79-$119.** 3040 Eagandale Pl 55121. I-35E exit 98 (Lone Oak Rd), just sw. Ext corridors. **Pets:** Medium. $50 one-time fee/ room. Designated rooms, service with restrictions, supervision.
[SAVE] 🛰 ✖ 🔋 💻 🌊 ✖

▼▼▼ **Staybridge Suites** 🏠

(651) 994-7810. **Call for rates.** 4675 Rahncliff Rd 55122. I-35E exit 93 (Cliff Rd), just w, then just s. Int corridors. **Pets:** Accepted.
🛰 🔋 💻 🌊

▼▼▼ **TownePlace Suites Minneapolis St. Paul Airport/Eagan** 🏠

(651) 994-4600. **$89-$139.** 3615 Crestridge Dr 55122. I-35E exit 97A (Pilot Knob Rd), just se. Int corridors. **Pets:** Accepted.
🛰 ✖ 🔋 🔋 💻 🌊

EDEN PRAIRIE

▼▼▼ **Best Western Eden Prairie Inn** 🏠

(952) 829-0888. **$90-$110.** 11500 W 78th St 55344. I-494 exit 11A (Prairie Center Dr), just sw. Int corridors. **Pets:** Dogs only. $10 daily fee/pet. Service with restrictions, supervision. [SAVE] 🛰 🔋 💻 🌊

▼▼ **Extended StayAmerica Minneapolis-Eden Prairie** 🏠 ☼

(952) 941-1113. **$69-$79.** 7550 Office Ridge Cir 55344. I-494 exit 12, just se. Int corridors. **Pets:** Other species. $25 daily fee/pet. Service with restrictions. 🛰 🔋 💻

▼▼ **Homestead Studio Suites Hotel-Minneapolis-Eden Prairie** 🏠 ☼

(952) 942-6818. **$69-$79.** 11905 Technology Dr 55344. Just sw of jct I-494 and US 212 (Flying Cloud Dr). Int corridors. **Pets:** Other species. $25 daily fee/pet. Service with restrictions. 🛰 🔋 🔋 💻

▼▼▼ **Residence Inn by Marriott-Minneapolis SW** 🏠

(952) 829-0033. **$169-$186.** 7780 Flying Cloud Dr 55344. I-494 exit 11A (Prairie Center Dr), on US 169 S and 212 (Flying Cloud Dr). **Pets:** Accepted. 🛰 ✖ 🔋 💻 🌊

EDINA

▲▲▲ ▼▼▼ **Residence Inn Minneapolis-Edina** 🏠

(952) 893-9300. **$101-$152.** 3400 Edinborough Way 55435. I-494 exit 6B (France Ave), 0.3 mi n to Minnesota Dr, then just e. Int corridors. **Pets:** Accepted. [SAVE] 🛰 ✖ 🔋 💻

▲▲▲ ▼▼▼ **The Westin Edina Galleria** 🏠 ☼

(952) 567-5000. **$109-$429.** 3201 Galleria 55435. I-494 exit 6B (France Ave), 1.5 mi n, just e at the Galleria. Int corridors. **Pets:** Medium. Designated rooms, service with restrictions, supervision.
[SAVE] 🛰 ✖ 🔋 💻 🍴 🌊

FOREST LAKE

▼▼ **AmericInn Motel of Forest Lake** 🏠

(651) 464-1930. **$80-$110.** 1291 W Broadway Ave 55025. I-35 exit 131 (CR 2), just ne. Int corridors. **Pets:** Medium. $10 daily fee/pet. Designated rooms, service with restrictions, supervision. 🛰 🔋 💻 🌊

HASTINGS

▼▼ **AmericInn Lodge & Suites of Hastings** 🏠

(651) 437-8877. **Call for rates.** 2400 Vermillion St 55033. 1.5 mi s on US 61. Int corridors. **Pets:** Accepted. 🛰 🔋 🔋 💻 🌊

▼▼ **Hastings Country Inn** 🏠 ☼

(651) 437-8870. **$79-$97.** 300 33rd St 55033. 1.7 mi s on US 61, just e. Int corridors. **Pets:** Other species. $10 one-time fee/pet. Designated rooms, service with restrictions, crate. 🛰 🔋 💻 🌊

▼▼ **Regency Inn & Suites** 🏠

(651) 438-8888. **$55-$150, 14 day notice.** 2450 Vermillion St 55033. 1.5 mi s on US 61. Int corridors. **Pets:** Accepted. 🛰 🔋 💻

MAPLE GROVE

▼▼ **Extended StayAmerica Minneapolis-Maple Grove** 🏠 ☼

(763) 694-9747. **$69-$84.** 12970 63rd Ave N 55369. I-494 exit 26 (Bass Lake Rd), just ne. Int corridors. **Pets:** Other species. $25 daily fee/pet. Service with restrictions. 🛰 🔋 🔋 💻

▼▼ Select Inn ⊞
(763) 493-2277. **Call for rates.** 7285 Forestview Ln N 55369. I-94 exit 28 (CR 61/Hemlock Ln), just se. Int corridors. **Pets:** Accepted.

▼▼ Staybridge Suites Minneapolis-Maple Grove ⊞
(763) 494-8856. **$89-$145.** 7821 Elm Creek Blvd 55369. Just ne of jct I-94/494/694. Int corridors. **Pets:** Accepted.

MAPLEWOOD

ⒶⒶⒶ ▼▼ Emerald Inn ⊞
(651) 777-8131. **$50-$75.** 2025 County Rd D E 55109. I-694 exit 50 (White Bear Ave), just se. Int corridors. **Pets:** Accepted.

MINNEAPOLIS

ⒶⒶⒶ ▼▼ Aloft Minneapolis ⊞ ❀
(612) 455-8400. **$79-$299.** 900 Washington Ave S 55415. Jct 9th Ave. Int corridors. **Pets:** Medium, dogs only.

ⒶⒶⒶ ▼▼ Best Western Plus The Normandy Inn & Suites ⊞
(612) 370-1400. **$89-$209.** 405 S 8th St 55404. Corner of S 8th St and S 4th Ave. Int corridors. **Pets:** Dogs only. $100 deposit/room, $10 daily fee/room. Designated rooms, service with restrictions, crate.

ⒶⒶⒶ ▼▼ Days Hotel on University ⊞
(612) 623-3999. **$50-$153.** 2407 University Ave SE 55414. I-35W exit University Ave, 1 mi se. Int corridors. **Pets:** $20 one-time fee/pet. Designated rooms, service with restrictions, supervision.

ⒶⒶⒶ ▼▼▼▼ The Grand Hotel Minneapolis-A Kimpton Hotel ⊞ ❀
(612) 288-8888. **$149-$599.** 615 2nd Ave S 55402. Corner of 2nd Ave S and S 7th St. Int corridors. **Pets:** Other species.

ⒶⒶⒶ ▼▼▼▼ Graves 601 Hotel, Wyndham Grand Collection ⊞
(612) 677-1100. **$149-$359.** 601 1st Ave N 55403. Between 6th and 7th sts. Int corridors. **Pets:** Accepted.

ⒶⒶⒶ ▼▼▼ Hilton Minneapolis ⊞
(612) 376-1000. **$99-$309.** 1001 Marquette Ave S 55403. Between S 10th and S 11th sts. Int corridors. **Pets:** Accepted.

ⒶⒶⒶ ▼▼▼▼ Hotel Ivy ⊞
(612) 746-4600. **$389, 3 day notice.** 201 S 11th St 55404. 2nd Ave and 11th St. Int corridors. **Pets:** Accepted.

ⒶⒶⒶ ▼▼▼▼ The Marquette Hotel ⊞
(612) 333-4545. **$119-$409.** 710 Marquette Ave 55402. Jct Marquette Ave and S 7th St. Int corridors. **Pets:** Medium, other species. $50 one-time fee/pet. Designated rooms, service with restrictions, crate.

▼▼▼ Minneapolis Marriott City Center ⊞
(612) 349-4000. **$109-$319.** 30 S 7th St 55402. Between Hennepin and Nicollet aves; in City Center Shopping Complex. Int corridors. **Pets:** Accepted.

ⒶⒶⒶ ▼▼▼▼ Radisson Plaza Hotel Minneapolis ⊞
(612) 339-4900. **$99-$429.** 35 S 7th St 55402. Between Nicollet and Hennepin aves. Int corridors. **Pets:** Accepted.

ⒶⒶⒶ ▼▼▼ Residence Inn by Marriott Minneapolis Downtown City Center ⊞
(612) 677-1000. **$251-$307.** 45 S 8th St 55402. At 8th St and LaSalle Ave. Int corridors. **Pets:** Accepted.

▼▼▼ Residence Inn Milwaukee Road Depot ⊞ ❀
(612) 340-1300. **$129-$289.** 425 S 2nd St 55401. Jct S 2nd St and 5th Ave S. Int corridors. **Pets:** Other species. $100 one-time fee/room. Service with restrictions.

ⒶⒶⒶ ▼▼▼ Sheraton Minneapolis Midtown Hotel ⊞ ❀
(612) 821-7600. **$109-$299.** 2901 Chicago Ave S 55407. At Lake St. Int corridors. **Pets:** Medium, dogs only. Service with restrictions, supervision.

ⒶⒶⒶ ▼▼▼ The Westin Minneapolis ⊞
(612) 333-4006. **$129-$679.** 88 S 6th St 55402. At Marquette Ave. Int corridors. **Pets:** Accepted.

ⒶⒶⒶ ▼▼▼ ▼▼▼ W Minneapolis - The Foshay ⊞
(612) 215-3700. **$109-$699.** 821 Marquette Ave 55402. Between 9th and 8th sts. Int corridors. **Pets:** Accepted.

MINNETONKA

▼▼▼ Minneapolis Marriott-Southwest ⊞
(952) 935-5500. **$69-$209.** 5801 Opus Pkwy 55343. Just nw of jct US 169 and Cross Town SR 62 exit Bren Rd. Int corridors. **Pets:** Accepted.

ⒶⒶⒶ ▼▼▼ Sheraton Minneapolis West Hotel ⊞ ❀
(952) 593-0000. **$89-$199.** 12201 Ridgedale Dr 55305. I-394 exit 1C (Ridgedale Dr), 0.3 mi s. Int corridors. **Pets:** Medium. No service, supervision.

MONTICELLO

ⒶⒶⒶ ▼▼ Best Western Chelsea Inn & Suites ⊞
(763) 271-8880. **$90-$120.** 89 Chelsea Rd 55362. I-94 exit 193, 0.3 mi se. Int corridors. **Pets:** Medium, other species. $10 daily fee/room. Designated rooms, service with restrictions, supervision.

ⒶⒶⒶ ▼▼ Days Inn ⊞
(763) 295-1111. **$49-$75.** 200 E Oakwood Dr 55362. I-94 exit 193, 0.3 mi se. Int corridors. **Pets:** Accepted.

ⒶⒶⒶ ▼▼ Super 8 ⊞
(763) 295-5900. **Call for rates.** 1114 Cedar St 55362. I-94 exit 193, 0.3 mi se. Int corridors. **Pets:** Medium. $10 daily fee/room. Designated rooms, service with restrictions, supervision.

NEW BRIGHTON

▼▼▼ Homewood Suites New Brighton ⊞
(651) 631-8002. **$99-$171.** 1815 Old Hwy 8 NW 55112. I-35W exit 28A (CR 96). Int corridors. **Pets:** Medium. $150 one-time fee/room. Service with restrictions, crate.

NORTH BRANCH

▼▼ AmericInn Lodge & Suites of North Branch ⊞ ❀
(651) 674-8627. **$79-$180.** 38675 14th Ave 55056. I-35 exit 147 (SR 95), just e, just s on Oakview Ave, then w on Oak St. Int corridors. **Pets:** Other species. $30 one-time fee/room. Service with restrictions, supervision.

OAKDALE

▼▼ AmericInn Lodge & Suites of Oakdale ⊞
(651) 730-5700. **$79-$169.** 6630 Hudson Blvd N 55128. I-94 exit 247 (Century Ave), 0.7 mi n on Hudson Blvd (Frontage Rd). Int corridors. **Pets:** Medium, dogs only. $20 daily fee/room. Service with restrictions, crate.

AAA **WWWW** Best Western Regency Plaza Hotel 🏨 ❀
(651) 578-8466. **$69-$199.** 970 Helena Ave N 55128. I-694 exit 57, just e, then just s. Int corridors. **Pets:** Medium, dogs only. $20 daily fee/room. Service with restrictions, crate. [SAVE] 🛜 📶 🛗 💻 📺

OAK PARK HEIGHTS
WW AmericInn Lodge & Suites of Oak Park
Heights 🏨 ❀
(651) 275-0980. **Call for rates.** 13025 60th St N 55082. SR 36 at Still-water Blvd, just se. Int corridors. **Pets:** Other species. $15 daily fee/room. Service with restrictions, supervision. 🛜 ✕ 📶 💻 🏊 ✕

PLYMOUTH
AAA **WWWW** Best Western Plus Kelly Inn 🏨 ❀
(763) 553-1600. **$95-$110.** 2705 N Annapolis Ln 55441. I-494 exit 22 (SR 55), just e. Int corridors. **Pets:** Large, dogs only. Designated rooms, service with restrictions, supervision.
[SAVE] 🛜 📶 💻 🍴 🏊 ✕

WWW Comfort Inn 🏨
(763) 559-1222. **$69-$105.** 3000 Harbor Ln 55447. I-494 exit 22 (SR 55), 0.3 mi nw. Int corridors. **Pets:** Accepted. 🛜 📶 💻 🍴 🏊 ✕

AAA **WWWW** Crowne Plaza Minneapolis West 🏨
(763) 559-6600. **$79-$239.** 3131 Campus Dr 55441. I-494 exit 22 (SR 55), just e to CR 61 (Northwest Blvd), then 0.8 mi nw. Int corridors.
Pets: Accepted. [SAVE] 🛜 💻 🍴 🏊 ✕

AAA **WWW** Days Inn Minneapolis/West 🏨
(763) 559-2400. **$40-$84.** 2955 Empire Ln 55447. I-494 exit 22 (SR 55), just w. Int corridors. **Pets:** Other species. $10 daily fee/room. Service with restrictions, crate. [SAVE] 🛜 📶 📶 💻

AAA **WWW** Red Roof Inn 🅼
(763) 553-1751. **$50-$65.** 2600 Annapolis Cir N 55441. I-494 exit 22 (SR 55), just se. Ext corridors. **Pets:** Large, other species. No service, super-vision. [SAVE] 🛜 📶

WWWW Residence Inn by Marriott 🏨
(763) 577-1600. **$89-$279.** 2750 Annapolis Cir 55441. I-494 exit 22 (SR 55), just e to CR 61, just nw. Int corridors. **Pets:** Accepted.
🛜 ✕ 📶 💻 🏊

RICHFIELD
WWWW Candlewood Suites 🏨
(612) 869-7704. **$129-$169.** 351 W 77th St 55423. I-494 exit 4B (Lyn-dale Ave), just ne. Int corridors. **Pets:** $15 daily fee/room. Service with restrictions. 🛜 📶 📶 💻

ROGERS
WW AmericInn Lodge & Suites of Rogers 🏨
(763) 428-4346. **$79-$149.** 21800 Industrial Blvd 55374. I-94 exit 207 (SR 101), just sw. Int corridors. **Pets:** Accepted. 🛜 📶 💻 🏊

AAA **WWWW** Hampton Inn & Suites 🏨 ❀
(763) 425-0044. **$99-$199.** 13550 Commerce Blvd 55374. I-94 exit 207 (SR 101), 0.4 mi ne. Int corridors. **Pets:** Medium. Designated rooms, service with restrictions, supervision.
[SAVE] 🛜 ✕ 📶 📶 💻 🏊

ROSEVILLE
AAA **WWW** Days Inn St. Paul NW/Roseville 🏨
(651) 636-6730. **$43-$113.** 2550 Cleveland Ave N 55113. I-35W exit 24 (CR C), 0.3 mi se. Int corridors. **Pets:** Accepted. [SAVE] 🛜 📶 💻

WWW Residence Inn 🏨
(651) 636-0680. **$174-$192.** 2985 Centre Pointe Dr 55113. I-35W exit 25A (CR D), just se. Int corridors. **Pets:** Accepted.
🛜 ✕ 📶 📶 💻 🏊 ✕

ST. LOUIS PARK
AAA **WWWW** DoubleTree by Hilton Hotel Minneapolis - Park
Place 🏨 ❀
(952) 542-8600. **$89-$229.** 1500 Park Place Blvd 55416. I-394 exit 5 (Park Place Blvd), just sw. Int corridors. **Pets:** Small. $15 daily fee/pet. Service with restrictions, crate. [SAVE] 🛜 📶 💻 🍴 🏊

WWWW Homewood Suites St. Louis Park/Minneapolis
West 🏨
(952) 544-0495. **$99-$359.** 5305 Wayzata Blvd 55416. I-394 exit 5 (Park Place Blvd), just se. Int corridors. **Pets:** Accepted.
🛜 📶 📶 💻 🏊

WWWW TownePlace Suites Minneapolis West St. Louis
Park 🏨
(952) 847-6900. **$69-$259.** 1400 Zarthan Ave S 55416. I-394 exit 5 (Park Place Blvd), 0.3 mi w on 16th, then just n. Int corridors. **Pets:** Accepted.
🛜 ✕ 📶 💻 🏊

ST. PAUL
AAA **WWW** Best Western Bandana Square 🏨
(651) 647-1637. **Call for rates.** 1010 Bandana Blvd W 55108. I-94 exit 239B (Lexington Pkwy), 1.3 mi n, then 0.3 mi w on Energy Park Dr. Int corridors. **Pets:** Accepted. [SAVE] 🛜 📶 📶 💻 🏊 ✕

AAA **WWWW** Best Western Plus Kelly Inn 🏨
(651) 227-8711. **$99-$159.** 161 St. Anthony Ave 55103. Jct I-35E and 94. Int corridors. **Pets:** Medium, other species. Service with restrictions, crate. [SAVE] 🛜 📶 💻 🍴 🏊 ✕

WW Super 8 🏨
(651) 771-5566. **$53-$99.** 1739 Old Hudson Rd 55106. I-94 exit 245 (White Bear Ave), just nw. Int corridors. **Pets:** Accepted. 🛜 📶 💻

SHAKOPEE
WW Americas Best Value Inn & Suites 🏨
(952) 445-3644. **$49-$139.** 1244 Canterbury Rd 55379. Just nw of US 169. Int corridors. **Pets:** Accepted. 🛜 📶 💻 🍴 🏊

WWW Country Inn & Suites By Carlson 🏨
(952) 445-0200. **$89-$199.** 1204 Ramsey St 55379. Just ne of US 169. Int corridors. **Pets:** Accepted. 🛜 📶 📶 💻 🏊

WW Sandalwood Studios & Suites 🏨
(952) 277-0100. **$39-$109.** 3910 12th Ave E 55379. Just nw of US 169. Int corridors. **Pets:** Small, other species. $10 daily fee/room. Designated rooms, service with restrictions, supervision. 🛜 📶

SOUTH ST. PAUL
WW Clarion South Saint Paul Hotel & Conference
Center 🏨
(651) 455-3600. **$84-$149.** 701 Concord St S 55075. I-494 exit 64B (SR 56/Concord St), 0.3 mi n. Int corridors. **Pets:** Accepted.
🛜 📶 📶 💻 🍴 🏊 ✕

STILLWATER
WW Americas Best Value Inn 🏨
(651) 430-1300. **Call for rates.** 1750 W Frontage Rd 55082. SR 36 at Washington Ave, just ne. Int corridors. **Pets:** Accepted.
🛜 📶 📶 💻 🏊

WW Super 8 🏨
(651) 430-3990. **$41-$80.** 2190 W Frontage Rd 55082. SR 36 at Wash-ington Ave. Int corridors. **Pets:** Other species. $10 one-time fee/room. Supervision. 🛜 📶 💻

WACONIA
WWWW AmericInn Lodge & Suites of Waconia 🏨 ❀
(952) 442-8787. **Call for rates.** 550 Cherry Dr 55387. Just nw of jct SR 5. Int corridors. **Pets:** Small, dogs only. $10 daily fee/pet. Designated rooms, service with restrictions, crate. 🛜 ✕ 📶 💻 🏊

▼▼ Waconia Inn & Suites ⓜ

(952) 442-5147. **Call for rates.** 301 E Frontage Rd 55387. On SR 5 at jct CR 10. Int corridors. **Pets:** Other species. $10 daily fee/pet. Designated rooms, service with restrictions. 🛜 🔲 🖵

WHITE BEAR LAKE

▼▼ AmericInn Lodge & Suites of White Bear Lake Ⓗ

(651) 429-7131. **$79-$149.** 4675 White Bear Pkwy 55110. I-35E exit 117, just ne of jct SR 96. Int corridors. **Pets:** Small, dogs only. $10 one-time fee/pet. Designated rooms, service with restrictions, supervision.

🛜 ⊠ ⓛⓜ 🔲 🖵 ⊃ ⊠

Ⓐ ▼▼▼ Best Western Plus White Bear Country Inn Ⓗ

(651) 429-5393. **$80-$120.** 4940 N Hwy 61 55110. Jct SR 96, 1 mi n. Int corridors. **Pets:** Medium, other species. $10 one-time fee/room. Designated rooms, supervision. ⟨SAVE⟩ 🛜 🔲 🖵 🍽 ⊃ ⊠

WOODBURY

▼▼ Extended
StayAmerica-Minneapolis-Woodbury Ⓗ ☙

(651) 501-1085. **$69-$79.** 10020 Hudson Rd 55125. I-94 exit 251, just se. Int corridors. **Pets:** Other species. $25 daily fee/pet. Service with restrictions. 🛜 🔲 🖵

▼▼▼ Holiday Inn Express Hotel & Suites Ⓗ

(651) 702-0200. **$107-$189.** 9840 Norma Ln 55125. I-94 exit 251, just sw. Int corridors. **Pets:** Accepted. 🛜 ⊠ 🔲 🖵 ⊃

Ⓐ ▼▼▼ Red Roof Inn #7063 ⓜ

(651) 738-7160. **$49-$85.** 1806 Wooddale Dr 55125. I-494 exit 59 (Valley Creek Rd), just se. Ext corridors. **Pets:** Large, other species. No service, supervision. ⟨SAVE⟩ 🛜

Ⓐ ▼▼▼ Sheraton St. Paul Woodbury Hotel Ⓗ ☙

(651) 209-3280. **$99-$249.** 676 Bielenberg Dr 55125. I-494 exit 59C (Tamarack Rd), just ne. Int corridors. **Pets:** Dogs only. Service with restrictions, supervision. ⟨SAVE⟩ 🛜 ⊠ ⓛⓜ 🔲 🖵 🍽 ⊃

END METROPOLITAN AREA

MONTEVIDEO

Ⓐ ▼▼▼ Crossings by GrandStay Inn & Suites Ⓗ

(320) 269-8000. **$87-$152, 30 day notice.** 1805 E SR 7 56265. On SR 7; east of downtown. Int corridors. **Pets:** Other species. $200 deposit/room, $10 daily fee/room. Designated rooms, service with restrictions, supervision. ⟨SAVE⟩ 🛜 🔲 🖵 ⊃

MOORHEAD

▼▼ Travelodge & Suites Ⓗ

(218) 233-5333. **$72-$90.** 3027 S Frontage Rd 56560. Just s of US 10 E; east of downtown. Int corridors. **Pets:** Designated rooms, service with restrictions, supervision. 🛜 ⓛⓜ 🔲 🖵 ⊃

MOOSE LAKE

▼▼ AmericInn Lodge & Suites of Moose Lake Ⓗ

(218) 485-8885. **$70-$170.** 400 Park Place Dr 55767. I-35 exit 214 (SR 73), just sw. Int corridors. **Pets:** Medium. Designated rooms, crate.

🛜 🔲 🖵 ⊃

MOUNTAIN IRON

▼▼ AmericInn Lodge & Suites of Virginia Ⓗ ☙

(218) 741-7839. **$104-$158.** 5480 Mountain Iron Dr 55792. US 53, just s of jct US 169. Int corridors. **Pets:** Medium, dogs only. $15 daily fee/pet. Designated rooms, service with restrictions, supervision.

🛜 ⓛⓜ 🔲 🖵 ⊃ ⊠

▼▼▼ Holiday Inn Express & Suites Ⓗ

(218) 741-7411. **$99-$179.** 8570 Rock Ridge Dr 55768. On US 169, just w of jct US 53. Int corridors. **Pets:** Accepted. 🛜 🔲 🖵 ⊃

NEW ULM

▼▼▼ Holiday Inn Ⓗ

(507) 359-2941. **$90-$179.** 2101 S Broadway 56073. SR 15/68, 1.8 mi se. Int corridors. **Pets:** Accepted. 🛜 🔲 🖵 🍽 ⊃ ⊠

Ⓐ ▼▼▼ Microtel Inn & Suites Ⓗ

(507) 354-9800. **$54-$104.** 424 20th St S 56073. Just e of jct SR 15/68 and CR 37. Int corridors. **Pets:** $10 daily fee/room. Designated rooms, service with restrictions, crate. ⟨SAVE⟩ 🛜 ⓛⓜ 🔲 🖵 ⊃

NISSWA

Ⓐ ▼▼ Nisswa Motel ⓜ

(218) 963-7611. **$59-$102, 5 day notice.** 5370 Merrill Ave 56468. Just sw of Main St; center. Ext corridors. **Pets:** Medium, dogs only. $5 daily fee/pet. Designated rooms, service with restrictions, supervision.

⟨SAVE⟩ 🛜 🔲 🖵

NORTHFIELD

▼▼ Americas Best Value Inn & Suites Ⓗ

(507) 663-0371. **Call for rates.** 1420 Riverview Dr 55057. 1.3 mi w of jct SR 19 and 3. Int corridors. **Pets:** Accepted. 🛜 🔲 🖵 ⊃

ORR

▼▼ North Country Inn Ⓗ

(218) 757-3778. **Call for rates.** 4483 Hwy 53 55771. 0.3 mi s. Int corridors. **Pets:** Accepted. 🛜 ⊠ ⓛⓜ 🔲

OTTERTAIL

Ⓐ ▼▼▼ Thumper Pond Resort Ⓗ

(218) 367-2000. **Call for rates.** 300 Thumper Lodge Rd 56571. Jct SR 108 and 78. Int corridors. **Pets:** Dogs only. $20 daily fee/pet. Service with restrictions, crate. ⟨SAVE⟩ 🛜 ⊠ 🔲 🖵 🍽 ⊠

OWATONNA

▼▼ AmericInn of Owatonna Ⓗ

(507) 455-1142. **Call for rates.** 245 Florence Ave 55060. I-35 exit 41 (Bridge St), 0.3 mi ne. Int corridors. **Pets:** Accepted.
🛜 🔲 🖵 ⊃ ⊠

▼▼▼ Comfort Inn Ⓗ

(507) 444-0818. **$99-$199.** 2345 43rd St NW 55060. I-35 exit 45 (Clinton Falls), just sw. Int corridors. **Pets:** Accepted. ⓛⓜ 🔲 🖵 ⊃

▼▼▼ Holiday Inn Hotel & Suites Ⓗ

(507) 446-8900. **$114-$149.** 2365 43rd St NW 55060. I-35 exit 45 (Clinton Falls), just sw. Int corridors. **Pets:** Accepted.
🛜 ⊠ 🔲 🖵 🍽 ⊃ ⊠

▼▼ Microtel Inn & Suites Ⓗ

(507) 446-0228. **$54-$72.** 150 St. John Dr NW 55060. I-35 exit 41 (Bridge St), just nw. Int corridors. **Pets:** Accepted. 🛜 ⓛⓜ 🔲 🖵

PARK RAPIDS

◆◆ C'mon Inn 🅷

(218) 732-1471. **$90-$174.** 1009 1st St E 56470. SR 34, 0.8 mi e of jct US 71. Int corridors. **Pets:** Accepted. 🛜 🛂 💻 🌊

PAYNESVILLE

◆◆ Paynesville Inn & Suites 🅷

(320) 243-4146. **Call for rates.** 700 W Hwy 23 56362. Jct SR 55, 0.3 mi s. Int corridors. **Pets:** Accepted. 🛜 🛂 💻 🌊

PEQUOT LAKES

AAA ◆◆ AmericInn Lodge & Suites of Pequot
Lakes 🅷

(218) 568-8400. **Call for rates.** 32912 Paul Bunyan Trail Dr (SR 371/CR 16) 56472. SR 371, 2 mi n of downtown. Int corridors. **Pets:** Dogs only. $10 daily fee/pet. Designated rooms, service with restrictions, supervision. SAVE 🛜 ✖ 🛂 💻 🌊 ✖

PERHAM

◆◆ Super 8 🅷

(218) 346-7888. **$58-$72.** 106 Jake St SE 56573. SR 78, just nw of jct US 10. Int corridors. **Pets:** Other species. $10 daily fee/pet. Service with restrictions, supervision. 🛜 🛂 💻

PINE RIVER

◆◆ Rodeway Inn Ⓜ

(218) 587-4499. **Call for rates.** 2684 SR 371 SW 56474. 1 mi s. Ext corridors. **Pets:** Small. $20 deposit/room. Supervision. 🛜 🛂 💻 ✖

RED WING

◆◆ Days Inn Ⓜ

(651) 388-3568. **$56-$86.** 955 E 7th St 55066. US 61/63, 1.7 mi se. Ext corridors. **Pets:** Dogs only. $7 daily fee/pet. Service with restrictions, supervision. 🛜 🛂 💻 🌊

ROCHESTER

◆◆ AmericInn Hotel & Suites Rochester Airport 🅷

(507) 536-7000. **$80-$150.** 7320 Airport View Dr SW 55902. On US 63 (Broadway), airport exit. Int corridors. **Pets:** $25 one-time fee/room. Designated rooms, service with restrictions, supervision. 🛜 ✖ 🛂 🛂 💻 🌊 ✖

AAA ◆◆◆ Best Western Plus Soldiers Field Tower &
Suites 🅷

(507) 288-2677. **$93-$121.** 401 6th St SW 55902. 4th Ave SW at 6th St; just s of Mayo Clinic. Ext/int corridors. **Pets:** $10 daily fee/pet. Designated rooms, service with restrictions, crate. SAVE 🛜 🛂 💻 🍽 🌊 ✖

◆◆◆ Clarion Inn 🅷

(507) 288-1844. **Call for rates.** 1630 S Broadway 55904. 0.5 mi s of jct US 14 and 63 (Broadway). Ext/int corridors. **Pets:** $15 daily fee/room. Service with restrictions. 🛜 🛂 💻 🍽 🌊 ✖

◆◆ Comfort Inn 🅷

(507) 289-3344. **Call for rates.** 5708 Bandel Rd NW 55901. US 52 exit 55th St, just n on E Frontage Rd. Int corridors. **Pets:** Medium, dogs only. $35 one-time fee/room. Service with restrictions, supervision. 🛜 ✖ 🛂 🛂 💻 🌊 ✖

◆◆ Extended StayAmerica-Rochester North 🅷 🐾

(507) 289-7444. **$59-$79.** 2814 43rd St NW 55901. Just nw from jct US 52. Int corridors. **Pets:** Other species. $25 daily fee/pet. Service with restrictions. 🛜 🛂 💻

◆◆ Extended StayAmerica-Rochester-South 🅷 🐾

(507) 536-7444. **$59-$79.** 55 Wood Lake Dr SE 55904. US 63 (Broadway) exit 49th St S, 0.7 mi ne. Int corridors. **Pets:** Other species. $25 daily fee/pet. Service with restrictions. 🛜 🛂 💻

◆◆ GuestHouse International Inn & Suites 🅷

(507) 288-9090. **Call for rates.** 435 16th Ave NW 55901. Just se of jct US 14 and 52; exit Civic Center Dr. Int corridors. **Pets:** Accepted. SAVE 🛜 ✖ 🛂 🛂 💻 🍽 🌊 ✖

AAA ◆◆◆ International Hotel 🅷

(507) 328-8000. **Call for rates.** 20 SW 2nd Ave 55902. Opposite Mayo Clinic and Methodist Hospital; 11th Floor of The Kahler Grand Hotel. Int corridors. **Pets:** Accepted. SAVE 🛜 ✖ 🛂 💻 🌊 ✖

◆◆◆ The Kahler Grand Hotel 🅷

(507) 280-6200. **Call for rates.** 20 SW 2nd Ave 55902. Opposite Mayo Clinic and Methodist Hospital. Int corridors. **Pets:** Accepted. 🛜 ✖ 🛂 💻 🍽 🌊 ✖

◆◆ Kahler Inn & Suites 🅷

(507) 285-9200. **Call for rates.** 9 NW 3rd Ave 55901. Just n of Mayo Clinic. Int corridors. **Pets:** Accepted. 🛜 ✖ 🛂 💻 🍽 🌊 ✖

◆◆◆ Marriott Hotel 🅷

(507) 280-6000. **$233-$289.** 101 1st Ave SW 55902. Just e of Mayo Clinic. Int corridors. **Pets:** $100 one-time fee/room. Designated rooms, service with restrictions, crate. 🛜 ✖ 🛂 💻 🍽 🌊 ✖

◆◆ Microtel Inn & Suites 🅷

(507) 286-8780. **$50-$117.** 4210 Hwy 52 N 55901. US 52 exit 58 (41st St NW), just w. Int corridors. **Pets:** Accepted. 🛜 🛂 🛂 💻

AAA ◆◆◆ Quality Inn & Suites 🅷 🐾

(507) 282-8091. **$68-$100.** 1620 1st Ave SE 55904. On US 63 (Broadway) from jct US 14, 0.5 mi s, just e on 16th St, then just s. Ext/int corridors. **Pets:** Other species. $15 daily fee/pet. Service with restrictions, crate. SAVE 🛜 ✖ 🛂 💻

◆◆◆ Residence Inn by Marriott 🅷

(507) 292-1400. **$113-$229.** 441 W Center St 55902. Just n of Mayo Clinic; downtown. Int corridors. **Pets:** Other species. $100 one-time fee/room. Designated rooms. 🛜 ✖ 🛂 🛂 💻

◆◆◆ Staybridge Suites 🅷

(507) 289-6600. **$121-$131.** 1211 2nd St SW 55902. US 52/14 exit 55B (2nd St SW), just e. Int corridors. **Pets:** Accepted. 🛜 ✖ 🛂 💻 🌊

◆◆◆ TownePlace Suites 🅷

(507) 281-1200. **$119-$199.** 2829 NW 43rd St 55901. US 52 exit 41st St NW, just w, just n on W Frontage Rd, then just w. Int corridors. **Pets:** $100 one-time fee/room. Service with restrictions. 🛜 ✖ 🛂 💻 🌊 ✖

ROSEAU

AAA ◆◆◆ AmericInn Lodge & Suites of Roseau 🅷

(218) 463-1045. **$70-$141.** 1110 3rd St NW 56751. 1 mi w on SR 11. Int corridors. **Pets:** $25 one-time fee/room. Supervision. SAVE 🛜 🛂 🛂 💻 🌊 ✖

◆◆ North Country Inn 🅷

(218) 463-9444. **$72-$120.** 902 3rd St NW 56751. 0.8 mi w on SR 11. Int corridors. **Pets:** Small. $7 daily fee/pet. Designated rooms, service with restrictions, supervision. 🛜 🛂 💻

ST. CLOUD

◆◆ AmericInn Lodge & Suites of St. Cloud 🅷

(320) 253-6337. **Call for rates.** 4385 Clearwater Rd 56301. I-94 exit 171 (CR 75), just ne. Int corridors. **Pets:** Accepted. 🛜 🛂 🛂 💻 🌊

AAA ◆◆◆ Best Western Americanna Inn & Conference
Center 🅷

(320) 252-8700. **$70-$95.** 520 S US Hwy 10 56304. Jct SR 23, 0.3 mi s. Ext/int corridors. **Pets:** Accepted. SAVE 🛜 🛂 💻 🍽 🌊 ✖

Best Western Plus Kelly Inn 🅷

(320) 253-0606. **$90-$120.** 100 4th Ave S 56301. SR 23 at 4th Ave S; center. Int corridors. **Pets:** Service with restrictions, supervision.

[SAVE] 🛜 [&M] 🛏 🖵 🍴 🏊 🚫

Country Inn & Suites By Carlson-St. Cloud West 🅷

(320) 259-8999. **$89-$140.** 235 S Park Ave 56301. Jct SR 15 and 23 W, just w. Int corridors. **Pets:** Small, dogs only. $15 one-time fee/room. Designated rooms, service with restrictions, supervision.

[SAVE] 🛜 [&M] 🛏 🖵 🏊

GrandStay Residential Suites Hotel 🅷

(320) 251-5400. **$77-$170.** 213 6th Ave S 56301. SR 23 at 6th Ave S; center. Int corridors. **Pets:** Medium, other species. $250 deposit/room, $10 daily fee/pet. Service with restrictions, crate.

[SAVE] 🛜 🛏 🖵 🏊 🚫

Holiday Inn Express & Suites 🅷 ❀

(320) 240-8000. **$99-$189.** 4322 Clearwater Rd 56301. I-94 exit 171 (CR 75), just ne. Int corridors. **Pets:** Large. Service with restrictions, supervision. 🛜 [&M] 🛏 🖵 🏊

Holiday Inn Hotel & Suites 🅷

(320) 253-9000. **$95-$230.** 75 S 37th Ave 56301. Jct SR 15 and 23. Int corridors. **Pets:** Service with restrictions. 🛜 🛏 🖵 🍴 🏊 🚫

Le St-Germain Suite Hotel 🅷

(320) 654-1661. **$89-$139.** 404 W St. Germain St 56301. Just n of SR 23; center. Int corridors. **Pets:** Accepted.

[SAVE] 🛜 🚫 [&M] 🛏 🖵 🏊 🚫

Quality Inn 🅷

(320) 251-1500. **$77-$90.** 4040 2nd St S 56301. Jct SR 15 and 23 W, just w. Int corridors. **Pets:** Accepted.

🛜 🚫 [&M] 🛏 🖵 🍴 🏊 🚫

SAUK CENTRE

AmericInn Lodge & Suites of Sauk Centre 🅷 ❀

(320) 352-2800. **$76-$149.** 1230 Timberlane Dr 56378. I-94 exit 127, just ne. Int corridors. **Pets:** Medium, dogs only. $10 daily fee/pet. Designated rooms, service with restrictions, crate. 🛜 🛏 🖵 🏊 🚫

GuestHouse International Hotel 🅷

(320) 351-7256. **$72-$86.** 322 12th St S 56378. I-94 exit 127, just ne. Int corridors. **Pets:** Medium, dogs only. $10 one-time fee/room. Designated rooms, service with restrictions, supervision. 🛜 🛏 🖵 🍴 🏊

SILVER BAY

AmericInn Lodge & Suites of Silver Bay 🅷 ❀

(218) 226-4300. **$100-$160.** 150 Mensing Dr 55614. On SR 61, 0.5 mi ne of jct SR 61 and Outer Dr. Int corridors. **Pets:** Dogs only. $10 daily fee/pet. Designated rooms, service with restrictions, crate.

🛜 🚫 [&M] 🛏 🖵 🏊 🚫

Mariner Motel Ⓜ ❀

(218) 226-4488. **$55-$75, 3 day notice.** 46 Outer Dr 55614. Just w off SR 61; at traffic signal. Ext corridors. **Pets:** Dogs only. $10 daily fee/pet. Service with restrictions, supervision. [SAVE] 🛜 🛏 🖵 🚫

SLEEPY EYE

Inn of Seven Gables 🅷

(507) 794-5390. **$59-$89.** 1100 E Main St 56085. US 14, 0.8 mi e of jct CR 4 and US 14. Int corridors. **Pets:** Accepted. 🛜 🛏 🖵 🏊

SPICER

Northern Inn Hotel & Suites 🅷

(320) 796-2091. **$60-$160.** 154 Lake Ave S 56288. Just e of jct SR 23 and CR 10. Int corridors. **Pets:** Other species. $10 one-time fee/pet. Designated rooms, service with restrictions, supervision. 🛜 🛏 🖵 🏊

SPRINGFIELD

Microtel Inn & Suites 🅷

(507) 723-8200. **$54-$67.** 502 E Rock St 56087. On US 14. Int corridors. **Pets:** Other species. Designated rooms, no service, supervision.

🛜 🚫 [&M] 🛏 🖵 🏊

SPRING VALLEY

Spring Valley Inn & Suites 🅷

(507) 346-7788. **Call for rates.** 745 N Broadway 55975. Just w on US 63. Int corridors. **Pets:** Other species. $10 daily fee/pet. Service with restrictions. 🛜 🚫 [&M] 🛏 🖵

STEWARTVILLE

Relax Inn Ⓜ

(507) 533-4747. **Call for rates.** 1700 2nd Ave NW 55976. I-90 exit 209A, 1 mi s on US 63. Int corridors. **Pets:** Very small. $10 daily fee/pet. Designated rooms, service with restrictions, supervision.

[SAVE] 🛜 [&M] 🛏 🖵

TOFTE

AmericInn Lodge & Suites of Tofte 🅷

(218) 663-7899. **$80-$130.** 7231 W SR 61 55615. On SR 61. Int corridors. **Pets:** Other species. $15 daily fee/pet. Designated rooms, service with restrictions, crate. [SAVE] 🛜 🛏 🖵 🏊 🚫

Bluefin Bay on Lake Superior 🆑 ❀

(218) 663-7296. **$69-$549, 7 day notice.** 7198 W Hwy 61 55615. SR 61. Ext corridors. **Pets:** $20 daily fee/room. Designated rooms, service with restrictions, crate. [SAVE] 🛜 🛏 🖵 🍴 🏊 🚫

Surfside on Lake Superior 🆑

(218) 663-6870. **$165-$549, 7 day notice.** 10 Surfside (Hwy 61) Dr 55615. On SR 61. Ext corridors. **Pets:** Accepted.

🛜 🚫 🛏 🖵 🍴 🏊 🚫

TWO HARBORS

AmericInn Lodge & Suites of Two Harbors 🅷 ❀

(218) 834-3000. **$105-$240.** 1088 SR 61 N 55616. On SR 61, 0.7 mi s. Int corridors. **Pets:** Medium, dogs only. $15 daily fee/room. Designated rooms, service with restrictions, supervision.

[SAVE] 🛜 [&M] 🛏 🖵 🏊 🚫

Superior Shores Resort 🆑 ❀

(218) 834-5671. **$49-$479.** 1521 Superior Shores Dr 55616. On SR 61, 1.5 mi n of center. Ext/int corridors. **Pets:** Dogs only. $15 daily fee/room. Designated rooms, service with restrictions, supervision.

🛜 🛏 🖵 🍴 🏊 🚫

VIRGINIA

Lakeshor Motor Inn Ⓜ

(218) 741-3360. **$40-$104.** 404 6th Ave N 55792. Just n of Chestnut St; center. Ext corridors. **Pets:** Accepted. 🛜 🛏 🖵

Pine View Inn Ⓜ

(218) 741-8918. **$59-$109.** 903 N 17th St 55792. Jct US 53 and 169, 0.5 mi n on US 53, 0.7 mi e on 9th St N, then 0.5 mi n on 9th Ave W. Ext/int corridors. **Pets:** Accepted. [SAVE] 🛜 🖵 🚫

WABASHA

AmericInn Lodge & Suites of Wabasha 🅷

(651) 565-5366. **$71-$180.** 150 Commerce Dr 55981. Just ne of jct US 61 and SR 60. Int corridors. **Pets:** Accepted.

🛜 [&M] 🛏 🖵 🏊 🚫

WALKER

Country Inn Walker 🅷

(218) 547-1400. **$76-$225.** 442 Walker Bay Blvd 56484. 1 mi s on SR 371. Int corridors. **Pets:** Medium, dogs only. $30 one-time fee/room. Designated rooms, service with restrictions, supervision.

🛜 [&M] 🛏 🖵

WARROAD

Can-Am Motel H

(218) 386-3807. **Call for rates.** 406 Main Ave NE 56763. 0.5 mi w on SR 11. Int corridors. **Pets:** Accepted.

The Patch Motel H

(218) 386-2723. **Call for rates.** 801 State St N 56763. 0.6 mi w on SR 11. Int corridors. **Pets:** Accepted.

WILLMAR

AmericInn Motel of Willmar H

(320) 231-1962. **$80-$120.** 2404 E US 12 56201. 2 mi e. Int corridors. **Pets:** Accepted.

Comfort Inn H

(320) 231-2601. **$80-$175.** 2200 E US 12 56201. 1.8 mi e. Int corridors. **Pets:** Medium. $10 daily fee/room. Service with restrictions, supervision.

Days Inn-Willmar H

(320) 231-1275. **$57-$72.** 225 28th St SE 56201. 2.3 mi e on US 12. Int corridors. **Pets:** Medium. $10 daily fee/room. Service with restrictions, supervision.

Holiday Inn & Willmar Conference Center H

(320) 235-6060. **$99-$150.** 2100 US 12 E 56201. 1.8 mi e. Int corridors. **Pets:** Medium. $10 daily fee/room. Service with restrictions, supervision.

WINDOM

Guardian Inn Motel M

(507) 831-1809. **$60-$100.** 1955 1st Ave 56101. Just ne on SR 60 from jct US 71. Ext/int corridors. **Pets:** $15 one-time fee/pet. Designated rooms, service with restrictions, supervision.

WINONA

Express Suites Riverport Inn H

(507) 452-0606. **$80-$170.** 900 Bruski Dr 55987. Jct US 14/61 and SR 43, just ne. Int corridors. **Pets:** $25 daily fee/pet. Service with restrictions, supervision.

Holiday Inn Express & Suites H

(507) 474-1700. **$129-$144.** 1128 Homer Rd 55987. Jct SR 43, just sw. Int corridors. **Pets:** Accepted.

The Plaza Hotel & Suites H

(507) 453-0303. **$99-$205.** 1025 Hwy 61 E 55987. Jct SR 43, just sw. Int corridors. **Pets:** Large, other species. $25 daily fee/room. Designated rooms, service with restrictions, supervision.

WORTHINGTON

AmericInn Lodge & Suites of Worthington H

(507) 376-4500. **$115-$155.** 1475 Darling Dr 56187. I-90 exit 43 (US 59), just se. Int corridors. **Pets:** Other species. $10 one-time fee/room. Service with restrictions, supervision.

MISSISSIPPI

CITY INDEX

ABERDEEN

Best Western Aberdeen Inn M

(662) 369-4343. **$75-$80.** 801 E Commerce St 39730. On US 45, just n of jct SR 25 and Tenn-Tom Bridge. Ext corridors. **Pets:** Accepted.

AMORY

Briarwood Inn M

(662) 256-2120. **$64-$75.** 915 Hwy 278 E 38821. Jct SR 25 (Main St), 0.6 mi e. Ext corridors. **Pets:** Accepted.

BATESVILLE

Quality Inn H

(662) 563-1188. **Call for rates.** 290 Power Dr 38606. I-55 exit 243B, just w on US 278, then just se. Ext corridors. **Pets:** Accepted.

BILOXI

Edgewater Inn H

(228) 388-1100. **$99-$495, 3 day notice.** 1936 Beach Blvd 39531. I-110 exit 1B, 3.4 mi w on US 90. Ext corridors. **Pets:** Medium, dogs only. $50 one-time fee/pet. Designated rooms, service with restrictions, supervision.

Hard Rock Hotel & Casino Biloxi H

(228) 374-7625. **$109-$499.** 777 Beach Blvd 39530. I-110 exit 1A (US 90), just e. Int corridors. **Pets:** Small. $75 one-time fee/room. Designated rooms, service with restrictions, supervision.

La Quinta Inn & Suites H

(228) 392-5978. **$67-$129.** 957 Cedar Lake Rd 39532. I-10 exit 44, just s. Int corridors. **Pets:** Medium, other species. Service with restrictions, supervision.

BOONEVILLE

Super 8 H

(662) 720-1688. **$40-$60.** 110 Hospitality Ave 38829. Jct US 45 and SR 4/30, 1.7 mi e to SR 145, then 0.5 mi s. Int corridors. **Pets:** Accepted.

CANTON

Americas Best Value Inn H

(601) 859-2643. **$50-$60.** 119 Soldier Colony Rd 39046. I-55 exit 119, just se. Ext corridors. **Pets:** Accepted.

Best Western Canton Inn H
(601) 859-8600. **Call for rates.** 137 Soldier Colony Rd 39046. I-55 exit 119, just se. Int corridors. **Pets:** Accepted. [SAVE] 🛜 🔲 💻 🌊

Brentwood Inn & Suites H
(601) 859-7575. **$63-$120.** 145 Soldier Colony Rd 39046. I-55 exit 119, just se. Int corridors. **Pets:** Other species. $25 one-time fee/pet. Service with restrictions. [SAVE] 🛜 🔲 💻 🌊

La Quinta Inn & Suites H
(601) 855-2121. **$84-$144.** 152 Soldiers Colony Rd 39046. I-55 exit 119, just se. Int corridors. **Pets:** Medium, other species. Service with restrictions, supervision. [SAVE] 🛜 ✖ 🔲 💻 🌊

CLARKSDALE

Americas Best Value Inn & Suites M
(662) 621-1110. **$70-$90.** 350 S State St 38614. 0.5 mi s of jct US 49 and SR 161. Ext corridors. **Pets:** Very small, dogs only. $10 daily fee/pet. Service with restrictions, supervision. [SAVE] 🛜 🔲

CLINTON

Best Western Ridgeland Inn H
(601) 926-4323. **$68-$78.** 102 Clinton Loop Dr 39056. I-20 exit 36, just s, then just w on Clinton Center Dr. Int corridors. **Pets:** Accepted.
[SAVE] 🛜 🔲 💻 🌊

COLUMBUS

Comfort Inn H
(662) 329-2422. **Call for rates.** 1210 US Hwy 45 N 39705. Jct US 82 Bypass and 45 N. Ext corridors. **Pets:** Accepted. 🛜 🔲 💻

CORINTH

Quality Inn H
(662) 287-4421. **Call for rates.** 2101 Hwy 72 W 38834. Jct US 72 and 45, just e. Ext corridors. **Pets:** Accepted. 🛜 🔲 💻 🌊

D'IBERVILLE

Wingate by Wyndham H
(228) 396-0036. **$98-$107.** 12009 Indian River Rd 39540. I-10 exit 46B, just ne. Int corridors. **Pets:** Accepted. 🛜 🔲 💻 🌊

FOREST

Econo Lodge Inn & Suites H
(601) 469-2100. **Call for rates.** 1250 Hwy 35 S 39074. I-20 exit 88, just n. Ext corridors. **Pets:** Accepted. 🛜 🔲 💻 🌊

GREENVILLE

Holiday Inn Express H
(662) 332-5800. **Call for rates.** 3090 Hwy 82 E 38701. 3 mi e of center. Int corridors. **Pets:** Accepted. 🛜 🔲 💻 🌊

GRENADA

Comfort Inn & Suites H
(662) 227-8444. **$86-$130.** 255 SW Frontage Rd 38901. I-55 exit 206, just sw. Int corridors. **Pets:** Other species. $25 one-time fee/room. Service with restrictions. 🛜 🔲 💻 🌊

GULFPORT

Americas Best Value Inn H
(228) 868-8500. **$69-$109.** 9375 Hwy 49 39503. I-10 exit 34A, just sw. Ext corridors. **Pets:** Accepted. 🛜 🔲 💻 🌊

Best Western Plus Seaway Inn H 🐾
(228) 864-0050. **$99-$119.** 9475 Hwy 49 39503. I-10 exit 34A, just sw. Ext corridors. **Pets:** Medium, other species. $15 daily fee/pet.
[SAVE] 🛜 🔲 💻 🌊

Hampton Inn H
(228) 868-3300. **$89-$199.** 9445 Hwy 49 39503. I-10 exit 34A, just sw. Ext corridors. **Pets:** Small. $100 deposit/room, $25 one-time fee/room. Service with restrictions, supervision. [SAVE] 🛜 🔲 💻 🌊

Motel 6 #416 M
(228) 863-1890. **$51-$65.** 9355 US Hwy 49 39503. I-10 exit 34A, just s. Ext corridors. **Pets:** Other species. Service with restrictions, supervision. 🛜 🌊

Quality Inn Gulfport H
(228) 864-7222. **$69-$129.** 9435 Hwy 49 39503. I-10 exit 34A, 0.6 mi s. Ext corridors. **Pets:** Accepted. 🛜 🔲 💻

Ramada Inn Hotel & Convention Center H
(228) 868-8200. **$59-$129.** 9415 Hwy 49 39503. I-10 exit 34A, 0.6 mi s. Ext corridors. **Pets:** Accepted. 🛜 🔲 💻 🍴 🌊

Residence Inn by Marriott Gulfport-Biloxi Airport H 🐾
(228) 867-1722. **$99-$219.** 14100 Airport Rd 39503. I-10 exit 34A, 0.8 mi s on US 49, then 1.2 mi e. Int corridors. **Pets:** Other species. $100 one-time fee/room. Designated rooms, service with restrictions.
🛜 ✖ ♿ 🔲 💻 🌊 ✖

HATTIESBURG

Candlewood Suites H
(601) 264-9666. **$99-$120.** 9 Gateway Dr 39402. I-59 exit 67B, just nw to Classic Dr, then just sw. Int corridors. **Pets:** Accepted.
🛜 ♿ 🔲 💻

Comfort Inn University H
(601) 264-1881. **Call for rates.** 6541 Hwy 49 39401. I-59 exit 67A, just s. Ext/int corridors. **Pets:** Accepted. 🛜 🔲 💻 🌊

Hampton Inn of Hattiesburg H
(601) 264-8080. **$89-$99.** 4301 Hardy St 39402. I-59 exit 65, just nw. Ext/int corridors. **Pets:** Medium. $25 one-time fee/room. Designated rooms, no service, supervision. 🛜 🔲 💻 🌊

Ramada Inn on the Hill H
(601) 599-2001. **Call for rates.** 6595 Hwy 49 N 39401. I-59 exit 67A, just se. Ext corridors. **Pets:** Accepted. 🛜 🔲 💻 🍴 🌊

La Quinta Inn H
(601) 268-2850. **$64-$162.** 6563 Hwy 49 N 39401. I-59 exit 67A, just se. Int corridors. **Pets:** Medium, other species. Service with restrictions, supervision. [SAVE] 🛜 🔲 💻 🌊

Residence Inn Hattiesburg H
(601) 264-9202. **$113-$142.** 116 Grand Dr 39401. I-59 exit 65, jct N 40th St, then just w. Int corridors. **Pets:** Accepted.
🛜 ✖ ♿ 🔲 💻 🌊 ✖

HOLLY SPRINGS

Econo Lodge H
(662) 252-5444. **Call for rates.** 100 Brooks Rd 38635. US 78 exit 30, just sw. Int corridors. **Pets:** Accepted. 🛜 🔲 💻 🌊

HORN LAKE

Best Western Plus Goodman Inn & Suites H
(662) 510-6999. **$80-$110.** 6910 Windchase Dr 38637. I-55 exit 289, just w, then just s. Int corridors. **Pets:** Medium. $50 deposit/pet. Service with restrictions, supervision. [SAVE] 🛜 ✖ ♿ 🔲 💻 🌊

Comfort Inn H
(662) 349-3493. **$80-$89.** 801 Desoto Cove 38637. I-55 exit 289, just w, then just n. Int corridors. **Pets:** Accepted. 🛜 ♿ 🔲 💻 🌊

▼▼▼▼ Drury Inn & Suites-Memphis South H

(662) 349-6622. **$100-$179.** 735 Goodman Rd W 38637. I-55 exit 289, just w, then just s. Int corridors. **Pets:** Accepted.
🛜 ⚡ 🍴 💻 🏊

▼▼▼ La Quinta Inn & Suites Horn Lake H

(662) 510-6500. **$98-$160.** 721 Southwest Dr 38637. I-55 exit 289, just sw. Int corridors. **Pets:** Medium, other species. Service with restrictions, supervision. 🛜 ✖ ⚡ 🍴 💻 🏊

▼▼ Sleep Inn H

(662) 349-2773. **$75-$109.** 708 Desoto Cove 38637. I-55 exit 289, just w, then just n. Int corridors. **Pets:** Accepted. 🛜 🍴 💻 🏊

JACKSON

AAA ▼▼▼ Best Western Executive Inn H

(601) 969-6555. **$68-$150.** 725 Larson St 39202. I-55 exit 96B (High St), e to Greymont Ave, then just n. Int corridors. **Pets:** Medium, other species. $20 daily fee/pet. Designated rooms, service with restrictions, supervision. SAVE 🛜 🍴 💻 🏊

▼▼▼ Clarion Hotel The Roberts Walthall H

(601) 948-6161. **$70-$200.** 225 E Capitol St 39201. I-55 exit 96A (Pearl St), 0.8 mi w; between West and Lamar sts; downtown. Ext/int corridors. **Pets:** Accepted. 🛜 🍴 💻 🍴 🏊 ✖

AAA ▼▼▼ Hilton Jackson H

(601) 957-2800. **Call for rates.** 1001 E County Line Rd 39211. I-55 exit 103 (County Line Rd), just e. Int corridors. **Pets:** Accepted.
SAVE 🛜 🍴 💻 🍴 🏊

▼▼▼ Jameson Inn H

(601) 206-8923. **$74-$94.** 585 E Beasley Rd 39206. I-55 exit 102, just w. Int corridors. **Pets:** Medium. $15 daily fee/room. Service with restrictions, supervision. 🛜 ⚡ 🍴 💻 🏊

▼▼▼ La Quinta Inn Jackson (North) H

(601) 957-1741. **$48-$104.** 616 Briarwood Dr 39211. I-55 exit 102A northbound, just ne on Frontage Rd. Ext corridors. **Pets:** Medium, other species. Service with restrictions, supervision. 🛜 ⚡ 🍴 💻 🏊

▼ Red Roof Inn Downtown Fairgrounds #131 M

(601) 969-5006. **$39-$99.** 700 Larson St 39202. I-55 exit 96B (High St), e to Greymont Ave, then just ne. Ext corridors. **Pets:** Large, other species. No service, supervision. 🛜 🍴

▼▼▼ Studio 6 Jackson H

(601) 355-3599. **Call for rates.** 881 E River Pl 39202. I-55 exit 96C, just e. Ext corridors. **Pets:** Other species. $10 daily fee/room. Service with restrictions, supervision. 🛜 ✖ 🍴 💻 🏊 ✖

KOSCIUSKO

AAA ▼▼▼ Americas Best Value Inn M

(662) 289-6252. **$57-$65.** 1052 Veterans Memorial Dr 39090. Just sw of jct SR 35 and Natchez Trace Pkwy. Ext corridors. **Pets:** Other species. $5 daily fee/pet. Service with restrictions, crate.
SAVE 🛜 🍴 💻 🏊

LUCEDALE

▼▼▼ Holiday Inn Express & Suites H

(601) 947-2099. **Call for rates.** 1287 Beaver Dam Rd 39452. Jct US 98 and SR 63, 1.5 mi se. Int corridors. **Pets:** Accepted. 🛜 🍴 💻 🏊

MACON

▼▼ River Chase Inn M

(662) 726-4334. **Call for rates.** 12710 Hwy 45 39341. Jct SR 14, just s. Ext corridors. **Pets:** Accepted. 🛜 ⚡ 🍴 💻 🏊

MCCOMB

AAA ▼▼▼ Ramada H

(601) 684-8655. **$65-$109.** 2001 Veteran's Blvd 39648. I-55 exit 18, just w. Int corridors. **Pets:** Medium. $25 one-time fee/room. Service with restrictions, crate. SAVE 🛜 ⚡ 🍴 💻 🏊

MERIDIAN

AAA ▼▼▼ Best Western of Meridian H

(601) 693-3210. **$61-$64.** 2219 S Frontage Rd 39301. I-20/59 exit 153, just sw. Ext/int corridors. **Pets:** Small. $10 daily fee/pet. Service with restrictions, crate. SAVE 🛜 🍴 💻 🏊

▼▼▼ Drury Inn & Suites H

(601) 483-5570. **$95-$189.** 112 US Hwy 11 & 80 N 39301. I-20/59 exit 154, jct US 11/80 N. Int corridors. **Pets:** Accepted.
🛜 ⚡ 🍴 💻 🏊

▼▼ Econo Lodge M

(601) 693-9393. **Call for rates.** 2405 S Frontage Rd 39301. I-20/59 exit 153, 0.5 mi sw. Ext corridors. **Pets:** Accepted. 🛜 🍴 💻

▼▼ Jameson Inn H

(601) 483-3315. **$69-$89.** 524 Bonita Lakes Dr 39301. I-20/59 exit 154 southbound; exit 154A northbound, just s. Ext corridors. **Pets:** Medium. $15 daily fee/room. Service with restrictions, supervision.
🛜 ⚡ 🍴 💻 🏊

▼▼ Microtel Inn & Suites H

(601) 553-8100. **$47-$59.** 518 Bonita Lakes Dr 39301. I-20/59 exit 154 westbound, 0.4 mi s to Bonita Lakes Dr, then just sw; exit 154A eastbound, just s. Int corridors. **Pets:** Accepted. 🛜 ⚡ 🍴 💻

▼ Motel 6 #0424 M

(601) 482-1182. **$41-$53.** 2309 S Frontage Rd 39301. I-20/59 exit 153, 0.5 mi sw. Ext corridors. **Pets:** Other species. Service with restrictions, supervision. 🛜 🏊

▼▼ Rodeway Inn M

(601) 482-4400. **Call for rates.** 146 Hwy 11 & 80 39301. I-20/59 exit 154B eastbound; exit 154 westbound, on northeast frontage road. Ext corridors. **Pets:** Accepted. 🛜 🍴 💻

AAA ▼▼▼ Super 8 M

(601) 482-8088. **$45-$67.** 124 Hwy 11 & 80 39301. I-20/59 exit 154 westbound; exit 154B eastbound, on northeast frontage road. Ext corridors. **Pets:** Accepted. SAVE 🛜 🍴 💻

MOSS POINT

AAA ▼▼▼ Best Western Flagship Inn H

(228) 475-5000. **$81.** 4830 Amoco Dr 39563. I-10 exit 69, just s. Ext corridors. **Pets:** Accepted. SAVE 🛜 🍴 💻 🏊

▼▼ Quality Inn H

(228) 475-2477. **$65-$90.** 6800 Hwy 63 N 39563. I-10 exit 69, just s. Ext corridors. **Pets:** Medium, other species. $15 daily fee/room. Designated rooms, service with restrictions, crate. 🛜 🍴 💻 🏊

NATCHEZ

▼▼ Eola Hotel H

(601) 445-6000. **$95-$600.** 110 N Pearl St 39120. Corner of Main and Pearl sts. Int corridors. **Pets:** Small. $50 one-time fee/room. Service with restrictions, crate. 🛜 🍴 💻 🍴

▼▼▼ Hampton Inn & Suites H

(601) 446-6770. **Call for rates.** 627 S Canal St 39120. US 84/65 exit just before Mississippi River. Int corridors. **Pets:** Small. $35 daily fee/room. Service with restrictions, supervision. 🛜 ⚡ 🍴 💻 🏊

OCEAN SPRINGS

 **Quality Inn Ocean Springs** 🅷
(228) 875-7555. **Call for rates.** 7304 Washington Ave 39564. I-10 exit 50, 0.4 mi s on SR 609. Ext corridors. **Pets:** Medium. $15 daily fee/pet. Service with restrictions, supervision. 🛜 ♿M 🛏 💻 🏊

Ramada Limited 🅷
(228) 872-2323. **$59-$99, 7 day notice.** 8011 Tucker Rd 39532. I-10 exit 50, just n. Ext corridors. **Pets:** $15 one-time fee/pet. No service. 🛜 🛏 💻 🏊

Super 8 🅷
(228) 875-2288. **$49-$86.** 13838 Wilfred Seymour Rd 39565. I-10 exit 50, just ne. Ext corridors. **Pets:** Accepted. 🛜 ♿M 🛏 💻 🏊

OLIVE BRANCH

Candlewood Suites 🅷 🐾
(662) 890-7491. **$65-$95.** 7448 Craft Goodman Rd 38654. US 78 exit 1 westbound, 0.5 mi se; exit 2 (SR 302) eastbound, 1.4 mi ne. Int corridors. **Pets:** Medium, other species. $10 daily fee/pet. Service with restrictions, supervision. 🛜 ♿M 🛏 💻

Comfort Inn 🅷
(662) 895-0456. **$77-$85.** 7049 Enterprise Dr 38654. US 78 exit 2 (SR 302), just w, then just n. Int corridors. **Pets:** Accepted. 🛜 🛏 💻 🏊

Holiday Inn Express Hotel & Suites 🅷
(662) 893-8700. **$80-$125, 3 day notice.** 8900 Expressway Dr 38654. US 78 exit 4, just n, then just w. Int corridors. **Pets:** Accepted. SAVE 🛜 ♿M 🛏 💻 🏊

Magnolia Inn & Suites 🅷
(662) 895-4545. **$55-$100.** 6935 W Hamilton Cir 38654. US 78 exit 2 (SR 302), 0.5 mi w. Int corridors. **Pets:** Medium, dogs only. $20 daily fee/pet. Service with restrictions, supervision. 🛜 🛏 💻 🏊

PEARL

 **Candlewood Suites** 🅷
(601) 936-3442. **$79-$109.** 632 S Pearson Rd 39208. I-20 exit 48, just s. Int corridors. **Pets:** Other species. $25 one-time fee/room. No service, crate. 🛜 ♿M 🛏 💻

Jameson Inn of Pearl 🅷
(601) 932-6030. **$74-$94.** 434 Riverwind Dr 39208. I-20 exit 48, just nw. Int corridors. **Pets:** Medium. $15 daily fee/room. Service with restrictions, supervision. 🛜 ♿M 🛏 💻 🏊

La Quinta Inn & Suites Jackson Airport 🅷
(601) 664-0065. **$89-$149.** 501 S Pearson Rd 39208. I-20 exit 48, just s. Int corridors. **Pets:** Medium, other species. Service with restrictions, supervision. 🛜 🛏 💻 🏊

Ramada Jackson Airport 🅷
(601) 933-1122. **$59-$89.** 341 Airport Rd 39208. I-20 exit 52, just nw. Int corridors. **Pets:** Other species. $25 one-time fee/room. Service with restrictions. 🛜 🛏 💻

PHILADELPHIA

Golden Moon Hotel & Casino 🅷
(601) 650-1234. **$69-$179.** 13541 Hwy 16 W 39350. Jct SR 15, 2 mi w. Int corridors. **Pets:** Accepted. 🛜 ♿M 🛏 💻 🍴 🏊 ❌

Silver Star Hotel & Casino 🅷
(601) 650-1234. **$69-$179.** 13540 Hwy 16 W 39350. Jct SR 15, 2 mi w. Int corridors. **Pets:** Accepted. 🛜 ♿M 🛏 💻 🍴 🏊 ❌

PICAYUNE

Days Inn 🅷
(601) 799-1339. **$63.** 450 S Lofton Ave 39466. I-59 exit 4, just nw. Ext corridors. **Pets:** Accepted. 🛜 🛏 💻 🏊

RICHLAND

Executive Inn & Suites 🅷
(601) 664-3456. **$51-$65.** 390 Hwy 49 S 39218. I-20 exit 47, just s. Ext corridors. **Pets:** Accepted. 🛜 🛏 💻 🏊

RIDGELAND

Drury Inn & Suites Ridgeland-Jackson 🅷
(601) 956-6100. **$95-$164.** 610 E County Line Rd 39157. I-55 exit 103 (County Line Rd), just w. Int corridors. **Pets:** Accepted. 🛜 ♿M 🛏 💻 ❌

Homewood Suites by Hilton 🅷
(601) 899-8611. **Call for rates.** 853 Centre St 39157. I-55 exit 103 (County Line Rd), just e to Ridgewood Rd, 0.4 mi ne, then just e. Int corridors. **Pets:** Accepted. 🛜 ♿M 🛏 💻 🏊

Residence Inn Jackson Ridgeland 🅷 🐾
(601) 206-7755. **$94-$180.** 855 Centre St 39157. I-55 exit 103 (County Line Rd), just e to Ridgewood Rd, then just e. Int corridors. **Pets:** Medium, other species. $75 one-time fee/room. Service with restrictions, supervision. 🛜 ❌ ♿M 🛏 💻 🏊 ❌

RIPLEY

Best Western Ripley Ⓜ
(662) 837-0002. **$74-$76.** 922 City Ave S 38663. Jct US 4 and 15, 0.5 mi s. Ext corridors. **Pets:** Accepted. SAVE 🛜 🛏 💻 🏊

SOUTHAVEN

Days Inn Southaven 🅷
(662) 342-5847. **Call for rates.** 8792 Hamilton Rd 38671. I-55 exit 291, just e, then just s. Ext corridors. **Pets:** Small, other species. $10 daily fee/pet. Service with restrictions, supervision. 🛜 🛏 💻 🏊

Magnolia Inn & Suites 🅷
(662) 280-5555. **$50-$95.** 5069 Pepper Chase Dr 38671. I-55 exit 287, just w. Int corridors. **Pets:** Small, dogs only. $20 daily fee/pet. Designated rooms, service with restrictions, supervision. 🛜 🛏

Residence Inn Memphis Southaven 🅷
(662) 996-1500. **$93-$171.** 7165 Sleepy Hollow Dr 38671. I-55 exit 289, just e to Southcrest Pkwy, just n, then just w. Int corridors. **Pets:** Other species. $100 one-time fee/room. Service with restrictions, crate. 🛜 ❌ ♿M 🛏 💻 🏊

STARKVILLE

Comfort Suites Starkville 🅷
(662) 324-9595. **$119-$299.** 801 Russell St 39759. 0.5 mi w of jct US 82 and SR 12. Int corridors. **Pets:** Accepted. 🛜 ❌ 🛏 💻 🏊

Hampton Inn 🅷
(662) 324-1333. **$89-$116.** 700 Hwy 12 E 39759. 1.1 mi sw of jct SR 182. Int corridors. **Pets:** Accepted. 🛜 ❌ ♿M 🛏 💻 🏊

TUNICA

Americas Best Value Inn 🅷
(662) 363-0030. **$45-$250.** 4250 Casino Center Dr 38664. Just n of jct US 61; near casinos. Ext/int corridors. **Pets:** Accepted. 🛜 🛏 💻 🏊

Key West Inn Tunica Ⓜ
(662) 363-0021. **$40-$150.** 11635 Hwy 61 N 38664. US 61, 0.3 mi n of SR 304. Ext corridors. **Pets:** Small, dogs only. $10 daily fee/pet. Service with restrictions, crate. 🛜 🛏 💻

TUPELO

▼▼ America's Best Inn Ⓜ
(662) 842-4403. **$52-$100, 3 day notice.** 897 Harmony Ln 38804. US 45 exit Barnes Crossing, 0.5 mi sw, then just e. Ext corridors.
Pets: Accepted. 🛜 🚼Ⓜ 🛏 💻 ⊳

▼▼ Comfort Inn Ⓗ
(662) 842-5100. **Call for rates.** 1190 N Gloster St 38804. Jct McCullough Blvd and SR 145, 1.3 mi s to McCullough Blvd, w to N Gloster St, then 0.3 mi n. Ext corridors. **Pets:** Small. $25 one-time fee/pet. Service with restrictions, crate. 🛜 🛏 💻

◈◈◈ ▼▼ Days Inn Ⓜ
(662) 842-0088. **$57-$103.** 1015 N Gloster St 38804. On SR 145, just n of McCullough Blvd. Ext corridors. **Pets:** Accepted.
ⓈAVE 🛜 🚼Ⓜ 🛏 💻

▼▼ Super 8 Ⓜ
(662) 842-0448. **$54-$127.** 3898 McCullough Blvd 38801. US 78 exit 81, just sw. Ext corridors. **Pets:** Accepted. 🛜 🛏 💻 ⊳

VICKSBURG

◈◈◈ ▼▼▼ Best Western Vicksburg Ⓗ 🐾
(601) 636-5800. **$75-$105.** 2445 N Frontage Rd 39180. I-20 exit 3, just w on NW Frontage Rd. Ext corridors. **Pets:** Medium. $15 daily fee/room. Service with restrictions, supervision. ⓈAVE 🛜 🛏 💻 ⊳

◈◈◈ ▼▼▼ Cedar Grove Mansion Inn & Restaurant Ⓒⓘ
(601) 636-1000. **$100-$215, 3 day notice.** 2200 Oak St 39180. I-20 exit 1A, 2.3 mi n on Washington St, then w on Klein St; to gated entrance. Ext/int corridors. **Pets:** Medium. $50 one-time fee/room. Designated rooms, service with restrictions, supervision.
ⓈAVE 🛜 ✕ 🛏 💻 🍴 ⊳

▼▼▼ Corners Mansion Inn, a Bed & Breakfast ⒷⒷ
(601) 636-7421. **$125-$210, 3 day notice.** 601 Klein St 39180. I-20 exit 1A, 2.3 mi n on Washington St, then just w. Ext/int corridors. **Pets:** Other species. Designated rooms, service with restrictions, crate.
🛜 ✕ 🛏 💻

▼▼ Econo Lodge Ⓗ
(601) 634-8438. **$47-$50.** 3959 E Clay St 39180. I-20 exit 4A eastbound; exit 5B westbound, 0.5 mi s of National Military Park. Ext corridors.
Pets: Accepted. 🛜 🛏 💻 ⊳

▼▼ Jameson Inn Ⓗ
(601) 619-7799. **$64-$84.** 3975 S Frontage Rd 39180. I-20 exit 4A, on southeast frontage road. Ext corridors. **Pets:** Medium. $15 daily fee/room. Service with restrictions, supervision. 🛜 🚼Ⓜ 🛏 💻 ⊳

▼ Motel 6 #4189 Ⓗ
(601) 638-5077. **$50-$80.** 4127 N Frontage Rd 39183. I-20 exit 4B (Clay St), just ne. Int corridors. **Pets:** Other species. Service with restrictions, supervision. 🛜 🛏 ⊳

▼▼ Rainbow Hotel Ⓗ
(601) 638-7111. **$59-$159.** 1350 Warrenton Rd 39180. I-20 exit 1A, 1.4 mi s. Int corridors. **Pets:** Medium. $35 daily fee/room. Service with restrictions, supervision. 🛜 🚼Ⓜ 🛏 💻 ⊳

▼▼ Travel Inn Ⓜ
(601) 630-0100. **$45-$100.** 1675 N Frontage Rd 39180. I-20 exit 1C; on northeast frontage road. Ext corridors. **Pets:** Small, dogs only. $20 daily fee/pet. Designated rooms, no service, supervision. 🛜 🛏

MISSOURI

ARNOLD

▼▼▼ Drury Inn & Suites Arnold 🄷
(636) 287-3111. **$85-$174.** 3800 SR 141 63010. I-55 exit 191 (SR 141), 0.3 mi e. Int corridors. **Pets:** Accepted. 🛜 ᰦM 🗋 💻 🏊

▼▼ Pear Tree Inn Arnold 🄷
(636) 296-9600. **$60-$129.** 1201 Drury Ln 63010. I-55 exit 191 (SR 141), 0.3 mi e. Int corridors. **Pets:** Accepted. 🛜 🗋 💻 🏊

AVA

▼▼ Ava Super 8 🄷
(417) 683-1343. **$58-$72.** 1711 S Jefferson St 65608. 1.8 mi s of jct SR 5, 14 and 76. Int corridors. **Pets:** Accepted. 🛜 ᰦM 🗋 💻

BETHANY

▼▼ Comfort Inn Bethany 🄷
(660) 425-8006. **Call for rates.** 496 S 39th St 64424. I-35 exit 92, just nw. Int corridors. **Pets:** Accepted. 🛜 🗋 💻

▼▼ Family Budget Inn 🄼
(660) 425-7915. **$45-$54.** 4014 Miller St 64424. I-35 exit 92, just se. Int corridors. **Pets:** Accepted. 🛜 🗋 💻

BOONVILLE

🅰🅰🅰 ▼▼ Boonville Comfort Inn 🄷 🐾
(660) 882-5317. **$55-$149.** 2427 Mid America Industrial Dr 65233. I-70 exit 101, just sw. Int corridors. **Pets:** Small. $10 daily fee/pet. Designated rooms, service with restrictions, supervision. [SAVE] 🛜 🗋 💻 🏊

BRANSON METROPOLITAN AREA

BRANSON

🅰🅰🅰 ▼▼▼ Baymont Inn & Suites 🄷
(417) 334-1985. **$59-$109.** 1000 W Main St 65616. Just sw of jct US 65 and SR 76 (Country Blvd). Int corridors. **Pets:** Small, dogs only. $25 one-time fee/room. Service with restrictions, crate.
[SAVE] 🛜 ⊗ 🗋 💻 🏊

🅰🅰🅰 ▼▼▼ Best Western Plus Landing View Inn & Suites 🄷
(417) 334-6464. **$89-$149.** 403 W Main (Hwy 76) 65616. 0.3 mi e of jct SR 76 (Country Blvd) and US 65. Ext corridors. **Pets:** Large, dogs only. $10 daily fee/pet. Designated rooms, service with restrictions, supervision.
[SAVE] 🛜 🗋 💻 🏊 ⊗

🅰🅰🅰 ▼▼▼ Chateau on the Lake Resort & Spa 🄷
(417) 334-1161. **$139-$359, 3 day notice.** 415 N State Hwy 265 65616. Just n of jct SR 165. Int corridors. **Pets:** Small, dogs only. $35 one-time fee/room. Designated rooms, service with restrictions, supervision. [SAVE] 🛜 ⊗ ᰦM 🗋 💻 🍽 🏊 ⊗

🅰🅰🅰 ▼▼ Fall Creek Inn & Suites 🄷 🐾
(417) 348-1683. **$42-$69.** 995 Hwy 165 65616. Jct SR 76 (Country Blvd), 1.5 mi s on SR 165. Ext corridors. **Pets:** Medium, other species. $50 deposit/pet, $10 daily fee/pet. Designated rooms, service with restrictions. [SAVE] 🛜 🗋 💻 🏊

▼▼ Foxborough Resort 🄼
(417) 335-4369. **$60.** 235 Expressway Ln 65616. US 65 exit Shepherd of the Hills Expwy, 2.3 mi w, then just sw. Ext corridors. **Pets:** Medium. $25 one-time fee/room. Service with restrictions, crate.
🛜 ᰦM 🗋 💻 🏊 ⊗

▼▼ Golden Arrow Resort 🄼
(417) 338-2245. **$47-$135, 21 day notice.** 2869 Indian Point Rd 65616. 2.7 mi s of jct SR 76 (Country Blvd). Ext corridors. **Pets:** Small. $10 daily fee/pet. Designated rooms, no service, crate. 🛜 🗋 💻 🏊 ⊗

▼▼▼ Grand Crowne Resorts 🅲🅾 🐾
(417) 332-8330. **Call for rates.** 300 Golf View Dr 65616. Jct US 65, 3 mi w on SR 76 (Country Blvd), then 1 mi s. Ext corridors. **Pets:** Small. Designated rooms, service with restrictions, supervision.
🛜 ᰦM 🗋 💻 🏊 ⊗

🅰🅰🅰 ▼▼▼ Grand Plaza Hotel 🄷
(417) 336-6646. **$75-$164.** 245 N Wildwood Dr 65616. Just n of jct SR 76 (Country Blvd). Int corridors. **Pets:** Accepted.
[SAVE] 🛜 ⊗ 🗋 💻 🍽 🏊 ⊗

🅰🅰🅰 ▼▼▼ Hampton Inn Branson Hills 🄷
(417) 243-7800. **$89-$109.** 200 Payne Stewart Dr 65616. 1.5 mi nw of jct US 65 and Branson Hills Pkwy. Int corridors. **Pets:** Accepted.
[SAVE] 🛜 ᰦM 💻

🅰🅰🅰 ▼▼▼ Hilton Branson Convention Center Hotel 🄷 🐾
(417) 336-5400. **$79-$199.** 200 E Main St 65616. Main St; at Branson Landing Shopping Complex. Int corridors. **Pets:** Medium, other species. $50 one-time fee/room. Service with restrictions, supervision.
[SAVE] 🛜 ᰦM 🗋 💻 🍽 🏊

▼▼▼ Hilton Promenade at Branson Landing 🄷 🐾
(417) 336-5500. **$79-$219.** 3 Branson Landing 65616. In Branson Landing Shopping District. Int corridors. **Pets:** Medium. $50 one-time fee/room. Service with restrictions, supervision. 🛜 🗋 💻 🍽 🏊

AAA ▽ HomeStay Inn Branson H ❀
(417) 336-2666. **$49-$89.** 3221 Shepherd of the Hills Expwy 65616. 0.3 mi e of jct SR 76 (Country Blvd). Ext corridors. **Pets:** Medium, other species. $5 one-time fee/pet. Designated rooms, crate.
[SAVE] 🛜 🛏 💻 🏊

AAA ▽▽ Hotel Grand Victorian H
(417) 336-2935. **$70-$130.** 2325 W Hwy 76 (Country Blvd) 65616. 2.3 mi w of jct US 65. Ext/int corridors. **Pets:** Small, dogs only. $35 one-time fee/room. Designated rooms, service with restrictions.
[SAVE] 🛜 🛏 💻 🏊 ✗

▽▽ La Quinta Inn Branson Music City Centre H
(417) 336-1600. **$62-$190.** 1835 W Hwy 76 65616. 1.6 mi w of jct US 65. Ext/int corridors. **Pets:** Medium, other species. Service with restrictions, supervision. 🛜 ✗ 🛏 💻 🏊 ✗

▽ Lazy Valley Resort M
(417) 334-2397. **$65-$230, 60 day notice.** 285 River Ln 65616. 2.5 mi s of jct SR 76 (Country Blvd); on Fall Creek Rd to River Valley Rd. Ext corridors. **Pets:** Small, dogs only. $10 daily fee/pet. No service, supervision. 🔇 🛏 💻 🏊 ✗ 🧺

AAA ▽▽ Lodge at the Falls H
(417) 336-3255. **$59-$79.** 3245 Falls Pkwy 65616. Jct SR 76 (Country Blvd), 0.9 mi s on SR 165. Ext corridors. **Pets:** Accepted.
[SAVE] 🛜 🛏 💻

▽ Quality Inn & Suites on the Strip H
(417) 334-1194. **$70-$100.** 2834 W Hwy 76 65616. Jct US 65, 2 mi w. Ext corridors. **Pets:** Other species. $10 daily fee/room. Service with restrictions. 🛜 🛏 💻 🏊

▽▽▽ Radisson Hotel Branson H
(417) 335-5767. **$105-$239, 3 day notice.** 120 S Wildwood Dr 65616. Just s of jct SR 76 (Country Blvd). Int corridors. **Pets:** Medium, other species. $30 one-time fee/pet. Designated rooms, service with restrictions, crate. 🛜 🔇 🛏 💻 🍴 🏊 ✗

▽▽ Ramada Resort & Conference Center H ❀
(417) 334-1000. **$49-$89.** 1700 Hwy 76 W 65616. 1.5 mi w of jct US 65. Ext corridors. **Pets:** $15 one-time fee/room. Service with restrictions, supervision. 🛜 🛏 💻 🍴 🏊 ✗

▽▽▽ Residence Inn by Marriott H ❀
(417) 336-4077. **$113-$142.** 280 Wildwood Dr S 65616. 2 mi w on SR 76 (Country Blvd), just s. Int corridors. **Pets:** Medium, other species. $100 one-time fee/room. Service with restrictions.
🛜 ✗ 🔇 🛏 💻 🏊 ✗

▽▽ Super 8 Central of Branson H
(417) 336-3300. **$41-$57.** 3470 Keeter St 65616. Just sw of jct SR 76 (Country Blvd). Ext corridors. **Pets:** Accepted. 🛜 🔇 🛏 💻 🏊

AAA ▽▽▽▽ The Village At Indian Point CO
(417) 338-8800. **$130-$295, 31 day notice.** 24 Village Tr 65616. 2.5 mi s of jct SR 76 (Country Blvd) on Indian Point Rd. Ext corridors. **Pets:** Small, dogs only. $10 daily fee/pet. Designated rooms, no service, crate. [SAVE] 🛜 ✗ 🛏 💻 🏊 ✗

HOLLISTER

AAA ▽▽▽▽ Westgate Branson Lakes at Emerald Pointe CO
(417) 334-4944. **$79-$259, 3 day notice.** 750 Emerald Pointe Dr 65672. Jct US 65 and SR 265, 1 mi w to Hill Haven Rd, then 2 mi s. Ext corridors. **Pets:** Accepted. [SAVE] ✗ 🔇 🛏 💻 🏊 ✗

END METROPOLITAN AREA

BROOKFIELD

AAA ▽▽ Best Western Brookfield H
(660) 258-4900. **$96-$116.** 28622 Hwy 11 64628. US 36 exit Business Rt 36, just se. Int corridors. **Pets:** Medium, dogs only. $20 daily fee/pet. Service with restrictions, crate. [SAVE] 🛜 🔇 🛏 💻

CAMERON

AAA ▽▽ Best Western Acorn Inn M
(816) 632-2187. **$75-$90.** 2210 E US 36 64429. I-35 exit 54, 0.3 mi e. Ext corridors. **Pets:** Accepted. [SAVE] 🛜 🛏 💻 🏊

▽▽ Days Inn H
(816) 632-6666. **$54-$70.** 601 E Bryan Rd 64429. I-35 exit 54, 0.5 mi w on US 36. Int corridors. **Pets:** Medium. $10 daily fee/pet. Service with restrictions, supervision. 🛜 🛏 💻 🏊

▽▽ Econo Lodge H
(816) 632-6571. **Call for rates.** 220 E Grand Ave 64429. I-35 exit 54, 0.5 mi w on US 36, then just s on US 69. Ext corridors. **Pets:** Accepted.
🛜 🛏 🏊

▽▽ Super 8 H
(816) 632-8888. **$51-$86.** 1710 N Walnut St 64429. I-35 exit 54, 0.5 mi w on US 36. Int corridors. **Pets:** Small. $10 daily fee/room. Designated rooms, service with restrictions, supervision. 🛜 🛏 💻 🏊

CANTON

▽▽ Comfort Inn Canton H
(573) 288-8800. **$80-$113.** 1701 Oak St 63435. US 61 exit US 61 business route/CR P, just e. Int corridors. **Pets:** Small. $15 daily fee/pet. Designated rooms, service with restrictions, supervision.
🛜 🛏 💻 🏊 ✗

CAPE GIRARDEAU

▽▽ Auburn Place Hotel & Suites H
(573) 651-4486. **$79-$139.** 3265 William St 63701. I-55 exit 96 (William St), just e. Ext/int corridors. **Pets:** Accepted.
🛜 🔇 🛏 💻 🏊 ✗

▽▽▽ Drury Lodge-Cape Girardeau H
(573) 334-7151. **$85-$139.** 104 S Vantage Dr 63701. I-55 exit 96 (William St), just e. Ext/int corridors. **Pets:** Accepted. 🛜 🛏 💻 🏊

▽▽▽ Drury Suites-Cape Girardeau H
(573) 339-9500. **$100-$144.** 3303 Campster Dr 63701. I-55 exit 96 (William St), just w. Int corridors. **Pets:** Accepted.
🛜 🔇 🛏 💻 🏊 ✗

▽▽ Hampton Inn-Cape Girardeau H
(573) 651-3000. **$98-$109.** 103 Cape W Pkwy 63701. I-55 exit 96 (William St), 0.3 mi sw. Int corridors. **Pets:** Accepted.
🛜 ✗ 🔇 🛏 💻

▽ Pear Tree Inn by Drury-Cape Girardeau H
(573) 334-3000. **$65-$119.** 3248 William St 63701. I-55 exit 96 (William St), just e. Int corridors. **Pets:** Other species. Service with restrictions, supervision. 🛜 💻 🏊

CARTHAGE

AAA ▽▽▽ Best Western Precious Moments Hotel H ❀
(417) 359-5900. **$77-$80.** 2701 Hazel St 64836. Just e of jct US 71 and SR HH. Int corridors. **Pets:** Medium, dogs only. $10 daily fee/pet. Designated rooms, service with restrictions, crate. [SAVE] 🛜 🛏 💻 🏊

▼▼ Econo Lodge H

(417) 358-3900. **$67-$139.** 1441 W Central Ave 64836. Just ne of jct US 71 and SR 96. Ext/int corridors. **Pets:** Accepted.

▼▼ Super 8 H

(417) 359-9000. **$54-$76.** 416 W Fir Rd 64836. Just e of jct US 71 and SR HH. Int corridors. **Pets:** Accepted.

CHILLICOTHE

▼ Chillicothe Super 8 H

(660) 646-7888. **$53-$63.** 580 Business Hwy 36 E 64601. Jct US 36 and 65 (Washington St), 0.8 mi e. Int corridors. **Pets:** $10 daily fee/pet. Service with restrictions, crate.

▼▼ Econo Lodge Inn & Suites Chillicothe H

(660) 646-0572. **$65-$100.** 1020 S Washington St 64601. Jct US 36 and 65 (Washington St), just nw. Ext/int corridors. **Pets:** $10 daily fee/pet. Designated rooms, service with restrictions, crate.

CLINTON

▼ M-Star Hotel Clinton M

(660) 885-2206. **$55-$80.** 106 S Baird St 64735. Jct SR 7 and 13, just n. Ext corridors. **Pets:** Medium, dogs only. $10 daily fee/pet. Designated rooms, service with restrictions, supervision.

COLUMBIA

▼▼ Candlewood Suites H

(573) 817-0525. **$72-$199.** 3100 Wingate Ct 65201. I-70 exit 128A (US 63), just s, just e on I-70 Dr SE, then just s on Keene St. Int corridors. **Pets:** Other species. $25 one-time fee/room. Service with restrictions, supervision.

▼▼▼ Drury Inn-Columbia H

(573) 445-1800. **$105-$184.** 1000 Knipp St 65203. I-70 exit 124 (Stadium Blvd), just s. Int corridors. **Pets:** Accepted.

▼▼ Extended StayAmerica-Columbia-Stadium Blvd H ✤

(573) 445-6800. **$59-$84.** 2000 Business Loop 70 W 65203. I-70 exit 124 (Stadium Blvd), just ne. Int corridors. **Pets:** Other species. $25 daily fee/pet. Service with restrictions.

AAA ▼▼▼ Holiday Inn Executive Center H ✤

(573) 445-8531. **$108-$130.** 2200 I-70 Dr SW 65203. I-70 exit 124 (Stadium Blvd), just w. Int corridors. **Pets:** $30 one-time fee/room. Designated rooms, service with restrictions, supervision.

SAVE

▼▼ Quality Inn H

(573) 449-2491. **$59-$129.** 1612 N Providence Rd 65202. I-70 exit 126 (Providence Rd), just n. Ext/int corridors. **Pets:** Other species. $15 daily fee/pet. Designated rooms, service with restrictions, crate.

▼▼ Ramada H

(573) 443-4141. **Call for rates.** 901 Conley Rd 65201. I-70 exit 128A (US 63), just sw. Int corridors. **Pets:** $15 one-time fee/pet. Designated rooms, service with restrictions, supervision.

▼ Super 8 Columbia Clark Lane M

(573) 474-8488. **$50-$95.** 3216 Clark Ln 65202. I-70 exit 128A (US 63); northeast corner. Int corridors. **Pets:** Small. $15 daily fee/pet. Designated rooms, service with restrictions, supervision.

CUBA

AAA ▼▼ Best Western Cuba Inn M

(573) 885-7707. **$80-$90.** 246 Hwy P 65453. I-44 exit 208 (SR 19), just n, then just e. Ext corridors. **Pets:** Small. $10 daily fee/pet. Designated rooms, service with restrictions, supervision. **SAVE**

▼▼ Super 8 H

(573) 885-2087. **$54-$68.** 28 Hwy P 65453. I-44 exit 208 (SR 19), just n, then just w. Ext/int corridors. **Pets:** $15 one-time fee/pet. Designated rooms, service with restrictions, supervision.

FESTUS

▼▼ Drury Inn-Festus H

(636) 933-2400. **$90-$144.** 1001 Veterans Blvd 63028. I-55 exit 175, just e. Int corridors. **Pets:** Accepted.

FULTON

▼▼▼ Loganberry Inn Bed & Breakfast BB

(573) 642-9229. **$99-$199, 14 day notice.** 310 W 7th St 65251. Jct US 54 exit CR F, 1 mi e, just n to Westminster Ave, then just e. Int corridors. **Pets:** Medium, dogs only. $15 one-time fee/room. Designated rooms, service with restrictions.

HANNIBAL

AAA ▼▼▼ Quality Inn & Suites H

(573) 221-4001. **$100-$199.** 120 Lindsey Dr 63401. 2 mi w on US 36 exit Shinn Ln to south service road, then 0.6 mi e. Int corridors. **Pets:** Small. $10 daily fee/pet. Designated rooms, no service, supervision. **SAVE**

▼ Super 8 M

(573) 221-5863. **$48-$86.** 120 Huckleberry Heights Dr 63401. Jct US 36, 1.5 mi s on US 61. Int corridors. **Pets:** $15 daily fee/pet. Designated rooms, service with restrictions, supervision.

HARRISONVILLE

▼▼ Comfort Inn & Suites H

(816) 884-4102. **Call for rates.** 2304 S Commercial St 64701. US 71 exit Commercial St, just e. Int corridors. **Pets:** Accepted.

HAYTI

▼▼ Drury Inn & Suites Hayti/Caruthersville H

(573) 359-2702. **$85-$144.** 1317 Hwy 84 63851. I-55 exit 19 (US 412/SR 84), just w. Int corridors. **Pets:** Accepted.

HIGGINSVILLE

▼▼ Super 8-Higginsville H

(660) 584-7781. **$54-$65.** 6471 Oakview Ln 64037. I-70 exit 49 (SR 13), just se. Int corridors. **Pets:** Accepted.

JACKSON

AAA ▼▼▼ Comfort Suites H

(573) 204-0014. **$80-$115.** 2904 Old Orchard Rd 63755. I-55 exit 99, 0.5 mi e, then just n. Int corridors. **Pets:** Medium, dogs only. $35 daily fee/pet. Designated rooms, service with restrictions. **SAVE**

▼▼▼ Drury Inn & Suites-Jackson, MO H

(573) 243-9200. **$80-$159.** 225 Drury Ln 63755. I-55 exit 105 (SR 61), 0.3 mi w. Int corridors. **Pets:** Accepted.

JANE

▼▼ Booneslick Lodge H

(417) 226-1888. **$55-$80.** 21140 US Hwy 71 64856. Just s on US 71. Int corridors. **Pets:** Accepted.

JEFFERSON CITY

▼▼▼ Capitol Plaza Hotel & Convention Center H

(573) 635-1234. **Call for rates.** 415 W McCarty St 65101. On US 50 and 63 S, just e of jct US 54. Int corridors. **Pets:** Accepted.

▼▼ Super 8 Jefferson City H
(573) 636-5456. **$53-$77.** 1710 Jefferson St 65109. US 54 exit Ellis Blvd, 0.3 mi nw on frontage road. Int corridors. **Pets:** Accepted. 📶 🛢 💻

JOPLIN

AAA ▼▼ Best Western Oasis Inn & Suites H
(417) 781-6776. **$69-$149.** 3508 S Range Line Rd 64804. I-44 exit 8B, just nw. Ext corridors. **Pets:** Accepted. SAVE 📶 🛢 💻 🏊

AAA ▼▼▼ Candlewood Suites H ❀
(417) 623-9595. **$89-$139.** 3512 S Range Line Rd 64804. I-44 exit 8B, just nw. Int corridors. **Pets:** $75 one-time fee/room.
SAVE 📶 🛢 💻

▼▼▼▼ Drury Inn & Suites-Joplin H
(417) 781-8000. **$105-$184.** 3601 S Range Line Rd 64804. I-44 exit 8B, just ne. Int corridors. **Pets:** Accepted. 📶 🛢 💻 🏊

▼▼▼▼ Holiday Inn and Convention Center Joplin H ❀
(417) 782-1000. **Call for rates.** 3615 S Range Line Rd 64804. I-44 exit 8B, just ne. Int corridors. **Pets:** Large. $25 deposit/pet. Service with restrictions, crate. 📶 🛢 💻 🍽 🏊

▼▼▼▼ La Quinta Inn Joplin H
(417) 781-0500. **$85-$145.** 3320 S Range Line Rd 64804. I-44 exit 8B, just n. Int corridors. **Pets:** Medium, other species. Service with restrictions, supervision. 📶 🛢 💻 🍽 🏊

▼▼▼▼ Residence Inn by Marriott-Joplin H ❀
(417) 782-0908. **$132-$180.** 3128 E Hammons Blvd 64804. I-44 exit 8B, just ne. Int corridors. **Pets:** Large, other species. $75 one-time fee/room. Service with restrictions. 📶 ✕ 🔊 🛢 💻 🏊 🏊

AAA ▼▼▼ Sleep Inn H
(417) 782-1212. **Call for rates.** 4100 Hwy 43 S 64803. I-44 exit 4, just s. Int corridors. **Pets:** Accepted. SAVE 📶 💻

▼▼▼▼ TownePlace Suites by Marriott Joplin H
(417) 659-8111. **$89-$93.** 4026 Arizona Ave 64804. I-44 exit 8A, just sw. Int corridors. **Pets:** Accepted. 📶 ✕ 🔊 🛢 💻 🏊

KANSAS CITY METROPOLITAN AREA

BLUE SPRINGS

AAA ▼▼ Americas Best Value Inn M
(816) 229-6363. **$60-$100.** 1110 N 7 Hwy 64014. I-70 exit 20, just n. Ext corridors. **Pets:** Accepted. SAVE 📶 🛢 🏊

▼▼▼▼ Hampton Inn Blue Springs H
(816) 220-3844. **$89-$99.** 900 NW South Outer Rd 64015. I-70 exit 20, just s on SR 7, then just w. Int corridors. **Pets:** Large, other species. Service with restrictions. 📶 🛢 💻 🏊

INDEPENDENCE

AAA ▼▼ Best Western Truman Inn H ❀
(816) 254-0100. **$60-$140.** 4048 S Lynn Court Dr 64055. I-70 exit 12, just n on Noland Rd, then just w. Ext corridors. **Pets:** Large. $50 deposit/room, $10 daily fee/pet. Service with restrictions, supervision.
SAVE 📶 🛢 💻 🏊

▼▼▼▼ Drury Inn & Suites Kansas City - Independence H
(816) 795-9393. **$100-$179.** 20300 E 42nd St S 64015. I-70 exit 17, just s. Int corridors. **Pets:** Accepted. 📶 ✕ 🔊 🛢 💻 🏊

▼▼ Fairfield Inn by Marriott H
(816) 795-1616. **$85-$150.** 18700 E 37th Terr S 64057. I-70 exit 15B (SR 291 N), just e on 39th St, then just n on Arrowhead Ave. Int corridors. **Pets:** Medium, other species. $50 one-time fee/room. Designated rooms, service with restrictions, crate. 📶 ✕ 🛢 💻 🏊

AAA ▼▼▼▼ Holiday Inn Express & Suites - Independence/ Kansas City H ❀
(816) 795-8889. **$89-$169.** 19901 E Valley View Pkwy 64057. I-70 exit 17 (Little Blue Pkwy), just s, then just w. Int corridors. **Pets:** Other species. $25 daily fee/room. Service with restrictions, crate.
SAVE 📶 ✕ 🔊 🛢 💻 🏊

AAA ▼▼▼ Quality Inn & Suites - East H
(816) 373-8856. **$65-$160.** 4200 S Noland Rd 64055. I-70 exit 12, just s. Int corridors. **Pets:** Small, other species. $10 daily fee/pet. Service with restrictions, supervision. SAVE 📶 🛢 💻 🏊

▼▼ Super 8 Independence H
(816) 833-1888. **$49-$103.** 4032 S Lynn Court Dr 64055. I-70 exit 12, just n on Noland Rd, then just w. Int corridors. **Pets:** Large. $50 deposit/room, $10 daily fee/pet. Service with restrictions, supervision.
📶 🛢 💻 🏊

KANSAS CITY

AAA ▼▼ Best Western Country Inn - North M
(816) 459-7222. **$54-$200.** 2633 NE 43rd St 64117. I-35 exit 8C (Antioch Rd), just s on SR 1, then just e. Ext corridors. **Pets:** Small, other species. $10 daily fee/pet. Designated rooms, service with restrictions, supervision.
SAVE 📶 🛢 💻 🏊

AAA ▼▼▼ Best Western Plus Seville Plaza Hotel H
(816) 561-9600. **Call for rates.** 4309 Main St 64111. Jct 43rd St, just s. Int corridors. **Pets:** Accepted. SAVE 📶 ✕ 🔊 🛢 💻

▼▼▼▼ Candlewood Suites Kansas City Airport H
(816) 886-9700. **Call for rates.** 11110 NW Ambassador Dr 64153. I-29 exit 12, just se. Int corridors. **Pets:** Accepted. 📶 🔊 🛢 💻

AAA ▼▼▼ Candlewood Suites Kansas City Northeast H ❀
(816) 886-9311. **$99-$149, 3 day notice.** 4450 N Randolph Rd 64117. I-435 exit 54, just s. Int corridors. **Pets:** Medium. $25 daily fee/pet. Designated rooms, service with restrictions, crate. SAVE 📶 🛢 💻 🏊

▼▼▼▼ Chase Suite Hotel H ❀
(816) 891-9009. **$99-$159.** 9900 NW Prairie View Rd 64153. I-29 exit 10, just w, then just n. Ext corridors. **Pets:** Medium. $150 deposit/room, $10 daily fee/pet. Service with restrictions, crate.
📶 ✕ 🛢 💻 🏊 🏊

▼▼▼▼ Clarion Hotel H
(816) 464-2423. **$69-$159.** 11828 NW Plaza Cir 64153. I-29 exit 13, just e on CR D, just s on Ambassador Dr, then just w. Int corridors. **Pets:** Accepted. 📶 🔊 🛢 💻 🍽 🏊

▼▼▼▼ Clarion Hotel Sports Complex H
(816) 353-5300. **$79-$219.** 4011 Blue Ridge Cutoff 64133. I-70 exit 9 (Blue Ridge Cutoff), just se. Int corridors. **Pets:** Accepted.
📶 ✕ 🔊 🛢 💻 🍽 🏊 🏊

▼▼▼▼ Country Hearth Inn & Suites Kansas City Northeast H
(816) 483-7900. **Call for rates.** 1051 N Cambridge St 64120. I-435 exit 57, just w, then just s. Int corridors. **Pets:** Accepted.
📶 🛢 💻 🏊 🏊

Drury Inn & Suites-Kansas City Airport H
(816) 880-9700. **$85-$194.** 7900 NW Tiffany Springs Pkwy 64153-2310. I-29 exit 10, just w. Int corridors. **Pets:** Accepted.

Drury Inn & Suites-Kansas City Stadium H
(816) 923-3000. **$85-$174.** 3830 Blue Ridge Cutoff 64133. I-70 exit 9 (Blue Ridge Cutoff), just nw. Int corridors. **Pets:** Accepted.

Embassy Suites Kansas City-International Airport H
(816) 891-7788. **$99-$211.** 7640 NW Tiffany Springs Pkwy 64153. I-29 exit 10, just e. Int corridors. **Pets:** Very small. $10 daily fee/pet.

Fairfield Inn & Suites Kansas City North Near Worlds of Fun H
(816) 452-6212. **$79-$149.** 4231 N Corrington Ave 64117. I-435 exit 54 northbound, just w on Parvin Rd; exit southbound, 1 mi s on service road, just w on Parvin Rd, then just n. Int corridors. **Pets:** Accepted.

Hilton Kansas City Airport H
(816) 891-8900. **$99-$169.** 8801 NW 112th St 64153. I-29 exit 12, just se. Int corridors. **Pets:** Accepted.

Hilton President Kansas City H 🐾
(816) 221-9490. **$125-$206.** 1329 Baltimore Ave 64105. Jct 14th St. Int corridors. **Pets:** Medium, dogs only. $50 one-time fee/pet. Service with restrictions, crate.

Holiday Inn Country Club Plaza H 🐾
(816) 753-7400. **$89-$149.** 1 E 45th St 64111. Jct Main St; in Country Club Plaza. Int corridors. **Pets:** Other species. $25 deposit/pet, $25 daily fee/pet. Designated rooms, service with restrictions, supervision.

Holiday Inn Kansas City Northeast H 🐾
(816) 455-1060. **$79-$129.** 7333 NE Parvin Rd 64117. I-435 exit 54, just w. Int corridors. **Pets:** Medium, other species. $20 one-time fee/room. Service with restrictions, crate.

Holiday Inn Kansas City SE - Water Park H
(816) 737-0200. **$79-$139.** 9103 E 39th St 64133. I-70 exit 9 (Blue Ridge Cutoff), just ne. Int corridors. **Pets:** Service with restrictions, supervision.

Holiday Inn KCI Airport & Expo Center H
(816) 801-8400. **$79-$149.** 11728 NW Ambassador Dr 64153. I-29 exit 13, just e on CR D, then just s. Int corridors. **Pets:** Large. $30 one-time fee/room. Designated rooms, service with restrictions, supervision.

Homestead Studio Suites-Kansas City/Country Club Plaza H 🐾
(816) 531-2212. **$84-$109.** 4535 Main St 64111. Jct 45th St, just s; just ne of Country Club Plaza. Int corridors. **Pets:** Other species. $25 daily fee/pet. Service with restrictions.

Homewood Suites by Hilton H
(816) 880-9880. **$89-$201.** 7312 NW Polo Dr 64153. I-29 exit 10, just e. Int corridors. **Pets:** Other species. $75 one-time fee/room. Service with restrictions.

The InterContinental Kansas City at the Plaza H 🐾
(816) 756-1500. **Call for rates.** 401 Ward Pkwy 64112. Jct Wornall Rd; in Country Club Plaza. Int corridors. **Pets:** Small, dogs only. $25 one-time fee/room. Service with restrictions, supervision.

Microtel Inn & Suites H
(816) 270-1200. **$40-$63.** 11831 NW Plaza Cir 64153. I-29 exit 13, just e on CR D, then just s. Int corridors. **Pets:** Accepted.

The Q Hotel + Spa H
(816) 931-0001. **$109-$139.** 560 Westport Rd 64111. Jct Main St, 0.4 mi w; in Westport Plaza area. Int corridors. **Pets:** Accepted.

Residence Inn by Marriott Downtown/Union Hill H
(816) 561-3000. **$116-$169.** 2975 Main St 64108. Jct 31st St, just n. Ext corridors. **Pets:** Other species. $100 one-time fee/room.

Residence Inn by Marriott, Kansas City Airport H
(816) 741-2300. **$79-$170.** 10300 N Ambassador Dr 64153. I-29 exit 10, 1.5 mi ne. Int corridors. **Pets:** Medium, other species. $100 one-time fee/room. Service with restrictions, crate.

Residence Inn by Marriott Kansas City Country Club Plaza H
(816) 753-0033. **$140-$180.** 4601 Broadway Blvd 64112. Jct JC Nichols Pkwy, just w on 46th Terr; in Country Club Plaza. Int corridors. **Pets:** Small. $100 one-time fee/room. Service with restrictions, crate.

The Sheraton Kansas City Hotel at Crown Center H
(816) 841-1000. **$89-$399.** 2345 McGee St 64108. In Crown Center area. Int corridors. **Pets:** Accepted.

Sheraton Suites Country Club Plaza H
(816) 931-4400. **$149-$329.** 770 W 47th St 64112. Jct Summit St; in Country Club Plaza. Int corridors. **Pets:** Medium. Service with restrictions, supervision.

Sleep Inn - KCI H
(816) 891-0111. **$53-$69.** 7611 NW 97th Terr 64153. I-29 exit 10, just sw. Int corridors. **Pets:** Medium. $20 daily fee/room. Designated rooms, service with restrictions, supervision.

Super 8 - KCI H
(816) 464-2002. **$41-$63.** 11900 NW Plaza Cir 64153. I-29 exit 13, just e on CR D, then just s. Ext corridors. **Pets:** Small. $15 daily fee/pet. Service with restrictions, supervision.

The Westin Crown Center H 🐾
(816) 474-4400. **$99-$359.** 1 E Pershing Rd 64108. 0.5 mi s. Int corridors. **Pets:** Dogs only. $25 one-time fee/room. Service with restrictions, crate.

KEARNEY

Kearney Super 8 H
(816) 628-6800. **$49-$130.** 210 Platte Clay Way 64060. I-35 exit 26, just e on SR 92, then just n. Int corridors. **Pets:** $10 daily fee/pet. Service with restrictions, supervision.

Quality Inn H
(816) 628-5000. **Call for rates.** 601 Centerville Ave 64060. I-35 exit 26, just w. Int corridors. **Pets:** Accepted.

LEE'S SUMMIT

Comfort Inn by Choice Hotels H
(816) 524-8181. **$65-$95.** 607 SE Oldham Pkwy 64081. Jct US 50 and SR 291 N. Int corridors. **Pets:** Medium. $25 one-time fee/pet. Service with restrictions, supervision.

NORTH KANSAS CITY

▼▼▼▼ Harrah's North Kansas City Casino and Hotel 🅷
(816) 472-7777. **Call for rates.** One Riverboat Dr 64116. I-29/35 exit 6A, 1.4 mi e on SR 210, then just s on Chouteau Thrwy. Int corridors.
Pets: Accepted. 🛜 🕭M 🛗 💻 🍴

▼▼ La Quinta Inn Kansas City North 🅷
(816) 221-1200. **$64-$122.** 2214 Taney Rd 64116. I-29/35 exit 6A, just e on SR 210, then just n. Int corridors. **Pets:** Medium, other species. Service with restrictions, supervision. 🛜 🛗 💻

OAK GROVE (JACKSON COUNTY)

▼ Econo Lodge 🅼
(816) 690-3681. **Call for rates.** 410 SE 1st St 64075. I-70 exit 28, just s on Broadway St, just e on SE 4th St, then just n. Ext corridors.
Pets: Accepted. 🛜 🛗 💻

PLATTE CITY

AAA ▼▼▼ Best Western Airport Inn & Suites/KCI North 🅷 🐾
(816) 858-0200. **$68-$72.** 2512 NW Prairie View Rd 64079. I-29 exit 18, just e, then just s. Int corridors. **Pets:** Medium. $25 one-time fee/pet. Designated rooms, service with restrictions, crate.
SAVE 🛜 🕭M 🛗 💻 🌊 ❌

END METROPOLITAN AREA

KIRKSVILLE

▼ Super 8-Kirksville 🅼 🐾
(660) 665-8826. **$50-$67.** 1101 Country Club Dr 63501. On US 63 and SR 6. Int corridors. **Pets:** $10 daily fee/pet. Designated rooms, service with restrictions, crate. 🛜 🛗 💻

LAKE OZARK

AAA ▼▼▼▼ The Lodge of Four Seasons Golf Resort & Spa Shiki 🅷
(573) 365-3000. **Call for rates.** 315 Four Seasons Dr 65049. US 54B, 2.5 mi to CR HH, then 2.5 mi w. Ext/int corridors. **Pets:** Medium, other species. $50 daily fee/pet. Designated rooms, service with restrictions.
SAVE 🛜 ❌ 🛗 💻 🍴 🌊 ❌

▼▼ The Resort at Port Arrowhead 🅷
(573) 365-2334. **$80-$140, 3 day notice.** 3080 Bagnell Dam Blvd 65049. 2.6 mi s of Bagnell Dam. Ext/int corridors. **Pets:** Accepted.
🛜 🕭M 🛗 💻 🍴 🌊 ❌

LAMAR

▼ Super 8-Lamar 🅷
(417) 682-6888. **$47-$90.** 45 SE 1st Ln 64759. Jct US 71 and 160. Ext/int corridors. **Pets:** Small, dogs only. $15 daily fee/pet. Designated rooms, service with restrictions, supervision. 🛜 🛗 💻 🌊

LEBANON

AAA ▼▼▼ Best Western Wyota Inn 🅷
(417) 532-6171. **$77.** 1221 Mill Creek Rd 65536. I-44 exit 130, just nw. Ext corridors. **Pets:** Medium. $15 daily fee/pet. Designated rooms, service with restrictions, crate. SAVE 🛜 🛗 💻 🌊

LICKING

▼ Scenic Rivers Inn 🅼
(573) 674-4809. **$55-$65.** 209 S Hwy 63 65542. On US 63. Ext corridors. **Pets:** Accepted. 🛜 🛗 💻 🌊

LINN

▼▼▼ Settle Inn & Suites 🅷
(573) 897-9903. **$79-$99.** 1639 US Hwy 50 E 65051. 1 mi e of jct US 50 and SR 89. Int corridors. **Pets:** Medium, dogs only. $15 daily fee/pet. Designated rooms, service with restrictions, supervision.
🛜 🛗 💻 🌊

MACON

▼ Super 8 🅷
(660) 385-5788. **$56-$75.** 203 E Briggs Dr 63552. Jct US 36 and 63. Int corridors. **Pets:** Accepted. 🛜 🛗 💻

MARSHFIELD

▼▼ Holiday Inn Express 🅷
(417) 859-6000. **$95-$105.** 1301 Banning St 65706. I-44 exit 100 (SR 38); on southeast corner. Int corridors. **Pets:** Other species. $25 one-time fee/room. Designated rooms, service with restrictions, supervision.
🛜 🕭M 🛗 💻 🌊

MARYVILLE

▼▼ Super 8 🅷
(660) 582-8088. **$54-$61.** 222 Summit Dr 64468. On Business Rt US 71; just n of US 71 Bypass. Int corridors. **Pets:** Other species. $25 deposit/room. Service with restrictions, supervision. 🛜 ❌ 🛗 💻

MINER

▼▼▼ Drury Inn & Suites - Sikeston 🅷
(573) 472-2299. **$105-$169.** 2608 E Malone Ave 63801. I-55 exit 67, just nw. Int corridors. **Pets:** Accepted. 🛜 🛗 💻 🌊

▼▼ Pear Tree Inn by Drury 🅷
(573) 471-4100. **$80-$144.** 2602 E Malone Ave 63801. I-55 exit 67, just nw. Int corridors. **Pets:** Accepted. 🛜 🕭M 🛗 💻 🌊

MOUND CITY

▼▼ Mound City Super 8 🅷
(660) 442-4000. **$66.** 109 W 8th St 64470. I-29 exit 84, just e. Int corridors. **Pets:** Accepted. 🛜 🛗 💻 🌊

OSAGE BEACH

▼▼ Dogwood Hills Golf Resort 🅷
(573) 348-1735. **$52-$114.** 1252 State Hwy KK 65065. 0.5 mi n, off US 54. Ext corridors. **Pets:** Other species. $25 one-time fee/pet. Service with restrictions, crate. 🛜 🛗 💻 🍴 🌊

PACIFIC

AAA ▼▼▼ Quality Inn Near Six Flags 🅷
(636) 257-8400. **$69-$109.** 1400 W Osage St 63069. I-44 exit 257, just se. Ext/int corridors. **Pets:** Medium. $10 daily fee/pet. Service with restrictions, crate. SAVE 🛜 🛗 💻 🌊

PERRYVILLE

▼▼ Americas Best Value Inn 🅼
(573) 547-1091. **$55-$80.** 1500 Liberty St 63775. I-55 exit 129 (SR 51). Int corridors. **Pets:** Accepted. 🛜 🛗 🌊

POPLAR BLUFF

▼▼ Drury Inn-Poplar Bluff 🅷
(573) 686-2451. **$95-$124.** 2220 N Westwood Blvd 63901. 1.4 mi se of jct US 60 and 67. Int corridors. **Pets:** Accepted.
🛜 🛗 💻 🌊 ❌

▼▼ **Super 8** 🅷
(573) 785-0176. **$58-$63.** 2831 N Westwood Blvd 63901. 0.7 mi se of jct US 60 and 67. Int corridors. **Pets:** $50 one-time fee/room. Designated rooms, service with restrictions, supervision. 🛰🚪🖵

POTOSI

▼ **Potosi Super 8** 🅷
(573) 438-8888. **$58-$64.** 820 E High St 63664. Jct SR 8 and 21. Ext/int corridors. **Pets:** $10 one-time fee/pet. Service with restrictions, supervision. 🛰🚪🖵

REPUBLIC

▼▼ **AmericInn Lodge & Suites of Republic** 🅷
(417) 732-5335. **$85-$140.** 950 N Austin Ln 65738. I-44 exit 67, 4.4 mi s to SR 174, then 0.7 mi e. Int corridors. **Pets:** Small. $10 daily fee/pet. Service with restrictions, crate. 🛰🚪🖵🛬

ROLLA

▼▼ **Baymont Inn & Suites** 🅷
(573) 364-7000. **$71-$119.** 1801 Martin Springs Dr 65401. I-44 exit 184, just sw. Int corridors. **Pets:** Accepted. 🛰🅜🚪🖵🛬

🆎 ▼▼ **Best Western Coachlight** 🅼
(573) 341-2511. **$75-$95.** 1403 Martin Springs Dr 65401. Jct I-44 and Business Rt 44 S exit 184. Ext corridors. **Pets:** Large, other species. $20 daily fee/pet. Designated rooms, service with restrictions, crate.
[SAVE] 🛰🚪🖵🛬

▼▼ **Drury Inn-Rolla** 🅷
(573) 364-4000. **$80-$124.** 2006 N Bishop Ave 65401. I-44 exit 186 (US 63), just ne. Int corridors. **Pets:** Accepted. 🛰🚪🖵🛬

🆎 ▼▼ **Super 8 Rolla** 🅷
(573) 426-6688. **$61-$90.** 1641 Martin Springs Dr 65401. I-44 exit 184, just sw. Int corridors. **Pets:** Accepted. [SAVE]🛰🅜🚪🖵🛬

ST. CLAIR

▼▼ **Budget Lodging** 🅼
(636) 629-1000. **$69-$79.** 866 S Outer Rd 63077. I-44 exit 240, just w. Ext corridors. **Pets:** Large. $10 daily fee/pet. Designated rooms, service with restrictions, supervision. 🛰🚪🖵🛬

ST. JOSEPH

▼▼▼ **Drury Inn & Suites-St. Joseph** 🅷
(816) 364-4700. **$95-$159.** 4213 Frederick Blvd 64506. I-29 exit 47, just e. Int corridors. **Pets:** Accepted. 🛰🅜🚪🖵🛬❌

▼▼▼ **St. Joseph Holiday Inn-Riverfront** 🅷
(816) 279-8000. **$89-$114.** 102 S Third St 64501. I-229 exit Edmond St northbound; exit Felix St southbound; downtown. Int corridors.
Pets: Accepted. 🛰🅜🚪🖵🍴🛬❌

ST. LOUIS METROPOLITAN AREA

BERKELEY

🆎 ▼▼▼▼ **Renaissance St. Louis Airport Hotel** 🅷
(314) 429-1100. **$79-$159.** 9801 Natural Bridge Rd 63134. I-70 exit 237 (Natural Bridge Rd), just n; I-170 exit 6 (Natural Bridge Rd), just n. Int corridors. **Pets:** Accepted. [SAVE]🛰❌🚪🖵🍴🛬

BRIDGETON

▼▼ **StudioPlus-St Louis-Earth City** 🅷 🌸
(314) 209-1011. **$59-$84.** 3125 Rider Tr S 63045. I-70 exit 231B (Earth City Expwy), just n, then 0.7 mi e. Int corridors. **Pets:** Other species. $25 daily fee/pet. Service with restrictions. 🛰🚪🖵

CHESTERFIELD

▼▼▼ **Drury Plaza Hotel-Chesterfield** 🅷
(636) 532-3300. **$105-$309.** 355 Chesterfield Center E 63017. I-64/US 40 exit 19B (Clarkson Rd/Olive Blvd); jct I-64/US 40 and Clarkson Rd; southwest corner. Int corridors. **Pets:** Accepted.
🛰🅜🚪🖵🍴🛬

▼▼▼ **Hampton Inn-Chesterfield** 🅷
(636) 537-2500. **$99-$129.** 16201 Swingley Ridge Rd 63017. I-64/US 40 exit 19B (Clarkson Rd/Olive Blvd). Int corridors. **Pets:** Accepted.
🛰🚪🖵🛬❌

▼▼▼ **Homewood Suites by Hilton** 🅷
(636) 530-0305. **$119-$149.** 840 Chesterfield Pkwy W 63017. I-64/US 40 exit 20 (Chesterfield Pkwy), 0.6 mi n. Int corridors. **Pets:** Accepted.
🛰🚪🖵🛬

CLAYTON

🆎 ▼▼▼▼ **Crowne Plaza St. Louis-Clayton** 🅷
(314) 726-5400. **$99-$279, 3 day notice.** 7750 Carondelet Ave 63105. I-64 exit 32B (Hanley Rd), 1.3 mi n, then just w. Int corridors.
Pets: Accepted. [SAVE]🛰🚪🖵🍴🛬❌

🆎 ▼▼▼▼ **The Ritz-Carlton, St. Louis** 🅷
(314) 863-6300. **Call for rates.** 100 Carondelet Plaza 63105. I-64 exit 32B (Hanley Rd), 1.2 mi n, then just e. Int corridors. **Pets:** Accepted.
[SAVE]🛰❌🖵🍴🛬❌

🆎 ▼▼▼▼ **Sheraton Clayton Plaza Hotel** 🅷
(314) 863-0400. **$99-$239, 3 day notice.** 7730 Bonhomme Ave 63105. I-64 exit 31 (Brentwood Blvd), 1.3 mi n, then 0.7 mi e. Int corridors.
Pets: Accepted. [SAVE]🛰❌🚪🖵🍴🛬

CREVE COEUR

▼▼▼ **Drury Inn & Suites-Creve Coeur** 🅷
(314) 989-1100. **$100-$184.** 11980 Olive Blvd 63141. I-270 exit 14 (Olive Blvd), just e. Int corridors. **Pets:** Accepted.
🛰🅜🚪🖵🛬❌

EARTH CITY

▼▼ **Candlewood Suites St. Louis** 🅷
(314) 770-2744. **$70-$130.** 3250 Rider Tr S 63045. I-70 exit 231B (Earth City Expwy N), just n, then just e. Int corridors. **Pets:** Accepted.
🚪🖵

▼▼▼ **Residence Inn St. Louis Airport/Earth City** 🅷
(314) 209-0995. **$119-$159.** 3290 Rider Tr S 63045. I-70 exit 231B (Earth City Expwy N), just n, then just e. Int corridors. **Pets:** Accepted.
🛰❌🅜🚪🖵🛬❌

EDMUNDSON

▼▼▼ **Drury Inn-St. Louis Airport** 🅷
(314) 423-7700. **$90-$189.** 10490 Natural Bridge Rd 63134. I-70 exit 236 (Lambert Airport), just s, then just e. Int corridors. **Pets:** Accepted.
🛰🅜🚪🖵🛬

🆎 ▼▼▼ **Marriott-St. Louis Airport** 🅷
(314) 423-9700. **$79-$209.** 10700 Pear Tree Ln 63134. I-70 exit 236 (Lambert Airport), just s. Int corridors. **Pets:** Accepted.
[SAVE]🛰❌🚪🖵🍴🛬

EUREKA

▼▼▼ **Holiday Inn at Six Flags** 🅷
(636) 938-6661. **$99-$299.** 4901 Six Flags Rd 63025. I-44 exit 261 (Allenton Rd). Ext/int corridors. **Pets:** Medium, other species. $10 daily fee/pet. Designated rooms, supervision. 🛰🚪🖵🍴🛬❌

FENTON

▼▼▼ Drury Inn & Suites-Fenton H
(636) 343-7822. **$85-$169.** 1088 S Highway Dr 63026. I-44 exit 274 (Bowles Ave), just se. Int corridors. **Pets:** Accepted. 🛜 🛑 💻 🏊

▼▼ Pear Tree Inn by Drury-Fenton H
(636) 343-8820. **$60-$129.** 1100 S Highway Dr 63026. I-44 exit 274 (Bowles Ave), just s. Int corridors. **Pets:** Accepted. 🛜 🛑 💻 🏊

▼▼ TownePlace Suites by Marriott H
(636) 305-7000. **$89-$109.** 1662 Fenton Business Park Ct 63026. I-44 exit 275 westbound; exit 274 eastbound to S Highway Dr, just s. Int corridors. **Pets:** Accepted. 🛜 ✖ ♿ 🛑 💻 🏊

FORISTELL

AAA ▼▼▼ Best Western West 70 Inn H
(636) 673-2900. **$67-$95.** 12 Hwy W 63348. I-70 exit 203 (CR W), just n. Int corridors. **Pets:** Medium. $15 daily fee/pet. Service with restrictions, supervision. SAVE 🛜 🛑 💻 🏊

HAZELWOOD

▼▼ La Quinta Inn St. Louis Airport H
(314) 731-3881. **$58-$115.** 5781 Campus Ct 63042. I-270 exit 23 (McDonnell Blvd), just s, just w on Campus Pkwy, then just n. Int corridors. **Pets:** Medium, other species. Service with restrictions, supervision.
🛜 🛑 💻 🏊

KIRKWOOD

AAA ▼▼▼ Best Western Kirkwood Inn H 🐾
(314) 821-3950. **$100-$130.** 1200 S Kirkwood Rd 63122. I-44 exit 277B (Lindbergh Blvd), just n. Int corridors. **Pets:** Large. $10 daily fee/pet. Designated rooms, service with restrictions, crate.
SAVE 🛜 ✖ 🛑 💻 🍴 🏊

MARYLAND HEIGHTS

AAA ▼▼▼▼ DoubleTree by Hilton Hotel St. Louis - Westport H
(314) 434-0100. **$63-$249.** 1973 Craigshire Rd 63146. I-270 exit 16A (Page Ave), just e to Lackland Rd, then 0.4 mi sw on Lackland and Craigshire rds. Int corridors. **Pets:** Accepted.
ECO SAVE 🛜 ♿ 🛑 💻 🍴 🏊 ✖

▼▼ Drury Inn & Suites-St. Louis-Westport H
(314) 576-9966. **$90-$174.** 12220 Dorsett Rd 63043. I-270 exit 17 (Dorsett Rd), just e. Int corridors. **Pets:** Accepted. 🛜 🛑 💻 🏊

AAA ▼▼▼▼ Harrah's Casino & Hotel H 🐾
(314) 770-8100. **Call for rates.** 777 Casino Center Dr 63043. I-70 exit 231A (Earth City Expwy S), 1 mi s, then 1.2 mi nw. Int corridors. **Pets:** Medium, dogs only. $40 daily fee/room. Designated rooms, service with restrictions, crate. SAVE 🛜 ♿ 🛑 💻 🍴

▼▼ Residence Inn by Marriott - Westport H
(314) 469-0060. **$86-$134.** 1881 Craigshire Rd 63146. I-270 exit 16A (Page Ave), 0.8 mi e, exit Lackland Rd, just w, just s on Craig Rd, then just w. Ext corridors. **Pets:** Accepted. 🛜 ✖ 🛑 💻 🏊 ✖

AAA ▼▼▼▼ Sheraton Westport Lakeside Chalet H
(314) 878-1500. **$89-$269.** 191 Westport Plaza Dr 63146. I-270 exit 16A (Page Ave), 0.8 mi e to Lackland Rd exit, just w, then 0.4 mi n. Int corridors. **Pets:** Accepted. SAVE 🛜 ✖ ♿ 🛑 💻 🍴 🏊 ✖

AAA ▼▼▼▼ Sheraton Westport Plaza Tower H
(314) 878-1500. **$99-$179.** 900 Westport Plaza 63146. I-270 exit 16A (Page Ave), 0.8 mi e; exit Lackland Rd, just w, then just n. Int corridors. **Pets:** Accepted. SAVE 🛜 ✖ ♿ 🛑 💻 🍴 🏊 ✖

▼▼▼▼ Staybridge Suites H
(314) 878-1555. **Call for rates.** 1855 Craigshire Rd 63146. I-270 exit 16A (Page Ave), 0.8 mi e, exit Lackland Rd, 1 mi w, 0.4 mi s on Craig Rd, then just e. Ext/int corridors. **Pets:** Accepted.
🛜 🛑 💻 🏊 ✖

MEHLVILLE

▼▼ Americas Best Value Inn H
(314) 894-9449. **$60-$120.** 6602 S Lindbergh Blvd 63123. I-55 exit 197 (Lindbergh Blvd), just w, just s on Rusty Rd, then just e on Feth St. Int corridors. **Pets:** Medium, other species. $10 daily fee/pet. Service with restrictions, crate. 🛜 🛑 💻 🏊

AAA ▼▼▼ Best Western St. Louis Inn H
(314) 416-7639. **$69-$89.** 6224 Heimos Industrial Park Dr 63129. I-55 exit 193, just e on Meramec Bottom Rd, then just n. Int corridors. **Pets:** Medium, other species. $10 daily fee/pet. Designated rooms, service with restrictions, crate. SAVE 🛜 🛑 💻 🏊

▼▼▼▼ Holiday Inn St. Louis-South I-55 H
(314) 894-0700. **$89-$189.** 4234 Butler Hill Rd 63129. I-55 exit 195 (Butler Hill Rd), just e, then just s. Ext/int corridors. **Pets:** $15 daily fee/pet. Service with restrictions, supervision. 🛜 🛑 💻 🍴 🏊 ✖

O'FALLON

▼▼▼ Hilton Garden Inn St. Louis/O'Fallon H
(636) 625-2700. **$79-$209.** 2310 Technology Dr 63368. US 40/61 exit 6 (Wing Haven Blvd/CR DD), just ne; I-70 exit 216 (Bryan Rd), 4.2 mi s. Int corridors. **Pets:** Accepted. 🛜 ✖ ♿ 🛑 💻 🍴 🏊

▼▼▼ Staybridge Suites O'Fallon H 🐾
(636) 300-0999. **$105-$159, 3 day notice.** 1155 Technology Dr 63368. I-64/US 40 exit 9 (CR K), just nw. Int corridors. **Pets:** Large. $50 one-time fee/room. Service with restrictions. 🛜 ♿ 🛑 💻 🏊

RICHMOND HEIGHTS

▼▼▼ Residence Inn By Marriott-St. Louis Galleria H
(314) 862-1900. **$95-$215.** 8011 Galleria Pkwy 63117. I-170 exit 1C (Brentwood Blvd) northbound; exit 1D southbound, just s, just e on Galleria Pkwy, then just s. Ext corridors. **Pets:** Accepted.
ECO 🛜 ✖ ♿ 🛑 💻 🏊 ✖

ST. ANN

▼▼▼ Hampton Inn-St. Louis Airport H
(314) 429-2000. **$89-$169.** 10820 Pear Tree Ln 63074. I-70 exit 236 (Airport Dr), just sw. Int corridors. **Pets:** Accepted. 🛜 🛑 💻 🏊

▼▼ Pear Tree Inn by Drury-St. Louis Airport H
(314) 427-3400. **$80-$144.** 10810 Pear Tree Ln 63074. I-70 exit 236 (Airport Dr), just sw. Int corridors. **Pets:** Accepted. 🛜 🛑 💻 🏊

ST. CHARLES

▼▼▼ Comfort Suites-St. Charles H
(636) 949-0694. **Call for rates.** 1400 S 5th St 63301. I-70 exit 229 (5th St), just ne. Int corridors. **Pets:** Accepted.
🛜 ✖ ♿ 🛑 💻 🏊

AAA ▼▼▼ Country Inn & Suites By Carlson H
(636) 724-5555. **Call for rates.** 1190 S Main St 63301. I-70 exit 229A (5th St S) to S Main St, then 0.7 mi ne. Int corridors. **Pets:** Accepted.
SAVE 🛜 🛑 💻 🏊

AAA ▼▼▼ Red Roof Inn H
(636) 947-7770. **$40-$100.** 2010 Zumbehl Rd 63303. I-70 exit 227 (Zumbehl Rd), just se. Ext corridors. **Pets:** Large, other species. No service, supervision. SAVE 🛜 ♿ 🛑

▼▼ TownePlace Suites by Marriott H 🐾
(636) 949-6800. **$80-$89.** 1800 Zumbehl Rd 63303. I-70 exit 227 (Zumbehl Rd), 0.6 mi s, then just se. Int corridors. **Pets:** Other species. $75 one-time fee/room. Service with restrictions, supervision.
🛜 ✖ 🛑 💻 🏊

ST. LOUIS

AAA ▼▼▼▼ The Cheshire H
(314) 647-7300. **Call for rates.** 6300 Clayton Rd 63117. I-64/US 40 exit 34A (Clayton Rd/Skinker Blvd), 0.4 mi w. Int corridors. **Pets:** Accepted.
SAVE 🛜 ✖ 🛑 💻 🍴 🏊

▼▼▼▼ **Drury Inn & Suites Near Forest Park** H
(314) 646-0770. **$110-$234.** 2111 Sulphur Ave 63139. I-44 exit 286, just s. Int corridors. **Pets:** Accepted.

▼▼▼▼ **Drury Inn & Suites-St. Louis-Convention Center** H
(314) 231-8100. **$100-$214.** 711 N Broadway 63102. I-70 exit 250B (Stadium/Memorial Dr), at convention center. Int corridors.
Pets: Accepted.

▼▼▼▼ **Drury Inn-St. Louis/Union Station** H
(314) 231-3900. **$115-$199.** 201 S 20th St 63103. Just e of Jefferson Ave; between Market St and Clark Ave. Int corridors. **Pets:** Accepted.

▼▼▼▼ **Drury Plaza Hotel-St. Louis At the Arch** H
(314) 231-3003. **$110-$304.** 2 S 4th St 63102. I-70 exit 250B (Stadium/Memorial Dr), just w on Pine St to Broadway, just s to Walnut St, just e to 4th St, then just n. Int corridors. **Pets:** Accepted.

AAA ▼▼▼▼ **Four Seasons Hotel St. Louis** H ❖
(314) 881-5800. **$195-$375.** 999 N 2nd St 63102. I-70 exit 250A, just s, 1.1 mi e, then just s. Int corridors. **Pets:** Service with restrictions, crate.

AAA ▼▼▼▼ **Hilton St. Louis at the Ballpark** H
(314) 421-1776. **$89-$295.** 1 S Broadway 63102. Between Walnut and Market sts. Int corridors. **Pets:** Accepted.

▼▼▼▼ **Hilton-St. Louis Downtown** H
(314) 436-0002. **$109-$229.** 400 Olive St 63102. I-70 exit 249C/251C (6th St) to N Broadway to Olive St. Int corridors. **Pets:** Accepted.

AAA ▼▼▼▼ **Holiday Inn Forest Park** H
(314) 645-0700. **Call for rates.** 5915 Wilson Ave 63110. I-44 exit 286, just n. Int corridors. **Pets:** Accepted.

AAA ▼▼▼▼ **Hyatt Regency St. Louis at The Arch** H
(314) 655-1234. **$79-$349.** 315 Chestnut St 63102. I-70 exit 250B (Stadium/Memorial Dr); at 4th and Chestnut sts. Int corridors.
Pets: Accepted. ECO SAVE

AAA ▼▼▼ **Millennium Hotel St. Louis** H
(314) 241-9500. **$99-$299.** 200 S 4th St 63102. Jct Market St, just s. Int corridors. **Pets:** Accepted. SAVE

AAA ▼▼▼▼ **Moonrise Hotel** H
(314) 721-1111. **Call for rates.** 6177 Delmar Blvd 63112. I-64 exit 38A, 2.4 mi on Forest Park Pkwy, 0.4 mi n on Skinker Blvd, then just e; in "The Loop". Int corridors. **Pets:** Accepted.

▼▼▼ **Omni Majestic Hotel** H
(314) 436-2355. **Call for rates.** 1019 Pine St 63101. Jct N Broadway, just w; at 10th St. Int corridors. **Pets:** Accepted.

AAA ▼▼▼ **The Parkway Hotel** H
(314) 256-7777. **$117-$269.** 4550 Forest Park Ave 63108. I-64 exit 36A (Kingshighway Blvd), 0.6 mi n, then just e. Int corridors. **Pets:** Medium. $20 daily fee/pet. Designated rooms, service with restrictions, crate.

▼▼▼▼ **Pear Tree Inn - St. Louis/Union Station** H
(314) 241-3200. **$90-$169.** 2211 Market St 63103. I-64/US 40 exit 39, just n on Jefferson Ave, then just e. Int corridors. **Pets:** Accepted.

▼▼▼▼ **Residence Inn St. Louis Downtown** H
(314) 289-7500. **$119-$189.** 525 S Jefferson Ave 63103. I-64/US 40 exit 38C westbound; exit 38A (Jefferson Ave) eastbound, just s. Int corridors. **Pets:** Other species. $75 one-time fee/pet. Service with restrictions.

AAA ▼▼▼▼ **St. Louis Union Station Marriott** H ❖
(314) 621-5262. **$129-$209.** 1820 Market St 63103. I-64 exit 38C eastbound; exit 39A westbound, just n on N Jefferson Ave, then 0.5 mi e on Market St. Int corridors. **Pets:** Dogs only. $50 one-time fee/room. Designated rooms, service with restrictions, crate.

AAA ▼▼▼▼ **Sheraton St. Louis City Center Hotel & Suites** H ❖
(314) 231-5007. **$89-$349.** 400 S 14th St 63103. I-64 exit 39B (14th St) eastbound, just n; exit 40A westbound, just n, just w on Clark Ave, then just s. Int corridors. **Pets:** Medium, dogs only. Service with restrictions, supervision. SAVE

AAA ▼▼▼▼ **The Westin St. Louis** H ❖
(314) 621-2000. **$132-$409.** 811 Spruce St 63102. I-64 exit 39C eastbound, just n on 11th St, then just e; exit 40A westbound, just n, just e on Clark Ave, just s on 8th St, then just w. Int corridors. **Pets:** Medium, other species. Service with restrictions. SAVE

ST. PETERS
▼▼▼ **Drury Inn St. Peters** H
(636) 397-9700. **$95-$179.** 170 Mid Rivers Mall Cir 63376. I-70 exit 222 (Mid Rivers Mall Dr), just se. Int corridors. **Pets:** Accepted.

VALLEY PARK
▼▼▼▼ **Drury Inn & Suites-St. Louis Southwest** H
(636) 861-8300. **$95-$159.** 5 Lambert Drury Pl 63088. I-44 exit 272 (SR 141), just sw. Int corridors. **Pets:** Accepted.

▼▼▼▼ **Hampton Inn-St. Louis Southwest near Six Flags** H ❖
(636) 529-9020. **Call for rates.** 9 Lambert Drury Pl 63088. I-44 exit 272 (SR 141), just sw. Int corridors. **Pets:** Service with restrictions.

WELDON SPRING
▼▼▼▼ **Wingate by Wyndham Weldon Spring** H
(636) 329-8503. **$76-$107.** 32 Research Park Cir 63304. I-64/40 exit 11 (Research Park Cir), just se. Int corridors. **Pets:** Accepted.

WOODSON TERRACE
AAA ▼▼▼▼ **Hilton St. Louis Airport** H
(314) 426-5500. **$89-$209.** 10330 Natural Bridge Rd 63134. I-70 exit 236 (Lambert Airport), 0.5 mi se. Int corridors. **Pets:** Accepted.

END METROPOLITAN AREA

ST. ROBERT

Americas Best Value Inn H
(573) 451-3100. **$71-$105.** 110 Carmel Valley Way 65584. I-44 exit 161, just nw. Int corridors. **Pets:** Other species. $10 daily fee/pet. Service with restrictions, supervision. [SAVE] 🛜 [&M] 🛏 🖵

Baymont Inn & Suites Ft. Leonard Wood-St. Robert H
(573) 336-5050. **$72-$81.** 139 Carmel Valley Way 65584. I-44 exit 161, just nw. Int corridors. **Pets:** Accepted. 🛜 🛏 🖵 ⇌

Best Western Montis Inn H
(573) 336-4299. **$75-$84.** 14086 Hwy Z 65584. I-44 exit 163, just s. Ext corridors. **Pets:** Small, dogs only. $10 daily fee/pet. Designated rooms, service with restrictions, supervision. [SAVE] 🛜 🛏 🖵 ⇌

MainStay Suites H
(573) 451-2700. **$110-$190.** 227 St. Robert Blvd 65584. I-44 exit 159, 0.8 mi nw. Ext/int corridors. **Pets:** Medium, other species. $15 daily fee/room. Service with restrictions, supervision. [ECO] 🛜 🛏 🖵 ⇌

STE. GENEVIEVE

Microtel Inn & Suites H
(573) 883-8884. **$63-$84.** 21958 Hwy 32 63670. I-55 exit 150 (SR 32), 3.9 mi e. Int corridors. **Pets:** $10 daily fee/pet. Service with restrictions.
[SAVE] 🛜 [&M] 🛏 🖵

SEDALIA

Best Western State Fair Inn H
(660) 826-6100. **$85-$150.** 3120 S Limit Ave 65301. Jct US 50, 1.5 mi s on US 65. Ext/int corridors. **Pets:** Medium. Designated rooms, service with restrictions, crate. [SAVE] 🛜 🛏 🖵 🍴 ⇌ ⊗

Hotel Bothwell, an Ascend Collection hotel H
(660) 826-5588. **$86-$150.** 103 E 4th St 65301. Corner of 4th and S Ohio sts; downtown. Int corridors. **Pets:** Accepted. 🛜 ⊠ 🖵 🍴

SEYMOUR

Americas Best Value Inn H
(417) 935-9888. **$63-$73.** 1000 E Clinton Rd 65746. Just s of jct US 60. Int corridors. **Pets:** Medium. $15 daily fee/pet. Designated rooms, service with restrictions, supervision. 🛜 🛏 🖵

SIKESTON

Comfort Inn & Suites H
(573) 472-0197. **$87-$170.** 109 Matthews Ln 63801. I-55 exit 67, just sw. Int corridors. **Pets:** Medium. $15 daily fee/pet. Service with restrictions, supervision. [SAVE] 🛜 🛏 🖵 ⇌

SPRINGFIELD

Baymont Inn & Suites H
(417) 889-8188. **$79-$149.** 3776 S Glenstone Ave 65804. On US 60 (James River Expwy). Int corridors. **Pets:** Medium. $10 daily fee/pet. Designated rooms, service with restrictions, supervision.
[SAVE] 🛜 [&M] 🛏 🖵 ⇌

Best Western Coach House Inn H ❀
(417) 862-0701. **$69-$139.** 2535 N Glenstone Ave 65803. I-44 exit 80A, just s. Ext corridors. **Pets:** Medium. $10 daily fee/pet. Service with restrictions, crate. [SAVE] 🛜 🛏 🖵 ⇌

Best Western Deerfield Inn H
(417) 887-2323. **$65-$90.** 3343 E Battlefield St 65804. US 65 exit Battlefield St, just w. Int corridors. **Pets:** Small, dogs only. $20 daily fee/pet. Designated rooms, service with restrictions, crate.
[SAVE] 🛜 🛏 🖵 ⇌ ⊗

Best Western Route 66 Rail Haven M
(417) 866-1963. **$69-$129.** 203 S Glenstone Ave 65802. I-44 exit 80A, 3 mi s. Ext corridors. **Pets:** Accepted. [SAVE] 🛜 [&M] 🛏 🖵 ⇌

Candlewood Suites South H ❀
(417) 881-8500. **$89-$139.** 1035 E Republic Rd 65807. US 60 (James River Expwy) exit National Ave, just s. Int corridors. **Pets:** Medium. $10 daily fee/pet. Service with restrictions, crate. [SAVE] 🛜 [&M] 🛏 🖵

Candlewood Suites Springfield I-44 H
(417) 866-4242. **$89-$139.** 1920 E Kerr St 65803. I-44 exit 80A, just e to Evergreen St. Int corridors. **Pets:** Accepted. [SAVE] 🛜 [&M] 🛏 🖵

Courtyard by Marriott Airport H
(417) 869-6700. **$112-$136.** 3527 W Kearney St 65803. I-44 exit 75 (US 160 W Bypass), just se to SR 744, then just w. Int corridors.
Pets: Accepted. 🛜 ⊠ [&M] 🛏 🖵 🍴 ⇌

Days Inn Battlefield H
(417) 882-9484. **$61-$90.** 3260 E Montclair St 65804. US 65 exit Battlefield Rd, just w to Moulder Ave, then just sw. Int corridors.
Pets: Accepted. 🛜 ⊠ [&M] 🛏 🖵 ⇌

DoubleTree by Hilton Hotel Springfield H
(417) 831-3131. **$69-$139.** 2431 N Glenstone Ave 65803. I-44 exit 80A, just s. Int corridors. **Pets:** Other species. $25 one-time fee/room. Designated rooms, service with restrictions, crate.
[SAVE] 🛜 [&M] 🛏 🖵 🍴 ⇌

Drury Inn & Suites-Springfield H
(417) 863-8400. **$95-$194.** 2715 N Glenstone Ave 65803. I-44 exit 80A (Glenstone Ave), just s. Int corridors. **Pets:** Accepted.
🛜 [&M] 🛏 🖵 ⇌

Quality Inn South H
(417) 889-6300. **Call for rates.** 3330 E Battlefield Rd 65804. US 65 exit Battlefield Rd. Ext corridors. **Pets:** Accepted. 🛜 🛏 🖵 ⇌

Greenstay Hotel & Suites H ❀
(417) 863-1440. **$89-$129, 14 day notice.** 222 N Ingram Mill Rd 65802. US 65 exit Chestnut Expwy, just sw. Ext/int corridors. **Pets:** Medium. $10 daily fee/pet. Service with restrictions, crate.
[SAVE] 🛜 ⊠ 🛏 🖵 ⇌

Hilton Garden Inn Springfield H
(417) 875-8800. **$69-$139.** 4155 S Nature Center Way 65804. US 60 exit Glenstone Ave (US 65 business route), just s. Int corridors.
Pets: Small, dogs only. $35 deposit/room. Designated rooms, service with restrictions, crate. [SAVE] 🛜 ⊠ 🛏 🖵 🍴 ⇌

La Quinta Inn & Suites Springfield Airport Plaza H
(417) 447-1466. **$67-$148.** 2445 N Airport Plaza Ave 65803. I-44 exit 75, just se. Int corridors. **Pets:** Medium, other species. Service with restrictions, supervision. 🛜 🛏 🖵 ⇌

La Quinta Inn Springfield South H
(417) 890-6060. **$80-$142.** 2535 S Campbell Ave 65807. Jct Battlefield Rd and Campbell Ave, 0.5 mi n. Int corridors. **Pets:** Medium, other species. Service with restrictions, supervision.
[SAVE] 🛜 ⊠ 🛏 🖵 ⇌

Quality Inn & Suites H ❀
(417) 888-0898. **$70.** 3930 S Overland Ave 65807. US 60 (James River Expwy) exit Kansas Expwy, just n to Chesterfield Blvd, then just w. Int corridors. **Pets:** Medium, dogs only. $10 daily fee/pet. Service with restrictions, crate. [SAVE] 🛜 [&M] 🛏 🖵 ⇌

Quality Inn & Suites North H
(417) 869-0001. **$65-$90.** 2745 N Glenstone Ave 65803. I-44 exit 80A, just sw. Ext/int corridors. **Pets:** $25 daily fee/pet. Service with restrictions, supervision. 🛜 🛏 🖵 ⇌

Sleep Inn of Springfield H
(417) 886-2464. **$80-$95.** 233 El Camino Alto 65810. US 60 (James River Expwy) exit Campbell Ave, just se. Int corridors. **Pets:** Medium, other species. $20 one-time fee/room. Designated rooms, service with restrictions, supervision. 🛜 🛏 🖵 ⇌

▼▼▼▼ **University Plaza Hotel and Convention Center** 🏨
(417) 864-7333. **$89-$189, 3 day notice.** 333 John Q Hammons Pkwy 65806. 0.5 mi e on St. Louis St. Int corridors. **Pets:** Accepted.
🛜 ✖ 🔥ᴹ 🛏 💻 🍽 ♨

SULLIVAN
▼▼ **Baymont Inn & Suites** 🏨
(573) 860-3333. **$72-$103.** 275 N Service Rd W 63080. I-44 exit 225. Int corridors. **Pets:** Accepted. 🛜 🛏 💻 ♨

△△△ ▼▼▼ **Comfort Inn** 🏨
(573) 468-7800. **$81-$99.** 736 S Service Rd W 63080. I-44 exit 225, just sw. Int corridors. **Pets:** Accepted. 🆂🅰🆅🅴 🛜 ✖ 🛏 💻 ♨

TRENTON
▼▼ **Country Home Inn** 🏨
(660) 359-2988. **$66-$79.** 1845A E 28th St 64683. US 65, 1 mi n of jct SR 6 and US 65. Int corridors. **Pets:** Accepted. 🛜 🛏

UNION
▼▼ **Super 8** 🏨
(636) 583-8808. **$71-$77.** 1015 E Main St 63084. I-44 exit 247 (US 50), 4.7 mi w; just w of jct SR 47. Int corridors. **Pets:** Small, dogs only. $10 daily fee/pet. Designated rooms, service with restrictions, supervision.
🛜 🔥ᴹ 🛏 💻 ♨

WASHINGTON
▼▼ **Sleep Inn & Suites** 🏨
(636) 390-8877. **Call for rates.** 2621 E 5th St 63090. I-44 exit 251, 8.5 mi w on SR 100. Int corridors. **Pets:** Accepted.
🛜 ✖ 🛏 💻 ♨

▼ **Super 8 Washington** 🏨
(636) 390-0088. **$71-$82.** 2081 Eckelkamp Ct 63090. I-44 exit 251, 10 mi w on SR 100, just s of SR 100 and 47. Int corridors. **Pets:** Small, dogs only. $10 daily fee/pet. Designated rooms, service with restrictions, supervision. 🛜 🛏 💻

WEST PLAINS
△△△ ▼▼▼ **Best Western Grand Villa** 🏨
(417) 257-2711. **$80-$85.** 220 Jan Howard Expy 65775. 0.5 mi nw of jct US 63 and 160. Int corridors. **Pets:** Small, other species. $10 daily fee/ room. Service with restrictions. 🆂🅰🆅🅴 🛜 🛏 💻 ♨

WILLOW SPRINGS
▼▼ **Comfort Inn of Willow Springs** 🏨
(417) 469-0410. **Call for rates.** 1204 E Main St 65793. Just n of US 60/63. Int corridors. **Pets:** Small, dogs only. $15 one-time fee/pet. Desig- nated rooms, service with restrictions, supervision. 🛜 🛏 💻

MONTANA

CITY INDEX

ALBERTON
▼▼ **The Ghost Rails Inn B & B** 🅱🅱
(406) 722-4990. **$79-$99, 3 day notice.** 702 Railroad Ave 59820. Downtown. Int corridors. **Pets:** Accepted. 🛜 ✖ 🆆 🆉

BELGRADE
▼▼▼ **Gallatin River Lodge** 🅒🅘 ❀
(406) 388-0148. **$170-$400, 7 day notice.** 9105 Thorpe Rd 59718. I-90 exit 298, 2.7 mi s on SR 85, 1 mi w on Valley Center Rd (gravel), then 0.5 mi s, follow signs. Int corridors. **Pets:** $20 daily fee/room. Designated rooms, service with restrictions. 🛜 ✖ 💻 🍽 🆇

▼▼ **La Quinta Inn & Suites Belgrade / Bozeman** 🏨
(406) 388-2222. **$98-$199.** 6445 Jackrabbit Ln 59714. I-90 exit 298, just s on SR 85. Int corridors. **Pets:** Medium, other species. Service with restrictions, supervision. 🛜 🛏 💻 ♨ 🆇

△△△ ▼▼▼ **Quality Inn** 🏨 ❀
(406) 388-0800. **$69-$159.** 6261 Jackrabbit Ln 59714. I-90 exit 298, just s on SR 85. Int corridors. **Pets:** Other species. $5 one-time fee/pet. Serv- ice with restrictions, crate. 🆂🅰🆅🅴 🛜 ✖ 🔥ᴹ 🛏 💻

△△△ ▼▼▼ **Super 8-Belgrade/Bozeman Airport** 🏨
(406) 388-1493. **$50-$104.** 6450 Jackrabbit Ln 59714. I-90 exit 298, just s on SR 85. Int corridors. **Pets:** $5 daily fee/pet. Designated rooms, supervision. 🆂🅰🆅🅴 🛜 🛏 💻 ♨

BIGFORK
△△△ ▼▼▼ **Mountain Lake Lodge** 🏨
(406) 837-3800. **$205-$285, 7 day notice.** 14735 Sylvan Dr 59911. On US 35, 5 mi s. Ext corridors. **Pets:** Other species. $15 one-time fee/pet. Designated rooms, service with restrictions, supervision.
🆂🅰🆅🅴 🛜 🔥ᴹ 🛏 💻 🍽 ♨ 🆇

△△△ ▼▼▼ **Timbers Motel** Ⓜ
(406) 837-6200. **Call for rates.** 8540 Hwy 35 59911. Just n on US 35 from jct SR 209. Ext corridors. **Pets:** Accepted.
🆂🅰🆅🅴 🛜 🛏 💻 ♨

BIG SKY
▼▼ **Buck's T-4 Lodge** 🏨
(406) 995-4111. **$99-$159.** 46625 Gallatin Rd 59716. US 191, 1 mi s of Big Sky entrance. Ext/int corridors. **Pets:** Accepted.
🛜 ✖ 🛏 💻 🍽 🆇

▼▼▼ **Rainbow Ranch Lodge** 🏨 ❀
(406) 995-4132. **Call for rates.** 42950 Gallatin Rd 59730. 5 mi s on US 191. Ext corridors. **Pets:** Dogs only. $40 one-time fee/pet. Designated rooms, service with restrictions. 🛜 ✖ 🛏 💻 🍽 🆇 🅐🅒

BIG TIMBER
▼▼ **Big Timber Super 8** 🏨 ❀
(406) 932-8888. **$58-$83.** 20A Big Timber Loop Rd 59011. I-90 exit 367. Int corridors. **Pets:** Medium, other species. $10 daily fee/pet. Designated rooms, service with restrictions, supervision. 🛜 🔥ᴹ 🛏 💻

◆ **River Valley Inn** H
(406) 932-4943. **$68-$90.** 600 W 2nd St 59011. I-90 exit 367, just n, then 0.6 mi e. Int corridors. **Pets:** Small, other species. $10 one-time fee/room. Service with restrictions, supervision. 🛜 ▯

BILLINGS

◆ ◆◆◆ **Best Western Plus Clocktower Inn** H ❀
(406) 259-5511. **$90-$160.** 2511 1st Ave N 59101. On I-90 business loop; downtown. Ext/int corridors. **Pets:** Other species. $20 daily fee/pet. Designated rooms, service with restrictions, supervision.
SAVE 🛜 ✕ ▯ ▱ ▯ ⌇

◆ ◆◆◆ **Best Western Plus Kelly Inn & Suites** H ❀
(406) 256-9400. **$110-$150.** 4915 Southgate Dr 59101. I-90 exit 447, just w. Ext/int corridors. **Pets:** Medium. Designated rooms, service with restrictions, supervision. SAVE 🛜 ✕ ▯M ▯ ▱ ⌇

◆◆◆ **Billings Hotel and Convention Center** H
(406) 248-7151. **$69-$169.** 1223 Mullowney Ln 59101. I-90 exit 446, just s. Int corridors. **Pets:** Small, dogs only. $20 daily fee/room. Designated rooms, service with restrictions, supervision.
🛜 ▯ ▱ ▯ ⌇ ✕

◆ ◆◆ **Billings Inn by Riversage** H ❀
(406) 252-6800. **$75-$85.** 880 N 29th St 59101. I-90 exit 450, 2 mi n on 27th St, then just w on 9th Ave. Int corridors. **Pets:** $7 daily fee/pet. Designated rooms, service with restrictions, supervision.
SAVE 🛜 ✕ ▯ ▱

◆ ◆◆ **Billings Sleep Inn** H
(406) 254-0013. **Call for rates.** 4904 Southgate Dr 59101. I-90 exit 447, just w. Int corridors. **Pets:** Accepted. SAVE 🛜 ▯M ▯ ▱

◆ ◆◆ **Billings Super 8** H
(406) 248-8842. **$55-$82.** 5400 Southgate Dr 59102. I-90 exit 447, just n on S Billings Blvd, 0.8 mi w on King Ave, then just s on Parkway Ln. Int corridors. **Pets:** Accepted. SAVE 🛜 ▯M ▯ ▱

◆ ◆◆ **Cherry Tree Inn** H
(406) 252-5603. **$63.** 823 N Broadway 59101. I-90 exit 450, 2 mi n on 27th St, then just w on 9th Ave. Int corridors. **Pets:** Accepted.
SAVE 🛜 ✕ ▯ ▱

◆◆ **Comfort Inn by Choice Hotels** H
(406) 652-5200. **$74-$94.** 2030 Overland Ave 59102. I-90 exit 446, 0.5 mi n, then just s. Int corridors. **Pets:** Accepted. 🛜 ▯M ▯ ▱ ⌇

◆◆ **Days Inn** H
(406) 252-4007. **$57-$84.** 843 Parkway Ln 59101. I-90 exit 447, just n on S Billings Blvd, 0.8 mi w on King Ave, then just s. Int corridors.
Pets: Accepted. 🛜 ▯ ▱

◆◆ **Econo Lodge** H
(406) 252-2700. **Call for rates.** 5425 Midland Rd 59101. I-90 exit 446, just se. Ext/int corridors. **Pets:** Accepted. 🛜 ▯ ▱ ⌇

◆◆ **Extended StayAmerica-Billings-West End** H ❀
(406) 245-3980. **$69-$89.** 4950 Southgate Dr 59101. I-90 exit 447, just w. Int corridors. **Pets:** Other species. $25 daily fee/pet. Service with restrictions. 🛜 ▯M ▯ ▱

◆ ◆◆ **Hilltop Inn by Riversage** H ❀
(406) 245-5000. **$75-$85.** 1116 N 28th St 59101. I-90 exit 450, 2 mi n on 27th St, just w on 11th Ave, then just n. Int corridors. **Pets:** $7 daily fee/pet. Designated rooms, service with restrictions, supervision.
SAVE 🛜 ✕ ▯M ▯ ▱

◆ ◆◆◆ **Holiday Inn Grand Montana Billings** H
(406) 248-7701. **$139-$159.** 5500 Midland Rd 59101. I-90 exit 446. Int corridors. **Pets:** $50 one-time fee/room. Designated rooms, service with restrictions, supervision. SAVE 🛜 ▯M ▯ ▱ ⌇ ✕

◆ **Kelly Inn** H ❀
(406) 248-9800. **$79-$129.** 5610 S Frontage Rd 59101. I-90 exit 446, just s. Ext/int corridors. **Pets:** Designated rooms, service with restrictions, supervision. 🛜 ▯M ▯ ▱ ⌇

◆ **Motel 6 # 1150 Billings North** H
(406) 248-7551. **$45-$65.** 5353 Midland Rd 59102. I-90 exit 446, just se. Int corridors. **Pets:** Other species. Service with restrictions, supervision. 🛜 ▯M ▯ ⌇

◆ **Motel 6 #178 Billings South** M
(406) 252-0093. **$45-$65.** 5400 Midland Rd 59101. I-90 exit 446, just se. Ext corridors. **Pets:** Other species. Service with restrictions, supervision. 🛜 ▯M

◆◆◆ **Quality Inn Homestead** H
(406) 652-1320. **$90-$95.** 2036 Overland Ave 59102. I-90 exit 446, 0.5 mi n, then just s. Int corridors. **Pets:** Medium. $5 daily fee/room. Designated rooms, service with restrictions, supervision.
🛜 ▯ ▱ ⌇ ✕

◆ ◆◆◆ **Residence Inn by Marriott** H ❀
(406) 656-3900. **$132-$170.** 956 S 25th St W 59102. I-90 exit 446, 1.5 mi w, just s on S 24th St, then just s; behind Home Depot. Int corridors. **Pets:** Other species. $75 one-time fee/room.
SAVE 🛜 ✕ ▯M ▯ ▱ ⌇ ✕

◆ ◆◆ **Western Executive Inn** H
(406) 294-8888. **$60-$200.** 3121 King Ave W 59102. I-90 exit 446, 2.5 mi w. Int corridors. **Pets:** $10 daily fee/pet. Service with restrictions, supervision. SAVE 🛜 ▯M ▯ ▱

◆ ◆ **Westwood's Rimview Inn** M
(406) 248-2622. **Call for rates.** 1025 N 27th St 59101. I-90 exit 450, 2 mi n. Ext/int corridors. **Pets:** Accepted. SAVE 🛜 ▯ ▱

BOZEMAN

◆ ◆◆◆ **Best Western Plus GranTree Inn** H
(406) 587-5261. **$89-$169.** 1325 N 7th Ave 59715. I-90 exit 306, just s. Int corridors. **Pets:** Service with restrictions, supervision.
SAVE 🛜 ✕ ▯ ▱ ▯ ⌇ ✕

◆◆ **Bozeman Days Inn & Suites** H
(406) 587-5251. **$45-$128.** 1321 N 7th Ave 59715. I-90 exit 306, just s. Int corridors. **Pets:** Accepted. 🛜 ▯ ▱ ⌇ ✕

◆ ◆ **Bozeman Inn** M
(406) 587-3176. **$55-$88.** 1235 N 7th Ave 59715. I-90 exit 306, just s. Ext corridors. **Pets:** Other species. $5 daily fee/room. Service with restrictions, supervision. SAVE 🛜 ▯ ▱

◆◆ **Bozeman's Western Heritage Inn** H ❀
(406) 586-8534. **$78-$158.** 1200 E Main St 59715. I-90 exit 309, 0.5 mi w. Int corridors. **Pets:** Dogs only. $10 daily fee/pet. Service with restrictions, supervision. 🛜 ✕ ▯ ▱

◆◆ **Comfort Inn of Bozeman** H
(406) 587-2322. **Call for rates.** 1370 N 7th Ave 59715. I-90 exit 306, just s. Int corridors. **Pets:** Medium. $10 daily fee/pet. Designated rooms, service with restrictions, supervision. 🛜 ✕ ▯ ▱ ⌇

◆◆◆ **Holiday Inn Bozeman** H
(406) 587-4561. **$59-$159.** 5 E Baxter Ln 59715. I-90 exit 306, just s. Int corridors. **Pets:** Accepted. 🛜 ▯ ▱ ▯ ⌇ ✕

◆◆◆ **La Quinta Inn & Suites** H
(406) 585-9300. **Call for rates.** 620 Nikles Dr 59715. I-90 exit 306, just ne. Int corridors. **Pets:** Medium, other species. Service with restrictions, supervision. 🛜 ✕ ▯M ▯ ▱ ⌇

◆◆ **Microtel Inn & Suites** H
(406) 586-3797. **$50-$99.** 612 Nikles Dr 59715. I-90 exit 306, just ne. Int corridors. **Pets:** Accepted. 🛜 ✕ ▯ ▱ ⌇

WWW MountainView Lodge & Suites H
(406) 522-8686. **$89-$179.** 1121 Reeves Rd W 59718. I-90 exit 305, just n. Int corridors. **Pets:** Dogs only. $10 daily fee/pet. Designated rooms, service with restrictions, supervision. (SAVE M) 🔊 🛏 💻 🏊 ⊗

AAA WW Rainbow Motel M
(406) 587-4201. **$50-$75.** 510 N 7th Ave 59715. I-90 exit 306, 0.8 mi s. Ext corridors. **Pets:** Accepted. (SAVE) 🔊 🛏 💻 🏊

AAA WW Ramada Limited H
(406) 585-2626. **$59-$129, 3 day notice.** 2020 Wheat Dr 59715. I-90 exit 306, just n, then just w. Ext/int corridors. **Pets:** Accepted. (SAVE) 🔊 ⊗ 🛏 💻 🏊 ⊗

WW Rodeway Inn H
(406) 585-7888. **Call for rates.** 817 Wheat Dr 59718. I-90 exit 306, just n. Int corridors. **Pets:** Accepted. 🔊 ⊗ (M) 🛏 💻 🏊

AAA WW Royal "7" Budget Inn M
(406) 587-3103. **$48-$58.** 310 N 7th Ave 59715. I-90 exit 306, 0.8 mi s. Ext corridors. **Pets:** Other species. $3 daily fee/pet. Designated rooms, service with restrictions, supervision. (SAVE) 🔊 ⊗ 🛏 💻

WW Super 8 H
(406) 586-1521. **$50-$109.** 800 Wheat Dr 59715. I-90 exit 306, just n, then just w. Int corridors. **Pets:** Accepted. 🔊 💻

BROWNING

AAA WW Western Motel LLC M
(406) 338-7572. **$70-$168, 4 day notice.** 121 Central Ave E 59417. On US 2; center. Ext corridors. **Pets:** Medium, other species. $10 daily fee/pet. Designated rooms, supervision. (SAVE) 🔊 ⊗ 🛏

BUTTE

AAA WWWW Best Western Plus Butte Plaza Inn H
(406) 494-3500. **$107-$150.** 2900 Harrison Ave 59701. I-90/15 exit 127 (Harrison Ave). Int corridors. **Pets:** Medium, other species. Designated rooms, service with restrictions, supervision.
(SAVE) 🔊 ⊗ 🛏 💻 🍴 🏊 ⊗

AAA WW Comfort Inn of Butte H ❀
(406) 494-8850. **$95-$135.** 2777 Harrison Ave 59701. I-90/15 exit 127 (Harrison Ave), just s. Int corridors. **Pets:** Other species. $25 daily fee/pet. Designated rooms, service with restrictions, supervision.
(ECO) (SAVE) 🔊 🛏 💻 🏊 ⊗

WW Days Inn H
(406) 494-7000. **$89-$158.** 2700 Harrison Ave 59701. I-90/15 exit 127 (Harrison Ave), just n. Int corridors. **Pets:** Accepted.
🔊 (M) 🛏 💻 🏊

WW Finlen Hotel H
(406) 723-5461. **$57-$90.** 100 E Broadway 59701. Jct of Wyoming St; in Historic Uptown. Ext/int corridors. **Pets:** Accepted. 🔊 ⊗ 🛏

WW Butte War Bonnet Hotel H
(406) 494-7800. **$85-$149.** 2100 Cornell Ave 59701. I-90/15 exit 127B (Harrison Ave), just n, then just e. Int corridors. **Pets:** Accepted.
🔊 ⊗ 🛏 💻 🍴 🏊 ⊗

AAA WW Rocker Inn M
(406) 723-5464. **$46-$61.** 122001 W Brown's Gulch Rd 59701. I-90/15 exit 122 (Rocker Rd). Int corridors. **Pets:** Medium. $10 daily fee/room. Designated rooms, service with restrictions, supervision. (SAVE) 🔊 🛏

AAA WW Super 8 of Butte H
(406) 494-6000. **$69-$99.** 2929 Harrison Ave 59701. I-90/15 exit 127 (Harrison Ave), just s. Int corridors. **Pets:** Large. $15 one-time fee/pet. Designated rooms, service with restrictions, supervision.
(SAVE) 🔊 🛏 💻

CHINOOK

AAA WW Chinook Motor Inn M
(406) 357-2248. **$69-$79.** 100 Indiana St 59523. On US 2. Int corridors. **Pets:** Other species. $10 daily fee/pet. Service with restrictions, supervision. (SAVE) 🔊 🛏 🍴

COLUMBUS

AAA WWW Super 8 of Columbus H ❀
(406) 322-4101. **$60-$101.** 602 8th Ave N 59019. I-90 exit 408, just s on SR 78. Int corridors. **Pets:** Large, dogs only. $10 daily fee/pet. Designated rooms, service with restrictions, supervision.
(SAVE) 🔊 (M) 🛏 💻

CONRAD

WW Super 8 H
(406) 278-7676. **$69-$78.** 215 N Main St 59425. I-15 exit 339, just w. Int corridors. **Pets:** Other species. $10 daily fee/pet. Service with restrictions, supervision. 🔊 🛏 💻

COOKE CITY

WW Elk Horn Lodge M
(406) 838-2332. **$79-$119, 7 day notice.** 103 Main St 59020. Center. Ext corridors. **Pets:** Dogs only. $10 daily fee/pet. Designated rooms, supervision. 🔊 🛏 💻 (K) (Z)

DARBY

WW Rye Creek Lodge CA
(406) 821-3366. **$200-$500, 60 day notice.** 458 Rye Creek Rd 59829. US 93, 4.5 mi s, 1.5 mi e. Ext corridors. **Pets:** $25 one-time fee/room. Designated rooms, no service, supervision. 🔊 ⊗ 🛏 💻 ⊗

DEER LODGE

AAA WWW Travelodge M
(406) 846-2370. **Call for rates.** 1150 N Main St 59722. I-90 exit 184, 0.3 mi s. Int corridors. **Pets:** Other species. $10 one-time fee/room. Service with restrictions, supervision. (SAVE) 🔊 ⊗ 🛏 💻

WW Western Big Sky Inn M
(406) 846-2590. **$50-$85.** 210 N Main St 59722. I-90 exit 184, 1 mi w. Ext corridors. **Pets:** Other species. $10 one-time fee/room. Designated rooms, service with restrictions, supervision. 🔊 ⊗ 🛏 💻

DILLON

AAA WWW Best Western Paradise Inn H
(406) 683-4214. **$77-$150.** 650 N Montana St 59725. I-15 exit 63, 0.3 mi s on SR 41. Ext corridors. **Pets:** Accepted.
(SAVE) 🔊 ⊗ 🛏 💻 🍴 🏊

WW Comfort Inn of Dillon H
(406) 683-6831. **$99-$110.** 450 N Interchange 59725. I-15 exit 63. Int corridors. **Pets:** Accepted. 🔊 ⊗ 🛏 💻 🏊

WW GuestHouse International Inn & Suites H
(406) 683-3636. **$74-$199.** 580 Sinclair St 59725. I-15 exit 63. Int corridors. **Pets:** Small, dogs only. $15 one-time fee/pet. Designated rooms, service with restrictions, supervision. 🔊 (M) 🛏 💻 🏊

EAST GLACIER PARK

AAA WW Dancing Bears Inn LLC M
(406) 226-4402. **$68-$172, 4 day notice.** 40 Montana Ave 59434. Just off US 2, follow signs; center. Ext/int corridors. **Pets:** Medium, other species. $10 daily fee/pet. Designated rooms, supervision.
(SAVE) 🔊 ⊗ 🛏

EMIGRANT

AAA WWW Paradise Gateway Bed & Breakfast & Guest Cabin BB
(406) 333-4063. **$85-$400, 14 day notice.** 2644 Hwy 89 S 59027. I-90 exit 333 (US 89), 4.5 mi s of town; between MM 26 and 27, 0.3 mi e on gravel road. Ext/int corridors. **Pets:** Accepted. (SAVE) 🔊 ⊗ 🛏 💻

ENNIS

▽ Riverside Motel & Outfitters Ⓜ

(406) 682-4240. **$50-$145, 14 day notice.** 346 Main St 59729. US 287, east of town. Ext corridors. **Pets:** Medium, dogs only. $15 daily fee/pet. Designated rooms, service with restrictions, supervision.

🤝 ✕ 🛏 🖥

FORSYTH

◇◇◇ ▽▽ Magnuson Hotels Sundowner Inn Ⓜ ❄

(406) 346-2115. **$95-$130.** 1018 Front St 59327. I-94 exit 95, 0.5 mi nw on north frontage road. Ext corridors. **Pets:** Large, other species. $10 daily fee/pet. Service with restrictions, crate. SAVE 🤝 🛏 🖥

◇◇◇ ▽ Rails Inn Motel ♓

(406) 346-2242. **$65-$75, 3 day notice.** 290 Front St 59327. I-94 exit 93, just n, then 0.5 mi e on frontage road. Int corridors. **Pets:** Other species. $6 daily fee/pet. Service with restrictions, supervision.

SAVE 🤝 🛏 🖥

◇◇◇ ▽ Restwel Motel Ⓜ

(406) 346-2771. **$67-$78.** 810 Front St 59327. I-94 exit 95, 0.8 mi nw on north frontage road. Ext corridors. **Pets:** Accepted. SAVE 🤝 🛏

◇◇◇ ▽ Westwind Motor Inn Ⓜ

(406) 346-2038. **$65-$75, 3 day notice.** 225 Westwind Ln 59327. I-94 exit 93, 0.3 mi n. Int corridors. **Pets:** Other species. $6 daily fee/pet. Service with restrictions, supervision. SAVE 🤝 ✕ 🛏 🖥

GARDINER

◇◇◇ ▽▽▽ Best Western Plus By Mammoth Hot Springs Ⓜ ❄

(406) 848-7311. **$85-$200, 3 day notice.** 905 Scott St W 59030. 0.5 mi n. Ext/int corridors. **Pets:** Other species. $20 daily fee/room. Designated rooms, service with restrictions, crate.

SAVE 🤝 ✕ 🛏 🖥 🍴 ≈ ✕

◇◇◇ ▽ Yellowstone River Motel Ⓜ

(406) 848-7303. **$62-$112.** 14 E Park St 59030. Just e of US 89. Ext corridors. **Pets:** Accepted. SAVE 🤝 ✕ 🛏 🖥

▽▽ Yellowstone Super 8-Gardiner ♓

(406) 848-7401. **$49-$121.** Hwy 89 S 59030. On US 89. Int corridors. **Pets:** Other species. $10 daily fee/pet. Designated rooms, supervision.

🤝 ✕ 🛏 ≈

GLASGOW

▽▽ Cottonwood Inn ♓

(406) 228-8213. **$85-$110.** 45 1st Ave NE 59230. 0.5 mi e on US 2. Int corridors. **Pets:** Accepted. 🤝 🛏 🖥 🍴 ≈

GLENDIVE

▽ Super 8 Glendive Ⓜ

(406) 365-5671. **$43-$58.** 1904 Merrill Ave 59330. I-94 exit 215, just n. Int corridors. **Pets:** Other species. $10 one-time fee/room. Service with restrictions, supervision. 🤝 🖥

GREAT FALLS

◇◇◇ ▽▽▽ Best Western Plus Heritage Inn ♓ ❄

(406) 761-1900. **$100-$150.** 1700 Fox Farm Rd 59404. I-15 exit 278, 0.8 mi e on 10th Ave S and US 87/89 and SR 3/200. Int corridors. **Pets:** $15 one-time fee/pet. SAVE 🤝 ✕ 🛏 🖥 🍴 ≈ ✕

◇◇◇ ▽ Central Motel Ⓜ

(406) 453-0161. **$65-$95, 3 day notice.** 715 Central Ave W 59404. I-15 exit 280 (Central Ave), 0.7 mi e. Ext corridors. **Pets:** Accepted.

SAVE 🤝 🛏

▽▽ Comfort Inn by Choice Hotels ♓

(406) 454-2727. **$89-$129.** 1120 9th St S 59405. I-15 exit 278, 3 mi e on 10th Ave S and US 87/89 and SR 3/200, then just s. Int corridors. **Pets:** Other species. $10 daily fee/pet. Designated rooms, service with restrictions, supervision. 🤝 🛏 🖥 ≈

▽▽ Crystal Inn ♓

(406) 727-7788. **$89-$129.** 3701 31st St SW 59404. I-15 exit 277, just e. Int corridors. **Pets:** Accepted. 🤝 🛏 🖥 ≈

▽▽ Days Inn of Great Falls ♓

(406) 727-6565. **$62-$84.** 101 14th Ave NW 59404. I-15 exit 280 (Central Ave), 1.3 mi e on Central Ave/Business Rt I-15, 0.8 mi n on 3rd St NW, then just w. Int corridors. **Pets:** Dogs only. $5 daily fee/room. Designated rooms, service with restrictions, supervision. 🤝 🛏 🖥

▽▽ Extended StayAmerica-Great Falls-Missouri River ♓ ❄

(406) 761-7524. **$64-$89.** 800 River Dr S 59405. I-15 exit 278, 1.7 mi e on 10th Ave S, then 0.7 mi n. Int corridors. **Pets:** Other species. $25 daily fee/pet. Service with restrictions. 🤝 🔛 🛏 🖥

◇◇◇ ▽▽▽ The Great Falls Inn by Riversage ♓ ❄

(406) 453-6000. **$75-$85.** 1400 28th St S 59405. I-15 exit 278, 5.3 mi e on 10th Ave S, 0.3 mi s on 26th St S, then just e on 15th Ave S. Int corridors. **Pets:** Other species. $7 daily fee/pet. Service with restrictions, supervision. SAVE 🤝 ✕ 🔛 🛏 🖥

▽▽▽ Hampton Inn ♓

(406) 453-2675. **$119-$225.** 2301 14th St SW 59404. I-15 exit 278, just sw. Int corridors. **Pets:** Medium, dogs only. $25 one-time fee/room. Service with restrictions, supervision. 🤝 🔛 🛏 🖥 ≈

▽▽▽ Holiday Inn ♓

(406) 727-7200. **$89-$179.** 400 10th Ave S 59405. I-15 exit 278, 2 mi e on 10th Ave S, then just s. Int corridors. **Pets:** Small, other species. $10 deposit/pet. Service with restrictions, supervision.

🤝 ✕ 🛏 🖥 🍴 ≈ ✕

▽▽▽ La Quinta Inn & Suites Great Falls ♓

(406) 761-2600. **$120-$184.** 600 River Dr S 59405. I-15 exit 278, 1.7 mi e on 10th Ave S, then 0.8 mi n. Int corridors. **Pets:** Medium, other species. Service with restrictions, supervision.

🤝 🔛 🛏 🖥 ≈ ✕

◇◇◇ ▽ Motel 6 #4238 Ⓜ

(406) 453-1602. **$67-$95.** 2 Treasure State Dr 59404. I-15 exit 278, 0.8 mi e on 10th Ave S and US 87/89 and SR 3/200. Int corridors. **Pets:** Other species. Service with restrictions, supervision. SAVE 🤝

▽▽▽ O'Haire Motor Inn Ⓜ

(406) 454-2141. **$69-$110.** 17 7th St S 59403. Center of downtown. Ext/int corridors. **Pets:** Accepted. 🤝 🛏 🖥 🍴 ≈

◇◇◇ ▽▽ Quality Inn ♓

(406) 761-3410. **$60-$120.** 220 Central Ave 59401. Downtown. Ext/int corridors. **Pets:** Accepted. SAVE 🤝 🛏 🖥 🍴 ≈

▽▽▽ Staybridge Suites ♓

(406) 761-4903. **$99-$199.** 201 3rd St NW (US 87) 59404. I-15 exit 280 (Central Ave), 1.2 mi w, then just n. Int corridors. **Pets:** Medium, other species. $30 one-time fee/pet. Service with restrictions, crate.

🤝 ✕ 🔛 🛏 🖥 ≈

◇◇◇ ▽▽ TownHouse Inn of Great Falls Ⓜ

(406) 761-4600. **$90-$150.** 1411 10th Ave S 59405. I-15 exit 278, 2.6 mi e on 10th Ave S and US 87/89 and SR 3/200. Int corridors. **Pets:** Other species. $10 daily fee/pet. Service with restrictions, supervision.

SAVE 🤝 ✕ 🛏 🖥 ≈ ✕

HAMILTON

◇◇◇ ▽▽▽ Best Western Hamilton Inn Ⓜ

(406) 363-2142. **$70-$101.** 409 S 1st St (US 93) 59840. On US 93, s of City Center, jct Madison. Ext corridors. **Pets:** Other species. $10 one-time fee/pet. Service with restrictions, supervision. SAVE 🤝 🔛 🛏 🖥

▼▼▼ **Bitterroot River Inn & Conference Center** 🅷 ✿
(406) 375-2525. **$69-$139.** 139 Bitterroot Plaza Dr 59840. US 93, 1 mi n, then just w. Ext/int corridors. **Pets:** Service with restrictions, supervision. 📶 ✖ ♿ 🛏 🐾 💻 🏊 ✖

▼▼▼ **Town House Inns** 🅷 🐾
(406) 363-6600. **Call for rates.** 1113 N 1st St 59840. On US 93, n of City Center. Int corridors. **Pets:** Other species. $10 one-time fee/pet. Service with restrictions, supervision. 📶 ♿ 🛏 💻

HARDIN

▼ **Rodeway Inn** 🅷
(406) 665-1870. **Call for rates.** 1324 N Crawford Ave 59034. I-90 exit 495, just s on SR 47. Ext corridors. **Pets:** Other species. $10 daily fee/pet. Designated rooms, service with restrictions, supervision.
📶 🛏 💻 🏊

▼ **Western Motel** Ⓜ
(406) 665-2296. **$65-$110.** 830 W 3rd St 59034. I-90 exit 495 eastbound, 1.3 mi s on SR 47 and CR 313, then just e; exit 497 westbound, 0.3 mi w on I-90 business loop, continue on 3rd St for 0.7 mi. Ext corridors. **Pets:** Accepted. 📶 🛏

HARLOWTON

▼ **Countryside Inn** Ⓜ
(406) 632-4119. **$54-$67.** 309 3rd St NE 59036. US 12 E. Ext corridors. **Pets:** Accepted. 🛏

HAVRE

▼▼ **AmericInn Lodge & Suites of Havre** 🅷
(406) 395-5000. **$83-$148.** 2520 Hwy 2 W 59501. On US 2, west side of town. Int corridors. **Pets:** Accepted. 📶 ✖ 🛏 💻 🏊

▼▼ **TownHouse Inn of Havre** 🅷
(406) 265-6711. **Call for rates.** 601 1st St W 59501. Just w of town center on US 2. Int corridors. **Pets:** Accepted. 📶 🛏 💻 🏊 ✖

HELENA

▼▼▼ **Barrister Bed & Breakfast** 🅱🅱 ✿
(406) 443-7330. **$130-$145, 4 day notice.** 416 N Ewing St 59601. I-15 exit 192 (Prospect Ave), 1.5 mi sw via Prospect and Montana aves to 9th Ave, 0.8 mi w, then just s. Int corridors. **Pets:** Dogs only. 📶 ✖ ☎

 ▼▼▼ **Best Western Premier Helena Great Northern Hotel** 🅷
(406) 457-5500. **$162-$190.** 835 Great Northern Blvd 59601. I-15 exit 193 (Cedar St), 2 mi w, just w on Lyndale Ave, then just s on Getchell St; downtown. Int corridors. **Pets:** Accepted.
[SAVE] 📶 ✖ ♿ 🛏 💻 🍴 🏊

▼▼ **Days Inn Helena** 🅷
(406) 442-3280. **$59-$99.** 2001 Prospect Ave 59601. I-15 exit 192 (Prospect Ave), just w. Int corridors. **Pets:** Accepted.
📶 ♿ 🛏 💻 ✖

▲▲▲ ▼▼▼ **Helena Super 8** 🅷
(406) 443-2450. **$59-$63.** 2200 11th Ave 59601. I-15 exit 192 northbound; exit west business district southbound on US 12. Int corridors. **Pets:** Other species. $10 one-time fee/pet. Service with restrictions, supervision. [SAVE] 📶 🛏

▼▼▼ **Holiday Inn Conference Center Downtown** 🅷
(406) 443-2200. **$99-$189.** 22 N Last Chance Gulch 59601. Jct Park and Broadway aves. Int corridors. **Pets:** Large. $10 daily fee/pet. Designated rooms, service with restrictions, crate. 📶 ✖ 🛏 💻 🍴 🏊

▲▲▲ ▼▼▼ **Red Lion Colonial Hotel** 🅷
(406) 443-2100. **$115-$155.** 2301 Colonial Dr 59601. I-15 exit 192 (Prospect Ave) southbound; exit 192B northbound. Int corridors.
Pets: Accepted. [SAVE] 📶 ✖ 🛏 💻 🍴 🏊 ✖

▼▼▼ **Residence Inn by Marriott** 🅷
(406) 443-8010. **$123-$161.** 2500 E Custer Ave 59602. I-15 exit 292 (Cedar Ave), just e, 1 mi on Washington St, then just e. Int corridors. **Pets:** $100 one-time fee/room. Service with restrictions.
📶 ✖ ♿ 🛏 🏊

▼▼▼ **Wingate by Wyndham** 🅷
(406) 449-3000. **$101-$133.** 2007 N Oakes St 59601. I-15 exit 193 (Cedar St), just sw. Int corridors. **Pets:** Large. $10 daily fee/pet. Designated rooms, service with restrictions, supervision.
📶 ♿ 🛏 💻 🏊

HUNGRY HORSE

▲▲▲ ▼▼▼ **Mini Golden Inns Motel** Ⓜ
(406) 387-4313. **$86-$160, 30 day notice.** 8955 US 2 E 59919. East end of town. Ext corridors. **Pets:** Accepted. [SAVE] 📶 ♿ 🛏 💻

KALISPELL

▲▲▲ ▼ **Aero Inn** 🅷 ✿
(406) 755-3798. **$49-$104.** 1830 US 93 S 59901. 1.3 mi s on US 93 from jct US 2. Int corridors. **Pets:** $10 deposit/room. Designated rooms, service with restrictions, supervision. [SAVE] 📶 🛏 🏊

▼▼ **Americas Best Value Glacier Peaks Inn** 🅷
(406) 756-3222. **$55-$105.** 1550 Hwy 93 N 59901. 1.3 mi n on US 93 from jct US 2. Int corridors. **Pets:** Large. $10 daily fee/room. Designated rooms, supervision. 📶 ✖ 🛏 💻

▼▼ **Comfort Inn** 🅷
(406) 755-6700. **$70-$250.** 1330 Hwy 2 W 59901. 1 mi w on US 2 from jct US 93. Int corridors. **Pets:** Medium. $20 one-time fee/room. Designated rooms, service with restrictions, supervision.
[SAVE] 📶 ✖ 🛏 💻 🍴 🏊

▼▼▼ **Holiday Inn Express & Suites** 🅷 ✿
(406) 755-7405. **$99-$209.** 275 Treeline Rd 59901. 3 mi n on US 93 from jct US 2, just w. Int corridors. **Pets:** Dogs only. $35 one-time fee/room. Supervision. 📶 ✖ ♿ 🛏 💻 🏊

▼▼ **Kalispell/Glacier Int'l Airport area Super 8** 🅷
(406) 755-1888. **$74-$96.** 1341 1st Ave E 59901. 1.2 mi s on US 93 from jct US 2. Int corridors. **Pets:** Other species. $10 one-time fee/pet. Service with restrictions, supervision. 📶 ✖ ♿ 🛏 💻

▼▼ **Kalispell Grand Hotel** 🅷 ✿
(406) 755-8100. **$80-$150.** 100 Main St 59901. On US 93; downtown. Int corridors. **Pets:** Other species. 📶 ✖ 🍴

▼▼▼▼ **La Quinta Inn & Suites Kalispell** 🅷
(406) 257-5255. **$80-$194.** 255 Montclair Dr 59901. Jct US 93 and 2, 1 mi e. Int corridors. **Pets:** Medium, other species. Service with restrictions, supervision. 📶 ✖ ♿ 🛏 💻 🏊

▲▲▲ ▼▼▼ **Red Lion Hotel Kalispell** 🅷
(406) 751-5050. **$69-$199.** 20 N Main St 59901. Just s on US 93 from jct of US 2; connected to Kalispell Center Mall. Int corridors.
Pets: Accepted. [SAVE] 📶 ✖ ♿ 🛏 💻 🏊 ✖

LAUREL

▲▲▲ ▼▼▼ **Best Western Yellowstone Crossing** 🅷
(406) 628-6888. **$99-$107.** 205 SE 4th St 59044. I-90 exit 434, just n, then just e. Int corridors. **Pets:** Medium. $10 daily fee/pet. Designated rooms, service with restrictions, supervision.
[SAVE] 📶 ♿ 🛏 💻 🏊

LEWISTOWN

▼ **B & B Motel** Ⓜ
(406) 535-5496. **$50-$90.** 520 E Main St 59457. Downtown. Ext corridors. **Pets:** Accepted. 📶 🛏 💻

LIBBY

▼▼ Sandman Motel M

(406) 293-8831. **$55-$85, 7 day notice.** 31901 US 2 59923. Just w on US 2 from jct SR 37. Ext corridors. **Pets:** Accepted.

LIVINGSTON

ᐯᐯᐯ ▼▼ Best Western Yellowstone Inn H

(406) 222-6110. **$86-$134.** 1515 W Park St 59047. I-90 exit 333, just n. Int corridors. **Pets:** Accepted. [SAVE]

▼▼ Livingston Rodeway Inn M

(406) 222-6320. **$60-$130.** 102 Rogers Ln 59047. I-90 exit 333, just n on US 89, then just w. Ext/int corridors. **Pets:** Large. $10 daily fee/pet. Designated rooms, service with restrictions, supervision.

LOLO

▼▼ Days Inn H

(406) 273-2121. **$59-$99, 3 day notice.** 11225 US 93 S 59847. North edge of town. Ext/int corridors. **Pets:** Accepted.

MALTA

ᐯᐯᐯ ▼ Maltana Motel M

(406) 654-2610. **Call for rates.** 138 S 1st Ave W 59538. Just s of US 2 via US 191, then just w; downtown. Ext corridors. **Pets:** Accepted.

MILES CITY

ᐯᐯᐯ ▼▼ Best Western War Bonnet Inn M ❀

(406) 234-4560. **$85-$200.** 1015 S Haynes Ave 59301. I-94 exit 138 (Broadus), 0.3 mi n. Ext corridors. **Pets:** Other species. $20 daily fee/room. Designated rooms, service with restrictions, supervision.

ᐯᐯᐯ ▼▼ GuestHouse International Inn & Suites H ❀

(406) 232-3661. **$90-$120.** 3111 Steel St 59301. I-94 exit 138 (Broadus), just s. Int corridors. **Pets:** $15 daily fee/pet. Designated rooms, service with restrictions, supervision. [SAVE]

MISSOULA

▼▼▼ AmericInn Hotel & Suites of Missoula H

(406) 542-0888. **$79-$129.** 4545 N Reserve St 59808. I-90 exit 101 (Reserve St), 0.5 mi s. Int corridors. **Pets:** Medium, dogs only. $15 daily fee/room. Service with restrictions, supervision.

ᐯᐯᐯ ▼▼▼▼ Best Western Plus Grant Creek Inn H ❀

(406) 543-0700. **$109-$169.** 5280 Grant Creek Rd 59808. I-90 exit 101 (Reserve St), just n. Int corridors. **Pets:** $10 daily fee/room. Designated rooms, service with restrictions, supervision. [SAVE]

▼▼▼ Broadway Inn Conference Center H

(406) 532-3300. **$70-$100.** 1609 W Broadway 59808. I-90 exit 104 (Orange St), 0.5 mi s, then 1 mi w. Int corridors. **Pets:** Accepted.

▼▼ Campus Inn M

(406) 549-5134. **$70-$135.** 744 E Broadway 59802. I-90 exit 105 (Van Buren St), just s to Broadway, then just w. Ext/int corridors. **Pets:** Other species. $6 daily fee/pet. Service with restrictions.

ᐯᐯᐯ ▼▼ Days Inn/Missoula Airport H ❀

(406) 721-9776. **$59-$99.** 8600 Truck Stop Rd 59808. I-90 exit 96, just n. Int corridors. **Pets:** Other species. $10 daily fee/pet. Designated rooms, service with restrictions, supervision. [SAVE]

▼▼ Days Inn University H

(406) 543-7221. **$75-$89.** 201 E Main St 59802. I-90 exit 104 (Orange St), 0.5 mi s to Broadway, 0.5 mi e to Washington St, just s to Main St, then just w. Ext corridors. **Pets:** Accepted.

ᐯᐯᐯ ▼▼▼ DoubleTree by Hilton Hotel Missoula - Edgewater H

(406) 728-3100. **$109-$199.** 100 Madison St 59802. I-90 exit 105 (Van Buren St), just s, then just w on Front St. Int corridors. **Pets:** Accepted. [SAVE]

▼▼ Econo Lodge H

(406) 542-7550. **$65-$80.** 4953 N Reserve St 59808. I-90 exit 101 (Reserve St), just s. Int corridors. **Pets:** $10 daily fee/pet. Designated rooms, service with restrictions, supervision.

ᐯᐯᐯ ▼▼ Family Inn M ❀

(406) 543-7371. **$72-$96.** 1031 E Broadway 59802. I-90 exit 105 (Van Buren St), just s, then just e. Ext corridors. **Pets:** Medium, dogs only. $50 deposit/room. [SAVE]

▼▼▼ GuestHouse Inn & Suites - Missoula H

(406) 251-2665. **$69-$99.** 3803 Brooks St 59804. I-90 exit 101 (Reserve St), 5 mi s to Brooks St, then just w. Int corridors. **Pets:** Accepted.

ᐯᐯᐯ ▼▼▼▼ Hampton Inn H ❀

(406) 549-1800. **$99-$149.** 4805 N Reserve St 59808. I-90 exit 101 (Reserve St), just s. Int corridors. **Pets:** Other species. $10 one-time fee/room. Service with restrictions, supervision. [SAVE]

ᐯᐯᐯ ▼▼▼▼ Holiday Inn Missoula-Downtown at the Park H

(406) 721-8550. **$129-$229.** 200 S Pattee St 59802. I-90 exit 104 (Orange St), 0.5 mi s to Broadway, just e to Pattee St, then just s. Int corridors. **Pets:** Accepted. [SAVE]

▼▼ La Quinta Inn Missoula H

(406) 549-9000. **$80-$194.** 5059 N Reserve St 59808. I-90 exit 101 (Reserve St), just s. Int corridors. **Pets:** Medium, other species. Service with restrictions, supervision.

▼▼ Red Lion Inn M

(406) 728-3300. **Call for rates.** 700 W Broadway 59802. I-90 exit 104 (Orange St), just s, then just w. Ext corridors. **Pets:** Accepted.

ᐯᐯᐯ ▼▼ Ruby's Inn & Convention Center H

(406) 721-0990. **$79-$125.** 4825 N Reserve St 59808. I-90 exit 101 (Reserve St), just s. Ext/int corridors. **Pets:** Other species. $10 daily fee/room. Service with restrictions, supervision. [SAVE]

▼▼ Sleep Inn by Choice Hotels H ❀

(406) 543-5883. **Call for rates.** 3425 Dore Ln 59801. I-90 exit 101 (Reserve St), 5 mi s, then just e on Brooks St. Int corridors. **Pets:** Other species. $25 one-time fee/room. Designated rooms, service with restrictions, supervision.

▼ Super 8-Brooks St H

(406) 251-2255. **$51-$85.** 3901 Brooks St 59804. I-90 exit 101 (Reserve St), 5 mi s to Brooks St, then just w. Int corridors. **Pets:** Accepted.

ᐯᐯᐯ ▼▼ Thunderbird Motel M ❀

(406) 543-7251. **$65-$120.** 1009 E Broadway 59802. I-90 exit 105 (Van Buren St), just s to Broadway, then just e. Ext/int corridors. **Pets:** Small, dogs only. $5 daily fee/pet. Designated rooms, service with restrictions, supervision. [SAVE]

AAA PetBook® Photo Contest Entries

Each year, the winning entry in AAA's PetBook Photo Contest, sponsored by Best Western® appears on a cover of *Traveling With Your Pet: The AAA PetBook®* and also receives other great prizes. You have already met the contest winners, but here are more great entries that we just had to make room for!

Check out AAA.com/PetBook for pictures, contest rules and an entry form for next year's contest. And keep traveling with your pet!

Elsa & Reese in Bretton Woods, New Hampshire
Owners: Kimberly & Christopher Palermo from
North Andover, Mass.

Ranger on vacation in Chicago, Illinois
Owner: Jeffrey Barr from Clifton Heights, Pa.

Molly at Lower Colorado River, Arizona
Owner: Melissa Westfall from Phoenix, Ariz.

Sunny at Channel Islands Harbor, California
Owners: Roxanne & Ryan Maley from
Thousand Oaks, Calif.

Sandy in Mammoth Lakes, California
Owner: John Plummer from Pasadena, Calif.

Cooper at Dead Horse Point State Park in Moab, Utah
Owner: Jean Younger from Perris, Calif.

Max & Linda at Hendrik Point, California
Owners: John & Diane Hollenbeck from
Tustin, Calif.

Eli vacationing in Yosemite, California
Owner: Dora Shaieb from
Huntington Beach, Calif.

Brandy at the O'Brien Country Store,
O'Brien, Oregon Owner: Christine Murphy
from Cave Junction, Ore.

Yoshi visiting Yosemite National Park, California
Owner: Jean Mumbleau from Rancho Cucamonga, Calif.

Tigger, Lilly & Winnie at Gay Head, Martha's Vineyard,
Massachusetts Owners: Leslie & Kevin Ganac from
South Kingstown, R.I.

Valarie at Crater Lake, Oregon
Owner: Christa Biddle from Lake Elsinore, Calif.

Dakota at San Gabriel Mtns, LA County,
California Owner: Jason Harper of
Huntington Beach, Calif.

Koko Bean at Alexander Ramsey Park,
Redwood Falls, Minnesota
Owner: Rita Vetsch from Monticello, Minn.

Keio at the Grand Canyon
Owner: Takako Muramatsu from Los Angeles, Calif.

Flynn at Bald Head Island, North Carolina
Owner: Lauren Robbins from Leland, N.C.

Trumper at Golden Gate Nat. Recreation
Area, San Francisco, California
Owner: Mick Gast from San Francisco, Calif.

Storm at Big Bear Lake, California
Owner: Cindy Bradford from Chino, Calif.

Gunner at Summerland Beach, California
Owner: Sabrina Gauss-Trinh from Stevenson
Ranch, Calif.

Happy visiting the Mayflower Ship in Plymouth, Massachusetts
Owner: William Austin from Cumberland, R.I.

Lucy vacationing in Sedona, Arizona
Owner: Diane Seitz from Yorba Linda, Calif.

Jackie vacationing in Wyoming
Owner: Christine Jones from La Quinta, Calif.

Lola at Curt Gowdy State Park, Wyoming
Owner: Ashley Clark from Cheyenne, Wyo.

Molly at Chesapeake Bay, Oxford, Maryland
Owner: Linda Niederst from Glenshaw, Pa.

Tiny Frau at Palm Beach, Florida
Owner: Craig Billington Smith from Lake Worth, Fla.

Zero at Triple Falls, Oregon
Owner: Keath McKenzie from Gresham, Ore.

Stuie & Chloe at Lake Erie, Pennsylvania
Owner: Trudy Cross from Pittsburgh, Pa.

Hana Pukana la at Harpersfield Covered Bridge,
Harpersfield, Ohio
Owner: Kathy Oravecz from Thompson, Ohio

Sarah at Cape San Blas, Florida
Owners: Chad & Faith Augustine from Louisville, Ky.

Breezy at Monument Valley Navajo Tribal Park, Utah
Owner: Jessica Smith from Ocala, Fla.

Nugget, at Badlands National Park, South Dakota
Owner: Janelle Thoma from Arlington Heights, Ill.

Hannah in Crawford Notch, New Hampshire
Owners: Karen & Dennis Macedo from
Mashpee, Mass.

Breeze relaxing in Key Biscayne, Florida
Owner: Grace Gems from Coral Gables, Fla.

Chase along the Strait of Juan de Fuca
Highway, Washington
Owner: Marie Baraldi from Seattle, Wash.

Riley at the Susquehanna River in Laceyville, Pennsylvania Owner: Lisa Granahan from Dunmore, Pa.

Rusty vacationing at Venice Beach, California
Owners: Star & Bobby Fields from Scottsdale, Ariz.

A few more tail-wagging travelers

1) Bailey at Mammoth Lakes (Lake Mary), California, Owners: Gary & Pam Garfield from Claremont, Calif. 2) Chevy in Blue Springs, Georgia, Owner: Brooke Hendrix from Savannah, Ga. 3) Ariel at Acadia National Park, Mount Desert Island, Maine, Owner: Linda Bates from North Easton, Mass. 4) Reveille & Sprocket at Bitterroot National Forest in Montana, Owner: Wendy Wolff from Teton Village, Wyo. 5) Bentley at Crater Lake National Park, Oregon, Owner: Danielle Lucas from San Francisco, Calif. 6) Fida & Tara in Escalante, Utah, Owner: Ajay Varma from Redmond, Wash. 7) Normie & Gunther at Lake Arrowhead, California, Owner: Jaimie Davis from Silverado, Calif.

▼ Travelers Inn Motel **M**
(406) 728-8330. **$65-$85.** 4850 N Reserve St 59808. I-90 exit 101
(Reserve St), just s. Ext corridors. **Pets:** Accepted. 🛜 🛗

MONTANA CITY

△△△ ▼▼ Elkhorn Mountain Inn **H** 🐾
(406) 442-6625. **$70-$90.** 1 Jackson Creek Rd 59634. I-15 exit 187
(Montana City), just w. Int corridors. **Pets:** Other species. $10 daily fee/
room. Designated rooms, service with restrictions, supervision.
SAVE 🛜 ✕ 🛗 🛗 🖵

POLSON

△△△ ▼▼▼ Best Western Plus KwaTaqNuk
Resort **H** 🐾
(406) 883-3636. **$110-$171, 3 day notice.** 49708 US Hwy 93 E 59860.
Just s of downtown. Int corridors. **Pets:** Medium, other species. $20 daily
fee/pet. Designated rooms, service with restrictions, supervision.
SAVE 🛜 🛗 🛗 🖵 🍴 🏊 ✕

RED LODGE

▼▼ Comfort Inn of Red Lodge **H**
(406) 446-4469. **$90-$180.** 612 N Broadway 59068. Jct US 212 and SR
78, north entrance. Int corridors. **Pets:** Other species. $10 daily fee/room.
Designated rooms, service with restrictions, supervision.
🛜 ✕ 🛗 🛗 🖵 🏊

▼▼ Lu Pine Inn **H**
(406) 446-1321. **$69-$149.** 702 S Hauser Ave 59068. 0.4 mi s, just w of
US 212. Int corridors. **Pets:** Designated rooms, service with restrictions,
supervision. 🛜 ✕ 🛗 🖵 🏊 ✕

▼ Yodeler Motel **M**
(406) 446-1435. **$69-$135.** 601 S Broadway Ave 59068. Just s on US
212. Ext corridors. **Pets:** $5 daily fee/pet. Designated rooms, service with
restrictions, supervision. 🛜 ✕ 🛗 🖵

RONAN

▼ Starlite Motel **M**
(406) 676-7000. **$47-$87.** 18 Main St SW 59864. Just w of jct US 93
and Main St. Ext corridors. **Pets:** Dogs only. $10 one-time fee/room. Des-
ignated rooms, service with restrictions, supervision. 🛜 🛗 🖵

ST. IGNATIUS

▼ Sunset Motel **M**
(406) 745-3900. **$60-$80.** 333 Mountain View 59865. Just s of downtown, exit US 93. Ext corridors. **Pets:** Dogs only. $5 daily fee/pet. Service
with restrictions, supervision. 🛜 ✕ 🛗

ST. REGIS

△△△ ▼ Little River Motel **M** 🐾
(406) 649-2713. **$45-$80.** 424 Little River Ln 59866. I-90 exit 33, just n
to flashing light, just w, then just sw. Ext corridors. **Pets:** $10 daily fee/
pet. Designated rooms, service with restrictions, supervision.
SAVE 🛜 🛗 🖵 🎾 ☎

△△△ ▼▼ Super 8-St. Regis **H**
(406) 649-2422. **$51-$76.** 9 Old Hwy 10 E 59866. I-90 exit 33, just n.
Ext/int corridors. **Pets:** $10 daily fee/pet. Service with restrictions, crate.
SAVE 🛜 🛗 🖵

SHELBY

▼▼ Comfort Inn of Shelby **H** 🐾
(406) 434-2212. **$95-$135.** 455 McKinley Ave 59474. I-15 exit 363, just
e, then just s. Int corridors. **Pets:** Large, dogs only. $10 daily fee/pet.
Designated rooms, service with restrictions, supervision.
🛜 🛗 🖵 ✕

△△△ ▼ O'Haire Manor Motel **M**
(406) 434-5555. **Call for rates.** 204 2nd St S 59474. Just s of Main St
via Maple St. Ext/int corridors. **Pets:** Medium. $5 daily fee/pet. Designated
rooms, supervision. SAVE 🛜 🛗

SIDNEY

△△△ ▼▼▼ Richland Motor Inn **M**
(406) 433-6400. **$107-$117.** 1200 S Central Ave 59270. 1.5 mi n of jct
SR 200 and 16. Int corridors. **Pets:** Other species. $10 one-time fee/pet.
Service with restrictions, supervision. SAVE 🛜 🛗 🖵

THREE FORKS

△△△ ▼ Broken Spur Motel **M**
(406) 285-3237. **$60-$120.** 124 W Elm (Hwy 2) 59752. I-90 exit 278
westbound, 1.3 mi sw; exit 274 eastbound, 1 mi s on SR 287 to jct SR
2, then 3 mi se. Ext corridors. **Pets:** Other species. $5 one-time fee/pet.
Designated rooms, service with restrictions, supervision. SAVE 🛜 🛗

▼ Fort Three Forks Motel & RV Park **M**
(406) 285-3233. **$48-$109.** 10776 Hwy 287 59752. I-90 exit 274. Ext
corridors. **Pets:** Other species. $5 daily fee/pet. Designated rooms, serv-
ice with restrictions, supervision. 🛜 🛗 🖵

WEST YELLOWSTONE

△△△ ▼▼◆ Best Western Cross-Winds Motor
Inn **M** 🐾
(406) 646-9557. **Call for rates.** 201 Firehole Ave 59758. Just w of US
191 and 287, on US 20 at Dunraven St and Firehole Ave. Ext corridors.
Pets: Designated rooms, service with restrictions, supervision.
SAVE 🛜 ✕ 🛗 🖵 🏊

△△△ ▼▼▼ Best Western Desert Inn **H** 🐾
(406) 646-7376. **$68-$255.** 133 Canyon St 59758. US 191 at US 20;
corner of Canyon St and Firehole Ave. Int corridors. **Pets:** Large. Designated rooms, service with restrictions, supervision.
SAVE 🛜 ✕ 🛗 🛗 🖵 🏊

△△△ ▼▼▼ Best Western Weston Inn **M**
(406) 646-7373. **$70-$180.** 108 Gibbon Ave 59758. US 191; jct Canyon
St. Ext/int corridors. **Pets:** Accepted. SAVE 🛜 ✕ 🛗 🖵 🏊

△△△ ▼▼▼ Brandin' Iron Inn **M**
(406) 646-9411. **$79-$149, 3 day notice.** 201 Canyon St 59758. Just w;
just n of park entrance. Ext corridors. **Pets:** Accepted.
SAVE 🛜 ✕ 🛗 🛗 🖵

△△△ ▼ City Center Motel **M**
(406) 646-7337. **$69-$109, 3 day notice.** 214 Madison Ave 59758.
West off US 191 at Madison Ave and Dunraven St; just nw of park
entrance. Ext corridors. **Pets:** $15 one-time fee/room. Service with restric-
tions, supervision. SAVE 🛜 ✕ 🖵 ☎

▼▼ ClubHouse Inn **H**
(406) 646-4892. **$100-$260.** 105 S Electric St 59758. Just sw of jct US
191, 187 and 20; just w of park entrance. Int corridors. **Pets:** Large, other
species. Designated rooms, service with restrictions, supervision.
🛜 ✕ 🛗 🛗 🖵 🏊

△△△ ▼▼▼ Gray Wolf Inn & Suites **H**
(406) 646-0000. **$69-$279, 3 day notice.** 250 S Canyon St 59758. Just
w of park entrance. Int corridors. **Pets:** Accepted.
SAVE 🛜 ✕ 🛗 🛗 🖵 🏊

△△△ ▼▼▼ Holiday Inn West Yellowstone **H**
(406) 646-7365. **$109-$299, 3 day notice.** 315 Yellowstone Ave 59758.
Just w of park entrance. Int corridors. **Pets:** Medium. $50 one-time fee/
pet. Designated rooms, supervision.
SAVE 🛜 ✕ 🛗 🛗 🛗 🖵 🍴 🏊 ✕

▼▼ Kelly Inn **H**
(406) 646-4544. **Call for rates.** 104 S Canyon St 59758. S of jct US
191, 287 and 20; just w of park entrance. Ext/int corridors. **Pets:** Designated rooms, service with restrictions, supervision.
🛜 ✕ 🛗 🖵 🏊

Stage Coach Inn 🅷
(406) 646-7381. **$59-$229.** 209 Madison Ave 59758. Corner of Dunraven St and Madison Ave, just w of park entrance. Int corridors.
Pets: Accepted. (SAVE) 🛜 ⊠ 📶 💻 ➰ ⊠

Three Bear Lodge 🅷
(406) 646-7353. **$59-$219.** 217 Yellowstone Ave 59758. Just w of park entrance. Ext/int corridors. **Pets:** Medium, other species. $25 daily fee/pet. Designated rooms, service with restrictions, crate.
(SAVE) 🛜 ⊠ 📶 💻 ➰ ⊠

Yellowstone Lodge 🅷
(406) 646-0020. **$69-$189.** 251 S Electric St 59758. Just w of park entrance. Int corridors. **Pets:** Other species. Designated rooms, service with restrictions, crate. (SAVE) 🛜 📶 💻 ➰

WHITEFISH

Best Western Rocky Mountain Lodge 🅷 🐾
(406) 862-2569. **$98-$161.** 6510 Hwy 93 S 59937. 1.3 mi s on US 93 from jct SR 487. Ext/int corridors. **Pets:** $20 one-time fee/room. Designated rooms, service with restrictions, crate.
(SAVE) 🛜 ⊠ 📶 📶 💻 ➰ ⊠

Grouse Mountain Lodge 🅷
(406) 862-3000. **$109-$399, 14 day notice.** 2 Fairway Dr 59937. 1 mi w on US 93 from jct SR 487. Int corridors. **Pets:** Accepted.
(SAVE) 🛜 📶 💻 🍽 ➰ ⊠

Kristianna Mountain Homes ⓒⓄ
(406) 862-2860. **Call for rates.** 331 Karrow Ave 59937. Jct US 93 and SR 487, 2.4 mi n on SR 487, at flashing light go 5.2 mi on Big Mountain Rd, just n on Gelande St, then just w on Kristianna Close. Ext/int corridors. **Pets:** Accepted. (SAVE) 🛜 ⊠ 📶 💻 ⊠ 🐾

North Forty Resort ⓒⒶ
(406) 862-7740. **$119-$269, 14 day notice.** 3765 Hwy 40 W 59912. 2.5 mi e on SR 40 from jct US 93. Ext corridors. **Pets:** Accepted.
🛜 ⊠ 📶 💻 ⊠ 🐾

Pine Lodge 🅷
(406) 862-7600. **$79-$170.** 920 Spokane Ave 59937. 1 mi s on US 93 from jct SR 487. Int corridors. **Pets:** Other species. Service with restrictions, supervision. (SAVE) 🛜 ⊠ 📶 📶 💻 ➰

WHITE SULPHUR SPRINGS

All Seasons Inn & Suites 🅷
(406) 547-8888. **$77-$140.** 808 3rd Ave SW 59645. On US 89/12, south end of town. Int corridors. **Pets:** $10 one-time fee/pet. Service with restrictions, supervision. (SAVE) 🛜 ⊠ 📶 📶

WIBAUX

Beaver Creek Inn & Suites Ⓜ
(406) 796-2666. **$78-$160.** 400 W 2nd Ave N 59353. I-94 exit 241 westbound; exit 242 eastbound. Int corridors. **Pets:** Accepted. 🛜 📶 💻

NEBRASKA

CITY INDEX

BELLEVUE

Best Western White House Inn 🅷
(402) 293-1600. **$69-$99.** 305 Fort Crook Rd N 68005. US 75, 1.8 mi n of jct SR 370 and Fort Crook Rd N. Int corridors. **Pets:** Other species. $25 one-time fee/room. Designated rooms, crate.
(SAVE) 🛜 ⊠ 📶 📶 💻 ⊠

Candlewood Suites-Bellevue 🅷
(402) 932-8144. **Call for rates.** 10902 S 15th St 68123. Jct US 75 and Cornhusker Rd, just e on Cornhusker Rd, then 0.3 mi s. Int corridors.
Pets: Accepted. 🛜 ⊠ 📶 📶 💻

Hampton Inn 🅷
(402) 292-1607. **$109-$219.** 3404 Samson Way 68123. US 75, 1 mi n on SR 370, just w on Golden Blvd, then 0.3 mi n. Int corridors.
Pets: Accepted. 🛜 ⊠ 📶 📶 💻 ➰

Microtel Inn & Suites 🅷
(402) 292-0191. **$67-$180.** 3008 Samson Way 68123. US 75, 1 mi w on SR 370, n on Golden Blvd, then just w. Int corridors. **Pets:** Other species. $25 one-time fee/room, $5 daily fee/pet. Service with restrictions, crate. (SAVE) 🛜 ⊠ 📶 📶 💻

Settle Inn & Suites 🅷 🐾
(402) 292-1155. **$69-$200.** 2105 Pratt Ave 68123. US 75 exit Cornhusker Rd, just w. Int corridors. **Pets:** Dogs only. $15 daily fee/room. Designated rooms, service with restrictions, crate.
🛜 ⊠ 📶 📶 💻 ➰

BROKEN BOW

The Arrow Hotel 🅷
(308) 872-6662. **$69-$155.** 509 S 9th Ave 68822. On SR 2/92; downtown. Int corridors. **Pets:** Other species. $10 daily fee/pet. Crate.
🛜 ⊠ 📶 💻 🍽

CENTRAL CITY

Super 8 🅷
(308) 946-5055. **$58-$67.** 1701 31st St 68826. SR 14, 1 mi s of jct US 30. Ext/int corridors. **Pets:** Accepted. 🛜 📶 📶 💻

CHADRON

Best Western West Hills Inn 🅷 🐾
(308) 432-3305. **$76-$104.** 1100 W 10th St 69337. Just s of jct US 385 and 20. Ext/int corridors. **Pets:** $10 daily fee/pet. Service with restrictions, crate. (SAVE) 🛜 ⊠ 📶 💻

Grand Westerner Motel Ⓜ
(308) 432-5595. **$55-$64.** 1050 W Hwy 20 69337. On US 20, 0.8 mi w; just e of jct US 385. Ext corridors. **Pets:** Dogs only. $10 one-time fee/room. No service, supervision. 🛜 ⊠ 📶

Westerner Motel Ⓜ
(308) 432-5577. **$55-$64.** 300 Oak St 69337. On US 20, 0.5 mi e of jct US 385 and SR 87. Ext corridors. **Pets:** Dogs only. $10 one-time fee/room. No service, supervision. (SAVE) 🛜 📶

COLUMBUS

▼▼ ▼▼ Sleep Inn & Suites Hotel 🄷 ❁

(402) 562-5200. **$74-$85.** 303 23rd St 68601. On US 30, 2 mi e of jct US 30 and 81; east side of town. Int corridors. **Pets:** Medium, other species. $25 daily fee/pet. Crate. 🛜 🕭ᴹ 🖥 🖵

COZAD

▼▼ Rodeway Inn 🄷

(308) 784-4900. **Call for rates.** 809 S Meridian 69130. I-80 exit 222, just n. Int corridors. **Pets:** Other species. Designated rooms, service with restrictions, supervision. 🛜 🗙 🕭ᴹ 🖥 🖵

FREMONT

▼▼ Oak Tree Inn 🄷

(402) 721-3700. **Call for rates.** 2700 N Diers Pkwy 68025. US 30, just n. Int corridors. **Pets:** Accepted. 🛜 🗙 🕭ᴹ 🖥 🖵

GERING

▼▼ Monument Inn & Suites 🄷

(308) 436-1950. **$70-$78.** 1130 M St 69341. Just w of corner M (SR 92) and 10th sts; 1 mi e of SR 71. Int corridors. **Pets:** Small, dogs only. $15 one-time fee/room. Designated rooms, service with restrictions, supervision. 🛜 🖥 🖵

GOTHENBURG

▼◆▼ Comfort Suites 🄷

(308) 537-7378. **Call for rates.** 315 Platte River Dr 69138. I-80 exit 211 (SR 47), just n, then just w. Int corridors. **Pets:** Accepted.
🛜 🗙 🕭ᴹ 🖥 🖵 🏊

▼▼ Gothenburg Super 8 🄷

(308) 537-2684. **$46-$54.** 401 Platte River Dr 69138. I-80 exit 211 (SR 47), just n. Int corridors. **Pets:** Accepted. 🛜 🕭ᴹ 🖥 🖵 🏊

GRAND ISLAND

▼◆▼ Quality Inn and Conference Center 🄷 ❁

(308) 384-7770. **$69-$130.** 7838 S US Hwy 281 68803. I-80 exit 312 (US 281), just s. Int corridors. **Pets:** Other species. $15 daily fee/room. Service with restrictions, crate. 🛜 🕭ᴹ 🖥 🖵 🍴 🏊 🗙

▼▼ Rodeway Inn 🄷 ❁

(308) 384-1333. **$55-$95.** 3205 S Locust St 68801. I-80 exit 314, 4 mi n. Int corridors. **Pets:** Large, other species. $50 deposit/pet. Service with restrictions, supervision. 🛜 🖥 🖵

▼▼ Super 8 🄷

(308) 384-4380. **$52-$62.** 2603 S Locust St 68801. I-80 exit 314, 4.7 mi n. Int corridors. **Pets:** Other species. $10 daily fee/room. Service with restrictions, supervision. 🛜 🕭ᴹ 🖥 🖵 🏊

▼▼ Travelodge 🄷

(308) 382-5003. **$45-$71.** 1311 S Locust St 68801. I-80 exit 314, 5.2 mi n. Int corridors. **Pets:** Accepted. 🛜 🗙 🕭ᴹ 🖥 🖵

HASTINGS

▼▼ Super 8 Ⓜ

(402) 463-8888. **$36-$90.** 2200 N Kansas Ave 68901. Jct US 34 and 281, 2 mi n. Int corridors. **Pets:** Large, other species. $10 daily fee/pet. Service with restrictions, supervision. 🛜 🕭ᴹ 🖥 🖵

HOLDREGE

▼▼ Super 8 🄷

(308) 995-2793. **$67.** 420 Broadway 68949. US 183, 0.5 mi w on US 6/34. Int corridors. **Pets:** $10 daily fee/pet. Service with restrictions, supervision. 🛜 🕭ᴹ 🖥 🖵 🏊

KEARNEY

🄰🄰🄰 ▼▼ ▼▼ AmericInn Lodge & Suites of Kearney 🄷

(308) 234-7800. **$105-$170.** 215 W Talmadge Rd 68845. I-80 exit 272 (SR 44), just n. Int corridors. **Pets:** Medium, dogs only. $10 daily fee/ room. Designated rooms, service with restrictions, supervision.
🅂🄰🅅🄴 🛜 🗙 🕭ᴹ 🖥 🖵 🏊

🄰🄰🄰 ▼▼ ▼▼ Best Western Inn of Kearney 🄷

(308) 237-5185. **$80-$100.** 1010 3rd Ave 68845. I-80 exit 272 (SR 44), 1 mi n, then just w. Ext/int corridors. **Pets:** Accepted.
🅂🄰🅅🄴 🛜 🕭ᴹ 🖥 🖵 🍴 🏊 🗙

▼▼ ▼▼ Econo Lodge 🄷

(308) 237-2671. **$56-$100.** 709 2nd Ave 68847. I-80 exit 272 (SR 44), 1 mi n. Int corridors. **Pets:** Large, other species. $15 daily fee/room. Service with restrictions, supervision. 🛜 🖥 🖵

▼▼ Microtel Inn & Suites 🄷

(308) 698-3003. **$50-$67.** 104 Talmadge St 68847. I-80 exit 272 (SR 44), just se. Int corridors. **Pets:** Accepted. 🛜 🗙 🕭ᴹ 🖥 🖵

▼▼ Quality Inn by Choice Hotels 🄷

(308) 237-0838. **$70-$200.** 121 3rd Ave 68845. I-80 exit 272 (SR 44), 0.3 mi n. Int corridors. **Pets:** Accepted. 🛜 🕭ᴹ 🖥 🖵 🏊

🄰🄰🄰 ▼▼ ▼▼ Ramada Kearney Hotel 🄷

(308) 237-3141. **$80-$130.** 301 2nd Ave 68847. I-80 exit 272 (SR 44), 0.7 mi n. Int corridors. **Pets:** Medium, other species. $25 one-time fee/ room. Designated rooms, service with restrictions, crate.
🅂🄰🅅🄴 🛜 🕭ᴹ 🖥 🖵 🍴 🏊 🗙

▼▼ ▼▼ Rodeway Inn & Suites 🄷

(308) 698-2810. **$60-$140.** 411 2nd Ave 68847. I-80 exit 272 (SR 44), 0.8 mi n. Int corridors. **Pets:** Large, other species. $15 daily fee/room. Service with restrictions, supervision. 🛜 🕭ᴹ 🖥 🖵

LEXINGTON

▼▼ Days Inn 🄷

(308) 324-6440. **$52-$63.** 2506 Plum Creek Pkwy 68850. I-80 exit 237 (US 283), 0.6 mi n. Int corridors. **Pets:** Dogs only. $10 one-time/pet. Designated rooms, service with restrictions, supervision.
🛜 🕭ᴹ 🖥 🖵

🄰🄰🄰 ▼▼ ▼▼ Holiday Inn Express Suites 🄷

(308) 324-9900. **$120-$160.** 2605 Plum Creek Pkwy 68850. I-80 exit 237 (US 283), 0.5 mi n. Int corridors. **Pets:** Other species. $15 daily fee/room. Designated rooms, service with restrictions, supervision.
🅂🄰🅅🄴 🛜 🗙 🕭ᴹ 🖥 🖵 🏊

▼▼▼ Lexington Comfort Inn 🄷

(308) 324-3747. **$70-$125, 5 day notice.** 2810 Plum Creek Pkwy 68850. I-80 exit 237 (US 283), 0.3 mi n. Ext/int corridors. **Pets:** Small, other species. $15 one-time fee/pet. Service with restrictions, supervision. 🛜 🕭ᴹ 🖥 🖵

LINCOLN

🄰🄰🄰 ▼▼ ▼▼ AmericInn Lodge & Suites of Lincoln North 🄷

(402) 435-1600. **$79-$199.** 6555 N 27th St 68521. I-80 exit 403 (27th St), 0.3 mi s, just w on Whitehead Dr, then just s. Int corridors. **Pets:** Accepted. 🅂🄰🅅🄴 🛜 🕭ᴹ 🖥 🖵 🏊

▼▼▼ AmericInn Lodge & Suites of Lincoln South 🄷

(402) 420-0027. **Call for rates.** 8701 Amber Hill Ct 68526. 5.8 mi se on SR 2 (Nebraska Hwy), just w at 87th St. Int corridors. **Pets:** Accepted.
🛜 🗙 🕭ᴹ 🖥 🖵 🏊

🄰🄰🄰 ▼▼ ▼▼ Best Western Crown Inn 🄷

(402) 438-4700. **$72-$140.** 6501 N 28th St 68504. I-80 exit 403 (27th St), just s to Wildcat Dr, then 0.3 mi s. Int corridors. **Pets:** Medium, dogs only. $15 daily fee/pet. Designated rooms, service with restrictions, supervision. 🅂🄰🅅🄴 🛜 🗙 🕭ᴹ 🖥 🖵 🏊

▼▼▼▼ **Candlewood Suites** 🏠 ❀
(402) 420-0330. **$85-$95.** 4100 Pioneer Woods Dr 68506. Jct SR 2 (Nebraska Hwy) and 70th St, 1.6 mi n, just e on Pioneers Blvd, then just n. Int corridors. **Pets:** Medium. $75 one-time fee/pet. Service with restrictions, crate.

▼▼▼ **Chase Suites Hotel** 🏠
(402) 483-4900. **Call for rates.** 200 S 68th Pl 68510. On US 34, 4.3 mi e, then just s. Ext corridors. **Pets:** Accepted.

▼▼▼ **Comfort Suites** 🏠
(402) 476-8080. **$74-$249.** 4231 Industrial Ave 68504. I-80 exit 403 (27th St), 2.3 mi s. Int corridors. **Pets:** Other species. $10 daily fee/pet. Service with restrictions, supervision.

▼▼▼ **Comfort Suites East** 🏠
(402) 325-8800. **$79-$200.** 331 N Cotner Blvd 68505. 3.3 mi e on US 6 city route, then 0.3 mi n. Int corridors. **Pets:** Medium, other species. $20 one-time fee/pet. Service with restrictions, crate.

🅐🅐🅐 ▼▼▼▼ **Country Inn & Suites By Carlson North** 🏠 ❀
(402) 476-5353. **$94-$200.** 5353 N 27th St 68521. I-80 exit 403 (27th St), 1.5 mi s. Int corridors. **Pets:** Other species. $20 daily fee/pet. Service with restrictions. SAVE

▼▼▼▼ **Holiday Inn Express & Suites** 🏠
(402) 464-0588. **Call for rates.** 1101 W Commerce Way 68521. I-80 exit 399, just n, then just e. Int corridors. **Pets:** Accepted.

🅐🅐🅐 ▼▼▼ **La Quinta Inn Lincoln** 🏠
(402) 476-2222. **$69-$134.** 4433 N 27th St 68521. I-80 exit 403 (27th St), 2.3 mi s. Int corridors. **Pets:** Medium, other species. Service with restrictions, supervision. SAVE

▼▼▼ **Lincoln Heights Hotel-Lincoln Airport** 🏠
(402) 474-2080. **Call for rates.** 1301 W Bond Cir 68521. I-80 exit 399 (Airport), just e. Int corridors. **Pets:** Other species. $10 daily fee/room. Service with restrictions.

🅐🅐🅐 ▼▼▼ **Microtel Inn & Suites** 🏠
(402) 476-2591. **$50-$99.** 2505 Fairfield St 68521. I-80 exit 403 (27th St), 2.7 mi s, then just w. Int corridors. **Pets:** Accepted. SAVE

▼▼▼ **New Victorian Suites** 🏠
(402) 464-4400. **$69-$149.** 225 N 50th St 68504. 2.5 mi e on US 6 and 34; just ne of jct O St; entrance off 48th St. Int corridors. **Pets:** Small, dogs only. $15 daily fee/pet. Service with restrictions, supervision.

🅐🅐🅐 ▼▼▼▼ **Residence Inn by Marriott - Lincoln South** 🏠
(402) 423-1555. **$107-$131.** 5865 Boboli Ln 68516. 1 mi s of SR 2 (Nebraska Hwy) via 56th St, then just e on Pine Lake Rd (Southeast Lincoln). Int corridors. **Pets:** Accepted. SAVE

▼▼▼ **Settle Inn & Suites** 🏠
(402) 435-8100. **Call for rates.** 7333 Husker Cir 68504. I-80 exit 403 (27th St), just s to Wildcat Dr, just e, then just n. Int corridors. **Pets:** Accepted.

▼▼▼▼ **Staybridge Suites Lincoln-I-80** 🏠
(402) 438-7829. **$99-$316.** 2701 Fletcher Ave 68504. I-80 exit 403 (27th St), 0.4 mi s, then just e. Int corridors. **Pets:** Other species. $25 one-time fee/room. Service with restrictions, crate.

▼ **Super 8-Lincoln/West "O" Street** 🏠
(402) 476-8887. **$40-$69.** 2635 West O St 68528. I-80 exit 396 eastbound, 0.5 mi e; exit 397 westbound, 0.5 mi w. Int corridors. **Pets:** Other species. $10 daily fee/pet. Service with restrictions, supervision.

MCCOOK

▼▼ **Days Inn-McCook** 🏠
(308) 345-7115. **$60-$65.** 901 N Hwy 83 69001. Jct US 6 and 34, 0.3 mi n. Int corridors. **Pets:** Accepted.

▼▼▼ **Horse Creek Inn** 🏠
(308) 345-4505. **Call for rates.** 1 Bison Holiday Dr 69001. On US 83, just n of jct US 6 and 34. Int corridors. **Pets:** Accepted.

MORRILL

▼▼ **Oak Tree Inn** 🏠
(308) 247-2111. **Call for rates.** 707 E Webster St 69358. 0.4 mi e of center on US 26. Ext/int corridors. **Pets:** $5 one-time fee/room. Service with restrictions, supervision.

NORTH PLATTE

🅐🅐🅐 ▼ **Americas Best Value Travelers Inn** Ⓜ
(308) 534-4020. **$40-$60.** 602 E 4th St 69101. I-80 exit 177 (US 83), 1.5 mi n, then 0.3 mi e. Ext corridors. **Pets:** Medium, other species. Service with restrictions, supervision. SAVE

▼▼ **Comfort Inn** 🏠
(308) 532-6144. **$88-$129.** 2901 S Jeffers St 69101. I-80 exit 177 (US 83), just s. Int corridors. **Pets:** Medium. $15 daily fee/pet. Designated rooms, no service, supervision.

▼▼▼▼ **Holiday Inn Express Hotel & Suites** 🏠
(308) 532-9500. **$114-$144.** 300 Holiday Frontage Rd 69101. I-80 exit 177 (US 83), just s. Int corridors. **Pets:** Accepted.

🅐🅐🅐 ▼▼▼ **La Quinta Inn & Suites North Platte** 🏠
(308) 534-0700. **$98-$179.** 2600 Eagles Wings Pl 69101. I-80 exit 179, just n, then just w. Int corridors. **Pets:** Medium, other species. Service with restrictions, supervision. SAVE

▼▼ **Oak Tree Inn** 🏠
(308) 535-9900. **$69-$129.** 451 Halligan Dr 69101. I-80 exit 177 (US 83), 0.3 mi n, then 0.3 mi e on service road. Int corridors. **Pets:** Other species. Service with restrictions, supervision.

OGALLALA

🅐🅐🅐 ▼▼▼ **Best Western Stagecoach Inn** 🏠 🐾
(308) 284-3656. **$70-$100.** 201 Stagecoach Tr 69153. I-80 exit 126 (US 26/SR 61), just n, then e on Frontage Rd. Ext corridors. **Pets:** Medium, other species. $10 daily fee/pet. Designated rooms, service with restrictions, crate. SAVE

🅐🅐🅐 ▼▼▼ **Days Inn** Ⓜ 🐾
(308) 284-6365. **$62-$80.** 601 Stagecoach Tr 69153. I-80 exit 126 (US 26/SR 61), just n, then e on Frontage Rd. Int corridors. **Pets:** Dogs only. $6 daily fee/pet. Service with restrictions, supervision. SAVE

OMAHA

🅐🅐🅐 ▼▼▼ **Best Western Plus Kelly Inn** 🏠 🐾
(402) 339-7400. **$79-$169.** 4706 S 108th St 68137. I-80 exit 445 (L St E), 0.3 mi e, then just s. Int corridors. **Pets:** Other species. Service with restrictions, supervision. SAVE

Best Western Settle Inn H
(402) 431-1246. **$80-$140.** 650 N 109th Ct 68154. I-680 exit 3 (Dodge St W), 0.7 mi w to 108th St and Old Mill Rd, then just w on Mill Valley Rd. Int corridors. **Pets:** Medium, dogs only. $15 daily fee/room. Designated rooms, service with restrictions, supervision.

Best Western Seville Plaza Hotel H
(402) 345-2222. **Call for rates.** 330 N 30th St 68131. I-480 exit 2B westbound; exit 2A northbound, just w on Dodge St, then just n on 30th St. Int corridors. **Pets:** Medium. $25 one-time fee/pet. Designated rooms, service with restrictions, supervision.

Candlewood Suites H
(402) 758-2848. **$64-$139.** 360 S 108th Ave 68154. I-680 exit 3 (Dodge St W), 0.7 mi to 108th Ave, then 0.8 mi s. Int corridors. **Pets:** Large. $10 daily fee/pet. Service with restrictions, crate.

Comfort Inn & Suites H
(402) 934-4900. **$80-$260.** 7007 Grover St 68106. I-80 exit 449 (72nd St), just n, then e. Int corridors. **Pets:** Medium. $10 one-time fee/pet. Designated rooms, service with restrictions, supervision.

Comfort Inn at the Zoo H
(402) 342-8000. **$70-$190.** 2920 S 13th Ct 68108. I-80 exit 454 (13th St) westbound; exit 454 (13th St N) eastbound, just w. Int corridors. **Pets:** Accepted.

Comfort Inn-Southwest H
(402) 593-2380. **$80-$150.** 10728 L St 68127. I-80 exit 445 (L St E), just n on 108th St, then e. Int corridors. **Pets:** Medium. $10 daily fee/pet. Designated rooms, service with restrictions, supervision.

Countryside Suites M
(402) 884-2644. **$55-$75.** 9477 S 142nd St 68138. I-80 exit 440, just ne. Ext corridors. **Pets:** Other species. $10 daily fee/pet. Service with restrictions.

DoubleTree by Hilton Hotel Omaha Downtown H
(402) 346-7600. **$107-$197.** 1616 Dodge St 68102. Downtown. Int corridors. **Pets:** Accepted.

DoubleTree Suites by Hilton Hotel Omaha H
(402) 397-5141. **$99-$189.** 7270 Cedar St 68124. I-80 exit 449 (72nd St), 1.3 mi n. Int corridors. **Pets:** Medium, other species. $50 one-time fee/room. Service with restrictions, crate.

Element Omaha Midtown Crossing H ❉
(402) 614-8080. **$99-$229.** 3253 Dodge St 68131. I-480 exit 2B westbound; exit 2A northbound, just w. Int corridors. **Pets:** Medium, dogs only. Designated rooms, service with restrictions, crate.

Hilton Omaha H ❉
(402) 998-3400. **$109-$329.** 1001 Cass St 68102. Jct Cass and 10th sts; downtown. Int corridors. **Pets:** Medium, dogs only. $75 one-time fee/room. Designated rooms, service with restrictions, crate.

Holiday Inn Express Hotel & Suites-West H
(402) 333-5566. **$105-$229.** 17677 Wright St 68130. I-80 exit 445 (L St W), 5.5 mi w, then just s. Int corridors. **Pets:** Accepted.

Homewood Suites Omaha Downtown H
(402) 345-5100. **$99-$199.** 1314 Cuming St 68102. Corner of 13th and Cuming sts; downtown. Int corridors. **Pets:** Accepted.

La Quinta Inn Omaha Southwest H
(402) 592-5200. **$62-$119.** 10760 M St 68127. I-80 exit 445 (L St E), 0.3 mi e, s on 108th St, then just e. Int corridors. **Pets:** Medium, other species. Service with restrictions, supervision.

Magnolia Hotel H
(402) 341-2500. **$109-$479, 30 day notice.** 1615 Howard St 68102. Jct 16th St. Int corridors. **Pets:** $50 one-time fee/pet. Service with restrictions, supervision.

Premiere Suites Omaha H
(402) 397-7500. **$72-$135.** 7010 Hascall St 68106. I-80 exit 449 (72nd St), just n, then just e. Ext/int corridors. **Pets:** $25 one-time fee/room. Service with restrictions.

Relax Inn Motel & Suites M ❉
(402) 731-7300. **$50-$60.** 4578 S 60th St 68117. I-80 exit 450 (60th St), 0.8 mi s. Ext corridors. **Pets:** Very small, dogs only. $20 deposit/pet, $10 daily fee/pet. Designated rooms, service with restrictions, supervision.

Residence Inn by Marriott Omaha-Central H
(402) 553-8898. **$98-$239.** 6990 Dodge St 68132. I-680 exit 3 (Dodge E), 3 mi e. Ext corridors. **Pets:** $100 one-time fee/room. Service with restrictions, crate.

Satellite Motel M ❉
(402) 733-7373. **$45-$55.** 6006 L St 68117. I-80 exit 450 (60th St), 0.8 mi s; just n of US 275 and SR 92. Ext/int corridors. **Pets:** Very small, dogs only. $20 deposit/pet, $10 daily fee/pet. Designated rooms, service with restrictions, supervision.

Sleep Inn & Suites H
(402) 342-2525. **$69-$159.** 2525 Abbott Dr 68110. I-480 E exit 14th St (Cuming St), 2 mi n, follow signs. Int corridors. **Pets:** Large. $10 daily fee/pet. Supervision.

TownePlace Suites Omaha West H
(402) 590-2800. **$94-$169.** 10865 W Dodge Rd 68154. I-680 exit 3 (Dodge St), 0.7 mi to 108th St to 108th Ave and N Old Mill Rd exits, then just s. Int corridors. **Pets:** Accepted.

SCOTTSBLUFF

Comfort Inn H
(308) 632-7510. **$70-$80.** 1902 21st Ave 69361. 1.8 mi e on US 26, just n. Ext/int corridors. **Pets:** Accepted.

Scottsbluff Super 8 H ❉
(308) 635-1600. **$57-$58.** 2202 Delta Dr 69361. 1.8 mi e on US 26. Int corridors. **Pets:** $10 one-time fee/pet. Designated rooms, service with restrictions, supervision.

SIDNEY

AmericInn Lodge & Suites of Sidney H ❉
(308) 254-0100. **$89-$199.** 645 Cabela Dr 69162. I-80 exit 59, just nw. Int corridors. **Pets:** Other species. $12 daily fee/pet. Service with restrictions, crate.

Days Inn H
(308) 254-2121. **$75-$135.** 3042 Silverberg Dr 69162. I-80 exit 59, just n. Int corridors. **Pets:** Medium. $10 daily fee/pet. Designated rooms, service with restrictions, supervision.

Holiday Inn & Conference Center H 🐾
(308) 254-2000. **$99-$309.** 664 Chase Blvd 69162. I-80 exit 59, just s. Int corridors. **Pets:** Large. $20 one-time fee/room. Service with restrictions.

SOUTH SIOUX CITY

▼▼▼▼ **Marina Inn Conference Center** H
(402) 494-4000. **$89-$149.** 385 E 4th St 68776. I-29 exit 149 southbound; exit 148 northbound, e at traffic light by Nebraska side of bridge; on banks of Missouri River. Int corridors. **Pets:** Accepted.
🛜 ⊠ ᴸᴹ 🛏 🖥 ⊓⊔ ⇌

VALENTINE

▼▼ **Dunes Lodge & Suites** M ❀
(402) 376-3131. **$54-$159.** 340 E Hwys 20 & 83 69201. Jct US 20/83, 0.3 mi e. Ext corridors. **Pets:** Medium. $10 daily fee/pet. Designated rooms, service with restrictions, supervision. 🛜 🛏 🖥

▼▼ **Trade Winds Motel** M
(402) 376-1600. **$61-$99.** 1009 E Hwy 20 69201. Jct US 20/83, 1 mi se. Ext corridors. **Pets:** $10 daily fee/pet. Designated rooms, service with restrictions, supervision. 🛜 🛏 🖥

YORK

ⒶⒶⒶ ▼▼ **Americas Best Value-Palmer Inn** M
(402) 362-5585. **$45-$95.** 2426 S Lincoln Ave 68467. I-80 exit 353 (US 81), 1 mi n. Ext corridors. **Pets:** Accepted.
🆂🅰🆅🅴 🛜 ᴸᴹ 🛏 🖥 ⇌

ⒶⒶⒶ ▼▼▼◆ **Comfort Inn** H
(402) 362-6555. **$80-$129.** 3815 S Lincoln Ave 68467. I-80 exit 353 (US 81), just n. Ext/int corridors. **Pets:** Other species. $20 daily fee/pet. Designated rooms, service with restrictions, supervision.
🆂🅰🆅🅴 🛜 ᴸᴹ 🛏 🖥 ⇌

ⒶⒶⒶ ▼▼▼◆ **Holiday Inn** H
(402) 362-6661. **Call for rates.** 4619 S Lincoln Ave 68467. I-80 exit 353 (US 81), just s. Int corridors. **Pets:** Other species. $25 one-time fee/room. Designated rooms, service with restrictions, supervision.
🆂🅰🆅🅴 🛜 ⊠ ᴸᴹ 🛏 🖥 ⊓⊔ ⇌

ⒶⒶⒶ ▼▼ **Yorkshire Inn Motel** M
(402) 362-6633. **$42-$89.** 3402 S Lincoln Ave 68467. I-80 exit 353 (US 81), 0.5 mi n. Ext/int corridors. **Pets:** Accepted. 🆂🅰🆅🅴 🛜 🛏

NEVADA

CITY INDEX

BEATTY

▼▼ **Death Valley Inn & RV Park** H
(775) 553-9400. **$63-$125.** 651 Hwy 95 S 89003. Just s. Ext corridors. **Pets:** Accepted. ⊠ 🛏 🖥 ⇌

ⒶⒶⒶ ▼▼ **Stagecoach Hotel Casino** M ❀
(775) 553-2419. **$62-$77.** 900 E Hwy 95 N 89003. North end of town; west side of US 95. Ext/int corridors. **Pets:** Medium. $10 deposit/pet, $5 one-time fee/pet. Designated rooms, service with restrictions, supervision.
🆂🅰🆅🅴 🛜 ᴸᴹ 🛏 🖥 ⊓⊔ ⇌

CARSON CITY

▼▼▼ **Holiday Inn Express & Suites** H
(775) 283-4055. **$100-$199.** 4055 N Carson St 89701. US 395 exit 43, 0.7 mi se. Int corridors. **Pets:** Other species. $20 one-time fee/pet. Designated rooms, service with restrictions, crate. 🛜 ᴸᴹ 🛏 🖥 ⇌

ELKO

ⒶⒶⒶ ▼▼▼ **Americas Best Value Gold Country Inn & Casino** H
(775) 738-8421. **$79-$159, 14 day notice.** 2050 Idaho St 89801. I-80 exit 303, just s; Americas Best Value Gold Country Inn & Casino. Ext corridors. **Pets:** Other species. $15 one-time fee/room. Designated rooms, service with restrictions, crate. 🆂🅰🆅🅴 🛜 🛏 🖥 ⊓⊔ ⇌

ⒶⒶⒶ ▼▼▼◆ **Best Western Elko Inn** H
(775) 738-8787. **$105-$140.** 1930 Idaho St 89801. I-80 exit 303, 0.3 mi sw. Int corridors. **Pets:** Accepted. 🆂🅰🆅🅴 🛜 🛏 🖥 ⇌

ⒶⒶⒶ ▼▼ **Oak Tree Inn** H
(775) 777-2222. **$89-$109.** 95 Spruce Rd 89801. I-80 exit 301, just n. Int corridors. **Pets:** $10 daily fee/pet. Service with restrictions, supervision.
🆂🅰🆅🅴 🛜 ⊠ ᴸᴹ 🛏 🖥 ⊠

ⒶⒶⒶ ▼▼▼◆ **Red Lion Hotel & Casino** H
(775) 738-2111. **$99-$259.** 2065 Idaho St 89801. I-80 exit 303, just s. Int corridors. **Pets:** Accepted. 🆂🅰🆅🅴 🛜 ᴸᴹ 🛏 🖥 ⊓⊔ ⇌

ⒶⒶⒶ ▼▼ **Rodeway Inn** M
(775) 738-7152. **$50-$140.** 736 Idaho St 89801. I-80 exit 301 or 303, Center. Ext corridors. **Pets:** Medium, dogs only. $20 daily fee/pet. Designated rooms, service with restrictions, supervision. 🆂🅰🆅🅴 🛜 🛏 🖥

▼▼ **Shilo Inn Suites - Elko** H
(775) 738-5522. **$110-$175.** 2401 Mountain City Hwy 89801. I-80 exit 301, just n. Int corridors. **Pets:** Dogs only. $25 one-time fee/room. Designated rooms, service with restrictions, crate.
🛜 ⊠ 🛏 🖥 ⇌ ⊠

ⒶⒶⒶ ▼▼ **Thunderbird Motel** M
(775) 738-7115. **$55-$100.** 345 Idaho St 89801. I-80 exit 301 or 303, 1 mi s. Ext corridors. **Pets:** Accepted. 🆂🅰🆅🅴 🛜 🛏 ⇌

ELY

ⒶⒶⒶ ▼▼▼ **Best Western Park Vue Motel** M
(775) 289-4497. **$70-$90.** 930 Aultman St 89301. 0.8 mi w of jct US 50 and 93. Ext corridors. **Pets:** Accepted. 🆂🅰🆅🅴 🛏 🖥

ⒶⒶⒶ ▼▼ **Four Sevens Motel** M
(775) 289-4747. **$35-$48, 7 day notice.** 500 High St 89301. Just n of 5th St; downtown. Ext corridors. **Pets:** Medium, other species. $10 daily fee/room. Service with restrictions, supervision. 🆂🅰🆅🅴 🛜 🛏 🖥

ⒶⒶⒶ ▼▼ **Historic Hotel Nevada & Gambling Hall** H ❀
(775) 289-6665. **$45-$55, 7 day notice.** 501 Aultman St 89301. 1.1 mi w of jct US 50 and 93. Int corridors. **Pets:** Other species. $10 one-time fee/pet. Service with restrictions, supervision. 🆂🅰🆅🅴 🛜 🛏 🖥 ⊓⊔

▼▼▼ **La Quinta Inn & Suites-Ely** H
(775) 289-8833. **$93-$164.** 1591 Great Basin Blvd 89301. 0.4 mi s of jct US 6, 50 and 93. Int corridors. **Pets:** Medium, other species. Service with restrictions, supervision. 🛜 ⊠ 🛏 🖥 🛆

🐾 ▼▼▼ **Prospector Hotel Gambling Hall** H 🐾
(775) 289-8900. **$59-$69.** 1501 E Aultman St 89301. 0.8 mi e of jct US 50 and 93. Int corridors. **Pets:** Medium. $10 daily fee/pet. Designated rooms, service with restrictions, supervision.
SAVE 🛜 ♿ 🛏 🖥 🍴 🛆

EUREKA

🐾 ▼▼▼ **Best Western Plus Eureka Inn** H
(775) 237-5247. **Call for rates.** 251 N Main St 89316. On east side of Main St; center. Int corridors. **Pets:** Accepted. SAVE 🛜 ♿ 🛏 🖥

FALLON

🐾 ▼▼ **Best Western Fallon Inn and Suites** H 🐾
(775) 423-6005. **$80-$100.** 1035 W Williams Ave 89406. 0.4 mi w of jct US 50 and 95. Ext corridors. **Pets:** $15 daily fee/pet. Designated rooms, service with restrictions, supervision. SAVE 🛜 ♿ 🛏 🖥 🛆

🐾 ▼ **Econo Lodge** M
(775) 423-2194. **$50-$99.** 70 E Williams Ave 89406. Just e of jct US 50 and 95. Ext corridors. **Pets:** Small, dogs only. $10 daily fee/pet. Service with restrictions, supervision. SAVE 🛜 🛏 🖥 🛆

▼▼▼ **Holiday Inn Express** H
(775) 428-2588. **$77-$139.** 55 Commercial Way 89406. At Williams Ave, 0.8 mi w of US 95. Int corridors. **Pets:** Accepted.
🛜 ♿ 🛏 🖥 🛆 ⊠

🐾 ▼ **Motel 6 #4140** M
(775) 423-2277. **$48-$89.** 1705 S Taylor St 89406. 0.8 mi s of jct US 50. Ext corridors. **Pets:** Other species. Service with restrictions, supervision. SAVE 🛜 🛏 🛆

🐾 ▼▼ **Super 8** H
(775) 423-6031. **$49-$58.** 855 W Williams Ave 89406. 0.4 mi w of jct US 50 and 95. Ext/int corridors. **Pets:** Large, other species. $20 one-time fee/room. Designated rooms, service with restrictions, supervision. SAVE 🛜 🛏 🖥 🍴

FERNLEY

🐾 ▼▼▼ **Best Western Fernley Inn** M 🐾
(775) 575-6776. **$90-$110, 7 day notice.** 1405 E Newlands Dr 89408. I-80 exit 48 (Craig Rd), 0.3 mi sw. Ext corridors. **Pets:** Other species. $10 daily fee/pet. Designated rooms, service with restrictions, crate.
SAVE 🛜 ♿ 🛏 🖥 🛆

GARDNERVILLE

🐾 ▼▼▼ **Best Western Topaz Lake Inn** H
(775) 266-4661. **$70-$100.** 3410 Sandy Bowers Ave 89410. US 395 at Topaz Lake, 20 mi s. Ext/int corridors. **Pets:** Accepted.
SAVE 🛜 ⊠ ♿ 🛏 🖥

🐾 ▼▼▼ **Super 8 Topaz Lodge** H
(775) 266-3338. **$59-$89, 3 day notice.** 1979 US 395 S 89410. US 395 S at Topaz Lake; 20 mi s. Ext corridors. **Pets:** Dogs only. $12 daily fee/pet. Designated rooms, service with restrictions.
SAVE 🛜 🖥 🍴 🛆

🐾 ▼ **Westerner Motel** M
(775) 782-3602. **$45-$89.** 1353 US Hwy S 395 89410. On US 395, south end of town. Ext corridors. **Pets:** Dogs only. Designated rooms, service with restrictions, crate. SAVE 🛜 🛏 🖥 🛆

HAWTHORNE

🐾 ▼▼▼ **America's Best Inn & Suites** M
(775) 945-2660. **$100-$110.** 1402 E 5th St 89415. US 95, 0.5 mi e. Ext corridors. **Pets:** Accepted. SAVE 🛜 🛏 🖥 🛆

JACKPOT

▼▼ **Horseshu Hotel & Casino** H
(775) 755-2321. **$55-$89.** 1385 Hwy 93 89825. On US 93; center. Int corridors. **Pets:** Other species. $5 one-time fee/room. Designated rooms, service with restrictions. 🖥 🍴 🛆 ⊠

LAKE TAHOE AREA

INCLINE VILLAGE

🐾 ▼▼▼▼ **Hyatt Regency Lake Tahoe Resort, Spa and Casino** H
(775) 832-1234. **$119-$479, 3 day notice.** 111 Country Club Dr at Lakeshore 89450. 0.4 mi w of SR 28, toward lake via Country Club Dr; 2 mi s of Mt. Rose Hwy. Int corridors. **Pets:** Accepted.
ECO SAVE 🛜 ♿ 🛏 🖥 🍴 🛆 ⊠

ZEPHYR COVE

🐾 ▼▼ **Zephyr Cove Resort** CA
(775) 589-4907. **Call for rates.** 760 Hwy 50 89449. 4 mi n of Stateline, NV. Ext/int corridors. **Pets:** Accepted.
SAVE 🛜 ⊠ 🛏 🖥 🍴 ⊠

END AREA

LAS VEGAS METROPOLITAN AREA

BOULDER CITY

🐾 ▼▼ **Boulder Inn & Suites** H
(702) 369-1000. **$79-$169.** 704 Nevada Way 89005. Center. Ext corridors. **Pets:** Medium, dogs only. $10 daily fee/pet. Service with restrictions, crate. SAVE 🛜 🛏 🖥 🍴 🛆

🐾 ▼▼▼ **Quality Inn** H
(702) 293-6444. **Call for rates.** 110 Ville Dr 89005. Jct US 93. Ext corridors. **Pets:** Accepted. SAVE 🛜 🛏 🖥 🛆

🐾 ▼ **Sands Motel** M 🐾
(702) 293-2589. **$59-$99, 3 day notice.** 809 Nevada Way 89005. On US 93. Ext corridors. **Pets:** Dogs only. $15 one-time fee/room. Designated rooms, service with restrictions, supervision. SAVE 🛜 🛏

ECHO BAY

⚅⚅ ▼ Echo Bay Marina Ⓜ
(702) 394-4000. **Call for rates.** North Shore Rd 89040. 4 mi e of SR 167; on Lake Mead. Int corridors. **Pets:** Accepted.
[SAVE] 🛜 [&M] 🛏 [🍴] [✕]

HENDERSON

⚅⚅ ▼▼▼ Best Western Plus Henderson Hotel Ⓗ
(702) 564-9200. **$69-$99.** 1553 N Boulder Hwy 89011. Jct Sunset Rd, 0.5 mi s. Int corridors. **Pets:** Accepted.
[SAVE] 🛜 [&M] 🛏 [💻] [🍴] [≈]

⚅⚅ ▼▼▼ Fiesta-Henderson Ⓗ 🐾
(702) 558-7000. **$30-$299.** 777 W Lake Mead Pkwy 89015. I-515 exit 61A southbound; exit 61 northbound, just e. Int corridors. **Pets:** Medium, dogs only. $50 one-time fee/room. Designated rooms, service with restrictions, supervision. [SAVE] 🛜 [&M] 🛏 [🍴] [≈]

▼▼▼ Hampton Inn & Suites Ⓗ
(702) 992-9292. **$79-$99.** 421 Astaire Dr 89014. I-215 exit 3A (Stephanie St) eastbound, 1.8 mi n, just e on Warm Springs Rd, then just n; exit 3 (Stephanie St) westbound. Int corridors. **Pets:** Other species. Service with restrictions, crate. 🛜 [&M] 🛏 [💻] [≈]

▼▼ Hawthorn Inn & Suites Ⓗ
(702) 568-7800. **$69-$189.** 910 S Boulder Hwy 89015. Jct Lake Mead Pkwy, 1.4 mi s. Int corridors. **Pets:** Medium, other species. $10 daily fee/room. Service with restrictions, supervision. 🛜 🛏 [💻] [≈]

⚅⚅ ▼▼▼▼ Loews Lake Las Vegas Ⓗ 🐾
(702) 567-6000. **Call for rates.** 101 Montelago Blvd 89011. I-515 exit 61A southbound; exit 61 northbound (Lake Mead Pkwy), 6.3 mi ne, then n, follow signs. Int corridors. **Pets:** Other species. $25 one-time fee/room. Designated rooms, service with restrictions, crate.
[SAVE] 🛜 [&M] 🛏 [💻] [🍴] [≈] [✕]

▼▼▼▼ Ravella A Dolce Hotel & Resort Ⓗ
(702) 567-4700. **$149-$799.** 1610 Lake Las Vegas Pkwy 89011. I-515 exit 61A southbound; exit 61 northbound (Lake Mead Pkwy), 6.3 mi ne, then n, follow signs. Int corridors. **Pets:** Accepted.
🛜 [✕] [&M] 🛏 [💻] [🍴] [≈] [✕]

▼▼▼ Residence Inn-Green Valley Ⓗ
(702) 434-2700. **$89-$199.** 2190 Olympic Ave 89014. I-215 exit 5 (Green Valley Pkwy N), 3 mi n at Sunset Rd. Int corridors. **Pets:** Accepted.
[ECO] 🛜 [✕] [&M] 🛏 [💻] [≈] [✕]

⚅⚅ ▼▼▼▼ Sunset Station Hotel & Casino Ⓗ
(702) 547-7777. **Call for rates.** 1301 W Sunset Rd 89014. I-515 exit 64A (Sunset Rd), just w. Int corridors. **Pets:** Accepted.
[SAVE] 🛜 🛏 [💻] [🍴] [≈]

⚅⚅ ▼▼▼▼ TownePlace Suites Las Vegas Henderson Ⓗ 🐾
(702) 896-2900. **$89-$129.** 1471 Paseo Verde Pkwy 89012. I-215 exit 3A (Stephanie St) eastbound; exit 3 westbound (S Stephanie St), just s. Int corridors. **Pets:** Other species. $100 one-time fee/room. Service with restrictions, crate. [SAVE] 🛜 [✕] 🛏 [💻] [≈]

LAS VEGAS

⚅⚅ ▼▼▼ Alexis Park All Suite Resort Ⓗ 🐾
(702) 796-3300. **$59-$289.** 375 E Harmon Ave 89169. Jct Las Vegas Blvd, just e. Ext corridors. **Pets:** Other species. $50 one-time fee/room. Designated rooms, service with restrictions, supervision.
[SAVE] 🛜 [&M] 🛏 [💻] [🍴] [≈] [✕]

⚅⚅ ▼▼▼ Ambassador Strip Inn Travelodge Ⓜ
(702) 736-3600. **Call for rates.** 5075 S Koval Ln 89119. I-15 exit 37 (Tropicana Ave), 0.5 mi n. Ext corridors. **Pets:** Medium, other species. $50 deposit/room. Service with restrictions, supervision.
[SAVE] 🛜 🛏 [💻] [≈]

▼▼▼ Artisan Hotel Ⓗ
(702) 214-4000. **Call for rates.** 1501 W Sahara Ave 89102. I-15 exit 40 (Sahara Ave), just s. Int corridors. **Pets:** Accepted.
🛜 [✕] 🛏 [🍴] [≈]

▼▼▼ ▼▼▼ Autograph Collection Cosmopolitan of Las Vegas Ⓗ
(702) 698-7000. **Call for rates.** 3708 Las Vegas Blvd S 89109. Between Flamingo Rd and Tropicana Ave, on the Strip. Int corridors.
Pets: Accepted. 🛜 [✕] [&M] 🛏 [💻] [🍴] [≈] [✕]

⚅⚅ ▼▼▼ Best Western Main Street Inn Ⓜ
(702) 382-3455. **$50-$150.** 1000 N Main St 89101. I-15 exit 43E northbound; exit 44E southbound. Ext corridors. **Pets:** Large, other species. $15 daily fee/pet. Service with restrictions, supervision.
[SAVE] 🛜 🛏 [💻] [🍴] [≈]

⚅⚅ ▼▼▼ Best Western Mardi Gras Hotel & Casino Ⓗ 🐾
(702) 731-2020. **$69-$129.** 3500 Paradise Rd 89169. 0.5 mi s of convention center. Ext corridors. **Pets:** Medium, dogs only. $50 deposit/pet, $15 daily fee/pet. Designated rooms, service with restrictions.
[SAVE] 🛜 🛏 [💻] [🍴] [≈]

⚅⚅ ▼▼▼ Best Western Plus Las Vegas West Ⓗ
(702) 256-3766. **$85-$160.** 8669 W Sahara Ave 89117. Jct Durango Dr. Int corridors. **Pets:** Small. $20 daily fee/pet. Service with restrictions, supervision. [SAVE] 🛜 🛏 [💻] [≈]

⚅⚅ ▼▼▼ Caesars Palace Ⓗ
(702) 731-7110. **Call for rates.** 3570 Las Vegas Blvd S 89109. I-15 exit 38 (E Flamingo Rd), just e at the Strip. Int corridors. **Pets:** Accepted.
[SAVE] 🛜 [&M] 🛏 [💻] [🍴] [≈] [✕]

▼▼ Candlewood Suites Ⓗ
(702) 836-3660. **$69-$159.** 4034 S Paradise Rd 89169. I-15 exit 38 (E Flamingo Rd) to Paradise Rd, just ne. Int corridors. **Pets:** Accepted.
🛜 [&M] 🛏 [💻] [≈]

▼▼ City Center Motel Ⓜ
(702) 382-4766. **Call for rates.** 700 E Fremont St 89101. Jct 7th and Fremont sts. Ext corridors. **Pets:** Medium, other species. $15 daily fee/pet. Designated rooms, crate. 🛜 🛏 [💻] [≈]

⚅⚅ ▼▼▼ Element by Westin Las Vegas Summerlin Ⓗ 🐾
(702) 589-2000. **$109-$329, 14 day notice.** 10555 Discovery Dr 89135. I-215 exit 23 (Town Center), just n. Int corridors. **Pets:** Medium, dogs only. $50 one-time fee/room. Designated rooms, service with restrictions, supervision. [SAVE] 🛜 [✕] [&M] 🛏 [💻] [≈]

▼▼▼ Embassy Suites Convention Center Ⓗ
(702) 893-8000. **$99-$189.** 3600 Paradise Rd 89169. 0.5 mi s of convention center. Int corridors. **Pets:** Accepted. 🛜 [&M] 🛏 [💻] [🍴] [≈]

▼▼▼ Emerald Suites Ⓜ
(702) 948-9999. **$49-$199.** 9145 Las Vegas Blvd S 89123. I-15 exit 31 (Silverado Ranch Blvd), just e, then 0.5 mi n. Ext corridors.
Pets: Accepted. 🛏 [💻] [≈]

▼▼▼ Flamingo Las Vegas Ⓗ 🐾
(702) 733-3111. **Call for rates.** 3555 Las Vegas Blvd S 89109. I-15 exit 38 (E Flamingo Rd), just n on the Strip. Int corridors. **Pets:** Medium, dogs only. Designated rooms, service with restrictions, crate.
🛜 [&M] 🛏 [🍴] [≈] [✕]

⚅⚅ ▼▼▼▼ Four Seasons Hotel Las Vegas Ⓗ 🐾
(702) 632-5000. **$229-$5000.** 3960 Las Vegas Blvd S 89119. I-15 exit 37 (E Tropicana Ave), just s on the Strip. Int corridors. **Pets:** Small, other species. $50 one-time fee/pet. Designated rooms, service with restrictions, supervision. [SAVE] 🛜 [✕] [&M] 🛏 [💻] [🍴] [≈] [✕]

▼▼▼▼ **Harrah's-Las Vegas** 🄷 🐾
(702) 369-5000. **$40-$499, 3 day notice.** 3475 Las Vegas Blvd S 89109. I-15 exit 38 (E Flamingo Rd), just n, on the Strip. Int corridors. **Pets:** Medium, dogs only. $50 daily fee/pet. Designated rooms, service with restrictions, crate. 🛜 🅂🄼 🔋 🖵 🍽 ⇆

🄰🄰🄰 ▼ **Highland Inn Motel** 🄼
(702) 896-4333. **$50-$200.** 8025 Dean Martin Dr 89139. I-15 exit W Blue Diamond Rd, just w. Ext corridors. **Pets:** Small. $10 daily fee/pet. Service with restrictions, supervision. (SAVE) 🛜 🔋 🖵

▼▼ **Homestead Studio Suites Hotel-Las Vegas/Midtown** 🄷 🐾
(702) 369-1414. **$50-$105.** 3045 S Maryland Pkwy 89109. I-15 exit 40 (Sahara Ave E), 1.7 mi e, then 0.6 mi s. Int corridors. **Pets:** Other species. $25 daily fee/pet. Service with restrictions. 🛜 🅂🄼 🔋 🖵

▼▼ **Homewood Suites by Hilton Las Vegas Airport** 🄷
(702) 407-0075. **$119-$159.** 230 Hidden Well Rd 89119. Jct E Sunset and Bermuda rds; 1 mi s, 0.5 mi w. Int corridors. **Pets:** Medium. $100 one-time fee/room. Service with restrictions, supervision.
🛜 🔋 🖵 ⇆ 🏋

🄰🄰🄰 ▼▼▼▼ **La Quinta Inn & Suites Airport South** 🄷
(702) 492-8900. **$93-$159.** 6560 Surrey St 89119. Jct Eastern Ave, just w. Int corridors. **Pets:** Medium, other species. Service with restrictions, supervision. (SAVE) 🛜 🏋 🅂🄼 🔋 🖵 ⇆

▼▼ **La Quinta Inn & Suites Las Vegas Redrock/Summerlin** 🄼
(702) 243-0356. **$107-$169.** 9570 W Sahara Ave 89117. Jct Fort Apache Rd, just w. Int corridors. **Pets:** Medium, other species. Service with restrictions, supervision. 🛜 🏋 🅂🄼 🔋 🖵 ⇆

🄰🄰🄰 ▼▼ **La Quinta Inn Las Vegas Nellis** 🄼
(702) 632-0229. **$125-$339.** 4288 N Nellis Blvd 89115. I-15 exit 48 (Craig Rd), e to N Las Vegas Blvd. Int corridors. **Pets:** Medium, other species. Service with restrictions, supervision.
(SAVE) 🛜 🅂🄼 🔋 🖵 ⇆

▼▼ **Microtel Inn & Suites** 🄷
(702) 273-2500. **$76-$153.** 55 E Robindale Rd 89123. I-15 exit 33 (Blue Diamond Rd), just e, then just n. Int corridors. **Pets:** Accepted.
🛜 🏋 🔋 🖵 ⇆

▼▼▼▼ **Paris Las Vegas** 🄷
(702) 946-7000. **Call for rates.** 3655 Las Vegas Blvd S 89109. I-15 exit 38 (E Flamingo Rd), e to the Strip, then just s. Int corridors.
Pets: Accepted. 🛜 🅂🄼 🔋 🖵 🍽 ⇆ 🏋

▼▼▼▼ **Planet Hollywood Resort & Casino** 🄷
(702) 785-5555. **Call for rates.** 3667 Las Vegas Blvd S 89109. I-15 exit 38 (E Flamingo Rd), just e to the Strip, then just s. Int corridors.
Pets: Accepted. 🛜 🔋 🖵 🍽 ⇆ 🏋

▼▼▼▼ **Platinum Hotel** 🄷
(702) 365-5000. **$99-$399, 3 day notice.** 211 E Flamingo Rd 89169. I-15 exit 38 (E Flamingo Rd), 1.2 mi e. Int corridors. **Pets:** Accepted.
🛜 🏋 🅂🄼 🔋 🖵 🍽 ⇆ 🏋

▼▼▼▼ **Residence Inn by Marriott Las Vegas South** 🄷
(702) 795-7378. **$116-$319.** 5875 Dean Martin Rd 89118. I-15 exit 36 (Russell Rd), just sw. Int corridors. **Pets:** Accepted.
🛜 🏋 🅂🄼 🔋 🖵 ⇆ 🏋

▼▼▼▼ **Residence Inn-Hughes Center** 🄷
(702) 650-0040. **$116-$359.** 370 Hughes Center Dr 89169. Jct Flamingo and Paradise rds, just n. Int corridors. **Pets:** Accepted.
🄴🄲🄾 🛜 🏋 🅂🄼 🔋 🖵 ⇆ 🏋

▼▼▼▼ **Residence Inn Las Vegas Convention Center** 🄷
(702) 796-9300. **$107-$449.** 3225 Paradise Rd 89109. Opposite convention center. Ext corridors. **Pets:** Accepted.
🄴🄲🄾 🛜 🏋 🅂🄼 🔋 🖵 ⇆ 🏋

▼▼▼▼ **Rio All Suite Hotel & Casino** 🄷 🐾
(702) 777-7777. **Call for rates.** 3700 W Flamingo Rd 89103. I-15 exit 38 (Flamingo Rd), 0.3 mi w. Int corridors. **Pets:** Medium, dogs only. $50 daily fee/pet. Designated rooms, service with restrictions.
🛜 🅂🄼 🔋 🖵 🍽 ⇆

▼▼▼▼ **Staybridge Suites Las Vegas South** 🄷
(702) 259-2663. **$149-$174.** 5735 Dean Martin Rd 89118. I-15 exit 36 (Russell Rd), just w. Int corridors. **Pets:** Accepted.
🛜 🅂🄼 🔋 🖵 ⇆

🄰🄰🄰 ▼▼▼ **Super 8** 🄼
(702) 794-0888. **$41-$179.** 4250 Koval Ln 89109. Jct Flamingo Rd and Koval Ln, just s. Int corridors. **Pets:** $15 daily fee/pet. Designated rooms, service with restrictions, crate. (SAVE) 🛜 🔋 🖵 ⇆

🄰🄰🄰 ▼▼▼ ▼▼▼ **THEhotel at Mandalay Bay** 🄷
(702) 632-7777. **$109-$1999.** 3950 Las Vegas Blvd S 89119. I-15 exit 36 (Russell Rd), e to the Strip, then just n. Int corridors. **Pets:** Accepted.
(SAVE) 🛜 🅂🄼 🔋 🖵 🍽 ⇆ 🏋

▼▼▼ ▼▼▼ **Trump International Hotel Las Vegas** 🄷 🐾
(702) 982-0000. **$99-$699, 3 day notice.** 2000 Fashion Show Dr 89109. Jct Las Vegas Blvd, just w. Int corridors. **Pets:** Small, dogs only. $200 one-time fee/room. Service with restrictions.
🛜 🏋 🔋 🖵 ⇆ 🏋

🄰🄰🄰 ▼▼▼ **Westgate Flamingo Bay** 🄲🄾
(702) 252-6000. **$79-$209, 3 day notice.** 5625 W Flamingo Rd 89103. Jct Jones Blvd, just e. Ext corridors. **Pets:** Accepted.
(SAVE) 🛜 🅂🄼 🔋 🖵 ⇆ 🏋

🄰🄰🄰 ▼▼▼ **The Westin Casuarina Las Vegas Hotel, Casino and Spa** 🄷 🐾
(702) 836-5900. **$100-$500.** 160 E Flamingo Rd 89109. I-15 exit 38 (Flamingo Rd E), 1.1 mi e. Int corridors. **Pets:** Medium, other species. $150 deposit/room, $35 one-time fee/room. Service with restrictions, supervision. (SAVE) 🛜 🏋 🅂🄼 🔋 🖵 🍽 ⇆ 🏋

LAUGHLIN

🄰🄰🄰 ▼▼▼ **Don Laughlin's Riverside Resort Hotel & Casino** 🄷
(702) 298-2535. **$45-$750.** 1650 S Casino Dr 89029. 2 mi s of Davis Dam. Int corridors. **Pets:** Accepted.
(SAVE) 🛜 🔋 🖵 🍽 ⇆ 🏋

▼▼▼ **Harrah's Casino Hotel** 🄷
(702) 298-4600. **Call for rates.** 2900 S Casino Dr 89029. 5 mi s of Davis Dam. Ext corridors. **Pets:** Accepted.
🛜 🅂🄼 🔋 🖵 🍽 ⇆ 🏋

MESQUITE

🄰🄰🄰 ▼▼▼ **Best Western Mesquite Inn** 🄼
(702) 346-7444. **$79-$125.** 390 N Sandhill Blvd 89027. I-15 exit 122. Ext corridors. **Pets:** Medium. $20 daily fee/room. Designated rooms, service with restrictions, supervision. (SAVE) 🛜 🔋 🖵 ⇆

▼▼▼ **Falcon Ridge Hotel** 🄷
(702) 346-2200. **$49-$149.** 1030 W Pioneer Blvd 89027. I-15 exit 120, just w. Int corridors. **Pets:** Accepted. 🛜 🔋 🖵 ⇆ 🏋

▼▼▼ **Virgin River Hotel Casino Bingo** 🄼
(702) 346-7777. **Call for rates.** 100 Pioneer Blvd 89027. I-15 exit 122, just w. Ext corridors. **Pets:** Accepted. 🛜 🅂🄼 🔋 🍽 ⇆

NORTH LAS VEGAS

🄰🄰🄰 ▼▼▼ ▼▼▼ **Aliante Station Casino & Hotel** 🄷
(702) 692-7777. **$49-$299.** 7300 Aliante Pkwy 89084. I-215 exit 43 (Aliante Pkwy), just n. Int corridors. **Pets:** Accepted.
(SAVE) 🛜 🅂🄼 🔋 🖵 🍽 ⇆

▼▼▼ **Nellis Motor Inn** Ⓜ

(702) 643-6111. **Call for rates.** 5330 E Craig Rd 89115. I-15 exit 48 (Craig Rd), 2.8 mi e; 0.3 mi from Nellis AFB. Ext corridors. **Pets:** Accepted. 🛜 🔌 💻 🏊

Ⓐ ▼▼▼▼ **Best Western Plus North Las Vegas Inn & Suites** Ⓗ

(702) 649-3000. **$90-$130.** 4540 Donovan Way 89081. I-15 exit 48 (Craig Rd), just w to Donovan Way. Int corridors. **Pets:** Accepted. 🅂🄰🅅🄴 🛜 🔌 💻 🏊

END METROPOLITAN AREA

MINDEN

Ⓐ ▼▼▼ **Best Western Minden Inn** Ⓜ ❀

(775) 782-7766. **Call for rates.** 1795 Ironwood Dr 89423. Just w of jct US 395. Ext corridors. **Pets:** Medium. $25 daily fee/pet. Designated rooms, service with restrictions, supervision. 🅂🄰🅅🄴 🛜 ✖ 🅶🄼 🔌 💻 🏊

▼▼▼▼ **Holiday Inn Express & Suites Minden** Ⓗ

(775) 782-7500. **$129-$350.** 1659 State Route 88 89423. Jct US 395 N. Int corridors. **Pets:** Accepted. 🛜 ✖ 🔌 💻 🏊

RENO

Ⓐ ▼▼▼▼ **Best Western Plus Airport Plaza Hotel** Ⓗ

(775) 348-6370. **$70-$170.** 1981 Terminal Way 89502. US 395 exit 65A southbound (E Plumb Ln/Villanova Dr), just e on Villanova Dr; exit 65 northbound, just e on E Plumb Ln. Int corridors. **Pets:** Accepted. 🅂🄰🅅🄴 🛜 ✖ 🅶🄼 🔌 💻 🍴 🏊 ✖

▼▼ **Extended StayAmerica-Reno-South Meadows** Ⓗ ❀

(775) 852-5611. **$69-$84.** 9795 Gateway Dr 89521. US 395 exit 60 (S Meadows Pkwy), just e, then n. Int corridors. **Pets:** Other species. $25 daily fee/pet. Service with restrictions. 🛜 🔌 💻

Ⓐ ▼▼▼▼ **Grand Sierra Resort & Casino** Ⓗ ❀

(775) 789-2000. **$69-$259.** 2500 E 2nd St 89595. 0.5 mi s of jct I-80 and US 395; US 395 exit 66 (Mill St). Int corridors. **Pets:** $30 daily fee/room. Designated rooms, service with restrictions, supervision. 🅂🄰🅅🄴 🛜 🅶🄼 🔌 💻 🍴 🏊 ✖

Ⓐ ▼▼▼▼ **Harrah's** Ⓗ ❀

(775) 786-3232. **Call for rates.** 219 N Center St 89501. I-80 exit Virginia St, 0.6 mi s; jct 2nd st; downtown. Int corridors. **Pets:** Medium, dogs only. $100 deposit/room. Designated rooms, service with restrictions, crate. 🅂🄰🅅🄴 🛜 🅶🄼 🔌 💻 🍴 🏊 ✖

▼▼▼▼ **Holiday Inn Express & Suites Reno Airport** Ⓗ

(775) 229-7070. **Call for rates.** 2375 Market St 89502. US 395 exit 66, just n. Int corridors. **Pets:** Medium, other species. $20 daily fee/pet. Service with restrictions, supervision. 🛜 ✖ 🅶🄼 🔌 💻 🏊

Ⓐ ▼▼▼▼ **Homewood Suites by Hilton Reno** Ⓗ

(775) 853-7100. **$119-$159.** 5450 Kietzke Ln 89511. US 395 exit 62, just sw. Int corridors. **Pets:** Small. $75 one-time fee/room. Service with restrictions. 🅂🄰🅅🄴 🛜 🔌 💻 🏊 ✖

▼▼▼ **La Quinta Inn Reno** Ⓜ

(775) 348-6100. **$64-$139.** 4001 Market St 89502-3110. US 395 exit 65A southbound (E Plumb Ln/Villanova Dr), just w on Villanova Dr; exit 65 northbound, just n, then just w on Villanova Dr. Ext corridors. **Pets:** Medium, other species. Service with restrictions, supervision. 🛜 🅶🄼 🔌 💻 🏊

▼▼▼ **Ramada Reno Hotel & Casino** Ⓗ

(775) 786-5151. **$49-$129.** 1000 E 6th St 89512. I-80 exit 14 (Wells Ave), just s, then just e. Int corridors. **Pets:** Accepted. 🛜 🅶🄼 🔌 💻 🍴 🏊

PAHRUMP

Ⓐ ▼▼▼ **Best Western Pahrump Station** Ⓜ ❀

(775) 727-5100. **$80-$100.** 1101 S Hwy 160 89048. Downtown. Ext/int corridors. **Pets:** Dogs only. $10 daily fee/pet. Designated rooms, service with restrictions, supervision. 🅂🄰🅅🄴 🛜 🅶🄼 🔌 💻 🍴 🏊

▼▼▼▼ **Residence Inn by Marriott** Ⓗ ❀

(775) 853-8800. **$101-$146.** 9845 Gateway Dr 89521. US 395 exit S Meadows Pkwy, just e. Int corridors. **Pets:** Medium, other species. $113 one-time fee/room. Service with restrictions. 🄴🄲🄾 🛜 ✖ 🅶🄼 🔌 💻 🏊 ✖

▼▼▼ **Sands Regency Casino Hotel** Ⓗ

(775) 348-2200. **$29-$169, 3 day notice.** 345 N Arlington Ave 89501. At 3rd St. Int corridors. **Pets:** Medium, dogs only. $15 daily fee/pet. Designated rooms, crate. 🛜 🔌 🍴 🏊 ✖

Ⓐ ▼▼ **Seasons Inn** Ⓜ ❀

(775) 322-6000. **$49-$109, 3 day notice.** 495 West St 89503. Corner of West and 5th sts. Ext corridors. **Pets:** Large, other species. $10 daily fee/pet. Service with restrictions, supervision. 🅂🄰🅅🄴 🛜

▼▼▼▼ **Staybridge Suites Reno** Ⓗ

(775) 657-8999. **$109-$239, 3 day notice.** 10559 Professional Cir 89511. US 395 exit 59 (Damonte Ranch Pkwy), just e, just n on Double R Blvd, then just w. Int corridors. **Pets:** Accepted. 🛜 ✖ 🔌 💻 🏊

SPARKS

Ⓐ ▼▼▼▼ **Holiday Inn Reno-Sparks** Ⓗ ❀

(775) 358-6900. **$99-$149.** 55 E Nugget Ave 89431. I-80 exit 19 (McCarran Blvd), just se. Int corridors. **Pets:** Large. $20 daily fee/pet. Designated rooms, service with restrictions, supervision. 🅂🄰🅅🄴 🛜 🔌 💻 🍴 🏊

Ⓐ ▼▼▼▼ **John Ascuaga's Nugget Hotel Tower** Ⓗ ❀

(775) 356-3300. **$49-$179.** 1100 Nugget Ave 89431. I-80 exit 17 (Nugget Ave) eastbound; exit 18 (Pyramid Way) westbound. Int corridors. **Pets:** Medium. $50 deposit/room, $20 daily fee/room. Designated rooms, service with restrictions, supervision. 🅂🄰🅅🄴 🛜 🔌 💻 🍴 🏊 ✖

Ⓐ ▼▼▼ **Sparks Super 8** Ⓗ

(775) 358-8884. **$81-$180.** 1900 E Greg St 89431. I-80 exit 20, 0.6 mi s, then just e. Int corridors. **Pets:** $10 one-time fee/pet. Designated rooms, service with restrictions, supervision. 🅂🄰🅅🄴 🛜 🔌 💻 🏊

TONOPAH

Ⓐ ▼▼▼ **Best Western Hi-Desert Inn** Ⓜ

(775) 482-3511. **$100-$139.** 320 Main St 89049. On US 6 and 95. Int corridors. **Pets:** Dogs only. Designated rooms, service with restrictions, supervision. 🄴🄲🄾 🅂🄰🅅🄴 🛜 🅶🄼 🔌 💻 🏊

Ⓐ ▼▼▼ **Ramada Inn-Tonopah Station** Ⓜ

(775) 482-9777. **$60-$70.** 1137 S Main St 89049. On US 6 and 95. Int corridors. **Pets:** Accepted. 🅂🄰🅅🄴 🛜 ✖ 🅶🄼 💻 🍴

WINNEMUCCA

Ⓐ ▼▼▼▼ **Best Western Plus Gold Country Inn** Ⓗ

(775) 623-6999. **$125-$180.** 921 W Winnemucca Blvd 89445. 0.6 mi sw of center. Int corridors. **Pets:** Accepted. 🅂🄰🅅🄴 🛜 🔌 💻 🏊

▼▼▼ **Holiday Inn Express** H

(775) 625-3100. **$129-$224.** 1987 W Winnemucca Blvd 89445. I-80 exit 176, just s. Int corridors. **Pets:** Accepted.

ECO 🛰 ✕ ᏜM 🛏 💻 🍽 🏊

▲▲▲ ▼▼▼ **Town House Motel** M

(775) 623-3620. **$82-$90.** 375 Monroe St 89445. 0.4 mi sw of center to Monroe St, then just se. Ext corridors. **Pets:** Small, dogs only. $10 one-time fee/pet. Designated rooms, service with restrictions, supervision.

SAVE 🛰 ✕ 🛏 💻 🏊

▲▲▲ ▼▼▼ **Winnemucca Holiday Motel** M

(775) 623-3684. **$79-$149.** 670 W Winnemucca Blvd 89445. 0.4 mi sw of center. Ext corridors. **Pets:** Other species. $25 deposit/pet. Service with restrictions, supervision. SAVE 🛰 🛏 💻 🏊

▲▲▲ ▼▼▼ **The Winnemucca Inn** H

(775) 623-2565. **$99-$149.** 741 W Winnemucca Blvd 89445. 0.5 mi sw of center. Ext/int corridors. **Pets:** Accepted.

SAVE 🛰 🛏 💻 🍽 🏊

NEW HAMPSHIRE

CITY INDEX

ASHLAND

▼▼▼▼ **Glynn House Inn** BB

(603) 968-3775. **$149-$299, 21 day notice.** 59 Highland St 03217. I-93 exit 24 (SR 25 and US 3), 0.8 mi e to flag pole in center of town (Highland St), then 0.3 mi nw. Ext/int corridors. **Pets:** Accepted.

ECO 🛰 ✕ 🗲

BARTLETT

▲▲▲ ▼▼▼ **The Bartlett Inn** BB

(603) 374-2353. **$109-$248, 14 day notice.** 1477 US Rt 302 03812. On US 302, 7 mi w of jct SR 16. Ext/int corridors. **Pets:** Dogs only. $15 one-time fee/pet. Designated rooms, service with restrictions, supervision.

SAVE 🛰 ✕ 🛏 💻 🏊 ✕ 🗲

▼▼ **The Villager Motel** M

(603) 374-2742. **Call for rates.** 1126 US 302 03812. 1 mi e on US 302; 1.3 mi w of Attitash Mountain. Ext corridors. **Pets:** Accepted.

🛰 ✕ 🛏 💻 🏊 ✕

BRETTON WOODS

▼▼▼▼ **Omni Bretton Arms Inn** CI

(603) 278-3000. **$139-$479, 3 day notice.** 173 Mount Washington Hotel Rd (US 302) 03575. Center. Int corridors. **Pets:** Accepted.

🛰 ✕ 🛏 🍽 ✕

CAMPTON

▼▼▼▼ **Days Inn Campton/Plymouth** H

(603) 536-3520. **$62-$125.** 1513 Daniel Webster Hwy 03223. I-93 exit 27, just e, then just n. Int corridors. **Pets:** Accepted.

🛰 🛏 💻 🏊 ✕

CHESTERFIELD

▼▼▼▼ **Chesterfield Inn** CI

(603) 256-3211. **$149-$345, 5 day notice.** 20 Cross Rd 03466. I-91 exit 3, 2 mi e on SR 9. Ext/int corridors. **Pets:** Medium, other species. Designated rooms, supervision. ECO 🛰 ✕ 🛏 💻 🍽

COLEBROOK

▲▲▲ ▼▼ **Northern Comfort Motel** M

(603) 237-4440. **$69-$89, 3 day notice.** 1 Trooper Scott Phillips Hwy 03576. 1.5 mi s on US 3. Ext corridors. **Pets:** Accepted.

SAVE 🛰 ✕ 🛏 🏊 ✕

CONCORD

▲▲▲ ▼▼▼ **Best Western Concord Inn & Suites** H

(603) 228-4300. **$90-$280.** 97 Hall St 03301. I-93 exit 13, just n on Main St, then 0.5 mi w. Int corridors. **Pets:** $15 daily fee/pet. Designated rooms, service with restrictions, supervision. SAVE 🛰 🛏 💻 🏊

▼▼▼▼ **Concord Comfort Inn** H

(603) 226-4100. **$79-$199.** 71 Hall St 03301. I-93 exit 13, just n on Main St, then 0.3 mi w. Int corridors. **Pets:** Accepted.

🛰 ᏜM 🛏 💻 🏊 ✕

▲▲▲ ▼▼▼ **Days Inn** M

(603) 224-2511. **$81-$270, 7 day notice.** 406 S Main St 03301. I-93 exit 12S, on SR 3A. Ext corridors. **Pets:** Dogs only. $15 one-time fee/pet.

SAVE 🛰 🛏 💻 🏊

▲▲▲ ▼▼▼ **Fairfield Inn Concord** H

(603) 224-4011. **$109-$153.** 4 Gulf St 03301. I-93 exit 13, just n on Main St, then immediate right turn. Int corridors. **Pets:** Accepted.

SAVE 🛰 ✕ ᏜM 🛏 💻 🏊 ✕

▼▼▼▼ **Residence Inn by Marriott Concord** H

(603) 226-0012. **$159-$208.** 91 Hall St 03301. I-93 exit 13, just n on Main St, then 0.5 mi w. Int corridors. **Pets:** Accepted.

🛰 ✕ ᏜM 🛏 💻 🏊

DOVER

▼▼▼▼ **Comfort Inn & Suites** H

(603) 750-7507. **$89-$229.** 10 Members Dr 03820. SR 16 exit 9, 0.4 mi ne. Int corridors. **Pets:** Accepted. 🛰 ᏜM 🛏 💻 🏊 ✕

▼▼▼ **Days Inn** M

(603) 742-0400. **$89-$143.** 481 Central Ave 03820. Spaulding Tpke exit 7, 2 mi n on SR 108; downtown. Ext/int corridors. **Pets:** $50 deposit/pet, $10 daily fee/pet. Service with restrictions, supervision.

🛰 ✕ 🛏 💻 🏊

▼▼▼▼ **Homewood Suites Dover** H

(603) 516-0929. **$119-$269.** 21 Members Way 03820. SR 16 exit 9, 0.4 mi w. Int corridors. **Pets:** Accepted. 🛰 ᏜM 🛏 💻 🏊 ✕

DURHAM

▲▲▲ ▼▼▼▼ **Three Chimneys Inn** CI 🐾

(603) 868-7800. **$139-$239, 7 day notice.** 17 Newmarket Rd 03824. On SR 108; center. Ext/int corridors. **Pets:** Designated rooms, service with restrictions. SAVE 🛰 ✕ 💻 🍽

EXETER

◇◇ ▼▼▼ Hampton Inn & Suites 🄷 ☘
(603) 658-5555. **$119-$214.** 59 Portsmouth Ave 03833. I-101 exit 11. Int corridors. **Pets:** Large. Designated rooms, service with restrictions, supervision. [SAVE] 🛰 ✖ 🛁ᴹ 🍴 💻 🏊

▼▼▼ The Inn by the Bandstand 🄱🄱
(603) 772-6352. **Call for rates.** 6 Front St 03833. Center; across from Bandstand. Int corridors. **Pets:** Accepted. 🛰 ✖ 🍴 🆉

FRANCONIA

◇◇ ▼▼▼ Best Western White Mountain Resort 🄷 ☘
(603) 823-7422. **$100-$200, 3 day notice.** 87 Wallace Hill Rd 03580. I-93 exit 38, just e. Int corridors. **Pets:** Large, other species. $20 daily fee/room. Designated rooms, service with restrictions, crate.
[SAVE] 🛰 ✖ 🍴 💻 🏊 ✖

▼▼▼ Gale River Motel 🄼 ☘
(603) 823-5655. **$60-$220, 7 day notice.** 1 Main St 03580. I-93 exit 38, 0.8 mi n on SR 18. Ext corridors. **Pets:** $10 daily fee/pet. Designated rooms, service with restrictions, supervision.
[ECO] 🛰 ✖ 🍴 💻 🏊 ✖

▼▼▼ Lovetts Inn by Lafayette Brook 🄲🄸
(603) 823-7761. **Call for rates.** 1474 Profile Rd 03580. I-93 exit 38, just w on Wallace Hill Rd, then 2.1 mi s on SR 18. Ext/int corridors.
Pets: Accepted. 🛰 ✖ 🍴 💻 🍴 🏊 ✖ 🆉

GILFORD

▼▼ Fireside Resort Inn & Suites 🄷 ☘
(603) 293-7526. **$90-$270.** 17 Harris Shore Rd 03249. Jct SR 11 and 11B, 2.5 mi e of jct US 3 N. Int corridors. **Pets:** Large. $20 daily fee/pet. Designated rooms, service with restrictions, supervision.
🛰 ✖ 🛁ᴹ 🍴 💻 🏊 ✖

▼▼▼ TownePlace Suites by Marriott Gilford 🄷 ☘
(603) 524-5533. **$139-$230.** 14 Sawmill Rd 03249. Just e of jct SR 3 and 11A. Int corridors. **Pets:** Large, other species. $100 one-time fee/room. Service with restrictions, supervision.
🛰 ✖ 🛁ᴹ 🍴 💻 🏊

GLEN

◇◇ ▼ Will's Inn 🄼
(603) 383-6757. **$49-$235, 10 day notice.** 440 US 302 03838. On US 302, 2 mi w of jct SR 16. Ext corridors. **Pets:** Accepted.
[SAVE] 🛰 ✖ 🍴 💻 🏊 ✖

GORHAM

▼ Moose Brook Motel 🄼
(603) 466-5400. **$59-$89, 7 day notice.** 65 Lancaster Rd 03581. Jct SR 16, 0.5 mi w on US 2. Ext corridors. **Pets:** $10 one-time fee/pet. Designated rooms, service with restrictions, crate. 🛰 ✖ 🍴 💻 🏊

▼▼ Royalty Inn 🄷
(603) 466-3312. **$65-$165.** 130 Main St 03581. On US 2 and SR 16; center. Ext/int corridors. **Pets:** Other species. $5 daily fee/pet. Designated rooms, no service. [ECO] 🛰 🛁ᴹ 🍴 💻 🍴 🏊 ✖

◇◇ ▼▼ Top Notch Inn 🄼
(603) 466-5496. **$69-$149.** 265 Main St 03581. On US 2 and SR 16; center. Ext/int corridors. **Pets:** Accepted. [SAVE] 🛰 ✖ 🍴 💻 🏊

▼▼ Town & Country Motor Inn 🄷
(603) 466-3315. **$68-$148.** 20 SR 2 03581. 0.5 mi e of jct SR 16. Ext/int corridors. **Pets:** $6 daily fee/pet. Designated rooms, service with restrictions, crate. 🛰 🍴 💻 🍴 🏊 ✖

HAMPTON

◇◇ ▼▼▼ Best Western Plus The Inn at Hampton 🄷
(603) 926-6771. **$100-$180.** 815 Lafayette Rd, US 1 03842. 0.5 mi n on US 1. Int corridors. **Pets:** Medium, dogs only. $30 one-time fee/pet. Designated rooms, service with restrictions, supervision.
[SAVE] 🛰 🛁ᴹ 🍴 💻 🏊 ✖

◇◇ ▼▼▼ Lamie's Inn and The Old Salt 🄲🄸 ☘
(603) 926-0330. **$99-$160, 3 day notice.** 490 Lafayette Rd 03842. Jct SR 27 on US 1. Int corridors. **Pets:** Medium, dogs only. $100 deposit/room, $10 daily fee/pet. Designated rooms, service with restrictions, supervision. [SAVE] 🛰 ✖ 🍴 🍴

◇◇ ▼▼ Seascape Inn 🄼 ☘
(603) 926-1750. **$79-$175, 7 day notice.** 955 Ocean Blvd 03842. On SR 1A. Ext corridors. **Pets:** Other species. $10 daily fee/room. Designated rooms, service with restrictions, crate. [SAVE] 🛰 ✖ 🍴

HANCOCK

▼▼▼ The Hancock Inn 🄲🄸
(603) 525-3318. **Call for rates.** 33 Main St 03449. Jct SR 123 and 137; center. Int corridors. **Pets:** Accepted. 🛰 ✖ 🍴

HARTS LOCATION

▼▼▼ Notchland Inn 🄲🄸
(603) 374-6131. **Call for rates.** 2 Morey Rd 03812. On US 302, 6.4 mi w of town. Ext/int corridors. **Pets:** Accepted.
[ECO] 🛰 ✖ 🍴 💻 🍴 ✖ 🎦

HEBRON

◇◇ ▼▼▼ Coppertoppe Inn & Retreat Center 🄱🄱 ☘
(603) 744-3636. **$135-$275, 14 day notice.** 8 Range Rd 03241. I-93 exit 23, 6 mi w on SR 104, 8.7 mi n on SR 3A, then 0.6 mi w on N Shore Rd. Int corridors. **Pets:** Other species. $15 daily fee/pet.
[ECO] [SAVE] 🛰 ✖ 🍴 💻 🆉

HENNIKER

▼▼ Henniker Motel 🄼
(603) 428-3536. **Call for rates.** 61 Craney Pond Rd 03242. I-89 exit 5, 6.5 mi w on US 202 and SR 9 to jct SR 114, 3 mi s to Flanders Rd, then 0.5 mi w, follow signs; adjacent to Pat's Peak. Ext/int corridors.
Pets: Accepted. 🛰 ✖ 🍴 💻 🏊

JACKSON

▼▼▼ Christmas Farm Inn & Spa 🄲🄸
(603) 383-4313. **Call for rates.** 3 Blitzen Way (Rt 16B) 03846. Jct SR 16, 0.6 mi e on SR 16A (through Jackson covered bridge), then 0.4 mi. Ext/int corridors. **Pets:** Accepted. 🛰 ✖ 🍴 💻 🍴 🏊 ✖

▼▼▼ The Eagle Mountain House & Golf Club 🄷
(603) 383-9111. **$69-$229, 3 day notice.** 179 Carter Notch Rd 03846. Jct SR 16B, from village center follow SR 16B across the Jackson covered bridge to immediate right turn, 0.7 mi n. Int corridors.
Pets: Accepted. [ECO] 🛰 ✖ 🍴 🍴 🏊 ✖ 🏌

◇◇ ▼▼▼ Nordic Village Resort 🄲🄾
(603) 383-9101. **$89-$869, 7 day notice.** Rt 16 03846. 1 mi n of jct US 302. Ext/int corridors. **Pets:** Other species. $25 daily fee/pet. Designated rooms, service with restrictions, supervision.
[SAVE] 🛰 ✖ 🍴 💻 🏊 ✖

▼▼▼ Snowflake Inn 🄱🄱 ☘
(603) 383-8259. **$169-$375, 14 day notice.** 95 Main St (SR 16A) 03846. On SR 16A; center. Int corridors. **Pets:** Dogs only. $30 daily fee/pet. Designated rooms. 🛰 ✖ 🏊

JEFFERSON

◇◇ ▼▼▼ Jefferson Inn 🄱🄱
(603) 586-7998. **$85-$165, 14 day notice.** 6 Renaissance Ln 03583. US 2, 0.5 mi e of SR 116. Int corridors. **Pets:** Dogs only. Designated rooms, crate. [SAVE] 🛰 ✖ 🍴 ✖ 🆉

KEENE

◇◇◇◇ Best Western Plus Sovereign Hotel H
(603) 357-3038. **$90-$200.** 401 Winchester St 03431. SR 10, just s of jct SR 12 and 101. Int corridors. **Pets:** Other species. $20 daily fee/pet. Designated rooms, service with restrictions, supervision.
SAVE ▵ ⊟ ⊡ ⊟ ⊳

◇◇◇◇ Courtyard by Marriott Keene Downtown H
(603) 354-7900. **$189-$230.** 75 Railroad St 03431. Just off Main St; downtown. Int corridors. **Pets:** Accepted.
ECO ▵ ⊠ ⊟ ⊡ ⊟ ⊳

◇◇◇ Days Inn of Keene H ✿
(603) 352-9780. **$90-$207.** 3 Ashbrook Rd 03431. Jct SR 9 and 12, just w. Int corridors. **Pets:** $20 one-time fee/room. Service with restrictions, supervision. SAVE ▵ ⊟ ⊡

◇◇◇ Holiday Inn Express H ✿
(603) 352-7616. **$99-$179.** 175 Key Rd 03431. SR 101, just n, via Winchester St, then 0.3 mi w. Int corridors. **Pets:** Medium, dogs only. $50 daily fee/pet. Designated rooms, service with restrictions, supervision.
▵ ⊠ ⊟ ⊟ ⊡ ⊳

LANCASTER

◇◇◇ Coos Motor Inn H
(603) 788-3079. **$49-$110.** 209 Main St 03584. On US 2 and 3; center. Int corridors. **Pets:** Medium, dogs only. $15 daily fee/pet. Designated rooms, service with restrictions, supervision. SAVE ▵ ⊟ ⊡

LEBANON

◇◇◇◇ Residence Inn Hanover Lebanon H ✿
(603) 643-4511. **$170-$229.** 32 Centerra Pkwy 03766. I-89 exit 18, 2.5 mi n on SR 120. Int corridors. **Pets:** $100 one-time fee/room. Service with restrictions. SAVE ▵ ⊠ ⊟ ⊟ ⊡ ⊳ ⊠

LINCOLN

◇◇◇◇ Comfort Inn & Suites H ✿
(603) 745-6700. **$84-$229.** 21 Railroad St 03251. I-93 exit 32, just e on SR 112; at Hobo Railroad. Int corridors. **Pets:** Other species. $15 daily fee/pet. Designated rooms, service with restrictions.
SAVE ▵ ⊠ ⊟ ⊟ ⊡ ⊳ ⊠

◇◇◇ Econo Lodge Inn & Suites M
(603) 745-3661. **$55-$250.** 381 US Rt 3 03251. I-93 exit 33 (US 3), 0.3 mi ne. Ext/int corridors. **Pets:** Medium, dogs only. $20 daily fee/pet. Designated rooms, service with restrictions, crate.
SAVE ▵ ⊠ ⊟ ⊳ ⊠

◇◇ Parker's Motel M
(603) 745-8341. **$59-$99, 3 day notice.** 750 US Rt 3 03251. I-93 exit 33 (US 3), 2 mi ne. Ext corridors. **Pets:** Medium. $10 daily fee/pet. Designated rooms, no service, supervision. SAVE ▵ ⊟ ⊟ ⊡ ⊳ ⊠

◇◇ Woodward's Resort M
(603) 745-8141. **$89-$139, 7 day notice.** 527 US 3 03251. I-93 exit 33 (US 3), 1.4 mi ne. Ext/int corridors. **Pets:** Large. Designated rooms, supervision. SAVE ▵ ⊟ ⊡ ⊟ ⊳ ⊠

LITTLETON

◇◇◇ Eastgate Motor Inn M
(603) 444-3971. **$69-$135.** 335 Cottage St 03561. I-93 exit 41, just e. Ext/int corridors. **Pets:** Dogs only. $10 daily fee/pet. Service with restrictions, supervision. SAVE ▵ ⊟ ⊡

◇◇ Thayers Inn H
(603) 444-6469. **Call for rates.** 111 Main St 03561. I-93 exit 42, 1.3 mi e on US 302 and SR 10; center. Int corridors. **Pets:** Accepted.
▵ ⊠ ⊟ ⊡ ⊟

LOUDON

◇◇◇ Red Roof Inn H
(603) 225-8399. **$69-$113.** 2 Staniels Rd 03307. I-393 exit 3, 1.5 mi n. Int corridors. **Pets:** Large, other species. No service, supervision.
SAVE ▵ ⊟M ⊟ ⊳

MANCHESTER

◇◇◇◇ Best Western Plus Executive Court Inn & Conference Center H
(603) 627-2525. **$105-$200.** 13500 S Willow St 03103. I-293 exit 1, 0.5 mi s on SR 28, then 1 mi e. Int corridors. **Pets:** Accepted.
SAVE ▵ ⊟ ⊡ ⊟ ⊠

◇◇◇ Comfort Inn H
(603) 668-2600. **$89-$259.** 298 Queen City Ave 03102. I-293 exit 4, just w. Int corridors. **Pets:** Accepted. SAVE ▵ ⊟ ⊡

◇◇◇ Four Points by Sheraton H
(603) 668-6110. **$89-$195, 3 day notice.** 55 John E Devine Dr 03103. I-293 exit 1, just nw on SR 28. Int corridors. **Pets:** Dogs only. $70 one-time fee/room. Service with restrictions, crate.
SAVE ▵ ⊠ ⊟M ⊟ ⊡ ⊟ ⊳

◇◇◇ Holiday Inn Express Hotel & Suites - Manchester Airport H
(603) 669-6800. **$99-$149.** 1298 S Porter St 03103. I-293 exit 1. Int corridors. **Pets:** Accepted. ▵ ⊟M ⊟ ⊡ ⊳

◇◇◇ Homewood Suites by Hilton H
(603) 668-2200. **$99-$129.** 1000 Perimeter Rd 03103. I-293 exit 2, follow signs to Manchester-Boston Regional Airport. Int corridors.
Pets: Accepted. ▵ ⊟M ⊟ ⊡ ⊳ ⊠

◇◇◇◇ Radisson Hotel Manchester Downtown H ✿
(603) 625-1000. **Call for rates.** 700 Elm St 03101. Jct Granite St; downtown. Int corridors. **Pets:** Medium, other species. $25 one-time fee/pet. Designated rooms, service with restrictions, supervision.
ECO ▵ ⊠ ⊟M ⊟ ⊡ ⊟ ⊳ ⊠

◇◇◇ TownePlace Suites Manchester-Boston Regional Airport H
(603) 641-2288. **$83-$103.** 686 Huse Rd 03103. I-293 exit 1, 0.5 mi se on SR 28. Int corridors. **Pets:** Accepted. ▵ ⊠ ⊟M ⊟ ⊡ ⊳

MEREDITH

◇◇◇ Church Landing at Mill Falls H
(603) 279-7006. **$239-$469, 3 day notice.** 281 Daniel Webster Hwy 03253. Jct US 3 and SR 104, 0.6 mi n. Ext/int corridors. **Pets:** Accepted.
▵ ⊠ ⊟ ⊡ ⊟ ⊳

◇◇◇ The Inn at Mill Falls H
(603) 279-7006. **$109-$299, 3 day notice.** 312 Daniel Webster Hwy 03253. Jct US 3 and SR 25; center. Int corridors. **Pets:** Accepted.
ECO ▵ ⊠ ⊟ ⊟ ⊳

MERRIMACK

◇◇◇ Comfort Inn M
(603) 429-4600. **$70-$180.** 242 Daniel Webster Hwy 03054. Everett Tpke exit 11, just e, then 0.7 mi s on US 3. Int corridors. **Pets:** Small. Service with restrictions, supervision. SAVE ▵ ⊟M ⊟ ⊡

◇◇◇ Residence Inn Nashua-Merrimack H
(603) 424-8100. **$89-$171.** 246 Daniel Webster Hwy 03054. Everett Tpke exit 11, just e, then 0.6 mi s on US 3. Ext/int corridors. **Pets:** Accepted.
ECO ▵ ⊠ ⊟M ⊟ ⊡ ⊳ ⊠

MOULTONBOROUGH

◇◇ Rodeway Inn M ✿
(603) 253-4314. **Call for rates.** 340 Whittier Hwy 03254. On SR 25, 3 mi w. Ext corridors. **Pets:** Medium. $10 one-time fee/pet. Designated rooms, service with restrictions, supervision. ▵ ⊟ ⊡ ⊳

NASHUA

Best Western Granite Inn M
(603) 883-7700. **$80-$200.** 10 St. Laurent St 03060. US 3 (Everett Tpke) exit 7E, just e. Int corridors. **Pets:** Accepted. [SAVE] 🔆 🖥 🖵 ➴

Hampton Inn Nashua H
(603) 883-5333. **$89-$169.** 407 Amherst St 03063. US 3 (Everett Tpke) exit 8. Int corridors. **Pets:** Accepted.
[ECO] 🔆 ✕ ⓜ 🖥 🖵 ➴

Holiday Inn & Suites Nashua H
(603) 888-1551. **$79-$179.** 9 Northeastern Blvd 03062. US 3 (Everett Tpke) exit 4, just w, then 0.3 mi n. Int corridors. **Pets:** Accepted.
🔆 ⓜ 🖥 🖵 🍽 ➴

Motel 6 #2019 M
(603) 888-1893. **$55-$65.** 77 Spitbrook Rd 03060. US 3 (Everett Tpke) exit 1, just e. Ext corridors. **Pets:** Other species. Service with restrictions, supervision. 🔆 ⓜ

NEWBURY

Best Western Sunapee Lake Lodge H
(603) 763-2010. **$110-$170.** 1403 SR 103 03255. Jct SR 103B, just e. Int corridors. **Pets:** Accepted. [SAVE] 🔆 ✕ ⓜ 🖥 🖵 ➴ ✕

NEW CASTLE

Wentworth By The Sea Marriott Hotel & Spa H
(603) 422-7322. **$199-$499, 3 day notice.** 588 Wentworth Rd 03854. On SR 1B, 2 mi e of SR 1A. Ext/int corridors. **Pets:** Small, dogs only. $30 one-time fee/room. Service with restrictions, supervision.
[SAVE] 🔆 ✕ 🖵 🍽 ➴ ✕

NEW LONDON

Fairway Motel at Lake Sunapee Country Club M
(603) 526-0202. **$69-$109, 14 day notice.** 344 Andover Rd 03257. I-89 exit 11, 3 mi e on SR 11. Ext corridors. **Pets:** Medium. $25 daily fee/room. Designated rooms, service with restrictions, supervision.
🔆 ✕ 🖥 ➴

New London Inn CI
(603) 526-2791. **$139-$259, 3 day notice.** 353 Main St 03257. Center. Int corridors. **Pets:** Accepted. [SAVE] 🔆 ✕ 🍽

NORTH CONWAY

North Conway Hampton Inn & Suites H 🐾
(603) 356-7736. **$89-$279.** 1788 White Mountain Hwy 03860. Jct US 302/SR 16, 1 mi n. Int corridors. **Pets:** Medium. Designated rooms, service with restrictions, crate. [ECO] 🔆 ✕ 🖥 🖵 ✕

North Conway Mountain Inn M
(603) 356-2803. **$79-$239.** 2114 White Mountain Hwy 03860. 1 mi s on US 302/SR 16. Ext corridors. **Pets:** $20 daily fee/pet. Designated rooms, service with restrictions, crate. [SAVE] 🔆 ✕ 🖥

Red Jacket Mountain View Resort and Indoor Water Park H
(603) 356-5411. **$109-$339.** 2251 White Mountain Hwy 03860. 1 mi s on US 302/SR 16. Ext/int corridors. **Pets:** Accepted.
[ECO] [SAVE] 🔆 ✕ ⓜ 🖥 🖵 🍽 ➴ ✕

Residence Inn by Marriott, North Conway H 🐾
(603) 356-3024. **$170-$229.** 1801 White Mountain Hwy 03860. Jct US 302/SR 16, 1 mi n. Int corridors. **Pets:** Medium, other species. $100 one-time fee/room. Designated rooms, service with restrictions, supervision.
[SAVE] 🔆 ✕ ⓜ 🖥 🖵 ➴ ✕

White Trellis Motel M
(603) 356-2492. **$49-$249, 3 day notice.** 3245 White Mountain Hwy 03860. 0.8 mi n on US 302/SR 16; village center. Ext corridors. **Pets:** Accepted. 🔆 🖥 🖵

PITTSBURG

The Glen CA
(603) 538-6500. **$232-$294 (no credit cards), 7 day notice.** 118 Glen Rd 03592. 9 mi n on US 3, from jct SR 145 to Varney Rd, then 0.3 mi s to Glen Rd, follow signs. Ext/int corridors. **Pets:** Accepted.
🔆 ✕ 🖥 🖵 🍽 ✕ 🐾 📺 🐾

PORTSMOUTH

Anchorage Inn & Suites H 🐾
(603) 431-8111. **$89-$349.** 417 Woodbury Ave 03801. Jct US 1 and I-95; at Portsmouth Traffic Circle. Int corridors. **Pets:** Small, dogs only. $20 daily fee/pet. Designated rooms, service with restrictions, supervision.
🔆 🖥 ➴ ✕

Hampton Inn-Portsmouth H
(603) 431-6111. **$99-$209.** 99 Durgin Ln 03801. I-95 exit 7, 1 mi w via Market St and Woodbury Ave to Durgin Ln, then 0.3 mi s. Int corridors.
Pets: Accepted. 🔆 ⓜ 🖥 🖵 ➴ ✕

Homewood Suites by Hilton H
(603) 427-5400. **$129-$259.** 100 Portsmouth Blvd 03801. I-95 exit 7, 0.5 mi w, then 0.3 mi n. Int corridors. **Pets:** Accepted.
🔆 ⓜ 🖥 🖵 ➴

Motel 6 Portsmouth #1424 H
(603) 334-6606. **$55-$85.** 3 Gosling Rd 03801. I-95 exit 4 to Spaulding Tpke (US 4 and SR 16) exit 1, then just e. Int corridors. **Pets:** Other species. Service with restrictions, supervision. 🔆 ⓜ 🖥 ➴

Residence Inn by Marriott H
(603) 436-8880. **$159-$279.** 1 International Dr 03801. SR 4/16 exit 1, just s. Int corridors. **Pets:** Accepted.
[ECO] 🔆 ✕ ⓜ 🖥 🖵 ➴ ✕

Residence Inn by Marriott Downtown/Waterfront H
(603) 422-9200. **$119-$299.** 100 Deer St 03801. Downtown. Int corridors.
Pets: Accepted. 🔆 ✕ ⓜ 🖥 🖵 🍽 ➴

Sheraton Portsmouth Harborside Hotel & Conference Center H
(603) 431-2300. **$139-$649.** 250 Market St 03801. Downtown. Int corridors. **Pets:** Accepted.
[ECO] [SAVE] 🔆 ✕ ⓜ 🖥 🖵 🍽 ➴ ✕

ROCHESTER

Anchorage Inn M
(603) 332-3350. **$89-$159.** 13 Wadleigh Rd 03867. Jct Spaulding Tpke and SR 125 exit 12. Ext corridors. **Pets:** Medium. $20 daily fee/room. Designated rooms, service with restrictions, supervision. 🔆 🖥 ➴

The Governor's Inn CI
(603) 332-0107. **Call for rates.** 78 Wakefield St 03867. On SR 125 and 108, just n of monument; center. Int corridors. **Pets:** Other species. Designated rooms, service with restrictions. 🔆 ✕ 🖥 🖵 🍽

Holiday Inn Express Hotel & Suites Rochester H
(603) 994-1175. **$89-$169.** 77 Farmington Rd 03867. I-16 exit 15, 1 mi w on SR 11. Int corridors. **Pets:** Accepted. [SAVE] 🔆 ⓜ 🖥 🖵 ➴

SALEM

▼▼▼▼ La Quinta Inn & Suites Salem H

(603) 893-4722. **$58-$143.** 8 Keewaydin Dr 03079. I-93 exit 2, just sw. Int corridors. **Pets:** Medium, other species. Service with restrictions, supervision. 🛜 ⫖M 🖥 💻 ⇌

▼▼▼ Red Roof Inn #151 M

(603) 898-6422. **$50-$110.** 15 Red Roof Ln 03079. I-93 exit 2, just se. Ext corridors. **Pets:** Large, other species. No service, supervision.

SAVE 🛜 ⫖M 🖥

SEABROOK

▼▼▼ Hampshire Inn M

(603) 474-5700. **$79-$189.** 20 Spur Rd 03874. I-95 exit 1 on SR 107. Int corridors. **Pets:** Accepted. SAVE 🛜 🖥 ⇌ ⊠

SUGAR HILL

▼▼▼▼ The Hilltop Inn BB 🐾

(603) 823-5695. **$110-$195, 8 day notice.** 9 Norton Ln 03586. I-93 exit 38, 0.5 mi n on SR 18, then 2.8 mi w on SR 117. Int corridors. **Pets:** Dogs only. $10 daily fee/room. Supervision.

🛜 ⊠ 🖥 ⫛ ⫚ ⊠

▼▼▼▼ Sunset Hill House-A Grand Inn CI

(603) 823-5522. **$139-$499, 14 day notice.** 231 Sunset Hill Rd 03586. I-93 exit 38, 0.5 mi n on SR 18, 2.2 mi w on SR 117, then 0.5 mi s. Int corridors. **Pets:** Accepted. ECO 🛜 ⊠ 🖥 ⫛ ⇌ ⊠

SUNAPEE

▼▼ Dexter's Inn CI 🐾

(603) 763-5571. **$110-$185, 7 day notice.** 258 Stagecoach Rd 03782. Jct SR 103B and 11, 0.4 mi w on SR 11, 1.8 mi s (Winn Hill Rd). Ext/int corridors. **Pets:** Other species. $20 daily fee/pet. Designated rooms, service with restrictions. 🛜 ⊠ 🖥 💻 ⫛ ⇌ ⊠

THORNTON

▼ Shamrock Motel M

(603) 726-3534. **$55-$85, 7 day notice.** 2913 US 3 03285. I-93 exit 29, 2.3 mi n. Ext corridors. **Pets:** Other species. $5 daily fee/room. Designated rooms, no service, supervision.

ECO 🛜 ⊠ 🖥 💻 ⇌ ⫛ ⊠

TILTON

▼▼▼ Black Swan Inn BB

(603) 630-6155. **Call for rates.** 354 W Main St 03276. I-93 exit 20 southbound, 1.5 mi w on SR 3 and 11. Int corridors. **Pets:** Accepted.

🛜 ⊠ 🖥 💻

TROY

▼▼▼ The Inn at East Hill Farm CI

(603) 242-6495. **$140-$302, 21 day notice.** 460 Monadnock St 03465. Jct SR 12 and Monadnock St, 2 mi e. Ext/int corridors. **Pets:** Other species. $10 daily fee/pet. Designated rooms.

ECO SAVE 🛜 ⊠ 🖥 ⫛ ⇌ ⊠ ⊠

WATERVILLE VALLEY

▼▼▼ Best Western Silver Fox Inn H

(603) 236-3699. **$119-$159.** 70 Packards Rd 03215. I-93 exit 28, 11 mi e on SR 49, just n. Int corridors. **Pets:** Accepted. SAVE 🛜 ⊠ 💻

WEST LEBANON

▼▼ A Fireside Inn and Suites H

(603) 298-5900. **$120-$200.** 25 Airport Rd 03784. I-89 exit 20 (SR 12A), just s. Int corridors. **Pets:** Accepted. 🛜 🖥 💻 ⫛ ⇌ ⊠

▼▼▼ Baymont Inn M

(603) 298-8888. **$72-$162.** 45 Airport Rd 03784. I-89 exit 20 (SR 12A), just s, then just e. Int corridors. **Pets:** Large. $10 one-time fee/room. Designated rooms, service with restrictions, supervision.

SAVE 🛜 ⫖M 🖥 💻 ⇌

WOODSVILLE

▼ All Seasons Motel M

(603) 747-2157. **$60-$125, 3 day notice.** 36 Smith St 03785. I-91 exit 17, 4.1 mi e on US 302, then just s. Ext corridors. **Pets:** $5 one-time fee/pet. Service with restrictions, supervision. SAVE 🛜 🖥 💻 ⇌

▼▼▼ Nootka Lodge M

(603) 747-2418. **$75-$235, 3 day notice.** 4982 Dartmouth College Hwy 03785. I-91 exit 17, 4.5 mi e on US 302. Ext corridors. **Pets:** $5 one-time fee/pet. Designated rooms, service with restrictions, supervision.

SAVE 🛜 🖥 ⇌ ⊠

NEW JERSEY

CITY INDEX

ATLANTIC CITY METROPOLITAN AREA

ABSECON

Quality Inn & Suites Atlantic City Marina District H

(609) 652-3300. **$40-$179.** 328 E White Horse Pike (US 30) 08205. Garden State Pkwy exit 40 southbound; exit northbound, U-turn through Atlantic City Service Plaza, s to exit 40, then just e. Ext corridors. **Pets:** Accepted.

ATLANTIC CITY

Sheraton Atlantic City Convention Center Hotel H

(609) 344-3535. **$99-$499, 3 day notice.** 2 Convention Blvd 08401. Garden State Pkwy exit 38 to Atlantic City Expwy to Arctic Ave, just e to Michigan Ave, then just n. Int corridors. **Pets:** Accepted.

SOMERS POINT

Residence Inn Atlantic City Somers Point H

(609) 927-6400. **$139-$219.** 900 Mays Landing Rd 08244. Garden State Pkwy exit 30 southbound; exit 29 northbound, 1 mi e. Ext corridors. **Pets:** Accepted.

WEST ATLANTIC CITY

Ramada-West Atlantic City H

(609) 646-5220. **$59-$269.** 8037 Black Horse Pike 08232. Garden State Pkwy exit 38 (Atlantic City Expwy), 2 mi e to exit 5, 0.5 mi s on US 9 to US 40/322, then 1.8 mi e. Ext/int corridors. **Pets:** Accepted.

END METROPOLITAN AREA

BASKING RIDGE

Hotel Indigo H

(908) 580-1300. **$99-$219.** 80 Allen Rd 07920. I-78 exit 33, 0.3 mi n on CR 525, then 0.3 mi w. Int corridors. **Pets:** $25 daily fee/pet. Service with restrictions.

BAY HEAD

Grenville Hotel H

(732) 892-3100. **$89-$359, 14 day notice.** 345 Main Ave (SR 35) 08742. SR 35 S; at Bridge Ave. Int corridors. **Pets:** Accepted.

BEACH HAVEN

Engleside Inn H

(609) 492-1251. **$170-$459, 30 day notice.** 30 Engleside Ave 08008. 6.9 mi s of SR 72 Cswy to Engleside Ave, then just e. Ext corridors. **Pets:** Other species. $15 daily fee/pet. Designated rooms.

BRIDGEWATER

Days Inn Conference Center H

(908) 526-9500. **$63-$90.** 1260 US 22 E 08807. I-287 exit 17 to US 202/206 S, just s exit US 22, then 2 mi e; exit 14B northbound, 1 mi w on US 22, U-turn at Adamsville Rd, then 1 mi e. Int corridors. **Pets:** Accepted.

Hyatt house Bridgewater H

(908) 725-0800. **$89-$229.** 530 US 22 E 08807. I-287 exit 14B northbound; exit 17 southbound to US 22 W, then 0.8 mi. Ext corridors. **Pets:** Accepted.

CAPE MAY

Madison Avenue Beach Club Motel M

(609) 884-8266. **Call for rates.** 605 Madison Ave 08204. Jct Columbia Ave. Ext corridors. **Pets:** $200 deposit/room. Designated rooms, service with restrictions, crate.

Marquis de Lafayette Hotel H

(609) 884-3500. **$132-$545, 10 day notice.** 501 Beach Ave 08204. Between Decatur and Ocean sts. Ext/int corridors. **Pets:** Other species. $100 deposit/pet, $25 daily fee/pet. Designated rooms, service with restrictions, supervision.

Palace Hotel of Cape May H

(609) 898-8100. **$89-$329, 7 day notice.** 1101 Beach Ave 08204. Jct Beach and Philadelphia aves. Int corridors. **Pets:** Medium. $25 one-time fee/pet. Designated rooms, service with restrictions, supervision.

White Dove Cottage BB

(609) 884-0613. **Call for rates.** 619 Hughes St 08204. Between Franklin and Ocean sts. Ext/int corridors. **Pets:** Accepted.

CAPE MAY COURT HOUSE

The Doctors Inn BB

(609) 463-9330. **$100-$350, 14 day notice.** 2 N Main St 08210. At Main (US 9) and Mechanic sts; just s of Garden State Pkwy. Int corridors. **Pets:** Medium. $25 daily fee/pet. Designated rooms, supervision.

CLINTON

▼▼▼ Hampton Inn H

(908) 713-4800. **Call for rates.** 16 Frontage Dr 08809. I-78 exit 15, 0.3 mi s on CR 513, then left at next light. Int corridors. **Pets:** $35 daily fee/pet. Designated rooms, service with restrictions, supervision.

SAVE 📶 ⓜ 🔒 🖥 ⊶

▼▼▼ Holiday Inn-Clinton H

(908) 735-5111. **$119-$129.** 111 Rt 173 08809. I-78 exit 15, just nw. Int corridors. **Pets:** Accepted. 📶 🔒 🖥 🍴 ⊶

CRANBURY

▼▼▼ Courtyard by Marriott Cranbury/South
Brunswick H

(609) 655-9950. **$109-$219.** 420 Forsgate Dr 08512. New Jersey Tpke exit 8A to SR 32 W toward town, just w. Int corridors. **Pets:** Medium. $75 one-time fee/room. Designated rooms, service with restrictions, supervision. 📶 ✖ ⓜ 🔒 🖥 🍴 ⊶

▼▼▼ Residence Inn by Marriott/Cranbury-South
Brunswick H

(609) 395-9447. **$94-$149.** 2662 US 130 08512. New Jersey Tpke exit 8A to SR 32 W toward town, 2 mi w on S River Rd. Int corridors. **Pets:** $100 one-time fee/pet. Designated rooms, service with restrictions, supervision. SAVE 📶 ✖ ⓜ 🔒 🖥 ⊶ ✖

▼▼▼ Staybridge Suites/Cranbury H

(609) 409-7181. **$99-$249.** 1272 S River Rd 08512. New Jersey Tpke exit 8A to SR 32 W toward town, 2 mi w. Int corridors. **Pets:** Accepted.

📶 ✖ 🔒 🖥 ⊶

DOVER

▼▼▼ Homewood Suites by Hilton Dover-Rockaway H

(973) 989-8899. **$109-$179.** 2 Commerce Center Dr 07801. 1.2 mi n on Mt Hope Ave, just w on Mt Pleasant Ave. Int corridors. **Pets:** Accepted.

📶 ⓜ 🔒 🖥 ⊶

EAST BRUNSWICK

▼▼▼ Best Western East Brunswick Inn H ❀

(732) 238-4900. **$85-$160.** 764 SR 18 N 08816. Between Rue Ln and Racetrack Rd; New Jersey Tpke exit 9 (SR 18 N), 4 mi s. Int corridors. **Pets:** Medium. $20 daily fee/pet. Designated rooms, service with restrictions, crate. SAVE 📶 ⓜ 🔒 🖥

▼▼ Motel 6, East Brunswick #1083 M

(732) 390-4545. **$55-$69.** 244 SR 18 N 08816. New Jersey Tpke exit 9 (SR 18), 1 mi s, U-turn at Edgeboro Rd, then just e. Ext/int corridors. **Pets:** Other species. Service with restrictions, supervision. 📶 ⓜ

▼▼▼ Studio 6 East Brunswick #6020 H

(732) 238-3330. **$69-$79.** 246 Rt 18 at Edgeboro Rd 08816. New Jersey Tpke exit 9 (SR 18), 1 mi s, U-turn at Edgeboro Rd, then just e. Int corridors. **Pets:** Other species. $10 daily fee/room. Service with restrictions, supervision. 📶 ⓜ 🔒 🖥

EAST RUTHERFORD

▼▼▼ Residence Inn East Rutherford Meadowlands H

(201) 939-0020. **$69-$309.** 10 Murray Hill Pkwy 07073. New Jersey Tpke exit 16W (from western spur) to SR 3 W to SR 17 N, 1.5 mi n to Paterson Plank Rd (SR 120), then just e. Int corridors. **Pets:** Accepted.

📶 ✖ ⓜ 🔒 🖥 ⊶ ✖

▼▼▼ Sheraton Meadowlands Hotel & Conference
Center H

(201) 896-0500. **$104-$850, 3 day notice.** 2 Meadowlands Plaza 07073. New Jersey Tpke exit 16W (from western spur), sports complex right after toll to Sheraton Plaza Dr. Int corridors. **Pets:** Accepted.

SAVE 📶 ✖ ⓜ 🔒 🖥 🍴 ⊶ ✖

EAST WINDSOR

▼▼▼ Quality Inn East Windsor H ❀

(609) 448-7399. **Call for rates.** 351 Franklin St 08520. New Jersey Tpke exit 8, just w. Ext/int corridors. **Pets:** Medium. $35 one-time fee/pet. Service with restrictions, crate. SAVE 📶 ⓜ 🔒 🖥

EATONTOWN

▼▼▼ Staybridge Suites Hotel Eatontown-Tinton
Falls H

(732) 380-9300. **$89-$209.** 4 Industrial Way E 07724. Garden State Pkwy exit 105, 0.7 mi e on SR 36, then 1 mi s on SR 35. Int corridors. **Pets:** Large. $75 one-time fee/pet. Service with restrictions, crate.

📶 ⓜ 🔒 🖥 ⊶

EDISON

▼▼▼ Courtyard by Marriott Edison/Woodbridge H

(732) 738-1991. **$79-$159.** 3105 Woodbridge Ave 08837. New Jersey Tpke exit 10, 0.5 mi se on CR 514, then just e. Int corridors.
Pets: Accepted. 📶 ✖ ⓜ 🔒 🖥 ⊶

▼▼ Red Roof Inn #7194 M

(732) 248-9300. **$61-$74.** 860 New Durham Rd 08817. I-287 exit 2A northbound, 0.3 mi w via Bridge St, then left; exit 3 southbound, just w. Ext corridors. **Pets:** Large, other species. No service, supervision.

SAVE 📶 ⓜ 🔒

▼▼▼ Sheraton Edison Hotel Raritan Center H

(732) 225-8300. **$99-$289.** 125 Raritan Center Pkwy 08837. New Jersey Tpke exit 10, 0.5 mi se on CR 514, keep right after tolls. Int corridors.
Pets: Accepted. SAVE 📶 ✖ ⓜ 🔒 🖥 🍴 ⊶ ✖

ELIZABETH

▼▼▼ Country Inn & Suites By Carlson H

(908) 282-0020. **$99-$189.** 100 Glimcher Realty Way 07201. New Jersey Tpke exit 13A, 1 mi se on Jersey Garden Blvd, just n on Kapkowski Rd, then just w. Int corridors. **Pets:** Accepted.

ECO 📶 ⓜ 🔒 🖥 ⊶

▼▼▼ Hilton Newark Airport H

(908) 351-3900. **$109-$229.** 1170 Spring St 07201. New Jersey Tpke exit 14, 2.3 mi s on US 1 and 9. Int corridors. **Pets:** Accepted.

SAVE 📶 ⓜ 🔒 🖥 🍴 ⊶

▼▼▼ Residence Inn Newark Elizabeth/Liberty International
Airport H

(908) 352-4300. **$199-$230.** 83 Glimcher Realty Way 07201. New Jersey Tpke exit 13A, 1 mi se on Jersey Garden Blvd, just n on Kapkowski Rd, then just w. Int corridors. **Pets:** Accepted.

📶 ✖ ⓜ 🔒 🖥 ⊶

EWING

▼▼▼ Element Ewing Hopewell H

(609) 671-0050. **$149-$329.** 1000 Sam Weinroth Rd E 08628. I-95 exit 3A, n on Sam Weinroth Rd, then just e. Int corridors. **Pets:** Accepted.

SAVE 📶 ✖ ⓜ 🔒 🖥 ⊶ ✖

FAIRFIELD

▼▼▼ La Quinta Inn & Suites Fairfield H

(973) 575-1742. **$62-$135.** 38 Two Bridges Rd 07004. I-80 exit 52 westbound; exit 47B (Caldwells) eastbound, 7 mi e on US 46 exit Passaic Ave. Int corridors. **Pets:** Medium, other species. Service with restrictions, supervision. 📶 ⓜ 🔒 🖥 🍴 ⊶

HASBROUCK HEIGHTS

▼▼▼ Hilton Hasbrouck Heights H

(201) 288-6100. **$109-$239.** 650 Terrace Ave 07604. I-80 exit 64B westbound; exit 64 eastbound, just s on SR 17 S. Int corridors.
Pets: Accepted. 📶 🔒 🖥 🍴 ⊶

HAZLET

▼▼▼ Holiday Inn/Hazlet ⊞

(732) 888-2000. **$89-$179.** 2870 SR 35 07730. Garden State Pkwy exit 117 to SR 35 S, 2.5 mi s. Int corridors. **Pets:** Accepted.

🛜 🛏 💻 🍽 🏊

HILLSBOROUGH

AAA ▼▼▼ Days Inn ⊞

(908) 685-9000. **$59-$72.** 118 Rt 206 S 08844. 2.6 mi s of jct SR 28, US 202 and 206; at circle. Int corridors. **Pets:** $20 daily fee/pet. Service with restrictions, crate. SAVE 🛜 ♿M 🛏 💻 🍽 🏊

HOBOKEN

AAA ▼▼▼▼ W Hoboken ⊞

(201) 253-2400. **$329-$929.** 225 River St 07030. Between 1st and 2nd sts. Int corridors. **Pets:** Accepted. SAVE 🛜 ✕ ♿M 🛏 💻 🍽

JERSEY CITY

AAA ▼▼▼ ▼▼▼ The Westin Jersey City Newport ⊞

(201) 626-2900. **$169-$599.** 479 Washington Blvd 07310. US 1 and 9 N, just before Holland Tunnel entrance, e on Jersey Ave toward Newport Mall, then s; at 6th St. Int corridors. **Pets:** Accepted.

SAVE 🛜 ✕ ♿M 🛏 💻 🍽 🏊 ✕

LAWRENCEVILLE

AAA ▼▼▼ Red Roof Inn-Princeton #10111 Ⓜ

(609) 896-3388. **$64-$109.** 3203 Brunswick Pike (US 1) 08648. I-295 exit 67A, just n. Ext corridors. **Pets:** Large, other species. No service, supervision. SAVE 🛜 🛏

LEDGEWOOD

AAA ▼▼▼ Quality Inn ⊞

(973) 347-5100. **Call for rates.** 1691 US 46 W 07852. I-80 exit 27, 2 mi e via US 206 N and 183 N. Int corridors. **Pets:** Accepted.

SAVE 🛜 🛏 💻 🏊

LONG BRANCH

▼▼▼ Ocean Place Resort & Spa ⊞

(732) 571-4000. **$125-$629, 7 day notice.** 1 Ocean Blvd 07740. Jct SR 71, 3 mi e on SR 36, then 0.5 mi s. Int corridors. **Pets:** Accepted.

🛜 ✕ 🛏 💻 🍽 🏊 ✕

MAHWAH

▼▼▼▼ Homewood Suites by Hilton ⊞ 🐾

(201) 760-9994. **$119-$209.** 375 Corporate Dr 07430. I-287 exit 66, 1.7 mi on SR 17 S to MacArthur Blvd, then 0.4 mi w. Int corridors. **Pets:** Other species. $150 one-time fee/room. Service with restrictions, crate. 🛏 💻 🏊

AAA ▼▼▼ Sheraton Mahwah Hotel ⊞

(201) 529-1660. **$109-$249.** 1 International Blvd (Rt 17) 07495. I-287 exit 66; at SR 17 N. Int corridors. **Pets:** Accepted.

SAVE 🛜 ✕ 🛏 💻 🍽 🏊 ✕

MIDDLETOWN

AAA ▼▼▼ Comfort Inn Middletown-Red Bank ⊞

(732) 671-3400. **$100-$200.** 750 State Rt 35 S 07748. Garden State Pkwy exit 114, 2 mi e on Red Hill Rd, 1 mi s on King's Hwy to SR 35, then 0.3 mi s. Int corridors. **Pets:** Large. $30 daily fee/room. Service with restrictions, supervision. SAVE 🛜 🛏 💻 🍽 🏊

MONMOUTH JUNCTION

AAA ▼ Red Roof Inn/North Princeton #7198 Ⓜ

(732) 821-8800. **$55-$133.** 208 New Rd 08852. On US 1 S. Ext corridors. **Pets:** Large, other species. No service, supervision.

SAVE 🛜 🛏 💻

Residence Inn Princeton-South Brunswick ⊞ 🐾

(732) 329-9600. **$159-$197.** 4225 US 1 S 08543. 0.5 mi s of Raymond Rd. Int corridors. **Pets:** Small. $100 one-time fee/room. Service with restrictions, crate. 🛜 ✕ ♿M 🛏 💻 🏊 ✕

MORRIS PLAINS

▼▼▼ Candlewood Suites Parsippany-Morris Plains ⊞

(973) 984-9960. **Call for rates.** 100 Candlewood Dr 07950. I-287 exit 39 northbound; exit 39B southbound, 2 mi w on SR 10. Int corridors. **Pets:** Accepted. ♿M 🛏 💻

MORRISTOWN

AAA ▼▼▼▼ Hyatt house Morristown ⊞

(973) 971-0008. **$89-$259.** 194 Park Ave 07960. SR 24 exit 2A (Morristown), stay in far left lane. Int corridors. **Pets:** Accepted.

SAVE 🛜 ✕ ♿M 🛏 💻 🍽 ✕

AAA ▼▼▼ The Westin Governor Morris ⊞

(973) 539-7300. **$119-$459.** 2 Whippany Rd 07960. I-287 exit 36 southbound, left lane to light, left to stop sign, then 1 mi e; exit 36A northbound thru Morris Ave, 0.8 mi e, follow signs. Int corridors.
Pets: Accepted. SAVE 🛜 ✕ 🛏 💻 🍽 🏊

MOUNT OLIVE

▼▼▼ Residence Inn Mt. Olive at The International Trade Center ⊞

(973) 691-1720. **$149-$179.** 271 Continental Dr 07828. I-80 exit 25, just n, follow signs for International Trade Center. Int corridors.
Pets: Accepted. 🛜 ✕ 🛏 💻 🏊 ✕

NEPTUNE

▼▼▼ Residence Inn by Marriott Neptune at Gateway Centre ⊞

(732) 643-9350. **$169-$219.** 230 Jumping Brook Rd 07753. Garden State Pkwy exit 100B, 0.5 mi e on SR 33, then 0.5 mi n. Int corridors.
Pets: Medium, other species. $100 one-time fee/room. Service with restrictions. 🛜 ✕ ♿M 🛏 💻 🏊 ✕

NEWARK

AAA ▼▼▼▼ DoubleTree by Hilton Newark Airport ⊞

(973) 690-5500. **Call for rates.** 128 Frontage Rd 07114. I-95 exit 14, 2nd right after toll booth, then just w. Int corridors. **Pets:** Accepted.

SAVE 🛜 ✕ ♿M 🛏 💻 🍽 🏊

AAA ▼▼▼▼ Hilton Newark Penn Station ⊞

(973) 622-5000. **$119-$499.** Gateway Center - 1048 Raymond Blvd 07102. New Jersey Tpke exit 15E, 3 mi w via Raymond Blvd. Int corridors. **Pets:** Accepted. SAVE 🛜 🛏 💻 💻

▼▼▼ SpringHill Suites Newark Liberty International Airport ⊞

(973) 624-5300. **$103-$170.** 652 Rt 1 & 9 S 07114. I-95 exit 14, 1 mi sw via US 1 and 9 S. Int corridors. **Pets:** Accepted.

✕ ♿M 🛏 💻 🏊

NEW BRUNSWICK

▼▼▼ The Heldrich Hotel & Spa ⊞

(732) 729-4670. **$89-$199.** 10 Livingston Ave 08901. At George and New sts; center. Int corridors. **Pets:** Accepted.

🛜 ✕ ♿M 🛏 💻 🍽 🏊

NORTH BRUNSWICK

▼▼▼ Brunswick Hotel ⊞

(732) 297-7400. **$89-$149.** 2880 US 1 N 08902. Between Finnegan and Black Horse lns. Int corridors. **Pets:** Medium. $20 daily fee/pet. Designated rooms, service with restrictions, supervision. 🛜 ♿M 🛏 💻

PARAMUS

▼▼ La Quinta Inn H

(201) 265-4200. **$100-$188.** 393 Rt 17 S 07652. Garden State Pkwy exit 163 northbound to SR 17 N, 0.6 mi to Midland Ave, then U-turn to SR 17 S; exit 165 southbound to Richwood Ave, 1 mi. Int corridors. **Pets:** Medium, other species. Service with restrictions, supervision.

🛜 🛏 💻

PARSIPPANY

▼▼▼ Embassy Suites H

(973) 334-1440. **$109-$299.** 909 Parsippany Blvd 07054. I-80 exit 42 to US 202 N; just ne of jct US 202 and 46 W. Int corridors. **Pets:** Accepted.

🛜 🛏 💻 🍴 🏊 ✕

▼▼▼ Hampton Inn Parsippany H

(973) 290-9058. **$89-$229.** One Hilton Ct 07054. I-287 exit 39 northbound; exit 39B southbound, 1.3 mi w on SR 10; in Hilton Court. Int corridors. **Pets:** Accepted. 🛜 ✕ ♿ 🛏 💻 ✕

▼▼▼ Hilton Parsippany H

(973) 267-7373. **$99-$289.** 1 Hilton Ct 07054. I-287 exit 39 northbound; exit 39B southbound, 1.3 mi w on SR 10; in Hilton Court. Int corridors. **Pets:** Accepted. 🛜 🛏 💻 🍴 🏊 ✕

▲▲▲ ▼▼▼ Red Roof Inn #7072 M

(973) 334-3737. **$55-$99.** 855 US 46 E 07054. I-80 exit 47 westbound; exit 45 eastbound, 0.5 mi e. Ext corridors. **Pets:** Large, other species. No service, supervision. SAVE 🛜 🛏 💻

▼▼▼ Residence Inn by Marriott Parsippany H ❀

(973) 984-3313. **$82-$239.** 3 Gatehall Dr 07054. I-287 exit 39 northbound; exit 39B southbound, 2 mi w on SR 10. Ext/int corridors. **Pets:** Large, other species. $100 one-time fee/room. Service with restrictions, supervision. 🛜 ✕ ♿ 🛏 💻 🏊 ✕

▲▲▲ ▼▼▼ Sheraton Parsippany Hotel H

(973) 515-2000. **$75-$369.** 199 Smith Rd 07054. I-287 exit 41A northbound; exit 42 to US 46 E, 0.4 mi s. Int corridors. **Pets:** Accepted.

ECO SAVE ✕ 🛏 💻 🍴 🏊 ✕

▼▼▼ Staybridge Suites Parsippany H

(973) 334-2907. **Call for rates.** 61 Interpace Pkwy 07054. I-80 exit 42, 0.3 mi s on Cherry Hill Rd, then just w. Int corridors. **Pets:** Accepted.

🛜 ♿ 🛏 💻 🏊

PHILADELPHIA METROPOLITAN AREA (NEARBY PENNSYLVANIA)

BORDENTOWN

▲▲▲ ▼▼ Days Inn-Bordentown M

(609) 298-6100. **$81-$135.** 1073 US 206 N 08505. New Jersey Tpke exit 7, 0.8 mi n. Ext corridors. **Pets:** Accepted.

SAVE 🛜 🛏 💻 🍴 🏊

BRIDGEPORT

▼▼▼ Hampton Inn-Bridgeport H

(856) 467-6200. **$113-$142.** 2 Pureland Dr 08085. I-295 exit 10, just se. Int corridors. **Pets:** Accepted. 🛜 ✕ ♿ 🛏 💻 🏊

CARNEYS POINT

▼▼▼ Comfort Inn & Suites H

(856) 299-8282. **Call for rates.** 634 Sodders Rd 08069. I-295 exit 2B, just e on Pennsville-Auburn Rd, then 0.3 mi s. Int corridors. **Pets:** Accepted. 🛜 ♿ 🛏 💻

▲▲▲ ▼▼▼ Holiday Inn Express Hotel & Suites H

(856) 351-9222. **$110-$135.** 506 Pennsville-Auburn Rd 08069. I-295 exit 2B, just e. Int corridors. **Pets:** Medium, other species. $10 daily fee/pet. Service with restrictions, supervision. SAVE 🛜 🛏 💻

CHERRY HILL

▼▼ Extended StayAmerica-Philadelphia/Cherry Hill H ❀

(856) 616-1200. **$82-$149.** 1653 E SR 70 (Marlton Pike) 08034. I-295 exit 34A, just e. Int corridors. **Pets:** Other species. $25 daily fee/pet. Service with restrictions. 🛜 🛏 💻

▲▲▲ ▼▼▼ Holiday Inn Philadelphia-Cherry Hill H

(856) 663-5300. **$95-$169.** 2175 W Marlton Pike 08002. I-295 exit 34B, 2.5 mi w. Int corridors. **Pets:** Other species. $75 deposit/room. Service with restrictions. SAVE 🛜 ✕ 🛏 💻 🍴 🏊

DEPTFORD

▼▼▼ Residence Inn Deptford H

(856) 686-9188. **$119-$259.** 1154 Hurffville Rd 08096. SR 42 exit Deptford, Runnemede, Woodbury to CR 544, just e to CR 415. Int corridors. **Pets:** Accepted. 🛜 ✕ 🛏 💻 ✕

HADDONFIELD

▼▼▼ Haddonfield Inn BB

(856) 428-2195. **Call for rates.** 44 W End Ave 08033. I-295 exit 28, 0.7 mi n on SR 168, 2.6 mi e on Kings Hwy, then just n. Int corridors. **Pets:** Medium, dogs only. $25 daily fee/pet. Designated rooms, service with restrictions, crate. 🛜 ✕ 🛏

MOUNT LAUREL

▼▼ Candlewood Suites H

(856) 642-7567. **$85-$100.** 4000 Crawford Pl 08054. New Jersey Tpke exit 4, 1 mi s on SR 73 S. Int corridors. **Pets:** Accepted. 🛏 💻

▼▼ Extended Stay Deluxe-Philadelphia-Mt. Laurel H ❀

(856) 608-9820. **$105-$149.** 500 Diemer Dr 08054. New Jersey Tpke exit 4, 1 mi se on SR 73, just n on Crawford Pl, then just e. Int corridors. **Pets:** Other species. $25 daily fee/pet. Service with restrictions. 🛜 🛏 💻

▲▲▲ ▼▼▼▼ Hyatt house Mt. Laurel H

(856) 222-1313. **$99-$249.** 3000 Crawford Pl 08054. New Jersey Tpke exit 4, 1 mi s on SR 73; I-295 exit 36A, 1.5 mi s on SR 73. Ext corridors. **Pets:** Accepted. SAVE 🛜 ✕ ♿ 🛏 💻 🏊

▼▼▼▼ Philadelphia/Mount Laurel Homewood Suites by Hilton H

(856) 222-9001. **$118-$159.** 1422 Nixon Dr 08054. I-295 exit 36B, follow ramp to end, then just n. Int corridors. **Pets:** Accepted.

🛜 ♿ 🛏 💻 🏊 ✕

▲▲▲ ▼▼▼ Red Roof Inn #7066 M

(856) 234-5589. **$53-$100.** 603 Fellowship Rd 08054. New Jersey Tpke exit 4, just nw on SR 73 to Fellowship Rd, then just s; I-295 exit 36A, just se on SR 73 to Fellowship Rd, then just s. Ext corridors. **Pets:** Large, other species. No service, supervision. SAVE 🛜 🛏

▼▼▼ Residence Inn by Marriott Mount Laurel at Bishop's Gate H

(856) 234-1025. **$199-$249.** 1001 Sunburst Ln 08054. I-295 exit 40A. Int corridors. **Pets:** Accepted. 🛜 ✕ ♿ 🛏 💻 🏊 ✕

▲▲▲ ▼▼▼ Staybridge Suites H ❀

(856) 722-1900. **$90-$180.** 4115 Church Rd 08054. New Jersey Tpke exit 4, 0.5 mi s on SR 73, then 0.5 mi w. Int corridors. **Pets:** Medium. $75 one-time fee/pet. Service with restrictions, crate.

SAVE 🛜 🛏 💻 🏊 ✕

▲▲▲ ▼▼▼▼ The Westin Mount Laurel H

(856) 778-7300. **$109-$299.** 555 Fellowship Rd 08054. New Jersey Tpke exit 4, just nw to Fellowship Rd, then just n; I-295 exit 36A, just se on SR 73 to Fellowship Rd, then just n. Int corridors. **Pets:** Medium, dogs only. Designated rooms, service with restrictions.

SAVE 🛜 ✕ ♿ 🛏 💻 🍴 🏊 ✕

Wyndham Philadelphia/Mount Laurel H
(856) 234-7000. **$108-$136.** 1111 SR 73 08054. New Jersey Tpke exit 4; I-295 exit 36A, 0.5 mi se. Int corridors. **Pets:** Medium. $100 deposit/pet, $50 one-time fee/pet. Designated rooms, service with restrictions, crate. SAVE 🛜 ✕ 🛗 💻 🍽 ⌦

SPRINGFIELD
Hotel 304 West H
(973) 376-9400. **$119-$125.** 304 US 22 W 07081. Garden State Pkwy exit 140 northbound, 4 mi w; exit 140A southbound. Int corridors. **Pets:** Service with restrictions, crate. 🛜 🛗 💻 🍽 ⌦ ✕

SWEDESBORO
Holiday Inn H
(856) 467-3322. **$102-$149.** 1 Pureland Dr 08085. I-295 exit 10, 0.4 mi e. Int corridors. **Pets:** Accepted. 🛜 ✕ 🛗 💻 🍽 ⌦

WESTAMPTON
Best Western Burlington Inn H
(609) 261-3800. **$115-$129.** 2020 Burlington Mt Holly Rd 08060. New Jersey Tpke exit 5, just n. Int corridors. **Pets:** Accepted.
SAVE 🛜 🛗 💻 ⌦

Holiday Inn Express Hotel & Suites H
(609) 702-5800. **$85-$135.** 18 Western Dr 08060. New Jersey Tpke exit 5, 0.3 mi n. Int corridors. **Pets:** Accepted. 🛜 🛗 💻 ⌦

END METROPOLITAN AREA

PISCATAWAY
Embassy Suites Hotel H
(732) 980-0500. **$101-$160.** 121 Centennial Ave 08854. I-287 exit 9 (Highland Park), just s to Centennial Ave. Int corridors. **Pets:** Accepted.
🛜 🛗 💻 🍽 ⌦

Extended Stay Deluxe Piscataway-Rutgers University H ✤
(732) 235-1000. **$105-$169.** 410 S Randolphville Rd 08854. I-287 exit 7, 0.4 mi s. Int corridors. **Pets:** Other species. $25 daily fee/pet. Service with restrictions. 🛜 ⓜ 🛗 💻 ⌦

Motel 6 Piscataway #1084 H
(732) 981-9200. **$55-$65.** 1012 Stelton Rd 08854. I-287 exit 5, just e. Ext/int corridors. **Pets:** Other species. Service with restrictions, supervision. 🛜

POMPTON PLAINS
Best Western Plus Regency House Hotel H
(973) 696-0900. **Call for rates.** 140 SR 23 N 07444. 6 mi n of jct I-80, US 46 and SR 23. Int corridors. **Pets:** Accepted.
SAVE 🛜 🛗 💻 🍽 ⌦

PRINCETON
Chauncey Hotel and Conference Center H
(609) 921-3600. **$119-$299.** 660 Rosedale Rd 08541. 0.5 mi w on Stockton Rd, 0.5 mi n on Elm Rd, 1.8 mi w on Rosedale Rd; enter through the ETS campus. Int corridors. **Pets:** Accepted.
🛜 ✕ 🛗 💻 🍽 ⌦ ✕

Clarion Hotel-The Palmer Inn H
(609) 452-2500. **Call for rates.** 3499 US 1 S 08540. 2 mi s of jct CR 526 and 571. Ext/int corridors. **Pets:** Accepted.
SAVE 🛜 🛗 💻 🍽 ⌦

Courtyard by Marriott Princeton H
(609) 716-9100. **$169-$208.** 3815 US 1 S 08540. 0.4 mi s of Scudders Mill Rd at Mapleton Rd. Int corridors. **Pets:** Accepted.
🛜 ✕ ⓜ 🛗 💻 🍽 ⌦

Hampton Inn Princeton H
(609) 951-0066. **$109-$179.** 4385 US 1 S 08540. Just past Ridge Rd. Int corridors. **Pets:** Accepted. 🛜 ✕ ⓜ 🛗 💻 ⌦

Holiday Inn Princeton H
(609) 520-1200. **$89-$155.** 100 Independence Way 08540. I-295 exit 67A (SR 1) northbound; exit 67 (SR 1) southbound, 7 mi n. Int corridors. **Pets:** Medium, other species. $50 one-time fee/pet. Designated rooms, service with restrictions, crate. 🛜 🛗 💻 🍽 ⌦ ✕

Nassau Inn H ✤
(609) 921-7500. **$229-$279.** 10 Palmer Square E 08542. Center. Int corridors. **Pets:** Medium. $75 one-time fee/room. Designated rooms, service with restrictions, crate. SAVE 🛜 🛗 💻 🍽

Residence Inn by Marriott-Princeton at Carnegie Center H
(609) 799-0550. **$125-$449.** 3563 US 1 S 08540. 1.5 mi s of jct CR 527 and 571. Int corridors. **Pets:** Accepted.
🛜 ✕ ⓜ 🛗 💻 ⌦ ✕

Staybridge Suites H
(609) 951-0009. **Call for rates.** 4375 US 1 S 08543. Just past Ridge Rd. Ext corridors. **Pets:** Accepted. 🛜 🛗 💻 ⌦ ✕

Westin Princeton at Forrestal Village H
(609) 452-7900. **$119-$359.** 201 Village Blvd 08540. On US 1 southbound, 1.5 mi n of CR 571. Int corridors. **Pets:** Accepted.
SAVE 🛜 ✕ ⓜ 🛗 💻 🍽 ⌦ ✕

RAHWAY
Hotel Indigo Rahway H
(732) 340-0076. **$144-$148.** 1 Carriage City Plaza 07065. Across from train station; center. Int corridors. **Pets:** Accepted. SAVE 🛜 ✕ 💻

RAMSEY
Best Western The Inn at Ramsey H ✤
(201) 327-6700. **$84-$104.** 1315 Rt 17 S 07446. Jct I-287 and SR 17 S, 3 mi s. Int corridors. **Pets:** Large, dogs only. $50 deposit/room, $20 daily fee/room. Designated rooms, service with restrictions, supervision.
SAVE 🛜 🛗 💻

RUTHERFORD
Extended StayAmerica-Meadowlands-Rutherford H ✤
(201) 635-0266. **$115-$199.** 750 Edwin L Ward Sr Memorial Hwy 07070. I-95 exit 16W, 1.5 mi w on SR 3 to SR 17 N service road exit, then 0.5 mi e. Int corridors. **Pets:** Other species. $25 daily fee/pet. Service with restrictions. 🛜 🛗 💻

SECAUCUS
La Quinta Inn & Suites Secaucus Meadowlands H
(201) 863-8700. **$104-$177.** 350 Lighting Way 07094. Between eastern and western spurs of New Jersey Tpke exits 16E, 17 or 16W via SR 3 W and Harmon Meadow Blvd; in Mill Creek Mall. Int corridors. **Pets:** Medium, other species. Service with restrictions, supervision.
🛜 🛗 💻 🍽 ⌦

SOMERSET

▼▼ **Candlewood Suites** H
(732) 748-1400. **Call for rates.** 41 Worlds Fair Dr 08873. I-287 exit 10 (CR 527), left on ramp (CR 527 S/Easton Ave), 0.3 mi, then 0.5 mi w. Int corridors. **Pets:** Medium, other species. $15 one-time fee/pet, $10 daily fee/pet. Service with restrictions, supervision. 🛜 🛗 💷

▼▼▼ **Crowne Plaza Somerset/Bridgewater** H
(732) 560-0500. **$99-$169.** 110 Davidson Ave 08873. I-287 exit 10 (CR 527), just n (direction Bound Brook) to Davidson Ave, then just sw. Int corridors. **Pets:** Accepted. 🛜 ⊠ 🛗ᴹ 🛗 💷 🍴 ⤵ ⊠

🅐🅐🅐 ▼▼▼ **Holiday Inn-Somerset** H
(732) 356-1700. **$119-$159, 3 day notice.** 195 Davidson Ave 08873. I-287 exit 10 (CR 527), just n (direction Bound Brook), then 0.5 mi sw. Int corridors. **Pets:** Accepted. 🆂🅰🆅🅴 🛜 🛗ᴹ 🛗 💷 🍴 ⤵

▼▼▼ **Homewood Suites by Hilton-Somerset** H
(732) 868-9155. **$89-$210.** 101 Pierce St 08873. I-287 exit 10 (CR 527), left on ramp (CR 527 S/Easton Ave), 0.3 mi, 0.7 mi w on Worlds Fair Dr, then just s. Int corridors. **Pets:** Accepted. 🛜 🛗ᴹ 🛗 💷 ⤵ ⊠

▼▼▼ **La Quinta Inn & Suites Somerset** H
(732) 560-9880. **$100-$188.** 60 Cottontail Ln 08873. I-287 exit 12, just sw via Weston Canal Rd (Cottontail Ln signage). Int corridors. **Pets:** Medium, other species. Service with restrictions, supervision. 🛜 🛗 💷 🍴 ⤵

▼▼▼ **Residence Inn by Marriott-Somerset** H
(732) 627-0881. **$118-$219.** 37 Worlds Fair Dr 08873. I-287 exit 10 (CR 527), 0.3 mi left on ramp (CR 527 S/Easton Ave), then 0.5 mi w. Int corridors. **Pets:** Accepted. 🛜 ⊠ 🛗ᴹ 🛗 💷 ⤵ ⊠

▼▼▼ **Staybridge Suites Somerset** H
(732) 356-8000. **Call for rates.** 260 Davidson Ave 08873. I-287 exit 10 (CR 527), just n (direction Bound Brook) to Davidson Ave, then 0.8 mi sw. Ext corridors. **Pets:** Medium, dogs only. $10 daily fee/room. Service with restrictions. 🛜 🛗 💷 ⤵ ⊠

SOUTH PLAINFIELD

🅐🅐🅐 ▼▼ **Best Western The Garden Executive Hotel** H
(908) 561-4488. **$82-$100.** 101 New World Way 07080. I-287 exit 5, just s. Int corridors. **Pets:** Small. $25 one-time fee/room. Service with restrictions, supervision. 🆂🅰🆅🅴 🛜 🛗 💷

TINTON FALLS

🅐🅐🅐 ▼▼ **Red Roof Inn #7211** M
(732) 389-4646. **$79-$145.** 11 Centre Plaza 07724. Garden State Pkwy exit 105, just right at 1st light after toll. Ext corridors. **Pets:** Large, other species. No service, supervision. 🆂🅰🆅🅴 🛜 🛗ᴹ 🛗 💷

▼▼▼ **Residence Inn Tinton Falls** H
(732) 389-8100. **$159-$189.** 90 Park Rd 07724. Garden State Pkwy exit 105, 1st jughandle after toll, immediate left before Courtyard by Marriott, just n, then e. Ext corridors. **Pets:** Accepted.
🛜 ⊠ 🛗 💷 ⤵ ⊠

TOMS RIVER

🅐🅐🅐 ▼▼▼ **Howard Johnson Hotel-Toms River** H
(732) 244-1000. **$116-$179.** 955 Hooper Ave 08753. Garden State Pkwy exit 82, 1 mi e on SR 37. Int corridors. **Pets:** Other species. $50 daily fee/pet. Designated rooms, service with restrictions, supervision.
🆂🅰🆅🅴 🛜 🛗 💷 🍴 ⤵

▼▼▼ **Quality Inn** H ❀
(732) 341-2400. **$86-$190.** 815 SR 37 W 08755. Garden State Pkwy exit 82A, 1.5 mi w. Int corridors. **Pets:** Medium, dogs only. $40 daily fee/pet. Service with restrictions, supervision. 🛜 ⊠ 🛗 💷 🍴 ⤵

VERNON

🅐🅐🅐 ▼▼◆ **Appalachian Motel** M
(973) 764-6070. **$55-$125, 3 day notice.** 367 Rt 94 N 07462. 1 mi n. Ext corridors. **Pets:** Medium. $25 daily fee/pet. Designated rooms, service with restrictions, supervision. 🆂🅰🆅🅴 🛜 🛗

WANTAGE

▼ **High Point Country Inn** M
(973) 702-1860. **$79-$89.** 1328 SR 23 N 07461. 1 mi n of Colesville Village Center. Ext corridors. **Pets:** Accepted. 🛜 ⊠ 🛗 ⤵ ⊘

WAYNE

▼▼ **La Quinta Inns & Suites** H
(973) 696-8050. **$55-$121.** 1850 SR 23 07470. I-80 exit 53 (Butler-Verona) westbound to SR 23 N, 3 mi to Ratzer Rd (service road), then just n; exit 54 eastbound to Minnisink Rd, U-turn for US 80 W exit 53. Int corridors. **Pets:** Medium, other species. Service with restrictions, supervision. 🛜 🛗ᴹ 🛗 💷 ⤵

▼▼▼ **Residence Inn by Marriott Wayne** H
(973) 872-7100. **$112-$256.** 30 Nevins Rd 07470. Jct CR 640 (Riverview Dr) and 681 (Valley Rd), 3.5 mi n, just w on Barbour Pond Dr, then just n. Int corridors. **Pets:** Accepted. 🛜 ⊠ 🛗ᴹ 🛗 💷 ⤵ ⊠

WEEHAWKEN

🅐🅐🅐 ▼▼◆ **Sheraton Lincoln Harbor Hotel** H
(201) 617-5600. **$149-$659.** 500 Harbor Blvd 07086. I-495 E toward Lincoln Tunnel exit Weehawken/Hoboken, bear right at bottom of hill, then 0.4 mi e to Lincoln Harbor Complex; on 19th St. Int corridors.
Pets: Accepted. 🆂🅰🆅🅴 🛜 ⊠ 🛗 💷 🍴 ⤵

WEST ORANGE

▼▼▼ **Residence Inn by Marriott-West Orange** H
(973) 669-4700. **$179-$219.** 107 Prospect Ave 07052. I-280 exit 8B, 1 mi n on CR 577 (Prospect Ave). Int corridors. **Pets:** Other species. $100 one-time fee/pet. Service with restrictions. ⊠ 🛗 💷 ⤵

▼◆▼ **The Wilshire Grand Hotel** H ❀
(973) 731-7007. **$199-$389, 3 day notice.** 350 Pleasant Valley Way 07052. I-280 exit 8B, just n to Eagle Rock Rd, 0.9 mi w, then just n. Int corridors. **Pets:** Other species. $10 daily fee/room. Service with restrictions, supervision. 🛜 ⊠ 🛗 💷 🍴

WHIPPANY

🅐🅐🅐 ▼▼▼ **Hyatt house Parsippany/Whippany** H
(973) 605-1001. **$79-$259.** 1 Ridgedale Ave N 07981. I-287 exit 39, just nw. Int corridors. **Pets:** Accepted. 🆂🅰🆅🅴 🛜 ⊠ 🛗 💷 ⤵

WOODBRIDGE

▼▼ **Homestead Studio Suites Woodbridge-Newark** H ❀
(732) 442-8333. **$95-$139.** 1 Hoover Way 07095. New Jersey Tpke exit 11, 1.4 mi to US 9 N, then just w on King Georges Post Rd. Int corridors. **Pets:** Other species. $25 daily fee/pet. Service with restrictions.
🛜 🛗ᴹ 🛗 💷

CITY INDEX

ALAMOGORDO

Best Western Desert Aire Inn ⓜ
(575) 437-2110. **$79-$126.** 1021 S White Sands Blvd 88310. 1.6 mi s of jct US 82/70 and 54. Ext corridors. **Pets:** Accepted.

Super 8-Alamogordo ⓗ
(575) 434-4205. **$54-$63.** 3204 N White Sands Blvd 88310. Just s of jct US 54/70 and 82. Int corridors. **Pets:** Other species. $10 daily fee/pet. Service with restrictions, supervision.

ALBUQUERQUE

Albuquerque Sheraton Uptown Hotel ⓗ
(505) 881-0000. **$99-$229.** 2600 Louisiana Blvd NE 87110. I-40 exit 162, 0.8 mi n. Int corridors. **Pets:** Accepted.

Best Western Airport Albuquerque InnSuites Hotel & Suites ⓗ
(505) 242-7022. **$69-$169.** 2400 Yale Blvd SE 87106. I-25 exit 222 (Gibson Blvd) northbound; exit 222A southbound, 1 mi e, then just s. Int corridors. **Pets:** Medium. $20 one-time fee/room. Service with restrictions, supervision.

Best Western Plus Rio Grande Inn ⓗ 🐾
(505) 843-9500. **$99-$169.** 1015 Rio Grande Blvd NW 87104. I-40 exit 157A (Rio Grande Blvd), just s. Int corridors. **Pets:** Medium, dogs only. $20 daily fee/pet. Designated rooms, service with restrictions, supervision.

Brittania & W E Mauger Estate Bed & Breakfast 🅱🅱 🐾
(505) 242-8755. **$99-$204, 10 day notice.** 701 Roma Ave NW 87102. I-25 exit 225, 1 mi w, then just s on 7th Ave. Int corridors. **Pets:** Dogs only. $20 one-time fee/room. Designated rooms, service with restrictions, crate.

Candlewood Suites ⓗ
(505) 888-3424. **$79-$149, 3 day notice.** 3025 Menaul Blvd NE 87107. I-40 exit 160, just n to Menaul Blvd, then 0.5 mi w. Int corridors. **Pets:** Large, other species. $10 daily fee/room. Service with restrictions.

ClubHouse Inn & Suites ⓗ
(505) 345-0010. **$89-$129.** 1315 Menaul Blvd NE 87107. I-25 exit 227A southbound, 1.5 mi s to Menaul Blvd, then just w; exit 225 northbound, 1.8 mi, then just w. Int corridors. **Pets:** Medium, other species. $10 daily fee/pet. Service with restrictions, supervision.

Comfort Inn-Airport ⓗ
(505) 243-2244. **$67-$135.** 2300 Yale Blvd SE 87106. I-25 exit 222A southbound; exit 222 (Gibson Blvd) northbound, 1 mi n, then just s. Ext/int corridors. **Pets:** Accepted.

Comfort Inn & Suites by Choice Hotels ⓗ
(505) 822-1090. **$63-$180.** 5811 Signal Ave NE 87113. I-25 exit 233, just e via Alameda Blvd. Int corridors. **Pets:** $15 daily fee/pet. Designated rooms, service with restrictions, supervision.

Country Inn & Suites Albuquerque Airport ⓗ
(505) 246-9600. **Call for rates.** 2601 Mulberry SE 87106. I-25 exit 222 (Gibson Blvd), just e. Int corridors. **Pets:** Accepted.

Crowne Plaza Albuquerque ⓗ
(505) 884-2500. **Call for rates.** 1901 University Blvd NE 87102. I-40 exit 160, just n to Menaul Blvd, then 1.1 mi w. Int corridors. **Pets:** Other species. $75 daily fee/room. Supervision.

Drury Inn & Suites-Albuquerque ⓗ
(505) 341-3600. **$95-$184.** 4310 The 25 Way NE 87109. I-25 exit Jefferson St NE; northwest quadrant of exchange. Int corridors. **Pets:** Accepted.

Econo Lodge Downtown ⓜ 🐾
(505) 243-1321. **$50.** 817 Central Ave NE 87102. I-25 exit 224A northbound; exit 224B southbound, just w. Ext corridors. **Pets:** Medium. $5 daily fee/pet. Service with restrictions, supervision.

Econo Lodge East ⓗ
(505) 292-7600. **$45-$55.** 13211 Central Ave NE 87123. I-40 exit 167 (Central Ave), just w. Ext corridors. **Pets:** Other species. $7 daily fee/pet. Service with restrictions, supervision.

Econo Lodge Midtown ⓗ
(505) 880-0080. **Call for rates.** 2412 Carlisle Blvd NE 87110. I-40 exit 160, just n. Ext corridors. **Pets:** Small, other species. $15 daily fee/pet. Service with restrictions, supervision.

Hacienda Antigua Inn 🅱🅱
(505) 345-5399. **$139-$209, 10 day notice.** 6708 Tierra Dr NW 87107. I-25 exit 230 (Osuna Dr), 2 mi w, then just n. Ext/int corridors. **Pets:** Accepted.

Hampton Inn-North ⓗ 🐾
(505) 344-1555. **$76-$89.** 5101 Ellison NE 87109. I-25 exit 231 (San Antonio Dr), just w. Ext corridors. **Pets:** Other species. Service with restrictions, supervision.

Holiday Inn Express ⓗ 🐾
(505) 275-8900. **$82-$92.** 10330 Hotel Ave NE 87123. I-40 exit 165 (Eubank Blvd), just e. Ext corridors. **Pets:** Medium, other species. $25 one-time fee/pet. Service with restrictions, supervision.

Hotel Andaluz ⓗ 🐾
(505) 242-9090. **$139-$329.** 125 2nd St NW St NW 87102. I-25 exit 224A northbound; exit 224B southbound, jct Copper Ave and 2nd St; downtown. Int corridors. **Pets:** Large. $50 one-time fee/room. Service with restrictions, crate.

The Hotel Blue ⓗ
(505) 924-2400. **Call for rates.** 717 Central Ave NW 87102. 8th St and Central Ave; downtown. Ext corridors. **Pets:** Accepted.

AAA ▼▼▼▼▼ **Hotel Parq Central** H ❀
(505) 242-0040. **$140-$420.** 806 Central Ave SE 87102. I-25 exit 224A northbound; exit 224B southbound, just w. Int corridors. **Pets:** Medium. $75 one-time fee/pet. Designated rooms, service with restrictions, crate.
[SAVE] 🛜 ✕ 🛢 🍽 ✕

AAA ▼▼▼▼ **Hyatt Regency Albuquerque** H ❀
(505) 842-1234. **$89-$240.** 330 Tijeras Ave NW 87102. I-25 exit 224B, 0.5 mi w; downtown. Int corridors. **Pets:** Medium. $75 daily fee/room. Service with restrictions, supervision.
[ECO] [SAVE] 🛜 � 🛢 🍽 ⇌ ✕

▼▼▼ **La Quinta Inn Albuquerque Airport** H
(505) 243-5500. **$68-$133.** 2116 Yale Blvd SE 87106. I-25 exit 222 (Gibson Blvd) northbound; exit 222A southbound, 1 mi e. Ext corridors. **Pets:** Medium, other species. Service with restrictions, supervision.
🛜 � 🛢 ⅏ ⇌

▼▼ **La Quinta Inn Albuquerque Northeast** M
(505) 821-9000. **$64-$133.** 5241 San Antonio Dr NE 87109. I-25 exit 231 (San Antonio Dr), just e. Ext corridors. **Pets:** Medium, other species. Service with restrictions, supervision. 🛜 ⅏M 🛢 ⅏ ⇌

▼▼▼ **La Quinta Inn & Suites Albuquerque Journal Ctr NW** H
(505) 345-7500. **$62-$122.** 7439 Pan American Frwy NE 87109. I-25 exit 231 (San Antonio Dr), just w. Int corridors. **Pets:** Medium, other species. Service with restrictions, supervision. 🛜 🛢 ⅏ ⇌

▼▼▼ **La Quinta Inn & Suites Albuquerque Midtown** H
(505) 761-5600. **$107-$214.** 2011 Menaul Blvd 87107. Jct University and Menaul blvds, just e. Int corridors. **Pets:** Medium, other species. Service with restrictions, supervision. 🛜 ⅏M 🛢 ⅏ ⇌

▼▼▼ **La Quinta Inn & Suites Albuquerque West** H
(505) 839-1744. **$74-$144.** 6101 Iliff Rd NW 87121. I-40 exit 155, just sw. Int corridors. **Pets:** Medium, other species. Service with restrictions, supervision. 🛜 ⅏M 🛢 ⅏ ⇌

▼▼▼ **Nativo Lodge** H
(505) 798-4300. **$89-$159.** 6000 Pan American Frwy NE 87109. I-25 exit 230, just e. Int corridors. **Pets:** Accepted. 🛜 🛢 ⅏ 🍽 ⇌ ✕

▼▼▼ **Residence Inn by Marriott Albuquerque Airport** H
(505) 242-2844. **$94-$169.** 2301 International Dr SE 87106. I-25 exit 222 northbound; exit 222A southbound, 1 mi e of jct Yale Blvd SE, then just n. Int corridors. **Pets:** Medium. $100 one-time fee/room. Service with restrictions. 🛜 ✕ ⅏M 🛢 ⅏ ⇌ ✕

AAA ▼▼▼ **Residence Inn Albuquerque- North** H
(505) 761-0200. **$109-$139.** 4331 The Lane at 25 NE 87109. I-25 exit 229 (Jefferson St), just w, just n to The Lane at 25 NE, then just e. Int corridors. **Pets:** Medium, other species. $100 one-time fee/room. Designated rooms, service with restrictions.
[SAVE] 🛜 ✕ ⅏M 🛢 ⅏ ⇌

▼▼▼ **Sandia Peak Inn** H
(505) 831-5036. **Call for rates.** 4614 Central Ave SW 87105. I-40 exit 157A (Rio Grande Blvd), just s, then 2 mi w. Ext corridors. **Pets:** Accepted. 🛜 🛢 ⅏ ⇌

AAA ▼▼▼ **Sheraton Albuquerque Airport Hotel** H
(505) 843-7000. **$89-$219.** 2910 Yale Blvd SE 87106. I-25 exit 225 northbound; exit 222A southbound, 1 mi e on Gibson Blvd, then 0.5 mi s. Int corridors. **Pets:** Accepted. [SAVE] 🛜 ✕ ⅏M 🛢 ⅏ 🍽 ✕

▼▼▼ **Staybridge Suites Albuquerque Airport** H
(505) 338-3900. **$99-$159.** 1350 Sunport Pl SE 87106. I-25 exit 221, 0.3 mi e to University Blvd exit, then just n to Woodward Rd. Int corridors. **Pets:** Accepted. 🛜 ✕ ⅏M 🛢 ⅏ ⇌ ✕

AAA ▼▼▼ **Staybridge Suites Albuquerque North** H
(505) 266-7829. **$89-$359, 3 day notice.** 5817 Signal Ave NE 87113. I-25 exit 233 (Alameda Blvd), just e; jct Alameda Blvd and Signal Ave. Int corridors. **Pets:** Accepted. [SAVE] 🛜 ✕ 🛢 ⅏ ⇌ ✕

▼▼ **Suburban Extended Stay Hotels** M
(505) 883-8888. **$60-$100.** 2401 Wellesley Dr NE 87107. I-40 exit 160, just n to Menaul Blvd, just w, then just s. Ext corridors. **Pets:** Accepted.
🛜 🛢 ⅏

AAA ▼▼▼ **Super 8 of Albuquerque** H
(505) 888-4884. **$39-$80.** 2500 University Blvd NE 87107. I-25 exit 225 northbound, 1.9 mi n on frontage road to Menaul Blvd, then just e; exit 227 (Comanche Rd) southbound, 0.9 mi s to Menaul Blvd, then just e. Int corridors. **Pets:** Accepted. [SAVE] 🛜 🛢 ⅏

AAA ▼▼▼ **TownePlace Suites by Marriott** H
(505) 232-5800. **$69-$109.** 2400 Centre Ave SE 87106. I-25 exit 222 (Gibson Blvd) northbound; exit 222A southbound, 1 mi e to Yale Blvd, at northeast jct Gibson and Yale blvds, then just e. Int corridors. **Pets:** Small, other species. $100 one-time fee/room. Service with restrictions, supervision. [SAVE] 🛜 ✕ ⅏M 🛢 ⅏ ⇌

ALGODONES
▼▼▼ **Hacienda Vargas Bed and Breakfast Inn** BB
(505) 867-9115. **Call for rates.** 1431 SR 313 (El Camino Real) 87001. I-25 exit 248, 0.3 mi w, then 0.3 mi s. Int corridors. **Pets:** Accepted.
ꟽ Ⓩ

ARROYO SECO
▼▼▼ **Adobe and Stars B & B** BB
(575) 776-2776. **Call for rates.** 584 State Hwy 150 87571. 1.1 mi ne of Arroyo Seco village, at Valdez Rd. Ext/int corridors. **Pets:** Medium. $10 daily fee/pet. Designated rooms, service with restrictions, crate.
🛜 ✕ 🛢 ⅏ Ⓩ

▼▼▼ **Cottonwood Inn Bed & Breakfast** BB
(575) 776-5826. **$125-$265, 14 day notice.** 2 SR 230 87514. On SR 150 at SR 230. Ext/int corridors. **Pets:** $20 daily fee/pet. Designated rooms, service with restrictions, supervision.
🛜 ✕ 🛢 ⅏ ✕ ⅏ Ⓩ

ARTESIA
AAA ▼ **Artesia Inn** M
(575) 746-9801. **$75-$110.** 1820 S 1st St 88210. 1.5 mi s on US 285. Ext corridors. **Pets:** $12 one-time fee/room. Service with restrictions, crate. [SAVE] 🛜 🛢 ⅏

AAA ▼▼▼ **Best Western Pecos Inn** H
(575) 748-3324. **$109-$129.** 2209 W Main St 88210. 1.5 mi w on US 82. Int corridors. **Pets:** Accepted. [SAVE] 🛜 🛢 ⅏ 🍽 ⇌ ✕

BERNALILLO
AAA ▼▼▼ **Days Inn Bernalillo** H
(505) 771-7000. **$58-$165.** 107 N Camino del Pueblo 87004. I-25 exit 242, just w. Int corridors. **Pets:** Small. $30 deposit/pet. Service with restrictions, supervision. [SAVE] 🛜 🛢 ⅏ ⇌

AAA ▼▼▼ **Hyatt Regency Tamaya Resort and Spa** H ❀
(505) 867-1234. **$99-$389, 7 day notice.** 1300 Tuyuna Tr 87004. I-25 exit 242, 1 mi w on SR 44 to Tamaya Blvd, then 1 mi n, follow signs. Int corridors. **Pets:** Medium, dogs only. $50 one-time fee/room. Designated rooms, service with restrictions.
[ECO] [SAVE] 🛜 ⅏M 🛢 ⅏ 🍽 ⇌ ✕

▼▼ **Motel 6 Bernalillo** H
(505) 771-9500. **Call for rates.** 210 N Hill Rd 87004. I-25 exit 242, just w. Int corridors. **Pets:** Other species. Service with restrictions, supervision.
🛜 🛢

BLOOMFIELD
▼▼ **Super 8** M
(505) 632-8886. **$49-$76, 10 day notice.** 525 W Broadway Blvd 87413. Jct of US 64 and 550. Int corridors. **Pets:** Accepted. 🛜 ⅏

CARLSBAD

AAA ♦♦♦ **Best Western Stevens Inn** H
(575) 887-2851. **$104-$126.** 1829 S Canal St 88220. 1 mi s on US 62, 180 and 285. Ext corridors. **Pets:** Medium. $20 daily fee/pet. Service with restrictions, supervision. SAVE 📶 🛁 💻 🍴 🏊

CHAMA

AAA ♦♦♦ **Vista del Rio Lodge** M
(575) 756-2138. **$65-$150, 3 day notice.** 2595 US Hwy 84/64 87520. 0.5 mi s of SR 17. Ext corridors. **Pets:** Accepted.
SAVE 📶 🛁 💻 ⊠

CHIMAYÓ

♦♦ **Casa Escondida Bed & Breakfast** BB ❀
(505) 351-4805. **$105-$165, 14 day notice.** 64 CR 100 87522. Jct SR 76 and 98, just w on SR 76, then 0.5 mi ne on CR 100, follow signs; 7.5 mi e of Espanola on SR 76. Ext/int corridors. **Pets:** Other species. $15 daily fee/pet. Designated rooms, service with restrictions, supervision.
📶 ⊠ 🛁 💻 🔳 ⊠

CIMARRON

AAA ♦♦ **Cimarron Inn & RV Park** M ❀
(575) 376-2268. **$49-$65 (no credit cards).** 212 10th St 87714. On US 64. Ext corridors. **Pets:** Large, other species. $10 one-time fee/room. Supervision. SAVE 📶 ⊠ 🛁 💻

CLAYTON

AAA ♦♦♦ **Best Western Kokopelli Lodge** H ❀
(575) 374-2589. **$110-$125.** 702 S 1st St 88415. US 87, 0.5 mi se of jct US 56 and 64. Ext corridors. **Pets:** Large, other species. $10 daily fee/pet. Service with restrictions, supervision. SAVE 📶 ⊠ 🛁 💻 🏊

AAA ♦♦♦ **Days Inn & Suites** H
(575) 374-0133. **$76-$134.** 1120 S 1st St 88415. US 87, 1 mi s of jct US 56 and 64. Int corridors. **Pets:** Small. $15 daily fee/pet. Designated rooms, service with restrictions, supervision. SAVE 📶 🛁 💻 🏊

CLOUDCROFT

AAA ♦♦♦♦ **The Lodge Resort** H
(575) 682-2566. **$115-$335, 14 day notice.** 601 Corona Pl 88317. US 82, 0.3 mi s on Curlew Pl/Corona Pl. Int corridors. **Pets:** $25 one-time fee/room. Designated rooms, service with restrictions, supervision.
SAVE 📶 ⊠ 🛁 💻 🍴 🏊 ⊠

CLOVIS

AAA ♦♦♦♦ **Comfort Inn & Suites** H
(575) 762-4536. **$99-$119.** 201 Schepps Blvd 88101. Jct US 60/70/84 and Schepps Blvd, just n. Int corridors. **Pets:** Accepted.
SAVE 📶 🛁 💻 🏊

♦♦♦ **Econo Lodge** M
(575) 763-3439. **$50-$99.** 1400 E Mabry Dr 88101. 0.5 mi e on US 60/70/84. Ext corridors. **Pets:** Small. $10 one-time fee/pet. Service with restrictions, supervision. 📶 🛁 💻 🏊

♦♦♦♦ **La Quinta Inn & Suites Clovis** H
(575) 763-8777. **$108-$204.** 4521 N Prince St 88101. Jct US 60/84 and Prince St, 3 mi n. Int corridors. **Pets:** Medium, other species. Service with restrictions, supervision. 📶 🛁 💻 🏊

DEMING

AAA ♦♦♦ **Best Western Mimbres Valley Inn** H ❀
(575) 546-4544. **$78-$130.** 1500 W Pine St 88030. I-10 exit 81, just e. Ext corridors. **Pets:** Medium. $15 daily fee/pet. Designated rooms, no service, supervision. SAVE 📶 🛁 💻 🏊

AAA ♦♦♦ **Days Inn** M ❀
(575) 546-8813. **$49-$79.** 1601 E Pine St 88030. I-10 exit 85 westbound, 2 mi w on business loop; exit 81 eastbound, 1 mi e on business loop. Ext corridors. **Pets:** Small. $7 daily fee/pet. Service with restrictions, supervision. SAVE 📶 🛁 💻 🏊

AAA ♦♦♦ **Grand Motor Inn** H
(575) 546-2632. **$50-$65.** 1721 E Pine St 88030. I-10 exit 85 westbound, 2 mi w on business loop; exit 82 eastbound, 1 mi e on business loop. Ext/int corridors. **Pets:** Accepted. SAVE 📶 🛁 💻 🏊

AAA ♦♦♦ **Holiday Inn** H
(575) 546-2661. **$70-$90.** 4600 E Pine St 88030. I-10 exit 85, just w. Ext corridors. **Pets:** Large. Service with restrictions, supervision.
SAVE 📶 🛁 🛁 💻 🍴 🏊

AAA ♦♦♦♦ **La Quinta Inn & Suites Deming** H
(575) 546-0600. **$75-$144.** 4300 E Pine St 88030. I-10 exit 85, just w. Int corridors. **Pets:** Medium, other species. Service with restrictions, supervision. SAVE 📶 ⊠ 🛁 🛁 💻 🏊

♦♦♦ **Super 8 - Deming** H
(575) 546-0481. **$63-$120.** 1217 W Pine St 88030. I-10 exit 81, just e. Ext/int corridors. **Pets:** Accepted. 📶 🛁 💻 🏊

DULCE

AAA ♦♦♦ **Best Western Jicarilla Inn & Casino** H
(505) 759-3663. **$105.** 13603 US Hwy 64 87528. Center. Int corridors. **Pets:** $20 deposit/pet, $20 daily fee/pet. Designated rooms, supervision.
SAVE 📶 🛁 💻 🍴

ELEPHANT BUTTE

AAA ♦♦♦ **Elephant Butte Inn & Spa** H ❀
(575) 744-5431. **$79-$150.** 401 Hwy 195 87935. I-25 exit 83, 4 mi e. Ext corridors. **Pets:** Large, other species. $25 one-time fee/pet. Designated rooms, service with restrictions, supervision.
SAVE 📶 ⊠ 🛁 🛁 💻 🍴 🏊

ESPAÑOLA

AAA ♦♦♦ **Comfort Inn** H
(505) 753-2419. **Call for rates.** 604-B S Riverside Dr 87532. US 84 and 285, just s of jct SR 68. Int corridors. **Pets:** $10 daily fee/pet. Service with restrictions, supervision. SAVE 📶 🛁 💻 🏊

♦♦♦ **Inn at the Delta** BB
(505) 753-9466. **Call for rates.** 243 Paseo de Onate 87532. US 84 and 285, 1 mi n of jct SR 68; 0.3 mi n of jct SR 30. Ext corridors.
Pets: Accepted. 📶 ⊠ 🛁 💻

FARMINGTON

AAA ♦♦♦♦ **Comfort Inn** H
(505) 325-2626. **$70-$120.** 555 Scott Ave 87401. 1 mi e on SR 516 (Main St), just s. Int corridors. **Pets:** Accepted. SAVE 📶 🛁 💻 🏊

♦♦♦ **Holiday Inn Express** H
(505) 325-2545. **$99-$169, 3 day notice.** 2110 Bloomfield Blvd 87401. 1.6 mi e on US 64 (Bloomfield Blvd), just past jct Broadway; on Frontage Rd. Int corridors. **Pets:** Accepted. 📶 ⊠ 🛁 💻 🏊

♦♦♦ **La Quinta Inn Farmington** H
(505) 327-4706. **$72-$144.** 675 Scott Ave 87401. 1 mi e on SR 516 (Main St), just s. Ext/int corridors. **Pets:** Medium, other species. Service with restrictions, supervision. 📶 🛁 💻 🏊

♦♦♦ **TownePlace Suites by Marriott** H
(505) 327-2442. **$76-$127.** 4200 Sierra Vista Dr 87402. 5 mi e on SR 516 (E Main St), just s. Int corridors. **Pets:** Medium, other species. $100 one-time fee/room. Designated rooms, service with restrictions.
📶 ⊠ 🛁 💻 🍴 🏊

GALLUP

AAA ♦♦♦ **Americas Best Value Inn & Suites** M
(505) 722-0757. **Call for rates.** 2003 Hwy 66 W 87301. I-40 exit 20, 1 mi w. Ext/int corridors. **Pets:** Accepted. SAVE 📶 🛁 💻 🍴

Comfort Suites H

(505) 863-3445. **$89-$129.** 3940 E Hwy 66 87301. I-40 exit 26, just e. Int corridors. **Pets:** Accepted.

La Quinta Inn & Suites Gallup H

(505) 722-2233. **$116-$179.** 3880 E Hwy 66 87301. I-40 exit 26, just e. Int corridors. **Pets:** Medium, other species. Service with restrictions, supervision.

Quality Inn & Suites M

(505) 726-1000. **$90-$130.** 1500 W Maloney Ave 87301. I-40 exit 20, just n on Muñoz Dr, then just w. Ext/int corridors. **Pets:** $15 daily fee/pet. Service with restrictions.

Red Lion Hotel Gallup H

(505) 722-2221. **$62-$109.** 3009 W US 66 87301. I-40 exit 16, 1 mi e. Int corridors. **Pets:** Accepted.

Red Rock Inn Gallup H

(505) 722-7600. **Call for rates.** 3010 E US 66 87301. I-40 exit 26, 1 mi w. Int corridors. **Pets:** Accepted.

Red Roof Inn M

(505) 722-7765. **$44-$59.** 3304 W Hwy 66 87301. I-40 exit 16, just se. Ext corridors. **Pets:** Large, other species. No service, supervision.

GRANTS

Comfort Inn H

(505) 287-8700. **$90-$109.** 1551 E Santa Fe Ave 87020. I-40 exit 85, 0.3 mi n. Int corridors. **Pets:** Accepted.

Quality Inn & Suites H

(505) 285-4676. **Call for rates.** 1496 E Santa Fe Ave 87020. I-40 exit 85, 0.3 mi n. Int corridors. **Pets:** Small. $20 daily fee/pet. Service with restrictions, supervision.

HOBBS

Best Western Executive Inn H

(575) 397-7171. **$90-$120.** 309 N Marland Blvd 88240. US 62, 180 and Snyder St. Ext corridors. **Pets:** Dogs only. $10 daily fee/pet. Service with restrictions, supervision.

Days Inn M

(575) 397-6541. **$66-$81.** 211 N Marland Blvd 88240. 2 mi e on US 62 and 180. Ext corridors. **Pets:** Small. $10 daily fee/pet. Service with restrictions, supervision.

Econo Lodge H

(575) 397-3591. **Call for rates.** 619 N Marland Blvd 88240. 2.5 mi e on US 62 and 180. Ext corridors. **Pets:** Accepted.

La Quinta Inn & Suites Hobbs H

(575) 397-8777. **$94-$160.** 3312 N Lovington Hwy 88240. SR 18 (Lovington Hwy), just s of jct Joe Harvey Blvd. Int corridors. **Pets:** Medium, other species. Service with restrictions, supervision.

Sleep Inn & Suites H ❀

(575) 393-3355. **$89-$139.** 4630 Lovington Hwy 88240. Jct SR 18 N (Lovington Hwy) and W Millen Dr, 0.8 mi s. Int corridors. **Pets:** Small. $10 daily fee/pet. Service with restrictions, crate.

LAS CRUCES

Best Western Mission Inn H

(575) 524-8591. **$90-$110.** 1765 S Main St 88005. I-10 exit 142 (University Ave), 1 mi n. Ext corridors. **Pets:** $10 daily fee/pet. Designated rooms, service with restrictions, supervision.

Comfort Inn & Suites de Mesilla H

(575) 527-1050. **Call for rates.** 1300 Avenida de Mesilla 88005. I-10 exit 140, just s. Int corridors. **Pets:** Accepted.

Comfort Inn of Las Cruces H

(575) 527-2000. **$79-$105.** 2585 S Valley Dr 88005. I-10 exit 142 (University Ave), just n. Int corridors. **Pets:** Small, dogs only. $20 one-time fee/pet. Designated rooms, service with restrictions, supervision.

Comfort Suites by Choice Hotels H

(575) 522-1300. **$81-$91.** 2101 S Triviz Dr 88001. I-25 exit 1 (University Ave), just w, then just n. Int corridors. **Pets:** Accepted.

DreamCatcher Inn Bed & Breakfast de Las Cruces BB

(575) 522-3035. **$115-$145, 7 day notice.** 10201 Starfly Rd 88011. US 70 E to NASA/Baylor Canyon Rd, 0.5 mi s, then 0.5 mi w. Ext corridors. **Pets:** Other species. $25 one-time fee/room.

Drury Inn & Suites Las Cruces H

(575) 523-4100. **$100-$144.** 1631 Hickory Loop 88005. I-10 exit 140, just e. Int corridors. **Pets:** Accepted.

Hampton Inn H

(575) 526-8311. **$80-$90.** 755 Avenida de Mesilla 88005. I-10 exit 140, just e. Ext corridors. **Pets:** Accepted.

Hilltop Hacienda B & B BB

(575) 382-3556. **$115-$155, 14 day notice.** 2600 Westmoreland Ave 88012. I-25 exit 6 (US 70), just e to Del Rey Blvd, 3 mi n, then 1 mi e. Int corridors. **Pets:** Dogs only. No service, supervision.

Hotel Encanto de Las Cruces H ❀

(575) 522-4300. **$89-$159.** 705 S Telshor Blvd 88011. I-25 exit 3 (Lohman Ave), just e, then just s. Int corridors. **Pets:** Medium, other species. $25 daily fee/pet. Designated rooms, service with restrictions, supervision.

La Quinta Inn & Suites Las Cruces Organ Mountain H

(575) 523-0100. **$64-$126.** 1500 Hickory Dr 88005. I-10 exit 140, just se of jct I-25 and Avenida de Mesilla. Int corridors. **Pets:** Medium, other species. Service with restrictions, supervision.

La Quinta Inn Las Cruces Mesilla Valley H

(575) 524-0331. **$68-$130.** 790 Avenida de Mesilla 88005. I-10 exit 140, just e. Int corridors. **Pets:** Medium, other species. Service with restrictions, supervision.

Lundeen's Inn of the Arts BB

(575) 526-3326. **$79-$125, 3 day notice.** 618 S Alameda Blvd 88005. Jct Lohman Ave, just s; center. Int corridors. **Pets:** Medium. $15 one-time fee/room. Service with restrictions, supervision.

Quality Inn & Suites H

(575) 524-4663. **Call for rates.** 2200 S Valley Dr 88005. I-10 exit 142 (University Ave), 2 blks w. Ext corridors. **Pets:** Accepted.

Ramada Palms de Las Cruces H

(575) 526-4411. **$69-$109.** 201 E University Ave 88005. I-10 exit 142 (University Ave), just n. Int corridors. **Pets:** Accepted.

Sleep Inn by Choice Hotels H

(575) 522-1700. **$69-$110.** 2121 S Triviz Dr 88001. I-25 exit 1 (University Ave), just w, then just n. Int corridors. **Pets:** Accepted.

Staybridge Suites H

(575) 521-7999. **Call for rates.** 2651 Northrise Dr 88011. I-25 exit 6 (US 70), just e. Int corridors. **Pets:** Accepted.

◆◆◆ **TownePlace Suites Las Cruces** 🅷 🐾
(575) 532-6500. **$102-$120.** 2143 Telshor Ct 88011. I-25 exit 6 (US 70), just s. Int corridors. **Pets:** Other species. $75 one-time fee/room. Service with restrictions, supervision. 📶 ✕ ⅃ 🛗 🔲 ➿

LAS VEGAS

◆◆◆ ◆◆◆◆ **Best Western Plus Montezuma Inn & Suites** 🅷
(505) 426-8000. **$79-$109.** 2020 N Grand Ave 87701. I-25 exit 347, just sw. Int corridors. **Pets:** Accepted.
SAVE 📶 ✕ ⅃ 🛗 🔲 ➿ ✕

◆◆◆ ◆◆◆ **Comfort Inn** 🅷
(505) 425-1100. **$75-$101.** 2500 N Grand Ave 87701. I-25 exit 347, just sw; US 85 and I-25 business route. Int corridors. **Pets:** Other species. $15 one-time fee/pet. Designated rooms, service with restrictions, supervision. SAVE 📶 🛗 🔲 ➿

◆◆◆ **Holiday Inn Express Hotel & Suites** 🅷
(505) 426-8182. **$91-$126.** 816 S Grand Ave 87701. I-25 exit 343, just n. Int corridors. **Pets:** Other species. $15 daily fee/room. Designated rooms, service with restrictions, supervision. 📶 ⅃ 🛗 🔲 ➿

◆◆◆ ◆◆ **Plaza Hotel** 🅷
(505) 425-3591. **$69-$132.** 230 Plaza St 87701. I-25 exit 343W, just w, follow signs to Old Town Plaza. Int corridors. **Pets:** Accepted.
SAVE 📶 ✕ 🛗 🔲 🍽

LORDSBURG

◆◆◆ ◆◆◆◆ **Comfort Inn & Suites** 🅷
(575) 542-3355. **$70-$120.** 400 W Wabash St 88045. I-10 exit 22, just n, then w. Int corridors. **Pets:** Small. $10 daily fee/pet. Service with restrictions, supervision. SAVE 📶 ⅃ 🛗 🔲 ➿ ✕

◆◆◆ ◆◆ **Days Inn & Suites** 🅷
(575) 542-3600. **$45-$80.** 1426 W Motel Dr 88045. I-10 exit 20, just n. Int corridors. **Pets:** $10 one-time fee/pet. Service with restrictions, supervision. 📶 🛗 🔲 ➿

◆◆◆ ◆◆ **Econo Lodge** 🅷
(575) 542-3666. **Call for rates.** 1408 S Main St 88045. I-10 exit 22, just s. Ext corridors. **Pets:** Accepted. 📶 🛗 🔲 ➿

◆◆◆◆ **Hampton Inn** 🅷
(575) 542-8900. **$89-$99.** 412 W Wabash 88045. I-10 exit 22, just w. Int corridors. **Pets:** Accepted. 📶 ✕ ⅃ 🛗 🔲 ➿

LOS ALAMOS

◆◆◆◆ **Holiday Inn Express & Suites** 🅷
(505) 661-2646. **$95-$179.** 60 Entrada Dr 87544. Jct Airport Basin Dr and SR 502. Int corridors. **Pets:** Accepted.
📶 ✕ ⅃ 🛗 🔲 ➿

LOS LUNAS

◆◆◆ ◆◆ **Western Skies Inn & Suites** 🅷
(505) 865-0001. **$65-$95.** 2258 Sun Ranch Village Loop 87031. I-25 exit 203, just w. Int corridors. **Pets:** Large, other species. $100 deposit/room, $10 daily fee/pet. Service with restrictions, supervision.
SAVE 📶 ⅃ 🛗 🔲 ➿

MORIARTY

◆◆◆ ◆◆◆ **Americas Best Value Inn** 🅷
(505) 832-4457. **$52-$85.** 1316 Route 66 W 87035. I-40 exit 194, 0.5 mi se on US 66 and I-40 business loop. Int corridors. **Pets:** Medium, other species. $10 daily fee/pet. Service with restrictions, supervision.
SAVE 📶 🛗 🔲

◆◆◆ ◆◆◆◆ **Best Western Moriarty Heritage Inn** 🅷
(505) 832-5000. **$89-$110.** 111 Anaya Blvd 87035. I-40 exit 194, 0.4 mi e. Int corridors. **Pets:** Other species. $15 one-time fee/room. Designated rooms, service with restrictions, supervision.
SAVE 📶 ✕ ⅃ 🛗 🔲 ➿ ✕

◆◆◆ ◆◆◆ **Comfort Inn** 🅷 🐾
(505) 832-6666. **Call for rates.** 119 Route 66 E 87035. I-40 exit 196, just s, then just e. Int corridors. **Pets:** Other species. Designated rooms, service with restrictions, supervision. 📶 ⅃ 🛗 🔲 ➿

◆◆◆ ◆◆◆◆ **Super 8** 🅷
(505) 832-6730. **$55-$85.** 1611 W Old Route 66 87035. I-40 exit 194, 0.5 mi e on Central Ave. Int corridors. **Pets:** Medium, other species. $10 daily fee/pet. Service with restrictions, supervision. SAVE 📶 🛗 🔲

PINOS ALTOS

◆◆◆ **Bear Creek Motel & Cabins** CA
(575) 388-4501. **$109-$189.** 88 Main St 88053. 1 mi n of town on SR 15. Ext corridors. **Pets:** Accepted. 📶 🛗 🔲 🐾

RATON

◆◆◆ ◆◆◆◆ **Best Western Plus Raton Hotel** 🅷
(575) 445-8501. **$99-$149.** 473 Clayton Rd 87740. I-25 exit 451, just w. Ext/int corridors. **Pets:** Dogs only. $10 daily fee/room. Designated rooms, service with restrictions, supervision.
SAVE 📶 ✕ ⅃ 🛗 🔲 🍽 ➿

◆◆◆ ◆◆◆ **Budget Host Raton** Ⓜ
(575) 445-3655. **$57-$84.** 136 Canyon Dr 87740. I-25 exit 454, 0.8 mi s on I-25 business loop. Ext corridors. **Pets:** Medium. $5 daily fee/pet. Service with restrictions, supervision. SAVE ⅃

◆◆◆ ◆◆◆◆ **Holiday Inn Express Hotel & Suites** 🅷
(575) 445-1500. **$129-$179.** 101 Card Ave 87740. I-25 exit 450, just w. Int corridors. **Pets:** Accepted. SAVE 📶 ✕ 🛗 🔲 ➿ ✕

◆◆◆ ◆◆ **Raton Microtel Inn** 🅷
(575) 445-9100. **$63-$76.** 1640 Cedar St 87740. I-25 exit 451, just w. Int corridors. **Pets:** Dogs only. $20 daily fee/pet. Designated rooms, service with restrictions, supervision. 📶 ✕ 🛗 🔲

◆◆ **Raton Pass Inn** Ⓜ
(575) 445-3641. **$48-$64.** 308 Canyon Dr 87740. I-25 exit 454, 0.8 mi s. Ext corridors. **Pets:** Dogs only. $2 daily fee/pet. Service with restrictions, supervision. 📶 ✕ 🛗

RED RIVER

◆◆◆ ◆◆◆ **Best Western Rivers Edge** 🅷
(575) 754-1766. **$60-$200, 7 day notice.** 301 W River St 87558. 1 blk s of W Main St (SR 38); center. Ext corridors. **Pets:** Accepted.
SAVE 🛗 🔲 ✕

RIO RANCHO

◆◆◆ ◆◆◆ **Days Inn Rio Rancho** 🅷
(505) 892-8800. **$55-$117.** 4200 Crestview Dr 87124. I-25 exit 233 (Alameda Blvd), 8 mi w on SR 528; I-40 exit 155, 8 mi n on Coors Rd (SR 448). Ext corridors. **Pets:** Small, other species. $15 one-time fee/pet. Service with restrictions, supervision. SAVE 📶 🛗 🔲 ➿

◆◆◆ **Extended StayAmerica Albuquerque-Rio Rancho** Ⓜ 🐾
(505) 792-1338. **$64-$99.** 2608 The American Rd NW 87124. Corner of SR 528 and Cottonwood Dr, just n, then just w. Int corridors. **Pets:** Other species. $25 daily fee/pet. Service with restrictions. 📶 🛗 🔲

◆◆◆ ◆◆◆ **Inn at Rio Rancho Hotel and Conference Center** 🅷 🐾
(505) 892-1700. **$59-$119.** 1465 Rio Rancho Dr SE 87124. I-25 exit 233 (Alameda Blvd), 6.5 mi w; I-40 exit 155, 10 mi n on Coors Rd/Coors Bypass to SR 528, then 1 mi n. Ext corridors. **Pets:** $25 daily fee/pet. Designated rooms, service with restrictions, crate.
SAVE 📶 🛗 🔲 🍽 ➿

◆◆ **Rio Rancho Super 8** 🅷
(505) 896-8888. **$40-$85.** 4100 Barbara Loop SE 87124. I-25 exit 233 (Alameda Blvd), 0.5 mi w, 3.8 mi nw on SR 528, then just e. Int corridors. **Pets:** Accepted. 📶 🛗 🔲

ROSWELL

Best Western El Rancho Palacio H
(575) 622-2721. **$70-$110.** 2205 N Main St 88201. 1.8 mi n on US 70 and 285. Ext corridors. **Pets:** Medium. Service with restrictions, crate.

Candlewood Suites Roswell H
(575) 623-4300. **$114-$144.** 4 Military Heights Dr 88201. Jct US 70 and 285, just n of US 385. Int corridors. **Pets:** Accepted.

Comfort Inn H
(575) 623-4567. **$90-$110.** 3595 N Main St 88201. 3 mi n on US 70 and 285. Int corridors. **Pets:** Medium, other species. Service with restrictions, crate.

Days Inn H
(575) 623-4021. **$77-$88.** 1310 N Main St 88201. 0.8 mi n on US 70 and 285. Ext corridors. **Pets:** Medium. Service with restrictions.

Holiday Inn Express H
(575) 627-9900. **$110-$170.** 2300 N Main St 88201. 1.8 mi n on US 70 and 285. Int corridors. **Pets:** Medium. $10 daily fee/pet. Service with restrictions, supervision.

La Quinta Inn & Suites Roswell H
(575) 622-8000. **$93-$189.** 200 E 19th St 88201. Jct N Main and 19th sts, 2 blks e. Int corridors. **Pets:** Medium, other species. Service with restrictions, supervision.

RUIDOSO

The Lodge at Sierra Blanca H
(575) 258-5500. **$99-$209.** 107 Sierra Blanca Dr 88345. Jct Sudderth Dr. Int corridors. **Pets:** Small, other species. $50 one-time fee/room. Service with restrictions, supervision.

Village Lodge CO
(575) 258-5442. **$89-$179, 7 day notice.** 1000 Mechem Dr 88345. 2 mi n on SR 48. Ext corridors. **Pets:** Accepted.

Whispering Pine Cabins CA
(575) 257-4311. **$99-$450, 30 day notice.** 422 Main Rd 88345. 0.9 mi w of jct SR 48 and Sudderth Dr. Ext corridors. **Pets:** Accepted.

RUIDOSO DOWNS

Best Western Pine Springs Inn H
(575) 378-8100. **Call for rates.** 1420 W Hwy 70 88346. Just e of jct US 70 and SR 48. Ext corridors. **Pets:** $10 deposit/room, $10 one-time fee/room. Service with restrictions, supervision.

La Quinta Inn & Suites H
(575) 378-3333. **$85-$215.** 2115 W Hwy 70 88346. Just e of jct US 70 and SR 48. Int corridors. **Pets:** Medium, other species. Service with restrictions, supervision.

SANTA FE

Best Western Plus Inn of Santa Fe H
(505) 438-3822. **$89-$110.** 3650 Cerrillos Rd 87507. I-25 exit 278, 2.8 mi n. Int corridors. **Pets:** Accepted.

Bishop's Lodge Ranch Resort & Spa H
(505) 983-6377. **$135-$1299, 3 day notice.** 1297 N Bishop's Lodge Rd 87501. 3.5 mi n of jct Paseo de Peralta. Ext/int corridors. **Pets:** Other species. $150 deposit/pet, $15 daily fee/pet. Service with restrictions, supervision.

DoubleTree by Hilton Santa Fe H
(505) 473-4646. **$99-$209.** 4048 Cerrillos Rd 87507. I-25 exit 278, 2.3 mi n; just n of Rodeo Dr. Int corridors. **Pets:** Accepted.

Eldorado Hotel & Spa H
(505) 988-4455. **$139-$419, 3 day notice.** 309 W San Francisco St 87501. Just w of The Plaza; at Sandoval St. Int corridors. **Pets:** $50 one-time fee/room. Service with restrictions.

El Paradero Bed & Breakfast BB
(505) 988-1177. **$100-$200, 14 day notice.** 220 W Manhattan Ave 87501. 0.3 mi s on Cerrillos Rd, 1/2 blk e. Ext/int corridors. **Pets:** Accepted.

Encantado, An Auberge Resort H
(505) 946-5700. **$275-$675, 14 day notice.** 198 SR 592 87506. US 285/84 N exit 172, 0.5 mi e, then 2 mi n. Ext corridors. **Pets:** Accepted.

Hacienda Nicholas BB
(505) 986-1431. **$110-$260, 14 day notice.** 320 E Marcy St 87501. Just e of jct Paseo de Peralta; 4 blks e of historic plaza. Ext/int corridors. **Pets:** Other species. $25 one-time fee/pet. Service with restrictions, crate.

Hampton Inn Santa Fe H
(505) 474-3900. **$89-$149.** 3625 Cerrillos Rd 87505. I-25 exit 278, 2.5 mi n. Int corridors. **Pets:** Medium. Designated rooms, service with restrictions, supervision.

Hilton Santa Fe Golf Resort & Spa at Buffalo Thunder H
(505) 455-5555. **$99-$339.** 20 Buffalo Thunder Tr 87506. N on US 285 exit Buffalo Thunder Rd, just e. Int corridors. **Pets:** Large. $50 one-time fee/room. Supervision.

Hilton Santa Fe Historic Plaza H
(505) 988-2811. **$139-$239.** 100 Sandoval St 87501. Just sw of The Plaza; between San Francisco and W Alameda sts. Ext/int corridors. **Pets:** Accepted.

Holiday Inn Express-Santa Fe H
(505) 474-7570. **$79-$119.** 3450 Cerrillos Rd 87507. I-25 exit 278, 3 mi n. Int corridors. **Pets:** Medium, other species. Designated rooms, service with restrictions.

Hotel St. Francis H
(505) 983-5700. **Call for rates.** 210 Don Gaspar Ave 87501. Just s of The Plaza. Int corridors. **Pets:** Accepted.

Hotel Santa Fe, The Hacienda & Spa H
(505) 982-1200. **$119-$500, 3 day notice.** 1501 Paseo de Peralta 87501. At Cerrillos Rd, 0.6 mi s of The Plaza. Int corridors. **Pets:** Dogs only. $20 daily fee/room. Designated rooms, service with restrictions.

The Inn & Spa at Loretto H
(505) 988-5531. **$189-$599, 3 day notice.** 211 Old Santa Fe Tr 87501. Just s of The Plaza. Int corridors. **Pets:** Medium. $25 daily fee/pet. Designated rooms, service with restrictions, supervision.

Inn at Santa Fe H
(505) 474-9500. **$89-$249, 3 day notice.** 8376 Cerrillos Rd 87507. I-25 exit 278, 0.3 mi n. Int corridors. **Pets:** Accepted.

Inn On The Alameda 🅷 ❀
(505) 984-2121. **$125-$390, 3 day notice.** 303 E Alameda St 87501. Just e of The Plaza; jct Paseo de Peralta. Ext/int corridors. **Pets:** Small, other species. $30 daily fee/pet. Designated rooms, service with restrictions. ⟨SAVE⟩ 📶 ➊ 🖥 ➌ ☒

La Fonda On the Plaza 🅷
(505) 982-5511. **$229-$799.** 100 E San Francisco St 87501. On The Plaza. Int corridors. **Pets:** Accepted.
⟨SAVE⟩ 📶 ☒ ⟨&M⟩ ➊ 🖥 ➌ ⟨¶⟩ ➋ ☒

La Posada de Santa Fe Resort & Spa 🅷
(505) 986-0000. **$169-$659, 3 day notice.** 330 E Palace Ave 87501. Jct Paseo de Peralta and E Palace Ave. Ext corridors. **Pets:** $75 one-time fee/pet. No service, supervision.
⟨SAVE⟩ 📶 ☒ 🖥 ⟨¶⟩ ➋ ☒

La Quinta Inn Santa Fe 🅷
(505) 471-1142. **$54-$152.** 4298 Cerrillos Rd 87507. I-25 exit 278, 1.8 mi n. Ext/int corridors. **Pets:** Medium, other species. Service with restrictions, supervision. 📶 ➊ 🖥 ➋

Las Palomas 🅷 ❀
(505) 982-5560. **$99-$498.** 460 W San Francisco St 87501. Just w of jct Guadalupe St. Ext corridors. **Pets:** Dogs only. $20 daily fee/pet. Designated rooms, service with restrictions. ⟨SAVE⟩ 📶 ☒ ➊ 🖥 ☒

The Lodge at Santa Fe 🅷
(505) 992-5800. **Call for rates.** 750 N St. Francis Dr 87501. Jct of Cerrillos Rd and St. Francis Dr (US 84/285), 1.1 mi nw to Alamo Dr, just w, then just n. Ext/int corridors. **Pets:** Accepted.
📶 ☒ ➊ 🖥 ⟨¶⟩ ➋

Motel 6 - 150 Ⓜ
(505) 473-1380. **$45-$65.** 3007 Cerrillos Rd 87507. I-25 exit 278, 3.8 mi n. Ext corridors. **Pets:** Other species. Service with restrictions, supervision. 📶 ➊ ➋

The Old Santa Fe Inn Ⓜ
(505) 995-0800. **$99-$390, 3 day notice.** 320 Galisteo St 87501. Just sw of The Plaza; center. Ext/int corridors. **Pets:** Large. $20 daily fee/pet. Service with restrictions, supervision. ⟨SAVE⟩ 📶 ☒ ➊ 🖥

Pecos Trail Inn Ⓜ ❀
(505) 982-1943. **$89-$155.** 2239 Old Pecos Tr 87505. I-25 exit 284, 0.8 mi n on CR 466 (Old Pecos Tr). Ext corridors. **Pets:** $25 one-time fee/room. Service with restrictions, supervision.
⟨SAVE⟩ 📶 ☒ ➊ 🖥 ⟨¶⟩ ➋

Red Roof Inn 🅷
(505) 438-8950. **$49-$149.** 4044 Cerrillos Rd 87507. I-25 exit 278, 1.5 mi n. Int corridors. **Pets:** Large, other species. No service, supervision.
⟨SAVE⟩ 📶 ➊ ➋

Rosewood Inn of the Anasazi 🅷
(505) 988-3030. **Call for rates.** 113 Washington Ave 87501. Just ne of The Plaza. Int corridors. **Pets:** Accepted. ⟨SAVE⟩ 📶 ☒ 🖥 ⟨¶⟩

Santa Fe Motel & Inn Ⓜ
(505) 982-1039. **$79-$199, 3 day notice.** 510 Cerrillos Rd 87501. 4 blks sw of The Plaza. Ext corridors. **Pets:** $15 daily fee/pet. Designated rooms, service with restrictions, crate. ⟨SAVE⟩ 📶 ➊ 🖥

Santa Fe Sage Inn Ⓜ
(505) 982-5952. **$45-$140.** 725 Cerrillos Rd 87505. 0.4 mi ne of St. Francis Dr. Ext corridors. **Pets:** Medium. $25 one-time fee/pet. Designated rooms, service with restrictions, supervision.
⟨SAVE⟩ 📶 ➊ 🖥 ➋

The Santa Fe Suites Ⓜ
(505) 989-3600. **$79-$99.** 3007 S St. Francis Dr 87505. 0.8 mi n on S St. Francis Dr, just e on Zia Rd via access drive. Ext corridors. **Pets:** Accepted. ⟨SAVE⟩ 📶 ⟨&M⟩ ➊ 🖥

SANTA ROSA

Best Western Adobe Inn 🅷
(575) 472-3446. **$69-$99.** 2255 Historic Route 66 88435. I-40 exit 275. Ext corridors. **Pets:** Medium. Service with restrictions, supervision.
⟨SAVE⟩ 📶 ➊ 🖥 ➋

Best Western Santa Rosa Inn Ⓜ
(575) 472-5877. **$72-$120.** 2491 Historic Route 66 88435. I-40 exit 277, 0.5 mi w. Ext corridors. **Pets:** Medium. $10 daily fee/pet. Designated rooms, service with restrictions, supervision. ⟨SAVE⟩ 📶 ➊ 🖥 ➋

Holiday Inn Express 🅷
(575) 472-5411. **$80-$199.** 2516 Historic Route 66 88435. I-40 exit 277, 0.4 mi w. Int corridors. **Pets:** Accepted. 📶 ⟨&M⟩ ➊ 🖥 ➋ ☒

La Quinta Inn Santa Rosa 🅷
(575) 472-4800. **$85-$150.** 2277 Historic Route 66 88435. I-40 exit 275, just e. Int corridors. **Pets:** Medium, other species. Service with restrictions, supervision. 📶 ➊ 🖥 ➋

Quality Inn 🅷
(575) 472-5570. **$59-$89.** 3343 E Historic Route 66 88435. I-40 exit 277, 0.3 mi w. Ext corridors. **Pets:** $10 one-time fee/pet. Service with restrictions, supervision. 📶 ➊ 🖥 ➋

Super 8-Santa Rosa Ⓜ
(575) 472-5388. **$58-$85.** 2075 Historic Route 66 88435. I-40 exit 275, just w. Int corridors. **Pets:** $10 daily fee/pet. Service with restrictions, supervision. 📶 ⟨&M⟩ ➊ 🖥

SILVER CITY

Comfort Inn 🅷
(575) 534-1883. **$95-$155.** 1060 E Hwy 180 88061. Just e of jct SR 15. Int corridors. **Pets:** Small. $30 deposit/pet, $10 daily fee/pet. Service with restrictions, supervision. ⟨SAVE⟩ 📶 ☒ ➊ 🖥 ➋

Econo Lodge Silver City 🅷
(575) 534-1111. **$69-$149.** 1120 Hwy 180 E 88061. 1.5 mi ne on US 180 and SR 90. Int corridors. **Pets:** $7 daily fee/pet. Designated rooms, service with restrictions, supervision. ⟨SAVE⟩ 📶 ⟨&M⟩ ➊ 🖥 ➋

Holiday Inn Express 🅷
(575) 538-2525. **$109-$134.** 1103 Superior St 88061. 3 mi ne on US 180 and SR 90. Int corridors. **Pets:** Other species. Designated rooms, service with restrictions, supervision. ⟨SAVE⟩ 📶 ☒ ➊ 🖥

SOCORRO

Best Western Socorro Hotel & Suites 🅷
(575) 838-0556. **$105, 3 day notice.** 1100 California Ave NE 87801. Center. Ext/int corridors. **Pets:** Large. $10 one-time fee/pet. Designated rooms, service with restrictions, supervision.
⟨SAVE⟩ 📶 ☒ ⟨&M⟩ ➊ 🖥 ➋ ☒

Comfort Inn & Suites 🅷
(575) 838-4400. **Call for rates.** 1259 Frontage Rd NW 87801. I-25 exit 150, just nw. Int corridors. **Pets:** Accepted. 📶 ⟨&M⟩ ➊ 🖥 ➋

Days Inn-Socorro 🅷
(575) 835-0230. **$56-$76.** 507 N California St 87801. I-25 exit 147, 1.7 mi n; exit 150, just s. Ext corridors. **Pets:** $10 daily fee/pet. Service with restrictions, supervision. ⟨SAVE⟩ 📶 ➊ 🖥 ➋

Econo Lodge Ⓜ 🐾
(575) 835-1500. **$55-$125.** 713 N California St NW 87801. I-25 exit 150, 1 mi s. Ext corridors. **Pets:** Medium, dogs only. $10 one-time fee/pet. Service with restrictions, supervision. 📶 ➊ 🖥 ➋ ☒

TAOS

American Artists Gallery House Bed & Breakfast BB
(575) 758-4446. **$95-$225, 14 day notice.** 132 Frontier Ln 87571. 1 mi s of jct US 64 and Taos Plaza, 0.3 mi e. Ext/int corridors. **Pets:** Dogs only. $25 one-time fee/pet. Designated rooms, service with restrictions, supervision.

An Inn On The Rio BB
(575) 758-7199. **$100-$145, 14 day notice.** 910 Kit Carson Rd 87571. US 64, 1.5 mi e of jct SR 68 and Taos Plaza. Ext corridors.
Pets: Accepted.

El Monte Sagrado, Autograph Collection H
(575) 828-8267. **$169-$309, 3 day notice.** 317 Kit Carson Rd 87571. 0.5 mi e of jct US 64 and SR 68. Ext corridors. **Pets:** Accepted.

Inn on La Loma Plaza BB ❖
(575) 758-1717. **$175-$450, 15 day notice.** 315 Ranchitos Rd 87571. 0.3 mi sw on Ranchitos Rd, just w of Taos Plaza; in La Loma Plaza Historic District. Ext/int corridors. **Pets:** Large, dogs only. $50 one-time fee/pet. Designated rooms, service with restrictions, supervision.

La Posada de Taos BB ❖
(575) 758-8164. **$129-$239, 3 day notice.** 309 Juanita Ln 87571. From Taos Plaza, just w on Don Fernando St, just s on Manzanares St, then just w. Ext/int corridors. **Pets:** Medium, dogs only. $50 one-time fee/room. Supervision.

Quality Inn H
(575) 758-2200. **Call for rates.** 1043 Paseo del Pueblo Sur 87571. SR 68, 2 mi sw of jct US 64 and Taos Plaza. Ext/int corridors.
Pets: Accepted.

Sagebrush Inn H
(575) 758-2254. **$79-$219.** 1508 Paseo del Pueblo Sur 87571. SR 68, 3 mi sw of jct US 64 and Taos Plaza. Ext corridors. **Pets:** Accepted.

San Geronimo Lodge BB
(575) 751-3776. **Call for rates.** 1101 Witt Rd 87571. 1.3 mi e of jct SR 68 and Taos Plaza on US 64, 0.6 mi s. Ext/int corridors. **Pets:** Dogs only. $20 one-time fee/room. Designated rooms, no service, supervision.

TRUTH OR CONSEQUENCES

Comfort Inn & Suites H
(575) 894-1660. **$80-$125.** 2250 N Date St 87901. I-25 exit 79, just e. Int corridors. **Pets:** Accepted.

Sierra Grande Lodge & Spa H
(575) 894-6976. **$99-$445.** 501 McAdoo St 87901. Just w of Foch St; center. Ext/int corridors. **Pets:** Small. $25 daily fee/pet. Designated rooms, service with restrictions, supervision.

TUCUMCARI

Best Western Discovery Inn H
(575) 461-4884. **$89-$120.** 200 E Estrella Ave 88401. I-40 exit 332, just n. Ext corridors. **Pets:** Accepted.

Days Inn H
(575) 461-3158. **$57-$72.** 2623 S 1st St 88401. I-40 exit 332, just n. Ext/int corridors. **Pets:** Accepted.

La Quinta Inn & Suites Tucumcari H
(575) 461-2233. **$98-$160.** 2516 S Adams St 88401. I-40 exit 332, just n. Int corridors. **Pets:** Medium, other species. Service with restrictions, supervision.

Rodeway Inn H ❖
(575) 461-4094. **$40-$110.** 2800 E Tucumcari Blvd 88401. I-40 exit 335, 0.5 mi w. Ext corridors. **Pets:** $8 one-time fee/room. Service with restrictions, supervision.

Super 8 M
(575) 461-4444. **$47-$50.** 4001 Old Route 66 88401. I-40 exit 335, just w. Int corridors. **Pets:** Accepted.

NEW YORK

ALBANY

▼▼▼ CrestHill Suites 🄷 ☙
(518) 454-0007. **$99-$209.** 1415 Washington Ave 12206. I-90 exit 2 westbound, just s on Fuller Rd, then just e; exit eastbound, just e. Int corridors. **Pets:** Other species. $15 daily fee/pet. Designated rooms, service with restrictions. 🛜 ⛟ 🍴 💻 ⇲

▼ ▼ Extended StayAmerica Albany-Capital 🄷 ☙
(518) 446-0680. **$85-$119.** 1395 Washington Ave 12206. I-90 exit 2 westbound, just s on Fuller Rd, then 0.5 mi e; exit eastbound, just e. Int corridors. **Pets:** Other species. $25 daily fee/pet. Service with restrictions. 🛜 🍴 💻

▼▼◆ TownePlace Suites Albany SUNY 🄷
(518) 435-1900. **$139-$229.** 1379 Washington Ave 12206. I-90 exit 2 westbound, just s on Fuller Rd, then 0.6 mi e; exit eastbound, just e. Int corridors. **Pets:** Accepted. 🛜 ⛟ 🍴 💻 ⇲

▼▼◆ TownePlace Suites by Marriott Albany Downtown/ Medical Center 🄷
(518) 860-1500. **$159-$239.** 22 Holland Ave 12209. I-90 exit 5 (Everett Rd), 2.6 mi on SR 5, then just e. Int corridors. **Pets:** Medium, other species. $100 one-time fee/room. Designated rooms, service with restrictions. 🛜 ⛟ 🍴 💻 ⇲

ALEXANDRIA BAY

△△△ ▼ The Ship Motel 🄼
(315) 482-4503. **$75-$135.** 6 Market St 13607. Center. Ext corridors. **Pets:** Small. $10 daily fee/room. Service with restrictions, crate. 🆂🅰🆅🅴 🛜 ⛟

ALLEGANY

▼ ▼ Microtel Inn & Suites-Olean/Allegany 🄷
(716) 373-5333. **$63-$108.** 3234 NYS Rt 417 14760. I-86 exit 25 westbound; exit 24 eastbound, 2.1 mi e on SR 417 (State St). Int corridors. **Pets:** Other species. $15 daily fee/pet. Service with restrictions, supervision. 🛜 ⛟ 🍴 💻

AMSTERDAM

▼▼ Super 8 🄷
(518) 843-5888. **$65-$81.** 5502 Rt 30 S 12010. I-90 exit 27 (SR 30 S). Int corridors. **Pets:** Accepted. 🛜 🍴 💻

ANGELICA

▼▼▼ Angelica Inn B & B 🅱🅱
(585) 466-3063. **Call for rates.** 64 W Main St 14709. I-86 exit 31, 0.5 mi w. Ext/int corridors. **Pets:** Accepted. 🛜 ✕ 🍴 💻 🎟 🚳

APALACHIN

▼▼ Quality Inn 🄷
(607) 625-4441. **Call for rates.** 7666 SR 434 13732. SR 17 exit 66, just e. Int corridors. **Pets:** Accepted. 🛜 🍴 💻

AUBURN

▼▼ Days Inn Auburn/Finger Lakes Region 🄷
(315) 252-7567. **$56-$100.** 37 William St 13021. Just s on SR 34, just w. Ext/int corridors. **Pets:** Accepted. 🛜 🍴

△△△ ▼▼▼ Holiday Inn-Auburn/Finger Lakes 🄷
(315) 253-4531. **$79-$189.** 75 North St 13021. On SR 34, just n of US 20/SR 5. Int corridors. **Pets:** Other species. $15 daily fee/room. Designated rooms, service with restrictions, supervision. 🆂🅰🆅🅴 🛜 ⛟ 🍴 💻 🍴 ⇲

▼▼ Inn at the Finger Lakes 🄷
(315) 253-5000. **$99-$189, 3 day notice.** 12 Seminary Ave 13021. Jct SR 34/38, just e on US 20/SR 5; center. Int corridors. **Pets:** Accepted. 🛜 ✕ ⛟ 🍴 💻

AVERILL PARK

▼▼◆ La Perla at the Gregory House Country Inn & Restaurant 🄲🄸
(518) 674-3774. **$120-$175, 7 day notice.** 3016 SR 43 12018. Center. Int corridors. **Pets:** Accepted. 🛜 ✕ 🍴 ⇲

BALDWINSVILLE

Microtel Inn & Suites [H]
(315) 635-9556. **$59-$104, 7 day notice.** 131 Downer St 13027. SR 690 exit SR 31 W, 0.4 mi e. Int corridors. **Pets:** Large, other species. $10 one-time fee/pet. Designated rooms, service with restrictions.

The Red Mill Inn [H]
(315) 635-4871. **$92-$299.** 4 Syracuse St 13027. Just w of jct SR 31 on SR 48; center. Int corridors. **Pets:** Medium, other species. $50 one-time fee/pet. Designated rooms, service with restrictions, crate.

BATAVIA

Budget Inn [M]
(585) 343-7921. **$49-$129.** 301 Oak St 14020. I-90 exit 48, just n. Int corridors. **Pets:** Medium. $10 daily fee/pet. Designated rooms, service with restrictions, supervision.

Clarion Hotel Palm Island Indoor Water Park [H]
(585) 344-2100. **$88-$149.** 8250 Park Rd 14020. I-90 exit 48, just w. Int corridors. **Pets:** $20 one-time fee/pet. Service with restrictions, supervision.

Quality Inn & Suites [H]
(585) 344-7000. **$79-$159.** 8200 Park Rd 14020. I-90 exit 48, just w. Int corridors. **Pets:** Medium. $10 daily fee/pet. Designated rooms, service with restrictions, supervision.

Super 8 [H]
(585) 345-0800. **$41-$244.** 202 Oak St 14020. I-90 exit 48, just s. Int corridors. **Pets:** Large, other species. $10 daily fee/pet. Designated rooms, service with restrictions, supervision.

BATH

Bath Super 8 [H]
(607) 776-2187. **$29-$126, 3 day notice.** 333 W Morris St 14810. I-86 exit 38, just n. Int corridors. **Pets:** $10 daily fee/pet. Service with restrictions, supervision.

Microtel Inn & Suites [H]
(607) 776-5333. **$40-$117.** 370 W Morris St 14810. I-86 exit 38, just n. Int corridors. **Pets:** Accepted.

BELLEROSE

Comfort Inn Bellerose [H]
(718) 343-4400. **Call for rates.** 249-05 Jericho Tpke 11426. Cross Island Pkwy exit 27 northbound; exit 27 E southbound. Int corridors. **Pets:** Accepted.

BINGHAMTON

Comfort Inn of Binghamton [H]
(607) 724-3297. **Call for rates.** 1000 Upper Front St 13905. I-81 exit 5, 1 mi n on US 11 (Front St). Int corridors. **Pets:** Accepted.

Grand Royale Hotel [H]
(607) 722-0000. **$79-$94.** 79 Collier St 13901. Just n of jct Hawley St; downtown. Int corridors. **Pets:** Accepted.

Holiday Inn Arena [H]
(607) 722-1212. **Call for rates.** 2-8 Hawley St 13901. Downtown. Int corridors. **Pets:** Accepted.

BOHEMIA

La Quinta Inn & Suites Islip Macarthur Airport [H]
(631) 881-7700. **$93-$198.** 10 Aero Rd 11716. I-495 exit 57, 5.1 mi se on SR 454, just s on Johnson Ave, then just e. Int corridors. **Pets:** Medium, other species. Service with restrictions, supervision.

BRIGHTON

La Quinta Inn & Suites Rochester South [H]
(585) 272-7800. **$109-$219.** 717 E Henrietta Rd 14623. I-390 exit 16B (Henrietta Rd) southbound; exit 16 (Henrietta Rd) northbound, just w. Int corridors. **Pets:** Medium, other species. Service with restrictions, supervision.

Towpath Motel [M]
(585) 271-2147. **$55-$105.** 2323 Monroe Ave (US 31) 14618. I-590 exit 2 northbound, just w; exit 2A southbound. Ext corridors. **Pets:** Small, other species. $10 one-time fee/pet. Service with restrictions, supervision.

BROCKPORT

Dollinger's Inn and Suites [H]
(585) 395-1000. **$100-$150.** 4908 Lake Rd S 14420. Just s of jct SR 31, on SR 19 S. Int corridors. **Pets:** Large, other species. $25 one-time fee/room. No service, supervision.

BUFFALO METROPOLITAN AREA

AMHERST

Candlewood Suites [H]
(716) 688-2100. **$79-$150.** 20 Flint Rd 14226. I-290 exit 5B, just n on SR 263 (Millersport Hwy). Int corridors. **Pets:** Large. $50 one-time fee/room. Service with restrictions.

Comfort Inn University [H]
(716) 688-0811. **$69-$159.** 1 Flint Rd 14226. I-290 exit 5B, just n on SR 263 (Millersport Hwy), then just w. Int corridors. **Pets:** Medium. $20 daily fee/pet. Designated rooms, service with restrictions, crate.

Homewood Suites Buffalo/Amherst [H]
(716) 833-2277. **Call for rates.** 1138 Millersport Hwy 14226. I-290 exit 5A, just w. Int corridors. **Pets:** Accepted.

Hotel Indigo Buffalo-Amherst [H]
(716) 689-4414. **$109-$269.** 10 Flint Rd 14226. I-290 exit 5B, just n on SR 263 (Millersport Hwy). Int corridors. **Pets:** Accepted.

Lord Amherst Hotel [M]
(716) 839-2200. **$69-$135.** 5000 Main St 14226. I-290 exit 7A, just w on SR 5. Ext/int corridors. **Pets:** Accepted.

Red Roof Inn #7104 [M]
(716) 689-7474. **$44-$129.** 42 Flint Rd 14226. I-290 exit 5B, just n on SR 263 (Millersport Hwy). Ext corridors. **Pets:** Large, other species. No service, supervision.

BLASDELL

Econo Lodge South [M]
(716) 825-7530. **$56-$102.** 4344 Milestrip Rd 14219. I-90 exit 56, just e on SR 179. Ext corridors. **Pets:** Medium. $10 daily fee/room. Designated rooms, service with restrictions, supervision.

BOWMANSVILLE

La Quinta Inn Buffalo Airport [H]
(716) 633-1011. **$66-$176.** 6619 Transit Rd 14026. I-90 exit 49, just n. Int corridors. **Pets:** Medium, other species. Service with restrictions, supervision.

AAA **▼▼▼** Red Roof Inn-Buffalo Airport #7137 **M**

(716) 633-1100. **$60-$119.** 146 Maple Dr 14026. Just e of SR 78; just n of entrance to I-90 (New York State Thruway) exit 49. Ext corridors. **Pets:** Large, other species. No service, supervision. [SAVE] 🛜 🔲

BUFFALO

AAA **▼▼▼** Best Western - On The Avenue **H**

(716) 886-8333. **$129-$166.** 510 Delaware Ave 14202. Between Virginia and Allen sts; downtown. Int corridors. **Pets:** Medium, dogs only. Designated rooms, service with restrictions, supervision.

[SAVE] 🛜 🔲 🔲 🔲

AAA **▼▼▼▼** Hyatt Regency Buffalo/Hotel and Conference
Center **H** 🐾

(716) 856-1234. **$89-$249.** 2 Fountain Plaza 14202. On Pearl St at W Huron St; downtown. Int corridors. **Pets:** Small, dogs only. $80 one-time fee/pet. Designated rooms, service with restrictions, supervision.

[SAVE] 🛜 🔲 🔲 🔲 🔲

CHEEKTOWAGA

AAA **▼▼▼▼** Comfort Inn-Cheektowaga **H**

(716) 896-2800. **$79-$149.** 475 Dingens St 14206. Just n of I-90 exit 53 (I-190); I-190 exit 1 (S Ogden St), just w. Int corridors. **Pets:** Small, dogs only. $10 daily fee/pet. Designated rooms, service with restrictions, supervision. [SAVE] 🛜 🔲 🔲 🔲 🔲

AAA **▼▼▼▼** Comfort Suites-Buffalo Airport **H**

(716) 633-6000. **$129-$179.** 901 Dick Rd 14225. SR 33 exit Dick Rd, just sw. Int corridors. **Pets:** Medium, dogs only. $15 daily fee/pet. Designated rooms, service with restrictions, supervision.

[SAVE] 🛜 🔲 🔲 🔲 🔲 🔲

▼▼▼▼ Holiday Inn-Buffalo Airport **H** 🐾

(716) 634-6969. **$119-$179.** 4600 Genesee St 14225. I-90 exit 51, 1 mi e on SR 33. Int corridors. **Pets:** $50 one-time fee/room. Service with restrictions, supervision. 🛜 🔲 🔲 🔲 🔲 🔲 🔲

▼▼▼▼ Holiday Inn Express Hotel & Suites-Buffalo
Airport **H**

(716) 631-8700. **$129-$179.** 131 Buell Ave 14225. I-90 exit 51, just e on Genesee St (SR 33), then just s. Int corridors. **Pets:** Medium. $40 one-time fee/pet. Service with restrictions, crate.

🛜 🔲 🔲 🔲 🔲 🔲 🔲

▼▼▼▼ Homewood Suites by Hilton **H**

(716) 685-0700. **$149-$199.** 760 Dick Rd 14225. SR 33 exit Dick Rd, 0.3 mi sw. Int corridors. **Pets:** Accepted. 🛜 🔲 🔲 🔲

AAA **▼▼** Oak Tree Inn **H**

(716) 681-2600. **$69-$150.** 3475 Union Rd 14225. I-90 exit 52, 0.3 mi e on Walden Ave, just n on SR 277 (Union Rd). Int corridors. **Pets:** Accepted. [SAVE] 🛜 🔲 🔲 🔲

▼▼▼▼ Residence Inn Buffalo-Cheektowaga **H**

(716) 892-5410. **$159-$219.** 107 Anderson Rd 14225. I-90 exit 52 westbound, stay to left off exit ramp. Int corridors. **Pets:** Large. $100 one-time fee/room. Service with restrictions. 🛜 🔲 🔲 🔲 🔲 🔲 🔲

CLARENCE

▼▼▼▼ Staybridge Suites-Buffalo Airport **H** 🐾

(716) 810-7829. **$169-$499, 3 day notice.** 8005 Sheridan Dr 14221. I-90 exit 49, 3 mi n on SR 78 (Transit Rd); jct SR 324; next to Eastern Hills Mall. Int corridors. **Pets:** Medium. $75 one-time fee/room. Service with restrictions, crate. 🛜 🔲 🔲 🔲 🔲 🔲

HAMBURG

AAA **▼▼▼** Comfort Inn & Suites **H**

(716) 648-2922. **$64-$129.** 3615 Commerce Pl 14075. I-90 exit 57, just w. Int corridors. **Pets:** Accepted. [SAVE] 🛜 🔲 🔲 🔲 🔲 🔲

AAA **▼▼▼** Quality Inn Hamburg **H**

(716) 649-0500. **Call for rates.** 5440 Camp Rd 14075. I-90 exit 57, 0.3 mi se on SR 75. Int corridors. **Pets:** Accepted.

[SAVE] 🛜 🔲 🔲 🔲 🔲

AAA **▼▼▼** Red Roof Inn #7055 **M**

(716) 648-7222. **$50-$120.** 5370 Camp Rd 14075. I-90 exit 57, just se on SR 75. Ext corridors. **Pets:** Large, other species. No service, supervision. [SAVE] 🛜 🔲

AAA **▼▼▼** Super 8 Hamburg **H**

(716) 649-0505. **$63-$108.** 5442 Camp Rd 14075. I-90 exit 57, 0.3 mi se on SR 75. Int corridors. **Pets:** Accepted. [SAVE] 🛜 🔲 🔲

KENMORE

▼▼▼ Super 8-Buffalo/Niagara Falls **H**

(716) 876-4020. **$53-$86.** 1288 Sheridan Dr 14217. I-190 exit 15, 1.5 mi e on SR 324 (Sheridan Dr). Int corridors. **Pets:** Medium. Service with restrictions, supervision. 🛜 🔲 🔲

SPRINGVILLE

▼▼ Microtel Inn & Suites **H**

(716) 592-3141. **$58-$80.** 270 S Cascade Dr 14141. Just s off SR 39 E. Int corridors. **Pets:** Large. $15 daily fee/room. Service with restrictions, crate. 🛜 🔲 🔲

TONAWANDA

▼▼ Econo Lodge **M**

(716) 694-6696. **Call for rates.** 2000 Niagara Falls Blvd 14150. I-290 exit 3 (Niagara Falls Blvd), 0.5 mi n on US 62. Ext/int corridors. **Pets:** Accepted. 🛜 🔲

WEST SENECA

▼▼▼ Staybridge Suites Buffalo-South **H**

(716) 939-3100. **Call for rates.** 16 Slade Ave 14224. I-90 exit 55 (Ridge Rd E), just n. Int corridors. **Pets:** Medium. $75 one-time fee/room. Designated rooms, service with restrictions, crate.

🛜 🔲 🔲 🔲 🔲 🔲

WILLIAMSVILLE

▼▼▼ Residence Inn by Marriott Buffalo/Amherst **H**

(716) 632-6622. **$116-$206.** 100 Maple Rd 14221. I-290 exit 5B, just n on Millersport Hwy exit Maple Rd, then just e. Ext corridors. **Pets:** Accepted. 🛜 🔲 🔲 🔲 🔲 🔲

▼▼ Super 8 Buffalo/Williamsville Airport **H**

(716) 634-1500. **Call for rates.** 7200 Transit Rd 14221. I-90 exit 49 (SR 78), 1.2 mi n. Int corridors. **Pets:** Medium. $10 one-time fee/room. Service with restrictions, supervision. 🛜 🔲 🔲

END METROPOLITAN AREA

CALCIUM

▼▼ Microtel Inn Watertown ⊞

(315) 629-5000. **$67-$77.** 8000 Virginia Smith Dr 13616. Jct SR 342 and US 11, just s. Int corridors. **Pets:** Other species. $10 daily fee/room. Service with restrictions, supervision. 📶 🛋 💻

CANANDAIGUA

🔶🔶 ▼▼▼▼ The Inn On The Lake ⊞

(585) 394-7800. **Call for rates.** 770 S Main St 14424. I-90 exit 44 (SR 332), just s of jct US 20 and SR 5. Int corridors. **Pets:** Accepted.
[SAVE] 📶 ✕ 🅼 🛋 💻 🍽 ≋ ✕

▼▼ Super 8 ⊞

(585) 396-7224. **$63-$101.** 4450 Eastern Blvd 14424. Jct SR 332, 5 and US 20, 0.5 mi e. Int corridors. **Pets:** Other species. $10 daily fee/room. Service with restrictions, supervision. 📶 🛋 💻

CANASTOTA

▼▼ Days Inn ⊞

(315) 697-3309. **$63-$126.** 377 N Peterboro St 13032. I-90 exit 34, on SR 13. Int corridors. **Pets:** Other species. $15 daily fee/room. Service with restrictions, crate. 📶 💻

CAZENOVIA

▼▼▼▼ Brae Loch Inn 🅲🅸 ❀

(315) 655-3431. **$115-$170, 10 day notice.** 5 Albany St 13035. On US 20. Int corridors. **Pets:** $25 one-time fee/room. Service with restrictions, crate. 📶 ✕ 💻 🍽

CHESTER

🔶 ▼▼▼▼ Holiday Inn Express Hotel & Suites ⊞

(845) 469-3000. **$99-$171.** 2 Bryle Pl 10918. SR 17 exit 126, just n on SR 94, then just w on SR 17M (Brookside Ave). Int corridors.
Pets: Accepted. [SAVE] 📶 🅼 🛋 💻 ≋ ✕

CICERO

🔶🔶 ▼ Budget Inn 🅼

(315) 458-3510. **$55-$145, 7 day notice.** 901 South Bay Rd 13039. I-481 exit 10, just n. Ext corridors. **Pets:** Small, dogs only. $10 daily fee/pet. Designated rooms, service with restrictions, supervision.
[SAVE] 📶 🛋 💻

🔶🔶 ▼▼▼▼ Comfort Suites Syracuse-Cicero ⊞

(315) 752-0150. **$89-$229.** 5875 Carmenica Dr 13039. I-80 exit 31, just e. Int corridors. **Pets:** Accepted. [SAVE] 📶 ✕ 🅼 🛋 💻 ≋

CLAY

▼▼▼▼ Hampton Inn-Syracuse/Clay ⊞

(315) 622-3443. **$129-$209.** 3948 SR 31 13090. SR 481 exit 12, just w. Int corridors. **Pets:** Medium, dogs only. $150 deposit/room. Designated rooms, service with restrictions, supervision.
📶 🅼 🛋 💻 ≋ ✕

CLAYTON

▼▼ Fair Wind Lodge 🅼

(315) 686-5251. **$50-$85, 3 day notice.** 38201 NYS Rt 12E 13624. 2.3 mi sw. Ext corridors. **Pets:** Accepted. 📶 🛋 💻 ≋ ✒

CLINTON

▼▼▼▼ Amidst the Hedges 🅱🅱

(315) 723-2035. **$95-$225, 20 day notice.** 180 Sanford Ave 13323. SR 412 (College St), 0.3 mi n on Elm St. Int corridors. **Pets:** Dogs only. $100 deposit/pet. Designated rooms, no service, supervision.
📶 ✕ 🛋 💻

COBLESKILL

🔶🔶🔶 ▼▼▼▼ Best Western Plus Inn of Cobleskill ⊞

(518) 234-4321. **$89-$169.** 121 Burgin Dr 12043. I-88 exit 21 eastbound on SR 7, 0.8 mi e of jct SR 10; exit 22 westbound, 2.9 mi w on SR 7. Int corridors. **Pets:** Other species. $15 daily fee/room. Designated rooms, service with restrictions. [SAVE] 📶 ✕ 🅼 🛋 💻 🍽 ≋

▼▼ Super 8 ⊞

(518) 234-4888. **$62-$113.** 955 E Main St 12043. I-88 exit 22 westbound, 2.4 mi w on SR 7; exit 21 eastbound, 3.1 mi e on SR 7. Int corridors. **Pets:** Other species. $10 daily fee/pet. Service with restrictions, supervision. 📶 🅼 🛋 💻

COLONIE

🔶🔶 ▼▼▼ Best Western Albany Airport Inn ⊞

(518) 458-1000. **Call for rates.** 200 Wolf Rd 12205. I-87 exit 4, just se to Wolf Rd, then just sw. Int corridors. **Pets:** Accepted.
[SAVE] 📶 🛋 💻 🍽 ≋

🔶🔶 ▼▼▼ Cocca's Inn & Suites, Wolf Rd 🅼

(518) 459-2240. **$59-$149.** 2 Wolf Rd 12205. I-87 exit 2E, just e. Ext/int corridors. **Pets:** Medium, other species. $10 daily fee/pet. Service with restrictions, supervision. [SAVE] 📶 🛋 💻

▼▼▼ Holiday Inn Albany on Wolf Road ⊞

(518) 458-7250. **$99-$199.** 205 Wolf Rd 12205. I-87 exit 4, 0.3 mi se. Int corridors. **Pets:** Medium. $35 daily fee/pet. Service with restrictions.
📶 🅼 🛋 💻 🍽 ≋ ✕

🔶🔶 ▼▼▼ Red Roof Inn #7112 🅼

(518) 459-1971. **$55-$130.** 188 Wolf Rd 12205. I-87 exit 4, just se to Wolf Rd, then just sw. Ext corridors. **Pets:** Large, other species. No service, supervision. [SAVE] 📶 🅼 🛋

🔶🔶 ▼▼▼ Travelodge Inn & Suites, Albany Airport ⊞

(518) 459-5670. **$45-$94.** 42 Wolf Rd 12205. I-87 exit 2E, just e, then just n. Int corridors. **Pets:** Small. $10 daily fee/pet. Service with restrictions, supervision. [SAVE] 📶 🛋 💻

CORNING

▼▼▼▼ Radisson Hotel Corning ⊞

(607) 962-5000. **$109-$399.** 125 Denison Pkwy E 14830. Downtown. Int corridors. **Pets:** Accepted. [ECO] 📶 🛋 💻 🍽 ≋

▼▼▼ Staybridge Suites ⊞ ❀

(607) 936-7800. **Call for rates.** 201 Townley Ave 14830. I-86/SR 17 exit 46, just s. Int corridors. **Pets:** Medium, other species. $75 one-time fee/room. Service with restrictions, crate. 📶 🅼 🛋 💻 ≋ ✕

CORTLAND

🔶🔶 ▼▼ Econo Lodge 🅼

(607) 756-2856. **Call for rates.** 10 S Church St 13045. I-81 exit 11, 0.8 mi s on SR 13/41 and US 11. Ext corridors. **Pets:** Accepted.
[SAVE] 📶 🛋 💻

▼▼ Quality Inn Cortland ⊞

(607) 756-5622. **Call for rates.** 188 Clinton Ave 13045. I-81 exit 11, just n. Int corridors. **Pets:** $20 daily fee/room. Service with restrictions, supervision. 📶 ✕ 🛋 💻

🔶🔶 ▼▼▼ Ramada Cortland ⊞

(607) 756-4431. **$66-$162.** 2 River St 13045. I-81 exit 11, just s on SR 13. Int corridors. **Pets:** Other species. $15 daily fee/room. Designated rooms, service with restrictions, supervision.
[SAVE] 📶 🛋 💻 🍽 ≋

CUBA

▼▼ Cuba Econo Lodge 🅼

(585) 968-1992. **Call for rates.** 1 N Branch Rd 14727. I-86 exit 28, just n to N Branch Rd, then e. Int corridors. **Pets:** Accepted. 📶 🛋

DEWITT

AAA ▼▼▼ Econo Lodge **M**

(315) 446-3300. **$70-$90.** 3400 Erie Blvd E 13214. I-481 exit 3, 1.2 mi w on SR 5; I-690 exit 17 S (Bridge St), just e on Erie Blvd (SR 5). Ext corridors. **Pets:** Medium. $15 daily fee/pet. Service with restrictions, supervision. (SAVE) 🛜 🔒 🖵

DIAMOND POINT

▼▼ ▼▼ Golden Sands Resort **M**

(518) 668-2203. **$75-$175, 30 day notice.** 3654 Lake Shore Dr 12845. I-87 exit 22, 3.3 mi n on SR 9N. Ext corridors. **Pets:** Small, other species. $10 daily fee/pet. Designated rooms, service with restrictions, supervision. 🛜 🔒 ⊠

DUNKIRK

AAA ▼▼▼▼ Best Western Plus Dunkirk & Fredonia Inn **H**

(716) 366-7100. **$90-$200.** 3912 Vineyard Dr 14048. I-90 exit 59, just w. Int corridors. **Pets:** Medium, other species. $15 daily fee/pet. Service with restrictions, supervision. (SAVE) 🛜 ⊠ 🔒 🖵 ⚓

AAA ▼▼▼▼ Comfort Inn **H**

(716) 672-4450. **$90-$160.** 3925 Vineyard Dr 14048. I-90 exit 59, just se on SR 75 (Camp Rd), then just w. Int corridors. **Pets:** Medium, other species. $15 daily fee/pet. Service with restrictions, supervision. (SAVE) 🛜 🔒 🖵

EAST GREENBUSH

▼▼▼▼ Residence Inn Albany East Greenbush/Tech Valley **H**

(518) 720-3600. **$169-$197.** 3 Tech Valley Dr 12061. I-90 exit 9, just e. Int corridors. **Pets:** Accepted. 🛜 ⊠ ♿M 🔒 🖵 ⚓ ⊠

EAST SYRACUSE

AAA ▼▼▼▼ Best Western Plus Carrier Circle Syracuse **H**

(315) 437-2761. **$99-$179.** 6555 Old Collamer Rd S 13057. I-90 exit 35 (Carrier Cir) to SR 298 E, just n. Ext/int corridors. **Pets:** $15 daily fee/pet. Service with restrictions, crate. (SAVE) 🛜 🔒 🖵 🍴 ⚓ ⊠

AAA ▼▼▼▼ Candlewood Suites Syracuse **H** ❀

(315) 432-1684. **$99-$129.** 6550 Baptist Way 13057. I-90 exit 35 (Carrier Cir) to SR 298 E to Old Collamer Rd, just n. Int corridors. **Pets:** Medium. $25 one-time fee/room. Service with restrictions, crate. (SAVE) 🛜 ♿M 🔒 🖵

▼▼▼ Comfort Inn-Carrier Circle **H**

(315) 437-0222. **$69-$155.** 6491 Thompson Rd S 13206. I-90 exit 35 (Carrier Cir), just s. Ext/int corridors. **Pets:** Medium. $10 daily fee/room. Designated rooms, service with restrictions, supervision. 🛜 🔒 🖵

▼▼▼▼ CrestHill Suites **H**

(315) 432-5595. **$109-$249.** 6410 New Venture Gear Dr 13057. I-90 exit 35 (Carrier Cir) to SR 298 E, 0.7 mi s, then just e. Int corridors. **Pets:** Large. $50 one-time fee/room. Designated rooms, service with restrictions, crate. 🛜 🔒 🖵 ⚓

▼▼▼ Quality Inn Syracuse **H**

(315) 432-9333. **$65-$145.** 6611 Old Collamer Rd S 13057. I-90 exit 35 (Carrier Cir) to SR 298 E, just n. Ext/int corridors. **Pets:** Accepted. 🛜 ♿M 🔒 🖵 ⚓

AAA ▼▼▼ Red Roof Inn #7157 **M**

(315) 437-3309. **$50-$150.** 6614 N Thompson Rd 13206. I-90 exit 35 (Carrier Cir), just n. Ext corridors. **Pets:** Large, other species. No service, supervision. (SAVE) 🛜

▼▼▼▼ Residence Inn Syracuse **H**

(315) 432-4488. **$161-$269.** 6420 Yorktown Cir 13057. I-90 exit 35 (Carrier Cir), SR 298 E to Old Collamer Rd, then just n. Ext/int corridors. **Pets:** Large, other species. $75 one-time fee/room. Service with restrictions, crate. 🛜 ⊠ ♿M 🔒 🖵 ⚓ ⊠

ELLICOTTVILLE

AAA ▼▼▼▼ The Jefferson Inn of Ellicottville **BB** ❀

(716) 699-5869. **$89-$269, 30 day notice.** 3 Jefferson St 14731. Just n of jct US 219 and SR 242. Ext/int corridors. **Pets:** Other species. $15 daily fee/pet. Designated rooms, no service. (SAVE) 🛜 ⊠ 🔒 🖵

▼▼▼▼ Sugar Pine Lodge **BB**

(716) 699-4855. **$109-$225, 30 day notice.** 6158 Jefferson St, Rt 219 S 14731. Jct US 219 and SR 242, 0.5 mi s on US 219. Ext/int corridors. **Pets:** Accepted. 🛜 ⊠ 🔒 🖵 ⚓

ELMIRA

AAA ▼▼▼ Coachman Motor Lodge **M** ❀

(607) 733-5526. **$90-$120.** 908 Pennsylvania Ave 14904. I-86/SR 17 exit 56, 0.7 mi w on SR 352 (Church St), 0.5 mi s on Madison Ave (becomes Pennsylvania Ave), then 1.4 mi s. Ext corridors. **Pets:** Medium. $15 daily fee/pet. Service with restrictions, supervision. (SAVE) 🛜 🔒 🖵

▼▼▼▼ Holiday Inn-Elmira Riverview **H**

(607) 734-4211. **$139-$259.** 760 E Water St 14901. I-86/SR 17 exit 56, 0.5 mi s. Int corridors. **Pets:** Dogs only. $25 one-time fee/room. Designated rooms, service with restrictions, supervision. 🛜 🔒 🖵 🍴 ⚓

EVANS MILLS

▼▼▼▼ Candlewood Suites Watertown/Fort Drum **H**

(315) 629-6990. **Call for rates.** 26513 Herrick Dr 13637. Jct US 11, just n. Int corridors. **Pets:** Medium. $75 one-time fee/room. Service with restrictions, crate. 🛜 ⊠ ♿M 🔒 🖵

FARMINGTON

AAA ▼▼▼ Budget Inn **M**

(585) 924-5020. **$49-$109, 3 day notice.** 6001 Rt 96 14425. I-90 exit 44, 1 mi s on SR 332, then just e. Ext corridors. **Pets:** Small, dogs only. $15 daily fee/pet. Service with restrictions, supervision. (SAVE) 🛜 🔒 🖵

FAYETTEVILLE

AAA ▼▼▼▼ Craftsman Inn and Conference Center **H**

(315) 637-8000. **Call for rates.** 7300 E Genesee St (SR 5) 13066. Across from Fayetteville Towne Center. Int corridors. **Pets:** Accepted. (SAVE) 🛜 ⊠ ♿M 🔒 🖵 🍴

FISHKILL

▼▼ ▼▼ Days Inn-Fishkill **H**

(845) 896-4995. **$79-$169.** 20 Schuyler Blvd 12524. I-84 exit 13, just n. Int corridors. **Pets:** Accepted. 🛜 ♿M 🔒 🖵

▼▼ ▼▼ Extended StayAmerica-Fishkill-Poughkeepsie **H** ❀

(845) 896-0592. **$110-$199.** 55 W Merritt Blvd 12524. I-84 exit 13, just n. Int corridors. **Pets:** Other species. $25 daily fee/pet. Service with restrictions. 🛜 ♿M 🔒 🖵

▼▼ ▼▼ Homestead Studio Suites-Fishkill-Poughkeepsie **H** ❀

(845) 897-2800. **$95-$199.** 25 Merritt Blvd 12524. I-84 exit 13, just n. Int corridors. **Pets:** Other species. $25 daily fee/pet. Service with restrictions. 🛜 🔒 🖵 ⊠

AAA ▼▼▼▼ Residence Inn Fishkill **H**

(845) 896-5210. **$116-$170.** 14 Schuyler Blvd 12524. I-84 exit 13, just n. Ext corridors. **Pets:** Other species. $100 one-time fee/room. Service with restrictions, crate. (SAVE) 🛜 ⊠ ♿M 🔒 🖵 ⚓ ⊠

FLORAL PARK

▼▼ ▼▼ Quality Inn Floral Park **H**

(718) 343-9600. **Call for rates.** 256-15 Jericho Tpke 11001. At Keene Ave. Int corridors. **Pets:** Large, other species. $25 daily fee/pet. Service with restrictions, crate. 🛜 ⊠ 🖵

GARDEN CITY

▼▼▼▼ La Quinta Inn & Suites Garden City
(516) 705-9000. **$125-$219.** 821 Stewart Ave 11530. Meadowbrook
Pkwy exit 3, 0.5 mi w. Int corridors. **Pets:** Medium, other species. Service
with restrictions, supervision. 🛜 ⓜ 🐾 💻

GATES

▼▼▼▼ Holiday Inn-Rochester Airport 🄷
(585) 328-6000. **$129-$179.** 911 Brooks Ave 14624. I-390 exit 18A (SR
204), just e. Int corridors. **Pets:** Medium, other species. $50 deposit/room.
Designated rooms, service with restrictions, supervision.
🛜 🐾 💻 🍴 ➰ ⊠

▼▼▼ Quality Inn-Rochester 🄷
(585) 464-8800. **$89-$169.** 1273 Chili Ave 14624. I-390 exit 19, just w on
SR 33. Int corridors. **Pets:** $25 deposit/room. Service with restrictions,
crate. 🛜 🐾 💻 🍴 ➰

GENESEO

▼▼▼ Quality Inn Geneseo 🄷
(585) 243-0500. **$99-$159.** 4242 Lakeville Rd 14454. I-390 exit 8, 3.4 mi
w on SR 20A. Int corridors. **Pets:** Small, other species. $25 daily fee/pet.
Service with restrictions, crate. 🛜 ⊠ 🐾 💻 ➰

GENEVA

🅰🅰🅰 ▼▼▼▼ Cobtree Vacation Rentals Resort 🆅🄷 🐾
(315) 789-1144. **$125-$430, 90 day notice.** 440-454 Armstrong Rd
14456. 3 mi n on SR 14. Ext corridors. **Pets:** Other species. $8 daily
fee/pet. No service, supervision. 🆂🅰🆅🅴 🛜 ⊠ 🐾 💻 ⊠

▼▼▼ Microtel Inn & Suites 🄷
(315) 789-7890. **$59-$129.** 550 Hamilton St 14456. Jct SR 14, 2 mi w
on US 20/SR 5. Int corridors. **Pets:** Accepted. 🛜 ⊠ ⓜ 🐾 💻

GLENS FALLS

🅰🅰🅰 ▼▼▼▼ Queensbury Hotel 🄷 🐾
(518) 792-1121. **$89-$189.** 88 Ridge St 12801. Corner of Maple St; center. Int corridors. **Pets:** $100 deposit/room, $25 daily fee/pet. Designated
rooms, service with restrictions, supervision.
🆂🅰🆅🅴 🛜 ⊠ 🐾 💻 🍴 ➰ ⊠

GREAT NECK

▼▼▼▼ The Andrew Hotel 🄷 🐾
(516) 482-2900. **$199-$309.** 75 N Station Plaza 11021. Jct SR 25A, 0.8
mi n on Middle Neck Rd, just e. Int corridors. **Pets:** Medium, other species. $150 one-time fee/pet. Service with restrictions, supervision.
🛜 ⊠ 🐾 💻

▼▼▼▼ Inn at Great Neck 🄷
(516) 773-2000. **Call for rates.** 30 Cutter Mill Rd 11021. Jct SR 25A,
0.8 mi n on Middle Neck Rd, just w. Int corridors. **Pets:** Accepted.
🛜 ⓜ 🐾 💻 🍴 ⊠

GREECE

▼▼▼ Comfort Inn West 🄷
(585) 621-5700. **$80-$160.** 1501 W Ridge Rd 14615. Jct I-390 and SR
104 (Ridge Rd), 0.5 mi e. Int corridors. **Pets:** Large, other species. $15
daily fee/pet. Designated rooms, service with restrictions, supervision.
🛜 🐾 💻

▼▼ Extended StayAmerica-Rochester-Greece 🄷 🐾
(585) 663-5558. **$75-$119.** 600 Center Place Dr 14615. I-390 exit 24A,
just e on SR 104 (Ridge Rd), just n on Buckman Rd. Int
corridors. **Pets:** Other species. $25 daily fee/pet. Service with restrictions.
🛜 ⓜ 🐾 💻

▼▼▼▼ Hampton Inn-Rochester North 🄷 🐾
(585) 663-6070. **$119-$149.** 500 Center Place Dr 14615. I-390 exit 24A,
just e on SR 104 (Ridge Rd), then just n on Buckman Rd. Int corridors.
Pets: Small, other species. Supervision. 🛜 ⓜ 🐾 💻 ➰ ⊠

▼▼▼ Residence Inn Rochester West/Greece 🄷
(585) 865-2090. **$130-$251.** 500 Paddy Creek Cir 14615. I-390 exit 24A,
just e on SR 104 (Ridge Rd), just s on Hoover Dr, then just w. Int corridors. **Pets:** Accepted. 🛜 ⊠ 🐾 💻 ➰ ⊠

GUILDERLAND

▼▼▼ Days Inn-Albany/Sunny 🄷
(518) 489-4423. **$71-$107.** 1230 Western Ave 12203. I-90 exit 1S, 0.7
mi e on US 20 (Western Ave). Int corridors. **Pets:** Large. $20 one-time
fee/room. Designated rooms, service with restrictions, supervision.
🛜 ⓜ 🐾 💻

HANCOCK

▼▼▼ Smith's Colonial Motel 🄼
(607) 637-2989. **$65-$130.** 23085 State Hwy 97 13783. SR 17 exit 87,
2.7 mi s. Ext corridors. **Pets:** Accepted. 🐾 💻

HAUPPAUGE

🅰🅰🅰 ▼▼▼▼ Hyatt Regency Long Island at Wind Watch
Golf Club, New York 🄷 🐾
(631) 784-1234. **$89-$299.** 1717 Motor Pkwy (SR 67) 11788. I-495 exit
57, just n to Long Island Motor Pkwy (SR 67), then 1.3 mi ne. Int corridors. **Pets:** Medium, dogs only. $30 daily fee/room. Designated rooms,
service with restrictions, supervision.
🄴🄲🄾 🆂🅰🆅🅴 🛜 ⓜ 🐾 💻 🍴 ➰ ⊠

▼▼▼ Residence Inn Long Island-Hauppauge/Islandia 🄷
(631) 724-4188. **$119-$299.** 850 Veterans Memorial Hwy 11788. I-495
exit 57, 1.2 mi nw. Int corridors. **Pets:** Other species. $100 one-time fee/
room. Service with restrictions. 🛜 ⊠ ⓜ 🐾 💻 ➰ ⊠

🅰🅰🅰 ▼▼▼ Sheraton Long Island Hotel 🄷
(631) 231-1100. **$109-$229.** 110 Vanderbilt Motor Pkwy 11788. I-495 exit
53 (Wicks Rd), just n, then 0.3 mi e. Int corridors. **Pets:** Accepted.
🆂🅰🆅🅴 🛜 ⊠ ⓜ 🐾 💻 🍴 ➰

HENRIETTA

▼▼▼ Homewood Suites by Hilton-Rochester 🄷
(585) 334-9150. **$149-$199.** 2095 Hylan Dr 14623. I-390 exit 13, just e.
Int corridors. **Pets:** $75 one-time fee/room. Service with restrictions.
🛜 ⓜ 🐾 💻

▼▼ Microtel-Rochester 🄷
(585) 334-3400. **$48-$129.** 905 Lehigh Station Rd 14467. I-390 exit 12
northbound; exit 12A southbound, just w on SR 253. Int corridors.
Pets: Accepted. 🛜 🐾

▼▼▼▼ Radisson Rochester Airport 🄷
(585) 475-1910. **$109-$189, 3 day notice.** 175 Jefferson Rd 14623.
I-390 exit 14A southbound; exit 14 northbound, 3 mi w on SR 252 (Jefferson Rd). Int corridors. **Pets:** Accepted. 🛜 ⓜ 🐾 💻 🍴 ➰

🅰🅰🅰 ▼▼▼ Red Roof Inn-Henrietta #7042 🄼
(585) 359-1100. **$56-$119.** 4820 W Henrietta Rd 14467. I-390 exit 12
northbound; exit 12A southbound, 0.5 mi w on SR 253, then just s on SR
15 (Henrietta Rd). Ext corridors. **Pets:** Large, other species. No service,
supervision. 🆂🅰🆅🅴 🛜 🐾

▼▼▼▼ Residence Inn Rochester 🄷
(585) 272-8850. **$109-$189.** 1300 Jefferson Rd 14623. I-390 exit 14A
southbound, 0.5 mi e on SR 252 (Jefferson Rd); exit 14 northbound, just
n on SR 15A, then 0.5 mi e on SR 252 (Jefferson Rd). Ext/int corridors.
Pets: Accepted. 🛜 ⊠ 🐾 💻 ➰ ⊠

▼▼▼▼ R I T Inn & Conference Center 🄷
(585) 359-1800. **$109-$189.** 5257 W Henrietta Rd 14586. I-390 exit 12
northbound; exit 12A southbound, 0.5 mi w on SR 253, then 0.7 mi s. Int
corridors. **Pets:** Accepted. 🄴🄲🄾 🛜 ⊠ 🐾 💻 🍴 ➰ ⊠

HERKIMER

AAA ▼▼▼ Herkimer Motel & Suites M
(315) 866-0490. **$78-$150.** 100 Marginal Rd 13350. I-90 exit 30, just n on SR 28. Ext/int corridors. **Pets:** Other species. $10 daily fee/pet. Service with restrictions, supervision. [SAVE] 🛜 🛗 💻 🏊

HIGHLAND

▼▼ Super 8 M
(845) 691-6888. **$64-$174.** 3423 Rt 9W 12528. Just s of jct SR 299 and US 9W. Int corridors. **Pets:** Accepted. 🛜 ♿M 🛗 💻

HOGANSBURG

AAA ▼▼▼ Comfort Inn & Suites Hogansburg H
(518) 358-1000. **$110-$299.** 865 State Route 37 13655. Jct SR 95, 0.3 mi w. Int corridors. **Pets:** Medium, other species. $10 daily fee/pet. Service with restrictions, supervision. [SAVE] 🛜 ✖ 🛗 💻 🏊

INLET

AAA ▼ Marina Motel M
(315) 357-3883. **$79-$189, 14 day notice.** 6 S Shore Rd 13360. Center. Ext corridors. **Pets:** $15 daily fee/pet. Designated rooms, supervision. [SAVE] 🛜 🛗

IRONDEQUOIT

▼▼▼ Holiday Inn Express H
(585) 342-0430. **$139-$179.** 2200 Goodman St N 14609. SR 104 exit Goodman St, just n. Int corridors. **Pets:** Medium, other species. $25 one-time fee/room. Service with restrictions, supervision.
🛜 ♿M 🛗 💻 🏊

ITHACA

AAA ▼▼▼ Best Western University Inn M
(607) 272-6100. **Call for rates.** 1020 Ellis Hollow Rd 14850. SR 79 E, 1 mi ne on Pine Tree Rd, just n; in East Hill Plaza. Int corridors. **Pets:** Accepted. [SAVE] 🛜 🛗 💻 🏊

AAA ▼▼ Comfort Inn H ♣
(607) 272-0100. **Call for rates.** 356 Elmira Rd 14850. Jct SR 96, 89 and 79, 1.5 mi sw on SR 13. Int corridors. **Pets:** Dogs only. $25 one-time fee/room. Designated rooms, service with restrictions, supervision. [SAVE] 🛜 ✖ ♿M 🛗 💻

AAA ▼▼▼ Country Inn & Suites By Carlson H ♣
(607) 256-1100. **$99-$359.** 1100 Danby Rd (SR 96B) 14850. 0.5 mi past entrance to Ithaca College and jct SR 96B. Int corridors. **Pets:** Large, other species. $25 daily fee/pet. Designated rooms, service with restrictions, supervision. [SAVE] 🛜 ✖ ♿M 🛗 💻 🏊

AAA ▼▼▼ Hampton Inn H
(607) 277-5500. **$116-$206.** 337 Elmira Rd 14850. On SR 13. Int corridors. **Pets:** Accepted. [SAVE] 🛜 ♿M 🛗 💻 🏊

▼▼▼ La Tourelle Resort and Spa CI
(607) 273-2734. **$149-$700, 3 day notice.** 1150 Danby Rd 14850. 2.7 mi s on SR 96B. Int corridors. **Pets:** Other species. Designated rooms, service with restrictions, supervision.
[ECO] 🛜 ✖ 🛗 💻 🍴 ✖

▼▼ Meadow Court Inn M
(607) 273-3885. **$65-$225.** 529 S Meadow St 14850. 1.5 mi s on SR 13 and 96. Ext/int corridors. **Pets:** Accepted. 🛜 ♿M 🛗 💻 🍴

AAA ▼▼ Rodeway Inn & Suites M
(607) 272-5252. **Call for rates.** 654 Elmira Rd 14850. On SR 13 S. Ext/int corridors. **Pets:** Medium, other species. $10 daily fee/pet. Designated rooms, service with restrictions, crate. [SAVE] 🛜 🛗 💻

JAMESTOWN

AAA ▼▼▼▼ Best Western Plus Downtown Jamestown H ♣
(716) 484-8400. **$115-$140.** 200 W 3rd St 14701. I-86/SR 17 exit 12, 2 mi s on SR 60 (Washington St). Int corridors. **Pets:** Medium. $15 daily fee/room. Designated rooms, service with restrictions.
[SAVE] 🛜 ✖ ♿M 🛗 💻 🏊

▼▼▼ Comfort Inn H
(716) 664-5920. **$99-$140.** 2800 N Main St 14701. I-86/SR 17 exit 12, just s on SR 60 (Main St). Int corridors. **Pets:** Accepted. 🛜 🛗 💻

JOHNSON CITY

AAA ▼▼▼ Best Western Plus of Johnson City H
(607) 729-9194. **$99-$129.** 569 Harry L Dr 13790. SR 17 exit 70N, 0.3 mi n. Int corridors. **Pets:** Accepted. [SAVE] 🛜 🛗 💻

AAA ▼▼▼ La Quinta Inn Binghamton - Johnson City H
(607) 770-9333. **$88-$176.** 581 Harry L Dr 13790. SR 17 exit 70N, 0.3 mi n. Int corridors. **Pets:** Medium, other species. Service with restrictions, supervision. [SAVE] 🛜 🛗 💻

AAA ▼▼▼ Red Roof Inn-Binghamton #7203 M
(607) 729-8940. **$65-$175.** 590 Fairview St 13790. SR 17 exit 70N, 0.3 mi n, then just n on Reynolds Rd. Ext corridors. **Pets:** Large, other species. No service, supervision. [SAVE] 🛜 🛗

JOHNSTOWN

▼▼▼ Holiday Inn H
(518) 762-4686. **$103-$155.** 308 N Comrie Ave 12095. Jct SR 30A and 29 E, 1.3 mi n. Int corridors. **Pets:** Accepted.
🛜 ♿M 🛗 💻 🍴 🏊

KINGSTON

AAA ▼▼▼ Holiday Inn H
(845) 338-0400. **$139-$209, 3 day notice.** 503 Washington Ave 12401. I-87 exit 19, just e of traffic circle. Int corridors. **Pets:** $25 daily fee/room. Service with restrictions, supervision.
[SAVE] 🛜 ✖ 🛗 💻 🍴 🏊 ✖

LAKE GEORGE

▼ Green Haven Resort M
(518) 668-2489. **$64-$139, 10 day notice.** 3136 Lake Shore Dr 12845. I-87 exit 22, 0.8 mi n on SR 9N. Ext corridors. **Pets:** Medium, dogs only. $20 one-time fee/pet. No service, supervision. 🛜 🛗 💻 🏊 ✖

▼▼ Lake George Inn M
(518) 668-2673. **$48-$175, 10 day notice.** 444 Canada St 12845. I-87 exit 22, 0.3 mi s on US 9. Ext corridors. **Pets:** Other species. $15 daily fee/pet. Designated rooms, service with restrictions. 🛜 🛗 💻 🏊

▼▼ Lake Haven Motel M
(518) 668-2260. **$49-$132, 10 day notice.** 442 Canada St 12845. I-87 exit 22, 0.4 mi s on US 9. Ext corridors. **Pets:** Medium, dogs only. $10 daily fee/pet. Designated rooms, service with restrictions, crate.
🛜 🛗 💻

▼▼ Roaring Brook Ranch & Tennis Resort H
(518) 668-5767. **$170-$246, 10 day notice.** 2206 Rt 9N S 12845. I-87 exit 21, 1 mi s. Ext/int corridors. **Pets:** Accepted.
🛜 🛗 🍴 🏊 ✖

▼▼ Travelodge of Lake George M
(518) 668-5421. **$65-$142.** 2011 SR 9 12845. I-87 exit 21, just s. Ext/int corridors. **Pets:** Medium, dogs only. $20 daily fee/pet. Designated rooms, service with restrictions, supervision. 🛜 🛗 🏊

LAKE LUZERNE

Luzerne Court

(518) 696-2734. **$80-$180, 14 day notice.** 508 Lake Ave 12846. I-87 exit 21, 8.7 mi s on SR 9N. Ext corridors. **Pets:** Dogs only. Service with restrictions, supervision.

LAKE PLACID

Art Devlin's Olympic Motor Inn, Inc.

(518) 523-3700. **$74-$498, 14 day notice.** 2764 Main St 12946. 0.5 mi e on SR 86. Ext corridors. **Pets:** Dogs only. $4 daily fee/pet. Designated rooms, supervision.

Comfort Inn on Lake Placid

(518) 523-9555. **Call for rates.** 2125 Saranac Ave 12946. 0.5 mi w on SR 86. Ext/int corridors. **Pets:** Large, other species. $15 daily fee/pet. Service with restrictions, supervision.

Crowne Plaza Resort & Golf Club Lake Placid

(518) 523-2556. **$119-$329.** 101 Olympic Dr 12946. Downtown. Ext/int corridors. **Pets:** Dogs only. $10 daily fee/pet. Service with restrictions, supervision.

Golden Arrow Lakeside Resort

(518) 523-3353. **Call for rates.** 2559 Main St 12946. On SR 86; center. Int corridors. **Pets:** Other species. $100 deposit/pet, $50 one-time fee/pet. Designated rooms, service with restrictions, supervision.

High Peaks Resort

(518) 523-4411. **$129-$349, 7 day notice.** 2384 Saranac Ave 12946. 0.3 mi w on SR 86. Int corridors. **Pets:** Large, dogs only. $100 deposit/pet. Designated rooms, service with restrictions, supervision.

Lakeview Motor Inn

(518) 523-4411. **$79-$229, 7 day notice.** 1 Mirror Lake Dr 12946. 0.3 mi w on SR 86. Int corridors. **Pets:** Large, dogs only. $100 deposit/room. Designated rooms, service with restrictions.

LAKEVILLE (LIVINGSTON COUNTY)

Rodeway Inn

(585) 346-2330. **Call for rates.** 6001 Big Tree Rd 14480. I-390 exit 8, 2.4 mi e on SR 20A; jct SR 15, 0.7 mi s. Int corridors. **Pets:** Accepted.

LANSING

Homewood Suites by Hilton

(607) 266-0000. **Call for rates.** 36 Cinema Dr 14850. SR 13 exit Triphammer Rd, just e, then just n on Sheraton Dr (which becomes Cinema Dr). Int corridors. **Pets:** Accepted.

Ramada Inn Ithaca

(607) 257-3100. **$95-$221.** 2310 N Triphammer Rd 14850. SR 13 exit Triphammer Rd, just w; adjoins Triphammer Mall. Int corridors. **Pets:** Large, other species. Service with restrictions, supervision.

LATHAM

The Century House, A Clarion Hotel & Conference Center

(518) 785-0931. **$110-$170.** 997 New Loudon Rd 12110. I-87 exit 7 (SR 7), just e, then 0.5 mi n on US 9. Int corridors. **Pets:** Accepted.

Comfort Inn Albany Airport & Conference Center

(518) 783-1900. **Call for rates.** 20 Airport Park Blvd 12110. I-87 exit 4, 2.2 mi nw on Albany Shaker Rd. Int corridors. **Pets:** Other species. $25 one-time fee/room. Designated rooms, service with restrictions, supervision.

Hotel Indigo

(518) 869-9100. **$149-$179.** 254 Old Wolf Rd 12110. I-87 exit 4, just w on Albany Shaker Rd. Int corridors. **Pets:** Accepted.

La Quinta Inn & Suites Latham Albany Airport

(518) 640-2200. **$100-$188.** 833 New Loudon Rd 12110. I-87 exit 7 (SR 7), just s on US 9 to Latham Cir, then just n on US 9. Int corridors. **Pets:** Medium, other species. Service with restrictions, supervision.

Microtel Inn, Albany Airport

(518) 782-9161. **$54-$108.** 7 Rensselaer Ave 12110. I-87 exit 6, just w. Int corridors. **Pets:** Medium. $10 daily fee/pet. Service with restrictions, supervision.

Residence Inn by Marriott Albany Airport

(518) 783-0600. **$116-$206.** 1 Residence Inn Dr 12110. I-87 exit 6, 2 mi w on SR 7. Ext corridors. **Pets:** Accepted.

LITTLE FALLS

Knights Inn of Little Falls

(315) 823-4954. **$66-$98, 3 day notice.** 20 Albany St 13365. On SR 5 and 167. Int corridors. **Pets:** Other species. $10 one-time fee/pet. Designated rooms, service with restrictions, crate.

LIVERPOOL

Best Western Plus Liverpool Grace Inn & Suites

(315) 701-4400. **$79-$279.** 136 Transistor Pkwy 13088. I-90 exit 37 (Electronics Pkwy), just n. Int corridors. **Pets:** Medium. $25 daily fee/pet. Service with restrictions, supervision.

Homewood Suites

(315) 451-3800. **$169-$189.** 275 Elwood Davis Rd 13088. I-81 exit 25 (7th North St), 1 mi w; I-90 exit 36. Int corridors. **Pets:** Large. $100 one-time fee/room. Designated rooms, service with restrictions, crate.

Knights Inn

(315) 453-6330. **$50-$143.** 430 Electronics Pkwy 13088. I-90 exit 37 (Electronics Pkwy), just w; I-81 exit 25 (7th North St), 1.3 mi nw, then just w. Ext corridors. **Pets:** Medium. $20 daily fee/pet. Designated rooms, no service, supervision.

Super 8 Route 57

(315) 451-8550. **$53-$107, 3 day notice.** 7360 Oswego Rd 13090. I-90 exit 38, 1 mi n on CR 57. Int corridors. **Pets:** Small, dogs only. $15 daily fee/pet. Designated rooms, service with restrictions, supervision.

MALONE

Econo Lodge of Malone

(518) 483-0500. **Call for rates.** 227 W Main St 12953. Just w of jct US 11 and SR 30. Ext/int corridors. **Pets:** Accepted.

Four Seasons Motel

(518) 483-3490. **$55-$99.** 206 W Main St 12953. 1 mi w on US 11. Ext corridors. **Pets:** Accepted.

△△△▽ ▽▽ Super 8 at Jons 🅷
(518) 483-8123. **$47-$107.** 42 Finney Blvd 12953. On SR 30, just s of jct US 11. Int corridors. **Pets:** Large, other species. Designated rooms, service with restrictions, supervision. 🆂🅰🆅🅴 🛜 ⊠ ＆M 🔌 💻 ⑪

MANCHESTER
△△△▽ ▽ Scottish Inns 🅼
(585) 289-3811. **$49-$139.** 4078 Rt 96 14504. I-90 exit 43, just s, then just w. Ext/int corridors. **Pets:** $10 one-time fee/pet. Service with restrictions, supervision. 🆂🅰🆅🅴 🛜 🔌

MASSENA
▽▽▽ Econo Lodge-Meadow View Motel 🅷
(315) 764-0246. **Call for rates.** 15054 State Hwy 37 13662. On SR 37, 2.7 mi sw. Int corridors. **Pets:** Accepted. 🛜 🔌 💻

MCGRAW
△△△▽ ▽▽ Cortland Days Inn 🅷
(607) 753-7594. **$49-$134.** 3775 US Rt 11 13101. I-81 exit 10 (McGraw/Cortland), just n. Int corridors. **Pets:** Small, other species. $20 daily fee/pet. Service with restrictions, supervision. 🆂🅰🆅🅴 🛜 🔌 💻

MELVILLE
▽▽ Extended StayAmerica-Long Island-Melville 🅷 🐾
(631) 777-3999. **$120-$299.** 100 Spagnoli Rd 11747. I-495 exit 49S eastbound, 0.5 mi e on south service road, then 1.1 mi s on SR 110; exit westbound, 1.5 mi s on SR 110. Int corridors. **Pets:** Other species. $25 daily fee/pet. Service with restrictions. 🛜 ＆M 🔌 💻

MIDDLETOWN
▽▽ ▽ Microtel Inn & Suites 🅷 🐾
(845) 692-0098. **$62-$143.** 19 Crystal Run Crossing 10941. SR 17 exit 122, just nw. Int corridors. **Pets:** Medium. $20 one-time fee/pet. Service with restrictions, crate. 🛜 ⊠ ＆M 🔌 💻

▽▽▽▽ Middletown Hampton Inn 🅷
(845) 344-3400. **$99-$179.** 20 Crystal Run Crossing 10941. SR 17 exit 122, just ne. Int corridors. **Pets:** Accepted. 🛜 ＆M 🔌 💻 🐾

MILFORD
△△△▽ ▽▽▽▽ Country Inn & Suites By Carlson, Cooperstown 🅷
(607) 286-7600. **$78-$299.** 4470 State Hwy 28 13807. 4 mi s of Cooperstown. Int corridors. **Pets:** Accepted.
🆂🅰🆅🅴 🛜 ⊠ ＆M 🔌 💻 🐾

MOUNT MORRIS
△△△▽ ▽▽▽▽ Country Inn & Suites By Carlson 🅷 🐾
(585) 658-4080. **$120-$190.** 130 N Main St 14510. On SR 36; center. Int corridors. **Pets:** $25 daily fee/room. Designated rooms, service with restrictions. 🆂🅰🆅🅴 🛜 ⊠ 🔌 💻 🐾

NEWARK
△△△▽ ▽▽▽ Quality Inn Finger Lakes Region 🅷
(315) 331-9500. **Call for rates.** 125 N Main St 14513. Jct SR 31, just n on SR 88. Int corridors. **Pets:** Accepted. 🆂🅰🆅🅴 🛜 🔌 💻 ⑪ 🐾

NEWBURGH
▽▽▽ Super 8 🅼
(845) 564-5700. **$54-$149.** 1287 Rt 300 12550. I-87 exit 17, just w; I-84 exit 6, 2 mi e. Int corridors. **Pets:** Accepted. 🛜 ＆M 🔌 💻

NEW HAMPTON
△△△▽ ▽▽▽ Days Inn 🅼
(845) 374-2411. **$67-$117.** 4939 Rt 17M 10958. I-84 exit 3, 0.8 mi e on US 6 and SR 17M; SR 17 exit 123, 4 mi w. Ext/int corridors. **Pets:** Medium. $10 daily fee/room. Designated rooms, supervision.
🆂🅰🆅🅴 🛜 🔌 💻 🐾

NEW HARTFORD
▽▽▽ Holiday Inn Utica 🅷
(315) 797-2131. **$89-$189.** 1777 Burrstone Rd 13413. I-90 (New York State Thruway) exit 31, 4.5 mi w on SR 5 W and 12 S exit Burrstone Rd, then 1 mi nw. Int corridors. **Pets:** Medium. $35 one-time fee/room. Service with restrictions, supervision. 🅴🅲🅾 🛜 ＆M 🔌 💻 ⑪ 🐾

▽▽ Ramada 🅷
(315) 735-3392. **$76-$136.** 141 New Hartford St 13413. SR 8, 12 and 5 exit French Rd, just w, then just n. Int corridors. **Pets:** Accepted.
🛜 🔌 💻 ⑪ 🐾

NEW WINDSOR
▽▽▽ Homewood Suites by Hilton Newburgh-Stewart Airport 🅷
(845) 567-2700. **$149-$179.** 180 Breunig Rd 12553. I-84 exit 5A, 2 mi s on SR 747 (International Dr), 1.4 mi e on SR 207, then just n. Int corridors. **Pets:** Accepted. 🛜 ＆M 🔌 💻 🐾 ⊠

NEW YORK CITY METROPOLITAN AREA

ARMONK
▽▽▽ La Quinta Inn & Suites Armonk 🅷
(914) 273-9090. **$83-$146.** 94 Business Park Dr 10504. I-684 exit 3S northbound; exit 3 southbound, 0.3 mi s on SR 22. Int corridors. **Pets:** Medium, other species. Service with restrictions, supervision.
🛜 ⊠ ＆M 🔌 💻 ⑪

BROOKLYN
△△△▽ ▽▽▽▽ Aloft New York Brooklyn 🅷
(718) 256-3833. **$129-$429, 3 day notice.** 216 Duffield St 11201. Between Willoughby St and Fulton Mall. Int corridors. **Pets:** Accepted.
🆂🅰🆅🅴 🛜 ⊠ ＆M 🔌 💻 ⑪ 🐾

▽▽▽▽ Fairfield Inn & Suites New York-Brooklyn 🅷
(718) 522-4000. **Call for rates.** 181 3rd Ave 11217. In Park Slope; jct Butler St. Int corridors. **Pets:** Accepted. 🛜 ⊠ 🔌 💻

▽▽▽ Holiday Inn Express Brooklyn 🅷
(718) 797-1133. **$149-$399.** 625 Union St 11215. Between 3rd and 4th aves. Int corridors. **Pets:** Medium. $50 one-time fee/room. Service with restrictions, supervision. 🛜 🔌 💻

▽▽▽ Holiday Inn Express Brooklyn Downtown 🅷
(718) 855-9600. **$139-$349.** 279 Butler St 11217. In Park Slope; between 3rd Ave and Nevins St. Int corridors. **Pets:** Accepted.
🛜 🔌 💻

△△△▽ ▽▽▽▽ Nu Hotel Brooklyn 🅷
(718) 852-8585. **Call for rates.** 85 Smith St 11201. Between Atlantic and State sts. Int corridors. **Pets:** Accepted. 🆂🅰🆅🅴 🛜 ⊠ 🔌

△△△▽ ▽▽▽▽ Sheraton Brooklyn New York Hotel 🅷 🐾
(718) 855-1900. **$149-$649.** 228 Duffield St 11201. Between Willoughby St and Fulton Mall. Int corridors. **Pets:** Medium. Service with restrictions, crate. 🆂🅰🆅🅴 🛜 ⊠ 🔌 💻 ⑪ 🐾

CROTON-ON-HUDSON

▼▼▼▼ Alexander Hamilton House BB

(914) 271-6737. **$142-$299, 14 day notice.** 49 Van Wyck St 10520. US 9 exit SR 129, just e on Municipal Place, just n on Riverside Ave, just e on Grand St, then just n on Hamilton Ave. Int corridors. **Pets:** Accepted.

ELMSFORD

▼▼ Extended StayAmerica-White Plains-Elmsford H ❖

(914) 347-8073. **$130-$249.** 118 Tarrytown Rd 10523. I-87 exit 8, just w. Int corridors. **Pets:** Other species. $25 daily fee/pet. Service with restrictions.

FLUSHING

▼▼ Extended StayAmerica-NY City-LaGuardia Airport H ❖

(718) 357-3661. **$145-$349.** 18-30 Whitestone Expwy 11357. In Flushing; I-678 (Van Wyck Expwy) exit 15, just w; in Whitestone. Int corridors. **Pets:** Other species. $25 daily fee/pet. Service with restrictions.

AAA ▼▼▼▼ Sheraton LaGuardia East Hotel H ❖

(718) 460-6666. **$159-$319.** 135-20 39th Ave 11354. In Flushing; Grand Central Pkwy to Northern Blvd, 1 mi e to Main St, 0.3 mi s to 39th Ave, then just w. Int corridors. **Pets:** Medium. Service with restrictions, crate.

JAMAICA

AAA ▼▼▼▼ DoubleTree by Hilton Hotel JFK Airport H

(718) 322-2300. **$229-$339.** 135-30 140th St 11436. In Jamaica; I-678 (Van Wyck Expwy) exit 2 (Rockaway Blvd), just e to 140th St, then s. Int corridors. **Pets:** Accepted.

AAA ▼▼▼▼ Sheraton JFK Airport Hotel H

(718) 322-7190. **$269-$349, 3 day notice.** 132-26 S Conduit Ave 11430. In Jamaica; between S Conduit and 149th aves; off Nassau Expwy. Int corridors. **Pets:** Accepted.

MOUNT KISCO

AAA ▼▼▼▼ Holiday Inn H

(914) 241-2600. **$159-$205, 3 day notice.** 1 Holiday Inn Dr 10549. Saw Mill River Pkwy exit 37, just e. Int corridors. **Pets:** Other species. $39 one-time fee/room. Service with restrictions, supervision.

NANUET

▼▼▼ Candlewood Suites H

(845) 371-4445. **Call for rates.** 20 Overlook Blvd 10954. I-287/87 (New York State Thruway) exit 14 (SR 59 W) to New Clarkstown Rd. Int corridors. **Pets:** Accepted.

▼▼▼ Comfort Inn & Suites H

(845) 623-6000. **$119-$169.** 425 E Rt 59 10954. Palisades Interstate Pkwy exit 8, just w. Int corridors. **Pets:** $100 deposit/room. Designated rooms, service with restrictions, supervision.

AAA ▼▼▼ Days Inn Nanuet M

(845) 623-4567. **Call for rates.** 367 W Rt 59 10954. I-287/87 (New York State Thruway) exit 14 (SR 59) northbound, just e; exit southbound, just w. Ext/int corridors. **Pets:** Small, other species. $20 daily fee/pet. Service with restrictions, supervision.

NEW YORK

AAA ▼▼▼▼ 70 Park Avenue Hotel H

(212) 973-2400. **$199-$899.** 70 Park Ave 10016. At 38th St. Int corridors. **Pets:** Accepted.

AAA ▼▼▼▼ Affinia 50 H ❖

(212) 751-5710. **Call for rates.** 155 E 50th St 10022. Between 3rd and Lexington aves. Int corridors. **Pets:** Medium. $25 one-time fee/pet. Service with restrictions, supervision.

AAA ▼▼▼▼ Affinia Dumont H ❖

(212) 481-7600. **$189-$699.** 150 E 34th St 10016. Between Lexington and 3rd aves. Int corridors. **Pets:** Large, other species. $25 one-time fee/room. Service with restrictions, supervision.

AAA ▼▼▼▼ Affinia Gardens H

(212) 355-1230. **Call for rates.** 215 E 64th St 10021. Between 2nd and 3rd aves. Int corridors. **Pets:** Accepted.

AAA ▼▼▼▼ Affinia Manhattan H ❖

(212) 563-1800. **$199-$519.** 371 7th Ave 10001. At 31st St. Int corridors. **Pets:** $25 one-time fee/room. Designated rooms, service with restrictions, crate.

AAA ▼▼▼▼ Affinia Shelburne H ❖

(212) 689-5200. **$189-$699.** 303 Lexington Ave 10016. Between 37th and 38th sts. Int corridors. **Pets:** Other species. $25 one-time fee/pet. Service with restrictions, crate.

AAA ▼▼▼▼ The Alex H ❖

(212) 867-5100. **$450-$3700, 3 day notice.** 205 E 45th St 10017. At 3rd Ave. Int corridors. **Pets:** Small. $250 one-time fee/room. Service with restrictions, supervision.

AAA ▼▼▼▼ Algonquin Hotel Autograph Collection H ❖

(212) 840-6800. **$419-$681.** 59 W 44th St 10036. Between 5th and 6th (Ave of the Americas) aves. Int corridors. **Pets:** Medium, other species. Service with restrictions, supervision.

AAA ▼▼▼▼ Aloft Harlem Hotel H ❖

(212) 749-4000. **$189-$369.** 2296 Frederick Douglass Blvd 10027. At W 124th St. Int corridors. **Pets:** Other species. Service with restrictions, supervision.

AAA ▼▼▼▼ Andaz 5th Avenue H

(212) 601-1234. **Call for rates.** 485 5th Ave 10017. At 41st St. Int corridors. **Pets:** Accepted.

AAA ▼▼▼▼ Andaz Wall Street H

(212) 590-1234. **Call for rates.** 75 Wall St 10005. Between Pearl and Water sts. Int corridors. **Pets:** $100 one-time fee/room. Service with restrictions, supervision.

▼▼▼▼ The Benjamin Hotel H

(212) 715-2500. **Call for rates.** 125 E 50th St 10022. Between Lexington and 3rd aves. Int corridors. **Pets:** Accepted.

AAA ▼▼▼ Best Western Plus Seaport Inn Downtown H

(212) 766-6600. **Call for rates.** 33 Peck Slip on Front St 10038. North end of South St Seaport. Int corridors. **Pets:** Accepted.

AAA ▼▼▼▼ Candlewood Suites Times Square H

(212) 967-2254. **$179-$289.** 339 39th St 10018. Between 8th and 9th aves. Int corridors. **Pets:** Medium, other species. $150 one-time fee/pet. Service with restrictions, crate.

AAA ▼▼▼▼ The Carlton Hotel H ❖

(212) 532-4100. **$269-$599.** 88 Madison Ave 10016. Between 28th and 29th sts. Int corridors. **Pets:** $50 one-time fee/room. Service with restrictions.

▼▼▼▼ The Carlyle, a Rosewood Hotel H

(212) 744-1600. **Call for rates.** 35 E 76th St 10021. At Madison Ave. Int corridors. **Pets:** Accepted.

▼▼▼ Cassa Hotel and Residences H
(212) 302-8700. **$199-$569.** 70 W 45th St 10036. Between 5th and 6th (Ave of the Americas) aves. Int corridors. **Pets:** Accepted.

AAA ▼▼▼▼ Comfort Inn Manhattan Bridge H
(212) 925-1212. **$129-$309.** 61-63 Chrystie St 10002. At Hester and Canal sts. Int corridors. **Pets:** Accepted.

AAA ▼▼▼▼ Comfort Inn Times Square South Area H
(212) 268-3040. **$109-$339.** 305 W 39th St 10018. At 8th Ave. Int corridors. **Pets:** Accepted.

AAA ▼▼▼▼ Courtyard by Marriott/Manhattan-Times Square South H
(212) 391-0088. **$199-$599.** 114 W 40th St 10018. Between Broadway and 6th Ave (Ave of the Americas). Int corridors. **Pets:** Accepted.

AAA ▼▼▼▼ DoubleTree by Hilton New York City - Chelsea H
(212) 564-0994. **Call for rates.** 128 W 29th St 10001. Between 6th (Ave of the Americas) and 7th aves. Int corridors. **Pets:** Accepted.

AAA ▼▼▼▼ DoubleTree Suites by Hilton Hotel New York City - Times Square H
(212) 719-1600. **$189-$699.** 1568 Broadway 10036. Jct 47th St and 7th Ave. Int corridors. **Pets:** Accepted.

AAA ▼▼▼▼ Duane Street Hotel H
(212) 964-4600. **$199-$599.** 130 Duane St 10013. Between Church St and W Broadway. Int corridors. **Pets:** Accepted.

▼▼ ▼▼ Eastgate Tower Hotel H
(212) 687-8000. **Call for rates.** 222 E 39th St 10016. Between 2nd and 3rd aves. Int corridors. **Pets:** Other species. $25 one-time fee/room.

AAA ▼▼▼▼ Element by Westin Times Square West H
(212) 643-0770. **$159-$699, 3 day notice.** 311 W 39th St 10018. Between 8th and 9th aves. Int corridors. **Pets:** Accepted.

AAA ▼▼▼ ▼▼▼ Eventi-A Kimpton Hotel H 🐾
(212) 564-4567. **$299-$599.** 851 6th Ave (Ave of the Americas) 10001. At 30th St. Int corridors. **Pets:** Other species. Designated rooms, service with restrictions, supervision.

AAA ▼▼▼▼▼ The Flatotel H
(212) 887-9400. **Call for rates.** 135 W 52nd St 10019. Between 6th (Ave of the Americas) and 7th aves. Int corridors. **Pets:** Accepted.

AAA ▼▼▼▼ Four Seasons Hotel New York H
(212) 758-5700. **$595-$1650.** 57 E 57th St 10022. Between Park and Madison aves. Int corridors. **Pets:** Accepted.

▼▼▼▼ The Franklin Hotel H
(212) 369-1000. **Call for rates.** 164 E 87th St 10128. Between 3rd and Lexington aves. Int corridors. **Pets:** Medium. Service with restrictions.

▼▼ ▼▼ ▼▼ Gansevoort Meatpacking NYC H
(212) 660-6700. **Call for rates.** 18 9th Ave 10014. At 13th St. Int corridors. **Pets:** Accepted.

▼▼ ▼▼ The Gracie Inn BB 🐾
(212) 628-1700. **$149-$399, 3 day notice.** 502 E 81st St 10028. Between York and East End aves. Int corridors. **Pets:** Small. $100 deposit/room. Service with restrictions, crate.

AAA ▼▼▼▼ Hampton Inn-Madison Square Garden Area H
(212) 947-9700. **$149-$429.** 116 W 31st St 10001. Between 6th (Ave of the Americas) and 7th aves. Int corridors. **Pets:** Accepted.

AAA ▼▼▼▼ Hampton Inn-Manhattan/Chelsea H
(212) 414-1000. **$149-$429.** 108 W 24th St 10011. Between 6th (Ave of the Americas) and 7th aves. Int corridors. **Pets:** Accepted.

AAA ▼▼▼▼ Hampton Inn-Manhattan/Seaport/Financial District H
(212) 571-4400. **$149-$429.** 320 Pearl St 10038. Between deck slip and Dover St. Int corridors. **Pets:** Accepted.

AAA ▼▼▼▼ Hampton Inn Manhattan/Times Square South H
(212) 967-2344. **$179-$389.** 337 W 39th St 10018. Between 8th and 9th aves. Int corridors. **Pets:** Accepted.

▼▼▼▼ Hampton Inn/New York-35th Street/Empire State Bldg H
(212) 564-3688. **Call for rates.** 59 W 35th St 10001. Between 5th and 6th (Ave of the Americas) aves. Int corridors. **Pets:** Accepted.

▼▼▼▼ Hilton Club New York H
(646) 459-6500. **$369-$899.** 1335 Ave of the Americas, 37th Floor 10019. At W 54th St; between 6th (Ave of the Americas) and 7th aves. Int corridors. **Pets:** Small. $75 one-time fee/pet. Service with restrictions, supervision.

▼▼▼▼ Hilton New York H
(212) 586-7000. **$239-$589.** 1335 Ave of the Americas 10019. Between 53rd and 54th sts. Int corridors. **Pets:** Accepted.

AAA ▼▼▼▼ Hilton Times Square H
(212) 840-8222. **$179-$799.** 234 W 42nd St 10036. Between 7th and 8th aves. Int corridors. **Pets:** Large, other species. $75 one-time fee/pet. Service with restrictions, crate.

▼▼▼▼ Holiday Inn Express Fifth Ave H
(212) 302-9088. **$159-$499.** 15 W 45th St 10036. At 5th Ave. Int corridors. **Pets:** Accepted.

▼▼▼▼ Holiday Inn NYC/Manhattan 6th Avenue H
(212) 430-8500. **$199-$599.** 125 W 26th St 10001. Between 6th (Ave of the Americas) and 7th aves. Int corridors. **Pets:** Accepted.

AAA ▼▼▼▼ Hotel 36 H
(212) 542-8990. **$159-$549.** 341 W 36th St 10018. Between 8th and 9th aves. Int corridors. **Pets:** Accepted.

AAA ▼▼ ▼▼ Hotel 373 Fifth Avenue H
(212) 213-3388. **Call for rates.** 373 Fifth Ave 10016. Jct 35th St. Int corridors. **Pets:** Accepted.

▼▼▼▼ Hotel Indigo New York City-Chelsea H
(212) 973-9000. **$199-$599.** 127 W 28th St 10001. Between 6th (Ave of the Americas) and 7th aves. Int corridors. **Pets:** Accepted.

AAA ▼▼▼ Hotel Mela H
(212) 710-7000. **Call for rates.** 120 W 44th St 10036. Between Broadway and 6th Ave (Ave of the Americas). Int corridors. **Pets:** Accepted.

▼▼▼ ▼▼▼ **Hotel Plaza Athenee** H
(212) 734-9100. **$920-$1390.** 37 E 64th St 10065. Between Madison and Park aves. Int corridors. **Pets:** Accepted. 🛰 🖪 🖵 🍴 ⌧

(AAA) ▼▼▼▼ **Hotel Wales** H
(212) 876-6000. **$195-$695.** 1295 Madison Ave 10128. Between 92nd and 93rd sts E. Int corridors. **Pets:** Accepted. SAVE 🛰 ⌧ 🖪 🍴

▼▼▼ ▼▼▼ **Ink 48 Hotel New York City** H
(212) 757-0088. **Call for rates.** 653 11th Ave 10036. Between 47th and 48th sts. Int corridors. **Pets:** Accepted. 🛰 ⌧ 🖵 🍴

(AAA) ▼▼▼▼ **InterContinental New York Barclay** H
(212) 755-5900. **Call for rates.** 111 E 48th St 10017. Between Park and Lexington aves. Int corridors. **Pets:** Accepted.
SAVE 🛰 ⌧ 🖪 🖵 🍴 ⌧

(AAA) ▼▼▼ ▼▼ **Intercontinental New York Times Square** H
(212) 803-4500. **Call for rates.** 300 W 44th St 10036. Between 8th and 9th aves. Int corridors. **Pets:** Accepted.
SAVE 🛰 ⌧ &M 🖪 🖵 🍴

▼▼▼ ▼▼▼ **Jumeirah Essex House** H
(212) 247-0300. **Call for rates.** 160 Central Park S 10019. Between 6th (Ave of the Americas) and 7th aves. Int corridors. **Pets:** Accepted.
🛰 ⌧ &M 🖪 🖵 🍴 ⌧

▼▼▼ ▼▼▼ **The Kimberly A Boutique Hotel** H
(212) 702-1600. **$299-$1650.** 145 E 50th St 10022. Between 3rd and Lexington aves. Int corridors. **Pets:** Accepted. 🛰 🖪 🖵 🍴 ⌧

▼▼▼ ▼▼▼ **Le Parker Meridien New York** H 🐾
(212) 245-5000. **$289-$1129.** 118 W 57th St 10019. Between 6th (Ave of the Americas) and 7th aves; vehicle entrance on 56th St. Int corridors. **Pets:** Other species. $50 daily fee/room. Service with restrictions, supervision. 🛰 ⌧ 🖪 🍴 ⇌ ⌧

(AAA) ▼▼▼ ▼▼ **Loews Regency Hotel** H 🐾
(212) 759-4100. **$519-$4500.** 540 Park Ave 10021. At 61st St. Int corridors. **Pets:** Other species. $25 one-time fee/room.
SAVE 🛰 ⌧ &M 🖪 🖵 🍴 ⌧

▼▼▼ ▼▼▼ **The London NYC** H
(212) 307-5000. **Call for rates.** 151 W 54th St 10019. Between 6th (Ave of the Americas) and 7th aves. Int corridors. **Pets:** Accepted.
🛰 🖪 🍴

▼▼▼ ▼▼▼ **The Lowell Hotel** H 🐾
(212) 838-1400. **$625-$985, 3 day notice.** 28 E 63rd St 10021. Between Park and Madison aves. Int corridors. **Pets:** Large. $200 one-time fee/room. 🛰 🖪 🖵 🍴 ⌧

(AAA) ▼▼▼▼▼ **Mandarin Oriental, New York** H 🐾
(212) 805-8800. **Call for rates.** 80 Columbus Cir at 60th St 10023. At 60th St. Int corridors. **Pets:** Small, dogs only. Designated rooms, crate.
SAVE 🛰 🍴 ⇌

(AAA) ▼▼▼ ▼▼ **The Manhattan at Times Square** H
(212) 581-3300. **$170-$579.** 790 7th Ave 10019. Between 51st and 52nd sts. Int corridors. **Pets:** Accepted. SAVE 🛰 ⌧ 🖪 🖵 ⇌

▼▼▼ ▼▼▼ **The Mansfield** H
(212) 277-8700. **$169-$899.** 12 W 44th St 10036. Between 5th and 6th (Ave of the Americas) aves. Int corridors. **Pets:** Accepted. 🛰 🍴

▼▼▼ ▼▼▼ **Millennium Broadway Hotel, Times Square, New York** H
(212) 768-4400. **$179-$599.** 145 W 44th St 10036. Between 6th Ave (Ave of the Americas) and Broadway; in Times Square. Int corridors. **Pets:** Accepted. 🛰 &M 🖵 🍴

▼▼▼ ▼▼▼ **Mondrian Soho** H
(212) 389-1000. **Call for rates.** 9 Crosby St 10013. Just s of Grand St. Int corridors. **Pets:** Accepted. 🛰 🖵

(AAA) ▼▼▼ ▼▼ **The Muse Hotel** H 🐾
(212) 485-2400. **Call for rates.** 130 W 46th St 10036. Between 6th (Ave of the Americas) and 7th aves. Int corridors. **Pets:** Other species. Service with restrictions. ECO SAVE 🛰 ⌧ 🖵 🍴 ⌧

(AAA) ▼▼▼ ▼▼ **The New York Helmsley Hotel** H 🐾
(212) 490-8900. **$199-$699.** 212 E 42nd St 10017. Between 2nd and 3rd aves. Int corridors. **Pets:** Medium, dogs only. $50 one-time fee/room. Service with restrictions. SAVE 🛰 ⌧ 🖪 🍴

▼▼▼ ▼▼▼ **New York Marriott Marquis** H
(212) 398-1900. **$279-$649.** 1535 Broadway 10036. Between 45th and 46th sts; motor entrance on 46th St. Int corridors. **Pets:** Accepted.
🛰 ⌧ 🖪 🖵 🍴

▼▼▼ ▼▼▼ **The New York Palace** H 🐾
(212) 888-7000. **Call for rates.** 455 Madison Ave 10022. Between 50th and 51st sts. Int corridors. **Pets:** Small, dogs only. Service with restrictions, supervision. 🛰 ⌧ &M 🖪 🖵 🍴 ⌧

(AAA) ▼▼▼▼ **Novotel New York Times Square** H
(212) 315-0100. **Call for rates.** 226 W 52nd St 10019. At Broadway. Int corridors. **Pets:** Accepted. SAVE 🛰 &M 🖪 🍴

(AAA) ▼▼▼ ▼▼ **Omni Berkshire Place** H
(212) 753-5800. **$259-$799.** 21 E 52nd St 10022. Between Madison and 5th aves. Int corridors. **Pets:** Accepted.
SAVE 🛰 ⌧ &M 🖪 🍴 ⌧

(AAA) ▼▼▼ ▼▼ **On The Ave Hotel** H 🐾
(212) 362-1100. **$169-$699.** 2178 Broadway 10024. At 77th St. Int corridors. **Pets:** Medium. $40 daily fee/pet. Designated rooms, service with restrictions, supervision. SAVE 🛰 ⌧ 🖵 🍴

(AAA) ▼▼▼ ▼▼ **The Paramount Hotel New York** H
(212) 764-5500. **$149-$599.** 235 W 46th St 10036. Between Broadway and 8th Ave. Int corridors. **Pets:** Accepted. SAVE 🛰 ⌧ 🍴

(AAA) ▼▼▼ ▼▼ **The Peninsula New York** H 🐾
(212) 956-2888. **$595-$995.** 700 5th Ave 10019. At 55th St. Int corridors. **Pets:** Medium. SAVE 🛰 🖪 🖵 🍴 ⇌ ⌧

(AAA) ▼▼▼ ▼▼ **The Pierre New York-A Taj Hotel** H
(212) 838-8000. **$795-$1045, 3 day notice.** 2 E 61st St 10065. At 5th Ave. Int corridors. **Pets:** Accepted. ECO SAVE 🛰 &M 🖪 🍴 ⌧

(AAA) ▼▼▼ ▼▼ **The Plaza Hotel** H
(212) 759-3000. **$595-$1295.** 5th Ave at Central Park S 10019. Corner of 5th Ave and Central Park S. Int corridors. **Pets:** Accepted.
SAVE 🛰 ⌧ &M 🖪 🖵 🍴 ⌧

(AAA) ▼▼▼ ▼▼ **Radisson Martinique on Broadway** H 🐾
(212) 736-3800. **$230-$499.** 49 W 32nd St 10001. Between Broadway and 5th Ave. Int corridors. **Pets:** Small, dogs only. $25 daily fee/pet. Service with restrictions, supervision.
SAVE 🛰 &M 🖪 🖵 🍴 ⌧

▼▼▼ ▼▼ **Renaissance New York Hotel 57** H
(212) 753-8841. **$199-$599.** 130 E 57th St 10022. At Lexington Ave. Int corridors. **Pets:** Accepted. 🛰 ⌧ 🖪 🖵 🍴

(AAA) ▼▼▼ ▼▼ **Renaissance New York Hotel Times Square** H
(212) 765-7676. **$399-$769.** 2 Times Square, 7th Ave at W 48th St 10036. At Broadway and 7th Ave; auto access from 7th Ave, s of W 48th St. Int corridors. **Pets:** Accepted. SAVE 🛰 ⌧ 🖵 🍴

Residence Inn by Marriott Manhattan/Times Square H
(212) 768-0007. **$229-$649.** 1033 6th Ave (Ave of the Americas) 10018. Between 38th and 39th sts. Int corridors. **Pets:** Accepted.

The Ritz-Carlton New York, Battery Park H
(212) 344-0800. **$295-$695, 3 day notice.** Two West St 10004. Jct Battery Pl. Int corridors. **Pets:** Accepted.

The Ritz-Carlton New York, Central Park H ❀
(212) 308-9100. **$625-$1905.** 50 Central Park S 10019. Jct 59th St (Central Park S) and 6th Ave (Ave of the Americas). Int corridors. **Pets:** Medium. $75 one-time fee/room.

Royalton Hotel H
(212) 869-4400. **Call for rates.** 44 W 44th St 10036. Between 5th and 6th (Ave of the Americas) aves. Int corridors. **Pets:** Accepted.

Sheraton New York Hotel & Towers H
(212) 581-1000. **$199-$699.** 811 7th Ave 10019. At 52nd St. Int corridors. **Pets:** Accepted.

Sheraton Tribeca New York Hotel H
(212) 966-3400. **$129-$599.** 370 Canal St 10013. Just e of Broadway. Int corridors. **Pets:** Accepted.

The Shoreham Hotel H
(212) 247-6700. **Call for rates.** 33 W 55th St 10019. Between 5th and 6th (Ave of the Americas) aves. Int corridors. **Pets:** Accepted.

Skyline Hotel H ❀
(212) 586-3400. **$119-$450.** 725 10th Ave 10019. At 49th and 50th sts. Int corridors. **Pets:** $200 deposit/room. Service with restrictions, crate.

Sofitel New York H ❀
(212) 354-8844. **Call for rates.** 45 W 44th St 10036. Between 5th and 6th (Ave of the Americas) aves. Int corridors. **Pets:** $300 deposit/pet.

The SoHo Grand Hotel H
(212) 965-3000. **Call for rates.** 310 W Broadway 10013. In SoHo; jct Grand St. Int corridors. **Pets:** Accepted.

Staybridge Suites Times Square H ❀
(212) 757-9000. **$199-$499.** 340 W 40th St 10018. Between 8th and 9th aves. Int corridors. **Pets:** Small, other species. $150 one-time fee/room. Service with restrictions, crate.

The Surrey H ❀
(212) 288-3700. **Call for rates.** 20 E 76th St 10021. Jct E 76th St and Madison Ave. Int corridors. **Pets:** Medium. $100 one-time fee/room. Service with restrictions, supervision.

Trump International Hotel & Tower H ❀
(212) 299-1000. **$825-$950, 3 day notice.** 1 Central Park W 10023. Jct Central Park S; at Columbus Cir. Int corridors. **Pets:** Small, dogs only. $250 one-time fee/room. No service.

The Waldorf=Astoria H
(212) 355-3000. **$279-$899.** 301 Park Ave 10022. Between E 49th and 50th sts. Int corridors. **Pets:** Accepted.

The Westin New York at Times Square H
(212) 201-2700. **$199-$899.** 270 W 43rd St 10036. Corner of 8th Ave. Int corridors. **Pets:** Accepted.

W New York H
(212) 755-1200. **$229-$849.** 541 Lexington Ave 10022. At 49th St. Int corridors. **Pets:** Accepted.

W New York Downtown H ❀
(646) 826-8600. **$249-$789.** 123 Washington St 10006. At Albany St. Int corridors. **Pets:** Medium. $100 one-time fee/room, $25 daily fee/room. Service with restrictions.

W New York Times Square H
(212) 930-7400. **$269-$899.** 1567 Broadway at 47th St 10036. Corner of 47th St. Int corridors. **Pets:** Accepted.

W New York-Union Square H ❀
(212) 253-9119. **$299-$999.** 201 Park Ave S 10003. At 17th St. Int corridors. **Pets:** Medium, other species. $100 one-time fee/room, $25 daily fee/room. Designated rooms.

ORANGEBURG

Holiday Inn H
(845) 359-7000. **$115-$195.** 329 Rt 303 10962. I-87/287 exit 12, 3.2 mi s; 1 mi n of Palisades Interstate Pkwy exit 5 northbound; 1 mi e of exit 6. Int corridors. **Pets:** Accepted.

RYE BROOK

Hilton Rye Town H ❀
(914) 939-6300. **Call for rates.** 699 Westchester Ave 10573. I-287 (Cross Westchester Expwy) exit 10 eastbound, 0.6 mi ne on SR 120A; exit westbound, 0.3 mi n on Webb Ave, then 0.4 mi ne on SR 120A. Int corridors. **Pets:** Medium, dogs only. $50 one-time fee/room. Designated rooms, service with restrictions, supervision.

STATEN ISLAND

Hilton Garden Inn Staten Island H
(718) 477-2400. **Call for rates.** 1100 South Ave 10314. I-278 exit 6 (South Ave) westbound, just s; exit 5 eastbound to SR 440 S to South Ave exit, just s, 1 mi n to Lois Ln, then just w. Int corridors. **Pets:** Accepted.

SUFFERN

Crowne Plaza Hotel and Conference Center H
(845) 357-4800. **$126-$159.** 3 Executive Blvd 10901. I-87 (New York State Thruway) exit 14B, just n. Int corridors. **Pets:** Medium, dogs only. $50 one-time fee/room. Designated rooms, service with restrictions.

TARRYTOWN

Sheraton Tarrytown Hotel H
(914) 332-7900. **$89-$299.** 600 White Plains Rd 10591. I-87 exit 9 northbound, 0.8 mi e on SR 119; exit southbound, just n on US 9, then 1 mi e on SR 119. Int corridors. **Pets:** Accepted.

Westchester Marriott Hotel H
(914) 631-2200. **$129-$299.** 670 White Plains Rd 10591. I-87 (New York State Thruway) exit 9 northbound, 0.8 mi e on SR 119; exit southbound, just n on US 9, then 1 mi e on SR 119. Int corridors. **Pets:** Accepted.

WHITE PLAINS

Hyatt house White Plains H

(914) 251-9700. **$119-$279.** 101 Corporate Park Dr 10604. I-287 (Cross Westchester Expwy) exit 9A eastbound, 0.6 mi e on Westchester Ave, then 0.3 mi n; exit 9N-S westbound, 0.9 mi w on Westchester Ave. Int corridors. **Pets:** Other species. $50 one-time fee/pet. Service with restrictions.

Residence Inn by Marriott White Plains H

(914) 761-7700. **$227-$239.** 5 Barker Ave 10601. I-287 exit 6 westbound, w on service road to SR 22 (Broadway), 0.8 mi s to Barker Ave, then 0.5 mi w; exit eastbound, s on Broadway. Int corridors.
Pets: Accepted.

The Ritz-Carlton, Westchester H

(914) 946-5500. **$229-$669.** 3 Renaissance Square 10601. Jct SR 22, just w on Main St, then just n. Int corridors. **Pets:** Accepted.

END METROPOLITAN AREA

NIAGARA FALLS METROPOLITAN AREA

LOCKPORT

Comfort Inn H

(716) 434-4411. **$60-$160.** 551 S Transit St 14094. 1 mi s on SR 78. Int corridors. **Pets:** Medium. $10 daily fee/pet. Service with restrictions, supervision.

Holiday Inn Lockport H

(716) 434-6151. **$95-$150, 3 day notice.** 515 S Transit St 14094. 1 mi s on SR 78. Int corridors. **Pets:** Accepted.

NEWFANE

Lake Ontario Motel M

(716) 778-5004. **$65-$100, 5 day notice.** 3330 Lockport-Olcott Rd 14108. 2.5 mi n of jct SR 104 on SR 78. Int corridors. **Pets:** Other species. $5 daily fee/room. Service with restrictions, supervision.

NIAGARA FALLS

Four Points by Sheraton Niagara Falls H

(716) 299-0344. **$65-$300.** 7001 Buffalo Ave 14304. I-190 exit 21 (Robert Moses Pkwy), just e. Int corridors. **Pets:** Accepted.

Holiday Inn Express Niagara Falls H

(716) 298-4500. **$89-$499.** 10111 Niagara Falls Blvd 14304. I-190 exit 22, 2.1 mi e on US 62. Int corridors. **Pets:** Accepted.

Motel 6 M

(716) 297-9902. **$45-$250.** 9100 Niagara Falls 14304. I-190 exit 22, 1.8 mi e. Int corridors. **Pets:** Other species. Service with restrictions, supervision.

Quality Hotel & Suites "At the Falls" H

(716) 282-1212. **$60-$160.** 240 First St 14303. I-190 exit 21 (Robert Moses Pkwy) eastbound to City Traffic exit, just w; downtown. Int corridors. **Pets:** Medium. $30 daily fee/pet. Service with restrictions, supervision.

Sheraton At The Falls H 🐾

(716) 285-3361. **$119-$299.** 300 3rd St 14303. I-190 exit 21 (Robert Moses Pkwy), to City Traffic exit, just w on Rainbow Blvd, then just n. Int corridors. **Pets:** Medium, dogs only. Service with restrictions.

END METROPOLITAN AREA

NORTH SYRACUSE

Best Western Syracuse Airport Inn H

(315) 455-7362. **$100-$160.** 900 Col. Eileen Collins Blvd 13212. I-81 exit 27 (Syracuse Hancock International Airport). Int corridors. **Pets:** Accepted.

Candlewood Suites Syracuse Airport H 🐾

(315) 454-8999. **$79-$189.** 5414 South Bay Rd 13212. I-90 exit 36; I-81 exit 26 (Mattydale Rd), follow South Bay Rd signs, just n. Int corridors. **Pets:** Other species. $10 daily fee/pet. No service.

Comfort Inn & Suites/Syracuse Airport H

(315) 457-4000. **$89-$189.** 6701 Buckley Rd 13212. I-81 exit 25 (7th North St), just w. Int corridors. **Pets:** Accepted.

NORWICH

Super 8 of Norwich H

(607) 336-8880. **$50-$81.** 6067 State Hwy 12 13815. On SR 12, 0.9 mi n. Int corridors. **Pets:** Accepted.

OGDENSBURG

Quality Inn Gran-View M

(315) 393-4550. **$101-$275.** 6765 State Hwy 37 13669. On SR 37, 3 mi sw. Ext/int corridors. **Pets:** Large, other species. $10 daily fee/pet. Designated rooms, service with restrictions, supervision.

The Stonefence Resort & Motel M

(315) 393-1545. **$70-$210.** 7191 SR 37 13669. Jct SR 68, 0.5 mi w. Ext/int corridors. **Pets:** Accepted.

Windjammer Lodge M

(315) 393-6300. **$80-$175.** 5843 SR 37 13669. On SR 37, 5 mi sw. Ext corridors. **Pets:** Large, other species. $10 daily fee/room. Service with restrictions, supervision.

OLD FORGE

Adirondack Lodge Old Forge M

(315) 369-6836. **$59-$299, 7 day notice.** 2752 SR 28 13420. 0.3 mi s. Ext/int corridors. **Pets:** Large, dogs only. $25 one-time fee/room. Designated rooms, service with restrictions, supervision.

ONEIDA

Super 8-Oneida H

(315) 363-5168. **$54-$108.** 215 Genesee St 13421. I-90 exit 33, 4 mi s on SR 365 to SR 5, then 0.5 mi w. Int corridors. **Pets:** Accepted.

ONEONTA

Holiday Inn Oneonta/Cooperstown Area H

(607) 433-2250. **$89-$239.** 5206 State Hwy 23 13820-0634. I-88 exit 15 (SR 23 and 28), 1.5 mi e. Int corridors. **Pets:** Accepted.

Super 8 H

(607) 432-9505. **$55-$94.** 4973 SR 23 13820. I-88 exit 15 (SR 23 and 28), 0.3 mi e. Int corridors. **Pets:** $15 daily fee/pet. Service with restrictions, supervision.

OSWEGO

Quality Inn & Suites - Riverfront H

(315) 343-1600. **$99-$190.** 70 E 1st St 13126. Just n on SR 481. Int corridors. **Pets:** Small. $10 daily fee/pet. Designated rooms, service with restrictions, supervision.

PAINTED POST

Americas Best Value Inn Lodge on the Green M

(607) 962-2456. **$76-$160.** 196 S Hamilton St 14870. I-86/SR 17 exit 44B eastbound; exit 44A westbound; US 15 exit 3, 1 mi n. Ext corridors. **Pets:** Dogs only. $10 one-time fee/room. Service with restrictions, supervision.

Econo Lodge H

(607) 962-4444. **$79-$149.** 200 Robert Dann Dr 14870. I-86/SR 17 exit 44A westbound; exit 44B eastbound; US 15 N exit 3 (Gang Mills), just n on Hamilton St, then just w. Int corridors. **Pets:** $10 daily fee/pet. Service with restrictions, supervision.

Erwin Motel M

(607) 962-7411. **$29-$129.** 806 Addison Rd 14870. US 15 exit 2, just e on SR 417. Ext corridors. **Pets:** Medium, dogs only. $10 daily fee/pet. Designated rooms, service with restrictions, supervision.

Ramada H

(607) 962-5021. **$52-$223, 7 day notice.** 304 S Hamilton St 14870. I-86/SR 17 exit 44, to US 15 S; exit 3 (Gang Mills), just n. Int corridors. **Pets:** Large, other species. $50 deposit/pet, $15 daily fee/pet. Service with restrictions, supervision.

PEMBROKE

Darien Lakes Econo Lodge H

(585) 599-4681. **$63-$160.** 8493 Alleghany Rd 14036. I-90 exit 48A, just s. Int corridors. **Pets:** Accepted.

PENN YAN

Best Western Plus Vineyard Inn & Suites H

(315) 536-8473. **$110-$153.** 142 Lake St 14527. I-90 exit 43, SR 14 S to SR 54 N; corner of SR 54 and 14A. Int corridors. **Pets:** Other species. $20 daily fee/pet. Designated rooms, service with restrictions, supervision.

PINE VALLEY

Rodeway Inn Marshall Manor M

(607) 739-3891. **$89-$180.** 3527 Watkins Rd 14845. I-86 exit 52B, 5 mi n on SR 14. Ext corridors. **Pets:** Other species. $20 daily fee/room. Designated rooms, service with restrictions, crate.

PITTSFORD

Brookwood Inn Rochester/Pittsford H

(585) 248-9000. **Call for rates.** 800 Pittsford-Victor Rd 14534. I-490 exit 27 (Bushnell's Basin/SR 96), just n. Int corridors. **Pets:** Large, dogs only. $75 one-time fee/room. Designated rooms, service with restrictions, supervision.

PLAINVIEW

Homewood Suites Long Island Melville H

(516) 293-4663. **$209-$249.** 1585 Round Swamp Rd 11803. I-495 exit 48, just s. Int corridors. **Pets:** Accepted.

Residence Inn Plainview Long Island H

(516) 433-6200. **$225-$235.** 9 Gerhard Rd 11803. I-495 exit 44, 1.6 mi s on SR 135 exit 10, then just e on Old Country Rd. Int corridors. **Pets:** Small, dogs only. $100 one-time fee/room. Service with restrictions, supervision.

PLATTSBURGH

Best Western The Inn at Smithfield H

(518) 561-7750. **$100-$180.** 446 Rt 3 12901. I-87 exit 37, just e. Int corridors. **Pets:** $5 daily fee/room. Designated rooms, service with restrictions, crate.

La Quinta Inn & Suites Plattsburgh H

(518) 562-4000. **$79-$156.** 16 Plaza Blvd 12901. I-87 exit 37, just w. Int corridors. **Pets:** Medium, other species. Service with restrictions, supervision.

Microtel Inn & Suites H

(518) 324-3800. **$80-$134.** 554 SR 3 12901. I-87 exit 37, just w. Int corridors. **Pets:** Medium. $10 daily fee/room. Supervision.

POUGHKEEPSIE

Clarion Hotel & Conference Center H

(845) 462-4600. **$80-$229.** 2170 South Rd (Rt 9) 12601. I-84 exit 13N, 4.7 mi s of Mid-Hudson Bridge. Int corridors. **Pets:** Medium, dogs only. $100 deposit/pet, $25 daily fee/pet. Designated rooms, service with restrictions, supervision.

Days Inn M

(845) 454-1010. **$99-$198.** 536 Haight Ave 12603. 2 mi e of Mid-Hudson Bridge on US 44 and SR 55. Ext/int corridors. **Pets:** $30 one-time fee/pet. Designated rooms, service with restrictions.

Poughkeepsie Inn M

(845) 452-6600. **$65-$130.** 2625 South Rd 12601. I-84 exit 13, 10.7 mi n on US 9. Ext corridors. **Pets:** Dogs only. $50 deposit/pet, $25 daily fee/pet. Service with restrictions, supervision.

QUEENSBURY

Quality Inn of Glens Falls H

(518) 793-3800. **Call for rates.** 547 Aviation Rd 12804. I-87 exit 19, just e. Int corridors. **Pets:** Accepted.

RHINEBECK

Beekman Arms & Delamater Inn and Conference Center CI

(845) 876-7077. **$120-$300, 14 day notice.** 6387 Mill St (Rt 9) 12572. Jct US 9 and SR 308; center of village. Ext/int corridors. **Pets:** Small, other species. $15 daily fee/pet. Designated rooms, service with restrictions, supervision.

RIVERHEAD

◆◆◆ Holiday Inn Express East End 🄷
(631) 548-1000. **Call for rates.** 1707 Old Country Rd (SR 58) 11901.
I-495 exit 73, 0.5 mi e. Int corridors. **Pets:** Accepted.
🖥 🄜 🛏 🖳 🏊

◆◆◆ Hotel Indigo East End 🄷
(631) 369-2200. **$149-$399, 3 day notice.** 1830 SR 25 11901. I-495
exit 72 (SR 25 E). Int corridors. **Pets:** Accepted.
🖥 ⊠ 🖳 🍴 🏊

ROCHESTER

◆◆ La Quinta Inn Rochester North 🄷
(585) 254-1000. **$82-$153.** 1956 Lyell Ave 14606. I-390 exit 21 (SR 31),
just e. Int corridors. **Pets:** Medium, other species. Service with restrictions,
supervision. 🖥 🛏 🖳

◆◆◆ Radisson Hotel Rochester Riverside 🄷
(585) 546-6400. **$99-$199.** 120 E Main St 14604. Downtown. Int corridors. **Pets:** Medium. $25 one-time fee/room. Designated rooms, service
with restrictions, crate. 🖥 🄜 🛏 🖳 🍴

◍ ◆◆◆ Rochester Plaza Hotel & Conference
Center 🄷
(585) 546-3450. **$99-$149.** 70 State St 14614. Jct Main St; downtown.
Int corridors. **Pets:** Accepted. SAVE 🖥 🛏 🖳 🍴 🏊

◍ ◆◆◆ Strathallan Hotel 🄷
(585) 461-5010. **$126-$169.** 550 East Ave 14607. I-490 exit 17, 0.8 mi n
on Goodman St, then just w. Int corridors. **Pets:** Accepted.
SAVE 🖥 ⊠ 🄜 🛏 🖳 🍴

ROCKVILLE CENTRE

◍ ◆◆◆ Best Western Mill River Manor 🄷
(516) 678-1300. **$100-$160.** 173 Sunrise Hwy 11570. On SR 27;
between N Village and N Centre aves. Ext corridors. **Pets:** $15 daily
fee/room. Service with restrictions, crate.
SAVE 🖥 🄜 🛏 🖳 🍴 🏊

ROME

◆◆ Econo Lodge 🄼
(315) 337-9400. **Call for rates.** 145 E Whitesboro St 13440. Just s of jct
SR 26 (Turin Rd) and 46. Ext corridors. **Pets:** Accepted. 🖥 🛏 🖳

◍ ◆◆◆ Inn at the Beeches 🄼 ☙
(315) 336-1775. **$95-$295.** 7900 Turin Rd 13440. Jct SR 46, 2 mi n on
SR 26 (Turin Rd). Ext corridors. **Pets:** Other species. $10 daily fee/pet.
Designated rooms, service with restrictions, crate.
SAVE 🖥 🛏 🖳 🍴 🏊

◍ ◆◆◆ Quality Inn of Rome 🄷
(315) 336-4300. **$90-$140.** 200 S James St 13440. On SR 49; downtown. Ext/int corridors. **Pets:** $25 daily fee/pet. Designated rooms, service
with restrictions, supervision. SAVE 🖥 🛏 🖳 🍴 🏊

ROSCOE

◍ ◆◆ Roscoe Motel 🄼
(607) 498-5220. **$70-$85, 7 day notice.** 2054 Old Rt 17 12776. SR 17
exit 94, 0.5 mi n on SR 206, then just w. Ext corridors. **Pets:** Accepted.
SAVE 🖥 ⊠ 🛏 🖳

SACKETS HARBOR

◆◆ Ontario Place Hotel 🄷 ☙
(315) 646-8000. **$89-$370.** 103 General Smith Dr 13685. Corner of W
Main St; center. Int corridors. **Pets:** Other species. $25 one-time fee/
room. Designated rooms, service with restrictions. 🖥 ⊠ 🛏 🖳

SALAMANCA

◆◆◆ Holiday Inn Express Hotel & Suites 🄷 ☙
(716) 945-7600. **$140-$229.** 779 Broad St 14779. I-86 exit 20, just n. Int
corridors. **Pets:** Other species. $25 one-time fee/room. Designated rooms,
service with restrictions, crate. 🖥 🄜 🛏 🖳 🏊

SARANAC LAKE

◆ Adirondack Motel 🄼
(518) 891-2116. **$79-$265.** 248 Lake Flower Ave 12983. 0.7 mi e on SR
86. Ext corridors. **Pets:** Dogs only. $10 daily fee/pet. Service with restric-
tions, supervision. 🖥 ⊠ 🛏 🖳 ⊠

◍ ◆◆◆ Best Western Mountain Lake Inn 🄷
(518) 891-1970. **$89-$239.** 487 Lake Flower Ave 12983. 0.8 mi e on SR
86. Int corridors. **Pets:** Other species. $20 one-time fee/room. Designated
rooms, service with restrictions, supervision.
SAVE 🖥 🄜 🛏 🖳 🍴 🏊

◆ Lake Flower Inn 🄼
(518) 891-2310. **Call for rates.** 234 Lake Flower Ave 12983. 0.6 mi e
on SR 86. Ext corridors. **Pets:** Accepted. 🖥 ⊠ 🛏 🏊 ⊠

◆ Lake Side Motel 🄼
(518) 891-4333. **$89-$149, 7 day notice.** 256 Lake Flower Ave 12983.
0.6 mi e on SR 86. Ext corridors. **Pets:** Accepted.
🖥 ⊠ 🛏 🏊 ⊠

SARATOGA SPRINGS

◆◆◆ Adelphi Hotel 🄷
(518) 587-4688. **$135-$570, 14 day notice.** 365 Broadway 12866.
Between Division and Washington sts; center. Int corridors.
Pets: Accepted. 🖥 ⊠ 🏊

◍ ◆◆◆ Best Western Plus Park Inn 🄷
(518) 584-2350. **$100-$370.** 3291 S Broadway 12866. I-87 exit 13N, 1.1
mi n on US 9. Int corridors. **Pets:** Accepted.
SAVE 🖥 🄜 🛏 🖳 🏊

◍ ◆◆◆ Comfort Inn & Suites 🄷
(518) 587-6244. **$95-$369.** 17 Old Gick Rd 12866. I-87 exit 15, just e,
then just n. Int corridors. **Pets:** Accepted.
SAVE 🖥 ⊠ 🄜 🛏 🖳 🏊

◆◆◆ Holiday Inn 🄷
(518) 584-4550. **$140-$400.** 232 Broadway 12866. On US 9, jct SR 50.
Int corridors. **Pets:** Accepted. 🖥 🛏 🖳 🍴 🏊

◆◆◆ Residence Inn by Marriott-Saratoga
Springs 🄷 ☙
(518) 584-9600. **$139-$409.** 295 Excelsior Ave 12866. I-87 exit 15, just
n, just s, then just e. Int corridors. **Pets:** Other species. $75 one-time
fee/room. Service with restrictions, crate.
🖥 ⊠ 🄜 🛏 🖳 🏊 ⊠

◆◆◆ Roosevelt Inn & Suites 🄷
(518) 584-0980. **$99-$495, 14 day notice.** 2961 S Broadway 12866.
I-87 exit 13N, just n. Ext/int corridors. **Pets:** Accepted.
🖥 🄜 🛏 🖳 🍴 🏊 ⊠

◆◆◆ The Saratoga Hilton 🄷
(518) 584-4000. **$99-$409.** 534 Broadway 12866. I-87 exit 15, on SR 50.
Int corridors. **Pets:** Accepted. 🖥 🛏 🖳 🍴 🏊

◆ Saratoga Motel 🄼
(518) 584-0920. **Call for rates.** 440 Church St 12866. On SR 9N, 2.3 mi
w of jct US 9/SR 50. Ext corridors. **Pets:** Accepted. 🛏 🖳

◆◆◆ Union Gables Bed & Breakfast 🄱🄱 ☙
(518) 584-1558. **$105-$225, 14 day notice.** 55 Union Ave 12866. I-87
exit 14, 1.5 mi w. Int corridors. **Pets:** $25 one-time fee/room. Service with
restrictions, supervision. 🖥 ⊠ 🛏 ✉

SAUGERTIES

AAA **WWW** Comfort Inn 🅷 ❄

(845) 246-1565. **Call for rates.** 2790 SR 32 12477. I-87 exit 20, just n. Int corridors. **Pets:** $10 daily fee/pet. Service with restrictions, supervision.
[SAVE] 🛜 🗄 💻

SCHENECTADY

WW Days Inn 🅷

(518) 370-3297. **$63-$251.** 167 Nott Terr 12308. Jct State St (SR 5) and Nott Terr, 2 blks e; downtown. Int corridors. **Pets:** Accepted.
🛜 🗄 💻

SCHOHARIE

WWWW Holiday Inn Express Hotel & Suites Schoharie 🅷

(518) 295-6088. **Call for rates.** 160 Holiday Way 12157. I-88 exit 23, just e to Park Pl, then just s. Int corridors. **Pets:** Accepted.
🛜 ♿M 🗄 💻

SENECA FALLS

AAA **WW** Microtel Inn & Suites 🅷

(315) 539-8438. **$54-$108.** 1966 Rt 5 & 20 13148. I-90 (New York State Thruway) exit 41, 4 mi s on SR 414, then just e. Int corridors. **Pets:** Other species. $15 daily fee/room. Supervision.
[SAVE] 🛜 ♿M 🗄 💻

SKANEATELES

WWWW Skaneateles Suites 🅼

(315) 685-7568. **$99-$175.** 4114 W Genesee St Rd 13152. On US 20, 2 mi w. Ext corridors. **Pets:** Other species. $35 one-time fee/pet. Service with restrictions, crate. 🛜 ✖ 🗄 💻

SOLVAY

WW Clarion Inn & Suites 🅷 ❄

(315) 457-8700. **$89-$139.** 100 Farrell Rd 13209. I-690 exit 4 (John Glenn Blvd). Int corridors. **Pets:** Medium. $25 one-time fee/room. Service with restrictions, supervision. 🛜 🗄 💻 🍴 ➿

SOUTHAMPTON

WW Southampton Inn 🅷 ❄

(631) 283-6500. **$159-$499, 30 day notice.** 91 Hill St 11968. 0.3 mi n from corner of Main St and Jobs Ln. Ext corridors. **Pets:** Other species. $40 daily fee/pet. Designated rooms, service with restrictions, supervision.
🛜 ✖ ♿M 🗄 ➿ ✖

SYLVAN BEACH

W Cinderella's Cafe & Suites 🅼

(315) 762-4280. **$59-$199, 15 day notice.** 1208 N Main St 13157. On SR 13; center. Ext corridors. **Pets:** Accepted. 🛜 ✖ 🗄 💻 🍴

SYRACUSE

AAA **WWWW** Crowne Plaza Hotel Syracuse 🅷

(315) 479-7000. **$149-$269.** 701 E Genesee St 13210. Jct Almond St; downtown. Int corridors. **Pets:** Accepted.
[SAVE] 🛜 ✖ ♿M 🗄 💻 🍴

AAA **WWWW** Sheraton Syracuse University Hotel & Conference Center 🅷

(315) 475-3000. **$145-$355.** 801 University Ave 13210. I-81 exit 18. Int corridors. **Pets:** Accepted. [ECO] [SAVE] 🛜 ✖ 🗄 💻 🍴 ➿

TICONDEROGA

WW Super 8-Ticonderoga 🅷 ❄

(518) 585-2617. **$56-$72.** 1144 Wicker St 12883. Jct SR 9N and 74. Int corridors. **Pets:** $20 one-time fee/pet. Designated rooms, service with restrictions, supervision. 🛜 🗄 💻

TROY

AAA **WWWW** Best Western Plus Franklin Square Inn 🅷 ❄

(518) 274-8800. **$60-$199.** One 4th St 12180. I-787 exit 8, just e on 23rd to Federal, just e to 4th St, then just s; downtown. Int corridors. **Pets:** Other species. $25 one-time fee/room. Service with restrictions.
[SAVE] 🛜 ✖ ♿M 🗄 💻

TULLY

AAA **WWWW** Best Western Tully Inn 🅷

(315) 696-6061. **$88-$200.** 5779 Rt 80 13159. I-81 exit 14, just e. Int corridors. **Pets:** Medium. $10 daily fee/pet. Designated rooms, service with restrictions, supervision. [SAVE] 🛜 💻

TUPPER LAKE

AAA **WW** Red Top Inn 🅼

(518) 359-9209. **$55-$95, 7 day notice.** 1562 SR 30 12986. 3 mi s. Ext/int corridors. **Pets:** Accepted. [SAVE] 🛜 🗄 💻 ✖

UTICA

WWWW Hotel Utica, an Ascend Collection hotel 🅷

(315) 724-7829. **$130-$180.** 102 Lafayette St 13502. I-90 (New York State Thruway) exit 31, 1.1 mi s on Genesee St; center. Int corridors. **Pets:** Small. $25 daily fee/pet. Service with restrictions, supervision.
🛜 🗄 💻 🍴

AAA **WWWW** Red Roof Inn #7180 🅼

(315) 724-7128. **$52-$150.** 20 Weaver St 13502. I-90 (New York State Thruway) exit 31. Ext corridors. **Pets:** Large, other species. No service, supervision. [SAVE] 🛜 💻

WWWW Rosemont Inn Bed & Breakfast 🅱🅱

(315) 797-9033. **$99-$179, 3 day notice.** 1423 Genesee St 13501. I-90 (New York State Thruway) exit 31, 2.5 mi s. Int corridors. **Pets:** Accepted.
🛜 ✖ 🧖

VALATIE

WW Blue Spruce Inn & Suites 🅼 ❄

(518) 758-9711. **$75-$105, 3 day notice.** 3093 Rt 9 12184. I-90 (New York State Thruway) exit 12, 4 mi s on US 9 via New York State Thruway Ext exit B1. Ext corridors. **Pets:** Medium. Service with restrictions, supervision. 🛜 🗄 ➿

VICTOR

AAA **WWWW** Best Western Plus Victor Inn & Suites 🅷

(585) 924-3933. **$80-$140.** 7449 SR 96 14564. I-90 (New York State Thruway) exit 45, 0.5 mi s. Int corridors. **Pets:** Small, dogs only. $35 daily fee/pet. Designated rooms, service with restrictions.
[SAVE] 🛜 ♿M 🗄 💻 ➿

AAA **WWWW** Hampton Inn & Suites-Rochester/Victor 🅷 ❄

(585) 924-4400. **$134-$199.** 7637 Pittsford-Victor Rd 14564. I-90 (New York State Thruway) exit 45, just n. Int corridors. **Pets:** Medium. Designated rooms, service with restrictions, supervision.
[SAVE] 🛜 ✖ 🗄 💻 ➿

WW Microtel Inn Victor 🅷

(585) 924-9240. **$53-$106.** 7498 Main St Fishers 14564. I-90 (New York State Thruway) exit 45, just s on SR 96, then just e. Int corridors. **Pets:** Accepted. 🛜 ✖ 🗄 💻

WARRENSBURG

WW Super 8 🅼 ❄

(518) 623-2811. **$63-$113.** 3619 SR 9 12845. I-87 exit 23, just w. Int corridors. **Pets:** Other species. $15 one-time fee/room. Crate.
🛜 🗄 💻

WATERLOO

△△△▽ **▼▼▼▼** Holiday Inn Waterloo-Seneca Falls **H**

(315) 539-5011. **$89-$199.** 2468 SR 414 13165. I-90 (New York State Thruway) exit 41, 4 mi s; just n of jct SR 414/5 and US 20. Int corridors. **Pets:** $15 daily fee/room. Service with restrictions, crate.
[SAVE] 🛜 [&M] 🔲 🖵 [†] 🏊 [✕]

WATERTOWN

△△△▽ **▼▼▼** Best Western Carriage House Inn **H** 🐾

(315) 782-8000. **Call for rates.** 300 Washington St 13601. Center. Int corridors. **Pets:** Other species. $15 daily fee/pet. Designated rooms, service with restrictions, supervision. [ECO] [SAVE] 🛜 🔲 🖵 [†] 🏊

▼▼▼▼ Comfort Inn & Suites **H** 🐾

(315) 782-2700. **$120-$150.** 110 Commerce Park Dr 13601. I-81 exit 45, 0.5 mi e. Int corridors. **Pets:** Medium, other species. $25 one-time fee/pet. Service with restrictions, crate. 🛜 🔲 🖵 🏊

WATKINS GLEN

△△△▽ **▼▼▼** Anchor Inn and Marina **M** 🐾

(607) 535-4159. **$69-$189, 10 day notice.** 3425 Salt Point Rd 14891. Just n on SR 14, 0.8 mi n. Ext corridors. **Pets:** Medium, dogs only. $25 deposit/pet. Service with restrictions, supervision.
[SAVE] 🛜 [✕] 🔲 [✕]

△△△▽ **▼▼▼** Chieftain Motel **M** 🐾

(607) 535-4759. **$69-$189, 10 day notice.** 3815 SR 14 14891. 3 mi n of town; on west side of SR 14. Ext corridors. **Pets:** Medium, dogs only. $25 deposit/pet. Service with restrictions, supervision.
[SAVE] 🛜 🔲 🖵

WELLSVILLE

▼▼▼ Microtel Inn & Suites **H**

(585) 593-3449. **$62-$109.** 30 W Dyke St 14895. Just n off SR 19 and 417. Int corridors. **Pets:** Accepted. 🛜 🔲 🖵

WEST COXSACKIE

△△△▽ **▼▼▼** Best Western New Baltimore Inn **H**

(518) 731-8100. **$80-$150.** 12600 Rt 9W 12192. I-87 (New York State Thruway) exit 21B, 0.5 mi s. Int corridors. **Pets:** Accepted.
[SAVE] 🛜 [✕] 🔲 🖵 🏊 [✕]

WILMINGTON

△△△▽ **▼▼▼** Hungry Trout Resort **M**

(518) 946-2217. **$79-$189, 7 day notice.** 5239 Rt 86 12997. On SR 86, 2 mi w. Ext corridors. **Pets:** Accepted.
[SAVE] 🛜 [✕] 🔲 🖵 [†] 🏊 [✕]

△△△▽ **▼▼▼** Ledge Rock at Whiteface **M**

(518) 946-2379. **$69-$179, 10 day notice.** 5078 NYS Rt 86 12997. On SR 86, 3 mi w. Ext corridors. **Pets:** $25 daily fee/pet. Designated rooms, service with restrictions, crate. [SAVE] 🛜 [✕] 🔲 🖵 🏊 [✕]

△△△▽ **▼▼▼** North Pole Inn **M** 🐾

(518) 946-7733. **$68-$199, 7 day notice.** 5636 NYS Rt 86 12997. On SR 86, just w of jct CR 431. Ext corridors. **Pets:** Dogs only. $2 one-time fee/pet. Designated rooms, service with restrictions, supervision.
[SAVE] 🛜 [✕] 🔲 🖵 🏊 [✕]

△△△▽ **▼▼▼** Willkommen Hof Bed & Breakfast **BB** 🐾

(518) 946-7669. **$70-$245, 14 day notice.** 5367 Rt 86 12997. On SR 86, 1.5 mi of jct CR 431. Int corridors. **Pets:** Other species. $50 deposit/pet, $10 daily fee/pet. Designated rooms, service with restrictions, crate.
[SAVE] 🛜 [✕] 🔲 🖵 [✕] [✑]

WOODBURY

△△△▽ **▼▼▼** Best Western Woodbury Inn **M**

(516) 921-6900. **$89-$179.** 7940 Jericho Tpke (SR 25) 11797. Jct SR 25 and 135, 0.9 mi e. Ext/int corridors. **Pets:** Accepted.
[SAVE] 🛜 [✕] 🔲 🖵 [†] 🏊

△△△▽ **▼▼▼** Executive Inn at Woodbury **M** 🐾

(516) 921-8500. **$99-$209.** 8030 Jericho Tpke (SR 25) 11797. Jct SR 25 and 135, 1 mi e. Ext corridors. **Pets:** Medium, dogs only. $50 deposit/room, $20 daily fee/room. Service with restrictions, supervision.
[SAVE] 🛜 🔲 🖵 🏊

ABERDEEN

Hampton Inn & Suites H
(910) 693-4330. **$109-$149.** 200 Columbus Dr 28315. Jct US 1, just n on US 15/501, then just s. Int corridors. **Pets:** Accepted.

Motel 6-1234 M
(910) 944-5633. **$43-$53.** 1408 Sandhills Blvd 28315. Jct US 15/501 N, just s on US 1. Ext corridors. **Pets:** Other species. Service with restrictions, supervision.

ALBEMARLE

Quality Inn M
(704) 983-6990. **$60-$140.** 735 Hwy 24/27 Bypass E 28001. Jct US 52 S, 1.4 mi e. Ext corridors. **Pets:** Medium. $25 daily fee/pet. Designated rooms, service with restrictions, crate.

Sleep Inn & Suites H
(704) 983-2770. **$90.** 621 Hwy 24/27 Bypass 28001. Jct US 52 S, 1.1 mi e. Int corridors. **Pets:** Accepted.

APEX

Candlewood Suites - Apex/Raleigh H
(919) 387-8595. **$90-$129.** 1005 Marco Dr 27502. US 1 exit 95, just w on SR 55. Int corridors. **Pets:** Medium, other species. $75 one-time fee/room. Service with restrictions, crate.

ARCHDALE

Comfort Inn H
(336) 434-4797. **$64-$129.** 10123 N Main St 27263. I-85 exit 111, just n on US 311, then just sw on Balfour Dr. Int corridors. **Pets:** Small. $25 one-time fee/pet. Service with restrictions, supervision.

Country Inn & Suites By Carlson, High Point H
(336) 861-2233. **$79-$89.** 10151 N Main St 27263. I-85 exit 111, just n on US 311. Int corridors. **Pets:** Accepted.

Innkeeper High Point M
(336) 434-5151. **Call for rates.** 10002 S Main St 27263. I-85 exit 111, just s on US 311. Ext/int corridors. **Pets:** Accepted.

Hampton Inn-High Point H
(336) 434-5200. **$99-$109.** 10066 N Main St 27263. I-85 exit 111, just n on US 311. Int corridors. **Pets:** Small. Designated rooms, service with restrictions, supervision.

Holiday Inn Express Hotel & Suites H
(336) 861-3310. **$91-$99.** 10050 N Main St 27263. I-85 exit 111, just n on US 311. Int corridors. **Pets:** Accepted.

Quality Inn - High Point H
(336) 861-3000. **Call for rates.** 1202 Liberty Rd 27263. I-85 exit 113, just s on SR 62. Int corridors. **Pets:** Accepted.

ARDEN

Quality Inn & Suites Biltmore South H
(828) 684-6688. **$89-$129.** 1 Skyland Inn Dr 28704. I-26 exit 37, just e. Int corridors. **Pets:** Medium, other species. $25 one-time fee/room. Designated rooms, service with restrictions.

ASHEBORO

Comfort Inn H
(336) 626-4414. **$60-$99.** 825 W Dixie Dr 27205. Jct US 220, just e on US 64. Int corridors. **Pets:** Accepted.

Quality Inn H
(336) 626-3680. **$65-$90.** 242 Lakecrest Rd 27203. US 64, just nw on SR 42. Ext corridors. **Pets:** Accepted.

ASHEVILLE

1889 WhiteGate Inn & Cottage BB
(828) 253-2553. **$169-$379, 14 day notice.** 173 E Chestnut St 28801. I-240 exit 5B (Charlotte St), just n, then just w; in historic district. Ext/int corridors. **Pets:** Dogs only. $50 one-time fee/room. Designated rooms, service with restrictions, crate.

1900 Inn on Montford BB
(828) 254-9569. **$145-$625, 14 day notice.** 296 Montford Ave 28801. I-240 exit 4C (Montford Ave/Haywood St), 0.7 mi n; in historic district. Ext/int corridors. **Pets:** Other species. Designated rooms.

Abbington Green Bed & Breakfast Inn BB
(828) 251-2454. **$150-$450, 30 day notice.** 46 Cumberland Cir 28801. I-240 exit 4C (Montford Ave/Haywood St), just n on Montford Ave, just e on W Chestnut St, just n on Cumberland Ave, then just ne; in historic district. Ext/int corridors. **Pets:** Accepted.

⬧⬧⬧ ▼▼▼ Applewood Manor Inn Bed & Breakfast BB
(828) 254-2244. **$160-$250, 7 day notice.** 62 Cumberland Cir 28801. I-240 exit 4C (Montford Ave/Haywood St), just n on Montford Ave, just e on W Chestnut St, just n on Cumberland Ave, then just ne; in historic district. Ext/int corridors. **Pets:** Dogs only. $15 daily fee/pet. Designated rooms, service with restrictions, crate. SAVE 📶 ✕ 🖨 🖵 🐾

⬧⬧⬧ ▼▼▼ Best Western of Asheville Biltmore East M
(828) 298-5562. **$60-$300.** 501 Tunnel Rd 28805. I-240 exit 7, 0.5 mi e on US 70 (Tunnel Rd). Ext corridors. **Pets:** Small, dogs only. $10 daily fee/pet. Service with restrictions, supervision. SAVE 📶 🖨 🖵 🐾

⬧⬧⬧ ▼▼▼ Biltmore Village Inn BB
(828) 274-8707. **$199-$335, 21 day notice.** 119 Dodge St 28803. I-40 exit 50/50B (US 25 N), 0.5 mi n, just e on Lula St, just n on Reed St, just e on Warren Ave, then just s. Ext/int corridors. **Pets:** Accepted.
SAVE 📶 ✕ 🖨 🖵

⬧⬧⬧ ▼▼▼ Cedar Crest Inn BB
(828) 252-1389. **$129-$300, 30 day notice.** 674 Biltmore Ave 28803. I-40 exit 50, 1.1 mi n. Ext/int corridors. **Pets:** Other species. $50 one-time fee/room. Designated rooms, no service. SAVE 📶 ✕ 🖾 🖨 🖵

▼▼ Comfort Inn-West H
(828) 665-6500. **Call for rates.** 15 Crowell Rd 28806. I-40 exit 44, just n on US 19 and 23, just w on Old Haywood Rd, then just s. Int corridors. **Pets:** Accepted. 📶 🖾 🖨 🖵 🐾

⬧⬧⬧ ▼▼▼ Comfort Suites Biltmore H ❀
(828) 665-4000. **$59-$179.** 890 Brevard Rd 28806. I-26 exit 33, 0.3 mi w. Int corridors. **Pets:** Other species. $25 daily fee/room. Designated rooms. SAVE 📶 ✕ 🖾 🖨 🖵 🐾

⬧⬧⬧ ▼▼▼ Crowne Plaza Resort H ❀
(828) 254-3211. **$89-$199.** 1 Resort Dr 28806. I-240 exit 3B (Resort Dr), just w. Int corridors. **Pets:** Other species. $25 daily fee/room. Designated rooms, service with restrictions, crate.
SAVE 📶 ✕ 🖾 🖨 🖵 🍴 🐾 ✕

⬧⬧⬧ ▼▼▼ Days Inn-Asheville Mall M
(828) 252-4000. **$53-$188.** 201 Tunnel Rd 28805. I-240 exit 6, 0.5 mi e, on south side of road. Ext corridors. **Pets:** Medium. $20 daily fee/pet. Designated rooms, service with restrictions, crate.
SAVE 📶 🖨 🖵 🐾

⬧⬧⬧ ▼▼▼ Days Inn-Biltmore East H
(828) 298-4000. **$54-$126.** 1435 Tunnel Rd 28805. I-40 exit 55, just n. Int corridors. **Pets:** Small, dogs only. $10 daily fee/pet. No service, supervision. SAVE 📶 🖾 🖨 🖵 🐾

⬧⬧⬧ ▼▼▼ Extended StayAmerica Asheville-Tunnel Rd H ❀
(828) 253-3483. **$60-$130.** 6 Kenilworth Knoll 28805. I-240 exit 6, 0.7 mi e on US 70 (Tunnel Rd), then just n. Int corridors. **Pets:** Other species. $25 daily fee/pet. Service with restrictions. 📶 🖾 🖨 🖵

⬧⬧⬧ ▼▼▼▼ Four Points by Sheraton Asheville Downtown H ❀
(828) 253-1851. **$89-$209.** 22 Woodfin St 28801. I-240 exit 5A (Merrimon Ave), just s, then just w. Int corridors. **Pets:** $50 one-time fee/room. Designated rooms, service with restrictions.
SAVE 📶 ✕ 🖾 🖨 🖵 🍴 🐾

⬧⬧⬧ ▼▼▼ ▼▼▼ Grand Bohemian Hotel Asheville, Autograph Collection H
(828) 505-2949. **$161-$449, 3 day notice.** 11 Boston Way 28803. I-40 exit 50/50B, 0.8 mi n on US 25, follow signs for Biltmore Estate Historic Biltmore Village. Int corridors. **Pets:** Accepted.
SAVE 📶 ✕ 🖾 🖨 🖵 🍴

⬧⬧⬧ ▼▼▼▼ Haywood Park Hotel & Promenade H ❀
(828) 252-2522. **Call for rates.** One Battery Park Ave 28801. I-240 exit 4C (Montford Ave/Haywood St), just s, 0.6 mi se on Haywood St, then just w. Int corridors. **Pets:** Medium, dogs only. $50 one-time fee/pet. No service. SAVE 📶 ✕ 🖨 🖵

⬧⬧⬧ ▼▼▼ ▼▼▼ Hilton Asheville Biltmore Park H ❀
(828) 209-2700. **$129-$259.** 43 Town Square Blvd 28803. I-26 exit 37, just e (Long Shoals Rd), then w; in Biltmore Town Square. **Pets:** Medium. $50 one-time fee/room. Service with restrictions.
ECO SAVE 📶 🖾 🖨 🖵 🍴 🐾 ✕

▼▼▼ Holiday Inn-Biltmore East at the Blue Ridge Parkway H
(828) 298-5611. **$79-$159.** 1450 Tunnel Rd 28805. I-40 exit 55, just n. Int corridors. **Pets:** Accepted. 📶 🖾 🖨 🖵 🍴 🐾

▼▼▼ Hotel Indigo H ❀
(828) 239-0239. **$149-$399.** 151 Haywood St 28801. I-240 exit 4C (Montford Ave/Haywood St), just s, then just w. Int corridors. **Pets:** Medium, other species. $50 one-time fee/room. Designated rooms, service with restrictions, crate. 📶 ✕ 🖾 🖨 🖵 🍴

⬧⬧⬧ ▼▼▼ Quality Inn & Suites M
(828) 298-5519. **$65-$149.** 1430 Tunnel Rd 28805. I-40 exit 55, just n. Ext corridors. **Pets:** Accepted. SAVE 📶 🖾 🖨 🖵 🐾

⬧⬧⬧ ▼▼▼ Ramada H ❀
(828) 298-9141. **$56-$133, 7 day notice.** 800 Fairview Rd 28803. I-240 exit 8; jct I-40 and US 74. Int corridors. **Pets:** Medium. $15 daily fee/pet. Designated rooms, no service, crate. SAVE 📶 🖨 🖵 🐾 ✕

▼▼▼ Red Roof Inn-West M
(828) 667-9803. **$47-$89.** 16 Crowell Rd 28806. I-40 exit 44, just n on US 19 and 23, just w on Old Haywood Rd, then just s. Ext corridors. **Pets:** Large, other species. No service, supervision. 📶 🖾 🖨

▼▼▼ Rodeway Inn Asheville M
(828) 667-8706. **$49-$149.** 8 Crowell Rd 28806. I-40 exit 44, just n on US 19 and 23. Int corridors. **Pets:** Medium, other species. $15 daily fee/pet. Service with restrictions, supervision. 📶 🖨 🖵

▼▼▼ Sleep Inn Biltmore H ❀
(828) 277-1800. **$59-$129.** 117 Hendersonville Rd 28803. I-40 exit 50 eastbound; exit 50B westbound, just n on US 25. Int corridors. **Pets:** Small, other species. $10 daily fee/pet. Designated rooms, service with restrictions. 📶 🖾 🖨 🖵

BANNER ELK

▼▼▼▼ The Banner Elk Inn B&B and Cottages BB
(828) 898-6223. **$95-$250, 30 day notice.** 407 Main St E 28604. Jct SR 184 and 194, just n on SR 194; center. Int corridors. **Pets:** Designated rooms, no service, supervision. 📶 ✕ 🖨 🖵

⬧⬧⬧ ▼▼▼▼ Best Western Plus Mountain Lodge at Banner Elk H
(828) 898-4571. **$80-$200, 3 day notice.** 1615 Tynecastle Hwy 28604. Jct SR 194, 1.3 mi s on SR 184. Ext corridors. **Pets:** Accepted.
SAVE 📶 ✕ 🖾 🖨 🖵 🍴 🐾

BLACK MOUNTAIN

⬧⬧⬧ ▼▼▼ Comfort Inn M
(828) 669-9950. **$70-$180.** 585 Hwy 9 28711. I-40 exit 64, just s. Ext corridors. **Pets:** $25 one-time fee/room. Designated rooms, service with restrictions, supervision. SAVE 📶 🖾 🖨 🖵 🐾

BLOWING ROCK

▼▼▼ Alpine Village Inn M
(828) 295-7206. **$49-$129, 7 day notice.** 297 Sunset Dr 28605. Jct US 321, just w. Ext corridors. **Pets:** Dogs only. $25 daily fee/pet. Designated rooms, service with restrictions, supervision. 📶 ✕ 🖨 🖵

▼▼▼ Cliff Dwellers Inn M
(828) 295-3121. **Call for rates.** 116 Lakeview Terr 28605. Jct US 221/321 business route, just s on US 321, then just e. Ext corridors. **Pets:** Accepted. 📶 ✕ 🖨 🖵

◇◇ ◇◇ **Hillwinds Inn** Ⓜ
(828) 295-7660. **$69-$299, 3 day notice.** 315 Sunset Dr 28605. Jct US 321, just w. Ext/int corridors. **Pets:** Accepted. 🛜 ❎ 🛏️ 💻

◈◈◇ ◇◇ ◇◇ **Holiday Inn Express** Ⓗ
(828) 295-4422. **$69-$174.** 8412 Valley Blvd 28605. Jct Sunset Dr, 0.5 mi s on US 321. Int corridors. **Pets:** Accepted.
SAVE 🛜 &M 🛏️ 💻 🏊

◇◇ ◇◇ **Homestead Inn** Ⓜ
(828) 295-9559. **$45-$99, 7 day notice.** 153 Morris St 28605. Jct US 321 business route (Main St), just e. Ext corridors. **Pets:** Accepted.
🛜 ❎ &M 🛏️ 💻

◇◇◇◇◇ **The Village Inn** Ⓜ
(828) 295-3380. **$65-$299, 3 day notice.** 7876 Valley Blvd 28605. Jct Sunset Dr, just s on US 321. Ext corridors. **Pets:** Accepted.
🛜 ❎ &M 🛏️ 💻

BOONE
◇◇◇◇◇ **La Quinta Inn & Suites Boone** Ⓗ
(828) 262-1234. **$69-$229.** 165 Hwy 105 Ext 28607. US 421, just s on SR 105. Int corridors. **Pets:** Medium, other species. Service with restrictions, supervision. 🛜 ❎ &M 🛏️ 💻 🏊

BREVARD
◇◇◇◇◇ **Hampton Inn-Brevard** Ⓗ
(828) 883-4800. **Call for rates.** 275 Forest Gate Dr 28768. Jct US 64, just e on SR 280, then just n. Int corridors. **Pets:** Accepted.
🛜 &M 🛏️ 💻 🏊

◈◈◇ ◇◇◇◇◇ **Holiday Inn Express** Ⓗ 🐾
(828) 862-8900. **$79-$179.** 2228 Asheville Hwy 28712. Jct SR 280, just w on US 64. Int corridors. **Pets:** Other species. $25 daily fee/room. Service with restrictions, crate. SAVE 🛜 ❎ &M 🛏️ 💻 🏊

◈◈◇ ◇◇ ◇◇ **The Inn at Brevard** 🅱️🅱️
(828) 884-2105. **$115-$235, 14 day notice.** 315 E Main St 28712. Jct Broad St, just e; center. Ext/int corridors. **Pets:** Other species. $25 one-time fee/room. Designated rooms, service with restrictions.
SAVE 🛜 ❎ 💻 🛡️

BRYSON CITY
◇◇ ◇◇ **Settlers Mountain** 🆅🅷
(828) 488-8622. **Call for rates.** 340 E Alarka Rd 28713. US 74 exit 64, 1.5 mi s on Alarka Rd, then 0.4 mi e. Ext corridors. **Pets:** Accepted.
🛜 ❎ 🛏️ 💻

BURLINGTON
◈◈◇ ◇◇ ◇◇ **Econo Lodge** Ⓗ
(336) 227-1270. **$43-$69.** 2133 W Hanford Rd 27215. I-40/85 exit 145, just s on SR 49, then just w. Int corridors. **Pets:** Accepted.
SAVE 🛜 🛏️ 🏊

◇◇ **Motel 6 - 1257** Ⓜ
(336) 226-1325. **$35-$47.** 2155 Hanford Rd 27215. I-40/85 exit 145, just s on SR 49, then just w. Ext corridors. **Pets:** Other species. Service with restrictions, supervision. 🛜 🛏️ 🏊

◈◈◇ ◇◇◇◇◇ **Quality Inn** Ⓗ
(336) 229-5203. **Call for rates.** 2444 Maple Ave 27215. I-40/85 exit 145, just n on SR 49. Int corridors. **Pets:** Other species. $25 one-time fee/pet. Service with restrictions, crate. SAVE 🛜 &M 🛏️ 💻 🍽️ 🏊

CANDLER
◈◈◇ ◇◇ ◇◇ **Days Inn Asheville West #6116** Ⓜ
(828) 667-9321. **$40-$85.** 2551 Smokey Park Hwy 28715. I-40 exit 37, just s, then w. Ext corridors. **Pets:** $10 daily fee/room. Designated rooms, service with restrictions, crate. SAVE 🛜 🛏️ 💻 🏊

CANTON
◇◇ ◇◇ **Comfort Inn** Ⓗ
(828) 648-4881. **Call for rates.** 737 Champion Dr 28716. I-40 exit 31, just s. Int corridors. **Pets:** Accepted. 🛜 🛏️ 💻 🏊

◇◇ ◇◇ **Days Inn** Ⓜ
(828) 648-0300. **$63-$116.** 1963 Champion Dr 28716. I-40 exit 31, just n. Ext corridors. **Pets:** Accepted. 🛜 🛏️ 💻 🏊

CARY
◈◈◇ ◇◇◇◇◇ **Best Western Plus Cary Inn & Extended Stay** Ⓗ
(919) 481-1200. **Call for rates.** 1722 Walnut St 27511. I-40 exit 293A, just s on US 1 exit 101A, then just e. Ext/int corridors. **Pets:** Accepted.
SAVE 🛜 🛏️ 💻 🏊

◇◇ ◇◇ **Candlewood Suites-Raleigh/Cary** Ⓗ
(919) 468-4222. **$89-$129.** 1020 Buck Jones Rd 27606. I-40 exit 293A, just s on US 1 exit 101B, 0.5 mi nw; in Buck Jones Village. Int corridors.
Pets: Accepted. 🛜 🛏️ 💻

◇◇ ◇◇ **Comfort Suites Hotel** Ⓗ 🐾
(919) 852-4318. **$79-$119.** 350 Asheville Ave 27518. US 1 exit 98A, 0.8 mi e on Tryon Rd, then just n. Int corridors. **Pets:** Large. $75 one-time fee/room. Designated rooms, service with restrictions, supervision.
🛜 ❎ &M 🛏️ 💻 🏊 ❎

◇◇ ◇◇ **Extended StayAmerica-Raleigh-Cary-Regency Pkwy** Ⓗ 🐾
(919) 468-5828. **$58-$83.** 1500 Regency Pkwy 27518. US 1 exit 98A, 0.5 mi e on Tryon Rd, then just s. Int corridors. **Pets:** Other species. $25 daily fee/pet. Service with restrictions. 🛜 🛏️ 💻

◇◇ ◇◇ **Extended Stay Deluxe Raleigh-Cary-Regency Parkway** Ⓗ 🐾
(919) 460-1161. **$65-$90.** 3100 Regency Pkwy 27518. US 1 exit 98A, 0.5 mi e on Tryon Rd, then just s. Int corridors. **Pets:** Other species. $25 daily fee/pet. Service with restrictions. 🛜 🛏️ 💻 🏊

◇◇◇◇◇ **Hampton Inn & Suites** Ⓗ
(919) 233-1798. **$85-$145.** 111 Hampton Woods Ln 27607. I-40 exit 290, just w on SR 54, then just s. Int corridors. **Pets:** Accepted.
🛜 ❎ &M 🛏️ 💻 🏊

◇◇◇◇◇ **La Quinta Inn & Suites Raleigh (Cary)** Ⓗ
(919) 851-2850. **$73-$159.** 191 Crescent Commons Dr 27511. US 1 exit 98A, 0.5 mi e on Tryon Rd, then just n. Int corridors. **Pets:** Medium, other species. Service with restrictions, supervision.
🛜 &M 🛏️ 💻 🏊

◇◇◇◇◇ **Residence Inn Raleigh Cary** Ⓗ
(919) 467-4080. **$89-$179.** 2900 Regency Pkwy 27518. US 1 exit 98A, 0.5 mi e on Tryon Rd, then just s. Int corridors. **Pets:** Accepted.
🅴🅲🅾 🛜 ❎ &M 🛏️ 💻 🏊 ❎

◇◇ ◇◇ **StudioPLUS-Raleigh-Cary-Harrison Ave** Ⓗ 🐾
(919) 677-9910. **$70-$95.** 600 Weston Pkwy 27513. I-40 exit 287, 0.5 mi s on Harrison Ave, then just w. Int corridors. **Pets:** Other species. $25 daily fee/pet. Service with restrictions. 🛜 🛏️ 💻 🏊

◈◈◇ ◇◇◇◇◇ **TownePlace Suites by Marriott - Raleigh/Cary/ Weston Parkway** Ⓗ
(919) 678-0005. **$69-$104.** 120 Sage Commons Way 27513. I-40 exit 287, 0.5 mi s on Harrison Ave, 2.3 w on Weston Pkwy, then just n. Int corridors. **Pets:** Accepted. SAVE 🛜 ❎ &M 🛏️ 💻 🏊

◈◈◇ ◇◇◇◇◇ **The Umstead Hotel & Spa** Ⓗ
(919) 447-4000. **$239-$619, 3 day notice.** 100 Woodland Pond Dr 27513. I-40 exit 287, just s on Harrison Ave, just e on SAS Campus Dr, then just n. Int corridors. **Pets:** Accepted.
SAVE 🛜 ❎ &M 💻 🍽️ 🏊 ❎

CASHIERS

AAA ▼▼▼▼ High Hampton Inn & Country Club H
(828) 743-2411. **$271-$380, 15 day notice.** 1525 Hwy 107 S 28717. Jct US 64, 1.5 mi s. Ext/Int corridors. **Pets:** Accepted.
[SAVE] 🛜 ✕ 🖥 💻 🍴 ✕ 🐾 W 🏊

CHAPEL HILL

AAA ▼▼▼▼ Aloft - Chapel Hill H 🐾
(919) 932-7772. **$99-$269.** 1001 S Hamilton Rd 27517. I-40 exit 273/273A, 2.6 mi w on SR 54, then just s. Int corridors. **Pets:** Medium, dogs only. Designated rooms, service with restrictions, supervision.
[SAVE] 🛜 ✕ 🖥 🖥 💻 🏊

AAA ▼▼▼ Chapel Hill University Inn M 🐾
(919) 929-2171. **$75-$115.** 1301 N Fordham Blvd 27514. I-40 exit 270, 2 mi s on US 15/501. Ext corridors. **Pets:** Medium, other species. $40 one-time fee/room. Designated rooms, service with restrictions.
[SAVE] 🛜 🖥 💻 🍴 🏊

AAA ▼▼▼▼ Residence Inn by Marriott-Chapel Hill H
(919) 933-4848. **$139-$159.** 101 Erwin Rd 27514. I-40 exit 270, 1.2 mi s on US 15/501, then just w. Int corridors. **Pets:** Accepted.
[SAVE] 🛜 ✕ 🖥 🖥 💻 🏊 ✕

AAA ▼▼▼▼ Sheraton Chapel Hill H 🐾
(919) 968-4900. **$89-$280.** 1 Europa Dr 27517. I-40 exit 270, 1 mi s, then just e. Int corridors. **Pets:** Other species. Service with restrictions.
[SAVE] 🛜 ✕ 🖥 💻 🍴 🏊

AAA ▼▼▼▼ The Siena Hotel H 🐾
(919) 929-4000. **$119-$300.** 1505 E Franklin St 27514. I-40 exit 270, 2 mi s on US 15/501, then 0.5 mi w. Int corridors. **Pets:** Large, dogs only. $75 one-time fee/pet. Designated rooms, service with restrictions.
[SAVE] 🛜 ✕ 🖥 💻 🍴

CHARLOTTE METROPOLITAN AREA

CHARLOTTE

AAA ▼▼▼▼ Aloft Charlotte-Ballantyne H 🐾
(704) 247-2222. **$99-$269.** 13139 Ballantyne Corporate Pl 28277. I-485 exit 61 or 61B, 0.5 mi s on US 521 (Johnston Rd), just e on Ballantyne Commons Pkwy, then just n. Int corridors. **Pets:** Medium, dogs only. Designated rooms, service with restrictions, supervision.
[ECO] [SAVE] 🛜 ✕ 🖥 🖥 💻 🏊

AAA ▼▼▼▼ Aloft Charlotte Uptown @ the EpiCentre H
(704) 333-1999. **$99-$399.** 210 E Trade St 28202. I-77 exit 10 or 10B, 0.9 mi e, then just n; jct College St. Int corridors. **Pets:** Accepted.
[SAVE] 🛜 ✕ 🖥 🖥 💻 🏊

▼▼ Candlewood Suites - Charlotte University H
(704) 598-9863. **$60-$399.** 8812 University East Dr 28213. I-85 exit 45A (W. T. Harris Blvd), 2.5 mi e on SR 24, then just s; in University East Business Park. Int corridors. **Pets:** Accepted. 🛜 🖥 💻

▼▼ Candlewood Suites I-77 South/Tyvola Rd H
(704) 529-7500. **$69-$599.** 5840 Westpark Dr 28217. I-77 exit 5 (Tyvola Rd), just e, then 0.5 mi s. Int corridors. **Pets:** Accepted.
🛜 🖥 🖥 💻

▼▼▼▼ Comfort Suites - Airport H
(704) 971-4400. **$79-$129.** 3425 Mulberry Church Rd 28208. I-85 exit 33, just e, then just n. Int corridors. **Pets:** Accepted.
🛜 ✕ 🖥 💻 🏊

▼▼▼▼ Comfort Suites-University H
(704) 547-0049. **$89-$199.** 7735 University City Blvd 28213. I-85 exit 45A (W. T. Harris Blvd), 1 mi e on SR 24, then 0.5 mi s on SR 49. Int corridors. **Pets:** Accepted. 🛜 ✕ 🖥 🖥 💻 🏊

AAA ▼▼▼▼ Country Inn & Suites By Carlson-Charlotte University H
(704) 549-8770. **Call for rates.** 131 E McCullough Dr 28262. I-85 exit 45A (W. T. Harris Blvd), 0.5 mi e on SR 24, 0.4 mi s on US 29 (N Tryon St), then just e. Int corridors. **Pets:** Accepted.
🛜 ✕ 🖥 🖥 💻 🏊

AAA ▼▼▼▼ Crowne Plaza - Charlotte H
(704) 372-7550. **$99-$189.** 201 S McDowell St 28204. I-277 exit 2A, just w on 4th St, then just s. Int corridors. **Pets:** Accepted.
[SAVE] 🛜 ✕ 🖥 💻 🍴 🏊

AAA ▼▼▼▼ DoubleTree Suites by Hilton Hotel Charlotte - SouthPark H
(704) 364-2400. **$89-$269.** 6300 Morrison Blvd 28211. I-77 exit 5 (Tyvola Rd), 3.3 mi e on Tyvola/Fairview rds, just n on Barclay Downs, then just e. Int corridors. **Pets:** Accepted. [SAVE] 🛜 🖥 💻 🍴 🏊

▼▼▼▼ Drury Inn & Suites-Charlotte North H
(704) 593-0700. **$95-$199.** 415 W W. T. Harris Blvd 28262. I-85 exit 45A (W. T. Harris Blvd), just e on SR 24. Int corridors. **Pets:** Accepted.
🛜 🖥 🖥 💻 🏊

▼▼▼▼ Drury Inn & Suites-Charlotte Northlake H
(704) 599-8882. **$105-$209.** 6920 Northlake Mall Dr 28216. I-77 exit 18 (W. T. Harris Blvd), just w on SR 24. Int corridors. **Pets:** Accepted.
🛜 🖥 🖥 💻 🏊

▼▼▼▼ Extended StayAmerica-Charlotte-Pineville H 🐾
(704) 341-0929. **$75-$100.** 10930 Park Rd 28226. I-485 exit 64A, just n on SR 51, then just e; behind Terraces at Park Place Shopping Center. Int corridors. **Pets:** Other species. $25 daily fee/pet. Service with restrictions. 🛜 🖥 🖥 💻

▼▼▼▼ Extended StayAmerica-Charlotte-University Place H 🐾
(704) 510-1636. **$65-$90.** 8211 University Executive Park Dr 28262. I-85 exit 45A (W. T. Harris Blvd), 0.5 mi e on SR 24, then 0.5 mi s on US 29 (N Tryon St). Int corridors. **Pets:** Other species. $25 daily fee/pet. Service with restrictions. 🛜 🖥 💻

▼▼▼▼ Extended Stay Deluxe-Charlotte/Pineville H 🐾
(704) 542-9521. **$115-$140.** 8405 Pineville-Matthews Rd 28226. I-485 exit 64A, 0.7 mi n on SR 51. Int corridors. **Pets:** Other species. $25 daily fee/pet. Service with restrictions. 🛜 🖥 🖥 💻 🏊

▼▼▼▼ Holiday Inn Airport H
(704) 394-4301. **$94-$174.** 2707 Little Rock Rd 28214. I-85 exit 32, just e. Int corridors. **Pets:** Accepted. 🛜 🖥 🖥 💻 🍴 🏊

▼▼▼▼ Holiday Inn at University Executive Park H
(704) 547-0999. **$94-$169.** 8520 University Executive Park Dr 28262. I-85 exit 45A (W. T. Harris Blvd), just e on SR 24, then just s. Int corridors. **Pets:** Medium. $25 one-time fee/pet. Designated rooms, service with restrictions, supervision. 🛜 🖥 🖥 💻 🍴 🏊

▼▼▼ Homestead Studio Suites Hotel-Charlotte/Airport M 🐾
(704) 676-0083. **$65-$90.** 710 Yorkmont Rd 28217. I-77 exit 6B northbound, just w, just s on S Tryon St, then just w; exit southbound, just s on S Tryon St, then just w. Ext corridors. **Pets:** Other species. $25 daily fee/pet. Service with restrictions. 🛜 🖥 💻

▼▼▼▼ Homewood Suites by Hilton Airport H
(704) 357-0500. **$99-$169.** 2770 Yorkmont Rd 28208. I-77 exit 6B, 2 mi nw on Billy Graham Pkwy exit Coliseum/Tyvola Rd, just se on Tyvola Rd, then just w. Int corridors. **Pets:** Medium, other species. $50 one-time fee/room. Designated rooms, service with restrictions, supervision.
🛜 🖥 🖥 💻

WWWW Homewood Suites by Hilton-University Research Park H
(704) 549-8800. **$90-$199.** 8340 N Tryon St 28262. I-85 exit 45A (W. T. Harris Blvd), 0.5 mi e on SR 24, then just s on US 29. Ext/int corridors.
Pets: Accepted. 🛜 🍸M 📧 💻 🏊 🐾

AAA WWWW Hyatt Summerfield Suites Charlotte Airport H
(704) 525-2600. **$79-$229.** 4920 S Tryon St 28217. I-77 exit 6B northbound, just w, then just s; exit southbound, just s. Int corridors.
Pets: Accepted. SAVE 🛜 ✕ 🍸M 📧 💻 🏊 🐾

WWWW La Quinta Inn & Suites Charlotte Airport North H
(704) 392-1600. **$62-$130.** 3127 Sloan Dr 28208. I-85 exit 33, just w, then just s. Int corridors. **Pets:** Medium, other species. Service with restrictions, supervision. 🛜 📧 💻

WWWW La Quinta Inn & Suites Charlotte Airport South H
(704) 523-5599. **$74-$137.** 4900 S Tryon St 28217. I-77 exit 6B northbound, just w, then just s; exit southbound, just s. Int corridors.
Pets: Medium, other species. Service with restrictions, supervision.
🛜 🍸M 📧 💻 🏊

WW MainStay Suites H
(704) 521-3232. **$79-$119.** 7926 Forest Pine Dr 28273. I-77 exit 3 southbound; exit 2 northbound, just e, then just s. Int corridors.
Pets: Accepted. 🛜 🍸M 📧 💻 🏊

AAA WWWW Omni Charlotte Hotel H 🌸
(704) 377-0400. **$129-$425.** 132 E Trade St 28202. I-77 exit 10 or 10B, 0.8 mi e; jct Tryon St. Int corridors. **Pets:** Small. $50 one-time fee/pet. Service with restrictions. SAVE 🛜 ✕ 📧 💻 🍴 🏊 🐾

WWWW Quality Inn & Suites Airport H
(704) 393-5306. **$54-$59.** 3100 Queen City Dr 28208. I-85 exit 33, just w, then just n. Ext/int corridors. **Pets:** Accepted.
🛜 🍸M 📧 💻 🏊

AAA WW Quality Inn-Executive Park H
(704) 525-0747. **$70-$190.** 440 Griffith Rd 28217. I-77 exit 5 (Tyvola Rd), just e, just s on Westpark Dr, then just e. Int corridors. **Pets:** Accepted.
SAVE 🛜 📧 💻 🏊

WWWW The Registry Hotel H
(704) 523-1400. **Call for rates.** 321 W Woodlawn Rd 28217. I-77 exit 6B northbound, just w; exit southbound, just s on S Tryon St. Int corridors. **Pets:** Accepted. 🛜 ✕ 🍸M 📧 💻 🍴 🏊

WWWW Residence Inn by Marriott-Charlotte University Research Park H
(704) 547-1122. **$67-$159.** 8503 N Tryon St 28262. I-85 exit 45A (W. T. Harris Blvd), 0.5 mi e on SR 24, then just s on US 29 (N Tryon St). Ext corridors. **Pets:** Accepted. 🛜 ✕ 🍸M 📧 💻 🏊 🐾

AAA WWWW Residence Inn by Marriott-Charlotte Uptown H 🌸
(704) 340-4000. **$89-$229.** 404 S Mint St 28202. I-77 exit 10 or 10B, 0.6 mi e on Trade St, then just s. Int corridors. **Pets:** Large, other species. $100 one-time fee/room. Designated rooms, service with restrictions, crate. ECO SAVE 🛜 ✕ 🍸M 📧 💻 🍴

WWWW Residence Inn by Marriott-Piper Glen H
(704) 319-3900. **$119-$154.** 5115 Piper Station Dr 28277. I-485 exit 59, just s on Rea Rd, then just e. Int corridors. **Pets:** Accepted.
🛜 ✕ 🍸M 📧 💻 🏊 🐾

WWWW Residence Inn Charlotte South at I-77 / Tyvola Rd H 🌸
(704) 527-8110. **$99-$169.** 5816 Westpark Dr 28217. I-77 exit 5 (Tyvola Rd), just e, then 0.4 mi s. Ext/int corridors. **Pets:** $75 one-time fee/room. Service with restrictions, supervision.
🛜 ✕ 🍸M 📧 💻 🏊 🐾

WWWW Residence Inn Charlotte SouthPark H
(704) 554-7001. **$137-$199.** 6030 Piedmont Row Dr S 28287. I-77 exit 5 (Tyvola Rd), 3.2 mi e on Tyvola/Fairview rds, then just s. Int corridors.
Pets: Accepted. 🛜 ✕ 🍸M 📧 💻 🏊 🐾

AAA WWWW Sheraton Charlotte Airport Hotel H
(704) 392-1200. **$89-$269.** 3315 Scott Futrell Dr 28208. I-85 exit 33, just e, then just s. Int corridors. **Pets:** Accepted.
SAVE 🛜 ✕ 📧 💻 🍴 🏊

AAA WW Sleep Inn H
(704) 549-4544. **$60-$159.** 8525 N Tryon St 28262. I-85 exit 45A (W. T. Harris Blvd), 0.5 mi e on SR 24, just s on US 29 (N Tryon St). Int corridors. **Pets:** Medium, other species. $25 one-time fee/room. Service with restrictions, crate. SAVE 🛜 🍸M 📧 💻 🏊

WW Sleep Inn - Billy Graham Parkway H
(704) 525-5005. **$80-$140.** 701 Yorkmont Rd 28217. I-77 exit 6B northbound, just w, just s on S Tryon St, then just w; exit southbound, just s on Tryon St, then just w. Int corridors. **Pets:** Accepted.
🛜 🍸M 📧 💻 🏊

AAA WWWW Sleep Inn Northlake H
(704) 399-7778. **$64-$99.** 6300 Banner Elk Dr 28216. I-77 exit 16B, just w on Sunset Rd, then just s. Int corridors. **Pets:** Small, other species. $20 daily fee/pet. Designated rooms, service with restrictions, supervision.
SAVE 🛜 ✕ 📧 💻 🏊

WWW Staybridge Suites-Arrowood H
(704) 527-6767. **$89-$169.** 7924 Forest Pine Dr 28273. I-77 exit 3 southbound; exit 2 northbound, just e, then just s. Int corridors.
Pets: Accepted. 🛜 🍸M 📧 💻 🏊

WWWW Staybridge Suites Charlotte-Ballantyne H
(704) 248-5000. **$100-$169.** 15735 John J Delaney Dr 28277. I-485 exit 61 or 61B, just s, then just w. Int corridors. **Pets:** Accepted.
🛜 ✕ 🍸M 📧 💻 🏊 🐾

WWW StudioPLUS - Charlotte/Tyvola Rd H 🌸
(704) 527-1960. **$63-$88.** 5830 Westpark Dr 28217. I-77 exit 5 (Tyvola Rd), just e, then 0.4 mi s. Int corridors. **Pets:** Other species. $25 daily fee/pet. Service with restrictions. 🛜 📧 💻 🏊

AAA WWWW TownePlace Suites by Marriott - University H
(704) 548-0388. **$89-$129.** 8710 Research Dr 28262. I-85 exit 45B (W. T. Harris Blvd), just w on SR 24, then just n. Int corridors.
Pets: Accepted. SAVE 🛜 ✕ 🍸M 📧 💻 🏊

WWWW TownePlace Suites Charlotte Arrowood H
(704) 227-2000. **$74-$209.** 7805 Forest Point Blvd 28217. I-77 exit 3 southbound; exit 2 northbound, just e. Int corridors. **Pets:** Accepted.
🛜 ✕ 🍸M 📧 💻 🏊

AAA WWWW The Westin Charlotte H
(704) 375-2600. **$199-$529.** 601 S College St 28202. I-277 exit College St, just n; jct E Stonewall St. Int corridors. **Pets:** Accepted.
SAVE 🛜 ✕ 🍸M 📧 💻 🍴 🏊 🐾

CONCORD

W Americas Best Value Inn M
(704) 788-8550. **$53-$145.** 2451 Kannapolis Hwy 28025. I-85 exit 58, just s on US 29, then just w. Ext corridors. **Pets:** Accepted.
🛜 📧 💻

WWW Comfort Suites-Concord Mills H
(704) 979-3800. **$99-$219.** 7800 Gateway Ln NW 28027. I-85 exit 49, just e, just n on Weddington Rd, then just w. Int corridors.
Pets: Accepted. 🛜 ✕ 📧 💻 🏊

▼▼▼▼ Embassy Suites Charlotte-Concord Golf Resort & Spa **H**

(704) 455-8200. **$109-$189.** 5400 John Q Hammons Dr 28027. I-85 exit 49, 1 mi e, then just n. Int corridors. **Pets:** Accepted.

▼▼▼▼ Hampton Inn **H** ❀

(704) 793-9700. **$89-$139.** 612 Dickens Pl NE 28025. I-85 exit 60, just e, then just s. Int corridors. **Pets:** Small, other species. Service with restrictions, supervision.

▼▼▼▼ Residence Inn Charlotte Concord **H**

(704) 454-7862. **$109-$139.** 7601 Scott Padgett Pkwy 28027. I-85 exit 49, 1 mi e, then just n. Int corridors. **Pets:** Accepted.

▲▲▲ ▼▼▼ Sleep Inn-Concord **H** ❀

(704) 788-2150. **$70-$120.** 1120 Copperfield Blvd 28025. I-85 exit 60, just e. Int corridors. **Pets:** Medium. $25 one-time fee/pet, $5 daily fee/pet. Designated rooms, service with restrictions, supervision.

▼▼▼▼ Wingate by Wyndham **H**

(704) 979-1300. **$89-$179, 7 day notice.** 7841 Gateway Ln NW 28027. I-85 exit 49, just e, just n on Weddington Rd, then just w. Int corridors. **Pets:** Medium. $50 one-time fee/pet. Designated rooms, service with restrictions, crate.

CORNELIUS

▲▲▲ ▼▼ Clarion Inn - Lake Norman **H**

(704) 896-0660. **$65-$90.** 19608 Liverpool Pkwy 28031. I-77 exit 28, just w, then s. Int corridors. **Pets:** Accepted.

▼▼▼▼ Comfort Inn & Suites **H**

(704) 896-7622. **$75-$190.** 19521 Liverpool Pkwy 28031. I-77 exit 28, just w, then s. Int corridors. **Pets:** Accepted.

▼▼ ▼▼ Econo Lodge Inn & Suites **M**

(704) 892-3500. **Call for rates.** 20740 Torrence Chapel Rd 28031. I-77 exit 28, just w, then just n. Ext corridors. **Pets:** $15 daily fee/pet. Service with restrictions, supervision.

HUNTERSVILLE

▲▲▲ ▼▼▼ Best Western Plus Huntersville Inn & Suites Near Lake Norman **H**

(704) 875-7880. **$86-$115.** 13830 Statesville Rd 28078. I-77 exit 23, just e, then s on US 21. Int corridors. **Pets:** Other species. $20 daily fee/room. Designated rooms, service with restrictions, supervision.

▼▼▼▼ Candlewood Suites **H**

(704) 895-3434. **$82-$110.** 16530 Northcross Dr 28078. I-77 exit 25, just w on SR 73, then just s. Int corridors. **Pets:** Accepted.

▼▼▼▼ Residence Inn by Marriott-Lake Norman **H**

(704) 584-0000. **$109-$149.** 16830 Kenton Dr 28078. I-77 exit 25, 1 mi w on SR 73, then just n. Int corridors. **Pets:** Other species. $100 one-time fee/room. Service with restrictions.

MATTHEWS

▲▲▲ ▼▼▼▼ Country Inn & Suites By Carlson-Matthews **H** ❀

(704) 846-8000. **$80-$119.** 2001 Mount Harmony Church Rd 28104. I-485 exit 51B, 0.5 mi e on US 74, just n on Independence Commerce Dr, then just w. Int corridors. **Pets:** $15 daily fee/pet. Service with restrictions, crate.

▼▼▼▼ Hampton Inn-Matthews **H** ❀

(704) 841-1155. **$89-$129.** 9615 Independence Point Pkwy 28105. I-485 exit 51A, 2 mi w on US 74, then just s. Int corridors. **Pets:** Medium. Designated rooms, service with restrictions, supervision.

END METROPOLITAN AREA

CHEROKEE

▼▼ ▼▼ Great Smokies Inn **M**

(828) 497-2020. **$49-$139.** 1636 Acquoni Rd 28719. US 441 N, 2.5 mi n; downtown. Ext corridors. **Pets:** Small. $25 daily fee/pet. Designated rooms, no service, crate.

▼▼ ▼▼ Microtel Inn & Suites **H** ❀

(828) 497-7800. **$63-$126.** 674 Casino Tr 28719. Jct US 441 and Business Rt US 441 S. Int corridors. **Pets:** Other species. $18 daily fee/room. Designated rooms, service with restrictions.

▲▲▲ ▼▼ Pioneer Motel **M**

(828) 497-2435. **$48-$80, 3 day notice.** 122 Tsalagi Rd 28719. 0.8 mi w on US 19 S. Ext corridors. **Pets:** Small, dogs only. $25 one-time fee/room. Designated rooms, no service, crate.

CHOCOWINITY

▼▼ ▼▼ Super 8 **M**

(252) 946-8001. **$50-$65.** 3635 US Hwy 17 S 27817. On US 17 business route. Ext corridors. **Pets:** Small. $10 daily fee/pet. No service, supervision.

CLEMMONS

▼▼ ▼▼ Super 8 Clemmons **H**

(336) 778-0931. **$40-$75.** 6204 Ramada Dr 27012. I-40 exit 184, just s, then just e. Int corridors. **Pets:** Medium. $10 daily fee/pet. Service with restrictions, supervision.

▼▼ ▼▼ The Village Inn Golf & Conference Center **H**

(336) 766-9121. **$68-$79, 3 day notice.** 6205 Ramada Dr 27012. I-40 exit 184, just s, then just e. Int corridors. **Pets:** Accepted.

COLUMBUS

▲▲▲ ▼▼▼ Days Inn **M**

(828) 894-3303. **$72-$77.** 626 W Mills St 28722. I-26 exit 67, just w on SR 108. Ext corridors. **Pets:** Accepted.

DUNN

▼▼ ▼▼ Jameson Inn **M**

(910) 891-5758. **$72-$92.** 901 Jackson Rd 28334. I-95 exit 73, just w, then just s. Ext corridors. **Pets:** Medium. $15 daily fee/room. Service with restrictions, supervision.

▼▼ ▼▼ Super 8 **M**

(910) 892-1293. **$44-$60.** 1125 E Broad St 28334. I-95 exit 73, just w, then just n. Ext corridors. **Pets:** Medium. $10 daily fee/pet. Service with restrictions, supervision.

DURHAM

▼▼ ▼▼ Candlewood Suites **H**

(919) 484-9922. **$74-$87.** 1818 E NC Hwy 54 27713. I-40 exit 278, just s, then just w. Int corridors. **Pets:** Accepted.

▼▼▼▼ Comfort Inn Medical Park **H**

(919) 471-6100. **$70-$200.** 1816 Hillandale Rd 27705. I-85 exit 174, just w. Int corridors. **Pets:** Accepted.

▼▼ ▼▼ Durham Skyland Inn, A Magnuson Hotel M
(919) 383-2508. **Call for rates.** 5400 US 70 W 27705. I-85 exit 170, 0.3 mi e on US 70, then just n. Ext corridors. **Pets:** Accepted.
🛜 🅿 💻 🏊

▼▼ ▼▼ Extended Stay Deluxe-Durham-RTP-Miami Blvd
North H 🐾
(919) 941-2878. **$75-$100.** 4610 S Miami Blvd 27703. I-40 exit 281, just n. Int corridors. **Pets:** Other species. $25 daily fee/pet. Service with restrictions. 🛜 🅿 💻 🏊

▼▼ ▼▼ Extended Stay Deluxe-Durham-RTP-Miami-S H 🐾
(919) 998-0400. **$75-$100.** 4919 S Miami Blvd 27703. I-40 exit 281, just s. Int corridors. **Pets:** Other species. $25 daily fee/pet. Service with restrictions. 🛜 🅗M 🅿 💻 🏊

▼▼ ▼▼▼ Four Points by Sheraton-Durham at
Southpoint H 🐾
(919) 806-8200. **$105-$210.** 7807 Leonardo Dr 27713. I-40 exit 274, just s on SR 751. Int corridors. **Pets:** $50 one-time fee/pet. Service with restrictions, crate. 💾 🛜 ⊠ 🅿 💻 🍴 🏊

▼▼ ▼▼▼ Hilton Durham near Duke
University H 🐾
(919) 383-8033. **$99-$209.** 3800 Hillsborough Rd 27705. I-85 exit 173, just e on Cole Mill Rd, then 0.5 mi w on US 70 business route. Int corridors. **Pets:** Medium, dogs only. $50 one-time fee/pet. Service with restrictions, crate. 💾 🛜 🅿 💻 🍴 🏊

▼▼ ▼▼▼ Hilton - Raleigh-Durham Airport at Research Triangle
Park H
(919) 941-6000. **Call for rates.** 4810 Page Creek Ln 27703. I-40 exit 282, just s on Page Rd, then just w on Creekstone Dr. Int corridors.
Pets: Accepted. 🛜 ⊠ 🅗M 🅿 💻 🍴 🏊

▼▼ ▼▼▼ Holiday Inn Express H
(919) 313-3244. **$94-$189.** 2516 Guess Rd 27705. I-85 exit 175, just e. Int corridors. **Pets:** Accepted. 🛜 🅿 💻 🏊

▼▼ ▼▼▼ Holiday Inn Express Hotel & Suites-RTP H
(919) 474-9800. **$85-$149.** 4912 S Miami Blvd 27703. I-40 exit 281, just s. Int corridors. **Pets:** Accepted. 🛜 🅗M 🅿 💻

▼▼ ▼▼ Homestead Studio Suites
Hotel-Durham/University M 🐾
(919) 402-1700. **$63-$88.** 1920 Ivy Creek Blvd 27707. I-40 exit 270, 2 mi n on US 15/501 exit 105B, just e on Martin Luther King Jr Pkwy, then just s; in University Place. Ext corridors. **Pets:** Other species. $25 daily fee/pet. Service with restrictions. 🛜 🅿 💻

▼▼ ▼▼ Hotel Indigo H
(919) 474-3000. **$79-$149.** 151 Tatum Dr 27703. I-40 exit 281, just s on Miami Blvd, then just e. Int corridors. **Pets:** Medium. $75 one-time fee/room. Service with restrictions, crate.
🛜 ⊠ 🅗M 🅿 💻 🍴 🏊

▼▼ ▼▼▼ La Quinta Inn & Suites Raleigh (Durham-Chapel
Hill) H
(919) 401-9660. **$83-$143.** 4414 Durham Chapel Hill Blvd 27707. I-40 exit 270, 1.7 mi n on US 15/501. Int corridors. **Pets:** Medium, other species. Service with restrictions, supervision. 🛜 🅗M 🅿 💻 🏊

▼▼ ▼▼▼ La Quinta Inn & Suites Raleigh (Research Triangle
Park) H
(919) 484-1422. **$84-$155.** 1910 W Westpark Dr 27713. I-40 exit 278, just n on SR 55, then just e. Int corridors. **Pets:** Medium, other species. Service with restrictions, supervision. 🛜 🅗M 🅿 💻 🏊

▼▼ ▼▼▼ Quality Inn & Suites H
(919) 382-3388. **$58-$169.** 3710 Hillsborough Rd 27705. I-85 exit 173, just e on Cole Mill Rd, then just w on US 70 business route. Ext/int corridors. **Pets:** Medium. $25 one-time fee/room. Service with restrictions, crate. 🛜 🅿 💻 🏊

(AAA) ▼▼ ▼▼ Residence Inn Durham/Research Triangle
Park H
(919) 361-1266. **$89-$139.** 201 Residence Inn Blvd 27713. I-40 exit 278, just s on SR 55, then just w. Ext/int corridors. **Pets:** Accepted.
💾 🛜 ⊠ 🅗M 🅿 💻 🏊 ⊠

▼▼ ▼▼▼ Staybridge Suites of Durham H
(919) 401-9800. **$109-$119.** 3704 Mt. Moriah Rd 27707. I-40 exit 270, just n on US 15/501, then just e. Int corridors. **Pets:** Accepted.
🛜 🅗M 🅿 💻 🏊

(AAA) ▼▼ ▼▼▼▼ Washington Duke Inn & Golf
Club H 🐾
(919) 490-0999. **$349-$379.** 3001 Cameron Blvd 27705. US 15/501 Bypass exit 107, 0.8 mi s on SR 751. Int corridors. **Pets:** Medium, dogs only. $50 one-time fee/room. Designated rooms, service with restrictions, supervision. 💾 🛜 ⊠ 🅿 💻 🍴 🏊 ⊠

EDEN

(AAA) ▼▼ ▼▼ Econo Lodge M
(336) 627-5131. **$58-$225.** 110 E Arbor Ln 27288. Jct SR 700/770, 1.4 mi s on SR 87/14, then just e. Ext corridors. **Pets:** Medium. $10 daily fee/pet. Designated rooms, service with restrictions, supervision.
💾 🛜 🅿

▼▼ ▼▼▼ Hampton Inn H
(336) 627-1111. **Call for rates.** 724 S Van Buren Rd 27288. Jct SR 700/770, 1.4 mi s on SR 87/14. Int corridors. **Pets:** Accepted.
🛜 🅿 💻 🏊

▼▼ ▼▼ Jameson Inn M
(336) 627-0472. **$70-$90.** 716 Linden Dr 27288. Jct SR 700/770, 1.4 mi s on SR 87/14, then just e. Ext corridors. **Pets:** Medium. $15 daily fee/room. Service with restrictions, supervision. 🛜 🅗M 🅿 💻 🏊

ELIZABETH CITY

▼▼ ▼▼ The Pond House Inn BB
(252) 335-9834. **$115-$165, 7 day notice.** 915 Rivershore Rd 27909. Jct US 17 business route, 2.1 mi se on Halstead Blvd, 1.2 mi n on Edgewood Dr, keep straight on Park Dr and Rivershore Rd. Ext/int corridors. **Pets:** Accepted. 🛜 ⊠ 🅗M 🅿 💻 ⊠ 🖾

FAYETTEVILLE

▼▼ ▼▼▼ Bordeaux Hotel & Conference Center H
(910) 323-0111. **Call for rates.** 1707 Owen Dr 28304. Jct I-95 business route/US 301 S, 2.3 mi w. Ext/int corridors. **Pets:** Accepted.
🛜 ⊠ 🅿 💻 🍴 🏊

▼▼ ▼▼▼ Comfort Inn near Fort Bragg H
(910) 867-1777. **$104-$135.** 1922 Skibo Rd 28314. All American Frwy exit US 401 Bypass, 0.8 mi s. Int corridors. **Pets:** Large, other species. $49 one-time fee/pet. Service with restrictions, supervision.
🛜 🅿 💻 🏊

(AAA) ▼▼ ▼▼ Country Hearth Inn & Suites M
(910) 438-0748. **$60-$90.** 1902 Cedar Creek Rd 28312. I-95 exit 49, just w. Ext corridors. **Pets:** Other species. $10 daily fee/pet. Service with restrictions, supervision. 💾 🛜 🅗M 🅿 💻 🏊

(AAA) ▼▼ ▼▼ Econo Lodge I-95 M
(910) 433-2100. **$60-$66.** 1952 Cedar Creek Rd 28312. I-95 exit 49, just w. Ext corridors. **Pets:** $10 daily fee/pet. Service with restrictions, supervision. 💾 🛜 🅿 🏊

▼▼ ▼▼ Extended StayAmerica Fayetteville-Owen
Dr. M 🐾
(910) 485-2747. **$90-$105.** 408 Owen Dr 28304. Jct All American Frwy. Ext corridors. **Pets:** Other species. $25 daily fee/pet. Service with restrictions. 🛜 🅿 💻

▼▼ Extended Stay Deluxe Fayetteville-Cross Creek Mall 🅗 ❀

(910) 868-5662. **$115-$140.** 4105 Sycamore Dairy Rd 28303. All American Frwy exit Morganton Rd, just e, then just n. Int corridors. **Pets:** Other species. $25 daily fee/pet. Service with restrictions. 📶 🛟 💻 ➳

▼▼▼ Holiday Inn I-95 🅗

(910) 323-1600. **Call for rates.** 1944 Cedar Creek Rd 28312. I-95 exit 49, just w. Ext/int corridors. **Pets:** Accepted. 📶 🛟 💻 🍴 ➳

▼▼▼ Home2 Suites by Hilton 🅗

(910) 223-1170. **$129-$154.** 4035 Sycamore Dairy Rd 28303. US 401 Bypass, just e on McPherson Church Rd, then just s. Int corridors. **Pets:** Accepted. 📶 ♿ 🛟 💻 ➳

▼▼ Innkeeper-Cross Creek Ⓜ

(910) 867-7659. **$55-$89, 3 day notice.** 1720 Skibo Rd 28303. All American Frwy exit US 401 Bypass, just s; enter thru Cross Creek Plaza entrance. Ext/int corridors. **Pets:** Accepted. 📶 🛟 💻 ➳

🅐🅐🅐 ▼▼▼ Quality Inn Ambassador Ⓜ

(910) 485-8135. **Call for rates.** 2035 Eastern Blvd 28306. Jct SR 87, 1.2 mi s on I-95 business route/US 301; jct Owen Dr. Ext corridors. **Pets:** Accepted. 💾 📶 🛟 💻

🅐🅐🅐 ▼▼▼ Red Roof Inn 🅗

(910) 321-1460. **$59-$159.** 1569 Jim Johnson Rd 28312. I-95 exit 49, just w on SR 53, then just n. Int corridors. **Pets:** Large, other species. No service, supervision. 💾 📶 ♿ 🛟 ➳

🅐🅐🅐 ▼▼▼▼ Residence Inn Fayetteville Cross Creek 🅗 ❀

(910) 868-9005. **$151-$169.** 1468 Skibo Rd 28303. Jct SR 24/87, just s on US 401 Bypass. Int corridors. **Pets:** Other species. $100 one-time fee/room. Service with restrictions.

💾 📶 ✖ ♿ 🛟 💻 ➳ ✖

🅐🅐🅐 ▼▼▼▼ TownePlace Suites Fayetteville Cross Creek 🅗 ❀

(910) 764-1100. **$122-$149.** 1464 Skibo Rd 28303. Jct SR 24/87, just s on US 401 Bypass. Int corridors. **Pets:** Other species. $100 one-time fee/room. Service with restrictions, crate. 💾 📶 ✖ 🛟 💻 ➳

FEARRINGTON VILLAGE

🅐🅐🅐 ▼▼▼▼▼ The Fearrington House Inn 🅒🅘

(919) 542-2121. **$299-$635.** 2000 Fearrington Village Center 27312. US 64 exit 383, 6 mi n on US 15/501. Ext/int corridors. **Pets:** Accepted.

💾 📶 ✖ ♿ 🍴 ➳ ✖

FLAT ROCK

▼▼ Highland Lake Inn 🅗

(828) 693-6812. **Call for rates.** 86 Lily Pad Ln 28731. I-26 exit 53 (Upward Rd), 2.1 mi w, just s on Highland Lake Dr, then just w. Ext/int corridors. **Pets:** Accepted. 📶 ✖ 🛟 💻 🍴 ➳ ✖

▼▼▼▼ Mountain Inn & Suites 🅗

(828) 692-7772. **$69-$139.** 755 Upward Rd 28731. I-26 exit 53 (Upward Rd), just e. Int corridors. **Pets:** Accepted. 📶 ♿ 🛟 💻

▼▼▼▼ Mountain Lodge 🅗

(828) 693-9910. **Call for rates.** 755 Upward Rd 28731. I-26 exit 53 (Upward Rd), just e. Int corridors. **Pets:** Accepted.

📶 ✖ ♿ 🛟 💻 ➳

FLETCHER

▼▼▼▼ Chateau On The Mountain 🅑🅑

(828) 651-9810. **$185-$350, 7 day notice.** 22 Vineyard Hill Dr 28732. I-26 exit 40, 2 mi e on SR 280, 1.3 mi s on US 25 (Hendersonville Rd), 2.3 mi e on Old Airport Rd/Mills Gap Rd, 3.7 mi e on Hooper's Creek Rd, then 1 mi up the hill. Ext/int corridors. **Pets:** Accepted.

📶 ✖ 🛟 💻 ➳ Ⓩ

▼▼ Comfort Inn Asheville Airport 🅗 ❀

(828) 687-9199. **$66-$120.** 15 Rockwood Rd 28732. I-26 exit 40, just e on SR 280, then just s. Int corridors. **Pets:** Medium, other species. $17 daily fee/room. Service with restrictions, supervision. 📶 🛟 💻 ➳

FOREST CITY

▼▼ Jameson Inn Ⓜ

(828) 287-8788. **$70-$90.** 164 Jameson Inn Dr 28043. US 74 Bypass exit 181, 1.8 mi nw on US 74A. Ext corridors. **Pets:** Medium. $15 daily fee/room. Service with restrictions, supervision. 📶 ♿ 🛟 💻 ➳

▼▼ Quality Inn Ⓜ

(828) 248-3400. **Call for rates.** 205 Commercial Dr 28043. US 74 Bypass exit 181, 1.8 mi nw on US 74A. Ext corridors. **Pets:** Accepted. 📶 🛟 💻 ➳

FRANKLIN

▼▼ Microtel Inn & Suites 🅗

(828) 349-9000. **$72-$99.** 81 Allman Dr 28734. Jct US 441 Bypass, 0.4 mi s on US 441 and 23. Int corridors. **Pets:** Small. $20 one-time fee/pet. Designated rooms, service with restrictions, supervision. 📶 ♿ 🛟 💻

GARNER

▼▼ Sleep Inn 🅗

(919) 772-7771. **Call for rates.** 105 Commerce Pkwy 27529. I-40 exit 312, just w on SR 42, then just s. Int corridors. **Pets:** Accepted. 📶 ♿ 🛟 💻 ➳

▼▼ Super 8 Ⓜ

(919) 661-1991. **$56-$65.** 101 Leone Ct 27529. I-40 exit 312, just e on SR 42, then just s. Ext corridors. **Pets:** Medium. $7 daily fee/pet. Service with restrictions, supervision. 📶 🛟 💻 ➳

GASTONIA

🅐🅐🅐 ▼▼▼▼ Best Western Plus Executive Inn 🅗

(704) 868-2000. **$79-$100.** 360 Best Western Ct 28054. I-85 exit 20, just n on SR 279, then just e. Ext/int corridors. **Pets:** Accepted.

💾 📶 🛟 💻 ➳

🅐🅐🅐 ▼▼▼ Days Inn Ⓜ ❀

(704) 864-9981. **$36-$67.** 1700 N Chester St 28052. I-85 exit 17, just s on US 321. Ext/int corridors. **Pets:** Other species. $10 daily fee/pet. Service with restrictions, supervision. 💾 📶 🛟 💻 🍴 ➳

▼▼▼ Hampton Inn 🅗

(704) 866-9090. **Call for rates.** 1859 Remount Rd 28054. I-85 exit 20, just n on SR 279, then just e. Int corridors. **Pets:** Accepted.

📶 ♿ 🛟 💻 ➳

GOLDSBORO

▼▼ Days Inn Goldsboro Ⓜ

(919) 735-7911. **$50-$150.** 801 US 70 E Bypass 27534. US 70 E Bypass exit Wayne Memorial Dr eastbound, just n, just w on 11th St, then 0.5 mi sw on Lincoln Mercury Dr; exit westbound, straight on 11th St, then 0.5 mi sw on Lincoln Mercury Dr. Ext corridors. **Pets:** Medium, dogs only. $15 daily fee/pet. Designated rooms, service with restrictions, supervision. 📶 🛟 💻 ➳

▼▼▼ Hampton Inn 🅗

(919) 778-1800. **$119-$179.** 905 N Spence Ave 27534. US 70 E Bypass exit Spence Ave, just s. Int corridors. **Pets:** Accepted.

📶 🛟 💻 ➳

▼▼▼ Holiday Inn Express Goldsboro 🅗

(919) 751-1999. **$90-$150.** 909 N Spence Ave 27534. US 70 E Bypass exit Spence Ave, just s. Int corridors. **Pets:** Accepted.

📶 🛟 💻 ➳

GREENSBORO

Baymont Inn & Suites H ❀
(336) 294-6220. **Call for rates.** 2001 Veasley St 27407. I-40 exit 217, just s on High Point Rd, then just w. Int corridors. **Pets:** Medium. $10 daily fee/room. Designated rooms, service with restrictions, crate.

Best Western Plus Windsor Suites H
(336) 294-9100. **$89-$149.** 2006 Veasley St 27407. I-40 exit 217, just s on High Point Rd, then just w. Int corridors. **Pets:** Medium. $200 deposit/room, $15 daily fee/pet. Designated rooms, service with restrictions, supervision.

Candlewood Suites H
(336) 454-0078. **Call for rates.** 7623 Thorndike Rd 27409. I-40 exit 210 (SR 68), just s, then just w. Int corridors. **Pets:** Accepted.

Comfort Inn Greensboro H
(336) 297-1055. **Call for rates.** 1103 Lanada Rd 27407. I-40 exit 214 or 214A, just sw on Wendover Ave, then just e on Stanley Rd. Int corridors. **Pets:** Accepted.

Comfort Suites Airport H
(336) 882-6666. **$89-$160.** 7619 Thorndike Rd 27409. I-40 exit 210 (SR 68), just s, then just w. Int corridors. **Pets:** Medium, other species. $150 deposit/pet, $20 daily fee/pet. Service with restrictions, supervision.

Crestwood Suites H
(336) 886-1250. **$40-$70.** 501 Americhase Dr 27409. I-40 exit 210 (SR 68), 0.5 mi s. Int corridors. **Pets:** Small. $15 daily fee/room. Designated rooms, service with restrictions.

Drury Inn & Suites-Greensboro H
(336) 856-9696. **$85-$162.** 3220 High Point Rd 27407. I-40 exit 217, just s. Int corridors. **Pets:** Accepted.

Econo Lodge Inn & Suites M
(336) 275-9575. **Call for rates.** 120 Seneca Rd 27406. I-40/85 business route exit 221, just s, then e. Ext/int corridors. **Pets:** Accepted.

Extended Stay Deluxe-Greensboro-Airport H ❀
(336) 454-0080. **$70-$85.** 7617 Thorndike Rd 27409. I-40 exit 210 (SR 68), just s, then just w. Int corridors. **Pets:** Other species. $25 daily fee/pet. Service with restrictions.

Fairfield Inn Greensboro/Airport H ❀
(336) 841-0140. **$75-$119.** 7615 Thorndike Rd 27409. I-40 exit 210 (SR 68), just s, then just w. Int corridors. **Pets:** Medium, other species. $50 one-time fee/room. Service with restrictions, supervision.

Holiday Inn Express & Suites - Airport H
(336) 882-0004. **$94-$109.** 645 S Regional Rd 27409. I-40 exit 210 (SR 68), just s, then just e. Int corridors. **Pets:** Accepted.

Holiday Inn Express - I-40 at Wendover H
(336) 854-0090. **$79-$109.** 4305 Big Tree Way 27409. I-40 exit 214 or 214B, just ne on Wendover Ave, then just w. Int corridors. **Pets:** Medium. $50 one-time fee/pet. Designated rooms, service with restrictions, crate.

Holiday Inn - Greensboro Airport H
(336) 668-0421. **$89-$169.** 6426 Burnt Poplar Rd 27409. I-40 exit 211, just n on Gallimore Dairy Rd, then just w. Int corridors. **Pets:** Medium. $10 daily fee/pet. Service with restrictions, crate.

Quality Inn & Suites M
(336) 697-4000. **$66-$130.** 3114 Cedar Park Rd 27401. I-85 business route exit 224, just w on SR 6, then just n. Ext corridors. **Pets:** Small. $25 one-time fee/room. Designated rooms, service with restrictions, supervision.

Quality Inn & Suites-Airpark East H
(336) 668-3638. **$69-$159, 3 day notice.** 7067 Albert Pick Rd 27409. I-40 exit 210 (SR 68) westbound, just s, then just e; exit eastbound, just e. Int corridors. **Pets:** Accepted.

Red Roof Inn Airport M
(336) 271-2636. **$34-$79.** 615 Regional Rd S 27409. I-40 exit 210 (SR 68), just s, then just e. Ext corridors. **Pets:** Large, other species. No service, supervision.

Residence Inn by Marriott-Greensboro Airport H ❀
(336) 632-4666. **$94-$228.** 7616 Thorndike Rd 27409. I-40 exit 210 (SR 68), just s, then just w. Int corridors. **Pets:** Small. $100 one-time fee/room. Designated rooms, service with restrictions, supervision.

GREENVILLE

Candlewood Suites H
(252) 317-3000. **Call for rates.** 1055 Waterford Commons Dr 27834. Just e of US 264; jct Stantonsburg and B's Barbeque rds; just w of Pitt County Memorial Hospital. Int corridors. **Pets:** Accepted.

City Hotel & Bistro H
(252) 355-8300. **Call for rates.** 203 W Greenville Blvd 27834. Jct SR 11/903, 1 mi e on US 264A. Int corridors. **Pets:** Accepted.

Hilton Greenville H ❀
(252) 355-5000. **$119-$199.** 207 SW Greenville Blvd 27834. Jct SR 11/903, 1 mi e on US 264 alternate route. Int corridors. **Pets:** Large. $75 one-time fee/pet. Designated rooms, service with restrictions.

Home-Towne Suites H
(252) 752-3411. **$59-$130.** 2111 W Arlington Blvd 27834. Jct US 13/SR 11, 0.4 mi w on Stantonsburg Rd, then just s. Int corridors. **Pets:** Medium. $25 daily fee/room. Service with restrictions, crate.

Jameson Inn M
(252) 752-7382. **$72-$92.** 920 Crosswinds St 27834. Jct US 264 alternate route, just s on US 13/SR 11, then just w. Ext corridors. **Pets:** Medium. $15 daily fee/room. Service with restrictions, supervision.

HAVELOCK

Quality Inn H
(252) 444-1111. **Call for rates.** 400 Hwy 70 W 28532. Jct SR 101, 1.9 mi w. Int corridors. **Pets:** Accepted.

HENDERSON

Budget Host Inn M
(252) 492-2013. **$49-$69.** 1727 N Garnett St 27536. I-85 exit 215, just e, then just w on US 158. Ext corridors. **Pets:** Small. $15 daily fee/pet. Designated rooms, service with restrictions, supervision.

Lamplight Inn B&B BB ❀
(252) 438-6311. **$90-$120, 7 day notice.** 1680 Flemingtown Rd 27537. I-85 exit 220, 1.5 mi nw. Int corridors. **Pets:** Medium, dogs only. Designated rooms, service with restrictions, crate.

Sleep Inn H
(252) 433-9449. **$70-$79.** 18 Market St 27537. I-85 exit 212, just w on Ruin Creek Rd, then just se on Zeb Robinson Rd. Int corridors. **Pets:** Small. $15 daily fee/pet. Designated rooms, service with restrictions, supervision.

HENDERSONVILLE

◈◈◈ **The Waverly Inn** BB
(828) 693-9193. **$189-$305, 7 day notice.** 783 N Main St 28792. I-26 exit 49B, 2 mi w on US 64, then just n. Int corridors. **Pets:** Medium, other species. Designated rooms, service with restrictions, crate.

ⒶⒶⒶ ◈◈◈ **Best Western Hendersonville Inn** M
(828) 692-0521. **$60-$110.** 105 Sugarloaf Rd 28792. I-26 exit 49A, just e on US 64. Ext corridors. **Pets:** Other species. $10 daily fee/pet. Service with restrictions. SAVE

◈◈◈ **Comfort Inn** M
(828) 693-8800. **$55-$109.** 206 Mitchelle Dr 28792. I-26 exit 49B, just w on US 64, just s on Orr Camp Dr, then just e. Ext corridors. **Pets:** Accepted. SAVE

◈ **Days Inn** M
(828) 697-5999. **$50-$99.** 102 Mitchelle Dr 28792. I-26 exit 49B, just w on US 64, then just s on Orr Camp Dr. Ext corridors. **Pets:** $15 daily fee/pet. Service with restrictions, supervision.

◈◈◈ **Inn on Church Street** CI
(828) 693-3258. **Call for rates.** 201 3rd Ave W 28739. I-26 exit 49B, 2 mi w on US 64, just s on Main St, then just w. Int corridors. **Pets:** Accepted.

ⒶⒶⒶ ◈◈◈ **Ramada** H
(828) 697-0006. **$43-$116.** 150 Sugarloaf Rd 28792. I-26 exit 49A, just e on US 64, then just s. Int corridors. **Pets:** Medium. $15 daily fee/pet. Designated rooms, service with restrictions, supervision.
SAVE

HICKORY

◈◈◈◈ **Crowne Plaza** H
(828) 323-1000. **$85-$135.** 1385 Lenoir Rhyne Blvd SE 28602. I-40 exit 125, just s. Ext/int corridors. **Pets:** $75 one-time fee/room. Designated rooms, service with restrictions, crate.

◈◈ **Jameson Inn** M
(828) 304-0410. **$71-$91.** 1120 13th Ave Dr SE 28602. I-40 exit 125, just s, then 0.4 mi w. Ext corridors. **Pets:** Medium. $15 daily fee/room. Service with restrictions, supervision.

◈◈ **Red Roof Inn Hickory** M
(828) 323-1500. **$47-$79.** 1184 Lenoir Rhyne Blvd 28602. I-40 exit 125, just n. Ext corridors. **Pets:** Large, other species. No service, supervision.

HIGHLANDS

◈◈ **Mountain High Lodge** M
(828) 526-2790. **$49-$189, 7 day notice.** 200 Main St 28741. Just w on US 64; downtown. Ext corridors. **Pets:** Accepted.

HILLSBOROUGH

ⒶⒶⒶ ◈◈◈ **Holiday Inn Express** H
(919) 644-7997. **$95-$179.** 202 Cardinal Dr 27278. I-85 exit 164, just se, then just s; I-40 exit 261, 1.2 mi n, then just w. Int corridors. **Pets:** Medium. $25 daily fee/pet. Designated rooms, service with restrictions, supervision. SAVE

JACKSONVILLE

◈◈◈ **Baymont Inn & Suites Jacksonville** H
(910) 347-6500. **$80-$87, 30 day notice.** 474 Western Blvd 28546. Jct US 17, just n. Ext corridors. **Pets:** Accepted.

◈◈◈ **Candlewood Suites** H
(910) 333-0494. **$89-$129.** 119 Penny Ln 28546. Jct Western Blvd, just n on US 17, then just w. Int corridors. **Pets:** Large. $75 one-time fee/room. Service with restrictions, crate.

◈◈ **Extended StayAmerica Jacksonville Camp Lejeune** H
(910) 347-7684. **$88-$110.** 20 McDaniel Dr 28546. Jct Western Blvd, just n on US 17, then just w. Int corridors. **Pets:** Other species. $25 daily fee/pet. Service with restrictions.

◈◈◈ **TownePlace Suites Jacksonville** H
(910) 478-9795. **$118-$134.** 400 Northwest Dr 28546. Jct US 17, 2 mi w on Western Blvd, then just s. Int corridors. **Pets:** Small. $100 one-time fee/room. Service with restrictions, supervision.

JONESVILLE

ⒶⒶⒶ ◈◈◈ **Best Western Yadkin Valley Inn & Suites** H
(336) 835-6000. **$86-$140.** 1713 NC Hwy 67 28642. I-77 exit 82, just e. Int corridors. **Pets:** Medium. $15 daily fee/pet. Designated rooms, service with restrictions, supervision. SAVE

◈◈ **Days Inn Jonesville-Elkin** M
(336) 526-6777. **$66-$108.** 1540 NC Hwy 67 28642. I-77 exit 82, just w. Ext corridors. **Pets:** Accepted.

ⒶⒶⒶ ◈◈◈ **Quality Inn** M
(336) 835-9400. **$79-$100.** 1633 Winston Rd 28642. I-77 exit 82, just w on SR 67. Ext corridors. **Pets:** Medium, other species. $20 daily fee/pet. Designated rooms, service with restrictions, supervision.
SAVE

KENLY

◈◈ **Econo Lodge** M
(919) 284-1000. **$45-$150.** 405 S Church St 27542. I-95 exit 107, just e. Ext corridors. **Pets:** Medium. $10 daily fee/pet. Designated rooms, service with restrictions.

LAKE TOXAWAY

◈◈◈ **Cabins at Seven Foxes** CA
(828) 877-6333. **$170-$285, 30 day notice.** Seven Foxes Ln 28747. Jct US 64 and SR 281 N, 0.5 mi n to Slick Fisher Rd, then 1.4 mi w. Ext corridors. **Pets:** Dogs only. $50 one-time fee/pet. No service, supervision.

LAURINBURG

◈◈ **Jameson Inn** M
(910) 277-0080. **$65-$85.** 14 Jameson Inn Ct 28352. Jct US 74 Bypass exit 183, just n on US 15/401 Bypass, then just e. Ext corridors. **Pets:** Medium. $15 daily fee/room. Service with restrictions, supervision.

LELAND

ⒶⒶⒶ ◈◈◈ **Best Western Plus Westgate Inn & Suites** H
(910) 371-2858. **$89-$119, 3 day notice.** 1120 Towne Lake Dr 28451. Jct US 74/76, 2 mi s on US 17. Int corridors. **Pets:** Dogs only. $20 daily fee/pet. Designated rooms, service with restrictions, supervision.
SAVE

◈◈◈◈ **Comfort Suites - Magnolia Greens** H
(910) 383-3300. **$79-$159.** 1020 Grandiflora Dr 28451. Jct US 74/76, 2 mi s on US 17, just w. Int corridors. **Pets:** Medium. $40 one-time fee/room. Designated rooms, service with restrictions.

LENOIR

◈◈ **Days Inn** M
(828) 754-0731. **$54-$82.** 206 Blowing Rock Blvd 28645. Jct US 64/SR 18, just n on US 321. Ext corridors. **Pets:** Small, dogs only. $10 daily fee/pet. Service with restrictions, supervision.

LEXINGTON

▼▼▽ **Days Inn** H

(336) 357-2333. **Call for rates.** 1620 Cotton Grove Rd 27292. I-85 exit 91, just s on SR 8, then just ne. Ext/int corridors. **Pets:** Medium. $10 daily fee/pet. Designated rooms, no service, supervision.

🛜 ᶦᴹ 🖥 💻

▼▼▽ **Quality Inn** H

(336) 243-2929. **$80-$110, 5 day notice.** 101 Plaza Pkwy 27292. I-85 exit 91, just n on SR 8, then 0.4 mi ne. Int corridors. **Pets:** Medium. $26 daily fee/pet. Designated rooms, service with restrictions, supervision.

🛜 ᶦᴹ 🖥 💻 ➿

LILLINGTON

▼▽ **Microtel Inn & Suites** H

(910) 893-2626. **$63-$81.** 300 E Cornelius Harnett Blvd 27546. Jct US 401/SR 210, just ne on US 421/SR 27. Int corridors. **Pets:** Accepted.

🛜 ᶦᴹ 🖥 💻

LITTLE SWITZERLAND

▽▽▽▽ **Switzerland Inn** CI

(828) 765-2153. **Call for rates.** 86 High Ridge Rd 28749. Jct SR 226A and Blue Ridge Pkwy, MM 334. Ext/int corridors. **Pets:** Accepted.

🛜 ✕ ᶦᴹ 🖥 💻 🍴 ➿ ✕

LUMBERTON

▲▲▲ ▼▼▼▼ **Best Western Inn** M

(910) 618-9799. **$90-$160.** 201 Jackson Ct 28358. I-95 exit 22, just e, then just s. Ext corridors. **Pets:** Medium. $10 daily fee/pet. Service with restrictions, supervision. SAVE 🛜 🖥 💻 ➿

MAGGIE VALLEY

▲▲▲ ▼▼ **Comfort Inn** H

(828) 926-9106. **$50-$130.** 3282 Soco Rd 28751. US 19, 3.3 mi w of US 276. Int corridors. **Pets:** Accepted. SAVE 🛜 ✕ 🖥 💻 ➿

▲▲▲ ▼▼ **Microtel Inn & Suites** H

(828) 926-8554. **$45-$144.** 3777 Soco Rd, Hwy 19 28751. US 19, 4 mi w of US 276. Int corridors. **Pets:** Accepted.

SAVE 🛜 ᶦᴹ 🖥 💻 ➿

MARION

▼▽ **Comfort Inn** H

(828) 652-4888. **$75-$150.** 178 Hwy 70 W 28752. I-40 exit 85, 5 mi n; jct US 221 N Bypass and 70. Int corridors. **Pets:** Accepted.

🛜 ᶦᴹ 🖥 💻 ➿

MILLS RIVER

▽▼▽ **Barkwells** CA

(828) 891-8288. **$198-$325, 30 day notice.** 234-333 Barkwells Ln 28759. I-26 exit 40, 0.8 mi n on US 25 (Boylston Hwy), 2.4 mi w on Old Fanning Bridge Rd, then 0.3 mi s, follow signs to gated entrance. Ext corridors. **Pets:** Accepted. 🛜 ✕ 🖥 💻 ✕

MOCKSVILLE

▼▼ **Quality Inn** M

(336) 751-7310. **$59-$79.** 1500 Yadkinville Rd 27028. I-40 exit 170, just s on US 601. Ext corridors. **Pets:** Accepted. 🛜 🖥 💻 ➿

MONROE

▼▼ **Super 8** M

(704) 289-1555. **$50-$69.** 608-E W Roosevelt Blvd 28110. Jct US 601, 1 mi e on US 74. Ext corridors. **Pets:** Accepted. 🛜 ᶦᴹ 🖥 💻 ➿

MOORESVILLE

▼▼▼ **Holiday Inn Express Hotel & Suites** H

(704) 662-6900. **$99-$159, 3 day notice.** 130 Norman Station Blvd 28117. I-77 exit 36, just e on SR 150, then just s. Int corridors. **Pets:** Accepted. 🛜 ᶦᴹ 🖥 💻 ➿

▼▼▼▼ **TownePlace Suites Charlotte Mooresville** H

(704) 659-8600. **$99-$129.** 139 Gateway Blvd 28117. I-77 exit 33, just ne on US 21, then just w. Int corridors. **Pets:** Medium, other species. $100 one-time fee/room. Service with restrictions, crate.

🛜 ✕ ᶦᴹ 🖥 💻 ➿

MOREHEAD CITY

▼▼▼ **Holiday Inn Express Hotel & Suites** H ✿

(252) 247-5001. **$89-$179.** 5063 Executive Dr 28557. Jct US 70 and SR 24. Int corridors. **Pets:** Medium, other species. $35 one-time fee/room. Designated rooms, service with restrictions, crate.

🛜 ✕ 🖥 💻 ➿

MORGANTON

▲▲▲ ▼▼▽ **Comfort Inn & Suites** H

(828) 430-4000. **$90-$140.** 1273 Burkemont Ave 28655. I-40 exit 103, just s. Int corridors. **Pets:** Medium. $25 daily fee/pet. Designated rooms, service with restrictions, supervision. SAVE 🛜 ᶦᴹ 🖥 💻 ➿

▼▼▼ **Quality Inn** H

(828) 437-0171. **$69-$139.** 2400 S Sterling St 28655. I-40 exit 105 (SR 18), just s. Ext corridors. **Pets:** Medium. $25 one-time fee/pet. Service with restrictions, supervision. 🛜 ᶦᴹ 🖥 💻 🍴 ➿

▼▼ **Sleep Inn** H

(828) 433-9000. **$69-$139.** 2400A S Sterling St 28655. I-40 exit 105 (SR 18), just s. Int corridors. **Pets:** Medium. $25 one-time fee/pet. Service with restrictions, supervision. 🛜 ᶦᴹ 🖥 💻

MORRISVILLE

▼▼ **Extended StayAmerica-Raleigh-RDU Airport** M ✿

(919) 380-1499. **$65-$85.** 2700 Slater Rd 27560. I-40 exit 284 or 284A, 0.4 mi s on Airport Blvd, then just w. Ext corridors. **Pets:** Other species. $25 daily fee/pet. Service with restrictions. 🛜 🖥 💻

▼▼▽ **Holiday Inn Express** H

(919) 653-2260. **$119-$139.** 1014 Airport Blvd 27560. I-40 exit 284 or 284A, just s. Int corridors. **Pets:** Accepted. 🛜 ᶦᴹ 🖥 💻 ➿

▼▼▼▼ **Holiday Inn - Raleigh-Durham Airport** H

(919) 465-1910. **$110-$130.** 930 Airport Blvd 27560. I-40 exit 284 or 284A, 0.5 mi s. Int corridors. **Pets:** Accepted.

🛜 ᶦᴹ 🖥 💻 🍴 ➿

▼▼▼▼ **La Quinta Inn & Suites Raleigh Durham Airport** S H

(919) 481-3600. **$64-$148.** 1001 Aerial Center Pkwy 27560. I-40 exit 284 or 284A, just s, then just e; in Aerial Center Park. Int corridors. **Pets:** Medium, other species. Service with restrictions, supervision.

🛜 ᶦᴹ 🖥 💻

▼▼▼▼ **La Quinta Inn & Suites (Raleigh-Durham Int'l Airport)** H

(919) 461-1771. **$88-$181.** 1001 Hospitality Ct 27560. I-40 exit 284 or 284A, just s, just e on Aerial Center Pkwy, then just ne; in Aerial Center Park. Int corridors. **Pets:** Medium, other species. Service with restrictions, supervision. 🛜 ᶦᴹ 🖥 💻

▼▼▼ **Residence Inn Raleigh - Durham Airport** H ✿

(919) 467-8689. **$79-$189.** 2020 Hospitality Ct 27560. I-40 exit 284 or 284A, just s on Airport Blvd, just e on Aerial Center Pkwy, then just ne. Int corridors. **Pets:** Large. $100 one-time fee/room. Service with restrictions, crate. ECO 🛜 ✕ ᶦᴹ 🖥 💻 ➿ ✕

▼▼▼▼ **Staybridge Suites Raleigh Durham Airport** H

(919) 468-0180. **$90-$113.** 1012 Airport Blvd 27560. I-40 exit 284 or 284A, just s; enter between Hampton Inn-RDU and Holiday Inn Express. Int corridors. **Pets:** Large. $50 one-time fee/room. Service with restrictions, crate. 🛜 ᶦᴹ 🖥 💻

MOUNT AIRY

▼▼▼▼ Holiday Inn Express & Suites

(336) 719-1731. **$95-$150.** 1320 EMS Dr 27030. Jct US 52, 0.5 mi s on US 601, then just w. Int corridors. **Pets:** Small. $25 daily fee/pet. Designated rooms, service with restrictions, supervision.

▼▼ Quality Inn M

(336) 789-2000. **$68-$130.** 2136 Rockford St 27030. Jct US 52, 0.6 mi s on US 601. Ext corridors. **Pets:** Medium, other species. $25 one-time fee/room. Designated rooms, service with restrictions, supervision.

MURPHY

AAA ▼▼▼ Best Western of Murphy M ❖

(828) 837-3060. **$64-$100.** 1522 Andrews Rd 28906. US 74, 19 and 129 exit Andrews Rd. Ext corridors. **Pets:** Medium, other species. $15 daily fee/room. Designated rooms.

AAA ▼▼▼ Days Inn M

(828) 837-8030. **$53-$89.** 754 Hwy 64 W 28906. US 64 W, 19 S, 74 W and 129 S. Ext corridors. **Pets:** Accepted.

NEW BERN

▼▼▼▼ Hilton New Bern Riverfront

(252) 638-3585. **Call for rates.** 100 Middle St 28560. On waterfront; downtown. Int corridors. **Pets:** Accepted.

OCEAN ISLE BEACH

AAA ▼▼▼ The Islander Inn

(910) 575-7000. **Call for rates.** 57 W First St 28469. Jct SR 904, just s. Int corridors. **Pets:** Accepted.

AAA ▼▼▼ The Winds Resort Beach Club

(910) 579-6275. **$71-$363, 30 day notice.** 310 E First St 28469. SR 904, 1.6 mi n. Ext/int corridors. **Pets:** Small. $25 daily fee/pet. Designated rooms, service with restrictions, crate.

OLD FORT

▼▼▼▼ Inn On Mill Creek BB ❖

(828) 668-1115. **$149-$199, 30 day notice.** 3895 Mill Creek Rd 28762. I-40 exit 66, just n, 0.9 mi e on Ridgecrest Rd, 0.9 mi n on Yates Ave, then 1.5 mi n. Ext/int corridors. **Pets:** Other species. $15 daily fee/pet. Designated rooms, service with restrictions, crate.

ORIENTAL

▼▼ Oriental Marina & Inn CO

(252) 249-1818. **$99-$234.** 103 Wall St 28571. Jct SR 55 (Broad St), just ne on Hodges St. Ext corridors. **Pets:** Accepted.

OUTER BANKS AREA

KILL DEVIL HILLS

▼▼▼ Comfort Inn North Oceanfront

(252) 441-6333. **$70-$260.** 1601 S Virginia Dare Tr 27948. SR 12, at MM 9.5. Int corridors. **Pets:** Other species. $25 daily fee/room. Designated rooms, service with restrictions, supervision.

AAA ▼▼▼▼ First Flight Retreat Condominiums CO

(252) 489-4747. **$145-$399.** 815 S Virginia Dare Tr 27948. SR 12, at MM 8.5. Int corridors. **Pets:** Medium, dogs only. $125 one-time fee/pet. Designated rooms, no service, supervision.

AAA ▼▼▼ John Yancey Oceanfront Inn M

(252) 441-7141. **Call for rates.** 2009 S Virginia Dare Tr 27948. SR 12, at MM 10.3. Ext/int corridors. **Pets:** Medium, other species. $20 daily fee/pet. Designated rooms, service with restrictions, supervision.

AAA ▼▼▼ Ramada Plaza Nags Head Beach  ❖

(252) 441-2151. **$66-$276, 3 day notice.** 1701 S Virginia Dare Tr 27948. SR 12, at MM 9.5. Int corridors. **Pets:** $25 daily fee/pet. Designated rooms, supervision.

AAA ▼▼▼ Travelodge-Nags Head Beach  ❖

(252) 441-0411. **$54-$198, 3 day notice.** 804 N Virginia Dare Tr 27948. SR 12, at MM 8.1. Ext/int corridors. **Pets:** Other species. $10 daily fee/pet. Designated rooms, service with restrictions.

NAGS HEAD

▼▼▼▼ Comfort Inn Oceanfront South

(252) 441-6315. **$80-$255.** 8031 Old Oregon Inlet Rd 27959. SR 12, at MM 17. Int corridors. **Pets:** Other species. $25 daily fee/pet. Designated rooms, service with restrictions, supervision.

▼▼ Dolphin Oceanfront Motel M

(252) 441-7488. **$49-$399, 30 day notice.** 8017 Old Oregon Inlet Rd 27959. Jct SR 12, just s, at MM 16.5. Ext corridors. **Pets:** Other species. $10 daily fee/pet. Service with restrictions.

OCRACOKE

AAA ▼▼▼ The Anchorage Inn M ❖

(252) 928-1101. **Call for rates.** 205 Irvin Garrish Hwy (SR 12) 27960. From Cedar Island Ferry, just n. Ext corridors. **Pets:** Other species. $25 daily fee/room. Designated rooms, service with restrictions, supervision.

END AREA

OXFORD

AAA ▼▼▼ Comfort Inn & Suites

(919) 692-1000. **$75-$140.** 1000 Linden Ave 27565. I-85 exit 204, just e. Int corridors. **Pets:** Accepted.

PEMBROKE

▼▼▼▼ Holiday Inn Express

(910) 521-1311. **Call for rates.** 605 Redmond Rd 28372. Jct SR 710, just se on SR 711, then just s. Int corridors. **Pets:** Accepted.

PINEHURST

AAA ▼▼▼▼ Homewood Suites by Hilton - Olmstead Village near Pinehurst

(910) 255-0300. **$107-$228.** 250 Central Park Ave 28374. Jct SR 5 and 211, just n; in Olmstead Village. Int corridors. **Pets:** Accepted.

▼▼▼▼ SpringHill Suites Pinehurst Southern Pines

(910) 695-0234. **$96-$142.** 10024 US 15/501 28374. Jct US 1, 2.3 mi n. Int corridors. **Pets:** Accepted.

PLYMOUTH

▼▼▼ Holiday Inn Express ⬛
(252) 793-4700. **$81-$86.** 840 US Hwy 64 W 27962. Jct SR 32 S, 1 mi w. Ext/int corridors. **Pets:** Accepted. 🛜 ⬛ ⬛ ⬛ ⬛

🅰🅰🅰 ▼▼▼ Port-o Plymouth Inn Ⓜ
(252) 793-5006. **$55-$150.** 510 Hwy 64 E 27962. On US 64. Ext corridors. **Pets:** Small. $10 daily fee/pet. Designated rooms, service with restrictions, supervision. ⬛ 🛜 ⬛ ⬛

RALEIGH

🅰🅰🅰 ▼▼▼ Americas Best Value Inn - Crabtree ⬛
(919) 277-8485. **$55-$65.** 3921 Arrow Dr 27612. I-440 exit 7 or 7B, just w on US 70, just s on Blue Ridge Rd, then 0.4 mi e on Summit Park Ln. Ext/int corridors. **Pets:** Other species. $15 daily fee/pet. Service with restrictions, supervision. ⬛ 🛜 ⬛ ⬛

🅰🅰🅰 ▼▼▼ Best Western Plus Raleigh North ⬛
(919) 872-5000. **Call for rates.** 2715 Capital Blvd 27604. I-440 exit 11 or 11B, just n on US 1. Int corridors. **Pets:** Accepted.
⬛ 🛜 ⬛ ⬛ ⬛

▼▼ ▼▼ Candlewood Suites-Crabtree ⬛ 🐾
(919) 789-4840. **$71-$81.** 4433 Lead Mine Rd 27612. I-440 exit 7 or 7B, just w, then just n. Int corridors. **Pets:** Large. $25 daily fee/room. Service with restrictions. 🛜 ⬛ ⬛ ⬛

▼▼▼▼ Comfort Inn & Suites Crabtree ⬛
(919) 782-1112. **$55-$90.** 6209 Glenwood Ave 27612. I-440 exit 7 or 7B, 2.5 mi w on US 70. Int corridors. **Pets:** Accepted.
🛜 ⬛ ⬛ ⬛ ⬛

🅰🅰🅰 ▼▼▼▼ Comfort Suites ⬛
(919) 876-2211. **$62-$142.** 4400 Capital Blvd 27604. I-440 exit 11 and 11B, just s on US 1. Int corridors. **Pets:** Medium, other species. $25 one-time fee/room, $10 daily fee/room. Service with restrictions, crate.
⬛ 🛜 ⬛ ⬛ ⬛ ⬛

▼▼ ▼▼ Days Inn Ⓜ
(919) 878-9310. **$45-$57.** 3201 Wake Forest Rd 27609. I-440 exit 10 (Wake Forest Rd), just n, then just w. Ext corridors. **Pets:** Accepted.
🛜 ⬛ ⬛ ⬛

▼▼ ▼▼ Extended StayAmerica-Raleigh-North Raleigh ⬛ 🐾
(919) 829-7271. **$62-$90.** 911 Wake Towne Dr 27609. I-440 exit 10 (Wake Forest Rd), just s, then w. Int corridors. **Pets:** Other species. $25 daily fee/pet. Service with restrictions. 🛜 ⬛ ⬛

🅰🅰🅰 ▼▼▼▼ Fairfield Inn & Suites Raleigh Crabtree Valley ⬛
(919) 881-9800. **$74-$124.** 2201 Summit Park Ln 27612. I-440 exit 7 or 7B, just w on US 70, just s on Blue Ridge Rd, then just e. Int corridors. **Pets:** Large. $75 one-time fee/room. Designated rooms, service with restrictions, crate. ⬛ 🛜 ⬛ ⬛ ⬛ ⬛ ⬛

▼▼▼▼ Hilton North Raleigh Midtown ⬛
(919) 872-2323. **$99-$219.** 3415 Wake Forest Rd 27609. I-440 exit 10 (Wake Forest Rd), 0.4 mi n. Int corridors. **Pets:** Accepted.
🛜 ⬛ ⬛ ⬛ ⬛ ⬛

▼▼▼▼ Holiday Inn Crabtree Valley ⬛
(919) 782-8600. **$69-$139.** 4100 Glenwood Ave 27612. I-440 exit 7 or 7B, just w on US 70. Int corridors. **Pets:** Accepted.
🛜 ⬛ ⬛ ⬛ ⬛ ⬛ ⬛

▼▼▼▼ Holiday Inn Express & Suites at NC State/Southwest ⬛ 🐾
(919) 854-0001. **$89-$129.** 3741 Thistledown Dr 27606. I-40 exit 295, just n on Gorman St, then just e. Int corridors. **Pets:** Small, dogs only. $25 daily fee/pet. Designated rooms, no service, supervision.
🛜 ⬛ ⬛ ⬛ ⬛ ⬛

▼▼▼▼ Holiday Inn Express Hotel & Suites ⬛
(919) 570-5550. **$80-$120.** 11400 Common Oaks Dr 27614. Jct SR 98, 1.2 mi s on US 1, then just w. Int corridors. **Pets:** Accepted.
🛜 ⬛ ⬛ ⬛ ⬛

🅰🅰🅰 ▼▼▼▼ Holiday Inn Raleigh-North ⬛ 🐾
(919) 872-3500. **$89-$129.** 2805 Highwoods Blvd 27604. I-440 exit 11 or 11B, just n on US 1, then just w. Int corridors. **Pets:** $35 one-time fee/room. No service, crate. ⬛ 🛜 ⬛ ⬛ ⬛ ⬛ ⬛ ⬛

▼▼ ▼▼ Homestead Studio Suites Hotel-Raleigh/Crabtree Valley ⬛ 🐾
(919) 510-8551. **$62-$87.** 4810 Bluestone Dr 27612. I-440 exit 7 or 7B, 1.6 mi w on US 70, then just s. Ext corridors. **Pets:** Other species. $25 daily fee/pet. Service with restrictions. 🛜 ⬛ ⬛

▼▼ ▼▼ Homestead Studio Suites Hotel-Raleigh/Northeast ⬛ 🐾
(919) 807-9970. **$65-$90.** 2601 Appliance Ct 27604. I-440 exit 11 or 11B, just n on US 1, then just e. Int corridors. **Pets:** Other species. $25 daily fee/pet. Service with restrictions. 🛜 ⬛ ⬛ ⬛

▼▼ ▼▼ Homestead Studio Suites Hotel-Raleigh/North Raleigh Ⓜ 🐾
(919) 981-7353. **$57-$85.** 3531 Wake Forest Rd 27609. I-440 exit 10 (Wake Forest Rd), 0.5 mi n. Ext corridors. **Pets:** Other species. $25 daily fee/pet. Service with restrictions. 🛜 ⬛ ⬛ ⬛

▼▼▼▼ La Quinta Inn & Suites Raleigh (Crabtree) ⬛
(919) 785-0071. **$88-$171.** 2211 Summit Park Ln 27612. I-440 exit 7 or 7B, just w on US 70, just s on Blue Ridge Rd, then just e. Int corridors. **Pets:** Medium, other species. Service with restrictions, supervision.
🛜 ⬛ ⬛ ⬛ ⬛

▼▼ ▼▼ Red Roof Inn - Convention Center ⬛
(919) 833-6005. **$49-$79.** 1813 S Saunders St 27603. I-40 exit 298B, just n. Int corridors. **Pets:** Large, other species. No service, supervision.
🛜 ⬛ ⬛

🅰🅰🅰 ▼▼▼▼ Residence Inn by Marriott-Raleigh Midtown ⬛
(919) 878-6100. **$76-$139.** 1000 Navaho Dr 27609. I-440 exit 10 (Wake Forest Rd), just n, then w. Ext corridors. **Pets:** Accepted.
⬛ 🛜 ⬛ ⬛ ⬛ ⬛ ⬛ ⬛

🅰🅰🅰 ▼▼▼▼ Residence Inn Raleigh Crabtree Valley ⬛
(919) 279-3000. **$94-$174.** 2200 Summit Park Ln 27612. I-440 exit 7 or 7B, just w on US 70, just s on Blue Ridge Rd, then just e. Int corridors. **Pets:** Accepted. ⬛ 🛜 ⬛ ⬛ ⬛ ⬛ ⬛ ⬛

REIDSVILLE

🅰🅰🅰 ▼▼▼ Quality Inn Ⓜ
(336) 634-1275. **$65-$199.** 2203 Barnes St 27320. US 29 exit 150 (Barnes St), just e. Ext corridors. **Pets:** Small. $15 daily fee/pet. Designated rooms, service with restrictions, supervision.
⬛ 🛜 ⬛ ⬛ ⬛ ⬛

RESEARCH TRIANGLE PARK

▼▼▼▼ Radisson Hotel in Research Triangle Park ⬛
(919) 549-8631. **Call for rates.** 150 Park Dr 27709. I-40 exit 280, just s, then just w. Int corridors. **Pets:** Accepted.
⬛ 🛜 ⬛ ⬛ ⬛ ⬛ ⬛ ⬛

ROANOKE RAPIDS

▼▼ ▼▼ Jameson Inn Ⓜ
(252) 533-0022. **$70-$90.** 101 S Old Farm Rd 27870. I-95 exit 173, 0.5 mi w on US 158, then just s. Ext corridors. **Pets:** Medium. $15 daily fee/room. Service with restrictions, supervision. 🛜 ⬛ ⬛ ⬛ ⬛

▼▼ ▼▼ Quality Inn Ⓜ
(252) 537-9927. **Call for rates.** 1914 Julian R Allsbrook Hwy 27870. I-95 exit 173, just w. Ext corridors. **Pets:** Medium, other species. $15 one-time fee/room. Service with restrictions, supervision. 🛜 ⬛ ⬛ ⬛ ⬛

ROBBINSVILLE

▼▼ ▼▼ **Microtel Inn & Suites** H
(828) 479-6772. **$67-$94.** 111 Rodney Orr Bypass (US 129) 28771. Center of downtown. Int corridors. **Pets:** Accepted. 🛜 ✕ 🛏 💻

ROCKY MOUNT

△△△ ▼▼▼ **Best Western Inn I-95/Goldrock** M
(252) 985-1450. **$50-$80.** 7095 NC 4 27809. I-95 exit 145, just e. Ext corridors. **Pets:** Other species. $20 one-time fee/room. Service with restrictions, supervision. SAVE 🛜 🛏 💻 🏊

▼▼▼▼ **Candlewood Suites** H 🐾
(252) 467-2550. **$85-$129.** 688 English Rd 27804. I-95 exit 138, 1 mi e on US 64 exit 466, just n on Winstead Ave, then just w. Int corridors. **Pets:** Other species. $25 one-time fee/room. Designated rooms, service with restrictions. 🛜 🛗M 🛏 💻 🏊

△△△ ▼▼▼▼ **Comfort Inn** H
(252) 937-7765. **$74-$85.** 200 Gateway Blvd 27804. I-95 exit 138, 1 mi e on US 64 exit 466, just s on Winstead Ave, just e on Curtis Ellis Dr, then just ne. Int corridors. **Pets:** Accepted. SAVE 🛜 🛏 💻 🏊

△△△ ▼▼▼▼ **Country Inn & Suites By Carlson** H 🐾
(252) 442-0500. **$79-$169, 14 day notice.** 672 English Rd 27804. I-95 exit 138, 1 mi e on US 64 exit 466, just n on Winstead Ave, just w. Int corridors. **Pets:** Other species. $15 one-time fee/room. Designated rooms, no service, crate. SAVE 🛜 ✕ 🛗M 🛏 💻 🏊

△△△ ▼▼▼▼ **Residence Inn Rocky Mount** H
(252) 451-5600. **$97-$144.** 230 Gateway Blvd 27804. I-95 exit 138, 1 mi e on US 64 exit 466, just s on Winstead Ave, just e on Curtis Ellis Dr, then just ne. Int corridors. **Pets:** Other species. $40 one-time fee/room. Service with restrictions, crate. SAVE 🛜 ✕ 🛗M 🛏 💻 🏊 ✕

△△△ ▼▼▼ **Best Western Rocky Mount Inn** M 🐾
(252) 442-8101. **$50-$80.** 1921 N Wesleyan Blvd 27804. US 64 exit 468A, 2.2 mi n on US 301 Bypass. Ext corridors. **Pets:** Small, other species. $20 one-time fee/room. Designated rooms.
SAVE 🛜 🛏 💻 🏊

ROXBORO

▼▼▼▼ **Hampton Inn** H
(336) 599-8800. **$103-$119.** 920 Durham Rd 27573. Jct US 158, n on US 501. Int corridors. **Pets:** Accepted. 🛜 🛏 💻 🏊

SALISBURY

▼▼▼▼ **Hampton Inn** H
(704) 637-8000. **$99-$199.** 1001 Klumac Rd 28144. I-85 exit 75, just n on US 601, then just sw. Int corridors. **Pets:** Accepted.
🛜 🛏 💻 🏊

▼▼▼▼ **Holiday Inn Hotel & Conference Center** H
(704) 637-3100. **$89-$159.** 530 Jake Alexander Blvd S 28147. I-85 exit 75, 0.5 mi n on US 601. Ext/int corridors. **Pets:** Medium. $40 one-time fee/room. Designated rooms, service with restrictions, supervision. 🛜 ✕ 🛗M 🛏 💻 🍴 🏊 ✕

SALUDA

▼▼▼▼ **The Oaks Bed & Breakfast** BB 🐾
(828) 749-2000. **$139-$209, 7 day notice.** 339 Greenville St 28773. I-26 exit 59, 1.1 mi sw, 0.5 mi w on US 176, then cross railway tracks. Ext/int corridors. **Pets:** Medium. $50 one-time fee/room. Designated rooms, service with restrictions, supervision. ✕ 🛏 💻 🍴

SANFORD

▼▼▼▼ **Hampton Inn** H
(919) 775-2000. **Call for rates.** 1904 S Horner Blvd 27330. Jct US 1 exit 69A, 3.2 mi s on US 421 and SR 87. Int corridors. **Pets:** Accepted.
🛜 ✕ 🛗M 🛏 💻 🏊

▼▼▼▼ **Holiday Inn Express Hotel & Suites** H 🐾
(919) 776-6600. **$85-$106.** 2110 Dalrymple St 27330. Jct US 1 exit 69A, 3.5 mi s on US 421 and SR 87, then just w. Int corridors. **Pets:** Other species. $35 one-time fee/room. Designated rooms, service with restrictions, crate. 🛜 🛗M 🛏 💻 🏊

▼▼▼▼ **Jameson Inn** M
(919) 708-7400. **$75-$95.** 2614 S Horner Blvd 27330. Jct US 1 exit 69A, 4.1 mi s on US 421 and SR 87. Ext corridors. **Pets:** Medium. $15 daily fee/room. Service with restrictions, supervision. 🛜 🛗M 🛏 💻 🏊

SCOTLAND NECK

▼▼▼▼ **Scotland Neck Inn** M
(252) 826-5141. **$70-$90.** 308 S Main St 27874. Jct SR 125 S, just s on US 258. Int corridors. **Pets:** Medium. $15 daily fee/pet. Designated rooms, service with restrictions, supervision. 🛜 🛏 💻 🏊

SELMA

▼▼ ▼▼ **Days Inn** H
(919) 965-4000. **Call for rates.** 115 US 70A 27576. I-95 exit 97, just e, then just n. Int corridors. **Pets:** Accepted. 🛜 🛗M 🛏 💻 🏊

▼▼ ▼▼ **Quality Inn** M
(919) 965-5200. **Call for rates.** 1705 Industrial Park Dr 27576. I-95 exit 97, just w, then just s. Ext corridors. **Pets:** Other species. $15 daily fee/room. Service with restrictions. 🛜 🛏 💻 🏊

SHELBY

▼▼ ▼▼ **Americas Best Value Inn** M
(704) 482-3821. **Call for rates.** 825 W Dixon Blvd 28152. Jct SR 18, 0.8 mi w on US 74 Bypass. Ext corridors. **Pets:** Accepted. 🛜 🛏 🏊

SMITHFIELD

▼▼ ▼▼ **Jameson Inn** M
(919) 989-5901. **$75-$95.** 125 S Equity Dr 27577. I-95 exit 95, just w on US 70 business route, just n on Industrial Park Blvd, then just w. Ext corridors. **Pets:** Medium. $15 daily fee/room. Service with restrictions, supervision. 🛜 🛗M 🛏 💻 🏊

△△△ ▼▼ ▼▼ **Super 8** H
(919) 989-8988. **$59-$96.** 735 Dick Fleming Blvd 27577. I-95 exit 95, just w on US 70 business route, then just n. Int corridors. **Pets:** Medium. $15 daily fee/room. Designated rooms, service with restrictions, supervision. SAVE 🛜 🛗M 🛏 💻 🏊

SOUTHERN PINES

△△△ ▼▼ ▼▼ **Best Western Pinehurst Inn** H 🐾
(910) 692-0640. **$80-$110.** 1675 US Hwy 1 S 28387. Jct US 15/501, 0.5 mi n on US 1. Ext corridors. **Pets:** Dogs only. $10 daily fee/pet. Service with restrictions, crate. SAVE 🛜 🛏 💻 🏊

▼▼ ▼▼ **Econo Lodge Inn & Suites** H
(910) 692-2063. **Call for rates.** 408 W Morganton Rd 28387. US 1 exit Morganton Rd, just w. Int corridors. **Pets:** Medium, other species. $20 daily fee/pet. Service with restrictions, crate. 🛜 🛏 💻

▼▼ ▼▼ **Residence Inn - Pinehurst/Southern Pines** H
(910) 693-3400. **$98-$190.** 105 Brucewood Rd 28387. Jct US 1, 1.2 mi n on US 15/501, then just e. Int corridors. **Pets:** Large, dogs only. $125 one-time fee/room. Designated rooms, service with restrictions, supervision. 🛜 ✕ 🛏 💻 🏊 ✕

SOUTHPORT

△△△ ▼▼ ▼▼ **Comfort Suites** H 🐾
(910) 454-7444. **$99-$149.** 4963 Southport Supply Rd (SR 211) 28461. Jct SR 87, 1.8 mi n. Int corridors. **Pets:** Small. $20 daily fee/room. Designated rooms, service with restrictions, crate.
SAVE 🛜 ✕ 🛏 💻 🏊

SPRUCE PINE

▼▼▼▼ Richmond Inn BB

(828) 765-6993. **Call for rates.** 51 Pine Ave 28777. Jct US 19E, just n on SR 226 business route (Highland Ave), just e on Oak St, just n on Walnut Ave, just w on Balsam Ave, then just ne. Int corridors. **Pets:** $25 daily fee/pet. Designated rooms, crate. 🛰 ⊠ 🛏 🕅 ⊠

STATESVILLE

AAA ▼▼▼ Best Western Statesville Inn M ❀

(704) 881-0111. **$70-$130.** 1121 Morland Dr 28677. I-77 exit 49A, just e on US 70. Ext corridors. **Pets:** Medium. $20 daily fee/pet. Designated rooms, service with restrictions, supervision.

(SAVE) 🛰 (&M) 🛏 🖵 🏊

AAA ▼▼▼▼ Courtyard Statesville Mooresville/Lake Norman H

(704) 768-2400. **$99-$229.** 1530 Cinema Dr 28625. I-77 exit 49B, just e on Salisbury Rd, 0.6 mi n on Folger Dr, then just e. Int corridors.
Pets: Accepted. (SAVE) 🛰 ⊠ (&M) 🛏 🖵 🍴 🏊

▼▼▼ Quality Inn & Suites M

(704) 878-2721. **Call for rates.** 715 Sullivan Rd 28677. I-40 exit 151, just s on US 21. Ext corridors. **Pets:** Accepted. 🛰 🛏 🖵 🏊

▼▼▼ Ramada Statesville H

(704) 878-9691. **Call for rates.** 1215 Garner Bagnal Blvd 28677. I-77 exit 49A, just e on US 70. Int corridors. **Pets:** Accepted.
🛰 (&M) 🛏 🖵 🍴 🏊

▼▼ Red Roof Inn M

(704) 878-2051. **$44-$74.** 1508 E Broad St 28625. I-77 exit 50, just e, then just s on Middleton St. Ext corridors. **Pets:** Large, other species. No service, supervision. 🛰 (&M) 🛏 🖵

THOMASVILLE

▼▼▼▼ Microtel Inn & Suites H

(336) 474-4515. **$54-$99.** 959 Lake Rd 27360. I-85 exit 102, just w, then just s. Int corridors. **Pets:** Small, dogs only. $20 daily fee/pet. Designated rooms, service with restrictions, supervision. 🛰 (&M) 🛏 🖵

AAA ▼▼▼ Piedmont Inn H

(336) 472-6600. **$42-$69.** 895 Lake Rd 27360. I-85 exit 102, just w, then just s. Int corridors. **Pets:** Medium, dogs only. $15 daily fee/pet. Designated rooms, service with restrictions, supervision.

(SAVE) 🛰 🛏 🖵 🍴 🏊

WAKE FOREST

▼▼▼ Hampton Inn H

(919) 554-0222. **$89-$119.** 12318 Wake Union Church Rd 27587. Jct SR 98, 0.5 mi n on US 1, then 0.5 mi w. Int corridors. **Pets:** Accepted.
🛰 🛏 🖵 🏊

WAYNESVILLE

▼▼ Days Inn-Waynesville M

(828) 452-9009. **$68-$99.** 232 Phillips Rd 28786. US 23/74 exit 102 (US 276), just sw. Ext corridors. **Pets:** Accepted. 🛰 (&M) 🛏 🖵 🏊

▼▼ Super 8 M

(828) 454-9667. **$37-$115.** 79 Liner Cove Rd 28786. I-40 exit 27, to US 23/74, 3 mi; exit 104 (Liner Cove Rd). Ext corridors. **Pets:** Accepted.
🛰 (&M) 🛏 🖵 🏊

AAA ▼▼▼▼ The Waynesville Inn Golf Resort & Spa H ❀

(828) 456-3551. **$79-$169.** 176 Country Club Dr 28786. US 23 S/74 W exit 100, 0.6 mi s on Hazelwood Ave, then 0.3 mi e on Virginia Ave. Ext/int corridors. **Pets:** Medium. $25 daily fee/room. Designated rooms, service with restrictions, crate. (SAVE) 🛰 (&M) 🛏 🖵 🍴 🏊

WELDON

AAA ▼▼▼ Days Inn M

(252) 536-4867. **$49-$72.** 1611 Julian R Allsbrook Hwy 27890. I-95 exit 173, just e on US 158. Ext corridors. **Pets:** Accepted.
(SAVE) 🛰 🛏 🖵 🏊

WEST JEFFERSON

▼▼ Nation's Inn M

(336) 246-2080. **Call for rates.** 107 Beaver Creek School Rd 28694. Jct US 221, just n on SR 194, then just w. Ext corridors. **Pets:** Accepted.
🛰 (&M) 🛏 🖵

WHITEVILLE

▼▼ Econo Lodge M

(910) 642-2378. **$80-$90.** 503 N J K Powell Blvd 28472. Jct US 74/76, 1 mi s on US 701 Bypass. Ext corridors. **Pets:** Accepted.
🛰 🛏 🖵 🏊

WILKESBORO

AAA ▼▼▼▼ Holiday Inn Express H

(336) 838-1800. **$69-$90.** 1700 Winkler St 28697. Jct SR 16 N, 2 mi nw on US 421/SR 16. Int corridors. **Pets:** Accepted.
(SAVE) 🛰 (&M) 🛏 🖵 🏊

WILLIAMSTON

▼▼ The Inn at Moratoc H

(252) 792-3184. **$69-$89.** 101 East Blvd 27892. US 64 exit 514, 1.5 mi n on US 17 business route. Ext/int corridors. **Pets:** Accepted.
🛰 🛏 🍴 🏊

WILMINGTON

▼▼ Baymont Inn M

(910) 392-6767. **$53-$93, 14 day notice.** 306 S College Rd 28403. Jct US 17 business route, just s on SR 132. Ext/int corridors.
Pets: Accepted. 🛰 🛏 🖵 🏊

▼▼▼▼ Best Western Plus Coastline Inn H ❀

(910) 763-2800. **$79-$169.** 503 Nutt St 28401. Jct Market St, just w on Front St, just s on Red Cross St, then just w. Ext corridors.
Pets: Medium, dogs only. $20 daily fee/room. Service with restrictions, crate. (SAVE) 🛰 ⊠ 🛏 🖵

▼▼ Innkeeper H

(910) 799-4292. **Call for rates.** 5345 W Market St 28405. Jct SR 132, just s on US 17 business route. Int corridors. **Pets:** Accepted.
🛰 🛏 🖵 🏊

AAA ▼▼▼ Comfort Inn Wilmington H

(910) 791-4841. **Call for rates.** 151 S College Rd 28403. Jct US 17 business route, just s on SR 132. Int corridors. **Pets:** Accepted.
(SAVE) 🛰 🛏 🖵 🏊

▼▼ Days Inn M ❀

(910) 799-6300. **$39-$81.** 5040 Market St 28405. Jct SR 132, 0.6 mi s on US 17 business route. Ext corridors. **Pets:** $15 daily fee/room. Designated rooms, service with restrictions, crate.  🛰 🛏 🖵 🍴 🏊

▼▼ Jameson Inn H

(910) 452-5660. **$79-$99.** 5102 Dunlea Ct 28405. Jct SR 132, 0.5 mi s on US 17 business route, just w on New Centre Dr. Int corridors.
Pets: Medium. $15 daily fee/room. Service with restrictions, supervision.
🛰 🛏 🖵 🏊

MainStay Suites H

(910) 392-1741. **$79-$199.** 5229 Market St 28405. Jct SR 132, just s on US 17 business route. Int corridors. **Pets:** Accepted.

Quality Inn M

(910) 791-8850. **Call for rates.** 4926 Market St 28405. Jct SR 132, 0.9 mi s on US 17 business route. Ext corridors. **Pets:** Medium. $25 one-time fee/pet, $5 daily fee/pet. Designated rooms, service with restrictions, supervision.

Residence Inn by Marriott Wilmington Landfall H

(910) 256-0098. **$109-$249.** 1200 Culbreth Dr 28405. Jct US 17 business route, 2.4 mi e on US 74, 0.4 mi n on Military Cutoff Rd, then just e. Int corridors. **Pets:** Medium, other species. $100 one-time fee/room. Service with restrictions.

TownePlace Suites Wilmington/Wrightsville Beach H

(910) 332-3326. **$65-$329.** 305 Eastwood Rd 28403. Jct US 17 business route, just e on US 74. Int corridors. **Pets:** Large. $75 one-time fee/room. Designated rooms, service with restrictions, crate.

WILSON

Days Inn M

(252) 291-2323. **$59-$72.** 1801 S Tarboro St 27893. US 264 exit 40, 3.3 mi e on SR 42. Ext corridors. **Pets:** Medium. $15 daily fee/pet. Service with restrictions, supervision.

WINDSOR

The Inn at Grays Landing CI

(252) 794-2255. **$70-$140.** 401 S King St 27983. US 17, just w on SR 308. Int corridors. **Pets:** Small. $25 one-time fee/pet. Designated rooms, service with restrictions.

WINSTON-SALEM

Augustus T Zevely Inn BB

(336) 748-9299. **Call for rates.** 803 S Main St 27101. I-40 business route exit 5D eastbound, 0.5 mi s on Liberty St to Old Salem Rd, just e on Academy St, then just s; exit 5C westbound, just n on Cherry St, just e on 2nd St, 1 mi s on Liberty St to Old Salem Rd, just e on Academy St, then just s. Ext/int corridors. **Pets:** Accepted.

Embassy Suites-Winston-Salem H

(336) 724-2300. **$139-$229.** 460 N Cherry St 27101. I-40 business route exit 5C (Cherry St), just n. Int corridors. **Pets:** Accepted.

Extended StayAmerica Winston-Salem-Hanes Mall Blvd M

(336) 768-0075. **$55-$80.** 1995 Hampton Inn Ct 27103. I-40 exit 189 (Stratford Rd), just s, just e on Hanes Mall Blvd, then just n. Ext corridors. **Pets:** Other species. $25 daily fee/pet. Service with restrictions.

Fairfield Inn & Suites Winston-Salem Hanes Mall H

(336) 714-3000. **$66-$132.** 1680 Westbrook Plaza 27103. I-40 exit 189 (Stratford Rd), 0.5 mi n, just w, then just s. Int corridors. **Pets:** Accepted.

The Hawthorne Inn & Conference Center H

(336) 777-3000. **$80-$165.** 420 High St 27101. I-40 business route exit 5C (Cherry St) eastbound, just e; exit westbound, just w on 1st St, then just s on Marshall St. Int corridors. **Pets:** Accepted.

Innkeeper M

(336) 721-0062. **$45-$99, 3 day notice.** 2115 Peters Creek Pkwy 27127. I-40 exit 192 (Peters Creek Pkwy), just ne on SR 150. Ext/int corridors. **Pets:** Accepted.

La Quinta Inns & Suites Winston-Salem H

(336) 765-8777. **$68-$130.** 2020 Griffith Rd 27103. I-40 exit 189 (Stratford Rd), just s, just e on Hanes Mall Blvd, then just s. Int corridors. **Pets:** Medium, other species. Service with restrictions, supervision.

Quality Inn & Suites-Hanes Mall H

(336) 765-6670. **$80-$90.** 2008 S Hawthorne Rd 27103. I-40 business route exit 2A, 0.5 mi s on Silas Creek Pkwy, then just e. Ext corridors. **Pets:** Small. $25 one-time fee/pet. No service, supervision.

Quality Inn-Coliseum H

(336) 767-8240. **$60-$100.** 531 Akron Dr 27105. US 52 exit 112, just e. Int corridors. **Pets:** Medium, other species. $15 daily fee/pet. Designated rooms, service with restrictions, supervision.

Residence Inn Winston-Salem H

(336) 759-0777. **$101-$149.** 7835 North Point Blvd 27106. US 52 N exit 115B, 2 mi s on University Pkwy, then just e. Ext corridors. **Pets:** Accepted.

Sleep Inn-Hanes Mall H

(336) 774-8020. **$60-$110.** 1985 Hampton Inn Ct 27103. I-40 exit 189 (Stratford Rd), just s, just e on Hanes Mall Blvd, then just n. Int corridors. **Pets:** Accepted.

Sundance Plaza Hotel, Spa & Wellness Center H

(336) 723-2911. **$90-$140.** 3050 University Pkwy 27105. I-40 business route exit 5C (Cherry St), 3 mi n. Int corridors. **Pets:** Accepted.

Wingate by Wyndham H

(336) 714-2800. **$98-$107.** 125 S Main St 27101. I-40 business route exit 5D, just n. Int corridors. **Pets:** $50 one-time fee/room. Service with restrictions, supervision.

YADKINVILLE

Days Inn H

(336) 679-5000. **$49-$112.** 220 Sharon Dr 27055. US 421 exit 257, just s on US 601, then just e. Int corridors. **Pets:** Accepted.

YANCEYVILLE

Days Inn M

(336) 694-9494. **$54-$162.** 1858 NC Hwy 86 N 27379. Jct SR 62, 1.6 mi nw on US 158/SR 86. Ext corridors. **Pets:** Medium. $20 daily fee/pet. Service with restrictions, supervision.

NORTH DAKOTA

CITY INDEX

BEULAH

◈◈ AmericInn Lodge & Suites of Beulah ⊞

(701) 873-2220. **$89-$166.** 2100 2nd Ave NW 58523. Jct SR 49/200, 1.2 mi s. Int corridors. **Pets:** Accepted. 🛜 &M 🛏 🖵 ⚊

BISMARCK

⨁ ◈◈◈ Best Western Doublewood Inn ⊞ ❀

(701) 258-7000. **$130.** 1400 E Interchange Ave 58501. I-94 exit 159 (US 83), just s. Int corridors. **Pets:** $20 one-time fee/room. Designated rooms, service with restrictions, supervision.

[SAVE] 🛜 ✕ &M 🛏 🖵 ⊟ ⚊ ✕

⨁ ◈◈◈ Best Western Plus Ramkota Hotel ⊞ ❀

(701) 258-7700. **$109-$149.** 800 S 3rd St 58504. Just s of jct I-94 business loop (Bismarck Expwy) and S 3rd St. Int corridors. **Pets:** Medium. $10 daily fee/pet. Designated rooms, service with restrictions, supervision.

[SAVE] 🛜 ✕ &M 🛏 🖵 ⊟ ⚊ ✕

◈◈◈ Candlewood Suites ⊞ 🐾

(701) 751-8900. **$129-$150.** 4400 Skyline Crossings 58503. I-94 exit 159 (US 83), 1.7 mi n, then just e. Int corridors. **Pets:** Medium, dogs only. $75 one-time fee/pet. Designated rooms, service with restrictions, supervision. 🛜 &M 🛏 🖵 ⚊

◈◈ Comfort Inn ⊞

(701) 223-1911. **Call for rates.** 1030 Interstate Ave 58503. I-94 exit 159 (US 83), 0.3 mi nw. Int corridors. **Pets:** Small, other species. Service with restrictions, supervision. 🛜 &M 🛏 🖵 ⚊ ✕

◈◈ Days Inn-Bismarck Ⓜ

(701) 223-9151. **$70-$150.** 1300 E Capitol Ave 58501. I-94 exit 159 (US 83), just s. Int corridors. **Pets:** Accepted. 🛜 &M 🛏 🖵 ⚊ ✕

⨁ ◈◈◈ Kelly Inn Ⓜ ❀

(701) 223-8001. **Call for rates.** 1800 N 12th St 58501. I-94 exit 159 (US 83), 0.3 mi s. Int corridors. **Pets:** Supervision.

[SAVE] 🛜 &M 🛏 🖵 ⊟ ⚊ ✕

◈◈◈ La Quinta Inn & Suites Bismarck ⊞

(701) 751-3313. **Call for rates.** 2240 N 12th St 58501. I-94 exit 159 (US 83), just s. Int corridors. **Pets:** Medium, other species. Service with restrictions, supervision. 🛜 ✕ &M 🛏 🖵 ⚊

⨁ ◈◈◈ Radisson Hotel Bismarck ⊞

(701) 255-6000. **$101-$115.** 605 E Broadway Ave 58501. Jct 6th St; center. Int corridors. **Pets:** Large, other species. $20 one-time fee/room. Designated rooms, supervision.

[SAVE] 🛜 ✕ &M 🛏 🖵 ⊟ ⚊ ✕

⨁ ◈◈◈ Ramada Limited Bismarck ⊞ 🐾

(701) 221-3030. **$97-$164.** 3808 E Divide Ave 58501. I-94 exit 161, just s on E Bismarck Expwy. Int corridors. **Pets:** Other species. $10 daily fee/room. Service with restrictions, supervision.

[SAVE] 🛜 &M 🛏 🖵 ⚊ ✕

⨁ ◈◈◈ Select Inn Ⓜ

(701) 223-8060. **$71-$114.** 1505 Interchange Ave 58501. I-94 exit 159 (US 83), just se. Int corridors. **Pets:** Other species. $5 daily fee/pet. Designated rooms, service with restrictions, supervision.

[SAVE] 🛜 &M 🛏 🖵

⨁ ◈◈◈ Super 8 Ⓜ

(701) 255-1314. **$60-$145, 7 day notice.** 1124 E Capitol Ave 58501. I-94 exit 159 (US 83), just s. Int corridors. **Pets:** Medium. $10 daily fee/pet. Designated rooms, service with restrictions, supervision.

[SAVE] 🛜 🛏 🖵

BOTTINEAU

◈◈ Super 8 of Bottineau ⊞

(701) 228-2125. **$66.** 1007 11th St E 58318. 0.5 mi e on SR 5. Int corridors. **Pets:** Accepted. 🛜 &M 🛏 🖵

CARRINGTON

◈◈ Carrington Inn & Suites Ⓜ

(701) 652-3982. **$60-$105.** 101 4th Ave S 58421. Jct US 52 and 281, 0.5 mi s on US 52; just s of jct SR 200. Int corridors. **Pets:** Medium. $10 daily fee/pet. Designated rooms, service with restrictions, supervision.

🛜 🛏

◈◈ Chieftain Conference Center Ⓜ

(701) 652-3131. **$71-$120.** 60 4th Ave S 58421. Jct US 52 and 281, 0.5 mi s on US 52; just s of jct SR 200. Ext/int corridors. **Pets:** Accepted.

🛜 &M 🛏 🖵

CASSELTON

◈◈ Days Inn/Governors Conference Center ⊞

(701) 347-4524. **$89-$159.** 2050 Governors Dr 58012. I-94 exit 331, just n on SR 18. Int corridors. **Pets:** Other species. $25 deposit/room. Designated rooms, service with restrictions, supervision.

🛜 &M 🛏 🖵 ⊟ ⚊ ✕

DICKINSON

◈◈ Comfort Inn ⊞

(701) 264-7300. **Call for rates.** 493 Elks Dr 58601. I-94 exit 61 (SR 22), just n, then w. Int corridors. **Pets:** Accepted.

🛜 ✕ &M 🛏 🖵 ⚊

◈◈◈ Holiday Inn Express Hotel & Suites ⊞

(701) 456-8000. **$129-$169.** 103 14th St W 58601. I-94 exit 61 (SR 22), just n, then just e. Int corridors. **Pets:** Medium, other species. $20 one-time fee/room. Designated rooms, service with restrictions, supervision.

🛜 ✕ &M 🛏 🖵 ⚊ ✕

◈◈ Microtel Inn & Suites Dickinson ⊞

(701) 465-2000. **Call for rates.** 1597 6th Ave W 58601. I-94 exit 61 (SR 22), just n, then w. Int corridors. **Pets:** Accepted.

🛜 ✕ &M 🛏 🖵 ⚊

⨁ ◈◈◈ Quality Inn & Suites-Dickinson ⊞

(701) 225-9510. **$125-$175.** 71 Museum Dr 58601. I-94 exit 61 (SR 22), just s, then just e. Int corridors. **Pets:** Accepted.

[SAVE] 🛜 &M 🛏 🖵 ⚊ ✕

FARGO

⨁ ◈◈◈ AmericInn Lodge & Suites of Fargo ⊞

(701) 234-9946. **$78-$142.** 1423 35th St SW 58103. I-29 exit 64, just e on 13th Ave SW, just s on 34th St SW, then just w. Int corridors. **Pets:** Medium. $10 daily fee/pet. Designated rooms, service with restrictions, supervision. [SAVE] 🛜 ✕ &M 🛏 🖵 ⚊ ✕

AAA ◈◈◈ **Best Western Fargo Doublewood Inn** H
(701) 235-3333. **$95-$115.** 3333 13th Ave S 58103. I-29 exit 64, 0.3 mi e. Int corridors. **Pets:** Accepted.
[SAVE] 🛜 ✕ 👤 🍴 ≈ ✕

AAA ◈◈◈◈ **Best Western Plus Kelly Inn &**
Suites H ✿
(701) 282-2143. **$100-$150.** 1767 44th St S 58103. I-94 exit 348 (45th St SW), just n, then just e on 18th Ave. Ext/int corridors. **Pets:** Small. Service with restrictions, supervision.
[SAVE] 🛜 ✕ 👤 🍴 ≈ ✕

◈◈◈◈ **Candlewood Suites** H
(701) 235-8200. **$104-$159.** 1831 NDSU Research Park Dr 58102. I-29 exit 67 (19th Ave), 1.6 mi e. Int corridors. **Pets:** Accepted.
🛜 👤 🍴

◈◈ **Comfort Inn Fargo East** H
(701) 280-9666. **Call for rates.** 1407 35th St SW 58103. I-29 exit 64, just e on 13th Ave SW, just s on 34th St SW, then just w. Int corridors. **Pets:** Accepted. 🛜 👤 🍴 ≈

◈◈ **Comfort Suites** H
(701) 237-5911. **$79-$129.** 1415 35th St SW 58103. I-29 exit 64, just e on 13th Ave SW, just s on 34th St SW, then just w. Int corridors. **Pets:** $10 daily fee/pet. Service with restrictions, crate.
🛜 ✕ 👤 🍴 ≈

AAA ◈◈◈◈ **Country Inn & Suites By Carlson** H
(701) 234-0565. **Call for rates.** 3316 13th Ave S 58103. I-29 exit 64, 0.3 mi e. Int corridors. **Pets:** Accepted.
[SAVE] 🛜 ✕ 👤 🍴 ≈ ✕

◈◈ **Econo Lodge** M ✿
(701) 232-3412. **$55-$199.** 1401 35th St SW 58103. I-29 exit 64, just e on 13th Ave SW, just s on 34th St SW, then just w. Int corridors. **Pets:** Other species. $10 daily fee/pet. Service with restrictions, supervision. 🛜 ✕ 👤 🍴

AAA ◈◈◈◈ **Holiday Inn of Fargo** H
(701) 282-2700. **$110-$179.** 3803 13th Ave S 58103. I-29 exit 64, just nw. Int corridors. **Pets:** Large, other species. $20 one-time fee/pet. Service with restrictions, supervision.
[SAVE] 🛜 👤 👤 🍴 🍴 ≈ ✕

◈◈ **Kelly Inn** H
(701) 281-9700. **$84-$139, 3 day notice.** 3800 Main Ave (US 10) 58103. I-29 exit 65, just sw on US 10. Ext/int corridors. **Pets:** Medium. Service with restrictions, supervision.
🛜 👤 👤 🍴 ≈ ✕

◈◈ **Kelly Inn 13th Avenue** H
(701) 277-8821. **$88-$134, 5 day notice.** 4207 13th Ave SW 58103. I-29 exit 64, 0.4 mi w. Ext/int corridors. **Pets:** Medium. Service with restrictions, supervision. 🛜 ✕ 👤 👤 🍴 ≈

◈◈◈ **La Quinta Inn & Suites Fargo** H
(701) 499-2000. **$89-$230.** 2355 46th St S 58104. I-94 exit 348 (45th St SW), just s, then just w. Int corridors. **Pets:** Medium, other species. Service with restrictions, supervision. 🛜 ✕ 👤 👤 🍴 ≈

AAA ◈◈◈◈ **MainStay Suites** H
(701) 277-4627. **$85-$180.** 1901 44th St SW 58103. I-94 exit 348 (45th St SW), just n, then just e. Int corridors. **Pets:** Accepted.
[SAVE] 🛜 👤 👤 🍴 ≈

AAA ◈ **Select Inn** M
(701) 282-6300. **$62-$89.** 1025 38th St SW 58103. I-29 exit 64, just n on west frontage road (38th St SW). Int corridors. **Pets:** Medium. $5 daily fee/pet. Designated rooms, service with restrictions, supervision.
[SAVE] 🛜 👤 👤 🍴

◈◈◈ **Settle Inn & Suites** H
(701) 235-4699. **Call for rates.** 4325 23rd Ave 58104. I-94 exit 348 (45th St SW), just se. Int corridors. **Pets:** Accepted.
🛜 ✕ 👤 👤 🍴 ≈ ✕

AAA ◈◈◈◈ **Sleep Inn** H
(701) 281-8240. **$60-$130.** 1921 44th St SW 58103. I-94 exit 348 (45th St SW), just n, just e on 19th Ave S, then just s. Int corridors.
Pets: Accepted. [SAVE] 🛜 🍴 👤 👤 🍴 ≈

AAA ◈◈◈◈ **Staybridge Suites** H
(701) 281-4900. **$89-$249.** 4300 20th Ave S 58103. I-94 exit 348 (45th St SW), just n, just e on 19th Ave, just s on 44th St S, then just e. Int corridors. **Pets:** Accepted. [SAVE] 🛜 🍴 👤 👤 🍴 ≈ ✕

◈◈◈ **Super 8 Fargo/I-29/West Acres Mall** H ✿
(701) 232-9202. **$53-$79.** 3518 Interstate Blvd 58103. I-29 exit 64, just n on east frontage road via 35th St. Int corridors. **Pets:** Medium, dogs only. $10 daily fee/pet. Designated rooms, service with restrictions, supervision.
🛜 🍴 👤 👤 🍴 ≈

GRAND FORKS

AAA ◈ **Americas Best Value Inn of Grand**
Forks M ✿
(701) 775-0555. **Call for rates.** 1000 N 42nd St 58203. I-29 exit 141, just e on US 2 (Gateway Dr), then just s. Int corridors. **Pets:** Other species. $10 deposit/pet. Designated rooms, service with restrictions, supervision. [SAVE] 🛜 ✕ 👤

AAA ◈◈◈ **Days Inn - Columbia Mall** H
(701) 775-0060. **$58-$90.** 3101 S 34th St 58201. I-29 exit 138, 0.4 mi e on 32nd Ave S, then just n. Int corridors. **Pets:** Small. $10 daily fee/pet. Designated rooms, service with restrictions, supervision.
[SAVE] 🛜 👤 👤 ≈

◈◈ **GuestHouse International Town House** H
(701) 746-5411. **$73-$130.** 710 1st Ave N 58203. I-29 exit 140, 2.8 mi e on DeMers Ave, then just n; downtown. Int corridors. **Pets:** Accepted.
🛜 👤 👤 🍴 ≈ ✕

AAA ◈◈◈ **Howard Johnson Grand Forks** H
(701) 772-7131. **Call for rates.** 1210 N 43rd St 58203. I-29 exit 141, just e on US 2 (Gateway Dr), then just s. Ext/int corridors.
Pets: Accepted. [SAVE] 🛜 👤 👤 🍴 ≈ ✕

◈◈ **Ramada Inn** H
(701) 775-3951. **$62-$109.** 1205 N 43rd St 58203. I-29 exit 141, just e on US 2 (Gateway Dr), then just s. Int corridors. **Pets:** Accepted.
🛜 👤 👤 🍴 ≈

◈◈ **Travelodge of Grand Forks** H
(701) 772-8151. **$53-$71, 14 day notice.** 2100 S Washington St 58201. I-29 exit 140, 2.2 mi e on DeMers Ave, then 1 mi s. Int corridors.
Pets: Accepted. 🛜 ✕ 👤 👤 ≈

JAMESTOWN

◈◈ **Quality Inn & Suites** H
(701) 252-3611. **$100-$120.** 507 25th St SW 58401. I-94 exit 258 (US 281), just se. Int corridors. **Pets:** Accepted.
🛜 👤 👤 🍴 ≈ ✕

AAA ◈◈ **Super 8** H
(701) 252-4715. **Call for rates.** 2623 Hwy 281 S 58401. I-94 exit 258 (US 81), just s. Int corridors. **Pets:** Accepted. [SAVE] 🛜 👤 👤

MANDAN

AAA ◈◈◈◈ **Best Western Plus Seven Seas Hotel &**
Waterpark H
(701) 663-7401. **$112-$147.** 2611 Old Red Tr 58554. I-94 exit 152, just n on Sunset Dr, then just w. Int corridors. **Pets:** Accepted.
[SAVE] 🛜 ✕ 👤 👤 👤 🍴 ≈

MINOT

Best Western Kelly Inn 🅜 ❀
(701) 852-4300. **$130-$210.** 1510 26th Ave SW 58701. US 2 and 52 Bypass, at 16th St SW. Ext/int corridors. **Pets:** Other species. Service with restrictions, crate. SAVE 🛜 ⊠ 🚱M 🔒 🖥 ⤳ 🚫

Candlewood Suites 🎫 ❀
(701) 858-7700. **Call for rates.** 900 37th Ave SW 58701. US 83, 0.6 mi s of US 2 and 52 Bypass, then just w. Int corridors. **Pets:** Medium. $150 one-time fee/room. Service with restrictions, crate.
🛜 ⊠ 🚱M 🔒 🖥

Comfort Inn 🎫
(701) 852-2201. **$120-$200.** 1515 22nd Ave SW 58701. US 2 and 52 Bypass, at 16th St SW. Int corridors. **Pets:** Medium. $10 daily fee/room. Designated rooms, service with restrictions, supervision.
SAVE 🛜 ⊠ 🚱M 🔒 🖥 ⤳ 🚫

Days Inn Minot 🅜
(701) 852-3646. **$62-$143.** 2100 4th St SW 58701. Jct US 2 and 52 Bypass, just n. Int corridors. **Pets:** Accepted. 🛜 🔒 🖥 ⤳

Holiday Inn Riverside Minot 🎫
(701) 852-2504. **Call for rates.** 2200 Burdick Expy E 58702. 1.3 mi e on US 2 business route (Burdick Expwy E). Int corridors. **Pets:** Accepted.
🛜 🚱M 🔒 🖥 🍽 ⤳ 🚫

MainStay Suites 🎫
(701) 852-6246. **Call for rates.** 1212 31st Ave SW Ave SW 58701. US 2 and 52 Bypass, 0.4 mi s on 16th St SW, then 0.4 mi e. Int corridors. **Pets:** Accepted. 🛜 ⊠ 🔒 🖥

Sleep Inn & Suites 🎫
(701) 837-3100. **Call for rates.** 2400 10th St SW 58701. US 2 and 52 Bypass, 0.4 mi s on 16th St SW, then 0.4 mi e. Int corridors. **Pets:** Small. $25 one-time fee/pet. Designated rooms, service with restrictions, supervision. SAVE 🛜 ⊠ 🚱M 🔒 🖥 ⤳ 🚫

VALLEY CITY

AmericInn Lodge & Suites of Valley City 🎫 ❀
(701) 845-5551. **$81-$140.** 280 Winter Show Rd SE 58072. I-94 exit 292, just ne. Int corridors. **Pets:** Other species. $10 one-time fee/room. Designated rooms, service with restrictions, supervision.
🛜 🚱M 🔒 🖥 ⤳ 🚫

WAHPETON

Rodeway Inn 🎫
(701) 642-1115. **Call for rates.** 209 13th St S 58075. SR 13, 0.3 mi e of jct SR 210 Bypass. Int corridors. **Pets:** Accepted. 🛜 🔒 🖥 ⤳

WATFORD CITY

Roosevelt Inn & Suites 🎫
(701) 842-3686. **$90-$105.** 600 2nd Ave SW 58854. US 85, 0.3 mi w. Int corridors. **Pets:** Other species. $10 daily fee/pet. Service with restrictions, supervision. SAVE 🛜 ⊠ 🔒 🖥 ⤳

WILLISTON

Candlewood Suites 🎫
(701) 572-3716. **Call for rates.** 3716 6th Ave W 58801. 1.3 mi n on US 2 and 85 Bypass, just w. Int corridors. **Pets:** Accepted.
🛜 ⊠ 🚱M 🔒 🖥

El Rancho Motor Hotel 🎫
(701) 572-6321. **Call for rates.** 1623 2nd Ave W 58801. 1 mi n on US 2 and 85 N Bypass. Ext/int corridors. **Pets:** Accepted.
SAVE 🛜 🚱M 🔒 🖥 🍽

HomStay Suites 🎫
(701) 577-3701. **Call for rates.** 3701 4th Ave W 58801. 1.3 mi n on US 2 and 85 Bypass, just w. Int corridors. **Pets:** Other species. $10 daily fee/pet. Service with restrictions, supervision. 🛜 ⊠ 🔒 🖥 🍽

Marquis Plaza & Suites 🎫
(701) 774-3250. **$125-$147.** 1525 9th Ave NW 58801. US 2 and 85 Bypass, 4 mi e of jct US 85 Bypass. Int corridors. **Pets:** Small. $15 daily fee/pet. Designated rooms, service with restrictions, supervision.
SAVE 🛜 ⊠ 🚱M 🔒 🖥 ⤳ 🚫

Microtel Inn & Suites Williston 🎫
(701) 577-4900. **$209-$299, 3 day notice.** 3820 4th Ave W 58801. 1.3 mi n on US 2 and 85 Bypass, just w. Int corridors. **Pets:** Small, dogs only. $25 one-time fee/room. Service with restrictions, crate.
🛜 ⊠ 🚱M 🔒 🖥 ⤳

Missouri Flats Inn 🅜
(701) 572-4242. **$108.** 213 35th St W 58801. 1.3 mi n on US 2 and 85 Bypass. Int corridors. **Pets:** Small, dogs only. $15 daily fee/pet. Designated rooms, service with restrictions, supervision.
SAVE 🛜 ⊠ 🚱M 🔒 🖥

OHIO

AKRON

 Red Roof Inn-Akron South #0207 M

(330) 644-7748. **$54-$80.** 2939 S Arlington Rd 44312. I-77 exit 120, just
n. Ext corridors. **Pets:** Large, other species. No service, supervision.
SAVE 🛰 🔧

ALLIANCE

Holiday Inn Express Hotel & Suites H

(330) 821-6700. **Call for rates.** 2341 W State St 44601. 2 mi w on US
62. Int corridors. **Pets:** Large, other species. $10 daily fee/pet. Designated
rooms, service with restrictions, supervision. 🛰 🅼 🔧 💻 ⇌

Super 8 M

(330) 821-5688. **$39-$81.** 2330 W State St 44601. 2 mi w on US 62. Ext
corridors. **Pets:** $5 daily fee/pet. Service with restrictions, crate.
SAVE 🛰 🔧 💻 ⇌

AMHERST

Days Inn M

(440) 985-1428. **$45-$113.** 934 N Leavitt Rd 44001. I-80 exit 140, 2.7 mi
n on SR 58. Ext/int corridors. **Pets:** Accepted. 🛰 🔧 💻 ⇌

ASHTABULA

Cedars Motel M

(440) 992-5406. **$50-$140.** 2015 W Prospect Rd 44004. Jct SR 11, 3 mi
w on US 20. Ext corridors. **Pets:** Accepted. 🛰 🔧

ATHENS

The Ohio University Inn & Conference Center H

(740) 593-6661. **$79-$399.** 331 Richland Ave 45701. 1 mi w on US 33
and 50. Int corridors. **Pets:** Accepted. 🛰 🅼 🔧 💻 🍴 ⇌

AUSTINBURG

Ramada H

(440) 275-2711. **Call for rates.** 1860 Austinburg Rd 44010. I-90 exit
223, just n. Int corridors. **Pets:** Accepted. 🛰 🔧 💻 🍴 ⇌

AUSTINTOWN

Austintown Super 8 M

(330) 793-7788. **$53-$71.** 5280 76 Dr 44515. I-80 exit 223, just s on SR
46. Int corridors. **Pets:** $10 daily fee/pet. Service with restrictions, supervi-
sion. SAVE 🛰 🔧

Best Western Meander Inn H

(330) 544-2378. **$80-$100.** 870 N Canfield-Niles Rd 44515. I-80 exit 223,
0.3 mi s on SR 46. Int corridors. **Pets:** Large, other species. $10 daily
fee/pet. Designated rooms, service with restrictions, supervision.
SAVE 🛰 🔧 💻 🍴 ⇌

Comfort Inn M

(330) 792-9740. **Call for rates.** 5425 Clarkins Dr 44515. I-80 exit 223B,
just n. Ext corridors. **Pets:** Accepted. 🛰 🔧 💻 ⇌

BEAVERCREEK

Residence Inn by Marriott Beavercreek H 🐾

(937) 427-3914. **$99-$145.** 2779 Fairfield Commons Blvd 45431. I-675
exit 17, just s on N Fairfield Rd, just w on Pentagon Rd, then just s. Int
corridors. **Pets:** Other species. $100 one-time fee/room. Service with
restrictions, crate. 🛰 ✕ 🅼 🔧 💻 ⇌ 🗙

BLUFFTON

Comfort Inn H

(419) 358-6000. **$80-$105.** 117 Commerce Ln 45817. I-75 exit 142, just
w on SR 103. Int corridors. **Pets:** Large, other species. $25 one-time
fee/pet. Service with restrictions, supervision. 🛰 🔧 💻 ⇌ 🗙

BOARDMAN

Americas Best Value Inn & Suites M 🐾

(330) 549-0157. **$49-$121.** 9988 Market St 44452. 0.5 mi n on SR 7. Int
corridors. **Pets:** Medium. $10 daily fee/room. Service with restrictions,
supervision. 🛰 🅼 🔧

BOSTON HEIGHTS

**Baymont Inn & Suites Hudson/Boston
Heights** M 🐾

(330) 650-2040. **$55-$79.** 6731 Industrial Pkwy 44236. I-80/90 exit 180,
0.3 mi n on SR 8 S, just e on Hines Hill Rd, then just n. Int corridors.
Pets: Large. $10 daily fee/pet. Crate. SAVE 🛰 🅼 🔧 💻 ⇌

◬▽ ▽▽ Clarion Inn and Conference Center 🅗 ✿
(330) 653-9191. **$79-$119.** 240 E Hines Hill Rd 44236. I-80/90 exit 180, 0.3 mi n on SR 8. Int corridors. **Pets:** Large. $10 daily fee/room. Service with restrictions, supervision. 🆂🅰🆅🅴 🛜 🅶🅼 📶 📺 🍴 🏊 🚫

BOTKINS

◬▽ ▽ Budget Host Inn 🅜
(937) 693-6911. **$43-$75, 14 day notice.** 505 E State St 45306. I-75 exit 104 (SR 219), just w. Ext corridors. **Pets:** Other species. $40 deposit/pet. Designated rooms, service with restrictions, crate.
🆂🅰🆅🅴 🛜 📶 🍴 🏊

BOWLING GREEN

▽▽▽ Holiday Inn Express 🅗
(419) 353-5500. **Call for rates.** 2150 E Wooster St 43402. I-75 exit 181, just e. Int corridors. **Pets:** Accepted. 🛜 🅶🅼 📶 📺 🏊

BROOKVILLE

◬▽ ▽▽▽ Holiday Inn Express Hotel & Suites Dayton West (Brookville) 🅗 ✿
(937) 833-9998. **$85-$199.** 95 N Parkview Dr 45309. I-70 exit 21, just s. Int corridors. **Pets:** Small. $25 daily fee/pet. No service, crate.
🆂🅰🆅🅴 🛜 🅶🅼 📶 🏊

BRYAN

◬▽ ▽▽ Colonial Manor Motel 🅜
(419) 636-3123. **$67-$97.** 924 E High St 43506. US 127, 0.8 mi e on SR 2/34. Ext corridors. **Pets:** Medium. Designated rooms, service with restrictions, crate. 🆂🅰🆅🅴 🛜 📶 📺 🍴

◬▽ ▽ Plaza Motel 🅜
(419) 636-3159. **$69-$93.** 1604 S Main St 43506. 1.3 mi s on US 127 and SR 15. Ext corridors. **Pets:** Service with restrictions, supervision.
🆂🅰🆅🅴 🛜 📶 📺

BUCYRUS

▽▽▽ Hideaway Country Inn 🅒🅘 ✿
(419) 562-3013. **$109-$289, 14 day notice.** 1601 SR 4 44820. 4.5 mi s. Ext/int corridors. **Pets:** Small. $75 daily fee/pet. Designated rooms, service with restrictions, supervision. 🛜 🚫 📶 📺 🍴

CAMBRIDGE

▽▽ Baymont Inn & Suites 🅜
(740) 439-1505. **$63-$117.** 61595 Southgate Pkwy 43725. I-70 exit 178, just s on SR 209. Int corridors. **Pets:** Accepted.
🛜 🅶🅼 📶 📺 🏊

▽ Budget Inn 🅜
(740) 432-2304. **$45-$60.** 6405 Glenn Hwy 43725. I-70 exit 176, just e on US 40. Ext/int corridors. **Pets:** Small. $10 daily fee/pet. Designated rooms, service with restrictions, supervision. 🛜 📶 📺

▽▽ Days Inn-Cambridge 🅜
(740) 432-5691. **$54-$108, 3 day notice.** 2328 Southgate Pkwy 43725. I-70 exit 178, just n on SR 209. Int corridors. **Pets:** Accepted.
🛜 📶 📺 🏊

CANTON

◬▽ ▽▽ Comfort Inn-Hall of Fame 🅗 ✿
(330) 492-1331. **$89-$259.** 5345 Broadmoor Cir NW 44709. I-77 exit 109, 0.5 mi e on Everhard Rd. Int corridors. **Pets:** Medium, other species. $10 one-time fee/pet. Service with restrictions, crate.
🆂🅰🆅🅴 🛜 📶 📺 🏊

▽▽ La Quinta Inn & Suites Canton 🅗
(330) 492-0151. **$85-$155.** 5335 Broadmoor Cir NW 44709. I-77 exit 109, 0.5 mi e on Everhard Rd. Int corridors. **Pets:** Medium, other species. Service with restrictions, supervision. 🛜 🅶🅼 📶 📺 🏊

◬▽ ▽▽ Red Roof Inn #7019 🅜
(330) 499-1970. **$55-$80.** 5353 Inn Circle Ct NW 44720. I-77 exit 109, just w on Everhard Rd. Ext corridors. **Pets:** Large, other species. No service, supervision. 🆂🅰🆅🅴 🛜 📶

▽▽▽ Residence Inn by Marriott 🅗
(330) 493-0004. **$105-$260.** 5280 Broadmoor Cir NW 44709. I-77 exit 109, 0.5 mi e on Everhard Rd. Int corridors. **Pets:** Accepted.
🛜 🚫 🅶🅼 📶 📺 🏊 🚫

CARROLLTON

▽▽ Carrollton Days Inn 🅗
(330) 627-9314. **$77-$119, 7 day notice.** 1111 Canton Rd 44615. On SR 43, 0.5 mi n of SR 39. Int corridors. **Pets:** Accepted.
🛜 📶 📺 🏊

CEDARVILLE

▽▽▽ Hearthstone Inn & Suites 🅗
(937) 766-3000. **$109-$169.** 10 S Main St 45314. I-70 exit 54, 11 mi s. Int corridors. **Pets:** Medium, dogs only. $15 daily fee/pet. No service, supervision. 🛜 🚫 📶 📺

CELINA

▽▽ Americas Best Value Inn-Celina 🅜
(419) 586-4656. **Call for rates.** 1421 SR 703 E 45822. Jct SR 29. Ext corridors. **Pets:** $10 daily fee/pet. Service with restrictions, supervision.
🛜 📶 📺

CHILLICOTHE

◬▽ ▽▽ Best Western Adena Inn 🅗
(740) 775-7000. **Call for rates.** 1250 N Bridge St 45601. US 35 exit Bridge St, 0.8 mi n. Int corridors. **Pets:** Accepted.
🆂🅰🆅🅴 🛜 📶 📺 🏊

▽▽ Christopher Inn & Suites 🅗
(740) 774-6835. **$100-$160.** 30 N Plaza Blvd 45601. US 35 exit Bridge St, just n on US 23. Int corridors. **Pets:** Accepted.
🛜 📶 📺 🏊 🚫

CINCINNATI METROPOLITAN AREA

BATAVIA

▽▽ ▽▽ Ameristay Inn & Suites 🅗
(513) 735-4678. **$76-$139.** 2188 Winemiller Ln 45103. I-275 exit 63B (SR 32), 7.3 mi e. Int corridors. **Pets:** Accepted. 🛜 📶 📺 🏊

▽▽▽ Hampton Inn-Cincinnati Eastgate 🅗
(513) 752-8584. **$84-$149.** 858 Eastgate North Dr 45245. I-275 exit 63B (SR 32), just e, just n on Gleneste Withamsville Rd, then just w. Int corridors. **Pets:** Accepted. 🛜 📶 📺 🏊

▽▽▽ Holiday Inn & Suites Cincinnati Eastgate 🅗
(513) 752-4400. **$69-$199.** 4501 Eastgate Blvd 45245. I-275 exit 63B (SR 32), 0.5 mi e to Eastgate Mall exit, then 0.5 mi n. Int corridors. **Pets:** Accepted. 🛜 📶 📺 🍴 🏊 🚫

BLUE ASH

▼▼▼ **Embassy Suites Hotel-Cincinnati Northeast** ﾋ
(513) 733-8900. **$119-$179.** 4554 Lake Forest Dr 45242. I-275 exit 47, 2.3 mi s; I-71 exit 15, 1 mi w on Pfeiffer Rd. Int corridors. **Pets:** Small. $50 one-time fee/pet. Designated rooms, service with restrictions, supervision.

▼ **Extended StayAmerica - Cincinnati - Blue Ash - Kenwood Road** ﾋ ✿
(513) 469-8900. **$50-$82.** 11145 Kenwood Rd 45242. I-71 exit 15, 0.5 mi w on Pfeiffer Rd, then 1.3 mi n. Int corridors. **Pets:** Other species. $25 daily fee/pet. Service with restrictions.

▼▼ **Extended StayAmerica - Cincinnati - Blue Ash - Reagan Highway** ﾋ ✿
(513) 793-6750. **$62-$79.** 4260 Hunt Rd 45242. I-71 exit 14, 1.3 mi w on Ronald Reagan Hwy exit Hunt Rd, then just e. Int corridors. **Pets:** Other species. $25 daily fee/pet. Service with restrictions.

▼▼ **Residence Inn by Marriott-Blue Ash** ﾋ ✿
(513) 530-5060. **$143-$175.** 11401 Reed-Hartman Hwy 45241. I-275 exit 47, 0.8 mi s. Ext/int corridors. **Pets:** Large, other species. $100 one-time fee/room. Service with restrictions.

▼▼ **TownePlace Suites by Marriott Blue Ash** ﾋ
(513) 469-8222. **$116-$142.** 4650 Cornell Rd 45241. I-275 exit 47, 0.9 mi s on Reed-Hartman Hwy, then just w. Int corridors. **Pets:** Accepted.

CHERRY GROVE

AAA ▼▼ **Best Western Clermont** Ⓜ
(513) 528-7702. **$65-$99.** 4004 Williams Dr 45255. I-275 exit 65, just w, then just s. Ext corridors. **Pets:** Medium. $20 one-time fee/room. Service with restrictions, supervision.

CINCINNATI

AAA ▼▼▼ **Holiday Inn Express Cincinnati West** ﾋ
(513) 574-6000. **$104-$199.** 5505 Rybolt Rd 45248. I-74 exit 11, just s. Int corridors. **Pets:** Accepted.

AAA ▼▼▼ **Hyatt Regency Cincinnati** ﾋ
(513) 579-1234. **$99-$359.** 151 W 5th St 45202. At Hyatt-Saks Fifth Avenue Center. Int corridors. **Pets:** Accepted.

▼▼▼ **Millennium Hotel Cincinnati** ﾋ
(513) 352-2100. **$69-$349.** 150 W 5th St 45202. Between Elm and Race sts. Int corridors. **Pets:** $65 deposit/pet, $35 one-time fee/pet. Designated rooms, service with restrictions, crate.

▼▼▼ **Residence Inn by Marriott Cincinnati Downtown** ﾋ
(513) 651-1234. **$189-$229.** 506 E Fourth St 45202. Center. Int corridors. **Pets:** Accepted.

AAA ▼▼▼▼ **The Westin Cincinnati** ﾋ ✿
(513) 621-7700. **$99-$309.** 21 E 5th St 45202. Between Vine and Walnut sts. Int corridors. **Pets:** Small. Designated rooms, service with restrictions, supervision.

HARRISON

▼▼ **Executive Inn & Suites Cincinnati** ﾋ
(513) 367-9666. **Call for rates.** 391 Comfort Dr 45030. I-74 exit 1, just n on New Haven Rd, then just e on Biggs Blvd. Int corridors. **Pets:** Accepted.

MASON

▼▼ **Kings Island Resort & Conference Center** ﾋ ✿
(513) 398-0115. **$49-$189.** 5691 Kings Island Dr 45040. I-71 exit 25, just e on Kings Mills Rd, then just s. Ext/int corridors. **Pets:** Dogs only. $25 one-time fee/room. Service with restrictions, crate.

▼▼ **La Quinta Inn & Suites Cincinnati Northeast** ﾋ
(513) 459-1111. **$62-$145.** 9918 Escort Dr 45040. I-71 exit 19, just w, then just s. Int corridors. **Pets:** Medium, other species. Service with restrictions, supervision.

▼▼ **TownePlace Suites by Marriott** ﾋ
(513) 774-0610. **$109-$129.** 9369 Waterstone Blvd 45249. I-71 exit 19, 0.5 mi e on Mason-Montgomery and Fields-Ertel rds, then 0.9 mi n. Int corridors. **Pets:** Accepted.

MIDDLETOWN

▼▼ **Middletown Drury Inn & Suites** ﾋ
(513) 425-6650. **$90-$164.** 3320 Village Dr 45005. I-75 exit 32, just w on SR 122. Int corridors. **Pets:** Accepted.

MILFORD

▼▼ **Homewood Suites by Hilton** ﾋ
(513) 248-4663. **$109-$169.** 600 Chamber Dr 45150. I-275 exit 59 southbound; exit 59A northbound, 0.5 mi w on Milford Pkwy, then 0.5 mi s. Int corridors. **Pets:** Accepted.

MOUNT ORAB

AAA ▼▼▼ **Best Western Plus Mt. Orab Inn** ﾋ
(937) 444-6666. **$75-$95.** 100 Leininger St 45154. Jct US 68 and SR 32, just n on US 68. Int corridors. **Pets:** Accepted.

SHARONVILLE

AAA ▼▼▼ **Crowne Plaza Cincinnati North-CoCo Key** ﾋ
(513) 771-2080. **$80-$161.** 11320 Chester Rd 45246. I-75 exit 15, just w on Sharon Rd, then 0.5 mi n. Int corridors. **Pets:** Small, dogs only. $75 one-time fee/room. No service, supervision.

▼▼▼ **Drury Inn & Suites-Cincinnati North** ﾋ
(513) 771-5601. **$105-$214.** 2265 E Sharon Rd 45241. I-75 exit 15, just e. Int corridors. **Pets:** Accepted.

AAA ▼▼▼ **Hawthorn Suites by Wyndham** ﾋ
(513) 354-1000. **$60-$130.** 11180 Dowlin Dr 45241. I-75 exit 15, just e on Sharon Rd, then just n. Int corridors. **Pets:** Medium, dogs only. $15 daily fee/pet. Service with restrictions, crate.

▼▼▼ **Holiday Inn Cincinnati I-275 North** ﾋ
(513) 563-8330. **$79-$119.** 3855 Hauck Rd 45241. I-275 exit 46, just n. Int corridors. **Pets:** Medium, dogs only. $35 one-time fee/room. Service with restrictions, crate.

▼▼▼ **Homewood Suites by Hilton-Cincinnati North** ﾋ ✿
(513) 772-8888. **$119-$149.** 2670 E Kemper Rd 45241. I-275 exit 44, jct Mosteller Rd. Int corridors. **Pets:** Large, other species. $25 daily fee/pet. Designated rooms, service with restrictions.

▼▼▼ **La Quinta Inn & Suites Cincinnati Sharonville** ﾋ
(513) 771-0300. **$85-$149.** 11029 Dowlin Dr 45241. I-75 exit 15, just e. Int corridors. **Pets:** Medium, other species. Service with restrictions, supervision.

▼▼▼ **Residence Inn by Marriott** ﾋ
(513) 771-2525. **$125-$153.** 11689 Chester Rd 45246. I-75 exit 15, just w on Sharon Rd, then 1 mi n. Ext corridors. **Pets:** Accepted.

SPRINGDALE

▼▼ **La Quinta Inn Cincinnati North** ﾋ
(513) 671-2300. **$62-$125.** 12150 Springfield Pike 45246. I-275 exit 41, just n on SR 4. Int corridors. **Pets:** Medium, other species. Service with restrictions, supervision.

WEST CHESTER

▼▼▼▼ Residence Inn by Marriott Cincinnati North/West Chester ⬚

(513) 341-4040. **$109-$209.** 6240 Muhlhauser Rd 45069. I-75 exit 19, just w on Union Centre Blvd, then just n. Int corridors. **Pets:** Accepted.
🛜 ⊠ ⓜ 🚪 🖥 ➰ ⊠

▼▼▼▼ Staybridge Suites Cincinnati North ⬚

(513) 874-1900. **$99-$250.** 8955 Lakota Dr W 45069. I-75 exit 19, just w on Union Centre Blvd, then 0.5 mi n. Int corridors. **Pets:** Accepted.
🛜 ⓜ 🚪 🖥 ➰ ⊠

WILMINGTON

▼▼▼▼ Holiday Inn Wilmington & Roberts Conference Centre ⬚

(937) 283-3200. **$110-$143.** 123 Gano Rd 45177. I-71 exit 50, just w. Int corridors. **Pets:** Accepted. 🛜 ⊠ ⓜ 🚪 🖥 ⑪ ➰

END METROPOLITAN AREA

CLEVELAND METROPOLITAN AREA

BEACHWOOD

▼▼▼▼ Embassy Suites ⬚

(216) 765-8066. **$119-$219.** 3775 Park East Dr 44122. I-271 exit 29, just w on Chagrin Blvd. Int corridors. **Pets:** Accepted.
🛜 🚪 🖥 ⑪ ➰ ⊠

▼▼ Extended

StayAmerica-Cleveland-Beachwood ⬚ ✿

(216) 595-9551. **$79-$114.** 3820 Orange Pl 44122. I-271 exit 29, 0.3 mi e on Chagrin Blvd, then 0.4 mi s. Int corridors. **Pets:** Other species. $25 daily fee/pet. Service with restrictions. 🛜 🚪 🖥

⟨AAA⟩ ▼▼▼▼ Hilton Cleveland East/Beachwood ⬚

(216) 464-5950. **$84-$227.** 3663 Park East Dr 44122. I-271 exit 29, just w on Chagrin Blvd, then just n. Int corridors. **Pets:** Accepted.
⟨SAVE⟩ 🛜 🚪 🖥 ⑪ ➰ ⊠

▼▼ Homestead Studio Suites

Hotel-Cleveland/Beachwood ⬚ ✿

(216) 896-5555. **$79-$114.** 3625 Orange Pl 44122. I-271 exit 29, 0.3 mi e on Chagrin Blvd, then 0.4 mi s. Int corridors. **Pets:** Other species. $25 daily fee/pet. Service with restrictions. 🛜 🚪 🖥

▼▼▼▼ Residence Inn by Marriott

Cleveland-Beachwood ⬚

(216) 831-3030. **$189-$209.** 3628 Park East Dr 44122. I-271 exit 29, just w on Chagrin Blvd. Int corridors. **Pets:** Accepted.
🛜 ⊠ ⓜ 🚪 🖥 ➰ ⊠

BROOKLYN

▼▼ Extended StayAmerica Cleveland-Brooklyn ⬚ ✿

(216) 267-7799. **$69-$104.** 10300 Cascade Crossing 44144. I-480 exit 13, just s. Int corridors. **Pets:** Other species. $25 daily fee/pet. Service with restrictions. 🛜 🚪 🖥

BROOK PARK

⟨AAA⟩ ▼▼▼ Best Western Airport Inn & Suites ⬚

(216) 267-9364. **$84-$89.** 16501 Snow Rd 44142. I-71 exit 237, just e. Int corridors. **Pets:** Accepted. ⟨SAVE⟩ 🛜 🚪 🖥 ➰

CLEVELAND

▼▼▼ Comfort Inn Downtown Cleveland ⬚

(216) 861-0001. **$89-$199.** 1800 Euclid Ave 44115. Corner of Euclid Ave and E 18th St. Int corridors. **Pets:** Accepted. 🛜 ⊠ 🚪 🖥

▼▼▼ La Quinta Inn Cleveland Airport North ⬚

(216) 251-8500. **$67-$139.** 4222 W 150th St 44135. I-71 exit 240, just n. Int corridors. **Pets:** Medium, other species. Service with restrictions, supervision. 🛜 🚪 🖥

▼▼▼ Residence Inn by Marriott ⬚

(216) 443-9043. **$197-$241.** 527 Prospect Ave E 44115. Between E 9th and Ontario sts. Int corridors. **Pets:** Accepted. 🛜 ⊠ 🚪 🖥

⟨AAA⟩ ▼▼▼▼ The Ritz-Carlton, Cleveland ⬚

(216) 623-1300. **$199-$399.** 1515 W 3rd St 44113. In Tower City Center (3rd St side). Int corridors. **Pets:** Dogs only. $75 one-time fee/pet. Service with restrictions, supervision. ⟨SAVE⟩ 🛜 ⊠ 🚪 🖥 ⑪ ➰ ⊠

⟨AAA⟩ ▼▼▼▼ Sheraton Cleveland Airport Hotel ⬚

(216) 267-1500. **$79-$209.** 5300 Riverside Dr 44135. I-71 exit 237, just s of I-480 on SR 237, follow signs. Int corridors. **Pets:** Accepted.
⟨SAVE⟩ 🛜 ⊠ ⓜ 🖥 ⑪ ➰

INDEPENDENCE

▼▼▼ La Quinta Inn Cleveland Independence ⬚

(216) 447-1133. **$71-$135.** 6161 Quarry Ln 44131. I-77 exit 155, just e on Rockside Rd, then just s. Int corridors. **Pets:** Medium, other species. Service with restrictions, supervision. 🛜 🚪 🖥

⟨AAA⟩ ▼▼▼ Red Roof Inn #0028 Ⓜ

(216) 447-0030. **$49-$99.** 6020 Quarry Ln 44131. I-77 exit 155, just e on Rockside Rd, then just s. Ext corridors. **Pets:** Large, other species. No service, supervision. ⟨SAVE⟩ 🛜 🚪

▼▼▼▼ Residence Inn by Marriott ⬚

(216) 520-1450. **$99-$259.** 5101 W Creek Rd 44131. I-77 exit 155, just w on Rockside Rd, then just n. Ext/int corridors. **Pets:** Accepted.
🛜 ⊠ 🚪 🖥 ➰ ⊠

LAKEWOOD

▼▼▼ Travelodge Ⓜ

(216) 221-9000. **$50-$89.** 11837 Edgewater Dr 44107. I-90 exit 166, 1.7 mi n on W 117th St, then just w. Int corridors. **Pets:** Accepted.
🛜 🚪 🖥

MAYFIELD HEIGHTS

⟨AAA⟩ ▼▼▼ Comfort Inn - Mayfield Heights ⬚

(440) 442-8400. **$94-$107.** 1421 Golden Gate Blvd 44124. I-271 exit 34, 0.3 mi w on US 322, then just n. Int corridors. **Pets:** Medium, other species. $10 daily fee/room. Service with restrictions.
⟨SAVE⟩ 🛜 ⊠ 🚪 🖥

▼▼▼ Staybridge Suites Cleveland East ⬚

(440) 442-9200. **$109-$169.** 6103 Landerhaven Dr 44124. I-271 exit 32, just e on Cedar Rd, 0.7 mi n on Lander Rd, then just e. Int corridors. **Pets:** Medium, dogs only. $75 one-time fee/pet. Designated rooms, service with restrictions. 🛜 ⓜ 🚪 🖥 ➰

MEDINA

▼▼▼ Quality Inn & Suites ⬚

(330) 723-4994. **$80-$150.** 2850 Medina Rd 44256. I-71 exit 218, just e. Int corridors. **Pets:** Accepted. 🛜 🚪 🖥 ➰

▼▼ Red Roof Inn **M**
(330) 725-1395. **$51-$85.** 5021 Eastpointe Dr 44256. I-71 exit 218, just w. Ext corridors. **Pets:** Large, other species. No service, supervision.
🛜 🛗 🏊

MIDDLEBURG HEIGHTS

🅰🅰🅰 ▼▼▼ Comfort Inn-Cleveland Airport **H**
(440) 234-3131. **$73-$130.** 17550 Rosbough Dr 44130. I-71 exit 235, 0.3 mi w to Engle Rd, then 0.3 mi n. Int corridors. **Pets:** Other species. $45 one-time fee/room. Service with restrictions, supervision.
SAVE 🛜 ♿ 🛗 🔲 🏊

🅰🅰🅰 ▼▼▼ Days Inn Cleveland Airport South **M**
(440) 243-2277. **$56-$65.** 7233 Engle Rd 44130. I-71 exit 235, just w. Ext corridors. **Pets:** Medium. $10 daily fee/room. Designated rooms, service with restrictions, supervision. SAVE 🛜 🛗 🔲 🏊

🅰🅰🅰 ▼▼▼ Red Roof Inn-Middleburg Heights #7060 **H**
(440) 243-2441. **$49-$79.** 17555 Bagley Rd 44130. I-71 exit 235, just w, then just s. Ext/int corridors. **Pets:** Large, other species. No service, supervision. SAVE 🛜 🛗

▼▼▼ Residence Inn by Marriott **H**
(440) 234-6688. **$161-$197.** 17525 Rosbough Dr 44130. I-71 exit 235, just w on Bagley Rd, then just n on Engle Rd. Ext/int corridors. **Pets:** Other species. $75 one-time fee/room. Service with restrictions, crate. 🛜 🔀 🛗 🔲 🏊 🔀

▼▼ StudioPLUS-Cleveland-Middleburg Heights **H** 🐾
(440) 243-7024. **$69-$104.** 17552 Rosbough Dr 44130. I-71 exit 235, 0.3 mi w to Engle Rd, then 0.3 mi n. Int corridors. **Pets:** Other species. $25 daily fee/pet. Service with restrictions. 🛜 🛗 🔲

▼▼ TownePlace Suites Cleveland Airport **H** 🐾
(440) 816-9300. **$69-$109.** 7325 S Engle Rd 44130. I-71 exit 235, just w on Bagley Rd, then just s. Int corridors. **Pets:** Other species. $75 one-time fee/room. Crate. ECO 🛜 🔀 🛗 🔲 🏊

NORTH OLMSTED

▼▼ Candlewood Suites Cleveland/North Olmsted **H**
(440) 716-0584. **$89-$104, 3 day notice.** 24741 Country Club Blvd 44070. I-480 exit 6B westbound; exit 6 eastbound, just n on SR 252. Int corridors. **Pets:** Accepted. 🛜 🛗 🔲

▼▼ Homestead Studio Suites Hotel-Cleveland/Airport/North Olmsted **H** 🐾
(440) 777-8585. **$69-$104.** 24851 Country Club Blvd 44070. I-480 exit 6B westbound; exit 6 eastbound, just n on SR 252. Int corridors. **Pets:** Other species. $25 daily fee/pet. Service with restrictions.
🛜 ♿ 🛗 🔲

🅰🅰🅰 ▼▼▼ La Quinta Inn & Suites Cleveland Airport West **H**
(440) 734-4477. **$66-$154.** 25105 Country Club Blvd 44070. I-480 exit 6B westbound; exit 6 eastbound, just n on SR 252. Int corridors. **Pets:** Medium, other species. Service with restrictions, supervision.
SAVE 🛜 ♿ 🛗 🔲 🏊

▼▼ StudioPLUS Cleveland-Airport-N Olmstead **H** 🐾
(440) 716-2412. **$69-$104.** 25801 Country Club Blvd 44070. I-480 6B westbound; exit 6 eastbound, just n on SR 252, then 0.3 mi w. Int corridors. **Pets:** Other species. $25 daily fee/pet. Service with restrictions.
🛜 🛗 🔲 🏊

RICHFIELD

▼▼ Days Inn & Suites Richfield **H**
(330) 659-6151. **$71-$116.** 4742 Brecksville Rd 44286. I-80 exit 173, just s; I-77 exit 145, 0.5 mi n. Int corridors. **Pets:** Accepted.
🛜 🛗 🔲 🍴 🏊 🔀

SOLON

▼▼▼ Hampton Inn **H** 🐾
(440) 542-0400. **$99-$139.** 6035 Enterprise Pkwy 44139. US 422 exit Harper Rd, 0.6 mi s, then 0.4 mi e. Int corridors. **Pets:** Large. $50 one-time fee/room. Designated rooms, service with restrictions, supervision.
🛜 🔀 ♿ 🛗 🔲 🏊

TWINSBURG

🅰🅰🅰 ▼▼▼ Comfort Suites-Twinsburg **H**
(330) 963-5909. **$85-$149.** 2715 Creekside Dr 44087. I-480 exit 37, just n. Int corridors. **Pets:** Dogs only. $25 one-time fee/room. Designated rooms, service with restrictions, supervision.
SAVE 🛜 🔀 ♿ 🛗 🔲 🏊

WESTLAKE

▼▼ Extended Stay Deluxe Cleveland-Westlake **H** 🐾
(440) 899-4160. **$79-$114.** 30360 Clemens Rd 44145. I-90 exit 156, just n. Int corridors. **Pets:** Other species. $25 daily fee/pet. Service with restrictions. 🛜 🛗 🔲

🅰🅰🅰 ▼▼▼ Holiday Inn Cleveland Westlake **H**
(440) 871-6000. **$89-$129.** 1100 Crocker Rd 44145. I-90 exit 156, just n. Int corridors. **Pets:** Accepted. SAVE 🛜 ♿ 🛗 🔲 🍴 🏊 🔀

🅰🅰🅰 ▼▼▼ Red Roof Inn-Westlake #7094 **M**
(440) 892-7920. **$49-$89.** 29595 Clemens Rd 44145. I-90 exit 156, just n. Ext corridors. **Pets:** Large, other species. No service, supervision.
SAVE 🛜 🛗 🔲

▼▼▼ Residence Inn by Marriott **H**
(440) 892-2254. **$161-$197.** 30100 Clemens Rd 44145. I-90 exit 156, just n. Ext corridors. **Pets:** Accepted. 🛜 🔀 🛗 🔲 🏊 🔀

WILLOUGHBY

🅰🅰🅰 ▼▼▼ Red Roof Inn-East #053 **M**
(440) 946-9872. **$50-$90.** 4166 SR 306 44094. I-90 exit 193, just s. Ext corridors. **Pets:** Large, other species. No service, supervision.
SAVE 🛜 🛗

END METROPOLITAN AREA

CLYDE

▼▼ Red Roof Inn **H**
(419) 547-6660. **$69-$129.** 1363 W McPherson Hwy 43410. 1 mi w on SR 20. Int corridors. **Pets:** Large, other species. No service, supervision.
🛜 ♿ 🛗 🔲 🏊

COLUMBUS METROPOLITAN AREA

CIRCLEVILLE

▼▼▼ Holiday Inn Express Hotel & Suites H
(740) 420-7711. **$99-$199.** 23911 US 23 S 43113. Jct US 22, 1.2 mi s. Int corridors. **Pets:** Accepted. 🛰 ⓖⓜ 🖥 💻 🏊

COLUMBUS

▼▼ Baymont Inn & Suites Columbus at Rickenbacker H
(614) 491-4400. **$53-$95.** 2323 Rickenbacker Pkwy W 43217. I-270 exit 49, 3.6 mi s, then just w. Int corridors. **Pets:** Medium. $25 one-time fee/room. Service with restrictions, supervision. 🛰 🖥 💻 🏊

⬥⬥⬥ ▼▼▼▼ Best Western Plus Columbus North H
(614) 888-8230. **$90.** 888 E Dublin Granville Rd 43229. I-71 exit 117, 0.5 mi w on SR 161. Int corridors. **Pets:** Accepted.
SAVE 🛰 🖥 💻 🏊 ✕

▼▼▼ Candlewood Suites Polaris H
(614) 436-6600. **Call for rates.** 8515 Lyra Dr 43240. I-71 exit 121, 0.3 mi w on SR 750. Int corridors. **Pets:** Accepted.
🛰 ⓖⓜ 🖥 🏊 ✕

⬥⬥⬥ ▼▼▼ Comfort Inn North Conference Center H
(614) 885-4085. **$65-$100.** 1213 E Dublin Granville Rd 43229. I-71 exit 117, just e. Int corridors. **Pets:** $10 daily fee/pet. No service, supervision.
SAVE 🛰 🖥 💻 🏊

▼▼ ▼▼ Comfort Inn Polaris H
(614) 791-9700. **$79-$139.** 8400 Lyra Dr 43240. I-71 exit 121, just w. Int corridors. **Pets:** Medium. $25 one-time fee/room. Designated rooms, service with restrictions. 🛰 ✕ ⓖⓜ 🖥 💻 🏊 ✕

▼▼ ▼▼ Comfort Suites Fairgrounds M
(614) 586-1001. **$85-$160.** 1690 Clara St 43211. I-71 exit 111, just w. Int corridors. **Pets:** Accepted. 🛰 ✕ 🖥 💻 🏊

⬥⬥⬥ ▼▼▼ Days Inn-Columbus Worthington H
(614) 436-0556. **$47-$95.** 7500 Vantage Dr 43235. I-270 exit 23, 0.4 mi n on US 23, just e on Dimension Dr, then just s. Int corridors.
Pets: Other species. $15 daily fee/room. Service with restrictions, crate.
SAVE 🛰 ⓖⓜ 🖥 💻

⬥⬥⬥ ▼▼▼▼ DoubleTree by Hilton Hotel Columbus - Worthington H
(614) 885-3334. **$79-$149.** 175 Hutchinson Ave 43235. I-270 exit 23, just n on US 23 N, just e on Dimension Dr, then just s on High Cross Blvd. Int corridors. **Pets:** Accepted. SAVE 🛰 ⓖⓜ 🖥 💻 🍽 🏊

▼▼▼▼ DoubleTree Suites by Hilton Hotel Columbus Downtown H
(614) 228-4600. **$152-$179.** 50 S Front St 43215. Corner of Front and State sts, just n. Int corridors. **Pets:** Accepted. 🛰 🖥 💻 🍽

▼▼▼▼ Drury Inn & Suites-Columbus Convention Center H
(614) 221-7008. **$130-$204.** 88 E Nationwide Blvd 43215. 0.3 mi n on US 23. Int corridors. **Pets:** Accepted. 🛰 ⓖⓜ 🖥 💻 🏊 ✕

▼▼ ▼▼ Extended StayAmerica-Columbus-Easton H ✿
(614) 428-6022. **$75-$100.** 4200 Stelzer Rd 43230. I-270 exit 32, just w on Morse Rd, then just n. Int corridors. **Pets:** Other species. $25 daily fee/pet. Service with restrictions. 🛰 🖥 💻

▼▼ ▼▼ Extended StayAmerica-Columbus-North H ✿
(614) 431-0033. **$55-$77.** 6255 Zumstein Dr 43229. I-71 exit 117, just w on SR 161, then 0.5 mi n. Int corridors. **Pets:** Other species. $25 daily fee/pet. Service with restrictions. 🛰 🖥 💻

▼▼ ▼▼ Extended Stay Deluxe Columbus/Polaris H ✿
(614) 431-5522. **$85-$105.** 8555 Lyra Dr 43240. I-71 N exit 121, just w on Polaris Pkwy. Int corridors. **Pets:** Other species. $25 daily fee/pet. Service with restrictions. 🛰 ⓖⓜ 🖥 💻 🏊

▼▼▼ Hawthorn Suites by Wyndham H
(614) 853-6199. **$89-$109.** 5505 Keim Cir 43228. I-70 exit 91B, just n on Renner Rd. Int corridors. **Pets:** Medium. $25 daily fee/pet. Service with restrictions, supervision. 🛰 ⓖⓜ 🖥 💻 🏊

⬥⬥⬥ ▼▼▼ Hawthorn Suites by Wyndham Airport Columbus East H
(614) 864-8844. **$79-$279.** 2084 S Hamilton Rd 43232. I-70 exit 107, 0.5 mi s, then just e. Ext corridors. **Pets:** Accepted.
SAVE 🛰 ✕ 🖥 💻 🏊 ✕

⬥⬥⬥ ▼▼▼ ▼▼▼ Hilton Columbus at Easton H
(614) 414-5000. **$189-$259.** 3900 Chagrin Dr 43219. I-270 exit 33, 0.5 mi w; at Easton Town Center. Int corridors. **Pets:** Medium. $50 one-time fee/room. Service with restrictions, supervision.
SAVE 🛰 ✕ ⓖⓜ 🖥 💻 🍽 🏊 ✕

⬥⬥⬥ ▼▼▼ ▼▼▼ Hilton Columbus/Polaris H
(614) 885-1600. **$129-$229.** 8700 Lyra Dr 43240. I-71 exit 121, just w on Polaris Pkwy, then just n. Int corridors. **Pets:** Medium, dogs only. $50 one-time fee/room. Service with restrictions, supervision.
SAVE 🛰 ✕ ⓖⓜ 🖥 💻 🍽 🏊 ✕

⬥⬥⬥ ▼▼▼▼ Holiday Inn Columbus Downtown Capitol Square H
(614) 221-3281. **$99-$179.** 175 E Town St 43215. I-70 exit 100B, 0.3 mi n on 4th St. Int corridors. **Pets:** Accepted.
SAVE 🛰 🖥 💻 🍽 🏊

⬥⬥⬥ ▼▼▼▼ Holiday Inn Express & Suites Columbus Southeast H
(614) 920-2400. **$90-$109.** 4041 Hamilton Square Blvd 43125. US 33 exit Hamilton Rd. Int corridors. **Pets:** Small. $25 one-time fee/pet. Designated rooms, service with restrictions, supervision.
SAVE 🛰 🖥 💻 🏊

▼▼▼▼ La Quinta Inns & Suites Columbus West H
(614) 878-8844. **$84-$154.** 5510 Trabue Rd 43228. I-70 exit 91 eastbound; exit 91B westbound, just n on Renner Rd, then just e. Int corridors. **Pets:** Medium, other species. Service with restrictions, supervision.
🛰 ✕ 🖥 💻 🏊

⬥⬥⬥ ▼▼▼▼ Red Roof Inn Columbus Downtown - Convention Center H
(614) 224-6539. **$80-$180.** 111 E Nationwide Blvd 43215. Jct 3rd St. Int corridors. **Pets:** Large, other species. No service, supervision.
SAVE 🛰 ✕ ⓖⓜ 🖥 💻

⬥⬥⬥ ▼▼ ▼▼ Red Roof Inn-OSU #7121 M
(614) 267-9941. **$70-$130.** 441 Ackerman Rd 43202. SR 315 exit Ackerman Rd, 0.6 mi e. Ext corridors. **Pets:** Large, other species. No service, supervision. SAVE 🛰 ⓖⓜ 🖥 💻

⬥⬥⬥ ▼▼ ▼▼ Red Roof Inn-West #7009 M
(614) 878-9245. **$50-$75.** 5001 Renner Rd 43228. I-70 exit 91 eastbound; exit 91B westbound, just nw. Ext corridors. **Pets:** Large, other species. No service, supervision. SAVE 🛰 ⓖⓜ 🖥

▼▼▼▼ Residence Inn by Marriott H
(614) 885-0799. **$125-$153.** 7300 Huntington Park Dr 43235. I-270 exit 23, 0.4 mi n on US 23, 0.3 mi e on E Campus View Blvd, then 0.5 mi s. Int corridors. **Pets:** Accepted. 🛰 ✕ ⓖⓜ 🖥 💻 🏊 ✕

▼▼▼▼ **Residence Inn by Marriott** H

(614) 222-2610. **$139-$199.** 36 E Gay St 43215. Between High and S 3rd sts. Int corridors. **Pets:** Large, other species. $100 one-time fee/room. Service with restrictions. 🛜 ⊠ 👤M 🔌 💻

▼▼▼▼ **Residence Inn by Marriott Easton** H

(614) 414-1000. **$175-$213.** 3999 Easton Loop W 43219. I-270 exit 33, 1 mi w, then just n. Int corridors. **Pets:** Accepted.
🛜 ⊠ 🔌 💻 ➔ ⊠

▲▲▲ ▼▼▼▼ **Sheraton Suites Columbus** H 🐾

(614) 436-0004. **$109-$189.** 201 Hutchinson Ave 43235. I-270 exit 23, 0.3 mi n on US 23, just e on Dimension Dr, then 0.4 mi se on Vantage Dr. Int corridors. **Pets:** Designated rooms, service with restrictions, supervision. SAVE 🛜 ⊠ 👤M 🔌 💻 🍴 ➔

▼▼▼▼ **TownePlace Suites by Marriott** H

(614) 885-1557. **$107-$131.** 7272 Huntington Park Dr 43235. I-270 exit 23, 0.4 mi n, 0.3 mi e on E Campus View Blvd, then 0.3 mi s. Int corridors. **Pets:** Accepted. ECO 🛜 ⊠ 🔌 💻 ➔

▲▲▲ ▼▼ **Varsity Inn North** M

(614) 267-4646. **Call for rates.** 3246 Olentangy River Rd 43202. SR 315 exit N Broadway, 0.3 mi s. Ext corridors. **Pets:** Accepted.
SAVE 🛜 🔌 💻 ➔

▲▲▲ ▼▼▼▼ **The Westin Columbus** H 🐾

(614) 228-3800. **$139-$239.** 310 S High St 43215. Corner of Main and High sts. Int corridors. **Pets:** Medium, other species. Service with restrictions, supervision. SAVE 🛜 ⊠ 🔌 💻 🍴

DELAWARE

▼▼ **Comfort Inn** H

(740) 363-8869. **Call for rates.** 1251 Columbus Pike 43015. 1.5 mi s on US 23. Int corridors. **Pets:** Small, dogs only. $30 one-time fee/room. Service with restrictions, supervision. 🛜 🔌 💻 ➔

DUBLIN

▼▼ **Chase Suite Hotel** H

(614) 766-7762. **$99-$179.** 4130 Tuller Rd 43017. I-270 exit 20, 0.3 mi s on Sawmill Rd via Village Pkwy and Dublin Center Dr. Ext corridors.
Pets: Accepted. 🛜 ⊠ 🔌 💻 ➔

▼▼▼▼ **Drury Inn & Suites-Columbus Northwest** H

(614) 798-8802. **$85-$159.** 6170 Parkcenter Cir 43017. I-270 exit 15 (Tuttle Crossing Blvd), 0.3 mi e, then just n on Blazer Pkwy. Int corridors.
Pets: Accepted. 🛜 👤M 🔌 💻 ➔

▼▼▼▼ **Dublin Homewood Suites by Hilton** H

(614) 791-9675. **$109-$179.** 5300 Parkcenter Ave 43017. I-270 exit 15 (Tuttle Crossing Blvd), just e, just n on Blazer Pkwy, then just e. Int corridors. **Pets:** Large, other species. $50 one-time fee/room. Service with restrictions, supervision. 🛜 👤M 🔌 💻 ➔ ⊠

▼▼ **Extended StayAmerica-Columbus-Dublin** H 🐾

(614) 760-0053. **$60-$82.** 450 Metro Pl N 43017. I-270 exit 17A, just e on SR 161, just s on Frantz Rd, then just w. Int corridors. **Pets:** Other species. $25 daily fee/pet. Service with restrictions. 🛜 🔌 💻

▼▼ **Extended Stay Deluxe (Columbus/Tuttle)** H 🐾

(614) 760-0245. **$75-$100.** 5530 Tuttle Crossing Blvd 43016. I-270 exit 15 (Tuttle Crossing Blvd), 0.3 mi w. Int corridors. **Pets:** Other species. $25 daily fee/pet. Service with restrictions. 🛜 🔌 💻

▼▼▼▼ **Holiday Inn Express** H 🐾

(614) 793-5500. **$104-$129.** 5500 Tuttle Crossing Blvd 43016. I-270 exit 15 (Tuttle Crossing Blvd), just w. Int corridors. **Pets:** $35 one-time fee/room. Service with restrictions, crate. 🛜 👤M 🔌 💻 ➔ ⊠

▼▼ **La Quinta Inn Columbus Dublin** H

(614) 792-8300. **$67-$135.** 6145 Parkcenter Cir 43017. I-270 exit 15 (Tuttle Crossing Blvd), just e, then just n on Blazer Pkwy. **Pets:** Medium, other species. Service with restrictions, supervision.
🛜 👤M 🔌 💻

▲▲▲ ▼▼▼ **Red Roof Inn-Dublin #127** M

(614) 764-3993. **$45-$110.** 5125 Post Rd 43017. I-270 exit 17A, just ne. Ext corridors. **Pets:** Large, other species. No service, supervision.
SAVE 🛜 👤M 🔌

▼▼▼▼ **Residence Inn by Marriott Dublin** H

(614) 791-0403. **$159-$174.** 435 Metro Pl S 43017. I-270 exit 17A, 0.5 mi e on SR 161, 0.5 mi s on Frantz Rd, then just w. Ext/int corridors.
Pets: Accepted. 🛜 ⊠ 👤M 🔌 💻 ➔ ⊠

GAHANNA

▼▼▼ **Candlewood Suites Columbus Airport** H 🐾

(614) 863-4033. **Call for rates.** 590 Taylor Rd 43230. I-270 exit 37, 0.4 mi e, 0.6 mi s on Morrison Rd, then just e. Int corridors. **Pets:** Large, other species. $15 one-time fee/room, $10 daily fee/room. 🛜 🔌 💻

▼▼▼ **TownePlace Suites by Marriott Columbus Airport** H

(614) 861-1400. **$89-$159.** 695 Taylor Rd 43230. I-270 exit 37, just e, 0.6 mi s on Morrison Rd, then just e. Int corridors. **Pets:** $100 one-time fee/room. Service with restrictions, crate. ECO 🛜 ⊠ 🔌 💻 ➔

GROVE CITY

▲▲▲ ▼▼▼ **Best Western Executive Inn** M

(614) 875-7770. **$76.** 4026 Jackpot Rd 43123. I-71 exit 100, just e. Ext corridors. **Pets:** Small, dogs only. $10 daily fee/pet. Designated rooms, service with restrictions, crate. SAVE 🛜 🔌 💻 ➔

▼▼▼ **Drury Inn & Suites-Columbus South** H

(614) 875-7000. **$100-$209.** 4109 Parkway Centre Dr 43123. I-71 exit 100, just e. Int corridors. **Pets:** Accepted. 🛜 👤M 🔌 💻 ➔

▼▼▼ **La Quinta Inn Grove City** H

(614) 539-6200. **$75-$189.** 3962 Jackpot Rd 43123. I-71 exit 100, just e. Int corridors. **Pets:** Medium, other species. Service with restrictions, supervision. 🛜 🔌 💻 ➔ ⊠

▼▼▼ **Red Roof Inn Columbus/Grove City** M

(614) 871-9617. **$54-$76.** 4055 Jackpot Rd 43123. I-71 exit 100, just e. Ext corridors. **Pets:** Large, other species. No service, supervision.
🛜 🔌 💻 ➔

HEBRON

▼▼▼ **Red Roof Inn** H

(740) 467-7663. **$50-$170.** 10668 Lancaster Rd SW 43025. I-70 exit 126, just s. Int corridors. **Pets:** Large, other species. No service, supervision. 🛜 👤M 🔌

HILLIARD

▼▼▼ **Comfort Suites by Choice Hotels-Columbus** H

(614) 529-8118. **$69-$129.** 3831 Park Mill Run Dr 43026. I-270 exit 13A northbound; exit 13 southbound, 0.3 mi e on Fishinger Blvd. Int corridors.
Pets: Accepted. 🛜 ⊠ 👤M 🔌 💻 ➔

▼▼▼▼ **Homewood Suites by Hilton-Columbus** H 🐾

(614) 529-4100. **$79-$111.** 3841 Park Mill Run Dr 43026. I-270 exit 13 southbound; exit 13A northbound, 0.4 mi e on Fishinger Blvd. Int corridors. **Pets:** Other species. $25 one-time fee/room, $10 daily fee/room. Service with restrictions, crate. 🛜 👤M 🔌 💻 ➔ ⊠

MARYSVILLE

▼▼ **Comfort Inn** H

(937) 644-0400. **$70.** 16420 Allenby Dr 43040. Jct US 33 and 36. Int corridors. **Pets:** Accepted. 🛜 🔌 💻 ➔

NEWARK

▼▼▼ **Cherry Valley Lodge** H

(740) 788-1200. **$99-$179.** 2299 Cherry Valley Rd 43055. 4.6 mi w on SR 16, 0.3 mi s. Int corridors. **Pets:** Accepted.
🛜 ⊠ 👤M 🔌 💻 🍴 ➔ ⊠

OBETZ

◇◇◇ ▼▼▼ Comfort Inn Obetz Rickenbacker 🅷 ✿
(614) 492-9000. **$65-$150.** 4870 Old Rathmell Ct 43207. I-270 exit 49, just e. Int corridors. **Pets:** Large. $20 daily fee/pet. Designated rooms, service with restrictions, crate. 🆂🅰🆅🅴 📶 ♿ 🛗 🍴 💻 ⊇

PICKERINGTON

◇◇◇ ▼▼▼ Comfort Inn 🅷
(614) 575-9900. **Call for rates.** 1800 Hill Rd N 43147. I-70 exit 112A, just s. Int corridors. **Pets:** Accepted. 🆂🅰🆅🅴 📶 ♿ 🛗 🍴 💻 ⊇

REYNOLDSBURG

▼▼▼ Days Inn & Suites Columbus East 🅷
(614) 864-1280. **$48-$59.** 2100 Brice Rd 43068. I-70 exit 110 westbound; exit 110B eastbound, just n. Int corridors. **Pets:** Accepted.
📶 🛗 💻 🍴 ⊇

▼▼▼ The Fairfield Inn & Suites Columbus East 🅷
(614) 864-4555. **$94-$104.** 2826 Taylor Rd Ext 43068. I-70 exit 112B eastbound; exit 112 westbound, just n, then just e. Int corridors. **Pets:** Medium. $75 one-time fee/room. Service with restrictions, supervision. 📶 ✕ ♿ 🛗 💻 ⊇ ✕

END METROPOLITAN AREA

CONNEAUT

◇◇◇ ▼▼▼ Days Inn of Conneaut 🅷
(440) 593-6000. **$63-$80.** 600 Days Blvd 44030. I-90 exit 241, 0.3 mi n. Int corridors. **Pets:** Accepted. 🆂🅰🆅🅴 📶 🛗 💻 🍴 ⊇

CUYAHOGA FALLS

◇◇◇ ▼▼▼ Sheraton Suites Akron-Cuyahoga Falls 🅷
(330) 929-3000. **$129-$329.** 1989 Front St 44221. SR 8 exit Broad Blvd, just w. Int corridors. **Pets:** Accepted.
🆂🅰🆅🅴 📶 ✕ ♿ 🛗 💻 🍴 ⊇ ✕

DANVILLE

▼▼▼ The White Oak Inn 🅱🅱 ✿
(740) 599-6107. **Call for rates.** 29683 Walhonding Rd (SR 715) 43014. 3 mi s on US 62, 1.3 mi se on US 36, then 2.7 mi e on SR 715. Ext/int corridors. **Pets:** Other species. $25 daily fee/room. Designated rooms, supervision. 📶 ✕ 🛗 💻 ✕

DAYTON

▼▼▼ Comfort Inn by Choice Hotels-North 🅷
(937) 890-9995. **$67-$135.** 7125 Miller Ln 45414. I-75 exit 59 (Wyse Rd/Benchwood Rd), just w on Benchwood Rd, then 0.6 mi n. Int corridors. **Pets:** Accepted. 📶 ♿ 🛗 💻 ⊇

▼▼▼ Dayton Inn South 🅷
(937) 291-0284. **$59.** 8099 Old Yankee St 45458. I-675 exit 2 northbound, just e on SR 725, then just s; exit southbound, just s. Int corridors. **Pets:** Accepted. 📶 ♿ 🛗 💻 ⊇

▼▼▼ Dayton Marriott Hotel 🅷
(937) 223-1000. **$179-$199.** 1414 S Patterson Blvd 45409. I-75 exit 51 (Edwin C Moses Blvd), 0.6 mi e on Edwin C Moses Blvd, just s on Stewart St, then just w. Int corridors. **Pets:** Accepted.
📶 ✕ ♿ 🍴 ⊇ ✕

▼▼▼ Drury Inn & Suites-Dayton North 🅷
(937) 454-5200. **$100-$244.** 6616 Miller Ln 45414. I-75 exit 59 (Wyse Rd/Benchwood Rd), just w on Benchwood Rd, then just n. Int corridors. **Pets:** Accepted. 📶 ♿ 🛗 💻 ⊇

▼▼▼ Extended StayAmerica Dayton South 🅷 ✿
(937) 439-2022. **$52-$110.** 7851 Lois Cir 45459. I-75 exit 44, just e on SR 725; opposite mall. Int corridors. **Pets:** Other species. $25 daily fee/pet. Service with restrictions. 📶 🛗 💻 ⊇

▼▼▼ Super 8 Reynoldsburg 🅼
(614) 864-3880. **$43-$166.** 2055 Brice Rd 43068. I-70 exit 110 westbound; exit 110B eastbound. Ext corridors. **Pets:** Accepted.
📶 🛗 💻 ⊇

SUNBURY

▼▼▼ Hampton Inn-Columbus/Delaware 🅷
(740) 363-4700. **$99-$159.** 7329 SR 36 & 37 43074. I-71 exit 131, just nw. Int corridors. **Pets:** Accepted. 📶 ♿ 🛗 💻 ⊇

WESTERVILLE

▼▼ Baymont Inn & Suites North East 🅼
(614) 890-1244. **$65.** 909 S State St 43081. I-270 exit 29, 0.4 mi n on SR 3, just w on Heatherdown Dr, then just s. Ext corridors.
Pets: Accepted. 🛗 💻 ⊇

▼▼ Fairfield Inn by Marriott Dayton North 🅷
(937) 898-1120. **$69-$129.** 6960 Miller Ln 45414. I-75 exit 59 (Wyse Rd/Benchwood Rd), just w on Benchwood Rd, then 0.5 mi n. Ext/int corridors. **Pets:** Accepted. 📶 ✕ ♿ 🛗 💻 ⊇

◇◇◇ ▼▼▼ Red Roof Inn-North #10023 🅼
(937) 898-1054. **$45-$99.** 7370 Miller Ln 45414. I-75 exit 59 (Wyse Rd/Benchwood Rd), just w on Benchwood Rd, then 0.8 mi n. Ext corridors. **Pets:** Large, other species. No service, supervision. 🆂🅰🆅🅴 📶 🛗

▼▼▼ TownePlace Suites by Marriott Dayton North 🅷
(937) 898-5700. **$98-$120.** 3642 Maxton Rd 45414. I-75 exit 59 (Wyse Rd/Benchwood Rd), just w on Wyse Rd, 0.5 mi n on Miller Ln. Int corridors. **Pets:** Accepted. 📶 ✕ ♿ 🛗 💻

DELPHOS

▼▼ Microtel Inn & Suites 🅷
(567) 765-1500. **$58-$67.** 480 Moxie Ln 45833. US 30 exit 5th St, 0.5 mi s. Int corridors. **Pets:** Small, dogs only. $20 one-time fee/pet. Service with restrictions, supervision. 📶 ✕ ♿ 🛗 💻

ENGLEWOOD

◇◇◇ ▼▼ Best Western Plus Dayton Northwest 🅷
(937) 832-2222. **Call for rates.** 20 Rockridge Rd 45322. I-70 exit 29, just n. Int corridors. **Pets:** Accepted. 🆂🅰🆅🅴 📶 🛗 💻

◇◇◇ ▼▼▼ Comfort Inn & Suites-Dayton 🅷 ✿
(937) 836-9400. **$69-$179.** 9305 N Main St 45415. I-70 exit 29, just s. Int corridors. **Pets:** Medium, other species. $25 daily fee/room. Service with restrictions, supervision. 🆂🅰🆅🅴 📶 ✕ 🛗 💻 ⊇

▼▼▼ Holiday Inn Dayton Airport 🅷
(937) 832-1234. **$85-$129.** 10 Rockridge Rd 45322. I-70 exit 29, just n. Int corridors. **Pets:** Accepted. 📶 🛗 💻 🍴 ⊇

FAIRBORN

▼▼ Baymont Inn & Suites Dayton-Fairborn 🅷 ✿
(937) 754-9109. **$71-$112.** 730 E Xenia Dr 45324. I-675 exit 22, 0.6 mi w. Int corridors. **Pets:** Large. $50 deposit/pet, $10 daily fee/pet. Service with restrictions. 📶 🛗 💻

▼▼▼ Holiday Inn Dayton/Fairborn/I-675 🅷
(937) 426-7800. **Call for rates.** 2800 Presidential Dr 45324. I-675 exit 17 (N Fairfield Rd), just w. Int corridors. **Pets:** Accepted.
📶 ♿ 🛗 💻 🍴 ⊇

▼▼▼▼ Homewood Suites by Hilton-Fairborn/Dayton **H**

(937) 429-0600. **$99-$199.** 2750 Presidential Dr 45324. I-675 exit 17 (N Fairfield Rd), just w. Ext/int corridors. **Pets:** Accepted.

▼▼ Ramada Limited & Suites-Fairborn Ohio **H**

(937) 490-2000. **$45-$95.** 2540 University Blvd 45324. I-675 exit 15 (Colonel Glenn Hwy), 1.5 mi e, then just s. Int corridors. **Pets:** Accepted.

▼▼ StudioPLUS Dayton-Fairborn **H** ❖

(937) 429-0140. **$45-$115.** 3131 Presidential Dr 45324. I-675 exit 15 (Colonel Glenn Hwy), 1.5 mi e, then just s. Int corridors. **Pets:** Other species. $25 daily fee/pet. Service with restrictions.

FAIRLAWN

▼▼▼ Extended StayAmerica Akron-Copley **H** ❖

(330) 668-9818. **$64-$99.** 185 Montrose West Ave 44321. I-77 exit 137B, just w on SR 18, then 0.6 mi s. Int corridors. **Pets:** Other species. $25 daily fee/pet. Service with restrictions.

△△△△ ▼▼▼▼ Hilton Akron/Fairlawn **H**

(330) 867-5000. **$109-$209.** 3180 W Market St 44333. I-77 exit 137A, 2 mi e on SR 18. Int corridors. **Pets:** Medium, dogs only. $50 one-time fee/room. Service with restrictions, supervision.

▼▼▼▼ InnPlace Suites Akron **H**

(330) 666-4811. **Call for rates.** 120 Montrose West Ave 44321. I-77 exit 137B, 0.3 mi w on SR 18, then 0.5 mi s. Ext corridors. **Pets:** Accepted.

▼▼ StudioPLUS-Akron-Copley **H** ❖

(330) 666-3177. **$64-$99.** 170 Montrose West Ave 44321. I-77 exit 137B, 0.3 mi w on SR 18, then 0.5 mi s. Int corridors. **Pets:** Other species. $25 daily fee/pet. Service with restrictions.

FINDLAY

▼▼▼ Country Inn & Suites By Carlson **H**

(419) 422-4200. **Call for rates.** 903 Interstate Dr 45840. I-75 exit 159, just w. Int corridors. **Pets:** Accepted.

▼▼▼ Drury Inn & Suites **H**

(419) 422-9700. **$100-$159.** 820 Trenton Ave 45840. I-75 exit 159, just e. Int corridors. **Pets:** Accepted.

▼▼▼ Extended Stay Deluxe Findlay-Tiffin Ave **H** ❖

(419) 425-9696. **$83-$100.** 2355 Tiffin Ave 45840. 3 mi e on US 224. Int corridors. **Pets:** Other species. $25 daily fee/pet. Service with restrictions.

▼▼▼▼ Holiday Inn Express Hotel & Suites **H**

(419) 420-1776. **Call for rates.** 941 Interstate Dr 45840. I-75 exit 159, just w. Int corridors. **Pets:** Medium. $25 one-time fee/pet. Designated rooms, service with restrictions, supervision.

△△△ ▼▼ Quality Inn **M** ❖

(419) 423-4303. **$62-$85.** 1020 Interstate Ct 45840. I-75 exit 159, just w. Ext corridors. **Pets:** Dogs only. $15 daily fee/pet. Service with restrictions, supervision.

▼▼▼ TownePlace Suites by Marriott Findlay **H**

(419) 425-9545. **$103-$125.** 2501 Tiffin Ave 45840. 3 mi e on US 224. Int corridors. **Pets:** Other species. $50 one-time fee/room. Service with restrictions, supervision.

FOSTORIA

△△△ ▼▼▼ Best Western Fostoria Inn & Suites **H**

(419) 436-3600. **$81-$89.** 1690 N County Line Rd 44830. SR 12, 2 mi n on SR 23. Int corridors. **Pets:** Medium, other species. $10 daily fee/pet. Designated rooms, service with restrictions, crate.

FREDERICKTOWN

▼▼▼ Heartland Country Resort **CA** ❖

(419) 768-9300. **$180-$240, 7 day notice.** 3020 Township Rd 190 43019. I-71 exit 151, 2 mi e on SR 95, 0.6 mi s on SR 314, then 1.3 mi e. Ext corridors. **Pets:** Other species. $15 daily fee/room.

FREMONT

▼▼ Comfort Inn & Suites **H**

(419) 355-9300. **$95-$140.** 840 Sean Dr 43420. I-80/90 exit 91, 2 mi s on SR 53. Int corridors. **Pets:** Large, other species. $25 one-time fee/pet. Service with restrictions, supervision.

▼▼ Days Inn **H**

(419) 334-9551. **$75-$129.** 3701 SR 53 N 43420. I-80/90 exit 91, just n. Int corridors. **Pets:** Small, dogs only. $50 deposit/room. Designated rooms, service with restrictions, supervision.

GENEVA

△△△ ▼ Motel 6 #4476 **H**

(440) 466-1168. **$50-$96.** 1715 SR 534 S 44041. I-90 exit 218, just n. Int corridors. **Pets:** Other species. Service with restrictions, supervision.

GENEVA-ON-THE-LAKE

△△△ ▼▼▼ The Lodge & Conference Center at Geneva-on-the-Lake **H** ❖

(440) 466-7100. **$89-$299, 3 day notice.** 4888 N Broadway (SR 534) 44041. I-90 exit 218, 6.1 mi n on SR 534. Int corridors. **Pets:** Medium. $25 one-time fee/room. Designated rooms, service with restrictions, crate.

GREEN

△△△ ▼▼▼ Super 8 **H**

(330) 899-9888. **$45-$171.** 1605 Corporate Woods Pkwy 44685. I-77 exit 118, just w. Int corridors. **Pets:** Medium. $10 daily fee/pet. Designated rooms, service with restrictions, supervision.

GREENVILLE

△△△ ▼▼ Greenville Inn **H**

(937) 548-3613. **$65-$115.** 851 Martin St 45331. Jct US 36 and 127, 0.3 mi w on SR 571. Int corridors. **Pets:** $10 daily fee/pet. Service with restrictions, supervision.

HILLSBORO

▼▼ Days Inn Hillsboro **H**

(937) 393-0299. **$63-$85.** 103 Harry Sauner Rd 45133. 1.9 mi ne on US 62. Int corridors. **Pets:** Accepted.

HOLLAND

▼ Extended StayAmerica Toledo-Holland **H** ❖

(419) 861-1133. **$55-$77.** 6155 W Trust Dr 43528. I-475 exit 8, 0.5 mi e to Holland-Sylvania Rd, then just n. Int corridors. **Pets:** Other species. $25 daily fee/pet. Service with restrictions.

HUBER HEIGHTS

▼▼▼ Holiday Inn Express Hotel & Suites **H**

(937) 235-2000. **$100-$120.** 5612 Merily Way 45424. I-70 exit 36, just se on SR 202. Int corridors. **Pets:** Small. $25 one-time fee/room. Service with restrictions, crate.

HURON

▼▼ Motel 6 Huron **H**

(419) 433-7829. **$39-$169, 3 day notice.** 601 Rye Beach Rd 44839. SR 2 exit Rye Beach, 2.5 mi w on US 6. Int corridors. **Pets:** Other species. Service with restrictions, supervision.

▼▼▼▼ River's Edge Inn 🅷
(419) 433-8000. **Call for rates.** 132 N Main St 44839. 3 blks n on Williams St to South St, just e. Int corridors. **Pets:** Accepted. [SAVE] 🛜 🏊

JACKSON

▼▼ Red Roof Inn Ⓜ
(740) 288-1200. **$73-$107.** 1000 Acy Ave 45640. US 35 exit McCarty Ln, just nw. Int corridors. **Pets:** Large, other species. No service, supervision. 🛜 🔋

KENT

▼▼ Days Inn-Akron Kent Ⓜ
(330) 677-9400. **$53-$140.** 4422 Edson Rd 44240. I-76 exit 33. Ext corridors. **Pets:** Accepted. 🛜 🔋 🖥 🏊

KINSMAN

▼▼▼ Dream Horse Guesthouse 🅱🅱
(330) 876-0428. **$75-$140, 14 day notice.** 9532 SR 7 44428. 0.5 mi n on SR 7. Int corridors. **Pets:** Medium, other species. $20 daily fee/pet. No service, supervision. 🛜 ✖ 🔋 🖥 ✖

LIMA

▼▼▼ Country Inn & Suites By Carlson 🅷
(419) 999-9992. **Call for rates.** 804 S Leonard Ave 45804. I-75 exit 125A southbound; exit 125 northbound, just w. Int corridors. **Pets:** Accepted. 🛜 🔋 🖥 🏊

▼▼▼ Holiday Inn & Suites 🅷
(419) 879-4000. **$114-$139.** 803 S Leonard Ave 45804. I-75 exit 125A southbound; exit 125 northbound, just w. Int corridors. **Pets:** Accepted. 🛜 ✖ ⌖ 🔋 🖥 🍴 🏊 ✖

▼▼▼▼ Wingate by Wyndham Downtown Lima 🅷
(419) 228-7000. **$43-$130.** 175 W Market St 45801. Jct Elizabeth St; downtown. Int corridors. **Pets:** Accepted. [SAVE] 🛜 🔋 🖥 ✖

LOGAN

▼▼ The Cabins at Cedar Grove 🅲🅰
(740) 380-2209. **Call for rates.** 19555 SR 664 S 43138. US 33 exit SR 664, 9.4 mi s. Ext corridors. **Pets:** Accepted. ✖ 🔋 🖥

▼▼▼▼ Holiday Inn Express Hocking Hills 🅷
(740) 385-7700. **Call for rates.** 12916 Grey St 43138. SR 664, just w to Lake Logan Rd, then just n. Int corridors. **Pets:** Accepted. [SAVE] 🛜 ⌖ 🏊

▼▼▼ The Inn & Spa At Cedar Falls 🅲🅸 ✿
(740) 385-7489. **$129-$289.** 21190 SR 374 43138. 9.5 mi s on SR 664, 1 mi e. Int corridors. **Pets:** Medium, dogs only. $45 one-time fee/pet. Designated rooms, service with restrictions, crate. 🛜 ✖ 🔋 🖥 🍴 ✖ 🅿 ⓩ

LOUDONVILLE

▼▼▼ Mohican Little Brown Inn Ⓜ
(419) 994-5525. **Call for rates.** 940 S Market St 44842. 1.3 mi s on SR 3. Ext/int corridors. **Pets:** Small, dogs only. $10 one-time fee/pet. Designated rooms, no service, supervision. [SAVE] 🛜 🔋

MANSFIELD

▼▼ Best Western Richland Inn-Mansfield 🅷 ✿
(419) 756-6670. **$70-$190.** 180 E Hanley Rd 44903. I-71 exit 169, jct SR 13. Int corridors. **Pets:** Large. $15 one-time fee/room. Service with restrictions, crate. [SAVE] 🛜 🔋 🖥 🏊

▼▼ La Quinta Inn & Suites Mansfield 🅷
(419) 774-0005. **$71-$129.** 120 Stander Ave 44903. I-71 exit 169. Int corridors. **Pets:** Medium, other species. Service with restrictions, supervision. 🛜 ⌖ 🔋 🖥 🏊

▼▼ Super 8 🅷
(419) 756-8875. **$49-$107.** 2425 Interstate Cir 44903. I-71 exit 169. Int corridors. **Pets:** Accepted. 🛜 🔋 🖥

▼▼ Travelodge Ⓜ
(419) 756-7600. **$41-$81.** 90 W Hanley Rd 44903. I-71 exit 169, just s. Ext corridors. **Pets:** Accepted. 🛜 🔋 🖥

MARIETTA

▼▼▼ Comfort Inn Marietta 🅷 ✿
(740) 374-8190. **$77-$110.** 700 Pike St 45750. I-77 exit 1, just e. Int corridors. **Pets:** Medium, dogs only. $10 one-time fee/pet. Designated rooms, service with restrictions, supervision. [SAVE] 🛜 ⌖ 🔋 🖥 🍴 🏊

▼▼ The Lafayette Hotel 🅷
(740) 373-5522. **$65-$195.** 101 Front St 45750. Center. Int corridors. **Pets:** $50 deposit/room. Service with restrictions, crate. 🛜 🔋 🖥

▼▼ Magnuson Hotel By The River Ⓜ
(740) 374-7211. **$66-$99.** 279 Muskingum Dr 45750. I-77 exit 6, 3.5 mi sw on SR 821, then 1 mi s on SR 60. Ext corridors. **Pets:** Medium, other species. $5 daily fee/room. Service with restrictions, supervision. 🛜 🔋 🖥 ✖

▼▼ Microtel Inn & Suites 🅷
(740) 373-7373. **$62-$130.** 506 Pike St 45750. I-77 exit 1, just w. Int corridors. **Pets:** Accepted. 🛜 ⌖ 🔋 🖥

▼▼▼ Super 8-Marietta Ⓜ
(740) 374-8888. **$42-$90.** 46 Acme St 45750. I-77 exit 1, just w. Int corridors. **Pets:** $10 daily fee/pet. Service with restrictions, supervision. [SAVE] 🛜 🔋 🖥

MARION

▼▼ Comfort Inn by Choice Hotels 🅷
(740) 389-5552. **$80-$120.** 256 Jamesway Dr 43302. Jct US 23 and SR 95, just w. Int corridors. **Pets:** Accepted. 🛜 🔋 🖥 🏊

MAUMEE

▼▼▼ Comfort Inn West Toledo/Maumee 🅷
(419) 893-2800. **$59-$99.** 1426 S Reynolds Rd 43537. I-80/90 exit 59, 0.5 mi s. Int corridors. **Pets:** Accepted. 🛜 🔋 🖥 🏊

▼▼▼ Homewood Suites by Hilton Toledo/Maumee 🅷
(419) 897-0980. **$99-$169.** 1410 Arrowhead Rd 43537. I-475 exit 6, just e. Int corridors. **Pets:** Accepted. 🛜 ⌖ 🔋 🖥 🏊 ✖

▼▼ Red Roof Inn-Maumee #7046 Ⓜ
(419) 893-0292. **$50-$85.** 1570 S Reynolds Rd 43537. I-80/90 exit 59, just s. Ext/int corridors. **Pets:** Large, other species. No service, supervision. [SAVE] 🛜 🔋 🖥

▼▼▼ Residence Inn by Marriott Maumee 🅷
(419) 891-2233. **$149-$169.** 1370 Arrowhead Dr 43537. I-475 exit 6, just e. Int corridors. **Pets:** Accepted. 🛜 ✖ 🔋 🖥 🏊 ✖

▼▼ StudioPLUS-Toledo-Maumee 🅷 ✿
(419) 891-1211. **$60-$90.** 542 W Dussel Dr 43537. I-475 exit 6, just e. Int corridors. **Pets:** Other species. $25 daily fee/pet. Service with restrictions. 🛜 🔋 🖥

▼▼▼ Super 8-Maumee/Toledo 🅷
(419) 897-3800. **$58-$67.** 1390 Arrowhead Rd 43537. I-475 exit 6, just e. Int corridors. **Pets:** Medium. $10 daily fee/pet. Service with restrictions, supervision. [SAVE] 🛜 ✖ 🔋 🖥

MENTOR

Best Western Plus Lawnfield Inn & Suites H ☼

(440) 205-7378. **$79-$149.** 8434 Mentor Ave 44060. I-90 exit 195, 1.5 mi n to SR 20 (Mentor Ave), then just e. Int corridors. **Pets:** $20 daily fee/room. Designated rooms, service with restrictions, supervision. (SAVE) 🛜 ⊠ 🔌M 📳 💻 🏊

Comfort Inn & Suites H

(440) 951-7333. **Call for rates.** 7701 Reynolds Rd 44060. On SR 306, just s of SR 2. Int corridors. **Pets:** Medium. $25 one-time fee/pet. Designated rooms, service with restrictions, crate. 🛜 📳 💻 🏊 ⊠

Residence Inn by Marriott H

(440) 392-0800. **$169-$189.** 5660 Emerald Ct 44060. Jct SR 2 and Heisley Rd, just s. Int corridors. **Pets:** Other species. $75 one-time fee/room. Service with restrictions, crate. 🛜 ⊠ 📳 💻 🏊 ⊠

Super 8 H

(440) 951-8558. **$40-$90.** 7325 Palisades Pkwy 44060. On SR 306, just s of SR 2. Int corridors. **Pets:** Accepted. (SAVE) 🛜 📳

MIAMISBURG

Homewood Suites by Hilton-Dayton South H

(937) 432-0000. **$134-$154.** 3100 Contemporary Ln 45342. I-75 exit 44, just e on SR 725, just se on Prestige Plaza Dr, then just s. Int corridors. **Pets:** Accepted. 🛜 🔌M 📳 💻 🏊

Quality Inn & Suites Dayton South H

(937) 865-0077. **Call for rates.** 250 Byers Rd 45342. I-75 exit 44, just w on SR 725, then just n. Int corridors. **Pets:** $10 daily fee/pet. Designated rooms, service with restrictions, crate. 🛜 📳 💻 🏊

Red Roof Inn-South #10006 M

(937) 866-0705. **$45-$99.** 222 Byers Rd 45342. I-75 exit 44, just w on SR 725. Ext corridors. **Pets:** Large, other species. No service, supervision. (SAVE) 🛜 📳

Super 8 Miamisburg/South Dayton H

(937) 866-5500. **$45-$67.** 155 Monarch Ln 45342. I-75 exit 44, 0.5 mi w on SR 725. Int corridors. **Pets:** Accepted. 🛜 📳 💻

MILAN

Motel 6 - 4016 H

(419) 499-8001. **$39-$169, 3 day notice.** 11406 US 250 Milan Rd 44846. I-80/90 exit 118, 1.5 mi n. Int corridors. **Pets:** Other species. Service with restrictions, supervision. (ECO) 🛜 🏊

Red Roof Inn H

(419) 499-4347. **$49-$159.** 11303 Rte 250 Milan Rd 44846. I-80/90 exit 118, 0.5 mi n. Int corridors. **Pets:** Large, other species. No service, supervision. 🛜 📳 💻 🏊 ⊠

Super 8 H

(419) 499-4671. **$49-$158.** 11313 US 250 Milan Rd 44846. I-80/90 exit 118, 0.5 mi n. Ext/int corridors. **Pets:** Small, dogs only. $50 deposit/pet. Service with restrictions, supervision. 🛜 🍴 🏊

MILLERSBURG

Comfort Inn Millersburg H ☼

(330) 674-7400. **Call for rates.** 1102 Glen Dr 44654. SR 39, 0.5 mi s on S Clay. Int corridors. **Pets:** Medium, dogs only. $20 daily fee/pet. Designated rooms, service with restrictions, supervision.
🛜 ⊠ 📳 💻 🏊 ⊠

Hotel Millersburg H

(330) 674-1457. **$70-$185.** 35 W Jackson St 44654. Just w of jct SR 83; downtown. Int corridors. **Pets:** Medium, dogs only. $12 daily fee/room. Designated rooms, service with restrictions, crate.
🛜 ⊠ 📳 💻 🍴

MONTPELIER

Holiday Inn Express Hotel & Suites Bryan/Montpelier H

(419) 485-0008. **$96-$220.** 13399 SR 15 43543. I-80/90 exit 13, just s. Int corridors. **Pets:** Other species. $10 daily fee/pet. Designated rooms, service with restrictions, supervision. 🛜 📳 💻 🏊

Ramada H

(419) 485-5555. **$71-$116.** 13508 SR 15 43543. I-80/90 exit 13, just s. Int corridors. **Pets:** Accepted. 🛜 📳 💻 🍴 🏊 ⊠

MOUNT VERNON

Comfort Inn H

(740) 392-6886. **$85-$200.** 150 Howard St 43050. Jct SR 13; south of downtown. Int corridors. **Pets:** Other species. $10 daily fee/pet. Service with restrictions, supervision. 🛜 📳 💻 🏊

Holiday Inn Express H

(740) 392-1900. **$119-$169.** 11555 Upper Gilchrist Rd 43050. 2.6 mi e on US 36, then just s. Int corridors. **Pets:** Small. Designated rooms, service with restrictions, crate. 🛜 ⊠ 📳 💻 🏊

NAPOLEON

Best Western Plus Napoleon Inn & Suites H ☼

(419) 599-0850. **$75-$100.** 1290 Independence Dr 43545. US 6 and 24, just se. Int corridors. **Pets:** Other species. $15 daily fee/pet. Service with restrictions, supervision. (SAVE) 🛜 📳 💻 🏊 ⊠

NEWCOMERSTOWN

Hampton Inn H

(740) 498-9800. **$89-$169.** 200 Morris Crossing 43832. I-77 exit 65, 0.8 mi w. Int corridors. **Pets:** Accepted. 🛜 🔌M 📳 💻 🏊

NEWTON FALLS

Econo Lodge M

(330) 872-0988. **Call for rates.** 4248 SR 5 44444. I-80 exit 209, just w. Ext corridors. **Pets:** Other species. $15 daily fee/pet. Service with restrictions, crate. (SAVE) 🛜 📳 💻

NORTH LIMA

Super 8 M ☼

(330) 549-9190. **Call for rates.** 10076 Market St 44452. I-76 exit 232, 0.5 mi n. Ext corridors. **Pets:** Medium, other species. $10 daily fee/pet. Service with restrictions, crate. 🛜 📳 💻

NORWALK

All American Inn & Suites H ☼

(419) 663-1922. **$59-$249, 7 day notice.** 415 Milan Ave 44857. 4 mi n on US 250; 5 mi s of I-80/90 (Ohio Tpke). Int corridors. **Pets:** Medium. $25 one-time fee/pet. Service with restrictions, crate.
(SAVE) 🛜 📳 💻 🏊

Best Western Norwalk H ☼

(419) 663-3501. **$80-$270, 7 day notice.** 351 Milan Ave 44857. 3.5 mi n on US 250; 5.5 mi s of I-80/90 (Ohio Tpke). Int corridors. **Pets:** Medium. $20 one-time fee/pet. Service with restrictions, crate.
(SAVE) 🛜 📳 💻 🏊

Econo Lodge M

(419) 668-5656. **$44-$139.** 342 Milan Ave 44857. 3 mi n on US 250; 6 mi s of I-80/90 (Ohio Tpke). Ext corridors. **Pets:** Small, dogs only. $50 deposit/pet. Service with restrictions, supervision. 🛜 📳 💻 🏊

OBERLIN

Oberlin Inn H

(440) 775-1111. **$109-$189.** 7 N Main St 44074. On SR 58; jct College and Main sts; center. Int corridors. **Pets:** Accepted. 🛜 📳 💻 🍴

OREGON

ᴬᴬᴬ⮞ ▼▼▼ Comfort Inn East �H 🐾
(419) 691-8911. **$77-$85.** 2930 Navarre Ave 43616. I-280 exit 7, just n on access road, then 0.5 mi e on SR 2 (Navarre Ave). Int corridors. **Pets:** Large, other species. $15 one-time fee/room. Designated rooms, service with restrictions, crate. (SAVE) 🛜 🍴 🖥 🏊

ᴬᴬᴬ⮞ ▼▼▼ Sleep Inn & Suites �H 🐾
(419) 697-7800. **$77-$85.** 1761 Meijer Cir 43616. I-280 exit 6 (Curtice Rd), just w. Int corridors. **Pets:** Large, other species. $15 one-time fee/room. Designated rooms, service with restrictions, crate.
(SAVE) 🛜 🍴 🖥 🏊

PAINESVILLE

▼▼▼ Quail Hollow Resort �H
(440) 497-1100. **Call for rates.** 11080 Concord-Hambden Rd 44077. I-90 exit 200, 0.3 mi s on SR 44, then just e on Auburn Rd. Int corridors. **Pets:** Small. $150 deposit/room, $50 one-time fee/room. Service with restrictions, crate. 🛜 ✕ ♿ 🍴 🖥 🍴 🏊 ✕

PERRYSBURG

▼▼▼ Candlewood Suites �H 🐾
(419) 872-6161. **$89-$99.** 27350 Lake Vue Dr 43551. I-75 exit 193, just e. Int corridors. **Pets:** Medium. $10 daily fee/pet. Designated rooms, service with restrictions, crate. 🛜 ♿ 🍴 🖥

▼▼▼ La Quinta Inn Toledo Perrysburg �H
(419) 872-0000. **$67-$129.** 1154 Professional Dr 43551. I-75 exit 193, just w. Int corridors. **Pets:** Medium, other species. Service with restrictions, supervision. 🛜 🍴 🖥

PIQUA

▼▼▼ Comfort Inn, Piqua, at Miami Valley Centre Mall �H
(937) 778-8100. **$74-$169.** 987 E Ash St 45356. I-75 exit 82, just w. Int corridors. **Pets:** Accepted. 🛜 🍴 🖥 🏊 ✕

▼▼▼ La Quinta Inn Piqua �H
(937) 615-0140. **$71-$149.** 950 E Ash St 45356. I-75 exit 82, just w. Int corridors. **Pets:** Medium, other species. Service with restrictions, supervision. 🛜 🍴 🖥 🏊

POLAND

▼▼▼ Residence Inn by Marriott-Youngstown �H
(330) 726-1747. **$140-$150.** 7396 Tiffany S 44514. I-680 exit 11, just w. Int corridors. **Pets:** Accepted. 🛜 ✕ 🍴 🖥 🏊 ✕

PORT CLINTON

ᴬᴬᴬ⮞ ▼ Best Budget Inn & Suites �H
(419) 734-5633. **$44-$179, 3 day notice.** 1735 E Perry St 43452. 1.5 mi e on SR 163, w of jct SR 2. Ext/int corridors. **Pets:** Accepted.
(SAVE) 🍴 🏊

ᴬᴬᴬ⮞ ▼▼ Best Western Port Clinton �H
(419) 734-2274. **$59-$169.** 1734 E Perry St 43452. 1.7 mi e on SR 163, w of jct SR 2. Int corridors. **Pets:** Small, dogs only. $50 deposit/pet. Service with restrictions, supervision. (SAVE) 🛜 🍴 🖥 🏊

▼▼ Comfort Inn, Waterfront �H
(419) 732-2929. **Call for rates.** 1723 E Perry St 43452. 1.5 mi e on SR 163, w of jct SR 2. Ext corridors. **Pets:** Accepted. 🛜 🍴 🖥 🏊

▼▼ Commodore Perry Inn & Business Center �H
(419) 732-2645. **$60-$220, 3 day notice.** 255 W Lakeshore Dr 43452. SR 2 exit 121A, 2.4 mi on SR 163. Int corridors. **Pets:** Accepted.
🛜 🍴 🖥 🍴 🏊

▼▼ Sleep Inn & Suites �H
(419) 732-7707. **Call for rates.** 947 SE Catawba Rd (SR 53) 43452. SR 2 exit 124, just n on SR 53. Int corridors. **Pets:** Accepted.
🛜 ♿ 🍴 🖥 🏊

▼▼ Super 8 �H
(419) 734-4446. **$54-$159.** 1704 E Perry St 43452. 1.7 mi e on SR 163, w of jct SR 2. Int corridors. **Pets:** Small, dogs only. $50 deposit/pet. Service with restrictions, supervision. 🛜 🖥

PORTSMOUTH

▼▼ Comfort Inn �M
(740) 353-3232. **$96.** 5100 Old Scioto Tr 45662. 3.8 mi n of downtown. Int corridors. **Pets:** Medium. $25 one-time fee/pet. Service with restrictions, supervision. 🛜 ♿ 🍴 🖥 🏊

ROSSFORD

ᴬᴬᴬ⮞ ▼▼▼ Country Inn & Suites By Carlson, Toledo South �H
(419) 872-9900. **$69-$169.** 9790 Clark Dr 43460. I-75 exit 195, just e. Int corridors. **Pets:** Large. $25 daily fee/pet. Designated rooms, service with restrictions, supervision. (SAVE) 🛜 ✕ ♿ 🍴 🖥 🏊

ST. CLAIRSVILLE

ᴬᴬᴬ⮞ ◆ Americas Best Value Inn St. Clairsville/Wheeling �M 🐾
(740) 695-5038. **$59-$129.** 51260 National Rd 43950. I-70 exit 218, 0.5 mi ne on US 40. Ext corridors. **Pets:** Other species. $10 one-time fee/room. Designated rooms, service with restrictions, crate.
(SAVE) 🛜 🍴 🖥 🏊

▼▼▼ Fairfield Inn & Suites by Marriott �H
(740) 699-4980. **$116-$169.** 67731 Mall Rd 43950. I-70 exit 218, just s. Int corridors. **Pets:** Accepted. 🛜 ✕ 🍴 🖥 🏊

ᴬᴬᴬ⮞ ▼▼ Red Roof Inn #7101 �M
(740) 695-4057. **$46-$96.** 68301 Red Roof Ln 43950. I-70 exit 218, just n. Ext corridors. **Pets:** Large, other species. No service, supervision. (SAVE) 🛜 🍴

ST. MARYS

▼▼ Americas Best Value Inn St Marys �H 🐾
(419) 394-2341. **Call for rates.** 1321 Celina Rd 45885. SR 66/29, 0.8 mi w on SR 703. Ext corridors. **Pets:** Small. $10 daily fee/pet. Designated rooms, service with restrictions, crate. 🛜 🍴 🖥 🏊

SALESVILLE

◆◆◆ Pine Lakes Lodge Bed & Breakfast Cabins and Conference Center 🇧🇧
(740) 679-3617. **Call for rates.** 61680 Buskirk Ln 43778. I-70 exit 193, 6.6 mi s on SR 513, then 6 mi w on SR 265. Int corridors.
Pets: Accepted. 🛜 ✕ 🍴 🖥 ✕ 🇿

SANDUSKY

ᴬᴬᴬ⮞ ▼▼ Best Budget Inn �M
(419) 626-3610. **$39-$119.** 2027 Cleveland Rd 44870. US 6, just e of Cedar Point Cswy. Ext/int corridors. **Pets:** Small, dogs only. $50 deposit/pet. Service with restrictions, supervision. (SAVE) 🛜 🍴 🖥 🏊

▼▼ Knights Inn Sandusky �M
(419) 621-9000. **$38-$124.** 2405 Cleveland Rd 44870. US 6, 2 mi e of Cedar Point Cswy. Ext/int corridors. **Pets:** Accepted. 🛜 🍴 🖥 🏊

SEAMAN

▼▼ Comfort Inn �M
(937) 386-2511. **$74-$120.** 55 Stern Dr 45679. Jct SR 32 and 247. Int corridors. **Pets:** Accepted. 🛜 🍴 🖥 🏊

SEVILLE

 **Hawthorn Suites by Wyndham** H
(330) 769-5025. **$79-$129, 4 day notice.** 5025 Park Ave W 44273. I-76/US 224 exit 2, just n. Int corridors. **Pets:** Accepted.

Super 8-Seville H
(330) 769-8880. **$54-$58.** 6116 Speedway Dr 44273. Jct US 224 and Lake Rd, just s. Int corridors. **Pets:** Medium. $25 one-time fee/pet. Service with restrictions, supervision.

SPRINGFIELD

 **Courtyard by Marriott Springfield Downtown** H
(937) 322-3600. **$89-$129.** 100 S Fountain Ave 45502. I-70 exit 54, 2 mi n on SR 72 (Limestone St), just w on Main St, then just s; downtown. Int corridors. **Pets:** Large. $75 one-time fee/room. Service with restrictions, crate.

Quality Inn and Conference Center H
(937) 323-8631. **$78-$116.** 383 E Leffel Ln 45505. I-70 exit 54, just n, then e. Int corridors. **Pets:** Medium, other species. $20 daily fee/pet. Designated rooms, service with restrictions, crate.

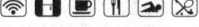 **Red Roof Inn** H
(937) 325-5356. **$59-$129.** 155 W Leffel Ln 45506. I-70 exit 54, just n, then w. Int corridors. **Pets:** Large, other species. No service, supervision.

STRASBURG

Ramada Limited Dover/Strasburg H
(330) 878-1400. **$55-$134.** 509 S Wooster Ave 44680. I-77 exit 87, 0.4 mi n on US 250 and SR 21. Int corridors. **Pets:** Large. $15 daily fee/room. Service with restrictions, supervision.

STREETSBORO

TownePlace Suites by Marriott H
(330) 422-1855. **$107-$139.** 795 Mondial Pkwy 44241. I-80 exit 187, 0.8 mi s. Int corridors. **Pets:** Accepted.

SWANTON

Days Inn H
(419) 865-2002. **$59-$68.** 10753 Airport Hwy 43558. I-80/90 exit 52, just s, then 0.5 mi e. Int corridors. **Pets:** Accepted.

TIFFIN

Holiday Inn Express H
(419) 443-5100. **$69-$99.** 78 Shaffer Park Dr 44883. Just n of US 224. Int corridors. **Pets:** Accepted.

TIPP CITY

La Quinta Inn & Suites Tipp City H
(937) 667-1574. **$71-$139.** 19 Weller Dr 45371. I-75 exit 68, just w. Int corridors. **Pets:** Medium, other species. Service with restrictions, supervision.

TOLEDO

Park Inn Hotel Toledo H
(419) 241-3000. **$99-$159, 3 day notice.** 101 N Summit St 43604. Between Jefferson and Monroe sts; downtown. Int corridors. **Pets:** Small. $15 daily fee/room. Service with restrictions, crate.

TROY

Holiday Inn Express Hotel & Suites H
(937) 332-1700. **Call for rates.** 60 Troy Town Dr 45373. I-75 exit 74, just w. Int corridors. **Pets:** Accepted.

Residence Inn by Marriott H
(937) 440-9303. **$116-$142.** 87 Troy Town Dr 45373. I-75 exit 74, just w. Int corridors. **Pets:** Accepted.

UHRICHSVILLE

Best Western Country Inn M
(740) 922-0774. **$60-$85.** 111 W McCauley Dr 44683. US 250 exit McCauley Dr. Ext corridors. **Pets:** Accepted.

VAN WERT

Comfort Inn H
(419) 232-6040. **Call for rates.** 840 N Washington St 45891. US 127, s of jct US 30 and 224. Int corridors. **Pets:** Small. $15 daily fee/pet. Designated rooms, service with restrictions, supervision.

VERMILION

Holiday Inn Express H
(440) 967-8770. **Call for rates.** 2417 SR 60 44089. Jct SR 2 and 60. Int corridors. **Pets:** Medium. $35 one-time fee/pet. Service with restrictions, supervision.

WAPAKONETA

Best Western Wapakoneta Inn H
(419) 738-2050. **$86-$106.** 1008 Lunar Dr 45895. I-75 exit 111, just w. Int corridors. **Pets:** Accepted.

WARREN

Fairfield Inn by Marriott-Warren/Niles H
(330) 544-5774. **$126-$154.** 1860 Niles-Cortland Rd 44484. Jct US 422 and SR 46, 1 mi n on SR 46. Int corridors. **Pets:** Medium. $50 one-time fee/room. Service with restrictions, crate.

WASHINGTON COURT HOUSE

Holiday Inn Express H
(740) 335-9310. **Call for rates.** 101 Courthouse Pkwy 43160. Jct US 35, 0.4 mi sw on US 62. Int corridors. **Pets:** Accepted.

WAUSEON

Best Western Del Mar H
(419) 335-1565. **$76-$86.** 8319 SR 108 43567. I-80/90 exit 34, just s. Ext corridors. **Pets:** $17 one-time fee/room. Service with restrictions, supervision.

WOOSTER

Econo Lodge M
(330) 264-8883. **$54-$99.** 2137 E Lincoln Way 44691. US 30, 3 mi e. Ext corridors. **Pets:** Accepted.

YOUNGSTOWN

Days Inn & Suites M
(330) 759-9820. **$57-$85, 3 day notice.** 1615 E Liberty St 44420. I-80 exit 229, just s. Int corridors. **Pets:** Small, other species. $25 one-time fee/pet. Service with restrictions, supervision.

ZANESVILLE

Baymont Inn & Suites Zanesville M
(740) 454-9332. **$54-$89.** 230 Scenic Crest Dr 43701. I-70 exit 155, just s. Int corridors. **Pets:** Accepted.

Best Western B. R. Guest H
(740) 453-6300. **$80.** 4929 East Pike 43701. I-70 exit 160, just s. Int corridors. **Pets:** Other species. $10 daily fee/pet. Service with restrictions, crate.

◇◇◇ ▽▽▽ Comfort Inn H

(740) 454-4144. **$90-$200.** 500 Monroe St 43701. I-70 exit 155 westbound; exit 7th St eastbound, e on Elberon to light, just n on Underwood St. Int corridors. **Pets:** Large, other species. $10 daily fee/pet. Designated rooms, service with restrictions, supervision.

SAVE 🛜 ᴹ ▤ ▣ ⇶

◇◇◇ ▽▽▽ Super 8-Zanesville M

(740) 455-3124. **$54-$81.** 2440 National Rd 43701. I-70 exit 152, just n. Int corridors. **Pets:** Medium. $10 daily fee/pet. Service with restrictions, supervision. SAVE 🛜 ▤ ▣

OKLAHOMA

ALTUS

◇◇◇ ▽▽▽ Best Western Altus H

(580) 482-9300. **$75-$95.** 2804 N Main St 73521. 2 mi n on US 283. Ext corridors. **Pets:** Accepted. SAVE 🛜 ▤ ▣ ⇶ ⊠

▽▽▽ Hampton Inn & Suites Altus H

(580) 482-1273. **$99-$169.** 3601 N Main St 73521. 2.2 mi n on US 283. Int corridors. **Pets:** Other species. Service with restrictions.

🛜 ⊠ ᴹ ▤ ▣ ⇶

ARDMORE

◇◇◇ ▽▽▽ Best Western Ardmore Inn H

(580) 223-7525. **$70-$175.** 136 Holiday Dr 73401. I-35 exit 31A, just e, then just n. Int corridors. **Pets:** Very small. $10 daily fee/pet. Designated rooms, service with restrictions, supervision. SAVE 🛜 ▤ ▣ ⇶

▽▽ La Quinta Inn Ardmore North H

(580) 223-7976. **$67-$125.** 2432 Veterans Blvd 73401. I-35 exit 33, just e. Ext corridors. **Pets:** Medium, other species. Service with restrictions, supervision. 🛜 ▤ ▣ ⇶

▽▽▽ Quality Hotel H

(580) 223-7130. **Call for rates.** 2705 W Broadway 73401. I-35 exit 31A, just e. Ext corridors. **Pets:** Very small, other species. $10 daily fee/room. Service with restrictions, supervision. 🛜 ▤ ▣ 🍴 ⇶

ATOKA

◇◇◇ ▽▽▽ Best Western Atoka Inn H

(580) 889-7381. **$70-$80.** 2101 S Mississippi Ave 74525. 1 mi s. Ext corridors. **Pets:** Medium, other species. $10 one-time fee/room. Service with restrictions, crate. SAVE 🛜 ▤ ▣ ⇶

◇◇◇ ▽▽▽ Comfort Inn & Suites H

(580) 889-8999. **Call for rates.** 1502 S Mississippi Ave 74525. Just s of center. Int corridors. **Pets:** Accepted. SAVE 🛜 ▤ ▣

BARTLESVILLE

▽▽ Candlewood Suites H

(918) 766-0044. **$69-$89.** 3812 SE Washington Pl 74006. Just s of jct US 60. Int corridors. **Pets:** Accepted. 🛜 ⊠ ᴹ ▤ ▣

▽▽ Microtel Inn & Suites of Bartlesville H

(918) 333-2100. **$56-$68.** 2696 SE Washington Blvd 74006. 1.4 mi s of jct US 60. Int corridors. **Pets:** Accepted. 🛜 ᴹ ▤ ▣

BIG CABIN

▽▽ Super 8-Big Cabin M

(918) 783-5888. **$49-$63.** 30954 S Hwy 69 74301. I-44 exit 283, just ne. Ext/int corridors. **Pets:** Accepted. 🛜 ▤ ▣ ⇶

BLACKWELL

◇◇◇ ▽▽▽ Best Western Blackwell Inn H 🐾

(580) 363-1300. **$84-$94.** 4545 W White Ave 74631. I-35 exit 222, just ne. Int corridors. **Pets:** Medium, dogs only. $10 daily fee/pet. Designated rooms, service with restrictions, supervision. SAVE 🛜 ▤ ▣ ⇶

◇◇◇ ▽▽▽ Quality Inn Blackwell H

(580) 363-7000. **$72-$80.** 1201 N 44th St 74631. I-35 exit 222, just ne. Int corridors. **Pets:** Medium, dogs only. $10 daily fee/pet. Designated rooms, service with restrictions, supervision.

SAVE 🛜 ⊠ ▤ ▣ ⇶

BROKEN BOW

◇◇◇ ▽▽▽▽ Best Western Broken Bow Inn & Suites H

(580) 584-7400. **$90-$120.** 1699 S Park Dr 74728. On US 70/259, 1 mi s of SR 3. Int corridors. **Pets:** Accepted. SAVE 🛜 ▤ ▣ ⇶

CHICKASHA

◇◇◇ ▽▽▽ Best Western Chickasha H

(405) 224-4890. **$95.** 2101 S 4th St 73018. I-44 exit 80, just nw. Ext/int corridors. **Pets:** Small. $40 one-time fee/pet. Service with restrictions, supervision. SAVE 🛜 ▤ ▣ 🍴 ⇶ ⊠

DURANT

▽▽▽ Comfort Inn & Suites H

(580) 924-8881. **$80-$99.** 2112 W Main St 74701. Just e of jct US 75/69 and 70. Int corridors. **Pets:** Accepted. 🛜 ▤ ▣ ⇶

ENID

▽▽ Baymont Inn & Suites-Enid H

(580) 234-6800. **$71-$113.** 3614 W Owen K Garriott Rd 73703. 2 mi w of jct US 81. Int corridors. **Pets:** Accepted. 🛜 ᴹ ▤ ▣ ⇶

▽▽▽ Holiday Inn Express Hotel & Suites H

(580) 237-7722. **$119-$134.** 4702 W Owen K Garriott Rd 73703. 2.3 mi w of jct US 81. Int corridors. **Pets:** Accepted. 🛜 ▤ ▣ ⇶

GROVE

◇◇◇ ▽▽▽ Best Western TimberRidge Inn H

(918) 786-6900. **$87.** 120 W 18th St 74344. Just w of jct US 59. Ext/int corridors. **Pets:** Dogs only. $10 daily fee/pet. Designated rooms, service with restrictions, supervision. SAVE 🛜 ⊠ ▤ ▣ ⇶

GUYMON

(AAA) ▼▼▼▼ Best Western Plus Guymon Hotel & Suites 🅷
(580) 338-0800. **$80-$100.** 1102 NE 6th St (Hwy 54) 73942. Just s of jct US 64. Ext/int corridors. **Pets:** Other species. $15 one-time fee/pet. Designated rooms, service with restrictions, supervision.
🆂🅰🆅🅴 📶 ♿ 🍴 🖥 🏊 ⊗

▼▼▼▼ Comfort Inn & Suites 🅷
(580) 338-0831. **Call for rates.** 501 Hwy 54 E 73942. Just s of jct US 64. Int corridors. **Pets:** Accepted. 📶 🍴 🖥 🏊

▼▼ Guymon Super 8 🅷
(580) 338-0507. **$53-$77.** 1201 Hwy 54 E 73942. Jct US 54 and 64. Int corridors. **Pets:** Small. $7 daily fee/pet. Designated rooms, service with restrictions, supervision. 📶 🍴 🖥

▼▼▼▼ Holiday Inn Express Hotel & Suites Guymon 🅷
(580) 338-4208. **$95-$114.** 701 SE Hwy 3 73942. Jct US 54/412, just e. Int corridors. **Pets:** Accepted. 📶 ⊗ 🅼 🍴 🖥 🏊

HENRYETTA

(AAA) ▼▼ Green Country Inn Ⓜ
(918) 652-9988. **$45-$58.** 2004 Old Hwy 75 W 74437. I-40 exit 237, just ne. Ext corridors. **Pets:** Medium. $10 daily fee/pet. Service with restrictions, supervision. 🆂🅰🆅🅴 📶 🍴 🏊

IDABEL

▼▼▼▼ Comfort Suites 🅷
(580) 286-9393. **$77-$149.** 400 SE Lincoln Rd 74745. Just s of jct US 70 and 259. Int corridors. **Pets:** Accepted. 📶 ⊗ 🍴 🖥 🏊

▼▼ Super 8 🅷
(580) 286-2888. **$54-$100.** 401 NE Lincoln Rd 74745. On US 259. Ext corridors. **Pets:** Accepted. 📶 🍴 🖥 🏊

LAWTON

(AAA) ▼▼▼▼ Best Western Plus Lawton Hotel & Convention Center 🅷 ✿
(580) 353-0200. **$79-$119.** 1125 E Gore Blvd 73501. I-44 exit 37, just e. Ext/int corridors. **Pets:** Medium. $40 one-time fee/pet. Service with restrictions, crate. 🆂🅰🆅🅴 📶 🍴 🖥 🍴 🏊

(AAA) ▼▼▼▼ Sleep Inn & Suites 🅷
(580) 353-5555. **$89-$110.** 421 SE Interstate Dr 73501. I-44 exit 37, just w, then just s. Int corridors. **Pets:** Medium. $25 one-time fee/room. Service with restrictions, supervision. 🆂🅰🆅🅴 📶 ⊗ 🅼 🍴 🖥 🏊

LOCUST GROVE

(AAA) ▼▼▼▼ Best Western Plus Locust Grove Inn & Suites 🅷
(918) 479-8082. **$77-$82.** 106 Holiday Ln 74352. Just nw of jct US 412 and SR 82. Int corridors. **Pets:** Small. $25 one-time fee/pet. Service with restrictions, supervision. 🆂🅰🆅🅴 📶 🍴 🖥 🏊

MCALESTER

(AAA) ▼▼▼ Best Western Inn of McAlester 🅷
(918) 426-0115. **$80-$90.** 1215 George Nigh Expy 74502. 3 mi s on US 69. Ext corridors. **Pets:** Accepted. 🆂🅰🆅🅴 📶 🍴 🖥 🏊

▼▼▼ Candlewood Suites 🅷
(918) 426-4171. **$72-$100.** 425 S George Nigh Expy 74501. 2 mi e on US 69. Int corridors. **Pets:** Accepted. 📶 ⊗ 🅼 🍴 🖥

▼▼▼▼ Comfort Suites 🅷
(918) 302-0001. **$71-$199.** 650 S George Nigh Expy 74501. 1.2 mi s on US 69. Int corridors. **Pets:** Accepted. 📶 ⊗ 🍴 🖥 🏊

(AAA) ▼▼▼ Econo Lodge Ⓜ
(918) 426-4420. **$60-$65.** 731 S George Nigh Expy 74501. 1.5 mi s on US 69. Ext corridors. **Pets:** Accepted. 🆂🅰🆅🅴 📶 🍴 🖥

(AAA) ▼▼ Happy Days Hotel 🅷
(918) 429-0910. **$50-$84.** 1400 S George Nigh Expy 74501. 3.3 mi s on US 69. Int corridors. **Pets:** Accepted. 🆂🅰🆅🅴 📶 ⊗ 🍴 🖥 🏊

MIAMI

▼▼▼▼ Holiday Inn Express & Suites 🅷
(918) 542-7424. **Call for rates.** 509 Henley St 74354. I-44 exit 313, just w. Int corridors. **Pets:** Accepted. 📶 ⊗ 🅼 🍴 🖥 🏊 ⊗

MUSKOGEE

(AAA) ▼▼▼▼ La Quinta Inn & Suites Muskogee 🅷
(918) 687-9000. **$102-$164.** 3031 Military Blvd 74401. Just se of jct US 62 and 69. Int corridors. **Pets:** Medium, other species. Service with restrictions, supervision. 🆂🅰🆅🅴 📶 ⊗ 🍴 🖥 🍴 🏊

OKLAHOMA CITY METROPOLITAN AREA

EDMOND

(AAA) ▼▼▼ Best Western Edmond Inn & Suites 🅷
(405) 216-0300. **$77-$89.** 2700 E 2nd St 73034. I-35 exit 141, 1.1 mi w. Int corridors. **Pets:** Accepted. 🆂🅰🆅🅴 📶 ⊗ 🍴 🖥 🏊

EL RENO

(AAA) ▼▼▼ Best Western Hensley's 🅷
(405) 262-6490. **$85-$105.** 2701 S Country Club Rd 73036. I-40 exit 123, just s. Ext corridors. **Pets:** Medium. $25 deposit/room, $5 daily fee/pet. Service with restrictions, supervision. 🆂🅰🆅🅴 📶 🍴 🖥 🏊

(AAA) ▼ Motel 6 # 4267 🅷
(405) 262-6060. **$69-$80.** 1506 Domino Dr 73036. I-40 exit 123, just ne. Int corridors. **Pets:** Other species. Service with restrictions, supervision. 🆂🅰🆅🅴 📶 🍴 🏊

GUTHRIE

▼▼▼▼ Holiday Inn Express 🅷
(405) 293-6464. **$95-$149.** 2227 E Oklahoma Ave 73044. I-35 exit 157, just s. Int corridors. **Pets:** Accepted. 📶 🅼 🍴 🖥 🏊

MIDWEST CITY

▼▼▼▼ Hawthorn Suites by Wyndham 🅷
(405) 737-7777. **$105-$125, 3 day notice.** 5701 Tinker Diagonal Rd 73110. I-40 exit 156A (Sooner Rd), just n. Int corridors. **Pets:** Accepted. 📶 🅼 🍴 🖥 🏊

(AAA) ▼▼▼▼ Sheraton Midwest City Hotel at the Reed Conference Center 🅷
(405) 455-1800. **$89-$139, 3 day notice.** 5750 Will Rogers Rd 73110. I-40 exit 156A (Sooner Rd), just ne. Int corridors. **Pets:** Accepted. 🆂🅰🆅🅴 📶 ⊗ 🍴 🖥 🍴 🏊

MOORE

Best Western Plus Greentree Inn & Suites H

(405) 912-8882. **$70-$95.** 1811 N Moore Ave 73160. I-35 exit 118, just n on west frontage road. Int corridors. **Pets:** Small, dogs only. $10 daily fee/pet. Service with restrictions, supervision.

NORMAN

Best Western Norman Inn & Suites H

(405) 701-4011. **$60-$140.** 2841 S Classen Blvd 73071. Just n of jct SR 9. Int corridors. **Pets:** Small. $10 daily fee/room. Designated rooms, no service, supervision.

Country Inn & Suites By Carlson H

(405) 360-0240. **$82-$174, 3 day notice.** 960 Ed Noble Pkwy 73072. I-35 exit 108B (Lindsey St), just nw. Int corridors. **Pets:** Accepted.

Econo Lodge M

(405) 364-5554. **$65-$95.** 100 SW 26th Dr 73069. I-35 exit 109 (Main St), just se. Ext corridors. **Pets:** Medium. $5 daily fee/pet. Service with restrictions, supervision.

Embassy Suites Norman - Hotel & Conference Center H ❖

(405) 364-8040. **$129-$239.** 2501 Conference Dr 73069. 0.7 mi n of jct 24th Ave NW and Robinson. Int corridors. **Pets:** Medium. $50 one-time fee/room. Service with restrictions.

La Quinta Inn & Suites Oklahoma City Norman H

(405) 579-4000. **$80-$139.** 930 Ed Noble Dr 73072. I-35 exit 108B (Lindsey St), just nw. Int corridors. **Pets:** Medium, other species. Service with restrictions, supervision.

OKLAHOMA CITY

Americas Best Value Inn Bricktown M

(405) 677-1000. **$50-$67.** 3030 S Prospect 73129. I-35 exit 124B northbound; exit 125A southbound, just n on service road. Ext corridors. **Pets:** Large, other species. $15 one-time fee/pet. Service with restrictions.

Baymont Inn & Suites H

(405) 943-4400. **Call for rates.** 4240 W I-40 Service Rd 73108. I-40 exit 145 (Meridian Ave), just e on south frontage road. Ext/int corridors. **Pets:** Medium. $10 daily fee/pet. Designated rooms, service with restrictions, supervision.

Best Western Plus Broadway Inn & Suites H ❖

(405) 848-1919. **$79-$99, 7 day notice.** 6101 N Santa Fe 73118. I-44 exit 127, just e on 63rd St, then just s. Int corridors. **Pets:** Medium. $25 daily fee/pet. Service with restrictions, supervision.

Best Western Plus Memorial Inn & Suites H

(405) 286-5199. **$85.** 1301 W Memorial Rd 73114. John Kilpatrick Tpke exit Western Ave, just nw. Int corridors. **Pets:** Medium. $10 daily fee/pet. Service with restrictions, supervision.

Best Western Plus Saddleback Inn & Conference Center H ❖

(405) 947-7000. **$100-$130.** 4300 SW 3rd St 73108. I-40 exit 145 (Meridian Ave), just ne. Ext/int corridors. **Pets:** Medium. $15 daily fee/room. Designated rooms, service with restrictions, crate.

Candlewood Suites Hotel H

(405) 680-8770. **Call for rates.** 4400 River Park Dr 73108. I-40 exit 145 (Meridian Ave), 1.1 mi s. Int corridors. **Pets:** Accepted.

Colcord Hotel H

(405) 601-4300. **$179-$199.** 15 N Robinson Ave 73102. Jct Sheridan and Robinson aves. Int corridors. **Pets:** Large, other species. Designated rooms, service with restrictions.

Comfort Inn North H

(405) 478-7282. **Call for rates.** 4625 NE 120th St 73131. I-35 exit 137 (122nd St), just sw. Int corridors. **Pets:** Large. $20 daily fee/pet. Service with restrictions, crate.

Country Inn & Suites By Carlson H

(405) 286-3555. **Call for rates.** 13501 Memorial Park Dr 73120. Just sw of jct Memorial Rd and Memorial Park Ln. Int corridors. **Pets:** Accepted.

Courtyard by Marriott-Downtown/Bricktown H

(405) 232-2290. **$118-$188.** 2 W Reno Ave 73102. Gaylord and Reno aves. Int corridors. **Pets:** $100 one-time fee/pet. Supervision.

Courtyard by Marriott-NW H

(405) 848-0808. **$99-$139.** 1515 Northwest Expwy 73118. I-44 exit 125C westbound; exit 125B eastbound, just e. Int corridors. **Pets:** Small. $75 one-time fee/room. Designated rooms, service with restrictions, supervision.

Crowne Plaza Hotel H

(405) 848-4811. **$115-$179.** 2945 Northwest Expwy 73112. 0.5 mi e of jct SR 74 and 3. Ext/int corridors. **Pets:** Accepted.

Econo Lodge H ❖

(405) 478-0400. **Call for rates.** 12001 N I-35 Service Rd 73131. I-35 exit 137 (122nd St), just sw. Ext corridors. **Pets:** Small, dogs only. $10 one-time fee/pet. Service with restrictions, supervision.

Embassy Suites H ❖

(405) 682-6000. **$109-$169.** 1815 S Meridian Ave 73108. I-40 exit 145 (Meridian Ave), 1 mi s. Int corridors. **Pets:** Large. $50 one-time fee/room. Service with restrictions, crate.

Four Points by Sheraton Oklahoma City Airport H

(405) 681-3500. **$90-$189.** 6300 Terminal Dr 73159. I-40 exit 145 (Meridian Ave), 4 mi s. Int corridors. **Pets:** Small. $30 one-time fee/room. Service with restrictions, supervision.

Homewood Suites Oklahoma City-West H

(405) 789-3600. **Call for rates.** 6920 W Reno Ave 73127. Just e of jct Rockwell Ave. Int corridors. **Pets:** Accepted.

La Quinta Inn & Suites OKC North - Quail Springs H

(405) 755-7000. **$107-$169.** 3003 W Memorial Rd 73134. John Kilpatrick Tpke exit May Ave, just nw. Int corridors. **Pets:** Medium, other species. Service with restrictions, supervision.

La Quinta Inn & Suites Oklahoma City NW Expwy H

(405) 773-5575. **$71-$129.** 4829 Northwest Expwy 73132. 1.9 mi w of jct SR 3 and 74. Int corridors. **Pets:** Medium, other species. Service with restrictions, supervision.

Quality Inn H

(405) 632-6666. **$60-$90.** 7800 CA Henderson Blvd 73139. I-240 exit 2A, just s. Ext corridors. **Pets:** Medium, dogs only. $20 daily fee/pet. Service with restrictions, supervision.

Residence Inn by Marriott H

(405) 601-1700. **$126-$189.** 400 E Reno Ave 73104. Just se of jct Joe Carter Ave; in Bricktown. Int corridors. **Pets:** Accepted.

▼▼▼ Residence Inn by Marriott Oklahoma City
South-Crossroads Mall 🇭 ❀
(405) 634-9696. **$139-$299.** 1111 E I-240 Service Rd 73149. I-240 exit 4C eastbound, 0.4 mi nw; exit 5 westbound, 0.8 mi nw. Int corridors. **Pets:** Other species. $75 one-time fee/room. Service with restrictions, supervision. 🛜 ⊠ 🍴 💻 ➰ ⊠

🐾 ▼▼▼ Residence Inn by Marriott-Oklahoma City West 🇭
(405) 942-4500. **$89-$179.** 4361 W Reno Ave 73107. I-40 exit 145 (Meridian Ave), 0.3 mi n, then just e. Ext corridors. **Pets:** Accepted.
SAVE 🛜 ⊠ 🍴 💻 ➰

🐾 ▼▼ ▼▼ Sheraton Oklahoma City 🇭
(405) 235-2780. **$149-$329.** 1 N Broadway Ave 73102. Jct Sheridan and Broadway aves. Int corridors. **Pets:** Accepted.
SAVE 🛜 ⊠ 🍴 💻 🍴 ➰

🐾 ▼▼ ▼▼ Skirvin Hilton 🇭
(405) 272-3040. **$99-$229.** 1 Park Ave 73102. Corner of N Broadway and Park aves. Int corridors. **Pets:** Medium, dogs only. $50 one-time fee/pet. Service with restrictions, supervision.
SAVE 🛜 ⊠ 🛒 🍴 💻 🍴 ➰ ⊠

▼▼ ▼▼ SpringHill Suites by Marriott 🇭
(405) 604-0200. **$94-$118.** 510 S MacArthur Blvd 73128. I-40 exit 144, just ne. Int corridors. **Pets:** Medium. $25 one-time fee/room. Service with restrictions, supervision. 🛜 ⊠ 🛒 🍴 💻 ➰

▼▼ ▼▼ Staybridge Suites 🇭
(405) 429-4400. **$79-$299.** 4411 SW 15th St 73108. I-40 exit 145 (Meridian Ave), 1 mi se. Int corridors. **Pets:** Accepted.
🛜 🛒 🍴 💻 ➰ ⊠

▼▼ ▼▼ Wyndham Garden Hotel Oklahoma City Airport 🇭
(405) 685-4000. **Call for rates.** 2101 S Meridian Ave 73108. I-40 exit 145 (Meridian Ave), 1.3 mi s. Int corridors. **Pets:** Small. $25 one-time fee/room. Service with restrictions, supervision. 🛜 🍴 💻 🍴 ➰

SHAWNEE

🐾 ▼▼ ▼▼ La Quinta Inn & Suites Shawnee 🇭
(405) 275-7930. **$94-$155.** 5401 Enterprise Ct 74804. I-40 exit 186, just ne. Int corridors. **Pets:** Medium, other species. Service with restrictions, supervision. SAVE 🛜 🛒 🍴 💻 ➰

YUKON

🐾 ▼▼ ▼▼ Best Western Plus Yukon 🇭
(405) 265-2995. **$95-$145.** 11440 W I-40 Service Rd 73099. I-40 exit 138, just sw. Ext/int corridors. **Pets:** Other species. $25 deposit/room, $6 daily fee/pet. Service with restrictions, supervision.
SAVE 🛜 🍴 💻 ➰

▼▼ ▼▼ Comfort Suites 🇭
(405) 577-6500. **Call for rates.** 11424 NW 4th St 73099. I-40 exit 138, just nw. Int corridors. **Pets:** Accepted. 🛜 ⊠ 🍴 💻 ➰

▼▼ ▼▼ La Quinta Inn & Suites Oklahoma City - Yukon 🇭
(405) 494-7600. **$72-$130.** 11500 W I-40 73099. I-40 exit 138, just s. Int corridors. **Pets:** Medium, other species. Service with restrictions, supervision. 🛜 🛒 🍴 💻 ➰

END METROPOLITAN AREA

OKMULGEE

🐾 ▼▼▼ Best Western Plus Okmulgee 🇭
(918) 756-9200. **$89-$102.** 3499 N Wood Dr 74447. Just n of jct US 75 and SR 56. Int corridors. **Pets:** Accepted. SAVE 🛜 🍴 💻 ➰

PAULS VALLEY

▼▼▼ Comfort Inn & Suites 🇭 ❀
(405) 207-9730. **$81-$95.** 103 S Humphrey Blvd 73075. I-35 exit 72, just e. Int corridors. **Pets:** Small, other species. $10 one-time fee/pet. Service with restrictions, supervision. 🛜 ⊠ 🛒 🍴 💻 ➰

🐾 ▼▼▼ Days Inn 🇭
(405) 238-7548. **$61.** 2606 W Grant Ave 73075. I-35 exit 72, just e. Int corridors. **Pets:** Small. Service with restrictions, crate.
SAVE 🛜 🍴 💻

PERRY

🐾 ▼▼▼ Comfort Inn & Suites 🇭
(580) 336-3800. **$90-$120.** 3112 W Fir St 73077. I-35 exit 186, just w. Int corridors. **Pets:** Small, dogs only. $20 daily fee/pet. Designated rooms, service with restrictions, supervision.
SAVE 🛜 ⊠ 🛒 🍴 💻 ➰

PONCA CITY

🐾 ▼▼▼ Comfort Inn & Suites 🇭 ❀
(580) 765-2322. **$80-$99.** 3101 N 14th St 74604. I-35 exit 214, 3 mi n on US 77. Int corridors. **Pets:** Small. $10 daily fee/pet. Service with restrictions, crate. SAVE 🛜 🛒 🍴 💻 ➰

POTEAU

▼▼▼ Holiday Inn Express & Suites-Poteau 🇭
(918) 649-0123. **Call for rates.** 201 Hillview Pkwy 74953. Just ne of jct US 59/271 and SR 112. Int corridors. **Pets:** Accepted.
🛜 ⊠ 🛒 🍴 💻 ➰

PRYOR

▼▼▼ Holiday Inn Express & Suites 🇭
(918) 476-5400. **$109-$159.** 271 Mid America Dr 74361. 5 mi s on US 69. Int corridors. **Pets:** Accepted. 🛜 🛒 🍴 💻 ➰

STILLWATER

🐾 ▼▼▼ Best Western Plus Cimarron Hotel & Suites 🇭
(405) 372-2878. **$120-$140.** 315 N Husband St 74074. Just w of jct Hall of Fame Blvd and Main St. Int corridors. **Pets:** Accepted.
SAVE 🛜 ⊠ 🛒 🍴 💻 ➰

▼▼▼ Residence Inn by Marriott 🇭 ❀
(405) 707-0588. **$103-$242.** 800 S Murphy St 74074. Just s of jct SR 51. Int corridors. **Pets:** Medium, other species. $75 one-time fee/room. Service with restrictions, supervision. 🛜 ⊠ 🛒 🍴 💻 ➰

STROUD

🐾 ▼▼ ▼ Best Western Stroud Motor Lodge 🇭
(918) 968-9515. **$73-$81.** 1200 N 8th Ave 74079. I-44 exit 179, just ne. Ext corridors. **Pets:** Medium, other species. $10 daily fee/pet. Designated rooms, service with restrictions, supervision. SAVE 🛜 💻 🍴 ➰

THACKERVILLE

▼▼ ▼ The Inn at WinStar 🇭
(580) 276-4487. **Call for rates.** Rt 1, Box 682 73459. I-35 exit 1, 1.2 mi n on E Service Rd. Int corridors. **Pets:** Accepted. 🛜 🍴 💻 ➰

TULSA METROPOLITAN AREA

BROKEN ARROW

▼▼▼▼ Clarion Hotel **H**
(918) 258-7085. **$62-$149.** 2600 N Aspen Ave 74012. Just s of jct SR 51. Int corridors. **Pets:** Accepted. 🛜 📶 💳 ➔

▼▼▼▼ Homewood Suites by Hilton Tulsa South **H**
(918) 392-7700. **$109-$159.** 4900 W Madison Pl 74012. Just ne of jct 71st St and Garnett Ave. Int corridors. **Pets:** Accepted.
🛜 ⓜ 📶 💳 ➔ ✕

▼▼▼▼ TownePlace Suites by Marriott **H**
(918) 355-9600. **$71-$87.** 2251 N Stonewood Cir 74012. Just ne of jct SR 51 and Elm Pl. Int corridors. **Pets:** Large, other species. $100 one-time fee/room. Service with restrictions, supervision.
🛜 ✕ ⓜ 📶 💳 ➔

CATOOSA

▼▼▼▼ Hampton Inn & Suites **H**
(918) 739-3939. **$98-$125.** 100 McNabb Field Rd 74015. I-44 exit 240A, just ne. Int corridors. **Pets:** Accepted. 🛜 ✕ ⓜ 📶 💳 ➔

CLAREMORE

ⒶⒶⒶ▼ Claremore Motor Inn **M**
(918) 342-4545. **$44-$89.** 1709 N Lynn Riggs Blvd 74017. 1.2 mi n on SR 66. Ext/int corridors. **Pets:** Accepted. 🆂🅰🆅🅴 🛜 📶

▼▼▼ Comfort Inn Claremore **H**
(918) 343-3297. **$80-$100.** 1720 S Lynn Riggs Blvd 74017. 1.6 mi s on SR 66. Int corridors. **Pets:** Medium. $15 daily fee/pet. Designated rooms, service with restrictions, supervision. 🛜 📶 💳 ➔

▼▼ Microtel Inn & Suites **H**
(918) 343-2868. **$54-$75.** 10600 E Mallard Lake Rd 74017. 2.6 mi s on SR 66. Int corridors. **Pets:** Accepted. 🛜 📶 💳 ➔

ⒶⒶⒶ ▼▼▼ Super 8 **H**
(918) 341-2323. **$54-$99.** 1100 E Will Rogers Blvd 74017. I-44 exit 255, just w. Ext/int corridors. **Pets:** Small. $10 daily fee/pet. Designated rooms, service with restrictions, supervision. 🆂🅰🆅🅴 🛜 📶 💳

GLENPOOL

ⒶⒶⒶ▼ ▼▼▼ Best Western Glenpool/Tulsa **H**
(918) 322-5201. **$83.** 14831 S Casper St 74033. I-44 exit 224, 9.5 mi s on US 75. Ext corridors. **Pets:** Accepted. 🆂🅰🆅🅴 🛜 📶 💳 ➔

OWASSO

ⒶⒶⒶ▼ ▼▼▼ Best Western Owasso Inn & Suites **H**
(918) 272-2000. **$80.** 7653 N Owasso Expwy 74055. Just ne of jct US 169 and 76th St. Ext/int corridors. **Pets:** Medium, other species. $25 one-time fee/pet. Service with restrictions, supervision.
🆂🅰🆅🅴 🛜 ✕ 📶 💳 ➔

▼▼◆▼ Candlewood Suites **H**
(918) 272-4334. **Call for rates.** 11699 E 96th St N 74055. 0.4 mi nw of jct US 169. Int corridors. **Pets:** Accepted. 🛜 ✕ ⓜ 📶 💳

▼▼◆▼ TownePlace Suites Tulsa North/Owasso **H**
(918) 376-4400. **$99-$109.** 9355 N Owasso 74055. Just se of jct US 169 and 96th St. Int corridors. **Pets:** Accepted.
🛜 ✕ ⓜ 📶 💳 ➔

TULSA

ⒶⒶⒶ▼ ▼▼▼ Aloft Tulsa **H**
(918) 949-9000. **$89-$159.** 6716 S 104th E Ave 74133. Just nw of jct US 169 and 71st St. Int corridors. **Pets:** Accepted.
🆂🅰🆅🅴 🛜 ✕ ⓜ 📶 💳 ➔ ✕

ⒶⒶⒶ ▼▼▼▼ Ambassador Hotel **H** 🐾
(918) 587-8200. **$209-$299.** 1324 S Main St 74119. Jct 14th and Main sts. Int corridors. **Pets:** Large, dogs only. Service with restrictions, supervision. 🆂🅰🆅🅴 🛜 ✕ 📶 💳 🍽

▼▼ Baymont Inn & Suites Tulsa **H**
(918) 488-8777. **$47-$67.** 4530 E Skelly Dr 74135. I-44 exit 229 (Yale Ave/SR 66), just sw. Int corridors. **Pets:** Accepted. 🛜 📶 💳 ➔

ⒶⒶⒶ ▼▼▼ Best Western Airport **H** 🐾
(918) 438-0780. **$70-$100.** 222 N Garnett Rd 74116. I-244 exit 14 (Garnett Rd), just s. Ext corridors. **Pets:** Other species. $20 one-time fee/room. Service with restrictions, crate. 🆂🅰🆅🅴 🛜 📶 💳 ➔

▼▼▼ Candlewood Suites **H**
(918) 294-9000. **Call for rates.** 10008 E 73rd St S 74133. Just sw of jct 71st St and 101st E Ave. Int corridors. **Pets:** Accepted.
🛜 ⓜ 📶 💳

▼▼ Comfort Inn Airport **H**
(918) 835-4444. **$60-$70.** 6730 E Archer St 74115. I-244 exit 11 (Sheridan Rd), just se. Ext/int corridors. **Pets:** Accepted. 🛜 📶 💳 ➔

▼▼ Comfort Suites-Tulsa Airport **H**
(918) 628-0900. **$70-$90.** 1737 S 101st E Ave 74128. I-44 exit 233 eastbound; exit 233B westbound, follow signs. Int corridors. **Pets:** Small, other species. $10 daily fee/pet. Service with restrictions, crate.
🛜 ✕ 📶 💳 ➔

▼▼◆▼ DoubleTree by Hilton Hotel Tulsa Downtown **H**
(918) 587-8000. **$69-$139.** 616 W 7th St 74127. Jct 7th St and Houston Ave. Int corridors. **Pets:** Other species. $50 one-time fee/room. Crate.
🛜 ✕ 📶 🍽 ➔ ✕

▼▼◆▼ DoubleTree by Hilton Hotel Tulsa - Warren Place **H**
(918) 495-1000. **$99-$149.** 6110 S Yale Ave 74136. I-44 exit 229 (Yale Ave/SR 66), 1.3 mi s. Int corridors. **Pets:** Accepted.
🛜 ⓜ 📶 💳 🍽 ➔ ✕

▼▼◆▼ Embassy Suites Hotel **H**
(918) 622-4000. **$105-$199.** 3332 S 79th E Ave 74145. I-44 exit 231 (31st St) eastbound; exit 232 (Memorial Dr) westbound, just sw. Int corridors. **Pets:** Accepted. 🛜 📶 💳 🍽 ➔

▼▼◆▼ Hilton Tulsa Southern Hills **H**
(918) 492-5000. **$89-$149.** 7902 S Lewis Ave 74136. I-44 exit 227, 3 mi s. Int corridors. **Pets:** Accepted. 🛜 📶 💳 🍽 ➔

ⒶⒶⒶ▼ ▼▼◆▼ Holiday Inn **H**
(918) 585-5898. **Call for rates.** 17 W 7th St 74119. Jct Boulder Ave. Int corridors. **Pets:** Accepted. 🆂🅰🆅🅴 🛜 ✕ ⓜ 📶 💳 🍽 ➔

▼▼◆▼ Holiday Inn & Suites **H**
(918) 994-5000. **$99-$129.** 10020 E 81st St 74133. Just w of jct US 169. Int corridors. **Pets:** Accepted. 🛜 ✕ 📶 💳 🍽 ➔

ⒶⒶⒶ▼ ▼▼◆▼ Hyatt Regency Tulsa **H**
(918) 582-9000. **$69-$299.** 100 E 2nd St 74103. Jct 2nd St and Boston Ave; downtown. Int corridors. **Pets:** Small. $25 deposit/room, $25 one-time fee/room. Service with restrictions, supervision.
🆂🅰🆅🅴 🛜 ⓜ 📶 💳 🍽 ➔

▼▼◆▼ La Quinta Inn & Suites Tulsa Airport / Expo Square **H**
(918) 949-3600. **$71-$154.** 23 N 67th E Ave 74115. I-244 exit 11 (Sheridan Ave), just se. Int corridors. **Pets:** Medium, other species. Service with restrictions, supervision. 🛜 ✕ ⓜ 📶 💳 ➔

▼▼▼▼ La Quinta Inn & Suites Tulsa Central H
(918) 665-2630. **$80-$144.** 6030 E Skelly Dr 74135. I-44 exit 230, just s. Int corridors. **Pets:** Medium, other species. Service with restrictions, supervision. 🛰 ✕ 🛏 💻 🏊

▼▼▼▼ McBirney Mansion Inn BB
(918) 585-3234. **Call for rates.** 1414 S Galveston Ave 74127. US 64 and SR 51 exit Denver Ave, 0.5 mi sw. Ext/int corridors. **Pets:** Accepted. 🛰 ✕

🆔 ▼▼▼▼ Park Inn Tulsa Airport H
(918) 835-9911. **$109-$119.** 2201 N 77th E Ave 74115. SR 11 exit airport terminal. Int corridors. **Pets:** Small, dogs only. $25 one-time fee/pet. Service with restrictions, crate. SAVE 🛰 ✕ 🛏 💻 🍴 🏊

▼▼▼▼ Ramada H
(918) 828-9128. **$65-$100, 10 day notice.** 8175 E Skelly Dr 74129. I-44 exit 231 (31st St) eastbound; exit 232 (Memorial Dr) westbound, just ne. Int corridors. **Pets:** Medium. $10 daily fee/pet. Service with restrictions, supervision. 🛰 🛏 💻 🏊

▼▼ Red Roof Inn M
(918) 622-6776. **$50-$100.** 4717 S Yale Ave 74135. I-44 exit 229 (Yale Ave), just s. Ext corridors. **Pets:** Large, other species. No service, supervision. 🛰 🛏 🏊

🆔 ▼▼▼▼ ▼▼▼▼ Renaissance Tulsa Hotel & Convention Center H 🐾
(918) 307-2600. **$146-$168.** 6808 S 107th E Ave 74133. Just ne of jct US 169 and 71st St. Int corridors. **Pets:** Large, dogs only. $75 one-time fee/room. Service with restrictions.
SAVE 🛰 ✕ 🛗 🛏 💻 🍴 🏊 ✕

▼▼▼ Residence Inn by Marriott H
(918) 250-4850. **$99-$159.** 11025 E 73rd St 74133. US 169 exit 71st St, just e. Int corridors. **Pets:** Medium. $75 one-time fee/room. Service with restrictions, crate. 🛰 ✕ 🛏 💻 🏊 ✕

▼▼ Sleep Inn & Suites Tulsa Central H 🐾
(918) 663-2777. **$75-$110.** 8021 E 33rd St S 74145. I-44 exit 231 (31st St) eastbound; exit 232 (Memorial Dr) westbound, just sw. Int corridors. **Pets:** Medium, dogs only. $15 daily fee/pet. Service with restrictions, supervision. 🛰 ✕ 🛏 💻 🏊 ✕

▼▼▼▼ Staybridge Suites H
(918) 461-2100. **$99-$155.** 11111 E 73rd St 74133. Just se of jct US 169 and 71st St. Int corridors. **Pets:** Accepted.
🛰 ✕ 🛗 🛏 💻 🏊 ✕

▼▼▼▼ Tulsa Square Hotel H
(918) 663-1000. **Call for rates.** 3209 S 79th E Ave 74145. I-44 exit 231 (31st St) eastbound; exit 232 (Memorial Dr) westbound, just sw. Int corridors. **Pets:** Accepted. 🛰 🛏 💻 🏊

▼▼▼▼ Wyndham Tulsa H
(918) 627-5000. **Call for rates.** 10918 E 41st St 74146. Just e of US 169. Int corridors. **Pets:** Small, dogs only. $75 one-time fee/room. Designated rooms, no service. 🛰 💻 🍴 🏊 ✕

WAGONER
▼▼▼▼ The Canebrake H
(918) 485-1810. **$99-$314, 7 day notice.** 33241 E 732nd Rd 74467. 1.7 mi n of jct SR 51 and S 330th Rd. Ext corridors. **Pets:** Accepted.
ECO 🛰 ✕ 🛗 🛏 💻 🍴 ✕

END METROPOLITAN AREA

WOODWARD
🆔 ▼▼▼▼ Northwest Inn H 🐾
(580) 256-7600. **$85-$119.** Hwy 270 S & 1st St 73802. 1.4 mi s of jct US 183 and 270, SR 3 and 34. Ext/int corridors. **Pets:** Medium. $10 daily fee/room. Designated rooms, service with restrictions, supervision.
SAVE 🛰 🛏 💻 🍴 🏊

OREGON

ALBANY

Comfort Suites - Linn County Fairgrounds and Expo H
(541) 928-2053. **$72-$126.** 100 Opal Ct NE 97322. I-5 exit 234A southbound; exit 234 northbound, just se. Int corridors. **Pets:** Accepted.
[SAVE] [icons]

Econo Lodge M
(541) 926-0170. **$65-$89.** 1212 SE Price Rd 97322. I-5 exit 233, just e on Santiam Hwy (US 20), then just n. Ext corridors. **Pets:** Small. $10 daily fee/room. Service with restrictions, supervision. [SAVE] [icons]

Holiday Inn Express Hotel & Suites H
(541) 928-8820. **$99-$159.** 105 Opal Ct NE 97322. I-5 exit 234A southbound; exit 234 northbound, just se. Int corridors. **Pets:** Accepted.
[SAVE] [icons]

La Quinta Inn Albany H
(541) 928-0921. **$80-$142.** 251 Airport Rd SE 97322. I-5 exit 234B southbound; exit 234 northbound, just sw. Int corridors. **Pets:** Medium, other species. Service with restrictions, supervision.
[icons]

Motel 6 #4124 M
(541) 926-4233. **$55-$111.** 2735 E Pacific Blvd 97321. I-5 exit 234B southbound; exit 234 northbound, 0.5 mi w. Ext corridors. **Pets:** Other species. Service with restrictions, supervision. [SAVE] [icons]

Phoenix Inn Suites-Albany H
(541) 926-5696. **Call for rates.** 3410 Spicer Rd SE 97322. I-5 exit 233, just se. Int corridors. **Pets:** Accepted. [SAVE] [icons]

Quality Inn H
(541) 928-5050. **$59-$109.** 1100 Price Rd SE 97322. I-5 exit 233, just e on Santiam Hwy (US 20), then just n. Int corridors. **Pets:** Accepted.
[SAVE] [icons]

Super 8 - Albany H
(541) 928-6322. **$57-$134.** 315 Airport Rd SE 97322. I-5 exit 234B southbound; exit 234 northbound, just sw. Ext corridors. **Pets:** Accepted.
[SAVE] [icons]

ASHLAND

Ashland Chanticleer Inn BB
(541) 482-1919. **$130-$199, 31 day notice.** 120 Gresham St 97520. Just se of downtown on SR 99 (Main St), just s. Int corridors. **Pets:** Dogs only. $20 daily fee/pet. Designated rooms, service with restrictions, crate.
[icons]

Ashland Springs Hotel H ❀
(541) 488-1700. **$89-$269, 3 day notice.** 212 E Main St 97520. Corner of 1st St; center. Int corridors. **Pets:** Medium, dogs only. $30 one-time fee/pet. Designated rooms, service with restrictions, crate.
[icons]

Best Western Bard's Inn H ❀
(541) 482-0049. **$99-$175.** 132 N Main St 97520. From Downtown Plaza, just nw on SR 99 (N Main St). Ext/int corridors. **Pets:** Large, other species. $15 daily fee/pet. Designated rooms, service with restrictions, supervision. [SAVE] [icons]

Best Western Plus Windsor Inn H
(541) 488-2330. **$80-$219.** 2520 Ashland St 97520. I-5 exit 14, just se on Ashland St (SR 66). Ext corridors. **Pets:** Medium. $15 daily fee/pet. Designated rooms, service with restrictions, supervision.
[SAVE] [icons]

Callahan's Lodge CI
(541) 482-1299. **$135-$260.** 7100 Old Hwy 99 S 97520. I-5 exit 6 (Mt. Ashland), just e; 8 mi s of town. Int corridors. **Pets:** $20 one-time fee/room. Service with restrictions, supervision.
[SAVE] [icons]

Cedarwood Inn M
(541) 488-2000. **$59-$119, 3 day notice.** 1801 Siskiyou Blvd 97520. I-5 exit 11 northbound, 2.6 mi nw; exit 14 southbound, just w on Ashland St (SR 66), 0.6 mi s on Tolman Creek Rd, then 0.6 mi w. Ext corridors. **Pets:** Small, dogs only. $10 daily fee/pet. Designated rooms, service with restrictions, supervision. [SAVE] [icons]

Flagship Inn of Ashland M
(541) 482-2641. **$59-$119, 3 day notice.** 1193 Siskiyou Blvd 97520. I-5 exit 14, 1.3 mi w on Ashland St (SR 66), then just n. Ext corridors. **Pets:** Accepted. [SAVE] [icons]

Holiday Inn Express Hotel & Suites - Ashland H
(541) 201-0202. **$116-$189.** 565 Clover Ln 97520. I-5 exit 14, just e on Ashland St (SR 66), then s. Int corridors. **Pets:** $15 daily fee/pet. Designated rooms, service with restrictions, supervision.
[SAVE] [icons]

La Quinta Inn & Suites Ashland H
(541) 482-6932. **$93-$172.** 434 S Valley View Rd 97520. I-5 exit 19, just sw. Int corridors. **Pets:** Medium, other species. Service with restrictions, supervision. [icons]

Mt Ashland Inn BB
(541) 482-8707. **$155-$230, 30 day notice.** 550 Mt. Ashland Rd 97520. I-5 exit 6 (Mt. Ashland), 0.6 mi w, 5.2 mi towards Mt. Ashland ski area, follow signs; 13 mi s of town. Int corridors. **Pets:** Accepted.
[icons]

Plaza Inn & Suites At Ashland Creek H ❖
(541) 488-8900. **$89-$289.** 98 Central Ave 97520. From Downtown Plaza, just nw on SR 99 (N Main St), just n on Water St, then just w. Int corridors. **Pets:** Medium. $25 daily fee/room. Designated rooms, service with restrictions, supervision. (SAVE) 📶 ⊠ 🛏 🖥

Timbers Motel of Ashland M ❖
(541) 482-4242. **$49-$135, 3 day notice.** 1450 Ashland St 97520. I-5 exit 14, 1.2 mi w on Ashland St (SR 66). Ext corridors. **Pets:** Other species. Designated rooms, service with restrictions, crate. (SAVE) 📶 ⊠ 🛏 🖥 🏊

Village Suites at Ashland Hills H
(541) 482-8310. **$129-$159.** 2525 Ashland St 97520. I-5 exit 14, just ne on Ashland St (SR 66). Int corridors. **Pets:** Accepted.
📶 ⊠ 🛏 🖥 🏊

ASTORIA

Astoria Dunes Motel M
(503) 325-7111. **$75-$135.** 288 W Marine Dr 97103. Just e of Astoria Bridge on US 30. Ext corridors. **Pets:** Dogs only. $10 daily fee/pet. Service with restrictions, supervision. (SAVE) 📶 🛏 🖥 🏊

Astoria Holiday Inn Express Hotel & Suites H ❖
(503) 325-6222. **$119-$339.** 204 W Marine Dr 97103. On US 30; west side of town. Int corridors. **Pets:** $15 daily fee/pet. Service with restrictions, supervision. 📶 ⊠ ♿M 🛏 🖥 🏊 ⊠

Best Western Lincoln Inn H ❖
(503) 325-2205. **$89-$299.** 555 Hamburg Ave 97103. On US 101/30; at east end of Young's Bay Bridge. Int corridors. **Pets:** Medium, dogs only. $15 daily fee/room. Designated rooms, service with restrictions, supervision. (SAVE) 📶 ⊠ 🛏 🖥 🏊 ⊠

Clementine's Bed & Breakfast BB
(503) 325-2005. **$89-$165, 7 day notice.** 847 Exchange St 97103. At 8th and Exchange sts; in historic downtown. Int corridors. **Pets:** $20 one-time fee/room. Designated rooms, no service, supervision.
📶 ⊠ 🛏 🖥 🐾 🐕

Comfort Suites Columbia River H
(503) 325-2000. **$100-$310.** 3420 Leif Erickson Dr 97103. 2.5 mi e of Astoria Bridge on US 30. Int corridors. **Pets:** Accepted.
(SAVE) 📶 ⊠ 🛏 🖥 🏊 ⊠

Crest Motel M
(503) 325-3141. **$68-$135.** 5366 Leif Erickson Dr 97103. 4 mi e of Astoria Bridge on US 30. Ext corridors. **Pets:** Service with restrictions, supervision. (SAVE) 📶 🛏 🖥 🐾

BAKER CITY

Best Western Sunridge Inn H ❖
(541) 523-6444. **Call for rates.** 1 Sunridge Ln 97814. I-84 exit 304, just w. Int corridors. **Pets:** Other species. $15 daily fee/room. Designated rooms, service with restrictions, supervision.
(SAVE) 📶 ⊠ 🛏 🖥 🍽 🏊

Geiser Grand Hotel H ❖
(541) 523-1889. **$99-$259, 3 day notice.** 1996 Main St 97814. I-84 exit 304, 0.9 mi w on Campbell St, then 0.3 mi s; downtown. Int corridors. **Pets:** Other species. $15 daily fee/pet. Service with restrictions, crate.
📶 ⊠ 🍽

BANDON

Bandon Beach Vacation Rentals VH
(541) 347-4801. **$100-$175, 30 day notice.** 54515 Beach Loop Rd 97411. 1 mi s on US 101, 0.8 mi w on Seabird Rd, then 1 mi s; registration in house behind property. Ext corridors. **Pets:** Dogs only. $20 one-time fee/pet. No service, supervision. 📶 ⊠ 🛏 🖥 🐕

Bandon Inn M ❖
(541) 347-4417. **$74-$149.** 355 US 101 97411. Center. Ext corridors. **Pets:** Medium. $15 daily fee/pet. Designated rooms, service with restrictions, supervision. (SAVE) 📶 ⊠ 🛏 🖥 🐕

Best Western Inn at Face Rock H
(541) 347-9441. **$115-$166.** 3225 Beach Loop Dr 97411. 1 mi s on US 101, 0.8 mi w on Seabird Rd, then just s. Ext corridors. **Pets:** Accepted.
(SAVE) 📶 ⊠ 🛏 🖥 🍽 🏊 🐕 🐕

BEND

Bend Riverside Motel & Suites H
(541) 389-2363. **$68-$159.** 1565 NW Wall St 97701. US 97 exit 137 (Revere Ave), just s. Ext corridors. **Pets:** Medium. $10 daily fee/room. Designated rooms, service with restrictions, supervision.
📶 🛏 🖥 🏊

Best Western Inn & Suites of Bend H
(541) 382-1515. **$80-$130.** 721 NE 3rd St 97701. Jct US 20 and Business Rt US 97 (NE 3rd St), just s. Ext corridors. **Pets:** Large, other species. $15 daily fee/pet. Designated rooms, service with restrictions, supervision. (SAVE) 📶 🛏 🖥 🏊

Cricketwood Country Bed & Breakfast BB ❖
(541) 330-0747. **$105-$145, 7 day notice.** 63520 Cricketwood Rd 97701. US 97 exit 136 (NE Butler Market Rd), 3.7 mi ne on Butler Market Rd (which becomes Hamehook Rd), 0.4 mi n on Hamehook Rd, 0.4 mi e on Repine Dr, then just n (0.7 mi of gravel road). Ext/int corridors. **Pets:** Dogs only. $10 daily fee/room. Designated rooms, no service. 📶 ⊠ 🛏 🖥

Days Inn H ❖
(541) 383-3776. **$42-$128.** 849 NE 3rd St 97701. Jct US 20 and Business Rt US 97 (NE 3rd St), just s. Ext corridors. **Pets:** $10 one-time fee/pet. Designated rooms, service with restrictions, supervision. (SAVE) 📶 🛏 🖥 🏊

Holiday Inn Express Hotel & Suites H ❖
(541) 317-8500. **$99-$249, 6 day notice.** 20615 Grandview Dr 97701. On US 97; north end of town. Int corridors. **Pets:** Other species. $10 daily fee/pet. No service, supervision. 📶 ⊠ ♿M 🛏 🖥 🏊

La Quinta Inn Bend H
(541) 388-2227. **$103-$175.** 61200 SE 3rd St (Business Rt US 97) 97702. From south end of jct US 97 and Business Rt US 97 (NE 3rd St), 0.5 mi n. Int corridors. **Pets:** Medium, other species. Service with restrictions, supervision. 📶 ⊠ 🛏 🖥 🐕

The Oxford Hotel H ❖
(541) 382-8436. **$189-$310.** 10 NW Minnesota Ave 97701. Jct NW Minnesota Ave and NW Lava Rd; downtown. Int corridors. **Pets:** Large, dogs only. $55 one-time fee/pet. Designated rooms, service with restrictions, supervision. 📶 ⊠ ♿M 🛏 🖥 🍽 🐕

Quality Inn H
(541) 318-0848. **$79-$139.** 20600 Grandview Dr 97701. On US 97; north end of town. Int corridors. **Pets:** Medium, other species. $10 daily fee/pet. Designated rooms, service with restrictions, supervision. (SAVE) 📶 ♿M 🛏 🖥 🏊

Red Lion Hotel Bend H
(541) 382-7011. **$95-$209.** 1415 NE 3rd St 97701. Jct US 20 and Business Rt US 97 (NE 3rd St), just n. Ext corridors. **Pets:** Accepted. (SAVE) 📶 ⊠ ♿M 🛏 🖥 🏊

The Riverhouse Hotel & Convention Center H
(541) 389-3111. **$99-$219.** 3075 N Business 97 97701. US 97 exit 137 (Revere Ave) northbound, just n on NE Division St, then just n; exit 136 (Butler Market Rd) southbound, just w. Ext/int corridors. **Pets:** Accepted.
(SAVE) 📶 🛏 🖥 🍽 🏊 🐕

▼▼▼ Seventh Mountain Resort [CO] ❀

(541) 382-8711. **$99-$499, 7 day notice.** 18575 SW Century Dr 97702. US 97 exit 139 (Reed Market Rd), 1.6 mi sw, then 3.5 mi sw. Ext corridors. **Pets:** Other species. $50 one-time fee/room. Designated rooms, service with restrictions, supervision.

[SAVE] 🛜 ✕ 🛏 📶 🖵 ⑪ ⚓ ✕

▼▼▼ Shilo Inn Suites Hotel - Bend [H]

(541) 389-9600. **$69-$210.** 3105 OB Riley Rd 97701. US 97 exit 137 (Revere Ave) northbound, just n on NE Division St, then just n; exit 136 (Butler Market Rd) southbound, just w. Ext corridors. **Pets:** Dogs only. $25 one-time fee/room. Designated rooms, service with restrictions, crate.

[SAVE] 🛜 ✕ 🛏 📶 🖵 ⑪ ⚓ ✕

▼▼ TownePlace Suites by Marriott [H]

(541) 382-5006. **$109-$189.** 755 SW 13th Pl 97702. US 97 exit 138 (Downtown/Mt Bachelor Dr), 1.6 mi sw on NW Colorado Ave. Int corridors. **Pets:** Accepted. 🛜 ✕ 🛏 📶 🖵 ⚓ ✕

BROOKINGS

▼▼▼ Best Western Plus Beachfront Inn [H]

(541) 469-7779. **$159-$219.** 16008 Boat Basin Rd 97415. US 101 exit Benham Ln, 0.6 mi w; 1.2 mi s of Chetco River Bridge. Ext corridors. **Pets:** Large, other species. $10 daily fee/pet. Designated rooms, service with restrictions, supervision. [SAVE] 🛜 ♿M 🛏 🖵 ⚓ 🔑

▼▼▼ Spindrift Motel [M]

(541) 469-5345. **$69-$89.** 1215 Chetco Ave (US 101) 97415. On US 101; north end of town. Ext corridors. **Pets:** Very small, dogs only. $10 daily fee/pet. Designated rooms, service with restrictions, supervision.

[SAVE] 🛜 🛏 🖵 🔑

▼▼ Westward Inn [M]

(541) 469-7471. **$55-$99, 3 day notice.** 1026 Chetco Ave (US 101) 97415. On US 101; just n of downtown. Ext corridors. **Pets:** Medium, dogs only. $12 daily fee/pet. Designated rooms, service with restrictions, supervision. [SAVE] 🛜 🛏 🖵

▼▼ Wild Rivers Motorlodge [M] ❀

(541) 469-5361. **$69-$119.** 437 Chetco Ave (US 101) 97415. On US 101; just n of Chetco River Bridge. Ext corridors. **Pets:** $20 one-time fee/room. Designated rooms, service with restrictions, supervision.

[SAVE] 🛜 🛏 🖵

BURNS

▼▼ America's Best Inn [M] ❀

(541) 573-1700. **$60-$77.** 999 Oregon Ave (US 395/20) 97720. 1 mi w on US 395/20 from jct SR 78. Ext/int corridors. **Pets:** Medium, dogs only. $10 daily fee/pet. Designated rooms, service with restrictions, supervision.

[SAVE] 🛜 🛏 🖵 ⚓

CANNON BEACH

▼▼ Cannon Beach Ecola Creek Lodge [M]

(503) 436-2776. **$79-$239, 7 day notice.** 208 E 5th St 97110. US 101 exit Ecola State Park northbound, just w; north end of downtown. Ext corridors. **Pets:** Large, other species. $20 one-time fee/pet. Designated rooms, service with restrictions, supervision.

🛜 ✕ ♿M 🛏 🖵 🔑

▼▼ Inn at Cannon Beach [H] ❀

(503) 436-9085. **$99-$289, 7 day notice.** 3215 S Hemlock St 97110. US 101 exit Tolovana Park, just w on Warren Way, then just n. Ext corridors. **Pets:** Dogs only. $15 daily fee/pet. Designated rooms, service with restrictions, supervision. 🛜 ✕ 🛏 🖵 🔑

▼▼▼ The Ocean Lodge [H] ❀

(503) 436-2241. **$199-$399, 7 day notice.** 2864 S Pacific St 97110. US 101 exit Tolovana Park, just w on Warren Way, just n on S Hemlock St, just w on W Chisana St, then just n. Ext/int corridors. **Pets:** Other species. $15 daily fee/pet. Designated rooms, service with restrictions, supervision. 🛜 ✕ 🛏 🖵

▼▼▼ Surfsand Resort [H] ❀

(503) 436-2274. **$129-$429, 3 day notice.** 148 W Gower St 97110. US 101 exit Cannon Beach (2nd exit); downtown. Ext corridors. **Pets:** Large, other species. $15 daily fee/pet. Designated rooms, service with restrictions, supervision. [SAVE] 🛜 ✕ 🛏 🖵 ⑪ ⚓ ✕

▼▼▼ Tolovana Inn [CO]

(503) 436-2211. **$69-$474, 3 day notice.** 3400 S Hemlock St 97145. US 101 exit Tolovana Park, just w on Warren Way, then just s. Ext corridors. **Pets:** Accepted. [SAVE] 🛜 ✕ 🛏 🖵 ⚓ ✕ 🔑

CANYONVILLE

▼▼▼ Holiday Inn Express & Suites Canyonville [H]

(541) 839-4200. **$109-$189.** 200 Creekside Dr 97417. I-5 exit 99, just w. Int corridors. **Pets:** Small. $10 daily fee/pet. Designated rooms, service with restrictions, supervision. [SAVE] 🛜 ✕ 🛏 🖵 ⚓

CASCADE LOCKS

▼▼▼ Best Western Plus Columbia River Inn [H]

(541) 374-8777. **$100-$180.** 735 WaNaPa St (US 30) 97014. I-84 exit 44 eastbound, 0.4 mi ne; exit westbound, 1.4 mi nw. Int corridors. **Pets:** Medium. $10 daily fee/pet. Designated rooms, service with restrictions, supervision. [SAVE] 🛜 ✕ ♿M 🛏 🖵 ⚓

CENTRAL POINT

▼▼▼ Holiday Inn Express Hotel & Suites [H]

(541) 423-1010. **$89-$149.** 285 Peninger St 97502. I-5 exit 33, just se. Int corridors. **Pets:** Medium, other species. $25 daily fee/room. Designated rooms, service with restrictions, supervision.

🛜 ♿M 🛏 🖵 ⚓

▼▼▼ Super 8 Inn & Suites [H]

(541) 664-5888. **$63-$94.** 4999 Biddle Rd 97502. I-5 exit 33, 0.5 mi e. Int corridors. **Pets:** Accepted. 🛜 ♿M 🛏 🖵 ⚓

CLATSKANIE

▼▼▼ Clatskanie River Inn [H]

(503) 728-9000. **$89-$149.** 600 E Columbia River Hwy (US 30) 97016. On US 30. Int corridors. **Pets:** Medium, other species. $25 one-time fee/room. Service with restrictions, supervision. [SAVE] 🛜 🛏 🖵 ⚓

COOS BAY

▼▼▼ Best Western Holiday Motel [H]

(541) 269-5111. **$100-$190.** 411 N Bayshore Dr 97420. On US 101; just n of downtown. Ext/int corridors. **Pets:** Dogs only. $15 daily fee/pet. Service with restrictions, crate. [SAVE] 🛜 ✕ 🛏 🖵

▼▼▼ Red Lion Hotel Coos Bay [H]

(541) 267-4141. **$89-$156.** 1313 N Bayshore Dr 97420. On US 101; 0.5 mi n of downtown. Ext corridors. **Pets:** Accepted.

[SAVE] 🛜 ✕ ♿M 🛏 🖵 ⑪ ⚓

▼▼▼ Super 8 Coos Bay [M]

(541) 808-0700. **Call for rates.** 1001 N Bayshore Dr 97420. On US 101; just n of downtown. Ext corridors. **Pets:** Other species. $15 one-time fee/room. Service with restrictions, supervision. [SAVE] 🛜 ✕ 🛏 🖵

COQUILLE

▼▼ Myrtle Lane Motel [M]

(541) 396-2102. **$55-$80.** 787 N Central Blvd 97423. SR 42, 0.4 mi n. Ext corridors. **Pets:** Accepted. 🛜 🛏 🖵 🔑

CORVALLIS

▼▼▼ Best Western Grand Manor Inn [H]

(541) 758-8571. **$79-$250.** 925 NW Garfield Ave 97330. Jct SR 34 and US 20, 0.3 mi w on NW Harrison Blvd, 1 mi n on NW 9th St, then just w. Int corridors. **Pets:** Small, dogs only. $10 daily fee/pet. Designated rooms, service with restrictions, supervision.

[SAVE] 🛜 ✕ ♿M 🛏 🖵 ⚓ ✕

 **Days Inn** 🅷

(541) 754-7474. **$46-$103.** 1113 NW NW 9th St 97330. Jct SR 34 and US 20, 0.3 mi w on NW Harrison Blvd, 0.5 mi n. Int corridors. **Pets:** $10 daily fee/pet. Designated rooms, service with restrictions, supervision.

 **Holiday Inn Express On The River** 🅷 🐾

(541) 752-0800. **$89-$199.** 781 NE 2nd St 97330. Jct SR 34 and US 20, 0.4 mi n. Int corridors. **Pets:** Other species. $25 daily fee/room. Designated rooms, service with restrictions, supervision.

Motel 6 #4243 🅷

(541) 758-9125. **$65-$199.** 935 NW Garfield Ave 97330. Jct SR 34 and US 20, 0.3 mi w on NW Harrison Blvd, 1 mi n on NW 9th St, then just w. Int corridors. **Pets:** Other species. Service with restrictions, supervision.

Rodeway Inn Willamette River 🅼

(541) 752-9601. **Call for rates.** 345 NW 2nd St 97330. Between NW Harrison Blvd and NW Van Buren St; downtown. Ext/int corridors. **Pets:** Medium, dogs only. $10 daily fee/pet. Designated rooms, service with restrictions, supervision.

Super 8 🅷

(541) 758-8088. **$41-$122.** 407 NW 2nd St 97330. Jct SR 34 and US 20, just n; downtown. Int corridors. **Pets:** Accepted.

COTTAGE GROVE

 Best Western Cottage Grove Inn 🅷

(541) 942-1000. **$100-$120.** 1601 Gateway Blvd 97424. I-5 exit 174, just sw. Int corridors. **Pets:** Medium, other species. $15 daily fee/pet. Designated rooms, service with restrictions, supervision.

Comfort Inn 🅷

(541) 942-9747. **$77-$140.** 845 Gateway Blvd 97424. I-5 exit 174, just sw. Ext/int corridors. **Pets:** Medium. $10 daily fee/pet. Designated rooms, service with restrictions, supervision.

CRESWELL

 **Comfort Inn & Suites** 🅷

(541) 895-4025. **$85-$124.** 247 Melton Rd 97426. I-5 exit 182, just ne. Int corridors. **Pets:** Other species. $20 one-time fee/room. Designated rooms, service with restrictions, supervision.

Super 8 Creswell Inn 🅼

(541) 895-3341. **$49-$189.** 345 E Oregon Ave 97426. I-5 exit 182, just sw. Ext corridors. **Pets:** Medium, other species. $15 one-time fee/pet. Designated rooms, service with restrictions, supervision.

DALLAS

 **Best Western Dallas Inn & Suites** 🅷

(503) 623-6000. **$90-$130.** 250 Orchard Dr 97338. SR 223, just n. Int corridors. **Pets:** Medium, other species. $15 daily fee/pet. Designated rooms, service with restrictions, supervision.

DEPOE BAY

Crown Pacifiq Motel 🅼

(541) 765-7773. **$59-$129.** 50 NE Bechill St 97341. Just n of downtown. Ext/int corridors. **Pets:** Accepted.

Surfrider Resort 🅷

(541) 764-2311. **$69-$199, 3 day notice.** 3115 NW US 101 97341. 2 mi n of Depoe Bay. Ext corridors. **Pets:** Medium, dogs only. $10 daily fee/pet. Designated rooms, service with restrictions, supervision.

ENTERPRISE

Best Western Rama Inn & Suites 🅷

(541) 426-2000. **$80-$180.** 1200 Highland Ave 97828. 0.5 mi w on SR 82. Int corridors. **Pets:** Dogs only. $15 one-time fee/pet. Designated rooms, service with restrictions, supervision.

Ponderosa Motel 🅼

(541) 426-3186. **$56-$72.** 102 E Greenwood St 97828. Center. Ext corridors. **Pets:** Accepted.

The Wilderness Inn 🅼

(541) 426-4535. **$51-$70.** 301 W North St 97828. Corner of NW 2nd St. Ext corridors. **Pets:** Dogs only. $10 daily fee/pet. Service with restrictions, supervision.

EUGENE

Americas Best Value Inn 🅼

(541) 343-0730. **$49-$149.** 1140 W 6th Ave 97402. I-5 exit 194B, 3.5 mi w on I-105, then 0.3 mi w on SR 99 N (6th Ave). Ext corridors. **Pets:** Large. $10 daily fee/pet. Service with restrictions, supervision.

Best Western Greentree Inn 🅷 🐾

(541) 485-2727. **$105-$135.** 1759 Franklin Blvd 97403. I-5 exit 194B southbound to I-105 exit University of Oregon, 0.9 mi e; exit 192 northbound, 1.2 mi w. Ext/int corridors. **Pets:** Large. $50 deposit/room, $20 daily fee/room. Designated rooms, service with restrictions, supervision.

Best Western New Oregon Motel 🅷 🐾

(541) 683-3669. **$105-$135.** 1655 Franklin Blvd 97403. I-5 exit 194B southbound to I-105 exit University of Oregon, 0.9 mi e; exit 192 northbound, 1.2 mi w. Ext/int corridors. **Pets:** Large. $50 deposit/room, $20 daily fee/room. Designated rooms, service with restrictions, supervision.

Broadway Inn 🅼

(541) 344-5233. **$55-$150, 3 day notice.** 476 E Broadway 97401. I-5 exit 194B southbound, 1.3 mi w on I-105 exit 2 (Coburg Rd), 1.5 mi n, follow University of Oregon signs; exit 192 northbound, 2.2 mi w. Ext corridors. **Pets:** Small. $15 one-time fee/pet. Designated rooms, service with restrictions, supervision.

Campus Inn & Suites 🅼

(541) 343-3376. **$81-$168.** 390 E Broadway 97401. I-5 exit 194B southbound, 1.3 mi w on I-105 exit 2 (Coburg Rd), 1.5 mi s, follow University of Oregon signs; exit 192 northbound, 2.2 mi w. Ext corridors. **Pets:** Medium. $50 deposit/room, $10 one-time fee/pet. Designated rooms, service with restrictions.

Express Inn & Suites 🅼

(541) 868-1520. **$59-$99, 3 day notice.** 990 W 6th Ave 97402. I-5 exit 194B, 3.5 mi w on I-105, then 0.3 mi w on SR 99 N (6th Ave). Ext corridors. **Pets:** Small, dogs only. $10 daily fee/pet. Designated rooms, service with restrictions, supervision.

Hilton Eugene 🅷

(541) 342-2000. **$99-$289.** 66 E 6th Ave 97401. At 6th Ave and Oak St; center. Int corridors. **Pets:** Accepted.

La Quinta Inn & Suites Eugene 🅷

(541) 344-8335. **$100-$195.** 155 Day Island Rd 97401. I-5 exit 194B, 1.3 mi w on I-105 exit 2 (Coburg Rd), straight through jct Coburg Rd to Southwood Ln, just w, then 0.5 mi se on Country Club Rd, follow signs for Autzen Stadium. Int corridors. **Pets:** Medium, other species. Service with restrictions, supervision.

Motel 6 - #36 🅼

(541) 687-2395. **$51-$65.** 3690 Glenwood Dr 97403. I-5 exit 191, just sw. Ext corridors. **Pets:** Other species. Service with restrictions, supervision.

AAA ◆◆◆◆ Red Lion Hotel Eugene H
(541) 342-5201. **$94-$150.** 205 Coburg Rd 97401. I-5 exit 194B, 1.3 mi
w on I-105 to exit 2 (Coburg Rd), then just n. Ext corridors.
Pets: Accepted. [SAVE] 📶 ✕ 👤M 🍴 💻 ⊇ ✕

◆◆◆◆ Residence Inn by Marriott Eugene Springfield H
(541) 342-7171. **$149-$319.** 25 Club Rd 97401. I-5 exit 194B, 1.3 mi w
on I-105 exit 2 (Coburg Rd), straight through jct Coburg Rd to Southwood
Ln, just w, then se on Country Club Rd; follow signs for Autzen Stadium.
Int corridors. **Pets:** Accepted. 📶 ✕ 👤M 🍴 💻 ⊇ ✕

AAA ◆◆◆◆ Valley River Inn H ✿
(541) 743-1000. **Call for rates.** 1000 Valley River Way 97401. I-5 exit
194B, 2.5 mi w on I-105 exit 1, follow signs for Valley River Center. Int
corridors. **Pets:** Medium. Designated rooms, service with restrictions,
supervision. [SAVE] 📶 ✕ 🍴 💻 🍴 ⊇ ✕

FLORENCE

AAA ◆◆◆◆ Best Western Plus Pier Point Inn H
(541) 997-7191. **$130-$260.** 85625 US 101 S 97439. Jct SR 126, 1.1 mi
s. Ext corridors. **Pets:** Accepted. [SAVE] 📶 ✕ 🍴 💻 ⊇ ✕

AAA ◆ Le Chateau Inn M
(541) 997-3481. **Call for rates.** 1084 US 101 N 97439. Jct SR 126, just
n. Ext corridors. **Pets:** Accepted. [SAVE] 📶 🍴 💻 ⊇ ✕ 🄰

AAA ◆◆◆ Ocean Breeze Motel M ✿
(541) 997-2642. **$59-$150.** 85165 US 101 S 97439. Jct SR 126, 2 mi s.
Ext corridors. **Pets:** Dogs only. $10 daily fee/pet. Designated rooms,
supervision. [SAVE] 📶 ✕ 🍴 💻 🄰

AAA ◆◆◆ Old Town Inn M ✿
(541) 997-7131. **$89-$99.** 170 US 101 S 97439. Jct SR 126, 0.4 mi s.
Ext corridors. **Pets:** $10 daily fee/pet. Designated rooms, supervision.
[SAVE] 📶 🍴 💻 🄰

AAA ◆ Park Motel M ✿
(541) 997-2634. **$55-$150, 7 day notice.** 85034 US 101 S 97439. Jct
SR 126, 2.2 mi s. Ext corridors. **Pets:** Medium, other species. $10 daily
fee/pet. Service with restrictions, supervision.
[SAVE] 📶 ✕ 🍴 💻 🄰

FOREST GROVE

**AAA ◆◆◆ Best Western University Inn &
Suites H ✿**
(503) 992-8888. **$89-$199.** 3933 Pacific Ave 97116. East end of town on
SR 8. Int corridors. **Pets:** Medium, dogs only. $20 daily fee/pet. Desig-
nated rooms, service with restrictions, supervision.
[SAVE] 📶 ✕ 👤M 🍴 💻 ⊇ ✕

GEARHART

AAA ◆◆◆ Gearhart By The Sea CO
(503) 738-8331. **$126-$300, 3 day notice.** 1157 N Marion Ave 97138.
US 101 exit City Center, 1 mi w. Ext corridors. **Pets:** Medium. $11 daily
fee/pet. Designated rooms, service with restrictions, supervision.
[SAVE] 📶 🍴 💻 🍴 ⊇ 🄰

GLENEDEN BEACH

◆◆◆◆ Salishan Spa & Golf Resort H
(541) 764-2371. **$159-$329, 3 day notice.** 7760 US 101 N 97388. Just
e of US 101; center. Ext corridors. **Pets:** Accepted.
📶 ✕ 🍴 💻 🍴 ⊇ ✕ 🄰

GLIDE

AAA ◆◆ Illahee Inn and Restaurant & Bakery M
(541) 496-4870. **Call for rates.** 170 Wild Thyme Ln 97443. Just e on
SR 138, then just s. Ext corridors. **Pets:** Accepted.
[SAVE] 📶 ✕ 🍴 💻 🍴

GOLD BEACH

AAA ◆◆ Gold Beach Inn M
(541) 247-7091. **Call for rates.** 29346 Ellensburg Ave (US 101) 97444.
On US 101; center. Ext corridors. **Pets:** Accepted.
[SAVE] 📶 ✕ 🍴 💻 🄰

AAA ◆◆◆ Gold Beach Resort and Condominiums H
(541) 247-7066. **$79-$185.** 29232 Ellensburg Ave (US 101) 97444. On
US 101; south end of town. Ext corridors. **Pets:** Dogs only. $15 daily
fee/pet. Designated rooms, service with restrictions, supervision.
[SAVE] 📶 ✕ 🍴 💻 ⊇

AAA ◆◆◆ Inn of the Beachcomber M ✿
(541) 247-6691. **$68-$179.** 29266 Ellensburg Ave (US 101) 97444. On
US 101; south end of town. Ext/int corridors. **Pets:** Other species. $15
daily fee/pet. Service with restrictions, supervision.
[SAVE] 📶 ✕ 🍴 💻 ⊇

AAA ◆◆◆ Jot's Resort M ✿
(541) 247-6676. **$65-$230, 3 day notice.** 94360 Wedderburn Loop
97491. Just w of US 101; north end of bridge. Ext corridors. **Pets:** Other
species. $15 daily fee/pet. Designated rooms, service with restrictions,
supervision. [SAVE] 📶 🍴 💻 ⊇ ✕ 🄰

◆◆ Motel 6 - 4047 M
(541) 247-4533. **Call for rates.** 94433 Jerry's Flat Rd 97444. Just e of
jct US 101; south end of bridge. Ext corridors. **Pets:** Other species. Service with restrictions, supervision. 📶 🍴 💻 🄰

AAA ◆◆◆ Pacific Reef Resort M ✿
(541) 247-6658. **$69-$210.** 29362 Ellensburg Ave (US 101) 97444. On
US 101; south end of town. Ext corridors. **Pets:** Other species. $15 daily
fee/pet. Designated rooms, supervision. [SAVE] 📶 ✕ 🍴 💻 🄰

GOVERNMENT CAMP

AAA ◆◆◆ Best Western Mt. Hood Inn H ✿
(503) 272-3205. **$109-$189.** 87450 E Government Camp Loop 97028.
0.5 mi w of center. Int corridors. **Pets:** Large, other species. $10 daily
fee/pet. Designated rooms, service with restrictions.
[SAVE] 📶 ✕ 🍴 💻 🄰

GRANTS PASS

AAA ◆ Bestway Inn M
(541) 479-2952. **$55-$75.** 1253 NE 6th St 97526. I-5 exit 58, 0.9 mi s on
SR 99. Ext corridors. **Pets:** Medium, dogs only. $10 daily fee/pet. Service
with restrictions, supervision. [SAVE] 📶 🍴 💻

AAA ◆◆◆ Best Western Grants Pass Inn H ✿
(541) 476-1117. **$79-$129.** 111 NE Agness Ave 97526. I-5 exit 55, just
nw. Ext corridors. **Pets:** Other species. $10 daily fee/pet. Service with
restrictions, supervision. [SAVE] 📶 👤M 🍴 💻 ⊇

AAA ◆◆◆ Best Western Inn at the Rogue H ✿
(541) 582-2200. **$85-$145.** 8959 Rogue River Hwy 97527. I-5 exit 48,
just nw. Int corridors. **Pets:** Other species. $10 one-time fee/room. Desig-
nated rooms, service with restrictions, supervision.
[SAVE] 📶 ✕ 🍴 💻 ⊇

◆◆◆ Holiday Inn Express Grants Pass H ✿
(541) 471-6144. **$119-$169.** 105 NE Agness Ave 97526. I-5 exit 55, just
nw. Int corridors. **Pets:** Large, other species. $10 daily fee/pet. Desig-
nated rooms, service with restrictions. 📶 🍴 💻

AAA ◆ Knights Inn Motel M
(541) 479-5595. **$50-$85.** 104 SE 7th St 97526. I-5 exit 58, 1.7 mi s on
SR 99, just e on G St, then just n. Ext corridors. **Pets:** Small, dogs only.
$10 one-time fee/pet. Designated rooms, service with restrictions, supervi-
sion. [SAVE] 📶 🍴

◆◆◆ La Quinta Inn & Suites Grants Pass H
(541) 472-1808. **$89-$169.** 243 NE Morgan Ln 97526. I-5 exit 58, 0.4 mi
s on SR 99, just e on Hillcrest Dr to SR 99 N, then just n. Int corridors.
Pets: Medium, other species. Service with restrictions, supervision.
📶 ✕ 👤M 🍴 💻 ⊇

▼ Motel 6 - #253 **M**
(541) 474-1331. **$45-$65.** 1800 NE 7th St 97526. I-5 exit 58, 0.3 mi s on SR 99. Ext corridors. **Pets:** Other species. Service with restrictions, supervision. 🛰️ 🗻M 🔋 🏊

ⓐⓐⓐ ▼▼ Redwood Motel **H** 🐾
(541) 476-0878. **$63-$210.** 815 NE 6th St 97526. I-5 exit 58, 1.2 mi s on SR 99. Ext corridors. **Pets:** Medium, dogs only. $200 deposit/room. Designated rooms, service with restrictions, supervision.
SAVE 🛰️ ✕ 🗻M 🔋 🖥️ 🏊

ⓐⓐⓐ ▼▼ Riverside Inn **H**
(541) 476-6873. **$125-$149, 3 day notice.** 986 SW 6th St 97526. I-5 exit 58, 2.5 mi s on SR 99. Ext corridors. **Pets:** Other species. $25 daily fee/room. Designated rooms, service with restrictions, supervision.
SAVE 🛰️ ✕ 🗻M 🔋 🖥️ 🏊

ⓐⓐⓐ ▼▼ Shilo Inn - Grants Pass **H**
(541) 479-8391. **$69-$130.** 1880 NW 6th St 97526. I-5 exit 58, 0.3 mi s on SR 99. Int corridors. **Pets:** Dogs only. $25 one-time fee/room. Designated rooms, service with restrictions, crate.
SAVE 🛰️ ✕ 🗻M 🔋 🖥️ 🏊

ⓐⓐⓐ ▼▼ Super 8 - Grants Pass **H**
(541) 474-0888. **$49-$92.** 1949 NE 7th St 97526. I-5 exit 58, 0.4 mi s on SR 99, just e on Hillcrest Dr to SR 99 N, then just n. Int corridors. **Pets:** Other species. $25 deposit/room. Service with restrictions, supervision. SAVE 🛰️ 🗻M 🔋 🖥️ 🏊

ⓐⓐⓐ ▼ Sweet Breeze Inn **M**
(541) 471-4434. **$60-$165.** 1627 NE 6th St 97526. I-5 exit 58, 0.5 mi s on SR 99. Ext/int corridors. **Pets:** Accepted. SAVE 🛰️ ✕ 🔋

ⓐⓐⓐ ▼▼ Travelodge **M** 🐾
(541) 479-6611. **$53-$135.** 1950 NW Vine St 97526. I-5 exit 58, just s on SR 99. Ext corridors. **Pets:** Medium. $10 daily fee/pet. Service with restrictions, supervision. SAVE 🛰️ 🗻M 🔋 🖥️ 🏊

HALSEY

▼ Pioneer Villa Travelodge **M**
(541) 369-2804. **$69-$78.** 33180 SR 228 97348. I-5 exit 216, just se. Ext corridors. **Pets:** $10 daily fee/room. Service with restrictions, crate.
🛰️ 🔋 🖥️ 🍴 🏊

HERMISTON

▼▼ Comfort Inn & Suites Hermiston **H**
(541) 564-5911. **Call for rates.** 77514 SR 207 97838. I-84 exit 182, just nw. Int corridors. **Pets:** Accepted. 🛰️ 🗻M 🔋 🖥️ 🏊

▼▼ Oak Tree Inn **H**
(541) 567-2330. **$69-$84.** 1110 SE 4th St 97838. 0.4 mi s on US 395, then just w. Int corridors. **Pets:** Small. $10 daily fee/pet. Service with restrictions, supervision. 🛰️ ✕ 🔋 🖥️

▼▼ Oxford Suites **H**
(541) 564-8000. **$129-$139.** 1050 N 1st St 97838. 0.5 mi n on US 395. Int corridors. **Pets:** Small, dogs only. $25 one-time fee/pet. Service with restrictions, supervision. 🛰️ 🗻M 🔋 🖥️ 🏊

HINES

ⓐⓐⓐ ▼▼ Best Western Rory & Ryan Inns **H**
(541) 573-5050. **$81-$100.** 534 US 20 N 97738. On US 20 (Central Oregon Hwy). Int corridors. **Pets:** Accepted.
SAVE 🛰️ ✕ 🔋 🖥️ 🏊

▼▼ Rory & Ryan Inns **H**
(541) 573-3370. **$49-$125.** 504 US 20 N 97738. On US 20 (Central Oregon Hwy). Int corridors. **Pets:** Accepted. 🛰️ ✕ 🔋 🖥️ 🏊

HOOD RIVER

ⓐⓐⓐ ▼▼▼ Best Western Plus Hood River Inn **H**
(541) 386-2200. **$91-$200, 3 day notice.** 1108 E Marina Way 97031. I-84 exit 64, just ne. Int corridors. **Pets:** Accepted.
SAVE 🛰️ ✕ 🔋 🖥️ 🍴 🏊 ✕

ⓐⓐⓐ ▼▼▼ Columbia Gorge Hotel **CI**
(541) 386-5566. **$159-$289.** 4000 Westcliff Dr 97031. I-84 exit 62, just sw of overpass. Int corridors. **Pets:** Accepted. SAVE 🛰️ ✕ 🔋 🖥️ 🍴

ⓐⓐⓐ ▼▼ Sunset Motel **M**
(541) 386-6322. **$69-$119, 3 day notice.** 2300 Cascade Ave 97031. I-84 exit 62, 0.7 mi se. Ext corridors. **Pets:** Accepted.
SAVE 🛰️ ✕ 🗻M 🔋 🖥️

ⓐⓐⓐ ▼ Vagabond Lodge **M** 🐾
(541) 386-2992. **$56-$129.** 4070 Westcliff Dr 97031. I-84 exit 62, 0.3 mi nw. Ext corridors. **Pets:** Other species. $5 daily fee/pet. Service with restrictions, supervision. SAVE 🛰️ 🔋 🖥️

JACKSONVILLE

ⓐⓐⓐ ▼▼▼ Jacksonville Inn **CI**
(541) 899-1900. **$159-$465, 3 day notice.** 175 E California St 97530. On California St (SR 238); between 3rd and 4th sts; center. Ext/int corridors. **Pets:** Dogs only. $15 daily fee/room. Designated rooms, service with restrictions, supervision. SAVE 🛰️ ✕ 🔋 🖥️ 🍴

ⓐⓐⓐ ▼▼▼ Jacksonville's Magnolia Inn **BB** 🐾
(541) 899-0255. **$99-$169, 7 day notice.** 245 N 5th St 97530. At 5th (SR 238) and D sts. Int corridors. **Pets:** Dogs only. $25 one-time fee/room. Designated rooms, supervision. SAVE 🛰️ ✕ 🗻M

▼▼ The Wine Country Inn **M**
(541) 899-3953. **$125-$295, 3 day notice.** 830 N 5th St 97530. 0.5 mi ne of downtown. Ext corridors. **Pets:** $25 daily fee/pet. Designated rooms, service with restrictions, supervision. 🛰️ ✕ 🔋 🖥️

JOHN DAY

ⓐⓐⓐ ▼▼▼ Best Western John Day Inn **H**
(541) 575-1700. **$95-$130.** 315 W Main St 97845. Just w of jct US 26 and 395. Ext corridors. **Pets:** Large. $15 daily fee/room. Designated rooms, service with restrictions, supervision.
SAVE 🛰️ ✕ 🔋 🖥️ 🏊 ✕

ⓐⓐⓐ ▼ Dreamers Lodge **M**
(541) 575-0526. **$42-$99.** 144 N Canyon Blvd 97845. Just n of jct US 26 and 395. Ext corridors. **Pets:** Medium, dogs only. $5 daily fee/pet. Designated rooms, supervision. SAVE 🛰️ ✕ 🔋 🖥️

KEIZER

ⓐⓐⓐ ▼▼▼ Keizer Renaissance Inn **H**
(503) 390-4733. **$79-$99.** 5188 Wittenberg Ln N 97303. I-5 exit 260B southbound; exit 260 northbound, 1.5 mi w via Chemawa Rd and Lockhaven Dr, just s on River Rd, just e on Claggett St NE, then just s. Int corridors. **Pets:** Accepted.
SAVE 🛰️ ✕ 🗻M 🔋 🖥️ 🍴 🏊 ✕

KLAMATH FALLS

ⓐⓐⓐ ▼ Econo Lodge **M** 🐾
(541) 884-7735. **$35-$105.** 75 Main St 97601. US 97 exit City Center Dr, just e. Ext corridors. **Pets:** Medium. $10 daily fee/pet. Designated rooms, service with restrictions, supervision. SAVE 🛰️ 🔋 🖥️

ⓐⓐⓐ ▼ Golden West Motel **M** 🐾
(541) 882-1758. **$42-$68.** 6402 S 6th St 97603. On S 6th St (SR 140); at eastern edge of town. Ext corridors. **Pets:** $10 one-time fee/room. Supervision. SAVE 🛰️ ✕ 🔋 🖥️

ⓐⓐⓐ ▼▼▼ The Lodge at Running Y Ranch **H**
(541) 850-5500. **$99-$159, 3 day notice.** 5500 Running Y Rd 97601. Jct US 97, 7.5 mi nw on SR 140. Int corridors. **Pets:** Dogs only.
SAVE 🛰️ ✕ 🗻M 🔋 🖥️ 🍴 🏊 ✕

Majestic Inn & Suites M
(541) 883-7771. **$35-$105.** 5543 S 6th St 97603. 1 mi e on 6th St (SR 140) from jct SR 140 E/39 S and SR 39 N/US 97 business route. Ext corridors. **Pets:** Accepted. SAVE 📶 🔌

Maverick Motel M
(541) 882-6688. **$39-$109.** 1220 Main St 97601. US 97 exit City Center Dr, 0.9 mi e on S Klamath Ave, just n on S 12th St, then just e. Ext corridors. **Pets:** Medium. $5 daily fee/pet. Designated rooms, service with restrictions, supervision. SAVE 📶 🔌

Microtel Inn & Suites H 🐾
(541) 273-0206. **$62-$80.** 2716 Dakota Ct 97603. US 97 exit 277, 2.7 mi e to SR 140 exit 3, 1 mi n on Washburn Way, just e on Laverne Ave, then just s on Brooke Dr. Int corridors. **Pets:** Other species. $35 one-time fee/room. Service with restrictions, crate.
SAVE 📶 ❌ 🔌 🏊

Motel 6 - #226 M
(541) 884-2110. **$45-$65.** 5136 S 6th St 97603. 0.5 mi e on 6th St (SR 140) from jct SR 140 E/39 S and SR 39 N/US 97 business route. Ext corridors. **Pets:** Other species. Service with restrictions, supervision.
📶 🔌 🏊

Oregon 8 Motel M 🐾
(541) 883-3431. **$35-$99.** 5225 US 97 N 97601. On US 97, 4 mi n of downtown; between MM 270 and 271. Ext corridors. **Pets:** Medium. $10 daily fee/pet. Designated rooms, service with restrictions, supervision.
SAVE 📶 🔌 🏊

Quality Inn H 🐾
(541) 882-4666. **$65-$135.** 100 Main St 97601. US 97 exit City Center Dr, just e. Ext corridors. **Pets:** Medium. $20 daily fee/pet. Designated rooms, service with restrictions, supervision.
SAVE 📶 🔌 🏊

Shilo Inn Suites Hotel-Klamath Falls H
(541) 885-7980. **$90-$180.** 2500 Almond St 97601. On US 97, 1.5 mi n of downtown. Int corridors. **Pets:** Dogs only. $25 one-time fee/room. Designated rooms, service with restrictions, crate.
SAVE 📶 ❌ 🔌 🏊

Super 8 H
(541) 884-8880. **$56-$76.** 3805 US 97 97601. On US 97, 2 mi n of downtown. Int corridors. **Pets:** Accepted. 📶 🔌

Vagabond Inn & Suites M 🐾
(541) 882-1200. **$69-$139.** 4061 S 6th St 97603. Just w on 6th St (SR 140) from jct SR 140 E/39 S and SR 39 N/US 97 business route. Ext corridors. **Pets:** Medium. $20 daily fee/pet. Designated rooms, service with restrictions, supervision. SAVE 📶 🔌 🏊

LA GRANDE

Americas Best Value Sandman Inn H
(541) 963-3707. **$79-$84.** 2410 E R Ave 97850. I-84 exit 261, just s on Island Ave, just e on N Albany St, then just n. Int corridors. **Pets:** Dogs only. $15 one-time fee/room. Designated rooms, service with restrictions, crate. SAVE 🔌 🏊

Royal Motor Inn M
(541) 963-4154. **$40-$69.** 1510 Adams Ave 97850. I-84 exit 265 (US 30) to La Grande exit; downtown. Ext corridors. **Pets:** Accepted.
SAVE 📶

LAKEVIEW

Best Western Skyline Motor Lodge M
(541) 947-2194. **$95-$139.** 414 N G St 97630. Jct US 395 and SR 140. Ext corridors. **Pets:** Accepted. SAVE 📶 🔌 🏊

LA PINE

Best Western Newberry Station H
(541) 536-5130. **$90-$125.** 16515 Reed Rd 97739. Just off US 97; north end of town. Int corridors. **Pets:** Medium, dogs only. $15 one-time fee/pet. Service with restrictions, supervision. SAVE 📶 🔌 🏊

LINCOLN CITY

Ashley Inn & Suites H 🐾
(541) 996-7500. **$69-$199.** 3430 NE US 101 97367. Just n of downtown. Int corridors. **Pets:** Medium, other species. $25 daily fee/pet. Designated rooms, supervision. SAVE 📶 ❌ 🔌 🏊 ❌

The Coho Oceanfront Lodge H 🐾
(541) 994-3684. **$99-$299.** 1635 NW Harbor Ave 97367. US 101 exit N 17th St, just w. Ext corridors. **Pets:** Small, dogs only. $20 daily fee/pet. Designated rooms, service with restrictions, supervision.
SAVE 📶 🔌 🏊 ❌ 🅰

Comfort Inn & Suites H
(541) 994-8155. **$89-$299.** 136 NE US 101 97367. Just n of D River. Int corridors. **Pets:** Small, dogs only. $20 daily fee/pet. Designated rooms, service with restrictions, supervision. SAVE 📶 ❌ 🔌 🏊

Econo Lodge H
(541) 994-5281. **$40-$160.** 1713 NW 21st St 97367. US 101 exit NW 21st St, just w. Int corridors. **Pets:** Small, dogs only. $15 one-time fee/pet. Designated rooms, supervision. SAVE 📶 🔌 🅰

Inn at Wecoma H 🐾
(541) 994-2984. **$59-$199.** 2945 NW US 101 97367. Just s of NW 30th St; n of downtown. Int corridors. **Pets:** Small, dogs only. $15 daily fee/pet. Designated rooms, service with restrictions, supervision.
SAVE 📶 ❌ 🔌 🏊 ❌ 🅰

Lincoln City Inn H 🐾
(541) 996-4400. **$65-$130.** 1091 SE 1st St 97367. On US 101 at D River. Int corridors. **Pets:** Dogs only. $10 daily fee/pet. Designated rooms, service with restrictions, supervision. SAVE 📶 ❌ 🔌

Looking Glass Inn H 🐾
(541) 996-3996. **$79-$259, 3 day notice.** 861 SW 51st St 97367. US 101 exit 51st St; south end of town. Ext corridors. **Pets:** Dogs only. $10 daily fee/pet. Designated rooms, service with restrictions, supervision.
📶 ❌ 🔌 🅰

Motel 6 - #4172 H
(541) 996-9900. **$46-$100.** 3517 NW US 101 97367. North end of downtown. Int corridors. **Pets:** Other species. Service with restrictions, supervision. 📶 🔌

O'dysius Hotel H
(541) 994-4121. **$109-$269.** 120 NW Inlet Ave 97367. On US 101 at D River. Int corridors. **Pets:** Small, dogs only. $25 daily fee/pet. Designated rooms, supervision. SAVE 📶 ❌ 🔌 🅰

Palace Inn & Suites H
(541) 996-9466. **$69-$209.** 550 SE US 101 97367. Center. Int corridors. **Pets:** Accepted. SAVE 📶 ❌ 🔌 ❌

MADRAS

Best Western Madras Inn M 🐾
(541) 475-6141. **$90-$110.** 12 SW 4th St 97741. On US 97/26 S; at B and 4th sts; downtown. Ext corridors. **Pets:** Large, other species. $20 daily fee/room. Designated rooms, service with restrictions, supervision.
SAVE 📶 🔌 🏊

Budget Inn M
(541) 475-3831. **$55-$99.** 133 NE 5th St 97741. On US 97/26 N; downtown. Ext corridors. **Pets:** Medium, other species. $10 daily fee/pet. Service with restrictions, supervision. SAVE 📶

Inn at Cross Keys Station H
(541) 475-5800. **$77-$185.** 66 NW Cedar St 97741. On US 26; north end of town. Int corridors. **Pets:** Medium, dogs only. $30 daily fee/pet. Designated rooms, service with restrictions, supervision.

Sonny's Motel M
(541) 475-7217. **$58-$135.** 1539 SW US 97 97741. South end of town. Ext corridors. **Pets:** $50 deposit/room, $10 daily fee/room. Designated rooms, service with restrictions, supervision.

MCMINNVILLE

Americas Best Value Inn & Suites M
(503) 472-5187. **$75-$100.** 381 NE SR 99 W 97128. North end of SR 99 W. Ext corridors. **Pets:** Medium, other species. $10 daily fee/pet. Designated rooms, service with restrictions, supervision.

Best Western Vineyard Inn Motel H
(503) 472-4900. **Call for rates.** 2035 S SR 99 W 97128. Jct SR 99 W and 18. Int corridors. **Pets:** Accepted.

Comfort Inn & Suites H
(503) 472-1700. **$119-$159.** 2520 SE Stratus Ave 97128. Jct SR 99 W; 2.3 mi ne on SR 18. Int corridors. **Pets:** Other species. $10 daily fee/pet. Designated rooms, service with restrictions, supervision.

Red Lion Inn & Suites H
(503) 472-1500. **$95-$136.** 2535 NE Cumulus Ave 97128. Jct SR 99 W, 2.3 mi ne on SR 18. Int corridors. **Pets:** Accepted.

MEDFORD

Best Western Horizon Inn H
(541) 779-5085. **$79-$129.** 1154 E Barnett Rd 97504. I-5 exit 27 (Barnett Rd), just ne. Ext corridors. **Pets:** $10 daily fee/pet. Designated rooms, service with restrictions, crate.

Candlewood Suites Medford Airport H
(541) 772-2800. **Call for rates.** 3548 Heathrow Way 97504. I-5 exit 33, 1.5 mi se via E Pine St and Biddle Rd, just w on O'Hare Pkwy, then just n. Int corridors. **Pets:** Other species. $10 daily fee/room. Supervision.

Comfort Inn North Medford H
(541) 772-9500. **$79-$149.** 2280 Biddle Rd 97504. I-5 exit 30 southbound, just ne on Crater Lake Hwy, follow signs to Biddle Rd/Airport, then just n; exit northbound, follow signs to Biddle Rd/Airport, then just ne. Int corridors. **Pets:** Small, dogs only. $10 daily fee/pet. Designated rooms, service with restrictions.

Comfort Inn South H
(541) 772-8000. **$75-$159.** 60 E Stewart Ave 97501. I-5 exit 27 (City Center), just w on Garfield St, 0.4 mi n on S Pacific Hwy, then just e. Int corridors. **Pets:** Small, dogs only. $10 daily fee/pet. Designated rooms, service with restrictions.

Homewood Suites by Hilton H
(541) 779-9800. **$109-$149.** 2010 Hospitality Way 97504. I-5 exit 27 (Barnett Rd), 0.4 mi e, just s on Ellendale Dr, then just w. Int corridors. **Pets:** Medium, other species. $75 one-time fee/room. Service with restrictions, crate.

Motel 6-Medford North - 739 M
(541) 779-0550. **$49-$65.** 2400 Biddle Rd 97504. I-5 exit 30 southbound, just ne on Crater Lake Hwy, follow signs to Biddle Rd/Airport, then just n; exit northbound, follow signs to Biddle Rd/Airport, then just n. Ext corridors. **Pets:** Other species. Service with restrictions, supervision.

Motel 6-Medford South - #89 M
(541) 773-4290. **$45-$61.** 950 Alba Dr 97504. I-5 exit 27 (Barnett Rd), just w, then just n. Ext corridors. **Pets:** Other species. Service with restrictions, supervision.

Quality Inn & Suites H
(541) 779-0050. **Call for rates.** 1950 Biddle Rd 97504. I-5 exit 30 southbound, just ne on Crater Lake Hwy, follow signs to Biddle Rd/Airport, then just s; exit northbound, follow signs to Biddle Rd/Airport, then just s. Int corridors. **Pets:** Accepted.

Ramada Medford and Convention Center H
(541) 779-3141. **$56-$103.** 2250 Biddle Rd 97504. I-5 exit 30 southbound, just ne on Crater Lake Hwy, follow signs, then just s; exit northbound, follow signs to Biddle Rd/Airport, then just s. Int corridors. **Pets:** $20 one-time fee/room. Designated rooms, service with restrictions.

Red Lion Hotel Medford H
(541) 779-5811. **$81-$129.** 200 N Riverside Ave 97501. I-5 exit 27 (City Center), 0.4 mi w on Garfield St, then 1.7 mi n on S Pacific Hwy. Ext corridors. **Pets:** Accepted.

Rogue Regency Inn & Suites H
(541) 770-1234. **$111-$126.** 2300 Biddle Rd 97504. I-5 exit 30 southbound, just ne on Crater Lake Hwy, follow signs, then just n; exit northbound, follow signs to Biddle Rd/Airport, then just n. Int corridors. **Pets:** Accepted.

Shilo Inn-Medford H
(541) 770-5151. **$69-$130.** 2111 Biddle Rd 97504. I-5 exit 30 southbound, just ne on Crater Lake Hwy, follow signs to Biddle Rd/Airport, then just s; exit northbound, follow signs to Biddle Rd/Airport, then just s. Int corridors. **Pets:** Dogs only. $25 one-time fee/room. Designated rooms, service with restrictions, crate.

TownePlace Suites by Marriott H
(541) 842-5757. **$79-$189.** 1395 Center Dr 97501. I-5 exit 27 (City Center), just w on Garfield St, then just n. Int corridors. **Pets:** Accepted.

MERLIN

Morrison's Rogue River Lodge CA
(541) 476-3825. **$69-$400, 45 day notice.** 8500 Galice Rd 97532. I-5 exit 61, 12 mi w on Merlin-Galice Rd. Ext/int corridors. **Pets:** Accepted.

MYRTLE POINT

Myrtle Trees Motel M
(541) 572-5811. **$65-$75, 5 day notice.** 1010 8th St (SR 42) 97458. On SR 42, 0.5 mi e. Ext corridors. **Pets:** Accepted.

NEWBERG

The Allison Inn & Spa H
(503) 554-2525. **$305-$1100.** 2525 Allison Ln 97132. Jct Portland Rd (SR 99), 1 mi n on Springbrook Rd; north of city center. Int corridors. **Pets:** Dogs only. $50 one-time fee/pet. Designated rooms.

Best Western Newberg Inn H
(503) 537-3000. **$75-$180.** 2211 Portland Rd 97132. Northeast of center. Int corridors. **Pets:** Large. $10 daily fee/pet. Designated rooms, service with restrictions, supervision.

Shilo Inn Suites - Newberg H
(503) 537-0303. **$69-$159.** 501 Sitka Ave 97132. Northeast of city on Portland Rd (SR 99 W). Int corridors. **Pets:** Dogs only. $25 one-time fee/room. Designated rooms, service with restrictions, crate.

NEWPORT

Best Western Plus Agate Beach Inn H
(541) 265-9411. **$85-$225.** 3019 N Coast Hwy (US 101) 97365. Jct US 20, 1.5 mi n on US 101. Int corridors. **Pets:** Accepted.

Elizabeth Street Inn H
(541) 265-9400. **$169-$319.** 232 SW Elizabeth St 97365. Jct US 20, 0.5 mi s on US 101, just w on SW Falls St, then just n. Int corridors.
Pets: Accepted.

Hallmark Resort Oceanfront H
(541) 265-2600. **$89-$294.** 744 SW Elizabeth St 97365. Jct US 20, 0.7 mi s on US 101, just w on SW Bay St. Ext corridors. **Pets:** Accepted.

The Landing at Newport CO
(541) 574-6777. **$109-$388.** 890 SE Bay Blvd 97365. Jct US 101, 0.5 mi e on US 20, 0.3 mi s on John Moore Rd. Ext corridors. **Pets:** $75 deposit/room, $25 one-time fee/room, $10 daily fee/room. Designated rooms, service with restrictions, supervision.

La Quinta Inn & Suites Newport H
(541) 867-7727. **$80-$174.** 45 SE 32nd St 97365. US 101, just s of Yaquina Bay Bridge. Int corridors. **Pets:** Medium, other species. Service with restrictions, supervision.

Newport Belle Riverboat Bed & Breakfast BB
(541) 867-6290. **$135-$165, 7 day notice.** 2126 SE OSU Dr 97365. South end of Yaquina Bay Bridge, follow signs to Marine Science Center, then just w; moored at dock H. Ext corridors. **Pets:** Small, dogs only. $25 daily fee/pet. Designated rooms, service with restrictions, supervision.

Shilo Inn Suites Oceanfront Hotel - Newport H
(541) 265-7701. **$95-$250.** 536 SW Elizabeth St 97365. Jct US 20, 0.5 mi s on US 101, then just w on SW Falls St. Ext/int corridors.
Pets: Dogs only. $25 one-time fee/room. Designated rooms, service with restrictions, crate.

Waves of Newport Motel and Vacation Rentals H
(541) 265-4661. **$68-$129, 3 day notice.** 820 NW Coast St 97365. Jct US 20, 0.5 mi n on US 101, just w on NW 11th St, then just s on Spring St. Ext corridors. **Pets:** Accepted.

The Whaler Motel M
(541) 265-9261. **$89-$179.** 155 SW Elizabeth St 97365. Jct US 20, just s on US 101, 0.4 mi w on SW 2nd St. Ext corridors. **Pets:** Dogs only. $10 daily fee/pet. Designated rooms, service with restrictions, supervision.

NORTH BEND

The Mill Casino & Hotel H
(541) 756-8800. **$108-$135.** 3201 Tremont Ave 97459. 0.7 mi n on US 101; on bayfront. Int corridors. **Pets:** Dogs only. $25 one-time fee/room. Service with restrictions, crate.

Quality Inn & Suites H
(541) 756-3191. **$89-$189.** 1503 Virginia Ave 97459. 0.5 mi w of US 101. Ext/int corridors. **Pets:** Accepted.

OAKLAND

Motel 6 - Rice Hill H
(541) 849-3335. **$54-$60.** 621 John Long Rd 97462. I-5 exit 148, just e. Ext corridors. **Pets:** Other species. Service with restrictions, supervision.

OAKRIDGE

Best Western Oakridge Inn H
(541) 782-2212. **$96-$106.** 47433 SR 58 97463. West end of downtown. Ext corridors. **Pets:** $15 one-time fee/pet. Designated rooms, service with restrictions, supervision.

Cascade Motel M
(541) 782-2489. **$56-$75.** 47487 SR 58 97463. Center. Ext corridors.
Pets: Medium, dogs only. $10 one-time fee/pet. Designated rooms, service with restrictions, supervision.

ONTARIO

Clarion Inn H
(541) 889-8621. **Call for rates.** 1249 Tapadera Ave 97914. I-84 exit 376B, just nw. Int corridors. **Pets:** Other species. $11 one-time fee/room. Designated rooms, service with restrictions, crate.

Rodeway Inn M
(541) 889-9188. **$54-$69.** 615 E Idaho Ave 97914. I-84 exit 376A, just sw. Ext corridors. **Pets:** Large, other species. $6 daily fee/room. Designated rooms, service with restrictions, crate.

Sleep Inn H
(541) 881-0007. **$59-$129.** 1221 SE 1st Ave 97914. I-84 exit 376B, just ne. Int corridors. **Pets:** Dogs only. $10 daily fee/pet. Designated rooms, service with restrictions, supervision.

PACIFIC CITY

Inn at Cape Kiwanda H
(503) 965-7001. **$129-$359.** 33105 Cape Kiwanda Dr 97135. Just w on Pacific Ave, 1 mi n. Ext corridors. **Pets:** Dogs only. $20 daily fee/pet. Designated rooms, service with restrictions, supervision.

Pacific City Inn M
(503) 965-6464. **$79-$99, 3 day notice.** 35280 Brooten Rd 97135. Center. Ext corridors. **Pets:** Large, dogs only. $16 daily fee/pet. Designated rooms, service with restrictions, supervision.

PENDLETON

Americas Best Value Inn M
(541) 276-1400. **$79-$99.** 201 SW Court Ave 97801. I-84 exit 210 (SR 11), 0.7 mi ne on SE 3rd Dr, then 0.6 mi w. Ext corridors. **Pets:** Other species. $15 one-time fee/room. Supervision.

Best Western Plus Pendleton Inn H
(541) 276-2135. **$95-$119.** 400 SE Nye Ave 97801. I-84 exit 210 (SR 11), just se. Int corridors. **Pets:** Small. $10 one-time fee/pet. Supervision.

Holiday Inn Express H
(541) 966-6520. **$109-$129.** 600 SE Nye Ave 97801. I-84 exit 210 (SR 11), just se. Int corridors. **Pets:** Other species. $20 daily fee/room. Supervision.

Motel 6 - #349 M
(541) 276-3160. **$45-$59.** 325 SE Nye Ave 97801. I-84 exit 210 (SR 11), just se. Ext corridors. **Pets:** Other species. Service with restrictions, supervision.

Oxford Suites H
(541) 276-6000. **$115-$195.** 2400 SW Court Pl 97801. I-84 exit 209, just n on SW Emigrant Ave, just nw on SW 20th St, then just sw to SW Court Pl. Int corridors. **Pets:** Small, dogs only. $25 one-time fee/pet. Service with restrictions, supervision.

Red Lion Hotel Pendleton H
(541) 276-6111. **$109-$169.** 304 SE Nye Ave 97801. I-84 exit 210 (SR 11), just sw. Ext/int corridors. **Pets:** Accepted.

Rodeway Inn H
(541) 276-6231. **$60-$75.** 310 SE Dorion Ave 97801. I-84 exit 210 (SR 11), 0.7 mi ne on SE 3rd Dr, 0.4 mi w on SE Court St, then just s on SE 3rd St. Ext corridors. **Pets:** $10 daily fee/pet. Service with restrictions.

▼▼ **Rugged Country Lodge** 🅗

(541) 966-6800. **Call for rates.** 1807 SE Court Ave 97801. I-84 exit 210 (SR 11), 0.7 mi ne on SE 3rd Dr, then 0.4 mi e. Ext/int corridors. **Pets:** Accepted. 🛜 ✕ 🛏 💷

▼▼ **Super 8 Pendleton** 🅗 🐾

(541) 276-8881. **$58-$90.** 601 SE Nye Ave 97801. I-84 exit 210 (SR 11), just se. Int corridors. **Pets:** Other species. $10 one-time fee/pet. Designated rooms, no service, supervision. 🛜 🛏 💷 🏊

🅐🅐🅐 ▼▼ **Travelodge** Ⓜ 🐾

(541) 276-7531. **$59-$80.** 411 SW Dorion Ave 97801. I-84 exit 209, 0.9 mi ne on SW Frazer Ave, then just nw on SW 4th St. Ext corridors. **Pets:** Large, dogs only. $10 daily fee/pet. Designated rooms, service with restrictions. 🆂🅰🆅🅴 🛜 🛏 💷

PORTLAND METROPOLITAN AREA

BEAVERTON

▼▼ **Comfort Inn & Suites** 🅗

(503) 643-9100. **$75-$130.** 13455 SW Tualatin Valley Hwy 97005. SR 217 exit 2A (Canyon Rd/SR 8), 1 mi w. Int corridors. **Pets:** Medium. $20 daily fee/pet. Service with restrictions, crate. 🛜 ✕ 🛏 💷 🏊

▼▼◈ **Homewood Suites by Hilton** 🅗

(503) 614-0900. **$129-$189.** 15525 NW Gateway Ct 97006. US 26 exit 65, just sw on NW Cornell Rd, just s on NW 158th Ave, just se on NW Waterhouse Ave, then just e. Int corridors. **Pets:** Accepted.

🛜 ♿ 🛏 💷 🏊

🅐🅐🅐 ▼▼◈ **Phoenix Inn Suites - Beaverton/Hillsboro** 🅗

(503) 614-8100. **Call for rates.** 15402 NW Cornell Rd 97006. US 26 exit 65, just ne. Int corridors. **Pets:** Accepted.

🆂🅰🆅🅴 🛜 ♿ 🛏 💷 🏊 ✕

🅐🅐🅐 ▼▼◈ **Shilo Inn Hotel & Suites-Portland/Beaverton** 🅗

(503) 297-2551. **$69-$170.** 9900 SW Canyon Rd 97225. SR 217 exit 2A (Canyon Rd/SR 8), 0.7 mi e. Int corridors. **Pets:** Dogs only. $25 one-time fee/room. Designated rooms, service with restrictions, crate.

🆂🅰🆅🅴 🛜 🛏 💷 🍽 🏊

CLACKAMAS

▼▼◈ **Comfort Suites** 🅗

(503) 723-3450. **Call for rates.** 15929 SE McKinley Ave 97015. I-205 exit 12 northbound; exit 12B southbound, just w. Int corridors. **Pets:** Large, other species. $10 daily fee/room. Designated rooms, service with restrictions, supervision. 🛜 ✕ 🛏 💷 🏊 ✕

🅐🅐🅐 ▼▼◈ **Howard Johnson Clackamas** 🅗 🐾

(503) 496-1000. **$59-$117.** 12855 SE 97th Ave 97015. I-205 exit 14, follow signs for Sunnyside Rd E, just e, then just s. Ext corridors. **Pets:** Large, other species. $10 daily fee/room. Service with restrictions, supervision. 🆂🅰🆅🅴 🛜 🛏 💷 🏊

GLADSTONE

▼▼ **Oxford Suites** 🅗 🐾

(503) 722-7777. **$89-$149.** 75 82nd Dr 97027. I-205 exit 11, 0.3 mi sw. Int corridors. **Pets:** Medium. $25 one-time fee/pet. Service with restrictions, supervision. 🛜 ✕ 🛏 💷 🏊 ✕

GRESHAM

🅐🅐🅐 ▼▼ **Days Inn & Suites** 🅗

(503) 465-1515. **$52-$113.** 24124 SE Stark St 97030. I-84 exit 16, 1.5 mi s on NE 238th and NE 242nd drs, then just w. Int corridors. **Pets:** Dogs only. $10 daily fee/pet. Designated rooms, service with restrictions, supervision. 🆂🅰🆅🅴 🛜 🛏 💷 🏊

▼▼ **Days Inn-Portland/Gresham** 🅗

(503) 618-8400. **$48-$77.** 2261 NE 181st Ave 97230. I-84 exit 13, just sw. Int corridors. **Pets:** Accepted. 🛜 ♿ 🛏 💷 🏊

▼▼ **Extended StayAmerica Portland/Gresham** 🅗 🐾

(503) 661-0226. **$65-$80.** 17777 NE Sacramento St 97230. I-84 exit 13, 0.3 mi s on NE 181st Ave, just w on NE San Rafael St, then just n on NE 178th Ave. Int corridors. **Pets:** Other species. $25 daily fee/pet. Service with restrictions. 🛜 ♿ 🛏 💷

▼▼▼ **Holiday Inn Portland/Gresham** 🅗

(503) 907-1777. **$95-$195.** 2752 NE Hogan Dr 97030. I-84 exit 16, 1.8 mi s on NE 238th, NE 242nd and NE Hogan drs. Int corridors. **Pets:** Small. $35 daily fee/pet. Service with restrictions, supervision.

🛜 ✕ ♿ 🛏 💷 🍽 🏊

🅐🅐🅐 ▼▼▼ **Howard Johnson Gresham** 🅗

(503) 666-9545. **$49-$121.** 1572 NE Burnside Rd 97030. I-84 exit 16, 2.7 mi s on NE 238th, NE 242nd and NE Hogan drs, just w on Division St, then just se; I-205 exit 19, 5.5 mi e on Division St, then just se. Int corridors. **Pets:** Accepted. 🆂🅰🆅🅴 🛜 🛏 💷 🏊

🅐🅐🅐 ▼▼ **Super 8** 🅗

(503) 661-5100. **$44-$63.** 121 NE 181st Ave 97230. I-84 exit 13, 1.3 mi s. Int corridors. **Pets:** Medium, dogs only. $10 daily fee/pet. Designated rooms, service with restrictions, supervision. 🆂🅰🆅🅴 🛜 🛏 💷

HILLSBORO

▼▼ **Extended StayAmerica-Portland-Beaverton** 🅗 🐾

(503) 439-1515. **$80-$95.** 18665 NW Eider Ct 97006. US 26 exit 64, 0.7 mi s on NW 185th Ave, then just w. Int corridors. **Pets:** Other species. $25 daily fee/pet. Service with restrictions. 🛜 🛏 💷

▼▼◈ **Residence Inn by Marriott Portland West** 🅗

(503) 531-3200. **$99-$199.** 18855 NW Tanasbourne Dr 97124. US 26 exit 64, just s on NW 185th Ave, then just w. Ext/int corridors. **Pets:** Accepted. 🛜 ✕ ♿ 🛏 💷 🏊 ✕

▼▼◈ **TownePlace Suites by Marriott-Portland Hillsboro** 🅗

(503) 268-6000. **$79-$159.** 6550 NE Brighton St 97124. US 26 exit 62A westbound; exit 62 eastbound, 1 mi s on Cornelius Pass Rd, 0.7 mi w on NE Cornell Rd, just n on NW 229th Ave, then just w. Ext corridors. **Pets:** Accepted. 🛜 ✕ 🛏 💷 🏊 ✕

LAKE OSWEGO

▼▼▼ **Crowne Plaza Hotel** 🅗

(503) 624-8400. **$79-$249.** 14811 Kruse Oaks Dr 97035. I-5 exit 292B northbound; exit 292 southbound, just e on Kruse Way, then just s. Int corridors. **Pets:** Accepted. 🛜 ✕ ♿ 🛏 💷 🍽 🏊 ✕

▼▼ **Lakeshore Inn** 🅗

(503) 636-9679. **$89-$199, 3 day notice.** 210 N State St 97034. Jct N State St and Foothills Rd; downtown. Ext corridors. **Pets:** Accepted.

🛜 ♿ 🛏 💷 🏊

🅐🅐🅐 ▼▼▼ **Phoenix Inn Suites-Lake Oswego** 🅗 🐾

(503) 624-7400. **Call for rates.** 14905 SW Bangy Rd 97035. I-5 292B northbound; exit 292 southbound, just s. Int corridors. **Pets:** Dogs only. $20 daily fee/room. Designated rooms, service with restrictions, supervision. 🆂🅰🆅🅴 🛜 ✕ ♿ 🛏 💷 🏊

▼▼▼ **Residence Inn by Marriott-Portland South** 🅗 🐾

(503) 684-2603. **$94-$159.** 15200 SW Bangy Rd 97035. I-5 exit 292B northbound; exit 292 southbound, just e, then 0.3 mi s. Ext corridors. **Pets:** Other species. $75 one-time fee/room. Service with restrictions, crate. 🛜 ✕ ♿ 🛏 💷 🏊 ✕

OREGON CITY

Best Western Plus Rivershore Hotel H ❖

(503) 655-7141. **$96-$116.** 1900 Clackamette Dr 97045. I-205 exit 9, just n. Int corridors. **Pets:** Other species. $10 daily fee/pet. Designated rooms, service with restrictions, supervision.

SAVE 📶 ✕ 📶 🛏 📺 🍽 🏊 ✕

PORTLAND

Aloft Portland Airport at Cascade Station H

(503) 200-5678. **$119-$229.** 9920 NE Cascades Pkwy 97220. I-205 exit 24A northbound; exit 24 southbound, 0.5 mi w on Airport Way, 0.5 mi s on NE Mt Hood Ave, then just e. Int corridors. **Pets:** Accepted.

ECO SAVE 📶 ✕ 📶 🛏 📺 🏊

The Benson Hotel, a Coast Hotel H ❖

(503) 228-2000. **$129-$359.** 309 SW Broadway 97205. At SW Broadway and Oak St. Int corridors. **Pets:** $25 one-time fee/room. Designated rooms, service with restrictions, supervision.

SAVE 📶 ✕ 📶 📺 🍽

Best Western Inn at the Meadows H

(503) 286-9600. **$90-$130.** 1215 N Hayden Meadows Dr 97217. I-5 exit 306B, just e. Int corridors. **Pets:** Other species. $20 daily fee/pet. Designated rooms, service with restrictions, supervision.

SAVE 📶 ✕ 🛏 📺

Best Western Pony Soldier Inn-Airport H ❖

(503) 256-1504. **$95-$112.** 9901 NE Sandy Blvd 97220. I-205 exit 23A, just e. Int corridors. **Pets:** $10 one-time fee/room. Designated rooms, service with restrictions, supervision.

SAVE 📶 📶 🛏 📺 🏊 ✕

Candlewood Suites - Portland Airport H

(503) 255-4003. **$99-$199.** 11250 NE Holman St 97220. I-205 exit 24B northbound; exit 24 southbound, 0.4 mi e on Airport Way, then just sw. Int corridors. **Pets:** Accepted. 📶 ✕ 📶 🛏 📺

Courtyard by Marriott Portland City Center H

(503) 505-5000. **$98-$134.** 550 SW Oak St 97204. At SW Oak St and SW 6th Ave. Int corridors. **Pets:** Accepted.

ECO SAVE 📶 ✕ 📶 🛏 📺 🍽

Days Inn-Portland H

(503) 289-1800. **$50-$78.** 9930 N Whitaker Rd 97217. I-5 exit 306B, just e. Int corridors. **Pets:** Accepted. SAVE 📶 🛏 📺

DoubleTree by Hilton Hotel Portland H

(503) 281-6111. **$79-$179.** 1000 NE Multnomah St 97232. I-5 exit 302A, just e, just s on 9th Ave, then just e; I-84 exit Lloyd Center westbound. Int corridors. **Pets:** Accepted.

ECO SAVE 📶 ✕ 📶 🛏 📺 🍽 🏊

Hampton Inn-Portland Airport H ❖

(503) 288-2423. **$109-$199.** 8633 NE Airport Way 97220. I-205 exit 24A northbound; exit 24 southbound, 1.4 mi w. Int corridors. **Pets:** Medium. Designated rooms, service with restrictions, supervision.

SAVE 📶 ✕ 📶 📺 🏊

The Heathman Hotel H ❖

(503) 241-4100. **$209-$1200, 3 day notice.** 1001 SW Broadway 97205. At SW Broadway and Salmon St. Int corridors. **Pets:** $35 one-time fee/room. Designated rooms, service with restrictions, supervision.

SAVE 📶 📶 📺 🍽

Hilton Portland & Executive Tower H ❖

(503) 226-1611. **$129-$219.** 921 SW 6th Ave 97204. I-405 exit 1B (6th Ave); at 6th Ave and Taylor St. Int corridors. **Pets:** Large. $25 one-time fee/room. Service with restrictions, supervision.

ECO SAVE 📶 ✕ 🛏 📺 🍽 🏊 ✕

Holiday Inn Portland Airport Hotel & Convention Center H

(503) 256-5000. **Call for rates.** 8439 NE Columbia Blvd 97220. I-205 exit 23B, 0.5 mi w. Int corridors. **Pets:** Accepted.

📶 ✕ 🛏 📺 🍽 🏊

Hospitality Inn H

(503) 244-6684. **$79-$129.** 10155 SW Capitol Hwy 97219. I-5 exit 295 southbound, just e; exit 294 northbound, 1 mi n on SW Barbur Blvd, then just e. Int corridors. **Pets:** Medium, dogs only. $10 daily fee/pet. Designated rooms, service with restrictions, supervision.

SAVE 📶 📶 🛏 📺

Hotel deLuxe H

(503) 219-2094. **$109-$299.** 729 SW 15th Ave 97205. I-5 to I-405 exit Salmon St northbound, just n on 14th Ave, w on Morrison St, then s; exit Couch St/Burnside St southbound; at SW 15th Ave and Yamhill St. Int corridors. **Pets:** Accepted. SAVE 📶 ✕ 📶 📺 🍽

Hotel Fifty H ❖

(503) 221-0711. **$129-$369.** 50 SW Morrison St 97204. At Morrison St and Naito Pkwy (formerly Front Ave). Int corridors. **Pets:** Medium, dogs only. $50 one-time fee/room. Designated rooms, service with restrictions, supervision.

SAVE 📶 ✕ 📶 🛏 📺 🍽

Hotel Lucia H

(503) 225-1717. **$139-$279.** 400 SW Broadway 97205. At SW Broadway and Stark St. Int corridors. **Pets:** Accepted.

SAVE 📶 ✕ 📶 📺 🍽

Hotel Monaco Portland H

(503) 222-0001. **$149-$309.** 506 SW Washington St 97204. At SW 5th Ave and SW Washington St. Int corridors. **Pets:** Accepted.

ECO SAVE 📶 📶 📺 🍽 ✕

Hotel Vintage Plaza H ❖

(503) 228-1212. **$139-$259.** 422 SW Broadway 97205. At Broadway and Washington St. Int corridors. **Pets:** Designated rooms, service with restrictions, supervision. ECO SAVE 📶 ✕ 📺 🍽

La Quinta Inn & Suites Portland Airport H

(503) 382-3820. **$63-$137.** 11207 NE Holman St 97220. I-205 exit 24B northbound; exit 24 southbound, 0.4 mi e on Airport Way, then just sw. Int corridors. **Pets:** Medium, other species. Service with restrictions, supervision. 📶 ✕ 📶 🛏 📺 🏊

La Quinta Inn & Suites Portland NW-Downtown H

(503) 497-9044. **$75-$148.** 4319 NW Yeon Ave 97210. I-5 to I-405 exit 3 (US 30), 2.5 mi w. Int corridors. **Pets:** Medium, other species. Service with restrictions, supervision. 📶 ✕ 🛏 📺 🏊

La Quinta Inn Portland Convention Center H

(503) 233-7933. **$103-$175.** 431 NE Multnomah St 97232. I-5 exit 302A, just e on NE Weidler St, just s on NE Martin Luther King Jr Blvd, then just e. Int corridors. **Pets:** Medium, other species. Service with restrictions, supervision. 📶 ✕ 🛏 📺 🏊

The Mark Spencer Hotel H ❖

(503) 224-3293. **$99-$249.** 409 SW 11th Ave 97205. At SW Stark St and SW 11th Ave. Int corridors. **Pets:** Other species. $15 daily fee/pet. Designated rooms, service with restrictions, crate.

ECO SAVE 📶 ✕ 🛏 📺

Motel 6 #4463 M

(503) 234-4391. **Call for rates.** 518 NE Holladay St 97232. I-5 exit 302A, just e on NE Weidler St, just s on NE Martin Luther King Jr Blvd, then just e. Ext corridors. **Pets:** Other species. Service with restrictions, supervision. SAVE 📶 🛏

▼ Motel 6 North Portland #4198 �H
(503) 247-3700. **$49-$80.** 1125 N Schmeer Rd 97217. I-5 exit 306B, 0.4 mi s on N Whitaker Rd, then just e. Int corridors. **Pets:** Other species. Service with restrictions, supervision. 🛜 🍽

AAA ▼▼ ▼▼ The Nines �H ❀
(503) 222-9996. **$169-$599.** 525 SW Morrison St 97204. At SW Morrison St and SW 5th Ave. Int corridors. **Pets:** Small, dogs only. $30 daily fee/room. Supervision. ᴇᴄᴏ SAVE 🛜 ✖ ᴍ 🍽

▼▼ ▼▼ Oxford Suites �H ❀
(503) 283-3030. **$85-$179.** 12226 N Jantzen Dr 97217. I-5 exit 308, just e on Hayden Island Dr. Int corridors. **Pets:** $25 one-time fee/room. Service with restrictions, crate. 🛜 ✖ ᴍ 🍽 🖥 ✖

AAA ▼▼ Park Lane Suites and Inn M
(503) 226-6288. **$99-$199.** 809 SW King Ave 97205. I-405 exit Couch St/Burnside St southbound, 0.5 mi w on Burnside St, then just s; exit Everett St northbound, 0.3 mi w on Glisan St, just s on NW 21st Ave, just w on Burnside St, then just s. Ext corridors. **Pets:** Accepted.
SAVE 🛜 ✖ ᴍ 🍽 🖥

AAA ▼▼ ▼▼ The Portlander Inn �H
(503) 345-0300. **$80-$120.** 10350 N Vancouver Way 97217. I-5 exit 307, follow signs for Marine Dr E, just ne, then 0.7 mi se. Int corridors. **Pets:** Accepted. SAVE 🛜 🍽 🖥 🍴 ✖

AAA ▼▼ ▼▼ Ramada Portland Airport �H
(503) 255-6511. **$47-$109.** 6221 NE 82nd Ave 97220. I-205 exit 23B (Killingsworth St), just w on Columbia Blvd, then just n on 80th Ave. Int corridors. **Pets:** Small. $20 daily fee/pet. Service with restrictions, supervision. SAVE 🛜 ᴍ 🍽 🖥 🍴 🖥 ✖

▼▼ ▼▼ Ramada Portland South I-205 �H
(503) 252-7400. **Call for rates.** 9707 SE Stark St 97216. I-205 exit 21A southbound, just e on Washington St, just n on SE 99th Ave, then just w. Int corridors. **Pets:** Medium. $25 one-time fee/room. Service with restrictions, supervision. 🛜 ✖ ᴍ 🍽 🖥

AAA ▼▼ ▼▼ Red Lion Hotel on the River Jantzen Beach-Portland �H
(503) 283-4466. **$99-$189.** 909 N Hayden Island Dr 97217. I-5 exit 308, just ne. Int corridors. **Pets:** Accepted.
ᴇᴄᴏ SAVE 🛜 ✖ ᴍ 🍽 🖥 🍴 🖥 ✖

▼▼ ▼▼ Red Lion Hotel Portland Airport �H
(503) 255-6722. **Call for rates.** 7101 NE 82nd Ave 97220. I-205 exit 24A northbound; exit 24 southbound, 1.3 mi w on NE Airport Way, then 0.5 mi s. Ext/int corridors. **Pets:** Accepted.
🛜 ✖ 🍽 🖥 🍴 🖥

AAA ▼▼ ▼▼ Red Lion Hotel Portland-Convention Center �H
(503) 235-2100. **$129-$199.** 1021 NE Grand Ave 97232. I-5 exit 302A, just e on NE Weidler St, just s on NE Martin Luther King Jr Blvd, then just e. Int corridors. **Pets:** Accepted. SAVE 🛜 ✖ 🍽 🖥 🍴

▼▼ ▼▼ Residence Inn by Marriott Portland Airport at Cascade Station �H
(503) 284-1800. **$113-$161.** 9301 NE Cascades Pkwy 97220. I-205 exit 24A northbound; exit 24 southbound, 0.5 mi w on Airport Way, 0.5 mi s on NE Mt Hood Ave, then just w. Int corridors. **Pets:** Accepted.
🛜 ✖ 🍽 🖥 🖥 ✖

▼▼ ▼▼ Residence Inn by Marriott Portland Downtown/Lloyd Center �H ❀
(503) 288-1400. **$113-$189.** 1710 NE Multnomah St 97232. I-5 exit 302A, 0.8 mi e on Weidler St, just s on 15th Ave; I-84 exit 1 (Lloyd Center) westbound, just n on 13th St, then just e. Ext corridors. **Pets:** Other species. $75 one-time fee/room. Service with restrictions, crate. 🛜 ✖ ᴍ 🍽 🖥 🖥 ✖

▼▼ ▼▼ Residence Inn by Marriott-Portland North Harbour �H
(503) 285-9888. **$93-$123.** 1250 N Anchor Way 97217. I-5 exit 307, follow signs to Marine Dr E, then just n. Int corridors. **Pets:** Accepted.
🛜 ✖ ᴍ 🍽 🖥 🖥 ✖

▼▼ ▼▼ Residence Inn Portland Downtown at RiverPlace �H
(503) 552-9500. **$99-$249.** 2115 SW River Pkwy 97201. At SW Moody Ave and SW River Pkwy; on Willamette River Waterfront. Int corridors. **Pets:** Accepted. 🛜 ✖ 🍽 🖥 🖥 ✖

AAA ▼▼ ▼▼ Sheraton Portland Airport Hotel �H ❀
(503) 281-2500. **$109-$309.** 8235 NE Airport Way 97220. I-205 exit 24A northbound; exit 24 southbound, 1.5 mi w. Int corridors. **Pets:** Medium, dogs only. $50 one-time fee/room. Service with restrictions.
SAVE 🛜 ✖ ᴍ 🍽 🍴 🖥 ✖

AAA ▼▼ ▼▼ Shilo Inn-Portland/Rose Garden �H
(503) 736-6300. **$79-$150.** 1506 NE 2nd Ave 97232. I-5 exit 302A, just e on NE Weidler St, then just s. Int corridors. **Pets:** Dogs only. $25 one-time fee/room. Designated rooms, service with restrictions, crate.
SAVE 🛜 ✖ 🍽 🖥

AAA ▼▼ ▼▼ Shilo Inn Suites Hotel-Portland Airport �H
(503) 252-7500. **$89-$179.** 11707 NE Airport Way 97220. I-205 exit 24B northbound; exit 24 southbound, 0.5 mi e. Int corridors. **Pets:** Dogs only. $25 one-time fee/room. Designated rooms, service with restrictions, crate.
SAVE 🛜 🍽 🖥 🍴 🖥 ✖

▼▼ ▼▼ Staybridge Suites Portland-Airport �H
(503) 262-8888. **$119-$159.** 11936 NE Glenn Widing Dr 97220. I-205 exit 24B northbound; exit 24 southbound, 0.7 mi e, then just nw. Int corridors. **Pets:** Medium, dogs only. $75 one-time fee/pet. Service with restrictions, supervision. 🛜 ✖ ᴍ 🍽 🖥 🖥 ✖

AAA ▼▼ ◈ University Place Hotel & Conference Center �H
(503) 221-0140. **$89-$169.** 310 SW Lincoln St 97201. I-5 to I-405 exit 4th Ave, just n, then just e. Ext/int corridors. **Pets:** Accepted.
SAVE 🛜 ✖ 🍽 🖥 🍴 🖥

AAA ▼▼ ▼▼ The Westin Portland �H
(503) 294-9000. **$159-$369.** 750 SW Alder St 97205. At Park Ave and SW Alder St. Int corridors. **Pets:** Accepted.
SAVE 🛜 ✖ ᴍ 🍽 🍴

TIGARD

AAA ▼▼ ▼▼ Embassy Suites Hotel-Portland Washington Square �H ❀
(503) 644-4000. **$109-$189.** 9000 SW Washington Square Rd 97223. SR 217 exit 4 (Progress/Scholls Ferry Rd), just ne on SW Scholls Ferry Rd, just e on SW Hall Blvd, then just s. Int corridors. **Pets:** Small, dogs only. $25 one-time fee/room. Designated rooms, service with restrictions, supervision. SAVE 🛜 ᴍ 🍽 🖥 🍴 🖥

▼▼ ▼▼ Homestead Studio Suites Hotel Portland-Tigard �H ❀
(503) 670-0555. **$76-$91.** 13009 SW 68th Pkwy 97223. I-5 exit 293 (Haines St) southbound, 0.5 mi s on SW 68th Ave; exit 293 northbound, just w on Atlanta Ave, then 0.7 mi s; SR 217 exit 7 (72nd Ave), just ne, just e on Hampton St, then just s. Ext corridors. **Pets:** Other species. $25 daily fee/pet. Service with restrictions. 🛜 🍽 🖥

AAA ▼▼ ▼▼ Phoenix Inn Suites-Tigard �H
(503) 624-9000. **$99-$159.** 9575 SW Locust St 97223. SR 217 exit 5 (Greenburg Rd), just ne on SW Greenburg Rd, then just e. Int corridors. **Pets:** Small, other species. $25 one-time fee/pet. Designated rooms, service with restrictions, supervision. SAVE 🛜 ᴍ 🍽 🖥 🖥 ✖

▼▼ ◈ Shilo Inn-Tigard/Washington Square �H
(503) 620-4320. **$69-$199.** 10830 SW Greenburg Rd 97223. SR 217 exit 5 (Greenburg Rd), just sw. Int corridors. **Pets:** Dogs only. $25 one-time fee/room. Designated rooms, service with restrictions, crate.
🛜 ✖ 🍽 🖥 ✖

TROUTDALE

AAA ▼▼▼ **Comfort Inn & Suites, Columbia Gorge West** H

(503) 669-6500. **$86-$165.** 477 NW Phoenix Dr 97060. I-84 exit 17, just s off Frontage Rd; south side of interstate. Int corridors. **Pets:** Accepted.

SAVE 🛜 ✕ 🛏 🖵 🌊

▼▼ **Holiday Inn Express-Portland East** H

(503) 492-2900. **$99-$129.** 1000 NW Graham Rd 97060. I-84 exit 17 eastbound, e on Frontage Rd, then just n; exit westbound, just n. Int corridors. **Pets:** Accepted. 🛜 🛏 🖵

▼ **Motel 6-Portland Troutdale - 407** M

(503) 665-2254. **$43-$55.** 1610 NW Frontage Rd 97060. I-84 exit 17 eastbound, just sw; exit westbound, just w on Frontage Rd, then just sw. Ext corridors. **Pets:** Other species. Service with restrictions, supervision.

🛜 ♿ 🛏 🖵

TUALATIN

AAA ▼▼▼ **Comfort Inn & Suites** H ❀

(503) 612-9952. **$89-$199.** 7640 SW Warm Springs St 97062. I-5 exit 289, just w on Nyberg St, just s on Martinazzi Ave, then just e; just behind Fred Meyer. Int corridors. **Pets:** Medium, dogs only. $15 daily fee/pet. Designated rooms, service with restrictions, supervision.

SAVE 🛜 ✕ ♿ 🛏 🖵 🌊

WILSONVILLE

▼▼ **GuestHouse Inn & Suites** H

(503) 682-9000. **$56-$69.** 8855 SW Citizens Dr 97070. I-5 exit 283, just e on Wilsonville Rd, just n on Town Center Loop West, then just w. Int corridors. **Pets:** Accepted. 🛜 🛏 🖵

AAA ▼▼▼ **Holiday Inn-Wilsonville** H ❀

(503) 682-2211. **$69-$139.** 25425 SW 95th Ave 97070. I-5 exit 286, just w on Boones Ferry Rd, then just se. Int corridors. **Pets:** Medium. $15 daily fee/room. Designated rooms, service with restrictions, supervision.

SAVE 🛜 ✕ 🛏 🖵 🍴 🌊

AAA ▼▼▼ **La Quinta Inn Wilsonville** H

(503) 682-3184. **$74-$160.** 8815 SW Sun Pl 97070. I-5 exit 286, just e on Elligsen Rd, just n on Parkway Ave, then just w. Int corridors. **Pets:** Medium, other species. Service with restrictions, supervision.

SAVE 🛜 ✕ ♿ 🛏 🖵 🌊

AAA ▼▼▼ **Quality Inn Wilsonville & Conference Center** H

(503) 682-2288. **$69-$109.** 30800 SW Parkway Ave 97070. I-5 exit 283, just e on Wilsonville Rd, just s on Town Center Loop W, just w on Main St, then 0.4 mi s. Int corridors. **Pets:** Large, other species. $10 daily fee/pet. Designated rooms, service with restrictions, supervision.

SAVE 🛜 🛏 🖵 🌊

AAA ▼▼▼ **Super 8 - Wilsonville** H

(503) 682-2088. **Call for rates.** 25438 SW Parkway Ave 97070. I-5 exit 286, just e on Elligsen Rd, then just n. Int corridors. **Pets:** Accepted.

SAVE 🛜 🛏 🖵

AAA ▼▼▼ **Wilsonville Inn & Suites** H

(503) 570-9700. **$69-$159, 3 day notice.** 29769 SW Boones Ferry Rd 97070. I-5 exit 283, just w on Wilsonville Rd, then just n. Int corridors. **Pets:** Accepted. SAVE 🛜 ♿ 🛏 🖵 🌊 ✕

END METROPOLITAN AREA

PORT ORFORD

▼ **Castaway by the Sea** M

(541) 332-4502. **Call for rates.** 545 W 5th St 97465. Jct US 101, 1 blk w on Harbor Dr, 1 blk n. Ext corridors. **Pets:** Accepted.

🛜 ✕ 🛏 🖵 AC

PRINEVILLE

AAA ▼▼▼ **Best Western Prineville Inn** H

(541) 447-8080. **$78-$116.** 1475 NE 3rd St 97754. 0.8 mi e on US 26. Int corridors. **Pets:** Small, dogs only. $15 daily fee/room. Designated rooms, service with restrictions, supervision.

SAVE 🛜 ✕ ♿ 🛏 🖵 🌊

▼ **Econo Lodge** M

(541) 447-6231. **$56-$100.** 123 NE 3rd St 97754. Downtown. Int corridors. **Pets:** Accepted. 🛜 🛏 🖵

▼▼▼ **Stafford Inn** H ❀

(541) 447-7100. **$82-$117.** 1773 NE 3rd St 97754. 1 mi e on US 26. Int corridors. **Pets:** $20 one-time fee/room. Service with restrictions, supervision. 🛜 ♿ 🛏 🖵 🌊

PROSPECT

▼▼ **Prospect Historic Hotel-Motel & Dinner House** M ❀

(541) 560-3664. **$70-$205, 7 day notice.** 391 Mill Creek Dr 97536. Jct SR 62 (0.7 mi e of MM 43), 0.3 mi s on 1st St, then just w. Ext/int corridors. **Pets:** Other species. $15 one-time fee/pet. Designated rooms, supervision. 🛜 ✕ 🛏 🖵 🍴 ✕

REDMOND

▼▼▼ **Comfort Suites-Redmond Airport** H

(541) 504-8900. **$88-$159.** 2243 SW Yew Ave 97756. US 97 exit 124 (Yew Ave/Airport Way/Redmond Airport), just nw; 2 mi s of jct SR 126. Int corridors. **Pets:** $27 one-time fee/room. Service with restrictions, supervision. 🛜 ✕ 🛏 🖵 🌊

AAA ▼ **Motel 6 Redmond #4076** H

(541) 923-2100. **$60-$100.** 2247 S US 97 97756. 1.1 mi s on US 97 from jct SR 126, just w. Int corridors. **Pets:** Other species. Service with restrictions, supervision. ECO SAVE 🛜 ♿ 🛏

AAA ▼▼▼ **Redmond Inn** M ❀

(541) 548-1091. **$45-$125.** 1545 S US 97 97756. Jct SR 126, 0.7 mi s. Ext corridors. **Pets:** Medium. $7 daily fee/pet. Designated rooms, service with restrictions, supervision. SAVE 🛜 🛏 🖵

AAA ▼▼▼ **Sleep Inn & Suites-Redmond** H ❀

(541) 504-1500. **$89-$119.** 1847 NW US 97 97756. US 97 exit 119, 0.6 mi s on Business Rt US 97; 1 mi n of downtown. Int corridors. **Pets:** Medium. $10 daily fee/pet. Service with restrictions, crate.

SAVE 🛜 ✕ ♿ 🛏 🖵 🌊

REEDSPORT

AAA ▼▼▼ **Best Western Plus Salbasgeon Inn & Suites of Reedsport** H

(541) 271-4831. **$99-$235.** 1400 US 101 S 97467. Jct SR 38, 0.4 mi s. Ext corridors. **Pets:** Small, dogs only. $15 daily fee/pet. Designated rooms, service with restrictions, supervision. SAVE 🛜 🛏 🖵 🌊

AAA ▼▼▼ **Salbasgeon Inn of the Umpqua** M

(541) 271-2025. **$85-$325.** 45209 SR 38 97467. Jct US 101, 7.5 mi e. Ext corridors. **Pets:** Accepted. SAVE ✕ 🛏 🖵

ROCKAWAY BEACH

AAA ▼▼▼ **Silver Sands Oceanfront Motel** H ❀

(503) 355-2206. **$72-$166.** 215 S Pacific St 97136. US 101, just w on SW 2nd Ave. Ext corridors. **Pets:** Dogs only. $10 daily fee/pet. Designated rooms, service with restrictions, supervision.

SAVE 🛜 🛏 🖵 🌊 ✕ AC

AAA ▼▼▼ Tradewinds Motel M
(503) 355-2112. **$58-$169, 7 day notice.** 523 N Pacific St 97136. US 101, just w on NW 6th Ave, just s. Ext corridors. **Pets:** Large, dogs only. $15 daily fee/pet. Designated rooms, service with restrictions, supervision.
SAVE 🛰 ✕ 📠 💻 📶

ROSEBURG

AAA ▼▼▼ Best Western Garden Villa Inn M 🐾
(541) 672-1601. **$80-$130.** 760 NW Garden Valley Blvd 97471. I-5 exit 125, just nw. Ext corridors. **Pets:** Large, other species. $15 daily fee/room. Service with restrictions, supervision.
SAVE 🛰 ✕ 📠 💻 🏊

▼▼▼ Holiday Inn Express H 🐾
(541) 673-7517. **Call for rates.** 375 W Harvard Blvd 97470. I-5 exit 124, just se. Ext/int corridors. **Pets:** $15 one-time fee/room. Designated rooms, service with restrictions, supervision. 🛰 ✕ ♿ 📠 💻 🏊

▼ Motel 6 #4108 H
(541) 464-8000. **$49-$82.** 3100 NW Aviation Dr 97470. I-5 exit 127, just se. Int corridors. **Pets:** Other species. Service with restrictions, supervision. 🛰 ♿ 📠

AAA ▼▼ Quality Inn M
(541) 673-5561. **$63-$110.** 427 NW Garden Valley Blvd 97470. I-5 exit 125, just se. Ext corridors. **Pets:** Dogs only. $50 deposit/room, $10 daily fee/room. Designated rooms, service with restrictions, supervision.
SAVE 🛰 📠 💻 🏊

AAA ▼▼ Roseburg Travelodge M 🐾
(541) 672-4836. **$63-$90.** 315 W Harvard Ave 97470. I-5 exit 124, just se. Ext corridors. **Pets:** $10 daily fee/pet. Designated rooms, service with restrictions, supervision. SAVE 🛰 📠 💻 🏊

AAA ▼ Shady Oaks Motel M 🐾
(541) 672-2608. **$45-$79.** 2954 Old Hwy 99 S 97471. I-5 exit 120, 0.5 mi n. Ext corridors. **Pets:** Medium, dogs only. $10 daily fee/pet. Designated rooms, service with restrictions, supervision. SAVE 🛰 📠

▼▼ Sleep Inn & Suites H
(541) 464-8338. **$65-$95.** 2855 NW Edenbower Blvd 97471. I-5 exit 127, just sw. Int corridors. **Pets:** Large. $10 one-time fee/room. Service with restrictions, crate. 🛰 ♿ 📠 💻 🏊

▼▼ Super 8 H
(541) 672-8880. **$54-$85.** 3200 NW Aviation Dr 97470. I-5 exit 127, just ne. Int corridors. **Pets:** $10 daily fee/room. Service with restrictions, supervision. 🛰 ♿ 📠 💻 🏊

AAA ▼▼ Windmill Inn of Roseburg H 🐾
(541) 673-0901. **$76-$109.** 1450 NW Mulholland Dr 97470. I-5 exit 125, just ne. Int corridors. **Pets:** Other species. Designated rooms, service with restrictions, supervision. SAVE 🛰 ✕ 📠 💻 🏊 ✕

ST. HELENS

AAA ▼▼ Best Western Oak Meadows Inn H
(503) 397-3000. **$100-$126.** 585 S Columbia River Hwy (US 30) 97051. South end of town. Int corridors. **Pets:** Accepted.
SAVE 🛰 ✕ 📠 💻 🏊

SALEM

AAA ▼▼▼ Best Western Pacific Highway Inn H 🐾
(503) 390-3200. **$86-$106.** 4646 Portland Rd NE 97305. I-5 exit 258, 0.3 mi e. Ext corridors. **Pets:** Dogs only. $20 daily fee/room. Designated rooms, service with restrictions, supervision. SAVE 🛰 📠 💻 🏊

AAA ▼▼▼ Best Western Plus Mill Creek Inn H 🐾
(503) 585-3332. **$112-$163.** 3125 Ryan Dr SE 97301. I-5 exit 253, just w on Mission St (SR 22), just n on Hawthorne Ave SE, then just w. Int corridors. **Pets:** Large, dogs only. $20 daily fee/room. Supervision.
SAVE 🛰 ✕ 📠 💻 🏊 ✕

▼▼▼ Comfort Suites Airport H
(503) 585-9705. **$95-$175.** 630 Hawthorne Ave SE 97301. I-5 exit 253, just w on Mission St (SR 22), 0.4 mi n on Hawthorne Ave SE, then just e. Int corridors. **Pets:** Accepted. 🛰 ✕ ♿ 📠 💻 🏊 ✕

▼▼ Crossland Studios Salem North M 🐾
(503) 363-7557. **$60-$75.** 3535 Fisher Rd NE 97305. I-5 exit 258, just e on Portland Rd NE, 0.3 mi s on Ward Dr, then 0.8 mi s. Ext corridors. **Pets:** Other species. $25 daily fee/pet. Service with restrictions.
🛰 📠 💻

AAA ▼▼ Days Inn Black Bear H 🐾
(503) 581-1559. **$59-$86.** 1600 Motor Ct NE 97301. I-5 exit 256, just e on Market St NE, then just s. Ext corridors. **Pets:** Medium. $11 daily fee/room. Designated rooms, service with restrictions, supervision.
SAVE 🛰 📠 💻 🏊 ✕

AAA ▼▼ Howard Johnson Inn H
(503) 375-7710. **$49-$79.** 2250 Mission St SE 97302. I-5 exit 253, 1.4 mi w. Int corridors. **Pets:** Small, dogs only. $15 daily fee/pet. Designated rooms, service with restrictions, supervision.
SAVE 🛰 ✕ 📠 💻 🏊

AAA ▼▼ La Quinta Inn & Suites Salem H
(503) 391-7000. **$93-$154.** 890 Hawthorne Ave SE 97301. I-5 exit 253, just w on Mission St (SR 22), then just n. Int corridors. **Pets:** Medium, other species. Service with restrictions, supervision.
SAVE 🛰 ✕ ♿ 📠 💻 🏊

AAA ▼▼▼ Phoenix Inn Suites-North Salem H
(503) 581-7004. **Call for rates.** 1590 Weston Ct NE 97301. I-5 exit 256, just w on Market St, then just s. Int corridors. **Pets:** Accepted.
SAVE 🛰 ♿ 📠 💻 🏊

AAA ▼▼ Phoenix Inn Suites-South Salem H 🐾
(503) 588-9220. **$89-$139.** 4370 Commercial St SE 97302. I-5 exit 252, 1.5 mi w on Kuebler Rd, then 0.7 mi n. Int corridors. **Pets:** Medium, other species. $20 daily fee/room. Designated rooms, service with restrictions.
SAVE 🛰 ♿ 📠 💻 🏊 ✕

▼▼ Red Lion Hotel Salem H
(503) 370-7888. **$124-$169.** 3301 Market St NE 97301. I-5 exit 256, just w. Int corridors. **Pets:** Accepted.
SAVE 🛰 ✕ ♿ 📠 💻 🍴 🏊

▼▼▼ Residence Inn by Marriott H
(503) 585-6500. **$110-$150.** 640 Hawthorne Ave SE 97301. I-5 exit 253, just w on Mission St (SR 22), 0.4 mi n on Hawthorne Ave SE, then just e. Int corridors. **Pets:** Accepted. 🛰 ✕ ♿ 📠 💻 🏊 ✕

AAA ▼▼ Shilo Inn Suites-Salem H
(503) 581-4001. **$81-$130.** 3304 Market St NE 97301. I-5 exit 256, just w. Int corridors. **Pets:** Dogs only. $25 one-time fee/room. Designated rooms, service with restrictions, crate.
SAVE 🛰 ✕ 📠 💻 🏊 ✕

▼▼ Super 8 Salem H
(503) 370-8888. **$54-$67.** 1288 Hawthorne Ave NE 97301. I-5 exit 256, just w on Market St, then just s. Int corridors. **Pets:** Accepted.
🛰 📠 💻 🏊

AAA ▼ Travelodge Salem Capital M
(503) 581-2466. **$49-$69.** 1555 State St 97301. I-5 exit 253, 1.8 mi w on Mission St (SR 22), 0.4 mi n on 17th St SE, then just w. Ext corridors. **Pets:** Medium. $10 daily fee/pet. Designated rooms, service with restrictions, supervision. SAVE 🛰 📠 💻 🏊

SANDY

AAA ▼▼ Best Western Sandy Inn H 🐾
(503) 668-7100. **$80-$152.** 37465 US 26 97055. West side of town. Int corridors. **Pets:** Medium, dogs only. $20 daily fee/room. Service with restrictions, crate. SAVE 🛰 ✕ 📠 💻 🏊

SEASIDE

Best Western Ocean View Resort H ❖
(503) 738-3334. **$79-$269, 3 day notice.** 414 N Prom 97138. US 101 exit 1st Ave, just w, just n on Necanicum Dr, then just w on 4th Ave. Ext/int corridors. **Pets:** Medium, dogs only. $20 one-time fee/room. Designated rooms, service with restrictions.
SAVE ⊗ ⊗ 🖥 💻 🍴 ➳

Comfort Inn & Suites by Seaside Convention Center/Boardwalk H ❖
(503) 738-3011. **$89-$399.** 545 Broadway St 97138. US 101, just w on Ave A; downtown. Int corridors. **Pets:** Medium, dogs only. $25 daily fee/pet. Designated rooms, service with restrictions, supervision.
SAVE ⊗ ⊗ 📶 🖥 💻 ➳

Ebb-Tide Resort H
(503) 738-8371. **$120-$220, 3 day notice.** 300 N Prom 97138. US 101 exit 1st Ave, 0.4 mi w, just n on Columbia St, then just w on 2nd Ave. Ext/int corridors. **Pets:** Medium, other species. $20 one-time fee/pet. Designated rooms, service with restrictions, supervision.
SAVE ⊗ 🖥 💻 ➳ ⊗ ℀

Holiday Inn Express Hotel & Suites-Seaside Convention Center H
(503) 717-8000. **$89-$249, 3 day notice.** 34 N Holladay Dr 97138. US 101 exit Broadway St, just w, then just n. Int corridors. **Pets:** Medium, dogs only. $25 daily fee/pet. Designated rooms, service with restrictions, supervision.
SAVE ⊗ ⊗ 📶 🖥 💻 ➳ ⊗

Inn at Seaside H ❖
(503) 738-9581. **$65-$209, 3 day notice.** 441 2nd Ave 97138. US 101 exit 1st Ave, then just w. Ext/int corridors. **Pets:** Other species. $15 daily fee/pet. No service. SAVE ⊗ ⊗ 🖥 💻

Inn At The Shore M ❖
(503) 738-3113. **$69-$249, 3 day notice.** 2275 S Prom 97138. US 101 exit Ave U, just w. Ext corridors. **Pets:** $20 one-time fee/pet. Designated rooms, supervision. ⊗ ⊗ 🖥 💻 ℀

Microtel Inn & Suites H
(503) 738-8971. **$53-$98.** 2455 S Roosevelt Dr (US 101) 97138. Just s of downtown on US 101. Int corridors. **Pets:** Accepted.
⊗ ⊗ 📶 🖥 💻

Rivertide Suites H ❖
(503) 717-1100. **$95-$525, 3 day notice.** 102 N Holladay Dr 97138. US 101, just w on Broadway St, just n. Int corridors. **Pets:** Medium, dogs only. $25 daily fee/pet. Designated rooms, service with restrictions, supervision. SAVE ⊗ ⊗ 📶 🖥 💻 ➳

Seashore Inn...on the Beach H
(503) 738-6368. **$75-$249.** 60 N Prom 97138. US 101 exit 1st Ave, 0.4 mi w. Ext/int corridors. **Pets:** Small. $20 daily fee/pet. Designated rooms, service with restrictions, supervision. SAVE ⊗ 🖥 💻 ➳ ℀

The Seaside Oceanfront Inn & Restaurant H ❖
(503) 738-6403. **$99-$299, 5 day notice.** 581 S Prom 97138. US 101 exit Ave G, 0.6 mi w, then just n. Int corridors. **Pets:** Large. $25 one-time fee/pet. Designated rooms, service with restrictions, supervision.
⊗ ⊗ 💻 🍴

Shilo Inn Suites Oceanfront Hotel-Seaside H
(503) 738-9571. **$81-$400.** 30 N Prom 97138. US 101 exit Broadway St, 0.4 mi w. Ext corridors. **Pets:** Dogs only. $25 one-time fee/room. Designated rooms, service with restrictions, crate.
SAVE ⊗ ⊗ 🖥 💻 🍴 ➳ ⊗ ℀

SISTERS

Best Western Ponderosa Lodge H ❖
(541) 549-1234. **$100-$180, 7 day notice.** 500 US 20 W 97759. Jct SR 242; just w on US 20; at Barclay Dr; west end of town. Ext corridors. **Pets:** Large, other species. $15 daily fee/room. Designated rooms, service with restrictions, supervision. SAVE ⊗ ⊗ 🖥 💻 ➳

FivePine Lodge & Spa Resort CA
(541) 549-5900. **$149-$244, 7 day notice.** 1021 Desperado Tr 97759. Jct SR 126 and US 20, just e on US 20; east end of town. Int corridors. **Pets:** Accepted. SAVE ⊗ ⊗ 🖥 💻 🍴 ➳ ⊗

Sisters Inn & Suites M ❖
(541) 549-7829. **$109-$129.** 605 N Arrow Leaf Tr 97759. Just w on US 20 from jct SR 242; west end of town. Ext corridors. **Pets:** $15 one-time fee/room. Service with restrictions, supervision.
SAVE ⊗ ⊗ 📶 🖥 💻

SPRINGFIELD

Best Western Grand Manor Inn H
(541) 726-4769. **$99-$140.** 971 Kruse Way 97477. I-5 exit 195A, just se. Int corridors. **Pets:** Accepted. SAVE ⊗ 📶 🖥 💻 ➳

Comfort Suites Eugene/Springfield H
(541) 746-5359. **$109-$149.** 969 Kruse Way 97477. I-5 exit 195A, just se. Int corridors. **Pets:** Dogs only. $25 one-time fee/room. Designated rooms, service with restrictions, supervision. ⊗ ⊗ 🖥 💻 ➳

Holiday Inn Express Hotel & Suites H ❖
(541) 746-8471. **$119-$169.** 3480 Hutton St 97477. I-5 exit 195A, just se. Int corridors. **Pets:** $20 daily fee/pet. Designated rooms, service with restrictions, supervision. ⊗ ⊗ 🖥 💻 ➳

Motel 6 #418 M
(541) 741-1105. **$49-$65.** 3752 International Ct 97477. I-5 exit 195A, just e on Beltline Rd, just nw on Gateway St, then just n. Ext corridors. **Pets:** Other species. Service with restrictions, supervision.
ECO ⊗ 📶 🖥 ➳

Quality Inn & Suites H
(541) 726-9266. **$79-$129.** 3550 Gateway St 97477. I-5 exit 195A, just e on Beltline Rd, then just nw. Int corridors. **Pets:** Large, other species. $5 daily fee/pet. Designated rooms, supervision. ⊗ 📶 🖥 💻 ➳

Super 8 H
(541) 746-1314. **$63-$147.** 3315 Gateway St 97477. I-5 exit 195A, just e on Beltline Rd, then just s. Int corridors. **Pets:** Small. $22 one-time fee/pet. Designated rooms, service with restrictions, supervision.
SAVE ⊗ 🖥 💻

Village Inn M
(541) 747-4546. **$69-$79.** 1875 Mohawk Blvd 97477. I-5 exit 194A, 2.5 mi e on SR 126 exit Mohawk Blvd, then just n. Ext corridors. **Pets:** $10 daily fee/pet. Designated rooms, service with restrictions, supervision.
SAVE ⊗ 🖥 💻 ➳

SUNRIVER

Discover Sunriver Vacation Rentals VH
(541) 593-2482. **$99-$180, 60 day notice.** Sunriver Village Mall, Bldg #9 97707. US 97 exit 153 (S Century Dr), 2 mi w to Abbott Dr, then just n on Beaver Dr. Int corridors. **Pets:** Accepted.
SAVE ⊗ ⊗ 🖥 💻 ➳ ⊗

Sunriver Resort H
(541) 593-1000. **$139-$304, 21 day notice.** 17600 Center Dr 97707. US 97 exit 153 (S Century Dr), 1.5 mi w to Abbott Dr, then 0.6 mi w. Ext corridors. **Pets:** Accepted. SAVE ⊗ 🖥 💻 🍴 ➳ ⊗

SUTHERLIN

Best Western Plus Hartford Lodge H
(541) 459-1424. **$120-$150.** 150 Myrtle St 97479. I-5 exit 136, just ne. Ext corridors. **Pets:** Accepted. SAVE ⊗ ⊗ 🖥 💻 ➳

Microtel Inn & Suites H ❖
(541) 459-6800. **$53-$80.** 1400 Hospitality Pl 97479. I-5 exit 136, just se. Int corridors. **Pets:** Other species. $10 daily fee/room. Designated rooms, service with restrictions, supervision. ⊗ 📶 🖥

SWEET HOME

AAA ◈◈ Sweet Home Inn **M**
(541) 367-5137. **$69-$155.** 805 Long St 97386. Just e of jct US 20 and SR 228; just s on 10th Ave, then just w. Ext corridors. **Pets:** Medium, dogs only. $15 daily fee/pet. Service with restrictions, supervision.
SAVE 🛜 🖥 📺

THE DALLES

◈◈ Celilo Inn **M**
(541) 769-0001. **Call for rates.** 3550 E 2nd St 97058. I-84 exit 87, just s on US 197, just w on US 30, then 0.8 mi ne on SE Frontage Rd/E 2nd St. Ext corridors. **Pets:** Accepted. 🛜 ✕ 🖥 📺 ⊛

◈◈ Comfort Inn Columbia Gorge **H**
(541) 298-2800. **$104-$220.** 351 Lone Pine Dr 97058. I-84 exit 87, just nw. Int corridors. **Pets:** Accepted. 🛜 ✕ 🖥 📺 ⊛ ✕

◈◈ Cousins' Country Inn **H** 🐾
(541) 298-5161. **$89-$189.** 2114 W 6th St 97058. I-84 exit 83 eastbound, just nw; exit 84 westbound, just nw on W 2nd St, just sw on Webber St, then just n. Ext corridors. **Pets:** Dogs only. $10 daily fee/pet. Designated rooms, service with restrictions, supervision.
🛜 ♿ 🖥 📺 🍴 ⊛

◈◈ The Dalles Inn **H** 🐾
(541) 296-9107. **$84-$169.** 112 W 2nd St 97058. I-84 exit 84 eastbound, 0.6 mi se; exit 85 westbound, 0.8 mi nw; at Liberty and W 2nd sts; downtown. Ext/int corridors. **Pets:** Dogs only. $10 daily fee/pet. Designated rooms, crate. 🛜 🖥 📺 ⊛

◈ Motel 6 #4268 **H**
(541) 296-1191. **Call for rates.** 2500 W 6th St 97058. I-84 exit 83 eastbound, just nw; exit 84 westbound, just nw on W 2nd St, just sw on Webber St, then just n. Int corridors. **Pets:** Other species. Service with restrictions, supervision. 🛜 🖥 ⊛

AAA ◈◈ Shilo Inn Suites Hotel-The Dalles **H**
(541) 298-5502. **$80-$189.** 3223 Bret Clodfelter Way 97058. I-84 exit 87, just ne. Int corridors. **Pets:** Dogs only. $25 one-time fee/room. Designated rooms, service with restrictions, crate.
SAVE 🛜 ✕ 🖥 📺 🍴 ⊛ ✕

◈◈ Super 8 **H**
(541) 296-6888. **$58-$90.** 609 Cherry Heights Rd 97058. I-84 exit 84 eastbound, just se on W 2nd St, then just sw; exit 84 westbound, just nw on W 2nd St, just sw on Webber St, then just se on W 8th St. Int corridors. **Pets:** Accepted. 🛜 🖥 📺 ⊛

TILLAMOOK

AAA ◈◈◈ Ashley Inn of Tillamook **H**
(503) 842-7599. **$90-$200.** 1722 N Makinster Rd 97141. 1 mi n on US 101. Int corridors. **Pets:** Small. $20 daily fee/pet. Designated rooms, service with restrictions, supervision. SAVE 🛜 ✕ 🖥 📺 ⊛ ✕

◈ Mar-Clair Inn **M** 🐾
(503) 842-7571. **$86-$106.** 11 Main Ave 97141. US 101, just n of jct SR 6. Ext/int corridors. **Pets:** Small, dogs only. $10 daily fee/pet. Service with restrictions, supervision. 🛜 🖥 📺 🍴 ⊛ ✕

AAA ◈◈ Shilo Inn Suites Hotel-Tillamook **H**
(503) 842-7971. **$69-$199.** 2515 N Main Ave 97141. 1 mi n on US 101. Int corridors. **Pets:** Dogs only. $25 one-time fee/room. Designated rooms, service with restrictions, crate. SAVE 🛜 ✕ 🖥 📺 🖥 🍴 ⊛ ✕

WARRENTON

AAA ◈◈◈ Shilo Inn Suites Hotel - Warrenton/Astoria **H**
(503) 861-2181. **$69-$199.** 1609 E Harbor Dr 97146. On US 26/101; near west end of Youngs Bay Bridge. Int corridors. **Pets:** Dogs only. $25 one-time fee/room. Designated rooms, service, crate.
SAVE 🛜 ✕ 🖥 📺 🍴 ⊛ ✕

WELCHES

AAA ◈◈◈ The Resort at The Mountain **H** 🐾
(503) 622-3101. **$119-$379, 5 day notice.** 68010 E Fairway Ave 97067. 0.6 mi s of US 26 on E Welches Rd. Ext corridors. **Pets:** Medium, dogs only. $50 one-time fee/room. Designated rooms, service with restrictions, supervision. SAVE 🛜 ✕ 🖥 📺 🍴 ⊛ ✕

WHITE CITY

◈◈◈ La Quinta Inn & Suites White City **H**
(541) 826-0800. **$80-$144.** 2020 Leigh Way 97503. I-5 exit 30, 5.6 mi ne on Crater Lake Hwy (SR 62), then just w. Int corridors. **Pets:** Medium, other species. Service with restrictions, supervision.
🛜 ✕ ♿ 🖥 📺 ⊛

WOODBURN

AAA ◈◈◈ Best Western Woodburn **H** 🐾
(503) 982-6515. **$88-$113.** 2887 Newberg Hwy 97071. I-5 exit 271, just ne. Int corridors. **Pets:** Medium, dogs only. $10 daily fee/pet. Designated rooms, service with restrictions, supervision.
SAVE 🛜 ♿ 🖥 📺 ⊛

◈◈ La Quinta Inn & Suites Woodburn **H**
(503) 982-1727. **$71-$139.** 120 Arney Rd NE 97071. I-5 exit 271, just nw. Int corridors. **Pets:** Medium, other species. Service with restrictions, supervision. 🛜 🖥 📺 ⊛

◈◈ Super 8 - Woodburn **H**
(503) 981-8881. **$49-$72.** 821 Evergreen Rd 97071. I-5 exit 271, just se. Int corridors. **Pets:** Small, dogs only. $10 daily fee/pet. Service with restrictions, supervision. 🛜 🖥 📺 ⊛

YACHATS

AAA ◈◈ The Adobe Resort **H** 🐾
(541) 547-3141. **$75-$405.** 1555 US 101 97498. 0.5 mi n; just w of US 101. Int corridors. **Pets:** Other species. $10 daily fee/pet. Designated rooms, service with restrictions.
SAVE 🛜 ✕ 🖥 📺 🍴 ⊛ ✕ 🐾

◈ The Dublin House **M**
(541) 547-3703. **Call for rates.** 251 W 7th St 97498. US 101 at 7th St; downtown. Ext corridors. **Pets:** Dogs only. $10 daily fee/pet. Designated rooms, service with restrictions, supervision. 🛜 🖥 📺 ⊛ 🐾

AAA ◈◈ Fireside Motel **M** 🐾
(541) 547-3636. **$70-$160.** 1881 US 101 N 97498. 0.6 mi n; just w of US 101. Ext corridors. **Pets:** Other species. $10 daily fee/pet. Service with restrictions, supervision. SAVE 🛜 ✕ 🖥 📺 ✕ 🐾

PENNSYLVANIA

ABBOTTSTOWN

▽▽▽▽ The Altland House Inn and Suites 🅲🅸
(717) 259-9535. **Call for rates.** 35 Fleet St 17301. Jct SR 194. Int corridors. **Pets:** Accepted. 🛜 ⊠ 🛢 🍴

ALLENTOWN

🔺🔺🔺 ▽▽▽▽ Allentown Howard Johnson Inn & Suites 🅷
(610) 439-4000. **$62-$170.** 3220 Hamilton Blvd 18103. I-78 exit 54 (Hamilton Blvd), 0.8 mi n. Int corridors. **Pets:** Medium. $25 one-time fee/pet. Service with restrictions, supervision. 🆂🅰🆅🅴 🛜 🚹 🛢 🖵 🏊

▽▽▽▽ Comfort Inn Lehigh Valley-West 🅷
(610) 391-0344. **$79-$129.** 7625 Imperial Way 18106. I-78 exit 49B (SR 100), just n. Int corridors. **Pets:** Medium, other species. $25 one-time fee/room. Service with restrictions, crate. 🛜 🛢 🖵

🔺🔺🔺 ▽▽▽▽ Four Points by Sheraton Hotel & Suites
Allentown Airport 🅷
(610) 266-1000. **$79-$299.** 3400 Airport Rd 18109. On SR 987 N (Airport Rd), 0.5 mi n of jct US 22. Int corridors. **Pets:** Accepted.
🆂🅰🆅🅴 🛜 ⊠ 🚹 🛢 🖵 🍴 🏊

▽▽▽▽ Holiday Inn-Allentown Center City 🅷
(610) 433-2221. **$89-$159.** 904 Hamilton St 18101. At 9th and Hamilton sts; downtown. Int corridors. **Pets:** Other species. $50 one-time fee/pet. Service with restrictions. 🛜 🚹 🛢 🖵 🍴 🏊

🔺🔺🔺 ▽▽▽ Knights Inn 🅷
(610) 266-9070. **$49-$81.** 1880 Steelstone Rd 18109. US 22 exit Airport Rd S. Int corridors. **Pets:** Medium. $25 one-time fee/pet. Service with restrictions, supervision. 🆂🅰🆅🅴 🛜 🚹 🛢 🖵

🔺🔺🔺 ▽▽▽ Quality Inn-Allentown 🅷
(610) 435-7880. **Call for rates.** 1715 Plaza Ln 18104. US 22 exit 15th St, just n. Int corridors. **Pets:** Accepted. 🆂🅰🆅🅴 🛜 🚹 🛢 🖵

▽▽▽▽ Staybridge Suites Allentown Airport Lehigh
Valley 🅷
(610) 443-5000. **$89-$199.** 1787-A Airport Rd 18109. US 22 exit Airport Rd S, 0.3 mi s. Int corridors. **Pets:** Large, other species. $100 one-time fee/room. Service with restrictions. 🛜 🚹 🛢 🖵 🏊

ALTOONA

▽▽▽▽ Holiday Inn Express Altoona 🅷 🐾
(814) 944-9661. **Call for rates.** 3306 Pleasant Valley Blvd 16602. I-99/US 220 exit 32 (Frankstown Rd), 0.5 mi w, then just n. Int corridors. **Pets:** Small. $75 one-time fee/room. Designated rooms, service with restrictions, crate. 🛜 🚹 🛢 🖵

▽▽▽ Motel 6 #1415 🅼
(814) 946-7601. **$51-$61.** 1500 Sterling St 16602. I-99/US 220 exit 31 (Plank Rd), just w. Ext corridors. **Pets:** Other species. Service with restrictions, supervision. 🛜 🚹 🏊

▽▽▽ Super 8 Altoona 🅼
(814) 942-5350. **$53-$83.** 3535 Fairway Dr 16602. I-99/US 220 exit 32 (Frankstown Rd), just w. Int corridors. **Pets:** Medium. $15 daily fee/pet. Designated rooms, service with restrictions, supervision.
🛜 🚹 🛢 🖵

BARKEYVILLE

🔺🔺🔺 ▽▽▽ Comfort Inn-Barkeyville 🅼
(814) 786-7901. **Call for rates.** 137 Gibb Rd 16038. I-80 exit 29, just n on SR 8. Ext corridors. **Pets:** Accepted. 🆂🅰🆅🅴 🛜 🚹 🛢 🖵

BEDFORD

🔺🔺🔺 ▽▽▽ Best Western Bedford Inn 🅷 🐾
(814) 623-9006. **$77-$93.** 4517 Business Rt 220 15522. I-70/76 (Pennsylvania Tpke) exit 146, 0.3 mi n. Ext/int corridors. **Pets:** Other species. $15 daily fee/room. Supervision. 🆂🅰🆅🅴 🛜 🚹 🛢 🖵 🍴 🏊 ⊠

▽▽▽▽▽ Omni Bedford Springs Resort & Spa 🅷 🐾
(814) 623-8100. **$279-$459, 3 day notice.** 2138 Business Rt 220 15522. I-70/76 (Pennsylvania Tpke) exit 146, 3.9 mi s. Int corridors. **Pets:** Small. $50 one-time fee/room. Service with restrictions, crate. 🛜 ⊠ 🚹 🛢 🖵 🍴 🏊 ⊠

🔺🔺🔺 ▽▽▽ Quality Inn Bedford 🅷
(814) 623-5188. **$55-$155.** 4407 Business Rt 220 N 15522. I-70/76 (Pennsylvania Tpke) exit 146, just n. Ext/int corridors. **Pets:** Medium, other species. $20 one-time fee/room. Designated rooms, service with restrictions, supervision. 🆂🅰🆅🅴 🛜 🚹 🛢 🖵 🍴 🏊

BETHEL

Comfort Inn-Bethel/Midway H
(717) 933-8888. **$75-$125.** 41 Diner Dr 19507. I-78 exit 16, just w. Int corridors. **Pets:** Other species. $10 daily fee/pet. Designated rooms, service with restrictions, crate. SAVE

BETHLEHEM

Best Western Plus Lehigh Valley Hotel & Conference Center H
(610) 866-5800. **$99-$159.** 300 Gateway Dr 18017. US 22 exit Center St and SR 512. Ext/int corridors. **Pets:** $20 one-time fee/pet. Designated rooms, service with restrictions, supervision.

Comfort Inn H
(610) 865-6300. **$99-$149.** 3191 Highfield Dr 18020. US 22 exit SR 191, just s. Ext/int corridors. **Pets:** $10 daily fee/pet. Service with restrictions.

Comfort Suites H
(610) 882-9700. **$99-$199.** 120 W 3rd St 18015. SR 378 exit 3rd St, at W 3rd and Brodhead sts; center. Int corridors. **Pets:** Medium. $20 daily fee/room. Designated rooms, service with restrictions, crate.

Extended StayAmerica-Allentown/Bethlehem H
(610) 866-8480. **$73-$119.** 3050 Schoenersville Rd 18017. US 22 exit SR 378/Schoenersville Rd, follow signs for Schoenersville Rd, just n. Int corridors. **Pets:** Other species. $25 daily fee/pet. Service with restrictions.

Historic Hotel Bethlehem H
(610) 625-5000. **$129-$199.** 437 Main St 18018. SR 378 S exit 3 (City Center), just n on 3rd Ave, 0.3 mi e on Union, then 0.3 mi s. Int corridors. **Pets:** $75 one-time fee/room. Designated rooms, service with restrictions, supervision.

Homewood Suites - Allentown/Bethlehem Airport H
(610) 264-7500. **$109-$179.** 2031 Avenue C 18017. US 22 exit SR 378/Schoenersville Rd, follow signs for Schoenersville Rd, then 0.7 mi n. Int corridors. **Pets:** $75 one-time fee/room. Service with restrictions.

Residence Inn Allentown Bethlehem/Lehigh Valley Airport H
(610) 317-2662. **$85-$196.** 2180 Motel Dr 18018. US 22 exit Airport Rd S, 0.8 mi se on Catasauqua Rd. Int corridors. **Pets:** Accepted.

BLOOMSBURG

Econo Lodge at Bloomsburg H
(570) 387-0490. **$75-$159.** 189 Columbia Mall Dr 17815. I-80 exit 232 (SR 42), just n. Int corridors. **Pets:** Medium. $100 deposit/pet, $15 daily fee/pet. Designated rooms, service with restrictions, supervision.

The Inn at Turkey Hill CI
(570) 387-1500. **$135-$245.** 991 Central Rd 17815. I-80 exit 236 eastbound; exit 236A westbound, just s. Ext/int corridors. **Pets:** Other species. $20 daily fee/room. Designated rooms, service with restrictions, supervision.

BLUE MOUNTAIN

Kenmar Motel M
(717) 423-5915. **$65-$90.** 17788 Cumberland Hwy 17240. I-76 exit 201, just e on SR 997 N. Ext corridors. **Pets:** Dogs only. $10 daily fee/pet. Designated rooms, service with restrictions, supervision. SAVE

BRADFORD

Best Western Plus Bradford Inn H
(814) 362-4501. **$115-$130.** 100 Davis St S 16701. US 219 exit Forman St southbound, just w to Davis St, then 0.3 mi s; exit Elm St northbound, just w. Ext/int corridors. **Pets:** $10 daily fee/pet. Designated rooms, service with restrictions, crate. SAVE

Comfort Inn-Bradford H
(814) 368-6772. **$109-$129.** 76 Elm St 16701. US 219 exit Forman St southbound, just w to Davis St, then 0.3 mi s; exit Elm St northbound, just w. Int corridors. **Pets:** Accepted.

Glendorn CI
(814) 362-6511. **$299-$1349, 30 day notice.** 1000 Glendorn Dr 16701. US 219 exit Forman St, just s on Mechanic St, then 4.3 mi w on W Corydon. Ext/int corridors. **Pets:** Accepted.

BREEZEWOOD

Best Western Plaza Inn M
(814) 735-4352. **$59-$69, 7 day notice.** 16407 Lincoln Hwy 15533. I-76 (Pennsylvania Tpke) exit 161, just w on US 30; I-70 exit 147. Ext corridors. **Pets:** Accepted. SAVE

Wiltshire Motel M
(814) 735-4361. **$44-$54.** 140 S Breezewood Rd 15533. I-76 (Pennsylvania Tpke) exit 161, just w on US 30; I-70 exit 147. Ext corridors. **Pets:** Other species. Service with restrictions, supervision.

BROOKVILLE

Super 8 M
(814) 849-8440. **$49-$76.** 251 Allegheny Blvd 15825. I-80 exit 78, just n on SR 36. Int corridors. **Pets:** Large, other species. $10 daily fee/pet. Service with restrictions, supervision. SAVE

CAMP HILL

Radisson Hotel Harrisburg H
(717) 763-7117. **$85-$189.** 1150 Camp Hill Bypass 17011. Jct US 11, 15 and Erford Rd. Ext/int corridors. **Pets:** Accepted.

CARLISLE

Comfort Suites Hotel H
(717) 960-1000. **$111-$260.** 10 S Hanover St 17013. I-81 exit 47, 0.8 mi n on SR 34, just s of the square; downtown. Int corridors. **Pets:** Medium. $20 daily fee/pet. Designated rooms, service with restrictions.

Country Inn & Suites By Carlson H
(717) 241-4900. **$90-$199.** 1529 Commerce Ave 17015. I-81 exit 44 (Plainfield Rd), s on SR 465 (Allen Rd), then left. Int corridors. **Pets:** Medium. $25 one-time fee/room. Designated rooms, service with restrictions, crate. SAVE

Days Inn Carlisle-South H
(717) 258-4147. **$71-$135, 14 day notice.** 101 Alexander Spring Rd 17015. I-81 exit 45, just sw. Int corridors. **Pets:** Other species. $15 daily fee/room. Service with restrictions, supervision. SAVE

Fairfield Inn & Suites Carlisle H
(717) 243-2080. **$125-$168.** 1528 E Commerce Ave 17015. I-81 exit 44 (Plainfield Rd), just n, then just left. Int corridors. **Pets:** Other species. $75 deposit/room. Service with restrictions.

Hampton Inn Carlisle H
(717) 240-0200. **$89-$189.** 1164 Harrisburg Pike 17013. I-76 (Pennsylvania Tpke) exit 226, just n; I-81 exit 52 (US 11) southbound; exit 52B northbound, 0.8 mi s. Int corridors. **Pets:** Accepted. SAVE

AAA ▼▼▼▼ **Hotel Carlisle & Embers Convention Center** H ❀

(717) 243-1717. **$85-$175, 30 day notice.** 1700 Harrisburg Pike 17015. I-81 exit 52 (US 11) southbound; exit 52A northbound, 0.4 mi n; I-76 (Pennsylvania Tpke) exit 226, 1.2 mi n. Int corridors. **Pets:** Large, other species. $25 daily fee/pet. Designated rooms, service with restrictions, supervision. SAVE 🛜 🖬 🖵 🍽 🏊 ⊠

AAA ▼▼▼▼ **Pheasant Field Bed & Breakfast** BB ❀

(717) 258-0717. **$129-$239, 7 day notice.** 150 Hickorytown Rd 17015. I-76 (Pennsylvania Tpke) exit 226, 0.4 mi n on US 11, 2.3 mi right on S Middlesex Rd, 0.4 mi left on Ridge Dr, then right. Ext/int corridors. **Pets:** Other species. $10 daily fee/room. Designated rooms, service with restrictions, supervision. SAVE 🛜 ⊠ 🖬 ⊠

AAA ▼▼▼ **Quality Inn Carlisle** H

(717) 243-6000. **$68-$153.** 1255 Harrisburg Pike 17013. I-81 exit 52 (US 11) southbound; exit 52B northbound; I-76 (Pennsylvania Tpke) exit 226, 0.8 mi n. Int corridors. **Pets:** Small. $20 daily fee/pet. Designated rooms, service with restrictions, supervision. SAVE 🛜 🖬 🖵 🏊

AAA ▼▼▼▼ **Residence Inn by Marriott Harrisburg Carlisle** H

(717) 610-9050. **$134-$188.** 1 Hampton Ct 17013. I-76 (Pennsylvania Tpke) exit 226, just n; I-81 exit 52 (US 11) southbound; exit 52B northbound, 0.8 mi s. Int corridors. **Pets:** Large, other species. $100 one-time fee/room. Service with restrictions, crate.
SAVE 🛜 ⊠ 🗄 🖬 🖵 🏊

AAA ▼▼ **Super 8/Carlisle South** M ❀

(717) 245-9898. **$40-$114.** 100 Alexander Spring Rd 17015. I-81 exit 45, just se. Int corridors. **Pets:** Medium. $10 daily fee/pet. Service with restrictions, supervision. SAVE 🛜 🗄M 🖬 🖵

CHAMBERSBURG

▼▼ **Americas Best Value Inn Chambersburg** M

(717) 264-8005. **$49-$129.** 1110 Sheller Ave 17201. I-81 exit 14, just w on SR 316. Int corridors. **Pets:** Accepted. 🛜 🖬 🖵

AAA ▼▼▼ **Best Western Chambersburg** H

(717) 262-4994. **$70-$165.** 211 Walker Rd 17201. I-81 exit 16, just w on US 30, then just n. Int corridors. **Pets:** Large. $15 daily fee/pet. Designated rooms, service with restrictions, supervision.
SAVE 🛜 🖬 🖵 🏊

▼▼▼ **Country Inn & Suites By Carlson** H

(717) 261-0900. **$89-$189.** 399 Bedington Blvd 17201. I-81 exit 17 (Walker Rd), 0.6 mi s, then just w. Int corridors. **Pets:** Small, other species. $15 one-time fee/room. Designated rooms, service with restrictions, crate. 🛜 🗄M 🖬 🖵 🏊

▼▼ **Days Inn** H

(717) 263-1288. **$54-$116.** 30 Falling Spring Rd 17202. I-81 exit 16, just e on US 30. Int corridors. **Pets:** Accepted. 🛜 🖬 🖵 🏊

▼▼▼▼ **La Quinta Inn & Suites** H

(717) 446-0770. **$85-$194.** 199 Walker Rd 17201. I-81 exit 16, just w on US 30, then just n. Int corridors. **Pets:** Medium, other species. Service with restrictions, supervision. 🛜 ⊠ 🖬 🖵 🏊

▼▼ **Red Carpet Inn** M

(717) 267-2323. **Call for rates.** 1175 Wayne Ave 17201. I-81 exit 14, just e on SR 316. Ext corridors. **Pets:** Accepted. 🛜 🖬

▼▼▼ **Sleep Inn & Suites** H

(717) 263-0596. **$63-$77.** 1435 Doron Dr 17202. I-81 exit 20, just w. Int corridors. **Pets:** Accepted. 🛜 🗄M 🖬 🖵 🏊

AAA ▼▼ ▼ **Super 8** H

(717) 264-6288. **$30-$62.** 3648 Old Scotland Rd 17202. I-81 exit 20, just e, then just n on SR 696. Int corridors. **Pets:** Medium. $10 daily fee/pet. Service with restrictions, supervision. SAVE 🛜 🖬 🖵

CLARION

▼▼ ▼ **Comfort Inn-Clarion** H

(814) 226-5230. **Call for rates.** 129 Dolby St 16214. I-80 exit 62, 0.6 mi n on SR 68. Int corridors. **Pets:** Accepted. 🛜 🖬 🖵 🏊

▼▼▼ **Holiday Inn Clarion** H ❀

(814) 226-8850. **$99-$149.** 45 Holiday Inn Rd 16214. I-80 exit 62, 0.5 mi n on SR 68. Int corridors. **Pets:** Other species. $25 one-time fee/room. Service with restrictions, crate. 🛜 🖬 🖵 🍽 🏊

▼▼▼ **Microtel Inn & Suites-Clarion** H

(814) 227-2700. **$53-$67.** 151 Hotel Dr 16214. I-80 exit 62, just n on SR 68, then just e. Int corridors. **Pets:** Accepted. 🛜 🖬 🖵

AAA ▼▼▼▼ **Quality Inn & Suites Clarion** M

(814) 226-8682. **$59-$175.** 24 United Dr 16214. I-80 exit 62, just n on SR 68. Int corridors. **Pets:** Other species. $5 daily fee/pet. Service with restrictions, supervision. SAVE 🛜 🖬 🖵 🍽 🏊

CLARKS SUMMIT

AAA ▼▼▼ **Econo Lodge of Clarks Summit/Scranton North** M

(570) 586-1211. **Call for rates.** 649 Northern Blvd 18411. I-81 exit 194, on US 6 and 11; I-476 (Pennsylvania Tpke) exit 131, just e. Ext corridors. **Pets:** Medium, other species. $10 daily fee/pet. Service with restrictions, supervision. SAVE 🛜 🖬 🖵

AAA ▼▼▼ **Nichols Village Hotel & Spa** H

(570) 587-1135. **$99-$179.** 1101 Northern Blvd 18411. I-81 exit 194, just w; I-476 (Pennsylvania Tpke) exit 131, 0.7 mi w on US 6 and 11. Int corridors. **Pets:** Accepted. SAVE 🛜 ⊠ 🖬 🖵 🏊 ⊠

CLEARFIELD

AAA ▼▼ **Budget Inn** M ❀

(814) 765-2639. **$36-$79.** 6321 Clearfield Woodland Hwy (US 322 E) 16830. I-80 exit 120, 1.5 mi sw on SR 879, then 1.2 mi e. Ext/int corridors. **Pets:** Medium. $11 daily fee/pet. Designated rooms, service with restrictions, supervision. SAVE 🛜 🖬 🖵

▼▼ **Super 8-Clearfield** M

(814) 768-7580. **$61-$82.** 14597 Clearfield/Shawville Hwy (Rt 879) 16830. I-80 exit 120, just s. Int corridors. **Pets:** Other species. $5 daily fee/room. Designated rooms, service with restrictions, supervision. 🛜 🗄M 🖵

COUDERSPORT

▼▼ **Westgate Inn** H

(814) 274-0400. **$79-$99.** 307 Rt 6 W 16915. On US 6, 1 mi w. Int corridors. **Pets:** Small, dogs only. $15 daily fee/pet. Designated rooms, service with restrictions, supervision. 🛜 🖬 🖵

DANVILLE

AAA ▼▼▼ **Best Western Plus Danville Inn** H ❀

(570) 275-5750. **$120-$140, 3 day notice.** 79 Old Valley School Rd 17821. I-80 exit 224, just s. Int corridors. **Pets:** Other species. $15 daily fee/pet. Designated rooms, service with restrictions, supervision. SAVE 🛜 🖬 🖵 🏊

AAA ▼▼▼ **Danville Super 8** M ❀

(570) 275-4640. **$50-$180, 3 day notice.** 35 Sheraton Rd 17821. I-80 exit 224, just sw on SR 54. Ext corridors. **Pets:** Medium, other species. $15 one-time fee/room. Designated rooms, service with restrictions, crate. SAVE 🛜 🖬 🖵

AAA ▼▼▼▼ **Quality Inn & Suites Danville** M

(570) 275-5100. **$89-$159.** 15 Valley West Rd 17821. I-80 exit 224, just n on SR 54. Int corridors. **Pets:** Medium. $25 one-time fee/room. Designated rooms, service with restrictions, supervision. SAVE 🛜 🖬 🖵 🏊

DICKSON CITY

 **Days Inn Scranton** H
(570) 383-9979. **$52-$134.** 1946 Scranton-Carbondale Hwy 18508. I-81 exit 191A, 2 mi e on US 6; I-476 (Pennsylvania Tpke NE Ext) exit 131 (Clarks Summit), 4.5 mi e on US 6. Int corridors. **Pets:** $10 daily fee/pet. Service with restrictions, supervision.

Residence Inn by Marriott-Scranton H
(570) 343-5121. **$179-$208.** 947 Viewmont Dr 18519. I-81 exit 190, just e, follow signs to Viewmont Dr. Int corridors. **Pets:** Accepted.

DU BOIS

 **Best Western Plus Inn & Conference Center** H ❧
(814) 371-6200. **$110-$149.** 82 N Park Pl 15801. I-80 exit 97 eastbound, 2.5 mi e on DuBois Ave (US 219/SR 255), then just s; exit 101 westbound, 2.7 mi w on DuBois Ave (US 219/SR 255), then just s on US 219. Int corridors. **Pets:** $12 daily fee/pet. Service with restrictions, crate.

DUNMORE

Best Western Plus Scranton East Hotel & Convention Center H
(570) 343-4771. **$100-$140.** 200 Tigue St 18512. I-84/380 exit 1 (Tigue St), 0.3 mi e of jct I-81. Int corridors. **Pets:** Accepted.

Quality Inn H
(570) 348-6101. **$49-$99.** 1226 O'Neill Hwy 18512. I-81 exit 188 (Throop), just e at SR 347 N (O'Neill Hwy). Int corridors. **Pets:** $10 daily fee/pet. Service with restrictions, supervision.

Sleep Inn & Suites H
(570) 961-1116. **$89-$129.** 102 Monahan Ave 18512. I-81 exit 188 (Throop), just e at SR 347 N (O'Neill Hwy), then just s. Int corridors. **Pets:** Large. $15 daily fee/pet. Designated rooms, service with restrictions, crate.

EASTON

Grand Eastonian Suites Hotel H
(610) 258-6350. **$109-$239.** 140 N Northampton St 18042. US 22 exit 4th St (SR 611), just e to 3rd St, just s to downtown square, then just e towards river. Int corridors. **Pets:** Medium. $25 daily fee/room. Designated rooms, service with restrictions.

The Lafayette Inn BB ❧
(610) 253-4500. **$150-$250.** 525 W Monroe St 18042. US 22 exit 4th St (SR 611), just n on 3rd St, 0.3 mi ne on College Ave, then 0.3 mi n on Cattell St to jct Monroe St. Ext/int corridors. **Pets:** $20 daily fee/room. Designated rooms, service with restrictions, supervision.

TownePlace Suites by Marriott - Bethlehem/Easton H
(610) 829-2000. **$99-$219.** 3800 Easton Nazareth Hwy 18045. SR 33 exit SR 248 (Nazareth/Wilson), 0.6 mi w. Int corridors. **Pets:** Accepted.

EBENSBURG

Comfort Inn H
(814) 472-6100. **Call for rates.** 111 Cook Rd 15931. Jct US 219, just e on US 22. Int corridors. **Pets:** Accepted.

ERIE

Fairfield Inn by Marriott Erie H ❧
(814) 868-0985. **$139-$164.** 2082 Interchange Rd 16506. I-79 exit 180, just e; in Pavilion Marketplace. Int corridors. **Pets:** Other species. $25 one-time fee/room. Service with restrictions, crate.

Glass House Inn M
(814) 833-7751. **$79-$131.** 3202 W 26th St 16506. I-79 exit 182, 1.4 mi w on US 20. Ext corridors. **Pets:** Dogs only. $25 one-time fee/pet. Service with restrictions, supervision.

Homewood Suites by Hilton H
(814) 866-8292. **$139-$199.** 2084 Interchange Rd 16565. I-79 exit 180, just e; in Pavilion Marketplace. Int corridors. **Pets:** Accepted.

La Quinta Inn & Suites H
(814) 864-1812. **$84-$195.** 7820 Perry Hwy 16509. I-90 exit 27, just n. Int corridors. **Pets:** Medium, other species. Service with restrictions, supervision.

Microtel Inn-Erie M
(814) 864-1010. **$53-$98.** 8100 Peach St 16509. I-90 exit 24, just s. Int corridors. **Pets:** Accepted.

Quality Inn & Suites Conference Center H
(814) 864-4911. **$50-$200.** 8040 Perry Hwy 16509. I-90 exit 27, just s. Ext corridors. **Pets:** $25 one-time fee/room. Designated rooms, service with restrictions, supervision.

Red Roof Inn #7054 M
(814) 868-5246. **$60-$150.** 7865 Perry Hwy 16509. I-90 exit 27, just n on SR 97. Ext/int corridors. **Pets:** Large, other species. No service, supervision.

Sheraton Erie Bayfront Hotel H ❧
(814) 454-2005. **$109-$459, 3 day notice.** 55 West Bay Dr 16507. I-90 exit 22B to Bayfront Connector; I-79 to Bayfront Pkwy. Int corridors. **Pets:** Large, dogs only. $50 deposit/room. Designated rooms, service with restrictions, supervision.

TownePlace Suites Erie H
(814) 866-7100. **$110-$154.** 2090 Interchange Rd 16565. I-79 exit 180, just e; in Pavilion Marketplace. Int corridors. **Pets:** Accepted.

Wingate by Wyndham H
(814) 860-3050. **$78-$164.** 8060 Old Oliver Rd 16509. I-90 exit 24, just s on Peach St, just w, just n, then just e. Int corridors. **Pets:** Accepted.

FOGELSVILLE

Glasbern CI
(610) 285-4723. **$150-$485, 7 day notice.** 2141 Packhouse Rd 18051. I-78 exit 49B (SR 100), 0.3 mi n to 1st traffic light, 0.3 mi w on Main St, 0.6 mi n on Church St, then 0.8 mi ne. Ext corridors. **Pets:** Dogs only. $25 daily fee/pet. Service with restrictions, supervision.

Holiday Inn Conference Center H
(610) 391-1000. **$129-$169, 3 day notice.** 7736 Adrienne Dr 18031. I-78 exit 49A, 0.3 mi s on SR 100. Int corridors. **Pets:** Accepted.

Sleep Inn H
(610) 395-6603. **$70-$160.** 327 Star Rd 18106. I-78 exit 49A, 0.3 mi s on SR 100, e at 1st traffic light, then n on service road. Int corridors. **Pets:** Medium. $15 daily fee/pet. Designated rooms, no service, supervision.

Staybridge Suites-Allentown West H
(610) 841-5100. **Call for rates.** 327 Star Rd 18106. I-78 exit 49A, 0.3 mi s on SR 100, e at traffic light, then n on service road. Int corridors. **Pets:** Accepted.

GETTYSBURG

▼▼▼▼▼ **1863 Inn of Gettysburg** **H**
(717) 334-6211. **$99-$275.** 516 Baltimore St 17325. Jct US 15 business route and SR 97. Ext/int corridors. **Pets:** Other species. $20 daily fee/room. Designated rooms, service with restrictions, supervision.
🛜 ⊠ 🛗 💻 ➿

▲▲▲ **▼▼▼** **Americas Best Value Inn** **M**
(717) 334-1188. **$58-$158.** 301 Steinwehr Ave 17325. 1 mi s on US 15 business route, just s of jct SR 134. Ext/int corridors. **Pets:** Other species. Service with restrictions, supervision. SAVE 🛜 ⊠ 🛗 ➿

▼▼▼▼▼ **Battlefield Bed & Breakfast Inn** **BB**
(717) 334-8804. **Call for rates.** 2264 Emmitsburg Rd 17325. 4 mi s on Steinwehr Ave and Baltimore Pike. Int corridors. **Pets:** Accepted.
🛜 ⊠ 🗷

▼▼ ▼▼ **Comfort Inn-Gettysburg** **M**
(717) 337-2400. **Call for rates.** 871 York Rd 17325. 1 mi e on US 30. Int corridors. **Pets:** Other species. $20 daily fee/pet. Service with restrictions, crate. 🛜 🛗 💻 ➿

▲▲▲ **▼▼▼▼** **Country Inn & Suites By Carlson** **H** ❀
(717) 337-9518. **$69-$165.** 1857 Gettysburg Village Dr 17325. US 15 exit SR 97, just e. Int corridors. **Pets:** Other species. $20 daily fee/room. Service with restrictions, crate. SAVE 🛜 ⊠ 🛗 💻 ➿

▼▼ ▼▼ **Gettysburg Travelodge** **M**
(717) 334-9281. **$62-$152.** 613 Baltimore St 17325. On SR 97; at US 15 business route. Ext/int corridors. **Pets:** Medium. $10 daily fee/room. Designated rooms, service with restrictions. 🛜 ⊠ 🛗 💻

▲▲▲ **▼▼ ▼▼** **Motel 6 Gettysburg #4462** **H**
(717) 334-4274. **$75-$160.** 606 York St 17325. 0.5 mi e on US 30 from the square. Int corridors. **Pets:** Other species. Service with restrictions, supervision. SAVE 🛜 🛗 ➿

▲▲▲ **▼▼ ▼▼** **Super 8** **M** ❀
(717) 337-1400. **$45-$189.** 869 York Rd 17325. 1 mi e on US 30. Int corridors. **Pets:** Other species. $10 daily fee/pet. Service with restrictions, supervision. SAVE 🛜 🛗M 🛗 💻

▲▲▲ **▼▼▼▼▼** **Wyndham Gettysburg** **H**
(717) 339-0020. **$89-$199.** 95 Presidential Cir 17325. US 15 exit York St, just e on US 30. Int corridors. **Pets:** Accepted.
SAVE 🛜 ⊠ 🛗M 🛗 💻 🍽 ➿

GRANTVILLE

▲▲▲ **▼▼ ▼▼** **Days Inn Grantville-Hershey** **M**
(717) 469-0631. **$81-$90.** 252 Bow Creek Rd 17028. I-81 exit 80. Ext corridors. **Pets:** Medium. $10 daily fee/pet. Service with restrictions, supervision. SAVE 🛜 🛗 💻

▲▲▲ **▼▼▼** **Holiday Inn Harrisburg-Hershey Area, I-81** **H**
(717) 469-0661. **$99-$199.** 604 Station Rd 17028. I-81 exit 80. Int corridors. **Pets:** Other species. $25 one-time fee/room. Designated rooms, service with restrictions, crate. SAVE 🛜 🛗M 🛗 💻 🍽 ➿ 🗷

GREENCASTLE

▲▲▲ **▼▼▼** **Comfort Inn** **H**
(717) 597-8164. **$80-$140.** 50 Pine Dr 17225. I-81 exit 3, just s on US 11. Int corridors. **Pets:** Other species. $20 daily fee/room. Service with restrictions. SAVE 🛜 🛗 💻 🍽 🗷

HAMBURG

▼▼ ▼▼ **Microtel Inn & Suites** **H**
(610) 562-4234. **$66-$106.** 50 Industrial Dr 19526. I-78 exit 29B, 0.3 mi n on SR 61, then just e. Int corridors. **Pets:** Other species. $10 daily fee/pet. Service with restrictions, supervision. 🛜 🛗M 🛗 💻 🍽

HARRISBURG

▲▲▲ **▼▼ ▼▼** **Comfort Inn Harrisburg/Hershey** **H**
(717) 657-2200. **$65-$169.** 5680 Allentown Blvd 17112. I-81 exit 72, just s on N Mountain Rd, then just w on US 22. Int corridors. **Pets:** Medium. $25 daily fee/pet. Service with restrictions, crate.
SAVE 🛜 🛗M 🛗 💻 ➿

▼▼ ▼▼ **Comfort Inn Riverfront** **H**
(717) 233-1611. **$80-$199.** 525 S Front St 17104. I-83 exit 43, 0.5 mi n. Int corridors. **Pets:** Small. $25 daily fee/room. Designated rooms, service with restrictions, supervision. 🛜 ⊠ 🛗 💻 🍽 ➿

▲▲▲ **▼▼ ▼▼** **Econo Lodge** **H**
(717) 540-9100. **Call for rates.** 7930 Linglestown Rd 17112. I-81 exit 77. Int corridors. **Pets:** Medium. $10 daily fee/pet. Designated rooms, service with restrictions, supervision. SAVE 🛜 🛗 💻

▲▲▲ **▼▼▼▼** **Hilton Harrisburg** **H**
(717) 233-6000. **$129-$229.** One N 2nd St 17101. Jct Market St; downtown. Int corridors. **Pets:** Accepted.
SAVE 🛜 🛗M 🛗 💻 🍽 ➿ 🗷

▲▲▲ **▼▼▼▼** **Holiday Inn Express East** **H**
(717) 561-8100. **$89-$179.** 4021 Union Deposit Rd 17109. I-83 exit 48, just w. Int corridors. **Pets:** Medium, dogs only. $25 one-time fee/room. Service with restrictions, crate. SAVE 🛜 🛗 💻 ➿

▲▲▲ **▼▼▼▼** **Holiday Inn Harrisburg East-Airport** **H**
(717) 939-7841. **$99-$169.** 4751 Lindle Rd 17111. I-283 exit 2, just e. Int corridors. **Pets:** Small, other species. $75 deposit/room, $25 one-time fee/room. Service with restrictions, crate.
SAVE 🛜 ⊠ 🛗M 🛗 💻 🍽 ➿ 🗷

▲▲▲ **▼▼▼▼** **Ramada Harrisburg** **H**
(717) 652-7180. **Call for rates.** 300 N Mountain Rd 17112. I-81 exit 72 southbound; exit 72B northbound. Int corridors. **Pets:** Other species. $25 daily fee/room. Service with restrictions, crate. SAVE 🛜 🛗 💻 ➿

▲▲▲ **▼▼ ▼▼** **Red Roof Inn- Harrisburg/Hershey #7027** **M**
(717) 939-1331. **$59-$79.** 950 Eisenhower Blvd 17111. I-283 exit 2, just e. Ext/int corridors. **Pets:** Large, other species. No service, supervision. SAVE 🛜 🛗

▲▲▲ **▼▼ ▼▼** **Red Roof Inn-North #7037** **M**
(717) 657-1445. **$49-$109.** 400 Corporate Cir 17110. I-81 exit 69 (Progress Ave), just n. Ext/int corridors. **Pets:** Large, other species. No service, supervision. SAVE 🛜 🛗

▼▼▼▼ **Residence Inn by Marriott Harrisburg-Hershey** **H**
(717) 561-1900. **$152-$205.** 4480 Lewis Rd 17111. US 322 exit Penhar Dr, just e. Ext/int corridors. **Pets:** $100 one-time fee/room. Designated rooms, service with restrictions, crate. 🛜 ⊠ 🛗 💻 ➿ 🗷

▲▲▲ **▼▼▼▼** **Sheraton Harrisburg Hershey** **H**
(717) 564-5511. **$125-$249, 3 day notice.** 4650 Lindle Rd 17111. I-283 exit 2, just e. Int corridors. **Pets:** Accepted.
SAVE 🛜 ⊠ 🛗M 🛗 💻 🍽 ➿ 🗷

▲▲▲ **▼▼▼▼** **Staybridge Suites Harrisburg** **H** ❀
(717) 233-3304. **Call for rates.** 920 Wildwood Park Dr 17110. I-81 exit 67 A/B. Int corridors. **Pets:** Medium, other species. $75 one-time fee/room. Designated rooms, service with restrictions, supervision.
SAVE 🛜 ⊠ 🛗 💻 ➿

▲▲▲ **▼▼▼▼** **TownePlace Suites by Marriott Harrisburg Hershey** **H**
(717) 558-0200. **$122-$275.** 450 Friendship Rd 17111. I-83 exit 45, 0.7 mi on Paxton St, then 0.3 mi s. Int corridors. **Pets:** Small, other species. $100 one-time fee/pet. Designated rooms, service with restrictions.
SAVE 🛜 ⊠ 🛗 💻 ➿ 🗷

HAZLETON

▲▲▲ ▼▼▼ **Best Western Genetti Inn & Suites**
(570) 454-2494. **$93-$110, 3 day notice.** 1341 N Church St 18202. I-80 exit 262, 6 mi s on SR 309; I-81 exit 145, 0.5 mi s on SR 93, 1 mi e on Airport Rd, then 0.6 mi s. Ext/int corridors. **Pets:** $10 one-time fee/pet. Service with restrictions, supervision. [SAVE] 🛜 🖥 🖥 🏊

▼▼ **Ramada Inn Hazleton**
(570) 455-2061. **$72-$126.** 1213 N Church St 18202. I-80 exit 262, 6 mi s on SR 309; I-81 exit 145, 0.5 mi s on SR 93, 1 mi e on Airport Rd, then 0.7 mi s. Ext/int corridors. **Pets:** Accepted.
🛜 🖥 🖥 🍴 🏊

▼▼▼ **Residence Inn by Marriott - Hazleton**
(570) 455-9555. **$209-$259.** 1 New St 18202. I-81 exit 143, just s on SR 924 S; at Humboldt Station, just e on Commerce Dr. Int corridors. **Pets:** Other species. $20 one-time fee/room. Service with restrictions, supervision. 🛜 ✖ 🖥 🖥 🖥 🏊 ✖

HERSHEY

▲▲▲ ▼▼▼ **Best Western Inn Hershey**
(717) 533-5665. **$99-$199.** US 422 & Sipe Ave 17033. Jct US 322, just e. Ext/int corridors. **Pets:** Other species. $20 daily fee/pet. Designated rooms, service with restrictions, crate.
[SAVE] 🛜 ✖ 🖥 🖥 🏊 ✖

▲▲▲ ▼▼▼ **Days Inn Hershey**
(717) 534-2162. **$99-$225.** 350 W Chocolate Ave 17033. On US 422; center. Int corridors. **Pets:** Medium, dogs up to $20 one-time fee/pet. Designated rooms, service with restrictions, supervision.
[SAVE] 🛜 ✖ 🖥 🖥 🖥 🏊 ✖

▲▲▲ ▼▼▼▼ **Hampton Inn & Suites**
(717) 533-8400. **$109-$289.** 749 E Chocolate Ave 17033. 0.9 mi e on US 422. Int corridors. **Pets:** Small, dogs only. Designated rooms, service with restrictions, crate. [SAVE] 🛜 🖥 🖥 🖥 🏊 ✖

▼▼ **Hershey Econo Lodge**
(717) 533-2515. **$53-$153.** 115 Lucy Ave 17036. Jct US 322, just e on US 422. Ext corridors. **Pets:** Large, other species. $15 daily fee/pet. Crate. 🛜 🖥 🖥

HUNTINGDON

▼▼ **Huntingdon Motor Inn**
(814) 643-1133. **$51-$85, 3 day notice.** 6920 Motor Inn Dr 16652. On US 22 at SR 26. Ext corridors. **Pets:** Medium. $10 daily fee/pet. Service with restrictions, supervision. 🛜 🖥 🖥

INDIANA (INDIANA COUNTY)

▼▼▼▼ **Holiday Inn**
(724) 463-3561. **$99-$159.** 1395 Wayne Ave 15701. US 422 exit Wayne Ave, 1 mi n. Ext/int corridors. **Pets:** Accepted. 🛜 🖥 🖥 🍴 🏊

JOHNSTOWN

▼▼▼ **Comfort Inn & Suites**
(814) 266-3678. **$90-$150.** 455 Theatre Dr 15904. US 219 exit Elton (SR 756), just e. Int corridors. **Pets:** Large. $50 deposit/pet, $15 daily fee/pet. Designated rooms, service with restrictions, supervision.
🛜 🖥 🖥 🖥 🏊

▼▼ **Econo Lodge**
(814) 536-1114. **Call for rates.** 430 Napoleon Pl 15901. Jct SR 271 and 403; downtown. Int corridors. **Pets:** Large. $10 daily fee/room. Designated rooms, service with restrictions, supervision. 🛜 🖥 🖥

▼▼ **Holiday Inn Downtown**
(814) 535-7777. **Call for rates.** 250 Market St 15901. Corner of Market and Vine sts; downtown. Int corridors. **Pets:** Accepted.
🛜 🖥 🖥 🍴 🏊 ✖

▼▼ **Holiday Inn Express Johnstown**
(814) 266-8789. **Call for rates.** 1440 Scalp Ave 15904. US 219 exit Windber (SR 56 E), just e. Int corridors. **Pets:** Accepted.
🛜 🖥 🖥 🖥

▼▼ **Sleep Inn**
(814) 262-9292. **$81-$135.** 453 Theatre Dr 15904. US 219 exit Elton (SR 756), just e. Int corridors. **Pets:** Large. $50 deposit/pet, $15 daily fee/pet. Designated rooms, service with restrictions, supervision.
🛜 🖥 🖥 🖥

▲▲▲ ▼▼ **Super 8 Johnstown**
(814) 535-5600. **$63-$225.** 627 Solomon Run Rd 15904. US 219 exit Galleria Dr, just w. Int corridors. **Pets:** Small, dogs only. $10 daily fee/pet. Designated rooms, service with restrictions, supervision.
[SAVE] 🛜 🖥 🖥

JONESTOWN

▼▼ **Days Inn Lebanon/Lickdale**
(717) 865-4064. **$54-$134.** 3 Everest Ln 17038. I-81 exit 90. Int corridors. **Pets:** Accepted. 🛜 🖥 🖥

▼▼ **Quality Inn Jonestown/Lebanon**
(717) 865-6600. **Call for rates.** 16 Marsanna Ln 17038. I-81 exit 90, just w. Int corridors. **Pets:** Accepted. 🛜 🖥 🖥 🏊

KITTANNING

▼▼ **Quality Inn Royle**
(724) 543-1159. **Call for rates.** 405 Butler Rd 16201. SR 28 exit US 422 W. Ext/int corridors. **Pets:** Accepted. 🛜 🖥 🖥

LAMAR

▼▼▼ **Comfort Inn of Lamar**
(570) 726-4901. **Call for rates.** 31 Hospitality Ln 17751. I-80 exit 173, just n on SR 64. Int corridors. **Pets:** Accepted. 🛜 🖥 🖥 🏊

LAUREL HIGHLANDS AREA

CHALK HILL

▲▲▲ ▼▼▼ **The Lodge at Chalk Hill**
(724) 438-8880. **$60-$140.** Rt 40 E 15421. I-40 exit 14B, just w. Ext corridors. **Pets:** Medium, dogs only. $10 daily fee/pet. Service with restrictions, crate. [SAVE] 🛜 🖥 🖥 ✖

FARMINGTON

▼▼▼ **Historic Summit Inn**
(724) 438-8594. **$139-$299, 3 day notice.** 101 Skyline Dr 15437. On US 40; center. Int corridors. **Pets:** Small, dogs only. $20 daily fee/pet. Service with restrictions, supervision. 🛜 🖥 🖥 🍴 🏊 ✖

▲▲▲ ▼▼▼▼ **Nemacolin Woodlands Resort**
(724) 329-8555. **$265-$885, 14 day notice.** 1001 Lafayette Dr 15437. 1 mi e on US 40. Ext/int corridors. **Pets:** Small, dogs only. $150 one-time fee/room. Designated rooms, service with restrictions, supervision.
[SAVE] 🛜 🖥 🍴 🏊 ✖

GREENSBURG

▲▲▲ ▼▼▼▼ **Four Points by Sheraton Greensburg**
(724) 836-6060. **$89-$139.** 100 Sheraton Dr 15601. I-76 (Pennsylvania Tpke) exit 75, 5.6 mi on US 119 N, 3 mi e on US 30, then just n. Int corridors. **Pets:** Accepted. [SAVE] 🛜 ✖ 🖥 🖥 🖥 🍴 🏊

NEW STANTON

◊◊◊◊ ▼▼ Super 8-New Stanton M
(724) 925-8915. **$62-$68.** 103 Bair Blvd 15672. I-76 exit 75, 0.5 mi se; I-70 exit 57B westbound; exit 57 eastbound. Int corridors. **Pets:** Medium, dogs only. $25 one-time fee/pet, $25 daily fee/pet. Service with restrictions, crate. SAVE 📶 🔒 💻 💻

SOMERSET

▼ Budget Host Inn M
(814) 445-7988. **$45-$95, 3 day notice.** 799 N Center Ave 15501. I-70/76 (Pennsylvania Tpke) exit 110, 0.3 mi s. Ext corridors. **Pets:** Small. $10 daily fee/pet. No service, supervision. 📶 🔒

◊◊◊◊ ▼▼▼ Comfort Inn H
(814) 445-9611. **$95-$115.** 202 Harmon St 15501. I-70/76 (Pennsylvania Tpke) exit 110, just s. Int corridors. **Pets:** Small, other species. $35 one-time fee/room. Designated rooms, service with restrictions, supervision.
SAVE 📶 ♿ 🔒 💻 🏊

▼ Dollar Inn M
(814) 445-2977. **$40-$95.** 1146 N Center Ave 15501. I-70/76 (Pennsylvania Tpke) exit 110, 0.3 mi s, then just n on SR 601/N Central Ave; at top of hill. Ext corridors. **Pets:** Medium. $10 daily fee/pet. Designated rooms, service with restrictions, supervision. 📶 🔒

▼▼ Glades Pike Inn BB
(814) 443-4978. **Call for rates.** 2684 Glades Pike Rd 15501. I-70/76 (Pennsylvania Tpke) exit 110, 6 mi w on SR 31; exit 91, 13 mi e on SR 31. Int corridors. **Pets:** Other species. No service, supervision.
📶 ✖ 🔒

UNIONTOWN

▼▼▼ Uniontown Holiday Inn H
(724) 437-2816. **$109-$179.** 700 W Main St 15401. 1.8 mi w on US 40. Int corridors. **Pets:** Small. $10 daily fee/room. Designated rooms, service with restrictions, supervision. 📶 ♿ 🔒 💻 ⏹ 🏊 ✖

END AREA

LEBANON (LEBANON COUNTY)

▼▼◊▼ Berry Patch Bed and Breakfast BB
(717) 865-7219. **$125-$229, 14 day notice.** 115 Moore Rd 17046. I-81 exit 90, 2.8 mi s on SR 72, 1 mi e on New Bunker Hill St, 0.8 mi s on S Lancaster St, just e, then follow signs. Ext/int corridors. **Pets:** Medium. $25 one-time fee/pet. Designated rooms, service with restrictions, supervision. 📶 ✖ 🔒

LINCOLN FALLS

▼▼▼ Morgan Century Farm BB
(570) 924-4909. **$99-$149, 5 day notice.** 7043 Rt 154 18616. In village. Ext/int corridors. **Pets:** Medium. $10 one-time fee/pet. Designated rooms, service with restrictions, supervision. 📶 🔒 💻 ⏹

LOCK HAVEN

◊◊◊ ▼▼◊ Best Western Lock Haven H ❀
(570) 748-3297. **$109-$179.** 101 E Walnut St 17745. US 220 exit 111 (SR 120 W), just w. Int corridors. **Pets:** $12 daily fee/pet. Service with restrictions, crate. SAVE 📶 🔒 💻

MANSFIELD

◊◊◊ ▼▼ Comfort Inn H ❀
(570) 662-3000. **Call for rates.** 300 Gateway Dr 16933. Jct US 6 and 15. Int corridors. **Pets:** Large, other species. $15 daily fee/room. Service with restrictions, supervision. SAVE 📶 🔒 💻 ✖

◊◊◊ ▼ Mansfield Inn M
(570) 662-2136. **$55-$110, 3 day notice.** 26 S Main St 16933. US 15 exit Mansfield, jct US 6, just s on Business Rt US 15; downtown. Ext corridors. **Pets:** Dogs only. $10 daily fee/pet. No service, crate.
SAVE 📶 🔒 💻

MARIENVILLE

▼ The Forest Lodge & Campground M ❀
(814) 927-8790. **$40-$85, 14 day notice.** 44078 Rt 66 16239. 6 mi n of town. Ext/int corridors. **Pets:** Medium. $12 daily fee/pet. Designated rooms, service with restrictions, supervision. 🔒 💻

MEADVILLE

▼▼ Quality Inn Meadville M
(814) 333-8883. **$63-$90.** 17259 Conneaut Lake Rd 16335. I-79 exit 147B, just w on US 322. Ext/int corridors. **Pets:** Other species. $10 daily fee/pet. Designated rooms, service with restrictions, supervision.
📶 🔒 💻

MECHANICSBURG

▼▼ Comfort Inn Capital City H
(717) 766-3700. **$69-$169.** 1012 Wesley Dr 17055. I-76 (Pennsylvania Tpke) exit 236 (US 15), 1 mi n to Wesley Dr exit, then just w. Int corridors. **Pets:** Accepted. 📶 ♿ 🔒 💻 🏊

◊◊◊ ▼▼▼ Comfort Inn West H
(717) 790-0924. **Call for rates.** 6325 Carlisle Pike 17050. Jct Carlisle Pike and US 11, 1 mi w on US 11. Int corridors. **Pets:** Small, other species. $20 one-time fee/pet. Designated rooms, service with restrictions, supervision. SAVE 📶 🔒 💻

▼▼▼ Hampton Inn-Harrisburg West H ❀
(717) 691-1300. **$89-$169.** 4950 Ritter Rd 17055. I-76 (Pennsylvania Tpke) exit 236 (US 15), 1 mi n to Rossmoyne Rd exit. Int corridors. **Pets:** Other species. Designated rooms, service with restrictions, supervision. 📶 ♿ 🔒 💻 🏊

▼▼▼ Homewood Suites by Hilton-Harrisburg West H
(717) 697-4900. **$99-$199.** 5001 Ritter Rd 17055. I-76 (Pennsylvania Tpke) exit 236 (US 15), 1 mi n to Rossmoyne Rd exit. Int corridors. **Pets:** Accepted. 📶 ♿ 🔒 💻 🏊 ✖

◊◊◊ ▼▼▼ Park Inn by Radisson Harrisburg West H
(717) 697-0321. **$99-$179.** 5401 Carlisle Pike 17050. Jct Carlisle Pike and US 11, just w. Ext/int corridors. **Pets:** Accepted.
SAVE 📶 🔒 💻 ⏹ 🏊 ✖

MERCER

▼ Comfort Inn Mercer H
(724) 748-3030. **Call for rates.** 835 Perry Hwy 16137. I-80 exit 15, just n on US 19. Int corridors. **Pets:** Other species. Designated rooms, service with restrictions, supervision. 📶 🔒 💻 🏊 ✖

MIFFLINVILLE

▼▼ Super 8 - Mifflinville M
(570) 759-6778. **$45-$125.** 450 W 3rd St 18631. I-80 exit 242 (SR 339), just n. Ext corridors. **Pets:** Accepted. 📶 🔒 💻

MILROY

◊◊◊ ▼▼▼ Best Western Nittany Inn Milroy H
(717) 667-9595. **$75-$96.** 5 Commerce Dr 17063. US 322 exit Milroy, just e. Int corridors. **Pets:** Small, dogs only. $20 daily fee/pet. Designated rooms, service with restrictions, supervision.
SAVE 📶 ✖ 🔒 💻 ⏹ 🏊

MONTGOMERY

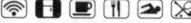 White Deer Motel **M**

(570) 547-1007. **$50-$120, 3 day notice.** 6967 SR 15 17752. Jct SR 54, 1.4 mi s. Ext corridors. **Pets:** Small. $10 deposit/pet. Designated rooms, service with restrictions, supervision. 🛰️ ❌ 🛏️ 💻

MORGANTOWN

Holiday Inn **H**

(610) 286-3000. **$85-$145.** 6170 Morgantown Rd 19543. I-76 exit 298, just s on SR 10. Int corridors. **Pets:** Medium. $25 daily fee/pet. Designated rooms, service with restrictions, supervision.

🛰️ 🛏️ 💻 🍴 🏊 ❌

MYERSTOWN

Quality Inn & Suites at The Lantern Lodge **H**

(717) 866-6536. **$70-$250.** 411 N College St 17067. Just n of US 422 on SR 501. Ext/int corridors. **Pets:** Other species. $50 deposit/pet, $10 daily fee/pet. Designated rooms, service with restrictions, supervision. 🛰️ 🛏️ 💻 🍴

NEW CASTLE

Comfort Inn-New Castle **H**

(724) 658-7700. **Call for rates.** 1740 New Butler Rd (US Business 422) 16101. Jct SR 65, 1 mi e on US 422, then 1 mi w on US 422 business route. Int corridors. **Pets:** Accepted. 🛰️ 🛏️ 💻

NEW COLUMBIA

Holiday Inn Express **H**

(570) 568-1100. **$99-$189.** 160 Commerce Park Dr 17856. I-80 exit 210A (US 15/New Columbia), just s. Int corridors. **Pets:** Medium, other species. $20 daily fee/pet. Designated rooms, service with restrictions, supervision. SAVE 🛰️ 🛏️ 💻 🏊

New Columbia Comfort Inn **H** ❀

(570) 568-8000. **$85-$145.** 330 Commerce Park Dr 17856. I-80 exit 210A (US 15/New Columbia), just s. Int corridors. **Pets:** Other species. SAVE 🛰️ ❌ 🛏️ 💻 🍴 🏊

NEW CUMBERLAND

Days Inn Harrisburg South **H**

(717) 774-4156. **$51-$93.** 353 Lewisberry Rd 17070. I-83 exit 39A, just ne. Int corridors. **Pets:** Accepted. 🛰️ 🛏️ 💻 🏊

Harrisburg Holiday Inn Hotel & Conference Center **H**

(717) 774-2721. **$99-$149.** 148 Sheraton Dr 17070. I-83 exit 40A, just se. Int corridors. **Pets:** Accepted. SAVE 🛰️ 🛏️ 💻 🍴 🏊

PENNSYLVANIA DUTCH COUNTRY AREA

AKRON

Boxwood Inn **BB**

(717) 859-3466. **$110-$235, 7 day notice.** 1320 Diamond St 17501. SR 272, 0.4 mi se on Main St to Diamond St, then 0.3 mi s. Ext/int corridors. **Pets:** Accepted. 🛰️ ❌ 🛏️ 💻 🔌

BIRD-IN-HAND

Amish Country Motel **M**

(717) 768-8396. **$76-$109.** 3013 Old Philadelphia Pike (Rt 340) 17505. On SR 340, 1 mi e. Ext corridors. **Pets:** Small, other species. $100 deposit/room, $50 one-time fee/pet. Designated rooms, service with restrictions, crate. 🛰️ ❌ 🛏️ 🏊

DENVER

Black Horse Lodge and Suites **H**

(717) 336-7563. **$59-$199, 3 day notice.** 2180 N Reading Rd 17517. I-76 (Pennsylvania Tpke) exit 286, 1 mi w to SR 272, then 0.3 mi n. Ext/int corridors. **Pets:** Accepted. 🛰️ 🛏️ 💻 🍴 🏊

Comfort Inn Lancaster County North **H**

(717) 336-7541. **$80-$140.** 1 Denver Rd 17517. I-76 (Pennsylvania Tpke) exit 286, 1 mi w to SR 272, then just s. Int corridors. **Pets:** Other species. $5 daily fee/pet. Service with restrictions, supervision. 🛰️ 🛏️ 💻 🍴 🏊

Red Roof Inn **H**

(717) 336-4649. **$54-$139.** 2017 N Reading Rd 17517. I-76 (Pennsylvania Tpke) exit 286, 1 mi w to SR 272, then just s. Int corridors. **Pets:** Large, other species. No service, supervision. 🛰️ 🛏️ 💻

ELIZABETHTOWN

Holiday Inn Express Elizabethtown (Hershey Area) **H**

(717) 367-4000. **$136-$162.** 147 Merts Dr 17022. SR 283 exit Elizabethtown/Rheems. Int corridors. **Pets:** Large, other species. $25 daily fee/pet. Designated rooms, service with restrictions, crate. SAVE 🛰️ 🛏️ 💻

GORDONVILLE

Motel 6-Lancaster #4174 **M**

(717) 687-3880. **$50-$200.** 2959 Lincoln Hwy E 17529. On US 30 (Lincoln Hwy); center. Int corridors. **Pets:** Other species. Service with restrictions, supervision. SAVE 🛰️ 🛏️

LANCASTER

Best Western Premier Eden Resort & Suites **H**

(717) 569-6444. **$90-$400.** 222 Eden Rd 17601. Jct US 30 (Lincoln Hwy) and SR 272 (Oregon Pike). Ext/int corridors. **Pets:** Medium, other species. $15 daily fee/pet. Designated rooms, service with restrictions, crate. SAVE 🛰️ ❌ 🛏️ 💻 🍴 🏊 ❌

Hawthorn Suites by Wyndham **H**

(717) 290-7100. **$89-$159.** 2045 Lincoln Hwy 17602. Jct US 30 (Lincoln Hwy E). Int corridors. **Pets:** Medium, dogs only. $50 one-time fee/room. Designated rooms, service with restrictions, supervision. SAVE 🛰️ ❌ 🛏️ 💻

Lancaster Host Resort & Conference Center **H**

(717) 299-5500. **$109-$199.** 2300 Lincoln Hwy E 17602. On US 30 (Lincoln Hwy), 5 mi e. Int corridors. **Pets:** Accepted. SAVE 🛰️ 🛏️ 💻 🍴 🏊 ❌

Red Roof Inn of Lancaster **M**

(717) 299-9700. **$59-$139.** 2307 Lincoln Hwy E 17602. On US 30 (Lincoln Hwy), 5 mi e. Ext/int corridors. **Pets:** Large, other species. No service, supervision. SAVE 🛰️ ❌ 🛏️ 💻 🏊

Willow Valley Inn & Suites **H** ❀

(717) 464-2716. **Call for rates.** 2416 Willow St Pike 17602. On US 222, 3.8 mi s. Ext/int corridors. **Pets:** Small, dogs only. $25 daily fee/pet. Designated rooms, service with restrictions, supervision.

🛰️ 🛏️ 💻 🍴 🏊 ❌

LITITZ

Holiday Inn Express Hotel & Suites **H**

(717) 625-2366. **$110-$175.** 101 Crosswinds Dr 17543. 1.4 mi s on SR 501 (Lititz Pike), then just w on Trolley Run Rd. Int corridors. **Pets:** Medium. $25 one-time fee/pet. No service, crate. SAVE 🛰️ 🛏️ 💻 🏊

NEW HOLLAND

Comfort Inn H

(717) 355-9900. **$100-$170.** 626 W Main St 17557. 0.5 mi w on SR 23. Int corridors. **Pets:** Large. $20 daily fee/pet. Designated rooms, service with restrictions, crate.

STRASBURG

Carriage House Motor Inn M

(717) 687-7651. **$49-$109.** 144 E Main St 17579. 0.3 mi e on SR 896 and 741. Ext corridors. **Pets:** Medium, dogs only. $50 deposit/pet, $10 daily fee/room. Designated rooms, service with restrictions, crate.

END AREA

PHILADELPHIA METROPOLITAN AREA

AUDUBON

Homewood Suites by Hilton H

(610) 539-7300. **$109-$219.** 681 Shannondell Blvd 19403. I-422 exit Trooper Rd, 1.2 mi n. Int corridors. **Pets:** Other species. $75 one-time fee/room. Service with restrictions, supervision.

BENSALEM

Extended

StayAmerica-Philadelphia/Bensalem H ❀

(215) 633-6900. **$95-$139.** 3216 Tillman Dr 19020. I-95 exit 37 (SR 132/ Street Rd), 2.5 mi w, then just s; I-276 exit 351, 0.9 mi on US 1, 1.4 mi e, then just s. Int corridors. **Pets:** Other species. $25 daily fee/pet. Service with restrictions.

Holiday Inn-Philadelphia Northeast H

(215) 637-1500. **$99-$129.** 3499 Street Rd 19020. I-276 (Pennsylvania Tpke) exit 351, just s on US 1, then 0.3 mi e on SR 132. Ext/int corridors. **Pets:** Small, other species. $20 one-time fee/pet. Designated rooms, service with restrictions, crate.

Sleep Inn & Suites-Bensalem H

(215) 244-2300. **Call for rates.** 3427 Street Rd 19020. I-276 (Pennsylvania Tpke) exit 351, just s on US 1, then 0.3 mi e on SR 132. Int corridors. **Pets:** Accepted.

BERWYN

Residence Inn Philadelphia-Valley Forge H ❀

(610) 640-9494. **$97-$226.** 600 W Swedesford Rd 19312. US 202 exit Paoli/SR 252, 1 mi n. Ext corridors. **Pets:** Large. $100 one-time fee/pet. Designated rooms, service with restrictions.

CHADDS FORD

Brandywine River Hotel H

(610) 388-1200. **Call for rates.** 1609 Baltimore Pike 19317. Jct US 1 (Baltimore Pike) and SR 100, 2 mi w of US 202 (Wilmington Pike). Int corridors. **Pets:** Accepted.

CHESTER

Best Western Plus Philadelphia Airport South at Widener University H ❀

(610) 872-8100. **$129-$219.** 1450 Providence Ave (SR 320) 19013. I-95 exit 6, just e to SR 320, follow signs. Int corridors. **Pets:** Medium. $40 one-time fee/pet. Service with restrictions, crate.

CONSHOHOCKEN

Residence Inn by Marriott Philadelphia/Conshohocken H

(610) 828-8800. **$159-$289.** 191 Washington St 19428. I-76 (Schuylkill Expwy) exit 332 (SR 23); I-476 exit 16 (SR 23), 0.3 mi over Fayette Bridge to Elm St, then just se along the river. Int corridors. **Pets:** Accepted.

EAST NORRITON

Hyatt house Philadelphia/Plymouth Meeting H

(610) 313-9990. **$99-$229.** 501 E Germantown Pike 19401. I-476 exit 20; I-276 (Pennsylvania Tpke) exit 333, 2.5 mi w. Int corridors. **Pets:** Medium. $75 one-time fee/room. Service with restrictions, supervision.

ERWINNA

Golden Pheasant Inn CI ❀

(610) 294-9595. **$95-$225, 21 day notice.** 763 River Rd 18920. SR 32, 0.5 mi n of jct Dark Hollow Rd. Int corridors. **Pets:** Medium, other species. $25 daily fee/pet. Designated rooms, service with restrictions, supervision.

ESSINGTON

Red Roof Inn-Airport #7119 M

(610) 521-5090. **$81-$95.** 49 Industrial Hwy 19029. I-95 exit 9A, 0.3 mi sw on SR 291. Ext corridors. **Pets:** Large, other species. No service, supervision.

FORT WASHINGTON

Best Western Fort Washington Inn H

(215) 542-7930. **$95-$105, 3 day notice.** 285 Commerce Dr 19034. I-276 (Pennsylvania Tpke) exit 339 (SR 309 S), just w on Pennsylvania Ave, just n to Commerce Dr, then 0.3 mi e. Int corridors. **Pets:** Large. $15 daily fee/pet. Designated rooms, service with restrictions, supervision.

Hilton Garden Inn Philadelphia/Fort Washington H

(215) 646-4637. **$109-$199.** 530 W Pennsylvania Ave 19034. I-276 (Pennsylvania Tpke) exit 339 (SR 309 S). Int corridors. **Pets:** Accepted.

Holiday Inn Fort Washington Hotel & Conference Center H

(215) 643-3000. **$99-$149.** 432 W Pennsylvania Ave 19034. I-276 (Pennsylvania Tpke) exit 339 (SR 309 S), just w. Int corridors. **Pets:** Medium. $45 one-time fee/room. Service with restrictions, supervision.

GLEN MILLS

Sweetwater Farm Bed & Breakfast BB

(610) 459-4711. **$150-$370, 14 day notice.** 50 Sweetwater Rd 19342. US 1, 2 mi w on Valley Rd, then 0.6 mi s. Int corridors. **Pets:** Other species. $35 daily fee/pet. Designated rooms, service with restrictions, supervision.

HORSHAM

Days Inn-Horsham/Philadelphia H

(215) 674-2500. **$71-$98.** 245 Easton Rd 19044. I-276 (Pennsylvania Tpke) exit 343 (SR 611), 1 mi n. Int corridors. **Pets:** Accepted.

▼▼ Extended

StayAmerica-Philadelphia/Horsham 🅗 ❖
(215) 784-9045. **$89-$134.** 114 Welsh Rd 19044. I-276 (Pennsylvania Tpke) exit 343 (SR 611), s toward Jenkintown, 0.6 mi w on Maryland Rd, 0.5 mi sw on Computer Ave, then just n. Int corridors. **Pets:** Other species. $25 daily fee/pet. Service with restrictions. 📶 🐾 🅗 📺

▼▼▼ Residence Inn by Marriott-Willow Grove 🅗
(215) 443-7330. **$103-$285.** 3 Walnut Grove Dr 19044. I-276 (Pennsylvania Tpke) exit 343 (SR 611), 1 mi n on Easton Rd, then 1.3 mi w on Dresher Rd; in Pennsylvania Business Campus. Ext corridors. **Pets:** Accepted. 📶 🗙 🅗 🅜 🅗 📺 🏊 🚫

KULPSVILLE
▼▼▼ Holiday Inn Lansdale 🅗
(215) 368-3800. **$99-$149.** 1750 Sumneytown Pike 19443. I-476 exit 31, just e. Int corridors. **Pets:** Accepted. 📶 🅗 🅜 🅗 📺 🍴 🏊

LANGHORNE
🆎 ▼▼▼ Residence Inn Langhorne 🅗
(215) 946-6500. **$219-$329.** 15 E Cabot Blvd 19047. I-95 exit 46A (Oxford Valley Rd), just e off US 1 N; 0.5 mi n of Sesame Place. Int corridors. **Pets:** Accepted. 🆂🅰🆅🅴 📶 🗙 🅜 🅗 📺 🏊 🚫

🆎 ▼▼▼ Sheraton Bucks County Hotel 🅗 ❖
(215) 547-4100. **$99-$259.** 400 Oxford Valley Rd 19047. I-95 exit 46A (Oxford Valley Rd), just e off US 1 N. Int corridors. **Pets:** Medium, dogs only. Designated rooms, service with restrictions, supervision. 🆂🅰🆅🅴 📶 🗙 🅜 🅗 📺 🍴 🏊 🚫

LIONVILLE
▼▼ Extended StayAmerica-Philadelphia/Exton 🅗 ❖
(610) 524-7185. **$104-$139.** 877 N Pottstown Pike (Rt 100) 19353. I-76 (Pennsylvania Tpke) exit 312, 1.8 mi s on SR 100. Int corridors. **Pets:** Other species. $25 daily fee/pet. Service with restrictions. 📶 🅗 📺

▼▼▼ Hampton Inn Exton 🅗 ❖
(610) 363-5555. **$129-$189.** 4 N Pottstown Pike 19341. I-76 (Pennsylvania Tpke) exit 312, 0.5 mi s; jct SR 113 and 100. Int corridors. **Pets:** Other species. Service with restrictions, crate. 📶 🅜 🅗 📺 🏊

▼▼▼ Residence Inn Philadelphia Great Valley/Exton 🅗
(610) 594-9705. **$170-$210.** 10 N Pottstown Pike 19341. I-76 (Pennsylvania Tpke) exit 312, 1 mi s on SR 100. Int corridors. **Pets:** Other species. $100 one-time fee/room. Service with restrictions. 📶 🗙 🅗 📺 🏊 🚫

MALVERN
▼▼ Extended StayAmerica-Philadelphia/Malvern 🅗 ❖
(610) 240-0455. **$104-$139.** 300 Morehall Rd (SR 29) 19355. US 202 exit SR 29 N. Int corridors. **Pets:** Other species. $25 daily fee/pet. Service with restrictions. 📶 🅜 🅗 📺

▼▼▼ Homestead Studio Suites Hotel
Philadelphia-Malvern 🅗 ❖
(610) 695-9200. **$99-$149.** 8 E Swedesford Rd 19355. Just w of US 202 and SR 29 N. Int corridors. **Pets:** Other species. $25 daily fee/pet. Service with restrictions. 📶 🅗 📺 🏊

▼▼▼ Homewood Suites by Hilton 🅗 ❖
(610) 296-3500. **$99-$139.** 12 E Swedesford Rd 19355. US 202 exit SR 29, follow signs. Int corridors. **Pets:** $50 one-time fee/pet. Service with restrictions, crate. 📶 🅜 🅗 📺 🏊

🆎 ▼▼▼ Sheraton Great Valley Hotel 🅗 ❖
(610) 524-5500. **$119-$279.** 707 Lancaster Pike 19355. Jct US 202 and 30 E. Int corridors. **Pets:** Medium, dogs only. Service with restrictions, crate. 🆂🅰🆅🅴 📶 🗙 🅜 🅗 📺 🍴 🏊

▼▼▼ Staybridge Suites 🅗
(610) 296-4343. **$109-$229, 3 day notice.** 20 Morehall Rd 19355. Jct US 30 and SR 29, just nw. Ext/int corridors. **Pets:** Accepted. 📶 🅗 📺 🏊 🚫

MONTGOMERYVILLE
▼▼▼ Residence Inn Philadelphia/Montgomeryville 🅗
(267) 468-0111. **$109-$289.** 1110 Bethlehem Pike 19454. I-276 (Pennsylvania Tpke) exit 339, 6.5 mi n on SR 309. Int corridors. **Pets:** Accepted. 📶 🗙 🅗 📺 🏊 🚫

▼▼ Rodeway Inn 🅗
(215) 699-8800. **$72-$119.** 969 Bethlehem Pike 18936. I-276 (Pennsylvania Tpke) exit 339, 8 mi n on SR 309. Ext corridors. **Pets:** Medium. $25 daily fee/room. Designated rooms, service with restrictions, supervision. 📶 🅜 🅗 📺

NEW HOPE
▼▼▼ 1870 Wedgwood Inn of New Hope 🅱🅱
(215) 862-2570. **$95-$295, 10 day notice.** 111 W Bridge St (SR 179) 18938. 0.5 mi w of SR 32; downtown. Int corridors. **Pets:** Small, dogs only. $20 daily fee/pet. Designated rooms, service with restrictions, supervision. 📶 🗙 🅗 📺

PHILADELPHIA
🆎 ▼▼▼ Aloft Philadelphia 🅗
(267) 298-1700. **$109-$309.** 4301 Island Ave 19153. Jct I-95 and SR 291 exit 13 northbound; exit 15 southbound. Int corridors. **Pets:** Accepted. 🆂🅰🆅🅴 📶 🗙 🅜 🅗 📺 🏊

🆎 ▼▼▼ Best Western Center City Hotel 🅗
(215) 557-0259. **$149-$159.** 501 N 22nd St 19130. I-95 exit 22, just n on Benjamin Franklin Pkwy. Int corridors. **Pets:** Medium. $15 daily fee/room. Designated rooms, service with restrictions. 🆂🅰🆅🅴 📶 🅜 🅗 📺 🍴

▼▼▼ Chestnut Hill Hotel 🅗
(215) 242-5905. **Call for rates.** 8229 Germantown Ave 19118. I-476 exit 19, 5.5 mi e. Int corridors. **Pets:** Accepted. 📶 🗙 🅗 🍴

▼▼ Extended StayAmerica-Philadelphia Airport 🅗 ❖
(215) 492-6766. **$74-$149.** 9000 Tinicum Blvd 19153. I-95 exit 12B (airport), just n on Essington Ave, then just w on Bartram Ave. Int corridors. **Pets:** Other species. $25 daily fee/pet. Service with restrictions. 📶 🅜 🅗 📺

🆎 ▼▼▼ Four Points by Sheraton Philadelphia Airport 🅗
(215) 492-0400. **$100-$260.** 4101 Island Ave 19153. Jct I-95 and SR 291 exit 13 northbound; exit 15 southbound. Int corridors. **Pets:** Accepted. 🆂🅰🆅🅴 📶 🗙 🅗 📺 🍴 🏊

🆎 ▼▼▼ Four Points by Sheraton Philadelphia Northeast 🅗 ❖
(215) 671-9600. **$99-$169.** 9461 E Roosevelt Blvd 19114. I-276 (Pennsylvania Tpke) exit 351, 5 mi s on US 1. Int corridors. **Pets:** Medium. $100 one-time fee/room. Designated rooms, service with restrictions, supervision. 🆂🅰🆅🅴 📶 🗙 🅗 📺 🍴 🏊

🆎 ▼▼▼▼ Four Seasons Hotel Philadelphia 🅗
(215) 963-1500. **Call for rates.** 1 Logan Square 19103. Corner of 18th St and Benjamin Franklin Pkwy. Int corridors. **Pets:** Accepted. 🆂🅰🆅🅴 📶 🅜 🅗 📺 🍴 🏊 🚫

🆎 ▼▼ ▼▼ The Hilton Inn at Penn 🅗
(215) 222-0200. **Call for rates.** 3600 Sansom St 19104. I-76 exit 345 eastbound; exit 346A (Sansom St) westbound; between 36th and 37th sts. Int corridors. **Pets:** Accepted. 🆂🅰🆅🅴 📶 🗙 🅗 📺

▼▼▼ Hotel Palomar-Philadelphia 🅗 ❖
(215) 563-5006. **Call for rates.** 117 S 17th St 19103. Corner of 17th and Samson sts. Int corridors. **Pets:** Other species. Designated rooms, service with restrictions, supervision. 📶 🗙 🅜 🅗 📺 🍴

◇◇◇ ▼▼▼ ▼▼▼ Hyatt at The Bellevue H
(215) 893-1234. **$149-$449, 3 day notice.** 200 S Broad St 19102. Between Walnut and Locust sts. Int corridors. **Pets:** Accepted.
SAVE 📶 🌙 🔌 🍴 🐾 ⊠

◇◇◇ ▼▼▼ ▼▼▼ Hyatt Regency Philadelphia At Penn's Landing H
(215) 928-1234. **$99-$499.** 201 S Columbus Blvd 19106. Jct S Columbus Blvd and Dock St. Int corridors. **Pets:** Accepted.
SAVE 📶 🌙 🔌 💺 🍴 🐾 ⊠

◇◇◇ ▼▼▼ ▼▼▼ Loews Philadelphia Hotel H
(215) 627-1200. **Call for rates.** 1200 Market St 19107. Corner of 12th and Market sts. Int corridors. **Pets:** Accepted.
SAVE 📶 ⊠ 🌙 🔌 💺 🍴 🐾 ⊠

▼▼▼ ▼▼▼ Philadelphia Airport Residence Inn by Marriott H ❖
(215) 492-1611. **$229-$263.** 4630 Island Ave 19153. I-95 exit 13 northbound; exit 15 southbound, 0.5 mi e; just e of SR 291. Ext corridors. **Pets:** Other species. $150 one-time fee/room, $5 daily fee/room. Service with restrictions, crate. 📶 ⊠ 🌙 🔌 💺

◇◇◇ ▼▼▼ ▼▼▼ Radisson Plaza-Warwick Hotel Philadelphia H ❖
(215) 735-6000. **$149-$499.** 1701 Locust St 19103. On 17th St; between Walnut and Locust sts; main entrance on Walnut St. Int corridors. **Pets:** Small, dogs only. $50 one-time fee/room, $10 daily fee/room. Designated rooms, service with restrictions, supervision.
ECO SAVE 📶 ⊠ 🔌 💺 🍴

▼▼◇▼▼ Residence Inn by Marriott Philadelphia City Center H
(215) 557-0005. **$161-$325.** 1 E Penn Square 19107. Jct Market and Juniper sts. Int corridors. **Pets:** Accepted. 📶 ⊠ 🔌 💺

◇◇◇ ▼▼◇▼▼▼ The Rittenhouse Hotel and Condominium Residences H ❖
(215) 546-9000. **$525-$565, 3 day notice.** 210 W Rittenhouse Square 19103. On Rittenhouse Square. Int corridors. **Pets:** $50 one-time fee/room. Service with restrictions, supervision.
SAVE 📶 ⊠ 🌙 💺 🍴 🐾 ⊠

▼▼◇▼▼ The Ritz-Carlton Philadelphia H ❖
(215) 523-8000. **Call for rates.** Ten Avenue of the Arts 19102. On Broad St; between Market and Chestnut sts. Int corridors. **Pets:** Small, dogs only. $150 one-time fee/room. Service with restrictions, supervision.
📶 ⊠ 💺 🍴 ⊠

◇◇◇ ▼▼◇▼▼▼ Sheraton Philadelphia Downtown Hotel H ❖
(215) 448-2000. **$100-$360, 3 day notice.** 201 N 17th St 19103. Jct 17th and Race sts. Int corridors. **Pets:** Medium, dogs only. Designated rooms, service with restrictions, supervision.
SAVE 📶 ⊠ 🔌 💺 🍴 🐾

◇◇◇ ▼▼◇▼▼▼ Sheraton Society Hill H
(215) 238-6000. **$149-$369.** One Dock St 19106. Just s of jct 2nd and Walnut sts. Int corridors. **Pets:** Accepted.
SAVE 📶 ⊠ 🔌 💺 🍴 🐾

◇◇◇ ▼▼▼ ▼▼▼ Sheraton Suites Philadelphia Airport H
(215) 365-6600. **$109-$289.** 4101 Island Ave 19153. Jct I-95 and SR 291 exit 13 northbound; exit 15 southbound. Int corridors. **Pets:** Accepted.
SAVE 📶 ⊠ 🔌 💺 🍴 🐾

◇◇◇ ▼▼▼ ▼▼▼ Sofitel Philadelphia H
(215) 569-8300. **$175-$460.** 120 S 17th St 19103. Jct Sansom and 17th sts. Int corridors. **Pets:** Accepted. ECO SAVE 📶 ⊠ 🌙 🍴

◇◇◇ ▼▼▼ ▼▼▼ The Westin Philadelphia H ❖
(215) 563-1600. **$139-$599.** 99 S 17th St at Liberty Pl 19103. Between Market and Chestnut sts. Int corridors. **Pets:** Medium, dogs only. $50 one-time fee/room. Designated rooms, service with restrictions, supervision. SAVE 📶 ⊠ 💺 🍴 ⊠

POTTSTOWN

◇◇◇ ▼▼▼▼ Comfort Inn & Suites H
(610) 326-5000. **$95-$135.** 99 Robinson St 19464. SR 100, 1 mi n of jct US 422. Int corridors. **Pets:** Accepted.
SAVE 📶 ⊠ 🌙 🔌 💺 🐾

QUAKERTOWN

◇◇◇ ▼▼▼▼ Comfort Inn & Suites H ❖
(215) 538-3000. **$89-$159.** 1905 John Fries Hwy (SR 663) 18951. I-476 (Pennsylvania Tpke) exit 44, just e. Ext corridors. **Pets:** Other species. $10 daily fee/room. Service with restrictions, crate. SAVE 📶 🔌 💺

▼▼▼▼ Hampton Inn-Quakertown H
(215) 536-7779. **$109-$139.** 1915 John Fries Hwy (SR 663) 18951. I-476 (Pennsylvania Tpke) exit 44, just e. Int corridors. **Pets:** Accepted.
📶 🌙 🔌 💺 🐾

ROYERSFORD

▼▼▼▼ Staybridge Suites Royersford/Valley Forge H
(610) 792-9300. **$119-$169.** 88 Anchor Pkwy 19468. I-422 exit Royersford, just n. Int corridors. **Pets:** Accepted. 📶 🌙 🔌 💺 🐾

TREVOSE

◇◇◇ ▼▼ ▼▼ Comfort Inn Trevose Northeast Philadelphia H
(215) 638-4554. **Call for rates.** 2779 Lincoln Hwy N 19053. I-276 (Pennsylvania Tpke) exit 351, 0.5 mi s. Int corridors. **Pets:** Accepted.
SAVE 📶 🔌 💺 🐾

◇◇◇ ▼▼ ▼▼ Red Roof Inn #7185 M
(215) 244-9422. **$67-$84.** 3100 Lincoln Hwy 19053. I-276 (Pennsylvania Tpke) exit 351, 0.5 mi s on US 1 at US 132. Ext corridors. **Pets:** Large, other species. No service, supervision. SAVE 📶 🌙 🔌

UPPER BLACK EDDY

▼▼▼▼ The Bridgeton House on the Delaware BB
(610) 982-5856. **$189-$479, 30 day notice.** 1525 River Rd 18972. On SR 32; center. Int corridors. **Pets:** Small, dogs only. $100 deposit/pet. Designated rooms, supervision. 📶 ⊠ 🔌 💺

END METROPOLITAN AREA

PINE GROVE

▼▼ ▼▼ Comfort Inn H ❖
(570) 345-8031. **$69-$145.** 433 Suedberg Rd 17963. I-81 exit 100, just e. Int corridors. **Pets:** Other species. $10 daily fee/room. Designated rooms, service with restrictions, crate. 📶 🌙 🔌 💺 🐾

▼▼▼▼ Hampton Inn Pine Grove H ❖
(570) 345-4505. **$99-$179.** 481 Suedberg Rd 17963. I-81 exit 100, just w. Int corridors. **Pets:** Other species. $25 one-time fee/pet. Designated rooms, service with restrictions, supervision. 📶 🌙 🔌 💺 🐾

PITTSBURGH METROPOLITAN AREA

BEAVER FALLS

▼▼▼ Holiday Inn H
(724) 846-3700. $99-$189. 7195 Eastwood Rd 15010. I-76 (Pennsylvania Tpke) exit 13, just n. Int corridors. Pets: Medium. $35 one-time fee/room. Service with restrictions, supervision. 🛜 🛅 💻 🍽 🌊 ⊠

BETHEL PARK

▼▼▼ Crowne Plaza Pittsburgh South H ❀
(412) 833-5300. $119-$199. 164 Ft Couch Rd 15241. 1 mi n on US 19. Int corridors. Pets: $35 one-time fee/room. Service with restrictions, supervision. 🛜 ⊠ 🛅 💻 🍽 🌊

BUTLER

▼▼ Butler Days Inn Conference Center H
(724) 287-6761. $76-$85. 139 Pittsburgh Rd 16001. 2 mi s. Int corridors. Pets: Accepted. 🛜 🛅 💻 🍽 🌊

▼▼ Locust Brook Lodge BB
(724) 283-8453. $85-$150. 179 Eagle Mill Rd 16001. 5 mi w on US 422 to jct Eagle Mill Rd, then 0.8 mi s; I-79 exit 99, 10 mi e on US 422 to jct Eagle Mill Rd, then 0.8 mi s. Ext/int corridors. Pets: Accepted. 🛜 ⊠

▼▼ Super 8 M
(724) 287-8888. $46-$60. 138 Pittsburgh Rd 16001. 2 mi s. Int corridors. Pets: Medium. $15 daily fee/pet. Service with restrictions, supervision. 🛜 🛅 💻

CORAOPOLIS

⟨AAA⟩ ▼▼▼ Crowne Plaza Hotel Pittsburgh International H
(412) 262-2400. $99-$299. 1160 Thorn Run Rd 15108. Business Rt SR 60 exit Thorn Run Rd. Int corridors. Pets: $50 one-time fee/pet. Service with restrictions, supervision. SAVE 🛜 🛅 💻 🍽 🌊

⟨AAA⟩ ▼▼▼ Embassy Suites-Pittsburgh International Airport H
(412) 329-2617. $139-$239. 550 Cherrington Pkwy 15108. Business Rt SR 60 exit Thorn Run Rd. Int corridors. Pets: Accepted.
SAVE 🛜 ⊠ 🔽M 🛅 💻 🍽 🌊 ⊠

▼▼▼ Hampton Inn Pittsburgh Airport H
(412) 264-0020. $99-$159. 8514 University Blvd 15108. Business Rt SR 60, 0.5 mi n. Int corridors. Pets: Accepted. 🛜 🛅 💻

⟨AAA⟩ ▼▼▼ Holiday Inn-Pittsburgh Airport H
(412) 262-3600. $89-$199. 8256 University Blvd 15108. Business Rt SR 60, 1 mi n. Int corridors. Pets: Medium. $50 one-time fee/room. Designated rooms, service with restrictions, crate.
SAVE 🛜 ⊠ 🔽M 🛅 💻 🍽 🌊

⟨AAA⟩ ▼▼▼ Hyatt Regency Pittsburgh International Airport H
(724) 899-1234. $89-$359. 1111 Airport Blvd 15231. SR 60 exit 6 (Airport Blvd). Int corridors. Pets: Accepted.
ECO SAVE 🛜 🛅 💻 🍽 🌊 ⊠

▼▼ La Quinta Inn Pittsburgh Airport H
(412) 269-0400. $72-$125. 8507 University Blvd 15108. 1 mi n of Business Rt SR 60. Int corridors. Pets: Medium, other species. Service with restrictions, supervision. 🛜 🔽M 🛅 💻

▼▼ Pittsburgh Airport Super 8 M
(412) 264-7888. $45-$63. 8991 University Blvd 15108. Business Rt SR 60, 1 mi n. Int corridors. Pets: Accepted. 🛜 🛅 💻

CRANBERRY TOWNSHIP

▼▼▼ Holiday Inn Express H ❀
(724) 772-1000. $99-$159. 20003 Rt 19 16066. I-76 (Pennsylvania Tpke) exit 28, jct US 19 and I-76 (Pennsylvania Tpke); I-79 exit 76 northbound; exit 78 southbound, just s. Int corridors. Pets: $25 daily fee/pet. Service with restrictions. 🛜 🛅 💻

⟨AAA⟩ ▼▼▼ Red Roof Inn-Cranberry Township-Pittsburgh North #7079 M
(724) 776-5670. $70-$85. 20009 Rt 19 16066. I-76 (Pennsylvania Tpke) exit 28; I-79 exit 76 northbound; exit 78 southbound. Ext corridors. Pets: Large, other species. No service, supervision. SAVE 🛜 🛅

▼▼▼ Residence Inn Pittsburgh Cranberry Township H
(724) 779-1000. $148-$198. 1308 Freedom Rd 16066. I-76 (Pennsylvania Tpke) exit 28, 0.5 mi n on US 19, then 0.3 mi w; I-79 exit 78 southbound, 0.5 mi w. Int corridors. Pets: Accepted.
🛜 ⊠ 🛅 💻 🌊 ⊠

DELMONT

▼▼ Super 8 M
(724) 468-4888. $62-$71. 180 Sheffield Dr 15626. SR 66, just s of US 22. Int corridors. Pets: Accepted. 🛜 🔽M 🛅 💻

FRANKLIN (VENANGO COUNTY)

▼▼ Franklin Super 8 H
(814) 432-2101. $49-$112. 847 Allegheny Blvd 16323. 2 mi n on SR 8. Int corridors. Pets: Accepted. 🛜 🛅 💻

GIBSONIA

▼▼ Quality Inn & Suites Pittsburgh-Gibsonia M
(724) 444-8700. $85-$195. 5137 William Flynn Hwy 15044. I-76 (Pennsylvania Tpke) exit 39, just n. Ext corridors. Pets: Large, other species. $10 daily fee/pet. Service with restrictions, supervision. 🛜 🛅 💻

GREEN TREE

⟨AAA⟩ ▼▼▼ DoubleTree by Hilton Pittsburgh-Green Tree H
(412) 922-8400. $109-$359. 101 DoubleTree Dr 15205. I-376 exit 67, 1.1 mi nw via Mansfield Ave. Int corridors. Pets: Service with restrictions, crate. SAVE 🛜 ⊠ 🔽M 🛅 💻 🍽 🌊 ⊠

▼▼▼ Hampton Inn Pittsburgh Green Tree H
(412) 922-0100. $99-$199. 555 Trumbull Dr 15205. I-376 exit 4A northbound; exit 4B southbound; jct US 22 and 30, 1 mi nw via Mansfield Ave. Int corridors. Pets: Accepted. 🛜 🛅 💻 🌊

MARS

▼▼ Comfort Inn Cranberry Township H
(724) 772-2700. $89-$103. 924 Sheraton Dr 16046. I-76 (Pennsylvania Tpke) exit 28; I-79 exit 76 (US 19 N) northbound; exit 78 southbound, 0.5 mi s on US 19. Int corridors. Pets: Accepted. 🛜 🛅 💻

▼▼ Super 8-Cranberry H
(724) 776-9700. $67-$143. 929 Sheraton Dr 16046. I-76 (Pennsylvania Tpke) exit 28; I-79 exit 76 (US 19 N) northbound; exit 78 southbound, 0.5 mi s on US 19. Int corridors. Pets: Accepted. 🛜 🛅 💻

MONACA

▼▼▼ Hampton Inn Beaver Valley/Pittsburgh H ❀
(724) 774-5580. $124-$132. 202 Fairview Dr 15061. SR 60 exit 12, just n. Int corridors. Pets: Medium, other species. Service with restrictions, supervision. 🛜 🔽M 🛅 💻 🌊

▼▼▼ **Holiday Inn Express Hotel & Suites-Center Township** H

(724) 728-5121. **$99-$179.** 105 Stone Quarry Rd 15061. SR 60 exit 12, just n. Int corridors. **Pets:** Small, dogs only. $20 daily fee/room. Service with restrictions, supervision. 🛜 🅗 💻 🏊

▼▼ **The Inn** H

(724) 728-9270. **$79-$129.** 1525 Old Brodhead Rd 15061. SR 60 exit 12, 1 mi e. Int corridors. **Pets:** Accepted. 🛜 🅗 💻

MONROEVILLE

ⒶⒶⒶ ▼▼▼ **DoubleTree by Hilton Hotel Pittsburgh - Monroeville Convention Center** H

(412) 373-7300. **$116-$155.** 101 Mall Blvd 15146. I-76 (Pennsylvania Tpke) exit 57, 2 mi w on US 22. Int corridors. **Pets:** Accepted.
SAVE 🛜 ❌ 🅗 💻 🍴 🏊

▼▼ **Extended StayAmerica-Pittsburgh-Monroeville** H ❖

(412) 856-8400. **$89-$129.** 3851 Northern Pike 15146. I-76 (Pennsylvania Tpke) exit 57, 1.2 mi w on Business Rt US 22. Int corridors. **Pets:** Other species. $25 daily fee/pet. Service with restrictions. 🛜 🅗 💻

▼▼▼ **Hampton Inn Monroeville/Pittsburgh** H

(412) 380-4000. **$109-$139.** 3000 Mosside Blvd 15146. I-76 (Pennsylvania Tpke) exit 57; I-376 exit 14A, 0.3 mi s on SR 48. Int corridors. **Pets:** Accepted. 🛜 ❌ 💻 🏊

ⒶⒶⒶ ▼▼▼ **Red Roof Inn-Monroeville #7174** M

(412) 856-4738. **$50-$70.** 2729 Mosside Blvd 15146. I-76 (Pennsylvania Tpke) exit 57; I-37 exit 14A, 0.8 mi s on SR 48. Ext corridors. **Pets:** Large, other species. No service, supervision. SAVE 🛜 🅗

▼▼ **Super 8 Pittsburgh/Monroeville** M

(724) 733-8008. **$54-$441.** 1807 Golden Mile Hwy (Rt 286) 15239. I-76 (Pennsylvania Tpke) exit 57; I-376 exit 14A, 2 mi w on US 22 E, then 2 mi e. Int corridors. **Pets:** Other species. $10 daily fee/pet. Designated rooms, service with restrictions, supervision. 🛜 🅗 💻

MOON RUN

▼▼ **Extended Stay Deluxe Pittsburgh Airport** H ❖

(412) 490-0979. **$94-$134.** 200 Chauvet Dr 15275. SR 60 exit 1 (Robinson Town Center Blvd), just s. Int corridors. **Pets:** Other species. $25 daily fee/pet. Service with restrictions. 🛜 🅗 💻 🏊

ⒶⒶⒶ ▼▼▼ **Four Points by Sheraton Pittsburgh Airport** H

(724) 695-0002. **$99-$215.** 1 Industry Ln 15275. SR 60 exit 2 (Montour Run Rd). Int corridors. **Pets:** $50 one-time fee/room. Designated rooms, service with restrictions, crate. SAVE 🛜 ❌ 🅗 💻 🍴 🏊

▼▼▼ **Holiday Inn Express & Pittsburgh Airport** H

(412) 788-8400. **$89-$169.** 5311 Campbells Run Rd 15205. US 22 and 30 W near jct SR 60 S (Crafton), just w. Int corridors. **Pets:** Accepted.
🛜 ❌ 🅗 💻 🏊

▼▼ **MainStay Suites Pittsburgh Airport** H

(412) 490-7343. **Call for rates.** 1000 Park Lane Dr 15275. SR 60 exit 2 (Montour Run Rd), just w on Cliff Mine Rd, then just s. Int corridors. **Pets:** Accepted. 🛜 🅗 💻 ❌

ⒶⒶⒶ ▼▼▼ **Pittsburgh Airport Marriott** H

(412) 788-8800. **$251-$338.** 777 Aten Rd 15108. SR 60 exit 2 (Montour Run Rd). Int corridors. **Pets:** Accepted.
SAVE 🛜 ❌ 🅗 💻 🍴 🏊

ⒶⒶⒶ ▼▼▼ **Red Roof Inn South Airport #7030** M

(412) 787-7870. **$64-$89.** 6404 Steubenville Pike 15205. I-79 exit 60A, 3.2 mi w on SR 60 (Steubenville Pike). Ext/int corridors. **Pets:** Large, other species. No service, supervision. SAVE 🛜 🅗

▼▼▼ **Residence Inn Pittsburgh Airport Coraopolis** H

(412) 787-3300. **$90-$280.** 1500 Park Lane Dr 15275. SR 60 exit 2 (Montour Run Rd), just w on Cliff Mine Dr to Summit Park Dr, just s to Park Lane Dr, then just e. Int corridors. **Pets:** Accepted.

🛜 ❌ 🅗ᴹ 🅗 💻 🏊 ❌

OAKDALE

ⒶⒶⒶ ▼▼ **Quality Inn Pittsburgh Airport** H

(412) 787-2600. **$90-$150.** 7011 Old Steubenville Pike 15071. US 22 and 30, jct SR 60; 4 mi w of jct I-279 and 79. Ext/int corridors. **Pets:** Large. $10 daily fee/pet. Designated rooms, service with restrictions, supervision. SAVE 🛜 🅗 💻

PITTSBURGH

▼▼▼ **DoubleTree by Hilton Hotel & Suites Pittsburgh Downtown** H

(412) 281-8800. **$189-$289.** One Bigelow Square 15219. Jct Bigelow Square and 6th St; just n of Grant St. Int corridors. **Pets:** Accepted.

ECO 🛜 ❌ 🅗 💻 🍴 🏊

ⒶⒶⒶ ▼▼▼ **Fairmont Pittsburgh** H ❖

(412) 773-8800. **Call for rates.** 510 Market St 15222. Between Market St and 5th Ave; in cultural district. Int corridors. **Pets:** Other species. $25 daily fee/room. Service with restrictions, supervision.

ECO SAVE 🛜 ❌ 🅗ᴹ 🅗 💻 🍴 ❌

▼▼▼ **Omni William Penn Hotel** H

(412) 281-7100. **Call for rates.** 530 William Penn Pl 15219. Jct 6th St and William Penn Pl. Int corridors. **Pets:** Accepted. 🛜 🅗 💻 ❌

▼▼▼ **Residence Inn by Marriott Pittsburgh University/ Medical Center** H

(412) 621-2200. **$199-$230.** 3896 Bigelow Blvd 15213. On SR 380. Int corridors. **Pets:** Accepted. 🛜 ❌ 🅗 💻 🏊 ❌

▼▼▼ **Residence Inn-Wilkins** H ❖

(412) 816-1300. **$143-$193.** 3455 William Penn Hwy 15235. I-76 exit 57, 3.5 mi n on William Penn Hwy. Int corridors. **Pets:** Large, other species. $100 one-time fee/room. Designated rooms, service with restrictions, crate. 🛜 ❌ 🅗 💻 🏊

ⒶⒶⒶ ▼▼▼ **Sheraton Station Square Hotel** H

(412) 261-2000. **$189-$389.** 300 W Station Square Dr 15219. I-376 exit Grant St, south end of Smithfield St Bridge; across river. Int corridors. **Pets:** Accepted. SAVE 🛜 ❌ 🅗 💻 🍴 🏊 ❌

ⒶⒶⒶ ▼▼▼ **The Westin Convention Center Pittsburgh** H

(412) 281-3700. **$161-$500.** 1000 Penn Ave 15222. Jct 10th St; at Liberty Center. Int corridors. **Pets:** Accepted.
SAVE 🛜 ❌ 🅗 💻 🍴 🏊 ❌

ⒶⒶⒶ ▼▼▼ **Wyndham Grand Pittsburgh Downtown** H

(412) 391-4600. **$99-$459.** 600 Commonwealth Pl 15222. Jct I-279/376/SR 885; in Gateway Center. Int corridors. **Pets:** Accepted.
SAVE 🛜 🅗ᴹ 💻 🍴

WASHINGTON

ⒶⒶⒶ ▼▼ **Ramada** H

(724) 225-9750. **$85-$109.** 1170 W Chestnut St 15301. I-70 exit 15, 0.5 mi e on US 40. Ext/int corridors. **Pets:** Small. $35 daily fee/room. Designated rooms, service with restrictions, supervision.
SAVE 🛜 🅗 💻 🍴 🏊

ⒶⒶⒶ ▼▼ **Red Roof Inn #10048** M

(724) 228-5750. **$69-$106.** 1399 W Chestnut St 15301. I-70 exit 15, just e on US 40. Ext/int corridors. **Pets:** Large, other species. No service, supervision. SAVE 🛜 🅗

WEST MIFFLIN

▼▼ ▼▼ **Extended StayAmerica-Pittsburgh-West Mifflin** H ❖

(412) 650-9096. **$94-$134.** 1303 Lebanon Church Rd 15122. 0.5 mi e of jct SR 51. Int corridors. **Pets:** Other species. $25 daily fee/pet. Service with restrictions. 🐾 (M) 🔒 💻

▼▼▼ **Holiday Inn Express Hotel & Suites** H

(412) 469-1900. **$128-$148.** 3122 Lebanon Church Rd 15122. 1.5 mi e of jct SR 51. Int corridors. **Pets:** Accepted. 🐾 🔒 💻

END METROPOLITAN AREA

POCONO MOUNTAINS AREA

BARTONSVILLE

AAA ▼▼▼▼ **Comfort Inn Bartonsville** H

(570) 476-1500. **Call for rates.** SR 611 18321. I-80 exit 302B, 0.4 mi n. Int corridors. **Pets:** Other species. Designated rooms, service with restrictions, supervision. (SAVE) 🐾 🔒 💻 🍴 🏊 ⊠

BLAKESLEE

AAA ▼▼▼▼ **Best Western Inn at Blakeslee-Pocono** H ❖

(570) 646-6000. **$85-$195.** New Ventures Business Park 18610. I-80 exit 284, just n. Int corridors. **Pets:** $50 deposit/room. Service with restrictions, supervision. (SAVE) 🐾 (M) 💻 🏊

EAST STROUDSBURG

AAA ▼▼▼▼ **Budget Inn & Suites** H ❖

(570) 424-5451. **$67-$115.** 308 Greentree Dr 18301. I-80 exit 308, just se. Ext/int corridors. **Pets:** Designated rooms, service with restrictions, crate. (SAVE) 🐾 🔒 💻 🍴

▼▼ ▼▼ **Super 8 East Stroudsburg** M

(570) 424-7411. **$42-$118.** 340 Greentree Dr 18301. I-80 exit 308, just se. Int corridors. **Pets:** $10 daily fee/pet. Designated rooms, service with restrictions, supervision. 🐾 (M) 🔒 💻

HAMLIN

AAA ▼▼ ▼▼ **Comfort Inn-Pocono Lakes Region** H

(570) 689-4148. **$80-$209.** 117 Twin Rocks Rd 18427. I-84 exit 17, just n on SR 191. Int corridors. **Pets:** Accepted. (SAVE) 🐾 🔒 💻

MATAMORAS

AAA ▼▼ ▼▼ **Best Western Inn at Hunt's Landing** H

(570) 491-2400. **$99-$169.** 120 Rt 6 & 209 18336. I-84 exit 53. Int corridors. **Pets:** Accepted. (SAVE) 🐾 🔒 💻 🍴 🏊 ⊠

MILFORD

▼▼▼▼ **Hotel Fauchere** H ❖

(570) 409-1212. **$195-$425, 14 day notice.** 401 Broad St 18337. In historic downtown. Int corridors. **Pets:** Dogs only. $25 daily fee/pet. Designated rooms, service with restrictions, supervision.

🐾 ⊠ 🔒 💻 🍴

AAA ▼▼ ▼▼ **Milford Motel** M ❖

(570) 296-6411. **$45-$110, 3 day notice.** 591 Rt 6 & 209 18337. US 6 and 209 N, 0.7 mi e. Ext corridors. **Pets:** Dogs only. $5 daily fee/pet. Designated rooms, service with restrictions, supervision. (SAVE) 🐾 🔒

AAA ▼▼ ▼▼ **Scottish Inns** M

(570) 491-4414. **$50-$110, 3 day notice.** 274 Rt 6 & 209 18337. I-84 exit 53, 1 mi s. Ext corridors. **Pets:** Accepted. (SAVE) 🐾 🔒 💻

STARLIGHT

▼▼ ▼▼ **The Inn at Starlight Lake** CI

(570) 798-2519. **$115-$195, 14 day notice.** 289 Starlight Lake Rd 18461. Off SR 370, 1 mi n, follow signs. Ext/int corridors. **Pets:** Other species. $10 daily fee/room. Designated rooms.

⊠ 🍴 ⊠ (K) (P) ☕

TANNERSVILLE

AAA ▼▼ ▼▼ **Chateau Resort & Conference Center** H

(570) 629-5900. **Call for rates.** 300 Camelback Rd 18372. I-80 exit 299, 1 mi w on Sullivan Tr, then 1.7 mi on Camelback Rd, follow signs to Camelback Ski area or Camelback Beach Water Park. Int corridors. **Pets:** Accepted. (SAVE) 🐾 🔒 💻 🍴 🏊 ⊠

END AREA

SAYRE

AAA ▼▼ ▼▼ **Best Western Grand Victorian Inn** H

(570) 888-7711. **$139.** 255 Spring St 18840. SR 17 exit 61, just s. Int corridors. **Pets:** Accepted. (SAVE) 🐾 🔒 💻 🍴 🏊 ⊠

SCRANTON

▼▼▼▼ **Hilton Scranton & Conference Center** H ❖

(570) 343-3000. **$109-$259.** 100 Adams Ave 18503. I-81 exit 185, just w of jct Lackawanna Ave, Jefferson Ave and Spruce St; downtown. Int corridors. **Pets:** Medium. $50 deposit/pet. Designated rooms, service with restrictions, crate. (ECO) 🐾 (M) 🔒 💻 🍴 🏊

▼▼▼▼ **Radisson Lackawanna Station Hotel Scranton** H ❖

(570) 342-8300. **$119-$289.** 700 Lackawanna Ave 18503. I-81 exit 185, jct Lackawanna and Jefferson aves and Spruce St; downtown. Int corridors. **Pets:** Medium, dogs only. $70 one-time fee/pet, $10 daily fee/pet. Designated rooms, service with restrictions, crate.

🐾 🔒 💻 🍴 ⊠

▼▼▼▼ **TownePlace Suites Scranton Wilkes-Barre** H

(570) 207-8500. **$123-$143.** 26 Radcliffe Dr 18507. I-81 exit 182A southbound, just e to Montage Mountain Rd, just se to Glenmaura Blvd, just e on National Blvd, then just n; exit 182 northbound. Int corridors. **Pets:** Accepted. 🐾 ⊠ (M) 🔒 💻 ☕

SELINSGROVE

▼▼ ▼▼ **Comfort Inn** H

(570) 374-8880. **$89-$189.** 613 N Susquehanna Tr 17870. US 11 and 15, just n of US 522. Int corridors. **Pets:** Small. $25 daily fee/pet. Service with restrictions, crate. 🐾 🔒 💻 🍴 ☕

SHAMOKIN DAM

▼▼ Econo Lodge Inn & Suites ℍ ❀

(570) 743-1111. **$60-$169.** 3249 N Susquehanna Tr 17876. US 11 and 15, just n of jct SR 61. Ext corridors. **Pets:** Small, other species. $10 daily fee/pet. Designated rooms, service with restrictions, crate.
🛜 🖬 🖵 🍽 ⇔

▼▼ Phillips Motel Ⓜ

(570) 743-3100. **Call for rates.** 2943 N Susquehanna Tr 17876. 3 mi n of Selingsgrove. Ext corridors. **Pets:** Accepted. 🛜 🖬 🖵

SHICKSHINNY

▼▼ The Blue Heron Bed & Breakfast 🅱🅱

(570) 864-9930. **Call for rates.** 1266 Bethel Hill Rd 18655. Jct US 11, 6.2 mi n on SR 239, then 2 mi n on CR 4016 (Harveyville/Bethel Hill Rd). Int corridors. **Pets:** Accepted. 🛜 ✖ 🐾 🐾 📵

SHILLINGTON

AAA ▼▼▼ Best Western Plus Reading Inn & Suites ℍ ❀

(610) 777-7888. **$50-$129.** 2299 Lancaster Pike 19607. US 422 exit Penn Ave, 1.5 mi e on SR 724, then 0.5 mi s on US 222; I-76 (Pennsylvania Tpke) exit 286, 9 mi n on US 222. Int corridors. **Pets:** Large, other species. $50 deposit/room, $14 daily fee/pet. Service with restrictions, supervision. 🅢🅐🅥🅔 🛜 🖬 🖵 ⇔

SHIPPENSBURG

AAA ▼▼ Best Western Shippensburg Hotel ℍ

(717) 532-5200. **$63-$121.** 125 Walnut Bottom Rd 17257. I-81 exit 29, 0.5 mi w on SR 174. Int corridors. **Pets:** Medium. $10 daily fee/pet. Service with restrictions, supervision. 🅢🅐🅥🅔 🛜 🖬 🖵 ⇔ ✖

SOUTH WILLIAMSPORT

▼▼ Ridgemont Motel Ⓜ

(570) 321-5300. **$49-$59.** 637 US Hwy 15 S 17702. 1.2 mi s on US 15. Ext corridors. **Pets:** Accepted. 🛜 ✖ 🖬 🖵

STATE COLLEGE

▼▼ The Autoport Motel & Restaurant Ⓜ

(814) 237-7666. **Call for rates.** 1405 S Atherton St 16801. US 322 business route, 1.4 mi e of jct SR 26. Ext/int corridors. **Pets:** Accepted.
🛜 ✖ 🖬 🖵 🍽 ⇔

AAA ▼▼▼ Days Inn Penn State ℍ

(814) 238-8454. **$80-$129.** 240 S Pugh St 16801. Just e SR 26 northbound; 0.4 mi n of jct US 322 business route; downtown. Int corridors. **Pets:** Accepted. 🅢🅐🅥🅔 🛜 🖬 🖵 🍽 ⇔

AAA ▼ Nittany Budget Motel Ⓜ ❀

(814) 238-0015. **$49-$225, 30 day notice.** 2070 Cato Ave 16801. SR 26, 2.6 mi s of jct US 322 business route. Ext corridors. **Pets:** Other species. $5 daily fee/pet. Service with restrictions, supervision.
🅢🅐🅥🅔 🛜

AAA ▼▼▼ Quality Inn Penn State Ⓜ ❀

(814) 234-1600. **Call for rates.** 1274 N Atherton St 16803. US 322 business route, 1 mi w of jct SR 26. Int corridors. **Pets:** Other species. $10 one-time fee/room. Service with restrictions, supervision.
🅢🅐🅥🅔 🛜 ✖ 🔥 🖬 🖵

▼▼▼ Residence Inn State College ℍ

(814) 235-6960. **$109-$219.** 1555 University Dr 16801. US 322 business route, 1.5 mi e of jct SR 26. Int corridors. **Pets:** Accepted.
🛜 ✖ 🖬 🖵 ⇔ ✖

AAA ▼▼▼ Super 8 State College ℍ

(814) 237-8005. **$43-$273, 14 day notice.** 1663 S Atherton St 16801. US 322 business route, 1.6 mi e of jct SR 26. Int corridors. **Pets:** $25 one-time fee/room. Service with restrictions, supervision.
🅢🅐🅥🅔 🛜 🖬 🖵

▼▼▼ Toftrees Golf Resort & Conference Center ℍ

(814) 234-8000. **$69-$399.** One Country Club Ln 16803. US 322/I-99 exit 71 (Toftrees/Woodycrest). Int corridors. **Pets:** Accepted.
🅢🅐🅥🅔 🛜 🖬 🖵 🍽 ⇔ ✖

WARREN

AAA ▼▼▼ Holiday Inn of Warren ℍ

(814) 726-3000. **$119-$129.** 210 Ludlow St 16365. Jct US 6, just n on Ludlow St (US 62 N). Int corridors. **Pets:** Other species. Designated rooms. 🅢🅐🅥🅔 🛜 🔥 🖬 🖵 🍽 ⇔

▼▼ Warren Super 8 ℍ

(814) 723-8881. **$58-$67.** 204 Struthers St 16365. 1.5 mi w on US 6 exit Ludlow St, w on Allegheny, then s. Ext/int corridors. **Pets:** Medium. $25 deposit/room. Designated rooms, service with restrictions, crate.
🛜 🖬 🖵

WEST HAZLETON

▼▼▼ Candlewood Suites ℍ

(570) 459-1600. **$99-$119.** 9 Bowman's Mill Rd 18202. I-81 exit 145 southbound; exit SR 93 S northbound to Tom Hicken Rd. Int corridors. **Pets:** Other species. $10 daily fee/pet. Service with restrictions, crate.
🛜 🔥 🖬 🖵

WEST READING

▼▼▼ Candlewood Suites ℍ

(610) 898-1910. **$119-$219.** 55 S 3rd Ave 19611. Jct Penn Ave. Int corridors. **Pets:** Medium. $75 one-time fee/room. Service with restrictions, crate. 🛜 🔥 🖬 🖵

WHITE HAVEN

AAA ▼▼ Comfort Inn-Pocono Mountain ℍ

(570) 443-8461. **Call for rates.** Rt 940 at I-80 & 476 18661. I-476 exit 95, just e; I-80 exit 277 (Lake Harmony). Int corridors. **Pets:** Accepted.
🅢🅐🅥🅔 🛜 🖬 🖵 ⇔ ✖

WILKES-BARRE

AAA ▼▼ Best Western Genetti Hotel & Conference Center ℍ ❀

(570) 823-6152. **$85-$150.** 77 E Market St 18701. Jct Washington St; downtown. Int corridors. **Pets:** Large, dogs only. $10 daily fee/pet. Designated rooms, service with restrictions, crate.
🅢🅐🅥🅔 🛜 🖬 🖵 🍽 ⇔

AAA ▼▼ Days Inn ℍ

(570) 826-0111. **$57-$208.** 760 Kidder St 18702. I-81 exit 170B, to exit 1 (SR 309 S business route), just w; I-76 (Pennsylvania Tpke) exit 105 to exit 1 (SR 115 N). Int corridors. **Pets:** Accepted. 🅢🅐🅥🅔 🛜 🖬

AAA ▼▼ Econo Lodge Arena ℍ ❀

(570) 823-0600. **$54-$200.** 1075 Wilkes-Barre Township Blvd 18702. I-81 exit 165 southbound; exit 165B northbound, on SR 309 business route. Int corridors. **Pets:** Large. $100 deposit/room, $10 daily fee/pet. Designated rooms, service with restrictions, supervision. 🅢🅐🅥🅔 🛜 🖬 🖵

▼▼▼ Extended Stay Deluxe Wilkes-Barre Hwy 315 ℍ ❀

(570) 970-2500. **$100-$149.** 1067 Hwy 315 18702. I-81 exit 170B to exit 1 (SR 309 S business route), 0.3 mi n. Int corridors. **Pets:** Other species. $25 daily fee/pet. Service with restrictions. 🛜 🔥 🖬 🖵

AAA ▼▼▼ Host Inn All Suites Hotel ℍ

(570) 270-4678. **$109-$149.** 860 Kidder St 18702. I-81 exit 170B to exit 1 (SR 309 S business route), then 0.5 mi w. Int corridors. **Pets:** $15 daily fee/pet. Service with restrictions, crate. 🅢🅐🅥🅔 🛜 🔥 🖬 🖵 ⇔

▼▼ Quality Inn & Suites ℍ

(570) 824-8901. **$69-$129.** 880 Kidder St 18702. I-81 exit 170B to exit 1 (SR 309 S business route) off expressway, then 0.5 mi w. Ext corridors. **Pets:** Accepted. 🛜 🖬 🖵 🍽

◆◆◇ ◇◇◇◇ Red Roof Inn #7139 **M**
(570) 829-6422. **$49-$79.** 1035 Hwy 315 18702. I-81 exit 170B to exit 1 (SR 309 S business route) to SR 315, then just n. Ext corridors. **Pets:** Large, other species. No service, supervision. (SAVE) 🛜 📠

◇◇◇◇◇◇ The Woodlands Inn, An Ascend Collection by Choice Hotels **H**
(570) 824-9831. **$109-$189.** 1073 Hwy 315 18702. I-81 exit 170B to exit 1 (SR 309 S business route), then 0.3 mi n. Int corridors.
Pets: Accepted. 🛜 📠 🖥 🍴 🏊 ✕

WILLIAMSPORT

◆◆◆ ◇◇◇◇ Best Western Williamsport Inn **H**
(570) 326-1981. **Call for rates.** 1840 E 3rd St 17701. I-180 exit 25 (Faxon St), 0.5 mi e. Ext corridors. **Pets:** Medium, dogs only. $15 daily fee/pet. Designated rooms, service with restrictions, supervision.
(SAVE) 🛜 📠 🖥 🍴 🏊

◇◇◇◇ Candlewood Suites **H**
(570) 601-9100. **$169-$279.** 1836 E 3rd St 17701. I-180 exit 25 (Faxon St), 0.5 mi e. Int corridors. **Pets:** Medium, other species. $10 daily fee/pet. Designated rooms, service with restrictions, supervision.
🛜 📠 🖥 🏊

◆◆◆ ◇◇◇◇ Genetti Hotel & Suites **H** 🐾
(570) 326-6600. **$139-$220, 7 day notice.** 200 W 4th St 17701. Jct William St; downtown. Ext/int corridors. **Pets:** Dogs only. $15 daily fee/pet. Designated rooms, service with restrictions, supervision.
(SAVE) 🛜 📠 🖥 🍴 🏊

WIND GAP

◆◆◆ ◇◇◇◇ Red Carpet Inn **M**
(610) 863-7782. **$59-$130.** 1395 Jacobsburg Rd 18091. SR 33 exit Wind Gap/Bath (SR 512 S), just s on Jacobsburg Rd, follow signs. Ext/int corridors. **Pets:** Small. $20 daily fee/pet. Designated rooms, service with restrictions, supervision. (SAVE) 🛜 📠

WYOMISSING

◆◆◆ ◇◇◇◇◇ Crowne Plaza Reading Hotel **H**
(610) 376-3811. **$129-$189, 3 day notice.** 1741 W Papermill Rd 19610. US 422 exit Papermill Rd. Int corridors. **Pets:** Accepted.
(SAVE) 🛜 ✕ 🖥 📠 🖥 🍴 🏊

◇◇◇ Econo Lodge Inn & Suites **H**
(610) 378-5105. **Call for rates.** 635 Spring St 19610. Just off US 422 to exit Papermill Rd. Int corridors. **Pets:** Accepted. 🛜 📠 🖥

◇◇◇◇ Homewood Suites-Reading/Wyomissing **H**
(610) 736-3100. **$119-$209.** 2801 Papermill Rd 19610. US 422 exit Papermill Rd, 1.8 mi nw; US 222 exit Spring Ridge Rd. Int corridors. **Pets:** Medium. $75 one-time fee/pet. Service with restrictions, supervision.
🛜 🖥 📠 🖥 🏊

◆◆◆ ◇◇◇◇ The Inn at Reading **H**
(610) 372-7811. **$89-$199.** 1040 N Park Rd 19610. US 222 exit on N Wyomissing Blvd, just n, then 0.3 mi e. Int corridors. **Pets:** Large. $10 daily fee/pet. Designated rooms, service with restrictions, crate.
(SAVE) 🛜 🖥 📠 🖥 🍴 🏊 ✕

WYSOX

◇◇◇◇ Comfort Inn **H**
(570) 265-5691. **Call for rates.** US 6 18854. On US 6; center. Int corridors. **Pets:** Accepted. 🛜 ✕ 📠 🖥 🏊 ✕

YORK

◇◇◇◇ Comfort Inn & Suites **H**
(717) 699-1919. **Call for rates.** 2250 N George St 17402. I-83 exit 22, just n. Int corridors. **Pets:** Large. $50 one-time fee/room. Designated rooms, service with restrictions, crate. 🛜 🖥 📠 🖥

◇◇◇◇ Holiday Inn Conference Center of York **H**
(717) 846-9500. **$139-$179.** 2000 Loucks Rd 17408. I-83 exit 21B northbound, 2.5 mi w on US 30, then just n; exit 22 southbound, 0.5 mi s on SR 181, 2.2 mi w on US 30, then just n. Int corridors. **Pets:** Accepted.
🛜 📠 🖥 🍴 🏊 ✕

◇◇◇◇ Holiday Inn Express **H** 🐾
(717) 741-1000. **$95-$180.** 140 Leader Heights Rd 17403. I-83 exit 14, just w on SR 182. Int corridors. **Pets:** Large, dogs only. $50 one-time fee/room. Service with restrictions, crate. 🛜 ✕ 📠 🖥

◇◇◇◇ Red Roof Inn #315 **H**
(717) 843-8181. **$59-$114.** 125 Arsenal Rd 17404. I-83 exit 21B northbound, 0.3 mi w on US 30; exit 21 southbound, 0.5 mi s on SR 181 to US 30. Int corridors. **Pets:** Large, other species. No service, supervision.
🛜 📠 🖥

◆◆◆ ◇◇◇◇ The Yorktowne Hotel **H**
(717) 848-1111. **$109-$279.** 48 E Market St 17401. SR 462 eastbound and I-83 business route, just e of square, follow signs. Int corridors. **Pets:** Medium, other species. $25 daily fee/pet. Designated rooms, service with restrictions, crate. (SAVE) 🛜 📠 🖥 🍴

RHODE ISLAND

CITY INDEX

EAST PROVIDENCE

◇◇◇ Extended StayAmerica Providence-East Providence **H** 🐾
(401) 272-1661. **$92-$199.** 1000 Warren Ave 02914. I-195 exit 8 eastbound, just e; exit 6 westbound, 1.1 mi e via Warren Ave. Int corridors. **Pets:** Other species. $25 daily fee/pet. Service with restrictions.
🛜 🖥 📠 🖥

MIDDLETOWN

◆◆◆ ◇◇◇◇ The Ambassador Inn & Suites **M**
(401) 849-2718. **Call for rates.** 1359 W Main Rd 02842. On SR 114, just n of jct SR 214. Int corridors. **Pets:** Accepted.
(SAVE) 🛜 ✕ 📠 🏊

◆◆◆ ◇◇◇◇ Howard Johnson Inn-Newport **H** 🐾
(401) 849-2000. **$71-$220.** 351 W Main Rd 02842. On SR 114, 0.3 mi s of jct SR 138. Int corridors. **Pets:** Other species. $10 daily fee/pet. Designated rooms, service with restrictions, supervision.
(SAVE) 🛜 🖥 📠 🖥 🍴 🏊 ✕

◆◆◆ ◇◇◇◇ Residence Inn by Marriott-Newport/Middletown **H** 🐾
(401) 845-2005. **$119-$349, 3 day notice.** 325 W Main Rd 02842. On SR 114, 0.3 mi s of jct SR 138. Int corridors. **Pets:** Other species. $75 one-time fee/room. Designated rooms, service with restrictions.
(SAVE) 🛜 ✕ 🖥 📠 🖥 🏊 ✕

NEWPORT

AAA ◆◆◆ **Beech Tree Inn** BB
(401) 847-9794. **$99-$359, 14 day notice.** 34 Rhode Island Ave 02840. Just e of SR 114; 0.8 mi s of jct SR 138. Int corridors. **Pets:** Other species. $25 one-time fee/pet. Designated rooms, no service.
SAVE ◎ ✕ 🛢

AAA ◆◆◆ **Best Western The Mainstay Inn** H
(401) 849-9880. **$50-$250, 3 day notice.** 151 Admiral Kalbfus Rd 02840. SR 138; from Newport Bridge, 2nd exit. Int corridors.
Pets: Accepted. SAVE ◎ 🛢 💻 🍽 ⊠

◆◆◆ **The Burbank Rose** BB
(401) 849-9457. **$89-$240, 7 day notice.** 111 Memorial Blvd W 02840. Just e on SR 138A. Int corridors. **Pets:** Accepted.
◎ ✕ 🛢 💻 ⊠

AAA ◆◆◆◆ **Hyatt Regency Newport Hotel & Spa** H ❖
(401) 851-1234. **$109-$449, 3 day notice.** 1 Goat Island 02840. 0.8 mi w of America's Cup Ave, follow signs to Goat Island. Int corridors. **Pets:** Dogs only. $75 one-time fee/room. Service with restrictions, crate.
ECO SAVE ◎ ♿M 🛢 💻 🍽 ⊠ ⊠

◆◆◆ **Pelham Court Hotel** H
(401) 619-4950. **Call for rates.** 14 Pelham St 02840. Just n of Memorial Blvd (SR 138A) via Spring St, then just w. Int corridors. **Pets:** Accepted.
◎ ✕ 🛢 💻

AAA ◆◆◆◆ **Vanderbilt Grace** H ❖
(401) 846-6200. **$275-$1600, 21 day notice.** 41 Mary St 02840. Just n of Thames St; downtown. Int corridors. **Pets:** Dogs only. $100 one-time fee/pet. Designated rooms, service with restrictions, supervision.
SAVE ◎ ✕ 🛢 💻 ⊠ ⊠

NORTH KINGSTOWN

◆◆◆ **Hamilton Village Inn** M
(401) 295-0700. **$79-$139, 7 day notice.** 642 Boston Neck Rd 02852. SR 1A, 1.3 mi s of jct SR 102. Ext corridors. **Pets:** Other species. Designated rooms, service with restrictions, supervision. ◎ 🛢 💻 🍽

PAWTUCKET

◆◆ **Comfort Inn-Providence/Pawtucket** H
(401) 723-6700. **$110-$125.** 2 George St 02860. I-95 exit 27, just e, then just n. Int corridors. **Pets:** Medium. $15 daily fee/pet. Service with restrictions, crate. ◎ ♿M 🛢 💻 🍽 ⊠

PROVIDENCE

AAA ◆◆◆◆ **The Hotel Providence** H ❖
(401) 861-8000. **Call for rates.** 139 Mathewson St 02903. Corner of Westminster St; downtown. Int corridors. **Pets:** Medium, dogs only. $75 one-time fee/room. Supervision. ECO SAVE ◎ ✕ 🛢 💻 🍽

AAA ◆◆◆◆ **Marriott Providence Downtown** H
(401) 272-2400. **$144-$208.** 1 Orms St 02904. I-95 exit 23 to state offices. Int corridors. **Pets:** Accepted.
ECO SAVE ◎ ✕ ♿M 🛢 💻 🍽 ⊠ ⊠

AAA ◆◆◆◆ **Providence Biltmore Hotel** H
(401) 421-0700. **$119-$299.** 11 Dorrance St 02903. Between Washington and Worcester sts. Int corridors. **Pets:** Medium. $75 one-time fee/room. Service with restrictions, supervision.
ECO SAVE ◎ ♿M 🛢 💻 🍽

AAA ◆◆◆◆ **The Westin Providence** H
(401) 598-8000. **$149-$509.** One W Exchange St 02903. I-95 exit 22A; downtown. Int corridors. **Pets:** Accepted.
ECO SAVE ◎ ✕ ♿M 🛢 💻 🍽 ⊠ ⊠

SMITHFIELD

AAA ◆◆◆ **Hampton Inn & Suites Smithfield** H
(401) 232-9200. **$139-$189.** 945 Douglas Pike 02917. I-295 exit 8B, 0.6 mi nw on SR 7. Int corridors. **Pets:** Accepted.
SAVE ◎ ✕ ♿M 🛢 💻 ⊠

AAA ◆◆◆ **Quality Inn Smithfield** H
(401) 232-2400. **$100-$250, 7 day notice.** 355 George Washington Hwy 02917. I-295 exit 8B, 0.3 mi n on SR 7, then 0.6 mi e on SR 116. Int corridors. **Pets:** Medium, dogs only. $25 daily fee/pet. Designated rooms, service with restrictions, supervision.
SAVE ◎ ♿M 🛢 💻 ⊠

WAKEFIELD

◆◆◆ **The Kings' Rose Inn** BB ❖
(401) 783-5222. **$110-$145.** 1747 Mooresfield Rd (SR 138) 02879. I-95 exit 3A, 1 mi e on SR 138; 3.3 mi w of US 1. Int corridors. **Pets:** Service with restrictions, crate. ◎ ✕

WARWICK

AAA ◆◆◆ **Best Western Airport Inn** H
(401) 737-7400. **$80-$150.** 2138 Post Rd 02886. I-95 exit 13, e to US 1, then just ne. Int corridors. **Pets:** Accepted. SAVE ◎ 🛢 💻

◆◆◆ **Comfort Inn-Airport** H
(401) 732-0470. **$55-$129.** 1940 Post Rd 02886. I-95 exit 13, e to US 1, then 0.5 mi n. Int corridors. **Pets:** Medium, other species. $50 one-time fee/pet. Supervision. ◎ 🛢 💻

◆◆◆ **Crowne Plaza Hotel at the Crossings** H
(401) 732-6000. **Call for rates.** 801 Greenwich Ave 02886. I-95 exit 12A southbound; exit 12 northbound, 0.3 mi se on SR 5. Int corridors.
Pets: Accepted. ECO ◎ ♿M 🛢 💻 🍽 ⊠ ⊠

◆◆ **Extended StayAmerica Providence-Airport-Warwick** H ❖
(401) 732-2547. **$80-$169.** 245 W Natick Rd 02886. I-295 exit 2 northbound, just sw; exit 3A southbound, 1.1 mi e on SR 37, 2 mi s on SR 2, then just sw. Int corridors. **Pets:** Other species. $25 daily fee/pet. Service with restrictions. ◎ ♿M 🛢 💻

AAA ◆◆◆ **Hampton Inn & Suites Providence-Warwick Airport** H
(401) 739-8888. **$119-$149.** 2100 Post Rd 02886. I-95 exit 13, e to US 1, then just n. Int corridors. **Pets:** Medium. Service with restrictions, supervision. SAVE ◎ ♿M 🛢 💻 ⊠ ⊠

◆◆◆ **Holiday Inn Express Hotel & Suites** H
(401) 736-5000. **Call for rates.** 901 Jefferson Blvd 02886. I-95 exit 13, 0.4 mi on Airport Connector Rd, then exit Jefferson Blvd. Int corridors. **Pets:** Dogs only. $50 deposit/pet. Designated rooms, service with restrictions, supervision. ECO ◎ ✕ ♿M 🛢 💻 ⊠

◆◆ **Homestead Studio Suites Hotel-Providence/Airport/Warwick** H ❖
(401) 732-6667. **$85-$159.** 268 Metro Center Blvd 02886. I-95 exit 12A, 0.4 mi e on SR 113, 0.4 mi n on SR 5, then 0.4 mi e. Int corridors. **Pets:** Other species. $25 daily fee/pet. Service with restrictions.
◎ ♿M 🛢 💻 ⊠

◆◆◆ **Homewood Suites by Hilton** H
(401) 738-0008. **$79-$259.** 33 International Way 02886. I-95 exit 13, 0.4 mi n on Jefferson Blvd, 0.5 mi nw on Kilvert St, then 0.4 mi sw on Metro Center Blvd. Int corridors. **Pets:** Accepted.
◎ ♿M 🛢 💻 ⊠ ⊠

◆◆ **La Quinta Inn & Suites Warwick Providence Airport** H
(401) 941-6600. **$62-$146.** 36 Jefferson Blvd 02888. I-95 exit 15, just se. Int corridors. **Pets:** Medium, other species. Service with restrictions, supervision. ◎ 🛢 💻 ⊠

◆◆◆ Residence Inn by Marriott **H**
(401) 737-7100. **$89-$339.** 500 Kilvert St 02886. I-95 exit 13 to Jefferson Blvd, 0.4 mi n, then 0.6 mi w. Ext corridors. **Pets:** Accepted.
🛜 ⊗ 🅱 🛗 💻 🏊 ⊗

◆◆◆ Sheraton Providence Airport Hotel **H**
(401) 738-4000. **$89-$209.** 1850 Post Rd 02886. I-95 exit 13, 0.6 mi n on US 1. Int corridors. **Pets:** Small, dogs only. $50 one-time fee/pet. Service with restrictions, crate. [SAVE] 🛜 ⊗ 🅱 🛗 💻 🍴 🏊

WATCH HILL
◆◆◆ ◆◆◆◆ Ocean House **H** 🐾
(401) 584-7000. **$260-$1500, 3 day notice.** 1 Bluff Ave 02891. Jct SR 1A, 0.4 mi sw via Westerly Rd. Int corridors. **Pets:** Small, dogs only. $150 one-time fee/pet. Service with restrictions.
[SAVE] 🛜 ⊗ 🛗 🅱 💻 🍴 🏊 ⊗

WESTERLY
◆◆◆◆ Shelter Harbor Inn **CI**
(401) 322-8883. **$106-$258, 7 day notice.** 10 Wagner Rd 02891. 4 mi ne of jct SR 78 on US 1. Ext/int corridors. **Pets:** Accepted.
🛜 ⊗ 🍴 ⊗

WEST GREENWICH
◆◆◆ Residence Inn by Marriott Providence / Coventry **H**
(401) 828-1170. **$160-$210.** 755 Center of New England Blvd 02817. I-95 exit 7, just ne. Int corridors. **Pets:** Other species. $100 one-time fee/ room. Service with restrictions, crate.
🛜 ⊗ 🛗 🅱 💻 🏊 ⊗

WEST WARWICK
◆◆ Extended StayAmerica Providence-Airport-West Warwick **H** 🐾
(401) 885-3161. **$80-$199.** 1235 Division Rd 02893. I-95 exit 8A northbound, just s on SR 2, then just w; exit 8 southbound, just s on SR 2, then just w. Int corridors. **Pets:** Other species. $25 daily fee/pet. Service with restrictions. 🛜 🛗 🅱 💻

WYOMING
◆◆◆ ◆◆◆◆ Stagecoach House Inn **BB**
(401) 539-9600. **$100-$199.** 1136 Main St (SR 138) 02898. I-95 exit 3B northbound, 0.7 mi nw; exit southbound, 0.4 mi nw. Ext/int corridors. **Pets:** Dogs only. $25 daily fee/room. Designated rooms, service with restrictions, supervision. [SAVE] 🛜 ⊗ 🅱 💻

SOUTH CAROLINA

CITY INDEX

AIKEN
◆◆ ◆◆ Clarion Inn **M**
(803) 648-0999. **Call for rates.** 155 Colony Pkwy/Whiskey Rd 29803. Jct US 1/78 and SR 19 (Whiskey Rd), 1.8 mi s on SR 19. Ext corridors. **Pets:** Accepted. 🛜 🅱 💻 🏊

◆◆ ◆◆◆ Quality Inn & Suites **M**
(803) 641-1100. **$70-$90.** 3608 Richland Ave W 29801. Jct US 1/78 and SR 19 (Whiskey Rd), 2.9 mi w on US 1/78. Ext corridors. **Pets:** Large. $15 daily fee/pet. Service with restrictions, supervision.
[SAVE] 🛜 🅱 💻 🏊

◆◆ ◆◆ Super 8-Aiken **H**
(803) 641-8800. **$51-$135, 3 day notice.** 2577 Whiskey Rd 29803. Jct US 1/78 and SR 19 (Whiskey Rd), 4.3 mi s on SR 19. Int corridors. **Pets:** Accepted. 🛜 🅱 💻 🏊

ANDERSON
◆◆◆◆ Country Inn & Suites By Carlson **H**
(864) 622-2200. **Call for rates.** 116 Interstate Blvd 29621. I-85 exit 19B, just n, then just se. Int corridors. **Pets:** Medium. $25 one-time fee/pet. Designated rooms, service with restrictions, crate.
🛜 🛗 🅱 💻 🏊

◆◆ ◆◆ Days Inn **M**
(864) 375-0375. **$62-$135.** 1007 Smith Mill Rd 29625. I-85 exit 19A, just se. Ext corridors. **Pets:** Accepted. [SAVE] 🛜 🛗 🅱 💻 🏊

◆◆ ◆◆◆ Holiday Inn Express **H**
(864) 231-0231. **$79-$119.** 410 Alliance Pkwy 29621. I-85 exit 27, just s on SR 81. Int corridors. **Pets:** Accepted. [SAVE] 🛜 🛗 🅱 💻 🏊

◆◆ Home-Towne Suites **H**
(864) 226-1112. **Call for rates.** 151 Civic Center Blvd 29625. I-85 exit 19A, 2.2 mi se on US 76, then 0.6 mi s. Int corridors. **Pets:** Accepted.
🛜 🅱 💻 🏊

◆◆ Jameson Inn **M**
(864) 375-9800. **$71-$91.** 128 Interstate Blvd 29621. I-85 exit 19B, just n, then just se. Ext corridors. **Pets:** Medium. $15 daily fee/room. Service with restrictions, supervision. 🛜 🛗 🅱 💻 🏊

◆◆ La Quinta Inn Anderson **M**
(864) 225-3721. **$58-$119.** 3430 Clemson Blvd 29621. I-85 exit 19A, 2.9 mi se on US 76/SR 28 (Clemson Blvd); exit 21 southbound, 2.6 mi s on US 178. Ext corridors. **Pets:** Medium, other species. Service with restrictions, supervision. 🛜 🅱 💻 🏊

BEAUFORT
◆◆◆◆ City Loft Hotel **H**
(843) 379-5638. **Call for rates.** 311 Carteret St 29902. Jct Port Republic St. Ext corridors. **Pets:** Accepted. 🛜 ⊗ 🅱

◆◆◆ Quality Inn at Town Center **M**
(843) 524-2144. **$50-$80.** 2001 Boundary St 29902. Jct SR 170/US 21, 1 mi e. Ext corridors. **Pets:** Medium. $10 daily fee/pet. Designated rooms, service with restrictions, supervision. 🛜 🅱 💻 🏊

BENNETTSVILLE
◆◆◆ ◆◆◆ Best Western Bennettsville Inn **M**
(843) 479-1700. **$80-$150.** 213 US Hwy 15 & 401 Bypass E 29512. 0.6 mi s of center, just ne on US 15/401/SR 9. Ext corridors. **Pets:** Medium. $25 daily fee/pet. Service with restrictions, crate.
[SAVE] 🛜 🅱 💻 🏊

BISHOPVILLE

▼▼ **Econo Lodge** Ⓜ

(803) 428-3200. **$49-$125.** 1135 Sumter Hwy 29010. I-20 exit 116, just sw. Ext corridors. **Pets:** Accepted. 🛜 🔋 🖥️

BLUFFTON

Ⓐⓐⓐ ▼▼▼ **Candlewood Suites** Ⓗ

(843) 705-9600. **$79-$129.** 5 Young Clyde Ct 29909. I-95 exit 8 (US 278), 7.2 mi e to Okatie Center Blvd S, then just s. Int corridors. **Pets:** Large. $50 one-time fee/room. Designated rooms, service with restrictions. 🆂🅰🆅🅴 🛜 Ⓜ 🔋 🖥️ ⮑

Ⓐⓐⓐ ▼▼▼ **Holiday Inn Express Hotel & Suites** Ⓗ ❀

(843) 757-2002. **$79-$129.** 35 Bluffton Rd 29910. Jct William Hilton Pkwy (US 278/46/Bluffton Rd), just se. Int corridors. **Pets:** Large, other species. $50 one-time fee/room. Designated rooms, service with restrictions, supervision. 🆂🅰🆅🅴 🛜 Ⓜ 🔋 🖥️ ⮑

Ⓐⓐⓐ ▼▼▼▼ **The Inn at Palmetto Bluff** 🅒🅐 ❀

(843) 706-6500. **$475-$900, 7 day notice.** 476 Mount Pelia Rd 29910. Jct US 278/SR 170, 4.4 mi sw on SR 170, then 2.2 mi e on SR 46 (Bluffton Rd) to Palmetto Bluff Rd; check-in at gatehouse. Ext corridors. **Pets:** $25 daily fee/room. Service with restrictions.

🆂🅰🆅🅴 🛜 ❌ 🔋 🖥️ 🍴 ⮑ 🐾

CAYCE

Ⓐⓐⓐ ▼▼ **Riverside Inn** Ⓜ

(803) 939-4688. **$62.** 111 Knox Abbott Dr 29033. US 21, just w of Congaree River Bridge. Ext corridors. **Pets:** Medium. $20 one-time fee/room. Service with restrictions, crate. 🆂🅰🆅🅴 🛜 🔋 🖥️ ⮑ 🐾

CHARLESTON METROPOLITAN AREA

CHARLESTON

Ⓐⓐⓐ ▼▼▼ **Best Western Plus Charleston Downtown Hotel** Ⓗ ❀

(843) 722-4000. **$90-$270.** 146 Lockwood Dr (Blvd) 29403. I-26 exit 221A (US 17 S), 1.2 mi sw; just e of Ashley River. Int corridors. **Pets:** Other species. $20 daily fee/room. Service with restrictions.

🆂🅰🆅🅴 🛜 ❌ 🔋 🖥️ 🍴 ⮑

Ⓐⓐⓐ ▼▼▼ **Best Western Sweetgrass Inn** Ⓜ ❀

(843) 571-6100. **$60-$260.** 1540 Savannah Hwy 29407. US 17 S, 3.6 mi w of Ashley River Bridge; jct I-526 W terminus and US 17 N, 1.7 mi e. Ext corridors. **Pets:** Large, other species. $20 daily fee/room. Service with restrictions, supervision. 🆂🅰🆅🅴 🛜 🔋 🖥️ ⮑

Ⓐⓐⓐ ▼▼▼ **The Inn at Middleton Place** 🅒🅘 ❀

(843) 556-0500. **$149-$749, 3 day notice.** 4290 Ashley River Rd 29414. I-526 exit 11B (Ashley River Rd/SR 61), 2.8 mi nw on Paul Cantrell Blvd/Glenn McConnell Pkwy to Bees Ferry Rd, 1.8 mi ne to Ashley River Rd/SR 61, then 9.2 mi nw, follow signs to historic plantations, adjacent to Middleton Place, National Historic Landmark. Ext corridors. **Pets:** Medium, other species. $50 one-time fee/room. Service with restrictions, crate. 🆂🅰🆅🅴 🛜 ❌ 🔋 🖥️ 🍴 ⮑ 🐾

Ⓐⓐⓐ ▼▼▼ **John Rutledge House Inn** 🅑🅑 ❀

(843) 723-7999. **$209-$365, 3 day notice.** 116 Broad St 29401. Corner of King St. Int corridors. **Pets:** Large, dogs only. $25 daily fee/room. Designated rooms, service with restrictions. 🆂🅰🆅🅴 🛜 ❌ 🔋

Ⓐⓐⓐ ▼▼▼ **Kings Courtyard Inn** Ⓗ

(843) 723-7000. **$169-$280, 3 day notice.** 198 King St 29401. Between Market St and Horlbeck Alley. Ext/int corridors. **Pets:** Medium, dogs only. $25 daily fee/pet. Designated rooms, service with restrictions.

🆂🅰🆅🅴 🛜 🔋

▼▼▼ **La Quinta Inn & Suites Charleston Riverview** Ⓗ

(843) 556-5200. **$88-$188.** 11 Ashley Point Dr 29407. US 17 S, just over Ashley River Bridge to Albemarle Rd, 0.4 mi s to Ashley Pointe Dr. Ext/int corridors. **Pets:** Medium, other species. Service with restrictions, supervision. 🛜 🔋 🖥️ ⮑

▼▼▼ **Residence Inn by Marriott Charleston Downtown/Riverview** Ⓗ ❀

(843) 571-7979. **$109-$216.** 90 Ripley Point Dr 29407. US 17 S, just over Ashley River Bridge to Albemarle Rd, then just s. Int corridors. **Pets:** Medium, other species. $100 one-time fee/room. Service with restrictions. 🛜 ❌ Ⓜ 🔋 🖥️ ⮑ 🐾

Ⓐⓐⓐ ▼▼▼ **Town & Country Inn & Suites** Ⓜ

(843) 571-1000. **Call for rates.** 2008 Savannah Hwy 29407. US 17 S, 3.5 mi nw of Ashley River Bridge; jct I-526 W to terminus and US 17 N, just se. Ext corridors. **Pets:** Large, other species. $100 deposit/pet. Designated rooms, service with restrictions.

🆂🅰🆅🅴 🛜 🔋 🖥️ 🍴 ⮑ 🐾

Ⓐⓐⓐ ▼▼▼ **Vendue Inn** 🅒🅘 ❀

(843) 577-7970. **$199-$459, 3 day notice.** 19 Vendue Range 29401. Off E Bay St, 1 blk from Waterfront Park; in historic district. Int corridors. **Pets:** Medium. $50 one-time fee/pet. Designated rooms, service with restrictions, supervision. 🆂🅰🆅🅴 🛜 ❌ 🔋 🍴

FOLLY BEACH

Ⓐⓐⓐ ▼▼▼ **Tides Folly Beach** Ⓗ

(843) 588-6464. **$169-$299, 3 day notice.** 1 Center St 29439. Terminus of SR 171; center. Ext corridors. **Pets:** $85 one-time fee/room. Service with restrictions. 🆂🅰🆅🅴 🛜 ❌ 🔋 🖥️ 🍴 ⮑

KIAWAH ISLAND

▼▼▼ **Kiawah Island Golf Resort - Courtside Villas** 🅒🅞

(843) 768-2121. **Call for rates.** 1401 Shipwatch Rd 29455. Just e of main gate to Kiawah Beach Dr, then just s; in West Beach Village area. Ext corridors. **Pets:** Accepted. ❌ 🔋 🖥️ ⮑ 🐾

▼▼▼ **Kiawah Island Golf Resort - Fairway Oaks Villas** 🅒🅞

(843) 768-2121. **Call for rates.** 1301 Kiawah Beach Dr 29455. Just e of main gate, just s; in West Beach Village area. Ext corridors. **Pets:** Accepted. ❌ 🔋 🖥️ ⮑ 🐾

▼▼▼ **Kiawah Island Golf Resort - Mariners Watch Villas** 🅒🅞

(843) 768-2121. **Call for rates.** 4200 Sea Forest Dr 29455. 1.6 mi e of main gate, then just s; in East Beach Village area. Ext corridors. **Pets:** Accepted. ❌ 🔋 🖥️ ⮑ 🐾

▼▼▼ **Kiawah Island Golf Resort - Parkside Villas** 🅒🅞

(843) 768-2121. **Call for rates.** 4501 Park Lake Dr 29455. 2 mi e of main gate, then just s; in East Beach Village area. Ext corridors. **Pets:** Accepted. ❌ 🔋 🖥️ ⮑ 🐾

▼▼▼ **Kiawah Island Golf Resort - Seascape Villas** 🅒🅞

(843) 768-2121. **Call for rates.** 3510 Shipwatch Rd 29455. Just e of main gate, then just s; in West Beach Village area. Ext corridors. **Pets:** Accepted. ❌ 🔋 🖥️ ⮑ 🐾

▼▼▼ **Kiawah Island Golf Resort - Shipwatch Villas** 🅒🅞

(843) 768-2121. **Call for rates.** 2200 Shipwatch Rd 29455. Just e of main gate, then just s; in West Beach Village area. Ext corridors. **Pets:** Accepted. ❌ 🔋 🖥️ ⮑ 🐾

▼▼▼▼ **Kiawah Island Golf Resort - Tennis Club Villas** co
(843) 768-2121. **Call for rates.** 4659 Tennis Club Ln 29455. 2.2 mi e of main gate, then just s; at Roy Barth Tennis Center. Ext corridors.
Pets: Accepted. ✕ 🗋 ▭ 🏊 ✕

▼▼▼▼ **Kiawah Island Golf Resort - Turtle Cove Villas** co
(843) 768-2121. **Call for rates.** 5501 Green Dolphin Way 29455. 2.4 mi e of main gate, then just se; at Roy Barth Tennis Center. Ext corridors.
Pets: Accepted. ✕ 🗋 ▭ 🏊 ✕

▼▼▼▼ **Kiawah Island Golf Resort - Turtle Point Villas** co
(843) 768-2121. **Call for rates.** 4901 Green Dolphin Way 29455. 2.4 mi e of main gate, then just se; at Roy Barth Tennis Center and Turtle Point Golf Club. Ext corridors. **Pets:** Accepted. ✕ 🗋 ▭ 🏊 ✕

▼▼▼▼ **Kiawah Island Golf Resort - Windswept Villas** co
(843) 768-2121. **Call for rates.** 4300 Sea Forest Dr 29455. 1.6 mi e of main gate, then just s; in East Beach Village area. Ext corridors.
Pets: Accepted. ✕ 🗋 ▭ 🏊 ✕

LADSON

AAA ▼▼▼▼ **Best Western Plus Magnolia Inn and Suites** H
(843) 553-8888. **$69-$129.** 747 Treeland Dr 29456. I-26 exit 203 (College Park Rd), just ne. Int corridors. **Pets:** $20 daily fee/pet. Designated rooms, service with restrictions, supervision.
SAVE 🛜 ⑤M 🗋 ▭ 🏊

MOUNT PLEASANT

AAA ▼◈▼ **Days Inn Patriots Point** M
(843) 881-1800. **$62-$152, 3 day notice.** 261 Johnnie Dodds Blvd 29464. Just e of base of Cooper River Bridge on US 17 (Johnnie Dodds Blvd). Ext corridors. **Pets:** Very small, dogs only. $10 daily fee/pet. Designated rooms, service with restrictions, supervision.
SAVE 🛜 🗋 ▭ 🏊

▼▼▼ **Extended StayAmerica-Charleston-Mount Pleasant** H 🐾
(843) 884-4453. **$70-$140.** 304 Wingo Way 29464. Just e of Cooper River Bridge on US 17 (Johnnie Dodds Blvd), then just n. Int corridors. **Pets:** Other species. $25 daily fee/pet. Service with restrictions.
🛜 🗋 ▭

▼▼▼▼ **Hampton Inn-Patriots Point** H
(843) 881-3300. **$79-$179.** 255 Sessions Way 29464. Just ne of base of Cooper River Bridge to McGrath-Darby Blvd, then just s. Int corridors.
Pets: Accepted. 🛜 ⑤M 🗋 ▭ 🏊

▼▼▼▼ **Holiday Inn Charleston/Mt. Pleasant** H
(843) 884-6000. **$79-$209.** 250 Johnnie Dodds Blvd 29464. US 17 (Johnnie Dodds Blvd), just e of base of Cooper River Bridge. Int corridors. **Pets:** Accepted. 🛜 ⑤M 🗋 ▭ 🍴 🏊

▼▼▼▼ **Homewood Suites by Hilton** H
(843) 881-6950. **Call for rates.** 1998 Riviera Dr 29464. I-526 exit 32 (Georgetown/US 17 N), 1.4 mi ne on US 17, 1 mi se on Isle of Palms Connector (SR 517), then just sw. Int corridors. **Pets:** Other species. $75 one-time fee/room. Service with restrictions, crate.
🛜 ⑤M 🗋 ▭ 🏊 ✕

▼▼▼ **Red Roof Inn** M
(843) 884-1411. **$54-$109.** 301 Johnnie Dodds Blvd 29464. Just e of base of Cooper River Bridge on US 17 (Johnnie Dodds Blvd), then just s on McGrath-Darby Blvd. Ext corridors. **Pets:** Large, other species. No service, supervision. 🛜 🗋 🏊

▼▼▼▼ **Residence Inn Charleston Mt. Pleasant** H
(843) 881-1599. **$170-$228.** 1116 Isle of Palms Connector 29464. I-526 exit 30 (Georgetown/US 17 N), 1.4 mi ne on US 17 to Isle of Palms Connector (SR 517), then just se. Int corridors. **Pets:** Accepted.
🛜 ✕ ⑤M 🗋 ▭ 🏊

▼▼▼ **Rodeway Inn Charleston/Mt Pleasant** M
(843) 884-5853. **$65-$150.** 310 Hwy 17 Bypass 29464. 0.7 mi ne of base of Cooper River Bridge. Ext corridors. **Pets:** Dogs only. $30 one-time fee/pet. Service with restrictions. 🛜 🗋 ▭

▼◈▼ **Sleep Inn Mt. Pleasant** H
(843) 856-5000. **$79-$169.** 299 Wingo Way 29464. Just ne of base of Cooper River Bridge to McGrath Darby Blvd, then just n. Int corridors.
Pets: Accepted. 🛜 ⑤M 🗋 ▭ 🏊

NORTH CHARLESTON

AAA ▼▼▼▼ **Aloft Charleston Airport & Convention Center** H 🐾
(843) 566-7300. **$99-$209.** 4875 Tanger Outlet Blvd 29418. I-26 exit 213A, follow signs to Tanger Outlet Mall. Int corridors. **Pets:** Medium. Designated rooms, service with restrictions, crate.
SAVE 🛜 ✕ 🗋 ▭ 🏊

▼▼▼▼ **Candlewood Suites** H 🐾
(843) 797-3535. **$89-$169.** 2177 Northwoods Blvd 29406. I-26 exit 209 (Ashley Phosphate Rd), just e, then just n. Int corridors. **Pets:** Other species. $12 daily fee/room. Designated rooms, service with restrictions, crate. 🛜 🗋 ▭

▼▼▼▼ **Comfort Suites Charleston/N Charleston, SC** H
(843) 725-5400. **$89-$169.** 2520 N Forest Dr 29420. I-26 exit 209 (Ashley Phosphate Rd), just w of Northside Dr. Int corridors. **Pets:** Accepted.
🛜 ✕ ⑤M 🗋 ▭ 🏊

▼▼▼▼ **Residence Inn Charleston** H
(843) 572-5757. **$136-$164.** 7645 Northwoods Blvd 29406. I-26 exit 209 (Ashley Phosphate Rd), just e, then n. Ext corridors. **Pets:** Accepted.
🛜 ✕ 🗋 ▭ 🏊 ✕

▼▼▼▼ **Homestead Charleston-Airport-N Charleston** H 🐾
(843) 740-3440. **$65-$130.** 5045 N Arco Ln 29418. I-26 exit 213 westbound; exit 213A eastbound; enter through Tanger Outlet access roads. Int corridors. **Pets:** Other species. $25 daily fee/pet. Service with restrictions. 🛜 ⑤M 🗋 ▭ 🏊

▼▼ **La Quinta Inn Charleston North** M
(843) 797-8181. **$62-$137.** 2499 La Quinta Ln 29420. I-26 exit 209 (Ashley Phosphate Rd), just w. Ext/int corridors. **Pets:** Medium, other species. Service with restrictions, supervision. 🛜 🗋 ▭ 🏊

AAA ▼▼▼▼ **Radisson Hotel Charleston Airport** H
(843) 744-2501. **$69-$189.** 5991 Rivers Ave 29406. I-26 exit 211B (Aviation Ave), just ne. Int corridors. **Pets:** Small. $50 one-time fee/pet. Designated rooms, service with restrictions, supervision.
SAVE 🛜 🗋 ▭ 🍴 🏊 ✕

▼▼ **Red Roof Inn** M
(843) 572-9100. **$44-$69.** 7480 Northwoods Blvd 29406. I-26 exit 209 (Ashley Phosphate Rd), just e, then just n. Ext corridors. **Pets:** Large, other species. No service, supervision. 🛜 🏊

▼▼▼▼ **Residence Inn Charleston Airport** H
(843) 266-3434. **$138-$156.** 5035 International Blvd 29418. I-26 exit 213 westbound; exit 213A eastbound, just s; I-526 exit 16 (International Blvd), 0.7 mi e. Int corridors. **Pets:** Accepted.
🛜 ✕ ⑤M 🗋 ▭ 🏊 ✕

AAA ▼▼▼▼ **Sheraton Charleston Airport Hotel** H 🐾
(843) 747-1900. **$89-$159.** 4770 Goer Dr 29406. I-26 exit 213 westbound; exit 213B eastbound, just n. Int corridors. **Pets:** Medium, dogs only. $100 deposit/room, $40 one-time fee/room. Designated rooms, service with restrictions, supervision. SAVE 🛜 ✕ 🗋 ▭ 🍴 🏊

▼▼▼ **Sleep Inn Charleston North** H
(843) 572-8400. **$69-$139.** 7435 Northside Dr 29420. I-26 exit 209 (Ashley Phosphate Rd), just w. Int corridors. **Pets:** Accepted. 🛜 🗋 ▭

▼▼▼ **Staybridge Suites North Charleston** H
(843) 377-4600. **$129-$149.** 7329 Mazyck Rd 29406. I-26 exit 209A (Ashley Phosphate Rd), just sw, then just s. Int corridors. **Pets:** Accepted.
🛜 🗋 ▭

▼▼ ▼▼ **StudioPLUS Charleston-North Charleston** 🏨 ❖
(843) 553-0036. **$60-$110.** 7641 Northwoods Blvd 29406. I-26 exit 209 (Ashley Phosphate Rd), just e, then just n. Int corridors. **Pets:** Other species. $25 daily fee/pet. Service with restrictions. 📶 🛡 💻 🏊

SUMMERVILLE
▼▼▼▼ **Country Inn & Suites By Carlson** 🏨
(843) 285-9000. **$99-$109.** 220 Holiday Dr 29483. I-26 exit 199A, just w on US 17 alternate route to Holiday Dr, then just n. Int corridors. **Pets:** Medium, other species. $10 daily fee/pet. Service with restrictions, supervision. 📶 🛡 💻 🏊

▼▼▼▼ **Holiday Inn**
Express-Charleston/Summerville 🏨 ❖
(843) 875-3300. **$89-$149, 3 day notice.** 120 Holiday Dr 29483. I-26 exit 199A, just w. Int corridors. **Pets:** Other species. Service with restrictions, supervision. 📶 ♿M 🛡 💻 🏊

🅰🅰🅰 ▼▼▼▼ **Woodlands Inn** 🆑
(843) 875-2600. **Call for rates.** 125 Parsons Rd 29483. I-26 exit 199A, 2 mi sw on US 17 alternate route, to W Richardson Ave (SR 165), 1.4 mi nw to Parsons Rd, then just s. Int corridors. **Pets:** Accepted.
(SAVE) 📶 ❌ 🍴 🏊 ❌

END METROPOLITAN AREA

CHARLOTTE METROPOLITAN AREA (NEARBY NORTH CAROLINA)

ROCK HILL
🅰🅰🅰 ▼▼▼▼ **Baymont Inn & Suites** 🏨
(803) 329-1330. **$68-$80.** 1106 N Anderson Rd 29730. I-77 exit 82B (US 21), 0.4 mi sw to US 21 Bypass, then just s. Int corridors. **Pets:** Medium. $10 daily fee/pet. Service with restrictions, supervision.
(SAVE) 📶 🛡 💻 🏊

▼▼▼▼ **The Book & the Spindle** 🅱🅱 ❖
(803) 328-1913. **$90-$105, 10 day notice.** 626 Oakland Ave 29730. I-77 exit 82B (US 21), 3.1 mi s; between Sumter and Aiken aves. Int corridors. **Pets:** Small, other species. $15 deposit/room. Crate.
📶 🛡 💻

▼▼▼▼ **Comfort Suites** 🏨
(803) 326-3300. **$99-$108.** 1323 Old Springdale Rd 29732. I-77 exit 79, just se. Int corridors. **Pets:** Accepted. 📶 ❌ 🛡 💻 🏊

▼▼ ▼▼ **Howard Johnson Inn** 🇲
(803) 329-7900. **$40-$85.** 911 Riverview Rd 29730. I-77 exit 82B (US 21), just sw, then just s. Ext corridors. **Pets:** Accepted. 📶 🛡 💻

▼▼ ▼▼ **Super 8** 🏨
(803) 980-0400. **$37-$63.** 888 Riverview Rd 29730. I-77 exit 82B (US 21), just sw, then just s. Int corridors. **Pets:** Accepted.
📶 ♿M 🛡 💻

▼▼▼▼ **TownePlace Suites by Marriott Rock Hill** 🏨 ❖
(803) 327-0700. **$85-$133.** 2135 Tabor Dr 29730. I-77 exit 79, just e on Dave Lyle Blvd to Galleria Blvd, then just n. Int corridors. **Pets:** Medium. $100 one-time fee/room. Supervision. 📶 ❌ ♿M 🛡 💻 🏊

END METROPOLITAN AREA

CHERAW
▼▼ ▼▼ **Jameson Inn** 🇲
(843) 537-5625. **$83-$88.** 885 Chesterfield Hwy 29520. Jct US 1/52/SR 9, 1.6 mi w on SR 9. Ext corridors. **Pets:** Medium. $15 daily fee/room. Service with restrictions, supervision. 📶 🛡 💻 🏊

CLEMSON
🅰🅰🅰 ▼▼ ▼▼ **Comfort Inn-Clemson** 🏨 ❖
(864) 653-3600. **$90-$150.** 1305 Tiger Blvd 29631. Jct SR 133 (College Ave) and US 76/123, 0.5 mi e. Int corridors. **Pets:** Medium, other species. $15 daily fee/room. Service with restrictions, crate.
(SAVE) 📶 🛡 💻 🏊

CLINTON
▼▼ ▼▼ **Days Inn** 🇲 ❖
(864) 833-6600. **$50-$72.** 12374 Hwy 56 N 29325. I-26 exit 52, just s. Ext corridors. **Pets:** $10 one-time fee/room. Service with restrictions, supervision. 📶 🛡 💻 🏊

▼▼ ▼▼ **Quality Inn** 🇲
(864) 833-5558. **Call for rates.** 105 Trade St 29325. I-26 exit 52, just n. Ext corridors. **Pets:** Medium. $10 daily fee/pet. Service with restrictions, supervision. 📶 🛡 💻 🏊

COLUMBIA
▼▼▼▼ **Affordable Suites Delux** 🏨
(803) 779-7000. **Call for rates.** 150 Stoneridge Dr 29210. I-126 exit Greystone Blvd, just n, then just e. Ext corridors. **Pets:** Accepted.
📶 ❌ 🛡 💻 🏊 ❌

🅰🅰🅰 ▼▼▼▼ **Candlewood Suites Columbia-Fort Jackson** 🏨
(803) 727-1299. **$99-$139.** 921 Atlas Rd 29209. I-77 exit 9A (Garners Ferry Rd), 0.9 mi se to Atlas Rd, then just sw. Int corridors. **Pets:** Accepted. (SAVE) 📶 ♿M 🛡 💻 🏊

▼▼▼▼ **Chesnut Cottage Bed & Breakfast** 🅱🅱 🐾
(803) 256-1718. **Call for rates.** 1718 Hampton St 29201. SR 12 (Taylor St), just s; between Henderson and Barnwell sts; downtown. Int corridors. **Pets:** Other species. 📶 ❌ 🛡 💻

🅰🅰🅰 ▼▼ ▼▼ **Comfort Inn Columbia** 🏨 ❖
(803) 798-5101. **$69-$109.** 911 Bush River Rd 29210. I-26 exit 108A, just e. Int corridors. **Pets:** Medium. $15 daily fee/pet. Designated rooms, service with restrictions, crate. (SAVE) 📶 🛡 💻 🏊

🅰🅰🅰 ▼▼▼▼ **DoubleTree by Hilton Columbia** 🏨
(803) 731-0300. **$99-$179.** 2100 Bush River Rd 29210. I-20 exit 63 (Bush River Rd), just e; I-26 exit 108 (Bush River Rd), 0.7 mi w. Int corridors. **Pets:** Accepted. (SAVE) 📶 🛡 💻 🍴 🏊

▼▼ ▼▼ **Extended StayAmerica Columbia-Fort Jackson** 🇲 ❖
(803) 782-2025. **$60-$90.** 5430 Forest Dr 29206. I-77 exit 12, just ne, then just s along service road; behind mall. Ext corridors. **Pets:** Other species. $25 daily fee/pet. Service with restrictions. 📶 🛡 💻

▼▼▼▼ ▼▼▼▼ **Hilton Columbia Center** 🏨
(803) 744-7800. **$129-$239.** 924 Senate St 29201. Jct US 1/SR 48, just s; downtown. Int corridors. **Pets:** Accepted.
📶 ❌ ♿M 🛡 💻 🍴 🏊

▼▼▼ **Jameson Suites**

(803) 736-6666. **$90-$110.** 7525 Two Notch Rd 29223. I-20 exit 74 (Two Notch Rd), just ne; I-77 exit 17 (Two Notch Rd), 0.5 mi sw. Int corridors. **Pets:** Medium. $15 daily fee/room. Service with restrictions, supervision.

📶 🛏 💻 🏊

▼▼ **La Quinta Inn & Suites Columbia NE/Ft. Jackson Area**

(803) 736-6400. **$71-$139.** 1538 Horseshoe Dr 29223. I-20 exit 74 (Two Notch Rd), just n; I-77 exit 17 (Two Notch Rd), 0.5 mi s. Int corridors. **Pets:** Medium, other species. Service with restrictions, supervision.

📶 🛏 💻 🏊

▼▼ **La Quinta Inn-Maingate Ft. Jackson**

(803) 783-5410. **$93-$154.** 7333 Garners Ferry Rd 29209. I-77 exit 9A (Garners Ferry Rd), just se. Int corridors. **Pets:** Medium, other species. Service with restrictions, supervision. 📶 🛏 💻 🏊

🆎 ▼▼▼ **Quality Inn**

(803) 451-2400. **Call for rates.** 1335 Garner Ln 29210. I-20 exit 65, just s on US 176, then just ne. Ext corridors. **Pets:** Accepted.

SAVE 📶 🛏 💻 🏊

▼▼▼▼ **Residence Inn Columbia Northeast** H

(803) 788-8850. **$99-$129.** 2320 Legrand Rd 29223. I-77 exit 19 southbound, just ne on Farrow Rd to Rabon Rd, then just se; exit 18 northbound. Int corridors. **Pets:** Accepted. 📶 ❌ 🛏 💻 🏊 ❌

🆎 ▼▼▼▼ **Sheraton Columbia Downtown Hotel** H

(803) 988-1400. **$99-$269.** 1400 Main St 29201. Jct Washington St; downtown; center. Int corridors. **Pets:** Accepted.

SAVE 📶 ❌ 💻 🍽

▼▼▼▼ **Staybridge Suites Columbia** H 🐾

(803) 451-5900. **$99-$199.** 1913 Huger St 29201. I-126 exit 3B (US 21/Huger St), just s. Int corridors. **Pets:** Large, other species. $50 one-time fee/room. Service with restrictions, crate. 📶 🛏 💻 🏊

▼ **Super 8** M

(803) 735-0008. **$39-$64.** 5719 Fairfield Rd 29203. I-20 exit 70, just s. Ext corridors. **Pets:** Accepted. 🛏 💻

▼▼▼▼ **TownePlace Suites Columbia Northwest/Harbison** H

(803) 781-9391. **$79-$99.** 350 Columbiana Dr 29212. I-26 exit 103 (Harbison Blvd), just sw to Columbiana Dr, then 0.7 mi nw. Int corridors. **Pets:** Accepted. 📶 ❌ 📶 🛏 💻 🏊

DUNCAN

▼▼ **Jameson Inn** M

(864) 433-8405. **$65-$85.** 1546 E Main St 29334. I-85 exit 63, 0.4 mi se on SR 290. Ext corridors. **Pets:** Medium. $15 daily fee/room. Service with restrictions, supervision. 📶 🛏 💻 🏊

EASLEY

▼▼▼ **Jameson Inn** M

(864) 306-9000. **$65-$85.** 211 Dayton School Rd 29642. Jct US 123/SR 93, 0.6 mi e on US 123; jct US 123/SR 153, 1.4 mi w. Ext corridors. **Pets:** Medium. $15 daily fee/room. Service with restrictions, supervision.

📶 🛏 💻 🏊

🆎 ▼▼▼ **Quality Inn** M

(864) 859-7520. **$62-$69.** 5539 Calhoun Memorial Hwy 29640. Jct US 123/SR 93, just e on US 123. Ext corridors. **Pets:** Small, dogs only. $25 daily fee/pet. Designated rooms, service with restrictions, supervision.

SAVE 📶 🛏 💻 🏊

FLORENCE

🆎 ▼▼▼ **Baymont Inn & Suites** M

(843) 468-9994. **$53-$152, 4 day notice.** 1826 W Lucas St 29501. I-95 exit 164, just e on US 52. Ext corridors. **Pets:** Large, other species. $10 daily fee/pet. Service with restrictions. SAVE 📶 🛏 💻 🏊

🆎 ▼▼▼ **Econo Lodge** M

(843) 665-4558. **$50-$60.** 1920 W Lucas St 29501. I-95 exit 164, just se. Ext/int corridors. **Pets:** Other species. $10 daily fee/pet. Designated rooms, service with restrictions, supervision. SAVE 📶 🛏 💻 🏊

🆎 ▼▼▼ **Howard Johnson Express Inn & Suites** M 🐾

(843) 664-9494. **$49-$167.** 3821 Bancroft Rd 29501. I-95 exit 157, just ne on US 76. Ext corridors. **Pets:** Medium. $10 one-time fee/pet. Service with restrictions, supervision. SAVE 📶 🛏 💻 🏊

▼ **Motel 6 #1250** M

(843) 667-6100. **$35-$45.** 1834 W Lucas St 29501. I-95 exit 164, just sw. Ext corridors. **Pets:** Other species. Service with restrictions, supervision.

📶 🏊

🆎 ▼▼▼ **Quality Inn & Suites** M

(843) 664-2400. **$60-$300.** 150 Dunbarton Dr 29501. I-95 exit 160A, just e, then just n. Ext corridors. **Pets:** $20 one-time fee/room. Service with restrictions, crate. SAVE 📶 🛏 💻 🏊

🆎 ▼▼▼ **Ramada** M 🐾

(843) 665-4555. **$59-$99.** 1819 W Lucas St 29501. I-95 exit 164, just se. Ext corridors. **Pets:** Other species. $15 one-time fee/room. Designated rooms, service with restrictions. SAVE 📶 🛏ᴹ 🛏 💻 🍽 🏊

▼▼ **Red Roof Inn** M

(843) 678-9000. **$39-$69.** 2690 David McLeod Blvd 29501. I-95 exit 160A, just e on service road. Ext corridors. **Pets:** Large, other species. No service, supervision. 📶 🛏ᴹ 🛏

▼▼▼ **Residence Inn by Marriott Florence** H

(843) 468-2800. **$142-$179.** 2660 Hospitality Blvd 29501. I-95 exit 160A, just e, then s. Int corridors. **Pets:** Accepted. 📶 ❌ 🛏 💻 🏊

🆎 ▼▼▼ **Super 8** M

(843) 661-7267. **$43-$225.** 1832 1/2 W Lucas St 29501. I-95 exit 164, just se. Ext corridors. **Pets:** Small, other species. $10 daily fee/pet. Service with restrictions, supervision. SAVE 📶 🛏 💻 🏊

GAFFNEY

▼▼ **Jameson Inn** M

(864) 489-0240. **$75-$95.** 101 Stuard St 29341. I-85 exit 92, 0.5 mi se on SR 11/W Floyd Baker Blvd. Ext corridors. **Pets:** Medium. $15 daily fee/room. Service with restrictions, supervision. 📶 🛏 💻 🏊

▼▼ **Sleep Inn** H

(864) 487-5337. **Call for rates.** 834 Windslow Ave 29341. I-85 exit 90, just se, then ne on frontage road. Int corridors. **Pets:** Large, other species. $15 daily fee/pet. Service with restrictions, crate.

📶 🛏ᴹ 🛏 💻 🏊

🆎 ▼▼▼ **Super 8** M

(864) 489-1699. **$54-$89.** 100 Ellis Ferry Ave 29341. I-85 exit 92, 0.7 mi se on SR 11/W Floyd Baker Blvd. Ext corridors. **Pets:** Medium. $10 one-time fee/pet. Service with restrictions, supervision.

SAVE 📶 🛏 💻 🏊

THE GRAND STRAND AREA

CONWAY

◆◆◆ Comfort Suites at the University ⊞
(843) 347-9292. **$59-$189.** 2480 Hwy 501 E 29526. Jct US 501/501 business route, 1.6 mi se on US 501. Int corridors. **Pets:** Accepted.

GEORGETOWN

◆◆ Jameson Inn Georgetown M
(843) 546-6090. **$75-$95.** 120 Church St 29440. Jct US 17/17 alternate route/701, 1.2 mi se on US 17; just w of ICW Bridge at Georgetown Landing. Ext corridors. **Pets:** Medium. $15 daily fee/room. Service with restrictions, supervision.

LITTLE RIVER

◆◆◆ Holiday Inn Express Hotel and Suites-North Myrtle Beach ⊞
(843) 281-9400. **$59-$299.** 722 Hwy 17 N 29566. Jct SR 9/US 17, 1 mi e; at Coquina Harbor. Int corridors. **Pets:** Medium, dogs only. $25 daily fee/pet. Designated rooms, service with restrictions.

MURRELLS INLET

◆◆◆ Holiday Inn Express Hotel & Suites ⊞ ❖
(843) 357-0100. **$69-$189.** 1303-A Tadlock Dr 29576. Jct US 17 Bypass and 17 S business route. Int corridors. **Pets:** Large, other species. $50 one-time fee/room. Service with restrictions.

MYRTLE BEACH

◆◆◆ Compass Cove Oceanfront Resort ⓒⓞ
(843) 448-8373. **Call for rates.** 2311 S Ocean Blvd 29577. Jct 24th Ave S. Ext corridors. **Pets:** Accepted.

◆◆◆ La Quinta Inn & Suites Myrtle Beach At 48th Avenue ⊞
(843) 449-5231. **$83-$247.** 4709 N Kings Hwy 29577. Jct 48th Ave N and US 17 business route. Int corridors. **Pets:** Medium, other species. Service with restrictions, supervision.

◆◆◆ La Quinta Inn & Suites Myrtle Beach Broadway Area ⊞
(843) 916-8801. **$83-$247.** 1561 21st Ave N 29577. Jct US 17 Bypass, just se. Int corridors. **Pets:** Medium, other species. Service with restrictions, supervision.

◆◆ Ocean Dunes Resort & Villas ⓒⓞ
(843) 449-7441. **Call for rates.** 201 75th Ave N 29578. Jct N Ocean Blvd, just se. Ext/int corridors. **Pets:** Accepted.

◆◆◆ Ocean Park Resort ⊞ ❖
(843) 448-1915. **$45-$259.** 1905 S Ocean Blvd 29588. Jct 20th Ave S. Int corridors. **Pets:** Small. $15 daily fee/pet. Service with restrictions, crate.

◆◆◆ Patricia Grand Resort Hotel ⊞ ❖
(843) 448-8453. **$48-$210.** 2710 N Ocean Blvd 29577. Jct 27th Ave N. Ext corridors. **Pets:** Small, other species. $15 daily fee/pet. Designated rooms, service with restrictions, crate.

◆◆ Red Roof Inn & Suites Myrtle Beach ⊞
(843) 626-4444. **$44-$139.** 2801 S Kings Hwy 29577. Between 27th and 29th Ave S on US 17 business route. Int corridors. **Pets:** Large, other species. No service, supervision.

◆◆ Sea Mist Oceanfront Resort ⊞
(843) 448-1551. **$32-$199, 14 day notice.** 1200 S Ocean Blvd 29577. Jct 12th Ave S. Ext/int corridors. **Pets:** Medium. $50 one-time fee/pet. Designated rooms, service with restrictions, supervision.

◆◆◆ Sheraton Myrtle Beach Convention Center Hotel ⊞
(843) 918-5000. **$89-$259, 3 day notice.** 2101 N Oak St 29577. Jct 21st Ave N and US 17 business route, just nw on 21st Ave N. Int corridors. **Pets:** Accepted.

◆◆◆◆ Staybridge Suites At Fantasy Harbour ⊞ ❖
(843) 903-4000. **$65-$179.** 303 Fantasy Harbour Blvd 29579. Jct US 17 Bypass, 0.7 mi n on US 501 exit River Oaks Rd/George Bishop Pkwy, just w on River Oaks Rd, then 0.4 mi s. Int corridors. **Pets:** Medium. $20 daily fee/room. Service with restrictions, crate.

◆◆◆ Westgate Myrtle Beach Oceanfront Resort ⊞
(843) 448-4481. **$49-$299, 3 day notice.** 415 S Ocean Blvd 29577. Jct 6th Ave S, just ne. Int corridors. **Pets:** Medium. $80 one-time fee/room. Designated rooms, supervision.

SURFSIDE BEACH

◆◆◆ Holiday Inn Oceanfront at Surfside Beach ⊞ ❖
(843) 238-5601. **$99-$229, 3 day notice.** 1601 N Ocean Blvd 29575. Jct 16th Ave N and N Ocean Blvd. Int corridors. **Pets:** Medium, other species. $100 one-time fee/room. Service with restrictions.

END AREA

GREENVILLE

◆◆◆ Best Western Greenville Airport Inn M ❖
(864) 297-5353. **$63-$70.** 5009 Pelham Rd 29615. I-85 exit 54 (Pelham Rd), just se. Ext corridors. **Pets:** Other species. $15 daily fee/pet. Designated rooms, service with restrictions, supervision.

◆◆◆ Clarion Inn & Suites M ❖
(864) 254-6383. **$55-$99.** 50 Orchard Park Dr 29615. I-385 exit 39 (Haywood Rd), just n, just e on Orchard Park Rd, then just s. Ext corridors. **Pets:** Other species. $20 one-time fee/room. Service with restrictions.

◆◆ Comfort Inn & Suites Downtown Greenville ⊞
(864) 283-0370. **$75-$150.** 10 Mills Ave 29605. Jct US 29 and 25 business. Int corridors. **Pets:** Accepted.

◆◆◆ Drury Inn & Suites-Greenville ⊞
(864) 288-4401. **$90-$194.** 10 Carolina Point Pkwy 29607. I-85 exit 51A (Woodruff Rd), just se; I-385 exit 35 (Woodruff Rd), 0.6 mi nw. Int corridors. **Pets:** Accepted.

◆◆ Extended StayAmerica-Greenville Airport ⊞ ❖
(864) 213-9698. **$60-$90.** 3715 Pelham Rd 29615. I-85 exit 54 (Pelham Rd), 0.5 mi w. Int corridors. **Pets:** Other species. $25 daily fee/pet. Service with restrictions.

▼▼▼ **Hawthorn Suites** H
(864) 297-0099. **Call for rates.** 48 McPrice Ct 29615. I-385 exit 39 (Haywood Rd), just n, just e on Orchard Park Rd, then just s. Ext corridors. **Pets:** Medium. $50 one-time fee/pet. Service with restrictions.
🛜 🛗 💻 🏊 ⊠

▲▲▲ ▼▼▼ **Hilton Greenville** H 🐾
(864) 232-4747. **$89-$139.** 45 W Orchard Park Dr 29615. I-385 exit 39 (Haywood Rd), just n, then w. Int corridors. **Pets:** Large. $50 one-time fee/pet. Designated rooms, service with restrictions.
[SAVE] 🛜 🕭M 🛗 💻 🍽 🏊 ⊠

▼▼▼ **Holiday Inn I-85 @ Augusta Rd** H
(864) 277-8921. **$84-$85.** 4295 Augusta Rd 29605. I-85 exit 46A, just s. Int corridors. **Pets:** Accepted. 🛜 🕭M 🛗 💻 🏊

▲▲▲ ▼▼▼ **Hyatt Regency Greenville** H
(864) 235-1234. **$79-$269.** 220 N Main St 29601. Just n of center. Int corridors. **Pets:** Accepted. [ECO] [SAVE] 🛜 🛗 💻 🍽 🏊

▼▼▼ **La Quinta Inn & Suites Greenville Haywood** H
(864) 233-8018. **$68-$148.** 65 W Orchard Park Dr 29615. I-385 exit 39 (Haywood Rd), just n, then w. Int corridors. **Pets:** Medium, other species. Service with restrictions, supervision. 🛜 🛗 💻 🏊 ⊠

▼▼▼ **La Quinta Inn Greenville (Woodruff Rd)** M
(864) 297-3500. **$58-$115.** 31 Old Country Rd 29607. I-85 exit 51A (Woodruff Rd), just nw on SR 146; I-385 exit 37, just sw on Roper Mountain Rd, then 0.9 mi se. Ext/int corridors. **Pets:** Medium, other species. Service with restrictions, supervision. 🛜 🛗 💻 🏊

▼▼▼ **The Phoenix Greenville's Inn** H
(864) 233-4651. **$79-$295.** 246 N Pleasanturg Dr 29607. I-385 exit 40B, 0.6 mi s on SR 291. Ext corridors. **Pets:** Accepted.
[SAVE] 🛜 🛗 💻 🍽 🏊

▼▼▼ **Red Roof Inn** M
(864) 297-4458. **$39-$64.** 2801 Laurens Rd 29607. I-85 exit 48A, just se to Millennium Blvd, then just nw on Vision Ct. Ext corridors. **Pets:** Large, other species. No service, supervision. 🛜 🕭M 🛗

▼▼▼ **Residence Inn by Marriott Greenville-Spartanburg Airport** H
(864) 627-0001. **$99-$129.** 120 Milestone Way 29615. I-85 exit 54 (Pelham Rd), 0.6 mi w to Milestone Way, then just n. Int corridors.
Pets: Accepted. 🛜 ⊠ 🕭M 🛗 💻 🏊

▲▲▲ ▼▼▼ **Sleep Inn Carolina First Center** H 🐾
(864) 240-2006. **$49-$109.** 231 N Pleasanburg Dr 29607. I-385 exit 40B, 0.6 mi s on SR 291. Int corridors. **Pets:** Medium. $20 one-time fee/room. Designated rooms, no service, supervision. [SAVE] 🛜 🕭M 🛗 💻

▼▼▼ **Staybridge Suites Greenville/Spartanburg** H
(864) 288-4448. **$84-$179.** 31 Market Point Dr 29607. I-85 exit 51A (Woodruff Rd), 0.5 mi se to Miller Rd, 0.5 mi s to S Oak Forest Dr, then just nw; I-385 exit 35 (Woodruff Rd), nw to Miller Rd, 0.5 mi s to S Oak Forest Dr, then just nw. Int corridors. **Pets:** Accepted.
🛜 🛗 💻 🏊

▼▼ **StudioPLUS-Greenville-Haywood Mall** H 🐾
(864) 288-4300. **$70-$100.** 530 Woods Lake Rd 29607. I-385 exit 39 (Haywood Rd), just s, then just w. Int corridors. **Pets:** Other species. $25 daily fee/pet. Service with restrictions. 🛜 🛗 💻

▼▼▼ **TownePlace Suites Greenville Haywood Mall** H
(864) 675-1670. **$94-$109.** 75 Mall Connector Rd 29607. I-385 exit 39 (Haywood Rd), just s to Woods Crossing Rd, just se to Mall Connector Rd, then just s. Int corridors. **Pets:** Accepted.
🛜 ⊠ 🕭M 🛗 💻

▼▼ **Vintel Inn & Suites** H
(864) 297-3811. **Call for rates.** 1024 Woodruff Rd 29607. I-85 exit 51A (Woodruff Rd), 0.5 mi nw; I-385 exit 37, just nw on Roper Mountain Rd, then just se. Int corridors. **Pets:** Accepted. 🛜 🛗 💻

▲▲▲ ▼▼▼ **The Westin Poinsett** H
(864) 421-9700. **$99-$319.** 120 S Main St 29601. Just s of center. Int corridors. **Pets:** Accepted. [ECO] [SAVE] 🛜 ⊠ 🛗 💻 🍽

GREENWOOD

▼ **Econo Lodge** M
(864) 229-5329. **$65-$100.** 719 Bypass 25 NE 29646. Jct US 25 Bypass NE/221, just se. Ext corridors. **Pets:** Medium. $10 one-time fee/pet. Service with restrictions, supervision. 🛜 🛗 💻 🏊

GREER

▼▼▼ **Holiday Inn Express Hotel & Suites Greenville Airport** H
(864) 213-9331. **$89-$119.** 2681 Dry Pocket Rd 29650. I-85 exit 54 (Pelham Rd), just w to The Parkway, just n to Parkway E, then just se. Int corridors. **Pets:** Accepted. 🛜 🛗 💻 🏊

▼▼ ▼ **MainStay Suites-Greenville** H 🐾
(864) 987-5566. **$60-$100.** 2671 Dry Pocket Rd 29650. I-85 exit 54 (Pelham Rd), just w to The Parkway, just n to Parkway E, then just se. Int corridors. **Pets:** Medium, other species. $10 daily fee/pet. Service with restrictions, crate. 🛜 🛗 💻 🏊

HARDEEVILLE

▼▼▼ **Holiday Inn Express & Suites** H 🐾
(843) 784-2800. **$81-$159.** 145 Independence Blvd 29927. I-95 exit 8, just w. Int corridors. **Pets:** Medium. $25 one-time fee/room. Designated rooms, service with restrictions. 🛜 🕭M 🛗 💻 🏊

HILTON HEAD ISLAND

▲▲▲ ▼▼▼ **Comfort Inn South Forest Beach** H
(843) 842-6662. **$79-$229.** 2 Tanglewood Dr 29928. Sea Pines Cir, 1.1 mi se on Pope Ave, just sw on Coligny Plaza. Int corridors.
Pets: Accepted. [SAVE] 🛜 🛗 💻 🏊

▲▲▲ ▼▼▼ ▼▼▼ **Hilton Oceanfront Resort Hilton Head Island** H 🐾
(843) 842-8000. **$99-$359.** 23 Ocean Ln 29928. Jct US 278 business route/Queens Folly Rd, 0.9 mi se to Ocean Ln, then just sw; in Palmetto Dunes Plantation. Ext/int corridors. **Pets:** Medium. $100 one-time fee/pet. Designated rooms, service with restrictions, crate.
[SAVE] 🛜 ⊠ 🕭M 🛗 💻 🍽 🏊 ⊠

▲▲▲ ▼▼▼ **Park Lane Hotel & Suites** CO
(843) 686-5700. **$80-$190.** 12 Park Ln 29928. 10 mi of J Wilton Graves Bridge on US 278 business route. Int corridors. **Pets:** Accepted.
[SAVE] 🛜 🛗 💻 🏊 ⊠

▼▼ ▼ **Red Roof Inn-Hilton Head** M
(843) 686-6808. **$39-$149.** 5 Regency Pkwy 29928. 9 mi e of J Wilton Grave Bridge on US 278 business route; between Shipyard Plantation and Palmetto Dunes. Ext corridors. **Pets:** Large, other species. No service, supervision. 🛜 🛗 🏊

▲▲▲ ▼▼▼ ▼▼▼ **Westin Hilton Head Island Resort & Spa** H
(843) 681-4000. **$99-$559, 5 day notice.** Two Grasslawn Ave 29928. 5.6 mi from J Wilton Graves Bridge on US 278 business route to Coggins Point Rd, then just e, follow signs. Int corridors. **Pets:** Accepted.
[SAVE] 🛜 ⊠ 🛗 💻 🍽 🏊 ⊠

LANCASTER

▼▼ **Jameson Inn** M
(803) 283-1188. **$70-$90.** 114 Commerce Blvd 29720. Jct SR 9 Bypass and US 521, 1.3 mi w on SR 9 Bypass. Ext corridors. **Pets:** Medium. $15 daily fee/room. Service with restrictions, supervision.
🛜 🕭M 🛗 💻 🏊

LANDRUM

▼▼▼▼ The Red Horse Inn Cottages CA ❀
(864) 895-4968. **$210-$325, 30 day notice.** 45 Winstons Chase Ct 29356. Jct SR 14/414, 1.5 mi w on SR 414 to Campbell Rd, then 0.7 mi n. Ext corridors. **Pets:** $25 one-time fee/pet. Designated rooms, service with restrictions, supervision. 🛰 ✕ 📶 💻 ✕

MANNING

AAA▷ ▼▼▼ Baymont Inn & Suites M
(803) 473-5334. **Call for rates.** 2284 Raccoon Rd 29102. I-95 exit 119 (SR 261), just se, then s. Ext corridors. **Pets:** Accepted.
SAVE 🛰 📶 💻 ⚊

AAA▷ ▼▼▼ Days Inn of Manning M
(803) 473-4021. **$50-$81.** 2825 Paxville Hwy 29102. I-95 exit 119 (SR 261), just se. Ext corridors. **Pets:** Medium. $10 daily fee/pet. Service with restrictions, supervision. SAVE 🛰 📶 💻 ⚊

AAA▷ ▼▼▼ Ramada Inn M
(803) 473-5135. **$49-$89.** 2816 Paxville Hwy 29102. I-95 exit 119 (SR 261), just se. Ext corridors. **Pets:** Accepted. SAVE 🛰 📶 💻 ⚊

NEWBERRY

AAA▷ ▼▼▼ Americas Best Value Inn M
(803) 276-5850. **Call for rates.** 11701 Hwy 34 29108. I-26 exit 74 (SR 34), just ne. Ext corridors. **Pets:** Medium. $10 daily fee/pet. Service with restrictions, supervision. SAVE 📶 💻

ORANGEBURG

▼▼▼▼ Country Inn & Suites By Carlson H
(803) 928-5300. **$105-$190.** 731 Citadel Rd 29118. I-26 exit 145A (US 601), just s. Int corridors. **Pets:** Other species. $10 one-time fee/room. Service with restrictions, crate. 🛰 ⑤M 📶 💻 ⚊

▼▼▼ Jameson Inn Orangeburg M
(803) 534-1611. **$70-$90.** 2350 Chestnut St NE 29115. I-26 exit 145A (US 601), 3.9 mi sw to jct US 601 and 21/178 Bypass, then 2 mi nw. Ext corridors. **Pets:** Medium. $15 daily fee/room. Service with restrictions, supervision. 🛰 📶 💻 ⚊

RICHBURG

AAA▷ ▼▼▼ Super 8 M
(803) 789-7888. **$32-$76.** 3085 Lancaster Hwy 29729. I-77 exit 65, just w on SR 9. Ext corridors. **Pets:** Small, other species. $10 one-time fee/pet. Designated rooms, service with restrictions, supervision.
SAVE 🛰 📶 💻 ⚊

RIDGELAND

AAA▷ ▼▼▼ Comfort Inn H ❀
(843) 726-2121. **Call for rates.** Hwy 336 & I-95 29936. I-95 exit 21 (US 336), just nw. Ext/int corridors. **Pets:** Large, other species. $10 one-time fee/room. Service with restrictions, crate. SAVE 🛰 📶 💻 ⚊

ST. GEORGE

AAA▷ ▼▼▼ Comfort Inn M
(843) 563-4180. **$65-$89.** 139 Motel Dr 29477. I-95 exit 77 (US 78), just e. Ext corridors. **Pets:** $10 daily fee/pet. Designated rooms, service with restrictions, supervision. SAVE 🛰 📶 💻 ⚊

AAA▷ ▼ Econo Lodge M
(843) 563-4195. **$50-$75.** 5971 W Jim Bilton Blvd 29477. I-95 exit 77 (US 78), just e. Ext corridors. **Pets:** Small. $5 daily fee/pet. Designated rooms, service with restrictions, supervision. SAVE 🛰 📶 💻 ⚊

SANTEE

▼▼▼▼ Holiday Inn Santee H
(803) 854-9800. **$89-$165.** 139 Bradford Blvd 29142. I-95 exit 98 (SR 6), just nw, then just sw. Int corridors. **Pets:** Small, other species. $25 daily fee/pet. Designated rooms, service with restrictions, supervision.
🛰 ⑤M 📶 💻 🍴 ⚊

AAA▷ ▼▼▼ Howard Johnson Express Inn M
(803) 854-3870. **$54-$58.** 9112 Old Hwy 6 29142. I-95 exit 98 (SR 6), 0.4 mi se. Ext corridors. **Pets:** Medium. $10 daily fee/pet. Designated rooms, service with restrictions. SAVE 🛰 📶 💻 ⚊

AAA▷ ▼▼▼ Quality Inn & Suites Santee M ❀
(803) 854-2121. **Call for rates.** 8929 Old Number 6 Hwy 29142. I-95 exit 98 (SR 6), just nw. Ext corridors. **Pets:** Medium, other species. $10 one-time fee/pet. Designated rooms, service with restrictions, supervision. SAVE 🛰 📶 💻 🍴 ⚊ ✕

AAA▷ ▼▼▼ Super 8 M
(803) 854-3456. **$25-$72.** 9125 Old Hwy 6 29142. I-95 exit 98 (SR 6), 0.4 mi se. Ext corridors. **Pets:** $10 daily fee/pet. Designated rooms, service with restrictions, crate. SAVE 🛰 📶 💻 ⚊

AAA▷ ▼▼▼ Travelodge M
(803) 854-3122. **$47-$51.** 9091 Old Hwy 6 29142. I-95 exit 98 (SR 6), 0.4 mi se. Ext corridors. **Pets:** Accepted. SAVE 🛰 📶 💻

SENECA

▼▼▼ Jameson Inn M
(864) 888-8300. **$75-$95.** 226 Hi-Tech Rd 29678. Jct SR 28 and US 76/123, 0.9 mi w on US 76/123, just se. Ext corridors. **Pets:** Medium. $15 daily fee/room. Service with restrictions, supervision.
🛰 ⑤M 📶 💻 ⚊

SIMPSONVILLE

▼▼▼ Days Inn M ❀
(864) 963-7701. **$54-$67.** 45 Ray E Talley Ct 29680. I-385 exit 27, just s, then just e. Ext corridors. **Pets:** Small. $15 daily fee/pet. Service with restrictions, supervision. 🛰 📶 💻 ⚊

▼ Motel 6 Greenville - Simpsonville #4266 H
(864) 962-8484. **Call for rates.** 3706 Grandview Dr 29680. I-385 exit 27, just s, then just w. Int corridors. **Pets:** Other species. Service with restrictions, supervision. 🛰 ⑤M 📶

▼▼ Quality Inn M
(864) 963-2777. **Call for rates.** 3755 Grandview Dr 29680. I-385 exit 27, just s. Ext corridors. **Pets:** Accepted. 🛰 📶 💻 ⚊

SPARTANBURG

▼▼ Extended StayAmerica-Spartanburg-Asheville Hwy M ❀
(864) 573-5949. **$45-$70.** 130 Mobile Dr 29303. I-85 business route exit 4/4B, just se, then just ne on service road. Ext corridors. **Pets:** Other species. $25 daily fee/pet. Service with restrictions. 🛰 📶 💻

AAA▷▼▼▼ Holiday Inn Express Hotel & Suites H
(864) 699-7777. **Call for rates.** 895 Spartan Blvd 29301. I-26 exit 21B (US 29), just e to W Blackstock Rd, then 0.7 mi n. Int corridors. **Pets:** Large, other species. $50 one-time fee/room. Designated rooms, service with restrictions. SAVE 🛰 ⑤M 📶 💻 ⚊

SUMMERTON

AAA▷ ▼▼▼ Days Inn of Summerton M
(803) 485-2865. **$41-$68.** 400 Bluff Blvd 29148. I-95 exit 108, just n. Ext corridors. **Pets:** Accepted. SAVE 🛰 📶 💻 ⚊

SUMTER

▼▼▼▼ Candlewood Suites H
(803) 469-4000. **$119-$159.** 2541 Broad St 29150. 1.1 mi w of jct US 76/378/521. Int corridors. **Pets:** Accepted. 🛰 ✕ 📶 💻 ⚊

AAA▷ ▼▼ Travelers Inn & Suites M
(803) 469-9210. **$55-$99.** 1210 Camden Rd 29151. Jct US 521/76. Ext corridors. **Pets:** Accepted. SAVE 🛰 📶 💻 ⚊

TRAVELERS REST

▼▼ Sleep Inn **H**

(864) 834-7040. **Call for rates.** 110 Hawkins Rd 29690. Jct US 25, just e. Int corridors. **Pets:** Accepted.

WALTERBORO

AAA ▼▼ Best Western of Walterboro **M** ✿

(843) 538-3600. **$80-$90.** 1428 Sniders Hwy 29488. I-95 exit 53 (SR 63), just e. Ext corridors. **Pets:** Small. $15 daily fee/pet. Service with restrictions, supervision.

AAA ▼▼ Microtel Inn & Suites **H**

(843) 539-5656. **$48-$71.** 130 Cane Branch Rd 29488. I-95 exit 53 (SR 63), just w, then just s. Int corridors. **Pets:** Other species. $15 one-time fee/room. Service with restrictions, crate.

AAA ▼ Rice Planters Inn **M**

(843) 538-8964. **$44.** 97 Ladson Ln 29488. I-95 exit 53 (SR 63), just e. Ext corridors. **Pets:** Small, other species. $5 daily fee/pet. Service with restrictions, supervision.

AAA ▼▼ Super 8 **M**

(843) 538-5383. **$45-$66.** 1972 Bells Hwy 29488. I-95 exit 57 (SR 64), just nw. Ext corridors. **Pets:** Medium. $10 daily fee/pet. Designated rooms, service with restrictions, supervision.

WEST COLUMBIA

▼▼ Days Inn & Suites Airport **M**

(803) 796-0044. **$45-$111.** 110 Branch Rd 29169. I-26 exit 113 (Airport Blvd), just sw. Ext corridors. **Pets:** Accepted.

▼▼ Quality Inn **M**

(803) 791-5160. **$60-$120.** 2516 Augusta Rd 29169. I-26 exit 111B (US 1 N), just e. Ext/int corridors. **Pets:** Medium. $15 daily fee/pet. Designated rooms, service with restrictions, supervision.

WINNSBORO

▼▼ Days Inn **M**

(803) 635-1447. **$45-$51.** 1894 US Hwy 321 Bypass 29180. I-77 exit 34 (SR 34), 6.5 mi w; jct US 321/SR 34/213. Ext corridors. **Pets:** Small. $10 daily fee/pet. Designated rooms, service with restrictions, supervision.

YEMASSEE

AAA ▼▼ Best Western Point South **M**

(843) 726-8101. **$70-$80.** 3536 Point South Dr 29945. I-95 exit 33 (US 17), just ne. Ext corridors. **Pets:** Accepted.

SOUTH DAKOTA

CITY INDEX

ABERDEEN

▼▼ Aberdeen East Super 8 **H**

(605) 229-5005. **$67-$108.** 2405 6th Ave SE 57401. 1.8 mi e on US 12. Int corridors. **Pets:** Accepted.

▼▼ Aberdeen North Super 8 **M**

(605) 226-2288. **$58-$99.** 1023 8th Ave NW 57401. On US 281, 1.5 mi nw. Int corridors. **Pets:** Accepted.

▼▼ Aberdeen West Super 8 **M**

(605) 225-1711. **$58-$99.** 714 S Hwy 281 57401. Just s of jct US 12. Int corridors. **Pets:** Accepted.

▼▼▼ AmericInn Lodge & Suites of Aberdeen **H**

(605) 225-4565. **Call for rates.** 301 Centennial St 57401. 2.2 mi e on US 12, just n. Int corridors. **Pets:** Medium, dogs only. $25 one-time fee/pet. Service with restrictions, supervision.

AAA ▼▼▼ Best Western Ramkota Hotel **H**

(605) 229-4040. **$99-$120.** 1400 8th Ave NW 57401. 1.5 mi nw on US 281. Ext/int corridors. **Pets:** Large. Service with restrictions, supervision.

▼▼▼ Holiday Inn Express Hotel & Suites **H** ✿

(605) 725-4000. **$110-$150.** 3310 7th Ave SE 57401. 2.1 mi e on US 12. Int corridors. **Pets:** Medium, dogs only. $20 one-time fee/room. Service with restrictions, crate.

ARLINGTON

▼▼ Arlington Inn **M**

(605) 983-4609. **$66-$98.** 402 S Hwy 81 57212. 1 mi s on US 81. Int corridors. **Pets:** $15 one-time fee/pet. Designated rooms, service with restrictions, supervision.

BLACK HILLS AREA

BELLE FOURCHE

▼ Ace Motel **M**

(605) 892-2612. **$38-$78.** 109 6th Ave 57717. 0.5 mi n via US 85, just e; just s of US 212 Bypass. Ext corridors. **Pets:** Dogs only. $8 daily fee/room. Designated rooms, service with restrictions, supervision.

CUSTER CITY

AAA ▼▼ Bavarian Inn Motel **M**

(605) 673-2802. **$59-$139, 3 day notice.** 907 N 5th St 57730. 1 mi n on US 16 and 385. Ext/int corridors. **Pets:** Accepted.

▼▼▼▼ **Creekside Lodge** H
(605) 255-4388. **Call for rates.** 13389 US Hwy 16A 57730. On Alternate Rt US 16, 14 mi e. Int corridors. **Pets:** Accepted.
[icons]

▼▼▼▼ **Custer Days Inn** H
(605) 673-4500. **$51-$202, 3 day notice.** 519 Crook St 57730. Just n of downtown on US 16 and 385. Int corridors. **Pets:** Accepted.
[icons]

AAA▽ ▼▼▼ **Rock Crest Lodge and Cabins** CA
(605) 673-4323. **$75-$305, 15 day notice.** 15 W Mt. Rushmore Rd 57730. US 16, 0.5 mi w. Ext/int corridors. **Pets:** Accepted.
[icons]

AAA▽ ▼▼ **Rocket Motel** M
(605) 673-4401. **$59-$99, 3 day notice.** 211 Mt. Rushmore Rd 57730. On US 16; center. Ext corridors. **Pets:** Medium, dogs only. $10 daily fee/pet. Service with restrictions, supervision. [icons]

▼▼▼ **State Game Lodge** M
(605) 255-4541. **$99-$995, 15 day notice.** 13389 US 16A 57730. On Alternate Rt US 16, 14 mi e. Ext/int corridors. **Pets:** Other species. $10 daily fee/pet. Designated rooms, service with restrictions, supervision.
[icons]

AAA▽ ▼▼▼ **Super 8 Custer** H ❀
(605) 673-2200. **$54-$198.** 535 W Mt. Rushmore Rd 57730. US 16, 0.8 mi w. Int corridors. **Pets:** Dogs only. $10 daily fee/pet. Designated rooms, service with restrictions, supervision.
[icons]

DEADWOOD

▼▼ **Black Hills Inn & Suites** M
(605) 578-7791. **$43-$85, 3 day notice.** 206 Mountain Shadow Ln 57732. 0.3 mi s of jct US 385 and 85. Ext/int corridors. **Pets:** $20 one-time fee/room. Designated rooms, service with restrictions, supervision.
[icons]

AAA▽ ▼▼▼▼ **Cadillac Jacks Gaming Resort** H ❀
(605) 578-1500. **$39-$299.** 360 Main St 57732. 0.6 mi n on US 85. Int corridors. **Pets:** Medium, other species. $25 daily fee/room. Designated rooms, service with restrictions, supervision.
[icons]

AAA▽ ▼▼▼ **Deadwood Gulch Gaming Resort** H
(605) 578-1294. **$59-$169.** 304 Cliff St 57732. 0.7 mi s on US 85 S. Ext/int corridors. **Pets:** Dogs only. $500 deposit/pet, $25 daily fee/pet. Designated rooms. [icons]

AAA▽ ▼▼▼ **First Gold Hotel & Gaming** H
(605) 578-9777. **$79-$299, 7 day notice.** 270 Main St 57732. 0.7 mi n on US 85. Int corridors. **Pets:** Medium. $25 one-time fee/room. Designated rooms, service with restrictions, supervision.
[icons]

▼▼▼▼ **Holiday Inn Express Hotel & Suites-Gold Dust Casino** H ❀
(605) 578-3330. **$79-$499.** 22 Lee St 57732. Jct Main St; center. Int corridors. **Pets:** $25 one-time fee/room. Designated rooms, supervision.
[icons]

AAA▽ ▼▼▼ **The Lodge at Deadwood** H ❀
(605) 584-4800. **$89-$540, 3 day notice.** 100 Pine Crest Ln 57732. Jct US 14, 1 mi n on US 85. Ext/int corridors. **Pets:** Other species. Service with restrictions, crate. [icons]

HILL CITY

AAA▽ ▼▼▼▼ **Best Western Plus Golden Spike Inn & Suites** H ❀
(605) 574-2577. **$80-$120.** 601 E Main St 57745. Just n on US 16 and 385. Ext/int corridors. **Pets:** Large. $15 daily fee/pet. Designated rooms, service with restrictions, supervision.
[icons]

AAA▽ ▼▼▼ **Lantern Inn** M
(605) 574-2582. **$64-$150.** 580 E Main St 57745. On US 16 and 385; north side of town. Ext corridors. **Pets:** Very small. $10 daily fee/pet. Supervision. [icons]

AAA▽ ▼▼▼ **The Lodge at Palmer Gulch** H ❀
(605) 574-2525. **$50-$695, 10 day notice.** 12620 SR 244 57745. On SR 244, 5 mi w of Mt. Rushmore. Int corridors. **Pets:** Dogs only. $20 daily fee/pet. No service, supervision.
[icons]

HOT SPRINGS

AAA▽ ▼▼▼ **Best Western Sundowner Inn** H
(605) 745-7378. **$59-$180.** 737 S 6th St 57747. 0.5 mi se off US 18 and 385. Int corridors. **Pets:** Accepted. [icons]

AAA▽ ▼▼▼ **Budget Host Hills Inn** M
(605) 745-3130. **$49-$154.** 640 S 6th St 57747. 0.5 mi se off US 18 and 385. Ext corridors. **Pets:** Medium. Designated rooms, service with restrictions, supervision. [icons]

AAA▽ ▼▼▼ **Dollar Inn Hot Springs** M
(605) 745-3182. **$50-$200.** 402 Battle Mountain Ave 57747. 1 mi n on US 385. Ext corridors. **Pets:** Accepted. [icons]

▼▼ **Hot Springs Super 8** M
(605) 745-3888. **$48-$156.** 800 Mammoth St 57747. Jct US 18 and 385, 1 mi w on US 18 Bypass. Int corridors. **Pets:** Accepted.
[icons]

AAA▽ ▼▼▼▼ **Stay USA Hotel and Suites** H
(605) 745-4411. **$56-$280.** 1401 Hwy 18 57747. Jct US 18 and 385, 0.7 mi w on US 18 Bypass. Int corridors. **Pets:** Accepted.
[icons]

KEYSTONE

AAA▽ ▼▼▼ **Econo Lodge of Mt. Rushmore** H
(605) 666-4417. **Call for rates.** 908 Madill St 57751. SR 40, 1 mi e of jct US 16A. Int corridors. **Pets:** Accepted. [icons]

AAA▽ ▼▼▼ **Holy Smoke Resort** CA
(605) 666-4616. **$50-$145, 3 day notice.** 24105 Hwy 16A 57751. On US 16A, 1 mi n. Ext corridors. **Pets:** Accepted.
[icons]

AAA▽ ▼▼▼ **Mt. Rushmore's Washington Inn** H
(605) 666-5070. **$49-$99, 3 day notice.** 231 Winter St 57751. On US 16A; downtown. Ext/int corridors. **Pets:** Medium, dogs only. Designated rooms, service with restrictions, supervision.
[icons]

AAA▽ ▼▼▼ **Mt. Rushmore's White House Resort** H
(605) 666-4917. **$49-$99, 3 day notice.** 115 Swanzey St 57751. Jct US 16A and SR 40. Ext/int corridors. **Pets:** Medium, dogs only. Designated rooms, service with restrictions, supervision.
[icons]

AAA▽ ▼▼▼ **Powder House Lodge** CA
(605) 666-4646. **$80-$300, 3 day notice.** 24125 Hwy 16A 57751. On US 16A, 1.5 mi n. Ext corridors. **Pets:** Accepted.
[icons]

RAPID CITY

▼▼ **Americas Best Value Inn** H ❀
(605) 343-5434. **$59-$259, 7 day notice.** 620 Howard St 57701. I-90 exit 58, just nw of Haines Ave. Int corridors. **Pets:** Medium, other species. $10 daily fee/pet. Designated rooms, service with restrictions, supervision.
[icons]

AAA ◆◆◆ **AmericInn Lodge & Suites of Rapid City** H ❀

(605) 343-8424. **$39-$299, 3 day notice.** 1632 Rapp St 57701. I-90 exit 59 (LaCrosse St), just se. Int corridors. **Pets:** Large, dogs only. $20 one-time fee/room. Designated rooms, service with restrictions.

SAVE 🛜 ✕ &M ⬛ 💻 ⇌ ✕

AAA ◆◆◆ **Best Western Ramkota Hotel** H ❀

(605) 343-8550. **$90-$230.** 2111 N LaCrosse St 57701. I-90 exit 59 (LaCrosse St), just n. Ext/int corridors. **Pets:** Medium, other species. Designated rooms, service with restrictions, supervision.

SAVE 🛜 ✕ &M ⬛ 💻 🍴 ⇌ ✕

AAA ◆◆◆ **Best Western Town 'N Country** H ❀

(605) 343-5383. **$50-$260.** 2505 Mt. Rushmore Rd 57701. 1.3 mi s on US 16. Ext corridors. **Pets:** Large, dogs only. $20 one-time fee/room. Service with restrictions, supervision. SAVE 🛜 &M ⬛ 💻 ⇌

AAA ◆◆ **Big Sky Lodge** M

(605) 348-3200. **$59-$159.** 4080 Tower Rd 57701. 3 mi s on US 16, 0.3 mi n on Skyline Dr, take service road off US 16. Ext corridors. **Pets:** Accepted. SAVE 🛜 ✕ &M ⬛ 💻 🐾

◆◆◆ **Comfort Suites & Convention Center** H

(605) 791-2345. **$69-$289.** 1333 N Elk Vale Rd 57703. I-90 exit 61 (Elk Vale Rd), just s. Int corridors. **Pets:** Accepted.

🛜 ✕ &M ⬛ 💻 ⇌

AAA ◆◆◆ **Country Inn & Suites By Carlson** H ❀

(605) 394-0017. **Call for rates.** 2321 N LaCrosse St 57701. I-90 exit 59 (LaCrosse St), 0.3 mi n. Int corridors. **Pets:** Dogs only. $20 one-time fee/pet. Designated rooms, service with restrictions.

SAVE 🛜 ✕ &M ⬛ 💻 ⇌ ✕

◆◆ **Days Inn I-90** H

(605) 348-8410. **$72-$261.** 1570 N LaCrosse St 57701. I-90 exit 59 (LaCrosse St), just s. Int corridors. **Pets:** Accepted.

🛜 ✕ &M ⬛ 💻 ⇌ ✕

AAA ◆◆ **Gold Star Motel** M

(605) 341-7051. **$45-$150.** 801 E North St 57701. I-90 exit 60, 1.5 mi sw on I-90 business loop, 1.2 mi s, then just e, from exit 59 (LaCrosse St). Ext corridors. **Pets:** Accepted. SAVE 🛜 &M ⬛ 💻

AAA ◆◆◆ **GrandStay Residential Suites Hotel** H

(605) 341-5100. **$89-$299.** 660 Disk Dr 57701. I-90 exit 58C (Haines Ave), just n, then just w. Int corridors. **Pets:** Medium. $100 deposit/pet, $10 daily fee/pet. Service with restrictions, supervision.

SAVE 🛜 ✕ &M ⬛ 💻 ⇌ ✕

◆◆◆ **Holiday Inn Express** H

(605) 341-9300. **$95-$160.** 750 Cathedral Dr 57701. 1.4 mi s on US 16, just e. Int corridors. **Pets:** Accepted. 🛜 &M ⬛ 💻 ⇌

◆◆◆ **Holiday Inn Express Hotel & Suites, I-90** H

(605) 355-9090. **$99-$209.** 645 E Disk Dr 57701. I-90 exit 59 (LaCrosse St), just ne. Int corridors. **Pets:** Large. $10 daily fee/pet. Designated rooms, service with restrictions. 🛜 &M ⬛ 💻 ⇌

◆◆◆ **Holiday Inn-Rushmore Plaza** H

(605) 348-4000. **$99-$209.** 505 N 5th St 57701. I-90 exit 58, 1.3 mi s on Haines. Int corridors. **Pets:** Accepted.

🛜 ✕ &M ⬛ 💻 🍴 ⇌ ✕

AAA ◆◆◆◆ **The Hotel Alex Johnson, an Ascend Collection hotel** H ❀

(605) 342-1210. **$49-$270.** 523 6th St 57701. I-190 exit 57 (I-190), left at Omaha St; downtown. Int corridors. **Pets:** Dogs only. $25 one-time fee/pet. Designated rooms, service with restrictions, crate.

SAVE 🛜 ✕ ⬛ 💻

AAA ◆◆◆ **Howard Johnson Inn & Suites** H

(605) 737-4656. **$53-$365.** 950 North St 57701. I-90 exit 57 (I-190) exit 1C, then just e. Int corridors. **Pets:** Medium, dogs only. $10 daily fee/room. Designated rooms, service with restrictions, supervision.

SAVE 🛜 ✕ &M ⬛ 💻 ⇌ ✕

AAA ◆◆◆ **La Quinta Inn & Suites Rapid City** H

(605) 718-7000. **$143-$230.** 1416 N Elk Vale Rd 57703. I-90 exit 61 (Elk Vale Rd), just s, then just e. Int corridors. **Pets:** Medium, other species. Service with restrictions, supervision.

SAVE 🛜 ✕ &M ⬛ 💻 🍴

AAA ◆ **Lazy U Motel** M

(605) 343-4242. **$42-$72.** 2215 Mt. Rushmore Rd 57701. 1 mi s on US 16. Ext corridors. **Pets:** Accepted. SAVE 🛜 ⬛

AAA ◆◆◆ **Microtel Inn & Suites** H

(605) 348-2523. **$43-$242.** 1740 Rapp St 57701. I-90 exit 59 (LaCrosse St), just se. Int corridors. **Pets:** Accepted.

SAVE 🛜 ✕ &M ⬛ 💻 ⇌

AAA ◆◆◆ **Rapid City Ramada** H

(605) 342-3322. **$40-$275.** 1902 N LaCrosse St 57701. I-90 exit 59 (LaCrosse St), just s. Ext/int corridors. **Pets:** Accepted.

SAVE 🛜 ✕ &M ⬛ 💻 🍴 ⇌ ✕

◆◆ **Sleep Inn & Suites** H

(605) 791-5678. **$59-$199.** 4031 Cheyenne Blvd 57703. I-90 exit 61 (Elk Vale Rd), just s. Int corridors. **Pets:** Medium, other species. $10 daily fee/pet. Service with restrictions, supervision.

🛜 ✕ &M ⬛ 💻 ⇌

AAA ◆◆ **Super 8 LaCrosse St** M

(605) 348-8070. **$41-$176.** 2124 LaCrosse St 57701. I-90 exit 59 (LaCrosse St), just n. Int corridors. **Pets:** Medium, other species. $10 daily fee/pet. Service with restrictions, crate. SAVE 🛜 &M ⬛ 💻

◆◆ **Super 8 Mt. Rushmore Rd** M

(605) 342-4911. **$38-$216.** 2520 Tower Rd 57701. 1.4 mi s on US 16, then just e. Int corridors. **Pets:** Accepted. 🛜 ⬛ 💻

AAA ◆ **Thrifty Motor Inn** M

(605) 342-0551. **$45-$150.** 1303 LaCrosse St 57701. I-90 exit 59 (LaCrosse St), 0.5 mi s. Ext corridors. **Pets:** Medium, dogs only. $5 daily fee/pet. Designated rooms, service with restrictions, supervision.

SAVE 🛜 ⬛ 💻

SPEARFISH

◆ **Bell's Motor Lodge Motel** M

(605) 642-3812. **$40-$88.** 230 N Main St 57783. 0.5 mi s of center. Ext corridors. **Pets:** Small. $2 daily fee/pet. Designated rooms, supervision.

🛜 ⬛ 💻 ⇌

AAA ◆◆◆ **Best Western Black Hills Lodge** H ❀

(605) 642-7795. **$64-$139.** 540 E Jackson Blvd 57783. I-90 exit 12, just s. Ext/int corridors. **Pets:** Large, dogs only. $15 daily fee/pet. Designated rooms, supervision. SAVE 🛜 ✕ &M ⬛ 💻 ⇌ ✕

◆◆ **Days Inn** H ❀

(605) 642-7101. **$49-$261.** 240 Ryan Rd 57783. I-90 exit 10, 1.2 mi s. Ext/int corridors. **Pets:** Other species. $11 daily fee/pet. Designated rooms, service with restrictions, supervision. 🛜 ✕ &M ⬛ 💻

AAA ◆◆◆ **Holiday Inn Hotel & Convention Center** H ❀

(605) 642-4683. **$89-$149.** 305 N 27th St 57783. I-90 exit 14 (Spearfish Canyon), just n. Ext/int corridors. **Pets:** Other species. $100 deposit/room, $25 one-time fee/room. Designated rooms, service with restrictions, supervision. SAVE 🛜 &M ⬛ 💻 🍴 ⇌ ✕

▼▼ Howard Johnson Express Inn 🄷
(605) 642-8105. **$50-$239.** 323 S 27th St 57783. I-90 exit 14 (Spearfish Canyon), just s. Int corridors. **Pets:** Accepted.
📶 ☒ 🅂ᴍ 🍴 🖵 🛏 🏊

🄰🄰🄰 ▼▼▼▼ Spearfish Canyon Lodge 🄷 ❀
(605) 584-3435. **$89-$275, 5 day notice.** 10619 Roughlock Falls Rd 57754. I-90 exit 14 (Spearfish Canyon), 13 mi s. Int corridors. **Pets:** Other species. $25 daily fee/pet. Service with restrictions, supervision.
🆂🅰🆅🅴 📶 ☒ 🅂ᴍ 🍴 🖵 🍴 ☒

▼▼ Spearfish Super 8 🄷
(605) 642-4721. **$49-$225.** 440 Heritage Dr 57783. I-90 exit 14 (Spearfish Canyon), just s, just e, then just s. Int corridors. **Pets:** Other species. $10 daily fee/pet. Designated rooms, service with restrictions, supervision. 📶 🅂ᴍ 🍴 🖵 🏊

STURGIS

🄰🄰🄰 ▼▼▼ Best Western Sturgis Inn 🄷
(605) 347-3604. **$49-$149.** 2431 S Junction Ave 57785. I-90 exit 32, just n. Ext/int corridors. **Pets:** Other species. $10 daily fee/room. Designated rooms, service with restrictions, crate.
🆂🅰🆅🅴 📶 🅂ᴍ 🍴 🖵 🍴 🛏 ☒

▼▼▼ Holiday Inn Express & Suites - Sturgis 🄷 ❀
(605) 347-4140. **$99-$159.** 2721 Lazelle St 57785. I-90 exit 30 (US 14A), just s. Int corridors. **Pets:** Other species. $25 one-time fee/pet. Service with restrictions, supervision. 📶 ☒ 🍴 🖵 🏊 ☒

🄰🄰🄰 ▼ Star Lite Motel 🄼
(605) 347-2506. **$55-$90.** 2426 Junction Ave 57785. I-90 exit 32, just n. Ext corridors. **Pets:** Very small, dogs only. $10 daily fee/pet. Designated rooms, service with restrictions, crate. 🆂🅰🆅🅴 📶 🍴 🖵

END AREA

BRANDON

▼▼ Comfort Inn 🄷
(605) 582-5777. **Call for rates.** 1105 N Splitrock Blvd 57005. I-90 exit 406, just s. Int corridors. **Pets:** Accepted. 📶 🅂ᴍ 🍴 🖵 🏊

▼▼▼▼ Holiday Inn Express & Suites 🄷
(605) 582-2901. **$99-$159.** 1103 N Splitrock Blvd 57005. I-90 exit 406, just s. Int corridors. **Pets:** $15 daily fee/pet. Service with restrictions, crate. 📶 ☒ 🅂ᴍ 🍴 🖵 🏊 ☒

BROOKINGS

▼▼ Brookings Super 8 🄷
(605) 692-6920. **$58-$103.** 3034 Lefevre Dr 57006. I-29 exit 132, just e. Int corridors. **Pets:** Medium, other species. $10 daily fee/pet. Service with restrictions, supervision. 📶 🅂ᴍ 🍴 🖵 🏊

▼▼▼▼ Holiday Inn Express Hotel & Suites 🄷
(605) 692-9060. **$115-$169.** 3020 Lefevre Dr 57006. I-29 exit 132, just se. Int corridors. **Pets:** Other species. $10 daily fee/room. Service with restrictions, supervision. 📶 🅂ᴍ 🍴 🖵 🏊 ☒

BUFFALO

▼ Tipperary Lodge 🄼
(605) 375-3721. **$54.** 604 1st St W 57720. 0.5 mi n on US 85, turn at sign. Int corridors. **Pets:** Other species. Designated rooms, service with restrictions, supervision. 📶 ☒ 🍴

CHAMBERLAIN

▼▼ AmericInn Lodge & Suites of Chamberlain 🄷
(605) 734-0985. **Call for rates.** 1981 E King St 57325. I-90 exit 265, just e. Int corridors. **Pets:** Accepted. 📶 🅂ᴍ 🍴 🖵 🏊 ☒

🄰🄰🄰 ▼▼ Best Western Lee's Motor Inn 🄷
(605) 734-5575. **$70-$99.** 220 W King St 57325. US 16 and I-90 business loop; downtown. Ext/int corridors. **Pets:** Accepted.
🆂🅰🆅🅴 ☒ 🅂ᴍ 🖵 🏊 ☒

🄰🄰🄰 ▼▼▼▼ Cedar Shore Resort 🄷 ❀
(605) 734-6376. **$90-$200.** 1500 Shoreline Dr 57365. I-90 exit 260, 2.5 mi e on Business Rt I-90, then 1 mi ne on George S Mickelson Shoreline Dr, follow signs. Int corridors. **Pets:** $10 daily fee/room. Service with restrictions, supervision. 🆂🅰🆅🅴 📶 ☒ 🅂ᴍ 🍴 🖵 🍴 🏊 ☒

🄰🄰🄰 ▼▼ Oasis Inn 🄷
(605) 734-6061. **$59-$130, 7 day notice.** 1100 E Hwy 16 57365. I-90 exit 260, 0.4 mi e on US 16 and I-90 business loop. Ext/int corridors. **Pets:** Other species. Service with restrictions, supervision.
🆂🅰🆅🅴 📶 ☒ 🅂ᴍ 🍴 🖵

🄰🄰🄰 ▼▼▼ Quality Inn 🄷
(605) 734-5593. **Call for rates.** 100 W Hwy 16 57365. I-90 exit 260, just n. Int corridors. **Pets:** Accepted. 🆂🅰🆅🅴 📶 ☒ 🅂ᴍ 🍴 🖵 🏊

DELL RAPIDS

▼▼ Bilmar Inn & Suites 🄷
(605) 428-4288. **Call for rates.** 510 N Hwy 77 57022. I-29 exit 98 (SR 115), 3 mi e, then just n. Int corridors. **Pets:** Accepted. 📶 🅂ᴍ 🍴

DE SMET

▼▼ De Smet Super Deluxe Inn & Suites 🄷
(605) 854-9388. **$74-$94.** 288 Hwy 14 E 57231. US 14, just e. Int corridors. **Pets:** Accepted. 📶 ☒ 🍴 🖵 🏊

FAITH

🄰🄰🄰 ▼▼ Prairie Vista Inn 🄷
(605) 967-2343. **$78-$90.** Hwy 212 & E 1st St 57626. On US 212; east end of town. Int corridors. **Pets:** $15 daily fee/pet. Designated rooms, service with restrictions, supervision. 🆂🅰🆅🅴 📶 🅂ᴍ 🍴 🖵 ☒

FLANDREAU

🄰🄰🄰 ▼▼ Royal River Casino & Hotel 🄷
(605) 997-3746. **$71-$205.** 607 S Veterans St 57028. I-29 exit 114, 7 mi e, follow signs. Int corridors. **Pets:** Accepted.
🆂🅰🆅🅴 📶 🅂ᴍ 🍴 🖵 🍴 🏊 ☒

FORT PIERRE

▼▼▼ AmericInn Lodge & Suites of Fort Pierre 🄷
(605) 223-2358. **$106-$199.** 312 Island Dr 57532. Jct US 14 and SR 34, just w of Missouri River Bridge, then just s. Int corridors. **Pets:** Accepted.
📶 ☒ 🅂ᴍ 🍴 🖵 🏊

▼▼ Fort Pierre Motel 🄼
(605) 223-3111. **$58-$78, 3 day notice.** 211 S 1st St 57532. On US 83, 1.2 mi s of jct US 14. Ext corridors. **Pets:** Dogs only. Service with restrictions, supervision. 📶 🅂ᴍ 🍴

FREEMAN

▼▼ Freeman Country Inn 🄷
(605) 925-4888. **$75-$116.** 1019 S Hwy 81 57029. On US 81, just s. Int corridors. **Pets:** Accepted. 📶 ☒ 🅂ᴍ 🍴

HURON

🄰🄰🄰 ▼▼▼ Best Western Of Huron 🄷
(605) 352-2000. **$79-$99.** 2000 Dakota Ave 57350. 1.3 mi s on SR 37. Ext/int corridors. **Pets:** Medium, dogs only. $10 daily fee/room. Service with restrictions, supervision. 🆂🅰🆅🅴 📶 🅂ᴍ 🍴 🖵 ☒

INTERIOR

▲▲▲ 🚩 **Badlands Budget Host Inn** **M**
(605) 433-5335. **$59-$69.** 900 SD Hwy 377 57750. Jct SR 44 and 377, 2 mi s of Badlands National Park. Ext corridors. **Pets:** Accepted.
[SAVE] 🛜 🖥 〠 🏊

KADOKA

▲▲▲ 🚩 **Budget Host Sundowner Motor Inn** **M**
(605) 837-2296. **$50-$110.** 510 SD Hwy 73 57543. I-90 exit 150, just s. Ext corridors. **Pets:** Small. Designated rooms, service with restrictions.
[SAVE] 🛜 ⓜ 🖥 🏊

▲▲▲ 🚩🚩 **Rodeway Inn** **M** ❀
(605) 837-2287. **$69-$109.** 915 Hwy 248 57543. 1.5 mi w on I-90 business route from exit 152, 1.3 mi e from exit 150. Ext corridors. **Pets:** Other species. Designated rooms, service with restrictions, crate.
[SAVE] 🛜 ⓜ 🖥 🖥 🍽 🏊

MADISON

💎💎 **AmericInn Lodge & Suites of Madison** **H**
(605) 256-3076. **Call for rates.** 504 10th St SE 57042. SR 34, 0.5 mi se; south side of town. Int corridors. **Pets:** Accepted.
🛜 ⓜ 🖥 🖥 🏊

MITCHELL

▲▲▲ 🚩🚩 **AmericInn Lodge & Suites of Mitchell** **H**
(605) 996-9700. **$75-$150.** 1421 S Burr St 57301. I-90 exit 332, just n. Int corridors. **Pets:** Accepted. [SAVE] 🛜 ✕ 🖥 🖥 🏊

▲▲▲ 🚩🚩 **Best Western Motor Inn** **M** ❀
(605) 996-5536. **$55-$99.** 1001 S Burr St 57301. I-90 exit 332, 0.6 mi n. Ext corridors. **Pets:** $7 one-time fee/pet. Service with restrictions, crate.
[SAVE] 🛜 ⓜ 🖥 🖥 🏊

▲▲▲ 🚩🚩 **Days Inn Mitchell** **H**
(605) 996-6208. **$58-$104.** 1506 S Burr St 57301. I-90 exit 332, just n. Int corridors. **Pets:** $20 deposit/room, $10 daily fee/pet. Designated rooms, service with restrictions, supervision.
[SAVE] 🛜 ⓜ 🖥 🖥 🏊 ✕

▲▲▲ 🚩🚩🚩 **Hampton Inn** **H** ❀
(605) 995-1575. **Call for rates.** 1920 Highland Way 57301. I-90 exit 332, just se. Int corridors. **Pets:** Dogs only. $20 one-time fee/room. Service with restrictions. [SAVE] 🛜 ✕ ⓜ 🖥 🖥 🏊 ✕

▲▲▲ 🚩🚩🚩 **Kelly Inn & Suites** **H**
(605) 995-0500. **$75-$130.** 1010 Cabela Dr 57301. I-90 exit 332, just sw. Ext/int corridors. **Pets:** Large. Service with restrictions, supervision.
[SAVE] 🛜 ✕ 🖥 🖥 🏊

🚩🚩🚩 **Ramada Inn & Suites Conference Center** **H**
(605) 996-6501. **$99-$134.** 1525 W Havens St 57301. I-90 exit 330, 0.8 mi n. Int corridors. **Pets:** Accepted. 🛜 ✕ 🖥 🖥 🍽 🏊 ✕

MOBRIDGE

🚩🚩 **Wrangler Inn** **H**
(605) 845-3641. **$67-$149.** 820 W Grand Crossing 57601. 0.5 mi w on US 12. Ext/int corridors. **Pets:** Accepted. 🛜 🖥 🖥 🍽 🏊 ✕

MURDO

▲▲▲ 🚩🚩 **Best Western Graham's** **M**
(605) 669-2441. **$60-$140.** 301 W 5th 57559. On I-90 business loop, 0.5 mi w of jct US 83; I-90 exit 191 or 192. Ext corridors. **Pets:** Medium, other species. $10 one-time fee/pet. Designated rooms, service with restrictions, supervision. [SAVE] 🛜 ✕ ⓜ 🖥 🖥 🏊

▲▲▲ 🚩🚩 **Days Inn Range Country** **H**
(605) 669-2425. **$65-$131.** 302 W 5th 57559. I-90 business loop, 0.5 mi w of jct US 83 exit 192 or 191. Ext/int corridors. **Pets:** Other species. $50 deposit/room. Designated rooms, service with restrictions, supervision.
[SAVE] 🛜 ⓜ 🖥 🖥 🏊

NORTH SIOUX CITY

🚩🚩🚩 **Hampton Inn** **H**
(605) 232-9739. **$79-$139.** 101 S Sodrac Dr 57049. I-29 exit 2, just w. Int corridors. **Pets:** Accepted. 🛜 ⓜ 🖥 🖥 🏊

PIERRE

▲▲▲ 🚩🚩🚩🚩 **Best Western Ramkota Hotel** **H** 🐾
(605) 224-6877. **$107-$115.** 920 W Sioux Ave 57501. 1 mi w on US 14/83. Ext/int corridors. **Pets:** Other species. Service with restrictions, supervision. [SAVE] 🛜 ✕ ⓜ 🖥 🖥 🍽 🏊 ✕

🚩🚩🚩 **Comfort Inn of Pierre** **H**
(605) 224-0377. **$75-$110.** 410 W Sioux Ave 57501. 0.3 mi w on US 14/83 and SR 34. Int corridors. **Pets:** Accepted.
🛜 ✕ ⓜ 🖥 🖥 🏊

🚩🚩 **Governor's Inn** **H**
(605) 224-4200. **$75-$140.** 700 W Sioux Ave 57501. 0.8 mi w on US 14/83 and SR 34. Ext/int corridors. **Pets:** Other species. $10 one-time fee/room. Service with restrictions, supervision.
🛜 ✕ ⓜ 🖥 🖥 🏊

🚩🚩 **River Lodge** **H**
(605) 224-4140. **$63-$85.** 713 W Sioux Ave 57501. 0.8 mi w on US 14/83. Int corridors. **Pets:** Other species. $8 daily fee/room. Service with restrictions, supervision. 🛜 ⓜ 🖥 🖥

PLANKINTON

🚩🚩 **Smart Choice Inn & Suites** **H**
(605) 942-7722. **$40-$80.** 801 S Main St 57368. I-90 exit 308, just n. Int corridors. **Pets:** Accepted. 🖥

SIOUX FALLS

🚩🚩 **Baymont Inn & Suites** **H**
(605) 362-0835. **$66-$142.** 3200 Meadow Ave 57106. I-29 exit 77 (41st St), just w, then just n. Int corridors. **Pets:** Other species. $15 one-time fee/room. Service with restrictions, supervision. 🛜 ⓜ 🖥 🖥 🏊

▲▲▲ 🚩🚩🚩 **Best Western Empire Towers** **H**
(605) 361-3118. **$80-$120.** 4100 W Shirley Pl 57106. I-29 exit 77 (41st St), just ne. Int corridors. **Pets:** Other species. $15 daily fee/room. Designated rooms, service with restrictions, supervision.
[SAVE] 🛜 ⓜ 🖥 🖥 🏊

▲▲▲ 🚩🚩🚩 **Best Western Plus Ramkota Hotel** **H**
(605) 336-0650. **$89-$129.** 3200 W Maple St 57107. I-29 exit 81 (Airport/Russell St), just e. Ext/int corridors. **Pets:** Accepted.
[SAVE] 🛜 ✕ ⓜ 🖥 🖥 🍽 🏊 ✕

▲▲▲ 🚩🚩🚩 **ClubHouse Hotel & Suites** **H**
(605) 361-8700. **$119-$159.** 2320 S Louise Ave 57106. I-29 exit 78 (26th St), just e. Ext/int corridors. **Pets:** Accepted.
[SAVE] 🛜 ✕ ⓜ 🖥 🖥 🏊 ✕

🚩🚩 **Comfort Inn by Choice Hotels South** **H**
(605) 361-2822. **$70-$140.** 3216 S Carolyn Ave 57106. I-29 exit 77 (41st St), just e, then n. Int corridors. **Pets:** Accepted.
🛜 ⓜ 🖥 🖥 🏊

🚩🚩 **Comfort Suites by Choice Hotels** **H**
(605) 362-9711. **$82-$150.** 3208 S Carolyn Ave 57106. I-29 exit 77 (41st St), just e, then n. Int corridors. **Pets:** Accepted.
🛜 ✕ ⓜ 🖥 🖥 🏊

🚩🚩 **Country Inn & Suites By Carlson** **H**
(605) 373-0153. **Call for rates.** 200 E 8th St 57103. Just e of Phillips Ave; downtown. Int corridors. **Pets:** Accepted.
🛜 ⓜ 🖥 🖥 🍽 🏊

▲▲▲ 🚩🚩🚩 **Days Inn Airport** **H** 🐾
(605) 331-5959. **$63-$94.** 5001 N Cliff Ave 57104. I-90 exit 399 (Cliff Ave), just s. Int corridors. **Pets:** Other species. $10 daily fee/room. Service with restrictions, supervision. [SAVE] 🛜 ⓜ 🖥 🖥

AAA **Days Inn-Empire** H
(605) 361-9240. **$63-$99.** 3401 Gateway Blvd 57106. I-29 exit 77 (41st St), just w. Int corridors. **Pets:** Other species. $10 daily fee/pet. Designated rooms, service with restrictions, supervision.
SAVE 🛜 ⛎ 🖥 🖵

AAA **Holiday Inn Sioux Falls City Centre** H
(605) 339-2000. **$104-$179.** 100 W 8th St 57104. Just w of Phillips Ave; downtown. Int corridors. **Pets:** Small, dogs only. $15 one-time fee/room. Service with restrictions, supervision.
SAVE 🛜 ✕ ⛎ 🖥 🖵 ⍗ ⇆ ✕

Homewood Suites By Hilton H ✿
(605) 338-8585. **$69-$229.** 3620 W Avera Dr 57108. I-229 exit 1C (Louise Ave), just s. Int corridors. **Pets:** Other species. $15 one-time fee/room, $5 daily fee/room. Service with restrictions, crate.
🛜 ⛎ 🖥 🖵 ⇆ ✕

AAA **Quality Inn & Suites** H ✿
(605) 336-1900. **$90-$170.** 5410 N Granite Ln 57107. I-29 exit 83 (SR 38), just e, then 0.3 mi n. Int corridors. **Pets:** Medium, other species. $10 daily fee/pet. Designated rooms, service with restrictions, supervision.
SAVE 🛜 ⛎ 🖥 🖵 ⇆

Red Roof Inn H
(605) 361-1864. **$42-$82, 7 day notice.** 3500 S Gateway Blvd 57106. I-29 exit 77 (41st St), just w. Int corridors. **Pets:** Large, other species. No service, supervision. 🛜 ⛎ 🖥 🖵

Residence Inn by Marriott H
(605) 361-2202. **$99-$229.** 4509 W Empire Pl 57106. I-29 exit 77 (41st St), 0.5 mi se. Int corridors. **Pets:** Accepted.
🛜 ✕ ⛎ 🖥 🖵 ⇆ ✕

AAA **Sheraton Sioux Falls** H ✿
(605) 331-0100. **$79-$159.** 1211 N West Ave 57104. I-29 exit 81 (Airport/Russell St), 1.3 mi e. Int corridors. **Pets:** Medium, dogs only. Service with restrictions, supervision.
SAVE 🛜 ✕ ⛎ 🖥 🖵 ⍗ ⇆

Staybridge Suites H ✿
(605) 361-2298. **$99-$319.** 2505 S Carolyn Ave 57106. I-29 exit 78 (26th St), just se. Int corridors. **Pets:** Medium, other species. $50 daily fee/pet. Designated rooms, service with restrictions, supervision.
🛜 ⛎ 🖥 🖵 ⇆ ✕

Super 8-East H
(605) 338-8881. **$63-$81.** 2616 E 10th St 57103. I-229 exit 6, just e. Int corridors. **Pets:** Accepted. 🛜 ⛎ 🖥 🖵 ⇆

AAA **Super 8/I-90/Airport East** H
(605) 339-9212. **$54-$90, 3 day notice.** 4808 N Cliff Ave 57104. I-90 exit 399 (Cliff Ave), 0.3 mi s. Int corridors. **Pets:** Small. $10 one-time fee/pet. Service with restrictions, supervision. SAVE 🛜 🖥 🖵

AAA **TownePlace Suites by Marriott** H
(605) 361-2626. **$89-$179.** 4545 W Homefield Dr 57106. I-29 exit 78 (26th St), just w. Int corridors. **Pets:** Medium. $75 one-time fee/room. Service with restrictions, crate. SAVE 🛜 ✕ ⛎ 🖥 🖵 ⇆ ✕

SUMMERSET
Ramada H
(605) 787-4844. **$59-$300.** 7900 Stagestop Rd 57718. I-90 exit 48, just s. Int corridors. **Pets:** Accepted. 🛜 ✕ ⛎ 🖥 🖵 ⇆

VERMILLION
AAA **Comfort Inn** H
(605) 624-8333. **Call for rates.** 701 W Cherry St 57069. I-29 exit 26 (SR 50), 7.5 mi w on Business Rt SR 50. Int corridors. **Pets:** Medium. $10 daily fee/pet. Service with restrictions, supervision.
SAVE 🛜 ⛎ 🖥 🖵 ⇆ ✕

Prairie Inn H
(605) 624-2824. **Call for rates.** 916 N Dakota St 57069. I-29 exit 26 (SR 50), 7 mi w, then 0.3 mi n. Int corridors. **Pets:** Accepted.
🛜 ✕ 🖥 🖵 ⍗

WALL
AAA **Best Western Plains Motel** M ✿
(605) 279-2145. **$69-$179.** 712 Glenn St 57790. I-90 exit 110, just n. Ext corridors. **Pets:** Other species. $10 one-time fee/pet. Service with restrictions, supervision. SAVE 🛜 ⛎ 🖥 🖵 ⇆ ✕

AAA **Econo Lodge** M
(605) 279-2121. **Call for rates.** 804 Glenn St 57790. I-90 exit 110, just n. Ext corridors. **Pets:** Other species. Designated rooms, service with restrictions, supervision. SAVE 🛜 ⛎ 🖥 🖵 ⇆

AAA **Sunshine Inn** M
(605) 279-2178. **$51-$71.** 608 Main St 57790. Downtown. Ext corridors. **Pets:** Other species. $5 one-time fee/room. Service with restrictions.
SAVE 🛜

WATERTOWN
AAA **Best Western Ramkota Hotel** H ✿
(605) 886-8011. **$95-$140.** 1901 9th Ave SW 57201. I-29 exit 177 (US 212), 4 mi w. Int corridors. **Pets:** Large. Designated rooms, service with restrictions, supervision. SAVE 🛜 ✕ ⛎ 🖥 🖵 ⍗ ⇆ ✕

Country Inn & Suites By Carlson H
(605) 886-8900. **$96-$140.** 3400 8th Ave SE 57201. I-29 exit 177 (US 212), just w. Int corridors. **Pets:** Accepted. 🛜 ⛎ 🖥 🖵 ⇆

AAA **Days Inn** H
(605) 886-3500. **$67-$94.** 2900 9th Ave SE 57201. I-29 exit 177 (US 212), 0.5 mi w. Ext/int corridors. **Pets:** $15 one-time fee/room. Service with restrictions, crate. SAVE 🛜 ⛎ 🖥 🖵 ⇆

Holiday Inn Express Hotel & Suites H
(605) 882-3636. **Call for rates.** 3901 9th Ave SE 57201. I-29 exit 177 (US 212), just e. Int corridors. **Pets:** $10 one-time fee/room. Service with restrictions, supervision. 🛜 ⛎ 🖥 🖵 ⇆ ✕

Quality Inn & Suites H ✿
(605) 886-3010. **$75-$125.** 800 35th St Cir 57201. I-29 exit 177 (US 212), just w. Ext/int corridors. **Pets:** $15 one-time fee/room. Supervision.
🛜 ⛎ 🖥 🖵 ⇆

Super 8-Watertown H
(605) 882-1900. **$26-$71.** 503 14th Ave SE 57201. On US 81, 0.3 mi s of jct US 212. Int corridors. **Pets:** Accepted. 🛜 ⛎ 🖥 🖵 ⇆

AAA **Travelers Inn Motel** H
(605) 882-2243. **$55-$75.** 920 14th St SE 57201. I-29 exit 177 (US 212), 1.5 mi w, then just s. Int corridors. **Pets:** Accepted. SAVE 🛜 🖥 🖵

WINNER
Holiday Inn Express Hotel & Suites H
(605) 842-2255. **$100-$110.** 1360 E Hwy 44 57580. Just ne of jct US 18 and 183. Int corridors. **Pets:** Accepted. 🛜 ✕ ⛎ 🖥 🖵 ⇆

YANKTON
AAA **Best Western Kelly Inn** H ✿
(605) 665-2906. **$80-$120.** 1607 Hwy 50 E 57078. On US 50, 1.8 mi e. Ext/int corridors. **Pets:** Other species. Service with restrictions, supervision. SAVE 🛜 ✕ ⛎ 🖥 🖵 ⍗ ⇆ ✕

AAA ▼▼▼ **Days Inn** 🅷

(605) 665-8717. **$55-$61.** 2410 Broadway St 57078. US 81, 1.7 mi n. Int corridors. **Pets:** Accepted. 🆂🅰🆅🅴 📶 🛄 🍴 🖥 🏊

▼▼ **Lewis & Clark Resort** 🅼

(605) 665-2680. **$70-$125, 30 day notice.** 43496 Shore Dr 57078. 4 mi w on SR 52; in Lewis and Clark State Park, turn into park, just w of marina. Ext corridors. **Pets:** Dogs only. $5 daily fee/pet. Service with restrictions, supervision. 📶 ✖ 🛄 📶 🖥 🏊 ✖ 🐾

TENNESSEE

CITY INDEX

ALCOA

 **Candlewood Suites Knoxville Airport/Alcoa** 🅷 🐾

(865) 233-4411. **$74-$599.** 176 Cusick Rd 37701. US 129, just e. Int corridors. **Pets:** Small. $75 one-time fee/pet. Service with restrictions. 📶 🛄 🍴 🖥 🏊

AAA ▼▼ **Family Inns of America** 🅼

(865) 970-2006. **$49-$59, 7 day notice.** 2450 Airport Hwy 37701. US 129, just e. Ext corridors. **Pets:** Accepted. 🆂🅰🆅🅴 📶 🍴 🏊

▼▼ **Jameson Inn Alcoa** 🅷

(865) 984-6800. **$79-$99.** 206 Corporate Pl 37701. US 129, just s. Int corridors. **Pets:** Medium. $15 daily fee/room. Service with restrictions, supervision. 📶 📶 🍴 🖥 🏊 ✖

▼▼ **MainStay Suites** 🅷

(865) 379-7799. **$75-$130.** 361 Fountain View Cir 37701. US 129, just n on SR 35, just se on Associates Blvd, then just w. Int corridors. **Pets:** Accepted. 📶 📶 🍴 🖥 🏊

ATHENS

▼▼ **Days Inn-Athens** 🅼

(423) 745-5800. **$50-$54.** 2541 Decatur Pike 37303. I-75 exit 49, just e on SR 30. Ext corridors. **Pets:** $10 daily fee/pet. Service with restrictions, crate. 📶 📶 🍴 🖥 🏊

BRENTWOOD

▼▼ **Baymont Inn & Suites** 🅷

(615) 376-4666. **$67-$90.** 111 Penn Warren Dr 37027. I-65 exit 74B, 1.5 mi w, then just s on West Park. Int corridors. **Pets:** Accepted. 📶 📶 🍴 🖥 🏊

▼▼ **Candlewood Suites** 🅷

(615) 309-0600. **$69-$109.** 5129 Virginia Way 37027. I-65 exit 74B, 0.5 mi w, 0.5 mi s on Franklin Rd (US 31), 1.2 mi w on Maryland Way, just s on Ward Cir, then just s. Int corridors. **Pets:** Accepted. 📶 🍴 🖥

▼▼ **MainStay Suites-Brentwood** 🅷

(615) 371-8477. **$60-$100.** 107 Brentwood Blvd 37027. I-65 exit 74B, 1 mi w. Int corridors. **Pets:** Accepted. 📶 📶 🍴 🖥 🏊

▼▼▼ **Residence Inn Nashville - Brentwood** 🅷

(615) 371-0100. **$71-$169.** 206 Ward Cir 37027. I-65 exit 74B, 0.3 mi s on Franklin Rd (US 31 S), then 0.5 mi w on Maryland Way. Ext/int corridors. **Pets:** Accepted. 📶 ✖ 🍴 🖥 🏊 ✖

▼▼ **Sleep Inn** 🅷 🐾

(615) 376-2122. **$80-$89.** 1611 Galleria Blvd 37027. I-65 exit 69, 0.4 mi w, then just n. Int corridors. **Pets:** Medium. $15 daily fee/pet. Designated rooms, supervision. 📶 📶 🍴 🖥 🏊

BULLS GAP

AAA ▼▼▼ **Best Western Executive Inn** 🅷

(423) 235-9111. **$80-$90.** 50 Speedway Ln 37711. I-81 exit 23. Int corridors. **Pets:** $15 daily fee/pet. Designated rooms, service with restrictions, supervision. 🆂🅰🆅🅴 📶 📶 🍴 🖥 🏊

BURNS

▼▼ **Montgomery Bell State Park Inn** 🅷

(615) 797-3101. **Call for rates.** 1000 Hotel Ave 37029. 3.7 mi e of jct US 70 and SR 96, follow signs. Int corridors. **Pets:** $15 daily fee/pet. Designated rooms, service with restrictions, supervision. 📶 ✖ 📶 🍴 🖥 🍴 🏊 ✖

BUTLER

▼▼▼ **Iron Mountain Inn B&B and Creekside Chalet** 🅱🅱

(423) 768-2446. **Call for rates.** 138 Moreland Dr 37640. 1.6 mi w on Pine Orchard Rd from SR 67 at Stout Store, follow signs; 13 mi w on SR 67 from US 421 in Mountain City, follow sign at Stout Store area; 15.1 mi from Shell Station in Hampton to Pine Orchard Rd, 1.6 mi to Moreland Dr. Ext/int corridors. **Pets:** Dogs only. $50 one-time fee/pet. Designated rooms, no service, supervision. 📶 🍴 🖥 ✖

CHATTANOOGA

▼▼ **America's Best Inn-Hamilton Mall Area** 🅼

(423) 894-5454. **Call for rates.** 7717 Lee Hwy 37421. I-75 exit 7B northbound; exit 7 southbound. Ext corridors. **Pets:** Accepted. 📶 🍴 🖥 🏊

▼▼▼ **Baymont Inn & Suites-Chattanooga** 🅷

(423) 821-1090. **$59-$90.** 3540 Cummings Hwy 37419. I-24 exit 174, 0.4 mi s. Int corridors. **Pets:** Accepted. 📶 📶 🍴 🖥 🏊

AAA ▼▼▼ **Best Western Heritage Inn** 🅷

(423) 899-3311. **$69-$99.** 7641 Lee Hwy 37421. I-75 exit 7B northbound; exit 7 southbound, just w. Ext corridors. **Pets:** Small, dogs only. $10 daily fee/pet. Service with restrictions, crate. 🆂🅰🆅🅴 📶 🍴 🖥 🍴 🏊

▼▼▼▼ Chattanooga Choo-Choo 🅷 ❀
(423) 266-5000. **$109-$229.** 1400 Market St 37402. I-24 exit 178 (Broad St) eastbound; exit Market St westbound, 0.5 mi n. Ext/int corridors. **Pets:** $25 one-time fee/room. Service with restrictions, supervision.
ⒺⒸⓄ ⓢⒶⓋⒺ 🛜 &M 🛏 🖵 ¶ 🏊 ✕

▼▼▼▼ The Chattanoogan 🅷
(423) 756-3400. **$139-$199.** 1201 Broad St 37402. I-24 exit 178 (Market St), follow signs to Broad St/US 11, then 0.6 mi n. Int corridors.
Pets: Accepted. ⒺⒸⓄ ⓢⒶⓋⒺ 🛜 ✕ &M 🛏 🖵 ¶ 🏊 ✕

▼▼▼▼ Country Inn & Suites By Carlson,
Chattanooga I-24 West 🅷
(423) 825-6100. **$109-$199.** 3725 Modern Industries Blvd 37419. I-24 exit 174, just s. Int corridors. **Pets:** Medium, dogs only. $25 one-time fee/room. Designated rooms, service with restrictions, crate.
ⓢⒶⓋⒺ 🛜 &M 🛏 🖵 🏊

▼▼▼ Days Inn-Lookout Mountain/Tiftonia 🅷
(423) 821-6044. **$49-$77.** 3801 Cummings Hwy 37419. I-24 exit 174, just n. Ext corridors. **Pets:** $10 daily fee/pet. Service with restrictions, supervision. ⓢⒶⓋⒺ 🛜 &M 🛏 🖵 🏊

▼▼▼ Extended StayAmerica-Chattanooga-Airport 🅷 ❀
(423) 892-1315. **$50-$100.** 6240 Airpark Dr 37421. SR 153 exit 1 (Lee Hwy), 0.3 mi s to Vance Rd, then just w to cul de sac. Ext corridors. **Pets:** Other species. $25 daily fee/pet. Service with restrictions.
🛜 &M 🛏 🖵

▼▼▼▼ GuestHouse International Inn 🅷
(423) 510-0800. **Call for rates.** 2201 Park Dr 37421. I-75 exit 5 (Shallowford Rd), 0.5 mi w. Ext corridors. **Pets:** Accepted. 🛜 🛏 🖵

▼▼▼▼ Homewood Suites by Hilton 🅷
(423) 510-8020. **$119-$169.** 2250 Center St 37421. I-75 exit 5 (Shallowford Rd), 0.5 mi w. Int corridors. **Pets:** Accepted. 🛜 🛏 🖵 🏊

▼▼▼▼ La Quinta Inn Chattanooga 🅷
(423) 265-3151. **$107-$169.** 100 W 21st St 37408. I-24 exit 178, US 11 to Lookout Mountain, w to 20th St, w to Williams St, then w. Int corridors. **Pets:** Medium, other species. Service with restrictions, supervision.
ⓢⒶⓋⒺ 🛜 &M 🛏 🖵 🏊

▼▼▼ La Quinta Inn Chattanooga/Hamilton Place 🅷
(423) 855-0011. **$64-$122.** 7015 Shallowford Rd 37421. I-75 exit 5 (Shallowford Rd), just w. Ext corridors. **Pets:** Medium, other species. Service with restrictions, supervision. 🛜 &M 🛏 🖵 🏊

▼▼▼ MainStay Suites-Chattanooga 🅷
(423) 485-9424. **$69-$129.** 7030 Amin Dr 37421. I-75 exit 5 (Shallowford Rd), just w, then s. Int corridors. **Pets:** Medium. $15 daily fee/pet. Designated rooms, service with restrictions, crate. 🛜 &M 🛏 🖵

▼▼ Microtel Inn-Chattanooga 🅷
(423) 510-0761. **$40-$52.** 7014 McCutcheon Rd 37421. I-75 exit 5 (Shallowford Rd), just w, 0.3 mi n on Shallowford Village Dr, then just w. Int corridors. **Pets:** Accepted. 🛜 &M 🛏

▼ Motel 6 Downtown #4145 🅷
(423) 265-7300. **Call for rates.** 2440 Williams St 37408. I-24 exit 178 (Market St), just s. Int corridors. **Pets:** Other species. Service with restrictions, supervision. 🛜 🛏

▼▼▼ Quality Inn 🅷
(423) 821-1499. **$70-$96.** 3109 Parker Ln 37419. I-24 exit 175, just s. Ext corridors. **Pets:** $15 daily fee/pet. Designated rooms, service with restrictions. ⓢⒶⓋⒺ 🛜 🛏 🖵 🏊

▼▼▼ Quality Suites 🅷 ❀
(423) 892-1500. **$75-$85.** 7324 Shallowford Rd 37421. I-75 exit 5 (Shallowford Rd), just e. Ext corridors. **Pets:** $10 daily fee/pet. Service with restrictions, supervision. ⓢⒶⓋⒺ 🛜 🛏 🖵 🏊

▼▼ Ramada Limited-Lookout Mountain West 🅷
(423) 821-7162. **$41-$109.** 30 Birmingham Hwy 37419. I-24 exit 174, just s. Ext/int corridors. **Pets:** Medium, dogs only. $15 daily fee/pet. Designated rooms, no service, supervision. 🛜 🛏 🖵 🏊

▼▼▼ Red Roof Inn-Chattanooga 🅼
(423) 899-0143. **$39-$89.** 7014 Shallowford Rd 37421. I-75 exit 5 (Shallowford Rd), just w. Ext corridors. **Pets:** Large, other species. No service, supervision. ⓢⒶⓋⒺ 🛜 &M 🛏 🖵

▼▼▼ Residence Inn Chattanooga - Downtown 🅷
(423) 266-0600. **$142-$151.** 215 Chestnut St 37402. US 27 exit 1C (4th St), just n. Int corridors. **Pets:** Accepted.
ⒺⒸⓄ 🛜 ✕ &M 🛏 🖵 🏊

▼▼▼▼ The Sheraton Read House Hotel
Chattanooga 🅷 ❀
(423) 266-4121. **$129-$500.** 827 Broad St 37402. US 27 exit 1A (Dr Martin Luther King Blvd), just e. Int corridors. **Pets:** Large, dogs only. $50 one-time fee/room. Designated rooms, service with restrictions, supervision. ⓢⒶⓋⒺ 🛜 ✕ &M 🛏 🖵 ¶ 🏊

▼▼▼▼ Staybridge Suites 🅷
(423) 267-0900. **$129-$169.** 1300 Carter St 37402. US 27 N exit 1A (Dr Martin Luther King Blvd), just e to Carter St, then 0.3 mi s. Int corridors. **Pets:** Accepted. ⒺⒸⓄ 🛜 &M 🛏 🖵 🏊

▼▼▼▼ Staybridge Suites-Hamilton Place 🅷
(423) 826-2700. **$129-$249.** 7015 Shallowford Rd 37421. I-75 exit 5 (Shallowford Rd), just w. Int corridors. **Pets:** Small. $75 one-time fee/pet. Designated rooms, service with restrictions. 🛜 &M 🛏 🖵 🏊

▼▼▼ Super 8 🅷
(423) 490-8560. **$41-$68.** 7024 McCutcheon Rd 37421. I-75 exit 5 (Shallowford Rd), just w, then 0.3 mi n on Shallowford Village Dr. Int corridors. **Pets:** Accepted. ⓢⒶⓋⒺ 🛜 &M 🛏 🖵 🏊

▼▼▼ Super 8/Lookout Mountain 🅷
(423) 821-8880. **$41-$72.** 20 Birmingham Hwy 37419. I-24 exit 174, just s. Int corridors. **Pets:** Accepted. 🛜 🛏 🖵 🏊

CLARKSVILLE

▼▼▼ Candlewood Suites 🅷
(931) 906-0900. **$109-$139.** 3050 Clay Lewis Rd 37040. I-24 exit 4, just s. Int corridors. **Pets:** Accepted. 🛜 🛏 🖵

▼▼▼ MainStay Suites 🅷
(931) 648-3400. **$89-$159.** 115 Fairbrook Pl 37043. I-24 exit 4, just sw. Int corridors. **Pets:** Accepted. 🛜 ✕ &M 🛏 🖵 🏊

▼▼▼ Quality Inn-Exit 4 🅷
(931) 648-4848. **$77-$99.** 3095 Wilma Rudolph Blvd 37040. I-24 exit 4, just se. Ext corridors. **Pets:** Medium, other species. $25 one-time fee/room, $15 daily fee/room. Service with restrictions.
ⓢⒶⓋⒺ 🛜 🛏 🖵 ¶ 🏊 ✕

▼▼ Red Roof Inn 🅷
(931) 905-1555. **$41-$79.** 197 Holiday Dr 37040. I-24 exit 4, just se. Ext corridors. **Pets:** Large, other species. No service, supervision.
🛜 🛏 🏊

CLEVELAND

▼ Colonial Inn 🅼
(423) 472-6845. **$35-$45, 7 day notice.** 1555 25th St 37311. I-75 exit 25, 0.3 mi e. Ext corridors. **Pets:** Very small, dogs only. $10 daily fee/pet. Service with restrictions, supervision. 🛜 🛏 🖵 🏊

▼▼▼ Douglas Inn & Suites 🅷
(423) 559-5579. **$55-$115.** 2600 Westside Dr NW 37312. I-75 exit 25, just e. Ext/int corridors. **Pets:** Medium. $10 daily fee/pet. Service with restrictions, supervision. ⓢⒶⓋⒺ 🛜 &M 🛏 🖵

▼▼ **Howard Johnson Chalet** H
(423) 476-8511. **$50-$64.** 2595 Georgetown Rd 37311. I-75 exit 25, just e. Ext corridors. **Pets:** Accepted. 🛜 👤M 🖥 💻 🍴 🏊

▼▼ **Jameson Inn** H
(423) 614-5583. **$74-$94.** 360 Paul Huff Pkwy 37312. I-75 exit 27, 1 mi e. Ext corridors. **Pets:** Medium. $15 daily fee/room. Service with restrictions, supervision. 🛜 ✖ 👤M 🖥 💻 🏊

▼▼ **Mountain View Inn** H
(423) 472-1500. **Call for rates.** 2400 Executive Park Dr 37312. I-75 exit 25, just w. Ext/int corridors. **Pets:** Accepted.
🛜 👤M 🖥 💻 🍴 🏊

▼▼ **Quality Inn** H
(423) 478-5265. **$60-$100.** 153 James Asbury Dr 37312. I-75 exit 27, just w. Ext/int corridors. **Pets:** Accepted. 🛜 🖥 💻 🏊

▼▼ **Super 8** M
(423) 476-5555. **$50-$99.** 163 Bernham Dr 37312. I-75 exit 27, just w. Ext/int corridors. **Pets:** Accepted. 🛜 🖥 💻 🏊

CLINTON
▼▼▼ **Red Roof Inn & Suites** H
(865) 457-9070. **$54-$99.** 141 Buffalo Rd 37716. I-75 exit 122, just w. Ext corridors. **Pets:** Large, other species. No service, supervision.
🛜 👤M 🖥 💻 🏊

COLUMBIA
▼▼ **Jameson Inn** H
(931) 388-3326. **$90-$110.** 715 James M Campbell Blvd 38401. 0.9 mi w of jct SR 50 and US 31. Int corridors. **Pets:** Medium. $15 daily fee/room. Service with restrictions, supervision. 🛜 🖥 💻 🏊

▼▼ **Super 8 Columbia** H
(931) 380-1227. **$50-$99.** 1554 Bear Creek Pike 38401. I-65 exit 46, just w. Ext corridors. **Pets:** Accepted. 🛜 👤M 🖥 💻 🏊

COOKEVILLE
▼▼▼ **Baymont Inn & Suites Cookeville** H
(931) 525-6668. **$59-$75.** 1151 S Jefferson Ave 38506. I-40 exit 287, just s. Int corridors. **Pets:** Other species. $25 daily fee/pet. Service with restrictions, supervision. 🛜 👤M 🖥 💻 🏊 ✖

AAA ▼▼ **Best Western Thunderbird Motel** H 🐾
(931) 526-7115. **$63-$73.** 900 S Jefferson Ave 38501. I-40 exit 287, just n. Ext corridors. **Pets:** $20 daily fee/room. Designated rooms, service with restrictions, crate. SAVE 🛜 👤M 🖥 💻 🍴 🏊

AAA ▼▼ **Clarion Inn** H
(931) 526-7125. **$69.** 970 S Jefferson Ave 38501. I-40 exit 287, just n. Ext/int corridors. **Pets:** Accepted.
SAVE 🛜 👤M 🖥 💻 🍴 🏊 ✖

▼▼ **Hampton Inn** H
(931) 520-1117. **$89-$116.** 1025 Interstate Dr 38501. I-40 exit 287, 0.5 mi n. Ext corridors. **Pets:** Medium, other species. Service with restrictions.
🛜 👤M 🖥 💻 🏊

AAA ▼▼ **Red Roof Inn Cookeville** M
(931) 528-2020. **$50-$125.** 1292 S Walnut Ave 38501. I-40 exit 287. Ext corridors. **Pets:** Large, other species. No service, supervision.
SAVE 🛜 🖥 💻 🏊

CROSSVILLE
AAA ▼▼ **La Quinta Inn-Crossville** H
(931) 456-9338. **$80-$145.** 4038 Hwy 127 N 38571. I-40 exit 317 (US 127), just n. Int corridors. **Pets:** Medium, other species. Service with restrictions, supervision. SAVE 🛜 👤M 🖥 💻 🏊

DANDRIDGE
AAA ▼▼▼ **Holiday Inn Express** H
(865) 397-1910. **Call for rates.** 119 Sharon Dr 37725. I-40 exit 417, just s. Int corridors. **Pets:** Medium. $50 one-time fee/room. Service with restrictions, supervision. SAVE 🛜 👤M 🖥 💻

▼▼ **Jefferson Inn** H
(865) 940-5042. **$50-$80.** 127 Sharon Dr 37725. I-40 exit 417, just s. Int corridors. **Pets:** Small, dogs only. $10 daily fee/pet. Designated rooms, service with restrictions, supervision. 👤M 🖥 💻 🏊

▼▼ **Super 8** H
(865) 397-1200. **$40-$90.** 125 Sharon Dr 37725. I-40 exit 417, just s. Int corridors. **Pets:** Accepted. 🛜 👤M 🖥 💻 🏊

DAYTON
AAA ▼▼ **Best Western Dayton** H
(423) 775-6560. **$70-$95.** 7835 Rhea County Hwy 37321. 1 mi n on US 27. Ext corridors. **Pets:** Medium. $10 daily fee/pet. Service with restrictions, supervision. SAVE 🛜 🖥 💻 🏊

DECHERD
▼▼ **Jameson Inn** H
(931) 962-0130. **$74-$94.** 1838 Decherd Blvd 37324. Jct Main St and SR 41A, just s. Ext corridors. **Pets:** Medium. $15 daily fee/room. Service with restrictions, supervision. 🛜 🖥 💻 🏊

DICKSON
AAA ▼▼ **Best Western Executive Inn** H
(615) 446-0541. **$50-$80.** 2338 Hwy 46 37055. I-40 exit 172, just n. Ext corridors. **Pets:** Medium, dogs only. $10 daily fee/pet. Designated rooms, service with restrictions, supervision. SAVE 🛜 🖥 💻 🏊

AAA ▼▼ **Comfort Inn** H
(615) 740-1000. **$55-$99.** 1085 E Christi Dr 37055. I-40 exit 172, just ne. Int corridors. **Pets:** Accepted. SAVE 🛜 👤M 🖥 💻 🏊

▼▼ **Econo Lodge Inn & Suites** M
(615) 441-5252. **Call for rates.** 1025 E Christi Dr 37055. I-40 exit 172, just ne. Int corridors. **Pets:** Accepted. 🛜 🖥 💻 🏊

AAA ▼▼▼ **Holiday Inn Express** H
(615) 446-2781. **$90-$120, 3 day notice.** 100 Barzani Blvd 37055. I-40 exit 172, just se. Int corridors. **Pets:** Small, dogs only. $20 daily fee/pet. Service with restrictions, supervision. SAVE 🛜 👤M 🖥 💻

AAA ▼▼ **Quality Inn** H
(615) 740-0074. **Call for rates.** 1055 E Christi Dr 37055. I-40 exit 172, just ne. Ext corridors. **Pets:** Small, other species. $10 daily fee/pet. Service with restrictions. SAVE 🛜 🖥 💻

AAA ▼▼ **Super 8** H
(615) 446-1923. **$41-$59, 3 day notice.** 150 Suzanne Dr 37055. I-40 exit 172, just ne. Int corridors. **Pets:** Accepted. SAVE 🛜 🖥 💻 🏊

DYERSBURG
AAA ▼▼ **Best Western Dyersburg Inn** H
(731) 285-8601. **Call for rates.** 770 Hwy 51 Bypass W 38024. I-155 exit 13, 0.5 mi s; jct US 51 Bypass and SR 78. Ext corridors. **Pets:** Small, other species. $15 daily fee/pet. Service with restrictions, crate.
SAVE 🛜 🖥 💻 🍴 🏊

▼▼ **Days Inn** H
(731) 287-0888. **$57-$63.** 2600 Lake Rd 38024. I-155 exit 13, just s. Int corridors. **Pets:** Accepted. 🛜 👤M 🖥 💻

▼▼ **Executive Inn & Suites** H
(731) 287-0044. **$45-$65.** 2331 Lake Rd 38024. I-155 exit 13, 0.5 mi s. Ext corridors. **Pets:** Large. $10 daily fee/pet. Designated rooms, service with restrictions, supervision. 🛜 🖥

▼▼▼ Hampton Inn H

(731) 285-4778. **$69-$89.** 2750 Mall Loop Rd 38024. I-155 exit 13, just s. Int corridors. **Pets:** Medium, other species. Service with restrictions, supervision. 🛜 ⓜ ▣ ⌦

▼▼▼ Holiday Inn Express & Suites H

(731) 286-1021. **$90-$95.** 822 Reelfoot Dr 38024. I-155 exit 13, just s. Int corridors. **Pets:** Accepted. 🛜 ⓜ ▣ ⌦

▼▼▼ Sleep Inn & Suites H ❀

(731) 287-0248. **Call for rates.** 824 Reelfoot Dr 38024. I-155 exit 13, just s. Int corridors. **Pets:** Very small. $10 daily fee/pet. Service with restrictions, crate. 🛜 ✕ ⓜ ▣ ▣ ⌦

FARRAGUT

AAA ▼▼▼ Econo Lodge Knoxville M

(865) 288-3641. **$70-$110.** 11717 Campbell Lakes Dr 37934. I-40/75 exit 373 (Campbell Station Rd), just s. Ext corridors. **Pets:** Small, other species. $10 daily fee/pet. Designated rooms, service with restrictions, supervision. SAVE 🛜 ⓜ ▣ ▣ ⌦

FAYETTEVILLE

AAA ▼▼▼ Best Western Fayetteville Inn H

(931) 433-0100. **$95-$107.** 3021 Thornton Taylor Pkwy 37334. 0.7 mi e of US 431, on US 64 and 231 Bypass. Ext corridors. **Pets:** Accepted. SAVE 🛜 ▣ ▣ ⌦

FRANKLIN

AAA ▼▼▼ Aloft Nashville-Cool Springs H ❀

(615) 435-8700. **$89-$199.** 7109 S Springs Dr 37067. I-65 exit 68B, just w, 0.3 mi n on Mallory Ln, then just e. Int corridors. **Pets:** Small, dogs only. Designated rooms, service with restrictions, supervision. SAVE 🛜 ✕ ⓜ ▣ ▣ ⌦

AAA ▼▼▼ Best Western Franklin Inn H

(615) 790-0570. **$60-$70.** 1308 Murfreesboro Rd 37064. I-65 exit 65, just w. Ext corridors. **Pets:** Accepted. SAVE 🛜 ▣ ▣ ⌦

AAA ▼▼▼ Days Inn H

(615) 790-1140. **$58-$77.** 3915 S Carothers Pkwy 37064. I-65 exit 65, just se. Ext corridors. **Pets:** Accepted. SAVE 🛜 ▣ ▣ ⌦

▼▼▼ Embassy Suites Nashville South/Cool Springs H ❀

(615) 515-5151. **$119-$229.** 820 Crescent Centre Dr 37067. I-65 exit 68A to Carothers Rd. Int corridors. **Pets:** $50 one-time fee/room. Designated rooms, service with restrictions, supervision. 🛜 ⓜ ▣ ▣ 🍴 ⌦ ✕

▼▼▼ Holiday Inn Express Hotel & Suites H

(615) 591-6660. **Call for rates.** 4202 Franklin Commons Ct 37067. I-65 exit 65, just e. Int corridors. **Pets:** Small, dogs only. $30 daily fee/pet. Designated rooms, service with restrictions, supervision. 🛜 ⓜ ▣ ▣ ⌦

▼▼ Homestead Studio Suites Hotel-Nashville/Franklin-Cool Springs H ❀

(615) 771-7600. **$50-$70.** 680 Bakers Bridge Ave 37067. I-65 exit 69 (Galleria Blvd), 0.3 mi e on Moores Ln to Carothers Pkwy, 0.5 mi s, then 0.3 mi w. Ext corridors. **Pets:** Other species. $25 daily fee/pet. Service with restrictions. 🛜 ▣ ▣

▼▼ La Quinta Inn & Suites Nashville-Franklin H

(615) 791-7700. **$71-$129.** 4207 Franklin Commons Ct 37067. I-65 exit 65, just e. Int corridors. **Pets:** Medium, other species. Service with restrictions, supervision. 🛜 ⓜ ▣ ▣ ⌦

AAA ▼▼▼ Residence Inn by Marriott Franklin Cool Springs H

(615) 778-0002. **$129-$199.** 2009 Meridian Blvd 37067. I-65 exit 68A, just e on Cool Springs Blvd, then just n on Carothers Pkwy. Int corridors. **Pets:** Medium. $100 one-time fee/room. Designated rooms, service with restrictions. SAVE 🛜 ✕ ⓜ ▣ ▣ ⌦ ✕

GALLATIN

▼▼ Jameson Inn M

(615) 451-4494. **$79-$99.** 1001 Village Green Crossing 37066. 2 mi s on US 31. Ext corridors. **Pets:** Medium. $15 daily fee/room. Service with restrictions, supervision. 🛜 ⓜ ▣ ▣ ⌦

GATLINBURG

AAA ▼▼▼ Cobbly Nob Rentals CA

(865) 436-5298. **$100-$155, 30 day notice.** 3722 E Parkway 37738. On US 321, 10.3 mi n of jct US 441. Ext corridors. **Pets:** Accepted. SAVE 🛜 ✕ ▣ ▣ ⌦ ✕

AAA ▼▼▼ Greenbrier Valley Resorts at Cobbly Nob CA

(865) 436-2015. **$100-$1000, 30 day notice.** 3629 E Parkway 37738. Jct US 441, 10.1 mi n on US 321. Ext corridors. **Pets:** Medium. $15 daily fee/pet. Service with restrictions, crate. SAVE 🛜 ▣ ▣ ⌦

AAA ▼▼ Microtel Inn & Suites Gatlinburg H ❀

(865) 436-0107. **$49-$269, 3 day notice.** 211 Historic Nature Tr 37738. Just e of US 441 at traffic light 8. Int corridors. **Pets:** Medium. $10 daily fee/pet. Service with restrictions, supervision. SAVE 🛜 ⓜ ▣ ▣

▼▼▼ Outback Resort Rentals & Sales VH

(865) 430-9385. **$120-$799, 30 day notice.** 902 Street of Dreams Way 37738. Jct US 441 on north end of town at Great Smoky Mountains Welcome Center, 1 mi sw on Wiley Oakley Dr, then 0.5 mi w on N Woodland Dr. Ext corridors. **Pets:** Small. $80 deposit/pet. Designated rooms, no service, crate. 🛜 ▣ ▣ ⌦

▼▼ Red Roof Inn M

(865) 436-7813. **$39-$199.** 309 Ownby St 37738. Traffic light 10, (Ski Mountain Rd), 0.4 mi n. Ext corridors. **Pets:** Large, other species. No service, supervision. 🛜 ▣ ▣ ⌦

AAA ▼▼▼ Westgate Smoky Mountain Resort & Spa CA

(865) 430-4800. **$79-$339, 3 day notice.** 915 Westgate Resort Rd 37738. I-40 exit 407, SR 66 to US 441; across from Gatlinburg Welcome Center. Ext corridors. **Pets:** Accepted. SAVE 🛜 ✕ ▣ ▣ 🍴 ⌦ ✕

GREENEVILLE

▼ Andrew Johnson Inn M

(423) 638-8124. **$42-$55, 7 day notice.** 2145 E Andrew Johnson Hwy 37745. US 11 E, 3.1 mi ne. Ext corridors. **Pets:** Very small. $15 daily fee/pet. Designated rooms, service with restrictions, supervision. ▣ ▣ ⌦

AAA ▼▼▼ Comfort Inn of Greeneville H

(423) 639-4185. **$77-$215.** 1790 E Andrew Johnson Hwy 37745. US 11 E, 2.9 mi ne. Ext/int corridors. **Pets:** Accepted. SAVE 🛜 ▣ ▣ ⌦

▼▼ Days Inn M

(423) 639-2156. **$49-$171.** 935 E Andrew Johnson Hwy 37745. US 11 E, 2 mi ne. Ext corridors. **Pets:** Accepted. 🛜 ▣ ▣

▼▼ Jameson Inn H

(423) 638-7511. **$74-$94.** 3160 E Andrew Johnson Hwy 37745. US 11 E Bypass, 3.6 mi ne. Int corridors. **Pets:** Medium. $15 daily fee/room. Service with restrictions, supervision. 🛜 ⓜ ▣ ▣ ⌦

HARRIMAN

AAA ▼▼▼ Days Inn Harriman M

(865) 882-6200. **Call for rates.** 120 Childs Rd 37748. I-40 exit 347, just n on US 27. Ext corridors. **Pets:** Medium. $10 one-time fee/pet. Service with restrictions, supervision. SAVE 🛜 ⓜ ▣ ▣

▼▼ Quality Inn M ❀

(865) 882-5340. **$55-$150.** 1845A S Roane St 37748. I-40 exit 347, just s on US 27/SR 61. Ext corridors. **Pets:** Other species. $15 one-time fee/pet. No service, supervision. 🛜 ⓜ ▣ ▣ ⌦

▼▼ **Rodeway Inn** Ⓜ ❀
(865) 882-5400. **$55-$130.** 1845B S Roane St 37748. I-40 exit 347, just s on US 27/SR 61. Int corridors. **Pets:** Other species. $15 one-time fee/pet. No service, supervision. 📶 🔲 📱

HURRICANE MILLS

Ⓐ ▼▼ **Best Western of Hurricane Mills** ℍ ❀
(931) 296-4251. **$100-$120.** 15542 Hwy 13 S 37078. I-40 exit 143, just n. Ext corridors. **Pets:** $10 daily fee/pet. Designated rooms, service with restrictions, crate. (SAVE) 📶 🔲 📱 ⤳

JACKSON

Ⓐ ▼▼ **Best Western Carriage House Inn & Suites** ℍ
(731) 664-3030. **$80-$90.** 1936 Hwy 45 Bypass 38305. I-40 exit 80A, just s. Ext corridors. **Pets:** Accepted. (SAVE) 📶 🔲 📱 ⤳

▼▼▼ **Courtyard by Marriott** ℍ
(731) 422-1818. **$89-$209.** 200 Campbell Oaks Dr 38305. I-40 exit 83, just sw. Int corridors. **Pets:** Medium, other species. Service with restrictions, supervision. 📶 ✕ 🔲 📱 🍴 ⤳

▼▼▼ **Hampton Inn & Suites** ℍ
(731) 427-6100. **$109-$139.** 150 Campbell Oaks Dr 38305. I-40 exit 83, just s. Int corridors. **Pets:** Medium. Service with restrictions, crate. 📶 🔲 📱 ⤳

▼▼ **Jameson Inn** ℍ
(731) 660-8651. **$89-$109.** 1292 Vann Dr 38305. I-40 exit 80B, 0.6 mi w. Int corridors. **Pets:** Medium. $15 daily fee/room. Service with restrictions, supervision. 📶 🔲 📱 ⤳

▼▼ **Quality Inn** ℍ
(731) 668-1400. **$68-$80.** 535 Wiley Parker Rd 38305. I-40 exit 80A, just s, then e on Carriage House Dr. Ext/int corridors. **Pets:** Medium, other species. $15 daily fee/pet. Service with restrictions, supervision. 📶 🔲 📱 ⤳

JOHNSON CITY

Ⓐ ▼▼▼ **Best Western Johnson City Hotel & Conference Center** ℍ
(423) 282-2161. **$60-$275.** 2406 N Roan St 37601. I-26 exit 20A westbound; exit 20 eastbound, just n. Ext/int corridors. **Pets:** Accepted. (SAVE) 📶 🔲 📱 🍴 ⤳

Ⓐ ▼▼▼ **Carnegie Hotel** ℍ
(423) 979-6400. **$104-$124.** 1216 W State of Franklin Rd 37604. I-26 exit 24, 2.2 mi se on US 321 S. Int corridors. **Pets:** Dogs only. $25 daily fee/pet. Designated rooms, service with supervision. (SAVE) 📶 🔲 📱 🍴 ⤳

▼▼ **Comfort Inn of Johnson City** ℍ
(423) 928-9600. **$69-$275.** 1900 S Roan St 37604. I-26 exit 24, just w on US 321. Ext corridors. **Pets:** Accepted. 📶 🔲 📱 ⤳

▼▼▼ **DoubleTree by Hilton Hotel Johnson City** ℍ
(423) 929-2000. **$89-$199.** 211 Mockingbird Ln 37604. I-26 exit 20A westbound; exit 20 eastbound, just w on N Roan St. Int corridors. **Pets:** Accepted. (ECO) 📶 🔲 📱 🍴 ⤳

▼▼▼ **Holiday Inn-Johnson City** ℍ
(423) 282-4611. **$108-$119.** 101 W Springbrook Dr 37604. I-26 exit 20A westbound; exit 20 eastbound, just e on N Roan St, then just n. Int corridors. **Pets:** Small. $25 one-time fee/pet. Service with restrictions, supervision. 📶 🔲 📱 🍴 ⤳ .

▼▼ **Jameson Inn** ℍ
(423) 282-0488. **$97-$117.** 119 Pinnacle Dr 37615. I-26 exit 17, just w on CR 354, then just s. Ext corridors. **Pets:** Medium. $15 daily fee/room. Service with restrictions, supervision. 📶 🔲 📱 ⤳

▼▼ **Motel 6 Johnson City #4620** ℍ
(423) 282-3335. **$40-$46.** 207 E Mountcastle Dr 37601. I-26 exit 20B westbound; exit 20 eastbound, 0.5 mi w on N Roan St, then 0.3 mi s. Ext/int corridors. **Pets:** Other species. Service with restrictions, supervision. 📶 ✕ 🔲 📱 ⤳

▼▼ **Red Roof Inn-Johnson City** Ⓜ
(423) 282-3040. **$50-$90.** 210 Broyles Dr 37601. I-26 exit 20A westbound; exit 20 eastbound, just w on N Roan St. Ext corridors. **Pets:** Large, other species. No service, supervision. 📶 🔲

▼▼ **Sleep Inn & Suites** ℍ
(423) 915-0081. **Call for rates.** 2020 Franklin Terrace Ct 37604. I-26 exit 19, just w, then just n, follow signs; entrance on Oakland Ave at light. Int corridors. **Pets:** Accepted. 📶 🔲 📱

JONESBOROUGH

Ⓐ ▼▼▼ **AmericInn Lodge & Suites of Jonesborough** ℍ
(423) 753-3100. **$70-$100.** 376 E Jackson Blvd 37659. I-26 exit 17 (Boones Creek Rd); jct E Jackson Blvd (US 11 E). Int corridors. **Pets:** Medium, other species. $25 one-time fee/room. Designated rooms, service with restrictions, supervision. (SAVE) 📶 🔲 📱 ⤳

KIMBALL

Ⓐ ▼▼ **Super 8 - Kimball** ℍ
(423) 837-7185. **$50-$85.** 395 Main St 37347. I-24 exit 152, 0.5 mi n. Ext corridors. **Pets:** $10 one-time fee/pet. Service with restrictions, supervision. (SAVE) 📶 🔲 📱 ⤳

KINGSPORT

▼▼ **Colonial Inn** Ⓜ
(423) 239-3400. **$50-$210.** 4234 Fort Henry Dr 37663. I-81 exit 59, 0.7 mi n on SR 36. Ext corridors. **Pets:** Medium. $10 daily fee/pet. Designated rooms, service with restrictions, supervision. 📶 🔲 📱

▼▼▼ **Jameson Inn** ℍ
(423) 230-0534. **$81-$101.** 3004 Bay Meadow Pl 37664. I-26 exit 4, just n. Int corridors. **Pets:** Medium. $15 daily fee/room. Service with restrictions, supervision. 📶 🔲 📱 ⤳

▼▼▼ **La Quinta Inn & Suites Kingsport Tri-Cities Airport** ℍ
(423) 323-0500. **$68-$126.** 10150 Airport Pkwy 37663. I-81 exit 63, just e. Int corridors. **Pets:** Medium, other species. Service with restrictions, supervision. 📶 🔲 📱 ⤳

▼▼ **Sleep Inn** ℍ
(423) 279-1811. **Call for rates.** 200 Hospitality Pl 37663. I-81 exit 63, just s. Int corridors. **Pets:** Accepted. 📶 🔲 📱

KINGSTON

▼▼ **Motel 6 #4403** Ⓜ
(865) 376-2069. **$43-$90.** 495 Gallaher Rd 37763. I-40 exit 356, just n. Ext corridors. **Pets:** Other species. Service with restrictions, supervision. 📶 🔲 ⤳

Ⓐ ▼▼▼ **Super 8 of Kingston** Ⓜ
(865) 376-4965. **Call for rates.** 905 N Kentucky St 37763. I-40 exit 352, 0.3 mi s. Ext corridors. **Pets:** Medium. $10 daily fee/pet. Designated rooms, service with restrictions, supervision. (SAVE) 📶 🔲 📱

KINGSTON SPRINGS

Ⓐ ▼▼▼ **Best Western Harpeth Inn** ℍ
(615) 952-3961. **$55-$105.** 116 Luyben Hills Rd 37082. I-40 exit 188, just n. Ext corridors. **Pets:** Other species. $10 daily fee/pet. Service with restrictions, supervision. (SAVE) 📶 🔲 📱 ⤳

KNOXVILLE

▼▼ Baymont Inn & Suites East Knoxville ⊞
(865) 246-3600. **$58-$94.** 814 Brakebill Rd 37914. I-40 exit 398 (Strawberry Plains Pike), just n, then w. Ext corridors. **Pets:** Accepted.
🛜 📶 💻 🌊

⟨AAA⟩ ▼▼ Best Western Knoxville Suites ⊞
(865) 687-9922. **$79-$150.** 5317 Pratt Rd 37912. I-75 exit 108 (Merchants Dr), just e, then n. Int corridors. **Pets:** Accepted.
[SAVE] 🛜 📶 📶 💻 🌊

▼▼ Candlewood Suites-Knoxville ⊞
(865) 777-0400. **$89-$119.** 10206 Parkside Dr 37922. I-40/75 exit 374 (Lovell Rd), 0.5 mi s, then 1 mi e. Int corridors. **Pets:** Medium. $15 daily fee/room. Service with restrictions. 📶 📶 💻

⟨AAA⟩ ▼▼▼ The Clarion Inn ⊞
(865) 687-8989. **$70-$130.** 5634 Merchants Center Blvd 37912. I-75 exit 108 (Merchants Dr), just w, then just n. Int corridors. **Pets:** Small. $20 daily fee/pet. Service with restrictions, supervision.
[SAVE] 🛜 📶 📶 💻 🌊

▼▼▼ Crowne Plaza Knoxville ⊞ ✿
(865) 522-2600. **$134-$137.** 401 W Summit Hill Dr 37902. Corner of Walnut St; downtown. Int corridors. **Pets:** Large, other species. $25 one-time fee/room. Service with restrictions. 🛜 📶 📶 💻 🍴 🌊

⟨AAA⟩ ▼▼▼ Econo Lodge Inn & Suites - East Knoxville Ⓜ
(865) 932-1217. **$45-$149.** 7424 Strawberry Plains Pike 37924. I-40 exit 398 (Strawberry Plains Pike), just n. Ext corridors. **Pets:** Medium, other species. $10 daily fee/room. Designated rooms, service with restrictions, crate. [SAVE] 🛜 📶 💻 🌊

⟨AAA⟩ ▼▼▼ Econo Lodge-North Ⓜ
(865) 687-5680. **$50-$90.** 5505 Merchants Center Blvd 37912. I-75 exit 108 (Merchants Dr), just w, then just n. Ext corridors. **Pets:** Very small, dogs only. $10 daily fee/pet. Service with restrictions, supervision.
[SAVE] 🛜 📶

▼▼ Extended StayAmerica Knoxville-Cedar Bluff Ⓜ ✿
(865) 769-0822. **$60-$100.** 214 Langley Pl 37922. I-40/75 exit 378 (Cedar Bluff Rd), just s, then 1 mi w on N Peters Rd. Ext corridors. **Pets:** Other species. $25 daily fee/pet. Service with restrictions.
🛜 📶 📶 💻

▼▼ Extended StayAmerica Knoxville-West Hills ⊞ ✿
(865) 694-4178. **$60-$120.** 1700 Winston Rd 37919. I-40/75 exit 380 (West Hills), just w on Kingston Pike, then just s. Int corridors. **Pets:** Other species. $25 daily fee/pet. Service with restrictions.
🛜 📶 💻 🌊

▼▼▼ Hilton Knoxville Downtown ⊞
(865) 523-2300. **$100-$360.** 501 W Church Ave 37902. Between Locust and Walnut sts; downtown. Int corridors. **Pets:** Accepted.
🛜 📶 📶 💻 🍴 🌊

▼▼▼ Holiday Inn Cedar Bluff ⊞ ✿
(865) 693-1011. **$99-$149.** 304 Cedar Bluff Rd 37923. I-40/75 exit 378 (Cedar Bluff Rd) eastbound; exit 378B westbound, just n to Executive Park Dr. Int corridors. **Pets:** Other species. $50 one-time fee/room. Designated rooms, service with restrictions, supervision.
🛜 📶 📶 💻 🍴 🌊 ⊠

⟨AAA⟩ ▼▼▼ Holiday Inn Express Knoxville-East ⊞
(865) 525-5100. **$99-$159.** 730 Rufus Graham Rd 37924. I-40 exit 398 (Strawberry Plains Pike), just n. Int corridors. **Pets:** Accepted.
[SAVE] 🛜 📶 📶 💻 🌊

▼▼▼ Homewood Suites by Hilton ⊞
(865) 777-0375. **$129-$169.** 10935 Turkey Dr 37922. I-40/75 exit 374 (Lovell Rd), just s to Parkside Dr, then 0.5 mi n on Snow Goose Dr. Int corridors. **Pets:** Accepted. 🛜 📶 📶 💻 🌊 ⊠

▼▼▼ La Quinta Inn & Suites Knoxville Strawberry Plains ⊞
(865) 633-5100. **$75-$134.** 7210 Saddle Rack St 37914. I-40 exit 398 (Strawberry Plains Pike), just s, just e on Region Ln, then just se on Shumard Ave. Int corridors. **Pets:** Medium, other species. Service with restrictions, supervision. 🛜 📶 📶 💻 🌊

▼▼▼ La Quinta Inn Knoxville (West) Ⓜ
(865) 690-9777. **$55-$79.** 258 N Peters Rd 37923. I-40/75 exit 378 (Cedar Bluff Rd), just s, then just e. Ext corridors. **Pets:** Medium, other species. Service with restrictions, supervision. 🛜 📶 💻 🌊

▼▼▼ MainStay Suites Knoxville ⊞
(865) 247-0222. **$79-$199.** 144 Merchant Dr 37912. I-75 exit 108 (Merchants Dr), just n. Int corridors. **Pets:** Small. $15 daily fee/pet. Designated rooms, service with restrictions, supervision. 🛜 📶 📶 💻

▼▼ Quality Inn Merchants Dr Ⓜ
(865) 342-3701. **$50-$110.** 117 Cedar Ln 37912. I-75 exit 108 (Merchants Dr), just e. Ext corridors. **Pets:** Accepted.
🛜 📶 📶 💻 🌊

▼▼ Red Roof Inn Ⓜ
(865) 688-1010. **$50-$99.** 5334 Central Ave Pike 37912. I-75 exit 108 (Merchants Dr), just e. Ext corridors. **Pets:** Large, other species. No service, supervision. 🛜 💻 🌊

▼▼ Red Roof Inn Knoxville Central-Papermill Road ⊞
(865) 584-3911. **$64-$175.** 1315 Kirby Rd 37909. I-40/75 exit 383 (Papermill Rd), 0.5 mi e. Int corridors. **Pets:** Large, other species. No service, supervision. 🛜 📶 📶 💻 🍴 🌊

▼▼ Red Roof Inn-West Ⓜ
(865) 691-1664. **$50-$120.** 209 Advantage Pl 37922. I-40/75 exit 378 (Cedar Bluff Rd), just s to N Peters Rd, then w. Ext corridors. **Pets:** Large, other species. No service, supervision. 🛜 📶 📶

▼▼▼ Residence Inn Knoxville Cedar Bluff ⊞
(865) 539-5339. **$107-$161.** 215 Langley Pl 37922. I-40 exit 378 (Cedar Bluff Rd), just s, then 1 mi w on N Peters Blvd. Int corridors. **Pets:** Accepted. 🛜 ⊠ 📶 📶 💻 🌊 ⊠

KODAK

▼ Big Bear Extended Stay Suites ⊞
(865) 225-1719. **$45-$100.** 2162 Parkway 37764. I-40 exit 407, just s on SR 66, then w. Ext corridors. **Pets:** Medium. $10 daily fee/room. Designated rooms, service with restrictions, crate. 🛜 📶 💻

LAWRENCEBURG

▼▼ Americas Best Value Inn Ⓜ
(931) 762-4467. **Call for rates.** 1940 N Hwy 43 38464. Jct US 43 and 64, 1.6 mi n. Ext corridors. **Pets:** Very small. $10 daily fee/pet. Designated rooms, supervision. 🛜 📶 📶 💻 🌊

⟨AAA⟩ ▼▼▼ Best Western Villa Inn ⊞
(931) 762-4448. **Call for rates.** 2126 N Locust Ave 38464. On US 43, 2.2 mi n of jct US 64. Ext corridors. **Pets:** Medium. $10 daily fee/pet. Designated rooms, service with restrictions, supervision.
[SAVE] 📶 💻 🌊

LEBANON

▼▼ Americas Best Value Inn & Suites Ⓜ ✿
(615) 449-5781. **$44-$99.** 822 S Cumberland St 37087. I-40 exit 238, just n. Ext corridors. **Pets:** Small. $12 daily fee/pet. Designated rooms, service with restrictions, supervision. 🛜 📶 💻 🌊

▼▼ Econo Lodge Ⓜ
(615) 444-1001. **$49.** 829 S Cumberland St 37087. I-40 exit 238, just n. Ext corridors. **Pets:** Accepted. 🛜 📶 💻 🌊

▼▼ Quality Inn **M** ❀
(615) 444-7020. **$55-$110.** 641 S Cumberland St 37087. I-40 exit 238, just n. Ext corridors. **Pets:** Small. $10 daily fee/pet. Service with restrictions, supervision. 🛜 ⬛ 🖥 🏊

▼▼▼ Sleep Inn & Suites-Lebanon/Nashville **H**
(615) 449-7005. **$90-$109.** 150 S Eastgate Ct 37090. I-40 exit 232. Int corridors. **Pets:** Medium. $25 one-time fee/room. Service with restrictions, supervision. 🛜 ⬛ 🖥 🏊

LENOIR CITY
▼▼ Days Inn **H**
(865) 986-2011. **$56-$62.** 1110 Hwy 321 N 37771. I-75 exit 81, just e. Ext corridors. **Pets:** Small. $10 daily fee/pet. Service with restrictions, supervision. 🛜 ⬛ 🖥 🏊

▲▲▲ ▼▼ Econo Lodge **H**
(865) 986-0295. **$55-$85.** 1211 Hwy 321 N 37771. I-75 exit 81, just w. Ext corridors. **Pets:** Medium. $10 daily fee/pet. Service with restrictions, supervision. (SAVE) 🛜 ⬛ 🏊

LOUDON
▲▲▲ ▼ Americas Best Value Inn **M**
(865) 458-5855. **$55-$69.** 15100 Hwy 72 37774. I-75 exit 72, just w. Ext corridors. **Pets:** Large. $7 daily fee/pet. Service with restrictions, supervision. (SAVE) 🛜 ⬛

MANCHESTER
▼▼▼ Comfort Suites **H**
(931) 728-1301. **$77-$210.** 152 Hospitality Blvd 37355. I-24 exit 114, just e. Int corridors. **Pets:** Accepted. 🛜 ✖ ⬛ 🖥 🏊

▼▼▼ Microtel Inn & Suites **H**
(931) 723-7001. **Call for rates.** 201 Expressway Dr 37355. I-24 exit 114, 0.5 mi nw on SR 41, then just n. Int corridors. **Pets:** Accepted.
🛜 ⬛ 🖥 🏊

▲▲▲ ▼▼▼ Ramada Limited **H**
(931) 728-0800. **$59-$129.** 2314 Hillsboro Blvd 37355. I-24 exit 114, just n. Ext corridors. **Pets:** Medium. $10 daily fee/pet. Service with restrictions, supervision. (SAVE) 🛜 ⬛ 🖥

▼▼▼ Sleep Inn & Suites **H**
(931) 954-0580. **Call for rates.** 84 Relco Dr 37355. I-24 exit 114, just se. Int corridors. **Pets:** Medium, other species. $15 daily fee/pet. Designated rooms, service with restrictions, supervision.
🛜 ✖ ⬛ 🖥 🏊

MARTIN
▼▼ Days Inn **H**
(731) 587-9577. **$51-$85.** 800 University St 38237. Jct SR 431. Ext corridors. **Pets:** Medium. $10 daily fee/pet. Service with restrictions, supervision. 🛜 ⬛ 🖥 🏊

MARYVILLE
▼▼ LuxBury Inn & Suites **M** ❀
(865) 983-9839. **$59-$129.** 805 Foothills Mall Dr 37801. Jct US 321 (Lamar Alexander Hwy). Ext corridors. **Pets:** Small, dogs only. $25 one-time fee/pet. Designated rooms, service with restrictions, supervision.
🛜 ⬛ 🖥

MCKENZIE
▲▲▲ ▼▼▼ Best Western McKenzie **H**
(731) 352-1083. **$72-$120.** 16180 N Highland Ave 38201. Jct US 79 and SR 22, just s. Ext corridors. **Pets:** Very small. $10 daily fee/pet. Designated rooms, service with restrictions, supervision.
(SAVE) 🛜 ⬛ 🖥 🏊

MCMINNVILLE
▲▲▲ ▼▼▼ Best Western Tree City Inn **H**
(931) 473-2159. **$75-$85.** 809 Sparta Hwy 37110. Jct US 70 S Bypass and Red Rd, 1 mi s, follow signs. Ext corridors. **Pets:** Small, dogs only. $10 daily fee/pet. Service with restrictions, supervision.
(SAVE) 🛜 ⬛ 🖥 🏊

MEMPHIS METROPOLITAN AREA

ATOKA
▼▼▼ Comfort Inn & Suites **H**
(901) 837-7729. **$80-$90.** 10772 Hwy 51 S 38004. 0.5 mi n of jct SR 206. Int corridors. **Pets:** Accepted. 🛜 ⬛ 🖥 🏊

COLLIERVILLE
▼▼▼ Hampton Inn Collierville **H**
(901) 854-9400. **$99-$199.** 1280 W Poplar Ave 38017. 0.9 mi w of jct CR 175 on US 72. Int corridors. **Pets:** Accepted.
🛜 ✖ ⬛ 🖥 🏊

CORDOVA
▼▼▼ StudioPLUS-Memphis-Cordova **H** 🐾
(901) 754-4030. **$45-$65.** 8110 Cordova Centre Dr 38016. I-40 exit 16A, 0.8 mi s. Int corridors. **Pets:** Other species. $25 daily fee/pet. Service with restrictions. 🛜 ⬛ 🖥 🏊

GERMANTOWN
▲▲▲ ▼▼▼ Comfort Inn & Suites-Germantown **H**
(901) 757-7800. **$90-$110.** 7787 Wolf River Blvd 38138. I-40 exit 16, 5 mi s on Germantown Pkwy to Wolf River Blvd, then just w. Int corridors. **Pets:** Medium. $25 one-time fee/pet. Service with restrictions, supervision.
(SAVE) 🛜 ✖ ⬛ 🖥 🏊

▼▼▼ Homewood Suites by Hilton-Germantown **H**
(901) 751-2500. **$99-$159.** 7855 Wolf River Blvd 38138. I-40 exit 16, 5.7 mi s on Germantown Pkwy, then just e. Int corridors. **Pets:** Accepted.
🛜 ⬛ 🖥 🏊

▼▼▼ Residence Inn Memphis/Germantown **H**
(901) 752-0900. **$92-$129.** 9314 Poplar Pike 38138. I-240 exit 15 (Poplar Ave), 7 mi e. Int corridors. **Pets:** Accepted.
🛜 ✖ ⬛ 🖥 🏊 ✖

MEMPHIS
▼▼ Baymont Inn & Suites Memphis East **H**
(901) 377-2233. **$53-$77.** 6020 Shelby Oaks Dr 38134. I-40 exit 12, just n. Int corridors. **Pets:** Medium. Service with restrictions, crate.
🛜 ⬛ 🖥 🏊

▲▲▲ ▼▼▼ Best Western Travelers Inn **H**
(901) 363-8430. **$70-$80.** 5024 US Hwy 78 38118. I-240 exit 21 (US 78), 6 mi s. Ext corridors. **Pets:** Medium. $25 daily fee/pet. Designated rooms, service with restrictions. (SAVE) 🛜 ⬛ 🖥 🏊

▼▼▼ Drury Inn & Suites-Memphis Northeast **H**
(901) 373-8200. **$85-$164.** 1556 Sycamore View 38134. I-40 exit 12, just n. Int corridors. **Pets:** Accepted. 🛜 ⬛ 🖥 🏊

▼▼▼ Hampton Inn Walnut Grove **H**
(901) 747-3700. **$89-$115.** 33 Humphreys Center Dr 38120. I-240 exit 13 (Walnut Grove E), just e. Int corridors. **Pets:** Accepted.
🛜 ⬛ 🖥 🏊

▼▼▼ Hilton Memphis **H**
(901) 684-6664. **$99-$239.** 939 Ridge Lake Blvd 38120. I-240 exit 15 (Poplar Ave), just e, then n under overpass. Int corridors. **Pets:** Accepted.
🛜 ⬛ 🖥 🍴 🏊

▼▼▼▼ **Homewood Suites by Hilton-Hacks Cross** H
(901) 758-5018. **$89-$152.** 3583 Hacks Cross Rd 38125. I-240 exit 16, 4 mi e on SR 385, then 1 mi n. Int corridors. **Pets:** Medium, dogs only. $50 one-time fee/room. Designated rooms, service with restrictions, supervision. 🛜 🕭M 🛏 📺 ≈

▼▼▼▼ **Homewood Suites by Hilton-Poplar** H
(901) 763-0500. **$87-$183.** 5811 Poplar Ave 38119. I-240 exit 15 (Poplar Ave), just e. Ext/int corridors. **Pets:** Accepted. 🛜 🛏 📺 ≈

◆◆◆ ▼▼▼▼ **La Quinta Inn & Suites Memphis East-Sycamore View** H
(901) 381-0044. **$64-$150.** 6069 Macon Cove Rd 38134. I-40 exit 12, just s. Int corridors. **Pets:** Medium, other species. Service with restrictions, supervision. [SAVE] 🛜 ✕ 🕭M 🛏 📺 ≈

▼▼▼▼ **La Quinta Inn & Suites Memphis (Primacy Parkway)** H
(901) 374-0330. **$68-$126.** 1236 Primacy Pkwy 38119. I-240 exit 15 (Poplar Ave), 0.5 mi e, s on Ridgeway Rd, just w, then just s. Int corridors. **Pets:** Medium, other species. Service with restrictions, supervision. 🛜 🕭M 🛏 📺 ≈

◆◆◆ ▼▼▼ ▼▼▼ **Madison Hotel** H
(901) 333-1200. **Call for rates.** 79 Madison Ave 38103. Just w of jct Main St. Int corridors. **Pets:** Very small, dogs only. $250 deposit/pet, $30 daily fee/pet. Service with restrictions, supervision.
[SAVE] 🛜 ✕ 🛏 📺 🍽

◆◆◆ ▼▼▼ ▼▼▼ **Peabody Memphis** H 🐾
(901) 529-4000. **$199-$550, 3 day notice.** 149 Union Ave 38103. Just se of jct 2nd St. Int corridors. **Pets:** Medium. $50 one-time fee/room. Designated rooms. [SAVE] 🛜 ✕ 🛏 📺 🍽 ≈ ✕

▼▼▼▼ **Residence Inn by Marriott Memphis Downtown** H
(901) 578-3700. **$142-$199.** 110 Monroe Ave 38103. Just e of jct Main St. Int corridors. **Pets:** Accepted. 🛜 ✕ 🕭M 🛏 📺 ✕

▼▼▼▼ **Residence Inn by Marriott Memphis East** H 🐾
(901) 685-9595. **$108-$132.** 6141 Poplar Pike 38119. I-240 exit 15 (Poplar Ave), 0.5 mi e. Int corridors. **Pets:** Small. $100 one-time fee/room. Service with restrictions, supervision. 🛜 ✕ 🕭M 🛏 📺 ≈

▼▼▼ **Sleep Inn** H
(901) 312-7777. **Call for rates.** 2855 Old Austin Peay Hwy 38128. I-40 exit 8A, 0.8 mi ne. Int corridors. **Pets:** Accepted.
🛜 🕭M 🛏 📺 ≈

▼▼▼ **Staybridge Suites** H
(901) 682-1722. **$109-$119, 3 day notice.** 1070 Ridge Lake Blvd 38120. I-240 exit 15 (Poplar Ave), just e, then n under overpass. Int corridors. **Pets:** Accepted. 🛜 🕭M 🛏 📺 ≈ ✕

◆◆◆ ▼▼▼ ▼▼▼ **The Westin Memphis Beale Street** H 🐾
(901) 334-5900. **$199-$399.** 170 Lt. George W. Lee Ave 38103. Jct S 3rd St. Int corridors. **Pets:** Small. Designated rooms, service with restrictions, supervision. [SAVE] 🛜 ✕ 🕭M 📺 🍽

MILLINGTON
▼▼ **Plantation Oaks Suites & Inn** H
(901) 872-8000. **Call for rates.** 6656 Hwy 51 N 38053. 1.5 mi s of jct SR 385. Ext/int corridors. **Pets:** Medium. $40 one-time fee/room. Designated rooms, service with restrictions, crate. 🛜 🛏 📺 ≈

END METROPOLITAN AREA

MONTEAGLE
◆◆◆ ▼▼ ▼▼ **Best Western Smoke House Lodge** H
(931) 924-2091. **$60-$100.** 850 W Main St 37356. I-24 exit 134, just s. Ext corridors. **Pets:** Accepted. [SAVE] 🛜 🛏 📺 🍽 ≈ ✕

▼▼▼▼ **Edgeworth Inn** BB
(931) 924-4000. **Call for rates.** 19 Wilkins Ave 37356. I-24 exit 134, 0.4 mi e on US 41A, 2nd left through assembly gates, follow signs. Ext/int corridors. **Pets:** Medium. $25 one-time fee/pet. Designated rooms, service with restrictions, crate. 🛜 ✕ 🛏 📺 🍽 ≈ ✓

MORRISTOWN
◆◆◆ ▼▼▼▼ **Best Western Plus Morristown Conference Center Hotel** H 🐾
(423) 587-2400. **$105-$300, 3 day notice.** 5435 S Davy Crockett Pkwy 37813. I-81 exit 8, just n. Int corridors. **Pets:** Medium. $20 daily fee/room. Service with restrictions, supervision.
[SAVE] 🛜 🕭M 🛏 📺 🍽 ≈

◆◆◆ ▼▼ ▼ **Days Inn** M
(423) 587-2200. **$45-$180, 7 day notice.** 2512 E Andrew Johnson Hwy 37814. I-81 exit 8, 6 mi n on US 25 E to exit 2B (Greeneville-Morristown), then just w. Ext corridors. **Pets:** Medium, other species. $10 daily fee/pet. Designated rooms, service with restrictions, supervision.
[SAVE] 🕭M 🛏 📺 ≈

▼▼ **Super 8** M 🐾
(423) 318-8888. **$42-$80.** 5400 S Davy Crockett Pkwy 37813. I-81 exit 8, just n. Int corridors. **Pets:** Medium. $9 one-time fee/pet. Service with restrictions, supervision. 🛜 🕭M 🛏 📺

▼▼ **Travelodge** M
(423) 581-8700. **$58-$134.** 3304 W Andrew Johnson Hwy 37814. 2.5 mi w on US 11 E. Ext corridors. **Pets:** Other species. $10 one-time fee/pet. Service with restrictions. 🛜 🕭M 🛏 📺 ≈

MOUNT JULIET
◆◆◆ ▼▼▼ **Quality Inn & Suites** H
(615) 773-3600. **$80-$90.** 1000 Hershel Dr 37122. I-40 exit 226, just s. Int corridors. **Pets:** Small. $25 one-time fee/room. Service with restrictions, crate. [SAVE] 🛜 🛏 📺 ≈

MURFREESBORO
▼▼▼ **Baymont Inn & Suites** M 🐾
(615) 896-1172. **$67-$108.** 2230 Armory Dr 37129. I-24 exit 78B, just n. Ext corridors. **Pets:** $15 daily fee/room. Designated rooms, service with restrictions, supervision. 🛜 🕭M 🛏 📺 ≈

◆◆◆ ▼▼▼ ▼▼▼ **Best Western Chaffin Inn** M
(615) 895-3818. **$60-$140.** 168 Chaffin Pl 37129. I-24 exit 78B. Ext corridors. **Pets:** Medium. $15 daily fee/room. Designated rooms, service with restrictions, supervision. [SAVE] 🛜 🛏 📺 ≈

◆◆◆ ▼▼▼▼ **DoubleTree by Hilton Hotel Murfreesboro** H
(615) 895-5555. **$89-$134.** 1850 Old Fort Pkwy 37129. I-24 exit 78B, 0.6 mi n. Int corridors. **Pets:** $50 one-time fee/room. Service with restrictions, crate. [ECO] [SAVE] 🛜 🕭M 🛏 📺 🍽 ≈

◆◆◆ ▼▼▼ ▼▼▼ **Econo Lodge Inn & Suites** M
(615) 890-2811. **Call for rates.** 110 N Thompson Ln 37129. I-24 exit 78B, just n. Ext corridors. **Pets:** Accepted.
[SAVE] 🛜 🕭M 🛏 📺 ≈

▼▼▼ Hampton Inn & Suites ⊞
(615) 890-2424. **Call for rates.** 325 N Thompson Ln 37129. I-24 exit 78B, just n. Int corridors. **Pets:** Accepted. 🛜 ⓑM 🍴 💻 🏊

◈◈/ ▼▼▼ Quality Inn Murfreesboro ⊞ ❀
(615) 890-1006. **$60-$109.** 2135 S Church St 37130. I-24 exit 81 westbound; exit 81B eastbound. Int corridors. **Pets:** Other species. $10 one-time fee/room. Service with restrictions. SAVE 🛜 ⓑM 🍴 💻 🏊

NASHVILLE METROPOLITAN AREA

ANTIOCH

▼▼▼ Holiday Inn-The Crossings ⊞
(615) 731-2361. **$89-$119.** 201 Crossings Pl 37013. I-24 exit 60, 0.5 mi e. Int corridors. **Pets:** Medium. $50 one-time fee/room. Service with restrictions, supervision. 🛜 ⓑM 🍴 💻 🍴 🏊

GOODLETTSVILLE

◈◈/ ▼▼▼ Best Western Fairwinds Inn ⊞
(615) 851-1067. **$60-$150.** 100 Northcreek Blvd 37072. I-65 exit 97 (Long Hollow Pike), 0.5 mi e. Ext corridors. **Pets:** Small. $15 daily fee/pet. Service with restrictions. SAVE 🛜 🍴 💻 🏊

◈◈/ ▼▼▼▼ Holiday Inn Express & Suites ⊞
(615) 851-1891. **Call for rates.** 120 S Cartwright Ct 37072. I-65 exit 97 (Long Hollow Pike), just w. Int corridors. **Pets:** Small, other species. $25 one-time fee/room. Designated rooms, service with restrictions.
SAVE 🛜 ⓑM 🍴 💻 🏊

◈◈/ ▼▼▼ Quality Inn ⊞
(615) 859-5400. **$62-$125.** 925 Conference Dr 37072. I-65 exit 97 (Long Hollow Pike), 0.6 mi e. Ext corridors. **Pets:** Small. $10 daily fee/pet. Designated rooms, service with restrictions, supervision.
SAVE 🛜 ⓑM 🍴 💻 🏊

◈◈/ ▼▼▼ Rodeway Inn Ⓜ
(615) 859-1416. **Call for rates.** 650 Wade Cir 37072. I-65 exit 96, just ne. Ext corridors. **Pets:** Accepted. SAVE 🛜 🍴 💻 🏊

HERMITAGE

◈◈/ ▼▼▼ Super 8 ⊞
(615) 871-4545. **$41-$90.** 1414 Princeton Pl 37076. I-40 exit 221 westbound; exit 221B eastbound, just n. Ext corridors. **Pets:** Small. $10 daily fee/pet. Service with restrictions, supervision. SAVE 🛜 🍴 💻 🏊

NASHVILLE

▼▼▼ Airport Super 8 Nashville ⊞
(615) 889-8887. **$62-$119.** 720 Royal Pkwy 37214. I-40 exit 216C (Donelson Pike N), 0.5 mi n, then just e. Int corridors. **Pets:** Accepted.
🛜 ✕ ⓑM 🍴 💻 🏊

◈◈/ ▼▼▼ Best Western Airport Inn ⊞
(615) 889-9199. **$47-$150.** 701 Stewarts Ferry Pike 37214. I-40 exit 219 (Stewarts Ferry Pike), just s. Ext corridors. **Pets:** Accepted.
SAVE 🛜 🍴 💻 🏊

◈◈/ ▼▼▼ Best Western Music City Inn Ⓜ ❀
(615) 641-7721. **$70-$120.** 13010 Old Hickory Blvd 37013. I-24 exit 62, just n. Ext corridors. **Pets:** Medium, dogs only. $15 daily fee/room. Designated rooms, service with restrictions, supervision.
SAVE 🛜 ⓑM 🍴 💻 🏊

◈◈/ ▼▼▼▼ Best Western Plus Music Row ⊞
(615) 242-1631. **$79-$249.** 1407 Division St 37203. I-40 exit 209B (Broadway), just w around circle, then just e. Int corridors. **Pets:** Small, other species. $10 daily fee/pet. Service with restrictions.
SAVE 🛜 🍴 💻 🏊

◈◈/ ▼▼▼ Comfort Inn ⊞
(615) 356-0888. **$70-$135.** 412 White Bridge Pl 37209. I-40 exit 204B, just s. Int corridors. **Pets:** Small. $10 daily fee/pet. Service with restrictions, supervision. SAVE 🛜 ⓑM 🍴 💻 🏊

▼▼▼ Comfort Inn Downtown ⊞
(615) 255-9977. **$90-$160.** 1501 Demonbreun St 37203. I-40 exit 209B (Broadway), just w. Ext corridors. **Pets:** Accepted.
🛜 ⓑM 🍴 💻 🏊

◈◈/ ▼▼▼ Comfort Inn Opryland ⊞
(615) 889-0086. **$70-$119.** 2516 Music Valley Dr 37214. I-40 exit 215 (Briley Pkwy), 4 mi n; I-65 exit 90 to McGavock Pike exit, off Briley Pkwy. Int corridors. **Pets:** Small. $25 one-time fee/room. Service with restrictions, crate. SAVE 🛜 🍴 💻 🏊

◈◈/ ▼▼▼ Days Inn ⊞
(615) 889-0090. **$60-$111.** 2460 Music Valley Dr 37214. I-40 exit 215B (Briley Pkwy), 4 mi n to exit 11 (McGavock Pike). Int corridors.
Pets: Accepted. SAVE 🛜 🍴 💻 🏊

▼▼▼▼ Drury Inn & Suites-Nashville Airport ⊞
(615) 902-0400. **$90-$169.** 555 Donelson Pike 37214. I-40 exit 216 (Donelson Pike), just n. Int corridors. **Pets:** Accepted.
🛜 ⓑM 🍴 💻 🏊

▼▼▼ Embassy Suites ⊞ ❀
(615) 871-0033. **$109-$159.** 10 Century Blvd 37214. I-40 exit 215 (Briley Pkwy N) to exit 7 (Elm Hill Pike), 0.3 mi e to McGavock Pike, 0.3 mi s to Century Blvd, then 0.3 mi w. Int corridors. **Pets:** Large. $75 one-time fee/pet. Service with restrictions, supervision.
🛜 ⓑM 🍴 💻 🍴 🏊 ✕

▼▼▼ Extended StayAmerica-Nashville-Vanderbilt ⊞ ❀
(615) 383-7490. **$80-$200.** 3311 West End Ave 37203. I-440 exit 1A, just e. Int corridors. **Pets:** Other species. $25 daily fee/pet. Service with restrictions. 🛜 ⓑM 🍴 💻

▼▼▼ GuestHouse International Inn & Suites ⊞
(615) 885-4030. **$89-$169.** 2420 Music Valley Dr 37214. Briley Pkwy exit 12 (McGavock Pike), 0.3 mi w, then 0.3 mi n. Int corridors. **Pets:** Other species. $25 one-time fee/room. Designated rooms, service with restrictions, crate. 🛜 ✕ 🍴 💻 🏊

◈◈/ ▼▼▼▼ The Hermitage Hotel ⊞
(615) 244-3121. **Call for rates.** 231 6th Ave N 37219. Corner of Union St; center. Int corridors. **Pets:** Accepted.
SAVE 🛜 ✕ ⓑM 🍴 💻 🍴 ✕

◈◈/ ▼▼▼▼ Hilton Nashville Downtown ⊞ ❀
(615) 620-1000. **$217-$313.** 121 4th Ave S 37201. Center. Int corridors. **Pets:** Medium, other species. $75 one-time fee/room. Service with restrictions, supervision. SAVE 🛜 ✕ ⓑM 🍴 💻 🍴 🏊 ✕

◈◈/ ▼▼▼▼ Holiday Inn Express-Airport/Opryland Area ⊞
(615) 883-1366. **$79-$129.** 1111 Airport Center Dr 37214. I-40 exit 216C (Donelson Pike N), 1 mi n, then 0.5 mi e. Int corridors. **Pets:** Accepted.
SAVE 🛜 ⓑM 🍴 💻 🏊

▼▼▼ Homestead Studio Suites Hotel-Nashville/Airport Ⓜ ❀
(615) 316-9020. **$50-$70.** 727 McGavock Pike 37214. I-40 exit 215B (Briley Pkwy), 1 mi n to exit 7 (Elm Hill Pike), then just e. Ext corridors. **Pets:** Other species. $25 daily fee/pet. Service with restrictions.
🛜 ⓑM 🍴 💻

▼▼▼ Homewood Suites Nashville Downtown ⊞
(615) 742-5550. **$129-$149.** 706 Church St 37203. Jct 7th Ave N and Church St. Int corridors. **Pets:** Accepted. 🛜 ⓑM 🍴 💻

▼▼▼ **Hotel Indigo-Nashville Downtown** H

(615) 891-6000. **$109-$399.** 301 Union St 37201. I-40 exit 209A (Church St), 0.8 mi e on Charlotte Ave, then just s. Int corridors. **Pets:** Accepted.

▼▼▼ **Hotel Indigo-Nashville West End** H

(615) 329-4200. **$109-$399.** 1719 West End Ave 37203. I-40 exit 209B (Broadway), 0.4 mi w. Int corridors. **Pets:** Accepted.

AAA ▼▼▼▼ **Hotel Preston** H

(615) 361-5900. **$119-$249, 3 day notice.** 733 Briley Pkwy 37217. I-40 exit 215 (Briley Pkwy), just s. Int corridors. **Pets:** Small. $49 one-time fee/room. Designated rooms, service with restrictions.

AAA ▼▼▼▼ **Hutton Hotel** H ❀

(615) 340-9333. **Call for rates.** 1808 W End Ave 37203. I-40 W exit 209B (Broadway), 1 mi w. Int corridors. **Pets:** Other species. $50 one-time fee/room. Designated rooms.

▼▼ ▼▼ **La Quinta Inn & Suites Nashville-Airport** H

(615) 885-3100. **$64-$122.** 531 Donelson Pike 37214. I-40 exit 216C (Donelson Pike), 0.3 mi n. Int corridors. **Pets:** Medium, other species. Service with restrictions, supervision.

AAA ▼▼▼ ▼▼▼ **Loews Vanderbilt Hotel Nashville** H ❀

(615) 320-1700. **Call for rates.** 2100 West End Ave 37203. I-40 exit 209B (Broadway), 1.3 mi w. Int corridors. **Pets:** $25 daily fee/room. Designated rooms, service with restrictions, supervision.

AAA ▼▼ ▼▼ **Microtel Inn & Suites** H

(615) 662-0004. **$50-$71.** 100 Coley Davis Ct 37221. I-40 exit 196, just se. Int corridors. **Pets:** Small. $25 daily fee/pet. Service with restrictions, supervision.

AAA ▼▼▼ **Radisson Hotel Opryland** H

(615) 889-0800. **$109-$119.** 2401 Music Valley Dr 37214. Briley Pkwy exit 12B. Ext/int corridors. **Pets:** Accepted.

▼▼ ▼▼ **Red Roof Inn Airport** M

(615) 872-0735. **$50-$100.** 510 Claridge Dr 37214. I-40 exit 216C (Donelson Pike), 0.3 mi n. Ext corridors. **Pets:** Large, other species. No service, supervision.

AAA ▼▼▼▼ **Residence Inn Nashville Airport** H

(615) 889-8600. **$92-$161.** 2300 Elm Hill Pike 37214. I-40 exit 215B (Briley Pkwy), 1.5 mi n. Int corridors. **Pets:** Other species. $100 one-time fee/room. Service with restrictions.

AAA ▼▼▼▼ **Sheraton Music City Hotel** H

(615) 885-2200. **$105-$299.** 777 McGavock Pike 37214. I-40 exit 215B (Briley Pkwy), 1 mi n to exit 7 (Elm Hill Pike), 0.5 mi e, then s. Int corridors. **Pets:** Accepted.

AAA ▼▼▼▼ **Sheraton Nashville Downtown Hotel** H

(615) 259-2000. **$109-$329.** 623 Union St 37219. I-40 exit 209, just s of State Capitol. Int corridors. **Pets:** Accepted.

AAA ▼▼ ▼▼ **Super 8-West** M

(615) 356-6005. **$50-$97.** 6924 Charlotte Pike 37209. I-40 exit 201B, just n. Ext corridors. **Pets:** Medium. $10 daily fee/pet. Service with restrictions, supervision.

END METROPOLITAN AREA

NEWPORT

AAA ▼▼ ▼▼ **Best Western Newport Inn** M ❀

(423) 623-8713. **$50-$150.** 1015 Cosby Hwy 37821. I-40 exit 435, just w. Ext corridors. **Pets:** Medium. $10 daily fee/room. Service with restrictions, supervision.

AAA ▼▼ ▼▼ **Comfort Inn** H

(423) 623-5355. **$50-$180.** 1149 Smokey Mountain Ln 37821. I-40 exit 432B, just n. Int corridors. **Pets:** Medium. $10 one-time fee/pet. Service with restrictions, supervision.

AAA ▼▼ **Motel 6-#4090** M

(423) 623-1850. **$35-$60.** 255 Heritage Blvd 37822. I-40 exit 435, just n. Int corridors. **Pets:** Other species. Service with restrictions, supervision.

OAK RIDGE

▼▼▼▼ **DoubleTree by Hilton Hotel Oak Ridge** H

(865) 481-2468. **$104-$179.** 215 S Illinois Ave 37830. 0.3 mi se of SR 95 on SR 62. Int corridors. **Pets:** Accepted.

▼▼▼▼ **Jameson Inn** H

(865) 483-6809. **$84-$104.** 216 S Rutgers Ave 37830. Jct SR 95 and 62, 0.9 mi se on SR 62 (Oak Ridge Hwy) to Rutgers Ave, then 0.7 mi n. Int corridors. **Pets:** Medium. $15 daily fee/room. Service with restrictions, supervision.

▼▼▼ **Staybridge Suites** H

(865) 298-0050. **$129-$159.** 420 S Illinois Ave 37830. Jct Lafayette St and SR 62 (Oak Ridge Hwy). Int corridors. **Pets:** Accepted.

OOLTEWAH

▼▼ **Super 8** M

(423) 238-5951. **$41-$54.** 8934 Lee Hwy 37363. I-75 exit 11, just w. Ext corridors. **Pets:** Accepted.

PARIS

▼▼ ▼▼ **Super 8** H

(731) 644-7008. **$52-$66.** 1309 E Wood St 38242. 1.6 mi ne of jct US 79 and 641. Ext/int corridors. **Pets:** Accepted.

PICKWICK DAM

▼▼▼▼ **Pickwick Landing State Resort Park Inn** H

(731) 689-3135. **Call for rates.** 220 Playground Loop 38365. Jct US 57 and SR 128; in State Park. Ext/int corridors. **Pets:** Accepted.

PIGEON FORGE

▼▼▼ **Blackberry Ridge-Accommodations by Sunset Cottage** CA

(865) 429-8478. **Call for rates.** 3630 S River Rd 37863. Just e of jct US 441 at traffic light 8, then just n. Ext corridors. **Pets:** Other species. $100 deposit/pet. Designated rooms, no service, crate.

◆ **Country Hearth Inn & Suites** **M**
(865) 429-3000. **Call for rates.** 117 Pinoak View Dr 37863. Between traffic lights 0 and 1. Ext corridors. **Pets:** Accepted.

AAA ◆◆◆ **Eden Crest Vacation Rentals** **CA** ☙
(865) 774-0059. **$100-$1000.** 652 Wears Valley Rd 37863. US 321 to light 3, just w. Ext corridors. **Pets:** Small, dogs only. $100 one-time fee/pet. Designated rooms, service with restrictions, crate.

◆◆◆ **Hampton Inn & Suites** **H** ☙
(865) 428-1600. **$99-$229.** 2025 Parkway 37863. On US 441, at traffic light 0. Int corridors. **Pets:** Medium. $20 daily fee/room. Service with restrictions, crate.

AAA ◆ **Motel 6 #4021** **M**
(865) 908-1244. **$29-$99.** 336 Henderson Chapel Rd 37863. Jct US 441, just w at traffic light 1. Int corridors. **Pets:** Other species. Service with restrictions, supervision.

AAA ◆◆◆ **RiverStone Resort & Spa** **CO**
(865) 908-0660. **$110-$380, 7 day notice.** 212 Dollywood Ln 37863. I-40 exit 407, just e of jct US 441, at traffic light 8. Ext corridors. **Pets:** Small, dogs only. $25 daily fee/pet. Designated rooms, service with restrictions, supervision.

POWELL
◆◆ **Super 8 of Powell** **M**
(865) 938-5501. **$40-$86.** 323 E Emory Rd 37849. I-75 exit 112. Ext corridors. **Pets:** Accepted.

PULASKI
◆◆ **Richland Inn** **H**
(931) 363-0006. **Call for rates.** 1020 W College St 38478. On US 64, 1 mi w of jct US 31. Ext corridors. **Pets:** Accepted.

ROGERSVILLE
◆◆ **Comfort Inn & Suites** **H**
(423) 272-8700. **$89-$199.** 128 James Richardson Ln 37857. US 11 W. Int corridors. **Pets:** Accepted.

◆◆ **Quality Inn** **H**
(423) 272-1842. **$90.** 7139 Hwy 11 W 37857. Jct SR 66 and US 11, 0.5 mi sw. Int corridors. **Pets:** Accepted.

SELMER
◆◆ **America's Best Inn** **H**
(731) 645-8880. **$50-$65.** 644 Mulberry Ave 38375. Jct SR 64 and 45, just s on SR 45. Ext corridors. **Pets:** Dogs only. $10 daily fee/pet. Designated rooms, service with restrictions, supervision.

SEVIERVILLE
◆◆◆ **Baymont Inn & Suites** **H**
(865) 933-9448. **$58-$126.** 2863 Winfield Dunn Pkwy 37764. I-40 exit 407, 2.3 mi s on SR 66. Int corridors. **Pets:** Large, other species. $10 daily fee/pet. Designated rooms, service with restrictions.

◆◆◆ **La Quinta Inn & Suites Sevierville / Kodak** **H**
(865) 933-3339. **$62-$125.** 2428 Winfield Dunn Pkwy 37764. I-40 exit 407, 3.2 mi on SR 66. Int corridors. **Pets:** Medium, other species. Service with restrictions, supervision.

AAA ◆◆◆ **Quality Inn & Suites River Suites** **M**
(865) 428-5519. **$49-$119.** 860 Winfield Dunn Pkwy 37876. I-40 exit 407, 7 mi s on SR 66; 1.3 mi n of jct US 411. Ext corridors. **Pets:** Medium. $10 daily fee/pet. Designated rooms, service with restrictions, supervision.

◆◆◆ **Sleep Inn** **H**
(865) 429-0484. **$44-$112.** 1020 Parkway 37862. On US 441, 1.2 mi s of jct US 411. Int corridors. **Pets:** Accepted.

SHELBYVILLE
AAA ◆◆◆ **Best Western Plus Celebration Inn & Suites** **H**
(931) 684-2378. **$70-$300.** 724 Madison St 37160. Jct US 231 and 41. Ext corridors. **Pets:** Medium. $20 daily fee/room. Designated rooms, service with restrictions, supervision.

SMYRNA
◆◆◆ **La Quinta Inn & Suites** **H**
(615) 220-8845. **$84-$149.** 2537 Highwood Blvd 37167. I-24 exit 66A, just w. Int corridors. **Pets:** Medium, other species. Service with restrictions, supervision.

◆◆◆ **Sleep Inn & Suites** **H**
(615) 220-2260. **$79-$109.** 2689 Highwood Blvd 37167. I-24 exit 66A, just w. Int corridors. **Pets:** Accepted.

SWEETWATER
AAA ◆◆◆ **Comfort Inn West** **H**
(423) 337-3353. **$65-$75.** 249 Hwy 68 37874. I-75 exit 60, just e. Ext/int corridors. **Pets:** Small. $10 daily fee/pet. Designated rooms, service with restrictions, supervision.

AAA ◆◆◆ **Econo Lodge** **M**
(423) 337-6646. **$56-$66.** 731 S Main St 37874. On US 11, jct SR 68. Ext/int corridors. **Pets:** Small. $10 daily fee/pet. Designated rooms, service with restrictions, supervision.

◆◆ **Magnuson Hotel** **H**
(423) 337-3541. **$80-$100.** 1421 Murray's Chapel Rd 37874. I-75 exit 60, just w. Ext/int corridors. **Pets:** Accepted.

AAA ◆◆◆ **Quality Inn & Suites** **H**
(423) 337-4900. **Call for rates.** 1116 Hwy 68 37874. I-75 exit 60, just w. Int corridors. **Pets:** Accepted.

TOWNSEND
◆◆ **Econo Lodge** **M**
(865) 448-9000. **$70-$200.** 7824 E Lamar Alexander Pkwy 37882. On US 321, 0.7 mi s of jct SR 73. Ext corridors. **Pets:** Accepted.

◆◆ **Valley View Lodge** **M**
(865) 448-2237. **Call for rates.** 7726 E Lamar Alexander Pkwy 37882. On US 321, 1.1 mi s of jct SR 73. Ext corridors. **Pets:** Accepted.

TULLAHOMA
◆◆ **Jameson Inn** **H**
(931) 455-7891. **$75-$95.** 2113 N Jackson St 37388. 3 mi n on SR 41A (N Jackson St). Ext corridors. **Pets:** Medium. $15 daily fee/room. Service with restrictions, supervision.

VONORE
◆◆ **Grand Vista Hotel & Suites** **H**
(423) 884-6200. **Call for rates.** 117 Grand Vista Dr 37885. I-75 exit 72, 14 mi e on SR 72, just e into Tellico West Industrial Park southern entrance, just n onto Deer Crossing, then just nw. Int corridors. **Pets:** Accepted.

WHITE HOUSE
◆◆◆ **Holiday Inn Express** **H**
(615) 672-7200. **$79-$109.** 206 Knight Cir 37188. I-65 exit 108, just e. Int corridors. **Pets:** Accepted.

TEXAS

CITY INDEX

ABILENE

Americas Best Value Inn
(325) 673-5424. **$55-$60.** 1633 W Stamford St 79601. I-20 exit 285, 1 mi e on S Frontage Rd. Ext corridors. **Pets:** Accepted.

Best Western Mall South
(325) 695-1262. **$90-$100.** 3950 Ridgemont Dr 79606. US 83/84 exit Buffalo Gap Rd to Ridgemont Dr, just w. Ext corridors. **Pets:** Medium. $30 daily fee/pet. Designated rooms, service with restrictions, crate.

Frontier Inn & Suites
(325) 677-2683. **Call for rates.** 3210 Pine St 79601. Jct I-20 and US 83 business route exit 286A. Ext/int corridors. **Pets:** Accepted.

Holiday Inn Express Mall South
(325) 695-0500. **$89-$139.** 3112 S Clack St 79606. US 83/277 and Southwest Dr, just e to Catclaw Dr, then just n. Int corridors. **Pets:** Accepted.

La Quinta Inn Abilene
(325) 676-1676. **$76-$145.** 3501 W Lake Rd 79601. I-20 exit 286C. Ext corridors. **Pets:** Medium, other species. Service with restrictions, supervision.

Quality Inn
(325) 676-0203. **$80-$130 (no credit cards).** 1758 E I-20 79601. I-20 exit 288, on N Frontage Rd. Ext corridors. **Pets:** Accepted.

Residence Inn by Marriott
(325) 677-8700. **$123-$180.** 1641 Musgrave Blvd 79601. I-20 exit 288, on N Frontage Rd. Int corridors. **Pets:** Accepted.

Sleep Inn & Suites
(325) 437-1525. **$77-$159 (no credit cards).** 3225 S Danville Dr 79605. US 83/84/277S exit Buffalo Gap Rd, on E Frontage Rd. Int corridors. **Pets:** Medium, other species. $25 one-time fee/pet. Designated rooms, service with restrictions, supervision.

Super 8
(325) 701-4779. **$54-$90.** 4397 Sayles Blvd 79605. US 83/84 southbound exit Buffalo Gap Rd, just e to Industrial Blvd, 0.5 mi e to Sayles Blvd, then just s; northbound exit Buffalo Gap Rd, just e. Int corridors. **Pets:** $20 daily fee/pet. Designated rooms, service with restrictions, supervision.

ALAMO

La Quinta Inn & Suites Alamo At East McAllen
(956) 783-6955. **$89-$163.** 909 E Frontage Rd 78516. US 83 exit Alamo Rd. Int corridors. **Pets:** Medium, other species. Service with restrictions, supervision.

Super 8 **M**

(956) 787-9444. **$44-$62.** 714 N Alamo Rd 78516. US 83 exit FM 907, just n. Ext corridors. **Pets:** Accepted. 🛜 ⊠ 🖥 🏊

ALICE

Days Inn **H**

(361) 664-6616. **$54-$90.** 555 N Johnson St 78332. On US 281 business route, n of Johnson St. Int corridors. **Pets:** Accepted.

🛜 🖥 💻 🏊

La Quinta Inn & Suites Alice **H**

(361) 661-1777. **$127-$221.** 2400 E Main St 78332. 0.8 mi e of downtown. Int corridors. **Pets:** Medium, other species. Service with restrictions, supervision. 🛜 ⊠ 🔊M 🖥 💻 🏊

ALPINE

Best Western Alpine Classic Inn **H**

(432) 837-1530. **Call for rates.** 2401 E Hwy 90 79830. Jct SR 118 and US 67/90, 1.5 mi e. Int corridors. **Pets:** Accepted.

SAVE 🛜 ⊠ 🔊M 🖥 💻 🏊

Oak Tree Inn **H**

(432) 837-5711. **Call for rates.** 2407 E Holland (Hwy 90/67) 79830. US 90, 2 mi e. Int corridors. **Pets:** Accepted. SAVE 🛜 ⊠ 🔊M 🖥 💻

Ramada of Alpine **H** 🐾

(432) 837-1100. **Call for rates.** 2800 W Hwy 90 79830. On US 90, 2 mi n. Int corridors. **Pets:** $25 one-time fee/room. Designated rooms, service with restrictions, supervision. SAVE 🛜 🔊M 🖥 💻 🍽 🏊

ALVARADO

La Quinta Inn & Suites Alvarado **H**

(817) 783-8700. **$85-$145.** 1165 Hwy 67 W 76009. I-35W exit 26B, just e. Int corridors. **Pets:** Medium, other species. Service with restrictions, supervision. 🛜 ⊠ 🔊M 🖥 💻 🏊

Super 8 **H**

(817) 790-7378. **$49-$90.** 5445 S I-35W 76009. I-35W exit 27A (US 67), just e to 1st traffic light on US 67, then 0.4 mi n on access road. Int corridors. **Pets:** Accepted. 🛜 🔊M 🖥 💻 🏊

ALVIN

Americas Best Value Inn & Suites **M**

(281) 331-0335. **$60-$70.** 1588 S Hwy 35 Loop 77511. SR 35 Bypass, 0.5 mi sw of SR 6. Ext corridors. **Pets:** Accepted. 🛜 🖥 💻 🏊

AMARILLO

Ambassador Hotel **H**

(806) 358-6161. **$99-$169.** 3100 I-40 W 79102. I-40 exit 68 (Georgia St), just w on north frontage road. Int corridors. **Pets:** Accepted.

🛜 ⊠ 🖥 💻 🍽 🏊 ⊠

Baymont Inn & Suites **H**

(806) 356-6800. **$54-$99.** 3411 I-40 W 79109. I-40 exit 67, 0.3 mi e on south frontage road. Int corridors. **Pets:** Other species. $15 daily fee/pet. Service with restrictions. SAVE 🛜 🖥 💻 🏊

Best Western Medical Center Inn **H**

(806) 358-7861. **$100-$120.** 1610 Coulter Dr 79106. I-40 exit 65 (Coulter Dr), 0.6 mi n. Ext/int corridors. **Pets:** Medium. $20 one-time fee/pet. Designated rooms, service with restrictions, supervision.

SAVE 🛜 🖥 💻 🏊

Best Western Santa Fe **H** 🐾

(806) 372-1885. **$70-$78.** 4600 I-40 E 79103. I-40 exit 73 (Eastern St) eastbound; exit Bolton St westbound, U-turn on south frontage road. Int corridors. **Pets:** Medium. $20 daily fee/pet. Service with restrictions. supervision. SAVE 🛜 🖥 💻 🏊

Country Inn & Suites By Carlson, I-40 West **H** 🐾

(806) 356-9977. **$79-$229.** 2000 Soncy Rd 79121. I-40 exit 64 (Soncy Rd), just n. Int corridors. **Pets:** $20 one-time fee/pet. Service with restrictions, supervision. 🛜 🖥 💻 🏊

Days Inn East Amarillo **H**

(806) 379-6255. **$56-$62.** 1701 I-40 E 79102. I-40 exit 71 (Ross-Osage), just w on north frontage road. Int corridors. **Pets:** Other species. $10 one-time fee/pet. Designated rooms, service with restrictions, supervision.

SAVE 🛜 🖥 💻 🏊

Days Inn South **H**

(806) 468-7100. **Call for rates.** 8601 Canyon Dr 79110. I-27 exit 116 (Hollywood Rd), just n on east frontage road. Int corridors.
Pets: Accepted. 🛜 🖥 🏊

Drury Inn & Suites-Amarillo **H**

(806) 351-1111. **$105-$164.** 8540 W I-40 79121. I-40 exit 64 (Soncy Rd). Int corridors. **Pets:** Accepted. 🛜 🔊M 🖥 💻 🏊

Extended StayAmerica Amarillo West **H** 🐾

(806) 351-0117. **$64-$79.** 2100 Cinema Dr 79124. I-40 exit 64 (Soncy Rd), just n. Int corridors. **Pets:** Other species. $25 daily fee/pet. Service with restrictions. 🛜 🖥 💻

Hampton Inn **H**

(806) 372-1425. **$96-$101.** 1700 I-40 E 79103. I-40 exit 71 (Ross-Osage), just e on south frontage road. Int corridors. **Pets:** Medium, other species. Designated rooms, service with restrictions, supervision.

SAVE 🛜 🖥 💻 🏊

Holiday Inn Express & Suites **H**

(806) 335-2500. **$139-$159.** 9401 I-40 E 79118. I-40 exit 76 (Airport Blvd), just w on north frontage road. Int corridors. **Pets:** Accepted.

🛜 ⊠ 🔊M 🖥 💻 🏊

La Quinta Inn Amarillo East Airport Area **H**

(806) 373-7486. **$62-$125.** 1708 I-40 E 79103. I-40 exit 71 (Ross-Osage), just e on south frontage road. Ext corridors. **Pets:** Medium, other species. Service with restrictions, supervision. 🛜 🔊M 🖥 💻 🏊

La Quinta Inn Amarillo West Medical Center **H**

(806) 352-6311. **$62-$125.** 2108 S Coulter Dr 79106. I-40 exit 65 (Coulter Dr), just n. Ext corridors. **Pets:** Medium, other species. Service with restrictions, supervision. 🛜 🔊M 🖥 💻 🏊

Microtel Inn & Suites **H**

(806) 372-8373. **$63-$72.** 1501 S Ross St 79102. I-40 exit 71 (Ross-Osage), just n. Int corridors. **Pets:** Dogs only. $10 one-time fee/pet. Designated rooms, service with restrictions, supervision.

SAVE 🛜 🔊M 🖥 💻 🏊

Quality Inn & Suites West **H**

(806) 358-7943. **$55-$139.** 6800 I-40 W 79106. I-40 exit 66 (Bell St), 0.5 mi w on north frontage road. Ext corridors. **Pets:** Medium. $20 daily fee/pet. Service with restrictions, supervision. SAVE 🛜 🖥 💻 🏊

Residence Inn by Marriott **H**

(806) 354-2978. **$114-$133.** 6700 I-40 W 79106. I-40 exit 66 (Bell St), 0.5 mi w on north frontage road. Int corridors. **Pets:** Accepted.

🛜 ⊠ 🔊M 🖥 💻 🏊 ⊠

ANGLETON

Best Western Angleton Inn **H**

(979) 849-5822. **$77-$115.** 1809 N Velasco St 77515. Jct SR 35 and Business Rt SR 288, 1 mi n. Ext corridors. **Pets:** Small. $25 one-time fee/pet. Service with restrictions, supervision. SAVE 🛜 🖥 💻 🏊

La Quinta Inn & Suites Angelton **H**

(979) 864-3383. **$93-$154.** 2400 W Mulberry 77515. Jct SR 35 and 288; on northwest corner. Int corridors. **Pets:** Medium, other species. Service with restrictions, supervision. 🛜 🔊M 🖥 💻 🏊

ARLINGTON

Best Western Cooper Inn & Suites H
(817) 784-9490. **$79-$149.** 4024 Melear Dr 76015. I-20 exit 449B (Cooper St), just n, then just w. Ext corridors. **Pets:** Accepted.

Comfort Suites Six Flags in Arlington H
(817) 460-8700. **$100-$700.** 411 W Road To Six Flags St 76011. I-30 exit 27 (Cooper St) eastbound; exit 28 (Cooper St) westbound, just s, then just e. Int corridors. **Pets:** Accepted.

Hawthorn Suites by Wyndham H
(817) 640-1188. **$79-$299.** 2401 Brookhollow Plaza Dr 76006. I-30 exit 30 (SR 360), just n to Lamar Blvd, just w to Brookhollow Plaza Dr, then just n. Ext corridors. **Pets:** Medium. $50 one-time fee/pet. Service with restrictions, crate.

Hilton Arlington H
(817) 640-3322. **$119-$269.** 2401 E Lamar Blvd 76006. Just w of SR 360 exit Ave H/Lamar Blvd; just nw of I-30 exit 30 (SR 360/Six Flags Dr). Int corridors. **Pets:** Accepted.

Homewood Suites by Hilton H
(817) 633-1594. **$109-$149.** 2401 East Rd to Six Flags Dr 76011. I-30 exit 30 (SR 360), 0.5 mi s on southbound frontage road, then just w. Int corridors. **Pets:** Accepted.

Howard Johnson Express Inn H
(817) 461-1122. **$45-$148.** 2001 E Copeland Rd 76011. I-30 exit 30 (SR 360) westbound, just s to Six Flags Dr, just w to Copeland Rd, then 0.9 mi w; exit 29 (Ball Pkwy) eastbound. Int corridors. **Pets:** Medium. $25 daily fee/pet. Service with restrictions, supervision.

La Quinta Inn & Suites Dallas/Arlington 6 Flags Dr H
(817) 640-4142. **$98-$195.** 825 N Watson Rd 76011. SR 360 exit Six Flags Dr northbound; exit Ave H/Lamar Blvd southbound, on southbound frontage road. Int corridors. **Pets:** Medium, other species. Service with restrictions, supervision.

Microtel Inn H
(817) 557-8400. **$50-$71.** 1740 Oak Village Blvd 76017. I-20 exit 449B (Cooper St) westbound; exit 449A (Cooper St) eastbound, just s, just w. Int corridors. **Pets:** Other species. $15 daily fee/pet. Designated rooms, service with restrictions, supervision.

Sheraton Arlington Hotel H
(817) 261-8200. **$139-$429.** 1500 Convention Center Dr 76011. I-30 exit 29 (Ballpark Way), 0.4 mi e on Copeland Rd to Convention Center Dr, then just s. Int corridors. **Pets:** Accepted.

Sleep Inn Main Gate-Six Flags H
(817) 649-1010. **$59-$149.** 750 Six Flags Dr 76011. I-30 exit 30 (SR 360), 0.5 mi s. Int corridors. **Pets:** Medium, other species. $35 one-time fee/pet. Service with restrictions, supervision.

Studio 6-South Arlington #6036 H
(817) 465-8500. **$43-$63.** 1980 W Pleasant Ridge Rd 76015. I-20 exit 449 (Cooper St), 0.3 mi n, then just w. Ext corridors. **Pets:** Other species. $10 daily fee/room. Service with restrictions, supervision.

TownePlace Suites Arlington Near Six Flags H
(817) 861-8728. **$98-$123.** 1709 E Lamar Blvd 76006. 2 mi w of SR 360. Int corridors. **Pets:** Accepted.

AUSTIN

Aloft Austin at the Domain H
(512) 491-0777. **$119-$259.** 11601 Domain Dr 78758. Loop 1 (Mo-Pac Expwy) exit Burnett/Duval Rd, just e; in The Domain. Int corridors. **Pets:** Accepted.

Best Western Atrium North H
(512) 339-7311. **$99-$139.** 7928 Gessner Dr 78753. I-35 exit 240A, 0.4 mi w on US 183. Int corridors. **Pets:** Accepted.

Best Western Plus Austin Airport Inn & Suites H
(512) 386-5455. **$99-$219.** 1805 Airport Commerce Dr 78741. Jct SR 71 (E Ben White Blvd) and Riverside Dr, just n; in Airport Commerce Park. Int corridors. **Pets:** Medium. $20 daily fee/room. Service with restrictions.

Candlewood Suites Austin Northwest H
(512) 338-1611. **$109-$135.** 9701 Stonelake Blvd 78759. Jct SR 360 (Capital of Texas Hwy) and Stonelake Blvd, just s. Int corridors. **Pets:** Accepted.

Candlewood Suites-South H
(512) 444-8882. **$109-$159.** 4320 S I-35 78745. I-35 exit 230 northbound; exit 230B (Ben White Blvd/SR 71) southbound, on southbound frontage road. Int corridors. **Pets:** Medium. $15 daily fee/room. Service with restrictions, crate.

Clarion Inn & Suites Conference Center H
(512) 444-0561. **$99-$199.** 2200 S I-35 78704. I-35 exit 232A (Oltorf Blvd), on west side access road. Ext/int corridors. **Pets:** Accepted.

Comfort Suites Airport H
(512) 386-6000. **$109.** 7501 E Ben White Blvd 78741. I-35 exit 230B (Ben White Blvd/SR 71), 3.6 mi e. Int corridors. **Pets:** Medium. $50 one-time fee/pet. Service with restrictions, crate.

Crossland Studios Austin West H ✿
(512) 331-4747. **$34-$49.** 12621 Hymeadow Rd 78729. US 183 N exit Lake Creek Pkwy, just n, then just e. Ext corridors. **Pets:** Other species. $25 daily fee/pet. Service with restrictions.

DoubleTree Suites by Hilton Hotel Austin H
(512) 478-7000. **$179-$349.** 303 W 15th St 78701. Just nw of state capitol building. Int corridors. **Pets:** Accepted.

The Driskill H
(512) 474-5911. **$189-$999, 3 day notice.** 604 Brazos St 78701. Jct 6th St. Int corridors. **Pets:** Accepted.

Drury Inn & Suites-Austin North H
(512) 467-9500. **$104-$174.** 6711 I-35 N 78752. I-35 exit 238A, on east frontage road. Int corridors. **Pets:** Accepted.

Econo Lodge H
(512) 835-7070. **$69-$170.** 9102 Burnet Rd 78758. US 183 and Burnet Rd; on northeast corner. Ext corridors. **Pets:** Accepted.

Embassy Suites Austin North H
(512) 454-8004. **$99-$159.** 5901 I-35 N 78723. I-35 exit 238A, on east frontage road. Int corridors. **Pets:** Accepted.

Extended StayAmerica Austin Arboretum H ✿
(512) 231-1520. **$69-$89.** 10100 Capital of Texas Hwy 78759. Jct Loop 1 (Mo-Pac Expwy) and Capital of Texas Hwy (SR 360), just w. Int corridors. **Pets:** Other species. $25 daily fee/pet. Service with restrictions.

Extended StayAmerica Austin Northwest Lakeline Mall H ✿
(512) 258-3365. **$54-$69.** 13858 US Hwy 183 N 78750. Jct US 183 and SR 620; on southwest corner. Int corridors. **Pets:** Other species. $25 daily fee/pet. Service with restrictions.

▼▼ ▼▼ **Extended StayAmerica Austin Southwest** 🅷 ❀
(512) 892-4272. **$65-$79.** 5100 US Hwy 290 W 78735. I-35 exit 230, US 290 W exit Brodie Ln, then 1 mi w. Int corridors. **Pets:** Other species. $25 daily fee/pet. Service with restrictions. 📶 ⓜ 🅗 💻 🐾

▼▼▼▼ **Extended StayAmerica Deluxe Austin-North Central** 🅷 ❀
(512) 339-6005. **$54-$69.** 8221 N I-35 78753. I-35 exit 241, on east frontage road. Int corridors. **Pets:** Other species. $25 daily fee/pet. Service with restrictions. 📶 🅗 💻 🐾

▼▼▼ **Extended Stay Deluxe Austin-Arboretum-North** 🅷 ❀
(512) 833-0898. **$69-$84.** 2700 Gracy Farms Ln 78758. 2 mi n of US 183 on Loop 1 (Mo-Pac Expwy) exit Burnet Rd. Int corridors. **Pets:** Other species. $25 daily fee/pet. Service with restrictions. 📶 🅗 💻 🐾

▼▼ **Extended Stay Deluxe Austin Metro** 🅷 ❀
(512) 452-0880. **$54-$69.** 6300 US Hwy 290 E 78723. Jct I-35 and US 290 E. Int corridors. **Pets:** Other species. $25 daily fee/pet. Service with restrictions. 📶 🅗 💻 🐾

▼▼ **Extended Stay Deluxe (Austin/Northwest/Research Park)** 🅷 ❀
(512) 219-6500. **$66-$79.** 12424 Research Blvd 78759. US 183 exit Oak Knoll Dr, on eastbound frontage road. Int corridors. **Pets:** Other species. $25 daily fee/pet. Service with restrictions. 📶 ⓜ 🅗 💻 🐾

▼▼▼▼ **Fairfield Inn & Suites Austin NW** 🅷
(512) 527-0734. **$74-$149.** 11201 N Mo-Pac Expwy 78759. US 183 N, 1.5 mi n on Loop 1 (Mo-Pac Expwy) exit Braker Ln, on east frontage road. Int corridors. **Pets:** Accepted. 📶 ✕ ⓜ 🅗 💻 🐾 ✕

🆔 ▼▼▼▼ **Four Seasons Hotel** 🅷
(512) 478-4500. **$445-$2600.** 98 San Jacinto Blvd 78701. Bordering lake. Int corridors. **Pets:** Accepted. SAVE 📶 ✕ 🅗 💻 🍴 🐾 ✕

▼▼▼▼ **Hampton Inn Northwest** 🅷
(512) 349-9898. **$129-$179.** 3908 W Braker Ln 78759. 1 mi n of US 183 on Loop 1 (Mo-Pac Expwy) exit W Braker Ln. Int corridors. **Pets:** Accepted. 📶 ⓜ 💻 🐾

🆔 ▼▼▼▼ **Hilton Austin** 🅷 ❀
(512) 482-8000. **$125-$369.** 500 E 4th St 78701. Jct 4th and Neches sts. Int corridors. **Pets:** Medium, other species. $50 one-time fee/room. Service with restrictions, supervision.
SAVE 📶 ⓜ 🅗 💻 🍴 🐾 ✕

▼▼▼▼ **Hilton Austin Airport** 🅷
(512) 385-6767. **Call for rates.** 9515 Hotel Dr 78719. SR 71, service road exit at airport. Int corridors. **Pets:** Accepted.
ECO SAVE 📶 ✕ ⓜ 🅗 💻 🍴 🐾

▼▼▼ **Holiday Inn Express** 🅷
(512) 386-7600. **$109-$500.** 7601 E Ben White Blvd 78741. I-35 exit 230B (Ben White Blvd/SR 71), 3.2 mi e. Int corridors. **Pets:** Accepted.
📶 ⓜ 🅗 💻 🐾

▼▼▼ **Holiday Inn Express Hotel & Suites** 🅷
(512) 251-9110. **$100-$140.** 14620 N I-35 78728. I-35 exit 247, on west frontage road. Int corridors. **Pets:** Accepted. 📶 ⓜ 🅗 💻 🐾

▼▼ **Homestead Studio Suites Hotel-Austin/Arboretum-South** 🅷 ❀
(512) 837-6677. **$49-$59.** 9100 Waterford Centre Blvd 78758. US 183 exit Burnet Rd, on westbound frontage road. Ext corridors. **Pets:** Other species. $25 daily fee/pet. Service with restrictions. 📶 🅗 💻

▼▼▼▼ **Homestead Studio Suites Hotel-Austin/Downtown/Town Lake** 🅷 ❀
(512) 476-1818. **$74-$99.** 507 S 1st St 78704. I-35 exit 234B southbound; exit 234A northbound, 1.8 mi w on Cesar Chavez/E 1st St, then 0.5 mi s. Int corridors. **Pets:** Other species. $25 daily fee/pet. Service with restrictions. 📶 🅗 💻

▼▼▼▼ **Homewood Suites-Austin South** 🅷
(512) 445-5050. **$139-$169.** 4143 Governor's Row 78744. I-35 exit 231 (Ben White Blvd/SR 71) southbound; exit 229 northbound, at Ben White Blvd. Int corridors. **Pets:** Small, other species. $75 one-time fee/room. Service with restrictions, crate. 📶 ⓜ 🅗 💻 🐾

▼▼▼▼ **Homewood Suites by Hilton Arboretum NW** 🅷
(512) 349-9966. **$129-$209.** 10925 Stonelake Blvd 78759. US 183 N to Loop 1 (Mo-Pac Expwy), 1.5 mi n to Braker Ln; on northwest corner. Int corridors. **Pets:** Medium. Service with restrictions.
📶 ⓜ 🅗 💻 🐾 ✕

▼▼▼▼ **Hotel Allandale** 🅷
(512) 452-9391. **$139-$149.** 7685 Northcross Dr 78757. Loop 1 (Mo-Pac Expwy) exit Anderson Rd, just e to Northcross Dr, then just s. Ext corridors. **Pets:** Dogs only. $50 one-time fee/room. Designated rooms, service with restrictions, crate. 📶 🅗 💻 🐾

▼▼▼▼ **Hotel Saint Cecelia** 🅷
(512) 852-2400. **Call for rates.** 112 Academy Dr 78704. Jct S Congress Ave and Riverside Dr, 2 blks s. Ext corridors. **Pets:** Accepted.
📶 ✕ 🅗 🐾

▼▼ **Howard Johnson** 🅷
(512) 462-9201. **$58-$99.** 2711 I-35 S 78741. I-35 exit 231 (Woodward Ave) southbound; exit 232A (Oltorf St) northbound, on northbound frontage road; just n of jct I-35 and US 290/SR 71. Int corridors.
Pets: Accepted. 📶 🅗 💻 🐾

🆔 ▼▼▼▼ **Hyatt Summerfield Suites Austin/Arboretum** 🅷
(512) 342-8080. **$89-$229.** 10001 N Capital of Texas Hwy 78759. US 183, N Capital of Texas Hwy (SR 360), just e. Int corridors.
Pets: Accepted. SAVE 📶 🅗 💻 🐾

🆔 ▼▼▼▼ **Hyatt Regency Austin** 🅷
(512) 477-1234. **$99-$399.** 208 Barton Springs Rd 78704. At south end of Congress Avenue Bridge; on south bank of Town Lake. Int corridors.
Pets: Accepted. ECO SAVE 📶 ✕ 🅗 💻 🍴 🐾 ✕

🆔 ▼▼▼▼ **Hyatt Regency Lost Pines Resort and Spa** 🅷
(512) 308-1234. **$129-$499, 3 day notice.** 575 Hyatt Lost Pines Rd 78612. SR 71, 13 mi e of Austin-Bergstrom International Airport; 9 mi w of Bastrop. Int corridors. **Pets:** Accepted.
ECO SAVE 📶 ✕ ⓜ 🅗 💻 🍴 🐾 ✕

▼▼▼▼ **La Quinta Inn & Suites Austin Airport** 🅷
(512) 386-6800. **$121-$203.** 7625 E Ben White Blvd 78741. I-35 exit 230B (Ben White Blvd/SR 71), 8.8 mi e. Int corridors. **Pets:** Medium, other species. Service with restrictions, supervision.
📶 ⓜ 🅗 💻 🐾

🆔 ▼▼▼ **La Quinta Inn & Suites-Austin/Cedar Park-Lakeline** 🅷
(512) 568-3538. **$84-$154.** 10701 Lakeline Mall Dr 78717. Jct US 183 and Lakeline Dr, 0.5 mi e, then just s on Lake Creek Dr. Int corridors. **Pets:** Medium, other species. Service with restrictions, supervision.
SAVE 📶 ✕ 🅗 💻 🐾

▼▼▼▼ **La Quinta Inn & Suites Austin Mopac North** 🅷
(512) 832-2121. **$94-$177.** 11901 N Mo-Pac Expwy 78759. US 183, 2 mi n on Loop 1 (Mo-Pac Expwy) exit Duval Rd. Int corridors. **Pets:** Medium, other species. Service with restrictions, supervision. 📶 ⓜ 🅗 💻 🐾

▼▼▼ **La Quinta Inn & Suites Austin Southwest at Mopac** 🅷
(512) 899-3000. **$134-$207.** 4424 S Loop 1 (Mo-Pac Expwy) 78735. Jct Loop 1 (Mo-Pac Expwy), US 290 and SR 71 E, on southbound frontage road. Int corridors. **Pets:** Medium, other species. Service with restrictions, supervision. 📶 ⓜ 🅗 💻 🐾

▼▼▼ **La Quinta Inn & Suites Round Rock South** 🅷
(512) 246-2800. **$84-$148.** 150 Parker Dr 78728. I-35 exit 250, on west frontage road. Int corridors. **Pets:** Medium, other species. Service with restrictions, supervision. 📶 ⓜ 🅗 💻 🐾

▼▼▼▼ **La Quinta Inn Austin Capitol** H
(512) 476-1166. **$127-$203.** 300 E 11 St 78701. Just e of state capitol building. Ext/int corridors. **Pets:** Medium, other species. Service with restrictions, supervision. 🛜 🛗 💻 🏊

▼▼▼▼ **La Quinta Inn Austin Highland Mall** H
(512) 459-4381. **$78-$144.** 5812 I-35 N 78751. I-35 exit 238A, on west frontage road. Ext corridors. **Pets:** Medium, other species. Service with restrictions, supervision. 🛜 🛗 💻 🏊

🅐🅐🅐 ▼▼▼▼ **La Quinta Inn Austin North** H
(512) 467-1701. **$98-$159.** 7622 N I-35 & 183 78752. I-35 exit 240A, on west frontage road. Int corridors. **Pets:** Medium, other species. Service with restrictions, supervision. SAVE 🛜 🛗 💻 🏊

▼▼▼▼ **La Quinta Inn Austin Oltorf** H
(512) 447-6661. **$94-$159.** 1603 E Oltorf Blvd 78741. I-35 exit 232A (Oltorf Blvd), just s. Ext/int corridors. **Pets:** Medium, other species. Service with restrictions, supervision. 🛜 🛗 💻 🏊

▼▼▼▼ **La Quinta Inn Austin South/Ih35** H
(512) 443-1774. **$84-$148.** 4200 I-35 S 78745-1202. I-35 exit 231 (St. Edwards Dr/Woodward St) southbound; exit 230 northbound, just s of jct I-35, US 290 and SR 71, on frontage road. Ext corridors. **Pets:** Medium, other species. Service with restrictions, supervision.
🛜 🛗 🛗 💻 🏊

🅐🅐🅐 ▼▼▼▼ **Mansion at Judges' Hill** H 🐾
(512) 495-1800. **$139-$599, 3 day notice.** 1900 Rio Grande St 78705. Jct Rio Grande St and Martin Luther King Jr Blvd. Int corridors. **Pets:** Other species. $50 one-time fee/room. Service with restrictions, supervision. SAVE 🛜 🍴

🅐🅐🅐 ▼▼▼▼ **Omni Austin Hotel & Suites** H 🐾
(512) 476-3700. **$169-$599.** 700 San Jacinto Blvd 78701. 8th St and San Jacinto Blvd. Int corridors. **Pets:** Small. $50 one-time fee/room. Service with restrictions, crate. SAVE 🛜 🛗 🛗 💻 🍴 🏊 ✖

🅐🅐🅐 ▼▼▼▼ **Omni Austin Hotel Southpark** H 🐾
(512) 448-2222. **$109-$499.** 4140 Governor's Row 78744. I-35 exit 230B (Ben White Blvd/SR 71) southbound, on east frontage road. Int corridors. **Pets:** Small. $50 one-time fee/room. Designated rooms, service with restrictions, supervision.
SAVE 🛜 🛗 🛗 💻 🍴 🏊 ✖

🅐🅐🅐 ▼▼▼▼ **Renaissance Austin Hotel** H
(512) 343-2626. **$161-$229.** 9721 Arboretum Blvd 78759. Jct US 183 and Capital of Texas Hwy (SR 360); southwest corner. Int corridors.
Pets: Accepted. SAVE 🛜 ✖ 🛗 🛗 💻 🍴 🏊 ✖

▼▼▼▼ **Residence Inn by Marriott Austin Airport/South** H
(512) 912-1100. **$110-$200.** 4537 S I-35 78744. I-35 exit 229 (Stassney Rd) southbound; exit 230 (Ben White Blvd/SR 71) northbound, on northbound frontage road. Int corridors. **Pets:** Accepted.
🛜 ✖ 🛗 💻 🏊 ✖

▼▼▼▼ **Residence Inn by Marriott Austin/Downtown/Convention Center** H
(512) 472-5553. **$130-$320.** 300 E 4th St 78701. Between Trinity St and San Jacinto Blvd. Int corridors. **Pets:** Accepted.
🛜 ✖ 🛗 💻 🍴 🏊

▼▼▼ **Residence Inn by Marriott-Austin North/Parmer Lane** H
(512) 977-0544. **$98-$200.** 12401 N Lamar Blvd 78753. I-35 exit 245, just w. Int corridors. **Pets:** Accepted.
🛜 ✖ 🛗 🛗 💻 🏊 ✖

▼▼▼ **Staybridge Suites Austin Airport** H
(512) 389-9767. **$126-$136.** 1611 Airport Commerce Dr 78741. Jct SR 71 (E Ben White Blvd) and Riverside Dr, just n; in Airport Commerce Park. Int corridors. **Pets:** Accepted. 🛜 🛗 🛗 💻 🏊

▼▼▼ **Staybridge Suites Austin Arboretum** H
(512) 349-0888. **$169-$199.** 10201 Stonelake Blvd 78759. Jct Capital of Texas Hwy (SR 360) and Stonelake Blvd, 1 blk n. Int corridors.
Pets: Accepted. 🛜 🛗 🛗 💻 🏊 ✖

▼▼▼ **Staybridge Suites Austin Northwest** H
(512) 336-7829. **$99-$179.** 13087 Hwy 183 N, Lot 3 78750. US 183 N exit Anderson Mill Rd, just n of exit on east frontage road and s of Anderson Mill Rd. Int corridors. **Pets:** Medium. $75 one-time fee/pet. Service with restrictions, crate. 🛜 🛗 🛗 💻 🏊

▼▼▼ **Studio 6-Northwest #6032** M
(512) 258-3556. **$43-$63.** 11901 Pavilion Blvd 78759. US 183 exit Oak Knoll Dr westbound; exit Duval Rd/Balcones Woods Dr eastbound, on eastbound frontage road. Ext corridors. **Pets:** Other species. $10 daily fee/room. Service with restrictions, supervision. 🛜 🛗 💻

🅐🅐🅐 ▼▼▼ **Super 8 Austin North** H
(512) 339-1300. **$45-$170.** 8128 N I-35 78753. I-35 exit 241, on west frontage road. Int corridors. **Pets:** $25 one-time fee/pet. Designated rooms, service with restrictions, supervision. SAVE 🛜 🛗 🛗 💻 🏊

▼▼▼ **Super 8 University Austin** H
(512) 451-7001. **$41-$117.** 5526 I-35 N 78751. I-35 exit 238A southbound; exit 238B northbound, on southbound frontage road. Ext corridors.
Pets: Accepted. 🛜 🛗 💻

🅐🅐🅐 ▼▼▼▼ **Westin Austin at the Domain** H 🐾
(512) 832-4197. **$139-$329.** 11301 Domain Dr 78758. Jct Braker and Burnet rds; on northwest corner; in The Domain. Int corridors.
Pets: Medium, dogs only. Designated rooms, service with restrictions, supervision. SAVE 🛜 ✖ 🛗 🛗 💻 🍴 🏊

▼▼▼ **Wyndham Garden Hotel** H 🐾
(512) 448-2444. **$99-$189.** 3401 I-35 S 78741. I-35 exit 231 (Woodward St) southbound; exit 230 (Ben White Blvd/SR 71) northbound; on northbound frontage road. Ext/int corridors. **Pets:** $35 one-time fee/room. Designated rooms, service with restrictions.
🛜 🛗 🛗 💻 🍴 🏊 ✖

BASTROP

▼▼ **Days Inn Bastrop** H
(512) 321-1157. **$54-$135.** 4102 Hwy 71 E 78602. On SR 71, 2 mi e of river at Loop 150 E. Ext corridors. **Pets:** Small. $25 daily fee/pet. Service with restrictions, crate. 🛜 🛗 💻 🏊

▼▼ **Quality Inn** H
(512) 321-3303. **$49-$295.** 106 Hasler Blvd 78602. Jct SR 71 and Hasler Blvd. Int corridors. **Pets:** Medium, dogs only. $20 daily fee/pet. Designated rooms, service with restrictions, crate. 🛜 🛗 🛗 💻 🏊

BAY CITY

🅐🅐🅐 ▼▼▼ **Best Western Matagorda Hotel & Conference Center** H
(979) 244-5400. **$89-$110.** 407 7th St 77414. SR 35 (7th St), 1 mi s of jct SR 35 (7th St) and 60. Ext corridors. **Pets:** Accepted.
SAVE 🛜 🛗 💻 🏊

▼▼▼ **Comfort Suites** H
(979) 245-9300. **$85-$129.** 5100 7th St 77414. SR 35 (7th St), 2.2 mi e. Int corridors. **Pets:** Accepted. 🛜 ✖ 🛗 💻 🏊

▼▼▼ **La Quinta Inn & Suites Bay City** H
(979) 323-9095. **$94-$155.** 5300 7th St 77414. On SR 35 (7th St), 3 mi e of downtown. Int corridors. **Pets:** Medium, other species. Service with restrictions, supervision. 🛜 ✖ 🛗 🛗 💻 🏊

BEAUMONT

🅐🅐🅐 ▼▼▼ **Best Western Jefferson Inn** H 🐾
(409) 842-0037. **$59-$89.** 1610 I-10 S 77707. I-10 exit 851 (College St), westbound frontage road; 0.5 mi s of jct US 90. Ext corridors.
Pets: Medium. $25 one-time fee/room. Service with restrictions, crate.
SAVE 🛜 🛗 💻 🏊

AAA ▼◆ Days Inn H ❀
(409) 898-8150. **Call for rates.** 2155 N 11th St 77703. I-10 exit 853B (11th St), just n. Ext corridors. **Pets:** Medium. $25 one-time fee/room. Service with restrictions, supervision. [SAVE] 🛜 🛏 🖵 ⅌

▼▼ Econo Lodge Inn & Suites M
(409) 835-8800. **$60-$70.** 50 I-10 N 77702. I-10 exit 852A westbound, on eastbound frontage road; exit 852B eastbound. Ext corridors.
Pets: Accepted. 🛜 ⅏ 🛏 🖵

▼◆▼◆ Holiday Inn Hotel & Suites Beaumont Plaza H
(409) 842-5995. **$99-$149.** 3950 I-10 S 77705. I-10 exit 848 (Walden Rd), just n. Int corridors. **Pets:** Medium, other species. $25 one-time fee/room. Service with restrictions, crate. 🛜 ✕ 🛏 🖵 🍴 ⅌

▼◆▼◆ Homewood Suites by Hilton H
(409) 842-9990. **$99-$179.** 3745 IH-10 S 77705. I-10 exit 848 (Walden Rd), on eastbound frontage road. Int corridors. **Pets:** Accepted.
🛜 ⅏ 🛏 🖵 ⅌

▼▼ Ramada Beaumont H
(409) 842-4420. **$62-$82.** 3985 College St 77707. I-10 exit 851A (College St), on westbound frontage road. Int corridors. **Pets:** Accepted.
🛜 🛏 🖵 ⅌

▼▼ Red Roof Inn & Suites - Beaumont H
(409) 842-8200. **$79-$150.** 2310 S I-10 77707. I-10 exit 850 (Washington Blvd) westbound; exit 851 (College St) eastbound. Int corridors.
Pets: Large, other species. No service, supervision. 🛜 🛏 🖵 ⅌

BEDFORD

▼▼ Extended Stay Deluxe Dallas-Bedford H ❀
(817) 354-5210. **$69-$99.** 1908 Forest Ridge Dr 76021. SR 183 exit Forest Ridge Dr, just n. Int corridors. **Pets:** Other species. $25 daily fee/pet. Service with restrictions. 🛜 🛏 🖵 ⅌

▼▼ Motel 6 H
(817) 545-2555. **$45-$110.** 2904 Crystal Springs St 76021. SR 121 exit Harwood Rd. Ext/int corridors. **Pets:** Other species. Service with restrictions, supervision. 🛜 ✕ 🛏 🖵

BEEVILLE

AAA ▼▼ Best Western Texan Inn H
(361) 358-9999. **$105.** 2001 Hwy 59 78102. US 181 at US 59, just e. Ext/int corridors. **Pets:** Accepted. [SAVE] 🛜 🛏 🖵 ⅌

▼▼ Motel 6 - Beeville #4296 H
(361) 358-4000. **Call for rates.** 400 S US 181 Bypass 78102. 0.3 mi s of jct US 59 and 181. Ext corridors. **Pets:** Other species. Service with restrictions, supervision. 🛜 🛏 ⅌

BELTON

AAA ▼▼ Budget Host Inn H ❀
(254) 939-0744. **$49-$75.** 1520 S I-35 76513. I-35 exit 292 southbound; exit 293A northbound. Ext corridors. **Pets:** Medium. $7 daily fee/pet. Service with restrictions, supervision. [SAVE] 🛜 🛏 🖵 ⅌

▼◆▼◆ La Quinta Inn & Suites Belton H
(254) 939-2772. **$84-$159.** 229 W Loop 121 76513. I-35 exit 292, just w. Int corridors. **Pets:** Medium, other species. Service with restrictions, supervision. 🛜 🛏 🖵 ⅌

BENBROOK

AAA ▼◆▼◆ Best Western Winscott Inn & Suites H
(817) 249-0076. **$100-$190.** 590 Winscott Rd 76126. I-20 exit 429B. Int corridors. **Pets:** Small. $10 daily fee/pet. Designated rooms, no service, supervision. [SAVE] 🛜 🛏 🖵 ⅌

AAA ▼◆▼◆ Comfort Suites H
(817) 249-8008. **Call for rates.** 8004 Winbrook Dr 76126. I-20 exit 429B, just n. Int corridors. **Pets:** Accepted. [SAVE] 🛜 ✕ 🛏 🖵 ⅌

◆ Motel 6 - 4051 H
(817) 249-8885. **$62-$74.** 8601 Benbrook Blvd (Hwy 377 S) 76126. I-20 exit 429A, 0.7 mi s. Int corridors. **Pets:** Other species. Service with restrictions, supervision. ⅏ 🛏 ⅌

BIG SPRING

▼◆▼◆ Holiday Inn Express H
(432) 263-5400. **Call for rates.** 1109 N Aylesford St 79720. I-20 exit 177, on eastbound frontage road. Int corridors. **Pets:** Accepted.
🛜 ⅏ 🛏 🖵 ⅌

▼◆▼◆ La Quinta Inns & Suites Big Spring H
(432) 264-0222. **$78-$164.** 1102 I-20 W 79720. I-20 exit 177, on N Frontage Rd. Int corridors. **Pets:** Medium, other species. Service with restrictions, supervision. 🛜 ✕ ⅏ 🛏 🖵 ⅌

BOERNE

AAA ▼▼ Americas Best Value Inn M
(830) 249-9791. **$69-$103.** 35150 I-10 W 78006. I-10 exit 540 (SR 46), westbound access road. Ext corridors. **Pets:** Medium. $20 one-time fee/pet. Service with restrictions, crate. [SAVE] 🛜 🛏 🖵 ⅌

▼▼▼ Comfort Inn & Suites H
(830) 249-6800. **Call for rates.** 35000 I-10 W 78006. I-10 exit 540 (SR 46), just e to Norris Ln, then just s. Int corridors. **Pets:** Small, other species. $25 one-time fee/room. Service with restrictions, crate.
🛜 🛏 🖵 ⅌

▼▼▼ La Quinta Inn & Suites Boerne H
(830) 249-1212. **$71-$189.** 36756 IH-10 W 78006. I-10 exit 539 (Johns Rd), exit 540 (Bandera Rd) eastbound, U-turn back; on westbound access road. Int corridors. **Pets:** Medium, other species. Service with restrictions, supervision. 🛜 ✕ ⅏ 🛏 🖵 ⅌

▼ Spinelli Country Inn M
(830) 249-9563. **Call for rates.** 911 S Main St 78006. I-10 exit 542 (US 87/Main St), 1.5 mi n. Ext corridors. **Pets:** Accepted.
🛜 ✕ 🍴 🏷

BONHAM

AAA ▼▼▼ Americas Best Value Inn M
(903) 583-3121. **$51-$67.** 1515 Old Ector Rd 75418. Jct SR 56 W and 121 S. Ext corridors. **Pets:** Medium. $15 one-time fee/room. Designated rooms, service with restrictions, supervision. [SAVE] 🛜 🛏 🖵 ⅌

BORGER

AAA ▼▼▼ Best Western Plus Borger Inn H
(806) 274-7050. **$80-$110.** 206 S Cedar St 79007. Jct SR 136 and 207, just n. Int corridors. **Pets:** Other species. $15 one-time fee/pet. Designated rooms, service with restrictions, supervision.
[SAVE] 🛜 🛏 🖵 ⅌

BOWIE

AAA ▼◆▼◆ Best Western Bowie Inn & Suites H
(940) 872-9595. **$80-$90.** 900 W US Hwy 287 S 76230. Jct SR 59. Int corridors. **Pets:** Medium. $15 one-time fee/pet. Service with restrictions, supervision. [SAVE] 🛜 ✕ 🛏 🖵 ⅌

AAA ▼ Park's Inn M
(940) 872-1111. **$60-$70.** 708 W Wise St 76230. 0.5 mi n of jct SR 59; downtown. Ext corridors. **Pets:** Small. $5 daily fee/pet. Service with restrictions, supervision. [SAVE] 🛜 🛏 ⅌

BRADY

AAA ▼▼ Best Western Brady Inn H
(325) 597-3997. **$77-$85.** 2200 S Bridge St 76825. 1.1 mi s on US 87/377. Ext corridors. **Pets:** Small. $5 daily fee/pet. Service with restrictions, supervision. [SAVE] 🛜 🛏 🖵 ⅌

Days Inn M
(325) 597-0789. **$58-$90.** 2108 S Bridge St 76825. 1 mi s on US 87/377 at US 190. Ext corridors. **Pets:** Small. $5 daily fee/pet. Service with restrictions, supervision. [SAVE] [icons]

BRENHAM

Best Western Plus Inn of Brenham H ❀
(979) 251-7791. **$80-$150.** 1503 Hwy 290 E 77833. Eastbound, 0.7 mi w of jct US 290 E and SR 577; westbound, 1.3 mi e of jct SR 36 and US 290. Ext corridors. **Pets:** Large. $20 daily fee/pet. Service with restrictions, supervision. [SAVE] [icons]

Comfort Suites H ❀
(979) 421-8100. **$100-$110.** 2350 S Day St 77833. US 290 exit SR 36 S, just n on Business Rt SR 36. Int corridors. **Pets:** Medium. $20 daily fee/pet. Service with restrictions, supervision.
[SAVE] [icons]

La Quinta Inn & Suites Brenham H
(979) 836-5551. **$107-$189.** 2950 Woodridge Blvd 77833. Jct US 290 and SR 36, just s. Int corridors. **Pets:** Medium, other species. Service with restrictions, supervision. [icons]

BRIDGEPORT

Comfort Suites H
(940) 683-5777. **$75-$90.** 2302 10th St 76426. 0.6 mi e of jct US 380 and SR 114. Int corridors. **Pets:** Accepted. [icons]

BROWNFIELD

Best Western Caprock Inn H
(806) 637-9471. **$86-$100, 3 day notice.** 321 Lubbock Rd 79316. Jct US 385 and 82, 2 blks n. Ext corridors. **Pets:** Accepted.
[SAVE] [icons]

BROWNSVILLE

Holiday Inn H
(956) 547-1500. **$77-$85.** 3777 N Expwy 78520. US 77 and 83 exit Ruben Torres Sr Blvd (FM 802), on southbound frontage road. Int corridors. **Pets:** Small. $100 one-time fee/pet. Designated rooms, crate.
[SAVE] [icons]

Homewood Suites by Hilton H
(956) 574-6900. **$99-$139.** 3759 N Expwy 78520. US 77 and 83 exit Ruben Torres Sr Blvd (FM 802); on southbound frontage road. Int corridors. **Pets:** Small. $75 one-time fee/pet. Service with restrictions, crate.
[SAVE] [icons]

Staybridge Suites H
(956) 504-9500. **$99-$159, 3 day notice.** 2900 Pablo Kisel Blvd 78526. US 77 and 83 exit Ruben Torres Sr Blvd (FM 802), 0.8 mi n on frontage road to Pablo Kisel Blvd, then 0.5 mi e. Int corridors. **Pets:** Accepted.
[icons]

BROWNWOOD

La Quinta Inn and Suites H
(325) 641-1731. **$116-$179.** 103 Market Place Blvd 76801. US 183, just e. Int corridors. **Pets:** Medium, other species. Service with restrictions, supervision. [icons]

BUFFALO

Craigs Inn Buffalo H
(903) 322-5831. **$75-$90.** IH-45 & US 79 75831. I-45 exit 178, just n on NW Frontage Rd. Ext/int corridors. **Pets:** Accepted. [icons]

BURKBURNETT

Burkburnett Hampton Inn H
(940) 569-8109. **$89-$125.** 1008 Sheppard Rd 76354. I-44 exit 12, just e. Int corridors. **Pets:** $30 one-time fee/room. Service with restrictions, supervision. [icons]

BURLESON

Best Western Plus Burleson Inn & Suites H
(817) 744-7747. **$80-$100, 3 day notice.** 516 Memorial Plaza 76028. I-35W exit 36 northbound; exit 35 southbound, on northbound access road. Int corridors. **Pets:** Accepted. [SAVE] [icons]

Comfort Suites H
(817) 426-6666. **$70-$140.** 321 S Burleson Blvd 76028. I-35W exit 34 southbound, 2 mi s to crossover, U-turn; exit 36 northbound, on northbound access road. Int corridors. **Pets:** Medium. $30 daily fee/pet. Service with restrictions, supervision. [SAVE] [icons]

La Quinta Inn & Suites H
(817) 447-6565. **$85-$145.** 225 E Alsbury Blvd 76028. I-35E exit 38 (E Alsbury Blvd), just e. Int corridors. **Pets:** Medium, other species. Service with restrictions, supervision. [icons]

BURNET

Best Western Post Oak Inn M
(512) 756-4747. **$70-$115.** 908 Buchanan Dr 78611. Jct US 281 and FM 29, 1 mi w. Ext corridors. **Pets:** Accepted. [SAVE] [icons]

Log Country Cove VH
(512) 756-9132. **Call for rates.** 617 Log Country Cove 78611. Jct FM 1431 and 2342, 2 mi n; Park Rd 4 and FM 2342, 3 mi s. Ext corridors. **Pets:** Accepted. [icons]

CAMERON

Budget Host Inn & Suites H
(254) 605-0610. **$89-$200.** 102 Lafferty Ave 76520. US 77/190, 0.5 mi s. Int corridors. **Pets:** Medium. $15 daily fee/pet. Designated rooms, no service, supervision. [SAVE] [icons]

CANTON

Best Western Canton Inn H
(903) 567-6591. **$80-$170, 3 day notice.** 2251 N Trade Days Blvd 75103. Jct I-20 and SR 19 exit 527. Ext corridors. **Pets:** Other species. $5 daily fee/pet. Service with restrictions, supervision.
[SAVE] [icons]

Quality Inn & Suites H
(903) 567-0909. **Call for rates.** 2406 N Trade Days Blvd 75103. I-20 exit 527, just n. Ext corridors. **Pets:** Accepted. [icons]

Super 8 H
(903) 567-6567. **$45-$104.** 17350 I-20 75103. I-20 exit 527. Ext corridors. **Pets:** Accepted. [icons]

CANYON

Best Western Palo Duro Canyon Inn & Suites H
(806) 655-1818. **$100-$111.** 2801 4th Ave 79015. I-27 exit 106, 1 mi w. Int corridors. **Pets:** Medium, dogs only. $15 one-time fee/pet. Service with restrictions, supervision. [SAVE] [icons]

Holiday Inn Express Hotel & Suites H
(806) 655-4445. **$99-$149.** 2901 4th Ave 79015. I-27 exit 106, 2 mi w. Int corridors. **Pets:** Other species. $25 one-time fee/pet. Service with restrictions, supervision. [SAVE] [icons]

CARTHAGE

Baymont Inn & Suites H
(903) 694-9075. **$103-$144, 3 day notice.** 2313 SE Loop 75633. Just n of jct E US 59 Loop and SR 699. Int corridors. **Pets:** Small. $25 one-time fee/pet. Designated rooms, service with restrictions, supervision.

CEDAR PARK

▽▽▽▽ Candlewood Suites 🅷 ❀
(512) 610-5700. **$79-$149.** 1100 Cottonwood Creek Tr 78613. Jct US 183A and CR 1431, 1 mi e. Int corridors. **Pets:** Medium. $75 one-time fee/pet. Service with restrictions, crate. 🛜 🅼 📶 💻

🅰🅰🅰 ▽▽ Comfort Inn 🅷
(512) 259-1810. **Call for rates.** 300 E Whitestone Blvd 78613. Jct US 183 and CR 1431, just e. Int corridors. **Pets:** Other species. $10 daily fee/pet. Service with restrictions, supervision.
SAVE 🛜 🅼 📶 💻 🏊

▽▽▽▽ La Quinta Inn & Suites Austin - Cedar Park 🅷
(512) 528-9300. **$116-$179.** 1010 E Whitestone Blvd 78613. Jct US 183A and CR 1431, on southwest corner. Int corridors. **Pets:** Medium, other species. Service with restrictions, supervision.
🛜 🅼 📶 💻 🏊

CHILDRESS

🅰🅰🅰 ▽▽ Best Western Childress 🅷
(940) 937-6353. **$90.** 1801 Ave F NW (Hwy 287) 79201. On US 287, just s of jct US 62/83. Ext corridors. **Pets:** Accepted.
SAVE 🛜 📶 💻 🏊

🅰🅰🅰 ▽▽ Comfort Inn 🅷 🐾
(940) 937-6363. **$69-$99.** 1804 Ave F NW (Hwy 287) 79201. On US 287, just s of jct US 62/83. Ext corridors. **Pets:** Medium, other species. $10 daily fee/pet. Service with restrictions, supervision.
SAVE 🛜 🅼 📶 💻 🏊 ❌

▽▽▽ Hampton Inn & Suites 🅷
(940) 937-3500. **$95-$99.** 400 Madison Ave 79201. Jct US 298/83/62, just w. Int corridors. **Pets:** Accepted. 🛜 ❌ 🅼 📶 💻 🏊

▽ Rodeway Inn 🅷
(940) 937-3695. **Call for rates.** 1612 Ave F NW 79201. On US 287, just s of jct US 62/83. Ext corridors. **Pets:** Accepted. 🛜 📶 💻

🅰🅰🅰 ▽▽ Super 8 Childress 🅼
(940) 937-8825. **$50-$100.** 411 Ave F NE (Hwy 287 S) 79201. Jct US 83/287, 1.5 mi e. Ext corridors. **Pets:** Other species. $13 daily fee/pet. Service with restrictions, crate. SAVE 🛜 📶 💻

CISCO

▽▽ Americas Best Value Inn 🅼
(254) 442-3735. **Call for rates.** 1898 Hwy 206 W 76437. I-20 exit 330, just n. Ext corridors. **Pets:** Accepted. 🛜 📶 💻 🏊

CLARENDON

🅰🅰🅰 ▽▽▽ Best Western Plus Red River Inn 🅷
(806) 874-0160. **$99-$109.** 902 W 2nd St 79226. Jct US 287 and SR 70. Int corridors. **Pets:** Accepted. SAVE 🛜 ❌ 🅼 📶 💻 🏊

🅰🅰🅰 ▽▽ Western Skies Motel 🅼
(806) 874-3501. **$45-$99.** 800 W 2nd St 79226. 0.5 mi nw on US 287 and SR 70. Ext corridors. **Pets:** $10 one-time fee/room. Service with restrictions, supervision. SAVE 📶

CLAUDE

🅰🅰🅰 ▽ L A Motel 🅼
(806) 226-4981. **$35-$65, 5 day notice.** 300 E 1st St 79019. 0.3 mi s. Ext corridors. **Pets:** Small. $5 one-time fee/room. No service, supervision.
SAVE 🛜 📶 💻

CLEAR LAKE CITY

▽▽ Candlewood Suites-Houston-Clear Lake 🅷
(281) 461-3060. **$99-$149.** 2737 Bay Area Blvd 77058. I-45 exit 26 (Bay Area Blvd), 3.7 mi e. Int corridors. **Pets:** Accepted. 🛜 📶 💻

▽▽▽▽ Residence Inn-Houston Clear Lake 🅷 ❀
(281) 486-2424. **$84-$139.** 525 Bay Area Blvd 77058. I-45 exit 26 (Bay Area Blvd) southbound, 1.2 mi e. Ext/int corridors. **Pets:** Other species. $100 one-time fee/room. Service with restrictions.
🛜 ❌ 📶 💻 🏊 ❌

CLEBURNE

▽▽▽ Budget Host Inn-Sagamar Inn 🅼
(817) 556-3631. **$65-$80.** 2107 N Main St 76033. US 67 exit SR 174, just e. Ext corridors. **Pets:** Small, dogs only. $15 daily fee/pet. Designated rooms, service with restrictions, supervision. 🛜 📶 💻

▽▽▽ Comfort Inn 🅷
(817) 641-4702. **$86-$149.** 2117 N Main St 76033. On SR 174, just s of jct US 67. Int corridors. **Pets:** Other species. $10 daily fee/pet. Designated rooms, service with restrictions. 🛜 🅼 📶 💻 🏊

🅰🅰🅰 ▽▽▽ Hampton Inn & Suites 🅷 ❀
(817) 641-7770. **$79-$109.** 1966 W Henderson St 76033. US 67, just e of US 67 S. Int corridors. **Pets:** Medium, other species. $25 one-time fee/pet. Service with restrictions, supervision.
SAVE 🛜 🅼 📶 💻 🏊

▽▽▽ La Quinta Inn & Suites Cleburne 🅷
(817) 641-4455. **$75-$144.** 107 E Kilpatrick Ave 76033. Just n of jct SR 171/174 and FM 4. Int corridors. **Pets:** Medium, other species. Service with restrictions, supervision. 🛜 🅼 📶 💻 🏊

CLUTE

🅰🅰🅰 ▽▽▽▽ Best Western Clute Inn & Suites 🅷
(979) 388-0055. **$83-$89.** 900 Hwy 332 77531. Just w of jct Business Rt SR 288. Int corridors. **Pets:** Small, dogs only. $15 daily fee/pet. Service with restrictions, supervision. SAVE 🛜 📶 💻 🏊

▽▽ La Quinta Inn Clute Lake Jackson 🅼
(979) 265-7461. **$62-$119.** 1126 Hwy 332 W 77531. On SR 288/332, just w of jct Business Rt SR 288. Ext corridors. **Pets:** Medium, other species. Service with restrictions, supervision. 🛜 📶 💻 🏊

COLLEGE STATION

▽▽ Econo Lodge 🅷
(979) 260-9150. **$60-$210.** 901 University Dr E 77840. Jct SR 6, 1 mi e. Ext corridors. **Pets:** Accepted. 🛜 🅼 📶 💻 🏊

▽▽ Hawthorn Suites 🅷
(979) 695-9500. **Call for rates.** 1010 University Dr E 77840. SR 6 exit University Dr, 0.5 mi w. Int corridors. **Pets:** Accepted.
🛜 🅼 📶 💻 🏊

▽▽▽ Hilton College Station & Conference Center 🅷
(979) 693-7500. **$89-$249.** 801 University Dr E 77840. SR 6 exit University Dr, 1.1 mi w. Int corridors. **Pets:** Accepted.
🛜 📶 🍽 🏊

▽▽▽ Holiday Inn Express Hotel & Suites 🅷
(979) 846-8700. **$124-$134.** 1203 University Dr E 77840. SR 6 exit University Dr, 1 mi w. Int corridors. **Pets:** Accepted.
🛜 🅼 📶 💻 🏊

🅰🅰🅰 ▽▽▽ Homewood Suites-College Station 🅷
(979) 846-0400. **$179-$279.** 950 University Dr E 77840. Jct SR 6 and 60 (Texas Ave), 1.5 mi e. Int corridors. **Pets:** Medium, other species. $100 one-time fee/room. Service with restrictions, crate.
SAVE 🛜 🅼 📶 💻 🏊 ❌

🅰🅰🅰 ▽▽▽ Howard Johnson Express 🅷
(979) 693-6810. **$54-$150.** 3702 Hwy 6 S 77845. SR 6 exit Rock Prairie Rd southbound. Ext corridors. **Pets:** Accepted. SAVE 🛜 📶 💻 🏊

▼▼▼▼ **La Quinta Inn College Station** 🅷
(979) 696-7777. **$88-$155.** 607 Texas Ave 77840. Just s on jct SR 60 and 6 business route to Live Oak St, then just e. Ext corridors. **Pets:** Medium, other species. Service with restrictions, supervision.
🛜 📠 🖥 🌊

▼▼▼ **Manor Inn College Station** 🅷
(979) 764-9540. **$55-$145, 14 day notice.** 2504 Texas Ave S 77840. 2.4 mi s of jct SR 60. Ext corridors. **Pets:** $40 one-time fee/pet. Designated rooms, service with restrictions, supervision. 🛜 📠 🖥 🌊

🅰🅰🅰 ▼▼▼ **Residence Inn by Marriott College Station** 🅷
(979) 268-2200. **$159-$169.** 720 University Dr E 77840. Jct Texas Ave, 0.5 mi e. Int corridors. **Pets:** Accepted.
(SAVE) 🛜 ✖ ♿ 📠 🖥 🌊 ✖

▼▼▼ **TownePlace Suites By Marriott** 🅷
(979) 260-8500. **$94-$188.** 1300 University Dr E 77840. SR 6 exit University Dr, 1 mi w. Ext corridors. **Pets:** Accepted.
(ECO) 🛜 ✖ 📠 🖥 🌊

COLUMBUS

▼▼▼▼ **Comfort Inn & Suites** 🅷
(979) 732-3785. **$89-$98, 4 day notice.** 2535 Hwy 71 S 78934. I-10 exit 696 (SR 71), just s. Int corridors. **Pets:** Accepted.
🛜 ✖ ♿ 📠 🖥 🌊

🅰🅰🅰 ▼▼▼ **Country Hearth Inn** 🅷
(979) 732-6293. **$78-$150.** 2436 Hwy 71 S 78934. I-10 exit 696 (SR 71). Ext corridors. **Pets:** Small, dogs only. $20 daily fee/pet. Designated rooms, service with restrictions, supervision. (SAVE) 🛜 📠 🖥 🌊

🅰🅰🅰 ▼▼▼▼ **Holiday Inn Express Hotel & Suites** 🅷
(979) 733-9300. **$99-$123.** 4321 I-10 78934. I-10 exit 696 (SR 71), just w on westbound service road. Int corridors. **Pets:** Other species. $25 daily fee/pet. Service with restrictions, supervision.
(SAVE) 🛜 ✖ 📠 🖥 🌊

CORPUS CHRISTI

🅰🅰🅰 ▼▼▼ **Best Western Marina Grand Hotel** 🅷
(361) 883-5111. **$119-$169.** 300 N Shoreline Blvd 78401. Center of downtown. Int corridors. **Pets:** Medium, dogs only. $25 daily fee/pet. Designated rooms, service with restrictions, crate. (SAVE) 🛜 📠 🖥 🌊

▼▼ **Budget Inn & Suites** 🅼
(361) 884-2485. **$60-$150.** 801 S Shoreline Blvd 78401. I-37 exit Shoreline Blvd, between Park and Furnan aves. Ext corridors. **Pets:** Small. $15 daily fee/pet. Designated rooms, service with restrictions, supervision.
🛜 📠 🖥 🌊

🅰🅰🅰 ▼▼▼ **Econo Lodge Inn & Suites** 🅷
(361) 883-7400. **$70-$100.** 722 N Port Ave 78408. I-37 exit 1D (Port Ave), on southbound access road. Ext corridors. **Pets:** Small. $150 deposit/room, $10 daily fee/pet. Service with restrictions, crate.
(SAVE) 🛜 📠 🖥 🌊

▼▼▼ **Extended Stay Deluxe - Corpus Christi-Staples** 🅷 🐾
(361) 991-1967. **$89-$129.** 6218 S Staples St 78413. SR 358 southbound exit S Staples St, 0.3 mi, then 1.5 mi s. Int corridors. **Pets:** Other species. $25 daily fee/pet. Service with restrictions. 🛜 📠 🖥 🌊

🅰🅰🅰 ▼▼▼ **Holiday Inn-Airport and Conference Center** 🅷
(361) 289-5100. **$99-$179.** 5549 Leopard St 78408. Jct SR 358 and Leopard St, 5.5 mi w. Int corridors. **Pets:** Accepted.
(SAVE) 🛜 📠 🖥 🍽 🌊

▼▼▼ **Holiday Inn-Emerald Beach** 🅷 🐾
(361) 883-5731. **$125-$199.** 1102 S Shoreline Blvd 78401. 1.5 mi s on bay from downtown marina. Ext/int corridors. **Pets:** Medium. $30 one-time fee/room. Service with restrictions, supervision.
🛜 ♿ 📠 🖥 🍽 🌊 ✖

▼▼▼ **Homewood Suites by Hilton** 🅷
(361) 854-1331. **$129-$249.** 5201 Crosstown Expwy (SR 286) 78417. I-37 exit SR 358 E (Greenwood Dr), 0.6 mi e on eastbound access road. Int corridors. **Pets:** Accepted. 🛜 📠 🖥 🌊

▼▼▼ **La Quinta Inn & Suites Corpus Christi Airport** 🅷
(361) 299-2600. **$103-$175.** 546 S Padre Island Dr 78405. SR 358 exit Old Brownsville Rd, on access road. Int corridors. **Pets:** Medium, other species. Service with restrictions, supervision.
🛜 ✖ ♿ 📠 🖥 🌊

▼▼▼ **La Quinta Inn Corpus Christi North** 🅷
(361) 888-5721. **$71-$159.** 5155 I-37 N 78408. I-37 exit 3A (Navigation Blvd), on southbound access road. Ext corridors. **Pets:** Medium, other species. Service with restrictions, supervision. 🛜 📠 🖥 🌊

▼▼▼ **La Quinta Inn Corpus Christi South** 🅷
(361) 991-5730. **$71-$159.** 6225 S Padre Island Dr 78412. SR 358 exit Airline Rd. Ext corridors. **Pets:** Medium, other species. Service with restrictions, supervision. 🛜 📠 🖥 🌊

▼ **Motel 6 #231** 🅼
(361) 289-9397. **$43-$55.** 845 Lantana St 78408. I-37 exit 4B (Lantana St), on southbound access road. Ext corridors. **Pets:** Other species. Service with restrictions, supervision. 🛜 📠 🌊

🅰🅰🅰 ▼▼▼ **Omni Corpus Christi Hotel-Bayfront Tower** 🅷
(361) 887-1600. **$129-$199.** 900 N Shoreline Blvd 78401. Across from bay; downtown; in marina district. Int corridors. **Pets:** Accepted.
(SAVE) 🛜 ✖ ♿ 📠 🖥 🍽 🌊 ✖

▼▼▼ **Omni Corpus Christi Hotel-Marina Tower** 🅷
(361) 887-1600. **$129-$179.** 707 N Shoreline Blvd 78401. Just n across from bay. Int corridors. **Pets:** Accepted. 🛜 📠 🖥 🍽 🌊 ✖

▼▼ **Plaza Inn Corpus Christi** 🅷
(361) 289-8200. **$69-$159.** 2021 N Padre Island Dr 78408. I-37 exit SR 358, just se at Leopard St. Int corridors. **Pets:** Other species. $25 one-time fee/pet. Designated rooms, service with restrictions, crate.
🛜 📠 🖥 🌊

▼▼ **Quality Inn & Suites Sandy Shores** 🅷
(361) 883-7456. **$80-$210, 3 day notice.** 3202 Surfside Blvd 78402. 1 mi n on US 181; at north end of Harbor Bridge exit Bridge St. Ext/int corridors. **Pets:** Accepted. 🛜 📠 🖥 🌊

▼▼ **Red Roof Inn** 🅷
(361) 992-9222. **$45-$85.** 6805 S Padre Island Dr 78412. SR 358 exit Nile Dr. Ext corridors. **Pets:** Large, other species. No service, supervision.
🛜 📠 🖥 🌊

🅰🅰🅰 ▼▼▼ **Surfside Condominiums** 🅲🅾
(361) 949-8128. **$140-$215, 3 day notice.** 15005 Windward Dr 78418. Park Rd 22 on N Padre Island Dr, jct Whitecap Blvd, 0.6 mi n to Windward Dr, then 0.8 mi w. Ext corridors. **Pets:** Medium. $20 daily fee/pet. Designated rooms, service with restrictions.
(SAVE) 🛜 ✖ 📠 🖥 🌊

CORSICANA

🅰🅰🅰 ▼▼▼ **Best Western Plus Executive Inn** 🅷
(903) 872-0020. **$80-$150.** 2100 E Hwy 31 75109. I-45 exit 231, just e. Int corridors. **Pets:** Medium. $10 daily fee/pet. Service with restrictions, supervision. (SAVE) 🛜 ♿ 📠 🖥 🌊

▼▼▼ **La Quinta Inn & Suites Corsicana** 🅷
(903) 874-6292. **$71-$129.** 2020 Regal Dr 75110. I-45 exit 231, just e. Int corridors. **Pets:** Medium, other species. Service with restrictions, supervision. 🛜 📠 🖥 🌊

COTULLA

🅰🅰🅰 ▼▼▼ **Best Western Cowboy Inn** 🅷
(830) 879-3100. **$110.** 145 W FM 468 78014. I-35 exit 57 (FM 468), just w. Ext/int corridors. **Pets:** Accepted. (SAVE) 🛜 ✖ 📠 🖥 🌊

CRESSON

▽▽▽▽ Best Western Cresson Inn ▣

(817) 396-4480. **Call for rates.** 9120 E Hwy 377 76035. 0.4 mi s of jct US 377 and SR 171. Int corridors. **Pets:** Accepted.

[SAVE] 🛜 🛏 🖵 ⊃

DALHART

▽▽▽▽ Best Western Nursanickel Motel ▣ 🐾

(806) 244-5637. **$80-$100.** 102 Scott Ave (Hwy 87 S) 79022. Just s of jct US 54 and 87. Ext corridors. **Pets:** Large. $10 daily fee/pet. Service with restrictions, supervision. [SAVE] 🛜 🛏 🖵 ⊃

▽▽ Budget Inn Ⓜ

(806) 244-4557. **$45-$60.** 415 Liberal St (Hwy 54) 79022. On US 54, just e of US 87 and 385. Ext corridors. **Pets:** Small. $25 deposit/pet. Service with restrictions, supervision. [SAVE] 🛜 🛏

▽▽ ◇ Days Inn ▣ 🐾

(806) 244-5246. **$67-$85.** 701 Liberal St (Hwy 54) 79022. On US 54, 0.5 mi e. Int corridors. **Pets:** Large, other species. $25 one-time fee/pet. No service, supervision. 🛜 🛏 🖵 ⊃

▽▽▽ Rodeway Inn Ⓜ

(806) 249-8585. **$70.** 918 Liberal St (Hwy 54 E) 79022. 0.5 mi e of jct US 54 and 87. Ext corridors. **Pets:** Accepted. [SAVE] 🛜 🛏 🖵 ⊃

▽ Sands Motel Ⓜ

(806) 244-4568. **$30-$70.** 301 Liberal St (Hwy 54) 79022. On US 54, just e of US 87 and 385. Ext corridors. **Pets:** Service with restrictions. [SAVE] 🛜 🛏

▽▽▽ Super 8 Ⓜ

(806) 249-8526. **$50-$88.** 403 Tanglewood Rd (Hwy 54 E) 79022. Jct US 87 and 54, 0.5 mi e. Int corridors. **Pets:** Small. $25 deposit/pet. Designated rooms, service with restrictions, supervision. [SAVE] 🛜 🛏 🖵

DALLAS METROPOLITAN AREA

ADDISON

▽▽▽▽ Comfort Suites by Choice Hotels ▣ 🐾

(972) 503-6500. **$74-$104.** 4555 Belt Line Rd 75001. Just w of Addison Rd; behind Macaroni Grill. Int corridors. **Pets:** Medium. $50 deposit/room, $10 daily fee/pet. Service with restrictions, crate.

[SAVE] 🛜 ✖ 🛏 🖵 ⊃

▽▽▽ Homewood Suites by Hilton ▣

(972) 788-1342. **$99-$179.** 4451 Belt Line Rd 75001. Just e of jct Belt Line and Midway rds. Ext/int corridors. **Pets:** Accepted.

🔸 🛏 🖵 ⊃ ✖

▽▽▽▽ Hyatt Summerfield Suites Dallas/Addison ▣

(972) 661-3113. **$79-$169.** 4900 Edwin Lewis Dr 75001. Just n of jct Belt Line Rd and Quorum Dr to Edwin Lewis Dr, then just w. Ext/int corridors. **Pets:** Small. $150 one-time fee/pet. Service with restrictions, supervision. [SAVE] 🛜 ✖ 🔸 🛏 🖵 ⊃ ✖

▽▽▽▽ La Quinta Inn & Suites Dallas Addison Galleria ▣

(972) 404-0004. **$67-$159.** 14925 Landmark Blvd 75254. Jct Belt Line Rd and Landmark Blvd, just s. Int corridors. **Pets:** Medium, other species. Service with restrictions, supervision. 🛜 🔸 🛏 🖵 ⊃

▽▽▽ Quality Inn & Suites ▣

(972) 991-8888. **$49-$129.** 4103 Belt Line Rd 75001. Between Midway Rd and Marsh Ln. Ext corridors. **Pets:** Accepted. 🛜 🛏 🖵 ⊃

▽▽▽ Residence Inn by Marriott-Addison ▣

(972) 866-9933. **$99-$149.** 14975 Quorum Dr 75254. Just s of jct Belt Line Rd and Quorum Dr. Int corridors. **Pets:** Medium. $100 one-time fee/room. Service with restrictions, supervision.

🛜 ✖ 🛏 🖵 ⊃ ✖

ALLEN

▽▽▽ Courtyard by Marriott Dallas Allen at the John Q Hammons Center ▣

(214) 383-1151. **$109-$169.** 210 E Stacy Rd 75002. US 75 exit 36, just e; in Village at Allen. Int corridors. **Pets:** Medium, other species. $50 one-time fee/room. Service with restrictions, crate.

🛜 ✖ 🛏 🖵 🍴 ⊃ ✖

▽▽▽ La Quinta Inn & Suites Allen At The Village ▣

(214) 667-6772. **$80-$165.** 1220 N Central Expy 75013. US 75 exit 36 (Exchange Pkwy), just e. Int corridors. **Pets:** Medium, other species. Service with restrictions, supervision. [SAVE] 🛜 ✖ 🛏 🖵 ⊃

▽▽ Pyramids Hotel ▣

(972) 396-9494. **$89-$149.** 407 Central Expwy S 75013. US 75 exit 33 (Bethany Dr), just n on frontage road. Int corridors. **Pets:** Medium. $30 one-time fee/room. Designated rooms, service with restrictions, supervision. 🛜 ✖ 🛏 🖵 ⊃ ✖

CARROLLTON

▽▽▽ Rodeway Inn ▣

(972) 245-9900. **Call for rates.** 1832 N I-35 E 75006. I-35E exit 443C (Frontage Rd) northbound; exit 443B southbound (Belt Line Rd), U-turn, just 1 mi n. Int corridors. **Pets:** Accepted. 🛜 🛏

CEDAR HILL

▽▽▽▽ La Quinta Inn & Suites ▣

(972) 291-0008. **$85-$169.** 1419 N Hwy 67 75104. US 67 exit Wintergreen Rd, on southbound frontage road. Int corridors. **Pets:** Medium, other species. Service with restrictions, supervision.

🛜 ✖ 🔸 🛏 🖵 ⊃

COMMERCE

▽▽▽▽ Holiday Inn Express Hotel & Suites ▣

(903) 886-4777. **$92-$159, 3 day notice.** 2207 Culver St 75428. 0.9 mi e of jct SR 224, 24 and 50. Int corridors. **Pets:** Accepted.

[SAVE] 🛜 ✖ 🔸 🛏 🖵 ⊃

DALLAS

▽▽▽ ▽▽▽ The Adolphus ▣

(214) 742-8200. **$129-$279.** 1321 Commerce St 75202. Between Field and Akard sts. Int corridors. **Pets:** Small, dogs only. $100 deposit/pet, $50 one-time fee/pet. Designated rooms, service with restrictions, supervision. [SAVE] 🛜 ✖ 🔸 🛏 🖵 🍴 ✖

▽▽▽ Aloft Downtown Dallas ▣

(214) 761-0000. **$129-$219.** 1033 Young St 75202. Northeast corner of Griffin and Young sts. Int corridors. **Pets:** Accepted.

[SAVE] 🛜 ✖ 🔸 🛏 🖵 ⊃

▽▽ Baymont Inn & Suites Dallas Love Field ▣

(214) 350-5577. **$62-$67.** 2370 W Northwest Hwy 75220. I-35E exit 436 Northwest Hwy (Loop 12), 0.8 mi e. Int corridors. **Pets:** Accepted.

🛜 🛏 🖵 ⊃

▽▽▽ Best Western Cityplace Inn ▣

(214) 827-6080. **$60-$120.** 4150 N Central Expwy 75204. US 75 exit 1B (Fitzhugh Ave) southbound; exit 2 (Fitzhugh Ave) northbound. Ext corridors. **Pets:** Accepted. [SAVE] 🛜 🛏 🖵 🍴 ⊃

▽▽ Candlewood Suites-Dallas by the Galleria ▣

(972) 233-6888. **$58-$119.** 13939 Noel Rd 75240. Jct Dallas Pkwy and Spring Valley, just e to Noel Rd, then just s. Int corridors. **Pets:** Accepted. 🔸 🛏 🖵

Candlewood Dallas Market Center H
(214) 631-3333. **$89-$109.** 7930 N Stemmons Frwy 75247. I-35 exit 433B (Mockingbird Ln), on northbound frontage road. Int corridors. **Pets:** Small. $75 one-time fee/pet. Service with restrictions, supervision.

Candlewood Suites Dallas North/Richardson H
(972) 669-9606. **$54-$100.** 12525 Greenville Ave 75243. I-635 exit 18A (Greenville Ave), just n, then just w on Amberton Pkwy. Int corridors. **Pets:** Large. $15 daily fee/pet. Service with restrictions, crate.

Comfort Inn & Suites Market Center H
(214) 461-2677. **$80-$150.** 7138 N Stemmons Frwy 75247. I-35E exit 433B (Mockingbird Ln) northbound; exit 432B (Commonwealth Dr) southbound, turn under freeway, 0.7 mi on north access road. Int corridors. **Pets:** $25 one-time fee/pet. Service with restrictions, crate.

Crowne Plaza Hotel Dallas Market Center H
(214) 630-8500. **Call for rates.** 7050 Stemmons Frwy 75247. I-35E exit 433B northbound; exit 432B southbound. Int corridors. **Pets:** Accepted.

Crowne Plaza Suites Hotel Dallas Park Central H
(972) 233-7600. **$79-$129.** 7800 Alpha Rd 75240. I-635 exit 19C (Coit Rd) eastbound; exit 19B (Coit Rd) westbound, just n, then just w. Int corridors. **Pets:** Medium. $100 deposit/room, $25 one-time fee/room. Service with restrictions, crate.

Dallas Marriott Suites Market Center H
(214) 905-0050. **$71-$199.** 2493 N Stemmons Frwy 75207. I-35E exit 431 (Motor St), on southbound frontage road. Int corridors.
Pets: Accepted.

Extended StayAmerica Dallas-North-Park Central H
(972) 671-7722. **$54-$89.** 9019 Vantage Point Rd 75243. I-635 exit 18A (Greenville Ave), just s, then just w. Ext corridors. **Pets:** Other species. $25 daily fee/pet. Service with restrictions.

Extended StayAmerica Dallas-Richardson H
(972) 238-1133. **$59-$89.** 12270 Greenville Ave 75243. I-635 exit 18A (Greenville Ave), just s. Int corridors. **Pets:** Other species. $25 daily fee/pet. Service with restrictions.

Extended Stay Deluxe Dallas-Market Center H
(214) 630-0154. **$69-$119.** 2979 N Stemmons Frwy 75247. I-35E exit 432B, on southbound access road. Int corridors. **Pets:** Other species. $25 daily fee/pet. Service with restrictions.

The Fairmont Dallas H
(214) 720-2020. **Call for rates.** 1717 N Akard St 75201. Corner of Ross Ave and N Akard St. Int corridors. **Pets:** Accepted.

Hilton Dallas Lincoln Centre H
(972) 934-8400. **$129-$399.** 5410 LBJ Frwy 75240. Jct I-635 and North Dallas Tollway/Dallas Pkwy; I-635 exit 22D (Dallas Pkwy) eastbound; exit 22B (Dallas Pkwy/Inwood Rd) westbound, just e on frontage road. Int corridors. **Pets:** Medium. $50 one-time fee/pet. Service with restrictions.

Hilton Dallas Park Cities H
(214) 368-0400. **$107-$249.** 5954 Luther Ln 75225. North Dallas Tollway exit Northwest Hwy (Loop 12), just e to Douglas Ave, then just s. Int corridors. **Pets:** Accepted.

Holiday Inn Dallas Market Center H
(214) 219-3333. **$89-$209.** 4500 Harry Hines Blvd 75219. I-35E exit 430B (Market Center Blvd), just e. Int corridors. **Pets:** Accepted.

Homestead Studio Suites Hotel-Dallas/Plano H
(972) 248-2233. **$74-$99.** 18470 N Dallas Pkwy 75287. North Dallas Tollway exit Frankford Rd, on northbound frontage road. Int corridors. **Pets:** Other species. $25 daily fee/pet. Service with restrictions.

Homewood Suites by Hilton - I-635 H
(972) 437-6966. **$119-$189.** 9169 Markville Dr 75243. I-635 exit 18A (Greenville Ave S), just s, then just e. Int corridors. **Pets:** Large. $75 one-time fee/pet. Service with restrictions.

Homewood Suites Dallas Market Center H
(214) 819-9700. **$89-$169.** 2747 N Stemmons Frwy 75207. I-35E exit 432A (Inwood Rd), just s. Int corridors. **Pets:** Accepted.

Hotel Indigo Dallas Downtown H
(214) 741-7700. **$89-$149.** 1933 Main St 75201. Main and Harwood sts; northwest corner. Int corridors. **Pets:** Large. $75 one-time fee/pet. Service with restrictions, crate.

Hotel Palomar H
(214) 520-7969. **Call for rates.** 5300 E Mockingbird Ln 75206. US 75 exit 3 (Mockingbird Ln), on southeast corner. Int corridors. **Pets:** Other species. Designated rooms, service with restrictions.

Hotel St. Germain CI
(214) 871-2516. **$305-$700, 7 day notice.** 2516 Maple Ave 75201. I-35 exit 430A (Oak Lawn Ave), 0.5 mi e, then 1 mi s. Int corridors. **Pets:** Small, dogs only. $50 daily fee/pet. Designated rooms, service with restrictions, supervision.

Hotel ZaZa H
(214) 468-8399. **$295-$415.** 2332 Leonard St 75201. Jct Maple Ave/ Routh St and McKinney Ave; southeast corner. Int corridors.
Pets: Accepted.

Hyatt Summerfield Suites Dallas/Lincoln Park H
(214) 696-1555. **$99-$209.** 8221 N Central Expy 75225. US 75 exit 5A southbound; exit 4B northbound, just w on Caruth Haven to Lincoln Pl, then just n. Int corridors. **Pets:** Medium. $200 one-time fee/room. Service with restrictions, supervision.

Hyatt Summerfield Suites Dallas/Uptown H
(214) 965-9990. **$99-$209.** 2914 Harry Hines Blvd 75201. I-35 exit 430A (Oaklawn Ave), just n to Harry Hines Blvd, then 0.6 mi s. Int corridors. **Pets:** Large. $200 one-time fee/pet. Service with restrictions.

La Quinta Inn & Suites Dallas North Central H
(214) 361-8200. **$94-$169.** 10001 N Central Expwy 75231. US 75 exit 6 (Walnut Hill Ln/Meadow Rd) northbound, 0.5 mi n to Meadow Rd, then U-turn under highway; exit 7 (Royal St/Meadow Rd) southbound, 1 mi s on feeder. Int corridors. **Pets:** Medium, other species. Service with restrictions, supervision.

La Quinta Inn Dallas Uptown H
(214) 821-4220. **$94-$165.** 4440 N Central Expwy 75206. US 75 exit 2 (Knox St/Henderson Ave) northbound; exit 1B (Haskell Ave/Blackburn St) southbound. Ext corridors. **Pets:** Medium, other species. Service with restrictions, supervision.

Le Meridien Dallas by the Galleria H
(972) 503-8700. **$89-$399, 3 day notice.** 13402 Noel Rd 75240. Dallas Pkwy exit Alpha Rd, just e to Noel Rd, then just s. Int corridors.
Pets: Accepted.

Magnolia Hotel Dallas H

(214) 915-6500. **Call for rates.** 1401 Commerce St 75201. Corner of Commerce and Akard sts. Int corridors. **Pets:** Small, dogs only. $50 one-time fee/room. Service with restrictions, crate.

MCM Elegante Hotel & Suites H

(214) 351-4477. **$89-$139, 7 day notice.** 2330 W Northwest Hwy 75220. I-35E exit 436, just e. Ext/int corridors. **Pets:** Accepted.

Motel 6 - Dallas #4641 H

(214) 904-9955. **Call for rates.** 2380 W Northwest Hwy 75220. I-35 exit 436 Northwest Hwy (Loop 12), 0.8 mi e. Int corridors. **Pets:** Other species. Service with restrictions, supervision.

Motel 6 - Dallas - Forest Lane #4657 H

(972) 484-9111. **Call for rates.** 2660 Forest Ln 75234. I-635 exit 26 (Josey Ln) eastbound, 0.5 mi s to Forest Ln, then just w; exit 25 (Josey Ln) westbound, just s to Forest Ln, then just w. Ext corridors. **Pets:** Other species. Service with restrictions, supervision.

Motel 6 North Dallas #4549 H

(972) 907-9500. **Call for rates.** 13185 N Central Expwy 75243. US 75 N exit 22 (Midpark Rd), on southbound frontage road. Int corridors. **Pets:** Other species. Service with restrictions, supervision.

Park Inn by Radisson, Dallas-Love Field H

(214) 630-7000. **$99-$129.** 1241 W Mockingbird Ln 75247. I-35E exit 433B, just ne of jct I-35E and W Mockingbird Ln. Int corridors. **Pets:** Accepted.

Radisson Hotel Dallas Central/ University Park H

(214) 750-6060. **Call for rates.** 6070 N Central Expwy 75206. US 75 exit 3 (Mockingbird Ln), on northbound frontage road. Int corridors. **Pets:** Accepted.

Radisson Hotel Dallas East H

(214) 341-5400. **Call for rates.** 11350 LBJ Frwy 75238. I-635 exit 13 (Jupiter Rd/Kingsley Rd), just sw. Int corridors. **Pets:** Accepted.

Ramada Inn/Near Love Field H

(214) 638-6100. **$43-$240.** 1575 Regal Row 75247. I-35E exit 434B (Regal Row), just sw. Int corridors. **Pets:** Accepted.

Residence Inn by Marriott at Dallas Central H

(214) 750-8220. **$110-$161.** 10333 N Central Expwy 75231. US 75 exit 6 (Walnut Hill Ln/Meadow Rd) northbound, 0.5 mi n to Meadow Rd, U-turn under highway; exit 7 (Royal St/Meadow Rd) southbound, 1 mi s on access road. Ext/int corridors. **Pets:** Accepted.

Residence Inn by Marriott-Dallas Market Center H

(214) 631-2472. **$85-$170.** 6950 N Stemmons Frwy 75247. I-35E exit 432B (Commonwealth Ln), 0.6 mi n on northbound frontage road. Ext/int corridors. **Pets:** Accepted.

Residence Inn by Marriott-Dallas Park Central H

(972) 503-1333. **$80-$132.** 7642 LBJ Frwy 75251. I-635 exit 20 (Hillcrest Ave), on eastbound access road. Int corridors. **Pets:** Other species. $100 one-time fee/room. Service with restrictions.

The Ritz-Carlton, Dallas H

(214) 922-0200. **$399-$599, 3 day notice.** 2121 McKinney Ave 75201. SR 366 (Woodall Rodgers Frwy) exit Pearl St, just sw to Olive St, then just nw. Int corridors. **Pets:** Accepted.

Rosewood Crescent Hotel H

(214) 871-3200. **Call for rates.** 400 Crescent Ct 75201. Corner of Crescent Ct and McKinney Ave; uptown. Int corridors. **Pets:** Accepted.

Rosewood Mansion on Turtle Creek H 🐾

(214) 559-2100. **$695-$5000.** 2821 Turtle Creek Blvd 75219. 2 mi nw, entrance on Gillespie St, just e of jct Gillespie St and Oak Lawn Ave. Int corridors. **Pets:** Other species. $100 one-time fee/pet.

Sheraton Dallas Hotel H 🐾

(214) 922-8000. **$99-$369.** 400 N Olive St 75201. Live Oak and Olive sts, just w off Central Expwy. Int corridors. **Pets:** Medium, dogs only. Service with restrictions, supervision.

Sheraton Suites Market Center-Dallas H

(214) 747-3000. **$79-$269.** 2101 N Stemmons Frwy 75207. I-35E exit 430B (Market Center Blvd), just w. Int corridors. **Pets:** Accepted.

Staybridge Suites Dallas Near The Galleria H 🐾

(972) 391-0000. **$109-$179.** 7880 Alpha Rd 75240. I-635 exit 19B (Coit Rd), 0.3 mi s, then just w. Int corridors. **Pets:** Medium. $15 one-time fee/room, $10 daily fee/room. Designated rooms, service with restrictions, crate.

Staybridge Suites North Dallas H

(972) 726-9990. **$79-$169.** 16060 N Dallas Pkwy 75248. North Dallas Tollway exit Keller Springs, just e to Knoll Tr, then just s. Int corridors. **Pets:** Accepted.

The Stoneleigh Hotel & Spa H 🐾

(214) 871-7111. **$169-$480.** 2927 Maple Ave 75201. I-35E exit 430A (Oak Lawn Ave), 0.5 mi e, then 1.2 mi s. Int corridors. **Pets:** Medium. $50 one-time fee/room.

Super 8 H

(972) 572-1030. **$50-$100.** 8541 S Hampton Rd 75232. I-20 exit 465, 0.3 mi e to S Hampton Rd, then just s. Ext corridors. **Pets:** Accepted.

Warwick Melrose Hotel H

(214) 521-5151. **$149-$599.** 3015 Oak Lawn Ave 75219. I-35E exit 430 (Oak Lawn Ave), 0.8 mi n; entrance off Cedar Springs, just n. Int corridors. **Pets:** Medium. $50 one-time fee/room. Designated rooms, service with restrictions, supervision.

W Dallas - Victory H

(214) 397-4100. **$199-$529, 3 day notice.** 2440 Victory Park Ln 75219. Southwest corner of Olive and N Houston sts; uptown Dallas; across from American Airlines Center. Int corridors. **Pets:** Accepted.

The Westin Galleria, Dallas H 🐾

(972) 934-9494. **$119-$429.** 13340 Dallas Pkwy 75240. Just n of jct I-635 and N Dallas Pkwy. Int corridors. **Pets:** Medium, dogs only. Service with restrictions, supervision.

Westin Park Central H

(972) 385-3000. **$349-$424.** 12720 Merit Dr 75251. I-635 exit 19C (Coit Rd) eastbound; exit 19B (US 75/Coit Rd) westbound, 0.3 mi w of jct US 75. Int corridors. **Pets:** Accepted.

DENTON

Days Inn Denton North H

(940) 383-1471. **$41-$72.** 4211 I-35 N 76207. I-35 exit 469 (University Dr), just w, then just n. Int corridors. **Pets:** Small, other species. $25 daily fee/pet. Service with restrictions, crate.

ᵂᵂᵂ Homewood Suites by Hilton-Denton H
(940) 382-0420. **Call for rates.** 2907 Shoreline Dr 76210. I-35E exit 462 (State School Rd/Mayhill Rd), just w to Unicorn Lake, 0.4 mi n, then just w. Int corridors. **Pets:** Accepted. 🛜 🔧 💻 🏊 ⊠

ᵂᵂᵂ La Quinta Inn & Suites Denton H
(940) 808-0444. **$80-$145.** 4465 N I-35 76207. I-I35 exit 469 (University Dr), just w, n on Mesa Dr, w on Barcelona St, then around to hotel. Int corridors. **Pets:** Medium, other species. Service with restrictions, supervision. 🛜 ⊠ 🔧 💻 🏊

ᵂᵂ La Quinta Inn Denton H
(940) 387-5840. **$62-$122.** 700 Fort Worth Dr 76201. I-35E exit 465B (Fort Worth Dr), just n. Ext corridors. **Pets:** Medium, other species. Service with restrictions, supervision. 🛜 &M 🔧 💻 🏊

ᵂᵂ Quality Inn & Suites Denton H
(940) 387-3511. **$70-$120.** 1500 Dallas Dr 76205. I-35E 464 eastbound; exit 465A (Teasley Ln) westbound, 0.4 mi n to Dallas Dr, then 0.5 mi e. Ext corridors. **Pets:** Accepted. 🛜 🔧 💻 🏊

ᵂᵂ Super 8-Denton H
(940) 380-8888. **$49-$113.** 620 S I-35 76205. I-35 exit 465A (Teasley Ln). Int corridors. **Pets:** $25 daily fee/pet. Service with restrictions, supervision. 🛜 🔧 💻 🏊

DESOTO

ᵂᵂ Days Inn & Suites DeSoto H
(972) 224-7100. **Call for rates.** 1401 N I-35 E 75115. I-35E exit 416 (Wintergreen Rd), just s. Ext/int corridors. **Pets:** Accepted. 🛜 🔧

AAA ᵂᵂᵂ MCM Grande Hotel H
(972) 224-9100. **$79-$119.** 1515 N I-35 E 75115. I-35E exit 416 (Wintergreen Rd), just s. Ext/int corridors. **Pets:** Small. $25 one-time fee/room. Designated rooms, service with restrictions.
SAVE 🛜 🔧 💻 🍽 🏊

ᵂᵂᵂ TownePlace Suites Dallas DeSoto H 🐾
(972) 780-9300. **$80-$95.** 2700 Travis St 75115. US 67 exit Cockrell Hill, on northbound service road. Int corridors. **Pets:** Medium, other species. $100 one-time fee/room. Service with restrictions.
🛜 ⊠ &M 🔧 💻 🏊

ENNIS

ᵂᵂᵂ Comfort Suites H 🐾
(972) 872-9898. **$63-$80.** 400 S I-45 75119. I-45 exit 251A, 0.7 mi n on N Frontage Rd to Dolfie Ln, then just e. Int corridors. **Pets:** $15 daily fee/pet. Service with restrictions, supervision.
🛜 ⊠ &M 🔧 💻 🏊

FARMERS BRANCH

ᵂᵂᵂ Fairfield Inn & Suites by Marriott Dallas North H
(972) 661-9800. **$69-$109.** 13900 Parkside Center Blvd 75244. I-635 exit 23 (Midway Rd), 0.9 mi n to Spring Valley Rd, just w, then just s. Int corridors. **Pets:** Other species. $75 one-time fee/room. Service with restrictions, crate. 🛜 ⊠ 🔧 💻 🏊

ᵂᵂ La Quinta Inn Dallas Northwest Farmers Branch H
(972) 620-7333. **$55-$115.** 13235 Stemmons Frwy N 75234. I-35E exit 441 (Valley View Ln), on southbound frontage road. Ext corridors. **Pets:** Medium, other species. Service with restrictions, supervision.
🛜 🔧 💻 🏊

ᵂᵂ ᵂᵂ Omni Dallas Hotel Park West H
(972) 869-4300. **$90-$207.** 1590 LBJ Frwy 75234. I-I635 exit 29 (Luna Rd), just s. Int corridors. **Pets:** Accepted. 🛜 🔧 💻 🍽 🏊 ⊠

AAA ᵂᵂᵂ Sheraton Dallas North by the Galleria H
(972) 661-3600. **$79-$249, 3 day notice.** 4801 LBJ Frwy 75244. I-635 exit 22D (Dallas Pkwy) eastbound; exit 22B (Dallas Pkwy) westbound, on westbound frontage road. Int corridors. **Pets:** Medium. Service with restrictions, supervision. SAVE 🛜 ⊠ &M 🔧 💻 🍽 🏊 ⊠

ᵂᵂ ᵂᵂ StudioPLUS Hotel Dallas-Farmers Branch H 🐾
(972) 385-6006. **$64-$99.** 4022 Parkside Center Blvd 75244. I-635 exit 23 (Midway Rd), 0.9 mi n to Parkside Center Blvd. Int corridors. **Pets:** Other species. $25 daily fee/pet. Service with restrictions.
🛜 🔧 💻 🏊

ᵂᵂ Super 8 H
(972) 406-3030. **$41-$74.** 14040 Stemmons Frwy 75234. I-35E exit 442 (Valwood Pkwy). Int corridors. **Pets:** Medium. $15 daily fee/pet. Service with restrictions, supervision. 🛜 🔧 💻 🏊

FORNEY

AAA ᵂᵂᵂ Best Western Plus Christopher Inn & Suites H 🐾
(972) 552-1412. **$90-$120.** 752 Pinson Rd 75126. US 80 exit FM 740 (Pinson Rd), just ne. Int corridors. **Pets:** Large, other species. $10 daily fee/room. Service with restrictions, supervision.
SAVE 🛜 ⊠ &M 🔧 💻 🏊

FRISCO

AAA ᵂᵂᵂ Aloft Frisco H 🐾
(972) 668-6011. **$89-$289.** 3202 Parkwood Blvd 75034. N Dallas Tollway exit Warren Pkwy, 0.5 mi e to Parkwood Blvd, then just s. Int corridors. **Pets:** Medium. Designated rooms, service with restrictions, supervision.
SAVE 🛜 ⊠ &M 🔧 💻 🏊

AAA ᵂᵂᵂ Embassy Suites Dallas-Frisco Hotel, Convention Center & Spa H 🐾
(972) 712-7200. **$120-$260.** 7600 John Q Hammons Dr 75034. SR 121 exit Parkwood, just n. Int corridors. **Pets:** Large. $75 one-time fee/room. Designated rooms, service with restrictions, supervision.
SAVE 🛜 &M 🔧 💻 🍽 🏊 ⊠

AAA ᵂᵂᵂ Sheraton Stonebriar Hotel H 🐾
(972) 668-8700. **$99-$309.** 5444 State Hwy 121 75034. SR 121 exit Legacy Dr; northwest corner. Int corridors. **Pets:** Small, dogs only. Service with restrictions, supervision. SAVE 🛜 ⊠ &M 🔧 💻 🍽

AAA ᵂᵂᵂᵂ The Westin Stonebriar H 🐾
(972) 668-8000. **$109-$389.** 1549 Legacy Dr 75034. 0.3 mi n of jct SR 121. Int corridors. **Pets:** Medium, dogs only. Designated rooms, service with restrictions, supervision.
SAVE 🛜 ⊠ &M 🔧 💻 🍽 🏊 ⊠

GARLAND

AAA ᵂᵂ Best Western Lakeview Inn H
(972) 303-1601. **$60-$80.** 1635 E I-30 at Bass Pro Rd 75043. I-30 exit 62 (Bass Pro Rd) eastbound, s on Chaha and over bridge to north frontage road. Ext corridors. **Pets:** Accepted. SAVE 🛜 🔧 💻 🏊

ᵂᵂ La Quinta Inn Dallas Garland H
(972) 271-7581. **$58-$119.** 75041. I-635 exit 11B, on west frontage road. Ext/int corridors. **Pets:** Medium, other species. Service with restrictions, supervision. 🛜 🔧 💻 🏊

GRAND PRAIRIE

ᵂᵂᵂ Comfort Suites H
(214) 412-1022. **$79-$99.** 2504 I-20 W 75052. I-20 exit 454 (Great Southwest Pkwy), just n, then just e. Int corridors. **Pets:** Accepted.
🛜 ⊠ 🔧 💻 🏊

ᵂᵂᵂ La Quinta Inn & Suites South Grand Prairie H
(214) 412-3220. **$107-$169.** 2131 W I-20 75052. I-20 exit 454 (Great Southwest Pkwy), on eastbound frontage road. Int corridors. **Pets:** Medium, other species. Service with restrictions, supervision.
🛜 ⊠ 🔧 💻 🏊

ᵂᵂ Super 8 H
(972) 606-2800. **$49-$81.** 4020 Great Southwest Pkwy 75052. I-20 exit 454 (Great Southwest Pkwy), just s. Ext corridors. **Pets:** Accepted.
🛜 🔧 💻 🏊

GREENVILLE

Best Western Plus Monica Royale Inn & Suites H

(903) 454-3700. **$105-$110.** 3001 Mustang Crossing 75402. I-30 exit 93A. Int corridors. **Pets:** Small, dogs only. $10 daily fee/pet. Service with restrictions, supervision. [SAVE] 🛜 ✕ 🐾ᴹ 🛏 🖵 ⇆ ✕

Holiday Inn Express Hotel & Suites H

(903) 454-8680. **$104-$113.** 2901 Mustang Crossing 75402. I-30 exit 93A. Int corridors. **Pets:** Accepted. 🛜 🐾ᴹ 🛏 🖵 ⇆

HUTCHINS

La Quinta Inn & Suites H

(214) 269-1015. **$94-$155.** 1000 Dowdy Ferry Rd 75141. I-45 exit 274, just e. Int corridors. **Pets:** Medium, other species. Service with restrictions, supervision. 🛜 🛏 🖵 ⇆

IRVING

Aloft Las Colinas H 🐾

(972) 717-6100. **$89-$289.** 122 E John Carpenter Frwy 75062. SR 114 exit O'Connor Rd, just s. Int corridors. **Pets:** Medium, dogs only. Designated rooms, service with restrictions, supervision. [SAVE] 🛜 ✕ 🐾ᴹ 🛏 🖵 ⇆

Candlewood Dallas/Las Colinas H

(972) 714-9990. **$81-$126, 3 day notice.** 5300 Green Park Dr 75038. SR 114 exit Walnut Hill Ln, just s. Int corridors. **Pets:** Small, other species. $15 one-time fee/pet. Supervision. 🛜 🐾ᴹ 🖵 ⇆

Courtyard by Marriott-DFW Airport North H

(972) 929-4004. **$71-$159.** 4949 Regent Blvd 75063. I-635 exit 34 (Freeport Pkwy), 0.5 mi s, then 0.5 mi w. Int corridors. **Pets:** Accepted. 🛜 ✕ 🐾ᴹ 🛏 🖵 🍴 ⇆

DoubleTree by Hilton Hotel DFW Airport-North H

(972) 929-8181. **$99-$189.** 4441 Hwy 114 75063. N off SR 114 exit Esters Blvd. Int corridors. **Pets:** Other species. $50 one-time fee/room. Service with restrictions, crate. [SAVE] 🛜 ✕ 🛏 🖵 🍴 ⇆

Four Seasons Resort and Club H 🐾

(972) 717-0700. **$150-$500.** 4150 N MacArthur Blvd 75038. SR 114 exit MacArthur Blvd, 1.5 mi s. Int corridors. **Pets:** Very small. Service with restrictions, supervision. [SAVE] 🛜 🐾ᴹ 🛏 🖵 🍴 ⇆ ✕

Homewood Suites by Hilton Las Colinas H

(972) 556-0665. **$169-$209.** 4300 Wingren Dr 75039. SR 114 exit O'Connor Rd/Wingren Dr eastbound, just e on frontage road, then just n; exit Rochelle Rd westbound, just w on frontage road, then just n. Ext/int corridors. **Pets:** Accepted. 🛜 🐾ᴹ 🛏 🖵 ⇆ ✕

Hyatt Summerfield Suites Dallas/Las Colinas H

(972) 831-0909. **$89-$169.** 5901 N MacArthur Blvd 75039. SR 114 exit MacArthur Blvd; northwest corner. Ext/int corridors. **Pets:** Accepted. [SAVE] 🛜 ✕ 🐾ᴹ 🛏 🖵 ⇆ ✕

La Quinta Inn & Suites Dallas DFW Airport North H

(972) 915-4022. **$76-$165.** 4850 W John Carpenter Frwy 75063. SR 114 exit Freeport Pkwy, on eastbound service road. Int corridors. **Pets:** Medium, other species. Service with restrictions, supervision. 🛜 🐾ᴹ 🛏 🖵

La Quinta Inn & Suites Dallas DFW Airport South / Irving H

(972) 252-6546. **$80-$175.** 4105 W Airport Frwy 75062-5997. SR 183 exit Esters Rd westbound; exit North Beltline Rd eastbound; on westbound frontage road. Int corridors. **Pets:** Medium, other species. Service with restrictions, supervision. 🛜 🛏 🖵 ⇆

La Quinta Inn & Suites Dallas - Las Colinas H

(972) 261-4900. **$58-$149.** 4225 N MacArthur Blvd 75038. Se off SR 114 exit MacArthur Blvd, 1.4 mi s. Int corridors. **Pets:** Medium, other species. Service with restrictions, supervision. 🛜 ✕ 🛏 🖵 ⇆

Motel 6 #1274 DFW North M

(972) 915-3993. **$45-$57.** 7800 Heathrow Dr 75063. SR 114 exit Freeport Pkwy, just se. Int corridors. **Pets:** Other species. Service with restrictions, supervision. 🛜 ⇆

NYLO Dallas/Las Colinas H

(972) 373-8900. **$89-$499.** 1001 W Royal Ln 75039. SR 114 exit MacArthur, just n, then just w. Int corridors. **Pets:** Medium. $50 one-time fee/ pet. Designated rooms, service with restrictions, supervision. [SAVE] 🛜 ✕ 🖵 🍴 ⇆

Omni Mandalay Hotel at Las Colinas H

(972) 556-0800. **$119-$309.** 221 E Las Colinas Blvd 75039. SR 114 exit O'Connor Rd, just n, then just e. Int corridors. **Pets:** Accepted. 🛜 🛏 🖵 🍴 ⇆ ✕

Ramada Inn-DFW Airport H

(972) 929-0066. **$49-$120.** 8205 Esters Blvd 75063. Nw off SR 114 exit Esters Blvd. Int corridors. **Pets:** Accepted. 🛜 🛏 🖵 ⇆

Red Roof Inn/DFW Airport North M

(972) 929-0020. **$46-$75.** 8150 Esters Blvd 75063. SR 114 exit Esters Blvd, just n. Ext corridors. **Pets:** Large, other species. No service, supervision. 🛜 ⇆

Residence Inn by Marriott at Las Colinas H

(972) 580-7773. **$98-$134.** 950 W Walnut Hill Ln 75038. SR 114 exit MacArthur Blvd, 0.5 mi s, then just e. Ext corridors. **Pets:** Accepted. [ECO] ✕ 🐾ᴹ 🛏 🖵 ⇆ ✕

Residence Inn by Marriott-DFW/Irving H

(972) 871-1331. **$89-$229.** 8600 Esters Blvd 75063. SR 114 exit Esters Blvd, 0.9 mi n. Int corridors. **Pets:** Accepted. 🛜 ✕ 🛏 🖵 ⇆ ✕

Sheraton DFW Airport Hotel H

(972) 929-8400. **$99-$259.** 4440 W John Carpenter Frwy 75063. SR 114 exit Esters Blvd, just s. Int corridors. **Pets:** Accepted. [SAVE] 🛜 ✕ 🛏 🖵 🍴 ⇆

Staybridge Suites Dallas-Las Colinas H 🐾

(972) 465-9400. **$89-$229.** 1201 Executive Cir 75038. SR 114 exit MacArthur Blvd, just s to W Walnut Hill Ln, then just w. Int corridors. **Pets:** Medium. $10 daily fee/pet. Service with restrictions. 🛜 🛏 🖵 ⇆

The Westin Dallas Fort Worth Airport H

(972) 929-4500. **$109-$349.** 4545 W John Carpenter Frwy 75063. Nw off SR 114 exit Esters Blvd. Int corridors. **Pets:** Accepted. [SAVE] 🛜 ✕ 🛏 🖵 🍴 ⇆

Wyndham-Las Colinas H

(972) 650-1600. **$79-$199.** 110 W John Carpenter Frwy 75039. Sw off SR 114 exit O'Connor Rd. Int corridors. **Pets:** Accepted. [SAVE] 🛜 ✕ 🛏 🖵 🍴 ⇆

KAUFMAN

Best Western La Hacienda Inn M

(972) 962-6272. **$90-$108.** 200 E Hwy 175 75142. Just e of jct US 175 and SR 34. Ext corridors. **Pets:** Accepted. [SAVE] 🛜 🛏 🖵 ⇆

LAKE DALLAS

Best Western Plus Lake Dallas Inn & Suites H

(940) 497-1007. **$75-$145.** 305 Swisher Rd 75065. I-35E exit 458 (Swisher Rd), 0.6 mi on N Frontage Rd. Int corridors. **Pets:** Medium. $25 one-time fee/room. Service with restrictions, supervision. [SAVE] 🛜 ✕ 🛏 🖵 ⇆

LEWISVILLE

▼▼ ▼▼ Comfort Suites by Choice Hotels 🅷
(972) 315-6464. **$79-$99.** 755A Vista Ridge Mall Dr 75067. I-35E exit 448A (Round Grove Rd) southbound; 0.5 mi s of jct I-35 and Round Grove Rd on southbound service road to Vista Ridge Mall Dr, then just w; exit 447B northbound, just w on SR 121 Bypass. Int corridors.
Pets: Accepted. 📶 ✕ 🅱 🖵 🏊

▼▼ ▼▼ Extended StayAmerica Dallas-Lewisville 🅷 🐾
(972) 315-7455. **$59-$119.** 1900 Lakepointe Dr 75057. I-35E exit 449 (Corporate Dr), just e to Lakepointe Dr, then just s. Int corridors.
Pets: Other species. $25 daily fee/pet. Service with restrictions.
📶 🅱 🖵

▼▼▼▼ Homewood Suites by Hilton 🅷
(972) 315-6123. **$84-$125.** 700 Hebron Pkwy 75057. I-35E exit 448A (Round Grove Rd), just e. Int corridors. **Pets:** Small. $75 one-time fee/room. Service with restrictions, crate. 📶 ♿M 🅱 🖵 🏊 ✕

▼▼ ▼▼ La Quinta Inn Dallas Lewisville 🅷
(972) 221-7525. **$55-$119.** 1657 S Stemmons Frwy 75067-6401. I-35E exit 449 (Corporate Dr), just w. Ext corridors. **Pets:** Medium, other species. Service with restrictions, supervision. 📶 🅱 🖵 🏊

▼▼ Motel 6 - 1288 🅷
(972) 436-5008. **$43-$55.** 1705 Lakepointe Dr 75057. I-35E exit 449 (Corporate Dr), just n on access road. Int corridors. **Pets:** Other species. Service with restrictions, supervision. 📶 🅱 🖵

▼▼▼▼ Residence Inn by Marriott Dallas/Lewisville 🅷
(972) 315-3777. **$80-$143.** 755 C Vista Ridge Mall Dr 75067. I-35E exit 448A (Round Grove Rd) southbound, 0.5 mi s on frontage road, then just w; exit 447B northbound, just w to Lake Vista, just n. Int corridors.
Pets: Accepted. 📶 ✕ ♿M 🅱 🖵 🏊 ✕

▼▼▼▼ TownePlace Suites Dallas Lewisville 🅷
(972) 459-1275. **$100-$130.** 731 E Vista Ridge Mall Dr 75067. I-35 exit 447B northbound (SR 121); exit 448A southbound (SR 121), just w to Lake Vista, then just n. Int corridors. **Pets:** Medium, other species. $100 one-time fee/room. Service with restrictions, crate.
📶 ✕ 🅱 🖵 🏊

MCKINNEY

▼▼ Days Inn McKinney 🅷
(972) 548-8888. **$46-$179.** 2104 N Central Expy 75070. US 75 exit 41 0.5 mi n of jct US 380. Ext corridors. **Pets:** Small. $7 daily fee/pet. Designated rooms, service with restrictions, supervision. 📶 🅱 🖵 🏊

▲▲▲ ▼▼▼▼ La Quinta Inn & Suites 🅷
(972) 908-2370. **$64-$144.** 6501 Henneman Way 75070. SR 121 exit Stacy Rd, just n, then just w. Int corridors. **Pets:** Medium, other species. Service with restrictions, supervision. SAVE 📶 ✕ 🅱 🖵 🏊

▼▼ ▼▼ Super 8-McKinney 🅷
(972) 548-8880. **$49-$81.** 910 N Central Expwy 75070. US 75 exit 40A (Virginia St/Louisiana St), 0.5 mi n on northbound service road. Int corridors. **Pets:** Medium. $10 daily fee/pet. Service with restrictions, supervision. 📶 🅱 🖵 🏊

MESQUITE

▼▼▼▼ Comfort Inn 🅷
(972) 285-6300. **Call for rates.** 923 Windbell Cir 75149. I-635 exit 5, just e, then just s. Int corridors. **Pets:** Accepted. 📶 ♿M 🅱 🖵 🏊

▲▲▲ ▼▼▼▼ La Quinta Inn & Suites Dallas Mesquite 🅷
(972) 216-7460. **$85-$145.** 118 E Hwy 80 75149. US 80 E exit Belt Line Rd. Int corridors. **Pets:** Medium, other species. Service with restrictions, supervision. SAVE 📶 ♿M 🅱 🖵 🏊

◆◆ ▼▼ Super 8 🅷
(972) 289-5481. **$54-$90.** 121 Grand Junction Blvd 75149. I-635 exit 4 (Military Pkwy). Ext corridors. **Pets:** Accepted. 📶 🅱 🖵 🏊

MIDLOTHIAN

▼▼ ▼▼ Americas Best Value Inn & Suites 🅷
(972) 775-1891. **$79-$110.** 220 N Hwy 67 76065. On US 67, just n of jct US 287. Ext corridors. **Pets:** Medium. $10 one-time fee/pet. Service with restrictions, supervision. 📶 🅱 🖵

PLANO

▲▲▲ ▼▼▼▼ Aloft Plano 🅷
(214) 474-2520. **$89-$289.** 6853 N Dallas Pkwy 75024. North Dallas Tollway exit Spring Creek Pkwy/Tennyson Pkwy on frontage road, just s of Tennyson Pkwy. Int corridors. **Pets:** Accepted.
SAVE 📶 ✕ ♿M 🅱 🖵 🏊

▲▲▲ ▼▼▼▼ Best Western Park Suites Hotel 🅷
(972) 578-2243. **$95-$105.** 640 Park Blvd E 75074. US 75 exit 29A northbound, just e; exit 29 southbound, 0.5 mi s on access road, just e on 15th St, then 0.5 mi n on access road. Int corridors. **Pets:** Medium, dogs only. $25 daily fee/pet. Designated rooms, service with restrictions, supervision. SAVE 📶 ✕ ♿M 🅱 🖵

▲▲▲ ▼▼▼▼ Candlewood Suites Dallas/Plano/Richardson 🅷
(214) 474-2770. **$89-$199.** 2401 E President George Bush Tollway 75074. At Jupiter Rd exit, on westbound frontage road. Int corridors.
Pets: Accepted. SAVE 📶 🅱 🖵

▼▼▼▼ Candlewood Suites-Plano 🅷
(972) 618-5446. **$69-$129, 3 day notice.** 4701 Legacy Dr 75024. Jct SR 289 (Preston Rd) and Legacy Dr, just e. Int corridors.
Pets: Accepted. 📶 🅱 🖵

▼▼ ▼▼ Extended Stay Deluxe Dallas-Plano-Plano Parkway 🅷 🐾
(972) 398-0135. **$69-$109.** 4636 W Plano Pkwy 75093. Jct SR 289 (Preston Rd) and W Plano Pkwy, 0.4 mi e. Int corridors. **Pets:** Other species. $25 daily fee/pet. Service with restrictions. 📶 🅱 🖵 🏊

▼▼ ▼▼ Homestead Studio Suites Hotel-Dallas/Plano Parkway 🅷 🐾
(972) 596-9966. **$64-$99.** 4709 W Plano Pkwy 75093. Jct Plano Pkwy and SR 289 (Preston Rd), just e. Int corridors. **Pets:** Other species. $25 daily fee/pet. Service with restrictions. 📶 🅱 🖵 🏊

▼▼▼▼ Homewood Suites by Hilton 🅷
(972) 758-8800. **$85-$169.** 4705 Old Shepherd Pl 75093. Jct Plano Pkwy and SR 289 (Preston Rd), 0.4 mi n, then just e. Int corridors.
Pets: Accepted. ♿M 🅱 🖵 🏊 ✕

▼▼▼▼ La Quinta Inn & Suites Dallas Plano West 🅷
(972) 599-0700. **$76-$175.** 4800 W Plano Pkwy 75093. Just e of jct SR 289 (Preston Rd). Int corridors. **Pets:** Medium, other species. Service with restrictions, supervision. 📶 ♿M 🅱 🖵 🏊

▼▼▼▼ Nylo Plano at Legacy 🅷
(972) 624-6990. **$79-$209.** 8201 Preston Rd 75024. Just s of jct SR 121. Int corridors. **Pets:** Accepted. 📶 ✕ 🅱 🖵 🍽 🏊

▲▲▲ ▼▼▼▼ Southfork Hotel 🅷
(972) 578-8555. **Call for rates.** 1600 N Central Expwy 75074. US 75 exit 29A northbound; exit 29 southbound, on northbound frontage road. Int corridors. **Pets:** Accepted. SAVE 📶 ✕ 🅱 🖵 🍽 🏊

▼▼▼▼ Staybridge Suites Plano/Richardson 🅷
(972) 612-8180. **$99-$159.** 301 Silverglen Dr 75075. George Bush Toll Rd exit Coit Rd, n to Mapleshade, just e, then just s. Int corridors.
Pets: Medium. $75 one-time fee/pet. Service with restrictions, crate.
📶 ✕ ♿M 🅱 🖵 🏊 ✕

▼▼ ▼▼ Super 8-Plano 🅷
(972) 423-8300. **$45-$135.** 1704 N Central Expwy 75074. US 75 exit 29A (Park Blvd) northbound, just e; exit 29 southbound, 0.5 mi s on access road, just e on 15th St, then just n on access road. Int corridors.
Pets: Accepted. 📶 ♿M 🅱 🖵

▼▼ TowicePlace Suites by Marriott 🅷

(972) 943-8200. **$98-$107.** 5005 Whitestone Ln 75024. North Dallas Tollway exit Spring Creek Pkwy, 1.9 mi e, just n on SR 289 (Preston Rd) to Whitestone Ln, then just w. Int corridors. **Pets:** Accepted.

🛜 ❌ ♿ 🛏 💻 🏊

RICHARDSON

▼▼▼ Homestead Studio Suites
　Hotel-Dallas/Richardson 🅷 🐾

(972) 479-0500. **$69-$99.** 901 E Campbell Rd 75081. US 75 exit 26 (Campbell Rd), just e. Int corridors. **Pets:** Other species. $25 daily fee/pet. Service with restrictions. 🛜 ♿ 🛏 💻 🏊

⊗ ▼▼▼ Hyatt Summerfield Suites
　Dallas/Richardson 🅷

(972) 671-8080. **$79-$179.** 2301 N Central Expwy 75080. US 75 exit 26 (Campbell Rd), 0.5 mi w to Collins Blvd, then 0.6 mi n. Int corridors. **Pets:** Medium, other species. $200 one-time fee/room. Service with restrictions, crate. 〔SAVE〕 🛜 ❌ ♿ 🛏 💻 🏊 ⊗

⊗ ▼▼▼ Hyatt Regency North Dallas/Richardson 🅷

(972) 231-9600. **$79-$249.** 701 E Campbell Rd 75081. US 75 exit 26 (Campbell Rd) southbound; exit northbound, on access road. Int corridors. **Pets:** Accepted. 〔SAVE〕 🛜 ♿ 🛏 💻 🍽 🏊

⊗ ▼▼ ▼ Renaissance Dallas-Richardson
　Hotel 🅷

(972) 367-2000. **$93-$149.** 900 E Lookout Dr 75082. US 75 exit 27A (Gallatin Pkwy/Renner Rd) northbound; exit 26 (Gallatin Pkwy/Campbell Rd) southbound, just e. Int corridors. **Pets:** Medium, other species. $50 one-time fee/pet. Service with restrictions, supervision.

〔SAVE〕 🛜 ❌ 🛏 💻 🍽 🏊 ⊗

▼▼▼ Residence Inn by Marriott Richardson 🅷

(972) 669-5888. **$98-$179.** 1040 Waterwood Dr 75082. US 75 exit 26 (Campbell Rd), just e to Greenville Ave, 0.4 mi n to Glenville Rd, then just w. Int corridors. **Pets:** Accepted.

〔ECO〕 🛜 ❌ 🛏 💻 🏊 ⊗

ROANOKE

▼▼ Comfort Suites Alliance South 🅷

(817) 490-1455. **$89-$269.** 801 Byron Nelson Blvd 76262. I-35 exit 70 (SR 114), 2 mi e. Int corridors. **Pets:** Medium. $10 daily fee/pet. Designated rooms, service with restrictions, crate.

🛜 ❌ ♿ 🛏 💻 🏊

⊗ ▼▼ Speedway Sleep Inn & Suites 🅷

(817) 491-3120. **$90-$110.** 13471 Raceway Dr 76262. I-35 exit 70 (SR 114), just e, then just s. Int corridors. **Pets:** Medium, other species. $30 deposit/room. Service with restrictions, supervision.

〔SAVE〕 🛜 ♿ 🛏 💻 🏊

ROCKWALL

⊗ ▼▼▼ Best Western Plus Rockwall Inn &
　Suites 🅷

(972) 722-3265. **$85-$150.** 996 E I-30 75087. I-30 exit 68, on westbound frontage road. Int corridors. **Pets:** Medium, other species. $50 deposit/room, $10 daily fee/pet. Designated rooms, service with restrictions.

〔SAVE〕 🛜 ♿ 🛏 💻 🏊

▼▼▼ La Quinta Inn & Suites Rockwall 🅷

(972) 771-1685. **$93-$159.** 689 E I-30 75087. I-30 exit 67 (Ridge Rd) westbound; exit 67B (Horizon Rd) eastbound, on eastbound frontage road. Int corridors. **Pets:** Medium, other species. Service with restrictions, supervision. 🛜 ♿ 🛏 💻 🏊

ROWLETT

⊗ ▼▼▼ Comfort Suites Lake Ray Hubbard 🅷

(972) 463-9595. **$80-$89.** 8701 E I-30 75088. I-30 exit 64 (Dalrock Rd). Int corridors. **Pets:** Small. $10 daily fee/pet. Service with restrictions, supervision. 〔SAVE〕 🛜 ❌ ♿ 🛏 💻 🏊

TERRELL

⊗ ▼▼ Best Western Country Inn 🅷

(972) 563-1521. **$62-$90.** 1604 Hwy 34 S 75160. I-20 exit 501 (SR 34), just n. Ext corridors. **Pets:** Accepted. 〔SAVE〕 🛜 🛏 💻 🏊

THE COLONY

⊗ ▼▼▼ Comfort Suites 🅷

(972) 668-5555. **$80-$130.** 4796 Memorial Dr 75056. SR 121 exit Blair Oaks southbound; exit Main St northbound, just n to Memorial Dr, then just e. Int corridors. **Pets:** Accepted.

〔SAVE〕 🛜 ❌ ♿ 🛏 💻 🏊

▼▼▼ Residence Inn by Marriott-Plano/Frisco/The
　Colony 🅷 🐾

(214) 469-1155. **$99-$169.** 6600 Cascades Ct 75056. SR 121 exit Spring Creek Pkwy, on southwest frontage road. Int corridors. **Pets:** Medium, other species. $100 one-time fee/room. Service with restrictions.

🛜 ❌ 🛏 💻 🏊 ⊗

UNIVERSITY PARK

⊗ ▼▼▼ Hotel Lumen 🅷

(214) 219-2400. **Call for rates.** 6101 Hillcrest Ave 75205. Just n of jct Mockingbird Ln and Hillcrest Ave. Int corridors. **Pets:** Accepted.

〔ECO〕 〔SAVE〕 🛜 ❌ 🛏 🍽

WYLIE

⊗ ▼▼▼ Best Western Plus Wylie Inn 🅷 🐾

(972) 429-1771. **$79-$99.** 2011 Hwy 78 N 75098. 1.8 mi ne of SR 2514 (Ballard St); downtown. Int corridors. **Pets:** Other species. $20 one-time fee/pet. Service with restrictions, supervision.

〔SAVE〕 🛜 ♿ 🛏 💻 🏊

END METROPOLITAN AREA

DECATUR

⊗ ▼▼ Best Western Decatur Inn 🅼

(940) 627-5982. **$74-$79.** 1801 S Hwy 287 76234. 0.6 mi s of jct Business Rt US 380. Ext corridors. **Pets:** Accepted.

〔SAVE〕 🛜 🛏 💻 🏊

⊗ ▼▼▼ Holiday Inn Express Hotel & Suites 🅷

(940) 627-0776. **Call for rates.** 1051 N Hwy 287 76234. Just n of jct US 380 and 287. Int corridors. **Pets:** Small. $50 one-time fee/pet. Service with restrictions, crate. 〔SAVE〕 🛜 🛏 💻 🏊

DEL RIO

⊗ ▼▼ Best Western Inn of Del Rio 🅼

(830) 775-7511. **$70.** 810 Veterans Blvd 78840. Between E 6th and E 7th sts. Ext corridors. **Pets:** Accepted. 〔SAVE〕 🛜 🛏 💻 🏊

▼▼▼ La Quinta Inn Del Rio 🅷

(830) 775-7591. **$64-$126.** 2005 Veterans Blvd 78840. 1.8 mi nw on US 90, 277 and 377. Ext/int corridors. **Pets:** Medium, other species. Service with restrictions, supervision. 🛜 🛏 💻 🏊

⊗ ▼▼▼ Ramada Inn 🅷

(830) 775-1511. **$73-$106.** 2101 Veterans Blvd 78840. 1.8 mi nw on US 90, 277 and 377. Ext/int corridors. **Pets:** Medium, other species. Designated rooms, service with restrictions, crate.

〔SAVE〕 🛜 🛏 💻 🍽 🏊 ⊗

DONNA

Super 8 🅼
(956) 461-2226. **$47-$80.** 2005 E Expwy 83 78537. US 83 exit CR 493. Ext corridors. **Pets:** Accepted. 🛎️ 🖥️ 💻 ⊇

Victoria Palms Inn & Suites 🅷
(956) 464-7801. **$50-$140.** 602 N Victoria Rd 78537. US 83 exit Victoria Rd. Ext corridors. **Pets:** Small, other species. $5 daily fee/pet. Designated rooms, service with restrictions, supervision.
🛎️ ⊠ 🖥️ 💻 🍴 ⊇ ⊠

DUMAS

Best Western Windsor Inn 🅷
(806) 935-9644. **$79-$109.** 1701 S Dumas Ave 79029. US 287, 2 mi s of US 87 and SR 152. Ext corridors. **Pets:** Dogs only. $10 daily fee/pet. Service with restrictions, crate. SAVE 🛎️ 🖥️ 💻 ⊇ ⊠

Days Inn & Suites 🅷
(806) 935-2222. **$64-$144.** 1610 S Dumas Ave 79029. Just s on US 287. Int corridors. **Pets:** Medium, dogs only. $25 daily fee/pet. Service with restrictions, supervision. SAVE 🛎️ 🅼 🖥️ 💻 ⊇ ⊠

Econo Lodge 🅷
(806) 935-9098. **$50-$130.** 1719 S Dumas Ave 79029. US 287, 2 mi s of US 87 and SR 152. Int corridors. **Pets:** Accepted. SAVE 🛎️ 🖥️

Quality Inn 🅷
(806) 935-4000. **$81-$86.** 1525 S Dumas Ave 79029. US 287, 1.1 mi s of US 87 and SR 152. Int corridors. **Pets:** Other species. $30 one-time fee/pet. Service with restrictions, supervision. 🛎️ 🖥️ 💻 ⊇

Super 8 🅼
(806) 935-6222. **$71-$80.** 119 W 17th St 79029. US 287, 2 mi s of US 87 and SR 152. Ext corridors. **Pets:** Accepted. 🛎️ 🖥️ 💻

EAGLE PASS

Americas Best Value Inn 🅷
(830) 773-9531. **$61-$68.** 2150 N US Hwy 277 78852. On US 277, 4 mi n. Ext corridors. **Pets:** Accepted. 🛎️ 🖥️ 💻

La Quinta Inn Eagle Pass 🅼
(830) 773-7000. **$84-$155.** 2525 E Main St 78852-4498. US 57 and 277 (Loop 431). Ext corridors. **Pets:** Medium, other species. Service with restrictions, supervision. 🛎️ 🖥️ 💻 ⊇

EASTLAND

La Quinta Inn & Suites Eastland 🅷
(254) 629-1414. **$85-$145.** 10150 IH-20 76448. I-10 exit 343, on north service road. Int corridors. **Pets:** Medium, other species. Service with restrictions, supervision. 🛎️ ⊠ 🅼 🖥️ 💻 ⊇

Super 8 & RV Park 🅼
(254) 629-3336. **$49-$79.** 3900 I-20 E 76448. I-20 exit 343, on north service road. Ext corridors. **Pets:** Accepted. 🛎️ 🖥️ 💻 ⊇

EDINBURG

Best Western Plus Edinburg Inn & Suites 🅷
(956) 318-0442. **$80-$100.** 2708 S Bus Hwy 281 (Closner Rd) 78539. US 281 exit Canton Ave, 1 mi w to Business Rt US 281. Ext corridors. **Pets:** Small. $15 daily fee/pet. Designated rooms, service with restrictions, supervision. SAVE 🛎️ 🅼 🖥️ 💻 ⊇

Comfort Inn Edinburg 🅼
(956) 318-1117. **$59-$199.** 4001 S US Hwy 281 78539. US 281 exit Trenton Rd, just w, then just n. Int corridors. **Pets:** Accepted. SAVE 🛎️ 🖥️ 💻 ⊇

EL PASO

Best Western Airport Inn 🅷
(915) 779-7700. **$66-$76.** 7144 Gateway Blvd E 79915. I-10 exit 26 (Hawkins Blvd), on eastbound frontage road. Ext corridors. **Pets:** Medium. $15 daily fee/pet. Service with restrictions, supervision.
SAVE 🛎️ 🖥️ 💻 ⊇

Best Western Sunland Park Inn 🅼
(915) 587-4900. **$69-$89.** 1045 Sunland Park Dr 79922. I-10 exit 13, just s. Ext corridors. **Pets:** Very small. $20 daily fee/pet. Designated rooms, service with restrictions, supervision. SAVE 🛎️ 🖥️ 💻 ⊇

Chase Suites by Woodfin 🅷 🐾
(915) 772-8000. **$150-$299.** 6791 Montana Ave 79925. I-10 exit 25 (Airway Blvd), 1 mi n, then just e. Ext corridors. **Pets:** Small, other species. $250 deposit/room, $10 daily fee/pet. Designated rooms, service with restrictions, supervision. 🛎️ ⊠ 🖥️ 💻 ⊇ ⊠

Comfort Inn Airport East 🅷 🐾
(915) 594-9111. **$67-$75.** 900 Yarbrough Dr 79915. I-10 exit 28B, just s. Ext corridors. **Pets:** Other species. $20 one-time fee/room. Service with restrictions, supervision. 🛎️ 🖥️ 💻 ⊇

Comfort Suites by Choice Hotels 🅷
(915) 587-5300. **$69-$89.** 949 Sunland Park Dr 79922. I-10 exit 13, just s. Int corridors. **Pets:** Accepted. 🛎️ ⊠ 🖥️ 💻 ⊇

Days Inn Hotel East 🅼 🐾
(915) 595-1913. **$50-$58.** 10635 Gateway Blvd W 79935. I-10 exit 28B westbound; exit 29 (Lomaland Dr) eastbound, 1 mi w on frontage road. Ext corridors. **Pets:** $10 daily fee/room. Designated rooms, service with restrictions. 🛎️ 🖥️ 💻 ⊇

Embassy Suites Hotel 🅷
(915) 779-6222. **$109-$179.** 6100 Gateway Blvd E 79905. I-10 exit 24B (Geronimo Dr) eastbound; exit 24 (Geronimo Dr) westbound, 0.6 mi to Trowbridge, U-turn under interstate, then 0.5 mi e. Int corridors. **Pets:** Accepted. 🛎️ 🖥️ 💻 ⊇

GuestHouse International Suites 🅷
(915) 772-0395. **$79-$135.** 1940 Airway Blvd 79925. I-10 exit 25 (Airway Blvd), 1.2 mi n. Int corridors. **Pets:** Medium. $75 deposit/room, $10 daily fee/room. Designated rooms, service with restrictions, supervision.
🛎️ ⊠ 🅼 🖥️ 💻 ⊇

Holiday Inn El Paso Sunland Park 🅷
(915) 833-2900. **$99-$179.** 900 Sunland Park Dr 79922. I-10 exit 13 (Sunland Park Dr), just s. Ext corridors. **Pets:** Large. $25 one-time fee/pet. Service with restrictions, supervision. SAVE 🛎️ 🖥️ 💻 🍴 ⊇

Holiday Inn Express El Paso-Central 🅷 🐾
(915) 544-3333. **$89-$159.** 409 E Missouri St 79901. I-10 exit 19B westbound (downtown); exit 19 eastbound, just e. Int corridors. **Pets:** $25 one-time fee/pet. Service with restrictions, crate.
SAVE 🛎️ ⊠ 🖥️ 💻 ⊇

La Quinta Inn & Suites El Paso East 🅷
(915) 591-3300. **$74-$137.** 7944 Gateway Blvd E 79915. I-10 exit 28B. Int corridors. **Pets:** Medium, other species. Service with restrictions, supervision. 🛎️ 🅼 🖥️ 💻 ⊇

La Quinta Inn El Paso Lomaland 🅷
(915) 591-2244. **$62-$122.** 11033 Gateway Blvd W 79935. I-10 exit 29 eastbound; exit 30 westbound, 1 mi w. Ext corridors. **Pets:** Medium, other species. Service with restrictions, supervision. 🛎️ 🅼 🖥️ 💻 ⊇

La Quinta Inn El Paso West 🅼
(915) 833-2522. **$64-$126.** 7550 Remcon Cir 79912. I-10 exit 11 (Mesa St). Ext corridors. **Pets:** Medium, other species. Service with restrictions, supervision. 🛎️ 🖥️ 💻 ⊇

▼▼ **Microtel Inn & Suites** H
(915) 772-3650. **$54-$180.** 2001 Airway Blvd 79925. I-10 exit 25 (Airway Blvd), 1.3 mi n. Int corridors. **Pets:** Small, other species. $100 deposit/pet, $5 daily fee/pet. Service with restrictions. 📶 ♿ 🛗 💻 ⊟

▼▼ **Microtel Inn & Suites El Paso East** H
(915) 858-1600. **$45-$51.** 12211 Gateway Blvd W 79936. I-10 exit 34 (Joe Battle Blvd), on westbound frontage road. Int corridors. **Pets:** Medium, other species. $100 deposit/room. Service with restrictions. 📶 ♿ 🛗 💻 ⊟

▼▼ **Microtel Inn & Suites West** M
(915) 584-2026. **$45-$57.** 6185 S Desert Blvd 79932. I-10 exit 8 (Artcraft Rd/Paseo del Norte Rd); on eastbound frontage road. Int corridors. **Pets:** Accepted. 📶 ♿ 🛗 💻 ⊟

▼▼ **Motel 6 El Paso-Airport-Fort Bliss #4487** M
(915) 778-3311. **$45-$49.** 6363 Montana Ave 79925. I-10 exit 24 (Geronimo Dr) westbound; exit 24B (Geronimo Dr) eastbound, 0.5 mi n, then 0.5 mi e. Ext corridors. **Pets:** Other species. Service with restrictions, supervision. ECO 📶 🛗 ⊟

▼▼ **Motel 6 El Paso West #4583** H
(915) 584-4030. **$98-$169.** 7840 N Mesa St 79932. I-10 exit 11 (N Mesa St), just s. Ext corridors. **Pets:** Other species. Service with restrictions, supervision. 📶 🛗 ⊟

▼▼▼ **Quality Inn & Suites** H
(915) 772-3300. **$64-$74.** 6099 Montana Ave 79925. I-10 exit 24 (Geronimo Dr) westbound; exit 24B (Geronimo Dr) eastbound, 0.5 mi n. Ext corridors. **Pets:** Accepted. 📶 🛗 💻 🍴 ⊟

▼▼▼▼ **Residence Inn by Marriott El Paso** H
(915) 771-0504. **$98-$169.** 6355 Gateway Blvd W 79925. I-10 exit 24B (Geronimo Dr) eastbound, n to Edgemere, then just e; exit 25 (Airway Blvd) westbound, on westbound frontage road. Int corridors. **Pets:** Accepted. 📶 ✕ 🛗 💻 ⊟ ✕

▼▼ **Sleep Inn by Choice Hotels** H
(915) 585-7577. **$82.** 953 Sunland Park Dr 79922. I-10 exit 13, just w. Int corridors. **Pets:** $20 one-time fee/pet. Designated rooms, service with restrictions, supervision. 📶 🛗 ⊟

▼▼▼ **Wingate by Wyndham** H
(915) 772-4088. **$71-$125.** 6351 Gateway Blvd W 79925. I-10 exit 24B (Geronimo Dr) westbound; exit 25 (Airport Blvd) eastbound, U-turn, 0.5 mi. Int corridors. **Pets:** Other species. $10 daily fee/room. Service with restrictions, crate. 📶 ✕ ♿ 🛗 💻 ⊟

▼▼▼ **Wyndham El Paso Airport** H
(915) 778-4241. **$129-$172, 6 day notice.** 2027 Airway Blvd 79925. I-10 exit 25 (Airway Blvd), 1.3 mi n. Int corridors. **Pets:** Small. $25 one-time fee/pet. Service with restrictions.
📶 ✕ 🛗 💻 🍴 ⊟ ✕

EULESS

AAA ▼▼▼ **La Quinta Inn & Suites DFW Airport West - Euless** H
(817) 836-4000. **$98-$159.** 431 Airport Frwy 76040. SR 183 exit Ector Dr, on eastbound frontage road. Int corridors. **Pets:** Medium, other species. Service with restrictions, supervision.
SAVE 📶 ✕ 🛗 💻 ⊟

▼▼ **Microtel Inn & Suites** H
(817) 545-1111. **$44-$63.** 901 W Airport Frwy 76040. SR 183 exit Industrial Blvd (FM 157), on eastbound frontage road. Int corridors. **Pets:** Medium, dogs only. $25 one-time fee/room. Service with restrictions, supervision. 📶 ♿ 🛗 💻 ⊟

FALFURRIAS

▼▼ **Days Inn** M
(361) 325-2515. **$53-$63.** 2116 Hwy 281 S 78355. 1.5 mi s of SR 285. Ext corridors. **Pets:** Accepted. 📶 🛗 💻

FOREST HILL

AAA ▼▼ **Comfort Inn** H
(817) 551-5200. **$80-$100.** 3232 SE Loop 820 76140. I-20/SE Loop 820 exit 440A (Wichita St), on eastbound access road. Int corridors. **Pets:** Accepted. SAVE 📶 🛗 💻 ⊟

AAA ▼▼▼ **La Quinta Inn & Suites** H
(817) 293-5800. **$91-$152.** 3346 Forest Hill Cir 76140. I-20 exit 440B (Forest Hill), just s, then just w. Int corridors. **Pets:** Medium, other species. Service with restrictions, supervision.
SAVE 📶 ✕ 🛗 💻 ⊟

FORT DAVIS

▼▼ **Historical Prude Guest Ranch** RA
(432) 426-3202. **$61-$180, 3 day notice.** 6 mi n Hwy 118 79734. 4.5 mi n of jct SR 118 and 17. Ext corridors. **Pets:** Very small, dogs only. $10 daily fee/pet. No service, supervision.
📶 🛗 🛗 💻 🍴 ⊟ ✕ 🅿 ⊠

FORT STOCKTON

AAA ▼▼ **Days Inn** H
(432) 336-7500. **$71-$80.** 1408 N US Hwy 285 79731. I-10 exit 257, just s. Ext corridors. **Pets:** Medium. $12 daily fee/pet. Designated rooms, service with restrictions, supervision. SAVE 📶 🛗 💻 ⊟

AAA ▼▼ **La Quinta Inn Fort Stockton** H
(432) 336-9781. **$80-$139.** 1537 N US Hwy 285 79735. I-10 exit 257. Ext corridors. **Pets:** Medium, other species. Service with restrictions, supervision. 📶 🛗 💻 ⊟

AAA ▼▼ **Quality Inn** H
(432) 336-5955. **$79-$129.** 1308 N US Hwy 285 79735. I-10 exit 257, just s. Ext corridors. **Pets:** Accepted. SAVE 📶 🛗 💻 ⊟

AAA ▼▼ **Sleep Inn & Suites** H
(432) 336-8338. **$75-$150.** 3401 W Dickinson Blvd 79735. I-10 exit 256, just e. Int corridors. **Pets:** Medium. $35 daily fee/pet. Designated rooms, service with restrictions, supervision. SAVE 📶 ♿ 🛗 💻 ⊟

▼▼ **Swiss Clock Inn** H
(432) 336-8521. **Call for rates.** 3201 W Dickinson Blvd 79735. I-10 exit 256, 0.5 mi e. Ext corridors. **Pets:** Accepted. 📶 🛗 💻 ⊟

FORT WORTH

AAA ▼▼▼ **The Ashton Hotel** H 🐾
(817) 332-0100. **$199-$799.** 610 Main St 76102. Jct 6th and Main sts; center. Int corridors. **Pets:** Medium, dogs only. $150 deposit/room. Service with restrictions, supervision. SAVE 📶 ✕ 💻 🍴

▼▼ **Baymont Inn & Suites Fort Worth North** H
(817) 740-1099. **Call for rates.** 4681 Gemini Pl 76106. I-35W exit 56A, just w. Int corridors. **Pets:** Accepted. 📶 🛗 💻 ⊟

▼▼ **Candlewood Suites** H
(817) 838-8229. **$104-$124.** 5201 Endicott Ave 76137. I-820 exit 17B (Beach St), just s, then w. Int corridors. **Pets:** Accepted. 📶 🛗 💻

▼▼▼ **Comfort Suites North-Fossil Creek** H
(817) 222-2333. **$89-$144.** 3751 Tanacross Dr 76137. I-820 exit 17B (N Beach St), just s. Int corridors. **Pets:** Accepted.
📶 ✕ 🛗 💻 ⊟

AAA ▼▼▼ **Country Inn & Suites By Carlson** H
(817) 831-9200. **$109-$219.** 2200 Mercado Dr 76106. I-35W exit 53 (Northside Dr), just w. Int corridors. **Pets:** Other species. $25 one-time fee/pet. Service with restrictions, crate. SAVE 📶 ♿ 🛗 💻 ⊟

▼▼▼ **Crowne Plaza Fort Worth South** H
(817) 293-3088. **$89-$169.** 100 Altamesa Blvd E 76134. I-35W exit 44. Int corridors. **Pets:** Accepted. 📶 ✕ 🛗 💻 🍴 ⊟

▼▼ Extended Stay Deluxe Fort Worth-City View H ❖
(817) 263-8700. **$79-$109.** 4701 City Lake Blvd W 76132. I-20 exit 431 (Bryant Irvin Rd), just e on frontage road, then just s. Int corridors. **Pets:** Other species. $25 daily fee/pet. Service with restrictions.
🛜 🍴 💻 ➿

▼▼ Extended Stay Deluxe Hotel Fort Worth-Fossil Creek H ❖
(817) 232-1622. **$74-$139.** 3261 NE Loop 820 76137. I-820 exit 17B (N Beach St), 0.5 mi w on westbound frontage road. Int corridors. **Pets:** Other species. $25 daily fee/pet. Service with restrictions.
🛜 🍴 💻 ➿

▼▼ Aspen Suites H
(817) 731-9600. **Call for rates.** 6851 West Frwy 76116. I-30 exit 7B, 0.8 mi e on to Green Oaks Rd. Int corridors. **Pets:** Accepted.
🛜 ✕ ♿M 🍴 💻 ➿

▼▼▼ Historic Hilton Fort Worth H ❖
(817) 870-2100. **$139-$219.** 815 Main St 76102. Northeast corner of Main and 8th sts; center. Int corridors. **Pets:** Medium. $50 one-time fee/room. Service with restrictions, supervision. 🛜 ♿M 🍴 💻 🍴

▼▼▼ Holiday Inn Express Hotel & Suites H ❖
(817) 744-7755. **$109-$139.** 3541 NW Loop 820 76106. I-820 exit 10A eastbound; exit 10B westbound. Int corridors. **Pets:** Small. $20 daily fee/pet. Designated rooms, service with restrictions, crate.
🛜 ♿M 🍴 💻 ➿

▼▼▼ Holiday Inn Express Hotel & Suites-Fort Worth West H
(817) 560-4200. **$119-$159.** 2730 S Cherry Ln 76116. I-30 exit 7A (Cherry Ln), just s. Int corridors. **Pets:** Small. $150 deposit/room, $20 daily fee/pet. Designated rooms, service with restrictions, supervision.
🛜 🍴 💻 ➿

▼▼▼ Homewood Suites by Hilton H
(817) 834-7400. **$79-$249.** 3701 Tanacross Dr 76137. I-820 exit 17B (Beach St), just s, then just w. Int corridors. **Pets:** Accepted.
🛜 ♿M 🍴 💻 ➿

▼▼▼ La Quinta Inn & Suites Fort Worth North H
(817) 222-2888. **$98-$165.** 4700 North Frwy 76137. I-35W exit 56A, just n. Int corridors. **Pets:** Medium, other species. Service with restrictions, supervision. 🛜 🍴 💻 ➿

▼▼▼ La Quinta Inn & Suites Fort Worth Southwest H
(817) 370-2700. **$98-$175.** 4900 Bryant Irvin Rd 76132. I-20 exit 431 (Bryant Irvin Rd), just s. Int corridors. **Pets:** Medium, other species. Service with restrictions, supervision. 🛜 ♿M 🍴 💻 ➿

▼▼▼ La Quinta Inn & Suites Lake Worth H
(817) 237-9300. **$94-$155.** 5800 Quebec St 76135. I-820 exit 9 (Quebec), just sw. Int corridors. **Pets:** Medium, other species. Service with restrictions, supervision. 🛜 ✕ 🍴 💻 ➿

▼▼ Microtel Inn & Suites H
(817) 222-3740. **$59-$270.** 3740 Tanacross Dr 76137. I-820 exit 17B (N Beach St), just s, then just w. Int corridors. **Pets:** Accepted.
🛜 ✕ 🍴 💻 ➿

▼▼▼ Omni Hotel H
(817) 535-6664. **Call for rates.** 1300 Houston St 76102. Between 12th and 14th sts. Int corridors. **Pets:** Small. $50 one-time fee/room. Service with restrictions, supervision. 🛜 ✕ ♿M 💻 🍴 ➿ ✕

▼▼ Quality Inn & Suites H
(817) 560-4180. **Call for rates.** 2700 Cherry Ln 76116. I-30 exit 7A (Cherry Ln), just s. Ext corridors. **Pets:** Accepted. 🛜 🍴 💻 ➿

▼▼▼ Residence Inn by Marriott Fort Worth Cultural District H
(817) 885-8250. **$200-$240.** 2500 Museum Way 76107. I-30 exit 13B (Henderson St), 0.4 mi n to 7th St, 0.8 mi w to Stayton St, then just s. Int corridors. **Pets:** Accepted. 🛜 ✕ ♿M 🍴 💻 ➿ ✕

▼▼▼ Residence Inn by Marriott-Fossil Creek H
(817) 439-1300. **$103-$170.** 5801 Sandshell Dr 76137. I-35W exit 58 (Western Center Blvd) northbound to Sandshell Dr, 0.7 mi s; exit southbound, first road to right through strip center, just s to Sandshell Dr, then 0.7 mi s. Int corridors. **Pets:** Accepted.
🌿 🛜 ✕ ♿M 🍴 💻 ➿ ✕

▼▼▼ Residence Inn-Alliance Airport H
(817) 750-7000. **$98-$199.** 13400 North Frwy 76177. I-35W exit 66. Int corridors. **Pets:** Accepted. 🛜 ✕ 🍴 💻 ➿ ✕

▼▼▼ Residence Inn University by Marriott H
(817) 870-1011. **$119-$229.** 1701 S University Dr 76107. I-30 exit 12 (University Dr), 0.4 mi s. Ext corridors. **Pets:** Accepted.
🛜 ✕ ♿M 🍴 💻 ➿ ✕

▲▲▲ ▼▼▼▼ Sheraton Fort Worth Hotel & Spa H
(817) 335-7000. **$89-$399.** 1701 Commerce St 76102. Center. Int corridors. **Pets:** Accepted. 🆂🅰🆅🅴 🛜 ✕ 🍴 💻 🍴 ➿ ✕

▼▼▼ Staybridge Suites West Fort Worth H
(817) 935-6500. **$90-$179.** 229 Clifford Center Dr 76108. I-820 N exit 5A (Clifford Center Dr), just w. Int corridors. **Pets:** Accepted.
🛜 ✕ 🍴 💻 ➿

▼▼▼ TownePlace Suites Fort Worth Southwest H
(817) 732-2224. **$99-$159.** 4200 International Plaza Dr 76109. I-20 exit 433 (Hulen St), on westbound frontage road. Int corridors.
Pets: Accepted. 🌿 🛜 ✕ 🍴 💻 ➿

▲▲▲ ▼▼▼ ▼▼▼ The Worthington Renaissance Fort Worth Hotel H
(817) 870-1000. **$179-$320.** 200 Main St 76102. Northwest corner of 2nd and Main sts. Int corridors. **Pets:** Small, other species. $200 deposit/pet. Service with restrictions, crate. 🆂🅰🆅🅴 🛜 ✕ 🍴 💻 🍴 ➿ ✕

FREDERICKSBURG

▲▲▲ ▼▼▼▼ Best Western Plus Fredericksburg H ❖
(830) 992-2929. **$89-$229.** 314 E Highway St 78624. Jct US 87 and 290, 6 blks s. Int corridors. **Pets:** Medium. $20 daily fee/room. Designated rooms, service with restrictions, supervision. 🆂🅰🆅🅴 🛜 🍴 💻 ➿

▲▲▲ ▼▼▼ Dietzel Motel M
(830) 997-3330. **$52-$99.** 1141 W US 290 78624. On US 290, 1 mi w, at US 87. Ext corridors. **Pets:** Other species. $10 daily fee/pet. Designated rooms, service with restrictions. 🆂🅰🆅🅴 🛜 🍴 💻 ➿

▲▲▲ ▼▼▼ Fredericksburg Econo Lodge M
(830) 997-3437. **$50-$120.** 810 S Adams St 78624. Jct US 290 and SR 16 S, 1 mi s. Ext corridors. **Pets:** Other species. $10 daily fee/pet. Service with restrictions. 🆂🅰🆅🅴 🛜 🍴 💻 ➿

▲▲▲ ▼▼▼▼ Fredericksburg Inn & Suites H ❖
(830) 997-0202. **$79-$229.** 201 S Washington St 78624. US 290 and 87, 3 blks s. Ext corridors. **Pets:** Small, dogs only. $35 one-time fee/room. Designated rooms, service with restrictions, supervision.
🆂🅰🆅🅴 🛜 ✕ 🍴 💻 ➿

▼▼▼ Howard Johnson Hill Country H
(830) 990-4200. **Call for rates.** 1220 N Hwy 87 78624. 1 mi w on US 290 at US 87. Int corridors. **Pets:** Accepted. 🛜 ♿M 🍴 💻 ➿

▼▼▼ La Quinta Inn & Suites Fredericksburg H
(830) 990-2899. **$108-$184.** 1465 E Main St 78624. 1 mi e of downtown. Int corridors. **Pets:** Medium, other species. Service with restrictions, supervision. 🛜 ♿M 🍴 💻 ➿

▼▼▼ Quality Inn H
(830) 997-9811. **Call for rates.** 908 S Adams St 78624. 0.8 mi sw on SR 16; 0.8 mi sw of jct US 87 and 290. Ext corridors. **Pets:** Accepted.
🛜 🍴 💻 ➿

◆◆◆ Sunday House Inn & Suites **H**
(830) 997-4484. **$99-$249.** 501 E Main St 78624. 0.4 mi e on US 290.
Ext corridors. **Pets:** Small. $25 daily fee/pet. Designated rooms, service
with restrictions, supervision.

AAA ◆ Sunset Inn **M**
(830) 997-9581. **$55-$85.** 900 S Adams St 78624. 0.8 mi sw of jct US
290 and SR 16. Ext corridors. **Pets:** Accepted.

FREER

AAA ◆◆◆ Best Western Windwood Inn & Suites **M**
(361) 394-6200. **$100-$200.** 1172 E Riley St 78357. On US 59 and SR
44 E, just e of SR 16. Ext corridors. **Pets:** Accepted.

FULTON

AAA ◆◆◆ Best Western Inn by the Bay **H**
(361) 729-8351. **$65-$150.** 3902 N Hwy 35 78358. SR 35, 0.5 mi n of jct
Business Rt SR 35 and FM 3063. Ext corridors. **Pets:** Accepted.

GAINESVILLE

◆◆◆ Holiday Inn Express Hotel & Suites **H**
(940) 665-0505. **$99-$139.** 320 N I-35 76240. I-35 exit 496B (California
St), on northbound frontage road. Int corridors. **Pets:** Small. $15 daily
fee/pet. Service with restrictions, crate.

◆◆◆ La Quinta Inn & Suites Gainesville **H**
(940) 665-5700. **$103-$165.** 4201 N I-35 76240. I-35 exit 501, just w on
FM 1202, then just s on access road. Int corridors. **Pets:** Medium, other
species. Service with restrictions, supervision.

GALVESTON

◆◆◆ La Quinta Inn & Suites Galveston Seawall
West **H**
(409) 740-9100. **$107-$179.** 8710 Seawall Blvd 77554. Between 85th
and 89th sts. Int corridors. **Pets:** Medium, other species. Service with
restrictions, supervision.

AAA ◆◆◆ The San Luis Resort Spa & Conference
Center **H**
(409) 744-1500. **$119-$950, 3 day notice.** 5222 Seawall Blvd 77551.
Just e of jct Seawall Blvd and 53rd St. Int corridors. **Pets:** Accepted.

GATESVILLE

AAA ◆◆◆ Best Western Chateau Ville Motor Inn **H**
(254) 865-2281. **$76-$86, 14 day notice.** 2501 E Main St 76528. Jct
US 84 and SR 36, 0.5 mi w. Ext corridors. **Pets:** Small. Service with
restrictions, crate.

GEORGETOWN

◆◆◆ Country Inn & Suites By Carlson Georgetown **H**
(512) 868-8555. **Call for rates.** 600 San Gabriel Village Blvd 78626. I-35
exit 261A, 0.5 mi n on E Frontage Rd, then just e. Int corridors.
Pets: Accepted.

◆◆◆ La Quinta Inn Georgetown **H**
(512) 869-2541. **$72-$133.** 333 I-35 N 78628. I-35 exit 264 northbound;
exit 262 southbound, on west frontage road. Ext corridors. **Pets:** Medium,
other species. Service with restrictions, supervision.

GEORGE WEST

AAA ◆◆◆ Best Western George West Executive
Inn **M**
(361) 449-3300. **$119-$139.** 208 N Nueces St 78022. Just n of US 59
on US 281. Ext corridors. **Pets:** Accepted.

GLEN ROSE

AAA ◆◆◆ Best Western Dinosaur Valley Inn &
Suites **H**
(254) 897-4818. **$89-$112.** 1311 NE Big Bend Tr 76043. On US 67. Int
corridors. **Pets:** Accepted.

GRAHAM

◆◆◆ Wildcatter Ranch **RA**
(940) 549-3500. **Call for rates.** 6062 Hwy 16 S 76450. SR 16, 7 mi s.
Ext/int corridors. **Pets:** Accepted.

GRANBURY

◆◆◆ Baymont Inn & Suites **H** ❀
(817) 579-9977. **Call for rates.** 1515 N Plaza Dr 76048. On US 377
Bypass, 2.2 mi of jct SR 144 and US 377. Int corridors. **Pets:** Medium.
$10 daily fee/room. Service with restrictions, supervision.

AAA ◆◆◆ Best Western Granbury Inn &
Suites **H** ❀
(817) 573-4239. **$70-$100.** 1517 N Plaza Dr 76048. On US 377 Bypass;
2.2 mi n of jct SR 144 and US 377 Bypass. Int corridors. **Pets:** Other
species. $25 one-time fee/room. Service with restrictions, crate.

◆◆◆ Comfort Suites **H**
(817) 579-5559. **$90-$110.** 903 Harbor Lakes Dr 76048. Jct SR 144 and
US 377 Bypass, 1.9 mi n on US 377 Bypass. Int corridors.
Pets: Accepted.

◆◆◆ La Quinta Inns & Suites-Granbury **H**
(817) 573-2007. **$107-$179.** 880 Harbor Lakes Dr 76048. Jct US 377
and SR 144. Int corridors. **Pets:** Medium, other species. Service with
restrictions, supervision.

AAA ◆◆◆ Plantation Inn Granbury **H**
(817) 573-8846. **$60-$100.** 1451 E Pearl St 76048. 0.3 mi w of Business
Rt US 377; at US 377. Ext/int corridors. **Pets:** Accepted.

◆◆◆ Quality Inn & Suites **H** ❀
(817) 573-4411. **$50-$80.** 800 Harbor Lakes Dr 76048. Jct SR 144 and
US 377 Bypass, 1.9 mi n on US 377 Bypass. Int corridors.
Pets: Medium. $10 daily fee/pet. Designated rooms, no service, supervi-
sion.

GRAPEVINE

AAA ◆◆◆ Embassy Suites Outdoor World **H**
(972) 724-2600. **$139-$299.** 2401 Bass Pro Dr 76051. SR 121 exit Bass
Pro Dr, just w. Int corridors. **Pets:** Accepted.

◆◆◆ Homewood Suites by Hilton **H**
(972) 691-2427. **$109-$179.** 2214 Grapevine Mills Cir W 76051. SR 121
N exit Bass Pro Dr. Int corridors. **Pets:** Accepted.

AAA ◆◆◆ Hyatt Regency DFW **H**
(972) 453-1234. **$85-$319.** 2334 N International Pkwy 75261. In Dallas-
Fort Worth International Airport Terminal C area. Int corridors.
Pets: Accepted.

◆◆◆ Super 8-Grapevine **H** ❀
(817) 329-7222. **$73-$180.** 250 E Hwy 114 76051. SR 114 exit Main St.
Int corridors. **Pets:** Other species. $10 daily fee/pet. No service, supervi-
sion.

GROESBECK

AAA ◆◆◆ **Best Western Groesbeck Inn & Suites** H
(254) 729-0077. **Call for rates.** 1012 N Ellis St 76642. Jct SR 14 and 164, 1 mi n. Int corridors. **Pets:** Accepted.
[SAVE] 🛰 🕭M 🛏 🖵 🏊

GROOM

AAA ◆◆ **Chalet Inn** M
(806) 248-7524. **$39-$60.** I-40 FM 2300 79039. I-40 exit 113, just s. Ext corridors. **Pets:** Medium. $5 daily fee/pet. Designated rooms, service with restrictions, supervision. [SAVE] 🕭M 🛏

HALLETTSVILLE

◆◆ ◆◆ **Chaparral Motel** M
(361) 798-4385. **Call for rates.** 310 Hwy 77 S 77964. Jct US 77 S and Alternate US 90. Ext corridors. **Pets:** Accepted. 🛰 🛏 🖵 🏊

AAA ◆◆◆ **Hotel Texas** H
(361) 798-5900. **Call for rates.** 1632 N Texana St 77964. Just s of CR 200. Int corridors. **Pets:** Medium, other species. $10 daily fee/pet. Service with restrictions, crate. [SAVE] 🛰 ✖ 🛏 🖵 🏊

HARLINGEN

◆◆ ◆◆ **La Quinta Inn Harlingen** H
(956) 428-6888. **$71-$129.** 1002 S Expwy 83 78552. US 83 and 77 exit M St. Ext corridors. **Pets:** Medium, other species. Service with restrictions, supervision. 🛰 🕭M 🛏 🖵 🏊

HEARNE

AAA ◆◆◆ **Oak Tree Inn** H
(979) 279-5599. **$89-$120.** 1051 N Market St 77859. 0.6 mi n of jct US 79 and SR 6. Ext/int corridors. **Pets:** Accepted.
[SAVE] 🛰 🛏 🖵 🍴

HENDERSON

◆◆◆◆ **Baymont Inn & Suites Henderson** H
(903) 657-7900. **Call for rates.** 410 Hwy 79 S 75654. Just n of jct US 259. Int corridors. **Pets:** Small. $50 deposit/room, $10 daily fee/pet. Service with restrictions, supervision. 🛰 🛏 🖵 🏊

AAA ◆◆◆ **Best Western Inn of Henderson** H
(903) 657-9561. **Call for rates.** 1500 Hwy 259 S 75654. 2 mi s on US 259, 0.7 mi s of jct US 79 and 259 S. Ext/int corridors. **Pets:** Accepted.
[SAVE] 🛰 🛏 🖵 🏊

HEREFORD

AAA ◆◆◆ **Best Western Red Carpet Inn** H
(806) 364-0540. **$65-$70.** 830 W 1st St 79045. Just w of jct US 385 and 60. Ext corridors. **Pets:** Medium. Service with restrictions, crate.
[SAVE] 🛰 🛏 🖵 🏊

AAA ◆◆◆ **Holiday Inn Express** H
(806) 364-3322. **$119-$145.** 1400 W 1st St 79045. Jct US 385 and 60, just w. Int corridors. **Pets:** Medium. $20 daily fee/pet. No service, supervision. [SAVE] 🛰 🕭M 🛏 🖵 🏊

HILLSBORO

◆◆ ◆◆ **Comfort Inn of Hillsboro** H
(254) 582-3333. **Call for rates.** 1515 Old Brandon Rd 76645. I-35 exit 368A northbound; exit 368B southbound, just w. Ext corridors.
Pets: Accepted. 🛰 🕭M 🛏 🖵 🏊

AAA ◆◆◆ **Best Western Hillsboro Inn** H
(254) 582-8465. **Call for rates.** 307 I-35 Hwy NW 76645. I-35 exit 368A northbound; exit 368B southbound, just w. Ext corridors. **Pets:** Large, other species. $10 one-time fee/room. Service with restrictions.
[SAVE] 🛰 🛏 🖵 🏊

◆◆ **Motel 6 - 4136** H
(254) 580-9000. **$49-$61.** 1506 Hillview Dr 76645. I-35 exit 368 southbound; exit 368A northbound. Int corridors. **Pets:** Other species. Service with restrictions, supervision. 🛰 🕭M 🛏 🖵 🏊

◆◆ ◆◆ **Super 8** H
(254) 580-0404. **$59-$100.** 1512 Hillview Dr 76645. I-35 exit 368A northbound; exit 368 southbound, just e. Int corridors. **Pets:** Accepted.
🛰 🛏 🖵 🏊

HONDO

AAA ◆◆◆◆ **Best Western Hondo Inn** H
(830) 426-4466. **$80-$90.** 301 Hwy 90 E 78861. Just e of downtown. Int corridors. **Pets:** Accepted. [SAVE] 🛰 🕭M 🛏 🖵 🏊

HORSESHOE BAY

AAA ◆◆◆◆◆ **Horseshoe Bay Resort Marriott Hotel** H
(830) 598-8600. **$210-$362, 3 day notice.** 200 Hi Cir N 78657. Jct US 281 and SR 2147, 6.6 mi w. Ext/int corridors. **Pets:** Accepted.
[SAVE] 🛰 ✖ 🕭M 🛏 🖵 🍴 🏊 ✖

HOUSTON METROPOLITAN AREA

BAYTOWN

◆◆◆◆ **Baymont Inn & Suites by Wyndham** H
(281) 839-1400. **Call for rates.** 7212 E Point Blvd 77521. I-10 exit 792 (Garth Rd), just n. Int corridors. **Pets:** Small, other species. $15 daily fee/pet. Designated rooms, service with restrictions, supervision.
🛰 🛏 🖵 🏊

◆◆◆◆ **Comfort Suites** H
(281) 421-9764. **$79-$180.** 7209 Garth Rd 77521. I-10 exit 792 (Garth Rd), just n. Int corridors. **Pets:** Accepted. 🛰 ✖ 🕭M 🛏 🖵 🏊

AAA ◆◆◆ **Days Inn Baytown** H
(281) 421-2233. **Call for rates.** 5021 East Frwy 77521. I-10 exit 792 (Garth Rd). Ext corridors. **Pets:** Accepted. [SAVE] 🛰 🛏 🖵 🏊

◆◆◆◆ **La Quinta Inn & Suites Baytown East** H
(281) 421-5566. **$74-$133.** 5215 I-10 E 77521. I-10 exit 792 (Garth Rd), just ne. Int corridors. **Pets:** Medium, other species. Service with restrictions, supervision. 🛰 🕭M 🛏 🖵 🏊

BROOKSHIRE

◆◆◆◆ **La Quinta Inn & Suites Brookshire** H
(281) 375-8888. **$81-$169.** 721 FM 1489 77423. I-10 exit 731, on S Frontage Rd. Int corridors. **Pets:** Medium, other species. Service with restrictions, supervision. 🛰 ✖ 🕭M 🛏 🖵 🏊

CLEVELAND

◆◆ ◆◆ **Super 8** H
(281) 432-8800. **$60-$100, 3 day notice.** 427 W Southline St 77327. US 59 exit SR 105, just e to W Southline St, then just s. Int corridors.
Pets: Accepted. 🛰 🛏 🖵 🏊

CONROE

AAA ◆◆◆ **Baymont Inn & Suites-Conroe/Woodlands** H
(936) 539-5100. **$81-$90.** 1506 Interstate 45 S 77304. I-45 exit 85 (Gladstell St) northbound; exit 84 (Frazier St) southbound. Int corridors.
Pets: Medium, dogs only. $10 daily fee/pet. No service, crate.
[SAVE] 🛰 🛏 🖵 🏊

▼▼▼▼ La Quinta Inn & Suites Conroe 🄷
(936) 228-0790. **$102-$164.** 4006 Sprayberry Ln 77303. I-45 exit 91
(League Line Rd), just e. Int corridors. **Pets:** Medium, other species.
Service with restrictions, supervision. 🛰 ⟨&M⟩ 🛋 🖥 ⇔

DEER PARK
▼▼▼▼ La Quinta Inn & Suites Deer Park 🄷
(281) 476-5300. **$71-$149.** 1400 East Blvd 77536. Jct SR 225 and East
Blvd, 0.8 mi s. Int corridors. **Pets:** Medium, other species. Service with
restrictions, supervision. 🛰 ⟨✕⟩ ⟨&M⟩ 🛋 🖥 ⇔

HOUSTON
🆎 ▼▼▼▼ Aloft Houston by the Galleria 🄷 �
(713) 622-7010. **$89-$399.** 5415 Westheimer Rd 77056. I-610 exit 8C
(Westheimer Rd) northbound; exit 9A (San Felipe Rd/Westheimer Rd)
southbound, 0.8 mi w. Int corridors. **Pets:** Medium. Service with restrictions. SAVE 🛰 ✕ ⟨&M⟩ 🛋 🖥 ⇔

🆎 ▼▼ Athens Hotel Suites 🄷 🐾
(713) 739-1960. **$119-$139.** 1308 Clay St 77002. Between Caroline and
Austin sts; east end. Int corridors. **Pets:** Medium, dogs only. $50 one-time
fee/room. Designated rooms, service with restrictions, crate.
SAVE 🛰 ✕ 🛋 🖥

🆎 ▼▼▼▼ Best Western Plus Westchase
Mini-Suites 🄷 🌼
(713) 782-1515. **$59-$99.** 2950 W Sam Houston Pkwy S 77042. Just w
of Sam Houston Pkwy (Beltway 8) and Westheimer Rd, on southbound
frontage road. Int corridors. **Pets:** Small. Service with restrictions, crate.
SAVE 🛰 ✕ ⟨&M⟩ 🛋 🖥 ⇔

▼▼ Candlewood Suites at CITYCENTRE - Energy
Corridor 🄷
(713) 464-2677. **$110-$130.** 10503 Town & Country Way 77024. I-10
exit 755 eastbound, 1.1 mi on frontage road to Town & Country Blvd,
then 0.4 mi s; exit 756A westbound, U-turn under I-10, just e to Town &
Country Blvd, then 0.4 mi s. Int corridors. **Pets:** Accepted.
🛰 ⟨&M⟩ 🛋 🖥

▼▼ Candlewood Suites Houston by the Galleria 🄷
(713) 839-9411. **$69-$99.** 4900 Loop Central Dr 77081. I-610 exit 7 (Fur-
nace Rd) southbound; exit 7 (Westpark Dr) northbound, on northbound
frontage road. Int corridors. **Pets:** Accepted. 🛰 🛋 🖥

▼▼ Candlewood Suites-Westchase 🄷
(713) 780-7881. **$73-$103.** 4033 W Sam Houston Pkwy S 77042. Sam
Houston Pkwy (Beltway 8) exit Westpark Dr, southeast corner of Westpark Dr and Sam Houston Pkwy (Beltway 8) on northbound frontage
road. Int corridors. **Pets:** Accepted. 🛰 ⟨&M⟩ 🛋 🖥

🆎 ▼▼ Comfort Inn & Suites 🄷
(281) 444-5800. **$70-$125.** 3555 FM 1960 W 77068. I-45 exit 66 (FM
1960), 3.5 mi w. Int corridors. **Pets:** Accepted. SAVE 🛰 🛋 🖥 ⇔

🆎 ▼▼▼▼ Comfort Suites Galleria 🄷
(713) 787-0004. **$79-$139.** 6221 Richmond Ave 77057. US 59 exit Hill-
croft St, 1 mi n to Richmond Ave, then 0.6 mi e. Int corridors.
Pets: Accepted. SAVE 🛰 ✕ 🛋 🖥 ⇔

▼▼ Crossland Economy Studios
Houston-Northwest 🄷 🌼
(713) 934-7600. **$44-$59.** 5959 Guhn Rd 77040. US 290 exit Fairbanks
n Houston Rd, just e on eastbound frontage road, then just s. Ext corridors. **Pets:** Other species. $25 daily fee/pet. Service with restrictions.
🛰 ⟨&M⟩ 🛋 🖥

🆎 ▼▼▼▼ Crowne Plaza Northwest Hotel 🄷
(713) 462-9977. **$59-$179.** 12801 Northwest Frwy 77040. Nw on US 290
exit Hollister Rd, 0.7 mi e on south service road. Ext/int corridors.
Pets: Small, other species. $25 one-time fee/room. Service with restric-
tions, crate. SAVE 🛰 ✕ 🛋 🖥 ⟨🍴⟩ ⇔

🆎 ▼▼▼▼ Crowne Plaza Suites Houston
Southwest 🄷
(713) 995-0123. **$79-$299, 3 day notice.** 9090 Southwest Frwy 77074.
US 59 exit Beechnut St/Gessner Rd; on southbound frontage road. Int
corridors. **Pets:** Accepted. SAVE 🛰 ✕ ⟨&M⟩ 🛋 🖥 🍴 ⇔

▼▼▼▼ DoubleTree by Hilton Hotel Houston
Downtown 🄷
(713) 759-0202. **$89-$289.** 400 Dallas St 77002. At Dallas and Bagby
sts. Int corridors. **Pets:** Accepted. 🛰 ✕ 🛋 🖥 🍴

▼▼▼▼ DoubleTree Suites by Hilton Hotel Houston by the
Galleria 🄷
(713) 961-9000. **$129-$359.** 5353 Westheimer Rd 77056. I-610 exit 8C
(Westheimer Rd) northbound; exit 9A (San Felipe Rd/Westheimer Rd)
southbound, 0.8 mi w. Int corridors. **Pets:** Accepted.
🛰 🛋 🖥 🍴 ⇔ ✕

▼▼▼▼ Drury Inn & Suites-Houston Hobby 🄷
(713) 941-4300. **$75-$159.** 7902 Mosley Rd 77061. I-45 exit 36 (Airport
Blvd/College Rd) northbound, just w on Airport Blvd, then just n; exit
southbound, follow frontage road to Mosley Rd. Int corridors.
Pets: Accepted. 🛰 ⟨&M⟩ 🛋 🖥 ⇔

▼▼▼▼ Drury Inn & Suites-Houston Near the Galleria 🄷
(713) 963-0700. **$95-$249.** 1615 W Loop S 77027. I-610 exit 9 (San
Felipe Rd) northbound; exit 9A (San Felipe Rd/Westheimer Rd) southbound, on east service road. Int corridors. **Pets:** Accepted.
🛰 ⟨&M⟩ 🛋 🖥 ⇔

▼▼▼▼ Drury Inn & Suites-Houston West 🄷
(281) 558-7007. **$80-$149.** 1000 N Hwy 6 77079. I-10 exit 751 (Addicks
Rd/SR 6), just n on SR 6. Int corridors. **Pets:** Accepted.
🛰 ⟨&M⟩ 🛋 🖥 ⇔

🆎 ▼▼▼▼ Element by Westin Houston Vintage
Park 🄷 🌼
(281) 379-7300. **$79-$299.** 14555 Vintage Preserve Pkwy 77070. US
290 exit Louetta Rd, just e to Chasewood Park, then just s. Int corridors.
Pets: Other species. Designated rooms, service with restrictions, supervision. ECO SAVE 🛰 ✕ ⇔

🆎 ▼▼▼▼ Embassy Suites Houston Downtown 🄷
(713) 739-9100. **$129-$339.** 1515 Dallas St 77010. Between Crawford
and La Branch sts. Int corridors. **Pets:** Accepted.
SAVE 🛰 ✕ ⟨&M⟩ 🛋 🖥 🍴 ⇔

▼▼ Extended StayAmerica Houston-Greenway
Plaza 🄷 🌼
(713) 521-0060. **$74-$129.** 2330 Southwest Frwy 77098. US 59 exit
Greenbriar St/Shepherd Dr; on southbound frontage road. Int corridors.
Pets: Other species. $25 daily fee/pet. Service with restrictions.
🛰 🛋 🖥

▼▼ Extended Stay Deluxe Houston-Northwest 🄷 🌼
(713) 895-0965. **$89-$109.** 5454 Hollister St 77040. US 290 exit Tidwell
Rd/Hollister St, just s. Int corridors. **Pets:** Other species. $25 daily fee/pet.
Service with restrictions. 🛰 🛋 🖥

🆎 ▼▼▼▼ Four Points by Sheraton Houston, Memorial
City 🄷
(281) 501-4600. **$99-$175.** 10655 Katy Frwy 77024. I-10 exit 756A west-
bound; exit 755 eastbound, southeast corner of I-10 and Sam Houston
Pkwy (Beltway 8). Ext/int corridors. **Pets:** Accepted.
SAVE 🛰 ✕ 🛋 🖥 🍴 ⇔

🆎 ▼▼▼▼▼ Four Seasons Hotel Houston 🄷
(713) 650-1300. **$275-$4000.** 1300 Lamar St 77010. Jct Lamar and Austin sts. Int corridors. **Pets:** Accepted.
SAVE 🛰 ✕ 🛋 🖥 🍴 ⇔ ✕

▼▼▼▼ Hilton Houston Hobby Airport H ❀

(713) 645-3000. **$109-$249.** 8181 Airport Blvd 77061. I-45 exit 36 (Airport Blvd/College Rd), 1.5 mi w. Int corridors. **Pets:** Medium, dogs only. $50 one-time fee/room. Designated rooms, service with restrictions, supervision. 🛜 🖥 🖵 �🍽 ➰

▼▼▼▼ Hilton Houston North H

(281) 875-2222. **$79-$161.** 12400 Greenspoint Dr 77060. I-45 exit 61 (Greens Rd), 0.5 mi e. Int corridors. **Pets:** $50 deposit/room. Service with restrictions, supervision. 🛜 🖥M 🖥 🖵 🍽

♨♨ ▼▼▼▼ Hilton Houston Post Oak H

(713) 961-9300. **$129-$279.** 2001 Post Oak Blvd 77056. I-610 exit 8C (Westheimer Rd) northbound, just w; exit 9A (San Felipe Rd/Westheimer Rd) southbound; between San Felipe and Westheimer rds. Int corridors. **Pets:** Accepted. 🅂🄰🅅🄴 🛜 ✕ 🖥 🖵 🍽 ➰

▼▼▼▼ Hilton Houston Westchase H

(713) 974-1000. **$109-$269.** 9999 Westheimer Rd 77042. Sam Houston Pkwy (Beltway 8) exit Westheimer Rd and Briar Forest Dr northbound; exit Westheimer Rd and Richmond Ave southbound, 0.5 mi e. Int corridors. **Pets:** Accepted. 🛜 🖥M 🖥 🖵 🍽 ➰ ✕

♨♨ ▼▼▼▼ Holiday Inn Express Hotel & Suites Memorial Area H

(713) 688-2800. **$90-$130.** 7625 Katy Frwy 77024. I-10 exit 762 (Silber Rd), on eastbound frontage road. Int corridors. **Pets:** Accepted. 🅂🄰🅅🄴 🛜 ✕ 🖥M 🖥 🖵 ➰

♨♨ ▼▼▼▼ Holiday Inn Express Northwest H

(832) 237-4300. **$85-$169.** 12915 FM 1960 W 77065. US 290 exit FM 1960, just e. Int corridors. **Pets:** Accepted. 🅂🄰🅅🄴 🛜 🖥M 🖥 🖵 ➰

♨♨ ▼▼▼▼ Holiday Inn Houston Hobby Airport H

(713) 946-8900. **$79-$189, 3 day notice.** 8611 Airport Blvd 77061. I-45 exit 36 (Airport Blvd), 1.3 mi w. Int corridors. **Pets:** Small. $100 one-time fee/room. Designated rooms, service with restrictions, supervision. 🅂🄰🅅🄴 🛜 ✕ 🖥M 🖥 🖵 🍽 ➰

♨♨ ▼▼▼▼ Holiday Inn Houston Intercontinental Airport H

(281) 449-2311. **$89-$179.** 15222 John F Kennedy Blvd 77032. Jct N Sam Houston Pkwy (Beltway 8) E and John F Kennedy Blvd. Int corridors. **Pets:** Accepted. 🅂🄰🅅🄴 🛜 ✕ 🖥M 🖥 🖵 🍽 ➰ ✕

▼▼ Homestead Studio Suites Hotel-Houston/Galleria Area H ❀

(713) 960-9660. **$89-$149.** 2300 W Loop S 77027. I-610 exit 9A (San Felipe Rd) southbound; exit 9 (San Felipe Rd) northbound, on southbound frontage road. Int corridors. **Pets:** Other species. $25 daily fee/pet. Service with restrictions. 🛜 🖥 🖥

♨♨ ▼▼▼▼ Homewood Suites by Hilton Intercontinental Airport H

(281) 219-9100. **Call for rates.** 1340 N Sam Houston Pkwy E 77032. Sam Houston Pkwy (Beltway 8) exit Aldine Westfield Rd eastbound Rd, 0.8 mi e on frontage road; exit Hardy Toll Rd westbound, U-turn, then 1 mi e on frontage road. Int corridors. **Pets:** Accepted. 🅂🄰🅅🄴 🛜 🖥M 🖥 🖵 ➰ ✕

♨♨ ▼▼▼▼ Homewood Suites by Hilton Near the Galleria H

(713) 439-1305. **$109-$199.** 2950 Sage Rd 77056. I-610 exit 8C (Westheimer Rd), just w to Sage Rd, then just s. Int corridors. **Pets:** Accepted. 🅂🄰🅅🄴 🛜 🖥M 🖥 🖵

▼▼▼▼ Homewood Suites by Hilton-Westchase H

(713) 334-2424. **$89-$179.** 2424 Rogerdale Rd 77042. Sam Houston Pkwy (Beltway 8) exit Westheimer Rd, just w to Rogerdale Rd, then just n. Int corridors. **Pets:** Accepted. 🛜 🖥M 🖥 🖵 ➰ ✕

▼▼▼▼ Homewood Suites by Hilton-Willowbrook H

(281) 955-5200. **$99-$209.** 7655 W FM 1960 77070. Just e of jct SR 249 and FM 1960. Int corridors. **Pets:** Medium. $75 one-time fee/room. Service with restrictions, crate. 🛜 🖥M 🖥 🖵 ➰ ✕

▼▼▼▼ Hotel Icon H

(713) 224-4266. **Call for rates.** 220 Main St 77002. Between Travis and Main sts; entrance on Congress St. Int corridors. **Pets:** Small. No service, crate. 🅂🄰🅅🄴 🛜 ✕ 🖥 🖵 🍽

▼▼▼▼ Hotel Indigo Houston at the Galleria H

(713) 621-8988. **$99-$219.** 5160 Hidalgo St 77056. I-610 exit 9A (San Felipe Rd/Westheimer Rd) southbound; exit 8C (Westheimer Rd) northbound, s to Post Oak, just e to Hidalgo St, then just s. Int corridors. **Pets:** Medium. $85 one-time fee/room. Service with restrictions, supervision. 🛜 ✕ 🖥M 🖥 🖵 🍽

♨♨ ▼▼▼▼ Hotel ZaZa Houston Museum District H

(713) 526-1991. **$239-$379.** 5701 Main St 77005. US 59 exit Main St northbound, 0.5 mi s; exit Fannin St southbound, 0.5 mi s to Ewing St, then just w. Int corridors. **Pets:** Accepted. 🅂🄰🅅🄴 🛜 ✕ 🖥M 🖥 🍽 ➰ ✕

▼▼▼▼ Houston Marriott at the Texas Medical Center H

(713) 796-0080. **$101-$239.** 6580 Fannin St 77030. I-610 exit 2 (Main St), 2.5 mi ne to Holcombe St, 0.3 mi e, then just n. Int corridors. **Pets:** Other species. $75 deposit/room. Service with restrictions. 🛜 ✕ 🖥M 🖥 🖵 🍽 ➰ ✕

▼▼ Howard Johnson Inn Hobby M

(713) 910-8600. **Call for rates.** 8600 Gulf Frwy 77017. I-45 exit 38 (Monroe St), just w. Ext corridors. **Pets:** Accepted. 🛜 🖥 🖵 ➰

♨♨ ▼▼▼▼ Hyatt Summerfield Suites Houston/Galleria H

(713) 629-9711. **$89-$269.** 3440 Sage Rd 77056. I-610 exit 9A (San Felipe Rd/Westheimer Rd) southbound; exit 8C (Westheimer Rd) northbound, just w to Sage Rd, then 0.8 mi s. Int corridors. **Pets:** Accepted. 🅂🄰🅅🄴 🛜 ✕ 🖥 🖵 ➰

♨♨ ▼▼▼▼ Hyatt Summerfield Suites Houston-West/ Energy Corridor H

(281) 646-9990. **$89-$229.** 15405 Katy Frwy (I-10) 77094. I-10 exit 751 (SR 6), just s to Grisby Rd, then just w. Int corridors. **Pets:** Small, other species. $75 one-time fee/room. Designated rooms, service with restrictions, supervision. 🅂🄰🅅🄴 🛜 ✕ 🖥 🖵 ➰

▼▼▼▼ La Quinta Inn & Suites Energy Corridor H

(281) 668-1068. **$98-$199.** 2451 Shadow View Ln 77077. 2.5 mi w of Sam Houston Pkwy (Beltway 8) on Westheimer Rd, just n. Int corridors. **Pets:** Medium, other species. Service with restrictions, supervision. 🛜 ✕ 🖥M 🖥 🖵 ➰

▼▼▼▼ La Quinta Inn & Suites Houston Bush Intercontinental Airport South H

(281) 219-2000. **$68-$148.** 15510 John F Kennedy Blvd 77032. Sam Houston Pkwy (Beltway 8) exit John F Kennedy Blvd/Vickery Dr, just n. Int corridors. **Pets:** Medium, other species. Service with restrictions, supervision. 🛜 🖥M 🖥 🖵 ➰

▼▼▼▼ La Quinta Inn & Suites - Houston Clay Road H

(713) 939-1400. **$125-$189.** 4424 Westway Park Blvd 77041. Sam Houston Pkwy (Beltway 8) exit Clay Rd, just e. Int corridors. **Pets:** Medium, other species. Service with restrictions, supervision. 🛜 ✕ 🖥M 🖥 🖵 ➰

▼▼▼▼ La Quinta Inn & Suites Houston Galleria Area H

(713) 355-3440. **$84-$192.** 1625 W Loop S 77027. I-610 exit 9 (San Felipe Rd) northbound; exit 9A (San Felipe Rd/Westheimer Rd) southbound, on northbound service road. Int corridors. **Pets:** Medium, other species. Service with restrictions, supervision. 🛜 🖥M 🖥 🖵 ➰

La Quinta Inn & Suites Houston Hobby Airport H
(713) 490-1008. **$88-$192.** 8776 Airport Blvd 77061. I-45 exit 36 (Airport Blvd/College Rd), 1.3 mi w. Int corridors. **Pets:** Medium, other species. Service with restrictions, supervision. 🛰 ✕ ⓜ 🗎 💻 ➰

La Quinta Inn & Suites Houston I-45/1960 H
(281) 784-1112. **$88-$192.** 415 FM 1960 Rd E 77073. I-45 exit 66 (FM 1960), just e. Int corridors. **Pets:** Medium, other species. Service with restrictions, supervision. SAVE 🛰 🗎 💻 ➰

La Quinta Inn & Suites Houston - Normandy H
(713) 451-0009. **$88-$181.** 930 Normandy St 77015. I-10 exit 778B, just n. Int corridors. **Pets:** Medium, other species. Service with restrictions, supervision. 🛰 ✕ 🗎 💻 ➰

La Quinta Inn & Suites Houston - Westchase H
(281) 495-7700. **$111-$199.** 10850 Harwin Dr 77072. Sam Houston Pkwy (Beltway 8) exit Bellaire Blvd/Harwin Dr northbound; exit Westpark Dr/Harwin Dr southbound. Int corridors. **Pets:** Medium, other species. Service with restrictions, supervision. 🛰 ✕ 🗎 💻 ➰

La Quinta Inn & Suites Houston West Park 10 H
(281) 646-9200. **$74-$144.** 15225 Katy Frwy 77094. I-10 exit 748 (Barker Cypress Rd) eastbound, 2.6 mi on eastbound service road; exit 751 (SR 6) westbound, just s to Grisby Rd, then 0.5 mi w. Int corridors. **Pets:** Medium, other species. Service with restrictions, supervision. 🛰 🗎 💻 ➰

La Quinta Inn & Suites Willowbrook H
(281) 897-8868. **$71-$154.** 18828 State Hwy 249 (Tomball Pkwy) 77070. SR 249 exit Grant Rd/Schroeder Rd, on northbound frontage road. Int corridors. **Pets:** Medium, other species. Service with restrictions, supervision. 🛰 ✕ ⓜ 🗎 💻 ➰

La Quinta Inn Houston Cy-fair H
(281) 469-4018. **$64-$126.** 13290 FM 1960 W 77065. Just w of jct US 290 and FM 1960. Ext corridors. **Pets:** Medium, other species. Service with restrictions, supervision. 🛰 ⓜ 🗎 💻 ➰

La Quinta Inn Houston Wilcrest H
(713) 932-0808. **$58-$115.** 11113 Katy Frwy 77079. I-10 exit 754 (Kirkwood Dr) westbound; exit 755 (Wilcrest Rd) eastbound, on eastbound service road. Ext corridors. **Pets:** Medium, other species. Service with restrictions, supervision. 🛰 🗎 💻 ➰

Marriott Houston Hobby Airport H
(713) 943-7979. **$89-$189.** 9100 Gulf Frwy 77017. I-45 exit 36 (Airport Blvd/College Rd) southbound; exit 38 (Monroe Rd) northbound, on southbound frontage road. Int corridors. **Pets:** Accepted. 🛰 ✕ 🗎 💻 🍴 ➰

Omni Houston Hotel H ❀
(713) 871-8181. **$199-$499.** Four Riverway 77056. I-610 exit 10 (Woodway Dr), 0.3 mi w. Int corridors. **Pets:** Small. $50 one-time fee/room. Service with restrictions, supervision. 🛰 🗎 💻 🍴 ➰ ✕

Omni Houston Hotel Westside H
(281) 558-8338. **$109-$379.** 13210 Katy Frwy 77079. I-10 exit 753A (Eldridge St), just n. Int corridors. **Pets:** Small. $50 one-time fee/pet. Service with restrictions, crate. SAVE 🛰 🗎 💻 🍴 ➰

Quality Inn & Suites Houston West/Energy Corridor M ❀
(281) 493-0444. **$69-$170.** 715 Hwy 6 S 77079. I-10 exit 751 (Addicks/Howell Rd), 0.4 mi s. Ext corridors. **Pets:** Medium, other species. $15 daily fee/pet. Designated rooms, service with restrictions, supervision. SAVE 🛰 🗎 💻 ➰

Red Roof Inns H
(713) 785-9909. **$55-$75.** 2960 W Sam Houston Pkwy S 77042. Sam Houston Pkwy (Beltway 8) exit Westheimer Rd, on southbound frontage road. Ext/int corridors. **Pets:** Large, other species. No service, supervision. 🛰 🗎 ➰

Renaissance Houston Hotel Greenway Plaza H
(713) 629-1200. **$110-$299.** 6 Greenway Plaza E 77046. US 59 (Southwest Frwy) exit Buffalo Speedway. Int corridors. **Pets:** Accepted. ECO SAVE 🛰 ✕ 🗎 💻 🍴 ➰ ✕

Residence Inn by Marriott Houston by the Galleria H ❀
(713) 840-9757. **$84-$186.** 2500 McCue Rd 77056. I-610 exit 8C (Westheimer Rd) northbound; exit 9A (San Felipe Rd/Westheimer Rd) southbound, just w to McCue Rd, then just n. Ext/int corridors. **Pets:** Medium, other species. $100 one-time fee/room. Service with restrictions. SAVE 🛰 ✕ 🗎 💻 ➰ ✕

Residence Inn by Marriott Houston Downtown/ Convention Center H
(832) 366-1000. **$89-$339.** 904 Dallas St 77002. At Main St. Int corridors. **Pets:** Accepted. 🛰 ✕ ⓜ 🗎 💻 ➰

Residence Inn by Marriott-Medical Center/Reliant Park H
(713) 660-7993. **$95-$159.** 7710 Main St 77030. I-610 exit 2 (S Main St/Buffalo Speedway), 1.5 mi n. Ext corridors. **Pets:** Large, other species. $100 one-time fee/room. Service with restrictions. 🛰 ✕ ⓜ 🗎 💻 ➰

Residence Inn by Marriott-West University H ❀
(713) 661-4660. **$184-$227.** 2939 Westpark Dr 77005. US 59 exit Kirby Dr, just s, then just w. Int corridors. **Pets:** Large, other species. $100 one-time fee/room. Designated rooms, service with restrictions, crate. 🛰 ✕ ⓜ 🗎 💻 ➰ ✕

Residence Inn by Marriott Willowbrook H
(832) 237-2002. **$199-$219.** 7311 W Greens Rd 77064. SR 249 exit Greens Rd, just e. Int corridors. **Pets:** $100 one-time fee/room. Service with restrictions, crate. 🛰 ✕ 🗎 💻 ➰ ✕

The St. Regis Houston H ❀
(713) 840-7600. **$199-$885.** 1919 Briar Oaks Ln 77027. I-610 exit 9A (San Felipe Rd/Westheimer Rd), 0.3 mi e. Int corridors. **Pets:** Medium, dogs only. $250 deposit/room. Service with restrictions, supervision. SAVE 🛰 🗎 💻 🍴 ➰ ✕

Scottish Inn & Suites at Reliant Park-Medical Center M
(713) 795-9100. **$63-$250, 3 day notice.** 8510 Almeda Rd 77054. I-610 exit 1A (Almeda Rd) eastbound, just n; exit 1B (Fannin St) westbound, U-turn under I-610 to Almeda Rd, then just n. Ext corridors. **Pets:** Medium. $50 one-time fee/room. Service with restrictions, supervision. SAVE 🛰 🗎

Sheraton Houston Brookhollow H
(713) 688-0100. **$89-$249.** 3000 N Loop W 77092. I-610 exit 13C (TC Jester Blvd), on southbound frontage road. Int corridors. **Pets:** Accepted. SAVE 🛰 ✕ ⓜ 🗎 💻 🍴 ➰ ✕

Sheraton Houston West Hotel H
(281) 501-4200. **$109-$229.** 11191 Clay Rd 77041. Sam Houston Pkwy (Beltway 8) exit Clay Rd, just e. Int corridors. **Pets:** Accepted. SAVE 🛰 ✕ ⓜ 💻 🍴 ➰

Sheraton North Houston Hotel H ❀
(281) 442-5100. **$99-$270.** 15700 John F Kennedy Blvd 77032. Sam Houston Pkwy (Beltway 8) exit John F Kennedy Blvd, just n. Int corridors. **Pets:** Medium, other species. Service with restrictions, crate. SAVE 🛰 ✕ ⓜ 🗎 💻 🍴 ➰

Sheraton Suites Houston Near The Galleria H ❀
(713) 586-2444. **$99-$369.** 2400 W Loop S 77027. I-610 exit 9 (San Felipe Rd) northbound; exit 9A (San Felipe Rd/Westheimer Rd) southbound. Int corridors. **Pets:** Medium, dogs only. Service with restrictions, supervision. SAVE 🛰 ✕ 🗎 💻 🍴 ➰

Staybridge Suites Houston-Near The Galleria H
(713) 355-8888. **Call for rates.** 5190 Hidalgo St 77056. I-610 exit 9A (San Felipe Rd/Westheimer Rd) southbound; exit 8C (Westheimer Rd) northbound, 0.4 mi w to Sage Rd, then just s. Int corridors.
Pets: Accepted. 🛰 🅰 🔋 💻 ➿

Staybridge Suites Houston West Energy Corridor H
(281) 759-7829. **$129-$149.** 1225 Eldridge Pkwy 77077. I-10 exit 753A (Eldridge Pkwy), 1.8 mi s. Int corridors. **Pets:** $75 one-time fee/pet. Service with restrictions, supervision. 🛰 ✕ 🔋 💻 ➿

TownePlace Suites by Marriott-Central H
(713) 690-4035. **$117-$198.** 12820 Northwest Frwy (US 290) 77040. US 290 exit Bingle Rd/43rd St eastbound; exit Bingle Rd/Pinemont Dr/43rd St westbound, on westbound feeder. Int corridors. **Pets:** Accepted.
🛰 ✕ 🅰 🔋 💻

TownePlace Suites Houston I-10 West/Energy Corridor H
(281) 646-0058. **$96-$166.** 15155 Katy Frwy 77094. I-10 exit 751, just s on SR 6 to Grisby Rd, then w. Int corridors. **Pets:** Accepted.
🛰 ✕ 🔋 💻 ➿

The Westin Galleria, Houston H 🐾
(713) 960-8100. **$110-$331.** 5060 W Alabama St 77056. I-610 exit 8C (Westheimer Rd) northbound; exit 9A (San Felipe Rd/Westheimer Rd) southbound, 0.5 mi w on Westheimer Rd to Sage, just s, then just e. Int corridors. **Pets:** Medium, dogs only. Service with restrictions, supervision.
SAVE 🛰 ✕ 🅰 🔋 💻 🍴 ➿

Westin Oaks Houston at the Galleria H
(713) 960-8100. **$110-$331.** 5011 Westheimer Rd 77056. I-610 exit 8C (Westheimer Rd) northbound; exit 9A (San Felipe Rd/Westheimer Rd) southbound. Int corridors. **Pets:** Accepted.
SAVE 🛰 ✕ 🅰 🔋 💻 🍴 ➿

Wingate by Wyndham Houston Bush Intercontinental Airport IAH H
(281) 372-1000. **$99-$139.** 1330 N Sam Houston Pkwy E 77032. Off Sam Houston Pkwy (Beltway 8) exit Aldine Westfield Rd eastbound, 0.8 mi e on service road; exit Hardy Toll Rd westbound, U-turn, then 1 mi e on service road. Int corridors. **Pets:** Accepted. SAVE 🛰 🔋 💻 ➿

KATY

La Quinta Inn & Suites Katy H
(281) 392-9800. **$98-$159.** 22455 Katy Frwy (I-10) 77450. I-10 exit 743 (Grand Pkwy), on eastbound service road. Int corridors. **Pets:** Medium, other species. Service with restrictions, supervision.
SAVE 🛰 ✕ 🅰 🔋 💻 ➿

Residence Inn by Marriott Houston Katy Mills H
(281) 391-7501. **$121-$174.** 25401 Katy Mills Pkwy 77494. I-10 exit 740 (Pin Oak Rd) westbound; exit 741 (Pin Oak Rd) eastbound, just s, on south side of Kay Mills Mall. Int corridors. **Pets:** Accepted.
🛰 ✕ 🔋 💻 ➿ ✕

KINGWOOD

Comfort Suites Kingwood-Humble H 🐾
(281) 359-4448. **$80-$190.** 22223 Hwy 59 N 77339. US 59 exit Kingwood Dr northbound; exit McClellan southbound. Int corridors.
Pets: Medium, other species. $25 daily fee/pet. Service with restrictions, supervision. 🛰 ✕ 🅰 🔋 💻 ➿

Holiday Inn Express Hotel & Suites-Kingwood H
(281) 359-2700. **$70-$160.** 22675 US 59 N 77339. US 59 exit Kingwood Dr, on southbound access road. Int corridors. **Pets:** Small. $50 deposit/room. Designated rooms, service with restrictions, supervision.
SAVE 🛰 🔋 💻 ➿

MONTGOMERY

Best Western Lake Conroe Inn H
(936) 588-3030. **$80-$110.** 14643 Hwy 105 W 77356. Just w of McCaleb Rd. Ext corridors. **Pets:** Accepted. SAVE 🛰 🔋 💻 ➿

La Torretta Lake Resort & Spa H
(936) 448-4400. **$159-$499, 3 day notice.** 600 La Torretta Blvd 77356. SR 105, 2.5 mi n on Walden Rd to La Torretta Blvd. Ext/int corridors.
Pets: Accepted. SAVE 🛰 ✕ 🔋 💻 🍴 ➿ ✕

NASSAU BAY

Hilton Houston NASA Clear Lake H
(281) 333-9300. **$109-$179.** 3000 NASA Pkwy 77058. 2 mi e of NASA bypass road. Int corridors. **Pets:** Accepted.
🛰 ✕ 🔋 💻 🍴 ➿

ROSENBERG

Americas Best Value Inn & Suites H
(832) 595-6900. **Call for rates.** 28150 Southwest Frwy 77471. US 59 exit SR 36, on southbound frontage road. Ext corridors. **Pets:** Small, dogs only. $15 one-time fee/pet. Service with restrictions, supervision.
🛰 🔋 💻

La Quinta Inn & Suites Rosenberg H
(832) 595-6111. **$103-$165.** 28332 Southwest Frwy 77471. Jct US 59 and SR 36; on southbound Frontage Rd. Int corridors. **Pets:** Medium, other species. Service with restrictions, supervision. 🛰 🔋 💻 ➿

SEABROOK

Comfort Inn & Suites-NASA Clearlake H
(281) 326-3301. **$79-$109.** 2901 NASA Pkwy 77586. 1 mi w of jct W SR 146. Int corridors. **Pets:** Accepted. 🛰 ✕ 🔋 💻 ➿

Hampton Inn NASA/Johnson Space Center Houston H
(281) 532-9200. **$109-$159.** 3000 NASA Pkwy 77586. 1 mi w of jct SR 146. Int corridors. **Pets:** Accepted. 🛰 🔋 💻 ➿

La Quinta Inn & Suites Houston NASA Seabrook H
(281) 326-7300. **$84-$181.** 3636 NASA Pkwy 77586. I-45 exit 25 (NASA Rd One), 6 mi e; SR 146, 2 mi w. Int corridors. **Pets:** Medium, other species. Service with restrictions, supervision. 🛰 🔋 💻 ➿

SpringHill Suites Houston/NASA/Seabrook H
(281) 474-3456. **$85-$127.** 2120 NASA Pkwy 77586. Jct SR 146 and NASA Rd One, just w. Int corridors. **Pets:** Accepted.
🛰 ✕ 🅰 🔋 💻 ➿

SHENANDOAH

TownePlace Suites by Marriott The Woodlands H
(936) 273-7772. **$113-$143.** 107 Vision Park Blvd 77384. I-45 exit 79 (College Park/Needham Rd), 1 mi s; on southbound frontage road. Int corridors. **Pets:** Accepted. 🛰 ✕ 🅰 🔋 💻 ➿

STAFFORD

La Quinta Inn & Suites Houston Stafford Sugarland H
(281) 240-2300. **$68-$137.** 12727 Southwest Frwy 77477. US 59 exit Corporate Dr southbound; exit Airport Blvd/Kirkwood Rd northbound; eastbound service road. Int corridors. **Pets:** Medium, other species. Service with restrictions, supervision. 🛰 🔋 💻 ➿

Residence Inn by Marriott Houston/Sugar Land H
(281) 277-0770. **$84-$179.** 12703 Southwest Frwy 77477. US 59 exit Corporate Dr southbound; exit Airport Blvd/Kirkwood Rd northbound; on northbound service road. Int corridors. **Pets:** Accepted.
SAVE 🛰 ✕ 🔋 💻 ➿ ✕

▼▼▼ Staybridge Suites Stafford **H** ❀
(281) 302-6535. **Call for rates.** 11101 Fountain Lake Dr 77477. US 59 exit Kirkwood Rd, just nw. Int corridors. **Pets:** Small. $75 one-time fee/ pet. Service with restrictions, supervision. 🛰 ⌧ 🗄M 🔋 💻 ⇔

SUGAR LAND

▼▼▼ Drury Inn & Suites-Houston/Sugar Land **H**
(281) 277-9700. **$85-$174.** 13770 Southwest Frwy 77478. US 59 exit Dairy Ashford Rd/Sugar Creek Blvd, on N Frontage Rd. Int corridors. **Pets:** Accepted. 🛰 🔋 💻 ⇔

THE WOODLANDS

⚛ ▼▼▼ Best Western Plus The
Woodlands **H** ❀
(936) 271-2378. **$90-$100.** 17081 I-45 S 77385. I-45 exit 79 (College Park Dr/Needham Rd) northbound, northeast corner of SR 242; on north- bound frontage. Int corridors. **Pets:** Medium, other species. $20 daily fee/room. Service with restrictions. [SAVE] 🛰 🔋 💻 ⇔

▼▼▼ Drury Inn & Suites-Houston/The Woodlands **H**
(281) 362-7222. **$100-$174.** 28099 I-45 N 77380. I-45 exit 77 (Research Forest Dr/Tamina Rd) southbound, on southbound frontage road. Int corri- dors. **Pets:** Accepted. 🛰 🗄M 🔋 💻 ⇔

⚛ ▼▼▼ Holiday Inn Express Hotel & Suites **H**
(281) 681-8088. **$99-$129.** 24888 I-45 N 77386. I-45 exit 73 (Rayford Rd/Sawdust Rd), on northbound access road. Int corridors. **Pets:** Medium. $25 one-time fee/pet. Service with restrictions, supervision. [SAVE] 🛰 🔋 💻 ⇔ ⌧

▼▼▼ La Quinta Inn & Suites - The Woodlands
South **H**
(281) 681-9188. **$103-$185.** 24868 I-45 N 77386. I-45 exit 73 (Rayford Rd/Sawdust Rd), on northbound access road. Int corridors. **Pets:** Medium, other species. Service with restrictions, supervision.
🛰 ⌧ 🗄M 🔋 💻 ⇔ ⌧

▼▼▼ Residence Inn by Marriott Lake Front **H**
(281) 292-3252. **$181-$238.** 1040 Lake Front Cir 77380. I-45 exit 79 (College Park Dr/Needham Rd) northbound; exit 77 (Research Forest Dr/Tamina Rd) southbound; just off southbound frontage road. Int corri- dors. **Pets:** Other species. $100 one-time fee/room. Service with restric- tions, supervision. 🛰 ⌧ 🔋 💻 ⇔ ⌧

WEBSTER

▼▼ Nasa Parkway Inn **H**
(281) 333-3737. **Call for rates.** 904 E NASA Pkwy 77598. I-45 exit 25 (NASA Rd 1), 1.5 mi e. Ext corridors. **Pets:** Accepted.
🛰 🔋 💻 ⇔

⚛ ▼▼▼ Comfort Suites **H**
(281) 554-5400. **Call for rates.** 16931 N Texas Ave 77598. I-45 exit 26 (Bay Area Blvd), 0.5 mi e to Texas Ave, then just s. Int corridors. **Pets:** Medium. $25 one-time fee/pet. Designated rooms, service with restrictions, supervision. [SAVE] 🛰 ⌧ 🗄M 🔋 💻 ⇔

▼▼▼ Extended Stay Deluxe Houston NASA-Bay Area
Blvd **H** ❀
(281) 338-7711. **$69-$99.** 720 W Bay Area Blvd 77598. I-45 exit 26 (Bay Area Blvd), just e. Int corridors. **Pets:** Other species. $25 daily fee/pet. Service with restrictions. 🛰 🔋 💻 ⇔

▼▼▼ La Quinta Inn & Suites Clearlake/Webster **H**
(281) 554-5290. **$89-$179.** 520 W Bay Area Blvd 77598. I-45 exit 26 (Bay Area Blvd), just e. Int corridors. **Pets:** Medium, other species. Serv- ice with restrictions, supervision. 🛰 ⌧ 🗄M 🔋 💻 ⇔

▼▼▼ Staybridge Suites Houston/ Clear Lake **H**
(281) 338-0900. **$99-$159.** 501 W Texas Ave 77598. I-45 exit 26 (Bay Area Blvd), right, then left at 3rd light. Int corridors. **Pets:** Accepted.
🛰 ⌧ 🗄M 🔋 💻 ⇔ ⌧

⚛ ▼▼▼ Super 8-Houston-Webster-NASA **M**
(281) 333-5385. **$42-$95, 3 day notice.** 18103 Kingsrow Rd 77058. I-45 exit 25 (NASA Rd 1), 1.5 mi e. Ext corridors. **Pets:** Medium, other spe- cies. $25 one-time fee/pet. Designated rooms, service with restrictions, supervision. [SAVE] 🛰 🔋 💻 ⇔

WINNIE

▼▼▼ Comfort Inn & Suites **H**
(409) 296-6200. **Call for rates.** 338 Spur 5 77665. I-10 exit 829, just s. Int corridors. **Pets:** Accepted. 🛰 ⌧ 🔋 💻 ⇔

▼▼ Days Inn & Suites **H**
(409) 296-2866. **$71-$98.** 14932 FM 1663 77665. I-10 exit 829, just n. Ext corridors. **Pets:** Medium. $20 daily fee/pet. Service with restrictions, supervision. 🛰 🗄M 🔋 💻 ⇔

▼▼ Winnie Inn & Suites **H**
(409) 296-2947. **$50-$90.** 205 Spur 5, Hwy 124 77665. I-10 exit 829, just s. Ext corridors. **Pets:** Accepted. 🛰 🔋 💻 ⇔

END METROPOLITAN AREA

HUNTSVILLE

⚛ ▼▼▼ Best Western Plus Huntsville Inn &
Suites **H**
(936) 295-9000. **$79.** 201 W Hill Park Cir 77320. I-45 exit 116, just w on US 190. Ext corridors. **Pets:** Accepted. [SAVE] 🛰 🗄M 🔋 💻 ⇔

INGLESIDE

⚛ ▼▼ Best Western Naval Station Inn **M**
(361) 776-2767. **$80-$130.** 2025 State Hwy 361 78362. 1 mi e of jct SR 1069. Ext corridors. **Pets:** $10 daily fee/pet. Service with restrictions, supervision. [SAVE] 🛰 🔋 💻 ⇔

JACKSONVILLE

▼▼▼ Comfort Inn **H**
(903) 589-8500. **$89-$114.** 1848 S Jackson St 75766. On US 69, 2 mi s of jct US 69 and 79. Int corridors. **Pets:** Accepted.
🛰 🗄M 🔋 💻 ⇔

▼▼▼ La Quinta Inn & Suites Jacksonville **H**
(903) 586-6504. **$94-$155.** 1902 S Jackson St 75766. On US 69, 2.1 mi s of jct US 69 and 79. Int corridors. **Pets:** Medium, other species. Service with restrictions, supervision. 🛰 🗄M 🔋 💻 ⇔

JASPER

▼▼ Super 8 **H**
(409) 384-8600. **$56-$73.** 2100 N Wheeler St 75951. US 96, 1.8 mi n of jct US 190. Ext corridors. **Pets:** Accepted. 🛰 🔋 💻 ⇔

JOHNSON CITY

⚛ ▼▼▼ Best Western Johnson City Inn **H**
(830) 868-4044. **$80-$130.** 107 S Hwy 290/281 78636. Jct US 281 and 290 N. Ext corridors. **Pets:** Accepted. [SAVE] 🛰 🔋 💻 ⇔

JUNCTION

Classic Inn M

(325) 446-2505. **Call for rates.** 1611 Main St 76849. I-10 exit 456 eastbound, 1 mi s on US 377; exit 460 westbound, 3 mi w on Loop 481 to jct US 377, then just n. Ext corridors. **Pets:** Accepted.

Days Inn Junction Resort H

(325) 446-3730. **Call for rates.** 111 S Martinez St 76849. I-10 exit 457, 0.3 mi s. Ext corridors. **Pets:** Medium, dogs only. $20 daily fee/pet. Service with restrictions, crate.

Motel 6 Junction #4384 H

(325) 446-3572. **$65-$149.** 200 I-10 W 76849. I-10 exit 456, on N Frontage Rd. Ext corridors. **Pets:** Other species. Service with restrictions, supervision.

Rodeway Inn H

(325) 446-4588. **Call for rates.** 2343 N Main St 76849. I-10 exit 456, just s on US 377. Ext corridors. **Pets:** Accepted.

KERRVILLE

Best Western Sunday House Inn H

(830) 896-1313. **$79-$114.** 2124 Sidney Baker St 78028. I-10 exit 508 (SR 16), just s. Ext corridors. **Pets:** Medium, other species. $10 daily fee/pet. Service with restrictions, crate.

Comfort Inn H

(830) 792-7700. **$79-$149.** 2001 Sidney Baker St 78028. I-10 exit 508 (SR 16), 0.4 mi s. Int corridors. **Pets:** Small. $10 daily fee/pet. Service with restrictions, supervision.

Days Inn of Kerrville M

(830) 896-1000. **$44-$98.** 2000 Sidney Baker St 78028. I-10 exit 508 (SR 16), 0.5 mi s. Ext/int corridors. **Pets:** Accepted.

Y. O. Ranch Resort Hotel & Conference Center H

(830) 257-4440. **$79-$129.** 2033 Sidney Baker St 78028. I-10 exit 508 (SR 16), 0.3 mi s. Ext/int corridors. **Pets:** Accepted.

KILGORE

Best Western Inn of Kilgore H

(903) 986-1195. **$85-$120.** 1411 N Hwy 259 75662. I-20 exit 589, 3.9 mi s. Ext corridors. **Pets:** Accepted.

KILLEEN

Candlewood Suites - Ft. Hood/Killeen H 🐾

(254) 501-3990. **$79-$129.** 2300 Florence Rd 76542. US 90 exit Jasper Rd, just s. Int corridors. **Pets:** $150 one-time fee/room. Service with restrictions, supervision.

Days Inn Killeen Mall H

(254) 554-2727. **$62.** 1602 E Central Texas Expwy 76541. US 190 exit Trimmier Rd. Ext corridors. **Pets:** Other species. $25 one-time fee/room. Service with restrictions, supervision.

La Quinta Inn Killeen H

(254) 526-8331. **$80-$142.** 1112 S Fort Hood St 76541. US 190 exit Fort Hood St, on westbound access road. Ext corridors. **Pets:** Medium, other species. Service with restrictions, supervision.

Residence Inn by Marriott H

(254) 634-1020. **$94-$152.** 400 E Central Texas Expwy 76541. US 190 exit Fort Hood St/Jasper Rd (SR 195), on S Frontage Rd. Int corridors. **Pets:** Accepted.

Shilo Inn Suites Hotel - Killeen H

(254) 699-0999. **$115-$215.** 3701 S WS Young Dr 76542. US 190 exit WS Young Dr, 1 mi s. Int corridors. **Pets:** Dogs only. $25 one-time fee/room. Designated rooms, service with restrictions, crate.

TownePlace Suites by Marriott H

(254) 554-8899. **$85-$99.** 2401 Florence Rd 76542. US 190 exit Trimmier Rd to Jasper Rd, on south access road, 1 blk e to Florence Rd, then just s. Int corridors. **Pets:** Accepted.

KINGSLAND

Rio Vista Resort CO

(325) 388-6331. **$75-$880, 30 day notice.** 234 Rio Vista Dr 78639. Colorado River Bridge, 0.5 mi nw on FM 1431, 0.5 mi s on Reynolds St. Ext corridors. **Pets:** Accepted.

KINGSVILLE

Quality Inn H

(361) 592-5251. **$70-$100.** 221 S Hwy 77 Bypass 78363. On US 77, just s of jct SR 141. Ext corridors. **Pets:** Small, dogs only. $50 deposit/pet, $10 daily fee/pet. Designated rooms, service with restrictions, supervision.

Rodeway Inn M

(361) 595-5753. **Call for rates.** 3430 Hwy 77 78363. 4.5 mi s on US 77. Ext corridors. **Pets:** Accepted.

Super 8 M

(361) 592-6471. **$40-$126.** 105 S US Hwy 77 Bypass 78363. 0.8 mi e on US 77. Ext corridors. **Pets:** Small. $20 one-time fee/pet. No service, supervision.

KYLE

La Quinta Inn & Suites Kyle H

(512) 295-5599. **$98-$164.** 18869 IH-35 N 78640. I-35 exit 217, on east frontage road. Int corridors. **Pets:** Medium, other species. Service with restrictions, supervision.

LA GRANGE

Best Western Plus La Grange Inn & Suites H

(979) 968-6800. **Call for rates.** 600 E State Hwy 71 Bypass 78945. Jct US 77 and SR 71, just e on N Frontage Rd. Int corridors. **Pets:** $15 daily fee/room. Service with restrictions, crate.

LAJITAS

Lajitas Golf Resort and Spa H

(432) 424-5000. **Call for rates.** 1 Main St 79852. Center. Ext/int corridors. **Pets:** Accepted.

LAKE JACKSON

Candlewood Suites-Lake Jackson-Clute H

(979) 297-0011. **$129-$139.** 506 Hwy 332 77566. Jct SR 288/332 and Plantation Dr, just n. Int corridors. **Pets:** Medium. $150 one-time fee/room. Service with restrictions, crate.

Cherotel Brazosport Hotel & Conference Center H

(979) 297-1161. **$40-$120.** 925 Hwy 332 77566. On SR 288/332, just w of jct Business Rt SR 288. Int corridors. **Pets:** Accepted.

LAKEWAY

Lakeway Resort & Spa H 🐾

(512) 261-6600. **$119-$500, 3 day notice.** 101 Lakeway Dr 78734. Jct FM 620 and Lakeway Blvd W, 1.5 mi to Lakeway Dr, then 2.1 mi n. Int corridors. **Pets:** Small, dogs only. $25 one-time fee/pet. Designated rooms, service with restrictions, crate.

LAMESA

Shiloh Inn M

(806) 872-6721. **$53-$71, 3 day notice.** 1707 Lubbock Hwy 79331. Jct US 87 and 180, 1 mi n. Ext corridors. **Pets:** Accepted.

LAREDO

 **Americas Best Value Inn** **M**

(956) 723-1510. **$50-$110.** 5240 San Bernardo Ave 78041. I-35 exit 3B (Mann Rd), on southbound access road. Ext corridors. **Pets:** $10 daily fee/pet. Service with restrictions, supervision.

Days Inn & Suites **H**

(956) 724-8221. **$52-$56.** 7060 N San Bernardo Ave 78041. I-35 exit 4 (San Bernardo Ave), just s on southbound access road. Ext/int corridors. **Pets:** Small. $10 daily fee/pet. Service with restrictions, supervision.

Extended StayAmerica Laredo-Del Mar **H** ❀

(956) 724-1920. **$64-$79.** 106 W Village Blvd 78040. I-35 exit 3B (Mann Rd), just n on northbound access road to W Village, then just e. Int corridors. **Pets:** Other species. $25 daily fee/pet. Service with restrictions.

La Posada Hotel & Suites **H**

(956) 722-1701. **$99.** 1000 Zaragoza St 78040. I-35 exit downtown; just e of International Bridge 1. Ext/int corridors. **Pets:** Accepted.

La Quinta Inn & Suites Laredo Airport **H**

(956) 724-7222. **$85-$145.** 7220 Bob Bullock Loop 78041. I-35 exit 8 (Bob Bullock Loop E), 5.8 mi e on Loop 20. Int corridors. **Pets:** Medium, other species. Service with restrictions, supervision.

La Quinta Inn Laredo I-35 **M**

(956) 722-0511. **$72-$137.** 3610 Santa Ursula Ave 78041. I-35 exit 2 (Jefferson St). Ext corridors. **Pets:** Medium, other species. Service with restrictions, supervision.

Motel 6 South-142 **M**

(956) 725-8187. **$55-$69.** 5310 San Bernardo Ave 78041. I-35 exit 3B (Mann Rd). Ext corridors. **Pets:** Other species. Service with restrictions, supervision.

Red Roof Inn Laredo **M**

(956) 712-0733. **$49-$149.** 1006 W Calton Rd 78041. I-35 exit 3A (Hillside Rd), 0.3 mi w. Ext/int corridors. **Pets:** Large, other species. No service, supervision.

Residence Inn by Marriott Laredo **H**

(956) 753-9700. **$101-$143.** 310 Lost Oaks Blvd 78041. I-35 exit 3B (Mann Rd), just n on northbound access road. Int corridors. **Pets:** Large. $100 one-time fee/room. Service with restrictions, crate.

Staybridge Suites-Laredo **H**

(956) 722-0444. **$99-$145.** 7010 Bob Bullock Loop 78041. US 83 exit onto Loop 20 (Bob Bullock Loop); on west side. Int corridors. **Pets:** Accepted.

LEVELLAND

Holiday Inn Express Hotel & Suites **H** ❀

(806) 894-8555. **$109-$159.** 703 E SR 114 79336. Jct US 385 and SR 114, 0.5 mi e. Int corridors. **Pets:** Other species. $25 one-time fee/pet. Designated rooms, service with restrictions, supervision.

LITTLEFIELD

 Best Western Plus Littlefield Inn & Suites **H**

(806) 385-3400. **$110-$121.** 2600 Hall Ave 79339. Jct US 84 and 385, just s. Int corridors. **Pets:** Dogs only. $10 one-time fee/pet. Service with restrictions, crate.

LIVINGSTON

 **Best Western Plus Livingston Inn & Suites** **H**

(936) 327-8500. **$85-$95.** 335 Hwy 59 Loop S 77351. Just s of jct US 59 and 190, on southbound frontage road. Int corridors. **Pets:** $100 deposit/room. Designated rooms, service with restrictions, crate.

LLANO

 **Best Western Llano** **H**

(325) 247-4101. **$70-$110.** 901 W Young St 78643. 1 mi w on SR 71 and 29. Ext corridors. **Pets:** Accepted.

LONGVIEW

La Quinta Inn & Suites Longview North **H**

(903) 663-6611. **$94-$155.** 908 E Hawkins Pkwy 75605. Just w of jct US 259 (Eastman Rd). Int corridors. **Pets:** Medium, other species. Service with restrictions, supervision.

LUBBOCK

Americas Best Value Inn - Lubbock **M**

(806) 745-2515. **$50-$150.** 150 Slaton Rd 79404. I-27 exit 1B, just e on US 84. Ext corridors. **Pets:** Accepted.

Arbor Inn & Suites **H**

(806) 722-2726. **$89-$179.** 5310 Englewood Ave 79424. Loop 289 exit 50th St, just w. Int corridors. **Pets:** Dogs only. Service with restrictions, supervision.

Baymont Inn & Suites Lubbock **H**

(806) 792-5181. **$79-$95.** 3901 19th St 79410. Jct US 62/82 W and 19th St. Int corridors. **Pets:** Accepted.

Best Western Lubbock Windsor Inn **H**

(806) 762-8400. **$80-$200.** 5410 I-27 79404. 3.5 mi s on I-27 exit 1B southbound; U-turn at exit 1A (50th St) northbound. Int corridors. **Pets:** Large. $20 one-time fee/pet. Service with restrictions, supervision.

Extended StayAmerica Lubbock Southwest **H** ❀

(806) 785-9881. **$70-$149.** 4802 S Loop 289 79414. S Loop 289 exit Slide Rd, on north access road. Int corridors. **Pets:** Other species. $25 daily fee/pet. Service with restrictions.

Hawthorn Suites **H**

(806) 792-3600. **$110-$270.** 4435 Marsha Sharp Frwy 79407. W Loop 289 exit US 62/82, then 2.7 mi e. Int corridors. **Pets:** Medium, dogs only. $125 one-time fee/room. Service with restrictions, crate.

Holiday Inn Park Plaza **H**

(806) 797-3241. **$79-$109.** 3201 S Loop 289 79423. Loop 289 S exit Indiana Ave, on south frontage road. Ext/int corridors. **Pets:** Accepted.

La Quinta Inn & Suites Lubbock North **H**

(806) 749-1600. **$98-$179.** 5006 Auburn St 79416. Jct Loop 289 W and Quaker Ave, 1 mi s on W Frontage Rd. Int corridors. **Pets:** Medium, other species. Service with restrictions, supervision.

La Quinta Inn & Suites Lubbock West Medical Center **H**

(806) 792-0065. **$76-$135.** 4115 Marsha Sharp Frwy 79407. 3.3 mi sw; 2.5 mi ne of Loop 289 on US 62 and 82. Ext/int corridors. **Pets:** Medium, other species. Service with restrictions, supervision.

La Quinta Inn Lubbock Civic Center **H**

(806) 763-9441. **$67-$125.** 601 Ave Q 79401. 0.8 mi nw on US 84 (Ave Q). Ext corridors. **Pets:** Medium, other species. Service with restrictions, supervision.

▼▼ Lubbock Super 8 **M**

(806) 762-8726. **$49-$149.** 501 Ave Q 79401. 1 mi nw on US 84. Ext corridors. **Pets:** Medium, other species. $10 daily fee/pet. Designated rooms, service with restrictions. 🛜 🛏 📺 💻

▼▼ Radisson Hotel **H**

(806) 747-0171. **Call for rates.** 505 Ave Q 79401. I-27 exit 4, 0.9 mi w to US 84 (Ave Q), then just s. Int corridors. **Pets:** Accepted.
🛜 ✕ 🛏 💻 🍴 ➿

▼▼ Residence Inn by Marriott **H** 🐾

(806) 745-1963. **$126-$169.** 2551 S Loop 289 79423. Loop 289 exit University Ave, on south frontage road. Ext corridors. **Pets:** Large, other species. $100 one-time fee/room. 🛜 ✕ 🛏 💻 ➿ ✕

▼▼ Staybridge Suites **H**

(806) 765-8900. **$110-$170.** 2515 19th St 79410. Jct University Ave and 19th St; on southwest corner. Int corridors. **Pets:** Accepted.
🛜 ✕ 🛏 🛏 💻

▼▼ TownePlace Suites by Marriott **H**

(806) 799-6226. **$89-$149.** 5310 W Loop 289 79424. W Loop 289 exit US 62/82 (Brownfield Rd), 0.5 mi s on west frontage road. Int corridors. **Pets:** Accepted. 🛜 ✕ 🛏 🛏 💻 ➿

LUFKIN

AAA ▼▼▼ Best Western Plus Crown Colony Inn & Suites **H**

(936) 634-3481. **$109-$119.** 3211 S 1st St 75901. 2 mi s of jct US 59 and Loop 287. Int corridors. **Pets:** Medium. $20 one-time fee/pet. No service, crate. **SAVE** 🛜 🛏 💻 ➿

▼▼ La Quinta Inn Lufkin **H**

(936) 634-3351. **$75-$134.** 2119 S 1st St 75901. US 59 exit Carriage Way northbound, 0.3 mi s of jct S Loop 287 and US 59 business route. Ext corridors. **Pets:** Medium, other species. Service with restrictions, supervision. 🛜 🛏 💻 ➿

LUMBERTON

▼▼ Econo Lodge **M**

(409) 751-5557. **Call for rates.** 131 N LHS Dr 77657. On US 69, 1 mi n of jct US 96. Int corridors. **Pets:** Medium, dogs only. $10 daily fee/pet. Service with restrictions, crate. 🛜 🛏 💻 ➿

MADISONVILLE

AAA ▼▼ Best Western Executive Inn & Suites **H**

(936) 349-1700. **$105-$115.** 3307 E Main St 77864. I-45 exit 142, just e. Int corridors. **Pets:** Medium. $10 daily fee/pet. Designated rooms, service with restrictions, supervision. **SAVE** 🛜 🛏 🛏 💻 ➿

▼▼ Woodbine Hotel and Restaurant **CI**

(936) 348-3333. **$85-$165, 7 day notice.** 209 N Madison St 77864. I-45 exit 142, 2.2 mi w to town square, then 2 blks n. Ext/int corridors. **Pets:** Small. Crate. 🛜 🛏 🍴

MANSFIELD

AAA ▼▼▼ Best Western Plus Mansfield Inn & Suites **H**

(817) 539-0707. **$74-$84.** 775 N Hwy 287 76063. US 287 exit Walnut Creek Rd, on southbound frontage road. Int corridors. **Pets:** Medium. $20 daily fee/pet. Service with restrictions, supervision.
SAVE 🛜 🛏 🛏 💻 ➿

▼▼▼ Comfort Inn **H**

(817) 453-8848. **$63-$110.** 175 N Hwy 287 76063. US 287 S exit E Broad St. Int corridors. **Pets:** Other species. $15 one-time fee/pet. Service with restrictions. 🛜 🛏 🛏 💻 ➿

▼▼▼ Holiday Inn Express Hotel & Suites **H**

(817) 453-8722. **$85-$95.** 201 Hwy 287 N 76063. US 287 exit Walnut Creek Rd, just s on Frontage Rd. Int corridors. **Pets:** Accepted.
🛜 🛏 🛏 💻 ➿

▼▼▼ La Quinta Inn & Suites Mansfield **H**

(817) 453-5040. **$85-$149.** 1503 Breckenridge Rd 76063. US 287 exit Walnut Creek Rd/Debbie Ln, 1.2 mi n to Debbie Ln, then just e to Breckenridge Rd. Int corridors. **Pets:** Medium, other species. Service with restrictions, supervision. 🛜 ✕ 🛏 🛏 💻 ➿

MANVEL

AAA ▼▼▼ Best Western Plus Manvel Inn & Suites **H**

(281) 489-2266. **$78-$129.** 19301 Hwy 6 77578. 1.3 mi e of jct SR 288. Int corridors. **Pets:** Accepted. **SAVE** 🛜 ✕ 🛏 💻 ➿

MARBLE FALLS

AAA ▼▼▼ Best Western Plus Marble Falls Inn **H**

(830) 693-5122. **$59-$119.** 1403 US Hwy 281 78654. 0.4 mi n of jct SR 281 and FM 1431. Ext/int corridors. **Pets:** Medium. $10 daily fee/room. Designated rooms, service with restrictions, crate.
SAVE 🛜 🛏 🛏 💻 ➿

AAA ▼▼ Quality Inn-Marble Falls **H**

(830) 693-7531. **$59-$149.** 1206 Hwy 281 N 78654. 0.3 mi n of jct US 281 and FM 1431. Ext corridors. **Pets:** Medium. $50 deposit/pet, $10 daily fee/pet. Designated rooms, service with restrictions, supervision.
SAVE 🛜 🛏 💻 ➿

MARLIN

AAA ▼▼▼ Best Western Marlin Inn & Suites **H**

(254) 883-6000. **$80-$150.** 100 FM 147 76661. Jct SR 6 and 7, 1 mi n. Int corridors. **Pets:** Small, dogs only. $25 one-time fee/pet. Service with restrictions, supervision. **SAVE** 🛜 ✕ 🛏 💻 ➿

MARSHALL

AAA ▼▼ Best Western Executive Inn **H**

(903) 935-0707. **$79-$149.** 5201 E End Blvd S 75672. I-20 exit 617, 0.4 mi n on US 59. Ext corridors. **Pets:** Medium. $15 daily fee/pet. Service with restrictions, supervision. **SAVE** 🛜 🛏 💻 ➿

▼▼ La Quinta Inn Marshall **H**

(903) 927-0009. **$71-$149.** 5301 E End Blvd S 75672. I-20 exit 617, just n on US 59. Int corridors. **Pets:** Medium, other species. Service with restrictions, supervision. 🛜 🛏 💻 ➿

▼ Motel 6 Marshall #422 **M**

(903) 935-4393. **$43-$55.** 300 I-20 E 75670. I-20 exit 617, just s then just e. Ext corridors. **Pets:** Other species. Service with restrictions, supervision. 🛜 🛏 ➿

MCALLEN

▼▼▼ Drury Inn-McAllen **H**

(956) 687-5100. **$85-$149.** 612 W Expwy 83 78501. US 83 exit 2nd St, on northwest frontage road. Int corridors. **Pets:** Accepted.
🛜 🛏 💻 ➿

▼▼▼ Drury Suites-McAllen **H**

(956) 682-3222. **$95-$229.** 228 W Expwy 83 78501. At US 83 and 6th St. Int corridors. **Pets:** Accepted. 🛜 🛏 💻 ➿

▼ Motel 6 McAllen #212 **M**

(956) 687-3700. **$45-$59.** 700 W Expwy 83 78501. US 83 exit 2nd St, on northwest frontage road. Ext corridors. **Pets:** Other species. Service with restrictions, supervision. 🛜 ➿

▼▼▼ Pear Tree Inn by Drury **H**

(956) 682-4900. **$75-$119.** 300 W Expwy 83 78501. US 83 exit 2nd St, on northwest frontage road. Int corridors. **Pets:** Accepted.
🛜 🛏 💻 ➿

▼▼ Posada Ana Inn **H**

(956) 631-6700. **$77-$99.** 620 W Expwy 83 78501. US 83 exit 2nd St, on northwest frontage road. Int corridors. **Pets:** Accepted. 🛜 💻

◆◆◆ **Residence Inn by Marriott** 🅷
(956) 994-8626. **$139-$149.** 220 W Expwy 83 78501. US 83 exit 2nd St, just w, then just n on 2nd St. Int corridors. **Pets:** Medium, other species. $75 one-time fee/pet. Service with restrictions, crate.
📶 🚭 ▣ ☕ 🏊 ✂

◆◆◆ **Staybridge Suites McAllen-Airport** 🅷
(956) 213-7829. **$94-$190.** 620 Wichita Ave 78503. 0.4 mi s on US 83, just e. Int corridors. **Pets:** Accepted. 📶 🚭 ♿M ▣ ☕ 🏊

MIDLAND

◆◆ **Baymont Inn & Suites Midland Airport** 🅷
(432) 561-8000. **Call for rates.** 3312 S CR 1276 79706. I-20 exit 126, 0.8 mi n on I-20 business loop to W CR 117, then 0.4 mi e. Int corridors. **Pets:** Accepted. 📶 ▣ ☕ 🍴 🏊

◆◆ **Clarion Hotel & Conference Center** 🅷
(432) 697-3181. **Call for rates.** 4300 W Wall St 79703. I-20 exit 134 (Midkiff Rd), 1 mi n to I-20 business loop, then 0.7 mi w. Ext/int corridors. **Pets:** Accepted. 📶 ▣ ☕ 🏊 ✂

◆◆◆ **Hilton Midland Plaza** 🅷
(432) 683-6131. **Call for rates.** 117 W Wall St 79701. Jct Wall and Loraine sts; downtown. Int corridors. **Pets:** Accepted.
📶 ♿M ▣ ☕ 🍴 🏊 ✂

◆◆◆ **La Quinta Inn & Suites Midland North** 🅷
(432) 694-1200. **$137-$236.** 2606 N Loop 250 W 79707. Loop 250 W exit SR 158/191, 0.5 mi n on E Frontage Rd. Int corridors. **Pets:** Medium, other species. Service with restrictions, supervision.
📶 🚭 ♿M ▣ ☕ 🏊

◆◆◆ **La Quinta Inn Midland** 🅷
(432) 697-9900. **$71-$145.** 4130 W Wall St 79703. I-20 exit 131, 0.9 mi n on Loop 250 to exit 1A; 1.2 mi e on I-20 business route. Ext corridors. **Pets:** Medium, other species. Service with restrictions, supervision.
📶 ▣ ☕ 🏊

◆◆ **Plaza Inn** 🅷
(432) 686-8733. **$102-$122.** 4108 N Big Spring St 79705. I-20 exit 144, 6.1 mi on Loop 250 to SR 349 (Big Spring St), then just s on SR 349. Ext corridors. **Pets:** Accepted. 📶 ▣ ☕ 🏊

◆◆◆ **Residence Inn Midland** 🅷
(432) 689-3511. **$161-$179.** 5509 Deauville Blvd 79706. Loop 250 W exit SR 158/191 on S Frontage Rd. Int corridors. **Pets:** Accepted.
📶 🚭 ♿M ▣ ☕ 🏊

MINERAL WELLS

AAA ◆◆◆ **Best Western Club House Inn & Suites** 🅷 🐾
(940) 325-2270. **$70-$100.** 4410 Hwy 180 E 76067. Jct US 180 and SR 1195; in East Mineral Wells. Int corridors. **Pets:** Other species. $10 daily fee/pet. Service with restrictions, supervision.
SAVE 📶 ♿M ▣ ☕ 🏊

◆◆◆ **Comfort Suites** 🅷
(940) 327-0077. **$66-$79.** 105 Carl Kessler Blvd 76067. Jct US 281 and 180, 2.5 mi w. Int corridors. **Pets:** Accepted.
📶 🚭 ♿M ▣ ☕ 🏊

MISSION

◆◆◆ **El Rocio Retreat** BB
(956) 584-7432. **$75-$315, 3 day notice.** 2519 S Inspiration Rd 78572. Jct US 83 at Inspiration Rd, 2 mi s. Ext/int corridors. **Pets:** Accepted.
📶 🚭 ☕

MONAHANS

◆◆ **Americas Best Value Colonial Inn** 🅼
(432) 943-4345. **Call for rates.** 702 W I-20 79756. I-20 exit 80, just s. Ext/int corridors. **Pets:** Accepted. 📶 ▣ ☕ 🏊

AAA ◆◆◆ **Best Western Plus Monahans Inn & Suites** 🅷
(432) 943-3360. **$120-$160.** 2101 S Betty St 79756. I-20 exit 80, just s. Int corridors. **Pets:** Accepted. SAVE 📶 ▣ ☕ 🏊

MOUNT PLEASANT

AAA ◆◆ **Best Western Mt. Pleasant Inn** 🅼
(903) 572-5051. **$72-$80.** 102 E Burton Rd 75455. I-30 exit 162, just e. Ext corridors. **Pets:** Accepted. SAVE 📶 ▣ ☕ 🏊

◆◆◆ **Holiday Inn Express Hotel & Suites** 🅷
(903) 577-3800. **$84-$99, 3 day notice.** 2306 Greenhill Rd 75455. I-30 exit 162, just ne. Int corridors. **Pets:** Accepted. 📶 ♿M ▣ ☕ 🏊

◆◆◆ **La Quinta Inn & Suites Mt. Pleasant** 🅷
(903) 572-5514. **$67-$135.** 1620 Rotan Ave 75455. I-30 exit 160, just n. Int corridors. **Pets:** Medium, other species. Service with restrictions, supervision. 📶 🚭 ♿M ▣ ☕ 🏊

AAA ◆◆ **Quality Inn** 🅷
(903) 577-7553. **$62-$70.** 2515 W Ferguson Rd 75455. I-30 exit 160, just s. Ext corridors. **Pets:** $20 one-time fee/room. Service with restrictions, supervision. SAVE 📶 ▣ ☕ 🏊

MOUNT VERNON

AAA ◆◆ **Super 8 of Mount Vernon** 🅷
(903) 588-2882. **$45-$70.** 401 W I-30 75457. I-30 exit 147, on eastbound frontage road. Ext corridors. **Pets:** Small. $10 daily fee/pet. Service with restrictions, supervision. SAVE 📶 ▣ ☕

NACOGDOCHES

AAA ◆◆ **Best Western Northpark Inn** 🅷
(936) 560-1906. **$60-$120.** 4809 NW Stallings Dr 75964. Jct US 59 N and Loop 224 exit Westward Dr. Ext corridors. **Pets:** Small, dogs only. $20 one-time fee/pet. Service with restrictions, supervision.
SAVE 📶 ▣ ☕ 🏊

◆◆◆ **Super 8 Nacogdoches** 🅷
(936) 560-2888. **$76-$162.** 3909 South St 75964. On US 59, just s of jct Loop 224. Int corridors. **Pets:** Accepted. 📶 ▣ ☕ 🏊

NAVASOTA

◆◆◆ **Comfort Inn & Suites** 🅷
(936) 825-9464. **$90-$249.** 9345 State Hwy 6 Loop S 77868. SR 6 exit SR 105 and 90, 0.5 mi n on E Frontage Rd. Int corridors. **Pets:** Dogs only. $25 one-time fee/pet. Service with restrictions.
📶 🚭 ▣ ☕ 🏊

NEW CANEY

◆◆◆ **New Caney Inn & Suites** 🅷
(281) 354-7222. **$70-$150.** 22033 N Hwy 59 77357. US 59 northbound exit Community Dr, just e; southbound exit FM 1314, make U-turn, 1 mi n. Int corridors. **Pets:** Accepted. 📶 🚭 ▣ ☕ 🏊

◆◆◆ **La Quinta Inn & Suites-New Caney** 🅷
(281) 354-1904. **$84-$144.** 22025 US Hwy 59 77357. US 59 northbound exit Community Dr, just e; exit FM 1314 southbound, U-turn 1 mi n. Int corridors. **Pets:** Medium, other species. Service with restrictions, supervision. 📶 🚭 ▣ ☕ 🏊

NORTH RICHLAND HILLS

AAA ◆◆ **Best Western NE Mall Inn & Suites** 🅷 🐾
(817) 656-8881. **$70-$160.** 8709 Airport Frwy 76180. SR 121/183 exit Precinct Line Rd eastbound; exit Bedford Euless Rd westbound, on westbound frontage road. Ext corridors. **Pets:** Small. $30 daily fee/pet. Designated rooms, service with restrictions, supervision.
SAVE 📶 ▣ ☕ 🏊

ODESSA

Best Western Garden Oasis H
(432) 337-3006. **$130-$150.** 110 W I-20 79761-6838. Jct I-20 and US 385 exit 116, just w. Ext/int corridors. **Pets:** Other species. Service with restrictions, supervision. SAVE ⊚ 🛢 🖃 ⑪ ➷ ⊠

Comfort Suites H
(432) 362-1500. **$109-$169.** 4801 E 50th St 79762. Jct JBS Pkwy and 42nd St, 0.5 mi n. Int corridors. **Pets:** Medium. $50 deposit/pet. Service with restrictions. ⊚ ⊠ ⑤M 🛢 🖃 ➷

La Quinta Inn & Suites Odessa North H
(432) 288-9041. **$137-$236.** 4122 Faudree Rd 79765. Jct Loop 338 E and SR 191, 2 mi e. Int corridors. **Pets:** Medium, other species. Service with restrictions, supervision. ⊚ ⊠ ⑤M 🛢 🖃 ➷

La Quinta Inn Odessa H
(432) 333-2820. **$80-$155.** 5001 E Business Loop I-20 79761. I-20 exit 121, 0.8 mi n on Loop 338, then just w. Ext corridors. **Pets:** Medium, other species. Service with restrictions, supervision. ⊚ 🛢 🖃 ➷

MCM Grande Hotel H
(432) 362-2311. **Call for rates.** 6201 E Business Loop I-20 79762. I-20 exit 121, 0.8 mi n on Loop 338, then 1 mi e. Ext/int corridors.
Pets: Accepted. ⊚ 🛢 🖃 ⑪ ➷ ⊠

Motel 6 Odessa #439 M
(432) 333-4025. **$45-$65.** 200 E I-20 Service Rd 79766. I-20 exit 116, on eastbound frontage road. Ext corridors. **Pets:** Other species. Service with restrictions, supervision. ⊚ ➷

Quality Inn & Suites H
(432) 333-3931. **$89-$325.** 3001 E Business Loop I-20 79761. I-20 exit 121, 0.7 mi n on Loop 338, then 0.5 mi w. Ext/int corridors.
Pets: Accepted. SAVE ⊚ 🛢 🖃 ➷ ⊠

TownePlace Suites by Marriott H
(432) 362-1077. **$142-$170.** 4412 Tanglewood Ln 79762. Jct JBS Pkwy and 42nd St, 2 blks w to Tanglewood Ln, then just n. Int corridors.
Pets: Accepted. ⊚ ⊠ ⑤M 🛢 🖃 ➷

OLMITO

La Quinta Inn Brownsville H
(956) 350-8855. **$72-$130.** 8280 North Expy 78575. US 77/83 exit SR 511, just e. Int corridors. **Pets:** Medium, other species. Service with restrictions, supervision. ⊚ 🛢 🖃 ➷

ORANGE

Holiday Inn Express & Suites Orange H
(409) 882-9222. **$89-$129.** 2655 I-10 E 77630. I-10 exit 877 eastbound; exit 876 westbound, on eastbound frontage road. Int corridors.
Pets: Small. $100 deposit/room. Service with restrictions, supervision.
SAVE ⊚ ⑤M 🛢 🖃 ➷

OZONA

Hillcrest Motor Inn M
(325) 392-5515. **$50-$70.** 1204 Sheffield Rd/Loop 466 W 76943. I-10 exit 365, 2 blks n to Loop 466, then 1.0 mi w. Ext corridors. **Pets:** $10 one-time fee/pet. Designated rooms, service with restrictions, supervision.
SAVE ⊚ 🛢 🖃

Travelodge M
(325) 392-2656. **$54-$72.** 8 11th St 76943. I-10 exit 368 westbound, 2 mi w; exit 365 eastbound to Loop 466, 1 mi w. Ext corridors.
Pets: Accepted. SAVE ⊚ 🛢 🖃 ➷

PALESTINE

Best Western Palestine Inn H
(903) 723-4655. **$80-$150.** 1601 W Palestine Ave 75801. Jct US 287/SR 19, 0.7 mi sw on US 79. Ext corridors. **Pets:** Small. $10 daily fee/pet. Designated rooms, service with restrictions, supervision.
SAVE ⊚ 🛢 🖃 ⑪ ➷

La Quinta Inn & Suites Palestine H
(903) 723-1387. **$93-$154.** 3000 S Loop 256 75801. 1.8 mi e of jct US 79 and Loop 256. Int corridors. **Pets:** Medium, other species. Service with restrictions, supervision. ⊚ 🛢 🖃 ➷

PAMPA

AmericInn Lodge & Suites of Pampa H
(806) 665-4404. **Call for rates.** 1101 N Hobart St 79065. SR 70, Hobart and Somerville sts. Int corridors. **Pets:** Accepted.
SAVE ⊚ ⊠ ⑤M 🛢 🖃 ➷ ⊠

Best Western Northgate Inn H
(806) 665-0926. **$75-$100.** 2831 Perryton Pkwy 79065. SR 70, 3 mi n. Ext corridors. **Pets:** Accepted. SAVE ⊚ 🛢 🖃 ➷

PARIS

Americas Best Value Inn Paris H
(903) 785-2215. **$59-$79.** 3755 NE Loop 286 75460. Jct US 82 and E Loop 286, just n. Ext corridors. **Pets:** Accepted.
SAVE ⊚ 🛢 🖃 ➷

PEARLAND

Best Western Pearland Inn H
(281) 997-2000. **Call for rates.** 1855 N Main St 77581. Jct Loop 8 S and SR 35, 1.5 mi s. Ext corridors. **Pets:** Accepted.
SAVE ⊚ 🛢 🖃 ➷

La Quinta Inn & Suites Pearland H
(281) 412-5454. **$94-$192.** 9002 Broadway St 77584. Jct SR 288 and 518, 1.6 mi e. Int corridors. **Pets:** Medium, other species. Service with restrictions, supervision. SAVE ⊚ ⊠ ⑤M 🛢 🖃 ➷

PECOS

Best Western Swiss Clock Inn M 🐾
(432) 447-2215. **$85-$105.** 133 S Frontage Rd, I-20 79772. I-20 exit 40, just e. Ext corridors. **Pets:** Dogs only. $15 daily fee/room. Designated rooms, service with restrictions, supervision.
SAVE ⊚ 🛢 🖃 ⑪ ➷

Knights Inn Laura Lodge Motel & Suites M
(432) 445-4924. **$63-$99.** 1000 E Business I-20 79772. I-20 exit 42, 1 mi nw to Business Rt I-20, then 0.5 mi e. Ext corridors. **Pets:** Small. $10 daily fee/pet. Designated rooms, service with restrictions, supervision.
SAVE ⊚ 🛢 🖃 ➷

Oak Tree Inn H
(432) 445-1628. **Call for rates.** 22 N Frontage Rd 79772. I-20 exit 42, just w on north access road. Int corridors. **Pets:** Accepted.
SAVE ⊚ ⊠ 🛢 🖃

PERRYTON

Best Western Perryton Inn H
(806) 434-2850. **$80-$130.** 3505 S Main St (US 83) 79070. US 83, 2.2 mi s. Int corridors. **Pets:** Other species. $15 one-time fee/pet. Designated rooms, service with restrictions, supervision.
SAVE ⊚ ⑤M 🛢 🖃 ⑪ ➷

PHARR

La Quinta Inn & Suites Pharr H
(956) 787-2900. **$89-$150.** 4603 N Cage Blvd 78577. US 281 northbound exit Nolana Loop, just w. Int corridors. **Pets:** Medium, other species. Service with restrictions, supervision.
⊚ ⊠ ⑤M 🛢 🖃 ➷

PLAINVIEW

Best Western Conestoga H
(806) 293-9454. **$78.** 600 N I-27 79072. I-27 exit 49, just s of US 70, on eastbound access road. Ext corridors. **Pets:** Large. $15 daily fee/pet. No service, supervision. SAVE ⊚ 🛢 🖃 ➷

PORT ARANSAS

◆ Alister Square Inn **M**
(361) 749-3000. **Call for rates.** 122 S Alister St 78373. Just n of Ave C. Ext corridors. **Pets:** Accepted. 🛎 🛢 ➿

◆◆ Beachgate CondoSuites & Motel **CO**
(361) 749-5900. **$40-$610, 30 day notice.** 2000 On the Beach Dr 78373. Between beach markers 8 and 9; street access on Anchor Rd off 11th St. Ext/int corridors. **Pets:** Medium, dogs only. $15 daily fee/pet. Designated rooms, service with restrictions, supervision.
🛎 ⊠ 🛢 🖳 ➿ ⊠

◆◆◆ Best Western Ocean Villa **H**
(361) 749-3010. **$69-$209.** 400 E Ave G 78373. Just se of S Alister St (SR 361). Ext corridors. **Pets:** Accepted. (SAVE) 🛎 🛢M 🛢 🖳 ➿

◆ Mariner Inn & Suites **M**
(361) 749-8200. **Call for rates.** 2607 State Hwy 361 78373. 0.6 mi n of Gulf Beach Rd. Ext corridors. **Pets:** Accepted. 🛎 🛢 🖳 ➿

◆◆◆ Plantation Suites & Conference Center **M**
(361) 749-3866. **$80-$200.** 1909 Hwy 361 78373. On SR 361, 0.4 mi s. Ext corridors. **Pets:** Accepted. 🛎 🛢 🖳 ➿

PORT LAVACA

◆◆◆ Best Western Port Lavaca Inn **H** 🐾
(361) 553-6800. **$100-$120.** 2202 N Hwy 35 77979. Jct US 87 and SR 35, 2.5 mi e. Int corridors. **Pets:** Small, other species. $20 daily fee/room. Service with restrictions, supervision. (SAVE) 🛎 🛢 🖳 ➿

◆ ◆◆◆ La Quinta Inn & Suites Port Lavaca **H**
(361) 552-8800. **$93-$154.** 910 Hwy 35 77979. Jct US 87 and SR 35, 2 mi e. Int corridors. **Pets:** Medium, other species. Service with restrictions, supervision. (SAVE) 🛎 ⊠ 🛢M 🛢 🖳 ➿

POST

◆ ◆◆ Best Western Post Inn **H**
(806) 495-9933. **$87-$130.** 1011 N Broadway 79356. 1 mi n on US 84. Int corridors. **Pets:** Other species. $20 one-time fee/pet. Designated rooms, service with restrictions, supervision. (SAVE) 🛎 🛢 🖳 ➿

RAYMONDVILLE

◆ ◆◆ Best Western Executive Inn Raymondville **M**
(956) 689-4141. **$69-$109.** 118 N Expwy 77 78580. US 77, jct FM 186 on southbound access road. Ext corridors. **Pets:** Accepted.
(SAVE) 🛎 🛢 🖳 ➿

◆◆◆ La Quinta Inn & Suites Raymondville **H**
(956) 689-4000. **$80-$145.** 128 N Expwy 77 78580. US 77, jct FM 186 on southbound access road. Int corridors. **Pets:** Medium, other species. Service with restrictions, supervision. 🛎 ⊠ 🛢M 🛢 🖳 ➿

REFUGIO

◆ ◆◆◆ Best Western Refugio Inn **H**
(361) 526-4600. **$89-$107.** 1007 N Victoria St 78377. Just n of jct US 183 and 77. Int corridors. **Pets:** Accepted. (SAVE) 🛎 🛢 🖳 ➿

RICHLAND HILLS

◆◆◆ La Quinta Inn & Suites Fort Worth NE Mall **H**
(817) 595-4442. **$116-$179.** 653 NE Loop 820 76118. I-820 exit 23, just s of Glenview Dr. Int corridors. **Pets:** Medium, other species. Service with restrictions, supervision. 🛎 ⊠ 🛢M 🛢 🖳 ➿

ROBSTOWN

◆◆◆ Days Inn **M**
(361) 387-8600. **$72-$147.** 650 Hwy 77 S 78380. Just n of jct CR 892 and US 77. Ext corridors. **Pets:** Accepted. 🛎 🛢 🖳 ➿

◆ ◆◆◆ Executive Inn **M**
(361) 387-9416. **$56-$89.** 620 Hwy 77 S 78380. On US 77, 1 mi s. Ext corridors. **Pets:** $10 daily fee/pet. Service with restrictions, supervision.
(SAVE) 🛎 🛢 ➿

ROCKPORT

◆◆ Days Inn **M**
(361) 729-6379. **$59-$144.** 1212 Laurel St 78382. Jct Laurel St and Business Rt SR 35; center. Ext corridors. **Pets:** Accepted.
🛎 🛢 🖳 ➿

ROUND ROCK

◆◆◆ ◆◆ Best Western Executive Inn **H**
(512) 255-3222. **$79-$120.** 1851 N I-35 78664. I-35 exit 253 northbound; exit 253A (U-turn) southbound. Ext corridors. **Pets:** Large, other species. $5 daily fee/pet. Service with restrictions. (SAVE) 🛎 🛢M 🛢 🖳 ➿

◆◆◆◆ Candlewood Suites **H**
(512) 828-0899. **$66-$109.** 521 S I-35 78664. I-35 exit 252A, just n on northbound frontage road. Int corridors. **Pets:** Medium, other species. $50 daily fee/pet. Service with restrictions, supervision. 🛎 🛢 🖳

◆◆ Extended Stay America Austin-Round Rock-N **H** ☼
(512) 671-7872. **$54-$69.** 555 S I-35 City Centre Business Park 78664. I-35 exit 252A, on northbound frontage road. Int corridors. **Pets:** Other species. $25 daily fee/pet. Service with restrictions. 🛎 🛢 🖳

◆◆◆ Homewood Suites by Hilton **H**
(512) 394-9200. **$99-$299.** 2201 S Mays St 78664. I-35 exit 251, just n on E Access Rd to Hesters Crossing, then just e. Int corridors. **Pets:** Accepted. 🛎 ⊠ 🛢M 🛢 🖳 ➿ ⊠

◆◆◆ La Quinta Inn & Suites Austin Round Rock North **H**
(512) 255-6666. **$88-$155.** 2004 I-35 N 78681. I-35 exit 254, on west frontage road. Int corridors. **Pets:** Medium, other species. Service with restrictions, supervision. 🛎 🛢 🖳 ➿

◆◆◆◆ Residence Inn by Marriott Austin Round Rock **H**
(512) 733-2400. **$85-$186.** 2505 S I-35 78664. I-35 exit 250 southbound; exit 251 northbound, on east frontage road. Int corridors. **Pets:** Accepted.
🛎 ⊠ 🛢M 🛢 🖳 ➿ ⊠

◆◆◆ SpringHill Suites **H**
(512) 733-6700. **$84-$161.** 2960 Hoppe Tr 78681. I-35 exit 256 southbound; exit 254 northbound on west frontage road. Int corridors. **Pets:** Accepted. 🛎 ⊠ 🛢M 🛢 🖳 ➿

◆◆◆ Staybridge Suites Austin-Round Rock **H**
(512) 733-0942. **Call for rates.** 520 I-35 S 78681. I-35 exit 252B northbound; exit 252AB southbound, on west frontage road. Int corridors. **Pets:** Accepted. 🛎 🛢M 🛢 🖳 ➿

SALADO

◆◆◆ Holiday Inn Express Salado **H**
(254) 947-4004. **$99-$119.** 1991 N Stagecoach Rd 76571. I-35 exit 286. Int corridors. **Pets:** Accepted. 🛎 🛢M 🛢 🖳 ➿

◆ ◆◆◆ Stagecoach Inn **H**
(254) 947-5111. **Call for rates.** 401 S Stagecoach Rd 76571. I-35 and US 81 exit 284 southbound; exit 283 northbound. Ext corridors. **Pets:** Accepted. (SAVE) 🛎 🛢 🖳 🍴 ➿ ⊠

SAN ANGELO

◆ ◆◆◆ Best Western San Angelo **H**
(325) 223-1273. **$85-$105.** 3017 W Loop 306 76904. Loop 306 exit College Hills Blvd, just s. Ext corridors. **Pets:** Medium, dogs only. $15 daily fee/pet. Service with restrictions, supervision. (SAVE) 🛎 🛢 🖳 ➿

▼▼ Days Inn San Angelo ⚹
(325) 658-6594. **$57-$66.** 4613 S Jackson St 76903. Jct US 87 and Jackson St. Ext corridors. **Pets:** Accepted. 🛜 🛗 💻 🍴 ⚋

▼▼▼ La Quinta Inn & Conference Center San Angelo ⚹
(325) 949-0515. **$67-$135.** 2307 Loop 306 76904. Loop 306 exit Knickerbocker Rd, just s. Ext corridors. **Pets:** Medium, other species. Service with restrictions, supervision. 🛜 🛗 💻 ⚋

▼▼ Rodeway Inn ⚹
(325) 944-2578. **Call for rates.** 2502 Loop 306 76904. Loop 306 exit Knickerbocker Rd. Ext corridors. **Pets:** Small, dogs only. Service with restrictions, supervision. 🛜 🛗 💻 ⚋

▼▼▼ Staybridge Suites ⚹
(325) 653-1500. **Call for rates.** 1355 Knickerbocker Rd 76904. US 87 S, 1 mi w. Int corridors. **Pets:** Accepted. 🛜 🛗 💻 ⚋

SAN ANTONIO METROPOLITAN AREA

FLORESVILLE

🔶 ▼▼ Best Western Floresville Inn Ⓜ ⚹
(830) 393-0443. **$105-$110.** 1720 S 10th St 78114. US 181, just s of downtown. Ext corridors. **Pets:** Medium. $15 daily fee/pet. Service with restrictions, supervision. [SAVE] 🛜 🛗 💻 ⚋

LIVE OAK

▼▼ La Quinta Inn San Antonio I-35 North at Toepperwein ⚹
(210) 657-5500. **$78-$144.** 12822 I-35 N 78233. I-35 exit 170B (Toepperwein Rd), on northbound access road. Ext/int corridors. **Pets:** Medium, other species. Service with restrictions, supervision. 🛜 🛗 💻 ⚋

NEW BRAUNFELS

▼▼ Executive Inn & Suites Ⓜ
(830) 625-3932. **Call for rates.** 808 Hwy 46 S 78130. I-35 exit 189, 0.4 mi e. Ext corridors. **Pets:** Accepted. 🛜 🛗 💻 ⚋

▼▼▼ La Quinta Inn & Suites New Braunfels ⚹
(830) 627-3333. **$84-$159.** 365 Hwy 46 S 78130. I-35 exit 189, just s. Int corridors. **Pets:** Medium, other species. Service with restrictions, supervision. 🛜 ✖ 🛗 💻 ⚋

▼▼ Quality Inn & Suites ⚹
(830) 643-9300. **Call for rates.** 1533 IH-35 N 78130. I-35 exit 190, on southbound access road. Int corridors. **Pets:** Accepted.
🛜 🛗 💻 ⚋

▼▼ Ramada New Braunfels ⚹
(830) 625-8017. **$49-$180.** 1051 I-35 E 78130. I-35 exit 189, on southbound access road. Ext corridors. **Pets:** Small. $25 one-time fee/pet. Service with restrictions, supervision. 🛜 🛗 💻 ⚋

▼▼ Super 8-New Braunfels Ⓜ
(830) 629-1155. **$45-$180.** 510 Hwy 46 S 78130. I-35 exit 189, just e. Ext corridors. **Pets:** Small. $25 daily fee/pet. Service with restrictions, crate. 🛜 🛗 💻 ⚋

🔶 ▼▼▼ Wingate by Wyndham ⚹
(830) 515-4701. **$70-$189.** 245 FM 306 N 78130. I-35 exit 191 (FM 306), just w. Int corridors. **Pets:** Small. Service with restrictions, supervision. [SAVE] 🛜 ✖ 🛗 💻 ⚋

SAN ANTONIO

🔶 ▼▼ Alamo Inn Ⓜ
(210) 227-2203. **$45-$120.** 2203 E Commerce St 78203. I-37 exit 141A, 1.2 mi e at Commerce St and New Braunfels Ave. Ext corridors. **Pets:** Medium. $10 daily fee/pet. Designated rooms, service with restrictions, crate. [SAVE] 🛜 🛗 💻

🔶 ▼▼▼ Aloft San Antonio Airport ⚹
(210) 541-8881. **$99-$289.** 838 NW Loop 410 78216. I-410 exit Blanco Rd, just s. Int corridors. **Pets:** Accepted. [SAVE] 🛜 ✖ 🛗 💻 ⚋

🔶 ▼▼▼ Arbor House Suites Bed & Breakfast ⒷⒷ
(210) 472-2005. **$129-$207, 14 day notice.** 109 Arciniega St 78205. Just s of E Nueva; between S Presa and S St. Mary's sts; near La Villita Historic District. Ext/int corridors. **Pets:** Medium. Service with restrictions, crate. [SAVE] 🛜 ✖ 🛗 💻

▼▼ Baymont Inns & Suites ⚹
(210) 593-0338. **$53-$73.** 9542 I-10 W 78230. I-10 exit Wurzbach Rd, just e on eastbound access road. Ext corridors. **Pets:** Accepted.
🛜 🛗 💻 ⚋

🔶 ▼▼▼ Best Western Garden Inn ⚹
(210) 599-0999. **$59-$249.** 11939 N I-35 78236. I-35 exit 170, 0.5 mi s to exit Judson Rd; on southbound access road. Ext corridors.
Pets: Accepted. [SAVE] 🛗 💻 ⚋

🔶 ▼▼▼ Best Western Plus Posada Ana -Medical Center ⚹
(210) 691-9550. **Call for rates.** 9411 Wurzbach Rd 78240. I-10 exit 561 (Wurzbach Rd), on eastbound access road. Int corridors. **Pets:** Accepted.
[SAVE] 🛜 🛗 💻 ⚋

🔶 ▼▼▼ Best Western Posada Ana Inn-Airport ⚹
(210) 342-1400. **$88-$110.** 8600 Jones Maltsberger Rd 78216. I-410 exit 21A (Jones Maltsberger Rd), 0.5 mi s. Int corridors. **Pets:** Accepted.
[SAVE] 🛜 🛗 💻 ⚋

▼▼▼ Candlewood Suites Hotel ⚹ ⚹
(210) 615-0550. **$79-$99.** 9350 I-10 W 78230. I-10 W exit 561 (Wurzbach Rd), between Wurzbach Rd and Medical Dr; eastbound access road. Int corridors. **Pets:** Medium. $15 daily fee/room. Service with restrictions, supervision. 🛗 🛗 💻 ⚋

▼▼▼ Candlewood Suites San Antonio West SeaWorld Area ⚹
(210) 523-7666. **$49-$269.** 9502 Amelia Pass 78254. Loop 1604 at Braun Rd, on northbound access road. Int corridors. **Pets:** Accepted.
🛜 🛗 💻 ⚋

▼▼▼ Comfort Inn & Suites ⚹
(210) 733-8080. **$99-$149.** 6039 IH-10 W 78201. I-10 exit Vance Jackson Rd, on westbound access road. Int corridors. **Pets:** Accepted.
🛜 ✖ 🛗 💻 ⚋

🔶 ▼▼▼ Comfort Inn & Suites Airport ⚹
(210) 249-2000. **$70-$160.** 8640 Crownhill Blvd 78209. I-410 exit Airport Blvd, just off I-410 eastbound access road; just e of Broadway Ave. Int corridors. **Pets:** Small. $25 one-time fee/pet. Service with restrictions, supervision. [SAVE] 🛜 🛗 🛗 💻 ⚋

▼▼ Comfort Inn-Fiesta Ⓜ
(210) 696-4766. **Call for rates.** 6755 N Loop 1604 W 78249. I-10 exit CR 1604 W, 0.5 mi w of La Cantera Blvd. Int corridors. **Pets:** Accepted.
🛜 🛗 🛗 💻 ⚋

🔶 ▼▼▼ Crowne Plaza San Antonio Riverwalk ⚹
(210) 354-2800. **$89-$239.** 111 Pecan St E 78205. Corner of Pecan and Soledad sts. Int corridors. **Pets:** Accepted.
[SAVE] 🛜 ✖ 🛗 💻 🍴 ⚋ ✖

🔶 ▼▼▼ Howard Johnson Lackland Inn & Suites ⚹
(210) 675-9690. **$46-$66.** 6815 Hwy 90 W 78227. I-410 exit US 90 to Military Dr, 0.5 mi e on westbound access road. Ext corridors.
Pets: Other species. $25 one-time fee/room. [SAVE] 🛜 🛗 💻 ⚋

▼▼▼ Drury Inn & Suites Northeast H
(210) 657-1107. **$95-$159.** 4900 Crestwind Dr 78239. I-35 exit 165 (Walzem Rd), on northbound access road. Int corridors. **Pets:** Accepted.

▼▼▼ Drury Inn & Suites-San Antonio Airport H
(210) 308-8100. **$95-$194.** 95 NE Loop 410 78216. I-410 exit 21A (Jones Maltsberger Rd), 1.8 mi w of airport. Int corridors. **Pets:** Accepted.

▼▼▼ Drury Inn & Suites San Antonio-La Cantera H
(210) 696-0800. **$100-$209.** 15806 IH-10 W 78249. I-10 exit Loop 1604, on eastbound access road. Int corridors. **Pets:** Accepted.

▼▼▼ Drury Inn & Suites-San Antonio North H
(210) 404-1600. **$105-$209.** 801 N Loop 1604 E 78232. On Loop 1604, 0.4 mi w on US 281. Int corridors. **Pets:** Accepted.

▼▼▼ Drury Inn & Suites-San Antonio Northwest H
(210) 561-2510. **$115-$299.** 9806 I-10 W 78230. I-10 exit 561 (Wurzbach Rd), on southeast corner. Int corridors. **Pets:** Accepted.

▼▼▼ Drury Inn & Suites-San Antonio Riverwalk H
(210) 212-5200. **$130-$219.** 201 N St. Mary's St 78205. Just s of College St. Int corridors. **Pets:** Accepted.

◢◣ ▼▼▼ Drury Plaza Hotel-San Antonio Riverwalk H
(210) 270-7799. **$135-$274.** 105 S St. Mary's St 78205. Jct Commerce, St. Mary's and Market sts. Int corridors. **Pets:** Accepted.

▼▼ Drury Plaza San Antonio North H
(210) 494-2420. **$120-$194.** 823 N Loop 1604 E 78232. Jct Loop 1604 and US 281, just w. Int corridors. **Pets:** Accepted.

▼▼ Econo Lodge-East M
(210) 333-3346. **Call for rates.** 218 S WW White Rd 78219. I-10 exit 580, 0.3 mi s of jct WW White Rd. Ext corridors. **Pets:** Accepted.

◢◣ ▼▼ Econo Lodge Inn & Suites M
(210) 229-9220. **$55-$200.** 2755 N Panam Expwy 78208. I-35 N exit 159B (Walters Ave), on southbound access road. Ext corridors. **Pets:** Medium, dogs only. $15 daily fee/pet. Designated rooms, service with restrictions, crate.

◢◣ ▼▼ Econo Lodge Inn & Suites Fiesta Park M ✿
(210) 690-5500. **Call for rates.** 13575 I-10 W 78249. I-10 exit 557, westbound access road. Ext corridors. **Pets:** Very small, dogs only. $10 daily fee/pet. Service with restrictions, supervision.

◢◣ ▼▼▼ Emily Morgan Hotel H ✿
(210) 225-8486. **$109-$429.** 705 E Houston St 78205. Just n of Bonham St. Int corridors. **Pets:** Other species. $75 one-time fee/room. Service with restrictions.

▼▼▼ The Fairmount Hotel H
(210) 224-8800. **Call for rates.** 401 S Alamo St 78205. Opposite convention center and Hemisfair Plaza. Ext/int corridors. **Pets:** Accepted.

◢◣ ▼▼▼ Grand Hyatt San Antonio H ✿
(210) 224-1234. **$109-$499.** 600 E Market St 78205. I-37 exit 141A (Market St); between S Alamo St and I-37. Int corridors. **Pets:** Other species. $35 one-time fee/pet. Designated rooms, service with restrictions, crate.

▼▼▼ Hilton Hill Country Hotel & Spa H
(210) 509-9800. **$139-$199.** 9800 Westover Hills Blvd 78251. Between Loop 410 and 1604, just off CR 151. Int corridors. **Pets:** Accepted.

▼▼▼ Holiday Inn Express-San Antonio Airport H
(210) 308-6700. **$109-$129.** 91 NE Loop 410 78216. I-410 exit 21A (Jones Maltsberger Rd) eastbound; exit 20B westbound, on westbound access road; between San Pedro Ave and Jones Maltsberger Rd. Int corridors. **Pets:** Accepted.

◢◣ ▼▼▼ Holiday Inn Northwest-SeaWorld H
(210) 520-2508. **$85-$225.** 10135 State Hwy 151 78251. I-410 exit SR 151, 3 mi n on northbound access road. Int corridors. **Pets:** Medium. $75 one-time fee/room. Service with restrictions, crate.

▼▼▼ Holiday Inn San Antonio International Airport H
(210) 349-9900. **$99-$199.** 77 NE Loop 410 78216. I-410 exit 20B (McCullough St), on westbound access road. Int corridors. **Pets:** Other species. $100 deposit/room, $25 one-time fee/room. Service with restrictions.

▼▼ Homestead Studio Suites Hotel-San Antonio-Airport M ❀
(210) 491-9009. **$44-$59.** 1015 Central Pkwy S 78232. I-410 exit US 281 (San Pedro Ave), just n of Bitters Rd; on northbound access road. Ext corridors. **Pets:** Other species. $25 daily fee/pet. Service with restrictions.

◢◣ ▼▼▼▼ Hotel Contessa H ❀
(210) 229-9222. **$159-$299.** 306 W Market St 78205. Market St at St. Mary's. Int corridors. **Pets:** Medium. $50 one-time fee/room. Designated rooms, service with restrictions.

▼▼▼ The Hotel Havana CI
(210) 222-2008. **Call for rates.** 1015 Navarro St 78205. Just s of N St. Mary's St. Int corridors. **Pets:** Accepted.

▼▼▼ Hotel Indigo at the Alamo H
(210) 933-2000. **$109-$239.** 105 N Alamo Plaza 78205. I-37 exit Commerce St, just s. Int corridors. **Pets:** Accepted.

▼▼▼ Hotel Indigo Riverwalk H
(210) 527-1900. **$99-$199.** 830 N St. Mary's St 78205. Just n of Navarro St. Int corridors. **Pets:** Accepted.

◢◣ ▼▼▼▼ Hyatt Regency San Antonio H
(210) 222-1234. **$109-$479.** 123 Losoya St 78205. Between College and Crockett sts. Int corridors. **Pets:** Accepted.

▼▼ Inn on the Riverwalk BB
(210) 225-6333. **Call for rates.** 129 Woodward Pl 78204. Just n of W Cesar E Chavez Blvd. Ext/int corridors. **Pets:** Accepted.

▼▼ Knights Inn Northwest Fiesta M
(210) 558-9070. **$45-$90.** 9447 I-10 W 78230. I-10 exit 561 (Wurzbach Rd) westbound; exit Callaghan Rd, circle back eastbound. Ext corridors. **Pets:** Dogs only. $15 daily fee/pet. Service with restrictions, supervision.

◢◣ ▼▼▼ La Quinta Inn & Suites H
(210) 447-8000. **$116-$189.** 11155 W Loop 1604 N 78023. On W Loop 1604 access road, just w of Bandera Rd. Int corridors. **Pets:** Medium, other species. Service with restrictions, supervision.

▼▼▼ La Quinta Inn & Suites-Fiesta Texas H
(210) 696-0100. **$89-$159.** 5622 Utex Blvd 78249. I-10 exit Loop 1604, 0.7 mi e; on eastbound access road. Int corridors. **Pets:** Medium, other species. Service with restrictions, supervision.

▼▼▼▼ La Quinta Inn & Suites San Antonio Airport 🅷
(210) 342-3738. **$88-$170.** 850 Halm Blvd 78216. I-410 exit US 281 S, southwest corner. Int corridors. **Pets:** Medium, other species. Service with restrictions, supervision.

▼▼▼▼ La Quinta Inn & Suites San Antonio Convention Center 🅷
(210) 222-9181. **$167-$247.** 303 Blum St 78202. 0.5 mi ne. Ext/int corridors. **Pets:** Medium, other species. Service with restrictions, supervision.

▼▼▼▼ La Quinta Inn & Suites San Antonio Downtown 🅷
(210) 212-5400. **$108-$214.** 100 Cesar E Chavez Blvd 78204. I-35 exit 155B (Cesar E Chavez Blvd), 3 blks e of jct E Flores St. Int corridors. **Pets:** Medium, other species. Service with restrictions, supervision.

▼▼▼▼ La Quinta Inn & Suites San Antonio North Stone Oak 🅷
(210) 497-0506. **$120-$194.** 18502 Hardy Oak Blvd 78258. US 281, Loop 1604, on west bound access road. Int corridors. **Pets:** Medium, other species. Service with restrictions, supervision.

▼▼▼ La Quinta Inn San Antonio AlamoDome South 🅷
(210) 337-7171. **$89-$164.** 3180 Goliad Rd 78223. I-37 exit 135 (Brooks City Base/SE Military Dr), just w of interstate. Int corridors. **Pets:** Medium, other species. Service with restrictions, supervision.

▼▼▼▼ La Quinta Inn San Antonio I-10 East 🅷
(210) 661-4545. **$112-$175.** 6075 IH-10 E Foster Rd 78219. I-10 exit 583 (Foster Rd), on westbound access road. Int corridors. **Pets:** Medium, other species. Service with restrictions, supervision.

▼▼▼ La Quinta Inn San Antonio I-35 North At Rittman Rd 🅷
(210) 653-6619. **$78-$144.** 6410 I-35 78218. I-35 exit 163B northbound, on I-35 northbound access road; between Rittman and Eisenhauer rds; exit 164A (Rittiman Rd) southbound. Ext corridors. **Pets:** Medium, other species. Service with restrictions, supervision.

▼▼ ▼ La Quinta Inn San Antonio Lackland 🅷
(210) 674-3200. **$68-$155.** 6511 Military Dr W 78227. Sw of jct US 90 and Military Dr W. Ext corridors. **Pets:** Medium, other species. Service with restrictions, supervision.

▼▼ ▼ La Quinta Inn San Antonio Market Square 🅷
(210) 271-0001. **$78-$188.** 900 Dolorosa St 78207. I-10/35 exit Cesar E Chavez Blvd, just n on Santa Rosa St, then just w on Nueva St. Ext corridors. **Pets:** Medium, other species. Service with restrictions, supervision.

▼▼ ▼ La Quinta Inn San Antonio SeaWorld/Ingram Park 🅷
(210) 680-8883. **$62-$199.** 7134 NW Loop 410 78238. I-410 exit 10 (Culebra Rd), on eastbound access road. Ext corridors. **Pets:** Medium, other species. Service with restrictions, supervision.

▼▼ ▼ La Quinta Inn San Antonio South Park 🅷
(210) 922-2111. **$74-$155.** 7202 S Pan Am Expwy 78224. I-35 exit 150A (Military Dr) northbound; exit 150B southbound, se of jct I-35 and Military Dr SW. Ext corridors. **Pets:** Medium, other species. Service with restrictions, supervision.

▼▼ ▼ La Quinta Inn San Antonio Vance Jackson Ⓜ
(210) 734-7931. **$78-$170.** 5922 I-10 W 78201. I-10 exit 565B eastbound; exit 565C (Vance Jackson Rd) westbound, on eastbound access road. Ext corridors. **Pets:** Medium, other species. Service with restrictions, supervision.

ⒶⒶⒶ ▼▼▼▼ Marriott San Antonio Plaza 🅷
(210) 229-1000. **$210-$240.** 555 S Alamo St 78205. Opposite convention center and Hemisfair Plaza. Int corridors. **Pets:** Accepted.

ⒶⒶⒶ ▼▼▼▼ Mokara Hotel & Spa 🅷 🐾
(210) 396-5800. **$209-$459, 3 day notice.** 212 W Crockett 78205. Between St. Mary's and Navarro sts; on Riverwalk. Int corridors. **Pets:** Small, other species. $50 one-time fee/room. No service.

▼▼ ▼ Motel 6 - 1122 Ⓜ
(210) 225-1111. **$55-$75.** 211 N Pecos St 78207. I-10/35 exit 155B (Pecos St), on south access road. Ext corridors. **Pets:** Other species. Service with restrictions, supervision.

▼▼ ▼ Motel 6 - 4341 🅷
(210) 447-9000. **$45-$75.** 126 Kenley Pl 78232. US 281 exit Brook Hollow Blvd, just n on northbound access road. Int corridors. **Pets:** Other species. Service with restrictions, supervision.

▼ Motel 6 - 651 🅷
(210) 673-9020. **$43-$61.** 2185 SW Loop 410 78227. I-410 exit 7 (Marbach Rd), 0.7 mi w; on westbound access road. Ext corridors. **Pets:** Other species. Service with restrictions, supervision.

▼ Motel 6 East #183 Ⓜ
(210) 333-1850. **$41-$53.** 138 N WW White Rd 78219. I-10 exit 580 (WW White Rd), just off westbound access road. Ext corridors. **Pets:** Other species. Service with restrictions, supervision.

▼ Motel 6 Fort Sam Houston #1350 Ⓜ
(210) 661-8791. **$43-$53.** 5522 N Pan Am Expwy 78218. I-35/410 exit 164 (Rittiman Rd), just s on northbound access road; just off Goldfield St. Ext corridors. **Pets:** Other species. Service with restrictions, supervision.

▼▼ ▼ Motel 6 - Medical Center South #4429 🅷
(210) 616-0030. **$69-$175, 7 day notice.** 7500 Louis Pasteur Dr 78229. I-410 exit 14C (Babcock Rd), 1 mi nw, then 0.5 mi n. Int corridors. **Pets:** Other species. Service with restrictions, supervision.

ⒶⒶⒶ ▼▼▼▼ Omni La Mansión del Rio 🅷
(210) 518-1000. **$169-$309, 3 day notice.** 112 College St 78205. Just s on the Riverwalk. Ext/int corridors. **Pets:** Small. $50 one-time fee/room. Designated rooms, no service, supervision.

ⒶⒶⒶ ▼▼▼▼ Omni San Antonio Hotel 🅷 🐾
(210) 691-8888. **$109-$299.** 9821 Colonnade Blvd 78230. I-10 exit Wurzbach Rd, 12 mi nw on westbound access road. Int corridors. **Pets:** Small. $50 one-time fee/room. Service with restrictions, crate.

▼▼ ▼ Pear Tree Inn by Drury-San Antonio Northeast 🅷
(210) 654-1144. **$80-$144.** 8300 I-35 N 78239. I-35 exit 165 (Walzem Rd), northbound access road. Ext/int corridors. **Pets:** Accepted.

▼▼ ▼ Pear Tree Inn San Antonio Airport 🅷
(210) 366-9300. **$75-$139.** 143 NE Loop 410 78216. I-410 W exit 21 (Jones Maltsberger Rd), on westbound access road; between Airport Blvd and Jones Maltsberger Rd. Int corridors. **Pets:** Accepted.

▼▼ ▼ Clarion Inn & Suites 🅷
(210) 226-4361. **$60-$110.** 3855 I-35 N 78219. I-35 exit 162 (Binz-Engleman Rd) southbound; exit 161 northbound, on southbound access road. Ext corridors. **Pets:** Accepted.

ⒶⒶⒶ ▼▼▼ Quality Inn & Suites Ⓜ
(210) 359-7200. **Call for rates.** 222 S WW White Rd 78219. I-10 exit 580 (WW White Rd), 0.4 mi s. Ext corridors. **Pets:** Accepted.

Quality Inn & Suites North Airport 🅷
(210) 545-5400. **$70-$119.** 1505 Bexar Crossing 78232. US 281, Loop 1604 (Anderson Loop), 0.5 mi s on southbound access road. Int corridors. **Pets:** Small. $25 one-time fee/pet. Designated rooms, service with restrictions, supervision.

Quality Inn Downtown South 🅷
(210) 927-4800. **$53-$199.** 606 Division Ave 78214. I-35 exit 152 (Division Ave), on northbound access road. Ext corridors. **Pets:** Small. $75 deposit/room, $25 one-time fee/room. Service with restrictions, supervision.

Quality Inn Medical 🅷
(210) 684-8606. **$69-$99.** 4 Piano Pl 78228. I-410 exit Evers Rd westbound, U-turn; exit 14 (Callahan/Babcock Rd) eastbound. Ext corridors. **Pets:** Small, dogs only. $25 daily fee/pet. No service, supervision.

Quality Inn Six Flags Area 🅷
(210) 561-9058. **$89-$109.** 11010 I-10 W 78230. I-10 exit 560 westbound; exit 559 (Huebner Rd) eastbound. Int corridors. **Pets:** Accepted.

Red Roof Inn 🅷
(210) 333-9430. **$55-$120.** 4403 I-10 E 78219. I-10 exit 580 (WW White Rd), on westbound access road. Ext corridors. **Pets:** Large, other species. No service, supervision.

Red Roof Inn Lackland 🅷
(210) 675-4120. **$60-$140.** 6861 Hwy 90 W 78227. Ne of jct US 90 and Military Dr W; access via Renwick St, off Military Dr, just n of jct US 90. Ext corridors. **Pets:** Large, other species. No service, supervision.

Red Roof Inn-San Antonio Airport 🅷
(210) 340-4055. **$50-$100.** 333 Wolfe Rd 78216. Just s of US 281 at Isom Rd; on southbound access road. Ext/int corridors. **Pets:** Large, other species. No service, supervision.

Red Roof Inn San Antonio (Downtown) 🅷
(210) 229-9973. **$59-$169.** 1011 E Houston St 78205. I-37 exit 141 northbound; exit 141B southbound. Int corridors. **Pets:** Large, other species. No service, supervision.

Red Roof Inn San Antonio (NW-SeaWorld) 🅷
(210) 509-3434. **$49-$89.** 6880 NW Loop 410 78238. I-410 exit 11 (Alamo Downs Pkwy), on eastbound access road. Ext/int corridors. **Pets:** Large, other species. No service, supervision.

Residence Inn Alamo Plaza 🅷
(210) 212-5555. **$149-$209.** 425 Bonham St 78205. I-37/281 exit Commerce St, just w to Bowie St, then 4 blks n. Int corridors. **Pets:** Medium, other species. $100 one-time fee/room. Service with restrictions.

Residence Inn by Marriott San Antonio Downtown/Market Square 🅷
(210) 231-6000. **$130-$190.** 628 S Santa Rosa Blvd 78204. I-10/35 exit Cesar E Chavez Blvd, 0.5 mi e. Int corridors. **Pets:** Other species. $100 one-time fee/room. Service with restrictions, crate.

Residence Inn North San Antonio 🅷
(210) 490-1333. **$97-$134.** 1115 N SR 1604 E 78232. Loop 1604, just w of US 281, on westbound access road. Int corridors. **Pets:** Other species. $75 one-time fee/room. Service with restrictions, crate.

Residence Inn San Antonio-Airport 🅷 🐾
(210) 805-8118. **$79-$249.** 1014 NE Loop 410 78209. Loop 410 exit Broadway St, 0.4 mi e on eastbound access road. Ext corridors. **Pets:** Large. $100 one-time fee/room. Service with restrictions, crate.

Residence Inn San Antonio Northwest at The RIM 🅷
(210) 561-0200. **$98-$161.** 5707 Rim Pass Dr 78257. I-10 exit 555 (La Cantera Pkwy), on westbound access road; in Rim Shopping Complex. Int corridors. **Pets:** Accepted.

Residence Inn SeaWorld/Lackland AFB 🅷 🐾
(210) 509-3100. **$110-$190.** 2838 Cinema Ridge 78238. I-410 exit 10 (Ingram Rd), on eastbound access road. Int corridors. **Pets:** $100 one-time fee/room. Service with restrictions.

Rodeway Inn-Six Flags Fiesta Ⓜ
(210) 698-3991. **$40-$99.** 19793 I-10 W 78257. I-10 exit 554 (Camp Bullis Rd), westbound exit 552 (Dominion) and U-turn onto eastbound access road. Ext corridors. **Pets:** Medium. $10 daily fee/pet. Service with restrictions, supervision.

The St. Anthony Hotel 🅷
(210) 227-4392. **$95-$459, 3 day notice.** 300 E Travis St 78205. Corner of Travis and Jefferson sts. Int corridors. **Pets:** Accepted.

Sheraton Gunter 🅷 🐾
(210) 227-3241. **$99-$329, 3 day notice.** 205 E Houston St 78205. Center. Int corridors. **Pets:** Medium, dogs only. Designated rooms, service with restrictions, supervision.

Staybridge Suites San Antonio-Airport 🅷
(210) 341-3220. **$119-$129.** 66 NE Loop 410 78216. I-410 exit 20B (McCullough St), on eastbound access road. Int corridors. **Pets:** Accepted.

Staybridge Suites San Antonio NW-Colonnade 🅷 🐾
(210) 558-9009. **$139-$249.** 4320 Spectrum One 78230. I-10 W exit 561 (Wurzbach Rd), just off westbound access road. Int corridors. **Pets:** Medium. $15 one-time fee/room, $10 daily fee/room. Service with restrictions, crate.

Staybridge Suites San Antonio-Stone Oak 🅷
(210) 497-0100. **$104-$129.** 808 N Loop 1604 E 78232. On Loop 1604, 0.4 mi w of US 281. Int corridors. **Pets:** Large. $150 one-time fee/room. Service with restrictions, supervision.

Staybridge Suites Sunset Station 🅷
(210) 444-2700. **Call for rates.** 123 Hoefgen 78205. In historic downtown Sunset Station. Int corridors. **Pets:** Accepted.

Sunbridge Suites 🅷
(210) 561-9660. **$79-$149.** 4041 Bluemel Rd 78240. I-10 exit 561 (Wurzbach Rd), 0.3 mi w on eastbound access road. Ext corridors. **Pets:** Accepted.

Super 8 on Roland 🅷
(210) 798-5500. **$36-$135.** 302 Roland Ave 78210. I-10 exit 577 (Roland Ave) eastbound. Ext corridors. **Pets:** Accepted.

Super 8-Six Flags Fiesta 🅷
(210) 696-6916. **$40-$90.** 5319 Casa Bella 78249. I-10 exit 557 westbound; exit 558 eastbound, on westbound access road. Int corridors. **Pets:** Accepted.

TownePlace Suites San Antonio Northwest 🅷
(210) 694-5100. **$79-$149.** 5014 Prue Rd 78240. I-10 exit Huebner Rd, 1 blk sw to Fredericksburg Rd, then just n. Int corridors. **Pets:** Other species. $100 one-time fee/room. Service with restrictions.

The Westin Riverwalk 🅷
(210) 224-6500. **$179-$539, 3 day notice.** 420 W Market St 78205. 2 blks w of Navarro St. Int corridors. **Pets:** Accepted.

SEGUIN

▼▼▼ Quality Inn Seguin M
(830) 372-0860. **Call for rates.** 2950 N 123 Bypass 78155. I-10 exit 610 (SR 123). Ext corridors. **Pets:** Accepted. 🐾 📧 💻 🏊

▼▼▼▼ La Quinta Inn & Suites Seguin H
(830) 372-0567. **$84-$154.** 1501 Hwy 46 N 78155. I-10 exit 607 (SR 46). Int corridors. **Pets:** Medium, other species. Service with restrictions, supervision. 🛜 ⓜ 📧 💻 🏊

▼▼ Super 8 of Seguin H
(830) 379-6888. **$59-$131.** 1525 N Hwy 46 78155. I-10 exit 607 (SR 46), on eastbound access road. Int corridors. **Pets:** Accepted. 🛜 📧 💻

UNIVERSAL CITY

▼▼▼▼ Hawthorn Suites-San Antonio Northeast H
(210) 655-9491. **$89-$149, 3 day notice.** 13101 E Loop 1604 N 78233. Loop 1604 at Pat Booker Rd; 0.8 mi e of I-35. Ext corridors.
Pets: Accepted. 🛜 📧 💻 🏊

END METROPOLITAN AREA

SAN MARCOS

▼▼ Days Inn H
(512) 353-5050. **$54-$99.** 1005 I-35 N 78666. I-35 exit 205 northbound; exit 204B southbound, jct SR 80; on southbound frontage road. Ext corridors. **Pets:** Small, dogs only. $10 daily fee/pet. Designated rooms, service with restrictions, supervision. 🛜 📧 💻 🏊

AAA ▼▼▼ Econo Lodge H
(512) 353-5300. **$39-$139.** 811 S Guadalupe St 78666. I-35 exit 204 northbound; exit 204A southbound, on west frontage road. Ext corridors. **Pets:** Medium, other species. $20 one-time fee/room. Service with restrictions, crate. 🅂🄰🅅🄴 🛜 📧 💻 🏊

▼▼▼▼ Embassy Suites-San Marcos Hotel, Spa and Conference Center H 🐾
(512) 392-6450. **$159-$239.** 1001 E McCarty Ln 78666. I-35 exit 201, on east frontage road. Int corridors. **Pets:** Medium, other species. $50 daily fee/pet. Designated rooms, service with restrictions, crate.
🛜 ⓜ 📧 💻 🍴 🏊 ✖

▼▼▼▼ La Quinta Inn San Marcos H
(512) 392-8800. **$68-$192.** 1619 I-35 N 78666. I-35 exit 206 southbound, 0.5 mi s, on west frontage road; exit northbound, 1 mi n to turnaround to west frontage road, then 1.5 mi s. Ext/int corridors. **Pets:** Medium, other species. Service with restrictions, supervision. 🛜 ⓜ 📧 💻 🏊

▼▼ Rodeway Inn H
(512) 353-8011. **Call for rates.** 1635 Aquarena Springs Dr 78666. I-35 exit 206, 0.5 mi s. Ext corridors. **Pets:** Small, dogs only. $10 daily fee/pet. Designated rooms, service with restrictions, supervision. 📧 🏊

SCHULENBURG

AAA ▼▼▼ Best Western Plus Schulenburg Inn & Suites H
(979) 743-2030. **$97-$149.** 101 Huser Blvd 78956. I-10 exit 674, just s. Int corridors. **Pets:** Medium. $20 daily fee/pet. Service with restrictions, supervision. 🅂🄰🅅🄴 🛜 ✖ ⓜ 📧 💻 🏊

SEALY

AAA ▼▼▼ Americas Best Value Inn of Sealy H
(979) 885-3707. **$70-$95, 3 day notice.** 2107 Hwy 36 S 77474. I-10 exit 720. Ext corridors. **Pets:** Accepted. 🅂🄰🅅🄴 🛜 📧 💻 🏊

▼▼ Super 8 H 🐾
(979) 885-2121. **$45-$90.** 267 Gebhardt Rd 77474. I-10 exit 720. Ext corridors. **Pets:** Small, other species. $5 daily fee/pet. Designated rooms, service with restrictions, supervision. 🛜 ⓜ 📧 💻 🏊

SEMINOLE

AAA ▼▼▼ Seminole Inn M
(432) 758-9881. **Call for rates.** 2200 Hobbs Hwy 79360. 1.5 mi w on US 62 and 180. Ext corridors. **Pets:** Accepted. 🅂🄰🅅🄴 🛜 📧

SHAMROCK

AAA ▼▼▼ Best Western Plus Shamrock Inn & Suites H
(806) 256-1001. **$90-$159.** 1802 N Main St 79079. I-40 exit 163, just n. Int corridors. **Pets:** Medium, other species. $10 one-time fee/pet. Designated rooms, service with restrictions, supervision.
🅂🄰🅅🄴 🛜 ✖ ⓜ 📧 💻 🏊

▼▼▼ Holiday Inn Express & Suites H
(806) 256-5022. **Call for rates.** 101 E 13th St 79079. I-40 exit 163, just s. Int corridors. **Pets:** Accepted. 🛜 ✖ ⓜ 📧 💻 🏊

AAA ▼ Western Motel M
(806) 256-3244. **$59-$109.** 104 E 12th St 79079. Business Rt I-40 and US 83. Ext corridors. **Pets:** Medium. $10 daily fee/pet. Designated rooms, service with restrictions, supervision. 🅂🄰🅅🄴 🛜 📧 💻

SHERMAN

▼▼▼ Comfort Suites of Sherman H
(903) 893-0499. **$90-$126.** 2900 US Hwy 75 N 75090. US 75 exit 63, 0.3 mi s of jct US 82. Int corridors. **Pets:** Accepted.
🛜 ✖ 📧 💻 🏊

▼▼▼ La Quinta Inn & Suites Sherman Denison H
(903) 870-1122. **$80-$149.** 2912 US 75 N 75090. US 75 exit 63, on southbound frontage road. Int corridors. **Pets:** Medium, other species. Service with restrictions, supervision. 🛜 📧 💻 🏊

SINTON

AAA ▼▼▼ Best Western Sinton M
(361) 364-2882. **$90-$99.** 8108 US Hwy 77 78387. US 77 at CR 36A. Ext corridors. **Pets:** Accepted. 🅂🄰🅅🄴 🛜 📧 💻 🏊

SMITHVILLE

▼▼▼ Americas Best Value Inn & Suites H
(512) 237-2040. **Call for rates.** 1503 Dorothy Nichol Ln 78957. Jct SR 71 and Dorothy Nichol Ln. Ext corridors. **Pets:** Accepted.
🛜 📧 💻 🏊

SNYDER

AAA ▼▼▼ Purple Sage Motel M
(325) 573-5491. **$55-$75.** 1501 E Coliseum Dr 79549. 1 mi w on US 180 from jct US 84. Ext corridors. **Pets:** Other species. Service with restrictions, crate. 🅂🄰🅅🄴 🛜 📧 💻 🏊

SONORA

AAA ▼▼▼ Best Western Sonora Inn H
(325) 387-9111. **$89-$109.** 270 Hwy 277 N 76950. I-10 exit 400, just s. Ext corridors. **Pets:** Accepted. 🅂🄰🅅🄴 🛜 📧 💻 🏊

Holiday Host Motel **M**
(325) 387-2532. **$45-$55.** 127 Loop 467 (Hwy 290) 76950. Loop 467 exit 404 westbound, 3 mi w; exit 399 eastbound, 3 mi e. Ext corridors.
Pets: Service with restrictions, supervision. (SAVE)

SOUTH PADRE ISLAND
Howard Johnson Inn **H**
(956) 761-5658. **$62-$270.** 1709 Padre Blvd 78597. 0.9 mi n of Queen Isabella Cswy; corner of W Palm St. Int corridors. **Pets:** Other species. $25 one-time fee/room. Service with restrictions.

La Copa Inn Beach Hotel **H**
(956) 761-6000. **$50-$400, 3 day notice.** 350 Padre Blvd 78597. Just s of Queen Isabella Cswy. Int corridors. **Pets:** Medium. $25 daily fee/pet. Service with restrictions, supervision.

La Quinta Inn & Suites South Padre Beach **H**
(956) 772-7000. **$130-$310.** 7000 Padre Blvd 78597. 3 mi n of Queen Isabella Cswy. Int corridors. **Pets:** Medium, other species. Service with restrictions, supervision.

Motel 6 South Padre Island #1237 **M**
(956) 761-7911. **$51-$95.** 4013 Padre Blvd 78597. 2 mi n of Queen Isabella Cswy. Ext corridors. **Pets:** Other species. Service with restrictions, supervision.

Super 8 **H**
(956) 761-6300. **$32-$210.** 4205 Padre Blvd 78597. 2.7 mi n of Queen Isabella Cswy. Ext corridors. **Pets:** Small, dogs only. $25 daily fee/pet. Designated rooms, no service, supervision.

Travelodge **H**
(956) 761-4744. **$63-$207.** 6200 Padre Blvd 78597. 3 mi n of Queen Isabella Cswy. Ext corridors. **Pets:** Medium, other species. $10 daily fee/room. Service with restrictions, crate.

STEPHENVILLE
Americas Best Value Inn - Cross Timbers **H**
(254) 968-2114. **Call for rates.** 1625 W South Loop (US 377) 76401. 1.8 mi sw on US 377 Bypass and 67. Ext corridors. **Pets:** Other species. $20 daily fee/room. Service with restrictions, supervision.

La Quinta Inn & Suites Stephenville **H**
(254) 918-2444. **$107-$169.** 105 Christy Plaza 76401. US 67/377 S, 5 mi s of jct US 281. Int corridors. **Pets:** Medium, other species. Service with restrictions, supervision.

Stephenville Hampton Inn & Suites **H**
(254) 918-5400. **$99-$159.** 910 S Harbin Dr 76401. US 67/377 S, 3 mi s of jct US 281. Int corridors. **Pets:** Accepted.

SULPHUR SPRINGS
Best Western Trail Dust Inn & Suites **H**
(903) 885-7515. **$70-$80.** 1521 Shannon Rd 75482. Jct I-30 and Loop 301 exit 127. Ext/int corridors. **Pets:** Medium. $10 daily fee/pet. Designated rooms, service with restrictions. (SAVE)

Comfort Suites **H**
(903) 438-0918. **$80-$109.** 1521 E Industrial Dr 75482. I-30 exit 127, just n. Int corridors. **Pets:** Accepted.

SWEETWATER
Best Western Plus Sweetwater Inn & Suites **H**
(325) 236-6512. **$99-$129.** 300 NW Georgia Ave 79556. I-20 exit 244, jct US 70. Int corridors. **Pets:** Accepted. (SAVE)

Ranch House Motel & Restaurant **H**
(325) 236-6341. **Call for rates.** 301 SW Georgia Ave 79556. I-20 exit 244, just w of jct SR 70 on south access road. Ext/int corridors.
Pets: Accepted.

TEMPLE
La Quinta Inn & Suites Temple **H**
(254) 771-2980. **$67-$129.** 1604 W Barton Ave 76504. SR 53, just e; jct I-35 and US 81 exit 301. Ext/int corridors. **Pets:** Medium, other species. Service with restrictions, supervision.

Residence Inn by Marriott **H**
(254) 773-8400. **$79-$149.** 4301 S General Bruce Dr 76502. I-35 exit 298, on E Frontage Rd. Int corridors. **Pets:** Accepted.

TERLINGUA
Big Bend Resort & Adventures **M**
(432) 371-2218. **$108-$179, 3 day notice.** Hwy 118/170 79852. SR 118, 2 mi from entrance of Big Bend National Park. Ext corridors.
Pets: Accepted.

TEXARKANA
Candlewood Suites **H**
(903) 334-7418. **$89-$99.** 2901 S Cowhorn Creek Loop 75503. I-30 exit 222 (Summerhill Rd), just w on frontage road to Cowhorn Creek Rd, then just s. Int corridors. **Pets:** Medium. $25 daily fee/pet. Service with restrictions, supervision.

Fairfield Inn & Suites **H**
(903) 306-0473. **$94-$113.** 4209 Mall Dr 75501. I-30 exit 220B (Richmond Rd) westbound, on eastbound service road; exit 218 eastbound. Int corridors. **Pets:** $75 one-time fee/room. Service with restrictions, supervision.

TownePlace Suites by Marriott **H**
(903) 334-8800. **$89-$146.** 5020 N Cowhorn Creek Loop 75503. I-30 exit 222 (Summerhill Rd), w on frontage road, then just n. Int corridors.
Pets: Accepted. (SAVE)

THREE RIVERS
Best Western Inn-Three Rivers **M**
(361) 786-2000. **$99-$159, 3 day notice.** 900 N Harborth Ave 78071. I-37 exit 72 (US 281), 1.8 mi s; jct US 281 and SR 72. Ext corridors.
Pets: Accepted. (SAVE)

TULIA
Executive Inn **M**
(806) 995-3248. **$55-$65.** 1591 I-27 79088. I-27 exit 74, on W Frontage Rd. Ext corridors. **Pets:** Accepted.

TYLER
Candlewood Suites **H**
(903) 509-4131. **$79-$119.** 315 E Rieck Rd 75703. 1.1 mi s of jct Loop 323 and US 69 to Rieck Rd, just e. Int corridors. **Pets:** Large, other species. $150 one-time fee/room. Service with restrictions, crate.

Holiday Inn South Broadway **H**
(903) 561-5800. **$99-$119.** 5701 S Broadway Ave 75703. 1.1 mi s of jct Loop 323 and US 69. Int corridors. **Pets:** $50 one-time fee/room. Service with restrictions, supervision.

La Quinta Inn Tyler **H**
(903) 561-2223. **$64-$125.** 1601 W SW Loop 323 75701. 1 mi w of S US 69. Ext corridors. **Pets:** Medium, other species. Service with restrictions, supervision.

▼▼▼▼ Residence Inn by Marriott H
(903) 595-5188. **$85-$94.** 3303 Troup Hwy 75701. 0.3 mi n of jct E Loop 323 and SR 110. Ext corridors. **Pets:** Large, other species. $100 one-time fee/room. Designated rooms, service with restrictions, supervision.
📶 ✕ 🛏 💻 ≈ ⊠

UVALDE

▼▼ Quality Inn of Uvalde H
(830) 278-4511. **$100-$126.** 920 E Main St 78801. 0.5 mi e on US 90. Ext corridors. **Pets:** Accepted. 📶 🛏 💻 🍴 ≈

VAN HORN

▼ Budget Inn M
(432) 283-2019. **$34-$39.** 1303 W Broadway St 79855. I-10 exit 138, 0.7 mi e. Ext corridors. **Pets:** Accepted. 📶 🛏

▲▲▲ ▼▼ Days Inn M
(432) 283-1007. **$50-$70.** 600 E Broadway St 79855. I-10 exit 140B, just w. Ext corridors. **Pets:** Medium. $10 one-time fee/pet, $10 daily fee/pet. Designated rooms, service with restrictions, supervision.
SAVE 📶 🛏 💻 ≈

▲▲▲ ▼▼ Econo Lodge H
(432) 283-2211. **$62-$95.** 1601 W Broadway St 79855. I-10 exit 138, 0.5 mi e on Business Rt I-10. Ext corridors. **Pets:** Medium. $10 daily fee/pet. Designated rooms, service with restrictions, supervision.
SAVE 📶 🛏 💻 ≈

▲▲▲ ▼ Economy Inn M
(432) 283-2754. **$35-$40.** 1500 W Broadway St 79855. I-10 exit 138, 0.5 mi e on US 80. Ext corridors. **Pets:** Small. $5 one-time fee/pet. Service with restrictions, supervision. SAVE 📶 🛏

▲▲▲ ▼▼▼ Hampton Inn H 🐾
(432) 283-0088. **$99-$149.** 1921 SW Frontage Rd 79855. I-10 exit 138, just w on S Frontage Rd. Int corridors. **Pets:** Medium, other species. Designated rooms, service with restrictions, supervision.
SAVE 📶 ✕ 🛏 💻 ≈

▲▲▲ ▼ Motel 6 #4024 M
(432) 283-2992. **$46-$56, 5 day notice.** 1805 W Broadway St 79855. I-10 exit 138. Ext corridors. **Pets:** Other species. Service with restrictions, supervision. SAVE 📶 🛏 ≈

▲▲▲ ▼▼ Van Horn Super 8 M
(432) 283-2282. **$50-$70.** 1807 E Service Rd 79855. I-10 exit 138. Ext corridors. **Pets:** Accepted. SAVE 📶 🛏 💻

VEGA

▲▲▲ ▼▼▼ Best Western Country Inn M 🐾
(806) 267-2131. **$72-$90.** 1800 W Vega Blvd 79092. 0.5 mi w on US 40 business loop. Ext corridors. **Pets:** Large. $10 daily fee/pet. Designated rooms, service with restrictions, supervision. SAVE 📶 🛏 💻 ≈

▼▼▼ Days Inn Vega H
(806) 267-0126. **$72.** 1005 S Main St 79092. I-40 exit 36. Int corridors. **Pets:** Accepted. 📶 🛏 💻

VERNON

▲▲▲ ▼▼▼ Best Western Village Inn H
(940) 552-5417. **$70-$85.** 1615 US Hwy 287 E 76384. US 287 exit Main St, just w. Ext/int corridors. **Pets:** Accepted.
SAVE 📶 🛏 💻 🍴 ≈

▼▼ GreenTree Inn M
(940) 552-5421. **$45-$95.** 3029 Morton St 76384. US 287 exit Bentley St, just w. Ext corridors. **Pets:** Small. $10 daily fee/pet. No service, supervision. 📶 🛏 💻 ≈

▼▼▼ Holiday Inn Express Hotel & Suites H
(940) 552-0200. **$99-$109.** 700 Hillcrest Dr 76384. Jct US 287 and 70. Int corridors. **Pets:** Accepted. 📶 ✕ 🛏 🛏 💻 ≈

VICTORIA

▲▲▲ ▼▼▼ Best Western Plus Victoria Inn & Suites H
(361) 485-2300. **$135-$145.** 8106 NE Zac Lenz Pkwy 77904. Jct Zac Lenz Pkwy and Invitational Dr. Int corridors. **Pets:** Small. $20 daily fee/pet. Service with restrictions, supervision. SAVE 📶 ✕ 🛏 💻 ≈

▼▼ La Quinta Inn Victoria H
(361) 572-3585. **$98-$169.** 7603 N Navarro St (US 77 N) 77904. 4 mi n; at Loop 463. Ext corridors. **Pets:** Medium, other species. Service with restrictions, supervision. 📶 🛏 💻 ≈

▲▲▲ ▼▼ Lone Star Inn & Suites H
(361) 579-0225. **$85-$150.** 1907 US 59 N 77905. US 59 exit Bloomington (US 185); on northeast corner. Ext corridors. **Pets:** $25 one-time fee/pet, $5 daily fee/pet. Supervision. SAVE 📶 🛏 💻 ≈

▼ Motel 6 Victoria #225 M
(361) 573-1273. **$49-$61.** 3716 Houston Hwy 77901. On Business Rt US 59. Ext corridors. **Pets:** Other species. Service with restrictions, supervision. 📶 🛏 ≈

▼▼ Quality Inn-Victoria H
(361) 578-2030. **Call for rates.** 3112 E Houston Hwy (Business Rt 59) 77901. On Business Rt US 59, 2 mi ne. Ext corridors. **Pets:** Accepted. 📶 🛏 💻 ≈

VIDOR

▼▼ La Quinta Inn Vidor H
(409) 783-2600. **$66-$124.** 165 E Courtland St 77662. I-10 exit 860, just s. Int corridors. **Pets:** Medium, other species. Service with restrictions, supervision. 📶 ✕ 🛏 💻 ≈

WACO

▲▲▲ ▼▼▼ Best Western Old Main Lodge H
(254) 753-0316. **$70-$85.** I-35 & 4th St 76706. I-35 and US 81 exit 335A southbound (4th St and 5th St). Ext corridors. **Pets:** Medium. Service with restrictions, supervision. SAVE 📶 🛏 💻 ≈

▲▲▲ ▼▼▼▼ Clarion Hotel H
(254) 757-2000. **$70-$180.** 801 S 4th St 76706. I-35 exit 335A. Ext/int corridors. **Pets:** Accepted. SAVE 📶 🛏 💻 🍴 ≈

▲▲▲ ▼▼▼ Days Inn H
(254) 799-8585. **$53-$113.** 1504 I-35 N 76705. I-35 exit 338B (Behrens Cir), just n. Ext corridors. **Pets:** Accepted. SAVE 📶 🛏 💻 ≈

▼▼▼▼ Hilton-Waco H
(254) 754-8484. **$99-$199.** 113 S University Parks Dr 76701. I-35 exit 335B, 0.5 mi w. Int corridors. **Pets:** Accepted. 📶 🛏 💻 🍴 ≈

▼▼ La Quinta Inn Waco University H
(254) 752-9741. **$67-$139.** 1110 S 9th St 76706. I-35 exit 334 (17th St) southbound; exit 334A (18th St) northbound on E Frontage Rd. Ext corridors. **Pets:** Medium, other species. Service with restrictions, supervision. 📶 🛏 💻 ≈

▼▼ Econo Lodge Inn & Suites H
(254) 752-1991. **Call for rates.** 1430 I-35 S 76706. I-35 exit 334 (17th St), on northbound access road. Ext corridors. **Pets:** Small. $10 daily fee/pet. Designated rooms, service with restrictions, supervision.
📶 🛏 💻 ≈

▼▼▼ Residence Inn by Marriott H
(254) 714-1386. **$133-$219.** 501 S University Parks Dr 76706. I-35 exit 335B, 0.3 mi w. Int corridors. **Pets:** Accepted.
📶 ✕ 🛏 💻 ≈ ⊠

▼ Super 8-Waco H
(254) 754-1023. **$45-$115.** 1320 S Jack Kultgen Frwy 76706. I-35 exit 334, just e. Int corridors. **Pets:** Accepted. 📶 🛏 💻

WASHINGTON

▼▼▼▼ The Inn at Dos Brisas ▣
(979) 277-7750. **$500-$1400, 30 day notice.** 10000 Champion Dr 77880. US 290 exit Chapel Hill to FM 1155, 6.5 mi n. Ext corridors.
Pets: Accepted. 🛜 ⊠ 🛏 🖥 🍴 ≈

WAXAHACHIE

⨺ ▼▼▼▼ Comfort Suites ▣
(469) 517-1600. **$69-$89.** 131 RVG Plaza 75165. US 287 exit Hwy 77, on northbound frontage road. Int corridors. **Pets:** Medium. $10 daily fee/room. Designated rooms, service with restrictions, crate.
SAVE 🛜 ⊠ 🛏 🖥 ≈

▼▼ Super 8 ▣
(972) 938-9088. **$45-$59.** 400 N I-35 E 75165. I-35E exit 401B. Int corridors. **Pets:** Accepted. 🛜 🛏 🖥 ≈

WEATHERFORD

▼▼▼ Hampton Inn ▣
(817) 599-4800. **$90-$170.** 2524 S Main St 76087. I-20 exit 408. Int corridors. **Pets:** Small. $10 daily fee/pet. No service, supervision.
🛜 🛏 🖥

▼▼▼ La Quinta Inn & Suites Weatherford ▣
(817) 594-4481. **$103-$165.** 1915 Wall St 76086. I-20 exit 408, just ne. Int corridors. **Pets:** Medium, other species. Service with restrictions, supervision. 🛜 🛏 🖥 ≈

▼▼▼ Quality Inn & Suites ▣
(817) 599-3700. **Call for rates.** 2500 S Main St 76087. I-20 exit 408, just s. Ext/int corridors. **Pets:** Small. $10 daily fee/pet. No service, supervision. 🛜 ⅏M 🛏 🖥 ≈

▼▼▼ Weatherford Comfort Suites ▣
(817) 599-3300. **Call for rates.** 210 Alford Dr 76086. I-20 exit 408, just s on SR 171, then just w. Int corridors. **Pets:** Accepted.
🛜 ⊠ ⅏M 🛏 🖥 ≈

⨺ ▼▼▼ Best Western Santa Fe Inn ▣
(817) 594-7401. **$59-$79, 7 day notice.** 1927 Santa Fe Dr 76086. I-20 exit 409 (Clear Lake Rd/FM 2552), 0.3 mi nw. Ext corridors.
Pets: Accepted. SAVE 🛜 🛏 🖥 ≈

WESLACO

⨺ ▼▼▼ Best Western Palm Aire Motor Inn & Suites ▣
(956) 969-2411. **$65-$79.** 415 S International Blvd 78596. US 83 exit International Blvd, just s. Ext corridors. **Pets:** Accepted.
SAVE 🛜 🛏 🖥 🍴 ≈ ⊠

▼▼ Super 8 ▣
(956) 969-9920. **$41-$70.** 1702 E Expwy 83 78596. US 83 exit Airport Dr. Ext corridors. **Pets:** Accepted. 🛜 🛏 🖥 ≈

WICHITA FALLS

⨺ ▼▼▼▼ Best Western Plus University Inn & Suites ▣
(940) 687-2025. **$90-$100.** 4540 Maplewood Ave 76308. Jct Southwest Pkwy (CR 369). Int corridors. **Pets:** Medium, other species. $15 daily fee/pet. Service with restrictions, supervision.
SAVE 🛜 ⊠ ⅏M 🛏 🖥 ≈

▼▼▼ Holiday Inn ▣ 🐾
(940) 761-6000. **Call for rates.** 100 Central Frwy 76306. I-287 exit 1C, on west side access road. Int corridors. **Pets:** Medium. $25 one-time fee/pet. Service with restrictions, supervision.
🛜 ⅏M 🛏 🖥 🍴 ≈

▼▼▼ La Quinta Inn Wichita Falls Airport Area ▣
(940) 322-6971. **$58-$115.** 1128 Central Frwy N 76306. I-44 exit 2 (Maurine St), just w. Ext corridors. **Pets:** Medium, other species. Service with restrictions, supervision. 🛜 🛏 🖥 ≈

▼▼▼ Lexington Suites of Wichita Falls ▣
(940) 692-7900. **Call for rates.** 1917 Elmwood Ave N 76308. US 281 S exit Southwest Pkwy (CR 369), 2.3 mi w to Kemp Blvd, 2 blks n to Elmwood Ave, then just e. Int corridors. **Pets:** Accepted.
🛜 ⊠ ⅏M 🛏 🖥 ≈ ⊠

⨺ ▼▼▼ Red Roof Inn ▣
(940) 766-6881. **$60-$80.** 1032 Central Frwy 76306. I-44 exit 2, just w. Ext corridors. **Pets:** Large, other species. No service, supervision.
SAVE 🛜 🛏 🖥 ≈

WOODWAY

▼▼ Extended StayAmerica Waco-Woodway ▣ 🐾
(254) 399-8836. **$59-$109.** 5903 Woodway Dr 76712. I-35 exit 330 (SR 6), 5 mi sw; Loop 340 exit 330 to jct SR 84. Int corridors. **Pets:** Other species. $25 daily fee/pet. Service with restrictions. 🛜 ⅏M 🛏 🖥

▼▼▼ La Quinta Inn & Suites ▣
(254) 772-0200. **$116-$189.** 6003 Woodway Dr 76712. I-35 exit 330, 2.5 mi w on SR 6 to jct US 84, then just s on N Frontage Rd. Int corridors. **Pets:** Medium, other species. Service with restrictions, supervision.
🛜 ⊠ ⅏M 🛏 🖥 ≈

⨺ ▼▼▼ Super 8 Waco Mall ▣
(254) 776-3194. **$50-$94.** 6624 Woodway Dr (Hwy 84 W) 76712. Jct US 84 and SR 6, just w. Ext corridors. **Pets:** Medium. $10 one-time fee/room. Service with restrictions, supervision. SAVE 🛜 🛏 🖥 ≈

ZAPATA

⨺ ▼▼▼ Best Western Inn by the Lake ▣
(956) 765-8403. **$80-$95.** 1896 S US Hwy 83 78076. On US 83, 0.5 mi se. Ext corridors. **Pets:** Accepted. SAVE 🛜 🛏 🖥 ≈ ⊠

UTAH

AMERICAN FORK

▼▼▼▼ Holiday Inn Express & Suites American Fork - North Provo 🅷

(801) 763-8500. $89-$159. 712 S Utah Valley Dr 84003. I-15 exit 276, 0.3 mi n on S 500 E, just e on E 620 S, then just s. Int corridors. Pets: Medium. $15 daily fee/pet. Designated rooms, service with restrictions, supervision. 🛰 ✕ 🛏 💻 🏊

BEAVER

◆◆◆ ▼▼▼ Best Western Butch Cassidy Inn Ⓜ ❀

(435) 438-2438. $80-$86. 161 S Main St 84713. I-15 exit 112, 1.8 mi e. Ext corridors. Pets: Large. $10 one-time fee/pet. Designated rooms, supervision. [SAVE] 🛰 🛏 💻 🏊

◆◆◆ ▼▼▼ Best Western Paradise Inn 🅷 ❀

(435) 438-2455. $80. 314 W 1425 N 84713. I-15 exit 112, just e. Ext corridors. Pets: Large, other species. $9 one-time fee/pet. Designated rooms, service with restrictions, supervision. [SAVE] 🛰 🛏 💻 🏊

▼▼ Quality Inn 🅷

(435) 438-5426. Call for rates. 781 W 1800 S 84713. I-15 exit 109, just w. Int corridors. Pets: Large. $10 daily fee/pet. Designated rooms, service with restrictions. 🛰 🛏 💻 🏊

BLANDING

▼▼ Gateway Inn Ⓜ

(435) 678-2278. $55-$85. 88 E Center St 84511. On US 191. Ext corridors. Pets: Accepted. 🛰 🛏 💻 🏊

▼▼ Super 8 Ⓜ

(435) 678-3880. $60-$129. 755 S Main St 84511. On US 191. Int corridors. Pets: Accepted. 🛰 ✕ 🛏 💻

BLUFF

◆◆◆ ▼ Kokopelli Inn Ⓜ

(435) 672-2322. $65-$75. 160 E Main St 84512. On US 191 (Main St). Int corridors. Pets: Medium. $11 daily fee/pet. Designated rooms, service with restrictions, supervision. [SAVE] 🛰 ✕

◆◆◆ ▼▼▼ Recapture Lodge Ⓜ

(435) 672-2281. $75. 220 E Main St 84512. On US 191 (Main St). Ext corridors. Pets: Other species. Service with restrictions, supervision. [SAVE] 🛰 🛏 💻 🏊 ✕ 🗲

BOULDER

▼▼◆▼▼ Boulder Mountain Lodge 🅷 ❀

(435) 335-7460. $79-$200, 30 day notice. 20 N Hwy 12 84716. Just s on SR 12. Ext/int corridors. Pets: Large, other species. $15 daily fee/pet. Designated rooms, service with restrictions, supervision. 🛰 ✕ 🛏 💻 🍽 ✕

BRIAN HEAD

◆◆◆ ▼▼▼▼ The Grand Lodge at Brian Head 🅷

(435) 677-9000. Call for rates. 314 Hunter Ridge Rd 84719. On SR 143. Int corridors. Pets: Accepted.

[SAVE] 🛰 ✕ 🛡 🛏 💻 🍽 🏊 ✕

BRIGHAM CITY

▼▼ Crystal Inn 🅷

(435) 723-0440. $75-$119. 480 Westland Dr 84302. I-15 exit 362, 1 mi e. Int corridors. Pets: Other species. $25 one-time fee/pet. Designated rooms, service with restrictions, supervision. 🛰 🛏 💻 🏊

BRYCE CANYON CITY

◆◆◆ ▼▼▼ Best Western Plus Ruby's Inn 🅷

(435) 834-5341. $65-$150. 26 S Main St 84764. On SR 63, 1 mi s of SR 12. Ext/int corridors. Pets: Accepted.

[SAVE] 🛰 ✕ 🛏 💻 🍽 🏊 ✕

◆◆◆ ▼▼▼ Bryce View Lodge Ⓜ

(435) 834-5180. $60-$110. 991 S SR 63 84764. 1 mi s of SR 12. Ext corridors. Pets: Accepted. [SAVE] 🛰 ✕ 🛏 💻 ✕

CAINEVILLE

◆◆◆ ▼ Rodeway Inn Capitol Reef Ⓜ

(435) 456-9900. $68-$110. 25 E SR 24 84775. West end of town. Ext corridors. Pets: $15 one-time fee/pet. Designated rooms, service with restrictions, supervision. [SAVE] 🛰 ✕ 🛏 💻 🏊

CEDAR CITY

▼▼ Americas Best Value Inn Ⓜ

(435) 867-4700. $43-$95. 333 N 1100 W 84720. I-15 exit 59, just e. Int corridors. Pets: Medium, other species. $10 daily fee/room. Service with restrictions, supervision. 🛰 ✕ 🛏 💻 🏊

◆◆◆ ▼▼▼ Best Western El Rey Inn & Suites 🅷

(435) 586-6518. $60-$100. 80 S Main St 84720. I-15 exit 57, 2 mi n; center. Ext corridors. Pets: Accepted.

[SAVE] 🛰 ✕ 🛏 💻 🍽 🏊 ✕

▼▼ Crystal Inn Cedar City 🅷

(435) 586-8888. $69-$119. 1575 W 200 N 84720. I-15 exit 59, just w. Ext/int corridors. Pets: Other species. $15 one-time fee/room. Designated rooms, service with restrictions, crate. 🛰 🛏 💻 🍽 🏊 ✕

◆◆◆ ▼▼▼ Days Inn Ⓜ

(435) 867-8877. $45-$111. 1204 S Main St 84720. I-15 exit 57, 0.4 mi ne. Ext corridors. Pets: Small, other species. $10 daily fee/pet. Designated rooms, service with restrictions, supervision.

[SAVE] 🛰 🛏 💻 🏊

▼▼◆▼▼ Holiday Inn Express Hotel & Suites 🅷

(435) 865-7799. $89-$139. 1555 S Old Hwy 91 84720. I-15 exit 57, just e, then s. Int corridors. Pets: Large, other species. $15 daily fee/room. Designated rooms, service with restrictions, supervision.

🛰 ✕ 🛏 💻 🏊

▼▼ Motel 6 of Cedar City - 4041 [M]
(435) 586-9200. **Call for rates.** 1620 W 200 N 84720. I-15 exit 59, just w. Int corridors. **Pets:** Other species. Service with restrictions, supervision.

▼▼ Quality Inn [M]
(435) 586-2082. **$59-$129, 7 day notice.** 250 N 1100 W 84720. I-15 exit 59, just e. Ext corridors. **Pets:** Medium, other species. $10 daily fee/room. Designated rooms, service with restrictions, supervision.

▼▼ Super 8 [M]
(435) 586-8880. **$43-$85.** 145 N 1550 W 84720. I-15 exit 59, just w. Int corridors. **Pets:** Accepted.

COALVILLE

AAA ▼▼ Best Western Holiday Hills [H]
(435) 336-4444. **$80-$90.** 200 S 500 W 84017. I-80 exit 162, just w. Int corridors. **Pets:** Large, other species. $20 daily fee/room. Designated rooms, service with restrictions, supervision.

DELTA

▼▼ Days Inn [M]
(435) 864-3882. **$63-$90.** 527 E Topaz Blvd 84624. Jct US 6 and 50. Ext corridors. **Pets:** Accepted.

EDEN

▼▼ Red Moose Lodge [H]
(801) 745-6667. **Call for rates.** 2547 N Valley Junction Dr 84310. I-15 exit 344 (12th St), 10 mi e to Pineview Reservoir bridge, 4.3 mi n, then just nw of jct SR 158 and SR 162. Int corridors. **Pets:** Accepted.

ESCALANTE

▼▼ Rainbow Country Bed & Breakfast [BB]
(435) 826-4567. **$79-$109, 3 day notice.** 585 E 300 S 84726. Just s of SR 12; east end of town. Int corridors. **Pets:** $10 daily fee/pet. Service with restrictions, supervision.

FILLMORE

AAA ▼▼ Best Western Paradise Inn & Resort [M]
(435) 743-6895. **$80-$90.** 905 N Main St 84631. I-15 exit 167, just e. Ext corridors. **Pets:** Medium. Service with restrictions, crate.

▼▼ Comfort Inn & Suites [H]
(435) 743-4334. **$90-$140.** 940 S Hwy 99 84631. I-15 exit 163, just e. Int corridors. **Pets:** Accepted.

GLENDALE

▼▼ Historic Smith Hotel Bed & Breakfast [BB]
(435) 648-2156. **$48-$98, 4 day notice.** 295 N Main St 84729. US 89; north end of town. Int corridors. **Pets:** Large, other species. $10 one-time fee/room. Designated rooms, no service.

GREEN RIVER

▼▼ Holiday Inn Express [H]
(435) 564-4439. **$69-$199.** 1845 E Main St 84525. I-70 exit 160 eastbound, 3 mi e; exit 164 westbound, 1.7 nw. Int corridors. **Pets:** Dogs only. $10 one-time fee/pet. Designated rooms, service with restrictions, supervision.

AAA ▼▼ Super 8 [M]
(435) 564-8888. **$58-$90.** 1248 E Main St 84525. I-70 exit 164, 1.3 mi n. Int corridors. **Pets:** Large. $5 daily fee/pet. Designated rooms, service with restrictions, supervision.

HEBER CITY

AAA ▼▼ Swiss Alps Inn [M]
(435) 654-0722. **$60-$110.** 167 S Main St 84032. I-80 exit 146 (US 40), 15 mi s. Ext corridors. **Pets:** $10 daily fee/room. Service with restrictions, supervision.

HUNTSVILLE

▼ Jackson Fork Inn [M]
(801) 745-0051. **$85-$160, 3 day notice.** 7345 E 900 S 84317. I-15 exit 344 (12th St), 12 mi e. Int corridors. **Pets:** $20 one-time fee/room. Designated rooms, supervision.

HURRICANE

▼▼ Super 8 [M]
(435) 635-0808. **$40-$99.** 65 S 700 W 84737. Just s of SR 9. Ext corridors. **Pets:** Accepted.

KANAB

AAA ▼▼ Best Western Red Hills [H]
(435) 644-2675. **$60-$130.** 125 W Center St 84741. Center. Ext/int corridors. **Pets:** Other species. $10 one-time fee/room. Designated rooms, service with restrictions, supervision.

AAA ▼ Bob-Bon Inn [M]
(435) 644-3069. **Call for rates.** 236 Hwy 89 N 84741. On US 89. Ext corridors. **Pets:** Accepted.

▼ Comfort Inn Kanab [H]
(435) 644-8888. **Call for rates.** 815 E 300 S 84741. On US 89, just e. Int corridors. **Pets:** Accepted.

AAA ▼▼▼ Holiday Inn Express Hotel & Suites [H]
(435) 644-3100. **$89-$154.** 217 S 100 E 84741. On US 89; jct 200 S. Int corridors. **Pets:** Medium. $20 daily fee/room. Designated rooms, service with restrictions, supervision.

▼ Parry Lodge [M]
(435) 644-2601. **$49-$115.** 89 E Center St 84741. On US 89; corner of 100 E; center. Ext/int corridors. **Pets:** Accepted.

AAA ▼▼ Quail Park Lodge [M]
(435) 215-1447. **$69-$149.** 125 N 300 W (Hwy 89) 84741. On US 89. Ext corridors. **Pets:** Medium, dogs only. Designated rooms, service with restrictions, supervision.

AAA ▼▼ Shilo Inn Suites-Kanab [H]
(435) 644-2562. **$69-$199.** 296 W 100 N 84741. On US 89; north of downtown. Int corridors. **Pets:** Dogs only. $25 one-time fee/room. Designated rooms, service with restrictions, crate.

▼▼▼ Victorian Inn [H]
(435) 644-8660. **$89-$199.** 190 N 300 W 84741. North end of town. Int corridors. **Pets:** Other species. $20 daily fee/room. Designated rooms, supervision.

LAYTON

AAA ▼▼▼ Comfort Inn [H]
(801) 544-5577. **$69-$149.** 877 N 400 W 84041. I-15 exit 331, just e. Int corridors. **Pets:** Accepted.

▼▼▼ Hampton Inn [H]
(801) 775-8800. **$89-$139.** 1700 Woodland Park Dr 84041. I-15 exit 332 (Antelope Dr), 0.3 mi e, then just s. Int corridors. **Pets:** Dogs only. Service with restrictions, supervision.

WWW Home2 Suites by Hilton Layton **H** ❀
(801) 820-9222. **$99-$119.** 803 W Heritage Park Blvd 84041. I-15 exit 331, 0.6 mi n to Heritage Blvd, then 0.4 mi w. Int corridors. **Pets:** Large, other species. $75 one-time fee/room. Service with restrictions.
📶 🍴 🖥 🏊

WW La Quinta Inn & Suites Salt Lake City Layton **H**
(801) 776-6700. **$72-$148.** 1965 N 1200 W 84041. I-15 exit 332 (Antelope Dr), just e. Int corridors. **Pets:** Medium, other species. Service with restrictions, supervision. 📶 🍴 🖥 🏊

WW TownePlace Suites by Marriott **H**
(801) 779-2422. **$116-$142.** 1743 Woodland Park Dr 84041. I-15 exit 332 (Antelope Dr), 0.3 mi se. Int corridors. **Pets:** Accepted.
📶 ✖ 🍴 🖥 🏊

LEHI

AAA WWWW Best Western Plus Timpanogos Inn **H**
(801) 768-1400. **Call for rates.** 195 S 850 E 84043. I-15 exit 279, just w, then just s. Int corridors. **Pets:** Accepted. SAVE 📶 🍴 🖥 🏊

WW Super 8 **M**
(801) 766-8800. **$54-$130.** 125 S 850 E 84043. I-15 exit 279, just w, then just s. Int corridors. **Pets:** Accepted. 📶 🍴 🖥 🏊

LOGAN

AAA WW Best Western Baugh Motel **M**
(435) 752-5220. **$80-$160, 3 day notice.** 153 S Main St 84321. Just s of center. Ext corridors. **Pets:** Accepted. SAVE 📶 🍴 🖥 🏊

AAA WWW Best Western Weston Inn **H** ❀
(435) 752-5700. **$90-$130.** 250 N Main St 84321. 0.3 mi n of center. Ext corridors. **Pets:** Medium. $15 daily fee/room. Service with restrictions, supervision. ECO SAVE 📶 🍴 🖥 🏊 ✖

WWW Holiday Inn Express & Suites **H**
(435) 752-3444. **$95-$299.** 2235 N Main St 84341. 2.8 mi n of center. Int corridors. **Pets:** Other species. $25 one-time fee/pet. Designated rooms, service with restrictions, supervision. 📶 🍴 🖥 🏊

WW Super 8 **M**
(435) 753-8883. **$46-$86.** 865 S Hwy 89/91 84321. 2 mi s of center. Int corridors. **Pets:** Other species. $10 daily fee/pet. Service with restrictions, supervision. 📶 🍴 🖥 🏊

MANTI

WW Manti Country Village Motel **M**
(435) 835-9300. **$69-$99.** 145 N Main St 84642. On US 89; just n of center. Ext corridors. **Pets:** Medium, dogs only. $75 deposit/room. Designated rooms, service with restrictions, supervision. 📶 🍴 🍽

MEXICAN HAT

WW San Juan Inn & Trading Post **M**
(435) 683-2220. **Call for rates.** Hwy 163 & San Juan River 84531. Center. Ext corridors. **Pets:** Accepted. 📶 🍴 🍽

MIDWAY

AAA WWWW Homestead Resort **H**
(435) 654-1102. **$89-$769, 7 day notice.** 700 N Homestead Dr 84049. I-80 exit 146 (US 40), 13 mi s to River Rd traffic light, 2.9 mi w to roundabout, 1.2 mi w, follow signs to Homestead Dr, then 0.4 mi s. Ext/int corridors. **Pets:** Accepted. SAVE 📶 ✖ 🍴 🖥 🍽 🏊 ✖

MOAB

AAA WWW Big Horn Lodge **M** ❀
(435) 259-6171. **$50-$130.** 550 S Main St 84532. 0.5 mi s. Ext corridors. **Pets:** Other species. $5 daily fee/pet. Designated rooms, service with restrictions, supervision. SAVE 📶 🍴 🖥 🍴 🏊

AAA WW Bowen Motel **M**
(435) 259-7132. **$50-$134.** 169 N Main St 84532. Just n. Ext corridors. **Pets:** Small. $10 daily fee/room. Service with restrictions, supervision.
SAVE 📶 🍴 🏊

AAA WWWW The Gonzo Inn **H**
(435) 259-2515. **$101-$329.** 100 W 200 S 84532. Just w of 200 S and S Main St. Ext/int corridors. **Pets:** Accepted. SAVE 📶 🍴 🖥 🏊

AAA WWWW La Quinta Inn Moab **H**
(435) 259-8700. **$89-$209.** 815 S Main St 84532. 0.8 mi s. Int corridors. **Pets:** Medium, other species. Service with restrictions, supervision.
SAVE 📶 ✖ 🍴 🖥 🏊

AAA WWW Moab Valley Inn **H**
(435) 259-4419. **$69-$199.** 711 S Main St 84532. 0.7 mi s. Int corridors. **Pets:** Accepted. 📶 🍴 🖥 🏊 ✖

WWW Motel 6 Moab #4119 **M**
(435) 259-6686. **$59-$199.** 1089 N Main St 84532. 1.5 mi n. Int corridors. **Pets:** Other species. Service with restrictions, supervision. 📶 🏊

AAA WWWW Red Cliffs Lodge - Moab's Adventure
Headquarters **RA**
(435) 259-2002. **$99-$320, 30 day notice.** Milepost 14 Hwy 128 84532. 2.3 mi n to jct US 191 and SR 128, then 14 mi e to MM 14. Ext corridors. **Pets:** Medium. $20 daily fee/pet. Designated rooms, service with restrictions, supervision. SAVE 📶 ✖ 🍴 🖥 🍴 🏊 ✖

AAA WWW Red Stone Inn **M** ❀
(435) 259-3500. **$45-$125.** 535 S Main St 84532. 0.5 mi s. Int corridors. **Pets:** $5 daily fee/room. Designated rooms, service with restrictions, supervision. SAVE 📶 🍴

AAA WWW River Canyon Lodge, An Extended Stay Inn &
Suites **M**
(435) 259-8838. **$59-$290.** 71 W 200 N 84532. Just w of 200 N and Main St. Int corridors. **Pets:** Small. $20 one-time fee/room. Designated rooms, no service, supervision. SAVE 📶 ✖ 🍴 🖥 🏊

AAA WW Silver Sage Inn **M**
(435) 259-4420. **$45-$100.** 840 S Main St 84532. 0.9 mi s. Int corridors. **Pets:** Medium. $10 daily fee/room. Designated rooms, service with restrictions, supervision. SAVE 📶 🍴

WWW Sleep Inn **H** ❀
(435) 259-4655. **Call for rates.** 1051 S Main St 84532. 1.3 mi s. Int corridors. **Pets:** $50 deposit/room. Designated rooms, service with restrictions, supervision. 📶 🍴 🖥 🏊

AAA WWWW WWW Sorrel River Ranch Hotel & Spa
Resort **H** ❀
(435) 259-4642. **$329-$699, 45 day notice.** Hwy 128 at MM 17 84532. 17 mi e of jct US 191 and SR 128; at MM 17. Ext corridors. **Pets:** Medium, dogs only. $50 daily fee/pet. Designated rooms, service with restrictions, supervision. SAVE 📶 ✖ 🍴 🖥 🍴 🏊 ✖

MONTICELLO

AAA WW Inn at the Canyons **M**
(435) 587-2458. **$40-$150.** 533 N Main St 84535. On US 191; north end of town. Int corridors. **Pets:** Other species. $50 deposit/room. Designated rooms, service with restrictions, supervision.
SAVE 📶 ✖ 🔉 🍴 🏊

WWW Rodeway Inn & Suites **H**
(435) 587-2489. **$76-$120.** 649 N Main St 84535. On US 191; north end of town. Int corridors. **Pets:** Medium. $10 daily fee/pet. Service with restrictions, supervision. 📶 🍴 🖥 🏊

WWW Wayside Inn **M**
(435) 587-2261. **Call for rates.** 197 E Central St 84535. On US 491, just e of US 191. Ext corridors. **Pets:** Accepted.
📶 ✖ 🍴 🖥 🏊

MONUMENT VALLEY

Goulding's Trading Post & Lodge H
(435) 727-3231. **$85-$218, 3 day notice.** 1000 Main St 84536. 2 mi w of US 163; 0.5 mi n of Arizona border. Ext corridors. **Pets:** $20 daily fee/pet. Service with restrictions, supervision.

NEPHI

Best Western Paradise Inn of Nephi M
(435) 623-0624. **$81-$130.** 1025 S Main St 84648. I-15 exit 222, 0.5 mi n. Ext corridors. **Pets:** Accepted.

OGDEN

Best Western Plus High Country Inn H
(801) 394-9474. **$82-$139.** 1335 W 12th St 84404. I-15 exit 344 (12th St), just e. Ext/int corridors. **Pets:** Other species. Designated rooms, service with restrictions, crate.

Comfort Inn Farr West H
(801) 737-5660. **Call for rates.** 1776 W 2550 N 84404. I-15 exit 349 (Farr West), 0.3 mi e to 1850 W, then just s. Int corridors. **Pets:** Accepted.

Comfort Suites H
(801) 621-2545. **$88-$135.** 2250 S 1200 W 84401. I-15 exit 343 (21st St), just se. Int corridors. **Pets:** Other species. $25 one-time fee/room. Designated rooms, service with restrictions, supervision.

Holiday Inn Express & Suites H
(801) 392-5000. **$95-$118, 3 day notice.** 2245 S 1200 W 84401. I-15 exit 343 (21st St), 0.3 mi e. Int corridors. **Pets:** Accepted.

Ogden Marriott H
(801) 627-1190. **$170-$208.** 247 24th St 84401. I-15 exit 342 (24th St), 1.5 mi e. Int corridors. **Pets:** Other species. $50 one-time fee/room. Designated rooms, service with restrictions, supervision.

Sleep Inn M
(801) 731-6500. **$70-$100.** 1155 S 1700 W 84404. I-15 exit 344 (12th St), just w. Int corridors. **Pets:** Accepted.

OREM

Holiday Inn Express & Suites Orem - North Provo H
(801) 655-1515. **$99-$179.** 1290 W University Pkwy 84058. I-15 exit 269 (University Pkwy), 0.5 mi w. Int corridors. **Pets:** Accepted.

La Quinta Inn & Suites Orem University Parkway H
(801) 226-0440. **$78-$163.** 521 W University Pkwy 84058. I-15 exit 269, 0.4 mi e. Int corridors. **Pets:** Medium, other species. Service with restrictions, supervision.

La Quinta Inn Orem H
(801) 235-9555. **$64-$139.** 1100 W 780 N 84057. I-15 exit 272 (800 N), 0.3 mi e. Int corridors. **Pets:** Medium, other species. Service with restrictions, supervision.

TownePlace Suites by Marriott Orem H
(801) 225-4477. **$89-$139.** 873 N 1200 W 84057. I-15 exit 272 (800 N), just e. Int corridors. **Pets:** Medium, other species. $100 one-time fee/room. Service with restrictions.

PANGUITCH

Color Country Motel M
(435) 676-2386. **$39-$84.** 526 N Main St 84759. 0.3 mi n of center. Ext corridors. **Pets:** Accepted.

Harold's Place Cabins CA
(435) 676-2350. **$85-$95.** 3066 Hwy 12 84759. Jct US 89 and SR 12, 0.5 mi e. Ext corridors. **Pets:** Medium, other species. Designated rooms, service with restrictions, supervision.

Harold's Place Inn M
(435) 676-2350. **$75-$95.** 3090 Hwy 12 84759. Jct US 89 and SR 12, 0.5 mi e. Int corridors. **Pets:** Medium, other species. Designated rooms, service with restrictions, supervision.

Horizon Motel M
(435) 676-2651. **Call for rates.** 730 N Main St 84759. 0.4 mi n of center. Ext corridors. **Pets:** Accepted.

PARK CITY

Best Western Plus Landmark Inn & Pancake House H
(435) 649-7300. **$59-$299.** 6560 N Landmark Dr 84098. I-80 exit 145 (Kimball Jct), 0.3 mi s, then 0.3 mi nw. Int corridors. **Pets:** Other species. $10 daily fee/room. Designated rooms, service with restrictions, supervision.

Holiday Inn Express Hotel & Suites H
(435) 658-1600. **$89-$199.** 1501 W Ute Blvd 84098. I-80 exit 145 (Kimball Jct), just s, then 0.3 mi e. Int corridors. **Pets:** Accepted.

St. Regis Deer Valley Resort H
(435) 940-5700. **$199-$3449.** 2300 Deer Valley Dr E 84060. I-80 exit 145 (Kimball Jct), 6 mi se to Deer Valley Dr/SR 224, 1 mi e to roundabout, exit Deer Valley Dr, then 1.2 mi se; I-40 exit 4, 2.7 mi sw on SR 248/Kearns Blvd to Bonanza Dr, 0.5 mi to Deer Valley Dr/SR 224, then 1 mi se to roundabout. Int corridors. **Pets:** Medium, dogs only. $150 one-time fee/room. Service with restrictions, supervision.

PAROWAN

Days Inn Parowan M
(435) 477-3326. **Call for rates.** 625 W 200 S 84761. I-15 exit 75, 1.5 mi e. Ext corridors. **Pets:** Accepted.

PRICE

Legacy Inn M
(435) 637-2424. **$59-$125.** 145 N Carbonville Rd 84501. US 6 exit 240 (Business Loop), 0.6 mi se, then just e on N Carbonville Rd (at traffic light). Ext corridors. **Pets:** Medium, dogs only. $15 daily fee/pet. Designated rooms, service with restrictions, supervision.

PROVO

Best Western Plus CottonTree Inn H
(801) 373-7044. **$89-$112, 30 day notice.** 2230 N University Pkwy 84604. I-15 exit 269 (University Pkwy), 3.2 mi e, then just n; in CottonTree Square. Int corridors. **Pets:** Medium. $25 one-time fee/room. Service with restrictions, supervision.

Days Inn M
(801) 375-8600. **$41-$113.** 1675 N 200 W 84604. I-15 exit 269 (University Pkwy), 3.7 mi e, then just s at Freedom Blvd; in Village Green Square. Ext corridors. **Pets:** Medium. $25 one-time fee/room. Service with restrictions, supervision.

Econo Lodge M
(801) 373-0099. **$59-$89.** 1625 W Center St 84601. I-15 exit 265 (Center St), just w. Ext corridors. **Pets:** Large, other species. $10 one-time fee/pet. Designated rooms, service with restrictions, supervision.

▼▼▼▼ **La Quinta Inn Provo Town Center** H
(801) 374-9750. **$80-$140.** 1460 S University Ave 84601. I-15 exit 263 (University Ave), 0.5 mi e. Int corridors. **Pets:** Medium, other species. Service with restrictions, supervision. 🛜 🍴 💻 🍴 🏊

▼▼▼ **Residence Inn by Marriott Provo** H
(801) 374-1000. **$152-$186.** 252 W 2230 N 84604. I-15 exit 269 (University Pkwy), 3.2 mi e, then just n. Int corridors. **Pets:** Accepted.
🛜 ❌ 📶 🍴 💻 🏊 🍴

▼▼ **Sleep Inn** H
(801) 377-6597. **Call for rates.** 1505 S 40 E 84606. I-15 exit 263 (University Ave), just e. Int corridors. **Pets:** Accepted.
🛜 ❌ 🍴 💻 🏊

RICHFIELD

Ⓐ▼▼▼ **Best Western Richfield Inn** M
(435) 893-0100. **$80-$90.** 1275 N Main St 84701. I-70 exit 40, just s. Int corridors. **Pets:** Medium, other species. $15 daily fee/pet. Service with restrictions, supervision. SAVE 🛜 🍴 💻 🏊

▼▼▼ **Holiday Inn Express & Suites** H
(435) 896-8552. **$89-$189.** 20 W 1400 N 84701. I-70 exit 40, just s. Int corridors. **Pets:** Accepted. 🛜 🍴 💻 🏊

▼▼ **Super 8** M
(435) 896-9204. **$50-$64, 7 day notice.** 1377 N Main St 84701. I-70 exit 40, just s. Ext/int corridors. **Pets:** Accepted. 🛜 🍴 💻

ST. GEORGE

▼▼ **America's Best Inn & Suites** M
(435) 652-3030. **$54-$145, 3 day notice.** 245 N Red Cliffs Dr 84790. I-15 exit 8, just e. Ext corridors. **Pets:** Accepted. 🛜 🍴 💻 🏊

Ⓐ▼▼▼ **Americas Best Value Inn** M
(435) 688-8383. **Call for rates.** 915 S Bluff St 84770. I-15 exit 6 (Bluff St), just w. Int corridors. **Pets:** Other species. $10 daily fee/pet. Service with restrictions. SAVE 🛜 ❌ 🍴 💻 🏊

▼▼ **Budget Inn & Suites** H
(435) 673-6661. **$89-$120.** 1221 S Main St 84770. I-15 exit 6 (Bluff St), just w. Ext corridors. **Pets:** Other species. $15 daily fee/pet. Designated rooms, service with restrictions. 🛜 🍴 💻 🏊 ❌

▼▼▼◆ **Comfort Inn** H
(435) 628-8544. **Call for rates.** 138 E Riverside Dr 84790. I-15 exit 6 (Bluff St), just e. Int corridors. **Pets:** Accepted. 🛜 ❌ 🍴 💻 🏊

▼▼ **Crystal Inn St. George** H
(435) 688-7477. **$79-$139.** 1450 S Hilton Dr 84770. I-15 exit 6 (Bluff St), just w. Int corridors. **Pets:** Small. $25 one-time fee/pet. Designated rooms, service with restrictions, supervision. 🛜 ❌ 🍴 💻 🏊 ❌

Ⓐ ▼ **Dixie Palm Motel** M
(435) 673-3531. **$29-$89.** 185 E St. George Blvd 84770. I-15 exit 8, 0.9 mi w; downtown. Ext corridors. **Pets:** Dogs only. $10 daily fee/pet. Service with restrictions, supervision. SAVE 🛜 ❌ 🍴

Ⓐ ▼▼▼ ▼▼▼ **The Green Valley Spa & Resort** H ❖
(435) 628-8060. **$149-$650, 3 day notice.** 1871 W Canyon View Dr 84770. Jct Bluff and S Main sts, 4 mi sw via Hilton Dr to Dixie Dr, then just w to Canyon View Dr. Ext corridors. **Pets:** Medium. $500 deposit/room, $5 daily fee/room. Service with restrictions, supervision.
SAVE 🛜 ❌ 📶 🍴 💻 🍴 🏊 ❌

Ⓐ ▼▼ **Howard Johnson Inn** M
(435) 628-8000. **$44-$113.** 1040 S Main St 84770. I-15 exit 6 (Bluff St), just w, then just e. Ext corridors. **Pets:** $15 daily fee/pet. Designated rooms, service with restrictions, supervision.
SAVE 🛜 ❌ 🍴 💻 🏊

▼▼▼▼ **La Quinta Inn & Suites - St. George** H
(435) 674-2664. **$71-$179.** 91 E 2680 S 84790. I-15 exit 4, just e on Brigham Rd. Int corridors. **Pets:** Medium, other species. Service with restrictions, supervision. 🛜 ❌ 📶 🍴 💻 🏊

▼▼▼◆ **Lexington Hotel** H
(435) 628-4235. **$79-$199.** 850 S Bluff St 84770. I-15 exit 6 (Bluff St), just w. Ext/int corridors. **Pets:** Dogs only. $25 one-time fee/room. Designated rooms, service with restrictions, supervision.
🛜 🍴 💻 🍴 🏊 ❌

▼▼ **Quality Inn St. George** M
(435) 628-4481. **Call for rates.** 1165 S Bluff St 84770. I-15 exit 6 (Bluff St), just w. Ext corridors. **Pets:** Accepted. 🛜 🍴 💻 🏊

▼▼ **Ramada** M
(435) 628-2828. **$69-$139.** 1440 E St. George Blvd 84790. I-15 exit 8, just e. Int corridors. **Pets:** Small. $15 daily fee/pet. Designated rooms, service with restrictions, supervision. 🛜 🍴 💻 🏊

▼▼ **Red Cliffs Inn & Suites** H
(435) 673-3537. **Call for rates.** 912 W Red Cliffs Dr 84780. I-15 exit 10, just e. Ext/int corridors. **Pets:** Accepted. 🛜 🍴 💻 🍴 🏊

▼▼▼◆ **Seven Wives Inn** BB
(435) 628-3737. **$99-$195, 7 day notice.** 217 N 100 W 84770. I-15 exit 8, 2.1 mi w, then n. Ext/int corridors. **Pets:** Large. $20 one-time fee/pet. Designated rooms, service with restrictions, crate. 🛜 ❌ 🍴 🏊

Ⓐ ▼▼▼◆ **TownePlace Suites by Marriott** H
(435) 986-9955. **$109-$159.** 251 S 1470 E 84790. I-15 exit 8, just e. Int corridors. **Pets:** Other species. $100 one-time fee/room. Service with restrictions, supervision. SAVE 🛜 ❌ 📶 🍴 💻 🏊

SALINA

Ⓐ ▼▼▼ **Scenic Hills Super 8** M
(435) 529-7483. **$54-$90.** 375 E 1620 S 84654. I-70 exit 56, just n. Ext corridors. **Pets:** Accepted. SAVE 🛜 🍴 💻 🏊

SALT LAKE CITY METROPOLITAN AREA

COTTONWOOD HEIGHTS

▼▼ **Candlewood Suites Fort Union** H
(801) 567-0111. **Call for rates.** 6990 S Park Centre Dr 84121. I-15 exit 297 (7200 S), 2.6 mi e to Park Centre Dr, then just s. Int corridors. **Pets:** Accepted. 🛜 🍴 💻

MIDVALE

▼▼ **La Quinta Inn Salt Lake City Midvale** H
(801) 566-3291. **$68-$126.** 7231 S Catalpa St 84047. I-15 exit 297 (7200 S), just e, then just s. Int corridors. **Pets:** Medium, other species. Service with restrictions, supervision. 🛜 🍴 💻 🏊

Ⓐ ▼▼▼ **Magnuson Hotel Salt Lake - Midvale** H
(801) 566-4141. **$59-$90.** 280 W 7200 S 84047. I-15 exit 297 (7200 S), just e. Int corridors. **Pets:** Medium. $15 daily fee/room. Designated rooms, service with restrictions, supervision. SAVE 🛜 ❌ 🍴 💻 🏊

Ⓐ ▼▼▼ **Super 8 Midvale** M
(801) 255-5559. **$49-$62.** 7048 S 900 E 84047. I-15 exit 297 (7200 S), 2.4 mi e via 7200 S (Fort Union Blvd) to 900 E, then just n. Int corridors. **Pets:** Large, dogs only. $10 one-time fee/room. Service with restrictions, supervision. SAVE 🛜 🍴 💻

MURRAY

▼▼▼▼ Holiday Inn Express Murray 🅷
(801) 268-2533. **Call for rates.** 4465 S Century Dr 84123. I-15 exit 301 (4500 S), just w to 4500 S, then just n. Int corridors. **Pets:** Accepted.
🛜 ⊠ 🖥 🖵

▼▼ Pavilion Inn 🅷
(801) 506-8000. **Call for rates.** 5335 S College Dr 84123. I-15 exit 300 (5300 S), 0.3 mi w. Int corridors. **Pets:** Accepted. 🛜 🖥 🌊

NORTH SALT LAKE

AAA ▼▼▼ Best Western Plus CottonTree Inn 🅷
(801) 292-7666. **$105-$155.** 1030 N 400 E 84054. I-15 exit 315 (Woods Cross) northbound, just e to Onion St, then just s; southbound, 0.3 mi e to 500 E, just s, then just w. Int corridors. **Pets:** Medium, other species. Designated rooms, service with restrictions, supervision.
SAVE 🛜 🖥 🖵 🌊

SALT LAKE CITY

▼▼ Candlewood Suites Airport 🅷
(801) 359-7500. **$109-$159.** 2170 W N Temple 84116. 3 mi w of Temple Square. Int corridors. **Pets:** Accepted. 🛜 🖥 🖵

AAA ▼▼▼ Comfort Inn Airport 🅷
(801) 746-5200. **$79-$179.** 200 N Admiral Byrd Rd 84116. I-80 exit 113 (5600 W), 0.6 mi n, just e, then just s. Int corridors. **Pets:** Accepted.
SAVE 🛜 🖥 🖵 🍽 🌊 ⊠

▼▼ Comfort Inn Downtown 🅷
(801) 325-5300. **$80-$310.** 171 W 500 S 84101. Cross streets 100 W and 500 S. Ext/int corridors. **Pets:** Accepted. 🛜 🖥 🖵

▼▼ Crystal Inn Downtown 🅷 🐾
(801) 328-4466. **$89-$199.** 230 W 500 S 84101. Cross streets 500 S and 200 W. Int corridors. **Pets:** Other species. $25 one-time fee/pet. Designated rooms, service with restrictions, supervision.
🛜 🖥 🖵 🌊 ⊠

AAA ▼▼▼ Hilton Salt Lake City Airport 🅷 🐾
(801) 539-1515. **$79-$232.** 5151 Wiley Post Way 84116. I-80 exit 114 westbound, just n off ramp, then 0.4 mi w; exit 113 (5600 W), 0.5 mi n, 0.3 mi e on Amelia Earhart Dr, just s on Jimmy Doolittle Rd, then 0.3 mi e. Int corridors. **Pets:** $50 one-time fee/room. Designated rooms, service with restrictions, crate.
SAVE 🛜 🖥 🖵 🍽 🌊 ⊠

AAA ▼▼▼ Hilton Salt Lake City Center 🅷
(801) 328-2000. **$99-$249.** 255 S West Temple 84101. Just s of cross streets 200 S and S West Temple. Int corridors. **Pets:** Accepted.
SAVE 🛜 🖥 🖵 🍽 🌊 ⊠

▼▼▼ Holiday Inn & Suites Airport West 🅷
(801) 741-1800. **$75-$219.** 5001 W Wiley Post Way 84116. I-80 exit 114 (Wright Brothers Dr), just n off ramp, then 0.4 mi w; exit 113 (5600 W) eastbound, 0.5 mi n on 5600 W, 0.3 mi e on Amelia Earhart Dr, just s on Jimmy Doolittle Rd, then 0.5 mi e. Int corridors. **Pets:** Accepted.
🛜 🖥 🖵 🍽 🌊

▼▼▼ Holiday Inn Express Airport East 🅷 🐾
(801) 741-1500. **$129-$209, 3 day notice.** 200 N 2100 W 84116. I-80 exit 118 (Redwood Rd) westbound; exit 115 (N Temple) eastbound, 3.1 mi w of Temple Square. Int corridors. **Pets:** $20 daily fee/pet. Service with restrictions, crate. 🛜 🖥 🖵 🌊

AAA ▼▼▼▼ Hotel Monaco 🅷
(801) 595-0000. **Call for rates.** 15 W 200 S 84101. Cross streets 200 S and Main St. Int corridors. **Pets:** Accepted.
ECO SAVE 🛜 ⊠ 🖵 🍽

AAA ▼▼▼ Howard Johnson Express Inn Downtown Ⓜ
(801) 521-3450. **$58-$107.** 121 N 300 W 84103. 0.4 mi w of Temple Square; corner of W North Temple and 300 W. Ext/int corridors. **Pets:** $15 daily fee/room. Designated rooms, service with restrictions, supervision. SAVE 🛜 ⊠ 🖥 🖵 🌊

▼▼▼ Metropolitan Inn Downtown Ⓜ
(801) 531-7100. **Call for rates.** 524 S West Temple 84101. Cross streets 500 S and S West Temple. Ext corridors. **Pets:** Accepted.
🛜 ⊠ 🖥 🖵

AAA ▼▼▼ Peery Hotel 🅷 🐾
(801) 521-4300. **Call for rates.** 110 W Broadway (300 S) 84101. Cross streets W Temple and 300 S. Int corridors. **Pets:** Other species. $25 daily fee/room. Service with restrictions. SAVE 🛜 ⊠ 🖥 🍽

▼▼▼ Quality Inn & Suites Airport 🅷
(801) 539-5005. **Call for rates.** 315 N Admiral Byrd Rd 84116. I-80 exit 113 (5600 W), 0.6 mi n, then just e. Int corridors. **Pets:** Accepted.
🖥 🖵 🌊

AAA ▼▼▼ Radisson Hotel Salt Lake City Downtown 🅷
(801) 531-7500. **$79-$299.** 215 W South Temple 84101. Cross streets 200 S and W South Temple. Int corridors. **Pets:** Accepted.
ECO SAVE 🛜 ⊠ 🖥 🖵 🍽 🌊 ⊠

AAA ▼▼▼ Red Lion Hotel Salt Lake Downtown 🅷
(801) 521-7373. **$80-$170.** 161 W 600 S 84101. Cross streets S West Temple and 600 S. Int corridors. **Pets:** Accepted.
SAVE 🛜 🖥 🖵 🍽 🌊

▼▼▼ Residence Inn by Marriott Airport 🅷
(801) 532-4101. **$79-$149.** 4883 W Douglas Corrigan Way 84116. I-80 exit 114 (Wright Brothers Dr), just n off ramp. Int corridors. **Pets:** Other species. $25 daily fee/room. Service with restrictions.
🛜 ⊠ 🕭 🖥 🖵 🌊 ⊠

▼▼▼ Residence Inn by Marriott City Center 🅷
(801) 355-3300. **$99-$329.** 285 W Broadway (300 S) 84101. Corner of 300 W and 300 S. Int corridors. **Pets:** Accepted.
🛜 ⊠ 🖥 🖵 🌊 ⊠

AAA ▼▼▼▼ Sheraton Salt Lake City Hotel 🅷 🐾
(801) 401-2000. **$219-$359, 4 day notice.** 150 W 500 S 84101. Cross streets 200 W and 500 S. Int corridors. **Pets:** $25 one-time fee/room. Supervision. SAVE 🛜 ⊠ 🖥 🖵 🍽 🌊 ⊠

SANDY

AAA ▼▼▼ Best Western Plus CottonTree Inn 🅷
(801) 523-8484. **$99-$124.** 10695 S Auto Mall Dr 84070. I-15 exit 293 (10600 S), 0.3 mi e, then just s. Int corridors. **Pets:** Accepted.
SAVE 🛜 ⊠ 🖥 🖵 🌊

▼▼▼ Holiday Inn Express & Suites Sandy 🅷 🐾
(801) 495-1317. **Call for rates.** 10680 S Auto Mall Dr 84070. I-15 exit 293 (10600 S), 0.3 mi e, then just s. Int corridors. **Pets:** Other species. $10 daily fee/room. Designated rooms, service with restrictions, supervision. 🛜 🖥 🖵 🌊

▼▼▼ Residence Inn by Marriott Sandy 🅷
(801) 561-5005. **$99-$279.** 270 W 10000 S 84070. I-15 exit 293 (10600 S), 0.4 mi e to State St, 0.7 mi n to 10000 S, then 0.3 mi w. Int corridors. **Pets:** Other species. $100 one-time fee/room. Service with restrictions, crate. 🛜 ⊠ 🖥 🖵 🌊 ⊠

WEST VALLEY CITY

▼▼▼ Baymont Inn & Suites West Valley 🅷
(801) 886-1300. **$44-$89.** 2229 W City Center Ct 84119. I-215 exit 18 (3500 S), just e, then just w. Int corridors. **Pets:** Accepted.
🛜 🖥 🖵 🌊

▼▼ Country Inn & Suites By Carlson West Valley 🅷
(801) 908-0311. **$89-$129.** 3422 S Decker Lake Dr 84119. I-215 exit 18 (3500 S), just e, then just n. Int corridors. **Pets:** Other species. $10 daily fee/room. Designated rooms, service with restrictions.
🛜 🖥 🖵 🌊

▼▼▼ Holiday Inn Express Waterpark West Valley 🅷 ✿

(801) 517-4000. **$90-$150.** 3036 S Decker Lake Dr 84119. I-215 exit 18A (3500 S), just e, 0.6 mi n, then just w. Int corridors. **Pets:** $15 daily fee/pet. Service with restrictions, supervision. 🛜 🅷 💻 🏊 ✖

▼▼ La Quinta Inn Salt Lake City West 🅷

(801) 954-9292. **$84-$144.** 3540 S 2200 W 84119. I-215 exit 18 (3500 S), just e, then just s. Int corridors. **Pets:** Medium, other species. Service with restrictions, supervision. 🛜 🅷 💻 🏊

▼▼ Sleep Inn West Valley 🅼

(801) 975-1888. **$69-$139.** 3440 S 2200 W 84119. I-215 exit 18 (3500 S), just e, then just n. Int corridors. **Pets:** Accepted. 🛜 🅷 💻

▼▼▼ Staybridge Suites West Valley 🅷

(801) 746-8400. **$99-$169.** 3038 S Decker Lake Dr 84119. I-215 exit 18A (3500 S), just e, 0.6 mi n, then just w. Int corridors. **Pets:** Accepted. 🛜 ⬛ 🅷 💻 🏊 ✖

WOODS CROSS

▼▼▼ Hampton Inn Salt Lake City North - Woods Cross 🅷

(801) 296-1211. **$79-$99.** 2393 S 800 W 84087. I-15 exit 315, just w, then just n. Int corridors. **Pets:** Accepted. 🛜 ✖ 🅷 💻 🏊

END METROPOLITAN AREA

SPANISH FORK

🆎 ▼▼▼ Western Inn 🅼

(801) 798-9400. **$50-$80.** 632 Kirby Ln 84660. I-15 exit 257 northbound (US 6/Price), exit 258 southbound (US 6/Price), 1 mi se. Int corridors. **Pets:** Other species. $50 deposit/room, $6 daily fee/pet. Designated rooms, service with restrictions, supervision. SAVE 🛜 🅷

SPRINGDALE

🆎 ▼▼▼ Best Western Zion Park Inn 🅷

(435) 772-3200. **$89-$150.** 1215 Zion Park Blvd 84767. 2 mi s of park entrance. Int corridors. **Pets:** Medium. $25 one-time fee/room. Designated rooms, service with restrictions, crate.

SAVE 🛜 🅷 💻 🍽 🏊 ✖

▼▼ Canyon Ranch Motel 🅼

(435) 772-3357. **Call for rates.** 668 Zion Park Blvd 84767. SR 9, just s of south gate to Zion National Park. Ext corridors. **Pets:** Accepted.

🛜 ✖ 🅷 💻 🏊

SPRINGVILLE

🆎 ▼▼▼ Best Western Mountain View Inn 🅷

(801) 489-3641. **$70-$160.** 1455 N 1750 W 84663. I-15 exit 261, just e. Int corridors. **Pets:** Medium, other species. $10 daily fee/pet. Designated rooms, service with restrictions, supervision.

SAVE 🛜 ✖ 🅷 💻 🏊

TOOELE

▼▼▼ Holiday Inn Express & Suites Tooele 🅷

(435) 833-0500. **$129-$205, 3 day notice.** 1531 N Main St 84074. I-80 exit 99, 11 mi s. Int corridors. **Pets:** Accepted. 🛜 🅷 💻 🏊

TORREY

🆎 ▼▼▼ Best Western Capitol Reef Resort 🅼

(435) 425-3761. **$100-$120.** 2600 E Hwy 24 84775. 2 mi e of jct SR 12 and 24. Ext corridors. **Pets:** Small. $10 daily fee/room. Designated rooms, service with restrictions, supervision.

SAVE 🛜 🅷 💻 🍽 🏊 ✖

▼▼ Howard Johnson 🅷

(435) 425-3866. **$62-$98.** 877 N SR 24 84775. 1.5 mi ne of jct SR 12 and 24. Ext corridors. **Pets:** Accepted. 🛜 ✖ 🅷 💻 🍽

🆎 ▼▼▼ Red Sands Hotel 🅷

(435) 425-3688. **Call for rates.** 670 E Hwy 24 84775. 0.3 mi w of jct SR 12 and 24. Int corridors. **Pets:** Accepted. SAVE 🛜 🅷 🏊

🆎 ▼ Rim Rock Inn 🅼

(435) 425-3398. **$59-$79.** 2523 E Hwy 24 84775. 2.5 mi ne of jct SR 12 and 24. Ext corridors. **Pets:** Other species. $10 daily fee/room. Service with restrictions, supervision. SAVE 🛜 🍽

TREMONTON

▼▼▼ Hampton Inn 🅷

(435) 257-6000. **$89-$109.** 2145 W Main St 84337. I-84 exit 40, 0.4 mi e. Int corridors. **Pets:** Small. $25 one-time fee/room. Designated rooms, service with restrictions, supervision. 🛜 ✖ 🅷 💻 🏊

WASHINGTON

▼▼▼ Holiday Inn Express & Suites 🅷

(435) 986-1313. **$89-$149.** 2450 N Town Center Dr 84780. I-15 exit 16, just e. Int corridors. **Pets:** Accepted. 🛜 🅷 💻 🏊

VERMONT

ALBURG

Ransom Bay Inn & Restaurant BB
(802) 796-3399. **$80-$130.** 4 Center Bay Rd 05440. Jct SR 78, 0.5 mi s on US 2, just e. Int corridors. **Pets:** Accepted.

ARLINGTON

Candlelight Motel M
(802) 375-6647. **$59-$115, 14 day notice.** 4893 SR 7A 05250. Historic SR 7A, 1 mi n. Ext corridors. **Pets:** Medium, dogs only. $10 daily fee/pet. Designated rooms, service with restrictions, supervision.

BENNINGTON

Bennington Motor Inn M
(802) 442-5479. **$65-$169, 3 day notice.** 143 W Main St 05201. Jct US 7, 0.4 mi w on SR 9. Ext corridors. **Pets:** Medium, dogs only. $10 daily fee/pet. Designated rooms, service with restrictions, supervision.

Harwood Hill Motel M
(802) 442-6278. **$67-$99, 3 day notice.** 864 Harwood Hill Rd (SR 7A) 05201. Jct SR 9, 1.2 mi n on US 7, then 1.7 mi n on Historic SR 7A. Ext corridors. **Pets:** Accepted.

Knotty Pine Motel M
(802) 442-5487. **$79-$98.** 130 Northside Dr (SR 7A) 05201. Jct SR 9, 1.2 mi n on US 7, then just n on Historic SR 7A. Ext corridors. **Pets:** Service with restrictions, supervision.

BRANDON

Brandon Motor Lodge M
(802) 247-9594. **$69-$139.** 2095 Franklin St 05733. 2 mi s on US 7. Ext corridors. **Pets:** $10 one-time fee/room. Designated rooms, service with restrictions, supervision.

The Lilac Inn CI
(802) 247-5463. **$145-$375, 30 day notice.** 53 Park St 05733. Just e on SR 73. Int corridors. **Pets:** Dogs only. $35 one-time fee/room. Service with restrictions, supervision.

BRATTLEBORO

Colonial Motel & Spa H
(802) 257-7733. **$79-$145.** 889 Putney Rd 05301. I-91 exit 3, just e on SR 9, then 0.5 mi s on US 5. Ext corridors. **Pets:** Dogs only. $15 daily fee/room. Service with restrictions, crate.

Econo Lodge M
(802) 254-2360. **Call for rates.** 515 Canal St 05301. I-91 exit 1, 0.3 mi n on US 5. Ext/int corridors. **Pets:** Medium. $15 daily fee/pet. Designated rooms, service with restrictions, crate.

Meadowlark Inn BB
(802) 257-4582. **$145-$245, 7 day notice.** 13 Gibson Rd 05301. I-91 exit 2, just w on SR 9, then 1.5 mi n on Orchard St. Int corridors. **Pets:** Accepted.

BURLINGTON

Hilton Burlington H
(802) 658-6500. **$119-$309.** 60 Battery St 05401. At Battery and College sts; just n of ferry terminal; center. Int corridors. **Pets:** Other species. $25 daily fee/pet. Designated rooms, service with restrictions, supervision.

CAVENDISH

The Pointe at Castle Hill Resort & Spa H
(802) 226-7688. **Call for rates.** 2940 SR 103 05142. On SR 103, just n of jct SR 131. Int corridors. **Pets:** Accepted.

COLCHESTER

Days Inn Colchester H
(802) 655-0900. **$54-$126.** 124 College Pkwy 05446. I-89 exit 15 northbound, just e on SR 15 exit 16 southbound, 1.1 mi s on US 7, then 1 mi e on SR 15. Int corridors. **Pets:** Dogs only. $10 daily fee/pet. Designated rooms, service with restrictions, crate.

Hampton Inn & Conference Center H
(802) 655-6177. **$109-$329.** 42 Lower Mountain View Dr 05446. I-89 exit 16, just n on US 7. Int corridors. **Pets:** Other species. Designated rooms, service with restrictions, supervision.

Motel 6 #1407 H
(802) 654-6860. **$55-$65.** 74 S Park Dr 05446. I-89 exit 16, just s on US 7. Int corridors. **Pets:** Other species. Service with restrictions, supervision.

Quality Inn Colchester Burlington Area H
(802) 655-1400. **$79-$199.** 84 S Park Dr 05446. I-89 exit 16, just s on US 7. Ext/int corridors. **Pets:** Small. $10 daily fee/pet. Designated rooms, service with restrictions.

Residence Inn, Burlington-Colchester H
(802) 655-3100. **$149-$197.** 71 Rathe Rd 05446. I-89 exit 16, 0.6 mi n on US 2 W/7 N, then just w. Int corridors. **Pets:** $100 one-time fee/room. Designated rooms, service with restrictions, crate.

ESSEX JUNCTION

The Essex Resort & Spa H
(802) 878-1100. **$169-$349, 7 day notice.** 70 Essex Way 05452. SR 289 exit 10, 0.3 mi s. Int corridors. **Pets:** Accepted.

Handy Suites-Essex H
(802) 872-5200. **$69-$249.** 27 Susie Wilson Rd 05452. I-89 exit 15 northbound, 2 mi e, then just n. Int corridors. **Pets:** Medium, dogs only. $50 deposit/room. Designated rooms, service with restrictions, supervision.

FAIRLEE

AAA ▽▽ Silver Maple Lodge & Cottages BB

(802) 333-4326. **$79-$119, 14 day notice.** 520 US 5 S 05045. I-91 exit 15, 0.5 mi s. Ext/int corridors. **Pets:** Other species. Designated rooms.

[SAVE] 🛜 ✕ 🔋 💻 ✉

FLETCHER

▽▽▽ The Inn at Buck Hollow Farm BB

(802) 849-2400. **$100-$130, 14 day notice.** 2150 Buck Hollow Rd 05454. From Fairfax, 6 mi n of jct SR 104 via Buck Hollow Rd. Int corridors. **Pets:** Accepted. 🛜 ✕ ✉ ✕ ✉

JAMAICA

▽▽ Three Mountain Inn CI

(802) 874-4140. **Call for rates.** 3732 Main St/Rt 100/30 05343. On SR 30; center. Ext/int corridors. **Pets:** Accepted. 🛜 ✕ 🍴 ✉ ✕

KILLINGTON

AAA ▽▽▽ The Cascades Lodge H

(802) 422-3731. **$105-$299, 21 day notice.** 58 Old Mill Rd 05751. 3.6 mi s on Killington Rd, from jct SR 100/US 4, just e. Int corridors. **Pets:** $50 daily fee/pet. Designated rooms, service with restrictions, crate.

[SAVE] 🛜 ✕ 🔋 💻 🍴 ✉ ✕

LONDONDERRY

▽ Snowdon Motel M

(802) 824-6047. **$65-$125, 7 day notice.** 4071 VT Rt 11 05148. Jct SR 100, 2 mi e. Ext corridors. **Pets:** Accepted. 🛜 ✕ 🔋 ✉

LUDLOW

AAA ▽▽ All Seasons Motel M

(802) 228-8100. **$79-$249, 14 day notice.** 112 Main St 05149. On SR 103; center. Ext/int corridors. **Pets:** Accepted.

[SAVE] 🛜 ✕ 🔋 💻 ✉

▽▽ The Andrie Rose Inn BB

(802) 228-4846. **$110-$364, 20 day notice.** 13 Pleasant St 05149. Corner of Depot St; center. Int corridors. **Pets:** Accepted.

🛜 ✕ 🔋 🍴 ✉

MANCHESTER

▽▽ Weathervane Motel M

(802) 362-2444. **Call for rates.** 2212 Main St, Historic SR 7A 05254. Jct SR 11/30, 2.3 mi s. Ext corridors. **Pets:** Accepted.

🛜 ✕ 🔋 💻 ✉

MANCHESTER CENTER

▽▽ Casablanca Motel M ❀

(802) 362-2145. **$72-$125, 14 day notice.** 5927 Main St (Rt 7A) 05255. Jct SR 11/30, 1 mi n on Historic SR 7A. Ext corridors. **Pets:** Other species. $15 daily fee/pet. Service with restrictions.

[ECO] 🛜 ✕ 🔋 💻 ✉

MANCHESTER VILLAGE

AAA ▽▽▽▽ The Equinox, a Luxury Collection Golf Resort & Spa H

(802) 362-4700. **$199-$569, 21 day notice.** 3567 Main St 05254. 1.3 mi s on Historic SR 7A, from jct SR 11/30. Int corridors. **Pets:** Accepted.

[ECO] [SAVE] 🛜 ✕ ✉M 🔋 🍴 ✉ ✕

MENDON

AAA ▽▽ Econo Lodge-Killington Area H

(802) 773-6644. **Call for rates.** 4293 US Rt 4 05701. Jct US 7, 5.3 mi e. Int corridors. **Pets:** Other species. $15 daily fee/room. Designated rooms, service with restrictions, supervision.

[ECO] [SAVE] 🛜 🔋 💻 ✉

▽▽ Mendon Mountainview Lodge H

(802) 773-4311. **$69-$259, 7 day notice.** 78 US 4 05751. On US 4, 6 mi e of jct US 7. Int corridors. **Pets:** Accepted.

🛜 🔋 💻 🍴 ✉ ✕

MIDDLEBURY

▽▽▽ The Middlebury Inn H ❀

(802) 388-4961. **$119-$299, 3 day notice.** 14 Court Square 05753. On US 7; center. Ext/int corridors. **Pets:** Large, other species. $25 one-time fee/room. Designated rooms, supervision. [ECO] 🛜 ✕ 🔋 💻 🍴

▽▽▽ Swift House Inn CI

(802) 388-9925. **$129-$299, 7 day notice.** 25 Stewart Ln 05753. 0.3 mi n on US 7 from jct SR 125 W. Ext/int corridors. **Pets:** Accepted.

[ECO] 🛜 ✕ 💻 🍴 ✕

MONTGOMERY CENTER

▽▽▽ Phineas Swann Bed & Breakfast Inn BB

(802) 326-4306. **$99-$395, 30 day notice.** 195 Main St 05471. Center. Ext/int corridors. **Pets:** Accepted. 🛜 🔋 💻 ✕

MONTPELIER

▽ Econo Lodge M

(802) 229-5766. **Call for rates.** 101 Northfield St 05602. Just s of jct US 302/SR 12. Ext corridors. **Pets:** Accepted. 🛜 🔋 💻

MORRISVILLE

AAA ▽▽ Sunset Motor Inn M

(802) 888-4956. **$85-$142, 7 day notice.** 160 SR 15W 05661. Jct SR 100, just w on SR 15. Ext/int corridors. **Pets:** $50 deposit/room. Designated rooms, service with restrictions, crate.

[SAVE] 🛜 ✉M 🔋 🍴 ✉

NORTH HERO

▽▽▽ Shore Acres Inn CI

(802) 372-8722. **$95-$250, 21 day notice.** 237 Shore Acres Dr 05474. 0.5 mi s on US 2. Ext/int corridors. **Pets:** Dogs only. $20 deposit/pet. Crate. 🛜 ✕ 🔋 🍴 ✕ ✉

PUTNEY

▽▽ The Putney Inn H ❀

(802) 387-5517. **$98-$198.** 57 Putney Landing Rd 05346. I-91 exit 4, just e. Ext corridors. **Pets:** $10 daily fee/pet. Designated rooms, service with restrictions, supervision. 🛜 ✕ 🔋 💻 🍴

RANDOLPH

AAA ▽▽▽ Three Stallion Inn CI

(802) 728-5575. **$125-$275.** 665 Stock Farm Rd 05060. I-89 exit 4 (SR 66), 2 mi w on SR 66; jct SR 12, just e on SR 66, then just s. Ext/int corridors. **Pets:** Accepted. [SAVE] 🛜 ✕ 🍴 ✉ ✕

RUTLAND

▽▽ Comfort Inn at Trolley Square H

(802) 775-2200. **$79-$189.** 19 Allen St 05701. On US 7, 1 mi s from jct US 4 W; 1.5 mi n from US 4 E. Int corridors. **Pets:** Medium, other species. $35 one-time fee/room. Supervision. 🛜 ✕ ✉M 🔋 💻 ✉

▽▽▽ Holiday Inn Rutland/Killington H

(802) 775-1911. **$129-$249, 3 day notice.** 476 US Rt 7 S 05701. 2.4 mi s on US 7 from US 4 W; 0.4 mi n on US 7 from US 4 E. Int corridors. **Pets:** Other species. $25 daily fee/room. Designated rooms, service with restrictions, supervision. 🛜 ✉M 🔋 💻 🍴 ✉ ✕

AAA ▽▽▽ Red Roof Inn Rutland-Killington H

(802) 775-4303. **$60-$250.** 401 US Hwy 7 S 05701. 0.8 mi s on US 7 and US 4. Int corridors. **Pets:** Large, other species. No service, supervision. [SAVE] 🛜 🔋 💻 ✉

 Rodeway Inn **M**

(802) 775-2575. **Call for rates.** 138 N Main St 05701. 0.5 mi n of jct US 4 E. Ext corridors. **Pets:** Small, dogs only. $10 daily fee/pet. Supervision.

SAVE 🛰 🛅 💻 ➳

 Rodeway Inn **M**

(802) 773-9176. **Call for rates.** 115 Woodstock Ave 05701. Jct US 7, 0.5 mi e on US 4. Ext/int corridors. **Pets:** Small, dogs only. $10 daily fee/pet. Designated rooms, service with restrictions, supervision.

SAVE 🛰 🛅 💻 ➳

ST. ALBANS

Econo Lodge **M**

(802) 524-5956. **Call for rates.** 287 S Main St (US 7) 05478. I-89 exit 19, 1 mi w on Interstate Access Rd, then 0.5 mi s. Ext/int corridors. **Pets:** Accepted. SAVE 🛰 🛅 💻

ST. JOHNSBURY

Fairbanks Inn **M**

(802) 748-5666. **Call for rates.** 401 Western Ave 05819. I-91 exit 21, 0.8 mi e on US 2. Ext corridors. **Pets:** Accepted. 🛰 ✕ 🛅 ➳

SHAFTSBURY

Hillbrook Motel **M**

(802) 447-7201. **Call for rates.** 2629 Rt 7A 05262. SR 7 exit 2, 2 mi n. Ext corridors. **Pets:** Accepted. ✕ 🛅 ➳

Serenity Motel **CA**

(802) 442-6490. **$70-$90.** 4379 Rt 7A 05262. 3.3 mi n on Historic SR 7A from jct SR 67. Ext corridors. **Pets:** Other species. Designated rooms, service with restrictions, supervision. ✕ 🛅 💻

SHELBURNE

Quality Inn **M**

(802) 985-8037. **$69-$199.** 2572 Shelburne Rd 05482. I-89 exit 13 (I-189/US 7), 2.1 mi s. Ext/int corridors. **Pets:** $10 daily fee/pet. Service with restrictions, supervision. SAVE 🛰 🛅 💻 ➳ ✕

SOUTH BURLINGTON

Best Western Windjammer Inn & Conference Center **H**

(802) 863-1125. **$105-$180.** 1076 Williston Rd 05403. I-89 exit 14E, 0.3 mi e on US 2. Int corridors. **Pets:** Accepted.

ECO SAVE 🛰 ✕ 🛅 💻 🍴 ➳

DoubleTree by Hilton Hotel Burlington **H** ✿

(802) 658-0250. **Call for rates.** 1117 Williston Rd 05403. I-89 exit 14E, just e on US 2. Int corridors. **Pets:** Large, other species. $75 deposit/pet. Service with restrictions, supervision.

ECO SAVE 🛰 🛅 🛅 💻 🍴 ➳

Green Mountain Suites Hotel **H** ✿

(802) 860-1212. **$149-$489, 3 day notice.** 401 Dorset St 05403. I-89 exit 14E, just e on US 2, then 0.8 mi s. Int corridors. **Pets:** Medium. $25 daily fee/room. Designated rooms, service with restrictions, supervision.

ECO 🛰 🛅 🛅 💻 ➳

La Quinta Inn & Suites South Burlington **H**

(802) 865-3400. **$62-$194.** 1285 Williston Rd 05403. I-89 exit 14E, 0.5 mi e on US 2. Int corridors. **Pets:** Medium, other species. Service with restrictions, supervision. 🛰 🛅 🛅 💻 ➳

Sheraton Burlington Hotel & Conference Center **H**

(802) 865-6600. **$299-$329.** 870 Williston Rd 05403. I-89 exit 14W, just w on US 2. Int corridors. **Pets:** Accepted.

ECO SAVE 🛰 ✕ 🛅 💻 🍴 ➳

Smart Suites **H**

(802) 860-9900. **$99-$199.** 1700 Shelburne Rd 05403. I-89 exit 13 (I-189/US 7) to US 7, 1.5 mi s. Int corridors. **Pets:** Small. $25 one-time fee/pet. Designated rooms. 🛰 🛅 💻

SOUTH WOODSTOCK

Kedron Valley Inn **CI**

(802) 457-1473. **$129-$259, 15 day notice.** 10671 South Rd 05071. Jct US 4, 5 mi s. Ext/int corridors. **Pets:** $15 daily fee/pet. Designated rooms, service with restrictions, supervision. 🛰 ✕ 🛅 🍴 🛅

SPRINGFIELD

Holiday Inn Express **H**

(802) 885-4516. **$109-$199.** 818 Charlestown Rd 05156. I-91 exit 7. Int corridors. **Pets:** Accepted. 🛰 ✕ 🛅 🛅 💻 ➳

STOWE

1066 Ye Olde England Inne **CI** ✿

(802) 253-7558. **Call for rates.** 433 Mountain Rd 05672. Jct SR 100, 0.4 mi w on SR 108. Ext/int corridors. **Pets:** Large, other species. $20 daily fee/pet. Designated rooms, service with restrictions, crate.

ECO 🛰 ✕ 🛅 💻 🍴 ➳ ✕

Commodores Inn **H** ✿

(802) 253-7131. **$98-$198.** 823 S Main St 05672. Jct SR 108, 0.8 mi s on SR 100. Int corridors. **Pets:** Other species. $10 daily fee/room. Designated rooms. SAVE 🛰 ✕ 🛅 🍴 ➳ ✕

Edson Hill Manor **CI**

(802) 253-7371. **$139-$239, 15 day notice.** 1500 Edson Hill Rd 05672. Jct SR 100, 3.4 mi w on SR 108, 1.3 mi n. Ext/int corridors. **Pets:** Accepted. 🛰 ✕ 🍴 ➳ ✕

Golden Eagle Resort **M** ✿

(802) 253-4811. **$99-$299, 7 day notice.** 511 Mountain Rd 05672. Jct SR 100, 0.5 mi w on SR 108. Ext corridors. **Pets:** Other species. $25 one-time fee/room. Designated rooms, service with restrictions.

ECO SAVE 🛰 ✕ 🛅 💻 🍴 ➳ ✕

Hob Knob Inn & Restaurant **M**

(802) 253-8549. **$90-$300, 14 day notice.** 2364 Mountain Rd 05672. Jct SR 100, 2.5 mi w on SR 108. Ext/int corridors. **Pets:** Other species. $20 daily fee/pet. Designated rooms.

ECO 🛰 ✕ 🛅 💻 🍴 ➳

Honeywood Country Lodge **M**

(802) 253-4124. **$109-$189, 15 day notice.** 4527 Mountain Rd 05672. Jct SR 100, 4.7 mi w on SR 108. Ext corridors. **Pets:** Dogs only. $10 daily fee/pet. Service with restrictions, supervision.

🛰 ✕ 🛅 💻 ➳ ✕

Innsbruck Inn at Stowe **M**

(802) 253-8582. **$79-$199, 15 day notice.** 4361 Mountain Rd 05672. Jct SR 100, 4.5 mi w on SR 108. Ext/int corridors. **Pets:** Accepted.

ECO SAVE 🛰 ✕ 🛅 💻 ➳ ✕

The Mountain Road Resort at Stowe **M**

(802) 253-4566. **Call for rates.** 1007 Mountain Rd 05672. Jct SR 100, 1 mi w on SR 108. Ext corridors. **Pets:** Accepted.

🛰 ✕ 🛅 💻 ➳ ✕

The Snowdrift Motel **M**

(802) 253-7305. **$80-$150, 7 day notice.** 2135 Mountain Rd 05672. Jct SR 100, 2.1 mi w on SR 108. Ext/int corridors. **Pets:** Dogs only. $12 daily fee/pet. Designated rooms, service with restrictions, crate.

🛰 🛅 💻 ➳ ✕

Stoweflake Mountain Resort & Spa **H** ✿

(802) 253-7355. **$199-$559, 15 day notice.** 1746 Mountain Rd 05672. Jct SR 100, 1.4 mi w on SR 108. Int corridors. **Pets:** Medium, dogs only. $40 daily fee/room. Designated rooms, service with restrictions, crate.

SAVE 🛰 ✕ 🛅 💻 🍴 ➳ ✕

▲▲▲ ▼▼▼ The Stowe Inn & Tavern BB
(802) 253-4030. **$109-$459, 3 day notice.** 123 Mountain Rd 05672. Jct SR 100, just n. Ext/int corridors. **Pets:** Medium. $20 daily fee/pet. Designated rooms, service with restrictions, supervision.
SAVE ☎ 🖥 📺 ⑪ ⊷

▲▲▲ ▼▼▼ ▼▼▼ Stowe Mountain Lodge H ✿
(802) 253-3560. **$199-$829, 14 day notice.** 7412 Mountain Rd 05672. Jct SR 100, 7.3 mi w on SR 108. Int corridors. **Pets:** Large, dogs only. $50 one-time fee/room. Designated rooms, service with restrictions, supervision. ECO SAVE ☎ ✕ 🖥 📺 ⑪ ⊷ ✕

▲▲▲ ▼▼▼ Sun & Ski Inn and Suites M
(802) 253-7159. **$79-$350, 15 day notice.** 1613 Mountain Rd 05672. Jct SR 100, 1.7 mi w on SR 108. Ext corridors. **Pets:** Accepted.
SAVE ☎ ✕ 🖥 📺 ⊷ ✕

▲▲▲ ▼▼▼ ▼▼▼ Topnotch Resort and Spa H ✿
(802) 253-8585. **$175-$595, 14 day notice.** 4000 Mountain Rd 05672. Jct SR 100, 4.2 mi w on SR 108. Ext/int corridors. **Pets:** Dogs only. Designated rooms, service with restrictions, crate.
SAVE ☎ ✕ 🖥 ⑪ ⊷ ✕

▼▼▼ Trapp Family Lodge H ✿
(802) 253-8511. **$193-$504, 14 day notice.** 700 Trapp Hill Rd 05672. Jct SR 100, 2.1 mi w on SR 108, 1.4 mi s on Luce Hill Rd, follow signs. Int corridors. **Pets:** Large, dogs only. Designated rooms, service with restrictions, supervision. ECO ☎ ✕ 🖥 📺 ⑪ ⊷ ✕

SUNDERLAND

▼▼▼ Arcady at the Sunderland M
(802) 362-1176. **$80-$175, 3 day notice.** 6249 Rt 7A 05250. On Historic SR 7A, 6.3 mi s of jct SR 11. Ext corridors. **Pets:** Dogs only. $18 daily fee/pet. Designated rooms, service with restrictions, crate.
☎ ✕ 🖥 📺 ⊷

SWANTON

▲▲▲ ▼▼▼ Swanton Motel M
(802) 868-4284. **$75-$183.** 112 Grand Ave (US 7) 05488. I-89 exit 21, 0.8 mi w on SR 78, then 0.5 mi s. **Pets:** Large, other species. $150 deposit/room, $15 daily fee/pet. Designated rooms, service with restrictions, supervision. SAVE ☎ ✕ 🖥 📺 ⊷

WARREN

▼▼▼ ▼▼▼ The Pitcher Inn CI
(802) 496-6350. **Call for rates.** 275 Main St 05674. Center. Ext/int corridors. **Pets:** Accepted. ☎ ✕ 🖥 📺 ⑪ ✕

WEST BRATTLEBORO

▼▼▼ Molly Stark Motel M
(802) 254-2440. **$45-$95.** 829 Marlboro Rd 05301. I-91 exit 2, 3.3 mi w on SR 9. Ext corridors. **Pets:** Medium, dogs only. $5 one-time fee/room. Crate. ☎ 🖥 📺

WEST DOVER

▼▼▼ The Gray Ghost Inn M
(802) 464-2474. **$98-$212, 14 day notice.** 290 Rt 100 N 05356. 7.8 mi n on SR 100, from jct SR 9. Int corridors. **Pets:** Dogs only. Service with restrictions, supervision. ☎ ✕ ⊷ ☒

WESTMORE

▼▼▼ WilloughVale Inn on Lake Willoughby CI
(802) 525-4123. **Call for rates.** 793 SR 5A 05860. Jct SR 16 and 5A, just s. Ext/int corridors. **Pets:** Accepted. ☎ ✕ 🖥 📺 ⑪ ✕

WHITE RIVER JUNCTION

▼▼▼ Comfort Inn H
(802) 295-3051. **$100-$220.** 56 Ralph Lehman Dr 05001. I-91 exit 11, just e. Int corridors. **Pets:** Service with restrictions, supervision.
☎ ⌨ 🖥 📺 ⊷

▼▼▼ Super 8-White River Junction H
(802) 295-7577. **$56-$129.** 442 N Hartland Rd 05001. US 5, just w of jct I-89 and 91. Ext corridors. **Pets:** Large, other species. Service with restrictions, supervision. ☎ 🖥 📺 ⊷

WILLISTON

▼▼▼ Residence Inn Burlington Williston H
(802) 878-2001. **$99-$359.** 35 Hurricane Ln 05495. I-89 exit 12, just s on SR 2A, then just e. Ext corridors. **Pets:** Accepted.
☎ ✕ 🖥 📺 ⊷ ✕

▼▼▼ TownePlace Suites Burlington Williston H
(802) 872-5900. **$129-$164.** 66 Zephyr Rd 05495. I-89 exit 12, 1.1 mi n on SR 2A. Int corridors. **Pets:** Accepted. ☎ ✕ ⌨ 🖥 📺 ⊷

WINDSOR

▼▼▼ Juniper Hill Inn CI
(802) 674-5273. **Call for rates.** 153 Pembroke Rd 05089. I-91 exit 9, 2.9 mi s on US 5 to Juniper Hill Rd, then 0.5 mi w. Int corridors.
Pets: Accepted. ☎ ✕ ⑪ ✕ ☒

WOODSTOCK

▼▼▼ Ottauquechee Motor Lodge M
(802) 672-3404. **Call for rates.** 529 US Rt 4 (Woodstock Rd) 05091. On US 4, 4.5 mi w. Ext/int corridors. **Pets:** Accepted. ☎ ✕ 🖥

▲▲▲ ▼▼▼ ▼▼▼ Woodstock Inn & Resort H
(802) 457-1100. **$195-$864, 3 day notice.** 14 The Green 05091. On US 4; center. Int corridors. **Pets:** Accepted.
ECO SAVE ☎ ✕ ⌨ 🖥 📺 ⑪ ⊷ ✕

VIRGINIA

ABINGDON

 Holiday Inn Express 🅷 ❀
(276) 676-2829. **$99-$189.** 940 E Main St 24210. I-81 exit 19 (US 11), just w. Int corridors. **Pets:** Medium. $27 one-time fee/room. Designated rooms, service with restrictions, supervision.
SAVE 🛜 ♿ 🍴 💻 🏊

ALTAVISTA

Comfort Inn 🅷
(434) 369-4000. **Call for rates.** 1558 Main St 24517. US 29 business route, jct US 29. Int corridors. **Pets:** Accepted. 🛜 🍴 💻 🏊 ✕

Days Inn 🅷
(434) 369-4070. **$69-$99.** 1557 Main St 24517. US 29 business route, jct US 29. Int corridors. **Pets:** Other species. $10 daily fee/pet. Designated rooms, service with restrictions, supervision. 🛜 ♿ 🍴 💻

APPOMATTOX

Super 8 🅼
(434) 352-2339. **$44-$74.** 7571 Richmond Hwy 24522. US 460, just w of jct US 26. Int corridors. **Pets:** Accepted. 🛜 🍴 💻

ARRINGTON

Harmony Hill Bed and Breakfast 🅱🅱
(434) 263-7750. **$119-$169.** 929 Wilson Hill Rd 22922. US 29, 0.9 mi e on SR 665. Int corridors. **Pets:** Accepted. 🛜 ✕ 🍴 🅩

BEDFORD

Super 8 🅷
(540) 587-0100. **$59-$79.** 842 Sword Beach Ln 24523. 1.5 mi w on US 221 and 460. Int corridors. **Pets:** Accepted. 🛜 ♿ 🍴 💻

BLACKSBURG

Comfort Inn 🅷
(540) 951-1500. **Call for rates.** 3705 S Main St 24060. 3.5 mi s on US 460, jct US 460 Bypass. Int corridors. **Pets:** Accepted.
🛜 🍴 💻 🏊

Days Inn Blacksburg 🅷 ❀
(540) 951-1330. **$67-$189.** 3503 Holiday Ln 24060. 3.8 mi s on US 460; jct US 460 Bypass. Ext corridors. **Pets:** Other species. $50 deposit/room, $10 daily fee/pet. No service, supervision.
SAVE 🛜 🍴 💻 🏊

BRISTOL

Holiday Inn Hotel & Suites 🅷
(276) 466-4100. **$85-$93, 3 day notice.** 3005 Linden Dr 24202. I-81 exit 7, just w. Int corridors. **Pets:** Accepted.
ECO 🛜 ♿ 🍴 💻 🍴 🏊

La Quinta Inn Bristol 🅷
(276) 669-9353. **$62-$119.** 1014 Old Airport Rd 24201. I-81 exit 7, just e. Ext corridors. **Pets:** Medium, other species. Service with restrictions, supervision. 🛜 ♿ 🍴 💻 🏊

Motel 6 #4125 🅼
(276) 466-6060. **$55-$200.** 21561 Clear Creek Rd 24202. I-81 exit 7, 0.3 mi w. Int corridors. **Pets:** Other species. Service with restrictions, supervision. 🛜 ♿ 🍴

BUCHANAN

Wattstull Inn 🅼
(540) 254-1551. **$58-$75, 7 day notice.** 130 Arcadia Rd 24066. I-81 exit 168, just e on SR 614. Ext corridors. **Pets:** $10 daily fee/pet. Designated rooms, service with restrictions, supervision.
SAVE 🛜 🍴 💻 🍴 🏊

BURKEVILLE

Comfort Inn Burkeville 🅷
(434) 767-3750. **Call for rates.** 419 N Agnew St 23922. On US 460, just e of jct US 360. Int corridors. **Pets:** Accepted.
SAVE 🛜 ✕ 🍴 💻 🍴 🏊

CHARLOTTESVILLE

The Cavalier Inn at the University 🅷
(434) 296-8111. **$75-$350, 30 day notice.** 105 N Emmet St 22903. Jct US 29 (Emmet St) and 250 Bypass, 1.3 mi s on US 29 business route. Ext/int corridors. **Pets:** Accepted. ECO SAVE 🛜 ✕ 🍴 💻 🏊

Comfort Inn University 🅷
(434) 293-6188. **$89-$169.** 1807 Emmet St 22901. Jct US 250 Bypass, just n on US 29 (Emmet St). Int corridors. **Pets:** Accepted.
SAVE 🛜 🍴 💻 🏊

DoubleTree by Hilton Hotel 🅷 ❀
(434) 973-2121. **$99-$219.** 990 Hilton Heights Rd 22901. I-64 exit 118B (US 29/Emmet St), 4 mi n of jct US 250 Bypass. Int corridors.
Pets: Medium, dogs only. $25 one-time fee/room. Designated rooms, service with restrictions, crate. ECO SAVE 🛜 🍴 💻 🍴 🏊

▼▼▼ Fairfield Inn by Marriott �H

(434) 964-9411. **$123-$132.** 577 Branchlands Blvd 22901. US 29 (Emmet St), 1.3 mi n of US 250 Bypass. Int corridors. **Pets:** Accepted.
🛜 ❌ 🛑 🖥 ⮆

▼▼▼ Holiday Inn-Monticello/Charlottesville �H

(434) 977-5100. **$89-$229.** 1200 5th St SW 22902. I-64 exit 120, just n on SR 631. Int corridors. **Pets:** Accepted. 🛜 🛑 🖥 🍽 ⮆

▼▼▼ Omni Charlottesville Hotel �H

(434) 971-5500. **$115-$229.** 235 W Main St 22902. I-64 exit 120, 2.3 mi n on SR 631; downtown. Int corridors. **Pets:** Small. $50 one-time fee/room. Service with restrictions. 🅴🅲🅾 🛜 🛑 🖥 🍽 ⮆ ❌

AAA▷ ▼▼▼ Red Roof Inn of Charlottesville �H

(434) 295-4333. **$80-$249.** 1309 W Main St 22903. US 29 (Emmet St), 1 mi e on US 250 (University Ave). Int corridors. **Pets:** Large, other species. No service, supervision. 🆂🅰🆅🅴 🛜 🛑 🖥

AAA▷ ▼▼▼ Residence Inn by Marriott �H

(434) 923-0300. **$139-$229.** 1111 Millmont St 22903. I-64 exit 118B (US 29/Emmet St), 2.5 mi n on US 29/250 E, just s on Barracks Rd, then just se. Int corridors. **Pets:** $100 one-time fee/room. Service with restrictions. 🅴🅲🅾 🆂🅰🆅🅴 🛜 ❌ 🛑 🖥 ⮆ ❌

AAA▷ ▼▼▼ Sleep Inn & Suites Monticello �H

(434) 244-9969. **Call for rates.** 1185 5th St 22902. I-64 exit 120, just n. Int corridors. **Pets:** Accepted. 🆂🅰🆅🅴 🛜 🛑 🖥 ⮆

CHINCOTEAGUE

AAA▷ ▼▼▼ Americas Best Value Inn & Suites 🅼

(757) 336-6562. **$50-$199, 10 day notice.** 6151 Maddox Blvd 23336. Just e on Maddox Blvd. Ext corridors. **Pets:** Accepted.
🆂🅰🆅🅴 🛜 🛑 🖥 ⮆

▼▼ Rodeway Inn Chincoteague �H

(757) 336-6565. **$49-$349.** 6273 Maddox Blvd 23336. Just e on Maddox Blvd. Ext corridors. **Pets:** Accepted. 🛜 🅶🅼 🛑 🖥 ⮆

CHRISTIANSBURG

AAA▷ ▼▼▼ Econo Lodge 🅼

(540) 382-6161. **Call for rates.** 2430 Roanoke St 24073. I-81 exit 118, just w on US 11/460. Ext corridors. **Pets:** Medium. $10 daily fee/pet. Designated rooms, service with restrictions, supervision.
🆂🅰🆅🅴 🛜 🅶🅼 🛑 🖥 ⮆

AAA▷ ▼▼▼ Quality Inn 🅼 ❀

(540) 382-2055. **$53-$200.** 50 Hampton Blvd 24073. I-81 exit 118C, just e. Ext corridors. **Pets:** Other species. $10 daily fee/room. Designated rooms, service with restrictions. 🆂🅰🆅🅴 🛜 🛑 🖥 ⮆

AAA▷ ▼▼ Super 8-Christiansburg East 🅼

(540) 382-7421. **$59-$99, 3 day notice.** 2780 Roanoke Rd 24073. I-81 exit 118C, just e. Ext corridors. **Pets:** $10 daily fee/pet. Designated rooms, service with restrictions, supervision. 🆂🅰🆅🅴 🛜 🛑 🖥 ⮆

▼▼ Super 8-Christiansburg West 🅼

(540) 382-5813. **$49-$99.** 55 Laurel St NE 24073. I-81 exit 118, 1 mi w on US 11/460, then 3.5 mi nw on US 460 Bypass; jct SR 114. Int corridors. **Pets:** Medium. $10 daily fee/pet. Designated rooms, service with restrictions, supervision. 🛜 🛑

CLARKSVILLE

AAA▷ ▼▼▼ Best Western on the Lake �H

(434) 374-5023. **$85-$130, 3 day notice.** 103 Second St 23927. Just n of US 58 business route; downtown. Int corridors. **Pets:** Other species. $100 deposit/room, $20 daily fee/pet. Designated rooms, service with restrictions. 🆂🅰🆅🅴 🛜 🅶🅼 🛑 🖥 ⮆

COLLINSVILLE

▼▼ Knights Inn 🅼

(276) 647-3716. **$50-$70.** 2357 Virginia Ave 24078. Jct US 58, 3 mi n on US 220 business route. Ext corridors. **Pets:** Accepted. 🛜 🛑 ⮆

▼▼▼ Quality Inn-Dutch Inn Hotel and Convention Center �H

(276) 647-3721. **Call for rates.** 2360 Virginia Ave 24078. Jct US 58, 3 mi n on US 220 business route. Ext corridors. **Pets:** Dogs only. $20 daily fee/room. Service with restrictions, crate. 🛜 🛑 🖥 🍽 ⮆

COVINGTON

AAA▷ ▼▼▼ Best Western Mountain View �H

(540) 962-4951. **$113.** 820 E Madison St 24426. I-64 exit 16, just n. Ext corridors. **Pets:** Accepted. 🆂🅰🆅🅴 🛜 🛑 🖥 ⮆

AAA▷ ▼▼▼ Compare Inn & Suites �H

(540) 962-2141. **Call for rates.** 203 Interstate Dr 24426. I-64 exit 16, just sw. Int corridors. **Pets:** Accepted. 🆂🅰🆅🅴 🛜 🛑 🖥 ⮆

CULPEPER

▼▼▼ Comfort Inn-Culpeper 🅼

(540) 825-4900. **Call for rates.** 890 Willis Ln 22701. 2 mi s on Main St (US 29 business route); jct US 29, just e. Ext corridors. **Pets:** Accepted.
🛜 🛑 🖥 ⮆

DANVILLE

▼▼▼ Comfort Inn & Suites �H ❀

(434) 793-2000. **$81-$189.** 100 Tower Dr 24540. US 58, just w of jct US 29 business route. Int corridors. **Pets:** Small, other species. $15 daily fee/pet. Designated rooms, service with restrictions, supervision.
🛜 🛑 🖥 🍽 ⮆

▼▼▼ Courtyard by Marriott �H

(434) 791-2661. **$85-$118.** 2136 Riverside Dr 24540. On US 58, just w of jct US 29 business route. Int corridors. **Pets:** Accepted.
🛜 ❌ 🅶🅼 🛑 🖥 🍽 ⮆

▼▼▼ Innkeeper Danville North 🅼

(434) 836-1700. **$45-$99, 3 day notice.** 1030 Piney Forest Rd 24540. US 29 N business route, 0.5 mi n of US 58. Ext corridors. **Pets:** Medium. $50 one-time fee/pet. No service, crate. 🛜 🛑 ⮆

▼▼ Super 8 🅼

(434) 799-5845. **$49-$99, 3 day notice.** 2385 Riverside Dr 24541. On US 58, just e of jct US 29 business route. Int corridors. **Pets:** Accepted.
🛜 🛑 🖥

EMPORIA

AAA▷ ▼▼▼ Best Western Emporia �H

(434) 634-3200. **$63-$75.** 1100 W Atlantic St 23847. I-95 exit 11B, just w on US 58. Ext corridors. **Pets:** Accepted. 🆂🅰🆅🅴 🛜 🛑 🖥 ⮆

▼▼▼ Country Inn & Suites By Carlson Emporia �H

(434) 336-0001. **$79-$149.** 107 Sadler Ln 23847. I-95 exit 11A, just e on US 58. Int corridors. **Pets:** Accepted. 🛜 ❌ 🛑 🖥 ⮆

AAA▷ ▼▼▼ Days Inn-Emporia �H

(434) 634-9481. **$54-$63.** 921 W Atlantic St 23847. I-95 exit 11B, just w on US 58. Ext corridors. **Pets:** $10 daily fee/pet. Service with restrictions, supervision. 🆂🅰🆅🅴 🛜 🛑 🖥 🍽 ⮆

AAA▷ ▼▼▼ Hampton Inn �H ❀

(434) 634-9200. **$99-$119.** 898 Wiggins Rd 23847. I-95 exit 11B, just w on US 58. Int corridors. **Pets:** Other species. Designated rooms, service with restrictions, supervision. 🅴🅲🅾 🆂🅰🆅🅴 🛜 🅶🅼 🛑 🖥 ⮆

▼▼ Quality Inn �H

(434) 348-8888. **Call for rates.** 1207 W Atlantic St 23847. I-95 exit 11B, just w on US 58. Ext corridors. **Pets:** Accepted. 🛜 🛑 🖥 ⮆

◇◇◇ ▼▼▼ **Sleep Inn** H
(434) 348-3900. **$70-$120.** 899 Wiggins Rd 23847. I-95 exit 11B, just e on US 58, then just s. Int corridors. **Pets:** $10 daily fee/pet. Service with restrictions, supervision. [SAVE] 🛜 [&M] 🔒 🖵

EXMORE

◇◇◇ ▼▼▼ **Best Western Eastern Shore** H
(757) 442-7378. **$90-$140.** 2543 Lankford Hwy 23350. US 13, just n of SR 178. Ext/int corridors. **Pets:** Accepted.
[SAVE] 🛜 [&M] 🔒 🖵 �

▼▼▼ **Holiday Inn Express & Suites** H
(757) 442-5522. **Call for rates.** 3446 Lankford Hwy 23350. On US 13. Int corridors. **Pets:** Accepted. 🛜 ✕ [&M] 🔒 🖵 🌟

FANCY GAP

▼▼ **Doe Run Lodging at Groundhog Mountain** CO
(276) 398-4099. **$89-$425, 3 day notice.** 27 Buck Hollar Rd 24328. Blue Ridge Parkway at MM 189.2; 10 mi n from US 52. Ext corridors. **Pets:** Other species. $25 one-time fee/room. Designated rooms.
🔒 🖵 ✕

FLOYD

▼▼ **Hotel Floyd** M
(540) 745-6080. **$79-$109.** 120 Wilson St 24091. Just e; center. Ext corridors. **Pets:** Designated rooms, service with restrictions, supervision.
🛜 ✕ 🔒 🖵

FRANKLIN

▼ **Super 8** M
(757) 562-2888. **$49-$72.** 1599 Armory Dr 23851. Jct US 58 Bypass and SR 671. Int corridors. **Pets:** Accepted. 🛜 🔒 🖵

FREDERICKSBURG

◇◇◇ ▼▼▼ **Best Western Central Plaza** M
(540) 786-7404. **$69-$89.** 3000 Plank Rd 22401. I-95 exit 130B (SR 3). Ext corridors. **Pets:** Small, other species. $10 daily fee/pet. Service with restrictions, supervision. [ECO] [SAVE] 🛜 [&M] 🔒 🖵

◇◇◇ ▼▼▼ **Best Western Fredericksburg** H ❀
(540) 371-5050. **$79-$99.** 2205 Plank Rd 22401. I-95 exit 130A (SR 3), 0.3 mi e. Ext corridors. **Pets:** $10 daily fee/pet. Designated rooms, service with restrictions, supervision. [ECO] [SAVE] 🛜 [&M] 🔒 🖵 🌟

◇◇◇ ▼▼▼ **Clarion Inn Fredericksburg** H
(540) 371-5550. **$75-$89.** 564 Warrenton Rd 22406. I-95 exit 133, just nw on US 17. Ext corridors. **Pets:** Medium, other species. Service with restrictions, supervision. [SAVE] 🛜 🔒 🖵 🍴 🌟 ✕

◇◇◇ ▼▼▼ **Country Inn & Suites By Carlson, South** H
(540) 898-1800. **$89-$159.** 5327 Jefferson Davis Hwy 22408. I-95 exit 126 southbound; exit 126A northbound; just n on US 1 (Jefferson Davis Hwy). Int corridors. **Pets:** Accepted. [SAVE] 🛜 ✕ 🔒 🖵 🌟

◇◇◇ ▼▼▼ **Fredericksburg Hospitality House Hotel & Conference Center** H
(540) 786-8321. **$79-$169.** 2801 Plank Rd 22401. I-95 exit 130B (SR 3). Int corridors. **Pets:** Accepted. [SAVE] 🛜 ✕ [&M] 🔒 🖵 🍴 🌟

◇◇◇ ▼▼▼ **Quality Inn Fredericksburg** M
(540) 373-0000. **$50-$79.** 543 Warrenton Rd 22406. I-95 exit 133, just n on US 17. Ext corridors. **Pets:** Accepted. [SAVE] 🛜 ✕ 🔒 🖵

◇◇◇ ▼▼▼ **Quality Inn near Central Park** H
(540) 371-0330. **$69-$99.** 2310 Plank Rd 22401. I-95 exit 130A (SR 3). Ext corridors. **Pets:** Accepted. [ECO] [SAVE] 🛜 🔒 🖵 🌟

▼▼▼ **Residence Inn by Marriott** H
(540) 786-9222. **$124-$143.** 60 Town Centre Blvd 22407. I-95 exit 130B (SR 3), just w to Spotsylvania Towne Centre (Mall Dr), then just s. Int corridors. **Pets:** Accepted. 🛜 ✕ [&M] 🔒 🖵 🌟 ✕

▼▼▼ **TownePlace Suites by Marriott** H ❀
(540) 891-0775. **$94-$114.** 4700 Market St 22408. I-95 exit 126 southbound; exit 126A northbound, just n on US 1 (Jefferson Davis Hwy), then just e. Int corridors. **Pets:** Other species. $10 daily fee/pet. Service with restrictions. 🛜 ✕ 🔒 🖵

FRONT ROYAL

▼ **Budget Inn** M
(540) 635-2196. **Call for rates.** 1122 N Royal Ave 22630. I-66 exit 6, 2.2 mi s on US 340/522 and SR 55. Ext corridors. **Pets:** Accepted. 🔒

GLADE SPRING

▼ **Swiss Inn Motel & Suites** M
(276) 429-5191. **$39-$120.** 33361 Lee Hwy 24340. I-81 exit 29, just e. Ext corridors. **Pets:** Accepted. 🛜 🔒

GRETNA

▼▼▼ **Hampton Inn Altavista/Chatham** H
(434) 656-9000. **$89-$139.** 200 McBride Ln 24557. US 29, just e on SR 40. Int corridors. **Pets:** Accepted. 🛜 [&M] 🔒 🖵 🌟

GRUNDY

▼▼▼ **Comfort Inn** H
(276) 935-5050. **Call for rates.** 22006 Riverside Dr 24614. On US 460, 0.5 mi e. Int corridors. **Pets:** Accepted. 🛜 [&M] 🔒 🖵

HAMPTON ROADS AREA

CHESAPEAKE

◇◇◇ ▼▼▼▼ **Aloft Chesapeake** H
(757) 410-9562. **$99-$250, 3 day notice.** 1454 Crossways Blvd 23320. I-64 exit 289B (Greenbrier Pkwy), just s to Jarman Rd (at Crossways Center) to Crossways Blvd, then 0.7 mi n. Int corridors. **Pets:** Accepted.
[ECO] [SAVE] ✕ 🔒 🖵

▼▼▼ **Candlewood Suites** H
(757) 405-3030. **$75-$119.** 4809 Market Pl 23321. I-664 exit 11A (E Portsmouth Blvd/SR 337). Int corridors. **Pets:** Accepted.
[ECO] 🛜 [&M] 🔒 🖵

▼▼ **Extended StayAmerica Chesapeake-Greenbrier Circle** H ❀
(757) 523-7377. **$55-$65.** 809 Greenbrier Cir 23320. I-64 exit 289A (Greenbrier Pkwy), just n. Int corridors. **Pets:** Other species. $25 daily fee/pet. Service with restrictions. 🛜 [&M] 🔒 🖵

◇◇◇ ▼▼▼ **Hampton Inn & Suites** H
(757) 819-5230. **$79-$179.** 1421 N Battlefield Blvd 23320. I-64 exit 290B, just s; jct Coastal Way. Int corridors. **Pets:** Medium, dogs only. Service with restrictions, supervision. [SAVE] 🛜 ✕ [&M] 🔒 🖵 🌟

◇◇◇ ▼▼▼ **Hampton Inn Chesapeake/Greenbrier** H
(757) 420-1550. **$79-$179.** 701A Woodlake Dr 23320. I-64 exit 289A (Greenbrier Pkwy), just n to Woodlake Dr. Int corridors. **Pets:** Medium, dogs only. Designated rooms, service with restrictions, supervision.
[SAVE] 🛜 🔒 🖵 🌟

▼▼▼ **Residence Inn by Marriott, Chesapeake-Greenbrier** H
(757) 502-7300. **$109-$189.** 1500 Crossways Blvd 23320. I-64 exit 289B (Greenbrier Pkwy), just s to Jarman Rd (at Crossways Center) to Crossways Blvd, then 0.6 mi n. Int corridors. **Pets:** Accepted.
[ECO] 🛜 ✕ 🔒 🖵 🌟 ✕

▼▼▼▼ Staybridge Suites Greenbrier 🄷 ✿

(757) 420-2525. **$119-$179.** 709 Woodlake Dr 23320. I-64 exit 289A (Greenbrier Pkwy), just n. Int corridors. **Pets:** Medium. $75 one-time fee/pet. Designated rooms, service with restrictions.
🛜 ♿ 🛏 🖥 🏊

▼ Super 8 🄼

(757) 686-8888. **$42-$72.** 3216 Churchland Blvd 23321. I-664 exit 9B, 1 mi s on SR 17. Int corridors. **Pets:** Accepted. 🛜 🛏 🖥

▼ ▼ TownePlace Suites By Marriott 🄷

(757) 523-5004. **$79-$229.** 2000 Old Greenbrier Rd 23320. I-64 exit 289A (Greenbrier Pkwy), just n. Int corridors. **Pets:** Other species. $75 one-time fee/room. Service with restrictions, crate.
🄴🄲🄾 🛜 🗙 ♿ 🛏 🖥 🏊

GLOUCESTER

▼▼▼▼ Comfort Inn Gloucester 🄷

(804) 695-1900. **Call for rates.** 6639 Forest Hill Ave 23061. US 17, just s. Int corridors. **Pets:** Accepted. 🛜 🛏 🖥 🏊

HAMPTON

🆎 ▼▼▼▼ Best Western Plus Coliseum Inn & Suites 🄷

(757) 838-5011. **$59-$99.** 1809 W Mercury Blvd 23666. I-64 exit 263B (Mercury Blvd), jct SR 58. Int corridors. **Pets:** Accepted.
🆂🅰🆅🅴 🛜 ♿ 🛏 🖥 🍴 🏊

▼▼ Candlewood Suites 🄷

(757) 766-8976. **$69-$99.** 401 Butler Farm Rd 23666. I-64 exit 261B (Hampton Roads Center Pkwy) eastbound; exit 262B (Magruder Blvd) westbound, then n. Int corridors. **Pets:** Accepted.
🄴🄲🄾 🛜 ♿ 🛏 🖥

▼▼ Extended StayAmerica-Hampton Coliseum 🄼 ✿

(757) 896-3600. **$59-$69.** 1915 Commerce Dr 23666. I-64 exit 263 (Mercury Blvd), just n, then just e. Int corridors. **Pets:** Other species. $25 daily fee/pet. Service with restrictions. 🛜 ♿ 🛏 🖥

NEWPORT NEWS

▼▼▼ Comfort Inn 🄷

(757) 249-0200. **$89-$104.** 12330 Jefferson Ave 23602. I-64 exit 255A, just s on Clarie Ln; in mall parking lot. Int corridors. **Pets:** Accepted.
🛜 ♿ 🛏 🖥

▼▼ Crestwood Suites 🄼

(757) 951-1017. **$55-$75.** 11 Old Oyster Point Rd 23602. I-64 exit 256A, just s on Oyster Point Rd to Canon Blvd, just e, then just n. Int corridors. **Pets:** Accepted. 🛜 ♿ 🛏 🖥

▼▼ Microtel Inn 🄷

(757) 249-8355. **$56-$98.** 501 Operations Dr 23602. I-64 exit 255A, 0.5 mi s to Operations Dr, then just w. Int corridors. **Pets:** Accepted.
🛜 ♿ 🛏

🆎 ▼▼▼▼ Mulberry Inn 🄷

(757) 887-3000. **$79-$139.** 16890 Warwick Blvd 23603. I-64 exit 250A (SR 105/Ft Eustis Blvd S), s to US 60, then 0.3 mi w. Ext/int corridors. **Pets:** Medium. $50 one-time fee/room. Designated rooms, service with restrictions, crate. 🄴🄲🄾 🆂🅰🆅🅴 🛜 🛏 🖥 🏊

▼▼▼▼ Omni Newport News Hotel 🄷

(757) 873-6664. **Call for rates.** 1000 Omni Blvd 23606. I-64 exit 258A (US 17), just s to Oyster Point Rd. Int corridors. **Pets:** Small. $50 one-time fee/room. Service with restrictions, crate.
🛜 ♿ 🛏 🖥 🍴 🏊

🆎 ▼▼▼▼ Point Plaza-Suites at City Center 🄷 ✿

(757) 599-4460. **$69-$159.** 950 J Clyde Morris Blvd 23601. I-64 exit 258B (US 17), just n. Ext/int corridors. **Pets:** $50 one-time fee/room. Designated rooms, service with restrictions, crate.
🄴🄲🄾 🆂🅰🆅🅴 🛜 🛏 🖥 🏊

▼▼▼ Residence Inn by Marriott Newport News Airport 🄷

(757) 842-6214. **$116-$169.** 531 St Johns Rd 23602. I-64 exit 255A, just s on Jefferson Ave to Freedom Way, then just nw. Int corridors.
Pets: Accepted. 🛜 🗙 ♿ 🛏 🖥 🏊

▼▼ StudioPLUS-Newport News - I-64 - Jefferson Ave 🄷 ✿

(757) 882-8847. **$65-$75.** 12359 Hornsby Ln 23602. I-64 exit 255A, just s on Jefferson Ave. Int corridors. **Pets:** Other species. $25 daily fee/pet. Service with restrictions. 🛜 🛏 🖥 🏊

NORFOLK

▼▼▼ Candlewood Suites Norfolk Airport 🄷

(757) 605-4001. **$79-$159.** 5600 Lowery Rd 23502. I-264 exit 13B (US 13/Military Hwy), 1.3 mi n, then just w. Int corridors. **Pets:** Medium. $75 one-time fee/pet. Designated rooms, service with restrictions, supervision.
🛜 ♿ 🛏 🖥

🆎 ▼▼▼ Hilton Norfolk Airport 🄷

(757) 466-8000. **$99-$209.** 1500 N Military Hwy 23502. I-64 exit 281 (Military Hwy), just s; jct US 13 and SR 165. Int corridors. **Pets:** Medium, dogs only. $50 one-time fee/room. Designated rooms, service with restrictions, supervision. 🄴🄲🄾 🆂🅰🆅🅴 🛜 ♿ 🛏 🖥 🍴 🏊

🆎 ▼▼▼ La Quinta Inn & Suites Norfolk Airport 🄷

(757) 466-7001. **$98-$190.** 1387 N Military Hwy 23502. I-64 exit 281 (Military Hwy), just s. Int corridors. **Pets:** Medium, other species. Service with restrictions, supervision. 🆂🅰🆅🅴 🛜 🛏 🖥 🏊

🆎 ▼▼▼▼ Page House Inn Bed & Breakfast 🄱🄱

(757) 625-5033. **$150-$230, 7 day notice.** 323 Fairfax Ave 23507. I-264 exit 9, 1.4 mi n on Waterside Dr to Olney Rd, just w to Mowbray Arch, then just s; in Ghent historic district. Int corridors. **Pets:** Accepted.
🆂🅰🆅🅴 🛜 🗙 🛏

🆎 ▼▼▼▼ Quality Suites Lake Wright 🄷 🐾

(757) 461-6251. **$99-$149.** 6280 Northampton Blvd 23502. I-64 exit 282, just w on US 13. Int corridors. **Pets:** $35 one-time fee/room. Service with restrictions. 🄴🄲🄾 🆂🅰🆅🅴 🛜 🛏 🖥 🍴 🏊

▼▼▼ Residence Inn by Marriott Downtown 🄷 ✿

(757) 842-6216. **$119-$269.** 227 W Brambleton Ave 23510. Jct Duke St; downtown. Int corridors. **Pets:** Medium. $100 one-time fee/room. Designated rooms, service with restrictions, crate.
🄴🄲🄾 🛜 🗙 ♿ 🛏 🖥 🏊

▼▼▼ Residence Inn by Marriott Norfolk Airport 🄷

(757) 333-3000. **$109-$269.** 1590 N Military Hwy 23502. I-64 exit 281B (Military Hwy). Int corridors. **Pets:** Accepted.
🄴🄲🄾 🛜 🗙 ♿ 🛏 🖥 🏊 🗙

▼▼▼ Sheraton Norfolk Waterside Hotel 🄷

(757) 622-6664. **$99-$399.** 777 Waterside Dr 23510. I-264 exit 9 (Waterside Dr); downtown. Int corridors. **Pets:** Accepted.
🄴🄲🄾 🆂🅰🆅🅴 🛜 🗙 ♿ 🛏 🖥 🍴 🏊

🆎 ▼▼▼ Sleep Inn Lake Wright 🄷 ✿

(757) 461-1133. **$79-$129.** 6280 Northampton Blvd 23502. I-64 exit 282, just w on US 13. Int corridors. **Pets:** $25 one-time fee/room. Service with restrictions. 🄴🄲🄾 🆂🅰🆅🅴 🛜 ♿ 🛏 🖥 🍴 🏊

🆎 ▼▼▼ Tazewell Hotel and Suites, an Ascend Collection hotel 🄷

(757) 623-6200. **$79-$139.** 245 Granby St 23510. Jct Tazewell St; downtown. Int corridors. **Pets:** Medium. $25 daily fee/pet. Service with restrictions, supervision. 🆂🅰🆅🅴 🛜 🛏 🖥 🍴

SUFFOLK

 **TownePlace Suites by Marriott** 🅷
(757) 483-5177. **$69-$159.** 8050 Harbour View Blvd 23435. I-664 exit 8A (College Dr), just n. Int corridors. **Pets:** Accepted.
ECO 🛜 ✕ 🔥M 🔋 💻 🏊

VIRGINIA BEACH

△△△  **Alamar Resort Inn** 🅼
(757) 428-7582. **$49-$328, 21 day notice.** 311 16th St 23451. I-264 terminus to Pacific Ave, just s. Ext corridors. **Pets:** Accepted.
SAVE 🛜 ✕ 🔋 💻 🏊

▽▽▽ **Candlewood Suites** 🅷
(757) 213-1500. **$99-$199.** 4437 Bonney Rd 23462. I-264 exit 17B (Independence Blvd/Pembroke Area), just n to Bonney Rd, then just e. Int corridors. **Pets:** Accepted. ECO 🛜 🔋 💻

△△△ ▽▽▽ **DoubleTree by Hilton Hotel Virginia Beach** 🅷 🐾
(757) 422-8900. **$69-$249.** 1900 Pavilion Dr 23451. I-264 exit 22 (Birdneck Rd), just e. Int corridors. **Pets:** Medium, other species. $25 daily fee/room. Service with restrictions, crate.
ECO SAVE 🛜 🔋 💻 🍴 🏊

▽▽▽▽ **The Founders Inn and Spa** 🅷
(757) 424-5511. **$119-$239, 3 day notice.** 5641 Indian River Rd 23464. I-64 exit 286B, just e; on campus of Christian Broadcasting Network & Regent University. Int corridors. **Pets:** Accepted.
ECO 🛜 ✕ 🔋 💻 🍴 🏊 ✕

▽▽▽▽ **Homewood Suites by Hilton** 🅷
(757) 552-0080. **$109-$299.** 5733 Cleveland St 23462. I-264 exit 15 (Newtown Rd N), just n. Int corridors. **Pets:** Other species. $75 one-time fee/room. Service with restrictions, crate. ECO 🛜 🔋 💻 🏊 ✕

▽▽▽▽ **La Quinta Inn & Suites Virginia Beach** 🅷
(757) 428-2203. **$83-$306.** 2800 Pacific Ave 23451. I-264 0.5 mi n of terminus. Int corridors. **Pets:** Medium, other species. Service with restrictions, supervision. 🛜 🔥M 🔋 💻 🏊

▽▽ ▽▽ **Red Roof Inn VA Beach (Norfolk Airport)** 🅼
(757) 460-6700. **$50-$170.** 5745 Northampton Blvd 23455. I-64 exit 282, 1 mi n on US 13 (Northampton Blvd). Ext corridors. **Pets:** Large, other species. No service, supervision. 🛜 🔋 💻 🏊

▽▽▽ **Residence Inn Virginia Beach Oceanfront** 🅷
(757) 425-1141. **$129-$339, 3 day notice.** 3217 Atlantic Ave 23451. I-264 1.5 mi n of terminus; jct 33rd St. Int corridors. **Pets:** Accepted.
ECO 🛜 ✕ 🔥M 🔋 💻 🏊

△△△ ▽▽▽▽ **Sheraton Virginia Beach Oceanfront Hotel** 🅷
(757) 425-9000. **$259-$329, 3 day notice.** 3501 Atlantic Ave 23451. I-264 1 mi n of terminus; jct 36th St. Int corridors. **Pets:** Accepted.
ECO SAVE 🛜 ✕ 🔋 💻 🍴 🏊 ✕

△△△ ▽▽ ▽▽ **TownePlace Suites By Marriott** 🅷
(757) 490-9367. **$109-$179.** 5757 Cleveland St 23462. I-64 exit 284B to I-264 (Virginia Beach-Norfolk Expwy) exit Newtown Rd N. Int corridors. **Pets:** Medium. $100 one-time fee/room. Service with restrictions.
ECO SAVE 🛜 ✕ 🔥M 🔋 💻 🏊

△△△ ▽▽▽▽ **The Westin Virginia Beach Town Center** 🅷
(757) 557-0550. **$99-$299.** 4535 Commerce St 23462. I-264 exit 17B (Independence Blvd), just n, then just e. Int corridors. **Pets:** Small, dogs only. Service with restrictions, supervision.
ECO SAVE 🛜 ✕ 🔋 💻 🍴 🏊

△△△ ▽▽▽▽ **Wyndham Virginia Beach Oceanfront** 🅷
(757) 428-7025. **$79-$289, 3 day notice.** 5700 Atlantic Ave 23451. I-264 2.2 mi n of terminus. Int corridors. **Pets:** Medium, dogs only. $25 daily fee/pet. Designated rooms, service with restrictions.
ECO SAVE 🛜 ✕ 🔥M 🔋 💻 🍴 🏊 ✕

END AREA

HARRISONBURG

▽▽ ▽▽ **Candlewood Suites Harrisonburg** 🅷
(540) 437-1400. **$99-$299, 7 day notice.** 1560 Country Club Rd 22802. I-81 exit 247, just e. Int corridors. **Pets:** Medium. $50 one-time fee/room. Service with restrictions, supervision. ECO 🛜 🔋 💻

▽▽▽▽ **Comfort Inn** 🅷
(540) 433-6066. **$75-$109.** 1440 E Market St 22801. I-81 exit 247A, just e. Int corridors. **Pets:** Other species. $15 daily fee/room. Service with restrictions, supervision. ECO 🛜 🔋 💻 🏊

▽▽▽ **Days Inn Harrisonburg** 🅼
(540) 433-9353. **$61-$203.** 1131 Forest Hill Rd 22801. I-81 exit 245, just e; truck parking on premises. Int corridors. **Pets:** Medium. $10 one-time fee/pet. Service with restrictions, supervision. 🛜 🔋 💻 🏊

▽▽ ▽▽ **Harrisonburg Econo Lodge** 🅼
(540) 433-2576. **$60-$200.** 1703 E Market St 22801. I-81 exit 247A, 0.5 mi e on US 33. Ext/int corridors. **Pets:** Accepted. 🛜 🔋 💻 🏊

▽▽ ▽▽ **Microtel Inn & Suites** 🅷
(540) 437-3777. **$84-$130.** 85 Pleasant Valley Rd 22801. I-81 exit 243, just w. Int corridors. **Pets:** Accepted. 🛜 ✕ 🔋 💻

▽▽ ▽▽ **Ramada** 🅷
(540) 434-9981. **$59-$161.** 1 Pleasant Valley Rd 22801. I-81 exit 243, just w, then just n on US 11. Ext corridors. **Pets:** Accepted.
🛜 🔋 💻 🏊

△△△ ▽▽ ▽▽ **Residence Inn by Marriott Harrisonburg** 🅷
(540) 437-7426. **$113-$180.** 1945 Deyerle Ave 22801. I-81 exit 245, just e. Int corridors. **Pets:** Other species. $100 one-time fee/room. Service with restrictions. SAVE 🛜 ✕ 🔋 💻 🏊 ✕

△△△ ▽▽ ▽▽ **Sleep Inn & Suites** 🅷
(540) 433-7100. **$67-$259.** 1891 Evelyn Byrd Ave 22801. I-81 exit 247A, 0.5 mi e on US 33 to University Blvd, 0.3 mi s to Evelyn Byrd Ave, then just w. Int corridors. **Pets:** Accepted. ECO SAVE 🛜 🔋 💻

△△△ ▽▽ ▽▽ **Super 8** 🅼
(540) 433-8888. **$49-$89, 3 day notice.** 3330 S Main St 22801. I-81 exit 243, just e, then just s on US 11. Int corridors. **Pets:** Medium. $10 daily fee/pet. Designated rooms, no service, supervision. SAVE 🛜 🔋

△△△ ▽▽▽▽ **The Village Inn** 🅷
(540) 434-7355. **$75-$89.** 4979 S Valley Pike 22801. I-81 exit 240 southbound, 0.6 mi w on US 11; exit 243 northbound, just w to US 11, then 1.7 mi s. Ext corridors. **Pets:** Other species. $10 daily fee/pet. Service with restrictions, supervision.
ECO SAVE 🛜 🔋 💻 🍴 🏊 ✕

HILLSVILLE

△△△ ▽▽▽ **Best Western Four Seasons South** 🅼 🐾
(276) 728-4136. **$50-$150.** 57 Airport Rd 24343. I-77 exit 14, just w on US 58 and 221. Ext corridors. **Pets:** Other species. $13 daily fee/room. Designated rooms. SAVE 🛜 🔋 💻 🏊

AAA ▼▼▼▼ Quality Inn **H**
(276) 728-2120. **$79-$169.** 85 Airport Rd 24343. I-77 exit 14, just w on US 58 and 221. Ext corridors. **Pets:** Medium, other species. $10 daily fee/pet. Designated rooms, service with restrictions, supervision.
(SAVE) 📶 🅱 🖥 🏊

HOPEWELL

▼▼ Candlewood Suites **H**
(804) 541-0200. **Call for rates.** 5113 Plaza Dr 23860. I-295 exit 9B (SR 36), just w. Int corridors. **Pets:** Large, other species. $25 daily fee/pet. Service with restrictions. 📶 🅱 🖥

▼▼▼ Fairfield Inn & Suites by Marriott **H**
(804) 458-2600. **$98-$108.** 3952 Courthouse Rd 23860. I-295 exit 9A (SR 36), just e. Int corridors. **Pets:** Medium, other species. $50 one-time fee/pet. Designated rooms, service with restrictions, crate.
📶 ✕ 🅱 🖥 🏊

HOT SPRINGS

▼▼▼ ▼▼▼ The Homestead **H**
(540) 839-1766. **$185-$400, 7 day notice.** 1766 Homestead Dr 24445. Center. Int corridors. **Pets:** Accepted. (ECO) 📶 ✕ 🍽 🏊 ✕

HUDDLESTON

▼▼▼ Mariners Landing **CO**
(540) 297-4900. **$99-$269, 7 day notice.** 1217 Graves Harbor Tr 24104. On SR 626; on Smith Mountain Lake. Ext/int corridors.
Pets: Accepted. 📶 ✕ 🅱 🖥 🍽 🏊 ✕

IRVINGTON

AAA ▼▼▼▼ The Tides Inn **H**
(804) 438-5000. **$210-$395, 7 day notice.** 480 King Carter Dr 22480. 0.3 mi w of SR 200. Ext/int corridors. **Pets:** Accepted.
(ECO) (SAVE) 📶 ✕ 🅱 🖥 🍽 🏊 ✕

KESWICK

▼▼▼▼ Keswick Hall at Monticello **H**
(434) 979-3440. **$195-$765, 7 day notice.** 701 Club Dr 22947. I-64 exit 129, just n. Int corridors. **Pets:** Medium. $75 one-time fee/pet. Designated rooms, service with restrictions, crate.
📶 ✕ 🅱 🍽 🏊 ✕

LAWRENCEVILLE

▼▼▼▼ Brunswick Mineral Springs B & B Circa 1785 **BB**
(434) 848-4010. **Call for rates.** 14910 Western Mill Rd 23868. 5 mi e on US 58, 1 mi s on SR 712, then just e. Int corridors. **Pets:** Accepted.
📶 ✕ 🅱 🖥 🏊

LEBANON

▼▼ Lebanon Super 8 **M**
(276) 889-1800. **$65-$85.** 71 Townview Dr 24266. Just e on SR 654 from US 19 Bypass. Int corridors. **Pets:** Accepted. 📶 🅱 🖥

LEXINGTON

AAA ▼▼▼ Best Western Lexington Inn **M**
(540) 458-3020. **$69-$180.** 850 N Lee Hwy 24450. I-64 exit 55, just s on US 11; I-81 exit 191, 1.6 mi w. Ext corridors. **Pets:** Accepted.
(SAVE) 📶 🅱 🖥

AAA ▼▼▼▼ Best Western Plus Inn at Hunt
Ridge **H** ❧
(540) 464-1500. **$100-$200.** 25 Willow Spring Rd 24450. I-64 exit 55, just n on US 11 to SR 39; I-81 exit 191, 0.6 mi w. Int corridors. **Pets:** Medium, other species. $20 one-time fee/room. Service with restrictions, supervision. (SAVE) 📶 ✕ 🅱 🖥 🍽 🏊

▼▼ Comfort Inn-Virginia Horse Center **H**
(540) 463-7311. **Call for rates.** 62 Comfort Way 24450. I-64 exit 55, just s on US 11; I-81 exit 191, 0.6 mi w. Int corridors. **Pets:** Medium, other species. $25 one-time fee/room. Service with restrictions, supervision. 📶 🅱 🖥 🏊

▼▼ Economy Inn **M**
(540) 463-7371. **Call for rates.** 65 Econo Ln 24450. I-81 exit 191, just s on US 11. Ext corridors. **Pets:** Accepted. 📶 🅱 🖥

▼▼▼ Holiday Inn Express **H** ❧
(540) 463-7351. **$99-$149.** 880 N Lee Hwy 24450. I-64 exit 55, just s on US 11; I-81 exit 191, 1 mi w. Int corridors. **Pets:** Large, other species. $25 one-time fee/room. Service with restrictions, supervision.
📶 🅱 🖥

AAA ▼▼▼ Howard Johnson Inn **H**
(540) 463-9181. **$63-$189.** 2836 N Lee Hwy 24450. I-81 exit 195, just s on US 11. Int corridors. **Pets:** Accepted. (SAVE) 📶 🅱 🖥 🏊

AAA ▼▼▼ Quality Inn & Suites **H**
(540) 463-6400. **$60-$250.** 2814 N Lee Hwy 24450. I-81 exit 195, just sw on US 11. Int corridors. **Pets:** Medium, other species. $10 daily fee/pet. Designated rooms, service with restrictions, supervision.
(SAVE) 📶 🅱 🖥 🏊

AAA ▼▼▼ Sleep Inn & Suites **H**
(540) 463-6000. **$77-$250, 3 day notice.** 95 Maury River Rd 24450. I-64 exit 55, just n. Int corridors. **Pets:** Medium. $15 daily fee/pet. Service with restrictions, supervision. (SAVE) 📶 ✕ 🅱 🖥 🏊

▼▼ Super 8 Lexington **M**
(540) 463-7858. **$69-$99.** 1139 N Lee Hwy 24450. I-64 exit 55, just n. Int corridors. **Pets:** Accepted. 📶 🅱 🖥

LOW MOOR

▼▼ Oak Tree Inn **M**
(540) 965-0090. **$79-$89.** 123 Westvaco Rd 24457. I-64 exit 21, just s. Int corridors. **Pets:** Accepted. 📶 🅱 🖥

LURAY

▼▼ Days Inn-Luray **M**
(540) 743-4521. **$63-$144.** 138 Whispering Hill Rd 22835. US 211 Bypass, 1.7 mi e of jct US 340. Ext/int corridors. **Pets:** Accepted.
📶 🅱 🖥 🏊 ✕

LYNCHBURG

AAA ▼▼▼ Best Western Lynchburg **M** ❧
(434) 237-2986. **$85-$90.** 2815 Candlers Mountain Rd 24502. Jct US 29 and 460. Ext corridors. **Pets:** Large, dogs only. $10 daily fee/room. Service with restrictions. (SAVE) 📶 🅱 🖥 🏊

▼▼ Econo Lodge **M**
(434) 847-1045. **Call for rates.** 2400 Stadium Rd 24501. US 29 business route exit 4 southbound; exit 6 northbound, just w on James St, then just n. Ext corridors. **Pets:** Accepted. 📶 🅱 🖥

▼▼ Extended StayAmerica - Lynchburg - University
Blvd **M** ❧
(434) 239-8863. **$62-$75.** 1910 University Blvd 24502. US 460 exit Candlers Mountain Rd/University Blvd. Int corridors. **Pets:** Other species. $25 daily fee/pet. Service with restrictions. 📶 🅱 🖥

▼▼ Hampton Inn **H**
(434) 237-2704. **$104-$108.** 5604 Seminole Ave 24502. US 460 exit Candlers Mountain Rd, 0.3 mi w; US 29 exit Candlers Mountain Rd. Ext/int corridors. **Pets:** Accepted. 📶 🅱 🖥

▼▼▼ Holiday Inn Downtown **H**
(434) 528-2500. **$89-$139.** 601 Main St 24504. US 29 business route exit 1 (Main St), just w; downtown. Int corridors. **Pets:** Accepted.
📶 ✕ 🅱 🖥 🍽 🏊

▼▼▼▼ **Holiday Inn Express** Ⓗ
(434) 237-7771. **$95-$129.** 5600 Seminole Ave 24502. US 460 exit Candlers Mountain Rd, 0.3 mi w; US 29 business route exit Candlers Mountain Rd. Int corridors. **Pets:** Medium, other species. $50 one-time fee/room. Designated rooms, service with restrictions, crate.

🛜 ✕ 🔋 💻 ⇆

▼▼▼▼ **Kirkley Hotel & Conference Center** Ⓗ
(434) 237-6333. **$89-$199.** 2900 Candlers Mountain Rd 24502. US 29 business route exit 8A, just w. Int corridors. **Pets:** Accepted.

🅴🅲🅾 🛜 🔋 💻 🍽 ⇆

🅰🅰🅰 ▼▼▼ **Quality Inn Lynchburg** Ⓗ
(434) 847-9041. **$80-$200.** 3125 Albert Lankford Dr 24501. US 29 business route exit 7, just s. Int corridors. **Pets:** Medium. $25 one-time fee/pet. Designated rooms, service with restrictions, supervision.

ⓈⒶⓋⒺ 🛜 🔋 💻 ⇆

MARTINSVILLE

▼▼▼▼ **Comfort Inn Martinsville** Ⓗ
(276) 666-6835. **$89-$95.** 1895 Virginia Ave 24112. Jct US 58, 2.4 mi n on US 220 business route. Int corridors. **Pets:** Accepted.

🛜 🔋 💻 ⇆

▼▼ **Econo Lodge** Ⓗ
(276) 632-5611. **Call for rates.** US 220 Business Rt S 24112. Jct US 58, 2.3 mi n. Ext corridors. **Pets:** Accepted. 🛜 🔋 💻 🍽 ⇆

▼▼▼▼ **Hampton Inn** Ⓗ
(276) 647-4700. **$94-$104.** 50 Hampton Dr 24112. Jct US 58, 2.5 mi n on US 220 business route. Int corridors. **Pets:** Accepted.

🛜 🔋 💻 ⇆

MAX MEADOWS

▼▼ **Super 8** Ⓜ
(276) 637-4141. **$49-$79.** 194 Ft Chiswell Rd 24360. I-77/81 exit 80, just e. Ext corridors. **Pets:** Accepted. 🛜 🔋 💻

MIDDLETOWN

▼▼ **Super 8** Ⓗ
(540) 868-1800. **$52-$72.** 91 Reliance Rd 22645. I-81 exit 302. Int corridors. **Pets:** Accepted. 🛜 🔋 💻 ⇆

MINT SPRING

▼▼ **Days Inn-Staunton** Ⓜ
(540) 337-3031. **$63-$135.** 372 White Hill Rd 24401. I-81 exit 217, just e on SR 654. Ext corridors. **Pets:** Accepted. 🛜 🔋 💻 ⇆

MOUNT JACKSON

🅰🅰🅰 ▼▼▼ **Super 8 - Mt. Jackson** Ⓜ
(540) 477-2911. **$59-$89.** 250 Conicville Blvd 22842. I-81 exit 273, just e. Ext corridors. **Pets:** Accepted. ⓈⒶⓋⒺ 🛜 🔋 💻 ⇆

▼▼▼▼ **The Widow Kip's** ⒷⒷ 🐾
(540) 477-2400. **$110-$135, 5 day notice.** 355 Orchard Dr 22842. I-81 exit 273, 1.5 mi s on US 11, just w on SR 263, then just sw on SR 698. Int corridors. **Pets:** Other species. $20 daily fee/pet. Designated rooms, no service. 🅴🅲🅾 🛜 ✕ 🔋 💻 ⇆

NEW CHURCH

▼▼▼▼ **The Garden & The Sea Inn** ⒷⒷ 🐾
(757) 894-9097. **$110-$235, 10 day notice.** 4188 Nelson Rd 23415. US 13, 0.3 mi n, just w on CR 710 (Nelson Rd). Int corridors. **Pets:** Other species. $25 one-time fee/room. 🅴🅲🅾 🛜 ✕ 🔋 💻 ⇆ 🄯

NORTON

▼▼ **Super 8-Norton** Ⓜ
(276) 679-0893. **$49-$99.** 425 Wharton Ln 24273. Jct US 58 and 23. Int corridors. **Pets:** Accepted. 🛜 🔋 💻

ONANCOCK

🅰🅰🅰 ▼▼▼ **1890 Spinning Wheel Bed & Breakfast** ⒷⒷ 🐾
(757) 787-7311. **$85-$125, 5 day notice.** 31 North St 23417. Just n of jct Market (SR 179) and North sts. Int corridors. **Pets:** Large, other species. $15 daily fee/room. Designated rooms, service with restrictions, supervision. 🅴🅲🅾 ⓈⒶⓋⒺ 🛜 ✕ 🆆 🄯

ORANGE

▼▼▼▼ **Mayhurst Inn** ⒷⒷ 🐾
(540) 672-5597. **$179-$245, 10 day notice.** 12460 Mayhurst Ln 22960. On US 15, 0.5 mi s of town from SR 20 at the divided highway. Int corridors. **Pets:** Other species. $25 one-time fee/room. Designated rooms.

🅴🅲🅾 🛜 ✕ 🔋 💻 🄯

POUNDING MILL

▼▼▼ **Claypool Hill Holiday Inn Express Hotel & Suites** Ⓗ
(276) 596-9880. **$96-$151.** 180 Clay Dr 24637. 0.5 mi e of US 19/460. Int corridors. **Pets:** Accepted. 🛜 🔋 💻 ⇆

▼ **Claypool Hill Super 8** Ⓜ
(276) 964-9888. **$59-$89.** 12367 Governor GC Peery Hwy 24637. 0.3 mi w on US 19/460. Int corridors. **Pets:** Accepted. 🛜 🔋 💻

RADFORD

🅰🅰🅰 ▼▼▼▼ **Best Western Radford Inn** Ⓗ 🐾
(540) 639-3000. **$79-$129.** 1501 Tyler Ave 24141. I-81 exit 109, 2.7 mi nw on SR 177. Int corridors. **Pets:** $10 one-time fee/pet. Designated rooms, service with restrictions, supervision.

ⓈⒶⓋⒺ 🛜 🔋 💻 🍽 ⇆ ✕

🅰🅰🅰 ▼▼▼ **La Quinta Inn Radford** Ⓜ
(540) 633-6800. **$84-$174.** 1450 Tyler Ave 24141. I-81 exit 109, 2.6 mi w on SR 177. Int corridors. **Pets:** Medium, other species. Service with restrictions, supervision. ⓈⒶⓋⒺ 🛜 ✕ 🔋 💻 🍽

▼▼▼ **Super 8-Radford** Ⓜ
(540) 731-9355. **$49-$99.** 1600 Tyler Ave 24141. I-81 exit 109, just w. Int corridors. **Pets:** Accepted. 🛜 🔋 💻

RAPHINE

🅰🅰🅰 ▼▼▼ **Days Inn-Shenandoah Valley** Ⓜ
(540) 377-2604. **$67-$126.** 584 Oakland Cir 24472. I-81 exit 205, just sw. Int corridors. **Pets:** Medium, other species. $10 daily fee/pet. Designated rooms, service with restrictions, supervision.

ⓈⒶⓋⒺ 🛜 🔋 💻 ⇆

RICHMOND METROPOLITAN AREA

CHESTER

🅰🅰🅰 ▼▼▼▼ **Fairfield Inn By Marriott** Ⓗ
(804) 778-7500. **$80-$103.** 12400 Redwater Creek Rd 23831. I-95 exit 61B, just w of jct SR 10. Int corridors. **Pets:** Medium. $25 one-time fee/room. Designated rooms, service with restrictions, supervision.

ⓈⒶⓋⒺ 🛜 ✕ 🅶🅼 🔋 💻 ⇆

▼▼▼▼ **Residence Inn by Marriott** Ⓗ
(804) 530-5501. **$129-$169.** 800 Bermuda Hundred Rd 23836. I-295 exit 15, just w; in River's Bend. Int corridors. **Pets:** Accepted.

🅴🅲🅾 🛜 ✕ 🔋 💻 ⇆ ✕

CHESTERFIELD

▼▼▼ La Quinta Inn Richmond South ⊞
(804) 743-0770. **$93-$184.** 9040 Pams Ave 23237. I-95 exit 64, just w. Int corridors. **Pets:** Medium, other species. Service with restrictions, supervision. [SAVE] 🛜 ⛫ 📟

COLONIAL HEIGHTS

▼▼▼ Candlewood Suites ⊞
(804) 526-0111. **$99-$119.** 15820 Woods Edge Rd 23834. I-95 exit 58 northbound; exit 58B southbound, just w. Int corridors. **Pets:** Accepted.
🛜 ⛫ ⊟ 📟

DOSWELL

▼▼▼ Best Western Kings Quarters ⊞ ❖
(804) 876-3321. **$70-$150, 3 day notice.** 16102 Theme Park Way 23047. I-95 exit 98, just e on SR 30; entrance to theme park. Ext corridors. **Pets:** Other species. Designated rooms, service with restrictions, supervision. [SAVE] 🛜 ⊟ 📟 🍴 ⚊ ⊠

▼▼▼ Days Inn Kings Dominion ⊞
(804) 612-8680. **$49-$94.** 16220 International St 23047. I-95 exit 98, just e on SR 30. Int corridors. **Pets:** Accepted. [SAVE] 🛜 ⊟ 📟 ⚊

▼▼▼▼ Comfort Suites ⊞
(804) 876-6900. **Call for rates.** 16280 International St 23047. I-95 exit 98, just e on SR 30. Int corridors. **Pets:** Accepted.
[SAVE] 🛜 ⊠ ⛫ ⊟ 📟 ⚊

GLEN ALLEN

▼▼▼▼ Aloft Richmond West ⊞
(804) 433-1888. **$99-$250.** 3939 Duckling Dr 23060. I-64 exit 178B, just w on W Broad St. Int corridors. **Pets:** Accepted.
[SAVE] 🛜 ⊠ ⊟ 📟 ⚊

▼▼▼▼ Best Western Plus Glen Allen Inn ⊞
(804) 266-3500. **$70-$140.** 8507 Brook Rd 23060. I-95 exit 83B, 0.5 mi w to Brook Rd, then just n. Int corridors. **Pets:** Medium. $20 daily fee/pet. Designated rooms, service with restrictions, supervision.
[SAVE] 🛜 ⛫ ⊟ 📟 ⚊

▼▼▼▼ Candlewood Suites ⊞
(804) 262-2240. **$89-$129.** 10609 Telegraph Rd 23059. I-295 exit 43C, 1.7 mi n to JEB Stuart Pkwy, just w to Telegraph Rd; I-95 exit 86B (SR 656/Elmont), just w, 1 mi s. Int corridors. **Pets:** Accepted.
🛜 ⛫ ⊟ 📟

▼▼▼ Candlewood Suites Richmond-West ⊞
(804) 364-2000. **$75-$109.** 4120 Brookriver Dr 23060. I-64 exit 178, just w on W Broad St. Int corridors. **Pets:** Medium. $50 one-time fee/pet. Service with restrictions, supervision. 🛜 ⛫ ⊟ 📟

▼▼▼ Holiday Inn Express ⊞
(804) 934-9300. **$89-$109.** 9933 Mayland Dr 23233. I-64 exit 180B, just n to Mayland Dr, then just w. Int corridors. **Pets:** Accepted.
🛜 ⛫ ⊟ 📟 ⚊

▼▼▼ Residence Inn by Marriott ⊞
(804) 762-9852. **$90-$152.** 3940 Westerre Pkwy 23233. I-64 exit 180, n on Gaskins Rd to W Broad St. Int corridors. **Pets:** $75 one-time fee/room. Designated rooms, service with restrictions.
🛜 ⊠ ⛫ ⊟ 📟 ⚊ ⊠

▼▼▼ TownePlace Suites by Marriott ⊞
(804) 747-5253. **$85-$110.** 4231 Park Place Ct 23060. I-64 exit 178B, just e on W Broad St to Cox Rd, then just n to Innslake Dr; in Innsbrook Corporate Center. Int corridors. **Pets:** Cats only. $75 one-time fee/room. Service with restrictions. [ECO] [SAVE] 🛜 ⊠ ⛫ ⊟ 📟 ⚊

MECHANICSVILLE

▼▼▼ Hampton Inn ⊞
(804) 559-0559. **$99-$229.** 7433 Bell Creek Rd 23111. I-295 exit 37A (US 360 E) to Bell Creek Rd, just n. Int corridors. **Pets:** Accepted.
🛜 ⛫ ⊟ 📟 ⚊

RICHMOND

▼▼▼▼ The Berkeley Hotel ⊞
(804) 780-1300. **$150-$289.** 1200 E Cary St 23219. Just s of State Capitol; jct 12th St. Int corridors. **Pets:** Small, other species. $50 one-time fee/room. Designated rooms, service with restrictions, crate.
[SAVE] 🛜 ⊠ ⊟ 📟 🍴

▼▼▼▼ Best Western Plus Governors Inn ⊞
(804) 323-0007. **$90-$150.** 9826 Midlothian Tpke 23235. US 60, 1.5 mi w of jct Powhite Pkwy. Int corridors. **Pets:** Accepted.
[SAVE] 🛜 ⊟ 📟 ⚊

▼▼▼ Candlewood Suites ⊞
(804) 271-0016. **$72-$92.** 4301 Commerce Rd 23234. I-95 exit 69, just n. Int corridors. **Pets:** Accepted. 🛜 ⛫ ⊟ 📟

▼▼▼▼ Comfort Inn Midlothian Turnpike ⊞
(804) 320-8900. **$79-$119.** 8710 Midlothian Tpke 23235. Jct Powhite Pkwy (US 76) and Midlothian Tpke (US 60), just e. Int corridors.
Pets: Accepted. [SAVE] 🛜 ⊟ 📟

▼▼▼▼ Commonwealth Park Suites ⊞
(804) 343-7300. **$139-$159.** 901 Bank St 23219. Jct 9th and Bank sts. Int corridors. **Pets:** Dogs only. $50 daily fee/room. Designated rooms, service with restrictions, supervision.
[ECO] [SAVE] 🛜 ⊟ 📟 🍴 ⊠

▼▼ Extended Stay Deluxe Richmond- I-64 - W Broad St ⊞ ❖
(804) 285-7050. **$75-$90.** 6807 Paragon Pl 23230. I-64 exit 183C (W Broad St), just w to Glenside Dr, just n. Int corridors. **Pets:** Other species. $25 daily fee/pet. Service with restrictions. 🛜 ⊟ 📟 ⚊

▼▼▼▼ Hilton Richmond Hotel & Spa/Short Pump ⊞ ❖
(804) 364-3600. **Call for rates.** 12042 W Broad St 23233. I-64 exit 178, 2 mi w. Int corridors. **Pets:** Medium. $50 one-time fee/room. Designated rooms, service with restrictions, crate.
[ECO] [SAVE] 🛜 ⛫ ⊟ 🍴 ⚊ ⊠

▼▼ Homestead Studio Suites Hotel-Richmond/Midlothian ⊞ ❖
(804) 272-1800. **$60-$70.** 241 Arboretum Pl 23236. Jct Powhite Pkwy (US 76) and Midlothian Tpke (US 60), just w. Int corridors. **Pets:** Other species. $25 daily fee/pet. Service with restrictions. 🛜 ⛫ ⊟ 📟

▼▼▼▼ The Jefferson Hotel ⊞ ❖
(804) 788-8000. **$235-$395.** 101 W Franklin St 23220. Jct Franklin and Adams sts; center. Int corridors. **Pets:** Dogs only. $50 daily fee/pet. Service with restrictions. [ECO] [SAVE] 🛜 ⊠ ⊟ 🍴 ⚊ ⊠

▼▼▼ Omni Richmond Hotel ⊞
(804) 344-7000. **$139-$309.** 100 S 12th St 23219. I-95 exit 74A (downtown expwy I-195) exit Canal St; in James Center. Int corridors.
Pets: Accepted. [ECO] 🛜 ⛫ ⊟ 📟 🍴 ⚊

▼▼ Quality Inn West End ⊞
(804) 346-0000. **$89-$99.** 8008 W Broad St 23294. I-64 exit 183C (W Broad St) westbound; exit 183 eastbound, 1.5 mi w. Int corridors.
Pets: Accepted. 🛜 ⊟ 📟 ⚊

▼▼▼ Ramada Plaza Richmond West ⊞
(804) 285-2000. **Call for rates.** 6624 W Broad St 23230. I-64 exit 183 eastbound; exit 183B westbound. Int corridors. **Pets:** Accepted.
🛜 ⊠ ⛫ ⊟ 📟 🍴 ⚊

▼▼ Red Roof Inn-Richmond South Ⓜ
(804) 271-7240. **$50-$100.** 4350 Commerce Rd 23234. I-95 exit 69. Ext corridors. **Pets:** Large, other species. No service, supervision.
[SAVE] 🛜 ⊟

 **Sheraton Richmond Park South Hotel** 🏨 ❀

(804) 323-1144. **$89-$309.** 9901 Midlothian Tpke 23235. US 60, 1 mi w of Powhite Pkwy (US 76). Int corridors. **Pets:** Other species. Service with restrictions, supervision.

[ECO] [SAVE] 🛜 ✕ 👤M 🛏 💻 🍽 🏊 ✕

Super 8 M

(804) 262-8880. **$59-$89.** 5615 Chamberlayne Rd 23227. I-95 exit 82. Int corridors. **Pets:** Other species. $10 daily fee/pet. Service with restrictions, supervision. 🛜 🛏 💻

The Westin Richmond 🏨 ❀

(804) 282-8444. **$189-$219, 3 day notice.** 6631 W Broad St 23230. I-64 exit 183 eastbound; exit 183B westbound; in Reynolds Crossing. Int corridors. **Pets:** Medium, dogs only. Designated rooms, service with restrictions, supervision.

[ECO] [SAVE] 🛜 ✕ 👤M 🛏 💻 🍽 🏊 ✕

SANDSTON

Candlewood Suites Richmond Airport 🏨

(804) 652-1888. **$72-$90, 3 day notice.** 5400 Audubon Dr 23231. I-64 exit 197A (Sandston-RIC Airport), 1 mi w. Int corridors. **Pets:** $150 one-time fee/room. Service with restrictions, crate. [ECO] 🛜 👤M 🛏 💻

END METROPOLITAN AREA

ROANOKE

 **Best Western Plus Inn at Valley View** 🏨

(540) 362-2400. **$65-$140.** 5050 Valley View Blvd 24012. I-581 exit 3E, just e, then just s via shopping center exit. Int corridors. **Pets:** Large, dogs only. $25 one-time fee/room. Designated rooms, service with restrictions, crate. [SAVE] 🛜 ✕ 🛏 💻 🏊

Comfort Inn Airport 🏨

(540) 527-2020. **$89-$169.** 5070 Valley View Blvd 24012. I-81 exit 143 to I-581 exit 3, e to Hershberger Rd. Int corridors. **Pets:** Accepted.

🛜 ✕ 🛏 💻 🏊

Days Inn M

(540) 366-0341. **$63-$225.** 8118 Plantation Rd 24019. I-81 exit 146, just e on SR 115. Ext/int corridors. **Pets:** Other species. $15 one-time fee/room. Service with restrictions, supervision. [SAVE] 🛜 🛏 💻 🏊

Holiday Inn Roanoke Valley View 🏨 ❀

(540) 362-4500. **$79-$139.** 3315 Ordway Dr 24017. I-581 exit 3W, just w to Ordway Dr, then 0.6 mi n via service road. Int corridors. **Pets:** $25 one-time fee/room, $10 daily fee/room. Service with restrictions, crate.

[ECO] 🛜 🛏 💻 🍽 🏊 ✕

Holiday Inn Tanglewood/Roanoke 🏨

(540) 774-4400. **$99-$149.** 4468 Starkey Rd 24018. I-581 exit US 220 (Franklin Rd/Salem), 0.8 mi s on SR 419 (Electric Rd). Int corridors. **Pets:** Medium. $35 one-time fee/room. Designated rooms, service with restrictions, supervision. [ECO] 🛜 🛏 💻 🍽 🏊

MainStay Suites Roanoke Airport 🏨

(540) 527-3030. **$99-$130.** 5080 Valley View Blvd 24012. I-581 exit 3E, just n. Int corridors. **Pets:** Medium, dogs only. $40 one-time fee/room. Service with restrictions, supervision. 🛜 🛏 💻

Quality Inn Roanoke-Airport M

(540) 366-8861. **Call for rates.** 6626 Thirlane Rd 24019. I-581 exit 2 southbound, just s on SR 117 (Peters Creek Rd), then just w. Ext corridors. **Pets:** Accepted. [SAVE] 🛜 🛏 💻 🍽 🏊 ✕

Quality Inn/Tanglewood M

(540) 989-4000. **Call for rates.** 3816 Franklin Rd SW 24014. I-581 exit US 220 (Franklin Rd/Salem), just n on US 220 business route, then w on Frontage Rd. Ext corridors. **Pets:** Large. $15 daily fee/pet. Service with restrictions. [SAVE] 🛜 🛏 💻

Residence Inn Roanoke Airport 🏨

(540) 265-1119. **$143-$161.** 3305 Ordway Dr NW 24017. I-581 exit 3W, just s. Int corridors. **Pets:** Accepted.

🛜 ✕ 👤M 🛏 💻 🏊 ✕

Sleep Inn Tanglewood 🏨

(540) 772-1500. **$80-$100.** 4045 Electric Rd 24018. I-581 exit US 220 (Franklin Rd/Salem), 0.7 mi n on SR 419. Int corridors. **Pets:** Small, dogs only. $25 daily fee/pet. Designated rooms, service with restrictions, supervision. [SAVE] 🛜 🛏 💻

Super 8 M

(540) 563-8888. **$54-$79, 7 day notice.** 6616 Thirlane Rd 24019. I-581 exit 25, s on SR 117 (Peters Creek Rd), then just w. Int corridors. **Pets:** Medium. $10 daily fee/pet. Service with restrictions, crate.

🛜 🛏 💻

ROCKY MOUNT

Comfort Inn-Rocky Mount 🏨

(540) 489-4000. **Call for rates.** 1730 N Main St 24151. 1.5 mi n on US 220 business route. Int corridors. **Pets:** $25 one-time fee/room. Service with restrictions, supervision. 🛜 🛏 💻 🏊

Holiday Inn Express Hotel & Suites 🏨

(540) 489-5001. **$90-$140.** 395 Old Franklin Tpke 24151. US 220 S, just e on SR 40. Int corridors. **Pets:** Accepted. 🛜 🛏 💻 🏊

RUTHER GLEN

Super 8-Ruther Glen M

(804) 448-2608. **$44-$74.** 24011 Ruther Glen Rd 22546. I-95 exit 104 (SR 207), just e on Rogers Clark Blvd. Ext corridors. **Pets:** Accepted.

🛜 🛏 💻 🏊

SALEM

Comfort Suites Inn at Ridgewood Farm 🏨

(540) 375-4800. **$78-$129.** 2898 Keagy Rd 24153. I-81 exit 141, 4.7 mi s on SR 419, then just w. Int corridors. **Pets:** Accepted.

🛜 ✕ 🛏 💻 🏊

Days Inn M

(540) 986-1000. **$67-$180.** 1535 E Main St 24153. I-81 exit 141, 2 mi s on SR 419, then just w on US 460. Ext/int corridors. **Pets:** $15 one-time fee/room. Service with restrictions, supervision. [SAVE] 🛜 🛏 💻

La Quinta Inn Roanoke Salem 🏨

(540) 562-2717. **$84-$144.** 140 Sheraton Dr 24153. I-81 exit 141, 0.5 mi se on SR 419. Int corridors. **Pets:** Medium, other species. Service with restrictions, supervision. 🛜 🛏 💻 🏊

Quality Inn M

(540) 387-1600. **Call for rates.** 151 Wildwood Rd 24153. I-81 exit 137, 0.3 mi e on SR 112. Ext corridors. **Pets:** Accepted.

[SAVE] 🛜 🛏 💻 🏊

SOUTH BOSTON

The Berry Hill Resort and Conference Center 🏨

(434) 517-7000. **$139-$279.** 3105 River Rd S 24592. From US 501, 2.1 mi w on Greens Folly Rd (SR 654), 0.9 mi s on River Rd. Ext/int corridors. **Pets:** Accepted. 🛜 ✕ 👤M 🛏 💻 🍽 🏊 ✕

Holiday Inn Express 🏨

(434) 575-4000. **$82-$86.** 1074 Bill Tuck Hwy 24592. Just e on US 58, from jct US 501. Int corridors. **Pets:** Accepted. 🛜 👤M 🛏 💻 🏊

▼▼ Super 8 M
(434) 572-8868. **$59-$79, 3 day notice.** 1040 Bill Tuck Hwy 24592. Just e on US 58, from jct US 501. Int corridors. **Pets:** Medium. $10 daily fee/pet. Service with restrictions, supervision. 🛜 📠 💻

SOUTH HILL

▲▲▲ ▼▼▼▼ Comfort Inn & Suites H
(434) 447-2200. **$60-$90.** 250 Thompson St 23970. I-85 exit 12A, just n. Int corridors. **Pets:** Medium, other species. $20 daily fee/pet. Service with restrictions, supervision. SAVE 🛜 &M

▼▼▼▼ Fairfield Inn & Suites South Hill I-85 H
(434) 447-6800. **$85-$89.** 150 Arnold Dr 23970. I-85 exit 12A, just e on US 58. Int corridors. **Pets:** Accepted.
ECO 🛜 ✕ &M 📠 💻 ≈

▲▲▲ ▼▼▼ Quality Inn H
(434) 447-2600. **Call for rates.** 918 E Atlantic St 23970. I-85 exit 12B, just w. Ext corridors. **Pets:** Other species. $10 daily fee/pet. No service, crate. SAVE 🛜 📠 💻

STAFFORD

▲▲▲ ▼▼▼▼ Best Western Plus Aquia/Quantico Inn H
(540) 659-0022. **$99-$109.** 2868 Jefferson Davis Hwy 22554. I-95 exit 143A, jct US 1 and SR 610. Ext corridors. **Pets:** Accepted.
SAVE 🛜 📠 💻 ≈

▼▼▼ Quality Inn & Suites H 🐾
(540) 657-5566. **Call for rates.** 28 Greenspring Dr 22554. I-95 exit 143B, just w on Garrisonville Rd. Int corridors. **Pets:** Medium. $20 daily fee/pet. Service with restrictions, supervision. 🛜 📠 💻

▼▼▼▼ Staybridge Suites Stafford/Quantico H
(540) 720-2111. **$129-$169.** 2996 Jefferson Davis Hwy 22554. I-95 exit 143A, just n on US 1. Int corridors. **Pets:** Accepted.
🛜 ✕ &M 📠 💻 ≈

▲▲▲ ▼▼▼▼ TownePlace Suites by Marriott
Stafford H 🐾
(540) 657-1990. **$104-$119.** 2772 Jefferson Davis Hwy 22554. I-95 exit 143A, just s on US 1. Int corridors. **Pets:** Other species. $10 daily fee/pet. SAVE 🛜 ✕ &M 📠 💻 ≈

STAUNTON

▲▲▲ ▼▼▼ Best Western Staunton Inn H
(540) 885-1112. **$86-$125.** 92 Rowe Rd 24401. I-81 exit 222, just e on US 250. Int corridors. **Pets:** Accepted.
ECO SAVE 🛜 ✕ 📠 💻 ≈

▲▲▲ ▼▼▼ Comfort Inn H 🐾
(540) 886-5000. **$85-$139.** 1302 Richmond Ave 24401. I-81 exit 222, just w on US 250. Int corridors. **Pets:** $10 daily fee/pet. Crate.
SAVE 🛜 📠 💻 ≈

▲▲▲ ▼▼▼ Econo Lodge Staunton M
(540) 885-5158. **Call for rates.** 1031 Richmond Ave 24401. I-81 exit 222, 0.7 mi w on US 250. Ext/int corridors. **Pets:** Medium. $10 daily fee/pet. Service with restrictions, supervision. SAVE 🛜 📠 💻

▲▲▲ ▼▼▼▼ Holiday Inn Golf & Conference Center H
(540) 248-6020. **$99-$199.** 152 Fairway Ln 24401. I-81 exit 225, 0.3 mi w on SR 275 (Woodrow Wilson Pkwy). Int corridors. **Pets:** Large. $25 one-time fee/pet. Designated rooms, service with restrictions, crate.
SAVE 🛜 📠 💻 ¶ ≈

▼▼ Red Roof Inn #706 M
(540) 885-3117. **$50-$110.** 42 Sangers Ln 24401. I-81 exit 222, just e on US 250. Ext corridors. **Pets:** Large, other species. No service, supervision. 🛜 📠 💻

▼▼ Sleep Inn H 🐾
(540) 887-6500. **Call for rates.** 222 Jefferson Hwy 24401. I-81 exit 222, just e on US 250. Int corridors. **Pets:** Other species. Service with restrictions, supervision. 🛜 📠 💻

▲▲▲ ▼▼▼▼ Stonewall Jackson Hotel & Conference
Center H 🐾
(540) 885-4848. **$112-$199.** 24 S Market St 24401. Between Beverly and Johnson sts; downtown. Int corridors. **Pets:** $25 daily fee/room. Service with restrictions, supervision.
ECO SAVE 🛜 ✕ 💻 ¶ ≈ ✕

STEPHENS CITY

▲▲▲ ▼▼▼ Comfort Inn-Stephens City H
(540) 869-6500. **Call for rates.** 167 Town Run Ln 22655. I-81 exit 307, just se. Int corridors. **Pets:** Other species. $10 daily fee/pet. Service with restrictions, supervision. SAVE 🛜 📠 💻 ≈

STONY CREEK

▼▼▼ Hampton Inn-Stony Creek H
(434) 246-5500. **$80-$128.** 10476 Blue Star Hwy 23882. I-95 exit 33, 0.3 mi s on SR 301. Int corridors. **Pets:** Medium, dogs only. $25 daily fee/pet. Designated rooms, service with restrictions, supervision.
🛜 &M 📠 💻 ≈

▼▼▼ Sleep Inn & Suites H
(434) 246-5100. **$65-$130.** 11019 Blue Star Hwy 23882. I-95 exit 33, 0.3 mi s on SR 301. Int corridors. **Pets:** Small, dogs only. $15 daily fee/pet. Designated rooms, service with restrictions, supervision.
🛜 📠 💻 ≈

STRASBURG

▼▼▼ Hotel Strasburg CI
(540) 465-9191. **Call for rates.** 213 S Holliday St 22657. I-81 exit 298, 2.2 mi s on US 11, then just s. Int corridors. **Pets:** Accepted. 🛜 ¶

▼▼ Ramada H
(540) 465-2444. **$61-$99.** 21 Signal Knob Dr 22657. I-81 exit 298, just e. Int corridors. **Pets:** Accepted. 🛜 📠 💻 ¶ ≈ ✕

TAPPAHANNOCK

▼▼▼ The Essex Inn BB
(804) 443-9900. **$175-$205, 7 day notice.** 203 Duke St 22560. 0.3 mi s on US 17, then just e. Ext/int corridors. **Pets:** Accepted.
ECO 🛜 ✕ 📠 💻

▼▼ Super 8 M
(804) 443-3888. **Call for rates.** 1800 Tappahannock Blvd 22560. US 17 and 360. Int corridors. **Pets:** Accepted. 🛜 📠 💻

TROUTVILLE

▲▲▲ ▼▼▼ Comfort Inn H
(540) 992-5600. **$70-$140.** 2545 Lee Hwy S 24175. I-81 exit 150A, just s on US 11. Int corridors. **Pets:** Small. $25 one-time fee/room. Service with restrictions, crate. SAVE 🛜 📠 💻 ≈

▼▼ Red Roof Inn H
(540) 992-5055. **$50-$66.** 3231 Lee Hwy 24175. I-81 exit 150, just e. Int corridors. **Pets:** Large, other species. No service, supervision.
🛜 📠 💻 ≈

WARRENTON

▼▼▼ Holiday Inn Express Hotel & Suites H 🐾
(540) 341-3461. **$99-$239.** 410 Holiday Ct 20186. US 15/29 and 17 exit Meetze Rd (SR 643), just w, then 0.8 mi n on Walker Rd. Int corridors. **Pets:** Medium, other species. $25 daily fee/pet. Designated rooms, service with restrictions, crate. 🛜 ✕ &M 📠 💻 ≈

 **Nuevo Inn & Suites** **M**
(540) 349-8900. **$99-$139.** 7379 Comfort Inn Dr 20187. 1.5 mi n on US 15/29; on service road. Ext/int corridors. **Pets:** Small. $15 daily fee/pet. Designated rooms, service with restrictions, supervision.
[SAVE] 🛜 🚪 🖵 ⇉

WARSAW

Best Western Plus Warsaw **H**
(804) 333-1700. **$90-$103.** 4522 Richmond Rd 22572. US 360, just w of town. Int corridors. **Pets:** Small. $10 daily fee/pet. Service with restrictions, supervision. [SAVE] 🛜 🚪 🖵 ⇉

WASHINGTON

Middleton Inn **BB** ✿
(540) 675-2020. **$295-$850, 14 day notice.** 176 Main St 22747. 0.5 mi w on US 211 business route. Ext/int corridors. **Pets:** Dogs only. $60 one-time fee/pet. Designated rooms, service with restrictions, crate.
[SAVE] 🛜 ✕ 🚪 🖵

WASHINGTON, D.C. METROPOLITAN AREA

ALEXANDRIA

Comfort Inn & Suites Alexandria **H**
(703) 922-9200. **$90-$190.** 5716 S Van Dorn St 22310. I-95/495 exit 173, 2 mi e of jct I-395 and 495. Int corridors. **Pets:** Small. $25 daily fee/pet. Designated rooms, service with restrictions, supervision.
[SAVE] 🛜 🚪 🖵 ⇉

Extended StayAmerica-Washington, DC-Alexandria **M** ✿
(703) 941-9440. **$119-$339.** 205 N Breckinridge Pl 22312. I-395 exit 3B, 0.3 mi w on SR 236, 0.4 mi ne on Beauregard St, just e on Gloucester Rd, then just s. Int corridors. **Pets:** Other species. $25 daily fee/pet. Service with restrictions. 🛜 ⚴ 🚪 🖵

Hawthorn Suites by Wyndham Alexandria **H**
(703) 370-1000. **$99-$259.** 420 N Van Dorn St 22304. I-395 exit 3A, 0.3 mi e on SR 236 to S Van Dorn St, then 0.5 mi n. Int corridors.
Pets: Accepted. [SAVE] 🛜 ✕ 🚪 🖵 ⇉

Hilton Alexandria Mark Center **H**
(703) 845-1010. **$89-$399.** 5000 Seminary Rd 22311. I-395 exit 4, just w. Int corridors. **Pets:** Accepted. 🛜 ⚴ 🚪 🖵 🍴 ⇉ ✕

Holiday Inn Hotel & Suites-Historic District Alexandria **H**
(703) 548-6300. **$89-$245.** 625 First St 22314. George Washington Memorial Pkwy, just e of jct 1st and Washington sts. Int corridors.
Pets: Accepted. [ECO] [SAVE] 🛜 ✕ 🚪 🖵 🍴 ⇉ ✕

Homestead Studio Suites Hotel-Washington DC-Alexandria **H** ✿
(703) 329-3399. **$119-$339.** 200 Bluestone Rd 22304. I-95/495 exit 174 (Eisenhower Ave Connector), just n, then 1.2 mi e. Int corridors.
Pets: Other species. $25 daily fee/pet. Service with restrictions.
🛜 ⚴ 🚪 🖵

Hotel Monaco Alexandria-A Kimpton Hotel **H**
(703) 549-6080. **$149-$339.** 480 King St 22314. On SR 7; between S Pitt and S Royal sts; just sw of City Hall. Int corridors. **Pets:** Accepted.
[ECO] [SAVE] 🛜 ✕ 🚪 🖵 🍴 ✕

Lorien Hotel & Spa-A Kimpton Hotel **H**
(703) 894-3434. **Call for rates.** 1600 King St 22314. Between Harvard and Peyton sts. Int corridors. **Pets:** Accepted. [ECO] 🛜 ✕ 🍴 ✕

Morrison House-A Kimpton Hotel **H**
(703) 838-8000. **Call for rates.** 116 S Alfred St 22314. Jct King and S Alfred sts, just s. Int corridors. **Pets:** Accepted.
[ECO] [SAVE] 🛜 ✕ 🚪 🖵 🍴

Red Roof Inn-Alexandria **M**
(703) 960-5200. **$83-$125.** 5975 Richmond Hwy 22303. I-95/495 exit 177A, 0.5 mi s on US 1. Ext corridors. **Pets:** Large, other species. No service, supervision. [SAVE] 🛜 ⚴ 🚪

Residence Inn by Marriott Alexandria at Carlyle **H**
(703) 549-1155. **$98-$289.** 2345 Mill Rd 22314. I-95/495 exit 176B, just n on Telegraph Rd (SR 241 N), just e on Pershing Ave and Stovall St, then just n; in Carlyle area. Int corridors. **Pets:** Accepted.
🛜 ✕ ⚴ 🚪 🖵

Residence Inn by Marriott Alexandria-Old Town **H**
(703) 548-5474. **$107-$269.** 1456 Duke St 22314. I-95/495 exit 176, 0.5 mi n on SR 241, then 0.7 mi e on SR 236. Int corridors. **Pets:** Accepted.
🛜 ✕ ⚴ 🚪 🖵 ⇉

Sheraton Suites Old Town Alexandria **H**
(703) 836-4700. **$109-$389.** 801 N St. Asaph St 22314. Just e of Washington St. Int corridors. **Pets:** Accepted.
[ECO] [SAVE] 🛜 ✕ 🚪 🖵 🍴 ⇉ ✕

Washington Suites-Alexandria **H**
(703) 370-6200. **$99-$409.** 100 S Reynolds St 22304. I-395 exit 3A, 0.8 mi e on SR 236 E (Duke St), then just s. Int corridors. **Pets:** Medium. $20 daily fee/pet. Designated rooms.
[SAVE] 🛜 ⚴ 🚪 🖵 🍴 ⇉ ✕

The Westin Alexandria **H** ✿
(703) 253-8600. **$79-$475.** 400 Courthouse Square 22314. I-95/495 exit 176B, just n on Telegraph Rd (SR 241 N), 0.4 mi e on SR 236, then just s on Dulany St. Int corridors. **Pets:** Medium. Service with restrictions, supervision. [SAVE] 🛜 ✕ ⚴ 🚪 🖵 🍴 ⇉ ✕

ARLINGTON

Arlington Court Suites Hotel, A Clarion Collection **H**
(703) 524-4000. **$99-$249.** 1200 N Courthouse Rd 22201. 1.5 mi sw of Theodore Roosevelt Bridge on US 50. Int corridors. **Pets:** Medium. $75 one-time fee/room, $10 daily fee/room. Designated rooms, service with restrictions, crate. [SAVE] 🛜 ✕ ⚴ 🚪 🖵

Hilton Crystal City at Reagan National Airport **H**
(703) 418-6800. **$89-$269.** 2399 Jefferson Davis Hwy 22202. 1.8 mi s of 14th St Bridge on US 1. Int corridors. **Pets:** Accepted.
[SAVE] 🛜 🚪 🖵 🍴 ⇉

Hotel Palomar Arlington at Waterview **H**
(703) 351-9170. **Call for rates.** 1121 N 19th St 22209. I-66 exit 73, just sw of Key Bridge. Int corridors. **Pets:** Accepted.
[SAVE] 🛜 ✕ ⚴ 🍴

▼▼▼ Residence Inn by Marriott Arlington Capital View 🅷

(703) 415-1300. **$93-$287.** 2850 S Potomac Ave 22202. 2 mi s of 14th St Bridge on US 1; just s of jct SR 233. Int corridors. **Pets:** Accepted.
🛜 ✕ 🔊 🛏 💻 🌊

▼▼▼ Residence Inn by Marriott Arlington Courthouse 🅷 ❄

(703) 312-2100. **$89-$152.** 1401 N Adams St 22201. Jct of Clarendon Blvd and N Adams St; 1 blk from Courthouse Metro Stop (Orange Line). Int corridors. **Pets:** Medium, other species. $100 one-time fee/pet. Service with restrictions. 🅴🄲🄾 🛜 ✕ 🔊 🛏 💻 🌊 ✕

▼▼▼ Residence Inn by Marriott Arlington Rosslyn 🅷

(703) 812-8400. **$149-$289.** 1651 N Oak St 22209. I-66 exit 73, 0.3 mi s on Fort Myer Dr, 0.3 mi w on Wilson Blvd to N Pierce St, then 2 blks e on Clarendon Blvd; 2 blks from Rosslyn Metro Station. Int corridors. **Pets:** Accepted. 🛜 ✕ 🛏 💻 🌊

▼▼▼ Residence Inn by Marriott-Pentagon City 🅷

(703) 413-6630. **$97-$319.** 550 Army Navy Dr 22202. I-395 exit 8C, just 1 mi s of 14th St Bridge. Int corridors. **Pets:** Accepted.
🅴🄲🄾 ✕ 🔊 🛏 💻 🌊 ✕

▼▼▼ ▼▼▼ The Ritz-Carlton, Pentagon City 🅷 ❄

(703) 415-5000. **Call for rates.** 1250 S Hayes St 22202. 1 mi s of 14th St Bridge. Int corridors. **Pets:** Medium, dogs only. $125 one-time fee/room. Service with restrictions, supervision.
🅴🄲🄾 🛜 ✕ 🔊 🛏 💻 🍽 🌊 ✕

🅐🅐🅐 ▼▼▼ Sheraton Crystal City Hotel 🅷

(703) 486-1111. **$89-$289.** 1800 Jefferson Davis Hwy 22202. I-395 exit 8C, 1.4 mi s of 14th St Bridge on US 1; hotel entrance corner of Eads St. Int corridors. **Pets:** Large, dogs only. Service with restrictions, supervision. 🆂🅰🆅🅴 🛜 ✕ 🛏 💻 🍽

🅐🅐🅐 ▼▼▼ Sheraton National Hotel 🅷

(703) 521-1900. **$329.** 900 S Orme St 22204. I-395 exit 8A, at SR 27 and 244; 1.3 mi s of 14th St Bridge. Int corridors. **Pets:** Accepted.
🆂🅰🆅🅴 🛜 ✕ 🛏 💻 🍽 🌊

🅐🅐🅐 ▼▼▼ The Virginian Suites, an Ascend Collection hotel 🅷

(703) 522-9600. **Call for rates.** 1500 Arlington Blvd 22209. 1 mi w of Theodore Roosevelt Bridge on US 50. Int corridors. **Pets:** Accepted.
🆂🅰🆅🅴 🛜 ✕ 🛏 💻 🍽 🌊

🅐🅐🅐 ▼▼▼ The Westin Arlington Gateway 🅷

(703) 717-6200. **$139-$559.** 801 N Glebe Rd 22203. I-66 exit 71, just e on Fairfax Dr to Vermont Ave; just n of jct SR 120 and Wilson Blvd; 2 blks from Ballston Metro Station. Int corridors. **Pets:** Accepted.
🅴🄲🄾 🆂🅰🆅🅴 🛜 ✕ 🔊 🛏 💻 🍽 🌊 ✕

ASHBURN

🅐🅐🅐 ▼▼▼ Aloft Dulles North 🅷 ❄

(703) 723-6969. **$79-$239.** 22390 Flagstaff Plaza 20148. On Loudoun County Pkwy (CR 607), just s of jct SR 267 (Toll Rd) exit 7. Int corridors. **Pets:** Dogs only. Designated rooms, service with restrictions, crate.
🅴🄲🄾 🆂🅰🆅🅴 🛜 ✕ 🔊 🛏 💻 🌊

🅐🅐🅐 ▼▼▼ Homewood Suites by Hilton/Dulles North 🅷

(703) 723-7500. **$89-$239.** 44620 Waxpool Rd 20147. 1.7 mi w of jct SR 28 and Waxpool Rd (CR 625); SR 7, 3.4 mi s on Loudoun County Pkwy (CR 607), 0.3 mi w. Int corridors. **Pets:** Accepted.
🆂🅰🆅🅴 🛜 🔊 🛏 💻 🌊

CENTREVILLE

▼▼ Extended StayAmerica-Washington DC-Centreville/Manassas 🅷 ❄

(703) 988-9955. **$99-$299.** 5920 Fort Dr 20121. I-66 exit 53, 0.9 mi s on SR 28; off SR 28, 0.3 mi s of jct US 29. Int corridors. **Pets:** Other species. $25 daily fee/pet. Service with restrictions. 🛜 🛏 💻

CHANTILLY

▼▼▼ Extended Stay Deluxe Washington DC-Chantilly 🅷 ❄

(703) 263-7200. **$119-$309.** 4506 Brookfield Corporate Dr 20151. I-66 exit 53, 3 mi n on SR 28; 1 mi s of jct SR 28 and US 50. Int corridors. **Pets:** Other species. $25 daily fee/pet. Service with restrictions.
🛜 🔊 🛏 💻 🌊

🅐🅐🅐 ▼▼▼ Hampton Inn Washington Dulles International Airport South 🅷 ❄

(703) 818-8200. **$79-$209.** 4050 Westfax Dr 20151. 1 mi w on US 50 from jct SR 28. Int corridors. **Pets:** Large. Designated rooms, service with restrictions, supervision. 🅴🄲🄾 🆂🅰🆅🅴 🛜 🔊 🛏 💻 🌊 ✕

▼▼▼ Holiday Inn Chantilly-Dulles Expo Center 🅷

(703) 815-6060. **$179-$249.** 5920 Fort Dr 20151. I-66 exit 53, 3 mi n on SR 28; 1 mi s of jct US 50 and SR 28. Int corridors. **Pets:** Medium, other species. $100 one-time fee/room. Designated rooms, service with restrictions. 🛜 ✕ 🔊 🛏 💻 🍽 🌊 ✕

▼▼▼ Residence Inn by Marriott Chantilly Dulles South 🅷 ❄

(703) 263-7200. **$71-$219.** 14440 Chantilly Crossing Ln 20151. I-66 exit 57B, on US 50, just w of jct SR 28. Int corridors. **Pets:** Large, other species. $100 one-time fee/room. Service with restrictions, crate.
🅴🄲🄾 🛜 ✕ 🔊 🛏 💻 🌊 ✕

▼▼▼ Staybridge Suites Hotel Chantilly/Dulles International Airport 🅷 ❄

(703) 435-8090. **$79-$299.** 3860 Centerview Dr 20151. Jct SR 28, just e on US 50. Int corridors. **Pets:** Medium, other species. $75 one-time fee/room. Designated rooms, service with restrictions, crate.
🅴🄲🄾 🛜 🔊 🛏 💻 🌊

▼▼▼ TownePlace Suites by Marriott-Chantilly Dulles South 🅷

(703) 709-0453. **$89-$199.** 14036 Thunderbolt Pl 20151. Jct SR 28, just e on US 50. Int corridors. **Pets:** Accepted.
🅴🄲🄾 🛜 ✕ 🛏 💻 🌊 ✕

▼▼▼ Wingate by Wyndham Dulles Airport-Chantilly 🅷

(571) 203-0999. **$62-$143.** 3940 Centerview Dr 20151. Jct SR 28, just e on US 50. Int corridors. **Pets:** Small. $75 one-time fee/room. Service with restrictions, supervision. 🛜 🔊 🛏 💻 🌊 ✕

FAIRFAX

▼▼▼ Candlewood Suites Fairfax-Washington, D.C. 🅷

(703) 359-4490. **Call for rates.** 11400 Random Hills Rd 22030. I-66 exit 57A, 0.5 mi e on US 50, just s on Waples Mill Rd, then 0.4 mi w. Int corridors. **Pets:** Medium. $150 one-time fee/room. Service with restrictions, crate. 🛜 🔊 🛏 💻

▼▼ Comfort Inn University Center 🅷 ❄

(703) 591-5900. **$69-$169.** 11180 Fairfax Blvd 22030. I-66 exit 57A, 0.8 mi se on US 50; 0.5 mi nw of jct US 29 and US 50. Int corridors. **Pets:** Medium, other species. $25 daily fee/pet. Service with restrictions, crate. 🅴🄲🄾 🛜 ✕ 🛏 💻 🍽 🌊 ✕

▼▼▼ Extended Stay Deluxe Washington DC-Fairfax 🅷 ❄

(703) 359-5000. **$119-$319.** 3997 Fair Ridge Dr 22033. I-66 exit 57B, 1.2 mi w on US 50. Int corridors. **Pets:** Other species. $25 daily fee/pet. Service with restrictions. 🛜 🔊 🛏 💻 🌊

▼▼ **Homestead Studio Suites Hotel-Washington**
DC-Fairfax-Fair Oaks Ⓜ ❀

(703) 273-3444. **$99-$299.** 12104 Monument Dr 22033. I-66 exit 57B, 0.8 mi w on US 50, 0.3 mi s on SR 620 (W Ox Rd), then just se. Ext corridors. **Pets:** Other species. $25 daily fee/pet. Service with restrictions.

🛜 &M 🗄 💻

▼▼ **Homestead Studio Suites Washington DC-Falls**
Church-Merrifield Ⓗ ❀

(703) 204-0088. **$99-$299.** 8281 Willow Oaks Corporate Dr 22031. I-495 exit 50A, just w on US 50 to Gallows Rd, then just s. Ext corridors. **Pets:** Other species. $25 daily fee/pet. Service with restrictions.

🛜 &M 🗄 💻

ⒶⒶⒶ ▼▼▼ **Hyatt Fairfax at Fair Lakes** Ⓗ

(703) 818-1234. **$59-$299.** 12777 Fair Lakes Cir 22033. I-66 exit 55 (Fairfax County Pkwy N), just w, then just s. Int corridors. **Pets:** Accepted.

ECO SAVE 🛜 &M 🗄 💻 ⑪ 🌊 ✕

▼▼▼▼ **Residence Inn by Marriott Fairfax City** Ⓗ

(703) 267-2525. **$80-$199.** 3565 Chain Bridge Rd 22030. I-66 exit 60, 0.5 mi s on SR 123; jct US 29/50. Int corridors. **Pets:** Medium, other species. $150 one-time fee/room. Service with restrictions.

🛜 ✕ &M 🗄 💻 🌊

▼▼▼▼ **Residence Inn by Marriott-Fair Lakes** Ⓗ

(703) 266-4900. **$170-$219.** 12815 Fair Lakes Pkwy 22033. I-66 exit 55 (Fairfax County Pkwy N), just w. Int corridors. **Pets:** Medium, other species. $150 one-time fee/room. Service with restrictions, supervision.

ECO 🛜 ✕ &M 🗄 💻 🌊 ✕

FALLS CHURCH

▼▼▼▼ **Homewood Suites by Hilton-Falls Church** Ⓗ

(703) 560-6644. **$109-$249.** 8130 Porter Rd 22042. I-495 exit 50A, just w to SR 650; 0.4 mi n of SR 650. Int corridors. **Pets:** Accepted.

🛜 &M 🗄 💻 🌊 ✕

▼▼▼▼ **Residence Inn by Marriott Fairfax-Merrifield** Ⓗ

(703) 573-5200. **$85-$259.** 8125 Gatehouse Rd 22042. I-495 exit 50A, just w to SR 650 N. Int corridors. **Pets:** Accepted.

🛜 ✕ &M 🗄 💻 🌊 ✕

▼▼ **TownePlace Suites by Marriott-Falls Church** Ⓗ

(703) 237-6172. **$89-$279.** 205 Hillwood Ave 22046. I-495 exit 50B, 2.5 mi e on US 50, 0.6 mi n on Annandale Rd (CR 649), then e; just s of US 29. Int corridors. **Pets:** Accepted.

ECO 🛜 ✕ &M 🗄 💻 🌊

ⒶⒶⒶ ▼▼▼ **The Westin Tysons Corner** Ⓗ

(703) 893-1340. **$89-$419.** 7801 Leesburg Pike 22043. I-495 exit 47B, just e on SR 7. Int corridors. **Pets:** Accepted.

ECO SAVE 🛜 ✕ 🗄 💻 ⑪ 🌊 ✕

HERNDON

▼▼ **Candlewood Suites Washington Dulles-Herndon** Ⓗ

(703) 793-7100. **Call for rates.** 13845 Sunrise Valley Dr 20171. SR 28, 0.4 mi e on Frying Pan Rd, 0.7 mi nw. Int corridors. **Pets:** Small. $75 one-time fee/pet. Service with restrictions, crate. 🛜 &M 🗄 💻

ⒶⒶⒶ ▼▼▼ **Comfort Inn Dulles International Airport** Ⓗ

(703) 437-7555. **$69-$129.** 200 Elden St 20170. Just w on CR 606 from jct CR 7100 (Fairfax County Pkwy). Int corridors. **Pets:** Accepted.

SAVE 🛜 🗄 💻

▼▼ **Extended StayAmerica-Washington**
DC-Herndon Ⓜ ❀

(703) 481-5363. **$109-$299.** 1021 Elden St 20170. 0.8 mi n on SR 657 of jct SR 267 (Dulles Toll Rd) exit 10. Int corridors. **Pets:** Other species. $25 daily fee/pet. Service with restrictions. 🛜 &M 🗄 💻

▼▼▼▼ **Hilton Washington Dulles Airport** Ⓗ

(703) 478-2900. **$79-$289.** 13869 Park Center Rd 20171. SR 267 (Dulles Toll Rd) exit 9, 3 mi s on SR 28; at McLearen Blvd (SR 668). Int corridors. **Pets:** Accepted. ECO 🛜 &M 🗄 💻 ⑪ 🌊 ✕

ⒶⒶⒶ ▼▼▼ **Hyatt Summerfield Suites Herndon** Ⓗ

(703) 437-5000. **$79-$249.** 467 Herndon Pkwy 20170. SR 267 (Dulles Toll Rd) exit 11 CR 7100 (Fairfax County Pkwy), just n to Spring St exit, just s to Herndon Pkwy (CR 606), then just w on CR 606. Int corridors. **Pets:** Accepted. SAVE 🛜 🛜 ✕ 🗄 💻 🌊 ✕

▼▼▼▼ **Residence Inn by Marriott-Herndon/Reston** Ⓗ

(703) 435-0044. **$65-$78.** 315 Elden St 20170. 0.4 mi w on CR 606 from jct CR 7100 (Fairfax County Pkwy). Int corridors. **Pets:** Accepted.

🛜 ✕ 🗄 💻 🌊 ✕

ⒶⒶⒶ ▼▼▼▼ **Sheraton Herndon Dulles Airport**
Hotel Ⓗ ❀

(571) 643-0950. **$89-$299.** 13715 Sayward Blvd 20170. Jct SR 657 and 267 (Dulles Toll Rd) exit 10, 0.5 mi s on Centreville Rd (SR 657), then 1.1 mi w on Sunrise Valley Dr. Int corridors. **Pets:** Medium, dogs only. Service with restrictions, supervision.

SAVE 🛜 ✕ &M 🗄 💻 ⑪ 🌊 ✕

▼▼▼▼ **Staybridge Suites Herndon Dulles** Ⓗ

(703) 713-6800. **$99-$259.** 13700 Coppermine Rd 20171. SR 267 (Dulles Toll Rd) exit 10, 0.7 mi s on Centreville Rd (SR 657), then 0.4 mi w. Ext corridors. **Pets:** Medium. $15 daily fee/room. Service with restrictions, crate. 🛜 🗄 💻 🌊 ✕

ⒶⒶⒶ ▼▼▼▼ **The Westin Washington Dulles**
Airport Ⓗ ❀

(703) 793-3366. **$79-$269.** 2520 Wasser Terrace 20171. SR 28, 0.4 mi e on Frying Pan Rd, 0.8 mi nw. Int corridors. **Pets:** Medium, dogs only. Service with restrictions, supervision.

ECO SAVE 🛜 ✕ &M 🗄 💻 ⑪ 🌊 ✕

LEESBURG

ⒶⒶⒶ ▼▼▼ **Best Western Leesburg Hotel & Conference**
Center Ⓗ ❀

(703) 777-9400. **$89-$129.** 726 E Market St 20176. Off SR 7 business route, just w of jct US 15. Int corridors. **Pets:** Medium, dogs only. $10 daily fee/pet. Service with restrictions, supervision.

SAVE 🛜 🗄 💻 🌊

LORTON

ⒶⒶⒶ ▼▼▼ **Comfort Inn Gunston Corner** Ⓗ

(703) 643-3100. **$89-$199.** 8180 Silverbrook Rd 22079. I-95 exit 163, just w. Int corridors. **Pets:** Accepted. SAVE 🛜 ✕ 🗄 💻 🌊 ✕

MANASSAS

ⒶⒶⒶ ▼▼▼ **Best Western Battlefield Inn** Ⓗ ❀

(703) 361-8000. **$79-$175.** 10820 Balls Ford Rd 20109. I-66 exit 47A westbound; exit 47 eastbound, just s on SR 234 business route. Ext corridors. **Pets:** Medium, dogs only. $10 daily fee/pet. Service with restrictions, supervision. SAVE 🛜 🗄 💻 ⑪ 🌊

▼▼▼ **Candlewood Suites Manassas** Ⓗ ❀

(703) 530-0550. **$99-$129.** 11220 Balls Ford Rd 20109. I-66 exit 47A westbound; exit 47 eastbound, just s on SR 234 business route, then 0.7 mi w. Int corridors. **Pets:** Medium. $75 one-time fee/room. Service with restrictions, supervision. 🛜 &M 🗄 💻

▼▼▼▼ **Comfort Suites Manassas** Ⓗ

(703) 686-1100. **$109-$169.** 7350 Williamson Blvd 20109. I-66 exit 47A westbound; exit 47 eastbound, 0.5 mi s on SR 234 business route, then just e. Int corridors. **Pets:** Accepted. 🛜 ✕ 🗄 💻 🌊 ✕

ⒶⒶⒶ ▼▼▼ **Red Roof Inn-Manassas** Ⓜ

(703) 335-9333. **$70-$90.** 10610 Automotive Dr 20109. I-66 exit 47 eastbound; exit 47A westbound, just s on SR 234 business route, then just e on Balls Ford Rd. Ext corridors. **Pets:** Large, other species. No service, supervision. SAVE 🛜 &M 🗄

▼▼▼▼ **Residence Inn by Marriott Manassas Battlefield** Ⓗ

(703) 330-8808. **$200-$210.** 7345 Williamson Blvd 20109. I-66 exit 47A westbound; exit 47 eastbound, 0.5 mi s on SR 234 business route, then just e. Int corridors. **Pets:** Accepted.

🛜 ✕ &M 🗄 💻 🌊 ✕

MCLEAN

AAA **WW** Best Western Tysons Westpark **H**
(703) 734-2800. **$80-$190.** 8401 Westpark Dr 22102. I-495 exit 47A, 1.3 mi w on SR 7. Int corridors. **Pets:** Other species. $10 daily fee/pet. Service with restrictions. ▣ ▣ ▣ ▣ ▣ ▣ ▣

AAA **WWW** Crowne Plaza Tysons Corner **H**
(703) 893-2100. **$79-$299.** 1960 Chain Bridge Rd 22102. I-495 exit 46A, 0.5 mi s on SR 123, just nw on International Dr, then just sw on Greensboro Dr. Int corridors. **Pets:** Accepted.
▣ ▣ ▣ ▣ ▣ ▣ ▣ ▣ ▣ ▣

AAA **WWWW** The Ritz-Carlton, Tysons Corner **H**
(703) 506-4300. **Call for rates.** 1700 Tysons Blvd 22102. I-495 exit 46A, 0.3 mi sw on SR 123, then just nw. Int corridors. **Pets:** Accepted.
▣ ▣ ▣ ▣ ▣ ▣ ▣ ▣ ▣ ▣

AAA **WWW** Staybridge Suites-McLean-Tysons Corner **H**
(703) 448-5400. **$109-$349.** 6845 Old Dominion Dr 22101. I-495 exit 46B, 2 mi n on SR 123, then 0.3 mi e on SR 309. Int corridors. **Pets:** Accepted. ▣ ▣ ▣ ▣ ▣ ▣ ▣ ▣

RESTON

WW Homestead Studio Suites Washington DC-Reston **M** ⚘
(703) 707-9700. **$119-$339.** 12190 Sunset Hills Rd 20190. SR 267 (Dulles Toll Rd) exit 12 (Reston Pkwy), just n, then just w. Ext corridors. **Pets:** Other species. $25 daily fee/pet. Service with restrictions.
▣ ▣ ▣

AAA **WWW** Sheraton Reston Hotel **H**
(703) 620-9000. **$99-$429.** 11810 Sunrise Valley Dr 20191. SR 267 (Dulles Toll Rd) exit 12 (Reston Pkwy), just s. Int corridors.
Pets: Accepted. ▣ ▣ ▣ ▣ ▣ ▣ ▣ ▣

AAA **WWW** The Westin Reston Heights **H**
(703) 391-9000. **$129-$489.** 11750 Sunrise Valley Dr 20191. SR 267 (Dulles Toll Rd) exit 12 (Reston Pkwy), just s. Int corridors.
Pets: Accepted. ▣ ▣ ▣ ▣ ▣ ▣ ▣ ▣ ▣

SPRINGFIELD

WW Comfort Inn Washington DC/Springfield **H**
(703) 922-9000. **$79-$159.** 6560 Loisdale Ct 22150. I-95 exit 169A, just e on SR 644 E; jct I-395 and 495, 0.8 mi s. Int corridors. **Pets:** Medium, other species. Service with restrictions, crate. ▣ ▣ ▣

WWW Hampton Inn Washington DC/Springfield **H**
(703) 924-9444. **$80-$170.** 6550 Loisdale Ct 22150. I-95 exit 169A, just e on SR 644 E; jct I-395 and 495, 0.8 mi s. Int corridors. **Pets:** Medium, other species. Service with restrictions, crate. ▣ ▣ ▣ ▣ ▣

WWW Motel 6 Washington DC SW-Springfield #1400 **H**
(703) 644-5311. **$65-$85.** 6868 Springfield Blvd 22150. I-95 exit 169B, just sw of SR 644; jct I-395 and 495, 0.8 mi s. Int corridors. **Pets:** Other species. Service with restrictions, supervision. ▣ ▣ ▣

WWW Residence Inn by Marriott Springfield Old Keene Mill **H**
(703) 644-0020. **$89-$249.** 6412 Backlick Rd 22150. I-95 exit 169A, just nw of SR 644; jct I-395 and 495, 0.8 mi s. Int corridors. **Pets:** Accepted.
▣ ▣ ▣ ▣ ▣ ▣ ▣

WWW TownePlace Suites by Marriott Springfield **H**
(703) 569-8060. **$180-$216.** 6245 Brandon Ave 22150. I-95 exit 169B, just nw of SR 644; jct I-395 and 495, 0.8 mi s. Int corridors. **Pets:** Other species. $75 one-time fee/room. Service with restrictions.
▣ ▣ ▣ ▣ ▣ ▣

STERLING

AAA **WW** Best Western Dulles Airport Inn **M**
(703) 471-8300. **$79-$179.** 45440 Holiday Dr 20166. 1.7 mi n on SR 28 from jct SR 267 (Dulles Toll Rd), just e on CR 846, then just s on Shaw Rd. Ext corridors. **Pets:** Accepted. ▣ ▣ ▣ ▣ ▣

WW Candlewood Suites Washington Dulles/Sterling **H**
(703) 674-2288. **Call for rates.** 45520 Severn Way 20166. 1.3 mi s on SR 28 from jct SR 7, 0.3 mi e on Nokes Blvd, then 0.4 mi s on Atlantic Blvd. Int corridors. **Pets:** Accepted. ▣ ▣ ▣ ▣

AAA **WWW** Hampton Inn-Dulles/Cascades **H**
(703) 450-9595. **$99-$219.** 46331 McClellan Way 20165. 1.7 mi e on SR 7 from jct SR 28, 0.5 mi n on CR 1794 (Cascades Pkwy) to Palisade Pkwy, just e, then 0.4 mi s on Whitfield Pl. Int corridors. **Pets:** Accepted.
▣ ▣ ▣ ▣ ▣ ▣ ▣ ▣

AAA **WWW** Holiday Inn Washington Dulles International Airport **H**
(703) 471-7411. **$79-$229.** 45425 Holiday Dr 20166. 1.7 mi n on SR 28 from jct SR 267 (Dulles Toll Rd), just e on CR 846, then just s on Shaw Rd. Int corridors. **Pets:** Accepted.
▣ ▣ ▣ ▣ ▣ ▣ ▣ ▣ ▣

WWW Residence Inn by Marriott Dulles Airport @ Dulles 28 Centre **H**
(703) 421-2000. **$71-$229.** 45250 Monterey Pl 20166. SR 28 exit CR 625 (Waxpool Rd), just w, just n on Pacific Blvd, then just e on Commercial Dr. Int corridors. **Pets:** Medium, other species. $150 one-time fee/room. Service with restrictions, supervision.
▣ ▣ ▣ ▣ ▣ ▣ ▣

WW Suburban Extended Stay Hotel Washington-Dulles/Sterling **H**
(703) 674-2299. **$80-$100.** 45510 Severn Way 20166. 1.3 mi s on SR 28 from jct SR 7, 0.3 mi e on Nokes Blvd, then 0.4 mi s on Atlantic Blvd. Int corridors. **Pets:** Accepted. ▣ ▣ ▣

AAA **WWW** TownePlace Suites by Marriott at Dulles Airport **H**
(703) 707-2017. **$79-$229.** 22744 Holiday Park Dr 20166. 1.7 mi n on SR 28 from jct SR 267 (Dulles Toll Rd), just e on CR 846, then just s on Shaw Rd. Int corridors. **Pets:** Accepted.
▣ ▣ ▣ ▣ ▣ ▣ ▣

WWW TownePlace Suites by Marriott Sterling **H**
(703) 421-1090. **$99-$161.** 21123 Whitfield Pl 20165. 1.7 mi e on SR 7 from jct SR 28, 0.5 mi n on SR 1794 (Cascades Pkwy) to Palisades Pkwy, just e, then just s. Int corridors. **Pets:** Accepted.
▣ ▣ ▣ ▣ ▣

VIENNA

AAA **WWW** Comfort Inn Tysons Corner **M**
(703) 448-8020. **$79-$169.** 1587 Spring Hill Rd 22182. I-495 exit 47A, 1.8 mi w on SR 7, then just s; just e of jct SR 267 (Dulles Toll Rd). Ext corridors. **Pets:** Small. $25 one-time fee/room. Service with restrictions, supervision. ▣ ▣ ▣ ▣ ▣

WW Homestead Studio Suites Hotel-Washington DC-Tysons Corner **H** ⚘
(703) 356-6300. **$119-$339.** 8201 Old Courthouse Rd 22182. I-495 exit 47A, 0.6 mi w on SR 7, then just s on Gallows Rd. Int corridors. **Pets:** Other species. $25 daily fee/pet. Service with restrictions.
▣ ▣ ▣ ▣

AAA **WWW** Residence Inn by Marriott-Tysons Corner **H**
(703) 893-0120. **$209-$249.** 8616 Westwood Center Dr 22182. I-495 exit 47A, 1.9 mi w on SR 7, then just s. Ext corridors. **Pets:** Accepted.
▣ ▣ ▣ ▣ ▣ ▣ ▣

▼▼▼ **Residence Inn by Marriott Tysons Corner Mall** ▪ ❀

(703) 917-0800. **$109-$299.** 8400 Old Courthouse Rd 22182. I-495 exit 46A, 1.1 mi s on SR 123; 0.3 mi s of jct SR 7 and 123. Int corridors. **Pets:** $75 one-time fee/room. Service with restrictions.

📶 ✖ 🔱 🛎 💻 🏊 ❌

▼▼▼▼ **Sheraton Premiere At Tysons Corner** ▪

(703) 448-1234. **$99-$349.** 8661 Leesburg Pike 22182. SR 7, just e of jct SR 267 (Dulles Toll Rd). Int corridors. **Pets:** Accepted.

ECO SAVE 📶 ✖ 🔱 🛎 💻 🍴 🏊 ❌

WOODBRIDGE

▼▼▼ **Residence Inn by Marriott Potomac Mills** ▪

(703) 490-4020. **$145-$177.** 14301 Crossing Pl 22192. I-95 exit 158B (Prince William Pkwy), 0.5 mi sw. Int corridors. **Pets:** Accepted.

📶 ✖ 🔱 🛎 💻 🏊 ❌

END METROPOLITAN AREA

WAYNESBORO

▼▼▼▼ **Best Western Plus Waynesboro Inn & Suites Conf Ctr** ▪

(540) 942-1100. **$99-$139.** 109 Apple Tree Ln 22980. I-64 exit 94, just n. Int corridors. **Pets:** Accepted. ECO SAVE 📶 ✖ 🛎 💻 🏊

▼▼▼▼ **Comfort Inn Waynesboro** ▪

(540) 932-3060. **Call for rates.** 15 Windigrove Dr 22980. I-64 exit 94, 0.5 mi n on US 340, then just e. Int corridors. **Pets:** Accepted.

SAVE 📶 🛎 💻 🏊

▼▼ **Days Inn Waynesboro** Ⓜ

(540) 943-1101. **$63-$94.** 2060 Rosser Ave 22980. I-64 exit 94, 0.5 mi n on US 340. Ext corridors. **Pets:** Other species. $10 daily fee/room. Service with restrictions, supervision. SAVE 📶 🛎 💻 🏊

▼▼▼ **Quality Inn Waynesboro** Ⓜ

(540) 942-1171. **Call for rates.** 640 W Broad St 22980. I-64 exit 96, 3 mi w on SR 624; jct US 250 and 340. Ext/int corridors. **Pets:** Medium. $10 daily fee/pet. Service with restrictions. SAVE 📶 🛎 💻 🏊

▼▼▼ **Residence Inn by Marriott Waynesboro** ▪ ❀

(540) 943-7426. **$109-$269.** 44 Windigrove Dr 22980. I-64 exit 94, 0.5 mi n on US 340, then just e. Int corridors. **Pets:** Medium, other species. $100 one-time fee/room. Designated rooms, service with restrictions, crate. 📶 ✖ 🛎 💻 🏊 ❌

▼▼ **Super 8 Waynesboro** Ⓜ

(540) 943-3888. **$59-$79.** 2045 Rosser Ave 22980. I-64 exit 94, n on US 340 to Lew Dewitt Blvd, then just w to Apple Tree Ln. Int corridors. **Pets:** $5 daily fee/pet. Service with restrictions, supervision. SAVE 📶 🛎 💻

WILLIAMSBURG, JAMESTOWN & YORKTOWN AREA

WILLIAMSBURG

▼▼▼ **Clarion Hotel Historic District** ▪

(757) 229-4100. **$59-$139.** 351 York St 23185. US 60 E, 0.3 mi se of jct SR 5 and 31. Int corridors. **Pets:** Accepted.

SAVE 📶 ✖ 🔱 🛎 💻 🍴 🏊 ❌

▼▼▼ **Crowne Plaza Williamsburg at Fort Magruder** ▪ ❀

(757) 220-2250. **$69-$189, 3 day notice.** 6945 Pocahontas Tr 23185. US 60, 0.8 mi e of jct SR 5 and 31. Int corridors. **Pets:** Medium. $45 one-time fee/pet. Designated rooms, service with restrictions, crate.

ECO SAVE 📶 ✖ 🛎 💻 🍴 🏊 ❌

▼▼▼ **Holiday Inn Patriot-Williamsburg** ▪

(757) 565-2600. **$79-$149, 3 day notice.** 3032 Richmond Rd 23185. I-64 exit 234 (SR 199 E) to US 60, 2.5 mi e. Int corridors. **Pets:** Small. $15 daily fee/pet. Service with restrictions, supervision.

📶 🛎 💻 🍴 🏊

▼▼▼ **Patrick Henry Inn & Suites** ▪

(757) 229-9540. **$59-$99.** 249 York St 23185. E on US 60 (Richmond Rd) of jct SR 5 and 31; 1 blk from Colonial Williamsburg. Int corridors. **Pets:** Accepted. ECO SAVE 📶 ✖ 🔱 🛎 💻 🏊 ❌

▼▼ **Quality Suites Williamsburg** ▪

(757) 220-9304. **Call for rates.** 1406 Richmond Rd 23185. US 60, jct Bypass Rd. Int corridors. **Pets:** Accepted. 📶 🛎 💻 🏊

▼▼▼ **Residence Inn by Marriott Williamsburg** ▪ ❀

(757) 941-2000. **$99-$179.** 1648 Richmond Rd 23185. US 60, just w of jct Bypass Rd. Int corridors. **Pets:** Medium, other species. $75 one-time fee/room. Service with restrictions, crate.

SAVE 📶 ✖ 🔱 🛎 💻 🏊 ❌

▼▼ **Super 8-Williamsburg/Historic Area** Ⓜ

(757) 229-0500. **$39-$89.** 304 2nd St 23185. I-64 exit 242 (SR 199 W), 0.6 mi w to SR 143, 1.6 mi w to SR 162, then just w. Ext corridors. **Pets:** Medium, dogs only. $10 daily fee/pet. Service with restrictions, crate. SAVE 📶 🛎 💻 🏊

▼▼▼ **Williamsburg Inn** ▪

(757) 220-7978. **$299-$799, 3 day notice.** 136 E Francis St 23185. In Colonial Williamsburg restored area. Int corridors. **Pets:** Accepted.

📶 ✖ 🔱 🛎 🍴 🏊 ❌

YORKTOWN

▼▼ **Candlewood Suites-Yorktown** ▪

(757) 952-1120. **Call for rates.** 329 Commonwealth Dr 23693. I-64 exit 256B, just n, then just e. Int corridors. **Pets:** Accepted.

📶 🔱 🛎 💻 🏊

▼▼ **Days Inn** ▪

(757) 283-1111. **$58-$140.** 4531 George Washington Memorial Hwy 23692. I-64 exit 256B, 0.8 mi ne on Victory Blvd (SR 171), then 2.4 mi n on US 17. Int corridors. **Pets:** Accepted. 📶 🛎 💻 🏊

Staybridge Suites H
(757) 251-6644. **$99-$259, 3 day notice.** 401 Commonwealth Dr 23693. I-64 exit 256B, just n, then just e. Int corridors. **Pets:** Medium. $75 one-time fee/pet. Designated rooms, service with restrictions, crate.
ECO 📶 ♿M 🛏 💻 🏊

TownePlace Suites by Marriott H
(757) 874-8884. **$99-$149.** 200 Cybernetics Way 23693. I-64 exit 256B, e to Kiln Creek Pkwy. Int corridors. **Pets:** Accepted.
ECO SAVE 📶 ✕ ♿M 🛏 💻 🏊

END AREA

WINCHESTER

Best Western Lee-Jackson Inn & Conference Center H
(540) 662-4154. **$64-$70.** 711 Millwood Ave 22601. I-81 exit 313B, just nw on US 50/522/17. Ext corridors. **Pets:** Accepted.
SAVE 📶 🛏 💻 🍴 🏊

Candlewood Suites H
(540) 667-8323. **$65-$139.** 1135 Millwood Pike 22602. I-81 exit 313 northbound; exit 313A southbound, just se. Int corridors. **Pets:** Accepted.
ECO 📶 🛏 💻

Comfort Inn H 🐾
(540) 667-8894. **$69-$99.** 1601 Martinsburg Pike 22603. I-81 exit 317, just s on US 11. Int corridors. **Pets:** Medium, other species. $10 daily fee/pet. Designated rooms, service with restrictions, supervision.
SAVE 📶 🛏 💻 🏊 ✕

Country Inn & Suites By Carlson H
(540) 869-7657. **$79-$129.** 141 Kernstown Commons Blvd 22602. I-81 exit 310. Int corridors. **Pets:** Accepted. 📶 ✕ 🛏 💻 🏊

Days Inn M
(540) 667-1200. **$54-$70.** 2951 Valley Ave 22601. I-81 exit 310, just w, then 1.8 mi n on US 11. Ext/int corridors. **Pets:** Other species. $5 daily fee/pet. Designated rooms, service with restrictions.
SAVE 📶 🛏 💻 🏊

Econo Lodge North M
(540) 662-4700. **Call for rates.** 1593 Martinsburg Pike 22603. I-81 exit 317, 0.3 mi sw on US 11. Int corridors. **Pets:** Accepted.
SAVE 📶 🛏 💻 🏊

Quality Inn of Winchester H
(540) 545-8121. **Call for rates.** 1017 Millwood Pike 22602. I-81 exit 313 northbound; exit 313A southbound, just se on US 50/17, at US 522. Ext/int corridors. **Pets:** Other species. Designated rooms, service with restrictions, supervision. 📶 🛏 💻 🏊

Red Roof Inn M
(540) 667-5000. **$50-$80.** 991 Millwood Pike 22602. I-81 exit 313 northbound; exit 313A southbound, just se on US 50/17. Ext corridors. **Pets:** Large, other species. No service, supervision. SAVE 📶 🛏

Super 8 Winchester M
(540) 665-4450. **$49-$79.** 1077 Millwood Pike 22602. I-81 exit 313 northbound; exit 313A southbound, 0.3 mi se on US 50/17. Int corridors. **Pets:** Medium. $10 daily fee/pet. Designated rooms, no service, supervision. SAVE 📶 🛏 💻

TownePlace Suites Winchester H
(540) 722-2722. **$80-$94.** 170 Getty Ln 22602. I-81 exit 315, just e. Int corridors. **Pets:** Accepted. 📶 ✕ 🛏 💻 🏊

Travelodge of Winchester H
(540) 665-0685. **$54-$77, 7 day notice.** 160 Front Royal Pike 22602. I-81 exit 313 northbound; exit 313A southbound, just s on US 522. Int corridors. **Pets:** $10 daily fee/pet. Service with restrictions, supervision.
SAVE 📶 🛏 💻 🏊

WOODSTOCK

Comfort Inn Woodstock H 🐾
(540) 459-7600. **$79-$129.** 1011 Motel Dr 22664. I-81 exit 283, just e. Int corridors. **Pets:** $10 one-time fee/pet. Designated rooms, service with restrictions, supervision. SAVE 📶 🛏 💻 🏊

WYTHEVILLE

Best Western Wytheville Inn H
(276) 228-7300. **$70-$200.** 355 Nye Rd 24382. I-77 exit 41, just e. Int corridors. **Pets:** Accepted. SAVE 📶 🛏 💻 🏊

Budget Host Inn/Interstate Inn M
(276) 228-8618. **$45-$145, 3 day notice.** 705 Chapman Rd 24382. I-77/81 exit 73, just w. Ext corridors. **Pets:** Small. $10 daily fee/pet. Service with restrictions, supervision. 📶 🛏

Comfort Inn H
(276) 637-4281. **Call for rates.** 2594 E Lee Hwy 24382. I-77/81 exit 80, just w. Int corridors. **Pets:** Accepted. 📶 ♿M 🛏 💻 🏊

Days Inn M 🐾
(276) 228-5500. **$52-$131.** 150 Malin Dr 24382. I-77/81 exit 73, just w. Ext corridors. **Pets:** Medium. $10 daily fee/room. Service with restrictions, supervision. 📶 🛏 💻

Econo Lodge M
(276) 228-5525. **$55-$175.** 280 Lithia Rd 24382. I-77/81 exit 73, just w. Ext corridors. **Pets:** Medium, other species. $10 daily fee/pet. Service with restrictions, supervision. 📶 🛏

La Quinta Inn Wytheville H
(276) 228-7400. **$80-$169.** 1800 E Main 24382. I-77/81 exit 73, just w. Int corridors. **Pets:** Medium, other species. Service with restrictions, supervision. SAVE 📶 ✕ 🛏 💻 🏊

Red Roof Inn & Suites M
(276) 223-1700. **$44-$149.** 1900 E Main St 24382. I-77/81 exit 73, just w. Ext corridors. **Pets:** Large, other species. No service, supervision. SAVE 📶 🛏 💻 🏊

Super 8 M
(276) 228-6620. **$49-$89.** 130 Nye Cir 24382. I-77 exit 41, just e. Ext corridors. **Pets:** Accepted. 📶 🛏 💻

ZION CROSSROADS

Best Western Plus Crossroads Inn & Suites H 🐾
(540) 832-1700. **$100-$160.** 135 Wood Ridge Terr 22942. I-64 exit 136, just n. Int corridors. **Pets:** Large, other species. $20 daily fee/room. No service, crate. ECO SAVE 📶 ✕ ♿M 🛏 💻 🏊

WASHINGTON

AIRWAY HEIGHTS

▼▼▼ Days Inn & Suites H

(509) 244-0222. **$59-$94.** 1215 S Garfield Rd 99001. I-90/US 2 exit 277 to US 2, 4 mi w. Int corridors. **Pets:** Accepted.

ANACORTES

AAA ▼▼▼ Anacortes Inn M

(360) 293-3153. **$72-$128.** 3006 Commercial Ave 98221. Just s of downtown. Ext corridors. **Pets:** Dogs only. $50 deposit/room, $10 daily fee/pet. Service with restrictions, supervision.

▼▼▼ Anacortes Ship Harbor Inn M ☂

(360) 293-5177. **$79-$179, 3 day notice.** 5316 Ferry Terminal Rd 98221. 0.3 mi s of ferry landing. Ext corridors. **Pets:** Large, other species. $25 one-time fee/room. Service with restrictions, supervision.

AAA ▼▼▼ Cap Sante Inn M ☂

(360) 293-0602. **$65-$140.** 906 9th St 98221. On 9th St, just e. Ext corridors. **Pets:** Dogs only. $10 one-time fee/pet. Designated rooms, service with restrictions, supervision.

▼▼ Fidalgo Country Inn & Suites H

(360) 293-3494. **$89-$149.** 7645 SR 20 98221. Jct Fidalgo Bay Rd. Ext/int corridors. **Pets:** Dogs only. $20 daily fee/room. Designated rooms, service with restrictions, supervision.

▼▼ Islands Inn M

(360) 293-4644. **$64-$149.** 3401 Commercial Ave 98221. Just s of downtown. Ext corridors. **Pets:** Dogs only. $5 daily fee/pet. Supervision.

▼▼▼ Majestic Inn & Spa H

(360) 299-1400. **Call for rates.** 419 Commercial Ave 98221. At 5th Ave; downtown. Int corridors. **Pets:** Accepted.

ASHFORD

▼▼ Mountain Meadows Inn Bed & Breakfast BB

(360) 569-2788. **$119-$195, 14 day notice.** 28912 SR 706 E 98304. West end of town. Ext/int corridors. **Pets:** Medium, other species. $10 daily fee/pet. Designated rooms, supervision.

BELLINGHAM

AAA ▼▼▼ Baymont Inn & Suites H ☂

(360) 671-6200. **$78-$149.** 125 E Kellogg Rd 98226. I-5 exit 256A, 1 mi ne via Meridian St. Int corridors. **Pets:** Medium. Designated rooms, service with restrictions, supervision.

▼▼▼ Bellingham GuestHouse Intl Inn H

(360) 671-9600. **$69-$130.** 805 Lakeway Dr 98229. I-5 exit 253 (Lakeway Dr), just ne. Int corridors. **Pets:** Accepted.

AAA ▼▼▼ Best Western Plus Heritage Inn H ☂

(360) 647-1912. **$90-$180.** 151 E McLeod Rd 98226. I-5 exit 256A, just e. Int corridors. **Pets:** Large. $20 daily fee/room. Designated rooms, service with restrictions, supervision.

AAA ▼▼▼ Best Western Plus Lakeway Inn H

(360) 671-1011. **$130-$250.** 714 Lakeway Dr 98229. I-5 exit 253 (Lakeway Dr), just se. Int corridors. **Pets:** Accepted.

AAA ▼▼▼ Econo Lodge Inn & Suites H ☂

(360) 671-4600. **$69-$129.** 3750 Meridian St 98225. I-5 exit 256A, just w. Ext corridors. **Pets:** Dogs only. $10 daily fee/pet. Designated rooms, service with restrictions, supervision.

AAA ▼▼▼ Holiday Inn Express-Bellingham H ☂

(360) 671-4800. **$98-$168.** 4160 Meridian St 98226. I-5 exit 256A, 0.7 mi e. Int corridors. **Pets:** Medium. $15 one-time fee/room. Service with restrictions, supervision.

AAA ▼▼▼ Quality Inn Baron Suites H

(360) 647-8000. **Call for rates.** 100 E Kellogg Rd 98226. I-5 exit 256A, 1 mi ne via Meridian St. Ext/int corridors. **Pets:** Accepted.

BLAINE

AAA ▼▼▼▼ Semiahmoo Resort H

(360) 318-2000. **$119-$439, 3 day notice.** 9565 Semiahmoo Pkwy 98230. I-5 exit 270, 9.5 mi nw on Semiahmoo Spit. Int corridors. **Pets:** Accepted.

CASHMERE

AAA ▼▼▼ Village Inn Motel M

(509) 782-3522. **$59-$94, 7 day notice.** 229 Cottage Ave 98815. On Business Rt US 2 and 97; downtown. Ext corridors. **Pets:** Accepted.

CASTLE ROCK

◆◆◆◆ Blue Heron Inn B & B BB
(360) 274-9595. $170, 7 day notice. 2846 Spirit Lake Hwy 98611. I-5 exit 49, 5 mi e on US 504. Int corridors. Pets: Accepted.
[icons]

▲▲▲ ◆◆◆ Timberland Inn & Suites M ❀
(360) 274-6002. $60-$200. 1271 Mount St. Helens Way 98611. I-5 exit 49, just ne. Ext corridors. Pets: Small, dogs only. $10 daily fee/pet. Designated rooms, service with restrictions, supervision. SAVE [icons]

CENTRALIA

◆ Motel 6 - #394 M
(360) 330-2057. $41-$55. 1310 Belmont Ave 98531. I-5 exit 82, just w on Harrison Ave, then just n. Ext corridors. Pets: Other species. Service with restrictions, supervision. [icons]

CHEHALIS

▲▲▲ ◆◆◆◆ Best Western Plus Park Place Inn & Suites H ❀
(360) 748-4040. $98-$127. 201 SW Interstate Ave 98532. I-5 exit 76, just se. Int corridors. Pets: Large, dogs only. $20 daily fee/room. Designated rooms, service with restrictions, supervision.
SAVE [icons]

CHELAN

▲▲▲ ◆◆◆◆ Best Western Plus Lakeside Lodge & Suites H
(509) 682-4396. $89-$329, 7 day notice. 2312 W Woodin Ave 98816. West end of town. Ext corridors. Pets: Accepted.
SAVE [icons]

CHEWELAH

▲▲▲ ◆◆◆ Nordlig Motel M
(509) 935-6704. $59-$64. W 101 Grant Ave 99109. North edge of town on US 395. Ext corridors. Pets: Dogs only. $5 one-time fee/pet. Designated rooms, service with restrictions, supervision. SAVE [icons]

CLARKSTON

▲▲▲ ◆◆◆ Best Western RiverTree Inn H ❀
(509) 758-9551. $109-$149. 1257 Bridge St 99403. 0.9 mi w of Snake River Bridge on US 12. Ext corridors. Pets: Small. $20 one-time fee/room. Designated rooms, service with restrictions, supervision.
SAVE [icons]

◆ Motel 6 Clarkston #4256 M
(509) 758-1631. $49-$54. 222 Bridge St 99403. Just w of Snake River Bridge. Ext corridors. Pets: Other species. Service with restrictions, supervision. [icons]

▲▲▲ ◆◆◆◆ Quality Inn & Suites Conference Center H
(509) 758-9500. $95-$160. 700 Port Dr 99403. Just w of Snake River Bridge on US 12, then 0.3 mi n via 5th St. Int corridors. Pets: $10 daily fee/pet. Designated rooms, service with restrictions, supervision.
SAVE [icons]

CLE ELUM

◆◆ Econo Lodge M
(509) 674-2380. Call for rates. 906 E 1st St 98922. I-90 exit 85, 1 mi nw. Int corridors. Pets: Accepted. [icons]

▲▲▲ ◆◆◆ Stewart Lodge M
(509) 674-4548. $65-$94. 805 W 1st St 98922. I-90 exit 84 eastbound, just n; exit 85 westbound, 0.6 mi w. Ext corridors. Pets: Other species. $10 daily fee/pet. Designated rooms, service with restrictions, supervision.
SAVE [icons]

◆◆ Timber Lodge Inn M
(509) 674-5966. $70-$90. 301 W 1st St 98922. I-90 exit 84 eastbound, 1 mi ne; exit westbound, just w; downtown. Int corridors. Pets: Accepted. [icons]

COLFAX

▲▲▲ ◆◆◆ Best Western Plus Wheatland Inn H
(509) 397-0397. $100-$120, 3 day notice. 701 N Main 99111. Downtown. Int corridors. Pets: Medium, dogs only. $15 daily fee/pet. Designated rooms, service with restrictions, supervision.
[icons]

DAYTON

◆◆◆ The Weinhard Hotel H
(509) 382-4032. $125-$180, 7 day notice. 235 E Main St 99328. Downtown. Int corridors. Pets: Dogs only. $20 one-time fee/pet. Supervision. [icons]

EAST WENATCHEE

◆◆ Cedars Inn, East Wenatchee H
(509) 886-8000. $59-$179. 80 9th St NE 98802. Just e of SR 28. Int corridors. Pets: Accepted. [icons]

EATONVILLE

▲▲▲ ◆◆ Mill Village Motel M
(360) 832-3200. $80-$100. 210 Center St E 98328. Just e of jct SR 161; center. Ext corridors. Pets: Small. $10 one-time fee/pet. Service with restrictions, supervision. SAVE [icons]

ELLENSBURG

▲▲▲ ◆◆◆ Best Western Plus Lincoln Inn & Suites H ❀
(509) 925-4244. $89-$199. 211 W Umptanum Rd 98926. I-90 exit 109, just n, then just w. Int corridors. Pets: Medium, dogs only. $15 daily fee/pet. Designated rooms, service with restrictions.
SAVE [icons]

▲▲▲ ◆◆◆ Cedars Inn Ellensburg M
(509) 925-9844. $64-$84. 1390 N Dollarway Rd 98926. I-90 exit 106, just n. Ext corridors. Pets: Accepted. SAVE [icons]

◆◆ Ellensburg Comfort Inn H
(509) 925-7037. $70-$140. 1722 Canyon Rd 98926. I-90 exit 109. Int corridors. Pets: Accepted. [icons]

▲▲▲ ◆◆◆ Holiday Inn Express H ❀
(509) 962-9400. $99-$179. 1620 Canyon Rd 98926. I-90 exit 109, just n. Int corridors. Pets: Other species. $15 daily fee/room. Designated rooms, service with restrictions, supervision.
SAVE [icons]

ELMA

◆◆ Microtel Inn & Suites H
(360) 482-6868. $71-$99. 800 E Main St 98541. Just ne of jct US 12 and SR 8. Int corridors. Pets: Accepted. [icons]

EPHRATA

▲▲▲ ◆◆ Best Western Rama Inn H ❀
(509) 754-7111. Call for rates. 1818 Basin St SW 98823. On SR 28; west end of town. Int corridors. Pets: Large, other species. $25 one-time fee/room. Service with restrictions, supervision.
SAVE [icons]

FERNDALE

◆◆ Ferndale Super 8 H
(360) 384-8881. $72-$112. 5788 Barrett Rd 98248. I-5 exit 262, just ne. Int corridors. Pets: Large. $15 one-time fee/room. Designated rooms, service with restrictions, supervision. [icons]

▲▲▲ ◆◆◆ Silver Reef Hotel Casino & Spa H ❀
(360) 383-0777. $116-$269. 4876 Haxton Way 98248. I-5 exit 260, 3.6 mi w. Int corridors. Pets: Medium, other species. $15 one-time fee/pet. Designated rooms, service with restrictions.
SAVE [icons]

FORKS

AAA **WWW** **Forks Motel M**
(360) 374-6243. **$63-$158.** 351 US 101 98331. On US 101 (S Forks Ave), just s of Division St. Ext corridors. **Pets:** Other species. $15 daily fee/pet. Designated rooms. [SAVE] [icons]

WWW **Manitou Lodge BB** ❀
(360) 374-6295. **$99-$179, 14 day notice.** 813 Kilmer Rd 98331. 7.7 mi sw on SR 110 (LaPush Rd), 0.7 mi w on Mora Rd, then 0.8 mi n. Ext/int corridors. **Pets:** Other species. $10 daily fee/room. Designated rooms, supervision. [icons]

WWW **Miller Tree Inn Bed & Breakfast BB**
(360) 374-6806. **$115-$225, 7 day notice.** 654 E Division St 98331. 0.3 mi e of US 101 (S Forks Ave). Ext/int corridors. **Pets:** Other species. $10 daily fee/pet. Designated rooms, service with restrictions.
[icons]

AAA **WWW** **Olympic Suites Inn M** ❀
(360) 374-5400. **$49-$139.** 800 Olympic Dr 98331. North end of town; just ne off US 101 (S Forks Ave). Ext corridors. **Pets:** Dogs only. $10 one-time fee/pet. Designated rooms, service with restrictions, supervision. [SAVE] [icons]

GOLDENDALE

WW **Quality Inn & Suites H**
(509) 773-5881. **Call for rates.** 808 E Simcoe Dr 98620. US 97 exit Simcoe Dr, just sw. Ext corridors. **Pets:** Accepted. [icons]

ILWACO

AAA **W** **Heidi's Inn M**
(360) 642-2387. **$59-$89, 7 day notice.** 126 E Spruce St 98624. Downtown. Ext corridors. **Pets:** Small, dogs only. $6 daily fee/pet. Service with restrictions, supervision. [SAVE] [icons]

KALALOCH

AAA **WWW** **Kalaloch Lodge CA**
(360) 962-2271. **Call for rates.** 157151 Hwy 101 98331. In Kalaloch; at MM 157. Ext/int corridors. **Pets:** Accepted.
[SAVE] [icons]

KELSO

AAA **WWW** **Best Western Aladdin Motor Inn - Kelso H**
(360) 425-9660. **$80-$140.** 310 Long Ave 98626. I-5 exit 39, 1.1 mi w via Allen and W Main sts, then just n on 5th Ave NW. Int corridors.
Pets: Accepted. [SAVE] [icons]

WWWW **GuestHouse Inn & Suites H**
(360) 414-5953. **Call for rates.** 501 Three Rivers Dr 98626. I-5 exit 39, 0.3 mi w on Allen St, then 0.3 mi s. Int corridors. **Pets:** Accepted.
[icons]

WWW **Motel 6 - #43 M**
(360) 425-3229. **$45-$65.** 106 Minor Rd 98626. I-5 exit 39, just ne. Ext corridors. **Pets:** Other species. Service with restrictions, supervision.
[icons]

WWWW **Red Lion Hotel & Conference Center Kelso/Longview H**
(360) 636-4400. **$153-$265.** 510 Kelso Dr 98626. I-5 exit 39, 0.3 mi se. Int corridors. **Pets:** Accepted. [icons]

WW WW **Super 8 H**
(360) 423-8880. **$54-$139.** 250 Kelso Dr 98626. I-5 exit 39, just se. Int corridors. **Pets:** $10 daily fee/room. Service with restrictions, supervision. [icons]

KENNEWICK

WW WW **Baymont Inn & Suites H**
(509) 736-3326. **$61-$86.** 4220 W 27th Pl 99337. I-82 exit 113 (US 395), 0.8 mi n. Int corridors. **Pets:** Accepted.
[icons]

AAA **WWWW** **Best Western Plus Kennewick Inn H** ❀
(509) 586-1332. **$110-$150.** 4001 W 27th Ave 99337. I-82 exit 113 (US 395), 0.8 mi n. Int corridors. **Pets:** $10 one-time fee/room. Service with restrictions, supervision. [SAVE] [icons]

AAA **WWW** **Cedars Inn & Suites Kennewick H**
(509) 396-9979. **$85-$199, 3 day notice.** 602 N Young St 99336. 1 mi s of SR 240, just e. Int corridors. **Pets:** Accepted.
[SAVE] [icons]

WWW **Clover Island Inn H** ❀
(509) 586-0541. **$89-$349.** 435 Clover Island Dr 99336. US 395 exit Port of Kennewick, 1 mi e on Columbia Dr, then 0.7 mi n. Int corridors.
Pets: Other species. $10 one-time fee/pet. Service with restrictions, supervision. [icons]

WWW **Comfort Inn M**
(509) 783-8396. **$70-$159.** 7801 W Quinault Ave 99336. 0.5 mi s on Columbia Center Blvd from SR 240. Int corridors. **Pets:** Medium, dogs only. $10 daily fee/pet. Designated rooms, service with restrictions, supervision. [icons]

AAA **WWW** **Days Inn Kennewick H**
(509) 735-9511. **$59-$114.** 2811 W 2nd Ave 99336. Jct US 395 and Clearwater Ave, just s, then just w. Ext/int corridors. **Pets:** Other species. $10 daily fee/pet. Designated rooms, service with restrictions.
[SAVE] [icons]

WWWW **Fairfield Inn by Marriott H** ❀
(509) 783-2164. **$118-$151.** 7809 W Quinault Ave 99336. 0.5 mi s on Columbia Center Blvd from SR 240. Int corridors. **Pets:** Medium. $15 daily fee/pet. Service with restrictions, supervision.
[icons]

AAA **WWW** **Guesthouse International Suites H**
(509) 735-2242. **Call for rates.** 5616 W Clearwater Ave 99336. US 395, 1.9 mi w. Int corridors. **Pets:** Accepted. [SAVE] [icons]

AAA **WWW** **Kennewick Super 8 H**
(509) 736-6888. **$58-$72, 10 day notice.** 626 N Columbia Center Blvd 99336. 1.1 mi s of SR 240. Int corridors. **Pets:** Other species. $10 daily fee/room. Service with restrictions, supervision.
[SAVE] [icons]

WWWW **La Quinta Inn & Suites Kennewick H**
(509) 736-3656. **$107-$189.** 2600 S Quillan Pl 99338. I-82 exit 113 (US 395), 0.8 mi n. Int corridors. **Pets:** Medium, other species. Service with restrictions, supervision. [icons]

WWWW **Quality Inn Kennewick H**
(509) 735-6100. **Call for rates.** 7901 W Quinault Ave 99336. 0.5 mi s on Columbia Center Blvd from SR 240. Int corridors. **Pets:** Accepted.
[icons]

AAA **WWWW** **Red Lion Hotel Columbia Center-Kennewick H**
(509) 783-0611. **$99-$139.** 1101 N Columbia Center Blvd 99336. SR 240, 0.5 mi s. Int corridors. **Pets:** Accepted.
[SAVE] [icons]

LACEY

AAA **WWWW** **Best Western Plus Lacey Inn & Suites H** ❀
(360) 456-5655. **$99-$199.** 8326 Quinault Dr NE 98516. I-5 exit 111 (Marvin Rd), just ne. Int corridors. **Pets:** Medium. $15 daily fee/pet. Designated rooms, service with restrictions, supervision.
[SAVE] [icons]

WWWW **Candlewood Suites Olympia/Lacey H**
(360) 491-1698. **$140-$186.** 4440 3rd Ave SE 98503. I-5 exit 108 northbound, just n; exit 109 southbound, just s on Martin Ave E, just e on College Way, then just s. Int corridors. **Pets:** Accepted. [icons]

LA CONNER

▼▼ La Conner Country Inn 🅷 ❖
(360) 466-3101. **$129-$239.** 107 S 2nd St 98257. Jct 2nd and Morris sts; downtown. Ext/int corridors. **Pets:** $50 one-time fee/room. Designated rooms, service with restrictions, supervision. 🛜 ⊠ 🛢 💻 🍽

LANGLEY

▼▼▼ Boat Yard Inn 🅷
(360) 221-5120. **Call for rates.** 200 Wharf St 98260. East end of town on the waterfront. Ext corridors. **Pets:** Accepted.
🛜 ⊠ ♿ 🛢 💻 🐾

▼▼▼▼ The Inn at Langley 🅷
(360) 221-3033. **$290-$595, 7 day notice.** 400 1st St 98260. Center. Ext corridors. **Pets:** Accepted. 🛜 ⊠ 🛢 💻 🐾

LEAVENWORTH

▼▼ Alpine Rivers Inn 🅷
(509) 548-8888. **$99-$129, 7 day notice.** 1505 Alpensee Strasse 98826. East edge of town. Ext corridors. **Pets:** Medium, dogs only. $20 one-time fee/pet. Designated rooms, service with restrictions, supervision.
🛜 ⊠ 🛢 💻 🏊

AAA ▼▼ Bavarian Ritz Hotel 🅷
(509) 548-5455. **$89-$269, 3 day notice.** 633 Front St 98826. Center. Int corridors. **Pets:** Accepted. SAVE 🛜 ⊠ 🛢 💻

AAA ▼▼▼ Best Western Plus Icicle Inn 🅷
(509) 548-7000. **$150-$290, 7 day notice.** 505 W US 2 98826. West side of town. Int corridors. **Pets:** Large, dogs only. $20 daily fee/room. Designated rooms, service with restrictions, supervision.
SAVE 🛜 ⊠ 🛢 💻 🍽 🏊 🐾

AAA ▼▼ Der Ritterhof Motor Inn 🅷 ❖
(509) 548-5845. **$81-$182, 3 day notice.** 190 US 2 98826. 0.3 mi w. Ext corridors. **Pets:** Large, dogs only. $15 daily fee/pet. No service, supervision. SAVE 🛜 ⊠ ♿ 🛢 💻 🏊

AAA ▼▼ Obertal Inn Ⓜ ❖
(509) 548-5204. **$89-$299, 3 day notice.** 922 Commercial St 98826. Off US 2; center. Ext corridors. **Pets:** Other species. $15 daily fee/pet. Service with restrictions. SAVE 🛜 ⊠ 🛢 💻

LIBERTY LAKE

AAA ▼▼▼▼ Best Western Plus Peppertree Liberty Lake Inn 🅷
(509) 755-1111. **$79-$250.** 1816 N Pepper Ln 99019. I-90 exit 296 (Liberty Lake), just n. Int corridors. **Pets:** Accepted.
SAVE 🛜 ⊠ ♿ 🛢 💻 🏊

AAA ▼▼ Cedars Inn Spokane at Liberty Lake 🅷
(509) 340-3333. **$69-$110.** 2327 N Madson Rd 99019. I-90 exit 296 (Liberty Lake), 1 mi e on Appleway Ave, then just n. Int corridors. **Pets:** Dogs only. $15 daily fee/pet. Designated rooms, service with restrictions, supervision. SAVE 🛜 ♿ 🛢 💻 🏊

LONG BEACH

▼▼ Anchorage Cottages ⒸⒶ
(360) 642-2351. **$80-$138, 14 day notice.** 2209 Boulevard N 98631. Just w of SR 103; just n of downtown. Ext corridors. **Pets:** $10 daily fee/pet. No service, supervision. 🛜 ⊠ 🛢 💻 🅺 🐾

AAA ▼▼ The Breakers Ⓒ❂ ❖
(360) 642-4414. **$78-$328, 20 day notice.** 210 26th St NW 98631. North end of downtown. Ext corridors. **Pets:** Dogs only. $15 daily fee/room. Designated rooms, supervision.
SAVE 🛜 ⊠ 🛢 💻 🏊 🅺 🅺

▼▼ Our Place at the Beach 🅷
(360) 642-3793. **$75-$170, 3 day notice.** 1309 Ocean Beach Blvd S 98631. Just w of SR 103; south end of town. Ext corridors. **Pets:** $7 daily fee/pet. Service with restrictions, supervision.
🛜 ⊠ 🛢 💻 ⊠ 🅺

▼▼ Rodeway Inn & Suites 🅷
(360) 642-3714. **Call for rates.** 115 3rd St SW 98631. Downtown. Ext corridors. **Pets:** Accepted. 🛜 🛢 💻 🏊 🅺

AAA ▼▼ Super 8 🅷
(360) 642-8988. **$80-$179.** 500 Ocean Beach Blvd 98631. On SR 103; downtown. Int corridors. **Pets:** Accepted.
SAVE 🛜 ⊠ ♿ 🛢 💻 🅺

LONGVIEW

▼▼ Hudson Manor Inn & Suites Ⓜ
(360) 425-1100. **Call for rates.** 1616 Hudson St 98632. Downtown. Ext corridors. **Pets:** Accepted. 🛜 🛢 💻

AAA ▼▼ Longview Travelodge Ⓜ
(360) 423-6460. **$63-$122.** 838 15th Ave 98632. Downtown; opposite Medical Center. Ext corridors. **Pets:** $15 daily fee/room. Service with restrictions, supervision. SAVE 🛜 🛢 💻

AAA ▼ The Townhouse Motel Ⓜ
(360) 423-7200. **$55-$95, 3 day notice.** 744 Washington Way 98632. Downtown. Ext corridors. **Pets:** Other species. $7 daily fee/pet. Service with restrictions, supervision. SAVE 🛜 🛢 💻 🏊

MOCLIPS

AAA ▼▼▼ Ocean Crest Resort 🅷 ❖
(360) 276-4465. **$67-$217, 4 day notice.** 4651 SR 109 98562. South edge of town. Ext corridors. **Pets:** Other species. $20 daily fee/pet. Designated rooms, service with restrictions, supervision.
SAVE 🛜 ⊠ 🛢 💻 🏊 ⊠ 🅺

MORTON

AAA ▼▼ The Seasons Motel Ⓜ
(360) 496-6835. **$80-$100.** 200 Westlake Ave 98356. On US 12; jct SR 7. Ext corridors. **Pets:** Small. $10 one-time fee/pet. Service with restrictions, supervision. SAVE 🛜 🛢 💻

MOSES LAKE

▼▼ AmeriStay Inn & Suites 🅷
(509) 764-7500. **$89-$259.** 1157 N Stratford Rd 98837. I-90 exit 179, 1 mi n to SR 17, 2.8 mi nw, exit Stratford Rd, just n, then just e. Int corridors. **Pets:** Accepted. 🛜 ♿ 🛢 💻

AAA ▼▼ Best Western Plus Lake Front Hotel 🅷
(509) 765-9211. **$100-$140.** 3000 Marina Dr 98837. I-90 exit 176, just nw. Int corridors. **Pets:** Accepted.
SAVE 🛜 ⊠ ♿ 🛢 💻 🍽 🏊 ⊠

AAA ▼▼▼ Comfort Suites Moses Lake 🅷 ❖
(509) 765-3731. **$99-$249.** 1700 E Kittleson Rd 98837. I-90 exit 179, just nw. Int corridors. **Pets:** Small, dogs only. $25 daily fee/pet. Designated rooms, service with restrictions, supervision.
SAVE 🛜 ⊠ ♿ 🛢 💻 🏊

▼▼ Inn at Moses Lake 🅷
(509) 766-7000. **$80-$120.** 1741 E Kittleson Rd 98837. I-90 exit 179, just n. Int corridors. **Pets:** Accepted. 🛜 ⊠ 🛢 💻

AAA ▼▼ Moses Lake Super 8 🅷
(509) 765-8886. **$84-$163.** 449 Melva Ln 98837. I-90 exit 176, just n. Int corridors. **Pets:** Large, other species. $10 daily fee/pet. Service with restrictions, supervision. SAVE 🛜 🛢 💻 🏊

▦ ▧▧▧ Shilo Inn Suites-Moses Lake 🅷
(509) 765-9317. **$72-$113.** 1819 E Kittleson Rd 98837. I-90 exit 179, just n. Int corridors. **Pets:** Dogs only. $25 one-time fee/room. Designated rooms, service with restrictions, crate.
[SAVE] 🛜 ✕ 🖥 🔌 📺 ⊃ ✕

MOUNT RAINIER NATIONAL PARK
▦ ▧▧▧ Alta Crystal Resort at Mt Rainier 🅷 ❀
(360) 663-2500. **$149-$299, 30 day notice.** 68317 SR 410 E 98022. 2 mi outside northeast entrance. Ext corridors. **Pets:** Dogs only. $50 one-time fee/pet. Designated rooms, service with restrictions, supervision.
[SAVE] 🛜 ✕ 🔌 📺 ⊃ ✕ ⓚ

MOUNT VERNON
▦ ▧▧ Best Western College Way Inn 🅷
(360) 424-4287. **Call for rates.** 300 W College Way 98273. I-5 exit 227, just w. Ext corridors. **Pets:** $20 daily fee/room. Designated rooms, service with restrictions, supervision. [SAVE] 🛜 ✕ 🔌 📺 ⊃

▦ ▧▧▧ Best Western Plus CottonTree Inn 🅷
(360) 428-5678. **$115-$150.** 2300 Market St 98273. I-5 exit 227, 0.3 mi e on College Way, then 0.5 mi n on Riverside Dr. Int corridors.
Pets: Accepted. [SAVE] 🛜 ✕ 🔌 📺 ⊃

▦ ▧▧▧ Quality Inn-Mount Vernon 🅷
(360) 428-7020. **Call for rates.** 1910 Freeway Dr 98273. I-5 exit 227, just w on College Way, then just n. Ext corridors. **Pets:** Accepted.
[SAVE] 🛜 🔌 📺 ⊃

▦ ▧▧▧ Tulip Inn Ⓜ ❀
(360) 428-5969. **$65-$109.** 2200 Freeway Dr 98273. I-5 exit 227, just w on College Way, then just n. Ext corridors. **Pets:** Medium, other species. $10 daily fee/pet. Designated rooms, service with restrictions, supervision.
[SAVE] 🛜 🔌 📺

OAK HARBOR
▦ ▧▧▧▧ Candlewood Suites 🅷 ❀
(360) 279-2222. **$109-$169.** 33221 SR 20 98277. Just n of town. Int corridors. **Pets:** Large. $75 deposit/room, $10 daily fee/pet. Service with restrictions, crate. [SAVE] 🛜 ✕ 🔌 📺

▦ ▧▧▧ Coachman Inn 🅷
(360) 675-0727. **$84-$209.** 32959 SR 20 98277. Jct Goldie Rd and Midway Blvd. Ext corridors. **Pets:** Large. $8 daily fee/pet. Designated rooms, service with restrictions, supervision. [SAVE] 🛜 🔌 📺 ⊃ ✕

OCEAN PARK
▧ Ocean Park Resort Ⓜ
(360) 665-4585. **$67-$191, 10 day notice.** 25904 R St 98640. Just e of SR 103; downtown. Ext corridors. **Pets:** Medium. $7 daily fee/pet. Designated rooms, service with restrictions, supervision.
🛜 ✕ 🔌 📺 ⊃ ✕ ⓚ 🐾

OCEAN SHORES
▧▧ Canterbury Inn Ⓒ
(360) 289-3317. **$84-$202.** 643 Ocean Shores Blvd NW 98569. 0.3 mi s of Chance A La Mer Blvd. Int corridors. **Pets:** Large, dogs only. $150 deposit/room, $15 daily fee/pet. Designated rooms, supervision.
🛜 ✕ 🔌 📺 ⊃ ⓚ

▦ ▧▧▧ The Polynesian Condominium Resort Ⓒ
(360) 289-3361. **$99-$429.** 615 Ocean Shores Blvd NW 98569. 0.3 mi s of Chance A La Mer Blvd. Ext/int corridors. **Pets:** Accepted.
[SAVE] 🛜 🔌 📺 ⍾ ⊃ ✕ ⓚ

▦ ▧▧▧▧ Shilo Inn Suites Hotel - Ocean Shores 🅷
(360) 289-4600. **$108-$260.** 707 Ocean Shores Blvd NW 98569. Northwest corner of Chance A La Mer and Ocean Shores blvds NW. Int corridors. **Pets:** Dogs only. $25 one-time fee/room. Designated rooms, service with restrictions, crate. [SAVE] 🛜 ✕ 🔌 📺 ⍾ ⊃ ✕

OLYMPIA
▦ ▧▧▧▧ Red Lion Hotel Olympia 🅷
(360) 943-4000. **$99-$150, 3 day notice.** 2300 Evergreen Park Dr SW 98502. I-5 exit 104, 0.7 mi w on US 101, just n on Cooper Point Rd N, 0.7 mi e on S Evergreen Park Dr SW, then just n on Lakeridge Way SW. Int corridors. **Pets:** Accepted. [SAVE] 🛜 ✕ 🔌 📺 ⍾ ⊃

OLYMPIC NATIONAL PARK
▦ ▧▧▧ Lake Crescent Lodge 🅷
(360) 928-3211. **$105-$239, 3 day notice.** 416 Lake Crescent Rd 98363. 22 mi w of Port Angeles on US 101. Ext/int corridors.
Pets: Accepted. [SAVE] 🛜 ✕ 🔌 📺 ⍾ ✕ ⓚ Ⓦ ⓩ

▧ Log Cabin Resort Ⓒ
(360) 928-3325. **$40-$161, 7 day notice.** 3183 E Beach Rd 98363. 3.3 mi nw of US 101 (MM 232). Ext corridors. **Pets:** Accepted.
🛜 🔌 📺 ⍾ ✕ ⓚ Ⓦ ⓩ

OMAK
▦ ▧▧▧▧ Best Western Plus Peppertree Inn at Omak 🅷
(509) 422-2088. **$79-$250.** 820 Koala Dr 98841. US 97, just n of Riverside Dr. Int corridors. **Pets:** Accepted.
[SAVE] 🛜 ✕ 🔌 📺 ⊃

▦ ▧▧▧ Omak Inn LLC 🅷 ❀
(509) 826-3822. **$75-$130.** 912 Koala Dr 98841. On US 97, just n of Riverside Dr. Int corridors. **Pets:** Other species. $25 one-time fee/room. Designated rooms, service with restrictions, supervision.
[SAVE] 🛜 🔌 📺 ⊃

OTHELLO
▦ ▧▧▧ Best Western Othello Inn 🅷 ❀
(509) 488-5671. **$100-$160.** 1020 E Cedar St 99344. Just off Main St; jct 10th St. Int corridors. **Pets:** Dogs only. $20 one-time fee/room. Supervision. [SAVE] 🛜 🔌 📺 ⊃

PACIFIC BEACH
▧ Sandpiper Beach Resort Ⓒ
(360) 276-4580. **Call for rates.** 4159 SR 109 98571. 1.8 mi s. Ext corridors. **Pets:** $15 daily fee/pet. Service with restrictions, supervision.
🛜 ✕ 🔌 📺 ⓚ Ⓦ ⓩ

PACKWOOD
▧▧ Cowlitz River Lodge Ⓜ
(360) 494-4444. **$60-$100, 7 day notice.** 13069 US 12 98361. East end of town. Ext corridors. **Pets:** $20 one-time fee/pet. Designated rooms, service with restrictions, crate. 🛜 ✕ 🔌

▦ ▧▧▧ Crest Trail Lodge 🅷
(360) 494-4944. **$70-$100.** 12729 US 12 98361. Just w of town. Int corridors. **Pets:** Small. $10 one-time fee/pet. Service with restrictions, supervision. [SAVE] 🛜 🔌 📺

PASCO
▦ ▧▧▧ Best Western Plus Pasco Inn & Suites 🅷 ❀
(509) 543-7722. **$125-$160.** 2811 N 20th Ave 99301. I-182 exit 12B, just n. Int corridors. **Pets:** Large. $10 one-time fee/room. Service with restrictions, supervision. [SAVE] 🛜 ✕ 🔌 📺 ⊃

▦ ▧▧▧ Holiday Inn Express Pasco at TRAC 🅷 🐾
(509) 543-7000. **$109-$230, 7 day notice.** 4525 Convention Pl 99301. I-182 exit 9 (Rd 68), just n, then just e. Int corridors. **Pets:** Medium, dogs only. $20 daily fee/pet. Designated rooms, service with restrictions, supervision. [SAVE] 🛜 ✕ 🔌 📺 ⊃

Red Lion Hotel Pasco H
(509) 547-0701. **Call for rates.** 2525 N 20th Ave 99301. I-182 exit 12B, just n. Int corridors. **Pets:** Accepted.

Sleep Inn H
(509) 545-9554. **$89-$110.** 9930 Bedford St 99301. I-182 exit 7, just ne. Int corridors. **Pets:** Accepted.

PORT ANGELES

A Hidden Haven & Water Garden Cottages CA
(360) 452-2719. **$169-$389, 21 day notice.** 1428 Dan Kelly Rd 98363. 5.5 mi s of downtown on US 101, 2.2 mi sw on SR 112, then 1.4 mi e. Ext corridors. **Pets:** Accepted.

Days Inn H
(360) 452-4015. **$54-$127.** 1510 E Front St 98362. Front St at Alder St; on east side. Ext corridors. **Pets:** $25 one-time fee/pet. Designated rooms, no service, supervision.

Red Lion Hotel Port Angeles H
(360) 452-9215. **$119-$299.** 221 N Lincoln St 98362. On US 101 westbound; at ferry landing. Ext/int corridors. **Pets:** Accepted.

Super 8 M
(360) 452-8401. **$72-$117.** 2104 E 1st St 98362. 1.8 mi e of downtown, just s of US 101. Int corridors. **Pets:** Large, dogs only. $10 daily fee/pet. Service with restrictions, supervision.

PORTLAND METROPOLITAN AREA (NEARBY OREGON)

VANCOUVER

Comfort Inn & Suites Downtown Vancouver H
(360) 696-0411. **$90-$130.** 401 E 13th St 98660. I-5 exit 1C (E Mill Plain Blvd), just w, just s on C St, then just e. Int corridors. **Pets:** Small, dogs only. $20 one-time fee/room. Service with restrictions, supervision.

Comfort Suites H 🐾
(360) 253-3100. **$79-$109.** 4714 NE 94th Ave 98662. I-205 exit 30 (SR 500 W), 0.6 mi w to Thurston Way, just n to Vancouver Mall Dr, then 0.5 mi e; southeast edge of Westfield Shopping Center. Int corridors. **Pets:** Medium, dogs only. $20 one-time fee/pet. Service with restrictions, supervision.

Days Inn H
(360) 574-6000. **$34-$104.** 13207 NE 20th Ave 98686. I-5 exit 7, just e; I-205 exit 36, just w. Int corridors. **Pets:** Accepted.

Days Inn & Suites H
(360) 253-5000. **$50-$95.** 9107 NE Vancouver Mall Dr 98662. I-205 exit 30 (SR 500 W), 0.6 mi w to Thurston Way, just n to Vancouver Mall Dr, then 0.5 mi e; southeast edge of Westfield Shopping Center. Int corridors. **Pets:** Small, dogs only. $15 one-time fee/pet. Designated rooms, service with restrictions.

Hilton Vancouver Washington and Vancouver Convention Center H 🐾
(360) 993-4500. **$125-$169.** 301 W 6th St 98660. I-5 exit 1C (E Mill Plain Blvd) southbound, 0.3 mi w, then 0.3 mi s on W Columbia St; exit 1B northbound, 0.5 mi, follow signs to City Center/6th St. Int corridors. **Pets:** Medium. $35 one-time fee/room. Service with restrictions.

Homewood Suites by Hilton H
(360) 750-1100. **$139-$229.** 701 SE Columbia Shores Blvd 98661. SR 14 exit 1, just s. Ext/int corridors. **Pets:** Large, other species. $25 daily fee/pet. Designated rooms, service with restrictions, supervision.

La Quinta Inn & Suites Vancouver H
(360) 566-1100. **$75-$139.** 1500 NE 134th St 98685. I-5 exit 7, just w; I-205 exit 36, 0.5 mi w. Int corridors. **Pets:** Medium, other species. Service with restrictions, supervision.

Phoenix Inn Suites-Vancouver H
(360) 891-9777. **Call for rates.** 12712 SE 2nd Cir 98684. I-205 exit 28 (E Mill Plain Blvd), 0.8 mi e, then just n on SE 126th Ave. Int corridors. **Pets:** Accepted.

Red Lion Hotel Vancouver at the Quay H
(360) 694-8341. **$89-$149.** 100 Columbia St 98660. 0.5 mi s of dock at foot of Columbia St. Int corridors. **Pets:** Accepted.

Residence Inn Portland-North Vancouver H
(360) 253-4800. **$89-$125.** 8005 NE Parkway Dr 98662. I-205 exit 30 (SR 500 W), 0.5 mi w to Thurston Way, just n to NE Parkway Dr, then just w. Ext corridors. **Pets:** Other species. $75 one-time fee/room. Service with restrictions.

Shilo Inn & Suites-Salmon Creek H
(360) 573-0511. **$69-$149.** 13206 Hwy 99 98686. I-5 exit 7, just e; I-205 exit 36, just w. Int corridors. **Pets:** Dogs only. $25 one-time fee/room. Designated rooms, service with restrictions, crate.

Staybridge Suites Vancouver-Portland H
(360) 891-8282. **$79-$189.** 7301 NE 41st St 98662. I-205 exit 30 (SR 500 W), 1.5 mi w to NE Andresen Rd, just n to NE 40th St, just e to NE 72nd St, just n to NE 41st St, then just e. Int corridors. **Pets:** Accepted.

END METROPOLITAN AREA

PORT LUDLOW

The Resort at Port Ludlow H
(360) 437-7000. **Call for rates.** 1 Heron Rd 98365. 8 mi n of Hood Canal Floating Bridge; in town. Int corridors. **Pets:** Accepted.

PORT TOWNSEND

Ann Starrett Mansion H
(360) 385-3205. **$115-$225, 14 day notice.** 744 Clay St 98368. On the bluff; corner of Adams St. Ext/int corridors. **Pets:** Large, dogs only. $20 one-time fee/room. Designated rooms, service with restrictions, supervision.

Bishop Victorian Hotel H 🐾
(360) 385-6122. **$120-$275, 3 day notice.** 714 Washington St 98368. Corner of Washington and Quincy sts. Int corridors. **Pets:** Dogs only. $20 daily fee/pet. Designated rooms, supervision.

Palace Hotel H 🐾
(360) 385-0773. **$59-$289.** 1004 Water St 98368. Downtown. Int corridors. **Pets:** $20 one-time fee/pet. Supervision.

AAA ▼▼▼ The Swan Hotel **M** ❀
(360) 385-1718. **$100-$325, 3 day notice.** 216 Monroe St 98368. Downtown. Ext corridors. **Pets:** Dogs only. $20 daily fee/pet. Designated rooms, service with restrictions, supervision.
[SAVE] 🛰 ✕ ☎ 🖥 ℀

PROSSER
AAA ▼▼▼ Best Western Plus The Inn at Horse
                    Heaven **H**
(509) 786-7977. **$120-$150.** 259 Merlot Dr 99350. I-82 exit 80, just s. Int corridors. **Pets:** Dogs only. $10 daily fee/pet. Designated rooms, service with restrictions, supervision. [SAVE] 🛰 ✕ ☎M ☎ 🖥 ➹

PULLMAN
AAA ▼▼ Hilltop Inn **H** ❀
(509) 332-0928. **$70-$249, 3 day notice.** 928 NW Olsen St 99163. 1.6 mi e on SR 270 from US 195. Int corridors. **Pets:** Other species. $15 daily fee/pet. Designated rooms, service with restrictions, supervision.
[SAVE] 🛰 ✕ ☎M ☎ 🖥 ❙❙ ➹ ✕

▼▼▼ Holiday Inn Express Hotel & Suites **H** ❀
(509) 334-4437. **$109-$189.** SE 1190 Bishop Blvd 99163. Jct US 195 business route, 0.5 mi s, 1 mi e on SR 270. Int corridors. **Pets:** Medium, dogs only. $20 daily fee/pet. Designated rooms, service with restrictions, crate. 🛰 ✕ ☎M ☎ 🖥 ➹

AAA ▼▼▼ Quality Inn Paradise Creek **H**
(509) 332-0500. **Call for rates.** 1400 SE Bishop Blvd 99163. Jct US 195 business route, just s, 1 mi e on SR 270. Int corridors. **Pets:** Accepted.
[SAVE] 🛰 ✕ ☎ 🖥 ➹ ✕

QUINAULT
AAA ▼▼▼ Lake Quinault Lodge **H**
(360) 288-2900. **$99-$300, 3 day notice.** 345 S Shore Rd 98575. 2 mi off US 101. Ext/int corridors. **Pets:** Accepted.
[SAVE] 🛰 ✕ ☎ 🖥 ❙❙ ➹ ✕ ℀ ☏

REPUBLIC
AAA ▼▼ Prospector Inn **H**
(509) 775-3361. **$51-$150.** 979 S Clark Ave 99166. Downtown. Int corridors. **Pets:** Accepted. [SAVE] 🛰 ✕ ☎ 🖥 ✕

RICHLAND
AAA ▼▼▼ Days Inn **M**
(509) 943-4611. **$54-$84.** 615 Jadwin Ave 99352. I-182 exit 5B, 0.9 mi n; just w of SR 240 business route; downtown. Ext corridors.
Pets: Accepted. [SAVE] 🛰 ☎ 🖥 ➹

▼▼▼ Holiday Inn Express Hotel & Suites **H**
(509) 737-8000. **$119-$159.** 1970 Center Pkwy 99352. Just s on Columbia Center Blvd from SR 240, just w. Int corridors. **Pets:** Accepted.
🛰 ✕ ☎M ☎ 🖥 ➹

AAA ▼▼▼ Red Lion Hotel Richland Hanford
                    House **H**
(509) 946-7611. **Call for rates.** 802 George Washington Way 99352. I-182 exit 5B, 1.3 mi n on SR 240 business route. Ext/int corridors.
Pets: Accepted. [SAVE] 🛰 ✕ ☎M ☎ 🖥 ❙❙ ➹ ✕

AAA ▼▼▼ Shilo Inn Suites Hotel - Richland **H**
(509) 946-4661. **$65-$199.** 50 Comstock St 99352. I-182 exit 5B, 0.5 mi n. Ext corridors. **Pets:** Dogs only. $25 one-time fee/room. Designated rooms, service with restrictions, crate.
[SAVE] 🛰 ✕ ☎ 🖥 ❙❙ ➹ ✕

RITZVILLE
AAA ▼▼▼ Best Western Plus Bronco Inn **H**
(509) 659-5000. **$80-$200.** 105 W Galbreath Way 99169. I-90 exit 221, cross overpass, then second left. Int corridors. **Pets:** Accepted.
[SAVE] 🛰 ☎ 🖥 ➹

AAA ▼▼▼ Cedars Inn & Suites Ritzville **H**
(509) 659-1007. **$51-$149.** 1513 Smitty's Blvd 99169. I-90 exit 221, just n. Int corridors. **Pets:** $10 one-time fee/room. Designated rooms, service with restrictions, supervision. [SAVE] 🛰 ☎M ☎ 🖥 ➹

▼▼ Top Hat Motel **M** ❀
(509) 659-1100. **$42-$64.** 210 E 1st Ave 99169. I-90 exit 221, 1 mi ne via Division St. Ext corridors. **Pets:** Dogs only. $20 deposit/room. Designated rooms, service with restrictions, supervision. 🛰 ☎

SAN JUAN ISLANDS AREA

DEER HARBOR
▼▼ Deer Harbor Inn **CI**
(360) 376-4110. **Call for rates.** 33 Inn Ln 98243. In Deer Harbor; 7 mi sw of ferry landing; 3.5 mi sw of Westsound. Ext/int corridors.
Pets: Accepted. 🛰 ✕ ☎ 🖥 ❙❙ ℀ ☏

EASTSOUND
AAA ▼▼▼ Eastsound Landmark Inn **CO** ❀
(360) 376-2423. **$99-$254, 7 day notice.** 67 Main St 98245. In Eastsound; downtown. Ext corridors. **Pets:** $25 daily fee/pet. Designated rooms, supervision. [SAVE] 🛰 ☎ 🖥 ℀

AAA ▼▼▼ Turtleback Farm Inn **BB**
(360) 376-4914. **$100-$260, 15 day notice.** 1981 Crow Valley Rd 98245. 4 mi sw of Eastsound; 6 mi n of ferry landing; 2.5 mi n of Westsound Marina. Int corridors. **Pets:** Medium. $15 daily fee/room. Designated rooms, service with restrictions, supervision.
[SAVE] 🛰 ✕ ☎ 🖥 ℀ ▨ ☏

FRIDAY HARBOR
▼▼ Argyle House Bed & Breakfast **BB** ❀
(360) 378-4084. **$110-$275, 14 day notice.** 685 Argyle Ave 98250. In Friday Harbor; 0.3 mi e of jct Spring St. Ext/int corridors. **Pets:** Dogs only. $25 one-time fee/room. Supervision. 🛰 ✕ ☎ 🖥 ℀ ☏

AAA ▼▼▼ Best Western Plus Friday Harbor
                    Suites **H**
(360) 378-3031. **$165-$425, 7 day notice.** 680 Spring St 98250. In Friday Harbor; 0.7 mi w of ferry dock. Int corridors. **Pets:** $25 daily fee/pet. Designated rooms, service with restrictions, supervision.
[SAVE] 🛰 ✕ ☎M ☎ 🖥 ✕ ℀

▼▼ Earthbox Motel & Spa **H** ❀
(360) 378-4000. **$147-$407, 10 day notice.** 410 Spring St 98250. In Friday Harbor; 0.5 mi w of ferry dock. Ext corridors. **Pets:** $15 daily fee/pet. Designated rooms, service with restrictions, supervision.
🛰 ✕ ☎ 🖥 ➹ ✕

AAA ▼▼▼ Friday Harbor House **H**
(360) 378-8455. **Call for rates.** 130 West St 98250. In Friday Harbor; just w of Spring St; at the waterfront. Ext/int corridors. **Pets:** $50 one-time fee/room. Designated rooms, service with restrictions.
[SAVE] 🛰 ☎ 🖥 ❙❙ ℀

▼▼▼ Lakedale Resort at Three Lakes
(360) 378-2350. **Call for rates.** 4313 Roche Harbor Rd 98250. 4 mi n of Friday Harbor via Tucker Ave. Ext/int corridors. **Pets:** Accepted.
🛰 ✕ ☎ 🖥 ✕ ℀

▼▼/▼▼ States Inn & Ranch 🅱🅱 ❀
(360) 378-6240. **$99-$280, 7 day notice.** 2687 W Valley Rd 98250. 7 mi nw of Friday Harbor via 2nd St, Guard St and Beaverton Valley Rd. Int corridors. **Pets:** Dogs only. $25 daily fee/pet. Service with restrictions, supervision. 📶 ✖ 🛢 🎦 📮 🗲

🅰🅰🅰 ▼▼/▼▼ Trumpeter Inn Bed & Breakfast 🅱🅱 ❀
(360) 378-3884. **$130-$199, 7 day notice.** 318 Trumpeter Way 98250. 1.5 mi w of Friday Harbor via Spring St and San Juan Valley Rd. Int corridors. **Pets:** Dogs only. $25 one-time fee/pet. Designated rooms, supervision. 🆂🅰🆅🅴 📶 ✖ 🎦 📮 🗲

END AREA

SEATTLE METROPOLITAN AREA

ARLINGTON
🅰🅰🅰 ▼▼▼▼ Medallion Hotel 🅷
(360) 657-0500. **$109-$119.** 16710 Smokey Point Blvd 98223. I-5 exit 206, just e on 172nd St NE, then just s. Int corridors. **Pets:** Small. $25 daily fee/room. Designated rooms, supervision.
🆂🅰🆅🅴 📶 ✖ 🔥🅼 🛢 📮 🍴 🏊 🚫

AUBURN
▼▼/▼▼ Auburn GuestHouse Inn 🅷 ❀
(253) 735-9600. **$89-$99.** 9 14th St NW 98001. SR 167 exit 15th St NW, 0.8 mi e, just s on A St NE, then just w. Int corridors. **Pets:** Large, dogs only. $10 one-time fee/pet. Designated rooms, service with restrictions, supervision. 📶 🛢 📮

🅰🅰🅰 ▼▼▼▼ Best Western Plus Peppertree Auburn Inn 🅷 ❀
(253) 887-7600. **$89-$220.** 401 8th St SW 98001. SR 18 exit C St, just s, then just w. Int corridors. **Pets:** Dogs only. Service with restrictions, supervision. 🆂🅰🆅🅴 📶 ✖ 🛢 📮 🏊 🚫

▼▼ Cedars Inn Auburn 🅷
(253) 833-8007. **$50-$70.** 102 15th St NE 98002. SR 167 exit 15th St NW, 0.8 mi e. Int corridors. **Pets:** Accepted. 📶 🛢

▼▼/▼▼ Travelodge Inn & Suites 🅷
(253) 833-7171. **$63-$117.** 9 16th St NW 98001. SR 167 exit 15th St NW, 0.8 mi e, then just n on A St NE. Int corridors. **Pets:** Accepted.
📶 🔥🅼 🛢 📮

BAINBRIDGE ISLAND
🅰🅰🅰 ▼▼▼▼ Best Western Plus Bainbridge Island Suites 🅷 ❀
(206) 855-9666. **$130-$140.** 350 NE High School Rd 98110. 0.8 mi n of ferry dock on SR 305, then just w. Int corridors. **Pets:** Medium, other species. $20 daily fee/pet. Designated rooms, service with restrictions, crate. 🆂🅰🆅🅴 📶 ✖ 🛢 📮

BELLEVUE
🅰🅰🅰 ▼▼▼▼ Embassy Suites Hotel Bellevue 🅷
(425) 644-2500. **$99-$219.** 3225 158th Ave SE 98008. I-90 exit 11 westbound; exit 11A (156th Ave SE) eastbound, just ne. Int corridors.
Pets: Accepted. 🆂🅰🆅🅴 📶 🔥🅼 🛢 📮 🍴 🏊 🚫

▼▼▼▼ Extended StayAmerica-Seattle-Bellevue 🅷 ❀
(425) 453-8186. **$90-$105.** 11400 Main St 98004. I-405 exit 13A, just se. Int corridors. **Pets:** Other species. $25 daily fee/pet. Service with restrictions. 📶 🔥🅼 🛢 📮

▼▼▼▼ Fairfield Inn 🅷
(425) 869-6548. **$99-$189.** 14595 NE 29th Pl 98007. I-405 exit 14 (SR 520), 2.3 mi e to 148th Ave NE (north exit), then just nw. Int corridors.
Pets: Accepted. 📶 ✖ 🔥🅼 🛢 📮 🏊

▼▼▼▼ Hilton Bellevue 🅷 ❀
(425) 455-1300. **$129-$249.** 300 112th Ave SE 98004. I-405 exit 12, just nw. Int corridors. **Pets:** Medium. $75 one-time fee/room. Designated rooms, service with restrictions, crate. 📶 🔥🅼 📮 🍴 🏊

🅰🅰🅰 ▼▼/▼▼ Hotel Bellevue 🅷
(425) 454-4424. **$169-$1659.** 11200 SE 6th St 98004. I-405 exit 12, 0.4 mi nw. Int corridors. **Pets:** Accepted.
🆂🅰🆅🅴 📶 ✖ 🔥🅼 🍴 🏊 🚫

🅰🅰🅰 ▼▼/▼▼ Hyatt Regency Bellevue 🅷 ❀
(425) 462-1234. **$129-$419.** 900 Bellevue Way NE 98004. I-405 exit 13B, 1.5 mi w on NE 8th St. Int corridors. **Pets:** Medium, dogs only. $30 daily fee/room. Designated rooms, service with restrictions, crate.
🅴🅲🅾 🆂🅰🆅🅴 📶 🔥🅼 🛢 📮 🍴 🏊

🅰🅰🅰 ▼▼/▼▼ La Residence Suite Hotel 🅷
(425) 455-1475. **$125-$199.** 475 100th Ave NE 98004. I-405 exit 13B, 0.9 mi w on NE 8th St, then just s. Int corridors. **Pets:** Other species. $15 daily fee/pet. Designated rooms, service with restrictions, crate.
🆂🅰🆅🅴 📶 ✖ 🛢 📮

🅰🅰🅰 ▼▼/▼▼ Red Lion Hotel Bellevue 🅷
(425) 455-5240. **$69-$189.** 11211 Main St 98004. I-405 exit 12, 0.4 mi n on 114th St. Int corridors. **Pets:** Accepted.
🆂🅰🆅🅴 📶 🛢 📮 🍴 🏊

▼▼/▼▼ Residence Inn by Marriott, Bellevue-Redmond 🅷
(425) 882-1222. **$93-$143.** 14455 NE 29th Pl 98007. I-405 exit 14 (SR 520), 2.3 mi e to 148th Ave NE (north exit), then just nw. Ext corridors.
Pets: Accepted. 📶 ✖ 🔥🅼 🛢 📮 🏊 🚫

▼▼/▼▼ Residence Inn by Marriott Seattle-Bellevue/Downtown 🅷
(425) 637-8500. **$89-$179.** 605 114th Ave SE 98004. I-405 exit 12, just sw. Int corridors. **Pets:** Accepted. 📶 ✖ 🔥🅼 🛢 📮 🏊

🅰🅰🅰 ▼▼/▼▼ Sheraton Bellevue Hotel 🅷
(425) 455-3330. **$107-$359.** 100 112th Ave NE 98004. I-405 exit 12 northbound; exit 13 southbound, just s. Int corridors. **Pets:** Accepted.
🆂🅰🆅🅴 📶 ✖ 📮 🍴

🅰🅰🅰 ▼▼/▼▼ The Westin Bellevue 🅷
(425) 638-1000. **$169-$429.** 600 Bellevue Way NE 98004. I-405 exit 13B, 1.5 mi w on NE 8th St. Int corridors. **Pets:** Accepted.
🆂🅰🆅🅴 📶 ✖ 🛢 📮 🚫

BOTHELL
▼▼/▼▼ Country Inn & Suites By Carlson 🅷
(425) 485-5557. **Call for rates.** 19333 N Creek Pkwy 98011. I-405 exit 24, just e. Int corridors. **Pets:** Accepted.
🅴🅲🅾 📶 🔥🅼 🛢 📮 🍴 🏊 🚫

▼▼/▼▼ Extended StayAmerica-Seattle-Bothell 🅷 ❀
(425) 402-4252. **$75-$95.** 923 228th St SE 98021. I-405 exit 26, just sw. Int corridors. **Pets:** Other species. $25 daily fee/pet. Service with restrictions. 📶 🔥🅼 🛢 📮

▼▼/▼▼ Residence Inn by Marriott Seattle NE 🅷 ❀
(425) 485-3030. **$84-$162.** 11920 NE 195th St 98011. I-405 exit 24, 0.4 mi ne. Ext corridors. **Pets:** Other species. $75 one-time fee/room. Service with restrictions. 📶 ✖ 🔥🅼 🛢 📮 🏊 🚫

BREMERTON

Flagship Inn
(360) 479-6566. **$75-$150.** 4320 Kitsap Way 98312. 3.5 mi w of ferry terminal; SR 3 exit Kitsap Way, 0.5 mi e. Int corridors. **Pets:** Small, dogs only. $6 daily fee/pet. Supervision.

Midway Inn
(360) 479-2909. **$84-$160.** 2909 Wheaton Way 98310. SR 303, 2 mi n. Int corridors. **Pets:** Dogs only. $25 one-time fee/pet. Designated rooms, service with restrictions.

Quality Inn & Suites
(360) 405-1111. **$78-$169.** 4303 Kitsap Way 98312. 3.5 mi w of ferry terminal; SR 3 exit Kitsap Way, 0.5 mi e. Ext corridors. **Pets:** Accepted.

Super 8
(360) 377-8881. **$63-$81.** 5068 Kitsap Way 98312. 4.2 mi w of ferry terminal; SR 3 exit Kitsap Way, just ne. Int corridors. **Pets:** $10 daily fee/pet. Designated rooms, service with restrictions, supervision.

DUPONT

GuestHouse Inn & Suites
(253) 912-8900. **$99-$179.** 1609 McNeil St 98327. I-5 exit 118, just nw on Center Dr, then just w. Int corridors. **Pets:** Accepted.

EDMONDS

Best Western Plus Edmonds Harbor Inn
(425) 771-5021. **$100-$126.** 130 W Dayton St 98020. Just s at Port of Edmonds. Ext/int corridors. **Pets:** Large. $20 daily fee/room. Designated rooms, service with restrictions, supervision.

EVERETT

Best Western Cascadia Inn
(425) 258-4141. **$89-$109.** 2800 Pacific Ave 98201. I-5 exit 193 northbound; exit 194 southbound, just w. Int corridors. **Pets:** Accepted.

Best Western Plus Navigator Inn & Suites
(425) 347-2555. **$119-$149.** 10210 Evergreen Way 98204. I-5 exit 189, 1 mi w on SR 526 to Evergreen Way, then 1.6 mi s. Int corridors. **Pets:** Medium, dogs only. $20 daily fee/room. Designated rooms, service with restrictions, supervision.

Days Inn Seattle/Everett
(425) 355-1570. **$67-$180.** 1602 SE Everett Mall Way 98208. I-5 exit 189 northbound, 0.5 mi w on SR 527, then 0.5 mi s; exit southbound, 0.7 mi s. Ext corridors. **Pets:** Accepted.

Extended StayAmerica-Seattle-Everett
(425) 355-1923. **$65-$85.** 8410 Broadway 98208. I-5 exit 189, follow signs to Broadway, just nw. Int corridors. **Pets:** Other species. $25 daily fee/pet. Service with restrictions.

Extended Stay Deluxe-Seattle-Everett
(425) 337-1341. **$85-$105.** 1431 112th St SE 98208. I-5 exit 189, 1.5 mi se on 19th Ave SE, then 0.3 mi w. Int corridors. **Pets:** Other species. $25 daily fee/pet. Service with restrictions.

Holiday Inn Downtown Everett
(425) 339-2000. **$99-$169.** 3105 Pine St 98201. I-5 exit 193 northbound; exit 194 southbound, just sw. Int corridors. **Pets:** Medium, other species. $40 one-time fee/pet. Service with restrictions, supervision.

Inn at Port Gardner
(425) 252-6779. **$109-$249.** 1700 W Marine View Dr 98201. I-5 exit 193 northbound, 1.2 mi w on Pacific Ave, then 1.2 mi n; exit 194 southbound, 1.2 mi w on Everett Ave, then 1 mi n; in Everett Marina Village. Int corridors. **Pets:** Medium, other species. $25 one-time fee/room. Service with restrictions, supervision.

La Quinta Inn Everett
(425) 347-9099. **$78-$154.** 12619 4th Ave W 98204. I-5 exit 186, just w. Int corridors. **Pets:** Medium, other species. Service with restrictions, supervision.

Quality Inn & Suites
(425) 609-4550. **$90-$150.** 101 128th St SE 98208. I-5 exit 186, just e. Int corridors. **Pets:** Accepted.

FEDERAL WAY

Clarion Hotel Federal Way
(253) 941-6000. **$73-$130.** 31611 20th Ave S 98003. I-5 exit 143, 0.5 mi w on 320th St, then just n. Int corridors. **Pets:** Medium, dogs only. $15 daily fee/pet. Supervision.

Quality Inn & Suites
(253) 835-4141. **Call for rates.** 1400 S 348th St 98003. I-5 exit 142B, 0.5 mi w. Int corridors. **Pets:** Accepted.

FIFE

Emerald Queen Hotel & Casino
(253) 922-2000. **$89-$129.** 5700 Pacific Hwy E 98424. I-5 exit 137, just ne. Int corridors. **Pets:** Accepted.

Extended StayAmerica-Tacoma-Fife
(253) 926-6316. **$76-$91.** 2820 Pacific Hwy E 98424. I-5 exit 136B northbound; exit 136 southbound, just nw. Int corridors. **Pets:** Other species. $25 daily fee/pet. Service with restrictions.

GIG HARBOR

Best Western Plus Wesley Inn & Suites
(253) 858-9690. **$175-$299.** 6575 Kimball Dr 98335. SR 16 exit City Center, just e on Pioneer Way, then 0.3 mi s. Int corridors. **Pets:** Other species. $15 daily fee/pet. Designated rooms, service with restrictions, supervision.

The Inn at Gig Harbor
(253) 858-1111. **$169-$232, 3 day notice.** 3211 56th St NW 98335. SR 16 exit Olympic Dr, just w, then 0.4 mi n. Int corridors. **Pets:** $25 one-time fee/room, $10 daily fee/room. Designated rooms, service with restrictions, supervision.

KENT

Comfort Inn Kent
(253) 872-2211. **$75-$130.** 22311 84th Ave S 98032. SR 167 exit 84th Ave S, just n. Int corridors. **Pets:** Accepted.

Hawthorn Suites
(253) 395-3800. **$129-$199.** 6329 S 212th St 98032. I-5 exit 152, 2.6 mi se via Orilla Rd and 212th St. Ext corridors. **Pets:** Accepted.

TownePlace Suites by Marriott-Seattle Southcenter
(253) 796-6000. **$79-$149.** 18123 72nd Ave S 98032. I-405 exit 1 (SR 181), 1.6 mi s on W Valley Hwy, just e on S 180th St, then just s. Ext corridors. **Pets:** $10 daily fee/pet. Service with restrictions, supervision.

KIRKLAND

AAA ▼▼▼ Baymont Inn & Suites H
(425) 822-2300. **$85-$86.** 12223 NE 116th St 98034. I-405 exit 20A
northbound; exit 20 southbound, just e; in Totem Lake area. Ext corridors.
Pets: Medium, dogs only. $25 one-time fee/pet. Designated rooms, serv-
ice with restrictions, crate. [SAVE] 🛜 📶 ⓜ 🛏 🖳 ⊷

AAA ▼▼▼ The Heathman Hotel H
(425) 284-5800. **$149-$399.** 220 Kirkland Ave 98033. I-405 exit 18 (NE
85th St), 1 mi w, then just s on 3rd St. Int corridors. **Pets:** Accepted.
[SAVE] 🛜 ✕ ⓜ 🖳 ¶¶

**▼▼▼▼ La Quinta Inn & Suites Seattle Bellevue /
Kirkland H**
(425) 828-6585. **$72-$196.** 10530 NE Northup Way 98033. I-405 exit 14
(SR 520) via 108th Ave exit, 1 mi n on 108th Ave, then just w. Int corridors. **Pets:** Medium, other species. Service with restrictions, supervision.
🛜 ⓜ 🛏 🖳 ⊷

▼▼▼ ▼▼▼ Woodmark Hotel, Yacht Club & Spa H ❖
(425) 822-3700. **$179-$379.** 1200 Carillon Point 98033. On Lake Washington Blvd, 1 mi n of SR 520. Int corridors. **Pets:** Dogs only. No service.
🛜 ✕ ⓜ 🖳 ⊷ ⊠

LAKEWOOD

▼▼▼▼ La Quinta Inn & Suites Lakewood H
(253) 582-7000. **$125-$189.** 11751 Pacific Hwy SW 98499. I-5 exit 125,
just nw. Int corridors. **Pets:** Medium, other species. Service with restrictions, supervision. 🛜 ✕ 🛏 🖳 ⊷

LYNNWOOD

AAA ▼▼▼ Best Western Alderwood H ❖
(425) 775-7600. **$79-$105.** 19332 36th Ave W 98036. I-5 exit 181B
northbound, just n on Poplar Way, just w on 196th St SW, then just n;
exit 181 (SR 524 W) southbound, just nw. Int corridors. **Pets:** Very small,
dogs only. $25 one-time fee/pet. Designated rooms, service with restric-
tions, crate. [SAVE] 🛜 ⓜ 🛏 🖳 ⊷

▼▼▼ Embassy Suites Hotel Seattle North/Lynnwood H
(425) 775-2500. **$109-$229.** 20610 44th Ave W 98036. I-5 exit 181A
northbound, just se; exit 181 (SR 524 W) southbound, 0.5 w on 196th St
SW, then 0.6 mi s. Int corridors. **Pets:** Small, dogs only. $50 daily fee/
room. Designated rooms, service with restrictions.
🛜 ⓜ 🛏 🖳 ¶¶ ⊷ ⊠

AAA ▼▼▼▼ La Quinta Inn Lynnwood H
(425) 775-7447. **$89-$189.** 4300 Alderwood Mall Blvd 98036. I-5 exit
181A northbound, just w; exit 181 (SR 524 W) southbound, 0.5 mi w on
196th St SW, just s on 44th Ave SW, then just e. Int corridors.
Pets: Medium, other species. Service with restrictions, supervision.
[SAVE] 🛜 ✕ 🛏 🖳 ⊷

**▼▼▼ Residence Inn by Marriott-Seattle
North/Lynnwood H ❖**
(425) 771-1100. **$109-$179.** 18200 Alderwood Mall Pkwy 98037. I-5 exit
183 southbound, just w on 164th St SW, then 1.5 mi se on 28th St W;
exit 182 northbound on SR 525 exit 1, then just s; just n of Alderwood
Mall. Ext corridors. **Pets:** Other species. $75 one-time fee/room. Service
with restrictions, crate. 🛜 ✕ ⓜ 🛏 🖳 ⊷ ⊠

MONROE

AAA ▼▼▼ Best Western Sky Valley Inn H
(360) 794-3111. **$110-$140.** 19233 US 2 98272. West end of town. Int
corridors. **Pets:** Dogs only. $20 daily fee/pet. Service with restrictions,
supervision. [SAVE] 🛜 ✕ ⓜ 🛏 🖳 ⊷

AAA ▼▼▼ GuestHouse International Inn & Suites H
(360) 863-1900. **$114-$144.** 19103 US 2 98272. West end of town. Int
corridors. **Pets:** Other species. $20 daily fee/room. Supervision.
[SAVE] 🛜 ✕ ⓜ 🛏 🖳 ⊷

MUKILTEO

AAA ▼▼▼▼ Staybridge Suites Seattle North-Everett H
(425) 493-9500. **$119-$249, 3 day notice.** 9600 Harbour Pl 98275. Jct
Paine Field Blvd and SR 525 (Mukilteo Speedway). Int corridors.
Pets: Accepted. [SAVE] 🛜 ✕ ⓜ 🛏 🖳 ⊷ ⊠

▼▼▼ TownePlace Suites by Marriott-Mukilteo H ❖
(425) 551-5900. **$79-$149.** 8521 Mukilteo Speedway 98275. Just se of
jct 84th St SW and SR 525 (Mukilteo Speedway). Ext corridors.
Pets: Other species. $10 daily fee/pet. Service with restrictions, crate.
🛜 ✕ ⓜ 🛏 🖳 ⊷ ⊠

PORT ORCHARD

AAA ▼▼▼ Comfort Inn Port Orchard M
(360) 895-2666. **$85-$120.** 1121 Bay St 98366. SR 16 exit Tremont St,
0.9 mi e to Sidney Ave, 1.2 mi n to Bay St, then just e. Ext corridors.
Pets: Large, dogs only. $10 daily fee/pet. Designated rooms, service with
restrictions, supervision. [SAVE] 🛜 ✕ ⓜ 🛏 🖳

▼▼▼ Days Inn Port Orchard H
(360) 895-7818. **$60-$113.** 220 Bravo Terrace 98366. SR 16 exit SR
160 E (Sedgwick Rd), just se. Int corridors. **Pets:** Accepted.
🛜 ⓜ 🛏 🖳 ⊷

POULSBO

▼▼▼ GuestHouse International Inn & Suites H ❖
(360) 697-4400. **$109-$179.** 19801 7th Ave NE 98370. On SR 305. Int
corridors. **Pets:** Medium. $30 daily fee/pet. Service with restrictions,
supervision. 🛜 ⓜ 🛏 🖳

AAA ▼▼▼▼ Poulsbo Inn & Suites M
(360) 779-3921. **$99-$130, 7 day notice.** 18680 SR 305 NE 98370. SR
3, 2.3 mi e. Ext corridors. **Pets:** Medium. $15 daily fee/pet. Designated
rooms, service with restrictions, supervision.
[SAVE] 🛜 ⓜ 🛏 🖳 ⊷ ⊠

PUYALLUP

AAA ▼▼▼▼ Best Western Plus Park Plaza H ❖
(253) 848-1500. **$139-$169.** 620 S Hill Park Dr 98373. SR 512 exit S
Hill Park Dr southbound, just w; exit 9th St SW northbound, just w. Int
corridors. **Pets:** Dogs only. $20 one-time fee/room. Service with restric-
tions, crate. [SAVE] 🛜 ⓜ 🛏 🖳

▼ Crossland Economy Suites-Tacoma-Puyallup M ❖
(253) 445-5945. **$59-$69.** 2101 N Meridian 98371. SR 512 exit Milton/
Tacoma, just w on SR 167, then just n. Ext corridors. **Pets:** Other species. $25 daily fee/pet. Service with restrictions. 🛜 ⓜ 🛏 🖳

▼▼▼ Holiday Inn Express Hotel & Suites Puyallup H
(253) 848-4900. **$149-$189.** 812 S Hill Park Dr 98373. SR 512 exit S
Hill Park Dr southbound, just w; exit 9th St SW northbound, just w. Int
corridors. **Pets:** Accepted. 🛜 ✕ 🛏 🖳 ⊷

REDMOND

AAA ▼▼▼▼ Redmond Marriott Town Center H ❖
(425) 498-4000. **$107-$240.** 7401 164th Ave NE 98052. I-405 exit 14
(SR 520), 4.5 mi e to W Lake Sammamish Pkwy, just n to Leary Way,
just e to Bear Creek Pkwy, just s to NE 74th Ave, then just w. Int corridors. **Pets:** Medium, other species. $75 one-time fee/room. Designated
rooms, service with restrictions, supervision.
[ECO] [SAVE] 🛜 ✕ ⓜ 🛏 🖳 ¶¶ ⊷ ⊠

**▼▼▼ Residence Inn by Marriott Seattle East /
Redmond H ❖**
(425) 497-9226. **$98-$219.** 7575 164th Ave NE 98052. I-405 exit 14 (SR
520), 4.5 mi e to W Lake Sammamish Pkwy, just n to Leary Way, just e
to Bear Creek Pkwy, just s to NE 74th Ave, just w to 164th Ave NE, then
just n; center. Int corridors. **Pets:** Medium. $100 one-time fee/room. Serv-
ice with restrictions, crate. [ECO] 🛜 ✕ ⓜ 🛏 🖳 ⊷

RENTON

▼▼▼▼ **Holiday Inn-Renton** H
(425) 226-7700. **$79-$169.** One S Grady Way 98057. I-405 exit 2 (SR 167/Rainier Ave), jct SR 167 N. Int corridors. **Pets:** Accepted.
📶 🖥 🅿 🍽 📺 ⋙

▼▼▼ **Quality Inn Renton** H
(425) 226-7600. **$89-$99.** 1850 SE Maple Valley Hwy 98057. I-405 exit 4 (Bronson Way) northbound, follow Maple Valley Hwy; exit southbound, 0.6 mi s to 2nd light, then just e. Int corridors. **Pets:** Accepted.
📶 🖥 🅿

▼▼▼ **TownePlace Suites Seattle South/Renton** H
(425) 917-2000. **$71-$189.** 300 SW 19th St 98057. SR 167 exit E Valley Rd, 1 mi nw, then just w. Int corridors. **Pets:** Accepted.
📶 ⋙ ♿ 🅿 📺 ⋙

SEATAC

ⒶⒶⒶ ▼▼▼▼ **Cedarbrook Lodge** H 🐾
(206) 901-9268. **$129-$299.** 18525 36th Ave S 98188. SR 99, just e on 188th St, then just n. Int corridors. **Pets:** Medium, dogs only. $50 one-time fee/room. Service with restrictions. SAVE 📶 ⋙ ♿ 🅿 📺 🍽

▼▼▼ **Clarion Hotel** H
(206) 242-0200. **$98-$125.** 3000 S 176th St 98188. Just e of SR 99. Int corridors. **Pets:** Accepted. 📶 ⋙ ♿ 🅿 📺 🍽 ⋙

▼▼▼▼ **DoubleTree by Hilton Hotel Seattle Airport** H
(206) 246-8600. **$99-$145.** 18740 International Blvd 98188. On SR 99. Int corridors. **Pets:** Accepted. 📶 🅿 📺 🍽 ⋙

▼▼▼ **Hilton Seattle Airport & Conference Center** H
(206) 244-4800. **$115-$199.** 17620 International Blvd 98188. On SR 99. Int corridors. **Pets:** Accepted. 📶 ⋙ 📺 🍽 ⋙

▼▼▼▼ **Holiday Inn Express Hotel & Suites-Seattle Sea-Tac Airport** H
(206) 824-3200. **$89-$159.** 19621 International Blvd 98188. On SR 99. Int corridors. **Pets:** $50 one-time fee/room. Service with restrictions, supervision. 📶 🅿 📺

▼▼▼▼ **Holiday Inn Seattle SeaTac International Airport** H
(206) 248-1000. **$99-$209.** 17338 International Blvd 98188. On SR 99. Int corridors. **Pets:** Accepted. 📶 ⋙ ♿ 🅿 📺 🍽 ⋙

▼ **Motel 6 - 1332** M
(206) 246-4101. **$49-$65.** 16500 International Blvd 98188. On SR 99. Ext corridors. **Pets:** Other species. Service with restrictions, supervision.
ECO 📶

▼ **Motel 6 - 736** M
(206) 824-9902. **$41-$55.** 20651 Military Rd 98198. I-5 exit 151, just se. Ext corridors. **Pets:** Other species. Service with restrictions, supervision.
ECO 📶 🅿 ⋙

▼▼▼ **Radisson Hotel Seattle Airport** H
(206) 244-6666. **$99-$259.** 18118 International Blvd 98188. On SR 99. Int corridors. **Pets:** Accepted. ECO 📶 ⋙ ♿ 📺 🍽 ⋙ ⋙

ⒶⒶⒶ ▼▼▼ **Red Lion Hotel Seattle Airport** H
(206) 246-5535. **$89-$239.** 18220 International Blvd 98188. On SR 99. Int corridors. **Pets:** Accepted. SAVE 📶 📺 🍽 ⋙

▼▼ **Super 8 Sea-Tac** H
(206) 433-8188. **$62-$75.** 3100 S 192nd St 98188. Just e of SR 99. Int corridors. **Pets:** Small. $10 daily fee/pet. Service with restrictions, supervision. 📶 📺

SEATTLE

ⒶⒶⒶ ▼▼▼ ▼▼▼ **Alexis Hotel** H
(206) 624-4844. **$139-$349.** 1007 1st Ave 98104. Corner of Madison St and 1st Ave. Int corridors. **Pets:** Accepted.
ECO SAVE 📶 ⋙ 🅿 📺 ⋙

ⒶⒶⒶ ▼▼▼ **Comfort Inn & Suites Seattle** H
(206) 361-3700. **$75-$180.** 13700 Aurora Ave N 98133. I-5 exit 175, 1.1 mi w on NE 145th St, then 0.3 mi s. Int corridors. **Pets:** Accepted.
SAVE 📶 ⋙ 🅿 📺 ⋙

▼▼▼ **Crowne Plaza Seattle-Downtown** H
(206) 464-1980. **$99-$259.** 1113 6th Ave 98101. Corner of 6th Ave and Seneca St. Int corridors. **Pets:** $50 one-time fee/room. Designated rooms, service with restrictions. 📶 ⋙ ♿ 🅿 📺 🍽

ⒶⒶⒶ ▼▼▼ ▼▼▼ **The Edgewater** H
(206) 728-7000. **$229-$729.** 2411 Alaskan Way, Pier 67 98121. On waterfront at Pier 67; at base of Wall St. Int corridors. **Pets:** Designated rooms, service with restrictions, supervision.
SAVE 📶 ⋙ 🅿 📺 🍽

▼▼▼ **Executive Hotel Pacific** H 🐾
(206) 623-3900. **$129-$249.** 400 Spring St 98104. Between 4th and 5th aves. Int corridors. **Pets:** Small, other species. $40 deposit/room, $40 one-time fee/room. Designated rooms, service with restrictions, supervision. 📶 ⋙ 📺

ⒶⒶⒶ ▼▼▼ ▼▼▼ **The Fairmont Olympic Hotel** H
(206) 621-1700. **Call for rates.** 411 University St 98101. Corner of 4th Ave and University St. Int corridors. **Pets:** Accepted.
ECO SAVE 📶 🅿 📺 🍽 ⋙ ⋙

ⒶⒶⒶ ▼▼▼ ▼▼▼ **Four Seasons Hotel Seattle** H
(206) 749-7000. **$365-$545.** 99 Union St 98101. Southwest corner of 1st Ave and Union St. Int corridors. **Pets:** Accepted.
SAVE 📶 ⋙ ♿ 🍽 ⋙ ⋙

ⒶⒶⒶ ▼▼▼ ▼▼▼ **Grand Hyatt Seattle** H
(206) 774-1234. **$179-$419, 3 day notice.** 721 Pine St 98101. Corner of 7th Ave and Pine St. Int corridors. **Pets:** Accepted.
ECO SAVE 📶 🅿 📺 🍽 ⋙

▼▼▼ ▼▼▼ **Homewood Suites by Hilton-Seattle Downtown** H
(206) 281-9393. **$199-$239.** 206 Western Ave W 98119. I-5 exit 167 (Mercer St), 0.3 mi w, 0.5 mi s on Fairview Ave, 1.2 mi w on Denny Way, then just n. Int corridors. **Pets:** Medium, other species. $20 daily fee/pet. 📶 🅿 📺

▼▼▼ ▼▼▼ **Hotel 1000** H 🐾
(206) 957-1000. **$199-$449.** 1000 1st Ave 98104. Northeast corner of 1st Ave and Madison St. Int corridors. **Pets:** Medium, other species. $25 deposit/room. Service with restrictions, supervision. 📶 ⋙ 📺 🍽

▼▼ ▼▼ **Hotel Five** H
(206) 441-9785. **$105-$195.** 2200 5th Ave 98121. Corner of Blanchard St and 5th Ave. Int corridors. **Pets:** Accepted. 📶 ⋙ ♿ 📺 🍽

ⒶⒶⒶ ▼▼▼ **Hotel Max** H
(206) 728-6299. **$119-$269.** 620 Stewart St 98101. Corner of 7th Ave and Stewart St. Int corridors. **Pets:** Accepted.
SAVE 📶 ⋙ ♿ 🅿 📺 🍽

ⒶⒶⒶ ▼▼▼ **Hotel Monaco** H
(206) 621-1770. **$139-$349.** 1101 4th Ave 98101. Corner of 4th Ave and Spring St. Int corridors. **Pets:** Accepted. ECO SAVE 📶 ⋙ 🍽 ⋙

ⒶⒶⒶ ▼▼▼ **Hotel Nexus Seattle** H 🐾
(206) 365-0700. **$109-$209.** 2140 N Northgate Way 98133. I-5 exit 173, just nw. Ext corridors. **Pets:** $15 daily fee/room. Service with restrictions.
SAVE 📶 ⋙ ♿ 🅿 📺 ⋙

Hotel Vintage Park 🅷
(206) 624-8000. **$149-$699.** 1100 5th Ave 98101. Corner of Spring St and 5th Ave. Int corridors. **Pets:** Accepted.
ᴇᴄᴏ ꜱᴀᴠᴇ 🛜 ✕ 🍴 ⊠

Inn at Harbor Steps 🅷 🐾
(206) 748-0973. **$225-$375, 3 day notice.** 1221 1st Ave 98101. Corner of Seneca St and 1st Ave. Int corridors. **Pets:** Medium, dogs only. $65 one-time fee/pet. Designated rooms, service with restrictions, supervision.
🛜 ✕ 🛏 🖥 ⊅ ⊠

La Quinta Inn & Suites Seattle Downtown 🅷
(206) 624-6820. **$86-$180.** 2224 8th Ave 98121. Corner of 8th Ave and Blanchard St. Int corridors. **Pets:** Medium, other species. Service with restrictions, supervision. 🛜 ✕ 🖥 🖳

The Maxwell Hotel 🅷
(206) 286-0629. **$139-$359.** 300 Roy St 98109. Corner of Roy St and 3rd Ave N. Int corridors. **Pets:** Accepted. 🛜 ✕ 🔊 🛏 🖳 ⊅

Pan Pacific Hotel Seattle 🅷 🐾
(206) 264-8111. **$169-$525.** 2125 Terry Ave 98121. Just s of jct E Denny Way. Int corridors. **Pets:** $50 one-time fee/room. Service with restrictions, supervision. ꜱᴀᴠᴇ 🛜 ✕ 🖳 🍴 ⊠

Red Lion Hotel on Fifth Avenue-Seattle 🅷
(206) 971-8000. **Call for rates.** 1415 5th Ave 98101. Between Pike and Union sts. Int corridors. **Pets:** Accepted. ꜱᴀᴠᴇ 🛜 ✕ 🛏 🖳 🍴

Renaissance Seattle Hotel 🅷
(206) 583-0300. **$145-$252.** 515 Madison St 98104. Corner of Madison St and 6th Ave. Int corridors. **Pets:** Accepted.
ꜱᴀᴠᴇ 🛜 ✕ 🔊 🛏 🖳 🍴 ⊅ ⊠

Residence Inn by Marriott Seattle Downtown/Lake Union 🅷 🐾
(206) 624-6000. **$109-$249.** 800 Fairview Ave N 98109. I-5 exit 167 (Mercer St), just ne; south end of Lake Union. Int corridors. **Pets:** Other species. $10 daily fee/pet. Service with restrictions, supervision.
🛜 ✕ 🛏 🖳 ⊅ ⊠

The Roosevelt, A Coast Hotel 🅷
(206) 621-1200. **$149-$289.** 1531 7th Ave 98101. Corner of 7th Ave and Pine St. Int corridors. **Pets:** Accepted. ꜱᴀᴠᴇ 🛜 ✕ 🛏 🖳 🍴

Sheraton Seattle Hotel 🅷 🐾
(206) 621-9000. **$149-$249.** 1400 6th Ave 98101. Between Pike and Union sts. Int corridors. **Pets:** Medium, dogs only. Designated rooms, service with restrictions, supervision.
ꜱᴀᴠᴇ 🛜 ✕ 🔊 🖳 🍴 ⊅ ⊠

Sorrento Hotel 🅷 🐾
(206) 622-6400. **$145-$345.** 900 Madison St 98104. I-5 exit Madison St, just e; at 9th Ave and Madison St. Int corridors. **Pets:** Medium. $60 one-time fee/room. Service with restrictions, supervision.
ꜱᴀᴠᴇ 🛜 ✕ 🔊 🖳 🍴

University Inn 🅷
(206) 632-5055. **$125-$209.** 4140 Roosevelt Way NE 98105. I-5 exit 169, 0.5 mi e, then just s. Int corridors. **Pets:** Accepted.
🛜 ✕ 🛏 🖳 🍴 ⊅

Watertown 🅷
(206) 826-4242. **$155-$239.** 4242 Roosevelt Way NE 98105. I-5 exit 169, just e, then just s. Int corridors. **Pets:** Accepted.
🛜 ✕ 🔊 🛏 🖳

The Westin Seattle 🅷
(206) 728-1000. **$159-$399.** 1900 5th Ave 98101. Corner of 5th Ave and Stewart St. Int corridors. **Pets:** Accepted.
ᴇᴄᴏ ꜱᴀᴠᴇ 🛜 ✕ 🔊 🛏 🖳 🍴 ⊅

W Seattle 🅷
(206) 264-6000. **$229-$559.** 1112 4th Ave 98101. Corner of 4th Ave and Seneca St. Int corridors. **Pets:** Accepted. ꜱᴀᴠᴇ 🛜 ✕ 🔊 🍴 ⊠

SILVERDALE

Oxford Inn 🅷 🐾
(360) 692-7777. **$72-$90.** 9734 NW Silverdale Way 98383. SR 3 exit Newberry Hill Rd, just e, then 1.2 mi n. Int corridors. **Pets:** Small. $25 daily fee/pet. Designated rooms, service with restrictions, crate.
🛜 🛏 🖳

Oxford Suites Silverdale 🅷
(360) 698-9550. **$113-$189.** 9550 NW Silverdale Way 98383. SR 3 exit Newberry Hill Rd, 1.5 mi e. Int corridors. **Pets:** Small. $25 daily fee/pet. Designated rooms, service with restrictions, crate.
🛜 ✕ 🔊 🛏 🖳 🍴 ⊅ ⊠

Silverdale Beach Hotel 🅷
(360) 698-1000. **$115-$199.** 3073 NW Bucklin Hill Rd 98383. SR 3 exit Newberry Hill Rd, just e, 1 mi n on Silverdale Way, then just e. Int corridors. **Pets:** Medium, other species. $25 one-time fee/room. Service with restrictions, crate. ꜱᴀᴠᴇ 🛜 ✕ 🛏 🖳 🍴 ⊅ ⊠

SNOHOMISH

Inn At Snohomish 🅼
(360) 568-2208. **$80-$135.** 323 2nd St 98290. East end of town. Ext corridors. **Pets:** Other species. $50 deposit/room. Service with restrictions, crate. ꜱᴀᴠᴇ 🛜 🔊 🛏 🖳

SNOQUALMIE

Salish Lodge & Spa 🅷
(425) 888-2556. **$209-$999, 7 day notice.** 6501 Railroad Ave SE 98065. I-90 exit 27 eastbound, 5 mi ne via North Bend Way, Meadowbrook Way and SR 202; exit 31 westbound, 7 mi nw via SR 202. Int corridors. **Pets:** Accepted. ꜱᴀᴠᴇ 🛜 ✕ 🛏 🖳 🍴 ⊠

SUQUAMISH

Suquamish Clearwater Casino Resort 🅷
(360) 598-8700. **$79-$249.** 15347 Suquamish Way 98392. SR 3 exit SR 305, 6.2 mi se. Ext/int corridors. **Pets:** Accepted.
🛜 🛏 🖳 🍴 ⊅ ⊠

TACOMA

Comfort Inn Tacoma 🅷
(253) 538-7998. **$120-$170.** 8620 S Hosmer St 98444. I-5 exit 128 northbound; exit 129 southbound, follow signs to 84th St, just e to Hosmer St, then just s. Int corridors. **Pets:** Medium, other species. $25 daily fee/room. Designated rooms, service with restrictions, supervision.
ꜱᴀᴠᴇ 🛜 ✕ 🛏 🖳 ⊅

Hotel Murano 🅷
(253) 238-8000. **Call for rates.** 1320 Broadway Plaza 98402. I-5 exit 133 (City Center) to I-705 N exit A St, just w on 11th St, then just s; downtown. Int corridors. **Pets:** Accepted.
ꜱᴀᴠᴇ 🛜 ✕ 🛏 🖳 🍴 ⊠

La Quinta Inn & Suites Tacoma Seattle 🅷
(253) 383-0146. **$93-$188.** 1425 E 27th St 98421. I-5 exit 135 southbound; exit 134 northbound, just n. Int corridors. **Pets:** Medium, other species. Service with restrictions, supervision. 🛜 🛏 🖳 🍴 ⊅

Red Lion Hotel Tacoma 🅷
(253) 548-1212. **$109-$149.** 8402 S Hosmer St 98444. I-5 exit 128 northbound, just ne; exit 129 southbound, just e on 72nd St, then 1 mi s. Int corridors. **Pets:** Accepted. ꜱᴀᴠᴇ 🛜 ✕ 🛏 🖳 ⊅

Shilo Inn & Suites - Tacoma 🅷
(253) 475-4020. **$89-$199.** 7414 S Hosmer St 98408. I-5 exit 129, just se. Int corridors. **Pets:** Dogs only. $25 one-time fee/room. Designated rooms, service with restrictions, crate. ꜱᴀᴠᴇ 🛜 🛏 🖳 ⊅ ⊠

TUKWILA

▼▼▼ **Embassy Suites Hotel** 🅷
(425) 227-8844. **$99-$229.** 15920 W Valley Hwy 98188. I-405 exit 1 (SR 181), just s. Int corridors. **Pets:** Accepted.
🛜 🛏 💻 🍴 ➿ ✕

▼▼ **Extended StayAmerica-Seattle-Tukwila** 🅷 🐾
(206) 244-2537. **$65-$80.** 15451 53rd Ave S 98188. I-5 exit 153 northbound, just n on Southcenter Pkwy, just n on 61st St, just w on Southcenter Blvd, then just sw; exit 154B (Southcenter Mall) southbound, just sw. Ext corridors. **Pets:** Other species. $25 daily fee/pet. Service with restrictions. 🛜 🛏 💻

▼▼▼ **Homewood Suites by Hilton** 🅷
(206) 433-8000. **$119-$199.** 6955 Fort Dent Way 98188. I-405 exit 1 (SR 181), just ne. Ext/int corridors. **Pets:** Large. $75 one-time fee/room. Service with restrictions. 🛜 🛏 💻 ➿ ✕

▼▼ **Ramada Limited Sea-Tac Airport** 🅷
(206) 244-8800. **$46-$114.** 13900 Tukwila International Blvd 98168. I-5 exit 158 southbound, 2 mi s; exit 154A (SR 518 W) northbound, 1 mi n on SR 99. Int corridors. **Pets:** Large, other species. $40 daily fee/room. Designated rooms, service with restrictions, supervision. 🛜 🛏 💻

▼▼▼ **Residence Inn by Marriott-Seattle South** 🅷
(425) 226-5500. **$99-$189.** 16201 W Valley Hwy 98188. I-405 exit 1 (SR 181), just s. Ext corridors. **Pets:** Accepted.
🛜 ✕ 🛁M 🛏 💻 ➿ ✕

VASHON

▼ **The Swallow's Nest Guest Cottages** 🅲🅰 🐾
(206) 463-2646. **$105-$280.** 6030 SW 248th St 98070. North end Ferry Landing, 7.8 mi s on Vashon Hwy; south end (Tahlequah) Ferry Landing, 5.8 mi n on Vashon Hwy, 1.4 mi e on Quartermaster Dr, 1.5 mi s on Dockton Rd, 0.4 mi s on 75th Ave, then 1 mi e. Ext corridors. **Pets:** Other species. $15 daily fee/pet. Designated rooms, service with restrictions, supervision. ✕ 🛏 💻 🅰C

WOODINVILLE

▼▼▼ ▼▼▼ **Willows Lodge** 🅷
(425) 424-3900. **$179-$599, 3 day notice.** 14580 NE 145th St 98072. I-405 exit 20B (NE 124th St), 0.9 mi e, 1.3 mi n on 132nd Ave NE, 0.6 mi e on NE 143rd Pl, then just e. Int corridors. **Pets:** Accepted.
🛜 ✕ 🛏 💻 🍴 ✕

END METROPOLITAN AREA

SEQUIM

▼▼▼ **Juan de Fuca Cottages** 🅲🅰
(360) 683-4433. **$110-$325, 14 day notice.** 182 Marine Dr 98382. 7 mi n via Sequim Ave and E Anderson Rd; downtown. Ext corridors. **Pets:** Medium, dogs only. $20 daily fee/pet. Designated rooms, service with restrictions, supervision. 🛜 ✕ 🛏 💻 🅰C 🔁

▼▼▼ **Quality Inn & Suites - Sequim** 🅷
(360) 683-2800. **$120-$180.** 134 River Rd 98382. US 101 exit River Rd, just nw. Int corridors. **Pets:** Accepted. 🅴🅲🅾 🛜 ✕ 🛏 💻 ➿

▲▲▲ ▼▼▼ **Sequim West Inn** 🅼
(360) 683-4144. **$54-$125, 3 day notice.** 740 W Washington St 98382. US 101 exit River Rd, 0.9 mi ne via River Rd and W Washington St. Ext corridors. **Pets:** Small. $10 daily fee/pet. Service with restrictions, supervision. 🆂🅰🆅🅴 🛜 🛏 💻

SHELTON

▲▲▲ ▼▼▼▼ **Little Creek Casino Resort** 🅷
(360) 427-7711. **$89-$439.** 91 W SR 108 98584. Jct US 101 and SR 108. Int corridors. **Pets:** $50 one-time fee/room. Service with restrictions.
🆂🅰🆅🅴 🛜 🛁M 🛏 💻 🍴 ➿ ✕

▼▼ **Super 8 of Shelton** 🅷 🐾
(360) 426-1654. **$55-$71.** 2943 Northview Cir 98584. US 101 exit Wallace-Kneeland Blvd, just se. Int corridors. **Pets:** $15 daily fee/pet. Service with restrictions, supervision. 🛜 🛏 💻

SNOQUALMIE PASS

▼▼ **Summit Inn** 🅷
(425) 434-6300. **$89-$159, 3 day notice.** 603 SR 906 98068. I-90 exit 52 eastbound, 0.3 mi e; exit 53 westbound, 0.3 mi w. Int corridors. **Pets:** Medium. $25 one-time fee/pet. Designated rooms, service with restrictions, supervision. 🛜 ✕ 🛏 💻 🍴 ✕

SOAP LAKE

▼▼ **Notaras Lodge** 🅼
(509) 246-0462. **$85-$145.** 236 E Main Ave 98851. Just w of SR 17. Ext corridors. **Pets:** Accepted. 🛜 ✕ 🛏 💻

SPOKANE

▲▲▲ ▼▼▼ **Apple Tree Inn** 🅼
(509) 466-3020. **$44-$69.** 9508 N Division St 99218. Jct US 2 and 395, just n. Ext/int corridors. **Pets:** Small, dogs only. $10 daily fee/pet. Designated rooms, service with restrictions, supervision. 🆂🅰🆅🅴 🛜 🛏 ➿

▲▲▲ ▼▼▼ **Best Western Plus Peppertree Airport Inn** 🅷
(509) 624-4655. **$79-$250.** 3711 S Geiger Blvd 99224. I-90 exit 276 (Geiger Field), 1.3 mi n, 0.8 mi s, 0.4 mi e, then just s. Int corridors.
Pets: Accepted. 🆂🅰🆅🅴 🛜 ✕ 🛏 💻 ➿ ✕

▼▼ **Comfort Inn North** 🅷
(509) 467-7111. **Call for rates.** 7111 N Division St 99208. I-90 exit 281 (Division St), 4.6 mi n. Int corridors. **Pets:** Medium, other species. $10 daily fee/pet. Designated rooms, no service, supervision.
🛜 🛏 💻 ➿ ✕

▲▲▲ ▼▼ **Comfort Inn University District/Downtown** 🅷 🐾
(509) 535-9000. **$80-$150.** 923 E 3rd Ave 99202. I-90 exit 281 (Division St), just n to E 3rd Ave, then 0.7 mi e. Int corridors. **Pets:** $15 one-time fee/room. Service with restrictions, supervision.
🆂🅰🆅🅴 🛜 🛁M 🛏 💻 ➿

▲▲▲ ▼▼▼ ▼▼▼ **The Davenport Hotel and Tower** 🅷
(509) 455-8888. **$139-$299.** 10 S Post St 99201. Downtown. Int corridors. **Pets:** Accepted. 🅴🅲🅾 🆂🅰🆅🅴 🛜 ✕ 🛁M 🛏 🍴 ➿ ✕

▲▲▲ ▼▼▼ **DoubleTree by Hilton Spokane City Center** 🅷 🐾
(509) 455-9600. **$109-$249.** 322 N Spokane Falls Ct 99201. I-90 exit 281 (Division St), just n; downtown. Int corridors. **Pets:** $25 one-time fee/room. Service with restrictions, supervision.
🆂🅰🆅🅴 🛜 🛏 💻 🍴 ➿ ✕

▼▼ **Fairbridge Inn Express** 🅷
(509) 838-6630. **$70-$100.** 211 S Division St 99202. I-90 exit 281 (Division St), just n. Int corridors. **Pets:** Accepted. 🛜 🛏 💻

▼▼▼ **Holiday Inn Express-Downtown** 🅷
(509) 328-8505. **$129-$199.** 801 N Division St 99202. I-90 exit 281 (Division St), 0.8 mi n. Ext/int corridors. **Pets:** Accepted.
🛜 ✕ 🛁M 🛏 💻

▼▼▼ **Holiday Inn Spokane Airport** �H ❖
(509) 838-1170. **$103-$149.** 1616 S Windsor Dr 99224. I-90 exit 277
westbound; exit 277B eastbound, just w on US 2, then just s. Int corridors. **Pets:** Medium. $50 deposit/room. Service with restrictions, supervision. 🛜 ✕ ♨ ♿ 🍴 ➳

▼▼ **Howard Johnson Inn North** Ⓜ
(509) 326-5500. **$60-$152.** 3033 N Division St 99207. I-90 exit 281 (Division St), 2.3 mi n on US 2 and 395. Int corridors. **Pets:** Medium, other species. $10 daily fee/pet. Designated rooms, service with restrictions, supervision. 🛜 ✕ ♨ ♿ ➳

🅐🅐🅐 ▼▼▼ **The Madison Inn by Riversage** �H ❖
(509) 474-4200. **$78-$95.** 15 W Rockwood Blvd 99204. I-90 exit 281 (Division St) eastbound, just e to Cowley St, 0.4 mi s, then just w; exit westbound, just n to 2nd Ave, just w to Browne St, 0.5 mi s to 9th Ave, then just e. Int corridors. **Pets:** $10 daily fee/pet. Designated rooms, service with restrictions, supervision. 🆂🅰🆅🅴 🛜 ✕ ♨ ♿ 🍴

▼▼▼ **Oxford Suites-Downtown Spokane** �H
(509) 353-9000. **$117-$158.** 115 W North River Dr 99201. I-90 exit 281 (Division St), 1 mi n, then just n. Int corridors. **Pets:** Accepted.
🛜 ✕ ♨ ♿ ➳ 🗶

▼▼ **Quality Inn Oakwood** �H
(509) 467-4900. **$80-$149.** 7919 N Division St 99208. I-90 exit 281 (Division St), 6.5 mi n. Int corridors. **Pets:** $30 one-time fee/room. Designated rooms, service with restrictions, supervision. 🛜 ♿ ♨ ♿ ➳

▼▼▼ **Ramada Spokane Airport & Indoor
Waterpark** �H ❖
(509) 838-5211. **$49-$221.** 8909 Airport Dr 99224. I-90 exit 277B eastbound; exit 277 westbound, 3.4 mi n. Int corridors. **Pets:** Medium. $20 daily fee/pet. Designated rooms, service with restrictions, supervision. 🛜 ✕ ♨ ♿ 🍴 ➳ 🗶

🅐🅐🅐 ▼▼▼▼ **Red Lion Hotel at the Park-Spokane** �H
(509) 326-8000. **$99-$249.** 303 W North River Dr 99201. I-90 exit 281 (Division St), 1.5 mi n on US 195, then just w. Int corridors.
Pets: Accepted. 🆂🅰🆅🅴 🛜 ✕ ♨ ♿ 🍴 ➳ 🗶

🅐🅐🅐 ▼▼▼▼ **Red Lion River Inn-Spokane** �H
(509) 326-5577. **$99-$199.** 700 N Division St 99202. I-90 exit 281 (Division St), 0.8 mi n; downtown. Int corridors. **Pets:** Accepted.
🆂🅰🆅🅴 🛜 ✕ ♿ ♨ ♿ 🍴 ➳ 🗶

🅐🅐🅐 ▼▼▼ **Super 8 Airport West** Ⓜ
(509) 838-8800. **$54-$108.** 11102 W Westbow Blvd 99224. I-90 exit 272 (Medical Lake Rd), just s. Int corridors. **Pets:** Other species. $15 one-time fee/room. Designated rooms, service with restrictions, supervision.
🆂🅰🆅🅴 🛜 ♿ ♨ ♿ ➳

▼▼ **Travelodge Spokane at the Convention
Center** �H ❖
(509) 623-9727. **$80-$170.** W 33 Spokane Falls Blvd 99201. I-90 exit 281 (Division St), 0.5 mi n, then just w. Int corridors. **Pets:** Dogs only. $12 daily fee/pet. Supervision. 🛜 ✕ ♿ ♨ ♿

▼▼▼ **Wingate by Wyndham Spokane Airport** �H
(509) 838-3226. **$90-$117.** 2726 S Flint Rd 99201. I-90 exit 277B eastbound; exit 277 westbound, 3 mi w, then just s. Int corridors. **Pets:** Other species. $150 deposit/room. Designated rooms, service with restrictions, crate. 🛜 ✕ ♿ ♨ ♿ ➳

SPOKANE VALLEY

▼▼▼ **Holiday Inn Express-Valley** �H ❖
(509) 927-7100. **$119-$229.** 9220 E Mission Ave 99206. I-90 exit 287, just s. Ext/int corridors. **Pets:** Other species. Designated rooms, supervision. 🛜 ♿ ♨ ♿ ➳

▼▼▼ **La Quinta Inn & Suites Spokane** �H
(509) 893-0955. **$75-$174.** 3808 N Sullivan Rd 99216. I-90 exit 291B, 1.3 mi n. Int corridors. **Pets:** Medium, other species. Service with restrictions, supervision. 🛜 ♿ ♨ ♿ ➳

▼▼▼ **Mirabeau Park Hotel & Convention Center** �H
(509) 924-9000. **$85-$169.** 1100 N Sullivan Rd 99037. I-90 exit 291B, just s. Int corridors. **Pets:** Accepted. 🛜 ♨ ♿ 🍴 ➳ 🗶

▼▼▼ **Oxford Suites Spokane Valley** �H
(509) 847-1000. **$115-$199.** 15015 E Indiana Ave 99216. I-90 exit 291A eastbound; exit 291B westbound, just nw. Int corridors. **Pets:** Accepted.
🛜 ♿ ♨ ♿ ➳ 🗶

▼▼▼ **Pheasant Hill Inn & Suites** �H ❖
(509) 926-7432. **$80-$190.** 12415 E Mission Ave 99216. I-90 exit 289, just se. Int corridors. **Pets:** Medium. $15 daily fee/pet. Designated rooms, service with restrictions, supervision.
🛜 ✕ ♿ ♨ ♿ ➳ 🗶

▼▼▼ **Quality Inn Valley Suites** �H ❖
(509) 928-5218. **$110-$190.** 8923 E Mission Ave 99212. I-90 exit 287. Int corridors. **Pets:** Medium, dogs only. $20 one-time fee/room. Designated rooms, service with restrictions, supervision.
🛜 ✕ ♨ ♿ ➳ 🗶

🅐🅐🅐 ▼▼▼▼ **Residence Inn by Marriott** �H ❖
(509) 892-9300. **$125-$154.** 15015 E Indiana Ave 99216. I-90 exit 291 westbound, just e; exit 291B eastbound, just n, then just e. Int corridors. **Pets:** Other species. $25 daily fee/room. Designated rooms, service with restrictions, supervision. 🆂🅰🆅🅴 🛜 ✕ ♿ ♨ ♿ ➳ 🗶

🅐🅐🅐 ▼▼ **Rodeway Inn & Suites** �H
(509) 535-7185. **$50-$80, 7 day notice.** 6309 E Broadway 99212. I-90 exit 286, just w. Ext/int corridors. **Pets:** Medium. $10 daily fee/pet. Designated rooms, service with restrictions, supervision.
🆂🅰🆅🅴 🛜 ♿ ♨ ➳

🅐🅐🅐 ▼▼▼ **Super 8** Ⓜ
(509) 928-4888. **$48-$107.** 2020 N Argonne Rd 99212. I-90 exit 287, just n. Int corridors. **Pets:** Other species. $25 deposit/room, $15 one-time fee/room. Designated rooms, service with restrictions, supervision.
🆂🅰🆅🅴 🛜 ♿ ♨ ➳ 🗶

STEVENSON

🅐🅐🅐 ▼▼▼▼ **Skamania Lodge** �H
(509) 427-7700. **$149-$289, 5 day notice.** 1131 SW Skamania Lodge Way 98648. 1 mi w on SR 14, just n on Rock Creek Dr, then just w. Int corridors. **Pets:** Accepted. 🆂🅰🆅🅴 🛜 ✕ ♿ ♨ ♿ 🍴 ➳ 🗶

SULTAN

🅐🅐🅐 ▼▼ **Dutch Cup Motel** Ⓜ
(360) 793-2215. **$71-$86, 3 day notice.** 817 Main St 98294. Jct US 2 and Main St. Ext corridors. **Pets:** Medium, other species. $9 daily fee/pet. Designated rooms, service with restrictions, supervision.
🆂🅰🆅🅴 🛜 ♿ ♨

SUNNYSIDE

🅐🅐🅐 ▼▼▼▼ **Best Western Plus Grapevine Inn** �H
(509) 839-6070. **$70-$160.** 1849 Quail Ln 98944. I-82 exit 69, just n, then just w. Int corridors. **Pets:** Large, dogs only. $20 one-time fee/room. Designated rooms, service with restrictions, supervision.
🆂🅰🆅🅴 🛜 ✕ ♿ ♨ ♿ ➳

🅐🅐🅐 ▼▼▼ **Country Inn & Suites Sunnyside** Ⓜ ❖
(509) 837-7878. **$49-$79.** 408 Yakima Valley Hwy 98944. Downtown. Ext corridors. **Pets:** Medium. $10 daily fee/pet. Service with restrictions, supervision. 🆂🅰🆅🅴 🛜 ♿ ♨ ➳

TOPPENISH

▼▼ **Days Inn & Suites** �H
(509) 865-7444. **$70-$110.** 515 S Elm St 98948. I-82 exit 50, 3.1 mi e. Int corridors. **Pets:** $10 daily fee/pet. Service with restrictions, supervision.
🛜 ✕ ♿ ♨ ♿ ➳

⟨AAA⟩ ▼▼▼ Quality Inn & Suites H
(509) 865-5800. **$95-$120.** 511 S Elm St 98948. I-82 exit 50, 3.2 mi e. Int corridors. **Pets:** Dogs only. $10 daily fee/pet. Designated rooms, no service, supervision. (SAVE) 📶 🐾ᴹ 📶 💻 📺

TUMWATER

⟨AAA⟩ ▼▼▼ Best Western Tumwater Inn H 🐾
(360) 956-1235. **$90-$120.** 5188 Capitol Blvd 98501. I-5 exit 102, just e. Int corridors. **Pets:** Other species. $15 daily fee/room. Designated rooms, service with restrictions, supervision. (SAVE) 📶 ✕ 📶 💻 📺 ⊠

▼▼ Comfort Inn Conference Center H 🐾
(360) 352-0691. **$100-$150.** 1620 74th Ave SW 98501. I-5 exit 101, just se. Int corridors. **Pets:** Medium, other species. $15 daily fee/pet. Service with restrictions, supervision. 📶 ✕ 📶 💻 📺

▼▼ Extended StayAmerica-Olympia-Tumwater H 🐾
(360) 754-6063. **$80-$95.** 1675 Mottman Rd SW 98512. I-5 exit 104, 0.4 mi nw on US 101, just s on Crosby Blvd, then just se. Int corridors. **Pets:** Other species. $25 daily fee/pet. Service with restrictions. 📶 📶 💻

▼▼▼ GuestHouse Inn & Suites H
(360) 943-5040. **$79-$139.** 1600 74th Ave SW 98501. I-5 exit 101, just se. Int corridors. **Pets:** Accepted. 📶 🐾ᴹ 📶 💻 📺

UNION

▼▼▼ Alderbrook Resort & Spa H
(360) 898-2200. **Call for rates.** 7101 E SR 106 98592. Just e of town. Ext/int corridors. **Pets:** $30 daily fee/pet. Service with restrictions. 📶 ✕ 📶 💻 🍴 📺 ⊠

UNION GAP

⟨AAA⟩ ▼▼▼ Best Western Plus Ahtanum Inn H 🐾
(509) 248-9700. **$70-$140.** 2408 Rudkin Rd 98903. I-82 exit 36, just n. Int corridors. **Pets:** Medium, dogs only. $20 daily fee/pet. Designated rooms, service with restrictions, supervision. (SAVE) 📶 🐾ᴹ 📶 💻 📺 ⊠

▼▼ Quality Inn-Yakima Valley M
(509) 248-6924. **$79-$89.** 12 E Valley Mall Blvd 98903. I-82 exit 36, just s. Ext corridors. **Pets:** Medium, dogs only. $10 daily fee/pet. Service with restrictions, crate. 📶 🐾ᴹ 📶 💻 📺

▼▼ Super 8 Yakima H
(509) 248-8880. **$69-$83.** 2605 Rudkin Rd 98903. I-82 exit 36, just s. Int corridors. **Pets:** Accepted. 📶 🐾ᴹ 📶 💻 📺

WALLA WALLA

⟨AAA⟩ ▼▼▼ Best Western Plus Walla Walla Suites Inn H 🐾
(509) 525-4700. **$110-$150.** 7 E Oak St 99362. US 12 exit 2nd Ave, just s. Int corridors. **Pets:** Dogs only. $10 daily fee/pet. Service with restrictions. (SAVE) 📶 ✕ 🐾ᴹ 📶 💻 📺

⟨AAA⟩ ▼ Budget Inn M
(509) 529-4410. **$55-$140.** 305 N 2nd Ave 99362. US 12 exit 2nd Ave, 0.3 mi s. Ext corridors. **Pets:** Medium. $10 daily fee/pet. Service with restrictions, supervision. (SAVE) 📶 ✕ 🐾ᴹ 📶 📺

▼▼▼ Comfort Inn & Suites H 🐾
(509) 522-3500. **Call for rates.** 1419 W Pine St 99362. US 12 exit Pendleton/Prescott. Int corridors. **Pets:** Medium, dogs only. $15 daily fee/pet. Designated rooms, service with restrictions, supervision. 📶 ✕ 📶 💻 🍴 📺

▼▼▼ Holiday Inn Express H
(509) 525-6200. **$99-$199.** 1433 W Pine St 99362. US 12 exit Pendleton/Prescott. Int corridors. **Pets:** Accepted. 📶 ✕ 📶 💻 📺

▼▼ La Quinta Inn Walla Walla H
(509) 525-2522. **$75-$179.** 520 N 2nd Ave 99362. US 12 exit 2nd Ave, 0.3 mi s. Int corridors. **Pets:** Medium, other species. Service with restrictions, supervision. 📶 ✕ 📶 💻 📺

⟨AAA⟩ ▼▼▼ Marcus Whitman Hotel & Conference Center H
(509) 525-2200. **$119-$299.** 6 W Rose St 99362. Corner of N 2nd Ave and W Rose St. Int corridors. **Pets:** Accepted.
(SAVE) 📶 ✕ 📶 💻 🍴

▼▼▼ Walla Walla Super 8 H
(509) 525-8800. **$60-$82.** 2315 Eastgate St N 99362. US 12 exit Wilbur Ave, just se. Int corridors. **Pets:** Accepted. 📶 🐾ᴹ 📶 📺

⟨AAA⟩ ▼▼▼ Walla Walla Travelodge M
(509) 529-4940. **$54-$144.** 421 E Main St 99362. US 12 exit 2nd Ave, 0.5 mi s, then just e. Ext/int corridors. **Pets:** $7 daily fee/pet. Service with restrictions, supervision. (SAVE) 📶 📶 💻 📺

WENATCHEE

⟨AAA⟩ ▼ Avenue Motel M
(509) 663-7161. **$45-$125.** 720 N Wenatchee Ave 98801. On US 2 business loop; just nw of downtown. Ext/int corridors. **Pets:** Accepted. (SAVE) 📶 📶 💻

⟨AAA⟩ ▼▼▼ Coast Wenatchee Center Hotel H 🐾
(509) 662-1234. **$79-$165.** 201 N Wenatchee Ave 98801. Jct 2nd St; downtown. Int corridors. **Pets:** $10 one-time fee/room. Designated rooms, service with restrictions, supervision. (SAVE) 📶 📶 💻 🍴 📺

⟨AAA⟩ ▼▼▼ Comfort Inn Downtown H
(509) 662-1700. **Call for rates.** 815 N Wenatchee Ave 98801. Downtown. Int corridors. **Pets:** Accepted. (SAVE) 📶 📶 💻 📺 ⊠

⟨AAA⟩ ▼ Econo Lodge M
(509) 663-7121. **$51-$110.** 232 N Wenatchee Ave 98801. Downtown. Ext corridors. **Pets:** Medium, dogs only. $10 daily fee/pet. Service with restrictions, supervision. (SAVE) 📶 📶 💻 📺

▼▼▼ Holiday Inn Express H
(509) 663-6355. **$109-$169.** 1921 N Wenatchee Ave 98801. Northwest side of town. Int corridors. **Pets:** Accepted.
📶 ✕ 🐾ᴹ 📶 💻 📺

▼▼▼ La Quinta Inn & Suites Wenatchee H
(509) 664-6565. **$71-$184.** 1905 N Wenatchee Ave 98801. Northwest side of town. Int corridors. **Pets:** Medium, other species. Service with restrictions, supervision. 📶 ✕ 🐾ᴹ 📶 💻 📺 ⊠

⟨AAA⟩ ▼▼▼ Red Lion Hotel Wenatchee H
(509) 663-0711. **$89-$199.** 1225 N Wenatchee Ave 98801. Just nw of downtown. Int corridors. **Pets:** Accepted.
(SAVE) 📶 ✕ 📶 💻 🍴 📺

⟨AAA⟩ ▼▼▼ Super 8 Wenatchee H
(509) 662-3443. **$44-$80.** 1401 N Miller St 98801. 1.5 mi n on US 2. Int corridors. **Pets:** $50 deposit/room, $10 daily fee/pet. Designated rooms, service with restrictions, supervision. (SAVE) 📶 📶 💻 📺

⟨AAA⟩ ▼▼▼ Travelodge-Wenatchee M
(509) 662-8165. **$49-$81.** 1004 N Wenatchee Ave 98801. Downtown. Ext corridors. **Pets:** Accepted. (SAVE) 📶 🐾ᴹ 📶 💻 📺

WESTPORT

⟨AAA⟩ ▼▼▼ Chateau Westport H 🐾
(360) 268-9101. **$99-$299.** 710 W Hancock St 98595. Just w of SR 105 Spur N; 1.5 mi n of Twin Harbors State Park. Int corridors. **Pets:** Medium, dogs only. $20 daily fee/pet. Designated rooms, service with restrictions, supervision. (SAVE) 📶 ✕ 📶 💻 📺 ⊠ 🐾

WINTHROP

River Run Inn M

(509) 996-2173. **$75-$165, 10 day notice.** 27 Rader Rd 98862. 0.5 mi w on SR 20. Ext corridors. **Pets:** Dogs only. $15 daily fee/pet. Service with restrictions, supervision. SAVE ⊡ ⊠ ⊡ ⊡ ⊡ ⊡

Winthrop Inn M ☸

(509) 996-2217. **$70-$135, 7 day notice.** 960 Hwy 20 98862. 0.9 mi e. Int corridors. **Pets:** Medium, dogs only. $10 daily fee/pet. Designated rooms, supervision. SAVE ⊡ ⊠ ⊡ ⊡ ⊡

WOODLAND

Lewis River Inn M

(360) 225-6257. **$64-$110.** 1100 Lewis River Rd 98674. I-5 exit 21, just e. Ext corridors. **Pets:** Accepted. SAVE ⊡ ⊡ ⊡

YAKIMA

Best Western Plus Lincoln Inn H

(509) 453-8898. **$89-$199.** 1614 N 1st St 98901. I-82 exit 31, just s. Int corridors. **Pets:** Accepted. SAVE ⊡ ⊠ ⊡ ⊡ ⊡ ⊡

Birchfield Manor Country Inn CI

(509) 452-1960. **Call for rates.** 2018 Birchfield Rd 98901. I-82 exit 34, 2 mi e to Birchfield Rd, then just s. Int corridors. **Pets:** Accepted.
⊡ ⊠ ⊡ ⊡ ⊡ ⊡ ⊡ ⊡

Clarion Hotel & Conference Center H

(509) 248-7850. **$69-$119.** 1507 N 1st St 98901. I-82 exit 31, 0.5 mi s. Int corridors. **Pets:** Medium, dogs only. $10 daily fee/pet. Service with restrictions, supervision. ⊡ ⊠ ⊡ ⊡ ⊡ ⊡ ⊡ ⊡

Comfort Suites H

(509) 249-1900. **$89-$199.** 3702 Fruitvale Blvd 98902. US 12 exit 40th Ave, just s. Int corridors. **Pets:** Small, dogs only. $20 daily fee/pet. Designated rooms, service with restrictions, supervision.
SAVE ⊡ ⊠ ⊡ ⊡ ⊡ ⊡

Fairfield Inn & Suites by Marriott H ☸

(509) 452-3100. **$122-$160.** 137 N Fair Ave 98901. I-82 exit 33A eastbound, just s; exit 33 westbound, just w to 9th St, just n to B St, then just e. Int corridors. **Pets:** Medium. $25 daily fee/room. Designated rooms, service with restrictions, supervision.
SAVE ⊡ ⊠ ⊡ ⊡ ⊡ ⊡

GuestHouse Inn-Yakima M

(509) 452-8101. **$59-$109.** 1010 E A St 98901. I-82 exit 33B eastbound; exit 33 westbound, just w to 9th St, just n to A St, then just e. Ext corridors. **Pets:** Accepted. SAVE ⊡ ⊡

Holiday Inn Downtown Yakima H

(509) 494-7000. **$115-$159.** 802 E Yakima Ave 98901. I-82 exit 33 westbound; exit 33B eastbound, 0.7 mi w. Int corridors. **Pets:** Medium. $20 one-time fee/room. Designated rooms, service with restrictions, supervision. ⊡ ⊠ ⊡ ⊡ ⊡ ⊡ ⊡

Holiday Inn Express Yakima H

(509) 249-1000. **$119-$149.** 1001 E A St 98901. I-82 exit 33B eastbound; exit 33 westbound, just w to 9th St, just n to A St, then just e. Int corridors. **Pets:** Medium. $20 daily fee/pet. Designated rooms, service with restrictions, supervision. SAVE ⊡ ⊠ ⊡ ⊡ ⊡ ⊡

Howard Johnson Plaza Yakima H

(509) 452-6511. **$76-$125.** 9 N 9th St 98901. I-82 exit 33 westbound; exit 33B eastbound, just s. Int corridors. **Pets:** Accepted.
⊡ ⊠ ⊡ ⊡ ⊡ ⊡

Oxford Inn H ☸

(509) 457-4444. **$79-$99.** 1603 E Yakima Ave 98901. I-82 exit 33 westbound, just e; exit 33B eastbound. Int corridors. **Pets:** Medium. $25 one-time fee/pet. Designated rooms, service with restrictions, supervision.
⊡ ⊡ ⊡ ⊡ ⊡ ⊡

Oxford Suites H

(509) 457-9000. **Call for rates.** 1701 E Yakima Ave 98901. I-82 exit 33 westbound; exit 33B eastbound. Int corridors. **Pets:** Accepted.
⊡ ⊡ ⊡ ⊡ ⊡ ⊡

Red Lion Hotel Yakima Center H

(509) 248-5900. **$90-$120, 3 day notice.** 607 E Yakima Ave 98901. I-82 exit 33 westbound; exit 33B eastbound, 0.8 mi w. Ext/int corridors. **Pets:** Accepted. SAVE ⊡ ⊠ ⊡ ⊡ ⊡ ⊡ ⊡

ZILLAH

Comfort Inn H

(509) 829-3399. **Call for rates.** 911 Vintage Valley Pkwy 98953. I-82 exit 52, just n. Int corridors. **Pets:** Other species. $10 daily fee/pet.
⊡ ⊠ ⊡ ⊡ ⊡ ⊡ ⊡

WEST VIRGINIA

BARBOURSVILLE

AAA ◈◈◈ **Best Western Huntington Mall Inn** **M**
(304) 736-9772. **$79-$99.** 3441 US 60 E 25504. I-64 exit 20A eastbound; exit 20 westbound, 0.3 mi s. Int corridors. **Pets:** Other species. $15 one-time fee/room. Service with restrictions, crate. [SAVE] ⊚ 🖥 💻 🏊

◈◈◈ **Comfort Inn by Choice Hotels** **H**
(304) 733-2122. **$77-$125.** 249 Mall Rd 25504. I-64 exit 20, 0.4 mi n. Int corridors. **Pets:** Accepted. ⊚ ⓜ 🖥 💻 🏊

BECKLEY

AAA ◈◈◈ **Americas Best Value Inn** **M**
(304) 252-0671. **$67-$110.** 1939 Harper Rd 25801. I-64/77 exit 44, just e on SR 3. Ext/int corridors. **Pets:** Other species. $7 daily fee/pet. Service with restrictions, supervision. [SAVE] ⊚ 💻

◈◈◈◈ **Country Inn & Suites By Carlson** **H** 🐾
(304) 252-5100. **Call for rates.** 2120 Harper Rd 25801. I-64/77 exit 44, just w on SR 3. Int corridors. **Pets:** $30 one-time fee/room. Designated rooms, supervision. ⊚ ⓜ 🖥 💻 🏊 ⊠

AAA ◈◈◈ **Econo Lodge** **M**
(304) 255-2161. **$70-$129.** 1909 Harper Rd 25801. I-64/77 exit 44, 0.3 mi e on SR 3. Ext/int corridors. **Pets:** Other species. Service with restrictions, supervision. [SAVE] ⊚ 💻

◈◈◈ **Fairfield Inn** **H**
(304) 252-8661. **$94-$114.** 125 Hylton Ln 25801. I-64/77 exit 44, just e. Int corridors. **Pets:** Large, other species. $75 one-time fee/room. Designated rooms, service with restrictions, crate. ⊚ ⊠ 🖥 💻 🏊

AAA ◈◈◈ **Microtel Inn** **M**
(304) 256-2000. **$58-$112, 3 day notice.** 2130 Harper Rd 25801. I-64/77 exit 44, just w. Int corridors. **Pets:** Accepted. [SAVE] ⊚ 🖥 🏊

AAA ◈◈◈ **Super 8** **M**
(304) 253-0802. **$59-$89.** 2014 Harper Rd 25801. I-64/77 exit 44, just e. Int corridors. **Pets:** Medium. $15 one-time fee/room. Service with restrictions, supervision. [SAVE] ⊚ 🖥 💻

BLUEFIELD

◈◈◈ **Quality Hotel and Conference Center** **H**
(304) 325-6170. **Call for rates.** 3350 Big Laurel Hwy 24701. I-77 exit 1, 3.8 mi nw via US 52/460. Int corridors. **Pets:** Small, dogs only. $10 daily fee/pet. Designated rooms, service with restrictions, supervision. ⊚ 🖥 💻 🏊

BRADLEY

AAA ◈◈◈ **Days Inn** **M**
(304) 877-6455. **$53-$75.** 127 Ontario Dr 25880. I-64/77 exit 48, 1 mi ne on US 19. Int corridors. **Pets:** Small, dogs only. $15 one-time fee/pet. Designated rooms, service with restrictions, supervision.

[SAVE] ⊚ 🖥 💻 🏊

BRIDGEPORT

AAA ◈◈◈ **Best Western Bridgeport Inn** **H**
(304) 842-5411. **$100-$170.** 100 Lodgeville Rd 26330. I-79 exit 119, just e on US 50. Int corridors. **Pets:** Medium, other species. $5 daily fee/pet. Service with restrictions, crate. [SAVE] ⊚ 🖥 💻 🍴 🏊

◈◈◈ **Sleep Inn** **M**
(304) 842-1919. **$76-$81.** 115 Tolley Dr 26330. I-79 exit 119, just e on US 50. Int corridors. **Pets:** Service with restrictions, crate. ⊚ 🖥 💻

BRUCETON MILLS

◈◈◈ **Microtel Inn & Suites** **M**
(304) 379-7900. **$62-$113.** 886 Casteel Rd 26525. I-68 exit 29 (Hazelton), just n. Int corridors. **Pets:** Accepted. ⊚ 🖥 💻

CHARLESTON

AAA ◈◈◈ **Best Western Charleston Plaza Hotel** **H**
(304) 345-9779. **$69-$109.** 1010 Washington St E 25301. I-64/77 exit 100, 0.3 mi w. Int corridors. **Pets:** Accepted. [SAVE] ⊚ 🖥 💻 🏊

AAA ◈◈◈ **Charleston Residence Inn by Marriott** **H**
(304) 345-4200. **$89-$149.** 200 Hotel Cir 25311. I-64/77 exit 99, just e. Int corridors. **Pets:** Accepted. [SAVE] ⊚ ⊠ 🖥 💻 🏊 ⊠

◈◈◈ **Country Inn & Suites By Carlson South** **H** 🐾
(304) 925-4300. **$110-$130.** 105 Alex Ln 25304. I-77 exit 95, just s on SR 61. Int corridors. **Pets:** Medium. $25 one-time fee/pet. Designated rooms, supervision. ⊚ 🖥 💻

◈◈◈ **Holiday Inn Express Charleston-Kanawha City** **H**
(304) 925-1171. **$119-$190.** 107 Alex Ln 25304. I-77 exit 95, just s on SR 61. Int corridors. **Pets:** Accepted. ⊚ ⊠ 🖥 💻 🏊

◈◈◈ **Red Roof Inn-Kanawha City** **M**
(304) 925-6953. **$56-$81.** 6305 SE MacCorkle Ave 25304. I-77 exit 95, just s on SR 61. Ext corridors. **Pets:** Large, other species. No service, supervision. [SAVE] ⊚ 🖥

CROSS LANES

◈◈ **Comfort Inn Charleston West** **M** 🐾
(304) 776-8070. **$85-$148.** 102 Racer Dr 25313. I-64 exit 47, just s. Int corridors. **Pets:** Large. $75 deposit/room. Designated rooms, service with restrictions, supervision. ⊚ 🖥 💻 🏊

DANIELS

AAA ◈◈◈ **The Resort at Glade Springs** **H**
(304) 763-2000. **$152-$442, 7 day notice.** 255 Resort Dr 25832. I-64 exit 125, 1.5 mi w on SR 307, then 2.8 mi w on US 19. Ext/int corridors. **Pets:** Accepted. [SAVE] ⊚ 🖥 💻 🍴 🏊 ⊠

DAVIS

▼▼▼▼ Black Bear Resort CA
(304) 866-4391. **$100-$560.** Cortland Rd, Canaan Valley 26260. 4.5 mi s on SR 32. Ext corridors. **Pets:** Accepted. 🛰️ 🍴 🖵 🌊 ⊠

DUNBAR

▼ Dunbar Super 8 M
(304) 768-6888. **$55-$85.** 911 Dunbar Ave 25064. I-64 exit 53, just w. Int corridors. **Pets:** Medium. $10 daily fee/pet. Service with restrictions, supervision. 🛰️ 🍴 🖵

EDRAY

AAA▷ ▼▼▼ Marlinton Motor Inn M
(304) 799-4711. **$65-$140, 3 day notice.** US 219 N 24954. Center. Ext corridors. **Pets:** Small, dogs only. $15 daily fee/pet. Designated rooms, no service, crate. SAVE 🍴 🖵 ▢ 🌊

ELKINS

▼▼▼▼ Cheat River Lodge CA
(304) 636-2301. **$64-$88.** Rt 1, Box 115 26241. 4.8 mi e on US 33, then 1.5 mi ne. Ext corridors. **Pets:** Accepted. ⊠ 🍴 🖵 ⊠ 🐾

AAA▷ ▼▼▼ Elkins Super 8 M
(304) 636-6500. **$52-$79.** 350 Beverly Pike 26241. 0.8 mi s on SR 219. Int corridors. **Pets:** Medium, other species. $10 daily fee/room. Designated rooms, service with restrictions, crate. SAVE 🛰️ 🍴 🖵

ELKVIEW

AAA▷ ▼▼▼▼ Country Inn & Suites By Carlson, Charleston North H
(304) 965-9200. **$89-$94.** 101 The Crossings Shopping Center 25071. I-79 exit 9, just e. Int corridors. **Pets:** Very small. $20 one-time fee/pet. Designated rooms, service with restrictions, supervision.
SAVE 🛰️ 🍴 🖵 🌊

FAIRMONT

AAA▷ ▼▼▼▼ Clarion Inn Fairmont H
(304) 366-5500. **$84-$189.** 930 E Grafton Rd 26554. I-79 exit 137, just e. Int corridors. **Pets:** Accepted. SAVE 🛰️ 🖐M 🍴 🖵 🍴 🌊

▼▼ Super 8 M
(304) 363-1488. **$54-$100.** 2208 Pleasant Valley Rd 26554. I-79 exit 133, just e. Int corridors. **Pets:** Accepted. 🛰️ 🍴 🖵

FALLING WATERS

▼▼▼▼ Holiday Inn Express Martinsburg North H
(304) 274-6100. **Call for rates.** 1220 TJ Jackson Dr 25419. I-81 exit 20, just w. Int corridors. **Pets:** Accepted. 🛰️ 🍴 🖵 🌊

FROST

▼▼▼▼ The Inn at Mountain Quest CI
(304) 799-7267. **$117-$130.** Rt 92 Frost 24954. On SR 92, 0.4 mi n. Ext corridors. **Pets:** Other species. $10 one-time fee/pet. Designated rooms.
🛰️ ⊠ ⊠

HARPERS FERRY

▼▼▼▼ Quality Hotel Conference Center H
(304) 535-6302. **Call for rates.** 4328 William L Wilson Frwy 25425. Just w on US 340. Int corridors. **Pets:** Accepted. 🛰️ 🍴 🖵 🍴 🌊

HUNTINGTON

▼▼▼▼ Ramada Limited and Conference Center H
(304) 523-4242. **$85-$105.** 3094 16th Street Rd 25701. I-64 exit 11, just n. Int corridors. **Pets:** Other species. $20 daily fee/pet. Designated rooms, service with restrictions, crate. 🛰️ 🍴 🖵 🌊 ⊠

AAA ▼▼ Red Roof Inn M
(304) 733-3737. **$50-$79.** 5190 US Rt 60 E 25705. I-64 exit 15, just s. Ext corridors. **Pets:** Large, other species. No service, supervision.
SAVE 🛰️ 🍴

▼▼ Super 8 H
(304) 525-1410. **$75-$120.** 3090 16th Street Rd 25701. I-64 exit 11, just n. Int corridors. **Pets:** Accepted. 🛰️ 🍴 🖵 🌊 ⊠

▼▼▼▼ Towne Place Suites by Marriott Huntington H
(304) 525-4877. **$134-$189.** 157 Kinetic Dr 25701. I-64 exit 11, just n. Int corridors. **Pets:** Other species. $100 one-time fee/room. Service with restrictions, crate. 🛰️ ⊠ 🍴 🖵 🌊

JANE LEW

AAA▷ ▼▼▼ Plantation Inn & Suites M
(304) 884-7806. **$65-$100.** 1322 Hackers Creek Rd 26378. I-79 exit 105, just e. Ext corridors. **Pets:** Accepted. SAVE 🛰️ 🍴 🖵

KEYSER

AAA▷ ▼▼▼ Keyser Inn M
(304) 788-0913. **$58-$72.** 51 Josie Dr 26726. On US 220, 2.3 mi s. Int corridors. **Pets:** Small. $27 one-time fee/room. Designated rooms, service with restrictions, supervision. SAVE 🛰️ 🍴 🖵

▼▼▼ Microtel Inn & Suites Keyser H
(304) 597-1400. **$90-$120, 3 day notice.** 70 N Tornado Way 26726. On US 220, 2.1 mi s. Int corridors. **Pets:** Small, dogs only. $25 one-time fee/room. Service with restrictions, crate. 🛰️ 🍴 🖵

LEWISBURG

▼▼▼▼ Lewisburg Holiday Inn Express Hotel & Suites H
(304) 645-5750. **Call for rates.** 222 Hunter Ln 24901. I-64 exit 169, just s. Int corridors. **Pets:** Small. $25 daily fee/pet. Designated rooms, service with restrictions, supervision. 🛰️ 🍴 🖵 🌊

AAA▷ ▼▼▼ Quality Inn Lewisburg Conference Center H
(304) 645-7722. **Call for rates.** 540 N Jefferson St 24901. I-64 exit 169, just s on US 219. Ext corridors. **Pets:** Medium. $50 daily fee/pet. Designated rooms, service with restrictions, supervision.
SAVE 🛰️ 🍴 🖵 🍴 🌊

▼▼ Super 8 M
(304) 647-3188. **$59-$89.** 550 N Jefferson St 24901. I-64 exit 169, just s on US 219. Int corridors. **Pets:** $10 daily fee/pet. Service with restrictions, supervision. 🛰️ 🍴 🖵

LOGAN

▼ Super 8-Logan M
(304) 752-8787. **$54-$74.** 316 Riverview Ave 25601. 1.8 mi e on SR 73. Int corridors. **Pets:** Accepted. 🛰️ 🍴 🖵

MARTINSBURG

▼▼ Days Inn Martinsburg M
(304) 263-1800. **$55-$77.** 209 Viking Way 25404. I-81 exit 13, just e on W King St (CR 15). Ext/int corridors. **Pets:** Accepted. 🛰️ 🍴 🖵

▼▼▼ Holiday Inn Martinsburg H
(304) 267-5500. **$109-$169.** 301 Foxcroft Ave 25401. I-81 exit 13, just e on W King St (CR 15). Int corridors. **Pets:** Other species. $25 one-time fee/room. Service with restrictions, supervision. 🛰️ 🍴 🖵 🍴 🌊

▼ Knights Inn-Martinsburg M
(304) 267-2211. **$45-$49.** 1997 Edwin Miller Blvd 25404. I-81 exit 16E, 0.4 mi e on SR 9. Ext corridors. **Pets:** Accepted. 🛰️ 🍴

▼ Super 8-Martinsburg M
(304) 263-0801. **$54-$79.** 2048 Edwin Miller Blvd 25404. I-81 exit 16E, just e on SR 9. Int corridors. **Pets:** Accepted. 🛰️ 🍴 🖵

MINERAL WELLS

△△△ ▽▽▽ Comfort Suites Parkersburg South H ❀
(304) 489-9600. **$85-$139.** 167 Elizabeth Pike 26150. I-77 exit 170, 0.3 mi se. Ext/int corridors. **Pets:** Other species. $10 daily fee/pet. Service with restrictions, crate. [SAVE] 📶 ⊠ 🗄 💻 ⊲ ⊠

▽▽▽ Holiday Inn Express Hotel & Suites Parkersburg/ Mineral Wells H ❀
(304) 489-4111. **Call for rates.** 80 Old Nicholette Rd 26150. I-77 exit 170. Int corridors. **Pets:** Small. $35 daily fee/room. Designated rooms, no service, supervision. 📶 🗄 💻 ⊲

MORGANTOWN

▽▽ Comfort Inn-Morgantown M
(304) 296-9364. **Call for rates.** 225 Comfort Inn Dr 26508. I-68 exit 1, 0.3 mi n on US 119. Int corridors. **Pets:** Accepted.
📶 🗄 💻 🍴 ⊲

△△△ ▽▽▽ Ramada Conference Center H
(304) 296-3431. **$79-$155.** 20 Scott Ave 26508. I-68 exit 1, 0.3 mi n. Int corridors. **Pets:** Accepted. [SAVE] 📶 🗄 💻 🍴 ⊲

▽▽▽ Residence Inn by Marriott Morgantown H
(304) 599-0237. **$151-$165.** 1046 Willowdale Rd 26505. I-79 exit 155, 2 mi s on US 19, then 0.9 mi e on SR 705. Int corridors. **Pets:** Accepted.
📶 ⊠ ⏳ 💻 ⊲ ⊠

OAK HILL

△△△ ▽▽▽ Holiday Lodge Hotel and Conference Center H
(304) 465-0571. **$79-$120.** 340 Oyler Ave 25901. US 19 exit Oyler Ave, just w. Int corridors. **Pets:** Accepted.
[SAVE] 📶 ⏳ 💻 🍴 ⊲ ⊠

PARKERSBURG

▽▽▽ The Blennerhassett H
(304) 422-3131. **$129-$279.** 320 Market St 26101. Between 4th and 5th sts; downtown. Int corridors. **Pets:** Accepted. 📶 🗄 💻 🍴

▽▽ Red Roof Inn M
(304) 485-1741. **$49-$72.** 3714 E 7th St 26104. I-77 exit 176, just w on US 50. Ext corridors. **Pets:** Large, other species. No service, supervision.
📶 🗄 💻

△△△ ▽▽ Travelodge Parkersburg M ❀
(304) 424-5100. **$37-$158.** 3604 E 7th St 26104. I-77 exit 176, just w. Ext corridors. **Pets:** Large, other species. $5 daily fee/pet. Service with restrictions, crate. [SAVE] 📶 🗄 💻 ⊲

PHILIPPI

△△△ ▽ Budget Inn Philippi M
(304) 457-5888. **$49-$85.** Rt 4, Box 155 26416. 2.5 mi s on US 250. Int corridors. **Pets:** Accepted. [SAVE] 📶 ⏳ 🗄

PRINCETON

▽▽ Comfort Inn-Princeton M
(304) 487-6101. **$89-$99.** 136 Ambrose Ln 24740. I-77 exit 9, 0.3 mi w on US 460. Int corridors. **Pets:** Accepted. 📶 🗄 💻

△△△ ▽▽ Days Inn M ❀
(304) 425-8100. **$59-$70, 3 day notice.** 347 Meadowfield Ln 24740. I-77 exit 9, 0.3 mi w on US 460, just s on Ambrose Ln, then just e. Ext corridors. **Pets:** Small, other species. $20 daily fee/pet. Service with restrictions, supervision. [SAVE] 📶 🗄 💻 ⊲

△△△ ▽▽▽ Holiday Inn Express Princeton H ❀
(304) 425-8156. **$85-$180.** 805 Oakvale Rd 24740. I-77 exit 9, just w. Int corridors. **Pets:** Small, other species. $20 daily fee/pet. Designated rooms, service with restrictions, supervision. [SAVE] 📶 🗄 💻 ⊲

△△△ ▽▽▽ Microtel Inn & Suites M
(304) 487-3885. **$67-$90.** 250 Ambrose Ln 24740. I-77 exit 9, just w. Int corridors. **Pets:** $15 one-time fee/pet. Service with restrictions, supervision. [SAVE] 📶 ⊠ 🗄 💻 ⊲

RIPLEY

▽▽▽ Holiday Inn Express & Suites Ripley H
(304) 372-4444. **Call for rates.** 110 Memorial Dr 25271. I-77 exit 138, e on US 33, then s on New Stone Ridge Rd. Int corridors. **Pets:** $25 daily fee/pet. Service with restrictions, supervision. 📶 🗄 💻 ⊲

△△△ ▽▽▽ McCoys Inn & Conference Center H ❀
(304) 372-9122. **$81-$100.** 701 W Main St 25271. I-77 exit 138, just e. Ext/int corridors. **Pets:** Medium, other species. $15 daily fee/room. Designated rooms, service with restrictions, supervision.
[SAVE] 📶 💻 ⊲ ⊠

△△△ ▽▽▽ Quality Inn H
(304) 372-5000. **$71-$99.** 1 Hospitality Dr 25271. I-77 exit 138, just w on US 33, then 0.3 mi n. Ext/int corridors. **Pets:** Other species. Service with restrictions, supervision. [SAVE] 📶 🗄 💻

▽▽ Ripley Super 8 M
(304) 372-8880. **$54-$79.** 102 Duke Dr 25271. I-77 exit 138, just e on US 33. Int corridors. **Pets:** Accepted. 📶 🗄 💻

ROANOKE

△△△ ▽▽▽ ▽▽▽ Stonewall Resort H
(304) 269-7400. **Call for rates.** 940 Resort Dr 26447. I-79 exit 91, just e. Ext/int corridors. **Pets:** Accepted. [SAVE] 📶 🗄 💻 🍴 ⊲ ⊠

SHEPHERDSTOWN

▽▽ Comfort Inn Shepherdstown M ❀
(304) 876-3160. **$89-$99.** 70 Maddex Square Dr 25443. Just w on SR 45; center. Int corridors. **Pets:** $10 daily fee/room. 📶 🗄 💻

SOUTH CHARLESTON

△△△ ▽▽▽ Holiday Inn & Suites H
(304) 744-4641. **$85-$104.** 400 2nd Ave 25303. I-64 exit 56, just nw. Int corridors. **Pets:** Accepted. [SAVE] 📶 🗄 💻 🍴 ⊲

SUMMERSVILLE

△△△ ▽▽▽ Baymont Inn & Suites Summersville M
(304) 872-6500. **Call for rates.** 903 Industrial Dr N 26651. US 19, 1.9 mi n of jct SR 39. Int corridors. **Pets:** Large, other species. $10 daily fee/pet. Designated rooms, service with restrictions, supervision.
[SAVE] 📶 🗄 💻 ⊲ ⊠

△△△ ▽▽▽ Best Western Summersville Lake Motor Lodge H
(304) 872-6900. **$62-$99.** 1203 S Broad St 26651. US 19 and Broad St; 0.6 mi s of jct SR 39. Ext corridors. **Pets:** Other species. $15 daily fee/pet. Service with restrictions, supervision. [SAVE] 📶 🗄 💻

△△△ ▽▽▽ Country Inn & Suites By Carlson H
(304) 872-0555. **$89-$150.** 106 Merchants Walk 26651. US 19, just w. Int corridors. **Pets:** Accepted. [SAVE] 🗄 💻 ⊲

▽▽▽ Hampton Inn H
(304) 872-7100. **$80-$120.** 5400 Webster Rd 26651. Just s on SR 41 from US 19. Int corridors. **Pets:** Accepted. 📶 ⏳ 💻 ⊲ ⊠

◆◆◆ ▼▼ Sleep Inn of Summersville **M**

(304) 872-4500. **Call for rates.** 701 Professional Park Dr 26651. US 19, 1.7 mi n of jct SR 39. Int corridors. **Pets:** Accepted.

[SAVE] 🛜 🔌 💻 ⌁

▼ Super 8-Summersville **M**

(304) 872-4888. **$54-$79.** 306 Merchants Walk 26651. US 19, just n. Int corridors. **Pets:** Small. $10 daily fee/pet. Service with restrictions, supervision. 🛜 🔌

TRIADELPHIA

▼▼▼ Comfort Inn-Wheeling **M**

(304) 547-0610. **$100-$150.** 675 Fort Henry Rd 26059. I-70 exit 11, just n. Int corridors. **Pets:** Accepted. 🛜 🔌 💻 ⌁

▼▼▼ Econo Lodge Inn Suites Conference Center Wheeling East **M**

(304) 547-1380. **$99-$159.** 87 Jenkins Ln 26059. I-70 exit 11. Int corridors. **Pets:** Accepted. 🛜 🔌 💻 ⌁

WEIRTON

▼▼ Holiday Inn **H**

(304) 723-5522. **$114-$149.** 350 Three Springs Dr 26062. 4.5 mi e on US 22 exit Three Springs Dr. Int corridors. **Pets:** $50 one-time fee/room. Service with restrictions, supervision. 🛜 🔌 💻 🍴 ⌁ ✖

WESTON

◆◆◆ ▼▼▼ Comfort Inn **H**

(304) 269-7000. **$80-$105.** 2906 US Hwy 33 E 26452. I-79 exit 99, just e. Ext corridors. **Pets:** Medium. $15 daily fee/room. Designated rooms, service with restrictions, supervision. [SAVE] 🛜 🔌 💻 ⌁

▼▼▼ Holiday Inn Express Hotel & Suites **H**

(304) 269-3550. **Call for rates.** 215 Staunton Dr 26452. I-79 exit 99, just e. Int corridors. **Pets:** Accepted. 🛜 🔌 💻 ⌁

▼▼ Weston Super 8 **M**

(304) 269-1086. **$59-$79.** 100 Market Place Mall, Suite 12 26452. I-79 exit 99, just e. Int corridors. **Pets:** Very small, other species. $10 daily fee/pet. Service with restrictions, supervision. 🛜 🔌 💻

WHEELING

▼▼ Wheeling Super 8 **M**

(304) 243-9400. **$60-$99.** 2400 National Rd 26003. I-70 exit 5, just e. Int corridors. **Pets:** Accepted. 🛜 🔌 💻

WHITE SULPHUR SPRINGS

◆◆◆ ▼▼▼▼ The Greenbrier **H**

(304) 536-1110. **Call for rates.** 300 W Main St 24986. I-64 exit 181 westbound, 1.8 mi w on US 60; exit 175 eastbound, just n, then 3.2 mi e on US 60. Ext/int corridors. **Pets:** Accepted.

[SAVE] 🛜 ✖ ᴸᴹ 🔌 🍴 ⌁ ✖

WISCONSIN

CITY INDEX

ABBOTSFORD

Rodeway Inn
(715) 223-3337. **Call for rates.** 300 E Elderberry Rd 54405. SR 29 exit 132 (SR 13), just se. Int corridors. **Pets:** $100 deposit/pet, $10 daily fee/pet. Designated rooms, service with restrictions, crate.

ALGOMA

Algoma Beach Motel
(920) 487-2828. **$59-$199, 3 day notice.** 1500 Lake St 54201. Jct SR 54, 0.4 mi s on SR 42. Ext/int corridors. **Pets:** Dogs only. $15 daily fee/pet. Designated rooms, service with restrictions, supervision.

Scenic Shore Inn
(920) 487-3214. **$55-$71, 3 day notice.** 2221 Lake St 54201. Jct SR 54, 0.8 mi s on SR 42. Ext corridors. **Pets:** Large, dogs only. $5 daily fee/pet. Designated rooms, service with restrictions, supervision.

ANTIGO

Days Inn
(715) 623-0506. **$55-$91.** 525 Memory Ln 54409. 0.4 mi n of jct SR 64 E and US 45, just w. Int corridors. **Pets:** Accepted.

Holiday Inn Express & Suites Antigo
(715) 627-7500. **$79-$99.** 2407 Neva Rd 54409. Just n of jct SR 64 E and US 45, just e. Int corridors. **Pets:** Dogs only. $25 one-time fee/pet. Designated rooms, no service, crate.

Super 8-Antigo
(715) 623-4188. **$59-$103.** 535 Century Ave 54409. On US 45 at SR 64 E. Int corridors. **Pets:** Accepted.

APPLETON

Best Western Fox Valley Inn
(920) 731-4141. **$80-$200.** 3033 W College Ave 54914. US 41 exit 137 (SR 125), 0.5 mi e. Int corridors. **Pets:** Medium, dogs only. $10 daily fee/pet. Designated rooms, service with restrictions.

Candlewood Suites
(920) 739-8000. **$59-$99.** 4525 W College Ave 54914. US 41 exit 137 (SR 125), just w. Int corridors. **Pets:** Large, other species. $75 one-time fee/room. Service with restrictions, crate.

Comfort Suites Appleton Airport
(920) 730-3800. **$79-$159.** 3809 W Wisconsin Ave 54914. US 41 exit 138 (Wisconsin Ave), just e. Int corridors. **Pets:** Large. Service with restrictions, supervision.

Country Inn & Suites By Carlson
(920) 830-3240. **$110-$170, 3 day notice.** 355 Fox River Dr 54913. US 41 exit 137 (SR 125), just nw. Int corridors. **Pets:** $20 one-time fee/pet. Designated rooms, no service, supervision.

Days Inn
(920) 733-5551. **$44-$161.** 210 Westhill Blvd 54914. US 41 exit 137 (SR 125), just e. Int corridors. **Pets:** $10 daily fee/pet. Service with restrictions, supervision.

Extended StayAmerica-Appleton-Fox Cities
(920) 830-9596. **$50-$80.** 4141 Boardwalk Ct 54915. US 41 exit 137 (SR 125), just w on College Ave, then just s on Nicolet Rd. Int corridors. **Pets:** Other species. $25 daily fee/pet. Service with restrictions.

Fairfield Inn by Marriott
(920) 954-0202. **$95-$163.** 132 N Mall Dr 54913. US 41 exit 137 (SR 125), just nw. Int corridors. **Pets:** Medium, other species. $30 one-time fee/room. Designated rooms, service with restrictions, crate.

La Quinta Inn & Suites Appleton College Avenue
(920) 734-7777. **$84-$152.** 3730 W College Ave 54914. US 41 exit 137 (SR 125), just e. Int corridors. **Pets:** Medium, other species. Service with restrictions, supervision.

La Quinta Inn Appleton Fox River Mall Area
(920) 734-6070. **$54-$122.** 3920 W College Ave 54914. US 41 exit 137 (SR 125), just e. Ext/int corridors. **Pets:** Medium, other species. Service with restrictions, supervision.

Microtel Inn & Suites
(920) 997-3121. **$49-$144.** 321 Metro Dr 54913. US 41 exit 137 (SR 125), just nw. Int corridors. **Pets:** Accepted.

WWW Residence Inn by Marriott H

(920) 954-0570. **$170-$200.** 310 Metro Dr 54913. US 41 exit 137 (SR 125), just nw on Mall Dr. Int corridors. **Pets:** Accepted.

ARKDALE

WWW Northern Bay Condos & Castle Course CO

(608) 339-2090. **$190-$429.** 1844 20th Ave 54613. 2.9 mi w on SR 21, 3 mi s on CR Z, 0.9 mi w on Czech Ave, then 0.4 mi se. Int corridors. **Pets:** Accepted.

ASHLAND

WW AmericInn of Ashland H

(715) 682-9950. **$64-$199.** 3009 Lake Shore Dr E 54806. On US 2, 2.1 mi e of jct SR 13 S. Int corridors. **Pets:** Accepted.

AAA WWW Ashland Lake Superior Lodge H

(715) 682-5235. **Call for rates.** 30600 US Hwy 2 54806. 2.5 mi w. Ext/int corridors. **Pets:** $15 one-time fee/pet, $10 daily fee/pet. Designated rooms, service with restrictions, supervision.

BALDWIN

WW AmericInn Lodge & Suites of Baldwin H

(715) 684-5888. **$70-$185.** 500 Baldwin Plaza Dr 54002. I-94 exit 19 (US 63), just ne. Int corridors. **Pets:** Accepted.

WW Super 8 H

(715) 684-2700. **$58-$71.** 805 Energy Dr 54002. I-94 exit 19 (US 63), just se. Int corridors. **Pets:** Large. $15 one-time fee/pet. Supervision.

BARABOO

WWW Clarion Hotel & Convention Center H

(608) 356-6422. **$71-$148.** 626 W Pine St 53913. On US 12, 0.3 mi n of SR 33. Int corridors. **Pets:** Small, other species. $50 one-time fee/room. Designated rooms, service with restrictions, supervision.

BEAVER DAM

WW Super 8 H

(920) 887-8880. **$57-$81.** 711 Park Ave 53916. US 151 exit 132 (SR 33), just w. Int corridors. **Pets:** Medium. $10 one-time fee/pet. Service with restrictions, supervision.

BELOIT

AAA WWW Beloit Inn H ✿

(608) 362-5500. **$109-$219.** 500 Pleasant St 53511. Downtown. Int corridors. **Pets:** Other species. $100 deposit/room, $10 daily fee/pet. Service with restrictions, crate.

WW Comfort Inn of Beloit H

(608) 362-2666. **Call for rates.** 2786 Milwaukee Rd 53511. I-90 exit 185A, just w; at I-43 and SR 81. Int corridors. **Pets:** Accepted.

WW Econo Lodge H

(608) 365-8680. **Call for rates.** 3002 Milwaukee Rd 53511. I-90 exit 185A, just sw; at I-43 and SR 81. Int corridors. **Pets:** Medium. $15 one-time fee/pet. Service with restrictions, supervision.

WWW Fairfield Inn & Suites H

(608) 365-2200. **$109-$122.** 2784 Milwaukee Rd 53511. I-90 exit 185A, just sw; at I-43 and SR 81. **Pets:** Accepted.

AAA WW Rodeway Inn M

(608) 364-4000. **$50-$80.** 2956 Milwaukee Rd 53511. I-90 exit 185A, 0.3 mi w. Ext/int corridors. **Pets:** $10 daily fee/pet. Designated rooms, service with restrictions. SAVE

BERLIN

WW Countryside Lodge M

(920) 361-4411. **$74-$125.** 227 Ripon Rd 54923. On SR 49, at CR F. Int corridors. **Pets:** Accepted.

BLACK RIVER FALLS

AAA WWW Best Western Arrowhead Lodge & Suites H

(715) 284-9471. **$65-$140.** 600 Oasis Rd 54615. I-94 exit 116 (SR 54), just ne. Int corridors. **Pets:** Medium. $15 daily fee/room. Designated rooms, service with restrictions, supervision. SAVE

WW Days Inn H

(715) 284-4333. **$57-$123.** 919 Hwy 54 E 54615. I-94 exit 116 (SR 54), just w. Int corridors. **Pets:** Accepted.

BURLINGTON

WW AmericInn Lodge & Suites of Burlington H

(262) 534-2125. **$82-$112, 7 day notice.** 2709 Browns Lake Dr 53105. 3 mi n on SR 36 and 83, jct CR W. Int corridors. **Pets:** Accepted.

CADOTT

WW Countryside Motel M

(715) 289-4000. **$60-$100.** 545 Lavorata Rd 54727. SR 29 exit 91 (SR 27), just s. Int corridors. **Pets:** Small, dogs only. $5 daily fee/pet. Designated rooms, service with restrictions, supervision.

CHILTON

AAA WWW Best Western Stanton Inn H

(920) 849-3600. **$90-$160.** 1101 E Chestnut St 53014. Jct US 151 and SR 32/57. Int corridors. **Pets:** Accepted. SAVE

CHIPPEWA FALLS

WW AmericInn Motel & Suites of Chippewa Falls H

(715) 723-5711. **$85-$146.** 11 W South Ave 54729. 2 mi s on SR 124, access via CR J. Int corridors. **Pets:** Accepted.

CLINTONVILLE

WW Cobblestone Inn & Suites H

(715) 823-2000. **$80-$110.** 175 Waupaca St 54929. Jct US 45 and CR C. Int corridors. **Pets:** Medium, dogs only. $15 daily fee/room. Designated rooms, service with restrictions, supervision.

COLUMBUS

WW Super 8-Columbus H

(920) 623-8800. **$61-$106.** 219 Industrial Dr 53925. US 151 exit 118 (SR 16/60), just ne. Int corridors. **Pets:** Medium. $10 one-time fee/room. Designated rooms, service with restrictions, supervision.

CRANDON

AAA WWW Best Western Crandon Inn & Suites H

(715) 478-4000. **$90-$120, 7 day notice.** 9075 E Pioneer St 54520. 0.5 mi e on US 8 and SR 32. Int corridors. **Pets:** Medium. $20 daily fee/room. Designated rooms, service with restrictions, crate. SAVE

WW Four Seasons Motel M

(715) 478-3377. **$55-$80.** 304 W Glen St 54520. 0.5 mi w on US 8. Ext/int corridors. **Pets:** Medium. $25 deposit/pet. Service with restrictions, supervision.

DE FOREST

▽▽▽▽ Comfort Inn & Suites **H**
(608) 846-9100. **$79-$129.** 5025 County Hwy V 53532. I-90/94 exit 126 (CR V), just w. Int corridors. **Pets:** Accepted.
🛜 ⊠ ⅏ 🛏 💻 ⇌ ⊠

▽▽▽▽ Holiday Inn Express **H**
(608) 846-8686. **$89-$139.** 7184 Morrisonville Rd 53532. I-90/94 exit 126 (CR V), just e. Int corridors. **Pets:** Accepted.
ECO 🛜 ⊠ ⅏ 🛏 💻 ⇌

DELAVAN

▽▽ Super 8-Delavan **H**
(262) 728-1700. **$72-$126.** 518 Borg Rd 53115. I-43 exit 21 (SR 50), just w. Int corridors. **Pets:** Accepted. 🛜 ⊠ ⅏ 🛏 💻

DE PERE

▽▽▽▽ Kress Inn, an Ascend Collection hotel **H** ❀
(920) 403-5100. **Call for rates.** 300 Grant St 54115. US 41 exit 163 (Main Ave), 1 mi e, then just s on 3rd St. Int corridors. **Pets:** Medium, dogs only. $15 daily fee/pet. Designated rooms, service with restrictions, crate. 🛜 ⊠ ⅏ 🛏 💻

DODGEVILLE

AAA ▽▽▽ Best Western Quiet House & Suites **H**
(608) 935-7739. **$90-$149.** 1130 N Johns St 53533. On US 18, just e of jct SR 23. Int corridors. **Pets:** Large. $15 daily fee/pet. Designated rooms, service with restrictions, supervision. SAVE 🛜 ⊠ 🛏 💻 ⇌

AAA ▽▽ Pine Ridge Motel **M** ❀
(608) 935-3386. **$35-$85, 3 day notice.** 405 CR YZ 53533. 0.5 mi e of jct SR 23. Ext corridors. **Pets:** Very small, dogs only. $10 daily fee/pet. Designated rooms, service with restrictions, crate.
SAVE 🛜 ⊠ 🛏 💻

AAA ▽▽▽ Super 8 of Dodgeville **H**
(608) 935-3888. **$50-$86, 14 day notice.** 1308 Johns St 53533. Just n of US 18. Int corridors. **Pets:** Dogs only. $50 deposit/room. Supervision.
ECO SAVE 🛜 ⊠ ⅏ 🛏 💻

DOOR COUNTY AREA

EGG HARBOR

AAA ▽▽▽ The Shallows **M**
(920) 868-3458. **$75-$425, 30 day notice.** 7353 Horseshoe Bay Rd, Hwy G 54209. On CR G, 2.5 mi s. Ext corridors. **Pets:** Medium, dogs only. $20 daily fee/pet. Service with restrictions, supervision.
SAVE 🛜 ⊠ 🛏 💻 ⇌ ⊠

FISH CREEK

▽ Julie's Park Cafe & Motel **M**
(920) 868-2999. **Call for rates.** 4020 Hwy 42 54212. On SR 42, 0.3 mi n. Ext corridors. **Pets:** Accepted. 🛜 ⊠ 🛏 🍴

GILLS ROCK

▽ Maple Grove Motel **M**
(920) 854-2587. **Call for rates.** 809 SR 42 54210. On SR 42, 0.3 mi e; 1.5 mi w of car ferry. Ext corridors. **Pets:** Accepted. ⊠ 🛏 💻 ⊠

SISTER BAY

AAA ▽▽▽ Country House Resort **M** ❀
(920) 854-4551. **$72-$179, 14 day notice.** 2468 Sunnyside Rd 54234. Jct SR 42 and 57, 0.3 mi s on SR 42 to Highland Ave, just w. Ext corridors. **Pets:** Medium, dogs only. $20 daily fee/pet. Designated rooms, service with restrictions, supervision.
ECO SAVE 🛜 ⊠ 🛏 💻 ⇌ ⊠

STURGEON BAY

AAA ▽▽▽ Best Western Maritime Inn **H**
(920) 743-7231. **$63-$200.** 1001 N 14th Ave 54235. 1 mi n on Business Rt SR 42/57 at jct N 14th Ave. Int corridors. **Pets:** Accepted.
SAVE 🛜 ⊠ ⅏ 🛏 💻 ⇌ ⊠

END AREA

EAGLE RIVER

▽▽ Days Inn **H**
(715) 479-5151. **$62-$131.** 844 Railroad St N 54521. On US 45, 0.5 mi n. Int corridors. **Pets:** Accepted. 🛜 ⊠ 🛏 💻 ⇌ ⊠

▽▽ Super 8 **H**
(715) 477-0888. **$61-$122.** 200 W Pine St 54521. On SR 70; center. Int corridors. **Pets:** Accepted. 🛜 ⊠ ⅏ 🛏 💻 ⇌ ⊠

EAU CLAIRE

▽▽ AmericInn Motel & Suites of Eau Claire **H**
(715) 874-4900. **$75-$175.** 6200 Texaco Dr 54703. I-94 exit 59, jct US 12. Int corridors. **Pets:** Accepted. 🛜 ⊠ ⅏ 🛏 💻 ⇌

AAA ▽▽▽▽ Best Western Plus Trail Lodge Hotel & Suites **H**
(715) 838-9989. **$100-$110.** 3340 Mondovi Rd 54701. I-94 exit 65, just n. Int corridors. **Pets:** Medium. $20 daily fee/pet. Designated rooms, service with restrictions, supervision.
SAVE 🛜 ⊠ ⅏ 🛏 💻 ⇌ ⊠

▽▽ Days Inn **H**
(715) 834-3193. **$49-$80.** 2305 Craig Rd 54701. I-94 exit 65, 1.3 mi n on SR 37; just w of jct US 12. Int corridors. **Pets:** Accepted.
🛜 ⊠ ⅏ 🛏 💻

▽▽ Econo Lodge **H**
(715) 833-8818. **Call for rates.** 4608 Royal Dr 54701. I-94 exit 68, just n on SR 93, just w on Golf Rd, then just s. Int corridors. **Pets:** Accepted.
🛜 ⊠ ⅏ 🛏 💻

AAA ▽▽▽▽ GrandStay Residential Suites Hotel **H**
(715) 834-1700. **$100-$169.** 5310 Prill Rd 54701. I-94 exit 70, 0.8 mi n on US 53. Int corridors. **Pets:** Accepted.
SAVE 🛜 ⊠ ⅏ 🛏 💻 ⇌ ⊠

▽▽▽▽ Holiday Inn Campus Area **H**
(715) 835-2211. **$70-$159.** 2703 Craig Rd 54701. I-94 exit 65, 1.3 mi n on SR 37; just w of jct US 12. Int corridors. **Pets:** Accepted.
🛜 ⊠ ⅏ 🛏 💻 🍴 ⇌ ⊠

▽▽ Ramada Convention Center **H**
(715) 835-6121. **$59-$119.** 205 S Barstow St 54701. Jct S Barstow and Gibson sts; downtown. Int corridors. **Pets:** Accepted.
🛜 ⊠ ⅏ 🛏 💻 🍴 ⇌

▼▼▼▼ **Sleep Inn & Suites Conference Center** 🅷
(715) 874-2900. **$72-$125.** 5872 N 33rd Ave 54703. SR 29 exit 69 (CR T), just sw. Int corridors. **Pets:** Medium. $10 daily fee/room. Designated rooms, service with restrictions, crate.
🛜 ✕ 🅼 🛗 🖵 🍽 ➰ ✕

ELKHORN
▼▼▼ **AmericInn Lodge & Suites of Elkhorn** 🅷
(262) 723-7799. **$65-$112.** 210 E Commerce Ct 53121. I-43 exit 25, just s. Int corridors. **Pets:** Accepted. 🛜 ✕ 🅼 🛗 🖵 ➰ ✕

FITCHBURG
▼▼▼ **Candlewood Suites** 🅷
(608) 271-3400. **Call for rates.** 5421 Caddis Bend 53711. US 12/18 exit 260 (Fish Hatchery/CR D), 1.5 mi s. Int corridors. **Pets:** Accepted.
🛜 ✕ 🅼 🛗 🖵 ➰ ✕

▼▼◆ **Quality Inn & Suites** 🅷
(608) 274-7200. **$89-$126.** 2969 Cahill Main 53711. US 12/18 exit 260 (Fish Hatchery/CR D), 1.5 mi s at CR PD (McKee Rd). Int corridors.
Pets: Accepted. 🛜 ✕ 🅼 🛗 🖵 🍽 ➰ ✕

FOND DU LAC
▼▼ **Comfort Inn Fond du Lac** 🅷
(920) 921-4000. **$54-$260.** 77 Holiday Ln 54937. US 41 exit 97 (Military Rd), just sw. Int corridors. **Pets:** Other species. Service with restrictions, supervision. 🛜 ✕ 🅼 🛗 🖵 ➰ ✕

▼ **Executive Lodge of Fond du Lac** 🅷
(920) 923-2020. **$49-$89.** 649 W Johnson St 54935. US 41 exit 99 (Johnson St), 0.3 mi e on SR 23. Int corridors. **Pets:** Other species. $5 daily fee/pet. Service with restrictions, supervision. 🛜 ✕ 🛗 ➰

▼▼▼ **Holiday Inn** 🅷
(920) 923-1440. **$95-$379.** 625 W Rolling Meadows Dr 54937. US 41 exit 97 (Military Rd), just sw. Int corridors. **Pets:** $10 daily fee/pet. Service with restrictions, supervision.
🅔🅒🅞 🛜 ✕ 🅼 🛗 🖵 🍽 ➰ ✕

▼▼ **Microtel Inn & Suites** 🅷
(920) 929-4000. **$58-$114.** 920 S Military Rd 54935. US 41 exit 97 (Military Rd). Int corridors. **Pets:** Accepted. 🛜 ✕ 🅼 🛗 🖵

▼▼ **Super 8-FOND DU LAC** 🅷
(920) 922-1088. **$45-$162, 3 day notice.** 391 N Pioneer Rd 54935. US 41 exit 99 (SR 23), just n on east frontage road (CR VV). Int corridors.
Pets: Accepted. 🛜 ✕ 🅼 🛗 🖵

FORT ATKINSON
▼▼▼ **Holiday Inn Express Hotel & Suites** 🅷
(920) 563-3600. **$114-$194.** 1680 Madison Ave 53538. Jct SR 26 Bypass and US 12. Int corridors. **Pets:** Small, other species. $30 one-time fee/room. Designated rooms, service with restrictions, supervision.
🛜 ✕ 🅼 🛗 🖵 ➰ ✕

GRANTSBURG
▼ **Wood River Motel** 🅼
(715) 463-2541. **$68-$125, 3 day notice.** 703 W SR 70 54840. On SR 70, 1 mi w. Ext corridors. **Pets:** Medium. $10 one-time fee/pet. Designated rooms, service with restrictions, supervision. 🛜 ✕ 🅼 🛗

GREEN BAY
Ⓐ⅃ ▼▼▼ **Aloft Green Bay** 🅷 ❀
(920) 884-0800. **$89-$189.** 465 Pilgrim Way 54304. US 41 exit 163B, just e. Int corridors. **Pets:** Small, dogs only. Designated rooms, service with restrictions, supervision. 🆂🅰🆅🅴 🛜 ✕ 🅼 🛗 🖵 ➰ ✕

▼▼▼◆ **AmericInn Lodge & Suites Green Bay East** 🅷
(920) 964-0177. **$75-$155.** 2628 Manitowoc Rd 54311. I-43 exit 181, just w. Int corridors. **Pets:** $20 one-time fee/room. Designated rooms, crate.
🛜 ✕ 🅼 🛗 🖵 ➰ ✕

▼▼ ◆◆ **AmericInn Lodge & Suites of Green Bay West** 🅷 ❀
(920) 434-9790. **Call for rates.** 2032 Velp Ave 54303. US 41 exit 170, 0.3 mi w. Int corridors. **Pets:** $15 daily fee/pet. Designated rooms, supervision. 🛜 ✕ 🛗 🖵

▼▼◆ **Baymont Inn-Green Bay** 🅷
(920) 494-7887. **$53-$284.** 2840 S Oneida St 54304. US 41 exit 164 (Oneida St), just e. Int corridors. **Pets:** Accepted. 🛜 ✕ 🛗 🖵

Ⓐ🅐🅐 ◆ **Bay Motel** 🅼
(920) 494-3441. **$49-$75.** 1301 S Military Ave 54304. US 41 exit 167 (Lombardi Ave), 0.4 mi e to Marlee, then 0.6 mi n. Ext corridors.
Pets: Accepted. 🆂🅰🆅🅴 🛜 ✕ 🛗 🖵 🍽

Ⓐ🅐🅐 ▼▼◆ **Best Western Green Bay Inn Conference Center** 🅷
(920) 499-3161. **$59-$399.** 780 Armed Forces Dr 54304. US 41 exit 167 (Lombardi Ave), 1.4 mi e to Holmgren Way, then just s. Int corridors.
Pets: Small. $20 daily fee/pet. Designated rooms, no service, crate.
🆂🅰🆅🅴 🛜 ✕ 🛗 🖵 🍽 ➰ ✕

▼▼◆ **Clarion Hotel** 🅷
(920) 437-5900. **Call for rates.** 201 Main St 54301. Jct Adams St; downtown. Int corridors. **Pets:** $35 one-time fee/room. Service with restrictions, supervision. 🛜 ✕ 🛗 🖵 🍽 ➰ ✕

▼▼◆ **Comfort Inn by Choice Hotels** 🅷
(920) 498-2060. **$80-$200.** 2841 Ramada Way 54304. US 41 exit 164 (Oneida St), just e to Ramada Way, then just n. Int corridors.
Pets: Accepted. 🛜 ✕ 🛗 🖵 ➰

▼▼▼ **Country Inn & Suites By Carlson** 🅷
(920) 336-6600. **$99-$150, 3 day notice.** 2945 Allied St 54304. US 41 exit 164 (Oneida St), just nw. Int corridors. **Pets:** Small, other species. $15 daily fee/room. Designated rooms, service with restrictions, supervision. 🛜 ✕ 🛗 🖵 ➰ ✕

▼▼◆ **Days Inn Lambeau Field** 🅷
(920) 498-8088. **$54-$224.** 1978 Holmgren Way 54304. US 41 exit 167 (Lombardi Ave), 1.4 mi e, then just s. Int corridors. **Pets:** Accepted.
🛜 ✕ 🛗 🖵 ➰

▼▼◆ **Extended Stay Airport** 🅷
(920) 499-3600. **$60-$75, 10 day notice.** 1639 Commanche Ave 54313. US 41 exit 165, 1 mi w on SR 172, then just s. Int corridors.
Pets: Medium, dogs only. $75 one-time fee/pet. Designated rooms, service with restrictions, crate. 🛜 ✕ 🛗 🖵

▼▼◆ **Quality Inn & Suites** 🅷
(920) 437-8771. **$64-$250.** 321 S Washington St 54301-4214. On east side of Fox River, just s of Walnut St (SR 29); downtown. Int corridors.
Pets: Medium, other species. $10 one-time fee/pet. Designated rooms, service with restrictions, supervision. 🛜 ✕ 🛗 🖵 ➰ ✕

Ⓐ🅐🅐 ▼▼▼▼ **Ramada Plaza Hotel & Conference Center** 🅷
(920) 499-0631. **$89-$289.** 2750 Ramada Way 54304. US 41 exit 164 (Oneida St), just e. Int corridors. **Pets:** Accepted.
🆂🅰🆅🅴 🛜 ✕ 🅼 🛗 🖵 🍽 ➰ ✕

▼▼◆ **Residence Inn by Marriott** 🅷
(920) 435-2222. **$143-$175.** 335 W St. Joseph St 54301. SR 172 exit Riverside Dr, 1.1 mi n on SR 57, then just e. Ext corridors.
Pets: Accepted. 🛜 ✕ 🛗 🖵 ➰ ✕

▼▼◆ **Suburban Extended Stay Hotel** 🅷
(920) 430-7040. **$69-$159.** 1125 E Mason St 54301. US 41 exit 168 (Mason St), 4 mi e. Int corridors. **Pets:** Medium. $25 one-time fee/pet. Designated rooms, service with restrictions. 🛜 ✕ 🅼 🛗 🖵

Ⓐ🅐🅐 ▼▼▼ **Super 8** 🅷 ❀
(920) 494-2042. **$44-$175.** 2868 S Oneida St 54304. US 41 exit 164 (Oneida St), just e. Int corridors. **Pets:** Other species. $15 one-time fee/room. Supervision. 🆂🅰🆅🅴 🛜 ✕ 🛗 🖵

▼▼ Super 8 Green Bay I-43 H

(920) 406-8200. **$44-$116, 30 day notice.** 2911 Voyager Dr 54311. I-43 exit 183 (Mason St), just e. Int corridors. **Pets:** Accepted.

▼ Travelodge Green Bay/Lambeau H

(920) 499-3599. **$53-$179.** 2870 Ramada Way 54304. US 41 exit 164 (Oneida St), just e. Int corridors. **Pets:** Small. Service with restrictions, supervision.

HAYWARD

▼▼ AmericInn of Hayward H

(715) 634-2700. **$88-$195, 3 day notice.** 15601 US Hwy 63 54843. Just n of jct SR 77. Int corridors. **Pets:** Medium. $10 daily fee/pet. Designated rooms, service with restrictions, supervision.

▼▼▼ Comfort Suites H

(715) 634-0700. **$109-$169.** 15586 CR B 54843. 0.5 mi s of jct SR 27. Int corridors. **Pets:** Accepted.

AAA ▼▼▼ The Flat Creek Inn & Suites H ❀

(715) 634-4100. **$77-$165.** 10290 Hwy 27 S 54843. On SR 27 S, 0.7 mi s of jct US 63. Int corridors. **Pets:** Medium, dogs only. $15 daily fee/pet. Designated rooms, service with restrictions, supervision.

▼▼▼ Ross' Teal Lake Lodge and Teal Wing Golf Club CA ❀

(715) 462-3631. **$170-$270, 21 day notice.** 12425 N Ross Rd 54843. On SR 77, 20 mi ne of jct US 63. Ext corridors. **Pets:** $10 daily fee/pet. Designated rooms, service with restrictions, supervision.

HILLSBORO

AAA ▼▼▼ Hotel Hillsboro H

(608) 489-3000. **$75-$125.** 1235 Water Ave (Hwy 33) 54634. SR 33 and 80/82, just w. Int corridors. **Pets:** $15 one-time fee/room. Designated rooms, service with restrictions, crate.

HUDSON

▼▼ Fairfield Inn by Marriott H

(715) 386-6688. **$89-$143.** 2400 Center Dr 54016. I-94 exit 2 (CR F), 0.3 mi s. Int corridors. **Pets:** Accepted.

▼▼ Quality Inn H

(715) 386-6355. **Call for rates.** 811 Dominion Dr 54016. I-94 exit 2 (CR F), 1 mi w on south frontage road (Crestview Dr). Int corridors. **Pets:** Accepted.

AAA ▼▼▼ Super 8 of Hudson H

(715) 386-8800. **$56-$144.** 808 Dominion Dr 54016. I-94 exit 2 (CR F), 1 mi w on south frontage road (Crestview Dr). **Pets:** Medium, dogs only. $15 daily fee/pet. Designated rooms, service with restrictions, supervision.

HURLEY

▼▼ Days Inn of Hurley H

(715) 561-3500. **$77-$117.** 13355 N US Hwy 51 54534. Jct US 2 and 51, 0.4 mi s on US 51. Int corridors. **Pets:** Medium, other species. $15 one-time fee/room. No service, supervision.

JANESVILLE

▼▼ Baymont Inn & Suites H

(608) 758-4545. **Call for rates.** 616 Midland Rd 53546. I-90 exit 175B (SR 11), just ne. Int corridors. **Pets:** Accepted.

▼▼ Econo Lodge - Janesville H

(608) 754-0251. **$50-$120.** 3520 Milton Ave 53545. I-90/39 exit 171A, just sw via Frontage Rd. Int corridors. **Pets:** Accepted.

JOHNSON CREEK

▼▼▼ Days Inn-Johnson Creek H

(920) 699-8000. **$63-$108.** W4545 Linmar Ln 53038. I-94 exit 267 (SR 26), just ne. Int corridors. **Pets:** $100 deposit/room, $10 daily fee/pet. Designated rooms, service with restrictions, supervision.

KENOSHA

AAA ▼▼▼ Best Western Harborside Inn & Kenosha Conference Center H

(262) 658-3281. **$80-$150.** 5125 6th Ave 53140. Just ne of jct SR 32 and 158; downtown. Int corridors. **Pets:** Accepted.

AAA ▼▼▼ Candlewood Suites H

(262) 842-5000. **$99-$149.** 10200 74th St 53142. SR 50 exit 104th Ave, just n. Int corridors. **Pets:** Accepted.

▼▼ Country Inn & Suites By Carlson H

(262) 857-3680. **$99-$140.** 7011 122nd Ave 53142. I-94 exit 344 (SR 50), just nw. Int corridors. **Pets:** Small, dogs only. $25 daily fee/pet. Service with restrictions, crate.

KIMBERLY

▼▼ Super 8 - Kimberly H

(920) 788-4400. **$59-$126.** 761 Truman St 54136. US 41 exit 145 (SR 441), 2.7 mi s to CR CE, then 0.4 mi e. Int corridors. **Pets:** Medium, dogs only. $15 daily fee/pet. No service, supervision.

KOHLER

AAA ▼▼▼ Inn on Woodlake H ❀

(920) 452-7800. **$165-$300, 7 day notice.** 705 Woodlake Rd 53044. I-43 exit 126, 0.5 mi w on SR 23, 0.5 mi s on CR Y and Highland Dr; in Woodlake Shopping Center. Int corridors. **Pets:** Medium, dogs only. $75 one-time fee/room. Designated rooms, service with restrictions, crate.

LA CROSSE

AAA ▼▼▼ Best Western Plus Riverfront Hotel H ❀

(608) 781-7000. **$100-$145.** 1835 Rose St 54603. I-90 exit 3, 1 mi s on US 53. Int corridors. **Pets:** Large, dogs only. $15 daily fee/pet. Designated rooms, service with restrictions, supervision.

AAA ▼▼▼ Candlewood Suites H ❀

(608) 785-1110. **$89-$149.** 56 Copeland Ave 54603. I-90 exit 3, 2 mi s on US 53. Int corridors. **Pets:** $75 one-time fee/room. Service with restrictions, crate.

AAA ▼▼ Days Hotel & Conference Center H

(608) 783-1000. **$58-$116.** 101 Sky Harbour Dr 54603. I-90 exit 2, just sw; on French Island. Int corridors. **Pets:** $15 daily fee/room. Designated rooms, service with restrictions, crate.

AAA ▼▼ Econo Lodge H

(608) 781-0200. **$60-$139.** 1906 Rose St 54603. I-90 exit 3, 0.9 mi s on US 53. Int corridors. **Pets:** Small. $25 deposit/room. Designated rooms, service with restrictions, supervision.

AAA ▼▼▼ GrandStay Residential Suites Hotel of La Crosse H

(608) 796-1615. **$89-$209.** 525 Front St N 54601. I-90 exit 3; downtown. Int corridors. **Pets:** Accepted.

▼▼▼▼ Holiday Inn Hotel & Suites H

(608) 784-4444. **$99-$159, 3 day notice.** 200 Pearl St 54601. Downtown. Int corridors. **Pets:** Accepted.
📶 ⊠ ᯤ 🛄 🖥 ¶ 🏊 ⊠

▼▼▼ Howard Johnson Hotel La Crosse H

(608) 781-0400. **$53-$107.** 2150 Rose St 54603. I-90 exit 3, 0.8 mi s on US 53. Int corridors. **Pets:** Accepted. 📶 ⊠ ᯤ 🛄 🖥

▼▼▼ Settle Inn H ❀

(608) 781-5100. **$60-$120.** 2110 Rose St 54603. I-90 exit 3, 0.9 mi s on US 53. Int corridors. **Pets:** Small, dogs only. $15 daily fee/pet. Designated rooms, service with restrictions, supervision.
📶 ⊠ ᯤ 🛄 🖥

LADYSMITH
▼▼▼ FairBridge Inn Express H

(715) 532-6650. **Call for rates.** 800 W College Ave 54848. On SR 27, 0.5 mi s of US 8. Int corridors. **Pets:** Accepted.
📶 ⊠ ᯤ 🛄 🖥 🏊

LAKE GENEVA
▼▼ Budget Host Diplomat Motel M

(262) 248-1809. **$58-$106, 7 day notice.** 1060 Wells St 53147. 1 mi s of SR 50. Ext corridors. **Pets:** Accepted. 📶 ⊠ 🛄 🏊

▲▲▲ ▼▼▼▼ Grand Geneva Resort & Spa H ❀

(262) 248-8811. **$139-$449, 3 day notice.** 7036 Grand Geneva Way 53147. On SR 50, just e of jct US 12. Int corridors. **Pets:** Small, dogs only. $35 daily fee/room. Service with restrictions.
ECO SAVE 📶 ⊠ ᯤ 🛄 🖥 ¶ 🏊 ⊠

LAKE MILLS
▼▼ Americas Best Value Inn H

(920) 648-3800. **$60-$120.** W 7614 Oasis Ln 53551. I-94 exit 259 (SR 89), just n. Int corridors. **Pets:** Medium. $15 one-time fee/pet, $15 daily fee/pet. Service with restrictions, supervision.
📶 ⊠ 🛄 🖥 🏊

LAND O'LAKES
▼▼ Sunrise Lodge CA

(715) 547-3684. **$89-$235, 21 day notice.** 5894 W Shore Dr 54540. 2 mi s on US 45, 2.8 mi e on CR E, then 1 mi n. Ext corridors.
Pets: Accepted. 📶 ⊠ 🛄 🖥 ¶ ⊠ 🐾

LODI
▲▲▲ ▼▼▼▼ Best Western Countryside Inn H

(608) 592-1450. **$80-$150.** W 9250 Prospect Dr 53555. I-90/94 exit 119, just w. Int corridors. **Pets:** $15 daily fee/pet. Designated rooms, service with restrictions, crate. SAVE 📶 ⊠ ᯤ 🛄 🖥 🏊

MADISON
▲▲▲ ▼▼▼▼ AmericInn Madison West H

(608) 662-1990. **$77-$120.** 516 Grand Canyon Dr 53719. US 12 and 14 exit 255 (Gammon Rd), just n, then 0.5 mi e on Odana Rd. Int corridors.
Pets: Accepted. SAVE 📶 ⊠ ᯤ 🛄 🖥 🏊

▼▼▼ Baymont Inn & Suites H

(608) 241-3861. **$49-$121.** 4202 E Towne Blvd 53704. I-90/94 exit 135A (US 151), 0.5 mi w. Int corridors. **Pets:** Accepted. 📶 ⊠ 🛄 🖥

▲▲▲ ▼▼▼▼ Best Western Plus East Towne Suites H

(608) 244-2020. **Call for rates.** 4801 Annamark Dr 53704. I-90/94 exit 135A (US 151) southbound; exit 135C (High Crossing Blvd) northbound, just sw on US 151. Int corridors. **Pets:** Medium, other species. $20 daily fee/room. Service with restrictions, supervision.
SAVE 📶 ⊠ 🛄 🖥 🏊

▲▲▲ ▼▼▼ Best Western West Towne Suites H ❀

(608) 833-4200. **$80-$100.** 650 Grand Canyon Dr 53719. US 12 and 14 exit 255 (Gammon Rd), just e on Odana Rd, then just sw. Int corridors.
Pets: Medium. $25 deposit/room, $15 daily fee/room. Designated rooms, service with restrictions, supervision. SAVE 📶 ⊠ 🛄 🖥

▲▲▲ ▼▼▼▼ Clarion Suites Madison-Central H

(608) 284-1234. **$89-$239.** 2110 Rimrock Rd 53713. US 12 and 18 exit 262 (Rimrock Rd), just nw. Int corridors. **Pets:** Accepted.
SAVE 📶 ⊠ ᯤ 🛄 🖥 🏊

▼▼▼ Comfort Inn & Suites - Airport H

(608) 244-6265. **$70-$170.** 4822 E Washington Ave 53704. I-90/94 exit 135A (US 151), just w. Int corridors. **Pets:** Medium. $15 daily fee/pet. Designated rooms, service with restrictions.
📶 ⊠ ᯤ 🛄 🖥 🏊

▼▼▼ Comfort Suites-Madison H

(608) 836-3033. **$69-$159.** 1253 John Q Hammons Dr 53717. US 12 and 14 exit 252 (Greenway Blvd), just sw. Int corridors. **Pets:** Accepted.
ECO 📶 ⊠ ᯤ 🛄 🖥 🏊 ⊠

▲▲▲ ▼▼▼▼ Crowne Plaza Hotel Madison H ❀

(608) 244-4703. **$99-$299.** 4402 E Washington Ave 53704. I-90/94 exit 135A (US 151), 0.4 mi w. Int corridors. **Pets:** Medium. $25 one-time fee/room. Designated rooms, service with restrictions, crate.
ECO SAVE 📶 ⊠ ᯤ 🛄 🖥 ¶ 🏊 ⊠

▲▲▲ ▼▼▼ Days Inn of Madison H ❀

(608) 223-1800. **$65-$116.** 4402 E Broadway Service Rd 53716. US 12 and 18 exit 266 (US 51), just ne. Int corridors. **Pets:** Dogs only. $10 one-time fee/pet. Service with restrictions, supervision.
ECO SAVE 📶 ⊠ ᯤ 🛄 🖥 🏊

▲▲▲ ▼▼▼ Econo Lodge of Madison H

(608) 241-4171. **Call for rates.** 4726 E Washington Ave 53704. I-90/94 exit 135A (US 151), just w. Int corridors. **Pets:** Small. $10 daily fee/pet. Designated rooms, service with restrictions, supervision.
SAVE 📶 ⊠ ᯤ 🛄 🖥

▼▼▼▼ The Edgewater H ❀

(608) 256-9071. **$129-$419.** 666 Wisconsin Ave 53703. On Lake Mendota, 0.3 mi n of Capitol Square. Int corridors. **Pets:** Service with restrictions. 📶 ⊠ ᯤ 🛄 🖥 ¶

▼▼▼ Extended Stay Deluxe Madison West H ❀

(608) 833-2121. **$57-$115.** 45 Junction Ct 53717. US 12 exit 253 (Old Sauk Rd), just w. Int corridors. **Pets:** Other species. $25 daily fee/pet. Service with restrictions. 📶 ⊠ ᯤ 🛄 🖥 🏊

▲▲▲ ▼▼▼▼ GrandStay Residential Suites Hotel H

(608) 241-2500. **Call for rates.** 5317 High Crossing Blvd 53718. I-90/94 exit 135C (US 151/High Crossing Blvd), 0.5 mi e. Int corridors.
Pets: Other species. $200 deposit/room, $10 daily fee/room. Service with restrictions. SAVE 📶 ⊠ ᯤ 🛄 🖥 🏊 ⊠

▲▲▲ ▼▼▼▼ Hilton Madison Monona Terrace H

(608) 255-5100. **$134-$399.** 9 E Wilson St 53703. 2 blks e of Capitol Square; downtown. Int corridors. **Pets:** Accepted.
ECO SAVE 📶 ⊠ ᯤ 🛄 🖥 ¶ 🏊

▼▼▼▼ Homewood Suites by Hilton Madison West H

(608) 271-0600. **$99-$149.** 479 Commerce Dr 53719. US 12 exit 254 (Mineral Point Rd), just se. Int corridors. **Pets:** Accepted.
📶 ⊠ ᯤ 🛄 🖥 ⊠

▲▲▲ ▼▼▼▼ Hotel Red H ❀

(608) 819-8228. **Call for rates.** 1501 Monroe St 53711. Downtown. Int corridors. **Pets:** Other species. $50 one-time fee/room. Service with restrictions, crate. SAVE 📶 ⊠ ᯤ 🛄 🖥 ¶

▼▼▼▼ La Quinta Inn & Suites Madison American Center 🄷

(608) 245-0123. **$83-$155.** 5217 E Terrace Dr 53718. US 151 exit 98B (American Pkwy), just sw. Int corridors. **Pets:** Medium, other species. Service with restrictions, supervision. 🛜 ✕ ♿ 🖥 🖵 🚬

🅰🅰🅰 ▼▼▼ Magnuson Grand Hotel Madison 🄷

(608) 224-1500. **$67-$159.** 3510 Mill Pond Rd 53718. I-90 exit 142B, just e on US 12 and 18, then w on south frontage road. Int corridors.
Pets: Accepted. 🆂🅰🆅🅴 🛜 ✕ ♿ 🖥 🖵 🚬

▼▼▼ Microtel Inn & Suites 🄷

(608) 242-9000. **$50-$67.** 2139 E Springs Dr 53704. I-90/94 exit 135A (US 151), just s, then 0.5 mi ie. Int corridors. **Pets:** Small. $10 daily fee/pet. Designated rooms, service with restrictions, supervision.
🛜 ✕ ♿ 🖥 🖵

🅰🅰🅰 ▼▼▼ Red Roof Inn-Madison #7052 🄼

(608) 241-1787. **$55-$94.** 4830 Hayes Rd 53704. I-90/94 exit 135A (US 151), just sw. Ext corridors. **Pets:** Large, other species. No service, supervision. 🆂🅰🆅🅴 🛜 ✕ ♿ 🖥 🖵

▼▼▼ Residence Inn by Marriott 🄷

(608) 244-5047. **$145-$160.** 4862 Hayes Rd 53704. I-90/94 exit 135A (US 151), just sw to Hayes Rd, then just ne. Int corridors.
Pets: Accepted. 🛜 ✕ ♿ 🖥 🖵 🚬 ✕

🅰🅰🅰 ▼▼▼▼ Sheraton Madison Hotel 🄷 🐾

(608) 251-2300. **$89-$209.** 706 John Nolen Dr 53713. US 12 and 18 exit 263 (John Nolen Dr), just n. Int corridors. **Pets:** Medium, other species. $25 one-time fee/room. Service with restrictions, crate.
🄴🄲🄾 🆂🅰🆅🅴 🛜 ✕ ♿ 🖥 🖵 🍴 🚬

▼▼▼ Sleep Inn & Suites 🄷

(608) 221-8100. **$69-$99.** 4802 Tradewinds Pkwy 53718. US 12/14/18/ 151 exit 266, 0.5 mi se, then 0.6 mi on Dutch Mill Rd. Int corridors.
Pets: Large. $5 daily fee/pet. Designated rooms, service with restrictions, supervision. 🛜 ✕ ♿ 🖥 🖵 🚬 ✕

▼▼▼ Staybridge Suites 🄷

(608) 241-2300. **$89-$199.** 3301 City View Dr 53718. I-90/94 exit 135C (US 151/High Crossing Blvd), just e. Int corridors. **Pets:** Other species. $75 one-time fee/pet. Designated rooms, service with restrictions, crate.
🛜 ✕ ♿ 🖥 🖵 🚬

◆◆ Super 8-Madison 🄷

(608) 258-8882. **$59-$99.** 1602 W Beltline Hwy 53713. US 12 and 18 exit 260B (CR D), just w on N Frontage Rd. Int corridors.
Pets: Accepted. 🛜 ✕ 🖥 🖵 🚬

MANITOWOC

▼▼ AmericInn Lodge & Suites of Manitowoc 🄷

(920) 684-3344. **Call for rates.** 5020 Hecker Rd 54220. I-43 exit 149, just sw. Int corridors. **Pets:** Accepted. 🛜 ✕ 🖥 🖵 🚬 ✕

🅰🅰🅰 ▼▼◆ Best Western Lakefront Hotel 🄷 🐾

(920) 682-7000. **$100-$130.** 101 Maritime Dr 54220. I-43 exit 152, 4.2 mi e on SR 42 N, then 1 mi s. Int corridors. **Pets:** $20 one-time fee/room. Service with restrictions. 🆂🅰🆅🅴 🛜 ✕ 🖥 🖵 🍴 🚬 ✕

▼▼ Comfort Inn by Choice Hotels 🄷 🐾

(920) 683-0220. **$74-$104.** 2200 S 44th St 54220. I-43 exit 149, just e. Int corridors. **Pets:** Other species. $25 one-time fee/room. Service with restrictions, crate. 🛜 ✕ ♿ 🖥 🖵

▼ Econo Lodge 🄷

(920) 682-8271. **Call for rates.** 908 Washington St 54220. On US 151 business route; downtown. Int corridors. **Pets:** Accepted.
🛜 ✕ 🖥 🖵 🍴

▼▼▼ Holiday Inn Manitowoc 🄷 🐾

(920) 682-6000. **$119-$159.** 4601 Calumet Ave 54220. I-43 exit 149, just e. Int corridors. **Pets:** Other species. $150 deposit/room. Service with restrictions, crate. 🛜 ✕ ♿ 🖥 🖵 🍴 🚬 ✕

MARSHFIELD

▼▼ Baymont Inn & Suites-Marshfield 🄷

(715) 384-5240. **$76-$112.** 2107 N Central Ave 54449. On SR 97; 1.6 mi n of SR 13. Int corridors. **Pets:** Accepted.
🛜 ✕ ♿ 🖥 🖵 🚬 ✕

▼▼ Comfort Inn 🄷

(715) 387-8691. **$77-$90.** 114 E Upham St 54449. On SR 97; 0.8 mi n of jct SR 13. Int corridors. **Pets:** Dogs only. $40 deposit/room, $15 daily fee/pet. Designated rooms, service with restrictions, supervision.
🛜 ✕ ♿ 🖥 🖵 🚬

MAUSTON

🅰🅰🅰 ▼▼▼ Best Western Park Oasis Inn 🄷

(608) 847-6255. **$80-$111.** W5641 Hwy 82 E 53948. I-90/94 exit 69, just se. Int corridors. **Pets:** Large. $5 daily fee/pet. Designated rooms, service with restrictions, crate. 🆂🅰🆅🅴 🛜 ✕ 🖥 🖵 🍴 🚬 ✕

▼▼ DJ's Inn 🄷

(608) 847-5959. **$77-$150.** 1001 SR 82 53948. I-90/94 exit 69, just ne. Int corridors. **Pets:** Accepted. 🛜 ✕ 🖥 🖵 🚬

▼▼ Super 8 🄼 🐾

(608) 847-2300. **$55-$124.** 1001A Hwy 82 E 53948. I-90/94 exit 69, just ne. Int corridors. **Pets:** Other species. $10 daily fee/pet. Service with restrictions, supervision. 🛜 ✕ 🖥 🖵 🚬

MEDFORD

▼▼ AmericInn Motel of Medford 🄷

(715) 748-2330. **$74-$100.** 435 S 8th St 54451. On SR 13, 0.5 mi s of jct SR 64. Int corridors. **Pets:** $25 one-time fee/room. Designated rooms, service with restrictions, supervision.
🛜 ✕ ♿ 🖥 🖵 🚬 ✕

▼▼ Woodlands Inn & Suites 🄼

(715) 748-3995. **$65-$124.** 854 N 8th St 54451. On SR 13, 0.6 mi n of jct SR 64. Int corridors. **Pets:** $25 one-time fee/room. Designated rooms, service with restrictions, supervision. 🛜 ✕ 🖥 🖵 🚬

MENOMONIE

▼ Menomonie Motel 6 #4109 🄷

(715) 235-6901. **$48-$69.** 2100 Stout St 54751. I-94 exit 41 (SR 25), just se. Int corridors. **Pets:** Other species. Service with restrictions, supervision. 🛜 🖥

🅰🅰🅰 ▼▼▼ Quality Inn & Suites 🄷

(715) 233-1500. **Call for rates.** 1721 Plaza Dr NE 54751. I-94 exit 45 (CR B), just sw. Int corridors. **Pets:** Accepted.
🆂🅰🆅🅴 🛜 ✕ ♿ 🖥 🖵 🚬

▼▼ Super 8-Menomonie 🄷

(715) 235-8889. **$52-$58.** 1622 N Broadway 54751. I-94 exit 41 (SR 25), just s. Int corridors. **Pets:** Accepted. 🛜 ✕ 🖥 🖵 🚬

MERRILL

▼▼ AmericInn Lodge & Suites of Merrill 🄷

(715) 536-7979. **$89-$149.** 3300 E Main St 54452. US 51 exit 208, 0.5 mi w on SR 64. Int corridors. **Pets:** Other species. $20 daily fee/pet. Service with restrictions, supervision.
🛜 ✕ ♿ 🖥 🖵 🚬 ✕

▼▼ Super 8 🄷

(715) 536-6880. **$47-$108.** 3209 E Main St 54452. US 51 exit 208, 0.5 mi w on SR 64. Int corridors. **Pets:** Accepted.
🛜 ✕ ♿ 🖥 🖵 🚬 ✕

MIDDLETON

AAA ▼▼▼▼ **Country Inn & Suites By Carlson, Madison West** H

(608) 831-6970. **$114-$169.** 2212 Deming Way 53562. US 12/14 exit 251A, 0.3 mi w on University Ave, then just n. Int corridors. **Pets:** Small, dogs only. $35 daily fee/pet. Designated rooms, no service, supervision.

SAVE 🛜 ✕ 𝄐 🛏 🖥 ➿ ✕

▼▼▼ **Marriott Madison West** H

(608) 831-2000. **$152-$186.** 1313 John Q Hammons Dr 53562. US 12/14 exit 252 (Greenway Blvd), just w. Int corridors. **Pets:** Accepted.

🛜 ✕ 𝄐 🛏 🖥 🍴 ➿

▼▼▼ **Residence Inn by Marriott-Madison West/Middleton** H

(608) 662-1100. **$143-$175.** 8400 Market St 53562. US 12/14 exit 252 (Greenway Blvd), just w, then just n; in Greenway Station. Int corridors. **Pets:** Accepted. 🛜 ✕ 𝄐 🛏 🖥 ➿ ✕

▼▼▼ **Staybridge Suites** H

(608) 664-5888. **$139-$229.** 7790 Elmwood Ave 53562. US 12/14 exit 251 (University Ave), just nw. Int corridors. **Pets:** Medium. $75 one-time fee/room. 🛜 ✕ 𝄐 🛏 🖥 ➿

MILWAUKEE METROPOLITAN AREA

BROOKFIELD

AAA ▼▼▼ **Best Western Plus Midway Hotel & Suites-Brookfield** H

(262) 786-9540. **$99-$159.** 1005 S Moorland Rd 53005. I-94 exit 301A (Moorland Rd), just s. Int corridors. **Pets:** Medium. $15 one-time fee/ room. Service with restrictions, crate.

SAVE 🛜 ✕ 🛏 🖥 🍴 ➿ ✕

AAA ▼▼▼▼ **Brookfield Suites Hotel & Convention Center** H

(262) 782-2900. **$99-$395.** 1200 S Moorland Rd 53005. I-94 exit 301A (Moorland Rd), just s. Int corridors. **Pets:** Medium, dogs only. $25 one-time fee/pet. Designated rooms, service with restrictions, supervision.

SAVE 🛜 ✕ 𝄐 🛏 🖥 🍴 ➿ ✕

AAA ▼▼▼▼ **Country Inn & Suites By Carlson, Milwaukee-West** H

(262) 782-1400. **$99-$269.** 1250 S Moorland Rd 53005. I-94 exit 301A (Moorland Rd), just se. Int corridors. **Pets:** Accepted.

SAVE 🛜 ✕ 𝄐 🛏 🖥 🍴 ➿ ✕

▼▼ **Homestead Studio Suites Hotel-Milwaukee/Brookfield** H ❄

(262) 782-9300. **$55-$95.** 325 N Brookfield Rd 53045. I-94 exit 297, 1.1 mi e on US 18, then just e. Int corridors. **Pets:** Other species. $25 daily fee/pet. Service with restrictions. 🛜 ✕ 𝄐 🛏 🖥

▼▼ **La Quinta Inn Milwaukee West Brookfield** H

(262) 782-9100. **$64-$144.** 20391 W Bluemound Rd 53045. I-94 exit 297, just e on US 18. Int corridors. **Pets:** Medium, other species. Service with restrictions, supervision. 🛜 ✕ 𝄐 🛏 🖥

AAA ▼▼ **Quality Inn-Milwaukee/Brookfield** H

(262) 785-0500. **$65-$139.** 20150 W Bluemound Rd 53045. I-94 exit 297, just e on US 18. Ext/int corridors. **Pets:** Accepted.

SAVE 🛜 ✕ 🛏 🖥 ➿

AAA ▼▼▼ **Residence Inn by Marriott Milwaukee-Brookfield** H ❄

(262) 782-5990. **$99-$379.** 950 S Pinehurst Ct 53005. I-94 exit 301A, just s. Ext corridors. **Pets:** Other species. $100 one-time fee/room. Service with restrictions, crate. SAVE 🛜 ✕ 𝄐 🛏 🖥 ➿ ✕

AAA ▼▼▼▼ **Sheraton Milwaukee Brookfield** H ❄

(262) 364-1100. **$89-$269.** 375 S Moorland Rd 53005. I-94 exit 301B (Moorland Rd), just n. Int corridors. **Pets:** Medium, dogs only. Designated rooms, service with restrictions, supervision.

SAVE 🛜 ✕ 𝄐 🛏 🖥 🍴 ➿

▼▼▼ **TownePlace Suites by Marriott** H

(262) 784-8450. **$89-$199.** 600 N Calhoun Rd 53005. I-94 exit 297 eastbound, 2.1 mi e on US 18; exit 301B (Moorland Rd) westbound, 1.5 mi n, then 0.4 mi w on US 18. Int corridors. **Pets:** Accepted.

🛜 ✕ 🛏 🖥 ➿

DELAFIELD

AAA ▼▼▼▼ **The Delafield Hotel** H ❄

(262) 646-1600. **Call for rates.** 415 Genesee St 53018. I-94 exit 285, 0.4 mi n on CR C (Genesee St). Int corridors. **Pets:** Medium. $50 daily fee/pet. Designated rooms, service with restrictions, crate.

SAVE 🛜 ✕ 🖥 🍴

▼▼▼ **La Quinta Inn & Suites Milwaukee Delafield** H

(262) 395-1162. **$74-$159.** 2801 Hillside Dr 53018. I-94 exit 287, just s on SR 83, then just e. Int corridors. **Pets:** Medium, other species. Service with restrictions, supervision. 🛜 ✕ 𝄐 🛏 🖥 ➿

FRANKLIN

▼▼▼ **Staybridge Suites Milwaukee Airport South** H ❄

(414) 761-3800. **$99-$159.** 9575 S 27th St 53132. I-94 exit 322 (Ryan Rd), 0.6 mi w at jct 27th St. Int corridors. **Pets:** Medium, other species. $50 one-time fee/room. Service with restrictions, crate.

ECO 🛜 ✕ 𝄐 🛏 🖥 ➿ ✕

GERMANTOWN

▼▼▼ **Holiday Inn Express Milwaukee NW-Germantown** H

(262) 255-1100. **Call for rates.** W177 N9675 Riversbend Ln 53022. US 41 and 45 exit CR Q (County Line Rd), just w. Int corridors.
Pets: Accepted. 🛜 ✕ 𝄐 🛏 🖥 ➿

AAA ▼▼▼ **Super 8-Germantown/Milwaukee** H

(262) 255-0880. **$61-$70.** N96 W17490 County Line Rd 53022. US 41 and 45 exit CR Q (County Line Rd), just w. Int corridors. **Pets:** $10 daily fee/pet. Service with restrictions, supervision.

SAVE 🛜 ✕ 🛏 🖥 ➿

GLENDALE

▼▼ **Baymont Inn & Suites Glendale/Milwaukee Northeast** H

(414) 961-7272. **$49-$73.** 5485 N Port Washington Rd 53217. I-43 exit 78A (Silver Spring Dr), just se. Int corridors. **Pets:** Accepted.

🛜 ✕ 🛏 🖥

▼▼▼ **La Quinta Inn & Suites Milwaukee Bayshore Area** H

(414) 962-6767. **$98-$192.** 5423 N Port Washington Rd 53217. I-43 exit 78A (Silver Spring Dr), just se. Int corridors. **Pets:** Medium, other species. Service with restrictions, supervision. 🛜 ✕ 🛏 🖥 ➿ ✕

▼▼ **La Quinta Inn Milwaukee Glendale Hampton Ave** H

(414) 964-8484. **$54-$133.** 5110 N Port Washington Rd 53217. I-43 exit 78A (Silver Spring Dr), 0.4 mi se. Int corridors. **Pets:** Medium, other species. Service with restrictions, supervision. 🛜 ✕ 🛏 🖥

▼▼▼ **Residence Inn by Marriott Milwaukee/Glendale** H ❄

(414) 352-0070. **$134-$164.** 7275 N Port Washington Rd 53217. I-43 exit 80 (Good Hope Rd), just e. Ext corridors. **Pets:** Other species. $100 one-time fee/room. Service with restrictions, supervision.

🛜 ✕ 🛏 🖥 ➿

GRAFTON

▼▼ Baymont Inn & Suites Milwaukee-Grafton 🅷
(262) 387-1180. **$61-$179.** 1415 Port Washington Rd 53024. I-43 exit 92 (SR 60), just w, then just s. Int corridors. **Pets:** Accepted.
🛰 ☒ 🔥 📲 💻 🏊 ☒

JACKSON

▼▼ Comfort Inn & Suites of Jackson 🅷
(262) 677-1133. **$79-$159.** N W227 16890 Tillie Lake Ct 53037. US 41 exit 64 (SR 60), 2.9 mi e, jct US 45. Int corridors. **Pets:** Accepted.
🛰 ☒ 🔥 📲 🏊 ☒

MEQUON

🅰🅰🅰 ▼▼ Best Western Quiet House & Suites 🅷
(262) 241-3677. **$76-$274.** 10330 N Port Washington Rd 53092. I-43 exit 85 (Mequon Rd), just w on SR 167, then 1 mi s. Int corridors. **Pets:** $15 daily fee/pet. Service with restrictions, supervision.
🆂🅰🆅🅴 🛰 ☒ 🔥 📲 🏊

▼▼ The Chalet Motel of Mequon 🅼 🐾
(262) 241-4510. **$59-$159.** 10401 N Port Washington Rd 53092. I-43 exit 85 (Mequon Rd), just w on SR 167, then 1 mi s. Ext corridors. **Pets:** Other species. $10 daily fee/room. Designated rooms, service with restrictions, crate. 🛰 ☒ 🔥 📲 💻 🍽

MILWAUKEE

🅰🅰🅰 ▼▼ Aloft Milwaukee Downtown 🅷 🐾
(414) 226-0122. **$99-$229.** 1230 N Old World Third St 53212. I-43 exit 73A, just se. Int corridors. **Pets:** Medium, dogs only. Designated rooms, service with restrictions, crate. 🆂🅰🆅🅴 🛰 ☒ 🔥 📲 💻 🏊

▼▼▼ Ambassador Hotel 🅷
(414) 345-5000. **$119-$399.** 2308 W Wisconsin Ave 53233. I-94 exit 308 (US 41), just n to Wisconsin Ave (US 18) exit, then 1.5 mi e; jct N 24th St. Int corridors. **Pets:** Accepted. 🛰 ☒ 🔥 💻 🍽 ☒

🅰🅰🅰 ▼▼ Best Western Inn Towne Hotel 🅷
(414) 224-8400. **$89-$169.** 710 N Old World 3rd St 53203. Corner of Wisconsin Ave and N Old World 3rd St. Int corridors. **Pets:** Accepted.
🆂🅰🆅🅴 🛰 ☒ 🔥 📲 🍽

▼▼▼ Comfort Suites at Park Place 🅷
(414) 979-0250. **$99-$189.** 10831 W Park Pl 53224. US 41/45 exit 47B (Good Hope Rd), just e. Int corridors. **Pets:** Medium, dogs only. $15 one-time fee/pet. Service with restrictions, supervision.
🛰 ☒ 🔥 📲 💻 🏊 ☒

🅰🅰🅰 ▼▼▼ Hilton Milwaukee City Center 🅷
(414) 271-7250. **$149-$249.** 509 W Wisconsin Ave 53203. Corner of W Wisconsin Ave and 5th St. Int corridors. **Pets:** Accepted.
🅴🅲🅾 🆂🅰🆅🅴 🛰 ☒ 🔥 📲 💻 🍽 ☒

🅰🅰🅰 ▼▼▼ Holiday Inn & Suites Milwaukee Airport 🅷
(414) 482-4444. **$109-$179.** 545 W Layton Ave 53207. I-94 exit 317, 1.3 mi e. Int corridors. **Pets:** Accepted.
🆂🅰🆅🅴 🛰 ☒ 🔥 📲 💻 🍽 ☒

▼▼▼ Holiday Inn Express & Suites Milwaukee Airport 🅷 🐾
(414) 563-4000. **Call for rates.** 1400 W Zellman Ct 53221. I-94 exit 319, 0.4 mi e on College Ave (CR ZZ) to S 13th St, then just s. Int corridors. **Pets:** Medium, other species. Designated rooms, service with restrictions, supervision. 🅴🅲🅾 🛰 ☒ 🔥 📲 💻 🏊 ☒

▼▼▼ Hotel Metro 🅷
(414) 272-1937. **$159-$299.** 411 E Mason St 53202. Corner of Mason and Milwaukee sts. Int corridors. **Pets:** Accepted.
🅴🅲🅾 🛰 ☒ 🔥 💻 🍽 ☒

🅰🅰🅰 ▼▼ ▼▼ The Iron Horse Hotel 🅷
(414) 374-4766. **$149-$349.** 500 W Florida St 53204. Jct 6th St. Int corridors. **Pets:** Accepted. 🆂🅰🆅🅴 🛰 ☒ 🔥 📲 💻 🍽

▼▼ La Quinta Inn Milwaukee Northwest 🅷
(414) 535-1300. **Call for rates.** 5442 N Lovers Lane Rd 53225. US 45 exit 46 (Silver Spring Dr), just se. Int corridors. **Pets:** Medium, other species. Service with restrictions, supervision. 🛰 ☒ 🔥 📲 💻

🅰🅰🅰 ▼▼ ▼▼ The Pfister Hotel 🅷
(414) 273-8222. **$139-$2000.** 424 E Wisconsin Ave 53202. Corner of E Wisconsin Ave and Jefferson St. Int corridors. **Pets:** Other species. $100 one-time fee/room. Service with restrictions.
🅴🅲🅾 🆂🅰🆅🅴 🛰 ☒ 🔥 📲 💻 🍽 ☒

🅰🅰🅰 ▼▼▼ Sleep Inn & Suites 🅷
(414) 831-2000. **$84-$139.** 4600 S 6th St 53221. I-94/US 41 exit 317 (Layton Ave), 1.5 mi e. Int corridors. **Pets:** Medium, dogs only. $10 daily fee/pet. Designated rooms, service with restrictions.
🆂🅰🆅🅴 🛰 ☒ 🔥 📲 💻 🏊

NEW BERLIN

▼▼ La Quinta Inn & Suites Milwaukee SW New Berlin 🅷
(262) 717-0900. **$68-$166.** 15300 W Rock Ridge Rd 53151. I-43 exit 57 (Moorland Rd), just se. Int corridors. **Pets:** Medium, other species. Service with restrictions, supervision. 🛰 ☒ 🔥 📲 💻 🏊

OAK CREEK

▼▼▼ Candlewood Suites- Milwaukee 🅷 🐾
(414) 570-9999. **Call for rates.** 6440 S 13th St 53154. I-94 exit 319 (College Ave), just e on CR 22, then just s. Int corridors. **Pets:** Medium. $25 one-time fee/pet. Service with restrictions, crate.
🛰 ☒ 🔥 📲 💻

▼▼▼ Comfort Suites Milwaukee Airport 🅷
(414) 570-1111. **$79-$169.** 6362 S 13th St 53154. I-94 exit 319 (College Ave), just e on CR 22, then just s. Int corridors. **Pets:** Accepted.
🅴🅲🅾 🛰 ☒ 🔥 📲 💻 🏊 ☒

▼▼ Days Inn Milwaukee Airport 🅷
(414) 764-1776. **$49-$74.** 1201 W College Ave 53154. I-94 exit 319 (College Ave), just e. Int corridors. **Pets:** Accepted.
🛰 ☒ 🔥 📲 💻

▼▼ La Quinta Inn Milwaukee Airport / Oak Creek 🅷
(414) 762-2266. **$64-$141.** 7141 S 13th St 53154. I-94 exit 320 (Rawson Ave), just se. Int corridors. **Pets:** Medium, other species. Service with restrictions, supervision. 🛰 ☒ 🔥 📲 💻

▼▼ MainStay Suites Oak Creek 🅷
(414) 571-8800. **$59-$185.** 1001 W College Ave 53154. I-94 exit 319 (College Ave), just e. Int corridors. **Pets:** Large. $25 one-time fee/pet. Service with restrictions, crate. 🛰 ☒ 🔥 📲 💻

OCONOMOWOC

🅰🅰🅰 ▼▼▼ Olympia Resort, Spa & Conference Center 🅷 🐾
(262) 369-4999. **$99-$250.** 1350 Royale Mile Rd 53066. I-94 exit 282 (SR 67), 1 mi n. Int corridors. **Pets:** Other species. $10 daily fee/room. Service with restrictions.
🅴🅲🅾 🆂🅰🆅🅴 🛰 ☒ 🔥 📲 💻 🍽 🏊 ☒

🅰🅰🅰 ▼▼▼ Staybridge Suites Milwaukee West 🅷
(262) 200-2900. **$99-$139.** 1141 Blue Ribbon Dr 53066. I-94 exit 282 (SR 67), just s. Int corridors. **Pets:** $10 daily fee/pet. Service with restrictions. 🆂🅰🆅🅴 🛰 ☒ 🔥 📲 💻 🏊 ☒

PEWAUKEE

▼▼▼ Holiday Inn Pewaukee/Milwaukee West 🅷 🐾
(262) 506-6300. **Call for rates.** N14 24140 W Tower Pl 53072. I-94 exit 294 (CR J), just nw. Int corridors. **Pets:** Medium, dogs only. $50 one-time fee/room. Designated rooms, service with restrictions, crate.
🛰 ☒ 🔥 📲 💻 🍽 🏊 ☒

PORT WASHINGTON

AAA ▼▼▼ Holiday Inn Harborview 🅷
(262) 284-9461. **$109-$259.** 135 E Grand Ave 53074. On SR 33; waterfront of Lake Michigan; downtown. Int corridors. **Pets:** Small. $25 one-time fee/room. Designated rooms, service with restrictions, supervision.
SAVE 🛜 ✖ ⓜ 🛗 💻 🍽 ⌁ 🚭

SAUKVILLE

AAA ▼▼▼ Super 8- Saukville 🅷
(262) 284-9399. **$59-$95.** 180 S Foster Rd 53080. I-43 exit 96, just s. Int corridors. **Pets:** $15 daily fee/pet. Designated rooms, supervision.
SAVE 🛜 ✖ ⓜ 🛗 💻

WAUKESHA

AAA ▼▼▼ Best Western Waukesha Grand 🅷
(262) 524-9300. **$80-$90.** 2840 N Grandview Blvd 53072. I-94 exit 293, just s on CR T. Int corridors. **Pets:** Accepted.
SAVE 🛜 ✖ ⓜ 🛗 💻 ⌁ 🚭

▼▼ Extended

StayAmerica-Milwaukee-Waukesha 🅷 ❀
(262) 798-0217. **$45-$90.** 2520 Plaza Ct 53186. I-94 exit 297, just w on CR JJ (Bluemound Rd). Int corridors. **Pets:** Other species. $25 daily fee/pet. Service with restrictions. 🛜 ✖ ⓜ 🛗 💻

▼▼ Super 8 - Waukesha 🅷
(262) 786-6015. **$53-$68.** 2510 Plaza Ct 53186. I-94 exit 297, just w on CR JJ (Bluemound Rd). Int corridors. **Pets:** Medium. $10 daily fee/pet. Designated rooms, service with restrictions, supervision.
🛜 ✖ ⓜ 🛗 💻

WAUWATOSA

▼▼ Extended

StayAmerica-Milwaukee-Wauwatosa 🅷 ❀
(414) 443-1909. **$58-$100.** 11121 W North Ave 53226. US 45 exit 42A, just n. Int corridors. **Pets:** Other species. $25 daily fee/pet. Service with restrictions. 🛜 ✖ ⓜ 🛗 💻

▼▼ Holiday Inn Express Milwaukee West-Medical Center 🅷
(414) 778-0333. **$79-$159.** 11111 W North Ave 53226. US 45 exit 42A, just n on SR 100, then just w. Int corridors. **Pets:** Medium. $65 one-time fee/room. Designated rooms, service with restrictions, supervision.
🛜 ✖ ⓜ 🛗 💻

▼▼ Super 8 of Milwaukee West 🅷
(414) 257-0140. **$36-$135.** 115 N Mayfair Rd 53226. I-94 exit 304B, just n on SR 100. Int corridors. **Pets:** Medium, other species. $25 one-time fee/pet. Service with restrictions, crate. 🛜 ✖ ⓜ 🛗 💻

WEST BEND

▼▼ AmericInn of West Bend 🅷
(262) 334-0307. **$75-$90.** 2424 W Washington St 53095. US 45 exit Washington St/SR 33, just w. Int corridors. **Pets:** Medium, dogs only. $30 one-time fee/room. Designated rooms, service with restrictions, supervision. 🛜 ✖ 🛗 💻

END METROPOLITAN AREA

MINOCQUA

▼▼ AmericInn of Minocqua 🅷 ❀
(715) 356-3730. **$59-$169.** 700 Hwy 51 54548. On US 51; downtown. Int corridors. **Pets:** Other species. $10 daily fee/room. Service with restrictions, supervision. 🌿 🛜 ✖ ⓜ 🛗 💻 ⌁ 🚭

AAA ▼▼▼ Best Western Plus Concord Inn 🅷 ❀
(715) 356-1800. **$80-$141.** 320 Front St 54548. On US 51; downtown. Int corridors. **Pets:** Medium, dogs only. $10 daily fee/pet. Designated rooms, service with restrictions, supervision.
SAVE 🛜 ✖ ⓜ 🛗 💻 ⌁

AAA ▼▼ Quality Inn 🅷
(715) 358-2588. **$55-$135.** 8729 Hwy 51 N 54548. On US 51 at SR 70 W. Int corridors. **Pets:** Other species. $10 daily fee/room. Designated rooms, service with restrictions, crate. SAVE 🛜 ✖ 🛗 💻 ⌁

▼▼ The Waters of Minocqua 🅷
(715) 358-4000. **$69-$406, 5 day notice.** 8116 Hwy 51 S 54548. On US 51, 1 mi s. Int corridors. **Pets:** Other species. $10 daily fee/pet. No service, supervision. 🌿 🛜 ✖ ⓜ 🛗 💻 🍽 ⌁ 🚭

MONONA

▼▼ AmericInn of Madison South/Monona 🅷
(608) 222-8601. **$89-$179.** 101 W Broadway 53716. US 12/18 exit 265 (Monona Dr), just nw. Int corridors. **Pets:** Accepted.
🛜 ✖ ⓜ 🛗 💻 ⌁ 🚭

▼▼▼ Country Inn & Suites By Carlson, Madison 🅷
(608) 221-0055. **$99-$140.** 400 River Pl 53716. US 12/18 exit 265 (Monona Dr), just nw. Int corridors. **Pets:** Accepted.
🛜 ✖ ⓜ 🛗 💻 ⌁ 🚭

MONROE

AAA ▼▼▼ Gasthaus Motel 🅼
(608) 328-8395. **$59-$99.** 685 30th St 53566. 1.5 mi s on SR 69. Ext corridors. **Pets:** Medium, other species. $10 daily fee/pet. Service with restrictions, supervision. SAVE 🛜 ✖ ⓜ 🛗 💻

▼▼ Super 8 of Monroe 🅷
(608) 325-1500. **$50-$93.** 500 6th St 53566. On SR 69 S, 0.5 mi s of jct SR 81/11. Int corridors. **Pets:** Accepted. 🌿 🛜 ✖ 🛗 💻 ⌁

NEILLSVILLE

▼▼ Super 8-Neillsville 🅷
(715) 743-8080. **$59-$81.** 1000 E Division St 54456. US 10, jct Boon Blvd and Division St. Int corridors. **Pets:** Accepted.
🛜 ✖ ⓜ 🛗 💻 ⌁

NEW GLARUS

AAA ▼▼▼ Chalet Landhaus Inn 🅷
(608) 527-5234. **$85-$225.** 801 SR 69 53574. On SR 69. Int corridors.
Pets: Accepted. SAVE 🛜 ✖ 🛗 💻 🍽 ⌁ 🚭

▼▼ Swiss Aire Motel 🅷
(608) 527-2138. **$70-$110.** 1200 SR 69 53574. Just s of jct SR 39/69. Ext/int corridors. **Pets:** Accepted. 🛜 ✖ 🛗 💻

NEW LISBON

▼▼ Travelers Inn & Convention Center 🅷
(608) 562-5141. **Call for rates.** 1700 E Bridge St 53950. I-90/94 exit 61 (SR 80), just ne. Int corridors. **Pets:** Accepted. 🛜 ✖ ⓜ 🛗 ⌁

NEW LONDON

▼▼ AmericInn Lodge & Suites of New London 🅷 ❀
(920) 982-5700. **$59-$189.** 1404 N Shawano St 54961. US 45 exit US 54, just n. Int corridors. **Pets:** Medium, other species. $10 one-time fee/pet. Service with restrictions, supervision. 🛜 ✖ ⓜ 🛗 💻 ⌁

NEW RICHMOND

◇◇ AmericInn Motel & Suites of New Richmond ◫
(715) 246-3993. **$69-$109.** 1020 S Knowles Ave 54017. Just s on SR 65. Int corridors. **Pets:** Accepted. ⛇ ⊠ 🛏 🖳 ⤳

ONALASKA

◇◇ Baymont Inn & Suites LaCrosse-Onalaska ◫
(608) 783-7191. **$80-$179.** 3300 Kinney Coulee Rd N 54650. I-90 exit 5, just ne. Int corridors. **Pets:** Accepted. ⛇ ⊠ 🖳ᴹ 🛏 🖳 ⤳

◇◇◇ Holiday Inn Express ◫
(608) 783-6555. **Call for rates.** 9409 Hwy 16 54650. I-90 exit 5, 1 mi e. Int corridors. **Pets:** Service with restrictions, supervision.
⛇ ⊠ 🖳ᴹ 🛏 🖳 ⤳

◇◇ Microtel Inn ◫
(608) 783-0833. **$49-$113.** 3240 N Kinney Coulee Rd 54650. I-90 exit 5, just ne. Int corridors. **Pets:** Accepted. ⛇ ⊠ 🛏 🖳

◇◇◇ Stoney Creek Inn ◫
(608) 781-3060. **$89-$101.** 3060 S Kinney Coulee Rd 54650. I-90 exit 5, just se. Int corridors. **Pets:** Accepted.
⛇ ⊠ 🖳ᴹ 🛏 🖳 ⤳ ⊠

OSCEOLA

◭◭ ◇◇ River Valley Inn & Suites ◫
(715) 294-4060. **$80-$145.** 1030 Cascade St 54020. Just n on SR 35. Int corridors. **Pets:** Small. $10 daily fee/pet. Designated rooms, service with restrictions, supervision. 🆂🅰🆅🅴 ⛇ ⊠ 🛏 🖳 ⤳

OSHKOSH

◇◇◇ Comfort Suites ◫
(920) 230-7378. **$70-$170.** 400 S Koeller St 54902. US 41 exit 117 (9th Ave), just e. Int corridors. **Pets:** Dogs only. $15 daily fee/room. Designated rooms, service with restrictions.
⛇ ⊠ 🖳ᴹ 🛏 🖳 ⤳ ⊠

◇◇ Fairfield Inn by Marriott ◫
(920) 233-8504. **$85-$119.** 1800 S Koeller St 54902. US 41 exit 117 (9th Ave), 0.8 mi s on east frontage road. Int corridors. **Pets:** Accepted.
⛇ ⊠ 🖳ᴹ 🛏 🖳

◇◇◇ Hawthorn Suites by Wyndham ◫
(920) 303-1133. **$109-$449.** 3105 S Washburn St 54904. US 41 exit 116 (SR 44), just w, then just s. Int corridors. **Pets:** Accepted.
⛇ ⊠ 🖳ᴹ 🛏 🖳 🍴 ⤳ ⊠

◇◇◇ Holiday Inn Express Hotel & Suites ◫
(920) 303-1300. **$114-$189.** 2251 Westowne Ave 54904. US 41 exit 119, 0.4 mi w of jct SR 21. Int corridors. **Pets:** Accepted.
🄴🄲🄾 ⛇ ⊠ 🖳ᴹ 🛏 🖳 ⤳

◇◇ La Quinta Inn Oshkosh ◫
(920) 233-4190. **$48-$122.** 1950 Omro Rd 54902. US 41 exit 119, jct SR 21. Int corridors. **Pets:** Medium, other species. Service with restrictions, supervision. ⛇ ⊠ 🖳ᴹ 🛏 🖳

PLATTEVILLE

◇◇ Mound View Inn ◫
(608) 348-9518. **$65-$150, 3 day notice.** 1755 E Business Hwy 151 53818. On US 151 exit 21, just w. Int corridors. **Pets:** Accepted.
⛇ ⊠ 🛏 ⊠

◭◭ ◇◇◇ Super 8 ◫
(608) 348-8800. **$50-$137.** 100 Hwy 80/81 S 53818. Jct US 151 and SR 80. Int corridors. **Pets:** Other species. $10 daily fee/pet. Service with restrictions. 🆂🅰🆅🅴 ⛇ ⊠ 🖳ᴹ 🛏 🖳 ⊠

PLEASANT PRAIRIE

◇◇ La Quinta Inn Pleasant Prairie Kenosha ◫
(262) 857-7911. **$62-$148.** 7540 118th Ave 53158. I-94 exit 344 (SR 50), just e. Int corridors. **Pets:** Medium, other species. Service with restrictions, supervision. ⛇ ⊠ 🖳ᴹ 🛏 🖳

PLOVER

◇◇ AmericInn of Plover ◫
(715) 342-1244. **$64-$109.** 1501 American Dr 54467. I-39 exit 153 (CR B), just nw. Int corridors. **Pets:** Accepted.
⛇ ⊠ 🖳ᴹ 🛏 🖳 ⤳ ⊠

◇◇◇ Comfort Inn ◫
(715) 342-0400. **$67-$77.** 1560 American Dr 54467. I-39 exit 153 (CR B), just w. Int corridors. **Pets:** Accepted. ⛇ ⊠ 🛏 🖳 ⤳

PORTAGE

◭◭◭ ◇◇◇ Comfort Suites ◫
(608) 745-4717. **$74-$199.** N5780 Kinney Rd 53901. I-90/94 exit 108A (SR 78). Int corridors. **Pets:** Medium, dogs only. $10 daily fee/pet. Designated rooms, service with restrictions, supervision.
🆂🅰🆅🅴 ⛇ ⊠ 🖳ᴹ 🛏 🖳 ⤳ ⊠

◇◇ Super 8-Portage ◫ 🐾
(608) 742-8330. **$53-$58.** 3000 New Pinery Rd 53901. I-39 exit 92, just s. Int corridors. **Pets:** Other species. $10 daily fee/room. Service with restrictions, supervision. ⛇ ⊠ 🛏 🖳

PRAIRIE DU CHIEN

◭◭◭ ◇◇◇ Best Western Bluffview Inn & Suites ◫
(608) 326-4777. **$80-$120.** 37268 US Hwy 18 S 53821. On US 18, 1.9 mi e of jct SR 27 N. Ext/int corridors. **Pets:** Small. $20 daily fee/pet. Designated rooms, supervision. 🆂🅰🆅🅴 ⛇ ⊠ 🖳ᴹ 🛏 🖳 ⤳

◭◭◭ ◇◇◇ Country Inn & Suites By Carlson ◫
(608) 326-5700. **Call for rates.** 1801 Cabela's Ln 53821. On SR 35, 2 mi n of jct US 18/SR 35 S and 27 N. Int corridors. **Pets:** Accepted.
🆂🅰🆅🅴 ⛇ ⊠ 🖳ᴹ 🛏 🖳 🍴 ⤳ ⊠

◇◇ Super 8-Prairie Du Chien ◫
(608) 326-8777. **$54-$90.** 1930 S Marquette Rd 53821. On US 18, 1.9 mi e of jct SR 27 N. Ext/int corridors. **Pets:** Accepted.
⛇ ⊠ 🖳ᴹ 🛏 🖳

RACINE

◇◇ Comfort Inn Racine ◫
(262) 886-6055. **$60-$160.** 1154 Prairie Dr 53406. I-94 exit 333, 4.3 mi e on SR 20. Int corridors. **Pets:** Accepted. ⛇ ⊠ 🖳ᴹ 🛏 🖳

◇◇◇ Racine Marriott Hotel ◫
(262) 886-6100. **$158-$193.** 7111 Washington Ave 53406. I-94 exit 333, 4 mi e on SR 20. Int corridors. **Pets:** Accepted.
⛇ ⊠ 🖳ᴹ 🛏 🖳 🍴 ⤳ ⊠

REEDSBURG

◇◇ Quality Inn ◫
(608) 524-8535. **Call for rates.** 2115 E Main St 53959. 1.5 mi e on SR 23 and 33. Int corridors. **Pets:** Accepted. ⛇ ⊠ 🛏 🖳 ⤳

RHINELANDER

◭◭◭ ◇◇◇ Best Western Claridge Motor Inn ◫
(715) 362-7100. **$69-$119.** 70 N Stevens St 54501. Between Davenport and Rives sts; downtown. Int corridors. **Pets:** Other species. $5 daily fee/pet. Designated rooms, service with restrictions, supervision.
🆂🅰🆅🅴 ⛇ ⊠ 🖳ᴹ 🛏 🖳 🍴 ⤳ ⊠

◇◇ Comfort Inn ◫
(715) 369-1100. **Call for rates.** 1490 Lincoln St 54501. On Business Rt US 8, 2.6 mi e of jct SR 47. Int corridors. **Pets:** Accepted.
⛇ ⊠ 🖳ᴹ 🛏 🖳 ⤳ ⊠

▼▼ ▼▼ **Quality Inn** 🅷 ✻
(715) 369-3600. **Call for rates.** 668 W Kemp St 54501. On Business Rt US 8, just e of jct SR 47. Int corridors. **Pets:** Medium. $10 one-time fee/pet. Service with restrictions, supervision.
🛜 ✖ 📶 🛏 💻 🛝 ✖

RICE LAKE

▼▼ ▼▼ **Microtel Inn & Suites** 🅷
(715) 736-2010. **$62-$80.** 2771 Decker Dr 54868. US 53 exit 140 (CR O), just ne. Int corridors. **Pets:** $10 one-time fee/room. Supervision.
🛜 ✖ 🛏 💻

RICHLAND CENTER

▼▼ ▼▼ **The Center Lodge** 🅷
(608) 647-8988. **$70-$90, 10 day notice.** 100 Foundry Dr 53581. 0.9 mi e on US 14. Int corridors. **Pets:** Other species. $50 deposit/room. Service with restrictions, supervision. 🛜 ✖ 📶 🛏 💻 🛝

RIPON

▼▼ ▼▼ **Boulders by Cobblestone Inn & Suites** 🅷
(920) 748-7578. **$69-$199.** 1219 W Fond du Lac St 54971. 1.8 mi w on SR 23. Int corridors. **Pets:** Other species. $15 daily fee/room. Designated rooms, service with restrictions, crate.
🛜 ✖ 📶 🛏 💻 🛝 ✖

▼▼▼▼ **Comfort Suites at Royal Ridges** 🅷
(920) 748-5500. **Call for rates.** 2 Westgate Dr 54971. 2 mi w on SR 23. Int corridors. **Pets:** Medium. $15 daily fee/room. Service with restrictions, crate. 🛜 ✖ 📶 🛏 💻 🛝 ✖

RIVER FALLS

🅰🅰🅰 ▼▼ ▼▼ **Crossings by GrandStay Inn & Suites** 🅷
(715) 425-9500. **Call for rates.** 1525 Commerce Ct 54022. Just n of jct SR 65 and 35. Int corridors. **Pets:** $10 daily fee/pet. Designated rooms, service with restrictions, crate. [SAVE] 🛜 ✖ 📶 🛏 💻 🛝 ✖

▼▼▼▼ **Riverview Hotel & Suites** 🅷
(715) 425-1045. **Call for rates.** 100 Spring St 54022. Downtown. Int corridors. **Pets:** Accepted. 🛜 ✖ 📶 🛏 💻 🍽 🛝

ROTHSCHILD

▼▼ ▼▼ **Candlewood Suites - Wausau** 🅷
(715) 355-8900. **Call for rates.** 803 Industrial Park Dr 54474. I-39 exit 185 (Business Rt US 51), just se. Int corridors. **Pets:** Accepted.
🛜 ✖ 📶 🛏 💻

▼▼ ▼▼ **Econo Lodge** 🅷
(715) 355-4449. **$54-$110.** 1510 County Hwy XX 54474. I-39 exit 185 (Business Rt US 51), just se. Int corridors. **Pets:** Accepted.
🛜 ✖ 🛏 💻 🛝

▼▼▼▼ **Holiday Inn Hotel & Suites** 🅷
(715) 355-1111. **$94-$159, 3 day notice.** 1000 Imperial Ave 54474. I-39 exit 185 (Business Rt US 51), just se. Int corridors. **Pets:** Medium. $35 one-time fee/room. Service with restrictions, supervision.
🛜 ✖ 📶 🛏 💻 🍽 🛝 ✖

▼▼ ▼▼ **Motel 6 Rothschild** 🅷
(715) 355-3030. **Call for rates.** 904 Industrial Park Ave 54474. I-39 exit 185 (Business Rt US 51), just se. Int corridors. **Pets:** Other species. Service with restrictions, supervision. 🛜 ✖ 🛏 🛝

▼▼ ▼▼ **Stoney Creek Inn** 🅷 ✻
(715) 355-6858. **$69-$180.** 1100 Imperial Ave 54474. I-39 exit 185 (Business Rt US 51), just e. Int corridors. **Pets:** Other species. $25 one-time fee/room. Supervision. 🛜 ✖ 📶 🛏 💻 🛝 ✖

SHAWANO

▼▼▼▼ **Comfort Inn & Suites** 🅷
(715) 524-9090. **$74-$149.** W7393 River Bend Rd 54166. SR 29 exit 225, just n on SR 22. Int corridors. **Pets:** Medium, dogs only. $25 daily fee/pet. Designated rooms, service with restrictions, supervision.
🛜 ✖ 📶 🛏 💻 🛝

▼▼ ▼▼ **Super 8-Shawano** Ⓜ
(715) 526-6688. **$49-$72.** 211 Waukechon St 54166. 1.2 mi e on SR 29 business route; SR 29 exit 227, 1.8 mi n, then 1.1 mi w. Int corridors. **Pets:** Other species. $10 daily fee/pet. Service with restrictions, supervision. 🛜 🛏 💻

SHEBOYGAN

🅰🅰🅰 ▼▼▼▼ **GrandStay Residential Suites Hotel** 🅷
(920) 208-8000. **$90-$170.** 708 Niagara Ave 53081. Jct N 7th St; downtown. Int corridors. **Pets:** Other species. $10 daily fee/room. Service with restrictions. [SAVE] 🛜 ✖ 📶 🛏 💻 🛝 ✖

▼▼▼▼ **La Quinta Inn Sheboygan** 🅷
(920) 457-2321. **$68-$155.** 2932 Kohler Memorial Dr 53081. I-43 exit 126, 1 mi e on SR 23. Int corridors. **Pets:** Medium, other species. Service with restrictions, supervision. 🛜 ✖ 📶 🛏 💻

🅰🅰🅰 ▼▼ ▼▼ **Quality Inn** 🅷
(920) 457-7724. **$69-$130.** 4332 N 40th St 53083. I-43 exit 128, 0.3 mi e on Business Rt SR 42. Int corridors. **Pets:** Medium, other species. $10 daily fee/pet. Designated rooms, service with restrictions, supervision.
[SAVE] 🛜 ✖ 📶 🛏 💻 🛝

SHEBOYGAN FALLS

▼▼▼▼ **The Rochester Inn, A Historic Hotel** 🅱🅱
(920) 467-3123. **Call for rates.** 504 Water St 53085. Just e of downtown via CR PP. Int corridors. **Pets:** Accepted. 🛜 ✖ 🛏 💻

SHELL LAKE

▼▼ ▼▼ **America's Best Inn & Suites** 🅷
(715) 468-4494. **$69-$189.** 315 Hwy 63 S 54871. On SR 63, just s. Int corridors. **Pets:** Accepted. 🛜 ✖ 🛏 💻 🛝 ✖

SIREN

🅰🅰🅰 ▼▼▼▼ **The Lodge at Crooked Lake** 🅷
(715) 349-2500. **$89-$275.** 24271 SR 35 N 54872. On SR 35, 0.5 mi n of jct SR 70. Int corridors. **Pets:** Medium, dogs only. $50 deposit/pet, $15 daily fee/pet. Designated rooms, service with restrictions, supervision.
[SAVE] 🛜 ✖ 🛏 💻 🛝 ✖

▼▼ **Pine Wood Motel** Ⓜ
(715) 349-5225. **$35-$65.** 23862 Hwy 35 S 54872. On SR 35, 0.3 mi s of jct SR 70 W and CR B E. Ext corridors. **Pets:** Medium, dogs only. No service, supervision. ✖ 🛏 💻

SPARTA

🅰🅰🅰 ▼▼▼▼ **Best Western Plus Sparta Trail Lodge** 🅷
(608) 269-2664. **$89-$129.** 4445 Theatre Rd 54656. I-90 exit 28 (SR 16), just w. Int corridors. **Pets:** Accepted.
[SAVE] 🛜 ✖ 📶 🛏 💻 🍽 🛝 ✖

▼▼ ▼▼ **Country Inn & Suites By Carlson** 🅷 ✻
(608) 269-3110. **$89-$150.** 737 Avon Rd 54656. I-90 exit 25 (SR 27), just n. Int corridors. **Pets:** Other species. $10 daily fee/pet. Service with restrictions, supervision. 🛜 ✖ 📶 🛏 💻 🛝

▼▼ ▼▼ **Super 8 Sparta** 🅷
(608) 269-8489. **$50-$125.** 716 Avon Rd 54656. I-90 exit 25 (SR 27), just n. Int corridors. **Pets:** Large, other species. $10 daily fee/pet. Service with restrictions, supervision. 🛜 ✖ 🛏 💻 🛝

SPOONER

 Best Western American Heritage Inn 🄷

(715) 635-9770. **$80-$140.** 101 W Maple St 54801. On SR 70, just e of US 63, 1 mi w of US 53. Int corridors. **Pets:** Accepted.

SAVE 🛜 ✕ 🛏 💻 ➿ 🏊

Country House Motel & RV Park 🄼

(715) 635-8721. **Call for rates.** 717 S River St 54801. On US 63, 0.5 mi s of jct SR 70. Ext/int corridors. **Pets:** Medium. $5 daily fee/pet. Designated rooms, service with restrictions, crate.

SAVE 🛜 ✕ 🛏 💻 ➿

Inn Town Motel 🄼

(715) 635-3529. **$40-$70, 3 day notice.** 801 River St 54801. 0.8 mi n of jct US 63 and SR 70. Ext corridors. **Pets:** Dogs only. $10 daily fee/pet. Designated rooms, service with restrictions, supervision.

🛜 ✕ 🛏 💻

STEVENS POINT

 Country Inn & Suites By Carlson 🄷

(715) 345-7000. **$81-$144.** 301 Division St N 54481. I-39 exit 161 (US 51 business route), 0.6 mi s. Int corridors. **Pets:** Other species. $25 one-time fee/room. No service, supervision.

🛜 ✕ 🛏 💻 ➿ 🏊

Fairfield Inn by Marriott 🄷

(715) 342-9300. **$60-$170.** 5317 Hwy 10 E 54481. I-39 exit 158A (US 10), just se. Int corridors. **Pets:** Other species. $50 one-time fee/room. Service with restrictions. 🛜 ✕ 🛏 💻 ➿

Holiday Inn Express 🄷

(715) 344-0000. **Call for rates.** 1100 Amber Ave 54481. I-39 exit 158 (US 10), 1 mi e, then just n. Int corridors. **Pets:** Other species. $25 daily fee/room. Designated rooms, service with restrictions.

🛜 ✕ 🛏 💻 ➿

La Quinta Inn & Suites Stevens Point 🄷

(715) 344-1900. **$68-$148.** 4917 Main St 54481. I-39 exit 158B (US 10), just sw. Int corridors. **Pets:** Medium, other species. Service with restrictions, supervision. 🛜 ✕ 🛏 💻 ➿

Super 8 🄷

(715) 341-8888. **Call for rates.** 247 N Division St 54481. I-39 exit 161 (US 51 business route), 0.6 mi s. Int corridors. **Pets:** Accepted.

🛜 ✕ 🛏 💻

STOUGHTON

Quality Inn & Suites 🄷

(608) 877-9000. **Call for rates.** 660 Nygaard St 53589. On US 51 business route, 0.7 mi nw of jct SR 138 S. Int corridors. **Pets:** Accepted.

🛜 ✕ 🛏 💻 ➿

SUN PRAIRIE

 Quality Inn & Suites-Sun Prairie 🄷

(608) 834-9889. **$69-$179.** 105 Business Park Dr 53590. US 151 exit 103 (CR N), just n. Int corridors. **Pets:** Medium, dogs only. $10 daily fee/pet. Designated rooms, service with restrictions, supervision.

SAVE 🛜 ✕ 🛏 💻 ➿

SUPERIOR

Barkers Island Inn 🄷

(715) 392-7152. **$79-$189.** 300 Marina Dr 54880. Just ne of US 2/53; on Barkers Island. Int corridors. **Pets:** Other species. $10 daily fee/room. Designated rooms, service with restrictions, supervision.

SAVE 🛜 ✕ 🛏 💻 🍴 ➿ 🏊

Best Western Bay Walk Inn 🄷

(715) 392-7600. **$60-$170.** 1405 Susquehanna Ave 54880. Just e of US 2 on Belknap St. Int corridors. **Pets:** Accepted.

SAVE 🛜 ✕ 🛏 💻 ➿ 🏊

Best Western Bridgeview Motor Inn 🄷

(715) 392-8174. **$60-$189.** 415 Hammond Ave 54880. 0.8 mi n at south end of Blatnik Bridge. Int corridors. **Pets:** Accepted.

SAVE 🛜 ✕ 🛦 🛏 💻 ➿ 🏊

THORP

Fairbridge Inn 🄷

(715) 669-5959. **Call for rates.** 203 1/2 W Hill St 54771. US 29 exit 108 (SR 73), just nw. Int corridors. **Pets:** Accepted.

🛜 ✕ 🛦 🛏 💻 ➿ 🏊

TOMAH

AmericInn Lodge & Suites of Tomah 🄷

(608) 372-4100. **$79-$159.** 750 Vandervort St 54660. I-94 exit 143 (SR 21), just e. Int corridors. **Pets:** Small. $10 daily fee/pet. Service with restrictions, crate. 🛜 ✕ 🛦 🛏 💻 ➿

Best Western Tomah Hotel 🄷 🐾

(608) 372-3211. **$90-$130.** 1017 E McCoy Blvd 54660. I-94 exit 143 (SR 21), just e. Int corridors. **Pets:** Large, other species. Crate.

SAVE 🛜 ✕ 🛏 💻 🍴 ➿

Comfort Inn by Choice Hotels 🄷

(608) 372-6600. **$79-$191.** 305 Wittig Rd 54660. I-94 exit 143 (SR 21), just w. Int corridors. **Pets:** Accepted. 🛜 ✕ 🛏 💻 ➿

Econo Lodge 🄷

(608) 372-9100. **$102-$185.** 2005 N Superior Ave 54660. I-94 exit 143 (SR 21), just w. Ext/int corridors. **Pets:** $10 daily fee/pet. Service with restrictions. 🛜 ✕ 🛏 💻 ➿

Lark Inn 🄼

(608) 372-5981. **$55-$129.** 229 N Superior Ave 54660. I-94 exit 143 (SR 21), 1.5 mi s on US 12; 1-90 exit 41, 2 mi n on US 12. Ext/int corridors. **Pets:** Accepted. SAVE 🛜 ✕ 🛦 🛏 💻

Super 8-Tomah 🄷 🐾

(608) 372-3901. **$59-$139.** 1008 E McCoy Blvd 54660. I-94 exit 143 (SR 21), just e. Int corridors. **Pets:** Other species. $10 one-time fee/room. Service with restrictions, crate. SAVE 🛜 ✕ 🛏 💻

TOMAHAWK

Rodeway Inn & Suites 🄷

(715) 453-8900. **$70-$109.** 1738 Comfort Dr 54487. US 51 exit 229, just nw. Int corridors. **Pets:** Other species. $25 one-time fee/room. Service with restrictions, supervision. 🛜 ✕ 🛦 🛏 💻 ➿ 🏊

Super 8-Tomahawk 🄷

(715) 453-5210. **$63-$86.** 108 W Mohawk Dr 54487. US 51 exit 231, 1.4 mi w, then 0.6 mi s. Int corridors. **Pets:** $10 daily fee/pet. Designated rooms, service with restrictions, supervision.

🛜 ✕ 🛦 🛏 💻 ➿ 🏊

TWO RIVERS

 Lighthouse Inn on Lake Michigan 🄷

(920) 793-4524. **$89-$151.** 1515 Memorial Dr 54241. 0.3 mi s on SR 42. Int corridors. **Pets:** Accepted.

SAVE 🛜 ✕ 🛦 🛏 💻 🍴 ➿ 🏊

VERONA

Holiday Inn Express Hotel & Suites Madison-Verona 🄷

(608) 497-4500. **$139-$209.** 515 W Verona Ave 53593. On US 51 business route exit 81, 1.8 mi w. Int corridors. **Pets:** Medium. $25 daily fee/pet. Designated rooms, service with restrictions, supervision.

🛜 ✕ 🛦 🛏 💻 ➿

VIROQUA

⚡ **Hickory Hill Motel** Ⓜ

(608) 637-3104. **$54-$75.** US 14 S 3955 54665. On US 14 and SR 27 and 82, 1.8 mi se. Ext corridors. **Pets:** Small. $10 one-time fee/pet. Designated rooms, service with restrictions, supervision. 🛜 ⊠ 🔒 ➥

WATERFORD

⚡⚡ **Baymont Inn & Suites-Waterford** Ⓗ

(262) 534-4100. **$76-$188.** 750 Fox Ln 53185. On SR 36, 1 mi s of jct SR 164. Int corridors. **Pets:** Accepted.
🛜 ⊠ Ⓜ 🔒 💻 ➥ 🐾

WATERTOWN

⚡⚡ **Super 8** Ⓗ

(920) 261-1188. **$64-$85.** 1730 S Church St 53094. On SR 26, 1.5 mi s of jct SR 19. Int corridors. **Pets:** Accepted.
🛜 ⊠ Ⓜ 🔒 💻 ➥ 🐾

WAUPACA

🅰🅰🅰 ⚡⚡⚡ **Best Western Plus Grand Seasons Hotel** Ⓗ ❀

(715) 258-9212. **$86-$140.** 110 Grand Seasons Dr 54981. Jct US 10 and SR 54 W. Int corridors. **Pets:** Large. $12 daily fee/pet. Designated rooms, service with restrictions, crate.
SAVE 🛜 ⊠ Ⓜ 🔒 💻 ➥ 🐾

WAUPUN

⚡ **Inn Town Motel** Ⓜ

(920) 324-4211. **$49-$69.** 27 S State St 53963. US 151 exit 146 (SR 49), 1 mi w on Main St, then just s. Ext corridors. **Pets:** Accepted.
🛜 ⊠ Ⓜ 🔒 💻

WAUSAU

🅰🅰🅰 ⚡⚡ **Best Western Midway Hotel** Ⓗ ❀

(715) 842-1616. **$56-$120.** 2901 Hummingbird Rd 54401. I-39 exit 190 (CR NN), just sw. Int corridors. **Pets:** Other species. $20 daily fee/room. Designated rooms, service with restrictions, crate.
SAVE 🛜 ⊠ Ⓜ 🔒 💻 🍴 ➥ 🐾

⚡⚡ **Days Inn** Ⓜ

(715) 842-0641. **$49-$85.** 116 S 17th Ave 54401. I-39 exit 192, just ne. Int corridors. **Pets:** Accepted. 🛜 ⊠ 🔒 💻

🅰🅰🅰 ⚡⚡⚡ **Jefferson Street Inn** Ⓗ 🐾

(715) 845-6500. **$109-$325.** 201 Jefferson St 54403. Just w of jct 2nd St; center. Int corridors. **Pets:** $40 daily fee/pet. Service with restrictions, crate. ECO SAVE 🛜 ⊠ Ⓜ 🔒 💻 🍴 ➥ 🐾

⚡⚡ **La Quinta Inn Wausau** Ⓗ

(715) 842-0421. **$54-$130.** 1910 Stewart Ave 54401. I-39 exit 192, just se. Int corridors. **Pets:** Medium, other species. Service with restrictions, supervision. 🛜 ⊠ 🔒 💻 ➥

⚡⚡ **Rib Mountain Inn** Ⓗ

(715) 842-5663. **$69-$499, 3 day notice.** 2900 Rib Mountain Way 54401. I-39 exit 190 (CR NN), 1.2 mi w on N Mountain Rd (CR NN), then just s. Ext/int corridors. **Pets:** Accepted. 🛜 ⊠ 🔒 💻 🐾

⚡⚡⚡ **Stewart Inn Bed and Breakfast** Ⓑ 🐾

(715) 849-5858. **$170-$225, 30 day notice.** 521 Grant St 54403. Between 5th and 6th sts; center. Int corridors. **Pets:** Other species. Designated rooms, crate. ECO 🛜 ⊠

🅰🅰🅰 ⚡⚡ **Super 8 Wausau** Ⓗ

(715) 848-2888. **$49-$72.** 2006 Stewart Ave W 54401. I-39 exit 192, just se. Int corridors. **Pets:** Dogs only. $10 daily fee/pet. Designated rooms, service with restrictions, supervision. SAVE 🛜 ⊠ 🔒 💻 ➥

WAUTOMA

⚡⚡ **AmericInn Lodge & Suites of Wautoma** Ⓗ

(920) 787-5050. **$88-$189.** W7696 SR 21/73 54982. On SR 21 and 73, 1.2 mi e. Int corridors. **Pets:** Other species. $10 one-time fee/pet. Designated rooms, service with restrictions.
🛜 ⊠ Ⓜ 🔒 💻 ➥ 🐾

⚡⚡ **Super 8-Wautoma** Ⓗ

(920) 787-4811. **$54-$91.** W7607 SR 21/73 54982. On SR 21 and 73, 1.5 mi e. Int corridors. **Pets:** Large, other species. $10 one-time fee/room. Designated rooms, service with restrictions, supervision.
🛜 ⊠ Ⓜ 🔒 💻 ➥

WEST SALEM

⚡◆ **AmericInn Motel & Suites of West Salem** Ⓗ

(608) 786-3340. **$83-$153.** 125 Buol Rd 54669. I-90 exit 12, just sw on CR C. Int corridors. **Pets:** Accepted.
🛜 ⊠ Ⓜ 🔒 💻 ➥ 🐾

WINDSOR

⚡⚡ **Days Inn** Ⓗ

(608) 846-7473. **$56-$126.** 6311 Rostad Cir 53598. I-90/94 exit 131 (SR 19). Int corridors. **Pets:** Medium, dogs only. $10 daily fee/pet. Designated rooms, service with restrictions, supervision.
🛜 ⊠ Ⓜ 🔒 💻 ➥ 🐾

WISCONSIN DELLS

🅰🅰🅰 ◆ **Americas Best Value Day's End Motel** Ⓜ

(608) 254-8171. **$34-$152, 3 day notice.** N 504 Hwy 12-16 53965. I-90/94 exit 85 (US 12), 0.8 mi nw. Ext corridors. **Pets:** Other species. $10 daily fee/pet. Designated rooms.
SAVE 🛜 ⊠ 🔒 💻 ➥ 🐾

⚡⚡ **Super 8-Wisconsin Dells** Ⓗ

(608) 254-6464. **$43-$103.** 800 CR H 53965. I-90/94 exit 87 (SR 13), just e. Int corridors. **Pets:** Accepted. 🛜 ⊠ 🔒 💻 ➥

WISCONSIN RAPIDS

⚡⚡⚡ **Hotel Mead** Ⓗ ❀

(715) 423-1500. **$89-$199.** 451 E Grand Ave 54494. Just e of downtown. Int corridors. **Pets:** Other species. $100 deposit/room, $15 daily fee/room. Designated rooms, service with restrictions, supervision.
🛜 ⊠ Ⓜ 🔒 💻 🍴 ➥ 🐾

⚡⚡ **Quality Inn** Ⓗ

(715) 423-5506. **$68-$85.** 3120 8th St S 54494. 1.5 mi s on SR 13. Int corridors. **Pets:** Dogs only. $10 one-time fee/pet. Service with restrictions, supervision. 🛜 ⊠ 🔒 💻 ➥

⚡⚡ **Sleep Inn & Suites** Ⓗ

(715) 424-6800. **$72-$95.** 4221 8th St S 54494. 1.3 mi s on SR 13 from jct SR 54. Int corridors. **Pets:** Medium, dogs only. $15 daily fee/pet. Service with restrictions, supervision. 🛜 ⊠ Ⓜ 🔒 💻 ➥

WITTENBERG

🅰🅰🅰 ⚡⚡⚡ **Best Western Wittenberg Inn** Ⓗ 🐾

(715) 253-3755. **$69-$149.** W17267 Red Oak Ln 54499. US 29 exit 198, just se. Int corridors. **Pets:** Medium. $20 one-time fee/room. Designated rooms, service with restrictions, supervision.
SAVE 🛜 ⊠ Ⓜ 🔒 💻 ➥ 🐾

WYOMING

AFTON

♨ ▽ Lazy B Motel M

(307) 885-3187. **$65-$95.** 219 Washington St (US 89) 83110. On US 89; center. Ext corridors. **Pets:** Accepted. [SAVE]

BUFFALO

♨ ▽▽ Best Western Crossroads Inn H

(307) 684-2256. **Call for rates.** 75 N Bypass Rd 82834. I-25 exit 299 (US 16), just w. Ext/int corridors. **Pets:** $15 one-time fee/pet. Designated rooms, service with restrictions, supervision.

[SAVE]

▽▽ Comfort Inn H ✿

(307) 684-9564. **$74-$124.** 65 US Hwy 16 E 82834. I-25 exit 299 (US 16 E), just e; I-90 exit 58, 1.3 mi w. Ext/int corridors. **Pets:** Medium, other species. $10 daily fee/pet. Designated rooms, service with restrictions, supervision.

♨ ▽▽▽ The Occidental Hotel H

(307) 684-0451. **$75-$285, 14 day notice.** 10 N Main St 82834. Center. Int corridors. **Pets:** Other species. $10 one-time fee/pet. Designated rooms, service with restrictions, supervision. [SAVE]

♨ ▽ Super 8 of Buffalo H

(307) 684-2531. **$53-$107.** 655 E Hart St 82834. I-25 exit 299 (US 16), just w; I-90 exit 58, 1.3 mi w. Int corridors. **Pets:** Other species. $10 one-time fee/pet. Designated rooms, service with restrictions, supervision. [SAVE]

♨ ▽ WYO Motel M ✿

(307) 684-5505. **$49-$169.** 610 E Hart St 82834. I-25 exit 299 (US 16), just w; I-90 exit 58, 1.3 mi w. Ext corridors. **Pets:** $10 daily fee/room. Designated rooms, service with restrictions, supervision. [SAVE]

CASPER

♨ ▽▽▽ Best Western Ramkota Hotel H ✿

(307) 266-6000. **$90-$110.** 800 N Poplar St 82601. I-25 exit 188B (N Poplar St), just ne. Int corridors. **Pets:** Other species. $50 deposit/room. Designated rooms, service with restrictions, supervision. [SAVE]

▽▽ Days Inn Casper H

(307) 234-1159. **$67-$96, 7 day notice.** 301 East E St 82601. I-25 exit 188A, just s, then just e. Int corridors. **Pets:** Accepted.

▽▽ La Quinta Inn Casper H

(307) 265-1200. **$71-$159, 30 day notice.** 400 W 'F' St 82601. I-25 exit 188A, just e. Int corridors. **Pets:** Medium, other species. Service with restrictions, supervision.

♨ ▽▽▽ Quality Inn & Suites Casper H ✿

(307) 266-2400. **$89-$149.** 821 N Poplar St 82601. I-25 exit 188B (N Poplar St), just e. Int corridors. **Pets:** Dogs only. $15 daily fee/pet. Designated rooms, no service, supervision. [SAVE]

♨ ▽▽▽ Ramada Plaza Riverside H

(307) 235-2531. **$79-$119.** 300 W 'F' St 82601. I-25 exit 188A, just e. Int corridors. **Pets:** Accepted. [SAVE]

▽▽ Skyler Inn H

(307) 232-5100. **Call for rates.** 111 S Wilson St 82601. I-25 exit 186, 0.5 mi s to Yellowstone Hwy, then 1 mi w, jct 1st St. Int corridors. **Pets:** Accepted.

▽▽ Super 8 Casper West M

(307) 266-3480. **$71-$98.** 3838 CY Ave 82604. I-25 exit 188B (N Poplar St), 1.7 mi w on S Poplar St (SR 220), then 1.8 mi n. Int corridors. **Pets:** Accepted.

CHEYENNE

▽▽ Cheyenne Super 8 M

(307) 635-8741. **$62-$152.** 1900 W Lincolnway 82001. I-25 exit 9, 0.7 mi e. Int corridors. **Pets:** Other species. $10 daily fee/pet. Service with restrictions, crate.

▽▽▽ Days Inn Cheyenne H

(307) 778-8877. **$43-$243.** 2360 W Lincolnway 82001. I-25 exit 9, just e. Int corridors. **Pets:** $5 daily fee/pet. Designated rooms, service with restrictions, supervision.

♨ ▽▽▽ Historic Plains Hotel H

(307) 638-3311. **$109-$299.** 1600 Central Ave 82001. I-80 exit 362, 1 mi n on I-180/I-25 business loop/US 85/87 business route, then just w on I-80 business loop/US 30; downtown. Int corridors. **Pets:** Accepted. [SAVE]

♨ ▽▽ La Quinta Inn Cheyenne H

(307) 632-7117. **$78-$174.** 2410 W Lincolnway 82009. I-25 exit 9, just e. Int corridors. **Pets:** Medium, other species. Service with restrictions, supervision.

♨ ▽▽▽ Nagle Warren Mansion B & B BB ✿

(307) 637-3333. **$158-$192, 3 day notice.** 222 E 17th St 82001. I-80 exit 362, 1.2 mi n on I-25 business loop/US 85/87 business route, then just e; jct House St; downtown. Int corridors. **Pets:** Medium. $25 daily fee/pet. Designated rooms. [SAVE]

♨ ▽ Oak Tree Inn H

(307) 778-6620. **Call for rates.** 1625 Stillwater Ave 82009. 1.2 mi e of jct Dell Range Blvd and Yellowstone Rd, 0.4 mi s. Ext/int corridors. **Pets:** Accepted. [SAVE]

▽▽ Sleep Inn & Suites H

(307) 638-8891. **$75-$220.** 8101 Hutchins Dr 82007. I-80 exit 367, just n. Int corridors. **Pets:** Large, other species. $15 daily fee/pet. Designated rooms, service with restrictions, supervision.

▽▽▽ Windy Hills Guest House BB ✿

(307) 632-6423. **$139-$310, 3 day notice.** 393 Happy Jack Rd 82009. I-25 exit 10B, 22 mi w on SR 210 (Happy Jack Rd), then 1 mi s on private gravel road. Ext corridors. **Pets:** Dogs only. $50 one-time fee/room. Designated rooms, service with restrictions, supervision.

CODY

▽▽▽▽ Best Western Sunset Motor Inn 🏍 ❀
(307) 587-4265. **Call for rates.** 1601 8th St 82414. 0.8 mi w on US 14/16/20. Ext corridors. **Pets:** Small, other species. $25 one-time fee/pet. Designated rooms, service with restrictions, supervision.
[SAVE] 📶 ⊠ 🛢 💻 🍴 ➳ ⊠

▽▽ Carriagehouse Villas 🏠 ❀
(307) 272-0546. **$100-$210, 7 day notice.** 2144 Shoshone Tr N 82414. Jct Sheridan Ave, 0.5 mi s on 17th St, just e on Stampede Ave, then just s. . **Pets:** Medium, dogs only. $25 deposit/pet. Crate.
📶 ⊠ 🛢 💻 🏊

▽▽▽ The Cody 🏨 ❀
(307) 587-5915. **$110-$285.** 232 W Yellowstone Ave 82414. 2 mi w on US 14/16/20. Int corridors. **Pets:** Dogs only. $18 daily fee/pet. Designated rooms, service with restrictions, supervision.
[SAVE] 📶 ⊠ 🛢 💻 ➳ ⊠

▽▽ Cody Motor Lodge 🏍 ❀
(307) 527-6291. **Call for rates.** 1455 Sheridan Ave 82414. Just w on US 14/16/20 and SR 120. Int corridors. **Pets:** Large, other species. Designated rooms, service with restrictions, supervision. [SAVE] 📶 🛢 💻

DOUGLAS

▽▽ Clarion Hotel 🏨
(307) 358-9790. **$117-$190.** 1450 Riverbend Dr 82633. I-25 exit 140, 0.8 mi e. Int corridors. **Pets:** Accepted. 📶 🖐️ 🛢 💻 🍴 ➳ ⊠

DUBOIS

▽▽▽ The Longhorn Ranch Lodge and RV Resort 🏍 ❀
(307) 455-2337. **$50-$130, 3 day notice.** 5810 US Hwy 26 82513. 3 mi e on US 26 and 287. Ext corridors. **Pets:** Service with restrictions, supervision. [SAVE] 📶 ⊠ 🛢 💻 🏊

▽▽ Rocky Mountain Lodge 🏍
(307) 455-2844. **$60-$115, 3 day notice.** 1349 W Ramshorn St 82513. 1.6 mi w on US 26 and 287. Ext corridors. **Pets:** Other species. $5 daily fee/pet. Designated rooms, service with restrictions, supervision.
📶 ⊠ 🛢 💻 🐾

▽▽▽ Stagecoach Motor Inn 🏍 ❀
(307) 455-2303. **$58-$98.** 103 Ramshorn St 82513. On US 26 and 287; center. Ext corridors. **Pets:** Small. $10 daily fee/pet. Designated rooms, no service, supervision. [SAVE] 📶 🛢 💻 ➳ ⊠ 🐾

EVANSTON

▽▽▽ Best Western Dunmar Inn 🏍
(307) 789-3770. **$80-$110.** 1601 Harrison Dr 82930. I-80 exit 3 (Harrison Dr), just n. Ext corridors. **Pets:** Small. $25 deposit/room. Designated rooms, service with restrictions, supervision.
[SAVE] 📶 🖐️ 🛢 💻 🍴 🏊 ⊠

▽▽ Comfort Inn 🏨
(307) 789-7799. **$90-$130.** 1931 Harrison Dr 82930. I-80 exit 3 (Harrison Dr), just n. Int corridors. **Pets:** Other species. $10 daily fee/pet. Service with restrictions, supervision. 📶 🛢 💻 ➳

▽▽ Prairie Inn 🏍 ❀
(307) 789-2920. **$50-$77.** 264 Bear River Dr 82930. I-80 exit 6, 0.3 mi n. Ext/int corridors. **Pets:** $150 deposit/room, $10 daily fee/room. Designated rooms, service with restrictions, supervision. [SAVE] 📶 🛢

EVANSVILLE

▽▽ Baymont Inn and Suites of Casper 🏨
(307) 235-3038. **$80-$120.** 480 Lathrop Rd 82636. I-25 exit 185, just n to Lathrop Rd, then 0.3 mi e. Int corridors. **Pets:** Accepted.
📶 🖐️ 🛢 💻 ➳

▽▽▽ Sleep Inn & Suites Casper-Evansville 🏨
(307) 235-3100. **Call for rates.** 6733 Bonanza 82636. I-25 exit 182, just n on Hat Six Rd. Int corridors. **Pets:** Medium, dogs only. Designated rooms, service with restrictions, supervision. 📶 ⊠ 🛢 💻 🏊

▽▽▽ Super 8 Casper-Evansville 🏨 ❀
(307) 237-8100. **$80-$107.** 269 Miracle St 82636. I-25 exit 185, just n to Lathrop Rd, then just e. Int corridors. **Pets:** $10 one-time fee/room. Service with restrictions, supervision. 📶 🖐️ 🛢 💻 ➳

GILLETTE

▽▽▽ Best Western Tower West Lodge 🏨
(307) 686-2210. **$80-$230.** 109 N US Hwy 14-16 82716. I-90 exit 124, just n. Int corridors. **Pets:** Accepted. [SAVE] 📶 🛢 💻 🍴 ➳

▽▽ Budget Inn Express 🏍
(307) 686-1989. **$49-$199.** 2011 Rodgers Dr 82716. I-90 exit 124, just n. Int corridors. **Pets:** Medium. $10 daily fee/pet. Designated rooms, service with restrictions, supervision. [SAVE] 📶 🛢 ➳

▽▽▽ Candlewood Suites 🏨 ❀
(307) 682-6100. **$139-$159.** 904 Country Club Rd 82718. I-90 exit 126, 0.5 mi s, then just e. Int corridors. **Pets:** Medium, other species. $150 one-time fee/pet. Service with restrictions, crate. 📶 ⊠ 🛢 💻

▽▽▽ Comfort Inn & Suites of Gillette 🏨
(307) 685-2223. **$90-$200.** 1607 W 2nd Ave 82716. I-90 exit 124, 0.3 mi ne, then just se. Int corridors. **Pets:** Small, other species. $15 daily fee/pet. Designated rooms, supervision. [SAVE] 📶 ⊠ 🖐️ 🛢 💻 ➳

▽▽ Holiday Inn Express & Suites 🏨 ❀
(307) 686-9576. **$149-$209.** 1908 Cliff Davis Dr 82718. I-90 exit 126, just s to Boxelder Rd, then just e to Cliff Davis Dr. Int corridors. **Pets:** $15 one-time fee/room. Designated rooms, service with restrictions, supervision. 📶 🛢 💻 ➳

GREEN RIVER

▽▽▽ Hampton Inn & Suites Green River 🏨
(307) 875-5300. **$89-$139.** 1055 Wild Horse Canyon Rd 82935. I-80 exit 89, 0.4 mi s, then 0.8 mi n. Int corridors. **Pets:** Medium, dogs only. Designated rooms, service with restrictions, supervision.
📶 🖐️ 🛢 💻 ➳

▽▽▽ Oak Tree Inn 🏨
(307) 875-3500. **Call for rates.** 1170 W Flaming Gorge Way 82935. I-80 exit 89, 0.3 mi s. Ext/int corridors. **Pets:** Accepted.
[SAVE] 📶 ⊠ 🖐️ 🛢 💻 🍴

GUERNSEY

▽▽ Bunkhouse Motel 🏍
(307) 836-2356. **$65-$139.** 350 W Whalen St 82214. On US 26; center. Ext corridors. **Pets:** Medium, dogs only. $10 one-time fee/pet. Service with restrictions, supervision. [SAVE] 📶 🛢

HULETT

▽▽▽ Best Western Devils Tower Inn 🏨
(307) 467-5747. **$70-$180.** 229 Hwy 24 82720. Center. Int corridors. **Pets:** Dogs only. $20 daily fee/room. Designated rooms, service with restrictions, supervision. [SAVE] 📶 ⊠ 🖐️ 🛢 💻 ➳

▽▽ Hulett Motel 🏍
(307) 467-5220. **$70-$105.** 202 Main St 82720. On SR 24 (Main St); at north end of town. Ext corridors. **Pets:** Dogs only. $20 one-time fee/room. Designated rooms, service with restrictions, supervision.
[SAVE] 📶 ⊠ 🛢 💻

JACKSON HOLE AREA

ALPINE

⚠️ 💎 Alpen Haus Hotel Resort 🅷
(307) 654-7545. **$55-$150.** 50 W Hwy 26 83128. Jct US 26 and 89. Int corridors. **Pets:** Medium. $10 daily fee/pet. Designated rooms, service with restrictions, supervision. SAVE 🛜 🍴

GRAND TETON NATIONAL PARK

💎💎 Flagg Ranch Resort 🅷
(307) 543-2861. **Call for rates.** Hwy 89 83013. US 89 and 191; 2 mi s of Yellowstone National Park south entrance; 5 mi n of Grand Teton National Park north entrance. Ext corridors. **Pets:** Accepted.
🅼 📺 🍴 ❎ 🐾 🎫

💎💎💎 Jackson Lake Lodge 🅷
(307) 543-2811. **Call for rates.** US Hwy 89 83013. 5 mi nw of Moran. Ext/int corridors. **Pets:** Accepted.
ECO 🛜 ❎ 🅼 🍴 📺 ❎ 🐾 🎫

⚠️ 💎💎 Signal Mountain Lodge 🅷
(307) 543-2831. **$136-$315, 7 day notice.** 1 Inner Park Rd 83013. Teton Park Rd, 2 mi s of US 89, 191 and 287. Ext corridors. **Pets:** Other species. $20 daily fee/room. Designated rooms, service with restrictions, crate. ECO SAVE 🛜 ❎ 🍴 📺 ❎ 🐾 🎫

⚠️ 💎💎 Togwotee Mountain Lodge 🆑
(307) 543-2847. **Call for rates.** 27655 Hwy US 26 & 287 83013. 16.5 mi e of Moran, jct US 26 and 287. Ext/int corridors. **Pets:** Accepted.
SAVE 🛜 ❎ 🍴 ❎

JACKSON

⚠️ 💎💎💎 49'er Inn and Suites (Quality Inn and Suites) 🅷
(307) 733-7550. **$89-$339.** 330 W Pearl St 83001. Just w; just s of town square. Ext/int corridors. **Pets:** Service with restrictions, supervision.
SAVE 🛜 📺 ❎

⚠️ 💎💎 Antler Inn 🅷
(307) 733-2535. **$86-$275, 4 day notice.** 43 W Pearl St 83001. Just s of town square. Ext/int corridors. **Pets:** Accepted.
SAVE 🛜 📺 ❎

⚠️ 💎💎 Cowboy Village Resort 🆑
(307) 733-3121. **$86-$278.** 120 S Flat Creek Dr 83002. 0.3 mi w on Broadway to Flat Creek Dr, just s; downtown. Ext corridors. **Pets:** Other species. Supervision. SAVE 🛜 ❎ 📺 ❎

⚠️ 💎💎💎 Elk Country Inn 🅼 🐾
(307) 733-2364. **$76-$220.** 480 W Pearl St 83001. Just w, then just s of town square. Ext/int corridors. **Pets:** Other species. Designated rooms, service with restrictions, supervision. SAVE 🛜 ❎ 📺 ❎

💎💎💎 Homewood Suites by Hilton 🅷
(307) 739-0808. **$99-$369.** 260 N Millward St 83001. Just nw of town square, n on Millward St or w on Mercill Ave, from US 26/89/191. Int corridors. **Pets:** Accepted. 🛜 🅼 📺 ❎

⚠️ 💎💎💎 Jackson Hole Lodge 🅷
(307) 733-2992. **$89-$339, 15 day notice.** 420 W Broadway 83001. 0.3 mi w on US 26/89/191. Ext corridors. **Pets:** Large. $10 daily fee/pet. Designated rooms, supervision. SAVE 🛜 📺 ❎

💎💎💎 Painted Buffalo Inn 🅼 🐾
(307) 733-4340. **$80-$220.** 400 W Broadway 83001. Just w of town square. Ext corridors. **Pets:** Other species. $20 one-time fee/pet. Designated rooms, supervision. SAVE 🛜 🅼 📺 ❎

💎💎💎 Snow King Resort 🅷
(307) 733-5200. **$111-$985, 7 day notice.** 400 E Snow King Ave 83001. Just se of town square. Ext/int corridors. **Pets:** Accepted.
🛜 ❎ 📺 🍴 ❎

TETON VILLAGE

⚠️ 💎💎💎💎 Four Seasons Resort Jackson Hole 🅷
(307) 732-5000. **$375-$6750, 30 day notice.** 7680 Granite Loop Rd 83025. At base of Jackson Hole Mountain Resort. Int corridors.
Pets: Accepted. SAVE 🛜 ❎ 🅼 📺 🍴 ❎

💎💎💎💎 Inn at Jackson Hole 🅷 🐾
(307) 733-2311. **$79-$489, 14 day notice.** 3345 W Village Dr 83025. Center. Ext corridors. **Pets:** Medium. $10 daily fee/room. Designated rooms, service with restrictions. 🛜 ❎ 📺 🍴 ❎

END AREA

KEMMERER

⚠️ 💎💎💎 Best Western Plus Fossil Country Inn & Suites 🅷
(307) 877-3388. **$86-$125.** 760 US 30/189 83101. Jct US 30 and 189. Int corridors. **Pets:** Medium. $10 daily fee/room. Designated rooms, service with restrictions, supervision. SAVE 🛜 🅼 📺 ❎

LANDER

⚠️ 💎💎💎 Best Western The Inn at Lander 🅷
(307) 332-2847. **$90-$106.** 260 Grand View Dr 82520. Jct US 287 and SR 789. Int corridors. **Pets:** Accepted.
SAVE 🛜 ❎ 📺 🍴 ❎

💎💎💎 Holiday Inn Express & Suites Lander 🅷
(307) 332-4005. **$79-$169.** 1002 11th St 82520. 1 mi w on US 287, just w on Lincoln St. Int corridors. **Pets:** Accepted. 🛜 🅼 📺 ❎

⚠️ 💎 Holiday Lodge 🅼 🐾
(307) 332-2511. **$65-$75.** 210 McFarlane Dr 82520. Just e of jct US 287 and SR 789. Ext corridors. **Pets:** Other species. $10 daily fee/pet. Designated rooms, service with restrictions, crate. SAVE 🛜 📺

⚠️ 💎💎 Rodeway Inn & Suites/Pronghorn Lodge 🅼
(307) 332-3940. **$70-$90.** 150 E Main St 82520. Just n of jct US 287 and SR 789. Ext corridors. **Pets:** Accepted. SAVE 🛜 📺 🍴

LARAMIE

⚠️ 💎💎💎 AmericInn Lodge & Suites of Laramie 🅷
(307) 745-0777. **$90-$150.** 4712 E Grand Ave 82070. I-80 exit 316 (Grand Ave), just n. Int corridors. **Pets:** $25 one-time fee/room. Designated rooms, service with restrictions, supervision.
SAVE ❎ 🅼 📺 ❎

⚠️ 💎💎💎 Best Western Laramie Inn & Suites 🅷
(307) 745-5700. **$95-$139.** 1767 N Banner Rd 82072. I-80 exit 310 (Curtis St), just n. Int corridors. **Pets:** Accepted.
SAVE 🛜 ❎ 📺 ❎

💎💎 Days Inn 🅷
(307) 745-5678. **$56-$113.** 1368 McCue St 82072. I-80 exit 310 (Curtis St), 0.3 mi e to McCue St, then just s. Int corridors. **Pets:** Medium. $17 daily fee/pet. Designated rooms, service with restrictions, supervision.
🛜 📺 ❎

▼▼▼▼ **Holiday Inn** H ❀
(307) 721-9000. **$139-$189.** 204 S 30th St 82070. I-80 exit 316 (Grand Ave), 2.5 mi w to 30th St. Int corridors. **Pets:** Other species. $25 one-time fee/pet. Designated rooms, service with restrictions.
📶 ✕ 🕭M 🛏 💻 🍽 ⚊

▼▼ **Royal Super 8** M
(307) 745-8901. **$51-$86.** 1987 Banner Rd 82072. I-80 exit 310 (Curtis St), just n. Int corridors. **Pets:** Accepted. 📶 🛏 💻

LITTLE AMERICA

▲▲▲ ▼▼ **Little America Hotel & Travel Center** M
(307) 875-2400. **$69-$124.** I-80, exit 68 82929. I-80 exit 68, just n. Ext/int corridors. **Pets:** $20 daily fee/pet. Designated rooms, service with restrictions, supervision. 🆂🅰🆅🅴 📶 🕭M 🛏 💻 🍽 ⚊

LUSK

▲▲▲ ▼▼ **Americas Best Value Inn Covered Wagon** M
(307) 334-2836. **$72-$155.** 730 S Main St 82225. Just n of jct US 20/85. Ext/int corridors. **Pets:** Accepted. 🆂🅰🆅🅴 📶 🛏 💻 ⚊ ✕

▲▲▲ ▼ **Best Western Pioneer** M
(307) 334-2640. **$100-$220.** 731 S Main St 82225. Just n of jct US 20/85. Ext corridors. **Pets:** $20 daily fee/room. Designated rooms.
🆂🅰🆅🅴 📶 🛏 💻 ⚊

NEWCASTLE

▲▲▲ ▼▼ **Auto Inn Motel** M
(307) 746-2734. **$59-$195.** 2503 W Main St 82701. West end of town on US 16. Ext corridors. **Pets:** $6 daily fee/pet. Designated rooms, no service, supervision. 🆂🅰🆅🅴 📶 🛏 💻

▲▲▲ ▼ **Sage Motel** M
(307) 746-2724. **$60-$100, 3 day notice.** 1227 S Summit Ave 82701. 0.3 mi s of jct US 16 on US 85, then just w. Ext corridors. **Pets:** Small, dogs only. $10 daily fee/pet. Designated rooms, service with restrictions, supervision. 🆂🅰🆅🅴 📶 🛏 💻

PAINTER

▼ **Hunter Peak Ranch** RA
(307) 587-3711. **$150-$220, 91 day notice.** 4027 Crandall Rd 82414. SR 296, 5 mi s of US 212; 40 mi n of SR 120. Ext corridors. **Pets:** Dogs only. $15 daily fee/pet. Designated rooms, no service, supervision.
✕ 🛏 💻 🍽 ✕ 🅺 🅿 ⚿

PINEDALE

▼▼ **Baymont Inn & Suites** H
(307) 367-8300. **$98-$116.** 1624 W Pine St 82941. 1 mi n on US 191. Int corridors. **Pets:** Accepted. 📶 🕭M 🛏 💻 ⚊

▲▲▲ ▼▼ **Best Western Pinedale Inn** H
(307) 367-6869. **$90-$160.** 850 W Pine St 82941. 0.5 mi n on US 191. Int corridors. **Pets:** Large, other species. Designated rooms, service with restrictions, crate. 🆂🅰🆅🅴 📶 🛏 💻 ⚊

▲▲▲ ▼ **The Lodge at Pinedale** H
(307) 367-8800. **$80-$139.** 1054 W Pine St 82941. 0.7 mi n on US 191. Int corridors. **Pets:** Dogs only. $10 daily fee/pet. Designated rooms, service with restrictions, supervision. 🆂🅰🆅🅴 📶 ✕ 🛏 💻 ⚊

POWELL

▲▲▲ ▼▼ **Americas Best Value Inn** M
(307) 754-5117. **$80-$175.** 777 E 2nd St 82435. 0.3 mi e on US 14A. Ext corridors. **Pets:** Medium, other species. $10 daily fee/pet. Designated rooms, service with restrictions. 🆂🅰🆅🅴 📶 🛏 💻 ⚊

RAWLINS

▲▲▲ ▼▼ **Best Western CottonTree Inn** H
(307) 324-2737. **$99-$159.** 2221 W Spruce St 82301. I-80 exit 211, just n. Ext/int corridors. **Pets:** Accepted. 🆂🅰🆅🅴 📶 🛏 💻 ⚊ ✕

▲▲▲ ▼▼▼ **Comfort Inn & Suites** H
(307) 324-3663. **$89-$179.** 2366 Cedar St 82301. I-80 exit 215 (Cedar St), 0.3 mi w. Int corridors. **Pets:** Accepted.
🆂🅰🆅🅴 📶 ✕ 🛏 💻 ⚊

▼▼▼ **Hampton Inn** H
(307) 324-2320. **Call for rates.** 406 Airport Rd 82301. I-80 exit 215 (Cedar St), 0.8 mi nw. Int corridors. **Pets:** Other species. Designated rooms, service with restrictions, supervision.
📶 ✕ 🕭M 🛏 💻 ⚊

▼▼▼ **Holiday Inn Express** H
(307) 324-3760. **Call for rates.** 201 Airport Rd 82301. I-80 exit 215 (Cedar St), 0.8 mi nw. Int corridors. **Pets:** Accepted.
📶 🕭M 🛏 💻 ⚊

▼▼ **Microtel Inn & Suites** H
(307) 324-5588. **$81-$116.** 812 Locust St 82301. I-80 exit 214, 0.4 mi n on Higley Blvd, then just e. Int corridors. **Pets:** Accepted. 📶 🛏 💻

▲▲▲ ▼▼ **Oak Tree Inn** H
(307) 324-4700. **$69-$129.** 2005 E Daley St 82301. I-80 exit 215 (Cedar St), 1.2 mi w to N Higley Blvd, then 0.3 mi nw. Int corridors.
Pets: Accepted. 🆂🅰🆅🅴 📶 ✕ 🕭M 🛏 💻 🍽

▼▼ **Quality Inn of Rawlins** H
(307) 324-2783. **Call for rates.** 1801 E Cedar St 82301. I-80 exit 215 (Cedar St), 0.5 mi nw. Int corridors. **Pets:** Medium. $15 daily fee/pet. Service with restrictions, supervision. 📶 🛏 💻 🍽 ⚊

RIVERTON

▼▼ **Comfort Inn & Suites** H
(307) 856-8900. **$107-$119.** 2020 N Federal Blvd 82501. 1.5 mi ne on US 26/SR 789. Int corridors. **Pets:** Accepted.
📶 🕭M 🛏 💻 ⚊ ✕

▼▼ **Days Inn** M
(307) 856-9677. **$51-$130.** 909 W Main St 82501. 0.5 mi nw on US 26. Ext corridors. **Pets:** Medium. $15 daily fee/pet. Service with restrictions, supervision. 📶 🛏 💻

▼▼▼ **Hampton Inn & Suites-Riverton** H ❀
(307) 856-3500. **$89-$189.** 2500 N Federal Blvd (US 26) 82501. US 26, 2 mi ne on US 26/SR 789. Int corridors. **Pets:** Medium, other species. Service with restrictions, supervision. 📶 ✕ 🕭M 🛏 💻 ⚊

▼▼ **Super 8** M
(307) 857-2400. **$41-$89, 7 day notice.** 1040 N Federal Blvd 82501. 1 mi ne on US 26/SR 789. Int corridors. **Pets:** $10 one-time fee/pet. Service with restrictions, supervision. 📶 🛏 💻

ROCK SPRINGS

▲▲▲ ▼▼▼ **Americas Best Value Inn - The Inn** H
(307) 362-9600. **$55-$165.** 2518 Foothill Blvd 82901. I-80 exit 102 (Dewar Dr), just n. Int corridors. **Pets:** Small. $25 one-time fee/pet. Designated rooms, service with restrictions, supervision.
🆂🅰🆅🅴 📶 🛏 💻 🍽 ⚊

▲▲▲ ▼▼▼ **Best Western Outlaw Inn** H ❀
(307) 362-6623. **$90-$140.** 1630 Elk St 82901. I-80 exit 104 (Elk St), just n. Ext/int corridors. **Pets:** $15 daily fee/room. Designated rooms, service with restrictions, supervision. 🆂🅰🆅🅴 📶 ✕ 🛏 💻 🍽 ⚊

▼▼▼ **Hampton Inn** H
(307) 382-9222. **$139-$169.** 1901 Dewar Dr 82901. I-80 exit 102 (Dewar Dr), 1 mi s. Int corridors. **Pets:** Accepted. 📶 🕭M 🛏 💻 ⚊

▼▼▼ **Holiday Inn** H ❀
(307) 382-9200. **$109-$135.** 1675 Sunset Dr 82901. I-80 exit 102 (Dewar Dr), 0.3 mi sw. Ext/int corridors. **Pets:** Other species. $10 daily fee/room. Designated rooms, service with restrictions, supervision.
📶 🛏 💻 🍽 ⚊

▼▼▼▼ **Holiday Inn Express & Suites** 🅷

(307) 362-9200. **Call for rates.** 1660 Sunset Dr 82901. I-80 exit 102 (Dewar Dr), 0.4 mi s. Int corridors. **Pets:** Accepted.

🛜 ⊠ 🔊 🛏 💻 🏊

▼▼ **La Quinta Inn Rock Springs** 🅷

(307) 362-1770. **$75-$144.** 2717 Dewar Dr 82901. I-80 exit 102 (Dewar Dr), just n. Int corridors. **Pets:** Medium, other species. Service with restrictions, supervision. 🛜 🛏 💻 🏊

▼▼ **Quality Inn** Ⓜ

(307) 382-9490. **$90-$130.** 1670 Sunset Dr 82901. I-80 exit 102 (Dewar Dr), 0.3 mi s, then just w. Ext corridors. **Pets:** Accepted.

🛜 🛏 💻 🏊 ⊠

SARATOGA

▼▼ **Hacienda Motel** Ⓜ

(307) 326-5751. **$79-$94.** 1500 S First St 82331. 0.4 mi s of center on SR 130. Int corridors. **Pets:** Medium. $10 daily fee/pet. Designated rooms, service with restrictions, supervision. 🛜 🛏

SHERIDAN

🅰🅰🅰 ▼ **Americas Best Value Inn** Ⓜ

(307) 672-9757. **$59-$99.** 580 E 5th St 82801. I-90 exit 23 (5th St), 0.4 mi w. Ext corridors. **Pets:** Other species. Designated rooms, service with restrictions, supervision. [SAVE] 🛜 🛏 💻

🅰🅰🅰 ▼▼▼ **Best Western Sheridan Center** 🅷 🐾

(307) 674-7421. **$80-$140.** 612 N Main St 82801. I-90 exit 23 (5th St), 1 mi w, then just s. Ext/int corridors. **Pets:** Other species. $25 one-time fee/room. Designated rooms, service with restrictions, supervision.

[SAVE] 🛜 🛏 💻 🍽 🏊

🅰🅰🅰 ▼ **Budget Host Inn** Ⓜ

(307) 674-7496. **$70-$129.** 2007 N Main St 82801. I-90 exit 20, 0.7 mi s. Ext corridors. **Pets:** Accepted. [SAVE] 🛜 🛏 💻

▼▼ ▼▼ **Candlewood Suites** 🅷 🐾

(307) 675-2100. **$109-$159.** 1709 Sugarland Dr 82801. I-90 exit 25, just w, then just n. Int corridors. **Pets:** $75 one-time fee/room. Service with restrictions, supervision. 🛜 🔊 🛏 💻

🅰🅰🅰 ▼▼▼▼ **Holiday Inn Atrium & Convention Center** 🅷

(307) 672-8931. **$109-$159.** 1809 Sugarland Dr 82801. I-90 exit 25, 0.3 mi nw. Int corridors. **Pets:** Medium. $100 deposit/room. Service with restrictions, supervision. [SAVE] 🛜 🛏 💻 🍽 🏊 ⊠

🅰🅰🅰 ▼▼▼▼ **Mill Inn** Ⓜ

(307) 672-6401. **$65-$130.** 2161 Coffeen Ave 82801. I-90 exit 25, 0.3 mi w. Ext/int corridors. **Pets:** Large. $15 one-time fee/pet. Designated rooms, service with restrictions, crate. [SAVE] 🛜 🛏 💻

SUNDANCE

🅰🅰🅰 ▼▼▼ **Best Western Inn at Sundance** 🅷

(307) 283-2800. **$74-$200.** 2719 E Cleveland Ave 82729. I-90 exit 189, just n, then just w on I-90 business loop. Int corridors. **Pets:** Accepted. [SAVE] 🛜 ⊠ 🔊 💻 🏊

🅰🅰🅰 ▼▼ **Budget Host Arrowhead Motel** Ⓜ

(307) 283-3307. **$49-$79.** 214 Cleveland Ave 82729. I-90 business loop and US 14. Ext corridors. **Pets:** Accepted. [SAVE] 🛜 🛏

THERMOPOLIS

▼▼ **Days Inn** 🅷

(307) 864-3131. **$65-$133.** 115 E Park St 82443. In Hot Springs State Park. Ext/int corridors. **Pets:** Other species. $15 one-time fee/pet. Service with restrictions. 🛜 💻 🍽 🏊 ⊠

▼▼ **Hot Springs Super 8** 🅷

(307) 864-5515. **$54-$94.** Lane 5 Hwy 20 S 82443. On US 20, just se. Int corridors. **Pets:** Accepted. 🛜 🔊 🛏 💻 🏊 ⊠

TORRINGTON

▼▼▼ **Holiday Inn Express Hotel & Suites** 🅷 🐾

(307) 532-7600. **$95-$215.** 1700 E Valley Rd 82240. On US 26/E Valley Rd, 0.4 mi e of Main St. Int corridors. **Pets:** Dogs only. $15 daily fee/pet. Designated rooms, service with restrictions, supervision.

🛜 ⊠ 🔊 🛏 💻 🏊

UCROSS

🅰🅰🅰 ▼▼▼▼ **The Ranch at Ucross** 🆁🅰

(307) 737-2281. **$150, 3 day notice.** 2673 US Hwy 14 E 82835. Jct US 14/16, 0.5 mi w. Ext/int corridors. **Pets:** Dogs only. $100 deposit/room. No service, supervision. [SAVE] 🛜 ⊠ 🍽 🏊 ⊠ 📺

WAPITI

🅰🅰🅰 ▼ **Green Creek Inn** Ⓜ 🐾

(307) 587-5004. **$65-$180, 7 day notice.** 2908 Northfork Hwy 82414. 2.8 mi w on US 14/16/20; between Cody and Yellowstone National Park. Ext corridors. **Pets:** $10 daily fee/pet. Service with restrictions, supervision. [SAVE] 🛜 ⊠ 🛏 🗁

▼ **Yellowstone Valley Inn** Ⓜ

(307) 587-3961. **$59-$169, 21 day notice.** 3324 Yellowstone Park Hwy 82450. 3.3 mi w on US 14/16/20; halfway between Cody and Yellowstone National Park. Ext corridors. **Pets:** Accepted.

🛜 ⊠ 🛏 💻 🍽 🏊 ⊠ 🗁

WHEATLAND

🅰🅰🅰 ▼▼▼ **Best Western Torchlite Motor Inn** 🅷 🐾

(307) 322-4070. **$90-$150.** 1809 16th St 82201. I-25 exit 78, just e; 1.5 mi n on US 87/I-25 business loop (16th St). Ext corridors. **Pets:** Large, other species. $10 daily fee/pet. Service with restrictions, supervision.

[SAVE] 🛜 🛏 💻 🏊

WRIGHT

▼▼▼ **Wright Hotel** 🅷

(307) 464-6060. **$129-$139, 3 day notice.** 300 Reata Dr 82732. Just w of jct SR 59 and 387. Int corridors. **Pets:** $25 daily fee/pet. Designated rooms, service with restrictions, supervision.

🛜 ⊠ 🔊 🛏 💻 🍽

YELLOWSTONE NATIONAL PARK

🅰🅰🅰 ▼▼▼ **Elephant Head Lodge** 🅲🅰

(307) 587-3980. **$150-$350, 30 day notice.** 1170 Yellowstone Hwy 82414. 11.7 mi e of Yellowstone National Park east gate on US 14/16/20. Ext corridors. **Pets:** $20 one-time fee/pet. Supervision.

[SAVE] ⊠ 🛏 💻 🍽 ⊠ 🐾 📺 🗁

▼▼ **Shoshone Lodge** 🅲🅰

(307) 587-4044. **$110-$325, 30 day notice.** 349 North Fork Hwy 82190. 3.5 mi e of Yellowstone National Park East Gate on US 14/16/20. Ext corridors. **Pets:** Accepted. 🛜 🛏 💻 🍽 ⊠ 🐾 🗁

Canadian Lodgings

ALBERTA

ATHABASCA

▼▼▼ Days Inn Athabasca H
(780) 675-7020. **$125.** 2805 48th Ave T9S 0A4. Jct Hwy 2 and 55, 1.6 mi (2.7 km) e; east end of town. Int corridors. **Pets:** Small. $15 daily fee/room. Designated rooms, no service, crate.

BANFF

▼▼ Banff Ptarmigan Inn H
(403) 762-2207. **$99-$229, 3 day notice.** 337 Banff Ave T1L 1B1. Between Moose and Elk sts. Int corridors. **Pets:** Accepted.

▼▼▼ Banff Rocky Mountain Resort CO
(403) 762-5531. **$109-$219, 3 day notice.** 1029 Banff Ave T1L 1A2. Banff Ave and Tunnel Mountain Rd; just s of Trans-Canada Hwy 1. Ext corridors. **Pets:** Accepted.

CAA ▼▼▼ Best Western Plus Siding 29 Lodge H
(403) 762-5575. **$100-$221.** 453 Marten St T1L 1B3. 0.6 mi (1 km) ne, just off Banff Ave. Int corridors. **Pets:** Accepted.

▼▼ Castle Mountain Chalets CA
(403) 762-3868. **Call for rates.** Bow Valley Pkwy (Hwy 1A) T1L 1B5. 20 mi (32 km) w on Trans-Canada Hwy 1, jct Castle, 0.6 mi (1 km) ne on Hwy 1A (Bow Valley Pkwy). Ext corridors. **Pets:** Accepted.

CAA ▼▼▼ Douglas Fir Resort & Chalets CO 🐾
(403) 762-5591. **$118-$459.** 525 Tunnel Mountain Rd T1L 1B2. Jct Banff Ave and Wolf St, 1 mi (1.6 km) ne. Ext/int corridors. **Pets:** $25 daily fee/pet. Designated rooms, supervision.

CAA ▼▼▼ ▼▼▼ The Fairmont Banff Springs H
(403) 762-2211. **$250-$593, 3 day notice.** 405 Spray Ave T1L 1J4. Just s on Banff Ave over the bridge, 0.3 mi (0.5 km) e. Int corridors. **Pets:** Accepted.

▼▼▼ Hidden Ridge Resort CO
(403) 762-3544. **Call for rates.** 901 Hidden Ridge Way T1L 1B7. 1.5 mi (2.4 km) ne at Tunnel Mountain Rd. Ext corridors. **Pets:** Accepted.

▼ Homestead Inn M 🐾
(403) 762-4471. **$99-$149, 3 day notice.** 217 Lynx St T1L 1A7. Banff Ave, just w on Caribou St, then just n; downtown. Ext corridors. **Pets:** Medium. $25 daily fee/pet. Designated rooms, service with restrictions, supervision.

CAA ▼▼▼ Irwin's Mountain Inn H
(403) 762-4566. **$109-$209.** 429 Banff Ave T1L 1B2. N of Rabbit St. Int corridors. **Pets:** $15 daily fee/pet. Designated rooms, service with restrictions, supervision.

CAA ▼▼▼ Johnston Canyon Resort CA
(403) 762-2971. **Call for rates.** Hwy 1A T1L 1A9. 15 mi (24 km) nw on Hwy 1A (Bow Valley Pkwy). Ext corridors. **Pets:** Accepted.

▼▼▼ The Juniper H
(403) 762-2281. **$89-$289, 3 day notice.** 1 Mt. Norquay Rd T1L 1E1. Trans-Canada Hwy 1 exit Mt. Norquay Rd, just n. Int corridors. **Pets:** Accepted.

CAA ▼▼▼ Red Carpet Inn H
(403) 762-4184. **$79-$149.** 425 Banff Ave T1L 1B6. Between Beaver and Rabbit sts. Ext/int corridors. **Pets:** $15 daily fee/room. Designated rooms, service with restrictions, supervision.

CAA ▼▼▼ ▼▼▼ The Rimrock Resort Hotel H 🐾
(403) 762-3356. **$218-$395, 3 day notice.** 300 Mountain Ave T1L 1J2. 2.4 mi (4 km) s via Sulphur Mountain Rd; adjacent to Upper Hot Springs Pool. Int corridors. **Pets:** Medium. $35 daily fee/pet. Designated rooms, service with restrictions, supervision.

BONNYVILLE

CAA ▼▼▼ Best Western Bonnyville Inn & Suites H
(780) 826-6226. **$135.** 5401 43rd St T9N 0H3. Hwy 28, just n at 44th St. Int corridors. **Pets:** Accepted.

BROOKS

CAA ▼▼▼ Brooks Super 8 H
(403) 363-0080. **Call for rates.** 115 15th Ave W T1R 1C4. Just s off Trans-Canada Hwy 1. Ext/int corridors. **Pets:** Accepted.

▼▼ Heritage Inn H
(403) 362-6666. **$114-$180.** 1217 2nd St W T1R 1P7. Trans-Canada Hwy 1 exit Hwy 873, 0.5 mi (0.8 km) s. Int corridors. **Pets:** Medium, dogs only. $20 daily fee/pet. Designated rooms, service with restrictions, crate.

CAA ▼▼▼ Lakeview Inns & Suites H
(403) 362-7440. **Call for rates.** 1307 2nd St W T1R 1P7. Trans-Canada Hwy 1 exit Hwy 873, 0.5 mi (0.8 km) s. Int corridors. **Pets:** Medium. $25 one-time fee/pet. Designated rooms, service with restrictions, supervision.

▼▼▼ Ramada H 🐾
(403) 362-6440. **$132-$159.** 1319 2nd St W T1R 1P7. Trans-Canada Hwy 1 exit Hwy 873, 0.5 mi (0.8 km) s. Ext/int corridors. **Pets:** Other species. $15 daily fee/pet. Designated rooms, service with restrictions, supervision.

CALGARY METROPOLITAN AREA

AIRDRIE

▼▼▼▼ Holiday Inn Express & Suites Airdrie-Calgary North ⊞

(403) 912-1952. **$129-$189, 3 day notice.** 64 E Lake Ave NE T4A 2G8. Hwy 2 exit E Airdrie, 0.6 mi (1 km) n. Int corridors. **Pets:** Accepted.

ECO 🛜 ✕ 🔥M 🛗 💻 ➿ ✕

▼▼▼ Ramada Inn & Suites ⊞

(403) 945-1288. **$128-$259.** 191 E Lake Crescent T4A 2H7. Hwy 2 exit E Airdrie. Int corridors. **Pets:** Medium. $15 daily fee/pet. Designated rooms, service with restrictions, supervision.

ECO 🛜 ✕ 🔥M 🛗 💻 ➿ ✕

▼▼ Super 8 Airdrie ⊞

(403) 948-4188. **$113-$126.** 815 E Lake Blvd T4A 2G4. Hwy 2 exit E Airdrie, just e. Int corridors. **Pets:** Accepted. 🛜 ✕ 🛗 💻

CALGARY

▼▼ 5 Calgary Downtown Suites ⊞

(403) 263-0520. **$149-$229.** 618 5th Ave SW T2P 0M7. Corner of 5th Ave SW and 5th St SW. Int corridors. **Pets:** Accepted.

ECO 🛜 🛗 💻 🍴 ➿ ✕

⊕ ▼▼▼ Best Western Plus Port O'Call Hotel ⊞ ❀

(403) 291-4600. **$129-$169.** 1935 McKnight Blvd NE T2E 6V4. 1.6 mi (2.5 km) ne of jct Hwy 2 (Deerfoot Tr); at 19th St NE. Int corridors. **Pets:** Large. $20 daily fee/pet. Designated rooms, service with restrictions, supervision. ECO SAVE 🛜 ✕ 🔥M 🛗 💻 🍴 ➿ ✕

▼▼▼ Blackfoot Inn ⊞ ❀

(403) 252-2253. **$99-$289.** 5940 Blackfoot Tr SE T2H 2B5. At 58th Ave SE. Int corridors. **Pets:** Other species. $25 daily fee/room. Service with restrictions. ECO 🛜 🔥M 🛗 💻 ➿ ✕

⊕ ▼▼▼ Calgary Marriott Downtown ⊞

(403) 266-7331. **$139-$619.** 110 9th Ave SE T2G 5A6. Jct 9th Ave and Centre St; adjacent to TELUS Convention Centre. Int corridors. **Pets:** Medium. Service with restrictions.

ECO SAVE 🛜 ✕ 🛗 💻 🍴 ➿

▼▼▼ Calgary Westways Guest House BB ❀

(403) 229-1758. **$109-$180, 4 day notice.** 216 25th Ave SW T2S 0L1. 1.1 mi (1.7 km) s on Hwy 2A (Macleod Tr S), then just w. Int corridors. **Pets:** Other species. $8 daily fee/pet. 🛜 ✕

⊕ ▼▼▼ Carriage House Inn ⊞ ❀

(403) 253-1101. **$135-$249.** 9030 Macleod Tr S T2H 0M4. On Hwy 2A (Macleod Tr); corner of 90th Ave SW. Int corridors. **Pets:** $20 daily fee/pet. Designated rooms, service with restrictions, crate.

ECO SAVE 🛜 ✕ 🛗 💻 🍴 ➿ ✕

▼▼▼ Coast Plaza Hotel & Conference Centre ⊞ ❀

(403) 248-8888. **$134-$324.** 1316 33rd St NE T2A 6B6. Just s of jct 16th Ave (Trans-Canada Hwy 1) and 36th St NE, just w on 12th Ave NE. Int corridors. **Pets:** Medium. $20 daily fee/room. Designated rooms, service with restrictions, supervision. ECO 🛜 🛗 💻 🍴 ➿ ✕

▼▼▼ Delta Bow Valley ⊞

(403) 266-1980. **$109-$409.** 209 4th Ave SE T2G 0C6. 1st St SE and 4th Ave SE. Int corridors. **Pets:** Small. $35 one-time fee/pet. Designated rooms, service with restrictions, supervision.

ECO 🛜 ✕ 🔥M 🛗 💻 🍴 ➿ ✕

▼▼▼ Delta Calgary Airport ⊞ ❀

(403) 291-2600. **$149-$329.** 2001 Airport Rd NE T2E 6Z6. At Calgary International Airport. Int corridors. **Pets:** Medium, other species. $35 one-time fee/room. Service with restrictions, supervision.

ECO 🛜 ✕ 🔥M 🛗 💻 🍴 ➿

▼▼▼ Delta Calgary South ⊞

(403) 278-5050. **$89-$389.** 135 Southland Dr SE T2J 5X5. On Hwy 2A (Macleod Tr); corner of Southland Dr. Int corridors. **Pets:** Accepted.

ECO 🛜 ✕ 🔥M 🛗 💻 🍴 ➿ ✕

▼▼ Econo Lodge Motel Village M

(403) 289-2561. **$69-$189.** 2440 16th Ave NW T2M 0M5. Jct 16th Ave NW (Trans-Canada Hwy 1) and Banff Tr NW. Ext/int corridors. **Pets:** Small, other species. $10 daily fee/pet. Designated rooms, service with restrictions, crate. 🛜 🛗 💻

⊕ ▼▼▼ Econo Lodge South M

(403) 252-4401. **$90-$270.** 7505 Macleod Tr SW T2H 0L8. Corner of Hwy 2A (Macleod Tr) and 75th Ave. Ext/int corridors. **Pets:** Accepted.

ECO SAVE 🛜 🛗 💻 ➿

▼▼▼▼ Executive Royal Inn North Calgary ⊞

(403) 291-2003. **Call for rates.** 2828 23rd St NE T2E 8T4. Barlow Tr NE, just w; at 27th Ave NE. Int corridors. **Pets:** Accepted.

ECO 🛜 ✕ 🔥M 🛗 💻 🍴 ✕

▼▼▼▼ The Fairmont Palliser ⊞

(403) 262-1234. **Call for rates.** 133 9th Ave SW T2P 2M3. 9th Ave SW and 1st St SW. Int corridors. **Pets:** Accepted.

ECO 🛜 🔥M 💻 🍴 ➿ ✕

▼▼▼ Holiday Inn Calgary-Airport ⊞

(403) 230-1999. **Call for rates.** 1250 McKinnon Dr NE T2E 7T7. 0.6 mi (1 km) e of jct Hwy 2 (Deerfoot Tr) and 16th Ave NE (Trans-Canada Hwy 1). Int corridors. **Pets:** $20 daily fee/room. Designated rooms, service with restrictions, supervision. 🛜 ✕ 🔥M 🛗 💻 🍴 ➿

⊕ ▼▼▼ Holiday Inn Calgary-Macleod Trail South ⊞

(403) 287-2700. **$119-$249.** 4206 Macleod Tr S T2G 2R7. Corner of 42nd Ave SW and Macleod Tr S. Int corridors. **Pets:** Accepted.

ECO SAVE 🛜 ✕ 🔥M 🛗 💻 🍴 ➿

▼▼▼ Holiday Inn Express Hotel & Suites Calgary Downtown ⊞

(403) 269-8262. **$179-$289.** 1020 8th Ave SW T2P 1J2. At 10th St SW. Int corridors. **Pets:** Accepted. 🛜 🛗 💻

▼▼▼ Holiday Inn Express Hotel & Suites Calgary-South ⊞ ❀

(403) 225-3000. **$139-$259.** 12025 Lake Fraser Dr SE (Macleod Tr S) T2J 7G5. Hwy 2 (Deerfoot Tr) exit Anderson Rd W, just s on Macleod Tr, just e on Lake Fraser Gate, then 0.4 mi (0.7 km) n. Int corridors. **Pets:** Other species. $20 daily fee/pet. Designated rooms, service with restrictions, crate. 🛜 🛗 💻 ➿ ✕

▼▼▼ Hotel Arts ⊞

(403) 266-4611. **$139-$319.** 119 12th Ave SW T2R 0G8. At 1st St SW; centre. Int corridors. **Pets:** Accepted.

🛜 ✕ 🔥M 🛗 💻 🍴 ➿

▼▼▼ Hotel Le Germain Calgary ⊞ ❀

(403) 264-8990. **$199-$539.** 899 Centre St SW T2G 1B8. Corner of 1st St SW and 9th Ave SW; centre. Int corridors. **Pets:** Other species. $35 daily fee/pet. Service with restrictions, supervision. 🛜 ✕ 💻 🍴

⊕ ▼▼▼ Lakeview Signature Inn ⊞

(403) 735-3336. **$149-$309.** 2622 39th Ave NE T1Y 7J9. Barlow Tr NE, just e. Int corridors. **Pets:** Small, other species. $100 one-time fee/room. Designated rooms, service with restrictions, crate.

ECO SAVE 🛜 ✕ 🔥M 🛗 💻 ➿ ✕

⊕ ▼▼▼ Radisson Hotel Calgary Airport ⊞ ❀

(403) 291-4666. **Call for rates.** 2120 16th Ave NE T2E 1L4. Just e of jct 16th Ave NE (Trans-Canada Hwy 1) and Hwy 2 (Deerfoot Tr). Int corridors. **Pets:** $25 one-time fee/room. Designated rooms, service with restrictions, crate. ECO SAVE 🛜 ✕ 🔥M 🛗 💻 🍴 ➿

▼▼▼▼ Sandman Hotel Downtown Calgary �H

(403) 237-8626. **$149-$229.** 888 7th Ave SW T2P 3J3. Corner of 7th Ave SW and 8th St SW. Int corridors. **Pets:** Accepted.

🔟 🛜 🔋 🍴 ➰

▼▼▼ Sandman Hotel Suites & Spa Calgary Airport �H

(403) 219-2475. **$129-$199.** 25 Hopewell Way NE T3J 4V7. Just n of jct Barlow Tr and McKnight Blvd. Int corridors. **Pets:** Accepted.

🔟 🛜 🚹 🔋 🔲 🍴 ➰

ⒶⒶ ▼▼▼ Service Plus Inn & Suites Calgary �H

(403) 256-5352. **$129-$159.** 3503 114th Ave SE T2Z 3X2. South end of Barlow Tr, just w. Int corridors. **Pets:** Accepted.

🆂🅰🆅🅴 🛜 ✖ 🔋 🔲 ➰ 🗙

ⒶⒶ ▼▼▼ Sheraton Cavalier Hotel �H 🐾

(403) 291-0107. **$139-$469.** 2620 32nd Ave NE T1Y 6B8. Barlow Tr at 32nd Ave NE. Int corridors. **Pets:** Service with restrictions, supervision.

🔟 🆂🅰🆅🅴 🛜 ✖ 🔲 🍴 ➰ 🗙

ⒶⒶ ▼▼▼▼ Sheraton Suites Calgary Eau Claire �H 🐾

(403) 266-7200. **$149-$549.** 255 Barclay Parade SW T2P 5C2. At 3rd St SW and 2nd Ave SW. Int corridors. **Pets:** Medium, dogs only. Designated rooms, service with restrictions, supervision.

🔟 🆂🅰🆅🅴 🛜 ✖ 🔋 🔲 🍴 ➰ 🗙

ⒶⒶ ▼▼▼ Travelodge Calgary University �H 🐾

(403) 289-6600. **$89-$179.** 2227 Banff Tr NW T2M 4L2. 16th Ave NW (Trans-Canada Hwy 1) and Banff Tr NW. Int corridors. **Pets:** Medium, other species. $10 one-time fee/pet. Designated rooms, service with restrictions, supervision.

🔟 🆂🅰🆅🅴 🛜 🔋 🔲 ➰

ⒶⒶ ▼▼▼ Travelodge Hotel Calgary Airport �H

(403) 291-1260. **$94-$166.** 2750 Sunridge Blvd NE T1Y 3C2. Just se of jct 32nd Ave NE and Barlow Tr NE. Int corridors. **Pets:** Accepted.

🔟 🆂🅰🆅🅴 🛜 🔋 🔲 🍴 ➰

ⒶⒶ ▼▼▼▼ The Westin Calgary �H 🐾

(403) 266-1611. **$139-$489.** 320 4th Ave SW T2P 2S6. Corner of 4th Ave SW and 3rd St. Int corridors. **Pets:** Other species. Service with restrictions, supervision.

🔟 🆂🅰🆅🅴 🛜 ✖ 🔲 🍴 ➰ 🗙

▼▼▼ Wingate by Wyndham Calgary �H 🐾

(403) 514-0099. **$78-$491.** 400 Midpark Way SE T2X 3S4. Hwy 2A (Macleod Tr), 0.3 mi (0.5 km) e on Sun Valley Blvd SE, just n on Midpark Blvd SE, then just s. Int corridors. **Pets:** Large. $25 daily fee/pet. Service with restrictions, supervision.

🔟 🛜 ✖ 🔋 🔲 ➰ 🗙

COCHRANE

ⒶⒶ ▼▼▼ Best Western Harvest Country Inn �H

(403) 932-1410. **Call for rates.** 11 West Side Dr T4C 1M1. Jct Hwy 1A, 0.3 mi (0.5 km) s on Hwy 22, just e on Quigley Dr, then just s. Ext/int corridors. **Pets:** Accepted. 🆂🅰🆅🅴 🛜 ✖ 🔋 🔲 ➰ 🗙

▼▼▼ Days Inn & Suites Cochrane �H

(403) 932-5588. **$71-$143.** 5 West Side Dr T4C 1M1. Jct Hwy 1A, 0.3 mi (0.5 km) s on Hwy 22, just e on Quigley Dr, then just s. Int corridors. **Pets:** Accepted. 🛜 🔋 🔲 ➰

▼▼▼ Super 8-Cochrane �H

(403) 932-6355. **$133-$161.** 10 West Side Dr T4C 1M1. Jct Hwy 1A, 0.3 mi (0.5 km) s on Hwy 22, just e on Quigley Dr, then just s. Int corridors. **Pets:** Medium, other species. $15 daily fee/pet. Designated rooms, service with restrictions, supervision. 🔟 🛜 ✖ 🔋 🔲 ➰ 🗙

OKOTOKS

ⒶⒶ ▼▼▼ Lakeview Inns & Suites �H

(403) 938-7400. **$125-$130.** 22 Southridge Dr T1S 1N1. Hwy 2 exit 2A, 2.5 mi (4 km) s to Southridge Dr. Int corridors. **Pets:** Accepted.

🔟 🆂🅰🆅🅴 🛜 🔋 🔲

STRATHMORE

ⒶⒶ ▼▼▼ Best Western Strathmore Inn �H

(403) 934-5777. **$106-$126.** 550 Hwy 1 T1P 1M6. Trans-Canada Hwy 1, jct Hwy 817; centre. Int corridors. **Pets:** $10 daily fee/room. Designated rooms, service with restrictions, supervision.

🆂🅰🆅🅴 🛜 ✖ 🔋 🔲 ➰

ⒶⒶ ▼▼▼ Days Inn & Suites �H

(403) 934-1134. **Call for rates.** 400 Ranch Market T1P 0B2. Trans-Canada Hwy 1, just n at Lakeside Blvd (Centre St). Int corridors. **Pets:** Medium. $15 daily fee/pet. Designated rooms, service with restrictions, supervision. 🆂🅰🆅🅴 🛜 ✖ 🔋 🔲 ➰ 🗙

▼▼▼ Travelodge Strathmore �H 🐾

(403) 901-0000. **$107-$125.** 350 Ridge Rd T1P 1B5. Just n of Trans-Canada Hwy 1 at Ridge Rd. Int corridors. **Pets:** Medium, other species. $15 daily fee/room. Designated rooms, service with restrictions, supervision. 🛜 🔋 🔲 ➰ 🗙

END METROPOLITAN AREA

CAMROSE

▼▼ Norsemen Inn �H

(780) 672-9171. **$105-$199.** 6505 48th Ave T4V 3K3. Hwy 13 (48th Ave) at 65th St; west end of town. Int corridors. **Pets:** Other species. $20 daily fee/room. Designated rooms. 🛜 ✖ 🔋 🔲 🍴

▼▼▼ Ramada Camrose �H

(780) 672-5220. **Call for rates.** 4702 73rd St T4V 0E5. Hwy 13 (48th Ave), just s. Int corridors. **Pets:** Accepted.

🛜 ✖ 🔋 🔲 ➰ 🗙

▼▼▼ Super 8 Camrose �H

(780) 672-7303. **Call for rates.** 4710 73rd St T4V 0E5. Hwy 13 (48th Ave), just s. Int corridors. **Pets:** Accepted.

🛜 ✖ 🔋 🔲 ➰ 🗙

CANMORE

ⒶⒶ ▼▼▼ Banff Boundary Lodge 🅲🅾

(403) 678-9555. **$84-$189, 3 day notice.** 1000 Harvie Heights Rd T1W 2W2. Trans-Canada Hwy 1 exit 86, just n. Ext corridors. **Pets:** $15 daily fee/pet. No service. 🆂🅰🆅🅴 🛜 ✖ 🔋 🔲 🅰🅺

ⒶⒶ ▼▼▼ Best Western Plus Pocaterra Inn �H

(403) 678-4334. **$120-$210.** 1725 Mountain Ave T1W 2W1. Trans-Canada Hwy 1 exit 86, 1.3 mi (2.1 km) e. Int corridors. **Pets:** Accepted.

🆂🅰🆅🅴 🛜 ✖ 🔋 🔲 ➰ 🗙

▼▼▼ Blackstone Mountain Lodge �H

(403) 609-8098. **Call for rates.** 170 Kananaskis Way T1W 0A8. Trans-Canada Hwy 1 exit 89, 1.2 mi (2 km) s. Int corridors. **Pets:** Accepted.

🔟 🛜 ✖ 🔋 🔲 ➰ 🗙

▼▼ Bow Valley Motel Ⓜ

(403) 678-5085. **$75-$110.** 610 8th St T1W 2B5. Trans-Canada Hwy 1 exit 89, 1.1 mi (1.8 km) se. Ext corridors. **Pets:** Medium, dogs only. $10 daily fee/pet. Designated rooms, service with restrictions, supervision.

🛜 ✖ 🔋 🔲

ⒶⒸⒶ ♦♦ Canadian Rockies Chalets ⓒⓞ
(403) 678-3799. **$89-$249, 3 day notice.** 1206 Bow Valley Tr T1W 1N6. Trans-Canada Hwy 1 exit 89, 0.9 mi (1.5 km) se. Ext corridors. **Pets:** $15 daily fee/pet. No service. ⓈⒶⓋⒺ 🛜 ☒ 🛏 💻 Ⓚ

ⒶⒸⒶ ♦♦ Econo Lodge Canmore Ⓗ
(403) 678-5488. **$90-$200.** 1602 2nd Ave T1W 1M8. Trans-Canada Hwy 1 exit 89, 1.3 mi (2.1 km) e. Int corridors. **Pets:** Accepted.
ⓈⒶⓋⒺ 🛜 ☒ 🛏 💻 🍴

♦♦♦ Mystic Springs Chalets & Hot Pools ⓒⓞ ❀
(403) 609-0333. **Call for rates.** 140 Kananaskis Way T1W 2X2. Trans-Canada Hwy 1 exit 89, 1.1 mi (1.8 km) s. Ext corridors. **Pets:** Large, other species. $25 daily fee/room. Service with restrictions, supervision.
ⒺⒸⓄ 🛜 ☒ 🛏 💻 🥤 ☒

ⒶⒸⒶ ♦♦♦ Quality Resort-Chateau Canmore Ⓗ ❀
(403) 678-6699. **$89-$119.** 1720 Bow Valley Tr T1W 2X3. Trans-Canada Hwy 1 exit 86, 0.5 mi (0.8 km) s. Int corridors. **Pets:** $25 daily fee/pet. Designated rooms, service with restrictions, crate.
ⓈⒶⓋⒺ 🛜 ☒ 🛏 💻 🍴 🥤 ☒

ⒶⒸⒶ ♦♦♦ Radisson Hotel & Conference Centre Ⓗ
(403) 678-3625. **$89-$249, 3 day notice.** 511 Bow Valley Tr T1W 1N7. Trans-Canada Hwy 1 exit 89, 1.4 mi (0.8 km) s. Ext/int corridors. **Pets:** Accepted. ⒺⒸⓄ ⓈⒶⓋⒺ 🛜 ☒ ♿ 🛏 💻 🍴 🥤 ☒

ⒶⒸⒶ ♦♦♦ Rocky Mountain Ski Lodge Ⓜ
(403) 678-5445. **$119-$209.** 1711 Bow Valley Tr T1W 2T8. Trans-Canada Hwy 1 exit 86, 0.5 mi (0.8 km) s. Ext corridors. **Pets:** Medium. $10 daily fee/pet. Designated rooms, service with restrictions, supervision.
ⒺⒸⓄ ⓈⒶⓋⒺ 🛜 ☒ 🛏 💻 ☒

♦♦♦ Solara Resort & Spa ⓒⓞ
(403) 609-3600. **Call for rates.** 187 Kananaskis Way T1W 0A3. Trans-Canada Hwy 1 exit 89, 1.2 mi (2 km) s. Int corridors. **Pets:** Accepted.
🛜 ☒ 🛏 💻

♦♦ Windtower Lodge & Suites ⓒⓞ
(403) 609-6600. **Call for rates.** 160 Kananaskis Way T1W 3E2. Trans-Canada Hwy 1 exit 89, 1.1 mi (1.8 km) s. Int corridors. **Pets:** Accepted.
🛜 ☒ 🛏 💻 ☒ Ⓚ

CLARESHOLM

♦♦ Bluebird Motel Ⓜ
(403) 625-3395. **$69-$109, 3 day notice.** 5505 1st St W T0L 0T0. 0.3 mi (0.5 km) n on Hwy 2. Ext corridors. **Pets:** Accepted.
🛜 ☒ 🛏 💻

♦♦ Motel 6 Claresholm #5710 Ⓗ
(403) 625-4646. **Call for rates.** 11 Alberta Rd (Hwy 2) T0L 0T0. North end of town. Int corridors. **Pets:** Other species. Service with restrictions, supervision. 🛜 ♿ 🛏

COLD LAKE

ⒶⒸⒶ ♦♦ Best Western Cold Lake Inn Ⓗ
(780) 594-4888. **$140-$186.** 4815 52nd St T9M 1P1. Corner of 55th Ave (Hwy 26 and 55) and 52nd St; south end of city. Ext/int corridors. **Pets:** Small, dogs only. $25 daily fee/room. Designated rooms, service with restrictions, supervision.
ⓈⒶⓋⒺ 🛜 ☒ ♿ 🛏 💻 🍴 🥤 ☒

DEAD MAN'S FLATS

ⒶⒸⒶ ♦♦♦ Copperstone Resort Hotel ⓒⓞ ❀
(403) 678-0303. **$129-$279.** 250 2nd Ave T1W 2W4. Trans-Canada Hwy 1 exit 98, just n on 2nd St, then just e. Int corridors. **Pets:** $20 daily fee/room. Service with restrictions. ⓈⒶⓋⒺ 🛜 ☒ 🛏 💻

DRAYTON VALLEY

♦♦♦ Drayton Valley Ramada Inn Ⓗ
(780) 514-7861. **$125-$165.** 2051 50th St T7A 1S5. Just n on Hwy 39; south end of town. Ext/int corridors. **Pets:** Accepted.
ⒺⒸⓄ 🛜 ☒ ♿ 🛏 💻 🥤 ☒

ⒶⒸⒶ ♦♦♦ Holiday Inn Express Hotel & Suites Ⓗ
(780) 515-9888. **$109-$169.** 5001 Brougham Dr T7A 0A1. Hwy 22 exit Drayton Valley, 1.5 mi (2.4 km) n. Int corridors. **Pets:** Accepted.
ⓈⒶⓋⒺ 🛜 ♿ 🛏 💻

ⒶⒸⒶ ♦♦ Lakeview Inns & Suites Ⓗ
(780) 542-3200. **Call for rates.** 4302 50th St T7A 1M4. Hwy 22 exit Drayton Valley, 1.5 mi (2.4 km) n. Int corridors. **Pets:** Accepted.
ⓈⒶⓋⒺ 🛜 🛏 💻

DRUMHELLER

♦♦♦ Inn and Spa at Heartwood Ⓗ
(403) 823-6495. **$99-$299, 3 day notice.** 320 N Railway Ave E T0J 0Y4. Jct Hwy 9 and 575 (S Railway Ave SE), just n, then just e. Ext/int corridors. **Pets:** Other species. $25 one-time fee/room. Designated rooms, no service, supervision. 🛜 ☒ 🛏 💻

♦♦♦ Jurassic Inn Ⓗ
(403) 823-7700. **Call for rates.** 1103 Hwy 9 S T0J 0Y0. Hwy 9, southeast access to town. Ext/int corridors. **Pets:** Accepted.
ⒺⒸⓄ 🛜 ☒ 🛏 💻 🍴 ☒

♦♦♦ Ramada Inn & Suites Ⓗ
(403) 823-2028. **$119-$170.** 680 2nd St SE T0J 0Y0. Jct Hwy 9 and 575 (S Railway Ave SE), just ne. Ext/int corridors. **Pets:** Accepted.
ⒺⒸⓄ 🛜 ☒ ♿ 🛏 💻 🥤 ☒

♦♦ Super 8 Ⓗ
(403) 823-8887. **$126-$162.** 600-680 2nd St SE T0J 0Y0. Jct Hwy 9 and 575 (S Railway Ave SE), just ne. Ext/int corridors. **Pets:** Accepted.
ⒺⒸⓄ 🛜 ☒ 🛏 💻 🥤 ☒

EDMONTON METROPOLITAN AREA

EDMONTON

ⒶⒸⒶ ♦♦ Alberta Place Suite Hotel Ⓗ
(780) 423-1565. **$99-$139.** 10049 103rd St T5J 2W7. Between Jasper and 100th aves. Int corridors. **Pets:** Other species. $20 one-time fee/room. Supervision. ⒺⒸⓄ ⓈⒶⓋⒺ 🛜 ☒ 🛏 💻 🥤

ⒶⒸⒶ ♦♦ Best Western Cedar Park Inn Ⓗ ❀
(780) 434-7411. **$120-$140.** 5116 Gateway Blvd T6H 2H4. Hwy 2 (Gateway Blvd) at 51st Ave. Int corridors. **Pets:** Other species. $20 daily fee/room. Designated rooms, service with restrictions, supervision.
ⓈⒶⓋⒺ 🛜 ♿ 🛏 💻 🍴 🥤

ⒶⒸⒶ ♦♦♦ Best Western Plus Westwood Inn Ⓗ
(780) 483-7770. **$115-$140.** 18035 Stony Plain Rd T5S 1B2. Hwy 16A (Stony Plain Rd) at 180th St. Int corridors. **Pets:** Accepted.
ⓈⒶⓋⒺ 🛜 🛏 💻 🍴 🥤

♦♦♦ Coast Edmonton House ⓒⓞ
(780) 420-4000. **$129-$300.** 10205 100th Ave T5J 4B5. Just se of jct 102nd St and 100th Ave. Int corridors. **Pets:** Accepted.
ⒺⒸⓄ 🛜 🛏 💻 🍴 🥤

ⒶⒸⒶ ♦♦ Comfort Inn West Ⓗ
(780) 484-4415. **$99-$154.** 17610 100th Ave T5S 1S9. At 176th St. Int corridors. **Pets:** Accepted. ⒺⒸⓄ ⓈⒶⓋⒺ 🛜 ♿ 🛏 💻 🍴

ⒶⒸⒶ ♦♦ Continental Inn Ⓗ
(780) 484-7751. **$110-$145, 6 day notice.** 16625 Stony Plain Rd T5P 4A8. On Hwy 16A (Stony Plain Rd) at 166th St. Int corridors. **Pets:** Small. $5 one-time fee/pet. Designated rooms, service with restrictions, supervision. ⓈⒶⓋⒺ 🛜 🛏 💻 🍴

▼▼▼▼ **Courtyard by Marriott Edmonton** 🅷
(780) 423-9999. **$123-$161.** 1 Thornton Ct T5J 2E7. Just off Jasper Ave; between 99th and 97th sts. Int corridors. **Pets:** Large, other species. $35 one-time fee/room. Designated rooms, service with restrictions, supervision. 🛜 ✖ ⅏ 🍴 ▥

🅐🅐 ▼▼▼▼ **Delta Edmonton Centre Suite Hotel** 🅷 ❀
(780) 429-3900. **$109-$156.** 10222 102nd St NW T5J 4C5. At 102nd St NW and 103rd Ave NW. Int corridors. **Pets:** Large, other species. $35 one-time fee/pet. Service with restrictions, crate.
🄴🄲🄾 🅂🄰🅅🄴 🛜 ✖ ⅏ 🗄 🖥 🍴 ▥

🅐🅐 ▼▼▼▼ **Delta Edmonton South Hotel and Conference Centre** 🅷
(780) 434-6415. **$100-$300.** 4404 Gateway Blvd T6H 5C2. Jct Calgary Tr (Hwy 2) and Whitemud Dr. Int corridors. **Pets:** Medium, other species. $35 daily fee/room. Service with restrictions, supervision.
🄴🄲🄾 🅂🄰🅅🄴 🛜 ✖ 🗄 🖥 🍴 ☭

🅐🅐 ▼▼▼▼ **Edmonton Hotel and Convention Centre** 🅷
(780) 468-5400. **$119-$249.** 4520 76th Ave T6B 0A5. Hwy 14, just s via 50th St exit, then just e. Int corridors. **Pets:** Small, dogs only. $15 daily fee/pet. Designated rooms, service with restrictions, supervision.
🅂🄰🅅🄴 🛜 🗄 🖥 🍴 ☭ ▥

▼▼ ▼▼ **Executive Royal Inn West Edmonton** 🅷 ❀
(780) 484-6000. **$120.** 10010 178th St T5S 1T3. Corner of 178th St and 100th Ave. Int corridors. **Pets:** $25 daily fee/room. Designated rooms, service with restrictions, supervision. 🄴🄲🄾 🛜 ✖ 🗄 🖥 🍴

🅐🅐 ▼▼▼▼▼ **The Fairmont Hotel Macdonald** 🅷 ❀
(780) 424-5181. **$199-$399, 3 day notice.** 10065 100th St T5J 0N6. Just s of Jasper Ave. Int corridors. **Pets:** Small, other species. $25 daily fee/pet. Designated rooms, service with restrictions, supervision.
🄴🄲🄾 🅂🄰🅅🄴 🛜 ⅏ 🖥 🍴 ☭ ▥

🅐🅐 ▼▼▼▼▼ **Four Points by Sheraton Edmonton South** 🅷
(780) 465-7931. **$125, 7 day notice.** 7230 Argyll Rd T6C 4A6. Hwy 2 (Gateway Blvd), 2.3 mi (3.7 km) e at 63rd Ave (which becomes Argyll Rd); at 75th St. Int corridors. **Pets:** Accepted.
🅂🄰🅅🄴 🛜 ✖ ⅏ 🗄 🖥 🍴 ☭ ▥

▼▼▼▼ **Holiday Inn Express & Suites Edmonton South** 🅷
(780) 440-5000. **$129-$159.** 2440 Calgary Tr T6J 5J6. Hwy 2, just w at 31st Ave, then 0.5 mi (0.9 km) s on 104th St; Hwy 2 northbound, just w at 23 Ave, then just n. Int corridors. **Pets:** Accepted.
🛜 ✖ ⅏ 🗄 🖥 ☭

🅐🅐 ▼▼▼▼ **Holiday Inn Express Edmonton Downtown** 🅷
(780) 423-2450. **$149-$199.** 10010 104th St T5J 0Z1. Corner of 100th Ave; centre. Int corridors. **Pets:** Small. $25 one-time fee/pet. Designated rooms, service with restrictions, supervision.
🄴🄲🄾 🅂🄰🅅🄴 🛜 ✖ ⅏ 🗄 🖥 ☭ ▥

🅐🅐 ▼▼▼▼ **Mayfield Inn & Suites at West Edmonton** 🅷
(780) 484-0821. **$129-$225.** 16615 109th Ave T5P 4K8. 1 mi (1.6 km) n of jct Hwy 2 (170th St) and 16A (Stony Plain Rd). Int corridors. **Pets:** $35 daily fee/pet. Designated rooms, service with restrictions, supervision.
🄴🄲🄾 🅂🄰🅅🄴 🛜 ✖ 🗄 🖥 🍴 ☭ ▥

▼▼▼▼ **Metterra Hotel on Whyte** 🅷
(780) 465-8150. **$139-$359.** 10454 82nd Ave (Whyte Ave) T6E 4Z7. Just e of 105th St. Int corridors. **Pets:** Accepted. 🛜 ✖ ⅏ 🗄 🖥

▼▼ ▼▼ **Quality Inn West Harvest** 🅷 ❀
(780) 484-8000. **$109-$119.** 17803 Stony Plain Rd NW T5S 1B4. Hwy 16A (Stony Plain Rd) at 178th St. Int corridors. **Pets:** Large, other species. $20 daily fee/pet. Designated rooms, service with restrictions, supervision. 🛜 ✖ 🗄 🖥 🍴

🅐🅐 ▼▼▼▼ **Radisson Hotel Edmonton South** 🅷
(780) 437-6010. **$165-$250.** 4440 Gateway Blvd NW T6H 5C2. Between Whitemud Dr and 45th Ave. Int corridors. **Pets:** Other species. $10 daily fee/pet. Service with restrictions, supervision.
🄴🄲🄾 🅂🄰🅅🄴 🛜 🗄 🖥 🍴 ☭ ▥

🅐🅐 ▼▼▼▼ **Sawridge Inn Edmonton South** 🅷
(780) 438-1222. **$109-$189.** 4235 Gateway Blvd T6J 5H2. Just s of Whitemud Dr. Int corridors. **Pets:** Accepted.
🄴🄲🄾 🅂🄰🅅🄴 🛜 ✖ 🗄 🖥 🍴 ▥

▼▼ ▼▼ **Super 8 Edmonton South** 🅷
(780) 433-8688. **$114-$132.** 3610 Gateway Blvd T6J 7H8. Jct 36th Ave. Int corridors. **Pets:** Accepted. 🛜 ✖ ⅏ 🗄 🖥 ☭ ▥

▼▼▼▼ **The Sutton Place Hotel Edmonton** 🅷
(780) 428-7111. **$259-$450.** 10235 101st St T5J 3E9. 102nd Ave at 101st St. Int corridors. **Pets:** Accepted.
🄴🄲🄾 🛜 ✖ 🗄 🖥 🍴 ☭ ▥

🅐🅐 ▼▼ ▼▼ **Travelodge Edmonton East** 🅷
(780) 474-0456. **$71-$89.** 3414 118th Ave T5W 0Z4. 5 mi (8 km) e of Capilano Dr, 0.6 mi (1 km) s from W Hwy 16 (Yellowhead Tr) exit Victoria Tr. Int corridors. **Pets:** Medium, dogs only. $100 deposit/room, $25 one-time fee/room, $15 daily fee/room. Designated rooms, service with restrictions, supervision. 🄴🄲🄾 🅂🄰🅅🄴 🛜 🗄 🖥 🍴

🅐🅐 ▼▼ ▼▼ **Travelodge Edmonton South** 🅷
(780) 436-9770. **$90-$144.** 10320 45th Ave S T6H 5K3. Jct Calgary Tr (Hwy 2) and 45th Ave, just n of Whitemud Dr. Int corridors.
Pets: Accepted. 🄴🄲🄾 🅂🄰🅅🄴 🛜 🗄 🖥 ☭

▼▼▼▼ **Varscona Hotel on Whyte** 🅷
(780) 434-6111. **$125-$400.** 8208 106th St T6E 6R9. Corner of 82nd Ave (Whyte Ave) and 106th St. Int corridors. **Pets:** Accepted.
🄴🄲🄾 🛜 ✖ 🗄 🖥 🍴

▼▼ ▼▼ **West Edmonton Mall Inn** 🅷
(780) 444-9378. **$119-$194.** 17504 90th Ave T5T 6L6. From Whitemud Dr exit 170th St N, just w. Int corridors. **Pets:** Accepted.
🛜 ✖ ⅏ 🗄 🖥

🅐🅐 ▼▼▼▼ **The Westin Edmonton** 🅷
(780) 426-3636. **$119-$489.** 10135 100th St T5J 0N7. 101st Ave at 100th St. Int corridors. **Pets:** Accepted.
🄴🄲🄾 🅂🄰🅅🄴 🛜 ✖ 🗄 🖥 🍴 ☭ ▥

▼▼▼▼ **Wingate Inn Edmonton West** 🅷
(780) 443-1000. **$129-$147.** 18220 100th Ave T5S 2V2. From Anthony Henday Dr, 0.9 mi (1.5 km) e at 182nd St. Int corridors. **Pets:** Accepted.
🛜 ✖ 🗄 🖥 🍴 ☭ ▥

FORT SASKATCHEWAN

🅐🅐 ▼▼ ▼▼ **Lakeview Inns & Suites** 🅷
(780) 998-7888. **$125-$179.** 10115 88th Ave T8L 2T1. Just w of Hwy 15/21 and 101st St. Int corridors. **Pets:** Accepted.
🄴🄲🄾 🅂🄰🅅🄴 🛜 🗄 🖥 🍴

🅐🅐 ▼▼▼▼ **Musgrave's Hospitality Inns & Suites** 🅷 ❀
(780) 998-2770. **$139-$199.** 9820 86th Ave T8L 4P4. Just sw of Hwy 15/21 and 101st St. Int corridors. **Pets:** Small, dogs only. $25 daily fee/pet. Designated rooms, service with restrictions, crate.
🅂🄰🅅🄴 🛜 ✖ ⅏ 🗄 🖥

ST. ALBERT

🅐🅐 ▼▼▼▼ **Best Western Plus The Inn at St. Albert** 🅷 ❀
(780) 470-3800. **$145-$165.** 460 St. Albert Tr T8N 5J9. Hwy 2 (St. Albert Tr), just w at Lennox Dr. Int corridors. **Pets:** Medium. $20 daily fee/room. Designated rooms, service with restrictions, crate.
🅂🄰🅅🄴 🛜 ✖ 🗄 🖥 ☭

SHERWOOD PARK

▼▼▼▼ Coast Edmonton East Hotel H
(780) 464-4900. **Call for rates.** 2100 Premier Way T8H 2G4. Hwy 16 exit Broadmoor Blvd, 0.6 mi (1 km) sw. Int corridors. **Pets:** Accepted.
🛰 ✕ 📦 💻 🍽

◑ ▼▼ Franklin's Inn H
(780) 467-1234. **$129-$169, 3 day notice.** 2016 Sherwood Dr T8A 3X3. At Granada Blvd. Int corridors. **Pets:** Accepted.
SAVE 🛰 📦 💻 🍽

◑ ▼▼▼▼ MainStay Suites East Edmonton/Sherwood Park H
(780) 570-8080. **Call for rates.** 201 Palisades Way T8H 0N3. Hwy 16 exit 403 (Sherwood Dr), 0.9 mi (1.5 km) s. Int corridors. **Pets:** Accepted.
SAVE 🛰 📦 💻

▼▼ Ramada Limited-Edmonton East/Sherwood Park H
(780) 467-6727. **$112-$142.** 30 Broadway Blvd T8H 2A2. Hwy 16 exit Broadmoor Blvd, 1.2 mi (2 km) s. Int corridors. **Pets:** Accepted.
🛰 ✕ 📦 💻

◑ ▼▼ ▼▼ Super 8 Sherwood Park/Edmonton Area H
(780) 464-1000. **Call for rates.** 26 Strathmoor Dr T8H 2B6. Hwy 16 exit Broadmoor Blvd, just sw. Int corridors. **Pets:** Accepted.
SAVE 🛰 📦 💻 🍽

STONY PLAIN

◑ ▼▼▼▼ Best Western Sunrise Inn & Suites H
(780) 968-1716. **$149-$160.** 3101 43rd Ave T7Z 1L1. Hwy 16A (Township Rd 530), just s at S Park Dr, then just e. Int corridors.
Pets: Medium, other species. $25 one-time fee/room. Designated rooms, service with restrictions, supervision.
SAVE 🛰 ✕ 📦 💻 🏊 ✕

▼▼ Motel 6 Stony Plain #5707 H
(780) 968-5123. **Call for rates.** 66 Boulder Blvd T7Z 1V7. Just off Hwy 16A (Township Rd 530). Int corridors. **Pets:** Other species. Service with restrictions, supervision. ECO ✕ 📦

▼▼ Ramada Inn & Suites H
(780) 963-0222. **$99-$185.** 3301 43rd Ave T7Z 1L1. Hwy 16A (Township Rd 530), just s on S Park Dr, then just e. Ext/int corridors. **Pets:** Medium, other species. $25 one-time fee/room. Designated rooms, service with restrictions, supervision. 🛰 📦 💻 🍽 🏊

END METROPOLITAN AREA

EDSON

◑ ▼▼▼▼ Best Western High Road Inn H
(780) 712-2378. **$129-$139.** 300 52nd St T7E 1V8. On 2nd Ave; centre. Int corridors. **Pets:** Accepted. SAVE 🛰 ⬛ 📦 💻 🍽 🏊 ✕

▼▼ Guest House Inn & Suites M
(780) 723-4486. **Call for rates.** 4411 4th Ave T7E 1B8. 0.6 mi (1 km) e on Hwy 16. Ext/int corridors. **Pets:** Accepted. 🛰 📦 💻 🍽 ✕

◑ ▼▼▼▼ Lakeview Inn & Suites Edson Airport West H
(780) 723-7508. **Call for rates.** 528 63rd St T7E 1M1. Hwy 16, west end of town. Int corridors. **Pets:** $25 one-time fee/room. Designated rooms, service with restrictions, supervision.
ECO SAVE 🛰 ⬛ 📦 💻

◑ ▼▼▼▼ Lakeview Inns & Suites East H
(780) 723-2500. **Call for rates.** 4300 2nd Ave T7E 1B8. 0.6 mi (1.1 km) e on Hwy 16. Int corridors. **Pets:** Accepted. ECO SAVE 🛰 📦 💻

FORT MACLEOD

◑ ▼▼ Sunset Motel M
(403) 553-4448. **$80-$88.** 104 Hwy 3 W T0L 0Z0. 0.6 mi (1 km) w on Hwy 2 and 3. Ext corridors. **Pets:** Accepted. SAVE 🛰 📦 💻

FORT MCMURRAY

▼▼ Vantage Inn & Suites H
(780) 713-4111. **Call for rates.** 200 Parent Way T9H 5E6. 3.1 mi (5 km) s on Hwy 63 (Sakitawaw Tr). Int corridors. **Pets:** Accepted.
ECO 📦 💻

FOX CREEK

▼▼▼▼ Sandbrar Inn & Suites H
(780) 622-4434. **$150-$170.** 70 1st Ave T0H 1P0. Hwy 43, just n on Keybob Dr, then just e. Int corridors. **Pets:** Accepted.
🛰 ⬛ 📦 💻

GRANDE PRAIRIE

◑ ▼▼▼▼ Best Western Grande Prairie Hotel & Suites H
(780) 402-2378. **$140-$165, 3 day notice.** 10745 117th Ave T8V 7N6. Corner of Hwy 43 (100th Ave) and 117th Ave. Int corridors.
Pets: Accepted. ECO SAVE 🛰 📦 💻 🍽 🏊

▼▼▼▼ Days Inn Grande Prairie H
(780) 532-2773. **Call for rates.** 10218-162nd Ave T8V 0P2. Jct Hwy 2 and 43 (100th Ave), just s. Int corridors. **Pets:** Accepted. 🛰 📦 💻

▼▼ Grande Prairie Inn H
(780) 532-5221. **$119-$129.** 11633 100th St T8V 3Y4. Jct Hwy 43 (100th Ave) and 116th Ave. Int corridors. **Pets:** Accepted.
ECO 🛰 📦 💻 🍽 🏊 ✕

◑ ▼▼▼▼ Holiday Inn Hotel & Suites H 🐾
(780) 402-6886. **$135-$165.** 9816-107th St T8V 8E7. Jct Hwy 43 (100th Ave) and 40 (108th St). Int corridors. **Pets:** $25 daily fee/room. Designated rooms, service with restrictions, supervision.
ECO SAVE 🛰 ⬛ 📦 💻 🍽 🏊 ✕

▼▼▼▼ Motel 6 Grande Prairie #5709 H
(780) 830-7744. **Call for rates.** 15402 101st St T8V 0P7. Jct Hwy 2 and 43 (100th Ave), just s. Int corridors. **Pets:** Other species. Service with restrictions, supervision. ECO ⬛ 📦 💻

▼▼▼▼ Podollan Inn & Spa H
(780) 830-2000. **$159-$199.** 10612 99th Ave T8V 8E8. Jct Hwy 43 (100th Ave) and 40 (108th St), just e. Int corridors. **Pets:** Other species. $25 daily fee/pet. Service with restrictions, crate. 🛰 📦 💻 🍽

◑ ▼▼ ▼▼ Pomeroy Inn & Suites, Grande Prairie H 🐾
(780) 831-2999. **$150-$160.** 11710 102nd St T8V 7S7. 102nd St at 117th Ave. Int corridors. **Pets:** Other species. $30 one-time fee/room. Service with restrictions, crate. ECO SAVE 🛰 📦 💻 🏊 ✕

◑ ▼▼ ▼▼ Quality Hotel & Conference Centre Grande Prairie H 🐾
(780) 539-6000. **$99-$149.** 11201 100th Ave T8V 5M6. 1.8 mi (2.9 km) w on Hwy 2. Int corridors. **Pets:** Other species. $10 daily fee/pet. Designated rooms, service with restrictions, supervision.
ECO SAVE 📦 💻 🍽

▼▼▼▼ Service Plus Inns and Suites H
(780) 538-3900. **$159-$300.** 10810 107A Ave T8V 7A9. 1.4 mi (2.2 km) w on Hwy 2, just n. Int corridors. **Pets:** Accepted.
🛰 📦 💻 🏊 ✕

◆ Stanford Inn H
(780) 539-5678. **$99-$120.** 11401 100th Ave T8V 5M6. Hwy 2 and 43 (100th Ave), just e of 116 St. Ext/int corridors. **Pets:** Accepted.
ECO 🛰 🛏 💻 🍴

CAA ◆◆ Stonebridge Hotel H
(780) 539-5561. **$129-$189.** 12102 100th St T8V 5P1. 100th St at 121st Ave. Int corridors. **Pets:** Accepted. SAVE 🛰 🛏 💻 🍴

◆◆ Super 8 H
(780) 532-8288. **$117-$144.** 10050 116th Ave T8V 4K5. 102nd St at 117th Ave. Int corridors. **Pets:** Accepted. ECO 🛰 🛏 💻 🏊 ✕

GRIMSHAW

◆◆◆ Pomeroy Inn & Suites H
(780) 332-2000. **Call for rates.** 4311 51st St T0H 1W0. Hwy 2, south end of town. Int corridors. **Pets:** Accepted.
ECO 🛰 🛏 💻 🏊 ✕

HANNA

◆◆ Super 8 Hanna H
(403) 854-2400. **$117-$126.** 113 Palliser Tr T0J 1P0. Hwy 9, just n. Ext/int corridors. **Pets:** Accepted. ECO 🛰 🛏 💻

HIGH LEVEL

CAA ◆◆◆ Best Western Plus Mirage Hotel & Resort H
(780) 821-1000. **$160-$170.** 9616 Hwy 58 T0H 1Z0. Jct Hwy 35 and 58. Ext/int corridors. **Pets:** Other species. $10 daily fee/pet. Designated rooms, service with restrictions. SAVE 🛰 🛏 💻 🍴 🏊 ✕

CAA ◆◆◆ Super 8 High Level H 🐾
(780) 841-3448. **$50-$100.** 9502 114th Ave T0H 1Z0. Hwy 35, just se, south end of town. Ext/int corridors. **Pets:** $25 one-time fee/room. Service with restrictions, supervision. ECO SAVE 🛰 🛦M 🛏 💻 🏊 ✕

HIGH PRAIRIE

◆◆◆ Peavine Inn & Suites H
(780) 523-2398. **$149-$169.** 3905 51st Ave T0G 1E0. Hwy 2, just n; east end of town. Ext/int corridors. **Pets:** Accepted.
🛰 🛏 💻 🍴 🏊 ✕

HIGH RIVER

◆◆ Heritage Inn H
(403) 652-3834. **$129-$190.** 1104 11th Ave SE T1V 1M4. Trans-Canada Hwy 2 exit 23, 0.5 mi (0.8 km) w of Hwy 2. Int corridors. **Pets:** Medium, dogs only. $20 daily fee/pet. Designated rooms, service with restrictions, crate. 🛰 🛏 💻 🍴 🏊

◆◆◆ Super 8 H
(403) 652-4448. **$108-$126.** 1601 13th Ave SE T1V 2B1. Trans-Canada Hwy 2 exit High River, just w. Int corridors. **Pets:** Accepted.
ECO 🛰 ✕ 🛏 💻 🏊 ✕

HINTON

CAA ◆◆◆ Best Western White Wolf Inn H
(780) 865-7777. **Call for rates.** 828 Carmichael Ln T7V 1T1. At west end of town; just off Hwy 16. Ext corridors. **Pets:** Accepted.
SAVE 🛰 🛏 💻

◆◆◆ Holiday Inn Hinton H
(780) 865-3321. **$129-$149.** 393 Gregg Ave T7V 1N1. 0.3 mi (0.5 km) w on Hwy 16. Int corridors. **Pets:** Accepted.
ECO 🛰 🛦M 🛏 💻 🍴 🏊 ✕

CAA ◆◆◆ Lakeview Inns & Suites H
(780) 865-2575. **Call for rates.** 500 Smith St T7V 2A1. 1.1 mi (1.7 km) e on Hwy 16. Ext/int corridors. **Pets:** Accepted.
ECO SAVE 🛰 🛏 💻

◆◆ Overlander Mountain Lodge CI
(780) 866-2330. **Call for rates.** Hwy 16 T7V 1X5. Hwy 16, 15 mi (24 km) w; just outside Jasper National Park gates. Ext/int corridors.
Pets: Accepted. 🛰 ✕ 🛏 💻 🍴 🐟

◆◆ Super 8 H
(780) 817-2228. **$81-$128.** 284 Smith St T7V 2A1. 1 mi (1.6 km) e on Hwy 16. Int corridors. **Pets:** Accepted. 🛰 🛏 💻 🏊

JASPER

CAA ◆◆◆ Amethyst Lodge H 🐾
(780) 852-3394. **$85-$285.** 200 Connaught Dr T0E 1E0. 0.3 mi (0.5 km) e. Ext/int corridors. **Pets:** Other species. $15 daily fee/room. Service with restrictions, crate. ECO SAVE 🛰 ✕ 🛏 💻 🍴

CAA ◆◆◆◆ Best Western Jasper Inn & Suites H 🐾
(780) 852-4461. **Call for rates.** 98 Geikie St T0E 1E0. Corner of Geikie and Bonhomme sts. Ext/int corridors. **Pets:** Dogs only. $25 daily fee/room. Designated rooms, service with restrictions, supervision.
SAVE 🛰 ✕ 🛏 💻 🍴 🏊 ✕ 🐾

CAA ◆◆◆◆ Chateau Jasper H 🐾
(780) 852-5644. **$109-$295.** 96 Geikie St T0E 1E0. Corner of Juniper and Geikie sts. Int corridors. **Pets:** Other species. $15 daily fee/room. Service with restrictions, crate. ECO SAVE 🛰 ✕ 🛏 💻 🍴 🏊

CAA ◆◆◆◆ The Coast Pyramid Lake Resort H
(780) 852-4900. **$161-$368, 3 day notice.** Pyramid Lake Rd T0E 1E0. Jct Connaught Dr and Cedar St, 3.8 mi (6 km) nw via Pyramid Lake Rd. Ext corridors. **Pets:** $25 one-time fee/pet. Designated rooms, service with restrictions, crate. ECO SAVE 🛰 ✕ 🛏 💻 🍴 🏊 ✕ 🐾

CAA ◆◆◆◆ The Fairmont Jasper Park Lodge H 🐾
(780) 852-3301. **$229-$499, 3 day notice.** 1 Old Lodge Rd T0E 1E0. 3 mi (4.8 km) ne via Hwy 16, 2 mi (3.2 km) se off highway via Maligne Rd, follow signs. Ext corridors. **Pets:** Other species. $50 daily fee/room. Service with restrictions, supervision.
ECO SAVE 🛰 ✕ 🛦M 🛏 💻 🍴 🏊 ✕ 🐾

CAA ◆◆◆◆ Lobstick Lodge H 🐾
(780) 852-4431. **$99-$255.** 94 Geikie St T0E 1E0. Corner of Geikie and Juniper sts. Int corridors. **Pets:** Other species. $15 daily fee/room. Service with restrictions, crate.
ECO SAVE 🛰 ✕ 🛏 💻 🍴 🏊 ✕ 🐾

CAA ◆◆◆ Marmot Lodge M 🐾
(780) 852-4471. **$89-$255.** 86 Connaught Dr T0E 1E0. 1 mi (1.6 km) ne. Ext corridors. **Pets:** Other species. $15 daily fee/room. Service with restrictions, crate. ECO SAVE 🛰 ✕ 🛦M 🛏 💻 🏊

◆◆ Patricia Lake Bungalows CA
(780) 852-3560. **$87-$325, 7 day notice.** Pyramid Lake Rd T0E 1E0. 3 mi (4.8 km) nw via Pyramid Lake Rd. Ext corridors. **Pets:** Medium, dogs only. $10 daily fee/pet. Designated rooms, service with restrictions, supervision. 🛰 ✕ 🛏 💻 ✕ 🐟

CAA ◆◆◆ The Sawridge Inn and Conference Centre H
(780) 852-5111. **$87-$281, 3 day notice.** 76 Connaught Dr T0E 1E0. 1.1 mi (1.7 km) e. Int corridors. **Pets:** Accepted.
ECO SAVE 🛰 ✕ 🛦M 🛏 💻 🍴 🏊 ✕

CAA ◆◆◆ Sunwapta Falls Rocky Mountain Lodge CA
(780) 852-4852. **$99-$379.** Hwy 93 T0E 1E0. 34.7 mi (55 km) s on Icefields Pkwy (Hwy 93). Ext corridors. **Pets:** Accepted.
SAVE 🛰 ✕ 🛏 💻 🍴 ✕ 🐾 🐟

◆◆ Tonquin Inn M 🐾
(780) 852-4987. **$135-$400, 3 day notice.** 100 Juniper St T0E 1E0. Corner of Juniper and Geikie sts. Ext/int corridors. **Pets:** Medium. $25 one-time fee/pet. Designated rooms, service with restrictions, supervision.
🛰 ✕ 🛏 💻 🍴 🏊 ✕

KANANASKIS

(CAA) ▼▼▼▼ Delta Lodge at Kananaskis H ❀

(403) 591-7711. **$139-$309, 3 day notice.** Kananaskis Village T0L 2H0. Trans-Canada Hwy 1, 14.7 mi (23.5 km) s on Hwy 40 (Kananaskis Tr), then 1.8 mi (3 km) on Kananaskis Village access road, follow signs. Int corridors. **Pets:** Other species. $35 one-time fee/room. Service with restrictions. ⟦ECO⟧ ⟦SAVE⟧ 🛜 ⨯ 📶 💻 🍴 ⇌ ⊠

LAKE LOUISE

(CAA) ▼▼▼ ▼▼▼ The Fairmont Chateau Lake Louise H ❀

(403) 522-3511. **$279-$2123, 3 day notice.** 111 Lake Louise Dr T0L 1E0. 1.8 mi (3 km) up the hill from the village. Int corridors. **Pets:** Medium. $25 daily fee/room. Designated rooms, service with restrictions, supervision. ⟦ECO⟧ ⟦SAVE⟧ 🛜 ⨯ 📶 💻 🍴 ⇌ ⊠

▼▼ ▼▼ Lake Louise Inn H

(403) 522-3791. **$113-$176, 7 day notice.** 210 Village Rd T0L 1E0. Just w of 4-way stop. Ext/int corridors. **Pets:** $50 one-time fee/room. Designated rooms. 🛜 ⨯ 📶 💻 🍴 ⇌ ⊠

LETHBRIDGE

▼▼ ▼▼ Comfort Inn H

(403) 320-8874. **$119-$199.** 3226 Fairway Plaza Rd S T1K 7T5. Hwy 3 (Crowsnest Tr) exit Mayor Magrath Dr S, 1.8 mi (3 km) s, then just e on 24th Ave. Int corridors. **Pets:** Accepted. 🛜 📶 💻 ⇌

▼▼ ▼▼ Days Inn Lethbridge H

(403) 327-6000. **$94-$117.** 100 3rd Ave S T1J 4L2. Corner of 3rd Ave and Scenic Dr; centre. Ext/int corridors. **Pets:** Medium, other species. $10 daily fee/pet. Designated rooms, service with restrictions, crate. ⟦ECO⟧ 🛜 📶 💻 ⇌

▼▼ ▼▼ ▼▼ Holiday Inn Express Hotel & Suites Lethbridge H

(403) 394-9292. **$139-$229.** 120 Stafford Dr S T1J 4W4. Hwy 3 (Crowsnest Tr) exit Stafford Dr, just s; downtown. Int corridors. **Pets:** Accepted. 🛜 ⨯ 📶 💻 ⇌ ⊠

▼▼ ▼▼ ▼▼ Holiday Inn Hotel Lethbridge H

(403) 380-5050. **$89-$199.** 2375 Mayor Magrath Dr S T1K 7M1. Hwy 3 (Crowsnest Tr) exit Mayor Magrath Dr S, 1.8 mi (3 km) s, then just e on 22nd St. Int corridors. **Pets:** Accepted. ⟦ECO⟧ 🛜 ⨯ 📶 💻 🍴 ⇌ ⊠

(CAA) ▼▼ ▼▼ ▼▼ Lethbridge Lodge Hotel and Conference Centre H

(403) 328-1123. **$109-$199.** 320 Scenic Dr T1J 4B4. Scenic Dr at 4th Ave S; centre. Int corridors. **Pets:** Accepted. ⟦ECO⟧ ⟦SAVE⟧ 🛜 ⨯ 📶 💻 🍴 ⇌

(CAA) ▼▼ ▼▼ Quality Inn & Suites H

(403) 331-6440. **$120-$202.** 4040 2nd Ave S T1J 3Z2. Hwy 3 (Crowsnest Tr), just s on WT Hill Blvd, then just e. Int corridors. **Pets:** Designated rooms, service with restrictions, supervision. ⟦SAVE⟧ 🛜 ⟦&M⟧ 📶 💻 ⇌ ⊠

▼▼ ▼▼ Sandman Hotel Lethbridge H

(403) 328-1111. **$114-$179.** 421 Mayor Magrath Dr S T1J 3L8. Hwy 3 (Crowsnest Tr) exit Mayor Magrath Dr S, just s. Int corridors. **Pets:** Other species. $10 daily fee/pet. Designated rooms, service with restrictions. ⟦ECO⟧ 🛜 📶 💻 🍴 ⇌

MEDICINE HAT

(CAA) ▼▼ ▼▼ Best Western Plus Sun Country H ❀

(403) 527-3700. **$112-$142.** 722 Redcliff Dr T1A 5E3. On Trans-Canada Hwy 1, 0.3 mi (0.4 km) w of jct Hwy 3, access 7th St SW. Ext/int corridors. **Pets:** Small. $14 daily fee/pet. Designated rooms, service with restrictions, supervision. ⟦ECO⟧ ⟦SAVE⟧ 🛜 ⟦&M⟧ 📶 💻 ⇌ ⊠

▼▼ ▼▼ ▼▼ Holiday Inn Express Hotel & Suites H

(403) 504-5151. **$159-$199.** 9 Strachan Bay SE T1B 4Y2. Trans-Canada Hwy 1, just s on Dunmore Rd, then just e; east end of city. Int corridors. **Pets:** Accepted. ⟦ECO⟧ 🛜 ⟦&M⟧ 📶 💻 ⇌ ⊠

▼▼ ▼▼ ▼▼ Medicine Hat Lodge Resort, Casino & Spa H

(403) 529-2222. **$109-$189.** 1051 Ross Glen Dr SE T1B 3T8. Trans-Canada Hwy 1, just n on Dunmore Rd. Int corridors. **Pets:** Other species. $10 daily fee/pet. Designated rooms, service with restrictions, crate. 🛜 ⨯ ⟦&M⟧ 📶 💻 ⇌ ⊠

▼▼ Motel 6-Medicine Hat #5700 H

(403) 527-1749. **$85-$95.** 20 Strachan Ct SE T1B 4R7. Trans-Canada Hwy 1, just s on Dunmore Rd, then just w; southeast end of city. Int corridors. **Pets:** Other species. Service with restrictions, supervision. ⟦ECO⟧ 🛜 📶

▼▼ ▼▼ Super 8 H

(403) 528-8888. **$86-$91.** 1280 Trans-Canada Way SE T1B 1J5. Trans-Canada Hwy 1 at 13th Ave SE; just n off Trans-Canada Hwy 1. Ext/int corridors. **Pets:** Medium. $10 daily fee/room. Designated rooms, service with restrictions, crate. 🛜 📶 💻 ⇌

MORLEY

▼▼ ▼▼ Stoney Nakoda Resort H

(403) 881-2830. **Call for rates.** Jct Trans-Canada Hwy 1 and Hwy 40 T0L 1N0. Jct Hwy 40, just s. Int corridors. **Pets:** Accepted. 🛜 📶 💻 🍴 ⇌ ⊠

PINCHER CREEK

▼▼ ▼▼ Heritage Inn H

(403) 627-5000. **$125-$277.** 919 Waterton Ave (Hwy 6) T0K 1W0. Hwy 3 (Crowsnest Tr), 1.3 mi (2.1 km) s, follow Hwy 6 (Waterton Ave) e, then 1.6 mi (2.6 km) s. Int corridors. **Pets:** Medium, dogs only. $20 daily fee/pet. Designated rooms, service with restrictions, crate. 🛜 📶 💻 🍴 ⇌

▼▼ ▼▼ ▼▼ Ramada Inn & Suites H

(403) 627-3777. **$132-$239.** 1132 Table Mountain St T0K 1W0. Hwy 3 (Crowsnest Tr), 1.3 mi (2.1 km) s on Hwy 6. Ext/int corridors. **Pets:** Other species. $15 daily fee/pet. Service with restrictions, supervision. ⟦ECO⟧ 🛜 ⨯ 📶 💻 ⇌ ⊠

RED DEER

(CAA) ▼▼ ▼▼ ▼▼ Best Western Plus Red Deer Inn & Suites H

(403) 346-3555. **$135-$155.** 6839 66th St T4P 3T5. Hwy 2 exit 67th St, just e. Int corridors. **Pets:** Accepted. ⟦ECO⟧ ⟦SAVE⟧ 🛜 ⟦&M⟧ 📶 💻 ⇌

(CAA) ▼▼ ▼▼ ▼▼ Comfort Inn & Suites H ❀

(403) 348-0025. **$105-$159.** 6846 66th St T4P 3T5. Hwy 2 exit 67th St, just e. Int corridors. **Pets:** Small. $20 one-time fee/room. Designated rooms. ⟦SAVE⟧ 📶 💻 ⇌ ⊠

▼▼ ▼▼ ▼▼ Hampton Inn & Suites by Hilton Red Deer H

(403) 346-6688. **$121-$158.** 37400 Hwy 2, #130 T4N 5E2. Hwy 2 exit 391 (Gasoline Alley), just w. Int corridors. **Pets:** Accepted. 🛜 ⨯ 📶 💻 ⇌

(CAA) ▼▼ ▼▼ ▼▼ Holiday Inn 67th Street H

(403) 342-6567. **$129-$149.** 6500 67th St T4P 1A2. Hwy 2 exit 67th St, 0.5 mi (0.8 km) e. Int corridors. **Pets:** Very small. $25 daily fee/pet. Designated rooms, service with restrictions, supervision. ⟦SAVE⟧ 🛜 ⟦&M⟧ 📶 💻 🍴 ⇌ ⊠

▼▼ Motel 6 - Red Deer H

(403) 340-1749. **$75-$109.** 900-5001 19th St T4R 3R1. Hwy 2 exit 394 (Gaetz Ave), just w; in Southpointe Common Shopping District. Int corridors. **Pets:** Other species. Service with restrictions, supervision. ⟦ECO⟧ 📶

(CAA) ▼▼ ▼▼ ▼▼ Quality Inn North Hill H

(403) 343-8800. **$129-$139.** 7150 50th Ave T4N 6A5. Hwy 2 exit 401 (67th St), 1.7 mi (2.9 km) e, then 0.5 mi (0.8 km) n. Int corridors. **Pets:** $200 deposit/room, $10 daily fee/room. Designated rooms, service with restrictions, crate. ⟦SAVE⟧ 🛜 📶 💻 🍴 ⇌

Ⓐ ▼▼▼ Red Deer Lodge Hotel and Conference
     Centre ❚
(403) 346-8841. **Call for rates.** 4311-49th Ave T4N 5Y7. Hwy 2 exit 394
(Gaetz Ave), 2.6 mi (4.2 km) n. Int corridors. **Pets:** Accepted.
ECO SAVE 🛜 ❚ 🖵 🍴 ⤢ ⊠

▼▼▼ Sandman Hotel Red Deer ❚
(403) 343-7400. **Call for rates.** 2818 Gaetz Ave T4R 1M4. 1 mi (1.6
km) n on Hwy 2A (Gaetz Ave). Int corridors. **Pets:** Accepted.
ECO 🛜 ❚ 🖵 🍴 ⤢

Ⓐ ▼▼▼ Sheraton Red Deer Hotel ❚ ❀
(403) 346-2091. **$159-$219.** 3310 50th Ave T4N 3X9. 1.3 mi (2 km) n
on Hwy 2A (Gaetz Ave). Int corridors. **Pets:** Medium, dogs only. Service
with restrictions, supervision. SAVE 🛜 ❚ 🖵 🍴 ⤢ ⊠

RIMBEY

Ⓐ ▼▼▼ Best Western Rimstone Ridge Hotel ❚ ❀
(403) 843-2999. **$120-$160.** 5501 50th Ave T0C 2J0. Hwy 20, 1.2 mi (2
km) e. Int corridors. **Pets:** Medium, dogs only. $20 daily fee/room. Service
with restrictions, supervision. SAVE 🛜 ⊠ ❚ 🖵 🍴 ⤢ ⊠

ROCKY MOUNTAIN HOUSE

Ⓐ ▼▼▼ Best Western Rocky Mountain House Inn &
     Suites ❚ ❀
(403) 844-3100. **$145-$165.** 4407 41st Ave T4T 1A5. Hwy 11 and 22,
just w on 42nd Ave, then just s; east end of town. Int corridors.
Pets: Other species. $20 daily fee/room. Service with restrictions, crate.
ECO SAVE 🛜 ❚ 🖵 ⤢ ⊠

▼▼ Rocky Inn Express ❚
(403) 845-2871. **Call for rates.** 4715 45th St T4T 1B1. Hwy 11 and 22,
just e on 47th Ave, then just n. Int corridors. **Pets:** Accepted.
ECO 🛜 ᴍ ❚ 🖵

▼▼ Super 8 ❚
(403) 846-0088. **$128-$147.** 4406 41st Ave T4T 1J6. Hwy 11 and 22,
just w on 42nd Ave, then just s; east end of town. Ext/int corridors.
Pets: Accepted. ECO 🛜 ⊠ ᴍ ❚ 🖵 ⤢ ⊠

SLAVE LAKE

Ⓐ ▼▼▼ Lakeview Inns & Suites ❚
(780) 849-9500. **$121-$190.** 1550 Holmes Tr SE T0G 2A3. Hwy 2, just
n, east end of town. Int corridors. **Pets:** Accepted.
ECO SAVE 🛜 ❚ 🖵

STETTLER

▼▼▼ Stettler Canalta ❚
(403) 742-3371. **$119-$149.** 6020 50th Ave T0C 2L2. Hwy 12 (50th
Ave); at 61st St. Ext/int corridors. **Pets:** Accepted.
🛜 ⊠ ᴍ ❚ 🖵 🍴 ⤢ ⊠

TABER

▼▼ Heritage Inn Taber ❚
(403) 223-4424. **$100-$165.** 4830 46th Ave T1G 2A4. Jct Hwy 3 and 36
S, 1.5 mi (2.5 km) se. Int corridors. **Pets:** Medium, dogs only. $20 daily
fee/pet. Designated rooms, service with restrictions, crate.
🛜 ❚ 🖵 🍴 ⊠

▼▼ Super 8 Taber ❚
(403) 223-8181. **$95-$107.** 5700 46th Ave T1G 2B1. Jct Hwy 3 and 36
S, 0.5 mi (0.9 km) se. Ext/int corridors. **Pets:** Accepted. 🛜 ❚ 🖵

THREE HILLS

Ⓐ ▼▼▼ Best Western Diamond Inn ❚
(403) 443-7889. **Call for rates.** 351 7th Ave N T0M 2A0. Hwy 21 and
27, 1.1 mi (1.9 km) w. Int corridors. **Pets:** Accepted.
SAVE 🛜 ❚ 🖵 🍴

VALLEYVIEW

Ⓐ ▼▼ Western Valley Inn Ⓜ
(780) 524-4000. **$79-$139.** 5402 Highway St T0H 3N0. Just w of jct Hwy
43 and 49. Ext corridors. **Pets:** Dogs only. $20 one-time fee/room. Serv-
ice with restrictions, supervision. SAVE 🛜 ❚ 🖵

WAINWRIGHT

Ⓐ ▼▼▼ Best Western Wainwright Inn & Suites ❚
(780) 845-9934. **$130-$150.** 1209 27th St T9W 0A2. Jct Hwy 14 and 41,
just e. Int corridors. **Pets:** Medium. $20 daily fee/pet. Designated rooms,
service with restrictions, supervision. SAVE 🛜 ᴍ ❚ 🖵 ⤢

WATERTON PARK

Ⓐ ▼▼▼ Bayshore Inn Resort & Spa Ⓜ
(403) 859-2211. **$122-$282, 3 day notice.** 111 Waterton Ave T0K 2M0.
Centre. Ext/int corridors. **Pets:** Accepted.
SAVE 🛜 ⊠ ᴍ ❚ 🖵 🍴

▼▼▼ Waterton Lakes Resort ❚
(403) 859-2150. **Call for rates.** 101 Clematis Ave T0K 2M0. Centre.
Ext/int corridors. **Pets:** Accepted. 🛜 ⊠ ❚ 🖵 🍴 ⤢ ⊠

WESTEROSE

▼▼ Village Creek Country Inn ❚
(780) 586-0006. **Call for rates.** 15 Village Dr, RR 2 T0C 2V0. Hwy 2
exit 482, 17.5 mi (28 km) w on Hwy 13; in Village at Pigeon Lake. Ext/int
corridors. **Pets:** Accepted. 🛜 ❚ 🖵

WESTLOCK

Ⓐ ▼▼▼ Best Western Westlock ❚
(780) 349-4102. **Call for rates.** 10520 100th St T7P 2C6. Jct Hwy 18
and 44, just e. Ext/int corridors. **Pets:** Accepted.
SAVE 🛜 ❚ 🖵 🍴

WETASKIWIN

Ⓐ ▼▼▼ Best Western Wayside Inn ❚
(780) 312-7300. **$125-$135.** 4103 56th St T9A 1V2. On Hwy 2A, just n
of jct Hwy 13 W. Int corridors. **Pets:** Accepted.
SAVE 🛜 ⊠ ❚ 🖵 🍴

▼▼ Super 8 ❚ ❀
(780) 361-3808. **$108-$129.** 3820 56th St T9A 2B2. On Hwy 2A, just s
of jct Hwy 13 W. Ext/int corridors. **Pets:** Dogs only. Designated rooms,
service with restrictions, supervision. 🛜 ❚ 🖵

WHITECOURT

▼▼▼ Holiday Inn Express & Suites Whitecourt ❚
(780) 778-2516. **$147-$167.** 4721-49th St T7S 1N5. Hwy 43, just n on
51st St, just e. Int corridors. **Pets:** Accepted. 🛜 ᴍ ❚ 🖵

Ⓐ ▼▼▼ Super 8 ❚
(780) 778-8908. **$117-$126.** 4121 Kepler St T7S 0A3. On Hwy 43, just e
of Hwy 32. Int corridors. **Pets:** Accepted. ECO SAVE 🛜 ❚ 🖵

BRITISH COLUMBIA

CITY INDEX

100 MILE HOUSE

▼▼ ▼▼ **100 Mile House Super 8** **M**
(250) 395-8888. **$120-$150.** 989 Alder Ave V0K 2E0. 0.6 mi (1 km) s on Hwy 97. Ext corridors. **Pets:** Accepted. 🛜 ✕ ᴧM 🛗 💻

ABBOTSFORD

Ⓐ ▼▼ ▼▼ **Abbotsford Super 8** **H**
(604) 853-1141. **$107-$116.** 1881 Sumas Way V2S 4L5. Trans-Canada Hwy 1 exit 92 (Town Centre), just n on Hwy 11. Ext/int corridors. **Pets:** Accepted. SAVE 🛜 ᴧM 🛗 💻 ⇌ ✕

Ⓐ ▼▼ ▼▼ **Best Western Bakerview Inn** **M** 🐾
(604) 859-1341. **$116-$146.** 1821 Sumas Way V2S 4L5. Trans-Canada Hwy 1 exit 92 (Town Centre), just n on Hwy 11. Ext corridors. **Pets:** Other species. Service with restrictions, supervision.
ECO SAVE 🛜 🛗 💻 ⇌

Ⓐ ▼▼ ▼▼ ▼▼ **Coast Abbotsford Hotel & Suites** **H**
(604) 853-1880. **$112-$122.** 2020 Sumas Way V2S 2C7. Trans-Canada Hwy 1 exit 92 (Town Centre), just n on Hwy 11. Int corridors. **Pets:** Accepted. ECO SAVE 🛜 ✕ ᴧM 🛗 💻 ⇌

BARRIERE

▼▼ ▼▼ **Mountain Springs Motel & RV Park** **M**
(250) 672-0090. **$75-$80, 7 day notice.** 4253 Yellowhead Hwy V0E 1E0. 0.6 mi (1 km) s on Hwy 5 (Yellowhead Hwy). Ext corridors. **Pets:** Accepted. 🛜 ✕ ᴧM 🛗 💻

BLUE RIVER

▼▼ ▼▼ **Glacier Mountain Lodge** **H**
(250) 673-2393. **$99-$209.** 869 Shell Rd V0E 1J0. On Hwy 5 (Yellowhead Hwy); at Shell Rd, follow signs. Int corridors. **Pets:** Accepted. 🛜 ✕ 🛗

CACHE CREEK

Ⓐ ▼▼ ▼▼ **Bonaparte Motel** **M**
(250) 457-9693. **$59-$129.** 1395 Hwy 97 N V0K 1H0. Just n of jct Trans-Canada Hwy 1. Ext corridors. **Pets:** Small, dogs only. $10 daily fee/pet. Designated rooms, service with restrictions, supervision. SAVE 🛜 ✕ 🛗 💻 ⇌

CAMPBELL RIVER

▼▼ ▼▼ **Anchor Inn & Suites** **H**
(250) 286-1131. **$99-$149.** 261 Island Hwy V9W 2B3. On Island Hwy 19A, 1.3 mi (2 km) s. Int corridors. **Pets:** Accepted. 🛜 ᴧM 🛗 💻 ⇌ 🍴 ⇌ ℀

Ⓐ ▼▼ ▼▼ ▼▼ **Best Western Plus Austrian Chalet** **M**
(250) 923-4231. **$90-$140.** 462 S Island Hwy V9W 1A5. 2 mi (3.2 km) s on Island Hwy 19A. Ext/int corridors. **Pets:** Other species. $20 one-time fee/room. Designated rooms, service with restrictions, supervision.
SAVE 🛜 ᴧM 🛗 💻 ⇌ ✕

▼▼ ▼▼ **Ocean Resort** **M**
(250) 923-4281. **Call for rates.** 4834 S Island Hwy V9H 1E8. 11 mi (18 km) s on Island Hwy 19A. Int corridors. **Pets:** Accepted.
🛜 ✕ 🛗 ✕ ℀

▼▼ ▼▼ **Town Centre Inn** **M**
(250) 287-8866. **Call for rates.** 1500 Dogwood St V9W 3A6. Follow Island Hwy 19A through town, watch for signs, just e; corner of 16th Ave. Ext corridors. **Pets:** Accepted. 🛜 🛗 💻 ℀

▼▼ ▼▼ **Travelodge Campbell River** **M**
(250) 286-6622. **$63-$86.** 340 S Island Hwy V9W 1A5. 1.9 mi (3 km) s on Island Hwy 19A. Int corridors. **Pets:** Accepted.
ECO 🛜 ᴧM 🛗 💻 ⇌

CASTLEGAR

▼▼ ▼▼ **Quality Inn Castlegar** **H**
(250) 365-2177. **$90-$179.** 1935 Columbia Ave V1N 2W8. Jct Hwy 3A and 3B, just s. Ext/int corridors. **Pets:** Accepted.
🛜 ✕ 🛗 💻 🍴

▼▼ ▼▼ **Super 8-Castlegar** **H**
(250) 365-2700. **$113-$122.** 651 18th St V1N 2N1. Jct Hwy 3, just n on Hwy 22. Int corridors. **Pets:** Other species. $10 daily fee/pet. Designated rooms. ECO 🛜 ✕ 🛗 💻 🍴 ⇌

CHASE

▼▼ ▼▼ **Chase Country Inn Motel** **M** 🐾
(250) 679-3333. **$69-$99.** 576 Coburn St V0E 1M0. Trans-Canada Hwy 1 and Coburn St. Ext corridors. **Pets:** Medium. $5 daily fee/pet. Service with restrictions, supervision. 🛜 ᴧM 🛗 💻 🍴

Ⓐ ▼▼ ▼▼ ▼▼ **Quaaout Lodge & Spa, Talking Rock Golf** **H**
(250) 679-3090. **$100-$350, 3 day notice.** 1663 Little Shuswap Lake Rd W V0E 1M0. Trans-Canada Hwy 1 exit Squilax Bridge, 1.5 mi (2.5 km) w on Little Shuswap Rd. Int corridors. **Pets:** Large. $25 daily fee/room. Designated rooms.
SAVE 🛜 ✕ ᴧM 🛗 💻 🍴 ⇌ ✕

CHEMAINUS

Ⓐ ▼▼ ▼▼ ▼▼ **Best Western Plus Chemainus Inn** **H** 🐾
(250) 246-4181. **$125-$200.** 9573 Chemainus Rd V0R 1K5. Trans-Canada Hwy 1 exit Henry Rd, 0.9 mi (1.4 km) e. Int corridors. **Pets:** Medium. $20 daily fee/room. Designated rooms, service with restrictions, supervision. ECO SAVE 🛜 ✕ ᴧM 🛗 💻 ⇌

CHETWYND

ⒸAA ▼▼▼ Lakeview Inns & Suites Ⓗ
(250) 788-3000. **$129.** 4820 N Access Rd V0C 1J0. Hwy 29 and 97, just n on 48th St, then just e. Int corridors. **Pets:** $25 one-time fee/room. Service with restrictions, supervision. ⒺⒸⓄ ⓈAⓋE 🛜 ☒ ⓜ 🖥️ 💻 🏊

▼▼▼ Pomeroy Inn & Suites Ⓗ
(250) 788-4800. **Call for rates.** 5200 N Access Rd V0C 1J0. Hwy 29 and 97, just n on 52nd St. Int corridors. **Pets:** Accepted.
🛜 ☒ 🖥️ 💻 🏊 ⊠

CHILLIWACK

ⒸAA ▼▼ ▼ Best Western Rainbow Country Inn Ⓗ
(604) 795-3828. **$105-$130.** 43971 Industrial Way V2R 3A4. Trans-Canada Hwy 1 exit 116 (Lickman Rd). Int corridors. **Pets:** Accepted.
ⒺⒸⓄ ⓈAⓋE 🛜 ☒ 🖥️ 🖥️ 💻 🍴 🏊

ⒸAA ▼▼ ▼ The Coast Chilliwack Hotel Ⓗ
(604) 792-5552. **$99-$154.** 45920 First Ave V2P 7K1. Trans-Canada Hwy 1 exit 119, 1.8 mi (2.9 km) n on Vedder Rd, then just e. Int corridors. **Pets:** Accepted.
ⒺⒸⓄ ⓈAⓋE 🛜 ☒ 🖥️ 🖥️ 💻 🍴 🏊 ⊠

▼▼ ▼ Comfort Inn Ⓜ ❀
(604) 858-0636. **$104-$150.** 45405 Luckakuck Way V2R 3C7. Trans-Canada Hwy 1 exit 119, s on Vedder Rd, then 0.6 mi (1 km) w. Int corridors. **Pets:** Medium, other species. $5 daily fee/room. Designated rooms, service with restrictions, crate. ⒺⒸⓄ 🛜 🖥️ 🖥️

ⒸAA ▼▼ ▼ Travelodge Hotel, Chilliwack Ⓗ
(604) 792-4240. **$100-$225, 7 day notice.** 45466 Yale Rd W V2R 3Z8. Trans-Canada Hwy 1 exit 119, just n. Int corridors. **Pets:** Accepted.
ⒺⒸⓄ ⓈAⓋE 🛜 ☒ 🖥️ 💻 🍴 🏊

CLEARWATER

ⒸAA ▼▼ ▼ Clearwater Valley Resort & KOA Kampground ⒸA
(250) 674-3909. **$110-$170.** 373 Clearwater Valley Rd V0E 1N0. Jct Hwy 5 (Yellowhead Hwy) and Clearwater Valley Rd. Ext corridors. **Pets:** Medium. $10 daily fee/pet. Designated rooms, service with restrictions, supervision. ⓈAⓋE 🛜 ☒ 🖥️ 💻 🍴 🏊 ⊠

COMOX

ⒸAA ▼▼ ▼ Port Augusta Inn & Suites Ⓜ ❀
(250) 339-2277. **$75-$150.** 2082 Comox Ave V9M 1P8. Hwy 19A (Cliffe Ave), follow signs to Comox Ave, then 2.5 mi (4 km) e. Ext/int corridors. **Pets:** $10 daily fee/room. Designated rooms, service with restrictions, supervision. ⓈAⓋE 🛜 🖥️ 🖥️ 💻 🍴 🏊

COURTENAY

ⒸAA ▼▼▼▼ Best Western Plus The Westerly Hotel & Convention Centre Ⓗ
(250) 338-7741. **$120-$200.** 1590 Cliffe Ave and Island Hwy 19A N. Int corridors. **Pets:** Large, dogs only. $10 daily fee/pet. Designated rooms, service with restrictions, supervision.
ⒺⒸⓄ ⓈAⓋE 🛜 ☒ 🖥️ 🖥️ 💻 🍴 🏊 ⊠

▼▼▼▼ Crown Isle Resort & Golf Community Ⓗ
(250) 703-5050. **Call for rates.** 399 Clubhouse Dr V9N 9G3. Island Hwy 19A N, 0.9 mi (1.5 km) n on Comox Ave, then 1.6 mi (2.5 km) ne on Ryan Rd, follow signs. Ext corridors. **Pets:** $25 one-time fee/room. Designated rooms, service with restrictions, crate.
🛜 ☒ 🖥️ 🖥️ 💻 🍴 ⊠

▼▼▼▼ Holiday Inn Express & Suites Comox Valley Ⓗ ❀
(778) 225-0010. **$109-$159.** 2200 Cliffe Ave V9N 2L4. 0.6 mi (1.1 km) s on Island Hwy 19A. Int corridors. **Pets:** Other species. $15 one-time fee/room. Designated rooms, service with restrictions, supervision.
🛜 ☒ 🖥️ 🖥️ 💻 🏊 ⊠

▼▼▼ Kingfisher Oceanside Resort & Spa Ⓗ ❀
(250) 338-1323. **$119-$445, 7 day notice.** 4330 S Island Hwy V9N 9R9. 3.8 mi (6 km) s on Island Hwy 19A S, follow signs. Ext corridors. **Pets:** Other species. $25 daily fee/room. Designated rooms, service with restrictions, supervision. 🛜 ☒ 🖥️ 🖥️ 💻 🍴 🏊 ⊠ ⒶⓀ

▼▼ ▼ Travelodge Courtenay Ⓜ ❀
(250) 334-4491. **$76-$81.** 2605 Cliffe Ave V9N 2L8. 0.8 mi (1.2 km) s on Island Hwy 19A S. Ext corridors. **Pets:** Large, other species. $10 daily fee/pet. Service with restrictions, supervision. ⒺⒸⓄ 🛜 🖥️ 💻 🏊

CRANBROOK

ⒸAA ▼▼▼▼ Best Western Cranbrook Hotel Ⓗ
(250) 417-4002. **$150-$210.** 1019 Cranbrook St N V1C 3S4. Hwy 3 and 95; centre. Int corridors. **Pets:** Accepted.
ⒺⒸⓄ ⓈAⓋE 🛜 🖥️ 🖥️ 💻 🍴 🏊 ⊠

▼▼ ▼ Days Inn Cranbrook Ⓗ
(250) 426-6683. **$98-$107.** 600 Cranbrook St N V1C 3R7. Corner of 6th St and Cranbrook St N. Int corridors. **Pets:** Accepted.
ⒺⒸⓄ 🛜 🖥️ 💻 🍴 🏊

▼▼ ▼ Heritage Inn Cranbrook Ⓗ
(250) 489-4301. **$112-$220.** 803 Cranbrook St N V1C 3S2. Hwy 3 and 95; centre. Int corridors. **Pets:** Medium, dogs only. $20 daily fee/pet. Designated rooms, service with restrictions, crate.
🛜 🖥️ 🖥️ 💻 🍴 🏊

ⒸAA ▼▼▼▼ St. Eugene Golf Resort & Casino Ⓗ
(250) 420-2000. **$142-$182.** 7731 Mission Rd V1C 7E5. Hwy 3 exit Kimberley/Airport (Hwy 95A) to Mission Rd, 2.8 mi (4.5 km) n. Int corridors. **Pets:** Accepted. ⒺⒸⓄ ⓈAⓋE 🛜 ☒ 🖥️ 💻 🍴 🏊 ⊠

CRESTON

ⒸAA ▼▼ ▼ Skimmerhorn Inn Ⓜ
(250) 428-4009. **$65-$155.** 2711 Hwy 3 V0B 1G0. Hwy 3, 0.8 mi (1.3 km) e. Ext corridors. **Pets:** Accepted. ⓈAⓋE 🛜 ☒ 🖥️ 💻 🏊

ⒸAA ▼▼ ▼ Sunset Motel Ⓜ
(250) 428-2229. **$79-$109.** 2705 Canyon St (Hwy 3 E) V0B 1G0. Hwy 3, 0.8 mi (1.3 km) e. Ext corridors. **Pets:** Accepted.
ⓈAⓋE 🛜 ☒ 🖥️ 💻 🏊

DAWSON CREEK

ⒸAA ▼▼▼▼ Best Western Dawson Creek Inn Ⓗ
(250) 782-6226. **$189.** 500 Hwy 2 V1G 0A4. Jct Hwy 49, 1.6 mi (2.6 km) s on 8th St (Hwy 2), then just e; south end of town. Int corridors. **Pets:** Accepted. ⒺⒸⓄ ⓈAⓋE 🛜 🖥️ 🖥️ 💻 🍴 🏊 ⊠

▼▼▼▼ Pomeroy Inn & Suites Ⓗ
(250) 782-3700. **$170-$329.** 540 Hwy 2 V1G 0A4. Jct Hwy 49, 1.6 mi (2.6 km) s on 8th St (Hwy 2), then just e; south end of town. Int corridors. **Pets:** Accepted. 🛜 🖥️ 🖥️ 💻 🏊 ⊠

DUNCAN

ⒸAA ▼▼ ▼ Best Western Cowichan Valley Inn Ⓗ ❀
(250) 748-2722. **$119-$149.** 6474 Trans-Canada Hwy 1 V9L 6C6. 1.8 mi (3 km) n. Int corridors. **Pets:** Medium, dogs only. $20 one-time fee/room. Designated rooms, service with restrictions, supervision.
ⓈAⓋE 🛜 ☒ 🖥️ 💻 🍴 🏊

ⒸAA ▼▼ ▼ Super 8 Hotel Ⓗ
(250) 748-0661. **Call for rates.** 5325 Trans Canada Hwy V9L 5J2. 1 mi (1.6 km) s at Chaster Rd. Int corridors. **Pets:** Medium. $10 one-time fee/pet. Service with restrictions. ⓈAⓋE 🛜 🖥️ 💻 🍴

▼▼ ▼ Travelodge Duncan Ⓗ
(250) 748-4311. **$98-$152.** 140 Trans-Canada Hwy 1 V9L 3P7. Just n of the Silver Bridge. Ext corridors. **Pets:** $10 daily fee/pet. Designated rooms, service with restrictions, supervision. ⒺⒸⓄ 🛜 🖥️ 💻 🍴

FERNIE

(CAA) ▼▼▼▼ Best Western Plus Fernie Mountain Lodge 🅗 ❀

(250) 423-5500. **$150-$200.** 1622 7th Ave V0B 1M0. Jct Hwy 3 and 7th Ave; east end of town. Int corridors. **Pets:** Other species. $20 daily fee/room. Designated rooms, service with restrictions.

[ECO] [SAVE] 🛰 ✕ 🔋 🖵 🍴 ⇝ ✕

(CAA) ▼▼▼▼ Park Place Lodge 🅗

(250) 423-6871. **$128-$270.** 742 Hwy 3 V0B 1M0. At 7th St. Int corridors. **Pets:** Other species. Designated rooms, service with restrictions, supervision. [SAVE] 🛰 🔋 🖵 🍴 ⇝ ✕

(CAA) ▼▼▼ Super 8-Fernie 🅗 ❀

(250) 423-6788. **$75-$103.** 2021 Hwy 3 V0B 1M1. On Hwy 3; west end of town. Int corridors. **Pets:** Dogs only. $15 daily fee/pet. Designated rooms, service with restrictions, supervision. [SAVE] 🛰 ✕ 🔋 🖵

FORT NELSON

(CAA) ▼▼▼ Lakeview Inn & Suites 🅗

(250) 233-5001. **$140-$150.** 4507 50th Ave S V0C 1R0. Just off Hwy 97 (Alaska Hwy); at 44th St. Int corridors. **Pets:** Accepted.

[ECO] [SAVE] 🛰 🔋 🖵 ✕

FORT ST. JOHN

(CAA) ▼▼▼ Lakeview Inns & Suites 🅗

(250) 787-0779. **$109-$129.** 10103 98th Ave V1J 1P8. Corner of 100th Ave; centre of downtown. Int corridors. **Pets:** Accepted.

[ECO] [SAVE] 🛰 🔋 🖵 🍴

(CAA) ▼▼▼▼ Pomeroy Hotel 🅗

(250) 262-3233. **$179-$249, 14 day notice.** 11308 Alaska Rd V1J 5T5. Just w on Hwy 97 (Alaska Hwy). Int corridors. **Pets:** Accepted.

[SAVE] 🛰 ✕ ᴹ 🔋 🖵 🍴 ⇝ ✕

▼▼ Pomeroy Inn & Suites 🅗

(250) 262-3030. **$129-$159.** 9304 Alaska Rd V1J 6Z5. Just s on Hwy 97 (Alaska Hwy). Int corridors. **Pets:** Accepted. 🛰 🔋 🖵

▼▼▼ Quality Inn Northern Grand 🅗

(250) 787-0521. **$179.** 9830 100th Ave V1J 1Y5. Centre. Int corridors. **Pets:** Accepted. [ECO] 🛰 🔋 🖵 🍴 ⇝ ✕

(CAA) ▼▼▼ Super 8-Fort St. John 🅗 ❀

(250) 785-7588. **$135-$144.** 9500 W Alaska Rd V1J 6L5. Just s on Hwy 97 (Alaska Hwy). Int corridors. **Pets:** Medium. $25 daily fee/pet. Designated rooms, service with restrictions, supervision.

[ECO] [SAVE] 🛰 ᴹ 🔋 🖵 🍴 ⇝ ✕

FORT STEELE

▼▼▼▼ Bull River Guest Ranch 🆁🅰

(250) 429-3760. **Call for rates.** 2975 Bull River Rd V1C 4H7. Hwy 95, 12.9 mi (21.4 km) se of town on Ft Steele-Wardner Rd, 7.2 mi (12 km) ne on gravel road; Hwy 3 W, 24.6 mi (41 km) e of Cranbrook, 5 mi (8.2 km) n on Ft Steele-Wardner Rd, 7.2 mi (12 km) ne on gravel road. Ext corridors. **Pets:** Accepted. 🛰 ✕ 🔋 🖵 ✕ 🅜 🐾 ✇

GIBSONS

▼▼▼ Bonniebrook Lodge Oceanfront Inn 🅒🅘

(604) 886-2887. **$139-$328, 7 day notice.** 1532 Ocean Beach Esplanade V0N 1V5. Hwy 101, 3.8 mi (6 km) s on Veterans Rd to Fichett St, just sw to King St, 0.6 mi (1 km) sw to Chaster, then 5 mi (8 km) sw to Gowers Pt Rd, follow signs. Ext/int corridors. **Pets:** Accepted.

🛰 ✕ 🔋 🖵 🍴 🅜

GOLD BRIDGE

▼▼▼ Tyax Wilderness Resort 🅗

(250) 238-2221. **$169-$280, 30 day notice.** 1 Tyaughton Lake Rd V0K 1P0. 5 mi (8 km) n from the Tyaughton Lake turnoff, follow signs. Int corridors. **Pets:** Accepted. 🛰 ✕ ᴹ 🖵 🍴 ✕ 🅜

GOLDEN

▼▼ Golden Rim Motor Inn 🅜

(250) 344-2216. **$79-$185.** 1416 Golden View Rd V0A 1H1. On Trans-Canada Hwy 1, 1 mi (1.6 km) e of jct Hwy 95. Ext corridors. **Pets:** Small, dogs only. $15 daily fee/pet. Designated rooms, service with restrictions, supervision. 🛰 🔋 🖵 🍴 ⇝ ✕

GRAND FORKS

(CAA) ▼▼▼ Western Traveller Motel 🅜

(250) 442-5566. **$69-$139.** 1591 Central Ave V0H 1H0. West end of town on Hwy 3. Ext corridors. **Pets:** Medium, dogs only. $7 daily fee/pet. Designated rooms, no service, supervision. [SAVE] 🛰 ᴹ 🔋 🖵

GULF ISLANDS AREA

GALIANO ISLAND

▼▼▼ Galiano Oceanfront Inn & Spa 🅗 ❀

(250) 539-3388. **$199-$425, 7 day notice.** 134 Madrona Dr V0N 1P0. From Sturdies Bay Ferry Terminal, just ne on Sturdies Bay Rd. Ext/int corridors. **Pets:** Other species. $50 one-time fee/room. Designated rooms, service with restrictions, crate. 🛰 ✕ ᴹ 🔋 🖵 🍴 🅜

PENDER ISLANDS

(CAA) ▼▼▼▼ Poets Cove Resort & Spa 🅗

(250) 629-2100. **$169-$299, 3 day notice.** 9801 Spalding Rd V0N 2M3. From Otter Bay Ferry Terminal, follow signs to South Pender Island, then 10 mi (16 km) s; Otter Bay Rd to Bidwell Harbour Rd to Canal Rd. Ext/int corridors. **Pets:** Accepted.

[SAVE] 🛰 ✕ 🔋 🖵 🍴 ⇝ ✕ 🅜

QUADRA ISLAND

▼▼ Taku Resort & Marina 🅜 ❀

(250) 285-3031. **$99-$325, 30 day notice.** 616 Taku Rd V0P 1H0. From Campbell River ferry terminal, 4.1 mi (6.6 km) n on West Rd, then just e on Heriot Bay Rd, follow signs to Heriot Bay. Ext corridors. **Pets:** Dogs only. $15 daily fee/pet. Designated rooms, service with restrictions, supervision. 🛰 ✕ 🔋 🖵 ✕ 🅜 ✇

SALT SPRING ISLAND

▼▼ Harbour House Hotel 🅗

(250) 537-5571. **$99-$239.** 121 Upper Ganges Rd V8K 2S2. 0.6 mi (1 km) n on Lower Ganges Rd, then just e, towards Long Harbour Ferry Terminal. Ext/int corridors. **Pets:** $20 daily fee/pet. Designated rooms, service with restrictions, supervision.

[ECO] 🛰 ✕ ᴹ 🔋 🖵 🍴

▼▼ Salt Springs Spa Resort 🅒🅰

(250) 537-4111. **Call for rates.** 1460 N Beach Rd V8K 1J4. From Ganges Township, 4.9 mi (8 km) n on North End Rd, 0.6 mi (1 km) ne on Fernwood Rd, then 0.6 mi (1.8 km) nw. Ext corridors. **Pets:** Accepted. 🛰 ✕ 🔋 🖵 🅜 🐾 ✇

END AREA

HARRISON HOT SPRINGS

(CAA) ▼▼▼ Harrison Beach Hotel 🅗

(604) 796-1111. **$99-$269, 3 day notice.** 160 Esplanade Ave V0M 1K0. Just w; on lakefront. Int corridors. **Pets:** Accepted.

[SAVE] 📶 ✕ 🅼 🔋 💻 🍴 🏊

(CAA) ▼▼▼▼ Harrison Hot Springs Resort & Spa 🅗

(604) 796-2244. **$119-$289, 3 day notice.** 100 Esplanade Ave V0M 1K0. Just w; on lakefront. Int corridors. **Pets:** Accepted.

[ECO] [SAVE] 📶 ✕ 🅼 🔋 💻 🍴 🏊 ✕

HOPE

(CAA) ▼▼▼ Alpine Motel 🅜

(604) 869-9931. **$72-$115.** 505 Old Hope-Princeton Way V0X 1L0. Trans-Canada Hwy 1 exit 173 westbound; exit 170 eastbound, just n from lights. Ext corridors. **Pets:** Small. $50 deposit/room, $10 daily fee/room. No service, supervision. [SAVE] 📶 🔋 💻

(CAA) ▼ Best Continental Motel 🅜

(604) 869-9726. **$69-$125.** 860 Fraser Ave V0X 1L0. Trans-Canada Hwy 1 exit 170 to downtown; at Fort St. Ext corridors. **Pets:** Accepted.

[SAVE] 📶 🔋 💻

(CAA) ▼▼▼ Heritage Inn 🅜

(604) 869-7166. **$75-$116.** 570 Old Hope-Princeton Way V0X 1L0. Trans-Canada Hwy 1 exit 173 westbound; exit 170 eastbound, just n from lights. Ext corridors. **Pets:** Medium. $10 one-time fee/pet. No service, supervision. [SAVE] 📶 ✕ 🅼 🔋 💻

(CAA) ▼▼▼ Skagit Motor Inn 🅜 ✿

(604) 869-5220. **$98-$118, 3 day notice.** 655 3rd Ave V0X 1L0. Trans-Canada Hwy 1 exit 170 to downtown, just e of Water Ave. Ext corridors. **Pets:** Medium. $10 daily fee/pet. Service with restrictions, supervision. [SAVE] 📶 🅼 🔋 💻

(CAA) ▼▼▼ Travelodge 🅜

(604) 869-9951. **$87-$140.** 350 Old Hope-Princeton Way V0X 1L0. Trans-Canada Hwy 1 exit 173 westbound; exit 170 eastbound, just n from lights. Int corridors. **Pets:** Medium. Service with restrictions, supervision. [SAVE] 📶 🅼 🔋 💻 🏊

HUDSON'S HOPE

(CAA) ▼▼▼ Best Western Hudson's Hope Inn & Suites 🅗

(250) 783-2300. **Call for rates.** 9006 Clark Ave V0C 1V0. Hwy 29, north end of town. Int corridors. **Pets:** $25 one-time fee/room. Service with restrictions, crate. [SAVE] 📶 🅼 🔋 💻

INVERMERE

(CAA) ▼▼ Best Western Invermere Inn 🅗

(250) 342-9246. **$120-$200.** 1310 7th Ave V0A 1K0. Hwy 93 and 95 exit Invermere, 1.8 mi (3 km) w; centre. Int corridors. **Pets:** Accepted.

[SAVE] 📶 ✕ 🔋 💻 🍴

KAMLOOPS

(CAA) ▼▼▼ Accent Inns 🅜 ✿

(250) 374-8877. **$99-$179.** 1325 Columbia St W V2C 6P4. Trans-Canada Hwy 1 exit 369 (Columbia St) eastbound, at Notre Dame Dr; exit 370 (Summit Dr) westbound. Ext corridors. **Pets:** Large. $20 daily fee/pet. Designated rooms, service with restrictions, supervision.

[ECO] [SAVE] 📶 ✕ 🅼 🔋 💻 🏊 ✕

(CAA) ▼▼▼ Best Western Plus Kamloops Hotel 🅗 ✿

(250) 374-7878. **$135-$250.** 660 Columbia St W V2C 1L1. Trans-Canada Hwy 1 exit 369 (Columbia St) eastbound, 1.3 mi (2 km) n; exit 370 (Summit Dr) westbound to Columbia St via City Centre, then just n. Int corridors. **Pets:** Medium, other species. $20 one-time fee/room. Designated rooms, service with restrictions, supervision.

[ECO] [SAVE] 📶 ✕ 🅼 🔋 💻

(CAA) ▼▼▼ The Coast Kamloops Hotel & Conference Centre 🅗

(250) 828-6660. **$130-$185.** 1250 Rogers Way V1S 1N5. Trans-Canada Hwy 1 exit 368 (Hillside Ave), just s. Int corridors. **Pets:** Accepted.

[ECO] [SAVE] 📶 ✕ 🅼 🔋 💻 🍴 🏊 ✕

(CAA) ▼▼▼ Econo Lodge Inn & Suites 🅜 ✿

(250) 372-8533. **$89-$109.** 1773 Trans-Canada Hwy E V2C 3Z6. 1.5 mi (2.4 km) e on Trans-Canada Hwy 1, south side of service access road. Ext corridors. **Pets:** Small. $10 daily fee/pet. Designated rooms, service with restrictions, supervision. [SAVE] 📶 🔋 💻 🏊

(CAA) ▼▼▼ Hampton Inn by Hilton 🅗 ✿

(250) 571-7897. **Call for rates.** 1245 Rogers Way V1S 1R9. Trans-Canada Hwy 1 exit 368 (Hillside Ave), just s via Hillside Way. Int corridors. **Pets:** Dogs only. $20 daily fee/pet. Designated rooms, service with restrictions, supervision. [ECO] [SAVE] 📶 ✕ 🅼 🔋 💻 🏊 ✕

(CAA) ▼▼▼ Holiday Inn & Suites 🅗

(250) 376-8288. **$99-$119.** 675 Tranquille Rd V2B 3H7. Trans-Canada Hwy 1 exit 374 (Jasper Ave), 2.5 mi (4 km) w on Halston Connector Rd, 1.8 mi (3 km) s on 8th St to Fortune Dr, then just s. Int corridors. **Pets:** Accepted. [SAVE] 📶 ✕ 🅼 🔋 💻 🏊

▼▼▼ Holiday Inn Express Kamloops 🅗

(250) 372-3474. **$130-$183.** 1550 Versatile Dr V1S 1X4. Trans-Canada Hwy 1 exit 367 (Pacific Way), just w. Int corridors. **Pets:** Other species. $30 one-time fee/pet. Designated rooms, service with restrictions, supervision. [ECO] 📶 ✕ 🅼 🔋 💻 🏊

▼▼▼ Kamloops Super 8 🅜

(250) 374-8688. **$72-$82.** 1521 Hugh Allan Dr V1S 1P4. Trans-Canada Hwy 1 exit 367 (Pacific Way). Int corridors. **Pets:** Accepted.

📶 🅼 🔋 💻

(CAA) ▼▼▼ Pacific Host Inn & Suites 🅗

(250) 372-0952. **$120-$170.** 1820 Rogers Pl V1S 1T7. Trans-Canada Hwy 1 exit 368 (Hillside Ave), just w. Int corridors. **Pets:** Accepted.

[SAVE] 📶 ✕ 🅼 🔋 💻 🍴 🏊

(CAA) ▼▼▼ Quality Inn 🅜

(250) 851-0111. **$79-$159.** 1860 Rogers Pl V1S 1T7. Trans-Canada Hwy 1 exit 368 (Hillside Ave). Int corridors. **Pets:** Accepted.

[SAVE] 📶 🅼 🔋 💻 🏊 ✕

▼▼ Ranchland Motel 🅜

(250) 828-8787. **$69-$99.** 2357 Trans-Canada Hwy E V2C 4A8. 2.8 mi (4.5 km) e on Trans-Canada Hwy 1 exit River Rd, then just w along service access road. Ext corridors. **Pets:** Small. $10 daily fee/pet. Designated rooms, service with restrictions, supervision. 📶 🅼 🔋 💻

(CAA) ▼▼▼ Scott's Inn & Restaurant 🅜

(250) 372-8221. **$80-$120.** 551 11th Ave V2C 3Y1. Trans-Canada Hwy 1 exit 369 (Columbia St) eastbound, 3.1 mi (5 km) n; exit City Centre westbound, 1 mi (1.6 km) s on Columbia St. Ext corridors. **Pets:** $10 daily fee/pet. Service with restrictions, supervision.

[SAVE] 📶 ✕ 🅼 🔋 💻 🍴 🏊

KIMBERLEY

(CAA) ▼▼▼▼ Trickle Creek Lodge 🅗

(250) 427-5175. **$163-$272, 7 day notice.** 500 Stemwinder Dr V1A 2Y6. From Gerry Sorensen Way, follow signs. Int corridors. **Pets:** Accepted. [SAVE] ✕ 🔋 💻 🍴 🏊 ✕

MADEIRA PARK

▼▼▼ Sunshine Coast Resort & Marina 🅒🅞 ✿

(604) 883-9177. **$99-$445, 21 day notice.** 12695 Sunshine Coast Hwy V0N 2H0. Just n of Madeira Park Rd, follow signs. Ext/int corridors. **Pets:** $20 daily fee/pet. Service with restrictions, supervision.

📶 ✕ 🅼 🔋 💻 ✕

MCBRIDE

(CAA) ▼▼▼ North Country Lodge 🅼

(250) 569-0001. **Call for rates.** 868 N Frontage Rd V0J 2E0. Just w of village main exit, on Hwy 16 north service road. Ext corridors. **Pets:** Other species. $15 daily fee/pet. Service with restrictions.

SAVE 🛜 🔒 🍴

MERRITT

(CAA) ▼▼▼ Best Western Nicola Inn 🅷

(250) 378-4253. **$96-$130.** 4025 Walters St V1K 1K1. Hwy 5 exit 290, 0.6 mi (1 km) w. Ext corridors. **Pets:** Accepted.

SAVE 🛜 🖐M 🔒 🖵 🍴 🏊

(CAA) ▼▼ Ramada 🅼

(250) 378-3567. **Call for rates.** 3571 Voght St V1K 1C5. Hwy 5 exit 290, just w. Ext corridors. **Pets:** Medium. $10 daily fee/pet. Designated rooms, service with restrictions, supervision.

SAVE 🛜 🔒 🖵 🏊 🚫

▼▼ Super 8 Merritt 🅼

(250) 378-9422. **$68-$98.** 3561 Voght St V1K 1C5. Hwy 5 exit 290, just w. Ext corridors. **Pets:** Accepted. 🛜 🖐M 🔒 🖵 🍴 🏊

NAKUSP

(CAA) ▼▼▼ The Selkirk Inn 🅼

(250) 265-3666. **$65-$105.** 210 W 6th Ave V0G 1R0. Centre. Int corridors. **Pets:** Medium. $20 deposit/room, $10 daily fee/pet. Designated rooms, service with restrictions, supervision.

SAVE 🛜 🚫 🖐M 🔒 🖵

NANAIMO

(CAA) ▼▼▼ Best Western Northgate Inn 🅷

(250) 390-2222. **$110-$200.** 6450 Metral Dr V9T 2L8. Hwy 19A (Island Hwy), just w on Aulds Rd, then just s. Int corridors. **Pets:** Accepted.

SAVE 🛜 🚫 🔒 🖵 🍴 🚫

(CAA) ▼▼▼ Best Western Plus Dorchester Hotel 🅷 🐾

(250) 754-6835. **$140-$200.** 70 Church St V9R 5H4. Hwy 19A (Island Hwy) to Comox Rd; downtown. Int corridors. **Pets:** Medium, dogs only. $20 daily fee/pet. Designated rooms, service with restrictions, supervision.

ECO SAVE 🛜 🚫 🔒 🖵 🍴

▼▼▼ Days Inn Nanaimo Harbourview 🅷

(250) 754-8171. **$90-$103.** 809 Island Hwy S V9R 5K1. On Island Hwy 1, 1.3 mi (2 km) s. Int corridors. **Pets:** Accepted.

ECO 🛜 🚫 🖐M 🔒 🖵 🍴 🏊

▼▼▼ The Grand Hotel Nanaimo 🅷 🐾

(250) 758-3000. **$119-$320.** 4898 Rutherford Rd V9T 4Z4. 3.8 mi (6 km) n on Hwy 19A (Island Hwy) from Departure Bay ferry terminal, then just e. Int corridors. **Pets:** $20 daily fee/pet. Designated rooms, service with restrictions, supervision. 🚫 🖐M 🔒 🖵 🍴 🏊

(CAA) ▼▼▼ Inn on Long Lake 🅷 🐾

(250) 758-1144. **$109-$299.** 4700 Island Hwy N V9T 1W6. 3.1 mi (5 km) n on Hwy 19A (Island Hwy) from Departure Bay ferry terminal. Ext corridors. **Pets:** $20 one-time fee/room. Designated rooms, service with restrictions, supervision. ECO SAVE 🛜 🖐M 🔒 🖵 🚫

(CAA) ▼▼▼ Travelodge Nanaimo 🅷

(250) 754-6355. **$95-$139.** 96 Terminal Ave N V9S 4J2. Jct Terminal Ave and Hwy 19A (Island Hwy). Int corridors. **Pets:** Large, other species. $15 daily fee/pet. Designated rooms, service with restrictions, supervision.

ECO SAVE 🛜 🚫 🔒 🖵

NELSON

(CAA) ▼▼▼ Best Western Plus Baker Street Inn & Convention Centre 🅷 🐾

(250) 352-3525. **$125-$175.** 153 Baker St V1L 4H1. Jct Hwy 6 and 3A. Int corridors. **Pets:** Medium, other species. $15 daily fee/pet. Designated rooms, service with restrictions, supervision.

ECO SAVE 🛜 🚫 🖐M 🔒 🖵 🍴

▼▼ North Shore Inn 🅼 🐾

(250) 352-6606. **$62-$85.** 687 Hwy 3A V1L 5P7. 1.9 mi (3 km) n on Hwy 3A via Nelson Bridge. Int corridors. **Pets:** Dogs only. $10 daily fee/room. Designated rooms, service with restrictions, supervision.

🛜 🚫 🔒

NEW DENVER

▼▼ Sweet Dreams Guesthouse 🅲🅸

(250) 358-2415. **Call for rates.** 702 Eldorado St V0G 1S0. Just w of Hwy 6 on Slocan Ave. Int corridors. **Pets:** Accepted.

🛜 🚫 🐾 🖵 🏊

OKANAGAN VALLEY AREA

ENDERBY

(CAA) ▼▼ Howard Johnson Inn Fortunes Landing 🅷

(250) 838-6825. **$76-$98.** 1510 George St V0E 1V0. 0.6 mi (1 km) n on Hwy 97A (Harvey Ave). Ext corridors. **Pets:** Other species. $10 daily fee/pet. Designated rooms, service with restrictions, supervision.

SAVE 🛜 🚫 🔒 🖵 🍴 🏊

KELOWNA

(CAA) ▼▼▼ Accent Inns 🅷 🐾

(250) 862-8888. **$99-$189.** 1140 Harvey Ave V1Y 6E7. Corner of Hwy 97 N (Harvey Ave) and Gordon Dr. Ext corridors. **Pets:** $20 daily fee/room. Designated rooms, service with restrictions.

ECO SAVE 🛜 🚫 🖐M 🔒 🖵 🍴 🏊 🚫

(CAA) ▼▼▼ Best Western Plus Kelowna Hotel & Suites 🅷 🐾

(250) 860-1212. **$139-$219.** 2402 Hwy 97 N V1X 4J1. 0.6 mi (1 km) s of jct Hwy 33 and 97 N (Harvey Ave); corner of Leckie Rd. **Pets:** Medium. $20 daily fee/pet. Designated rooms, service with restrictions, crate. ECO SAVE 🛜 🚫 🖐M 🔒 🖵 🍴 🏊 🚫

(CAA) ▼▼▼ Days Inn 🅼

(250) 868-3297. **$74-$130.** 2649 Hwy 97 N V1X 4J6. Jct Hwy 97 (Harvey Ave) and 33, just n. Ext/int corridors. **Pets:** Medium. $10 daily fee/pet. Designated rooms, service with restrictions, crate.

ECO SAVE 🛜 🚫 🖐M 🔒 🖵 🏊

▼▼▼ Delta Grand Okanagan Resort & Conference Centre 🅷 🐾

(250) 763-4500. **Call for rates.** 1310 Water St V1Y 9P3. Hwy 97 (Harvey Ave), 0.6 mi (1 km) w along Water St. Int corridors. **Pets:** Small. $35 one-time fee/room. Designated rooms, service with restrictions, supervision. ECO 🛜 🚫 🖐M 🔒 🖵 🍴 🏊 🚫

(CAA) ▼▼▼ Econo Lodge 🅼

(250) 762-3221. **$94-$239.** 1780 Gordon Dr V1Y 3H2. Hwy 97 N (Harvey Ave), just s. Ext corridors. **Pets:** Small, other species. $10 one-time fee/pet. Supervision. SAVE 🛜 🚫 🔒 🖵 🏊

▼▼▼▼ Fairfield Inn & Suites by Marriott Kelowna 🅷 🐾

(250) 763-2800. **$120-$240.** 1655 Powick Rd V1X 4L1. Just s of jct Hwy 97 N (Harvey Ave) and 33 W. Int corridors. **Pets:** $15 daily fee/room. Designated rooms, service with restrictions.

ECO 🛜 🚫 🖐M 🔒 🖵 🏊 🚫

▼▼▼ Kelowna Inn & Suites 🅼

(250) 762-2533. **$95-$195.** 1070 Harvey Ave V1Y 8S4. Corner of Hwy 97 N (Harvey Ave) and Gordon Dr. Ext/int corridors. **Pets:** Small, dogs only. $10 daily fee/pet. Designated rooms, service with restrictions, supervision. ECO 🛜 🖐M 🔒 🖵 🍴 🏊

▼▼ ▼▼ **Ramada Hotel & Conference Centre** 🏠 🐾
(250) 860-9711. **Call for rates.** 2170 Harvey Ave V1Y 6G8. Hwy 97 N (Harvey Ave) at Dilworth Dr. Ext/int corridors. **Pets:** Other species. $15 daily fee/room. Designated rooms, service with restrictions, supervision.
📶 ✕ ⅏M 🛢 🍴 ⇄

▼▼ ▼▼ **Recreation Inn & Suites** Ⓜ
(250) 860-3982. **$79-$262.** 1891 Parkinson Way V1Y 7V6. Hwy 97 N (Harvey Ave), just n on Spall Rd. Ext corridors. **Pets:** Accepted.
📶 🛢 💻 🍴 ⇄

Ⓐ ▼▼ ▼▼ **The Royal Anne Hotel** 🏠 🐾
(250) 763-2277. **$89-$199.** 348 Bernard Ave V1Y 6N5. Corner of Pandosy St and Bernard Ave; downtown. Int corridors. **Pets:** Medium. $20 daily fee/pet. Designated rooms, service with restrictions, crate.
SAVE 📶 ✕ 🛢 💻

▼▼ ▼▼ **Vineyard Inn** Ⓜ
(250) 860-5703. **Call for rates.** 2486 Hwy 97 N V1X 4J3. Southwest corner of jct Hwy 97 (Harvey Ave) and 33. Ext corridors. **Pets:** Accepted.
📶 ✕ 🛢 💻 ⇄ ✕

OSOYOOS

Ⓐ ▼▼ ▼▼ **Best Western Plus Sunrise Inn** 🏠 🐾
(250) 495-4000. **$99-$259.** 5506 Main St V0H 1V0. Jct Hwy 97, 1.9 mi (3 km) on Hwy 3 (Main St). Int corridors. **Pets:** Large, other species. $20 daily fee/pet. Designated rooms, service with restrictions, supervision.
ECO SAVE 📶 ✕ ⅏M 🛢 💻 🍴 ⇄

Ⓐ ▼▼ ▼▼ **Holiday Inn & Suites** 🏠
(250) 495-7223. **$119-$219, 3 day notice.** 7906 Main St V0H 1V0. Jct Hwy 97, 1 mi (1.6 km) e on Hwy 3. Int corridors. **Pets:** Accepted.
ECO SAVE 📶 ✕ ⅏M 🛢 💻 🍴 ⇄

▼▼ ▼▼ ▼▼ **Spirit Ridge Vineyard Resort & Spa** Ⓒ
(250) 495-5445. **$95-$275.** 1200 Rancher Creek Rd V0H 1V6. Hwy 97 S, e on Hwy 3 (Main St), cross bridge, left on 45th St, then 0.9 mi (1.5 km) e. Ext/int corridors. **Pets:** Accepted.
ECO 📶 ✕ ⅏M 🛢 💻 🍴 ⇄ ✕

▼▼ ▼▼ ▼▼ **Watermark Beach Resort** Ⓒ
(250) 495-5500. **$99-$699.** 15 Park Pl V0H 1V0. Corner of Park Pl and Main St; downtown. Ext/int corridors. **Pets:** Accepted.
ECO 📶 ✕ 🛢 💻 🍴 ⇄ ✕

PENTICTON

Ⓐ ▼▼ ▼▼ **Best Western Plus Inn at Penticton** 🏠
(250) 493-0311. **$100-$200.** 3180 Skaha Lake Rd V2A 6G4. From downtown, 2.5 mi (4 km) s. Ext corridors. **Pets:** Accepted.
ECO SAVE 📶 ✕ 🛢 💻 ⇄

Ⓐ ▼▼ ▼▼ **Coast Penticton Hotel** 🏠
(250) 492-0225. **$79-$269.** 950 Westminster Ave W V2A 1L2. Hwy 97 (Eckhardt Ave W), just n to Westminster Ave W, then just e. Ext/int corridors. **Pets:** $10 daily fee/pet. Designated rooms, service with restrictions, supervision. SAVE 📶 ✕ 🛢 💻 🍴 ⇄

▼▼ ▼▼ **Days Inn & Conference Centre Penticton** 🏠
(250) 493-6616. **$89-$299.** 152 Riverside Dr V2A 5Y4. Hwy 97, just n. Int corridors. **Pets:** Accepted.
ECO 📶 ✕ ⅏M 🛢 💻 🍴 ⇄ ✕

Ⓐ ▼▼ ▼▼ ▼▼ **Penticton Lakeside Resort, Convention Centre & Casino** 🏠 🐾
(250) 493-8221. **$120-$225, 7 day notice.** 21 Lakeshore Dr W V2A 7M5. Main St at Lakeshore Dr W. Int corridors. **Pets:** Other species. $25 one-time fee/room. Designated rooms, service with restrictions, supervision. ECO SAVE 📶 ✕ 🛢 💻 🍴 ⇄ ✕

Ⓐ ▼▼ ▼▼ ▼▼ **Ramada Inn & Suites** 🏠
(250) 492-8926. **$79-$239.** 1050 Eckhardt Ave W V2A 2C3. 0.8 mi (1.2 km) w on Hwy 97. Ext/int corridors. **Pets:** Accepted.
ECO SAVE 📶 ✕ ⅏M 🛢 💻 🍴 ⇄ ✕

Ⓐ ▼▼ **Spanish Villa Resort** Ⓜ
(250) 492-2922. **$68-$350, 14 day notice.** 890 Lakeshore Dr W V2A 1C1. Corner of Power St and Lakeshore Dr W. Ext corridors. **Pets:** Medium, dogs only. $10 daily fee/pet. Designated rooms, service with restrictions, supervision. SAVE 📶 ✕ 🛢 💻 ⇄

▼▼ ▼▼ **Super 8 Penticton** Ⓜ 🐾
(250) 492-3829. **$108-$235.** 1706 Main St V2A 5G8. Jct Main St and Industrial Ave. Ext/int corridors. **Pets:** Dogs only. $15 daily fee/pet. Designated rooms, service with restrictions, supervision.
📶 ✕ ⅏M 🛢 💻 ⇄

SUMMERLAND

Ⓐ ▼▼ ▼▼ **Summerland Motel** Ⓜ
(250) 494-4444. **$80-$150, 10 day notice.** 2107 Tait St V0H 1Z4. 3.1 mi (5 km) s on Hwy 97 (32nd St). Ext corridors. **Pets:** $10 daily fee/room. Designated rooms, service with restrictions, crate.
SAVE 📶 ✕ ⅏M 🛢 💻 ⇄

▼▼ ▼▼ ▼▼ **Summerland Waterfront Resort & Spa** 🏠
(250) 494-8180. **Call for rates.** 13011 Lakeshore Dr S V0H 1Z1. Hwy 97, just n, follow signs. Ext/int corridors. **Pets:** Accepted.
📶 ✕ ⅏M 🛢 💻 🍴 ⇄ ✕

VERNON

Ⓐ ▼▼ ▼▼ ▼▼ **Best Western Plus Vernon Lodge & Conference Centre** 🏠 🐾
(250) 545-3385. **$112-$157.** 3914 32nd St V1T 5P1. 1 mi (1.6 km) n on Hwy 97 (32nd St). Int corridors. **Pets:** $15 daily fee/room. Designated rooms, service with restrictions, supervision.
SAVE 📶 ✕ ⅏M 🛢 💻 🍴 ⇄

Ⓐ ▼▼ ▼▼ **Best Western Villager Motor Inn** Ⓜ 🐾
(250) 549-2224. **$100-$125.** 5121 26th St V1T 8G4. 1.5 mi (2.5 km) n on 27th St. Ext corridors. **Pets:** Medium, other species. $20 daily fee/room. Supervision. SAVE 📶 ⅏M 🛢 💻 ⇄

Ⓐ ▼▼ ▼▼ **Holiday Inn Express Hotel & Suites Vernon** 🏠
(250) 550-7777. **$119-$209, 3 day notice.** 4716 34th St V1T 5Y9. Hwy 97 (32nd St) northbound at 48th Ave. Int corridors. **Pets:** Accepted.
SAVE 📶 ⅏M 🛢 💻 ⇄

WEST KELOWNA (WESTBANK)

Ⓐ ▼▼ ▼▼ **Comfort Inn Kelowna-Westside** 🏠
(250) 769-2355. **Call for rates.** 1655 Westgate Rd V1Z 3P1. Jct Hwy 97 (Harvey Ave) and Bartley Rd, s to Ross Rd. Int corridors. **Pets:** Dogs only. $25 daily fee/pet. Designated rooms, service with restrictions, supervision. SAVE 📶 ✕ ⅏M 🛢 💻 🍴 ⇄

▼▼ ▼▼ ▼▼ **The Cove Lakeside Resort** 🏠
(250) 707-1800. **$155-$889, 3 day notice.** 4205 Gellatly Rd V4T 2K2. Hwy 97 (Dobbin Rd), 1 mi (1.6 km) s, follow signs. Int corridors. **Pets:** Medium, dogs only. $20 daily fee/pet. Designated rooms, service with restrictions, supervision.
ECO 📶 ✕ ⅏M 🛢 💻 🍴 ⇄ ✕

END AREA

PARKSVILLE

♦♦ Arbutus Grove Motel M

(250) 248-6422. **Call for rates.** 1182 E Island Hwy V9P 1W3. Island Hwy 19 exit 46 (Parksville), 1 mi (1.6 km) n on Hwy 19A. Ext corridors. **Pets:** Accepted. ⊠ 🛏 💻 🐾

♦♦ Oceanside Village Resort CA

(250) 248-8961. **Call for rates.** 1080 Resort Dr V9P 2E3. Island Hwy 19 exit 46 (Parksville), 1.8 mi (2.5 km) n on Hwy 19A. Ext corridors. **Pets:** Accepted. 📶 ⊠ 🛏 💻 🐾 🦮

AAA ♦♦ Quality Resort Bayside H

(250) 248-8333. **$99-$199.** 240 Dogwood St V9P 2H5. Island Hwy 19 exit 51 (Parksville/Coombs), 1.3 mi (2 km) e, then 0.6 mi (1 km) n on Hwy 19A. Int corridors. **Pets:** Dogs only. $15 daily fee/room. Designated rooms, service with restrictions, crate.

SAVE 📶 ⊠ 🛏 💻 🍽 🐾

AAA ♦♦♦ Tigh-Na-Mara Seaside Spa Resort & Conference Centre H 🐾

(250) 248-2072. **$119-$359, 5 day notice.** 1155 Resort Dr V9P 2E3. Island Hwy 19 exit 46 (Parksville), 1.3 mi (2 km) n on Hwy 19A. Int corridors. **Pets:** Dogs only. $30 one-time fee/room. Designated rooms, service with restrictions, crate. SAVE 📶 ⊠ 🛏 💻 🍽 🐾 🦮 🦮

♦♦ Travelodge Parksville H 🐾

(250) 248-2232. **$116-$158.** 424 W Island Hwy V9P 1K8. Island Hwy 19 exit 51 (Parksville/Coombs), 1.3 mi (2 km) e, then just n on Hwy 19A. Int corridors. **Pets:** Other species. Designated rooms, service with restrictions, supervision. ECO 📶 ⊠ 🛏 🛏 💻 🐾

AAA ♦♦ V.I.P. Motel M

(250) 248-3244. **$69-$169.** 414 W Island Hwy V9P 1K8. Island Hwy 19 exit 51 (Parksville/Coombs), 1.3 mi (2 km) e, then just n on Hwy 19A. Ext corridors. **Pets:** Accepted. SAVE 📶 🛏 💻

PARSON

♦♦ Alexa Chalets-Timber Inn & Restaurant H

(250) 348-2228. **$89-$270, 30 day notice.** 3483 Hwy 95 V0A 1L0. Just off Hwy 95; 21.3 mi (34 km) s of Golden. Ext/int corridors. **Pets:** Accepted. 📶 ⊠ 🛏 💻 🍽 🦮 🦮 ☎

PEMBERTON

♦♦♦ Pemberton Valley Lodge H 🐾

(604) 894-2000. **$139-$409.** 1490 Portage Rd V0N 2L1. Just e on Hwy 99 from Pioneer Junction. Int corridors. **Pets:** Medium, dogs only. $45 one-time fee/room. Designated rooms, service with restrictions, supervision. ECO 📶 ⊠ 🛏 🛏 💻 🐾

PORT ALBERNI

AAA ♦♦♦ Best Western Plus Barclay Hotel H

(250) 724-7171. **$109-$159.** 4277 Stamp Ave V9Y 7X8. Johnston Rd (Hwy 4), just s on Gertrude St. Int corridors. **Pets:** Accepted.
SAVE 📶 ⊠ 🛏 💻 🍽 🐾 🦮

♦♦ The Hospitality Inn H 🐾

(250) 723-8111. **$99-$165.** 3835 Redford St V9Y 3S2. 2 mi (3.2 km) sw of jct Hwy 4 via City Centre/Port Alberni South Route. Int corridors. **Pets:** Other species. $10 daily fee/pet. Designated rooms, service with restrictions, supervision. ECO 📶 🛏 💻 🍽 🐾

♦ Riverside Motel M

(250) 724-9916. **Call for rates.** 5065 Roger St V9Y 3Y9. Johnston Rd (Hwy 4), just s on Gertrude St, then just w. Ext corridors. **Pets:** Accepted. 📶 ⊠ 🛏 💻

♦♦ Somass Motel M

(250) 724-3236. **$62-$132.** 5279 River Rd V9Y 6Z3. 2 mi (3.2 km) on River Rd (Hwy 4) from Johnston Rd. Ext corridors. **Pets:** Medium, other species. $10 daily fee/pet. Designated rooms, service with restrictions, supervision. 📶 ⊠ 🛏 💻 🐾

PORT HARDY

♦♦ Glen Lyon Inn H

(250) 949-7115. **$85-$160, 3 day notice.** 6435 Hardy Bay Rd V0N 2P0. Hwy 19, 0.9 mi (1.5 km) n, follow signs. Ext corridors. **Pets:** Accepted.
📶 ⊠ 🛏 🛏 💻 🍽 🦮

♦♦ Quarterdeck Inn & Marina H

(250) 902-0455. **$109-$145.** 6555 Hardy Bay Rd V0N 2P0. Hwy 19, 0.9 mi (1.5 km) n. Int corridors. **Pets:** Accepted.
📶 ⊠ 🛏 🛏 💻 🍽 🦮

POWELL RIVER

♦♦ Powell River Town Centre Hotel H

(604) 485-3000. **Call for rates.** 4660 Joyce Ave V8A 3B6. 0.5 mi (0.8 km) e on Duncan St (BC ferry terminal), then 0.6 mi (1 km) n. Int corridors. **Pets:** Accepted. 📶 ⊠ 🛏 💻 🍽

PRINCE GEORGE

AAA ♦♦♦ Best Western City Centre M 🐾

(250) 563-1267. **$100-$110.** 910 Victoria St V2L 2K8. Just n of Victoria St (Hwy 16) and Patricia Blvd; downtown. Ext corridors. **Pets:** $20 daily fee/room. Service with restrictions. SAVE 📶 🛏 💻 🍽 🐾

PRINCE RUPERT

♦ Aleeda Motel M

(250) 627-1367. **$60-$105.** 900 3rd Ave W V8J 1M8. Corner of 3rd Ave W and 8th St. Int corridors. **Pets:** $10 one-time fee/pet. Service with restrictions, supervision. 📶 🛏 💻 🦮

♦♦ The Coast Prince Rupert Hotel H

(250) 624-6711. **$89-$197.** 118 6th St V8J 3L7. Between 1st and 2nd aves W. Int corridors. **Pets:** Accepted. ECO 🛏 💻 🍽

♦ Inn on the Harbour M

(250) 624-9107. **$99-$165.** 720 1st Ave W V8J 3V6. Corner of 6th St. Int corridors. **Pets:** Accepted. 📶 ⊠ 🛏 🛏 💻 🦮

AAA ♦ Totem Lodge Motel M

(250) 624-6761. **$69-$99.** 1335 Park Ave V8J 1K3. 1 mi (1.6 km) w on Hwy 16 (2nd Ave W) from downtown. Int corridors. **Pets:** Other species. $10 daily fee/room. Designated rooms, service with restrictions, crate.
SAVE 📶 🛏 💻 🦮

PRINCETON

AAA ♦♦♦ Canadas Best Value Princeton Inn & Suites H 🐾

(250) 295-3537. **$99-$149.** 169 Hwy 3 V0X 1W0. Hwy 3, just n on Vermilion Ave. Ext corridors. **Pets:** Medium, other species. $10 one-time fee/room. Designated rooms. SAVE 📶 🛏 🛏 💻 🐾

AAA ♦ Villager Inn M

(250) 295-6996. **$69-$99.** 244 4th St V0X 1W0. Hwy 3, just w. Ext corridors. **Pets:** Medium, other species. $10 daily fee/pet. Service with restrictions, crate. SAVE 📶 ⊠ 🛏 💻 🐾

QUALICUM BEACH

♦♦ Old Dutch Inn (By The Sea) H

(250) 752-6914. **Call for rates.** 2690 Island Hwy W V9K 1G8. Hwy 19 exit 60 (Qualicum Beach/Port Alberni), 2.5 mi (4 km) on Memorial Ave, jct Hwy 19A. Int corridors. **Pets:** Accepted.
📶 ⊠ 🛏 💻 🍽 🐾 🦮

QUESNEL

AAA ♦♦ Quality Inn M

(250) 992-7247. **Call for rates.** 753 Front St V2J 2L2. Hwy 97, 0.6 mi (1 km) n of Carson Ave. Int corridors. **Pets:** Accepted.
SAVE 📶 🛏 🛏 💻

ⓐ ▼▼ Travelodge Ⓜ

(250) 992-7071. **$72.** 524 Front St V2J 2K6. Hwy 97, 0.5 mi (0.8 km) n of Carson Ave. Ext corridors. **Pets:** Large. $20 daily fee/pet. Designated rooms, service with restrictions, crate.

ECO SAVE 🛜 🖨 Ꮪᴹ 🛏 💻 ⩫

RADIUM HOT SPRINGS

▼▼ Lido Motel Ⓜ

(250) 347-9533. **$65-$95, 7 day notice.** 4876 McKay St V0A 1M0. Jct Hwy 93 and 95, just e, just s along Main St, then just e. Ext corridors. **Pets:** $10 daily fee/pet. Supervision. 🛜 ⨯ 🛏 💻 ⩫

ⓐ ▼▼▼ Prestige Radium Hot Springs Ⓗ

(250) 347-2300. **$129-$209.** 7493 Main St W V0A 1M0. Jct Hwy 93 and 95. Int corridors. **Pets:** Accepted.

SAVE 🛜 ⨯ 🛏 💻 ⑪ ⩫ ⨯

REVELSTOKE

ⓐ ▼▼▼▼ Best Western Plus Revelstoke Ⓗ ❀

(250) 837-2043. **$130-$210.** 1925 Laforme Blvd V0E 2S0. Trans-Canada Hwy 1, just n. Int corridors. **Pets:** Large. $20 daily fee/room. Designated rooms, service with restrictions, supervision.

SAVE 🛜 ⨯ Ꮪᴹ 🛏 💻 ⩫ ⨯

ⓐ ▼▼▼▼ The Hillcrest Hotel a Coast Resort Ⓗ ❀

(250) 837-3322. **$131-$181.** 2100 Oak Dr V0E 2S0. 2.7 mi (4.3 km) e on Trans-Canada Hwy 1, 0.6 mi (0.9 km) sw. Int corridors. **Pets:** $15 daily fee/room. Designated rooms, service with restrictions, supervision.

ECO SAVE 🛜 ⨯ Ꮪᴹ 🛏 💻 ⑪ ⨯

ⓐ ▼▼ Swiss Chalet Motel Ⓜ

(250) 837-4650. **$89-$155.** 1101 W Victoria Rd V0E 2S0. 0.6 mi (1 km) s from Trans-Canada Hwy 1; downtown. Ext corridors. **Pets:** Accepted.

SAVE 🛜 ⨯ 🛏 💻

SALMON ARM

ⓐ ▼▼▼ Best Western Salmon Arm Inn Ⓜ ❀

(250) 832-9793. **$109-$220.** 61 10th St SW V1E 1E4. 0.7 mi (1.1 km) w on Trans-Canada Hwy 1. Ext corridors. **Pets:** Medium. $20 one-time fee/pet. Designated rooms, service with restrictions, supervision.

ECO SAVE 🛜 Ꮪᴹ 🛏 💻 ⩫

▼▼▼ Holiday Inn Express Hotel & Suites Salmon Arm Ⓗ

(250) 832-7711. **$123-$176.** 1090 22nd St NE V1E 2V5. 0.5 mi (0.8 km) e on Trans-Canada Hwy 1. Int corridors. **Pets:** Accepted.

ECO 🛜 Ꮪᴹ 🛏 💻 ⩫ ⨯

SMITHERS

▼▼ Aspen Inn & Suites Ⓜ

(250) 847-4551. **Call for rates.** 4628 Yellowhead Hwy V0J 2N0. 0.9 mi (1.5 km) w on Hwy 16. Ext corridors. **Pets:** Accepted.

🛜 ⨯ Ꮪᴹ 🛏 💻 ⑪ ⩫

SQUAMISH

ⓐ ▼▼▼ Best Western Mountain Retreat Hotel Ⓗ

(604) 815-0883. **$110-$160.** 38922 Progress Way V8B 0K5. 0.9 mi (1.5 km) n on Hwy 99 at Industrial Way. Int corridors. **Pets:** Other species. $20 daily fee/room. Designated rooms, crate.

SAVE 🛜 Ꮪᴹ 🛏 💻 ⑪ ⩫ ⨯

SUN PEAKS

ⓐ ▼▼▼ Coast Sundance Lodge Ⓗ ❀

(250) 578-0200. **Call for rates.** 3160 Creekside Way V0E 5N0. Hwy 5, 19.5 mi (31 km) ne on Todd Mountain Rd, follow signs to village. Int corridors. **Pets:** Dogs only. $20 daily fee/room. Service with restrictions, supervision. ECO SAVE 🛜 ⨯ Ꮪᴹ 🛏 💻 ⑪ ⨯ ⨯

▼▼▼▼ Delta Sun Peaks Resort Ⓗ

(250) 578-6000. **$89-$599.** 3240 Village Way V0E 5N0. Hwy 5, 19.4 mi (31 km) ne on Todd Mountain Rd, follow signs to village. Int corridors. **Pets:** Accepted. ECO 🛜 ⨯ Ꮪᴹ 🛏 💻 ⑪ ⩫ ⨯

TERRACE

ⓐ ▼▼▼▼ Best Western Plus Terrace Inn Ⓗ

(250) 635-0083. **$124-$134.** 4553 Greig Ave V8G 1M7. Hwy 16, just e on Greig Ave, follow City Centre signs. Int corridors. **Pets:** Accepted.

ECO SAVE 🛜 ⨯ 🛏 💻

ⓐ ▼▼▼ Coast Inn of the West Ⓗ

(250) 638-8141. **Call for rates.** 4620 Lakelse Ave V8G 1R1. Hwy 16 to City Centre; between Emerson and Kalum sts; downtown. Int corridors. **Pets:** Dogs only. $20 daily fee/room. Crate.

ECO SAVE 🛜 🛏 💻

TOFINO

ⓐ ▼▼▼▼ Best Western Tin Wis Resort Lodge Ⓗ ❀

(250) 725-4445. **Call for rates.** 1119 Pacific Rim Hwy V0R 2Z0. 1.8 mi (3.5 km) s on Hwy 4. Ext corridors. **Pets:** Small, dogs only. $25 daily fee/room. Designated rooms, supervision.

ECO SAVE 🛜 ⨯ Ꮪᴹ 🛏 💻 ⑪ ⨯ ⨯

▼▼▼ Long Beach Lodge Resort Ⓗ

(250) 725-2442. **$169-$639, 7 day notice.** 1441 Pacific Rim Hwy V0R 2Z0. 4.7 mi (7.5 km) s on Hwy 4. Ext/int corridors. **Pets:** Accepted.

🛜 ⨯ 🛏 💻 ⨯

ⓐ ▼▼▼ Pacific Sands Beach Resort Ⓗ ❀

(250) 725-3322. **$185-$740, 7 day notice.** 1421 Pacific Rim Hwy V0R 2Z0. 4.7 mi (7.5 km) s on Hwy 4. Ext corridors. **Pets:** Large. $200 deposit/room, $40 one-time fee/pet. Supervision.

SAVE 🛜 ⨯ Ꮪᴹ 🛏 💻 ⨯

ⓐ ▼▼▼▼ Wickaninnish Inn Ⓗ ❀

(250) 725-3100. **$300-$580, 14 day notice.** 500 Osprey Ln at Chesterman Beach V0R 2Z0. 2.7 mi (4.3 km) e on Hwy 4. Int corridors. **Pets:** Other species. $40 daily fee/pet. Designated rooms, service with restrictions, crate. ECO SAVE 🛜 ⨯ Ꮪᴹ 🛏 💻 ⑪ ⨯ ⨯

UCLUELET

▼▼▼ Black Rock Oceanfront Resort Ⓗ

(250) 726-4800. **Call for rates.** 596 Marine Dr V0R 3A0. 1 mi (1.6 km) e on Peninsula Rd, just s on Matterson Rd, then just w. Ext/int corridors. **Pets:** Accepted. ECO 🛜 ⨯ 🛏 💻 ⑪ ⩫ ⨯ ⨯

VALEMOUNT

ⓐ ▼▼▼ Best Western Plus Valemount Inn & Suites Ⓗ ❀

(250) 566-0086. **$120-$224.** 1950 Hwy 5 S V0E 2Z0. 0.9 mi (1.5 km) s on Hwy 5 (Yellowhead Hwy). Int corridors. **Pets:** Other species. $20 one-time fee/room. Designated rooms, service with restrictions.

SAVE 🛜 ⨯ Ꮪᴹ 🛏 💻 ⩫ ⨯

▼▼ Chalet Continental Motel Ⓜ

(250) 566-9787. **Call for rates.** 1450 5th Ave V0E 2Z0. Off Hwy 5 (Yellowhead Hwy), just e. Int corridors. **Pets:** Accepted.

🛜 ⨯ Ꮪᴹ 🛏 💻 ⩫

▼▼ Ramada Valemount Ⓗ

(250) 566-8222. **Call for rates.** 1501 Swift Creek Rd V0E 2Z0. Just e of Hwy 5 (Yellowhead Hwy). Int corridors. **Pets:** Accepted.

🛜 Ꮪᴹ 🛏 💻 ⩫ ⨯

VANCOUVER METROPOLITAN AREA

ALDERGROVE

ⒶⒶ ▼▼▼▼ **Best Western Plus Country Meadows
Inn** 🅗 ❀

(604) 856-9880. **$100-$160.** 3070 264th St V4W 3E1. Trans-Canada Hwy 1 exit 73 (264th St/Aldergrove), 3.1 mi (5 km) s on 264th St (Hwy 13). Int corridors. **Pets:** Medium. $15 daily fee/room. Designated rooms, service with restrictions, supervision.
ECO SAVE 🛜 ✕ ♨M 🖥 🖥 ⑪ 🏊

BURNABY

ⒶⒶ ▼▼▼ **Accent Inns** 🅗 ❀

(604) 473-5000. **$109-$179.** 3777 Henning Dr V5C 6N5. Trans-Canada Hwy 1 exit 28 (Grandview Hwy), just n on Boundary Rd. Ext corridors. **Pets:** Dogs only. $20 daily fee/pet. Designated rooms, service with restrictions, supervision. ECO SAVE 🛜 ✕ ♨M 🖥 🖥 ⑪ 🏊

ⒶⒶ ▼▼▼▼ **Best Western Plus Kings Inn & Conference
Center** 🅗

(604) 438-1383. **$89-$139.** 5411 Kingsway V5H 2G1. Trans-Canada Hwy 1 exit 29 (Willingdon Ave), 1.9 mi (3 km) s to Kingsway, then 1.2 mi (2 km) e. Ext corridors. **Pets:** Accepted.
SAVE 🛜 ♨M 🖥 🖥 ⑪ 🏊

ⒶⒶ ▼▼▼ ▼▼▼ **Delta Burnaby Hotel and Conference
Centre** 🅗

(604) 453-0750. **$129-$1300.** 4331 Dominion St V5G 1B2. Trans-Canada Hwy 1 exit 29 (Willingdon Ave), just w on Canada Way, then n on Sumner St. Int corridors. **Pets:** Accepted.
ECO SAVE 🛜 ✕ ♨M 🖥 🖥 ⑪ 🏊

▼▼▼▼ **Hilton Vancouver Metrotown** 🅗

(604) 438-1200. **$125-$161.** 6083 McKay Ave V5H 2W7. Trans-Canada Hwy 1 exit 29 (Willingdon Ave), 1.8 mi (3 km) s to Kingsway, then just e. Int corridors. **Pets:** Accepted. ECO 🛜 ♨M 🖥 🖥 ⑪ 🏊

▼▼▼▼ **Holiday Inn Express Metrotown** 🅗

(604) 438-1881. **$148-$194.** 4405 Central Blvd V5H 4M3. Trans-Canada Hwy 1 exit 29 (Willingdon Ave), 3.1 mi (5 km) s to Central Blvd, then just e. Int corridors. **Pets:** Medium. $25 one-time fee/room. Designated rooms, service with restrictions, crate. ECO 🛜 ✕ ♨M 🖥 🖥 🏊

COQUITLAM

▼▼▼ **Ramada Coquitlam** 🅗

(604) 931-4433. **$89-$152.** 631 Lougheed Hwy V3K 3S5. Trans-Canada Hwy 1 exit 44 (Coquitlam), 1.9 mi (3 km) w on Lougheed Hwy (Hwy 7). Ext/int corridors. **Pets:** Other species. $10 daily fee/pet. Designated rooms, service with restrictions. 🛜 ✕ 🖥 🖥 ⑪ 🏊

DELTA

ⒶⒶ ▼▼▼▼ **The Coast Tsawwassen Inn** 🅗 ❀

(604) 943-8221. **$109-$149.** 1665 56th St V4L 2B2. Hwy 99 exit 28 (Tsawwassen Ferries), 5 mi (8 km) w on Hwy 17; 3.1 mi (5 km) from the BC ferry terminal. Int corridors. **Pets:** Other species. $15 daily fee/pet. Service with restrictions, supervision.
ECO SAVE 🛜 ✕ ♨M 🖥 🖥 ⑪ 🏊 ✕

▼▼▼▼ **River Run Cottages** 🅑🅑 ❀

(604) 946-7778. **$149-$225, 21 day notice.** 4551 River Rd W V4K 1R9. Hwy 17, 1.6 mi (2.5 km) n on Ladner Trunk Rd (which becomes 47A St, then becomes River Rd W). Ext corridors. **Pets:** Dogs only. $25 daily fee/pet. Designated rooms, service with restrictions, supervision.
🛜 ✕ 🖥 🖥 🎬 🎞 🐾

LANGLEY

ⒶⒶ ▼▼▼▼ **Best Western Plus Langley Inn** 🅗

(604) 530-9311. **$109-$139.** 5978 Glover Rd V3A 4H9. Trans-Canada Hwy 1 exit 66 (232nd St), 3.6 mi (6 km) s, follow signs. Int corridors. **Pets:** Small, dogs only. $15 daily fee/pet. Designated rooms, service with restrictions, supervision. SAVE 🛜 ✕ ♨M 🖥 🖥 ⑪ 🏊

ⒶⒶ ▼▼▼ **Canadas Best Value Westward Inn** Ⓜ

(604) 534-9238. **$89-$99.** 19650 Fraser Hwy V3A 4C7. Trans-Canada Hwy 1 exit 58 (200th St/Langley City), 3.1 mi (5 km) s on 200th St, 0.6 mi (1 km) w on Hwy 10, then just w. Ext corridors. **Pets:** $4 daily fee/room. Service with restrictions, supervision. SAVE 🖥 🖥

ⒶⒶ ▼▼▼▼ **Coast Hotel & Convention Centre** 🅗

(604) 530-1500. **$113-$149.** 20393 Fraser Hwy V3A 7N2. Trans-Canada Hwy 1 exit 58 (200th St/Langley City), 3.9 mi (6.3 km) s on 200th St, then just e. Int corridors. **Pets:** Medium. $15 daily fee/room. Designated rooms, service with restrictions. ECO SAVE 🛜 ✕ ♨M 🖥 🖥 ⑪

ⒶⒶ ▼▼▼▼ **Holiday Inn Express Hotel & Suites
Langley** 🅗

(604) 882-2000. **$99-$179.** 8750 204th St V1M 2Y5. Trans-Canada Hwy 1 exit 58 (200th St/Langley City), just e on 88th Ave. Int corridors. **Pets:** Small. $10 daily fee/pet. Designated rooms, service with restrictions, supervision. ECO SAVE 🛜 ✕ ♨M 🖥 🖥 ⑪ 🏊 ✕

▼▼ ▼▼ **Sandman Hotel Langley** 🅗

(604) 888-7263. **Call for rates.** 8855 202nd St V1M 2N9. Trans-Canada Hwy 1 exit 58 (200th St/Langley City), just e on 88th Ave. Int corridors. **Pets:** Accepted. ECO 🛜 ♨M 🖥 🖥 ⑪

MAPLE RIDGE

▼▼ ▼▼ **Maple Ridge Hotel** Ⓜ

(604) 467-1511. **$76-$99.** 21650 Lougheed Hwy V2X 2S1. 1.2 mi (2 km) w on Lougheed Hwy (Hwy 7). Int corridors. **Pets:** Accepted.
🛜 ✕ ♨M 🖥 🖥 🏊 ✕

ⒶⒶ ▼▼▼▼ **Quality Inn** 🅗

(604) 463-5111. **$89-$279.** 21735 Lougheed Hwy V2X 2S2. 1.2 mi (2 km) w on Lougheed Hwy (Hwy 7). Ext corridors. **Pets:** Medium, dogs only. $20 daily fee/pet. Designated rooms, service with restrictions, supervision. SAVE 🛜 ♨M 🖥 🖥 ⑪

MISSION

ⒶⒶ ▼▼▼▼ **Best Western Plus Mission City
Lodge** 🅗 ❀

(604) 820-5500. **$89-$125.** 32281 Lougheed Hwy V2V 1A3. Just w of Hwy 11; corner of Lougheed Hwy (Hwy 7) and Hurd St. Int corridors. **Pets:** Large. $15 daily fee/pet. Designated rooms, service with restrictions, supervision. SAVE 🛜 ✕ ♨M 🖥 🖥 ⑪ 🏊 ✕

NORTH VANCOUVER

ⒶⒶ ▼▼▼ **Comfort Inn & Suites** Ⓜ

(604) 988-3181. **$99-$130.** 1748 Capilano Rd V7P 3B4. Trans-Canada Hwy 1 exit 14 (Capilano Rd), 0.9 mi (1.5 km) s; from north end of Lions Gate Bridge, 0.6 mi (1 km) e on Marine Dr, then just n. Ext corridors. **Pets:** Accepted. ECO SAVE 🛜 ✕ ♨M 🖥 🖥 🏊

ⒶⒶ ▼▼▼▼ **Holiday Inn & Suites North
Vancouver** 🅗 ❀

(604) 985-3111. **$169-$199.** 700 Old Lillooet Rd V7J 2H5. Trans-Canada Hwy 1 exit 22 (Mt Seymour Pkwy), follow signs. Int corridors. **Pets:** Medium, dogs only. $25 daily fee/pet. Designated rooms, service with restrictions, supervision.
ECO SAVE 🛜 ♨M 🖥 🖥 ⑪ 🏊 ✕

▼▼ **Lionsgate Travelodge** Ⓜ

(604) 985-5311. **$60-$125.** 2060 Marine Dr V7P 1V7. Trans-Canada Hwy 1 exit 14 (Capilano Rd), 0.9 mi (1.5 km) s, then just w; from north end of Lions Gate Bridge, just e. Ext corridors. **Pets:** Designated rooms, service with restrictions. 🛜 🖥 🖥 🏊

ⒶⒶ ▼▼▼ **North Vancouver Hotel** Ⓜ ❀

(604) 987-4461. **$79-$149.** 1800 Capilano Rd V7P 3B6. Trans-Canada Hwy 1 exit 14 (Capilano Rd), 0.9 mi (1.5 km) s; from north end of Lions Gate Bridge, 0.6 mi (1 km) e on Marine Dr, then just n. Ext corridors. **Pets:** Medium. $20 daily fee/room. Designated rooms, service with restrictions, crate. SAVE ✕ ♨M 🖥 🖥 🏊

▼▼▼▼ **Pinnacle Hotel at the Pier** H ❧
(604) 986-7437. **$129-$199.** 138 Victory Ship Way V7L 0B1. Corner of Esplanade St and Lonsdale Ave. Int corridors. **Pets:** Other species. $25 daily fee/room. Designated rooms, service with restrictions, supervision.
ECO 🛜 ❌ &M 🖥 🖵 ❌ ⛵ ❌

PITT MEADOWS
▼▼ **Ramada Inn** H
(604) 460-9859. **$89-$199.** 19267 Lougheed Hwy V3Y 2J5. Lougheed Hwy (Hwy 7) and Harris Rd. Int corridors. **Pets:** Accepted.
🛜 🖥 🖵 ❌ ⛵

RICHMOND
CAA ▼▼▼ **Accent Inns** H
(604) 273-3311. **$89-$179.** 10551 Edwards Dr V6X 3L8. Hwy 99 exit 39 (Bridgeport Rd/Airport) northbound to St Edwards Dr; exit 39A (Richmond/ Airport) southbound to St Edwards Dr. Ext corridors. **Pets:** Accepted.
ECO SAVE 🛜 ❌ &M 🖥 🖵 ❌

CAA ▼▼▼ **Best Western Abercorn Inn** H
(604) 270-7576. **$130-$190.** 9260 Bridgeport Rd V6X 1S1. Hwy 99 exit 39 (Bridgeport Rd/Airport) northbound; exit 39A (Richmond/Airport) southbound. Int corridors. **Pets:** Accepted.
ECO SAVE 🛜 ❌ &M 🖥 🖵 ❌

CAA ▼▼▼▼ **Delta Vancouver Airport** H ❧
(604) 278-1241. **$129-$329.** 3500 Cessna Dr V7B 1C7. Corner of Russ Baker Way and Cessna Dr; near Moray Bridge. Int corridors. **Pets:** Medium, other species. $40 one-time fee/room. Service with restrictions, supervision. ECO SAVE 🛜 ❌ &M 🖵 ❌ ⛵

CAA ▼▼▼ ▼▼▼ **The Fairmont Vancouver Airport** H
(604) 207-5200. **$329-$459.** 3111 Grant McConachie Way V7B 0A6. In Vancouver International Airport. Int corridors. **Pets:** Accepted.
ECO SAVE &M 🖵 ❌ ⛵ ❌

CAA ▼▼▼ **Hilton Vancouver Airport** H
(604) 273-6336. **$179-$259.** 5911 Minoru Blvd V6X 4C7. Corner of Minoru Blvd and Westminster Hwy. Int corridors. **Pets:** Accepted.
ECO SAVE 🛜 &M 🖥 🖵 ❌ ⛵ ❌

▼▼▼▼ **Holiday Inn Express Vancouver-Airport** H
(604) 273-8080. **$119-$189.** 9351 Bridgeport Rd V6X 1S3. Hwy 99 exit 39 (Bridgeport Rd/Airport) northbound; exit 39A (Richmond/Airport) southbound. Int corridors. **Pets:** Accepted. ECO 🛜 ❌ &M 🖥 🖵

▼▼▼▼ **Holiday Inn Vancouver Airport - Richmond** H
(604) 821-1818. **$115-$189.** 10720 Cambie Rd V6X 1K8. Hwy 99 exit 39A (Bridgeport Rd/Airport) northbound to St. Edwards Dr, then 0.6 mi (1 km) n; exit 39B (No 4 Rd) southbound, just e. Int corridors.
Pets: Accepted. ECO 🛜 ❌ &M 🖥 🖵 ❌

CAA ▼▼▼ ▼▼▼ **River Rock Casino Resort** H ❧
(604) 247-8900. **$139-$189.** 8811 River Rd V6X 3P8. Hwy 99 exit 39 (Bridgeport Rd/Airport) northbound; exit 39A (Richmond/Airport) southbound, just w on Bridgeport Rd, then just n on Great Canadian Way. Int corridors. **Pets:** Other species. $25 daily fee/room. Service with restrictions, supervision. SAVE 🛜 ❌ &M 🖥 🖵 ❌ ⛵ ❌

▼▼ ▼▼ **Sandman Hotel Vancouver Airport** H
(604) 303-8888. **$99-$169.** 3233 St Edwards Dr V6X 3K4. Hwy 99 exit 39 (Bridgeport Rd/Airport) northbound to St Edwards Dr; exit 39A (Richmond/Airport) southbound. Int corridors. **Pets:** Large. $10 daily fee/ pet. Designated rooms, service with restrictions, supervision.
ECO 🛜 &M 🖥 🖵 ❌ ⛵

CAA ▼▼▼ ▼▼▼ **Sheraton Vancouver Airport Hotel** H ❧
(604) 273-7878. **$139-$359.** 7551 Westminster Hwy V6X 1A3. Corner of Minoru Blvd and Westminster Hwy. Int corridors. **Pets:** Other species. Service with restrictions, supervision.
ECO SAVE 🛜 ❌ &M 🖥 🖵 ❌ ⛵

CAA ▼▼ **Travelodge Hotel Vancouver Airport** H
(604) 278-5155. **$74-$117.** 3071 St Edwards Dr V6X 3K4. Hwy 99 exit 39 (Bridgeport Rd/Airport) northbound to St Edwards Dr; exit 39A (Richmond Rd/Airport) southbound. Int corridors. **Pets:** Small. $25 one-time fee/pet, $10 daily fee/pet. Designated rooms, service with restrictions, supervision. ECO SAVE 🛜 &M 🖥 🖵 ❌ ⛵

▼▼▼▼ **Vancouver Airport Marriott** H
(604) 276-2112. **$159-$269.** 7571 Westminster Hwy V6X 1A3. Corner of Minoru Blvd and Westminster Hwy. Int corridors. **Pets:** Other species. $20 daily fee/room. Service with restrictions, supervision.
🛜 ❌ &M 🖥 🖵 ❌ ⛵

CAA ▼▼▼ ▼▼▼ **The Westin Wall Centre Vancouver Airport** H ❧
(604) 303-6565. **$149-$409.** 3099 Corvette Way V6X 4K3. Hwy 99 exit 39 (Bridgeport Rd/Airport) northbound; exit 39A (Richmond/Airport) southbound, just w to No 3 Rd. Int corridors. **Pets:** Medium, dogs only. $60 one-time fee/room. Service with restrictions, supervision.
SAVE 🛜 ❌ &M 🖥 🖵 ❌ ⛵ ❌

SURREY
▼▼▼ **Coast Surrey Guildford Hotel** H
(604) 930-4700. **$99-$135.** 10410 158th St V4N 5C2. Trans-Canada Hwy 1 exit 50 (160th St), just w on 104th Ave. Int corridors. **Pets:** Small, dogs only. $20 daily fee/pet. Designated rooms, service with restrictions, supervision. 🛜 ❌ &M 🖥 ⛵

▼▼▼ **Comfort Inn & Suites Surrey** H
(604) 576-8888. **$96-$107.** 8255 166th St V4N 5R8. Trans-Canada Hwy 1 exit 53 (176th St/Hwy 15), 2.9 mi (4.8 km) s to Fraser Hwy (Hwy 1A), then 1.6 mi (2.6 km) nw. Int corridors. **Pets:** Accepted.
🛜 ❌ &M 🖥 🖵

▼▼▼ **Compass Point Inn** H
(604) 588-9511. **$99-$129, 3 day notice.** 9850 King George Hwy V3T 4Y3. Jct Fraser Hwy (Hwy 1A) and Hwy 99A (King George Hwy). Int corridors. **Pets:** Accepted. 🛜 ❌ &M 🖥 🖵 ❌ ⛵

CAA ▼▼▼ ▼▼ **Ramada Langley-Surrey** H ❧
(604) 576-8388. **$89-$179.** 19225 Hwy 10 V3S 8V9. Trans-Canada Hwy 1 exit 58 (200th St/Langley City), 3.1 mi (5 km) s on 200th St, then 1.2 mi (2 km) w on Rt 10; corner of 192nd St and Rt 10. Int corridors. **Pets:** Dogs only. $15 daily fee/pet. Designated rooms, service with restrictions. SAVE 🛜 ❌ &M 🖥 🖵 ❌ ⛵

CAA ▼▼▼ ▼▼ **Sheraton Vancouver Guildford Hotel** H ❧
(604) 582-9288. **$125-$185.** 15269 104th Ave V3R 1N5. Trans-Canada Hwy 1 exit 48 eastbound, 0.6 mi (1 km) s on 152nd St, then just e; exit 50 westbound, then just w. Int corridors. **Pets:** Medium, dogs only. Designated rooms, service with restrictions, supervision.
ECO SAVE 🛜 ❌ &M 🖥 🖵 ❌ ⛵

VANCOUVER
CAA ▼▼ **2400 Motel** M
(604) 434-2464. **$89-$189.** 2400 Kingsway V5R 5G9. 4.5 mi (7.2 km) se on Hwy 1A and 99A (Kingsway and 33rd Ave). Ext corridors.
Pets: Accepted. SAVE 🛜 🖥 🖵 ❌

CAA ▼▼ **Best Western Plus Downtown Vancouver** H ❧
(604) 669-9888. **$103-$180.** 718 Drake St V6Z 2W6. Between Howe and Granville sts. Int corridors. **Pets:** Large, dogs only. $20 daily fee/pet. Designated rooms, service with restrictions, crate.
ECO SAVE 🛜 ❌ &M 🖥 🖵 ❌

CAA ▼▼▼ ▼▼ **Best Western Plus Sands** H ❧
(604) 682-1831. **$99-$259.** 1755 Davie St V6G 1W5. Between Bidwell and Denman sts. Int corridors. **Pets:** Other species. $15 daily fee/pet. Designated rooms, no service.
ECO SAVE 🛜 ❌ &M 🖥 🖵 ❌

▼▼▼ Cascadia Hotel & Suites H

(604) 688-1234. **Call for rates.** 1234 Hornby St V6Z 1W2. Between Drake and Davie sts. Int corridors. **Pets:** Accepted.

⊕ ▼▼▼▼ Delta Vancouver Suites H

(604) 689-8188. **$159-$299.** 550 W Hastings St V6B 1L6. Between Seymour and Richards sts; entrance in alley way. Int corridors.
Pets: Accepted.

⊕ ▼▼▼ ▼▼▼ The Fairmont Hotel Vancouver H ❀

(604) 684-3131. **$199-$429.** 900 W Georgia St V6C 2W6. Corner of Burrard at W Georgia St; enter from Hornby St. Int corridors. **Pets:** $25 daily fee/room. Supervision.

⊕ ▼▼▼ ▼▼▼ Fairmont Pacific Rim H ❀

(604) 695-5300. **$229-$499.** 1038 Canada Place V6C 0B9. Between Burrard and Thurlow sts. Int corridors. **Pets:** Other species. $30 daily fee/room. Service with restrictions, supervision.

⊕ ▼▼▼ ▼▼▼ The Fairmont Waterfront H

(604) 691-1991. **$199-$429.** 900 Canada Place Way V6C 3L5. Howe St at Cordova St. Int corridors. **Pets:** $50 one-time fee/room. Service with restrictions, supervision.

⊕ ▼▼▼ ▼▼▼ Four Seasons Hotel Vancouver H

(604) 689-9333. **$255-$2750.** 791 W Georgia St V6C 2T4. Between Howe and Granville sts. Int corridors. **Pets:** Accepted.

⊕ ▼▼▼ ▼▼▼ Georgian Court Hotel H ❀

(604) 682-5555. **$159-$399.** 773 Beatty St V6B 2M4. Between Georgia and Robson sts. Int corridors. **Pets:** Other species. $20 daily fee/pet. Designated rooms, service with restrictions, supervision.

⊕ ▼▼▼ ▼▼▼ Granville Island Hotel H ❀

(604) 683-7373. **$189-$550.** 1253 Johnston St V6H 3R9. Granville Island; below the bridge, follow signs. Int corridors. **Pets:** Other species. $25 daily fee/room. Designated rooms, service with restrictions.

▼▼▼ ▼▼▼ Holiday Inn Express Vancouver H

(604) 254-1000. **$119-$309.** 2889 E Hastings St V5K 2A1. Between Renfrew and Kaslo sts. Int corridors. **Pets:** Accepted.

⊕ ▼▼▼ ▼▼▼ Hotel Le Soleil H

(604) 632-3000. **$375-$475.** 567 Hornby St V6C 2E8. Between Dunsmuir and Pender sts. Int corridors. **Pets:** Accepted.

⊕ ▼▼▼ ▼▼▼ Howard Johnson Hotel Downtown Vancouver H

(604) 688-8701. **$71-$152.** 1176 Granville St V6Z 1L8. Between Davie and Helmcken sts. Int corridors. **Pets:** Accepted.

⊕ ▼▼▼ ▼▼▼ Hyatt Regency Vancouver H ❀

(604) 683-1234. **$139-$439.** 655 Burrard St V6C 2R7. Between W Georgia and Melville sts. Int corridors. **Pets:** Medium, dogs only. $50 one-time fee/pet. Designated rooms, service with restrictions, supervision.

▼▼▼ ▼▼▼ L'Hermitage Hotel H

(778) 327-4100. **$180-$495.** 788 Richards St V6B 3A4. Between Robson and W Georgia sts. Int corridors. **Pets:** Accepted.

⊕ ▼▼▼ ▼▼▼ Pan Pacific Vancouver H ❀

(604) 662-8111. **$179-$439.** 300-999 Canada Pl V6C 3B5. Motor entrance off Burrard St. Int corridors. **Pets:** Other species. $30 daily fee/pet. Service with restrictions, supervision.

▼▼▼ ▼▼▼ Quality Hotel Downtown-The Inn at False Creek H

(604) 682-0229. **$79-$199.** 1335 Howe St V6Z 1R7. Between Drake and Pacific sts. Int corridors. **Pets:** Medium. $15 daily fee/pet. Designated rooms, service with restrictions.

⊕ ▼▼▼ ▼▼▼ Ramada Inn & Suites Downtown Vancouver H

(604) 685-1111. **$79-$199.** 1221 Granville St V6Z 1M6. Between Davie and Drake sts. Int corridors. **Pets:** Accepted.

⊕ ▼▼▼ ▼▼▼ Renaissance Vancouver Harbourside Hotel H

(604) 689-9211. **$169-$329.** 1133 W Hastings St V6E 3T3. Between Bute and Thurlow sts. Int corridors. **Pets:** Accepted.

⊕ ▼▼▼ ▼▼▼ Rosewood Hotel Georgia H

(604) 682-5566. **$215-$395.** 667 W Howe St V6C 1P7. Between W Georgia and Dunsmuir sts. Int corridors. **Pets:** Accepted.

▼▼▼ ▼▼▼ Sandman Hotel Vancouver City Centre H

(604) 681-2211. **$109-$209.** 180 W Georgia St V6B 4P4. Between Cambie and Beatty sts. Int corridors. **Pets:** Accepted.

⊕ ▼▼▼ ▼▼▼ Shangri-La Hotel Vancouver H ❀

(604) 689-1120. **$405-$525.** 1128 W Georgia St V6E 0A8. Between Thurlow and Bute sts. Int corridors. **Pets:** Medium. $50 one-time fee/room. Service with restrictions, supervision.

⊕ ▼▼▼ ▼▼▼ Sheraton Vancouver Wall Centre Hotel H ❀

(604) 331-1000. **$159-$449.** 1088 Burrard St V6Z 2R9. Between Helmcken and Nelson sts. Int corridors. **Pets:** Medium. $60 one-time fee/room. Service with restrictions, crate.

⊕ ▼▼▼ ▼▼▼ The Sutton Place Hotel H ❀

(604) 682-5511. **Call for rates.** 845 Burrard St V6Z 2K6. Between Smithe and Robson sts. Int corridors. **Pets:** Medium, other species. $40 one-time fee/room. Service with restrictions.

▼▼▼ ▼▼▼ Sylvia Hotel H ❀

(604) 681-9321. **$80-$400.** 1154 Gilford St V6G 2P6. Between Pendrell St and Beach Ave. Int corridors. **Pets:** Other species. Service with restrictions, supervision.

⊕ ▼▼▼ ▼▼▼ Vancouver Marriott Pinnacle Downtown H

(604) 684-1128. **$169-$329.** 1128 W Hastings St V6E 4R5. Between Thurlow and Bute sts. Int corridors. **Pets:** Accepted.

⊕ ▼▼▼ ▼▼▼ The Westin Bayshore Vancouver H ❀

(604) 682-3377. **$189-$460.** 1601 Bayshore Dr V6G 2V4. W Georgia and Cardero sts. Int corridors. **Pets:** Dogs only. Service with restrictions, supervision.

Ⓐ ▼▼▼ **The Westin Grand, Vancouver** H

(604) 602-1999. **$169-$679.** 433 Robson St V6B 6L9. Between Homer and Richards sts. Int corridors. **Pets:** Accepted.

ECO SAVE 🛜 ✕ 🛆M ⬛ 🖥 ¶ 🏊 ✕

WHITE ROCK

▼▼▼ **Ocean Promenade Hotel** H

(604) 542-0102. **$109-$469.** 15611 Marine Dr V4B 1E1. Hwy 99 exit 2B southbound; exit 2 (White Rock/8th Ave) northbound, 1.3 mi (2 km) w. Ext/int corridors. **Pets:** Accepted. 🛜 ✕ 🛆M ⬛ 🖥

END METROPOLITAN AREA

VICTORIA METROPOLITAN AREA

SAANICH

Ⓐ ▼▼ **Howard Johnson Hotel & Suites** H ❀

(250) 704-4656. **$116-$170.** 4670 Elk Lake Dr V8Z 5M2. Blanshard St (Hwy 17), just w on Royal Oak Dr, then just n. Ext/int corridors. **Pets:** Large, other species. $15 daily fee/pet. Designated rooms, service with restrictions, supervision. ECO 🛜 ✕ 🛆M ⬛ 🖥 ¶ 🏊

SAANICHTON

Ⓐ ▼▼▼ **Quality Inn Waddling Dog** H

(250) 652-1146. **$99-$149.** 2476 Mt Newton Crossroad V8M 2B8. Corner of Blanshard St (Hwy 17) and Mt Newton Crossroad. Int corridors. **Pets:** Dogs only. $15 daily fee/pet. Service with restrictions, supervision.

SAVE 🛜 ✕ 🖥 ¶

SIDNEY

Ⓐ ▼▼▼▼ **Best Western Plus Emerald Isle Motor Inn** H ❀

(250) 656-4441. **$109-$349.** 2306 Beacon Ave V8L 1X2. Hwy 17 exit 28 (Sidney), just e. Int corridors. **Pets:** Large, other species. $15 daily fee/pet. Designated rooms, supervision.

ECO SAVE 🛜 🛆M ⬛ 🖥 ¶ ✕

Ⓐ ▼▼▼ **The Cedarwood Inn & Suites** H

(250) 656-5551. **$95-$255.** 9522 Lochside Dr V8L 1N8. Hwy 17 exit 26, just e on McTavish Rd, then 0.8 mi (1.4 km) n. Ext corridors. **Pets:** Other species. $15 daily fee/pet. Designated rooms, service with restrictions, supervision. SAVE 🛜 ✕ 🛆M ⬛ 🖥 ✗

Ⓐ ▼▼▼ **The Sidney Pier Hotel & Spa** H ❀

(250) 655-9445. **$139-$369.** 9805 Seaport Pl V8L 4X3. Hwy 17 exit 28 (Beacon Ave), 0.6 mi (1 km) e. Int corridors. **Pets:** Dogs only. $30 daily fee/room. Designated rooms, service with restrictions, supervision.

ECO SAVE 🛜 ✕ 🛆M ⬛ 🖥 ¶ ✕

Ⓐ ▼▼▼ **Victoria Airport Travelodge Sidney** H ❀

(250) 656-1176. **$76-$128.** 2280 Beacon Ave V8L 1X1. Hwy 17 exit 28 (Beacon Ave), just e. Int corridors. **Pets:** Other species. $15 daily fee/room. Designated rooms, service with restrictions, supervision.

SAVE 🛜 🛆M ⬛ 🖥 🏊

SOOKE

▼▼▼ **Ocean Wilderness Inn** BB

(250) 646-2116. **$130-$220, 7 day notice.** 9171 W Coast Rd V9Z 1G3. 8.6 mi (14 km) w on Hwy 14. Ext/int corridors. **Pets:** $25 daily fee/pet. Designated rooms, no service, supervision.

🛜 ✕ ⬛ ✗ 𝒲 ✗

Ⓐ ▼▼▼▼ **Sooke Harbour House** CI ❀

(250) 642-3421. **$318-$758, 7 day notice.** 1528 Whiffen Spit Rd V9Z 0T4. 1.2 mi (2 km) w on Hwy 14. Ext/int corridors. **Pets:** Other species. $40 daily fee/pet. ECO SAVE 🛜 ✕ 🛆M ⬛ 🖥 ¶ ✗ 𝒲

VICTORIA

▼▼▼ **Abbeymoore Manor Bed & Breakfast Inn** BB

(250) 370-1470. **$129-$249, 14 day notice.** 1470 Rockland Ave V8S 1W2. Blanshard St (Hwy 17), 1.2 mi (2 km) e on Fort St, just s on St Charles St, then just w. Ext/int corridors. **Pets:** Accepted.

🛜 ✕ ⬛ 🖥 ✗

▼▼▼ **Abigail's Hotel** H ❀

(250) 388-5363. **$172-$349, 14 day notice.** 906 McClure St V8V 3E7. Blanshard St (Hwy 17), just e on Fairfield Rd, then just n on Vancouver St. Int corridors. **Pets:** Dogs only. $30 one-time fee/pet. Designated rooms, service with restrictions, supervision. 🛜 ✕ ⬛ 🖥

Ⓐ ▼▼▼ **Accent Inns** H

(250) 475-7500. **$99-$189.** 3233 Maple St V8X 4Y9. 1.9 mi (3 km) n on Blanshard St (Hwy 17); corner of Blanshard St and Cloverdale Ave. Ext corridors. **Pets:** Accepted. ECO SAVE 🛜 ✕ 🛆M ⬛ 🖥 ¶

Ⓐ ▼▼▼ **Admiral Inn** M ❀

(250) 388-6267. **$109-$229, 45 day notice.** 257 Belleville St V8V 1X1. Corner of Belleville and Quebec sts. Ext corridors. **Pets:** Other species. $15 daily fee/pet. Designated rooms, service with restrictions, crate.

SAVE 🛜 ✕ ⬛ 🖥

Ⓐ ▼▼▼ **Best Western Plus Carlton Plaza Hotel** H ❀

(250) 388-5513. **$89-$259.** 642 Johnson St V8W 1M6. Between Douglas and Broad sts. Int corridors. **Pets:** Large. $10 one-time fee/pet. Designated rooms, service with restrictions, supervision.

ECO SAVE 🛜 ✕ 🛆M ⬛ 🖥 ¶

Ⓐ ▼▼ **Blue Ridge Inns** M

(250) 388-4345. **$59-$109.** 3110 Douglas St V8Z 3K4. Between Finlayson St and Speed Ave. Ext corridors. **Pets:** Accepted.

ECO SAVE ⬛ 🖥 ¶ 🏊 ✗

▼▼▼ **Chateau Victoria Hotel and Suites** H ❀

(250) 382-4221. **$89-$229.** 740 Burdett Ave V8W 1B2. Between Douglas and Blanshard (Hwy 17) sts. Int corridors. **Pets:** Dogs only. $15 daily fee/pet. Designated rooms, service with restrictions, crate.

ECO 🛜 ✕ ⬛ 🖥 ¶ 🏊

Ⓐ ▼▼▼ **Comfort Inn & Suites** M

(250) 388-7861. **$80-$260.** 101 Island Hwy V9B 1E8. Douglas St, 3.1 mi (5 km) w on Gorge Rd, then just s on Admirals Rd. Ext/int corridors. **Pets:** Dogs only. $15 daily fee/pet. Service with restrictions, supervision.

SAVE 🛜 ⬛ 🖥 🏊

Ⓐ ▼▼▼ **Days Inn Victoria on the Harbour** H ❀

(250) 386-3451. **$110-$173.** 427 Belleville St V8V 1X3. Between Oswego and Menzies sts. Int corridors. **Pets:** $10 daily fee/room. Designated rooms, service with restrictions.

ECO SAVE 🛜 ✕ ⬛ 🖥 ¶ 🏊 ✗

Ⓐ ▼▼▼▼ **Delta Victoria Ocean Pointe Resort and Spa** H ❀

(250) 360-2999. **$129-$328.** 45 Songhees Rd V9A 6T3. Just w of Johnson St Bridge; Esquimalt at Tyee Rd. Int corridors. **Pets:** Medium, other species. $35 one-time fee/room. Designated rooms, supervision.

ECO SAVE 🛜 ✕ 🛆M ⬛ 🖥 ¶ 🏊 ✕

Executive House Hotel H

(250) 388-5111. **$99-$215.** 777 Douglas St V8W 2B5. Between Blan-shard (Hwy 17) and Douglas sts; downtown. Int corridors. **Pets:** Medium, other species. $15 daily fee/pet.

The Fairmont Empress H

(250) 384-8111. **$199-$499, 3 day notice.** 721 Government St V8W 1W5. Between Belleville and Humboldt sts. Int corridors. **Pets:** Accepted.

Harbour Towers Hotel & Suites H

(250) 385-2405. **$94-$450.** 345 Quebec St V8V 1W4. Between Oswego and Pendray sts. Int corridors. **Pets:** Accepted.

Howard Johnson Hotel-City of Victoria H

(250) 382-2151. **$71-$116.** 310 Gorge Rd E V8T 2W2. From Douglas St, 0.6 mi (1.4 km) w; between Jutland St and Washington Ave. Int corridors. **Pets:** Accepted.

Huntingdon Hotel & Suites H

(250) 381-3456. **$79-$389.** 330 Quebec St V8V 1W3. Between Oswego and Pendray sts. Int corridors. **Pets:** Accepted.

The Magnolia Hotel & Spa H

(250) 381-0999. **$189-$369.** 623 Courtney St V8W 1B8. Corner of Court-ney and Gordon sts. Int corridors. **Pets:** Accepted.

Prior House B&B Inn BB

(250) 592-8847. **$159-$259, 14 day notice.** 620 St. Charles St V8S 3N7. Blanshard St (Hwy 17), 1.2 mi (2 km) e on Fort St, then just s. Int corridors. **Pets:** Accepted.

Quality Inn Downtown Inner Harbour H

(250) 385-6787. **$99.** 850 Blanshard St V8W 2H2. Between Courtney St and Burnett Ave; downtown. Int corridors. **Pets:** Accepted.

Ramada Victoria H

(250) 386-1422. **$59-$139.** 123 Gorge Rd E V9A 1L1. From Douglas St, 1.2 mi (2.4 km) w. Int corridors. **Pets:** Large, dogs only. $15 daily fee/pet. Designated rooms, service with restrictions, crate.

Robin Hood Motel M

(250) 388-4302. **$66-$109.** 136 Gorge Rd E V9A 1L4. From Douglas St, 1.2 mi (2.4 km) w. Ext corridors. **Pets:** Dogs only. $5 daily fee/pet. Desig-nated rooms, service with restrictions, supervision.

Royal Scot Hotel & Suites H

(250) 388-5463. **$120-$299.** 425 Quebec St V8V 1W7. Between Menzies and Oswego sts. Int corridors. **Pets:** Medium, dogs only. $50 one-time fee/pet. Designated rooms, service with restrictions, supervision.

Travelodge Victoria H

(250) 388-6611. **$62-$130.** 229 Gorge Rd E V9A 1L1. From Douglas St, 1.2 mi (2 km) w at Washington Ave. Ext corridors. **Pets:** $10 daily fee/ pet. Service with restrictions, crate.

Victoria Marriott Inner Harbour H

(250) 480-3800. **$134-$224.** 728 Humboldt St V8W 3Z5. Between Blan-shard (Hwy 17) and Douglas sts. Int corridors. **Pets:** Medium, other spe-cies. $50 one-time fee/room. Service with restrictions, supervision.

The Westin Bear Mountain Golf Resort & Spa H

(250) 391-7160. **$109-$599.** 1999 Country Club Way V9B 6R3. Trans-Canada Hwy 1 exit 14 (Langford/Highlands), 1.1 mi (1.7 km) n on Mill-stream Rd, then 1.9 mi (3 km) ne on Bear Mountain Pkwy, follow signs. Int corridors. **Pets:** Medium, dogs only. $20 daily fee/room. Designated rooms, service with restrictions, supervision.

END METROPOLITAN AREA

WHISTLER

The Coast Blackcomb Suites at Whistler CO

(604) 905-3400. **$125-$799, 60 day notice.** 4899 Painted Cliff Rd V0N 1B4. Hwy 99, 0.6 mi (1 km) e on Lorimer Rd (Upper Village), just se on Blackcomb Way, then just w, follow road all the way to the end. Int corri-dors. **Pets:** Accepted.

Crystal Lodge & Suites H

(604) 932-2221. **$99-$339, 3 day notice.** 4154 Village Green V0N 1B4. Hwy 99, just e on Village Gate Blvd, then follow road to Whistler Way. Int corridors. **Pets:** Accepted.

Delta Whistler Village Suites H

(604) 905-3987. **$109-$409, 30 day notice.** 4308 Main St V0N 1B4. Hwy 99, just e on Village Gate Blvd, just n on Northlands Blvd, then just e. Int corridors. **Pets:** Accepted.

Edgewater Lodge H

(604) 932-0688. **$135-$339, 14 day notice.** 8020 Alpine Way V0N 1B0. 2.5 mi (4 km) n of Whistler Village via Hwy 99, then just e. Ext corridors. **Pets:** Dogs only. $20 daily fee/pet. Designated rooms, service with restric-tions, supervision.

The Fairmont Chateau Whistler H

(604) 938-8000. **$179-$900, 3 day notice.** 4599 Chateau Blvd V0N 1B4. Hwy 99, 0.6 mi (1 km) e on Lorimer Rd (Upper Village), just w on Blackcomb Way. Int corridors. **Pets:** Accepted.

Four Seasons Resort Whistler H

(604) 935-3400. **$305-$920, 30 day notice.** 4591 Blackcomb Way V0N 1B4. Hwy 99, 0.6 mi (1 km) e on Lorimer Rd (Upper Village). Int corri-dors. **Pets:** Accepted.

Hilton Whistler Resort & Spa H

(604) 932-1982. **$139-$399.** 4050 Whistler Way V0N 1B4. Hwy 99, just e on Village Gate Blvd, then follow Whistler Way. Int corridors. **Pets:** Accepted.

The Listel Hotel Whistler H

(604) 932-1133. **Call for rates.** 4121 Village Green V0N 1B4. Hwy 99, just e on Village Gate Blvd, then follow Whistler Way. Int corridors. **Pets:** Accepted.

Nita Lake Lodge H

(604) 966-5700. **Call for rates.** 2131 Lake Placid Rd V0N 1B2. 1.8 mi (3 km) s on Hwy 99, just w. Int corridors. **Pets:** Accepted.

Pan Pacific Whistler Village Centre H

(604) 966-5500. **Call for rates.** 4299 Blackcomb Way V0N 1B4. Hwy 99, just e on Village Gate Blvd. Int corridors. **Pets:** Accepted.

Summit Lodge & Spa H

(604) 932-2778. **$150-$599, 30 day notice.** 4359 Main St V0N 1B4. Hwy 99, just n on Village Gate Blvd, then just w on Northlands Blvd. Int corridors. **Pets:** Accepted.

◆◆ Tantalus Resort Lodge **CO** ❖

(604) 932-4146. **$139-$599, 3 day notice.** 4200 Whistler Way V0N 1B4. Hwy 99, just e on Village Gate Blvd, then follow Whistler Way to the end. Int corridors. **Pets:** Medium. $35 one-time fee/room. Service with restrictions, supervision. **ECO** 🛜 ✕ 🛏 🖥 ⊶ ✕ 🅰️

Ⓒ ◆◆◆ The Westin Resort & Spa, Whistler **H**

(604) 905-5000. **$149-$949, 21 day notice.** 4090 Whistler Way V0N 1B4. Hwy 99, just e on Village Gate Blvd, then s. Int corridors. **Pets:** Accepted. **ECO** **SAVE** 🛜 ✕ 🅼 🛏 🖥 ⦀ ⊶ ✕

WILLIAMS LAKE

◆ Drummond Lodge Motel **M**

(250) 392-5334. **$82-$145.** 1405 Cariboo Hwy V2G 2W3. 0.6 mi (1 km) s on Hwy 97. Ext corridors. **Pets:** Accepted. 🛜 🛏 🖥

Ⓒ ◆◆ Williams Lake Super 8 **M**

(250) 398-8884. **$83-$92.** 1712 Broadway Ave S V2G 2W4. 1.2 mi (2 km) s on Hwy 97. Int corridors. **Pets:** Small, other species. $15 daily fee/pet. Designated rooms, service with restrictions, supervision. **SAVE** 🛜 ✕ 🅼 🛏 🖥

MANITOBA

BEAUSEJOUR

▼▼ ▼▼ Superior Inn H

(204) 268-9050. **Call for rates.** 1055 Park Ave R0E 0C0. On Hwy 215; jct Hwy 12/44/302. Int corridors. **Pets:** Accepted.

BRANDON

ⒶⒶ ▼▼▼▼ Canad Inns-Destination Centre Brandon H

(204) 727-1422. **$115-$235.** 1125 18th St R7A 7C5. On Hwy 10 (18th St); jct Brandon Ave. Int corridors. **Pets:** Accepted.

▼▼ ▼▼ Comfort Inn Brandon M ❖

(204) 727-6232. **$114-$165.** 925 Middleton Ave R7C 1A8. Trans-Canada Hwy 1; between Hwy 10 (18th St) N and Hwy 10 S; on northside of service road. Int corridors. **Pets:** Other species. $10 daily fee/room. Service with restrictions, supervision.

▼▼ ▼▼ Days Inn Brandon H

(204) 727-3600. **$98-$166.** 2130 Currie Blvd R7B 4E7. Jct Trans-Canada Hwy 1, 4.9 mi (7.9 km) s on Hwy 10 (18th St). Int corridors. **Pets:** Small. $15 daily fee/pet. Designated rooms, service with restrictions, supervision.

▼▼ ▼▼ Royal Oak Inn & Suites H

(204) 728-5775. **Call for rates.** 3130 Victoria Ave R7B 0N2. Jct Trans-Canada Hwy 1 and 10 (18 St), 3.1 mi (5 km) s, then 1.1 mi (0.8 km) w. Int corridors. **Pets:** Accepted.

▼▼ ▼▼ Victoria Inn H

(204) 725-1532. **$116-$199.** 3550 Victoria Ave R7B 2R4. Jct Trans-Canada Hwy 1 and 10 (18 St), 3.1 mi (5 km) s, then 0.9 mi (1.4 km) w. Int corridors. **Pets:** Small, other species. $10 daily fee/room. Service with restrictions, supervision.

FLIN FLON

▼▼ ▼▼ Victoria Inn North H

(204) 687-7555. **Call for rates.** 160 Hwy 10A N R8A 0C6. Jct Hwy 10 and 10A, 0.6 mi (1 km) nw (eastern approach to city). Int corridors. **Pets:** Accepted.

PORTAGE LA PRAIRIE

▼▼ ▼▼ Super 8 H ❖

(204) 857-8883. **Call for rates.** 2668 Hwy 1A W R1N 3B2. On Hwy 1A, 0.9 mi (1.5 km) w. Int corridors. **Pets:** Other species. $10 daily fee/pet. Designated rooms, service with restrictions, supervision.

RUSSELL

▼▼ ▼▼ The Russell Inn Hotel & Conference Centre H ❖

(204) 773-2186. **$100-$196, 14 day notice.** Hwy 16 R0J 1W0. 0.8 mi (1.2 km) se on Hwy 16 and 83. Ext/int corridors. **Pets:** Small. Supervision.

STEINBACH

▼▼ ▼▼ Days Inn H

(204) 320-9200. **$90-$100.** 75 Hwy 12 N R5G 1T3. 0.5 mi (0.8 km) n of jct Hwy 52. Int corridors. **Pets:** Accepted.

SWAN RIVER

▼▼ ▼▼ Swan Valley Super 8 H

(204) 734-7888. **$80-$89.** 115 Kelsey Tr R0L 1Z0. Corner of Hwy 10 and 83. Int corridors. **Pets:** Accepted.

THE PAS

▼▼ ▼▼ Kikiwak Inn H

(204) 623-1800. **Call for rates.** Hwy 10 N R0B 2J0. On Hwy 10, 0.4 mi (0.6 km) n. Int corridors. **Pets:** Accepted.

▼▼ ▼▼ Super 8 H

(204) 623-1888. **$94-$120.** 1717 Gordon Ave R9A 1K3. At southern approach to town. Int corridors. **Pets:** Accepted.

THOMPSON

ⒶⒶ ▼▼ ▼▼ Lakeview Inn & Suites H

(204) 778-8879. **Call for rates.** 70 Thompson Dr N R8N 1Y8. Just w of Hwy 6. Int corridors. **Pets:** Small. $10 one-time fee/pet. Service with restrictions, supervision.

WINNIPEG METROPOLITAN AREA

WINNIPEG

ⒶⒶ ▼▼▼ Best Western Plus Pembina Inn & Suites H ❖

(204) 269-8888. **$116-$123.** 1714 Pembina Hwy R3T 2G2. 0.6 mi (1 km) n of jct Bishop Grandin Blvd. Int corridors. **Pets:** $12 daily fee/pet. Designated rooms, service with restrictions, supervision.

ⒶⒶ ▼▼▼ Canad Inns Destination Centre Polo Park H

(204) 775-8791. **$105-$259.** 1405 St. Matthews Ave R3G 0K5. Just e of St James St. Int corridors. **Pets:** Accepted.

▼▼▼▼ Clarion Hotel & Suites H

(204) 774-5110. **$144-$250.** 1445 Portage Ave R3G 3P4. Jct Empress St. Int corridors. **Pets:** Accepted.

ⒶⒶ ▼▼ ▼▼ Comfort Inn Airport M

(204) 783-5627. **$75-$140.** 1770 Sargent Ave R3H 0C8. At King Edward St. Int corridors. **Pets:** Accepted.

ⒶⒶ ▼▼ ▼▼ Comfort Inn South M

(204) 269-7390. **$114-$165.** 3109 Pembina Hwy R3T 4R6. Just n of jct Perimeter Hwy 100 and 75. Int corridors. **Pets:** Medium. $15 daily fee/pet. Designated rooms, service with restrictions, supervision.

▼▼ ▼▼ Country Inn & Suites By Carlson H

(204) 783-6900. **$110-$140, 4 day notice.** 730 King Edward St R3H 1B4. Just s of Wellington Ave. Int corridors. **Pets:** Accepted.

▼▼▼▼ Delta Winnipeg H ❖

(204) 942-0551. **$99-$399.** 350 St. Mary Ave R3C 3J2. At Hargrave St. Int corridors. **Pets:** $35 one-time fee/pet. Service with restrictions, supervision.

The Fairmont Winnipeg H
(204) 957-1350. **Call for rates.** 2 Lombard Pl R3B 0Y3. Just e of Portage Ave and Main St. Int corridors. **Pets:** Accepted.
ECO 🛜 &M 🖵 ⊤⊤ 🛥 ⊠

Greenwood Inn & Suites H
(204) 775-9889. **Call for rates.** 1715 Wellington Ave R3H 0G1. At Century St. Int corridors. **Pets:** Accepted.
ECO 🛜 &M 🔋 🖵 ⊤⊤ 🛥 ⊠

CAA **Hilton Suites Winnipeg Airport** H 🐾
(204) 783-1700. **$89-$229.** 1800 Wellington Ave R3H 1B2. At Berry St. Int corridors. **Pets:** Other species. Service with restrictions, crate.
ECO SAVE 🛜 ⊠ &M 🔋 🖵 ⊤⊤ 🛥 ⊠

Holiday Inn Winnipeg South H
(204) 452-4747. **$120-$199.** 1330 Pembina Hwy R3T 2B4. At McGillivray Blvd. Int corridors. **Pets:** Accepted. ECO 🛜 &M 🔋 🖵 ⊤⊤ 🛥

CAA **MainStay Suites Winnipeg** H
(204) 594-0500. **Call for rates.** 670 King Edward St R3H 0P2. Between Sargent and Ellice aves. Int corridors. **Pets:** Medium, other species. $10 daily fee/pet. Designated rooms, service with restrictions, crate.
SAVE 🛜 ⊠ &M 🔋 🖵

CAA **Place Louis Riel Suite Hotel** H
(204) 947-6961. **$150-$440.** 190 Smith St R3C 1J8. At St. Mary Ave. Int corridors. **Pets:** Accepted.
ECO SAVE 🛜 ⊠ &M 🔋 🖵 ⊤⊤ ⊠

CAA **Quality Inn & Suites** H 🐾
(204) 453-8247. **$90-$300.** 635 Pembina Hwy R3M 2L4. Jct s of Grant Ave. Int corridors. **Pets:** Large, other species. $15 daily fee/pet.
SAVE 🛜 🔋 🖵 ⊤⊤

Sandman Hotel & Suites Winnipeg Airport H
(204) 775-7263. **Call for rates.** 1750 Sargent Ave R3H 0C7. Between King Edward and Century sts. Int corridors. **Pets:** Accepted.
ECO 🛜 &M 🔋 🖵 ⊤⊤ 🛥

CAA **Travelodge Winnipeg** H 🐾
(204) 255-6000. **$85-$108.** 20 Alpine Ave R2M 0Y5. Just e of jct Fermor Ave and St. Anne's Rd. Int corridors. **Pets:** Other species. $10 daily fee/room. Designated rooms, service with restrictions, supervision.
ECO SAVE 🛜 ⊠ &M 🔋 🖵 ⊤⊤ 🛥 ⊠

CAA **Victoria Inn Hotel & Convention Centre** H
(204) 786-4801. **$134-$174.** 1808 Wellington Ave R3H 0G3. At Berry St. Int corridors. **Pets:** Accepted.
ECO SAVE 🛜 ⊠ &M 🔋 🖵 ⊤⊤ 🛥 ⊠

Viscount Gort Hotel H
(204) 775-0451. **$120-$180.** 1670 Portage Ave R3J 0C9. Jct Rt 90. Int corridors. **Pets:** Small. $25 one-time fee/room, $10 daily fee/room. Designated rooms, service with restrictions, supervision.
🛜 ⊠ &M 🔋 🖵 ⊤⊤ 🛥 ⊠

END METROPOLITAN AREA

NEW BRUNSWICK

BATHURST

◆◆ **Atlantic Host Hotel** 🅷

(506) 548-3335. **$110-$160.** 1450 Vanier Blvd E2A 4H7. Rt 11 exit 310 (Vanier Blvd). Int corridors. **Pets:** Accepted. 🛜 🖥 🍽 🏊 ⊠

◆◆ **Comfort Inn** 🅷

(506) 547-8000. **$90-$100.** 1170 St Peter's Ave E2A 2Z9. 2.1 mi (3.4 km) n on Rt 134 (St Peter's Ave). Int corridors. **Pets:** Other species. Designated rooms, service with restrictions, supervision. 🛜 🔒 🖥

◆◆ **Danny's Inn & Conference Centre** 🅷 ❀

(506) 546-6621. **$89-$159.** Rt 134 E2A 3Z2. Rt 11 exit 310 (Vanier Blvd) northbound to Rt 134 (St Peter's Ave), 2.5 mi (4 km) n; exit 318 southbound to Rt 134 (St Peter's Ave), 2.3 mi (3.8 km) s. Ext/int corridors. **Pets:** Designated rooms, service with restrictions, crate.
🛜 ⊠ 🔒 🖥 🍽 🏊 ⊠

CAA ◆◆ **Lakeview Inns & Suites** 🅷

(506) 548-4949. **$102-$192.** 777 St Peter's Ave E2A 2Y9. 1.8 mi (3 km) n on Rt 134 (St Peter's Ave). Int corridors. **Pets:** Accepted.
ECO SAVE 🛜 ⊠ ♿ 🔒 🖥

BLOOMFIELD

◆◆ **Evelyn's Bed & Breakfast** 🅱🅱

(506) 832-7788. **$99-$119, 7 day notice.** 374 Rt 121 E5N 4T4. Hwy 1 exit 166, follow signs. Int corridors. **Pets:** Accepted. 🛜 ⊠ 🏊 🅺

BOUCTOUCHE

◆◆ **Auberge Bouctouche Inn & Suites** 🅷

(506) 743-5003. **$85-$165.** 50 Industrielle St E4S 3H9. Rt 11 exit 32A/B. Int corridors. **Pets:** Medium, dogs only. $10 daily fee/pet. Designated rooms, service with restrictions, supervision. 🛜 ⊠ ♿ 🔒 🖥

CAMPBELLTON

◆◆ **Comfort Inn** 🅷

(506) 753-4121. **$120-$200.** 111 Val D'Amour Rd E3N 5B9. Hwy 11 exit 415, 0.6 mi (1 km) e on Sugarloaf St W. Ext/int corridors.
Pets: Accepted. ECO 🛜 🔒 🖥

CAA ◆◆ **Howard Johnson Hotel** 🅷

(506) 753-4133. **$87-$125.** 157 Water St E3N 3H2. Hwy 134; in City Centre Complex. Int corridors. **Pets:** Accepted. SAVE 🛜 🔒 🖥 🍽

◆◆ **Super 8-Campbellton** 🅷 ❀

(506) 753-8080. **$99-$126.** 26 Duke St E3N 2K3. Just s of Roseberry St; jct George and Duke sts; downtown. Ext/int corridors. **Pets:** $200 deposit/room, $20 daily fee/room. Designated rooms, service with restrictions, supervision. ECO 🛜 ⊠ ♿ 🔒 🖥 🏊 ⊠

CARAQUET

◆◆ **Super 8** 🅷

(506) 727-0888. **$88-$149.** 9 Carrefour Ave E1W 1B6. Just e of jct Rt 11 and St Pierre Blvd E. Int corridors. **Pets:** Accepted.
🛜 ⊠ ♿ 🔒 🖥 🏊 ⊠

COCAGNE

◆◆ **Cocagne Motel** 🅼

(506) 576-6657. **Call for rates.** 1718 Rt 535 E4R 1N6. Rt 11 exit 15, 0.6 mi (1 km) n. Ext corridors. **Pets:** Accepted. 🛜 🔒

DALHOUSIE

CAA ◆◆◆ **Best Western Plus Manoir Adelaide** 🅷

(506) 684-5681. **$109-$119.** 385 Adelaide St E8C 1B4. Centre at Brunswick St. Int corridors. **Pets:** Medium, other species. $10 deposit/room. Designated rooms, service with restrictions, crate.
SAVE 🛜 ⊠ 🔒 🖥 🍽

DOAKTOWN

◆◆◆ **The Ledges Inn** 🅲🅸

(506) 365-1820. **$100-$150, 7 day notice.** 30 Ledges Inn Ln E9C 1A7. On Rt 8; centre. Int corridors. **Pets:** Accepted. 🛜 ⊠ 🍽

EDMUNDSTON

◆◆ **Auberge Les Jardins Inn** 🅷

(506) 739-5514. **$89-$179.** 60 Principale St E7B 1V7. Trans-Canada Hwy 2 exit 8. Ext/int corridors. **Pets:** Designated rooms, service with restrictions, crate. 🛜 🔒 🖥 🍽 🏊

CAA ◆◆◆ **Best Western Plus Edmundston Hotel** 🅷

(506) 739-0000. **$140-$170.** 280 Hebert Blvd E3V 0A3. Trans-Canada Hwy 2 exit 18 (Hebert Blvd). Int corridors. **Pets:** Accepted.
ECO SAVE 🛜 ⊠ 🔒 🖥 🏊 ⊠

CAA ◆◆◆ **Clarion Hotel & Conference Centre** 🅷

(506) 739-7321. **Call for rates.** 100 rue Rice E3V 1T4. Trans-Canada Hwy 2 exit 18 (Hebert Blvd), 1 mi (1.6 km) sw, then just w on Church Rd. Int corridors. **Pets:** Accepted. SAVE 🛜 🔒 🖥 🍽 🏊

CAA ◆◆◆ **Comfort Inn** 🅷

(506) 739-8361. **$80-$180.** 5 Bateman Ave E3V 3L1. Trans-Canada Hwy 2 exit 18 (Hebert Blvd). Int corridors. **Pets:** Other species. Service with restrictions, crate. ECO SAVE 🛜 🔒 🖥

◆◆ **Days Inn Edmundston** 🅷

(506) 263-0000. **$81-$140.** 10 rue Mathieu E7C 3E1. Trans-Canada Hwy 2 exit 26. Int corridors. **Pets:** Accepted. ECO 🛜 🔒 🖥

◆◆ **Quality Inn** 🅷

(506) 735-5525. **$72-$135.** 919 Canada Rd E3V 3X2. Trans-Canada Hwy 2 exit 13B eastbound; exit 13BA westbound. Ext/int corridors. **Pets:** Medium. Designated rooms, service with restrictions, supervision.
🛜 ♿ 🔒 🖥 🍽 🏊 ⊠

FREDERICTON

CAA ◆◆◆ **Best Western Plus Fredericton Hotel & Suites** 🅷

(506) 455-8448. **$130-$170.** 333 Bishop Dr E3C 2M6. Rt 8 exit 6A eastbound; exit 6B westbound, just w of Regent Mall. Int corridors. **Pets:** Small. $20 daily fee/room. Designated rooms, supervision.
ECO SAVE 🛜 ⊠ ♿ 🔒 🖥 🏊

◆◆ **City Motel** 🅷

(506) 450-9900. **$85-$135.** 1216 Regent St E3B 3Z4. Trans-Canada Hwy 2 exit 285A eastbound; exit 285B westbound, 2 mi (3.3 km) n on Rt 101 (Regent St). Int corridors. **Pets:** Accepted. 🛜 🔒 🖥 🍽

CAA ◆◆◆ **Comfort Inn** 🅷 ❀

(506) 453-0800. **$108-$200.** 797 Prospect St E3B 5Y4. Trans-Canada Hwy 2 exit 281, 2.5 mi (4 km) ne on Rt 640 (Hanwell Rd). Int corridors. **Pets:** Other species. Designated rooms. ECO SAVE 🛜 🔒 🖥

(AA) ▼▼▼▼ **Crowne Plaza Fredericton Lord Beaverbrook** 🄷
(506) 455-3371. **$129-$249.** 659 Queen St E3B 5A6. Corner of Regent St. Int corridors. **Pets:** Accepted.
[ECO] [SAVE] 🛜 ✕ 📶 🖥 ❰❙ 🏊 🐾

(AA) ▼▼▼▼ **Delta Fredericton** 🄷 🐾
(506) 457-7000. **$129-$210.** 225 Woodstock Rd E3B 2H8. 1 mi (1.6 km) n on Rt 102; downtown. Int corridors. **Pets:** Other species. Service with restrictions, crate. [ECO] [SAVE] 🛜 🛗 📶 🖥 ❰❙ 🏊 🐾

▼▼ ▼▼ **Howard Johnson Plaza Hotel Fredericton** 🄷
(506) 462-4444. **$77-$107.** 958 Prospect St E3B 2T8. Rt 8 exit 3 (Hanwell Rd) eastbound; exit 5 (Smythe St) westbound. Ext/int corridors.
Pets: Accepted. 🛜 📶 🖥 ❰❙ 🏊 🐾

(AA) ▼▼ ▼▼ **Lakeview Inns & Suites-Fredericton** 🄷 🐾
(506) 459-0035. **$107-$140.** 665 Prospect St E3B 6B8. Rt 8 exit 3 (Hanwell Rd) eastbound; exit 5 (Smythe St) westbound. Int corridors.
Pets: Small. $10 daily fee/pet. Service with restrictions, supervision.
[ECO] [SAVE] 🛜 ✕ 📶 🖥

▼▼ ▼▼ ▼▼ **Ramada Hotel Fredericton** 🄷
(506) 460-5500. **$89-$171.** 480 Riverside Dr E3A 8C2. On Rt 105; at north end of Princess Margaret Bridge. Int corridors. **Pets:** Accepted.
[ECO] 🛜 ✕ 🛗 📶 🖥 ❰❙ 🏊 🐾

GRAND FALLS

(AA) ▼▼▼▼ **Best Western Plus Grand Sault Hotel & Suites** 🄷
(506) 473-6200. **$140-$170.** 187 Ouellette St E3Z 3E8. Trans-Canada Hwy 2 exit 79. Int corridors. **Pets:** Medium, dogs only. $20 daily fee/room. Designated rooms, service with restrictions, supervision.
[ECO] [SAVE] 🛜 ✕ 🛗 📶 🖥 🏊

▼▼ ▼▼ **Quality Inn Grand Falls** 🄷
(506) 473-1300. **$119-$189.** 10039 Rt 144 E3Y 3H5. Trans-Canada Hwy 2 exit 75, just w. Ext/int corridors. **Pets:** Very small. $15 one-time fee/ room. Designated rooms, service with restrictions, supervision.
🛜 🛗 📶 🖥 ❰❙ 🏊 🐾

MIRAMICHI

(AA) ▼▼ ▼▼ **Canadas Best Value Inn & Suites** 🄷 🐾
(506) 622-1215. **$79-$139.** 201 Edward St E1V 2Y7. 0.6 mi (1 km) w on Rt 8. Int corridors. **Pets:** Medium, dogs only. $10 daily fee/pet. Designated rooms, service with restrictions, supervision.
[ECO] [SAVE] 🛜 📶 🖥

▼▼ ▼▼ **Howard Johnson Inn & Suites Miramichi** 🄷
(506) 622-0302. **Call for rates.** 1 Jane St E1V 2S6. Just s off King George Hwy. Int corridors. **Pets:** Accepted.
🛜 ✕ 📶 🖥 ❰❙ 🏊

(AA) ▼▼ ▼▼ **Lakeview Inns & Suites** 🄷
(506) 627-1999. **Call for rates.** 333 King George Hwy E1V 1L2. 1.1 mi (1.8 km) w on Rt 8. Int corridors. **Pets:** Accepted.
[ECO] [SAVE] 🛜 📶 🖥

▼▼▼▼ **Rodd Miramichi River-A Rodd Signature Hotel** 🄷
(506) 773-3111. **$124-$175.** 1809 Water St E1N 1B2. Hwy 11 exit 120, 0.4 mi (0.6 km) e. Int corridors. **Pets:** Accepted.
[ECO] 🛜 ✕ 🛗 📶 🖥 ❰❙ 🏊 🐾

MONCTON

(AA) ▼▼ ▼▼ **Coastal Inn** 🄷
(506) 857-9686. **$99-$154.** 502 Kennedy St E1A 5Y7. At Paul St. Ext/int corridors. **Pets:** Accepted. [ECO] [SAVE] 🛜 📶 🖥 ❰❙ 🏊

▼▼ ▼▼ **Colonial Inns** 🄷
(506) 382-3395. **Call for rates.** 42 Highfield St E1C 8T6. 1 blk n of Main St; centre. Ext/int corridors. **Pets:** Accepted. 🛜 📶 ❰❙ 🏊

▼▼ ▼▼ **Comfort Inn** 🄷 🌼
(506) 384-3175. **$99-$275.** 2495 Mountain Rd E1G 2W4. Trans-Canada Hwy 2 exit 450. Int corridors. **Pets:** Other species. $100 deposit/room. Supervision. [ECO] 📶 🖥

(AA) ▼▼ ▼▼ **Comfort Inn** 🄷
(506) 859-6868. **$99-$160.** 20 Maplewood Dr E1A 6P9. Trans-Canada Hwy 2 exit 459A on Hwy 115 S, left on Rt 134 E (Lewisville Rd). Int corridors. **Pets:** Accepted. [ECO] [SAVE] 📶 🖥

(AA) ▼▼ ▼▼ **Crowne Plaza Moncton Downtown** 🄷
(506) 854-6340. **$99-$139.** 1005 Main St E1C 1G9. At Highfield and Main sts; downtown. Int corridors. **Pets:** Accepted.
[ECO] [SAVE] 🛜 ✕ 📶 🖥 ❰❙ 🏊 🐾

▼▼▼▼ **Delta Beausejour** 🄷
(506) 854-4344. **$209-$329.** 750 Main St E1C 1E6. Jct Main St and Sommet Ln; downtown. Int corridors. **Pets:** Accepted.
[ECO] 🛜 ✕ 📶 🖥 ❰❙ 🏊 🐾

▼▼▼▼ **Future Inns Moncton Hotel & Conference Centre** 🄷
(506) 852-9600. **$119-$189.** 40 Lady Ada Blvd E1G 0E3. Trans-Canada Hwy 2 exit 454. Int corridors. **Pets:** Accepted.
🛜 ✕ 🛗 📶 🖥 ❰❙

(AA) ▼▼▼▼ **Hampton Inn & Suites Moncton** 🄷 🐾
(506) 855-4819. **$129-$199.** 700 Mapleton Rd E1G 0L7. Trans-Canada Hwy 2 exit 454. Int corridors. **Pets:** Other species. Designated rooms, no service, supervision. [SAVE] 🛜 ✕ 🛗 📶 🖥 🏊

(AA) ▼▼▼▼ **Holiday Inn Express Hotel & Suites Moncton** 🄷
(506) 384-1050. **$109-$159.** 2515 Mountain Rd E1G 2W4. Trans-Canada Hwy 2 exit 450. Ext/int corridors. **Pets:** Accepted.
[ECO] [SAVE] 🛜 ✕ 📶 🖥 ❰❙ 🏊 🐾

(AA) ▼▼▼▼ **Hotel Casino New Brunswick** 🄷
(506) 861-4661. **$149-$999.** 21 Casino Dr E1G 0R7. Trans-Canada Hwy 2 exit 450. Int corridors. **Pets:** Large. $30 daily fee/room. Service with restrictions, supervision. [SAVE] 🛜 ✕ 📶 🖥 ❰❙ 🏊 🐾

▼▼▼▼ **Hotel St. James** 🄷
(506) 388-4283. **$159-$289.** 14 Church St E1C 4Y9. Corner of Main and Church sts. Int corridors. **Pets:** Accepted. 🛜 ✕ ❰❙

▼▼▼▼ **Howard Johnson Inn Moncton** 🄼
(506) 384-1734. **$85-$145.** 1062 Mountain Rd E1C 2T1. Trans-Canada Hwy 2 exit 454 (Mapleton Rd), 1.7 mi (2.8 km) to Rt 126 (Mountain Rd), then just s. Ext/int corridors. **Pets:** $10 daily fee/pet. Designated rooms, service with restrictions, supervision. 🛜 📶 🖥

(AA) ▼▼ ▼▼ **Motel 6 Moncton** 🄷
(506) 386-6749. **$75-$120.** 2530 Mountain Rd E1G 1B4. Trans-Canada Hwy 2 exit 450. Int corridors. **Pets:** Other species. Service with restrictions, supervision. [SAVE] 🛜 ✕ 🛗 📶 🖥

(AA) ▼▼▼▼ **Ramada Plaza Crystal Palace & Convention Centre** 🄷
(506) 858-8584. **$123-$261.** 499 Paul St E1A 6S5. Trans-Canada Hwy 2 exit 459A eastbound, s on Rt 115 to Lewisville Rd, then left; exit 467A westbound, 4.8 mi (8 km) w on Rt 15 to rotary. Int corridors.
Pets: Accepted. [ECO] [SAVE] 🛜 ✕ 📶 🖥 ❰❙ 🏊 🐾

(AA) ▼▼▼▼ **Residence Inn by Marriott Moncton** 🄷
(506) 854-7100. **$170-$229.** 600 Main St E1C 0M6. At Assomption Blvd. Int corridors. **Pets:** $75 one-time fee/room. Designated rooms, supervision. [ECO] [SAVE] 🛜 ✕ 🛗 📶 🖥 🏊

▼▼ ▼▼ **Rodd Moncton** 🄷
(506) 382-1664. **$99-$159.** 434 Main St E1C 1B9. On Rt 106 (Main St) at King St. Ext/int corridors. **Pets:** Accepted. [ECO] 🛜 ✕ 🖥 🏊

CAA ▼▼▼▼ **Super 8 Moncton/Dieppe** H
(506) 858-8880. **$81-$160.** 370 Dieppe Blvd E1A 8H4. Hwy 15 exit 16, 0.6 mi (1 km) s. Int corridors. **Pets:** Accepted.
ECO SAVE 🛜 ✕ ⛖M 🛏 🖵 ⛵ ✕

CAA ▼▼▼ **Travelodge Suites Moncton** H ❀
(506) 852-7000. **Call for rates.** 2475 Mountain Rd E1G 2J5. Trans-Canada Hwy 2 exit 450. Int corridors. **Pets:** Large, other species. $25 one-time fee/room. Service with restrictions, crate.
ECO SAVE 🛜 🛏 🖵

OROMOCTO

CAA ▼▼▼▼ **Days Inn Oromocto** H
(506) 357-5657. **$104-$130.** 60 Brayson Blvd E2V 4T9. Trans-Canada Hwy 2 exit 301 eastbound; exit 303 westbound, just s to Pioneer Ave, then 1 mi (1.6 km) w. Int corridors. **Pets:** Accepted.
ECO SAVE 🛜 ⛖M 🛏 🖵 ⛵

PERTH-ANDOVER

CAA ▼▼▼▼ **The Castle Inn** CI
(506) 273-9495. **Call for rates.** 21 Brentwood Dr E7H 1P1. Trans-Canada Hwy 2 exit 115, follow signs over St. John River. Int corridors. **Pets:** Accepted. SAVE 🛜 ✕ 🖵 ⛏ ⛵ ✕

SACKVILLE

▼▼ **Coastal Inn Sackville** H
(506) 536-0000. **$99-$155.** 15 Wright St E4L 4P8. Trans-Canada Hwy 2 exit 504. Int corridors. **Pets:** Designated rooms, service with restrictions, supervision. ECO 🛜 ✕ 🛏

CAA ▼▼▼▼ **Marshlands Inn** CI
(506) 536-0170. **$94-$225.** 55 Bridge St E4L 3N8. On Hwy 106; centre. Int corridors. **Pets:** Accepted. SAVE 🛜 ✕ ⛏

ST. ANDREWS

▼▼▼▼ **The Algonquin Hotel & Resort** H ❀
(506) 529-8823. **$119-$569, 3 day notice.** 184 Adolphus St E5B 1T7. Off Hwy 127. Int corridors. **Pets:** $25 daily fee/pet. Service with restrictions. ECO 🛜 🖵 ⛏ ⛵ ✕

CAA ▼▼▼▼ **Tara Manor Inn** BB
(506) 529-3304. **$99-$169, 7 day notice.** 559 Mowat Dr E5B 2P2. 1.7 mi (2.8 km) n on Hwy 127. Ext corridors. **Pets:** Accepted.
SAVE 🛜 ✕ 🛏 ⛵

SAINT JOHN

CAA ▼▼▼▼ **Best Western Plus Saint John Hotel & Suites** H
(506) 657-9966. **$100-$160.** 55 Majors Brook Dr E2J 0B2. Hwy 1 exit 129 westbound, 1 mi (1.6 km) s on Rt 100 (Rothesay Ave) to McAllister Dr, then just e; exit 128 eastbound, 1 mi (1.6 km) n on Rt 100 (Rothesay Ave), just n to McAllister Dr, then just e. Int corridors. **Pets:** Medium, dogs only. $15 daily fee/pet. Designated rooms, service with restrictions, supervision. SAVE 🛜 ✕ ⛖M 🛏 🖵 ⛵

CAA ▼▼ **Colonial Inn Saint John** H
(506) 652-3000. **$114-$130.** 175 City Rd E2L 3M9. Hwy 1 exit 123. Ext/int corridors. **Pets:** $10 daily fee/pet. Service with restrictions, crate.
SAVE 🛜 🛏 ⛏ ⛵ ✕

CAA ▼▼▼ **Comfort Inn** H
(506) 674-1873. **$114-$140.** 1155 Fairville Blvd E2M 5T9. Hwy 1 exit 117 westbound; exit 119 eastbound, then left. Int corridors.
Pets: Accepted. ECO SAVE 🛏 🖵

▼▼▼▼ **Delta Brunswick** H
(506) 648-1981. **$99-$199.** 39 King St E2L 4W3. Centre of downtown; in Brunswick Square Mall. Int corridors. **Pets:** Accepted.
ECO 🛜 ✕ ⛖M 🛏 🖵 ⛏ ⛵ ✕

CAA ▼▼▼▼ **Hampton Inn & Suites** H
(506) 657-4600. **$100-$169.** 51 Fashion Dr E2J 0A7. Hwy 1 exit 129, 1.5 mi (2.4 km) s on Rothesay Ave to Retail Dr; behind Home Depot. Int corridors. **Pets:** Accepted. SAVE 🛜 ✕ ⛖M 🛏 🖵 ⛵ ✕

CAA ▼▼▼▼ **Hilton Saint John** H
(506) 693-8484. **$99-$199.** 1 Market Square E2L 4Z6. Hwy 1 exit 122; at Market Square. Int corridors. **Pets:** Accepted.
ECO SAVE 🛜 ✕ 🛏 🖵 ⛏ ⛵

CAA ▼▼▼▼ **Holiday Inn Express & Suites** H
(506) 642-2622. **$119-$189.** 400 Main St/Chesley Dr E2K 4N5. 0.6 mi (1 km) w on Hwy 1; north end of Chesley Dr exit 121; off Harbour Bridge. Int corridors. **Pets:** Accepted. ECO SAVE 🛜 ✕ 🛏 🖵 ⛵

▼▼▼▼ **Homeport Historic Inn Circa 1858** BB ❀
(506) 672-7255. **$109-$175, 4 day notice.** 80 Douglas Ave E2K 1E4. Hwy 1 exit 121 eastbound; exit 123 westbound. Int corridors. **Pets:** Dogs only. Service with restrictions, supervision. 🛜 ✕ 🛏

CAA ▼▼▼ **Howard Johnson Fort Howe Plaza & Convention Center** H
(506) 657-7320. **Call for rates.** 10 Portland St E2K 4H8. Hwy 1 exit 121 eastbound off Harbour Bridge; exit 123 westbound. Int corridors. **Pets:** Medium. $25 one-time fee/room. Designated rooms, service with restrictions, supervision. ECO SAVE 🛜 🛏 🖵 ⛏ ⛵

CAA ▼▼▼ **Inn on the Cove and Spa** CI
(506) 672-7799. **$110-$225, 7 day notice.** 1371 Sand Cove Rd E2M 4Z9. Hwy 1 exit 119A, just s on Bleury St to Sand Cove Rd, then 1.2 mi (2 km) w. Int corridors. **Pets:** Accepted. SAVE ✕ ⛖M 🖵 ⛏

CAA ▼▼▼ **Travelodge Suites, Saint John** H ❀
(506) 635-0400. **Call for rates.** 1011 Fairville Blvd E2M 5T9. Hwy 1 exit 119B eastbound, left on Catherwood Dr, left at lights; exit 119A westbound. Int corridors. **Pets:** Medium, other species. $10 daily fee/room. Service with restrictions, crate. ECO SAVE 🛜 🛏

ST-LEONARD

CAA ▼▼ **Daigle's Motel** H
(506) 423-6351. **$83-$104.** 68 rue DuPont E7E 1Y1. Hwy 17, 0.6 mi (1 km) s of Trans-Canada Hwy 2 exit 58. Ext corridors. **Pets:** Accepted.
SAVE 🛜 ⛏ ⛵

ST. STEPHEN

▼▼ **St. Stephen Inn** M
(506) 466-1814. **$55-$130.** 99 King St E3L 2C6. Just n of Prince William St; centre. Ext/int corridors. **Pets:** Accepted. 🛜 🛏

CAA ▼▼ **Winsome Inn** M
(506) 466-2130. **$92-$129.** 198 King St E3L 2E2. Hwy 1 exit King St, just s on Rt 3. Ext corridors. **Pets:** $10 daily fee/room. Designated rooms, service with restrictions, supervision. SAVE 🛜 🛏 ⛵

SHEDIAC

▼▼ **Gaudet Chalets & Motel** M
(506) 533-8877. **Call for rates.** 14 Bellevue Heights E4P 1H2. On Rt 133, 1.4 mi (2.4 km) w of Rt 15 exit 37. Ext corridors. **Pets:** Accepted.
🛜 🛏 🖵

CAA ▼▼▼ **Seely's Motel** M
(506) 532-6193. **$80-$185, 3 day notice.** 21 Bellevue Heights E4P 1G9. On Rt 133, 1.5 mi (2.4 km) w of Rt 15 exit 37. Ext corridors. **Pets:** Small. $15 daily fee/pet. Designated rooms, service with restrictions, supervision.
SAVE 🛜 ✕ 🛏 🖵 ⛵

SUSSEX

▼▼ **All Seasons Inn** M
(506) 433-2220. **$69-$139, 3 day notice.** 1015 Main St E4E 2M6. Hwy 1 exit 192 eastbound; exit 198 westbound, left towards Sussex Corner; centre. Ext corridors. **Pets:** Medium. $10 one-time fee/pet. Designated rooms, service with restrictions, supervision. 🛜 🛏 ⛏

◆◆ **Fairway Inn** H

(506) 433-3470. **$125-$175.** 216 Roachville Rd E4E 5L6. Hwy 1 exit 193. Ext/int corridors. **Pets:** Medium. $10 daily fee/pet. Designated rooms, service with restrictions, supervision.

◆ **Pine Cone Motel** M

(506) 433-3958. **Call for rates.** 12808 Rt 114 E4E 5L9. Hwy 1 exit 198, 1.2 mi (2 km) e on Rt 114 towards Penobsquis. Ext corridors. **Pets:** Accepted. 🛜 🖪

WOODSTOCK

◆◆ **Canadas Best Value Inn & Suites** H

(506) 328-8876. **$70-$120.** 168 Rt 555 E7M 6B5. Trans-Canada Hwy 2 exit 188 (Houlton Rd). Ext/int corridors. **Pets:** Accepted. 🛜 🖵 🍴 ⇌

◆◆ **Howard Johnson Inn** H

(506) 328-3315. **$59-$125.** 159 Rt 555 exit 188 TCH E7M 6B5. Trans-Canada Hwy 2 exit 188 (Houlton Rd). Ext/int corridors. **Pets:** $10 daily fee/pet. Designated rooms, service with restrictions, supervision. 🛜 🖪 🖵 ⇌ ⊠

YOUNGS COVE

◆ **McCready's Motel** M

(506) 362-2916. **Call for rates.** 10995 Rt 10 E4C 2G5. Trans-Canada Hwy 2 exit 365, just w at Irving One Stop. Ext corridors. **Pets:** Accepted. 🛜 🍴 ⊠ ☎

NEWFOUNDLAND AND LABRADOR

CHANNEL-PORT AUX BASQUES

Hotel Port Aux Basques

(709) 695-2171. **$115.** 1 Grand Bay Rd A0M 1C0. Jct Trans-Canada Hwy 1. Int corridors. **Pets:** Other species. $10 one-time fee/pet. Service with restrictions, supervision.

St. Christopher's Hotel

(709) 695-7034. **Call for rates.** 146 Caribou Rd A0M 1C0. Trans-Canada Hwy 1 exit Port Aux Basques, follow signs 1.2 mi (2 km); downtown. Int corridors. **Pets:** Accepted.

CLARENVILLE

Restland Motel

(709) 466-7636. **$109-$139.** 262 Memorial Dr A5A 1N9. Centre. Ext/int corridors. **Pets:** Accepted.

St. Jude Hotel

(709) 466-1717. **$109-$130.** 247 Trans-Canada Hwy A5A 1Y4. On Trans-Canada Hwy 1; centre. Int corridors. **Pets:** Accepted.

CORNER BROOK

Comfort Inn

(709) 639-1980. **$140-$170.** 41 Maple Valley Rd A2H 6T2. Trans-Canada Hwy 1 exit 5 eastbound; exit 6 westbound, via Confederation Ave. Int corridors. **Pets:** Designated rooms, service with restrictions, supervision.

Glynmill Inn

(709) 634-5181. **$121-$205.** 1B Cobb Ln A2H 6E6. Just w of W Valley Rd; centre. Int corridors. **Pets:** Accepted.

Greenwood Inn & Suites-Corner Brook

(709) 634-5381. **Call for rates.** 48 West St A2H 2Z2. At Chestnut St; centre. Int corridors. **Pets:** Accepted.

Mamateek Inn

(709) 639-8901. **Call for rates.** 64 Maple Valley Rd A2H 6G7. Trans-Canada Hwy 1 exit 5 eastbound; exit 6 westbound, via Confederation Ave. Int corridors. **Pets:** Accepted.

COW HEAD

Shallow Bay Motel & Cabins

(709) 243-2471. **$105-$135.** Rt 430 Tr, The Viking Tr A0K 2A0. Hwy 430, 2.5 mi (4 km) w towards the ocean, follow signs. Ext/int corridors. **Pets:** Other species. $10 daily fee/room. Designated rooms, service with restrictions, supervision.

GANDER

Albatross Hotel

(709) 256-3956. **$108-$141.** Trans-Canada Hwy A1V 1W8. On Trans-Canada Hwy 1. Ext/int corridors. **Pets:** Accepted.

Comfort Inn

(709) 256-3535. **$144-$154.** 112 Trans-Canada Hwy 1 A1V 1P8. Centre. Ext/int corridors. **Pets:** Accepted.

Sinbad's Hotel & Suites

(709) 651-2678. **$101-$262.** 133 Bennett Dr A1V 1W8. Centre; opposite Gander Mall. Ext corridors. **Pets:** Other species. Service with restrictions.

GRAND FALLS-WINDSOR

Mount Peyton Hotel

(709) 489-2251. **Call for rates.** 214 Lincoln Rd A2A 1P8. 0.6 mi (1 km) ne on Trans-Canada Hwy 1. Ext/int corridors. **Pets:** Accepted.

HAPPY VALLEY-GOOSE BAY

Goose River Lodges

(709) 896-2600. **Call for rates.** NW River Rd A0P 1C0. Jct Rt 500, 10.6 mi (17 km) nw on Rt 520. Ext corridors. **Pets:** Accepted.

LABRADOR CITY

Carol Inn

(709) 944-7736. **Call for rates.** 215 Drake Ave A2V 2B6. Centre. Int corridors. **Pets:** Accepted.

L'ANSE AU CLAIR

Northern Light Inn

(709) 931-2332. **$109-$129.** Rt 510 A0K 3K0. Centre. Int corridors. **Pets:** Accepted.

PORT BLANDFORD

Terra Nova Golf Resort

(709) 543-2525. **Call for rates.** Trans-Canada Hwy 1 A0C 2G0. Centre. Int corridors. **Pets:** Accepted.

ST. JOHN'S

Comfort Inn Airport

(709) 753-3500. **$114-$140.** 106 Airport Rd A1A 4Y3. Trans-Canada Hwy 1 exit 47A, 0.6 mi (1 km) n on Rt 40 (Portugal Cove Rd). Int corridors. **Pets:** Accepted.

Delta St. John's Hotel and Conference Centre

(709) 739-6404. **Call for rates.** 120 New Gower St A1C 6K4. At Barter's Hill Rd; centre. Int corridors. **Pets:** Accepted.

Extended Stay Deluxe St. John's - Downtown

(709) 754-7888. **$124-$165.** 222 LeMarchant Rd A1C 2H9. Corner of Pleasant St. Int corridors. **Pets:** Other species. $25 daily fee/pet. Service with restrictions.

The Guv'nor Inn

(709) 726-0092. **$110-$230.** 389 Elizabeth Ave A1B 1V1. 2 blks n of Freshwater Rd. Ext/int corridors. **Pets:** Accepted.

Holiday Inn St. John's-Govt Centre

(709) 722-0506. **$159-$219.** 180 Portugal Cove Rd A1B 2N2. Trans-Canada Hwy 1 exit 47A, 0.9 mi (1.4 km) s. Ext/int corridors. **Pets:** Accepted.

Sheraton Hotel Newfoundland

(709) 726-4980. **$125-$318.** 115 Cavendish Square A1C 3K2. At Duckworth and Ordnance sts. Int corridors. **Pets:** Medium, dogs only. Service with restrictions, supervision.

▼▼ Super 8 **H** ❀

(709) 739-8888. **$122-$135.** 175 Higgins Line A1B 4N4. Trans-Canada Hwy 1 exit 47A, just s on Rt 40 (Portugal Cove Rd). Int corridors. **Pets:** Large. Service with restrictions, supervision.

ECO 📶 🏋M 🛏 💻 🚗

▼▼ Travellers Inn St. John's **H**

(709) 722-5540. **Call for rates.** 199 Kenmount Rd A1B 3P9. Trans-Canada Hwy 1 exit 45, 1 mi (1.6 km) s on Team Gushue Hwy to Kenmount Rd. Ext/int corridors. **Pets:** Accepted.

ECO 📶 🛏 💻 🍴 🚗

STEPHENVILLE

▼▼ Holiday Inn Stephenville **H**

(709) 643-6666. **$128-$143.** 44 Queen St A2N 2M5. Centre. Int corridors. **Pets:** Accepted. **ECO** 📶 ✕ 🛏 💻 🍴

NORTHWEST TERRITORIES

YELLOWKNIFE

(CAA) ▼▼▼ Chateau Nova Hotel & Suites **H**

(867) 873-9700. **$149-$199.** 4401 50th Ave X1A 2N2. Downtown. Int corridors. **Pets:** Accepted. **SAVE** 🛏 💻 🍴

▼▼▼ Coast Fraser Tower **H**

(867) 873-8700. **Call for rates.** 5303 52nd St X1A 1V1. Corner of 52nd St and 53rd Ave. Int corridors. **Pets:** Accepted.

ECO 📶 🛏 💻 🎾

▼▼▼ The Explorer Hotel **H**

(867) 873-3531. **Call for rates.** 4825 49th Ave X1A 2R3. Downtown. Int corridors. **Pets:** Accepted. 📶 🛏 💻 🍴

▼▼ Yellowknife Super 8 **M** ❀

(867) 669-8888. **$161-$199.** 308 Old Airport Rd X1A 3G3. 1.2 mi (2 km) s on Franklin Ave, 0.6 mi (1 km) w; in Wal-Mart Plaza. Int corridors. **Pets:** Large, other species. $25 one-time fee/room. Designated rooms, service with restrictions, crate. **ECO** 📶 ✕ 🛏 💻

NOVA SCOTIA

AMHERST

▼▼ Amherst Wandlyn Meeting & Convention Hotel 🅗
(902) 667-3331. **$105-$145.** 1539 Southampton Rd B4H 3Z2. Trans-Canada Hwy 104 exit 3, 0.6 mi (1 km) w. Ext/int corridors.
Pets: Accepted. 🛜 🔌 💻 🍴 🏊

▼▼ Comfort Inn 🅗
(902) 667-0404. **$113-$145.** 143 Albion St S B4H 2X2. Trans-Canada Hwy 104 exit 4, 1 mi (1.6 km) n on Rt 2. Int corridors. **Pets:** Large. Service with restrictions, supervision. 🌱 🛜 🔌 💻

▼▼ Super 8 🅗
(902) 660-8888. **$94-$144.** 40 Lord Amherst Dr B4H 4W6. Trans-Canada Hwy 104 exit 4. Int corridors. **Pets:** Medium. $10 daily fee/pet. Service with restrictions, supervision. 🌱 🛜 🔌 💻 🏊

ANNAPOLIS ROYAL

▼▼ Annapolis Royal Inn 🅜
(902) 532-2323. **$89-$150, 30 day notice.** 3924 Hwy 1 B0S 1A0. 0.6 mi (1 km) w. Ext corridors. **Pets:** Accepted. 🛜 💻

🅒🅐 ▼▼▼ Hillsdale House Inn 🅑🅑
(902) 532-2345. **$85-$160.** 519 St George St B0S 1A0. Just e of Rt 1; centre. Int corridors. **Pets:** Accepted. 💰 🛜 ✖

▼▼▼ The King George Inn 🅑🅑
(902) 532-5286. **$80-$160.** 548 Upper St George St B0S 1A0. Jct Rt 1 and 8, just e on Rt 8. Int corridors. **Pets:** Accepted. 🛜 ✖ 💻

ANTIGONISH

🅒🅐 ▼▼▼ Maritime Inn Antigonish 🅗
(902) 863-4001. **$115-$195.** 158 Main St B2G 2B7. Between St. Mary's and Court sts; centre. Ext/int corridors. **Pets:** Accepted.
💰 🛜 ✖ 🔌 💻 🍴

AULD'S COVE

🅒🅐 ▼▼ Cove Motel & Restaurant/Gift Shop 🅜
(902) 747-2700. **$105-$130.** 227 Auld's Cove Rd B0H 1P0. 0.6 mi (1 km) n off Trans-Canada Hwy 104; 1.9 mi (3 km) w of Canso Cswy. Ext corridors. **Pets:** Medium. Designated rooms, service with restrictions, supervision. 💰 🛜 🔌 💻 🍴

BADDECK

▼▼▼ Hunter's Mountain Chalets 🅒🅐
(902) 295-3392. **$78-$138, 4 day notice.** 562 Cabot Tr B0E 1B0. Trans-Canada Hwy 105 exit 7, 1.6 mi (2.6 km) n. Ext corridors. **Pets:** Dogs only. $10 daily fee/pet. No service, supervision.
🛜 ✖ 🔌 📵 ✂

🅒🅐 ▼▼ Inverary on Baddeck Bay 🅗
(902) 295-3500. **$99-$159, 3 day notice.** 368 Shore Rd B0E 1B0. Trans-Canada Hwy 105 exit 8, 1 mi (1.6 km) e on Rt 205 (Shore Rd). Ext/int corridors. **Pets:** Medium. $25 one-time fee/pet. Designated rooms, service with restrictions, supervision.
💰 🛜 ✖ 🔌 🔌 💻 🍴 🏊 ✖

▼▼ McIntyre's Housekeeping Cottages 🅒🅐
(902) 295-1133. **$80-$350, 4 day notice.** 8908 Hwy 105 B0E 1B0. Trans-Canada Hwy 105, 3 mi (5 km) w. Ext corridors. **Pets:** $10 daily fee/pet. Designated rooms, service with restrictions, supervision.
🛜 ✖ 🔌 🔌 💻

🅒🅐 ▼▼▼ Silver Dart Lodge & MacNeil House 🅗
(902) 295-2340. **$99-$240.** 257 Shore Rd B0E 1B0. Trans-Canada Hwy 105 exit 8, 0.6 mi (1 km) e on Rt 205 (Shore Rd). Ext/int corridors.
Pets: Accepted. 💰 🛜 ✖ 🔌 🔌 💻 🍴 🏊 ✖

BAYFIELD

▼▼ Sea'Scape Cottages 🅒🅐
(902) 386-2825. **$115-$145, 30 day notice.** 6 Sea Scape Cottage Ln B0H 1R0. Trans-Canada Hwy 104 exit 36, 3.2 mi (5.3 km) n on Sunrise Tr, then 1.1 mi (1.8 km) w on Ferry Rd. Ext corridors. **Pets:** Dogs only. $50 deposit/room. Service with restrictions, supervision.
✖ 🔌 🔌 ✖ 📵 🔌

BRIDGETOWN

▼▼ Bridgetown Motor Inn 🅜
(902) 665-4403. **Call for rates.** 396 Granville St B0S 1C0. Hwy 101 exit 20, 0.6 mi (1 km) w on Rt 1. Ext corridors. **Pets:** Accepted.
🛜 🔌 🏊

BRIDGEWATER

🅒🅐 ▼▼▼ Best Western Plus Bridgewater Hotel & Convention Centre 🅗 🐾
(902) 530-0101. **$120-$170.** 527 Hwy 10 B4V 7P4. Hwy 103 exit 12, just n. Int corridors. **Pets:** $20 daily fee/pet. Designated rooms, service with restrictions, supervision. 💰 🛜 ✖ 🔌 🔌 💻 🍴 🏊 ✖

▼▼ The Bridgewater Hotel 🅗
(902) 543-8171. **Call for rates.** 35 High St B4V 1V8. Hwy 103 exit 13, just e. Int corridors. **Pets:** Accepted. 🛜 💻 🍴 🏊

▼▼ Comfort Inn 🅗
(902) 543-1498. **$89-$129.** 49 North St B4V 2V7. Hwy 103 exit 12, 1.1 mi (1.7 km) s on Rt 10. Int corridors. **Pets:** Accepted.
🌱 🛜 🔌 🔌 💻

▼▼ Days Inn & Conference Centre Bridgewater 🅗
(902) 543-7131. **$81-$121.** 50 North St B4V 2V6. Hwy 103 exit 12, 1.1 mi (1.7 km) s on Rt 10. Int corridors. **Pets:** Accepted.
🛜 🔌 💻 🍴 🏊

CHARLOS COVE

▼▼▼ Seawind Landing Country Inn 🅒🅘 🐾
(902) 525-2108. **$99-$169.** 159 Wharf Rd B0H 1T0. Rt 316, 0.5 mi (0.8 km) se on gravel road. Ext/int corridors. **Pets:** Designated rooms.
🛜 ✖ 🔌 🍴 🔌

CHESTER

▼▼ Windjammer Motel 🅜
(902) 275-3567. **$65-$85.** 4070 Rt 3 B0J 1J0. 0.6 mi (1 km) w. Ext corridors. **Pets:** Medium, other species. Service with restrictions, supervision.
🛜 🔌

CHESTER BASIN

▼▼ ▼▼ **The Sword & Anchor Bed & Breakfast** BB
(902) 275-2478. **Call for rates.** 5306 Hwy 3 B0J 1K0. Centre. Int corridors. **Pets:** Accepted. 📶 ✕ 🛡 🎟 ☎

CHÉTICAMP

▼▼ ▼▼ **Cabot Trail Sea & Golf Chalets** CA
(902) 224-1777. **$139-$179, 7 day notice.** 71 Fraser Doucet Ln B0E 1H0. Centre. Ext corridors. **Pets:** Accepted.
📶 ✕ 🚹 🛡 🖵 ✕ 🎟 ☎

CAA ▼▼ ▼▼ **Laurie's Motor Inn** H
(902) 224-2400. **$90-$249, 3 day notice.** 15456 Laurie Rd B0E 1H0. Centre. Ext/int corridors. **Pets:** Accepted. SAVE 📶 ✕ 🛡 🖵 🎟

CHURCH POINT

▼▼ ▼▼ **Le Manoir Samson** M
(902) 769-2526. **$80-$110.** 1768 Rt 1 B0W 1M0. On Hwy 1; centre. Ext corridors. **Pets:** Medium. Service with restrictions, crate.
📶 ✕ 🛡 🎟

DARTMOUTH

CAA ▼▼ ▼▼ **Comfort Inn** H
(902) 463-9900. **$99-$149.** 456 Windmill Rd B3A 1J7. Hwy 111 exit Shannon Park. Int corridors. **Pets:** Accepted. ECO SAVE 📶 🛡 🖵

CAA ▼▼ ▼▼ **Days Inn** H
(902) 465-6555. **$89-$125.** 20 Highfield Park Dr B3A 4S8. From A. Murray MacKay Bridge, 0.8 mi (1.2 km) n on Hwy 111 exit 3 (Burnside Dr). Ext/int corridors. **Pets:** Other species. $100 deposit/room. Designated rooms, service with restrictions, supervision.
ECO SAVE 📶 🛡 🖵 🎟 ☂

CAA ▼▼ ▼▼ ▼▼ **Hampton Inn & Suites by Hilton-Halifax/Dartmouth** H ✿
(902) 406-7700. **Call for rates.** 65 Cromarty Dr B3B 0G2. Hwy 118 (Lakeview Dr) exit Wright Ave; in Dartmouth Crossing Outlet Mall. Int corridors. **Pets:** Medium. Service with restrictions, supervision.
ECO SAVE 📶 ✕ 🛡 🖵 🎟 ☂ ✕

CAA ▼▼ ▼▼ **Holiday Inn Halifax-Harbourview** H
(902) 463-1100. **$109-$209.** 101 Wyse Rd B3A 1L9. Adjacent to Angus L Macdonald Bridge. Int corridors. **Pets:** Accepted.
ECO SAVE 📶 ✕ 🛡 🖵 🎟 ☂

CAA ▼▼ ▼▼ **Park Place Hotel & Conference Centre Ramada Plaza** H
(902) 468-8888. **$99-$194.** 240 Brownlow Ave B3B 1X6. From A. Murray MacKay Bridge, 0.7 mi (1.2 km) n on Hwy 111 exit 3 (Burnside Dr). Int corridors. **Pets:** Accepted.
ECO SAVE 📶 🛡 🖵 🎟 ☂ ✕

CAA ▼▼ ▼▼ **Quality Inn Halifax/Dartmouth** H
(902) 469-5850. **$85-$125.** 313 Prince Albert Rd B2Y 1N3. Hwy 111 exit 6A, 1 blk s. Int corridors. **Pets:** Other species. Designated rooms, service with restrictions, supervision. SAVE 📶 ✕ 🛡 🖵 🎟

▼▼ ▼▼ **Super 8 Hotel-Dartmouth** H ✿
(902) 463-9520. **$77-$166.** 65 King St B2Y 4C2. Corner of King and Queen sts; centre of downtown. Int corridors. **Pets:** Other species. Designated rooms, service with restrictions, supervision. ECO 📶 🛡 🖵

CAA ▼▼ ▼▼ **Travelodge Suites** H
(902) 465-4000. **Call for rates.** 101 Yorkshire Ave Ext B2Y 3Y2. Hwy 111 exit Princess Margaret Blvd; at toll booth for A. Murray MacKay Bridge. Int corridors. **Pets:** Accepted. ECO SAVE 📶 ✕ 🛡 🖵

DIGBY

CAA ▼▼ ▼▼ **Admiral Digby Inn & Cottages** H
(902) 245-2531. **$85-$150.** 441 Shore Rd B0V 1A0. Hwy 101 exit 26, 1.5 mi (2.5 km) n, follow Saint John Ferry signs, 3 mi (5 km) w on Victoria Rd, just e of ferry terminal. Ext corridors. **Pets:** Dogs only. $10 daily fee/pet. Designated rooms, service with restrictions, supervision.
SAVE 📶 ✕ 🛡 🖵 🎟 ☂

CAA ▼▼ ▼▼ ▼▼ **Digby Pines Golf Resort and Spa** H
(902) 245-2511. **$182-$338, 3 day notice.** 103 Shore Rd B0V 1A0. Hwy 101 exit 26, 1.5 mi (2.5 km) n, follow Saint John Ferry signs, 1.5 mi (2.5 km) w on Victoria Rd, follow signs; 1.2 mi (2 km) e of ferry terminal. Ext/int corridors. **Pets:** $100 deposit/room. Designated rooms, service with restrictions. ECO SAVE 📶 ✕ 🚹 🛡 🖵 🎟 ☂ ✕

▼▼ ▼▼ **Dockside Suites** H
(902) 245-4950. **$89-$159.** 34 Water St B0V 1A0. Centre; in Fundy Complex. Ext/int corridors. **Pets:** Accepted. 📶 ✕ 🛡 🖵 🎟

HALIFAX

CAA ▼▼ ▼▼ ▼▼ **Atlantica Hotel Halifax** H ✿
(902) 423-1161. **$119-$230.** 1980 Robie St B3H 3G5. Jct Quinpool St. Int corridors. **Pets:** Medium. Service with restrictions, supervision.
ECO SAVE 📶 ✕ 🛡 🖵 🎟 ☂ ✕

CAA ▼▼ ▼▼ ▼▼ **Best Western Plus Chocolate Lake Hotel** H ✿
(902) 477-5611. **$99-$199.** 20 St. Margaret's Bay Rd B3N 1J4. 0.4 mi (0.7 km) e of Armdale Rotary. Ext/int corridors. **Pets:** Medium. Designated rooms, service with restrictions, supervision.
ECO SAVE 📶 ✕ 🚹 🛡 🖵 🎟 ☂ ✕

CAA ▼▼ ▼▼ ▼▼ **Cambridge Suites Hotel** H ✿
(902) 420-0555. **$119-$219.** 1583 Brunswick St B3J 3P5. Corner of Brunswick and Sackville sts. Int corridors. **Pets:** Other species. $25 one-time fee/room. Service with restrictions, supervision.
ECO SAVE 📶 ✕ 🚹 🛡 🖵 🎟 ✕

▼▼ **Chebucto Inn** H
(902) 453-4330. **Call for rates.** 6151 Lady Hammond Rd B3K 2R9. Jct Hwy 111 and Rt 2 (Bedford Hwy), 0.4 mi (0.7 km) e. Ext corridors. **Pets:** Accepted. 📶 🎟

CAA ▼▼ ▼▼ **Comfort Inn Halifax** H ✿
(902) 443-0303. **$79-$149.** 560 Bedford Hwy B3M 2L8. On Rt 2 (Bedford Hwy), 6 mi (9.6 km) w. Int corridors. **Pets:** $10 one-time fee/pet. Service with restrictions, supervision. SAVE 📶 🚹 🛡 🖵 ☂

▼▼ ▼▼ **Delta Barrington** H ✿
(902) 429-7410. **$139-$239.** 1875 Barrington St B3J 3L6. Between Cogswell and Duke sts. Int corridors. **Pets:** Medium, other species. $35 one-time fee/room. Service with restrictions, supervision.
ECO 📶 ✕ 🛡 🖵 🎟 ☂ ✕

▼▼ ▼▼ **Delta Halifax** H ✿
(902) 425-6700. **$115-$209.** 1990 Barrington St B3J 1P2. Corner of Cogswell and Barrington sts. Int corridors. **Pets:** Medium, other species. $35 one-time fee/room. Service with restrictions, supervision.
ECO 📶 🚹 🛡 🖵 🎟 ☂ ✕

CAA ▼▼ **Esquire Motel** M ✿
(902) 835-3367. **$69-$145.** 771 Bedford Hwy B4A 1A1. Hwy 102 exit 4A, 3.3 mi (5.3 km) e on Rt 2 (Bedford Hwy). Ext corridors. **Pets:** Other species. $10 daily fee/pet. Designated rooms, service with restrictions, supervision. SAVE 🛡 🛡 🖵 ☂ 🎟

▼▼ ▼▼ **Future Inns Halifax** H
(902) 443-4333. **$119-$179.** 30 Fairfax Dr B3S 1P1. Hwy 102 exit 2A. Int corridors. **Pets:** Accepted. 📶 ✕ 🚹 🛡 🖵 🎟

CAA ▼▼ ▼▼ ▼▼ **Halifax Marriott Harbourfront** H
(902) 421-1700. **$189-$270.** 1919 Upper Water St B3J 3J5. Adjacent to historic properties and Casino Nova Scotia. Int corridors. **Pets:** Accepted.
ECO SAVE 📶 ✕ 🚹 🛡 🖵 🎟 ☂ ✕

(CAA) ▼▼▼▼ Holiday Inn Express Halifax Airport H ❀
(902) 576-7600. $139-$199. 180 Pratt & Whitney Dr B2T 0A2. Hwy 102 exit 5A, 0.8 mi (1.2 km) e, then just n. Int corridors. Pets: Designated rooms, service with restrictions, supervision.
[SAVE] 🛜 ✕ 🅼 🖥 🖵

(CAA) ▼▼▼▼ Holiday Inn Express Halifax/Bedford H ❀
(902) 445-1100. $99-$149. 133 Kearney Lake Rd B3M 4P3. Hwy 102 exit 2. Int corridors. Pets: Medium. $25 one-time fee/room. Designated rooms, service with restrictions, supervision.
[ECO] [SAVE] 🛜 ✕ 🅼 🖥 🖵 ≈

(CAA) ▼▼▼ Lakeview Inns & Suites H ❀
(902) 450-3020. $139-$299. 98 Chain Lake Dr B3S 1A2. Hwy 102 exit 2A eastbound; Hwy 103 exit 2. Int corridors. Pets: Large. $100 deposit/room. Service with restrictions, crate.
[ECO] [SAVE] 🛜 ✕ 🅼 🖥 🖵 ≈

(CAA) ▼▼▼▼ The Lord Nelson Hotel & Suites H
(902) 423-6331. $129-$189, 3 day notice. 1515 S Park St B3J 2L2. Corner of Park St and Spring Garden Rd. Int corridors. Pets: Accepted.
[ECO] [SAVE] 🛜 ✕ 🅼 🖥 🖵 ¶

(CAA) ▼▼▼▼ The Prince George Hotel H ❀
(902) 425-1986. $149-$279. 1725 Market St B3J 3N9. Between Prince and Carmichael sts. Int corridors. Pets: Other species. $20 one-time fee/pet. Service with restrictions, supervision.
[ECO] [SAVE] 🛜 ✕ 🅼 🖥 🖵 ¶ ≈ ✕

▼▼▼ Quality Inn & Suites Halifax H
(902) 444-6700. $100-$160. 980 Parkland Dr B3M 4Y7. Hwy 102 exit 2. Int corridors. Pets: Accepted. [ECO] 🛜 ✕ 🅼 🖥 🖵 ≈ ✕

▼▼▼ Quality Inn Halifax Airport H
(902) 873-3000. $109-$170. 60 Sky Blvd B2T 1K3. Hwy 102 exit 6. Int corridors. Pets: Accepted. [ECO] 🛜 ✕ 🖥 🖵 ¶ ≈ ✕

(CAA) ▼▼▼▼ Residence Inn Halifax Downtown H
(902) 422-0493. $169-$229. 1599 Grafton St B3J 2C3. Corner of Sackville St. Int corridors. Pets: Accepted.
[ECO] [SAVE] 🛜 ✕ 🅼 🖥 🖵

(CAA) ▼▼▼▼ The Westin Nova Scotian H
(902) 421-1000. $139-$395. 1181 Hollis St B3H 2P6. Between Barrington and Lower Water sts. Int corridors. Pets: Accepted.
[ECO] [SAVE] 🛜 ✕ 🅼 🖵 ¶ ≈ ✕

INGONISH BEACH

(CAA) ▼▼▼▼ Keltic Lodge Resort & Spa H
(902) 285-2880. $155-$345, 3 day notice. Middle Head Peninsula B0C 1L0. In Cape Breton Highlands National Park; off Cabot Tr. Ext/int corridors. Pets: Accepted. [SAVE] 🛜 ✕ 🅼 🖥 🖵 ¶ ≈ ✕

KEMPTVILLE

▼▼▼ Trout Point Lodge CI
(902) 761-2142. Call for rates. 189 Trout Point Rd B0W 1Y0. 6.6 mi (11 km) e on Rt 203, 2.1 mi (3.5 km) n on gravel entry road. Ext corridors. Pets: Accepted. 🛜 ✕ 🖥 🖵 ¶ ✕ 🎿

KENTVILLE

▼ Sun Valley Motel M
(902) 678-7368. Call for rates. 843 Park St B4N 3V7. Hwy 101 exit 14, 0.5 mi (0.8 km) e on Rt 1. Ext corridors. Pets: Accepted.
🛜 🖥 🖵 🎿 🗲

KINGSTON

(CAA) ▼▼ Best Western Aurora Inn H
(902) 765-3306. $135-$140. 831 Main St B0P 1R0. Hwy 101 exit 17 to Rt 1, follow signs. Ext corridors. Pets: $10 one-time fee/pet. Supervision.
[SAVE] 🛜 ✕ 🖥 🖵 ¶

LISCOMB

(CAA) ▼▼▼ Liscombe Lodge Resort & Conference Centre H
(902) 779-2307. $139-$209, 3 day notice. 2884 Hwy 7 (RR 1) B0J 2A0. On Hwy 7. Ext/int corridors. Pets: Designated rooms, service with restrictions, crate. [SAVE] ✕ 🅼 🖥 🖵 ¶ ≈ ✕

LIVERPOOL

(CAA) ▼▼▼▼ Best Western Plus Liverpool Hotel & Conference Centre H ❀
(902) 354-2377. $130-$140. 63 Queens Place Dr B0T 1K0. Hwy 103 exit 19, just e. Int corridors. Pets: $20 one-time fee/room. Designated rooms, service with restrictions, crate. [ECO] [SAVE] 🛜 ✕ 🅼 🖥 🖵 ≈

(CAA) ▼▼▼ Lane's Privateer Inn H
(902) 354-3456. $85-$142. 27 Bristol Ave B0T 1K0. Hwy 103 exit 19, 1.2 mi (2 km) se on Rt 8 and 3. Ext/int corridors. Pets: Accepted.
[SAVE] 🛜 ✕ ¶

LOWER ARGYLE

(CAA) ▼▼▼▼ Ye Olde Argyler Lodge CI
(902) 643-2500. $100-$215, 3 day notice. Rt 3 B0W 1W0. Hwy 103 exit 32, 4.5 mi (7.5 km) e. Int corridors. Pets: Accepted.
[SAVE] 🛜 ✕ ¶

LUNENBURG

▼▼ The Homeport Motel M
(902) 634-8234. Call for rates. 167 Victoria Rd B0J 2C0. 0.6 mi (1 km) w on Rt 3. Ext corridors. Pets: Accepted. 🛜 ✕ 🖥 🖵

▼▼▼ Lunenburg Arms Hotel & Spa H ❀
(902) 640-4040. $129-$299. 94 Pelham St B0J 2C0. Corner of Pelham and Duke sts; centre. Int corridors. Pets: Medium. $25 one-time fee/room. Supervision. 🛜 ✕ 🅼 🖥 🖵 ¶

MAHONE BAY

▼▼▼ Bayview Pines Country Inn BB ❀
(902) 624-9970. $100-$165, 5 day notice. 678 Oakland Rd B0J 2E0. Hwy 103 exit 10, 1.2 mi (2 km) w on Rt 3 to Kedy's Landing, 3.6 mi (6 km) e of Mahone Bay. Ext/int corridors. Pets: Medium. Designated rooms, service with restrictions, supervision.
🛜 ✕ 🖥 🖵 🎥 🗲

▼▼▼ Fisherman's Daughter Bed & Breakfast BB
(902) 624-0483. $115-$145. 97 Edgewater St B0J 2E0. On Rt 3; centre. Int corridors. Pets: Accepted. 🛜 ✕ 🎥 🗲

MAVILLETTE

▼ Cape View Motel & Cottages M
(902) 645-2258. Call for rates. 124 John Doucette Rd B0W 2Y0. Rt 1, 19.2 mi (32 km) ne of Yarmouth; centre. Ext corridors. Pets: Accepted.
🛜 ✕ 🖥 🖵 🎥 🗲

MIDDLETON

▼▼ ▼ Mid-Valley Motel M
(902) 825-3433. Call for rates. 121 Main St B0S 1P0. Hwy 101 exit 18, 0.6 mi (1 km) w on Rt 1. Ext corridors. Pets: Accepted. 🛜 🖥 ≈

MUSQUODOBOIT HARBOUR

▼▼▼ Elephant's Nest Bed & Breakfast BB
(902) 827-3891. $110-$150, 3 day notice. 127 Pleasant Dr B0J 1N0. Jct Hwy 107 and 7, 1.8 mi (3 km) w, follow signs. Int corridors.
Pets: Accepted. 🛜 ✕ ✕ 🎥

NEW GLASGOW

▼▼ Comfort Inn H
(902) 755-6450. $110-$150. 740 Westville Rd B2H 2J8. On Hwy 289, just e of jct Trans-Canada Hwy 104 exit 23. Int corridors. Pets: Service with restrictions, supervision. [ECO] 🛜 🖥 🖵

▼▼ ▼▼ Country Inn & Suites By Carlson 🄷 ❀

(902) 928-1333. **$124-$137.** 700 Westville Rd B2H 2J8. On Hwy 289, just e of jct Trans-Canada Hwy 104 exit 23. Int corridors. **Pets:** Medium. $25 one-time fee/room. Designated rooms, service with restrictions.

🄴🄲🄾 🛜 ✖ 🗄 💻 📺

NEW HARBOUR

▼▼ ▼▼ ▼▼ Lonely Rock Seaside Bungalows 🄲🄰

(902) 387-2668. **$90-$230, 14 day notice.** 150 New Harbour Rd B0H 1T0. Rt 316, 0.4 mi (0.7 km) s. Ext corridors. **Pets:** Dogs only. $10 daily fee/pet. Designated rooms, supervision. 🛜 ✖ 🗄M 🗄 💻 🄺

NORTH SYDNEY

🄲🄰🄰 ▼▼ ▼▼ Clansman Motel 🄼

(902) 794-7226. **$89-$125.** 9 Baird St B2A 0A9. Hwy 125 exit 2, just e on King St. Ext/int corridors. **Pets:** Accepted.

🅂🄰🅅🄴 🛜 🗄M 🗄 💻 🍴 ⇌

PARRSBORO

🄲🄰🄰 ▼▼ ▼▼ Gillespie House Inn 🄱🄱 ❀

(902) 254-3196. **$99-$139.** 358 Main St B0M 1S0. On Rt 2; centre. Int corridors. **Pets:** $25 deposit/room. Designated rooms, service with restrictions, supervision. 🅂🄰🅅🄴 🛜 ✖ 🗄M 🄺 🄿🄽 🗄

▼▼ ▼▼ The Sunshine Inn 🄼

(902) 254-3135. **$89-$175.** Rt 2 B0M 1S0. 2 mi (3.2 km) n. Ext corridors. **Pets:** Accepted. 🛜 🗄 ✖ 🗄

PICTOU

▼▼ ▼▼ Caribou River Cottage 🄲🄰

(902) 485-6352. **Call for rates.** 1308 Shore Rd B0K 1H0. From PEI ferry terminal, 2.7 mi (4.5 km) w on Three Brooks Rd to Shore Rd. Ext corridors. **Pets:** Accepted. 🛜 ✖ 🗄 ✖ 🄺 🗄

🄲🄰🄰 ▼▼ ▼▼ ▼▼ Pictou Lodge Beach Resort 🄷

(902) 485-4322. **$89-$499, 3 day notice.** 172 Lodge Rd B0K 1H0. 4.3 mi (7 km) nw on Braeshore Rd; midway between Pictou and PEI ferry terminal at Caribou. Ext corridors. **Pets:** Large, dogs only. $30 one-time fee/pet. Service with restrictions, crate.

🅂🄰🅅🄴 🛜 ✖ 🗄 💻 🍴 ⇌ ✖

▼▼ ▼▼ Willow House Inn 🄱🄱

(902) 485-5740. **$60-$120.** 11 Willow St B0K 1H0. Corner of Willow and Church sts; centre. Int corridors. **Pets:** Accepted. 🛜 ✖

PORT HASTINGS

▼▼ ▼▼ Econo Lodge MacPuffin 🄼

(902) 625-0621. **$90-$140.** 373 Hwy 4 B9A 1M8. 1 mi (1.6 km) n on Hwy 4; 1 mi (1.6 km) s of Canso Cswy. Ext corridors. **Pets:** Large, other species. Designated rooms, service with restrictions.

🛜 ✖ 🗄M 💻 ⇌

PORT HAWKESBURY

🄲🄰🄰 ▼▼ ▼▼ Maritime Inn Port Hawkesbury 🄷

(902) 625-0320. **$117-$199.** 717 Reeves St B9A 2S2. 4.2 mi (6.4 km) n of Canso Cswy on Hwy 4; opposite shopping centre. Ext/int corridors. **Pets:** Accepted. 🅂🄰🅅🄴 🛜 ✖ 🗄 💻 🍴 ⇌

PORT HOOD

▼▼ ▼▼ Haus Treuburg Country Inn & Cottages 🄲🄸

(902) 787-2116. **$105-$210, 7 day notice.** 175 Main St B0E 2W0. Centre. Ext/int corridors. **Pets:** Other species. Designated rooms, service with restrictions, supervision. 🛜 ✖ 🗄 💻 🍴 🄺

SCOTSBURN

▼▼ ▼▼ ▼▼ Stonehame Lodge & Chalets 🄲🄰

(902) 485-3468. **$85-$240, 14 day notice.** 310 Fitzpatrick Mountain Rd B0K 1R0. Rt 256, 7.5 mi (12 km) w of Pictou via Rt 376, last 1.2 mi (2 km) on gravel entry road. Ext corridors. **Pets:** Large. $10 daily fee/pet. Designated rooms, service with restrictions, crate.

🛜 ✖ 🗄M 🗄 💻 ⇌ ✖

SMITHS COVE

🄲🄰🄰 ▼▼ ▼▼ ▼▼ Harbourview Inn 🄱🄱 ❀

(902) 245-5686. **$119-$179, 7 day notice.** 25 Harbourview Rd B0S 1S0. Hwy 101 exit 25 eastbound; exit 24 westbound. Ext/int corridors. **Pets:** Dogs only. Supervision. 🅂🄰🅅🄴 🛜 ✖ 🗄 💻 ⇌ ✖

▼▼ ▼▼ Hedley House Inn By The Sea 🄼

(902) 245-2500. **Call for rates.** RR 1 B0S 1S0. Hwy 101 exit 25 eastbound; exit 24 westbound. Ext corridors. **Pets:** Accepted.

🛜 🗄 💻 🄺 🗄

STELLARTON

🄲🄰🄰 ▼▼ ▼▼ ▼▼ Holiday Inn Express Stellarton-New Glasgow 🄷 ❀

(902) 755-1020. **$129-$169.** 86 Lawrence Blvd B0K 1S0. Hwy 104 exit 24, just s, then 0.6 mi (1 km) w. Int corridors. **Pets:** Large, other species. $25 deposit/room. Service with restrictions, crate.

🅂🄰🅅🄴 🛜 ✖ 🗄M 🗄 💻 ⇌ ✖

SYDNEY

🄲🄰🄰 ▼▼ ▼▼ ▼▼ Cambridge Suites Hotel 🄷 ❀

(902) 562-6500. **$111-$220, 30 day notice.** 380 Esplanade B1P 1B1. Hwy 4, 3.1 mi (5 km) e of jct Hwy 125 exit 6E; downtown. Int corridors. **Pets:** Other species. $25 one-time fee/pet. Designated rooms, service with restrictions, supervision. 🄴🄲🄾 🅂🄰🅅🄴 🛜 ✖ 🗄 💻 🍴 ✖

▼▼ ▼▼ Comfort Inn 🄷

(902) 562-0200. **$111-$163.** 368 Kings Rd B1S 1A8. Hwy 4, 2.1 mi (3.5 km) e of jct Hwy 125 exit 6E. Int corridors. **Pets:** Accepted.

🄴🄲🄾 🛜 🗄 💻

🄲🄰🄰 ▼▼ ▼▼ Days Inn Sydney 🄷

(902) 539-6750. **$98-$158.** 480 Kings Rd B1S 1A8. Hwy 4, 1.7 mi (2.8 km) e of jct Hwy 125 exit 6E. Int corridors. **Pets:** Large, other species. Designated rooms, service with restrictions, supervision.

🅂🄰🅅🄴 🛜 🗄 💻 🍴 ⇌ ✖

▼▼ ▼▼ Delta Sydney 🄷

(902) 562-7500. **Call for rates.** 300 Esplanade B1P 1A7. At Prince St; centre. Int corridors. **Pets:** Medium. $35 one-time fee/room. Service with restrictions, supervision. 🄴🄲🄾 🛜 ✖ 🗄 💻 🍴 ⇌ ✖

🄲🄰🄰 ▼▼ ▼▼ Quality Inn Sydney 🄷

(902) 539-8101. **$95-$135.** 560 Kings Rd B1S 1B8. Hwy 4, 2 mi (3.3 km) e of jct Hwy 125. Int corridors. **Pets:** Accepted.

🅂🄰🅅🄴 🛜 ✖ 🗄 💻 🍴 ⇌

TRURO

▼▼ ▼▼ Comfort Inn 🄷

(902) 893-0330. **$81-$119.** 12 Meadow Dr B2N 5V4. Hwy 102 exit 14. Int corridors. **Pets:** Accepted. 🄴🄲🄾 🛜 🗄 💻

▼▼ ▼▼ Holiday Inn Hotel & Conference Centre Truro 🄷

(902) 895-1651. **$99-$159.** 437 Prince St B2N 1E6. Just e of Willow St; centre. Int corridors. **Pets:** Accepted.

🄴🄲🄾 🛜 ✖ 🗄 💻 🍴 ⇌

▼▼ ▼▼ Super 8 🄷 ❀

(902) 895-8884. **$99-$136.** 85 Treaty Tr B2N 5A9. Hwy 102 exit 13A. Int corridors. **Pets:** Medium, other species. $10 daily fee/pet. Designated rooms, service with restrictions, supervision.

🄴🄲🄾 🛜 🗄M 🗄 💻 ⇌

WESTERN SHORE

🄲🄰🄰 ▼▼ ▼▼ ▼▼ Atlantica Hotel & Marina Oak Island 🄷

(902) 627-2600. **$109-$169.** 36 Treasure Dr B0J 3M0. Hwy 103 exit 9 or 10, follow signs on Rt 3; 6 mi (10 km) e of Mahone Bay. Int corridors. **Pets:** Accepted. 🄴🄲🄾 🅂🄰🅅🄴 🛜 ✖ 🗄M 🗄 💻 🍴 ⇌ ✖

WHYCOCOMAGH

◆◆◆ Keltic Quay Bayfront Lodge & Cottages 🄲🄰

(902) 756-1122. **$149-$299, 3 day notice.** 90 Main St B0E 3M0. Just se off Trans-Canada Hwy 105; centre. Ext corridors. **Pets:** Accepted.

WINDSOR

◆◆◆ Super 8 🄷

(902) 792-8888. **$51-$136.** 63 Cole Dr B0N 2T0. Hwy 101 exit 5A, just s. Int corridors. **Pets:** Accepted.

WOLFVILLE

🄒🄐 ◆◆◆ Tattingstone Inn 🄱🄱

(902) 542-7696. **$108-$188.** 620 Main St B4P 1E8. 0.4 mi (0.6 km) w on Rt 1. Ext/int corridors. **Pets:** Accepted. [SAVE] 🖥 ☒ ⤳

YARMOUTH

🄒🄐 ◆◆◆ Best Western Mermaid 🄼

(902) 742-7821. **$99-$140.** 545 Main St B5A 1J6. Corner of Main St and Starrs Rd. Ext corridors. **Pets:** Other species. $10 daily fee/room. Designated rooms, service with restrictions, supervision.

◆◆ Comfort Inn 🄷

(902) 742-1119. **$101-$138.** 96 Starrs Rd B5A 2T5. Jct Hwy 101 E and 3. Int corridors. **Pets:** Accepted. [ECO] 🖥 🖥 🖥

◆ Lakelawn Motel 🄼 ❀

(902) 742-3588. **$59-$79.** 641 Main St B5A 1K2. 0.6 mi (1 km) n on Hwy 1. Ext/int corridors. **Pets:** $5 daily fee/pet. Service with restrictions, supervision. 🖥 ☒ 🖥 🍽 🖥 🖥

◆◆ Rodd Grand Yarmouth 🄷

(902) 742-2446. **$111-$151.** 417 Main St B5A 4B2. Corner of Grand St. Int corridors. **Pets:** Accepted. [ECO] 🖥 ☒ 🖥 🖥 🍽 ⤳ ☒

◆◆ Voyageur Motel 🄼

(902) 742-7157. **$79-$189, 3 day notice.** RR 1 B5A 4A5. 3 mi (4.8 km) ne on Hwy 1. Ext corridors. **Pets:** Accepted. 🖥 🖥 🖥

ONTARIO

CITY INDEX

AJAX

Super 8-Ajax

(905) 428-6884. **$58-$119.** 210 Westney Rd S L1S 7P9. Hwy 401 exit Westney Rd, 0.6 mi (1 km) s; jct Bayly St. Int corridors. **Pets:** Small. $10 daily fee/pet. Service with restrictions, supervision.

ALGONQUIN PROVINCIAL PARK

Killarney Lodge

(705) 633-5551. **$338-$688, 3 day notice.** Hwy 60-Lake of Two Rivers-Algonquin P1H 2G9. 21 mi (33 km) into park from west gate; 14 mi (23 km) from east gate. Ext corridors. **Pets:** Large, dogs only. $25 daily fee/pet. Designated rooms, service with restrictions, supervision.

ALLISTON

Red Pine Inn & Conference Centre

(705) 435-4381. **Call for rates.** 497 Victoria St E L9R 1T9. 1.8 mi (3 km) e of King St. Ext/int corridors. **Pets:** Accepted.

ALTON

Millcroft Inn & Spa

(519) 941-8111. **$199-$299, 5 day notice.** 55 John St L7K 0C4. 2.5 mi (4 km) n off Hwy 136 from Hwy 24, 0.6 mi (1 km) w on Queen St E, then just n. Ext/int corridors. **Pets:** Accepted.

ARNPRIOR

Country Squire Motel

(613) 623-6556. **$59-$135, 3 day notice.** 111 Staye Court Dr K7S 0E8. Hwy 17 exit White Lake Rd, just n to Staye Court Dr, then just w. Ext corridors. **Pets:** Small, dogs only. $15 daily fee/pet. Service with restrictions, supervision.

Quality Inn

(613) 623-7991. **$113-$175.** 70 Madawaska Blvd K7S 1S5. Hwy 417 exit 180, 0.4 mi (0.7 km) n on CR 29, then 1.4 mi (2.3 km) w. Int corridors. **Pets:** $10 daily fee/pet. Service with restrictions, supervision.

BANCROFT

Best Western Sword Motor Inn

(613) 332-2474. **$136.** 146 Hastings St K0L 1C0. On Hwy 62 N; center. Ext/int corridors. **Pets:** Accepted.

BARRIE

Comfort Inn

(705) 722-3600. **$90-$150.** 75 Hart Dr L4N 5M3. Hwy 400 exit 96A E (Dunlop St). Int corridors. **Pets:** Medium. $6 daily fee/pet. Designated rooms, service with restrictions, supervision.

Comfort Inn & Suites

(705) 721-1122. **Call for rates.** 210 Essa Rd L4N 3L1. Hwy 400 exit 94 (Essa Rd), just e. Int corridors. **Pets:** Accepted.

Days Inn Barrie

(705) 733-8989. **$99-$216.** 60 Bryne Dr L4N 9Y4. Hwy 400 exit 94 (Essa Rd), just s, then just e. Int corridors. **Pets:** Accepted.

Holiday Inn Barrie-Hotel & Conference Centre

(705) 728-6191. **$99-$149.** 20 Fairview Rd L4N 4P3. Hwy 400 exit 94 (Essa Rd), just e. Int corridors. **Pets:** Small, other species. Designated rooms, service with restrictions, crate.

Holiday Inn Express Hotel & Suites Barrie

(705) 725-1002. **$112-$185.** 506 Bryne Dr L4N 9P6. Hwy 400 exit 90 (Mapleview Dr), just sw. Int corridors. **Pets:** Medium. $15 one-time fee/room. Designated rooms, service with restrictions, supervision.

Horseshoe Resort

(705) 835-2790. **Call for rates.** 1101 Horseshoe Valley Rd W L4M 4Y8. Hwy 400 exit 117 (Horseshoe Valley Rd), 3.8 mi (6 km) e. Int corridors. **Pets:** Accepted.

Super 8

(705) 814-8888. **$74-$154.** 441 Bryne Dr L4N 6C8. Hwy 400 exit 90 (Mapleview Dr), just nw. Int corridors. **Pets:** Large, other species. $15 daily fee/pet. Designated rooms, service with restrictions.

Travelodge Barrie

(705) 734-9500. **$72-$99.** 55 Hart Dr L4N 5M3. Hwy 400 exit 96A E (Dunlop St). Int corridors. **Pets:** Accepted.

BARRY'S BAY

Mountain View Motel

(613) 756-2757. **$75-$190, 7 day notice.** 18508 Hwy 60 E K0J 1B0. 2.5 mi (4 km) e of town. Ext corridors. **Pets:** Other species. Supervision.

BAYFIELD

ⓐⓐ ◈◈◈◈ The Little Inn of Bayfield CI ✿
(519) 565-2611. **Call for rates.** 26 Main St N0M 1G0. Hwy 21 exit Main St; jct Catherine St. Int corridors. **Pets:** Dogs only. $50 one-time fee/pet. Designated rooms, supervision. (SAVE) 📶 ✕ 💻 ⍩

BELLEVILLE

ⓐⓐ ◈◈◈ Best Western Belleville H ✿
(613) 969-1112. **$119-$179.** 387 N Front St K8P 3C8. Hwy 401 exit 543A, 0.3 mi (0.5 km) s on Hwy 62. Int corridors. **Pets:** Designated rooms, service with restrictions, supervision.
(ECO) (SAVE) 📶 🛏 💻 ⌇

ⓐⓐ ◈◈◈ Comfort Inn H
(613) 966-7703. **$110-$135.** 200 N Park St K8P 2Y9. Hwy 401 exit 543A, 0.6 mi (1 km) s on Hwy 62. Int corridors. **Pets:** Accepted.
(SAVE) 📶 🛏 💻

◈◈◈ Hotel Quinte H
(613) 962-4531. **Call for rates.** 211 Pinnacle St K8N 3A7. Hwy 401 exit 543A, 1.8 mi (3 km) s on Hwy 62; corner of Bridge St; downtown. Int corridors. **Pets:** Large, other species. $10 daily fee/room. Service with restrictions, crate. (ECO) 📶 🛏 💻 ⍩

ⓐⓐ ◈◈◈ Travelodge Hotel Belleville H
(613) 968-3411. **$65-$169.** 11 Bay Bridge Rd K8P 3P6. 0.3 mi (0.5 km) s of Hwy 2 (Dundas St). Int corridors. **Pets:** $15 daily fee/room. Service with restrictions, supervision.
(ECO) (SAVE) 📶 ✕ 🛏 💻 ⍩ ⌇ ✕

BLIND RIVER

◈◈ Lakeview Inn M
(705) 356-0800. **$89-$110, 3 day notice.** 143 Causley St P0R 1B0. On Hwy 17, just e of Hwy 557. Ext corridors. **Pets:** Small. $10 daily fee/pet. Designated rooms, service with restrictions, supervision.
📶 ✕ 🛏 💻 ⍩

BOWMANVILLE

◈◈◈ Holiday Inn Express & Suites Bowmanville H
(905) 697-8089. **$129-$159.** 37 Spicer Square L1C 5M2. Jct Hwy 401 and Waverly Rd N. Int corridors. **Pets:** $25 daily fee/pet. Service with restrictions, supervision. 📶 ✕ ⍓ 🛏 💻 ⌇

ⓐⓐ ◈◈◈ Howard Johnson Bowmanville H
(905) 623-8500. **$71-$116.** 160 Liberty St S L1C 2W4. Hwy 401 exit 432 (Liberty St), just n. Int corridors. **Pets:** Designated rooms, service with restrictions, supervision. (ECO) (SAVE) 📶 ✕ 🛏 💻 ⌇

BRACEBRIDGE

ⓐⓐ ◈◈◈ Travelodge Bracebridge M
(705) 645-2235. **$89-$269.** 320 Taylor Rd P1L 1K1. Hwy 11 exit 189 (Hwy 42/Taylor Rd), 0.6 mi (1 km) w. Ext corridors. **Pets:** Accepted.
(SAVE) 📶 🛏 💻 ⌇

BRAMPTON

◈◈ Motel 6 Brampton #1902 H
(905) 451-3313. **$61-$71.** 160 Steelwell Rd L6T 5T3. Hwy 410 exit Steeles Ave E, s on Tomken Rd, then just w. Int corridors. **Pets:** Other species. Service with restrictions, supervision. (ECO) 📶 🛏

BRANTFORD

ⓐⓐ ◈◈◈ Best Western Plus Brant Park Inn & Conference Centre H ✿
(519) 753-8651. **$125-$144.** 19 Holiday Dr N3R 7J4. Jct Hwy 403 and Wayne Gretzky Pkwy. Int corridors. **Pets:** Medium, other species. $100 deposit/room, $20 daily fee/pet. Designated rooms, service with restrictions, crate. (ECO) (SAVE) 📶 ✕ ⍓ 🛏 💻 ⍩ ⌇ ✕

ⓐⓐ ◈◈◈ Comfort Inn H
(519) 753-3100. **$90-$140.** 58 King George Rd N3R 5K4. Just s of jct Hwy 403 and 24. Int corridors. **Pets:** Accepted. (SAVE) 📶 🛏 💻

◈◈ Days Inn H
(519) 759-2700. **$84-$126.** 460 Fairview Dr N3R 7A9. Hwy 403 exit Wayne Gretzky Pkwy, 0.5 mi (0.8 km) n. Int corridors. **Pets:** Accepted.
(ECO) 📶 🛏 💻 ⍩

BRIGHTON

ⓐⓐ ◈◈◈◈ Timber House Country Inn CI
(613) 475-3304. **$130-$160.** 116 Cedardale Rd K0K 1H0. Jct 2 and 64, just w over swing bridge, follow signs. Int corridors. **Pets:** Accepted.
(SAVE) 📶 ✕ 💻 ⌇

BROCKVILLE

ⓐⓐ ◈◈◈ Best Western White House Inn M
(613) 345-1622. **$99-$139.** 1843 Hwy 2 E K6V 5T1. Hwy 401 exit 698, 1.2 mi (1.9 km) s on N Augusta Rd, then 0.9 mi (1.5 km) e. Ext corridors. **Pets:** Medium. $15 daily fee/pet. Designated rooms.
(SAVE) 📶 🛏 💻 ⌇

ⓐⓐ ◈◈◈ Comfort Inn H
(613) 345-0042. **$100-$200.** 7777 Kent Blvd K6V 6N7. Hwy 401 exit 696, just nw. Int corridors. **Pets:** Other species. $15 daily fee/pet. Designated rooms, service with restrictions, crate. (SAVE) 📶 🛏 💻

BURLINGTON

ⓐⓐ ◈◈◈ Admiral Inn H
(905) 639-4780. **$89-$99.** 3500 Billings Ct L7N 3N6. QEW exit Walker's Line Rd westbound, just s to Harvester Rd, then just w to S Service Rd; exit Guelph Line Rd eastbound, just s to Harvester Rd, then just e to S Service Rd. Int corridors. **Pets:** Accepted. (SAVE) 📶 🛏 💻

ⓐⓐ ◈◈ Comfort Inn H ✿
(905) 639-1700. **$85-$140.** 3290 S Service Rd L7N 3M6. QEW exit Walker's Line Rd westbound, just s to Harvester Rd, then just w; exit Guelph Line Rd eastbound, just s to Harvester Rd, then just e. Int corridors. **Pets:** Designated rooms, service with restrictions, crate.
(ECO) (SAVE) 📶 🛏 💻

ⓐⓐ ◈◈◈ Homewood Suites by Hilton H ✿
(905) 631-8300. **$134-$180.** 975 Syscon Rd L7L 5S3. QEW exit Burloak Dr S, w on Harvester Rd. Int corridors. **Pets:** Small. $100 one-time fee/room. Designated rooms, service with restrictions, crate.
(SAVE) 📶 🛏 💻 ⌇

◈◈ Motel 6 Burlington #1900 H
(905) 331-1955. **$65-$75.** 4345 N Service Rd L7L 4X7. QEW exit Walker's Line Rd N to N Service Rd, 0.9 mi (1.4 km) e. Int corridors. **Pets:** Other species. Service with restrictions, supervision. (ECO) 📶 🛏

◈◈◈ Quality Hotel Burlington H
(905) 639-9290. **Call for rates.** 950 Walker's Line Rd L7N 2G2. QEW exit Walker's Line Rd, just s. Int corridors. **Pets:** Accepted.
(ECO) 📶 🛏 💻 ⍩ ⌇ ✕

ⓐⓐ ◈◈◈ Waterfront Hotel - Downtown Burlington H
(905) 681-5400. **Call for rates.** 2020 Lakeshore Rd L7R 4G8. Corner of Brant St; downtown. Int corridors. **Pets:** Accepted.
(ECO) (SAVE) 📶 ✕ 🛏 💻 ⍩ ⌇

CAMBRIDGE

ⓐⓐ ◈◈◈◈ Cambridge Hotel Conference Centre H
(519) 622-1505. **$105-$140.** 700 Hespeler Rd N3H 5L8. Hwy 401 exit 282, just s. Int corridors. **Pets:** Accepted. (SAVE) 📶 ✕ 🛏 💻 ⍩

ⓐⓐ ◈◈ Comfort Inn H ✿
(519) 658-1100. **$95-$130.** 220 Holiday Inn Dr N3C 1Z4. Hwy 401 exit 282, just n to Groh Ave. Int corridors. **Pets:** Other species. Service with restrictions. (ECO) (SAVE) 📶 🛏 💻 ✕

▼▼▼▼ **Homewood Suites by Hilton Cambridge/Waterloo** 🄷 ❄

(519) 651-2888. **$164-$184.** 800 Jamieson Pkwy N3C 4N6. Hwy 401 exit 286 (Townline Rd), just n. Int corridors. **Pets:** Other species. $75 one-time fee/room. Supervision. 🛜 🔊M 🔲 💻 🌊 ⌧

Ⓐ ▼▼▼▼ **Langdon Hall Country House Hotel & Spa** 🄲🄸

(519) 740-2100. **$259-$649, 3 day notice.** 1 Langdon Dr N3H 4R8. Hwy 401 exit 275, 0.8 mi (1.3 km) se on Fountain St, then 0.6 mi (1 km) s on Blair Rd, follow signs. Ext/int corridors. **Pets:** Accepted.

SAVE 🛜 ⌧ 🔲 💻 🍴 🌊 ⌧

▼▼ **Super 8 Cambridge** 🄷

(519) 622-1070. **$70-$99.** 650 Hespeler Rd N1R 6J8. Hwy 401 exit 282, 0.6 mi (1 km) s. Int corridors. **Pets:** Very small, dogs only. $5 daily fee/pet. Designated rooms, service with restrictions, supervision.

🛜 🔲 💻 🍴 🌊

CHATHAM

▼▼ **Comfort Inn** 🄷

(519) 352-5500. **$92-$115.** 1100 Richmond St N7M 5J5. Hwy 401 exit 81 (Bloomfield Rd), 3.1 mi (5 km) n. Int corridors. **Pets:** Other species. Service with restrictions, crate. ECO 🛜 🔲 💻

▼▼▼▼ **Holiday Inn Express & Suites** 🄷

(519) 351-1100. **$135-$175.** 575 Richmond St N7M 1R2. Hwy 401 exit 81 (Bloomfield Rd) to jct Hwy 2, 0.9 mi (1.5 km) e, then 0.9 mi (1.5 km) w. Int corridors. **Pets:** Accepted. 🛜 🔊M 🔲 💻 🌊

CHATSWORTH

▼▼ **Key Motel** 🄼 ❄

(519) 794-2350. **$65-$85.** 317051 Hwy 6/10 N0H 1G0. On SR 6 and 10. Ext/int corridors. **Pets:** Other species. $5 daily fee/room. Service with restrictions, supervision. 🛜 🔲 🌊 ⌧

COBOURG

Ⓐ ▼▼▼▼ **Best Western Plus Cobourg Inn & Convention Centre** 🄷 ❄

(905) 372-2105. **$167.** 930 Burnham St K9A 2X9. Hwy 401 exit 472 (Burnham St S). Int corridors. **Pets:** Other species. Service with restrictions, supervision. ECO SAVE 🛜 🔲 💻 🍴 🌊

▼▼ **Comfort Inn** 🄷

(905) 372-7007. **$90-$135.** 121 Densmore Rd K9A 4J9. Hwy 401 exit 474, just se. Int corridors. **Pets:** Accepted. ECO 🛜 🔲 💻

CORNWALL

Ⓐ ▼▼▼▼ **Best Western Plus Parkway Inn & Conference Centre** 🄷

(613) 932-0451. **$136-$160.** 1515 Vincent Massey Dr K6H 5R6. Hwy 401 exit 789 (Brookdale Ave), 1.8 mi (2.8 km) s, then just w. Int corridors. **Pets:** Medium. $10 daily fee/room. Designated rooms, service with restrictions, supervision. ECO SAVE 🛜 ⌧ 🔲 💻 🍴 🌊

▼▼ **Comfort Inn-Cornwall** 🄷

(613) 937-0111. **$114-$129.** 1625 Vincent Massey Dr K6H 5R6. Hwy 401 exit 789 (Brookdale Ave), 1.8 mi (2.8 km) s, then 0.4 mi (0.7 km) w. Int corridors. **Pets:** $20 one-time fee/room. Designated rooms.

🛜 🔲 💻 🌊

DRYDEN

Ⓐ ▼▼▼▼ **Best Western Plus Dryden Hotel & Conference Centre** 🄷

(807) 223-3201. **$132.** 349 Government St P8N 2P4. On Hwy 17. Int corridors. **Pets:** Other species. $10 one-time fee/room. Designated rooms, service with restrictions. ECO SAVE 🛜 ⌧ 🔲 💻 🍴 🌊 ⌧

▼▼ **Comfort Inn** 🄼

(807) 223-3893. **$123-$134.** 522 Government St P8N 2P7. On Hwy 17. Int corridors. **Pets:** Accepted. ECO 🛜 🔲 💻

FONTHILL

▼▼ **Hipwell's Motel** 🄼

(905) 892-3588. **$45-$75.** 299 Reg Rd 20 W L0S 1E0. 1 mi (1.6 km) w; center. Ext corridors. **Pets:** Medium, dogs only. $10 daily fee/pet. Service with restrictions, supervision. 🛜 🔲 🌊

FORT FRANCES

Ⓐ ▼▼▼▼ **La Place Rendez-Vous** 🄷

(807) 274-9811. **$104-$114.** 1201 Idylwild Dr, B2-RR2 P9A 3M3. Hwy 11, just w on Lake Rd; west end of town. Int corridors. **Pets:** Other species. $10 daily fee/pet. Designated rooms, service with restrictions, supervision. SAVE 🛜 ⌧ 🔲 💻 🍴 ⌧

▼▼ **Super 8** 🄷

(807) 274-4945. **$95-$120.** 810 Kings Hwy P9A 2X4. On Hwy 11. Int corridors. **Pets:** Accepted. 🛜 🔊M 🔲 💻 🌊 ⌧

FRENCH RIVER

Ⓐ ▼▼ **French River Trading Post Motel** 🄼

(705) 857-2115. **$77-$90.** 20112 Hwy 69 P0M 1A0. Trans-Canada Hwy 69, 0.6 mi (1 km) n of French River Bridge. Ext corridors. **Pets:** $10 daily fee/pet. Designated rooms, service with restrictions, supervision.

SAVE 🛜 🔲 💻 🍴 🎿 🌊

GANANOQUE

Ⓐ ▼▼▼▼ **Best Western Country Squire Resort** 🄷

(613) 382-3511. **Call for rates.** 715 King St E K7G 1H4. Hwy 401 exit 647 eastbound; exit 648 westbound, 0.6 mi (1 km) w on Hwy 2. Ext/int corridors. **Pets:** Accepted. SAVE 🛜 ⌧ 🔲 💻 🍴 🌊 ⌧

Ⓐ ▼▼▼ **Clarion Inn & Conference Centre 1000 Islands** 🄷

(613) 382-7272. **Call for rates.** 50 Main St K7G 2L7. Corner of Hwy 2 (King St); center. Int corridors. **Pets:** Medium, other species. $15 daily fee/pet. Service with restrictions, supervision.

SAVE 🛜 🔲 💻 🍴 🌊

Ⓐ ▼▼▼ **Comfort Inn 1000 Islands** 🄼

(613) 382-4728. **Call for rates.** 785 King St E K7G 1H4. Hwy 401 exit 647 eastbound; exit 648 westbound, 0.3 mi (0.5 km) w on Hwy 2 (King St). Ext/int corridors. **Pets:** Medium, other species. $15 daily fee/pet. Designated rooms, service with restrictions, supervision.

SAVE 🛜 ⌧ 🔲 💻 🌊

Ⓐ ▼▼▼▼ **Holiday Inn Express & Suites 1000 Islands** 🄷

(613) 382-8338. **$99-$299.** 777 King St E K7G 1H4. Just w of jct Hwy 2 (King St), 401 and 1000 Islands Pkwy. Int corridors. **Pets:** Medium, other species. $15 daily fee/pet. Designated rooms, service with restrictions, supervision. ECO SAVE ⌧ 🔲 💻 🌊

Ⓐ ▼▼▼ **Quality Inn & Suites 1000 Islands** 🄼

(613) 382-1453. **Call for rates.** 650 King St E K7G 1H3. Hwy 401 exit 647 eastbound; exit 648 westbound, 0.6 mi (1 km) w on Hwy 2 (King St). Ext corridors. **Pets:** Medium, other species. $15 daily fee/pet. Designated rooms, service with restrictions, supervision.

SAVE 🛜 🔲 💻 🍴 🌊

▼▼ ▼▼ **Ramada Provincial Inn** 🄼

(613) 382-2038. **$74-$161.** 846 King St E K7G 1H3. Hwy 401 exit 647 eastbound; exit 648 westbound, 0.3 mi (0.5 km) w on Hwy 2 (King St). Ext corridors. **Pets:** $10 daily fee/room. Designated rooms, service with restrictions. 🛜 ⌧ 🔲 💻 🍴 🌊

▼▼ ▼▼ **Trinity House Inn** 🄲🄸

(613) 382-8383. **$99-$250, 7 day notice.** 90 Stone St S K7G 1Z8. Corner of Pine St; center. Int corridors. **Pets:** Other species. Designated rooms, service with restrictions. 🛜 ⌧ 🔲 💻 🍴 🎿

GRAVENHURST

▼▼▼ **Residence Inn by Marriott Gravenhurst Muskoka Wharf** 🏠 ❀

(705) 687-6600. **Call for rates.** 285 Steamship Bay Rd P1P 1Z9. Hwy 11 exit 169 (Bethune Dr), follow signs. Int corridors. **Pets:** Large, other species. $100 one-time fee/room. Service with restrictions, supervision.

🛜 ⊠ ⅃M 🛏 💻 ⇔

GRIMSBY

Ⓐ ▼▼▼ **Super 8-Grimsby** 🏠

(905) 309-8800. **$81-$118.** 11 Windward Dr L3M 4E9. QEW exit 74 (Casablanca Blvd N). Int corridors. **Pets:** Medium, other species. $10 daily fee/pet. Service with restrictions, supervision.

SAVE ⊠ 🛏 💻 ⇔

GUELPH

Ⓐ ▼▼▼▼ **Best Western Plus Royal Brock Hotel & Conference Centre** 🏠

(519) 836-1240. **$107-$110.** 716 Gordon St N1G 1Y6. Jct Stone Rd; 5 mi (8 km) n of Hwy 401 via Brock Rd. Int corridors. **Pets:** Accepted.

SAVE 🛜 ⊠ 🛏 💻 ⅃⅃ ⇔

Ⓐ ▼▼▼ **Comfort Inn Guelph** 🏠 ❀

(519) 763-1900. **$85-$130.** 480 Silvercreek Pkwy N1H 7R5. Jct Hwy 6 and 7. Int corridors. **Pets:** Medium. Service with restrictions, supervision.

ECO SAVE 🛜 🛏 💻

Ⓐ ▼▼▼ **Days Inn-Guelph** 🏠

(519) 822-9112. **$85-$144.** 785 Gordon St N1G 1Y8. Hwy 401 exit 299 (Brock Rd), 7 mi (11.5 km) n. Int corridors. **Pets:** $100 deposit/room. Service with restrictions, supervision. ECO SAVE 🛜 🛏 💻

▼▼▼ **Delta Guelph Hotel and Conference Centre** 🏠 ❀

(519) 780-3700. **$129-$219.** 50 Stone Rd W N1G 0A9. Jct Gordon St. Int corridors. **Pets:** Medium, other species. $35 one-time fee/room. Designated rooms, service with restrictions, supervision.

ECO 🛜 ⊠ ⅃M 🛏 💻 ⅃⅃

▼▼▼ **Hampton Inn & Suites by Hilton Guelph** 🏠

(519) 821-2144. **$109-$249.** 725 Imperial Rd N N1K 1X4. Hwy 401 exit 295 (Hwy 6 N) to Woodlawn Rd, w to Imperial Rd, then n. Int corridors. **Pets:** Accepted. 🛜 🛏 💻 ⇔

Ⓐ ▼▼▼ **Holiday Inn Express Hotel & Suites Guelph** 🏠

(519) 824-2400. **$99-$169.** 540 Silvercreek Pkwy N N1H 6N3. Jct Hwy 6 and 7. Int corridors. **Pets:** Accepted. SAVE 🛜 🛏 💻 ⇔

Ⓐ ▼▼▼ **Holiday Inn Guelph Hotel & Conference Centre** 🏠 ❀

(519) 836-0231. **$99-$169.** 601 Scottsdale Dr N1G 3E7. Jct Hwy 6 N and Stone Rd E; 5 mi (8 km) n of jct Hwy 401. Int corridors. **Pets:** Other species. $35 one-time fee/room. Designated rooms, service with restrictions, crate. ECO SAVE 🛜 🛏 💻 ⅃⅃ ⇔ ⊠

Ⓐ ▼▼▼ **Staybridge Suites** 🏠

(519) 767-3300. **$119-$209.** 11 Corporate Ct N1G 5G5. Jct Hwy 6 and Laird St, just e. Int corridors. **Pets:** Other species. $35 one-time fee/room. Service with restrictions. ECO SAVE 🛜 ⅃M 🛏 💻 ⇔

Ⓐ ▼▼▼ **Super 8-Guelph** 🅜

(519) 836-5850. **$79-$159.** 281 Woodlawn Rd W N1H 7K7. Jct Hwy 6 and 7. Ext/int corridors. **Pets:** Medium, dogs only. $10 one-time fee/pet. Designated rooms, service with restrictions, supervision.

SAVE 🛜 🛏 💻 ⅃⅃

HALIBURTON

▼▼ **Lakeview Motel** 🅜

(705) 457-1027. **$124-$260, 5 day notice.** 4951 CR 21 K0M 1S0. Jct Hwy 118, 1.6 mi (2.5 km) w. Ext corridors. **Pets:** Medium. $12 daily fee/pet. Designated rooms, service with restrictions, crate.

🛜 ⊠ 🛏 💻 ⅃⅃ ⇔

Ⓐ ▼▼▼ **Pinestone Resort, Conference Centre, Spa & Golf Course** 🏠 ❀

(705) 457-1800. **$129-$259, 3 day notice.** 4252 County Rd 21 K0M 1S0. 3.8 mi (6 km) s of town. Ext/int corridors. **Pets:** Medium. $50 one-time fee/room. Designated rooms, service with restrictions, supervision.

ECO SAVE 🛜 🛏 💻 ⅃⅃ ⇔ ⊠

HAMILTON

Ⓐ ▼▼▼ **Sheraton Hamilton Hotel** 🏠

(905) 529-5515. **$139-$359.** 116 King St W L8P 4V3. Between Bay and James sts; downtown. Int corridors. **Pets:** Accepted.

SAVE 🛜 ⊠ ⅃M 🛏 💻 ⅃⅃ ⇔

▼▼ **Super 8-Hamilton Airport/Mount Hope** 🏠

(905) 679-3355. **$61-$113.** 2975 Homestead Dr L0R 1W0. Jct Hwy 6 S (Upper James St) and Homestead Dr. Int corridors. **Pets:** $10 daily fee/pet. Designated rooms, service with restrictions, supervision.

🛜 🛏 💻

HUNTSVILLE

▼▼ **Comfort Inn** 🏠 ❀

(705) 789-1701. **$78-$148.** 86 King William St P1H 1E4. Jct Hwy 60. Int corridors. **Pets:** Other species. Service with restrictions, supervision.

ECO 🛜 🛏 💻

Ⓐ ▼▼▼ **Holiday Inn Express Hotel & Suites** 🏠

(705) 788-9500. **Call for rates.** 100 Howland Dr P1H 2P9. Jct Hwy 11 and 60, just se. Int corridors. **Pets:** Accepted. SAVE 🛜 🛏 💻 ⇔

▼▼ **HV Hidden Valley Resort** 🏠

(705) 789-2301. **$89-$239, 3 day notice.** 1755 Valley Rd P1H 1Z8. Jct Hwy 11, 4 mi (6.5 km) e on Hwy 60 to Canal, follow signs. Int corridors. **Pets:** Medium. $35 daily fee/room. Designated rooms, service with restrictions, supervision. 🛜 ⊠ 🛏 💻 ⅃⅃ ⇔ ⊠

▼▼ **Motel 6 Huntsville #5705** 🏠

(705) 787-0118. **Call for rates.** 70 Howland Dr P1H 2P9. Jct Hwy 11 and 60, just se. Int corridors. **Pets:** Other species. Service with restrictions, supervision. ECO 🛜 🛏 ⇔

▼ **Travelodge** 🏠

(705) 789-5504. **$72-$153.** 225 Main St W P1H 1Y1. Hwy 11 exit 219 (Muskoka Rd 3), just e. Int corridors. **Pets:** Accepted.

🛜 ⊠ 🛏 💻

▼ **Tulip Inn** 🅜

(705) 789-4001. **$60-$130, 3 day notice.** 211 Arrowhead Park Rd P1H 2J4. Hwy 11 exit 226 (Muskoka Rd 3), follow signs for Arrowhead Park. Ext corridors. **Pets:** Accepted. 🛜 🛏 💻

INGERSOLL

▼▼ **Comfort Inn & Suites** 🏠

(519) 425-1100. **$90-$150.** 20 Samnah Cres N5C 3J7. Hwy 401 exit 216 (Culloden Rd). Int corridors. **Pets:** Accepted. 🛜 🛏 💻 ⇔

JACKSONS POINT

Ⓐ ▼▼▼ **The Briars Resort and Spa** 🏠

(905) 722-3271. **$159-$450, 21 day notice.** 55 Hedge Rd, RR 1 L0E 1L0. Hwy 48, through Sutton to Jacksons Point, 0.6 mi (1 km) e. Ext/int corridors. **Pets:** Accepted. SAVE 🛜 ⊠ 🛏 💻 ⅃⅃ ⇔ ⊠

KAPUSKASING

Comfort Inn H

(705) 335-8583. **$99-$135.** 172 Government Rd E P5N 2W9. Hwy 11; corner of Brunelle Rd. Int corridors. **Pets:** Accepted. ECO 🛜 🖨 💻

Super 8 H

(705) 335-8887. **$108-$126.** 430 Government Rd P5N 2X7. Hwy 11. Int corridors. **Pets:** Accepted. SAVE 🛜 ✖ 🖨 💻 🏊 ✖

KENORA

Best Western Lakeside Inn & Conference Centre H ✿

(807) 468-5521. **$124-$164.** 470 1st Ave S P9N 1W5. Just s on 4th Ave S from jct Hwy 17. Int corridors. **Pets:** Other species. $100 deposit/room. Designated rooms, service with restrictions, supervision. ECO SAVE 🛜 ✖ 🖨 💻 🍴 🏊

Comfort Inn M

(807) 468-8845. **$97-$125.** 1230 Hwy 17 E P9N 1L9. 0.9 mi (1.5 km) e of town. Int corridors. **Pets:** Other species. $9 daily fee/room. Designated rooms, service with restrictions, supervision. 🛜 🖨 💻

Kenora Travelodge H

(807) 468-3155. **$81-$134.** 800 Hwy 17 E P9N 1L9. 0.6 mi (1 km) e of town. Int corridors. **Pets:** $15 daily fee/room. Designated rooms, service with restrictions, supervision. ECO SAVE 🛜 🖨 💻 🍴 🏊 ✖

KILLALOE

Annie's Inn Bed & Breakfast BB

(613) 757-0950. **$75-$200 (no credit cards), 7 day notice.** 67 Roche St K0J 2A0. Hwy 60 exit Maple St, 1 blk to Roche St, then w; driveway entrance is at the end of the street. Int corridors. **Pets:** Accepted. ✖ 🖨 🔈

KINCARDINE

Best Western Plus Governor's Inn H

(519) 396-8242. **$165-$200.** 791 Durham St N2Z 1M4. Jct Hwy 21. Int corridors. **Pets:** Accepted. SAVE 🛜 ✖ 🖨 💻 ✖

Holiday Inn Express and Suites-Kincardine H

(519) 395-3545. **Call for rates.** 2 Millenium Way N2Z 0B5. Jct Hwy 21. Int corridors. **Pets:** Accepted. 🛜 ✖ 🔈M 🖨 💻 🏊

KINGSTON

Best Western Plus Fireside Inn H ✿

(613) 549-2211. **$167-$178.** 1217 Princess St K7M 3E1. Hwy 401 exit 615 (Sir John A MacDonald Blvd), 2.5 mi (4 km) sw. Int corridors. **Pets:** Medium, dogs only. $10 daily fee/pet. Designated rooms, service with restrictions, supervision. SAVE 🛜 ✖ 🖨 💻 🍴 🏊

Comfort Inn Midtown H

(613) 549-5550. **$80-$150.** 1454 Princess St K7M 3E5. Hwy 401 exit 613 (Sydenham Rd), 2.5 mi (4 km) se. Int corridors. **Pets:** Accepted. ECO 🛜 🖨 💻

Confederation Place Hotel H

(613) 549-6300. **$89-$209.** 237 Ontario St K7L 2Z4. Center of downtown. Int corridors. **Pets:** Accepted. 🛜 🖨 💻 🏊

Days Inn Conference Centre Kingston H

(613) 546-3661. **$98-$152.** 33 Benson St K7K 5W2. Hwy 401 exit 617 (Division St), south side. Int corridors. **Pets:** Accepted. ECO SAVE 🛜 ✖ 🖨 💻 🍴 🏊

The Executive Inn & Suites M

(613) 549-1620. **$99-$149, 3 day notice.** 794 Hwy 2 E K7L 4V1. Hwy 401 exit 623, 5 mi (8 km) s, then 1.3 mi (2 km) e. Ext corridors. **Pets:** Accepted. SAVE 🛜 ✖ 🖨 💻 🏊

Holiday Inn Kingston-Waterfront H ✿

(613) 549-8400. **$129-$249.** 2 Princess St K7L 1A2. Corner of Ontario St; center of downtown. Int corridors. **Pets:** Other species. $20 daily fee/pet. Designated rooms, service with restrictions, supervision. ECO SAVE 🛜 ✖ 🔈M 🖨 💻 🍴 🏊 ✖

Motel 6 - Kingston #5712 H

(613) 507-6666. **$69-$119.** 1542 Robinson Ct K7L 4V2. Hwy 401 exit 611, just s. Int corridors. **Pets:** Other species. Service with restrictions, supervision. ECO 🛜 ✖ 🔈M 🖨

Peachtree Inn H ✿

(613) 546-4411. **$79-$159.** 1187 Princess St K7M 3E1. Hwy 401 exit 615 (Sir John A MacDonald Blvd), 2.5 mi (4 km) sw. Int corridors. **Pets:** Large, other species. $20 one-time fee/room. SAVE 🛜 🖨 💻

Residence Inn by Marriott Kingston Water's Edge H ✿

(613) 544-4888. **$159-$239.** 7 Earl St K7L 0A4. Hwy 401 exit 617 (Division St) to Princess St, right on King St, then left, 2 blks w of city hall. Int corridors. **Pets:** Medium. $100 one-time fee/room. 🛜 ✖ 🔈M 🖨 💻 🍴 🏊 ✖

KIRKLAND LAKE

Comfort Inn H

(705) 567-4909. **$145-$210.** 455 Government Rd W P0K 1A0. On Rt 66. Int corridors. **Pets:** Accepted. ECO 🛜 🖨 💻

KITCHENER

Delta Kitchener-Waterloo H ✿

(519) 744-4141. **$119-$189.** 105 King St E N2G 2K8. Corner of King and Benton sts; downtown. Int corridors. **Pets:** Small, other species. $35 one-time fee/room. Service with restrictions, supervision. ECO 🛜 ✖ 🖨 💻 🍴 🏊 ✖

Radisson Hotel Kitchener-Waterloo H

(519) 894-9500. **$129-$189.** 2960 King St E N2A 1A9. Hwy 401 exit 278, 3.8 mi (6 km) w on Hwy 8 exit Weber St. Int corridors. **Pets:** Accepted. ECO SAVE 🛜 🖨 💻 🍴 🏊

The Walper Hotel H ✿

(519) 745-4321. **$109-$119.** 20 Queen St S N2G 1V6. Corner of King and Queen sts; downtown. Int corridors. **Pets:** $100 deposit/room, $35 one-time fee/room. Service with restrictions. SAVE 🛜 ✖ 🖨 💻 🍴

LEAMINGTON

Comfort Inn H ✿

(519) 326-9071. **$100-$135.** 279 Erie St S N8H 3C4. 0.6 mi (1 km) s of jct Talbot and Erie sts; on direct route to Point Pelee National Park. Int corridors. **Pets:** Small. $10 daily fee/room. Designated rooms, service with restrictions, supervision. ECO 🛜 🖨 💻

Howard Johnson Inn Leamington H

(519) 325-0260. **$94-$152, 3 day notice.** 201 Erie St N N8H 3A5. 0.6 mi (1 km) n of Talbot St. Int corridors. **Pets:** Accepted. ECO 🛜 🖨 💻 🏊 ✖

LONDON

Airport Inn & Suites H

(519) 457-1200. **$96-$103, 7 day notice.** 2230 Dundas St E N5V 1R5. Hwy 401 exit Veteran's Memorial Pkwy, 4.8 mi (7.7 km) n; corner of Airport Rd and Dundas St E. Int corridors. **Pets:** Other species. $15 daily fee/pet. Service with restrictions. 🛜 🖨 💻

Best Western Plus Lamplighter Inn & Conference Centre H ✿

(519) 681-7151. **$119-$169.** 591 Wellington Rd S N6C 4R3. Hwy 401 exit 186 (Wellington Rd), 2.3 mi (3.7 km) n. Int corridors. **Pets:** Medium. $10 daily fee/pet. Designated rooms, service with restrictions, supervision. ECO SAVE 🛜 ✖ 🖨 💻 🍴 🏊 ✖

CAA ▼▼▼ **Comfort Inn** H
(519) 685-9300. **$86-$97.** 1156 Wellington Rd N6E 1M3. Hwy 401 exit 186B (Wellington Rd), just n. Int corridors. **Pets:** Accepted.
ECO SAVE 🛜 🛢 🖵

CAA ▼▼▼ **Days Inn London** H
(519) 681-1240. **$71-$128.** 1100 Wellington Rd S N6E 1M2. Hwy 401 exit 186B (Wellington Rd), 0.9 mi (1.5 km) n. Int corridors. **Pets:** Large. Designated rooms, service with restrictions, supervision.
ECO SAVE 🛜 🛢 🖵 🍽 ≋

CAA ▼▼▼▼ **Delta London Armouries** H
(519) 679-6111. **$119-$199.** 325 Dundas St N6B 1T9. Between Wellington and Waterloo sts. Int corridors. **Pets:** Accepted.
ECO SAVE 🛜 ✕ 🛢 🖵 🍽 ≋ ✕

CAA ▼▼▼ **Hilton London Ontario** H
(519) 439-1661. **Call for rates.** 300 King St N6B 1S2. Jct King St and Wellington Rd. Int corridors. **Pets:** Accepted.
ECO SAVE 🛜 ᴹ 🛢 🖵 🍽 ≋ ✕

CAA ▼▼▼▼ **Holiday Inn Hotel & Suites-London** H
(519) 680-0077. **$99-$144.** 864 Exeter Rd N6E 1L5. Hwy 401 exit 186B (Wellington Rd), just n. Int corridors. **Pets:** Accepted.
SAVE 🛜 🛢 🖵 🍽 ≋

CAA ▼▼▼▼ **Homewood Suites by Hilton London** H
(519) 686-7700. **$118-$174.** 45 Bessemer Rd N6E 0A2. Hwy 401 exit 186B (Wellington Rd), just n. Int corridors. **Pets:** Accepted.
SAVE 🛜 ᴹ 🛢 🖵

CAA ▼▼▼▼ **London Hotel and Suites** H
(519) 668-7900. **$99-$169.** 855 Wellington Rd S N6E 3N5. Jct Wellington and Southdale rds. Int corridors. **Pets:** Accepted.
ECO SAVE 🛜 🛢 🖵 🍽 ≋

▼▼ **Motel 6 London #5703** H
(519) 680-0900. **Call for rates.** 810 Exeter Rd N6E 1L5. Hwy 401 exit 186 (Wellington Rd), just n. Int corridors. **Pets:** Other species. Service with restrictions, supervision. ECO 🛜 ᴹ 🛢 ≋

CAA ▼▼▼▼ **Quality Suites** H ☷
(519) 680-1024. **$85-$125.** 1120 Dearness Dr N6E 1N9. Hwy 401 exit 186B (Wellington Rd), 1 mi (1.6 km) n. Int corridors. **Pets:** Service with restrictions, supervision. ECO SAVE 🛜 🛢 🖵

▼▼▼▼ **Residence Inn by Marriott London** H
(519) 433-7222. **$159-$259.** 383 Colborne St N6B 3P5. Jct King St. Int corridors. **Pets:** Accepted. ECO 🛜 ✕ 🛢 🖵

CAA ▼▼▼▼ **StationPark All Suite Hotel** H
(519) 642-4444. **$129-$204.** 242 Pall Mall St N6A 5P6. Hwy 401 exit 186B (Wellington Rd), 5.6 mi (9 km) n. Int corridors. **Pets:** Accepted.
SAVE 🛜 ✕ 🛢 🖵 🍽 ✕

CAA ▼▼▼▼ **Staybridge Suites** H
(519) 649-4500. **Call for rates.** 824 Exeter Rd N6E 1L5. Hwy 401 exit 186B (Wellington Rd), just n. Int corridors. **Pets:** $40 one-time fee/room. Service with restrictions, supervision.
ECO SAVE 🛜 ᴹ 🛢 🖵 ≋

MARATHON

CAA ▼▼▼ **Peninsula Inn** M
(807) 229-0651. **$91-$110, 6 day notice.** Hwy 17 P0T 2E0. 1.5 mi (2.4 km) w of jct Hwy 626. Ext corridors. **Pets:** Small. $10 daily fee/pet. Designated rooms, service with restrictions, supervision. SAVE 🛢 🍽

▼▼ **Travelodge Marathon** H
(807) 229-1213. **$87-$98.** Hwy 17 P0T 2E0. On Hwy 17, jct Peninsula Rd. Int corridors. **Pets:** Accepted. 🛜 🛢 🖵 🍽

MASSEY

▼ **Mohawk Motel Inc** M
(705) 865-2722. **$82-$155.** 335 Sable St P0P 1P0. Center. Ext/int corridors. **Pets:** Large, dogs only. $10 daily fee/pet. Designated rooms, service with restrictions, supervision. 🛜 ✕ 🛢 🖵

MIDLAND

▼▼ **Comfort Inn** H ☷
(705) 526-2090. **Call for rates.** 980 King St L4R 4K3. Jct Hwy 12 and King St. Int corridors. **Pets:** Medium. $10 one-time fee/room. Designated rooms, service with restrictions, supervision. ECO 🛜 🛢 🖵

CAA ▼▼▼ **Super 8 Midland** H ☷
(705) 526-8288. **$88-$154.** 1144 Hugel Ave L4R 0B1. Jct Hwy 93 N. Int corridors. **Pets:** Other species. $9 daily fee/room. Designated rooms, service with restrictions, crate. ECO SAVE 🛜 ✕ 🛢 🖵 ≋

MILTON

CAA ▼▼▼▼ **Best Western Plus Milton** H
(905) 875-3818. **$120-$180.** 161 Chisholm Dr L9T 4A6. Jct Hwy 401 and 25 S. Int corridors. **Pets:** $50 one-time fee/room. Designated rooms, service with restrictions, crate. SAVE 🛜 🛢 🖵 🍽 ≋

MINDEMOYA

▼ **Mindemoya Motel** M
(705) 377-4779. **$89-$139, 3 day notice.** 6375 Hwy 542 P0P 1S0. In Mindemoya; 0.6 mi (1 km) w of jct Hwy 551 and 542. Ext corridors. **Pets:** Accepted. 🛜 🛢 🖵

MISSISSAUGA

▼▼ **Comfort Inn Airport West** H
(905) 624-6900. **$80-$169.** 1500 Matheson Blvd L4W 3Z4. Hwy 401 exit Dixie Rd, then s. Int corridors. **Pets:** Accepted. ECO 🛜 🛢 🖵 🍽

CAA ▼▼ **Comfort Inn Toronto Airport** H
(905) 677-7331. **$89-$129.** 6355 Airport Rd L4V 1E4. 1.3 mi (2 km) s of Derry Rd. Int corridors. **Pets:** Other species. $10 daily fee/pet. Service with restrictions, crate. SAVE 🛜 🛢 🖵 🍽

CAA ▼▼▼▼ **Delta Meadowvale Resort and Conference Centre** H
(905) 821-1981. **$99-$229.** 6750 Mississauga Rd L5N 2L3. Hwy 401 W exit 336 (Mississauga Rd), just s. Int corridors. **Pets:** Accepted.
ECO SAVE 🛜 ✕ ᴹ 🛢 🖵 🍽 ≋ ✕

CAA ▼▼▼▼ **Delta Toronto Airport West** H
(905) 624-1144. **$99-$219.** 5444 Dixie Rd L4W 2L2. 0.6 mi (1 km) s of jct Hwy 401 and Dixie Rd. Int corridors. **Pets:** Medium. $35 one-time fee/room. Service with restrictions, crate.
ECO SAVE 🛜 ✕ 🛢 🖵 🍽 ≋ ✕

CAA ▼▼▼ **Four Points by Sheraton Mississauga Meadowvale** H
(905) 858-2424. **$99-$220.** 2501 Argentia Rd L5N 4G8. Hwy 401 exit 336 (Mississauga Rd), just s on Erin Mills Pkwy, then 1 mi (1.6 km) w. Int corridors. **Pets:** Accepted.
ECO SAVE 🛜 ✕ ᴹ 🛢 🖵 🍽 ≋

▼▼▼ **Holiday Inn Express Hotel & Suites, Mississauga** H
(905) 795-1011. **$115-$139, 3 day notice.** 40 Admiral Blvd L5T 2W1. Hwy 401 exit Hwy 10 (Hurontario St), 0.9 mi (1.5 km) n; just s of Derry Rd. Int corridors. **Pets:** Accepted. 🛜 ✕ 🛢 🖵 ≋

CAA ▼▼▼▼ **Holiday Inn Mississauga Toronto West** H
(905) 890-5700. **$99-$199.** 100 Britannia Rd E L4Z 2G1. Hwy 401 exit Hwy 10 S (Hurontario St). Int corridors. **Pets:** Accepted.
ECO SAVE 🛜 🛢 🖵 🍽 ≋

Holiday Inn Toronto-Mississauga 🏨
(905) 855-2000. **$89-$169.** 2125 N Sheridan Way L5K 1A3. QEW exit Erin Mills Pkwy. Int corridors. **Pets:** Accepted.

Motel 6 Mississauga #1910 🏨
(905) 814-1664. **$69-$79.** 2935 Argentia Rd L5N 8G6. Hwy 401 exit 333 (Winston Churchill Blvd), just s. Int corridors. **Pets:** Other species. Service with restrictions, supervision.

Novotel Toronto Mississauga Centre 🏨
(905) 896-1000. **$249.** 3670 Hurontario St L5B 1P3. Hwy 403 exit 344, 0.8 mi s (1.2 km) on Hwy 10 (Hurontario St); at Burnhamthorpe Rd. Int corridors. **Pets:** Accepted.

Residence Inn by Marriott Mississauga Airport Corporate Centre West 🏨
(905) 602-7777. **$113-$180.** 5070 Creekbank Rd L4W 5R2. Hwy 401 W exit Dixie Rd S, 0.9 mi (1.5 km) to Eglinton Ave, then 0.6 mi (1 km). Int corridors. **Pets:** Accepted.

Residence Inn Toronto-Mississauga/Meadowvale 🏨
(905) 567-2577. **$107-$180.** 7005 Century Ave L5N 7K2. Hwy 401 exit Erin Mills Pkwy/Mississauga Rd, s to Argentia Rd. Int corridors. **Pets:** Accepted.

Sheraton Gateway Hotel in Toronto International Airport 🏨 ❀
(905) 672-7000. **$139-$309.** Terminal 3, Toronto AMF L5P 1C4. In Toronto Pearson International Airport. Int corridors. **Pets:** Service with restrictions, supervision.

Staybridge Suites Mississauga 🏨
(905) 564-6892. **$139-$179, 7 day notice.** 6791 Hurontario St L5T 2W1. Hwy 401 W exit Hwy 10 (Hurontario St), 0.9 mi (1.5 km) n; just s of Derry Rd. Int corridors. **Pets:** Small. $75 daily fee/pet. Designated rooms, service with restrictions, supervision.

Studio 6 Mississauga #1908 🅼
(905) 502-8897. **$73-$83.** 60 Britannia Rd E L4Z 2T2. Hwy 401 exit Hwy 10 (Hurontario St). Int corridors. **Pets:** Other species. $10 daily fee/room. Service with restrictions, supervision.

MONETVILLE

Memquisit Lodge 🅲🅰
(705) 898-2355. **$135-$380, 90 day notice.** 506 Memquisit Rd P0M 2K0. 13 mi (20.8 km) ne on west arm of Lake Nipissing, on Hwy 64 and Memquisit Lodge Rd; 23 mi (36.8 km) sw off Hwy 17, on Hwy 64. Ext corridors. **Pets:** Accepted.

MORRISBURG

The McIntosh Country Inn & Conference Centre 🏨
(613) 543-3788. **$89-$199.** 12495 Hwy 2 E K0C 1X0. Hwy 401 exit 750, 1.2 mi (2 km) s on Rt 31, then 0.6 mi (1 km) e. Int corridors. **Pets:** Medium. $10 daily fee/pet. Service with restrictions.

NEWMARKET

Comfort Inn 🏨 ❀
(905) 895-3355. **$115-$132.** 1230 Journey's End Cir L3Y 8Z6. Hwy 404 exit 51 (Davis Dr), just w, then just n on Harry Walker Pkwy. Int corridors. **Pets:** Other species. $5 daily fee/room. Service with restrictions.

NIAGARA FALLS METROPOLITAN AREA

FORT ERIE

Clarion Hotel & Conference Centre 🏨
(905) 871-8333. **$86-$198.** 1485 Garrison Rd L2A 1P8. QEW exit Gilmore Rd. Int corridors. **Pets:** Accepted.

LINCOLN

Best Western Beacon Harbourside Inn & Suites Conf. Centre 🏨 ❀
(905) 562-4155. **$90-$200.** 2793 Beacon Blvd L0R 1S0. QEW exit 55. Int corridors. **Pets:** Dogs only. $20 daily fee/room. Designated rooms, service with restrictions, supervision.

Inn on the Twenty 🅲🅸
(905) 562-5336. **$159-$389, 7 day notice.** 3845 Main St L0R 1S0. QEW exit 57 (Victoria Ave/Reg Rd 24), 1.9 mi (3 km) s, 1.9 mi (3 km) e on Reg Rd 81, then just n. Ext/int corridors. **Pets:** Accepted.

NIAGARA FALLS

Best Western Fallsview 🏨 ❀
(905) 356-0551. **$80-$300, 3 day notice.** 6289 Fallsview Blvd L2G 3V7. Jct Niagara River Pkwy, just n on Murray St. Ext/int corridors. **Pets:** Other species. $25 daily fee/pet. Service with restrictions.

Days Inn Clifton Hill Casino 🏨
(905) 356-2461. **$44-$314.** 5657 Victoria Ave L2G 3L5. Just e on Hwy 20. Ext/int corridors. **Pets:** Accepted.

Falls Manor Resort & Restaurant 🅼 ❀
(905) 358-3211. **$49-$149.** 7104 Lundy's Ln L2G 1W2. On Hwy 20, 2.1 mi (3.4 km) w. Ext corridors. **Pets:** $100 deposit/pet. Designated rooms, service with restrictions, supervision.

Howard Johnson Express Inn 🅼
(905) 358-9777. **$40-$189.** 8100 Lundy's Ln L2H 1H1. QEW exit Hwy 20, 3.1 mi (5 km) w. Ext corridors. **Pets:** Medium, other species. $15 daily fee/pet. Designated rooms, service with restrictions, supervision.

Howard Johnson Hotel by the Falls 🏨
(905) 357-4040. **$54-$261.** 5905 Victoria Ave L2G 3L8. On Hwy 20; 0.4 mi (0.6 km) from the falls. Int corridors. **Pets:** Small. $20 daily fee/pet. Designated rooms, service with restrictions, supervision.

Imperial Hotel & Suites 🏨
(905) 356-2648. **$39-$259.** 5851 Victoria Ave L2G 3L6. On Hwy 20, 0.3 mi (0.5 km) from the falls. Int corridors. **Pets:** Accepted.

Niagara Parkway Court Motel 🅼
(905) 295-3331. **$39-$149.** 3708 Main St (Niagara Pkwy S) L2G 6B1. 1.6 mi (2.5 km) s of the falls. Ext corridors. **Pets:** Accepted.

Peninsula Inn & Resort 🏨
(905) 354-8812. **$59-$339.** 7373 Niagara Square Dr L2E 6S5. QEW exit McLeod Rd, just w. Int corridors. **Pets:** Small. $10 daily fee/pet. Designated rooms, service with restrictions, supervision.

🆎 ▼▼▼ **Super 8 Hotel & Suites Niagara Falls** 🅷
(905) 356-0052. **$53-$234.** 5706 Ferry St L2G 1S7. On Hwy 20, 0.9 mi (1.5 km) from the falls. Int corridors. **Pets:** Small, dogs only. $25 daily fee/room. Designated rooms, supervision.
🆂🅰🆅🅴 📶 📵 💻 🍴 🏊 ⊗

NIAGARA-ON-THE-LAKE

🆎 ▼▼▼▼ **Harbour House Hotel** 🅷 ❀
(905) 468-4683. **$199-$475, 10 day notice.** 85 Melville St L0S 1J0. Jct Ricardo St. Int corridors. **Pets:** Dogs only. $25 daily fee/room. Designated rooms, service with restrictions, supervision. 🆂🅰🆅🅴 📶 ⊗ 💻

🆎 ▼▼▼▼ **The Oban Inn, Spa and Restaurant** 🅷
(905) 468-2165. **$150-$495, 7 day notice.** 160 Front St L0S 1J0. Jct Gate St. Ext/int corridors. **Pets:** Accepted.
🆂🅰🆅🅴 📶 ⊗ 💻 🍴 🏊 ⊗

🆎 ▼▼▼▼ **Pillar and Post Hotel** 🅲🅸
(905) 468-2123. **$159-$409.** 48 John St L0S 1J0. Just n on Hwy 55 (Mississauga St), just e; 13 mi from QEW. Ext/int corridors. **Pets:** Small, dogs only. $35 daily fee/pet. Designated rooms, supervision.
🆂🅰🆅🅴 📶 ⊗ 🅗 💻 🍴 🏊 ⊗

🆎 ▼▼▼▼ **Prince of Wales Hotel & Spa** 🅷 ❀
(905) 468-3246. **$189-$429.** 6 Picton St L0S 1J0. Jct Picton and King sts; 9 mi (14.4 km) e of jct QEW and Hwy 55, via Hwy 55. Ext/int corridors. **Pets:** Small, other species. $35 daily fee/pet. Designated rooms, service with restrictions. 🆂🅰🆅🅴 📶 ⊗ 🅗 💻 🍴 🏊 ⊗

▼▼▼ ▼▼▼ **Shaw Club Hotel and Spa** 🅷 ❀
(905) 468-5711. **$99-$510, 10 day notice.** 92 Picton St L0S 1J0. Jct Wellington St. Int corridors. **Pets:** Dogs only. $25 daily fee/room. Designated rooms, service with restrictions, supervision.
📶 ⊗ 🅗 💻 🍴 ⊗

ST. CATHARINES

🆎 ▼▼▼ **Best Western St. Catharines Hotel & Conference Centre** 🅷
(905) 934-8000. **$110-$250, 30 day notice.** 2 N Service Rd L2N 4G9. QEW exit 46 (Lake St), just e. Int corridors. **Pets:** Accepted.
🅴🅲🅾 🆂🅰🆅🅴 📶 ⊗ 🅗 💻 🍴 🏊 ⊗

🆎 ▼▼▼ **Comfort Inn** 🅷 ❀
(905) 687-8890. **$95-$140.** 2 Dunlop Dr L2R 1A2. QEW exit 46 (Lake St); between Lake and Geneva sts. Int corridors. **Pets:** Designated rooms, service with restrictions, supervision.
🅴🅲🅾 🆂🅰🆅🅴 📶 🦽 🅗 💻

🆎 ▼▼▼ **Days Inn St. Catharines Niagara** 🅷
(905) 934-5400. **$98-$126.** 89 Meadowvale Dr L2N 3Z8. QEW exit 46 (Lake St). Int corridors. **Pets:** Other species. $15 daily fee/pet. Designated rooms, service with restrictions, crate.
🆂🅰🆅🅴 📶 🅗 💻 🍴 🏊 ⊗

🆎 ▼▼▼ **Holiday Inn & Suites Parkway Conference Center** 🅷 ❀
(905) 688-2324. **Call for rates.** 327 Ontario St L2R 5L3. QEW exit 47 (Ontario St), 0.5 mi (0.8 km) s. Int corridors. **Pets:** Medium. $15 daily fee/room. Service with restrictions, supervision.
🆂🅰🆅🅴 📶 ⊗ 🦽 🅗 💻 🍴 🏊 ⊗

THOROLD

🆎 ▼▼▼▼ **Four Points by Sheraton St. Catharines Niagara Suites** 🅷
(905) 984-8484. **$110-$220.** 3530 Schmon Pkwy L2V 4Y6. Hwy 406 exit St. David's Rd W; just s of Brock University. Int corridors. **Pets:** $10 daily fee/room. Designated rooms, service with restrictions, supervision.
🆂🅰🆅🅴 📶 ⊗ 🅗 💻 🍴 🏊 ⊗

WELLAND

▼▼ ▼▼ **Comfort Inn-Niagara Falls/Welland** 🅷
(905) 732-4811. **Call for rates.** 870 Niagara St L3C 1M3. 1.5 mi (2.5 km) n. Int corridors. **Pets:** Accepted. 📶 🅗 💻

END METROPOLITAN AREA

NORTH BAY

🆎 ▼▼▼▼ **Best Western North Bay Hotel and Conference Centre** 🅷
(705) 474-5800. **$109-$159.** 700 Lakeshore Dr P1A 2G4. Hwy 11 exit 338, 2.5 mi (4 km) w. Int corridors. **Pets:** Accepted.
🅴🅲🅾 🆂🅰🆅🅴 📶 🅗 💻 🍴 🏊 ⊗

🆎 ▼▼▼▼ **Clarion Resort Pinewood Park** 🅷
(705) 472-0810. **$79-$148.** 201 Pinewood Park Dr P1B 8Z4. Hwy 11 exit 338, just w on Lakeshore Dr, then 0.4 mi (0.7 km) s. Int corridors.
Pets: Accepted. 🆂🅰🆅🅴 📶 ⊗ 🅗 💻 🍴 🏊 ⊗

🆎 ▼▼▼ **Comfort Inn-Airport** 🅷
(705) 476-5400. **$105-$165.** 1200 O'Brien St P1B 9B3. On Hwy 11/17; jct O'Brien St. Int corridors. **Pets:** Medium. Service with restrictions, supervision. 🆂🅰🆅🅴 🅗 💻

🆎 ▼▼▼ **Holiday Inn Express Hotel & Suites** 🅷
(705) 476-7700. **$125-$175.** 1325 Seymour St P1B 9V6. Jct Hwy 11/17. Int corridors. **Pets:** Designated rooms, no service, supervision.
🅴🅲🅾 🆂🅰🆅🅴 📶 ⊗ 🅗 💻 🏊

▼▼ ▼▼ **Super 8 North Bay** 🅷
(705) 495-4551. **$72-$122.** 570 Lakeshore Dr P1A 2E6. Hwy 11 exit 338, 2.8 mi (4.5 km) w. Int corridors. **Pets:** Service with restrictions, supervision. 📶 🅗 💻

🆎 ▼▼ **Travelodge Airport North Bay** 🅷
(705) 495-1133. **$95-$171.** 1525 Seymour St P1B 8G4. Jct Hwy 11/17. Int corridors. **Pets:** Accepted. 🅴🅲🅾 🆂🅰🆅🅴 📶 🅗 💻 🏊

🆎 ▼▼ **Travelodge Lakeshore** 🅷
(705) 472-7171. **$81-$126.** 718 Lakeshore Dr P1A 2G4. Hwy 11 exit 338, 2.5 mi (4 km) w. Int corridors. **Pets:** Accepted.
🅴🅲🅾 🆂🅰🆅🅴 📶 🅗 💻

OAKVILLE

🆎 ▼▼▼▼ **Holiday Inn Oakville Centre** 🅷
(905) 842-5000. **$99-$140.** 590 Argus Rd L6J 3J3. QEW exit 118 (Trafalgar Rd), just s. Int corridors. **Pets:** Other species. $25 one-time fee/room. Service with restrictions, supervision.
🅴🅲🅾 🆂🅰🆅🅴 📶 🦽 🅗 💻 🍴 🏊

🆎 ▼▼▼▼ **Staybridge Suites Oakville Burlington** 🅷
(905) 847-2600. **$119-$184.** 2511 Wyecroft Rd L6L 6P8. QEW exit 111 (Bronte Rd/Hwy 25), 0.3 mi (0.5 km) s, then just e. Int corridors.
Pets: Accepted. 🆂🅰🆅🅴 📶 🦽 🅗 💻 🏊

ORILLIA

🆎 ▼▼▼▼ **Best Western Plus Mariposa Inn & Conference Centre** 🅷
(705) 325-9511. **$120-$180.** 400 Memorial Ave L3V 6J3. Jct Hwy 12 and Memorial Ave, just s. Int corridors. **Pets:** Accepted.
🅴🅲🅾 🆂🅰🆅🅴 📶 🅗 💻 🍴 🏊 ⊗

(AA) ▼▼ Comfort Inn H

(705) 327-7744. **$100-$136.** 75 Progress Dr L3V 6H1. Hwy 11 N exit Hwy 12, s on Memorial Ave; corner of Progress Dr and Memorial Ave. Int corridors. **Pets:** Small. $10 daily fee/pet. Designated rooms, service with restrictions, supervision. ECO SAVE 🛜 🛢 🖥

(AA) ▼▼ Highwayman Inn & Conference Centre H

(705) 326-7343. **$89-$129.** 201 Woodside Dr L3V 6T4. Hwy 11 exit Hwy 12 (Coldwater Rd), just e, then just s. Int corridors. **Pets:** Dogs only. $40 one-time fee/pet. Service with restrictions, supervision.
SAVE 🛜 🛢 🖥 🍴 ≥ 🏊

OSHAWA

▼▼ Comfort Inn H

(905) 434-5000. **$89-$149.** 605 Bloor St W L1J 5Y6. Hwy 401 exit 415 (Stevenson Rd), s to Bloor St, then 0.5 mi (0.8 km) w. Int corridors. **Pets:** Accepted. ECO 🛢 🖥

OTTAWA METROPOLITAN AREA

KANATA

(AA) ▼▼▼▼ Brookstreet Hotel H

(613) 271-1800. **$149-$499.** 525 Legget Dr K2K 2W2. Hwy 417 exit 138 (March Rd), 2.3 mi (3.7 km) n, just e on Solandt Dr to Legget Dr, then just n. Int corridors. **Pets:** Large. $250 deposit/pet, $25 daily fee/pet. Designated rooms, service with restrictions, supervision.
ECO SAVE 🛜 🖥 🍴 ≥ 🏊

(AA) ▼▼ Comfort Inn Ottawa West Kanata H ❀

(613) 592-2200. **$99-$159.** 222 Hearst Way K2L 3A2. Hwy 417 exit 138 (Eagleson Rd), 0.4 mi (0.6 km) s, just w on Katimavik Rd, then 0.5 mi (0.8 km) n. Int corridors. **Pets:** Other species. Designated rooms, service with restrictions, supervision. ECO SAVE 🛜 🛢 🖥

OTTAWA

(AA) ▼▼▼ Albert House Inn BB

(613) 236-4479. **$125-$180, 3 day notice.** 478 Albert St K1R 5B5. Between Bay St and Bronson Ave; at west end. Int corridors. **Pets:** Accepted. SAVE 🛜 ✕

(AA) ▼▼▼ ARC The.Hotel H

(613) 238-2888. **$139-$399.** 140 Slater St K1P 5H6. Between Metcalfe and O'Connor sts. Int corridors. **Pets:** Accepted.
ECO SAVE 🛜 🖥 🍴

(AA) ▼▼▼ Best Western Barons Plus Hotel & Conference Centre H

(613) 828-2741. **$130-$160, 30 day notice.** 3700 Richmond Rd K2H 5B8. Hwy 417 exit 130, 1.8 mi (2.9 km) s. Int corridors. **Pets:** Other species. $20 daily fee/room. Designated rooms, service with restrictions, supervision. SAVE 🛜 ✕ 🛢 🖥 🍴 ≥ 🏊

▼▼ Cartier Place Suite Hotel H ❀

(613) 236-5000. **$159-$350.** 180 Cooper St K2P 2L5. Between Elgin and Cartier sts. Int corridors. **Pets:** Other species. $35 daily fee/room.
🛜 🛢 🖥 🍴 ≥ 🏊

(AA) ▼▼▼ Comfort Inn H

(613) 744-2900. **$100-$145.** 1252 Michael St K1J 7T1. Hwy 417 exit 115 (St. Laurent Blvd), just ne. Int corridors. **Pets:** Medium. Service with restrictions, supervision. ECO SAVE 🛜 🛢 🖥

(AA) ▼▼ Days Inn-Downtown Ottawa H

(613) 789-5555. **$89-$188.** 319 Rideau St K1N 5Y4. Between Nelson St and King Edward Ave. Ext/int corridors. **Pets:** Designated rooms, service with restrictions, supervision. ECO SAVE 🛜 🛢 🖥 🍴

▼▼ The Days Inn Ottawa West H

(613) 726-1717. **$108-$117.** 350 Moodie Dr K2H 8G3. Hwy 417 exit 134, 0.9 mi (1.5 km) s. Int corridors. **Pets:** Accepted.
ECO 🛜 ✕ 🛢 🖥 🍴

(AA) ▼▼▼ Quality Hotel & Conference Centre H ❀

(905) 576-5101. **$115-$135.** 1011 Bloor St E L1H 7K6. Hwy 401 exit 419 (Harmony Rd). Int corridors. **Pets:** $15 daily fee/pet. Designated rooms, service with restrictions, crate.
SAVE 🛜 🛢 🖥 🍴 ≥ 🏊

(AA) ▼▼▼ Travelodge Oshawa H

(905) 436-9500. **$92-$113.** 940 Champlain Ave L1J 7A6. Hwy 401 exit 412 (Thickson Rd N). Int corridors. **Pets:** $25 one-time fee/room. Designated rooms, service with restrictions, supervision.
ECO SAVE 🛜 🛢 🖥 ≥ 🏊

(AA) ▼▼▼ Delta Ottawa City Centre H

(613) 237-3600. **$129-$269.** 101 Lyon St K1R 5T9. Entrance at corner of Albert St. Int corridors. **Pets:** Accepted.
ECO SAVE 🛜 🛢 🖥 🍴 ≥ 🏊

▼▼▼ Extended Stay Deluxe Ottawa Downtown H ❀

(613) 236-7500. **$121-$134.** 141 Cooper St K2P 0E8. Between Elgin and Cartier sts. Int corridors. **Pets:** Other species. $25 daily fee/pet. Service with restrictions. 🛜 🛢 🖥 🍴 🏊

(AA) ▼▼▼ Fairmont Château Laurier H

(613) 241-1414. **$179-$339.** 1 Rideau St K1N 8S7. Just e of Parliament buildings. Int corridors. **Pets:** Very small. $25 daily fee/room. Service with restrictions, supervision. ECO SAVE 🛜 &M 🛢 🖥 🍴 ≥ 🏊

▼▼▼ Holiday Inn & Suites Ottawa Downtown H ❀

(613) 238-1331. **$130-$175.** 111 Cooper St K2P 2E3. Corner of Cartier St. Int corridors. **Pets:** Other species. Designated rooms, service with restrictions, crate. ECO 🛜 ✕ 🛢 🖥 🍴

▼▼▼ Holiday Inn Express & Suites Ottawa West - Nepean H

(613) 690-0100. **Call for rates.** 45 Robertson Rd K2H 5Y9. Hwy 417 exit 134, 0.9 mi (1.5 km) s on Moodie Ave, then just e. Int corridors. **Pets:** Accepted. 🛜 ✕ &M 🛢 🖥 ≥

▼▼▼ Hotel Indigo Ottawa H ❀

(613) 231-6555. **$139-$269.** 123 Metcalfe St K1P 5L9. Corner of Laurier Ave W. Int corridors. **Pets:** Other species. $75 one-time fee/pet. Service with restrictions, supervision. ECO 🛜 ✕ 🛢 🖥 🍴 ≥ 🏊

(AA) ▼▼▼ Les Suites Hotel Ottawa H ❀

(613) 232-2000. **$149-$259.** 130 Besserer St K1N 9M9. Between Nicholas and Waller sts. Int corridors. **Pets:** $35 one-time fee/pet. Service with restrictions, crate. ECO SAVE 🛜 ✕ &M 🛢 🖥 🍴 ≥ 🏊

▼▼▼ Lord Elgin Hotel H

(613) 235-3333. **$149-$329.** 100 Elgin St K1P 5K8. Between Laurier Ave and Slater St. Int corridors. **Pets:** Accepted.
ECO 🛜 ✕ 🛢 🖥 🍴 ≥ 🏊

(AA) ▼▼▼▼ Marriott Ottawa Hotel H

(613) 238-1122. **$119-$299.** 100 Kent St K1P 5R7. Corner of Queen St. Int corridors. **Pets:** Service with restrictions, crate.
ECO SAVE 🛜 ✕ 🛢 🖥 🍴 ≥ 🏊

(AA) ▼▼▼▼ Monterey Inn Resort & Conference Centre H ❀

(613) 288-3500. **$109-$139.** 2259 Prince of Wales Dr K2E 6Z8. 0.5 mi (0.8 km) s of Hunt Club Rd. Ext corridors. **Pets:** Medium. Designated rooms, service with restrictions, supervision.
ECO SAVE 🛢 🖥 🍴 ≥ 🏊

(CAA) ▼▼▼▼ **National Hotel & Suites Ottawa** H
(613) 238-6000. **$290-$350.** 361 Queen St K1R 7S9. Corner of Lyon St. Int corridors. **Pets:** Accepted.
ECO SAVE 📶 ✕ 🛏 💻 🍴 ≋ 🐾

(CAA) ▼▼▼▼ **Novotel Ottawa Hotel** H ❁
(613) 230-3033. **$129-$299.** 33 Nicholas St K1N 9M7. Corner of Daly Ave. Int corridors. **Pets:** Small. Service with restrictions, supervision.
ECO SAVE 📶 🛏 💻 🍴 ≋ 🐾

(CAA) ▼▼▼ **Quality Hotel Downtown Ottawa** H ❁
(613) 789-7511. **$89-$149.** 290 Rideau St K1N 5Y3. Corner of King Edward Ave. Int corridors. **Pets:** Designated rooms, service with restrictions, supervision. ECO SAVE 📶 🛏 💻 🍴

(CAA) ▼▼▼▼ **Radisson Hotel Ottawa Parliament Hill** H
(613) 236-1133. **$129-$179.** 402 Queen St K1R 5A7. Corner of Bay and Queen sts. Int corridors. **Pets:** Accepted. ECO SAVE 📶 🛏 💻 🍴

▼▼▼▼ **Residence Inn Ottawa** H
(613) 231-2020. **$129-$329.** 161 Laurier Ave W K1P 5J2. Corner of Elgin St. Int corridors. **Pets:** Medium. $85 one-time fee/pet. Service with restrictions, supervision. ECO 📶 ✕ 🛏 💻 ≋ 🐾

(CAA) ▼▼▼ **Rideau Heights Inn** M
(613) 226-4152. **$99-$129.** 72 Rideau Heights Dr K2E 7A6. Hwy 16 (Prince of Wales Dr), 0.3 mi (0.5 km) n of Hunt Club Rd. Ext corridors. **Pets:** Small. $10 daily fee/room. Designated rooms, supervision.
SAVE ✕ 🛏 💻

(CAA) ▼▼▼▼ **Sheraton Ottawa Hotel** H ❁
(613) 238-1500. **$139-$450.** 150 Albert St K1P 5G2. Corner of O'Connor St. Int corridors. **Pets:** Medium. Service with restrictions.
ECO SAVE 📶 ✕ 🛏 💻 🍴 ≋

(CAA) ▼▼▼▼ **Southway Hotel & Conference Centre** H ❁
(613) 737-0811. **$145-$160.** 2431 Bank St K1V 8R9. On Hwy 31; jct Hunt Club Rd. Int corridors. **Pets:** Large. $30 daily fee/pet. Designated rooms, service with restrictions, supervision.
SAVE 📶 ✕ 🛏 💻 🍴 ≋ 🐾

(CAA) ▼▼▼ **Travelodge Ottawa East** H
(613) 745-1133. **$93-$110.** 1486 Innes Rd K1B 3V5. Hwy 417 exit 112 (Innes Rd), just e. Int corridors. **Pets:** Accepted.
ECO SAVE 📶 🛏 💻 🍴 ≋

(CAA) ▼▼▼ **Travelodge Ottawa Hotel & Conference Centre** H
(613) 722-7600. **$99-$153.** 1376 Carling Ave K1Z 7L5. Hwy 417 exit 124, just s. Int corridors. **Pets:** Accepted.
ECO SAVE 📶 ✕ 🛏 💻 🍴 ≋ 🐾

(CAA) ▼▼ **Webb's Motel** M
(613) 728-1881. **$85-$125.** 1705 Carling Ave K2A 1C8. Hwy 417 exit 126, 0.3 mi (0.5 km) n on Maitland Ave, then 0.3 mi (0.5 km) e. Ext/int corridors. **Pets:** Accepted. SAVE 📶 🛏 💻

▼▼ **WelcomINNS** H
(613) 748-7800. **$110-$130.** 1220 Michael St K1J 7T1. Hwy 417 exit 115 (St. Laurent Blvd), just ne. Int corridors. **Pets:** Small. $20 daily fee/pet. Designated rooms, service with restrictions, supervision.
ECO 📶 ✕ 🛏 💻

(CAA) ▼▼▼▼ **The Westin Ottawa** H ❁
(613) 560-7000. **$199-$599.** 11 Colonel By Dr K1N 9H4. Corner of Rideau St. Int corridors. **Pets:** Service with restrictions, crate.
ECO SAVE 📶 ✕ 🛏 💻 🍴 ≋ 🐾

END METROPOLITAN AREA

OWEN SOUND

▼▼ **Comfort Inn** H ❁
(519) 371-5500. **$80-$200.** 955 9th Ave E N4K 6N4. Jct Hwy 6, 10, 21 and 28. Int corridors. **Pets:** Medium, other species. $10 one-time fee/room. Service with restrictions, supervision. ECO 📶 🛏 💻

(CAA) ▼▼▼ **Days Inn and Conference Centre** H
(519) 376-1551. **$71-$151, 7 day notice.** 950 6th St E N4K 1H1. Jct Hwy 6 and 10. Int corridors. **Pets:** Small. $20 daily fee/room. Designated rooms, service with restrictions, supervision.
ECO SAVE 📶 🛏 💻 🍴 ≋ 🐾

(CAA) ▼▼▼ **Owen Sound Inn** H
(519) 371-3011. **Call for rates.** 485 9th Ave E N4K 3E2. Jct Hwy 6, 10, 26 and 21; follow Hwy 6 and 10, 0.6 mi (1 km) s. Int corridors. **Pets:** Accepted. SAVE 📶 🛏

PARRY SOUND

▼▼ **Comfort Inn** H
(705) 746-6221. **$110-$170.** 120 Bowes St P2A 2L7. Hwy 69 exit 224 (Bowes St), just w. Int corridors. **Pets:** Accepted. ECO 📶 🛏 💻

▼▼ **Microtel Inn & Suites** H
(705) 746-2700. **$89-$125.** 292 Louisa St P2A 0A1. Hwy 69 exit 224 (Bowes St), just w. Int corridors. **Pets:** Accepted. 📶 ✕ 🛏 💻

PEMBROKE

▼ **Colonial Fireside Inn** M
(613) 732-3623. **$59-$120.** 1350 Pembroke St W K8A 7A3. 2.7 mi (4.3 km) n on Forest Lea Rd (CR 42) from jct Hwy 17, just e. Ext corridors. **Pets:** Small. $10 one-time fee/pet. No service, supervision.
📶 🛏 💻 ≋

(CAA) ▼▼▼ **Comfort Inn** H
(613) 735-1057. **$129-$179.** 959 Pembroke St E K8A 3M3. 1 mi (1.6 km) e of town centre. Int corridors. **Pets:** Accepted.
ECO SAVE 📶 🛏 💻

PETAWAWA

(CAA) ▼▼▼ **Petawawa River Inn & Suites** H
(613) 687-4686. **$115-$200.** 3520 Petawawa Blvd K8H 1W9. Hwy 17 exit Paquette Rd, 1.5 mi (2.4 km) e, then just s. Int corridors. **Pets:** Other species. $10 daily fee/pet. Designated rooms, service with restrictions, supervision. ECO SAVE 📶 🛏 💻 🍴

(CAA) ▼▼▼ **Quality Inn & Suites Petawawa** H ❁
(613) 687-2855. **Call for rates.** 3119-B Petawawa Blvd K8H 1X9. Hwy 17 exit Murphy Rd (Hwy 37), 1.8 mi (3 km) ne. Int corridors. **Pets:** Medium. $10 daily fee/pet. Designated rooms, service with restrictions. SAVE 📶 ✕ 📶 🛏 💻 ≋ 🐾

PETERBOROUGH

(CAA) ▼▼▼▼ **Comfort Hotel & Suites** H
(705) 740-7000. **$80-$120.** 1209 Lansdowne St W K9J 7M2. 0.4 mi (0.6 km) w of jct Hwy 28. Int corridors. **Pets:** Accepted.
ECO SAVE 📶 🛏 💻 🍴 ≋

▼▼ **King Bethune House, Guest House & Spa** BB
(705) 743-4101. **$139-$399, 14 day notice.** 270 King St K9J 2S2. From Charlotte and George sts (clock tower), 1 blk s on George St to King St, then just w. Int corridors. **Pets:** Other species. $25 daily fee/pet. Supervision. 📶 ✕ 🛏 💻

▼▼ **Motel 6 - Peterborough** H
(705) 748-0550. **$69-$109.** 133 Landsdowne St E K9J 7P7. 1.6 mi (2.6 km) e of The Parkway. Int corridors. **Pets:** Other species. Service with restrictions, supervision. ECO 📶 🛏

▼▼ **Quality Inn** 🅗 ❀
(705) 748-6801. **$69-$119.** 1074 Lansdowne St W K9J 1Z9. 1.9 mi (3 km) from jct Hwy 115. Int corridors. **Pets:** Service with restrictions.
ECO 🛰 🛏 🖥

🅐 ▼▼▼▼ **Super 8 Peterborough** 🅗 ❀
(705) 876-8898. **$99-$129.** 1257 Lansdowne St W K9J 7M2. 0.3 mi (0.5 km) e from jct Hwy 28. Int corridors. **Pets:** Medium, other species. $25 one-time fee/room. Designated rooms, service with restrictions, crate.
ECO SAVE 🛰 ✖ 🛏 🖥 🏊

PICKERING

🅐 ▼▼▼ **Comfort Inn** 🅗
(905) 831-6200. **$95-$135.** 533 Kingston Rd L1V 3N7. Hwy 401 exit 394N (White's Rd) to Hwy 2, 0.3 mi (0.5 km) w. Int corridors.
Pets: Accepted. ECO SAVE 🛰 🛏 🖥

PLANTAGENET

▼▼ **Motel de Champlain** Ⓜ
(613) 673-5220. **Call for rates.** 5999 Hwy 17 K0B 1L0. Jct CR 9. Ext/int corridors. **Pets:** Accepted. 🛰 ✖ 🛏 🍴

PORT HOPE

▼▼ **Comfort Inn** 🅗
(905) 885-7000. **$89-$129.** 2201 County Rd 28 L1A 3V6. Hwy 401 exit 464 (Hwy 28), just n. Int corridors. **Pets:** Accepted. 🛰 🛏 🖥

PROVIDENCE BAY

🅐 ▼▼ **Aux Huron Sands Motel** Ⓜ
(705) 377-4616. **$80-$160, 3 day notice.** 5216 Hwy 551 P0P 1T0. In Providence Bay; on Hwy 551; center. Ext corridors. **Pets:** Accepted.
SAVE 🛰 🛏 🔁

RENFREW

🅐 ▼▼▼ **Best Western Renfrew Inn & Conference Centre** 🅗
(613) 432-8109. **$109-$129.** 760 Gibbons Rd K7V 3Z4. Hwy 17 exit O'Brien Rd, just s to Wrangler Rd, then just w. Int corridors.
Pets: Accepted. SAVE 🛰 🛏 🖥 🍴 🏊

▼▼ **The Rocky Mountain Lodge** Ⓜ
(613) 432-5801. **Call for rates.** 409 Stewart St N K7V 1Y4. Hwy 17 exit Bruce St, 1.9 mi (3.1 km) s. Ext corridors. **Pets:** Accepted.
🛰 🛏 🖥 🍴

ST. THOMAS

▼▼ **Comfort Inn** 🅗
(519) 633-4082. **$90-$140.** 100 Centennial Ave N5R 5B2. On Hwy 3, 4.1 mi (6.5 km) e. Int corridors. **Pets:** Accepted. 🛰 🛏 🖥

SARNIA

▼▼▼ **Comfort Inn** 🅗
(519) 383-6767. **$110-$175.** 815 Mara St N7V 1X4. Jct Church St. Int corridors. **Pets:** Small. $20 one-time fee/room. Designated rooms, service with restrictions, crate. 🛰 🛏 🖥

▼▼ **Super 8-Sarnia** 🅗
(519) 337-3767. **Call for rates.** 420 Christina St N N7T 5W1. Between Exmouth St and London Rd. Ext/int corridors. **Pets:** Accepted.
🛰 🖑 🛏 🖥 🍴

SAULT STE. MARIE

▼▼ **Adams Motel** Ⓜ
(705) 254-4345. **$69-$99.** 647 Great Northern Rd (Hwy 17) P6B 5A1. Hwy 17, 2.8 mi (4.4 km) n. Ext corridors. **Pets:** Accepted. 🛰 🛏 🖥

🅐 ▼▼▼▼ **Algoma's Water Tower Inn & Suites** 🅗
(705) 949-8111. **$129-$189, 7 day notice.** 360 Great Northern Rd P6B 4Z7. Jct Hwy 17 and Second Line. Int corridors. **Pets:** Accepted.
ECO SAVE 🛰 ✖ 🛏 🖥 🍴 🏊 🐾

▼▼ **Ambassador Motel** Ⓜ
(705) 759-6199. **$59-$99.** 1275 Great Northern Rd P6A 5K7. 4 mi (6.4 km) n on Hwy 17. Ext corridors. **Pets:** Accepted.
🛰 🛏 🖥 🏊 🐾

🅐 ▼▼ **Bel-Air Motel** Ⓜ
(705) 945-7950. **$55-$99.** 398 Pim St P6B 2V1. 1.3 mi (2 km) n on Hwy 17B. Ext corridors. **Pets:** Dogs only. $10 daily fee/pet. Designated rooms, service with restrictions. SAVE 🛰 🛏 🖥

🅐 ▼▼ **Catalina Motel** Ⓜ
(705) 945-9260. **$97-$120.** 259 Great Northern Rd P6B 4Z2. 2 mi (3.2 km) n on Hwy 17B. Ext corridors. **Pets:** Accepted.
SAVE 🛰 ✖ 🛏 🖥

🅐 ▼▼▼ **City Centre Travelodge** 🅗
(705) 759-1400. **$95-$200.** 332 Bay St P6A 1X1. Between Elgin and Bruce sts; downtown; opposite Station Mall. Int corridors. **Pets:** Medium. Designated rooms, service with restrictions, supervision.
ECO SAVE 🛰 🛏 🖥 🍴

🅐 ▼▼▼ **Comfort Inn** 🅗
(705) 759-8000. **$89-$169.** 333 Great Northern Rd P6B 4Z8. 2.3 mi (3.6 km) n on Hwy 17B. Int corridors. **Pets:** Medium, dogs only. $10 daily fee/pet. Service with restrictions, supervision. ECO SAVE 🛰 🛏 🖥

▼▼▼▼ **Delta Sault Ste. Marie Waterfront Hotel and Conference Centre** 🅗
(705) 949-0611. **$129-$179.** 208 St. Marys River Dr P6A 5V4. On the waterfront. Int corridors. **Pets:** Accepted.
ECO 🛰 ✖ 🛏 🖥 🍴 🏊 🐾

▼▼ **Glenview Cottages** 🅒🅐 ❀
(705) 759-3436. **$109-$195.** 2611 Great Northern Rd P6A 5K7. 6 mi (9.6 km) n on Hwy 17. Ext corridors. **Pets:** Medium, dogs only. $10 daily fee/room. Designated rooms, service with restrictions, crate.
ECO 🛰 🛏 🖥 🏊 🐾

▼▼ **Holiday Motel** Ⓜ
(705) 759-8608. **$55-$75.** 435 Trunk Rd P6A 3T1. On Hwy 17, just e of jct Hwy 17B. Ext corridors. **Pets:** Service with restrictions, supervision.
🛰 🛏 🖥

🅐 ▼▼ **Northlander Motel** Ⓜ
(705) 254-6452. **$55-$80.** 243 Great Northern Rd P6B 4Z2. 1.9 mi (3 km) n on Hwy 17B. Ext corridors. **Pets:** Accepted. SAVE ✖ 🛏 🖥

▼▼ **Satelite Motel** Ⓜ
(705) 759-2897. **$55-$95, 5 day notice.** 248 Great Northern Rd P6B 4Z6. 1.9 mi (3 km) n on Hwy 17B. Ext corridors. **Pets:** Accepted.
🛰 🛏 🖥

🅐 ▼▼ **Skyline Motel** Ⓜ
(705) 942-1240. **$65-$85, 5 day notice.** 232 Great Northern Rd P6B 4Z5. 1.9 mi (3 km) n on Hwy 17B. Ext corridors. **Pets:** Accepted.
SAVE 🛰 🛏 🖥

🅐 ▼▼▼ **Super 8** 🅗
(705) 254-6441. **$80-$99.** 184 Great Northern Rd P6B 4Z3. 1.3 mi (2 km) n on Hwy 17B. Int corridors. **Pets:** Accepted. SAVE 🛰 🛏 🖥

▼▼ **Villa Inn Motel** Ⓜ
(705) 942-2424. **Call for rates.** 724 Great Northern Rd P6B 5A3. 2.9 mi (4.6 km) n on Hwy 17B. Ext corridors. **Pets:** Accepted. 🛰 🛏 🖥

SIMCOE

(CAA) ▼▼▼ Best Western Little River Inn �H ❀
(519) 426-2125. **$112-$122.** 203 Queensway W N3Y 2M9. Jct Hwy 24, just w on Hwy 3. Int corridors. **Pets:** Medium. $20 one-time fee/room. Designated rooms, service with restrictions, supervision.
[SAVE] 🛜 🛅 🖵 🍴 🏊

▼▼ Comfort Inn �H ❀
(519) 426-2611. **$99-$180.** 85 Queensway E N3Y 4M5. 0.3 mi (0.5 km) e on Hwy 3. Int corridors. **Pets:** Designated rooms, service with restrictions, supervision. [ECO] 🛜 🛅 🖵

▼▼ Travelodge Simcoe �H
(519) 426-4751. **$105-$139.** 385 Queensway W (Hwy 3) N3Y 2M9. 0.6 mi (1 km) w. Ext/int corridors. **Pets:** $10 daily fee/pet. Designated rooms, service with restrictions, supervision.
[ECO] 🛜 🛅 🛅 🖵 🏊 🍴

SMITHS FALLS

(CAA) ▼▼▼ Best Western Colonel by Inn �H
(613) 284-0001. **$90-$140.** 88 Lombard St K7A 4G5. On Hwy 15, just w of jct Hwy 29. Int corridors. **Pets:** Medium, dogs only. $10 daily fee/pet. Designated rooms, service with restrictions, supervision.
[SAVE] 🛜 🍴 🛅 🖵 🏊

SOUTH BAYMOUTH

(CAA) ▼ Huron Motor Lodge 🅼
(705) 859-3131. **$111-$175.** 24 Water St N P0P 1Z0. In South Baymouth; center. Ext corridors. **Pets:** Accepted. [SAVE] 🛅 🏊 🅚 🕿

STRATFORD

▼▼▼ Arden Park Hotel �H
(519) 275-2936. **$99-$199.** 552 Ontario St (Hwy 7 & 8) N5A 3J3. Jct Romeo St. Int corridors. **Pets:** Accepted.
🛜 🍴 🛅 🛅 🖵 🍴 🏊

STURGEON FALLS

▼▼▼ Comfort Inn �H
(705) 753-5665. **$99-$120.** 11 Front St P2B 3L3. On Hwy 17 at western approach to town. Int corridors. **Pets:** Accepted.
🛜 🍴 🛅 🖵 🏊

SUDBURY

(CAA) ▼▼▼▼ Best Western Downtown Sudbury Centreville �H ❀
(705) 673-7801. **$120-$130, 14 day notice.** 151 Larch St P3E 1C3. Just w of Paris St; center. Int corridors. **Pets:** Medium. $20 daily fee/pet. Designated rooms, service with restrictions, supervision.
[SAVE] 🛜 🛅 🖵 🍴

(CAA) ▼▼▼ Comfort Inn �H
(705) 522-1101. **$83-$180.** 2171 Regent St P3E 5V3. Trans-Canada Hwy 17 exit Hwy 69/RR 46, 1.8 mi (2.8 km) n. Int corridors. **Pets:** Designated rooms, service with restrictions, crate. [ECO] [SAVE] 🛜 🛅 🖵

(CAA) ▼▼▼ Comfort Inn East �H ❀
(705) 560-4502. **$100-$145.** 440 2nd Ave N P3B 4A4. Just s of Kingsway Rd. Int corridors. **Pets:** Other species. $15 one-time fee/room. Service with restrictions, crate. [ECO] [SAVE] 🛜 🍴 🛅 🖵

▼▼ Days Inn-Sudbury �H ❀
(705) 674-7517. **$94-$106.** 117 Elm St P3C 1T3. Corner of Lorne St; downtown. Int corridors. **Pets:** Medium, other species. $20 one-time fee/room. Designated rooms, service with restrictions.
[ECO] 🛜 🍴 🛅 🖵 🍴 🏊 🍴

(CAA) ▼▼▼▼ Holiday Inn Hotel Sudbury �H
(705) 522-3000. **$124-$154.** 1696 Regent St P3E 3Z8. Trans-Canada Hwy 17 exit Hwy 69/RR 46, 2.4 mi (3.9 km) n. Int corridors.
Pets: Medium. Designated rooms, service with restrictions.
[SAVE] 🛜 🛅 🖵 🍴 🏊 🍴

(CAA) ▼▼▼ Homewood Suites by Hilton Sudbury �H
(705) 523-8100. **$139-$269.** 2270 Regent St P3E 0B4. Trans-Canada Hwy 17 exit Hwy 69/RR 46, 1.6 mi (2.5 km) n. Int corridors.
Pets: Accepted. [SAVE] 🛜 🍴 🛅 🖵 🏊

▼▼▼ Quality Inn & Conference Centre �H ❀
(705) 675-1273. **$110-$140.** 390 Elgin St S P3B 1B1. 0.6 mi (0.9 km) s on Paris St from jct Kingsway Rd and Elm St. Int corridors. **Pets:** $10 daily fee/room. Designated rooms, service with restrictions, supervision.
[ECO] 🛜 🍴 🛅 🖵 🍴 🏊

(CAA) ▼▼▼▼ Radisson Hotel Sudbury Downtown �H
(705) 675-1123. **$109-$249.** 85 Ste. Anne Rd P3E 4S4. Jct Notre Dame Ave; downtown. Int corridors. **Pets:** Accepted.
[SAVE] 🛜 🛅 🖵 🍴 🏊 🍴

▼▼▼ TownePlace Suites Sudbury �H ❀
(705) 525-7700. **$140-$188.** 1710 The Kingsway Ave P3B 0E4. Just e of jct Falconbridge Rd. Int corridors. **Pets:** $50 one-time fee/room. Designated rooms, service with restrictions, crate.
🛜 🍴 🍴 🛅 🖵 🏊

(CAA) ▼▼▼ Travelodge Hotel Sudbury �H ❀
(705) 522-1100. **$142-$151.** 1401 Paris St P3E 3B6. Trans-Canada Hwy 17 exit Hwy 69/RR 46, 2 mi (3.2 km) n on Regent St, then 0.9 mi (1.5 km) e. Int corridors. **Pets:** Large. Designated rooms, service with restrictions. [ECO] [SAVE] 🛜 🛅 🖵 🍴 🏊

THESSALON

(CAA) ▼ Carolyn Beach Motor Inn 🅼 ❀
(705) 842-3330. **$97-$140.** 1 Lakeside Dr P0R 1L0. On Hwy 17B, just s of jct Hwy 17. Ext corridors. **Pets:** $12 daily fee/pet. Service with restrictions, supervision. [SAVE] 🛜 🍴 🛅 🖵 🍴 🍴

THUNDER BAY

(CAA) ▼▼▼ Best Western Crossroads Motor Inn �H
(807) 577-4241. **$144.** 655 W Arthur St P7E 5R6. Just e of jct Hwy 61. Int corridors. **Pets:** Small, dogs only. $15 daily fee/pet. Designated rooms, service with restrictions, supervision. [SAVE] 🛜 🍴 🛅 🖵

(CAA) ▼▼▼▼ Best Western Plus Nor'Wester Hotel & Conference Centre �H ❀
(807) 473-9123. **$130-$150, 3 day notice.** 2080 Hwy 61 P7J 1B8. On Hwy 61 at Loch Lomond Rd. Int corridors. **Pets:** Medium, dogs only. $20 one-time fee/room. Designated rooms, service with restrictions, crate.
[SAVE] 🛜 🍴 🛅 🖵 🍴 🏊 🍴

(CAA) ▼▼▼ Comfort Inn 🅼 ❀
(807) 475-3155. **$100-$145.** 660 W Arthur St P7E 5R8. Just e of jct Hwy 61. Int corridors. **Pets:** Large, other species. Service with restrictions, supervision. [ECO] [SAVE] 🛜 🛅 🖵

(CAA) ▼▼▼ Super 8 �H
(807) 344-2612. **$40-$92.** 439 Memorial Ave P7B 3Y6. Jct Hwy 11, 17 and Harbour Expwy, 1.9 mi (3 km) e on Harbour Expwy, 1.3 mi (2 km) n. Int corridors. **Pets:** Medium, other species. $20 one-time fee/room. Designated rooms, service with restrictions, supervision. [SAVE] 🛜 🛅 🖵

▼▼ Victoria Inn Hotel & Convention Centre �H
(807) 577-8481. **$121-$145.** 555 W Arthur St P7E 5R5. 0.5 mi (0.8 km) e of jct Hwy 11B, 17B and 61 (western access to town). Int corridors.
Pets: Medium, other species. $10 daily fee/pet. Designated rooms, service with restrictions, supervision. 🛜 🍴 🛅 🖵 🍴 🏊 🍴

TILLSONBURG

▼▼ Howard Johnson/Tillsonburg �H
(519) 842-7366. **$95-$108.** 92 Simcoe St N4G 2J1. Hwy 19, just e. Int corridors. **Pets:** Accepted. [ECO] 🛜 🍴 🛅 🖵 🍴

TIMMINS

 Comfort Inn 🅗

(705) 264-9474. **$89-$199.** 939 Algonquin Blvd E P4N 7J5. Hwy 101, 0.3 mi (0.5 km) e of Hwy 655. Int corridors. **Pets:** Accepted.
🅔🅒🅞 📶 🖥 💻

🔻🔻 Travelodge 🅗

(705) 360-1122. **$88-$103.** 1136 Riverside Dr P4R 1A2. Hwy 101, 2.8 mi (4.4 km) w of Hwy 655. Int corridors. **Pets:** Accepted.
🅔🅒🅞 📶 🖥 💻

TOBERMORY

🔻 Coach House Inn 🅜

(519) 596-2361. **$59-$129.** 7189 Hwy 6 N0H 2R0. Hwy 6, 1.2 mi (2 km) s of ferry docks. Ext corridors. **Pets:** Accepted.
📶 ✖ 🖥 ➡ ✖ 🎫

TORONTO METROPOLITAN AREA

MARKHAM

🔻🔻🔻 Comfort Inn 🅗

(905) 477-6077. **$89-$129.** 8330 Woodbine Ave L3R 2N8. Hwy 401 exit 375, 5.6 mi (9 km) n; Hwy 404 exit Hwy 7, just e, then s. Int corridors. **Pets:** Accepted. 📶 🖥 💻 ➡ ✖

🔻🔻🔻 Delta Markham 🅗 🐾

(905) 477-2010. **$99-$179.** 50 E Valhalla Dr L3R 0A3. Hwy 404 exit Hwy 7, then e. Int corridors. **Pets:** Medium, other species. $35 one-time fee/ room. Service with restrictions, crate.
🅔🅒🅞 🖥 💻 🍴 ➡ ✖

Ⓒ 🔻🔻🔻🔻 Hilton Suites Toronto/Markham Conference Centre & Spa 🅗

(905) 470-8500. **$107-$171.** 8500 Warden Ave L6G 1A5. Hwy 404 exit Hwy 7, 2 mi (3.2 km) e. Int corridors. **Pets:** Accepted.
🅔🅒🅞 🆂🅰🆅🅴 📶 🖥 💻 🍴 ➡ ✖

Ⓒ 🔻🔻🔻🔻 Holiday Inn Hotel & Suites Toronto-Markham 🅗

(905) 474-0444. **$95-$169.** 7095 Woodbine Ave L3R 1A3. Just n of Steeles Ave. Int corridors. **Pets:** Accepted.
🆂🅰🆅🅴 📶 ✖ 🖥 💻 🍴 ➡ ✖

🔻🔻🔻 Homewood Suites by Hilton Toronto/Markham 🅗

(905) 477-4663. **$119-$129.** 50 Bodrington Ct L6G 0A9. Hwy 407 exit 84 (Woodbine Ave), just ne. Int corridors. **Pets:** Accepted.
📶 ♿🅼 🖥 💻 ➡

Ⓒ 🔻🔻🔻🔻 Howard Johnson Hotel Toronto-Markham 🅗

(905) 479-5000. **$71-$107.** 555 Cochrane Dr L3R 8E3. Hwy 404 N exit Hwy 7 E to E Valhalla Dr. Int corridors. **Pets:** Accepted.
🅔🅒🅞 🆂🅰🆅🅴 📶 🖥 💻 🍴 ➡ ✖

🔻🔻🔻 Residence Inn by Marriott Toronto-Markham 🅗

(905) 707-7933. **$179-$208.** 55 Minthorn Blvd L3T 7N5. Hwy 404 exit Hwy 7, 0.7 mi (1.1 km) w. Int corridors. **Pets:** Accepted.
📶 ✖ 🖥 💻 ➡ ✖

🔻🔻🔻 Staybridge Suites Toronto-Markham 🅗

(905) 771-9333. **$109-$239.** 355 S Park Rd L3T 7W2. Hwy 404 exit Hwy 7, 0.9 mi (1.4 km) w, 0.3 mi (0.5 km) s on Commerce Valley Dr W, then just e. Int corridors. **Pets:** Accepted. 📶 🖥 💻 ➡

RICHMOND HILL

Ⓒ 🔻🔻🔻🔻 Holiday Inn Express & Suites Toronto-Markham 🅗

(905) 695-5990. **$115-$179.** 10 E Pearce St L4B 0A8. Just n of jct Leslie St and Hwy 7. Int corridors. **Pets:** Small. $50 one-time fee/room. Service with restrictions, supervision.
🅔🅒🅞 🆂🅰🆅🅴 📶 ✖ ♿🅼 🖥 💻 ➡

Ⓒ 🔻🔻🔻🔻 Sheraton Parkway Toronto North Hotel and Suites 🅗

(905) 881-2121. **$119-$179.** 600 Hwy 7 E L4B 1B2. Hwy 404 exit 27, 0.6 mi (1 km) w. Int corridors. **Pets:** Accepted.
🅔🅒🅞 🆂🅰🆅🅴 📶 ✖ 💻 🍴 ➡ ✖

TORONTO

Ⓒ 🔻🔻🔻 Best Western Plus Roehampton Hotel & Suites 🅗

(416) 487-5101. **$120-$200.** 808 Mt. Pleasant Rd M4P 2L2. Just n of Eglinton Ave. Int corridors. **Pets:** Small. $50 one-time fee/pet. Service with restrictions, supervision. 🅔🅒🅞 🆂🅰🆅🅴 📶 🖥 💻 🍴 ➡

Ⓒ 🔻🔻 Comfort Inn 🅗

(416) 736-4700. **$85-$105.** 66 Norfinch Dr M3N 1X1. Hwy 400 exit Finch Ave E, just n. Int corridors. **Pets:** Medium. Designated rooms, service with restrictions, supervision. 🅔🅒🅞 🆂🅰🆅🅴 📶 🖥 💻

Ⓒ 🔻🔻🔻 Cosmopolitan Hotel & Residences 🅗

(416) 350-2000. **Call for rates.** 8 Colborne St M5E 1E1. Between King and Wellington sts. Int corridors. **Pets:** Accepted.
🆂🅰🆅🅴 📶 🖥 💻 🍴 ✖

Ⓒ 🔻🔻🔻 Crowne Plaza Toronto Airport 🅗 🐾

(416) 675-1234. **$115-$325.** 33 Carlson Ct M9W 6H5. Just w of jct Hwy 27, n of Dixon Rd. Int corridors. **Pets:** Medium, other species. $25 daily fee/room. Designated rooms, service with restrictions, supervision.
🅔🅒🅞 🆂🅰🆅🅴 📶 🖥 💻 🍴 ➡ ✖

🔻🔻🔻 Days Hotel & Conference Centre Toronto Don Valley 🅗

(416) 493-9000. **$108-$159.** 185 Yorkland Blvd M2J 4R2. Just s of Sheppard Ave. Int corridors. **Pets:** Medium. $35 daily fee/pet. Service with restrictions, supervision. 🅔🅒🅞 📶 ✖ 🖥 💻 🍴 ➡ ✖

Ⓒ 🔻🔻🔻 Delta Chelsea Hotel 🅗 🐾

(416) 595-1975. **$119-$299.** 33 Gerrard St W M5G 1Z4. Just w of Yonge St; just s of College St. Int corridors. **Pets:** Small. $35 one-time fee/pet. Service with restrictions, supervision.
🅔🅒🅞 🆂🅰🆅🅴 📶 ✖ 🖥 💻 🍴 ➡ ✖

🔻🔻🔻 Delta Toronto East 🅗 🐾

(416) 299-1500. **$119-$299.** 2035 Kennedy Rd M1T 3G2. Just ne of jct Hwy 401 and Kennedy Rd exit 379. Int corridors. **Pets:** Medium. $35 one-time fee/room. Service with restrictions, supervision.
🅔🅒🅞 📶 ✖ 🖥 💻 🍴 ➡ ✖

Ⓒ 🔻🔻🔻 DoubleTree by Hilton Hotel Toronto Airport 🅗

(416) 244-1711. **$109-$229.** 655 Dixon Rd M9W 1J3. Jct Hwy 27 N, just w of jct Hwy 401. Int corridors. **Pets:** Small. Service with restrictions, supervision. 🅔🅒🅞 🆂🅰🆅🅴 📶 ♿🅼 🖥 💻 🍴 ➡ ✖

Ⓒ 🔻🔻🔻🔻 The Fairmont Royal York 🅗

(416) 368-2511. **$169-$389.** 100 Front St W M5J 1E3. QEW/Gardiner Expwy, exit n on York or Bay sts; entrance on Wellington St. Int corridors. **Pets:** Accepted. 🅔🅒🅞 🆂🅰🆅🅴 📶 ♿🅼 🖥 💻 🍴 ➡ ✖

🔻🔻🔻 The Grand Hotel & Suites Toronto 🅗

(416) 863-9000. **$159-$169.** 225 Jarvis St M5B 2C1. Jct Dundas St. Int corridors. **Pets:** Accepted. 📶 🖥 💻 🍴 ➡ ✖

(CAA) ▼▼▼ **Holiday Inn Express Toronto Downtown** H ☙

(416) 367-5555. **$129-$189.** 111 Lombard St M5C 2T9. Gardiner Expwy exit Jarvis St, 0.6 mi (1 km) n, then just w; between Adelaide and Richmond sts. Int corridors. **Pets:** Medium. Service with restrictions, supervision. ECO SAVE 🛜 🖥 🖵

(CAA) ▼▼▼ **Holiday Inn Express Toronto-North York** H

(416) 665-3500. **$99-$139.** 30 Norfinch Dr M3N 1X1. Hwy 400 exit Finch Ave E. Int corridors. **Pets:** Large. $25 daily fee/room. Service with restrictions, supervision. SAVE 🛗M 🖥 🖵

(CAA) ▼▼▼ **Holiday Inn Toronto Downtown Centre** H

(416) 977-6655. **Call for rates.** 30 Carlton St M5B 2E9. Adjacent to Maple Leaf Gardens. Int corridors. **Pets:** Accepted.
ECO SAVE 🛜 🗙 🖥 🖵 🍽 🗙

▼▼▼ **Hotel Carlingview Toronto Airport** H

(416) 675-3303. **$79-$99.** 221 Carlingview Dr M9W 5E8. QEW exit Hwy 427 N to Dixon Rd E, 0.6 mi (1 km) to Carlingview Dr, then just s. Ext/int corridors. **Pets:** $40 one-time fee/room. Designated rooms, service with restrictions, crate. ECO 🖥 🖵 🍽

(CAA) ▼▼▼ **Hotel Indigo** H

(416) 637-7000. **$89-$149.** 135 Carlingview Dr M9W 5E7. Just n of Dixon Rd. Int corridors. **Pets:** Medium, other species. $25 daily fee/pet.
SAVE 🛜 🗙 🖥 🖵 🍽 🛶 🗙

▼▼▼ ▼▼ **Hotel Le Germain Maple Leaf Square** H ☙

(416) 649-7575. **$224-$544.** 75 Bremner Blvd M5J 0A1. Jct York St, just w of Air Canada Centre. Int corridors. **Pets:** $35 daily fee/room. Service with restrictions, supervision. 🛜 🗙 🖵

▼▼▼ ▼▼ **Hotel Le Germain Toronto** H

(416) 345-9500. **$235-$2900.** 30 Mercer St M5V 1H3. Between John St and Blue Jays Way. Int corridors. **Pets:** Accepted.
🛜 🗙 🖥 🖵 🍽 🗙

(CAA) ▼▼▼ ▼▼ **InterContinental Toronto Centre** H ☙

(416) 597-1400. **$189-$309.** 225 Front St W M5V 2X3. Between Spadina and University aves. Int corridors. **Pets:** Large. $50 one-time fee/room. Service with restrictions, crate. ECO SAVE 🛜 🖥 🖵 🍽 🛶 🗙

(CAA) ▼▼▼ **InterContinental Toronto Yorkville** H ☙

(416) 960-5200. **$195-$405.** 220 Bloor St W M5S 1T8. Just w of Avenue Rd. Int corridors. **Pets:** $25 daily fee/pet. Service with restrictions, crate.
ECO SAVE 🛜 🖥 🖵 🍽 🛶 🗙

(CAA) ▼▼▼ ▼▼ **Le Meridien King Edward Hotel** H

(416) 863-9700. **$159-$725.** 37 King St E M5C 1E9. Just e of Yonge St. Int corridors. **Pets:** Accepted. SAVE 🛜 🖥 🍽

(CAA) ▼▼▼ **Metropolitan Hotel** H ☙

(416) 977-5000. **$119-$359.** 108 Chestnut St M5G 1R3. Just s of Dundas St. Int corridors. **Pets:** $25 daily fee/pet. Designated rooms, service with restrictions, crate. ECO SAVE 🛜 🖥 🖵 🍽 🛶 🗙

(CAA) ▼▼▼ **Montecassino Hotel & Event Venue** H

(416) 630-8100. **$90-$119.** 3710 Chesswood Dr M3J 2W4. Jct Sheppard Ave. Int corridors. **Pets:** Accepted. SAVE 🛜 🗙 🖥 🖵

(CAA) ▼▼▼ **Novotel Toronto Centre** H

(416) 367-8900. **$159-$285.** 45 The Esplanade M5E 1W2. Just ne of Gardiner Expy via Yonge St. Int corridors. **Pets:** Accepted.
ECO SAVE 🛜 🖥 🖵 🍽 🛶 🗙

(CAA) ▼▼▼ **Novotel Toronto North York** H ☙

(416) 733-2929. **$145-$335.** 3 Park Home Ave M2N 6L3. Hwy 401 exit Yonge St, 1.1 mi (1.7 km) n, then just w. Int corridors. **Pets:** Other species. Supervision. ECO SAVE 🛜 🗙 🖵 🍽 🛶

(CAA) ▼▼▼ ▼▼ **Pantages Hotel Toronto Centre** H

(416) 362-1777. **Call for rates.** 200 Victoria St M5B 1V8. Jct Shuter St. Int corridors. **Pets:** Accepted. ECO SAVE 🛜 🗙 🖥 🖵 🍽 🗙

(CAA) ▼▼▼ ▼▼ **Park Hyatt Toronto** H ☙

(416) 925-1234. **$235-$450, 3 day notice.** 4 Avenue Rd M5R 2E8. Corner of Bloor St W. Int corridors. **Pets:** Medium, dogs only. $50 one-time fee/pet. Designated rooms, supervision. SAVE 🛜 🛗M 🍽 🗙

(CAA) ▼▼▼ **Quality Hotel & Suites Toronto Airport East** H

(416) 240-9090. **$119-$169.** 2180 Islington Ave M9P 3P1. Hwy 401 exit 356, just s. Int corridors. **Pets:** $15 daily fee/pet. Designated rooms, service with restrictions, supervision. ECO SAVE 🛜 🗙 🖥 🖵 🍽

(CAA) ▼▼▼ **Quality Suites Toronto Airport** H

(416) 674-8442. **$95-$174.** 262 Carlingview Dr M9W 5G1. 0.6 mi (1 km) w of jct Hwy 27 N and Dixon Rd. Int corridors. **Pets:** Accepted.
ECO SAVE 🛜 🖥 🖵 🍽

(CAA) ▼▼▼ **Radisson Hotel Toronto East** H

(416) 493-7000. **$119-$275.** 55 Hallcrown Pl M2J 4R1. Hwy 401 exit Victoria Park N to Consumers Rd, then w. Int corridors. **Pets:** $25 daily fee/room. Designated rooms, service with restrictions, supervision.
ECO SAVE 🛜 🛗M 🖥 🖵 🍽 🛶

(CAA) ▼▼▼ **Radisson Suite Hotel Toronto Airport** H

(416) 242-7400. **$129-$189.** 640 Dixon Rd M9W 1J1. Just e of jct Hwy 27; just w of jct Hwy 401. Int corridors. **Pets:** Accepted.
ECO SAVE 🛜 🖥 🖵 🍽

(CAA) ▼▼▼ ▼▼ **Renaissance Toronto Downtown Hotel** H

(416) 341-7100. **Call for rates.** 1 Blue Jays Way M5V 1J4. Jct Front St. Int corridors. **Pets:** Medium. $50 one-time fee/room. Service with restrictions, crate. ECO SAVE 🛜 🗙 🖥 🖵 🛶 🗙

▼▼▼ **Residence Inn by Marriott Toronto Airport** H

(416) 798-2900. **$179-$241.** 17 Reading Ct M9W 7K7. Just w of jct Hwy 27 and Dixon Rd. Int corridors. **Pets:** Medium. $100 one-time fee/pet. Designated rooms, service with restrictions, crate.
ECO 🛜 🗙 🛗M 🖥 🖵 🗙

▼▼▼ **Residence Inn by Marriott Toronto Downtown/ Entertainment District** H

(416) 581-1800. **$169-$249.** 255 Wellington St W M5V 3P9. Jct Blue Jays Way. Int corridors. **Pets:** Accepted. ECO 🛜 🗙 🖥 🖵 🛶

(CAA) ▼▼▼ ▼▼ **The Ritz-Carlton, Toronto** H ☙

(416) 585-2500. **Call for rates.** 181 Wellington St W M5V 3G7. Between Simcoe and John sts. Int corridors. **Pets:** Small. $150 one-time fee/room. Service with restrictions. SAVE 🛜 🗙 🛗M 🖵 🍽 🛶 🗙

(CAA) ▼▼▼ ▼▼ **Sheraton Centre Toronto Hotel** H

(416) 361-1000. **$159-$629.** 123 Queen St W M5H 2M9. Opposite Toronto Civic Centre and City Hall. Int corridors. **Pets:** Accepted.
ECO SAVE 🛜 🗙 🛗M 🖥 🖵 🍽 🛶 🗙

(CAA) ▼▼▼ ▼▼ **Sheraton Toronto Airport Hotel & Conference Centre** H ☙

(416) 675-6100. **$109-$259.** 801 Dixon Rd M9W 1J5. Jct Hwy 27 N and Dixon Rd. Int corridors. **Pets:** Medium. Service with restrictions, supervision. ECO SAVE 🛜 🗙 🛗M 🖥 🖵 🍽 🛶

(CAA) ▼▼▼ ▼▼ **SoHo Metropolitan Hotel** H ☙

(416) 599-8800. **$250-$895.** 318 Wellington St W M5V 3T4. Jct Blue Jays Way. Int corridors. **Pets:** Medium. Service with restrictions, crate.
SAVE 🛜 🖥 🖵 🍽 🛶 🗙

(CAA) ▼▼ **Super 8 Downtown Toronto** H

(647) 426-8118. **$88-$201.** 222 Spadina Ave M5T 2C2. At Dundas St; at Chinatown Centre. Int corridors. **Pets:** Accepted.
ECO SAVE 🛜 🗙 🖥 🖵

△ ▼▼ ▼▼ **The Sutton Place Hotel** 🅷

(416) 924-9221. **$145-$565.** 955 Bay St M5S 2A2. Jct Wellesley St. Int corridors. **Pets:** Other species. $150 deposit/room, $50 one-time fee/room. Service with restrictions, supervision.

ECO SAVE 🛜 🔌 📺 🍽 ✕

▼▼ ▼▼ **Thompson Hotel Toronto** 🅷

(416) 640-7778. **$295-$495.** 550 Wellington St W M5V 2V4. Jct Bathurst St. Int corridors. **Pets:** Accepted. 🛜 🔌 🍽 ⊷ ✕

△ ▼▼ ▼▼ **Toronto Don Valley Hotel & Suites** 🅷 🐾

(416) 449-4111. **$109-$149.** 175 Wynford Dr M3C 1J3. Don Valley Pkwy exit 375 (Wynford Dr); jct Don Valley Pkwy and Eglinton Ave E. Int corridors. **Pets:** Very small. $25 daily fee/room. Designated rooms, service with restrictions, supervision.

ECO SAVE 🛜 ✕ 🔌 ♿ 📺 🍽 ⊷ ✕

△ ▼▼ ▼▼ **Toronto Marriott Bloor Yorkville** 🅷

(416) 961-8000. **$149-$339.** 90 Bloor St E M4W 1A7. Just e of Yonge St. Int corridors. **Pets:** $50 one-time fee/room.

ECO SAVE 🛜 ✕ ♿ 🔌 📺 🍽

△ ▼▼ ▼▼ **Travelodge Toronto Airport (Dixon Road)** 🅷 🐾

(416) 674-2222. **$77-$126.** 925 Dixon Rd M9W 1J8. Corner of Carlingview Dr. Int corridors. **Pets:** $25 daily fee/pet. Designated rooms, service with restrictions, supervision. ECO SAVE 🛜 🔌 📺 🍽 ⊷

▼▼ ▼▼ **Travelodge Toronto East** 🅷

(416) 299-9500. **$80-$116.** 20 Milner Business Ct M1B 3C6. Jct Hwy 401 exit 383 (Markham Rd), just n. Int corridors. **Pets:** Accepted.

ECO 🛜 🔌 📺 🍽 ⊷

▼▼ ▼▼ **Travelodge Toronto North (North York)** 🅷

(416) 663-9500. **$80-$140.** 50 Norfinch Dr M3N 1X1. Hwy 400 exit 25 (Finch Ave E). Int corridors. **Pets:** Accepted.

ECO 🛜 🔌 📺 🍽 ⊷

△ ▼▼ ▼▼ **The Westin Bristol Place Toronto Airport** 🅷 🐾

(416) 675-9444. **$109-$229.** 950 Dixon Rd M9W 5N4. 1.6 mi (2.6 km) w of jct Hwy 401. Int corridors. **Pets:** Medium, dogs only. $125 deposit/room. Designated rooms, service with restrictions, supervision.

SAVE 🛜 ✕ 🔌 📺 🍽

△ ▼▼ ▼▼ **The Westin Harbour Castle** 🅷

(416) 869-1600. **$159-$549.** One Harbour Sq M5J 1A6. At the foot of Bay St. Int corridors. **Pets:** Accepted.

ECO SAVE 🛜 ✕ 🔌 📺 🍽 ⊷ ✕

△ ▼▼ ▼▼ **The Westin Prince Toronto** 🅷 🐾

(416) 444-2511. **$129-$389.** 900 York Mills Rd M3B 3H2. Just s of Hwy 401 via Leslie St exit to York Mills Rd E. Int corridors. **Pets:** Medium, dogs only. Service with restrictions, supervision.

SAVE 🛜 ✕ ♿ 📺 🍽 ⊷ ✕

▼▼ ▼▼ **Windsor Arms Hotel** 🅷 🐾

(416) 971-9666. **$295-$2000.** 18 St. Thomas St M5S 3E7. Just s of Bloor St. Int corridors. **Pets:** Medium. $50 one-time fee/pet. Service with restrictions, crate. 🛜 ✕ 🍽 ⊷ ✕

VAUGHAN

▼▼ ▼▼ **Holiday Inn Express & Suites Vaughan-Southwest** 🅷

(905) 851-1510. **Call for rates.** 6100 Hwy 7 L4H 0R2. Jct Hwy 27. Int corridors. **Pets:** Other species. $20 daily fee/room. Service with restrictions, supervision. ECO 🛜 ✕ 🔌 📺 ⊷

△ ▼▼ ▼▼ **Novotel Toronto Vaughan Centre** 🅷

(905) 660-0212. **$99-$249.** 200 Bass Pro Mills Dr L4K 0B9. Hwy 400 S exit 33 Rutherford Rd; Hwy 400 N exit 32 Bass Pro Mills Dr. Int corridors. **Pets:** Medium, other species. Designated rooms, service with restrictions, supervision. ECO SAVE 🛜 ✕ ♿ 🔌 📺 🍽 ⊷

▼▼ ▼▼ **Residence Inn by Marriott Toronto/Vaughan** 🅷

(905) 695-4002. **$170-$229.** 11 Interchange Way L4K 5W3. Hwy 400 exit 29 (Hwy 7), 0.6 mi (1 km) e. Int corridors. **Pets:** Accepted.

🛜 ✕ ♿ 🔌 📺 ⊷ ✕

END METROPOLITAN AREA

TRENTON

▼▼ ▼▼ **Comfort Inn** 🅷 🐾

(613) 965-6660. **$90-$135.** 68 Monogram Pl K8V 6S3. Hwy 401 exit 526 (Glen Miller Rd), just s, then just e. Int corridors. **Pets:** Other species. Service with restrictions. ECO 🛜 ♿ 🔌 📺

△ ▼▼ ▼▼ **Holiday Inn Trenton** 🅷

(613) 394-4855. **Call for rates.** 99 Glen Miller Rd K8V 5P8. Hwy 401 exit 526 (Glen Miller Rd), just s. Int corridors. **Pets:** Small, other species. $15 daily fee/room. Service with restrictions, supervision.

ECO SAVE 🛜 ✕ 🔌 📺 🍽 ⊷

△ ▼▼ ▼▼ **Travelodge** 🅷 🐾

(613) 965-6789. **$88-$117.** 598 Old Hwy 2 K8V 5P5. Hwy 401 exit 538, 1.3 mi (2 km) s to Old Hwy 2, then 3.8 mi (6 km) w; 3.1 mi (4.9 km) e of jct Hwy 33. Int corridors. **Pets:** Service with restrictions, supervision.

ECO SAVE 🛜 🔌 📺

TWEED

▼▼ **Park Place Motel** 🅼

(613) 478-3134. **$90-$115, 4 day notice.** 43 Victoria St S K0K 3J0. Hwy 37, 0.3 mi (0.5 km) s of center. Ext corridors. **Pets:** Accepted.

🛜 🔌

WALLACEBURG

▼▼ ▼▼ **Days Inn Wallaceburg** 🅷

(519) 627-0781. **$90-$94.** 76 McNaughton Ave N8A 1R9. On Hwy 40 (McNaughton Ave), south side of town. Int corridors. **Pets:** Accepted.

🛜 🔌 📺

WATERLOO

△ ▼▼ ▼▼ **Comfort Inn** 🅷 🐾

(519) 747-9400. **$110-$160.** 190 Weber St N N2J 3H4. Jct University Ave, just s. Int corridors. **Pets:** Other species.

ECO SAVE 🛜 🔌 📺 🍽

▼▼ ▼▼ **The Waterloo Inn Conference Hotel** 🅷

(519) 884-0220. **$149-$209.** 475 King St N N2J 2Z5. 1.9 mi (3 km) n on King St, jct Hwy 85. Int corridors. **Pets:** Large. $15 daily fee/pet. Designated rooms, service with restrictions, crate.

🛜 ✕ ♿ 🔌 📺 🍽 ⊷ ✕

WAWA

△ ▼▼ ▼▼ **Best Northern Motel & Restaurant** 🅼

(705) 856-7302. **$89-$135.** 150 Hwy 17 S P0S 1K0. On Hwy 17, 3.3 mi (5.3 km) s of jct Hwy 101. Ext corridors. **Pets:** Other species. $8 daily fee/pet. Designated rooms, service with restrictions, supervision.

SAVE 🛜 ✕ 🔌 📺 🍽 ✕ 🐾

Northern Lights Motel & Breakfast M

(705) 856-1900. **$89-$119.** 1014 Hwy 17 P0S 1K0. On Hwy 17, 5 mi (8 km) n of jct Hwy 101. Ext corridors. **Pets:** Accepted.

Parkway Motel M

(705) 856-7020. **$89-$129.** 232 Hwy 17 S P0S 1K0. On Hwy 17, 2.5 mi (4 km) s of jct Hwy 101. Ext corridors. **Pets:** Medium, other species. $10 daily fee/pet. Designated rooms, service with restrictions, supervision.

Sportsman's Motel M

(705) 856-2272. **$75-$85.** 171 Mission Rd P0S 1K0. On Hwy 101, 1.5 mi (2.4 km) e of jct Hwy 17. Ext corridors. **Pets:** Accepted.

WHITBY

Canadiana Inn M

(905) 668-3686. **$70-$130.** 732 Dundas St E (Hwy 2) L1N 2J7. Hwy 401 exit 410 (Brock St/Hwy 12), 1 mi (1.6 km) n to Dundas St, then 0.6 mi (1 km) e. Ext corridors. **Pets:** Dogs only. $100 deposit/room. Service with restrictions, supervision.

Motel 6 Whitby #1907 H

(905) 665-8883. **$65-$79.** 165 Consumers Dr L1N 1C4. Hwy 401 exit 410 (Brock St/Hwy 12), just ne. Int corridors. **Pets:** Other species. Service with restrictions, supervision.

Quality Suites H

(905) 432-8800. **$109-$169.** 1700 Champlain Ave L1N 6A7. Hwy 401 exit 412 (Thickson Rd), 0.3 mi (0.5 km) n to Champlain Ave, then 0.6 mi (1 km) e. Int corridors. **Pets:** Accepted.

Residence Inn Whitby H

(905) 444-9756. **$99-$169.** 160 Consumers Dr L1N 9S3. Hwy 401 exit 410 (Brock St/Hwy 12). Int corridors. **Pets:** Other species. $75 one-time fee/room. Service with restrictions, supervision.

WIARTON

Glen Miller Motel M

(519) 534-0175. **Call for rates.** 143 Hwy 6 N0H 2T0. 1.6 mi (2.5 km) n of town; center. Ext corridors. **Pets:** Accepted.

WINDSOR

Cadillac Inn M

(519) 969-9340. **$79-$109, 7 day notice.** 2498 Dougall Ave N8X 1T2. 2.5 mi (4 km) s on Hwy 3B from Detroit-Windsor Tunnel, just w on Eugenie St, then just n. Ext corridors. **Pets:** Accepted.

Comfort Inn H

(519) 966-7800. **$80-$125.** 2955 Dougall Ave N9E 1S1. 3.3 mi (5.3 km) s on Hwy 3B, off Hwy 401 via Detroit-Windsor Tunnel exit. Int corridors. **Pets:** Accepted.

Comfort Inn & Suites Ambassador Bridge H ❀

(519) 972-1100. **$90-$126.** 2330 Huron Church Rd N9E 3S6. N of EC Row Expwy. Int corridors. **Pets:** Medium, other species. $20 one-time fee/room. Service with restrictions, supervision.

Hampton Inn & Suites by Hilton H

(519) 972-0770. **$146-$169.** 1840 Huron Church Rd N9C 2L5. 0.9 mi (1.5 km) n of EC Row Expwy. Int corridors. **Pets:** Accepted.

Hilton Windsor H

(519) 973-5555. **$119-$199.** 277 Riverside Dr W N9A 5K4. 0.6 mi (1 km) w of Detroit-Windsor Tunnel; 0.6 mi (1 km) e of Ambassador Bridge; downtown. Int corridors. **Pets:** Medium, other species. $50 one-time fee/room. Service with restrictions, supervision.

Holiday Inn & Suites Windsor (Ambassador Bridge) H

(519) 966-1200. **$105-$195.** 1855 Huron Church Rd N9C 2L6. Jct Huron Church and Malden rds; 0.9 mi (1.5 km) n of EC Row Expwy. Int corridors. **Pets:** Accepted.

Holiday Inn Downtown Windsor H ❀

(519) 256-4656. **$124-$279.** 430 Ouellette Ave N9A 1B2. 0.3 mi (0.5 km) s of Riverside Dr at Park St W. Int corridors. **Pets:** $30 one-time fee/room. Service with restrictions, supervision.

Howard Johnson Plaza Hotel - Windsor Central H ❀

(519) 966-1860. **Call for rates.** 2530 Ouellette Ave N8X 1L7. Jct Eugenie St. Int corridors. **Pets:** Large. $10 daily fee/pet. Designated rooms, service with restrictions, crate.

Ivy Rose Motor Inn M

(519) 966-1700. **$74-$99.** 2885 Howard Ave N8X 3Y4. 3 mi (4.8 km) s of downtown; just n of Devonshire Shopping Mall. Ext corridors. **Pets:** Accepted.

Quality Suites Windsor H ❀

(519) 977-9707. **$90-$200.** 250 Dougall Ave N9A 7C6. Jct Chatham St; downtown. Int corridors. **Pets:** Medium. Service with restrictions, supervision.

Stonecroft Inn H

(519) 969-7600. **$85-$95.** 3032 Dougall Ave N9E 1S4. 0.3 mi (0.5 km) s of EC Row Expwy. Int corridors. **Pets:** Accepted.

Travelodge Hotel Downtown Windsor H

(519) 258-7774. **$80-$180.** 33 Riverside Dr E N9A 2S4. Jct Ouellette Ave; downtown. Int corridors. **Pets:** Small. Designated rooms, service with restrictions, supervision.

Windsor Riverside Inn H ❀

(519) 977-9777. **$119-$189.** 333 Riverside Dr W N9A 5K4. 0.6 mi (1 km) w of Detroit-Windsor Tunnel; 0.6 mi (1 km) e of Ambassador Bridge; downtown. Int corridors. **Pets:** Large. Service with restrictions, supervision.

WOODSTOCK

Microtel Inn & Suites H

(519) 537-2320. **$77-$94.** 811 Athlone Ave N4V 0B6. Hwy 401 exit 232, just n, then just w on Juliana Ave. Int corridors. **Pets:** Accepted.

Quality Hotel and Suites H

(519) 537-5586. **$90-$260.** 580 Bruin Blvd N4V 1E5. Hwy 401 exit 232, just n; w of Hwy 59. Int corridors. **Pets:** Accepted.

Super 8 H

(519) 421-4588. **$89-$110.** 560 Norwich Ave N4V 1C6. Hwy 401 exit 232, just n; w of Hwy 59. Int corridors. **Pets:** Accepted.

PRINCE EDWARD ISLAND

ALBERTON

▼▼ Briarwood Inn, Cottages & Lodge **M**
(902) 853-2518. **$60-$125, 30 day notice.** 253 Matthews Ln C0B 1B0. 1.9 mi (3 km) e on Rt 12. Ext/int corridors. **Pets:** Accepted.

CAVENDISH

▼▼ Bay Vista Motel **M**
(902) 963-2225. **$59-$135.** 9517 Cavendish Rd C0A 1E0. Jct Rt 13, 2.8 mi (4.8 km) w on Rt 6. Ext corridors. **Pets:** Accepted.

▼▼ Cavendish Bosom Buddies Cottages & Suites **CA**
(902) 963-3449. **$90-$300, 14 day notice.** RR 1 C0A 1N0. Jct Rt 6 and 13, 0.4 mi (0.7 km) e on Rt 6. Ext corridors. **Pets:** $10 daily fee/pet. Supervision.

CAA ▼▼▼ Cavendish Maples Cottages **CA**
(902) 963-2818. **$79-$319, 30 day notice.** 73 Avonlea Blvd C0A 1M0. Jct Rt 6 and 13, 1.5 mi (2.5 km) w on Rt 6. Ext corridors.
Pets: Accepted.

CAA ▼▼▼ Sundance Cottages **CA**
(902) 963-2149. **$85-$300, 14 day notice.** 34 Mac Coubrey Ln C0A 1N0. Jct Rt 13, 0.4 mi (0.6 km) e on Rt 6. Ext corridors. **Pets:** Other species. $10 daily fee/pet. Service with restrictions, crate.

CHARLOTTETOWN

CAA ▼▼▼ Best Western Charlottetown **H** ❀
(902) 892-2461. **$117-$185.** 238 Grafton St C1A 1L5. Between Hillsborough and Weymouth sts; centre. Int corridors. **Pets:** Other species. Service with restrictions, supervision.

CAA ▼▼ Comfort Inn **H** ❀
(902) 566-4424. **Call for rates.** 112 Trans-Canada Hwy 1 C1E 1E7. Trans-Canada Hwy 1, 2.8 mi (4.5 km) w. Int corridors. **Pets:** Medium. Service with restrictions, supervision.

CAA ▼▼▼ Delta Prince Edward **H** ❀
(902) 566-2222. **$123-$339.** 18 Queen St C1A 8B9. At Water and Queen sts. Int corridors. **Pets:** Medium. $35 one-time fee/room. Service with restrictions, supervision.

▼▼ Econo Lodge **M**
(902) 368-1110. **$90-$160.** 20 Lower Malpeque Rd C1A 7J9. Jct Trans-Canada Hwy 1 and Lower Malpeque Rd, 2.8 mi (4.5 km) w. Ext/int corridors. **Pets:** Accepted.

CAA ▼▼▼ Holiday Inn Express Hotel & Suites
Charlottetown **H**
(902) 892-1201. **$129-$189.** 200 Capital Dr C1E 2E8. On Trans-Canada Hwy 1, 3 mi (5 km) w. Int corridors. **Pets:** Medium. $25 one-time fee/room. Service with restrictions, supervision.

▼▼ Quality Inn on the Hill **H**
(902) 894-8572. **Call for rates.** 150 Euston St C1A 1W5. Just e of University Ave. Int corridors. **Pets:** Accepted.

▼▼▼ Rodd Charlottetown-A Rodd Signature Hotel **H**
(902) 894-7371. **$125-$247.** 75 Kent St C1A 7K4. Corner of Kent and Pownal sts. Int corridors. **Pets:** Accepted.

▼▼ Rodd Royalty **H**
(902) 894-8566. **$125-$195.** Intersection Hwy 1 & 2 C1A 8C2. 2.5 mi (4 km) w on Trans-Canada Hwy 1. Ext/int corridors. **Pets:** Accepted.

CORNWALL

▼▼ Howard Johnson Hotel **H**
(902) 566-2211. **$80-$131.** 100 Trans-Canada Hwy C0A 1H0. On Hwy 1, 4.3 mi (7 km) w of Charlottetown. Ext/int corridors. **Pets:** $10 daily fee/room. Designated rooms, service with restrictions, crate.

▼ Sunny King Motel **M**
(902) 566-2209. **$54-$116, 3 day notice.** 3 Centennial Dr C0A 1H0. On Hwy 1; centre. Ext corridors. **Pets:** Accepted.

▼▼ Super 8 **H** ❀
(902) 892-7900. **$114-$127.** 15 York Point Rd C0A 1H0. On Hwy 1, 3.7 mi (6 km) w of Charlottetown. Int corridors. **Pets:** Small. Designated rooms, service with restrictions, supervision.

DALVAY BEACH

▼▼▼ Dalvay by-the-Sea Heritage Inn **CI**
(902) 672-2048. **$189-$399, 15 day notice.** 16 Cottage Cres PEI National Pkwy C0A 1P0. Off Rt 6; at east end of PEI National Park. Ext/int corridors. **Pets:** Accepted.

FRENCH RIVER

▼▼▼ The Beach House Inn **BB** ❀
(902) 886-2145. **$79-$189, 14 day notice.** Cape Rd C0B 1M0. Just off Rt 20; centre. Ext/int corridors. **Pets:** Medium. $10 daily fee/room. Designated rooms, service with restrictions, supervision.

MAYFIELD

▼▼ Cavendish Gateway Resort by Clarion Collection **H**
(902) 963-2213. **Call for rates.** 6596 Rt 13 C0A 1N0. On Rt 13, 3.6 mi (6 km) w of Cavendish; centre. Ext/int corridors. **Pets:** Accepted.

MORELL

▼▼▼▼ Rodd Crowbush Golf & Beach Resort **H**
(902) 961-5600. **$180-$246, 3 day notice.** Rt 350 Lakeside C0A 1S0. 3 mi (5 km) w on Rt 2, follow signs. Ext/int corridors. **Pets:** Accepted.

ROSENEATH

▼▼▼ Brudenell Chalets **CA**
(902) 652-2900. **Call for rates.** 1068 Georgetown Rd C0A 1L0. Jct Rt 4 and 3, 4 mi (6 km) e on Rt 3. Ext corridors. **Pets:** Accepted.

◆◆◆ **Rodd Brudenell River-A Rodd Signature Resort** **H**
(902) 652-2332. **$110-$189, 3 day notice.** 86 Dewars Ln, Rt 3 C0A 1L0. Jct Rt 4, 3.3 mi (5.5 km) e. Ext/int corridors. **Pets:** Accepted.
📶 ♿M 🧊 ☕ 🍴 🏊 ⛳

ST. PETERS

◆◆◆ **The Inn at St. Peters** **CI**
(902) 961-2135. **$150-$270, 7 day notice.** 1668 Greenwich Rd C0A 2A0. Jct Rt 16 and 313, 0.6 mi (1 km) w on Rt 313. Ext corridors. **Pets:** Large. Service with restrictions. 📶 🚭 ♿M 🧊 ☕ 🍴

STANLEY BRIDGE

◆◆◆ **Inn at the Pier** **CI**
(902) 886-3126. **Call for rates.** 9796 Cavendish Rd C0A 1E0. Rt 6, 3.6 mi (6 km) w of Cavendish; centre. Ext/int corridors. **Pets:** Accepted.
📶 🚭 🧊 ☕ 🍴 🏊 ⛳

SUMMERSIDE

◆◆ **Econo Lodge** **H**
(902) 436-9100. **Call for rates.** 80 All Weather Hwy C1N 4P3. Jct Hwy 1A and 2, 3.1 mi (5 km) w on Hwy 2. Int corridors. **Pets:** Accepted.
📶 🚭 🧊 ☕ 🍴 🏊

CAA ◆◆ **Quality Inn & Suites** **H**
(902) 436-2295. **$110-$329.** 618 Water St C1N 2V5. 1 mi (1.6 km) e on Hwy 11. Ext/int corridors. **Pets:** Medium. $10 one-time fee/pet. Designated rooms, service with restrictions, supervision.
SAVE 📶 🚭 🧊 ☕ 🏊 ⛳

CAA ◆◆ **Slemon Park Hotel & Conference Centre** **H**
(902) 432-1780. **$110-$143.** 12 Redwood Ave C0B 1T0. On Rt 2, 3 mi (5 km) w at Summerside Airport. Int corridors. **Pets:** Small, dogs only. $100 deposit/room. Service with restrictions, supervision.
SAVE 📶 🚭 ♿M 🧊 ☕ 🍴 ⛳

WOOD ISLANDS

◆ **Meadow Lodge Motel** **M**
(902) 962-2022. **Call for rates.** Trans-Canada Hwy 1, Civic 313 C0A 1B0. 1 mi (1.6 km) nw of Wood Islands ferry terminal. Ext corridors. **Pets:** Accepted. 🚭 ⊘ 📵

WOODSTOCK

◆◆ **Rodd Mill River** **H**
(902) 859-3555. **$100-$156, 3 day notice.** Rt 136 C0B 1V0. On Rt 136, just e of jct Rt 2. Int corridors. **Pets:** Accepted.
📶 🚭 🧊 ☕ 🍴 🏊 ⛳

QUEBEC

ALMA

▼▼ Comfort Inn H
(418) 668-9221. **$119-$124.** 870 ave du Pont S G8B 2V8. On Hwy 169; centre. Int corridors. **Pets:** Accepted. 🛜 🔒 💻

AMOS

CAA ▼▼▼ Amosphere Complexe Hotelier H
(819) 732-7777. **$93-$120.** 1031 Rt 111 est J9T 1N2. Centre. Ext/int corridors. **Pets:** Other species. Supervision. SAVE 🛜 🔒 🍽 ⊗

BAIE-COMEAU

▼▼ Comfort Inn H
(418) 589-8252. **$125-$175.** 745 boul Lafleche G5C 1C6. On Rt 138. Int corridors. **Pets:** Accepted. ECO 🛜 ⊗ 🔒 💻

▼▼▼ Hotel Le Manoir H
(418) 296-3391. **$115-$125, 30 day notice.** 8 ave Cabot G4Z 1L8. Rt 138, 2.6 mi (4.4 km) e, follow signs. Int corridors. **Pets:** Accepted.
🛜 ⊗ 🔒 💻 🍽 ⊗

BAIE-ST-PAUL

CAA ▼▼▼ Hotel Baie-Saint-Paul H
(418) 435-3683. **Call for rates.** 911 boul Mgr-de-Laval G3Z 1A1. On Rt 138, 0.3 mi (0.5 km) e of Rt 362. Int corridors. **Pets:** Accepted.
SAVE 🛜 🔒 💻 🍽 ⊗

BROMONT

▼▼▼ Le St-Martin Bromont Hotel & Suites H
(450) 534-0044. **$169-$400.** 111 boul du Carrefour J2L 3L1. Hwy 10 exit 78. Int corridors. **Pets:** Accepted. 🛜 ⊗ 🔒 💻 🏊

CHICOUTIMI

CAA ▼▼▼▼ Hotel La Saguenéenne H
(418) 545-8326. **$99-$172.** 250 des Saguenees G7H 3A4. Just w of jct Rt 175 (boul Talbot); in Saguenay sector. Int corridors. **Pets:** $25 one-time fee/room. Designated rooms, service with restrictions, supervision.
SAVE 🛜 🔒 💻 🍽 🏊 ⊗

COWANSVILLE

▼▼ Auberge des Carrefours H
(450) 263-7331. **Call for rates.** 111 Place Jean-Jacques Bertrand J2K 3R5. Hwy 10 exit 68, 9.9 mi (15.9 km) s on Rt 139. Int corridors.
Pets: Accepted. 🛜 🔒 💻 🍽

DRUMMONDVILLE

CAA ▼▼▼▼ Best Western Plus Hotel Universel Drummondville H
(819) 478-4971. **$99-$220.** 915 rue Hains J2C 3A1. Hwy 20 exit 177, just s on boul St-Joseph, then just e. Int corridors. **Pets:** Accepted.
SAVE 🛜 🔒 💻 🍽 🏊

▼▼ Comfort Inn H
(819) 477-4000. **$72-$135.** 1055 rue Hains J2C 6G6. Hwy 20 exit 177, 0.3 mi (0.5 km) s on boul St-Joseph, then just w. Int corridors.
Pets: Accepted. ECO 🛜 🔒 💻

▼▼▼ Hotel & Suites Le Dauphin H
(819) 478-4141. **$99-$150.** 600 boul St-Joseph J2C 2C1. Hwy 20 exit 177, 0.8 mi (1.3 km) s. Ext/int corridors. **Pets:** $15 daily fee/room. Supervision. ECO 🛜 ⊗ 🔒 💻 🍽 🏊

▼▼▼ Quality Suites H 🐾
(819) 472-2700. **$100-$169.** 2125 rue Canadien J2C 7V8. Hwy 20 exit 175, just s. Int corridors. **Pets:** Other species. $25 one-time fee/room. Designated rooms, service with restrictions, supervision.
ECO 🛜 ⊗ 🔒 💻 🏊

GATINEAU

CAA ▼▼▼ Comfort Inn Gatineau H
(819) 243-6010. **$117-$161.** 630 boul La Gappe J8T 7S8. Hwy 50 exit 140, 1.1 mi (1.9 km) e. Int corridors. **Pets:** Other species. $25 one-time fee/pet. Designated rooms, service with restrictions, supervision.
ECO SAVE 🛜 ⊗ 🔒 💻

CAA ▼▼▼▼ Four Points by Sheraton Hotel & Conference Centre Gatineau-Ottawa H
(819) 778-6111. **$99-$240.** 35 rue Laurier J8X 4E9. Corner of rue Victoria; across from Canadian Museum of Civilization; in Hull sector. Int corridors. **Pets:** Accepted. ECO SAVE 🛜 ⊗ 🔒 💻 🍽 🏊

CAA ▼▼▼▼ Hilton Lac-Leamy H 🐾
(819) 790-6444. **Call for rates.** 3 boul du Casino J8Y 6X4. In Casino du Lac Leamy; in Hull sector. Int corridors. **Pets:** Medium. $50 one-time fee/room. Service with restrictions, supervision.
ECO SAVE 🛜 🔒 💻 🍽 🏊 ⊗

CAA ▼▼▼▼ Holiday Inn Plaza La Chaudière Gatineau-Ottawa H
(819) 778-3880. **$129-$159.** 2 rue Montcalm J8X 4B4. 0.5 mi (0.8 km) w of Portage Bridge at Rt 148 and rue Montcalm; in Hull sector. Int corridors. **Pets:** Large. $35 one-time fee/room. Designated rooms, service with restrictions, supervision. SAVE 🛜 🔒 💻 🍽 🏊 ⊗

GRENVILLE-SUR-LA-ROUGE

CAA ▼▼▼▼ Hôtel du Lac Carling H
(450) 533-9211. **Call for rates.** 2255 Rt 327 nord J0V 1B0. 3.1 mi (5 km) n. Int corridors. **Pets:** Accepted.
SAVE 🛜 🔒 💻 🍽 🏊 ⊗

ISLE-AUX-COUDRES

▼▼ Hotel Motel La Roche Pleureuse H
(418) 438-2734. **Call for rates.** 2901 chemin des Coudriers G0A 2A0. On Ile aux Coudres, 4.8 mi (8 km) e of ferry dock, follow signs; in la Baleine sector; access by ferry boat. Ext/int corridors. **Pets:** Accepted.
🛜 ⊗ 🍽 🏊 ⊗

JONQUIÈRE

▼▼▼ Holiday Inn Saguenay Convention Centre ⊞
(418) 548-3124. **$123-$137.** 2675 boul du Royaume G7S 5B8. Hwy 70 exit 39, just ne, follow signs. Int corridors. **Pets:** Accepted.
⌂ 🛈 🖭 🍴 ⤚ ⊠

LAC-BROME (KNOWLTON)

▼▼▼ Auberge Knowlton ⒞
(450) 242-6886. **$130-$160.** 286 chemin Knowlton J0E 1V0. Corner of Hwy 104 and Rt 243; centre. Int corridors. **Pets:** Small, dogs only. Designated rooms, service with restrictions, supervision. ⌂ ⊠ 🍴

🅐 ▼▼▼ Auberge Quilliams Inn ⒞
(450) 243-0404. **$159-$350, 3 day notice.** 572 chemin Lakeside J0E 1R0. Hwy 10 exit 90, 3.1 mi (4.9 km) s on Rt 243. Int corridors. **Pets:** Dogs only. $15 deposit/pet. Designated rooms, service with restrictions, supervision. 💲 ⌂ ⊠ 🛈 🖭 🍴 ⤚ ⊠

LA MALBAIE

🅐 ▼▼▼▼ Fairmont Le Manoir Richelieu ⊞ 🐾
(418) 665-3703. **$139-$279.** 181 rue Richelieu G5A 1X7. On Rt 362, 2.6 mi (4.1 km) w of jct Rt 138. Int corridors. **Pets:** Dogs only. $25 daily fee/pet. Service with restrictions, supervision.
🌱 💲 ⌂ 🛈 🖭 🍴 ⤚ ⊠

▼▼▼ ▼▼▼ La Pinsonnière ⒞
(418) 665-4431. **$295-$495, 15 day notice.** 124 rue St-Raphael G5A 1X9. Just off Rt 138, follow signs; in Cap-a-L'Aigle sector. Int corridors. **Pets:** Accepted. ⌂ ⊠ 🖭 🍴 ⤚ ⊠

LA POCATIÈRE

▼▼ Motel Le Pocatois Ⓜ
(418) 856-1688. **$109-$189.** 235 Rt 132 G0R 1Z0. Hwy 20 exit 439, 0.5 mi (0.8 km) s. Ext/int corridors. **Pets:** Small. Designated rooms, service with restrictions, supervision. ⌂ 🛈 🖭 🍴

LOUISEVILLE

▼▼▼ Gite du Carrefour et Maison historique J.L.L. Hamelin ⒝⒝
(819) 228-4932. **$65-$95 (no credit cards), 15 day notice.** 11 ave St-Laurent ouest J5V 1J3. On Rt 138; Hwy 40 exit 174 westbound; exit 166 eastbound; centre. Int corridors. **Pets:** Very small. Supervision.
🐾 🖨 🗧

MONTEBELLO

🅐 ▼▼▼ ▼▼▼ Fairmont Le Château Montebello ⊞ 🐾
(819) 423-6341. **$179-$399, 3 day notice.** 392 rue Notre-Dame J0V 1L0. On Rt 148. Int corridors. **Pets:** $35 daily fee/pet. Service with restrictions, crate. 🌱 💲 ⌂ 🛈 🖭 🍴 ⤚ ⊠

MONT-LAURIER

🅐 ▼▼▼ Best Western Plus Hotel Mont-Laurier ⊞
(819) 623-5252. **Call for rates.** 1231 boul A-Paquette J9L 1M6. On Rt 117; centre. Ext/int corridors. **Pets:** Accepted. 💲 ⌂ 🛈 🖭 ⤚

▼▼ Comfort Inn ⊞
(819) 623-6465. **$114-$129.** 700 boul A-Paquette J9L 1L4. On Hwy 117; centre. Ext/int corridors. **Pets:** Accepted. ⌂ 🛈 🖭 🍴 ⊠

🅐 ▼▼▼ Quality Inn Mont-Laurier ⊞
(819) 623-3555. **Call for rates.** 111 boul A-Paquette J9L 1J2. On Rt 117; centre. Ext/int corridors. **Pets:** Small. $10 daily fee/pet. Supervision. 💲 ⌂ 🛈 🖭 🍴 ⤚ ⊠

MONTMAGNY

▼▼▼ Manoir des Érables 1814 ⒞
(418) 248-0100. **$99-$265, 10 day notice.** 220 boul Tache est (Rt 132) G5V 1G5. Hwy 20 exit 376, 1.4 mi (2.2 km) e on Rt 228, 0.9 mi (1.5 km) e. Ext/int corridors. **Pets:** Accepted. ⌂ ⊠ 🖭 🍴 ⤚ ⊠

MONTRÉAL METROPOLITAN AREA

ANJOU

🅐 ▼▼▼ Quality Hotel East ⊞
(514) 493-6363. **$90-$250.** 8100 ave Neuville H1J 2T2. Hwy 40 exit 78, just n on boul Langelier, 0.4 mi (0.7 km) e on rue Jarry, then s. Int corridors. **Pets:** Accepted. 🌱 💲 ⌂ 🛈 🖭 🍴

BROSSARD

▼▼▼▼ Alt Hotel Quartier Dix 30 ⊞
(450) 443-1030. **Call for rates.** 6500 boul de Rome J4Y 0B6. Jct Hwy 10 and 30, just w on Hwy 30 exit boul de Rome; in Quartier Dix 30 Mall. Int corridors. **Pets:** Accepted. 🌱 ⌂ ⊠ 🛈 🖭

▼▼ Comfort Inn ⊞
(450) 678-9350. **$90-$210.** 7863 boul Taschereau J4Y 1A4. Rt 134, 0.9 mi (1.5 km) w of Hwy 10 exit boul Taschereau ouest. Int corridors. **Pets:** Medium. $25 one-time fee/pet. Designated rooms, service with restrictions, crate. 🌱 ⌂ 🛈 🖭

▼▼ Econo Lodge Montreal - Brossard Ⓜ
(450) 466-2186. **$87-$200.** 8350 boul Taschereau J4X 1C2. Rt 134, 1.4 mi (2.3 km) w of Hwy 10 exit boul Taschereau ouest. Ext/int corridors. **Pets:** Very small. $10 daily fee/pet. Service with restrictions, supervision.
⌂ 🛈 🖭

DORVAL

🅐 ▼▼▼ Aloft Montreal Airport ⊞ 🐾
(514) 633-0900. **$99-$229.** 500 ave McMillan H9P 0A2. Just n of Hwy 520 on north side service road at airport entrance. Int corridors. **Pets:** Medium. Service with restrictions, supervision.
💲 ⌂ ⊠ 🗧 🛈 🖭 ⤚

🅐 ▼▼▼ Comfort Inn Dorval ⊞
(514) 636-3391. **$95-$225.** 340 ave Michel-Jasmin H9P 1C1. Hwy 520 exit 2 eastbound; exit 1 westbound, just e along service road to ave Marshall, follow to ave Michel-Jasmin. Int corridors. **Pets:** Accepted.
🌱 💲 ⌂ 🛈 🖭

🅐 ▼▼▼ Hampton Inn & Suites by Hilton Montreal (Dorval) ⊞
(514) 633-8243. **Call for rates.** 1900 Rt Transcanadienne (Hwy 40) H9P 2N4. Hwy 40 exit 55, 0.5 mi (0.8 km) e of boul des Sources on south side service road. Int corridors. **Pets:** Medium. $50 one-time fee/room. Designated rooms, service with restrictions, supervision.
💲 ⌂ 🗧 🛈 🖭 ⤚

🅐 ▼▼▼ Quality Inn & Suites Aeroport Montreal-Trudeau ⊞
(514) 631-4537. **$80-$143.** 1010 chemin Herron H9S 1B3. Hwy 20 exit 54 westbound, just s on boul Fenelon to ave Dumont, follow to chemin Herron; exit 56 eastbound, 1.1 mi (1.7 km) along service road. Int corridors. **Pets:** Accepted. 🌱 💲 ⌂ 🛈 🖭 ⊠

🅐 ▼▼▼ ▼▼▼ The Sheraton Montreal Airport Hotel ⊞ 🐾
(514) 631-2411. **$169-$249.** 12505 boul Cote-de-Liesse H9P 1B7. Just n of Hwy 520 on north side service road at airport entrance. Int corridors. **Pets:** Medium. $25 one-time fee/pet. Designated rooms, service with restrictions, supervision. 💲 ⌂ ⊠ 🗧 🛈 🖭 🍴 ⊠

LAVAL

Comfort Inn 🅷

(450) 686-0600. **$118-$173.** 2055 Autoroute des Laurentides H7S 1Z6. Hwy 15 exit 8 (boul St-Martin), e on boul St-Martin, 0.4 mi (0.7 km) n on boul Le Corbusier, then just w on boul Tessier. Int corridors. **Pets:** Medium. $10 daily fee/pet. Designated rooms, service with restrictions, supervision.

Econo Lodge 🅷

(450) 681-6411. **Call for rates.** 1981 boul Cure-Labelle H7T 1L4. Hwy 15 exit 8 (boul St-Martin) northbound; exit 10 southbound 1.3 mi (2 km) w on boul St-Martin ouest, then 0.3 mi (0.5 km) n. Ext/int corridors. **Pets:** Small. Designated rooms, service with restrictions, supervision.

Hotel Châteauneuf Laval 🅷

(450) 681-9000. **$100-$199.** 3655 Autoroute des Laurentides H7L 3H7. Hwy 15 exit 10, just n on east side service road. Int corridors. **Pets:** Accepted.

Quality Suites Laval 🅷

(450) 686-6777. **$128-$188.** 2035 Autoroute des Laurentides H7S 1Z6. Hwy 15 exit 8 (boul St-Martin), 0.4 mi (0.7 km) n on boul Le Corbusier, then just w on boul Tessier. Int corridors. **Pets:** Medium. $10 daily fee/pet. Designated rooms, service with restrictions, supervision.

Sheraton Laval Hotel 🅷 ❖

(450) 687-2440. **$129-$269.** 2440 Autoroute des Laurentides H7T 1X5. Hwy 15 exit 10. Int corridors. **Pets:** Medium, dogs only. Designated rooms, service with restrictions, supervision.

MONTRÉAL

Candlewood Suites 🅷 ❖

(514) 667-5002. **$99-$169.** 191 boul Rene-Levesque est H2X 3Z9. Corner of rue Hotel-de-ville. Int corridors. **Pets:** Other species. $50 one-time fee/room. Service with restrictions, crate.

Château Versailles Hotel 🅷 ❖

(514) 933-3611. **$155-$465.** 1659 rue Sherbrooke ouest H3H 1E3. Corner of rue St-Mathieu. Int corridors. **Pets:** Medium, other species. $20 daily fee/pet. Designated rooms, service with restrictions, supervision.

Crowne Plaza Montreal Airport 🅷

(514) 344-1999. **$119-$189.** 6600 Cote-de-Liesse H4T 1E3. Hwy 520 exit 5 eastbound on south side service road; exit westbound to rue Ness, follow signs for rue Hickmore and Hwy 520 E. Int corridors. **Pets:** Large. $35 daily fee/room. Service with restrictions, supervision.

Delta Montreal 🅷

(514) 286-1986. **$145-$322.** 475 ave President-Kennedy H3A 1J7. Corner of rue City Councillors. Int corridors. **Pets:** Accepted.

Embassy Suites Montreal par/by Hilton 🅷

(514) 288-8886. **$149-$579.** 208 rue St-Antoine ouest H2Y 0A6. Corner of rue St-Francois-Xavier. Int corridors. **Pets:** Accepted.

Fairmont The Queen Elizabeth 🅷 ❖

(514) 861-3511. **Call for rates.** 900 boul Rene-Levesque ouest H3B 4A5. Between rue University and Mansfield. Int corridors. **Pets:** Small, other species. $25 daily fee/pet. Service with restrictions, supervision.

Hilton Montréal Bonaventure 🅷 ❖

(514) 878-2332. **$190-$625.** 900 rue de la Gauchetiere ouest H5A 1E4. Corner of Mansfield. Int corridors. **Pets:** Medium. $50 one-time fee/room. Designated rooms, service with restrictions, crate.

Holiday Inn Express Hotel & Suites Montreal Centre-Ville 🅷 ❖

(514) 448-7100. **$107-$300.** 155 boul Rene-Levesque est H2X 3Z8. Corner of rue de Bullion. Int corridors. **Pets:** Other species. $50 one-time fee/room. Service with restrictions, crate.

Holiday Inn Montreal-Midtown 🅷

(514) 842-6111. **$109-$149, 3 day notice.** 420 rue Sherbrooke ouest H3A 1B4. Between rue de Bleury and Aylmer. Int corridors. **Pets:** Medium. $35 one-time fee/room. Service with restrictions, supervision.

Hotel de la Montagne 🅷

(514) 288-5656. **$179-$299.** 1430 rue de la Montagne H3G 1Z5. Between rue Ste-Catherine and boul de Maisonneuve. Int corridors. **Pets:** $35 one-time fee/room. Service with restrictions, supervision.

Hôtel Espresso Montréal Centre-Ville/Downtown 🅷

(514) 938-4611. **$99-$169.** 1005 rue Guy H3H 2K4. Just s of boul Rene-Levesque. Int corridors. **Pets:** Medium. $15 daily fee/pet. Designated rooms, service with restrictions, supervision.

Hotel Gault 🅷 ❖

(514) 904-1616. **$240-$720.** 449 rue Ste-Helene H2Y 2K9. Just s of rue Notre-Dame. Int corridors. **Pets:** Small. $50 daily fee/pet. Service with restrictions, crate.

Hotel Gouverneur Place Dupuis 🅷

(514) 842-4881. **$109-$399.** 1415 rue St-Hubert H2L 3Y9. Between boul de Maisonneuve and rue Ste-Catherine. Int corridors. **Pets:** Accepted.

Hôtel Le Crystal 🅷 ❖

(514) 861-5550. **$209-$2499.** 1100 rue de la Montagne H3G 0A1. Corner of boul Rene-Levesque. Int corridors. **Pets:** Small. $75 one-time fee/pet. Designated rooms, supervision.

Hôtel Le Germain Montréal 🅷

(514) 849-2050. **Call for rates.** 2050 rue Mansfield H3A 1Y9. Corner of ave President-Kennedy. Int corridors. **Pets:** Accepted.

Hotel Le Roberval 🅷

(514) 286-5215. **$90-$169.** 505 boul Rene-Levesque est H2L 5B6. Corner of rue Berri. Int corridors. **Pets:** Accepted.

Hôtel Le St-James 🅷

(514) 841-3111. **$320-$625.** 355 rue St-Jacques ouest H2Y 1N9. Corner of rue St-Pierre. Int corridors. **Pets:** Accepted.

Hôtel Omni Mont-Royal 🅷 ❖

(514) 284-1110. **$179-$279.** 1050 rue Sherbrooke ouest H3A 2R6. Corner of rue Peel. Int corridors. **Pets:** Small, dogs only. $50 one-time fee/room. Designated rooms, service with restrictions, supervision.

Hotel St-Paul 🅷

(514) 380-2222. **Call for rates.** 355 rue McGill H2Y 2E8. Corner of rue St-Paul. Int corridors. **Pets:** Accepted.

Hotel Terrasse Royale 🅷

(514) 739-6391. **Call for rates.** 5225 chemin Cote-des-Neiges H3T 1Y1. Just n of chemin Queen Mary. Int corridors. **Pets:** Accepted.

Hotel Travelodge Montreal Centre 🅷

(514) 874-9090. **$76-$242.** 50 boul Rene-Levesque ouest H2Z 1A2. Between rue Clark and St-Urbain. Int corridors. **Pets:** Medium, other species. $10 daily fee/pet. Designated rooms, service with restrictions, supervision.

Hyatt Regency Montreal H ❖
(514) 982-1234. **$89-$529.** 1255 Jeanne-Mance H5B 1E5. Corner of rue Ste-Catherine. Int corridors. **Pets:** Very small. $35 one-time fee/room. Service with restrictions, supervision.

InterContinental Montréal H
(514) 987-9900. **$159-$289.** 360 rue St-Antoine ouest H2Y 3X4. Corner of rue St-Pierre. Int corridors. **Pets:** Accepted.

L'Appartement Hotel H
(514) 284-3634. **$115-$245.** 455 rue Sherbrooke ouest H3A 1B7. Corner of rue Durocher. Int corridors. **Pets:** Accepted.

Le Centre Sheraton H ❖
(514) 878-2000. **$144-$699.** 1201 boul Rene-Levesque ouest H3B 2L7. Between rue Drummond and rue Stanley. Int corridors. **Pets:** Medium. Service with restrictions, supervision.

Le Meridien Versailles-Montreal H ❖
(514) 933-8111. **$149-$509.** 1808 rue Sherbrooke ouest H3H 1E5. Corner of rue St-Mathieu. Int corridors. **Pets:** Medium, other species. $20 daily fee/pet. Designated rooms, service with restrictions, supervision.

Le Saint-Sulpice Hôtel Montréal H ❖
(514) 288-1000. **$189-$539.** 414 rue St-Sulpice H2Y 2V5. Just n of rue St-Paul. Int corridors. **Pets:** Large. $50 one-time fee/room. Designated rooms, service with restrictions.

Le Square Phillips Hotel & Suites H
(514) 393-1193. **$145-$369.** 1193 Place Phillips H3B 3C9. Between rue Ste-Catherine and boul Rene-Levesque. Int corridors. **Pets:** Accepted.

Le Westin Montréal H
(514) 380-3333. **$159-$329.** 270 rue St-Antoine ouest H2Y 0A3. In Old Montreal. Int corridors. **Pets:** Accepted.

Loews Hôtel Vogue H ❖
(514) 285-5555. **$152-$764.** 1425 de la Montagne H3G 1Z3. Between rue Ste-Catherine and boul de Maisonneuve. Int corridors. **Pets:** Other species. $25 one-time fee/room.

Marriott Residence Inn Montreal Airport H
(514) 336-9333. **$128-$209.** 6500 Place Robert-Joncas H4M 2Z5. Hwy 40 exit 65 (boul Cavendish), 0.3 mi (0.5 km) w on north side service road, then just n on rue Beaulac. Int corridors. **Pets:** Accepted.

Novotel Montreal Airport H ❖
(514) 337-3222. **$129-$329.** 2599 boul Alfred-Nobel H4S 2G1. Hwy 40 exit 60 (boul Alfred-Nobel); in St-Laurent Technoparc, just s of south side service road. Int corridors. **Pets:** Other species. Designated rooms, service with restrictions, supervision.

Novotel Montreal Centre H ❖
(514) 861-6000. **$119-$499.** 1180 rue de la Montagne H3G 1Z1. Between rue Ste-Catherine and boul Rene-Levesque. **Pets:** Small. $25 daily fee/pet. Designated rooms, service with restrictions, supervision.

Opus Hotel Montreal H
(514) 843-6000. **Call for rates.** 10 rue Sherbrooke ouest H2X 4C9. Corner of boul St-Laurent. Int corridors. **Pets:** Accepted.

Quality Hotel Dorval H
(514) 731-7821. **$127-$195.** 7700 Cote-de-Liesse H4T 1E7. Hwy 520 exit 4 eastbound, on south side service road; exit 4 (Montee-de-Liesse) westbound. Int corridors. **Pets:** Small. $25 daily fee/pet. Designated rooms, service with restrictions, supervision.

Quality Hotel Downtown Montreal H
(514) 849-1413. **$89-$365.** 3440 ave du Parc H2X 2H5. Between rue Sherbrooke and Milton. Int corridors. **Pets:** Medium, dogs only. $40 one-time fee/pet. Service with restrictions, crate.

Residence Inn by Marriott
Montreal-Downtown H ❖
(514) 982-6064. **$169-$229.** 2045 rue Peel H3A 1T6. Between rue Sherbrooke and boul de Maisonneuve. Int corridors. **Pets:** Medium. $100 one-time fee/room. Service with restrictions, crate.

Residence Inn by Marriott Montreal
Westmount H
(514) 935-9224. **$179-$199.** 2170 Lincoln Ave H3H 2N5. Just e of rue Atwater. Int corridors. **Pets:** Accepted.

Sofitel Montréal Le Carré Doré H
(514) 285-9000. **$180-$350, 3 day notice.** 1155 rue Sherbrooke ouest H3A 2N3. Corner of rue Stanley. Int corridors. **Pets:** Accepted.

W Montréal H ❖
(514) 395-3100. **$169-$799.** 901 Square Victoria H2Z 1R1. Corner of rue St-Antoine. Int corridors. **Pets:** Medium, other species. $100 one-time fee/room, $25 daily fee/room. Designated rooms, service with restrictions, supervision.

POINTE-CLAIRE

Comfort Inn H
(514) 697-6210. **$85-$135.** 700 boul St-Jean H9R 3K2. Hwy 40 exit 52, just s. Int corridors. **Pets:** $15 one-time fee/room. Service with restrictions, supervision.

Quality Suites Montreal Aeroport,
Pointe-Claire H
(514) 426-5060. **$124-$169.** 6300 Rt Transcanadienne H9R 1B9. Hwy 40 exit 52 eastbound, south side service road; westbound, follow signs for boul St-Jean sud and Hwy 40 est to access south side service road. Int corridors. **Pets:** $25 one-time fee/room. Designated rooms, service with restrictions, supervision.

ST-JÉRÔME

Super 8 St-Jerome H
(450) 438-4388. **$79-$148.** 3 boul J. F. Kennedy J7Y 4B4. Hwy 15 exit 41 southbound, just n; on west side of autoroute. Int corridors. **Pets:** Accepted.

ST-LAURENT

Holiday Inn Montreal-Airport H
(514) 739-3391. **$95-$229, 3 day notice.** 6500 Cote-de-Liesse H4T 1E3. Hwy 520 exit 5 eastbound on south side service road; exit westbound to rue Ness, follow signs for rue Hickmore and Hwy 520 E. Ext/int corridors. **Pets:** $50 one-time fee/room. Designated rooms, service with restrictions, supervision.

Park Inn Hotel & Suites Montreal Airport H
(514) 733-8818. **$79-$249.** 7300 Cote-de-Liesse H4T 1E7. Hwy 520 exit 4 eastbound on south side service road; exit 4 (Montee-de-Liesse) westbound. Int corridors. **Pets:** Accepted.

TERREBONNE

▼▼▼▼ Super 8 Hotel Lachenaie Terrebonne 🄷
(450) 582-8288. **$105-$162.** 1155 ave Yves-Blais J6V 0A9. Hwy 640 exit 50, just s on Montee des Pionniers, then just e; in Lachenaie sector. Int corridors. **Pets:** Medium. $20 daily fee/pet. Service with restrictions, crate.
🄴🄲🄾 ⓢ ✕ ♿ 🖵 🍽 ⌫

VAUDREUIL-DORION

▼▼ Super 8 🄷
(450) 424-8898. **$77-$149.** 3200 boul de la Gare J7V 8W5. Hwy 40 exit 35, just s on ave St-Charles, 0.3 mi (0.4 km) w on boul de la Cite-des-Jeunes, then just w. Int corridors. **Pets:** Accepted.
🄴🄲🄾 ⓢ ✕ ♿ 🖵 ⌫

END METROPOLITAN AREA

MONT-TREMBLANT

🄰 ▼▼▼▼ Fairmont Tremblant 🄷 ✿
(819) 681-7000. **$169-$599, 7 day notice.** 3045 chemin de la Chapelle J8E 1E1. In Mont-Tremblant Resort Centre. Int corridors. **Pets:** Medium, dogs only. $25 daily fee/pet. Service with restrictions, supervision.
🄴🄲🄾 🅂🄰🅅🄴 ♿ 🖵 🍽 ⌫ ✕

🄰 ▼▼▼▼ Le Grand Lodge Mont-Tremblant 🄷
(819) 425-2734. **$134-$384, 8 day notice.** 2396 rue Labelle J8E 1T8. On Rt 327, 0.3 mi (0.4 km) s of Montee Ryan. Int corridors.
Pets: Accepted. 🅂🄰🅅🄴 ⓢ ✕ ♿ 🖵 🍽 ⌫ ✕

🄰 ▼▼▼▼ Le Westin Resort & Spa, Tremblant 🄷
(819) 681-8000. **$199-$559.** 100 chemin Kandahar J8E 1E2. Hwy 117 N exit 119 (Montee Ryan), 6 mi (10 km) e, follow signs. Int corridors.
Pets: Accepted. 🅂🄰🅅🄴 ⓢ ✕ ♿ 🖵 🍽 ⌫ ✕

ORFORD

▼▼▼ Hotel Cheribourg 🄷
(819) 843-3308. **$130-$260.** 2603 chemin du Parc J1X 8C8. Hwy 10 exit 118, 1.9 mi (3 km) n on Hwy 141. Ext/int corridors. **Pets:** Accepted.
ⓢ ✕ ♿ 🖵 🍽 ⌫ ✕

PERCÉ

▼ Au Pic de l'Aurore 🄲🄰
(418) 782-2151. **$65-$245, 3 day notice.** 1 Rt 132 G0C 2L0. 1.2 mi (2 km) e from village. Ext corridors. **Pets:** Medium, dogs only. $25 one-time fee/pet. Designated rooms, service with restrictions, supervision.
ⓢ ✕ ♿ 🖵

▼▼▼ Hotel La Normandie 🄷
(418) 782-2112. **$79-$259.** 221 Rt 132 ouest G0C 2L0. Centre. Int corridors. **Pets:** Small. $30 one-time fee/room. Designated rooms, service with restrictions, supervision. ⓢ ✕ ♿ 🖵 🍽 🄺

▼▼▼ Hotel/Motel Le Mirage 🄼
(418) 782-5151. **$82-$198.** 288 Rt 132 ouest G0C 2L0. On Rt 132. Ext corridors. **Pets:** Accepted. ⓢ ♿ 🍽 ⌫

▼▼ Hotel Motel Manoir de Percé 🄷
(418) 782-2022. **$68-$178.** 212 Rt 132 G0C 2L0. Centre. Ext/int corridors. **Pets:** Small. $25 one-time fee/room. Service with restrictions, supervision. ⓢ ✕ ♿ 🍽

QUÉBEC METROPOLITAN AREA

BOISCHATEL

🄰 ▼▼ Econo Lodge Montmorency 🄷
(418) 822-4777. **$75-$145.** 5490 boul Ste-Anne G0A 1H0. On Hwy 138. Int corridors. **Pets:** Medium. $15 daily fee/pet. Designated rooms, service with restrictions, supervision. 🅂🄰🅅🄴 ⓢ ✕ ♿

L'ANCIENNE-LORETTE

▼▼ Comfort Inn 🄷
(418) 872-5900. **$80-$120.** 1255 boul Duplessis G2G 2B4. Jct boul Duplessis and Wilfrid-Hamel (Hwy 138). Int corridors. **Pets:** Other species. $25 one-time fee/room. Service with restrictions. 🄴🄲🄾 ⓢ ♿ 🖵

LÉVIS

🄰 ▼▼ Comfort Inn 🄷
(418) 835-5605. **$85-$145.** 10 du Vallon est G6V 9J3. Hwy 20 exit 325S eastbound; exit 325 westbound. Int corridors. **Pets:** Accepted.
🄴🄲🄾 🅂🄰🅅🄴 ⓢ ♿ 🖵

▼▼▼ Comfort Inn & Suites Rive-Sud Quebec 🄷
(418) 836-3336. **Call for rates.** 495 Rte-du-Pont G7A 2N9. Hwy 20 exit 311, just ne on Rt 116; in St-Nicolas sector. Int corridors. **Pets:** Small, other species. $25 one-time fee/room. Designated rooms, service with restrictions, supervision. 🅂🄰🅅🄴 ⓢ ✕ ♿ 🖵

▼▼ Hotel Kennedy 🄷
(418) 837-0233. **$90-$190.** 129 Rte du President-Kennedy G6V 6C8. Hwy 20 exit 325N, just n. Ext/int corridors. **Pets:** Accepted.
ⓢ ♿ 🖵

QUÉBEC

▼▼▼▼ ALT Hotel-Quebec 🄷
(418) 658-1224. **Call for rates.** 1200 ave Germain-des-Pres G1V 3M7. Just n of boul Laurier; facing Place Laurier mall. Int corridors.
Pets: Accepted. ⓢ ✕ 🍽

▼▼ Appartements La Pergola 🄲🄾
(418) 681-1428. **Call for rates.** 405 boul Rene-Levesque ouest G1S 1S2. Between aves Moncton and des Erables. Int corridors.
Pets: Accepted. ⓢ ✕ ♿ 🖵

🄰 ▼▼▼▼ Best Western Plus City Centre/Centre-Ville 🄷 ✿
(418) 649-1919. **$130-$410.** 330 rue de la Couronne G1K 6E6. Corner of rue du Roi. Int corridors. **Pets:** $15 daily fee/pet. Service with restrictions, supervision. 🅂🄰🅅🄴 ⓢ ✕ ♿ 🖵 🍽 ⌫

🄰 ▼▼▼▼ Château Bonne Entente 🄷 ✿
(418) 653-5221. **$159-$499.** 3400 chemin Ste-Foy G1X 1S6. Hwy 540 (Autoroute Duplessis) exit chemin Ste-Foy, just w. Int corridors.
Pets: Other species. $35 one-time fee/room. Service with restrictions, crate. 🅂🄰🅅🄴 ⓢ ✕ ♿ 🖵 🍽 ⌫ ✕

▼▼ Comfort Inn Beauport 🄷
(418) 666-1226. **$86-$145.** 3390 boul Ste-Anne G1E 3L7. Hwy 440 exit Francois-de-Laval. Int corridors. **Pets:** Accepted. 🄴🄲🄾 ⓢ ♿ 🖵

🄰 ▼▼ Comfort Inn de l'Aeroport-Hamel 🄷
(418) 872-5038. **$86-$220.** 7320 boul Wilfrid-Hamel G2G 1C1. Hwy 138, 0.9 mi (1.5 km) w of boul Duplessis. Int corridors. **Pets:** Other species. $25 one-time fee/pet. Service with restrictions, supervision.
🄴🄲🄾 🅂🄰🅅🄴 ⓢ ♿ 🖵

🄰 ▼▼ Delta Quebec 🄷
(418) 647-1717. **$110-$299.** 690 boul Rene-Levesque est G1R 5A8. Just w of boul Honore-Mercier. Int corridors. **Pets:** Accepted.
🄴🄲🄾 🅂🄰🅅🄴 ⓢ ♿ 🖵 🍽 ⌫ ✕

CAA ◆◆◆◆ **Fairmont Le Château Frontenac** H
(418) 692-3861. **$179-$459.** 1 rue des Carrieres G1R 4P5. In Old Quebec. Int corridors. **Pets:** Accepted.
ECO SAVE 📶 ▣ 💻 🍴 🏊 🏋

CAA ◆◆◆◆ **Hilton Québec** H 🐾
(418) 647-2411. **$139-$299.** 1100 boul Rene-Levesque est G1R 4P3. Corner of ave Honore-Mercier. Int corridors. **Pets:** Other species. $25 one-time fee/pet. Supervision. ECO SAVE 📶 ▣ 💻 🍴 🏊 🏋

◆◆◆ **Hotel Champlain Vieux-Quebec** H
(418) 694-0106. **$119-$279.** 115 rue Ste-Anne G1R 3X6. Between rue Ste-Angele and St-Stanislas. Int corridors. **Pets:** Accepted.
📶 🚭 ▣

CAA ◆◆◆ **Hotel Clarion Quebec** H 🐾
(418) 653-4901. **$99-$229.** 3125 boul Hochelaga G1V 4A8. Hwy 73 exit 136 (Hochelaga ouest). Int corridors. **Pets:** Other species. Designated rooms, supervision. SAVE 📶 ▣ 💻 🍴 🏊 🏋

◆◆◆ **Hotel Dauphin Quebec City** H 🐾
(418) 688-3888. **$85-$152.** 400 rue du Marais G1M 3R1. Hwy 40 exit 312S (Pierre-Bertrand sud), just w of Rt 358. Int corridors. **Pets:** $15 daily fee/room. Designated rooms, service with restrictions, supervision.
ECO 📶 🚭 ♿M ▣ 💻

◆◆◆◆ **Hotel Le Germain Dominion** H
(418) 692-2224. **$209-$415.** 126 rue St-Pierre G1K 4A8. Corner of rue St-Paul. Int corridors. **Pets:** Accepted. 📶 🚭 💻

CAA ◆◆◆ **Hotel Pur** H
(418) 647-2611. **Call for rates.** 395 rue de la Couronne G1K 7X4. Corner of rue St-Joseph est. Int corridors. **Pets:** Accepted.
SAVE 📶 ♿M ▣ 💻 🍴 🏊 🏋

CAA ◆◆ **Hotel Quality Suites Quebec** H 🐾
(418) 622-4244. **$115-$195.** 1600 rue Bouvier G2K 1N8. Hwy 40 exit 312N (Pierre-Bertrand nord), 1.3 mi (2 km) w of jct Rt 358. Int corridors. **Pets:** Other species. $25 one-time fee/pet. Designated rooms, service with restrictions, supervision. ECO SAVE 📶 ▣ 💻

◆◆◆ **Hotel Super 8 Quebec Ste-Foy** H
(418) 877-6888. **$72-$159.** 7286 boul Wilfred Hamel G2G 1C1. Hwy 138, 0.7 mi (1.1 km) w of boul Duplessis. Int corridors. **Pets:** Accepted.
ECO 📶 ▣ 💻 🏊 🏋

CAA ◆◆◆ **L'Hotel du Vieux Quebec** H
(418) 692-1850. **$104-$328.** 1190 rue St-Jean G1R 1S6. Corner of rue de l'Hotel-Dieu. Int corridors. **Pets:** Accepted.
ECO SAVE 📶 ▣ 💻 🍴

CAA ◆◆◆◆ **Loews Hôtel Le Concorde** H 🐾
(418) 647-2222. **$129-$299.** 1225 Cours du General-de-Montcalm G1R 4W6. Corner of Grande Allee est. Int corridors. **Pets:** Other species. $25 one-time fee/room. Supervision.
ECO SAVE 📶 🚭 ▣ 💻 🍴 🏊 🏋

CAA ◆◆◆◆ **Relais & Chateaux Auberge Saint-Antoine** H
(418) 692-2211. **$169-$1500, 3 day notice.** 8 rue St-Antoine G1K 4C9. Corner of rue Dalhousie. Int corridors. **Pets:** Medium, dogs only. $150 one-time fee/room. Service with restrictions, crate.
SAVE 📶 🚭 ▣ 💻 🍴 🏋

ST-FERRÉOL-LES-NEIGES

◆◆ **Chalets Montmorency Condominiums Mont-Sainte-Anne Quebec** CO
(418) 826-2600. **$89-$159, 30 day notice.** 1768 ave Royale G0A 3R0. On Hwy 360. Ext corridors. **Pets:** Accepted.
📶 🚭 ▣ 💻 🏊 🏋

STE-ANNE-DE-BEAUPRÉ

CAA ◆◆ **Quality Suites Mont Sainte-Anne** H
(418) 827-1570. **Call for rates.** 9800 boul Ste-Anne G0A 3C0. On Hwy 138. Int corridors. **Pets:** Very small. $20 daily fee/pet. Designated rooms, service with restrictions, supervision. SAVE 📶 🚭 ▣ 💻

END METROPOLITAN AREA

RIGAUD

◆◆ **Howard Johnson** H
(450) 458-7779. **$62-$170.** 93 Montee Lavigne (Rt 201) J0P 1P0. Hwy 40 exit 17, just ne. Int corridors. **Pets:** Accepted.
📶 🚭 ▣ 💻 🍴

RIMOUSKI

◆◆ **Comfort Inn** H
(418) 724-2500. **$115-$125.** 455 boul St-Germain ouest G5L 3P2. On Rt 132. Int corridors. **Pets:** $25 one-time fee/pet. Service with restrictions, supervision. ECO 📶 ▣ 💻

CAA ◆◆ **Hotel Gouverneur Rimouski** H
(418) 723-4422. **$85-$149.** 155 boul Rene-Lepage E G5L 1P2. On Rt 132. Int corridors. **Pets:** Small, dogs only. $25 one-time fee/room. Designated rooms, supervision. SAVE 📶 ▣ 💻 🍴 🏊

RIVIÈRE-DU-LOUP

◆◆ **Comfort Inn** H
(418) 867-4162. **$93-$170.** 85 boul Cartier G5R 4X4. Hwy 20 exit 507, just se; Hwy 85 exit 96 (Fraserville), follow signs. Int corridors. **Pets:** Accepted. ECO 📶 ▣ 💻

◆◆ **Days Inn Riviere-du-Loup** H
(418) 862-6354. **Call for rates.** 182 rue Fraser G5R 1C8. Hwy 20 exit 503, 0.6 mi (1 km) e on Rt 132. Ext/int corridors. **Pets:** Accepted.
ECO 📶 ▣ 💻 🏊

ROUYN-NORANDA

CAA ◆◆◆ **Best Western Plus Albert Centre-Ville** H
(819) 762-3545. **$115-$125.** 84 Ave Principale J9X 4P2. Centre. Int corridors. **Pets:** Medium, other species. $25 daily fee/pet. Service with restrictions, crate. SAVE 📶 🚭 ▣ 💻 🍴 🏋

◆◆ **Comfort Inn** H
(819) 797-1313. **$88-$135.** 1295 ave Lariviere J9X 6M6. On Rt 117, 2.5 mi (4 km) s from town centre. Int corridors. **Pets:** Accepted.
ECO 📶 ▣ 💻

◆◆◆ **Hotel Gouverneur le Noranda** H
(819) 762-2341. **$105-$125.** 41 6ieme rue J9X 1Y8. Corner of rue Murdoch; centre. Ext/int corridors. **Pets:** Small, other species. $20 daily fee/room. Designated rooms, service with restrictions, supervision.
📶 🚭 ▣ 💻 🍴 🏋

ST-ANTOINE-DE-TILLY

◆◆◆ **Manoir De Tilly** CI
(418) 886-2407. **$115-$230, 3 day notice.** 3854 chemin de Tilly G0S 2C0. Jct Hwy 20 exit 291, 5.3 mi (8.5 km) n on Rt 273; centre. Int corridors. **Pets:** Accepted. 📶 🚭 🍴

ST-FAUSTIN-LAC-CARRÉ

◆ **Motel Tremblant sur la Colline** M 🐾
(819) 688-2102. **$79-$109, 7 day notice.** 357 Rt 117 J0T 1J2. On Rt 117, 2.5 mi (4 km) n of exit for city. Ext/int corridors. **Pets:** Other species. $20 daily fee/pet. Designated rooms, service with restrictions, supervision.
📶 ▣ 💻 🏊

ST-HYACINTHE

▼▼▼▼ Holiday Inn Express & Suites **H**
(450) 251-1111. **Call for rates.** 1500 rue Johnson est J2S 8W5. Hwy 20 exit 133, just sw on boul Casavant est. Int corridors. **Pets:** Accepted.
🛜 ✖ 🛏 💻 🏊

(AA) ▼▼▼▼ Hotel des Seigneurs Saint-Hyacinthe **H** ✿
(450) 774-3810. **$120-$240.** 1200 rue Johnson J2S 7K7. Hwy 20 exit 130S, just e on rue Gauvin from boul Laframboise. Int corridors. **Pets:** $25 one-time fee/pet. Service with restrictions, crate.
ECO SAVE 🛜 ✖ ♿ 🛏 💻 🍴 🏊 ✖

ST-JEAN-PORT-JOLI

▼▼ Auberge Du Faubourg **M**
(418) 598-6455. **$80-$275, 10 day notice.** 280 ave de Gaspe ouest (Rt 132) G0R 3G0. 1.4 mi (2.4 km) w on Rt 132 from jct Rt 204; Hwy 20 exit 414. Ext corridors. **Pets:** $15 daily fee/pet. Supervision.
🛜 ✖ 🛏 💻 🍴 🏊 🖋

ST-JEAN-SUR-RICHELIEU

▼▼▼ Holiday Inn Express **H**
(450) 359-4466. **$109-$199.** 700 rue Gadbois J3A 1V1. Hwy 35 exit 45, e on rue Pierre-Caisse. Int corridors. **Pets:** Medium, other species. Designated rooms, service with restrictions, supervision.
🛜 ✖ ♿ 🛏 💻 🏊

STE-AGATHE-DES-MONTS

▼▼ Super 8 Ste-Agathe
(819) 324-8880. **$83-$144.** 500 rue Leonard J8C 0A3. Hwy 15 exit 86, just w on Rt 117 to rue Leonard, then 0.3 mi (0.5 km) s. Int corridors. **Pets:** Accepted. ECO 🛜 🛏 💻 🏊 ✖

STE-EULALIE

▼▼ Motel Marie-Dan **M**
(819) 225-4604. **$50-$85.** 311 rue des Bouleaux (Rt 161) G0Z 1E0. Hwy 20 exit 210, follow signs to Rt 161, then just s. Ext corridors. **Pets:** Very small. $10 one-time fee/pet. Service with restrictions, supervision.
🛜 🛏 🏊

STE-MARTHE

▼▼▼ Auberge des Gallant **CI**
(450) 459-4241. **$125-$250, 7 day notice.** 1171 chemin St-Henri J0P 1W0. From Hwy 201, 5.3 mi (8.5 km) w. Int corridors. **Pets:** Large, other species. $50 one-time fee/pet. Designated rooms, service with restrictions.
🛜 ✖ 💻 🍴 🏊 ✖

SEPT-ÎLES

▼▼ Hotel Gouverneur Sept-Iles **H**
(418) 962-7071. **$109-$169.** 666 boul Laure G4R 1X9. On Rt 138. Int corridors. **Pets:** $30 one-time fee/pet. Designated rooms, service with restrictions, crate. 🛜 🛏 💻 🍴 🏊

SHAWINIGAN

▼▼ Auberge Escapade Inn **H**
(819) 539-6911. **Call for rates.** 3383 rue Garnier G9N 6R4. Hwy 55 exit 217, 0.3 mi (0.5 km) n on Rt 351. Ext/int corridors. **Pets:** Accepted.
🛜 ✖ 🛏 🍴

▼▼▼ Comfort Inn & Suites **H**
(819) 536-2000. **$81-$144.** 500 boul du Capitaine G9P 5J6. Hwy 55 N exit 211, 2.8 mi (4.4 km) n on Hwy 153, then 1.3 mi (2 km) s on Rt 157. Int corridors. **Pets:** Small. $25 daily fee/room. Designated rooms, no service, supervision. ECO 🛜 🛏 💻

SHERBROOKE

▼▼▼ Comfort Inn **H**
(819) 564-4400. **$98-$125.** 4295 boul Bourque J1N 1S4. Hwy 410 exit 4 W, 0.9 mi (1.5 km) w on Rt 112. Ext/int corridors. **Pets:** Accepted.
ECO 🛜 🛏 💻

▼▼▼ Delta Sherbrooke Hotel and Conference Centre **H**
(819) 822-1989. **$104-$279.** 2685 rue King ouest J1L 1C1. Hwy 410 exit 4 W, 0.6 mi (1 km) e on Rt 112. Int corridors. **Pets:** Accepted.
ECO 🛜 ✖ 🛏 💻 🍴 🏊 ✖

THETFORD MINES

▼▼ Comfort Inn **H**
(418) 338-0171. **$126-$132.** 123 boul Frontenac ouest G6G 7S7. On Rt 112. Int corridors. **Pets:** Accepted. ECO 🛜 🛏 💻

TROIS-RIVIÈRES

▼▼ Comfort Inn **H**
(819) 371-3566. **$101-$121.** 6255 rue Corbeil G8Z 4P9. Hwy 55 exit 183 (boul Jean XXIII); 1.3 mi (2 km) n of Laviolette Bridge, then 0.3 mi (0.5 km) e. Int corridors. **Pets:** Accepted. ECO 🛜 🛏 💻

(AA) ▼▼ Days Inn **H**
(819) 377-4444. **$80-$135.** 3155 boul St-Jean G9B 2M4. Hwy 55 exit 183 (boul Jean XXIII), 0.3 mi (0.5 km) w, then 0.3 mi (0.4 km) n. Int corridors. **Pets:** $10 daily fee/room. Service with restrictions, crate.
ECO SAVE 🛜 🛏 💻

(AA) ▼▼▼ Delta Trois-Rivieres Hotel and Conference Center **H**
(819) 376-1991. **$114-$275, 3 day notice.** 1620 rue Notre-Dame Centre G9A 6E5. Corner of rue St-Roch; centre. Int corridors. **Pets:** Accepted.
ECO SAVE 🛜 ✖ 🛏 💻 🍴 🏊 ✖

▼▼▼ Super 8 Trois-Rivieres **H**
(819) 377-5881. **$82-$163.** 3185 boul St-Jean G9B 2M4. Hwy 55 exit 183 (boul Jean XXIII), just nw. Int corridors. **Pets:** Accepted.
ECO 🛜 ✖ 🛏 💻 🏊 ✖

VAL-D'OR

▼▼ Comfort Inn **H**
(819) 825-9360. **$115-$145.** 1665 3ieme Ave J9P 1V9. In town centre. Int corridors. **Pets:** Accepted. ECO 🛜 🛏 💻

▼▼ L'Escale Hotel Motel Suite **H**
(819) 824-2711. **$125-$140.** 1100 rue L'Escale J9P 4G8. In town centre. Ext/int corridors. **Pets:** Large. No service, supervision.
🛜 ✖ 🛏 💻 🍴

WAKEFIELD

▼▼▼ Auberge Le Moulin Wakefield Mill Inn & Spa **CI**
(819) 459-1838. **Call for rates.** 60 chemin Mill J0X 3G0. 0.6 mi (1 km) w of Riverside Dr; centre. Int corridors. **Pets:** Accepted.
ECO 🛜 ✖ 💻 🍴 ✖

SASKATCHEWAN

ESTEVAN

ⒶⒶ ▼▼ Motel 6 Estevan 🅷

(306) 634-8666. **$106-$125.** 88 King St E S4A 2A4. Hwy 39, 1 mi (1.7 km) n at Kensington Ave, then just e. Int corridors. **Pets:** Other species. Service with restrictions, supervision. [SAVE] 🛜 🛃M 🖶

KINDERSLEY

▼▼ Nova Inn 🅷

(306) 463-4687. **Call for rates.** 100 12th Ave NW S0L 1S0. Jct of Hwy 7 and 21. Ext/int corridors. **Pets:** Accepted. 🛜 🖶 🖵 🍽

LANGENBURG

▼ Langenburg Country Inn Ⓜ

(306) 743-2638. **Call for rates.** 1041 Kaiser William Ave E S0A 2A0. Hwy 16, 0.6 mi (1 km) e. Ext corridors. **Pets:** Accepted. 🛜 🖶 🖵

MOOSE JAW

▼▼ Comfort Inn 🅷

(306) 692-2100. **$108-$122.** 155 Thatcher Dr W S6J 1M1. 0.8 mi (1.2 km) s on Hwy 2 from jct Trans-Canada Hwy 1, then just w. Int corridors. **Pets:** Other species. $15 one-time fee/room. Designated rooms, service with restrictions, crate. 🛜 🖶 🖵

▼▼ Heritage Inn Moose Jaw 🅷 🐾

(306) 693-7550. **$125-$258.** 1590 Main St N S6J 1L3. On Hwy 2, 0.9 mi (1.4 km) s of jct Trans-Canada Hwy 1. Int corridors. **Pets:** Medium, dogs only. $20 daily fee/pet. Designated rooms, service with restrictions, crate. 🛜 ✕ 🖶 🖵 🍽 ⇌

▼ Prairie Oasis Motel 🅷

(306) 692-4894. **$89-$99.** 955 Thatcher Dr E S6H 4N9. Just s of jct Trans-Canada Hwy 1. Ext corridors. **Pets:** Dogs only. Designated rooms, service with restrictions. 🛜 🖶 🖵 ⇌ ✕

▼▼ Super 8-Moose Jaw 🅷

(306) 692-8888. **$103-$121.** 1706 Main St N S6J 1L4. On Hwy 2, 0.7 mi (1.1 km) s of jct Trans-Canada Hwy 1. Int corridors. **Pets:** Other species. $15 daily fee/room. Designated rooms, service with restrictions, crate. [ECO] 🛜 🖶 🖵

NORTH BATTLEFORD

▼▼ Super 8 🅷

(306) 446-8888. **$86-$113.** 1006 Hwy 16 Bypass S9A 3W2. 0.3 mi (0.5 km) nw of jct Hwy 16. Int corridors. **Pets:** Other species. $25 one-time fee/room. Designated rooms, service with restrictions, supervision. 🛜 🖶 🖵

▼▼ Tropical Inn 🅷

(306) 446-4700. **Call for rates.** 1001 Hwy 16 Bypass S9A 3W2. Corner of Battleford Rd. Int corridors. **Pets:** Accepted. 🛜 🖶 🖵 🍽 ⇌ ✕

PRINCE ALBERT

ⒶⒶ ▼▼ Best Western Marquis Inn & Suites 🅷 🐾

(306) 922-9595. **$100-$110.** 602 36th St E S6V 7P2. Jct Hwy 3 (6th Ave E) and Marquis Rd. Int corridors. **Pets:** Other species. Designated rooms, service with restrictions, supervision. [SAVE] 🛜 🖶 🖵 🍽

▼▼ Comfort Inn 🅷

(306) 763-4466. **$115-$135.** 3863 2nd Ave W S6W 1A1. 1.6 mi (2.6 km) s on Hwy 2. Int corridors. **Pets:** Accepted. [ECO] 🛜 🖶 🖵

▼▼ Ramada Prince Albert 🅷

(306) 922-1333. **$108-$199.** 3245 2nd Ave W S6V 5G1. 1.2 mi (2 km) s on Hwy 2. Int corridors. **Pets:** Accepted. 🛜 🖶 🖵 🍽

▼▼ Super 8 🅷

(306) 953-0088. **$89-$98.** 4444 2nd Ave W S6V 5R7. 1.7 mi (2.7 km) s on Hwy 2. Int corridors. **Pets:** Accepted. 🛜 ✕ 🖶 🖵

▼▼ Travelodge Prince Albert 🅷

(306) 764-6441. **$87-$133.** 3551 2nd Ave W S6V 5G1. 1.4 mi (2.2 km) s on Hwy 2. Int corridors. **Pets:** Service with restrictions, supervision. [ECO] 🛜 🖶 🖵 🍽

REGINA

ⒶⒶ ▼▼▼ Best Western Seven Oaks Inn 🅷

(306) 757-0121. **$145.** 777 Albert St S4R 2P6. On Hwy 6; jct 2nd Ave. Int corridors. **Pets:** $10 one-time fee/pet. Designated rooms, no service, supervision. [SAVE] 🛜 ✕ 🛃M 🖶 🖵 🍽 ⇌ ✕

ⒶⒶ ▼▼ Chateau Regina Hotel & Suites 🅷 🌼

(306) 565-0455. **$119-$149.** 1110 Victoria Ave E S4N 7A9. On Trans-Canada Hwy 1, just w of Ring Rd; at eastern approach to city. Int corridors. **Pets:** $25 one-time fee/pet. Designated rooms, service with restrictions, crate. [SAVE] 🛜 🖶 🖵 ⇌

ⒶⒶ ▼▼ Comfort Inn 🅷

(306) 789-5522. **$129-$135.** 3221 E Eastgate Dr S4Z 1A4. Trans-Canada Hwy 1, 1.3 mi (2 km) e of Ring Rd; at eastern approach to city. Int corridors. **Pets:** Accepted. [ECO] [SAVE] 🛜 🖶 🖵

▼▼ Country Inn & Suites By Carlson 🅷 🌼

(306) 789-9117. **$115-$199, 3 day notice.** 3321 Eastgate Bay S4Z 1A4. Trans-Canada Hwy 1, 1.3 mi (2 km) e of Ring Rd; at eastern approach to city. Int corridors. **Pets:** Medium, other species. $100 deposit/room, $25 one-time fee/room. Service with restrictions, crate. [ECO] 🛜 ✕ 🖶 🖵

▼▼▼ Delta Regina 🅷

(306) 525-5255. **$165-$230.** 1919 Saskatchewan Dr S4P 4H2. At Rose St; centre. Int corridors. **Pets:** Accepted. [ECO] 🛜 🖶 🖵 🍽 ⇌ ✕

▼▼▼ Holiday Inn Express Hotel & Suites Regina 🅷

(306) 569-4600. **Call for rates.** 1907 11th Ave S4P 0J2. Corner of Rose St; centre. Int corridors. **Pets:** Accepted. 🛜 🛃M 🖶 🖵

ⒶⒶ ▼▼ Quality Hotel 🅷

(306) 569-4656. **$119-$159.** 1717 Victoria Ave S4P 0P9. Just e of Broad St; downtown. Int corridors. **Pets:** Accepted. [ECO] [SAVE] 🛜 🖶 🖵 🍽

ⒶⒶ ▼▼▼ Radisson Plaza Hotel Saskatchewan 🅷

(306) 522-7691. **$183-$290.** 2125 Victoria Ave S4P 0S3. At Scarth St; centre. Int corridors. **Pets:** $50 one-time fee/room. Service with restrictions, supervision. [ECO] [SAVE] 🛜 ✕ 🖶 🖵 🍽 ✕

▼▼ Ramada Hotel & Convention Centre 🅷

(306) 569-1666. **$104-$163.** 1818 Victoria Ave S4P 0R1. At Broad St; centre. Int corridors. **Pets:** Accepted. [ECO] 🛜 🖶 🖵 🍽 ⇌ ✕

♦♦♦♦ Regina Inn Hotel & Conference Centre 🅷

(306) 525-6767. **$135-$210.** 1975 Broad St S4P 1Y2. Jct Victoria Ave; centre. Int corridors. **Pets:** Other species. $45 one-time fee/room. Service with restrictions, crate. 🅴🅲🅾 ⓢⓐⓥⓔ ▯ 🖵 ⑪ 🎿

♦♦♦ Sandman Hotel Suites & Spa Regina 🅷

(306) 757-2444. **$145-$220.** 1800 Victoria Ave E S4N 7K3. On Trans-Canada Hwy 1, just e of Ring Rd; at eastern approach to city. Int corridors. **Pets:** Medium. $15 daily fee/pet. Designated rooms, service with restrictions, supervision. 🅴🅲🅾 ⓢ ⓧ ▯ 🖵 ⑪ 🏊 🎿

♦♦ Super 8 Regina 🅷

(306) 789-8833. **$103-$112.** 2730 Victoria Ave E S4N 6M5. On Trans-Canada Hwy 1, 1 mi (1.6 km) e of Ring Rd; at eastern approach to city. Int corridors. **Pets:** Accepted. ⓢ ▯ 🖵

♦♦ West Harvest Inn 🅷

(306) 586-6755. **$116-$119.** 4025 Albert St S S4S 3R6. On Hwy 6, 1.3 mi (2 km) n of jct Trans-Canada Hwy 1. Int corridors. **Pets:** $25 daily fee/room. Designated rooms. ⓢⓐⓥⓔ ⓢ ⓧ ▯ 🖵 ⑪

♦♦♦ Wingate by Wyndham 🅷

(306) 584-7400. **$109-$169.** 1700 Broad St S4P 1X4. Corner of Saskatchewan Dr; centre. Int corridors. **Pets:** Accepted.
🅴🅲🅾 ⓢ ⓜ ▯ 🖵

SASKATOON

♦♦♦ Best Western Harvest Inn 🅷 🐾

(306) 244-5552. **$140-$152.** 1715 Idylwyld Dr N S7L 1B4. On Hwy 11 (Idylwyld Dr), 0.4 mi (0.7 km) s of jct Circle Dr. Int corridors. **Pets:** Medium, dogs only. $50 deposit/room, $15 one-time fee/room, $10 daily fee/room. Designated rooms, service with restrictions, supervision.
🅴🅲🅾 ⓢⓐⓥⓔ ⓢ ⓧ ⓜ ▯ 🖵 ⑪

♦♦♦ Best Western Plus Blairmore 🅷 🐾

(306) 242-2299. **Call for rates.** 306 Shillington Crescent S7M 1L7. Jct Hwy 7 and 14. Int corridors. **Pets:** Other species. $30 one-time fee/room. Designated rooms. ⓢⓐⓥⓔ ⓢ ⓧ ▯ 🖵 🏊 🎿

♦♦♦ Colonial Square Inn & Suites 🅷

(306) 343-1676. **$109-$149.** 1301 8th St E S7H 0S7. 1.5 mi (2.4 km) e of jct Hwy 11 (Idylwyld Dr); 1.4 mi (2.3 km) w of jct Circle Dr. Int corridors. **Pets:** Accepted. ⓢⓐⓥⓔ ⓢ ⓧ ▯ 🖵

♦♦♦ Comfort Inn 🅷

(306) 934-1122. **$125-$150.** 2155 Northridge Dr S7L 6X6. Just ne of jct Hwy 11 (Idylwyld Dr) and Circle Dr. Int corridors. **Pets:** Accepted.
🅴🅲🅾 ⓢⓐⓥⓔ ⓢ ⓜ ▯ 🖵

♦♦ Country Inn & Suites By Carlson 🅷

(306) 934-3900. **$120-$160.** 617 Cynthia St S7L 6B7. Just w on Circle Dr from jct Hwy 11 (Idylwyld Dr), then just n on Ave CN. Int corridors. **Pets:** Accepted. 🅴🅲🅾 ⓢ ⓧ ▯ 🖵

♦♦♦♦ Delta Bessborough 🅷

(306) 244-5521. **$132-$349.** 601 Spadina Crescent E S7K 3G8. At 21st St E; centre. Int corridors. **Pets:** Accepted.
🅴🅲🅾 ⓢ ▯ 🖵 ⑪ 🏊 🎿

♦♦♦ Holiday Inn Express Hotel & Suites 🅷

(306) 384-8844. **$144-$189.** 315 Idylwyld Dr N S7L 0Z1. On Hwy 11 (Idylwyld Dr), just n of 23rd St. Int corridors. **Pets:** Accepted.
🅴🅲🅾 ⓢ ⓧ ⓜ ▯ 🖵

♦♦ Motel 6 Saskatoon 🅷

(306) 665-6688. **$106-$148.** 231 Marquis Dr S7R 1B7. E of jct Trans-Canada Hwy 16; 0.4 mi (0.7 km) w of Hwy 11 (Idylwyld Dr). Int corridors. **Pets:** Other species. Service with restrictions, supervision.
ⓢ ⓧ ⓜ ▯ 🖵 🎿

♦♦♦ Radisson Hotel Saskatoon 🅷

(306) 665-3322. **$159-$249, 3 day notice.** 405 20th St E S7K 6X6. At 4th Ave S; centre. Int corridors. **Pets:** Accepted.
🅴🅲🅾 ⓢⓐⓥⓔ ⓢ ⓧ ⓜ ▯ 🖵 ⑪ 🏊 🎿

♦♦♦ Sandman Hotel 🅷

(306) 477-4844. **Call for rates.** 310 Circle Dr W S7L 2Y5. Just w of Hwy 11 (Idylwyld Dr). Int corridors. **Pets:** Accepted.
🅴🅲🅾 ⓢ ⓧ ⓜ ▯ 🖵 ⑪ 🎿

♦♦♦ Saskatoon Inn Hotel and Conference Centre 🅷

(306) 242-1440. **$139-$199.** 2002 Airport Dr S7L 6M4. Jct Hwy 16 (Circle Dr) and 11 (Idylwyld Dr N), 0.6 mi (1 km) sw, then just nw. Int corridors. **Pets:** Accepted. 🅴🅲🅾 ⓢⓐⓥⓔ ⓢ ▯ 🖵 ⑪ 🎿

♦♦♦♦ Sheraton Cavalier Saskatoon Hotel 🅷

(306) 652-6770. **$149-$289.** 612 Spadina Crescent E S7K 3G9. At 21st St E; centre. Int corridors. **Pets:** Accepted.
🅴🅲🅾 ⓢⓐⓥⓔ ⓢ ⓧ ▯ 🖵 ⑪ 🏊 🎿

SWIFT CURRENT

♦♦ Comfort Inn 🅷

(306) 778-3994. **$122-$139.** 1510 S Service Rd E S9H 3X6. On south side service road of Trans-Canada Hwy 1, just w of 22nd Ave NE. Int corridors. **Pets:** Accepted. 🅴🅲🅾 ⓢ ▯ 🖵

♦♦ Super 8 🅷

(306) 778-6088. **$100-$191.** 405 N Service Rd E S9H 3X6. Trans-Canada Hwy 1, just e of Central Ave N; on north side of Service Rd. Int corridors. **Pets:** Accepted. 🅴🅲🅾 ⓢ ▯ 🖵 🎿

UNITY

♦♦♦ Prairie Moon Inn & Suites 🅷

(306) 228-3333. **Call for rates.** 103 2nd Ave S S0K 4L0. Hwy 14, west end of town. Int corridors. **Pets:** Small. $10 daily fee/pet. Designated rooms, crate. ⓢ ⓧ ▯ 🖵

WEYBURN

♦♦♦ Canalta Hotel 🅷

(306) 842-8000. **Call for rates.** 1360 Sims Ave S4H 3N9. On Hwy 39, just w of Hwy 35. Ext/int corridors. **Pets:** Accepted.
🅴🅲🅾 ⓢ ⓧ ⓜ ▯ 🖵 🎿

♦♦♦ Perfect Inns & Suites 🅼

(306) 842-2691. **$95-$250.** 238 Sims Ave S4H 2J8. 0.3 mi (0.5 km) w of jct Hwy 35 and 39. Ext/int corridors. **Pets:** Accepted.
ⓢⓐⓥⓔ ⓢ ▯ 🖵

♦♦♦ Ramada Inn & Suites 🅷

(306) 842-4994. **$130-$150.** 1420 Sims Ave S4H 3N9. On Hwy 39, just w of Hwy 35. Ext/int corridors. **Pets:** Accepted.
🅴🅲🅾 ⓢ ⓧ ▯ 🖵 🎿

YORKTON

♦♦ Ramada Yorkton 🅷

(306) 783-9781. **$109-$159.** 100 Broadway St E S3N 0K9. On Hwy 9, 10, and 16 (Yellowhead Hwy); downtown. Int corridors. **Pets:** Accepted.
ⓢ ▯ 🖵 ⑪ 🎿

YUKON

DAWSON CITY

◆ Bonanza Gold Motel M
(867) 993-6789. **$89-$189.** Bonanza Creek Rd Y0B 1G0. 1.5 mi (2.4 km) s on Hwy 2. Ext corridors. **Pets:** Other species. $20 one-time fee/room. Designated rooms, service with restrictions, supervision.
🛜 ⊠ 🖥 💻 🍽

◆◆ Klondike Kate's Cabins CA
(867) 993-6527. **$145-$195.** 1102 3rd Ave Y0B 1G0. Corner of 3rd Ave and King St. Ext corridors. **Pets:** Large, other species. $25 one-time fee/room. Service with restrictions. 🛜 ⊠ ⚒ 🖥 💻 🍽

CAA ◆◆ Westmark Inn Dawson City M
(867) 993-5542. **$144-$189.** 5th Ave & Harper St Y0B 1G0. At 5th Ave and Harper St; downtown. Ext/int corridors. **Pets:** Accepted.
SAVE 🛜 ⊠ 🖥 💻 🍽

HAINES JUNCTION

◆◆ Alcan Motor Inn M
(867) 634-2371. **Call for rates.** Alaska & Haines Hwys Y0B 1L0. Jct Hwy 1 (Alaska Hwy) and 3 (Haines Hwy). Ext corridors. **Pets:** Accepted.
🛜 ⊠ 🖥 💻 🍽

TESLIN

CAA ◆ Dawson Peaks Resort and RV Park CA 🐾
(867) 390-2244. **$89-$159.** KM 1232 Alaska Hwy Y0A 1B0. 7 mi (10 km) se. Ext corridors. **Pets:** Dogs only. $10 daily fee/pet. Designated rooms, service with restrictions, supervision.
SAVE 🛜 ⊠ 🖥 💻 🍽 ⊠ AC Z

WHITEHORSE

CAA ◆◆◆ Best Western Gold Rush Inn H
(867) 668-4500. **$140-$170.** 411 Main St Y1A 2B6. Centre. Int corridors. **Pets:** Accepted. ECO SAVE 🛜 ⊠ 🖥 💻

CAA ◆◆ High Country Inn H 🐾
(867) 667-4471. **$130-$170, 3 day notice.** 4051 4th Ave Y1A 1H1. 0.4 mi (0.6 km) e of Main St. Int corridors. **Pets:** $15 daily fee/room. Designated rooms, service with restrictions, crate.
ECO SAVE 🛜 ⊠ 🖥 💻 🍽

CAA ◆◆◆ Westmark Whitehorse Hotel & Conference Center H
(867) 393-9700. **$159-$179.** 201 Wood St Y1A 2E4. At 2nd Ave; centre. Int corridors. **Pets:** Designated rooms, service with restrictions, supervision. SAVE 🛜 ⊠ ⚒ 🖥 💻 🍽 AC

Pet-Friendly Campgrounds

United States
Canada

United States

Camping information provided by Woodall's®

Alabama

ELBERTA — LAKE OSPREY RV COUNTRY CLUB. (251) 986-3800. **$40-$45.** 12096 B Cty Rd 95 36530. From jct Hwy 59 & Hwy 98: Go 8-1/4 mi E on Hwy 98, then 2-1/2 mi S on CR 95.
🏕️ 🚐 ✂️ ♿M

FAIRHOPE — COASTAL HAVEN RV PARK. (251) 990-9011. **$25. (no credit cards).** 10151 County Road 32 36532. From jct I-10 (exit 38) & Hwy 181/27: Go 12 mi S on Hwy 181/27, then 1/8 mi W on Hwy 32. 🏕️

GULF SHORES — BELLA TERRA OF GULF SHORES. (866) 880-9522. **$35-$55.** 101 Via Bella Terra 36535. From jct Hwy 59 and Foley Beach Express: Go 9 mi SE on Foley Beach Express, then 1/4 mi W on Brinks Willis Rd. 🏕️ ✂️ ♿M

GULF SHORES — GULF BREEZE RESORT. (251) 968-8884. **$32.** 19800 Oak Road West 36542. From jct US 98 & Hwy 59: Go 6-1/2 mi S on Hwy 59, then 300 yards on CR 6. 🏕️ 🚐 ✂️ ♿M

GULF SHORES — LUXURY RV RESORT. (800) 982-3510. **$36.** 590 Gulf Shores Pkwy 36542. From jct US 98 & Hwy 59: Go 9 mi S on Hwy 59. 🏕️ 🚐 ✂️ ♿M

LANGSTON — LITTLE MOUNTAIN MARINA CAMPING RESORT. (256) 582-8211. **$30.** 1001 Murphy Hill Rd. 35755. From jct US 431 & Hwy 227: Go 12 mi S on Hwy 227 (Hwy 227 turns N), then 1/2 mi N on S Sauty Rd (Hwy 227 goes E at S Sauty Rd) 1/4 mi on Murphy Hill Rd. 🚐 ✂️ ♿M

MONTGOMERY — CAPITAL CITY RV PARK. (877) 271-8026. **$30.** 4655 Old Wetumpka Hwy 36110. From jct I-85 (exit 6) & US Hwy 231 East Blvd: Go 4 mi NW on East Blvd; or from jct I-65 (exit 173) & Hwy 152: Go 6-1/4 mi NE on Hwy 152, then 2-1/2 mi N on US Hwy 231, then 1 blk E on Old Wetumpka Hwy. 🏕️ ✂️ ♿M

ORANGE BEACH — HERITAGE MOTORCOACH & MARINA. (800) 730-7032. **$50-$90.** 28888 Canal Road 36561. From jct Hwy 182 & Hwy 161: Go 1-1/2 mi N on Hwy 161, then 3 mi E on Canal Road. 🏕️ 🚐 ✂️ ♿M

OZARK — OZARK TRAVEL PARK. 🅰️🅰️🅰️ (800) 359-3218. **$33.** 2414 N US Highway 231 36360. From jct Hwy 27 & US Hwy 231: Go 3 mi N on US Hwy 231 (mile marker 47-east side). 🚐 ✂️

PELHAM — BIRMINGHAM SOUTH CAMPGROUND. (205) 664-8832. **$38-$41.** 222 Hwy 33 35124. From jct I-65 (exit 242) & Hwy 52: Go 700 yards W on Hwy 52, then 300 yards N on Hwy 33. 🚐 ✂️ ♿M

TROY — DEER RUN RV PARK. (800) 552-3036. **$29.** 25629 US Hwy 231 36081. From jct US 29 & Hwy 231: Go 6-1/2 mi N on US 231 (between mile marker 83 & 84), at Cty Rd 1124. 🅂🄴 🏕️ 🚐 ✂️ ♿M

Alaska

HAINES — HAINES HITCH-UP RV PARK. (907) 766-2882. **$33-$45.** 851 Main St 99827. From jct Alaska Marine Hwy Ferry Terminal & Lutak Rd: Go 2-3/4 mi S on Lutak Rd, then 4 blks S on 2nd Ave, then 1/2 mi W on Main St. 🏕️ ♿M

Arizona

APACHE JUNCTION — LA HACIENDA RV RESORT. (480) 982-2808. **$40.** 1797 W 28th Ave 85120. From jct Fwy 202 Loop & US 60 (Superstition Fwy): Go 5 mi E on US 60 (exit 195/Ironwood), then 200 yds N on Ironwood Dr. 🏕️ 🚐 ✂️ ♿M

APACHE JUNCTION — SHIPROCK RV RESORT ARIZONA. (480) 505-1300. **$35.** 1700 W Shiprock St 85120. From jct Fwy 202 Loop & US 60 (Superstition Fwy): Go 5 mi E on US 60 (exit 195/ Ironwood Dr), then 2-3/4 mi N on Ironwood Dr, then 300 ft W on Shiprock St. 🏕️ 🚐 ✂️ ♿M

APACHE JUNCTION — SUNRISE RV RESORT. (877) 633-3133. **$39. (no credit cards).** 1403 W Broadway 85120. From jct Fwy 202 Loop & US 60 (Superstition Fwy): Go 5 mi E on US 60 (exit 195/ Ironwood Dr), then 1-1/2 mi N on Ironwood, then 500 ft E on Broadway. 🏕️ 🚐 ♿M

APACHE JUNCTION — SUPERSTITION LOOKOUT RV RESORT. (480) 982-2008. **$35.** 1371 E 4th Ave 85119. From jct Fwy 202 Loop & US 60 (Superstition Fwy): Go 7 mi E on US 60 (exit 197/ Tomahawk), then 1-3/4 mi N on Tomahawk, then 600 ft W on 4th Ave. 🏕️ 🚐 ✂️ ♿M

APACHE JUNCTION — SUPERSTITION SUNRISE RV RESORT. (800) 624-7027. **$50. (no credit cards).** 702 S Meridian Rd 85120. From jct Fwy 202 Loop & US 60 (Superstition Fwy): Go 3 mi E on US 60 (exit 193/Signal Butte Rd), then 1/2 mi N on Signal Butte Rd, then 1 mi E on Southern, then 1 mi N on Meridian. 🏕️ 🚐 ✂️ ♿M

APACHE JUNCTION — WEAVER'S NEEDLE TRAVEL TRAILER RESORT. (480) 982-3683. **$36.** 250 S Tomahawk Rd 85119. From jct Fwy 202 Loop & US 60 (Superstition Fwy): Go 7 mi E on US 60 (exit 197/Tomahawk Rd), then 2 mi N on Tomahawk Rd. 🏕️ 🚐 ✂️ ♿M

BENSON — BUTTERFIELD RV RESORT. 🅰️🅰️🅰️ (800) 863-8160. **$36.** 251 S Ocotillo Ave 85602. From jct Hwy 90 & I-10: Go 2 mi E on I-10 (exit 304) Ocotillo Rd, then 3/4 mi S on Ocotillo Rd. 🏕️ 🚐 ✂️ ♿M

BENSON — COCHISE TERRACE RV RESORT. (520) 720-0911. **$30.** 1030 S Barrel Cactus Ridge 85602. From jct I-10 (exit 302) & Hwy 90: Go 3/4 mi S on Hwy 90. 🏕️ 🚐 ✂️ ♿M

CAMP VERDE — DISTANT DRUMS RV RESORT. (877) 577-5507. **$25-$39.** 583 W. Middle Verde Rd. 86322. From jct of Hwy 260 & I-17: Go 2-1/2 mi N on I-17 to (exit 289), then 1/4 mi W on Middle Verde Rd. 🏕️ 🚐 ✂️ ♿M

CASA GRANDE — **PALM CREEK GOLF & RV RESORT.** (800) 421-7004. **$30-$54.** 1110 N. Henness Rd. 85122. From jct I-8 & I-10: Go 5 mi NW on I-10 (exit 194) Hwy 287, then 1/2 mi W on Hwy 287/ Florence Blvd. 🅰 ➤ 🆇 ⴺM

EL MIRAGE — **PUEBLO EL MIRAGE RV RESORT & COUN-TRY CLUB.** (800) 445-4115. **$45.** 11201 N El Mirage Rd 85335. From jct I-10 (exit 129) & Dysart Rd: Go 7-1/2 mi N on Dysart Rd, then 1 mi E on Olive, then 1 1/2 mi N on El Mirage Rd. 🅰 ➤ 🆇 ⴺM

FLAGSTAFF — **J AND H RV PARK.** (928) 526-1829. **$44.** 7901 N US Highway 89 86004. From jct I-17 & I-40: Go 6 mi E on I-40 (exit 201), then 3/4 mi N on road to US 89, then 3 mi NE on US 89. 🅰 🆇

GOLD CANYON — **CANYON VISTAS RV RESORT.** (480) 288-8844. **$39.** 6601 E US Hwy 60 85218. From jct US 88 & US 60: Go 6-1/2 mi E on US 60. 🅰 ➤ 🆇 ⴺM

GOLD CANYON — **GOLD CANYON RV & GOLF RESORT.** (480) 982-5800. **$45.** 7151 E US Highway 60 85118. From jct Fwy 202 Loop & US 60 (Superstition Fwy): Go 12-1/2 mi SE on US 60. 🅰 ➤ 🆇 ⴺM

LAKE HAVASU CITY — **HAVASU RV RESORT.** (928) 764-2020. **$50.** 1905 Victoria Farms Rd 86404. From jct I-40 (exit 9) & Hwy 95: Go S 14-1/10 mi on Hwy 95 toward Lake Havasu City, then E 2/10 mi on Chenoweth Rd, then N 4/10 mi on Victoria Farms Rd. 🅰 ➤ 🆇 ⴺM

LAKE HAVASU CITY — **ISLANDER RV RESORT.** (928) 680-2000. **$44-$89.** 751 Beachcomber Blvd 86403. From jct I-40 (exit 9) & Hwy 95: Go 19-1/4 mi S on Hwy 95, then 1 block E on Mesquite Ave, then 1 block S on Lake Havasu Ave, then 2 mi W on McCulloch Blvd/ Beachcomber Blvd to entrance. 🅰 ➤ 🆇 ⴺM

MESA — **APACHE WELLS RV RESORT.** ⒶⒶⒶ (888) 940-8989. **$55.** 2656 N 56th St 85215. From jct Loop 101 & US 60 (Superstition Fwy): Go 10 mi E on US 60 to exit 186/Higley Rd, then 5-1/2 mi N on Higley Rd, then 1/2 mi E on McDowell Rd, then 200 feet S on 56th St. 🅰 ➤ ⴺM

MESA — **GOOD LIFE RV RESORT.** (888) 940-8989. **$50.** 3403 E Main St 85213. From Loop 101 & US 60 (Superstition Fwy): Go 8 mi E on US 60 to (exit 184/Val Vista Dr), then 2 mi N on Val Vista Dr, then 1/4 mi W on Main. 🅰 ➤ 🆇 ⴺM

MESA — **MESA REGAL RV RESORT.** (888) 940-8989. **$39.** 4700 E Main St 85205. From jct Loop 101 & US 60 (Superstition Fwy): Go 9 mi E on US 60 to (exit 185/Greenfield Rd), then 2 mi N on Green-field Rd, then 1/4 mi E on Main St. 🅰 ➤ 🆇 ⴺM

MESA — **MESA SPIRIT RV RESORT.** ⒶⒶⒶ (877) 924-6709. **$29-$58.** 3020 E Main St 85213. From jct Loop 101 & US 60 (Superstition Fwy): Go 6 mi E on US 60 to (exit 182/Gilbert Rd), then 2 mi N on Gilbert Rd, then 1-1/4 mi E on Main St. 🅰 ➤ 🆇 ⴺM

MESA — **MONTE VISTA VILLAGE RESORT.** (800) 435-7128. **$48.** 8865 E Baseline Road 85209. From jct Loop 101 & US 60 (Superstition Fwy): Go 15 mi E on US 60 to (exit 191/Ellsworth Rd), then 1/2 mi S on Ellsworth Rd, then 1/4 mi W on Baseline Rd. 🅰 ➤ 🆇 ⴺM

MESA — **PALM GARDENS MHC & RV PARK.** (480) 832-0290. **$35. (no credit cards).** 2929 E. Main St 85213. From jct Loop 101 & US 60 (Superstition Fwy): Go 6 mi E on US 60 to (exit 182/Gilbert Rd), then 2 mi N on Gilbert Rd, then 1-1/4 mi E on Main St. 🅰 ➤ ⴺM

MESA — **SILVERIDGE RV RESORT.** (480) 373-7000. **$50.** 8265 E Southern 85209. From jct Loop 101 & US 60 (Superstition Fwy): Go 13-1/4 mi E on US 60 (exit 189/Sossaman), then 1/2 mi N on Sos-saman Rd, then 1 mi E on Southern. 🅰 ➤ 🆇 ⴺM

MESA — **SUN LIFE RV RESORT.** (888) 940-8989. **$45.** 5055 E University Dr 85205. From jct Loop 101 & US 60 (Superstition Fwy): Go 10 mi E on US 60 to (exit 186/Higley Rd), then 2-1/2 mi N on Hig-ley Rd, then 100 yards W on University Dr. 🅰 ➤ 🆇 ⴺM

MESA — **THE RESORT.** (480) 986-8404. **$50.** 1101 S Ellsworth Rd 85208. From jct Loop 101& US 60 (Superstition Fwy): Go 15-1/4 mi E on US 60 (exit 191/Ellsworth Rd), then 1/2 mi N on Ellsworth Rd. 🅰 ➤ 🆇 ⴺM

MESA — **TOWERPOINT RESORT.** ⒶⒶⒶ (888) 940-8989. **$40-$45.** 4860 E. Main St 85205. From jct Loop 101 & US 60 (Superstition Fwy): Go 9 mi E on US 60 to (exit 185/Greenfield Rd), then 2 mi N on Greenfield Rd, then 1/4 mi E on Main St. 🅰 ➤ 🆇 ⴺM

MESA — **VALLE DEL ORO RV RESORT.** (480) 984-1146. **$45.** 1452 S. Ellsworth 85209. From jct Loop 101 & US 60 (Superstition Fwy): Go 15-1/4 mi E on US 60 to (exit 191/Ellsworth), then 200 yards N on Ellsworth Rd. 🅰 ➤ 🆇 ⴺM

MESA — **VAL VISTA VILLAGE RV RESORT.** (888) 940-8989. **$39-$75.** 233 N Val Vista Dr. 85213. From jct Loop 101 & US 60 (Superstition Fwy): Go 8 mi E on US 60 to (exit 184/Val Vista Dr), then 2-1/2 mi N on Val Vista Dr. 🅰 ➤ 🆇 ⴺM

MESA — **VIEW POINT RV AND GOLF RESORT.** (800) 822-4404. **$59.** 8700 E. University 85207. From jct Loop 101 & US 60 (Super-stition Fwy): Go 15 mi E on US 60 to exit 191/Ellsworth Rd, then 2-1/2 mi N on Ellsworth Rd, then 3/4 mi W on University. 🅰 ➤ 🆇 ⴺM

PEORIA — **PLEASANT HARBOR RV RESORT.** (800) 475-3272. **$32-$39.** 8708 W Harbor Blvd 85383. From jct I-17 (exit 223) & Hwy 74 (Carefree Hwy): Go 8 mi W on Hwy 74, then 1-3/4 mi N on Pleas-ant Harbor Blvd. ➤ 🆇 ⴺM

SUN CITY — **PARADISE RV RESORT.** ⒶⒶⒶ (877) 362-6736. **$45.** 10950 W Union Hills Dr 85373. From jct I-17 (exit 215) & W Loop 101 (Aqua Fria Fwy): Go 7 mi W on Loop 101 (Exit 15), then 3 1/2 mi W on Union Hills Dr. 🅰 ➤ 🆇 ⴺM

SURPRISE — **SUNFLOWER RESORT.** (888) 940-8989. **$55.** 16501 El Mirage Rd 85374. From jct I-17 (exit 215 W) & Loop 101: Go 8 mi W on Loop 101 (exit 14), then 5-1/2 mi W on Bell Rd, then 1/4 mi S on El Mirage Rd. 🅰 ➤ 🆇 ⴺM

TEMPE — **APACHE PALMS RV PARK.** ⒶⒶⒶ (480) 966-7399. **$36-$40.** 1836 E Apache Blvd 85281. From jct I-10 (exit 147A) & Fwy 202 Loop (Red Mountain Fwy): Go 8 mi E on Fwy 202 Loop (exit 8), then 1 mi S on McClintock Dr, then 1/2 mi E on University, then 1/2 mi S on Smith, then 1/4 mi W on Apache Blvd. 🅰 ➤

TUCSON — **DESERT PUEBLO.** (520) 889-9557. **$26. (no credit cards).** 1302 W Ajo Way 85713. From jct I-10 & I-19: Go 1-1/2 mi S on I-19 to (exit 99/Ajo Way), then 1/4 mi W on Ajo Way. 🏕️ ➡️ ⊠ ♿M

TUCSON — **FAR HORIZONS TUCSON VILLAGE RV RESORT.** (800) 480-3488. **$27-$47.** 555 N Pantano Rd 85710. From jct I-19 & I-10: Go 10 mi E on I-10 (exit 270) Kolb Rd, then 8 mi N on Kolb Rd, 1 mi E on Broadway, then 1/2 mi N on Pantano Rd, W 50 feet at 5th. 🏕️ ➡️ ⊠ ♿M

TUCSON — **RINCON COUNTRY EAST.** (888) 401-8989. **$38-$40.** 8989 E Escalante Rd 85730. From jct I-19 & I-10: Go 9-1/2 mi SE on I-10, exit 270, then 4-3/4 mi N on Kolb Rd, then 2 mi E on Escalante Rd. 🏕️ ➡️ ⊠ ♿M

TUCSON — **RINCON COUNTRY WEST.** (800) 782-7275. **$40-$46.** 4555 S Mission Rd 85746. From jct of I-10 & I-19: Go 1-1/2 mi S on I-19 (exit 99) Ajo Way, then 1 mi W on Ajo Way, then 1/2 mi S on Mission Rd. 🏕️ ➡️ ⊠ ♿M

TUCSON — **VOYAGER RV RESORT.** ⍉ (800) 424-9191. **$25-$53.** 8701 S Kolb 85756. From jct I-19 & I-10: Go 10-1/4 mi E on I-10 (exit 270), then 1/2 mi S on Kolb Rd. 🏕️ ➡️ ⊠ ♿M

TUCSON — **WESTERN WAY RV RESORT.** (800) 292-8616. **$46.** 3100 S Kinney Rd 85713. From jct I-10 & I-19: Go 1-1/4 mi S on I-19 (exit Hwy 86) Ajo Way, then 5 mi W on Ajo Way, then 1-1/2 mi N on Kinney Rd. Turn W on Western Way for 200 feet. 🏕️ ➡️ ♿M

WILLIAMS — **GRAND CANYON RAILWAY RV PARK.** (800) 843-8724. **$42.** 601 W Franklin Ave 86046. From I-40 & (exit 163) Williams/Grand Canyon: Go 1/2 mi S on Grand Canyon Blvd, then 1/4 mile W. on W. Franklin Ave. (to RV Park Registration Bldg.) (Ent on L) 🏕️ ➡️ ⊠ ♿M

YUMA — **ARABY ACRES RV RESORT.** (800) 833-6046. **$46.** 6649 E 32nd St. 85365. From jct US 95 & I-8: Go 5 mi E on I-8 (exit 7) & Araby Rd, then 1/2 mi S on Araby Rd, then 1/4 mi E on 32nd St/Hwy 80. 🏕️ ➡️ ⊠ ♿M

YUMA — **COCOPAH RV & GOLF RESORT.** (800) 537-7901. **$46.** 6800 Strand Ave. 85364. From jct I-8 (exit Winterhaven/4th Ave) & 4th Ave: Go 1/2 mi S on 4th Ave, then 2-1/2 mi W on 1st St, then 3 blocks S on Ave C, then 2 mi W on Riverside Drive, then 1 mi N on Strand Ave. 🏕️ ➡️ ⊠ ♿M

YUMA — **DEL PUEBLO RV PARK AND TENNIS RESORT.** (928) 341-2100. **$45.** 14794 S Avenue 3 E 85365. From jct US 95 & I-8: Go 1 mi E on I-8 (exit 3) Ave 3E, then 5-1/4 mi S on Ave 3E. 🏕️ ➡️ ⊠ ♿M

YUMA — **SHANGRI-LA RV RESORT.** (928) 342-9123. **$33-$43.** 10498 N Frontage Rd 85365. From jct US 95 & I-8: Go 10 mi E on I-8 (exit 12) & Fortuna Rd, then 100 ft N on Fortuna Rd, then 1/2 mi W on North Frontage Rd. 🏕️ ➡️ ♿M

YUMA — **SUN VISTA RV RESORT.** ⍉ (800) 423-8382. **$46.** 7201 E 32nd St 85365. From jct US 95 & I-8: Go 7 mi E on I-8 (exit 9) & 32nd St/Hwy 80, then 1 mi W on 32nd St. 🏕️ ➡️ ⊠ ♿M

YUMA — **VILLA ALAMEDA RV RESORT.** (928) 344-8081. **$33. (no credit cards).** 3547 S Avenue 5 E 85365. From jct US 95 & I-8: Go 5 mi E on I-8 (exit 7), Araby Rd, then 1/2 mi S on Araby Rd, then 1-1/2 mi W on 32nd St (Hwy 80), then 1/2 mi S on Ave 5E. 🏕️ ➡️ ⊠ ♿M

YUMA — **WESTWIND RV & GOLF RESORT.** ⍉ (928) 342-2992. **$50.** 9797 E 32nd St 85365. From jct US 95 & I-8: Go 10 mi E on I-8 (exit 12) & Fortuna Rd, then 1 mi W on South Frontage Rd. 🏕️ ➡️ ⊠ ♿M

Arkansas

CAVE SPRINGS — **THE CREEKS RV RESORT.** (479) 248-1000. **$35.** 1499 S Main St 72718. From jct I-540 & W Monroe Ave/Hwy 264 (exit 78): Go 4-3/4 mi W on Hwy 264, then 1 mi S on AR 112. 🏕️ ⊠

HOT SPRINGS — **CATHERINE'S LANDING AT HOT SPRINGS.** ⍉ (501) 262-2550. **$39-$49.** 1700 Shady Grove Rd 71901. From jct US 270/70 & Hwy 128 (exit 7): Go 1/2 mi SW on Hwy 128, then 1-3/4 Mi E on Shady Grove Rd. 🏕️ ➡️ ⊠ ♿M

HOT SPRINGS — **CLOUD NINE RV PARK.** (501) 262-1996. **$28.** 136 Cloud Nine Dr 71901. From jct Hwy 7 & US 70B: Go 12 mi E on US 70B/US70. ⊠ ♿M

HOT SPRINGS — **HOT SPRINGS NATIONAL PARK - KOA.** (501) 624-5912. **$33-$70.** 838 McClendon Rd 71901. E'bnd from jct Hwy 7 & US 70B (Grand Ave): Go 3 mi E on US 70B (exit 4), then 100 yds N under overpass, then 200 yds E on Service Rd. Enter on L. W'bnd: From jct US 70 & US 70B: Go 1-1/4 mi W on US 70B (exit 4), then 3/4 mi W on Service Rd. Enter on R. ➡️ ⊠ ♿M

OAK GROVE — **OUTDOOR RESORTS OF THE OZARKS.** (888) 749-7396. **$55.** 1229 CR 663 72660. From jct US 62 & Hwy 311 (in Green Forest): Go 16 mi N on Hwy 311, then 1-1/2 mi E on CR 663. 🏕️ ➡️ ⊠ ♿M

RUSSELLVILLE — **IVY'S COVE RV RETREAT.** (479) 280-1662. **$29-$31.** 321 Bradley Cove Rd 72802. From jct I-40 (exit 84) & Hwy 331: Go 1/2 mi NE on Hwy 331/Bradley Cove Rd. 🆂 ⊠ ♿M

California

AGUANGA — **OUTDOOR RESORTS RANCHO CALIFORNIA RV RESORT.** (888) 767-0848. **$65.** 45525 Hwy 795 92536. From jct Hwy 371 & Hwy 79S: Go 1/4 mi E on Hwy 79S. 🏕️ ➡️ ⊠ ♿M

ANAHEIM — **ANAHEIM RESORT RV PARK.** ⍉ (714) 774-3860. **$50-$70.** 200 W. Midway Dr 92805. From jct Hwy 57 & I-5: Go 2 mi N on I-5, then 1/4 mi W on Katella Ave, then 1/2 mi N on Anaheim Blvd, then 100 yards W on Midway Dr. ➡️ ♿M

ARCATA — **MAD RIVER RAPIDS RV PARK.** ⍉ (800) 822-7776. **$38-$43.** 3501 Janes Rd 95521. From jct Hwy 299 & US 101: Go 1/4 mi N on US 101 (Janes Rd & Guintoli Lane exit), then 1/4 mi W on Janes Rd. 🏕️ ➡️ ⊠ ♿M

BAKERSFIELD — **BAKERSFIELD RIVER RUN RV PARK.** ⍉ (888) 748-7786. **$35-$59.** 3715 Burr St 93308. From jct Hwy 99 & Hwy 58 (Rosedale Hwy): Go 1/2 mi W on Hwy 58 (Rosedale Hwy), then 1/2 mi S on Gibson Street, then 1/2 mi E on Burr St. 🏕️ ➡️ ♿M

BAKERSFIELD — **BAKERSFIELD RV RESORT.** (661) 833-9998. **$35-$50.** 5025 Wibel Rd 93313. N'bnd: From jct US 99 & Panama Ln (exit): Go 1/4 mi W on Panama Ln, then 3/4 mi N on Wible Rd. S'bnd: From jct US 99 & White Ln (exit): Go 1 blk W on White Ln, then 3/4 mi S on Wible Rd. 🏕 🚐 🍴 ♿

BIG BEAR LAKE — **BIG BEAR SHORES RV RESORT & MARINA.** (909) 866-4151. **$60-$150.** 40751 N Shore Ln 92333. From west end Big Bear Lake Hwy 18 (Dam): Go E 5 mi on SR 38 to North Shore Ln, then SE 1/10 mi. 🏕 🚐 🍴 ♿

BORREGO SPRINGS — **THE SPRINGS AT BORREGO RV RESORT & GOLF COURSE.** (866) 330-0003. **$39-$69.** 2255 DiGiorgio Rd 92004. From the center of town: Go 1/4 mi E on Palm Canyon Dr, then 1/4 mi N on DiGiorgio Rd. 🏕 🚐 🍴 ♿

BUELLTON — **FLYING FLAGS RV PARK & CAMPGROUND.** 🄰🄰🄰 (877) 783-5247. **$22-$98.** 180 Ave of the Flags 93427. From jct US-101 & Hwy-246: Go 1/4 mi W on Hwy-246, then 2 blocks S on Avenue of the Flags. 🚐 🍴 ♿

CATHEDRAL CITY — **OUTDOOR RESORT PALM SPRINGS RV RESORT & COUNTRY CLUB.** (800) 843-3131. **$45-$77.** 69-411 Ramon Rd 92234. From jct Hwy 74 & I-10: Go 4-3/4 mi W on I-10, then 2 mi S on Date Palm Dr, then 1/2 mi E on Ramon Rd. 🏕 🚐 🍴 ♿

CHOWCHILLA — **THE LAKES RV & GOLF RESORT.** (866) 665-6980. **$40-$50.** 5001 E Robertson 93610. From jct Hwy 99 & Robertson Blvd (Avenue 26) Go E on Robertson Blvd 1-1/2 mi Park Entrance on the right 300 ft. past entrance to Pheasant Run Golf Club. 🏕 🚐 🍴 ♿

CHULA VISTA — **CHULA VISTA RV RESORT & MARINA.** 🄰🄰🄰 (800) 770-2878. **$50-$77.** 460 Sandpiper Way 91910. From jct I-8 & I-5: Go 10 mi S on I-5, then 1 block W on J St, then 1/4 mi N on Marina Pkwy, then 1 block W on Sandpiper Way. 🆂🄳 🏕 🚐 🍴 ♿

CHULA VISTA — **KOA-SAN DIEGO METROPOLITAN.** (619) 427-3601. **$43-$89.** 111 N 2nd Ave 91910. From jct I-5 & E St (CRS-17): Go 1-1/4 mi E on E St, then 1 mi N on 2nd Ave. 🚐 🍴 ♿

DESERT HOT SPRINGS — **SANDS RV RESORT & GOLF.** (800) 772-7808. **$38-$46.** 16400 Bubbling Wells Rd 92240. From jct Hwy 62 & I-10: Go 6 mi E on I-10, then 3 mi N on Palm Dr, then 1 mi on Dillon Rd, then 1/4 mi N on Bubbling Wells Rd. 🏕 🚐 🍴 ♿

EL CENTRO — **DESERT TRAILS RV PARK & GOLF COURSE.** (760) 352-7275. **$37-$45.** 225 Wake Ave 92243. From jct I-8 & Hwy 86 (4th St exit): Go 1 block S on 4th St, then 1 block E on Wake Ave. 🚐 🍴 ♿

EL CENTRO — **RIO BEND RV GOLF RESORT.** (760) 352-7061. **$45-$70.** 1589 Drew Rd 92243. From jct Hwy 86 & I-8: Go 7-3/4 mi W on I-8, then 1/2 mi S on Drew Rd. 🏕 🚐 🍴 ♿

ESCONDIDO — **ESCONDIDO RV RESORT-SUNLAND.** (866) 225-3620. **$39-$73.** 1740 Seven Oaks Rd 92026. From San Diego: Go 21 mi N on I-15 (El Norte Pkwy exit), then 1 block E on El Norte Pkwy, then 1 block N on Seven Oaks. 🏕 🚐 🍴 ♿

FORT BRAGG — **POMO RV PARK & CAMPGROUND.** 🄰🄰🄰 (707) 964-3373. **$40-$42.** 17999 Tregoning Ln 95437. From jct Hwy 20 & Hwy 1: Go 1 mi S on Hwy 1, then 500 feet E on Tregoning Lane. 🍴 ♿

FORTUNA — **RIVERWALK RV PARK & CAMPGROUND.** (800) 705-5359. **$36-$46.** 2189 Riverwalk Dr 95540. From jct Hwy 36 & Hwy 101: Go 1-1/2 mi N on Hwy 101, then take Fortuna Kenmar exit, then 1/4 mi W on Riverwalk Dr. 🚐 🍴 ♿

HEMET — **GOLDEN VILLAGE PALMS RV RESORT - SUNLAND.** 🄰🄰🄰 (866) 225-2239. **$42-$75.** 3600 W Florida Ave 92545. From Palm Springs: Go 28 mi W on I-10, then 7-3/4 mi S on Hwy 79, then 5-1/2 mi S across Ramona Expressway on Sanderson Ave, then 1 block W on Hwy 74/Florida Ave. 🏕 🚐 🍴 ♿

HORNBROOK — **BLUE HERON RV PARK.** (530) 475-3270. **$40-$59.** 6930 Copco Rd 96044. From jct Hwy 96 & I-5: Go 3 mi on I-5, then take Henley/Hornbrook (exit 789), then 6-1/2 mi E on Copco Rd (1/2 mi past R-Ranch, a member park) 🏕 🚐 🍴 ♿

IMPERIAL BEACH — **BERNARDO SHORES RV PARK.** (619) 429-9000. **Call for rates.** 500 Hwy 75 91932. From jct I-5 & Hwy 75 (Palm Ave): Go 2 mi W on Hwy 75 (Palm Ave). 🏕 🍴

INDIO — **INDIAN WELLS RV RESORT CAREFREE.** (800) 789-0895. **$55.** 47-34 Jefferson St 92201. From jct Hwy 74 & I-10: Go 7-1/2 mi E on I-10, then 3 mi S on Jefferson St. 🏕 🚐 🍴 ♿

INDIO — **MOTORCOACH COUNTRY CLUB.** (888) 277-0789. **$68-$100.** 80-50 Avenue 48 92201. From jct I-10 & Central Indio exit (Monroe St): Go 2-1/2 mi S on Monroe St, then 1 mi W on Avenue 48th. 🏕 🚐 🍴 ♿

INDIO — **OUTDOOR RESORT INDIO.** (800) 892-2992. **$57-$114.** 80-93 Avenue 48 92201. From jct I-10 & Central Indio exit (Monroe St): Go 2-1/2 mi S on Monroe St, then 1-1/4 mi W on Avenue 48. 🏕 🚐 🍴 ♿

INDIO — **SHADOW HILLS RV RESORT.** (760) 360-4040. **$32-$58.** 40-65 Jefferson Blvd 92203. From jct I-10 & Jefferson St (exit 139): Go 100 yds N on Jefferson, then 200 yds E on Varner, then 300 yds N on Jefferson. 🚐 🍴 ♿

JACKSON — **JACKSON RANCHERIA RV PARK.** (800) 822-9466. **$30-$55.** 12222 New York Ranch Rd 95642. From center of town (Jackson) on Hwy 88: Go 2-1/2 mi E on Hwy 88, then 1-1/2 mi N on Dalton Rd. 🏕 🚐 🍴

KLAMATH — **CAMPER CORRAL RIVER BEACH RESORT.** 🄰🄰🄰 (800) 701-7275. **$33-$40.** 18151 Hwy 101 95548. From jct US 101 & Hwy 169 (Terwer Valley Rd): Go 200 feet W on Hwy 169 (Terwer Valley Rd). 🚐 🍴 ♿

LA MESA — **SAN DIEGO RV RESORT - SUNLAND.** (866) 225-3556. **$40-$65.** 7407 Alvarado Rd 91941. From jct I-15 & I-8: Go 3 mi on I-8 to 70th St/Lake Murrray Blvd exit, then stay in the Lake Murray Blvd/Alvarado Rd left lane to south side of I-8, then 1/2 mi E on Alvarado Rd. 🏕 🚐 ♿

LODI — **FLAG CITY RV RESORT.** 🄰🄰🄰 (866) 371-4855. **$54.** 6120 Banner St 95242. From jct I-5 & Hwy 12: Go 1/4 mi E on Hwy 12, then 1 block S on Star St, then 200 yds E on Banner St. 🆂🄳 🏕 🚐 ♿

MORGAN HILL — COYOTE VALLEY RV & GOLF RESORT. ⟨AAA⟩ (866) 376-5500. **$55-$70.** 9750 Monterey Rd 95037. From jct of Hwy 101 & exit 367/Cochrane Rd: Go 1 mi W on Cochrane Rd, then 4 mi N on Monterey Rd. 🏕 🚤 ❎ ♿M

NAPA — NAPA VALLEY EXPO RV PARK. ⟨AAA⟩ (707) 253-4900. **$45.** 575 3rd St 94559. From jct Hwy 12 & Hwy 221, take the Downtown Napa/Lake Berryessa Exit: Go 2-3/4 mi N on Hwy 221 (Napa Valley Hwy) which changes to Soscol Ave, then 1 block N on Silverado Trail. 🏕 ♿M

NEEDLES — THE PALMS RIVER RESORT. (760) 326-0333. **$33-$35.** 4170 Needles Hwy 92363. E'bnd from I-40 & River Rd exit: Go 1/2 mi E on Park Rd, then 1/2 mi N on Needles Hwy (River Rd). W'bnd from I-40 & W Broadway/River Rd exit: Go 2-1/2 mi N on Needles Hwy (River Rd). 🏕 🚤 ❎

NEWPORT BEACH — NEWPORT DUNES WATERFRONT RESORT. (800) 765-7661. **$55-$240.** 1131 Back Bay Dr 92660. From jct I-5 & Hwy 55: Go 5 mi S on Hwy 55, then 1-3/4 mi SE on I-405, then 5 mi SW on Jamboree Rd, then 1 block NW on Back Bay Rd. 🚤 ❎ ♿M

OCEANO — PISMO SANDS RV PARK. (800) 404-7004. **$41-$57.** 2220 Cienaga St 93445. From jct US 101 & Grand Ave: Go 1/4 mi SW on Grand Ave, then 1-1/2 mi S on Halcyon Rd, then 3/4 mi W on Hwy 1. 🏕 🚤 ❎ ♿M

OCEANSIDE — PARADISE BY THE SEA RV RESORT. (760) 439-1376. **$49-$115.** 1537 S Coast Hwy 92054. From jct I-5 & Hwy 78 (Vista Way): Go 1/2 mi W on Vista Way, then 1/2 mi N on Coast Hwy. 🏕 🚤 ❎ ♿M

ORANGE — ORANGELAND RV PARK. ⟨AAA⟩ (714) 633-0414. **$65-$80.** 1600 W. Struck Ave. 92867. From jct I-5 & Katella Exit: Go 2 mi E on Katella Ave, then 150 ft SE on Struck Ave 🏕 🚤 ❎ ♿M

OROVILLE — FEATHER FALLS KOA. (800) 562-5079. **$37-$55.** #1 Alverda Dr 95966. From jct Hwy 99 & Hwy 149: Go 4-1/2 mi SE on Hwy 149, then 9 mi S on Hwy 70, then 3-1/2 mi E on Ophir Rd, then 100 yards NE on Alverda Dr. 🏕 🚤 ❎ ♿M

PALM DESERT — EMERALD DESERT GOLF & RV RESORT - SUNLAND. (866) 225-4982. **$47-$85.** 76000 Frank Sinatra Drive 92211. From jct I-10 & Cook St: Go 3/4 mi S on Cook St, then 1 mi E on Frank Sinatra Dr. 🏕 🚤 ❎ ♿M

PASO ROBLES — WINE COUNTRY RV RESORT. (866) 927-8669. **$46-$85.** 2500 Airport Rd 93446. From jct 101 & Hwy 46 E (exit 231B): Go 2 mi E on Hwy 46 E, then 1/2 mi N on Airport Rd. 🏕 🚤 ❎ ♿M

PETALUMA — KOA-SAN FRANCISCO NORTH/PETALUMA. (800) 992-2267. **$40-$80.** 20 Rainsville Rd 94952. From north end of Golden Gate Bridge in San Francisco: Go 34 mi N on US 101 to Petaluma Blvd North-Penngrove exit, then 1/4 mi W on Petaluma Blvd, then 1/4 mi N on Stony Point Rd, then 200 yds W on Rainsville Rd. 🚤 ❎ ♿M

PISMO BEACH — PISMO COAST VILLAGE RV RESORT. (888) 782-3224. **$42-$58.** 165 S Dolliver St 93449. Southbound: From jct US 101 & Hwy 1 (Pismo Beach exit): Go 3/4 mi S on Hwy 1 (Dolliver St). Northbound: From jct US 101 & Price Street (Pismo Beach exit): Go 1 block W on Price St, then 3/4 mi S on Hwy 1 (Dolliver St). 🏕 🚤 ❎ ♿M

PLYMOUTH — FAR HORIZONS 49ER VILLAGE RV RESORT. (800) 339-6981. **$38-$75.** 18265 State Highway 49 95669. From jct Hwy 16 & Hwy 49: Go 2 mi N on Hwy 49. 🏕 ❎ ♿M

RED BLUFF — DURANGO RV RESORT. ⟨AAA⟩ (866) 770-7001. **$43-$58.** 810 Main St 96080. From jct I-5 & Hwy 36/99 (Antelope Blvd): Go 1/4 mi W on Hwy 36 (Antelope Blvd), then 1/4 mi N on Belle Mill Rd (East Ave). 🅂 🏕 🚤 ❎

RED BLUFF — RED BLUFF RV PARK. (530) 529-2929. **$33-$37.** 80 Chestnut Ave 96080. From jct I-5 & Hwy 99S (Susanville/Lassen Park Rd, exit 649): Go 3/4mi E on Hwy 99S, then 1/4 mi N on Chestnut. 🏕 🚤 ❎ ♿M

REDDING — JGW RV PARK. (800) 469-5910. **$35-$45.** 6612 Riverland Dr 96002. From jct Hwy 44 & I-5: Go 5-1/2 mi S on I-5 to Knighton Rd exit, then 100 feet W on Knighton Rd, then 2 mi S on Riverland Dr. 🏕 🚤 ❎ ♿M

REDDING — MOUNTAIN GATE RV PARK. (800) 404-6040. **$28-$35.** 14161 Holiday Rd 96003. From jct Hwy 44 & I-5: Go 7 mi N on I-5 (exit 687/Mountain Gate): Go 300 yds E, then 1/2 mi S on Holiday Rd. 🚤 ❎ ♿M

REDDING — PREMIER RV RESORT - REDDING. ⟨AAA⟩ (530) 246-0101. **$40-$44.** 280 N Boulder Dr 96003. From jct I-5 & Hwy 299: Go 1/4 mi W on Hwy 299 (Lake Blvd), then 100 ft N on Boulder Dr. 🚤 ❎ ♿M

SAN FRANCISCO — CANDLESTICK RV PARK. (800) 888-2267. **$69-$74.** 650 Gilman Ave 94124. From jct US 101 & Candlestick (429A) (Candlestick Point exit): Go 1 mi E and around stadium to Gate 4. ❎ ♿M

SANTA BARBARA — OCEAN MESA CAMPGROUND. (866) 410-5783. **$70-$90.** 100 El Capitan Terrace Ln 93117. From jct US 101 & El Capitan Beach Exit: Go 75 yds E on El Capitan St Beach Rd, then 1/2 mi N on Calle Real. 🅂 🚤 ❎ ♿M

SHINGLETOWN — KOA-MT. LASSEN. (530) 474-3133. **$36-$44.** 7749 KOA Rd 96088. From jct I-5 & Hwy 44 (Lassen Pk exit): Go 34 mi E on Hwy 44, then S on KOA Rd (14 mi W of Lassen Pk entrance). 🚤 ❎

TEMECULA — PECHANGA RV RESORT & CASINO. (877) 997-8386. **$45-$75.** 45000 Pechanga Pkwy 92592. From jct I-15 & Hwy 79 South (Temecula Pkwy): Go 3/4 mi E on Hwy 79 South (Temecula Pkwy), then 2 mi SE on Pechanga Pkwy, then 1/4 mi SW on Pechanga Resort Rd. 🅂 🏕 🚤 ♿M

TRINIDAD — SOUNDS OF THE SEA RV PARK & SPA. ⟨AAA⟩ (877) 489-6360. **$25-$45.** 3443 Patrick's Point Dr. 95570. From jct Hwy 299 & Hwy 101: Go 17-3/4 mi N on Hwy 101, then 1-1/4 mi S on Patrick's Point Dr. 🏕 🚤 ❎ ♿M

Colorado

BRECKENRIDGE — **TIGER RUN RV RESORT.** (970) 453-9690. **$40-$80.** 85 Tiger Run Rd 80424. From jct I-70 (exit 201) & Hwy 9: Go 6-1/2 mi S on Hwy 9.

CAÑON CITY — **ROYAL VIEW AT ROYAL GORGE CAMPGROUND.** (719) 275-1900. **$31-$45.** 43590 Hwy 50 Way 81212. From jct Hwy 115 (9th St) & US 50: Go 9 mi W on US 50.

CLIFTON — **RV RANCH AT GRAND JUNCTION.** (800) 793-0041. **$33-$37.** 3238 I-70 Business Loop 81520. From jct I-70 (exit 37) & Business I-70: Go 3/4 mi SW on Business I-70, then 100 feet W on F Rd, then 200 feet N on Frontage Rd.

COLORADO SPRINGS — **GARDEN OF THE GODS CAMPGROUND.** (800) 248-9451. **$42-$49.** 3704 W Colorado Ave 80904. From jct I-25 & US 24 (exit 141): Go 2-1/2 mi W on US 24, then 1 block N on 31st St, then 6 blocks W on Colorado Ave.

CREEDE — **MOUNTAIN VIEWS AT RIVERS EDGE RV RESORT.** (719) 658-2710. **$28-$37.** PO Box 680 81130. From southwest city limits: Go 1 mi SW on Hwy 149, then 1/2 mi S on Airport Rd.

DOLORES — **PRIEST GULCH CAMPGROUND & RV PARK.** (970) 562-3810. **$38.** 27646 Hwy 145 81323. From jct Hwy 184 & 145: Go 25 mi NE on Hwy 145.

FRUITA — **MONUMENT RV RESORT.** (888) 977-6777. **$30-$35.** 607 Hwy 340 81521. From I-70 (exit 19) & Hwy-340: Go 1/4 mi S on Hwy-340.

GOLDEN — **DAKOTA RIDGE RV PARK.** (800) 398-1625. **$40-$47.** 17800 W Colfax 80401. From jct I-70 & US 40 (exit 262): Go 1-1/2 mi SW on US 40.

GRAND JUNCTION — **GRAND JUNCTION KOA.** (970) 242-2527. **$35-$40.** 2819 Hwy 50 81503. From jct I-70 & US 50: Go 9 mi SE on US 50.

GUNNISON — **THE PALISADES SENIOR R-V PARK.** (970) 641-4951. **$32-$36.** 470 N Third 81230. From jct Hwy 135 & US 50: Go 1/2 mi W on US 50, then continue straight 1/2 mi W on Tomichi Ave, then 1/4 mi N on 3rd St.

MANCOS — **MESA VERDE RV RESORT.** (800) 776-7421. **$37-$45.** 35303 US Hwy 160 81328. From jct SR 184 & US 160: Go 6-1/2 mi W on US 160 (MM 49-1/2).

MONTROSE — **MONTROSE/BLACK CANYON NP KOA.** (970) 249-9177. **$42.** 200 N Cedar Ave 81401. From jct US 550 & US 50: Go 3/4 mi E on US 50, then 2 blocks N on Cedar Ave.

NATHROP — **CHALK CREEK CAMPGROUND & RV PARK.** (719) 395-8301. **$36-$52.** 11430 County Road 197 81236. From jct US 285 & US 24 : Go 5 mi S on US 285.

PAGOSA SPRINGS — **WOLF CREEK RUN.** (970) 264-0365. **$50-$60.** 1007 E Expressway 83 81147. From jct US 84 & US 160: Go 3/4 mi NE on US 160.

PUEBLO — **KOA-PUEBLO SOUTH/COLORADO CITY.** (800) 562-8646. **$37-$42.** 9040 I-25 S 81004. From jct I-25 & Hwy 165 (exit 74) & Hwy 165: Go 1/4 mi S on East Frontage Rd.

Connecticut

BOZRAH — **ODETAH CAMPING RESORT.** (860) 889-4144. **$40-$45.** 38 Bozrah St Ext 06334. N'b from jct I-395 (exit 81W) & Hwy 2: Go 3-1/2 mi W on Hwy 2 (exit 23) , then 1/4 mi S on Houghton Rd, straight at intrsctn & stop sign. S'b from jct I-395 (exit 82) & Hwy 2: Go 3-1/2 mi W on Hwy 2, then 100 yds S on Houghton Rd, then straight at intrsc. Enter on R.

EAST LYME — **ACES HIGH RV PARK.** (860) 739-8858. **$54-$59.** 301 Chesterfield Rd 06333. From jct I-95 (exit 74) & Hwy 161: Go 3 mi N on Hwy 161.

PRESTON — **STRAWBERRY PARK RESORT CAMPGROUND.** (888) 794-7944. **$40-$88.** 42 Pierce Rd 06365. From jct Hwy 164 & Hwy 165: Go 1 mi E on Hwy 165, then 1/2 mi N on Pierce Rd.

Delaware

LINCOLN — **DELAWARE BEACHES JELLYSTONE PARK.** (302) 491-6614. **$55-$65.** 8300 Brick Granary Rd 19960. From jct US 113 & Hwy 1: Go 6 mi S on Hwy 1, then 1/4 mi W on Brick Granary Rd.

MILLSBORO — **LEISURE POINT RESORT.** (302) 945-2000. **Call for rates. (no credit cards).** 25491 Dogwood Ln 19966. From jct Hwy 24 & Hwy 23: Go 1-1/2 mi SE on Hwy 23 then 1/4 mi NE on Radie Kay Lane, then 1 block SE on Dogwood Ln.

Florida

ARCADIA — **CROSS CREEK COUNTRY CLUB & RV RESORT.** (863) 494-7300. **$51.** 6837 NE Cubitis Ave. 34266. From jct Hwy 70 & US 17N: Go 5 mi N on US 17, then 1/4 mi W on CR 660, then 1 mi N on Cubitis Ave (Old Hwy 17).

AVON PARK — **ADELAIDE SHORES RV RESORT.** (800) 848-1924. **$22-$35.** 2881 US 27 N 33825. N'bnd from jct Hwy 64 & US 27: Go 4 mi N on US 27.

BOWLING GREEN — **TORREY OAKS RV & GOLF RESORT.** (863) 773-3157. **$30-$40.** 300 Bostick Rd NW 33834. From jct Hwy 62 & US 17: Go 1/2 mi N on US 17, then 1/2 mi W on Bostick Rd.

BRADENTON — **ENCORE MANATEE RV RESORT.** (800) 678-2131. **$27-$65.** 800 Kay Road NE 34212. From jct I-75 (exit 220) & Hwy 64: Go 3/4 mi W on Hwy 64, then 1 mi NE on 60th St Ct East.

BRADENTON — **HORSESHOE COVE RV RESORT.** (800) 291-3446. **$30-$60.** 5100 60th St. E 34203. From jct I-75 (exit 217) & Hwy 70: Go 1-1/4 mi W on Hwy 70, then 1/4 mi N on Caruso Rd.

BUSHNELL — **BLUEBERRY HILL RV RESORT (MORGAN RV RESORTS).** (877) 793-4112. **$40.** 6233 CR 609 33513. From jct I-75 (exit 314) & Hwy 48: Go 1 block E on Hwy 48.

BUSHNELL — PARADISE OAKS GOLF & RV RESORT. (352) 793-1823. **$23-$42.** 4628 CR 475 33513. From I-75 & SR 48 (exit 314): Go E on SR 48 for 1.8 mi, then N on CR 475/N Main for 1-1/2 mi. 🏕 🚐 🍴 🚿

CARRABELLE — SUNSET ISLE RV & YACHT CLUB RESORT. (850) 370-6223. **$48.** 260 Timber Island Rd 32322. From Hwy 67 & US 98/319: Go 1-3/10 mi W on US 98, then 3/4 mi E on Timber Island Rd. 🚐 🍴

CARRABELLE BEACH — CARRABELLE BEACH OUT-DOOR DESTINATIONS. 🅰🅰🅰 (850) 697-2638. **$40.** 1843 Hwy 98 W 32322. From jct Hwy 67 & US 98/319: Go 2-3/4 mi W on US 98/319. 🏕 🚐 🍴 🚿

CHOKOLOSKEE — OUTDOOR RESORTS/CHOKOLOSKEE ISLAND. (239) 695-3788. **$69-$89.** 150 Smallwood Dr, Hwy 29 S 34138. From jct US-41 & Hwy-29 (CR 29): Go 8 mi S on CR 29. 🏕 🚐 🍴 🚿

CLERMONT — ELITE RESORTS AT CITRUS VALLEY. (352) 432-5934. **$35-$50.** 2500 Hwy 27 S 34711. From jct Hwy-50 & US-27: Go 12 mi S on US-27, turn E into Citrus Valley Highlands for 1 block, then right to RV Resort. 🏕 🚐 🍴

CLERMONT — OUTDOOR RESORTS AT ORLANDO. (800) 531-3033. **$20-$30.** 9000 US Highway 192 W 34711. From jct I-4 & US-192: Go 6-1/2 mi W on US-192. 🏕 🚐 🍴 🚿

CORTEZ — HOLIDAY COVE RV RESORT. 🅰🅰🅰 (941) 792-1111. **$58-$110.** 11900 Cortez Rd W 34215. From jct I-75 (exit 217) & Hwy 70: Go 12 mi W on Hwy 70 (53rd Ave), then 4 mi W on Cortez Rd. 🏕 🚐 🍴 🚿

CRYSTAL RIVER — NATURE COAST LANDINGS RESORT. (352) 447-5820. **$39.** 10173 N Suncoast Blvd (US 19) 34428. From jct Hwy 40 & US 19: Go 2-1/4 mi S on US 19. 🏕 🚐 🍴 🚿

CRYSTAL RIVER — ROCK CRUSHER CANYON RV PARK. (877) 722-7875. **$32-$40.** 275 South Rock Crusher Road 34429. From US 19 & SR 44: Go 3-1/2 mi E on SR 44, then 1-1/4 mi S on Rock Crusher Road. 🏕 🚐 🍴 🚿

CUDJOE KEY — VENTURE OUT RESORT. (305) 745-2600. **$55-$85. (no credit cards).** 701 Spanish Main Dr 33042. US 1 at mile marker 23, then 3/4 mi S on Spanish Main. 🏕 🚐 🍴 🚿

DADE CITY — TRAVELERS REST RESORT. 🅰🅰🅰 (800) 565-8114. **$35.** 29129 Johnston Rd 33523. From jct I-75 (exit 293) & Hwy 41: Go 1/2 mi W on Hwy 41, then 1 mi S on Hwy 577, then 1-1/2 mi W on Johnston Rd. 🏕 🚐 🍴 🚿

DAVENPORT — DEER CREEK GOLF & RV RESORT. (800) 424-2931. **$59-$65.** 4200 US Hwy 27 N 33837. From jct I-4 (exit 55) & US 27: Go 1 mi S on US 27. 🏕 🚐 🍴 🚿

DEBARY — HIGHBANKS MARINA & CAMPRESORT. (386) 668-4491. **$45-$65.** 488 W Highbanks Rd 32713. From I-4 (exit 108) (circle under cloverleaf): Go 2 mi W on Dirksen Rd, then 1-3/4 mi N on US 17/92, then 2-1/2 mi W on Highbanks Rd. 🚐 🍴 🚿

DE FUNIAK SPRINGS — SUNSET KING LAKE RV RESORT. (800) 774-5454. **$36.** 366 Paradise Island Dr 32433. From jct I-10 (exit 85) & US 331: Go 2 mi N on US 331,then 2 mi W on US 90, then 5-1/2 mi N on US 331, then 1 mi SW on Kings Lake Rd, then 1/4 mi SE on Paradise Island Rd. 🚐 🍴 🚿

DESTIN — GERONIMO RV RESORT. 🅰🅰🅰 (850) 424-6801. **$42-$62.** 75 Arnett Ln 32550. From jct US 98 & Hwy 293 (Mid Bay Bridge): Go 4 mi E on US 98, then 1/2 mi S on South Geronimo St, then 500 ft W on Arnett Ln. 🏕 🚿

DESTIN — PANAMA CITY BEACH RV RESORT. (866) 637-3529. **$54-$69.** 4702 Thomas Dr 32541. From jct US 98 & Thomas Rd: Go 3-1/2 mi S on Thomas Rd, then 1/4 mi SE on CR-392. 🏕 🚐 🚿

DUNEDIN — DUNEDIN RV RESORT. (800) 345-7504. **$40-$66.** 2920 Alt 19 34698. From jct Hwy-586 & Alt US-19 N: Go 3/4 mi N on Alt US-19. 🚐 🍴 🚿

EVERGLADES CITY — EVERGLADES ISLE MOTORCOACH RETREAT. (239) 695-2600. **$79-$99.** 803 N Collier Ave 34139. From jct US 41 & Hwy 29: Go 3 mi S on Hwy 29. 🏕 🚐 🍴 🚿

FLAGLER BEACH — BEVERLY BEACH CAMPTOWN RV RESORT. 🅰🅰🅰 (800) 255-2706. **$50-$130.** 2816 N Ocean Shore Blvd 32136. From jct I-95 (exit 284) & Hwy 100: Go 3-1/4 mi E on Hwy 100, then 3 mi N on Hwy A1A. 🆂🅱 🚐 🍴 🚿

FORT MYERS — CYPRESS WOODS RV RESORT. (888) 299-6637. **$40-$80.** 5551 Luckett Rd 33905. From jct Hwy 82 & I-75: Go 1-1/2 mi N on I-75 (exit 139), then 1/2 mi E on Luckett Rd. 🏕 🚐 🍴 🚿

FORT MYERS BEACH — GULF WATERS RV RESORT. (239) 437-5888. **$42-$72.** 11301 Summerlin Sq Dr 33931. From Hwy 82 & I-75: Go 6 mi S on I-75 (exit 131), then 5-3/4 mi W on Daniels Rd/Cypress Lake Dr, then 5-1/2 mi S on Summerlin Rd, then 100 feet E on Pine Ridge Rd, then 500 feet S on Summerlin Sq Dr. 🏕 🚐 🍴 🚿

FORT MYERS BEACH — INDIAN CREEK RESORT. 🅰🅰🅰 (239) 466-6060. **$36-$51.** 17340 San Carlos Blvd 33931. From jct Hwy 82 & I-75: Go 6 mi S on I-75 (exit 131), then 2-1/4 mi W on Daniels Rd, then 3 mi W on Hwy 865, then 4 mi SW on Summerlin Rd, then 1/4 mi S on San Carlos Blvd. 🚐 🍴 🚿

FREEPORT — LIVE OAK LANDING. 🅰🅰🅰 (877) 436-5063. **$41.** 229 Pitts Ave 32439. From jct Hwy 20 & US 331: Go 3-1/2 mi S on US 331, then 1 mi E on Black Creek Hwy, then 1 mi N on McDaniels Fish Camp Rd, then 1/4 mi W on Pitts Ave. 🏕 🍴 🚿

FROSTPROOF — RAINBOW RESORT. (863) 635-7541. **$35. (no credit cards).** 700 County Road 630a 33843. From jct US 27 & Hwy 630A: Go 1/2 mi E on Hwy 630A. 🏕 🚐 🍴 🚿

HOMESTEAD — GOLDCOASTER MOBILE HOME & RV RESORT. (800) 828-6992. **$40-$60.** 34850 SW 187th Ave 33034. From jct US 1 & Hwy 9336 (Palm Dr): Go 1 mi W on Palm Dr, then 1 block S on SW 187th Ave. 🏕 🚐 🍴 🚿

INGLIS — RIVER LODGE RV RESORT. (352) 447-2900. **$30.** 13790 W Foss Groves Path 34449. From jct US 19 & Hwy 40: Go 3/4 mi S on US 19. 🏕 🚐 🍴 🚿

JACKSONVILLE — FLAMINGO LAKE RV RESORT. ⒶⒶⒶ (800) 782-4323. **$42-$65.** 3640 Newcomb Rd 32218. From jct I-95 & I-295: Go 3 mi S on I-295 (exit 32), then 200 yds N on Hwy 115 (Lem Turner Blvd), then 200 yds SE on Newcomb Rd. 🅰 ⮐ ⌧ ♿

JACKSONVILLE — PECAN PARK RV RESORT. (904) 751-6770. **$42.** 650 Pecan Park Rd 32218. From I-95 (exit 366) and Pecan Park Rd: Go 200 yds W on Pecan Park Rd. 🅢 🅰 ⮐ ⌧ ♿

JENSEN BEACH — NETTLES ISLAND RESORT & RV PARK. ⒶⒶⒶ (866) 229-1518. **$37-$64.** 9803 S Ocean Dr 34957. From jct Hwy 716 & US 1: Go 2 mi S on US 1, then 3 mi E on Jensen Beach Blvd, then 1/2 mi N on Indian River, then 2 mi E on Hwy 732, then 2-1/4 mi N on A-1-A. 🅰 ⮐ ⌧ ♿

JUNO BEACH — JUNO OCEAN WALK RV RESORT. (561) 622-7500. **$32-$75.** 900 Juno Ocean Walk 33408. From jct Hwy 786 (PGA Blvd) & I-95: Go 3 mi N on I-95 (exit 83), then 4-1/2 mi E on Donald Ross Rd, then 3/4 mi N on US 1, then 1/4 mi W on Juno Ocean Walk. 🅰 ⮐ ⌧ ♿

KEY WEST — BLUEWATER KEY RV RESORT. ⒶⒶⒶ (305) 745-2494. **$70-$150.** 2950 US Highway 1 33040. On US 1 at mile marker 14-1/2. 🅰 ⮐ ⌧ ♿

KISSIMMEE — KOA ORLANDO/KISSIMMEE. (407) 396-2400. **$37-$83.** 2644 Happy Camper Place 34746. From jct I-4 & US 192: Go 4-3/4 mi E on US 192, then left on Seven Dwarfs Lane (at Sam's Warehouse.) ⮐ ⌧ ♿

KISSIMMEE — TROPICAL PALMS RESORT. (800) 647-2567. **$29-$85.** 2650 Holiday Trail 34746. From jct I-4 & US 192: Go 1-1/2 mi E on US 192, then 1/2 mi S on Holiday Trail. ⌧ ♿

LABELLE — RIVERBEND MOTORCOACH RESORT. (863) 674-0085. **$50-$100.** 5800 W State Road 80 33935. From jct Hwy 82 & I-75: Go 3 mi N on I-75 (exit 141), then 17 mi E on Hwy 80. 🅰 ⮐ ⌧ ♿

LABELLE — WHISPER CREEK RV RESORT. (877) 545-6888. **$40. (no credit cards).** 3745 N State Road 29 SW 33935. From jct Hwy 80 & Hwy 29: Go 1.5 mi N on Hwy 29. 🅰 ⌧ ♿

LADY LAKE — THE RECREATION PLANTATION RV RESORT. (800) 448-5646. **$44.** 609 Hwy 466 32159. From jct US 27/441 & CR 466: Go 3/4 mi W on CR 466. ⮐ ⌧ ♿

LAKE BUENA VISTA — DISNEY'S FORT WILDERNESS RESORT & CAMPGROUND. ⒶⒶⒶ (407) 939-2267. **$61-$125.** 4600 N World Dr 32830. From jct I-4 & US 192: Go 1 mi W on US 192, then 1 mi N on World Dr. ⮐ ⌧ ♿

LAKE PLACID — CAMP FLORIDA RESORT. (863) 699-1991. **$40.** 100 Shoreline Dr 33852. From jct Hwy 70 & US 27: Go 4-1/2 mi N on US 27. 🅰 ⮐ ⌧ ♿

LEESBURG — HOLIDAY TRAVEL RESORT. ⒶⒶⒶ (800) 428-5334. **$41.** 28229 CR 33 34748. From jct FL Turnpike (exit 296) & CR 470: Go 3 mi E on CR 470, then 1 mi E on CR 33. ⮐ ⌧ ♿

MARATHON — GRASSY KEY RV PARK & RESORT. (305) 289-1606. **$50-$125.** 58671 Overseas Hwy 33050. On US 1 at mile marker 58-3/4. 🅰 ⮐ ⌧

MARGATE — AZTEC RV RESORT. ⒶⒶⒶ (954) 975-6411. **$61.** 1 Aztec Blvd 33068. From jct Hwy 814 & US 441: Go 1/2 mi S on US 441. 🅰 ⮐ ⌧ ♿

MILTON — AVALON LANDING RV PARK. (850) 995-5898. **$37-$39.** 2444 Avalon Blvd 32583. From jct I-10 (exit 22) & Hwy 281 (Avalon Blvd): Go 1/2 mi S on Hwy 281. 🅰 ⮐ ⌧ ♿

MIRAMAR BEACH — CAMP GULF. (877) 226-7485. **$55-$165.** 10005 W Emerald Coast Pkwy 32550. From Destin Mid Bay Bridge (293) & US 98: Go 5 mi E on US 98. ⮐ ⌧ ♿

NAPLES — CRYSTAL LAKE RV RESORT. ⒶⒶⒶ (239) 348-0017. **$35-$80.** 14960 Collier Blvd 34119. From jct I-75 (exit 101) & Hwy 951: Go 7 mi N on Hwy 951. 🅰 ⮐ ⌧ ♿

NAPLES — NEAPOLITAN COVE RV RESORT. (239) 793-0091. **$35-$75.** 3790 Tamiami Trl E 34112. From jct I-75 (exit 101) & Hwy 951: Go 1/4 mi S on Hwy 951, then 5 mi W on Hwy 84, then 3/4 mi S on Airport Rd, then 1/2 mi SE on US 41. 🅰 ⮐ ♿

NAPLES — PELICAN LAKE MOTORCOACH RESORT. (800) 835-4389. **$60-$125.** 4555 Southern Breeze Dr 34114. From jct I-75 (exit 101) & Hwy 951: Go 9 mi S on Hwy 951. 🅰 ⮐ ⌧ ♿

NAPLES — SIGNATURE MOTORCOACH RESORT AT NAPLES. (239) 530-0535. **$79-$100.** 13300 E Tamiami Trail 34114. From jct I-75 (exit 101) & Hwy 951: Go 7 mi S on Hwy 951, then 1/2 mi E on US 41. 🅰 ⮐ ⌧ ♿

NAPLES — SILVER LAKES RV RESORT AND GOLF CLUB. (800) 843-2836. **$45-$79.** 1001 Silver Lakes Blvd 34114. From jct I-75 (exit 101) & Hwy 951: Go 9 mi S on Hwy 951. 🅰 ⮐ ⌧ ♿

NAVARRE — EMERALD BEACH RV PARK. (866) 939-3431. **$42-$65.** 8885 Navarre Pkwy 32566. From jct Hwy 87 & US 98: Go 1 mi E on US 98. (Big Rigs coming from east-turn on Navarre Sound Circle to make right turn into park.) 🅰 ⮐

NAVARRE — NAVARRE BEACH CAMPGROUND. ⒶⒶⒶ (888) 639-2188. **$49-$85.** 9201 Navarre Pkwy 32566. From jct Hwy 87 & US 98: Go 2 mi E on US 98. ⮐ ⌧ ♿

NEW SMYRNA BEACH — NEW SMYRNA BEACH RV PARK. (800) 928-9962. **$30.** 1300 Old Mission Rd. 32168. S'bnd from jct I-95 (exit 249A) & Hwy 44: Go 2-1/2 mi E on Hwy 44, then 2 mi S on Mission Dr. Entrance on right. N'bnd from jct I-95 (exit 244) & Hwy 442: Go 3/4 mi E on Hwy 442, then 3 mi N on Old Mission Rd. Entrance on left. 🅢 ⮐ ⌧ ♿

NOKOMIS — ENCORE ROYAL COACHMAN. (941) 488-9674. **$43-$85.** 1070 Laurel Rd E 34275. From jct I-75 (exit 195) & Laurel Rd: Go 2-1/4 mi W on Laurel Rd. 🅰 ⮐ ⌧ ♿

NORTH FORT MYERS — RAINTREE RV RESORT. (800) 628-6095. **$52-$65.** 19250 N Tamiami Trail 33903. From jct Hwy 82 & I-75: Go 6 mi N on I-75 (exit 143), then 6-1/4 mi W on Hwy 78 (Bayshore Rd), then 4-1/2 mi N on US 41. 🅰 ⮐ ⌧ ♿

OKEECHOBEE — SILVER PALMS RV VILLAGE. (863) 467-5800. **$50-$70.** 4143 Hwy 441 S 34974. From jct Hwy 70 & Hwy 441: Go 2-1/2 mi S on Hwy 441. 🅰 ⮐ ⌧ ♿

OKEECHOBEE — WATER'S EDGE MOTOR COACH RESORT. (863) 357-5757. **$45-$90.** 12766 US Highway 441 SE 34974. From jct Hwy 78 & US 441/98: Go 10 mi S on US 441/98. 🅰 ⚊ ⊠ ♿M

ORANGE LAKE — GRAND LAKE RV & GOLF RESORT **(MORGAN RV RESORTS).** (800) 435-2291. **$25-$40.** 4555 W Hwy 318 32681. From jct I-75 (exit 368) & Hwy 318: Go 2-3/4 mi E on Hwy 318. 🆂 🅰 ⚊ ⊠ ♿M

PALMETTO — FROG CREEK RV RESORT & CAMPGROUND. (941) 722-6154. **$35-$48.** 8515 Bayshore Dr 34221. From jct I-75 (exit 228) & I-275: Go 1 mi W on I-275 (exit 1), then 3/4 mi N on US 41, then 1/4 mi SW on Bayshore Rd. 🅰 ⚊ ⊠ ♿M

PANAMA CITY BEACH — EMERALD COAST RV BEACH RESORT. (800) 232-2478. **$60-$80.** 1957 Allison Ave 32407. From Hathaway Bridge on Alt US 98: Go 2-1/4 mi W on Alt US 98, then 100 feet S on Allison Ave. 🅰 ⚊ ⊠ ♿M

PENSACOLA — PERDIDO COVE RV RESORT & MARINA. 🅰🅰🅰 (850) 492-7304. **$55-$95.** 13770 River Rd 32507. From jct I-10 (exit 7) & Hwy 297: Go 2-1/2 mi S on Hwy 297, then 10 mi SW on Hwy 173 (Blue Angle Pkwy), then 6 mi W on 292, then 350 ft E on Gongora Dr, then 1/10 mi N on Don Carlos Dr, then 1/10 mi W on River Rd. 🅰 ⚊ ⊠ ♿M

PORT CHARLOTTE — HARBOR LAKES. (800) 468-5022. **$33-$63.** 3737 El Jobean Rd 33953. From jct I-75 (exit 170) & Hwy 769 (Kings Hwy): Go 500 ft S on Hwy 769, then 10-1/2 mi W on Hwy 776. 🅰 ⚊ ⊠ ♿M

PORT CHARLOTTE — RIVERSIDE RV RESORT & CAMP-GROUND. (800) 795-9733. **$40-$55.** 9770 SW County Road 769 34269. From jct I-75 (exit 170) & Hwy 769 (Kings Hwy): Go 4-1/2 mi NE on Hwy 769. ⊠ ♿M

PORT ST. LUCIE — OUTDOOR RESORTS ST. LUCIE WEST MOTORCOACH RESORT. (866) 456-2303. **$65.** 800 NW Peacock Blvd 34986. From jct I-95 (exit 121) & St. Lucie W Blvd: Go 1 block E on St. Lucie W Blvd, then 1-1/2 mi N on NW Peacock Rd. 🅰 ⚊ ⊠ ♿M

ROCKLEDGE — SPACE COAST RV RESORT. (800) 982-4233. **$40-$55.** 820 Barnes Blvd 32955. S'bound from I-95 (exit 195): Go 200 yards N on Fiske Blvd, then 200 yards E on Barnes Blvd. N'bound from I-95 (exit 195): Go 300 yards straight ahead from light. 🆂 ⚊ ⊠ ♿M

RUSKIN — TAMPA SOUTH RV RESORT. (813) 645-1202. **$45-$55.** 2900 S US Highway 41 33570. From jct I-75 (exit 240) & Hwy 674: Go 3 mi W on Hwy 674,then 2 mi S on US 41. 🅰 ⚊ ⊠

SARASOTA — SUN-N-FUN RV RESORT. 🅰🅰🅰 (800) 843-2421. **$34-$75.** 7125 Fruitville Rd. 34240. From jct I-75 (exit 210) & Hwy 780 (Fruitville Rd): Go 1 mi E on Hwy 780. ⚊ ⊠ ♿M

SEBASTIAN — PELICAN'S LANDING RESORT. (772) 589-5188. **$40-$60.** 11330 Indian River Dr. 32958. From jct I-95 (exit 156) & Hwy 512: Go 6-1/4 mi E on Hwy 512, then 1 mi S on Indian River Dr. 🅰 ⊠

SEBRING — THE OUTBACK RV RESORT AT TANGLEWOOD. (888) 402-1501. **$37-$46.** 3000 Tanglewood Pkwy 33872. From jct Hwy 634A & US 27: Go 3/4 mi N on US 27. 🅰 ⚊ ⊠ ♿M

SEFFNER — LAZYDAYS RV CAMPGROUND. (866) 456-7015. **$25-$35.** 6210 County Road 579 33584. From jct I-75 & I-4: Go 1 mi E on I-4 (exit 10), then 1/4 mi N on Hwy 579. 🅰 ⚊ ⊠ ♿M

SILVER SPRINGS — WILDERNESS RV PARK ESTATES. (352) 625-1122. **$37-$40.** 10313 E Hwy 40 34488. From jct I-75 (exit 358) & Hwy 326: Go 9 mi E on Hwy 326, then 3 mi E on Hwy 40 (Just over bridge). 🅰 ⚊ ⊠ ♿M

STARKE — STARKE/GAINESVILLE NE KOA. (800) 562-8498. **$33-$46.** 1475 S Walnut St (US 301) 32091. From jct Hwy 100 & US 301: Go 1 mi S on US 301. 🅰 ⚊ ⊠ ♿M

TAMPA — BAY BAYOU RV RESORT. 🅰🅰🅰 (813) 855-1000. **$39-$62.** 12622 Memorial Hwy 33635. N'bnd from jct I-275 (exit 47) & Hillsborough Ave (SR 580): Go 10-1/2 mi W on Hillsborough Ave (SR 580), then 1/2 mi N on Countryway Blvd, then 3/4 mi W on Memorial Hwy, turn into Resort on Manatee Bay Dr. 🅰 ⚊ ⊠ ♿M

TITUSVILLE — SEASONS IN THE SUN. (877) 687-7275. **$28-$38.** 2400 Seasons in the Sun Blvd. 32754. From jct I-95 (exit 223) & Hwy 46: Go 1/2 mi W on Hwy 46. 🆂 🅰 ⊠ ♿M

TITUSVILLE — THE GREAT OUTDOORS RV-NATURE & GOLF RESORT. (800) 621-2267. **$40-$55.** 125 Plantation Dr 32780. From jct I-95 (exit 215) & Hwy 50 (Cheney Hwy): Go 1/2 mi W on Hwy 50 (Cheney Hwy) to entrance. 🅰 ⚊ ⊠ ♿M

VERO BEACH — SUNSHINE TRAVEL-ENCORE. (800) 628-7081. **$36-$55.** 9455 108th Ave 32967. From jct I-95 (exit 156) & Hwy 512: Go 1 block E on Hwy 512, then 1/2 block S on 108th St. ⚊ ⊠ ♿M

WEBSTER — FLORIDA GRANDE MOTOR COACH RESORT. (352) 569-1169. **$27-$35.** 9675 SE 47th Way 33597. From I-75 & exit 301: Go E on US 50 for 12-1/2 mi then N on CR 471 for 4 mi to Webster, then East on SE 1st Ave/CR 478 for 2 miles. 🅰 ⚊ ♿M

WESLEY CHAPEL — QUAIL RUN RV RESORT. (800) 582-7084. **$38-$44.** 6946 Old Pasco Rd. 33544. From jct I-75 (Zepher Hills exit 279) & SR 54: Go 1/2 mi W on SR 54, then 2 mi N on Old Pasco Rd. 🆂 🅰 ⚊ ⊠ ♿M

WEST PALM BEACH — VACATION INN RESORT. (561) 848-6170. **$40-$70.** 6500 N Military Tr 33407. From jct US 98/80 (Southern Blvd) & I-95: Go 8 mi N on I-95 (exit 76), then 1/2 mi W on Hwy 708 (Blue Heron Blvd), then 3/4 mi S on Hwy 809 (Military Rd). 🅰 ⚊ ⊠ ♿M

WILLISTON — WILLISTON CROSSINGS RV RESORT. 🅰🅰🅰 (352) 528-7100. **$22-$39.** 410 NW 5th St 32696. From W jct US 41 & Us 27A: Go 1 mi E on US 27A, then 300 ft N on NE 5th St. 🅰 ⊠ ♿M

ZEPHYRHILLS — MAJESTIC OAKS RV RESORT. (813) 783-7518. **$32.** 3751 Laurel Valley Blvd 33542. From jct SR 54 West & US 301: Go 2 mi S on US 301, then 1-1/2 mi E on Chancey Rd. 🅰 ⚊ ♿M

Georgia

ALBANY — **ALBANY RV RESORT.** (866) 792-1481. **$34-$36.** 1202 Liberty Expy SE 31705. From jct US 82 & US 19/Hwy 300: Go 4-1/2 mi S on US 19/Hwy 300. ⊠ ⅏ℳ

BRUNSWICK — **COASTAL GEORGIA RV RESORT.** (912) 264-3869. **$40.** 287 South Port Pkwy 31523. From jct I-95 (exit 29) & US 17: Go 1/2 mi W on US 17, then 1/4 mi S on US 17, then 1/2 mi E on Martin Palmer Dr. 🏕 ⇌ ⊠ ⅏ℳ

DILLARD — **RIVER VISTA MOUNTAIN VILLAGE.** (888) 850-7275. **$28-$60.** 960 Hwy 246 30537. From jct US 441/23 & Hwy 246: Go 1 mi E on Hwy 246. ⓢ 🏕 ⇌ ⊠ ⅏ℳ

HIAWASSEE — **BALD MOUNTAIN CAMPING RESORT.** (706) 896-8896. **$30-$35.** 751 Gander Gap Rd. 30546. From east jct US 76 & Hwys 75/17: Go 1/4 mi NW on US 76/Hwys 75/17, then 1/4 mi W on Hwy 288, then 3-1/2 mi S on Fodder Creek Rd, then on Gander Gap Rd. ⇌ ⊠ ⅏ℳ

HIAWASSEE — **ENOTA MOUNTAIN RETREAT.** (800) 990-8869. **$34-$39.** 1000 Hwy 180 30546. From jct Hwy 75/17 & Hwy 356: Go 10-3/4 mi N on Hwy 75/17, then 2-1/2 mi W on Hwy 180. ⇌ ⊠ ⅏ℳ

ROSSVILLE — **BEST HOLIDAY TRAV-L-PARK.** (800) 693-2877. **$37-$39.** 1623 Mack Smith Rd 30741. From jct I-24 & I-75: Go 1/2 mi S on I-75 (S'bnd exit 1; N'bnd 1B), then 1/4 mi W on US 41N, then 1/2 mi S on Mack Smith Rd. ⓢ ⇌ ⊠ ⅏ℳ

STONE MOUNTAIN — **STONE MOUNTAIN FAMILY CAMP-GROUND.** (800) 385-9807. **$33-$58.** 1900 Stonewall Jackson Drive 30083. From east jct I-285 (exit 39B) & US 78: Go 7-1/2 mi E on US 78 (Stone Mountain Fwy), to exit 8, then 500 ft S to East Gate. ⓢ ⇌ ⊠ ⅏ℳ

Idaho

BOISE — **HI-VALLEY RV PARK.** ⓐⓐⓐ (888) 457-5959. **$31.** 10555 Horseshoe Bend Rd 83714. From Jct I-84 & Hwy 55 (exit 46): Go 6.8 m N on Hwy 55, then 1.7 mi E on Hwy 44/55; then 1.5 mi N on Hwy 55, then 1 mi E on Floating Feather, then 1/4 mi S on N Horseshoe Bend. 🏕 ⊠ ⅏ℳ

CALDWELL — **AMBASSADOR RV RESORT.** ⓐⓐⓐ (888) 877-8307. **$34.** 615 S Smead Pkwy 83605. From jct I-84 (exit 29, US Hwy 20/26): Go 1/2 mi E. 🏕 ⇌ ⊠

COEUR D'ALENE — **BLACKWELL ISLAND RV RESORT.** (888) 571-2900. **$39-$55.** 800 S Marina Dr 83814. From I-90 & US 95: Go 1.5 mi S on US 95. 🏕 ⇌ ⊠ ⅏ℳ

MCCALL — **MCCALL RV RESORT.** ⓐⓐⓐ (208) 634-1418. **$44.** 200 Scott St 83638. From jct Hwy 55 & Deinhard St (S. side of town): Go 1/2 mi W on Deinhard St, then 1/10 mi S on Mission, then 4/10 mi W on Scott St. 🏕 ⇌ ⊠

MERIDIAN — **BOISE MERIDIAN KOA RV RESORT.** (866) 988-7003. **$33.** 184 W Pennwood St 83642. From I-84 take the Meridian Exit (exit 44): Go N approx 1/4 mi, then 1/4 mi NW on Meridian Rd, then 1/4 mi W on Pennwood St. ⓢ 🏕 ⇌ ⊠ ⅏ℳ

MOUNTAIN HOME — **MOUNTAIN HOME RV PARK.** ⓐⓐⓐ (208) 580-1211. **$33.** 2295 American Legion Blvd 83647. From jct I-84 (exit 95) and Hwy 51 (American Legion Blvd): Go S 1/2 mi on Hwy 51. 🏕 ⊠ ⅏ℳ

OROFINO — **CLEARWATER CROSSING RV PARK.** (208) 476-4800. **$24-$30.** 500 Riverfront Rd 83544. From jct Hwy 7 & Hwy 12: Go 1/10 mi SE on Hwy 7, then 1 block NW on Riverside Ave to Riverfront Rd. ⇌ ⊠ ⅏ℳ

POST FALLS — **COEUR D'ALENE RV PARK.** (208) 773-3527. **$34-$39.** 2600 E Mullan Ave 83854. From jct I-90 (exit 7) & Hwy 41: Go 1/4 mi N on Hwy 41, then 3/4 mi W on Mullan Ave. ⓢ 🏕 ⇌ ⊠ ⅏ℳ

Illinois

AMBOY — **O'CONNELL'S YOGI BEAR'S JELLYSTONE PARK CAMP-RESORT.** (815) 857-3860. **$41-$56.** 970 Green Wing Rd 61310. From jct US 30 & US 52: Go 1 mi S on US 52, then 1-1/2 mi E on Main St, then 2-1/2 mi SE on Shaw Rd, then 1 mi N on Green Wing Rd. ⇌ ⊠

HILLSDALE — **SUNSET LAKES RESORT.** (800) 747-5253. **$34-$59.** 2700 290th St N 61257. From jct I-88 (exit 6) & Hwy 92 : Go 1 mi E on Hwy 92, then 1/2 mi S on 290th St. ⇌ ⊠ ⅏ℳ

Indiana

BLOOMINGTON — **LAKE MONROE VILLAGE.** (812) 824-2267. **$45-$60.** 8107 S Fairfax Rd 47401. From jct SR 37 & Smithville Rd: Go 2 mi E on Smithville Rd, then 1-1/2 mi S on Fairfax Rd. ⇌ ⊠ ⅏ℳ

FLORENCE — **FOLLOW THE RIVER RV RESORT.** (812) 427-3330. **$34-$49.** 27 Markland Town Rd 47020. From jct of Hwy 101 Markland Locks/Dam Rd & SR 156: Go 1 mi S on Hwy 156. 🏕 ⇌ ⊠ ⅏ℳ

FREMONT — **YOGI BEAR'S JELLYSTONE PARK AT BARTON LAKE.** (800) 375-6063. **$21-$61.** 140 Lane 201 Barton Lake 46737. From I-80/90 (Indiana Turnpike) exit 144: Take exit to SR 120, then go 3-1/4 mi W on SR 120, then 1/2 mi N on CR N 300W. ⊠ ⅏ℳ

SANTA CLAUS — **LAKE RUDOLPH CAMPGROUND & RV RESORT.** (877) 478-3657. **$30-$54.** 78 N Holiday Blvd 47579. From jct I-64 & US 162 (exit 63): Go 7 mi S on US 162, then 1/4 mi N on Hwy 245/Holiday Blvd. ⇌ ⊠ ⅏ℳ

Iowa

ALTOONA — **GRIFFS VALLEY VIEW RV.** (515) 967-5474. **$28.** 6429 NE 46th St. 50009. From jct I-35 & Corporate Woods Dr becomes 62nd,(exit 89): Go 2-3/4 mi E on Corporate Woods Dr, then 1/4 mi N on NE 46th St. (sign in at office W 1/2 mi on 62nd). 🏕 ⅏ℳ

CENTER POINT — **LAZY ACRES RV PARK.** (319) 443-4000. **$26-$30.** 5486 32nd Ave 52213. From jct SR-150 & I-380: Go 1-1/2 mi S on I-380 (exit 41), then 100 yds E on 54th St Trail, then 100 yds NW on 32nd Ave. ⊠ ⅏ℳ

ELKADER — **DEER RUN RESORT.** (563) 245-3337. **$29-$32.** **(no credit cards).** 501 High St SE 52043. From jct Hwy 56 & Hwy 13: Go NE 1/2 mi on Hwy 13, then N 1/2 mi on S High St, then E 1/4 mi on Roberts. 🚗 ☒

Kansas

DODGE CITY — **GUNSMOKE TRAV-L-PARK.** (620) 227-8247. **$31-$33.** 11070 108 Rd 67801. From jct 283 (N'bnd) & US 56: Go N on 2nd Ave for 2 mi then 3 mi W on Bus US 50/Wyatt Earp Blvd. 🚤 ☒ ♿

LAWRENCE — **JELLYSTONE PARK CAMP RESORT W KANSAS CITY @ LAWRENCE.** (888) 703-3281. **$29-$55.** 1473 Hwy 40 66044. From jct I-70 (exit 204) & US-59/40: Go 1/2 mi N on US-59/40, then 1/4 mi E on US-24/40. 🚤 ☒

MAYETTA — **PRAIRIE BAND CASINO & RESORT RV PARK.** (877) 278-7275. **$21-$32.** 12305 150th Rd 66509. From jct US 75 & 150 Rd: Go 1-1/2 mi W on 150 Rd. 🚗

OAKLEY — **HIGH PLAINS CAMPING.** ⦿ (785) 672-3538. **$37.** 462 US Highway 83 67748. From jct I-70 (exit 70) & US-83: Go 200 yards S on US-83. ☒

TOPEKA — **DEER CREEK VALLEY RV PARK LLC.** (785) 357-8555. **$36.** 3140 SE 21st St 66607. From jct I-70 (exit 364B) & Carnahan Ave: Go S 1/8 mi to 21st St, then E 1/8 mi. 🚗 🚤 ☒ ♿

Kentucky

SHEPHERDSVILLE — **GRANDMA'S RV PARK.** (502) 543-7023. **$27.** 159 Dawson Drive 40165. From jct SR 44 & I-65: Go 1 mi S on I -65, then 200 yds W on SR 480. ⛽ 🚗 ♿

Louisiana

BREAUX BRIDGE — **CAJUN PALMS RV RESORT.** (337) 667-7772. **$32-$74.** 1055 N Barn Rd 70517. From jct I-10 (exit 115) & Hwy 347: Go 1/2 mi N on Hwy 347, then 1/4 mi E on N Barn Rd. 🚗 🚤 ☒

KINDER — **COUSHATTA LUXURY RV RESORT AT RED SHOES PARK.** (800) 584-7263. **$19-$24.** 777 Coushatta Dr 70648. From jct US 190 & US 165: Go 3 mi N on US 165. 🚗 🚤 ☒ ♿

MARKSVILLE — **PARAGON CASINO RV RESORT.** (800) 946-1946. **$17-$32.** 711 Paragon Pl 71351. From jct Hwy 452 & Hwy 1: Go 1 mi S on Hwy 1, then 1/4 mi E on Slim Lemoine Rd. 🚗 🚤 ☒ ♿

NEW ORLEANS — **FRENCH QUARTER RV RESORT.** ⦿ (504) 586-3000. **$69.** 500 N Claiborne Ave 70112. From jct I-10 (exit 235A) (Orleans St/Vieux Carre) & Basin St: Go 1/4 mi S on Basin St, then 100 ft W on Crozat St (follow signs), then S through parking lot to entrance. 🚗 ♿

SCOTT — **KOA-LAFAYETTE.** (800) 562-0809. **$38-$48.** 537 Apollo Rd 70583. From jct US-167 & I-10: Go 5-1/4 mi W on I-10 (exit 97), then 100 feet S on Hwy 93, then 1/4 mi W on entry road. 🚤 ☒

Maine

CASCO — **POINT SEBAGO GOLF AND BEACH RV RESORT.** (800) 872-7646. **$35-$90.** 261 Point Sebago Rd 04015. From jct Hwy 85 & US 302: Go 5 mi N on US 302, then 1 mi W at Casco Alliance Church (Pt. Sebago Rd). 🚤 ☒

HERMON — **PUMPKIN PATCH RV RESORT.** (866) 644-2267. **$30-$32.** 149 Billings Rd 04401. From jct I-95 (exit 180) & Cold Brook Rd: Go 2-1/2 mi W on Cold Brook Rd, then 1-1/2 mi W on Rt 2, then 1/2 mi N on Billings Rd. 🚗 ♿

KENNEBUNKPORT — **RED APPLE CAMPGROUND.** (207) 967-4927. **$47-$52. (no credit cards).** 111 Sinnott Rd 04046. From jct I-95 (exit 25) & Hwy 35: Go 1/2 mi E on Hwy 35, then 1-1/2 mi N on Ross Rd, then 1/4 mi N on US 1, then 2-1/4 mi E on Old Post Rd. ☒ ♿

OLD ORCHARD BEACH — **POWDER HORN FAMILY CAMPING RESORT.** (207) 934-4733. **$30-$65.** 48 Cascade Rd 04064. From jct I-95 (exit 36) & I-195: Go 1-3/4 mi E on I-195 (exit 2B), then 2-1/2 mi N on US 1, then 1-3/4 mi E on Hwy 98. 🚤 ☒ ♿

PINE POINT — **BAYLEY'S CAMPING RESORT.** (207) 883-6043. **$30-$86.** 275 Pine Point Rd 04074. From jct I-95 & I-195 (exit 36): Go 1-3/4 mi E on I-195, then 6 mi N on US 1, then 3 mi E on Hwy 9 to Pine Point. 🚤 ☒ ♿

SCARBOROUGH — **BAYLEY'S CAMPING RESORT.** ⦿ (207) 883-6043. **$30-$86.** 275 Pine Point Rd 04074. From jct I-95 Maine Tpk (exit 42) & Scarborough (US 1): Go 1-1/2 mi S on US 1, then 3 mi E on Hwy 9 West to Pine Point. 🚤 ☒ ♿

WELLS — **WELLS BEACH RESORT.** ⦿ (207) 646-7570. **$49-$77.** 1000 Post Rd 04090. From jct I-95 (exit 19) & Hwy 109: Go 1-1/2 mi E on Hwy 109, then 1-1/4 mi S on US 1. 🚤 ☒

Maryland

BERLIN — **CASTAWAYS RV RESORT & CAMPGROUND.** (410) 213-0097. **$42-$73.** 12612 Eagles Nest Rd 21811. From jct US 50 & Hwy 611: Go 5 mi S on Hwy 611, then 1-1/2 mi E on Eagles Nest Rd. 🚤 ☒ ♿

COLLEGE PARK — **CHERRY HILL PARK.** (800) 314-9308. **$58-$70.** 9800 Cherry Hill Rd 20740. N'bound from jct I-95 (exit 25) & US 1: Go 175 yds S on US 1, then 1 mi W on Cherry Hill Rd. Enter on left. S'bound from jct I-95 (exit 29B) & Hwy 212 (Powder Mill Rd): Go 1 mi W on Powder Mill Rd, then 1 mi S on Cherry Hill Rd. ⛽ 🚤 ☒ ♿

FREELAND — **MERRY MEADOWS RECREATION FARM.** ⦿ (410) 329-6636. **$41-$56.** 1523 Freeland Rd 21053. From I-83 (exit 36): Go 1/4 mi W on Hwy 439, then 1 mi N on Hwy 45, then 3 mi W on Freeland Rd. ⛽ 🚤 ☒ ♿

OCEAN CITY — **FRONTIER TOWN CAMPGROUND.** (800) 228-5590. **$38-$92.** 8428 Stephen Decatur Hwy 21843. From jct Hwy-528 & US-50: Go 1 mi W on US-50, then 3-3/4 mi S on Hwy-611. 🚤 ☒ ♿

WHALEYVILLE — **FORT WHALEY CAMPGROUND.** (410) 641-9785. **$30-$75.** 11224 Dale Rd 21872. From jct US 50 & Hwy 610: Go 1/4 mi S on Hwy 610. 🛶 ⊠ ♿

WILLIAMSPORT — **YOGI BEAR'S JELLYSTONE PARK CAMP-RESORT-WILLIAMSPORT-HAGERSTOWN.** (800) 421-7116. **$30-$72.** 16519 Lappans Rd 21795. From jct I-81 (exit 1) & Hwy 68: Go 1-1/4 mi E on Hwy 68. (Lappans Rd). 🔋 🛶 ⊠ ♿

WOODBINE — **RAMBLIN' PINES FAMILY CAMPGROUND & RV PARK.** ⨮ (800) 550-8733. **$53.** 801 Hoods Mill Rd 21797. From jct I-70 (exit 76) & Hwy-97: Go 2-1/2 mi N on Hwy-97, then 1/2 mi NW on Hoods Mill Rd. (Do not turn right on first Hoods Mill Rd; go across railroad tracks & up hill, then turn left on Hoods Mill Rd). 🔋 🛶 ⊠ ♿

Massachusetts

BOURNE — **BAY VIEW CAMPGROUNDS.** ⨮ (508) 759-7610. **$44-$60.** 260 MacArthur Blvd, Rt-28 02532. From jct I-495/Hwy 25 & Bourne Bridge: Cross Bourne Bridge to rotary, then 1 mi S on Hwy 28. 🛶 ⊠ ♿

EAST FALMOUTH — **CAPE COD CAMPRESORT & CABINS.** (508) 548-1458. **$34-$87.** 176 Thomas B. Landers Rd 02536. From jct Hwy 28 & Thomas B. Landers Rd: Go 2-1/2 mi E on Thomas B. Landers Rd. 🛶 ⊠ ♿

FOXBORO — **NORMANDY FARMS FAMILY CAMPING RESORT.** (866) 673-2767. **$35-$77.** 72 West Street 02035. From jct I-495 (exit 14A) & US 1: Go 1 mi N on US 1, then 1-1/2 mi E on Thurston-West Sts. 🔋 🛶 ⊠ ♿

OAKHAM — **PINE ACRES FAMILY CAMPING RESORT.** (508) 882-9509. **$41-$78.** 203 Bechan Rd 01068. From jct Hwy 122 & Hwy 148 (N Brookfield Rd): Go 2 mi SW on N Brookfield Rd, then 500 ft S on Spencer Rd, then 1/2 mi E on Bechan Rd. 🛶 ⊠ ♿

SALISBURY — **BEACH ROSE RV PARK.** (800) 382-2230. **$37-$56.** 147 Beach Rd 01952. From jct I-95 (exit 58) & Hwy 110: Go 2-1/2 mi E on Hwy110, then 500 ft N on US 1/US 1A, then 1-1/4 mi E on US 1A. 🏔 🏊 ⊠

SALISBURY — **BLACK BEAR CAMPGROUND.** (978) 462-3183. **$40-$45.** 54 Main St 01952. From jct I-95 (exit 60) & Hwy 286: Go down ramp to first traffic light, then 200 feet E on Main St. 🛶 ⊠ ♿

Michigan

CARSONVILLE — **LAKE HURON CAMPGROUND.** (866) 360-2267. **$21-$68.** 2353 N Lakeshore Rd 48419. From jct Hwy 46 & Hwy 25; Go 4-1/2 mi N on Hwy 25. 🛶 ⊠ ♿

EMPIRE — **INDIGO BLUFFS MOTORCOACH RESORT.** (231) 326-5050. **$60.** 6760 W Empire Hwy 49630. From jct Hwy 22 & Hwy 72: Go 3-1/2 mi E on Hwy 72. 🏔 🛶 ♿

FRANKENMUTH — **FRANKENMUTH JELLYSTONE PARK CAMP-RESORT.** (989) 652-6668. **$46-$68.** 1339 Weiss St 48734. From jct I-75 (exit 136) & Hwy 83: Go 2 mi E on Birch Run Rd, then 4-1/2 mi N on Hwy 83, then 1/4 mi N on Weiss St. 🔋 🛶 ⊠ ♿

HILLMAN — **THUNDER BAY RV & GOLF RESORT.** (800) 729-9375. **$29-$35.** 27800 M 32 W 49746. From jct Hwy 65 & Hwy 32: Go 6-1/2 mi W on Hwy 32. 🏔 ⊠

HOLLAND — **OAK GROVE CAMPGROUND RESORT.** (616) 399-9230. **$44-$50.** 2011 Ottawa Beach Rd 49424. From north jct Bus I-96 & US 31: Go 1/2 mi N on US 31, then 1-1/2 mi W on Lakewood Blvd, then 1-1/2 mi W on Douglas, then 3 mi W on Ottawa Beach Rd. 🏔 🛶 ⊠ ♿

HOPKINS — **HIDDEN RIDGE RV RESORT.** (877) 787-8297. **$39-$49.** 2306 12th St 49328. From jct Hwy 179 & US 131: Go 2 mi S on US 131 (exit 59), then 1/4 mi S on 12th St. 🏔 🛶 ⊠ ♿

HOWELL — **LAKE CHEMUNG OUTDOOR RESORT.** (517) 546-6361. **$38. (no credit cards).** 320 S Hughes Rd 48843. From jct US 23 & I-96: Go 3 mi W on I-96 (exit 145), then 3 mi NW on Grand River Ave, then 2 mi N on Hughes Rd. 🏔 🛶 ⊠ ♿

KIMBALL — **KOA-PORT HURON.** (810) 987-4070. **$30-$80.** 5111 Lapeer Rd 48074. From jct I-94 & I-69: Go 2-1/2 mi W on I-69 (exit 196), then 1/2 mi N on Wadhams Rd, then 1/4 mi E on Lapeer Rd. 🛶 ⊠ ♿

LAKE LEELANAU — **LAKE LEELANAU RV PARK.** (231) 256-7236. **$41-$69.** 3101 S Lake Shore Dr 49653. From jct Hwy 22 & Hwy 204: Go 4 mi W on Hwy 204, then 3-1/2 mi S on CR 643. 🔋 🛶 ⊠ ♿

LUDINGTON — **PONCHO'S POND.** (888) 308-6602. **$37-$49.** 5335 W Wallace Rd 49431. From west jct US 31 & US 10: Go 2 mi W on US 10, then 1 block south on Marquette St, then 1 block E on Wallace Rd. 🛶 ⊠ ♿

LUDINGTON — **VACATION STATION RV RESORT.** ⨮ (231) 845-0130. **$20-$50.** 4895 W US 10 49431. From west jct US 31 & US 10: Go 1 mi W on US 10. 🛶 ⊠ ♿

MANISTEE — **LITTLE RIVER RESORT.** (866) 572-4386. **$18-$38.** 2700 Orchard Hwy 49660. From jct Hwy 55 & US 31: Go 4 mi N on US 31, then 500 ft W o Hwy 22. 🔋 🏔 🛶 ⊠ ♿

MEARS — **SILVER CREEK RV RESORT.** ⨮ (866) 258-2541. **$20-$60.** 1441 N 34th Ave 49436. From jct Hwy 20 & US 31: Go 9 mi N on US 31 (exit 149), then 5 mi W on Polk Rd/56th Ave/Fox Rd. 🏔 🛶 ⊠ ♿

MONROE — **HARBORTOWN RV RESORT.** (734) 384-4700. **$37-$54.** 14931 Laplaisance Rd 48161. From jct I-275 & I-75: Go 9 mi S on I-75 (exit 11), then 3/4 mi NW on Laplaisance Rd. 🛶 ⊠ ♿

MUSKEGON — **DUCK CREEK RV RESORT.** (231) 766-3646. **$40-$55.** 1155 W Riley Thompson Road 49445. From jct Hwy 46 & US 31: Go 6-1/2 mi N on US 31, then 2 mi N on Russell Rd, then 3 mi W on Riley Thompson Rd. 🏔 🛶 ⊠ ♿

PETOSKEY — **HEARTHSIDE GROVE LUXURY MOTORCOACH RESORT.** (231) 347-0905. **$35-$159.** 2300 Hearthside Dr 49770. From jct US 131 & US 31: Go 5-1/2 mi N on US 31. 🏔 🛶 ⊠ ♿

PETOSKEY — **PETOSKEY KOA.** (AAA) (231) 347-0005. **$25-$69.** 1800 N US 31 49770. From jct US 131 & US 31: Go 4-1/2 mi N on US 31. 🏕 🚐 ⊠ ♿M

PETOSKEY — **SIGNATURE MOTORCOACH RESORT AT BAY HARBOR.** (877) 348-2401. **$49-$79.** 5505 US 31 S 49770. From jct US 131 & US 31: Go 4-1/4 mi S on US 31. 🏔 🚐 ⊠ ♿M

SOUTH HAVEN — **SUNNY BROOK RV RESORT.** (888) 499-5253. **$41-$56.** 315 Center St 49090. From north jct Bus I-196 & I-196 (exit 20): Go 3 mi E on Phoenix Rd (CR 388). 🏔 🚐 ⊠ ♿M

STANWOOD — **RIVER RIDGE RV RESORT & MARINA.** (AAA) (877) 287-4837. **$42-$50.** 22265 8 Mile Rd 49346. From jct US 131 & Hwy 20 (exit 131): Go 2 mi W on Hwy 20, then 1/4 mi S on Elder Rd. 🏕 🚐 ⊠ ♿M

TRAVERSE CITY — **HOLIDAY PARK CAMPGROUND.** (231) 943-4410. **$36-$53.** 4860 US 31 South 49685. From west jct Hwy 72 & US 31/Hwy 37: Go 6-3/4 mi S on US 31/Hwy 37, then 1 mi SW on US 31. 🚐 ⊠ ♿M

WILLIAMSBURG — **TRAVERSE BAY RV RESORT.** (231) 938-5800. **$45-$65.** 5555 M 72 E 49690. From north jct US 31 & Hwy 72: Go 1-1/2 mi E on Hwy 72. 🏔 🚐 ⊠ ♿M

Minnesota

AITKIN — **PETE'S RETREAT FAMILY CAMPGROUND & RV PARK.** (866) 578-7275. **$44-$54.** 22337 State Hwy 47 56431. From jct Hwy 18 & Hwy 47: Go 9 mi N on Hwy 47. 🚐 ⊠ ♿M

AUSTIN — **BEAVER TRAILS JELLYSTONE PARK CAMP-RESORT.** (800) 245-6281. **$38-$55.** 21943 630th Ave #7 55912. From jct US 218 (South at Austin) & I-90: Go 7-1/2 mi E on I-90 (exit 187), then 25 yards S on CR 20. 🆂🅳 ⊠ ♿M

GRANITE FALLS — **PRAIRIE VIEW RV PARK & CAMP-GROUND.** (866) 293-2121. **$24.** 5616 Prairie's Edge Ln 56241. From jct of Hwy 212 & Hwy 23: Go 3 mi S on Hwy 23, then 1/2 mi E on Hwy 274, then 1 mi E on Prairie's Edge Ln. 🚐 ⊠ ♿M

HINCKLEY — **GRAND CASINO HINCKLEY RV RESORT.** (AAA) (800) 995-4726. **$23-$28.** 1326 Fire Monument Rd 55037. From jct I-35 & Hwy 48: Go 1 mi E on Hwy 48. 🆂🅳 🏔 🚐 ⊠ ♿M

ST. CLOUD — **ST. CLOUD CAMPGROUND & RV PARK.** (320) 251-4463. **$33-$35.** 2491 2nd St SE 56304. From jct US 10 & Hwy 23: Go 1/4 mi E on Hwy 23, then 1 block S on 14th Ave SE, then 1 mi E on CR 8. 🚐 ⊠

WASECA — **KIESLER'S CAMPGROUND & R.V. RESORT.** (507) 835-3179. **$41-$62.** 14360 Hwy 14 E 56093. From jct I-35 & US 14 (exit 42): Go 12 mi W on US 14. 🚐 ⊠

WOODBURY — **ST. PAUL EAST RV PARK.** (651) 436-6436. **$33-$43.** 568 Cottage Grove Dr 55129. From jct I-694/494/94: Go 3 mi E on I-94 (exit 253), then 100 yds S on CR 15/Manning Ave S, then 1 mi W on Hudson Rd, then 1/4 mi S on CR 72/Settlers Ridge Pkwy. 🚐 ⊠ ♿M

Mississippi

BAY ST. LOUIS — **HOLLYWOOD CASINO RV PARK.** (866) 758-2591. **$35.** 711 Hollywood Blvd. 39520. From jct I-10 (exit 13) & Hwys 43/603: Go 6 mi S on Hwys 43/603, then 2 mi E on US 90 to jct Main St & Blue Meadow Rd, then 1/2 mi N on Blue Meadow Rd, then 1 mi E on Hollywood Blvd. (follow signs). 🏔 🚐 ⊠ ♿M

BILOXI — **CAJUN RV PARK.** (AAA) (877) 225-8699. **$40.** 1860 Beach Blvd 39531. From jct I-10 & I-110: Go 4 mi S on I-110, then 3 mi W on US 90. 🏔 🚐 ⊠

BILOXI — **MAJESTIC OAKS RV RESORT.** (228) 436-4200. **$39-$44.** 1750 Pass Rd 39531. From jct I-110 & Hwy 90 (Beach Rd): Go 2-3/4 mi W on Hwy 90, then 1 mi N on Rodenberg Ave, then 1/8 mi W on Pass Rd. 🏔 🚐 ♿M

BILOXI — **MAZALEA TRAVEL PARK.** (800) 877-8575. **$28-$30.** 8220 W Oaklawn Rd 39532. From jct I-110 & I-10 (exit 46): Go 4 mi W on I-10 (exit 41), then 300 yards S on Hwy 67.

BILOXI — **PARKER'S LANDING RV PARK.** (228) 392-7717. **$30-$32.** 7577 East Oaklawn Rd 39532. From jct I-110 & I-10 (exit 46): Go 4 mi W on I-10 (exit 41), then 500 ft S on Hwy 67, then 1/4 mi E on Oaklawn Rd. 🚐 ⊠ ♿M

GAUTIER — **INDIAN POINT RV RESORT.** (228) 497-1011. **$25-$30.** 1600 Indian Point Parkway 39553. From I-10 (exit 61) & Gautier/VanCleave Rd: Go 3/4 mi S on Gautier/VanCleave Rd, then E on Indian Point Rd to gate. 🏔 🚐 ⊠ ♿M

HORN LAKE — **MEMPHIS JELLYSTONE CAMP RESORT.** (662) 280-8282. **$45-$55.** 1400 Audubon Point Dr 38637. From jct I-55 & Church Rd (exit 287): Go 1 mi W on Church Rd, then 3/4 mi N on US 51, then 500 ft E on Audubon Point Dr. 🚐 ⊠ ♿M

PELAHATCHIE — **YOGI ON THE LAKE.** (AAA) (601) 854-6859. **$26-$46.** 143 Campgrounds Rd 39145. From I-20 (exit 68) & Hwy 43, then 2 mi N on Hwy 43, then 1/2 mi W on Lake Rd to Campgrounds Rd. 🚐 ⊠ ♿M

ROBINSONVILLE — **HARRAH'S CASINO RV RESORT.** (800) 946-4946. **$16-$20.** 111 Resort Village Rd 38664. From jct US 61 & Grand Casino Pkwy: Go 2-1/2 mi W on Grand Casino Pkwy. 🏔 🚐 ⊠ ♿M

ROBINSONVILLE — **HOLLYWOOD CASINO RV RESORT.** (800) 871-0711. **$18.** 1150 Casino Strip Resort Blvd 38664. From jct US 61 & Hwy 304: Go 5-1/2 mi W on Hwy 304. 🏔 🚐 ⊠ ♿M

ROBINSONVILLE — **SAM'S TOWN RV PARK.** (800) 456-0711. **$16.** 1477 Casino Strip Resort Blvd 38664. From jct 61 & Hwy 304 (Robinsonville exit): Go 5-1/2 mi W on Hwy 304 (Crossover Mississippi River Levee) Follow Signs 🏔 🚐 ⊠ ♿M

SOUTHAVEN — **EZ DAZE RV PARK.** (662) 342-7720. **$30-$33.** 536 WE Ross Pkway 38671. From jct I-55 (exit 287) & Church Rd: Go 1/8 mi W on Church Rd, then 3/4 mi N on Pepper Chase Dr, then 1 block W on WE Ross Parkway. 🏔 🚐 ♿M

VICKSBURG — **AMERISTAR RV PARK.** (800) 700-7770. **$25-$30.** 725 Lucy Bryson St 39182. From jct I-20 (exit 1A) & Washington St: Go 1/2 mi N on Washington St. 🏔 🚐

Missouri

BOWLING GREEN — COZY "C" RV CAMPGROUND. (573) 324-3055. **$27-$28.** 16733 Highway 54 63334. From jct US 61 & US 54: Go 2-1/2 mi E on US 54. ⊠

BRANSON — AMERICA'S BEST CAMPGROUND. (800) 671-4399. **$37.** 499 Buena Vista Rd 65616. From jct US 65 & Hwy 248 (Shepherd of the Hills Expwy): Go 1-3/4 mi W on Hwy 248 (Shepherd of the Hills Expwy), then keep right to Hwy 248 (1/2 mi N of Tri-Lake Center), then 1-1/4 mi N on Hwy 248, then 300 yards W on Buena Vista Rd. ⇗ ⊠ ♿

BRANSON — BRANSON KOA. (800) 467-7611. **$32-$50.** 397 Animal Safari Rd 65616. From jct US 65 & Hwy 76: Go 3-1/4 mi W on Hwy 76, then 1/2 mi S on Hwy 165, then 200 yards W on Animal Safari Rd. ⇗ ⊠ ♿

BRANSON — COMPTON RIDGE CAMPGROUND. (417) 338-2911. **$29-$43.** 5040 State Hwy 265 65616. From jct US 65 & US 465 (Ozark Mt High Rd): Go 7 mi S on US 465, then 1/4 mi W on US 76, then 1/2 mi S on Hwy 265. ⇗ ⊠ ♿

BRANSON — THE WILDERNESS AT SILVER DOLLAR CITY. (800) 477-5164. **$26-$35.** 5125 State Hwy 265 65616. From jct US 65 & US 465 (Ozark Mountain High Rd): Go 7 mi S on US 465, then 1/4 mi W on US 76, then 1/2 mi S on Hwy 265. ⇗ ⊠ ♿

BRANSON — TREASURE LAKE RV RESORT. (417) 334-1040. **Call for rates.** 1 Treasure Lake Drive 65616. From jct Hwy 248 & 65N: Go 2 mi W on Hwy 248, then 3-1/4 mi SW on Shepherd of the Hills Expwy to entrance. ⇗ ⊠ ♿

BRANSON WEST — ACORN ACRES RV PARK & VILLAS. (417) 338-2500. **$24-$52.** 159 Acorn Acres Lane 65737. From jct US 65 & US 465 (Ozark Mtn Highroad): Go 8 mi W on US 465 (Ozark Mtn Highroad), then 2-1/2 mi W on Hwy 76. ⇗ ⊠ ♿

CARTHAGE — COACHLIGHT CAMPGROUND. (417) 358-3666. **$25.** 5305 S Garrison Rd 64836. From jct I-44 (exit 18B) & US 71: Go 3/4 mi N on US 71 to Cedar Rd exit, then W 300 ft. ⛰

CARUTHERSVILLE — LADY LUCK RV PARK AND NATURE TRAIL. (573) 333-6000. **$20.** 777 East Third St 63830. From jct I-55 & Hwy 84 (exit 19): Go 5 mi E on Hwy 84. ⛰ ♿

COLUMBIA — COTTONWOODS RV PARK. ⒶⒶⒶ (888) 303-3313. **$30.** 5170 Oakland Gravel Rd 65202. From jct I-70 (exit 128A) & US 63: Go 3 mi N on US 63, then 1/4 mi NE on Oakland Gravel Rd. (paved road). ⇗ ⊠ ♿

EUREKA — KOA ST. LOUIS WEST/HISTORIC RT 66. (636) 257-3018. **$29-$50.** 18475 US Highway 66 63025. From jct I-44 (exit 261) & Six Flags Rd, then W'bnd 3/4 mi SW on Six Flags Rd to Bus Loop 44 (Hist Rt 66). E'bnd: 3/4 mi on bus Loop 44 (Hist Rt 66). ⇗ ⊠

KANSAS CITY — WORLDS OF FUN VILLAGE. (816) 454-4545. **$38-$40.** 4545 Worlds of Fun Ave 64161. From East Loop of I-435 (exit 54): Go 1/2 mi E on Parvin Rd. Enter RV Park through Oceans of Fun parking lot. ⛰ ⇗ ♿

MONROE CITY — MARK TWAIN LANDING RESORT. ⒶⒶⒶ (573) 735-9422. **$39.** 42819 Landing Ln 63456. From jct US 36 & US 61: Go 14 mi W on 36 to J Road, then 7-1/2 mi S on J Road. ⇗ ⊠

MONTGOMERY CITY — LAZY DAY CAMPGROUND. (573) 564-2949. **$30-$32.** 214 Highway J 63361. From jct I-70 (exit 170) & Hwy J: Go 1-1/4 mi S on Hwy J. ⛽ ⇗ ⊠ ♿

OWENSVILLE — LOST VALLEY LAKE RESORT. (573) 764-2129. **Call for rates. (no credit cards).** 2334 Hwy ZZ 65066. From jct I-44 (exit 247) & US 50: Go 25 mi W on US 50 to Hwy Y, then 3-1/2 mi N to Hwy ZZ, then 6 mi W on Hwy ZZ. ⛰ ⇗ ⊠ ♿

PECULIAR — PECULIAR PARK PLACE RV PARK. (816) 779-6300. **$30-$32. (no credit cards).** 22901 SE Outer Rd 64078. From jct Hwy 58 & US 71: Go 6 mi S on US 71, (Peculiar exit), then 300 ft E on CR J, then 1-1/2 mi S on E Outer Rd. ⛰ ⊠ ♿

PLATTE CITY — BASSWOOD COUNTRY RESORT. ⒶⒶⒶ (816) 858-5556. **$37-$49.** 15880 Interurban Rd 64079. From jct I-29 & Hwy 92 (exit 18): Go 3-3/4 mi E on Hwy 92, then 1-3/4 mi N on Winan Rd, then 2 blocks W on Interurban Rd. ⇗ ⊠ ♿

ST. CHARLES — SUNDERMEIER RV PARK & CONFERENCE CENTER. (800) 929-0832. **$53-$58.** 111 Transit St 63301-0949. From jct Hwy 370 & N 3rd St/Hwy 94 (exit 7): Go 3/10 mi W on Hwy 94, then 2 blocks E on Transit St. ⛰ ⊠

ST. JOSEPH — BEACON RV PARK. (816) 279-5417. **$26-$34.** 822 S Belt Hwy 64507. From jct I-29 (exit 46B) and US 36W: Go 1/4 mi W on US 36 (exit Belt Hwy), then 3/4 mi N on Belt Hwy. ⊠ ♿

Montana

BILLINGS — BILLINGS KOA. (800) 562-8546. **Call for rates.** 547 Garden Ave 59101. From jct I-90 (exit 450) & Hwy 3/27th St: Go 1 block S on 27th St, then 3/4 mi SW on Garden Ave. ⇗ ⊠ ♿

BILLINGS — YELLOWSTONE RIVER RV PARK & CAMP-GROUND. (800) 654-0878. **$22-$58.** 309 Garden Ave 59101. From jct I-90 (exit 450) & Hwy 3/27th St: Go 1 block S on 27th St, then 1/4 mi SW on Garden Ave. ⛽ ⇗ ⊠ ♿

ENNIS — ENNIS RV VILLAGE. ⒶⒶⒶ (866) 682-5272. **$26-$33.** 5034 US Highway 287 N 59729. From jct Hwy 287 & US 287: Go 3/4 mi N on US 287. ⊠ ♿

LIVINGSTON — YELLOWSTONE'S EDGE RV PARK. (800) 865-7322. **$44.** 3502 Hwy 89 S 59047. From jct I-90 (exit 333) & US 89: Go 18 mi S on US 89. ⛰ ⊠ ♿

POLSON — POLSON-FLATHEAD LAKE KOA. (888) 883-2151. **$39-$56.** 200 Irvine Flats Rd 59860. From jct Hwy 35 & US 93: Go 3 mi N on US 93, then 1/4 mi W on Irvine Flats Rd. ⛰ ⇗ ⊠ ♿

POLSON — POLSON MOTORCOACH & RV RESORT. (800) 985-0421. **$55-$65.** 200 Irvine Flats Rd 59860. From jct Hwy 35 & US 93: Go 3 mi N on US 93, then 1/4 mi W on Irvine Flats Rd. ⛰ ⇗ ⊠ ♿

WEST YELLOWSTONE — YELLOWSTONE GRIZZLY RV PARK. (406) 646-4466. $49-$60. 210 S Electric St 59758. From jct US 191/287 & US 20 South: Go 2 blks W on US 20 South, then 4 blks S on Electric St.

Nebraska

LINCOLN — CAMP-A-WAY. (866) 719-2267. $35-$49. 200 Campers Cir 68521. From jct I-80 (exit 401A) & I-180: Go 1/4 mi S on I-180, then 1/4 mi W on Superior St, then 1/4 mi NE on Camper Cir.

Nevada

ELKO — IRON HORSE RV RESORT. (775) 777-1919. $30-$45. 3400 E Idaho St 89801. From jct I-80 (exit 303) & Idaho St: Go 1/4 mi E on Idaho St (Hwy 140).

LAS VEGAS — LAS VEGAS RV RESORT. (702) 451-8005. $29. 3890 S Nellis Blvd 89121. From jct I-515 (US 93/95 Expressway) & Flamingo (exit 69): Go 1 mi E on Flamingo, then 1/4 mi N on Nellis Blvd.

LAS VEGAS — LVM RESORT. (866) 897-9300. $59-$99. 8175 Arville St 89139. From jct I-15 & Blue Diamond Road exit: Go 1 mi W on Blue Diamond Rd; then 1/4 mi N on Arville.

LAS VEGAS — OASIS LAS VEGAS RV RESORT. (800) 566-4707. $40-$72. 2711 W Windmill Lane 89123. Northbound: From jct I-15 (exit 33) & Hwy 160 (Blue Diamond) exit 33: Go 1/4 mi E on Blue Diamond, then S on first right turn into park.

MESQUITE — SOLSTICE MOTORCOACH RESORT & COUNTRY CLUB. (866) 762-0664. $40-$55. Corner of John Deere Dr & Bertha Howe Ln 89027. From I-15 (exit 120): Go N .5 mi on Falcon Ridge, then W .5 mi on Bertha Howe Way, then S .5 mi on John Deere Dr, then W .04 mi on Majestic Dr.

MINDEN — SILVER CITY RV RESORT. (800) 997-6393. $35. 3165 US Highway 395 N 89423. From south jct US 50 & US 395 (Carson St): Go 3-1/2 mi S on US 395 (Carson St) (8 mi N of Minden).

PAHRUMP — NEVADA TREASURE RV RESORT. (775) 751-1174. $40-$60. 301 W Leslie Rd 89060. From jct SR 372 & SR 160: Go 7-1/2 mi NW on SR 160.

PAHRUMP — TERRIBLE'S LAKESIDE CASINO & RV RESORT. (888) 558-5253. $29-$49. 5870 S Homestead Rd 89048. From jct Hwy 372 & Hwy 160: Go 2 mi S on Hwy 160; then 4 mi S on Homestead Rd.

SPARKS — SPARKS MARINA RV PARK. (775) 851-8888. $23-$44. 1200 E Lincoln Way 89434. From I-80 East & Sparks Blvd. (exit 20): Go 1 block N on Sparks Blvd to Lincoln Way, then go 2 blocks W on Lincoln Way.

New Hampshire

FREEDOM — DANFORTH BAY CAMPING & RV RESORT. (603) 539-2069. $48. 196 Shawtown Rd 03836. From jct Hwy 16 & Hwy 41: Go 1/2 mi N on Hwy 41, then 4-3/4 mi E on Ossipee Lake Rd, then 1 mi NE on Shawtown Rd.

FREEDOM — THE BLUFFS RV RESORT. (603) 539-2069. $48. 196 Shawtown Rd. 03836. From jct Hwy 16 & Hwy 41: Go 1/2 mi N on Hwy 41, then 4-3/4 mi E on Ossipee Lake Rd, then 1-1/4 m NE on Shawtown Rd.

NEW BOSTON — FRIENDLY BEAVER CAMPGROUND. (603) 487-5570. $36-$42. 88 Cochran Hill Rd 03070. From jct Hwy 77 & Hwy 136 & Hwy 13: Go 100 feet S on Hwy 13, then 2 mi W on Old Coach Rd.

TAMWORTH — CHOCORUA CAMPING VILLAGE KOA. (888) 237-8642. $32-$63. 893 White Mountain Hwy 03886. From north jct Hwy 25 & Hwy 16: Go 3 mi N on Hwy 16.

WEARE — COLD SPRINGS CAMP RESORT. (603) 529-2528. $52-$56. 62 Barnard Hill Rd 03281. From jct Hwy 149 & Hwy 114: Go 1 mi SE on Hwy 114, then 1/4 mi E on Barnard Hill Rd.

New Jersey

CAPE MAY — BEACHCOMBER CAMPING RESORT. (609) 886-6035. $33-$70. 462 Seashore Rd 08204. From jct Hwy 47 & US 9: Go 1-1/4 mi S on US 9, then 1 block W on Sally Marshall Crossing, then 1 block N on Seashore Rd.

CAPE MAY — HOLLY SHORES CAMPGROUND. (609) 886-1234. $34-$69. 491 Route 9 08204. From jct Hwy-47 & US-9: Go 1-1/4 mi S on US-9.

CAPE MAY — SEASHORE CAMPSITES. (609) 884-4010. $25-$62. 720 Seashore Rd 08204. From jct Garden State Parkway (exit 4A) & Hwy 47 N: Go 1 mi W on Hwy 47, then 2-3/4 mi S on Hwy 626 (Railroad Ave).

CAPE MAY COURT HOUSE — BIG TIMBER LAKE CAMPING RESORT. (609) 465-4456. $50-$74. 116 Swainton Goshen Rd 08210. From Garden State Pkwy (exit 13) & Avalon Blvd: Go 1/2 mi W on Avalon Blvd, then 3/4 mi S on US 9, then 1 mi W on Hwy 646.

New Mexico

GALLUP — USA RV PARK. (505) 863-5021. $29-$31. 2925 W. Hwy 66 87301. From jct I-40 (exit 16) & SR 118: Go E 1-1/4 mi on Hwy 66.

LAS CRUCES — HACIENDA RV RESORT. (888) 686-9090. $25-$55. 740 Stern Dr 88005. From jct I-10 & US 70: Go 5 mi E on I-10 to Hwy 28 (exit 140), then 1/4 mi S to Stern Dr, then 1/4 mi E on Stern Dr.

New York

BATH — HICKORY HILL CAMPING RESORT. (800) 760-0947. **$42-$65.** 7531 County Route 13 14810. From jct I-86/Hwy 17 (exit 38) & Hwy 54: Go 1 mi E on Hwy 54, (stop light), turn N on Hwy 54 for 1 block to fork in road, bear left onto Haverling St (CR 13) for 2 miles. ⛵ 🍴 ♿M

CHAUTAUQUA — CAMP CHAUTAUQUA CAMPING RESORT. (716) 789-3435. **$30-$65.** 3900 W Lake Rd 14785. E'bnd: From SE town limits: Go 2-3/4 mi SE on Hwy 394. W'bnd: From I-86/Hwy 17 (exit 8) & Hwy 394: Go 3 mi NW on Hwy 394 ⛵ 🍴 ♿M

COPAKE — KOA COPAKE. (518) 329-2811. **$49-$64.** 2236 County Rte. 7 12516. From jct I-87 & Hwy 23: Go 15 mi E on Hwy 23, then 5 mi S on Hwy 22, then 2 mi SW on Hwy 7A. ⛵ 🍴 ♿M

CORINTH — ALPINE LAKE RV RESORT, LLC. (518) 654-6260. **$52-$61.** 78 Heath Rd 12822. From south village limits: Go 1-1/4 mi S on Hwy 9N, then 1-1/4 mi E on Heath Rd. ⛵ 🍴 ♿M

DEWITTVILLE — CHAUTAUQUA LAKE KOA. (716) 386-3804. **$30-$55.** 5652 Thumb Rd 14728. From jct I-86 (exit 10) & Hwy 430: Go 6-1/2 mi W on Hwy 430, then 1/2 mi E on Thumb Rd. ⛵ 🍴 ♿M

FLORIDA — BLACK BEAR CAMPGROUND. ⓐⓐⓐ (845) 651-7717. **$45-$55.** 197 Wheeler Rd 10921. From jct Hwy 17 (exit 124) & Hwy 17A: Go 5-1/2 mi SW on Hwy 17A, turn right at light (Bridge St), then 1-1/2 mi W on CR 41. 🏕 ⛵ 🍴 ♿M

GARDINER — YOGI BEAR'S JELLYSTONE PARK CAMP-RESORT AT LAZY RIVER. (845) 255-5193. **$42-$68.** 50 Bevier Rd 12525. From jct Hwy-208 & Hwy-44/55: Go 2-1/2 mi W on Hwy-44/55, then 2/10 mi S on Albany Post Rd, then 1/2 mi E on Bevier Rd. ⛵ 🍴 ♿M

GREENFIELD PARK — SKYWAY CAMPING RESORT. (845) 647-5747. **$65.** 99 Mountaindale Rd 12435. From jct US 209 & Hwy 52: Go 5 mi W on Hwy 52, then 1 mi S on Skyway RV Rd (immediate right fork). ⛵ 🍴 ♿M

HENDERSON — ASSOCIATION ISLAND RV RESORT & MARINA. (800) 393-4189. **$30-$75.** 15530 Snowshoe Rd 13650. From I-81 (exit 41) & Hwy 178: Go 12 mi W on Hwy 178, then 2 mi N on Snowshoe Rd, cross bridge to 2nd Island. 🏕 ⛵ 🍴 ♿M

HERKIMER — KOA-HERKIMER DIAMOND RESORT. (800) 562-0897. **$34-$69.** 4621 State Route 28 13350. From I-90 (exit 30) & Hwy 2815: Go N on Hwy 28 (thru town) for 7 miles. ⛵ 🍴

LAKE GEORGE — LAKE GEORGE ESCAPE RESORT. (800) 327-3188. **$23-$70.** 175 E Schroon River Rd 12845. From jct I-87 (Exit 23) & Diamond Point Rd: Go 1/4 mi E on Diamond Point Rd, then 3/4 mi N on East Schroon River Rd. ⛵ 🍴 ♿M

LAKE GEORGE — LAKE GEORGE RV PARK. (518) 792-3775. **$52-$72.** 74 State Route 149 12845-3501. From jct I-87 (Exit 20-Northway) & Hwy-149/US-9: Go 3/4 mi N on Hwy-149/US-9, then 1/2 mi E on Hwy-149. 🏕 ⛵ 🍴 ♿M

NORTH HUDSON — YOGI BEAR'S JELLYSTONE PARK AT PARADISE PINES. (518) 532-7493. **$42-$61.** 4035 Blue Ridge RD 12855. From jct I-87 (exit 29-North Hudson) & Blue Ridge Rd: Go 750 feet E on Blue Ridge Rd. ⛵ 🍴 ♿M

NORTH JAVA — YOGI BEAR'S JELLYSTONE PARK OF WESTERN NEW YORK. (585) 457-9644. **$30-$84.** 5204 Youngers Rd 14113. From jct Hwy 98 & Hwy 78 (at Five Corners): Go 1-1/2 mi E on Pee Dee Rd, then 3/4 mi S Youngers Rd. ⛵ 🍴 ♿M

PLATTEKILL — NEW YORK CITY NORTH/NEWBURG KOA. (845) 564-2836. **$50-$67.** 119 Freetown Hwy 12568. From jct I-84 (exit 7N) & I-87 (exit 17): Go 4 mi N on Hwy-300, then 5 mi N on Hwy-32, then 1/2 mi NE on Freetown Hwy. ⛵ 🍴

VERONA — THE VILLAGES AT TURNING STONE RV PARK. (315) 361-7275. **$40-$55.** 5065 State Route 365 13478. From jct I-90 (NY Thruway) (exit 33) & Hwy 365: Go 1-1/2 mi W on Hwy 365. 🏕 ⛵ 🍴 ♿M

WATKINS GLEN — KOA-WATKINS GLEN/CORNING RESORT. (800) 562-7430. **$40-$80.** 1710 Route 414 14891. From South jct Hwy-14 & Hwy-414: Go 4-1/2 mi S on Hwy-414. ⛵ 🍴 ♿M

WOODRIDGE — YOGI BEAR'S JELLYSTONE PARK AT BIRCHWOOD ACRES. (800) 552-4724. **$66-$68.** 85 Martinfeld Rd 12789. From jct US-209 & Hwy-52: Go 8 mi W on Hwy-52, then 1 mi S on Martinfeld Rd. ⛵ 🍴 ♿M

North Carolina

EMERALD ISLE — HOLIDAY TRAV-L-PARK RESORT FOR CAMPERS. (252) 354-2250. **$50-$103.** 9102 Coast Guard Rd 28594. From jct Hwy 24 & Hwy 58: Go 2 mi SE on Hwy 58, then W on Coast Guard Rd. ⛵ 🍴 ♿M

JACKSON SPRINGS — SYCAMORE LODGE. (910) 652-5559. Call for rates. (no credit cards). 1059 Sycamore Lane 27281. From jct US 15/501 & NC211/US 1: Go 2/10 mi S on US 1, then 4-1/2 mi W on Roseland, then 5-1/4 mi SW on Rose Ridge Rd, then 2-3/4 mi NW on Sycamore Ln (NC 1465). ⛵ 🍴

SWANNANOA — MAMA GERTIE'S HIDEAWAY CAMP-GROUND. ⓐⓐⓐ (828) 686-4258. **$30-$46.** 15 Uphill Rd 28778. From jct I-40 (exit 59) & Patton Cove Rd: Go 1/2 mi S on Patton Cove Rd. 🍴 ♿M

Ohio

ANDOVER — BAY SHORE RESORT. (440) 293-7202. **$38-$46.** 7124 Pymatuning Lake Rd 44003. From jct US 6 / Hwy 7 & Hwy 85: Go 1-1/2 mi E on Hwy-85, then 4-1/4 mi S on Pymatuning Lake Rd. ⛵ 🍴 ♿M

BIG PRAIRIE — WHISPERING HILLS FAMILY CAMP-GROUND. (800) 992-2435. **$34-$48.** 8248 State Route 514 44611. From jct Hwy 226 & Hwy 514: Go 2 mi S on Hwy 514. ⛵ 🍴 ♿M

BROOKVILLE — KOA-DAYTON TALL TIMBERS RESORT. (937) 833-3888. **$42-$56.** 7796 Wellbaum Rd 45309. From jct I-70 (exit 24) & SR 49: Go 1/2 mi N on SR 49, then 1/2 mi W on Pleasant Plains Rd, then 1/4 mi S on Wellbaum Rd. ⛵ 🍴 ♿M

BUCKEYE LAKE — **BUCKEYE LAKE/COLUMBUS EAST KOA KAMPING RESORT.** (740) 928-0706. **$40-$91.** 4460 Walnut Road SE 43008. From jct I-70 (exit 129A) & SR 79: Go 1-1/2 mi S on SR 79. 🛶 ⊠ 🔥ᴹ

DELAWARE — **CROSS CREEK CAMPING RESORT.** (740) 549-2267. **$36-$60.** 3190 S Old State Rd 43015. From jct I-71 (exit 131) & SR 36/37: Go 3 mi W on SR 36/37, then 3 mi S on Lackey (Old State Rd.) ⑤🅳 🛶 ⊠ 🔥ᴹ

GENEVA-ON-THE-LAKE — **NASCAR RV RESORTS AT INDIAN CREEK.** (440) 466-8191. **$30-$58.** 4710 Lake Rd E 44041. From jct I-90 (exit 223) & Hwy 45: Go 6 mi N on Hwy 45, then 4 mi W on Hwy 531. 🛶 ⊠ 🔥ᴹ

GRANVILLE — **LAZY RIVER AT GRANVILLE.** ⒶⒶⒶ (740) 366-4385. **$28-$49.** 2340 Dry Creek Rd. NE 43023. From jct I-70 (exit 126) & SR 37: Go 8 mi N on SR 37, then 4-1/2 mi N on SR 661, then 1-1/4 mi E on Dry Creek Rd NE (CR 10). 🛶 ⊠ 🔥ᴹ

MANTUA — **YOGI BEAR'S JELLYSTONE PARK (MORGAN RV RESORTS).** (866) 617-8464. **$40-$59.** 3392 State Route 82 44255. From jct Hwy 43 & Hwy 82: Go 4-1/4 mi E on Hwy 82. 🛶 ⊠ 🔥ᴹ

MARENGO — **CARDINAL CENTER CAMPGROUND.** (419) 253-0800. **$26-$39.** 616 State Route 61 43334. From jct I-71 (exit 140) & SR 61: Go 1/2 mi N on SR 61. 🛶 ⊠ 🔥ᴹ

MOUNT EATON — **EVERGREEN PARK RV RESORT.** (888) 359-6429. **$50.** 16359 Dover Rd 44659. From jct Hwy 62 & US 250: Go 4 mi W on US 250. ⑤🅳 🛶 ⊠ 🔥ᴹ

NEW PHILADELPHIA — **WOOD'S TALL TIMBER LAKE RESORT.** ⒶⒶⒶ (330) 602-4000. **$31-$35.** 1921 Tall Timber Road NE 44663. From jct I-77 (exit 81) & SR 39: Go 7 mi E on SR 39, then 1/2 mi NE on Tall Timber Rd NE (County Road 88). ⑤🅳 🛶 ⊠ 🔥ᴹ

SANDUSKY — **CEDAR POINT CAMPER VILLAGE/ LIGHTHOUSE POINT.** (419) 627-2106. **$65-$90.** 1 Cedar Pointe Dr 44870. From jct Hwy 2 & US 250: Go 5 mi NW on US 250, then 1 mi E on US 6, then 4 mi N on Causeway Dr. 🏕 🛶 ⊠ 🔥ᴹ

SANDUSKY — **SANDUSKY BAYSHORE KOA.** (800) 562-2486. **$35-$67.** 2311 Cleveland Rd 44870. From jct US 250 & US 6: Go 1-3/4 mi E on US 6. 🛶 ⊠ 🔥ᴹ

SHELBY — **SHELBY/MANSFIELD KOA (WAGON WHEEL CAMPGROUND).** ⒶⒶⒶ (419) 347-1392. **$35-$77.** 6787 Baker 47 44875. From jct Hwy 61 & Hwy 39: Go 4 mi W on Hwy 39, then 4-1/2 mi N on Baker Rd. 🛶 ⊠ 🔥ᴹ

VAN BUREN — **PLEASANT VIEW RECREATION (FORMERLY FINDLAY/VAN BUREN KOA).** (419) 299-3897. **$30-$44.** 12611 Township Road 218 45889. From jct I-75 (exit 164) & SR 613: Go 3/4 mi E on SR 613, then 1/4 mi SE on Twp 218. 🛶 ⊠ 🔥ᴹ

WAPAKONETA — **WAPAKONETA/LIMA SOUTH - KOA.** (419) 738-6016. **$40-$55.** 14719 Cemetery Rd 45895. From jct I-75 N'bnd exit 110 & S'bnd exit 111: Go 1/2 block east to first intersection, then 3/4 mi N on Cemetery Rd. 🛶 ⊠ 🔥ᴹ

Oklahoma

ARDMORE — **HIDDEN LAKE RV PARK.** (580) 220-2900. **$28.** 4661 Hedges Rd 73401. From jct I-35 (exit 29) & US 70 E: Go 1000 ft W on US 70, then 1-1/4 mi S on Hedges Rd. 🏕 🛶 ⊠ 🔥ᴹ

CALUMET — **CHEROKEE KOA.** (800) 562-5736. **$34-$37.** 301 S Walbum 73014. From jct US-81 & I-40: Go 17-1/2 mi W on I-40 (exit 108), then 100 yards N on Spur US-281/North, then 1/4 mi E on access road beside Trading Post. 🛶 ⊠ 🔥ᴹ

CHECOTAH — **CHECOTAH/LAKE EUFAULA WEST KOA.** (800) 562-7510. **$35-$41.** HC 68 Box 750 74426. From jct US-69 & I-40 (exit 264): Go 9 mi W on I-40 (exit 255), then 1/2 mi W on N service road. 🛶 ⊠ 🔥ᴹ

CHOCTAW — **KOA-OKLAHOMA CITY EAST.** (405) 391-5000. **$35-$52.** 6200 S Choctaw Rd 73020. From jct I-44 & I-40: Go 19 mi E on I-40 (exit 166), then 3/4 mi N on Choctaw Rd. 🛶 ⊠

GORE — **MARVAL RESORT.** ⒶⒶⒶ (800) 340-4280. **$34-$60.** Rt 3 Box 60 74435. From jct I-40 (exit 287) & Hwy 100: Go 6 mi N on Hwy 100, then 1/4 mi E on Gore Landing Rd to MarVal Lane. 🛶 ⊠ 🔥ᴹ

NEWCASTLE — **A-AAA ADULT RV PARK.** (405) 387-3334. **$30. (no credit cards).** 3550 SW 24th St 73065. From jct I-44 (exit 108) & Hwy 37: Go 3 mi W on Hwy 37, then 5 mi S on Hwy 76, then 1/4 mi W on SW 24th St/NE 85th St. ⑤🅳 🏕

OKLAHOMA CITY — **ROCKWELL RV PARK.** (888) 684-3251. **$28-$30.** 720 S. Rockwell 73128. From jct I-44 & I-40: Go 3 mi W on I-40 (exit 143), then 800 feet S on Rockwell Ave. ⊠ 🔥ᴹ

OKLAHOMA CITY — **TWIN FOUNTAINS RV PARK.** (866) 693-1469. **$40.** 2727 NE 63rd St 73111. From jct I-40 & I-44: Go 9 mi E on I-44 (exit 129), then 1/2 mi E on NE 63rd St. 🏕 🛶 ⊠

SALLISAW — **SALLISAW/FT SMITH WEST KOA.** (800) 562-2797. **$28-$38.** 1900 KOA Power Drive 74955. From jct I-40 (exit 308) & US 59: Go 1/2 mi S on US 59, then 1/4 mi W on KOA Power Dr. 🛶 ⊠

THACKERVILLE — **WINSTAR RV PARK.** (580) 276-8900. **$25.** Exit 1, I-35 73459. From I-35 (exit 1): Go 1-1/4 mi N on E Feeder Rd, then 1/2 mi E on Scott. 🛶 ⊠ 🔥ᴹ

TULSA — **MINGO RV PARK.** (918) 832-8824. **$28.** 801 N. Mingo Rd 74116. From jct I-44/I-244: Go 1 mi W on I-244, 1/4 mi S on Garnett, then 1 mi W on Admiral, then 1/8 mi N on Mingo. From jct I-244/ Mingo (exit 13A): Go 1 blk N on Mingo. From jct I-44/US 169: Go 1-3/4 mi N on US 169, then 1/8 mi W on Admiral, 1/8 mi N on Mingo. 🏕 ⊠ 🔥ᴹ

VINITA — **WATER'S EDGE RV RESORT.** (918) 782-1444. **$25-$36.** 44671 E 355th 74301. From jct Hwy 85 & Hwy 82: Go 1 mi S on Hwy 82, then 1/2 mi E on E 350 Rd. 🏕 🛶 ⊠

Oregon

BEND — BEND/SISTERS GARDEN RV RESORT. (541) 549-3021. **$42-$63.** 67667 Hwy 20 97701. From jct Hwy-242 & US-20: Go 3-3/4 mi SE on US-20.

BEND — CROWN VILLA RV RESORT. (541) 388-1131. **$34-$89.** 60801 Brosterhous Rd. 97702. At the "South Junction" of Hwy 97 & Bus 97/Third Street Exit: Go 1/4 mi N on Bus 97/Third St, then 1 mi E on Murphy Rd, then 300 yds S on Brosterhous Rd.

BLUE RIVER — HOLIDAY FARM RV PARK. (541) 822-3726. **$35.** 54432 McKenzie Hwy 97413. From East town limits: Go 3-1/2 mi E on Hwy 126.

CANNON BEACH — RV RESORT AT CANNON BEACH. AAA (800) 847-2231. **$32-$44.** 340 Elk Creek Rd 97110. From jct US 26 & US 101: Go 4 mi S on US 101, then 100 yds E on Sunset Blvd, then 2 blocks E on Elk Creek Rd.

CANYONVILLE — SEVEN FEATHERS RV RESORT. AAA (877) 839-3599. **$38-$46.** 325 Creekside Dr 97417. From jct I-5 (exit 99) on W side of I-5 behind 7 Feathers Truck & Travel Ctr. Follow signs.

CHARLESTON — AAA MIDWAY RV PARK. (541) 888-9300. **$50.** 92478 Cape Arago Hwy 97420. From jct of US 101 & Newmark: Go 3 mi W on Newmark to Empire (Cape Arago Hwy), then 1.5 mi S on Empire.

EUGENE — PREMIER RV RESORT - EUGENE. (888) 710-8451. **$40-$47.** 33022 Van Duyn Rd 97408. From jct I-5 & Van Duyn Rd/Pearl St (exit 199): Go 2 blocks E on Van Duyn Rd.

FAIRVIEW — PORTLAND FAIRVIEW RV PARK. (877) 777-1047. **$35.** 21401 NE Sandy Blvd 97024. From jct I-84 (exit 14) Fairway Pkwy: Go 1/4 mi N on Fairway Pkwy, then 1/4 mi E on Sandy Blvd.

FLORENCE — PACIFIC PINES RV PARK & STORAGE. (541) 997-1434. **$27-$30.** 4044 Hwy 101 97439. From jct Hwy 126 & US 101: Go 2 mi N on US 101, then 1/2 block E on 42nd St.

FOSTER — FOSTER LAKE RV RESORT. (541) 367-5629. **$33-$37.** 6191 Hwy 20 E 97345. From east edge of town: Go 5 mi SE on Hwy 20 E.

GRANTS PASS — JACKS LANDING RV RESORT. (866) 785-2257. **$24-$30.** 247 NE Morgan Lane 97526. From jct I-5 North Grants Pass (exit 58) & 6th St (Hwy 99): Go 1/4 mi S on 6th St, then 1 block E on Hillcrest, then 1/4 mi N on 7th, then go 1 block E on Morgan Ln.

GRANTS PASS — MOON MOUNTAIN RV RESORT. (541) 479-1145. **$34.** 3298 Pearce Park Rd 97526. From jct I-5 (exit 55) & US 199: Go 200 yds W to signal, then 1/4 mi S on Agness, then 3/4 mi E on Foothill Blvd, then 3/4 mi E on Tom Pearce Park Rd.

LEBANON — MALLARD CREEK GOLF & RV RESORT. (541) 259-0070. **$40.** 31958 Bellinger Scale Rd 97355. From jct Hwy 34 & Denny School Rd (5 mi E of I-5 exit 228): Go 2-1/2 mi S on Denny School Rd, then 5 mi SE on Hwy 20, then 1-1/4 mi N on Waterloo Dr (go through Waterloo & across river), then 1/4 mi E on Berlin Rd, then 3/4 mi N on Bellinger Scale Rd.

LINCOLN CITY — LOGAN ROAD RV PARK. (877) 564-2678. **$32-$38.** 4800 NE Logan Rd 97367. From jct Hwy 18 & US 101: Go 3-1/4 mi S on US 101, then 3 blocks W on Logan Rd.

LINCOLN CITY — PREMIER RV RESORTS - LINCOLN CITY. (877) 871-0663. **$39-$41.** 4100 SE Highway 101 97367. From jct Hwy 18 & US 101: Go 6 mi S on US 101.

MCMINNVILLE — OLDE STONE VILLAGE RV PARK. (877) 472-4315. **$31.** 4155 Three Mile Lane 97128. From South jct Hwy 99 W & Hwy 18 (SW of McMinnville): Go 4 mi E on Hwy 18.

NEWPORT — OUTDOOR RESORTS PACIFIC SHORES MOTORCOACH RESORT. (800) 333-1583. **$50-$90.** 6225 N Coast Hwy 97365. From jct US 20 & US 101: Go 3 mi N on US 101.

NORTH BEND — THE MILL CASINO RV PARK. (800) 953-4800. **$20-$44.** 3201 Tremont Ave 97459. From jct US 101 & Commercial St: (Charleston/State Parks exit): Go 2 mi N on US 101.

OAKLAND — RICE HILL RV PARK. AAA (541) 849-2335. **$32.** 1120 John Long Rd 97462. From jct I-5 (exit 148) & John Long Rd: Go 1/4 mi N on John Long Rd.

PORTLAND — JANTZEN BEACH RV PARK. AAA (800) 443-7248. **$30.** 1503 N Hayden Is Dr 97217. From jct Bypass US-30 & I-5: Go 2-1/2 mi N on I-5 (exit 308 Jantzen Beach), then 1/2 mi W on Hayden Island Dr.

SALEM — HEE HEE ILLAHEE RV RESORT. (877) 564-7295. **$32-$36.** 4751 Astoria St NE 97305. From jct I-5 (exit 258) & Hwy 99 E (Portland Rd NE): Go 1/4 mi N on Hwy 99 E (Portland Rd), then 1/4 mi NW on Astoria St.

SALEM — PHOENIX RV PARK. AAA (800) 237-2497. **$33.** 4130 Silverton Rd NE 97305. S'bnd from I-5 (exit 256): Go left on Market Rd, then left on Lancaster Rd, then right on Silverton Rd. N'bnd from I-5 (exit 256): Go right on Market Rd, then left on Lancaster, then right on Silverton Rd.

SALEM — PREMIER RV RESORT - SALEM. AAA (877) 364-9990. **$36-$47.** 4700 Salem-Dallas Hwy 22 97304. From jct I-5 (exit 260A) & Hwy 99E: Go 3-1/4 mi Sw on Hwy 99E (Salem Hwy). then 1-1/2 mi S on Commercial St (Hwy 99E), then 4-3/4 mi W on Hwy 22 (follow ocean coast signs).

SUTHERLIN — HI-WAY HAVEN RV PARK. AAA (541) 459-4557. **$29-$31.** 609 Fort McKay Rd 97479. From jct I-5 (exit 136) & Hwy 138: Go 3/4 mi W on Hwy 138, then 1/4 mi W on Fort McKay Rd.

TUALATIN — ROAMERS REST RV PARK, LLC. (877) 478-7275. **$38.** 17585 SW Pacific Hwy (99W) 97062. S b'd from jct I-5 (Exit 294) & Hwy 99 W: Go 5 mi SW on Hwy 99 (R) N b'd. From jct I-5 & (Exit 289) Nyberg Rd: Go 2-3/4 mi W on Nyberg/Tualatin-Sherwood Rd, then 1-1/2 mi NW on 124th, then 1/4 mi N on Pacific Hwy/99 W (L). 🚗 ⴕM

WESTFIR — CASEY'S RIVERSIDE RV PARK. (541) 782-1906. **$38.** 46443 Westfir Rd. 97492. From jct I-5 (exit 188) & Hwy 58: Go 31 mi E on Hwy 58 to Westfir Rd, then 1/2 mi NE on Westfir Rd. Follow signs. 🚗 ⴄ ⴌ ⴕM

WILSONVILLE — PHEASANT RIDGE RV RESORT. ⴵ (503) 682-7829. **$39-$43.** 8275 SW Elligsen Rd 97070. From I-5 (exit 286 Stafford Rd): Go 1/4 mi E on Elligsen Rd. 🚗 ⴄ ⴌ ⴕM

WOODBURN — PORTLAND-WOODBURN RV PARK. ⴵ (888) 988-0002. **$37.** 115 N Arney Rd 97071. From jct I-5 & Hwy 214/219 (exit 271): Go 1/4 mi W on Hwy 219, then 1 block N on Arney Rd, then 1/2 block E at stop sign, then left at Starbucks. 🚗 ⴄ ⴌ ⴕM

YACHATS — SEA PERCH RV RESORT. (541) 547-3505. **$50-$70.** 95480 Hwy 101 S 97498. From south edge of town: Go 6-1/2 mi S on US 101. 🚗 ⴄ ⴌ ⴕM

Pennsylvania

BEDFORD — FRIENDSHIP VILLAGE CAMPGROUND & RV PARK. ⴵ (814) 623-1677. **$27-$43.** 348 Friendship Village Rd 15522. From jct PA Tpk & Bus US 220 (exit 146): Go 300 yds N on Bus US 220, then 1-1/2 mi S on US 220, then 1-1/2 mi NW on US 30, then 1/2 mi NE on Friendship Village Rd. ⴄ ⴌ ⴕM

BELLEFONTE — KOA-BELLEFONTE/STATE COLLEGE. (800) 562-8127. **$41-$60.** 2481 Jacksonville Rd 16823. From jct I-80 & SR-26 (exit 161): Go 2 mi N on SR-26 ⴄ ⴌ ⴕM

EAST STROUDSBURG — MOUNTAIN VISTA CAMPGROUND. (570) 223-0111. **$35-$56. (no credit cards).** 50 Taylor Dr 18301. From jct I-80 (exit 309) & US 209: Go 350 yds N on US 209, then 2 mi NW on SR-447, then 3 mi N on Business US 209, then 1 mi W on Craig's Meadow Rd, then 500 feet SW on Taylor Dr. ⴄ ⴌ ⴕM

EAST STROUDSBURG — OTTER LAKE CAMP RESORT. (800) 345-1369. **$39-$68.** 4805 Marshalls Creek Rd 18302. From jct I-80 & US 209 (exit 309): Go 4 mi N on US 209, then 300 feet NW on SR 402, then 7-1/2 mi N on Marshalls Creek Rd. ⴌ ⴕM

GETTYSBURG — DRUMMER BOY CAMPING RESORT. (800) 293-2808. **$36-$75.** 1300 Hanover Rd 17325. From jct US 30 & Bus US 15: Go 1/4 mi E on US 30, then 1 mi E on SR 116, then 1/8 mi N on Rocky Grove Rd. ⴄ ⴌ ⴕM

GETTYSBURG — GETTYSBURG CAMPGROUND. ⴵ (888) 879-2241. **$37-$53.** 2030 Fairfield Rd 17325. From jct Business US 15 & SR-116: Go 3 mi W on SR-116. ⴄ ⴌ

GETTYSBURG — KOA-GETTYSBURG. (800) 562-1869. **$28-$71.** 20 Knox Rd 17325. From jct US-30 & Business US-15: Go 3 mi W on US-30, then 2-1/2 mi S on Knoxlyn Rd, then 1/2 mi W on Knox Rd. ⴄ ⴌ ⴕM

HARRISVILLE — JELLYSTONE PARK AT KOZY REST. ⴵ (724) 735-2417. **$31-$48.** 449 Campground Rd 16038. From jct I-79 & SR-208 (exit 113): Go 4 mi E on SR-208, then 4 mi E on SR-58, then 2 mi N on Campground Rd. ⴄ ⴌ ⴕM

MANHEIM — PINCH POND FAMILY CAMPGROUND & RV PARK. ⴵ (800) 659-7640. **$38-$45.** 3075 Pinch Rd 17545. From jct PA Tpk (exit 266/20) & SR 72: Go 1 mi S on SR 72, then 1/2 mi W on Cider Press Rd, then 1 mi N on Pinch Rd. ⴌ ⴄ ⴌ ⴕM

MCKEAN — KOA-ERIE. (800) 562-7610. **$36-$68.** 6645 West Rd 16426. From jct I-79 (exit 174): Go 1 mi W on West Rd. ⴄ ⴌ ⴕM

MILL RUN — YOGI BEAR'S JELLYSTONE PARK CAMP-RESORT-MILL RUN. (800) 439-9644. **$62-$75.** 839 Mill Run Rd 15464. From south town limits: Go 1/8 mi S on SR-381. ⴄ ⴌ ⴕM

MUNCY VALLEY — PIONEER CAMPGROUND. (570) 946-9971. **$34-$45.** 307 Pioneer Tr 17758. From SR 154 & US 220: Go 2-1/2 mi S on US 220, then 1/2 mi W on Pioneer Trail. ⴄ ⴌ ⴕM

NARVON — LAKE IN WOOD RESORT. (717) 445-5525. **$35-$63.** 576 Yellow Hill Rd 17555. From SR-625 & E Maple Grove Rd: Go 3/4 mi E on Maple Grove Rd, then 1/2 mi S on Oaklyn Dr, then 1-1/2 mi E on Yellow Hill Rd. ⴄ ⴌ ⴕM

NEW TRIPOLI — KOA-ALLENTOWN-LEHIGH VALLEY KAMPGROUND. (610) 298-2160. **$38-$49.** 6750 KOA Drive 18066. From jct PA Tpk (exit 56) & US 22: Go 3 mi W on US 22/78 (exit 49B), then 6-1/2 mi N on SR-100, then 1/2 mi W on Narris Rd. ⴄ ⴌ ⴕM

NEWVILLE — DOGWOOD ACRES CAMPGROUND. (717) 776-5203. **$40-$50.** 4500 Enola Rd 17241. From jct I-81 & SR 233 (exit 37): Go 9 mi N on SR 233, then 2-1/2 mi E on SR 944. ⴄ ⴌ ⴕM

PINE GROVE — TWIN GROVE RESORT KOA AT PINE GROVE. (800) 562-5471. **$31-$60.** 1445 Suedberg Rd 17963. From jct I-81 & SR-443 (exit 100): Go 5 mi W on SR-443. ⴄ ⴌ ⴕM

PORTERSVILLE — BEAR RUN CAMPGROUND. ⴵ (888) 737-2605. **$40-$60.** 184 Badger Hill Rd 16051. From jct I-79 (exit 96) & Hwy 488: Go 50 yards E on Hwy 488, then 1/2 mi N on Badger Hill Rd. ⴌ ⴄ ⴌ ⴕM

QUARRYVILLE — YOGI BEAR'S JELLYSTONE PARK CAMP-RESORT-LANCASTER SOUTH/QUARRYVILLE. (717) 786-3458. **$42-$123.** 340 Blackburn Rd 17566. From east jct SR 372 & US 222: Go 2-1/2 mi S on US 222, then 1-1/2 mi E on Blackburn Rd. ⴄ ⴌ ⴕM

TRANSFER — SHENANGO VALLEY RV PARK. (724) 962-9800. **$40-$48.** 559 E Crestview Dr 16154. From jct of I-80 & SR18 (exit 4B): Go 11 mi N on SR 18 then 1/2 mi E on Reynolds Industrial Park Rd, then 1 mi SE on Crestview Dr, then left at Y intersection onto East Crestview Dr. ⴄ ⴌ ⴕM

South Carolina

CHARLESTON — OAK PLANTATION CAMPGROUND. (866) 658-2500. **$29-$36.** 3540 Savannah Hwy 29455. From west jct I-526 & US 17 South: Go 4 mi SW on US 17. 🏕️ 🛶 ⊠

HILTON HEAD ISLAND — HILTON HEAD ISLAND MOTORCOACH RESORT. Ⓐ (800) 722-2365. **$55-$75.** 133 Arrow Rd 29928. From jct I-95 (exit 8) & US 278: Go 22 mi E on US 278, then 5-1/2 mi E on Cross Island Pkwy, then 1/4 mi N on Target Rd, then E on Arrow Rd. 🏕️ 🛶 ⊠ ♿

LONGS — WILLOWTREE RESORT. (866) 207-2267. **$30-$93.** 520 Southern Sights Drive 29568. From jct SC-9 and SC 905: Go 1-3/4 mi NE on SC 905, then 1-1/2 mi N on Old Buck Creek Rd. 🏕️ 🛶 ⊠ ♿

MYRTLE BEACH — LAKEWOOD CAMPING RESORT. Ⓐ (843) 238-5161. **$25-$75.** 5901 S Kings Hwy 29575. From jct US 501 & 544: Go E 14 mi on Hwy 544, then N 1/2 mi on US 17 Bus. 🏊 🛶 ⊠ ♿

MYRTLE BEACH — MYRTLE BEACH TRAVEL PARK. Ⓐ (800) 255-3568. **$36-$67.** 10108 Kings Rd 29572. From jct US-501 & US-17: Go 9-3/4 mi N on US-17, then 1/2 mi E on Chestnut Rd, then 1/4 mi N on Kings Rd. 🛶 ⊠ ♿

MYRTLE BEACH — OCEAN LAKES FAMILY CAMP-GROUND. Ⓐ (800) 876-4306. **$28-$69.** 6001 S. Kings Highway 29575. From jct US-501 & SC Hwy 544: Go 14 mi E on SC Hwy 544. 🏊 🛶 ⊠ ♿

MYRTLE BEACH — PIRATELAND FAMILY CAMPING RESORT. (800) 443-2267. **$28-$74.** 5401 S Kings Hwy 29575. From jct US 17 & US 544: Go 2 mi E on US 544, then 1 mi N on US 17 Bus. 🛶 ⊠ ♿

South Dakota

HILL CITY — KOA-MOUNT RUSHMORE. (800) 562-8503. **$30-$74.** 12620 Highway 244 57745. From S Hill City limits: Go 2-1/2 mi S on US 16/385, then 3 mi E on Hwy 244. 🛶 ⊠ ♿

HILL CITY — RAFTER J BAR RANCH CAMPING RESORT. (888) 723-8375. **$42-$48.** 12325 Rafter J Bar Rd 57745. From South Hill City Limits: Go 2-3/4 mi S on US 16/385. ⊠ ♿

INTERIOR — BADLANDS/WHITE RIVER-KOA. (800) 562-3897. **$32-$45.** 20720 SD Highway 44 57750. From jct I-90 (exit 131) & Hwy 240: Go 9 mi S on Hwy 240, then 2 mi S on Hwy 377, then 4 mi E on Hwy 44. ⊠ ♿

RAPID CITY — HART RANCH RV RESORT. Ⓐ (800) 605-4278. **Call for rates.** 23756 Arena Dr 57702. From jct I-90 (exit 61) & US 16 Truck/Hwy 79: Go 5-1/4 mi S on US 16 Truck/Hwy 79, (North Elk Vale Rd) then 6 mi S on Hwy 79, then 2 mi W on Spring Creek Rd. 🛶 ⊠ ♿

RAPID CITY — KOA-RAPID CITY. (605) 348-2111. **$35-$80.** 3010 E Hwy 44 57703. From jct I-90 (exit 61) & US 16 Truck/Hwy 79: Go 2-1/2 mi S on US 16 Truck, then 1/4 mi NW on Hwy 44. 🛶 ⊠ ♿

RAPID CITY — RUSHMORE SHADOWS RESORT. Ⓐ (800) 231-0425. **$37.** 23680 Busted Five Ct 57702. From jct I-90 (exit 61) & US 16 Truck/Hwy 79: Go 9 mi S & W on US 16 Truck, then 6-1/2 mi W on US 16 W. 🏊 🛶 ⊠ ♿

SPEARFISH — ELKHORN RIDGE RV RESORT. Ⓐ (877) 722-1800. **$50.** 20189 US Hwy 85 57783. From jct US 85N & I-90 (exit 10): Go 7 mi E on I-90 (exit 17) then 3/4 mi S on US 85S. 🛶 ⊠ ♿

Tennessee

BLOUNTVILLE — ROCKY TOP CAMPGROUND & RV PARK. (800) 452-6456. **$36-$40.** 496 Pearl Lane 37617. From jct I-81 (exit 63 Tri-City Airport) & Browder Rd: Go 1/2 mi N on Browder Rd, then 3/4 mi SW on Pearl Lane. ⊠

COSBY — GREAT SMOKY JELLYSTONE PARK CAMP RESORT. (423) 487-5534. **$25-$49.** 4946 Hooper Hwy 37722. E'bnd from jct I-40 (exit 435) & Hwy 321: G0 15 mi S on Hwy 321. W'bnd from jct I-40 (exit 440) & Hwy 73: Go 15 mi S on Hwy 321. 🛶 ⊠ ♿

GATLINBURG — TWIN CREEK RV RESORT. Ⓐ (800) 252-8077. **$50-$54.** 1202 E. Parkway 37738. Go 2 1/4 mi E on US 321 N 🏕️ 🛶 ⊠ ♿

MANCHESTER — KOA-MANCHESTER. (800) 562-7785. **$32-$70.** 586 Campground Rd 37355. From jct I-24 (exit 114) & US 41: Go 100 yards on US 41, then 1/2 mi N on Campground Rd (Frontage Rd). 🛶 ⊠ ♿

PIGEON FORGE — KOA-PIGEON FORGE/GATLINBURG. (865) 453-7903. **$32-$82.** 3122 Veterans Blvd 37863. From center of town at jct US 441 & Dollywood Lane #8: Go 1/4 mi E on Dollywood Lane, then 1,000 feet N on Veterans Blvd. 🛶 ⊠ ♿

PIGEON FORGE — PINE MOUNTAIN RV PARK. (865) 453-9994. **$35-$56.** 411 Pine Mountain Rd 37863. From jct US 321 & US 441: Go S on US 441 to traffic light #6, then, 1/4 mi W on Pine Mountain Rd. 🏊 🏕️ 🛶

PIGEON FORGE — RIVEREDGE RV PARK. (800) 477-1205. **$41.** 4220 Huskey St 37863. South city limits at jct US 441 & Cates Ln (left exit before stop light #10): Go 1 blk E on Cates Ln. 🏕️ 🛶 ⊠ ♿

SEVIERVILLE — RIVER PLANTATION RV PARK. (865) 429-5267. **$23-$50.** 1004 Pkwy 37862. From jct Hwy 66 & US 441: Go 1 mi S on US 441. 🏕️ 🛶 ⊠

SEVIERVILLE — RIVERSIDE RV PARK & RESORT. (800) 341-7534. **$30-$32.** 4280 Boyds Creek Hwy 37876. From jct I-40 (exit 407) & Hwy 66: Go 4 mi S on Hwy 66, then 1/4 mi W on Boyds Creek Rd (turn right at Marathon). 🏕️ 🛶 ⊠

SEVIERVILLE — TWO RIVERS LANDING RESORT. (866) 727-5781. **$45-$65.** 2328 Business Center Cir 37876. From jct I-40 (exit 407) & Hwy 66: Go 3 mi S on Hwy 66, then 1/4 mi W on Knife Works Ln, then 1/4 mi N on Business Center Circle. 🏕️ 🛶 ⊠ ♿

TOWNSEND — BIG MEADOW FAMILY CAMPGROUND. (888) 497-0625. **$40-$50.** 8215 Cedar Creek Rd 37882. From jct Scenic Hwy 73 & US 321: Go 350 yds NE on US 321, then 100 yds W on Cedar Creek Rd (end of bridge). 🏕 🛶 ☒

Texas

ALPINE — LOST ALASKAN RV PARK. (432) 837-1136. **$32-$51.** 2401 North Hwy 118 79830. From jct US 90 & Hwy 118: Go 1-1/2 mi N on Hwy 118. 🛶 ☒ ♿

AMARILLO — FORT AMARILLO RV RESORT. (866) 431-7866. **$35.** 10101 Amarillo Blvd W 79124. From jct I-27 & I-40: Go 5-1/2 mi W on I-40 (exit 64), then 1/4 mi N on W Loop 335, then 1-1/4 mi W on Rt 66/Amarillo Blvd W, enter on left. E'bound I-40 (exit 62B), then 3/4 mi NE on Rt 66/Amarillo Blvd W, enter on right. 🆂 🏕 🛶 ☒ ♿

ARANSAS PASS — SOUTHERN OAKS LUXURY RV PARK, LLC. (361) 758-1249. **$35.** 1850 Highway 35 Byp 78336. From jct Hwy 188 & Hwy 35 bypass: Go 3-1/4 mi SW on Hwy 35 Bypass. 🏕 🛶

ARLINGTON — TREETOPS RV VILLAGE. (800) 747-0787. **$38-$45.** 1901 W Arbrook 76015. From I-20 (exit 449) & Hwy 157: Go 1/2 mi N on Hwy 157, then 1/4 mi W on Arbrook. 🏕 🛶 ♿

ATHENS — WINDSOR PLACE RV ESTATES. (903) 477-4001. **$35-$45.** 1506 W Corsicana 75751. From jct Bus US 175, Hwy 19 & Bus Hwy 31: Go 3/4 mi W on Bus Hwy 31 (Corsicana St). 🏕

AUSTIN — LA HACIENDA RV RESORT & COTTAGES. (512) 266-8001. **$44-$55.** 5320 Hudson Bend Rd 78734. From jct Hwy 71 & RM 620: Go 7-1/2 mi NE on RM 620, then 1-1/2 mi N on Hudson Bend. 🏕 🛶 ☒ ♿

AUSTIN — OAK FOREST RV PARK. (512) 926-8984. **$44.** 8207 Canoga Ave 78724. From jct I-35 (exit 230) & Hwy 71 E (Ben White Blvd): Go 5 mi E on Hwy 71, then 5-1/4 mi N on Hwy 183, then 1-1/2 E on FM 969/Martin Luther King Blvd, then 1/2 mi N on FM 3177 (Decker Lane) to Canoga Ave. 🆂 🏕 🛶 ☒ ♿

BASTROP — BASTROP RIVER RV PARK. (512) 321-7500. **$45.** 98 Hwy 71 78602. From W jct Hwy 21 & Hwy 71: Go 5-1/2 mi E on Hwy 71 (Service Road). 🆂 🏕 🛶 ☒ ♿

BAYTOWN — HOUSTON EAST RV RESORT. (281) 383-3618. **$36.** 11810 Interstate 10 E 77523. From jct Hwy 146 & I-10 Eastbound (exit 797) Westbound (exit 798): Go 1-1/2 mi E on South Frontage Rd. 🏕 🛶 ☒ ♿

BEAUMONT — GULF COAST RV RESORT. ⒶⒶⒶ (866) 410-7801. **$35.** 5175 Brooks Rd 77705. From jct US 69/96 S & I-10: Go 2-3/4 mi W on I-10 (exit 847), then 1/4 mi S on Brooks Rd. (E'bound I-10 exit 845). 🏕 🛶 ☒ ♿

BULLARD — KE BUSHMAN'S CAMP. (903) 894-8221. **$33-$40.** 3933 75757. From jct US 69 S & FM 344: Go S 1.8 mi on US 69. 🛶 ☒ ♿

CANTON — MILL CREEK RANCH RV PARK & COTTAGE RESORT. (903) 567-7275. **$35-$60.** 2102 Trade Days Blvd 75103. From jct I-20 (exit 527) & Hwy 19 (Trade Days Blvd): Go 1/4 mi S on Hwy 19. 🏕 🛶 ☒ ♿

CANYON LAKE — SUMMIT VACATION RESORT. (830) 964-3308. **Call for rates. (no credit cards).** 13105 River Rd 78132. From jct FM 306 & FM 2673: Go 1-1/2 mi S on FM 2673, then 1-1/2 mi E on River Rd. 🛶 ☒

CORPUS CHRISTI — COLONIA DEL REY RV PARK. (361) 937-2435. **$28-$37.** 1717 Waldron Rd 78418. From jct I-37 & Hwy 358 (S Padre Island Dr): Go 16 mi SE on S Padre Island Dr, then 3/4 mi S on Waldron. 🛶 ☒ ♿

DENTON — DALLAS DESTINY RV RESORT. (888) 238-1532. **$32-$41.** 7100 I-35 E 76210. From jct US 377 & I-35 E: Go 8-1/2 mi S on I-35 E (exit 460), then 1 mi S on W Service Road. 🏕 🛶 ☒ ♿

FREDERICKSBURG — FREDERICKSBURG RV PARK. (866) 324-7275. **$33.** 305 E Highway St 78624. From jct US 290 & Hwy 87: Go 7 blocks S on Hwy 87, then 1/2 block W on Highway St. 🏕 ☒ ♿

GALVESTON — JAMAICA BEACH RV PARK. ⒶⒶⒶ (409) 632-0200. **$47-$49.** 17200 FM 3005 77554. From jct I-45 (exit 1A) & 61st St: Go 2 mi S (R) on 61st St, then 11 mi SW on FM 3005. 🆂 🏕 🛶 ☒ ♿

GLADEWATER — SHALLOW CREEK RV RESORT. (903) 984-4513. **$33.** 5261 Hwy 135 N 75647. From jct I-20 & Hwy 135 (exit 583): Go 1-1/2 mi N on Hwy 135. 🏕 🛶 ☒ ♿

GRAND PRAIRIE — TRADERS VILLAGE RV PARK. ⒶⒶⒶ (972) 647-2331. **$30-$35.** 2602 Mayfield Rd 75052. From jct I-20 & exit 454 (Great Southwest Pkwy): Go 3/4 mi N on Great Southwest Pkwy, then 1/4 mi W on Mayfield Rd. 🛶 ☒

GRAPEVINE — THE VINEYARDS CAMPGROUND & CABINS ON LAKE GRAPEVINE. (888) 329-8993. **$42-$70.** 1501 N Dooley St 76051. From E jct Hwy 121 & Hwy 26 (Northwest Hwy): Go 2-1/2 mi SW on Hwy 26 (Northwest Hwy), then 1 mi N on Dooley. 🆂 🛶 ☒ ♿

HIGHLANDS — SAN JACINTO RIVERFRONT RV PARK. (281) 426-6919. **$35-$79.** 540 S Main St 77562. From jct E Loop I-610 & I-10: Go 10 mi E on I-10 (exit 787), then 1-1/4 mi N on Main St (Crosby-Lynchburg Rd) 🏕 🛶 ☒

HOUSTON — ADVANCED RV PARK. (888) 515-6950. **$44-$48.** 2850 S Sam Houston Pkwy East 77047. From jct Hwy 288 & Beltway 8: Go 1 block E on S Beltway 8 Access Rd. 🏕 🛶 ☒ ♿

HOUSTON — LAKEVIEW RV RESORT. (800) 385-9122. **$34-$51.** 11991 S Main St 77035. From jct S Loop I-610 & Alt US 90 (S Main St): Go 2 mi W on Alt US 90 (S Main St), then exit at Hiram-Clarke and U-turn. 🏕 🛶 ☒ ♿

HOUSTON — TRADERS VILLAGE RV PARK. (281) 890-8846. **$29-$32.** 7979 Eldridge Rd 77041. From W Beltway 8 & US 290: Go 3 mi NW on US 290, then 1/2 mi S on Eldridge Rd. 🛶 ☒ ♿

INGRAM — JOHNSON CREEK RV RESORT & PARK. (830) 367-3300. **$32-$42.** 4279 Junction Hwy 78025. From jct SH 16 and SH 27: Go 6 mi W on SH 27 to Ingram, stay in curb lane, continue W on SH 27 for 5 mi. 🏕 🛶 ☒ ♿

KEMAH — MARINA BAY RV RESORT. (281) 334-9944. **$45-$49.** 925 FM 2094 77565. From Jct I-45 (exit 23) & FM 518: Go 2-3/4 mi E on FM 518, then continue 3-1/2 mi E on FM 2094. 🏕️ 🚐 ✕ ♿M

KERRVILLE — BUCKHORN LAKE RESORT. (830) 895-0007. **$39-$49.** 2885 Goat Creek Rd 78028. From jct Hwy I-10 & exit 501 (FM 1338): Go 1/4 mi N on FM 1338. 🏕️ 🚐 ✕ ♿M

KERRVILLE — GUADALUPE RIVER RV RESORT. (800) 582-1916. **$35-$46.** 2605 Junction Highway 27 78028. From jct Hwy 16 & I-10: Go 2-1/2 mi W on I-10 (exit 505), then 2-1/2 mi S on FM 783, then 2-1/2 mi W on Hwy 27. 🏕️ 🚐 ✕ ♿M

LONGVIEW — FERNBROOK PARK. (903) 643-8888. **$33-$38.** PO 75603. From jct of I-20 & exit 591: Go S on FM 2011 for 2 mi to park. 🏕️ 🚐 ✕ ♿M

MANSFIELD — TEXAN RV RANCH. (817) 473-1666. **$32-$35.** 1961 Lone Star Rd 76063. From jct I-20 & US 287: Go 10-1/2 mi S on US 287, then 1/4 mi SW on Lone Star Rd (FM 157). 🏕️ 🚐 ✕ ♿M

MARBLE FALLS — SUNSET POINT ON LAKE LBJ. (830) 798-8199. **$43-$75.** 2322 N Wirtz Dam Rd 78654. From jct US 281 & FM 1431: Go 3-1/4 mi W on Hwy 1431, then 2-1/4 mi S on Wirtz Dam Rd. 🏕️ 🚐 ✕ ♿M

MATAGORDA — MATAGORDA BAY RV PARK. (979) 863-7120. **$25-$35.** 6430 FM 2031 77457. From jct Hwy 60 & FM 2031: Go 6 mi S on FM 2031. ✕ ♿M

MERCEDES — LLANO GRANDE LAKE PARK RESORT & COUNTRY CLUB. (956) 565-2638. **$30-$45.** 489 Yolanda 78570. From jct FM 491 & US 83: Go 1-1/2 mi W on US 83, then 1-3/4 mi S on Mile 2 W Rd. 🏕️ 🚐 ✕ ♿M

MISSION — BENTSEN PALM VILLAGE RV RESORT. (877) 247-3727. **$40-$51.** 2500 S Bentsen Palm Dr 78572. From jct 1016 & US 83: Go 3-1/2 mi W on US 83, then 3 mi S on Bentsen Palm Dr. 🏕️ 🚐 ✕ ♿M

MONTGOMERY — LAKE CONROE/HOUSTON NORTH KOA. (936) 582-1200. **$41-$50.** 19785 Hwy 105 W 77356. From jct Hwy 149 & Hwy 105: Go 1-3/4 mi E on Hwy 105. 🚐 ✕ ♿M

NEW BRAUNFELS — RIVER RANCH RV RESORT. (830) 625-7788. **$34-$53.** 420 Bus Loop 35 N 78130. S'bnd I-35 (exit 188) & Bus 35/46: Go 1/4 mi S on Bus 35/46. N'bnd I-35 (exit 189) & Hwy 46: Go 1/4 mi W on Hwy 46, then 1 mi S on Bus 35/46. 🏕️ 🚐 ✕ ♿M

NEW CANEY — FOREST RETREAT RV RESORT. (888) 354-9888. **$41-$47.** 21711 McCleskey Rd 77357. From South jct US 59 & FM 1485 (New Caney exit): Make a u-turn at FM 1485, then 1 mi S on W Service Rd, then 3/4 mi W on McCleskey Rd. From North US 59 & Community Drive exit: Go .2 N on exit ramp, then .8 mi E on McCleskey Road. 🏕️ 🚐 ♿M

ONALASKA — LAKESIDE RV RESORT & MARINA ON LAKE LIVINGSTON. (936) 646-3824. **$30-$40.** 15152 US Highway 190 W 77360. W'bound From jct US 59 & US 190 (in Livingston): Go 14 mi W on US 190. 🚐 ✕ ♿M

ONALASKA — NORTHSHORE RV PARK & MARINA. (936) 646-3124. **$25-$45.** 168 Butler 77360. From jct US 59 & US 190 (at Livingston): Go 12 mi W on US 190. 🏕️ 🚐 ✕ ♿M

PORT ARANSAS — PIONEER BEACH RESORT. (888) 480-3246. **$39-$45.** 120 Gulfwind Dr 78373. N'bound from jct Hwy 358 & Hwy 361: Go 14 mi N on Hwy 361. Entrance on right. S'bound from jct ferry landing & Hwy 361 (Cutoff Rd): Go 1 mi S on Hwy 361, then continue 3-1/2 mi S on Hwy 361. 🏕️ 🚐 ✕ ♿M

ROCKPORT — LAGOONS RV RESORT. (361) 729-7834. **$34-$36.** 600 Enterprise Blvd 78382. From jct Hwy 188 & Hwy 35: Go 6-1/2 mi N on Hwy 35 (Bypass), then 1 mi SE on FM 2165, then 500 feet N on Enterprise Blvd. 🏕️ 🚐 ✕ ♿M

RUSK — RUSK KOA CAMPGROUND. (903) 683-6641. **$36-$55.** PO Box 691 75785. From S jct US 69 & FM 343: Go 1/2 mi E on FM 343. 🚐 ✕ ♿M

SAN ANTONIO — ADMIRALTY RV RESORT. (210) 647-7878. **$36-$50.** 1485 N. Ellison 78251. From west Loop I-410 & Hwy 151: Go 2 mi W on Hwy 151 access road, then 1-1/4 mi SW on Potranco (FM 1957), then 3/4 mi N on Ellison. 🏕️ 🚐 ✕ ♿M

SAN ANTONIO — BLAZING STAR LUXURY RV RESORT. (210) 680-7827. **$42-$54.** 1120 W Loop 1604 N 78251. From W jct US 90 & Loop 1604: Go 4-1/2 mi N on Loop 1604. 🚐 ✕ ♿M

SAN ANTONIO — TRAVELER'S WORLD RV RESORT. (800) 755-8310. **$39-$42.** 2617 Roosevelt Ave 78214. From jct I-37 (exit 135) & SE Military Dr: Go 3 mi W on Military Dr, then 1-1/4 mi N on Roosevelt. 🚐 ✕ ♿M

SAN MARCOS — PECAN PARK CAMPGROUND. (888) 808-7181. **$35-$47.** 50 Squirrel Run 78666. From jct I-35 (exit 205) & Hwy 80: Go 2 mi SE on Hwy 80, (1 mi past Blanco River Bridge), then 1 block S on CR 101, then 1/2 mi E on CR 102. 🏕️ 🚐 ✕ ♿M

SPRING — RAYFORD CROSSING RV RESORT. (281) 298-8008. **$39-$52.** 29321 S. Plum Creek Dr 77386. From jct Hwy 242 & I-45: Go 5-1/2 mi S on I-45 (exit 73), then 1-1/2 mi E on Rayford Rd, then 1/2 mi S on Geneva Dr, then 1/4 mi E on South Plum Creek Dr. 🏕️ 🚐 ✕ ♿M

SPRING BRANCH — SPRING BRANCH RV RESORT. (866) 542-2110. **$41.** 10950 US Hwy 281 North 78070. N'bnd at jct Hwy 46 & US 281: Go 5 mi N on US 281. ✕ ♿M

SWEENY — STONEBRIDGE RV PARK I, LP. (979) 245-1200. **$35.** 15804 77480. From jct FM 1728 & Hwy 35: Go 2-3/4 mi NE on Hwy 35. 🏕️ 🚐

TERRELL — BLUEBONNET RIDGE RV PARK. (866) 419-0100. **$35.** 16543 FM 429 75161. From jct I-20 (exit 506) & FM 429: Go .6 mi N on FM 429, turn S into Park for 1/4 mi. 🏕️ 🚐 ✕ ♿M

TEXARKANA — SHADY PINES RV PARK. (903) 832-1268. **$30.** 10010 W 7th St 75501. S'bnd from jct I-30 & US 59S (exit 220A): Go 4-1/4 mi S on US 59, then 6 mi SW on 7th St (US 67 S). 🏕️ ✕ ♿M

TYLER — #1 RV PARK OF TYLER LLC. (903) 597-6966. **$40.** 12421 State Highway 31 W 75709. From jct W SW Loop 323 & State Hwy 31 W: Go 2 mi W on State Hwy 31 W. 🏕️ 🏕️ ♿M

VICTORIA — **LAZY LONGHORN RV PARK.** (877) 599-4676. **$28-$30. (no credit cards).** 1402 S Laurent 77901. From jct US 59 & Hwy 185: Go 1 mi N on Hwy 185. 🖼️ 🛶 🍴 ⑤M

WEATHERFORD — **OAK CREEK RV PARK.** (817) 594-0200. **$32-$35.** 7652 W. Interstate 20 76008. From jct FM 1189 & I-20 (exit 397): Go 1/2 mi W on N Service Rd. 🖼️ 🛶 ⑤M

WICHITA FALLS — **COYOTE RANCH RESORT.** (877) 767-6771. **$29-$46.** 14145 US Highway 287 N 76310. From jct US 82/287 & Exit Stephens Ranch Rd: Go E on Stephens Ranch Rd for 1.5 mi to Park (enter before sign) Right. 🛶 🍴 ⑤M

Utah

BRYCE CANYON CITY — **RUBY'S INN RV PARK & CAMP-GROUND.** 🆃 (866) 878-9373. **$35-$41.** 1280 S Hwy 63 84764. From jct Hwy 12 & Hwy 63: Go 1-1/2 mi S on Hwy 63. 🛶 🍴 ⑤M

HATCH — **MOUNTAIN RIDGE & RV PARK.** (435) 735-4300. **$30-$34.** 106 S Main St 84735. From Hwy 89 & Hwy 12: Go 8-1/4 mi S on Hwy 89. 🅂 🖼️ ⑤M

HENEFER — **EAST CANYON RESORT.** (801) 355-3460. **Call for rates.** Hwy 65. 84033. From jct I-84 (exit 115) & Hwy 65: Go 3/4 mi S to Hwy 65 S, then 12 mi S. 🖼️ 🛶 🍴 ⑤M

NORTH SALT LAKE — **PONY EXPRESS RV RESORT.** (800) 780-0170. **$29-$42.** 630 S Redwood Rd 84054. S-Bnd: From jct I-15/I-215 (exit 313): Go 3/4 mi W on I-215 to Redwood Rd (exit 27), then 1/4 mi S on Redwood Rd. N-Bnd: From jct I-80/I-215 (exit 117): Go 5 mi N on I-215 to Redwood Rd (exit 27), then 1/4 mi S on Redwood Rd. 🖼️ 🛶 🍴 ⑤M

SPRINGVILLE — **EAST BAY RV PARK.** 🆃 (801) 491-0700. **$34.** 1750 West 1600 North 84663. From jct I-15 (exit 261) & Hwy 75: Go 1/8 mi E on Hwy 75 🖼️ 🛶 🍴 ⑤M

VIRGIN — **ZION RIVER RESORT.** (800) 838-8594. **$48-$59.** 551 East Hwy 9 84779. N'bound from jct I-15 (exit 16) & Hwy 9: Go 19 mi E on Hwy 9. S'bound from jct I-15 (exit 27) & Hwy 17: Go 6 mi E on Hwy 17, then 7 mi E on Hwy 9 to mp 19. 🛶 🍴 ⑤M

Vermont

DANVILLE — **SUGAR RIDGE RV VILLAGE & CAMPGROUND.** (802) 684-2550. **$40-$42.** 24 Old Stagecoach Rd 05828. From jct I-91 (exit 21) & US 2: Go 4-1/2 mi W on US 2. 🛶 🍴 ⑤M

Virginia

CHERITON — **CHERRYSTONE FAMILY CAMPING RESORT.** 🆃 (757) 331-3063. **$17-$68.** 1511 Townfields Dr 23316. From jct US 13 & Hwy 680 (Townfields Dr): Go 1-1/2 mi W on Hwy 680 (Townfields Dr). 🛶 🍴 ⑤M

TOPPING — **GREY'S POINT CAMP.** (804) 758-2485. **$40-$83.** 3601 Grey's Point Rd 23169. From jct Hwy 33 & Hwy 3: Go 3 1/4 mi NE on Hwy 3. 🖼️ 🛶 🍴

URBANNA — **BETHPAGE CAMP-RESORT.** (804) 758-4349. **$40-$93.** 679 Browns Ln 23175. From jct US 17 & Hwy 602: Go 4 mi SE on Hwy 602, then 1/2 mi E on Browns Ln. 🖼️ 🛶 🍴 ⑤M

VIRGINIA BEACH — **HOLIDAY TRAV-L-PARK OF VIRGINIA BEACH.** (866) 850-9629. **$29-$80.** 1075 General Booth Blvd 23451. From Jct I-264 (exit 22) & Birdneck Rd: Go 3 mi SE on Birdneck Rd, then 1/4 mi S on General Booth Blvd. 🅂 🛶 🍴 ⑤M

WILLIAMSBURG — **AMERICAN HERITAGE RV PARK.** (888) 530-2267. **$46-$63.** 146 Maxton Ln 23188. From I-64 (exit 231A-Norge): Go 1/4 mi S on Hwy 607, then 1/4 mi E on Maxton Lane. 🅂 🛶 🍴 ⑤M

WILLIAMSBURG — **KOA-COLONIAL CENTRAL.** (800) 562-7609. **$35-$62.** 4000 Newman Rd 23188. From jct I-64 (Lightfoot exit 234) & Hwy 199W: Go 1 mi NE on Hwy 199W (becomes Newman Rd). 🛶 🍴

WILLIAMSBURG — **KOA-WILLIAMSBURG.** 🆃 (800) 562-1733. **$35-$62.** 5210 Newman Rd 23188. From jct I-64 (Lightfoot exit 234) & Hwy 199W: Go 1 mi NE on 199W (becomes Newman Rd). 🛶 🍴

Washington

BOTHELL — **LAKE PLEASANT RV PARK.** (425) 487-1785. **$44.** 24025 Bothell Everett Hwy S 98021. From jct I-405 (exit 26) & Hwy 527: Go 1 mi S on Hwy 527 (Bothell, Everett Hwy). 🖼️ 🍴 ⑤M

CASTLE ROCK — **TOUTLE RIVER RV RESORT.** (360) 274-8373. **$42.** 168 Dwight Rd 98611. From jct I-5 (exit 52) & Barnes Drive: Go 1 blk W on Barnes Drive, then 1/2 mi S on Happy Trails Rd. 🅂 🛶 🍴 ⑤M

CLARKSTON — **GRANITE LAKE PREMIER RV RESORT.** 🆃 (509) 751-1635. **$37-$46.** 306 Granite Lake Dr 99403. From Jct Snake River Bridge & US 12: Go 3/4 mi W on US 12, then 2-1/2 blocks N on Fifth St, then 100 ft E on Granite Lake Dr. 🖼️ 🍴 ⑤M

CLARKSTON — **HELLS CANYON RV RESORT & MARINA.** (509) 758-6963. **$30-$40.** 1550 Port Dr 99403. From Jct Snake River Bridge & US 12: Go 2 mi W on US 12, then 1/2 block N on 15th St, then 500 ft W on Port Dr. 🅂 🛶 🍴 ⑤M

DEER PARK — **SPOKANE RV RESORT AT DEER PARK GOLF CLUB.** (877) 276-1555. **$35.** 1205 A N. Country Club Dr 99006. From jct Hwy 395 & Crawford St: Go 1-3/4 mi E on Crawford St, then 1 mi N on Country Club Dr. From Hwy 2 & Milan-Deer Park Rd: Go 5 mi W on Milan-Deer Park Rd, then 1 mi N on Country Club Dr. 🖼️ 🛶 🍴 ⑤M

EVERETT — **MAPLE GROVE RV RESORT.** (866) 793-2200. **$39-$44.** 12417 Hwy 99 98204. From I-5 (exit 186): Go 1-1/2 mi W on 128th St SW, then 1/4 mi S on Hwy 99. 🅂 🖼️ ⑤M

MEAD — **ALDERWOOD RV RESORT.** (888) 847-0500. **$27-$37.** 14007 N Newport Hwy 99021. From I-90 (exit 287A): Go 8-1/4 mi N on Argonne Rd, then 2-1/4 mi W on Hwy 206 (Mt Spokane Rd), then cross intersection at Hwy 2 & follow Frontage Rd. 🛶 🍴 ⑤M

RICHLAND — HORN RAPIDS RV RESORT. (509) 375-9913. **$36.** 2640 Kingsgate Way 99354. From jct I-182 and Hwy 240 (exit #4): Go 6-1/4 mi NW on Hwy 240, then 200 ft N on Kingsgate Way. 🏕️ 🛶 ✖️ ♿

SEQUIM — GILGAL OASIS RV PARK. (888) 445-4251. **$31-$40.** 400 S Brown Rd 98382. From US 101 & River Rd: Go 1-1/4 mi E on US 101, then 1/2 mi N on Sequim Rd, then 1/2 mi E on Washington St, then 1 blck S on Brown Rd. 🏕️

SILVER CREEK — HARMONY LAKESIDE RV PARK. 🆔 (360) 983-3804. **$35-$53.** 563 State Route 122 98585. From jct I-5 (exit 68) & US 12: Go 21 mi E on US 12, then 2-1/2 mi N on Hwy 122. 🏕️ ✖️ ♿

WHITE SALMON — BRIDGE RV PARK & CAMPGROUND. (509) 493-1111. **$43-$45.** 65271 Highway 14 98672. From jct Hood River Bridge & Hwy 14: Go 600 feet E on Hwy 14. 🆔 ✖️ ♿

WOODLAND — COLUMBIA RIVERFRONT RV PARK. 🆔 (360) 225-2227. **$34-$42.** 1881 Dike Rd 98674. From jct I-5 (exit 22) & Dike Rd: Go 2-1/2 mi W and S on Dike Rd. 🏕️ 🛶 ✖️ ♿

West Virginia

HARPERS FERRY — HARPERS FERRY/CIVIL WAR BATTLEFIELDS KOA. (800) 562-9497. **$30-$52.** 343 Campground Rd 25425. From jct Hwy 230 & US 340: Go 2 mi N on US 340, then 25 feet S on Harpers Ferry entrance road, then 1/4 mi W on Campground Rd. 🛶 ✖️ ♿

SUTTON — FLATWOODS KOA. (866) 700-7284. **$38-$42.** 2000 Sutton Ln 26601. From jct I-79 (exit 67) & US 19: Go 100 yards E on US 19, then 1 block S on Hwy 4, then 1 block NE on Days Dr, then 1 block E on Sutton Ln (behind Days Hotel). 🆔 🏕️ 🛶 ✖️ ♿

Wisconsin

BANCROFT — VISTA ROYALLE CAMPGROUND. (715) 335-6860. **$39-$42.** 8025 Isherwood Rd 54921. From jct I-39/US 51 (exit 143) & CR W: Go 3/4 mi E on CR W, then 1 mi N on Isherwood Rd. ✖️ ♿

BARABOO — YOGI BEAR'S JELLYSTONE PARK CAMP-RESORT. (800) 462-9644. **$39-$115.** S 1915 Ishnala Rd 53913. From jct I-90/94 (exit 92) & US 12: Go 1/2 mi NW on US 12, then 1 mi W on Gasser Rd. 🛶 ✖️ ♿

BOWLER — MOHICAN RV PARK. (715) 787-2751. **$25-$35.** W12180 County Road A 54416. From jct CR G & CR A in Gresham: Go 3 mi W on CR A: Check in at "Bus Stop" in casino. 🏕️ ♿

CALEDONIA — YOGI BEAR JELLYSTONE CAMP-RESORT. (262) 835-2565. **$24-$49.** 8425 Hwy 38 53108. From I-94 (exit 326): Go 2 mi E on Seven Mile Rd, then 1/4 mi N on WI 38. 🛶 ✖️ ♿

LODI — SMOKEY HOLLOW CAMPGROUND. (608) 635-4806. **$45-$52.** W9935 McGowan Rd 53555. From jct Hwy-60 & I-90/94: Go 4 mi N on I-90/94 (exit 115), then 3/4 mi W on County CS, then 1-1/2 mi S on County J, then 200 yards E on McGowan Rd. 🛶 ✖️ ♿

MILTON — HIDDEN VALLEY RV RESORT & CAMPGROUND. (800) 469-5515. **$38-$68.** 872 E Hwy 59 53563. From I-90 (exit 163) & Hwy 59: Go 3/4 mi E on Hwy 59. 🛶 ✖️ ♿

OSSEO — STONEY CREEK RV RESORT. (715) 597-2102. **$27-$48.** 50483 Oak Grove Rd 54758. From jct I-94 (exit 88) & US 10: Go 100 yds E on US 10, then 1/4 mi S on Oak Grove Rd. 🛶 ✖️ ♿

PARDEEVILLE — PRIDE OF AMERICA CAMPING RESORT. (800) 236-6395. **$38-$58.** W7520 W Bush Rd 53954. From jct I-90/94 (exit 106) & Hwy 33: Go 4 mi E on Hwy 33, then 2-3/4 mi SE on CR P, then 1/2 mi S on CR G, then 1/8 mi E on W Bush Rd. 🛶 ✖️ ♿

RIO — SILVER SPRINGS CAMPSITES, INC. (920) 992-3537. **$38-$49.** N5048 Ludwig Rd 53960. From jct Hwy 16 & CR B: Go 4-1/4 mi N & E on CRB, then 1 mi N on Ludwig Rd. 🛶 ✖️ ♿

TWO RIVERS — BADGER RV PARK @ VILLAGE INN ON THE LAKE. (920) 794-8818. **$35-$45.** 3310 Memorial Dr 54241. From jct Hwy 147 & Hwy 42: Go 1-1/2 mi S. 🏕️ 🛶 ✖️ ♿

WILD ROSE — EVERGREEN CAMPSITES & RESORT. (866) 450-2267. **$49.** W5449 Archer Lane 54984. From jct Hwy 22 & CR H: Go 3 mi E on Hwy H, then 1-1/2 mi E on Archer Ln. 🛶 ✖️ ♿

WISCONSIN DELLS — HOLIDAY SHORES CAMPGROUND & RESORT. 🆔 (608) 254-2717. **$40-$49.** 3901 River Rd 53965. From jct I-90/94 (exit 87) & Hwy 13: Go 7 mi E & N on Hwy 13, then 100 ft NW (left) on CR-Q, then 500 feet N on River Rd. 🛶 ✖️ ♿

Wyoming

LARAMIE — KOA-LARAMIE. (800) 562-4153. **$33-$39.** 1271 W Baker 82072. From jct I-80 & 287 S: Go 2 1/2 mi W on I-80 to Curtis St. (exit 310), then 1/2 mi E on Curtis, then 1 block S on McCue St (Follow signs). ✖️ ♿

Canada

Camping information provided by Woodall's®

Alberta

COCHRANE — BOW RIVERSEDGE CAMPGROUND. (877) 932-4675. **$37-$47.** 900 Griffin Rd E T4C 2B8. From jct Hwy 1A & Hwy 22: Go 1.5 km/ 1 mi S on Hwy 22, then 3.2 km/2 mi E on Griffin Rd, then .5 km/1/4 mi W on Campground/Arena.

GRANDE PRAIRIE — CAMP TAMARACK RV PARK. CAA (877) 532-9998. **$30-$42.** RR2 Site 8 T8V 2Z9. From jct Hwy 43 & Hwy 40: Go 8.7 km/5-1/2 mi S on Hwy 40, then 100 m/110 yds E on Twp Rd 704 A, then 200 m/220 yds N on frontage road (Range Rd 62).

LETHBRIDGE — BRIDGEVIEW RV RESORT. (403) 381-2357. **$47-$52.** 1501-2nd Ave West T1J 4S5. From jct Hwy 5 & Hwy 3: Go 4.2 km/2-1/2 mi W on Hwy 3, then .5 km/1/4 mi NW on Bridgeview Campground access road.

SUNDRE — COYOTE CREEK GOLF & RV RESORT. (403) 638-1215. **$40.** PO Box 1499 T0M 1X0. From jct Hwy 22 & Hwy 584: Go 1.6 km/1 mi W on Hwy 584, then 3.9 km/2-1/2 mi S on Range Rd 55.

VALLEYVIEW — SHERK'S RV PARK. (780) 524-4949. **$30.** From Jct of PH-43 & 38th Ave, T0H 3N0. From jct Hwy 49 & Hwy 43: Go .8 km/1/2 mi S on Hwy 43, then 680 m/745 yds W on Twp Rd 702 (38th Ave).

British Columbia

ALDERGROVE — EAGLE WIND RV PARK. (604) 856-6674. **$37-$52.** 26920 52 Ave V4W 1N6. From jct Hwy 1 & Hwy 13 (264 St): Go 500m/550 yds S on Hwy 13, then 1.1 km/3/4 mi E on 52 Ave.

BURNABY — BURNABY CARIBOO RV PARK. CAA (604) 420-1722. **$60-$65.** 8765 Cariboo Place V3N 4T2. From jct Hwy 15 & Hwy 1: Go 16 km /10 mi W on Hwy 1, (exit 37), then .3 km/1/4 W on exit ramp, then 100 m/110 yds N on Gaglardi Wy, then 100 m/110 yds E on S Cariboo Rd, then .4 km/1/4 mi N on Stormont Ave/N Cariboo Rd, then 200 m/220 yds SE on Cariboo Pl.

CAMPBELL RIVER — RIPPLE ROCK RV PARK & MARINA. (250) 287-7108. **$30-$44.** 15011 Browns Bay Rd V9W 5B1. From jct Hwy 19A & Hwy 19 (Campbell River): Go 18.6 km/11-1/2 mi N on Hwy 19, then 5.3 km/ 3-1/4 mi E on Browns Bay Rd.

CAMPBELL RIVER — SALMON POINT RESORT RV PARK & MARINA. (866) 246-6605. **$27-$46.** 2176 Salmon Point Rd V9H 1E5. From jct Hwy 19 & Hwy 19A (Campbell River): Go 21.4 km/13-1/4 mi S on Hwy 19A, then .6 km/ 1/4 mi E on Salmon Point Rd.

CHILLIWACK — COTTONWOOD MEADOWS RV COUNTRY CLUB. CAA (604) 824-7275. **$36-$42.** 44280 Luckakuck Way V2R 4A7. From jct Hwy 9 & Hwy 1: Go 18.4 km/11-1/2 mi W on Hwy 1 (exit 116), then .3 km/1/4 mi S on Lickman Rd, then .5 km/ 1/4 mi E on Luckakuck Way.

HARRISON HOT SPRINGS — SPRINGS RV RESORT. (604) 796-9767. **$45-$59.** 670 Hot Springs Rd V0M 1K0. From jct Hwy 7 & Hwy 9: Go 5.2 km/3-1/4 mi N on Hwy 9.

KELOWNA — HOLIDAY PARK RESORT. (250) 766-4255. **$45-$70.** 1-415 Commonwealth Rd V4V 1P4. From jct Hwy 33 & Hwy 97: Go 14.5 km/9 mi N on Hwy 97, then .7 km/1/2 mi E on Commonwealth Rd.

OLIVER — DESERT GEM RV RESORT. (888) 925-9966. **$30-$44.** 34037 Hwy 97 V0H 1T0. From jct Hwy 3 & Hwy 97:Go 18.8 km/11-3/4 mi N on Hwy 97.

OSOYOOS — ISLAND VIEW RV RESORT. (250) 495-7696. **$30-$60.** 5005 E Lakeshore Dr V0H 1V6. From jct Hwy 97 & Hwy 3: Go 3 km/2 mi E on Hwy 3, then 1 km/1/2 mi S on Lakeshore Dr.

OSOYOOS — WALTON'S LAKEFRONT RESORT. CAA (800) 964-1148. **$45-$90.** 3207 Lakeshore Dr V0H 1V6. From jct Hwy 97 & Hwy 3: Go 3 km/2 mi E on Hwy 3, then 1.8 km/1 mi S on Lakeshore Dr.

PARKSVILLE — PARADISE SEA SIDE RESORT. (250) 248-6612. **$25-$42.** 375 Island Hwy W V9P 1A1. From jct Hwy 19 & Hwy 19A: Go 6.4 km/4 mi N on Hwy 19A.

PARKSVILLE — SURFSIDE RV RESORT. (866) 642-2001. **$35-$63.** 200 Corfield St N V9S 2H5. From jct Hwy 19 & Hwy 19A: Go 5 km/3 mi N on Hwy 19A, then 200 m/220 yds N on Corfield St.

RADIUM HOT SPRINGS — RADIUM VALLEY VACATION RESORT. (800) 663-9906. **$30-$65.** 7274 Radium Valley Rd V0A 1M0. From jct Hwy 93/95 & Hwy 95: Go 1.2 km/3/4 mi N on Hwy 95.

ROSEDALE — BRIDAL FALLS CAMPERLAND RV RESORT. (604) 794-7361. **$42-$52.** 53680 Bridal Falls Rd V0X 1X1. From jct Hwy 1 & Hwy 9: Go 150 m/165 yds S on Hwy 9, then 1.9 km/1-1/4 mi E on Bridal Falls Rd.

SAANICHTON — OCEANSIDE RV RESORT. CAA (250) 544-0508. **$24-$50.** 3000 Stautw Rd V8M 2K5. From E jct Hwy 1A (Gorge Rd) & Hwy 1 (Douglas St): Go 1.3 km/ 3/4 mi N on Hwy 1, then 300 m/350 yds E on Cloverdale Ave, then 16.5 km/10-1/4 mi N on Hwy 17 (Blanshard St), then .6 km/ 1/4 mi E on Mt. Newton Cross Rd, then 1.3 km/ 3/4 mi SE on Stautw Rd.

SURREY — HAZELMERE RV PARK & CAMPGROUND. CAA (877) 501-5007. **$33-$40.** 18843 - 8th Ave V3S 9R9. From E city limits: Go 24.3 km / 15-1/4 mi E on Hwy 1, then 18.5 km / 11-1/2 mi S on Hwy 15, then 2.5 km / 1-1/2 mi E on 8th Ave.

SURREY — PACIFIC BORDER RV PARK. (866) 333-1727. **$40-$45.** 67-175A St V3S 9T7. From jct Hwy 10 & Hwy 15/176 St (Cloverdale): Go 10.6 km/6-1/2 mi S on Hwy 15, then 100 metres/110 yds W on 4th Ave, then 500 metres/550 yds S on 175A St.

VICTORIA — **WEIR'S BEACH RV RESORT.** (866) 478-6888. **$35-$55.** 5191 William Head Rd V9C 4H5. From E jct Hwy 1A (Gorge Rd) & Hwy 1 (Douglas St): Go 7.1 km/4-1/2 mi W on Hwy 1 (exit 10), then 300 m/350 yds on exit ramp, then 5.3 km/3-1/4 mi SW on Burnside Rd West/Sooke Rd, then 11.9 km/7-1/2 mi S on Metchosin Rd/William Head Rd. 🏕 ⊠ ⴟᴹ

WHISTLER — **RIVERSIDE RESORT.** (604) 905-5533. **$35-$57.** 8018 Mons Road V0N 1B8. From jct Hwy 7A & Hwy 99: Go 123 km/6-1/2 mi N on Hwy 99, then 20 m/22 yds E on Spruce Grove Way, then .5 km/1/4 mi N on Mons Rd. ⊶ ⊠ ⴟᴹ

New Brunswick

MONCTON — **CAMPER'S CITY RV/RESORT.** (877) 512-7868. **$27-$46.** 138 Queensway Dr E1G 2L2. From Hwy 2 & Mapleton Rd (exit 454): Go 100 meters/300 ft N on Mapleton Rd, then .04 km/1/4 mi E on Queens Way Dr. ⊶ ⊠ ⴟᴹ

Nova Scotia

BADDECK — **BADDECK CABOT TRAIL CAMPGROUND.** ⓐⓐ (902) 295-2288. **$24-$41.** 9584 Hwy 105 B0E 1B0. From W Town City Limit at Baddeck on Hwy 105: Go 8 km/5 mi W on Hwy 105 (between exit 7 & 8). ⊶ ⊠

Ontario

BARRIE — **KOA-BARRIE.** ⓐⓐ (705) 726-6128. **$43-$82.** 3138 Penetanguishene Rd RR 1 L4M 4Y8. From jct Hwy 11 & Hwy 93: Go 11.2 km/7 mi N on Hwy 93. ⊶ ⊠ ⴟᴹ

BELWOOD — **HIGHLAND PINES CAMPGROUND.** (519) 843-2537. **$48-$55.** RR 1 8523 Wellington Rd 19 N0B 1J0. From jct Hwy 6 & CR 19: Go 9 km/5-1/2 mi E on CR 19. 🏊 ⊠ ⴟᴹ

CHERRY VALLEY — **QUINTE'S ISLE CAMPARK.** ⓐⓐ (613) 476-6310. **$50-$58.** RR 1 237 Salmon Pt Rd K0K 1P0. From town at jct CR 10 (Lake St) & CR 18: Go 9.6 km/6 mi S on CR 18, then .4 km/1/4 mi E on Salmon Point Rd (follow signs). ⊶ ⊠ ⴟᴹ

COOKSTOWN — **KOA-TORONTO NORTH COOKSTOWN.** (705) 458-2267. **$57.** RR 1, 139 Reive L0L 1L0. From jct Hwy 400 (exit 75) & Hwy 89: Go .4 km/1/4 mi N on Reive Blvd (NE corner). ⊶ ⊠ ⴟᴹ

KINCARDINE — **FISHERMAN'S COVE TENT & TRAILER PARK.** (519) 395-2757. **$47-$57.** 13 Southline Ave RR 4 N2Z 2X5. From jct Hwy 21 & Hwy 9: Go 18 km/11-1/4 mi E on Hwy 9,then 1.6 km/1 mi S on Bruce Rd 1, then 1.6 km/1 mi E on Southline Ave. ⊶ ⊠ ⴟᴹ

LEAMINGTON — **STURGEON WOODS CAMPGROUND & MARINA.** (877) 521-4990. **$38-$43.** 1129 Mersea Rd C RR 1 N8H 3V4. From jct Hwy 3 & Hwy 77: Go 1.6 km/1 mi S on CR 20, then 3.2 km/2 mi SE on Essex CR 33 to Point Pelee, look for signs. ⊶ ⊠ ⴟᴹ

MCGREGOR — **WILDWOOD GOLF & RV RESORT.** (866) 994-9699. **$42.** RR 1 N0R 1J0. From the Jct of Hwy 401 (exit 21) & Cty Rd 19 (Manning Rd) Go S on Cty Rd 19 4.6 km/3 mi to the Jct of Cty Rd 3, then Go SE on Cty Rd 3 4.8 km/3 mi to N Malden Rd, then Go SW on N Malden Rd 9.1 km/5-3/4 mi to Conc 11, then Go W on Conc 11 0.6 km/1/2 mi. 🏕 ⊶ ⊠ ⴟᴹ

MILLER LAKE — **SUMMER HOUSE PARK.** ⓐⓐ (800) 265-5557. **$40-$45.** 197 Miller Lake Shore Rd N0H 1Z0. From jct Hwy 6 & Miller Lake Rd: Go 3.2 km/2 mi E on Miller Lake Rd. ⊶ ⊠ ⴟᴹ

MOUNT ELGIN — **SPRING LAKE R.V. RESORT.** (877) 877-9265. **$38-$44.** RR 1 263459 Prouse Rd N0J 1N0. From jct Hwy 401 (exit 216) & Culloden Rd: Go 10.4 km/6-1/2 mi S on Culloden Rd, then .4 km/1/4 mi W on CR 27 (Prouse Rd). 🏕 ⊶ ⊠

NIAGARA FALLS — **CAMPARK RESORTS.** ⓐⓐ (877) 226-7275. **$42-$54.** 9387 Lundy's Lane RR 1 L2E 6S4. From jct Queen Elizabeth Way & Hwy 420 (exit Lundy's Lane, Hwy 20): Go 100 yards W, then .8 km/1/2 mi S on Montrose, then 2.4 km/1-1/2 mi W on Lundy's Lane. ⊶ ⊠

NIAGARA FALLS — **KOA-NIAGARA FALLS.** (800) 562-6478. **$50-$90.** 8625 Lundys Lane L2H 1H5. From jct Queen Elizabeth Way & Hwy 20 (Lundys Lane): Go 100 yards W, then .8 km/1/2 mi S on Montrose, then 2 km/1-1/4 mi W on Hwy 20. ⊶ ⊠

NIAGARA FALLS — **YOGI BEAR'S JELLYSTONE PARK CAMP-RESORT.** ⓐⓐ (905) 354-1432. **$36-$64.** 8676 Oakwood Dr L2E 6S5. From jct Hwy 420 & QEW: Go 3.2 km/2 mi S on QEW, then 183 meters/200 yards E on McLeod Rd, then 2.4 km/1-1/2 mi S on Oakwood Dr. ⊶ ⊠

PUSLINCH — **EMERALD LAKE TRAILER RESORT & WATER PARK.** (800) 679-1853. **$60-$75.** 7248 Gore Rd RR 2 N0B 2J0. From jct Hwy 401 and Hwy 6: Go 5 km/3 mi S on Hwy 6, then go 5 km/3 mi W on Con Rd 11. (Gore Rd). 🏊 ⊶ ⊠ ⴟᴹ

RIDGEVILLE — **BISSELL'S HIDEAWAY RESORT.** (888) 236-0619. **$45-$75.** RR 1 L0S 1M0. From west city limits: Go .4 km/1/4 mi W on Hwy 20, then 2.4 km/1-1/2 mi N on Effingham Rd, then .8 km/1/2 mi E on Metler Rd. 🏊 ⊶ ⊠

SAUBLE BEACH — **CARSON'S CAMP.** (519) 422-1143. **$40-$46. (no credit cards).** RR 1 110 Southhampton Pkwy N0H 2G0. From south city limits: Go 1 km/1/2 mi S on CR 13 (Southhampton Pkwy). ⊶ ⊠ ⴟᴹ

SAUBLE BEACH — **WOODLAND PARK.** (519) 422-1161. **$32-$52.** RR 1, 47 Sauble Falls Parkway N0H 2G0. From jct CR-8 & CR-13 (traffic light): Go .4 km/-1/4 mi N on CR 13 (Sauble Falls Rd). ⊶ ⊠ ⴟᴹ

SHERKSTON — **SHERKSTON SHORES.** (877) 482-3224. **$19-$91.** RR1 490 Empire Rd L0S 1R0. From jct Hwy 140 & Hwy 3: Go 8 km/5 mi E on Hwy 3, then 2.4 km/1-1/2 mi S on Empire Rd (Regional Rd 98). ⊶ ⊠ ⴟᴹ

THUNDER BAY — **KOA-THUNDER BAY.** (807) 683-6221. **$36-$47.** 162 Spruce River Road P7B 5E4. From jct Hwy 11-17 & Hwy 527: Go .4 km/1/4 mi S on Spruce River Rd. ⊶ ⊠

VINELAND — **N.E.T. CAMPING RESORT.** (866) 490-4745. **$36-$55.** 2325 Regional RD 24 L0R 2C0. From jct QEW (exit 57) & Regional Rd 24: Go 17.7 km/11 mi S on Regional Rd 24. ⊶ ⊠

WATERLOO — GREEN ACRE PARK. (877) 885-7275. **$31-$48.** 580 Beaver Creek Rd N2J 3Z4. From jct Hwy 401 & Hwy 8: Go 8 km/5 mi W on Hwy 8, then 10.4 km/6-1/2 mi N on Hwy 85, (frmly Hwy 86) then 3.2 km/2 mi W on Northfield Dr, then .8 km/1/2 mi N on Westmount Rd, then 1.6 km/1 mi W on Conservation Dr, then 90m/100 yards S on Beaver Creek Rd. 🏕 🏊 ⊠ ᶜᴹ

Prince Edward Island

KENSINGTON — TWIN SHORES CAMPING AREA. (877) 734-2267. **$33-$39.** 702 Lower Darnley Rd C0B 1M0. From jct Hwy 20 & Hwy 6: Go 17.3 km/10-3/4 mi W on Hwy 20, then 3.2 km/2 mi N on Darnley Point Rd. 🏊 ⊠ ᶜᴹ

Québec

BROMONT — CAMPING DU VILLAGE BROMONT RV RESORT. ⒶⒶ (450) 534-2404. **$40-$54.** 1699 SHEFFORD J2L 3N8. From I-10 (exit 74): Go 5.6 km/3-1/2 mi S on Boul Pierre Laporte, then 152 m/500 ft E on Shefford. 🏊 ⊠ ᶜᴹ

SAGUENAY-LA BAIE — CAMPING AU JARDIN DE MON PERE. (877) 544-6486. **$22-$39.** 3736 CH St Louis G7B 3P6. From jct Hwy 381 & Hwy 170: Go 2.5 km/1-1/2 mi W on Hwy 170, then 1.5 km/1 mi S on Ave du Port, then 150 meters/500 feet SE on Joseph-Gagne, then 1.3 km/1 mi S on St-Louis. 🏊 ⊠ ᶜᴹ

ST-MATHIEU-DE-BELOEIL — CAMPING ALOUETTE. ⒶⒶ (450) 464-1661. **$41-$45.** 3449 Rue de l'Industrie J3G 4S5. From Hwy I-20 (exit 105): Go 1.6 km/1 mi NE on service road (ch. de l'Industrie). 🏊 ⊠ ᶜᴹ

SAINT-NICOLAS — KOA-QUEBEC CITY. ⒶⒶ (418) 831-1813. **$43-$65.** 684 Chemin Olivier G7A 2N6. 1 mi W of I-73: Go W on I-20 (exit 311), then left at traffic light going E on I-20, (exit 311). Cross over I-20. Turn left at Oliver Rd (service road). 🏊 ⊠

ST-PHILIPPE — CAMPING LA CLE DES CHAMPS RV RESORT. (450) 659-3389. **$39-$48.** 415 Montee St-Claude J0L 2K0. From jct Hwy 30 & Rte 104 (exit 104): Go 1.7 mi E on Rte 104, then S 2 mi on Rang St Raphael, then W .5 mi on Montee St Claude. 🏊 ⊠ ᶜᴹ

VALCARTIER — CAMPING VALCARTIER. (888) 384-5524. **$22-$50.** 1860 Boulevard Valcartier G0A 4S0. From jct Hwy 40 (Henri IV) & Hwy 573: Go 11 Km/7 mi N on Hwy 573, then 10 Km/6-1/4 mi NE on Hwy 371 (Boul. Valcartier). 🏕 🏊 ⊠ ᶜᴹ

AAA PetBook Reader Questionnaire

We "paws-itively" want to hear from you! Your comments, opinions and suggestions are important to AAA. Please help us to improve the AAA PetBook® by taking a few minutes to complete this simple questionnaire.

> Please mail your completed questionnaire to: AAA PetBook, Mail Stop 64, 1000 AAA Drive, Heathrow, FL 32746-5063
>
> Or, email us your comments at PetBookFeedback@national.aaa.com

1. Where did you purchase the AAA PetBook®?
   - ☐ AAA Club _____ (club name)
   - ☐ Bookstore _____ (name of bookstore)
   - ☐ Online _____ (web site)

2. What specific pet-related information contained in the AAA PetBook is important to you when planning to travel with your pet? (Please check all that apply)
   - ☐ Lodgings
   - ☐ Campgrounds
   - ☐ National Public Lands
   - ☐ Attractions
   - ☐ Dog Parks
   - ☐ Emergency Animal Clinics
   - ☐ U.S. / Canada Border Crossing Procedures
   - ☐ Traveling by Car
   - ☐ Traveling by Air
   - ☐ Traveling with Disabilities

3. When traveling with your pet, what additional information would be helpful?
   _____

4. How well does the AAA PetBook® meet your expectations?
   - ☐ Exceeds
   - ☐ Meets all
   - ☐ Meets most
   - ☐ Falls below

5. Are you familiar with the annual photo contest at AAA.com/PetBook? ☐ Yes ☐ No

Additional feedback or comments about the AAA PetBook:
_____
_____

Which age group are you in? ☐ Under 25 ☐ 25-34 ☐ 35-44 ☐ 45-54 ☐ 55-64 ☐ 65+

On average, how many overnight leisure trips do you take a year?
   ☐ None ☐ One ☐ Two ☐ Three or more

How many trips/outings a year include traveling with your pet? _____

What is the average distance traveled? _____

In addition to the AAA PetBook, did you buy any other pet-travel or general travel guides for your trip? ☐ Yes ☐ No

If yes, which ones?
_____
_____

Optional:

Name (Mr/Mrs/Ms) _____

Address _____

City _____ State _____ Zip _____

Are you a AAA member? ☐ Yes ☐ No, If yes, name of AAA club: _____

Thank you for taking the time to complete this questionnaire. We appreciate your feedback.

All information including name and address is for AAA internal use only and will NOT be distributed outside the organization to any third parties.

14th edition

❖ Pet-Friendly Travel Notes ❖